ISBN 978-0-428-63759-0
PIBN 11272314


FB &c Ltd, Dalton House, 60 Windsor Avenue, London, SW19 2RR.
Company number 08720141. Registered in England and Wales.

# THE MANUAL OF STATISTICS

## STOCK EXCHANGE HAND-BOOK

# 1903

TWENTY FIFTH ANNUAL ISSUE

RAILROAD SECURITIES · INDUSTRIAL SECURITIES · GOVERNMENT SECURITIES · STOCK EXCHANGE QUOTATIONS · MINING · GRAIN AND PROVISIONS · COTTON · MONEY · BANKS AND TRUST COMPANIES

PRICE FIVE DOLLARS

THE MANUAL OF STATISTICS COMPANY

220 BROADWAY, NEW YORK

# INDEX

# INDEX

INDEX

# INDEX TO MAPS

# INDEX TO ADVERTISERS

# RAILROAD SECURITIES

**The Principal Railroad Companies of the United States, Canada and Mexico, with Details of Their Organization, Mileage, Capital Stock, Funded Debt and Earnings**

**Comprising all American Steam Railroad Corporations whose Securities are Quoted in the Leading Stock Markets. Concise Information regarding Them, with Detailed Accounts. Names of Officers and Directors and the Location of General and Financial Offices**

**Later Information Regarding the Companies Herein Represented and Other Railroad Corporations, either Organized or in Process of Formation, as well as Those not of Sufficient Importance to be Included, will be Furnished Free of Charge to Subscribers to the MANUAL on Application**

## AKRON & BARBERTON BELT RAILROAD CO.

A corporation formed under the laws of Ohio, May 6, 1902. The company is a consolidation of lines constituting a belt line around Barberton, O. Road owned, 22 miles. The company was organized in the interest of the Pennsylvania Company, Lake Shore & Michigan Southern Railroad Co., Erie Railroad Co. and Baltimore & Ohio Railroad Co., which corporations own all the stock.

Stock......Par $100..............................Authorized $100,000......Issued, $100,000

FUNDED DEBT.

1st mort., 4 per cent., due June, 1942, June and Dec................................ $1,000,000

The 1st mortgage is for $1,500,000, the unissued balance being reserved for improvements. There is a sinking fund of 1 per cent. per annum, and the bonds can be drawn at 105 and interest. Trustee of mortgage and agent for payment of interest, United States Mortgage & Trust Co., New York.

President, James McCrea; Secretary, S. B. Liggett; Treasurer, Robert R. Reed, Pittsburg.

Directors—James McCrea, Pittsburg; Eben B. Thomas, William H. Newman, New York; Oscar G. Murray, Baltimore; Charles Baird, Akron, O.

Main office, Akron, O.

## ALABAMA & VICKSBURG RAILWAY CO.

(Controlled by Alabama, New Orleans, Texas & Pacific Junction Railways Co., Limited.)

Road owned, Vicksburg to Meridian, Miss., 143 miles. Locomotives, 20; passenger cars, 20; freight cars, 680.

This company is controlled by the Alabama, New Orleans, Texas & Pacific Junction Railways Co., Limited, an English corporation.

Stock......Par $100..........................Authorized, $1,050,000......Issued, $1,050,000

Stock is transferred by the secretary of the company, New Orleans. Registrar, Central Trust Co., New York.

The company paid a dividend of 3 per cent. in 1890, 1891 and 1896, and 5 per cent. in 1897, 1898 and 1899, and 6 per cent. in 1900, 1901 and 1902. Dividends are yearly, in August.

FUNDED DEBT.

| | |
|---|---|
| Vicksburg & Meridian 1st mort., 6 per cent., due April, 1921, April and Oct......... | $1,000,000 |
| Ala. & Vicks. consol. 1st mort., 5 per cent., due April, 1921, April and Oct......... | 588,800 |
| 2d mort., income (non-cumulative), 5 per cent., due April, 1921..................... | 601,300 |
| Total............................................................ | $2,190,100 |

On March 19, 1900, the stock was increased from $700,000 to $1,050,000 to represent improvements since the present company took possession.

The company was formed in March, 1889, by the 2d mortgage bondholders of the Vicksburg & Meridian Railroad, who purchased the property of that company at foreclosure sale, retaining the Vicksburg & Meridian 1st mortgage as a continuing obligation. Of the consolidated bonds $1,000,000 additional are reserved to retire the Vicksburg & Meridian 1sts. The company has a land grant from which to June 30, 1902, 90,656 acres had been sold for $238,409. The acres unsold July 1, 1902, were 45,392.

EARNINGS.

Year ending June 30.

| | Gross. | Net. | Charges. | Surplus. |
|---|---|---|---|---|
| 1892–93 | $588,298 | $121,909 | $121,909 | ........ |
| 1893–94 | 565,780 | 129,447 | 128,186 | $1,260 |
| 1894–95 | 555,677 | 129,971 | 150,021 | 5,950 |
| 1895–96 | 575,072 | 160,958 | 125,811 | 35,147 |
| 1896–97 | 637,528 | 186,393 | 125,412 | 60,981 |
| 1897–98 | 682,053 | 203,523 | 123,136 | 80,386 |
| 1898–99 | 697,538 | 191,428 | 122,062 | 69,366 |
| 1899–00 | 812,778 | 228,581 | 142,180 | 86,401 |
| 1900–01 | 920,669 | 235,340 | 131,384 | 103,956 |
| 1901–02 | 1,019,843 | 254,281 | 108,024 | 146,257 |

In the year ending June 30, 1899, the dividend of 5 per cent. on the stock was $35,000. In the following three years the 6 per cent. dividends were $63,000 each year.

President, C. C. Harvey; Secretary and Treasurer, Henry W. Wenham; Auditor, Larz A. Jones, New Orleans.

Directors—George T. Bonner, New York; C. C. Harvey, New Orleans; Charles Schiff, London, Eng.; John F. Winslow, Cincinnati; T. A. McWillie, Jackson, Miss.

Main office, New Orleans. Annual meeting, first Monday in November, at Jackson, Miss.

## ALABAMA GREAT SOUTHERN RAILROAD CO.

(Controlled by Southern Railway Co.)

Line owned, Wauhatchie, Tenn., to Meridian, Miss., 291 miles; Attalla to Gadsden, Ala., 6 miles; leased, Wauhatchie to Chattanooga, 5 miles; Belt Line of Chattanooga, 43 miles; trackage, Woodstock to Blocton, Ala., 8 miles; other trackage, 21 miles; total, 374 miles; spurs and sidings additional, 77 miles; total, 451 miles. Locomotives, 48; passenger cars, 44; freight cars, 3,524.

The entire capital stock is owned by an English corporation, the Alabama Great Southern Railway Co., Limited. Control of this company is held by the Southern Railway Co. and the road is operated as part of the Southern Railway system, but under its own officials.

In 1895 this company leased for fifty years the Belt Railway of Chattanooga and acquired all of its $300,000 capital stock, guaranteeing sufficient revenue to Belt Line to meet its fixed charges. The Belt Line Co. has a 1st mortgage of $300,000, of which $275,000 is outstanding bearing 5 per cent. interest; also $24,000 4 per cent. non-cumulative income bonds, subject to call at par July 1, 1903.

This road was originally the Alabama & Chattanooga, and passed to the present company through foreclosure sale. It was controlled by the East Tennessee, Virginia & Georgia up to November, 1893, when control was resigned to the representatives of the English owners and a new board and officers representing their interests were installed. Under the reorganization plan for the Richmond Terminal and East Tennessee companies of May, 1893, holders of the $6,000,000 Cincinnati extension bonds of the latter company were offered an exchange for 25 per cent. of new 5 per cent. bonds of the reorganized company and 80 per cent. in new preferred stock. These terms being rejected, the property was excluded from the reorganization, and in March, 1894, interests connected with the Cincinnati, Hamilton & Dayton purchased a majority of the bonds. The Southern Railway in September, 1894, bought the minority of the bonds, and in July, 1895, bought a majority of the stock of the English company, which had been pledged to secure the Cincinnati Extension bonds of the East Tennessee, and which was sold by order of court to satisfy default in interest on the bonds. In May, 1895, an agreement was made between the Cincinnati, Hamilton & Dayton and the Southern Railway Co., regarding control of road, the operation of which was assumed by the latter company on October 3, 1895. This company and the English company own jointly $833,000 stock of the Southwest Construction Co., which controls the Cincinnati, New Orleans & Texas Pacific.

Stock..Par $100...Authorized { com., $7,830,000; pref., 4,000,000 } Issued { com., $7,830,000; pref., 3,380,350 } $11,210,350

The preferred stock is entitled to a preference of 6 per cent., cumulative, for 6 years. Arrears of dividends were funded in 1888 in form of 4 per cent. certificates redeemable in ten years in annual payments, of which $258,832 were outstanding as of June 30, 1902.

The share capital of the English company is divided into £1,566,000 ordinary or A and £800,000 preference or B stock, £123,930 of the preference stock being unissued. The Southern Railway owns £345,000 A and £908,010 B stock. The debenture bonds of the English company are £134,000, corresponding as to rate and maturity with those of the American company. Transfer office of the English company, 2 Prince's street, London.

A dividend of 3 per cent. was paid on the A English shares in January, 1893. On common B shares 1½ per cent. was paid in January, 1892. Six per cent. was paid on the A shares in 1895, 9 per cent. in 1897, 6 per cent. in 1898, 6 per cent. in 1899, 8 per cent. in 1900 and 9 per cent. in 1901, 3 per cent. being paid in May, 2 per cent. in September and 4 per cent. in December. In 1902 4 per cent. was paid in June and 5 per cent. December 16, 1902, making 9 per cent. for the year.

FUNDED DEBT.

| | |
|---|---|
| 1st mort., 6 per cent. bonds, due Jan., 1908, Jan. and July | $1,750,000 |
| Debentures, 6 per cent., due Aug. 15, 1906, Feb. and Aug. | 670,000 |
| Gen. mort., 5 per cent., due Dec., 1927, June and Dec. | 2,556,360 |
| Car trust notes, various | 156,600 |
| Total | $5,132,960 |

EARNINGS.

Year ending June 30.

| | Gross. | Net. | Fixed Charges. | Surplus. |
|---|---|---|---|---|
| 1892-93 | $1,818,229 | $321,651 | $279,430 | $42,221 |
| 1893-94 | 1,553,783 | 424,083 | 279,814 | 144,269 |
| 1894-95 | 1,528,407 | 499,800 | 277,996 | 221,804 |
| 1895-96 | 1,634,093 | 500,881 | 276,542 | 224,339 |
| 1896-97 | 1,605,546 | 502,505 | 292,548 | 209,921 |
| 1897-98 | 1,741,933 | 566,388 | 300,449 | 265,938 |
| 1898-99 | 1,816,523 | 577,417 | 302,244 | 275,173 |
| 1899-00 | 2,092,448 | 648,444 | 308,294 | 340,151 |
| 1900-01 | 2,198,738 | 658,996 | 312,831 | 346,165 |
| 1901-02 | 2,487,453 | 724,807 | 318,975 | 405,833 |

President, Samuel Spencer, New York; Vice-Presidents, A. B. Andrews, Raleigh, N. C.; W. W. Finley, Washington, D. C.; Secretary, R. D. Lankford, New York; Treasurer, H. C. Ansley, Washington, D. C.

Directors—Samuel Spencer, Francis Lynde Stetson, Walter G. Oakman, Charles Steele, R. D. Lankford, A. B. Andrews, William C. Lane, New York; S. M. Felton, Chicago; C. C. Harvey, New Orleans; W. W. Finley, H. Doughty Browne, London, England.

Main offices, Birmingham, Ala., and Washington, D. C.; New York office, 80 Broadway; office of English company, 2 Prince's street, London.

Annual meeting, first Wednesday in October, at Birmingham. Books close two weeks prior to meeting.

---

## ALASKA CENTRAL RAILWAY CO.

Road projected from Resurrection Bay, Alaska, to Rampart on the Yukon river, about 400 miles. The proposed line traverses a rich timber and mineral district.

Stock....Par $50....Authorized { com., $27,500,000 / pref., 2,500,000 } Issued { com., $27,500,000 / pref., 2,500,000 } $30,000,000

The preferred stock is 5 per cent., non-cumulative.

The company has authorized the creation of a mortgage bond issue at the rate of $35,000 per mile.

President, G. W. Dickinson; Vice-President, John H. McGraw; Treasurer, J. W. Goodwin; Secretary and Auditor, John E. Ballaine.

Directors—G. W. Dickinson, John H. McGraw, E. E. Caine, John E. Ballaine, J. W. Goodwin, Seattle, Wash.; George Turner, Spokane, Wash.; F. Aug. Heinze, New York.

Main office, Denny Building, Seattle, Wash.

---

## ALBANY & SUSQUEHANNA RAILROAD CO.

(Leased to Delaware & Hudson Co.)

Road owned, main line, Albany, N. Y., to Binghamton, 142 miles; branches leased and operated, 67 miles; total, 209 miles.

In 1870 this road was leased to the Delaware & Hudson Canal Co. for 150 years, lessee guaranteeing as rental interest on bonds and 7 per cent. on the stock (to be increased to 9 per cent. as stated below).

Stock......Par $100........................ Authorized, $3,500,000......Issued, $3,500,000

Transfer Agent and Registrar, National Bank of Commerce, New York.

Dividends are payable half-yearly, January 1 and July 1. The first semi-annual dividend at the new rate of 4½ per cent. was paid January 1, 1903.

FUNDED DEBT.

| | |
|---|---|
| Consolidated mort., 7 per cent. currency, due April, 1906, April and Oct............ | $3,000,000 |
| Consolidated mort., 6 per cent., due April, 1906, April and Oct..................... | 7,000,000 |
| Total................................................................ | $10,000,000 |

The company had a loan of $1,000,000 from the city of Albany, which was paid off in May, 1897. The sinking fund applicable for this purpose was $296,000 short of the amount required, and this sum was borrowed, payable in semi-annual instalments up to May, 1902, from a sinking fund of $70,000 per annum. When this payment was completed dividends under the lease, which were 7 per cent., or 3½ per cent. semi-annually, were to be increased to 9 per cent. per annum.

The consolidated mortgage bonds are guaranteed by the lessee.

EARNINGS.

Year ending June 30.

| | Div. Paid. | Gross. | Net. | Rental. | Gain to Lessee. |
|---|---|---|---|---|---|
| 1892-93.................... | 7 | $4,298,894 | $2,018,722 | $1,182,774 | $835,948 |
| 1893-94.................... | 7 | 3,998,795 | 1,782,796 | 1,171,652 | 611,144 |
| 1894-95.................... | 7 | 3,872,786 | 1,591,348 | 1,084,962 | 506,386 |
| 1895-96.................... | 7 | 4,212,762 | 1,890,053 | 1,185,039 | 705,014 |
| 1896-97.................... | 7 | 3,924,524 | 1,651,131 | 1,102,614 | 548,517 |
| 1897-98.................... | 7 | 4,125,187 | 1,822,427 | 1,113,184 | 709,243 |
| 1898-99.................... | 7 | 4,235,068 | 1,886,012 | 1,055,496 | 767,692 |
| 1899-00.................... | 7 | 4,803,246 | 2,607,247 | 1,056,632 | 1,478,997 |
| 1900-01.................... | 7 | 4,850,205 | 2,524,129 | 1,059,364 | 1,464,765 |
| 1901-02.................... | 7 | 4,643,964 | 2,163,146 | 1,033,152 | 1,140,218 |

Earnings are given as stated by lessee.

President, Robert Olyphant, New York; Secretary and Treasurer, William L. M. Phelps, Albany, N. Y.

Main office, Albany, N. Y. Annual meeting, third Tuesday in October, at Albany, N. Y.

## ALLEGHENY VALLEY RAILWAY CO.

(Leased to Pennsylvania Railroad Co.)

Road owned, River Division, Pittsburg, Pa., to Oil City, 132 miles; Low Grade Division, Red Bank to Driftwood, 110 miles; branches, 17 miles; total, 259 miles. Controls Brookville Ry., 13 miles. Locomotives, 87: passenger cars, 64; freight cars, 3,470.

In July, 1900, the Pennsylvania Railroad Co. leased this property from August 1, 1900. A portion of the Western New York & Pennsylvania Railroad is operated in connection with the road, forming the Buffalo & Allegheny Valley Division of the Pennsylvania Railroad Co., which division comprises 689 miles of road.

Stock............Authorized { com., $12,000,000 / pref., 18,000,000 } Issued { com., $10,544,200 / pref., 17,172,750 } $27,716,950

The preferred stock is 3 per cent. per annum, cumulative.

Transfer agency and Registrar, company's office, Broad Street Station, Philadelphia.

FUNDED DEBT.

| | |
|---|---|
| 1st mort. (Low Grade Div.), 7 per cent., due April, 1910, April and Oct............ | $9,998,000 |
| 2d mort. (Low Grade Div.), to State of Pa., 5 per cent., payable $100,000 yearly, Jan. | 600,000 |
| Gen. mort. gold, 4 per cent., due March, 1942, March and Sept..................... | 5,992,000 |
| Total.............................................................. | $16,590,000 |

This company is a reorganization, March, 1892, under title of the Allegheny Valley Railway Co., of the Allegheny Valley Railroad Co. The road was placed in the hands of a receiver April, 1884. Sold under foreclosure December, 1891, and reorganized under plan by which $18,000,000 preferred and $12,000,000 common stock were authorized to be exchanged for income bonds, overdue coupons and other securities. The 1st mortgage 7 per cent. bonds, due 1910, are guaranteed by the Pennsylvania Railroad Co. The general mortgage was authorized in the reorganization and is for $20,000,000, also guaranteed by the Pennsylvania Railroad Co. Of this $17,000,000 was reserved to take up prior liens.

The Pennsylvania Railroad Co. has a controlling interest, holding $11,876,655 preferred and $9,653,800 common stock.

EARNINGS.

| | Gross. | Net. | Fixed Charges. | | Deficit. |
|---|---|---|---|---|---|
| 1895 | $2,569,082 | $951,650 | $1,139,466 | | $187,816 |
| 1896 | 2,341,613 | 777,439 | 995,827 | | 218,387 |
| 1897 | 2,553,134 | 1,074,868 | 1,074,297 | Sur. | 571 |
| 1898 | 2,669,446 | 1,118,110 | 1,070,280 | " | 47,829 |
| 1899 | 3,183,044 | 1,106,894 | 1,081,631 | " | 25,263 |

Earnings are now included in those of the lessee.

President, William H. Barnes; Treasurer, Robert W. Smith; Secretary, John M. Harding, Philadelphia.

Main office, Pittsburg; President's office, Broad Street Station, Philadelphia. Annual meeting, first Monday in April, at Philadelphia.

## THE ANN ARBOR RAILROAD CO.

Road owned, Toledo, O., to Frankfort, Mich., 292 miles. Locomotives, 46; passenger cars, 27; freight cars, 2,331. Also 3 steam transfers, operated on Lake Michigan, between Frankford and Kewaunee, Wis., and Menominee, Gladstone, and Manistique, Mich.

This company is a reorganization, November, 1895, of the Toledo, Ann Arbor & North Michigan Railway Co. The latter was a consolidation, 1888, of the company of same name and the Toledo, Ann Arbor & Cadillac Railway. The company defaulted in May, 1893, and a Receiver was appointed. This was followed by litigation and efforts by several committees to reorganize the property. Finally, in July, 1895, the road was sold under foreclosure and purchased by bondholders' committee under a plan details of which were given in the MANUAL for 1899.

In 1902 control of the company was acquired by interests identified with the Wabash Railroad Co.

Stock...Par $100....Authorized { com., $3,250,000 / pref., 4,000,000 } Issued { com., $3,250,000 / pref., 4,000,000 } $7,250,000

The preferred stock is 5 per cent., non-cumulative. Common and preferred have equal voting rights.

Transfer agency, 66 Broadway, New York. Registrar, Metropolitan Trust Co., New York.

FUNDED DEBT.

1st mort., 4 per cent., gold, due July, 1995, quarterly, Jan., April, July, Oct.......... $7,000,000

EARNINGS.

| | Gross. | Net. | Charges. | Surplus. |
|---|---|---|---|---|
| 1893 | $1,088,793 | $244,052 | $469,560 | Def. $244,473 |
| 1894 | 1,029,624 | 164,998 | 416,039 | Def. 251,040 |
| 1895 | 1,085,348 | 185,346 | 417,301 | Def. 231,955 |
| 1896 | 1,155,765 | 34,253 | 287,871 | Def. 253,610 |
| 1897 | 1,229,436 | 192,268 | 185,483 | 6,786 |
| 1897–98 (year ending June 30) | 1,415,559 | 389,454 | 326,862 | 62,592 |
| 1898–99 ( " " " ) | 1,519,334 | 346,943 | 328,957 | 17,987 |
| 1899–00 ( " " " ) | 1,721,454 | 396,833 | 329,808 | 67,025 |
| 1900–01 ( " " " ) | 1,754,148 | 444,985 | 331,064 | 113,921 |
| 1901–02 ( " " " ) | 1,893,410 | 520,354 | 332,497 | 187,857 |

In 1899–1900 $279,461 was spent out of income for equipment and improvements, in 1900–01 $178,614, and in 1901–02 about $150,000 for the same purpose.

The following exhibits the freight traffic statistics of the company:

| | Average Mileage. | Total Tonnage. | Tons Carried One Mile. | Freight Density. | Rate per Ton per Mile. | Earnings per Train Mile. | Average Tons per Train. |
|---|---|---|---|---|---|---|---|
| 1897–98.... | 292 | 1,093,576 | 147,850,536 | 506,511 | 0.69 | $1,642 | 237 |
| 1898–99.... | 292 | 1,319,036 | 170,589,582 | 584,411 | 0.64 | 1,776 | 276 |
| 1899–00.... | 292 | 1,504,206 | 197,105,961 | 675,251 | 0.62 | 1,990 | 318 |
| 1900–01.... | 292 | 1,539,270 | 191,250,216 | 651,191 | 0.65 | 1,916 | 291 |
| 1901–02.... | 292 | 1,594,917 | 200,264,691 | 685,837 | 0.68 | 1,900 | 280 |

*President*, Joseph Ramsey, Jr.; Vice-President, Cyrus J. Lawrence; Secretary, Daniel C. Tate; *Treasurer*, H. B. Henson, New York.

Directors—Joseph Ramsey, Jr., George J. Gould, Cyrus J. Lawrence, Alvin W. Krech, J. Edward Simmons, Daniel C. Tate, Franklin B. Lord, New York; Henry W. Ashley, S. C. Reynolds, Toledo; Wellington R. Burt, Saginaw; Ammi W. Wright, Alma.

Main office, Toledo; Secretary's office, 66 Broadway; New York; Treasurer's office, 195 Broadway, New York. Annual meeting, third Saturday in September, at Durand, Mich.

## ARIZONA & UTAH RAILWAY CO.

A corporation formed under the laws of Arizona.

Road owned, McConnico to Chloride, Ariz., 25 miles; trackage on Atchison system, McConnico to Kingman, 4 miles; total operated, 29 miles. An extension of 63 miles from Chloride to Rioville on the Colorado River is planned. Locomotives, 3; passenger cars, 1; freight cars, 8.

Stock......Par $100..............................Authorized, $600,000......Issued, $467,000

Transfer office, 31 Nassau street, New York. Registrar, Continental Trust Co., New York.

FUNDED DEBT.

1st. mort., 6 per cent., due April, 1929, April and Oct........................?....... $334,000

The 1st mortgage, Continental Trust Co., New York, Trustee, is for $600,000. The balance of the bonds are to be issued as the extensions of the road are completed. There is a sinking fund of 1 per cent. annually after June 1, 1903, bonds to be drawn at 110.

EARNINGS.

Year ending June 30.

| | Gross. | Net. | Charges. | Deficit |
|---|---|---|---|---|
| 1901-02 | $31,811 | $6,885 | $20,040 | $13,155 |

President, F. L. Underwood, New York; Vice-President and General Manager, S. B McConnico, New Orleans; Secretary and Treasurer, R. H. Eggleston, New York.

Directors—F. L. Underwood, H. A. James, R. H. Eggleston, New York; S. B. McConnico, New Orleans; T. B. Comstock, Los Angeles, Cal.

Main office, 31 Nassau street, New York. Annual meeting, second Wednesday in March.

## ARKANSAS SOUTHERN RAILROAD CO.

Road owned, El Dorado, Ark., to Winfield, La., 100 miles. An extension to Sabine Pass, Tex., is planned. Locomotives, 11; passenger cars, 7; freight cars, 118.

Stock......Par $100..................... .....Authorized, $3,100,000......Issued, $1,262,000

Transfer Agent and Registrar, Mississippi Valley Trust Co., St. Louis.

A dividend of 5 per cent. was declared out of the earnings of the year 1902 on the amount of stock outstanding December 31, 1902, which was $750,000.

FUNDED DEBT.

1st. mort., 5 per cent., due July, 1929, Jan. and July.............................. $1,262,000

The trustee of the first mortgage is the Mississippi Valley Trust Co., St. Louis.

EARNINGS.

| | Gross. | Expenses and Charges. | Surplus. |
|---|---|---|---|
| 1902 | $378,266 | $327,215 | $51,051 |

President, J. W. Brown, Camden, Ark.; Vice-President, C. E. Neeley, St. Louis; Secretary, T. G. Gaughan; Treasurer, W. K. Ramsey, Camden, Ark.; General Manager, C. C. Henderson; General Auditor, R. W. Huie, Ruston, La.

Directors—C. C. Henderson, R. W. Huie, Ruston, La.; J. S. Cargile, Jonesboro, La.; J. W. Brown, W. W. Brown, W. K. Ramsey, W. H. Brown, T. J. Gaughan, Camden, Ark.; R. N. Garrett, Cargile, Ark.; Jesse B. Moore, Arkadelphia, Ark.; C. E. Neeley, St. Louis.

Main office, Junction City, Ark.

## THE ATCHISON, TOPEKA & SANTA FE RAILWAY CO.

A corporation formed under the laws of Kansas, December 12, 1895. The company acquired the Atchison, Topeka & Santa Fe Railroad sold under foreclosure December 10, 1895. This company took possession of the property January 1, 1896.

The original company which constructed this road was reorganized without foreclosure in 1889. Receivers were appointed in December, 1893, and a reorganization plan was issued in March, 1895, by a joint committee. The plan is given in detail in the MANUAL for 1901.

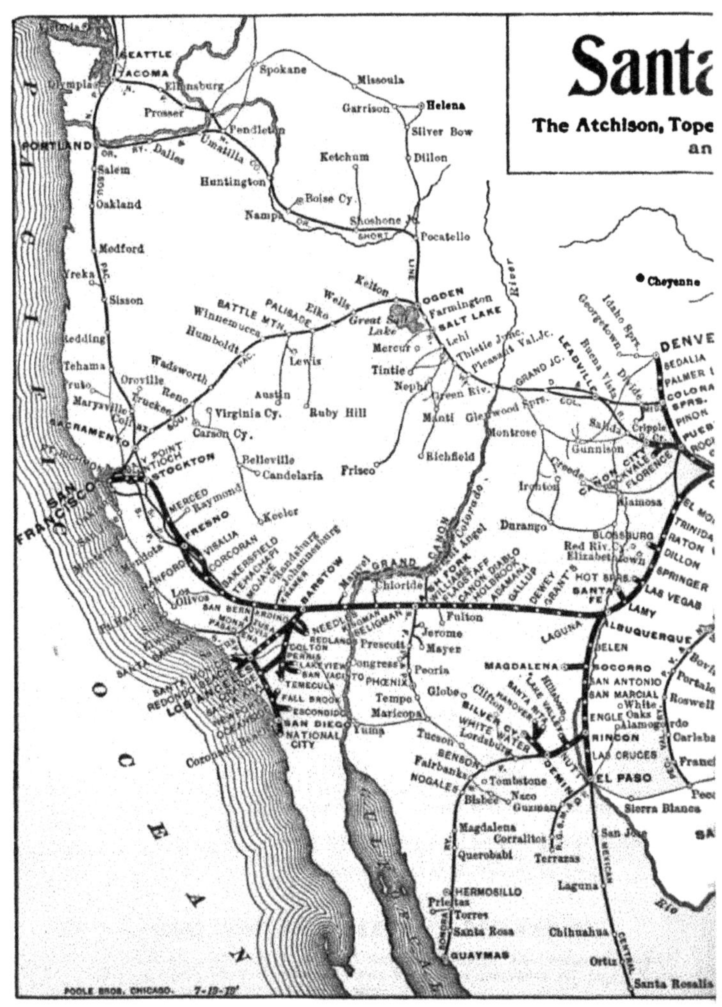
Santa
The Atchison, Tope
an
SEATTLE
TACOMA
Spokane
Missoula
Garrison
Helena
Silver Bow
Ellensburg
Prosser
Pendleton
Umatilla
PORTLAND
Dalles
Salem
Oakland
Medford
Yreka
Sisson
Redding
Tehama
Oroville
Marysville
SACRAMENTO
STOCKTON
SAN FRANCISCO
Ketchum
Dillon
Huntington
Boise Cy.
Nampa
Shoshone
Pocatello
SHORT
LINE
Kelton
OGDEN
Farmington
SALT LAKE
Great Salt Lake
Lehi
Wells
Elko
PALISADE
BATTLE MTN.
Winnemucca
Humboldt
Lewis
Wadsworth
Reno
Truckee
Austin
Virginia Cy.
Ruby Hill
Carson Cy.
Belleville
Candelaria
Keeler
Mercur
Tintic
Nephi
Thistle Junc.
Pleasant Val. Jc.
Green Riv.
Manti
Richfield
Frisco
Glenwood Sprs.
GRAND JC.
LEADVILLE
Montrose
Gunnison
Salida
Buena Vista
Georgetown
Idaho Sprs.
Divide
Cheyenne
DENVER
SEDALIA
PINON
Cripple Cr.
Creede
Ironton
CANON CITY
FLORENCE
Alamosa
Durango
BLOSSBURG
Red Riv. Cy.
Elizabethtown
TRINIDAD
RATON
DILLON
SPRINGER
LAS VEGAS
HOT SPRS.
SANTA FE
LAMY
River
Colorado
CANON
GRAND
Chloride
MERCED
Raymond
FRESNO
VISALIA
CORCORAN
HANFORD
Mendota
BAKERSFIELD
TEHACHAPI
MOJAVE
Randsburg
Johannesburg
BARSTOW
Marvel
Los Olivos
SAN BERNARDINO
MONROVIA
PASADENA
NEEDLES
KINGMAN
SELIGMAN
REDLANDS
COLTON
PERRIS
LAKEVIEW
SAN JACINTO
TEMECULA
FALL BROOK
ESCONDIDO
SAN DIEGO
NATIONAL CITY
Coronado Beach
SANTA MONICA
REDONDO BEACH
LOS ANGELES
ORANGE
SANTA ANA
NEWPORT
OCEANSIDE
SANTA BARBARA
WILLIAMS
FLAGSTAFF
CANON DIABLO
HOLBROOK
ADAMANA
GALLUP
DEWEY
GRANT'S
Fulton
Jerome
Mayer
Prescott
Congress
Peoria
PHOENIX
Tempe
Maricopa
Globe
Yuma
Tucson
BENSON
Fairbanks
NOGALES
Tombstone
Bisbee
Naco
Guzman
Clifton
SILVER CY.
WHITE WATER
Lordsburg
DEMING
LAGUNA
ALBUQUERQUE
BELEN
MAGDALENA
SOCORRO
SAN ANTONIO
SAN MARCIAL
ENGLE
RINCON
LAS CRUCES
EL PASO
White Oaks
Alamogordo
Roswell
Carlsbad
Sierra Blanca
San Jose
Magdalena
Corralitos
Querobabi
Terrazas
HERMOSILLO
Prietas
Torres
Santa Rosa
GUAYMAS
Laguna
Chihuahua
Ortiz
Santa Rosalia
MEXICAN CENTRAL
P A C I F I C
O C E A N
POOLE BROS. CHICAGO.

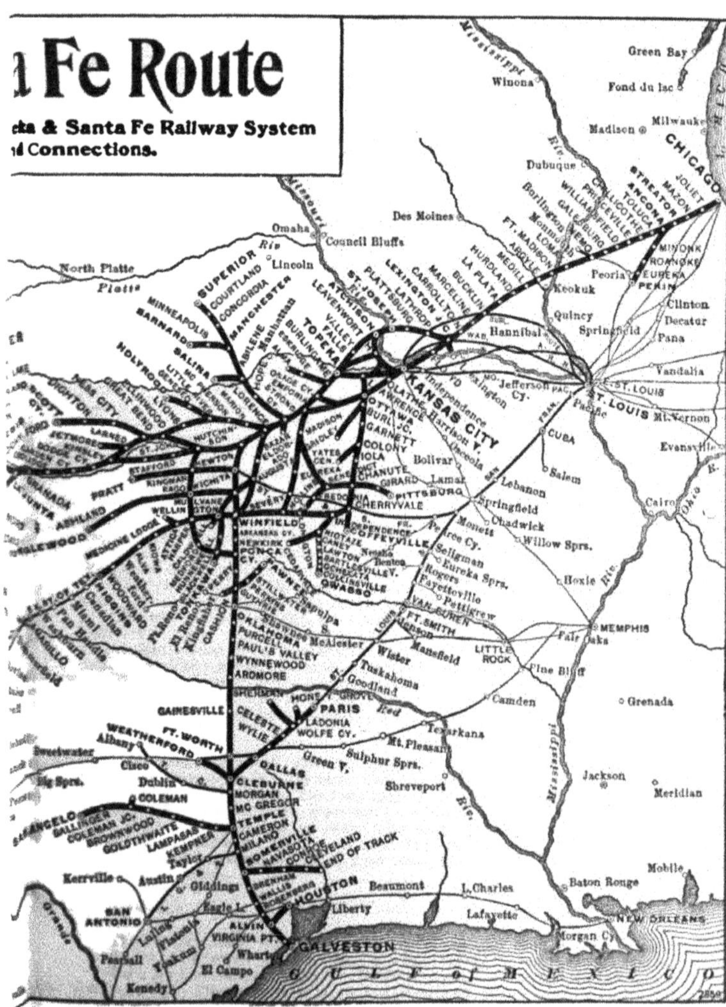

a Fe Route
eka & Santa Fe Railway System
d Connections.
Green Bay
Winona
Fond du lac
Madison
Milwaukee
CHICAGO
Dubuque
Des Moines
Omaha
Council Bluffs
Lincoln
North Platte
Platte
SUPERIOR
TOPEKA
KANSAS CITY
Hannibal
Keokuk
Quincy
Springfield
Peoria
Clinton
Decatur
Pana
Vandalia
ST. LOUIS
Mt. Vernon
Evansville
Jefferson Cy.
CUBA
Salem
Lebanon
Springfield
Chadwick
Willow Sprs.
Cairo
Bolivar
Lamar
PITTSBURG
CHERRYVALE
WINFIELD
COFFEYVILLE
PONCA CY.
Monett
Seligman
Eureka Sprs.
Rogers
Fayetteville
VAN BUREN
FT. SMITH
Hoxie
MEMPHIS
Fair Oaks
LITTLE ROCK
Pine Bluff
Mansfield
Wister
Tuskahoma
Goodland
McAlester
OKLAHOMA
PURCELL
PAUL'S VALLEY
WYNNEWOOD
ARDMORE
GAINESVILLE
PARIS
LADONIA
WOLFE CY.
Texarkana
Mt. Pleasant
Sulphur Sprs.
Camden
Grenada
Jackson
Meridian
Shreveport
FT. WORTH
WEATHERFORD
Albany
Sweetwater
Big Sprs.
Cisco
Dublin
DALLAS
CLEBURNE
MORGAN
MC GREGOR
TEMPLE
CAMERON
MILANO
SOMERVILLE
NAVASOTA
CLEVELAND
END OF TRACK
COLEMAN
SAN ANGELO
BROWNWOOD
GOLDTHWAITE
LAMPASAS
KEMPNER
Taylor
Austin
Giddings
Kerrville
SAN ANTONIO
Eagle L.
HOUSTON
Beaumont
L. Charles
Lafayette
Liberty
ALVIN
VIRGINIA PT.
GALVESTON
Wharton
El Campo
Yoakum
Pearsall
Kenedy
Baton Rouge
Mobile
NEW ORLEANS
Morgan Cy.
GULF of MEXICO
Mississippi
2859

This company's system of lines extends from Chicago via Kansas City to San Francisco and San Diego, Cal., with branches to Galveston, Tex., Denver, Col., and El Paso, Tex., besides local extensions in Kansas, Texas, California and other States. Total operated June 30, 1902, 7,876.70 miles, made up as follows: Atchison, Topeka & Santa Fe Railway, 4,843 miles; Gulf, Colorado & Santa Fe Railway (Galveston, Tex., to Purcell, I. T., and branches), 1,177 miles; Southern California Railway, 478 miles; Santa Fe Pacific Railroad, 815 miles; San Francisco & San Joaquin Valley Railway, 372 miles. The Southern Kansas Railway of Texas, 129 miles, is operated under its own organization, but for convenience its mileage is in the company's reports included in that of the Atchison, Topeka & Santa Fe. Of the mileage operated, 405 miles is not owned, and 350 miles is owned but not operated.

In April, 1886, the old company purchased the Gulf, Colorado & Santa Fe, exchanging stock, share for share. In 1887 the Chicago line, under title of Chicago, Santa Fe & California, was constructed.

In October, 1898, this company secured control of the San Francisco & San Joaquin Valley Railroad, Stockton, Cal., to Bakersfield, Cal., 235 miles, and branch, 69 miles, and in 1899-1900 constructed an extension of 70 miles, from Stockton to Point Richmond, on San Francisco Bay. Also in 1899 secured trackage over the Southern Pacific from Bakersfield, Cal., to Mojave, Cal., 68 miles. From Point Richmond to Market street, San Francisco, the company has a ferry, 7¾ miles. The new line is in all 372 miles, and was opened for traffic July 1, 1900.

The Santa Fe Pacific was formerly the Atlantic & Pacific, Western Division, Isleta, N. M., to The Needles, Cal., 563 miles. In 1897 the Atchison acquired this road and reorganized it under the present title. In the same year this company made an exchange of the Sonora Railway and the New Mexico & Arizona, 350 miles, for the Mojave Division of the Atlantic & Pacific, the Needles, Cal., to Mojave, Cal., 242 miles, which was owned by the Southern Pacific and operated since 1884 under lease by the Atlantic & Pacific.

In November, 1899, it acquired the Hutchinson Southern Railway, Hutchinson, Kan., to Cross, O. T., 142 miles. In July, 1900, purchased control of the Gulf, Beaumont & Kansas City Railroad, 71 miles. In January, 1901, a controlling interest in the Pecos Valley & Northeastern, 372 miles, was acquired.

Locomotives, 1,312; passenger cars, 752; freight cars, 34,201.

Stock..Par $100..Authorized { com., $102,000,000 / pref., 131,486,000 } Issued { com., $102,000,000 / pref., 114,199,530 } $216,199,530

The preferred stock is entitled to 5 per cent., non-cumulative, dividends. The unissued preferred stock, $17,286,470, is held in special trusts for the acquisition of auxiliary lines and for improvements and extensions.

Transfer agencies, 59 Cedar street, New York; Boston Safe Deposit & Trust Co., Boston. Registrars, Guaranty Trust Co., New York; Old Colony Trust Co., Boston.

The first dividend on the preferred stock of the present company was declared in December, 1898. It was 1 per cent., payable January 26, 1899. Another dividend of 1¼ per cent. on the preferred was paid July 26, 1899, and a semi-annual dividend of 1½ per cent. was declared payable February 1, 1900. A semi-annual dividend of 2½ per cent. on the preferred was paid August 1, 1900, and another of the same amount February 1, 1901, thus putting the preferred on a 5 per cent. basis. The preferred dividends are now 2½ per cent. semi-annual, February 1 and August 1.

The first dividend on the common stock was 1½ per cent. semi-annual, paid June 18, 1901. On December 2, 1901, 2 per cent. semi-annual was paid on the common, and dividends of the same amount have since been regularly paid on the common in June and December.

**Funded Debt.**

| | |
|---|---|
| New gen. mort., 4 per cent., due Oct., 1995, April and Oct. | $138,728,500 |
| Adjustment income bonds, 4 per cent., due July, 1995 | 51,728,000 |
| Serial debentures, 4 per cent., due Feb., 1903-14, Feb. and Aug. | 27,500,000 |
| Chicago & St. Louis, 1st mort., 6 per cent., due March, 1915, March and Sept. | 1,500,000 |
| Chic., Santa Fe & California, 1st mort., 5 per cent., due Jan., 1937, Jan. and July. | 629,000 |
| Hutchinson Southern, 1st mort., 5 per cent., due Jan., 1928, Jan. and July | 195,000 |
| San Fran. & San Joaquin, 1st mort., 5 per cent., due Oct., 1940, April and Oct. | 6,000,000 |
| Miscellaneous bonds | 4,810 |
| Total | $226,285,310 |

The reorganization of 1895 provided for $17,000,000 prior lien 4 per cent. bonds to be ssued prior to November 30, 1900, which time limit having expired the bonds cannot now be issued.

The 4 per cent. adjustment income bonds were non cumulative until July 1, 1900, and cumulative thereafter. Interest on these bonds was payable out of net earnings of each fiscal year up to 4 per cent., the rate to be determined in October each year. In 1899 at request of holders of a large amount of these bonds an agreement was formulated, dated September 14, 1899, by which semi-annual payments are made on bonds whose holders accept the agreement, the same being stamped on assenting bonds and semi-annual coupon sheets attached. A charge of 1 per cent. was at first made for such stamping, but the company in 1901 announced that holders of adjustment bonds could assent and have their bond stamped without expense.

The debenture bonds were issued February 1, 1902, and fall due—$2,500,000—on February 1 each year from 1903 to 1914. They were issued to pay for properties acquired and to provide for improvements and additional equipment.

There were $18,500,000 new general 4s reserved to retire old underlying bonds, guarantee fund notes and car trusts, $20,000,000 to acquire certain auxiliary properties and $30,000,000 for improvements at rate of $3,000,000 a year. Additional preferred stock to amount of $20,000,000 if necessary for acquisitions of auxiliary roads in the system was provided for.

In February, 1903, it was stated that the company contemplated an issue of $10,000,000 bonds secured on extensions and branch lines in Oklahoma and elsewhere to defray the cost of the same.

In January, 1897, the company purchased the $16,000,000 of Atlantic & Pacific 4 per cent. (Western Division) bonds held by the committees representing those bonds, for 52½ per cent. in Atchison 4 per cent. general mortgage bonds and 57½ per cent. in preferred stock, amounting to $8,400,000 of general 4s and $9,200,000 of preferred, the Atchison Company also paying $530,000 cash and assuming payment of the Atlantic & Pacific receivers' floating debt, amounting to $747,417. The acquisition of the Santa Fe & San Joaquin Valley Railway in October, 1898, involved the purchase of its $2,465,200 of capital stock at par and the assumption of its bonds.

## EARNINGS.

Year ending June 30.

| | Gross. | Per Cent. Oper. Exp. | Net. | Charges. | Surplus. |
|---|---|---|---|---|---|
| 1892–93 (7,480 miles)....... | $41,316,546 | 73.08 | $12,710,747 | $9,145,152 | $1,380,582 |
| 1893–94 (8,756 " )....... | 40,862,142 | 75.61 | 11,205,561 | ...... | ...... |
| 1894–95 (8,752 " )....... | 38,490,480 | 77.44 | 9,518,736 | ...... | ...... |
| 1895–96 (6,435 " )....... | 28,999,597 | 76.11 | 6,928,322 | ...... | ...... |
| 1896–97 (6,479 " )....... | 30,621,230 | 74.68 | 6,061,303 | 4,608,858 | 1,452,445 |
| 1897–98 (6,946 " )....... | 39,214,099 | 72.69 | 8,882,573 | 4,992,148 | 3,890,424 |
| 1898–99 (7,108 " )....... | 40,513,498 | 68.14 | 11,429,969 | 5,188,132 | 6,241,837 |
| 1899–00 (7,341 " )....... | 46,232,028 | 59.53 | 17,084,471 | 7,345,166 | 9,739,304 |
| 1900–01 (7,807 " )....... | 54,474,822 | 59.23 | 20,305,339 | 7,830,810 | 12,474,529 |
| 1901–02 (7,855 " )....... | 59,135,085 | 57.34 | 24,003,511 | 8,438,985 | 15,564,526 |

In November, 1897, company paid 3 per cent. on the adjustment bonds. In November, 1898, paid full 4 per cent. in same, amounting to $2,053,840, out of surplus for year ending June 30, 1898. In 1898-99 also paid full interest on the adjustments, $2,053,840, leaving a surplus of $4,187,997. Surplus from previous year, $226,494; total surplus June 30, 1899, $4,414,491. Dividend, 1¼ per cent., on preferred stock paid July 26, 1899, $1,427,071; balance surplus, $2,987,420. On June 30, 1900, the total surplus was $9,994,619, out of which 2 per cent. was paid in on the preferred stock, or $2,854,345, leaving a credit balance to profit and loss of $7,140,274. In 1901-02 the dividends of 5 per cent. on the preferred stock and 4 per cent. on the common amounted to $4,893,455, leaving a surplus of $10,671,071, out of which $2,750,000 was appropriated for constructions, improvements, etc. The total surplus credited to profit and loss June 30, 1902, was $16,027,415.

The following presents the comparative freight traffic statistics of the company:

| | Mileage. | Total Tonnage. | Tons Carried One Mile. | Freight Density. | Rate per Ton per Mile. | Earnings per Train Mile. | Average Tons per Train Mile. |
|---|---|---|---|---|---|---|---|
| 1896-97.... | 6,479 | 8,578,802 | 2,307,795,339 | 356,121 | 1.051c | $1.50 | 140 |
| 1897-98.... | 6,946 | 9,979,509 | 2,779,555,249 | 400,166 | 1.029 | 1.46 | 142 |
| 1898-99.... | 7,108 | 8,924,678 | 2,893,011,496 | 407,007 | 1.019 | 1.64 | 161 |
| 1899-00.... | 7,341 | 9,893,018 | 3,454,591,785 | 470,588 | 0.976 | 2.16 | 221 |
| 1900-01.... | 7,807 | 11,112,614 | 3,876,793,344 | 496,579 | 1.007 | 2.44 | 242 |
| 1901-02.... | 7,855 | 11,596,093 | 4,231,748,520 | 538,733 | 0.988 | 2.53 | 247 |

In 1898-99, 1899-1900, 1900-01 and 1901-02 all company's freight is excluded from the tonnage statistics.

## GROSS AND NET EARNINGS BY MONTHS FOR THREE YEARS.

| | 1900. | | 1901. | | 1902. | |
|---|---|---|---|---|---|---|
| | Gross. | Net. | Gross. | Net. | Gross. | Net. |
| January........ | $3,678,665 | $1,466,796 | $4,416,836 | $1,749,161 | $4,878,152 | $1,990,263 |
| February....... | 3,517,989 | 1,345,004 | 4,142,989 | 1,510,260 | 4,277,497 | 1,696,711 |
| March.......... | 3,869,138 | 1,632,336 | 4,638,722 | 1,752,942 | 4,794,270 | 2,059,142 |
| April........... | 3,808,402 | 1,561,697 | 4,874,745 | 2,010,215 | 4,953,237 | 2,105,739 |
| May ........... | 3,983,550 | 1,777,082 | 4,837,478 | 2,038,889 | 4,911,389 | 2,070,201 |
| June........... | 3,846,136 | 1,584,983 | 4,617,434 | 2,139,133 | 4,444,283 | 1,831,117 |

GROSS AND NET EARNINGS BY MONTHS FOR THREE YEARS.—*Continued.*

| | 1900. | | 1901. | | 1902. | |
|---|---|---|---|---|---|---|
| | Gross. | Net. | Gross. | Net. | Gross. | Net. |
| July ............ | $3,697,051 | $1,322,471 | $4,763,502 | $1,993,249 | $4,596,708 | $1,476,568 |
| August .......... | 4,253,840 | 1,526,336 | 4,941,078 | 2,069,277 | 4,858,285 | 1,600,523 |
| September ...... | 4,389,555 | 1,769,104 | 5,012,230 | 2,201,795 | 5,141,070 | 1,766,328 |
| October ........ | 5,070,447 | 2,241,454 | 5,390,922 | 2,407,696 | 5,910,930 | 2,487,690 |
| November...... | 4,779,095 | 2,071,004 | 5,439,579 | 2,489,228 | 5,648,192 | 2,331,347 |
| December.... .. | 4,756,629 | 2,080,905 | 5,328,953 | 2,311,395 | 5,539,866 | 2,215,363 |
| Totals ....... .. | $49,650,497 | $20,379,172 | $58,604,468 | $25,703,234 | 57,953,879 | 23,630,992 |
| Aver. per month. | 4,137,541 | 1,698,264 | 4,883,705 | 2,141,936 | 4,829,489 | 1,969,249 |

Chairman Executive Committee, Victor Morawetz, New York; President, Edward P. Ripley, Vice-Presidents, E. D. Kenna, Paul Morton, J. W. Kendrick, Chicago; Secretary and Treasurer, Edward Wilder, Topeka, Kan.; Comptroller, D. L. Gallup; Deputy Comptroller, D. J. Sheehan; Assistant Treasurer, H.W. Gardiner; Assistant Secretary, L. C. Deming, New Yok.

Directors—Edward P. Ripley, E. D. Kenna, Byron L. Smith, Chicago; Victor Morawetz, R. Somers Hayes, Edward J. Berwind, Charles Steele, H. Rieman Duval, Thomas P. Fowler, George G. Haven, New York; Howell Jones, Charles S. Gleed, Topeka; Andrew C. Jobes, Wichita, Kan.; Benjamin P. Cheney, Boston; John G. McCullough, Vermont.

Main office, Topeka, Kan.; New York office, 59 Cedar street; Chicago office, 77 Jackson boulevard. Annual meeting, second Thursday in December, at Topeka. Books close thirty days before.

## ATLANTA & WEST POINT RAILROAD CO.

Road owned, Atlanta to West Point, Ga., 86 miles. The company also leases and operates a belt line, 5 miles, around the city of Atlanta. Locomotives, 15; passenger cars, 23; freight cars, 378.

Stock......Par $100..........................Authorized, $1,232,200......Issued, $1,232,200

Dividends of 6 per cent. per annum were paid on the stock, the dividend periods being January and July. In October, 1899, the company paid an extra dividend of 25 per cent.

FUNDED DEBT.

Debenture certificates, redeemable at company's option, 6 per cent., Jan. and July.... $1,232,200

The Georgia Railroad owns $494,500 of the stock of this company and $388,900 of the debenture certificates.

EARNINGS.

| Year ending June 30. | Gross. | Net |
|---|---|---|
| 1899-00.................................................... | $702,475 | $267,705 |
| 1900-01.................................................... | 740,689 | 255,008 |
| 1901-02.................................................... | 788,637 | 317,814 |

President, Charles A. Wickersham; Secretary and Treasurer, F. H. Hill; Auditor, F. A. Healy, Atlanta, Ga.

Directors—Charles A. Wickersham, Atlanta, Ga.; John M. Egan, Savannah; W. B. Berry H. C. Fisher, Newman, Ga.; Milton H. Smith, Louisville; Harry Walters, Wilmington, N. C. J. F. Hanson, Macon, Ga.

Main office, Atlanta, Ga. Annual meeting, second Tuesday in September.

## ATLANTA, KNOXVILLE & NORTHERN RAILWAY CO.

(Controlled by Louisville & Nashville Railroad Co.)

Road owned, Marietta, Ga., to Knoxville, Tenn., 205 miles, branch, 26 miles; trackage, Marietta to Atlanta, 20 miles; total, 251 miles. Locomotives, 22; passenger cars, 17; freight cars, 290.

In 1902 control of the company was acquired by the Louisville & Nashville Railroad Co., which began the construction of a line from Jellico, Ky., to a connection with this company's line at Knoxville.

Stock......Par $100............. { com., $3,000,000 / pref., 1,500,000 } Issued { com., $3,000,000 / pref., 1,500,000 } $4,500,000

The preferred stock is 5 per cent., non-cumulative.

FUNDED DEBT.

1st mort., 5 per cent., due Dec., 1946, June and Dec. .............................. $1,000,000

Originally the Marietta & North Georgia, which company defaulted in 1891 and Receiver was appointed. The road was reorganized in 1896 and this company took possession November 1, 1896. For details of reorganization, see MANUAL for 1899.

Holders of $984,000 of 1st mortgage bonds funded their coupons from December, 1897, to June, 1899, inclusive, in 5 per cent. scrip, redeemable at company's option.

The company had an issue of $1,500,000 5 per cent. income bonds due 1947. In 1901 these bonds were exchanged for preferred stock. In March, 1902, an issue of 4 per cent. consolidated mortgage bonds, due 2002, interest March and September, was authorized at the rate of $10,000 per mile, $1,000,000 of the same being reserved to retire the 1st mortgage 5 per cent. bonds.

EARNINGS.

| Year ending June 30. | Gross. | Net. |
|---|---|---|
| 1897–98 | $328,097 | $113,184 |
| 1898–99 | 352,952 | 88,463 |
| 1899–00 | 418,354 | 113,111 |
| 1900–01 | 482,592 | 138,785 |

Net earnings in 1898 include miscellaneous income, $19,843; in 1899, $15,803; in 1900, $6,227.

President, Milton H. Smith, Louisville; Vice-President and General Manager, J. H. Ellis; Secretary and Treasurer, H. W. Oliver, Knoxville.

Directors—Milton H. Smith, J. H. Ellis, Louisville; Alexander W. Smith, Henry S. Johnson, George M. Brown, T. A. Hammond, Atlanta, Ga.; J. H. Ringgold, Knoxville.

Main office, Knoxville; New York office, 120 Broadway. Annual meeting, second Wednesday in January.

## ATLANTIC & BIRMINGHAM RAILROAD CO.

Road owned, Waycross, Ga., to Cordele, Ga., 108 miles. Extensions to Birmingham, Ala., and to Brunswick, Ga., are contemplated. Locomotives, 10; passenger cars, 11; freight cars, 100.

This company was formerly the Waycross Air Line Railroad, the name having been changed to the present style in 1901.

Stock ................Authorized { com., $3,540,000; pref., 3,540,000 } Issued { com., $666,400; pref., 700,000 } $1,366,400

The preferred stock is 5 per cent., non-cumulative.

Transfer Agent, W. J. Swain, Waycross, Ga.

FUNDED DEBT.

1st mort., 5 per cent., due July, 1920, Jan. and July .................................. $593,000

The authorized amount of the 1st mortgage is $1,400,000. Trustee, Farmers' Loan & Trust Co., New York, at which institution the interest is paid. It is provided that bonds in addition to the $500,000 outstanding can be issued only at the rate of $5,000 per mile for new road. Of this amount outstanding $150,000 have a prior lien and can be called after 5 years at 110. The company has $28,000 of car trust obligations.

EARNINGS.

| Year ending June 30. | Gross. | Net. |
|---|---|---|
| 1900–01 | $81,470 | $26,561 |
| 1901–02 | 147,400 | 65,405 |

The surplus over charges in 1900–01 was $3,288. In 1901–02 surplus $40,405.

President, W. G. Raoul, New York; Vice-President, George Dole Wadley; Secretary, W. J. Swain; Treasurer, First National Bank, Waycross, Ga.

Directors—W. G. Raoul, Percy R. Pyne, New York; George Dole Wadley, Alexander Bonnyman, W. J. Swain, Waycross, Ga.; B. H. Williams, James Swann, Atlanta, Ga.

Main office, Waycross, Ga.; President's office, 1 Nassau street, New York. Annual meeting, first Monday in August, at Waycross, Ga.

## ATLANTIC & DANVILLE RAILWAY CO.

(Leased to Southern Railway.)

Road owned, West Norfolk, Va., to Danville, Va., 205 miles; branch, James River Junction to Claremont, Va. (narrow gauge), 52 miles; other branches, 26 miles; total owned, 283 miles trackage, 1½ miles; total operated, 284½ miles.

In 1899, the Southern Railway Co. leased the road from September 1, 1899, to July 1, 1949.

Stock......Par $100..........................Authorized, $2,180,800.......Issued, $2,180,800

Transfer Agent, secretary of company, Norfolk, Va.

FUNDED DEBT.

1st mort., 4 per cent., due July, 1948, Jan. and July................................ $3,925,000

Trustee of mortgage and fiscal agent, Mercantile Trust Co., New York.

The 1st mortgage 4s were issued in 1900 in conformity with the lease to the Southern Railway, and the old 5 per cent. bonds, which were $1,238,000, and the $3,099,200 of 5 per cent. preferred stock were retired with the same; the retirement of the preferred to exten over a series of years. The bond issue authorized is $4,425,000, of which $500,000 may be used for improvements.

The Southern Railway paid under lease a rental of $127,000 until 1901; then $157,000 until 1904; $188,000 until 1909; and $218,000 until the end of the lease. Rental is to be increased if additional bonds are issued.

Road was built in 1883-1890. Defaulted and Receiver appointed 1891. Sold under foreclosure 1894, and purchased by English bondholders, who reorganized company in 1894.

Earnings are included in those of the lessee.

President, B. Newgass, London, Eng.; Vice-President, C. O. Haines; Secretary and Treasurer, Adam Treadwell, Norfolk, Va.

Main office, Norfolk, Va. Annual meeting, third Tuesday in November.

## ATLANTIC & LAKE SUPERIOR RAILWAY CO.

A corporation formed under an act of the Parliament of Canada in 1893. Road owned, Metapedia, Que., to Paspebiac, Que., 100 miles; branches, 32 miles; total, 132 miles. The company also has extensions in progress. Locomotives, 6; passenger cars, 5; freight cars, 58.

Stock......Par $100..........................Authorized, $10,000,000......Issued, $2,602,500

FUNDED DEBT.

1st mort., 4 per cent............................................................ $2,433,333

In the year ending June 30, 1902, the gross earnings of the company were $43,405. The road is operated by the Trustees for the bondholders.

President, J. R. Thibaudeau; Vice-President, William Owens; Secretary, Edgar N. Armstrong, Montreal.

Directors—J. R. Thibaudeau, William Owens, Alfred A. Thibaudeau, R. Mackay, Montreal; W. W. Larue, Quebec; George Ball, Nicolet, P. Q.; R. A. D. Fleming, L. H. de Friese, London, Eng.

Main office, 16 St. Sacrament street, Montreal.

## ATLANTIC & NORTH CAROLINA RAILROAD CO.

A corporation chartered by the State of North Carolina in 1853.

Road owned, Morehead City to Goldsboro, N. C., 95 miles. The company purchased the Atlantic Hotel at Morehead City in 1902. Locomotives, 17; passenger cars, 17; freight cars, 209.

The State of North Carolina owns $1,266,600 of the stock of the company, and the counties of Craven, Lenoir and Pamlico, N. C., also have interests in the stock.

Stock......Par $100..........................Authorized, $1,800,000......Issued, $1,797,200

The company has no preferred stock. Stock is transferred at the company's office, New Bern, N. C. Dividends of 2 per cent. per annum were formerly paid, but have been suspended since 1899.

FUNDED DEBT.

1st. mort., 6 per cent., due July, 1917, Jan. and July................................ $325,000

Interest on the bonds is paid at the National Farmers' & Planters' Bank, Baltimore. The company also has $26,000 of bills payable.

In the year ending June 30, 1901, the earnings of the company were: Gross, $294,878; net, $88,510; charges and improvements, $90,342; deficit, $1,832. In 1901-02, gross, $257,032; net, $85,271; charges and improvements, $75,335; surplus, $9,935.

President, James A. Bryan; Secretary and Treasurer, M. Manly; Auditor, M. L. Willis, New Bern, N. C.

Directors, James A. Bryan, C. M. Busbee, W. H. Smith, L. Harvey, J. C. Parker, T. W. Dewey, R. W. Taylor, R. D. Hooker, Henry Weil, C. E. Foy, Dempsey Wood, E. C. Duncan.

Main office, New Bern, N. C. Annual meeting, fourth Thursday in September.

## ATLANTIC COAST LINE CO.

A corporation formed under the laws of Connecticut, May 29, 1889. It controls through ownership of capital stock or a majority thereof and ownership of bonds a large system of Southern lines, extending from Richmond and Norfolk, Va., to Wilmington, N. C., Charleston, S. C., Augusta, Ga., Savannah, Jacksonville, Fla., Montgomery, Ala., and Tampa, Fla., with numerous branches. The companies controlled are the Atlantic Coast Line Railroad Co., 3,550 miles; Charleston & Western Carolina, 340 miles; Central South Carolina, 40 miles: branches, 50 miles; total controlled, about 4,000 miles. The Richmond, Fredericksburg & Potomac Railroad, 86 miles, was controlled, but this property was in 1901 transferred to the Richmond-Washington Company.

Among the roads controlled are several, formerly known by other titles, which were reorganized under the auspices of this company. See edition of the MANUAL for 1900. In April, 1900, the Atlantic Coast Line Railroad of Virginia was consolidated with the Atlantic Coast Line Railroad of South Carolina, the Wilmington & Weldon Railroad and the Norfolk & Carolina, forming a system of 1,770 miles. In 1902 the Savannah, Florida & Western Railway was consolidated with the Atlantic Coast Line Railroad Co., which added some 2,250 miles to the latter system of roads.

In December, 1898, this company purchased the Cape Fear & Yadkin Valley Railway at foreclosure sale and consolidated 177 miles of same, Wilmington, N. C., to Bennettsville, with the Wilmington & Weldon Railroad Co.

In October, 1902, an arrangement was ratified by which the Atlantic Coast Line Railroad Co. acquired a controlling interest in the stock of the Louisville & Nashville Railroad Co., but that system is operated separately through its own organization.

Stock......Par $100........................Authorized, $30,000,000......Issued $10,000,000

Certificates of indebtedness, 5 per cent. currency, irredeemable, June and Dec........ $5,000,000
Certificates of indebtedness of 1900, 4 per cent., Jan. and July...................... 5,000,000

The 5 per cent. certificates of indebtedness were authorized in 1897, and are $6,000,000 in amount. The $5,000,000 outstanding were issued to reduce the capital stock from $10,000,000 to $5,000,000. On November 1, 1898, a stock dividend of 100 per cent. was declared and issued to stockholders of record at that date, increasing the stock from $5,000,000 to $10,000,000.

The 4 per cent. certificates of indebtedness, of which $10,000,000 are authorized, were created in 1900, and the amount outstanding was distributed as a dividend to the stockholders in January, 1901. The dividend was 100 per cent., and included the $7,500,000 of this company's 4 per cent. certificates and $2,500,000 of Atlantic Coast Line Railroad Co.'s certificates held in this company's treasury. In 1901 the company purchased and retired $2,500,000 of the 4 per cent. certificates.

A dividend of 1½ per cent. was paid in October, 1895. In 1896 paid 3 per cent., in 1897 3½ per cent., in 1898 4 per cent., and 100 per cent. in stock. In 1899 paid 4½ per cent. In 1900 paid 5 per cent. in two half-yearly dividends, March (15) and September. A half-yearly dividend of 2 per cent. was paid March 11, 1901, and 2½ per cent. each was paid September 16, 1901, and March 10, 1902. The dividend paid September 10, 1902, was 2 per cent., quarterly, the same being the rate of the December, 1902, dividend.

Chairman, Henry Walters, New York; President, Warren G. Elliott; Vice-President, Michael Jenkins; Treasurer, Waldo Newcomer; Secretary, R. D. Cronley, Baltimore; Assistant Treasurer, A. Brandegee, New London, Conn.; Assistant Secretary, Goodwin Stoddard, Bridgeport, Conn.

Main office, Bridgeport, Conn.; Chairman's office, 71 Broadway, New York.

---

## ATLANTIC COAST LINE RAILROAD CO.

(Controlled by Atlantic Coast Line Co.)

A corporation chartered in Virginia in 1836 as the Richmond & Petersburg Railroad Co. The name was changed to its present style in April, 1900, as the Atlantic Coast Line Railroad of Virginia merged with it the Richmond & Petersburg Railroad and the Petersburg Railroad. On April 21, 1900, the company consolidated with the Wilmington & Weldon Railroad Co., the Norfolk & Carolina Railroad Co. and the Atlantic Coast Line Railroad Co. of South Carolina, and the name was changed by omission of the words "of Virginia."

In July, 1902, the company consolidated with the Savannah, Florida & Western Railway Co., known as the Plant system, which company controlled by stock ownership the Florida Southern and the Sanford & St. Petersburg Railways, which are operated separately.

In October, 1902, the company acquired ownership of a majority of the stock of the Louisville & Nashville Railroad Co., which system is operated separately by its own management. See below.

Road owned, Richmond, Va., to Tampa, Fla., 896 miles; Norfolk, Va., to Rocky Mount, N. C., 115 miles; Contentna, N. C., to Wilmington, N. C., 105 miles; Wilmington to Sanford, N. C., 116 miles; Sumter, S. C., to Columbia, S. C., 43 miles; Florence, S. C., to Robbins,

S. C., 138 miles; Waycross, Ga., to Montgomery, Ala., 314 miles; Brunswick, Ga., to Albany, Ala., 169 miles; branches, 1,570 miles; total owned, 3,466 miles; leased, Central of South Carolina, 42 miles; other leased lines, 69 miles; total operated, 3,577 miles; trackage, 54 miles; total of system, 3,631 miles. Locomotives, 432; passenger cars, 472; freight cars, 12,443.

This company also owns one-sixth interest in the Richmond-Washington Co., Richmond to Washington, 115 miles. It has a one-half interest in the lease of the Georgia Railroad, 626 miles, and controls both the Florida Southern, 246 miles, and the Sanford & St. Petersburg, 153 miles. The Louisville & Nashville system of over 5,542 miles is controlled, making the total of lines included in or affiliated with the Atlantic Coast Line Railroad Co.'s system about 10,300 miles.

| | | | |
|---|---|---|---|
| Stock....Par $100...Authorized, $100,000,000...Issued | com., | $35,650,000 | $59,770,000 |
| | " Class A, | 1,000,000 | |
| | pref., | 1,770,000 | |
| | 4 per ct. ctfs. | 21,350,000 | |

The preferred stock is entitled to 5 per cent. dividends. This stock, of which there was $18,850,000 was issued in exchange for the stocks of the constituent companies. A majority of the stock is owned by the Atlantic Coast Line Co. of Connecticut and most of it has been exchanged at 125 for the 4 per cent. irredeemable certificates of indebtedness.

The company assumed the A stock of the Richmond & Petersburg Railroad, which is $1,000,000 and which is given above as the common stock, Class A, of this company.

Transfer Agent, Safe Deposit & Trust Co., Baltimore.

The first dividend paid on the preferred stock was 2½ per cent. semi-annual, November 15, 1900. Preferred dividends are now paid semi-annually, 2½ per cent. each, in May (15) and November. An initial dividend of 1 per cent. on the common stock was declared paid January 10, 1901; 1½ per cent. was paid on the common July 10, 1901, and similar amounts January 10 and July 10, 1902; on January 10, 1903, 2 per cent. was paid.

In November an increase of $15,000,000 on the common stock was authorized for the purpose of acquiring the majority stock of the Louisville & Nashville Railroad Co. and $13,500,000 of the stock was issued.

FUNDED DEBT.

| | |
|---|---|
| 1st cons. mort., 4 per cent., due July, 1952, March and Sept | $23,589,000 |
| Collateral trust, L. & N. stock, 4 per cent., due 1952 | 35,000,000 |
| Richmond & Petersburg, 1st mort., 7 per cent., due May, 1915, May and Nov. | 24,500 |
| " " 1st mort., 6 per cent., due May, 1915, May and Nov. | 316,000 |
| " " cons. mort., 4½ per cent., due April, 1940, April and Oct. | 300,000 |
| Petersburg R. R., mort. "A," 5 per cent., due July, 1926, Jan. and July | 868,000 |
| " " mort. "B," 6 per cent., due Oct., 1926, April and Oct. | 800,000 |
| Norfolk & Carolina, 1st mort., 5 per cent., due April, 1939, April and Oct. | 1,320,000 |
| " " 2d mort., 5 per cent., due Jan., 1946, Jan. and July | 400,000 |
| Wilmington & Weldon, general mort., 5 per cent., due July, 1935, Jan. and July | 3,062,000 |
| " " general mort., 4 per cent. due July, 1935, Jan. and July | 938,000 |
| Albemarle & Raleigh, 1st mort., 4 per cent., due Jan., 1944, Jan. and July | 500,000 |
| Wilmington & New Berne, 1st. mort., 4 per cent., due Aug., 1947, Feb. and Aug. | 500,000 |
| Wil. & Weldon, Yadkin Div., 1st mort., 4 per cent., due June, 1949, June and Dec. | 1,800,000 |
| Wil., Col. & Aug. 1st mort. 6 per cent., due June 10, 1910, June and Dec. | 1,600,000 |
| Northeastern R. R. cons. mort., 6 per cent., due Jan., 1933, Jan. and July | 657,000 |
| Atlantic Coast Line of S. C. gen. 1st mort., gold 4 per cent., due July, 1948, Jan. & July. | 5,547,000 |
| Savannah, Florida & Western, 1st mort., 6 per cent., due April, 1924, April and Oct. | 4,056,000 |
| " " " 1st mort., 5 per cent., due April, 1934, April and Oct. | 2,444,000 |
| St. John's River Div., 1st mort., 4 per cent., due Jan., 1934 | 1,500,000 |
| Charleston & Savannah, gen. mort., 7 per cent., due Jan., 1936, Jan. and July | 1,500,000 |
| Brunswick & Western, 1st mort., 4 per cent., due Jan., 1938, Jan. and July. | 3,000,000 |
| Alabama Midland, 1st mort., 5 per cent., due Nov., 1928, May and Nov. | 2,800,000 |
| Silver Springs, Ocala & Gulf, 1st mort., 4 per cent., due 1918, Jan. and July | 1,107,000 |
| Manchester & Augusta, 1st mort., 5 per cent., due 1943, Jan. and July | 9,000 |
| Cheraw & Darlington, 1st mort., 5 per cent., due 1933, April and Oct. | 5,000 |
| Great Pond, W. & B., 1st mort., 7 per cent., due 1907, May | 15,000 |
| Ashley River R. R., 1st mort., 8 per cent., due 1915, Jan. and July | 33,500 |
| Total... | $93,691,000 |

The 1st consolidated mortgage is $80,000,000 authorized and is a first lien on nearly 600 miles of road. The issue was created in 1902, the first coupon being for eight months' interest, payable March 1, 1903. Of the total amount $35,102,000 was reserved to retire prior liens and $13,864,000 for improvements, etc. The bonds outstanding were issued to retire Savannah, Florida & Western 4 per cent. consols and to retire the Atlantic Coast Line 4 per cent. certificates of indebtedness and the 6 and 7 per cent. irredeemable certificates of indebtedness of the Wilmington & Weldon; also to purchase the $12,500,000 preferred stock of the Savannah, Florida & Western and to retire the Brunswick & Western and Charleston & Savannah income bond issues.

Prior to the issue of the 1st consolidated mortgage 4 per cent. bonds this company had $3,000,000 4 per cent. irredeemable income certificates of indebtedness issued to retire the preferred stock of the Atlantic Coast Line Co. of South Carolina. There were also $2,500,000 7 per cent. and $380,000 6 per cent. certificates of indebtedness of the Wilmington & Weldon which this company had assumed.

The collateral trust 4 per cent. mortgage, secured by the majority stock of the Louisville & Nashville Railroad, was created in November, 1902, to carry out the plan for the acquisition of control of that property. The arrangement included also the payment of $10,000,000 in cash, $5,000,000 in Atlantic Coast Line Railroad common stock and $35,000,000 of the collateral trust bonds, the Atlantic Coast Line Railroad Co. obtaining about 306,000 shares out of the total 600,000 shares of Louisville & Nashville stock outstanding.

EARNINGS.

Year ending June 30.

| | Gross. | Net. | Charges. | Surplus. |
|---|---|---|---|---|
| 1899-00 | $7,717,758 | $3,148,953 | $996,548 | $2,152,407 |
| 1900-01 | 7,978,015 | 3,001,186 | 1,235,528 | 1,765,658 |
| 1901-02 | 8,611,152 | 3,872,165 | 1,595,453 | 2,276,712 |

The earnings for 1901-02 do not include those of the Plant system.

Chairman, Henry Walters; President, Robert G. Irwin, New York; Vice-Presidents, Alexander Hamilton, Petersburg, Va.; C. S. Gadsden, Charleston, S. C.; T. M. Emerson, J. R. Kenly; Treasurer, James F. Post, Wilmington, N. C.; Secretary, Herbert L. Borden, New York.

Directors—Michael Jenkins, F. W. Scott, J. H. Estill, M. F. Plant, H. B. Short, Henry Walters, Waldo Newcomer, D. W. Lassiter, E. B. Borden, Donald MacRae, J. J. Lucas, Warren G. Elliott.

Main office, Wilmington, N. C.; New York office, 71 Broadway. Annual meeting, Tuesday after third Monday in November, at Richmond, Va.

---

## BALTIMORE & ANNAPOLIS SHORT LINE RAILROAD CO.

Road owned, Baltimore to Cliffords, Md., 22 miles; branch, 1 mile. Controls Annapolis, Washington & Baltimore Railway, 20 miles. Total operated, 43 miles. Locomotives, 4; passenger cars, 16; freight cars, 46.

Stock......Par $100..........................Authorized $358,000......Issued $358,000

The company also has $500,000 preferred stock, authorized, but has not issued the same.

Dividends are paid on the stock semi-annually, January and July. In 1898, paid 6 per cent.; in 1899, 5 per cent.; in 1900 and 1901, 6 per cent., and in 1902, 7½ per cent. The dividends are half-yearly, 3½ per cent., in January and July.

FUNDED DEBT.

1st mort., 5 per cent., due Dec., 1923, June and Dec................................ $334,000

The Annapolis, Washington & Baltimore was acquired in 1897. That road has no bonded debt.

The 1st mortgage is $400,000 authorized.

EARNINGS.

| Year ending June 30. | Gross. | Net. |
|---|---|---|
| 1900-01 | $93,022 | $34,151 |
| 1901-02 | 105,109 | 34,824 |

President, John Wilson Brown; Vice-President, W. W. Spence; Secretary, Austin McLanahan; Treasurer, William G. Bowdoin, Baltimore.

Directors—John Wilson Brown, Alexander Brown, Arthur George Brown, William G. Bowdoin, W. W. Spence, Austin McLanahan, F. S. Hambleton, H. Carroll Brown, Baltimore; J. L. Busk, New York.

Main office, Baltimore and Calvert streets, Baltimore. Annual meeting, second Wednesday in December.

# BALTIMORE & OHIO
# RAILROAD

**AND CONNECTIONS**

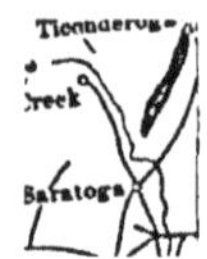
Ticonderoga
Creek
Saratoga

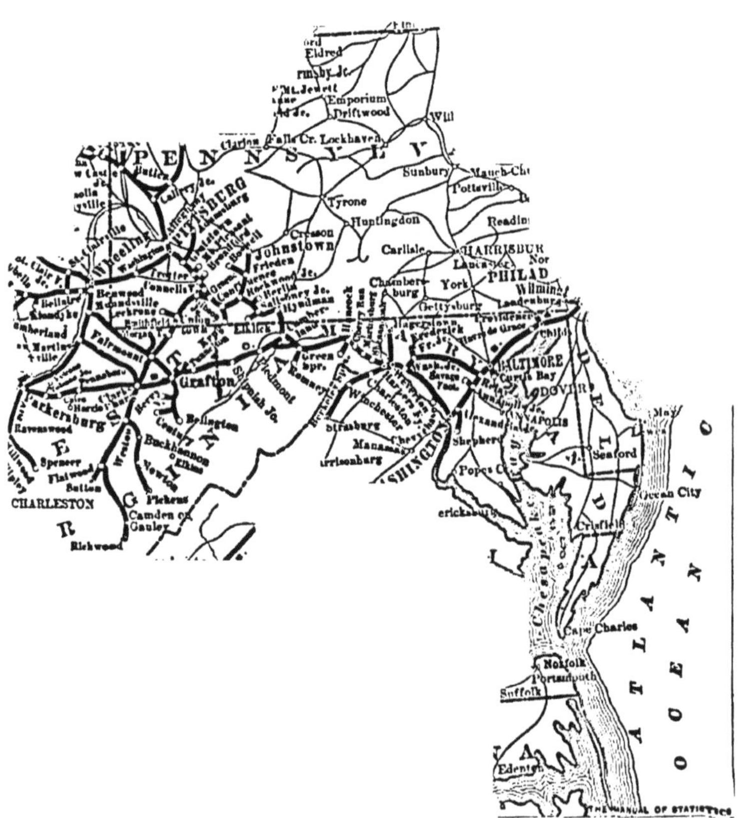
Eldred
Emporium
Driftwood
Lockhaven
PENNSYLV
Sunbury
Pottsville
Tyrone
Huntingdon
Reading
Cresson
Johnstown
Carlisle
HARRISBURG
PITTSBURG
Wheeling
York
PHILAD
Gettysburg
Benwood
Fairmont
Grafton
Piedmont
BALTIMORE
DOVER
Parkersburg
Ravenswood
Winchester
Strasburg
Manassas
Harrisonburg
Buckhannon
Spencer
Sutton
CHARLESTON
Camden on Gauley
Richwood
Seaford
Ocean City
Crisfield
Cape Charles
Norfolk
Portsmouth
Suffolk
Edenton
ATLANTIC
OCEAN
THE MANUAL OF STATISTICS

# BALTIMORE & OHIO RAILROAD CO.

A corporation chartered by the State of Maryland, by act approved February 28, 1827, and chartered by the Commonwealth of Virginia, March 8, 1827.

| Road owned—Main lines: | | Miles. |
|---|---|---|
| Baltimore to Wheeling | 379.42 | |
| Branches | 361.54 | 740.96 |
| Philadelphia Division | | 118.42 |
| Schuylkill River East Side Railroad | | 12.00 |
| Baltimore & New York R.R., Arthur Kill to Cranford, N. J. | | 5.30 |
| Washington Branch | | 31.00 |
| Bay Ridge & Annapolis Railroad | | 4.50 |
| West Virginia & Pittsburg Division | | 176.48 |
| Monongahela Division | | 31.20 |
| Pittsburg Division | | 404.93 |
| Middle Division | | 394.00 |
| Northwestern (Chicago) Division | | 395.39 |
| Southwestern Division (Baltimore & Ohio Southwestern) | | 918.42 |
| Total owned and operated directly | | 3,232.60 |

| Affiliated lines: | Miles. |
|---|---|
| Valley Railroad of Virginia | 62.00 |
| Ohio River Railroad and branches | 281.58 |
| Pittsburg Junction Railroad | 6.92 |
| Pittsburg & Western Railroad | 214.18 |
| Pittsburg, Cleveland & Toledo Railroad | 77.10 |
| Pittsburg, Painesville & Fairport Railway | 53.00 |
| Cleveland Terminal & Valley Railway | 75.47 |
| Cleveland, Loraine & Wheeling Railway | 192.30 |
| Ohio & Little Kanawha Railroad | 74.26 |
| Other lines | 69.23 |
| Total affiliated lines | 1,106.04 |
| Total mileage of system | 4,338.64 |

Controlled through ownership of all the capital stock: Staten Island Rapid Transit Railway, 24 miles. The company uses at Chicago the terminals of the Chicago Terminal Transfer Co. under rental. The company has a running arrangement with the Philadelphia & Reading and Central Railroad of New Jersey between Philadelphia and New York. Locomotives, 1,690; passenger cars, 1,112; freight cars, 82,927. Floating equipment, 139 steamers, tugs and barges. The above includes the equipment of the auxiliary companies.

Stock..Par $100...Authorized { com., $125,000,000; pref., 60 000,000 } Issued { com., $124,262,000; pref., 60,000,000 } $184,262,000

The preferred stock is 4 per cent., non-cumulative. Question having been raised as to whether the preferred was entitled to only 4 per cent. or should share with common in the surplus over that amount, a suit was brought in November, 1900, to test the question, and it was decided that only 4 per cent. could be claimed by the preferred. The dividend periods for both the common and preferred stocks are semi-annual, March 1 and September 1.

Both classes of stock were held in a voting trust, which was dissolved in 1901.

The amount of preferred stock originally authorized was $40,000,000, which was subsequently increased to $60,000,000. The common stock was originally $45,000,000, authorized, which was increased to $60,000,000 in February, 1901, to provide for the redemption of the convertible debentures. In November, 1901, it was increased to $100,000,000 to acquire the stocks of auxiliary roads and for improvements. In 1902 it was again increased to $125,000,000. In April, 1900, the common stockholders had the right to new common stock at 80 to the extent of one share for each six shares they held. In December, 1901, the stockholders subscribed for $22,537,200 new common at par, and in September, 1902, the stockholders subscribed at par for 30 per cent. of their holdings in new common stock, adding about $42,500,000 to the amount of the latter outstanding.

Transfer Agent, E. M. Devereux, 2 Wall street, New York. Registrar, Mercantile Trust Co., New York.

### Funded Debt.

| | |
|---|---|
| Prior lien mort., 3½ per cent., due July, 1925, Jan. and July | $71,000,000 |
| 1st mort., 4 per cent., due July, 1948, Jan. and July | 67,500,000 |
| Convertible debentures, 4 per cent., due March, 1911, March and Sept. | 592,000 |
| Pitts. Junc. & Mid. Div., 3½ per cent., due Nov., 1925, May and Nov. | 6,175,480 |
| Southwestern Div. 1st mort., 3½ per cent., gold, due July, 1925, Jan. and July | 43,000,000 |
| Pitts., L. E. & W. V. Sys. refunding mort., 4 per cent., due Nov., 1941, May and Nov. | 20,000,000 |
| Loan of 1853, extended, 4 per cent., due Oct., 1935, April and Oct. | 118,000 |
| Pittsburg & Connellsville, 1st mort. ext., 4 per cent., due July, 1946, Jan. and July | 69,000 |
| Total | $208,454,480 |

### Bonds of Other Companies Guaranteed or Underlying Baltimore & Ohio Bonds.

| | |
|---|---|
| Staten Island Rapid Transit, 1st mort., 6 per cent., due Jan., 1913, April and Oct. | 1,000,000 |
| " " " 2d mort., quar., 4 per cent., due July, 1904, Jan. and July | 2,500,000 |
| Monongahela River Coal mort., 5 per cent., due Dec., 1945, June and Dec. | 924,000 |
| Cent. Ohio, 1st mort., 4½ per cent., due Sept., 1930, May and Sept. | 1,009,000 |
| Sand. Man. & Newark, 1st mort., 7 per cent., due Jan., 1909, Jan. and July | 638,000 |

BONDS OF OTHER COMPANIES—*Continued.*

| | |
|---|---|
| Pittsburg Junction, 1st mort., 6 per cent., due July, 1922, Jan. and July............ | $959,000 |
| " " 2d mort., 5 per cent., due July, 1922, Jan. and July............ | 270,000 |
| " " terminal mort., 5 per cent., due Oct., 1907, April and Oct...... | 219,000 |
| Sch. River, E. Side, 1st mort., 5 per cent., due Dec., 1935, June and Dec.......... | 4,500,000 |
| West Va. & Pitts. 1st mort., 5 per cent., guar., due April, 1990, April and Oct..... | 4,000,000 |
| Monongahela River R. R. 1st mort., 5 per cent., due Feb., 1919, Feb. and Aug.... | 700,000 |
| Pitts., Clev. & Toledo, 1st mort., 6 per cent., due Oct., 1922, April and Oct........ | 2,400,000 |
| Pittsburg & Western, 1st con. mort., 4 per cent., due July, 1917, Jan. and July.... | 3,718,000 |

The prior lien 3½ per cent. bonds are a first lien on the main line and Pittsburg Division, aggregating 1,017 miles. The 1st mortgage 4s are a lien on the Philadelphia and the Chicago & Akron divisions and branches, altogether 570 miles. There are about $8,000,000 car trusts outstanding.

The 4 per cent. convertible debentures were created in February, 1901, to provide funds for construction and improvements. On March 1, 1902, or any subsequent interest date, on thirty days' notice in writing, these bonds were convertible, at the holder's option, into common stock. The company may on any interest day after March 1, 1902, retire these debentures at par and interest. Holders of the common and preferred stocks of record on February 21, 1901, were given the right of subscribing for the convertible debentures at par in the proportion of $1,000 of the same for each 70 shares of stock held. In October, 1902, all but $708,000 of the debentures had been exchanged for stock.

The Pittsburg, Lake Erie & West Virginia refunding 4 per cent. mortgage was issued in February, 1902, in connection with the reorganization of the Pittsburg & Western and the practical consolidation of it and other lines belonging to the system.

An account of the capitalization of the company prior to the reorganization under the plan of June, 1898, with full details of the receivership and reorganization, will be found in the MANUAL for 1902.

A feature of the arrangements in connection with the reorganization was the separate treatment of the leased lines of the system. To this end a supplementary plan was issued in October, 1889, covering the Central Ohio and leased lines, and in December, 1898, a plan for the Baltimore & Ohio Southwestern (see that company). The $15,000,000 of Baltimore & Ohio Pittsburg Junction & Middle Division 3½ per cent. bonds were to be issued in connection with the Central Ohio plan.

For details as to terms under which the Central Ohio bonds and those of its leased lines were exchanged for new securities, see MANUAL for 1900.

Arrangements were made, following the reorganization, with holders of other auxiliary roads in the system. In January, 1899, the holders of Schuylkill River East Side Railroad bonds agreed to give this company an option on their bonds at 110 for two years from December 1, 1898, the Baltimore & Ohio to guarantee 5 per cent. on the bonds to December, 1903, and if option was not exercised to guarantee interest and principal thereof. In 1899 the Staten Island Rapid Transit Railway was reorganized in the interest of this company. See separate statement of that company. In 1898 it was understood that the Pittsburg & Western would be separated from the Baltimore & Ohio system, but in 1899 the reorganization syndicate secured large holdings of that company's bonds and the property was reorganized in this company's interest in 1901. See above in regard to Pittsburg, Lake Erie & West Virginia system bonds of this company.

EARNINGS.

Year ending June 30.

| | | Main Stem and Branches | | | All Lines | |
|---|---|---|---|---|---|---|
| | Div. Paid. | Gross. | Net. | | Gross. | Net. |
| 1893-94........... | 5 | $10,685,629 | $4,107,707 | (2,065 miles) | $22,502,662 | $8,719,829 |
| 1894-95........... | .. | 10,806,337 | 4,142,107 | (2,094 miles) | 22,817,182 | 8,469,324 |
| 1895-96........... | .. | 11,249,986 | 3,714,062 | (2,094 miles) | 23,944,781 | 7,330,359 |
| 1896-97........... | .. | 12,870,977 | 3,583,611 | (2,046 miles) | 25,582,122 | 6,593,990 |
| 1897-98........... | .. | 13,152,222 | 4,304,613 | (2,046 miles) | 27,722,787 | 7,446,696 |
| 1898-99........... | .. | 13,604,312 | 4,399,962 | (2,046 miles) | 28,404,922 | 6,621,599 |

EARNINGS ENTIRE SYSTEM.

Year ending June 30.

| | Div. | | | Per Ct. | | | | |
|---|---|---|---|---|---|---|---|---|
| | Pfd. | Com. | Gross. | Op. Exp. | Net. | Charges. | Dividends. | Surplus. |
| 1899-00... | 4 | 4 | $42,117,405 | 64.58 | $15,468,414 | $8,561,258 | $4,073,560 | $2,833,595 |
| 1900-01... | 4 | 4 | 47,114,430 | 65.89 | 16,756,626 | 9,119,017 | 3,300,000 | 4,337,609 |
| 1901-02... | 4 | 4 | 51,178,060 | 64.26 | 20,374,580 | 9,939,598 | 5,439,848 | 5,005,134 |

The earnings of the entire system for 1899-1900 include the operations of the Baltimore & Ohio Southwestern. From the surplus of $2,833,595 shown for the year there is to be deducted

$293,365 for discount and commissions on securities sold, leaving a net surplus of $2,540,230, which was appropriated for additions and improvements. The net earnings, $15,468,414, include $995,139 representing miscellaneous income. In 1900-01 the net includes $856,793 for miscellaneous receipts, and $2,948,627 was charged to improvements, etc., leaving a surplus for the year of $1,388,985. In 1901-02 the miscellaneous income was $2,290,107, and the amount charged to improvements was $2,500,000.

GROSS AND NET EARNINGS BY MONTHS FOR THREE YEARS.

| | 1900. | | 1901. | | 1902. | |
|---|---|---|---|---|---|---|
| | Gross. | Net. | Gross. | Net. | Gross. | Net. |
| January..... | $3,387,015 | $1,175,106 | $3,995,159 | $1,400,582 | $4,295,374 | $1,448,619 |
| February.... | 3,106,325 | 949,780 | 3,515,683 | 1,092,938 | 3,696,165 | 1,088,669 |
| March....... | 3,616,622 | 1,226,983 | 4,062,500 | 1,464,999 | 4,139,408 | 1,264,483 |
| April....... | 3,469,388 | 1,025,290 | 3,839,615 | 1,238,597 | 4,207,342 | 1,339,445 |
| May......... | 3,636,506 | 1,138,764 | 3,988,649 | 1,255,801 | 4,454,363 | 1,495,189 |
| June........ | 3,677,426 | 1,153,060 | 4,033,036 | 1,454,504 | 4,431,834 | 1,616,257 |
| July........ | 3,542,931 | 916,148 | 4,050,697 | 1,517,725 | 5,176,625 | 2,010,675 |
| August...... | 3,744,578 | 1,224,053 | 4,454,003 | 1,749,435 | 5,549,757 | 2,141,502 |
| September... | 3,813,138 | 1,300,675 | 4,167,390 | 1,532,680 | 5,430,434 | 2,130,629 |
| October...... | 4,110,601 | 1,472,770 | 4,583,533 | 1,867,349 | 5,533,672 | 2,230,663 |
| November... | 3,832,324 | 1,254,268 | 4,274,611 | 1,585,462 | 5,028,634 | 1,874,571 |
| December... | 3,982,588 | 1,435,445 | 4,209,575 | 1,495,193 | 4,949,519 | 1,808,563 |
| Total... | $43,919,442 | $14,272,342 | $49,371,552 | $17,989,052 | $56,893,127 | $20,449,265 |
| Aver. per month | 3,659,953 | 1,189,361 | 4,114,296 | 1,449,087 | 4,741,094 | 1,704,105 |

The monthly figures from July, 1902, to December, 1902, include those of the Pittsburg & Western Pittsburg Junction, Ohio River and West Virginia Short Line roads.

The following presents the comparative freight traffic statistics of the company:

| | Average Mileage. | Total Tonnage | Tons Carried One Mile. | Freight Density. | Rate per Ton per Mile. | Earnings per Train Mile. | Average Tons per Train. |
|---|---|---|---|---|---|---|---|
| 1896-97.. | 2,046 | 18,716,665 | 3,499,075,760 | 1,744,304 | 0.524c | $1.274 | 235 |
| 1897-98.. | 2,046 | 21,986,220 | 4,362,241,046 | 2,144,686 | 0.458 | 1.474 | 314 |
| 1898-99.. | 2,046 | 25,057,178 | 5,137,367,360 | 2,510,932 | 0.390 | 1.412 | 342 |
| 1899-00.. | 2,277 | 28,366,696 | 5,846,897,698 | 2,984,294 | 0.455 | 1.723 | 366 |
| 1900-01.. | 3,220 | 33,528,513 | 7,140,897,000 | 2,217,669 | 0.498 | 1.901 | 381 |
| 1901-02.. | 3,233 | 38,710,216 | 7,495,527,780 | 2,318,443 | 0.515 | 2.012 | 406 |

The first dividend after the reorganization was 2 per cent. on the preferred, paid April 1, 1900. Since that time semi-annual dividends on the preferred have been regularly paid on March 1 and September 1. A dividend of 4 per cent. on the common stock out of the earnings of the fiscal year ending June 30, 1900, was declared payable, 2 per cent. September 4, 1900, and 2 per cent. March 1, 1901, and the common dividends have since been on the same basis with payments semi-annually in March and September.

The old company owned and operated an extensive telegraph system. It also operated an express business on all its lines. In October, 1887, the telegraph lines were sold to the Western Union Telegraph Co. for 50,000 shares of its stock, and the express business was sold to the United States Express Co.

President, L. F. Loree; Vice-President, Oscar G. Murray; Secretary, Custis W. Woolford; Treasurer, J. V. McNeal; General Counsel, John K. Cowen; Comptroller, H. D. Bulkley, Baltimore.

Directors—Jacob H. Schiff, Edward R. Bacon, James Stillman, Martin Erdmann, Edward H. Harriman, Charles Steele, New York; Samuel Rea, John P. Green, Sutherland M. Prevost, Philadelphia; Norman B. Ream, Chicago; James McCrea, Pittsburg; L. Victor Baughman, John K. Cowen, Arthur P. Gorman, Baltimore.

Main office, Baltimore and Calvert streets, Baltimore. Annual meeting, third Monday in November.

---

## BALTIMORE, CHESAPEAKE & ATLANTIC RAILWAY CO.

(Controlled by Pennsylvania Railroad Co.)

Road owned, Claiborne to Ocean City, Md., 87 miles; branch, 1 mile; total, 88 miles. In addition company operates a steam ferry between Baltimore and Claiborne of 45 miles and other steamboat routes on Chesapeake Bay and its affluents aggregating over 1,400 miles. Locomotives, 8; passenger cars, 21; freight cars, 74. Floating equipment comprises 15 steamboats of an aggregate tonnage of nearly 10,000 tons.

Company is a reorganization in 1894 of the Baltimore & Eastern Shore Railroad, sold under foreclosure, and acquired by purchase all the property of the Eastern Shore Steamboat Co., Maryland Steamboat Co., and Choptank Steamboat Co.

In September, 1899, the Pennsylvania Railroad acquired a controlling interest in the stock and $540,000 of the bonds and a management representing that company was elected.

Stock....Par $100.....Authorized { com., $1,000,000; pref., 1,500,000 } Issued { com., $1,000,000; pref., 1,500,000 } $2,500,000

The preferred stock is 5 per cent., cumulative.

Stock is transferred by the secretary of the company, Baltimore. Registrar, Atlantic Trust Co., New York.

FUNDED DEBT.

1st mort., 5 per cent., due Sept., 1934, March and Sept........................... $1,250,000

The trustee of the 1st mortgage is the Atlantic Trust Co., New York.

EARNINGS.

| Year ending August 31. | Gross. | Net. |
|---|---|---|
| 1894-95 | $514,108 | $128,806 |
| 1895-96 | 497,708 | 88,599 |
| 1896-97 | 489,005 | 83,803 |
| 1897-98 | 565,683 | 136,404 |
| 1898-99 | 607,420 | 148,053 |
| 1899-00 | 626,915 | 145,709 |
| 1900-01 | 675,090 | 152,501 |
| 1901-02 | 777,806 | 206,349 |

President, Sutherland M. Prevost, Philadelphia; Vice-President and General Manager, Willard Thompson, Baltimore; Secretary, James R. McClure; Treasurer, Robert W. Smith, Philadelphia.

Main office, Baltimore. Annual meeting, first Wednesday in November.

---

## BANGOR & AROOSTOOK RAILROAD CO.

Road owned, Brownville, Me., to Caribou, Me., 154 miles; Oldtown to Greenville, 76 miles; Ashland Junction to Ashland, 43 miles; Caribou to Van Buren, 33 miles; branches, 65 miles; total operated, 370 miles. In 1902 the company had extensions in progress. Locomotives, 57; passenger cars, 50; freight cars, 3,159.

Stock....Par $100.... Authorized { com., $1,050,000; pref., 1,328,000 } Issued { com., $1,050,000; pref., 64,400 } $1,114,000

The preferred stock is 5 per cent., non-cumulative. All but the amount given above has been retired.

Transfer Agent, Edward Stetson, Bangor, Me.

FUNDED DEBT.

| | |
|---|---|
| 1st mort., 5 per cent., due Jan., 1943, Jan. and July | $3,360,000 |
| 2d mort., 5 per cent., due July, 1945, Jan. and July | 157,000 |
| Cons. refunding mort., 4 per cent., due July, 1951, Jan. and July | 2,813,000 |
| Piscataquis Div. 1st mort., 5 per cent., due Jan., 1943, Jan. and July | 1,500,000 |
| Van Buren Ext., 1st mort., 5 per cent., due Jan., 1943, April and Oct. | 500,000 |
| Aroostook & Nor., 1st mort., 5 per cent., due Oct., 1947, April and Oct. | 225,000 |
| Aroostock County mort., guar. 4½ per cent., due Sept., 1912, March and Sept. | 500,000 |
| " " " " 4½ per cent., due July, 1915, Jan. and July | 228,000 |
| Total | $9,283,000 |

There were also outstanding car trusts for $860,000 at end of 1902.

Company was organized in 1891 and various sections completed, and opened between 1894 and 1896. In 1892 the Bangor & Piscataquis Railroad and its 18 mile branch, the Bangor & Katahdin Iron Works Railway, were leased for interest on the Bangor & Piscataquis bonds and loan from the city of Bangor. The Aroostook Northern is leased for 999 years for 5 per cent. on its bonds. In 1902 the above companies were consolidated with this company.

The second mortgage was created in 1895 to provide for cost of road in excess of 1st mortgage bonds and preferred stock subscriptions, and has been mainly retired with part of the consolidated refunding bonds.

In August, 1901, the consolidated 4 per cent. mortgage for $20,000,000 was created to retire the outstanding bonds and preferred stock and provide for improvements, of which amount $12,500,000 was reserved to retire old bonds and preferred stock, $3,000,000 was to be used for

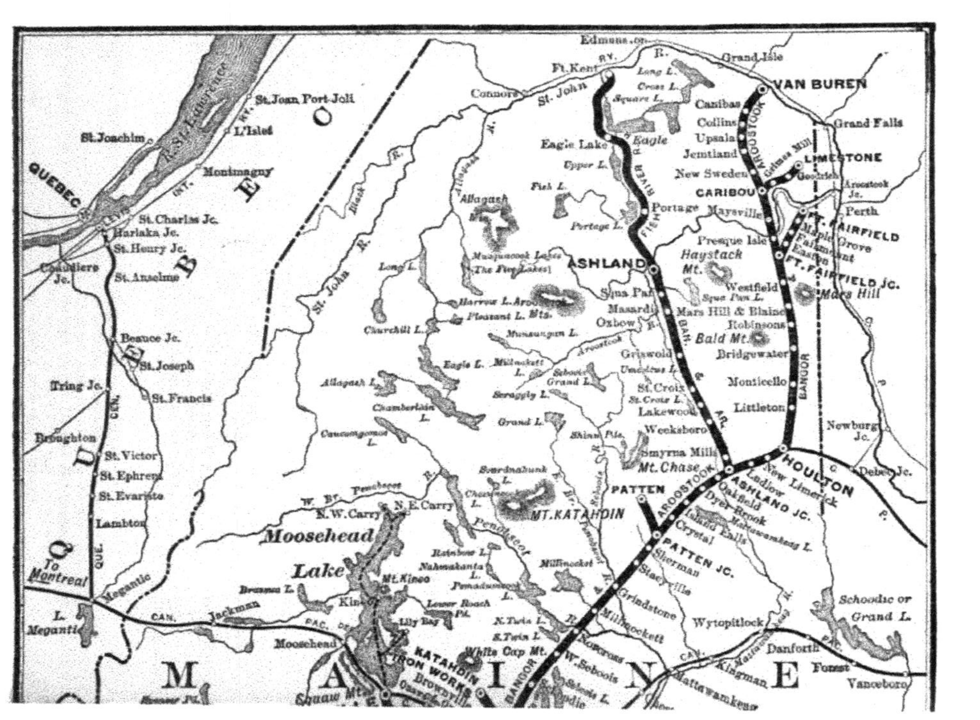

QUEBEC
St. Joachim
R. St. Lawrence
St. Joan Port Joli
L'Islet
Montmagny
St. Charles Jc.
Harlaka Jc.
St. Henry Jc.
St. Anselme
Beauce Jc.
St. Joseph
St. Francis
Tring Jc.
Broughton
St. Victor
St. Evariste
Lambton
To Montreal
Megantic
L. Megantic
Jackman
Moosehead
Moosehead Lake
Mt. Kineo
N. W. Carry
N. E. Carry
Connors
St. John
Ft. Kent
Edmunston
Grand Isle
VAN BUREN
Grand Falls
Caribou
Collins
Upsala
Jemtland
New Sweden
CARIBOU
LIMESTONE
Aroostook Jc.
Perth
Maysville
Presque Isle
FT. FAIRFIELD
Maple Grove
Easton
FT. FAIRFIELD JC.
Mars Hill
Haystack Mt.
Westfield
Mars Hill & Blaine
Robinsons
Bald Mt.
Bridgewater
Monticello
Littleton
Newburg Jc.
HOULTON
New Limerick
Ludlow
ASHLAND JC.
Oakfield
Dyer Brook
Island Falls
Crystal
PATTEN JC.
Sherman
Stacyville
Grindstone
Millinocket
Wytopitlock
Danforth
Forest
Vanceboro
Kingman
Mattawamkeag
Eagle Lake
Portage
Portage L.
ASHLAND
Masardis
Oxbow
Griswold
St. Croix
Lakewood
Weeksboro
Smyrna Mills
Mt. Chase
PATTEN
MT. KATAHDIN
KATAHDIN IRON WORKS
White Cap Mt.
W. Sebois
Allagash
Chamberlain L.
Churchill L.
Eagle L.
Long L.
Schoodic or Grand L.
AROOSTOOK
BANGOR
M A I N E
Q U E B E C

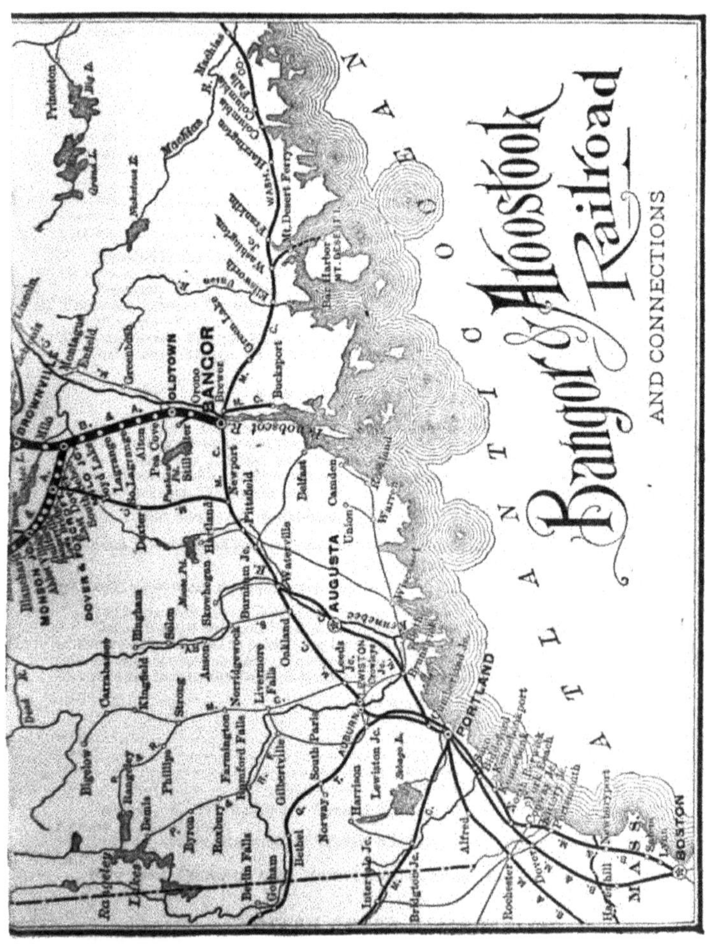
Bangor & Aroostook Railroad
AND CONNECTIONS
ATLANTIC OCEAN
BANGOR
OLDTOWN
AUGUSTA
PORTLAND
BOSTON
BROWNVILLE
LEWISTON
Bar Harbor
Mt. Desert Ferry
Bucksport
Belfast
Camden
Waterville
Pittsfield
Newport
Dexter
Skowhegan
Farmington
Rangeley
Kingfield
Bingham

improvements, and $4,500,000 for additional mileage. Interest on the consolidated refunding bonds is paid at the office of Brown Bros. & Co., New York.

In 1898 this company acquired control of the Bangor & Piscataquis and sold $1,500,000 5 per cent. bonds to retire $600,000 6 per cent. and $325,000 7 per cent. City of Bangor mortgages on the Bangor & Piscataquis maturing April, 1899, also $300,000 Greenville extension 5s due 1913, the balance of issue to be used for improvements. These bonds are secured by a first mortgage of the Bangor & Piscataquis road, now the Piscataquis Division.

EARNINGS.

Year ending June 30.

| | Gross. | Net. | Charges and Betterments. | Surplus. |
|---|---|---|---|---|
| 1895-96 | $699,662 | $256,480 | $229,283 | $27,197 |
| 1896-97 | 754,780 | 291,563 | 272,605 | 18,958 |
| 1897-98 | 779,205 | 324,388 | 292,408 | 31,980 |
| 1898-99 | 929,254 | 356,092 | 307,221 | 48,871 |
| 1899-00 | 1,230,423 | 488,084 | 434,963 | 53,121 |
| 1900-01 | 1,449,455 | 541,032 | 491,424 | 49,608 |
| 1901-02 | 1,708,936 | 607,052 | 552,821 | 54,231 |

Included in the charges were the following amounts for betterments: In 1899-00, $79,020; in 1900-01, $80,000; in 1901-02, $118,741.

President, F. W. Cram, Bangor, Me.; Vice-President, A. A. Burleigh, Houlton, Me.; Treasurer, Edward Stetson; Cashier, F. C. Plaisted, Bangor, Me.

Directors—F. W. Cram, B. B. Thatcher, F. H. Appleton, C. A. Gibson, H. P. Oliver, Edward Stetson, Bangor, Me.; A. A. Burleigh, Houlton, Me.

Main office, Bangor, Me. Annual meeting, third Tuesday in October.

## BAY OF QUINTE RAILWAY CO.

Road owned, Deseronto, Ont., to Deseronto Junction, Napanee to Tweed, Ont., Yarker Junction to Harrowsmith and Sydenham, a total of 65 miles. Has trackage on Grand Trunk between Deseronto Junction and Napanee, 4½ miles, and uses Kingston & Pembroke tracks between Harrowsmith Junction and Kingston, 19 miles; total operated, 88½ miles. Locomotives, 6; passenger cars, 11; freight cars, 148.

Stock......Par $100...... Authorized { com., $650,000 / pref., 325,000 } Issued { com., $650,000 / pref., 325,000 } $975,000

Stock is transferred by the Treasurer of the company.

FUNDED DEBT.

1st mort., 5 per cent., due Jan., 1927, Jan. and July........ $650,000

The preference stock is 6 per cent., non-cumulative.

The authorized amount of the 1st mortgage bonds is $1,000,000, or $10,000 per mile, $350,000 of the bonds being held to provide for future extensions. The bonds are subject to call at 105 and interest after January 2, 1902. Trustee of the mortgage, National Trust Co., Limited, Toronto. Coupons are paid by the Bank of Montreal and its agencies.

EARNINGS.

| | Gross. | Net. | Charges. | Surplus. |
|---|---|---|---|---|
| 1899 | $179,318 | $81,322 | $32,500 | $48,823 |
| 1900 | 193,077 | 93,112 | 32,500 | 60,612 |
| 1901 | 204,699 | 94,109 | 19,902 | 74,206 |
| 1902 | 216,200 | 92,807 | 32,500 | 60,307 |

President, E. W. Rathbun; General Manager, R. C. Carter; Secretary-Treasurer and Auditor, C. A. Millener.

Directors—E. W. Rathbun, E. Walter Rathbun, R. C. Carter, C. A. Millener, Deseronto, Ont.

Main office, Deseronto, Ont. Annual meeting, second Monday in September.

## BEECH CREEK RAILROAD CO.

(Leased to New York Central & Hudson River Railroad Co.)

Road owned, Jersey Shore to Mahaffey Junction, Pa., 113 miles; branches, 48 miles; total, 161 miles; trackage, 33 miles; total operated, 194 miles.

This property is part of the New York Central system. The latter company also leases the

Beech Creek Extension Railroad Co., Clearfield, Pa., to Keating, Pa., 60 miles, and trackage, 50 miles.

Stock......Par $50..........................Authorized, $6,000,000......Issued, $6,000,000

Transfer office, Grand Central Depot, New York.

Dividends of 4 per cent. per annum are paid on the stock, in quarterly payments of 1 per cent. each, in January, April, July and October.

FUNDED DEBT.

| | |
|---|---|
| 1st mort., 4 per cent., due July, 1936, Jan. and July | $5,000,000 |
| 2d mort., 5 per cent., due July, 1936, Jan. and July | 1,000,000 |
| Total | $6,000,000 |

In 1892 an additional issue of $1,000,000 stock and $1,000,000 5 per cent. 2d mort. bonds was authorized, both guaranteed by New York Central, to provide for extensions. In 1893 $500,000 additional stock and $250,000 bonds were issued, in 1894 $250,000 additional bonds, and in 1899 $165,000 new stock for the purchase of the Cambria County Railroad. This company guarantees interest on $749,000 4 per cent. 1st mortgage bonds of the Clearfield Bituminous Coal Co., and owns $825,000 of the latter's stock.

The Beech Creek Extension Railroad Co. has an authorized issue of $4,500,000 3½ per cent. bonds due April, 1951, April and October, which are guaranteed by the New York Central & Hudson River Railroad Co., of which $3,500,000 are outstanding.

EARNINGS.

| Year ending June 30. | Gross. | Net. |
|---|---|---|
| 1895 | $1,273,724 | $578,933 |
| 1896 | 1,376,000 | 718,350 |
| 1897 | 1,416,979 | 755,372 |
| 1898 | 1,540,890 | 772,004 |
| 1899 | 1,391,338 | 611,249 |

Since 1899 earnings are included in those of the New York Central.

In 1890 the New York Central bought all of the stock and leased the road for 999 years from January, 1890, guaranteeing 4 per cent. on the stock and interest on bonds.

President, M. E. Olmsted, Harrisburg, Pa.; Secretary, Warren S. Crane; Treasurer, E. V. W. Rossiter, New York.

Directors—George F. Baer, Reading; M. E. Olmsted, Harrisburg, Pa.; W. K. Vanderbilt, William H. Newman, New York; James Kerr, Clearfield, Pa.; W. D. Kelly, Philadelphia; Charles Miller, Franklin, Pa.

Main office, Jersey Shore, Pa. Annual meeting, first Friday after first Wednesday in May. Books close sixty days previous.

## BELLEFONTE CENTRAL RAILROAD CO.

A corporation formed under the laws of Pennsylvania, January 12, 1892. The company was a reorganization of the Buffalo Run, Bellefonte & Bald Eagle Railroad Co.

Road owned, Bellefonte, Pa., to Pine Grove Mills, Pa., 21 miles; branches, 9 miles; total operated, 30 miles. Locomotives, 3; passenger cars, 10; freight cars, 37.

Stock......Par $50..........................Authorized, $500,000......Issued, $500,000

The company has no preferred stock. Stock is transferred at the company's office, 209 South Third street, Philadelphia. Registrar, Real Estate Trust Co. of Philadelphia. No dividends have been paid on the stock.

FUNDED DEBT.

1st mort., 5 per cent., due Jan., 1924, Jan. and July.......... $48,000

The authorized amount of the 1st mortgage is $200,000. The bonds cover all the property of the company and are free from State tax. They are subject to call at 105. Trustee and agent for the payment of interest, Real Estate Trust Co., Philadelphia.

EARNINGS.

| | Gross. | Net. | Charges. | Surplus. |
|---|---|---|---|---|
| 1902 | $58,464 | $23,097 | $6,262 | $16,834 |

President, Robert Frazer; Vice-President, Theodore M. Etting; Secretary and Treasurer, Thomas R. Osbourn; Superintendent, F. H. Thomas.

Directors—F. F. Milne, R. Dale Benson, Byerly Hart, Theodore M. Etting, Walter Lippincott, Charles S. Whelen, Philadelphia.

Main office, 209 South Third street, Philadelphia. Annual meeting, first Monday in May, at Philadelphia.

## BELLINGHAM BAY & BRITISH COLUMBIA RAILROAD CO.

Road owned, Whatcom, Wash., to Maple Falls, Wash., 42 miles. Extensions are in progress. Locomotives, 5; passenger cars, 4; freight cars, 90.

Stock......Par $100..........................Authorized, $1,000,000......Issued, $1,000,000

FUNDED DEBT.

1st mort., 5 per cent., due Dec., 1932, June and Dec.............................. $500,000

The authorized amount of the 1st mortgage is $1,000,000. Trustee of mortgage, Mercantile Trust Co., San Francisco. A sinking fund of 3 per cent. of the amount of the bonds begins in 1911, but bonds cannot be called under the same.

For the year 1901 the company reported gross earnings, $120,134; net, $48,000.

President, Pierre B. Cornwall; Vice-President and Treasurer, S. P. Smith; Secretary, J. P. Hopkins.

Directors—Pierre B. Cornwall, A. Hayward, S. P. Smith, H. H. Taylor, J. P. Hopkins, Frank G. Dunn, San Francisco; Darius O. Mills, New York.

Main office, 204 Front Street, San Francisco.

## BELT RAILWAY CO. OF CHATTANOOGA

(Leased to Alabama Great Southern Railroad Co.)

Road owned, 25 miles, extending completely around the city of Chattanooga, Tenn., and connecting all the railroads centering there. The company's tracks altogether comprise about 45 miles, including spurs and sidings.

This company is a reorganization in 1895 of the Union Railway of Chattanooga, which was sold under foreclosure.

Stock......Par $100..............................Authorized, $300,000......Issued, $300,000

FUNDED DEBT.

1st mort., 5 per cent., due July, 1945, Jan. and July..... .............................. $275,000

All of the stock is owned by the lessee. The 1st mortgage bonds bore 3 per cent. until July, 1897, 4 per cent. for two succeeding years and 5 per cent. thereafter. They are redeemable after July 1, 1903. There are also $24,000 4 per cent. income bonds, non-cumulative, maturing 1945, which become a fixed charge in 1903.

Control of company was acquired by Alabama Great Southern, which leases property for 50 years from July 1, 1895, guaranteeing as rental interest on bonds and sufficient for taxes and maintenance. Interest is payable at Mercantile Trust & Deposit Co., Baltimore, trustee of mortgage.

President, H. S. Chamberlain, Chattanooga, Tenn.; Secretary, R. D. Lankford, New York; Treasurer, H. C. Ansley, Washington, D. C.

Main office, Chattanooga, Tenn.

## BELVIDERE DELAWARE RAILROAD CO.

(Leased to Pennsylvania Railroad Co.)

Road owned, Trenton to Manunka Chunk, N. J., 67 miles; branches, 15 miles; total, 82 miles.

Stock......Par $50..........................Authorized, $4,000,000......Issued, $1,253,000

Transfer agency, Camden, N. J.

Dividends are regularly paid, those for 1897, 1898, 1899, 1900, 1901 and 1902 being 5 per cent. annual in February.

FUNDED DEBT.

| | |
|---|---|
| Consolidated mort., 4 per cent., due Sept., 1925, March and Sept. | $500,000 |
| Consolidated mort., 4 per cent., due Feb., 1927, Feb. and Aug. | 749,000 |
| Consolidated mort., 4 per cent., due Jan., 1933, Jan. and July | 500,000 |
| Consolidated mort., 3½ per cent., due Jan., 1943, Jan. and July | 1,000,000 |
| Total | $2,749,000 |

First mortgage and 4 per cent. consolidated bonds, due 1925 and 1927, are guaranteed and a majority of stock is owned by United New Jersey Railroad & Canal Cos. The 4s, due 1933, are not guaranteed. Their original amount has been reduced by purchases for the sinking fund. Net earnings are paid as rental. The 1st mortgage extended 6 per cent. bonds matured June 1, 1902, and were paid off.

The 3½ per cent. bonds due 1943 are guaranteed by the United New Jersey Railroad & Canal Cos. and the Pennsylvania Railroad Co.

President, W. H. Wilson; Secretary, F. W. Schwarz; Treasurer, John M. Wood, Philadelphia.

Main office, Broad Street Station, Philadelphia. Annual meeting, third Monday in February.

## BESSEMER & LAKE ERIE RAILROAD CO.

(Controlled by United States Steel Corporation.)

Road owned, under construction in 1902, Salem, Pa., to Kremis, Pa., 10 miles; total owned, 10 miles; leases Pittsburg, Bessemer & Lake Erie Railroad and branches, 203 miles; total, 213 miles.

Stock......Par $100..............................Authorized, $500,000......Issued, $100,000

This corporation, of which all the stock is owned by the Carnegie Company, one of the constituent companies of the United States Steel Corporation, leased for 999 years from April 1, 1901, the entire property of the Pittsburg, Bessemer & Lake Erie Railroad Co. The lease provides for the payment as rental all charges of the leased company, 6 per cent. dividends on its preferred stock and 3 per cent. per annum on the common stock in the hands of the public. The lease is guaranteed by the Carnegie Company.

For further details see statement of the Pittsburg, Bessemer & Lake Erie in this edition of the MANUAL.

President, James H. Reed; Vice-President, D. M. Clemson; Secretary and Treasurer, George W. Kepler, Pittsburg.

Directors—James H. Reed, W. W. Blackburn, D. M. Clemson, Thomas Morrison, D. G. Kerr, George E. McCague, E. H. Utley, Pittsburg; R. A. Francks, Hoboken, N. J.; Elbert H. Gary, New York.

Main office, 434 Fifth avenue, Pittsburg.

## BOSTON & ALBANY RAILROAD CO.

(Leased to New York Central & Hudson River Railroad Co.)

Main line, Boston to Albany, 202 miles; branches owned, 104 miles; leased Pittsfield & North Adams Railroad, Ware River Railroad and North Brookfield Railroad, in all 88 miles; total, 394 miles. Locomotives, 247; passenger cars, 366; freight cars, 5,747.

Stock......Par $100........................Authorized, $30,000,000......Issued, $25,000,000

Stock is transferred at the office of the company, South Terminal Station, Boston.

Dividends of 8 per cent. were paid for many years in quarterly payments of 2 per cent. each in March (31), June, September and December. In declaring the December 30, 1900, dividend, the directors made the same 2¼ per cent., the additional ¼ per cent. being derived from the income of the $5,500,000 3½ per cent. bonds received from the New York Central in payment for surplus assets. It was also decided that the June dividends thereafter should be 2½ per cent., the extra ½ per cent. being the balance of the income from the above source.

FUNDED DEBT.

| | |
|---|---|
| Loan of 1902, 3½ per cent., due April, 1952, April and Oct........................ | $3,858,000 |
| Loan of 1893, 4 per cent., due Oct., 1913, April and Oct........................... | 3,627,000 |
| Loan of 1901, 3½ per cent., due Jan., 1951, Jan. and July.......................... | 1,000,000 |
| Total.................................................................... | $8,485,000 |

The company also guarantees 5 per cent. dividends on $450,000 stock of Pittsfield & North Adams Railroad and 7 per cent. on $750,000 stock of the Ware River Railroad.

The bonds are not secured by mortgage.

Company has an interest in Boston Terminal Railroad Co. and uses the South Terminal Station in Boston.

In June, 1899, a plan was formulated for a lease of the road to the New York Central for 999 years, the lessee assuming all charges, taxes, etc., and guaranteeing 8 per cent. annual dividends (2 per cent. quarterly) on this company's stock. The plan also reserved assets amounting to $4,000,000 for the Boston & Albany stockholders, the New York Central having an option to purchase the same with $4,000,000 of 3½ per cent. debenture bonds. Some stockholders objecting to these terms, a protection committee was formed and the stockholders' meeting called to ratify the lease adjourned without action.

After further postponement and negotiation a satisfactory agreement was reached and the opposition withdrawn. The new plan reduced the lease to 99 years and fixed the amount the New York Central was to pay for the reserved assets amounting to $5,500,000 in 3½ per cent. bonds. The income from this fund adds 77-100 of 1 per cent. to the 8 per cent. guaranteed dividend. The lessee also agreed to adequately maintain the property, and it was provided that $2,500,000 should be expended in the improvement of the terminals in Boston Harbor, this expense to extend over ten years' time. A meeting to ratify the new lease was held December, 1899, and a bill to authorize the lease was, in January, 1900, introduced in the Massachusetts Legislature. This was passed with some amendment, and the stockholders of both companies having ratified the lease the New York Central assumed the operation of the road November 15, 1900.

The issue of $2,500,000 3½ per cent. bonds was authorized in order that improvements to the terminals might be completed at once. The $3,858,000 5 per cent. bonds, which matured April 1, 1902, were retired with a like amount of new 50-year 3½ per cents.

**Earnings.**

Year ending June 30.

| | Div. Paid. | Gross. | Net. | Charges. | Surplus. |
|---|---|---|---|---|---|
| 1892-93 | 8 | $10,169,875 | $2,419,786 | $390,900 | $2,028,886 |
| 1893-94 | 8 | 9,190,276 | 2,469,988 | 459,410 | 2,010,578 |
| 1894-95 | 8 | 9,130,866 | 2,551,505 | 531,150 | 2,020,355 |
| 1895-96 | 8 | 9,350,632 | 2,438,766 | 415,980 | 2,022,786 |
| 1896-97 | 8 | 9,114,625 | 2,456,549 | 415,980 | 2,040,569 |
| 1897-98 | 8 | 9,241,568 | 2,446,566 | 415,980 | 2,030,586 |
| 1898-99 | 8 | 9,325,035 | 2,647,374 | 415,980 | 2,231,394 |
| 1899-00 | 8 | 9,956,138 | 2,439,666 | 415,980 | 2,023,686 |
| 1900-01 | 8¼ | 9,931,396 | 2,622,282 | 422,521 | 2,195,959 |

The earnings are now included in those of the lessee, the New York Central & Hudson River Railroad Co.

President, William Bliss; Secretary, E. D. Hayden; Treasurer, Frank H. Ratcliffe, Boston.

Directors—William Bliss, R. Foster, Boston; James A. Rumrill, Springfield, Mass.; C. S. Sargent, Brookline, Mass.; E. D. Hayden, Woburn, Mass.; Zenas Crane, Dalton, Mass.; E. L. Davis, A. G. Bullock, Stephen Salisbury, Worcester; Walter H. Barnes, Boston; A. C. Houghton, Adams, Mass.; S. Hoar, Concord, Mass.; E. S. Draper, Hopedale, Mass.

Main office, Boston. Annual meeting, fourth Wednesday in September.

---

## BOSTON & LOWELL RAILROAD

(Leased to Boston & Maine Railroad.)

Road owned, Boston to Lowell, 27 miles, and branches, 72 miles; leased, Manchester & Keene, 30 miles; Central Massachusetts, 104 miles; Connecticut & Passumpsic, 147 miles; total, 380 miles. The Boston & Maine has assumed nearly all the leases of the auxiliary roads.

Stock......Par $100..........................Authorized, $6,529,400......Issued, $6,529,400

Transfer agency, North Union Station, Boston.

The 8 per cent. dividends on the stock are paid semi-annually, 4 per cent. each in January and July.

**Funded Debt.**

| | |
|---|---|
| Bonds of 1883, 4½ per cent., due May, 1903, May and Nov. | $250,000 |
| Bonds of 1892, 4 per cent., due April, 1932, April and Oct. | 1,000,000 |
| Branch bonds, 4 per cent., due 1905, March and Sept. | 500,000 |
| 4 per cent. bonds, due 1906, May and Nov. | 500,000 |
| 4 per cent. bonds, due 1907, June and Dec. | 2,000,000 |
| 4 per cent. bonds, due 1907, Jan. and July | 325,000 |
| 4 per cent. bonds, due 1909, April and Oct. | 350,000 |
| 4 per cent. bonds, due Feb., 1913, Feb. and Aug. | 1,000,000 |
| 4 per cent. bonds, due March, 1915, March and Sept. | 500,000 |
| 4 per cent. bonds, due July, 1916, Jan. and July | 750,000 |
| 4 per cent. bonds, due Oct., 1917-18, April and Oct. | 414,000 |
| 3½ per cent. bonds, due 1919, Jan. and July | 620,000 |
| 3½ per cent. bonds, due 1921, Jan. and July | 319,000 |
| Total | $8,528,000 |

The bonds are plain bonds, not secured by mortgage.

The Central Massachusetts is leased on guarantee of interest; rental is 20 per cent. of gross receipts up to $1,000,000, and 25 per cent. over $1,000,000 per year, lessor to have all surplus over charges.

In 1887, the Boston & Lowell, with all its branches and leased lines, was leased to the Boston & Maine for 99 years, the latter guaranteeing all charges and 7 per cent. per year on

Boston & Lowell stock for the first ten years and 8 per cent. thereafter, payable semi-annually. Earnings are included in those of the lessee.

President, Walter C. Baylies, Boston; Treasurer and Clerk, Henry B. Cabot, Boston.

Main office, North Union Station, Boston. Annual meeting, first Wednesday in January.

## BOSTON & MAINE RAILROAD

Road operated, Western Division, Boston to Portland, Me., and branches, 209 miles, Eastern Division, Boston to Portland and branches, 210 miles; Northern Division, Conway Junction to Intervale Junction and branches, 134 miles; Worcester, Nashua & Portland Division, Worcester, Mass., to Portland, Me., and branches, 230 miles; Southern Division, Boston to Concord, N. H., and branches, 375 miles; White Mountain Division, Concord to Groveton, N. H., and branches, 246 miles; Concord Division, Concord to White River Junction, Vt., 172 miles; Connecticut & Passumpsic Division, Springfield, Mass., to Keene, N. H., 229 miles; Fitchburg Division (Fitchburg Railroad), Boston to Rotterdam, N. Y., and branches, 460 miles. Total operated, 2,265 miles, of which 619 miles are owned and 1,637 miles leased and 9 miles trackage.

The leased roads include the Fitchburg Railroad, 458 miles; Worcester, Nashua & Rochester Railroad, 94 miles; Connecticut & Passumpsic River Railroad, 110 miles; Massawippi Valley and branch, 35 miles; Nashua & Lowell Railroad, 15 miles; Connecticut River and branches, 80 miles; Concord & Montreal and branches, 450 miles; Northern Railroad and branches, 172 miles; Boston & Lowell Railroad and branches, 151 miles; other branches leased, 72 miles.

This company also controls the Maine Central, 816 miles; St. Johnsbury & Lake Champlain, 131 miles; Vermont Valley Railroad, 24 miles; Sullivan County Railroad, 26 miles; York Harbor & Beach Railroad, 11 miles. Total controlled, 1,008 miles. Total of system, 3,273 miles. Locomotives, 955; passenger cars, 1,550; freight cars, 17,489.

In 1899, the Eastern Railroad in New Hampshire, State Line to Portland, was merged in this company. The Concord & Montreal Railroad, 417 miles, was leased in June, 1895, for its charges and 7 per cent. on the road's capital stock. January 1, 1900, the Portsmouth & Dover, Portland, Saco & Portsmouth, and Portland & Rochester were merged with the Boston & Maine, additional stock of this company being exchanged for stocks of the merged corporations. In 1900 the Boston & Maine leased the Fitchburg Railroad for 99 years from July 1 of that year, having purchased all the outside holdings of the common stock of that company, amounting to $5,454,000, with the proceeds of an issue of 3 per cent. collateral trust bonds. In the same year an arrangement was proposed for the purchase of the stock of the Central Massachusetts Railroad Co., this plan being delayed by litigation, a final decision being reached in February, 1901, that this company should pay $65 per share for the Massachusetts Central preferred and $21 for its common, and nearly all the stock of that company has been acquired.

Stock..Par $100...Authorized { com., $23,653,125 / pref., 3,149,800 } Issued { com., $23,638,070 / pref., 3,149,800 } $26,787,870

The preferred stock is 6 per cent., non-cumulative. The 6 per cent. dividends on the preferred stock are paid semi-annually, 3 per cent. each, in March (1) and September. On the common stock 6 per cent. was paid from 1894 to 1898, both inclusive. The October, 1899, dividend was increased, making the annual rate 7 per cent., which has since been paid. Dividends on the common are 1¾ per cent. quarterly, January (1), April, July and October.

The common stock was increased by $4,641,400 in 1891 and by $865,300 in 1892, to provide for the purchase of leased roads. In 1899 the common stock was increased $2,683,538 to provide for merger of Portsmouth & Dover, Portland, Saco & Portsmouth and Portland & Rochester. In February, 1901, an increase of $1,735,200 was authorized to provide for purchase of the stock of the Central Massachusetts, the new stock to be offered to stockholders at 190. In October, 1902, an increase of $1,000,000 in the common stock was authorized.

Transfer Agent and Registrar, Old Colony Trust Co., Boston.

FUNDED DEBT.

| | |
|---|---|
| Improvement bonds, 4 per cent., due Feb., 1905–1907, Feb. and Aug. | $1,500,000 |
| Improvement bonds, 4 per cent., due Feb., 1937, Feb. and Aug. | 1,919,000 |
| Improvement bonds, 3½ per cent., due Nov., 1921, May and Nov. | 1,000,000 |
| Eastern Railroad certificates, 6 per cent., due Sept., 1906, March and Sept. | 8,110,941 |
| Plain bonds, 4 per cent., due Aug., 1942 Feb. and Aug. | 2,500,000 |
| Plain bonds, 4½ per cent., due Jan., 1944, Jan. and July | 6,000,000 |
| Plain bonds, Fitchburg purchase, 3 per cent., due July, 1950, Jan. and July | 5,454,000 |
| Ports. G. F. & Conway, 1st mort., 4½ per cent., due June, 1937, June and Dec. | 998,000 |
| Central Mass., 1st mort., assumed 5 per cent., due Oct., 1906, April and Oct. | 2,000,000 |
| Portland & Roch. Terminal bonds, 4 per cent., due Oct., 1907, April and Oct. | 113,500 |
| Total | $29,595,441 |

There are also $594,800 4 per cent. land mortgage notes. The $6,000,000 4½ per cent. bonds were issued in 1894 to retire $2,000,000 7 per cent. bonds maturing January 1, 1894, and to fund floating debt. The $1,000,000 of improvement 3½ per cent. bonds due 1921 were sold in 1901 to provide for betterments and additions on leased roads. This company is a joint guarantor of $300,000 4 per cent. Portland Union Railway Station Co. bonds.

The 3 per cent. bonds were created in 1900, and were given in exchange for the Fitchburg common stock owned by the State of Massachusetts and other holders.

For other bonds of system, see separate statements of the Fitchburg Railroad, Boston & Lowell Railroad, Concord & Montreal, etc.

The Eastern Railroad and its leased line, the Portsmouth, Great Falls & Conway, were consolidated in 1890 with the Boston & Maine on basis of $210 for Boston & Maine stock and $152.50 for the stocks of Eastern and Portsmouth, Gulf Falls & Conway. Rental of Kennebunk & Kennebunkport, $2,925, or 4½ per cent. on $65,000; Lowell & Andover, $52,500 per year; Worcester, Nashua & Rochester, $250,000. Dover & Winnipiseogee was purchased in 1892, and West Amesbury branch in 1893. Manchester & Lawrence leased for 50 years, from June, 1887, for all charges, and 10 per cent. on stock. Boston & Lowell leased for 99 years from 1887, for 7 per cent. on stock for first 10 years, and 8 per cent. thereafter, all charges guaranteed.

In February, 1893, leased the Connecticut River Railroad for 99 years for 10 per cent. annually on stock of that company.

The Fitchburg Railroad was leased in 1900 for 5 per cent. on its preferred and 1 per cent. on its common. See above for provisions regarding purchase of Fitchburg common with 3 per cent. bonds.

EARNINGS.

Year ending June 30.

| | Div. Paid. | Gross. | Net. | Interest and Rentals. | Surplus. |
|---|---|---|---|---|---|
| *1892-93 (1,293 miles)...... | 4 | $12,461,030 | $4,228,201 | $3,119,142 | $1,109,059 |
| 1893-94 ( " " )...... | 6½ | 15,962,276 | 5,754,571 | 4,414,061 | 1,340,510 |
| 1894-95 ( " " )...... | 6 | 16,892,313 | 5,705,539 | 4,399,258 | 1,306,281 |
| 1895-96 (1,717 " )...... | 6 | 20,460,092 | 6,597,361 | 5,291,892 | 1,305,469 |
| 1896-97 ( " " )...... | 6 | 19,556,687 | 6,638,982 | 5,369,687 | 1,269,295 |
| 1897-98 (1,715 " )...... | 6 | 19,742,945 | 6,759,475 | 5,496,051 | 1,263,424 |
| 1898-99 ( " " )...... | 6 | 19,890,607 | 6,841,184 | 5,561,769 | 1,279,415 |
| 1899-00 (1,787 " )...... | 7 | 22,148,602 | 7,260,959 | 5,573,638 | 1,687,321 |
| 1900-01 (2,264 " )...... | 7 | 30,406,906 | 9,856,835 | 8,166,422 | 1,690,413 |
| 1901-02 (2,265 " )...... | 7 | 31,840,694 | 9,997,443 | 8,210,717 | 1,786,726 |

* Nine months ending June 30.

In 1900-01 the surplus over dividends was $45,412.

The following presents the comparative freight traffic statistics of the company:

| | Average Mileage. | Total Tonnage. | Tons Carried One Mile. | Freight Density. | Rate per Ton per Mile. | Earnings per Train Mile. | Average Tons per Train. |
|---|---|---|---|---|---|---|---|
| 1896-97.. | 1,717 | 9,892,705 | 688,011,072 | 400,705 | 1.450c | $1.45 | 127 |
| 1897-98.. | 1,715 | 10,271,875 | 688,351,187 | 401,370 | 1.482 | 1.58 | 126 |
| 1898-99.. | 1,715 | 10,644,376 | 719,460,569 | 419,510 | 1.430 | 1.59 | 130 |
| 1899-00.. | 1,787 | 12,426,571 | 832,397,963 | 465,807 | 1.440 | 1.67 | 164 |
| 1900-01.. | 2,264 | 17,516,571 | 1,538,317,388 | 683,885 | 1.134 | 1.67 | 207 |
| 1901-02.. | 2,265 | 18,183,321 | 1,620,362,196 | 715,391 | 1,119 | .... | .... |

President, Lucius Tuttle; Comptroller and General Auditor, William J. Hobbs; Treasurer, Herbert E. Fisher; Clerk, W. B. Lawrence, Boston.

Directors—Lucius Tuttle, Richard Olney, Walter Hunnewell, Henry R. Reed, Alexander Cochrane, Boston; Joseph H. White, Henry M. Whitney, Brookline, Mass.; Lewis C. Ledyard, Henry F. Dimock, Charles M. Pratt, New York; Samuel C. Lawrence, Medford; A. W. Sulloway, Franklin, N. H.; William Whiting, Holyoke, Mass.

Main office, 92 Causeway street, Boston. Annual meeting, second Wednesday in October.

## BOSTON & PROVIDENCE RAILROAD CO.

(Leased to New York, New Haven & Hartford Railroad Co.)

Road owned, Boston to Providence, 44 miles; branches, 20 miles; total, 64 miles.

In 1887 this road was leased to the Old Colony for 99 years, with a guarantee of 10 per cent. yearly on the stock and all charges. This lease was transferred to the New York, New Haven & Hartford when that company acquired control of the Old Colony by lease.

Stock......Par $100........... ..............Authorized, $4,000,000......Issued, $4,000,000

Transfer agency, South Terminal Station, Boston.

Dividends are paid quarterly, 2½ per cent. each, in January (2), April, July and October.

FUNDED DEBT.

Plain bonds, coupon 4 per cent., due July, 1918, Jan. and July...................... $2,170,000

In 1893 $500,000 maturing 7 per cent. bonds were retired by issue of an equal amount of 4 per cent. bonds.

President, Royal C. Taft, Providence; Treasurer and Clerk, Benjamin B. Torrey, Boston.

Main office, South Terminal Station, Boston. Annual meeting, second Wednesday in October.

## BOSTON, REVERE BEACH & LYNN RAILROAD CO.

Road owned (3-feet gauge), East Boston to Lynn, Mass., 9 miles; East Boston to Winthrop, Mass., 4½ miles; total, 13½ miles. Also operates a ferry between Boston and the terminal at East Boston. Locomotives, 13; passenger cars, 67; ferryboats, 3.

Stock......Par $100............................Authorized, $1,125,000......Issued, $850,000

Stock is transferred at the office of the company's treasurer.

Prior to 1891-92 the company paid 7 per cent. dividends, payments being semi-annual, January and July. In the following year rate was reduced to 5½ per cent., and to 5 per cent. in 1892-93. In 1893-94 4½ per cent. was paid; in 1894-95, 4 per cent.; in 1895-96, 3 per cent. From June, 1897 to 1902, inclusive, the yearly rate has been 2 per cent., the dividends being 1 per cent. each in January and July.

FUNDED DEBT.

| | |
|---|---|
| 1st mort., 4½ per cent., due July 15, 1927, Jan. and July............................ | $561,000 |
| Boston, Winthrop & Shore 1st mort., 5 per cent., due Sept., 1906, March and Sept..... | 289,000 |
| Total.................................................................... | $850,000 |

The Winthrop Division 5 per cent. mortgage was assumed by this company. The 4½ per cent. mortgage is for $1,000,000. Sufficient of the issue is reserved to retire the 5s. The amount outstanding was issued to refund old 6s which fell due in 1897 and to discharge company's floating debt.

EARNINGS—Year ending June 30.

| | Gross. | Net. | Charges. | Surplus. |
|---|---|---|---|---|
| 1898-99.............................. | $288,815 | $65,314 | $48,314 | $17,000 |
| 1899-00.............................. | 374,340 | 70,024 | 53,024 | 17,000 |
| 1900-01.............................. | 407,395 | 73,085 | 56,085 | 17,000 |
| 1901-02.............................. | 485,139 | 75,162 | 57,561 | 17,601 |

President, Melvin O. Adams; Treasurer, John A. Fenno, Boston.

Directors—Henry R. Reed, Elijah B. Stoddard, Henry F. Hurlburt, Melvin O. Adams, William S. Spaulding, John A. Fenno.

Main office, 350 Atlantic avenue, Boston. Annual meeting, third Thursday in November.

## BROCKVILLE & NORTHWESTERN RAILROAD CO.

A corporation formed under the laws of Ontario, February 28, 1903. The company was created in pursuance of a plan for the reorganization of the Brockville, Westport & Sault Ste. Marie Railroad Co., which was sold under foreclosure January 20, 1903, and purchased by a syndicate formed to effect the reorganization.

Road owned, Brockville, Ont., to Westport, Ont., 45 miles. Locomotives, 4; passenger cars, 6; freight cars, 31.

Stock....Par $100.. ..Authorized { com., $500,000 / pref., 500,000 } Issued { com., $500,000 / pref., 500,000 } $1,000,000

The preferred stock is 6 per cent., non-cumulative.

FUNDED DEBT.

1st mort., 4 per cent., due 1913.............................................. $500,000

Trustee of the mortgage and agent for payment of interest on the bonds, Knickerbocker Trust Co., New York.

The bond issue, though authorized, remains in the treasury of the company.

The capitalization of the old Brockville, Westport & Sault Ste. Marie Railroad Co. consisted of $1,125,000 stock and $1,125,000 of bonds. The reorganization syndicate, managed by Holm & Smith, 61 Park Row, New York, provided $500,000 cash, with which all the old bonds were acquired, and purchased the road under foreclosure, as already stated, for $160,000.

The committee in charge of the reorganization consisted of Join Gerken, Henry W. Gennerich, Christoph F. Bode, William von Twistern, Frederick W. Saltzsieder, William F. Hencken, Gustav Schock, Charles F. Holm, William Volk, Henry von Minden, Diedrich W. Rohde, D. Werfelmann, Carsten Heilshorn, Benjamin Fox, P. J. Ryder, A. Bernard, Frank W. Bruns, Jacob Mattern, George Herbener, New York; Val Schmitt, Brooklyn, N. Y.; Clarence P. King, Philadelphia.

President, John Gerken; 1st Vice-President, Clarence P. King; 2d Vice-President, Charles F. Holm; Treasurer, Henry W. Gennerich; Secretary, Carsten Heilshorn.

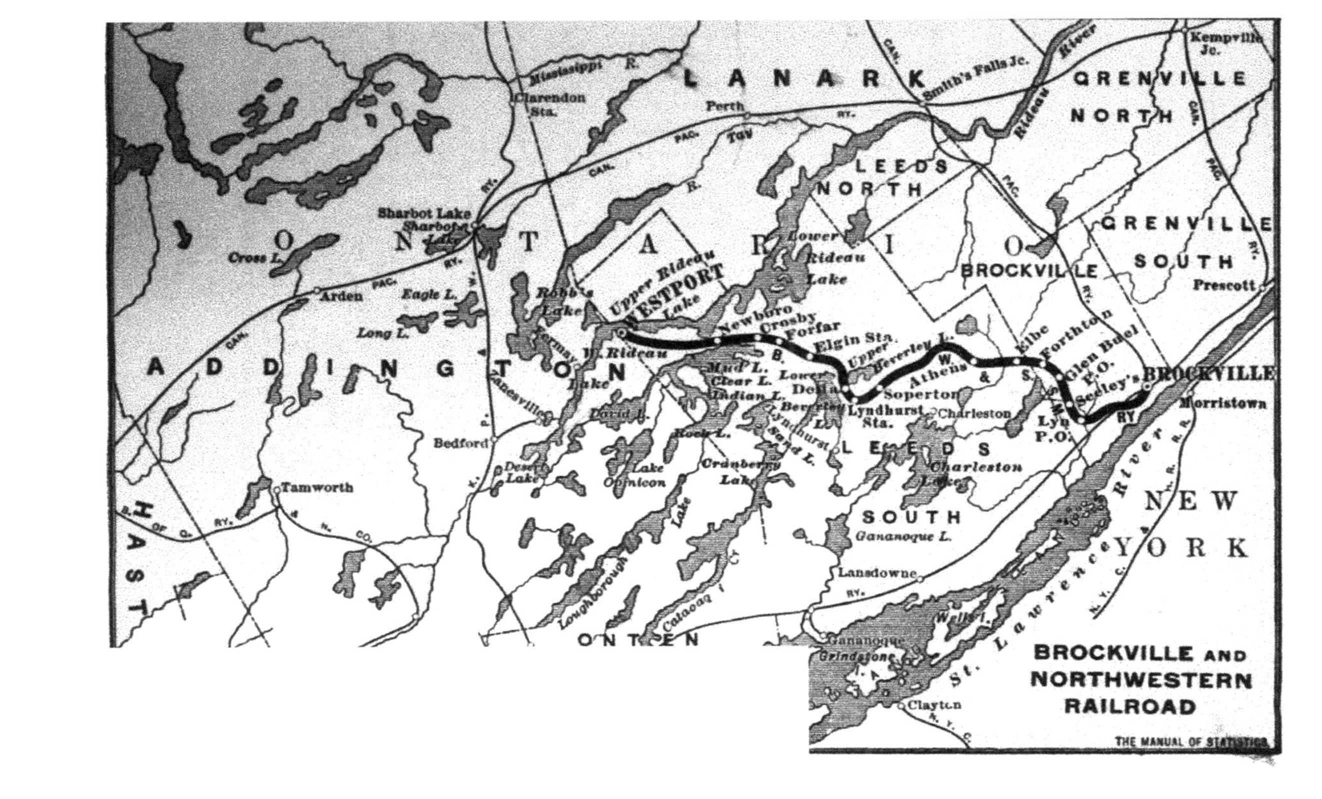
BROCKVILLE AND NORTHWESTERN RAILROAD
THE MANUAL OF STATISTICS
LANARK
GRENVILLE NORTH
GRENVILLE SOUTH
LEEDS NORTH
LEEDS SOUTH
BROCKVILLE
ADDINGTON
NEW YORK
Kempville Jc.
Smith's Falls Jc.
Perth
Clarendon Sta.
Mississippi R.
Rideau River
Sharbot Lake
Cross L.
Arden
Eagle L.
Long L.
Robb's Lake
Upper Rideau Lake
WESTPORT
Lower Rideau Lake
Newboro
Crosby
Forfar
Elgin Sta.
Upper Beverley L.
Athens
Soperton
Charleston
Lyndhurst Sta.
Elbe
Forthton
Glen Buel P.O.
Seeley's
Lyn P.O.
BROCKVILLE
Morristown
Prescott
Mud L.
Clear L.
Indian L.
Sand L.
Cranberry Lake
Lake Opinicon
Charleston Lake
Gananoque L.
Lansdowne
Gananoque
Grindstone
Clayton
Wellesl.
St. Lawrence River
Bedford
Tamworth
Loughborough Lake
Cataraqui
Zanesville

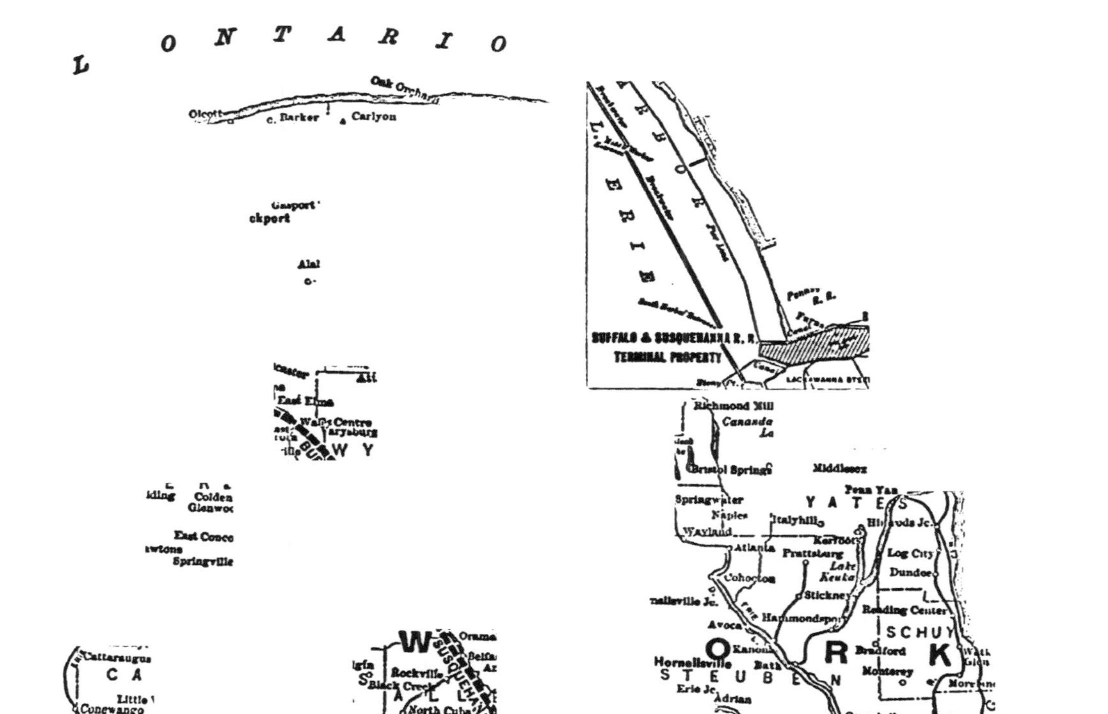

L. ONTARIO
Oak Orchard
Olcott
Barker
Carlyon
Gasport
East Elma
Wales Centre
Colden
East Concord
Springville
Cattaraugus
Little Conewango
Rockville
Black Creek
North Cuba
BUFFALO & SUSQUEHANNA R. R.
TERMINAL PROPERTY
L. ERIE
Richmond Mill
Bristol Springs
Middlesex
Penn Yan
YATES
Springwater
Naples
Italyhill
Wayland
Atlanta
Prattsburg
Lake Keuka
Log City
Dundee
Cohocton
Stickney
Reading Center
Avoca
Hammondsport
SCHUY
Kanona
Bradford
Monterey
Hornellsville
Bath
STEUBEN
Erie Jc.
Adrian
Campbell

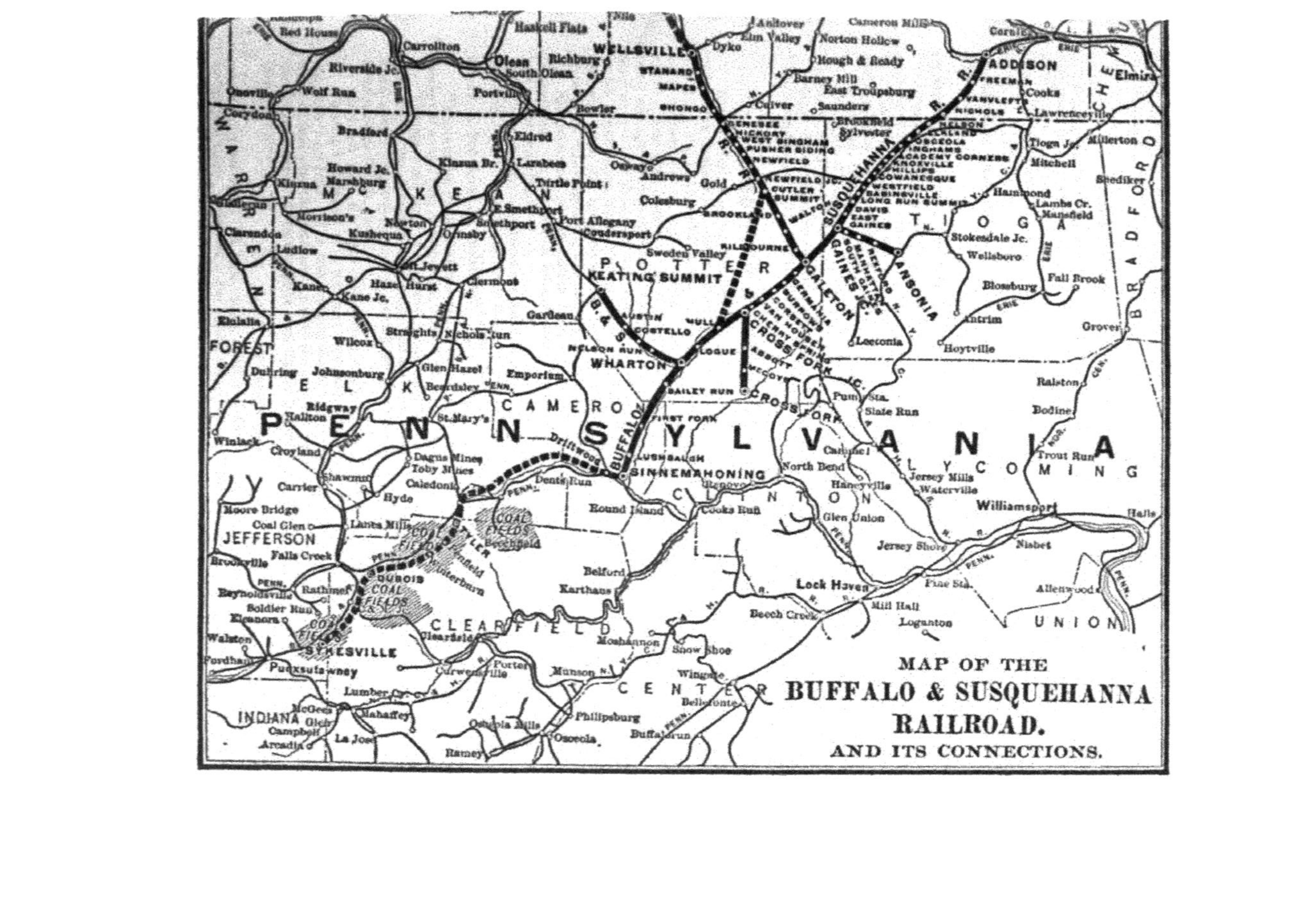

MAP OF THE
BUFFALO & SUSQUEHANNA
RAILROAD.
AND ITS CONNECTIONS.

Directors—John Gerken, Charles F. Holm, Henry W. Gennerich, Carsten Heilshorn, Christoph F. Bode, Fred W. Saltzsieder, William F. Hencken, Gustav Schock, William Volk, Henry C. Strahman, George Herbener, C. F. Gennerich, A. Bernard, New York; Val Schmitt, Brooklyn; Martin Zimmerman, Brockville, Ont.; Clarence P. King, Philadelphia.

Main office, Brockville, Ont.; New York office, 61 Park Row.

## BRUNSWICK & BIRMINGHAM RAILROAD CO.

Roa projected, Brunswick, Ga., to Birmingham, Ala., with branches, about 450 miles. Had completed in 1902 about 125 miles west from Brunswick. In July, 1902, purchased the Offerman & Western Railroad, 35 miles. A large amount of work has been done on the other parts of the line. Locomotives, 10; passenger cars, 13; freight cars, 652.

Stock......Par $100........................Authorized, $15,000,000......Issued, $2,160,000

Stock is transferred at the office of the company. Registrar, North American Trust Co., New York.

FUNDED DEBT.

1st mort., 4½ per cent., due July, 1952, Jan. and July......... ..................... $2,000,000

Trustee of the 1st mortgage bonds is the Knickerbocker Trust Co., New York. The total authorized issue is $12,000,000.

The first section of the road was opened for business in August, 1901. The company has traffic relation with the Seaboard Air Line.

President, Charles L. Hyde; Secretary, H. P. Condit; Treasurer, C. J. Bushnell, New York.

Directors—Charles L. Hyde, E. H. Mason, J. J. Lott, E. C. Macken, F. E. Twitty, R. A. Fairbairn, C. J. Bushnell.

Main office, Brunswick, Ga.; New York office, 71 Broadway. Annual meeting, second Wednesday in January, at Brunswick.

## BUFFALO & SUSQUEHANNA RAILROAD CO.

Road owned, Keating Summit, Pa., to New York State Line, 84.73 miles; Galeton, Pa., to New York State Line, 26.91 miles; Gaines Junction to Ansonia, Pa., 8.60 miles; Cross Fork Junction, Pa., to Cross Fork, Pa., 12.73 miles; Wharton, Pa., to Sinnemahoning, Pa., 19.45 miles; total mileage owned, 152.42 miles; leased lines, New York State Line to Addison, N. Y., 10 miles; New York State Line to Wellsville, N. Y., 10.11 miles; total mileage leased, 20.11 miles; total mileage owned and leased, 172.53 miles. The company is constructing a line from Sinnemahoning to Du Bois, and will also build from the latter point to Sykesville. A cut-off is also under construction from Hull to Cutler Summit, a distance of 22 miles, which will shorten the distance from the company's coal fields to Buffalo by about 16 miles, and reduce grades and curvatures. Locomotives, 21; passenger cars, 15; freight cars, 979.

An extension of the system from Wellsville to Buffalo has been undertaken by a separate corporation, the Buffalo & Susquehanna Railway Co., which has secured extensive terminal properties at Buffalo.

The company also owns extensive bituminous coal properties at Tyler and Du Bois, Pa., the capacity of the mines being about 600,000 tons per annum, which will be largely increased.

Stock....Par $100....Authorized { com., $16,037,500 / pref., 4,000,000 } Issued { com., $3,518,000 / pref., 3,000,000 } $6,518,000

The common stock is transferred at the company's office, Buffalo. Transfer Agents for the preferred stock, Fisk & Robinson, New York.

The preferred stock is 4 per cent., non-cumulative. It was authorized in 1902 and $3,000,000 sold to pay for additional coal properties and new lines to the same. Dividends on the preferred are quarterly, 1 per cent. each in September, December, March and June, three dividends having been paid to March, 1903.

In April, 1901, the stock outstanding was increased from $1,518,000 to $3,518,000.

In 1895 a dividend of 4 per cent. was paid, and from 1896 to 1902, inclusive, dividends of 5 per cent. were paid. The dividends on the common were paid yearly, in January, up to 1901. In April of that year the company adopted the policy of paying dividends of 1¼ per cent. each quarter, and such quarterly dividends have been regularly paid since that time in March, June, September and December.

FUNDED DEBT.

1st mort., 5 per cent., due Oct., 1913, April and Oct................................ $369,500
Refunding mort., 4 per cent., due April, 1951, Jan. and July......................... 2,218,000

Total.............................................................$3,587,500

The 1st mortgage refunding 4 per cent. gold bonds, dated April 1, 1901, were issued to refund the 5 per cent. bonds due 1913, for improvements, acquisition of coal fields and terminals, for new construction and for acquisition of stock and bonds of other railroad companies. These bonds are a first lien, subject only to $369,500 first 5s, which are being refunded from time to time. The 5s are also redeemed through the operation of the sinking fund, an annual amount equal to the outstanding bonds divisible by the number of years to maturity.

EARNINGS.

Year ending June 30.

| | Gross. | Net. | Charges. | Surplus. |
|---|---|---|---|---|
| 1893-94 | $276,433 | $117,263 | $95,517 | $21,746 |
| 1894-95 | 353,832 | 140,355 | 105,650 | 34,705 |
| 1895-96 | 487,844 | 217,746 | 147,262 | 70,485 |
| 1896-97 | 579,798 | 293,175 | 152,467 | 140,708 |
| 1897-98 | 625,692 | 261,942 | 152,092 | 109,850 |
| 1898-99 | 767,319 | 248,035 | 170,198 | 77,837 |
| 1899-00 | 732,991 | 347,990 | 166,480 | 181,510 |
| 1900-01 | 721,966 | 307,993 | 94,444 | 213,548 |
| 1901-02 | 835,748 | 394,941 | 149,725 | 245,216 |

Fixed charges in 1894 include $46,753 aid into sinking fund of 1st mortgage; in 1895, $57,019; in 1896, $78,921; in 1897, $78,926; in 1898, $79,443; in 1899, $79,579, and in 1900, $79,736 for same account.

In the seven months ending January 31, 1902, the gross earnings of the company were $558,490; net, $271,583; other income, $57,907; total income, $329,490.

President, M. E. Olmstead, Harrisburg, Pa.; 1st Vice-President and Chairman, F. H. Goodyear; 2d Vice-President and General Manager, C. W. Goodyear; Secretary and Treasurer, F. A. Lehr; Auditor, W. H. Baumes, Buffalo.

Directors—F. H. Goodyear, C. W. Goodyear, Buffalo; W. I. Lewis, Coudersport, Pa.; N. N. Metcalf, P. H. Farrell, Daniel Collins, W. H. Sullivan, Austin, Pa.; W. C. Park, Galeton, Pa.; M. E. Olmsted, Harrisburg, Pa.

Corporate office, Galeton, Pa.; main office, 960 Ellicott square, Buffalo. Annual meeting, second Monday in January. Fiscal Agents, Fisk & Robinson, 35 Cedar street, New York.

## BUFFALO, ROCHESTER & PITTSBURG RAILWAY CO.

Road owned, Buffalo, N. Y., to Lindsey, Pa., including 25 miles trackage, 166 miles; Rochester, N. Y., to Ashford, 94 miles; branches, 29 miles; total owned, 284 miles; controlled and leased, 20 miles; leased, Clearfield & Mahoning Railway, 26 miles; Allegheny & Western Railway, Punxsutawney, Pa., to Butler, Pa., 61 miles; Mahoning Valley Raiload, 2 miles; trackage, 100 miles; total operated, 472 miles. Locomotives, 185; passenger cars, 79; freight cars, 10,751.

In 1898 the Allegheny & Western Railway, Punxsutawney to Butler, Pa., 60 miles, was built in interest of this company. The company has trackage arrangements with the Pittsburg & Western from Butler to New Castle, Pa., and from Ribold Junction, Pa., to Allegheny City, Pa.

Formerly the Rochester & Pittsburg. The property was sold under foreclosure October 16, 1885, and was reorganized under the present name in March, 1887.

Stock...Par $100...Authorized { com., $9,000,000; pref., 6,000,000 } Issued { com., $8,300,000; pref., 6,000,000 } $14,300,000

Stock is transferred at the company's office, 36 Wall street, New York. Registrar, Union Trust Co., New York.

The preferred stock, 6 per cent., non-cumulative. After the common has also received 6 per cent., both classes of stock share pro rata in any further distribution of surplus earnings. The authorized common stock was increased from $6,000,000 to $9,000,000 in November, 1901, to provide funds for the construction of the Indiana branch, and $1,300,000 was sold to stockholders at par, the final payments for the same being in February, 1903.

FUNDED DEBT.

| | |
|---|---|
| 1st mort., R. & P. 6 per cent., due Feb., 1921, Feb. and Aug. | $1,300,000 |
| Consolidated 1st mort., 6 per cent., due Dec., 1922, June and Dec. | 3,920,000 |
| 1st general mort., gold B. R. & P. Ry., 5 per cent., due Sept., 1937, Mar. and Sept. | 4,427,000 |
| Car trust bonds, 5 per cent., various | 326,000 |
| Equipment bonds, Series A, 4½ per cent., due May, 1919, May and Nov. | 500,000 |
| " " Series B, 4½ per cent., due May, 1920, May and Nov. | 1,000,000 |
| " " Series C, 4½ per cent., due May, 1921, May and Nov. | 1,000,000 |
| Real estate mortgages, 5 per cent. | 304,000 |
| 1st mort. Lincoln Park & C., 5 per cent., due Jan., 1939, Jan. and July | 350,000 |
| Clearfield & Mahoning, 1st mort. guar., 5 per cent., due Jan., 1943, Jan. and July | 650,000 |
| Allegheny & Western 1st mort., 4 per cent., due Oct., 1998, April and Oct. | 2,000,000 |
| Total | $15,777,000 |

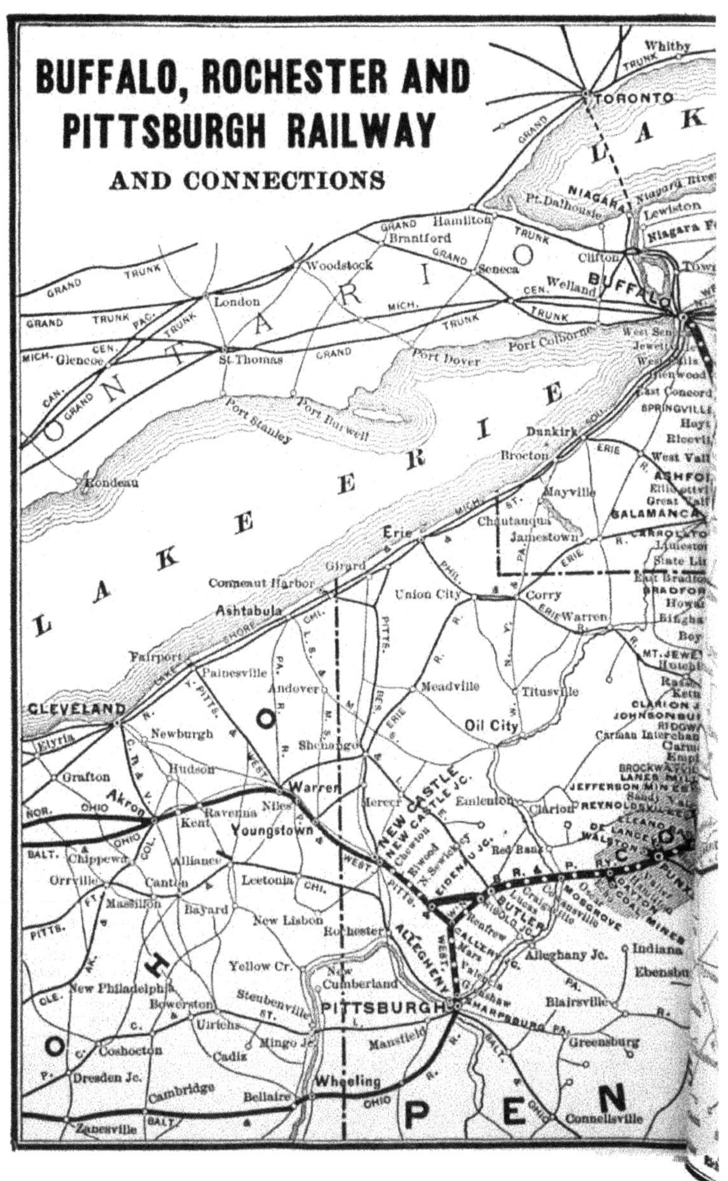
BUFFALO, ROCHESTER AND
PITTSBURGH RAILWAY
AND CONNECTIONS
LAKE ONTARIO
LAKE ERIE
OHIO
PENN
TORONTO
Whitby
Hamilton
Brantford
Woodstock
London
St. Thomas
Glencoe
Port Stanley
Port Burwell
Port Dover
Port Colborne
Rondeau
Seneca
Welland
Clifton
Pt. Dalhousie
NIAGARA
Lewiston
BUFFALO
Dunkirk
Brocton
Mayville
Chautauqua
Jamestown
SALAMANCA
Erie
Girard
Conneaut Harbor
Ashtabula
Fairport
Painesville
Union City
Corry
Warren
Titusville
Meadville
Oil City
Andover
Shenango
CLEVELAND
Elyria
Newburgh
Hudson
Grafton
Akron
Kent
Ravenna
Niles
Warren
Youngstown
Mercer
NEW CASTLE
NEW CASTLE JC.
Emlenton
Clarion
Chippewa
Alliance
Orrville
Canton
Leetonia
Massillon
Bayard
New Lisbon
Rochester
BUTLER
Renfrew
Mars
Valencia
Allegheny Jc.
Indiana
Blairsville
Yellow Cr.
New Cumberland
New Philadelphia
Bowerston
Steubenville
PITTSBURGH
Uhrichs
Mingo Jc.
Mansfield
Greensburg
Coshocton
Cadiz
Dresden Jc.
Cambridge
Bellaire
Wheeling
Zanesville
Connellsville
GRAND TRUNK
MICH. CEN.
LAKE SHORE
ERIE
BALT. & OHIO
PITTS.
ALLEGHENY

ONTARIO BEACH
CHARLOTTE
Sodus Point
ROCHESTER
Newark
Lyons
Clifton Sprs.
Geneva
Batavia
Avon
Canandaigua
Attica
Wyoming
WARSAW
Rock Glen
Perry
Silver Sprs.
Penn Yan
L. Keuka
Hammondsport
Bath
Watkins Glen
Hornellsville
Wellsville
Painted Post
Corning
Addison
Elmira
Cuba
Bolivar
Eldred
Tioga Jc.
Fall Brook
Hoytville
Port Allegany
Renovo
Lock Haven
Bellefonte
Lewistown
Altoona
Mt. Union
Gettysburg Jc.

In 1892–93 the company built a line under title of the Clearfield & Mahoning Railway, 26 miles, from Du Bois, Pa., to Clearfield, connecting there with the Beech Creek Railroad. This company guarantees the bonds of Clearfield & Mahoning Railroad and 6 per cent. dividends (semi-annual 3 per cent. January and July) on $750,000 of the latter's stock.

In 1897, debenture bonds for $3,000,000 were authorized, running 50 years at 6 per cent. with right to retire same at 105 at any interest period on twelve weeks notice. $1,000,000 debentures were sold to pay loans incurred for construction and for equipment. The interest rate on the debentures was reduced from 6 to 4 per cent. and the bonds made convertible into stock, and were all retired in 1902.

In connection with the construction of the Allegheny & Western Railway, in 1898, stockholders of this company were given privilege of subscribing at par for 4 shares of Allegheny & Western stock for each 25 shares of Buffalo, Rochester & Pittsburg. This company guarantees 6 per cent. dividends on $3,000,000 Allegheny & Western stock and interest and principal of its $2,000,000 4 per cent. 100-year bonds. The Allegheny & Western bond issue is $2,500,000 authorized, $500,000 being reserved for an extension from Butler Junction, Pa., to New Castle, Pa.

This company controls the Rochester & Pittsburg Coal and Iron Co., which has $802,000 1st mortgage 5 per cent. bonds and 5 per cent. purchase money bonds for $1,077,000.

The company is also interested in the Jefferson & Clearfield Coal & Iron Co., which has $1,683,000 1st mortgage 5 per cent. bonds and $1,000,000 5 per cent. seconds.

Dividend payments on preferred began in February, 1892, at the rate of 1¼ per cent. quarterly, but were suspended after February, 1893. In August, 1897, 1 per cent. was again paid on the preferred. In 1898 2 per cent. was paid on the preferred in semi-annual payments of 1 per cent. each in February and August, and in 1899 1 per cent. was again paid in February and August. On February 15, 1900, 3 per cent. was paid on the preferred, and the dividends have since been on that basis or 6 per cent. per annum, the payments being semi-annual in February and August. The first dividend on the common stock was 2 per cent., paid February 15, 1901. Similar dividends on the common were then regularly paid August 15 and February 15, but the February, 1903, dividend was increased to 2½ per cent.

EARNINGS.—Year ending June 30.

| | Gross. | Net. | Charges. | Surplus. |
|---|---|---|---|---|
| 1892-93 | $3,354,464 | $997,053 | $745,351 | $251,702 |
| 1893-94 | 2,819,825 | 769,390 | 848,416 | Def. 79,026 |
| 1894-95 | 3,066,440 | 894,012 | 851,343 | 42,669 |
| 1895-96 | 3,179,776 | 979,060 | 861,416 | 117,644 |
| 1896-97 | 3,347,276 | 1,093,821 | 862,934 | 230,887 |
| 1897-98 | 3,706,104 | 1,339,689 | 554,575 | 458,174 |
| 1898-99 | 3,801,968 | 1,360,574 | 970,624 | 389,951 |
| 1899-00 | 5,012,135 | 2,123,524 | 1,110,572 | 1,012,952 |
| 1900-01 | 5,830,618 | 2,553,411 | 1,338,003 | 1,215,438 |
| 1901-02 | 6,313,246 | 2,681,241 | 1,406,976 | 1,274,264 |

In 1891 $46,886 out of the earnings were expended in improvements; in 1892, $54,853; in 1893, $29,439; in 1894, $30,101; in 1895, $39,132; in 1896, $20,553; in 1897, $20,084; in 1898, $132,853. In 1899, $103,719 for this account is included in the charges, and in 1900 $138,269 for the same purpose was deducted from the surplus, making the net profit $874,683. Surplus in 1900 over dividends of 4 per cent. on preferred, $634,683. In 1900–01 improvements were charged with $530,134, dividends with $480,000, and the surplus was $205,304. In 1901-02 improvements $583,561, dividends $600,000, surplus $90,703.

The company controls a large coal property. In 1898 it transported 4,092,000 tons of coal and 548,000 tons of coke. In 1899 coal tonnage, 4,257,000 tons; coke, 579,000 tons. In 1900, coal tonnage, 4,561,000 tons; coke, 592,000 tons. In 1901, coal, 4,590,527 tons; coke, 553,070 tons. In 1902, coal, 4,655,783 tons; coke, 615,270 tons.

President, Arthur G. Yates, Rochester, N. Y.; Vice-President, Adrian Iselin, Jr., New York; Treasurer, J. F. Dinkey, Rochester, N. Y.; Secretary, John H. Hocart, New York.

Directors—J. Kennedy Tod, Arthur G. Yates, Adrian Iselin, Jr., Wheeler H. Peckham, Henry I. Barbey, Walter G. Oakman, C. O'D. Iselin, John H. Hocart, Auguste Richard, W. Emlen Roosevelt, Ernest Iselin, Oscar Grisch, John L. Riker.

Main office, Rochester, N. Y.; New York office, 36 Wall street. Annual meeting, third Monday in November, at New York.

---

## BURLINGTON, CEDAR RAPIDS & NORTHERN RAILWAY CO.

(Leased to Chicago, Rock Island & Pacific Railroad Co.)

Road chiefly owned. Burlington, Ia., to Erin, Minn., 296 miles; branches and extensions, 311 miles; leased and chiefly owned, 707 miles; trackage, 45 miles; total, 1,314 miles. In 1901 an extension from Germania, Ia., to Faribault, Minn., 95 miles, was commenced. The South St. Paul Belt Railway was acquired in 1901, giving the company an entrance to St. Paul. Locomotives, 135; passenger cars, 104; freight cars, 5,408.

The Chicago, Rock Island & Pacific owned $5,000,000 of the stock, and in June, 1902, leased the road for 999 years, with a guarantee of 6 per cent. on the stock. Minority stockholders were given the right to exchange their shares at par for Rock Island stock, and all but about $200,000 has been exchanged.

Stock......Par $100........................Authorized, $30,000,000......Issued, $7,121,740

Stock is transferred at the office of the treasurer, 17 Broad street, New York. Registrar and Fiscal Agent, Central Trust Co., New York.

In 1893, 1894 and 1895 dividends of 3 per cent. per annum were paid on the stock; in 1896, 1897 and 1898, 4 per cent., and in 1899, 4 per cent. and 4 per cent. extra. In 1900, 8 per cent. was paid, the dividends being 4 per cent. semi-annual, February 1 and August 1. The dividend paid February 1, 1901, was 2 per cent. and 1 per cent. extra. On August 1, 1901, 3 per cent. was paid, making 6 per cent. for the year. And the same rate was paid in 1902, this being the rate under the lease to the Rock Island referred to above.

**FUNDED DEBT.**

| | |
|---|---|
| 1st mort., 5 per cent., due June, 1906, June and Dec. | $6,500,000 |
| Consolidated 1st mort., and Col. trust, 5 per cent., due April, 1934, April and Oct. | 7,803,000 |
| Minn. & St. Louis bonds, assumed, 7 per cent., due June, 1927, June and Dec. | 150,000 |
| Cedar Rapids, Iowa Falls & N. W., guar., 5 per cent., due Oct., 1921, April and Oct. | 1,905,000 |
| Total | $16,358,000 |

**EARNINGS.**

| | Gross. | Net. | Charges. | Surplus. |
|---|---|---|---|---|
| 1892 (1,134 miles) | $4,354,789 | $1,161,648 | $788,180 | $431,015 |
| 1893 ( " " ) | 4,224,753 | 1,146,319 | 810,680 | 424,672 |
| 1894 ( " " ) | 3,748,829 | 1,026,612 | 811,280 | 414,131 |
| 1895 (1,136 " ) | 4,504,332 | 1,454,472 | 811,280 | 729,905 |
| 1896 ( " " ) | 4,450,036 | 1,083,304 | 807,673 | 690,328 |
| 1897 ( " " ) | 4,292,162 | 1,243,330 | 799,400 | 789,402 |
| 1898 ( " " ) | 4,545,643 | 1,430,821 | 799,400 | 631,421 |
| 1899 (1,171 " ) | 4,926,933 | 1,432,761 | 795,275 | 637,486 |
| 1900 (1,276 " ) | 4,848,277 | 1,511,823 | 811,127 | 700,696 |
| 1901 (1,299 " ) | 5,360,607 | 1,955,307 | 810,145 | 1,145,062 |

The outstanding stock was increased in 1900 from $5,500,000 to $7,150,000, the additional $1,650,000 being allotted to stockholders for subscription at par. The proceeds were used to build Faribault extension.

In 1884 the general mortgage bonds were authorized to take the place of divisional bonds. In 1896 $584,000 Iowa City & Western 7 per cent. bonds were thus retired and consols issued in their place. The $825,000 Cedar Rapids, Iowa Falls & Northwestern 6 per cent. bonds were called for redemption April 1, 1899, and replaced by consols.

Chairman, R. R. Cable, Chicago; President, C. J. Ives, Cedar Rapids, Ia.; Treasurer, H. H. Hollister, New York; Secretary, S. S. Dorwart, Cedar Rapids, Ia.

Directors—J. W. Blythe, C. P. Squires, Thomas Hedge, William Carson, Burlington, Ia.; C. J. Ives, Cedar Rapids, Ia.; F. H. Griggs, G. W. Cable, A. Kimball, Davenport, Ia.; J. Carskadden, Muscatine, Ia.; R. R. Cable, J. C. Peasley, W. G. Purdy, Robert Mather, Chicago.

Main office, Cedar Rapids, Ia. Annual meeting, last Tuesday in May.

## CALIFORNIA NORTHWESTERN RAILWAY CO.

Leases the San Francisco & North Pacific Railway Co., Tiburon, Cal., to Ukiah, Cal., 106 miles, and branches, 59 miles, together with ferry, Tiburon to San Francisco, 6½ miles. Total operated, 171½ miles. The company in 1900 began extension of 60 miles into the redwood timber country of Mendocino and Humboldt Counties, Cal., of which 30 miles was completed in the early part of 1902. Locomotives, 21; passenger cars, 62; freight cars, 457; floating equipment, 3 steamboats.

This company was incorporated in March, 1898, and leased the San Francisco & North Pacific for 20 years from September, 1898, the rental being the net profits of the leased line.

Stock......Par $100..........................Authorized, $3,000,000......Issued, $1,566,000

Stock is transferred at the office of the company, San Francisco.

**FUNDED DEBT.**

| | |
|---|---|
| San Francisco & North Pacific, 1st mort., 5 per cent., due Jan., 1919, Jan. and July | $3,970,000 |
| California Northwestern, 1st mort., 5 per cent., due April, 1928, April and Oct. | 750,000 |
| Total | $4,720,000 |

The San Francisco & North Pacific was a consolidation, 1889, of the Sonoma Valley, Cloverdale & Ukiah and San Francisco & San Rafael railroads with San Francisco & North Pacific. Narrow gauge portions of road were changed to standard gauge. Road opened to Ukiah in 1889. The San Francisco & North Pacific stock was $6,000,000 and its 1st mortgage was for $4,500,000, issuable at rate of $25,000 per mile, with a sinking fund of $25,000 per annum, bonds drawn at 110. Bonds outstanding were reduced to present amount by the operation of the sinking fund.

The California Northwestern 1st mortgage is for $2,000,000 5 per cent. gold bonds, due 1928, April and October, at rate of $25,000 per mile. The San Francisco & North Pacific guarantees the bonds which were authorized to provide for extensions.

EARNINGS.

| Year ending June 30. | Gross. | Net. | Charges. | Surplus. |
|---|---|---|---|---|
| 1892-93 | $876,277 | $323,271 | $261,526 | $61,745 |
| 1893-94 | 808,336 | 296,034 | 273,948 | 22,085 |
| 1894-95 | 826,700 | 315,551 | 261,763 | 53,788 |
| 1895-96 | 790,957 | 270,079 | 268,050 | 2,029 |
| 1896-97 | 737,094 | 274,991 | 264,781 | 10,210 |
| 1897-98 | 839,963 | 346,265 | 624,530 | 81,734 |
| 1898-99 | 922,245 | 355,096 | 265,712 | 89,383 |
| 1899-00 | 958,223 | 361,543 | 268,999 | 92,544 |
| 1900-01 | 1,038,999 | 379,406 | 266,339 | 113,066 |
| 1901-02 | 1,132,579 | 352,413 | 266,658 | 83,771 |

President, Arthur W. Foster; Vice-President, George A. Newhall; Secretary and Comptroller, Thomas Mellersh; Treasurer, Anglo-California Bank, San Francisco.

Directors—George A. Pope, J. V. Lilienthal J. P. Overton, George A. Newhall, Arthur W. Foster, San Francisco.

Main office, 222 Sansome street, San Francisco. Annual meeting, third Thursday in March.

## CANADA ATLANTIC RAILWAY CO.

A Canadian corporation formed in 1879 and amalgamated in August, 1899, with the Ottawa, Arnprior & Parry Sound Railway. Road owned, Parry Sound, Ont., to Alburg, Vt., via Ottawa, 400 miles; branches leased, 59 miles; trackage, 10 miles; total operated, 469 miles. The company has the use of the Grand Trunk tracks, Coteau to Montreal, 37 miles. The company controls the Canada Atlantic Transit Co., operating steamers between Parry Sound and other lake ports. Locomotives, 64; passenger cars, 43; freight cars, 2,709.

Stock....Par $100.....Authorized { com., $6,200,000; pref., 1,000,000 } Issued { com., $6,200,000; pref., 1,000,000 } $7,200,000

The preferred stock is entitled to 4 per cent. non-cumulative dividends. Stock is transferred at the company's office, Ottawa.

FUNDED DEBT.

| | |
|---|---|
| 1st mort., 5 per cent., due Jan., 1909, Jan. and July | $3,450,000 |
| Ottawa, Arnprior & Parry Sound 1st mort., 5 per cent | 1,000,000 |
| Total | $4,450,000 |

The 1st mortgage is $4,450,000 authorized. Trustee of bonds, Farmers' Loan & Trust Co., New York. The company pays interest on $380,000 5 per cent. bonds of the Central Counties Railway as rental.

EARNINGS.

| Year ending June 30. | Gross. | Net. |
|---|---|---|
| 1899-00 | $1,869,139 | $366,036 |
| 1900-01 | 1,786,338 | 411,554 |
| 1901-02 | 1,816,946 | 600,422 |

The net for 1901-02 includes $31,422, the earnings of the company's barges and lake steamers.

President, C. J. Booth; Vice-President, William Anderson; Secretary and Treasurer, A. W. Fleck; General Manager, E. J. Chamberlin, Ottawa.

Directors—C. J. Booth, William Anderson, N. McIntosh, J. F. Booth, J. A. Seybold, G. W. Mitchell, Ottawa; C. McLachlin, Arnprior, Ont.

Main office, Ottawa. Annual meeting, last Tuesday in September.

## CANADA SOUTHERN RAILWAY CO.

(Operated by Michigan Central Railroad Co.)

Road owned, Suspension Bridge, Niagara, to Windsor, Ont., 226 miles; Toledo to Detroit, 59 miles; other branches, 172 miles; total, 457 miles, including Canada Southern bridge, 4 miles.

Stock......Par $100........................ Authorized, $15,000,000......Issued, $15,000,000

Transfer office, Grand Central Station, New York. Registrar, Union Trust Co., New York.

Dividends have been as follows: In 1890, 3½ per cent.; in 1891, 2½ per cent.; in 1892, 1893 and 1894, 3 per cent.; in 1895 and 1896, 2½ per cent.; in 1897 and to 1900, inclusive, 2 per cent. Dividends are semi-annual, February 1 and August 1. In 1901, paid 2½ per cent. and in 1902 2 per cent.

FUNDED DEBT.

| | |
|---|---|
| 1st mort., 5 per cent., due Jan., 1908, Jan. and July | $14,000,000 |
| 2d mort., 5 per cent., due March, 1913, March and Sept. | 6,000,000 |
| Leamington & St. Clair 1st mort., 4 per cent., due Oct., 1945, April and Oct. | 130,000 |
| Total | $20,130,000 |

The company was reorganized in 1878, when the 1st mortgage bonds were issued; they bore only 3 per cent. up to 1881. The interest on the bonds was guaranteed by the New York Central & Hudson River Railroad Co. for 20 years. The 2d mortgage bonds, created in 1883, were issued under the agreement with the Michigan Central Railroad Co., to pay for improvements, new equipment and the bridge over the Niagara River.

By an agreement for working the property by the Michigan Central, the latter was to operate the road from January 1, 1883, for 21 years, applying the joint earnings to payment of working expenses and fixed charges of both roads, the surplus over these payments to be divided, two-thirds to the Michigan Central and one-third to the Canada Southern. In 1892, a reapportionment of earnings between the two companies was effected for the 5 years beginning January 1, 1893. By the new arrangement the Canada Southern Railway Co. is allowed in each year 40 per cent. of the first $1,000,000 and 33⅓ per cent. of any excess above $1,000,000 of earnings, after paying operating expenses and the fixed charges of both companies. This division of earnings has since been in force, the Michigan Central, however, receiving credit for the reduction of its fixed charges effected since the agreement has been in force.

For the year 1891 the Canada Southern's proportion of profit over all charges was $446,775; in 1892, $380,712; in 1893, $456,647; in 1894, $287,808; in 1895, $304,715; in 1896, $290,474; in 1897, $282,402; in 1898, $300,666; in 1899, $300,574; in 1900, $300,831, and in 1901, $375,238.

President and Treasurer, Charles F. Cox; Vice-President, Edward A. Wickes, New York; Secretary, Nicol Kingsmill, Toronto, Ont.

Directors—W. K. Vanderbilt, Frederick W. Vanderbilt, Charles F. Cox, Samuel F. Barger, Chauncey M. Depew, Edward A. Wickes, Joseph E. Brown, New York; Henry B. Ledyard, Detroit; Nicol Kingsmill, Toronto, Ont.

Main office, St. Thomas, Ont. Annual meeting, first Wednesday in June.

---

## CANADIAN NORTHERN RAILWAY CO.

This company is a consolidation, in 1898, of the Winnipeg Great Northern Railway, the Lake Manitoba Railway and Canal Co., and other companies. In 1901 this company sub-leased from the Province of Manitoba the lines in that Province owned by the Northern Pacific and which the Province leased from that company with an option to purchase the same for $7,000,000.

Road owned, Port Arthur to Saskatchewan River, 812 miles; branches, 128 miles; leased, 281 miles; total operated, 1,221 miles. In 1901 the Port Arthur, Duluth & Western Railway, 86 miles, was purchased.

Included in the above mileage is 356 miles of lines in Manitoba which belonged to the Northern Pacific Railway Co. and which were taken over by the Province and sub-leased to this company, which has an option to purchase the same for $7,000,000.

In February, 1903, it was reported that the company would be combined with the Great Northern Railway of Canada.

Stock......Par $100..........................Authorized, $24,750,000......Issued, $7,000,000

FUNDED DEBT.

| | |
|---|---|
| Ontario Div., mort. deb., 4½ per cent., due 1930 | £700,000 |
| Western & Saskatchewan Div., 1st mort., 4 per cent., due Feb., 1929, Feb. and Aug. | 718,300 |
| Total | £1,418,300 |

The Government of Manitoba agreed to guarantee the principal and interest of the bonds when the line should be completed and in operation. The contractors, Mackenzie, Mann & Co., of Toronto, also guaranteed interest on the bonds for one year after the line is completed. Trustee is the National Bank of Commerce, Toronto. A 1st mortgage of not more than $10,000 per mile may be created on the Ontario Division and the Western Division. The company will have a land grant of 2,455,000 acres, and has land grant mortgage bonds for $2,000,000.

President, William Mackenzie; Secretary and Treasurer, J. M. Smith, Toronto; Auditor, C. E. Friend, Winnipeg.

Main office, Church and King streets, Toronto.

## CANADIAN PACIFIC RAILWAY CO.

Incorporated February 17, 1881, under a charter from the Dominion of Canada. The company with its charter received from the Government $25,000,000 in cash as a subsidy, also 25,000,000 acres of land. The Government also conveyed to the company, free of all cost, 713 miles of road, including 435 miles from Winnipeg to Lake Superior. The company also acquired 440 miles of road and branches from Montreal west to Callendar.

Road owned, main line from Montreal to Vancouver, British Columbia, 2,905 miles; branches owned, including line from Quebec to Montreal, 1,872 miles; lines leased, 2,724 miles; trackage, 92 miles; worked for account of owners, 734 miles; under construction June 30, 1902, 321 miles; total 8,646 miles. The mileage included in the company's returns is 7,638 miles.

Locomotives, 745; passenger cars, 842; freight cars, 21,159; other cars, 1,376. The company owns 3 lake steamers, 20 river steamers, 2 ferryboats and 6 steamships.

Included in the leased lines are the St. Lawrence & Ottawa, 58 miles; Atlantic & Northwest, 349 miles; Ontario & Quebec Railway, including Toronto, Grey & Bruce Railway, 862 miles; New Brunswick Railway, 442 miles; Manitoba Southwestern, 215 miles; Montreal & Ottawa Railway, 23 miles; Guelph Junction Railway, 15 miles; Columbia & Kootenay, 27 miles; Shuswap & Okanagon, 51 miles; Montreal & Western Railway, 67 miles; Alberta Railway & Coal Co., 109½ miles, and other small branches, 76 miles. Also has running rights over 56 miles of Maine Central from Vanceboro to Mattawamkeag. The principal roads worked for owners under arrangement are the Qu'Appelle, Long Lake & Saskatchewan Railway, 254 miles; the Calgary & Edmunton Railway, 294 miles, and the Montreal & Atlantic Railway, 184 miles, the returns of all of which are not included in the Canadian Pacific earnings. In 1897 began the construction of the Crows Nest Pass line, Leithbridge, N. W. Territory, to Nelson, British Columbia, 393 miles, which was completed in 1899.

The company controls the Duluth, South Shore & Atlantic, 565 miles, and the Minneapolis, St. Paul & Sault Ste. Marie roads, 1,412 miles. See statements of those companies. It has also a line of steamships on the Pacific from Vancouver to China and Japan.

The company had on June 30, 1902, 18,603,023 acres in its land grants. The land sales for the year 1900-01 were 399,808 acres for $1,262,224. In 1901-02 there were sold 1,589,068 acres for $5,227,762.

Stock..Par $100...Authorized { com., $85,000,000 / pref., 42,500,000 } Issued { com., $84,500,000 / pref., 31,171,000 } $115,671,000

Stock is transferred at the secretary's office, Montreal. Transfer Agent in New York, the Bank of Montreal, 50 Wall street.

The preferred stock is 4 per cent., non-cumulative. It was authorized by the Canadian Parliament in 1892 to provide for extensions. The preferred is limited to one-half the amount of the common stock.

### Funded Debt.

| | |
|---|---|
| Land bonds, 3½ per cent., Dominion guar. due July, 1938, Jan. and July | $15,000,000 |
| Canada Central, 2d mort. bonds, 6 per cent., due Nov., 1910 | 973,333 |
| Q., M., O. & O. R. R. loan, 4 1-20 per cent., due 1904-6 and 1904, March 1 | 7,000,000 |
| Algoma Branch, 1st mort., 5 per cent., due 1937, Jan. and July (£750,000) | 3,650,000 |
| North Shore, 1st mort., 5 per cent. (£99,600), due April 20, 1904, April and Oct. | 616,119 |
| 1st mort. debentures, 5 per cent., due July, 1915, Jan. and July | 34,998,633 |
| Consolidated perpetual debenture stock, 4 per cent., Jan. and July | 63,532,415 |
| Total | $125,770,500 |

### Bonds of Leased Lines.

| | |
|---|---|
| Manitoba S. W. Colonization Ry., 1st mort., 5 per cent., due 1934, June and Dec. | $2,544,000 |
| Atlantic & N. W. 1st mort. 5 per cent., due 1937, Jan. and July | £1,330,000 |
| St. Lawrence & Ottawa 1st mort., reduced to 4 per cent., due 1910, June and Dec. | 200,000 |
| Ontario & Quebec debentures, irredeemable, 5 per cent., June and Dec. | £4,007,381 |
| Toronto, Grey & Bruce 1st mort., 4 per cent., due 2883, Jan. and July | 719,000 |
| New Brunswick Ry. 1st mort. 5 per cent., due 1934, Feb. and Aug. | 630,000 |
| New Brunswick Ry. perpetual debentures, 4 per cent., Jan. and July | 858,300 |

The common stock authorized was originally fixed at the sum of $100,000,000. In 1883 company purchased from the Dominion Government an annuity of 3 per cent. per annum for ten years, 1884 to 1893, on $65,000,000 of the stock outstanding; and the remaining $35,000,000 of stock was deposited with the Government, to be withdrawn by the company as the completion of its road called for it, and issued with the same guarantee. The Government modified the agreement February, 1884, and loaned the company $22,500,000, taking a lien on the company's property subject to the prior liens. In May, 1885, it was agreed to cancel the $35,000,000 of stock deposited as above, and issue instead mortgage bonds to an equivalent amount, of which $20,000,000 were to be held by the Government. In April, 1886, the company placed the $20,000,000 of bonds in London, and with the proceeds thereof and a transfer of lands at $1.50 per acre liquidated its entire debt to the Dominion of Canada.

In February, 1902, an increase of $20,000,000 in the common stock was authorized, and the stockholders were given the right to subscribe for $19,500,000 of the new stock at par to the extent of 30 per cent. of their holdings, and payments to be made in four installments—June 27, August 27, October 27, and December 27, 1902. This increased the issue of common stock to $84,500,000.

In May, 1888, the company surrendered its exclusive right to operate lines in Manitoba, the Government as consideration agreeing to guarantee $15,000,000 3½ per cent. new land grant bonds. The company guarantees 4 per cent. on the 1st mortgage bonds of the Minneapolis, Sault Ste. Marie & Atlantic and the Minneapolis & Pacific roads.

This company guarantees 6 per cent. dividends in perpetuity upon $2,000,000 stock of the Ontario & Quebec Railway. The land mortgage 5 per cent. bonds due 1931 and the land grant 3½ per cent. bonds due 1938 are not a lien on road or equipment, but are secured by company's lands.

EARNINGS.

| | Gross. | Net. | Charges. | Surplus. |
|---|---|---|---|---|
| 1891 (5,678 miles) | $20,241,095 | $8,009,659 | $4,664,493 | $3,345,166 |
| 1892 (5,958 " ) | 21,409,352 | 8,623,950 | 5,102,018 | 3,521,932 |
| 1893 (6,327 " ) | 20,962,317 | 7,951,232 | 5,338,597 | 2,612,682 |
| 1894 (6,343 " ) | 18,572,167 | 6,787,134 | 6,589,378 | 167,756 |
| 1895 (6,443 " ) | 18,941,037 | 8,033,864 | 6,659,478 | 1,374,386 |
| 1896 (6,476 " ) | 20,681,597 | 8,618,747 | 6,911,974 | 1,706,773 |
| 1897 (6,568 " ) | 24,049,535 | 10,644,482 | 6,783,367 | 3,861,115 |
| 1898 (6,681 " ) | 26,138,977 | 10,898,738 | 6,774,321 | 4,124,417 |
| 1899 (7,000 " ) | 29,230,038 | 13,380,364 | 6,816,676 | 5,563,687 |
| 1900-01 (7,563 miles) (year end. June 30) | 30,885,204 | 13,042,801 | 7,455,835 | 5,586,966 |
| 1901-02 (7,587 " ) ( " " ) | 37,503,053 | 15,044,739 | 7,334,825 | 7,709,913 |

No report for the calendar year 1900 was published, and the company has now changed its fiscal year to end June 30.

Dividends paid in 1896, 2½ per cent., $1,612,946; balance surplus, $93,827. In 1897 paid 4 per cent. on preferred and 2½ per cent. on common $2,964,026, balance surplus $897,089. In 1898 paid 4 per cent. on both stocks, balance surplus $1,051,708. In 1899 paid 4 per cent. on preferred stock and 5 per cent. on common, balance surplus $2,203,847. In 1900-01 surplus over dividends $1,114,460. In 1901-02 surplus $3,263,073.

GROSS AND NET EARNINGS BY MONTHS FOR THREE YEARS.

| | 1900. | | 1901. | | 1902. | |
|---|---|---|---|---|---|---|
| | Gross. | Net. | Gross. | Net. | Gross. | Net. |
| January | $2,152,071 | $691,570 | $2,054,016 | $648,197 | $2,621,792, | $820,461 |
| February | 1,954,087 | 622,732 | 1,917,189 | 620,680 | 2,349,039 | 674,361 |
| March | 2,294,787 | 799,101 | 2,500,619 | 948,336 | 2,953,770 | 1,054,915 |
| April | 2,491,194 | 1,027,068 | 2,681,312 | 1,180,809 | 3,263,849 | 1,291,707 |
| May | 2,602,898 | 1,079,670 | 2,654,847 | 1,010,284 | 3,237,082 | 1,166,892 |
| June | 2,612,760 | 1,057,806 | 2,702,177 | 1,121,432 | 3,179,971 | 846,737 |
| July | 2,471,170 | 884,374 | 2,851,455 | 1,095,867 | 3,246,620 | 1,175,711 |
| August | 2,637,983 | 1,054,475 | 3,118,551 | 1,305,632 | 3,554,184 | 1,362,901 |
| September | 2,663,492 | 1,058,700 | 3,264,024 | 1,352,732 | 3,651,482 | 1,410,755 |
| October | 2,774,826 | 1,078,174 | 3,552,403 | 1,467,039 | 4,127,402 | 1,616,135 |
| November | 2,748,660 | 1,065,548 | 3,583,383 | 1,440,878 | 3,976,069 | 1,558,241 |
| December | 2,988,911 | 1,438,366 | 3,497,733 | 1,568,691 | 3,959,146 | 1,672,442 |
| Totals | $30,452,839 | $11,857,584 | $34,407,711 | $13,760,578 | $40,120,406 | $14,651,258 |
| Aver. per month. | 2,621,069 | 988,132 | 2,867,309 | 1,146,714 | 3,343,367 | 1,220,938 |

Proportionate taxes for each month are deducted from the net.

Dividends of 4 per cent. on the preferred stock are regularly paid, 2 per cent. half-yearly, April 1 and October 1.

On the common 4 per cent. was paid in 1885; in 1886, 1887, 1888 and 1889 3 per cent. was paid; in 1894, 5 per cent.; in 1895, none; in 1896 and 1897, 2½ per cent.; in 1898, 4½ per cent.; in 1899, 4 per cent. In 1900 3 per cent. was pai in April and 2½ per cent. in October. The April, 1901, dividend was also 2½ per cent., which has since been the regular rate. Dividends on the common are half-yearly, April 1 and October 1.

Chairman, Sir William C. Van Horne; President, Sir Thomas G. Shaughnessy; Second Vice-President and General Manager, David McNicoll; Third Vice-President, I. G. Ogden; Treasurer, W. Sutherland Taylor; Secretary and Assistant to the President, Charles Drinkwater, Montreal.

Directors—Lord Strathcona and Mount Royal, London; Sir William C. Van Horne, Richard B. Angus. Sir Thomas G. Shaughnessy, Charles R. Hosmer, Montreal; Wilmot D. Matthews, Edmund B. Osler, Toronto; Sir Sanford Fleming, Ottawa; Thomas Skinner, London, Eng.; George R. Harris, Boston.

Main office, Windsor and Osborne streets, Montreal. Annual meeting, first Wednesday in October. Books close not less than two weeks previous.

## CANE BELT RAILROAD CO.

A corporation formed under the laws of Texas, March 8, 1898. Road owned, Sealey, Tex., to Bay City, Tex., 76 miles. At the end of 1902 an extension of 30 miles to Matagorda, Tex., was in progress. Locomotives, 7; passenger cars, 8; freight cars, 123.

Stock......Par $100..............................Authorized, $100,000......Issued, $100,000

The company has no preferred stock. Stock is transferred at the company's office, Eagle Lake, Tex.

FUNDED DEBT.

1st mort., 5 per cent., due June, 1921, June and Dec............................... $750,000

The 1st mortgage is for $3,000,000, bonds to be issued at the rate of $10,000 per mile of road actually constructed, with a discretion on the part of the trustee to increase the amount to $15,000 per mile if such additional amount is needed for betterments. Trustee of mortgage, Lincoln Trust Co., which institution is registrar of and agent for the payment of interest. Coupons are also paid by Kountze Brothers, New York.

In the year ending June 30, 1902, the earnings were: gross, $178,791; net, $55,768.

President, Jonathan Lane; Vice-President and General Manager, W. T. Eldridge, Houston, Tex.; Secretary and Treasurer, I. P. Fell, Eagle Lake, Tex.

Directors—Jonathan Lane, William T. Eldridge, I. P. Fell, A. A. B. Woerheide, Charles Boedker, George F. Durant, William Duncan, E. H. Coffin, J. H. A. Meyer.

Main office, Eagle Lake, Tex. Annual meeting, first Monday in June.

## THE CAPE BRETON RAILWAY CO., LIMITED

A corporation formed under a special charter granted by the Province of Nova Scotia, March 30, 1899, its original title being the Cape Breton Railway Extension Co. In July, 1901, the company was reorganized and the name changed to the present style. The company in 1902 began the construction of a line from Sydney and Louisbourg, Cape Breton Island, to Port Hawkesbury. At present 30 miles, Port Hawkesbury to St. Peter, are nearly completed. The line is being built by the Dominion Securities Co., which controls the road.

Stock......Par $100...........................Authorized, $1,000,000......Issued, $1,000,000

FUNDED DEBT.

1st mort., 5 per cent., due July, 2001, Jan. and July................................ $500,000

It was stated that the company has a subsidy of $6,400 per mile of road from the Province of Nova Scotia, and a like subsidy from the Dominion.

The trustee of the 1st mortgage is the Standard Trust Co., New York. It is $2,400,000 authorized. The bonds were to be issued at the rate of $20,000 per mile.

In October, 1902, a reorganization committee, James G. Cannon, New York, requested deposits of the securities with the Trust Co. of the Republic, New York.

President, Myron G. Evans; Vice-President, Robert J. Campbell; Secretary and Treasurer, George E. Johnson; General Counsel, White & Wing, New York.

Directors—Myron E. Evans, William A. Prendergast, Robert J. Campbell, James A. Minor, William C. White, William W. Orr, George E. Johnson, Arthur L. Meyer, Michael Guerin.

Main office, Montreal; New York office, 35 Nassau street.

## CAROLINA & NORTHWESTERN RAILWAY CO.

This company was formed February 28, 1890, and in January, 1897, acquired and consolidated with the Chester & Lenoir Railroad, which was sold under foreclosure.

Road owned, Chester, S. C., to Lenoir, N. C., 110 miles. Line was narrow gauge, but present company changed it to standard gauge, which work was to be completed in 1902. It is also proposed to build an extension of the road to East Tennessee. Locomotives, 8; passenger cars, 14; freight cars, 132.

Stock......Par $50 ..............................Authorized, $350,000......Issued, $350,000

Stock is transferred by the secretary of the company.

It has been reported that the syndicate which controls this company proposed to change the capitalization and issue $1,000,000 each of common and preferred stock.

FUNDED DEBT.

Gen mort., 5 per cent., due May, 1950, May and Nov.............................. $1,320,000

The mortgage is $14,000 per mile authorized. Trustee of the mortgage, Trust Co. of America, New York. Interest is paid at the company's office. The company retired about $440,000 of old 1st mortgage bonds with a like amount of new bonds.

In the year ending November 30, 1901, the gross earnings were $145,737; net, $42,720; charges, $19,250; balance, surplus, $23,470.

President, William A. Barber, New York; Treasurer, M. S. Lewis; Secretary, J. J. McLure; General Manager, L. T. Nichols, Chester, S. C.

Directors—J. L. Agurs, T. H. White, J. H. Marion, W. Holmes Hardin, Chester, S. C.; J. F. Wallace, Yorkville, S. C.; G. A. Gray, Gastonia, N. C.; J. H. Martin, Hickory, N. C.

Main office, Chester, S. C.; New York office, 35 Nassau street. Annual meeting, in September, at Chester, S. C.

## CARRABELLE, TALLAHASSEE & GEORGIA RAILWAY CO.

Road owned, Carrabelle to Tallahassee, Fla., 50 miles; an extension of 50 miles to Thomasville, Ga., is in progress.

Stock......Par $100..........................Authorized, $1,000,000......Issued, $1,000,000

FUNDED DEBT.

1st mort., 6 per cent., due 1914.................................................... $500,000

President, Charles M. Zeh, Newark, N. J.; Vice-President, S. D. Chittenden; Secretary and Treasurer, J. P. Contrell, Tallahassee.

Directors—Charles M. Zeh, J. William Clark, Newark, N. J.; S. D. Chittenden, F. T. Myers, R. L. Murray, Tallahassee.

Main office, Tallahassee, Fla.

## CENTRAL BRANCH RAILWAY CO.

(Controlled by Missouri Pacific Railway Co.)

A corporation formed under the laws of Kansas, July 7, 1899, in pursuance of a reorganization of the Central Branch Union Pacific Railway Co., the Atchison, Jewell County & Western and the Atchison, Colorado & Pacific roads, which, though owned by the Union Pacific, had been leased to and operated by the Missouri Pacific, the latter having acquired in 1898 the Union Pacific interests in the property, reorganized it under the present title, and owns all the stock of the company.

Road owned, Atchison to Lenora, Kan., 293 miles; branches, 95 miles; total, 388 miles. Locomotives, 21; passenger cars, 22; freight cars, 844.

Stock......Par $100..........................Authorized, $7,585,000......Issued, $7,585,000

FUNDED DEBT.

Central Branch Union Pac. Ry. 1st mort., 4 per cent., due June, 1948, June and Dec... $2,500,000
Central Branch Ry. 1st mort., 4 per cent. due Feb., 1919, Feb. and Aug............. 3,459,00

Total............................ .... .................................. $5,959,000

The old company guaranteed $4,070,000 6 per cent. bonds of Atchison, Colorado & Pacific and $542,000 6 per cent. bonds of Atchison, Jewell County & Western. Assenting holders of these bonds received in the reorganization 75 per cent. of their holdings in the new 4s, which are guaranteed by the Missouri Pacific.

This road was operated by the Missouri Pacific under a lease of 25 years from September, 1885, paying net earnings to the Union Pacific, which owned $874,200 of the old company's stock. Lease was terminable on six months' notice. The first mortgage and funded bond interest, due in 1895, was not paid. Committees representing various mortgages were appointed and foreclosure suits instituted. The bonds of this company held by government in Union Pacific sinking fund (about $1,000,000) were purchased at Union Pacific foreclosure sale by the Union Pacific reorganization committee, and sold in December, 1897, to interests identified with Missouri Pacific Railway. The road was sold under foreclosure, May 23, 1898, and reorganized as stated above.

EARNINGS.

| | Gross. | Net. | Charges. | | Surplus. |
|---|---|---|---|---|---|
| 1893 | $971,499 | $117,484 | $441,456 | Def. | $326,972 |
| 1894 | 731,988 | 54,550 | 440,319 | " | 385,769 |
| 1895 | 621,473 | Def. 24,697 | 346,283 | " | 363,485 |
| 1896 | 781,009 | 100,652 | ........ | | ........ |
| 1897 | 1,226,871 | 277,597 | ........ | | ........ |
| 1898 (6 months ending Dec. 31) | 294,219 | 100,563 | ........ | | ........ |
| 1899 | 1,263,052 | 366,213 | 313,857 | | 52,356 |
| 1900 | 1,335,615 | 359,035 | 327,134 | | 31,901 |
| 1901 | 1,315,996 | 355,681 | 325,488 | | 30,192 |
| 1902 | 1,091,792 | 279,013 | 329,318 | Def. | 50,305 |

In 1900, the company was credited with settlements under claims of Union Pacific purchased, amounting to $365,644.

President, C. G. Warner, St. Louis; Vice-President, H. B. Henson; Secretary and Treasurer, A. H. Calef, New York; Assistant Secretary and Treasurer, D. S. H. Smith, St. Louis.

Main office, Atchison, Kan.; New York office, 195 Broadway.

## CENTRAL FLORIDA & GULF COAST RAILROAD CO.

A corporation formed under the laws of Florida.

Road under construction, Plant City, Fla., to Gasparilla Island, via Braidentown, 110 miles, with branches of 25 miles in addition. Road completed at end of 1902, 15 miles.

Stock......Par $100......................Authorized, $15,000 per mile......Issued, $225,000

The company has no preferred stock.

FUNDED DEBT.

1st mort., 5 per cent., due April, 1932, April and Oct.................................. $90,000

The 1st mortgage bonds are at the rate of $15,000 per mile, with unauthorized maximum of $2,000,000. Trustee of mortgage and agent for the payment of interest, Standard Trust Co., New York.

President, Thomas H. McDonnell, Quincy, Mass.; Vice-President, Edward Page, Auburndale, Mass.; Secretary and Treasurer, Oscar Owen, Melrose, Mass.; General Manager, John H. Dawe, Boston.

Directors—Harold Page, Charles C. Loring, George G. Hackett, Boston; E. R. Gunby, Tampa, Fla.; R. A. Van Agnew, Kissimmee, Fla.; Thomas H. McDonnell, Quincy, Mass.; Edward Page, Auburndale, Mass.; Oscar Owen, Melrose, Mass.

Main office, 43 Milk street, Boston; secretary's office, 19 Doane street, Boston.

## CENTRAL NEW ENGLAND RAILWAY

This company, formed in 1899, is the successor under reorganization of the Philadelphia, Reading & New England Railroad Co., foreclosed in October, 1898.

Road owned, from Campbell Hall, N. Y., to Silvernails, N. Y., 58 miles, including the Poughkeepsie Bridge, 3 miles; leases Hartford & Connecticut Western, 109 miles; Dutchess County Railroad, Poughkeepsie to Hopewell, 12 miles; extension from Tariffville, Conn., to Springfield, Mass., completed in 1902, 18 miles; total operated, 197 miles. This company owns a majority of the stock of Hartford & Connecticut Western and Dutchess County roads. Locomotives, 36; passenger cars, 30; freight cars, 460.

Stock....Per $100.....Authorized { com., $3,450,000; pref., 3,150,000 } Issued { com., $3,450,000; pref., 3,150,000 } $6,600,000

The preferred stock is 4 per cent., non-cumulative. Both classes of stock are held in a voting trust for ten years, or until 4 per cent. interest has been paid on the general mortgage bonds for two consecutive years.

FUNDED DEBT.

| | |
|---|---|
| 1st mort., 5 per cent., due Feb., 1919, Feb. and Aug. | $650,000 |
| Gen. mort. income, 5 per cent., due Feb., 1949, Oct. | 7,250,000 |
| Dutchess Co. R.R., 1st mort., guar., 4½ per cent., due June 1, 1940, June and Dec. | 350,000 |
| Hartford & Conn. West., 1st mort., guar., 5 per cent., due July, 1903, Jan. and July. | 700,000 |
| Total | $8,950,000 |

In the reorganization the Dutchess County Railroad 6 per cent. bonds were reduced from 6 per cent. to 4½ per cent.

The lease of the Hartford & Connecticut Western is for 50 years from 1890 at 2 per cent. per annum on stock, $2,635,700, and interest on its bonds.

The new 5 per cent. first mortgage is for $1,250,000, of which $618,000 are issuable for assessments and balance reserved for Springfield extension and for improvements. The general 5 er cent. income mortgage is $8,500,000, of which $1,250,000 is reserved to retire the 1st mortgage bonds.

EARNINGS.

| Year ending June 30. | Gross. | Net. |
|---|---|---|
| 1892-93 (11 months) | $1,023,218 | Def. $4,365 |
| 1893-94 | 779,876 | 12,688 |
| 1894-95 | 724,114 | 201,661 |
| 1895-96 | 746,569 | 200,674 |
| 1896-97 | 647,474 | 195,177 |
| 1897-98 | 681,611 | 213,529 |
| 1898-99 | 677,206 | 205,266 |
| 1899-00 | 695,646 | 146,117 |
| 1900-01 | 711,759 | 176,656 |
| 1901-02 | 593,965 | 157,715 |

The old company was formed in 1892 by consolidation of the Central New England & Western, which was reorganized as the Philadelphia, Reading & New England in interest of Philadelphia & Reading and the Poughkeepsie Bridge. The Philadelphia & Reading practically owned all the common stock and controlled the road under a contract guaranteeing rentals and interest on 1st mortgage bonds. Total issue of 1st mortgage bonds was $7,250,000, of which $1,000,000 was reserved for improvements; $2,500,000 bore 4 per cent. interest until September, 1895, and 5 per cent. thereafter. Interest was defaulted in May and August, 1893, after appointment of receivers of the Philadelphia & Reading, and receiver was appointed for this road. No provision was made for company in the Reading reorganization and guarantee was cut off by foreclosure of lessee. Details of reorganization plan are given in MANUAL for 1900.

President, Chester W. Chapin, New York; Vice-President, Arthur Brock, Philadelphia; Treasurer, J. K. O. Sherwood, New York; Secretary, Clyde A. Heller, Philadelphia.

Directors—Arthur Brock, Lebanon, Pa.; H. O. Seixas, Chester W. Chapin, D. A. Geraty, Joseph B. Bourne, J. K. O. Sherwood, New York; John W. Brock, Clyde A. Heller, Joseph F. Sinnott, Philadelphia; James A. Rumrill, J. H. Appleton, Springfield, Mass.

Main office, Poughkeepsie, N. Y.; treasurer's office, 192 Broadway, New York.

---

## CENTRAL OF GEORGIA RAILWAY CO.

Road owned, Savannah, Ga., to Atlanta, 295 miles; Macon Junction, Ga., to Athens, Ga., 102 miles; Columbus, Ga., to Birmingham, Ala., 156 miles; Columbus, Ga., to Andalusia, Ala., 138 miles; Griffin, Ga., to Chattanooga, Tenn., 198 miles; Montgomery to Eufaula, Ala., 80 miles; other branches owned, 480 miles; total owned, 1,449 miles; leased, Augusta & Savannah Railroad, 53 miles; Southwestern Railroad of Georgia, 333 miles; Chattahoochee & Gulf, 68 miles; total of system, 1,903 miles; total operated, 1,845 miles. The line from Meldrim, Ga., to Lyons, Ga., 58 miles, is leased to Seaboard Air Line Railway. Also controls the Ocean Steamship Co., between New York and Savannah, and New England & Savannah Steamship Co., Savannah and Boston line, with 8 steel steamships.

In January, 1897, this company purchased the Middle Georgia & Atlantic Railway, Milledgeville to Covington, Ga., 64 miles. In 1898 purchased the Bruton & Pineora Railway, 58 miles, and in 1901 extended it 9 miles to Statesboro, Ga. In 1901 purchased the Dover & Statesboro Railroad, 10 miles; the Chattanooga & Durham, 18 miles, and the Chattanooga, Rome & Southern, 138 miles, which have all been merged with this company. In 1902 various extensions were understood to be under consideration. Locomotives, 224; passenger cars, 209; freight cars, 6,387.

The company is a reorganization in 1895 of the Central Railroad & Banking Co. of Georgia.

Stock......Par $100.......................... Authorized, $5,000,000.....Issued, $5,000,000

FUNDED DEBT.

| | |
|---|---|
| 1st mort., 5 per cent., due Nov., 1945, Feb. and Aug. | $7,000,000 |
| Cons. mort., 5 per cent., due Nov., 1945, May and Nov. | 17,200,000 |
| Mobile Div., 1st mort., 5 per cent., due Jan., 1946, Jan. and July | 1,000,000 |
| Macon & Nor. Div., 1st mort., 5 per cent., due Jan., 1946, Jan. and July | 840,000 |
| Middle Ga. & Atlantic, 1st mort., 5 per cent., due Jan., 1947, Jan. and July | 413,000 |
| Eatonton Br., 1st mort., 5 per cent., due June, 1926, June and Dec. | 168,000 |
| Chattanooga Div., purchase money mort., 4 per cent., due 1951, June and Dec. | 1,840,000 |
| Chattanooga, Rome & Southern, 1st mort., 5 per cent., due July, 1947, Jan. and July. | 343,000 |
| Oconee Div., 1st mort., 5 per cent., due Dec., 1945, June and Dec. | 462,000 |
| Cent. Railroad & Banking collateral trust, 5 per cent., due May, 1937, May and Nov. | 4,880,000 |
| Cent. of Ga. Ry., 1st pfd. incomes, 5 per cent., due 1945, Oct. | 4,000,000 |
| Cent. of Ga. Ry., 2d pfd. incomes, 5 per cent., due 1945, Oct. | 7,000,000 |
| Cent. of Ga. Ry., 3d pfd. incomes, 5 per cent., due 1945, Oct. | 4,000,000 |
| Chattahoochie & Gulf, 1st mort., 5 per cent., due July, 1930, Jan. and July. | 288,000 |
| Ocean S.S. Co., 1st mort., guar. 5 per cent., due July, 1920, Jan. and July. | 1,000,000 |
| Total | $50,434,000 |

The three classes of preferred income bonds are in order of priority entitled to 5 per cent. each when earned, non-cumulative. The Mobile Division 1st mortgage covers the former Mobile & Girard road, and the Macon & Northern Division firsts are a lien on the former Macon & Northern road, Macon Junction, Ga., to Athens, 102 miles. The company guarantees 5 per cent. dividends on $1,022,900 Augusta & Savannah stock, and the same on $5,191,100 Southwestern Railroad stock and 6 per cent. on $573,400 stock and bonds of the Chattahoochee & Gulf Railroad Co.

The consolidated mortgage is a first lien on 600 miles, comprising the old Savannah & Western, Montgomery & Eufaula and Savannah & Atlantic roads, and a second lien on the main and certain other lines. The issue may be increased to a maximum of $18,500,000, at the rate of not more than $500,000 a year for additions and improvements.

The Chattanooga Division 4 per cent. bonds were issued in 1901 to acquire the Chattanooga, Rome & Southern Railway and the Chattanooga & Durham. The mortgage is for $2,400,000, there being $343,000 of the bonds reserved to retire the Chattanooga, Rome & Southern 5s and $217,000 reserved for improvements.

The old company was chartered in 1835, and for many years paid regular dividends. Its charter provided for a bank at Savannah, which was operated with a capital of $500,000. The company acquired large interests in the Ocean Steamship Company, Savannah & Western Railway, Western Railway of Alabama, Montgomer & Eufaula, Port Royal & Western Carolina, and Port Royal & Augusta and other roads, the entire system at one time comprising over 2,600 miles of road.

In December, 1887, a proprietary corporation, The Georgia Co., was formed to hold a controlling interest ($4,000,000) of stock of the Central Railroad & Banking Co. October, 1888, the entire capital stock of the Georgia Co. was purchased by the Richmond & West Point Terminal Co. In 1891 the railroad and steamship lines were leased for 99 years to the Georgia Pacific, which road was leased to the Richmond & Danville.

On July 1, 1892, company defaulted on interest. E. P. Alexander, then President, was appointed Receiver of company March 4, 1892. On March 28 receivership was made permanent and a Board of Receivers, composed of the Directors, appointed. A decision was made in April, 1892, enjoining the Richmond Terminal from voting its stock, and on May 16 an election was held by order of Court, with a new Board of Directors, H. M. Comer, the Chairman of the Board of Receivers, becoming President, and was on July 15 appointed sole Receiver. In October, 1893, R. Somers Hayes of New York was appointed co-receiver. Litigation regarding the rights of the Richmond Terminal continued, and the Receiver of that company also instituted proceedings to recover from the syndicate which sold the stock of the Georgia Company to the Terminal Company the amount so paid. The Court decided in 1893 that the Richmond Terminal was entitled to vote its stock, and injunction was dissolved.

In 1894 a reorganization plan was announced and was carried out in 1895, the properties being foreclosed and purchased by the reorganization committee. The securities of the old Central Railroad & Banking Co. of Georgia affected by the plan, and terms of their exchange for the new, were given in the MANUAL for 1898.

In October, 1896, company paid 1¼ per cent. on 1st preference incomes; on October 1, 1897, paid 2½ per cent.; on October 1, 1898, 2 per cent.; October 1, 1899, 2 per cent.; October 1, 1900, 3½ per cent.; October 1, 1901, 5 per cent., and October 1, 1902, 3 per cent.

EARNINGS.

Year ending June 30.

| | Gross. | Net. | Net Income. | Charges. | Surplus. |
|---|---|---|---|---|---|
| 1892-93 (1,965 miles)....... | $7,823,125 | $855,272 | ........ | ........ | ...... |
| 1893-94 (1,417 " )... ... | 5,179,508 | 1,991,056 | ........ | ........ | ...... |
| 1894-95 (1,415 " )....... | 5,104,807 | 1,296,735 | ........ | ........ | ...... |
| 1895-96 (1,456 " )....... | 5,429,082 | 1,663,421 | ........ | ........ | ...... |
| 1896-97 (1,491 " )....... | 5,280,695 | 1,828,133 | $2,157,941 | $1,841,977 | $315,964 |
| 1897-98 (1,524 " )....... | 5,507,069 | 1,897,160 | 2,007,435 | 1,934,292 | 73,143 |
| 1898-99 (1,524 " )....... | 5,767,345 | 1,800,634 | 2,015,852 | 1,956,964 | 58,888 |
| 1899-00 (1,539 " )....... | 6,086,263 | 1,879,857 | 2,111,321 | 1,980,355 | 130,966 |
| 1900-01 (1,678 " )....... | 6,920,715 | 1,929,157 | 2,116,516 | 1,915,163 | 201,353 |
| 1901-02 (1,845 " )....... | 7,750,691 | 1,950,181 | 2,151,855 | 2,028,915 | 122,940 |

The net earnings are from the railroad lines only; the net income includes receipts from steamships.

The following exhibits the comparative freight traffic statistics of the company:

| | Average Mileage. | Total Tonnage. | Tons Carried One Mile. | Freight Density. | Rate per Ton per Mile. | Earnings per Train Mile. | Average Ton per Train. |
|---|---|---|---|---|---|---|---|
| 1896-99.. | 1,491 | 1,875,260 | 292,186,403 | 195,912 | 1.205c | $1.791 | 149 |
| 1897-98.. | 1,524 | 2,036,616 | 325,621,615 | 213,703 | 1.145 | 1.717 | 141 |
| 1898-99.. | 1,524 | 2,199,048 | 355,713,668 | 233,452 | 1.044 | 1.578 | 141 |
| 1899-00.. | 1,539 | 2,457,977 | 365,901,969 | 237,735 | 1.096 | 1.704 | 148 |
| 1900-01.. | 1,678 | 2,708,915 | 437,060,554 | 260,495 | 1.064 | 1.816 | 163 |
| 1901-02.. | 1,845 | 3,258,444 | 471,487,448 | 255,594 | 1.129 | 1.907 | 163 |

Chairman, J. F. Hanson, Macon, Ga.; President, John M. Egan; Treasurer, T. M. Cunningham; Auditor, W. D. Beymer, Savannah, Ga.

Directors—George J. Mills, Joseph Hull, Alexander R. Lawton, John M. Egan, Savannah, Ga.; E. P. Howell, J. W. English, Atlanta, Ga.; U. B. Harrold, Americus, Ga.; W. C. Bradley, Columbus, Ga.; E. T. Comer, J. F. Hanson, Samuel R. Jacques, Macon, Ga.; Samuel Spencer, G. G. Haven, Charles Steele, New York.

Main office, Savannah, Ga. Annual meeting, second Monday in October, at Savannah, Ga.

## CENTRAL PACIFIC RAILWAY CO.

(Leased to Southern Pacific Co.)

A corporation formed under the laws of Utah, July 29, 1899, as successor to railroad company of same name, the capital of which was in the above year readjusted and control of the property acquired by the Southern Pacific Co.

Road owned, San Francisco, Cal., to Ogden, Wash., 871 miles; Roseville, Cal., to Oregon State Line, 296 miles; Lathrop to Goshen, Cal., 146 miles; branches, 35 miles; total owned, 1,348 miles; trackage, 11 miles; grand total, 1,359 miles. Locomotives, 334; passenger cars, 324; freight cars, 8,082; floating equipment, 5 ferryboats, 5 river steamers, 1 tug, 2 car transfer steamers, 4 barges.

Stock Par $100..Authorized { com., $67,275,500 / pref., 20,000,000 } Issued { com., $67,275,500 / pref., 12,000,000 } $79,275,500

The preferred stock is 4 per cent., non-cumulative. The outstanding preferred was delivered to Southern Pacific Co. in consideration of an equal amount of its 4 per cent. collateral bonds. The balance can only be used to provide, if necessary, for meeting notes to the United States, and after they are all paid only for improvements. The Southern Pacific also holds the entire common stock of this company.

FUNDED DEBT (NEW COMPANY).

| | |
|---|---|
| 1st refunding mort., 4 per cent., due 1989, Feb. and Aug.................... ...... | $58,778,000 |
| New 3½ per cent. mort., due 1925, Jan. and Dec........................... ....... | 18,834,500 |
| Notes to United States Government, 3 per cent., due 1903-09..................... | 39,147,010 |
| California & Oregon 1st mort., extended 5 per cent., due Jan., 1918, Jan. and July | 515,000 |
| Old mort. bonds, 5 per cent., due April, 1939, April and October.................. | 99,000 |
| Fifty year bonds, 6 per cent., due 1936............................................ | 25,000 |
| Total............................................................... | $117,398,510 |

The Southern Pacific Co. endorses the new bond issues, principal and interest. The 1st refunding 4s are $100,000,000, of which $39,808,000 are held as collateral for notes to United

States Government, and the bonds thus held are released as the maturing notes are paid. In February, 1900, and February, 1901, two notes for $2,940,635 each were anticipated and an equal amount of 4s released; $51,253,500 of the refunding 4s were used in exchange for old bonds, and $1,690,500 purchased by reorganization syndicate. The 3½ per cent. mortgage is a second lien on property covered by 1st refunding 4s. The 3 per cent. notes issued to Government in settlement for its claims under subsidy were $58,812,714, payable in half yearly instalments of $2,940,635 within 10 years. They are secured by the deposit of refunding 4s against them. The syndicate paid the notes maturing from August 1, 1899, to February 1, 1901, inclusive. The company paid the notes maturing to August, 1902, inclusive.

Details regarding the government subsidy bonds of the old company, its relations to the Government and so forth are given in full in the MANUAL for 1900.

The old company had $67,225,500 stock. Last dividend on old stock, ½ per cent., January 3, 1899.

Property was leased from April 1, 1885, by the Southern Pacific Co., for 99 years, for interest on the bonded debt and $1,360,000 per year as a minimum, with three times that amount as a maximum, the rental subject to be applied first to retire floating debt. The floating debt was discharged in 1887, and a dividend of 1 per cent. paid in February, 1888; after which time 2 per cent. per annum was paid half yearly, February and August, until September, 1893, when it was made 1 per cent.; in 1894 no dividend was paid and in 1895 ½ per cent. under a new agreement, by which 1 per cent. per annum was guaranteed until settlement with the United States Goverment was reached, when 2 per cent. was to be paid for two years.

In 1899-1900 a dividend of 2 per cent. was paid on the new preferred stock.

In December, 1893, a new lease was executed to the Southern Pacific by which the rental was to be the net amount remaining after the payment of all charges.

In view of the situation of government debt and the failure of efforts to secure Congressional authority for a settlement a stockholders' committee was formed in London in 1897 with F. G. Banbury chairman, also one in New York, in co-operation with London committee, with August Belmont as chairman. The old 1st mortgage bonds were represented by Speyer & Co., New York, who issued their certificates of deposit for the bonds, nearly all of which were deposited with them. The gold 5s of 1939 were also represented by Speyer & Co.

In July, 1898, Congress appointed a commission consisting of the Secretaries of the Treasury and Interior with the Attorney-General to negotiate a settlement of the Central Pacific's debt to the government.

On February 18, 1899, it was announced that an agreement had been reached between the company and the commissioners on behalf of the United States for a settlement of the company's debt to the Government. The amount of the net claims on the Central Pacific and Western Pacific was fixed on February 1, 1899, at $58,812,714, and the agreement included payment thereof in twenty equal semi-annual instalments, with interest 3 per cent., the first payment maturing August 1, 1899. The company gave twenty notes for the same, secured by deposit of 4 per cent. refunding bonds, and the first four notes were to be taken up at once. On February 9, 1899, Speyer & Co., New York, issued a plan for financial readjustment of company and exchange of securities for the following, viz.: $20,000.000 4 per cent., cumulative, preferred stock; $67,275,500 common stock; $100,000,000 1st mortgage refunding 4 per cent. bonds, and $25,000,000 3½ per cent. thirty-year mortgage bonds. The common stock was sold to a syndicate, which offered for the old stock on payment of $2 per share an equal amount of stock of the Southern Pacific Co., with a bonus of 25 per cent. in Southern Pacific 4 per cent. collateral trust bonds, secured by a deposit of the Central Pacific preferred and common stock it had acquired. The new preferred stock was delivered to the Southern Pacific Co.

The terms on which the old stock and bonds were exchanged were given in full in the MANUAL for 1900.

A great majority of old bonds and stocks accepted the plan and were exchanged for the new securities. Plans were carried out and road reorganized as stated above.

EARNINGS.

| | Div. Paid. | Gross. | Net. | Charges. | Su |
|---|---|---|---|---|---|
| 1892 ........................ | 2 | $14,746,652 | $5,707,578 | ........ | ........ |
| 1893 ........................ | 2 | 14,319,907 | 5,739,335 | ........ | ........ |
| 1894 ........................ | .. | 13,118,245 | 4,949,387 | ........ | ........ |
| 1895 ........................ | ½ | 13,045,657 | 4,193,872 | ....... | ....... |
| 1896 ........................ | 1 | 12,527,084 | 4,171,490 | ........ | . |
| 1896-97 (6 mos. to June 30)..... | 1 | 5,806,720 | 2,180,450 | ........ | :::::::. |
| 1897-98 (year ending June 30).. | 1 | 15,766,348 | 6,544,679 | ........ | ........ |
| 1898-99 ( " " " ).. | .. | 16,401,026 | 6,362,378 | ........ | ........ |
| 1899-00 ( " " " ).. | *2 | 19,483,420 | 7,375,915 | $4,548,590 | $2,827,225 |
| 1900-01 ( " " " ).. | .. | 19,328,289 | 8,575,625 | 6,935,295 | 1,640,330 |
| 1901-02........ ............. | .. | 20,191,111 | 8,633,405 | 4,916,715 | 3,715,719 |

* On new preferred stock.

The company has a land grant estimated at 12,822,400 acres. The sales during the year 1890 were 53,601 acres for $194,768; in 1891, 71,313 acres for $290,103; in 1892, 16,714 acres for $50,963; in 1893, 39,258 acres for $88,562; in 1894, 48,107 acres for $96,767; in 1895, 259,692 acres for $223,816; in 1898, $308,362 was received from land department.

President, Edward H. Harriman; Vice-President, Charles H. Tweed, New York; Secretary, J. L. Willcutt; Treasurer, N. T. Smith, San Francisco.

Directors—Edward H. Harriman, David B. Hempstead, W. H. Chever, D. R. Gray, Thomas Marshall, J. S. Noble, H. E. Huntington, J. C. Royle, Charles H. Tweed.

Main office, Salt Lake City; New York office, 120 Broadway. Bonds registered at the company's New York office. Annual meeting, second Tuesday in April.

---

## CENTRAL RAILROAD CO. OF NEW JERSEY

(Controlled by the Reading Co.)

Road owned main line Jersey City to Phillipsburg, 72 miles; branches, 82 miles; controlled, 217 miles; leased, 248 miles; trackage, 20 miles; total operated, 638 miles. The controlled and leased lines include the New Jersey Southern Division, 199 miles; Lehigh & Susquehanna Division and branches, 229 miles. The New York & Long Branch road, 38 miles, owned, but is worked under a joint agreement with the Pennsylvania Railroad Co., both companies running trains over the road. Total mileage, 677 miles.

The company also has a ferry between New York and Jersey City, and operates steamboats between New York and Atlantic Highlands. Locomotives, 422; passenger cars, 453; freight cars, 17,202. The company has considerable floating equipment, including 3 steamboats, 7 ferry-boats, 9 steam tugs and 35 floats and coal barges.

Stock......Par $100........................Authorized, $30,000,000......Issued, $27,415,800

Stock is transferred at the company's office, New York. Registrar, Central Trust Co., New York.

The February 1, 1900, quarterly dividend was increased from 1 per cent. to 1¼ per cent., and 5 per cent. was paid in the year 1900. The February, 1902, dividend was increased to 2 per cent. The dividends are paid quarterly, February (1), May, August and November.

FUNDED DEBT.

| | |
|---|---|
| Deben. bds., convertible into stock after 1885, 6 per cent., due May, 1908, May and Nov. | $50,000 |
| General mort., 5 per cent., due July, 1987, Jan. and July..... | 45,091,000 |
| Equipment mort., 4 per cent., 1899-1909, June and Dec.... | 1,190,000 |
| " " " 1902-12, May and Nov.... | 2,500,000 |
| Real Estate mortgages.... | 179,100 |
| Total.... | $49,010,100 |

FUNDED DEBT—CONTROLLED LINES GUARANTEED.

| | |
|---|---|
| N. Y. & Long Branch, gen. mort., 4 per cent., due Sept., 1941, March and Sept..... | 1,535,000 |
| N. Y. & L. B., gen. mort., 5 per cent., due Sept., 1941, March and Sept.... | 192,000 |
| Amer. Dock & Imp't Co., 1st mort., gold, 5 per cent., due July, 1921, Jan. and July.. | 4,987,000 |

The Lehigh & Wilkes-Barre Coal Co. consolidated mortgage extended 4½ per cent. bonds, $12,175,000, issued in 1900, are guaranteed, principal and interest, by this company. The company is joint guarantor with the Lehigh Coal & Navigation Co. of $1,062,000 Lehigh & Hudson River 5 per cent. 1st mortgage bonds.

For history of the company see MANUAL for 1902.

In January, 1901, the Reading Co. acquired a majority interest in the stock of this company, paying $160 per share. Minority stockholders were given an option to sell one-half of their holdings to the Reading Co. at the same price, the option expiring January 21, 1901. Under this arrangement the Reading acquired in all $14,500,000 of this company's stock, which amount is deposited as security for the Reading Co.'s collateral trust 4 per cent. mortgage bonds.

EARNINGS.

| | Dividends. | Gross. | Per Cent. Oper. Exp. | Net. | Charges. | Surplus. |
|---|---|---|---|---|---|---|
| 1892 | 7 | $14,716,236 | 59.94 | $6,879,755 | $4,549,370 | $2,330,394 |
| 1893 | 7 | 14,967,956 | 60.91 | 6,874,439 | 4,735,649 | 2,138,790 |
| 1894 | 7 | 12,659,941 | 66.65 | 5,363,033 | 4,430,946 | 932,087 |
| 1895 | 5 | 13,568,024 | 61.14 | 6,474,545 | 4,646,258 | 1,828,288 |
| 1896 | 5 | 13,117,350 | 63.42 | 6,067,342 | 4,671,077 | 1,396,265 |
| 1897 | 4 | 13,212,772 | 61.82 | 5,742,240 | 4,655,623 | 1,086,617 |
| 1898 | 4 | 13,187,271 | 61.58 | 5,715,484 | 4,582,749 | 1,132,734 |
| 1899 | 4¼ | 15,591,198 | 59.94 | 6,904,537 | 4,842,188 | 2,062,348 |
| 1900 | 5 | 15,853,062 | 61.19 | 7,389,476 | 4,770,113 | 2,619,363 |
| 1901 | 5¼ | 18,616,307 | *51.19 | 9,364,587 | 6,141,104 | 3,223,484 |

——*Railroad lines only.

In 1902 the fiscal year was changed to end on June 30, and no report was issued for the calendar year 1902.

In 1894, after payment of dividends, there was a deficiency of $642,703. In 1895, surplus over dividends $703,438; in 1896, surplus $271,415; in 1897, surplus $186,737; in 1898, surplus $232,854; in 1899, surplus $957,864; in 1900, surplus $1,263,748; in 1901, surplus $1,652,968.

The company's coal tonnage has been: in 1894, 4,707,949 tons; in 1895, 5,121,797 tons; in 1896, 4,829,247 tons; in 1897, 4,894,890 tons; in 1898, 5,736,912 tons; in 1899, 6,304,801 tons; in 1900, 6,232,628 tons.

GROSS AND NET EARNINGS BY MONTHS FOR THREE YEARS.

| | 1900. | | 1901. | | 1902. | |
|---|---|---|---|---|---|---|
| | *Gross. | Net. | Gross. | Net. | Gross. | Net. |
| January | $1,303,419 | $556,037 | $1,406,018 | $654,343 | 1,309,512 | $542,077 |
| February | 1,089,955 | 380,777 | 1,164,482 | 444,394 | 1,217,279 | 462,874 |
| March | 1,143,823 | 401,859 | 1,363,104 | 586,549 | 1,138,671 | 285,530 |
| April | 1,236,991 | 474,194 | 1,340,189 | 519,823 | 1,580,377 | 654,853 |
| May | 1,262,185 | 521,790 | 1,316,044 | 543,381 | 1,196,124 | 320,641 |
| June | 1,353,217 | 546,344 | 1,503,780 | 647,221 | 990,874 | 186,141 |
| July | 1,309,234 | 560,147 | 1,404,737 | 651,838 | 1,038,917 | 186,225 |
| August | 1,572,490 | 675,528 | 1,574,597 | 714,431 | 1,190,549 | 337,359 |
| September | 1,247,128 | 471,201 | 1,443,845 | 651,435 | 997,552 | 134,490 |
| October | 1,028,815 | 238,534 | 1,543,880 | 633,108 | 1,087,387 | 128,149 |
| November | 1,380,266 | 583,192 | 1,513,047 | 751,394 | 1,730,695 | 871,717 |
| December | 1,925,539 | 743,455 | 1,273,892 | 780,382 | 1,629,724 | 647,200 |
| Totals | $15,853,062 | $6,153,158 | $15,286,710 | $9,364,588 | $15,107,661 | $4,757,256 |
| Aver. per month. | 1,321,089 | 512,763 | 1,273,892 | 780,382 | 1,258,972 | 396,438 |

Proportionate taxes for each month are deducted from the net.

President, George F. Baer; Vice-President and General Manager, W. G. Besler; Secretary and Treasurer, G. O. Waterman.

Directors—George F. Baer, Eben B. Thomas, Charles Steele, Harris C. Fahnestock, George F. Baker, Henry Graves, J. Rogers Maxwell, New York; Joseph S. Harris, J. Lowber Welsh, Philadelphia.

Main office, 143 Liberty street, New York. Annual meeting, Friday following the third Monday in September.

## CENTRAL RAILROAD CO. OF PENNSYLVANIA

A corporation formed under the laws of Pennsylvania in 1891.

Road owned, Bellefonte, Pa., to Mill Hill, Pa., 27 miles; branch, 5 miles; total operated, 32 miles. The road was completed in 1893. Further extensions are planned. Locomotives, 3; passenger cars, 6; freight cars, 11.

Stock......Par $50..........................Authorized, $1,200,000......Issued, $1,200,000

The company has no preferred stock. Transfer Agent, William J. McHugh, Philadelphia.

FUNDED DEBT.

1st mort., 6 per cent., due May, 1943, May and Nov.................................. $600,000

The authorized amount of the 1st mortgage is $1,200,000. Trustee of the mortgage and agent for the payment of interest, Fidelity Insurance Trust & Safe Deposit Co., Philadelphia.

In the year ending June 30, 1901, the company reported gross earnings $68,572, net $20,190.

President, Charles M. Clement, Bellefonte, Pa.; Vice-President, Edward L. Welsh, Reading Pa.; Secretary and Treasurer, William J. McHugh, Philadelphia.

Main office, 304 Walnut street, Philadelphia. Annual meeting, second Monday in January.

# CENTRAL VERMONT RAILWAY CO.

A company incorporated under special charter by Legislature of Vermont in November, 1898, to reorganize the railroad company of same title.

Road owned, Windsor, Vt., to St. Johns, P. Q., 178 miles; branches, 81 miles; Farnham to Dreighsburg, 18 miles; St. Albans to Richford, Vt., 28 miles; Essex Junction to Cambridge, Vt., 26 miles; total owned 331 miles; controlled, Montreal & Province Line Railway, 40 miles; leased, New London & Northern, 157 miles; Montville Branch, 3 miles; total system, 531 miles. Locomotives, 94; passenger cars, 115; freight cars, 2,130.

The Central Vermont Railroad, formed in 1892, was a consolidation of Vermont & Canada, Consolidated Railroad of Vermont, Central Vermont and Montpelier & White River Railroads. The Consolidated Railroad of Vermont was a reorganization, 1883, of the Vermont Central and Vermont & Canada.

Under the reorganization of 1898 several of the leased branches of the old company were acquired and consolidated with this company. The old company formerly leased the Rutland Railroad and the Ogdensburg & Lake Champlain Railroad.

Stock......Par $100..........................Authorized, $3,000,000......Issued, $3,000,000

Transfer Agent, American Loan & Trust Co., Boston.

FUNDED DEBT.

| | |
|---|---|
| 1st mort., Central Vermont Ry., 4 per cent., due May, 1920, quar., Feb............ | $11,000,000 |
| Montreal & Province Line, 1st mort., guar., 4 per cent., due Oct., 1910. April and Oct.. | 200,000 |
| Total............................................................ | $11,200,000 |

For details concerning the capitalization of the old company, see the MANUAL for 1901.

The Grand Trunk Railway Co. of Canada has a large interest in this property, and owns $2,185,100 of the stock of the company. The old company owed the Grand Trunk for considerable advances. In March, 1896, Grand Trunk brought a suit in equity against this company, under which Charles M. Hays, General Manager of the Grand Trunk Railway Co., and E. C. Smith, President of the Central Vermont Railroad, were named as Receivers. January, 1897, coupons of the consolidated 1st mortgage were not paid. A committee, B. P. Cheney of Boston chairman, was formed to represent interests of consolidated 5 per cent. mortgage bondholders. A new committee was also formed, headed by Ezra H. Baker and Henry L. Day, Boston.

In September, 1898, an agreement was reached by which a new plan was formed and accepted by bondholders. In pursuance of this the Central Vermont Railway Co. was incorporated by act of the Legislature of Vermont, and accepted by the Grand Trunk Railway Co. and the committee representing the Consolidated Railroad of Vermont 5 per cent. bonds. The authorized issue of the 21-year 1st mortgage 4 per cent. gold bonds of new company is $12,000,000, of which $1,000,000 are held in the treasury to be issued under restrictions for improvements, etc. Of the remaining $11,000,000, $7,000,000 retired the outstanding Consolidated Railroad of Vermont 5 per cent. bonds at par. The balance ($4,000,000) was issued in acquiring branch roads, or settlement of preferred claims, etc. Of the stock, part went to the 1st mortgage bondholders in payment of overdue interest, 8 per cent. on each bond. A majority of the stock, $2,185,100, is owned by the Grand Trunk Railway Co. The balance was issued for settlement of claims, etc. The new mortgage is a first lien on all the property of the company. The interest is guaranteed by the Grand Trunk Railway Co. under a traffic contract, by the terms of which the Grand Trunk Railway Co. agrees to set aside in any one year a sum not exceeding 30 per cent. of the gross business interchanged by the Grand Trunk Railway Co. and the Central Vermont Railway Co. This gross business has averaged from $1,200,000 to $1,500,000 per year. By the terms of mortgage the 1st mortgage bondholders name three directors in the new company, one of whom shall always be a member of the executive committee. In February, 1899, the road was sold under foreclosure and acquired by the present company in pursuance of above plan.

EARNINGS.

Year ending June 30.

| | Gross. | Net. | Charges. | Surplus. |
|---|---|---|---|---|
| 1898-99.................................. | $3,151,719 | $664,630 | $328,527 | $336,103 |
| 1899-00.................................. | 3,382,724 | 794,285 | 665,435 | 128,849 |
| 1900-01.................................. | 3,262,134 | 672,698 | 669,894 | 2,804 |
| 1901-02.................................. | 3,406,432 | 670,861 | 667,762 | 3,099 |

President, Charles M. Hays, Montreal; Vice-President and General Manager, E. H. Fitzhugh; Clerk and Treasurer, W. H. Chaffee; Auditor, W. G. Crabbe, St. Albans, Vt.

Directors—Charles M. Hays, Montreal; John Bell, Belleville, Ont.; Albert Tuttle, Fair Haven, Vt.; James L. Martin, Brattleboro, Vt.; Charles P. Smith, Burlington, Vt.; E. C.

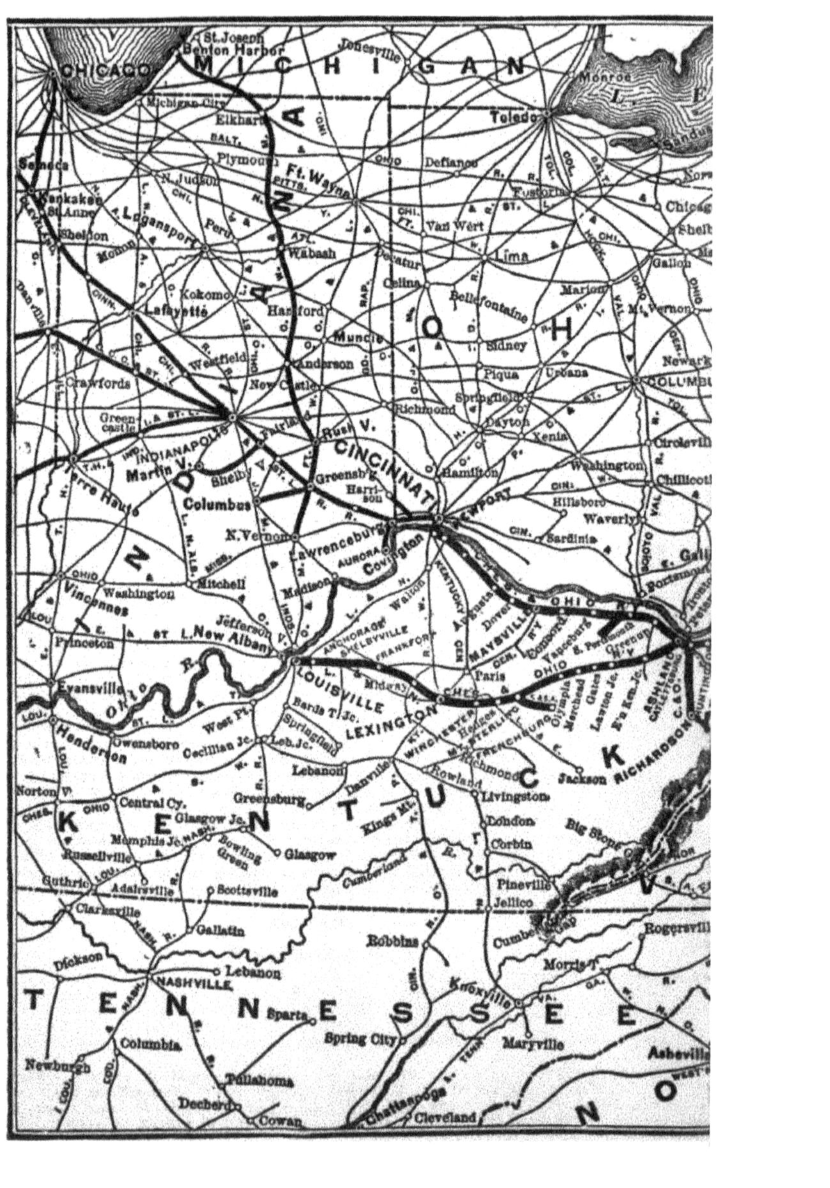

MICHIGAN
INDIANA
OHIO
KENTUCKY
TENNESSEE
CHICAGO
St. Joseph
Benton Harbor
Jonesville
Monroe
Toledo
Michigan City
Elkhart
Plymouth
Ft. Wayne
Defiance
Fostoria
Seneca
Kankakee
St. Anne
N. Judson
Logansport
Peru
Sheldon
Monon
Wabash
Van Wert
Lima
Decatur
Celina
Bellefontaine
Marion
Mt. Vernon
Galion
Kokomo
Lafayette
Danville
Hartford
Muncie
Sidney
Anderson
Westfield
Crawfords
New Castle
Piqua
Urbana
Newark
COLUMBUS
Springfield
Richmond
Dayton
Xenia
Green-castle
INDIANAPOLIS
Fairland
Rush V.
Circleville
Terre Haute
Martin V.
Shelby V.
Greensb'g
CINCINNATI
Hamilton
Washington
Chillicothe
Columbus
Harrison
NEWPORT
Hillsboro
Waverly
N. Vernon
Lawrenceburg
Sardinia
Aurora
Covington
Mitchell
Madison
Vincennes
Washington
Walton
Portsmouth
Augusta
Dover
MAYSVILLE
Jefferson V.
Princeton
New Albany
Anchorage
Shelbyville
Frankfort
Paris
Vanceburg
Greenup
Evansville
LOUISVILLE
Midway
Olympia
Morehead
Gates
Lawton Jc.
Ashland
Catlettsburg
Henderson
Owensboro
West Pt.
Bards T. Jc.
Springfield
Cecilian Jc.
Leb. Jc.
LEXINGTON
Winchester
Hedges
Mt. Sterling
Frenchburg
Lebanon
Danville
Richmond
Rowland
Jackson
RICHARDSON
Norton V.
Central Cy.
Greensburg
Livingston
Kings Mt.
Glasgow Jc.
London
Memphis Jc.
Bowling Green
Glasgow
Corbin
Big Stone Gap
Russellville
Cumberland R.
Guthrie
Adairsville
Scottsville
Pineville
Jellico
Clarksville
Gallatin
Cumberland Gap
Rogersville
Robbins
Dickson
Lebanon
Morristown
NASHVILLE
Knoxville
Sparta
Spring City
Maryville
Columbia
Asheville
Newburgh
Tullahoma
Decherd
Cowan
Chattanooga
Cleveland

Erie
Ashtabula
Cleveland
Warren
Akron
Alliance
New Castle
Butler
Homewood
Canton
Steuben v.
Pittsburg
Coshocton
Connellsville
Dresden
Bridgeport
Wheeling
Cambridge
Bellaire
Mounds V.
Marietta
Grafton
Parkersburg
Clarksburg
Mc Arthur
Pomeroy
Weston
Davis
Mt. Pleasant
Glenville
Buckhannon
Braxton
Addison
Clay C. H.
Gauley
OHIO RAILWAY
Pocahontas
Saltville
Glade Spr.
Stuart
Bristol
Jonesboro
Winston
Greensboro
Newton
Statesville
Salisbury
Lincolnton
Charlotte
Sanford
Elba

Smith, E. H. Fitzhugh, St. Albans; John W. Stewart, Middlebury, Vt.; W. Seward Webb, Shelburne, Vt.; Samuel E. Kilner, New York; Ezra H. Baker, Henry B. Day, Boston; John G. McCullough, Bennington, Vt.

Main office, St. Albans, Vt. Annual meeting, second Tuesday in October.

## CHARLESTON & WESTERN CAROLINA RAILWAY CO.

(Controlled by Atlantic Coast Line Co.)

Road owned, Port Royal, S. C., to Augusta, Ga., 112 miles; Augusta to Spartanburg, S. C., 133 miles; McCormick to Anderson, 58 miles; Laurens to Greenville, 36 miles; total, 339 miles. The Augusta Railway Terminal, 3 miles, is controlled. Locomotives, 29; passenger cars, 30; freight cars, 901.

This company, formed in 1896, is a reorganization of the Port Royal & Augusta and Port Royal & Western Carolina Railways, for the history of which see MANUAL for 1896.

In January, 1898, it was announced that a controlling interest had been sold to the Atlantic Coast Line Co.

Stock......Par $100........................Authorized, $1,200,000......Issued, $1,200,000

Transfer agency, 13 South street, Baltimore.

FUNDED DEBT.

| | |
|---|---|
| 1st mort., 5 per cent., due Oct., 1946, April and Oct. | $2,720,000 |
| Income mort., 5 per cent., non-cum., July | 2,380,000 |
| Augusta Railway Terminal, 1st mort., 6 per cent., due April, 1947, April and Oct. | 600,000 |
| Total | $5,700,000 |

First mortgage is $8,000 per mile, authorized. Income mortgage $7,000 per mile. This company guarantees by endorsement the principal and interest of the $600,000 Augusta Railway Terminal 1st mortgage bonds.

EARNINGS.

| Year ending June 30. | Gross. | Net. |
|---|---|---|
| 1896-97 | $635,717 | $208,012 |
| 1897-98 | 817,937 | 186,319 |
| 1898-99 | 841,520 | 197,493 |
| 1899-00 | 893,945 | 191,050 |
| 1900-01 | 963,297 | 190,053 |
| 1901-02 | 963,760 | 252,521 |

President, J. B. Cleveland, Spartanburg, S. C.; Vice-President, Henry Walters, New York; Treasurer, J. F. Post, Wilmington, N. C.; Secretary, R. D. Cronly, Baltimore.

General office, Augusta, Ga. Annual meeting, in November.

## CHARLESTON, CLENDENNIN & SUTTON RAILROAD CO.

Road owned, Charleston, W. Va., to Big Otter, 64 miles. An extension to Sutton, W. Va., is proposed. Locomotives, 4; passenger cars, 4; freight cars, 115.

Stock .....Par $100........................Authorized, $3,000,000......Issued, $1,867,300

FUNDED DEBT.

1st mort., 5 per cent., due April, 1944, April and Oct. .................... $1,500,000

The 1st mortgage is authorized at the rate of $30,000 per mile or $3,000,000 in all. The trustee of the mortgage is the West End Trust & Safe Deposit Co., Philadelphia.

In the year ending Dec. 31, 1901, the gross was $173,909 and the net earnings $90,438.

President, Thomas H. Given, Pittsburg; Vice-President, C. C. Lewis, Charleston, W. Va.; Secretary and Treasurer, Samuel L. Harman; General Manager, J. Wainright, Philadelphia.

Main office, Charleston, W. Va.; Philadelphia office, 32 South Broad street. Annual meeting, first Tuesday in March.

## CHESAPEAKE & OHIO RAILWAY CO.

A corporation formed under the laws of Virginia in 1868. The property was foreclosed and the company reorganized under the present title July 1, 1878. In 1888 it was again reorganized without foreclosure.

Road owned, Fort Monroe, Va., to Big Sandy River, Ky., 512 miles; James River Division formerly Richmond & Alleghany Railroad, Fulton, Va., to Clifton Forge, Va., 232 miles;

other branches owned, 181 miles; total owned, 924½ miles; controlled by stock ownership, Ashland, Ky., to Cincinnati, 146 miles; White House, Ky., to Lexington, Ky. (formerly Elizabethtown, Lexington & Big Sandy Railway), 185 miles; other controlled lines, 47 miles; total controlled, 377½ miles; leased, Greenbrier Railway, 95½ miles; Orange, Va., to Gordonsville, Va., 9 miles; other leased lines, 18 miles; total leased, 123 miles; operated under contract, 21 miles; operated jointly, Orange, Va., to Alexandria (Southern Railway), 78 miles; Alexandria to Washington (Washington Southern Railwa ), 7 miles; Lexington, Ky., to Louisville, Ky. (Louisville & Nashville Railroad), 84 miles; other trackage, 22 miles; total operated jointly 191 miles; total of all lines, 1,636 miles.

This company has one-sixth interest in the Richmond-Washington Co., controlling the Washington Southern Railway Co. In 1899 it began the construction of the Greenbrier Railway from Whitcomb, W. Va., northeasterly to Durhin, W. Va. Other branches and extensions were in progress in 1902. The company controls the Chesapeake & Ohio Steamship Co., operating an ocean line from Newport News to Liverpool.

Locomotives, 403; passenger cars, 243; freight cars, 20,084. Floating equipment consists of 20 passenger steamboats, tugs, ferryboats, floats, etc.

In 1900 the Pennsylvania Railroad Co. and the New York Central & Hudson River Railroad Co. obtained a large interest in this company's stock, with representation in the directory.

Stock......Par $100..........................Authorized, $86,000,000......Issued, $60,541,100

There was outstanding June 30, 1902, $10,800 of old 1st preferred and $800 of 2d preferred stock convertible into bonds. Under the reorganization in 1888 the stock issued was $46,000,000 common, $13,000,000 1st preferred and $12,000,000 2d preferred. In 1892 a proposition was submitted to preferred stockholders for conversion of their holdings, 1st preferred to receive two-thirds of its face value in 4½ per cent. bonds and one-third in common stock, and 2d preferred to receive one-third in 4½ per cent. bonds and two-thirds in common stock. This plan was accepted by practically all preferred stockholders. The common stock when conversion is completed will be the authorized amount.

Transfer Agents, J. P. Morgan & Co., New York. Registrar, Central Trust Co., New York.

On October 25, 1899, the company paid a dividend of 1 per cent. on its stock, being the first in its history. In 1900 a second dividend of 1 per cent. was declared, payable November 26, 1900, and similar dividends of 1 per cent. were also paid November 27, 1901, and November 26, 1902.

### Funded Debt.

| | |
|---|---|
| 1st mort. Peninsula extension bonds, 6 per cent., due June, 1911, April and Oct.... | $2,000,000 |
| Terminal 1st mort. bonds, 6 per cent., due June, 1922, June and Dec............... | 142,000 |
| 1st mort. "A" and "B" bonds, 6 per cent., due July, 1908, April and Oct......... | 2,013,354 |
| 1st con. mort., gold, 5 per cent. bonds, due May, 1939, Jan. and July.............. | 25,858,000 |
| Gen. mort., 4½ per cent., due March, 1992, March and Sept....... | 34,833,000 |
| Richmond & Allegheny div., 1st mort., 4 per cent., due Jan., 1989, Jan. and July.... | 6,000,000 |
| R. & A. div., 2d mort., 4 per cent., due Jan., 1989, Jan. and July.................. | 1,000,000 |
| Warm Springs Val., 1st mort., 5 per cent., due March, 1941, March and Sept....... | 400,000 |
| Craig Val., 1st mort., 5 per cent., due July, 1941, Jan. and July................ ... | 650,000 |
| Kineon Coal Co., 1st mort., 5 per cent., due Oct., 1915, April and Oct............ | 200,000 |
| Greenbrier & New River R.R., 1st mort., 5 per cent., due Aug., 1942, Feb. and Aug. | 555,000 |
| Equipment notes and car trusts, various.......................................... | 2,669,116 |
| Total ................................................................ | $76,310,470 |

### Guaranteed Bonds.

| | |
|---|---|
| Norfolk Term. & Trans. Co., 1st mort., 5 per cent., due Feb., 1948, Feb. and Aug... | $500,000 |
| C. & O. Grain Elevator Co., 1st mort., 4 per cent., due Oct., 1938, April and Oct... | 830,000 |
| C. & O. G. El. Co., 2d mort. (not guar.), income 4 per cent., due Oct., 1988, Oct... | 450,500 |
| Greenbrier Ry., 1st mort., 4 per cent., due Nov., 1940, May and Nov.............. | 2,000,000 |
| Pass. & Belt Ry., 1st mort., 5 per cent........................................... | 150,000 |
| L. & Jeffersonville Bridge, 1st mort., 4 per cent., due March, 1945, Mar. and Sept.. | 3,000,000 |
| C. & O. S. S. Co., 1st mort. debentures, 5 per cent., due Jan. 1909, Jan. and July.. | £70,000 |

The general 4½ per cent. mortgage, created in 1892, is for $70,000,000. Of this $15,000,000 was devoted to retiring preferred stocks and $32,700,000 reserved for prior liens, balance to be sold at the rate of $2,000,000 per annum, for additions to property, etc. In January, 1898, $2,287,000 additional consolidated mortgage 5s were issued to retire a like amount of purchase money 6 per cents. maturing July 1, 1898.

This company, with the Cleveland, Cincinnati, Chicago & St. Louis, controls the Louisville & Jeffersonville Bridge Co., and is joint guarantor (to extent of one-third) of $3,000,000 4 per cent. bonds of that company.

In October, 1887, a Receiver was appointed, and in February, 1888, reorganization was undertaken by a syndicate headed by Drexel, Morgan & Co. The reorganization having been agreed to by nearly all the security holders, Receiver was discharged October 1, 1888.

In August, 1888, the reorganized company absorbed the Richmond & Allegheny Railroad. The Elizabethtown, Lexington & Big Sandy was acquired in 1892 by purchase of its stock, this company guaranteeing the 1st mortgage bonds of that road, interest on which was reduced from 6 per cent. to 5 per cent. In 1902 the $3,007,000 1st mortgage 5 per cent. bonds of the Elizabethtown, Lexington & Big Sandy Railroad were retired at maturity by an issue of additional 4½ per cent. general mortgage bonds.

EARNINGS.

Year ending June 30.

| | Gross. | Per Cent. Operating Exp. | Net. | Charges. | Surplus. |
|---|---|---|---|---|---|
| 1892–93 (1,277 miles)........ | $10,349,765 | 66.50 | $3,204,049 | $2,780,289 | $423,760 |
| 1893–94 (1,362 " )........ | 9,044,108 | 63.30 | 3,016,980 | 3,002,920 | 14,060 |
| 1894–95 (1,360 " )........ | 9,596,030 | 64.20 | 3,131,502 | 3,112,796 | 18,706 |
| 1895–96 ( " " )........ | 10,221,131 | 65.20 | 3,257,978 | 3,110,637 | 147,341 |
| 1896–97 ( " " )........ | 10,708,182 | 64.80 | 3,421,413 | 3,118,871 | 302,541 |
| 1897–98 ( " " )........ | 11,788,557 | 64.90 | 3,806,250 | 3,187,741 | 618,509 |
| 1898–99 (1,445 " )........ | 12,009,839 | 63.70 | 3,932,455 | 3,226,324 | 706,130 |
| 1899–00 (1,476 " )........ | 13,402,070 | 64.90 | 4,462,802 | 3,306,220 | 1,156,580 |
| 1900–01 (1,562 " )........ | 15,371,541 | 62.20 | 5,554,287 | 3,552,390 | 2,001,897 |
| 1901–02 (1,636 " )........ | 16,524,378 | 62.90 | 5,838,475 | 3,778,066 | 2,060,408 |

In 1899–1900 the dividend of 1 per cent. was $605,278; amount devoted to extraordinary expenditures and equipment, $348,695; total, $953,973. In 1900–01, dividends, $605,288; expended for improvements and equipment, $1,304,172. In 1901–02, dividend, $605,291; improvements, etc., $1,440,814.

The following presents the comparative freight traffic statistics of the company:

| | Total Tonnage. | Tons Carried One Mile. | Freight Density. | Rate per Ton per Mile. | Earnings per Train mile. | Average Tons per Train. |
|---|---|---|---|---|---|---|
| 1896–97...... | 6,491,297 | 2,000,094,742 | 1,470,658 | 0.419c | $1.470 | 352 |
| 1897–98...... | 7,806,914 | 2,513,221,007 | 1,847,956 | 0.370 | 1.395 | 379 |
| 1898–99 ..... | 8,130,661 | 2,506,145,852 | 1,734,363 | 0.362 | 1.538 | 425 |
| 1899–00...... | 9,746,840 | 2,946,894,104 | 1,996,540 | 0.343 | 1.670 | 488 |
| 1900–01 ..... | 10,125,497 | 3,051,175,642 | 2,026,017 | 0.388 | 1.980 | 511 |
| 1901–02...... | 10,904,165 | 3,194,336,608 | 1,974,250 | 0.402 | 2.046 | 509 |

GROSS AND NET EARNINGS BY MONTHS FOR THREE YEARS.

| MONTH. | 1900. | | 1901. | | 1902. | |
|---|---|---|---|---|---|---|
| | Gross. | Net. | Gross. | Net. | Gross. | Net. |
| January........... | $1,101,250 | $289,859 | $1,228,199 | $399,288 | $1,339,845 | $453,615 |
| February.......... | 888,788 | 200,440 | 1,126,192 | 343,200 | 1,225,252 | 404,618 |
| March............ | 1,046,099 | 303,787 | 1,264,372 | 411,126 | 1,434,081 | 504,568 |
| April............ | 1,100,030 | 361,660 | 1,171,198 | 397,645 | 1,408,857 | 517,185 |
| May........ ........ | 1,124,546 | 325,102 | 1,310,902 | 432,452 | 1,442,673 | 502,746 |
| June............. | 1,273,061 | 414,843 | 1,313,710 | 544,702 | 1,194,023 | 413,599 |
| July............. | 1,198,633 | 485,605 | 1,346,706 | 517,358 | 1,041,652 | 301,340 |
| August........... | 1,364,179 | 545,628 | 1,499,278 | 629,228 | 1,167,084 | 364,799 |
| September........ | 1,358,602 | 542,513 | 1,456,053 | 605,005 | 1,181,846 | 367,159 |
| October.......... | 1,454,714 | 570,558 | 1,567,154 | 631,502 | 1,325,627 | 442,163 |
| November......... | 1,253,706 | 446,146 | 1,357,238 | 491,246 | 1,428,428 | 515,620 |
| December......... | 1,327,130 | 501,432 | 1,253,218 | 455,217 | 1,445,157 | 522,481 |
| Totals............ | $14,482,700 | $4,987,573 | $15,894,218 | $5,857,969 | $15,634,525 | $5,309,893 |
| Average per month | 1,206,891 | 415,631 | 1,324,518 | 488,164 | 1,302,877 | 442,491 |

President, George W. Stevens; Vice-President, Decatur Axtell; Treasurer, C. E. Potts; Secretary, C. E. Wellford, Richmond, Va.; Assistant Secretary, David C. Green, Philadelphia; Comptroller, L. F. Sullivan, Richmond, Va.

Directors—George W. Stevens, Henry T. Wickham, Decatur Axtell, Richmond, Va.; Chauncey M. Depew, Hamilton McK. Twombly, William H. Newman, New York; Sutherland M. Prevost, Samuel Rea, John P. Green, Philadelphia.

General office, 805 E. Main St., Richmond, Va. Annual meeting, Tuesday before last Tuesday in October.

---

## CHESAPEAKE BEACH RAILWAY CO.

A corporation formed in 1896, which took over the property of the Washington & Chesapeake Beach Railway Co., which was foreclosed.

Road owned, Washington to Chesapeake Beach, Md., 30 miles; trackage, 4 miles; total operated, 34 miles. Locomotives, 4; passenger cars, 36; freight cars, 18.

Stock......Par $100..........................Authorized, $1,000,000.... .Issued, $1,000,000

Stock is transferred by the secretary of the company, Washington.

FUNDED DEBT.

1st mort., 5 per cent., due Jan., 1923, Jan. and July.............................. $1,000,000

President and General Manager, Sylvester T. Smith, Chicago; Treasurer, Fred W. Moffatt; Secretary, Paul Y. Waters, Washington, D. D.

Directors—Sylvester T. Smith, Chicago; Fred W. Moffat, F. D. McKenney, Otto Mears, Washington, D. C.; Charles Popper, Chesapeake Beach, Md.

Main office, 1420 New York avenue, Washington, D. C. Annual meeting, in June, at Washington, D. C.

## CHESAPEAKE WESTERN RAILWAY CO.

Road owned, Bridgewater, Va., to North River Gap, 14 miles; leased Chesapeake & Western Railroad, Elkton, Va., to Bridgewater, 27 miles; total, 41 miles. Extensions to tidewater and westward to the West Virginia coal regions are planned. Locomotives, 3; passenger cars, 8; freight cars, 70.

Stock......Par $100......Authorized, $50,000,000.........Issued { com., $811,200 / pref., 608,400 } $1,419,600

The preferred stock is 5 per cent., non-cumulative. Registrar, Bowling Green Trust Co., New York.

The amount of capital stock authorized is $50,000,000. The stockholders have power, when stock shall be issued, to determine the character of the stock, whether it shall be common or preferred, or what proportion of each. The $50,000,000 represents the maximnm amount of stock of any character that is authorized.

FUNDED DEBT.

1st mort., new, 4 per cent., due Oct., 1951, April and Oct......................... $1,419,000

The Bowling Green Trust Co., New York, is trustee of the new mortgage. It was understood that the $660,000 1st mortgage 5 per cent. bonds, due 1945, of the Chesapeake & Western would be retired with part of the new issue. The Chesapeake & Western had $535,500 common and $50,000 preferred stock. All the securities were understood to be held by the construction company which is building the road.

In the year ending January 30, 1902, the earnings of 41 miles completed road were $37,125, net $6,138.

President, De Witt Smith; Vice-President, Edgar Madden; Secretary, J. C. Ward; Treasurer and General Manager, W. H. Hall, New York.

Directors—De Witt Smith, Edgar Madden, E. W. Mills, H. T. W. Huntting, F. P. Woodruff.

Main office, Harrisonburg, Va.; New York office, 141 Broadway.

## CHICAGO & ALTON RAILWAY CO.

A corporation organized in 1900, which on April 30, 1900, leased for 99 years the property of the Chicago & Alton Railroad Co.

Leases the road owned by the old company, Joliet to East St. Louis, 243 miles; branches owned, 300 miles; leased main line, Chicago to Joliet, 38 miles; Louisiana & Missouri River, 101 miles; Kansas City, St. Louis & Chicago, 162 miles; total leased, 844 miles. The new company acquired and owns in fee the portion of the St. Louis, Peoria & Northern Railway between Springfield, Ill., and Grove, Ill., 57 miles; trackage, 17 miles; total operated, 919 miles. Locomotives, 212; passenger cars, 182; freight cars, 9,846.

Stock..Par $100...Authorized { com., $20,000,000 / pref., 20,000,000 } Issued { com., $19,542,800 / pref., 19,544,000 } $39,086,800

The preferred stock is 4 per cent., non-cumulative.

The first dividend on the new preferred stock of the Railway Company was 2 per cent. semi-annual, paid January 10, 1901. The dividends on the preferred are paid semi-annually, 2 per cent. each, January 1 and July 1.

The stock of the old Chicago & Alton Railroad Co. consisted of $3,479,500 7 per cent., non-cumulative preferred and $18,751,100 common. See below for details regarding the purchase of this stock by the syndicate which organized the present company.

The old Railroad Company paid from 1885 to 1896, inclusive, 8 per cent. on both classes of its stock; in 1897 paid 7¼ per cent.; in 1898 and 1899, 7 per cent. In May, 1900, 30 per cent. was paid on the old stock to represent distribution of old company's surplus. Regular quarterly dividends of 1¾ per cent. each were paid in March and June, 1900, on the preferred, and in March, 1900, on the common. The dividend period on old stock has been changed to half-yearly, June and December, and the dividends on each class of that stock are at the rate of 7 per cent. per annum.

Transfer agency, 120 Broadway, New York. Registrar, United States Trust Co., New York.

FUNDED DEBT.

| | |
|---|---|
| Chicago & Alton Ry., 1st lien, 3½ per cent. bonds, due July, 1950, Jan. and July... | $22,000,000 |
| " " R. R., refund'g mort., cur., 3 per cent., due Oct., 1949, April and Oct. | 31,988,000 |
| " " " gen. mort., sterling, 6 per cent., due July, 1903, Jan. and July. | 4,379,850 |
| " " " sink. fund, 6 per cent., gold bonds, due May, 1903, M. and N.. | 1,663,000 |
| Total | $60,030,850 |

STOCKS OF LEASED LINES.

| | |
|---|---|
| Joliet & Chicago stock, guar. 7 per cent., quar., Jan | $1,500,000 |
| Kansas City, St. Louis & Chicago, common stock, 7 per cent. (contingent) | 271,800 |
| " " " guar. preferred stock, 6 per cent., quar., Feb.... | 1,750,000 |
| Louisiana & Missouri River, guar. preferred stock, 7 per cent., Feb. and Aug. | 329,000 |
| Total leased line stocks | $3,850,800 |

In February, 1899, a syndicate represented by Edward H. Harriman, George J. Gould, Jacob H. Schiff and James Stillman of New York made an offer of $200 per share for the preferred and $175 per share for the common stock of the old company. The sale was opposed by T. B. Blackstone, the company's president, but was approved by other large holders, and in March, 1899, it was announced that a considerable majority had accepted the terms offered. All but a small amount of the stock passed into the hands of the syndicate.

In May, 1899, the syndicate acquired the St. Louis, Peoria & Northern (St. Louis & Northern Short Line) road. A contract by the St. Louis, Peoria & Northern with the Chicago Terminal Transfer, for the use of the latter's terminal at Chicago, was also assumed.

The 3 per cent. refunding mortgage of the Railroad Company was created in October, 1899. The bonds authorized are $40,000,000. Of this amount the proceeds of $15,000,000 were reserved to retire the old sinking fund 6 per cent. bonds, the 6 per cent. sterling bonds and the Louisiana & Missouri River 1st and 2d mortgage bonds and the Mississippi River Bridge Co. 1st mortgage 6 per cent. bonds. Funds have been deposited to retire these issues at maturity. The company offered the stockholders the right to subscribe for 80 per cent. of the issue at 65, and $31,988,000 of the bonds were sold, including the $15,000,000 referred to above.

The Railway Company in April, 1900, created a 1st lien mortgage for $22,000,000 at 3½ per cent., secured on the 57 miles of the St. Louis, Peoria & Northern Railway acquired by the company, also by the lease of the Chicago & Alton Railroad and the further deposit of 34,722 shares of preferred and 183,224 shares of common stock of the Railroad Company. The purpose of this issue was to pay for the acquisition of the line from Springfield to Grove and for the shares of the Railroad Company deposited as additional security for the mortgage.

EARNINGS (OLD COMPANY).

| | Dividends Paid. Com. | Pref. | Gross. | Net. | Charges. | Surplus. |
|---|---|---|---|---|---|---|
| 1893 (843 miles) | 8 | 8 | $7,566,640 | $3,216,281 | $1,561,104 | $1,655,114 |
| 1894 ( " " ) | 8 | 8 | 6,292,236 | 2,663,549 | 1,193,914 | 1,469,635 |
| 1895 ( " " ) | 8 | 8 | 6,802,486 | 2,819,493 | 1,045,661 | 2,015,356 |
| 1896 ( " " ) | 8 | 8 | 6,840,283 | 3,035,993 | 1,155,169 | 1,880,824 |
| 1897 ( " " ) | 7¼ | 7¼ | 6,673,606 | 2,753,413 | 1,052,941 | 1,700,572 |
| 1898 ( " " ) | 7 | 7 | 6,532,860 | 2,663,064 | 1,274,737 | 1,388,327 |
| 1899 ( " " ) | 7 | 7 | 7,155,962 | 2,952,013 | 1,108,414 | 1,843,597 |
| *1900 (855 " ) | 7 | 8¾ | 7,801,358 | 3,570,266 | 1,709,281 | 1,860,985 |
| *1901 (920 " ) | 7 | 7 | 9,036,655 | 4,972,368 | 4,123,461 | 848,907 |

* Year ending June 30.

Net earnings include interest, rentals, etc., received. In 1890 the sum of $184,271 was charged for new construction, equipments, etc.; in 1891, $200,220; in 1892, $238,841; in 1894, $26,217; in 1895, $18,765; in 1896, $85,043; in 1897, $36,488, and in 1898, $32,309.

EARNINGS CHICAGO & ALTON RAILWAY.

Year ending June 30.

| | Gross. | Net. | Charges. | Surplus. |
|---|---|---|---|---|
| 1900-01 (919 miles) | $9,036,655 | $4,972,368 | $4,123,460 | $848,907 |
| 1901-02 ( " ) | 9,225,739 | 4,729,958 | 3,904,617 | 825,341 |

In 1900-01 the surplus over the dividends of 4 per cent. on the preferred stock was $67,147; in 1901-02 surplus $43,581.

Chairman of Executive Committee, Edward H. Harriman, New York; President, Samuel M. Felton, Chicago; Vice-President, William D. Cornish; Comptroller, William Mahl; Secretary, Alexander Millar; Treasurer, F. V. S. Crosby, New York; Assistant Treasurer, Horace E. R. Wood, Chicago; Assistant Comptroller, Herbert S. Bradt, New York.

Directors—Edward H. Harriman, James Stillman, George J. Gould, Mortimer L. Schiff, New York; Norman B. Ream, John J. Mitchell, Charles H. Chappell, James B. Forgan, David R. Francis, Samuel M. Felton, F. S. Winston, Chicago.

Main office, Chicago; New York office, 120 Broadway. Annual meeting, first Tuesday in October, at Chicago.

## CHICAGO & EASTERN ILLINOIS RAILROAD CO.

(Controlled by St. Louis & San Francisco Railroad Co.)

Road owned, Dolton, Ill., to Danville, Ill., 107 miles; Momence Junction, Ill., to Brazil, Ind., 130 miles; Danville Junction, Ill., to Thebes, Ill., and Joppa, Ill., 277 miles; Danville Junction to Brazil, 61 miles; branches owned, 140 miles; trackage, Chicago & Western Indiana, Dolton to Chicago, 17 miles; Evansville & Terre Haute, Otter Creek to Terre Haute, 6 miles; total operated, 738 miles. An extension of 62 miles to Thebes, Ill., was completed in January, 1900, connection being made with the St. Louis Southwestern, with which this company has made important traffic contracts. Locomotives, 179; passenger cars, 123; freight cars, 10,487.

In August, 1902, the St. Louis & San Francisco Railroad Co. acquired a majority of the common and preferred stocks of this company, giving in exchange its stock trust certificates as described below. Arrangements were made for trackage over the Cleveland, Cincinnati, Chicago & St. Louis for a connection via St. Louis between this company's lines and those of the San Francisco.

Stock....Par $100.....Authorized { com., $15,000,000 / pref., 10,000,000 } Issued { com., $7,217,800 / pref., 6,830,700 } $14,048,500

The preferred stock is entitled to 6 per cent. dividends, non-cumulative. In 1887 the old common $3,000,000 was exchanged for $3,000,000 preferred and $3,000,000 common. The company on June 30, 1902, had in its treasury $5,250,600 of common and $1,135,000 of preferred stock, which amounts are additional to the outstanding stock given above. In January, 1901, $1,000,000 each of additional preferred and common were sold to provide for improvements.

Transfer Agent, Metropolitan Trust Co., New York. Registrar, Central Trust Co., New York.

For dividends each year see above in earnings. The 6 per cent. dividends on the preferred are paid quarterly, 1½ per cent. each January (1), April, July and October. The first dividend on the common was 2½ per cent. July, 1898. In January, 1899, paid 1½ per cent. on the common and 2 per cent. in July. In January, 1900, paid 2 per cent. on the common and in July paid 2½ per cent., making 4½ per cent. for the calendar year. The January 2, 1901, dividend on common was 2 per cent. and ½ per cent. extra. In July, 1901, January, 1902, July, 1902, and January, 1903, 3 per cent. was paid on the common.

STOCK TRUST CERTIFICATES.

| | |
|---|---|
| St. L. & S. F., common stock trust ctfs., 10 per cent., due July, 1942, Jan. and July.. | $6,917,100 |
| " " preferred stock trust ctfs., 6 per cent., due July, 1912, quar., Jan..... | 4,112,500 |

The stock trust certificates were created in November, 1902, and were issued at par against the amounts of Chicago & Eastern Illinois common and preferred respectively acquired by the St. Louis & San Francisco Railroad Co. That company obligates itself to retire the same on or before July 1, 1942, at 250 for the common and 150 for the preferred trust certificates. The first payment of 5 per cent. semi-annual on the common and of 1½ per cent. quarterly on the preferred certificates was made January 2, 1903.

FUNDED DEBT.

| | |
|---|---|
| 1st mort., 6 per cent., due Dec., 1907, June and Dec. | $2,989,000 |
| 1st consolidated mort., 6 per cent., due Oct., 1934, April and Oct. | 2,788,000 |
| Coll. trust, 6 per cent., due Feb., 1912, Feb. and Aug. | 42,000 |
| Extension 1st mort., 6 per cent., due Dec., 1931, June and Dec. | 91,000 |
| Dan. & Grape Creek, 1st mort., 6 per cent., due May, 1920, May and Nov. | 97,000 |
| General consolidated mort., 5 per cent., due Nov., 1937, May and Nov. | 13,643,000 |
| Chic. & Ind. Coal Ry. consolidated 1st mort., 5 per cent., due Jan., 1936, Jan. and July. | 4,626,000 |
| Evansville, Terre Haute & Chic., 6 per cent. incomes, due May, 1920, May and Nov.. | 150,000 |
| Indiana Block Coal R. R. 1st mort., 7 per cent., due July, 1908, Jan. and July...... | 140,000 |
| Total | $24,566,000 |

The consolidated mortgage ($6,000,000 authorized) was created in May, 1884, of which $4,500,000 were to be exchanged for other issues. The general consolidated mortgage created in 1887 is a first lien on property acquired since consolidation. In 1892, Chicago & Indiana Coal Railway was leased in perpetuity and interest on its bonds guaranteed. Company uses Chicago terminal of Chicago & Western Indiana, and owns $1,000,000 of the latter's stock. It has a close traffic connection with Evansville & Terre Haute for a term of years. The company has terminal property in Chicago valued at over $1,200,000.

EARNINGS.—Year ending June 30.

| | Dividends. Pref. | Com. | Gross. | Per Cent. Oper. Ex. | Net. | Charges. | Surplus. |
|---|---|---|---|---|---|---|---|
| 1892-93........ | 6 | .. | $4,446,959 | 62.88 | $1,523,386 | $1,134,086 | $389,300 |
| 1893-94........ | 6 | .. | 3,860,114 | 58.30 | 1,576,091 | 1,181,543 | 394,548 |
| 1894-95........ | 6 | .. | 3,667,869 | 63.65 | 1,329,151 | 1,197,859 | 131,291 |
| 1895-96........ | 6 | .. | 4,014,623 | 56.60 | 1,735,379 | 1,203,473 | 531,905 |
| 1896-97........ | 6 | .. | 3,927,610 | 56.91 | 1,661,406 | 1,243,708 | 417,697 |
| 1897-98........ | 6 | 2½ | 4,221,438 | 56.97 | 1,768,092 | 1,312,703 | 455,389 |
| 1898-99........ | 6 | 3½ | 4,581,560 | 54.41 | 2,065,329 | 1,297,965 | 767,362 |
| 1899-00........ | 6 | 4½ | 5,148,897 | 55.53 | 2,300,159 | 1,309,787 | 990,373 |
| 1900-01........ | 6 | 5½ | 5,659,446 | 57.35 | 2,407,215 | 1,338,248 | 1,067,966 |
| 1901-02........ | 6 | 6 | 6,277,493 | 55.22 | 2,826,908 | 1,378,026 | 1,448,881 |

In 1896-97 surplus over 6 per cent. dividends on preferred stock, amounting to $289,842, was $127,855. In 1897-98 after 6 per cent. on preferred and 2½ per cent. (July, 1898) on common surplus was $10,602. In 1898-99 6 per cent. on the preferred and 3½ on the common were paid, leaving a surplus of $200,598, out of which $100,000 was charged to additional equipment. In 1899-1900 dividends paid amounted to $628,787, leaving a surplus balance of $361,629, out of which $129,205 was charged to additions and improvements. In 1900-01 dividends paid were $750,721, and $250,452 expended for betterments, the surplus of $66,793 being charged off for depreciation of equipment. In 1901-02 dividends were $841,710, balance $607,171, all of which was charged to improvements and new equipment.

The following exhibits the freight traffic statistics of the company:

| | Average Mileage. | Total Tonnage. | Tons Carried One Mile. | Freight Density. | Rate per Ton per Mile. | Earnings per Train Mile. | Average Tons per Train. |
|---|---|---|---|---|---|---|---|
| 1896-97...... | 648 | 4,582,668 | 612,368,345 | 895,275 | 0.50c | $1.840 | 361 |
| 1897-98...... | 648 | 4,784,375 | 660,143,108 | 1,018,289 | 0.51 | 1.890 | 369 |
| 1898-99...... | 648 | 5,538,429 | 750,399,337 | 1,158,023 | 0.48 | 2.010 | 414 |
| 1899-00...... | 711 | 5,876,261 | 850,501,320 | 1,196,204 | 0.45 | 2.250 | 466 |
| 1900-01...... | 722 | 5,914,394 | 917,170,653 | 1,263,320 | 0.49 | 2.400 | 487 |
| 1901-02...... | 737 | 7,411,362 | 1,096,645,035 | 1,487,985 | 0.45 | 2.78 | 605 |

President, B. F. Yoakum, St. Louis; Vice-President and Treasurer, Charles W. Hillard, New York; Vice-President and General Counsel, W. H. Lyford; Secretary, J. S. Ford; General Manager, R. R. Hammond, Chicago.

Directors—B. F. Yoakum, James Campbell, St. Louis; E. C. Henderson, F. S. Flower, Anson R. Flower, R. M. Hoe, Henry Seibert, Charles W. Hillard, New York; George H. Ball Boston; Henry H. Porter, Jr., W. H. Lyford, Chicago.

Main office, 355 Dearborn street, Chicago. Annual meeting, first Wednesday in June.

## CHICAGO & NORTHWESTERN RAILWAY CO.

A corporation formed in 1859 to acquire the Chicago, St. Paul & Fond du Lac Railroad, sold under foreclosure. By extensions and acquisitions of additional mileage the system has reached its present proportions.

Road owned 5,891 miles; leased, 62 miles; road operated May 31, 1902, Wisconsin division, 325 miles; Northern Wisconsin division, 333 miles; Galena division, 492 miles; Iowa division, 561 miles; Northern Iowa division, 357 miles; Madison division, 509 miles; Peninsula division, 464 miles; Sioux City division, 416 miles; Iowa & Minnesota division, 327 miles; Minnesota & Dakota division, 1,302 miles; Ashland division (formerly Milwaukee, Lake Shore & Western), 837 miles; total Chicago & Northwestern proper, 5,922 miles. In 1901 the company purchased the Sioux City & Pacific under an arrangement with the United States Government, the road being sold under the subsidy debt. The Chicago, St. Paul, Minneapolis & Omaha, controlled, comprising 1,538 miles; the Fremont, Elkhorn & Mo. Valley, 1,362 miles, which this company controls, are given under their respective titles.

Locomotives, 1,070; passenger cars, 980; freight cars, 43,559.

Stock ..Par $100..Authorized { com., $39,114,678 / pref., 22,395,120 } Issued { com., $39,114,678 / pref., 22,395,120 } $61,509,798

Transfer agency, 52 Wall street, New York. Registrar, Farmers Loan & Trust Co., New York.

The preferred stock is 7 per cent., non-cumulative. The preferred has a right to receive 3 per cent. additional after common stock has received 7 per cent.

Of the capital stock, $2,333,688 common and $3,834 preferred is in company's treasury.

Dividends on the preferred stock are paid quarterly, January, April, July and October. For many years 7 per cent. per annum was paid on the preferred. The July, 1902, dividend was, however, 1¾ per cent. and 1 per cent. extra, and the quarterly dividends on the preferred have since been 2 per cent. each or 8 per cent. per annum.

In January, 1900, the dividend on the common stock was increased from 2½ to 3 per cent. semi-annual. The July, 1902, dividend was 4 per cent. In January, 1903, 3½ per cent. was paid on the common. The dividends on the common are paid in January and July, usually about the 1st of the month.

FUNDED DEBT.

| | |
|---|---|
| Refunding mort. of 1897, 3½ per cent., due Nov., 1987, May and Nov | $20,538,000 |
| Consolidated sinking fund currency mort., 7 per cent., due Feb., 1915, quar., Feb | 12,832,000 |
| Madison Extension, 7 per cent., due April, 1911, April and Oct | 2,977,500 |
| Menominee River, 7 per cent., due July, 1906, Jan. and July | 400,000 |
| Menominee Extension, 7 per cent., due June, 1911, June and Dec | 2,546,500 |
| Menominee River R. R. ext., 1st mort., 7 per cent., due July, 1906, Jan. and July | 160,000 |
| Winona & St. Peter, 2d mort. (now 1st), 7 per cent., due Nov., 1907, May and Nov | 1,592,000 |
| " " Extension, 7 per cent., due Dec., 1916, June and Dec | 4,038,500 |
| Northwestern Union, 7 per cent., due June, 1917, March and Sept | 3,365,000 |
| Minnesota Valley, 7 per cent., due Oct., 1908, April and Oct | 150,000 |
| Rochester & Northern Minnesota, 7 per cent., due Sept., 1908, March and Sept | 200,000 |
| Plainview R. R., 7 per cent., due Sept., 1908, March and Sept | 100,000 |
| Chicago, Milwaukee & Northwestern, 6 per cent., due Nov., 1905, May and Nov | 601,000 |
| Chicago & Tomah, 6 per cent., due Nov., 1905, May and Nov | 1,528,000 |
| Milwaukee & Madison, 6 per cent., due Sept., 1905, March and Sept | 1,600,000 |
| Sinking fund bonds of 1879 on new lines, 6 per cent., due Oct., 1929, April and Oct | 5,809,000 |
| " " " " 5 per cent., due Oct., 1929, April and Oct | 6,921,000 |
| Des Moines & Minneapolis, 7 per cent., due Feb., 1907, Feb. and Aug | 600,000 |
| Dakota Central, 1st mort., 6 per cent., due Sept., 1907, March and Sept | 1,007,000 |
| " " Eastern Div., 1st mort., 6 per cent., due Nov., 1907, May and Nov | 2,000,000 |
| Debentures for C., St. P., M. & O. stock, 5 per cent., due May, 1933, May and Nov | 9,800,000 |
| Ottumwa, C. F. & St. P., 1st mort., 5 per cent., due March, 1909, March and Sept | 1,600,000 |
| Cedar Rapids & Missouri River, 1st mort., 7 per cent., due May, 1916, May and Nov | 2,332,000 |
| " " mort. of 1884, 7 per cent., due June, 1909, June and Dec | 769,000 |
| Twenty-five-year debenture bonds, 5 per cent., due Nov., 1909, May and Nov | 5,369,000 |
| Northern Illinois, 1st mort., 5 per cent., due March, 1910, March and Sept | 1,500,000 |
| C. & N. W. ext. bonds, 4 per cent., due Aug., 1926, Feb. and Aug | 17,489,000 |
| Thirty-year debentures, 5 per cent., due April 15, 1921, April and Oct | 9,819,000 |
| Minn. & Ia. R. R., 1st mort., 3½ per cent., due June, 1924, June and Dec | 1,904,000 |
| Iowa, Minn. & N.-Wn., 1st mort., 3½ per cent., due Jan., 1935, Jan. and July | 3,900,000 |
| Boyer Valley Ry., 1st mort., 3½ per cent., due Dec., 1923, June and Dec | 1,440,000 |
| Sioux City & Pac., 1st mort., 3½ per cent., due Aug., 1936, Feb. and Aug | 4,000,000 |
| Princeton & N. Wn., 1st mort., 3½ per cent., due Jan., 1926, Jan. and July | 1,940,000 |
| Peoria & Western, 1st mort., 3½ per cent., due March, 1926, March and Sept | 2,125,000 |
| Minn. & South Dakota, 1st mort., 3½ per cent., due Jan., 1935, Jan. and July | 528,000 |
| Mil., L. S. & Wn. 20-year deben., conv., 5 per cent., due Feb., 1907, Feb. and Aug | 436,000 |
| " " income bonds, 6 per cent., due May, 1911, May and Nov | 500,000 |
| " " cons., 1st mort., 6 per cent., due May, 1921, May and Nov | 5,000,000 |
| " " Marshfield, 1st mort., 5 per cent., due Oct., 1922, April and Oct | 400,000 |
| " " Mich. Div., 1st mort., 6 per cent., due July, 1924, Jan. and July | 1,281,000 |
| " " Ash. Div., 1st mort., 6 per cent., due March, 1925, Mar. and Sept | 1,000,000 |
| " " Ext. and Impt., mort., 5 per cent., due Feb., 1929, Feb. and Aug | 4,148,000 |
| Sioux City & Pacific pfd., stock mort., 7 per cent | 96,500 |
| Total | $146,342,000 |

In 1897 a new mortgage for $165,000,000, running 90 years, to refund existing bonds, was authorized. Bonds under this mortgage bear such interest, not over 5 per cent., as may be deemed advisable at time of issue. Enough of these bonds were reserved to retire $131,645,000 of underlying obligations, and the remainder was to be used for additions and improvements, the company receiving $1,000,000 thereafter per annum for betterments. The first issue, in 1897, of $20,000,000 of the new bonds bore 3½ per cent. interest.

In 1882 this company acquired a controlling interest of 93,200 common shares and 53,800 preferred shares in the stock of Chicago, St. Paul, Minneapolis & Omaha Railroad (see statement of that company), and issued the 5 per cent. debenture bonds of 1933 in payment for same.

In December, 1891, the company acquired control of the Milwaukee, Lake Shore & Western, purchasing the entire stock of the latter company in exchange for its own common stock. On September 1, 1893, the Milwaukee, Lake Shore & Western was merged with the Chicago & Northwestern and became the Ashland Division of the latter.

The Milwaukee, Lake Shore & Western guaranteed interest (not principal) on $1,120,000 St. Paul Eastern Grand Trunk 6 per cent. bonds, due 1913, which guarantee was assumed by Chicago & Northwestern.

In 1900 the company acquired the Boyer Valley Railway, Boone County Railway, Minnesota & Iowa Railway, Iowa, Minnesota & Northwestern Railway and Harlan & Kirkman Railway, and absorbed the Winona & St. Peter Railroad, Dakota Central Railway, Mankato & New Ulm Railway, and Minnesota & South Dakota Railway, which four latter roads were already controlled. In 1901 the Peoria & North Western, Princeton & North Western, Southern Iowa and Sioux City & Pacific were acquired, and in 1902 the Minnesota Western.

The company has a land grant from which 63,418 acres were sold in 1901-02, receipts from land being $984,649, not included in the net earnings. Unsold lands amount to 497,880 acres.

EARNINGS.

Year ending May 31.

| | Dividends Paid. Com. | Pref. | Gross. | Net. | Charges. | Surplus. |
|---|---|---|---|---|---|---|
| 1892-93 | 6 | 7 | $32,709,747 | $10,416,593 | $5,636,883 | $4,779,709 |
| 1893-94 | 6 | 7 | 31,986 182 | 11,078,252 | 6,770,708 | 4,307,543 |
| 1894-95 | 4 | 7 | 28,108,374 | 9,596,645 | 6,744,689 | 2,851,955 |
| 1895-96 | 5 | 7 | 33,488,701 | 12,038,789 | 6,671,707 | 5,368,082 |
| 1896-97 | 5 | 7 | 30,977,243 | 11,038,422 | 6,347,801 | 4,690,626 |
| 1897-98 | 5 | 7 | 36,050,561 | 12,304,075 | 6,548,929 | 5,755,145 |
| 1898-99 | 5 | 7 | 38,016,313 | 13,187,599 | 6,029,003 | 7,158,596 |
| 1899-00 | 6 | 7 | 42,950,805 | 15,956,792 | 5,895,263 | 10,061,529 |
| 1900-01 | 6 | 7 | 43,098,587 | 15,868,588 | 6,047,301 | 9,821,287 |
| 1901-02 | 7 | 8 | 46,644,121 | 16,638,199 | 6,063,654 | 10,574,825 |

Surplus over dividends in the respective fiscal year has been as follows: In 1892, $1,244,449; in 1893, $873,148; in 1894, $400,949; in 1895 (deficit), $273,590; in 1896, $1,851,024; in 1897, $1,171,970; in 1898, $2,235,322; in 1899, $3,635,366. In 1899-00, $4,542,041 was appropriated for construction and improvements, and dividends paid were $3,914,394; surplus, $1,605,119. In 1900,-01, appropriated for construction and improvements, $4,169,526; dividends, $3,914,394; surplus, $1,737,367. In 1901-02, dividends, $4,529,468; applied to improvements, $4,697,055; surplus, $1,348,302.

Dividends received on the company's holdings of Omaha stock are deducted from the charges. In 1900-01 and 1901-02 the company's revenue from investments was $577,080.

The following table shows the average mileage worked and the earnings per mile, etc.:

| | Miles Operated. | Gross Earnings per Mile. | Per Cent. of Expenses. | Net Earnings per Mile. |
|---|---|---|---|---|
| 1891-92 | 4,273 | $7,353 | 64.72 | $2,594 |
| 1892-93 | 4,273 | 7,654 | 68.15 | 2,437 |
| 1893-94 | 4,841 | 6,606 | 65.37 | 2,288 |
| 1894-95 | 5,030 | 5,587 | 65.86 | 1,907 |
| 1895-96 | 5,030 | 6,656 | 64.05 | 2,393 |
| 1896-97 | 5,030 | 6,157 | 64.37 | 2,194 |
| 1897-98 | 5,070 | 7,109 | 65.87 | 2,426 |
| 1898-99 | 5,077 | 7,488 | 65.31 | 2,597 |
| 1899-00 | 5,219 | 8,230 | 62.85 | 3,058 |
| 1900-01 | 5,507 | 7,825 | 63.18 | 2,881 |
| 1901-02 | 5,759 | 8,098 | 64.33 | 2,888 |

The following presents the comparative freight traffic statistics of the road:

| | Total Tonnage. | Tons Carried One Mile. | Freight Density. | Rate per Ton per Mile. | Earnings per Train Mile. | Tons to Train Mile. |
|---|---|---|---|---|---|---|
| 1896-97 | 15,225,138 | 2,254,027,285 | 448,116 | 0.990c | $1.51 | 151.57 |
| 1897-98 | 19,693,634 | 3,030,610,175 | 597,753 | 0.890 | 1.73 | 193.77 |
| 1898-99 | 21,081,613 | 3,229,327,820 | 636,070 | 0.870 | 1.82 | 208.48 |
| 1899-00 | 25,442,219 | 3,849,367,760 | 737,621 | 0.830 | 1.96 | 235.55 |
| 1900-01 | 25,271,726 | 3,701,417,722 | 672,111 | 0.850 | 1.98 | 232.37 |
| 1901-02 | 29,321,538 | 4,122,440,480 | 715,825 | 0.810 | 2.03 | 249.65 |

MONTHLY GROSS EARNINGS FOR SIX YEARS.

| Month. | 1897-98. 5,030 Miles. | 1898-99. 5,077 Miles. | 1899-00. 5,219 Miles. | 1900-01. 5,507 Miles. | 1901-02. 5,759 Miles. | 1902-03. 5,922 Miles. |
|---|---|---|---|---|---|---|
| June | $2,914,527 | $2,995,883 | $3,635,305 | $3,688,173 | $3,913,102 | $4,000,368 |
| July | 2,944,013 | 2,819,284 | 3,692,275 | 3,581,564 | 3,884,652 | 3,982,051 |
| August | 3,126,123 | 3,414,353 | 3,801,414 | 3,928,359 | 4,298,425 | 4,214,841 |
| September | 3,561,045 | 3,598,274 | 4,177,483 | 4,002,115 | 4,276,720 | 4,540,252 |
| October | 3,626,259 | 3,676,663 | 4,270,022 | 4,184,225 | 4,546,105 | 4,811,811 |
| November | 3,204,711 | 3,374,871 | 3,704,642 | 3,483,189 | 4,046,328 | 4,174,082 |
| December | 2,675,108 | 3,272,914 | 3,291,889 | 3,293,034 | 3,618,773 | 3,787,991 |
| January | 2,561,557 | 2,829,598 | 2,991,824 | 3,160,795 | 3,565,525 | ........ |
| February | 2,586,872 | 2,691,421 | 3,104,002 | 3,104,737 | 3,287,942 | .... |
| March | 3,051,836 | 3,152,812 | 3,449,050 | 3,531,113 | 3,474,204 | ........ |
| April | 2,711,697 | 2,853,015 | 3,374,641 | 3,478,050 | 3,772,224 | ........ |
| May | 3,086,809 | 3,337,223 | 3,458,257 | 3,663,231 | 3,960,122 | ........ |
| Totals for year | $36,050,557 | $38,016,314 | $42,950,804 | $43,098,587 | $46,644,122 | $........ |
| Av'ges per month | 3,002,216 | 3,168,026 | 3,579,233 | 3,591,548 | 3,887,010 | ........ |

In 1893-94 the Fremont, Elkhorn & Missouri Valley Railroad, the Trans-Missouri portion of the Chicago & Northwestern system, had a net profit of $65,544, and in 1894-95 a deficit of $332,195, and in 1895-96 a deficit of $128,799. In 1896-97 the deficit was $227,102. In 1897-98 profit was $217,041; in 1898-99, $253,807; in 1899-1900, $224,731, and in 1900-01, $285,836.

President, Marvin Hughitt, Chicago; Vice-President and Secretary, Eugene E. Osborn, New York; 2d Vice-President, M. M. Kirkman, Chicago; Treasurer and Assistant Secretary, S. O. Howe, New York; General Manager, William A. Gardner, Chicago.

Directors—William K. Vanderbilt, Frederick W. Vanderbilt, Hamilton McK. Twombly, Samuel F. Barger, James C. Fargo, Chauncey M. Depew, James Stillman, Martin L. Sykes, New York; Albert Keep, Marvin Hughitt, N. K. Fairbank, Byron L. Smith, Cyrus H. McCormick, Marshall Field, Chicago; David P. Kimball, Oliver Ames, Boston; Zenas Crane, Dalton, Mass.

Main office, 22 Fifth avenue, Chicago; New York office, 52 Wall street. Annual meeting, first Thursday in June.

## CHICAGO & WESTERN INDIANA RAILROAD CO.

Road owned, Dolton, Ill., to Chicago, 17 miles; also a branch to Hammond and a belt line around the city of Chicago, and numerous spurs to factories, lumber yards, etc., making with sidings 220 miles of track in all. The company owns over 900 acres of land, with stations, elevator, etc.; leases 75 miles track to the Belt Railway Co. of Chicago. Locomotives, 45; freight cars, 473.

The stock is owned by the Erie, the Chicago & Eastern Illinois, the Grand Trunk Western, the Chicago, Indianapolis & Louisville, and the Wabash companies, and the road is used as the Chicago entrance and terminus of those lines; also by the Atchison, Topeka & Santa Fe and Elgin, Joliet & Eastern Railway.

Stock......Par $100..........................Authorized, $5,000,000......Issued, $5,000,000

Dividends of 6 per cent. per annum have been paid on the stock except in 1895, when 7½ per cent. was paid. The dividends are quarterly, 1½ per cent. each, January (1), April, July and October.

FUNDED DEBT.

| | |
|---|---|
| General mort., 6 per cent., due 1932, quar., March | $9,868,666 |
| Cons. mort., 4 per cent., due 1952, Jan. and June | 7,100,000 |
| Total | $16,968,666 |

The general mortgage bonds are subject to redemption at 105 by a sinking fund.

The company has no earnings in the ordinary sense, its income being derived entirely from rentals paid by the companies using it. These rentals now amount to about $1,000,000 yearly.

The leases to the proprietary tenant companies are for 999 years, and provide for rentals covering all expenses, charges on the bonds and $200,000 in excess. They also contain a guaranty of interest and principal of the consolidated mortgage bonds.

In 1898 income was $945,432; interest, etc., $656,868; dividends (6 per cent.), $300,000; deficit for year, $11,435. In 1899, income, $943,305; deficit, $5,958. In 1900, income, $929,963; charges, $638,769; dividends, $300,000; deficit, $8,806. In 1901, income, $906,382; charges, $625,701; dividends, $300,000; deficit, $19,319.

The consolidated mortgage was created in 1902 and is for $50,000,000, of which $10,014,000 are held to retire the prior bonds, $4,500,000 were issued to the tenant companies for advances

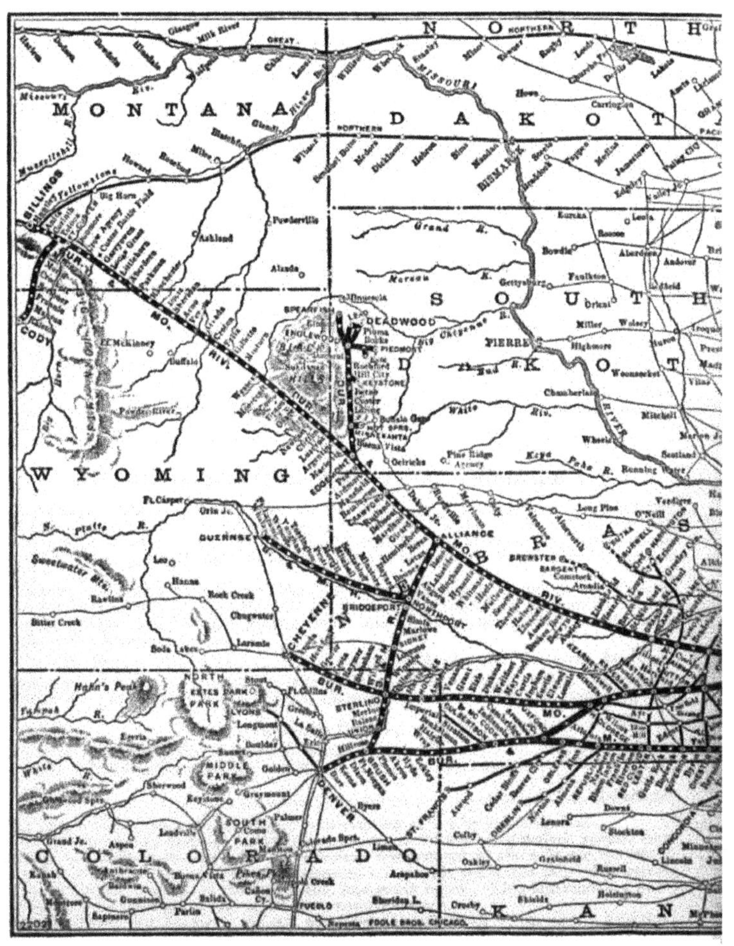
N O R T H
D A K O T
M O N T A N A
S O U T H
D A K O T
W Y O M I N G
N E B R A S
C O L O R A D O
K A N
Glasgow
Milk River
GREAT
NORTHERN
NORTHERN
PACIFIC
MISSOURI
Missouri
Musselshell
Yellowstone
BILLINGS
Big Horn
Powderville
Ashland
Alzada
CODY
Ft. McKinney
Buffalo
Powder River
BUR.
MO.
RIV.
SPEARFISH
DEADWOOD
PIEDMONT
KEYSTONE
Minnesela
Grand R.
Moreau R.
Bowdle
Aberdeen
Faulkton
Gettysburg
Miller
Highmore
PIERRE
Chamberlain
Woonsocket
Mitchell
White
Riv.
RIVER
Pine Ridge Agency
Oelrichs
Scotland
Running Water
Keya Paha R.
Howe
Carrington
Jamestown
Eureka
Leola
Roscoe
Andover
Hebron
Mandan
BISMARCK
Steele
Dickinson
Ft. Casper
Orin Jc.
GUERNSEY
N. Platte R.
Sweetwater Mts.
Leo
Hanna
Rock Creek
Chugwater
Rawlins
Bitter Creek
Laramie
Soda Lakes
CHEYENNE
ALLIANCE
BRIDGEPORT
NORTHPORT
BREWSTER
SARGENT
Comstock
Arcadia
Long Pine
O'Neill
Verdigre
DIV.
Hahn's Peak
NORTH PARK
ESTES PARK
LYONS
Ft. Collins
Greeley
Longmont
Boulder
MIDDLE PARK
Golden
STERLING
DENVER
Byers
Sherwood
Georgetown
Keystone
SOUTH PARK
Leadville
Aspen
Grand Jc.
Colorado Spgs.
Limon
Arapahoe
Buena Vista
Pikes Peak
Cripple Creek
Salida
Canon Cy.
Gunnison
Parlin
PUEBLO
Sheridan L.
Colby
Oakley
Grainfield
Russell
Lenora
Downs
Stockton
Lincoln
Hoisington
Shields
Crosby
ST. FRANCIS
Akron
Wray
Benkelman
POOLE BROS. CHICAGO

made by them and $4,000,000 were sold to a syndicate, of which in February, 1903, $2,600,000 had been delivered.

President and General Manager, Benjamin Thomas; Vice-President and General Solicitor, E. A. Bancroft; Treasurer, J. E. Murphy; Secretary, Michael J. Clark, Chicago.

Directors—Charles M. Hays, Montreal; E. B. Pryor, St. Louis; W. H. Lyford, E. P. Ripley, W. O. Johnson, W. H. McDoel, Chicago.

Main office, Dearborn Station, Chicago. Annual meeting, first Tuesday in June.

## CHICAGO, BURLINGTON & QUINCY RAILWAY CO.

(Controlled by Great Northern Railway Co. and Northern Pacific Railway Co.)

A corporation formed under the laws of Iowa in October, 1901, with an authorized capital of $100,000,000. The company, on November 20, leased the lines of the Chicago, Burlington & Quincy Railroad Co. for 99 years, from October 1, 1901, rental to include the payment of 7 per cent. dividends on the stock of the old company. The company was formed to facilitate the exercise of control by the Great Northern and Northern Pacific companies, which had acquired nearly all the stock of the old company and which own one-half each of the new company's stock.

Road leased 8,123 miles, including 186 miles leased and operated jointly with other companies. The principal lines extend from Chicago to Council Bluffs, Nebraska City to Denver, Omaha to Hastings, Rock Island to East St. Louis, Oregon, Ill., to St. Paul, Minn.; also extensions to Cheyenne, Wyo., Billings, Mont., and Deadwood, S. D. It also owns or controls 229 miles of narrow gauge lines. In 1899 the Chicago, Burlington & Northern, which had hitherto a separate corporate existence, was consolidated with the railroad company. In November, 1900, a number of controlled lines, including the Hannibal & St. Joseph Railroad, were formally merged with the parent company. Locomotives, 1,237; passenger cars, 1,101; freight cars, 45,868.

Stock (of Chi., Bur. & Q. R. R. Co.)..Par $100..Authorized, $111,200,000...Issued, $110,839,100
Stock (of Chi., Bur. & Q. Ry. Co.)...Par $100..Authorized, $100,000,000...Issued, $100,000,000

In April, 1884, capital stock of the old railroad company was increased $6,957,800, subscribed for by stockholders at par in the proportion of 10 per cent. of their holdings. Proceeds were devoted to construction and equipment. In January, 1893, stock was increased $5,876,300; stock, new issue, offered to stockholders at par. In 1890 debentures convertible into stock were issued to amount of $7,639,200, and in 1892 $7,639,500 of similar convertible bonds were created, which have been mainly exchanged for stock.

In January, 1901, the outstanding stock of the old company was $98,511,700. In that month the stock was increased to $109,206,400, and the stockholders of record February 7, 1901, were offered rights to subscribe at par for 10 per cent. of their holdings. Payments for the new stock could be made—20 per cent. on March 11, 50 per cent. May 31, and 30 per cent. August 1, 1901. The new stock was to be issued as of the latter date and to participate thereafter in dividends. The purpose of the issue was to refund sinking 5s, due October 1, 1901, and to provide for improvements.

For dividends paid in successive years, see tabulated earnings below. In September, 1898, the quarterly payment was increased to 1¾ per cent. Dividends were declared and paid quarterly, March (15), June, September and December. In June, 1901, 2 per cent. was paid for the four months ending July 1, 1901. Under the lease the dividends at the rate of 7 per cent. per annum are payable quarterly, in January (1), April, July and October.

In June, 1901, the Great Northern and the Northern Pacific jointly offered the holders of the stock of the Chicago, Burlington & Quincy Railroad Co. $200 per share for their stock, payable in joint 20-year 4 per cent. bonds, issued by the Great Northern and Northern Pacific companies, said bonds to be secured by a deposit of the stock thus acquired. In pursuance of this offer a very large majority of the old company's stock was exchanged for the bonds.

Transfer Agents of Railroad Company, National Bank of Commerce, New York; George C. Briggs, Boston. Registrars, Union Trust Co., New York; National Bank of Commerce, Boston.

FUNDED DEBT (INCLUDING CONTINGENT LIABILITIES FOR BRANCH LINES).

| | |
|---|---|
| Consolidated mort., 7 per cent., due July, 1903, Jan. and July | $21,699,200 |
| Trust mort., Iowa lines, 5 per cent., due Oct., 1919, April and Oct. | 2,566,000 |
| Trust mort., Iowa lines, 4 per cent., due Oct., 1919, April and Oct. | 8,390,000 |
| Bonds secured by Denver line bonds, 4 per cent., due Feb., 1922, Feb. and Aug. | 7,968,000 |
| Bonds issued for Bur. & Southwestern, 4 per cent., due Sept., 1921, March and Sept. | 4,300,000 |
| Deben. bonds for Hannibal & St. J. stock, 5 per cent., due May, 1913, May and Nov. | 9,000,000 |
| Bur. & Missouri River, in Nebraska, cons. 6 per cent., due July, 1918, Jan. and July. | 13,535,000 |
| Burlington & Missouri River bonds, 4 per cent., due Jan., 1910, Jan. and July | 3,347,000 |
| Chicago & Iowa Division, col. tr., 5 per cent., due Feb., 1905, Feb. and Aug. | 2,320,000 |
| Illinois Div. mort., 3½ per cent., due July, 1949, Jan. and July | 36,546,000 |
| Republican Valley bonds, 6 per cent., due July, 1919, Jan. and July | 1,078,000 |
| Atchison & Nebraska, 7 per cent., due March, 1908, March and Sept. | 1,125,000 |

FUNDED DEBT—*Continued.*

| | |
|---|---|
| Lincoln & N. W., 7 per cent., due Jan., 1910, Jan. and July | $600,000 |
| Nebraska extension sf. fund, 4 per cent., due May, 1927, May and Nov | 25,900,000 |
| Conv. deben., 5 per cent., due Sept., 1903, convertible into stock, March and Sept | 342,200 |
| Hannibal & St. Joe, mort., 6 per cent., due March, 1911, March and Sept | 8,000,000 |
| K. C., St. Joe & Council Bluffs, mort., 7 per cent., due Jan., 1907, Jan. and July | 5,000,000 |
| Tarkio Valley, mort., 7 per cent., due June, 1920, June and Dec | 188,000 |
| Nodaway Valley, 1st. mort., 7 per cent., due June, 1920, June and Dec | 168,000 |
| Total | $152,072,400 |

In April, 1899, the company created the Illinois Division mortgage, due 1949, covering lines east of the Mississippi. The issue is limited to $85,000,000. This mortgage covers the company's properties east of the Mississippi, and will become a first lien on payment of the $21,699,200 consolidated mortgage bonds, due 1903, and the $2,320,000 Chicago & Iowa 5s, due 1905. To retire the bonds of the Chicago, Burlington & Northern and the Ottawa, Oswego & Fox River Valley 8 per cents., due 1900, and to provide for improvements, the company, in April, 1899, issued $16,166,000 of the Illinois Division bonds, bearing 3½ per cent. interest, and offered same to stockholders at 75, together with $4,041,000 of new stock at par. The right was given to subscribe for $500 of bonds and $500 of new stock for each 60 shares held.

The authorized amount of consolidated mortgage is $30,000,000. The Nebraska extension bonds are a mortgage on 297 miles of road, and are secured by deposit of Nebraska branch 1st mortgage bonds at $20,000 per mile.

There has been paid into and accumulated in the various sinking funds $20,352,290. Sinking funds, exclusive of canceled securities, on June 30, 1902, amounted to $12,673,355.

EARNINGS.

| | Div. Paid. | Gross. | Net. | Charges. | Surplus. |
|---|---|---|---|---|---|
| 1894 (5,626 miles) | 4¼ | $24,667,132 | $10,321,918 | $7,530,786 | $2,791,131 |
| 1895 (5,730 " ) | 4 | 24,874,192 | 10,120,288 | 7,553,730 | 2,557,558 |
| 1896 (5,860 " ) | 4 | 25,553,073 | 10,533,874 | 7,703,986 | 2,829,888 |

EARNINGS ENTIRE SYSTEM.

| | Div. Paid. | Gross. | Net. | Charges. | Surplus. |
|---|---|---|---|---|---|
| 1896 (7,180 miles) | 4 | $34,176,456 | $11,906,308 | $9,439,837 | $2,466,470 |
| 1897 (6 months to June 30) | 2 | 16,941,848 | 5,338,332 | 4,738,876 | 599,456 |
| 1898 (year ending June 30) | 4½ | 42,800,162 | 1[illegible] 523,437 | 9,440,644 | 6,082,792 |
| 1899 ( " " " ) | 6 | 43,389,424 | 15,741,781 | 9,013,482 | 6,728,299 |
| 1900 ( " " " ) | 6 | 47,535,420 | 16,495,273 | 8,566,511 | 7,928,761 |
| 1901 ( " " " ) | 6½ | 50,051,988 | 16,363,878 | 8,238,471 | 8,125,407 |
| 1902 ( " " " ) | 6¼ | 53,795,245 | 18,453,174 | 8,370,064 | 10,083,110 |

The company in 1891 received for dividends and interest on securities of roads controlled by it $1,308,099, which amount is included in the surplus. In 1892 such receipts were $1,170,564; in 1893, $1,433,719; in 1894, $1,607,053; in 1895, $2,015,350; in 1896, $1,441,486; in 18 months, to June 30, 1898, $2,508,320; in 1898-99, $1,507,842; in 1899-1900, $2,077,746; in 1900-01, $82,431, and in 1901-02, $250,628.

In 1896, dividends paid, 4 per cent., were $3,280,111, leaving a deficit for year of $813,640. Fiscal year having been changed to end June 30, statement was issued covering operations of first six months of 1897, as given above. The 2 per cent. dividend payments for that period were $1,640,056 and deficit for the six months $1,040,599. In 1897-98, surplus over 4½ per cent. dividends was $2,392,666, out of which $1,000,000 was credited to renewal fund. In 1898-99, surplus over dividends, 6 per cent., was $1,489,928. In 1899-1900, surplus over dividends, $2,099,083, and in 1900-01, surplus, $1,472,849. In 1901-02, dividends on the stock of the public were $212,602, interest on the Northern Pacific-Great Northern, Chicago, Burlington & Quincy collateral bonds $8,606,120, surplus $1,263,388.

The following shows the average mileage worked, earnings per mile, etc.:

| Year | Miles Operated. | Gross Earnings per Mile. | Per Cent. of Expenses. | Net Earnings per Mile. |
|---|---|---|---|---|
| 1893 | 5,561 | $5,582 | 68.37 | $1,766 |
| 1894 | 5,626 | 4,384 | 66.02 | 1,490 |
| 1895 | 7,180 | 4,663 | 66.69 | 1,553 |
| 1896 | 7,180 | 4,731 | 66.30 | 1,599 |
| 1896-97 | 7,180 | 4,947 | 63.79 | 1,791 |
| 1897-98 | 7,180 | 5,961 | 64.98 | 2,087 |
| 1898-99 | 7,249 | 5,941 | 64.84 | 2,104 |
| 1899-00 | 7,546 | 6,251 | 66.10 | 2,130 |
| 1900 01 | 7,753 | 6,404 | 68.07 | 2,267 |
| 1901-02 | 8,109 | 6,634 | 66.63 | 2,234 |

GROSS AND NET EARNINGS BY MONTHS FOR THREE YEARS.

| | 1900. | | 1901. | | 1902. | |
|---|---|---|---|---|---|---|
| | Gross. | Net. | Gross. | Net. | Gross. | Net. |
| January........... | $3,510,243 | $1,230,932 | $3,734,661 | $1,232,056 | $4,214,017 | $1,524,733 |
| February.......... | 3,387,365 | 1,161,013 | 3,614,686 | 1,211,922 | 3,758,139 | 1,275,271 |
| March............ | 3,952,050 | 1,430,904 | 3,940,066 | 1,391,173 | 4,163,014 | 1,559,160 |
| April............. | 3,607,920 | 1,010,327 | 3,862,313 | 1,055,859 | 4,225,481 | 1,316,979 |
| May.............. | 3,571,255 | 944,618 | 4,345,886 | 1,161,710 | 4,477,262 | 1,399,407 |
| June.............. | 3,994,910 | 1,363,410 | 4,088,957 | 1,268,287 | 4,476,745 | 1,378,881 |
| July............... | 3,907,297 | 1,317,454 | 4,480,790 | 1,719,052 | 4,620,387 | 1,799,849 |
| August........... | 4,545,718 | 1,882,518 | 4,979,672 | 2,141,720 | 5,171,300 | 2,235,432 |
| September........ | 4,772,004 | 2,027,755 | 4,970,334 | 2,024,732 | ........ | ....... |
| October........... | 5,164,236 | 2,318,127 | 5,196,603 | 2,270,203 | ........ | ....... |
| November......... | 3,965,786 | 1,270,929 | 4,596,265 | 1,596,678 | ........ | ........ |
| December........ | 4,110,375 | 1,472,305 | 4,256,924 | 1,578,593 | ........ | ....... |
| Totals for year .... | $48,489,159 | $17,430,292 | $51,967,156 | $18,651,974 | $........ | $........ |
| Av'ges per month.. | 4,040,763 | 1,452,624 | 4,330,596 | 1,554,331 | ........ | ........ |

The company discontinued the publication of monthly earnings after August, 1902.

The following presents the comparative freight traffic statistics of the company:

| | Average Miles Operated. | Tons Carried One Mile. | Freight Density. | Rate per Ton per Mile. | Earnings per Train Mile. | Average Tons per Train |
|---|---|---|---|---|---|---|
| 1896-97............ | 7,180 | 2,75 ,736,618 | 383,111 | 0.867c | $1.508 | 171 |
| 1897-98............ | 7,180 | 3,295,586,072 | 445,067 | 0.919 | 1.562 | 170 |
| 1898-99............ | 7,249 | 3,373,480,389 | 465,372 | 0.861 | 1.603 | 184 |
| 1899-00............ | 7,546 | 3,793,008,334 | 502,651 | 0.851 | 1.640 | 197 |
| 1900-01............ | 7,753 | 3,870,529,358 | 499,243 | 0.862 | 1.756 | 201 |
| 1901-02............ | 8,109 | 4,613,072,546 | 568,881 | 0.772 | 1.967 | 251 |

This company does not include the train statistics of its narrow gauge lines in its reports, therefore the earnings per train mile and average train load given above are only approximately correct.

President, George B. Harris; 1st Vice-President, Darius Miller, Chicago; 2d Vice-President, Howard Elliott; Treasurer and Assistant Secretary, Thomas S. Howland; Secretary, Harry E. Jarvis, Burlington, Ia.; Assistant Treasurer, Arthur. G. Stanwood, Boston; Assistant Secretary, George H. Earl.

Directors—George B. Harris, Darius Miller, Charles E. Perkins, John S. Kennedy, James J. Hill, William H. McIntyre, James Stillman, William P. Clough, George W. Perkins, G. L. Briggs, Edward H. Harriman, Mortimer L. Schiff.

Main office, 209 Adams street, Chicago; Boston office, 199 Washington street. Annual meeting, first Wednesday in November, at Burlington, Ia.

---

## CHICAGO GREAT WESTERN RAILWAY CO.

A corporation formed under the laws of Illinois, January 5, 1892. The company was created for the purpose of reorganizing the Chicago, St. Paul & Kansas City Railway Co. on a stock basis.

Road owned, Chicago to St. Paul, 401 miles; Oelwein, Ia., to St. Joseph, Mo., 289 miles; branches, 155 miles; trackage, St. Paul to Minneapolis, 11 miles; Leavenworth to Kansas City, 46 miles; Chicago terminals, 10 miles; other trackage, 17 miles; total mileage, 929 miles. Company uses passenger terminals of the Chicago Terminal & Transfer Co., and has adequate freight terminals of its own in that city. Controls through stock ownership the Mason City & Fort Dodge Railroad, 251 miles, and the Wisconsin, Minnesota & Pacific Railroad, 272 miles. Total of system, 1,452 miles. Extensions to Omaha and Sioux City are in progress. Locomotives, 218; passenger cars, 106; freight cars, 6,677.

From 1896 to 1900 this company expended considerable sums on the reduction of grades, replacing wooden bridges with permanent structures of iron and stone and ballasting track. The Mason City & Fort Dodge and the Wisconsin, Minnesota & Pacific were acquired in 1902.

| Stock. Par $100..Auth'd | | | Issued | | | |
|---|---|---|---|---|---|---|
| | com., | $50,000,000 | | com., | $29,918,000 | $78,335,490 |
| | debent., | 30,000,000 | | 4 p. c. debent., | 27,577,000 | |
| | pref. A, | 15,000,000 | | 5 " pref. A, | 11,372,400 | |
| | " B, | 10,000,000 | | 4 " " B, | 9,468,090 | |

The authorized capital of the company was $15,000,000 4 per cent. debenture stock, interest payable half-yearly in gold; $15,000,000 5 per cent. preferred stock A, dividend contingent on earnings, payable half-yearly in gold; $10,000,000 4 per cent. preferred stock B, dividend contingent on earnings, payable in gold; $30,000,000 common stock. In February, 1903, the authorized common stock was increased from $30,000,000 to $50,000,000 to provide for the acquisition of the Mason City & Fort Dodge Railroad.

In January, 1898, the 4 per cent. debenture stock was increased from $15,000,000 to $30,000,000, the increase to be used to retire prior obligations and provide for improvements. In 1899 the issue of $8,000,000 of the increase was approved, and in August, 1899, the company issued $3,300,000 of this amount to take up the Chicago, St. Paul & Kansas City 5 per cent. priority loan of $2,823,000, which was paid off January 1, 1900. In 1899-1900 the outstanding 4 per cent. debentures were increased $4,245,898 to take up the priority loan, to retire car trust obligations for $163,000, and to provide for additions and improvements. In March, 1900, $2,400,000 of the debentures were issued to pay off $400,000 of equipment lease warrants and provide for improvements. In November, 1900, $1,500,000 more was issued to take up $1,293,309 of lease warrants. The balance of the $8,000,000 increase in the amount of debenture stock was to be issued to retire the remaining equipment lease warrants and the sterling and gold loans as soon as practicable.

Dividends of 2 per cent. semi-annual are regularly paid, January 15 and July 15, on the 4 per cent. debenture stock, such payments being made to European holders at the office of Robert Benson & Co., London, England. In December, 1898, the first dividend on preferred A was declared of 2 per cent., payable January 31, 1899. July 31, 1899, paid 2 per cent. on preferred A, and January 31, 1900, 2½ per cent., thus putting the preferred A on a 5 per cent. basis. Similar dividends of 2½ per cent. semi-annual have since been paid on the preferred A on each January 31 and July 31.

Transfer office, 31 Nassau street, New York. Registrar, Manhattan Trust Co., New York.

OBLIGATIONS.

| | |
|---|---|
| Gold notes, 5 per cent., due 1903 | $1,124,242 |
| " " 5 per cent., due 1904 | 808,333 |
| Wis., Minn. & Pac., 1st mort., 4 per cent., due Oct., 1950, April and Oct. | 3,960,000 |
| Total | $5,892,575 |

Under the reorganization plan the company has a finance committee in London, elected by the holders of 4 per cent. debenture and 5 per cent. preferred A stocks. Present finance committee consists of Howard Gilliat, chairman; Alexander F. Wallace, Sir Charles Tennant, Bart., and Edwin Waterhouse.

For the details of the reorganization of the Chicago, St. Paul & Kansas City Railway see the MANUAL for 1899 and preceding years.

EARNINGS.

Year ending June 30.

| | Gross. | Net. | Charges. | Surplus |
|---|---|---|---|---|
| 1892-93 (933 miles) | $5,083,014 | $1,127,839 | $733,246 | $393,593 |
| 1893-94 ( " " ) | 4,011,710 | 1,128,812 | 741,705 | 387,107 |
| 1894-95 ( " " ) | 3,636,098 | 819,349 | 736,135 | 83,214 |
| 1895-96 (927 " ) | 4,709,820 | 1,399,577 | 767,093 | 632,483 |
| 1896-97 (929 " ) | 4,680,859 | 1,253,271 | 797,958 | 455,313 |
| 1897-98 ( " " ) | 5,386,043 | 1,608,671 | 873,833 | 734,838 |
| 1898-99 ( " " ) | 5,867,739 | 1,720,224 | 758,170 | 962,054 |
| 1899-00 ( " " ) | 6,721,037 | 2,026,814 | 745,759 | 1,281,055 |
| 1900-01 ( " " ) | 7,013,861 | 1,978,246 | 638,222 | 1,340,124 |
| 1901-02 ( " " ) | 7,549,688 | 2,060,230 | 545,382 | 1,514,848 |

The proportion of operating expenses to gross earnings has been: In 1898-99, 67.21 per cent.; in 1899-00, 66.81 per cent.; in 1900-01, 68.88 per cent.; in 1901-02, 69.99 per cent.

Charges in 1895-96-97 and '98 include taxes, which in the latter year were $173,000. In 1899, 1900, 1901 and 1902 the taxes are deducted from net earnings.

| | 1897-98. | 1898-99. | 1899-00. | 1900-01. | 1901-02. |
|---|---|---|---|---|---|
| Net, after all fixed charges | $734,838 | $962,052 | $1,281,054 | $1,340,122 | $1,514,848 |
| 4 per cent. on debenture stock | 396,524 | 498,002 | 568,650 | 780,610 | 925,207 |
| Balances | $338,314 | $464,050 | $712,404 | $559,512 | $589,641 |
| Dividends on preferred A | ... .... | 454,896 | 568,620 | 568,620 | 568,620 |
| Surpluses | ........ | $9,154 | $143,783 | Def. $9,108 | $21,021 |

The following exhibits the comparative freight statistics of the company:

| | Average Miles Operated. | Total Tonnage. | Tons Carried One Mile. | Freight Density. | Rate per Ton per Mile. | Earnings per Train Mile. | Average Tons per Train Mile. |
|---|---|---|---|---|---|---|---|
| 1899-00.. | 929 | 2,340,965 | 706,924,174 | 760,956 | 0.72c | $1.89 | 261 |
| 1900-01.. | 929 | 2,651,054 | 833,799,170 | 897,947 | 0.64 | 2.00 | 319 |
| 1901-02.. | 929 | 2,753,675 | 804,613,173 | 865,632 | 0.75 | 2.02 | 269 |

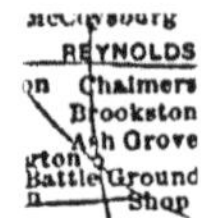
REYNOLDS
Chalmers
Brookston
Ash Grove
Battle Ground
Shop

Clayton
Martinsville
Harrodsburg

MAP OF THE
CHICAGO,
INDIANAPOLIS &
LOUISVILLE
RAILWAY.
Jasper
Huntingburg
Corydon Jc.
Cabel
Lincoln City
Kings Cave
Ohio
West Point
Bardstown Junc.
Irvington
Elizabeth-town
Munford-ville
Greensburg
Glasgow Jc.
Sadieville
K E N T U

President, A. B. Stickney; Vice-President, Ansel Oppenheim; Treasurer, C. O. Kalman; Auditor, W. B. Bend; Secretary, R. C. Wight, St. Paul, Minn.

Directors—A. B. Stickney, Ansel Oppenheim, Samuel C. Stickney, Frederick Weyhauser, J. W. Lusk, H. E. Fletcher, T. H. Wheeler, R. C. Wight, William A. Read.

Main office, St. Paul, Minn.; Chicago office, 115 Adams street. Annual meeting, first Thursday after first Tuesday in September. Books close thirty days previous.

## CHICAGO, INDIANA & EASTERN RAILWAY CO.

A corporation formed under the laws of Indiana March 8, 1893. Road owned, Converse, Ind., to Munice, Ind., 43 miles; projected, from Munice to Richmond, Ind., 40 miles. Locomotives, 9; passenger cars, 8; freight cars, 27.

Stock......Par $100..........................Authorized, $1,000,000......Issued, $1,000,000

In 1902 the stock was increased from $430,000 to $1,000,000.

Transfer Agent, Metropolitan Trust and Savings Bank, Chicago. Registrar, First National Bank, Chicago.

FUNDED DEBT.

1st mort., 5 per cent., due May, 1942, May and Nov.............................. $500,000

The 1st mortgage is $1,000,000 authorized, $500,000 of the bonds being reserved for extensions. Trustee of mortgage and agent for payment of interest, New York Security & Trust Co., New York. There is a sinking fund provision for the bonds, beginning in 1907.

In the year ending March 30, 1902, the company reported gross earnings, $98,238; net, $36,752.

President, Paul Brown; Vice-President and General Manager, H. E. Drew; Secretary-Treasurer, John H. Miller, Chicago.

Directors—Paul Brown, H. E. Drew, John H. Miller, Clarence A. Knight, Martin A. Devitt.

Main office, Matthews, Ind.; Chicago office, 100 Washington Street. Annual meeting, first Tuesday after first Monday in January, at Matthews.

## CHICAGO, INDIANAPOLIS & LOUISVILLE RAILWAY CO.

(Controlled jointly by the Louisville & Nashville and Southern Railway Companies.)

A corporation formed under the laws of Indiana, March 31, 1897. The company was created in pursuance of a plan to reorganize the Louisville, New Albany & Chicago Railway, the property of which was sold under foreclosure March 10, 1897, and transferred to this company, which took possession of the same July 1, 1897.

Road owned, New Albany, Ind., to Michigan City, 289 miles; State Line, Ind., to Indianapolis, 162 miles; Bedford to Switz City, 40 miles; Orleans to French Lick Springs, 18 miles; total, 509 miles. Leased, 38 miles, including use of track and bridge from New Albany to Louisville; also use of Chicago & Western Indiana, Hammond to Chicago, 20 miles, for $168,000 per year; total operated, 546 miles. The Indiana Stone Railroad, Clear Creek, Ind., to Harrodsburg, 9¼ miles, is operated by it. The company owns one-fifth of the Chicago & Western Indiana. In 1900 the company obtained joint ownership with the Baltimore & Ohio Southwestern and Southern Railway Co. in the Kentucky & Indiana Bridge and terminals at Louisville. Locomotives, 93; passenger cars, 82; freight cars, 5,945.

Litigation has been in progress growing out of a lease of the Beattyville road by a former management. In May, 1899, after all the testimony was taken by the Special Master in the Beattyville bond suit, a report was made to the United States Circuit Court for the district of Indiana, and on final hearing the Court confirmed all the contentions of this company, and the former sale, the confirmation of which had been suspended by order of the Circuit Court, was reconfirmed. An appeal from this decision was taken but in 1902 the matter was finally settled.

In July, 1902, the Louisville & Nashville and the Southern Railway acquired control of this company, the stockholders of which were offered $78 per share for the common and $90 per share for the preferred stock, payable in 50-year collateral trust 4 per cent. joint bonds of the two purchasing companies; 60 per cent. of the price being payable in cash, if desired. Under this arrangement a large majority of the stock was acquired, but the road is operated independently for the benefit of the two purchasing companies.

Stock..Par $100...Authorized { com., $10,500,000 / pref., 5,000,000 } Issued { com., $10,500,000 / pref., 5,000,000 } $15,500,000

Transfer office, 80 Broadway, New York. Registrar, Central Trust Co., New York.

The preferred stock is to 4 per cent., non-cumulative.

The first dividend on the preferred stock was 1 per cent., paid March 30, 1899. No further dividend was, however, paid until October 15, 1900, when a semi-annual dividend of 2 per cent. was paid on the preferred, and similar semi-annual dividends of 2 per cent. on the preferred have since been regularly paid April (15) and October. In March, 1902, 1 per cent. was paid on the common stock and 1¼ per cent. on January 29, 1903.

FUNDED DEBT.

| | |
|---|---|
| L., New Albany & C., 1st mort., main line, 6 per cent., due July, 1910, Jan. and July.. | $3,000,000 |
| " " " " C. & I. Div., 6 per cent., due Aug., 1911, Feb. and Aug. | 2,300,000 |
| Chic., Ind. & Louisville refunding mort., 5 per cent., due July, 1947, Jan. and July.. | 3,842,000 |
| " " " " 6 per cent., due July, 1947, Jan. and July.. | 4,700,000 |
| Total.................................................................. | $13,842,000 |

The authorized issue of refunding bonds is $15,000,000, of which the $4,700,000 bearing 6 per cent. were created in the reorganization to retire an equal amount of old company's 6 per cent. consols. Refunding bonds may be issued for additions and improvements to the extent of not over $300,000 in any year. In July, 1900, $300,000 refunding 5s were issued for such purposes.

In 1898 the company guaranteed $250,000 bonds of the Perry, Mathews, Buskirk Stone Co., $228,000 of which have been retired. It also guaranteed the bonds of the Indiana Stone Railroad Co. This company owns all the stock and bonds of the latter company. There were, on June 30, 1902, car trust obligations for $16,085.

In the spring of 1899 a controlling interest in this company was acquired by J. P. Morgan & Co., but it was announced that the property would be operated independently, but in harmony with other lines controlled by the same interest.

The stock of the old company was $6,995,000 6 per cent. non-cumulative preferred and $9,000,000 common. See MANUAL for 1897 for history and finances of the company.

EARNINGS.

Year ending June 30.

| | Gross. | Net. | Charges. | Surplus. |
|---|---|---|---|---|
| 1892-93 | $3,416,488 | $1,135,022 | $954,840 | $180,182 |
| 1893-94 | 3,195,882 | 1,077,272 | 999,287 | 77,985 |
| 1894-95 | 3,145,614 | 1,074,703 | 1,004,886 | 69,817 |
| 1895-96 | 3,362,772 | 1,182,384 | 1,019,486 | 162,897 |
| 1896-97 | 2,902,760 | 934,722 | 1,009,783 | Def. 75,061 |
| 1897-98 | 3,323,671 | 1,042,700 | 953,572 | 89,129 |
| 1898-99 | 3,501,121 | 1,232,857 | 958,109 | 274,747 |
| 1899-00 | 4,177,888 | 1,659,470 | 972,789 | 686,681 |
| 1900-01 | 4,150,470 | 1,496,927 | 979,930 | 652,773 |
| 1901-02 | 4,581,157 | 1,728,024 | 971,297 | 886,174 |

Net earnings, 1891-92, include $45,000 received as dividends on company's stock in the Chicago & Western Indiana, and in 1892-93 $60,000 from same source, with $14,400 dividend on Belt Railway of Chicago. In 1893-94 dividends from these sources were $60,000, and the company paid a dividend of 1½ per cent. on preferred stock, amounting to $57,252, and leaving surplus of $20,733. In 1894-95 the amount received from these sources was $78,600. In 1896 extraordinary expenses for improvements were $210,843, making deficit for year $47,946. In 1896-97 miscellaneous income was $74,400; in 1897-98, $75,037; in 1898-99, $86,686; in 1899-1900, $109,787; in 1900-01, $135,775, and in 1901-02, $129,447.

President and General Manager, William H. McDoel, Chicago; Vice-President, Anthony J. Thomas, New York; Treasurer, William H. Lewis, Chicago; Secretary, J. A. Hilton, New York.

Directors—R. M. Gallaway, Anthony J. Thomas, Temple Bowdoin, Amos T. French, Charles Steele, A. H. Gillard, New York; William H. McDoel, Gilbert B. Shaw, Henry A. Hickman, Chicago; James Murdock, Lafayette, Ind.; Volney T. Mallott, Indianapolis.

Main office, 198 Custom House place, Chicago. Annual meeting, third Wednesday in September, at Indianapolis.

## CHICAGO, MILWAUKEE & ST. PAUL RAILWAY CO.

Road owned, 6,578 miles; owned jointly with other companies, 25 miles; used under contracts, 150 miles; total mileage, 6,603 miles, which is located as follows: 347 miles in Illinois, 1,700 miles in Wisconsin, 1,120 miles in Minnesota, 1,794 miles in Iowa, 140 miles in Missouri, 118 miles in North Dakota, 1,224 miles in South Dakota, and 159 miles in Michigan, the principal lines being from Chicago to Milwaukee; Milwaukee via La Crosse to St. Paul; Milwaukee via Prairie du Chien to St. Paul; Calmar, Ia., to Chamberlain, So. Dak.; La Crosse, Wis., to Aberdeen, So. Dak.; Chicago by Sabula and Marion to Council Bluffs; Chicago to Kansas City. The Milwaukee & Northern, North Milwaukee, Wis., to Champion, Mich., and branches, 362 miles, was acquired in 1890 and absorbed by this company. Company also purchased in 1898 and controls the Des Moines, Northern & Western 147 miles. In October, 1900, the

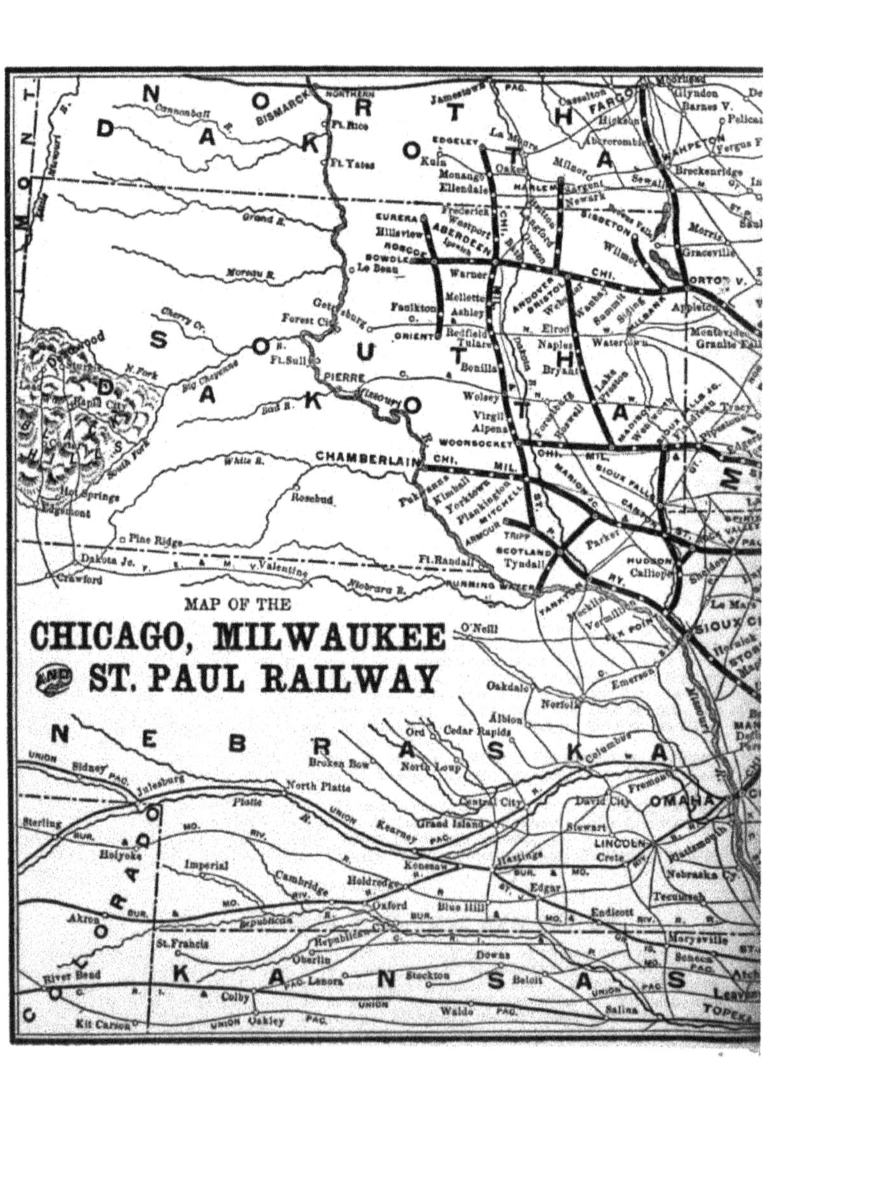
MAP OF THE
CHICAGO, MILWAUKEE
AND ST. PAUL RAILWAY

company acquired the Milwaukee & Superior Railway, Granville to North Lake, Wis. Various branches and extensions, including a Kansas City cut-off of 119 miles, are contemplated. Locomotives, 946; passenger cars, 873; freight cars, 38,752.

Stock...Par $100..Authorized { com., $58,183,900 / pref., 46,682,400 } Issued { com., $58,183,900 / pref., 46,682,400 } $104,866,300

The preferred stock is 7 per cent., non-cumulative. The preferred and common stocks share equally in any further division after 7 per cent. has been paid on both classes.

The company pays 7 per cent. per annum on the preferred stock in half-yearly payments of 3½ per cent. in April and October, about the 20th of each month. See below as to the convertibility of bonds into preferred stock.

Dividends on the common stock are also paid semi-annually in April and October. The October, 1888, dividend on common was passed and none was paid till October, 1892. In April, 1895, the dividend on common stock was reduced to 1 per cent. for the half year. In April, 1896, 2 per cent. was again paid. In October, 1897, 3 per cent. was paid, including 2 per cent. regular and 1 per cent. extra. In April, 1898, the dividend was 2 per cent. regular and ½ per cent. extra. The October, 1898, dividend was made 2½ per cent. regular, putting the common stock on a 5 per cent. basis. Regular payments were made at the same rate until the dividend payable April 25, 1901, which was increased to 3 per cent., which rate was maintained until the October, 1902, dividend, which was 3½ per cent., with ½ per cent. extra, making 7 per cent. on the common for the year.

In 1882 the common stock was increased by $7,500,000, of which $7,101,948 was issued at par to the subscribing stockholders, one-half payable in cash and one-half charged to income account. In 1883 the common stock was increased $3,000,000, issued to purchase coal lands. The preferred stock was increased $93,500, issued in exchange for bonds retired. In 1885 the preferred stock was increased $5,000,000, to retire floating debt and provide for improvements. In 1887 the common stock was increased $10,000,000, of which $7,000,000 was allotted to stockholders of record at $85 per share. In 1890 common stock was issued to amount of $6,346,000, most of which was used in acquiring the Milwaukee & Northern.

In February, 1901, an issue of $10,000,000 new common stock was authorized and $8,673,200 was issued, being an addition of 10 per cent. to the outstanding shares. Stockholders, both common and preferred, of record March 11, 1901, were given the right to subscribe for 10 per cent. of their holdings in the new stock at par, the right expiring April 18, 1901. The proceeds of this issue were to pay for extensions and for the Kansas City cut-off.

Transfer agency, 30 Broad street, New York. Registrar, Union Trust Co., New York.

FUNDED DEBT.

| | |
|---|---|
| Consolidated mort., 7 per cent., due 1904 and July, 1905, Jan. and July............ | $2,659,000 |
| Iowa & Dakota Div. Extension, 1st mort., 7 per cent., due July, 1908, Jan. and July. | 1,226,000 |
| La Crosse & Davenport Division, 5 per cent., due July, 1919, Jan. and July......... | 2,500,000 |
| Southwestern Division, 1st mort., 6 per cent., due July, 1909, Jan. and July........ | 4,000,000 |
| Chicago and Pacific Division, 1st mort., 6 per cent., due Jan., 1910, Jan. and July.. | 3,000,000 |
| Southern Minnesota Division, 1st mort., 6 per cent., due Jan., 1910, Jan. and July.. | 7,432,000 |
| Hastings & Dakota Div. Exten., 1st mort., 7 per cent., due Jan., 1910, Jan. and July.. | 5,680,000 |
| Hastings & Dakota Div. Exten., 1st mort., 5 per cent., due Jan., 1910, Jan. and July.. | 990,000 |
| Dubuque Division, 1st mort., 6 per cent., due July, 1920, Jan. and July............ | 6,007,000 |
| Wisconsin Valley Division, 1st mort., 6 per cent., due July, 1920, Jan. and July..... | 2,179,000 |
| Wisconsin Valley R. R., old bonds, 7 per cent., due Jan., 1909, Jan. and July...... | 1,106,500 |
| Mineral Point Division, 1st mort., 5 per cent., due July, 1910, Jan. and July........ | 2,840,000 |
| Chicago & Lake Superior Div., 1st mort., 5 per cent., due July, 1921, Jan. and July.. | 1,360,000 |
| Chicago & Pacific Western Div., 1st mort., 5 per cent., due Jan., 1921, Jan. and July. | 25,340,000 |
| Wisconsin & Minnesota Div., 1st mort., 5 per cent., due July, 1921, Jan. and July.. | 4,755,000 |
| Terminal mort., 5 per cent., due July, 1914, Jan. and July......................... | 4,748,000 |
| Fargo & Southern Ry., 1st mort., 6 per cent., due Jan., 1924, Jan. and July,....... | 1,250,000 |
| Dakota & Great Southern Ry., 1st mort., 5 per cent., due Jan., 1916, Jan. and July.. | 2,856,000 |
| Chicago & Missouri River Div., 1st mort., 5 per cent., due July, 1926, Jan. and July.. | 3,083,000 |
| General mort., 4 per cent., Series A, due May, 1989, Jan. and July................ | 24,000,000 |
| General mort., Series B, 3½ per cent., due May, 1989, Jan. and July............... | 10,263,000 |
| Milwaukee & Northern R. R., 1st mort., 6 per cent., due June, 1910, June and Dec.. | 2,155,000 |
| Milwaukee & Northern R. R., cons. mort., 6 per cent., due June, 1913, June and Dec. | 5,092,000 |
| Total.............................................................. | $124,521,500 |

During 1889 this company created a new issue of $150,000,000 general mortgage 100-year gold bonds, due May 1, 1989, to take up all outstanding issues and provide other funds as needed. Amount reserved to retire prior liens is $92,398,000. Of the $34,048,000 outstanding Decem er 31, 1900, $6,297,000 were in treasury of company. In January, 1899, the company sold $2,500,000 of general mortgage as general mortgage, Series B, 3½ per cent. bonds to provide for the purchase of the Des Moines, Northern & Western.

The Iowa & Dakota extension 7s, Chicago & Milwaukee 7s, Hastings & Dakota 7s and consolidated mortgage 7s can all be exchanged for preferred stock of the company. In 1894-95 bonds to the amount of $183,000 were so exchanged for stock; in 1896-97, $2,159,000; in 1897-98, $2,763,500; in 1898-99, $3,777,000; in 1899-1900, $4,859,500; in 1901, $4,750,500, and in 1902, $2,024,000. In 1902 the company sold $2,362,100 of its common stock, being the unissued balance of the authorized amount. Of the total bonds outstanding on June 30, 1901, $4,883,000 were unsold in treasury or due from trustees.

### Earnings.

Year ending June 30.

| | Dividends Paid. Com. | Pref. | Gross. | Net. | Charges. | Surplus. |
|---|---|---|---|---|---|---|
| 1892-93 (6,109 miles) | 4 | 7 | $33,975,055 | $11,587,616 | $7,065,216 | $4,522,400 |
| 1893-94 (6,147 " ) | 4 | 7 | 31,327,951 | 11,218,480 | 7,503,748 | 3,714,732 |
| 1894-95 (6,159 " ) | 3 | 7 | 27,335,369 | 10,426,263 | 7,629,377 | 2,796,886 |
| 1895-96 (6,153 " ) | 3 | 7 | 32,681,829 | 13,069,878 | 7,611,928 | 5,457,950 |
| 1896-97 (6,153 " ) | 4 | 7 | 30,486,767 | 12,072,051 | 7,488,747 | 4,583,304 |
| 1897-98 (6,154 " ) | 5 | 7 | 34,189,663 | 13,119,115 | 7,190,431 | 5,928,684 |
| 1898-99 (6,154 " ) | 5 | 7 | 38,310,632 | 14,465,206 | 6,890,120 | 7,575,086 |
| 1899-00 (6,347 " ) | 5 | 7 | 41,884,692 | 13,608,610 | 6,633,170 | 6,975,440 |
| 1900-01 (6,347 " ) | 5½ | 7 | 42,369,012 | 14,566,192 | 6,383,035 | 8,183,156 |
| 1901-02 (6,604 " ) | 6 | 7 | 45,613,124 | 15,850,544 | 6,210,086 | 9,640,458 |

The surplus over dividends was in 1898-99 $2,822,554, in 1899-00 $1,931,726, in 1900-01 $2,095,064, in 1901-02 $2,332,297.

The following table shows the average mileage worked, earnings per mile, etc.:

| | Average Miles Operated. | Gross Earnings per Mile. | Per Cent. of Expenses. | Net Earnings per Mile. |
|---|---|---|---|---|
| 1892-93 | 6,109 | $5,851 | 66.34 | $1,969 |
| 1893-94 | 6,147 | 5,096 | 64.21 | 1,824 |
| 1894-95 | 6,159 | 4,438 | 62.35 | 1,671 |
| 1895-96 | 6,153 | 5,311 | 60.21 | 2,114 |
| 1896-97 | 6,152 | 4,955 | 60.94 | 1,936 |
| 1897-98 | 6,152 | 5,555 | 62.01 | 2,110 |
| 1898-99 | 6,153 | 6,226 | 62.55 | 2,331 |
| 1899-00 | 6,347 | 6,598 | 67.85 | 2,121 |
| 1900-01 | 6,512 | 6,505 | 66.03 | 2,209 |
| 1901-02 | 6,604 | 6,906 | 66.20 | 2,334 |

The following presents the comparative freight traffic statistics of the company:

| | Total Tonage. | Tons Carried One Mile. | Freight Density. | Rate per Ton per Mile. | Earnings per Train Mile. | Average Tons per Train Mile. |
|---|---|---|---|---|---|---|
| 1896-97 | 11,554,153 | 2,193,241,080 | 356,450 | 1.008c | $1.683 | 167 |
| 1897-98 | 14,230,742 | 2,621,348,372 | 425,958 | 0.972 | 1.728 | 178 |
| 1898-99 | 15,830,156 | 3,079,579,710 | 500,419 | 0.937 | 1.748 | 187 |
| 1899-00 | 17,757,419 | 3,357,456,584 | 528,983 | 0.930 | 1.907 | 209 |
| 1900-01 | 18,010,683 | 3,639,977,919 | 558,964 | 0.861 | 2.038 | 236 |
| 1901-02 | 19,885,573 | 3,990,048,676 | 604,186 | 0.840 | 2.136 | 254 |

### Gross and Net Earnings by Months for Three Years.

| | 1900. | | 1901. | | 1902. | |
|---|---|---|---|---|---|---|
| | Gross. | Net. | Gross. | Net. | Gross. | Net. |
| January | $3,210,813 | $1,022,789 | $3,318,569 | $1,128,443 | $2,707,818 | $1,164,764 |
| February | 2,867,741 | 749,292 | 3,093,905 | 925,024 | 2,315,597 | 883,350 |
| March | 3,427,822 | 1,188,401 | 3,530,904 | 1,240,744 | 2,793,975 | 1,367,226 |
| April | 3,264,104 | 757,201 | 3,244,196 | 770,542 | 2,534,265 | 875,719 |
| May | 3,108,658 | 603,500 | 3,232,192 | 783,062 | 2,508,734 | 875,317 |
| June | 3,419,205 | 974,620 | 3,555,989 | 1,128,181 | 2,685,597 | 1,157,342 |
| July | 3,220,327 | 1,161,091 | 3,582,041 | 1,357,288 | 3,661,393 | 1,381,035 |
| August | 3,594,690 | 1,353,170 | 3,964,056 | 1,454,615 | 3,964,073 | 1,512,663 |
| September | 3,728,462 | 1,240,989 | 4,150,493 | 1,379,563 | 4,443,216 | 1,553,909 |
| October | 4,278,837 | 1,693,983 | 4,521,268 | 1,815,241 | 4,814,702 | 2,019,604 |
| November | 3,788,005 | 1,481,357 | 4,177,139 | 1,549,373 | 4,390,781 | 1,647,361 |
| December | 3,782,933 | 1,484,921 | 3,091,254 | 1,536,429 | 3,903,803 | 1,493,227 |
| Totals | $41,691,597 | $14,011,314 | $44,362,006 | $15,068,505 | $46,404,842 | $15,931,520 |
| Aver. per month. | 3,474,298 | 1,167,609 | 3,696,834 | 1,255,709 | 3,867,070 | 1,327,627 |

Proportionate taxes for the month are deducted from the net earnings.

Chairman, Roswell Miller, New York; President, Albert J. Earling; Treasurer, Frederic G. Ranney, Chicago; Secretary, P. M. Myers, Milwaukee.

Directors—Albert J. Earling, J. Ogden Armour, Chicago; Frederick Layton, Milwaukee; Roswell Miller, Frank S. Bond, Joseph Milbank, William Rockefeller, Peter Geddes, August Belmont, Samuel Spencer, Henry H. Rogers, Charles W. Harkness, James H. Smith, New York.

Main office, 84 Van Buren street, Chicago; New York office, 30 Broad street. Annual meeting, September, as directors may appoint. Books close fifteen days previous.

---

## CHICAGO, PEORIA & ST. LOUIS RAILWAY CO. OF ILLINOIS

A reorganization, in January, 1900, of the railroad of same name with which the St. Louis, Chicago & St. Paul Railway Co. was consolidated.

Road owned, Pekin, Ill., to Granite City, Ill., 180 miles; Madison to Bridge Junction, 3 miles; Havana, Ill., to Jacksonville, Ill., 42 miles; Grafton Branch, 8 miles; total owned, 233 miles. Controls by ownership of stock Litchfield & Madison Railway, Litchfield, Ill., to Madison, Ill., 44 miles; trackage, Peoria & Pekin Union Railway, 10 miles; other trackage, 13 miles; total operated, 300 miles. Locomotives, 42; passenger cars, 35; freight cars, 4,349.

Stock....Par $100...Authorized { com., $3,600,000 / pref., 3,750,000 } Issued { com., $3,600,000 / pref., 3,750,000 } $7,350,000

The preferred stock is 5 per cent., non-cumulative.

Stock is transferred at the office of the company, 27 Pine street, New York. Registrar, North American Trust Co., New York.

FUNDED DEBT.

| | |
|---|---|
| Prior lien mort., 4½ per cent., due March, 1930, March and Sept. | $1,500,000 |
| Cons. mort., 5 per cent., due July, 1930, Jan. and July | 2,000,000 |
| Income mort., 5 per cent., due July, 1930, Jan., if earned | 2,000,000 |
| Total | $5,500,000 |

The authorized issue of prior lien 4½ per cent. bonds is $2,000,000.

The railroad company to which this company succeeded was formed in February, 1896, and succeeded the railway company of same name sold under foreclosure in September, 1895. See MANUAL for 1896 and 1897 for details and history of legal and other complications. In July, 1898, Receivers were appointed. Reorganization plan, formulated in 1899, provided for the foreclosure of this property, its transfer to a new company and a consolidation with the St. Louis, Chicago & St. Paul Railway under the present title.

The reorganized company has $2,000,000 of 5 per cent. non-cumulative income bonds due 1930, and the Litchfield & Madison also has $500,000 of 5 per cent. non-cumulative incomes. It is proposed to exchange these incomes at par for 1st preferred stock, the original preferred becoming 2d preferred, the Litchfield & Madison incomes to be exchanged for preferred stock of this company. This proposition was generally accepted by the securityholders. A large majority of all the stock and income bonds has been deposited in trust with a committee, Thomas Carmichael, New York, chairman, with authority to sell the same prior to August, 1904, at 50 for the 1st preferred, 20 for the 2d preferred and 15 for the common stock.

The Chicago, Peoria & St. Louis owns one-quarter interest, or 2,500 shares, in the Peoria & Pekin Union Railroad.

EARNINGS.

Year ending June 30.

| | Gross. | Net. | Charges. | Surplus |
|---|---|---|---|---|
| 1900-01 (sixteen months ending June 30) | $1,778,052 | $327,931 | $271,026 | $56,905 |
| 1901-02 | 1,462,725 | 301,768 | 288,026 | 13,742 |

The charges in 1901-02 included expenditures for betterments.

For earnings of the predecessor company see MANUAL for 1900.

President, Charles E. Kimball, New York; Secretary and Treasurer, Ralph Blaisdell, Springfield, Ill.; Assistant Secretary and Assistant Treasurer, T. C. Wellman, New York.

Directors—Curtiss Millard, Ralph Blaisdell, Bluford Wilson, Springfield, Ill.; James Duncan, Alton, Ill.; Charles E. Kimball, Charles F. Dean, New York; Eleneious Smith, St. Louis.

Main office, Springfield, Ill.; New York office, 27 Pine street. Annual meeting, second Monday in December, at Springfield.

## CHICAGO, ST. PAUL, MINNEAPOLIS & OMAHA RAILWAY CO.

Road owned, Elroy, Wis., to St. Paul, 196 miles; St. Paul to Omaha, 397 miles; branches and extensions, 997 miles; total, 1,590 miles; of which 69 miles are leased. Locomotives, 277; passenger cars, 224; freight cars, 10,386.

Stock..Par $100...Authorized { com., $21,403,293 / pref., 12,646,833 } Issued { com., $18,558,933 / pref., 11,259,911 } $29,818,844

In addition to the above the company owns $2,844,339 of the common and $1,386,921 of the preferred stock.

The preferred stock is entitled to a preference of 7 per cent., non-cumulative, and the common shall not receive more than the preferred out of the earnings of any year.

Dividends of 7 per cent. per annum, half-yearly, 3½ per cent. February 20 and August 20, have been regularly paid on the preferred. A 2 per cent. annual dividend, the first in company's history, was paid on the common stock February 20, 1897. In 1899 the annual February dividend on common was increased to 3½ per cent., and February 20, 1900, 5 per cent. was paid on the common, which was also the rate in February, 1901, and February, 1902. In August, 1902, 3 per cent. semi-annual was paid on the common and the same rate in February, 1903.

Transfer agency, 52 Wall street, New York. Registrar, Central Trust Co., New York.

### Funded Debt.

| | |
|---|---|
| St. Paul, Stillwater & Taylor's Falls, 7 per cent., due Jan., 1908, Jan. and July...... | $134,800 |
| Hudson & River Falls, 8 per cent., due July, 1908, Jan. and July.................... | 125,000 |
| Minneapolis East, 1st mort., 7 per cent., due Jan., 1909, Jan. and July.............. | 75,000 |
| Sault Ste. Marie & S. W., 1st mort., 5 per cent. guar., due Nov., 1915, May and Nov. | 350,000 |
| Chicago, St. Paul & Min'apolis, 1st mort., 6 per cent., due May, 1918, May and Nov.. | 1,968,000 |
| St. Paul & Sioux City, 6 per cent., due April, 1919, April and Oct.................. | 6,070,000 |
| North Wisconsin, 6 per cent., due Jan., 1930, Jan. and July......................... | 789,000 |
| Consolidated mort., 6 per cent., due June, 1930, June and Dec....................... | 14,456,000 |
| Total.................................................................. | $24,167,800 |

The consolidated mortgage is for $30,000,000. It is intended to retire all prior bonds.

### Earnings.

| | Dividends, Pref. | Com. | Gross. | Per Ct. of Exp. | Net. | Charges. | Surplus. |
|---|---|---|---|---|---|---|---|
| 1891 (1,481 miles)...... | 5 | .. | $8,021,312 | 67.90 | $2,575,197 | $1,452,820 | $1,122,376 |
| 1892 ( " " )...... | 7 | .. | 9,196,942 | 69.24 | 2,828,646 | 1,473,980 | 1,354,667 |
| 1893 (1,485 " )...... | 7 | .. | 8,328,928 | 70.16 | 2,485,395 | 1,520,319 | 965,076 |
| 1894 ( " " )...... | 7 | .. | 7,297,618 | 67.78 | 2,351,435 | 1,521,436 | 829,998 |
| 1895 (1,492 " )...... | 7 | .. | 7,508,764 | 64.41 | 2,672,111 | 1,535,878 | 1,136,233 |
| 1896 ( " " )...... | 7 | 2 | 8,156,192 | 62.98 | 3,019,159 | 1,519,299 | 1,499,859 |
| 1897 ( " " )...... | 7 | 2 | 8,652,793 | 66.31 | 2,915,346 | 1,526,096 | 1,389,251 |
| 1898 ( " " )...... | 7 | 3½ | 9,590,993 | 63.51 | 3,499,429 | 1,505,374 | 1,994,054 |
| 1899 (1,498 " )...... | 7 | 5 | 10,488,814 | 62.14 | 3,970,678 | 1,479,344 | 2,491,334 |
| 1900 (1,543 " )...... | 7 | 5 | 10,342,000 | 62.75 | 3,852,846 | 1,454,721 | 2,398,124 |
| 1901 (1,578 " )...... | 7 | 5 | 11,196,403 | 59.62 | 4,182,133 | 1,452,882 | 2,729,250 |

Net receipts from land sales were: In 1897, $33,909; in 1898, $30,360; in 1899, $63,737; in 1900, $97,016. Land unsold December 31, 1900, 298,828 acres.

In 1898 the company appropriated $420,173 out of the surplus to improvement. The surplus after this payment and dividend for the year was $136,620. In 1899 $500,000 was appropriated for improvements, the surplus over the same and dividends being $275,630. In 1900, improvements, $500,000; dividends, $1,715,726; surplus, $182,398. In 1901, improvements, $600,000; dividends, $1,715,726; surplus, $413,524.

Present company was formed in 1880 by consolidation of the Chicago, St. Paul & Minneapolis, the North Wisconsin and the St. Paul & Sioux City. Of the stock, 93,200 shares of common and 53,800 of the preferred are now owned by the Chicago & Northwestern, and the road is operated in the interest of that company, although the organization is distinct. The Chicago & Northwestern paid $104 04 per share for the preferred and $48.40 per share for the common, the total cost being $10,503,959.

The following presents the freight traffic statistics of the company:

| | Average Mileage. | Total Tonnage. | Tons Carried One Mile. | Freight Density. | Rate per Ton per Mile. | Earnings per Train Mile. | Average Tons per Train. |
|---|---|---|---|---|---|---|---|
| 1896.... | 1,492 | 3,540,793 | 574,145,415 | 384,816 | 1.042c. | $1.78 | 170 |
| 1897.... | 1,492 | 3,772,439 | 647,845,804 | 434,213 | 1.007 | 1.88 | 187 |
| 1898.... | 1,492 | 4,337,958 | 731,347,471 | 490,782 | 0.967 | 2.12 | 219 |
| 1899.... | 1,498 | 4,792,950 | 789,701,170 | 527,170 | 0.977 | 2.31 | 236 |
| 1900.... | 1,543 | 4,707,105 | 755,737,001 | 489,719 | 0.971 | 2.35 | 242 |
| 1901.... | 1,574 | 5,073,440 | 823,144,727 | 522,328 | 0.961 | 2.37 | 247 |

President, Marvin Hughitt, Chicago; Vice-President and Assistant Secretary, E. E. Osborne, New York; 2d Vice-President and General Traffic Manager, James T. Clark, St. Paul; Treasurer and Assistant Secretary, S. O. Howe, New York; Secretary, E. E. Woodman, Hudson, Wis.

Directors—William K. Vanderbilt, Martin L. Sykes, Hamilton McK. Twombly, Chauncey M. Depew, Frederick W. Vanderbilt, New York; Albert Keep, Marvin Hughitt, Byron L. Smith, J. M. Whitman, Chicago; D. P. Kimball, Boston; J. A. Humbird, Thomas Wilson, St. Paul; H. G. Burt, Omaha.

Principal office, St. Paul, Minn.; New York office, 52 Wall street. Annual meeting, first Saturday after first Thursday in June, at Hudson, Wis.

---

## CHICAGO TERMINAL TRANSFER RAILROAD CO.

This company is a reorganization, June, 1897, of the Chicago & Northern Pacific and Chicago & Calumet Terminal Railway Companies.

The company owns extensive terminals in and about Chicago, comprising 760 acres, of which 50 acres are in the center of the business district, with 90¼ miles of road owned and 17 miles leased, second track spurs making the total tracks 273 miles. The company owns the Grand Central Passenger Station and 7,500 feet of docks on Chicago river. Nearly all its land, including that on which tracks have been built, is owned in fee. Locomotives, 42; passenger cars, 45; freight cars, 384.

Stock..Par $100...Authorized { com., $13,000,000; pref., 17,000,000 } Issued { com., $13,000,000; pref., 17,000,000 } $30,000,000

Preferred stock is 4 per cent., non-cumulative. Of the stock authorized and outstanding as given above $10,800 common is in the company's treasury. There were also on June 30, 1902, $265,000 of the new 1st mortgage bonds in company's treasury.

Transfer agency, 30 Broad street, New York. Registrar, Mercantile Trust Co., New York.

FUNDED DEBT.

| | |
|---|---|
| Chicago & Great Western, 1st mort., 5 per cent., due June, 1936, Jan. and Dec..... | $394,000 |
| Purchase Money Mort. to City of Chicago, 5 per cent., due May, 1938, May and Nov.. | 650,000 |
| Chicago Terminal Trans., 1st mort., 4 per cent., due July, 1947, Jan. and July..... | 13,635,000 |
| Total........ | $14,679,000 |

The Baltimore & Ohio, Chicago Great Western, Chicago, Hammond & Western, St. Louis, Peoria & Northern Railway, and Suburban Railroad make use of the terminals of the company. The Chicago, Rock Island & Pacific and the Lake Shore & Michigan Southern made temporary leases in 1901. The Wisconsin Central was also a tenant, but did not renew its lease in 1899.

In 1898–99 the St. Louis, Peoria & Northern Railway Co. contracted to become a tenant under a 99-year lease, which was modified in respect to the commuted rental payable thereunder, and Edward H. Harriman, Jacob H. Schiff, James Stillman and George J. Gould have jointly and severally agreed that on or before January 1, 1904, they will cause the Chicago & Alton Railroad Co., or some other corporation satisfactory to the Terminal Co. as to responsibility, to become the successor to the St. Louis Co. as lessee under said lease of October 1, 1898.

The 1st mortgage is for $16,500,000, of which $1,305,000 was reserved to retire underlying bonds and $2,195,000 to provide for new property, as provided in the mortgage

The following shows the results of the operations of this company for four years, ending June 30:

GROSS EARNINGS.

| | 1898–99. | 1899–00. | 1900–01. | 1901–02. |
|---|---|---|---|---|
| Rentals and trackage...... | $691,586 | $674,143 | $659,189 | $723,025 |
| Traffic....... | 529,520 | 591,817 | 771,799 | 916,091 |
| Total earnings.......... | $1,221,106 | $1,265,961 | $1,430,989 | $1,639,116 |
| Operating expenses and taxes.......... | 541,946 | 589,733 | 827,667 | 1,006,133 |
| | $679,160 | $676,227 | $603,321 | $632,983 |
| Less interest charges............ | 572,200 | 584,200 | 591,900 | 597,600 |
| Surplus earnings............... | $106,960 | $92,027 | $11,421 | $35,383 |

President and General Manager, J. N. Faithorn, Chicago; Secretary and Assistant Treasurer, W. T. Wisner, 2d., New York; Treasurer and Assistant Secretary, H. H. Hall; Comptroller, Samuel L. Prest, Chicago.

Directors—Henry W. DeForest, Otto T. Bannard, Henry R. Ickleheimer, Charles T. Parker, Charles W. Gould, Myles Tierney, New York; J. N. Faithorn, Jesse B. Barton, Henry S. Hawley, Kemper K. Knapp, Edward R. Knowlton, Henry A. Rust, E. S. Layman, Joseph Cooper, Chicago; F. G. Reighley, Summit, N. J.

Main office, Grand Central Station, Chicago; New York office, 30 Broad street. Annual meeting, second Wednesday in October.

## CHIHUAHUA & PACIFIC RAILROAD CO.

A corporation formed under the laws of New Jersey, December 13, 1897.

Road owned, Chihuahua, Mex., to Minaca, Mex., 125 miles. Locomotives, 6; passenger cars, 4; freight cars, 115.

Stock......Par $100..........................Authorized, $2,500,000......Issued, $2,500,000

The company has no funded debt.

President, Grant B. Schley, New York; Vice-President, Enrique C. Creel, Chihuahua, Mex.; Secretary, Thomas J. Brennan; Treasurer, Charles L. E. de Gaugue, New York; General Manager, C. L. Graves, Chihuahua, Mex.

Directors—Oliver H. Payne, Grant B. Schley, Herbert L. Terrell, Charles L. E. de Gaugue, New York; Enrique C. Creel, Chihuahua, Mex.; Rosendo Pineda, Augustin del Rio, City of Mexico.

Corporate office, Jersey City; main office, 80 Broadway, New York. Annual meeting, second Tuesday in April, at Jersey City.

## CHOCTAW, OKLAHOMA & GULF RAILROAD CO.

(Controlled by Chicago, Rock Island & Pacific.)

A corporation formed in 1894 as a reorganization of the Choctaw Coal & Railway Co.

| Road owned: | Miles. |
|---|---|
| Hopefield, Ark., to Texas-Oklahoma boundary | 646 |
| Haileyville, I. T., to Ardmore, I. T. | 117 |
| Geary, Okla., to Anthony, Kan., and Alva, Okla. | 137 |
| Hot Springs to Malvern, Ark. | 40 |
| Tecumseh Junction to Asher, Okla. | 25 |
| Total owned | 965 |
| Leased: | |
| White & Black River Valley Railroad, Brinkley to Jacksonport, Ark. | 64 |
| Little Rock Junction to Benton, Ark. | 23 |
| Total operated | 1,052 |

At the end of 1902 the company had under construction the Choctaw & Chickasaw Railroad from Ardmore, I. T., to the Red River, and other branch lines. The company also owns coal mines in the Indian Territory.

The Choctaw, Oklahoma & Texas Railroad, controlled by the Choctaw, Oklahoma & Gulf Railroad Co. under a financial and traffic agreement, extends from a connection with the latter road at the Texas-Oklahoma boundary to Amarillo, Tex., 114 miles, and there is under construction an extension of this line from Amarillo to the New Mexico boundary, a further distance of 72 miles.

Locomotives, 106; passenger cars, 65; freight cars, 4,938.

In 1898 this company obtained control of the Little Rock & Memphis Railroad, 133 miles, which was reorganized as the Choctaw & Memphis and extended to a connection with this road, in all 282 miles. In 1900 leased the White & Black River Valley Railroad for eighty years, the rental being interest on $500,000 5 per cent. bonds of the leased road. In 1901, the Hot Springs Railroad, 22 miles, was acquired, and an extension thereof of 20 miles was constructed. In 1902, the Choctaw Northern, Geary to Anthony, was absorbed by this company.

In June, 1902, practically all the common and preferred stock was sold to the Chicago, Rock Island & Pacific Railway, and the property is now operated as part of the Rock Island system. The prices paid were $80 per share for the common and $60 for the preferred.

Stock ...Par $50....Authorized { com., $10,000,000 / pref., 6,000,000 } Issued { com., $9,827,500 / pref., 6,000,000 } $15,827,500

The preferred stock is 5 per cent., cumulative. It was originally $4,000,000 authorized, and was created in 1896 to retire $1,100,000 of 5 per cent. income bonds, pay off car trusts and build a 6 mile extension, as well as to acquire $1,200,000 of general mortgage bonds.

In May, 1900, an issue of $2,000,000 new preferred and $2,250,000 new common was authorized, of which $1,762,500 preferred was exchanged for Choctaw & Memphis preferred, at par, on payment by holders of the latter of $5 per share, and of the new common $1,057,500 was exchanged for Choctaw & Memphis common on the basis of $5 of the latter for $3 in this company's stock. The balance of the issue was used to liquidate debts of the Choctaw & Memphis and for betterments. In 1901 $2,000,000 new common was sold to stockholders at par, making the total common $8,000,000, and in October, 1901, $800,000 additional common was distributed as a 10 per cent. stock dividend to the common shareholders.

On the preferred stock 5 per cent. was paid in 1898 and succeeding years. The preferred dividends are semi-annual, 2½ per cent. each, on April 30 and October 31. On the common the first dividend was 2 per cent., October 31, 1899. In 1900 the company paid 4 per cent. on the common, 2 per cent. in April and 2 per cent. in October (31). In April, 1901, 2 per cent. was paid on the common, and in October, 1901, 2½ per cent. with 10 per cent. in common stock.

### Funded Debt.

| | |
|---|---|
| Little Rock Bridge, 1st mort., 6 per cent., due July, 1919, Jan. and July | $375,000 |
| General, now 1st mort., 5 per cent., due Oct., 1919, Jan. and July | 5,500,000 |
| Choctaw & Memphis 1st mort., 5 per cent., due Jan., 1949, Jan. and July | 3,525,000 |
| Con. mort., 5 per cent., due May, 1952, May and Nov., issued May 1, 1902 | 5,062,000 |
| Car trusts, Series A, 5 per cent., due 1905 | 200,000 |
| Car trusts, series B, 5 per cent., due 1908 | 860,000 |
| Car trusts, Series C, gold, 4½ per cent., due 1909, issued May 1, 1902 | 1,750,000 |
| Total | $17,272,000 |

The first coupon due on general mortgage bonds was January 1, 1896. General mortgage is for $5,500,000.

To provide for the extensions to be built in 1901, the company in December, 1900, sold $500,000 general mortgage bonds to a syndicate, and $3,435,000 consolidated mortgage bonds, secured by a 1st mortgage on the extensions from the Oklahoma-Texas State Line to Elk City, and from Hartshorne to Ardmore, issued and to be issued at the rate of $1,000,000 for the coal estates of the company and $15,000 per mile for each mile of road now constructed or hereafter acquired or constructed. Bonds to the amount of the present issues of the general mortgage and of the Choctaw & Memphis bonds will be reserved to be used only for the retirement of those issues, so that the bonds outstanding under all mortgages shall not exceed in the aggregate the authorized issue of the consolidated bonds.

### Earnings.

Year ending October 31.

| | Gross. | Net. | Net Earnings, Mines. | Charges & Taxes. | Surplus. |
|---|---|---|---|---|---|
| 1892-93 (year ending June 30) | $235,180 | $68,585 | ...... | $82,072 | Def., $13,487 |
| 1893-94, " " " | 254,830 | 83,461 | ...... | 84,212 | Def., 751 |
| 1894-95 | 362,824 | 152,198 | $57,387 | 153,618 | 55,967 |
| 1895-96 | 546,061 | 205,241 | 33,596 | 234,690 | 4,174 |
| 1896-97 | 1,229,685 | 392,355 | ...... | 225,974 | 166,381 |
| 1897-98 | 1,634,932 | 597,791 | ...... | 242,208 | 355,583 |
| 1898-99 | 1,959,092 | 716,902 | ...... | 258,205 | 458,697 |
| 1899-00 | 3,463,505 | 1,228,738 | ...... | 497,835 | 730,903 |
| 1900-01 | 5,266,813 | 2,025,043 | ...... | 607,419 | 1,417,624 |

In 1894-95 and 1895-96 the net earnings of mines are shown separately, but in other years the operation of the company's mines are included in the earnings.

In 1900 the surplus over dividends was $282,496. The operations of the Choctaw & Memphis and the White & Black River Valley Railroad were included from July 1, 1900. In 1901 the coal mines showed a deficit of $62,316, making the net surplus $1,417,624.

Gross earnings of the mining department in 1896-97 were $511,727. In 1897-98 the gross of mining department was $567,398; in 1898-99, $606,964; in 1899-00, $741,485.

Coal mined in 1893 was 350,000 tons; in 1895, 358,655 tons; in 1896, 364,110 tons; in 1897, 365,769 tons; in 1898, 426,538 tons; in 1899, 419,813 tons; in 1900, 494,760 tons.

President, William B. Leeds; Secretary, George H. Crosby; Treasurer, F. E. Hayne; Comptroller, W. W. Stevenson, Chicago; Auditor, George H. Moore, Little Rock.

Directors—William B. Leeds, W. H. Moore, Daniel G. Reid, J. H. Moore, George T. Boggs, John J. Quinlan, New York; R. R. Cable, Robert Mather, Charles H. Warren, Chicago.

Main office, Grand Central Station, Chicago. Annual meeting, second Monday in January, at Philadelphia.

## CINCINNATI & MUSKINGUM VALLEY RAILROAD CO.

(Controlled by the Pennsylvania Company.)

A corporation formed under the laws of Ohio, June 8, 1898. The company took over the property of the railway company of the same title, which was sold under foreclosure.

Road owned, Trinway, O., to Morrow, O., 148 miles. Locomotives, 20; passenger cars, 17; freight cars, 366.

The company is controlled by the Pennsylvania Company through ownership of the stock, and the Pennsylvania Railroad Co. owns about $754,000 of the 1st mortgage 4 per cent. bonds. The road, though operated through its own organization, forms part of the Pennsylvania's Western system.

Stock......Par $100..........................Authorized, $2,000,000......Issued, $2,000,000

The company has no preferred stock. Stock is transferred by the secretary of the company, Pittsburg.

Dividends on the stock have been paid as follows: June 25, 1900, 2 per cent.; December 31, 1900, 4 per cent.; December, 1901, 2 per cent.

FUNDED DEBT.

1st mort., 4 per cent., due Aug., 1948, Feb. and Aug.......... ....................$1,500,000

The 1st mortgage, Farmers' Loan & Trust Co., New York, trustee, is $2,000,000, authorized. There is a sinking fund of 1 per cent. per annum, bonds to be purchased at par or under, but they cannot be drawn for redemption.

In the year 1901 the gross earnings were $574,032; net, $110,140; charges, $74,986; dividends, $40,000; balance, deficit, $4,845.

President, James McCrea; Vice-President, Joseph Wood; Secretary, S. B. Liggett; Treasurer, T. H. B. McKnight; Auditor, John W. Renner, Pittsburg.

Directors—James McCrea, Joseph Wood, J. J. Turner, L. L. Gilbert, F. A. Durbin, James Buckingham, John Hoge.

Main office, Pittsburg. Annual meeting, fourth Thursday in March, at Zanesville, O.

---

## CINCINNATI, HAMILTON & DAYTON RAILWAY CO.

Road owned, Cincinnati to Dayton, O., 60 miles; Dayton to Deans, O., 176 miles; Dayton to Delphos, O., 98 miles; total owned, 334 miles; leased, Dayton & Michigan, Dayton to Toledo, 142 miles; controlled, Cincinnati, Hamilton & Indianapolis, Hamilton to Indianapolis, 99 miles; other branches, 60 miles; trackage, 12½ miles; total operated, 651 miles. The company has a joint interest in the Dayton & Union, 47 miles, which is operated by the Cleveland, Cincinnati, Chicago & St. Louis. In December, 1895, control of the Indiana, Decatur & Western Railway was acquired. In 1901, acquired the Findlay, Fort Wayne & Western Railway, 80 miles. These two last named roads were operated separately. In August, 1902, it was decided to consolidate the Cincinnati, Hamilton & Indianapolis with the Indiana, Decatur & Western, under the title of the Cincinnati, Indianapolis & Western Railway Co. See statement of the latter company. Locomotives, 174; passenger cars, 161; freight cars, 8,868.

The present company was formed in 1895, being a consolidation of the railroad company of same name with the Cincinnati, Dayton & Ironton Railroad and the Cincinnati, Dayton & Chicago.

| Stock. Par $100. Au'ized | | | Issued | | | |
|---|---|---|---|---|---|---|
| | com., | $8,000,000 | | com., | $8,000,000 | |
| | pref., 4 p. c., | 1,074,000 | | pref., 4 p. c., | 1,074,500 | $16,000,000 |
| | " 5 " | 8,000,000 | | " 5 " | 6,925,500 | |

The $1,074,500 of preferred stock outstanding is entitled to 4 per cent. cumulative dividends and can be called at par. The new preferred is 5 per cent. non-cumulative. Old preferred shares, 4 per cent. cumulative, had option of exchange share for share for new, or of remaining undisturbed. The old common was exchanged on basis of two new common shares and $155 in new preferred for each old common share.

The company since 1895 has regularly paid 5 per cent. per annum on the new preferred stock in quarterly payments of 1¼ per cent. each in February, May, August and November. On the old preferred, 4 per cent. is paid in quarterly payments of 1 per cent. each on $612,100 of the old stock in January, April, July and October, and on $462,400 in March, June, September and December. No dividends have been paid on the common stock.

Stock is transferred by the Secretary of the company, Cincinnati. Registrar, Central Trust & Safe Deposit Co., Cincinnati.

FUNDED DEBT.

| | |
|---|---|
| Consolidated mort., 5 per cent., due Oct., 1905, April and Oct. | $376,000 |
| " " 7 per cent., due Oct., 1905, April and Oct. | 927,000 |
| " " 6 per cent., due Oct., 1905, April and Oct. | 1,292,000 |
| 2d mort. bonds, 4½ per cent., due Jan., 1937, Jan. and July | 2,000,000 |
| Gen. mort., 5 per cent., due June, 1942, June and Dec. | 3,000,000 |
| Cin., Dayton & Ironton 1st mort., 5 per cent., due May, 1941, May and Nov. | 3,500,000 |
| Dayton & Mich., con. mort., 5 per cent., due Jan, 1911, Jan. and July | 2,728,000 |
| Cin., Dayton & Chicago, 1st mort., 4 per cent., due April, 1942, April and Oct. | 1,200,000 |
| Total.. | $15,023,000 |

The company also guarantees 8 per cent. on the preferred stock, $1,211,250, and 3½ per cent. on $2,401,900 of the common stock of the Dayton & Michigan. In 1891 leased the Cincinnati, Dayton & Ironton, one of the divisions of the former Dayton, Fort Wayne & Chicago, and guaranteed its bonds. General mortgage was authorized in 1892 for $7,800,000, of which $4,800,000 was reserved to retire prior liens.

In 1894 a majority interest in securities of the Cincinnati, New Orleans & Texas Pacific, and the Alabama Great Southern was acquired in this company's interest, but litigation ensued with the Southern Railway in regard to those properties, the matter being arranged in May, 1895, by the surrender of the Alabama Great Southern to the Southern Railway while the latter and this company agreed to jointly control the Cincinnati Southern.

In 1900 a refunding 4 per cent. mortgage was authorized to refund and retire the existing bonds and obligations of the company.

The $1,800,000 1st mortgage 7 per cent. bonds of the Cincinnati, Hamilton & Indianapolis Railroad Co., maturing January 1, 1903, were retired by the issue of an equal amount of the 4 per cent. refunding bonds of the Cincinnati, Indianapolis & Western Railway Co. See the statement of the latter company.

EARNINGS.

Year ending June 30.

| | Dividends Pfd. Stocks. | Gross. | Net. | Charges. | Surplus. |
|---|---|---|---|---|---|
| 1892-93 | 4 & 5 | $5,412,912 | $1,844,280 | $981,250 | $863,030 |
| 1893-94 | 4 & 5 | 5,094,812 | 1,724,404 | 1,030,741 | 694,164 |
| 1894-95 | 4 & 5 | 5,039,136 | 1,627,986 | 1,027,988 | 599,998 |
| 1895-96 | 4 & 5 | 5,147,562 | 1,607,717 | 846,907 | 760,810 |
| 1896-97 | 4 & 5 | 4,627,352 | 1,398,670 | 1,027,750 | 370,920 |
| 1897-98 | 4 & 5 | 4,908,563 | 1,487,215 | 1,027,937 | 459,278 |
| 1898-99 | 4 & 5 | 5,241,503 | 1,582,096 | 1,031,396 | 550,700 |
| 1899-00 | 4 & 5 | 5,735,530 | 1,728,848 | 1,031,186 | 697,692 |
| 1900-01 | 4 & 5 | 5,837,915 | 1,806,002 | 1,049,637 | 756,364 |
| 1901-02 | 4 & 5 | 6,352,164 | 2,018,108 | 1,070,844 | 947,263 |

In 1896-97, after payment of dividends, $383,033, there was a deficit of $12,121. In 1897-98. surplus over dividends, $72,927. In 1898-99, surplus, $170,360. In 1899-1900, surplus, $310,554, In 1900-01, surplus, $367,364. In 1901-02, surplus, $558,038.

President, M. D. Woodford; Vice-President, Eugene Zimmerman; Secretary and Treasurer, Frederick H. Short; Auditor, George W. Lishawa, Cincinnati.

Directors—Alfred Kessler, Henry F. Shoemaker, Rush Taggart, Heman Dowd, George P. Benjamin, New York; Lawrence Maxwell, Jr., George R. Balch, M. D. Woodford, Frederic H. Short, W. A. Shoemaker, Eugene Zimmerman, Cincinnati; Robert C. Schenck, Dayton, O.; Charles A. Mayer, Lock Haven, Pa.

Main office, Cincinnati. Annual meeting, second Tuesday in October.

## *CINCINNATI, INDIANAPOLIS & WESTERN RAILWAY CO.*

(Controlled by Cincinnati, Hamilton & Dayton Railway Co.)

A corporation formed in August, 1902, as a consolidation of the Cincinnati, Hamilton & Indianapolis Railroad Co. and the Indiana, Decatur & Western Railroad Co. Both of these corporations were controlled through stock ownership by the Cincinnati, Hamilton & Dayton Railway Co. which owns all the stock of the present company.

Road owned, Hamilton, O., to Springfield, Ill., 291 miles; Sidell, Ill., to West Liberty, Ill., 78 miles; total, 369 miles.

Stock......Par $100..........................Authorized, $8,200,000......Issued, $8,200,000

The company has no preferred stock. The outstanding stock was issued in exchange for the stocks of the two constituent companies.

FUNDED DEBT.

| | |
|---|---|
| Ind., Decatur & West. 1st mort., guar. 5 per cent., due Jan., 1935, Jan. and July.... | $933,000 |
| " " " 1st mort. not guar., 5 per cent. due Jan., 1935, Jan. and July. | 2,215,000 |
| Cin., Ind. & West., 1st refunding mort., 4 per cent., due Jan., 1953, Jan. and July.. | 1,800,000 |
| Equipment trusts.......... | 429,000 |
| Total .......... | $5,377,000 |

The 4 per cent. refunding mortgage is $8,200,000 authorized and was created in 1902. Trustee of the mortgage and agent for the payment of interest, North American Trust Co., New York. The amount outstanding was issued to take up and retire the $1,800,000 7 per cent. 1st mortgage bonds of the Cincinnati, Hamilton & Indianapolis Railroad which matured January 1, 1903. There are also $2,700,000 of the issue in the Treasury of the Cincinnati, Hamilton & Dayton Railway Co. The latter company guarantees the bonds as to both principal and interest by endorsement. It is stated that the Indianapolis, Decatur & Western first 5 per cents. will also be retired. The latter bonds are redeemable at 110 on eight weeks' notice.

In the year ending June 30, 1901, the companies consolidated in this corporation earned gross $1,623,500, net $405,343.

See MANUAL for 1902 for statement of the Indiana, Decatur & Western Railroad Co.

President, M. D. Woodford, Cincinnati; Vice-President, Henry F. Shoemaker, New York; Secretary, George R. Balch; Treasurer, F. H. Short, Cincinnati.

Main office, Indianapolis.

## CINCINNATI, NEW ORLEANS & TEXAS PACIFIC RAILWAY CO.

"Queen & Crescent."

This company owns no road, but leases the Cincinnati Southern, Cincinnati to Chattanooga, Tenn., 336 miles, from the city of Cincinnati; trackage, 2 miles; total operated, 338 miles. It also has side tracks and spurs aggregating 158 miles. The lease dated from October 12, 1881, and expires October 12, 1906. A new lease was negotiated in 1901 and submitted to the voters of the city of Cincinnati in November, 1901, the same to run for 60 years from expiration of old lease. The lease having been approved was executed June 7, 1902. Locomotives, 113; passenger cars, 68; freight cars, 4,148.

A controlling interest in the company was acquired in 1890 by the East Tennessee, Virginia & Georgia system. In November, 1893, it was, however, announced that the property had been surrendered by the East Tennessee to the original owners, who were identified with the so-called Erlanger syndicate of English capitalists, and in January, 1894, it was stated that the property would not be included in the proposed reorganization of the Richmond Terminal and East Tennessee systems. In 1894 a controlling interest in the English company owning the stock was secured by the Cincinnati, Hamilton & Dayton. The Southern Railway representing the minority, however, opposed the carrying out of this plan, and in May, 1895, arrangement was concluded by which the two contesting companies agreed to a joint control of this line, a majority interest being vested in the Southwestern Construction Co., a corporation formed to carry out this purpose. In December, 1895, a new board, in which both companies were equally represented, was elected.

Samuel M. Felton, then the President of the company, was appointed Receiver in 1893, but in October, 1899, the company was taken out of the hands of the Receiver.

Stock......Par $100.....Authorized { com., $3,000,000; pref., 3,000,000 } Issued { com., $3,000,000; pref., 2,000,000 } $5,000,000

The preferred stock is 5 per cent., cumulative. This stock was created in 1902 and $2,000,000 sold to the holders of the common stock at par, the proceeds being used for improvements.

The dividends on the preferred stock are paid quarterly, 1¼ per cent. each in March, June, September and December. The first quarterly payment was on September 1, 1902.

Stock is transferred at the company's office. Registrar, Central Trust & Safe Deposit Co., Cincinnati.

The company had no funded debt. There were on June 30, 1902, $92,594 car trust obligations.

EARNINGS.

Year ending June 30.

| | Gross. | Net. | Charges. | Balance. |
|---|---|---|---|---|
| 1892-93.......... | $4,174,970 | $998,715 | $1,151,285 | Def. $152,569 |
| 1893-94.......... | 3,576,979 | 911,764 | 1,084,057 | " 172,293 |
| 1894-95.......... | 3,487,942 | 976,767 | 1,047,367 | " 70,600 |
| 1895-96.......... | 3,685,865 | 1,039,992 | 1,063,166 | " 23,174 |

EARNINGS—*Continued.*

| | Gross. | Net. | Charges. | | Balance. |
|---|---|---|---|---|---|
| 1896-97 | $3,440,505 | $1,097,325 | $1,091,642 | Sur. | $5,562 |
| 1897-98 | 4,128,118 | 1,389,682 | 1,115,404 | " | 274,278 |
| 1898-99 | 4,691,232 | 1,585,005 | 1,411,444 | " | 173,501 |
| 1899-00 | 5,124,241 | 1,424,725 | 1,102,000 | " | 322,725 |
| 1900-01 | 5,045,595 | 1,320,501 | 1,141,369 | " | 179,132 |
| 1901-02 | 5,660,404 | 1,446,659 | 1,237,525 | | 209,134 |

A dividend of 2 per cent. was paid in 1891.

The rental under the present contract was $812,000 yearly until 1886; then it was $912,000 until 1891; then $1,012,000 until 1896; then $1,102,000 until 1901; then $1,262,000 yearly until expiration of the lease in 1906. The new lease provides for a yearly rental of $1,050,000 for the first twenty years, $1,100,000 for the second twenty years and $1,200,000 for the last twenty years. The city is to provide $2,500,000 for improving the property, the company paying interest on the bonds issued for this purpose, while the company is to increase its stock to $5,000,000 and expend the proceeds of the additional $2,000,000 of stock on improvements. Charges for 1898-99 include $309,663 paid in judgment claims.

Chairman, Henry F. Shoemaker; President, Samuel Spencer, New York; Secretary, William A. Shoemaker; Treasurer, Charles Patton; General Manager, W. J. Murphy, Cincinnati.

Directors—M. D. Woodford, Lawrence Maxwell, Jr., Eugene Zimmerman, Melville E. Ingalls, Briggs S. Cunningham, Cincinnati; Samuel Spencer, Henry F. Shoemaker, Francis Lynde Stetson, New York; Samuel M. Felton, Chicago.

Main office, Elm and Seventh streets, Cincinnati. Annual meeting, third Tuesday in November.

## CINCINNATI NORTHERN RAILROAD CO.

(Controlled by Cleveland, Cincinnati, Chicago & St. Louis Railway Co.)

Road owned, Jackson, Mich., to Franklin, O., 205 miles; branches, 3 miles; trackage on Big Four, Franklin, O., to Cincinnati, 39 miles; on Lake Shore & Michigan Southern, at Jackson, Mich., 1 mile; total, 248 miles. Locomotives, 24; passenger cars, 23; freight cars, 1,173.

This company was formed in 1897 and took over the Ohio Division of the Cincinnati, Jackson & Mackinaw Railroad, which was foreclosed in that year. The Michigan Division of the Cincinnati, Jackson & Mackinaw was reorganized in the Detroit, Toledo & Milwaukee Railroad, Dundee, Mich., to Allegan, Mich., 132 miles, and the latter was leased to this company in 1899, but that road since January 1, 1902, has been operated by the Lake Shore & Michigan Southern Railway.

Stock......Par $100..........................Authorized, $3,000,000......Issued, $3,000,000

In September, 1901, the stock which was $6,800,000, consisting of common and preferred, was reduced to $3,000,000, all common.

FUNDED DEBT.

1st mortgage, 4 per cent., due July, 1951, Jan. and July..............................$1,000,000

In 1901 control of the company was acquired by the Cleveland, Cincinnati, Chicago and St. Louis Railway Co.

For details regarding the reorganization of the old company, see MANUAL for 1901.

The 1st mortgage was authorized in 1901 and is for $3,000,000. Trustee of mortgage, Guaranty Trust Co., New York.

President, Melville E. Ingalls; Vice-President, C. E. Schaff; Secretary, E. F. Osborn, Cincinnati; Treasurer, Charles F. Cox, New York.

Main office, Cincinnati.

## CINCINNATI, RICHMOND & MUNCIE RAILROAD CO.

Road owned, Indiana State line to Griffith, Ind., 220 miles. The line was completed and opened in 1902. The Cincinnati & Indiana Western Railroad is being built from Cincinnati to the Indiana line, 32½ miles, where it will connect with this company's road. Locomotives, 35; passenger cars, 25; freight cars, 375.

Stock......Par $100............................Authorized, $3,300,000......Issued, $3,300,000

Stock is transferred by the secretary of the company, 40 Water street, Boston.

FUNDED DEBT.

| | |
|---|---|
| 1st mort., 5 per cent., due Oct., 1950, April and Oct. | $1,804,000 |
| Chicago & Cincinnati Railroad, 1st mort., 5 per cent., due 1952, Feb. and Aug. | 750,000 |
| Total | $2,554,000 |

The trustee of the 1st mortgage is the Old Colony Trust Co., Boston. Bonds may be issued at the rate of $10,000 per mile of road.

President, W. A. Bradford, Jr.; Secretary and Treasurer, Roger N. Allen, Boston.

Directors—W. A. Bradford, Jr., Roger N. Allen, Boston; H. A. Christy, Sanger Brown, Chicago; J. A. S. Graves, Richmond, Ind.

Main office, Richmond, Ind. Annual meeting, first Monday in April.

## THE CLEVELAND, AKRON & COLUMBUS RAILWAY CO.

(Controlled by the Pennsylvania Co.)

Road owned, Columbus to Hudson, O., 144 miles; Killbuck to Trinway, O., 33 miles; branch, 9 miles; coal mine spurs, 11 miles; trackage, Trinway to Zanesville, 17 miles; total, 214 miles. Locomotives, 29; passenger cars, 40; freight cars, 2,627.

A reorganization, January, 1886, the road having been sold under foreclosure. In June, 1899, the Pennsylvania Co. purchased a controlling interest in the stock.

Stock......Par $100..........................Authorized, $4,000,000......Issued, $4,000,000

Stock is transferred by the secretary of the company, Pittsburg.

In September, 1901, 2 per cent. was paid on the stock. In 1902, semi-annual dividends of 1 per cent. each were paid in March and September, respectively.

FUNDED DEBT.

| | |
|---|---|
| Gen. mort., now 1st, 5 per cent., due March, 1927, March and Sept | $1,800,000 |
| 1st cons. mort., 4 per cent., due Aug., 1940, Feb. and Aug | 1,782,000 |
| Total | $3,582,000 |

EARNINGS.

Year ending June 30.

| | Gross. | Net. | Charges. | | Surplus. |
|---|---|---|---|---|---|
| 1892-93 | $1,030,240 | $248,145 | $168,193 | | $79,952 |
| 1893-94 | 896,089 | 219,906 | 168,051 | | 51,855 |
| 1894-95 | 857,930 | 238,300 | 179,238 | | 58,562 |
| 1895-96 | 874,920 | 243,958 | 181,393 | | 62,565 |
| 1896-97 | 718,051 | 140,137 | 179,197 | Def. | 39,060 |
| 1897-98 | 864,002 | 246,210 | 203,160 | | 41,050 |
| 1898-99 | 938,743 | 308,190 | 232,908 | | 75,282 |
| 1899-00 | 1,066,279 | 224,636 | 163,543 | | 61,093 |
| 1900-01 | 1,111,312 | 293,305 | 159,933 | | 133,371 |
| 1902 (year ending Dec. 31) | 1,417,574 | 411,270 | 282,345 | | 128,925 |

From the surplus earnings for 1900-01 there was deducted $40,532 for additions and improvements, making the net surplus for the year, $92,838.

In 1893 parties interested in Ohio Southern acquired control of the company and brought the two roads under same management. The company passed under control of interests identified it the Lake Erie & Western in 1895, but their holdings were in 1899 sold to the Pennsylvawiah

The consolidated 4 per cent. mortgage is for $4,000,000, and was created in 1900. Of the amount $1,800,000 is reserved to retire the general 1st mortgage bonds. Amount outstanding was issued to retire car trusts, and the $730,000 of old equipment and 2d mortgage bonds and the floating debt.

President, James McCrea, Pittsburg; Vice-President, John F. Miller, Akron, O.; Treasurer, T. H. B. McKnight; Secretary, S. B. Liggett, Pittsburg.

Directors—James McCrea, Joseph Wood, E. B. Taylor, J. J. Turner, Pittsburg; Andrew Squire, Charles T. Brooks, Cleveland; John F. Miller, Akron.

Main office, Cleveland. Annual meeting, third Thursday in March, at Cleveland.

## CLEVELAND & MARIETTA RAILWAY CO.

(Controlled by the Pennsylvania Company.)

Road owned, Marietta, O., to Canal Dover, O., 103 miles; leased, Canal Dover to Valley Junction, O., 8 miles; total operated, 111 miles. Locomotives, 23; passenger cars, 17; freight cars, 1,050.

Originally the; Marietta & Pittsburg. Name changed to Marietta, Cleveland & Pittsburg.

Sold under foreclosure in 1877 and again May 5, 1886. Present company formed by bondholders July 12, 1886. In 1893 a controlling interest was acquired by the Pennsylvania Company.

Stock......Par $100.........................Authorized, $2,000,000......Issued, $2,000,000

Transfer Agent, Farmers' Loan & Trust Co., New York.

FUNDED DEBT.

1st mort., 4½ per cent., due May, 1935, May and Nov.................................$1,250,000

EARNINGS.

| | Gross. | Net. | Charges. | Surplus. |
|---|---|---|---|---|
| 1895 | $367,752 | $98,592 | $96,369 | $2,223 |
| 1896 | 360,308 | 56,375 | 56,250 | 125 |
| 1897 | 355,720 | 9,775 | 62,995 | Def. 53,219 |
| 1898 | 421,988 | 66,822 | 56,252 | 10,572 |
| 1899 | 507,980 | 60,145 | 56,250 | 3,895 |
| 1900 | 639,595 | 134,320 | 130,871 | 3,449 |
| 1901 | 601,154 | 139,187 | 104,665 | 34,521 |
| 1902 | 696,051 | 135,116 | 101,682 | 33,433 |

The 1st mortgage was created in 1895, and is for $2,000,000. Principal and Interest of the $1,250,000 issued is guaranteed by the Pennsylvania Company. Coupons of the bonds are paid at the Farmers' Loan & Trust Co., New York.

President, William A. Baldwin, Cambridge, O.; Vice-President, James McCrea; Secretary, S. B. Liggett; Treasurer, T. H. B. McKnight; Auditor, John W. Renner, Pittsburg.

Directors — William. A. Baldwin, Cambridge, O.; A. J. Warner, Marietta, O.; James McCrea, Joseph Wood, J. J. Turner, Pittsburg.

Main office, Cambridge, O. Annual meeting, Thursday before second Friday in March, at Cambridge, O.

---

## CLEVELAND & PITTSBURG RAILROAD CO.

(Leased to Pennsylvania Railroad Co.)

Road owned, Rochester, Pa., to Cleveland, O., 124 miles; Bellaire to Yellow Creek, O.,
miles; branches, 35 miles; total, 202 miles. Leases use of Pittsburg, Fort Wayne & Chi-
43 track, Rochester, Pa., to Pittsburg, 26 miles. Total operated, 228 miles. Locomotives,
cago passenger cars, 72; freight cars, 5,171.

Stock......Par $50.........................Authorized, $11,261,865......Issued, $11,226,300

Transfer Agents, Winslow, Lanier & Co., 17 Nassau street, New York. Registrar, Farmers' Loan & Trust Co., New York.

The 7 per cent. dividends under the lease are paid quarterly, 1¾ each, in March (1), June, September and December.

FUNDED DEBT.

| | |
|---|---|
| Gen. mort., Series A and B, 4½ per cent., due Jan., 1942, Jan. and July............ | $4,561,000 |
| " " " B, reduced to 3½ per cent., due Oct., 1942, April and Oct......... | 439,000 |
| " " " C, 3½ per cent., due Nov. 1948, May and Nov.................... | 3,000,000 |
| " " " D, 3½ " " Aug., 1950, Feb. and Aug.................. | 1,933,000 |
| Total.................................................... | $9,933,000 |

The lessee pays interest on bonds, 7 per cent. on stock, sinking fund and $10,000 yearly for organization expenses.

General mortgage authorized in 1891 is for $10,000,000, and is guaranteed principal and interest by Pennsylvania Railroad. Series A, issued in 1892, was used to retire old 4th mortgage prior lien bonds for $1,104,000, and $1,010,000 construction 7s. The Series C bonds were issued to retire the 7 per cent. consolidated bonds which matured November 1, 1900. Of the Series D bonds, $1,933,000 were issued up to January, 1903, for improvements, etc.

EARNINGS.

| | Div. Paid. | Gross. | Net. | Rental. | Result to Lessee. |
|---|---|---|---|---|---|
| 1893 | 7 | $3,041,218 | $937,657 | $1,163,449 | Loss $225,791 |
| 1894 | 7 | 2,897,719 | 1,101,513 | 1,156,965 | " 55,452 |
| 1895 | 7 | 3,555,497 | 1,485,413 | 1,142,514 | Profit 342,900 |
| 1896 | 7 | 3,226,614 | 1,176,805 | 1,139,503 | " 37,302 |
| 1897 | 7 | 3,607,766 | 1,417,733 | 1,137,133 | " 280,599 |
| 1898 | 7 | 4,032,765 | 1,370,489 | 1,168,928 | " 201,560 |
| 1899 | 7 | 4,586,496 | 1,483,186 | 1,157,533 | " 325,653 |
| 1900 | 7 | 4,813,056 | 1,669,054 | 1,175,908 | " 493,146 |
| 1901 | 7 | 5,484,074 | 1,955,052 | 1,202,839 | " 752,213 |
| 1902 | 7 | 6,834,410 | 2,736,791 | 1,232,110 | " 1,504,680 |

In the year ending November 30, 1896, the company's total receipts, on account of rental from lessee, were $1,362,714. In 1897 they were $1,467,891; in 1898, $1,320,709; in 1899, $1,355,077; in 1900, $1,427,729, and in 1901, $1,157,300.

President, R. F. Smith; Vice-President, J. V. Painter; Secretary and Treasurer, John E Kloss, Cleveland.

Directors—H. Darlington, Pittsburg; Charles Lanier, William C. Egleston, J. S. Kennedy, New York; J. V. Painter, E. R. Perkins, H. C. Ranney, M. A. Hanna, R. F. Smith, Andrew Squire, Cleveland; John P. Green, Philadelphia; Frank J. Jones, Cincinnati.

Principal office, 93 Public Square, Cleveland. Annual meeting, Thursday following third Wednesday in May.

---

## CLEVELAND, CINCINNATI, CHICAGO & ST. LOUIS RAILWAY CO.

"Big Four."

A consolidation, 1889, of the Cincinnati, Indianapolis, St. Louis & Chicago Railway, the Cleveland, Columbus, Cincinnati & Indianapolis Railway and the Indianapolis & St. Louis Railway.

The total mileage owned and operated by company is 1,891 miles, under the following divisions: Cleveland, 138 miles; Cincinnati, 174 miles; Indianapolis, 203 miles; St. Louis, 266 miles; Cairo, 220 miles; Chicago, 320 miles; Whitewater, 70 miles; Sandusky, 146 miles; Michigan, 301 miles. Of this 835 miles are owned, including the original properties and the main line, St. Louis, Alton & Terre Haute Railroad, East St. Louis to Terre Haute, 190 miles, purchased in 1890. The controlled and leased roads include the Cairo, Vincennes & Chicago (all stock owned), 267 miles; Cincinnati, Sandusky & Cleveland (majority stock owned), 170 miles; other lines leased and controlled, 386 miles. The Michigan Division comprises the Cincinnati, Wabash & Michigan Railway. The company also controls and operates the Peoria & Eastern Railway, Springfield, O., to Peoria, Ill., 352 miles, the earnings of which are reported separately; Kankakee & Seneca Railroad, 42 miles; Cincinnati Northern, 248 miles, which is operated separately; other branches, 2½ miles; grand total owned, controlled and operated, including trackage Illinois Central, Kankakee to Chicago, 56 miles, and the Dayton & Union Railroad, 47 miles, in which company is part owner, 2,638 miles. Locomotives, 525; passenger cars, 463; freight cars, 20,756.

In 1900 and 1901 the New York Central and the Lake Shore & Michigan Southern acquired a controlling interest in the stock of the company.

| Stock...Par $100..Authorized | com., $28,700,000<br>pref., 10,000,000 | Issued | com., $27,989,310<br>pref., 10,000,000 | $37,989,310 |
|---|---|---|---|---|

The preferred stock is entitled to 5 per cent. non-cumulative dividends.

Transfer Agents, J. P. Morgan & Co., New York. Registrar, Central Trust Co., New York.

Dividends of 5 per cent. per annum have been paid on the preferred stock since 1890, except in 1897, when only 2½ per cent. was paid. The preferred dividends are paid quarterly, 1¼ per cent. each, in January (20), April, July and October. On the common stock 4 per cent. was paid in 1890; 3 per cent. in 1891, 1892 and 1893. No dividends were paid from 1894 to 1899, inclusive, but in March, 1900, they were resumed by a payment of 1½ per cent., semi-annual, another dividend of 1½ per cent. being paid September 1, 1900, making 3 per cent. on the common for 1900. The March, 1901, dividend on the common was also 1½ per cent., but the September 2 dividend on the common was 2 per cent., and the same rate was paid on the common, in March and September, 1902, and on March 2, 1903.

FUNDED DEBT.

| | |
|---|---|
| Cin., Ind., St. L. & Chicago, 1st mort., 4 per cent., due Aug., 1936, July and Feb... | $7,684,000 |
| " " " " 1st con., 6 per cent., due May, 1920, May and Nov.... | 675,000 |
| Cleve., Col., Cin. & Ind., 1st con. mort., 7 or 6, due June, 1914, June and Dec...... | 4,138,000 |
| " " " " gen. mort., 6 per cent., due Jan., 1934, Jan. and July..... | 3,205,000 |
| Indianapolis & St. Louis, 1st mort., 7 per cent. bonds, due July, 1919, various....... | 2,000,000 |
| " " 1st mort., 6 per cent. bonds, due Nov., 1912, May and Nov. | 500,000 |
| Cairo, Vin. & Chic. 1st mort., 4 per cent., due Jan., 1939, Jan. and July........... | 5,000,000 |
| C., C., C. & St. L. coll. t. (St. L. Div.), 4 per cent., due Nov., 1990, May and Nov.. | 10,000,000 |
| " " (Spring. & Col.) 1st mort., 4 per cent., due Sept., 1940, March and Sept.. | 1,103,730 |
| " " (Whitewater Div.) 1st mort., 4 per cent., due July, 1940, Jan. and July... | 650,000 |
| " " 100-year mort., 4 per cent., due June, 1993, June and Dec.............. | 16,657,000 |
| " " Cin., Wab. & Mich. Div. 1st mort., 4 per cent., due July, 1991, Jan. and July. | 4,000,000 |
| Cin., Sand. & Cleve., 1st cons. mort., 5 per cent., due Jan., 1928, Jan. and July.... | 2,571,000 |
| Total ........................................................... | $58,183,730 |

### Obligations of Peoria & Eastern Railway.

| | |
|---|---|
| Ind., Bloomington & Western 1st mort., pref., extended, 4 per cent., Jan. and July.. | $981,000 |
| Ohio, Indiana & Western 1st mort., pref., 5 per cent., due 1938, July, Q............ | 500,000 |
| Peoria & Eastern 1st cons. mort., 4 per cent., due 1940, April and Oct.............. | 8,500,000 |
| " " income mort., 4 per cent., due Jan., 1991, April................. | 4,000,000 |
| Total, Peoria & Eastern.................................................. | $13,981,000 |

The consolidation agreement provided that the consolidated company shall not issue any evidences of funded debt or execute any lease of railway property which may entail increased fixed charges, except by the consent of a majority in interest of the holders of the preferred stock, with the exception of the $5,000,000 4 per cent. 100-year bonds issued for the acquisition of the Cairo, Vincennes & Chicago Railway, which road was bought in 1889.

The main line of the St. Louis, Alton & Terre Haute was purchased in December, 1890, for $10,000,000 in 4 per cent. collateral trust bonds. In 1890 bought entire stock of Cincinnati, Wabash & Michigan Railway, and issued $4,000,000 4 per cent. bonds on that property. In 1890 purchased common stock of the Cincinnati, Sandusky & Cleveland, agreeing to pay 6 per cent. dividends on $428,850 preferred stock and interest on bonds of that company. Also acquired control of Cincinnati & Springfield. In 1890 leased the Peoria & Eastern, acquiring one-half of its stock and guaranteeing interest, but not principal, of that road's 1st consolidated mortgage bonds. In 1901 the company sold $397,000 Peoria & Eastern 1st consolidated mortgage bonds held in the treasury and bought control of the Cincinnati Northern Railroad for $377,851.

In 1890 a 100-year 4 per cent. mortgage for $50,000,000 was authorized. Of this $29,252,000 was reserved to retire existing liens, and $5,000,000 was sold for double tracking, equipment, etc., the balance, $15,748,000, to be issued only after July 1, 1894, for construction and improvements at the rate of $1,000,000 per year. Additional amounts have been issued to retire maturing underlying bonds. Company guarantees jointly with Chesapeake & Ohio, $3,000,000, the Louisville & Jeffersonville Bridge Co.'s 4 per cent. bonds.

### Earnings.

Year ending June 30.

| | Dividends. Pref. | Com. | Gross. | Per cent. Oper. Ex. | Net. | Charges. | Surplus. |
|---|---|---|---|---|---|---|---|
| 1892–93 (1,837 miles). | 5 | 3 | $14,669,855 | 74.74 | $3,704,269 | $2,652,961 | $1,051,307 |
| 1893–94 (1,850 " ). | 5 | .. | 13,034,049 | 71.69 | 3,283,545 | 2,759,171 | 524,373 |
| 1894–95 ( " " ). | 5 | .. | 13,625,027 | 71.38 | 3,370,959 | 2,844,705 | 526,253 |
| 1895–96 (1,838 " ). | 5 | .. | 13,704,534 | 70.86 | 3,410,831 | 2,844,509 | 566,321 |
| 1896–97 ( " " ). | 3¼ | .. | 13,117,111 | 70.78 | 3,252,446 | 2,883,926 | 368,520 |
| 1897–98 ( " " ). | 3¼ | .. | 14,320,094 | 72.42 | 3,351,726 | 2,905,024 | 446,702 |
| 1898–99 ( " " ). | 5 | .. | 14,719,362 | 68.39 | 4,073,807 | 2,873,709 | 1,200,098 |
| 1899–00 (1,891 " ). | 5 | 3 | 16,806,850 | 69.91 | 5,057,587 | 2,866,538 | 2,191,048 |
| 1900–01 ( " " ). | 5 | 3½ | 17,877,489 | 71.35 | 5,121,851 | 2,919,962 | 2,204,888 |
| 1901–02 ( " " ). | 5 | 4 | 18,717,071 | 73.43 | 4,972,151 | 2,799,650 | 2,172,500 |

In 1892 $11,342 was added to surplus, and $1,340,000 paid in dividends, leaving balance to credit profit and loss of $80,741. In 1893–94 balance, after dividends on preferred stock and accounts charged off, was $7,968. In 1895 it was $49,626. In 1896, $74,114. In 1897, $198,861. In 1898, $71,702. In 1899, $700,098. In 1900 dividends paid were $1,339,839; miscellaneous receipts, $82,934; appropriated for equipment, etc., $840,942; balance surplus, $93,200. In 1900–01 miscellaneous receipts were $127,654; dividends, $1,479,625; improvements, etc., $567,851; balance surplus, $285,064. In 1901–02 miscellaneous revenue, $78,360; dividends, $1,619,516; improvements, $600,371; balance surplus, $30,973.

The following presents the comparative freight traffic statistics of the company:

| | Average Mileage. | Total Tonnage. | Tons Carried One Mile. | Freight Density. | Rate Per Ton Per Mile. | Earnings Per Train Mile. | Average Tons Per Train. |
|---|---|---|---|---|---|---|---|
| 1896–97... | 1,838 | 8,223,347 | 1,343,484,916 | 730,949 | 0.614c | $1.52 | 247 |
| 1897–98... | 1,838 | 9,630,159 | 1,696,221,146 | 922,863 | 0.545 | 1.52 | 278 |
| 1898–99... | 1,838 | 10,043,126 | 1,704,824,779 | 927,543 | 0.541 | 1.65 | 305 |
| 1899–00... | 1,891 | 11,006,304 | 1,863,586,488 | 985,503 | 0.583 | 1.95 | 335 |
| 1900–01... | 1,891 | 11,098,315 | 1,909,086,365 | 1,009,511 | 0.610 | 2.03 | 333 |
| 1901–02... | 1,891 | 12,056,981 | 2,012,357,493 | 1,064,192 | 0.592 | 1.97 | 332 |

GROSS AND NET EARNINGS BY MONTHS FOR THREE YEARS.

| | 1900. | | 1901. | | 1902. | |
|---|---|---|---|---|---|---|
| | Gross. | Net. | Gross. | Net. | Gross. | Net. |
| January | $1,301,189 | $336,997 | $1,350,841 | $337,824 | $1,429,596 | $320,533 |
| February | 1,229,380 | 306,303 | 1,278,430 | 314,272 | 1,229,706 | 244,068 |
| March | 1,417,532 | 412,958 | 1,385,863 | 357,976 | 1,466,436 | 338,821 |
| April | 1,356,098 | 378,037 | 1,357,354 | 364,906 | 1,403,597 | 296,250 |
| May | 1,366,438 | 357,697 | 1,525,495 | 385,269 | 1,532,042 | 375,143 |
| June | 1,459,504 | 455,499 | 1,706,956 | 537,509 | 1,658,090 | 533,524 |
| July | 1,362,646 | 356,249 | 1,596,196 | 477,483 | 1,569,037 | 367,676 |
| August | 1,449,939 | 388,601 | 1,729,193 | 519,324 | 1,745,191 | 394,772 |
| September | 1,523,837 | 495,631 | 1,662,528 | 500,739 | 1,746,928 | 494,423 |
| October | 1,668,703 | 531,699 | 1,782,097 | 529,698 | 1,797,510 | 422,945 |
| November | 1,603,368 | 520,326 | 1,618,749 | 403,319 | 1,702,500 | 410,834 |
| December | 1,664,058 | 531,589 | 1,614,844 | 433,251 | 1,701,943 | 433,889 |
| Total for year | $17,402,692 | $5,071,546 | $18,608,546 | $5,161,570 | $18,976,576 | $4,632,878 |
| Average per month | 1,450,224 | 422,626 | 1,550,712 | 430,130 | 1,581,381 | 386,073 |

Proportionate taxes for each month are deducted from net earnings.

President, Melville E. Ingalls, Cincinnati; Vice-President, James D. Layng, New York; Secretary, E. F. Osborn, Cincinnati; Treasurer, Charles F. Cox, New York; Assistant Treasurer, F. Middlebrook, New York; Auditor, P. A. Hewitt, Cincinnati.

Directors—William K. Vanderbilt, Frederick W. Vanderbilt, Chauncey M. Depew, J. Pierpont Morgan, Walter E. Bliss, Hamilton McK. Twombly, James D. Layng, William H. Newman, New York; Alexander McDonald, Melville E. Ingalls, Cincinnati; James Barnett, Cleveland.

Main office, Cincinnati. Annual meeting, last Wednesday in October.

## CLEVELAND, LORAIN & WHEELING RAILWAY CO.

(Controlled by Baltimore & Ohio Railroad Co.)

Road owned, Lorain, O., to Bridgeport, O. (opposite Wheeling), 158 miles; branch, Medina, O., to Cleveland, 28 miles; other branches, 6 miles; total, 192 miles. Locomotives, 66; passenger cars, 34; freight cars, 4,560.

The present company succeeded in 1883 by purchase under foreclosure to the Cleveland, Tuscarawas Valley & Wheeling. In 1893 a consolidation with the Cleveland & Southwestern was effected, the arrangement involving an increase of the stock to $5,000,000 preferred and $8,000,000 common and an issue of $5,000,000 consolidated bonds.

In February, 1901, the Baltimore & Ohio Railroad Co. acquired a controlling interest in this company's stock, and from August 1, 1901, the property has been operated as part of the Baltimore & Ohio system. In 1902 the Baltimore & Ohio increased its holdings and had on June 30, 1902, 74 per cent. of the total stock outstanding. Nearly all its holdings are deposited under the mortgage for the Baltimore & Ohio, Pittsburg, Lake Erie & West Virginia system refunding bonds.

Stock....Par $100.....Authorized { com., $8,000,000 / pref., 5,000,000 } Issued { com., $8,000,000 / pref., 5,000,000 } $13,000,000

The preferred stock is 5 per cent., non-cumulative.

Transfer Agent, Continental Trust Co., New York. Registrar, Central Trust Co., New York.

In 1896 3 per cent. was paid on the preferred stock. No dividends since.

FUNDED DEBT.

| | |
|---|---|
| Cons. refunding mortgage, 4½ per cent., due Jan., 1930, Jan. and July | $950,000 |
| C., L. & W., cons. mort., 5 per cent., due Oct., 1933, April and Oct. | 5,000,000 |
| Gen. mort., 5 per cent., due June, 1936, June and Dec. | 893,000 |
| Total | $6,843,000 |

There are real estate mortgages outstanding for $100,000. The company also has about $23,228 car trusts outstanding.

The general mortgage was created in 1896 to provide for improvements. The consolidated refunding mortgage created in 1900 is for $10,000,000 (Colonial Trust Co., New York, Trustee), of which $5,000,000 is reserved to retire the 5 per cent. consols, $1,000,000 to retire the general 5s, and the remainder is available for improvements. In 1900 $950,000 of these bonds were sold to provide equipment.

EARNINGS.

Year ending June 30.

| | Gross. | Net. | Charges. | Surplus. |
|---|---|---|---|---|
| 1892-93 | $1,442,182 | $331,327 | $64,990 | $266,427 |
| 1893-94 | 1,182,044 | 329,617 | 152,719 | 176,898 |
| 1894-95 | 1,360,465 | 401,428 | 295,773 | 137,428 |
| 1895-96 | 1,586,917 | 440,172 | 280,228 | 158,944 |
| 1896-97 | 1,205,160 | 324,866 | 363,294 | Def. 33,503 |
| 1897-98 | 1,501,431 | 438,924 | 297,874 | 141,050 |
| 1898-99 | 1,621,981 | 491,086 | 296,571 | 194,515 |
| 1899-00 | 2,092,573 | 631,414 | 320,502 | 310,912 |
| 1900-01 | 2,063,653 | 685,285 | 374,815 | 310,470 |
| 1901-02 | 2,692,588 | 1,117,566 | 365,566 | 752,000 |

President, L. F. Loree; Secretary, Custis W. Woolford; Treasurer, J. V. McNeal, Baltimore.

Directors—L. F. Loree, Custis W. Woolford, Baltimore; James A. Blair, New York; S. T. Everett, J. M. Lessick, J. F. Whitelaw, Cleveland; Walter R. Woodford, Parks Foster, Elyria, O.; J. W. McClymonds, Massillon, O.

Main office, Cleveland. Annual meeting, first Tuesday in October.

## CLEVELAND TERMINAL & VALLEY RAILROAD CO.

(Controlled by Baltimore & Ohio Railroad Co.)

Road owned, Cleveland to Valley Junction, O., 75 miles. Locomotives, 32; passenger cars, 25; freight cars, 947.

This company is a reorganization of the Valley Railway Co. of Ohio, sold under foreclosure in September, 1895.

In 1889 Baltimore & Ohio obtained control by purchase of majority of stock of the Valley Railway, and has $4,594,300 of the common and $953,750 of the preferred stock of this company.

Stock..Par { com., $50 / pref., 100 } .. Authorized { com., $5,200,000 / pref., 2,200,000 } Issued { com., $5,200,000 / pref., 2,200,000 } $7,400,000

Transfer Agent and Registrar, Mercantile Trust Co., New York.

FUNDED DEBT.

1st mort., 4 per cent., due Nov. 1995, May and Nov. .......... $5,515,000

Company had considerable floating debt, and in June, 1892, Receivers were appointed. In 1894 committee representing 1st mortgage bonds proposed reorganization. A counter plan was offered in interest of Baltimore & Ohio. Litigation ensued, but after protracted negotiations it was agreed that the Baltimore & Ohio should reorganize the road and guarantee the new 1st mortgage bonds, principal and interest.

EARNINGS.

Year ending June 30.

| | Gross. | Net. | Charges. | Surplus |
|---|---|---|---|---|
| 1896-97 | $796,347 | $260,155 | $242,643 | $17,512 |
| 1897-98 | 855,844 | 285,231 | 240,751 | 44,479 |
| 1898-99 | 961,692 | 328,175 | 245,656 | 82,518 |
| 1899-00 | 1,102,733 | 376,240 | 259,703 | 116,537 |
| 1900-01 | 1,110,223 | 370,418 | 262,343 | 108,075 |
| 1901-02 | 1,218,959 | 443,027 | 235,950 | 207,077 |

President, L. F. Loree; Secretary, Custis W. Woolford; Treasurer, J. V. McNeal; Auditor, G. W. Booth, Baltimore.

Directors—L. F. Loree, Baltimore; S. T. Everett, J. H. McBride, Calvary Morris, F. H. Goff, Benjamin Rose, Harvey H. Brown, Robert R. Rhodes, Stewart R. Chisholm, Cleveland.

Main office, Baltimore and Calvert streets, Baltimore. Annual meeting, third Tuesday in October.

## COAHUILA & PACIFIC RAILROAD CO.

A corporation formed under the laws of New Jersey, May 23, 1899.

Road owned, Saltillo to Torreon, Coahuila, 210 miles. Entire line was completed and opened in August, 1902. The road connects at Saltillo with the Mexican National Railway and the Coahuila & Zacatecas Railroad, and at Torreon with the Mexican Central and the Mexican International Railroads. Locomotives, 9; passenger cars, 12; freight cars, 105.

Stock......Par $100...... ..........Authorized, $1,500,000......Issued, $1,500,000

Stock is transferred at the office of the secretary of the company, Jersey City.

FUNDED DEBT.

1st mort., 5 per cent., due Feb., 1930, Feb. and Aug................................ $2,500,000

Trustee of mortgage, New Jersey Title Guarantee & Trust Co., Jersey City, at which institution coupons are payable.

Under its concession from the Mexican Government this company is exempt from State and municipal taxes for thirty years.

President and General Manager, A. W. Lilliendahl, Saltillo, Mex.; Vice-President, Jacob J. Detwiller; Secretary and Treasurer, Henry T. Lilliendahl; Jersey City; Auditor, J. B. Tartt.

Directors—A. W. Lilliendahl, Saltillo, Mex.; J. J. Detwiller, H. T. Lilliendahl, R. S. Hudspeth, Jersey City; G. S. Lings, New York.

Main office, 15 Exchange place, Jersey City; operating office, Saltillo, Mex. Annual meeting, first Tuesday in February, at Jersey City.

---

## COLORADO & SOUTHERN RAILWAY CO.

A corporation formed under the laws of Colorado, December 20, 1898, to take over the property of the Union Pacific, Denver & Gulf Railway, which was sold under foreclosure November 19, 1898, and purchased by the reorganization committee.

Road owned, 1,062 miles, of which 386 miles are narrow gauge; trackage on Denver & Rio Grande Railway and Union Pacific, 59 miles. Total operated, 1,121 miles. This company also has a large interest in the Fort Worth & Denver City Railway. In 1900 purchased, with the Rio Grande Western, a joint control of the Colorado Midland Railway Co. Total of system, 1,910 miles. Locomotives, 173; passenger cars, 131; freight cars, 5,180.

| | Authorized | | Issued | | |
|---|---|---|---|---|---|
| Stock. Par $100. | common, | $31,000,000 | common, | $31,000,000 | $48,000,000 |
| | 1st pref., | 8,500,000 | 1st pref., | 8,500,000 | |
| | 2d pref., | 8,500,000 | 2d pref., | 8,500,000 | |

The 1st preferred stock is 4 per cent., non-cumulative, and the 2d preferred stock is 4 per cent., non-cumulative. All classes of stock are held in a voting trust for five years, from January 1, 1899, or until the 1st preferred shall have received 4 per cent. dividends for three consecutive years. Trustees—Grenville M. Dodge, Frederic P. Olcott, Henry Walters, Henry Budge, J. Kennedy Tod.

The company in January, 1900, began the payment of dividends on the 1st preferred by declaring 2 per cent. payable February 14, 1900, out of the earnings of the year 1899. An annual dividend of 2 per cent. was also paid on the 1st preferred February 14, 1901. On October 1, 1901, a semi-annual dividend of 1½ per cent. was paid on the 1st preferred, which was also the rate of the dividend paid April 1, 1902. The October, 1902, dividend was 2 per cent., putting the 1st preferred on a 4 per cent. basis.

Transfer Agents, Hallgarten & Co., 72 Broadway New York. Registrar, Central Trust Co., New York.

FUNDED DEBT.

1st mort., 4 per cent. gold, due Feb., 1929, Feb. and Aug........................... $18,503,000

The new 4 per cent. 1st mortgage bonds authorized are $20,000,000. The company on June 30, 1902, also had outstanding car trust notes for $567,367.

For details of the Union Pacific, Denver & Gulf bonded debt and its reorganization, see MANUAL for 1899.

EARNINGS.

Year ending June 30.

| | Gross. | Net. | Charges. | Surplus. |
|---|---|---|---|---|
| 1896–97 | $3,223,635 | $763,403 | ......... | ...... |
| 1897–98 | 3,787,001 | 1,026,102 | ......... | ...... |
| 1899 (6 months ending June 30) | 1,804,506 | 402,248 | $392,220 | $124,454 |
| 1899–00 | 4,237,742 | 1,143,314 | 897,969 | 245,344 |
| 1900–01 | 4,794,649 | 1,336,095 | 930,448 | 405,647 |
| 1901–02 | 5,580,326 | 1,595,541 | 968,783 | 626,758 |

In 1901–02 the 3 per cent. dividends on the 1st preferred stock were $255,000, balance surplus $371,758.

Chairman, Grenville M. Dodge, New York; President, Frank Trumbull, Denver; Secretary and Treasurer, Harry Bronner, New York.

Directors—Grenville M. Dodge, Frederic P. Olcott, Henry Budge, J. Kennedy Tod, John J. Emery, Edward C. Henderson, Edward J. Berwind, Harry Bronner, Adolph Lewisohn, Edwin Hawley, New York; Frank Trumbull, Denver; Henry Walters, Baltimore; Norman B. Ream, Chicago.

Main office, Denver; New York office, 74 Broadway. Annual meeting, third Thursday in November.

## THE COLORADO MIDLAND RAILWAY CO.

A corporation formed under the laws of Colorado, October 12, 1897, as successor to the railway of same name foreclosed and reorganized. Property was sold September 8, 1897, and new company took possession October 31, 1897.

Road owned, Colorado Springs to New Castle, Col., 226 miles; branches, 34 miles; Busk Tunnel, 2 miles; owned but not operated, 8 miles; total owned, 268 miles. Leased, New Castle to Rifle Creek, 14 miles, and leased jointly with Denver & Rio Grande, the Rio Grande Junction Railroad, 63 miles; total operated, 337 miles. Locomotives, 60; passenger cars, 51; freight cars, 1,741.

Stock....Par $100.....Authorized { com., $4,000,000; pref., 6,000,000 } Issued { com., $3,421,300; pref., 4,954,800 } $8,376,100

The preferred stock is 4 per cent., non-cumulative. Transfer Agent, Central Trust Co., New York.

**FUNDED DEBT.**

1st mort., 4 per cent., due July, 1947, Jan. and July.................................. $9,151,000

A prior lien mortgage, 4 per cent., was provided for by reorganization plan, but no such bonds were issued. The first mortgage is for $10,000,000, of which $2,500,000 bore 4 per cent. interest, and $7,500,000 bore 2 per cent. cash until July 1, 1900, and 3 per cent. cash to July 1, 1902, with preferred stock scrip for balance up to 4 per cent., but bore 4 per cent. cash after last named date. In January, 1900, the bonds were all made full 4 per cent., and the right to issue $500,000 of prior lien bonds was waived, the July, 1900, coupons being paid in full in cash. During 1902 interest is paid, $15 in January and $25 in July.

This company and the Denver & Rio Grande leased jointly the Rio Grande Junction Railway for 30 per cent. of the latter's gross earnings, and jointly and severally guarantee $1,850,000 of its 5 per cent. 1st mortgage bonds.

The old company guaranteed a rental equal to annual charge on the $1,250,000 of 7 per cent. Busk Tunnel bonds, but satisfactory terms not having been made with the bondholders of that property, the company in November, 1897, abandoned its use. In June, 1899, a compromise was reached, the Busk Tunnel bondholders accepting $1,250,000 Colorado Midland 4 per cent. bonds in payment for their property.

The stock was held in a voting trust; F. P. Olcott, Henry T. Rogers, A. H. Joline, William Lidderdale, and Cecil W. Boyle, Trustees, for six years, or until full 4 per cent. interest was paid in cash on 1st mortgage bonds for three successive years. In April, 1900, a syndicate submitted to stockholders of this company a proposition to purchase their stock at $30 per share for the preferred and $12.50 per share for the common, the purchase being in the interest of the Colorado & Southern and Rio Grande Western, which jointly control the property. The road is now controlled jointly by the Denver & Rio Grande and the Colorado & Southern, and those companies own all the stock.

Details of the reorganization of the old company are given in the MANUAL for 1900.

**EARNINGS.**

Year ending June 30.

| | Gross. | Net. | Charges. | Surplus. |
|---|---|---|---|---|
| 1891-92 (350 miles) | $2,103,599 | $563,582 | $763,733 | Def., $238,397 |
| 1892-93 ( " " ) | 2,140,006 | 341,628 | 830,994 | " 489,360 |
| 1893-94 ( " " ) | 1,463,256 | 121,667 | 853,845 | " 732,198 |
| 1894-95 ( " " ) | 1,592,457 | 368,947 | 859,636 | " 490,989 |
| 1895-96 ( " " ) | 1,906,280 | 558,067 | 329,385 | 228,682 |
| 1896-97 (336 " ) | 1,671,543 | 335,374 | 319,220 | 16,154 |
| 1897-98 (343 " ) | 1,731,443 | 345,758 | 322,180 | 23,578 |
| 1898-99 (345 " ) | 1,659,798 | 305,941 | 303,736 | 2,205 |
| 1899-00 ( " " ) | 2,197,037 | 641,440 | 565,001 | 76,439 |
| 1900-01 (348 " ) | 2,385,184 | 717,484 | 515,709 | 201,775 |
| 1901-02 (337 " ) | 2,162,286 | 534,480 | 514,451 | 20,023 |

Charges for 1899-1900 and for 1900-1901 include full 4 per cent. on all the 1st mortgage bonds.

President, Frank Trumbull, Denver; Vice-President, George W. Kramer, New York; Secretary, Harry Bronner, New York; Treasurer, H. B. Henson, New York.

Directors—Henry Budge, Grenville M. Dodge, Edward C. Henderson, J. Kennedy Tod, George J. Gould, Edwin Gould, Winslow S. Pierce, New York; George W. Kramer, E. T. Jeffrey, Frank Trumbull, Denver.

Main office, Denver; New York office, 74 Broadway. Annual meeting in November.

## COLORADO SPRINGS & CRIPPLE CREEK DISTRICT RAILWAY CO.

A corporation formed under the laws of Colorado April 18, 1897, as the Cripple Creek District Railway, the name being afterwards changed. The company is controlled by the owners of large mining interests in its territory.

Road owned, Colorado Springs to Cripple Creek, 46 miles; Cameron to Victor, Col., 5 miles. The company also has about 20 miles of branches operated by electricity. Total, 70 miles. Locomotives, 12; passenger cars, 6; freight cars, 300.

Stock....Par $100.....Authorized { com., $1,200,000 / pref., 800,000 } Issued { com., $1,200,000 / pref., 800,000 } $2,000,000

The preferred stock is 5 per cent., non-cumulative.

Stock is transferred by the Secretary of the company, Colorado Springs, Col.

FUNDED DEBT.

| | |
|---|---|
| 1st mort., 5 per cent., due Jan., 1930, Jan. and July | $1,977,000 |
| 2d mort., 5 per cent., due April, 1921, April and Oct. | 1,000,000 |
| Cons. mort., 5 per cent., due 1942 | 600,000 |
| Total | $3,577,000 |

The consolidated mortgage was created in 1902 and is for $3,600,000, of which $3,000,000 is reserved to retire the 1st and 2d mortgage bonds. Trustee of consolidated mortgage, Morton Trust Co., New York.

President, Irving Howbert; Vice-President, William Lennox; Secretary, E. F. Draper; Treasurer, F. M. Woods, Colorado Springs, Col.

Directors—Irving Howbert, William Lennox, F. M. Woods, E. W. Giddings, James F. Burns, T. F. Peck, K. R. Babbitt, H. G. Lunt, John G. Shields, Colorado Springs, Col.

Main office, Colorado Springs, Col. Annual meeting, second Tuesday in September, at Colorado Springs, Col.

## COLUMBIA, NEWBERRY & LAURENS RAILROAD CO.

A corporation formed under the laws of South Carolina, June 6, 1886. Road owned, Columbia to Laurens, S. C., 75 miles. Locomotives, 4; passenger cars, 4; freight cars, 17.

Stock......Par $25..........Authorized, $2,000,000......Issued, $500,000

FUNDED DEBT.

| | |
|---|---|
| 1st mort., 3 per cent., due 1937, Jan. and July | $899,000 |
| Income bonds | 77,453 |
| Certificates of indebtedness | 359,600 |
| Total | $1,336,053 |

The trustee of the 1st mortgage is the Safe Deposit & Trust Co., Baltimore.

EARNINGS.

| Year ending June 30. | Gross. | Net. |
|---|---|---|
| 1901-02 | $180,593 | $56,882 |

President and General Manager, W. G. Childs, Columbia, S. C.; Vice-President, H. C. Moseley, Prosperity, S. C.; Secretary and Treasurer, T. H. Gibbes, Columbia, S. C.

Directors—W. G. Childs, W. A. Clark, W. H. Lyle, James Woodrow, Columbia, S. C.; Henry Walters, Baltimore; John Skelton Williams, Richmond, Va.; Warren G. Elliott, J. R. Henley, Wilmington, N. C.; M. A. Carlisle, Newberry, S. C.; H. C. Moseley, Prosperity, S. C.

Main office, Columbia, S. C. Annual meeting in October at Columbia, S. C.

## THE COLUMBUS & LAKE MICHIGAN RAILROAD CO.

A corporation formed under the laws of Ohio, September 1, 1902. The company acquired and took over the road of the Columbus, Lima & Milwaukee Railway Co., which was sold in foreclosure. Road owned, Lima, O., to Defiance, O., 40 miles. Extensions are planned. Locomotives, 2; passenger cars, 1; freight cars, 10.

Stock......Par $100......Authorized { com., $400,000 / pref., 400,000 } Issued { com., $400,000 / pref., 400,000 } $800,000

The preferred stock is 4 per cent., non-cumulative. Both classes of stock are authorized at the rate of $10,000 per mile.

Stock is transferred at the company's office, 33 Wall street, New York.

FUNDED DEBT.

1st mort., 5 per cent., due Sept., 1922, March and Sept.................................. $800,000

The authorized issue of bonds is at the rate of $20,000 per mile. Trustee of mortgage, North American Trust Co., New York.

President, George A. Garretson, Cleveland; Vice-President, Elliott C. Smith; Treasurer, E. Hope Norton, New York; Secretary, William B. Whiting, Cleveland.

Directors—George A. Garretson, George S. Russell, William B. Whiting, Cleveland; Daniel Coolidge, George W. Boyd, Lorain, O.; E. Hope Norton, Elliott C. Smith, New York.

Main office, 103 Superior street, Cleveland; treasurer's office, 33 Wall street, New York. Annual meeting in September, at Cleveland.

## CONCORD & MONTREAL RAILROAD

(Leased to Boston & Maine.)

Road owned, Nashua, N. H., to Groveton Junction, 181 miles; Mt. Washington Branch, 20 miles; branches, 114 miles; total owned, 315 miles; controlled through ownership of all stock, 53 miles; leased, Pemigewasset Valley, 22 miles; Concord & Portsmouth, 40 miles; Suncook Valle , 17 miles; other branches leased, 5 miles; total leased, 84 miles; owned jointly, Manchester & Keene Railroad, 29 miles; Franklin & Tilton, 5 miles. Total of system, 486 miles. In 1900 a branch from Manchester to Milford, 18 miles, was constructed and another branch, Concord to Hudson, N. H., 35 miles, to be operated with electric power.

In June, 1895, the property of the company was leased to the Boston & Maine for 91 years, lessee to pay all charges and 7 per cent. per annum on the entire capital stock of this company.

| | Authorized | | | Issued | | |
|---|---|---|---|---|---|---|
| Stock..Par $100..Authorized | Class I., | $800,000 | Issued. | Class I., | $800,000 | $7,197,600 |
| | " II., | 540,400 | | " II., | 540,400 | |
| | " III., | 459,600 | | " III., | 459,600 | |
| | " IV., | 6,000,000 | | " IV., | 5,397,600 | |

Stock is transferred by the company's treasurer, Concord, N. H.

The company was formed 1889 by consolidation of the Concord and Boston, Concord & Montreal railroads, and the various classes of stock represent the shares of these two corporations. Under the lease to the Boston & Maine the 7 per cent. dividends are paid quarterly, 1¾ per cent. each, January (1), April, July and October.

FUNDED DEBT.

| | |
|---|---|
| Improvement bonds, 6 per cent., due Jan., 1911, Jan. and July..................... | $500,000 |
| Consolidated mortgage, 4 per cent., due June, 1920, June and Dec.................... | 5,000,000 |
| Debentures, currency, 4 per cent., due June, 1920, June and Dec...................... | 650,000 |
| " " 3½ per cent., due June, 1 June and Dec.................... | 400,000 |
| " " 3½ per cent., int. guar., 1920 June, 1920, June and Dec........ | 500,000 |
| Total ................................................................ | $7,050,000 |

The consolidated 4 per cent. mortgage is for $5,500,000 to provide for previous bond issues, improvements and floating debt. The debenture 4s were issued in 1897 to pay claim of the Manchester & Lawrence Railroad stockholders for $650,000. The currency debenture 3½ per cents. were authorized in October, 1900, to pay for construction of the Milford branch. The authorized amount of this issue is $500,000. An additional issue of $1,000,000 bonds was also authorized in 1900 to build the Hudson branch.

Earnings are included in those of the lessee company.

President, Benjamin A. Kimball; Treasurer, John F. Webster; Clerk, Frank S. Streeter, Concord.

Directors—Benjamin A. Kimball, George M. Kimball, B. C. White, Concord; C. E. Morrison, Boston; H. N. Turner, St. Johnsbury, Vt.; W. M. Parker, N. S. Clark, Arthur H. Hale, Frank P. Carpenter, Manchester, N. H.; Hiram A. Tuttle, Pittsfield, N. H.; Sumner Wallace, Rochester, N. H.; William H. Moses, Tilton, M. H.

Main office, Concord, N. H. Annual meeting, second Tuesday in October.

## CONNECTICUT RIVER RAILROAD CO.

(Leased to Boston & Maine.)

Road owned, Springfield, Mass., to Keene, N. H., 74 miles; branches, 6 miles; total, 80 miles.

The company also owns a portion of the stock of the Vermont Valley Railroad, 24 miles, which owns the Sullivan County Railroad, 26 miles. The Boston & Maine Railroad Co. operates those roads as agent. In May, 1888, the Ashuelot Railroad was consolidated with this company. On January 1, 1893, the road was leased for 99 years to the Boston & Maine for $258,000 per annum, equivalent to 10 per cent. on stock. Lessee pays interest on bonds and $2,000 per annum for organization expenses.

Stock......Par $100..........................Authorized, $2,670,000......Issued, $2,630,000

Stock is transferred at the office of the company, Springfield, Mass. Registrar, Hampden Trust Co., Springfield.

The 10 per cent. guaranteed dividends are paid semi-annually, 5 per cent. each, January (1) and July.

FUNDED DEBT.

| | |
|---|---|
| Gold bonds, 4 per cent., due Sept., 1943, March and Sept. | $1,000,000 |
| New bonds, 3½ per cent., due Jan., 1921, Jan. and July | 290,000 |
| " " 3½ per cent., due Jan., 1923, Jan. and July | 969,000 |
| Total | $2,259,000 |

The bonds are plain bonds, not mortgage. In December, 1900, $50,000 additional stock was issued.

Earnings are now included in those of lessee.

President, William Whiting, Holyoke, Mass.; Treasurer and Clerk, W. G. McIntyre, Springfield, Mass.

Main office, Springfield, Mass. Annual meeting, third Wednesday in September.

## CORNWALL & LEBANON RAILROAD CO.

Road owned. Lebanon, Pa., to Conewago, Pa., 22 miles; branches, 3 miles; total, 25 miles. Locomotives, 11; passenger cars, 17; freight cars, 571. This company is controlled by the Pennsylvania Steel Co.

Stock......Par $50..............................Authorized, $800,000 .....Issued, $800,000

Dividends on the stock are paid semi-annually in February and August.

In February, 1901, a dividend of 2½ per cent. was paid; the August, 1901, dividend was increased to 3 per cent., which has since been the semi-annual rate.

Stock is transferred at the office of the treasurer, Lebanon, Pa.

FUNDED DEBT.

1st mort., 5 per cent., due April, 1921, April and Oct.................... $766,400

EARNINGS.

| Year ending June 30. | Gross. | Net. |
|---|---|---|
| 1900-01 | $279,242 | $122,982 |
| 1901-02 | 332,848 | 155,786 |

☞ President, Allen D. Smith, Lebanon, Pa.; Vice-President, Edgar C. Felton, Philadelphia; Secretary, B. Dawson Coleman; Treasurer, Henry W. Siegrist, Lebanon, Pa.

Directors—B. Dawson Coleman, Edward R. Coleman, J. P. S. Gobin, B. H. Buckingham, Herbert B. Cox, Lebanon, Pa.; Walter Scranton, New York; Cornwall, Pa.; Edgar C. Felton, Theodore N. Ely, Philadelphia; Frank C. Smink, Reading, Pa.

Main office, Lebanon, Pa. Annual meeting, second Monday in January, at Lebanon, Pa.

## THE CUBA RAILROAD CO.

A corporation formed under the laws of New Jersey, May 1, 1902. The corporation was organized to build, own and operate railroads in the island of Cuba.

Road owned, 343 miles; leased, 57 miles; trackage, 32 miles. The main line extends from Santa Clara, Cuba, to San Luis, 334 miles, with control of line from San Luis to Santiago de Cuba, 20 miles, and of Ponupo branch, 12 miles; branch, Zaza Junction to Sancti Spiritus, 9 miles; leased, Jucaro to San Fernando, 57 miles; under construction, Nipe Bay to main line at Alto Cedro, 30 miles. Locomotives, 14; passenger cars, 24; freight cars, 484.

Stock...Par $100...Authorized { com., $10,000,000 / pref., 10,000,000 } Issued { com., $6,126,000 / pref., 8,000,000 } $14,126,000

The preferred stock is 6 per cent. non-cumulative.

Transfer Agent, Morton Trust Co., New York. Registrar, Guaranty Trust Co., New York.

FUNDED DEBT.

1st mort., 5 per cent., due July, 1952, Jan. and July................................ $4,000,000

The trustee of the mortgage and agent for the payment of interest on the bonds is the Morton Trust Co., New York. The bonds are authorized to the amount of $20,000 per mile of completed main line track and the same for branches.

President, Franklin B. Lord; Vice-President, Percival Farquhar; Secretary, Charles J. Fay; Treasurer, James I. Burke, New York.

Directors—Charles T. Barney, William L. Bull, Henry F. Dimock, Franklin B. Lord, New York; George Crocker, Ramsey, N. J.

Corporate and main office, 83 Montgomery street, Jersey City. Annual meeting, third Wednesday in September, at Jersey City.

## CUMBERLAND VALLEY RAILROAD CO.

(Controlled by Pennsylvania Railroad.)

Road owned, Harrisburg, Pa., to Potomac River, Md., 82 miles; leased and chiefly owned, 82 miles; total, 163 miles. The leased properties, which are chiefly controlled, include the Cumberland Valley & Martinsburg Railroad, Winchester, Va., to the Potomac River, 34 miles; Cumberland Valley & Waynesboro Railroad, Mt. Alto Junction to Waynesboro, Pa., 18 miles; Dillsburg & Mechanicsburg Railroad, Dillsburg Junction to Dillsburg, Pa., 8 miles, and Southern Pennsylvania Railway & Mining Co., Marion, Pa., to Richmond, Pa., 21 miles. Locomotrives, 33; passenger cars, 63; freight cars, 674.

| | | | | | | |
|---|---|---|---|---|---|---|
| Stock. Par $50...Authorized | com., | $1,515,100 | Issued | com., | $1,292,950 | $1,777,850 |
| | 1st pref., | 241,900 | | 1st pref., | 241,900 | |
| | 2d pref., | 243,000 | | 2d pref., | 243,000 | |

Stock is transferred at the office of the company, Chambersburg, Pa.

Dividends of 8 per cent. per annum are paid on all classes of the stock. The payments are made 2 per cent., quarterly, January (1), April, July and October.

FUNDED DEBT.

| | |
|---|---|
| 1st mort., 8 per cent., due April, 1904, April and Oct. | $139,500 |
| 2d mort., 8 per cent., due April, 1908, April and Oct. | 94,000 |
| Total | $233,500 |

EARNINGS.

| | Div. Paid. | Gross. | Net. | Charges and Taxes. | Surplus. |
|---|---|---|---|---|---|
| 1893 (165 miles) | 8 | $792,467 | $205,637 | $38,924 | $166,713 |
| 1894 (163 " ) | 8 | 719,240 | 249,096 | 43,018 | 206,078 |
| 1895 ( " " ) | 8 | 766,685 | 231,346 | 34,275 | 197,071 |
| 1896 ( " " ) | 8 | 743,640 | 226,767 | 42,842 | 183,924 |
| 1897 ( " " ) | 8 | 744,478 | 251,031 | 39,481 | 211,549 |
| 1898 ( " " ) | 8 | 774,769 | 245,175 | 40,594 | 204,581 |
| 1899 ( " " ) | 8 | 809,851 | 231,168 | 44,367 | 186,800 |
| 1900 ( " " ) | 8 | 898,406 | 250,360 | 42,536 | 207,823 |
| 1901 ( " " ) | 8 | 962,788 | 401,990 | 41,758 | 360,232 |
| 1902 ( " " ) | 8 | 1,084,505 | 372,163 | 43,347 | 328,816 |

Surplus over dividends was, in 1896, $46,405; betterments, $23,786. In 1897, surplus, $69,321; betterments, $11,432; 1898, surplus, $62,353; construction, $9,169; in 1899, surplus, $44,572; in 1900, surplus, $65,595; in 1900, surplus, $65,595; in 1901, surplus, $218,004, and in 1902, surplus, $186,588.

President, Thomas B. Kennedy; Vice-President, M. C. Kennedy; Treasurer and Secretary, William M. Biddle, Chambersburg, Pa.

Directors—Thomas B. Kennedy, Edward B. Watts, A. J. Cassatt, John Stewart, John P. Green, George H. Stewart, M. C. Kennedy, Spencer C. Gilbert, Samuel Rea, N. Parker Shortridge, Charles E. Pugh.

Main office, Chambersburg, Pa. Annual meeting, first Monday in October, at Harrisburg.

## DELAWARE & BOUND BROOK RAILROAD CO.

(Leased to Philadelphia & Reading.)

Road owned, Bound Brook, N. J., to Delaware River, 27 miles; Trenton Branch, 4 miles; total, 31 miles. The road forms a section of the Reading line between New York and Philadelphia.

Stock......Par $100..........................Authorized, $1,800,000......Issued, $1,800,000

The rental is interest on the bonds and 8 per cent. on stock. The 8 per cent. dividends are paid quarterly, 2 per cent. each, February 20, May, August and November.

Stock is transferred by the treasurer of the company, Philadelphia.

FUNDED DEBT.

| | |
|---|---|
| 1st mort., 7 per cent., due Aug., 1905, Feb. and Aug. | $1,500,000 |
| 2d mort., extended, 4 per cent. due Aug., 1905, May and Nov. | 300,000 |
| Total | $1,800,000 |

President, Edward C. Knight, Jr.; Vice-President, John H. Michener; Secretary and Treasurer, John S. Wise, Philadelphia.

Main office, Trenton; Philadelphia office, 240 South Third street. Annual meeting, second Thursday in May, at Trenton.

## THE DELAWARE & HUDSON CO.

A corporation chartered by the State of New York, April 23, 1823, as "The President, Managers and Company of the Delaware & Hudson Canal Company." This company built and operated a canal from Rondout, N. Y., to Honesdale, Pa., 108 miles. By Act of the Legislature, passed April 28, 1899, its title was changed to "The Delaware & Hudson Company," and the sale of its canal was authorized, which was effected in the following June.

Road owned, including branches, 170 miles. Leased, Albany & Susquehanna, 143 miles; New York & Canada Railroad, Whitehall, N. Y., to Rouse's Point, N. Y., 151 miles; Rensselaer & Saratoga Railroad and branches, 192 miles; Northern Coal & Iron Co., 22 miles; total leased, 508 miles; trackage, 39 miles; total, 717 miles. The Utica, Clinton & Binghamton and Rome & Clinton Railroads, 44 miles, are leased, but are sub-leased to the New York, Ontario & Western. The Adirondack Railway Co., which was controlled, was merged with this company in November, 1902. Locomotives, 352; passenger cars, 380; freight cars, 13,562; service cars, 205.

The company owns a large coal property, and nearly 200 miles of tramways and mine roads in its mines.

Statements for the leased lines will be found under their respective titles. See Albany & Susquehanna, Rensselaer & Saratoga and New York & Canada.

Stock......Par $100..........................Authorized, $35,000,000......Issued, $34,407,100

The directors of this company in January each year declare the dividend for the year out of the earnings of preceding years. The dividends are payable quarterly on the 15th day of March, June, September and December. In January, 1897, the dividend for the year was fixed at 5 per cent., which was also the rate in 1898, 1899 and 1900. In 1901 7 per cent. was paid, which has since been the annual rate.

Transfer Agent, National Bank of Commerce in New York.

FUNDED DEBT.

| | |
|---|---|
| 1st mort., Pennsylvania Division, 7 per cent., due Sept., 1917, March and Sept. | $5,000,000 |
| Equipment mort., 3½ per cent., due 1909, May 15 and Nov. | 1,050,000 |
| Equipment debentures, 4 per cent., due 1902-1914, Jan. and July | 2,100,000 |
| Total | $8,150,000 |

FUNDED DEBT.—GUARANTEED, LEASED AND CONTROLLED ROADS.

| | |
|---|---|
| Albany & Susquehanna, 1st., mort., 7 per cent., due April, 1906, April and Oct. | $3,000,000 |
| " " " " 6 per cent., due April, 1906, April and Oct. | 7,000,000 |
| N. Y. & Canada R. R., 1st mort., 6 per cent., due May, 1904, May and Nov. | 4,000,000 |
| " " debenture, 4½ per cent., due May, 1904, May and Nov. | 1,000,000 |
| Utica, Clinton & Binghamton R. R., 1st mort., 5 per cent., due July, 1939, Jan. and July. | 800,000 |
| Adirondack Ry. Co., 1st mort., 4½ per cent., due Dec., 1942, Jan. and July | 1,000,000 |
| Chateaugay Ore & Iron Co., 1st con. mort., 6 per cent., due Jan., 1929, Jan. and July. | 400,000 |
| Chateaugay Ry., 1st mort., 6 per cent., due Aug., 1907, Feb. and Aug. | 200,000 |
| Bluff Point Land & Imp't Co., 1st mort., 4 per cent., due Jan., 1940, Jan. and July... | 300,000 |
| Hudson Coal Co. debentures, 4 per cent , due 1902-1917, May and Nov. | 1,600,000 |
| Hudson Coal Co. debentures, guar., 4 per cent., due 1903-18, May and Nov | 1,850,000 |
| *Rensselaer & Saratoga R. R., 1st mort., 7 per cent., due May, 1921, May and Nov.. | 2,000,000 |
| *Schen. & Duanesb. R. R., 1st mort., 6 per cent., due Sept., 1924, March and Sept... | 500,000 |

*Interest only guaranteed.

Interest on the bonds is paid at the company's office.

The Delaware & Hudson Co. guarantees dividends as follows on stock of leased roads: Albany & Susquehanna, 7 per cent. on $3,500,000 stock; Rensselaer & Saratoga, 8 per cent. on $10,000,000 stock; Rome & Clinton, 6¼ per cent. on $350,000 stock.

In 1899 the equipment mortgage for $1,500,000 at 3½ per cent. was authorized for new equipment. These bonds are payable $150,000 per annum in May, and $1,050,000 are now outstanding. In 1900 the company created $2,500,000 4 per cent. debentures for equipment, payable $200,000 annually in January and $2,100,000 are now outstanding.

In 1899 the stockholders adopted a resolution establishing a sinking fund for the gradual retirement of the stock and bonds of the company contemporaneously with the mining and sale of its coal. This provides that at the end of each year there shall be credited to the sinking fund a sum not less than five cents for every ton of coal mined by the company, and any additional amount which the managers may deem expedient, which same shall be invested in the securities or stock of the company and said securities or stock forthwith retired and canceled. Pursuant thereto the company purchased and canceled 2,000 shares of its stock for 1899. For 1900, 1,418 more shares were thus retired, in 1901 1,511 shares, and in 1902 1,000 shares.

EARNINGS.

The earnings of the leased railroads have been as follows:

| | Gross. | Net. | Rental Paid. | Result to Lessee. | |
|---|---|---|---|---|---|
| 1893 | $6,995,073 | $2,356,874 | $2,445,459 | Gain | $11,415 |
| 1894 | 6,503,505 | 2,249,676 | 2,473,971 | Loss | 224,295 |
| 1895 | 6,920,994 | 2,459,124 | 2,487,771 | " | 28,647 |
| 1896 | 6,990,509 | 2,506,864 | 2,525,105 | " | 18,243 |
| 1897 | 7,067,580 | 2,684,848 | 2,575,341 | Gain | 109,507 |
| 1898 | 7,055,363 | 2,517,953 | 2,573,478 | Loss | 5,525 |
| 1899 | 7,762,313 | 3,220,942 | 2,529,575 | Gain | 691,367 |

The income statement is as follows:

| | Div. Paid. | Gross Receipts. | Net Receipts. | Charges. | Surplus. |
|---|---|---|---|---|---|
| 1893 | 7 | $12,692,018 | $3,902,579 | $688,030 | 3,214,549 |
| 1894 | 7 | 10,068,721 | 2,822,242 | 603,523 | 2,218,719 |
| 1895 | 7 | 10,753,324 | 2,714,393 | 350,000 | 2,364,393 |
| 1896 | 7 | 10,591,398 | 2,115,012 | 350,006 | 1,765,012 |
| 1897 | 5 | 11,171,923 | 2,491,420 | 350,000 | 2,141,420 |
| 1898 | 5 | 10,309,810 | 2,220,819 | 350,000 | 1,870,819 |
| 1899 | 5 | 10,728,551 | 2,990,846 | 350,000 | 2,640,846 |

For 1900, 1901 and 1902 the revenues and expenditures were stated in a different way, the results being as follows:

| | Div. Paid. | Gross. | Net. | Charges. | Surplus. |
|---|---|---|---|---|---|
| 1900 | 7 | $24,322,650 | $6,129,264 | $2,941,872 | $3,187,392 |
| 1901 | 7 | 29,497,454 | 7,602,748 | 2,998,072 | 4,604,076 |
| 1902 | 7 | 22,500,794 | 5,619,901 | 2,977,119 | 2,642,782 |

In 1901 there was deducted from surplus for depreciation and other items $1,333,369, leaving a balance of $3,370,700 or 9⅝ per cent. on the stock of the company.

The anthracite coal tonnage of the company was, in 1890, 4,915,376 tons; in 1891, 5,502,813 tons; in 1892, 6,225,295 tons; in 1893, 6,177,659 tons; in 1894, 5,751,386 tons; in 1895, 6,151,147 tons; in 1896, 5,835,621 tons; in 1897, 5,646,852 tons; in 1898, 5,613,000 tons; in 1899, 6,430,000 tons; in 1900, 6,614,002 tons; in 1901, 7,571,298 tons; in 1902, 4,640,772 tons.

The following exhibits the comparative freight traffic statistics of the company:

| | Average Mileage. | Total Tonnage. | Tons Carried One Mile. | Freight Density. | Rate per Ton per Mile. | Earnings per Train Mile. | Average Tons per Train Mile. |
|---|---|---|---|---|---|---|---|
| 1901 | 660 | 13,057,958 | 1,274,511,441 | 1,925,653 | 0.755c | $2.681 | ...... |
| 1902 | 717 | 10,659,444 | 1,159,831,753 | 1,682,598 | 0.711 | 2.454 | ...... |

President, Robert M. Olyphant; Vice-President and General Counsel, David Wilcox, New York; 2d Vice-President, Horace G. Young, Albany, N.Y.; Treasurer, Charles A. Walker; Secretary, F. Murray Olyphant; Comptroller, Abel I. Culver, New York.

Managers—Robert M. Olyphant, Alexander E. Orr, Chauncey M. Depew, James W. Alexander, Horace G. Young, John Jacob Astor, R. Somers Hayes, Frederic Cromwell, David Willcox, R. Suydam Grant, George I. Wilber, Charles A. Peabody.

Main office, 21 Cortlandt street, New York. Annual meeting, second Tuesday in May. Books close ten days previous.

## DELAWARE, LACKAWANNA & WESTERN RAILROAD CO.

A corporation formed in 1853 by the consolidation of other companies.

Road owned, Delaware River, via Scranton, Pa., to New York State line, 114 miles. branches, 80; total, 194 miles. Roads leased in New Jersey: Warren Railroad, 19 miles; Morris & Essex and branches, 157 miles; total, 176 miles. Leased in New York: Valley Railroad, 12 miles; Greene Railroad, 8 miles; Cayuga & Susquehanna, 34 miles; Utica, Chenango & Susquehanna Valley, 97 miles; Oswego & Syracuse, 35 miles; New York, Lackawanna & Western, 214 miles; total, 400 miles. Controlled: Syracuse, Binghamton & New York Railroad, 81 miles; Sussex Railroad, 31 miles. In 1900 purchased the Bangor & Portland Railroad, 38 miles. Total leased, controlled and operated, 947 miles. Rolling stock, all lines, locomotives, 649; passenger cars, 723; freight cars, 27,570. The company also owns large coal properties.

See separate statements of the following leased and controlled properties: Morris & Essex Railroad Co.; Syracuse, Binghamton & New York Railroad Co.; New York, Lackawanna & Western Railroad Co.

Stock......Par $50........................Authorized, $26,200,000......Issued, $26,200,000

Stock is transferred at the office of the company, New York. Registrar, Farmers' Loan & Trust Co. New York.

Dividends are paid quarterly, 1¾ per cent. each, in January (20) April, July and October.

FUNDED DEBT.

Consolidated mort., 7 per cent., due Sept., 1907, March and Sept.................. $3,067,000

In February, 1892, capitalists interested in the Central Railroad of New Jersey acquired large interests in this company, and were given representation in the directory. In 1893, it was announced the Vanderbilt interest had also acquired large holdings in this stock, and in 1899 the management was changed by the election of William H. Truesdale as president.

This company guarantees 5 per cent. dividends on the $10,000,000 stock of the New York, Lackawanna & Western, and interest on its $12,000,000 of 1st mortgage 6s, $5,000,000 of 5 per cent. 2ds and $5,000,000 of 3d mortgage terminal improvement 4 per cent. bonds.

Earnings and expenses of all kinds, including leased lines and coal property:

| | Div. Paid. | Gross Receipts. | Net Receipts. | Int. and Rents. | Surplus. |
|---|---|---|---|---|---|
| 1893 | 7 | $48,790,973 | $8,253,401 | $5,360,490 | $2,892,911 |
| 1894 | 7 | 43,058,862 | 7,049,667 | 5,412,322 | 1,637,348 |
| 1895 | 7 | 44,201,909 | 6,760,900 | 5,406,239 | 1,354,660 |
| 1896 | 7 | 44,206,352 | 6,730,978 | 5,406,239 | 1,324,739 |
| 1897 | 7 | 43,975,399 | 7,316,539 | 5,406,239 | 1,910,300 |
| 1898 | 7 | 43,696,482 | 6,730,504 | 5,406,239 | 1,324,264 |
| 1899 | 7 | 42,640,921 | 10,235,266 | 5,391,990 | 4,843,276 |
| 1900 | 7 | 43,149,650 | 9,307,591 | 5,377,277 | 3,930,314 |

EARNINGS—RAILROAD CO.

| | Gross. | Net. | Charges. | Dividends. | Surplus. |
|---|---|---|---|---|---|
| 1899 | $21,325,122 | $10,235,266 | $6,794,093 | $1,834,000 | $1,607,173 |
| 1900 | 20,887,763 | 8,107,509 | 5,377,277 | 1,834,000 | 896,232 |
| 1901 | 23,507,134 | 11,202,248 | 8,172,094 | 1,804,000 | 1,196,054 |
| 1902 | 21,398,764 | 8,115,337 | 8,461,989 | 1,834,000 | Def. 2,180,652 |

In 1896 dividends amounted to $1,834,000, and the debit balance for the year was $509,260. In 1897 the surplus over 7 per cent. dividends was $76,300. In 1898, deficit after dividends, $509,735. In 1899 $1,402,104 was charged off for various items and $1,834,000 paid for dividends, leaving a surplus for the year of $1,607,172. In 1900 $12,265 was charged for advances to other companies and $1,834,000 paid for dividends, leaving a surplus of $896,232. In 1901 $119,184 was advanced to leased lines, $2,523,127 charged to betterments and $1,834,000 paid for dividends, leaving a surplus of $1,196,054. In 1902, 3,058,145 was charged to betterments, which is included in the item of charges.

Coal tonnage was as follows: In 1893, 7,934,885; in 1894, 6,722,007; in 1895, 6,725,464; in 1896, 6,479,633; in 1897, 6,557,112; in 1898, 6,643,402; in 1899, 6,731,353; in 1900, 6,091,133 tons; in 1901, 7,398,057 tons. In 1902, 4,570,490.

Chairman, Samuel Sloan; President, William H. Truesdale; Vice-Presidents, E. E. Loomis, B. D. Caldwell: Secretary and Treasurer, Fred. F. Chambers; Assistant Secretary and Assistant Treasurer, Arthur D. Chambers; General Auditor, O. C. Post, New York.

Managers—Samuel Sloan, William W. Astor, Henry A. C. Taylor, Eugene Higgins, J. Rogers Maxwell, George F. Baker, William Rockefeller, James Stillman, Frank Work, Hamilton McK. Twombly, Harris C. Fahnestock, Frederick W. Vanderbilt, M. Taylor Pyne, John D. Rockefeller, Jr., New York.

Main office, 26 Exchange Place, New York. Annual meeting, Tuesday before the last Friday in February. Books close twenty days previously.

---

## DELAWARE, MARYLAND & VIRGINIA RAILROAD CO.

(Controlled by Philadelphia, Wilmington & Baltimore Railroad Co.)

Road owned, Rehoboth, Del., to Harrington, and Georgetown to Franklin City, 97½ miles. The road is operated by the Philadelphia, Wilmington & Baltimore Railroad Co., which supplies equipment.

Stock......Par $25..............................Authorized, $526,758......Issued, $526,758

Stock is transferred at the company's office, Philadelphia.

FUNDED DEBT.

1st mort., Breakwater & F. R. R., 3 per cent., due Jan., 1932, Jan. and July......... $200,000

The property is controlled by the Pennsylvania Railroad Co., and is operated by the Philadelphia, Baltimore & Wilmington. There is a 3 per cent. 1st mortgage of $185,000 on the Junction & Breakwater Railroad owned by State of Delaware.

President, H. F. Kenney; Vice-President, John P. Green; Treasurer, Robert W. Smith; Secretary, John M. Harding, Philadelphia.

Main office, Broad Street Station, Philadelphia. Annual meeting, last Wednesday in May, at Georgetown, Del.

## DELAWARE RIVER RAILROAD & BRIDGE CO.

(Controlled by the Pennsylvania Railroad Co.)

Road owned, Frankford Junction, Philadelphia, to Haddonfield, N. J., 10¼ miles, including the bridge across the Delaware River, connecting the lines of the Pennsylvania Railroad Co. in New Jersey with its Pennsylvania System. The property is operated by that company.

All of this company's stock is owned by the Pennsylvania Railroad Co.

Stock......Par $50..............................Authorized, $1,300,000......Issued $1,300,000

In 1900 the company paid 2 per cent. on its stock, and in 1901 the dividends were 4 per cent. for the year. In 1902 2 per cent. was paid in December.

FUNDED DEBT.

1st mort., old, 6 per cent., due Aug., 1936, Feb. and Aug............................ $1,300,000

The authorized amount of 1st mortgage bonds is $1,300,000. The bonds are guaranteed, principal and interest, by the Pennsylvania Railroad Co., at the office of which company interest is paid. There is a sinking fund of 1 per cent per annum, but bonds cannot be called. Trustee of mortgage, Girard Trust Co., Philadelphia.

Earnings are included in those of the Pennsylvania Railroad Co.

President, Samuel Rea; Secretary, John M. Harding; Treasurer, Taber Ashton, Philadelphia.

Main office, Broad Street Station, Philadelphia.

## DELAWARE, SUSQUEHANNA & SCHUYLKILL RAILROAD CO.

Road owned, Drifton, Pa., to Gowen, 31 miles; branches (part narrow gauge), 17 miles; total owned, 48 miles. Trackage on Lehigh Valley to Perth Amboy, etc., 133 miles; total operated, 181 miles. Locomotives, 23; passenger cars, 3; freight cars, 1,510.

This road was built by Coxe Bros. & Co., Incorporated, of Drifton, Pa., miners and shippers of anthracite coal, and is controlled by that organization.

Stock......Par $50..........................Authorized, $1,500,000......Issued, $1,500,000

In 1894 the company declared and paid a stock dividend of 50 per cent., increasing the stock from $1,000,000 to $1,500,000. The company paid cash dividends of 40 per cent. in 1892, 20 per cent. in 1893 and 26⅔ per cent. in 1894. No further dividends were paid until November, 1899, when 2 per cent. was paid, 2 per cent. being also paid in May, 1900, November, 1900, May, 1901, and November, 1901. In 1902 the semi-annual dividends were 2½ per cent. each in May and November.

EARNINGS.

| Year ending June 30. | Gross. | Net. |
|---|---|---|
| 1898 | $1,091,186 | $141,941 |
| 1899 | 1,123,398 | 183,064 |
| 1900 | 1,142,463 | 180,162 |
| 1901 | 1,145,262 | 152,062 |
| 1902 | 876,240 | 123,645 |

President, Irving A. Stearns, New York; Secretary, Arthur McClellan, Drifton, Pa.; Treasurer, J. Brinton White, New York.

Directors—Alexander B. Coxe, Eckley B. Coxe, Jr., Drifton, Pa.; Irving A. Stearns, New York; Henry B. Coxe, Henry B. Coxe, Jr., Philadelphia; S. P. Wolverton, Sunbury, Pa.; Alexander Brown Coxe, Paoli, Pa.

Main office, Drifton, Pa.; New York office, 143 Liberty street. Annual meeting, second Monday in January.

## DENVER & RIO GRANDE RAILROAD CO.

(Controlled by Missouri Pacific Railway Co.)

This company is a re-organization in 1886 of the railway company of same name.

Road operated, 2,390 miles; the chief lines being from Denver, Col., to Ogden, Utah, and to Leadville, Aspen, Santa Fe and Grand Junction; Pueblo to Alamosa and San Juan and Cuchara to El Moro. Of this 1,470 miles are standard gauge, of which 345 miles are laid with a third rail. Rio Grande Junction Railway, 62 miles, standard gauge, included in the above, is leased jointly to this company and the Colorado Midland. In 1901 this company acquired the Rio Grande Western, Grand River Junction to Ogden, and branches, 645 miles. The Rio Grande Southern Railroad, 180 miles, narrow gauge, was built and is operated in interest of this company. Locomotives, 451; passenger cars, 329; freight cars, 13,805.

In 1901 control of this company was acquired by the Missouri Pacific Railway Co.

Stock...Par $100....Authorized { com., $38,000,000 / pref., 44,400,000 } Issued { com. $38,000,000 / pref., 44,400,000 } $82,000,000

The preferred stock is entitled to 5 per cent., non-cumulative, dividends.

Transfer agency, 195 Broadway, New York. Registrar, United States Trust Co., New York.

Dividends on the preferred stock have been as follows: In 1890, 2½ per cent; in 1891, 2½ per cent.; in 1893, 2 per cent.; in 1896, 2 per cent.; in 1897, 2 per cent.; in 1898, 2½ per cent.; in 1899 and 1900, 4 per cent. The January, 1901, dividend on the preferred was increased to 2½ per cent., putting the stock on a 5 per cent. basis, which has since been the established rate Dividends on the preferred stock are paid half-yearly, January (15) and July.

In May, 1901, arrangements were concluded for the purchase of the stock of the Rio Grande Western Railway Co., which had $10,000,000 common and $7,500,000 preferred stock outstanding. The common was bought by this company at $80 per share and the preferred exchanged for preferred stock of this company in the proportion of ten shares of the Rio Grande Western preferred for eleven shares of Denver preferred.

To carry out this arrangement the preferred stock of this company was increased to $44,400,000 from $23,650,000. Of the new preferred stock $12,500,000 was taken by stockholders at 90 and proceeds used to buy the common stock of the Rio Grande Western. Nearly all of the latter's preferred has been exchanged on the terms above stated.

### FUNDED DEBT.

| | |
|---|---|
| Consolidated mort., 4 per cent., due Jan., 1936, Jan. and July | $33,450,000 |
| " " 4½ per cent., due Jan., 1936, Jan. and July | 6,382,500 |
| Improvement mort., 5 per cent., due June, 1928, June and Dec | 8,120,000 |
| Rio Grande Junction, 1st mort., 5 per cent. guar., due Dec., 1939, June and Dec | 1,850,000 |
| " " Southern, 1st mort., 5 per cent. guar., due July, 1940, Jan. and July | 2,277,000 |
| " " Western, 1st mort., 4 per cent., due July, 1939, Jan. and July | 15,200,000 |
| " " " 1st cons. mort., 4 per cent., due April, 1849, April and Oct | 12,276,600 |
| Utah Fuel Co., 1st mort., 5 per cent., due March, 1931, March and Sept | 750,000 |
| Pleasant Valley Coal, 1st mort., 5 per cent., due July, 1928, Jan. and July | 1,227,000 |
| Total | $81,533,000 |

In January, 1898, an arrangement was made with Kuhn, Loeb & Co. to refund the 7 per cent. 1st mortgage bonds into consols, an issue of which at 4½ per cent. was made for the purpose. By this the consolidated mortgage became a first lien on entire property. The larger part of the 1sts accepted the terms offered, and all the 1sts have now been retired.

This company is interested in Rio Grande Southern Railroad, which has $4,510,000 4 per cent. 1st mortgage bonds, due 1940. In 1900 the company guaranteed $2,227,000 of the same, preparatory to their sale. In 1896 this company acquired the Santa Fe Southern Railroad from Espanola to Santa Fe, 34 miles. This company, with Colorado Midland, leases and jointly guarantees principal and interest of $1,850,000 5 per cent. bonds of Rio Grande Junction Railway.

The consolidated mortgage is $42,000,000 authorized, and in May, 1901, authority was granted to issue $6,900,000 of the consolidated mortgage bonds theretofore reserved for acquiring the Rio Grande Western and for other capital requirements. $48,900,000 in 1901, to provide for improvements and additions. Improvement mortgage authorized June, 1888, at rate of $5,000 per mile.

The company on June 30, 1902, had securities in its treasury valued at $25,742,136, and a renewal fund comprising $281,651 in securities.

EARNINGS.

Year ending June 30.

| | Div. on Pfd. | Gross. | Net. | Charges and Div. | Surplus. Over Div. |
|---|---|---|---|---|---|
| 1892-93 (1,646 miles)....... | 2 | $9,317,647 | $4,090,137 | $3,160,829 | $929,308 |
| 1893-94 (1,654 " )....... | .. | 6,476,044 | 2,513,792 | 2,426,131 | 87,661 |
| 1894-95 (1,657 " )....... | .. | 6,916,841 | 2,940,229 | 2,411,539 | 528,690 |
| 1895-96 (1,663 " )....... | 2 | 7,551,187 | 3,259,741 | 3,041,349 | 218,392 |
| 1896-97 ( " " )....... | 2 | 6,945,115 | 2,921,461 | 2,890,265 | 31,196 |
| 1897-98 (1,666 " )....... | 2½ | 8,342,926 | 3,387,730 | 3,130,477 | 257,253 |
| 1898-99 (1,670 " )....... | 4 | 9,270,247 | 3,670,224 | 3,637,084 | 33,140 |
| 1899-00 (1,674 " )....... | 4 | 10,246,080 | 3,873,925 | 3,635,623 | 238,302 |
| 1900-01 (1,722 " )....... | 5 | 11,452,403 | 4,439,879 | 3,708,957 | 730,922 |
| 1901-02 (2,347 " )....... | 5 | 17,036,828 | 6,871,047 | 5,888,423 | 982,624 |

Expenditure for betterments in 1888, $240,906; 1889, $240,000; 1890-91, $259,816; 1891-92, $240,000; 1892-93, $240,000; 1895-96, $387,867; in 1896-97, surplus preferred over dividend, (2 per cent.), $31,196. In 1897-98, after dividends $591,250, $30,000 carried to renewal fund and $20,000 to bond conversion fund, the surplus was $257,253. In 1898-99 after dividends, $946,000, $60,000 carried to renewal fund and $120,000 to bond conversion fund and $177,589, appropriated for new locomotives, the surplus was $33,140. In 1899-1900 $130,161 was paid for new equipment and $60,000 carried to renewal fund and $120,000 to bond conversion account, which amounts are included in the charges given in above table. In 1900-01 the surplus over dividends and renewal fund was $730,922; in 1901-02, $862,624.

The following presents the comparative freight traffic statistics of the company:

| | Average Mileage. | Total Tonnage. | Tons Carried One Mile. | Freight Density. | Rate per Ton per Mile. | Earnings per Train Mile. | Av. Tons per Train. |
|---|---|---|---|---|---|---|---|
| 1900-01.. | 2,393 | 5,736,062 | 979,498,415 | 409,318 | 1.24c | $2.26 | 182 |
| 1901-02.. | 2,399 | 6,507,124 | 998,010,972 | 417,577 | 1.22 | 2.43 | 199 |

For purposes of comparison the traffic statistics of the Rio Grande Western are included in both years.

Chairman, George J. Gould; President, Edward T. Jeffery; Secretary and Comptroller, Stephen Little, New York; Treasurer, Joseph W. Gilluly, Denver; Assistant Treasurer, Jesse White, New York.

Directors—George J. Gould, Edward T. Jeffery, Winslow S. Pierce, Edward H. Harriman, Arthur Coppell, Mortimer L. Schiff, New York; Charles G. Warner, Russell Harding, St. Louis; Edward O. Wolcott, Denver.

General offices, Equitable Building, Denver; New York office, 195 Broadway. Annual meeting, third Tuesday in October, at Denver.

---

## DENVER & SOUTHWESTERN RAILWAY CO.

A corporation formed under the laws of New Jersey, November 18, 1889. Road owned, Divide to Cripple Creek and Florence, Col., 77 miles; Victor to Isabella, Col., 6 miles; branches, mainly spurs and mine extensions, 47 miles; total, 130 miles, of which 43 miles are standard gauge. Locomotives, 26; passenger cars, 16; freight cars, 504.

The company was a consolidation of the Midland Terminal Railway Co., Florence & Cripple Creek Railroad Co., and Golden Circle Railroad Co. The company also acquired the La Belle Mill, Water & Power Co. of Goldfield, Col., and the Colorado Trading & Transfer Co., and three-fourths of the stock of the Metallic Extraction Co., of Florence, Col. The company completed a 7-mile extension from Canon City to Ora Junta, Col., in 1900. The consolidation was financed by E. H. Rollins & Co., Boston, and Kessler & Co., New York.

Stock....Par $100.....Authorized { com., $3,000,000 / pref., 2,000,000 } Issued { com., $3,000,000 / pref., 2,000,000 } $5,000,000

The preferred stock is 5 per cent., non-cumulative.

The company began the payment of dividends in May, 1900, when 1¼ per cent. quarterly was paid on the preferred and 1½ per cent. quarterly on the common. Similar quarterly dividends at the rates of 5 per cent. per annum on the preferred and 6 per cent. per annum on the common were paid in February, May, August and November, until February 1, 1902, inclusive. The Ma , 1902, dividends on both common and preferred were suspended and none have been paid since.

Transfer Agents, Kessler & Co., 54 Wall street, New York. Registrar, Continental Trust Co., New York.

FUNDED DEBT.

| | |
|---|---|
| Gen. mort., 5 per cent., due Dec., 1929, June and Dec. | $4,923,000 |
| Midland Terminal, 1st mort., 5 per cent., due Dec., 1925, June and Dec. | 509,000 |
| Total | $5,432,000 |

The general mortgage, Continental Trust Co., New York, trustee, is secured by a deposit of securities of constituent companies, and is for $5,500,000, of which $577,000 is reserved to retire the Midland Terminal 1st mortgage bonds, and $100,000 is held in the company's treasury. There is a sinking fund of $95,000 per annum, bonds to be purchased at not above 110 and interest.

The Midland Terminal 1st mortgage, Farmers' Loan & Trust Co., New York, trustee, is for $1,000,000, of which issue $491,000 have been retired by a sinking fund.

EARNINGS.

Year ending November 30.

| | Gross. | Net. | Charges. | Surplus. |
|---|---|---|---|---|
| 1899-00 | $2,481,567 | $1,098,410 | $531,531 | $566,878 |
| 1900-01 | 1,840,069 | 660,650 | 396,401 | 264,259 |

In 1900-01, after the payment of dividends of 5 per cent. on the preferred and 6 per cent. on the common stock, there was a deficit of $15,751.

President, William K. Gillett, New York; Vice-President, Benjamin P. Cheney, Boston; Secretary and Treasurer, John P. Cobb, New York.

Directors—Charles F. Ayer, Benjamin P. Cheney, Montgomery Rollins, Boston; William K. Gillett, A. Kessler, John P. Cobb, G. Dunscomb, New York; Wilbur F. Day, New Haven, Conn.; Kenneth K. McLaren, Jersey City; E. W. Rollins, Denver; A. Jarvis, Toronto.

Main office, 54 Wall street, New York. Annual meeting, fourth Tuesday in February.

## DENVER, NORTHWESTERN & PACIFIC RAILWAY CO.

A corporation formed under the laws of Colorado, in July, 1902.

Road projected about 500 miles from Denver, Col., to Salt Lake City, Utah. A contract for the construction of the line was given to Colorado-Utah Construction Co., and it is expected that the road will be completed in two years.

Stock..Par $100...Authorized { com., $10,000,000 / pref., 10,000,000 } Issued { com., $10,000,000 / pref., 10,000,000 } $20,000,000

The preferred stock is 5 per cent. non-cumulative.

FUNDED DEBT.

| | |
|---|---|
| 1st mort., 4 per cent., due 1952 | $20,000,000 |

The 1st mortgage is for $22,500,000. Trustee of the mortgage, Mercantile Trust Co., New York. The $20,000,000 of bonds were placed by subscription in 1902.

The contract with the Colorado-Utah Construction Co. provides that it shall receive $40,000 in 1st mortgage bonds, $20,000 in common and $20,000 in preferred stock, for each mile of road.

President, David H. Moffatt, Denver.

Directors—David H. Moffatt, Walter Cheeseman, Charles Hughes, Jr., S. M. Perry, Frank B. Gibson, George E. Ross-Lewin, William G. Evans, Denver.

Main office, Denver.

## DES MOINES & FORT DODGE RAILROAD CO.

(Leased to Chicago, Rock Island & Pacific.)

Road owned, Des Moines, Ia., to Fort Dodge, 88 miles; extension, Tara to Ruthven, Ia., 56 miles; total, 144 miles; 5 miles, Tara to Fort Dodge, trackage leased.

Stock...Par $100....Authorized { com., $4,283,000 / pref., 763,500 } Issued { com., $4,283,000 / pref., 763,500 } $5,046,500

Preferred stock is 7 per cent., non-cumulative, and is entitled to an equal share in any profits after 7 per cent. has been paid on common stock.

Dividends of 6 per cent. were paid on the preferred from 1896 to 1898 inclusive. In 1899, 1900, 1901 and 1902, paid 7 per cent. on preferred. The preferred dividends are paid annually, August 1.

Transfer Agent, George T. Boggs, 13 William street, New York. Registrar, Central Trust Co., New York.

FUNDED DEBT.

| | |
|---|---|
| 1st mort., Series A, 4 per cent., due Jan., 1905, Jan. and July | $1,200,000 |
| 1st mort., Series B, 2½ per cent., due Jan., 1905, Jan. and July | 1,200,000 |
| Extension bonds, 4 per cent., due Jan., 1905, Jan. and July | 672,000 |
| Total | $3,072,000 |

In January, 1888, holders of the 1st mortgage, Series A, agreed to accept reduction of interest from 6 per cent. to 4 per cent., the extension bonds also being reduced from 6 to 4 per cent. The 1st mortgage, Series B, bonds, originally an income bond entitled to 6 per cent. when earned, was likewise reduced to 2½ per cent. and interest guaranteed. The road was at the same time leased from January 1, 1887, for eighteen years or until January 1, 1905, to the Chicago, Rock Island & Pacific Railway Co., which guarantees 4 per cent. on the 1st mortgage, Series A, and extension bonds, and 2½ per cent. on the 1st mortgage, Series B, bonds. The annual rental is 30 per cent. of the gross earnings.

EARNINGS.

| | Rentals, etc. | Int. and Exp's. | Net Income. | Dividends. | Surplus. |
|---|---|---|---|---|---|
| 1893 | $138,809 | $105,361 | $33,448 | $15,244 | $18,204 |
| 1894 | 143,642 | 109,994 | 33,648 | 30,492 | 3,156 |
| 1895 | 155,915 | 106,202 | 49,713 | 30,504 | 19,209 |
| 1896 | 155,643 | 106,029 | 49,614 | 45'756 | 3,858 |
| 1897 | 155,515 | 105,718 | 49,797 | 45,756 | 4,041 |
| 1898 | 162,249 | 106,083 | 56,166 | 45,756 | 10,410 |
| 1899 | 179,220 | 105,939 | 73,281 | 53,382 | 19,899 |
| 1900 | 191,619 | 106,084 | 85,535 | 53,382 | 32,153 |
| 1901 | 210,537 | 105,945 | 104,592 | 53,396 | 51,196 |

President, Charles N. Gilmore; Secretary, Carroll Wright, Des Moines; Treasurer, F. E. Hayne, Chicago.

Main office, Des Moines. Annual meeting, first Thursday in June.

## DES MOINES UNION RAILWAY CO.

A corporation formed under the laws of Iowa in January, 1884. The company owns in the city of Des Moines 25 acres of real estate, 5 miles of main track and 13 miles of second track sidings and yard track, a bridge across the Des Moines River, passenger and freight depots and other buildings. Its terminal facilities at Des Moines are rented by the Chicago, Milwaukee & St. Paul Railway Co., the Wabash Railroad Co., Chicago Great Western Railway Co., Chicago, Burlington & Quincy Railway Co. and Des Moines, Iowa Falls & Northern Railway Co.

Stock......Par $100..........................Authorized, $2,000,000......Issued, $400,000

Stock is transferred at the office of the company, Des Moines.

FUNDED DEBT.

| | |
|---|---|
| 1st mort., 5 per cent. bonds, due Nov., 1917, May and Nov. | $671,000 |

The amount of bonds authorized is $800,000. Trustee of the mortgage and agent for the payment of interest, Central Trust Co., New York.

The companies using the terminals pay as rental a sum equal to the interest on the outstanding bonds and the expenses of operation. In the fiscal year 1901 the interest was $34,750; taxes, $13,639; operating expenses, $161,376; total, $209,765.

President, F. C. Hubbell; Vice-President and Treasurer, H. D. Thompson; Secretary, F. M. Hubbell, Des Moines, Ia.

Directors—F. C. Hubbell, F. M. Hubbell, H. D. Thompson, A. B. Cumins, Cyrus Kirk, Des Moines, Ia.; J. Ramsey, Jr., New York; A. J. Earling, H. R. Williams, Chicago.

Main office, Des Moines, Ia. Annual meeting, first Thursday in January, at Des Moines.

## DETROIT & MACKINAC RAILROAD CO.

Road owned, Bay City to Tower, Mich., 174 miles; branches, 155 miles; total, 329 miles. Extensions to Mackinaw and Cheboygan are contemplated. System includes a number of temporary lumbering branches. Locomotives, 28; passenger cars, 26; freight cars, 1,061; service cars, 31.

Stock....Par $100.....Authorized { com., $2,000,000; pref., 1,000,000 } Issued { com., $2,000,000; pref., 950,000 } $2,950,000

Preferred stock may only be issued in exchange for mortgage bonds. In February, 1902, $750,000 of these bonds were converted into preferred stock.

Transfer Agents, J. P. Morgan & Co., New York. Registrar, Morton Trust Co., New York.

FUNDED DEBT.

1st lien bonds, 4 per cent., due June, 1995, June and Dec............................ $1,500,000
Mort. bonds, 4 per cent., due June, 1995, June and Dec............................ 1,250,000

Total ............................................................ $2,750,000

Originally Detroit, Bay City & Alpena, which road had several additional branches for lumbering purposes, which have been abandoned. In December, 1892, Drexel, Morgan & Co., New York, asked co-operation of bondholders in view of possible default. Default occurred on interest due July 1, 1893, and in November, 1893, Receiver was appointed on application of Farmers' Loan & Trust Co., Trustee of mortgage. In 1895 reorganization under present title was effected.

EARNINGS.

Year ending June 30.

| | Gross. | Net. | Charges. | Surplus. |
|---|---|---|---|---|
| 1895-96 | $434,462 | $131,070 | $105,362 | $25,708 |
| 1896-97 | 406,681 | 101,943 | 123,917 | Def. 21,975 |
| 1897-98 | 481,468 | 177,200 | 126,545 | 50,655 |
| 1898-99 | 601,440 | 203,899 | 118,160 | 72,630 |
| 1899-00 | 833,619 | 278,767 | 122,000 | 108,649 |
| 1900-01 | 865,747 | 275,362 | 160,918 | 114,443 |
| 1901-02 | 862,191 | 281,900 | 163,176 | 118,723 |

The total balance to credit of profit and loss June 30, 1902, was $558,470.

President and General Manager, James D. Hawks; Vice-President, George M. Crocker, Detroit; Secretary, A. H. Gillard, New York; Treasurer, J. H. Emanuel, Jr., New York.

Directors—Henry K. McHarg, Edward H. Bonner, Amedee D. Morgan, Walton Ferguson, New York; James D. Hawks, Detroit.

Main office, Detroit. Annual meeting, last Tuesday in October.

## DETROIT, GRAND HAVEN & MILWAUKEE RAILWAY CO.

Road owned, Detroit to Grand Haven, Mich., 189 miles. Locomotives, 21; passenger cars, 38; freight cars, 440.

The Grand Trunk of Canada owns the entire stock of the company and guarantees the principal and interest of the bonds.

Stock......Par $50............................Authorized, $1,500,000......Issued, $1,500,000

FUNDED DEBT.

1st mort. equipment, 6 per cent., due Nov., 1918, April and Oct..................... $2,000,000
Consolidated mort., 6 per cent, due Nov., 1918, April and Oct..................... 3,200,000

Total ............................................................ $5,200,000

Company has land mortgage of $146,000. The Grand Trunk provided for deficits to December 31, 1901, to the amount of $1,847,535. The company had a floating debt of $354,866 at the same date.

EARNINGS.

| | Gross. | Net. | Charges. | Deficit. |
|---|---|---|---|---|
| 1895 | $1,001,091 | $101,648 | $365,932 | $264,284 |
| 1896 | 964,357 | 93,743 | 371,010 | 277,266 |
| 1897 | 1,029,679 | 257,061 | 365,386 | 108,325 |
| 1898 | 938,232 | 238,359 | 365,686 | 127,327 |
| 1899 | 1,002,876 | 278,166 | 362,261 | 84,094 |
| 1900 | 1,006,323 | 225,599 | 363,427 | 137,848 |
| 1901 | 1,077,220 | 283,269 | 362,499 | 79,229 |

President and General Manager, Charles M. Hays, Montreal; Secretary and Treasurer, James H. Muir, Detroit.

Directors—Charles M. Hays, Frank W. Morse, F. H. McGuigan, John W. Loud, Joseph Hobson, Montreal; Elijah W. Meddaugh, A. P. Sherrill, John Pridgeon, Jr., W. J. Spicer, Detroit.

Main office, Detroit. Annual meeting, first Monday in October.

## DETROIT SOUTHERN RAILROAD CO.

A corporation formed under the laws of Michigan, May 25, 1901, which took over June 1, 1901, the lines of the Detroit & Lima Northern and the Ohio Southern Railroads, both of which roads were foreclosed and acquired by this company.

Road owned, Delray, Mich., to Dundee, Mich., 40 miles; Tecumseh, Mich., to Cornelia, O., 291 miles; Kingman, O., to Sedalia, O., 31 miles; total owned, 362 miles; trackage, 19 miles; total operated, 381 miles. The company enters the city of Detroit from Delray over the tracks of the Union Terminal Railway. Locomotives, 65; passenger cars, 35; freight cars, 4,870.

Stock ..........Authorized { com., $10,500,000 / pref., 6,500,000 } Issued { com., $10,013,000 / pref., 6,000,000 } $16,013,000

The preferred stock is entitled to 4 per cent., non-cumulative, dividends, and after 4 per cent. has been paid in, both preferred and common, both classes of stock share equally in any further division of the profits.

Transfer Agent, Continental Trust Co., New York. Registrar, Knickerbocker Trust Co., New York. Fiscal Agent, Colonial Trust Co., New York.

FUNDED DEBT.

| | |
|---|---|
| 1st mort., 4 per cent., due June, 1951, June and Dec...... .................. | $3,466,000 |
| 1st mort. Ohio Southern Division, 4 per cent., due March, 1941, March and Sept.... | 4,227,000 |
| Car trust notes........................................................... | 255,000 |
| Total ........................................................... | $7,948,000 |

A majority of the common and preferred stocks are held in a voting trust; Frederick J. Lisman, John E. Borne, Evans R. Dick, Cyrus J. Lawrence and Leopold Wallach, trustees. The voting trust is to continue until June 1, 1906, unless the trustees terminate it sooner.

The Detroit Southern Railroad 1st mortgage, Continental Trust Co., New York, trustee, is for $10,000,000. Of this amount $1,250,000 was issued to purchase the Detroit & Lima Northern Railroad, and $1,500,000 to acquire the Ohio & Southern Railroad. Of the remainder $4,500,000 are reserved to take up the Ohio Southern Division 1st mortgage 4s and $2,750,000 are held for the acquisition of additional mileage equipment, etc.

The Ohio Southern Division 1st mortgage, Central Trust Co., New York, trustee, is a purchase-money mortgage covering the lines of the former Ohio Southern Railroad, 224 miles and 51 miles of spurs with equipment. The total amount of the mortgage is $4,500,000, and the issue is redeemable at 105 with interest prior to March 1, 1906. There are $100,000 of the bonds reserved for improvements and $400,000 reserved to take up the equipment trust obligations, the last of which matures in February, 1905.

For the capital funded debts and receiverships of the Detroit & Lima Northern Railway Co. and the Ohio Southern Railroad Co. see the MANUAL for 1901.

The combined net earnings of both the old roads for 1899-00 were $301,666, and for 1900-01, $289,248.

EARNINGS.

Year ending June 30.

| | Gross. | Net | Charges. | Deficit. |
|---|---|---|---|---|
| 1901-02.............................. | $1,239,905 | $196,795 | $270,000 | $73,204 |

The net earnings are given with taxes deducted for the year.

President, Samuel Hunt, Detroit; Vice-President, Frederick J. Lisman, New York; Secretary-Treasurer, Thomas D. Rhodes; Auditor, W. D. Gray, Detroit; Assistant Secretary, William Goodman, New York.

Directors—John E. Borne, Cyrus J. Lawrence, Evans R. Dick, Leopold Wallach, Simon Borg, Frederick J. Lisman, George Crocker, New York; Samuel Hunt, Don M. Dickinson, William C. McMillan, Thomas D. Rhodes, Benjamin S. Warren, Detroit; A. B. Voorhees, Cincinnati; Myron B. Herrick, Cleveland.

Main office, 96 Griswold street, Detroit. Annual meeting, last Monday in October, at Detroit.

## DOMINION ATLANTIC RAILWAY CO.

A corporation formed under the laws of Novia Scotia.

Road owned, Windsor to Annapolis, N. S., 84 miles; Annapolis to Yarmouth, N. S., 87 miles; branches, 17 miles; operated under agreement, Windsor Branch of the Intercolonial Railway, Windsor, N. S., to Windsor Junction, with running rights over the Intercolonial Railway, Windsor Junction to Halifax, N. S., 32 miles. Total operated, 220 miles. Locomotives, 23; passenger cars, 42; freight cars, 394.

The company is a consolidation as of October 1, 1894, of the Windsor & Annapolis Railway Co. and the Yarmouth & Annapolis Railway Co.

Stock....Par $100.....Authorized { com., $1,119,333 / pref., 1,314,000 } Issued { com., $1,119,333 / pref., 1,314,000 } $2,433,333

The preference stock is 5 per cent., non-cumulative.

FUNDED DEBT.

Debenture bonds, 4 per cent., due Oct., 1944, April and Oct........................ $3,849,533

The authorized amount of bonds is $4,576,666, of which there has been subscribed $4,136,333, the amount given above being that which has been paid in thereon.

EARNINGS.

| Year ending June 30. | Gross. | Net. |
|---|---|---|
| 1901-02 | $1,044,975 | $255,420 |

President, C. Fitch Kemp, London; Vice-President, T. R. Ronald, Welling, Kent, England; General Manager, P. Gifkins; Traffic Superintendent, W. Frazer, Kentville, N. S.; Secretary, R. L. Campbell, London.

Directors—C. Fitch Kemp, London; T. R. Ronald, Welling, Kent, England; A. Denny, Dumbarton, Scotland.

Main office, Kentville, N. S.

## DUBUQUE & SIOUX CITY RAILROAD CO.

(Leased to Illinois Central Railroad Co.)

Road owned, Dubuque, Ia., to Iowa Falls, 143 miles; Iowa Falls to Sioux City, 184 miles; Onawa, Ia., to Sioux Falls, 155 miles; Manchester to Cedar Rapids, 42 miles; Cedar Falls to Minnesota line, 76 miles; Tara, Ia., to Council Bluffs, 130 miles, total operated, 730 miles. The Cedar Falls & Minnesota, formerly leased, was foreclosed and absorbed in 1896. The Omaha extension, Tara to Council Bluffs, was built in 1899.

The Illinois Central Railroad Co. owns practically all of this company's stock, and all of the bonds of the Cherokee & Dakota and the Cedar Rapids & Chicago Railroad Co.

Stock......Par $100........................Authorized, $15,000,000......Issued, $15,000,000

FUNDED DEBT.

Iowa Falls & Sioux City 1st mort., 7 per cent., due Oct., 1917, April and Oct......... $2,800,000

Dividends paid on the stock of the company have been as follows: In the calendar year ended December 31, 1898, 3½ per cent.; in 1899, 1½ per cent.; in 1900, 3 per cent.; in 1901, 3 per cent.; in 1902, 1 per cent.

This property is leased to the Illinois Central Railroad Co., rental being net earnings.

President, Stuyvesant Fish, New York; Vice-President, John C. Welling, Chicago; 2d Vice-President, E. C. Woodruff, Elizabeth, N. J.; Treasurer, Edmund T. H. Gibson, New York; Secretary, J. F. Merry, Dubuque, Ia.; Assistant Secretary, Charles H. Wenman, New York.

Main office, Dubuque, Ia. Annual meeting, Monday after fourth Wednesday in September.

## DULUTH & IRON RANGE RAILROAD CO.

(Controlled by United States Steel Corporation.)

Road owned, Duluth, Minn., via Two Harbors, to Ely, Minn., 119 miles; branches to mines, 65 miles; total, 184 miles. Locomotives, 70; passenger cars, 14; freight cars, 3,613.

Stock......Par $100........................Authorized, $10,000,000......Issued, $3,000,000

FUNDED DEBT.

1st mort., 5 per cent., due Oct., 1937, April and Oct.............................. $6,732,000
2d mort., 6 per cent., due Jan., 1916, Jan. and July.............................. 4,500,000

Total........................................................... $11,232,000

All the stock and $3,500,000 of the 2d mortgage bonds were owned by the Minnesota Iron Co., and by the purchase of its stock by the Federal Steel Co. the latter acquired control, which passed with the ownership of the Federal Steel's stock when it was acquired by the United States Steel Corporation. The second mortgage bonds were created in 1896 and are $5,000,000 authorized, $3,500,000 were issued to retire 6 per cent. income certificates and $1,000,000 for improvements. They are subject to call at 105. The land grant mortgage bonds created in 1897 have been retired.

EARNINGS.

Year ending June 30.

| | Gross. | Net. | Charges. | Surplus. |
|---|---|---|---|---|
| 1891-92 | $1,558,568 | $873,398 | $230,642 | $642,756 |
| 1892-93 | 1,227,073 | 634,224 | 255,564 | 378,660 |
| 1893-94 | 1,516,836 | 799,588 | 275,952 | 523,636 |
| 1894-95 | 2,205,455 | 1,209,851 | 290,202 | 919,648 |
| 1895-96 | 1,973,840 | 879,426 | 554,053 | 325,373 |
| 1896-97 | 2,644,539 | 1,182,270 | 574,384 | 607,886 |
| 1897-98 | 2,818,889 | 1,027,212 | 575,828 | 451,384 |
| 1898-99 | 3,036,450 | 1,583,065 | 606,600 | 976,465 |
| 1899-00 | 4,488,303 | 606,600 | 1,570,214 | 1,570,214 |
| 1900-01 | 4,200,581 | 2,318,473 | 993,578 | 1,324,895 |

President, F. E. House; Vice-President, A. H. Viele, Duluth, Minn.; Secretary and Treasurer, Charles P. Coffin, Chicago.

Main office, Duluth, Minn. Annual meeting, first Monday after first Wednesday in June.

## DULUTH, MISSABE & NORTHERN RAILWAY CO.

(Controlled by United States Steel Corporation.)

Road owned, Duluth to Mountain Iron, Minn., 77 miles; branches, 76 miles; trackage, 2 miles; total operated, 155 miles. Locomotives, 43; passenger cars, 9; freight cars, 3,850.

This road was built by the Lake Superior Consolidated Iron Mines, which corporation holds all the stock and a large part of the bonds. The United States Steel Corporation in 1901 obtained control of the Lake Superior Consolidated Iron Mines, and, consequently, of this company as well.

Stock......Par $100..........................Authorized, $5,000,000......Issued, $2,512,500

FUNDED DEBT.

| | |
|---|---|
| 1st mort., 6 per cent., due Jan., 1922, Jan. and July | $1,174,000 |
| 1st con. mort., 6 per cent., due Jan., 1923, Jan. and July | 1,850,000 |
| 2d mort., 5 per cent., due 1918, Jan. and July | 4,658,000 |
| Total | $7,682,000 |

The 1st consolidated mortgage is for $3,500,000 and the 2d mortgage is $5,000,000 in amount. The trustee is the Central Trust Co., New York, which pays the coupons of this company's bonds.

EARNINGS.

Year ending June 30.

| | Gross. | Net. | Charges. | Surplus. |
|---|---|---|---|---|
| 1899-00 | $3,640,313 | $2,110,462 | $659,373 | $1,451,089 |
| 1900-01 | ...... | ........ | ........ | ........ |
| 1901-02 | 3,755,416 | 1,307,556 | 762,630 | 544,926 |

President, William J. Olcott; Secretary, E. B. Ryan; Treasurer, Edward S. Kempton Duluth, Minn.

Main office, Duluth, Minn.

## DULUTH, SOUTH SHORE & ATLANTIC RAILWAY CO.

(Controlled by Canadian Pacific.)

Road owned, Sault Ste. Marie to West Superior, 408 miles; "Soo" Junction to St. Ignace 43 miles; Marquette, Mich., to Winthrop Junction, 17 miles; Nestoria to Houghton, Mich., 48 miles; branches, 47 miles; total 563 miles; trackage, 9½ miles; total operated, 575 miles. Locomotives, 91; passenger cars, 58; freight cars, 2,664.

The company purchased the Detroit, Mackinac & Marquette, sold in foreclosure in October, 1886. In December, 1886, bought the stock of the Marquette, Houghton & Ontonagon, and leased the property in perpetuity, February, 1887, but lease was rescinded and property of Marquette, Houghton & Ontonagon was bought in 1890.

Stock..Par $100...Authorized { com., $12,000,000 / pref., 10,000,000 }  Issued { com., $12,000,000 / pref., 10,000,000 } $22,000,000

The preferred stock is 6 per cent., non-cumulative.

Stock is transferred at the office of the company, 44 Wall street, New York. Registrar, Central Trust Co., New York.

FUNDED DEBT.

| | |
|---|---|
| 1st mort. ($12,000 per mile), 5 per cent., due Jan., 1937, Jan. and July | $3,816,000 |
| 1st con. 4 per cent. bonds, gold, due Aug., 1990, Feb. and Aug | 15,107,000 |
| Income ctfs., 4 per cent., due Dec., 1912 | 3,000,000 |
| Marquette, H. & O. 1st mort., 6 per cent., due 1925, April and Oct | 1,077,000 |
| Total | $23,000,000 |

There are also car trusts outstanding for about $323,000.

In 1887 a controlling interest in the company was acquired by the Canadian Pacific. The Canadian Pacific owns $5,100,000 preferred and $6,100,000 common stock. It guarantees interest on the consolidated 4 per cent. bonds of this company, and holds entire issue of same which are pledged among the collaterals for its debenture stock.

The issue of $20,000,000 of 4 per cent. bonds is guaranteed, principal and interest, by the Canadian Pacific. In 1892-93, the Marquette, Houghton & Ontonagon 8s and 6s were retired by an issue of consolidated 4s.

EARNINGS.

| | Gross. | Net. | Charges. | | Surplus. |
|---|---|---|---|---|---|
| 1893 | $2,088,913 | $571,312 | $870,166 | Def. | $298,854 |
| 1894 | 1,650,989 | 536,511 | 870,950 | " | 334,439 |
| 1895 | 1,811,823 | 704,794 | 893,121 | " | 188,327 |
| 1896 | 1,872,983 | 665,071 | 861,955 | " | 196,884 |
| 1897 | 1,549,465 | 505,967 | 868,122 | " | 362,155 |
| 1898 | 1,817,887 | 561,425 | 859,617 | " | 298,192 |
| 1899 | 2,407,437 | 889,827 | 875,768 | Sur. | 14,059 |
| 1900 | 2,557,973 | 855,590 | 859,700 | Def. | 4,110 |
| 1901-02 (year ending June 30) | 2,690,569 | 880,028 | 859,700 | Sur. | 20,327 |

President, William F. Fitch, Marquette, Mich.; 1st Vice-President, Sir Thomas G. Shaughnessy, Montreal; 2d Vice-President, George H. Church; Secretary, Arthur Starke, New York; Treasurer, E. W. Allen, Marquette, Mich.

Directors—E. V. Skinner, George H. Church, T. W. Pearsall, John W. Sterling, James O. Bloss, R. Y. Hebden, New York; Lord Strathcona and Mount Royal, London; Sir William C. Van Horne, Richard B. Angus, Sir Thomas G. Shaughnessy, Montreal; William F. Fitch, Marquette, Mich.

Main office, Marquette, Mich.; New York office, 44 Wall street. Annual meeting, third Thursday in September, at Marquette.

## EASTERN KENTUCKY RAILWAY CO.

A corporation formed under the the laws of Kentucky in 1870. Road owned, Riverton, Ky., to Webb, Ky., 36 miles. Locomotives, 4; passenger cars, 4; freight cars, 48.

The company has extensive real estate and mineral interests.

Stock...Par $100....Authorized { com., $10,000,000; pref., 3,000,000 } Issued { com., $1,667,800; pref., 1,779,500 } $3,447,300

The preferred stock is non-cumulative. Stock is transferred at the office of the Secretary and Treasurer.

The company has no funded debt.

In the year ending June 30, 1901, the gross earnings were $56,789, net $9,381; in 1901-02, gross $50,603, net $6,615. The net includes income from other sources.

President, Nathaniel Thayer, Boston; Vice-President, Sturgis G. Bates, Riverton, Ky.; Secretary and Treasurer, Edward B. Townsend, Boston.

Directors—Nathaniel Thayer, E. V. R. Thayer, Charles Merriam, H. H. Hunnewell, Edward B. Townsend, Boston; Edward F. Ripley, Cohasset, Mass.; Sturgis G. Bates, Riverton, Ky.

Main office, Riverton, Ky.; Secretary and Treasurer's office, 27 Kilby street, Boston. Annual meeting, first Wednesday in February.

## ELGIN, JOLIET & EASTERN RAILWAY CO.

(Controlled by United States Steel Corporation.)

Road owned, Waukegan, Ill., to Porter, Ind., 130 miles; Normantown, Ill., to Aurora, Ill., 10 miles; Walker to Coster, Ill., 33 miles; other branches, 19½ miles; spurs to mines and quarries, 20 miles; total owned, 212½ miles; trackage over Chicago & Western Indiana, and Belt Railway of Chicago, 7 miles; side tracks and yards, 104 miles; total operated, 323½ miles.

Company also owns extensive terminals and wharf property on the Calumet river, at South Chicago. Locomotives, 56; passenger cars, 3; freight cars, 1,981.

The lines of the company form an outer belt road around the city of Chicago, crossing and connecting with all railroads centering there.

In 1898 the Federal Steel Company acquired all the stock of the company, giving in exchange for each share of Elgin, Joliet & Eastern, on payment of $17.50, Federal Steel common stock for $70 and preferred for $87.50. The control of the Federal Steel Co. being acquired in 1901 by the United States Steel corporation, this property was included.

Stock .....Par $100........... ..............Authorized, $6,000,000......Issued, $6,000,000

FUNDED DEBT.

1st mort., 5 per cent., due May, 1941, May and Nov.................................... $8,500,000

The authorized amount of the 1st mortgage is $10,000,000; the balance of bonds can be issued for improvement or additional property only. Trustee of mortgage, Central Trust Co., New York. Interest is paid at the office of the United States Steel Corporation, 71 Broadway, New York.

EARNINGS.

Year ending June 30.

| | Gross. | Net. | Charges. | Surplus. |
|---|---|---|---|---|
| 1893-94 | $1,020,326 | $320,461 | $303,950 | $16,511 |
| 1894-95 | 1,080,685 | 349,934 | 335,418 | 14,516 |
| 1895-96 | 1,292,421 | 446,115 | 345,873 | 100,242 |
| 1896-97 | 1,184,646 | 412,581 | 356,329 | 56,252 |
| 1897-98 | 1,390,694 | 488,927 | 370,699 | 118,228 |
| 1898-99 | 1,674,342 | 686,412 | 376,915 | 309,497 |
| 1899-00 | 1,923,173 | 820,378 | 387,940 | 432,438 |
| 1900-01 | 2,041,516 | 760,810 | 392,600 | 377,210 |
| 1091-02 | 2,178,484 | 815,025 | 404,544 | 377,208 |

President, Alexander F. Banks; Secretary and Treasurer, Frederick D. Raymond, Chicago. Main office, 217 La Salle St., Chicago. Annual meeting, second Wednesday in June.

## EL PASO & SOUTH WESTERN RAILROAD CO.

A corporation formed in 1901, under the laws of Arizona. The company acquired a number of lines constructed by Phelps, Dodge & Co., of New York, for the purpose of affording an outlet for their various mining enterprises in the territory served by the roads. The El Paso Terminal Railroad Co. is controlled.

Road owned and operated, El Paso, Tex., to Benson, Ariz., 350 miles, with branches to Deming, N. M.; Douglas, Ariz.; Bisbee, Ariz.; Tombstone, Ariz., and other points. An extension into Mexico was in progress in 1902.

Stock......Par $100.........................Authorized, $7,000,000......Issued, $7,000,000

It is understood that this company has no funded debt.

President, James Douglas; Vice-President, Arthur C. James; Secretary, George Notman; Treasurer, Cleveland H. Dodge, New York.

Main office, 99 John street, New York; operating office, El Paso, Tex.

## ERIE & CENTRAL NEW YORK RAILROAD CO.

A corporation formed under the laws of New York, May 26, 1902. It acquired the property of the railway company of the same name, which was foreclosed in March, 1902. Road owned, Cortland, N. Y., to Cincinnatus, N. Y., 18 miles. Locomotives, 3; passenger cars, 3; freight cars, 6.

Stock......Par $100.............................Authorized, $250,000......Issued, $250,000

Stock is transferred at the company's office, New York.

FUNDED DEBT.

1st mort., 5 per cent., due May, 1922, May and Nov.................................. $250,000

Trustee of the mortgage, Trust Co. of America, New York.

President, William W. Montgomery, New York; Vice-President, L. N. Frederick, Cortland, N. Y.; Secretary and Treasurer, Sylvester J. O'Sullivan, New York.

Directors—William W. Montgomery, Sylvester J. O'Sullivan, Leonidas Dennis, W. C. Schryver, G. S. Terry, James P. Wright, C. W. Young, Thomas J. McGuire, W. H. Conroy, New York; L. N. Frederick, W. G. Tisdale, Irving N. Palmer, Cortland, N. Y.; Charles O. Scull, Baltimore.

Main office, Cortland, N. Y.; New York office, 140 Broadway. Annual meeting, second Monday in January.

## ERIE & PITTSBURG RAILROAD CO.

(Leased to the Pennsylvania Company.)

Road owned, Newcastle to Girard, Pa., 81 miles; branch, 3 miles; trackage, Girard to Erie, 17 miles; total operated, 101 miles. Locomotives, 29; passenger cars, 9; freight cars, 1,551.

The property is leased for 999 years from March 1, 1870, to the Pennsylvania Company for interest on the bonds and 7 per cent. on the stock.

Stock......Par $50..........................Authorized, $2,000,000......Issued, $2,000,000

Transfer Agent, Union Trust Co., New York.

The guaranteed dividends under the lease are paid quarterly, 1¾ per cent. each, in March (1) June, September and December.

FUNDED DEBT.

Gen. mort., 3½ per cent., due July, 1940, Jan. and July........................ ... $3,918,000

The 3½ per cent. general mortgage bonds are guaranteed by the Pennsylvania Railroad Co.

EARNINGS.

| | Gross. | Net. | Rental. | Result to Lessee. |
|---|---|---|---|---|
| 1895 | $1,022,217 | $414,234 | $406,759 | Profit $7,524 |
| 1896 | 804,829 | 79,503 | 401,258 | Loss. 321,755 |
| 1897 | 884,298 | 317,118 | 395,950 | " 78,831 |
| 1898 | 817,866 | 224,323 | 362,290 | " 137,966 |
| 1899 | 1,055,717 | 352,423 | 319,550 | Profit 32,873 |
| 1900 | 1,085,051 | 432,469 | 314,280 | " 118,216 |
| 1901 | 1,439,327 | 624,791 | 317,293 | " 307,498 |
| 1902 | 1,626,751 | 576,641 | 322,500 | " 254,141 |

President, Charles H. Strong; Vice-President, Matthew H. Taylor; Secretary and Treasurer, John P. Smart, Erie, Pa.

Directors—Matthew H. Taylor, George R. Metcalf, Charles H. Strong, Erie; John P. Green, Philadelphia; C. S. Fairchild, New York; James McCrea, Pittsburg; J. J. Spearman, Sharon, Pa.

Main office, Erie. Annual meeting, second Monday in January.

---

## ERIE RAILROAD CO.

A corporation formed under the laws of New York, November 13, 1895, as successor to the New York, Lake Erie & Western Railroad Co. The latter was sold under foreclosure November 6, 1895, in accordance with reorganization plan and property transferred to this company, which took possession December 1, 1895.

Road owned or controlled by ownership of entire stock: Main line, old New York, Lake Erie & Western and branches, old New York, Pennsylvania & Ohio Railroad and branches owned, and Chicago & Erie Railroad, 1,644 miles; controlled by ownership of a majority of stock, 158 miles; leased, 292 miles; trackage, 58 miles; total operated, 2,154 miles. Controlled or leased but not operated, 55 miles; restricted trackage, 109 miles: total of system, 2,318 miles. Also controls by stock ownership the New York, Susquehanna & Western Railroad, 238 miles, as well as the properties of the Hillsdale Coal & Iron Co., Blossburg Coal Co. and Northwestern Mining & Exchange Co., representing 10,500 acres of anthracite and 53,000 acres of bituminous coal lands in fee, and 14,000 acres under mineral rights. In 1901 acquired the whole capital stock of the Pennsylvania Coal Co. Also owns the Union Steamboat Co., with fleet of 8 lake steamers. The company also has a one-fifth ownership in the Chicago & Western Indiana Railroad Co. A steam ferry between New York and Jersey City is owned.

Locomotives, 1,154; passenger cars 951; freight cars, 52,592; service cars, 695. Also 8 ferryboats and numerous steamboats, tugs and barges. The equipment includes locomotives and cars held under car-trust agreements.

The New York, Lake Erie & Western Railroad Co. leased the New York, Pennsylvania & Ohio Railroad Co. (Salamanca, N. Y., to Cleveland and Dayton, O.). It also leased the Chicago & Erie. Under the reorganization plan the mortgages on the New York, Pennsylvania & Ohio were foreclosed and that road was reorganized as the Nypano Railroad Co., subject to $8,000,000 prior lien bonds of old company. All the stock and bonds of Nypano company were transferred to this company. The Erie company also owns the entire stock of Chicago & Erie. Under the reorganization during 1896 a number of branch lines were amalgamated with this company either by merger or acquisition of their capital stock, including the Buffalo & Southwestern Railroad, Buffalo, New York & Erie, etc. The company also controls the New Jersey & New York Railroad, 48 miles, which is operated by its own management. The New York & Greenwood Lake Railway, 51 miles, is leased for rental equal to its fixed charges and in 1899 the Northern Railroad of New Jersey, 26 miles, which was operated under contract, was leased and 4 per cent. guaranteed on its $1,000,000 of stock. In January, 1898, the control of the New York, Susquehanna & Western system was acquired and the preferred stock of that company at 90 was exchanged for Erie 1st preferred and the common stock at par for Erie common. To carry out this purchase the Erie 1st preferred stock was increased in March, 1898, from $30,000,000 to $43,000,000 and the common from $100,000,000 to $113,000,000.

In January, 1901, the company purchased from J. P. Morgan & Co. the entire capital stock of the Pennsylvania Coal Co. The company paid for this acquisition $32,000,000 in its collateral trust fifty-year 4 per cent. gold bonds and $5,000,000 in 1st preferred stock, the latter being increased by the amount in question for the purpose.

| Stock........Authorized | com., | $113,000,000 | Issued | com., | $112,378,900 | $176,271,300 |
|---|---|---|---|---|---|---|
| | 1st pref., | 48,000,000 | | 1st pref., | 47,892,400 | |
| | 2d pref., | 16,000,000 | | 2d pref., | 16,000,000 | |

The 1st preferred stock is 4 per cent., non-cumulative. The 2d preferred is also 4 per cent., non-cumulative, subject to the prior rights of the 1st preferred. Both classes of preferred can be retired at par at the company's option.

The company's entire stock is held in a voting trust for 5 years, or until 1st preferred receives 4 per cent. in a year. Trustees, J. Pierpont Morgan, Louis Fitzgerald, New York, and Sir Charles Tennant, Bart., London.

Transfer Agents, J. P. Morgan & Co., New York. Registrar, Mercantile Trust Co., New York.

The first dividend declared by the reorganized company was 1½ per cent. on the 1st preferred stock, paid August 30, 1901. Semi-annual dividends of 1½ per cent. each were also paid on the 1st preferred, February 28, 1902, and August 30, 1902.

### Funded Debt.

| | |
|---|---|
| Erie Ry., 1st mort., extended in 1897, 4 per cent., due May, 1947, May and Nov.... | $2,482,000 |
| " 2d mort., extended, 5 per cent., due Sept., 1919, March, and Sept.......... | 2,149,000 |
| " 3d mort., extended, 4½ per cent., due March, 1923, March and Sept........ | 4,617,000 |
| " 4th mort., extended, 5 per cent, due Oct., 1920. April and Oct.............. | 2,926,000 |
| " 5th mort., extended, 4 per cent., due June. 1928, June and Dec........... | 709,500 |
| Buffalo Branch mort., 4 per cent., due July 1931, Jan. and July.................... | 182,600 |
| 1st consolidated mort., 7 per cent., due Sept., 1920, March and Sept................ | 16,891,000 |
| N. Y., L. E. & W. R. R., 1st cons. mort., 7 per cent., due Sept., 1920, March and Sept. | 3,699,500 |
| Newburgh & New York Railroad mort., 5 per cent. due Jan., 1929, Jan. and July.. | 250,000 |
| Bergen County Railroad, 1st mort., 6 per cent., due April, 1911, April and Oct.. ... | 200,000 |
| N. Y., L. E. & W. Coal & R. R., 1st mort., 6 per cent., due May, 1922, May and Nov. | 1,100,000 |
| Elmira State Line Railroad, 1st mort., 7 per cent., due Oct., 1905, April and Oct.... | 160,000 |
| Long Dock bonds, 6 per cent., due Oct., 1935, April and Oct ...................... | 7,500,000 |
| Chicago & Erie, 1st mort., 5 per cent., due May, 1982, May and Nov.............. | 12,000,000 |
| Chicago & Atl. Terminal, 1st mort., 5 per cent., due July, 1918, Jan. and July...... | 300,000 |
| New York, Pa. & Ohio, prior lien, 4½ per cent., due March, 1935. March and Sept.. | 8,000,000 |
| Buffalo, New York & Erie, 1st mort., 7 per cent., due June, 1916, June and Dec.... | 2,380,000 |
| Jefferson R. R., 1st mort., 5 per cent., due Jan., 1909, Jan. and July................ | 2,800,000 |
| N. Y., L. E. & W. Docks and Impt. mort., 6 per cent., due July, 1913, Jan. and July. | 3,396,000 |
| Buffalo & Southwestern, 1st mort., 6 per cent., due July, 1908, Jan. and July....... | 1,500,000 |
| Tioga Railroad, 1st mort., 5 per cent., due Nov., 1915, May and Nov.............. | 239,500 |
| " extension mort., 7 per cent., due Oct., 1905, April and Oct......... | 265,000 |
| Honesdale Branch, 1st mort., 4½ per cent., due July, 1927, Jan. and July.......... | 204,000 |
| " 2d mort., 6 per cent., due Jan., 1929, Jan. and July............. | 96,000 |
| Erie Railroad cons. mort., prior lien, 4 per cent., due Jan., 1996, Jan. and July..... | 35,000,000 |
| " " gen. lien bonds, 4 per cent., due Jan., 1996, Jan. and July..... | 35,885,000 |
| " " conv. mort. bonds, 4 per cent., due April, 1953, April and Oct. | 10,000,000 |
| " " Buffalo B. & S. W., 2d lien, 5 per cent., due July, 1908, Jan. and July. | 1,000,000 |
| " " Pa. Coal collateral trust mort., 4 per cent., due Oct., 1951...... | 33,000,000 |
| Total.................................................................... | $188,932,100 |

### Funded Debt of Leased and Controlled Lines.

| | |
|---|---|
| Northern of New Jersey, 3d, now 1st mort., 6 per cent., due Jan., 1917, Jan. and July. | $654,000 |
| " " " gen. mort., guar. 4½ per cent., due Jan., 2000, Jan. and July | 154,000 |
| N.Y. & Greenw'd Lake, prior lien mort., 5 per cent., guar., due May, 1946, May and Nov. | 1,500,000 |
| New Jersey & New York, 1st mort., 6 per cent., due May, 1910, May and Nov....... | 400,000 |
| " " " general mort., 5 per cent., due Jan., 1932, Jan. and July... | 580,000 |
| Cleveland & Mahoning Val., con. 1st mort., 5 per cent., due Jan., 1938, Jan. and July. | 2,935,000 |
| Newcastle & Shenango Valley, 1st mort., 6 per cent., due July, 1917, Jan. and July... | 250,000 |
| Sharon Ry., 1st mort., 4½ per cent., due June, 1918, June and Dec.................. | 164,000 |

The balance sheet of company, June 30, 1902, gives car trusts as follows: New company's, $5,619,454; New York, Lake Erie & Western car trusts, $578,120; New York, Pennsylvania & Ohio car trusts, $1,015,203; total car trusts outstanding, $7,302,777.

See MANUAL for 1896 for old securities retired in reorganization, and MANUAL for 1896 and 1897 for terms of exchange and assessments for old bonds and stock under the plan.

The new first consolidated mortgage was created under the reorganization of 1895, and is for $175,000,000, divided into $35,000,000 prior lien and $140,000,000 3 to 4 per cent. general lien bonds. The latter's first coupon was payable January 1, 1897, and they bore 3 per cent. for two years and 4 per cent. thereafter. Of the prior lien bonds $14,400,000 were delivered as part payment for New York, Pennsylvania & Ohio Railroad, $15,000,000 were sold to a syndicate, and $5,000,000 reserved for improvements and contingencies. Of the general lien bonds $79,918,000 are reserved for ultimate retirement of old bonds and guaranteed stocks left undisturbed, and $17,000,000 for improvements after 1897, at rate of $1,000,000 per annum.

The Northern Railroad of New Jersey in 1899 created a general mortgage of $1,000,000 4½ per cent., of which $804,000 was reserved to retire prior bonds, the balance to be used for improvements and construction.

The collateral trust 4 per cent. mortgage was created in February, 1901, to pay for the acquisition of the Pennsylvania Coal Co. It is secured by a deposit of the majority of the latter's stock and 51 per cent. of the stock of the New York, Susquehanna & Western Railroad Co. The amount of bonds authorized is $36,000,000.

The convertible 4 per cent. bonds were created in 1903. They can be exchanged for common stock at 50 for the latter between April 1, 1905, and April 1, 1915. These bonds, of which the authorized issue is $50,000,000, were created in 1903 in order to provide for improvements and betterments. The stockholders, both common and preferred, were given the right to subscribe for the $10,000,000 issued at 92½.

EARNINGS.

Year ending June 30.

| | Div., 1st Pref. | Gross. | Per Ct. of Exp. | Net. | Income from Investments. | Total Inc. |
|---|---|---|---|---|---|---|
| 1894-95 | .. | $29,207,044 | .... | $6,982,124 | $542,403 | $7,524,527 |
| 1895-96* | .. | 17,017,376 | .... | 4,139,952 | 55,546 | 4,195,498 |
| 1896-97 (2,162 miles) | .. | 31,497,030 | 72.71 | 8,164,788 | 313,513 | 8,478,301 |
| 1897-98 (2,271 miles) | .. | 33,740,860 | 74.08 | 8,302,822 | 413,368 | 8,716,190 |
| 1898-99 ( " " ) | .. | 33,752,703 | 72.79 | 8,582,778 | 557,576 | 9,140,354 |
| 1899-00 ( " " ) | .. | 38,293,031 | 71.04 | 9,844,420 | 420,107 | 10,264,534 |
| 1900-01 ( " " ) | 1½ | 39,103,302 | 72.65 | 10,695,328 | 1,496,077 | 12,191,405 |
| 1901-02 (2,153 " ) | 3 | 40,894,433 | 68.90 | 12,717,833 | 2,485,208 | 14,663,041 |

* Seven months December 1, 1895, to June 30, 1896.

Income from investments in 1901-02 includes $1,702,490 received from the company's coal properties, including the Pennsylvania Coal Co.

The disposition of income for the 8 years has been as follows:

| | Income. | Charges. | Surplus. |
|---|---|---|---|
| 1894-95 | $7,524,527 | $8,637,700 | Def. $1,113,173 |
| 1895-96* | 4,195,498 | 4,043,789 | 151,709 |
| 1896-97 | 8,478,301 | 8,126,282 | 352,018 |
| 1897-98 | 8,716,190 | 8,032,271 | 633,918 |
| 1898-99 | 9,140,354 | 8,486,555 | 653,799 |
| 1899-00 | 10,264,534 | 8,601,104 | 1,663,430 |
| 1900-01 | 12,191,405 | 9,368,249 | 2,823,156 |
| 1901-02 | 14,663,041 | 10,278,364 | 4,384,677 |

* Seven months December 1, 1895, to June 30, 1896.

In the year 1901-02, the dividends of 3 per cent. on the 1st preferred were $1,436,772, and the net surplus $2,947,905.

The following presents the comparative freight traffic statistics of the company:

| | Average Mileage. | Total Tonnage. | Tons Carried One Mile. | Freight Density. | Rate Per Ton Per Mile. | Earnings Per Train Mile. | Average Tons Per Train. |
|---|---|---|---|---|---|---|---|
| 1896-97.. | 2,124 | 20,122,086 | 3,939,679,175 | 1,850,602 | 0.596c | $1.645 | 276 |
| 1897-98.. | 2,124 | 23,643,424 | 4,556,349,307 | 2,143,290 | 0.558 | 1.675 | 300 |
| 1898-99.. | 2,109 | 24,916,944 | 4,834,775,283 | 2,292,449 | 0.517 | 1.636 | 316 |
| 1899-00.. | 2,109 | 26,947,892 | 5,157,955,975 | 2,445,688 | 0.559 | 2.062 | 369 |
| 1900-01. | 2,155 | 25,999,602 | 4,989,381,988 | 2,315,351 | 0.587 | 2.201 | 375 |
| 1901-02.. | 2,153 | 27,697,159 | 4,756,339,949 | 2,209,169 | 0.635 | 2.389 | 376 |

In 1900-01 the tonnage of general freight carried was 13,725,395 tons, and of coal 12,274,207 tons. In 1901-02, general freight was 15,286,081 tons, and coal 12,411,078 tons.

Gross and Net Earnings by Months for Three Years.

| | 1900. | | 1901. | | 1902. | |
|---|---|---|---|---|---|---|
| | Gross. | Net. | Gross. | Net. | Gross. | Net. |
| January | $2,928,710 | $569,987 | $3,189,894 | $849,239 | $3,298,490 | $851,109 |
| February | 2,582,586 | 387,799 | 2,737,101 | 477,603 | 2,752,396 | 508,372 |
| March | 2,998,870 | 732,209 | 3,399,633 | 892,289 | 3,364,923 | 904,794 |
| April | 2,945,682 | 657,911 | 3,247,655 | 738,329 | 3,586,883 | 1,308,443 |
| May | 3,151,117 | 871,613 | 3,641,471 | 1,084,102 | 3,321,228 | 1,091,106 |
| June | 3,332,253 | 827,363 | 3,552,606 | 1,272,557 | 3,247,969 | 1,450,758 |
| July | 3,215,008 | 940,914 | 3,522,693 | 1,152,168 | 3,188,828 | 890,577 |
| August | 3,484,272 | 1,183,933 | 3,830,653 | 1,405,808 | 3,660,866 | 1,226,749 |
| September | 3,118,901 | 810,046 | 3,561,644 | 1,202,273 | 3,511,494 | 1,053,360 |
| October | 3,158,337 | 785,123 | 3,757,161 | 1,118,483 | 3,818,152 | 1,178,477 |
| November | 3,169,524 | 873,414 | 3,545,220 | 1,055,539 | 4,040,135 | 1,397,079 |
| December | 3,187,896 | 787,146 | 3,105,172 | 668,983 | 3,867,873 | 1,287,303 |
| Totals | $37,273,156 | $9,427,458 | $41,090,705 | $11,919,353 | $41,659,237 | $13,148,127 |
| Aver. per month | 3,106,096 | 785,621 | 3,424,225 | 993,279 | 3,471,603 | 1,095,677 |

President, Fred D. Underwood; 1st Vice-President and General Manager, Daniel Willard; 3d Vice-President, H. B. Chamberlain; Secretary, G. A. Richardson; Treasurer, John W. Platten; Auditor, M. P. Blauvelt, New York.

Directors—Samuel Spencer, Francis Lynde Stetson, Abram S. Hewitt, John G. McCullough, Darius O. Mills, Alexander E. Orr, Robert Bacon, Eben B. Thomas, Charles Steele, Hamilton McK. Twombly, James J. Goodwin, Fred D. Underwood, New York; J. Lowber Welsh, Philadelphia; James J. Hill, St. Paul; Norman B. Ream, Chicago.

Main office, 21 Cortlandt street, New York. Annual meeting, second Tuesday in October.

## EUREKA & PALISADE RAILWAY CO.

A corporation formed under the laws of Utah, July 10, 1901. The company is a reorganization of the Eureka & Palisade Railroad Co. and took possession of the property February 1, 1902.

Road owned, Palisade, Nev., to Eureka, Nev., 84 miles. Locomotives, 4; passenger cars, 4; freight cars, 94.

Stock......Par $100..............................Authorized, $300,000......Issued, $300,000

The company has no preferred stock or funded debt. Stock is transferred by the secretary of the company, Palisade, Nev.

A dividend of 4 per cent. was paid on July 1, 1902.

In the last five months of 1902 the company earned, gross $23,717, and net $7,514. Its balance sheet, December 31, 1902, showed a credit to profit and loss of $43,923.

President, M. L. Requa, San Francisco; Secretary and Treasurer, G. D. Abbott, Palisade, Nev.

Directors—M. L. Requa, H. H. Taylor, H. M. J. McMichael, San Francisco; Charles Read, C. L. Rood, Salt Lake City, Utah.

Corporate office, Masonic Block, Salt Lake City, Utah. Annual meeting, first Monday in June.

## EVANSVILLE & INDIANAPOLIS RAILROAD CO.

(Controlled by Evansville & Terre Haute.)

Road owned, Evansville to Terre Haute, Ind., 134 miles; leased, Saline City to Brazil, Ind., 12 miles; total, 146 miles. Consolidation, October, 1885, of Evansville & Indianapolis, Terre Haute & Southeastern, and Evansville, Washington & Brazil.

Stock......Par $100..........................Authorized, $2,000,000......Issued, $2,000,000

Funded Debt.

| | |
|---|---|
| 1st mort. Terre Haute & Southeastern, 7 per cent., due Sept., 1909, March and Sept... | $251,000 |
| 1st mort. guaranteed 6 per cent., due July, 1924, Jan. and July | 647,000 |
| 1st cons. mort., 6 per cent., due Jan., 1926, Jan. and July | 1,602,000 |
| Total | $2,500,000 |

EARNINGS.

Year ending June 30.

| | Gross. | Net. | Charges. | Deficit. |
|---|---|---|---|---|
| 1894-95 | $307,528 | $90,711 | $175,837 | $85,126 |
| 1895-96 | 278,428 | 68,020 | 174,444 | 106,424 |
| 1896-97 | 325,878 | 113,662 | 174,980 | 61,318 |
| 1897-98 | 332,691 | 123,776 | 177,097 | 53,321 |
| 1898-99 | 340,146 | 122,890 | 176,658 | 53,768 |
| 1900-01 | 355,653 | 89,433 | 176,035 | 86,604 |
| 1901-02 | 324,461 | 91,516 | 155,570 | 64,054 |

The bonds are guaranteed by the Evansville & Terre Haute, which owns all the stock.

President, Edwin S. Hooley; Treasurer, Charles A. Nones, New York; Secretary and Assistant Treasurer, Gilbert S. Wright, Evansville, Ind.

Main office, Evansville, Ind.; New York office, 49 Wall street. Annual meeting, third Monday in October.

## EVANSVILLE & TERRE HAUTE RAILROAD CO.

Road owned, Evansville, Ind., to Terre Haute, 109 miles; branches, 71 miles; total owned, 180 miles. The Evansville Belt Railroad, 4½ miles, is operated; the Rockville Branch, 23 miles, is leased to Terre Haute & Logansport Co. and Chicago and Eastern Illinois Railroad Co. jointly; total operated by the company, 161½ miles. Controls the Evansville & Indianapolis, 145 miles. Locomotives, 40; passenger cars, 39; freight cars, 3,501.

Stock....Par $100.....Authorized { com., $4,000,000 / pref., 1,283,333 } Issued { com., $3,987,383 / pref., 1,282,416 } $5,269,799

The preferred stock is 5 per cent., non-cumulative, and possesses no voting power. It was issued in pursuance of a compromise with the bondholders of the Evansville & Richmond Railroad.

Transfer Agents, Edwin S. Hooley & Co., 49 Wall street, New York. Registrar of common stock, Bowling Green Trust Co., New York. Registrar of preferred stock, New York Security & Trust Co., New York.

The directors meet annually in September for the declaration of dividends, though the latter are paid semi-annually on the preferred, April (15) and October. In 1896 and 1897 paid 1 per cent. on the preferred; in the fiscal year 1897-98, 4 per cent.; in 1898-99, 5 per cent. on the preferred and 2 per cent. on the common; in 1899-00, 5 per cent. on the preferred and 3 per cent. on the common, and in 1900-01 and 1901-02, 5 per cent. on the preferred. The dividends on the common were semi-annual, May and November, but after paying 1½ per cent. on the common in May, 1901, the November dividend was passed.

FUNDED DEBT.

| | |
|---|---|
| Consolidated mort., 6 per cent., due July, 1910, Jan. and July | $30,000 |
| 1st consolidated mort., 6 per cent., due July, 1921, Jan. and July | 3,000,000 |
| Gen. mort., 5 per cent., due April, 1942, April and Oct. | 2,223,000 |
| Mount Vernon branch, 6 per cent., due April, 1923, April and Oct. | 375,000 |
| Sullivan County branch mort., 5 per cent., due April, 1930, April and Oct. | 450,000 |
| Total | $6,078,000 |

Company guarantees also $2,500,000 bonds of the Evansville & Indianapolis.

This company guaranteed Evansville & Richmond bonds for $1,400,000, but default occurred on the interest thereof in March, 1894. That property was finally reorganized as the Southern Indiana Railway. See Southern Indiana Railway Co.'s statement in this edition of MANUAL.

There are also outstanding $251,000 7 per cent. bonds, due September, 1909, March and September, of the Terre Haute & Southeastern Railroad Co., one of the proprietary roads.

EARNINGS.

Year ending June 30.

| | Gross. | Net. | Charges. | Surplus. |
|---|---|---|---|---|
| 1894-95 | $1,038,273 | $451,085 | $385,122 | $79,133 |
| 1895-96 | 1,122,797 | 480,355 | 384,693 | 110,765 |
| 1896-97 | 1,003,430 | 464,813 | 385,573 | 79,239 |
| 1897-98 | 1,218,132 | 515,751 | 403,097 | 112,653 |
| 1898-99 | 1,259,434 | 611,619 | 407,221 | 204,398 |
| 1899-00 | 1,392,760 | 658,879 | 408,479 | 250,401 |
| 1900-01 | 1,393,942 | 647,556 | 415,202 | 232,354 |
| 1901-02 | 1,453,659 | 743,708 | 415,652 | 328,086 |

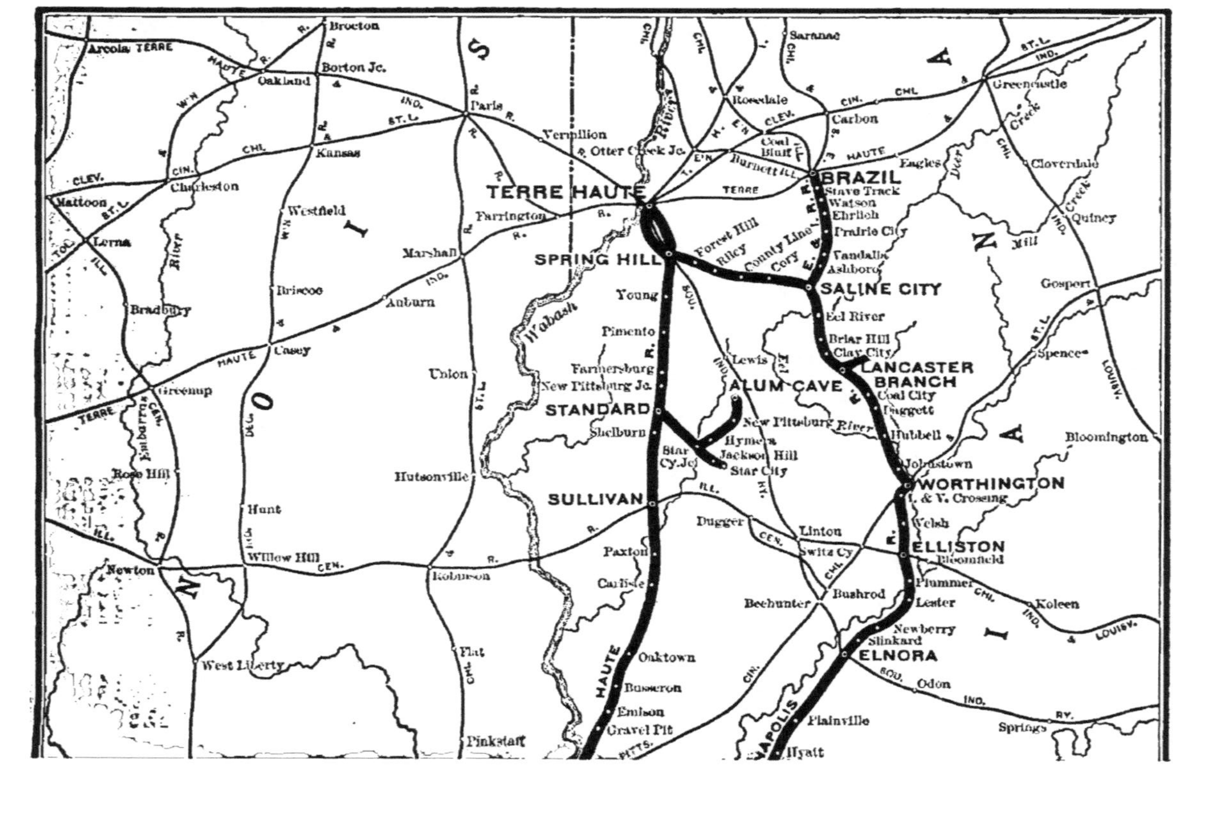
TERRE HAUTE
BRAZIL
SALINE CITY
SPRING HILL
STANDARD
ALUM CAVE
LANCASTER BRANCH
SULLIVAN
WORTHINGTON
ELLISTON
ELNORA
Arcola
Brocton
Oakland
Borton Jc.
Paris
Kansas
Charleston
Mattoon
Lerna
Westfield
Farrington
Marshall
Vermillion
Otter Creek Jc.
Briscoe
Auburn
Bradbury
Casey
Greenup
Union
Hutsonville
Rose Hill
Hunt
Willow Hill
Newton
Robinson
West Liberty
Flat
Pinkstaff
Young
Pimento
Farmersburg
New Pittsburg Jc.
Shelburn
Star Cy. Jc.
Paxton
Carlisle
Oaktown
Busseron
Emison
Gravel Pit
Forest Hill
Riley
County Line
Cory
Lewis
New Pittsburg
Hymera
Jackson Hill
Star City
Dugger
Linton
Switz Cy
Bushrod
Beehunter
Saranac
Rosedale
Carbon
Coal Bluff
Burnett
Stave Track
Watson
Ehrlich
Prairie City
Vandalia
Ashboro
Eel River
Briar Hill
Clay City
Coal City
Daggett
Hubbell
Johnstown
I. & V. Crossing
Welsh
Bloomfield
Plummer
Lester
Newberry
Slinkard
Odon
Plainville
Hyatt
Springs
Koleen
Bloomington
Spencer
Gosport
Quincy
Cloverdale
Greencastle
Eagles
Wabash
Eel
River
Deer
Mill
Creek

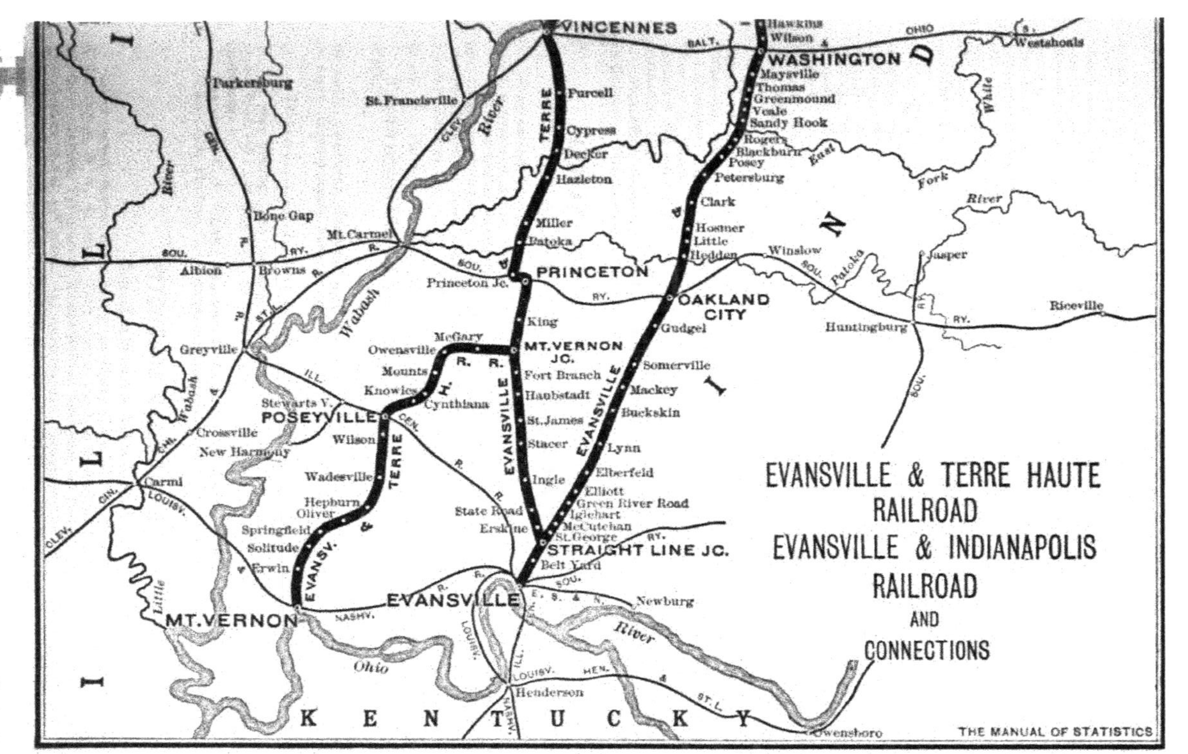
EVANSVILLE & TERRE HAUTE RAILROAD
EVANSVILLE & INDIANAPOLIS RAILROAD
AND CONNECTIONS
THE MANUAL OF STATISTICS
VINCENNES
WASHINGTON
PRINCETON
OAKLAND CITY
MT. VERNON JC.
POSEYVILLE
EVANSVILLE
MT. VERNON
STRAIGHT LINE JC.
Hawkins
Wilson
Maysville
Thomas
Greenmound
Veale
Sandy Hook
Rogers
Blackburn
Posey
Petersburg
Clark
Hosmer
Little
Hedden
Winslow
Gudgel
Somerville
Mackey
Buckskin
Lynn
Elberfeld
Elliott
Green River Road
Iglehart
McCutchan
St. George
Belt Yard
Newburg
Purcell
Cypress
Decker
Hazleton
Miller
Patoka
Princeton Jc.
King
Fort Branch
Haubstadt
St. James
Stacer
Ingle
State Road
Erskine
McGary
Owensville
Mounts
Knowles
Cynthiana
Stewarts V.
Wilson
Wadesville
Hepburn
Oliver
Springfield
Solitude
Erwin
Crossville
New Harmony
Carmi
Greyville
Albion
Browns
Bone Gap
Mt. Carmel
Parkersburg
St. Francisville
Westahoals
Jasper
Huntingburg
Riceville
Henderson
Owensboro
KENTUCKY
Ohio River
Wabash River
White River
East Fork
Patoka
Little Wabash
River

In 1895-96 additional miscellaneous revenues were $15,103, making total surplus $110,765 less deficit of Evansville & Indianapolis, $85,126, reducing surplus of system to $25,638. In 1896-97 dividend of 2 per cent. on preferred stock, $25,080; miscellaneous charges of $3,876 and Evansville & Indianapolis deficit of $106,688 were charges against the surplus, together with the company's accounts against the Evansville & Richmond, which were charged off as valueless. In 1897-98 deficit of $61,317 by the Evansville & Indianapolis reduced the surplus of system to $51,335. In 1898-99, deficit Evansville & Indianapolis, $53,320; net surplus, $151,077. In 1899-1900 Evansville & Terre Haute deficit, $53,768; net surplus, $196,633; dividends paid, $203,667; old accounts charged off, $109,831; debit to income for year, $116,865; total surplus June 30, 1900, $1,513,394. In 1900-01 the Evansville & Indianapolis deficit was $86,604, and after paying the dividends the surplus remaining was $85,955. In 1901-02 Evansville & Indianapolis deficit, $64,054; charged off for equipment, $189,379; balance surplus, $74,653.

The following presents the comparative freight traffic statistics of the company:

| | Average Mileage. | Total Tonnage. | Tons Carried One Mile. | Freight Density. | Rate per Ton per Mile. | Earnings per Train Mile. | *Average Tons per Train. |
|---|---|---|---|---|---|---|---|
| 1895-96.. | 167 | 1,039,242 | 64,224,412 | 384,553 | 1.027c | $2.042 | 205 |
| 1896-97.. | 167 | 942,330 | 59,869,714 | 358,502 | 0.958 | 1.909 | 205 |
| 1897-98.. | 167 | 1,404,477 | 89,012,441 | 533,008 | 0.829 | 2.006 | 249 |
| 1898 99.. | 167 | 1,052,192 | 86,664,728 | 518,950 | 0.877 | 2.098 | 246 |
| 1899-00.. | 162 | 1,718,539 | 100,445,054 | 620,031 | 0.868 | 2.242 | 265 |
| 1900-01.. | 162 | 1,708,558 | 101,196,986 | 624,672 | 0.870 | 2.221 | 262 |
| 1901-02.. | 162 | 1,810,435 | 109,344,068 | 674,963 | 0.848 | 2,327 | 281 |

* Includes company's freight.

President, Edwin S. Hooley, New York; Vice-President, George H. Ball, Boston; Treasurer, Charles A. Nones, New York; Assistant Secretary and Assistant Treasurer, Gilbert S. Wright, Evansville, Ind.

Directors—Edwin S. Hooley, W. F. arleton, Charles A. Nones, Thomas Honeymoon, Charles H. Sherill, H. H. Porter, Jr., Henry Seibert, Edwin W. Winter, Alfred Lauterbach, George S. Brewster, Joseph D. Donald, New York; George H. Ball, Boston; R. K. Dunkerson, Evansville, Ind.

Main office, Evansville, Ind. New York office, 49 Wall street. Annual meeting, third Monday in October. Books close ten days previous.

## FINDLAY, FORT WAYNE & WESTERN RAILWAY CO.

(Controlled by Cincinnati, Hamilton & Dayton Railway Co.)

Road owned, Findlay, O., to Fort Wayne, Ind., 80 miles. The company rents use of Pennsylvania terminals at Fort Wayne. Locomotives, 6; passenger cars, 8; freight cars, 125.

The road was originally the railroad company of same name, sold under foreclosure in 1894 and reorganized under the present title.

In November, 1901, control of this property was acquired by the Cincinnati, Hamilton & Dayton Railway Co.

Stock......Par $100..........................Authorized, $2,000,000......Issued, $2,000,000

Transfer agency, Fifth and Vine streets, Cincinnati. Registrar, Mercantile Trust Co., New York.

FUNDED DEBT.

| | |
|---|---|
| 1st mort., 5 per cent., due Jan., 1945, Jan. and July.................................. | $1,200,000 |
| 2d mort., income bonds, non-cumulative, 5 per cent., due Jan., 1945, Sept........... | 800,000 |
| Total.............................................................................. | $2,000,000 |

In year ending June 30, 1899, earnings were, gross, $98,994; net, $6,185. In 1899-1900, gross, $116,178; net, $15,897. In 1900-01, gross, $106,358; net, $17,111. No interest was paid on bonds.

President, T. J. Walsh; Secretary, F. H. Short; Treasurer, Clifford Resor, Cincinnati.

Main office, Findlay, O. Annual meeting, first Tuesday in February.

## FITCHBURG RAILROAD CO.

(Leased to Boston & Maine Railroad.)

Road owned, Boston to Fitchburg, 50 miles; Greenfield to Troy, N. Y., 85 miles; Vermont to Rotterdam, N. Y., 61 miles; Ashburnham Junction to Bellows Falls, Vt., 54 miles; branches, 144 miles; leased, Vermont & Massachusetts, Fitchburg to Greenfield, 56 miles; other leased lines, 8 miles; total, 458 miles. Locomotives, 221; passenger cars, 263; freight cars, 5,162.

In 1900 this company leased its property for 99 years from July 1, 1900, to the Boston & Maine Railroad for interest on the bonds and expenses and dividends of 5 per cent. per annum on the preferred stock and 1 per cent. per annum on the common stock. It was also provided that the Boston & Maine should purchase the common stock ($5,000,700) held by the State, with an issue of its 3 per cent. bonds, the same terms being offered with respect to the common stock in the hands of the public, and all of the common is now held by the Boston & Maine Railroad or by this company itself.

Stock...Par $100....Authorized { com., $7,000,000 / pref., 17,360,000 } Issued { com., $7,000,000 / pref., 17,360,000 } $24,360,000

Stock is transferred at the office of the company, Boston. Registrar, State Street Trust Co., Boston.

Preferred stock was increased $360,000 in 1895 to provide for the merger of the Brookline & Pepperell Railroad. Of the common stock $5,000,000 was owned by State of Massachusetts. See above for treatment of common stock in the lease. The common stock has no voting power (except on increases of preferred stock) until the common receives dividends for two consecutive years of not less than 4 per cent. per annum. No dividends were paid on the common stock prior to the lease.

Under the lease dividends on the preferred stock are paid quarterly, 1¼ per cent. each, in January (1), April, July and October. The payments on the common are also quarterly, ¼ per cent. each, in the same months, but no dividends are paid on stock held by the Boston & Maine Railroad or the Fitchburg Railroad Co. itself.

FUNDED DEBT.

| | |
|---|---|
| Plain bonds, 4 per cent., due 1904–05, March and Sept., Dec. and June | $1,000,000 |
| Plain bonds, 4 per cent., due 1920, June and Dec. | 500,000 |
| Plain bonds, 5 per cent., due 1908, May and Nov. | 2,000,000 |
| Plain bonds, 5 per cent., due 1903, March and Sept. | 378,000 |
| Plain bonds, 5 per cent., due 1903, May and Nov. | 1,000,000 |
| Plain bonds, 5 per cent., due 1903, June and Dec. | 500,000 |
| Plain bonds, 4½ per cent., due May, 1914, May and Nov. | 500,000 |
| Plain bonds, 4 per cent., due 1916, Jan. and July | 500,000 |
| Plain bonds, 3½ per cent., due Oct., 1920, April and Oct. | 500,000 |
| Plain bonds, 4 per cent., due April, 1907, April and Oct. | 1,500,000 |
| Plain bonds, 4 per cent., due 1927, March and Sept. | 2,750,000 |
| Plain bonds, 4 per cent., due 1915, March and Sept. | 1,359,000 |
| Bonds to State of Massachusetts, 4 per cent., due Feb., 1937, Feb. and Aug. | 5,000,000 |
| Plain bonds, 4 per cent., due 1928, Jan. and July | 1,450,000 |
| Plain bonds, 3½ per cent., due Oct., 1921, April and Oct. | 1,775,000 |
| Troy & Boston 1st mort., 7 per cent., due July, 1924, Jan. and July | 573,000 |
| Brookline & Pepperell R. R. bonds, 5 per cent., due Dec., 1911, June and Dec. | 100,000 |
| Total | $21,385,000 |

In 1887 this company purchased and absorbed the Troy & Greenfield, Troy & Boston and Boston, Hoosac Tunnel & Western roads, including the Hoosac Tunnel. In 1890 it acquired the Cheshire Railroad and the Southern Vermont Railroad. In 1894 the Brookline & Pepperell Railroad, the Brookline Railroad and the Brookline & Milford Railroad were consolidated with this company. The Boston, Barre & Gardner Railroad was absorbed in 1885.

The Vermont & Massachusetts Railroad is leased for guaranteed dividends of 6 per cent. on its $3,193,000 of stock.

The company from time to time increased its stock or issued bonds to effect the purchase and consolidation of the various roads it acquired, or to retire its own maturing bonds and those of its controlled roads, and to provide for improvements. Details of a number of such operations are given in the MANUAL for 1900.

EARNINGS.

Year ending June 30.

| | Pref. Div. Paid. | Gross. | Net. | Charges. | Surplus. |
|---|---|---|---|---|---|
| 1894–95 (457 miles) | 4 | $7,237,723 | $2,035,298 | $1,286,455 | $748,842 |
| 1895–96 ( " " ) | 4 | 7,606,765 | 1,894,895 | 1,262,168 | 632,726 |
| 1896–97 ( " " ) | 4 | 7,155,768 | 1,916,790 | 1,283,491 | 633,298 |
| 1897–98 ( " " ) | 4 | 7,359,470 | 2,002,867 | 1,294,618 | 708,246 |
| 1898–99 ( " " ) | 4 | 7,647,080 | 2,019,189 | 1,232,392 | 786,797 |
| 1899–00 ( " " ) | 4 | 8,071,440 | 2,703,573 | 1,526,118 | 1,177,454 |

Earnings are now included in those of the lessee.

President, Moses Williams; Treasurer, Daniel A. Gleason; Clerk, Paul Crocker, Boston.
Directors—Moses Williams, B. N. Bullock, Charles Lowell, Robert Winsor, J. J. Stimson, Boston; Rodney Wallace, Charles T. Crocker, Fitchburg, Mass.; W. Seward Webb, W. H. Hollister, New York; Francis Smith, Rockland, Me.; William E. Rice, Worcester; Joseph B. Russell, Belmont, Mass.
Main office, Boston. Annual meeting, last Wednesday in September.

---

## FLORIDA EAST COAST RAILWAY CO.

A corporation formed under the laws of Florida in 1895, as successor to the Jacksonville, St. Augustine & Indian River Railway Co.

Road owned, Jacksonville to Miami, Fla., 365 miles; branches, 69 miles. Locomotives, 30; passenger cars, 70; freight cars, 440.

Stock......Par $100..........................Authorized, $1,000,000.......Issued, $1,000,000

FUNDED DEBT.

1st mort........................................................................ $6,700,000

The company is owned by Henry M. Flagler, of New York, and information about its finances is scanty.

In the year ending June 30, 1901, the company earned gross, $1,583,856; net, $364,241.

President, Henry M. Flagler, New York; Vice-President, J. R. Parrott, St. Augustine, Fla.; Treasurer, W. H. Beardsley; Secretary, J. C. Salter, New York.

Main office, St. Augustine, Fla.; New York office, 26 Broadway.

---

## FLORIDA SOUTHERN RAILROAD CO.

(Controlled by Atlantic Coast Line Railroad Co.)

Road owned, Palatka, Fla., to Brooksville, Fla., 145 miles; Bartow, Fla., to Punta Gorda, Fla., 73 miles; branches, 28 miles; total, 246 miles. Locomotives, 9; passenger cars, 23; freight cars, 293.

This company was formed in 1892 as the successor of the railway company of same name, which was foreclosed and reorganized. In 1896 a controlling interest was acquired in the interest of the Plant system, and the road was transferred to the Atlantic Coast Line Railroad when that system, in 1902, absorbed the Savannah, Florida & Western and the roads of the Plant system. This road is operated separately, but in conjunction with the Atlantic Coast Line system.

Stock......Par $100..........................Authorized, $1,725,000......Issued, $1,725,000

FUNDED DEBT.

1st mort., 4 per cent., due 1945, Jan. and July...................................... $4,241,000

The bonds were issued in 1895 and bore 3½ per cent. until January 1, 1900, and after that time 4 per cent. They were guaranteed, principal and interest, by the Savannah, Florida & Western Railway Co.

EARNINGS.

| Year ending June 30. | Gross. | Net. |
|---|---|---|
| 1896-97 | $320,621 | Def. $33,157 |
| 1897-98 | 347,294 | Sur. 762 |
| 1898-99 | 366,118 | Def. 2,410 |
| 1899-00 | 356,628 | Sur. 8,636 |
| 1900-01 | 427,360 | " 113,768 |
| 1901-02 | 479,802 | " 122,776 |

President, F. Q. Brown; Secretary, Herbert L. Borden, New York; Treasurer, James F. Post, Wilmington, N. C.

Directors—M. F. Plant, F. Q. Brown, Henry Walters, Warren G. Elliott, Michael Jenkins, P. W. Scott, J. J. Kelligan, Waldo Newcomer, Robert G. Erwin.

Main office, Jacksonville; New York office, 71 Broadway. Annual meeting, Saturday following second Tuesday in January.

---

## FONDA, JOHNSTOWN & GLOVERSVILLE RAILROAD CO.

Road owned, Fonda, N. Y., to Northville, 26 miles; branches leased, 25 miles; total operated, 51 miles. The company controls the Amsterdam (N. Y.) Street Railway Co. Also leases the Johnstown, Gloversville & Kingsboro Horse Railroad and the Cayadutta Electric Railroad, both operated by electric power, and extensions of the company's electric division are planned. Locomotives, 9; passenger cars, 17; freight cars, 14.

Stock......Par $100..............................Authorized, $600,000......Issued, $600,000

In 1901-02 8 per cent. was paid on the stock of the company, the dividend periods being May and November.

Stock is transferred at the office of the company, Gloversville, N. Y.

FUNDED DEBT.

| | |
|---|---|
| Consolidated mort., 6 per cent., due April, 1921, April and Oct. | $200,000 |
| 1st cons. refunding bonds, 4½ per cent., due July, 1947, Jan. and July | 500,000 |
| General mortgage, 4 per cent., due July, 1950, Jan. and July | 400,000 |
| Johns., Glovers. & Kingsboro, 1st mort., guar. 6 per cent., due 1913, Jan. and July | 50,000 |
| Cayadutta R. R., 1st mort., guar. 6 per cent., due Oct., 1922, April and Oct. | 350,000 |
| Total | $1,500,000 |

The 4 per cent. general mortgage, New York Security & Trust Co., New York, Trustee, was created in 1900 and is for $1,500,000. Of this amount of bonds $200,000 were issued to retire $200,000 1st mortgage 7 per cent. bonds maturing July 1, 1900, $700,000 are held to retire the consols and 1st refunding bonds, and $600,000 are available for extensions, etc.

EARNINGS.

Year ending June 30.

| | Gross. | Net. | Charges. | Surplus. |
|---|---|---|---|---|
| 1900-01 | $344,927 | $96,381 | ...... | ...... |
| 1901-02 | 352,740 | 168,403 | 115,926 | $52,482 |

The net earnings for 1901-02 includes $59,203 miscellaneous receipts from rents, interest and dividends on securities owned by this company.

President, J. Ledlie Hees, Fonda, N.Y.; Secretary and Treasurer, George M. Place; Auditor, Lyman K. Brown, Gloversville.

Directors—J. Ledlie Hees, George M. Place, Chauncey M. Depew, John G. Ferres, James Stewart, Erastus Darling, A. J. Zimmer, G. Levor, R. T. McKeever, George F. Moore, James I. Younglove, S. H. Shotwell, Z. B. Whitney, William Harris, J. S. Friedman.

Main office, Gloversville, N. Y. Annual meeting, third Wednesday in January, at Gloversville.

## FORT SMITH & WESTERN RAILROAD CO.

Road pro e te , Fort Smith and Western Junction, I. T., to Guthrie, Okla., about 200 miles; road completed, junction to Indianola, I. T., 76 miles; trackage over Kansas City Southern Railway, junction to Fort Smith, 20 miles. The full line will be completed in 1903. Locomotives, 6; passenger cars, 10; freight cars, 375.

Stock......Par $100..........................Authorized, $5,000,000......Issued, $5,000,000

The company has no preferred stock.

FUNDED DEBT.

1st mort., 5 per cent., due April, 1932, April and Oct.............................. $2,150,000

The 1st mortgage is $5,000,000, authorized. Trustee and agent for payment of interest Mercantile Trust Co., New York. The bonds are subject to call at 105 and interest.

This road was planned to develop large coal deposits in the Indian Territory and Oklahoma.

President and Treasurer, Alton C. Duston, Cleveland; Auditor and Assistant Treasurer, H. B. Herendeen; General Manager, J. J. Mahoney, Fort Smith, Ark.

Directors—Henry C. Frick, Alton C. Duston, W. H. Canniff, William G. Mather, W. R. Woodford, J. H. Hoyt, George T. Sparks, J. J. Mahoney, H. B. Herendeen.

Main office, Fort Smith, Ark.; executive office, Superior and Water streets, Cleveland. Annual meeting, first Tuesday in February.

## FORT WORTH & DENVER CITY RAILWAY CO.

(Controlled by Colorado & Southern Railway Co.)

Road owned, Fort Worth, Tex., to Texas State line, 454 miles; branch, 14 miles; total, 468 miles. Locomotives, 37; passenger cars, 26; freight cars, 1,003.

The Colorado & Southern has a large interest in this company, which is operated as a portion of its system.

Stock....Par $100.....Authorized { com., $6,835,000 / pref., 2,555,000 } Issued { com., $6,835,000 / pref., 2,540,000 } $9,375,000

See below for details as to the preferred stock "stamped certificates."

Transfer Agent, Central Trust Co., New York.

In March, 1898, 2 per cent. was paid on the preferred stock; in March, 1899, 2 per cent., and on April 15, 1902, 2 per cent.

FUNDED DEBT.

1st mort., 6 per cent., due Dec., 1921, June and Dec. .............................. $8,176,000

The bonds were entitled to only 4 per cent. up to December 1, 1900, and after that date to the full 6 per cent. interest. As the company's earnings were not sufficient to provide for such payments, a bondholders' committee was constituted in December, 1900, Henry K. McHarg, Chairman, which invited bondholders to deposit bonds with the United States Trust Co., New York, under an agreement. In 1901 the payment of full interest at the rate of 6 per cent. on the bonds was resumed.

EARNINGS.

Year ending October 31.

| | Gross. | Net. | Charges. | | Surplus. |
|---|---|---|---|---|---|
| 1893 (469 miles)...................... | $1,498,731 | $346,646 | $520,876 | Def. | $174,229 |
| 1894 ( " " )...................... | 1,335,879 | 313,196 | 579,810 | " | 206,614 |
| 1895 ( " " )...................... | 1,087,702 | 210,778 | ...... | | ...... |
| 1896 ( " " )...................... | 1,010,878 | 248,220 | 440,363 | " | 192,143 |
| 1897 (470 " )...................... | 1,319,831 | 428,665 | 374,851 | | 53,814 |
| 1898 ( " " )...................... | 1,479,434 | 424,402 | 373,262 | | 51,139 |
| 1899 ( " " )...................... | 1,610,852 | 355,907 | 351,940 | | 3,967 |
| 1900 ( " " )...................... | 1,807,089 | 338,995 | 352,352 | | 3,726 |
| 1901 ( " " )...................... | 2,163,392 | 545,822 | 505,842 | | 39,981 |
| 1902 (6 months ending June 30)....... | 1,119,556 | 299,381 | 272,725 | | 26,656 |

A Receiver was appointed in 1893. In the same year a bondholders' committee was appointed; the December, 1893, and subsequent coupons not having been paid, a bondholders' committee, with Grenville M. Dodge, chairman, was appointed to protect their interests. Plan issued December, 1895, provided for reorganization without foreclosure. Coupons for 5 years, commencing December, 1895, were to be stamped at 4 per cent. per annum, and past due coupon paid 3 per cent. in cash. Remaining 4 past due coupons and 2 per cent. deferred on coupons for 5 years, amounting in aggregate to 22 per cent., to be converted into $275 of non-cumulative 4 per cent. preference stock. This plan was modified by circular of July 10, by which, instead of paying one past due coupon at 3 per cent. in cash, all 5 coupons past due were exchanged for preferred stock. Plan with this change was carried into effect in December, 1896.

President, Frank Trumbull, Denver; Vice-President, D. B. Keeler; Secretary and Treasurer, George Strong, Fort Worth, Tex.; Assistant Secretary, Harry Bronner, New York.

Directors—Grenville M. Dodge, New York; Henry Walters, Baltimore; Morgan Jones, Chicago; Frank Trumbull, Denver; D. B. Keeler, S. M. Hudson, W. R. Scott, R. M. Van Zandt, M. A. Spoonts, Fort Worth, Tex.

Main office, 510 Houston street, Fort Worth, Tex.; New York office, 74 Broadway. Annual meeting, first Tuesday in March, at Fort Worth.

## FORT WORTH & RIO GRANDE RAILWAY CO.

(Controlled by St. Louis & San Francisco Railroad Co.)

Road owned, Fort Worth to Brownwood, Tex., 144 miles; branch, 2½ miles; total owned and operated, 146½ miles. Locomotives, 13; passenger cars, 13; freight cars, 97.

In May, 1901, the majority of the stock was bought in the interest of the St. Louis & San Francisco Railroad Co., and the latter operates the road as part of its system.

Stock......Par $100.........................Authorized, $6,250,000... ..Issued, $6,250,000

An increase of the stock from $3,108,100 to the present amount was voted in June, 1901, to provide for an extension of the line to San Antonio.

Transfer Agent, H. B. Hollins & Co., 15 Wall street, New York.

FUNDED DEBT.

1st mort., 4 per cent., due July, 1928, Jan. and July................................ $2,923,000

In January, 1897, a readjustment of interest was proposed. The plan involved reduction of the 5 per cent. interest on the 1st mortgage bonds to 3 per cent. from January 1, 1897, to January 1, 1902, inclusive, and 4 per cent. thereafter. This was accepted by the bondholders.

EARNINGS.

Year ending June 30.

| | Gross. | Net. | Charges. | Surplus. |
|---|---|---|---|---|
| 1892-93 | $405,538 | $134,219 | $167,653 | Def. $33,434 |
| 1893-94 | 311,183 | 82,253 | 168,487 | " 86,234 |
| 1894-95 | 452,196 | 195,806 | 119,935 | 75,871 |
| 1895-96 | 387,127 | 145,762 | 117,810 | 27,952 |
| 1896-97 | 323,678 | 90,137 | 109,641 | Def. 19,504 |
| 1897-98 | 512,189 | 215,719 | 112,739 | 102,980 |
| 1898-99 | 556,414 | 267,296 | 105,679 | 161,617 |
| 1899-00 | 481,147 | 184,406 | 102,927 | 81,479 |
| 1900-01 | 661,308 | 293,196 | 139,927 | 153,269 |

The items of charges given above include coupons, interest and taxes. Earnings since 1900-1 are included in those of the St. Louis & San Francisco Railroad Co.

President, B. F. Yoakum, St. Louis; Vice-President, Luther B. Comer; Secretary, John S. Jones; Treasurer, L. O. Williams, Fort Worth, Tex.

Main office, 812 Main street, Fort Worth, Tex. Annual meeting in April, at Fort Worth.

## GALVESTON, HARRISBURG & SAN ANTONIO RAILWAY CO.

(Controlled by Southern Pacific Co.)

Road owned, Houston, Tex., to El Paso, 835 miles; Spofford to Eagle Pass, 35 miles; branches, 48 miles; total, 918 miles. Locomotives, 158; passenger cars, 69; freight cars, 3,762.

Stock......Par $100........................Authorized, $27,084,372......Issued, $27,084,372

FUNDED DEBT.

| | |
|---|---|
| 1st mort., Eastern Division 6 per cent., due Feb., 1910, Feb. and Aug. | $4,756,000 |
| 2d mort., " " 7 per cent., due June, 1905, June and Dec. | 1,000,000 |
| Western Division, 1st mort., 5 per cent., due May, 1931, May and Nov. | 13,418,000 |
| " " 2d mort. income, 6 per cent., due July, 1931, Jan. and July | 6,354,000 |
| Total | $25,528,000 |

In 1893 an agreement was made with holders of Western Division second mortgage 6 per cent. bonds, due 1931, by which interest thereon became payable only in case there is a surplus over prior charges. Interest, however, is to be non-cumulative.

The Southern Pacific Co. is the principal owner of the capital stock, but the company is operated by its own organization. The connection with the Southern Pacific of New Mexico was completed in 1883.

EARNINGS.

| | Gross. | Net. | Charges. | Surplus. |
|---|---|---|---|---|
| 1891 (937 miles) | $4,517,589 | $1,322,202 | $........ | $94,683 |
| 1892 ( " " ) | 4,556,423 | 1,168,666 | 1,215,916 | Def. 47,250 |
| 1893 ( " " ) | 4,204,754 | 1,078,590 | 1,232,127 | " 153,536 |
| 1894 ( " " ) | 4,293,714 | 1,382,719 | 1,248,836 | 133,883 |
| 1895 ( " " ) | 4,798,124 | 1,670,067 | 1,277,411 | 392,656 |
| 1896 ( " " ) | 5,127,630 | 1,719,859 | 1,151,743 | 568,116 |
| 1897 (18 months ending June 30) | 7,206,973 | 1,992,708 | 1,749,385 | 243,323 |
| 1898 (year ending June 30) | 5,002,173 | 1,387,206 | 1,117,498 | 269,708 |
| 1899 ( " " ) | 5,669,335 | 1,541,580 | 1,259,509 | 282,071 |
| 1900 ( " " ) | 6,292,693 | 1,109,248 | 1,206,854 | Def. 97,606 |
| 1901 ( " " ) | 6,698,292 | 1,292,606 | 1,192,066 | " 96,298 |

President, Edward H. Harriman, New York; Vice-President, C. H. Markham; Treasurer, E. B. C. Cushman; Secretary, C. B. Seger, Houston, Tex.

Main office, Houston, Tex.; New York office, 120 Broadway. Annual meeting, first Tuesday in July.

## GALVESTON, HOUSTON & HENDERSON RAILROAD CO.

Road owned, Galveston, Tex., to Houston, 50 miles. Locomotives, 11; passenger cars, 11; freight cars, 19.

Stock......Par $100.........................Authorized, $1,000,000......Issued, $1,000,000

FUNDED DEBT.

1st mort., 5 per cent., due 1913, April and Oct. .................................. $2,000,000

The stock of this company was acquired by the Missouri, Kansas & Texas and the road was leased January 1, 1883, to the International & Great Northern, both roads being at the time under the same control. Suit was brought by the Missouri, Kansas & Texas to annul the lease and regain possession of the road. Decision was rendered in favor of the Missouri, Kansas & Texas, but was overruled by a higher court. Legal proceedings continued until 1895, when a compromise was arrived at for a joint control and use of property by the contending companies. The two companies are to provide interest on bonds and $24,000 annually for dividends or other purposes and share expense of operation. The 99-year lease to International & Great Northern was abrogated, and stock divided between the two companies.

| Earnings. | Gross. | Net. |
|---|---|---|
| 1895 | 545,914 | 107,452 |
| 1896 | 317,985 | 148,405 |
| 1897 | 312,604 | 160,197 |
| 1898 | 380,599 | 176,311 |
| 1899 | 417,114 | 181,491 |
| 1900 | 332,740 | 155,548 |
| 1901 | 335,168 | 171,672 |
| 1902 | 375,823 | 182,214 |

President, Frederic P. Olcott, New York; Vice-President, J. H. Hawley; Secretary and Treasurer, A. A. Van Alstyne; Manager, J. H. Hill; Auditor, John E. O'Neill, Galveston.

Directors—Frederic P. Olcott, George J. Gould, Henry C. Rouse, New York; James A. Baker, Jr., Houston, Tex.; J. H. Hawley, R. B. Baer, Galveston; N. A. Stedman, Palestine, Tex.

Main office, Galveston. Annual meeting, first Monday in April.

## GENESSEE & WYOMING RAILROAD CO.

Road owned, Retsof, N. Y., to Pittsburg and Lehigh Junction, 11 miles; branches, 6 miles; total operated, 17 miles. An extension of 20 miles to Caledonia, N. Y., is planned.

Stock......Par $100..............................Authorized, $500,000......Issued, $500,000

Stock is transferred by the secretary of the company, New York.

The company pays dividend of 5 per cent. per annum on its stock in half-yearly payments, April (1) and October.

Funded Debt.

1st mort., 5 per cent., due April, 1929, April and Oct.................................. $500,000

The bonds outstanding are the full amounts authorized. Trustee of mortgage, Knickerbocker Trust Co., New York.

Earnings.

Year ending June 30.

| | Gross. | Net. | Charges. | Surplus |
|---|---|---|---|---|
| 1899-00 | $99,176 | $64,449 | $26,816 | $37,634 |
| 1900-01 | 110,362 | 35,023 | 27,864 | 7,159 |
| 1901-02 | 127,307 | 71,051 | 28,550 | 42,505 |

President Edward L. Fuller, Scranton, Pa.; Vice-President, Milo M. Belding, Jr.; Secretary, Henry D. Fuller, New York; Treasurer, M. B. Fuller, Scranton, Pa.

Main office, Retsof, N. Y.; New York office, 170 Broadway. Annual meeting, second Tuesday in April, at New York.

## GEORGIA, FLORIDA & ALABAMA RAILROAD CO.

A corporation formed under the laws of Georgia November 2, 1895.

Road owned, Bainbridge to Arlington, Ga., 40 miles; Tallahassee extension, 41 miles; branch, 9 miles; total, 90 miles. The company is building an extension to Columbus, Ga., which will add about 90 miles to the system. Further extensions are under consideration. Locomotives, 5; passenger cars, 5; freight cars, 30.

The name of this company was formerly the Georgia Pine Railroad Co. The name was changed to the present style in April, 1901.

Stock......Par $100..............................Authorized, $350,000......Issued, $350,000

Funded Debt.

1st mort., 5 per cent., due July, 1951, Jan. and July.................................. $315,000

The 1st mortgage was created in 1901 to provide for extensions of the line. The authorized amount of the mortgage is $550,000, the trustee being the Manhattan Trust Co., New York. Interest on the bonds is payable either at New York or Savannah.

EARNINGS.

Year ending June 30.

| | Gross. | Net. | Charges. | Suplus. |
|---|---|---|---|---|
| 1900-01 .................................. | $67,646 | $28,223 | $14,710 | $13,513 |

President, J. P. Williams, Savannah; Vice-President, R. B. Coleman, Bainbridge, Ga.; Secretary and Treasurer, J. O. Hatch, Savannah; Auditor, W. H. Carroll, Bainbridge, Ga.

Directors—J. P. Williams, Savannah; R. B. Coleman, J. W. Callahan, J. R. Sharpe, E. R. Bruton, Bainbridge, Ga.; J. W. Calhoun, Arlington, Ga.; J. S. Bush, Colquit, Ga.

Main office, Bainbridge, Ga.; branch office, Savannah. Annual meeting, third Tuesday in July, at Bainbridge, Ga.

## GEORGIA RAILROAD & BANKING CO.

(Leased to Louisville & Nashville Railroad Co., and Atlantic Coast Line Co.)

Road owned, Augusta, Ga., to Atlanta, 171 miles; branches, 136 miles; total, 307 miles.

The company owns one-half interest in the Western Railroad of Alabama and 47-100 in the Atlanta & West Point Railroad.

April, 1881, the road was leased for 99 years to W. M. Wadley, at $600,000 yearly. Mr. Wadley afterwards assigned the lease to the Central of Georgia and the Louisville & Nashville jointly, the latter subsequently acquiring the other road's interest in the lease. In 1899 the Atlantic Coast Line Co. of South Carolina acquired a half interest in the lease and assumed a joint obligation thereunder, the lessees each depositing with this company $500,000 of bonds as security.

Stock......Par $100........................Authorized, $4,200,000......Issued, $4,200,000

Stock is transferred at the office of the company, Augusta, Ga.

Dividends of 2¾ per cent. are paid quarterly on January, April, July and October 15. Since April 1, 1888, the yearly rate has been 11 per cent.

FUNDED DEBT.

| | |
|---|---|
| Plain bonds, 6 per cent., currency, due Jan., 1910, Jan. and July...... ............ | $1,000,000 |
| Plain bonds, 6 per cent., due Jan., 1922, Jan. and July.......................... ... | 300,000 |
| Plain bonds, 5 per cent., due Jan., 1922, Jan. and July.............................. | 200,000 |
| Plain bonds, refunding 5 per cent., due Jan., 1922, Jan. and July.................... | 1,000,000 |
| Total ......... .......................................................... | $2,500,000 |

EARNINGS.

Year ending March 30.

| | Div. Paid. | Gross. | Net. | Charges. | Result to Lessee. | |
|---|---|---|---|---|---|---|
| 1892-93. .......... .......... | 11 | $1,480,252 | $392,019 | $600,000 | Def. | $207,981 |
| 1893-94...................... | 11 | 1,367,185 | 589,952 | 600,000 | " | 10,048 |
| 1894-95...................... | 11 | 1,307,637 | 413,025 | 600,000 | " | 186,975 |
| 1895-96...................... | 11 | 1,479,792 | 431,120 | 600,000 | " | 168,880 |
| 1896-97....... .............. | 11 | 1,590,659 | 559,163 | 600,000 | " | 40,436 |
| 1897-98...................... | 11 | 1,616,146 | 455,556 | 600,000 | " | 144,443 |
| 1898-99....... .............. | 11 | 1,634,842 | 493,644 | 600,000 | " | 106,356 |
| *1899-00..................... | 11 | 1,658,338 | 632,110 | 600,000 | Sur. | 32,110 |
| *1900-01..................... | 11 | 1,834,679 | 550,306 | 600,000 | Def. | 50,694 |
| 1901-02...................... | 11 | 1,986,757 | 646,229 | 600,000 | " | 46,229 |

*Year ending June 30.

The company in 1892 discontinued its banking department, but became the principal owner of the Georgia Railroad Bank.

President, Jacob Phinizy; Cashier, C. G. Goodrich, Augusta, Ga.

Directors—H. H. Hickman, Thomas W. Coskery, W. A. Latimer, Leonard Phinizy, Henry B. King, James Tobin, Augusta, Ga.; Billups Phinizy, James White, W. W. Thomas, Athens, Ga.; G. A. Speer, A. W. Calhoun, R. D. Spalding, Atlanta, Ga.; Edward W. Butler, Madison, Ga.; H. D. McDaniel, Monroe, Ga.; Theodore M. Green, Washington, Ga.

Main office, Augusta, Ga. Annual meeting, second Wednesday in May.

## GEORGIA SOUTHERN & FLORIDA RAILWAY CO.

Road owned, Macon, Ga., to Palatka, Fla., 285 miles. In 1902 acquired the Atlantia, Valdosta & Western Railway, 118 miles. Locomotives, 36; passengers cars, 45; freight cars, 1,749.

This company was originally the Georgia Southern & Florida Railroad Co. Foreclosed and reorganized under its present title in 1895.

| Stock..Par $100...Authorized | com., $1,000,000<br>1st pref., 684,000<br>2d pref., 1,084,000 | Issued | com., $1,000,000<br>1st pref., 684,000<br>2d pref., 1,084,000 | $2,768,000 |
|---|---|---|---|---|

Preferred stocks are entitled to 5 per cent. dividends. The 1st preferred has a lien upon the property.

Transfer office, Mercantile Trust & Deposit Co., Baltimore.

In 1896 4 per cent. was paid on the 1st preferred. From 1897 to 1901, inclusive, 5 per cent. has been paid on the 1st preferred, dividends being semi-annual, 2½ per cent. in May and November. On the 2d preferred dividends paid have been: In 1897, 2 per cent.; in 1898 and 1899, 3 per cent.; in 1900 and 1901, 4 per cent. Dividends on the 2d preferred are paid annually, in November.

FUNDED DEBT.

1st mort., 5 per cent., due July, 1945, Jan. and July.................................. $3,801,000

The 1st mortgage is $4,000,000 authorized. Trustee and Agent for payment of interest, Mercantile Trust & Deposit Co., Baltimore. The company has a 4½ per cent. equipment trust for $360,000.

EARNINGS.

Year ending June 30.

| | Gross. | Net. | Charges. | Surplus. |
|---|---|---|---|---|
| 1895-96 | $869,115 | $258,787 | $179,200 | $79,587 |
| 1896-97 | 863,541 | 272,834 | 179,875 | 92,959 |
| 1897-98 | 949,627 | 300,276 | 177,950 | 122,329 |
| 1898-99 | 953,797 | 261,385 | 181,250 | 80,135 |
| 1899-00 | 1,180,411 | 322,467 | 187,550 | 134,917 |
| 1900-01 | 1,203,811 | 313,455 | 190,050 | 123,405 |
| 1901-02 | 1,250,875 | 309,058 | 190,050 | 119,008 |

In 1898-99 the surplus over dividends was $13,415; in 1899-1900, surplus $68,197; in 1900-01, surplus $24,165; in 1901-02, surplus $41,448.

President, Samuel Spencer, New York; Vice-President, W. Checkley Shaw; Secretary and Treasurer, Ben. C. Smith, Macon, Ga.

Main office, Macon, Ga.; President's office, 80 Broadway, New York. Annual meeting, third Thursday in October.

---

## GILA VALLEY, GLOBE & NORTHERN RAILWAY CO.

(Controlled by Southern Pacific Co.)

Road owned, Bowie, Ariz., to Globe, Ariz., 125 miles. Extensions projected, 40 miles; locomotives, 6; passenger cars, 4; freight cars, 4.

Stock......Par $100..........................Authorized, $2,000,000......Issued, $2,000,000

A dividend of 4 per cent. on the stock of this company was paid January 1, 1901, and 4 per cent. was also paid January 6, 1902.

FUNDED DEBT.

1st mort., 5 per cent., due 1924, May and Nov...................................... $1,514,000

The 1st mortgage is $15,000 per mile, and is guaranteed by the Southern Pacific Co., which owns $1,097,000 of the company's stock. Trustee of the mortgage, Manhattan Trust Co., New York. Interest is paid at the office of the Southern Pacific Co., New York.

EARNINGS.

Year ending June 30.

| | Gross. | Net. | Charges. | Surplus. |
|---|---|---|---|---|
| 1899-00 | $373,049 | $221,537 | $75,700 | $145,837 |
| 1900-01 | 365,835 | 196,385 | 75,700 | 120,685 |
| 1901-02 | 375,367 | 185,452 | 75,700 | 109,752 |

President, William Garland; Vice-President, R. H. Ingram; Secretary, A. C. Laird, Los Angeles, Cal.; Treasurer, T. Smith, San Francisco.

Main office, 313 Stimson Block, Los Angeles, Cal. Annual meeting in December, at Los Angeles.

## GRAND RAPIDS & INDIANA RAILWAY CO.

(Controlled by Pennsylvania Railroad Co.)

Road owned, Fort Wayne, Ind., to Mackinaw City, Mich., 367 miles; branches owned, 63 miles; total, 430 miles; branches operated, Cincinnati, Richmond & Fort Wayne, 86 miles; Traverse City Railroad, 26 miles; Muskegon, Grand Rapids & Indiana, 41 miles; total operated, 583 miles; trackage, 7 miles; total, 590 miles. Locomotives, 71; passenger cars, 90; freight cars, 3,067.

This company is successor to the railroad of the same name, foreclosed in June, 1896, and reorganized under the auspices of Pennsylvania Railroad Co., which owns a controlling interest, holding $2,644,540 of the stock of this company, $276,000 4½ per cent. extended guaranteed bonds, and $525,000 1st mortgage 3½ per cent. bonds. Present company was incorporated under laws of Michigan July 11, 1896, and those of Indiana July 13, 1896. It took possession of property August 1, 1896.

Stock......Par $100..........................Authorized, $6,000,000......Issued, $5,794,700

On April 16, 1900, the first dividend of 1 per cent. was paid on the stock of the reorganized company. In 1901 two dividends of 1 per cent. each were paid in April and October, respectively. In 1902 the semi-annual dividends were 1½ per cent. each.

FUNDED DEBT.

| | |
|---|---|
| 1st mort., 3½ per cent. extended, due July, 1941, guar. by Pa. R. R., Jan. and July. | $920,000 |
| 1st mort. extended, guar. by Pa. R. R., 4½ per cent., due July, 1941, Jan. and July. | 4,455,000 |
| 2d mort., 4 per cent., due Oct., 1936, April and Oct. | 3,962,000 |
| Total | $9,337,000 |

The Muskegon, Grand Rapids & Indiana has $750,000 5 per cent. 1st mortgage bonds, which, however, are not a debt of this company.

See previous editions of MANUAL for history of this company and its relations to Pennsylvania Railroad Co. and Pennsylvania Company. All debts to Pennsylvania were paid off when new company was formed. The Pennsylvania Company owns a controlling interest in the stock.

In 1895 suit to foreclose old 2d mortgage was begun and carried to completion. New company succeeded to property August 1, 1896. Of the new stock $1,075,000 was issued for overdue coupons. The new 2d mortgage is for $5,000,000. It bore 2 per cent. for one year from October, 1896; 3 per cent. for two succeeding years, and 4 per cent. thereafter.

EARNINGS.

| | Gross. | Net. | Interest. | Surplus. |
|---|---|---|---|---|
| 1897 | $1,978,567 | $525,086 | $455,009 | $70,077 |
| 1898 | 2,171,717 | 596,622 | 483,701 | 112,920 |
| 1899 | 2,464,284 | 634,847 | 458,922 | 175,925 |
| 1900 | 2,661,433 | 585,316 | 501,841 | 83,475 |
| 1901 | 2,871,782 | 700,713 | 562,055 | 138,658 |
| 1902 | 3,196,738 | 783,492 | 533,291 | 250,651 |

President, James McCrea, Pittsburg; Vice-President and Treasurer, W. R. Shelby; General Manager, J. H. P. Hughart; Secretary and Auditor, R. R. Metheany, Grand Rapids, Mich.

Directors—Harvey J. Hollister, J. J. Turner, W. R. Shelby, Grand Rapids, Mich.; James McCrea, Joseph Wood, J. J. Turner, E. B. Taylor, H. Darlington, Pittsburg.

Main office, Grand Rapids Mich. Annual meeting, first Wednesday in April. Books close ten days previous.

## GRAND TRUNK RAILWAY CO. OF CANADA

An English corporation having a large system of roads in Canada.

Road owned and operated, 3,561 miles, of which the principal lines are as follows: Portland, Me., via Montreal, Can., to Point Edward, Ontario, 799 miles; Niagara Falls to Detroit (Great Western), 230 miles; Fort Erie to Goderich, Ont., 162 miles. This company controls an extensive system of lines in the United States, including the Central Vermont, Grand Trunk Western and Detroit, Grand Haven & Milwaukee. Total of system, 4,659 miles. Locomotives, 803; passenger cars, 837; freight cars, 25,143.

The Chicago & Grand Trunk Railway, which this company controlled, was reorganized in 1900, being foreclosed and taken over by a new company, the Grand Trunk Western Railway, which is controlled by the Grand Trunk Railway Co. of Canada by ownership of all its stock. The Grand Trunk guarantees $15,000,000 of 4 per cent. 1st mortgage bonds of the Grand Trunk Western. The Grand Trunk Western also has an issue of $1,500,000 4 per cent. income bonds.

In August, 1882, the Grand Trunk absorbed the Great Western system, covering with its leases 825 miles, assuming all liabilities. In 1892 the Dominion Parliament authorized the consolidation and merger with this company of a number of branch roads owned or controlled. In 1898 company leased joint use of its line from Windsor, Ont., opposite Detroit, to near Buffalo, N. Y., to the Wabash Railroad for a long term. In 1898 the company took part in the reorganization of the Central of Vermont and made a traffic guarantee of the bonds of the new company. In 1901 the Cincinnati, Saginaw & Mackinaw, 53 miles, was leased to this company.

In 1902 it was proposed to build a line to the Pacific Coast under a separate organization to be controlled by this company.

CAPITAL STOCK.

| | Authorized | | Issued | |
|---|---|---|---|---|
| Stock..Par £100 | ordinary, | £23,318,309 | ordinary, | £22,475,984 |
| | guaranteed, | 5,220,000 | guaranteed, | 5,219,793 |
| | 1st preference, | 3,420,000 | 1st preference, | 3,420,000 |
| | 2d " | 2,530,000 | 2d " | 2,530,000 |
| | 3d " | 7,168,055 | 3d " | 7,168,055 |
| | | £41,656,364 | | £40,813,832 |

Stock is transferred at the offices of the company, Montreal and London.

The guaranteed stock is entitled to 4 per cent. per annum. The 1st and 2d preference stocks are 5 per cent. and the 3d preference 4 per cent.

From 1894 to 1897 nothing was paid on the 4 per cent. guaranteed stock. From 1898 the full 4 per cent. has been paid. The dividends on the guaranteed stock are 2 per cent., half yearly, in April and October. In 1898 3 per cent. was paid on the 1st preference stock, and since then the full dividend has been paid. A dividend of 3¼ per cent. on the 2d preference stock for the year 1899 was paid, the first for many years.

FUNDED DEBT.

| | |
|---|---|
| Canadian Government loan | £3,111,500 |
| Debenture stock, 5 per cent., irredeemable | 4,270,375 |
| Debenture stock, 4 per cent., irredeemable | 12,515,678 |
| Great Western debentures, 5 per cent., irredeemable | 2,723,080 |
| Equipment mort., 6 per cent., due July, 1919, Jan. and July | 414,300 |
| Total | £23,034,933 |

The divisional mortgages outstanding on lines leased to or consolidated with this company amount to over £8,800,000.

The company owns $26,950,397 of securities, including $6,000,000 Grand Trunk Western Railway stock; $693,000 International Bridge stock; $1,500,000 Detroit, Grand Haven & Milwaukee stock; $2,185,100 Central Vermont stock, and $1,583,300 of Vermont Central 4 per cent. bonds.

In May, 1895, a complete change was made in the management, Sir Henry Tyler, for many years its president, retiring, and was succeeded by Sir Charles Rivers Wilson, with a new board of directors.

EARNINGS.

| | Gross. | Net. | Payments. | Surplus. |
|---|---|---|---|---|
| 1892 (3,513 miles) | £4,028,865 | £1,162,293 | £986,316 | £175,977 |
| 1893 (3,502 " ) | 4,062,218 | 1,126,732 | 989,901 | 136,831 |
| 1894 (3,512 " ) | 3,649,957 | 1,024,481 | 940,829 | 83,652 |
| 1895 ( " " ) | 3,637,055 | 1,204,175 | 1,141,487 | 62,687 |
| 1896 ( " " ) | 3,787,285 | 1,287,079 | 1,150,999 | 136,080 |
| 1897 ( " " ) | 3,969,642 | 1,574,631 | 1,174,859 | 399,771 |
| 1898 ( " " ) | 4,012,314 | 1,548,932 | 1,154,327 | 364,604 |
| 1899 (3,506 " ) | 4,407,016 | 1,724,367 | 1,189,890 | 534,477 |
| 1900 ( " " ) | 4,558,910 | 1,690,701 | 1,200,863 | 489,838 |
| 1901 (3,507 " ) | 4,857,600 | 1,736,651 | 1,227,717 | 508,933 |

Receipts from investments, etc., in 1894 were £44,086; in 1895, £130,775; in 1896, £181,673; in 1897, £202,361; in 1898, £208,501; in 1899, £210,345; in 1900, £206,857.

President, Sir Charles Rivers Wilson; Vice-President, Joseph Price, London; 2d Vice-President and General Manager, Charles M. Hays, Montreal; Secretary, H. H. Norman, London; Treasurer, Frank Scott, Montreal.

Directors—Sir Charles Rivers Wilson, Joseph Price, George Allen, George Von Chauvin, John A. Clutton-Brock, Frederick Firebrace, Alexander Hubbard, Sir Henry Mather Jackson, Lewis J. Seargeant, Alfred A. Smithers, Lord Welby, Sir W. Lawrence Young, London.

Principal office, 94 McGill street, Montreal; London office, 9 New Broad street, E. C. Semi-annual meeting in April and October.

## GREAT NORTHERN RAILWAY CO.

(Controlled by Northern Securities Co.)

A corporation organized in 1889 to purchase various railroads in the Northwest. It leased the St. Paul, Minneapolis & Manitoba and owns the Duluth, Watertown & Pacific, Eastern of Minnesota, Montana Central, Wilmar & Sioux Falls and others; also the Seattle & Montana from Seattle to South Westminster, British Columbia.

MILEAGE.

| Leased: | Miles. | Proprietary roads: | Miles. |
|---|---|---|---|
| St. Paul, Minneapolis & Manitoba...... | 3,799 | Wilmar & Sioux Falls Railway......... | 437 |
| Eastern Railway of Minnesota......... | 470 | Duluth, Watertown & Pacific Railway.. | 70 |
| Duluth Terminal Railway............. | 2 | Montana Central Railway.. .......... | 260 |
| Dakota & Great Northern Railway..... | 40 | Minneapolis Union Railway........... | 2 |
| Park Rapids & Leech Lake Railway.... | 40 | Minneapolis Western....... ........ | 2 |
| Seattle & Montana Railroad (operated).. | 204 | | |
| Total operated directly............ | 4,555 | Total...................... ...... | 771 |

| | |
|---|---|
| Total operated June 30, 1902........................................................ | 5,326 |
| Operated separately and under construction.......................................... | 513 |
| Total of system.................................................................... | 5,839 |

The company controls the Northern Steamship Co., running between Buffalo and Duluth, and in 1897 instituted a trans-Pacific steamship line between Puget Sound, China and Japan. In 1898 completed extension from Duluth to Fosston, Minn., 229 miles, purchasing the Duluth, Superior & Western Railway, 99 miles, and amalgamating it with the Eastern Railway of Minnesota. In 1899 company also acquired the Spokane Falls & Northern and branches, and Sioux City & Northern and Sioux City & Western roads. Locomotives, 608; passenger cars, 486; freight cars, 26,545.

This company and the Northern Pacific in 1901 jointly purchased the stock of the Chicago, Burlington & Quincy Railroad, and leased that property to a new railway company which they jointly control. In payment for the Burlington stock the two purchasing companies issued their joint 4 per cent. collateral trust bonds at 200 for the Burlington shares.

In November, 1901, the stockholders of the company were offered the right to sell their stock at 180 to the Northern Securities Co., the price being payable in the stock of the Northern Securities Co. See statement of the latter company.

Stock......Par $100.......................Authorized, $125,000,000......Issued, $123,853,000

Transfer agency, 32 Nassau street, New York. Registrar, Central Trust Co., New York.

From 1892 to 1896 inclusive 5 per cent. dividends were paid. In August, 1897, the rate was increased, making 5½ per cent. paid in 1897. In 1898 the rate was further increased to 6¼ per cent., and in 1899 and 1900 7 per cent. was paid on the stock. Dividends are paid quarterly, 1¾ per cent. each, in February (1), May, August and November.

In 1898 stockholders also received a dividend of 50 per cent. in stock of the Seattle & Montana.

Originally, in 1890, $20,000,000 6 per cent. preferred non-cumulative stock was issued at 50 to St. Paul, Minneapolis & Manitoba stockholders, the other 50 per cent. being paid for by a transfer to this company of the St. Paul, Minneapolis & Manitoba treasury securities when this company leased the St. Paul, Minneapolis & Manitoba and guaranteed 6 per cent. on its $20,000,000 of stock. The Great Northern common stock authorized was $20,000,000, but none was issued. In 1893 $5,000,000 additional preferred was issued at par to pay for equipment, terminals, etc. In 1898 preferred stock was increased $25,000,000; of this $15,000,000 was sold to stockholders pro rata at par and proceeds used to retire the company's $15,000,000 of 4 per cent. collateral trust bonds and $10,000,000 was given to stockholders in exchange for the $12,500,000 stock of the Seattle & Montana which had been given to stockholders of the Great Northern as a 50 per cent. dividend. By these operations the Great Northern preferred stock was raised to $50,000,000.

In November company decided to surrender right to issue common stock and to increase outstanding stock to $75,000,000, making it of uniform character and having uniform rights. The $25,000,000 of stock was offerred to the holders of the St. Paul, Minneapolis & Manitoba, $20,000,000 stock in payment for their share at $125 each. A large majority of the St. Paul, Minneapolis & Manitoba stockholders accepted in advance. By this operation the complete unification of the system has been secured. On June 30, 1902, only $453,600 St. Paul, Minneapolis & Manitoba stock was outstanding.

In April, 1899, stock was increased $15,000,000, making authorized total $90,000,000, and increase was offered to stockholders at par, proceeds being used to acquire bonds and stock of Spokane Falls & Northern and other branches, and $7,500,000 new stock of Eastern Railway of Minnesota. In January, 1900, another increase of $10,000,000 was offered to stockholders at par, the purpose being to acquire additional mileage. This increased the authorized stock to $100,000,000. In

March, 1901, a further increase of $25,000,000 in the stock was announced, making the total $125,000,000. Stockholders were given the right to subscribe at par for the increase in the proportion of 25 per cent. of their holdings, being credited with $20 per share on such subscriptions, thus making the price paid by them for the new stock $80 per share.

FUNDED DEBT (LEASED AND PROPRIETARY LINES.)

| | |
|---|---|
| St. Paul, Minn. & Manitoba, 2d (now 1st) mort., 6 per cent., due 1909, April and Oct. | $7,503,000 |
| " Dakota extension mort., 6 per cent., due 1910, May and Nov. | 5,576,000 |
| " Consolidated mort., 6 per cent., due 1933, Jan. and July | 13,344,000 |
| " " " 4½ per cent., due 1933, Jan. and July | 20,176,000 |
| " Montana extension mort., 4 per cent., due 1937, June and Dec. | 10,185,000 |
| " Pacific extension sterling mort., 4 per cent., due 1940, June and Dec. | 14,545,454 |
| Eastern of Minnesota, 1st mort., 5 per cent., due 1908, April and Oct. | 4,700,000 |
| " " Northern Div. mort., 4 per cent., due 1948, April and Oct. | 5,000,000 |
| Montana Central, 1st mort., 6 per cent., due 1937, Jan. and July | 6,000,000 |
| " " " 5 per cent., due 1937, Jan. and July | 4,000,000 |
| Wilmar & Sioux Falls, 1st mort., 5 per cent., due 1938, June and Dec. | 3,646,000 |
| Minneapolis Union Railway, 1st mort., 6 per cent., due 1922, Jan. and July | 2,150,000 |
| " " " 1st mort., 5 per cent., due 1922, Jan. and July | 650,000 |
| Minneapolis Western Railway, 1st mort., 5 per cent., due 1911, Jan. and July | 500,000 |
| Total of leased and proprietary lines | $97,975,454 |

FUNDED DEBT (JOINTLY WITH NORTHERN PACIFIC).

Twenty-year joint collateral trust bonds, secured by Chicago, Burlington & Quincy stock, 4 per cent., gold, due July, 1921, Jan. and July .... $215,154,400

The bonded debt upon lines of the system covered by bonds in hands of the public is $20,696 per mile.

Great Northern guaranteed interest on the St. Paul, Minneapolis & Manitoba Railway debt, and 6 per cent. per annum on the $20,000,000 stock of that company. In 1898 the Eastern of Minnesota Northern Division 4 per cent. bonds for $5,000,000 were issued and guaranteed by this company to provide for the extension from Duluth to Fosston. The Great Northern 4 per cent. collateral trust 4 per cent. bonds for $15,000,000 were retired in 1898 with the proceeds of $15,000,000 of this company's stock as referred to above. This released £3,000,000 of Manitoba Pacific extension sterling 4s held in trust as security for the Great Northern bonds.

The Great Northern-Northern Pacific joint collateral trust 4 per cent. bonds, due 1921, are secured by the deposit of $107,576,500 out of a total of $111,200,000 of the Burlington stock. The bonds are subject to call at 105 after January 1, 1906.

EARNINGS, PROPERTIES LEASED FROM ST. PAUL, MINNEAPOLIS & MANITOBA.

Year ending June 30.

| | Gross. | Net. | Charges. | Surplus. |
|---|---|---|---|---|
| 1892–93 (3,352 miles) | $13,522,581 | $5,811,610 | $4,647,831 | $1,163,778 |
| 1893–94 (3,765 " ) | 11,345,356 | 4,444,634 | 5,352,804 | Def. 908,170 |
| 1894–95 ( " " ) | 13,109,939 | 5,504,262 | 5,372,590 | 131,672 |
| 1895–96 (3,770 " ) | 15,297,453 | 6,870,419 | 5,383,016 | 1,487,403 |
| 1896–97 (3,806 " ) | 14,994,541 | 6,318,445 | 5,380,729 | 937,715 |
| 1897–98 (3,854 " ) | 17,639,720 | 8,737,166 | 7,646,863 | 1,090,302 |
| 1898–99 ( " " ) | 19,057,813 | 8,902,224 | 5,937,824 | 2,964,400 |
| 1899–00 ( " " ) | 21,953,412 | 9,530,775 | 5,509,548 | 4,021,727 |
| 1900–01 ( " " ) | 20,881,051 | 8,026,870 | 3,687,656 | 4,339,214 |
| 1901–02 (4,555 " ) | 28,397,134 | 13,268,997 | 5,742,545 | 7,526,452 |

The figures for 1901–02 include the operations of the Seattle & Montana Railroad Co., and in the charges is included $2,000,000 transferred to the permanent improvement fund.

REVENUE, GREAT NORTHERN RAILWAY CO.

Year ending June 30.

| | Net from Leased Lines. | Other Income. | Total Income. | | Dividends Great Northern. | Surplus. |
|---|---|---|---|---|---|---|
| 1892–93 | $1,163,778 | $1,018,552 | $2,182,330 | (5) | $1,000,000 | $1,182,330 |
| 1893–94 | Def. 908,170 | 1,991,516 | 1,083,350 | (5) | 1,187,500 | Def. 104,150 |
| 1894–95 | 131,672 | 1,307,836 | 1,439,508 | (5) | 1,250,000 | 189,508 |
| 1895–96 | 1,487,403 | 805,143 | 2,292,547 | (5) | 1,250,000 | 1,042,547 |
| 1896–97 | 937,715 | 1,519,551 | 2,457,267 | (5) | 1,250,000 | 1,207,267 |
| 1897–98 | 1,090,302 | 2,481,465 | 3,571,768 | (6) | 1,500,000 | 2,071,768 |
| 1898–99 | 2,964,400 | 2,673,825 | 5,638,225 | (6¼) | 3,851,033 | 1,787,191 |
| 1899–00 | 4,021,227 | 4,605,314 | 8,626,541 | (7) | 6,408,777 | 2,217,763 |
| 1900–01 | 4,339,214 | 4,247,219 | 8,586,433 | (7) | 6,897,369 | 1,689,064 |
| 1901–02 | 7,526,452 | 2,816,458 | 10,342,918 | (7) | 8,225,920 | 2,116,990 |

Fixed charges in 1899 include $1,800,000 for permanent improvement, etc. In 1900 $1,800,000 for the same account is also included in charges.

EARNINGS, WHOLE SYSTEM.

Year ending June 30.

| | Miles. | Gross. | Net. | Per Cent. Expenses. | Gross Per Mile. | Net Per Mile. |
|---|---|---|---|---|---|---|
| 1895-96........... | 4,374 | $19,612,564 | $8,749,018 | 55.39 | $4,483 | $2,144 |
| 1896-97........... | 4,414 | 19,436,060 | 8,131,540 | 58.16 | 4,402 | 1,978 |
| 1897-98........... | 4,466 | 22,577,544 | 11,021,897 | 48.08 | 5,055 | 2,624 |
| 1898-99........... | 4,786 | 25,017,903 | 11,926,542 | 48.62 | 5,226 | 2,685 |
| 1899-00........... | 5,076 | 28,910,789 | 13,042,413 | 51.46 | 5,695 | 2,764 |
| 1900-01........... | 5,202 | 28,350,689 | 11,537,626 | 55.88 | 5,449 | 2,404 |
| 1901-02........... | 5,249 | 36,032,256 | 17,003,397 | 49.37 | 6,864 | 3,388 |

The following presents the comparative freight traffic statistics of the company:

| | Average Mileage. | Total Tonnage. | Tons Carried One Mile. | Freight Density. | Rate per Ton per Mile. | Earnings per Train Mile. | Average Tons per Train |
|---|---|---|---|---|---|---|---|
| 1896-97........ | 4,414 | 7,471,894 | 1,657,223,725 | 352,243 | 0.956c | $2.73 | 281 |
| 1897-98........ | 4,466 | 8,089,593 | 1,937,955,894 | 433,940 | 0.932 | 2.99 | 316 |
| 1898-99........ | 4,786 | 10,002,810 | 2,158,212,794 | 492,731 | 0.916 | 3.13 | 336 |
| 1899-00........ | 5,076 | 11,529,661 | 2,504,792,882 | 493,459 | 0.899 | 3.26 | 356 |
| 1900-01........ | 5,202 | 11,518,251 | 2,481,751,195 | 477,230 | 0.871 | 3.38 | 381 |
| 1901-02........ | 5,249 | 15,099,818 | 3,190,217,482 | 607,776 | 0.859 | 3.64 | 417 |

President, James J. Hill; 1st Vice-President, James N. Hill; 2d Vice-President, R. I. Farrington, St. Paul; 3d Vice-President and Secretary, E. T. Nichols, New York; 4th Vice-President, J. W. Blabon; Treasurer, Edward Sawyer, St. Paul; Assistant Secretary and Assistant Treasurer, Nicholas Terhune, New York; Comptroller, J. G. Drew, St. Paul.

Directors—James J. Hill, Frederick Weyerhaeuser, Edward Sawyer, M. D. Grover, James N. Hill, William B. Dean, R. I. Farrington, St. Paul; Henry W. Cannon, New York; Samuel Hill, Minneapolis.

Principal office, Third and Rosabel streets, St. Paul; New York office, 32 Nassau street. Annual meeting, second Thursday inOctober.

## GREAT NORTHERN RAILWAY CO. OF CANADA

Road owned, Riviere a Pierre, Que., to Hawkesbury, Ont., 175 miles; trackage on Quebec & Lake St. Johns Railroad into Quebec, 58 miles. Arrangements are made for entering Montreal over the Chateauguay & Northern Railway, 36 miles, which is being constructed in this company's interest. The company purchased a large terminal property at Quebec and improved the same with docks and warehouses. It owns the Great Northern Elevator at Quebec. It has a close traffic arrangement with the Canada Atlantic Railway, by which the two roads constitute a through line from Parry Sound on Georgian Bay of Lake Huron to deep water at Quebec. In 1900 arrangements were made for a steamship service between Quebec and London in connection with this company, and afterwards for a similar service to Liverpool and Manchester. A branch from Hawkesbury to Ottawa is projected. Locomotives, 19; passenger cars, 37; freight cars, 672.

In February, 1903, it was reported that this company would be combined with the Canadian Northern Railway Co.

| Stock....Par $100....Authorized | com., $4,500,000<br>pref., 450,000<br>deb., 3,000,000 | Issued | com., $3,000,000<br>pref., ........<br>deb., ..... . | $3,000,000 |
|---|---|---|---|---|

Although preferred and debenture stocks have been authorized for the amounts given above, they have not been issued.

FUNDED DEBT.

| | |
|---|---|
| 1st mort., 5 per cent., due Jan., 1950, Jan. and July.. .............................. | $4,002,000 |
| Car Trusts, 6 per cent., due 1902-05, Jan. and July.................................. | 274,000 |
| Quebec Terminal mort., 5 per cent., due 1950........................................ | 118,000 |
| Total ................................................................ | $4,394,000 |

The 1st mortgage, Trustee, Central Trust Co., New York, is for $6,000,000, authorized, at the rate of $20,000 per mile. Of the amount outstanding $500,000 was issued to pay for the bridge across the Ottawa River at Hawkesbury. The first coupon on the 1st mortgage bonds was due

July 1, 1901. The terminal mortgage was created in 1900, and is secured by the Quebec terminals of the company.

EARNINGS.

Year ending June 30.

| | Gross. | Net. | Charges. | Surplus. |
|---|---|---|---|---|
| 1901-02 | $524,764 | $207,963 | $157,417 | $50,546 |

President, Pierre Garneau, Quebec; Vice-Presidents, James McNaught, New York; H. H. Melville, Boston; Victor Chateauvert, General Manager, J. G. Scott; Treasurer, E. E. Ling; Secretary, Louis G. Scott, Quebec.

Directors—Pierre Garneau, Victor Chateauvert, John T. Ross, Jules Tessier, J. G. Scott, E. E. Ling, S. N. Parent, Quebec; James McNaught, William L. Bull, New York; H. H. Melville, John Joyce, Boston; H. E. Mitchell, Philadelphia.

Main office, St. Andrew street Terminal, Quebec. Annual meeting, first Tuesday in September.

## GREEN BAY & WESTERN RAILROAD CO.

Road owned, Green Bay, Wis., to East Winona, Wis., 212½ miles; branches, 12½ miles, including trackage, leased, 4 miles; total, 225 miles. Locomotives, 25; passenger cars, 20; freight cars, 450.

A corporation under the laws of Wisconsin June 16, 1896, and succeeded Green Bay, Winona & St. Paul Railroad Co., sold under foreclosure May 12, 1896.

Stock......Par $100..........................Authorized, $2,500,000......Issued, $2,500,000

Stock is transferred by the Secretary of the company, New York. Registrar, Farmers' Loan & Trust Co., New York.

In the formation of the company it was provided that after A debentures receive 2½ per cent. per annum if earned, stock shall receive up to 2½ per cent., after which the stock and A debentures share equally in surplus up to 5 per cent. each, after which B debentures are entitled to all surplus revenue.

The first dividend on company's stock was 1½ per cent., payable February 15, 1899. 2½ per cent. was also paid February 1, 1900; 3 per cent. February 1, 1901; 4 per cent. February 1, 1902, and 4 per cent. February 2, 1902.

FUNDED DEBT.

| | |
|---|---|
| Debentures A, income, 5 per cent., non-cumulative | $600,000 |
| " B, income, non-cumulative after stock | 7,000,000 |
| Total | $7,600,000 |

The Green Bay, Winona & St. Paul Railroad Co. defaulted on interest payable February 1, 1885, and passed into the hands of the Farmers' Loan & Trust Co., trustee for the 1st mortgage bondholders, bondholders agreeing to fund three overdue coupons. Interest payments were resumed August 1, 1886. Defaulted again in August, 1889, and was reorganized in 1892.

The old company again defaulted in August, 1894. Reorganization plan was adopted in 1895, by which road was foreclosed and securities exchanged for non-cumulative income debentures, Class A and Class B and stock. There are no fixed charges other than taxes, and consent of 75 per cent. of stock is necessary to sale or lease of property.

Dividends of 2½ per cent. were paid on A debentures February 15, 1898; 2½ per cent. February 15, 1899; 2½ per cent. February 1, 1900; 3 per cent. February 1, 1901, and 4 per cent. February 1, 1902.

EARNINGS.

| Year ending June 30. | Gross. | Net. |
|---|---|---|
| 1895-96 | $401,626 | $95,694 |
| 1896-97 | 419,759 | 77,945 |
| 1897-98 | 446,342 | 69,503 |
| 1898-99 | 459,342 | 69,503 |
| 1899-00 | 484,106 | 99,179 |
| 1900-01 | 481,629 | 122,790 |

President, S. S. Palmer, New York; Vice-President, J. A. Jordan, Green Bay, Wis.; Secretary and Treasurer, Mark T. Cox, New York.

Directors—S. S. Palmer, Mark T. Cox, C. Ledyard Blair, William J. Hunt, New York; J. A. Jordan, Green Bay, Wis.

Main office, Green Bay, Wis.; New York office, 40 Wall street. Annual meeting, second Thursday in March, at Green Bay.

## GULF & SHIP ISLAND RAILROAD CO.

A corporation chartered February 23, 1882, by the State of Mississippi with a perpetual charter.

Road owned, Gulfport to Jackson, Miss., 160½ miles; Maxie to Columbia, Miss., 48¾ miles; Saratoga to Laurel, 41¾ miles; total operated, 251 miles.

The completed line opened for operation in 1900. During 1902 the company authorized an issue of bonds for the purpose of acquiring land and constructing extensive terminals, docks, etc., at Gulfport, where the company has effected great improvements. These include the construction of a main pier about 1 mile long and the dredging of a ship canal about 6 miles long and 310 feet wide with a depth of from 23 to 24 feet. An anchorage basin of the depth of the main channel and one-quarter mile by one-half mile in area adjoining the main pier is being formed. The country tributary to the road is furnished with a large lumber tonnage, but the business of the company in transporting cotton and manufactures is increasing.

Stock......Par $100..........................Authorized, $5,000,000......Issued, $5,000,000

All of the capital stock of this company is held under a voting trust, the stock being deposited with the New York Security & Trust Co., Joseph T. Jones, Harvey Edward Fisk and Charles K. Beekman being the trustees.

FUNDED DEBT.

1st refunding and terminal mort., 5 per cent., due Jan., 1952, Jan. and July.......... $4,181,000

The 1st refunding and terminal mortgage was created in 1902 for the purpose of retiring the old 1st mortgage 5s, of which $16,000 remain outstanding. The authorized issue is $5,000,000. Of the new bonds $750,000 were reserved to build terminals at Gulfport, $500,000 are reserved for new equipment and $1,000,000 are held for future improvements or new property. There is a sinking fund of 1 per cent. of the bonds, beginning in 1904, the bonds to be purchased at 110, but not drawn.

EARNINGS.

Year ending June 30.

| | Gross. | Net. | Charges. | Surplus. |
|---|---|---|---|---|
| 1901 (250 miles)..................... | $1,030,849 | $235,289 | $230,742 | $4,547 |
| 1902 (251 " )..................... | 1,374,684 | 434,170 | 175,311 | 258,859 |

For the seven months ending January 31, 1903, the company reported net earnings of $377,464, as against $236,235 in 1902, and a surplus of $275,464 in 1903, as compared with $122,334 in 1902.

President, Joseph T. Jones; 1st Vice-President, Joseph A. Jones, Buffalo; 2d Vice-President, Thomas P. Hale, Gulfport, Miss.; Secretary and Treasurer, R. E. Powers, Buffalo; Auditor, Elisha Gee, Gulfport, Miss.

Directors—Joseph T. Jones, Joseph A. Jones, R. E. Powers, Buffalo; C. K. Beekman, New York; C. L. McClellan, Mt. Vernon, N. Y.; E. J. Bowers, Bay St. Louis, Miss.; T. P. Hale, Gulfport, Miss.; D. H. Jack, Bradford, Pa.; J. H. Thompson, Plainfield, N. J.

Main office, Gulfport, Miss.; President's office, Prudential Building, Buffalo. Annual meeting, first Monday in January. Fiscal Agents, Fish & Robinson, New York.

---

## THE HOCKING VALLEY RAILWAY CO.

A corporation formed under the laws of Ohio, February 25, 1899, to take over the property of the Columbus, Hocking Valley & Toledo Railway Co. The latter was a consolidation, 1881, of the Columbus & Hocking Valley, the Columbus & Toledo and the Ohio & West Virginia Railway Companies.

Road owned, Rockwell, O., to Pomeroy, O., 252 miles; Athens branch, 26 miles; other branches, 63 miles; trackage to Toledo, 6 miles; total, 347 miles. This company purchased the stock of the Toledo & Ohio Central and controls that road, which is operated separately. See its statement. In October, 1902, the company acquired all the stock and bonds of the Zanesville & Western Railway Co. Locomotives, 104; passenger cars, 65; freight cars, 14,387.

In December, 1902, a syndicate was formed which called for deposits of the common stock with J. P. Morgan & Co., with power to sell the control; the retirement of the preferred being also contemplated.

Stock..Par $100...Authorized { com., $11,000,000 / pref., 15,000,000 }  Issued { com., $11,000,000 / pref., 15,000,000 }  $26,000,000

The preferred stock is 4 per cent., non-cumulative, but after both classes of stock receive 4 per cent. in any year they share in any further division of surplus. The company has a statutory right to retire the preferred at par.

Transfer Agents, J. P. Morgan & Co., New York. Registrar, Central Trust Co., New York.

The first dividend on the new preferred stock was declared in November, 1899, 1½ per cent.,

THE
GULF & SHIP ISLAND
RAILROAD
AND ITS CONNECTIONS
MEMPHIS
Hernando
Tunica
Helena
Lula
Coahoma
Friar's Pt.
Eagles Nest
Riverside
Clarksdale
Senatobia
Abbeville
Batesville
Holly Springs
Ripley
Corinth
Iuka
Booneville
Myrtle
New Albany
Oxford
Pontotoc
Guntown
Tupelo
Nettleton
Watervalley
Coffeeville
Grenada
Okolona
Aberdeen Jc.
Egypt
Aberdeen
Muldon
West Point
Columbus
Starkville
Artesia
Wathall
Eupora
Winona
Greenwood
Itta Bena
Morehead
Minter City
Tutwiler
Webb
Duncan
Rosedale
Dockery
Boyle
Lamont
Wilczinski
Leland
Belzona
Hampton
Rolling Fork
Vaiden
Ackerman
Sturgis
Tchula Jc.
Lexington
Durant
Kosciusko
Macon
Wahalak
Yazoo City
Carthage
Philadelphia
Canton
McGehee
Tripp
Dermott
Huntington
Arkansas City
PIERS, TERMINALS
AND PROPOSED SLIPS
AT GULFPORT.

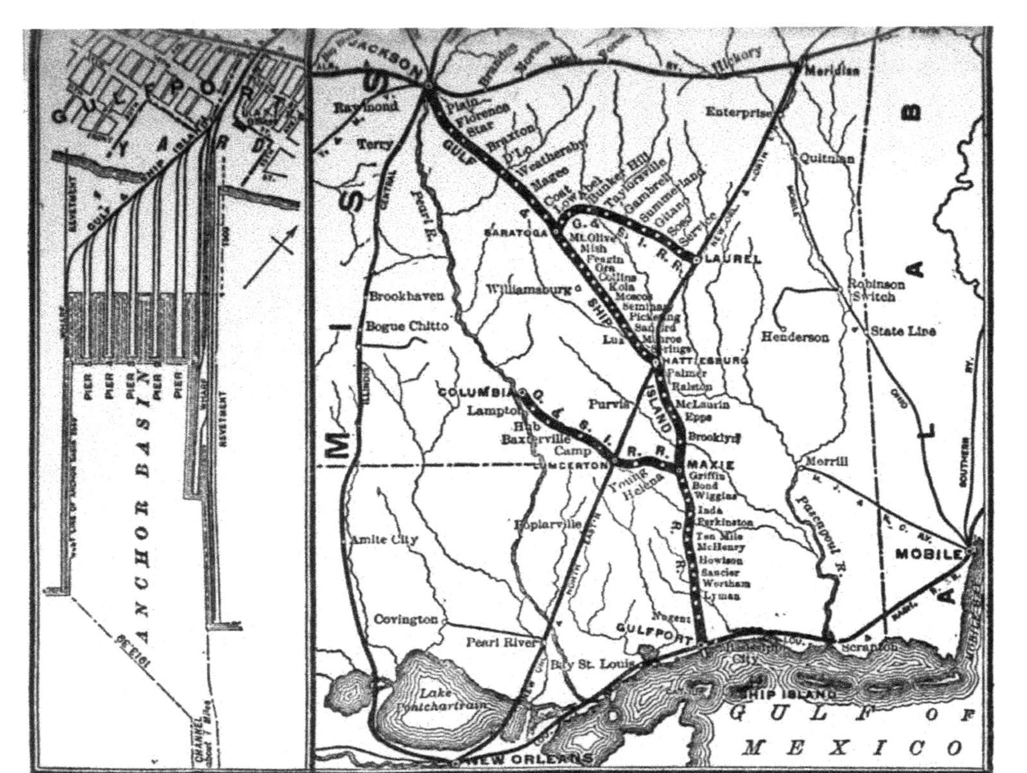
GULFPORT
ANCHOR BASIN
PIER
REVETMENT
WHARF
CHANNEL
JACKSON
Raymond
Terry
Plain
Florence
Star
Braxton
D'Lo
Weathersby
Magee
Mt. Olive
Mish
Pearl R.
Brookhaven
Bogue Chitto
Williamsburg
SARATOGA
Meridian
Enterprise
Quitman
LAUREL
Robinson Switch
State Line
Henderson
HATTIESBURG
Palmer
Ralston
McLaurin
Eppe
Purvis
COLUMBIA
Lampton
Hub
Baxterville
Camp
LUMBERTON
MAXIE
Griffin
Bond
Wiggins
Inda
Parkinston
Ten Mile
McHenry
Howison
Saucier
Wortham
Lyman
Young
Helena
Poplarville
Amite City
Covington
Pearl River
Bay St. Louis
Nugent
GULFPORT
Morrill
Pascagoul R.
MOBILE
Scranton
Lake Pontchartrain
NEW ORLEANS
SHIP ISLAND
GULF OF MEXICO
M I S S
A L A B
ILLINOIS CENTRAL
SOUTHERN RY.

MAP OF THE

HOCKING VALLEY

RAILWAY.

payable January 10, 1900. In July, 1900, 2 per cent., semi-annual, was paid on old preferred, and also 2 per cent., semi-annual, January 16, 1901. Since which time regular 2 per cent. semi-annual dividends have been paid on the preferred in January and July.

The first dividend on common stock was 1½ per cent. from the earnings of the year 1900-01, paid July 20, 1901, since which time regular 1½ per cent. semi-annual dividends have been paid on the common in January and July, 1902.

### Funded Debt.

| | |
|---|---|
| Hocking Valley Ry. 1st cons. mort., 4½ per cent., due Jan., 1999, Jan. and July..... | $11,397,000 |
| Col. & Hock. Val., extended, 1st mort., 4 per cent., due Oct., 1948, April and Oct... | 1,401,000 |
| Columbus & Toledo, 1st mort., 7 per cent., due Aug., 1905, Feb. and Aug.......... | 2,500,000 |
| Ohio & West Virginia, 1st mort., 7 per cent., due May, 1910, May and Nov........ | 1,584,000 |
| Total.............................................................. | $16,882,000 |

There are also car trust obligations for $3,157,992. The three bond issues given last in the above table were left undisturbed by the reorganization.

The old company suffered severely from the unfavorable condition of the coal trade, and no dividends were paid on the old preferred stock after July, 1896. In February, 1897, Vice-President Monsarrat was appointed Receiver. A majority of the 5 and 6 per cent. bonds were deposited with J. P. Morgan & Co., New York, who undertook the reorganization. Foreclosure under consolidated mortgage had been instituted, but a plan of reorganization was delayed by the state of the coal business. Foreclosure sale was made February 24, 1899.

The 1st mortgage, 7 per cent., bonds of the Columbus & Hocking Valley Railroad were extended at 4 per cent.

In December, 1899, this company acquired control of the Toledo & Ohio Central Railway. The stock of that company consists of $3,708,000 preferred and $5,895,000 common, all of which has been exchanged for stock of this company.

This company guarantees $2,750,000 5 per cent. bonds of the Kanawha & Hocking Coal & Coke Co., and $2,750,000 5s of the Continental Coal Co.

For details of the reorganization plan of the Columbus, Hocking Valley & Toledo Railway Co. and terms of exchange of old securities for new see Manual for 1900.

### Earnings.

| | Div. Pref. | Gross. | Net. | Charges. | Surplus. |
|---|---|---|---|---|---|
| 1893 (329 miles).......... | 5 | $3,270,362 | $1,378,930 | $948,676 | $430,254 |
| 1894 ( " " ).......... | 5 | 2,698,699 | 1,255,925 | 1,147,353 | 108,571 |
| 1895 ( " " ).......... | 5 | 2,656,162 | 1,158,627 | ........ | ...... |
| 1896 ( " " ).......... | 5 | 2,505,611 | 976,022 | ........ | ...... |
| 1897 ( " " ).......... | 5 | 2,580,467 | 908,499 | ........ | ...... |
| 1898 ( " " ).......... | .. | 2,756,552 | ........ | ........ | ...... |
| 1899 (4 mos. end'g June 30) | .. | 1,005,783 | 332,486 | 124,951 | 207,534 |
| 1900 (year ending June 30) | 3½ | 4,417,266 | 2,071,447 | 902,900 | 1,168,547 |
| 1901 ( " " ) | 4 | 4,653,258 | 1,867,972 | 513,794 | 1,354,177 |
| 1902 ( " " ) | 4 | 5,316,522 | 2,087,191 | 484,818 | 1,602,372 |

After payment of 3½ per cent. dividends on the preferred stock for the year 1899-1900 the balance to credit of profit and loss was $938,982. In 1900-01 the 4 per cent. dividends on preferred and 1½ per cent. on the common required $7:6,324. In 1901-02, after paying 4 per cent. on the preferred and 3 per cent. on the common, the surplus was $729,724.

The following presents the comparative freight traffic statistics of the company:

| | Average Mileage. | Total Tonnage. | Tons Carried One Mile. | Freight Density. | Rate per Ton per Mile. | Earnings per Train Mile. | Av. Tons per Train |
|---|---|---|---|---|---|---|---|
| 1899-00.. | 348 | 6,691,394 | 805,317,681 | 2,327,508 | 0.448c | $2.89 | 646 |
| 1900-01.. | 347 | 6,756,611 | 835,528,765 | 2,402,100 | 0.442 | 2.85 | 645 |
| 1901-02.. | 347 | 8,156,514 | 1,003,371,955 | 2,891,561 | 0.428 | 2.90 | 678 |

In 1899-1900 the total tonnage transported included 3,928,452 tons of bituminous coal, and in 1900-01, 4,171,502 tons.

President, Nicholas Monsarrat, Columbus, O.; 1st Vice-President, Ralph W. Hickox; 2d Vice-President, James H. Hoyt, Cleveland; Secretary and Treasurer, W. N. Cott; Auditor, Louis P. Ecker; Assistant to President, F. B. Sheldon, Columbus, O.; Assistant Secretary and Assistant Treasurer, A. H. Gillard, New York.

Directors—Charles Steele, Thomas F. Ryan, Charles B. Alexander, Nicholas Monsarrat, P. W. Huntington, W. F. Goodspeed, Robert M. Gallaway, James H. Hoyt, Myron T. Herrick, C. G. Hickox, Robert Bacon, R. S. Warner, Ralph W. Hickox.

Main office, 50 East Broad Street, Columbus, O. Annual meeting, first Tuesday in October, at Columbus.

## HOUSTON & TEXAS CENTRAL RAILROAD CO.

(Controlled by Southern Pacific Co.)

A corporation formed under the laws of Texas April 11, 1893, and succeeded the railway company of the same name, the road of which was sold under foreclosure.

Road owned, Houston, Tex., to Denison, Tex., 338 miles; branch, Hempstead to Austin, Tex., 115 miles; Bremond to Ross, Tex., 55 miles; total owned, 507 miles. In 1901 acquired and consolidated with the Fort Worth & New Orleans, 40 miles; Central Texas & Northwestern, 12 miles; Austin & Northwestern, 107 miles. The last named line is to be extended considerably. Total of system, 668 miles. Locomotives, 106; passenger cars, 100; freight cars, 2,965.

In February, 1901, the Legislature of Texas authorized the consolidation of the auxiliary roads with this company. In February, 1903, it was announced that the Rock Island Co. had obtained an interest in this company with joint rights in its operation with the Southern Pacific Co.

Stock......Par $100........................Authorized, $10,000,000......Issued, $10,000,000

Stock is transferred at the New York office of the company, 120 Broadway.

FUNDED DEBT.

| | |
|---|---|
| 1st mort., land grant, 5 per cent., due July, 1937, Jan. and July.................... | $5,960,000 |
| Consolidated mort., land grant, 6 per cent., due Oct., 1912, April and Oct.......... | 2,911,000 |
| General mort., 4 per cent., due April, 1921, April and Oct.......................... | 4,287,000 |
| Austin & Northwestern, 1st mort., 5 per cent., due July, 1941, Jan. and July...... | 1,920,000 |
| Waco & Northwestern Div., 1st mort., 6 per cent., due May, 1930, May and Nov.... | 1,105,000 |
| Fort Worth & N. O., 1st mort., 6 per cent., due Dec., 1925, Jan. and July.......... | 709,000 |
| Central Tex. & Northwestern, 1st mort., 6 per cent., due Oct., 1911, April and Oct.. | 180,000 |
| Total ........................................................................ | $17,072,000 |

The Southern Pacific Co. owns $9,596,000 of the stock.

The 1st mortgage on the Waco & Northwestern division is $1,225,000, authorized.

The company had a land grant from the State of Texas, of which about 2,600,000 acres remain unsold. Receipts from land sales not included below. They go to redeem the 1st mortgage consolidated and general mortgage bonds which may be called at 110 from proceeds of land sales. The 4 and 6 per cent. debentures, due October, 1897, were refunded till 1902 at 5 per cent.

The company defaulted on the interest on the 1st mortgage on January 1, 1885, and in February Receivers were appointed. The road was sold under foreclosure September 8, 1888. Under plan of reorganization of December 20, 1887, the Southern Pacific Co. guarantees the interest on the 1st mortgage, consolidated mortgage and general mortgage bonds, and principal and interest of the consolidated mortgage and debenture bonds. The plan required stockholders to pay an assessment of 71 4-10 per cent. of the par value of their holdings. Litigation against the payment of the assessment followed, and Receiver was not discharged until April, 1893.

EARNINGS.

Year ending June 30.

| | Gross. | Net. | Charges. | Surplus. |
|---|---|---|---|---|
| 1896-97 | $3,206,573 | $1,056,548 | $923,662 | $132,885 |
| 1897-98 | 3,164,529 | 1,039,429 | 993,202 | 46,227 |
| 1898-99 | 3,861,034 | 1,398,293 | 1,031,830 | 366,463 |
| 1899-00 | 4,475,570 | 1,160,093 | 962,903 | 187,190 |
| 1900-01 | 4,958,393 | 1,917,659 | 941,096 | 976,562 |
| 1901-02 | 5,156,171 | 1,575,302 | 1,003,074 | 572,228 |

President, Charles H. Tweed, New York; Vice-President, Charles H. Markham; Secretary and Treasurer, William H. Field, Houston, Tex.

Main offices, 120 Broadway, New York, and Houston, Tex. Annual meeting, first Monday in April.

---

## HOUSTON, EAST & WEST TEXAS RAILWAY CO.

(Controlled by Southern Pacific Co.)

Road owned, Houston to Logansport, Tex., 192 miles. Line was 3-foot gauge, but was changed to standard gauge in 1894. Locomotives, 18; passenger cars, 14; freight cars, 400. Company connects at Logansport, Tex., with the Houston & Shreveport Railroad, 40 miles, forming line to Shreveport, La. Locomotives, 18; passenger cars, 14; freight cars, 484.

In 1899 the Legislature of Texas authorized the consolidation of this company with the Houston & Shreveport. In July, 1900, the Southern Pacific Co. acquired control of the company by purchasing nearly all the stock.

Stock......Par $100..........................Authorized, $1,000,000......Issued, $1,920,000

FUNDED DEBT.

| | |
|---|---|
| 1st mort., 5 per cent., due May, 1933, May and Nov., guaranteed by Southern Pac... | $2,199,000 |
| 1st mort., 5 per cent., due May, 1933, May and Nov., not guaranteed............... | 501,000 |
| Total | $2,700,000 |

EARNINGS.

| Year ending June 30. | Gross. | Net. |
|---|---|---|
| 1894–95 | $569,553 | $226,883 |
| 1895–96 | 518,489 | 118,998 |
| 1896–97 | 571,150 | 121,196 |
| 1897–98 | 691,779 | 239,524 |
| 1898–99 | 685,817 | 244,722 |
| 1899–00 | 601,429 | 200,684 |
| 1900–01 | 847,113 | 245,480 |
| 1901–02 | 901,420 | 192,082 |

In 1900 the Southern Pacific Co. guaranteed $2,199,000 of the 1st mortgage 5 per cent. bonds, principal and interest, but the bonds may be redeemed at any time at 105 and interest, on six months' notice

Road went into hands of a Receiver in 1885 and was foreclosed in 1892. In 1896 company was again reorganized without foreclosure under plan of August, 1896. Old 1st mortgage bonds for $3,840,000 were exchanged, 55 per cent. for new 5s and 45 per cent. for new stock. The mortgage is $3,000,000.

The company has a land grant of 10,240 acres per mile.

President, C. H. Markham; Vice-President, Jeff. N. Miller; Treasurer, Eugene Dargan, Houston, Tex.

Main office, Houston, Tex. Annual meeting, first Tuesday in December.

---

## HUNTINGDON & BROAD TOP MOUNTAIN RAILROAD & COAL CO.

Road owned, Huntingdon, Pa., to Mt. Dallas, 45 miles; coal branches, 19 miles; total, 64 miles. Locomotives, 23; passenger cars, 11; freight cars, 2,920.

Stock......Par $50....Authorized { com., $1,500,000 / pref., 2,000,000 } Issued { com., $1,371,750 / pref., 2,000,000 } $3,371,750

Stock is transferred at the office of the company, Philadelphia.

The preferred stock is entitled to 7 per cent., non-cumulative.

Dividends of 7 per cent. were paid on the preferred stock from 1891 to 1896, inclusive. In 1897 paid 6 per cent. on the preferred; in 1898, 5 per cent.; in 1899, 5½ per cent.; in 1900, 7 per cent.; in 1901, 5 per cent., and in 1902, 6 per cent. Preferred dividends are half-yearly, January 25 and July 25. No dividends have been paid on the common stock since February, 1897.

FUNDED DEBT.

| | |
|---|---|
| 1st mort., extended, 4 per cent., due Sept., 1920, April and Oct..................... | $416,000 |
| 2d mort., extended 4 per cent., due Feb., 1925, Feb. and Aug............. | 367,500 |
| Consolidated mort., extended, 5 per cent., due March 31, 1925, April and Oct........ | 1,497,000 |
| Total | $2,280,500 |

There are also car trusts for $535,000 outstanding.

In 1894 arrangements were made to extend the consolidated 5 per cent. bonds to 1925.

EARNINGS.

| | Dividends. Pref. | Com. | Gross. | Net | Charges. | Surplus. |
|---|---|---|---|---|---|---|
| 1893 | 7 | 5 | $703,607 | $372,603 | $117,295 | $255,308 |
| 1894 | 7 | 5 | 580,718 | 313,812 | 117,635 | 196,179 |
| 1895 | 7 | 4½ | 648,004 | 352,021 | 110,650 | 241,371 |
| 1896 | 7 | 4 | 583,362 | 313,811 | 106,295 | 207,516 |
| 1897 | 6 | .. | 509,540 | 244,023 | 106,655 | 137,370 |
| 1898 | 5 | .. | 506,747 | 230,814 | 107,260 | 123,554 |
| 1899 | 5½ | .. | 624,841 | 274,051 | 106,190 | 167,861 |
| 1900 | 7 | .. | 643,904 | 247,443 | 106,190 | 141,243 |
| 1901 | 5 | .. | 754,632 | 324,963 | 106,105 | 218,868 |
| 1902 | 6 | .. | 860,246 | 345,609 | 106,190 | 239,417 |

In 1901 the company made large expenditures for betterments and equipments, the balance over preferred dividends and such expenditures being $56,642.

President, George H. Colket; Secretary and Treasurer, J. P. Donaldson, Philadelphia.

Directors—William Bault, Lewis A. Riley, William H. Shallcross, Harrison K. Caner Thomas R. Patton, Samuel Bancroft, Jr., Robert H. Crozer, Charles S. Farnum, Edward Bringhurst, Jr., Morris W. Stroud, James W. Paul, Jr., Charles D. Barney.

Main office, 4th and Walnut streets, Philadelphia. Annual meeting, first Tuesday in February. Books close sixty days previous.

## ILLINOIS CENTRAL RAILROAD CO.

Road owned, Chicago to Cairo, 365 miles; Centralia to East Dubuque, Ill., 341 miles; Dubuque & Sioux City Railroad, 730 miles; St. Louis, Peoria & Northern, Litchfield to East St. Louis, 98 miles; Switz City to Effingham, Ill., 88 miles; total owned, 1,622 miles; controlled and leased, Chicago, St. Louis & New Orleans Railroad, Cairo, Ill., to New Orleans, La., 547 miles; Memphis Division, Memphis to Grenada, Miss., 100 miles; Ohio Valley Railroad, 139 miles; Yazoo & Mississippi Valley Railroad, 1,001 miles; Louisville Division, formerly Chesapeake, Ohio & Southwestern, 396 miles; St. Louis, Alton & Terre Haute, East St. Louis to Eldorado, Ill., and branches, 239 miles; total controlled and leased, 2,422 miles. Controls branch lines, 1,096 miles, and leases 126 miles. Total operated June 30, 1902, 4,283 miles. The company also controls other lines not included in above. The operations of the Yazoo & Mississippi Valley are reported separately.

In 1892 the Illinois Central Railroad Co. acquired control of the Louisville, New Orleans & Texas, and consolidated it with the Yazoo & Mississippi Valley Railroad Co. In November, 1893, acquired the Chesapeake, Ohio & Southwestern. In 1896, leased the St. Louis, Alton & Terre Haute, and in 1897 the Chicago & Texas. In 1898 began the construction of a road, the Canton, Aberdeen & Nashville, to extend from West Point, Miss., to Windfield, Ala., 65 miles. In 1900 completed the construction of a line from Fort Dodge, Ia., to Council Bluffs, Ia., and Omaha, Neb., 130 miles, which is part of the Dubuque & Sioux City Railroad. In December, 1899, acquired 85 miles of the St. Louis, Peoria & Northern from Springfield, Ill., to Mt.Carbon, with trackage 17 miles to St. Louis. In 1900 the company completed an extension from Lyle, Minn., to Albert Lea, Minn. Also in 1900 took over the operation of the Peoria, Decatur & Evansville Railroad, 256 miles, having purchased control of that road from its bondholders. In 1901 the Cecilia branch of the Louisville & Nashville, 45 miles, which the company had operated under lease, was purchased. In 1901 it also acquired the Kentucky Western, 18 miles.

In 1902 a number of the leased and auxiliary roads were formally consolidated with the company.

Locomotives, 947; passenger cars, 726; freight cars, 42,419; service cars, 469.

Stock..............Par $100.................Authorized, $95,040,000......Issued, $95,040,000
Special stock..... Par $100.................Authorized, $10,000,000......Issued, $10,000,000

The special stock is entitled to 4 per cent. per annum. It was issued in June, 1883, when a dividend in this stock was paid to its stockholders in the proportion of 17 shares of special for each 100 shares of stock.

In July, 1887, stock was increased $10,000,000, the proceeds being devoted to the purchase of stocks of the Iowa Falls & Sioux City and the Dubuque & Sioux City roads; the balance, $3,700,000, being used for extensions. Another increase of $5,000,000 was made in 1890, and in 1892 $5,000,000 was authorized, making total stock $50,000,000. This stock was allotted to stockholders at par, unsubscribed balance being taken by a syndicate. In November, 1895, stock was increased $10,000,000, making total issue $60,000,000. Of increase $2,500,000 was allotted at par forthwith, and in 1899, balance, $7,500,000, was sold. In 1900 the stock was increased $6,000,000 for equipment and extensions, and in October, 1900, the authorized amount was increased to $79,200,000, part of the increase being offered to stockholders at par. A further increase of $15,840,000 was made in August, 1902. The stockholders of record, September 19, 1902, being allowed to subscribe for the increase at par in the proportion of 20 per cent. of their holdings.

Transfer agency, 214 Broadway, New York. Registrar, National Park Bank, New York.

For dividends paid see table of earnings below. September, 1900, the half-yearly dividend was increased to 3 per cent., putting the stock on a 6 per cent. basis. The dividends are paid semi-annually, 3 per cent. each, on March 1 and September 1. Dividends on the special leased line stock are paid semi-annually, 2 per cent. each, on January 1 and July 1.

### FUNDED DEBT.

| | |
|---|---|
| Sterling mort. bonds extended, 4 per cent., due April, 1951, April and Oct........... | $2,500,000 |
| Sterling mort. bonds, 5 per cent., due Dec., 1905, June and Dec..................... | 1,000,000 |
| Sterling sinking fund bonds, 5 per cent., due April, 1903, April and Oct............ | 3,150,000 |
| Springfield Division, refunding mort., 3½ per cent., due Jan., 1951, Jan. and July.. | 2,000,000 |
| Middle Division bonds, currency 5 per cent., due Aug., 1921, Feb. and Aug......... | 968,000 |
| Mortgage bonds, gold, 4 per cent., due Jan., 1951, Jan. and July.................... | 1,500,000 |
| Mortgage bonds, gold, 3½ per cent., due Jan., 1951, Jan. and July.................. | 2,499,000 |
| Sterling mort. bonds, 3½ per cent., due July, 1950, Jan. and July................... | 5,266,000 |

FUNDED DEBT—*Continued.*

| | |
|---|---|
| Sterling loan of 1895, 3 per cent., due March, 1951, March and Sept. | $2,500,000 |
| Collat. trust 4 per cent. gold bonds, due April, 1952, April and Oct. | 15,000,000 |
| Cairo bridge bonds, 4 per cent., due Dec., 1950, June and Dec. | 3,000,000 |
| Collat. trust, on Louisville, N. O. & Texas, 4 per cent., due Nov., 1953, May and Nov. | 25,000,000 |
| Chicago, St. L. & New Orleans, ref. mort., 3½ per cent., due 1951, June and Dec. | 1,359,000 |
| Chicago, St. L. & New Orleans, 2d mort., 6 per cent., due Dec., 1907, June and Dec. | 80,000 |
| C., St. L. & N. O. con. mt. ($18,000,000 auth.), 5 p. c., due June, 1951, June and Dec. | 11,289,000 |
| Memphis Division 4 per cent. gold bonds, due Dec., 1951, June and Dec. | 3,500,000 |
| Western lines, 1st mort., 4 per cent., due Aug., 1951, Feb. and Aug. | 5,425,000 |
| Louisville Division & Terminal, 1st mort., 3½ per cent., due July, 1953, Jan. and July. | 21,688,000 |
| St. Louis Division & Terminal, 1st mort., 3½ per cent., due July, 1951, Jan. and July. | 8,377,000 |
| " " " mort., 3 per cent., due July, 1951, Jan. and July. | 4,939,925 |
| Litch. Div., St. L., Peoria & Nor., 1st mort., 3 per cent., due Jan., 1951, Jan. and July. | 3,148,000 |
| Omaha Division, 3 per cent. due Aug., 1951, Feb. and Aug. | 5,000,000 |
| Total | $129,188,925 |

FUNDED DEBT ST. LOUIS, ALTON & TERRE HAUTE, ASSUMED.

| | |
|---|---|
| Belleville & El Dorado, 1st mort., 7 per cent., due July, 1910, Jan. and July. | $88,000 |
| Belleville & Carondelet, 1st mort., 6 per cent., due June, 1923, June and Dec. | 470,000 |
| St. Louis Southern, 1st mort., 4 per cent., due Sept., 1931, March and Sept. | 538,000 |
| Carb. & Shawnee., 1st guar. mort., 4 per cent., due March, 1932, March and Sept. | 241,000 |

The company pays the State of Illinois 7 per cent. on gross earnings of the original 705 miles in lieu of taxes. In 1901–02 this payment amounted to $911,365.

In 1894 company authorized $3,550,000 4 per cent. bonds to retire Cedar Falls & Minnesota 7s, mortgage to be secured on 143 miles of Dubuque & Sioux City main line. This issue in above table is noted as the Western lines 1st mortgage. The mortgage is for $10,000,000.

This company guaranteed under lease 2½ per cent. dividends on St. Louis, Alton & Terre Haute stock, but acquired nearly all same and that of the Belleville & Southern Illinois in exchange for Illinois Central 3 per cent. bonds. In 1897 created the St. Louis Division & Terminal 3½ per cent. mortgage for $15,000,000 upon the St. Louis, Alton & Terre Haute property. The St. Louis, Alton & Terre Haute 1st mortgage for $2,500,000 was paid off June 1, 1898.

In June, 1892, an issue of $25,000,000 collateral trust 4 per cent. bonds was authorized, $20,000,000 of which, with a cash payment of $5,000,000, was to be used to acquire securities of the Louisville, New Orleans & Texas, the purchased securities to be deposited as collateral therefor. The Louisville, New Orleans & Texas securities deposited aggregated, in par value, $35,524,000. These bonds were retired with the proceeds of the Louisville Division, 3½ per cent. mortgage. The Litchfield Division 3 per cent. mortgage is for $4,000,000, and was created in 1900 to acquire the portion of the St. Louis, Peoria & Northern from Litchfield at East St. Louis.

EARNINGS.

Year ending June 30.

| | Div. Paid. | Gross. | Net. | Charges. | Surplus. |
|---|---|---|---|---|---|
| 1892–93 (2,888 miles) | 5 | $20,095,190 | $7,363,082 | $4,509,088 | $2,853,993 |
| 1893–94 ( " " ) | 5 | 20,657,463 | 8,194,493 | 5,231,217 | 2,963,275 |
| 1894–95 ( " " ) | 5 | 19,056,994 | 7,430,905 | 4,927,989 | 2,502,611 |
| 1895–96 (3,067 " ) | 5 | 22,002,842 | 8,959,030 | 5,873,304 | 3,075,726 |
| 1896–97 (3,130 " ) | 5 | 22,110,937 | 8,539,248 | 5,760,698 | 3,699,461 |
| 1897–98 (3,775 " ) | 5 | 27,317,819 | 10,898,718 | 6,510,063 | 5,313,116 |
| 1898–99 (3,671 " ) | 5 | 28,114,689 | 11,133,506 | 6,802,004 | 4,331,501 |
| 1899–00 (3,845 " ) | 5½ | 32,611,967 | 12,184,382 | 6,427,107 | 5,757,274 |
| 1900–01 (4,214 " ) | 6 | 36,900,460 | 13,563,850 | 6,596,190 | 6,967,659 |
| 1901–02 (4,276 " ) | 6 | 40,821,030 | 16,358,495 | 6,568,034 | 9,790,461 |

In 1892-93 the credit from the surplus dividend fund was $236,708; in 1893-94, $353,993; in 1895-96, $920,910, $422,500 being also set aside in that year for betterments; in 1896-97, the credit from dividend fund was $920,910, and $15,000 charged for betterments. In 1897-98 credit from dividend fund, $924,461; charged to betterments, $1,726,451. In 1898-99, surplus to dividend fund, $1,005,626, and devoted to betterments, $1,475,040. In 1899-1900, surplus to dividend fund, $1,046,226; betterments, $2,416,675. In 1900-01, the $2,895,399 was charged for improvements and $1,088,486 carried to dividend fund. In 1901-02 betterments were credited with $4,340,172; dividends, $4,752,000, and a fund set apart for matured coupons, $654,329. The amount carried to surplus dividend fund being $1,132,446.

The Yazoo & Mississippi Valley Railroad, 807 miles, operated separately, earned in 1897-98, gross, $4,775,647; net income, $1,669,234; fixed charges, $785,202. Its surplus for the year, $884,031, was applied to payment of notes, past due interest on income bonds, etc. In 1898-99, mileage, 955; gross, $4,576,349; net, $1,257,601; surplus over charges, $340,921. In 1899-1900, mileage, 1,001; gross, $5,300,889; net, $1,905,539; surplus, $959,299. In 1900-01, mileage, 1,056; gross, $6,127,941; net, $2,070,385; surplus, $1,066,078.

GROSS AND NET EARNINGS BY MONTHS FOR THREE YEARS.

| | 1900. | | 1901. | | 1902. | |
|---|---|---|---|---|---|---|
| | Gross. | Net. | Gross. | Net. | Gross. | Net. |
| January | $2,912,379 | $1,093,681 | $3,220,473 | $1,403,967 | $3,493,554 | $1,332,831 |
| February | 2,634,415 | 848,112 | 2,959,355 | 1,135,706 | 3,114,907 | 994,428 |
| March | 2,875,475 | 910,027 | 3,226,434 | 1,323,340 | 3,509,116 | 1,232,531 |
| April | 2,411,206 | 307,156 | 2,953,757 | 942,629 | 3,305,236 | 886,970 |
| May | 2,625,499 | 418,712 | 3,173,306 | 964,167 | 3,462,870 | 905,138 |
| June | 2,771,759 | 642,707 | 2,910,434 | 650,743 | 3,300,318 | 765,763 |
| July | 2,636,890 | 399,732 | 3,175,752 | 969,017 | 3,348,770 | 733,622 |
| August | 1,990,439 | 686,677 | 3,383,178 | 1,003,162 | 3,400,469 | 719,346 |
| September | 3,112,621 | 934,883 | 3,425,279 | 1,007,933 | 3,734,456 | 1,055,303 |
| October | 3,414,924 | 1,118,129 | 3,752,331 | 1,288,184 | 4,044,808 | 1,358,301 |
| November | 3,142,838 | 1,022,026 | 3,486,304 | 1,141,370 | 3,741,380 | 1,223,341 |
| December | 3,267,706 | 1,275,568 | 3,413,125 | 1,279,363 | 3,787,102 | 1,428,963 |
| Total | $33,796,151 | $9,657,410 | $38,078,788 | $13,110,181 | $42,242,986 | $12,636,537 |
| Aver. per month. | 2,833,012 | 804,784 | 3,173,232 | 1,009,101 | 3,520,249 | 1,053,044 |

The proportion of taxes for each month is deducted from net.

The following presents the comparative freight traffic statistics of the road:

| | Average Mileage. | Total Tonnage. | Tons Carried One Mile. | Freight Density. | Rate per Ton per Mile. | Earnings per Train Mile. | Average Tons per Train. |
|---|---|---|---|---|---|---|---|
| 1896-97 | 3,130 | 9,948,367 | 2,258,388,132 | 721,529 | 0.671c | $1.294 | 193½ |
| 1897-98 | 3,775 | 12,694,058 | 2,722,540,585 | 721,202 | 0.695 | 1.432 | 206 |
| 1898-99 | 3,671 | 13,517,161 | 2,799,941,184 | 762,719 | 0.688 | 1.439 | 209 |
| 1899-00 | 3,845 | 16,020,835 | 3,425,794,698 | 890,986 | 0.650 | 1.442 | 221 |
| 1900-01 | 4,214 | 17,735,749 | 4,016,085,602 | 952,826 | 0.619 | 1.456 | 235 |
| 1901-02 | 4,276 | 19,096,441 | 4,452,073,927 | 1,041,211 | 0.622 | 1.711 | 274 |

President, Stuyvesant Fish; Secretary, Alexander G. Hackstaff; Treasurer, E. T. H. Gibson, New York.

Directors—Walther Luttgen, B. F. Ayer, James T. Harahan, Edward H. Harriman, Stuyvesant Fish, John W. Auchincloss, John C. Welling, Charles A. Peabody, Charles M. Beach, John Jacob Astor, W. Morton Grinnell, James D. W. Cutting, Richard Yates (*ex-officio*).

Main office, Chicago; New York office, 214 Broadway. Annual meeting, third Wednesday in October, at Chicago.

---

## *THE ILLINOIS SOUTHERN RAILWAY CO.*

Road owned, Chester, Ill., to Salem, Ill., 92 miles; Sparta, Ill., to Rosborough, 5 miles; total owned, 97 miles; trackage, 2 miles; total operated, 99 miles. Locomotives, 7; passenger cars, 7; freight cars, 108.

This company is the successor of the Centralia & Chester Railroad Co., sold in foreclosure, May 16, 1900. The present company took possession June 1, 1900.

Stock......Par $100..........................Authorized, $2,000,000......Issued, $2,000,000

Stock is transferred by the secretary of the company, Chicago. Registrar, Equitable Trust Co., Chicago.

FUNDED DEBT.

Bond certificates to be exchanged for 1st mort. bonds.............................. $825,000

The company has authorized a 1st mortgage, 4 per cent., due Oct., 1951, April and Oct., for $2,000,000. Trustee, Equitable Trust Co., Chicago.

In the year ending June 30, 1901, the gross earnings were $113,229; net, $16,951.

President, John W. Walsh; Treasurer, A. F. Williams; Secretary and Auditor, Charles F. Weinland, Chicago.

Directors—John W. Walsh, John R. Walsh, L. A. Walton, Azel F. Hatch, W. Burry, C. F. Weinland, Chicago; W. S. Ingraham, Bristol, Conn.

Main office, 204 Dearborn street, Chicago. Annual meeting, fourth Wednesday in September, at Chicago.

## THE INDIANA, ILLINOIS & IOWA RAILROAD CO.

(Controlled by Lake Shore & Michigan Southern Railroad Co.)

Road owned, main line, South Bend, Ind., to Seatonville, Ill., 192 miles; branches, 12 miles; total owned, 204 miles; leased St. Joseph, South Bend & Southern Railroad, South Bend to St. Joseph, Mich., 39½ miles. Trackage, 8 miles; total operated, 251½ miles; sidings and spurs, 77 miles; grand total, 328½ miles. Locomotives, 52; passenger cars, 15; freight cars, 1,337.

This company was formed in 1898 by consolidation of Indiana, Illinois & Iowa Railroad Co. with The Indiana, Illinois & Iowa Railway Co. of the State of Indiana.

At the beginning of 1902 a controlling interest in the company was acquired by the Lake Shore & Michigan Southern.

Stock......Par $100............. ............Authorized, $6,000,000......Issued, $5,000,000

The stock outstanding was increased in 1899 from $3,697,800 to $5,000,000, to pay for extensions.

Stock is transferred by the Treasurer, New York.

The 1st dividend on the stock was 1 per cent., paid October 2, 1899. Beginning in January, 1900, the company paid regular quarterly dividends of 1 per cent each, in January, April, July and October, until January, 1902, inclusive, when the dividend period was changed to semi-annually on January and July, 2 per cent. being regularly paid in those months.

FUNDED DEBT.

1st mort., 4 per cent., due July, 1950, Jan. and July............................... $4,850,000

The bonded debt of the old company was rearranged in 1890. In 1898 a 5 per cent. 1st mortgage was authorized to pay off the old funded debt of $1,800,000, consisting of $800,000 1st mortgage, 4 per cent. bonds; $500,000 1st mortgage 5s on South Bend extension, and $500,000 income bonds.

In 1900 the company created a new 1st mortgage 4 per cent. bond issue of $12,000,000, and sold $4,500,000 of the same. With the proceeds, the $3,000,000 of 5s outstanding were called for payment on February 1, 1901, the balance of the proceeds being used to pay for extensions and new equipment. Interest on the new 1st mortgage bonds is paid at the office of the Treasurer, Grand Central Depot, New York.

EARNINGS.

Year ending June 30.

| | Gross. | Net. | Charges. | Surplus. |
|---|---|---|---|---|
| 1892-93 | $782,880 | $190,440 | $91,686 | $98,754 |
| 1893-94 | 752,951 | 145,914 | 103,697 | 42,217 |
| 1894-95 | 739,618 | 177,630 | 102,388 | 75,242 |
| 1895-96 | 786,131 | 234,109 | 108,394 | 125,715 |
| 1896-97 | 738,289 | 195,077 | 108,398 | 86,679 |
| 1897-98 | 820,384 | 263,892 | 123,292 | 140,600 |
| 1898-99 | 902,305 | 340,209 | 163,778 | 176,431 |
| 1899-00 | 1,226,150 | 468,085 | 206,290 | 261,795 |
| 1900-01 | 1,419,116 | 562,143 | 264,716 | 297,427 |
| 1901-02 | 1,700,817 | 475,399 | 207,784 | 207,615 |

In the figures for 1901-02 taxes are deducted from the net. In previous years they were included in the item of charges.

President, William H. Newman; Vice-President and General Manager, William C. Brown; Secretary and Treasurer, Edwin D. Worcester, New York; Assistant Secretary and Assistant Treasurer, Rudolph P. Ahrens, Chicago.

Directors—William K. Vanderbilt, William H. Newman, William C. Brown, Edwin D. Worcester, Edward V. W. Rossiter, Hamilton McK. Twombly, New York; Henry B. Ledyard, Detroit; William J. Calhoun, Chicago; Edward A. Handy, Cleveland.

Main office, 217 La Salle St., Chicago; treasurer's office, Grand Central Station, New York. Annual meeting, third Wednesday in January, at Chicago.

---

## INDIANAPOLIS & VINCENNES RAILROAD CO.

(Controlled by Pennsylvania Company.)

Road owned, Indianapolis to Vincennes, Ind., 117 miles; branch, 16 miles; total, 133 miles. Locomotives, 7; passenger cars, 8; freight cars, 350.

Stock.... .Par, $50.......... ...............Authorized, $1,402,000......Issued, $1,402,000

Transfer Agent, Continental Trust Co., New York.

FUNDED DEBT.

1st mort., 7 per cent., due Feb., 1908, Feb. and Aug. ............ $1,700,000

The $1,400,000 of 6 per cent. 2d mortgage bonds which matured May 1, 1900, were paid by the Pennsylvania Railroad Co.

The Pennsylvania Company operates the road, advancing the interest deficiency, and there was due that company, January 1, 1898, $3,082,000. The Pennsylvania Company owns practically all the stock, and the Pennsylvania Railroad Co. guarantees interest on the bonds. Deficit under charges was, in 1893, $103,704; in 1894, $109,758; in 1895, $116,596; in 1896, $110,277; in 1897, $124,994; in 1898, $101,991; in 1899, $88,971; in 1900, $81,215; in 1901, $44,755.

| EARNINGS. | Gross. | Net. |
|---|---|---|
| 1895 | $518,447 | $91,988 |
| 1896 | 485,608 | 98,196 |
| 1897 | 489,304 | 84,403 |
| 1898 | 535,542 | 107,329 |
| 1899 | 595,051 | 114,028 |
| 1900 | 639,595 | 104,284 |
| 1901 | 709,434 | 125,245 |
| 1902 | 770,214 | 83,513 |

President, James McCrea; Secretary, S. B. Liggett; Treasurer, T. H. B. McKnight; Pittsburg. Main office, Indianapolis. Fiscal Agent, Farmers' Loan & Trust Co., New York. Annual meeting, second Thursday in May. Books close twenty days previous.

## INTERNATIONAL & GREAT NORTHERN RAILROAD CO.

Road owned, Longview, Tex., to Laredo, Tex., 494 miles; Palestine to Houston, Tex., 151 miles; branches, 332 miles; total, 977 miles; trackage, Houston to Galveston, 50 miles; other trackage, 26 miles; total operated, 1,053 miles. Company has equal rights in the Galveston, Houston & Henderson Railroad; 50 miles and to use of same. Locomotives, 82; passenger cars, 69; freight cars, 2,320.

Stock......Par $100..........Authorized, $25,000,000......Issued, $9,755,000

FUNDED DEBT.

| | |
|---|---|
| 1st mort., 6 per cent., due Nov., 1919, May and Nov. | $10,435,000 |
| 2d mort., 4½-5 per cent., due Sept., 1909 March and Sept. | 9,535,000 |
| 3d mort., 4 per cent. (income till 1897), due Sept., 1921, March and Sept. | 2,721,052 |
| Colorado bridge bonds, 7 per cent., due May, 1920, May and Nov. | 198,000 |
| Total | $22,889,052 |

This company is a reorganization, without foreclosure, 1892, of the same corporation. Control, through ownership of stock, is vested in interests identified with the Missouri Pacific. For details of the reorganization see MANUAL for 1900.

The International & Great Northern has no land grant, its lands having been acquired by the Texas Land Co.

| EARNINGS. | Gross. | Net. |
|---|---|---|
| 1892 | $3,655,439 | $744,814 |
| 1893 | 3,601,976 | 1,129,968 |
| 1894 | 3,244,759 | 937,911 |
| 1895 | 3,277,657 | 785,697 |
| 1896 | 3,528,177 | 830,695 |
| 1897 | 3,657,336 | 981,829 |
| 1898 | 3,990,855 | 1,201,355 |
| 1899 | 4,177,808 | 1,204,807 |
| 1900 | 4,138,576 | 1,206,351 |
| 1901 | 5,148,092 | 1,339,394 |

President, George J. Gould; 1st Vice-President, Frank Jay Gould, New York; 2d Vice-President, Leroy Trice; Secretary and Treasurer, A. R. Howard, Palestine, Tex.; Assistant Secretary and Assistant Treasurer, H. B. Henson, New York.

Directors—George J. Gould, Edwin Gould, Howard Gould, Frank Jay Gould, New York; Ira H. Evans, Austin, Tex.; Leroy Trice, A. R. Howard, W. L. Maury, N. A. Stedman, Palestine, Tex.

Main office, Palestine, Tex.; New York office, 195 Broadway. Annual meeting, first Monday in April. Books close 30 days before.

To the United States

ZACATECAS

Guadalupe

Soledad

Rincon de Romos

Pabellon

CHICALOTE

AGUAS CALIENTES

LAGOS

To the United States

LUIS

Allende

Patzcu

URUAPAN

Toluca

A C I F I C

O C E A N

ACAPULCO

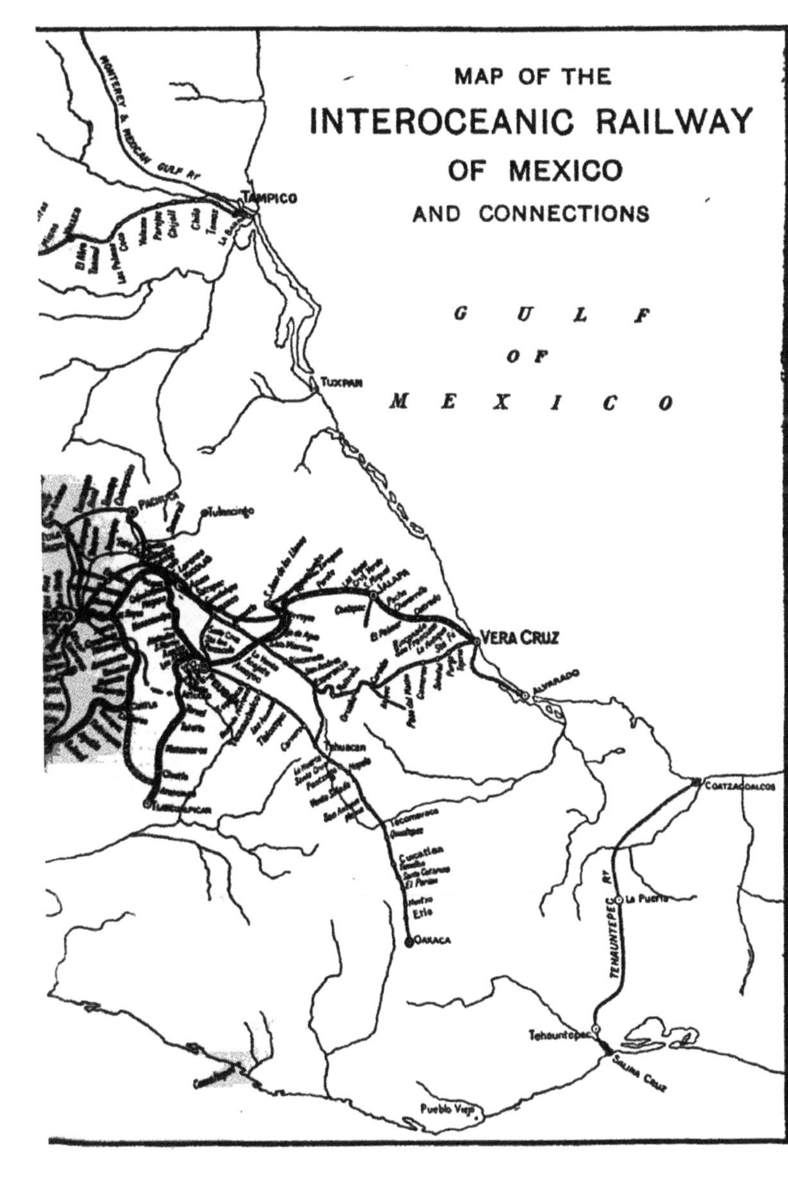

MAP OF THE
INTEROCEANIC RAILWAY
OF MEXICO
AND CONNECTIONS
G U L F
O F
M E X I C O
TAMPICO
TUXPAN
VERA CRUZ
ALVARADO
JALAPA
Tulancingo
OAXACA
Tehuacan
Tecomavaca
Cuicatlan
Etla
COATZACOALCOS
TEHAUNTEPEC RY
La Puerta
Tehauntepec
SALINA CRUZ
Pueblo Viejo
MONTEREY & MEXICAN GULF RY

## INTEROCEANIC RAILWAY OF MEXICO, LIMITED

A corporation, formed under the laws of Great Britain, in 1888, and acquired the concessions from the Government of Mexico for the building and operation of a railroad from Vera Cruz to Acapulco, via the City of Mexico, the concession being for 99 years from 1883. The line from Vera Cruz to the City of Mexico was completed in 1891.

Road owned, main line, Vera Cruz to the City of Mexico, 339.89 miles; branches, 215.18 miles, loop line, Cuantla to Ateucingo, 41.94 miles. Total, 597.01 miles.

In 1901 the company acquired the Nautla Railway, 79 miles, and began the construction of a cut-off of 61 miles from Virreyes to San Nicolas to reduce the distance and grades on its main line. The arrangements made in this connection include the creation of a company under the title of The Mexican Eastern Railway Co., to hold the Nautla Railway and build the extension, the line when completed to be leased to this company. The new line will reduce the distance from Vera Cruz to the City of Mexico by 48 miles, and reduce the maximum grade on the company's route from 2½ per cent. to 1½ per cent.

Locomotives, 79; passenger cars, 88; freight cars, 1,157.

Stock..Par £10...Authorized { ord., £1,700,000 / pref'ce., 1,000,000 } Issued { ord., £1,700,000 / pref'ce., 1,000,000 } £2,700,000

The preference share capital is 7 per cent., cumulative, but arrears are payable when and as the profits of the company will allow of such payments.

FUNDED DEBT.

| | |
|---|---|
| Prior lien 5 per cent. debentures, due 1912, Jan. and July | £400,000 |
| Four per cent. debenture stock, due 1950, March and Sept. | 699,886 |
| Four and one-half per cent. 2d debenture stock, due 1950 | 150,000 |
| Seven per cent. A debenture stock, income, Dec. | 735,390 |
| " " " B " " " Dec. | 469,459 |
| Total | £2,454,735 |

In 1896 the company was reorganized, the 6 per cent. debenture stock then outstanding being retired with the present issues.

In 1901 the second debenture 4½ per cent. stock was created, the total amount being £1,300,000, of which £150,000 was subscribed for by the stockholders at 86.

It was announced in November, 1901, that the Mexican Eastern Railway (see above) would create and issue £400,000 4 per cent. debenture stock to pay for the Nautla Railway and extensions.

EARNINGS.

| In Mexican Currency. Year ending June 30. | Gross. | Net. |
|---|---|---|
| 1892–93 | $2,036,613 | $401,307 |
| 1893–94 | 2,331,397 | 420,124 |
| 1894–95 | 2,316,463 | 460,737 |
| 1895–96 | 2,202,238 | 404,071 |
| 1896–97 | 2,539,447 | 581,725 |
| 1897–98 | 3,033,209 | 728,030 |
| 1898–99 | 3,612,592 | 842,521 |
| 1899–00 | 4,166,678 | 1,189,463 |
| 1900–01 | 4,211,085 | 993,993 |
| 1901–02 | 4,312,461 | 883,953 |

In December, 1901, 7 per cent. was paid on the A debenture stock out of the earnings of the year 1900–01, and at the same time 3 7-16 per cent. was paid on the B debenture stock.

In 1899–00 the equivalent of the net in English currency was £115,648; in 1900–01, £101,075.

Chairman, Harrison Hodgson, London; legal representative in Mexico, Pablo Martinez Del Rio; General Manager, William L. Morkill, City of Mexico; Secretary, C. E. Scruby, London; Treasurer, H. Friederichsen, City of Mexico.

Directors—Chandos S. Stanhope, H. T. Hodgson, Harrison Hodgson, G. W. Hoghton, G. M. Stewart, A. R. Robertson, London.

Mian office, City of Mexico; London office, 9 New Broad street. Annual meeting, in December.

---

## INVERNESS RAILWAY & COAL CO.

A corporation formed under a charter of the Province of Nova Scotia in 1887, with subsequent legislative amendments.

Road owned, Point Tupper, Cape Breton, to Inverness, Cape Breton, 61 miles. Locomotives 6; passenger cars, 4; freight cars, 187.

The former title of the company was the Inverness & Richmond Railway Co., Limited which, in June, 1902, absorbed the Inverness-Richmond Collieries & Railway Co. of Canada, Limited.

Stock......Par $100..........................Authorized, $7,500,000......Issued, $7,500,000

The company has no preferred stock.

FUNDED DEBT.

1st mort., 5 per cent., due May, 1922, May (1) and Nov.............................. $3,000,000

The trustee of the mortgage is the National Trust Co., Limited, Toronto. Interest on the bonds is payable through the Canadian Bank of Commerce, London, or at the office of the company, Toronto.

President, William Mackenzie; Vice-President, Donald D. Mann; Secretary-Treasurer, A. W. Mackenzie, Toronto; General Manager, James L. Brass, Inverness, Cape Breton.

Directors—William Mackenzie, Donald D. Mann, Edmund Bristol, Lewis Lukes, Toronto; R. M. Horne-Payne, London, England.

Main office, Railway Chambers, Toronto; operating office, Inverness, Cape Breton.

---

## IOWA CENTRAL RAILWAY CO.

This company is a reorganization in 1888 of the Central Iowa Railroad Co.

Road operated, Peoria, Ill., to Albert Lea, Minn., 371 miles; branches, 188 miles; total operated, 558 miles. Of this mileage 490 miles are owned, 28 miles are owned jointly and 40½ miles are leased. Trackage; Iowa Junction, Ill., to Peoria, Ill., 3 miles. Part of main line, Manly Junction, Ia., to Northwood, Ia., 12 miles, is leased to Burlington, Cedar Rapids & Northern Railway and operated jointly with that company. In 1899 an extension was built, under title of the Iowa Central & Western Railway, from Belmond, Ia., to Algona, Ia., 37 miles, making a connection with the Minneapolis & St. Louis Railway at Corwith, Ia. Locomotives, 76; passenger cars 41; freight cars, 2,736.

In 1900 interests identified with the Minneapolis & St. Louis obtained control of this company.

Stock..Par $100...Authorized { com., $11,000,000; pref., 7,400,000 } Issued { com., $8,519,688; pref., 5,674,236 } $14,193,924

The preferred stock is 5 per cent., non-cumulative, and after the common has received 5 per cent. both classes share equally in further surplus.

There is $3,688 common stock scrip outstanding and $3,036 preferred scrip, also $544 scrip for 1st mortgage bonds.

Stock is transferred at the office of the company, New York. Registrar, Mercantile Trust Co., New York.

In 1892 1 per cent. was pai on the preferred, but no further dividend was paid until the declaration of 1½ per cent., March 1, 1899. In September, 1899, 1½ per cent. was paid on the preferred, and a similar dividend in March, 1900. The September, 1900, dividend was passed, and no dividends have been declared since.

FUNDED DEBT.

| | |
|---|---|
| 1st mort., 5 per cent. bonds, due June, 1938, June and Dec. | $7,649,544 |
| Refunding mort., 4 per cent., due March, 1951, March and Sept. | 3,141,000 |
| Total | $10,790,544 |

EARNINGS.

Year ending June 30.

| | Gross. | Net. | Interest, etc. | Surplus. |
|---|---|---|---|---|
| 1892-93 (497 miles) | $1,942,564 | $581,903 | $505,297 | $76,606 |
| 1893-94 ( " " ) | 1,811,567 | 627,403 | 481,242 | 146,161 |
| 1894-95 ( " " ) | 1,569,221 | 535,150 | 465,188 | 69,962 |
| 1895-96 (499 " ) | 1,839,708 | 694,591 | 516,270 | 178,320 |
| 1896-97 (508 " ) | 1,564,205 | 471,831 | 468,329 | 3,502 |
| 1897-98 ( " " ) | 1,880,125 | 605,469 | 441,401 | 164,068 |
| 1898-99 (509 " ) | 2,135,550 | 639,871 | 452,371 | 187,499 |
| 1899-00 (513 " ) | 2,341,240 | 638,890 | 469,812 | 175,973 |
| 1900-01 (506 " ) | 2,284,123 | 514,641 | 507,593 | 7,048 |
| 1901-02 (558 " ) | 2,543,350 | 586,881 | 583,965 | 2,915 |

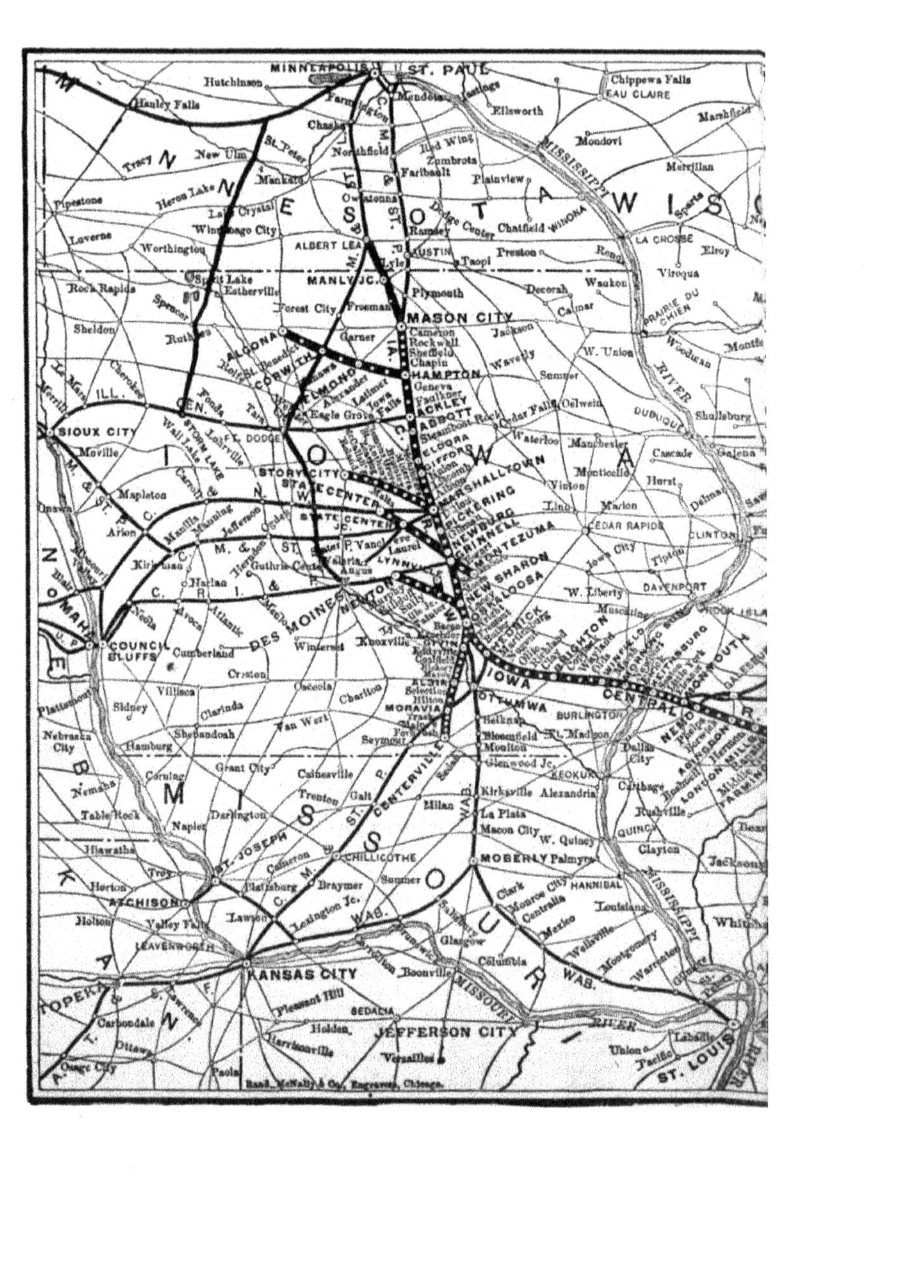

MINNEAPOLIS
ST. PAUL
Hutchinson
Hanley Falls
Chippewa Falls
EAU CLAIRE
Ellsworth
Marshfield
Mondovi
Red Wing
Zumbrota
Northfield
Faribault
Plainview
Tracy
New Ulm
Mankato
Owatonna
Merrillan
Pipestone
Heron Lake
Winnebago City
Dodge Center
Chatfield
WINONA
LA CROSSE
Loverne
Worthington
ALBERT LEA
AUSTIN
Preston
Elroy
Viroqua
Spirit Lake
Estherville
MANLY JC.
Plymouth
Decorah
Waukon
Rock Rapids
Forest City
MASON CITY
Calmar
PRAIRIE DU CHIEN
Sheldon
Garner
Jackson
ALGONA
W. Union
CORWITH
HAMPTON
Waverly
Sumner
Geneva
ACKLEY
ABBOTT
Eagle Grove
Iowa Falls
Cedar Falls
Oelwein
DUBUQUE
Shullsburg
SIOUX CITY
FT. DODGE
STORM LAKE
Waterloo
Manchester
Cascade
Galena
ELDORA
STORY CITY
MARSHALLTOWN
Monticello
Vinton
Hurst
Mapleton
STATE CENTER
PICKERING
Linn
Marion
CEDAR RAPIDS
CLINTON
NEWBURG
GRINNELL
MONTEZUMA
Arion
Manilla
Manning
Jefferson
Iowa City
Tipton
Guthrie Center
LYNNVILLE
Harlan
NEW SHARON
OSKALOOSA
W. Liberty
DAVENPORT
Muscatine
OMAHA
Neola
Avoca
Atlantic
DES MOINES
NEWTON
COUNCIL BLUFFS
Cumberland
Winterset
Knoxville
BRIGHTON
Creston
Osceola
Chariton
IOWA CENTRAL
Villisca
Sidney
Clarinda
MORAVIA
OTTUMWA
BURLINGTON
Nebraska City
Hamburg
Shenandoah
Van Wert
Seymour
Bloomfield
Moulton
Ft. Madison
Glenwood Jc.
Grant City
Corning
KEOKUK
Carthage
Nemaha
Trenton
Galt
CENTERVILLE
Kirksville
Alexandria
Milan
Table Rock
Darlington
La Plata
Rushville
Hiawatha
Napier
Macon City
W. Quincy
QUINCY
Clayton
ST. JOSEPH
CHILLICOTHE
MOBERLY
Palmyra
Troy
Cameron
Plattsburg
Braymer
Sumner
HANNIBAL
Horton
ATCHISON
Lexington Jc.
Louisiana
Holton
Valley Falls
Lawson
Glasgow
Mexico
Centralia
LEAVENWORTH
Columbia
Wellsville
Montgomery
KANSAS CITY
Boonville
Warrenton
TOPEKA
Pleasant Hill
SEDALIA
Carbondale
Holden
JEFFERSON CITY
MISSOURI
RIVER
Ottawa
Harrisonville
Versailles
Union
Labadie
Pacific
Osage City
Paola
ST. LOUIS
MISSISSIPPI
WAB.
Rand, McNally & Co., Engravers, Chicago.

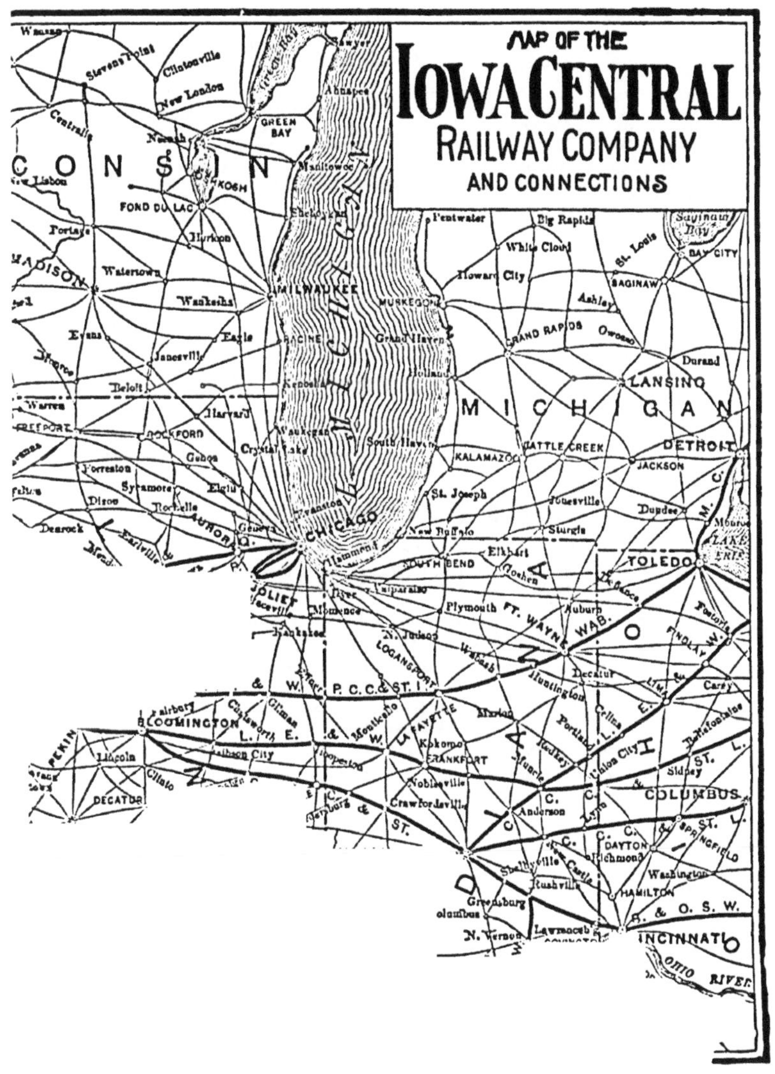
MAP OF THE
IOWA CENTRAL
RAILWAY COMPANY
AND CONNECTIONS
GREEN BAY
MILWAUKEE
CHICAGO
MICHIGAN
LANSING
DETROIT
JACKSON
GRAND RAPIDS
KALAMAZOO
BATTLE CREEK
SAGINAW
BAY CITY
TOLEDO
SOUTH BEND
LOGANSPORT
LA FAYETTE
FRANKFORT
BLOOMINGTON
DECATUR
COLUMBUS
DAYTON
HAMILTON
FOND DU LAC
MADISON
ROCKFORD
FREEPORT
AURORA
JOLIET
MUSKEGON
PEKIN
OHIO RIVER

The following presents the comparative freight traffic statistics of the company:

| | Average Mileage. | Total Tonnage. | Tons Carried One Mile. | Freight Density. | Rate per Ton per Mile. | Earnings per Train Mile. | Av'ge Tons per Train. |
|---|---|---|---|---|---|---|---|
| 1896-97.... | 508 | 1,123,147 | 134,719,786 | 265,196 | 0.880c | $1.522 | 172 |
| 1897-98.... | 508 | 1,323,342 | 155,993,134 | 307,073 | 0.940 | 1.508 | 159 |
| 1898-99.... | 509 | 1,540,716 | 205,650,328 | 404,660 | 0.823 | 1.434 | 174 |
| 1899-00.... | 513 | 1,742,379 | 265,417,072 | 517,382 | 0.696 | 1.539 | 221 |
| 1900-01.... | 506 | 1,667,202 | 252,497,682 | 498,971 | 0.709 | 1.602 | 226 |
| 1901-02.... | 558 | 1,866,971 | 296,184,406 | 530,796 | 0.668 | 1.460 | 218 |

Surplus, 1891-92, after paying 1 per cent. dividend on preferred stock, was $34,865. In 1898-99, surplus, after 1½ per cent. on preferred stock, was $102,481. In 1899-1900 3 per cent. was paid on the preferred stock, the surplus over dividends being $5,950. In 1900-01 the company received $93,409 on account of premium on bonds sold which added to the surplus from operations, make a total surplus of $100,457.

The Iowa Central & Western (see above) was built at a cost of $300,575 to the Iowa Central, which received bonds and stock of the new line to repay the advances.

The refunding mortgage created in 1900 is $25,000,000 authorized. With the $2,000,000 of these bonds which were issued the company retired the Keithsburg Bridge Co. and other maturing obligations.

President, Edwin Hawley; Vice-President and Treasurer, F. H. Davis, New York; Vice-President and General Manager, L. F. Day, Minneapolis; Secretary, A. C. Doan, New York; Assistant Treasurer, Joseph Gaskell; Auditor, Frank Nay, Minneapolis.

Directors—Robert J. Kimball, Edwin Hawley, George Crocker, Levi C. Weir, Edwin Langdon, E. C. Bradley, John E. Searles, F. H. Davis, Russell Sage, H. J. Morse, George R. Morse, New York; Paul Morton, Theodore P. Shonts, Henry A. Gardner, Chicago; L. F. Day, Minneapolis.

Main office, Minneapolis; New York office, 25 Broad street; Chicago office, 171 La Salle street. Annual meeting, first Friday after first Thursday in September. Books close ten days previous.

---

## *KANAWHA & MICHIGAN RAILWAY CO.*

(Controlled by Toledo & Ohio Central Railway Co.)

Road owned, Corning, O., to Gauley, W. Va., 173 miles, of which 18 miles are leased. Also owns Buckingham Branch, 11 miles, leased to Toledo & Ohio Central. Locomotives, 30; passenger cars, 15; freight cars, 1,676.

Formerly the Kanawha & Ohio Railroad, which was successor to River Division of Ohio Central Railroad, foreclosed 1885, and reorganized by bondholders, the road being controlled in the interest of the Toledo & Ohio Central, which company guarantees the bonds. An extension to a connection with the Chesapeake & Ohio was opened in 1893.

Stock......Par $100......................Authorized, $10,000,000......Issued, $10,000,000

Transfer Agents, J. P. Morgan & Co., New York. Registrar, Central Trust Co., New York.

FUNDED DEBT.

1st mort., 4 per cent., due April, 1990, April and Oct.............................. $2,469,000

The company also has car trust obligations for $1,568,677 and an equipment loan of $575,000.

EARNINGS.

Year ending June 30.

| | Gross. | Net. | Taxes and Rentals. | | Surplus. |
|---|---|---|---|---|---|
| 1894-95........................ | $420,624 | $108,260 | $124,847 | Def. | $16,586 |
| 1895-96........................ | 470,785 | 115,472 | 121,970 | Def. | 6,498 |
| 1896-97........................ | 479,488 | 119,335 | 122,482 | Def. | 3,147 |
| 1897-98........................ | 558,342 | 152,442 | 138,148 | | 14,294 |
| 1898-99........................ | 634,064 | 167,371 | 132,709 | | 34,661 |
| 1899-00........................ | 759,069 | 162,468 | 109,591 | | 52,877 |
| 1900-01........................ | 924,621 | 203,756 | 128,709 | | 75,047 |
| 1901-02........................ | 1,096,359 | 217,149 | 140,794 | | 76,355 |

President, Nicholas Monsarrat, Columbus, O.; Vice-Presidents, Decatur Axtell, Richmond, Va.; Ralph W. Hickox, Cleveland; Secretary and Treasurer, L. D. Kelley, Toledo, O.

Directors—Decatur Axtell, Richmond, Va.; Stevenson Burke, Charles G. Hickox, Ralph W. Hickox, James H. Hoyt, Nicholas Monsarrat, Columbus, O.; George M. Cumming, Charles H. Roberts, Charles Steele, New York.

Main office, Toledo, O. Annual meeting, Tuesday after first Monday in June.

## KANSAS CITY, FORT SCOTT & MEMPHIS RAILWAY CO.

(Controlled by St. Louis & San Francisco Railroad Co.)

A corporation formed under the laws of Kansas, June 14, 1901, to take over the property of the Kansas City, Fort Scott & Memphis Railroad Co., in the interest of the St. Louis & San Francisco, which had purchased control of that property. The St. Louis & San Francisco leased this road in 1901, and it is operated as part of the San Francisco system.

Road owned, Kansas City, Mo., to Memphis, Tenn., 485 miles; branches, 369 miles, total operated, 854 miles. The mileage includes a bridge over Mississippi at Memphis, Tenn., completed in 1892. The Kansas City, Clinton & Springfield, 162 miles, and Kansas City, Memphis & Birmingham, 285 miles, were also controlled in the interest of this company, which guaranteed bonds of former and made a traffic guarantee of bonds of the latter.

The Kansas City, Fort Scott & Memphis Railroad Co. was a consolidation on April 30, 1888, of Kansas City, Fort Scott & Gulf and Kansas City, Springfield & Memphis Railroad Companies. The Kansas City, Fort Scott & Gulf was the successor of the Missouri River, Fort Scott & Gulf, foreclosed and reorganized in 1879.

In February, 1901, it was announced that a majority interest of the stock of this company and of the stock and income bonds of the Kansas City, Memphis & Birmingham Railroad Co. had been sold to capitalists identified with the St. Louis & San Francisco Railroad Co. The terms of the sale were $150 per share, in cash, for the preferred stock of this company, and $75 cash and 25 per cent. in new securities for each share of common stock. All of the common stock is now held by the St. Louis & San Francisco Railroad Co.

Stock..Par $100...Authorized { com., $45,000,000 / pref., 15,000,000 } Issued { com., $15,000,000 / pref., 13,510,000 } $28,510,000

Preferred stock trust certificates, 4 per cent., guaranteed, quarterly, Jan....Par $100.. 13,510,000

The preferred stock is 8 per cent., non-cumulative.

All of the preferred stock is now held in trust, and the preferred stock 4 per cent. trust certificates, of which $15,000,000 are authorized, have been issued against the same. Interest on the trust certificates is paid quarterly, in January, April, July and October, at the Mercantile Trust Co., New York. The St. Louis & San Francisco Railroad Co. guarantees the certificates and can retire them at par at any time, and is obligated to do so within twenty years, that is to say, in 1921. The outstanding trust certificates were offered to the St. Louis & San Francisco stockholders for subscription in June, 1901.

Dividends paid in past years are shown in the table of earnings below. In 1900 5 per cent. was paid on the preferred stock, and 8 per cent. in 1901. The preferred dividends were paid semi-annually, February and August. A dividend of 4 per cent. was paid on the common stock, February 15, 1901, being the first since 1891.

### Funded Debt.

| | |
|---|---|
| K. C., F. S. & M. Ry. Co. refunding mort., 4 per cent., due 1936, April and Oct.... | $12,507,500 |
| 1st mort., land grant, sinking fund, 7 per cent., due June, 1908, June and Dec....... | 2,151,600 |
| Consol. mort., 6 per cent., due May, 1928, May and Nov.......................... | 13,736,000 |
| F. S., S. E. & M., 1st mort., 7 per cent., due Sept., 1910, March and Sept........... | 571,000 |
| Mem., Kan. & Col. Ry., 1st mort., 7 per cent., due Sept., 1910...................... | 492,000 |
| Kan. Equip. Co., 1st mort. on rolling stock, 5 per cent., due Jan., 1905............ | 761,000 |
| Fort Scott Equip. Co., 1st mort., 6 per cent., due July, 1909, Jan. and July......... | 233,000 |
| Ozark Equip. Co., 1st mort., 5 per cent., due May, 1910, May and Nov..... ........ | 834,000 |
| Kansas & Missouri R. R., 1st mort., 5 per cent., due Aug., 1922, Feb. and Aug...... | 390,000 |
| Total ........................................................... | $31,676,100 |

### Guaranteed Bonds of Consolidated Companies.

| | |
|---|---|
| K. C., Clinton & Springfield, 1st mort., 5 per cent., due Oct. 1925, April and Oct... | 3,192,000 |
| Current River, guar. 1st mort., 5 per cent., due Oct., 1927, April and Oct............. | 1,606,000 |
| K. C. & M. Bridge, 1st mort., 5 per cent., due Oct., 1929, April and Oct............ | 3,000,000 |
| K. C. Belt Ry. 1st mort., 6 per cent. ($534,000 guar.), due July, 1916, Jan. and July. | 2,050,000 |

The refunding mortgage is for $60,000,000. Of the issue $11,650,000 was offered for subscription in June, 1901. The bonds are guaranteed, principal and interest, by the St. Louis & San Francisco Railroad Co. Trustee and agent for payment of interest, Mercantile Trust Co., New York.

The sinking funds of the Fort Scott, Southeastern & Memphis bonds have retired $398,000 of that issue.

The Kansas City, Clinton & Springfield has gssumed $2,000,000 of the $13,736,000 consolidated mortgage 6 per cent. bonds of 1928. The same company is also responsible for $58,000 7 per cent. 1st mortgage bonds due October, 1907, April and October, of the Pleasant Hill & De 'o Railroad Co.

The consolidated 6 per cent. 40-year bonds at $25,000 per mile were created at time of the consolidation to retire prior bonds and provide for the construction of about 150 miles of new branches.

EARNINGS.

Year ending June 30.

| | Dividends. Com. | Pref. | Gross. | Net. | Charges. | Surplus. |
|---|---|---|---|---|---|---|
| 1892-93 (671 miles)... | .. | 5 | $5,111,151 | $1,297,638 | $1,094,027 | $203,610 |
| 1893-94 ( " " )... | .. | .. | 4,406,740 | 1,269,187 | 1,125,841 | 143,345 |
| 1894-95 ( " " )... | .. | .. | 3,985,635 | 1,191,488 | 1,099,277 | 92,211 |
| 1895-96 (708 " )... | .. | .. | 3,991,693 | 1,209,694 | 1,147,138 | 62,555 |
| 1896-97 (721 " )... | .. | .. | 4,137,124 | 1,310,556 | 1,139,448 | 171,118 |
| 1897-98 ( " " )... | .. | .. | 4,595,084 | 1,405,747 | 1,248,003 | 157,743 |
| 1898-99 ( " " )... | .. | .. | 4,346,276 | 1,372,326 | 1,165,266 | 207,060 |
| 1899-00 ( " " )... | .. | 5 | 5,328,106 | 1,732,626 | 1,346,738 | 385,887 |
| 1900-01 ( " " )... | 4 | 8 | 6,279,980 | 2,584,716 | 1,516,785 | 1,067,930 |

The earnings of the company are now included in those of the St. Louis & San Francisco Railroad Co.

In 1892, the company provided for deficits in interest payments of auxiliary roads, $94,988, of which $72,829 is not charged against above income. In 1893 such payments aggregated $53,596. In 1897, they were $120,785, and reduced the surplus revenue for the year to $50,332. In 1899 they were $139,316, making the surplus $67,743. In the same year $55,402 was also charged for improvements, leaving a net surplus of $12,341. In 1900 $200,000 was charged to the general improvement fund and dividends paid on the preferred stock were $137,490, leaving a surplus of $148,397.

President, Murray Carllton, St. Louis; Secretary and Treasurer, Corwin H. Spencer, St. Louis.

Main office, St. Louis; New York office, 25 Broad street. Annual meeting, second Wednesday in March.

## KANSAS CITY, MEMPHIS & BIRMINGHAM RAILROAD CO.

(Controlled by Kansas City, Fort Scott & Memphis Railway Co.)

Road owned, Memphis, Tenn., to Birmingham, Ala., 265 miles; branches, 20 miles; total, 285 miles. Locomotives, 46; passenger cars, 31; freight cars, 1,900.

The road was completed October, 1887. Built in the interest of the Kansas City, Springfield & Memphis, which gave a traffic guarantee of 10 per cent. of gross earnings from joint traffic to meet charges and retire bonds. The Kansas City, Fort Scott & Memphis owned one-half the stock.

Control of this company as well as of the Kansas City, Fort Scott & Memphis was acquired in February, 1901, by interests connected with the St. Louis & San Francisco Railroad Co. The price paid for the stock purchased was $50 cash, and the income bondholders received in exchange for their holdings 2d mortgage 5 per cent. bonds at 95. The property is operated as part of the St. Louis & San Francisco system.

Stock......Par $100.............. ..... .....Authorized, $5,976,000......Issued, $5,976,000

FUNDED DEBT.

| | |
|---|---|
| Gen. mort., 2-4 per cent., due March, 1934, March and Sept............ ............ | $3,323,300 |
| Income bonds, 5 per cent., due March, 1934, Sept.............................. .... | 6,322,780 |
| Birmingham Equipment Co., guar. bonds, 6 per ct., due March, 1934, March and Sept. | 913,000 |
| Memphis Equipment Co., guaranteed bonds, 6 per cent., due Aug., 1905............. | 189,000 |
| Total.............................................................. | $10,748,080 |

In 1902 the Kansas City, Fort Scott & Memphis guaranteed the interest and principal of all but $525,780 of the income bonds of this company; the bonds being stamped with a provision that they should be subject to call at 95 and interest within 10 years from September 1, 1902.

EARNINGS.

Year ending June 30.

| | Gross. | Net. | Charges. | Surplus. |
|---|---|---|---|---|
| 1894-95........................... | $1,035,605 | $187,687 | $145,314 | $42,373 |
| 1895-96........................... | 1,189,651 | 249,510 | 176,965 | 72,545 |
| 1896-97........................... | 1,241,393 | 340,973 | 198,085 | 142,888 |
| 1897-98........................... | 1,399,168 | 393,756 | 198,085 | 195,671 |
| 1898-99........................... | 1,433,294 | 403,852 | 197,743 | 206,109 |
| 1899-00........................... | 1,703,433 | 573,227 | 196,445 | 376,781 |
| 1900-01........................... | 2,032,192 | 717,209 | 270,466 | 446,743 |

Earnings are now included in those of the St. Louis & San Francisco Railroad Co.

A payment of 2 per cent. was made on the income bonds in September, 1897, and in September, 1898, 2½ per cent. was paid, amounting to $158,431, leaving net surplus for year 1897-98, $37,240. On September 1, 1899, 3 per cent. was paid on incomes, leaving the net surplus for the year $16,569. In 1900 5 per cent. was paid on incomes, September 1, and $15,000 was charged for new equipment, leaving a net surplus of $44,918 for the year. In September, 1901, 5 per cent. was also paid on the incomes.

A mortgage was executed in 1890 in favor of the Memphis Equipment Co. to secure $1,000,000 bonds at 6 per cent. to provide for new rolling stock. In 1891, 1st mortgage coupons for 5 years from September, 1891, were funded by issue of 6 per cent. notes, redeemable at par. In 1896-97, the company received $22,159, under traffic guarantee from Kansas City, Fort Scott & Memphis Co., in 1897-98, $21,569, and in 1898-99, $21,024.

In November, 1893, a plan for readjusting company's bonded debt was submitted. This plan was carried out in 1894-95.

President, B. F. Yoakum; Vice-President, B. L. Winchell, Kansas City; Secretary and Treasurer, F. H. Hamilton, St. Louis.

Main office, St. Louis; New York office, 25 Broad street. Annual meeting, first Wednesday in February, at Memphis.

## KANSAS CITY, MEXICO & ORIENT RAILROAD CO.

A corporation formed under the laws of Kansas in 1900. The company is constructing a road from Kansas City, Mo., to Port Stilwell, Topolobampo, Mexico, a total length of about 1,630 miles.

Road completed and in operation in March, 1903, Milton, Kan., to Carmen, Okla., 75 miles. East of Chihuahua, Mexico, 31 miles of track was laid at the same period. The company has an arrangement to use as part of its line the Chihuahua & Pacific Railway, Chihuahua to Minaca, Mexico, 125 miles. It was stated that by July 1, 1903, the road would be completed from Carmen, Okla., to a point beyond Fairview, Okla., making 125 miles in operation on that section of the line. Grading was in progress to Sweetwater, Tex. Work was also in progress east of Chihuahua and west of Minaca, Mexico, and also on 62 miles of track from Port Stilwell to El Puerto, Mexico, which had been graded and is to be completed early in 1903. Work is thus progressing simultaneously on the different portions of the line.

The contract for the construction of the section from Kansas City to Lone Wolf, Okla., was given to the Union Construction Co., a corporation formed in 1901, with an authorized capital of $3,000,000. The contract for the part of the line from Lone Wolf to the Pacific is held by the International Construction Co., a Delaware corporation formed in 1900, with an authorized capital of $7,000,000.

Stock...Par $100....Authorized { com., $12,500,000 / pref., 12,500,000 } Issued { com., $12,500,000 / pref., 12,500,000 } $25,000,000

The stock authorized is $20,000 per mile each of common and preferred. The preferred stock is 4 per cent., non-cumulative.

The company has authorized an issue of 4 per cent. 1st mortgage gold bonds, due 1950, interest January and July. Bonds are to be issued at the rate of $22,500 per mile; $2,500,000 extra in bonds are to be issued to cover heavy work in building the line through the Sierra Madras Mountains.

President, Arthur E. Stilwell, Kansas City; 1st Vice-President, Enrique C. Creel, Chihuahua, Mexico; 2d Vice-President, W. W. Sylvester; 3d Vice-President and General Manager, Edward Dickinson, Kansas City; 4th Vice-President, H. H. Melville, Boston; Secretary, Neal S. Doran, Kansas City; Assistant Secretary, J. Crosland Taylor, London; Treasurer, W. A. Rule, Kansas City; Assistant Treasurer, J. T. Nolthenius, New York; General Counsel, J. McD. Trimble, Kansas City.

Directors—Arthur E. Stilwell, Dr. W. S. Woods, William A. Rule, James J. Sylvester, Hugh C. Ward, C. C. Orthwein, R. A. Long, E. L. Martin, H. F. Hall, Edward Dickinson, J. S. Loose, Kansas City; George Crocker, J. T. Odell, George J. Gould, New York.; Russell Harding, St. Louis; Hermann Kuhn, Lewis Rendell, W. A. Simpson, London; Robert H. Law, Warren G. Purdy, Chicago; W. C. Edwards, Wichita, Kan.; J. R. Burton, Abilene, Kan.; David W. Mulvane, Topeka, Kan.

Main office, Eleventh and Grand avenue, Kansas City, Kan. Annual meeting, first Tuesday in May, at Kansas City.

## KANSAS CITY SOUTHERN RAILWAY CO.

A reorganization in 1900 of the Kansas City, Pittsburg & Gulf Railroad, sold in foreclosure March 19, 1900, and consolidated with other properties. See below.

Road operated, Kansas City, Mo., to Port Arthur, Tex., and branches, 833.39 miles. The properties acquired comprise the roads of the following former companies, viz.: Kansas City,

Pittsburg & Gulf, 372 miles; Texarkana & Fort Smith Railway, 190 miles; Kansas City, Shreveport & Gulf Railway, 245 miles; Kansas City Suburban Belt Railroad Co., 13 miles; Kansas City & Independence Air Line, 6¼ miles; Union Terminal Railroad Co., 5 miles. The company also owns the Port Arthur Channel & Dock Co., with a canal to Sabine Pass, 7 miles, and docks, warehouses and terminals. Locomotives, 131; passenger cars, 73; freight cars, 6,062; service cars, 576.

Stock..Par $100...Authorized { com., $30,000,000 / pref., 21,000,000 } Issued { com., $29,993,500 / pref., 21,000,000 } $50,993,500

The preferred stock is 4 per cent., non-cumulative.

Stock is transferred at the office of the company, New York. Registrar, Mercantile Trust Co., New York.

## Funded Debt.

1st. mort., 3 per cent., due April, 1950, April and Oct.......... .................... $30,000,500

The 1st mortgage (Mercantile Trust Co., New York, trustee), is $30,000,000 authorized, the unissued balance being available for improvements. Bonds are in denominations of $1,000 and $500. The bonds are a 1st lien on all the property of the company.

The company was originally organized as the Kansas City, Nevada & Fort Smith. Name was changed 1893, and company acquired the Kansas City, Fort Smith & Southern and Texarkana & Fort Smith Railway Companies. Company has a grant of right of way through Indian Territory. In April, 1899, Receivers were appointed. After some months of delay and negotiation between different committees of security holders, an arrangement was arrived at and a plan was issued in November, 1899, receiving the approval of both committees. Reorganization under this plan was completed early in 1900.

The plan involved foreclosure of the Kansas City, Pittsburg & Gulf Railroad and the combination with it of the Kansas City Suburban Belt Railroad and the Port Arthur Channel and Dock Co.'s property.

The voting power of both classes of stock was vested for five years in a trust. John W. Gates, Herman Sielcken, James Stillman, Louis Fitzgerald, Edward H. Harriman, O. H. Kahn, and George J. Gould, Trustees.

The Kansas City, Pittsburg & Gulf Railroad Co. had $23,000,000 of stock and $23,000,000 of 5 per cent. 1st mortgage bonds, due 1923. The Kansas City Suburban Belt Railroad had $4,750,000 stock and bond issues amounting to $4,050,000. The reorganization plan involved the unification of the entire system by the merger of the various companies. Details of the plan are given in the Manual for 1901.

## Earnings.

Year ending September 30.

| | Gross. | Net. | Charges. | Surplus. |
|---|---|---|---|---|
| 1896–97 | $1,773,243 | $461,575 | ........ | ........ |
| 1897–98 | 3,390,310 | 905,614 | ........ | ........ |
| 1898–99 | 4,174,300 | 972,901 | ........ | ........ |
| 1899–00 | 4,667,950 | 857,205 | ........ | ........ |
| 1900–01 (year ending June 30) | 4,753,066 | 1,269,586 | $790,902 | $478,684 |
| 1901–02 " " " | 5,450,871 | 1,821,270 | 904,936 | 916,334 |

In 1900–01 and 1901–02 taxes are deducted from the net earnings of the company.

The following presents the comparative freight traffic statistics of the company:

| | Average Mileage. | Total Tonnage. | Tons Carried One Mile. | Freight Density. | Rate per Ton per Mile | Earnings per Train Mile. | Av'ge Tons per Train. |
|---|---|---|---|---|---|---|---|
| 1900–01.... | 833 | 1,848,028 | 571,488,288 | 686,060 | 0.687c | $2.06 | 333 |
| 1901–02.... | 833 | 2,038,843 | 593,113,856 | 712,021 | 0.752 | 2.19 | 327 |

The average tons per train includes company's freight.

President, Stuart R. Knott, Kansas City; Vice-President, George J. Gould; Secretary, Alexander Millar; Treasurer, Frederic V. S. Crosby; Assistant Secretary, Joseph Hellen, New York; Assistant Secretary and Auditor, R. J. McCarty, Kansas City; Comptroller, William Mahl; Assistant Comptroller, Herbert S. Bradt, New York.

Directors—Edward H. Harriman, Otto H. Kahn, George J. Gould, Edwin Gould, H. P. Wertheim, Herman Sielcken, Lawrence Greer, New York; John W. Gates, John J. Mitchell, John Lambert, Chicago; Stuart R. Knott, Kansas City; H. C. Pierce, Julius S. Walsh, St. Louis.

Main office, Kansas City; New York office, 120 Broadway. Annual meeting in March.

## KEOKUK & DES MOINES RAILROAD CO.

(Leased to Chicago, Rock Island & Pacific Railway Co.)

Road owned, Keokuk, Ia., to Des Moines, 162 miles. The property is leased to the Rock Island for 45 years from October 1, 1878, at 25 per cent. of gross earnings, the lessee guaranteeing interest on bonds. The lessee owns a majority of the stock and provides equipment.

Stock...Par $100....Authorized { com., $2,600,000 pref., 1,524,600 } Issued { com., $2,600,400 pref., 1,524,600 } $4,125,000

Stock is transferred at the office of the company, New York.

Preferred stock is entitled to 8 per cent. dividends, non-cumulative. From 1896 to 1898, inclusive, no dividends were paid; in 1899 ½ per cent. was paid on preferred, and in 1900 50c per share. These dividends were paid annually on July 1. On September 1, 1901, 1 per cent. was paid and 1 per cent. September 1, 1902.

FUNDED DEBT.

1st mort., 5 per cent., due Oct., 1923, April and Oct. .............................. $2,750,000

President, Warren G. Purdy, Chicago; Treasurer and Secretary, George T. Boggs, New York.

Main office, Chicago; New York office, 71 Broadway. Annual meeting, first Wednesday in June, at Des Moines.

---

## KINGSTON & PEMBROKE RAILWAY CO.

Road owned, Kingston, Ont., to Renfrew, Ont., 104 miles; branches, 10 miles. Total, 114 miles. Locomotives, 9; passenger cars, 11; freight cars, 181.

The company has running rights on the Canadian Pacific from Renfrew to Pembroke and to Nipissing 175 miles.

The company is a reorganization under authority of an Act of the Parliament of Canada, dated June 30, 1898, of a company of the same name which defaulted on its interest charges in 1893, and was placed in the hands of a Receiver in 1894. It was stated in 1901 that the Canadian Pacific had acquired the property.

Stock... Par $50..Authorized { com., $2,500,000; 1st pref., 1,000,000; 2d " 150,000 } Issued { com., $2,250,000; 1st pref., 998,400; 2d " 145,150 } $3,393,550

The 1st preference stock is 5 per cent., non-cumulative, and the 2d preference stock 3 per cent., non-cumulative. All classes of stock have equal voting power.

Stock is transferred at the office of the company, 45 Broadway, New York. Registrar, Central Trust Co., New York.

The first dividend since the reorganization of the company, 1 per cent. on the 1st preferred stock, paid April 2, 1901. It was stated that this dividend was paid out of the earnings of the half year ending December 31, 1900.

FUNDED DEBT.

1st mort., 3 per cent., due Jan., 1912, Jan. and July............................ $572,000

Under the reorganization the old 6 per cent. bonds were exchanged for new 3 per cent. 1st mortgage bonds, and received 6 per cent. interest for 6½ years to January 1, 1899; the $150,000 of 3 per cent. 2d preference stock being also given to the bondholders in consideration of the reduction of the interest rate on the bonds to 3 per cent. until maturity. The 1st preference stock was sold to provide for the company's indebtedness, and the old stock was exchanged for half its face value in new common.

EARNINGS.

| Year ending June 30. | Gross. | Net. |
|---|---|---|
| 1899 | $137,996 | $34,530 |
| 1900 | 163,218 | 44,364 |
| 1901 | 164,286 | 23,994 |

President, M. H. Folger, Kingston, Ont.; Vice-President and General Manager, C. W. Spencer, Montreal; Secretary and Treasurer, John Whitebread, Kingston, Ont.

Directors—M. H. Folger, B. W. Folger, W. W. Hart, H. P. Timmerman, Kingston, Ont.; C. W. Spencer, Thomas Tait, A. R. Creelman, W. R. Baker, Montreal; W. D. Mathews.

Main office, Kingston, Ont.; New York office, 45 Broadway. Annual meeting, second Wednesday in February, at Kingston, Ont.

## KNOXVILLE & BRISTOL RAILROAD CO.

Road owned, Morristown, Tenn., to Corryton, Tenn., 40 miles. Extensions from Bean Station to Bristol, Tenn., and from Corryton to Knoxville are contemplated. This company is the successor of the Morristown & Cumberland Gap Railroad Co., which road was foreclosed in 1898. It was stated in December, 1902, that control of the road had been acquired in the interest of the Harriman & Northeastern Railway

Stock......Par $100.................................Authorized, $1,000,000......Issued, $100,000

A 1st mortgage at the rate of $20,000 per mile has been authorized.

President, Bird W. Robinson, New York; Vice-President and General Manager, H. M. Aiken, Morristown, Tenn.; Treasurer, J. B. Foster, Providence, R. I.

Main office, Morristown, Tenn.; New York office, 271 Broadway.

## LAKE ERIE & DETROIT RIVER RAILROAD CO.

(Controlled by Pere Marquette Railroad Co.)

A corporation formed under the laws of the Dominion of Canada in 1885. It was originally the Lake Erie, Essex & Detroit River Railway, the name being changed to the present title in 1891.

Road owned, Walkerville, Ont., to St. Thomas, Ont., 128 miles; Sarnia, Ont., to Rondeau, Ont. (formerly the Erie & Huron Railroad), 74 miles; leased, London, Ont., to Port Stanley, 24 miles; total operated, 226 miles. Locomotives, 33; passenger cars, 51; freight cars, 712.

In November, 1902, it was announced that the stock of this company had been acquired in the interest of the Pere Marquette Railroad Co., and that arrangements had been made for trackage over the Canada Southern Division of the Michigan Central, from St. Thomas to Buffalo, pending the construction of an independent line between those points.

Stock......Par $100..........................Authorized, $3,000,000......Issued, $3,000,000

All the stock is owned by the Pere Marquette Railroad Co.

FUNDED DEBT.

1st mort., 5 per cent., due May, 1932, May and Nov ................................ $3,000,000

The earnings of the company in 1901 were: Gross, $550,872; net, $190,504; charges, $115,816; surplus, $74,688.

President, Frederick H. Prince, Boston; Secretary and Treasurer, J. E. Howard, Walkerville, Ont.; Treasurer, J. H. Walker, Detroit.

Main office, Walkerville, Ont.

## LAKE ERIE & WESTERN RAILROAD CO.

(Controlled by Lake Shore & Michigan Southern Railroad Co.)

Road owned, Sandusky, O., to Peoria, Ill., 420 miles; branch, 10 miles; Fort Wayne to Connorsville and branch, 133 miles; Indianapolis to Michigan City, Ind., 162 miles; total, 725 miles. In September, 1895, purchased control of and leased the Northern Ohio, formerly the Pittsburg, Akron & Western Railway, Akron to Delphos, O., 165 miles, which road was to be extended from Akron to New Castle, Pa., 70 miles. This extension was, however, abandoned in 1899, the company selling to the Baltimore & Ohio Reorganization Committee a block of over $2,000,000 Pittsburg & Western bonds, which had been acquired in pursuance of the plan of extension. The company also had an interest in the Cleveland, Akron & Columbus Railway, which was disposed of in 1899. Locomotives, 119; passenger cars, 86; freight cars, 5,291.

In January, 1900, the Lake Shore & Michigan Southern acquired control of the road, and a directorate representing that interest was elected. A majority of the stock is owned by the Lake Shore, which holds $5,940,000 common and $5,930,000 of the preferred.

Stock. Par $100..Authorized { com., $20,000 per mile; pref., 20,000 " } Issued { com., $11,840,000; pref., 11,840,000 } $23,680,000

The preferred stock is 6 per cent., non-cumulative. Authorized capitalization is $10,000 per mile in bonds, and $20,000 each in common and preferred stock.

Transfer agency, Grand Central Station, New York. Registrar, Central Trust Co., New York.

The company paid dividends on the preferred stock as shown by the table of earnings. The preferred dividends were quarterly, February, May, August and November. The February, 1899, dividend was passed, and nothing was paid on the preferred until July, 1900, when 2 per cent. was paid, and 2 per cent. was also paid January 15, 1901. The July, 1901, January, 1902, July, 1902, and January, 1903, dividends were also 2 per cent. each, semi-annual.

FUNDED DEBT.

| | |
|---|---|
| 1st mort., 5 per cent., due 1937, Jan. and July | $7,250,000 |
| 2d mort., 5 per cent., due 1941, Jan. and July | 3,625,000 |
| Northern Ohio, 1st mort., 5 per cent. guar., due Oct. 1945, April and Oct | 2,500,000 |
| Total | $13,375,000 |

A Receiver of the old company, the predecessor of the present corporation, was appointed April 25, 1885, and road foreclosed December, 1886. Reorganized February 9, 1887. Purchased Indianapolis, Peru & Chicago, Indianapolis to Michigan City, in 1887 and the Fort Wayne, Cincinnati & Louisville in 1890.

In 1896 this company guaranteed the $2,500,000 5 per cent. 1st mortgage bonds of the Northern Ohio Railway.

EARNINGS.

| | Div. on Pref. | Gross. | Net. | Charges. | Surplus. |
|---|---|---|---|---|---|
| 1892 | 4¾ | $3,558,482 | $1,620,359 | $634,700 | $985,659 |
| 1893 | 5 | 3,512,620 | 1,463,877 | 650,470 | 813,407 |
| 1894 | 5 | 3,345,403 | 1,479,551 | 682,982 | 796,569 |
| 1895 | 5 | 3,519,104 | 1,602,960 | 701,786 | 901,174 |
| 1896 | 5 | 3,344,273 | 1,427,015 | 700,625 | 726,389 |
| 1897 | 5 | 3,439,397 | 1,463,282 | 846,636 | 616,646 |
| 1898 | 3½ | 3,485,378 | 1,482,693 | 745,427 | 737,267 |
| 1899 | 0 | 3,904,177 | 1,553,144 | 648,750 | 904,394 |
| 1900 | 4 | 4,284,780 | 1,359,918 | 643,750 | 716,168 |
| 1901 | 4 | 4,533,204 | 1,380,829 | 875,733 | 505,196 |

The estimated earnings for the year 1902 were: Gross, $4,690,354; net, $1,148,214, the latter not including miscellaneous income.

The operations of the Northern Ohio in 1896 resulted in gross, $146,160; net, $8,063; taxes $5,713; interest on bonds, $125,000; deficit, $122,650. In 1896-97 deficit was $118,911. In 1897-98, deficit, $119,142; in 1898-99, deficit, $110,029.

In 1892 the dividend on the preferred was increased to 5 per cent., and surplus after paying same was $393,659. In 1893 surplus over 5 per cent. dividend on preferred was $221,407. In 1894 same dividend rate was paid and surplus was $204,569. In 1895 the dividend was 5 per cent. and surplus $62,505, after devoting $246,669 to betterments. In 1896 company paid interest on the Northern Ohio 5 per cent. bonds amounting to $125,000, and $592,000 for 5 per cent. dividends on the preferred stock, leaving a balance of $134,389. In 1897 balance after Northern Ohio payment and preferred dividends was $149,647. In 1898 dividends on preferred were reduced to 3½ per cent., calling for $444,000, and $197,978 out of earnings was devoted to betterments. In 1899 the surplus was $201,144, and in 1900, after paying 4 per cent. on the preferred stock, there was a surplus of $242,568. In 1901 surplus over 4 per cent. on the preferred was $31,596.

President, William H. Newman; Vice-President, William C. Brown; Vice-President, Secretary and Treasurer, Charles F. Cox; Assistant Treasurer, F. Middlebrook, New York.

Directors—William K. Vanderbilt, Frederick W. Vanderbilt, Hamilton McK. Twombly, J. Pierpont Morgan, William H. Newman, George F. Baker, Henry W. Cannon, F. W. Whitridge, William C. Brown, New York.

Main office, Indianapolis. Annual meeting, first Wednesday in October, at Peoria, Ill.

---

## LAKE SHORE & MICHIGAN SOUTHERN RAILWAY CO.

(Controlled by New York Central & Hudson River Railroad Co.)

Road owned, Buffalo to Chicago, 540 miles; branches, 321 miles; branches owned, but under separate organizations, Detroit, Monroe & Toledo, 54 miles; Kalamazoo & White Pigeon, 37 miles; Findley to Goshen, 36 miles; Northern Central Michigan, 61 miles; Detroit & Chicago, 26 miles; Elkhart & Western, 11 miles; Central Trunk Railroad, 5 miles; total branches, 231 miles; leased, Kalamazoo, Allegan & Grand Rapids, 58 miles; Jamestown & Franklin, 51 miles; Mahoning Coal Railroad, 147 miles; Detroit, Hillsdale & Southwestern, 65 miles; Fort Wayne & Jackson Railroad, 98 miles; total leased, 319 miles; total operated, 1,411 miles. Also has a controlling interest in the stocks of the New York, Chicago & St. Louis, Pittsburg & Lake Erie and Lake Erie & Western. In 1901 purchased control of the Indiana, Illinois & Iowa Railroad Co. The company has large holdings of stocks of the Cleveland, Cincinnati, Chicago & St. Louis. Locomotives, 582; passenger cars, 431; freight cars, 21,564.

Stock..Par $100...Authorized { com., $49,466,500 / guar., 533,500 } Issued { com., $49,466,500 / guar., 533,500 } $50,000,000

The guaranteed stock is entitled to 10 per cent. dividends. It was issued in exchange for the stock of the Michigan Southern & North Indiana Railroad.

Transfer agency, Grand Central Station, New York. Registrar, Union Trust Co., New York.

Dividends of 10 per cent. per annum on the guaranteed stock are paid regularly, 5 per cent. each, in February and August. Dividends on the ordinary stock also paid half yearly, January 29 and July 29. The rate paid each year is shown in the table of earnings, the same having been increased to 7 per cent. per annum in 1898.

### Funded Debt.

| | |
|---|---|
| New consolidated refunding mort., 3½ per cent., due June, 1997, June and Dec..... | $43,844,000 |
| Consolidated 2d mort., 7 per cent., due Dec., 1903, June and Dec.................. | 6,098,000 |
| Total.............................................................. | $49,942,000 |

Registrar of the 3½ per cent. bonds, United States Trust Co., New York. Registrar of the consolidated 2d mortgage bonds, Union Trust Co., New York.

### Guaranteed Bonds of Controlled and Leased Companies.

| | |
|---|---|
| Detroit, Monroe & Toledo, 7 per cent., due Aug., 1906, Feb. and Aug.............. | $924,000 |
| Kalamazoo & White Pigeon, 5 per cent., due Jan., 1940, Jan. and July............ | 400,000 |
| Kalamazoo, Allegan & Grand Rapids, 5 per cent., due Jan., 1938, Jan. and July.... | 840,000 |
| Mahoning Coal R. R., 1st mort., 5 per cent., due July, 1934, Jan. and July......... | 1,500,000 |
| Sturgis, Goshen & St. Louis, 1st mort., 3 per cent., due Dec., 1989, June and Dec... | 322,000 |
| Total.............................................................. | $3,986,000 |

In February, 1898, the New York Central & Hudson River Railroad Co. made a proposition to Lake Shore stockholders to give them for each $500 of stock $1,000 in its own issue of 3½ per cent. collateral trust bonds, secured by a deposit of the stock so acquired. It was announced that the Vanderbilt interests and other large holders had accepted this offer, and 60 days were given for assents of other holders. At the end of 1902 the New York Central had acquired $45,289,200 of Lake Shore stock under this arrangement.

The new consolidated 3½ per cent. refunding mortgage of 1897 is for $50,000,000, sufficient bonds being reserved to retire the 2d mortgage 7s, due 1903. The saving of interest charges when the refunding is completed will be about $1,250,000 per annum.

Detroit, Hillsdale & Southern is leased for $54,000 per year; Fort Wayne & Jackson for $126,028 per year; Jamestown & Franklin for 40 per cent. of gross earnings; Kalamazoo, Allegan & Grand Rapids for $103,800 per year; Mahoning Coal Railroad for 40 per cent. of gross earnings, guaranteeing that this shall yield 5 per cent. per annum, $661,850, on its preferred stock and 5 per cent. per annum on $1,500,000 of 1st mortgage bonds.

In 1882 a controlling interest in the New York, Chicago & St. Louis Railroad was purchased, and the Lake Shore now holds 87,780 shares of its preferred and 62,400 shares of common stock. The company also has controlling interest in Pittsburg & Lake Erie, holding $3,050,000 of its stock, In 1900 the company acquired control of the Lake Erie & Western Railroad Co., purchasing $5,940,000 of the common, and $5,930,000 of the preferred stock of that company. It also in the same year acquired $11,224,000 of the common stock of the Cleveland, Cincinnati, Chicago & St. Louis Railway Co., and in 1902 $3,200,000 of the stock of the Lehigh Valley Railway Co.

In January, 1903, this company and the Baltimore & Ohio Railroad Co. acquired jointly a large interest in the stocks of the Reading Co. This company is understood to have made a loan of $25,000,000 for one year to finance this purchase.

### Earnings.

| | Div. Paid. | Gross. | Net. | Other Receipts. | Total. |
|---|---|---|---|---|---|
| 1893 (1,445 miles)........... | 6 | $23,685,932 | $6,562,019 | $459,131 | $7,021,140 |
| 1894 ( " " )........... | 6 | 19,557,870 | 6,371,802 | 409,356 | 6,781,158 |
| 1895 ( " " )........... | 6 | 21,016,035 | 6,447,816 | 412,978 | 6,860,794 |
| 1896 ( " " )........... | 6 | 20,193,958 | 6,467,803 | 354,812 | 6,822,614 |
| 1897 (1,404 " )........... | 6 | 20,297,722 | 6,755,231 | 395,621 | 7,150,852 |
| 1898 (1,410 " )........... | 7 | 20,753,683 | 7,520,554 | 346,810 | 7,867,364 |
| 1899 ( " " )........... | 7 | 23,613,945 | 7,781,801 | 376,051 | 8,157,852 |
| 1900 (1,413 " )........... | 7 | 26,466,514 | 8,829,305 | 329,414 | 9,158,719 |
| 1901 (1,411 " )........... | 7 | 29,272,673 | 9,770,364 | 1,329,290 | 10,391,736 |
| 1901–02 (year ending June 30). | 7 | 29,493,002 | 9,086,078 | 1,862,933 | 10,949,011 |

The disposition of the income was as follows:

| | Total Income. | Charges. | Surplus. | Dividends. |
|---|---|---|---|---|
| 1893 | $7,021,140 | $3,824,507 | $3,196,643 | $2,967,990 |
| 1894 | 6,781,158 | 3,812,219 | 2,968,939 | 2,967,990 |
| 1895 | 6,860,794 | 3,817,720 | 3,028,315 | 2,967,990 |
| 1896 | 6,822,614 | 3,800,214 | 3,022,400 | 2,967,990 |
| 1897 | 7,150,852 | 3,405,392 | 3,745,460 | 2,967,990 |
| 1898 | 7,867,364 | 3,790,789 | 4,076,575 | 3,516,005 |
| 1899 | 8,157,852 | 3,100,591 | 5,057,262 | 3,516,005 |
| 1900 | 9,158,719 | 3,196,559 | 5,962,160 | 3,516,005 |
| 1901 | 10,391,736 | 3,183,261 | 7,208,475 | 3,516,005 |
| 1901-02 (year ending June 30) | 10,949,011 | 3,941,229 | 7,007,782 | 3,516,005 |

In 1899 and 1900 the expenses included large amounts for new equipment.

The following shows the average mileage worked, earnings per mile, and percentage of expenses:

| | Mileage. | Gross Earnings per mile. | Per cent. of Expenses. | Net Earnings per mile. |
|---|---|---|---|---|
| 1893 | 1,440 | $16,449 | 72.29 | $4,557 |
| 1894 | 1,440 | 13,583 | 67.42 | 4,425 |
| 1895 | 1,440 | 14,595 | 69.32 | 4,478 |
| 1896 | 1,440 | 14,027 | 67.97 | 4,492 |
| 1897 | 1,403 | 14,128 | 66.72 | 4,701 |
| 1898 | 1,410 | 14,715 | 67.11 | 4,840 |
| 1899 | 1,413 | 16,707 | 67.05 | 5,505 |
| 1900 | 1,413 | 18,791 | 65.40 | 6,258 |
| 1901 | 1,411 | 20,745 | 66.62 | 6,924 |
| 1901-02 (year ending June 30) | 1,411 | 20,902 | 69.19 | 6,439 |

Chairman, Chauncey M. Depew; President, William H. Newman; Vice-President, William C. Brown; Vice-President, Secretary and Treasurer, Edwin D. Worcester, New York.

Directors—William K. Vanderbilt, Frederick W. Vanderbilt, Chauncey M. Depew, Samuel F. Barger, J. Pierpont Morgan, Edwin D. Worcester, Hamilton McK. Twombly, Darius O. Mills, W. Seward Webb, William H. Newman, William C. Brown, New York; Charles M. Reed, Erie, Pa.; James M. Schoonmaker, Pittsburg.

Operating office, Cleveland; executive office, Grand Central Depot, New York. Annual meeting, first Wednesday in May. Books usually close thirty days before.

---

## THE LARAMIE, HAHN'S PEAK & PACIFIC RAILWAY CO.

A corporation formed under the laws of Wyoming, February 1, 1901.

Road projected from Laramie, Wyo., to Grand Encampment, Wyo. Under construction from Laramie to Centennial, Wyo., 35 miles, which will be completed and in operation in 1903.

Stock......Par $10..........................Authorized, $9,000,000......Issued, $9,000,000

The stock of the company is issuable at the rate of 9,000 shares or $90,000 per mile for each mile of completed road. The amount given above as issued is nominal.

Transfer Agent, Federal Trust Co., Boston. Registrar, State Street Trust Co., Boston.

The company has no funded debt.

President, Isaac Van Horn, Boston; Vice-President, Fred A. Miller, Laramie, Wyo.; Secretary, E. S. Crawley, Boston; Treasurer, L. W. Thompson, Woburn, Mass.

Directors—Isaac Van Horn, Albert C. Smith, Boston; George M. Colby, Fred. A. Miller, Otto Gramm, Joseph B. McKee, Laramie, Wyo.; L. W. Thompson, Woburn, Mass.

Corporate office, Laramie, Wyo.; main office, 7 Congress street, Boston. Annual meeting, first Friday after first Thursday in September, at Laramie, Wy.

---

## LEHIGH & HUDSON RIVER RAILWAY CO.

Road owned, Belvidere, N. J., to Greycourt, N.Y., 63 miles; operates Orange County Railroad, Greycourt to Maybrook, 11 miles; Phillipsburg to Easton, Pa., ¾ mile; trackage, New York, Ontario & Western, Burnside to Campbell Hall, 2½ miles; Pennsylvania Railroad (Belvidere Division), Belvidere to Phillipsburg, N. J., 13 miles; total operated, 90¼ miles. Locomotives, 22; passenger cars, 11; freight cars, 743.

Stock......Par $100..........................Authorized, $1,340,000......Issued, $1,340,000

Stock is transferred at the company's office, Warwick, N. Y. Registrar, New York National Exchange Bank.

FUNDED DEBT.

| | |
|---|---|
| 1st mort., 5 per cent., due July, 1911, Jan. and July | $800,000 |
| 2d mort., 5 per cent., due July, 1917, Jan. and July | 164,000 |
| Gen. mort., 5 per cent., due July, 1920, Jan. and July | 1,124,000 |
| Warwick Val. R. R. 1st mort., 4½ per cent., due July, 1900, April and Oct. | 145,000 |
| " " " 2d mort., 6 per cent., due April, 1912, April and Oct. | 240,000 |
| Total | $2,473,000 |

The company has paid off its car trust obligations. General mortgage is for $3,000,000. The Central of New Jersey and Lehigh Coal & Navigation Cos. jointly guarantee $1,062,000 of the issue. The road affords the Central of New Jersey a connection with the Poughkeepsie bridge.

EARNINGS.

Year ending June 30.

| | Gross. | Net. | Charges. | Surplus. |
|---|---|---|---|---|
| 1892-93 | $507,169 | $184,749 | $133,444 | $51,305 |
| 1893-94 | 480,857 | 149,931 | 142,272 | 7,659 |
| 1894-95 | 392,912 | 153,221 | 140,337 | 12,884 |
| 1895-96 | 370,972 | 159,348 | 141,064 | 18,284 |
| 1896-97 | 327,078 | 144,747 | 142,090 | 2,652 |
| 1897-98 | 366,756 | 183,166 | 143,842 | 39,324 |
| 1898-99 | 422,108 | 210,031 | 145,075 | 64,956 |
| 1899-00 | 455,702 | 234,217 | 142,234 | 91,983 |
| 1900-01 | 414,029 | 175,640 | 137,286 | 38,354 |
| 1901-02 | 368,808 | 168,646 | 137,839 | 30,807 |

President, Lewis A. Riley, Philadelphia; Secretary and Treasurer, John Sayer, Warwick, N. Y.; Assistant Secretary, T. L. Hodge, Philadelphia.

Directors—George F. Baker, Charles Caldwell, James M. Duane, Harris C. Fahnestock, Henry Graves, William V. Martin, J. Roger Maxwell, W. R. Potts, Lewis A. Riley, George F. Baer, R. T. Davies, Alfred Ely, Joseph S. Harris.

Main office, Warwick, N. Y.; New York office, 143 Liberty street. Annual meeting, first Tuesday in December.

## LEHIGH & NEW ENGLAND RAILROAD CO.

Road operated, Campbell Hall, N. Y., to Slatington, Pa., 95½ miles; Glenwood to Glenwood Junction, 5 miles; branches, 2 miles; total operated, 102½ miles; total owned, 67½ miles. Has trackage as follows: New York, Susquehanna & Western, 18 miles; Erie Railroad, 17 miles; total trackage, 35 miles. Locomotives, 4; passenger cars, 2; freight cars, 22.

Was originally the Pennsylvania, Slatington & New England. Reorganized, 1887, as Pennsylvania, Poughkeepsie & Boston Railroad. Defaulted January 1, 1891, and Receiver appointed. In 1892 the Philadelphia & Reading assumed the operation of property, which furnished a connection between its system and the Poughkeepsie bridge lines which it controlled. It was understood that it would lease or otherwise control the property, but in July, 1893, another arrangement was made by which the Lehigh Valley and New York, Susquehanna & Western agreed to operate the line for a percentage of earnings.

Stock......Par $50..........Authorized, $1,500,000......Issued, $750,000

Stock is transferred at the company's office, Philadelphia. Registrar, Fidelity Insurance Trust & Safe Deposit Co.

FUNDED DEBT.

1st mort., 5 per cent., due July, 1945, Jan. and July.......... $731,000

EARNINGS.

| Year ending June 30. | Gross. | Net. |
|---|---|---|
| 1897-98 | $71,049 | $10,929 |
| 1898-99 | 78,140 | 26,336 |
| 1899-00 | 88,226 | 25,726 |
| 1900-01 | 85,714 | 466 |

There are $500,000 5 per cent. 1st mortgage bonds on the Campbell Hall Connecting Railroad (leased).

In December, 1894, road was sold under foreclosure and reorganized under present title April, 1895. First mortgage is for $1,000,000. Amount outstanding was issued for purchase price, the balance being held for improvements, etc.

President, W. Jay Turner; Vice-President, William B. Scott; Secretary, Joseph R. Sagee, Philadelphia; Treasurer, F. S. Fowler, Pen Argyle, Pa.

Directors—William B. Scott, W. W. Kurtz, Morris Pfaelzer, John W. Moffley, W. W. Gibbs, George W. Jackson, Philadelphia.

Main office, 929 Chestnut street, Philadelphia. Annual meeting, first Monday in May.

## LEHIGH VALLEY RAILROAD CO.

Road owned or controlled through ownership of the entire capital stock: main line, Jersey City to Phillipsburg, N. J., 75 miles; Phillipsburg to Wilkes-Barre, Pa., 99 miles, and Lehigh Valley Railway of New York, Pennsylvania State Line to Buffalo, 175 miles; branches, 631 miles; total owned, 980 miles; controlled by a majority ownership of stock, Pennsylvania & New York Canal & Railroad, 140 miles; Lehigh & New York Railroad, 115 miles; others, 69 miles; total, 325 miles. Leased, 28 miles; trackage, 49 miles; owned but not operated, 17 miles; total system, 1,399 miles. Locomotives, 760; passenger cars, 482; freight cars, 34,726; floating equipment, 6 lake steamers, 21 tugs, about 200 barges, canal boats, etc.

The company owns all the stock of the Easton & Amboy Railroad, and nearly all the stock of the Pennsylvania & New York Canal & Railroad Co. and of the Lehigh & New York Railroad. It controls the Morris Canal and absorbed the Geneva & Van Ettenville and the Lehigh Valley of New York. A company under the title of the Lehigh Valley Terminal was formed in 1891 to provide for the control of the line from South Plainfield, N. J., to Jersey City, where the company constructed large terminals. The company owns all the stock of the Lehigh Valley Coal Co., which controls valuable coal properties. It also controls a fleet of steamers on the lakes. In 1896 acquired the Elmira, Cortland & Northern. The Middlesex Valley Railroad is also controlled.

In 1892 the company's property was leased to the Philadelphia & Reading Railroad Co. In August, 1893, the lease to the Reading was dissolved.

Stock...Par $50...Authorized { com., $40,334,800 / pref., 106,300 } Issued { com., $40,334,800 / pref., 106,300 } $40,441,100

Stock is transferred at the company's office, Philadelphia.

Ten per cent. has been regularly paid on the preferred stock. For dividends on common stock, see table of earnings below. The dividends on the common were paid quarterly, but the October, 1893, dividend was passed, and none has been paid since.

FUNDED DEBT.

| | |
|---|---|
| 1st mort. extended, 4 per cent., due June, 1948, June and Dec. | $5,000,000 |
| 2d mort., 7 per cent., due Sept., 1910, March and Sept. | 6,000,000 |
| Consolidated mort., 4½ per cent., due Dec., 1923, June and Dec. | 4,762,000 |
| " " 6 per cent., due Dec., 1923, June and Dec. | 5,638,000 |
| " " annuity, irredeemable, 6 per cent. | 10,062,000 |
| " " " " 4½ per cent. | 2,538,000 |
| Collateral Trust mort., 5 per cent., due May, 1997, May and Nov. | 7,900,000 |
| Coal Trust certificates, 5 per cent., due Dec., 1912, June and Dec. | 3,000,000 |
| Equipment Trusts, 5 per cent., due 1902–1906 | 1,080,000 |
| Car Trusts, 4½ per cent. | 4,852,000 |
| National Storage Co. Trust certificates | 5,000,000 |
| Coal property purchase bonds | 1,170,000 |

GUARANTEED SECURITIES, SUBSIDIARY COMPANIES.

| | |
|---|---|
| Easton & Amboy, 5 per cent., due May, 1920, May and Nov. | $6,000,000 |
| Morris Canal 1st mort., 6 per cent., due Oct., 1920, April and Oct. | 500,000 |
| " pref. stock, guar., 10 per cent | 1,175,000 |
| " common stock, guar., 4 per cent | 1,025,000 |
| Penn. & N. Y. Canal & R. R., 4½ per cent. bonds, due April, 1939, April and Oct. | 1,500,000 |
| " " " 7 " " due June, 1906 | 1,500,000 |
| " " " 5 " " " April, 1939 | 4,000,000 |
| " " " 4 " " " April, 1939 | 3,000,000 |
| Lehigh & New York 1st mort., 4 per cent., due Sept., 1945, guar., March and Sept. | 2,000,000 |
| L. V. Ry. of N. Y., 1st mort., 4½ per cent., due July, 1940, Jan. and July | 15,000,000 |
| Lehigh Valley Terminal 1st mort., 5 per cent., due Oct., 1941, April and Oct. | 10,000,000 |
| Lehigh Valley Coal Co., mort., 5 per cent., due Jan., 1933, Jan. and July | 11,514,000 |
| Delano Land Co., 1st mort., 5 per cent., due Jan., 1932, Jan. and July | 1,102,000 |
| Lehigh Valley Coal Co., mort., 5 per cent., due 1947, May and Nov. | 5,000,000 |
| Easton & Northern, 1st mort., 4½ per cent., due Nov., 1935, May and Nov. | 51,000 |
| Middlesex Valley, 1st mort., 5 per cent., due Nov., 1942, May and Nov. | 375,000 |
| Elm., Court. & N., 1st pref. mort. (not guar.), 6 pr cent., due April, 1914, April and Oct. | 750,000 |
| " " 1st mort., 5 per cent., due April, 1914, April and Oct. (not guar.). | 1,250,000 |
| Canastota Nor., 1st mort. (not guar.), 6 per cent., due July, 1906, Jan. and July | 300,000 |

GUARANTEED SECURITIES—*Continued.*

| | |
|---|---|
| Greenville & Hudson Ry. Co., 1st mort., 5 per cent., due 1997, May and Nov........ | $350,000 |
| Schuylkill & Lehigh Val. R.R. Co., 1st mort., 5 per cent., due 1943, March and Sept.. | 2,000,000 |
| Rochester Southern R.R. Co., 1st mort., 5 per cent., due 1945, May and Nov........ | 425,000 |
| Hazleton Coal Co., 1st mort., 5 per cent., due 1936, March and Sept. .............. | 1,922,000 |
| Total............................................................... | $127,741,000 |

The collateral trust mortgage created in 1897 to provide for floating debt and future requirements is for $15,000,000. Of this amount $7,000,000, which may bear less than 5 per cent. interest, is for improvements and acquisition of securities of other companies in the system. The bonds are subject to call at 107½.

EARNINGS.

| Year ending November 30. | Gross. | Net. |
|---|---|---|
| 1892–93 | $18,610,777 | $5,905,417 |
| 1893–94 | 17,330,593 | 4,145,771 |
| 1894–95 | 18,564,454 | 4,728,066 |
| 1895–96 | 19,641,897 | 5,139,551 |
| 1896–97 | 19,559,166 | 5,305,973 |
| 1897–98 | 19,742,537 | 5,769,167 |
| 1898–99 | 22,659,161 | 5,098,219 |
| 1899–00 | 23,049,282 | 3,806,860 |
| 1900–01 | 26,683,533 | 6,613,657 |
| 1901–02 (year ending June 30.) | 24,272,254 | 4,620,136 |

The above are earnings from operation of road. The income statement, including miscellaneous receipts, is as follows:

| | Div. Paid. | Total Receipts. | Net Receipts. | Charges. | Surplus. |
|---|---|---|---|---|---|
| 1892–93 | 4 | $18,974,010 | $5,746,273 | $4,179,860 | $1,566,413 |
| 1893–94 | .. | 18,344,900 | 4,400,810 | 4,273,740 | 127,070 |
| 1894–95 | .. | 19,549,660 | 4,937,222 | 4,294,380 | 632,842 |
| 1895–96 | .. | 20,190,819 | 4,933,795 | 4,484,032 | 449,763 |
| 1896–97 | .. | 20,595,456 | 5,557,073 | 5,454,410 | 102,663 |
| 1897–98 | .. | 20,987,483 | 6,189,328 | 5,715,224 | 474,104 |
| 1898–99 | .. | 24,426,434 | 5,128,380 | 5,651,574 | Def. 523,194 |
| 1899–00 | .. | 24,956,716 | 3,684,273 | 5,762,070 | " 2,077,797 |
| 1900–01 | .. | 28,639,456 | 6,572,890 | 5,998,278 | Sur. 574,612 |
| 1901–02 (year ending June 30) | | 27,050,893 | 4,651,129 | 5,983,905 | Def. 1,332,776 |

Charges for 1897 include $710,204 for interest on Lehigh Coal Co. bonds. In 1898 the charge on this account is $831,058; in 1899, $827,304; in 1900, $825,700, and in 1901, $825,700. The amount of such interest to be deducted from surplus was $590,650 in 1896 and $596,625 in 1895.

In 1899 the gross earnings of the Lehigh Valley Coal Co. were $19,211,745; net loss from operation, $59,480; charges and improvements, $318,750; total debit for year, $259,270. In 1900 the Coal Co.'s gross was $18,279,559; net loss, $340,171; charges and improvements, $529,676; debit for year, $869,847. In 1901, deficit under charges, $491,576. In 1902, seven months to June 30, deficit, $568,682.

No statement of the company's earnings, etc., for the fiscal year ending November 30, 1892, was made public.

Coal tonnage for a series of years has been as follows: In 1890, 9,101,824 tons; in 1891, 10,332,954 tons; in 1892, 10,559,228 tons; in 1893, 11,477,630 tons; in 1894, 11,103,157 tons; in 1895, 12,045,368 tons; in 1896, 11,534,854 tons; in 1897, 10,278,410 tons; in 1898, 10,226,267 tons; in 1899, 11,375,555 tons; in 1900, 10,458,385 tons; in 1901, 12,538,387 tons; in 1902, 10,029,649 tons.

In 1897 the management readjusted the company's accounts, charging off the depreciation of equipment and other items, reducing the amount to the credit to profit and loss of the preceding year to $377,478 on November 30, 1897. Balance to debit profit and loss June 30, 1902, $3,372,147.

The following presents the comparative freight traffic statistics of the company:

| | Average Mileage. | Total Tonnage. | Tons Carried One Mile. | Freight Density. | Rate per Ton per Mile. | Earnings per Train Mile. | Average Tons per Train. |
|---|---|---|---|---|---|---|---|
| 1899–00.... | 1,381 | 17,430,470 | 3,278,236,232 | 2,373,813 | 0.542c. | $2.315 | 427 |
| 1900–01.... | 1,382 | 19,805,624 | 3,805,865,245 | 2,753,882 | 0.542 | 2.536 | 467 |
| 1901–02.... | 1,387 | 18,174,886 | 3,418,884,789 | 2,464,949 | 0.554 | 2.588 | 466 |

President, Eben B. Thomas, New York; 2d Vice-President, J. A. Middleton; Treasurer, W. C. Alderson; Secretary, D. G. Baird; Comptroller, Isaac McQuilkin, Philadelphia.

Directors—Beauveau Borie, Edward T. Stotesbury, Robert C. Lippincott, Irving A. Stearns, Abram Nesbit, Joseph Wharton, Philadelphia; Charles Steele, Norman B. Ream, George F. Baker, J. Rogers Maxwell, Hamilton McK. Twombly, New York; George F. Baer, Reading, Pa.

Main office, 228 South Third street, Philadelphia; New York office, 26 Cortlandt street. Annual meeting, third Tuesday in January.

## LEXINGTON & EASTERN RAILWAY CO.

Road owned, Lexington, Ky., to Jackson, Ky., 92 miles; operated, Ohio & Kentucky Railway, Jackson to Morgan County coal mines, 26 miles; total operated, 118 miles. Locomotives, 13, passenger cars, 15; freight cars, 462.

This company is a reorganization, without foreclosure, in 1901 of a company of the same name.

Stock......Par $100..............................Authorized, $500,000......Issued, $500,000

Transfer Agents, Kean & Van Cortlandt, New York. Registrar, Central Trust Co., New York.

FUNDED DEBT.

| | |
|---|---|
| 1st mort., extended, 5 per cent., due July, 1911, Jan. and July | $850,000 |
| General mort., 2-5 per cent., due Feb., 1933, Feb. and Aug. | 1,500,000 |
| Total | $2,350,000 |

In the readjustment of the company's affairs in 1901 the old 1st mortgage bonds were extended at the same rate as before, the company having a right to retire them at 102. Interest on the general mortgage bonds was waived until August 1, 1901, and after that date was to be 2 per cent. per annum for five years, then 3 per cent. for five years, and 5 per cent. thereafter. Deferred debentures will be issued for the balance of interest not paid in cash, these debentures being redeemable at the company's option, either in cash or in general mortgage bonds.

EARNINGS.

Year ending June 30.

| | Gross. | Net. | Charges. | Surplus. |
|---|---|---|---|---|
| 1900–01 | $357,881 | $131,241 | $74,437 | $57,804 |
| 1901–02 | 424,402 | 158,571 | 130,325 | 28,266 |

President, Arthur Cary; Vice-President, Secretary, Treasurer and Auditor, George Copland; General Manager, J. Rogers Barr, Lexington, Ky.

Directors—Robert E. Tod, New York; George Copland, Arthur Cary, J. R. Morton, J. Rogers Barr, Lexington, Ky.

Main office, Lexington, Ky.; New York office, 45 Wall street. Annual meeting, first Tuesday in October.

## LITTLE MIAMI RAILROAD CO.

(Leased to the Pittsburg, Cincinnati, Chicago & St. Louis Railway Co.)

Road owned, Cincinnati to Springfield, O., 84 miles; branch, 16 miles; leased, Columbus & Xenia, 55 miles; Dayton & Western, 38 miles; branch, 4 miles; Cincinnati street connecting railroad, 2 miles; total, 199 miles. Locomotives, 52; passenger cars, 56; freight cars, 711.

Leased, with all its leased lines, for 99 years to the Pittsburg, Cincinnati, Chicago & St. Louis from December 1, 1869, for 8 per cent. on stock, interest on the debt, $5,000 per annum additional, and all the lease obligations. The contract is guaranteed by the Pennsylvania Railroad Co. The lease was modified in 1900.

Stock......Par $50..........................Authorized, $8,000,000......Issued, $4,943,100

Stock is transferred at the company's office, Cincinnati. Registrar, Central Safe Deposit & Trust Co., Cincinnatid

Dividends are pai quarterly, 2 per cent. each in February and August and 2 1-5 per cent. each in June and December. The December, 1899, dividend was increased 1-5 per cent. and a similar extra amount is to be paid semi-annually out of the invested funds of company.

FUNDED DEBT.

| | |
|---|---|
| Renewal mort., 5 per cent., due Nov., 1912, May and Nov. | $1,500,000 |
| New mort., 3½ per cent., due Feb., 1951, Feb. and Aug. | 1,417,000 |
| D. & W., 6 per cent., guaranteed, due 1905, Jan. and July | 463,000 |
| " 7 per cent., guaranteed, due 1905, Jan. and July | 32,000 |
| Total | $3,412,000 |

$3,000,000 7 per cent. bonds, convertible into stock, were authorised in 1890. These were known as betterment bonds. In 1900 it was agreed with lessee that a new issue of $3,000,000 3½ per cent. non-convertible bonds should be created to pay lessee for improvements and redeem the 7 per cent. betterment bonds.

EARNINGS.

| | Div. Paid. | Gross. | Net. | Int. and Rental. | | Loss to Lessee. |
|---|---|---|---|---|---|---|
| 1896........................ | 8 | $1,750,960 | $400,531 | $706,426 | | $305,895 |
| 1897........................ | 8 | 1,874,361 | 475,981 | 706,626 | | 230,645 |
| 1898........................ | 8 1-5 | 1,977,166 | 440,401 | 662,626 | | 222,224 |
| 1899........................ | 8 2-5 | 2,249,209 | 621,938 | 659,626 | Profit | 54,724 |
| 1900........................ | 8 2-5 | 2,327,007 | 756,445 | 690,456 | Loss | 65,989 |
| 1901........................ | 8 2-5 | 2,567,098 | 774,890 | 707,738 | Profit | 67,151 |
| 1902........................ | 8 2-5 | 2,769,813 | 764,960 | 672,891 | Loss | 92,068 |

President, Frank J. Jones; Vice-President, Briggs S. Cunningham; Secretary and Treasurer, Henry C. Urner, Cincinnati.

Directors—Henry Hanna, William Worthington, Briggs S. Cunningham, Thomas J. Emery, J. N. Gamble, Charles Kruse, Charles P. Taft, M. M. White, Frank J. Jones, Stephen R. Burton, Cincinnati; A. S. Frazer, Xenia, O.; Joseph Wood, Pittsburg.

Main office, Third and Walnut streets, Cincinnati. Annual meeting, last Tuesday in January.

## LITTLE ROCK & HOT SPRINGS WESTERN RAILROAD CO.

Road owned, Little Rock, Ark., to Hot Springs, 57 miles. The line from Little Rock to Benton, Ark., 27 miles, was leased in 1901 to the Choctaw, Oklahoma & Gulf Railroad Co.

This company is a reorganization of the Little Rock, Hot Springs & Texas Railroad, the property of which was sold under foreclosure in 1899. The company has close traffic relations with the Choctaw, Oklahoma & Gulf Railroad Co.

Stock......Par $100.........................Authorized, $1,140,000......Issued, $1,140,000

FUNDED DEBT.

1st mort., 4 per cent., due July, 1929, Jan. and July................................ $1,140,000

In the reorganization it was provided that no interest should be paid on the bonds of the company until the coupon due January 1, 1901, matured.

President and Treasurer, William C. Fordyce, St. Louis; Vice-President, John G. Lonsdale, Hot Springs, Ark.; Secretary, William C. Mitchell, Little Rock, Ark.

Main office, Hot Springs, Ark.

## THE LONG ISLAND RAILROAD CO.

(Controlled by Pennsylvania Railroad Co.)

Road owned, Long Island City, N. Y., to Greenport, 95 miles; Long Island City to Great Neck, 14 miles; Bushwick to Sag Harbor, N. Y., 99 miles; branches, 81 miles; leased lines, 106 miles; total operated, 395 miles. This company controls the New York & Rockaway Beach Railroad, 13 miles, the earnings of which are kept separate; also controls the Prospect Park & Coney Island Railroad, 10 miles, but in 1899 the latter was leased to the Brooklyn Rapid Transit Co. Locomotives, 159; passenger cars, 536; freight cars, 1,207; floating equipment, 19 ferry-boats, tugs, etc.

In May, 1900, the Pennsylvania Railroad Co. purchased a controlling interest in the stock of this company and holds $6,797,900 of the same. It was announced in 1901 that the Long Island would build a tunnel under the East River and connect its lines with the Pennsylvania's proposed tunnel from Jersey City, using the Pennsylvania's terminal in New York.

Stock......Par $50..........................Authorized, $12,000,000......Issued, $12,000,000

Transfer Agent, United States Mortgage & Trust Co., New York. Registrar, Central Trust Co., New York.

Last dividend, 1 per cent., quarterly, November 2, 1896. The August, 1894, quarterly dividend was reduced from 1¼ to 1 per cent., and the February, 1897, dividend was passed, since which time no more have been paid.

FUNDED DEBT.

| | |
|---|---|
| 2d mort., 7 per cent., due Aug., 1918, Feb. and Aug.............................. | $268,703 |
| Consolidated mort., 5 per cent., due July, 1931, quarterly, Jan..................... | 3,610,000 |
| " " 4 per cent., due July, 1931, quarterly, Jan..................... | 1,121,000 |
| Gen. mort., 2d lien, 4 per cent., due June, 1938, June and Dec..................... | 3,000,000 |
| Mort. bonds, 4 per cent., due June, 1932, June and Dec............................ | 332,000 |

FUNDED DEBT—*Continued.*

| | |
|---|---|
| Unified mort., 4 per cent., due March, 1949, March and Sept | $6,860,000 |
| Debenture bonds, 5 per cent., due June, 1934, June and Dec | 1,500,000 |
| Brooklyn & Montauk, 1st mort., 6 per cent., due March, 1911, March and Sept | 250,000 |
| " " 1st mort., 5 per cent., due March, 1911, March and Sept | 750,000 |
| " " 2d mort., 5 per cent., due June, 1938, June and Dec | 600,000 |
| L. I. C. & Flushing, 1st mort., 6 per cent., due May, 1911, May and Nov | 600,000 |
| " " con. mort., 5 per cent., due May, 1937, May and Nov | 650,000 |
| N. Y. & Flushing, 1st mort., 6 per cent., due March, 1920, March and Sept | 125,000 |
| Ferry mort., L. I. R. R., 4½ per cent., due March, 1922, March and Sept | 1,494,000 |
| Met. Ferry Co., 1st mort., 5 per cent., due Nov., 1937, May and Nov | 1,250,000 |
| Total | $22,410,703 |

BONDS OF LEASED AND CONTROLLED LINES.

(Guaranteed Except as Noted.)

| | |
|---|---|
| New York & Rockaway, 1st mort., 7 per cent., due 1901, April and Oct., interest only. | $250,000 |
| North Shore Branch cons., 5 per cent., due Oct., 1932, quarterly, Jan | 1,425,000 |
| N. Y., B. & Man. Beach, 1st cons. mort., 5 per cent., due Oct., 1935, April and Oct. | 1,726,000 |
| Montauk Extension, 1st mort., 5 per cent., due Jan., 1945, Jan. and July | 600,000 |
| New York Bay Ext., 1st mort., 5 per cent., due Jan., 1943, Jan. and July | 200,000 |
| New York & Rockaway Beach, 1st mort., due Sept., 1927, March and Sept | 984,000 |
| " " " 2d mort. income, due 1927 | 1,000,000 |
| Prospect Park & Coney Isl., 2d, now 1st mort., 4½ per cent., due 1926, Feb. and Aug. | 340,000 |
| " " " 6 per cent., not guaranteed | 160,000 |
| " " " 3d, now 2d mort., 4½ per cent., due 1931. | 96,000 |
| " " " " " 6 per cent., not guaranteed | 104,000 |
| " " " incomes, 6 per cent | 250,000 |
| Total guaranteed bonds | $7,135,000 |
| Total bonded debt of system | 29,545,703 |

Dividends are guaranteed as rentals on the stock of leased lines as follows: New York, Brooklyn & Manhattan Beach, on $650,000, 5 per cent. dividends; Prospect Park & South Brooklyn Railroad, $50,000, 4½ per cent.; New York & Coney Island, $82,500, 4½ per cent., and $17,500, not guaranteed, 10 per cent.

The Long Island City & Flushing, the Newtown & Flushing and the Brooklyn & Montauk were merged with the Long Island in April, 1889, the latter assuming bonded debt and acquiring the stock of the former. The New York, Brooklyn & Manhattan Beach Railroad is leased and its bonds guaranteed. There are $281,237 real estate mortgages. The company owns stock and bonds of proprietary and leased roads to the amount of $2,793,969. On June 30, 1898, the company had outstanding $1,579,000 notes payable. These, all other floating debt and $150,000 equipment notes were discharged with part of proceeds of the unified mortgage bonds issued in 1899. Considerable amounts from same source were also devoted to improvements. The Prospect Park & Coney Island bonds are guaranteed so far as bondholders have accepted reduction of interest to 4½ per cent., and that road has been leased to the Brooklyn Rapid Transit Co.

EARNINGS.

Year ending June 30.

| | Div. Paid. | Gross. | Net. | Charges. | Surplus. |
|---|---|---|---|---|---|
| 1892-93 | 5 | $4,300,338 | $1,466,447 | $847,151 | $619,296 |
| 1893-94 | 4¾ | 4,143,433 | 1,453,349 | 933,694 | 519,655 |
| 1894-95 | 4 | 4,014,019 | 1,445,752 | 941,598 | 504,154 |
| 1895-96 | 4 | 3,962,799 | 1,576,817 | 1,146,933 | 429,884 |
| 1896-97 | 2 | 3,954,865 | 1,127,716 | 1,019,512 | 102,204 |
| 1897-98 | .. | 4,333,193 | 1,267,824 | 1,023,949 | 243,874 |
| 1898-99 | .. | 4,622,474 | 1,270,145 | 1,020,074 | 250,071 |
| 1899-00 | .. | 4,557,259 | 1,325,013 | 1,265,520 | 59,493 |
| 1900-01 | .. | 4,862,347 | 1,372,851 | 1,177,042 | 195,809 |
| 1901-02 | .. | 5,883,607 | 2,104,743 | 1,560,489 | 544,254 |

The earnings for 1901-02 include the figures of the New York & Rockaway Beach Railroad Co. for the year.

President, William H. Baldwin, Jr.; Secretary, Frank E. Haff, New York; Treasurer, Robert W. Smith, Philadelphia.

Directors—William H. Baldwin, Jr., Charles M. Pratt, Dumont Clarke, Lewis C. Ledyard, August Belmont, George W. Young, Walter G. Oakman, Frederick G. Bourne, R. Somers Hayes, New York; John P. Green, Charles E. Pugh, Sutherland M. Provost, Samuel Rea, Philadelphia.

Offices, Long Island City, N. Y., and 128 Broadway, New York. Annual meeting, second Tuesday in April.

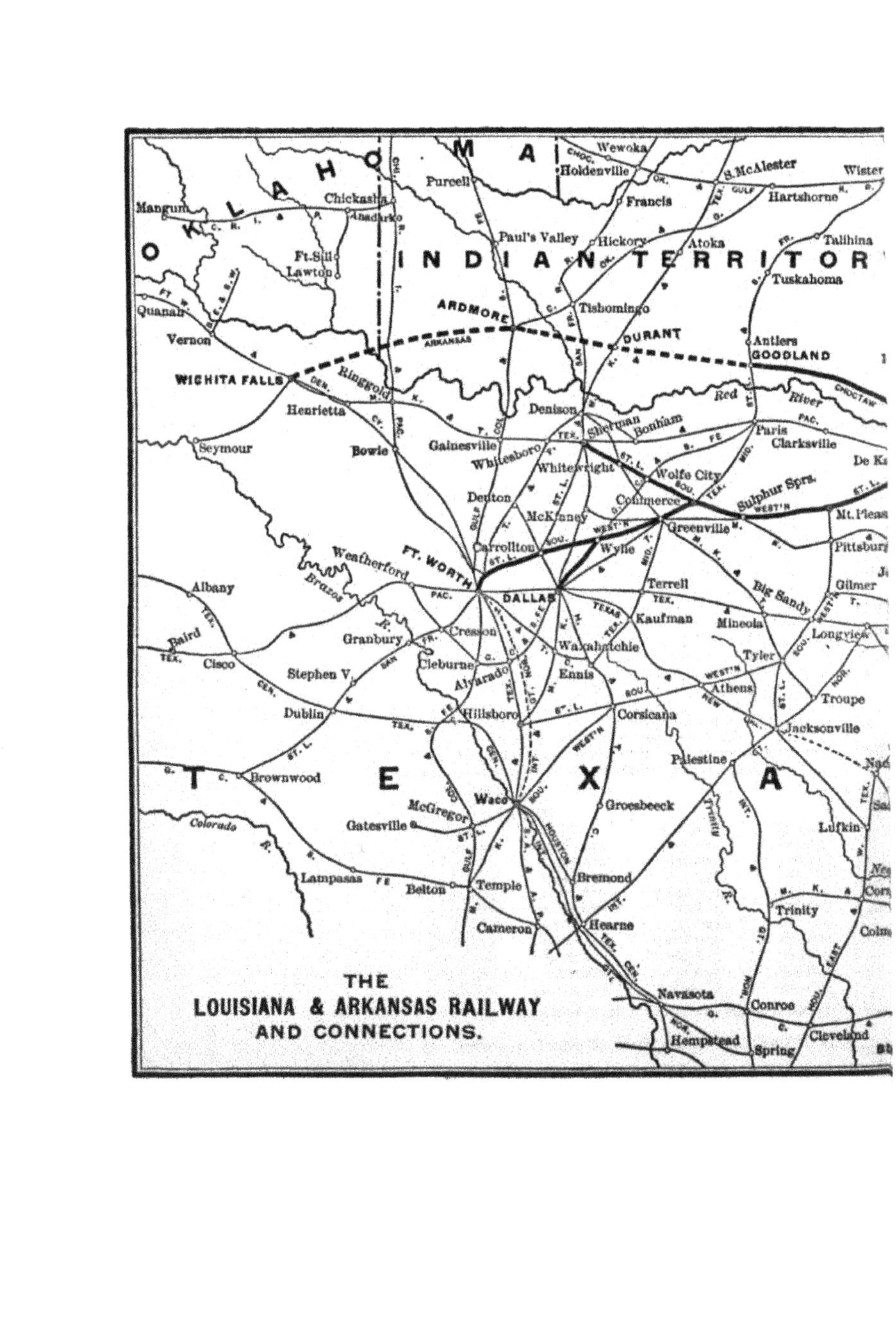


THE
LOUISIANA & ARKANSAS RAILWAY
AND CONNECTIONS.

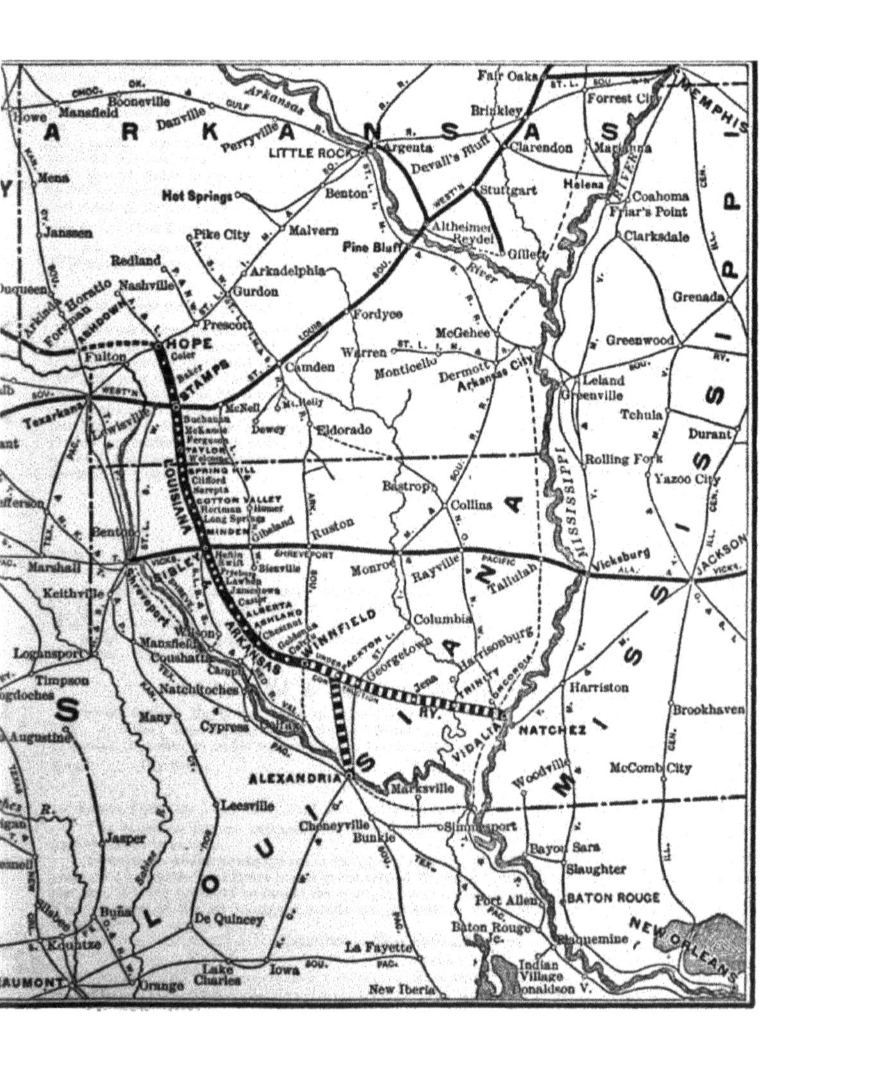

## LOUISIANA & ARKANSAS RAILWAY CO.

A corporation formed under the laws of Arkansas, June 10, 1902, to extend the charter of the Louisiana & Arkansas Railroad, and on August 18, 1902, all of the property and assets of the latter corporation were taken over and its outstanding liabilities assumed as of June 30, 1902. Both the capital stock and funded debt of the railroad have been retired and new securities of the railway company have been issued.

Road owned, Stamps, Ark., to Winnfield, La., 125.3 miles; road under construction, Stamps, Ark., to Hope, Ark., 23 miles; Winnfield, La., to Jena, La., 38 miles; under survey, Packton, La., to Alexandria, La., 42 miles; total operated, 125.3 miles; total mileage when completed, 228.3 miles. An extension of the Jena branch, eastward to Vidalia, La., on the Mississippi river, opposite Natchez, which city is reached by ferry, is contemplated. The road has a connection with the St. Louis Southwestern at Stamps, and when the extension now under construction to Hope is completed, it will have two very important connections, namely, the St. Louis, Iron Mountain & Southern and the Arkansas & Choctaw (St. Louis & San Francisco System).

Stock......Par $100..........................Authorized, $2,250,000......Issued, $1,750,000

All the stock of this company is held in a voting trust for ten years. The voting trustees are William Buchanan, Edward E. Porter, B. F. Yoakum, Harvey E. Fisk and Charles E. Pack.

FUNDED DEBT.

1st mort., 5 per cent., due Sept., 1927, March and Sept............................ $1,713,000

The 1st mortgage bonds were issued to acquire the property of the Louisiana & Arkansas Railroad, to acquire additional property for improvements, additions and extensions, and for bridges across the Black and Red rivers. The bonds are a first lien on all the property of the company now owned or hereafter acquired, and upon its equipment, franchises, etc. The entire issue, but no part, will be subject to redemption at 110 and accrued interest on any interest day after September 1, 1907. A sinking fund of $55,000 per annum, to be used by the trustees in the purchase of bonds at not to exceed 110 and accrued interest, will begin in 1907. If the bonds cannot be purchased at this price, the sinking fund may be invested in securities in which savings banks at that time are permitted to invest according to the laws of New York, New Jersey, Massachusetts or Connecticut.

EARNINGS.

Year ending June 30.

| | Gross. | Net. | Charges.* | Surplus. |
|---|---|---|---|---|
| 1900-01............................ | $316,746 | $140,514 | $37,157 | $102,357 |
| 1901-02............................ | 478,531 | 218,459 | 68,504 | 149,955 |

President and General Manager, William Buchanan, Texarkana, Tex.; Vice-President, F. H. Drake, Minden, La.; Secretary and Treasurer, J. A. Buchanan, Stamps, Ark.; Auditor, J. K. Wadley, Texarkana, Ark.

Main office, Stamps, Ark.; President's office, Texarkana, Tex. Fiscal Agents, Fisk & Robinson, New York.

---

## LOUISIANA & NORTHWEST RAILROAD CO.

Road owned, Magnolia, Ark., to Bienville, La., 82 miles; trackage, Magnolia to McNeill, Ark., 7 miles; total operated, 90 miles. Extension to junction with the Red River Valley Railroad, 23 miles, is under construction. Locomotives, 9; passenger cars, 8; freight cars, 106.

Stock......Par $100..........................Authorized, $3,000,000......Issued, $1,425,000

FUNDED DEBT.

1st mort., 5 per cent., due Jan., 1945, Jan. and July.............................. .. $100,000

The company has an extension to Natchitoches, La., under construction, which was to be completed early in 1902.

The trustee of the mortgage is the Peoples' Trust Co., Brooklyn. There is also an authorized issue of consolidated mortgage bonds at the rate of $7,500 per mile, but none of these bonds were put out, it being intended to cancel the mortgage and create one different in form and amount. The coupons of the 1st mortgage bonds are payable at the office of Boody, McLellen & Co., New York.

EARNINGS.—Year ending June 30.

| | Gross. | Net. | Charges. | Surplus. |
|---|---|---|---|---|
| 1900-01... ........................ .......... | $122,999 | $62,202 | $14,695 | $47,507 |
| 1901-02.................................. ..... | 154,331 | 75,676 | 59,609 | 16,067 |

President, (Vacancy); Vice-President, J. A. Richardson; Assistant Secretary, J. S. Richardson, Homer, La.; General Manager and Treasurer, J. D. Beardsley; General Superintendent, C. H. Beardsley, Gibsland, La.

Main office, Gibsland, La.

## LOUISIANA SOUTHERN RAILWAY CO.

This company is a reorganization of the New Orleans & Southern Railway, which was foreclosed in 1896. An English corporation, the United Railway Trading Co., acquired control of the company in 1901.

Road owned, New Orleans to Belair, La., 30 miles; Shell Beach branch, 15 miles; total operated, 45 miles. Locomotives, 5; passenger cars, 9; freight cars, 130.

Stock......Par $100..............................Authorized, $300,000......Issued, $300,000

FUNDED DEBT.

1st mort., 5 per cent., due March, 1950, March and Sept.. .......................... $250,000

The 1st mortgage was created in 1897. The bonds can be retired at 105 after 1902.

In the year ending June 30, 1901, the gross earnings of this company were reported as $91,780; net, $33,969.

President, E. A. Hopkins; Secretary and Treasurer, E. A. King, London, England; General Manager, P. Campbell, New Orleans.

Main office, New Orleans.

## LOUISIANA WESTERN RAILROAD CO.

(Leased to Southern Pacific Co.)

Road owned, Lafayette, La., to the Sabine River, 106 miles; branches, 58 miles; total, 164 miles. Locomotives, 24; passenger cars, 21; freight cars, 1,718.

Stock......Par $100..........................Authorized, $3,360,000......Issued, $3,360,000

FUNDED DEBT.

1st mort., 6 per cent., due July, 1921, Jan. and July............................... $2,240,000

Leased to the Southern Pacific Company (which see), from March 1, 1885, for charges and 7 per cent. of net profits, under omnibus lease. The Southern Pacific is the principal owner of the capital stock.

EARNINGS.

Year ending June 30.

| | Gross. | Net. | Charges. | Surplus |
|---|---|---|---|---|
| 1896-97 | $988,518 | $417,802 | $157,598 | $260,204 |
| 1897-98 | 1,034,288 | 460,552 | 189,017 | 271,535 |
| 1898-99 | 1,345,015 | 586,501 | 157,319 | 428,182 |
| 1899-00 | 1,349,537 | 438,101 | 173,716 | 264,385 |
| 1900-01 | 1,684,456 | 704,851 | 338,633 | 394,513 |
| 1901-02 | 1,969,887 | [illegible]42,121 | 272,840 | 769,290 |

President, Charles H. Tweed; Secretary, Alexander Millar, New York; Treasurer, J. B. Richardson, New Orleans.

Main office, 120 Broadway, New York. Annual meeting, first Monday in April.

## LOUISVILLE & NASHVILLE RAILROAD CO.

Road owned in fee or controlled by ownership of entire stock, 3,175 miles; operated but not owned, 269 miles; total operated, 3,335 miles. The company controls, by ownership of a majority of stock, the Nashville, Chattanooga & St. Louis, 941 miles, and has a joint interest in the lease of the Georgia Railroad and dependencies, 626 miles. In 1902 it bought the majority of stock of the Atlanta, Knoxville & Northern Railway, 228 miles. Owned, but not operated, 274 miles. Total mileage, 5,541 miles. The company practically owns the Henderson bridge and tracks, 10 miles. It also owned the Cecilian branch, 46 miles, leased to the Illinois Central, and sold the same to that company in February, 1902. The Clarkeville & Princeton branch, 21 miles, is leased to the Ohio Valley Railroad. The Tennessee Midland and Paducah, Tennessee & Alabama, now the Paducah & Memphis Division of this company, 254 miles, are owned, but are leased to the Nashville, Chattanooga & St. Louis. In 1899 the Atlantic Coast Line acquired a half interest in the Georgia Central lease. Locomotives, 589; passenger cars, 462; freight cars, 24,880.

In May, 1899, this company and the Southern Railway jointly acquired the Birmingham Southern Railway, 70 miles, from the Tennessee Coal & Iron Co. In 1901 this company and the Southern Railway Co. jointly acquired the Chicago, Indianapolis & Louisville Railway, issuing their joint bonds for the stock of that road. The Birmingham, Selma & New Orleans Railroad, 60 miles; the Shelby Railroad, 19 miles, and the Shelbyville, Bloomfield & Ohio Railroad, 92 miles, were bought in 1902. Various extensions were in progress at the end of 1902.

LONDON
CORBIN
Lowell
Barbour V.
GLASGOW
Oakland
Bowling Green
Willia
Celina
Richland
Gallatin
Gainesboro
Robbins
Carthage
Lebanon
HVILLE
Cokeville
Bon Air
Rockwood
Wartrace
Pikeville

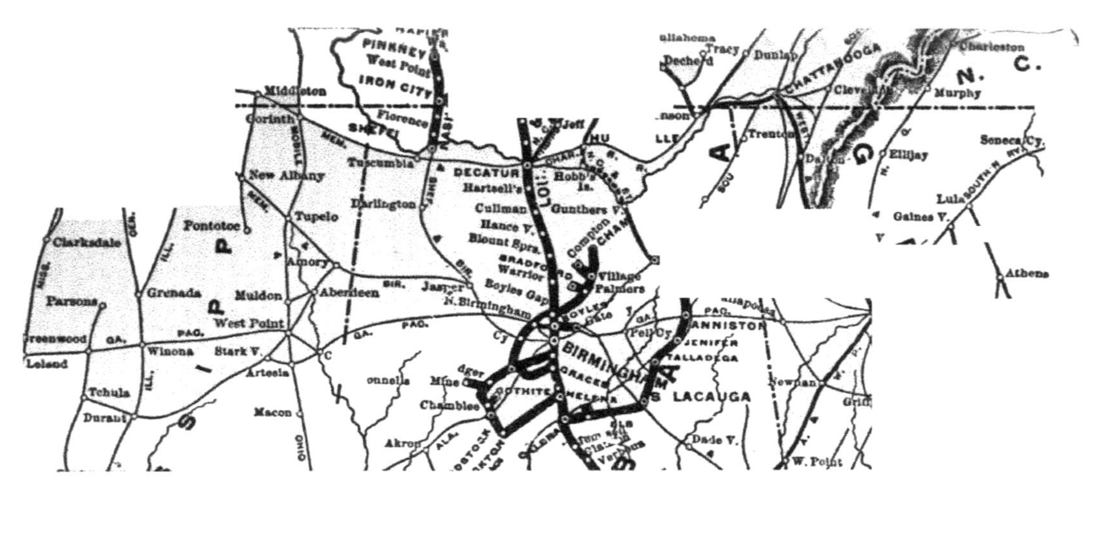

PINKNEY
West Point
IRON CITY
Middleton
Corinth
Florence
Tuscumbia
DECATUR
Hartsell's
Cullman
Gunthers V.
Hance V.
Blount Sprs.
Compton
Warrior
Village
Palmers
Boyles Gap
N. Birmingham
BIRMINGHAM
ANNISTON
JENIFER
TALLADEGA
LACAUGA
Pell Cy.
Newnan
Dade V.
W. Point
Chambles
Akron
Darlington
New Albany
Tupelo
Pontotoc
Amory
Aberdeen
Jasper
Muldon
West Point
Stark V.
Artesia
Macon
Clarksdale
Grenada
Parsons
Greenwood
Winona
Leland
Tchula
Durant
Tracy
Dunlap
Decherd
CHATTANOOGA
Cleveland
Murphy
Charleston
N. C.
Trenton
Ellijay
Seneca Cy.
Lula
Gaines V.
Athens

### EARNINGS.

Year ending June 30.

| | Div. Paid. | Gross. | Net. | Charges. | Surplus. |
|---|---|---|---|---|---|
| 1892-93 (2,942 miles)......... | 4 | $22,403,639 | $8,020,996 | $5,490,796 | $2,530,200 |
| 1893-94 (2,955 " )......... | .. | 18,974,336 | 7,110,552 | 5,665,636 | 1,552,490 |
| 1894-95 ( " " )......... | .. | 19,275,993 | 6,998,220 | 5,583,064 | 1,415,159 |
| 1895-96 (2,965 " )......... | .. | 20,390,711 | 6,885,505 | 5,563,057 | 1,322,448 |
| 1896-97 (2,981 " )......... | .. | 20,372,307 | 6,950,153 | 5,970,973 | 979,180 |
| 1897-98 (2,988 " )......... | .. | 21,996,653 | 7,665,698 | 6,032,797 | 1,632,901 |
| 1898-99 ( " " )......... | 3½ | 23,759,485 | 8,568,543 | 5,941,643 | 2,626,900 |
| 1899-00 (3,007 " )......... | 4 | 27,742,378 | 9,789,017 | 6,169,782 | 3,619,234 |
| 1900-01 (3,169 " )......... | 5 | 28,022,206 | 10,493,861 | 6,212,748 | 4,281,112 |
| 1901-02 (3,326 " )......... | 5 | 30,712,257 | 10,810,841 | 6,085,533 | 4,725,307 |

The following shows the average mileage worked, earnings per mile, and percentage of expenses:

| | Gross Earnings per Mile. | Per Cent. of Expenses. | Net Earnings per Mile. |
|---|---|---|---|
| 1892-93 (2,942 miles) .......................... | $7,615 | 64.20 | $2,726 |
| 1893-94 (2,955 " ).......................... | 6,418 | 62.53 | 2,405 |
| 1894-95 ( " " ).......................... | 6,521 | 63.69 | 2,367 |
| 1895-96 (2,965 " ).......................... | 6,877 | 66.23 | 2,322 |
| 1896-97 (2,981 " ).......................... | 6,834 | 67.98 | 2,188 |
| 1897-98 (2,988 " ).......................... | 7,361 | 67.84 | 2,367 |
| 1898-99 ( " " ).......................... | 7,951 | 66.21 | 2,686 |
| 1899-00 (3,007 " ).......................... | 9,224 | 67.06 | 3,038 |
| 1900-01 (3,169 " ).......................... | 8,841 | 65.07 | 3,088 |
| 1901-02 (3,326 " ).......................... | 9,231 | 68.06 | 2,948 |

To surplus is added, in 1890-91, $717,875; in 1891-92, $533,293; in 1892-93, $416,109; in 1893-94, $222,288, and in 1894-95, $363,273 for interest on investments. In 1895-96 income from investments, less losses on leaseholds, etc., $55,055. In 1896-97, such income was $353,130; charges for 1897 include losses on roads controlled. In 1897-98 income from investments was $353,883; losses on controlled roads, $175,100. In 1899, income from investments, $540,645; in 1900, $650,044; in 1901, $704,688; in 1902, $1,001,021.

The following presents the comparative freight traffic statistics of the company:

| | Average Mileage. | Total Tonnage. | Tons Carried One Mile. | Freight Density. | Rate per Ton per Mile. | Earnings per Train Mile. | Av'ge Tons per Train. |
|---|---|---|---|---|---|---|---|
| 1896-97.... | 2,981 | 11,391,942 | 1,757,230,703 | 589,476 | 0.805c. | $1.44 | 178 |
| 1897-98.... | 2,988 | 12,309,731 | 2,011,367,580 | 673,148 | 0.750 | 1.45 | 193 |
| 1898-99.... | 2,988 | 12,390,835 | 2,230,767,045 | 746,576 | 0.729 | 1.47 | 202 |
| 1899-00.... | 3,007 | 15,839,470 | 2,581,672,886 | 858,554 | 0.758 | 1.67 | 220 |
| 1900-01.... | 3,169 | 16,685,466 | 2,655,984,116 | 838,114 | 0.769 | 1.70 | 222 |
| 1901-02.... | 3,326 | 18,320,972 | 3,072,093,736 | 923,813 | 0.741 | 1.71 | 230 |

### GROSS AND NET EARNINGS BY MONTHS FOR THREE YEARS.

| | 1900. | | 1901. | | 1902. | |
|---|---|---|---|---|---|---|
| | Gross. | Net. | Gross. | Net. | Gross. | Net. |
| January ....... | $2,392,303 | $863,633 | $2,501,637 | $947,073 | $2,724,756 | $1,011,809 |
| February........ | 2,183,978 | 683,469 | 2,263,936 | 772,983 | 2,401,649 | 745,458 |
| March.......... | 2,452,227 | 805,918 | 2,498,243 | 878,577 | 2,606,375 | 807,780 |
| April........... | 2,148,371 | 571,127 | 2,243,519 | 592,647 | 2,520,550 | 684,178 |
| May............ | 2,260,768 | 616,089 | 2,386,873 | 764,914 | 2,625,300 | 826,116 |
| June........... | 2,177,312 | 675,447 | 2,271,180 | 637,710 | 2,662,200 | 844,977 |
| July............ | 2,189,988 | 710,154 | 2,311,390 | 546,989 | 2,709,244 | 804,559 |
| August .. ...... | 2,262,772 | 704,810 | 2,435,640 | 743,181 | 2,771,892 | 826,415 |
| September...... | 2,277,607 | 856,520 | 2,446,418 | 778,595 | 2,888,119 | 936,750 |
| October........ | 2,618,078 | 1,014,156 | 2,775,304 | 911,899 | 3,156,572 | 1,123,483 |
| November...... | 2,482,328 | 939,712 | 2,707,607 | 967,365 | 2,956,463 | 1,062,019 |
| December....... | 2,504,642 | 969,914 | 2,495,069 | 921,472 | 3,005,904 | 1,102,103 |
| Total for year... | $27,950,374 | $9,410,949 | $29,336,007 | $9,483,405 | $33,029,024 | $10,775,647 |
| Aver. per month. | 2,329,197 | 784,245 | 2,444,607 | 790,283 | 2,752,418 | 897,970 |

Chairman, August Belmont, New York; President, Milton H. Smith; Vice-Presidents, W. D. Hines, Louisville; A. W. Morriss, New York; William J. Dickinson; Treasurer, W. W. Thompson; Secretary, J. H. Ellis; Assistant Secretary, W. H. Bruce Louisville; Assistant Secretary and Assistant Treasurer, E. L. Smithers, New York.

Directors—August Belmont, W. G. Raoul, Walter G. Oakman, John I. Waterbury, R. G. Erwin, Henry Walters, New York; Milton H. Smith, Attilla Cox, Louisville; Gardiner M. Lane, Boston; D. P. Kingsley, Warren Delano, Jr., Warren G. Elliott, Michael Jenkins, Baltimore.

Main office, Main and Second streets, Louisville; New York office, 120 Broadway. Annual meeting, first Wednesday in October. Books close ten days before.

## LOUISVILLE, HENDERSON & ST. LOUIS RAILWAY CO.

Road owned, Henderson, Ky., to West Point, Ky., 121.4 miles; Fordsville branch, 43.8 miles; trackage, West Point to Louisville, 20.8 miles; Henderson to Evansville, 12 miles; total operated, 198 miles. Locomotives, 21; passenger cars, 23; freight cars, 800.

Stock....Par $100.....Authorized { com., $2,000,000 / pref., 2,000,000 } Issued { com., $2,000,000 / pref., 2,000,000 } $4,000,000

The preferred stock is 5 per cent., non-cumulative.

FUNDED DEBT.

1st mort., 5 per cent, due Jan., 1946, Jan. and July ................................ $2,200,000

This road was originally the Louisville, St. Louis & Texas Railway Co. That company defaulted on its August, 1893, interest and a Receiver was appointed. A bondholders' committee was constituted and plan of reorganization was submitted in January, 1896. Foreclosure was instituted and road sold and transferred to present company June 1, 1896. Stock is held in voting trust, J. J. McCook, Brayton Ives, Oscar Fenley, trustees, for 10 years, unless sooner terminated by trustees. New 1st mortgage is $2,500,000, $300,000 being reserved for betterments and extension to Louisville.

EARNINGS.

Year ending June 30.

| | Gross. | Net. | Charges. | Surplus. |
|---|---|---|---|---|
| 1896-97 | $484,793 | $121,234 | $........ | $........ |
| 1897-98 | 525,458 | 123,468 | ........ | ........ |
| 1898-99 | 532,220 | 151,174 | ........ | ........ |
| 1899-00 | 630,354 | 163,816 | ........ | ........ |
| 1900-01 | 668,484 | 155,516 | 121,926 | 33,589 |
| 1901-02 | 696,064 | 142,353 | 126,000 | 16,353 |

In 1900 the charges were $117,812; surplus, $46,003. In 1901 charges were $121,926; surplus, $33,589.

President, Attilla Cox; Treasurer, H. V. Sanders; Secretary, Ridgely Cayce, Louisville.

Directors—Attilla Cox, Harry Weissinger, Oscar Fenley, John Doerhoefer, Samuel A. Culbertson, J. D. Powers, J. D. Stewart, Louisville; John H. Barret, Henderson, Ky.; Charles B. Van Nostrand, New York.

Main office, Louisville. Annual meeting, first Tuesday in September, at Louisville.

## MACON & BIRMINGHAM RAILWAY CO.

A corporation formed under the laws of Georgia in 1896.

The company is a reorganization of the railroad company of the same name, which was foreclosed in that year.

Road owned, La Grange, Ga., to Sofkee, Ga., 97 miles; trackage, Sofkee to Macon, 8 miles; total operated, 105 miles. Locomotives, 4; passenger cars, 7; freight cars, 140.

Stock......Par $100..............................Authorized, $500,000......Issued, $500,000

FUNDED DEBT.

1st mort., 5 per cent., due July, 1946, Jan. and July................................ $500,000

Trustee of the 1st mortgage and agent for the payment of interest, Old Colony Trust Co., Boston.

EARNINGS.

| Year ending June 30. | Gross. | Net. |
|---|---|---|
| 1901-02 | $126,004 | $708 |

President, F. M. Edwards, Boston; Vice-President, T. Y. Crawford, Columbus, Ga.; Secretary, B. C. Parsons, Boston.

Directors—F. M. Edwards, Boston; L. F. Garrard, G. Y. Tygner, T. Y. Crawford, Columbus, Ga.; J. R. Lane, Macon, Ga.

Main office, Macon, Ga.

## MACON, DUBLIN & SAVANNAH RAILROAD CO.

A corporation formed under the laws of Georgia in 1885. Road owned, Macon, Ga., to Dublin, Ga., 54 miles. An extension of 99 miles to Savannah is planned, of which about 10 miles was completed at the end of 1902. Locomotives, 3; passenger cars, 4; freight cars, 40.

Stock......Par $100..........................Authorized, $3,200,000......Issued, $1,250,000

FUNDED DEBT.

1st mort., 5 per cent., due July, 1951, Jan. and July................................ $1,410,000

The 1st mortgage is for $1,500,000, and was created in 1901. The bonds were to be issued at the rate of $15,000 per mile on extensions of the road. Trustee of the mortgage and agent for the payment of interest, American Trust & Savings Bank, Chicago. Coupons are also payable by the First National Bank, New York.

EARNINGS.

| Year ending June 30. | Gross. | Net. |
|---|---|---|
| 1901-02 | $117,953 | $20,705 |

President, T. D. Catlin, Ottawa, Ill.; Vice-President, D. M. Hughes, Danville, Ga.; Vice-President and Treasurer, James T. Wright; Secretary, C. G. Smith, Macon, Ga.

Directors—T. D. Catlin, Ottawa, Ill.; J. M. Stubbs, Dublin, Ga.; C. G. Smith, James T. Wright, Macon, Ga.; D. M. Hughes, Danville, Ga.; A. C. Soper, Chicago; C. E. Luckey, Knoxville, Tenn.

Main office, Macon, Ga.

---

## MAINE CENTRAL RAILROAD CO.

Road owned, Portland to Bangor, Me., via Augusta, 137 miles; branches, Cumberland Junction to Skowhegan, 91 miles; Bath to Lewiston and Farmington, 71 miles; Woolwich to Rockland, 47 miles; Bar Harbor branch, 41 miles; branches, 7 miles; total owned, 394 miles. Leased, Belfast & Moosehead Lake, 33 miles; Newport to Dexter, 14 miles; Eastern Maine, 19 miles; European & North American, 114 miles; branches, 6 miles; Portland & Ogdensburg Railroad, Portland, Me., to Lunenburg, 110 miles; Hereford Railway, 53 miles; Dexter & Piscataquis Railroad, 16½ miles; Upper Coos Railroad, 55 miles; total leased, 421 miles; total operated, 815 miles of road. The company also operates steamboats in connection with its rail lines. The Knox & Lincoln, which had been leased, was absorbed by this company in February, 1901. Locomotives, 167; passenger cars, 242; freight cars, 3,914.

Stock......Par $100........................Authorized, $12,000,000......Issued, $4,988,000

In 1891 stock was increased by $900,000, the new stock being subscribed *pro rata* by stockholders at par. Proceeds applied to betterments and equipment. In January, 1893, $500,000 additional stock was issued for same purpose.

From 1884 to 1902, inclusive, 6 per cent. per annum was paid on the stock. The dividends are paid quarterly, 1½ per cent. each, in January (1), April, July and October.

FUNDED DEBT (ROAD OWNED).

| | |
|---|---|
| Maine Central consolidated, 7 per cent., due April, 1912, April and Oct. | $3,924,000 |
| " " 5 per cent., due April, 1912, April and Oct. | 269,500 |
| " " 4½ per cent., due April, 1912, April and Oct. | 1,525,000 |
| " " 4 per cent., due April, 1912, April and Oct. | 3,265,500 |
| " col. trust, 5 per cent., due June, 1923, June and Dec. | 669,000 |
| " improvement, A, 4½ per cent., due July, 1916, Jan. and July | 200,000 |
| " " B, 4½ per cent., due July, 1917, Jan. and July | 250,000 |
| " sinking fund bonds, 4½ per cent., due Feb., 1905, Feb. and Aug. | 600,000 |
| " 1st mort. bonds, 6 per cent., due June, 1923, June and Dec. | 81,000 |
| " interest scrip exchangeable for consols | 8,192 |
| Penobscot Shore Line 1st mort., assumed, 4 per cent., due Aug., 1920, Feb. and Aug. | 1,300,000 |
| Knox & Lincoln 2d mort., assumed, 5 per cent., due Feb., 1921, Feb. and Aug. | 400,000 |
| Total road owned | $12,492,192 |

FUNDED DEBT (ROADS LEASED).

| | |
|---|---|
| Portland & Ogdensburg bonds, 3½ per cent., due Nov., 1908, May and Nov. | $800,000 |
| " " 5 per cent., due Nov., 1908, May and Nov. | 1,319,000 |
| Dexter & Piscataquis, 4 per cent., due July, 1929, Jan. and July | 175,000 |
| Maine Central, refunding mort., European & North American, 4 per cent., due Jan., 1933, Jan. and July | 1,000,000 |
| Hereford Railway, 1st mort., guar. 4 per cent., due May, 1930, May and Nov. | 800,000 |

FUNDED DEBT.—*Continued.*

| | |
|---|---|
| Upper Coos R. R. 1st mort., guar., 4 per cent., due May, 1930, May and Nov....... | $350,000 |
| " " ext. mort., guar., 4½ per cent., due May, 1930 May and Nov............ | 693,000 |
| Dexter & Newport 1st mort., refunded, 4 per cent., due Sept., 1917, March and Sept. | 175,000 |
| Belfast & Moosehead Lake 1st mort., 4 per cent., due May 15, 1920, May and Nov.... | 114,500 |
| Total leased lines.......................................................... | $5,426,500 |
| Total for roads owned and leased......... ................................. | 17,918,692 |

This company guarantees jointly with Boston & Maine $300,000 Portland Union Station bonds. It also guarantees stock rentals as follows: 5 per cent. on $2,494,100 European & North American Railroad stock, 2 per cent. on $4,392,538 Portland & Ogdensburg stock, 5 per cent. on $122,000 Dexter & Piscataquis stock, 4 per cent. on $800,000 Hereford Railway, 6 per cent. on $350,000 Upper Coos Railroad, 4½ per cent. on $200,000 Eastern Maine, and 5 per cent. on $122,000 Dexter & Newport stock.

The leased line bonds, with the exception of the Belfast & Moosehead Lake 1sts, are guaranteed by the Maine Central.

EARNINGS.

Year ending September 30.

| | Div. Paid. | Gross. | Net. | Charges. | Surplus. |
|---|---|---|---|---|---|
| 1892-93 (822 miles).......... | 6 | $4,951,835 | $1,765,470 | $1,408,458 | $357,013 |
| 1893-94 ( " " ).......... | 6 | 4,561,138 | 1,769,229 | 1,427,997 | 341,232 |
| 1894-95 ( " " )*......... | 4½ | 3,488,046 | 1,332,367 | 1,057,243 | 275,124 |
| 1895-96 (year ending June 30) | 6 | 4,985,318 | 1,765,505 | 1,385,129 | 380,376 |
| 1896-97 ( " " " ) | 6 | 4,898,035 | 1,776,897 | 1,419,823 | 357,073 |
| 1897-98 ( " " " ) | 6 | 4,758,801 | 1,710,476 | 1,311,468 | 399,008 |
| 1898-99 ( " " " ) | 6 | 5,022,097 | 1,819,831 | 1,397,618 | 422,212 |
| 1899-00 ( " " " ) | 6 | 5,612,923 | 1,944,696 | 1,408,539 | 536,157 |
| 1900-01 ( " " " ) | 6 | 5,868,546 | 1,998,598 | 1,423,928 | 574,669 |
| 1901-02 ( " " " ) | 6 | 6,194,304 | 1,795,900 | 1,405,863 | 390,037 |

* 9 months ending June 30.

In 1900 charged to operating expenses $175,000 expended for new equipment, and also charged off $153,467 for depreciation of assets. Dividends in the same year were 6 per cent. on $298,543, leaving a net surplus of $84,146. In 1900-01 $200,000 from earnings was charged off and 6 per cent. dividends required $298,554, leaving a surplus of $76,115. In 1901-02 surplus over dividends, $62,031.

The Boston & Maine owns $2,516,000 of the company's stock.

President, Lucius Tuttle; Vice-President and General Manager, George F. Evans; Clerk, Henry B. Cleaves; Comptroller, George S. Hobbs; Treasurer, G. W. York, Portland, Me.

Directors—W. G. Davis, George F. Evans, George P. Wescott, Joseph W. Symonds, Portland, Me.; John Ware, Waterville; S. C. Lawrence, Medford, Mass.; Franklin A. Wilson, Bangor, Me.; Lucius Tuttle, Henry M. Whitney, Henry R. Reed, Boston; Lewis C. Ledyard, New York; William P. Frye, Lewiston, Me.; Joseph H. Manley, Augusta, Me.

Main office, 238 St. John street, Portland, Me. Annual meeting, third Wednesday in October.

## MARICOPA & PHŒNIX & SALT RIVER VALLEY RAILROAD CO.

A corporation formed under the laws of Arizona in 1895. The company is a consolidation of the Maricopa & Phœnix Railroad Co. and the Phœnix, Tempe & Mesa Railway Co.

Road owned, Maricopa Junction, Ariz., to Phœnix, Ariz., 34 miles; branch, 8 miles; total operated, 42 miles. Locomotives, 4; passenger cars, 4; freight cars, 20.

Stock......Par, $100..........................Authorized, $1,000,000......Issued, $1,000,000

The Southern Pacific Co. owns a majority of the stock of the company. Stock is transferred at the office of the Secretary and Treasurer, San Francisco.

FUNDED DEBT.

| | |
|---|---|
| Maricopa & Phœnix 1st mort., 6 per cent., due Nov., 1916, May and Nov........... | $540,000 |
| M. & P. & Salt Riv. Val. mort., 5 per cent., due Dec., 1925, May and Nov.......... | 78,000 |
| Total......... ............................................................ | $618,000 |

The mortgage of the Maricopa & Phœnix & Salt River Valley is for $750,000. Coupons of both bond issues are paid by the Farmers' Loan & Trust Co., New York.

In the year ending June 30, 1900, the company's earnings were: gross, $141,888; net, $54,228; charges, $41,282; surplus, $12,946.

President, Francis Cutting; Vice-President, Joseph M. Masten; Secretary and Treasurer, Frank I. Kendall, San Francisco.

Directors—Francis Cutting, Frank I. Kendall, Joseph M. Masten, C. E. Graham, San Francisco; S. Oberfelder, W. Talbot, Phœnix, Ariz.

Main office, Phœnix, Ariz. San Francisco office, 610 Market Street. Annual meeting, third Tuesday in January, at San Francisco.

## MARIETTA, COLUMBUS & CLEVELAND RAILROAD CO.

Road owned, Palos, O., to Moore's, O., 42 miles; branches, 7½ miles; total operated, 49½ miles. Trackage, 3 miles. Locomotives, 4; passenger cars, 6; freight cars, 30.

This company is a reorganization of the Toledo & Ohio Central Extension Railroad, which was foreclosed in 1900.

Stock....Par $100................................Authorized, $250,000......Issued, $250,000

FUNDED DEBT.

1st mort., 5 per cent., dated Oct. 31, 1900........................................... $250,000

Agent for the payment of interest, Knickerbocker Trust Co., New York.

The bonds of the Toledo & Ohio Central Extension Railroad were $850,000 at 5 per cent. The Toledo & Ohio Central guaranteed the interest on $300,000 of the issue. The company defaulted in 1894, and the guarantor provided for the part of the bonds of this issue for which it was responsible. Receiver was appointed in 1894, but foreclosure was deferred until 1900. The present company has issued no bonds, but an extension of the road is suggested.

In the year ending June 30, 1900, the earnings were: gross, $80,104; net, $2,874. In 1900-01, gross, $48,814; deficit, $6,636.

President, D. I. Roberts, New York; Secretary and Treasurer, James T. Blair, Greenville, Pa.; Auditor, R. B. Petriken, Marietta, O.

Main office, Marietta, O.; New York office, 21 Cortlandt St. Annual meeting, November 3.

## MARYLAND & PENNSYLVANIA RAILROAD CO.

Road owned, Baltimore to York, Pa., 80 miles; branch, 4 miles; total operated, 84 miles. Locomotives, 11; passenger cars, 26; freight cars, 116.

The company is a consolidation, February, 1901, of the Baltimore & Lehigh Railway Co. and the York Southern Railroad Co.

Stock......Par $100...........................Authorized, $3,600,000......Issued, $1,325,000

Transfer Agent, Continental Trust Co., Baltimore.

FUNDED DEBT.

| | |
|---|---|
| 1st mort., 4 per cent., due March, 1951, March and Sept. | $550,000 |
| Income bonds, 4 per. cent., cumulative, due April, 1951 | 900,000 |
| York & Peach Bottom R.R. 1st mort., A, 5 per cent., due April, 1932, April and Oct. | 49,500 |
| " " " " " B, 5 per cent., due April, 1932, May and Nov. | 202,450 |
| Total | $1,701,950 |

In 1901 3 per cent. was paid on the income bonds. In 1902, 4 per cent. was paid.

The 1st mortgage is for $1,200,000, of which amount $250,000 is reserved to retire the York & Peach Bottom 5 per cent. bonds at maturity, and $400,000 bonds are reserved for future requirements.

The Baltimore & Lehigh Railway Co. had $843,500 stock and no funded debt. The York Southern Railroad Co. had $600,000 stock and 2d mortgage 5 per cent. bonds for $150,000.

Under the consolidation plan, the Baltimore & Lehigh stock was purchased at 70 and the York Southern 2d mortgage bonds at par, the latter being cancelled. The York Southern stock was exchanged share for share for stock of this company.

The company sold $550,000 of the 1st mortgage bonds at 90 and sold the issue of income bonds at 75 and accrued interest, Baltimore & Lehigh stock at the above price being accepted in payment. Of the stock outstanding, $725,000 was offered as a bonus with subscriptions to the bond issues.

EARNINGS.

Year ending June 30.

| | Gross. | Net. | Charges. | Surplus |
|---|---|---|---|---|
| 1901-02 | $264,659 | $76,461 | $70,497 | $20,496 |

The Baltimore & Lehigh paid a dividend of 2½ per cent. on its stock in May, 1900.

MAP OF THE
Mexican Central
RAILWAY
and its
CONNECTIONS
SCALE OF MILES
ENGRAVED BY BORMAY & CO., N. Y.
PACIFIC OCEAN
GULF OF CALIFORNIA
LOWER CALIFORNIA
ARIZONA
NEW MEX.
EL PASO
CIUDAD JUAREZ
CHIHUAHUA
GOMEZ PALACIO
TORREON
DURANGO
ZACATECAS
MAZATLAN
CULIACAN
HERMOSILLO
GUAYMAS
LA PAZ
Cape San Lucas
TEPIC
SAN BLAS
MANZANILLO
COLIMA

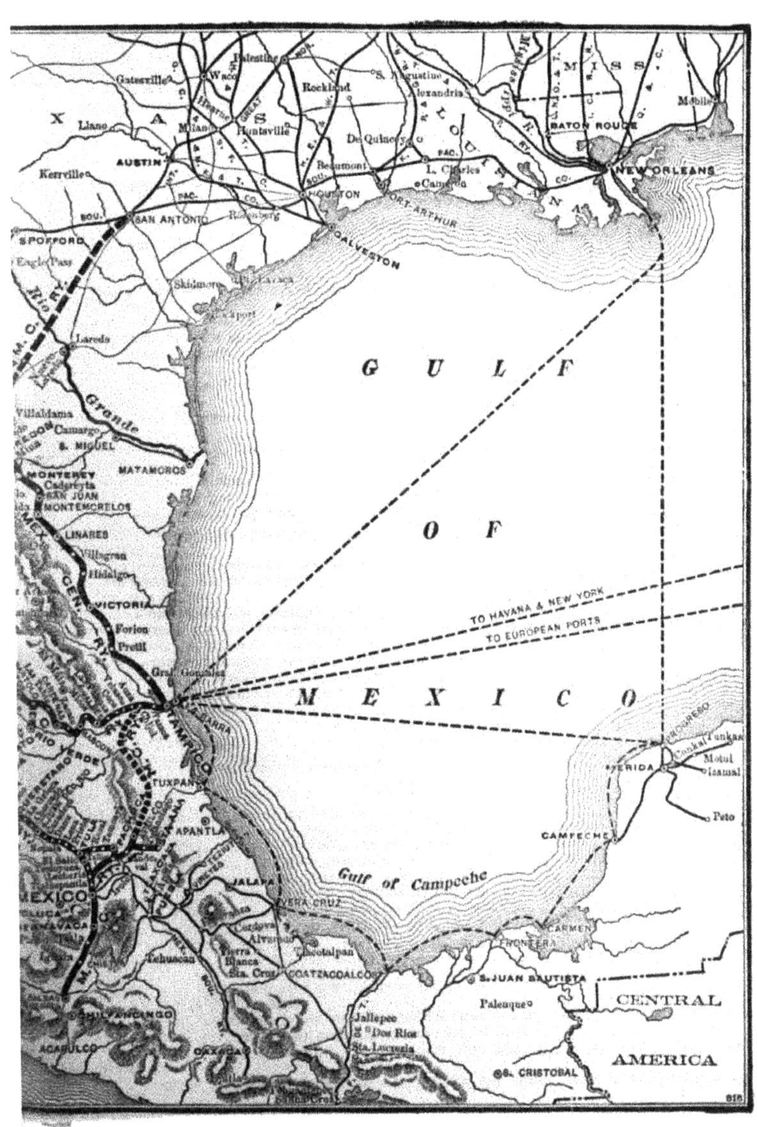
GULF OF MEXICO
Gulf of Campeche
TO HAVANA & NEW YORK
TO EUROPEAN PORTS
CENTRAL AMERICA
NEW ORLEANS
BATON ROUGE
Mobile
HOUSTON
GALVESTON
PORT ARTHUR
Beaumont
AUSTIN
SAN ANTONIO
Laredo
Rio Grande
MATAMOROS
MONTEREY
LINARES
VICTORIA
TAMPICO
TUXPAN
JALAPA
VERA CRUZ
MEXICO
CHILPANCINGO
ACAPULCO
OAXACA
COATZACOALCOS
CAMPECHE
MERIDA
PROGRESO
CARMEN
FRONTERA
S. JUAN BAUTISTA
S. CRISTOBAL
Palenque
Peto
Waco
Palestine
Huntsville
Kerrville
SPOFFORD
Eagle Pass
Villaldama
Camargo
S. MIGUEL
Tehuacan
Jaltipec
Dos Rios
816

President, John Wilson Brown; Vice-President, W. B. Brooks, Jr.; Secretary and Treasurer, John McHenry, Baltimore.

Directors—John Wilson Brown, W. W. Spence, George C. Jenkins, W. B. Brooks, Jr., John W. Hall, Solomon Frank, John K. Cowen, Baltimore; H. E. Young, Hanover, Pa.; Henry C. Niles, York, Pa.

Main office, North avenue and Oak street, Baltimore. Annual meeting, fourth Tuesday in January, at Baltimore.

---

## MEXICAN CENTRAL RAILWAY CO., LIMITED

A corporation formed under the laws of Massachusetts in 1880.

MILEAGE OWNED AND OPERATED JANUARY 1, 1903.

| | Miles. |
|---|---|
| Main Line, City of Mexico to Ciudad Juarez | 1,224.16 |
| Mexico City Belt Line | 5.95 |
| Santiago Branch, Mexico City to Santiago | 1.40 |
| Pachuca Branch, Tula to Pachuca | 43.81 |
| Guanajuato Branch, Silao to Marfil | 11.56 |
| Guadalajara Branch, Irapuato to Ameca | 217.06 |
| Zamora Extension, Yurecuaro to Los Reyes | 86.16 |
| San Marcos Extension, La Vega to San Marcos | 29.37 |
| Zapotlan Extension, Guadalajara to Tuxpan | 119.68 |
| San Luis Div., Chicalote to Tampico | 406.93 |
| Branch to Compania Metalurgica Mexicana Smelter, San Luis Potosi | 5.19 |
| Bar Extension, Tampico to La Barra | 6.21 |
| Monterey Division, Tampico to Trevino | 388.36 |
| Mexican Union Railway, Rincon de Romos to Cobre | 10.85 |
| Laguna Extension, Gomez Palacio to San Pedro | 39.78 |
| Parral Extension, Jimenez to Rosario | 95.79 |
| Santa Barbara Branch, Adrian to Santa Barbara | 5.47 |
| Mexico, Cuernavaca and Pacific Division, City of Mexico to Rio Balsas | 181.25 |
| Rio Verde Branch, San Bartolo to Rio Verde | 26.32 |
| Other branches | 9.46 |
| Total | 2,914.76 |

Locomotives, 251; passenger cars, 146; freight cars, 4,522; floating equipment, 2 tugs and 13 lighters.

In June, 1901, control of the Monterey & Mexican Gulf Railroad was acquired in this company's interest. In November, 1902, control of the Mexico, Cuernavaca & Pacific Railroad, 182 miles, was acquired.

The company had a subsidy from Mexican Government of $15,200 per mile, payable in certificates receivable for a portion of customs. In June, 1885, the Government stopped the payment of the subsidy, but it was resumed 1886, and in 1890 the Government agreed to pay a lump sum of about $14,900,000, Mexican currency, in liquidation of all subsidy claims. The amount was paid and applied to purchase of the priority bonds of the company. On January 1, 1902, there was a balance of $2,035,154 in hands of trustees of consolidated mortgage bonds and $6,122,646 priority bonds purchased for investment. Deficits in fixed charges can be made good from subsidy fund.

Stock......Par $100....................Authorized, $25,600 per mile......Issued, $47,962,100

Transfer Agents, Hanover National Bank, New York; Old Colony Trust Co., Boston.

FUNDED DEBT.

| | |
|---|---|
| Consol. mort., 4 per cent., due July, 1911, Jan. and July | $66,678,000 |
| 1st consol. income bonds (and scrip), 3 per cent., due Jan., 1939, non-cum., July | 20,563,400 |
| Registered income bonds, 3 per cent., not yet assented, due July, 1911 | 367,200 |
| 1st mort., unassented, 4 per cent., due July, 1911, and scrip, Jan. and July | 287,000 |
| 2d consol. income, 3 per cent., due Jan., 1939, July | 11,282,000 |
| Collateral trust mort., 4½ per cent., due Feb., 1907, Feb. and Aug | 10,000,000 |
| Equipment bonds, 5 per cent., due April, 1917, April and Oct | 750,000 |
| Equipment bonds, 5 per cent., 2d series, due Oct., 1919, April and Oct | 850,000 |
| Total | $110,777,600 |

There are $5,597,000 5 per cent. priority bonds outstanding, held, however, by the trustees of the consolidated mortgage.

Registered income bonds can be exchanged for stock at par. The 2d consolidated 3 per cent. income bonds, due 1939, can be retired at 50 per cent. of their face up to 1929.

In 1890 first incomes received 3 per cent., in 1891 and 1892 3 per cent. No interest has since been paid.

The 2d income bonds authorized are $36,400 per mile; consolidated mortgage bonds,

$32,000 per mile; 1st incomes, $9,600 per mile. The equipment bonds created in 1897 are to be paid off $50,000 each year. The 2d series equipment bonds were $1,000,000, of which $50,000 is to be paid each year.

At the annual meeting in May, 1901, representatives of new interests were elected to the company's directory, and alliances between the company and other systems of lines in the United States were reported as likely to be made. A readjustment of its capitalization has also been discussed.

The collateral trust 4½ per cent. bonds were created in January, 1902, and are secured by the deposit of $16,120,000 consolidated 4s, which had been held in the treasury. They were issued to pay for the acquisition of the Monterey & Mexican Gulf Railway and to provide for extensions of the same.

| Earnings. | Gross. | Net. |
|---|---|---|
| 1893 (1,847 miles) | $7,981,768 | $2,845,587 |
| 1894 (1,860 " ) | 8,426,025 | 2,966,350 |
| 1895 ( " " ) | 9,495,865 | 3,896,475 |
| 1896 (1,869 " ) | 10,208,020 | 3,463,747 |
| 1897 (1,956 " ) | 12,845,819 | 4,016,348 |
| 1898 ( " " ) | 13,588,966 | 4,427,533 |
| 1899 (2,016 " ) | 15,602,065 | 5,199,095 |
| 1900 (2,054 " ) | 17,223,878 | 5,373,683 |
| 1901 (2,135 " ) | 17,493,674 | 4,986,663 |

The earnings above are given in Mexican currency. The following gives the revenue of company in American currency:

| | Net Earnings U. S. Currency. | Charges. | Deficit. |
|---|---|---|---|
| 1893 | $1,764,823 | $2,243,349 | $478,525 |
| 1894 | 1,538,692 | 2,297,514 | 758,821 |
| 1895 | 2,063,156 | 2,328,409 | 265,252 |
| 1896 | 1,841,515 | 2,324,526 | 483,011 |
| 1897 | 1,937,483 | 2,476,430 | 538,947 |
| 1898 | 2,062,804 | 2,476,027 | 413,222 |
| 1899 | 2,516,961 | 2,417,763 | Sur. 99,198 |
| 1900 | 2,628,576 | 2,622,483 | " 6,092 |
| 1901 | 2,384,598 | 2,754,759 | Def. 370,161 |

There is an English corporation—the Mexican Central Railway Securities Co., Limited, organized in 1899—which accepts deposits of the 4 per cent. consols of the Mexican Central Railway, and issues against each $1,000 4 per cent. bond deposited £102 of A debentures and £102 B debentures. The office of this company is 3 Grace-church street, London, E. C.

Chairman, H. Clay Pierce; President, Albert A. Robinson; Vice-President and General Counsel, Eben Richards, St. Louis; Vice-President and General Manager, Hiram R. Nickerson, City of Mexico; Vice-President and Comptroller, Gabriel Morton, St. Louis; Vice-President, Frederick H. Prince, Boston; Clerk, James Piper; Treasurer, Charles A. Browne, St. Louis; General Auditor, W. A. Frost, City of Mexico.

Directors—H. Clay Pierce, Eben Richards, J. C. Van Blarcom, Gabriel Morton, B. Jones, St. Louis; Eugene N. Foss, Albert A. Robinson, Frederick H. Prince, Boston; Charles E. Perkins, Burlington, Ia.; Levi Z. Leiter, John J. Mitchell, Chicago; P. Martinez del Rio, Hiram R. Nickerson, Justino Fernandez, City of Mexico; C. D. Simpson, Scranton, Pa.; W. L. Stow, New York.

Main office, 422 Olive street, St. Louis. Annual meeting, first Wednesday in May.

---

## THE MEXICAN INTERNATIONAL RAILROAD CO.

(Controlled by National Railroad Co. of Mexico.)

Road owned, Ciudad Porfirio Diaz (formerly Piedras Negras), Mexico, to Durango, 540 miles; branches, 340 miles; total owned, 880 miles. Extension is projected to Mazatlan on the Pacific. Locomotives, 58; passenger cars, 29; freight cars, 1,710.

The road connects at Piedras Negras, opposite Eagle Pass, Tex., with the lines of Southern Pacific Co., which had a large interest in the stock of this company, and the road was built in the interest of the Southern Pacific. In 1901 the control was purchased in the interest of the National Railroad Co. of Mexico.

The company is a Connecticut corporation. The road was built under concessions from Mexican Government, exempting the company from taxation or payment of duties on material, etc., but it has no subsidy. The main line was constructed between 1883 and 1892. Considerable grading and other preliminary work has been done on extensions.

Stock......Par $100........................Authorized, $25,000,000......Issued, $20,708,200

Stock is transferred by the Secretary of the company.

FUNDED DEBT.

| | |
|---|---|
| Prior lien mort., sterling, 4½ per cent., due Sept., 1947, March and Sept............ | $5,850,000 |
| 1st cons. mort., 4 per cent., due Sept., 1977, guar. stamped, March and Sept........ | 3,621,000 |
| 1st cons. mort., 4 per cent., due Sept, 1977, not stamped, March and Sept.......... | 3,362,000 |
| Income bonds, 4 per cent., no mortgage, Sept.................................. | 4,499,000 |
| Total............................................................ | $17,332,000 |

In July, 1897, a proposition was made to exchange the $15,134,000 of 1st mortgage 4s for $6,000,000 prior lien 4½s, $4,635,000 1st consolidated 4s, and $4,499,000 income bonds. Consolidated 4s at the rate of $10,000 per mile were to be issued for further extensions. This proposition was accepted by bondholders. The annual fixed charges were reduced thereby from $600,000 to $448,650.

In 1902 the National Railroad Co. of Mexico stamped its guarantee on $3,621,000 of the consols, the stamped bonds being subject to call at 95 before March 1, 1907.

EARNINGS.

| | Gross. | Net. |
|---|---|---|
| 1893 (573 miles)........................ | $2,050,934 | $749,540 |
| 1894 ( " " )........................ | 2,169,121 | 887,306 |
| 1895 (588 " )........................ | 2,664,126 | 1,066,771 |
| 1896 (628 " )........................ | 2,912,107 | 1,065,022 |
| 1897 (659 " )........................ | 3,043,038 | 1,088,851 |
| 1898 ( " " )........................ | 3,497,075 | 1,430,564 |
| 1899 (773 " )........................ | 4,645,559 | 1,949,298 |
| 1900 (802 " )........................ | 5,378,977 | 2,131,237 |
| 1901 (848 " )........................ | 5,960,825 | 2,370,672 |

The earnings are given in Mexican currency. In 1895, net (United States currency) was $550,028; deficit after charges, $20,076. In 1896, net $546,463; deficit, $71,561. In 1897, net, $537,570; surplus, $38,289. In 1898, net, $652,051; surplus, $163,676. In 1899, net, $907,500; surplus, $409,231. In 1900, net, $1,002,533; surplus, $442,529. In 1901, net, $1,155,262; surplus, $595,602.

President, J. G. Metcalfe, Durango, Mex.; Vice-President, James Steuart Mackie; Secretary, Charles Knap, New York; General Manager, L. M. Johnson, Ciudad Porfirio Diaz, Mex.

Main office, Ciudad Porfirio Diaz, Mex.; New York office, 25 Broad street. Annual meeting, second Saturday in April, at New Haven, Conn.

## MEXICAN NORTHERN RAILWAY CO.

Road owned, Escalon, Mex., to Sierra Mojada, 81 miles. Locomotives, 7; passenger cars, 2; freight cars, 175.

Stock......Par $100........................Authorized, $3,000,000......Issued, $3,000,000

Stock is transferred in the company's office, 27 William street, New York. Registrar, Morton Trust Co., New York.

The company paid 6 per cent. on its stock in 1894, 4 per cent. each year from 1895 to 1899, inclusive. In 1900 paid 5 per cent. dividends and in 1901 4½ per cent. In 1902 1 per cent. was paid in March, but the subsequent dividends have been ½ per cent. each. Dividends are quarterly, in March (1), June, September and December.

FUNDED DEBT.

1st mort., gold, 6 per cent., due Dec., 1910, June and Dec.......................... $1,083,000

The authorized amount of bonds is $1,660,000, there being $577,000 in the sinking fund.

Control of the road was acquired in 1901 by interests identified with the Fort Worth & Rio Grande Railway Co., and it was said a connection with that line would be built.

EARNINGS.

Year ending June 30.

| | Gross. | Net. | Charges. | Surplus. |
|---|---|---|---|---|
| 1899–00.............................. | $638,552 | $286,411 | $131,804 | $154,607 |
| 1900–01.............................. | 642,132 | 301,982 | 137,285 | 164,697 |
| 1901–02.............................. | 262,149 | 159,350 | 112,707 | 46,643 |

In 1901–02 the deficit of the payment of the dividends was $58,357.

President and Treasurer, A. Foster Higgins; Vice-Presidents, George Foster Peabody, William J. Palmer; Secretary, C. J. Nourse, Jr., New York; Assistant Treasurer, T. J. Ryder, City of Mexico.

Main office, City of Mexico, Calle de Tiburcio No. 27; New York office, 27 William street.

## MEXICAN RAILWAY CO., LIMITED

An English corporation formed in 1864 as the Imperial Mexican Railway Co., Ltd. The company had a concession from the Government of Mexico with a subsidy of $560,000 per year. The Government also agreed not to subsidize any other railroad line between Vera Cruz and the City of Mexico.

Road owned, Vera Cruz to the City of Mexico, 264 miles; branches, Puebla to Apizaco, 29 miles; Ometusco to Pachuca, 28 miles; total operated, 321 miles. Locomotives, 71; passenger cars, 108; freight cars, 900.

| | Authorized | | | Issued | | |
|---|---|---|---|---|---|---|
| Stock. Par £10. Auth | Ordinary, | £2,254,720 | Issued | Ordinary, | £2,254,720 | £7,819,080 |
| | 1st pref., | 2,554,100 | | 1st pref., | 2,554,100 | |
| | 2d pref., | 1,010,960 | | 2d pref., | 1,010,260 | |
| | Perpetual debenture stock, | 2,000,000 | | Perpetual debenture stock, | 2,000,000 | |

The 1st preferred stock was issued in 1874 in exchange for the old 8 per cent. bonds of the company, which were in default. It is entitled to 8 per cent. per annum out of the earnings of each half year.

The 2d preferred stock is entitled to 6 per cent. per annum, and was issued in 1874 in settlement of past due coupons on the old bonds.

The perpetual debenture stock is entitled to 6 per cent. per annum. It was created in 1880 in order to retire outstanding bonds.

Dividends on the 1st preferred stock have varied from year to year, the recent payments having been as follows: In 1898, 2¼ per cent.; in 1899, 3⅛ per cent.; in 1900, 3⅜ per cent.; in 1901, 2⅞ per cent.; in 1902, 1⅜ per cent.

In the year 1901 the company reported earnings as £4,402,298 gross; net revenue, £164,287; surplus over interest on the perpetual debenture stock and dividends on the 1st preferred shares, £38,311.

Chairman, M. R. Pryor; Secretary, John T. Deniston, London.

Directors—M. R. Pryor, Henry Goschen, Lord Aldenham, William Barron, Thomas Braniff, Vincent W. Yorke, Pablo Escandon, Enerique Camacho-Guisasola, London; L. P. Figueros, Casimiro Pacheco, City of Mexico.

Main office, 45 New Broad street, London. Operating office, Buena Vista Station, City of Mexico.

## MICHIGAN CENTRAL RAILROAD CO.

(Controlled by New York Central & Hudson River Railroad Co.)

Road owned, Detroit to Kensington, Ill., 270 miles; trackage over Illinois Central to Chicago, 14 miles; Detroit to Bay City and branches, 176 miles; leased, Jackson to Mackinaw, 295 miles; other lines leased, 447 miles; total, 1,182 miles. The leased lines are chiefly owned and their bonds guaranteed. From January 1, 1883, the Canada Southern, covering 226 miles of main line and 231 miles of branches, has been operated under contract, this company paying all charges and turning over to the Canada Southern proportion of surplus as shown below. Total road operated, 1,639 miles. Locomotives, 461; passenger cars, 381; freight cars, 13,959. Rolling stock of Canada Southern is included.

Stock......Par $100........ ................Authorized, $18,738,000......Issued, $18,738,000

Transfer agency, Grand Central Station, New York. Registrar, Union Trust Co., New York.

For dividends paid each year see below in tabulation of earnings. Dividends are paid semi-annually, January (30) and July.

FUNDED DEBT.

| | |
|---|---|
| 1st mort., 3½ per cent., due May, 1952, May and Nov. | $10,000,000 |
| Air Line, 4 per cent., due Jan., 1940, Jan. and July | 2,600,000 |
| Grand River Valley, 1st mort., 6 per cent., due Sept., 1909, March and Sept. | 1,500,000 |
| Kalamazoo & South Haven, 1st mort., 5 per cent., due Nov., 1939, May and Nov. | 700,000 |
| Detroit & Bay City, 1st mort., 5 per cent., due March, 1931, March and Sept. | 3,850,000 |
| Michigan Central Terminal mort., 4 per cent., due July, 1941, Jan. and July | 725,000 |
| Jackson, Lansing & Saginaw, 1st mort., 3½ per cent. extended, March and Sept. | 1,900,000 |
| Total | $21,275,000 |

FUNDED DEBT (LEASED LINES).

| | |
|---|---|
| Detroit & Bay City Bridge, 8 per cent. bonds, due May, 1903, May and Nov......... | $150,000 |
| Battle Creek & Sturgis, 1st mort. guar., 3 per cent., due Dec., 1989, June and Dec... | 421,000 |
| Bay City and Battle Creek, 1st mort., 3 per cent., due Dec., 1989, June and Dec..... | 250,000 |
| Joliet & North Indiana, 1st mort., 7 per cent., due July, 1907, Jan. (10) and July.... | 800,000 |
| Total........ | $1,621,000 |

In 1898 holders of Michigan Central stock were given the privilege of exchanging the same for 3½ per cent. 100-year gold bonds of the New York Central & Hudson River Railroad Co. at the rate of $115 in bonds for $100 of stock, the stock thus acquired by the New York Central to be deposited as security for bonds. At latest accounts $16,814,300 of the stock had been exchanged.

This company guarantees 5 per cent. on $491,200 Grand River Valley stock, $70,000 per year on $2,000,000 Jackson, Lansing & Saginaw stock and $71,000 per annum to Joliet & Northern Indiana Railroad. It also pays 5 per cent. on $20,000,000 Canada Southern bonds and 5 per cent. on $130,000 Leamington & St. Clair bonds.

In 1892 a reapportionment of the net earnings between this company and the Canada Southern was agreed upon for a period of five years from January 1, 1893; sixty per cent. to the Michigan Central and forty per cent. to the Canada Southern Co. of the first million dollars of the net earnings of each year, any excess of such net earnings over and above one million dollars to be divided in the proportion of 66⅔ per cent. to the Michigan Central Railroad Co. and 33⅓ per cent. to the Canada Southern Railway Co.

The company had, January 1, 1903, 142,069 acres of land on hand. Proceeds from sales go to retire bonds of Jackson, Lansing & Saginaw.

EARNINGS.

| | Div. Paid. | Gross. | Net. | Mis. Income. | Total. |
|---|---|---|---|---|---|
| 1892 (1,638 miles)......... | 5½ | $15,908,292 | $3,862,198 | $46,798 | $3,908,996 |
| 1893 (1,633 " )......... | 5½ | 16,178,030 | 3,890,238 | 45,790 | 3,936,028 |
| 1894 ( " " )......... | 4 | 12,584,013 | 3,439,905 | 44,649 | 3,484,554 |
| 1895 (1,642 " )......... | 4 | 13,651,420 | 3,468,189 | 49,077 | 3,517,266 |
| 1896 ( " " )......... | 4 | 13,821,614 | 3,429,264 | 39,685 | 3,468,949 |
| 1897 (1,657 " )......... | 4 | 13,697,239 | 3,447,729 | 44,619 | 3,492,348 |
| 1898 ( " " )......... | 4 | 14,046,149 | 3,500,176 | 44,679 | 3,544,855 |
| 1899 ( " " )......... | 4 | 15,504,062 | 3,499,946 | 44,678 | 3,544,624 |
| 1900 ( " " )......... | 4 | 16,731,131 | 3,500,641 | 45,094 | 3,545,735 |
| 1901 ( " " )......... | 4 | 18,490,273 | 3,744,309 | 70,739 | 3,814,048 |

The disposition of the total net income was as follows:

| | Net Income. | Charges. | Surplus. | Dividends. |
|---|---|---|---|---|
| 1892........ | $3,908,996 | $2,785,075 | $1,123,921 | $1,030,601 |
| 1893........ | 3,936,028 | 2,858,451 | 1,077,577 | 1,030,601 |
| 1894........ | 3,484,554 | 2,688,992 | 795,562 | 749,528 |
| 1895........ | 3,517,266 | 2,706,916 | 810,350 | 749,520 |
| 1896........ | 3,468,949 | 2,691,039 | 777,910 | 749,520 |
| 1897........ | 3,492,348 | 2,697,426 | 794,922 | 749,520 |
| 1898........ | 3,544,855 | 2,720,602 | 824,253 | 749,520 |
| 1899........ | 3,544,624 | 2,790,185 | 829,765 | 749,520 |
| 1900........ | 3,545,735 | 2,705,070 | 840,665 | 749,520 |
| 1901........ | 3,814,048 | 2,830,798 | 983,296 | 749,500 |

The earnings for 1902, partly estimated, were: Gross, $18,650,000; net, $3,670,000.

Included in the surplus are the following amounts set aside for the construction of second tracks: In 1898, $70,000; in 1899, $65,000; in 1900, $80,000; in 1901, $210,000.

The amount paid Canada Southern as its proportion of net income as per agreement was in 1894, $287,808; in 1895, $304,715; in 1896, $296,474; in 1897, $282,902; in 1898, $300,666; in 1899, $300,574; in 1900, $300,852; in 1901, $375,238, the same being included in charges.

Chairman, Chauncey M. Depew, New York; President, Henry B. Ledyard, Detroit; Vice-President and Secretary, Edwin D. Worcester; Treasurer, Charles F. Cox, New York; Auditor, A. J. Burt, Detroit.

Directors—William K. Vanderbilt, Samuel F. Barger, Chauncey M. Depew, Hamilton McK. Twombley, Edwin D. Worcester, Frederick W. Vanderbilt, New York; Henry B. Ledyard, Ashley Pond, Detroit; Frederick S. Winston, Chicago.

Main office, foot of Third street, Detroit; New York office, Grand Central Station. Annual meeting, Thursday following first Wednesday in May. Books close thirty days before.

## MINERAL RANGE RAILROAD CO.

Road owned, Houghton, Mich., to Calumet, Mich., 14 miles; branches, 51 miles; total owned, 66 miles. Leased, Hancock & Calumet Railroad Co., 34 miles; trackage, 26 miles; total operated, 127 miles. Locomotives, 6; passenger cars, 13; freight cars, 366. The Hancock & Calumet Railroad was acquired and leased in 1901, this company assuming its obligations.

Stock......Par $100..........................Authorized, $1,200,000......Issued, $743,000

The stock was increased to $1,200,000 in 1901.

Dividends have been paid on the stock as follows: in 1895, 10½ per cent.; in 1896, 7 per cent.; in 1897, 7 per cent.; in 1898, 3½ per cent.; none since.

FUNDED DEBT.

| | |
|---|---|
| Consolidated mort., 5 per cent., due Jan., 1931, Jan. and July | $346,000 |
| " " 4 per cent., due Jan., 1931, Jan. and July | 254,000 |
| General mort., 4 per cent., due Jan., 1951, Jan. and July | 1,000,000 |
| Hancock & Calumet cons. mort., 5 per cent., due Jan., 1931, Jan. and July | 325,000 |
| Total | $1,925,000 |

The 4 per cent. consolidated mortgage bonds are held by the Canadian Pacific Railway Co. The latter company guarantees the interest on the general mortgage 4 per cent. bonds. There are $7,000 of the consols reserved to retire certain old bonds.

EARNINGS.

Year ending June 30.

| | Gross. | Net. | Charges. | Surplus. |
|---|---|---|---|---|
| 1901-02 | $592,648 | $103,522 | $98,014 | $5,508 |

The company's traffic is almost entirely composed of mineral products and ores.

President, William F. Fitch, Marquette, Mich.; Vice-President, William E. Parnall, Calumet, Mich.; Secretary, A. E. Miller; Treasurer, E. W. Allen, Marquette, Mich.; Assistant Secretary and Assistant Treasurer, George H. Church, New York.

Directors—William F. Fitch, E. W. Allen, Charles H. Schaffer, James E. Jopling, Marquette, Mich.; William E. Parnall, W. J. T. Reeder, W. E. Parnall, Jr., Calumet, Mich.

Main office, Marquette, Mich. New York office, 44 Wall street. Annual meeting,, second Thursday in September, at Marquette, Mich.

## MINNEAPOLIS & ST. LOUIS RAILROAD CO.

Road owned, Minneapolis, Minn., to Angus, Ia., 259 miles; Hopkins, Minn., to Watertown, S. D., 215 miles; Winthrop, Minn., to Storm Lake, Ia., 153 miles; branches, 3 miles; total owned, 630 miles; leased trackage, 10 miles; total operated, 640 miles. Owned, but leased to Burlington, Cedar Rapids & Northern, 13 miles. In 1900 the extension of 135 miles from New Ulm, Minn., to Storm Lake, Ia., was completed. In January, 1899, this company purchased the Wisconsin, Minnesota & Pacific's line from Morton to Watertown, 123 miles. Locomotives, 80; passenger cars, 64; freight cars, 3,139.

Control of the Iowa Central was acquired in 1900 by capitalists identified with this company.

Stock. Par $100. Au'd { com., $6,000,000; 2d pref., now pref., 4,000,000 } Issued { com., $6,000,000; pref., 4,000,000 } $10,000,000

First preferred stock was $2,500,000, 5 per cent., cumulative; second preferred, 5 per cent., non-cumulative. The first preferred stock was subject to retirement at par and accrued dividends, and in June, 1899, was paid off with part of proceeds of the issue of refunding 4 per cent. bonds. This made the 2d preferred the only preferred stock. It is 5 per cent., non-cumulative. The company on July 1, 1901, had in its treasury $282,000 of the consolidated 5s and $551,000 of the refunding 4s, which are included in the amount of these bonds given above.

Transfer Agent, Central Trust Co., New York. Registrar, United States Mortgage & Trust Co., New York.

In year 1894-95 the new company paid 3½ per cent. dividend on 1st preferred stock. In 1896, paid 5 per cent. on 1st preferred and 3 per cent. on 2d preferred. In 1897, 5 per cent. on 1st and 3 per cent. on 2d preferred. In 1898, 5 per cent. on 1st and 3½ per cent. on 2d preferred; the July, 1898, dividend on the latter increased from 1½ to 2 per cent. semi-annual, and in July, 1899, to 2½ per cent. semi-annual, at which rate the semi-annual January (15) and July dividends have since been paid. In July, 1900, the first dividend of 1½ per cent. was paid on the common. On January 15, 1901, a second dividend of 2 per cent. was paid on the common and 2 per cent. on July 15, 1901. The dividend on the common paid January 15, 1902, was increased to 2½ per cent., putting the common stock on a 5 per cent. basis.

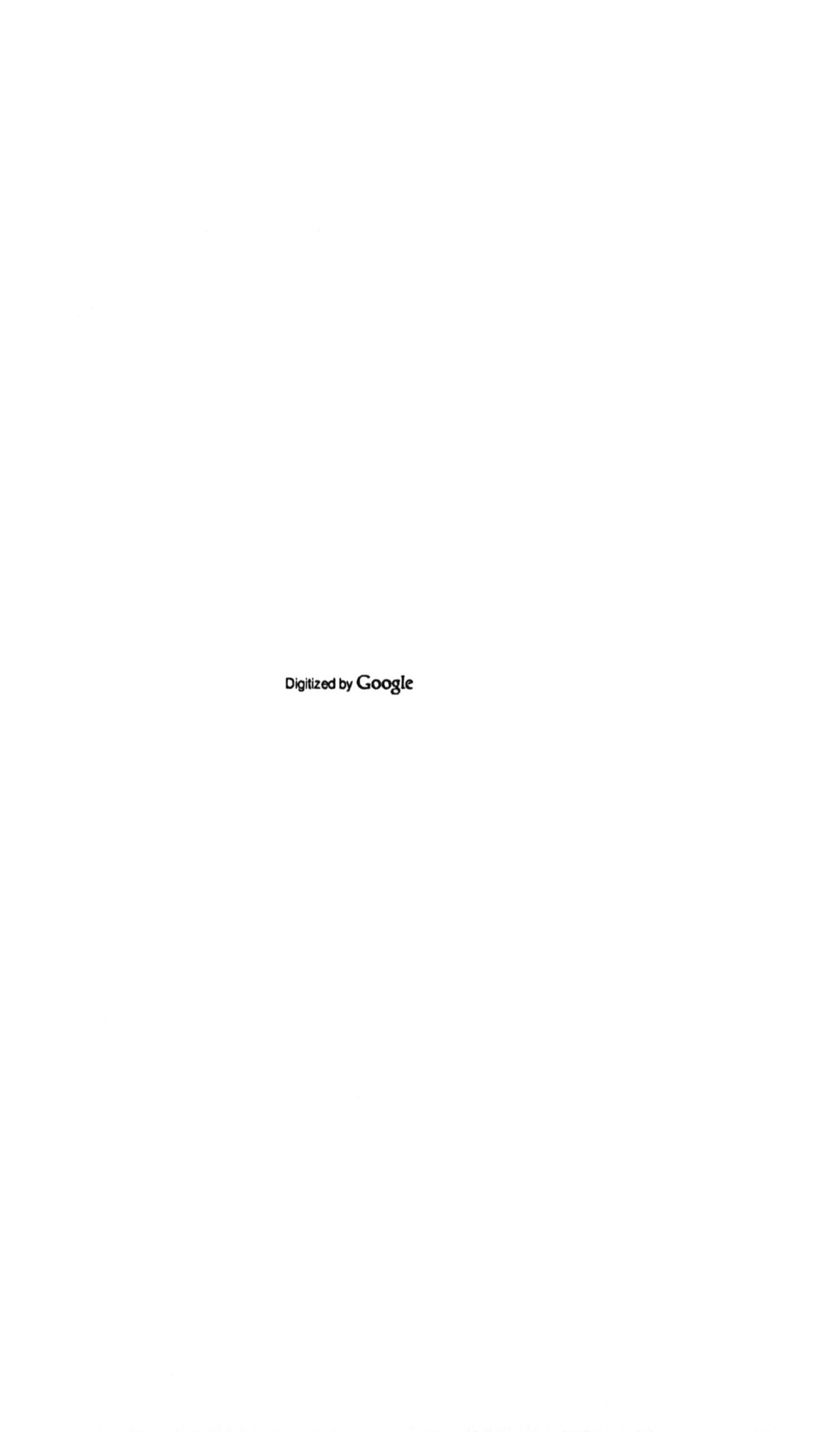

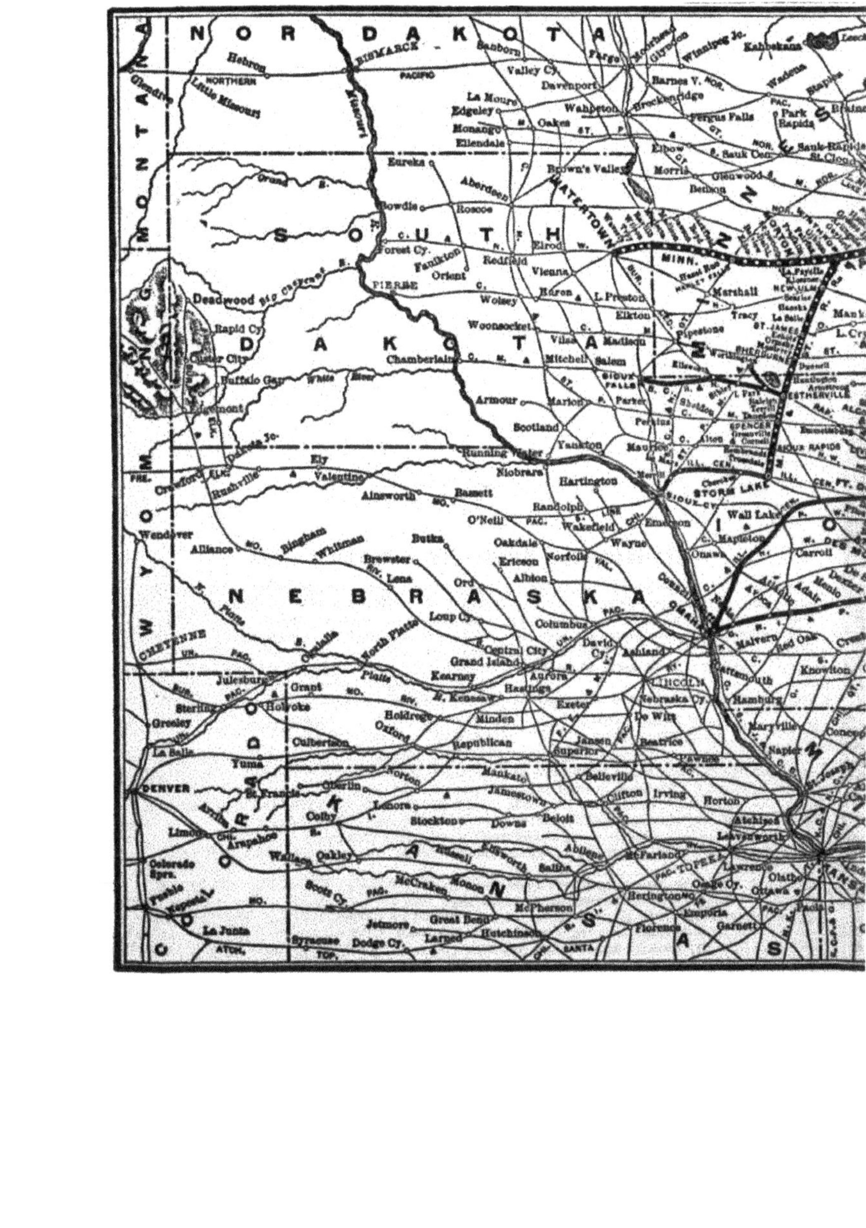
NORDAKOTA
MONTANA
SOUTH DAKOTA
NEBRASKA
WYOMING
COLORADO
KANSAS
Bismarck
Hebron
Glendive
Little Missouri
Northern Pacific
Missouri
Sanborn
Valley Cy.
Davenport
Fargo
Moorhead
Glyndon
Winnipeg Jc.
Kabbekana
Leech
La Moure
Edgeley
Monango
Ellendale
Oakes
Wahpeton
Breckenridge
Barnes V.
Fergus Falls
Wadena
Staples
Park Rapids
Sauk Rapids
St. Cloud
Sauk Cen.
Elbow
Morris
Glenwood
Benson
Eureka
Aberdeen
Brown's Valley
Watertown
Grand R.
Bowdle
Roscoe
Forest Cy.
Faulkton
Orient
Redfield
Elrod
Vienna
Minn.
Pierre
Wolsey
Huron
L. Preston
Marshall
Tracy
Deadwood
Big Cheyenne R.
Rapid Cy.
Custer City
Buffalo Gap
Edgemont
Woonsocket
Elkton
Pipestone
Madison
Mitchell
Salem
Chamberlain
White River
Sioux Falls
Armour
Marion
Parker
Scotland
Yankton
Running Water
Niobrara
Dakota Jc.
Crawford
Rushville
Ely
Valentine
Ainsworth
Bassett
Hartington
Storm Lake
Randolph
O'Neill
Wakefield
Emerson
Wall Lake
Sioux Cy.
Wendover
Alliance
Bingham
Whitman
Butka
Oakdale
Norfolk
Wayne
Onawa
Mapleton
Carroll
Brewster
Ericson
Albion
Lena
Ord
Loup Cy.
Columbus
Omaha
Council Bluffs
Avoca
Atlantic
Adair
Menlo
Malvern
Red Oak
Cheyenne
Julesburg
Grant
Ogalalla
North Platte
Kearney
Grand Island
Central City
David Cy.
Ashland
Aurora
Hastings
Lincoln
Plattsmouth
Knowlton
Sterling
Holyoke
Holdrege
Minden
Exeter
Nebraska Cy.
Hamburg
Greeley
Oxford
Republican
De Witt
Maryville
La Salle
Culbertson
Janson
Superior
Beatrice
Yuma
Napier
Denver
Oberlin
Norton
Mankato
Belleville
St. Joseph
St. Francis
Jamestown
Clifton
Irving
Horton
Lenora
Colby
Stockton
Downs
Beloit
Atchison
Leavenworth
Limon
Arapahoe
Abilene
McFarland
Topeka
Lawrence
Olathe
Colorado Sprs.
Wallace
Oakley
Russell
Ellsworth
Salina
Ottawa
Pueblo
Scott Cy.
McCracken
Herington
McPherson
Emporia
Garnett
La Junta
Jetmore
Great Bend
Hutchinson
Florence
Syracuse
Dodge Cy.
Larned
Atch.
Top.
Santa

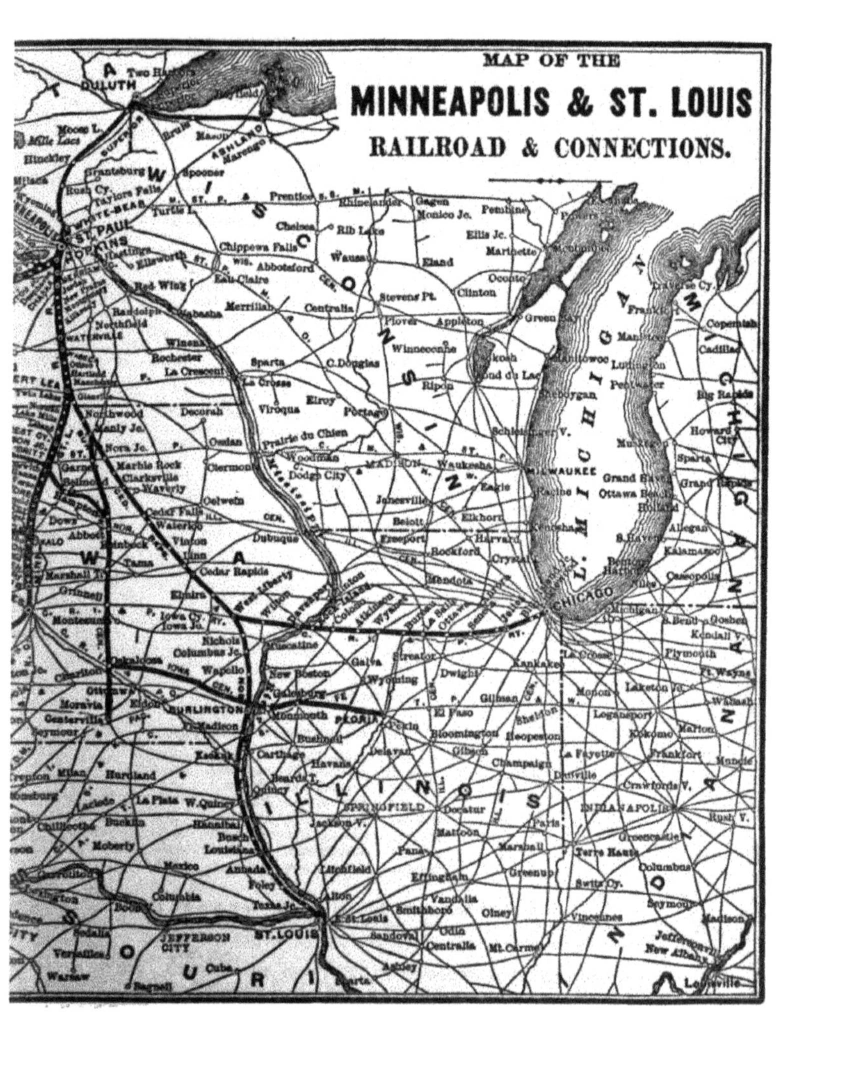

MAP OF THE
MINNEAPOLIS & ST. LOUIS
RAILROAD & CONNECTIONS.

FUNDED DEBT.

| | |
|---|---|
| 1st mort. (on 29 miles), 7 per cent., due Jan., 1907, Jan. and July | $455,000 |
| 1st mort. (on 80 miles), 7 per cent., due June, 1927, June and Dec. | 950,000 |
| 1st mort., Iowa Extension, 7 per cent., due June, 1909, June and Dec. | 1,015,000 |
| 1st mort., Southwestern Extension, 7 per cent., due Dec., 1910, June and Dec. | 636,000 |
| 1st mort., Pacific Division, 6 per cent., due April, 1921, April and Oct. | 1,382,000 |
| 1st cons. 5 per cent. gold bonds, due Nov., 1934, May and Nov. | 5,282,000 |
| 1st refunding mort., 4 per cent., due March, 1949, March and Sept. | 8,151,000 |
| Total | $17,871,000 |

In June, 1888, the old company defaulted on its interest charges and a Receiver was appointed on default in meeting interest on the equipment and improvement bonds. The road was reorganized in November, 1894. The equipment and improvement bonds and all coupons were paid in full; all underlying bonds were recognized and coupons, together with interest thereon, were paid in full.

In January, 1899, it was announced that this company had decided to create a 50-year, 4 per cent. refunding mortgage for $25,000,000, of which issue $10,000,000 was to retire the company's outstanding funded debt and $2,500,000 to retire the 1st preferred stock at par. An amount of $5,000,000 of the new bonds were sold, the proceeds to be used to pay for the Watertown branch of the Wisconsin, Minnesota & Pacific, which the company had arranged to purchase from the Chicago, Rock Island & Pacific, and to extend the New Ulm branch of this company's system to Storm Lake, Ia., a distance of 135 miles.

In November, 1901, the White Bear Lake Branch, 14 miles, was conveyed, subject to its liens, to the Northern Pacific Railway Co., which assumed principal and interest of the $280,000 7 per cent. bonds on the branch.

See MANUAL for 1898 for capital of old company and terms of reorganization plan.

Included in the amounts given as outstanding in the table of bonds this company has $282,000 5 per cent. consols and $551,000 refunding 4s in its treasury.

EARNINGS.

Year ending June 30.

| | Gross. | Net. | Charges. | Surplus. |
|---|---|---|---|---|
| 1892-93 | $1,974,498 | $845,174 | ...... | ...... |
| 1893-94 | 1,708,871 | 813,621 | ...... | ...... |
| 1894-95 | 1,823,998 | 838,201 | $457,817 | $380,384 |
| 1895-96 | 2,028,300 | 1,035,533 | 703,753 | 331,780 |
| 1896-97 | 2,006,505 | 1,030,023 | 706,236 | 323,786 |
| 1897-98 | 2,246,580 | 1,118,823 | 707,995 | 410,827 |
| 1898-99 | 2,500,004 | 1,258,596 | 799,934 | 458,662 |
| 1899-00 | 2,863,309 | 1,463,067 | 1,048,442 | 414,624 |
| 1900-01 | 3,275,503 | 1,615,625 | 1,061,863 | 553,762 |
| 1901-02 | 3,540,840 | 1,753,501 | 1,056,776 | 696,725 |

The following presents the comparative freight traffic statistics of the company:

| | Average Mileage. | Total Tonnage. | Tons Carried One Mile. | Freight Density. | Rate per Ton per Mile. | Earnings per Train Mile. | Average Tons per Train. |
|---|---|---|---|---|---|---|---|
| 1896-97 | 369 | 1,208,969 | 114,523,012 | 310,360 | 1.283c | $2.372 | 184 |
| 1897-98 | 385 | 1,342,286 | 140,901,750 | 365,978 | 1.171 | 2.466 | 211 |
| 1898-99 | 436 | 1,535,278 | 156,379,613 | 358,669 | 1.190 | 2.488 | 209 |
| 1899-00 | 514 | 1,605,383 | 174,654,187 | 339,794 | 1.212 | 3.047 | 251 |
| 1900-01 | 633 | 1,766,287 | 210,799,911 | 333,017 | 1.145 | 3.305 | 288 |
| 1901-02 | 641 | 1,940,268 | 204,515,108 | 319,056 | 1.235 | 3.160 | 255 |

In 1893-94 $36,215 was paid for improvements and $896,070 for accumulated interest in bonds. In 1894-95 surplus over dividends was $297,051; in 1895-96, $86,780; in 1896-97, $78,786; in 1897-98, $145,827; in 1898-99, $164,079; in 1899-1900, $124,624; in 1900-01, $113,762, and in 1901-02, $196,725.

President, Edwin Hawley, New York; Vice-President, L. F. Day; Secretary, Joseph Gaskell, Minneapolis; Treasurer, F. H. Davis, New York.

Directors—Edwin Hawley, Edwin Langdon, F. H. Davis, John E. Searles, Levi C. Weir, George Crocker, New York; H. E. Huntington, San Francisco; L. F. Day Minneapolis.

Main office, Minneapolis; New York office, 25 Broad street. Annual meeting, first Tuesday in October, at Minneapolis. Books close September 1.

## MINNEAPOLIS, ST. PAUL & SAULT STE. MARIE RAILWAY CO.

(Controlled by Canadian Pacific.)

Road owned, Sault Ste. Marie, Mich., via Minneapolis, Minn., to Portal, N. D., 1,038 miles; Hankinson, N. D., to Bismarck, N. D., 222 miles; branches, 168 miles; trackage, 18 miles; total, 1,448 miles. In addition the company has spurs and logging lines about 23 miles long. Locomotives, 106; passenger cars, 87; freight cars, 7,880.

Consolidation May, 1888, of the Minneapolis, Sault Ste. Marie & Atlantic, Minneapolis & Pacific, Aberdeen, Bismarck & Northwestern and Minneapolis & St. Croix.

A controlling interest in stock was acquired in 1888 by the Canadian Pacific, that company guaranteeing 4 per cent. on the bonds of this company. The extension northward to international boundary at Portal was completed in 1893. Connection is made at that point with Canadian Pacific.

Stock Par $100...Authorized { com., $14,000,000; pref., 7,000,000 } Issued { com., $14,000,000; pref., 7,000,000 } $21,000,000

Transfer Agent, Bank of Montreal, New York. Registrar, Central Trust Co., New York.

FUNDED DEBT.

| | |
|---|---|
| 1st mort., Minn., Sault Ste. Marie & Atl., 5 per cent., due Jan., 1926, Jan. and July. | $8,209,000 |
| Minn. & Pac., 1st mort., 5 per cent., due Jan., 1936, Jan. and July | 458,000 |
| Con. mort., 4 per cent., due July, 1938, Jan. and July | 22,482,000 |
| 2d mort. guar., 4 per cent., due Jan., 1949, Jan. and July | 3,500,000 |
| Total | $34,649,000 |

In 1888 consolidated mortgage, 5 per cent. bonds for $21,000,000 were authorized to retire outstanding bonds and provide for additional construction. There are $257,331 car trust obligations outstanding. The 2d mortgage is for $5,000,000, of which $3,500,000 was issued in 1899 to take up various indebtedness and provide for improvements.

EARNINGS.

Year ending June 30.

| | Gross. | Net. | Charges. | Surplus. |
|---|---|---|---|---|
| 1894-95 | $2,557,275 | $731,324 | $1,327,220 | Def. $513,909 |
| 1895-96 | 3,735,872 | 1,403,400 | 1,520,924 | Sur. 4,305 |
| 1896-97 | 3,611,469 | 1,334,980 | 1,456,406 | Def. 3,299 |
| 1897-98 | 4,175,718 | 1,767,062 | 1,538,450 | Sur. 402,187 |
| 1898-99 | 4,413,312 | 1,761,605 | 1,577,565 | 375,057 |
| 1899-00 | 5,191,122 | 2,470,210 | 1,718,498 | 880,872 |
| 1900-01 | 4,537,296 | 1,972,958 | 1,645,085 | 327,873 |
| 1901-02 | 6,223,387 | 3,280,760 | 1,924,259 | 1,286,501 |

Charges for 1901-02 include $300,000 appropriated for new equipment.

The following presents the comparative freight traffic statistics of the company:

| | Average Mileage. | Total Tonnage. | Tons Carried One Mile. | Freight Density. | Rate per Ton per Mile. | Earnings per Train Mile. | Average Tons per Train. |
|---|---|---|---|---|---|---|---|
| 1896-97 | 1,184 | 2,109,266 | 446,253,209 | 376,629 | 0.643c | $1.893 | 294 |
| 1897-98 | 1,195 | 2,661,344 | 546,093,524 | 457,982 | 0.602 | 1.914 | 317 |
| 1898-99 | 1,272 | 2,750,513 | 592,041,591 | 465,233 | 0.579 | 1.785 | 308 |
| 1899-00 | 1,285 | 3,102,244 | 603,856,370 | 469,656 | 0.658 | 1.985 | 301 |
| 1900-01 | 1,301 | 2,973,310 | 535,017,533 | 411,235 | 0.617 | 1.942 | 314 |
| 1901-02 | 1,396 | 3,234,023 | 617,746,549 | 441,795 | 0.739 | 2.330 | 314 |

President, Thomas Lowry; Vice-President, John Martin; 2d Vice-President and General Manager, E. Pennington; Secretary and Treasurer, Charles F. Clement; Auditor, C. W. Gardner, Minneapolis.

Directors—W. D. Washburn, E. Penington, John Martin, Thomas Lowry, C. H. Pettit, G. R. Newell, Minneapolis; Sir William C. Van Horne, Sir Thomas G. Shaughnessy, R. B. Angus, Montreal; E. A. Young, St. Paul.

Main office, Minneapolis. Annual meeting, third Tuesday in September.

---

## MISSOURI, KANSAS & TEXAS RAILWAY CO.

Road owned, 1,281 miles, comprising lines from St. Louis and Hannibal, Mo., to Denison, Tex., and branches; Missouri, Kansas & Texas Railway of Texas, 1,162 miles; Denison & Wachita Valley Railway, 20 miles; Wachita Falls Railway, 18 miles; Denison, Bonham & New Orleans Railroad, 24 miles; Galveston, Houston & Henderson Railroad (controlled jointly), 50

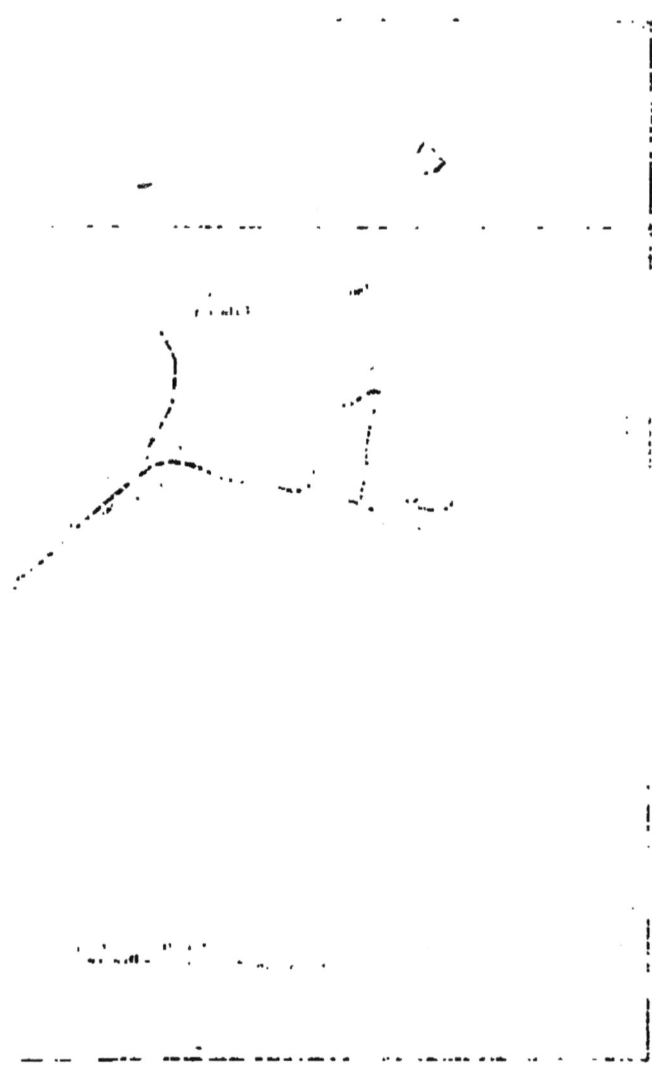

SOO LINE
SOO-PAC

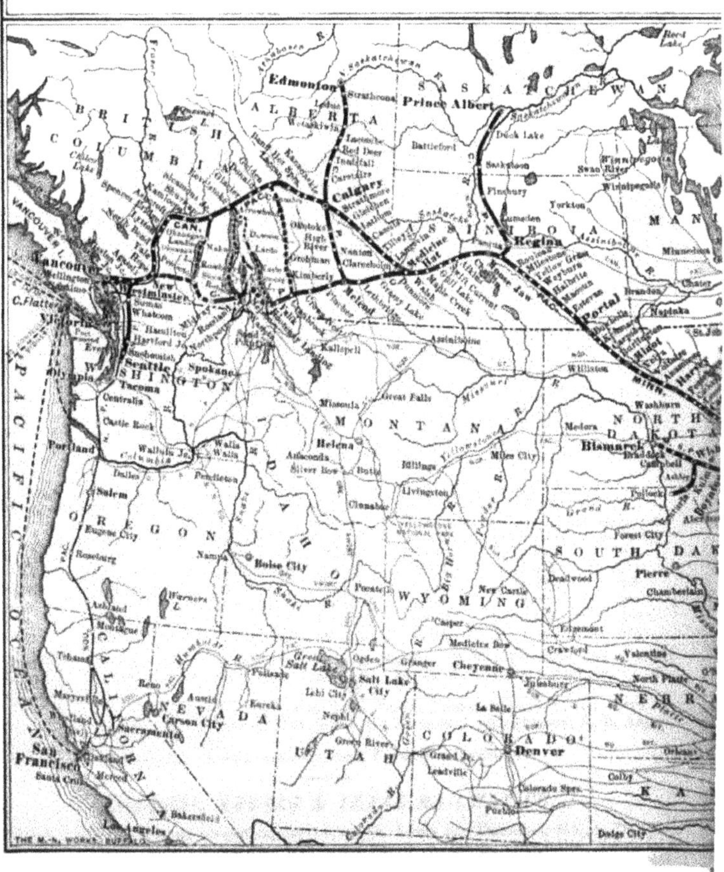
BRITISH COLUMBIA
ALBERTA
SASKATCHEWAN
ASSINIBOIA
WASHINGTON
OREGON
IDAHO
MONTANA
WYOMING
NORTH DAKOTA
SOUTH DAKOTA
NEVADA
UTAH
COLORADO
PACIFIC OCEAN
Edmonton
Strathcona
Prince Albert
Wetaskiwin
Lacombe
Red Deer
Innisfail
Battleford
Duck Lake
Saskatoon
Swan River
Winnipegosis
Calgary
Yorkton
Regina
Moose Jaw
Medicine Hat
Portal
Brandon
Minot
Vancouver
New Westminster
Whatcom
Victoria
Seattle
Tacoma
Olympia
Spokane
Kalispell
Assiniboine
Williston
Great Falls
Missoula
Helena
Anaconda
Silver Bow
Butte
Billings
Livingston
Miles City
Medora
Bismarck
Washburn
Portland
Walla Walla
Pendleton
Salem
Eugene City
Roseburg
Ashland
Nampa
Boise City
Pocatello
Warners L.
Deadwood
Pierre
Chamberlain
Forest City
New Castle
Casper
Cheyenne
Ogden
Salt Lake City
Reno
Carson City
Sacramento
San Francisco
Santa Cruz
Merced
Bakersfield
Los Angeles
Green River
Grand Jc.
Leadville
Denver
Colorado Spgs.
Pueblo
Julesburg
North Platte
Colby
Dodge City
THE M.-N. WORKS, BUFFALO

# IFIC LINE.

SOO
LINE


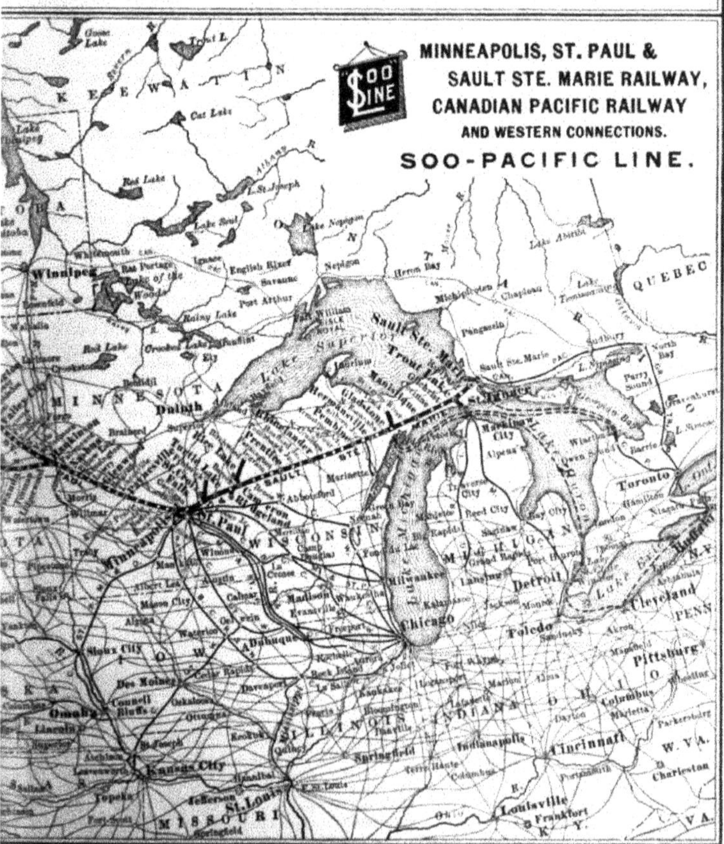

SOO
LINE
MINNEAPOLIS, ST. PAUL &
SAULT STE. MARIE RAILWAY,
CANADIAN PACIFIC RAILWAY
AND WESTERN CONNECTIONS.
SOO-PACIFIC LINE.
K E E W A T I N
QUEBEC
Winnipeg
Lake Superior
Sault Ste. Marie
MINNESOTA
Duluth
Minneapolis
St. Paul
WISCONSIN
MICHIGAN
Milwaukee
Chicago
Detroit
Toronto
Cleveland
Toledo
Pittsburg
OHIO
Columbus
Cincinnati
INDIANA
Indianapolis
ILLINOIS
Springfield
Louisville
Frankfort
KY.
St. Louis
MISSOURI
Kansas City
Omaha
Sioux City
Des Moines
IOWA
Dubuque
W. VA.
PENN.
VA.

miles; total of system, 2,555 miles. Company owns from Holden, Mo., to Paolo, 54 miles, leased to Missouri Pacific. The Sherman, Shreveport & Southern, Jefferson, Tex., to McKinney, 155 miles, which was operated separately, was, under authority granted in 1899 by the State of Texas, consolidated with this company. The company's lines were extended in 1901 from San Marcos to San Antonio, Tex. Formerly owned the Galveston, Houston & Henderson, 50 miles, which was leased to International & Great Northern. In 1895 arrangement was made with that company for joint control and use of the Galveston, Houston & Henderson. In 1902 the company bought the Fort Scott & Western Railroad, 15 miles, and the Missouri, Kansas & Northwestern, 29 miles. Locomotives, 330; passenger cars, 226; freight cars, 11,586.

In 1902 important extensions were commenced to points in Oklahoma under the titles of the Missouri, Kansas & Oklahoma Railroad and the Texas & Oklahoma Railroad, the new lines being about 375 miles.

Company was reorganized without foreclosure in 1890. The Dallas & Waco Railroad was built and leased to the company to connect its northern and southern divisions, and the Kansas City & Pacific was leased to afford an entrance to Kansas City. Extension to St. Louis was built by a company under name of Missouri, Kansas & Eastern, the Missouri, Kansas & Texas owning all its stock. All the company's lines in Texas are held, in conformity with the State law, by a company, the Missouri, Kansas & Texas Railway, of Texas, the stock of which, $2,468,900, is held in trust for the security holders of parent company.

Stock..Par $100...Authorized { com., $56,100,300 / pref., 13,000,000 } Issued { com., $56,100,300 / pref., 13,000,000 } $69,100,300

The preferred stock is 4 per cent., non-cumulative. Stock is transferred at the company's office, 40 Wall street, New York.

FUNDED DEBT.

| | |
|---|---|
| 1st mort., 4 per cent., due June, 1990, June and Dec. | $39,813,000 |
| 2d mort., 4 per cent., due June, 1990, Feb. and Aug. | 20,000,000 |
| 1st mort., extension bonds, 5 per cent., due Nov., 1944, May and Nov. | 2,548,000 |
| M., K. & T. of Texas, 1st mort., 5 per cent., due Sept., 1942, March and Sept. | 3,597,000 |
| M., K. & E. (St. Louis ex.), 1st mort., 4 per cent., due April, 2001, April and Oct. | 4,000,000 |
| St. Louis Div. 1st refunding mort., 4 per cent., due April, 2001, April and Oct. | 1,841,000 |
| " " 2d mort., 5 per cent., due Oct., 1942, April and Oct. | 121,000 |
| Kansas City & Pacific, 1st mort., guar., 4 per cent., due Aug., 1990, Feb. and Aug. | 2,500,000 |
| Tebo & Neosho R. R. Co., 1st mort., 7 per cent., due June, 1903, June and Dec. | 187,000 |
| Dallas & Waco, 1st mort., guar., 5 per cent., due Nov., 1940, May and Nov. | 1,340,000 |
| Boonville Bridge, new mort., 4 per cent., due 1951, May and Nov. | 1,000,000 |
| Sherman, Shreve. & So., 1st mort., guar., 5 per cent., due June, 1943, June and Dec. | 1,689,000 |
| S. W. Coal & Impt., 1st mort., guar., 6 per cent., due July, 1926, Jan. and July. | 968,000 |
| Total | $79,604,000 |

Interest on 2d mortgage bonds until August 1, 1895, was only to be paid if earned; at that date it became obligatory. In 1896 common stock was increased from $47,000,000 to $52,450,000 to carry out amalgamation of the Missouri, Kansas & Eastern and other branches with the parent company. In 1900 the common stock was again increased to $55,181,000 to provide for the acquisition of the Kansas City & Pacific and the Kansas City, Eldorado & Southern.

The St. Louis Division refunding bonds are $6,000,000 authorized, sufficient being reserved to retire the old Missouri, Kansas & Eastern bonds.

In 1902 an issue of 5 per cent. forty-year bonds of the Missouri, Kansas & Oklahoma Railroad was authorized, the same to be guaranteed as to principal and interest by this company.

EARNINGS.

Year ending June 30.

| | Gross. | Net. | Charges. | Surplus. |
|---|---|---|---|---|
| 1892-93 (1,712 miles) | $10,388,191 | $2,577,456 | $2,359,443 | $238,046 |
| 1893-94 (1,960 " ) | 9,877,290 | 2,671,348 | 2,680,870 | Def. 9,521 |
| 1894-95 (2,028 " ) | 11,544,363 | 3,123,179 | 2,898,440 | 224,739 |
| 1895-96 (2,147 " ) | 11,036,987 | 3,332,887 | 3,316,494 | 16,393 |
| 1896-97 (2,197 " ) | 11,478,315 | 3,277,913 | 3,427,267 | Def. 149,353 |
| 1897-98 ( " " ) | 12,047,236 | 3,933,938 | 3,427,169 | 506,769 |
| 1898-99 (2,200 " ) | 11,930,334 | 4,249,261 | 3,700,578 | 548,683 |
| 1899-00 (2,218 " ) | 12,626,511 | 3,904,251 | 3,453,384 | 450,866 |
| 1900-01 (2,265 " ) | 15,403,083 | 4,268,936 | 3,507,157 | 799,916 |
| 1901-02 (2,500 " ) | 16,391,399 | 4,519,835 | 3,644,708 | 908,939 |

Surplus for 1900-01 includes $38,136 of miscellaneous income, and in 1901-02 $33,813 from the same source.

The following presents the comparative freight traffic statistics of the company:

| | Average Mileage. | Total Tonnage. | Tons Carried One Mile. | Freight Density. | Rate per Ton per Mile. | Earnings per Train Mile. | Av'ge Tons per Train. |
|---|---|---|---|---|---|---|---|
| 1897-98.... | 2,197 | 3,568,825 | 1,040,700,027 | 473,691 | 0.918c | $1.588 | 172 |
| 1898-99.... | 2,200 | 3,594,500 | 1,005,776,939 | 457,122 | 0.934 | 1.645 | 176 |
| 1899-00.... | 2,218 | 3,936,957 | 1,176,879,464 | 531,956 | 0.840 | 1.655 | 197 |
| 1900-01.... | 2,265 | 4,884,976 | 1,304,692,564 | 576,022 | 0.927 | 1.967 | 212 |
| 1901-02.... | 2,500 | 5,014,429 | 1,396,710,077 | 558,684 | 0.904 | 1.860 | 206 |

Chairman and President, Henry C. Rouse, New York; Vice-President and General Manager, A. A. Allen, St. Louis; Vice-President and Treasurer, Charles G. Hedge; Secretary, S. Halline, New York.

Directors—John D. Rockefeller, William Rockefeller, Joel F. Freeman, Henry W. Poor, Herbert L. Satterlee, Colgate Hoyt, Henry C. Rouse, Charles G. Hedge, James Brown Potter, New York; T. N. Sedgwick, Parsons, Kan.; B. P. McDonald, Fort Scott, Kan.; Alfred J. Poor, Chapman, Kan.; H. J. de M. Oyens, Amsterdam, Holland; Myron T. Herrick, Cleveland; A. A. Allen, James Hagerman, St. Louis.

Main office, Parsons, Kan.; general office, 105 North Seventh street, St. Louis; executive offices, 40 Wall street, New York. Annual meeting, third Wednesday in May, at Parsons, Kan. Books close thirty days before.

---

## THE MISSOURI PACIFIC RAILWAY CO.

Road owned, main line, St. Louis to Kansas City, Mo., 283 miles; extensions to Atchison, Omaha and other points in Missouri, Kansas and Nebraska, 1,051 miles; branches of main line leased, 287 miles; total, main line system, 1,621 miles; branch line system, extending to Pueblo, Col., and other points in Missouri, Kansas and Colorado, 1,868 miles, of which 1,704 miles are ownec and 164 miles leased.

This company also controls, through ownership of stock, and operates the St. Louis, Iron Mountain & Southern Railway, St. Louis, Mo., to Texarkana, Ark., 490 miles, and branches, a total of 1,774 miles, of which 1,429 miles are owned and 345 miles leased; included in the latter are the Little Rock & Fort Smith Railway, 170 miles; Kansas & Arkansas Valley Railway, 171 miles; and Little Rock Junction Railway, 0.59 mile. The Missouri Pacific also operates the Central Branch Railway and leased lines, 388 miles.

Total of all lines operated by the Missouri Pacific Railway Co., 5,651 miles, of which 5,454 miles are owned or controlled by stock ownership and 112 miles leased. Equipment December 31, 1902: Locomotives, 772; passenger cars, 627; freight cars, 36,031; service cars, 2,365.

The Texas & Pacific is controlled, but is operated as an independent corporation. See below for arrangement whereby the 2d mortgage bonds of that road were exchanged for Iron Mountain unified gold 4s of 1899. In 1901 control of the Denver & Rio Grande and the Rio Grande Western roads was obtained by this company.

The statements below are for the Missouri Pacific proper and the companies operated directly by it; the other lines will be found under their respective titles.

The company exchanged its stock in 1881 for that of the St. Louis, Iron Mountain & Southern at the rate of three shares for four of Iron Mountain, and holds that stock in its treasury, of the par value of $25,723,845, out of a total of $25,788,435. This company leased the Missouri, Kansas & Texas in 1880, but the lease was dissolved in 1888.

The Central Branch Union Pacific was leased from the Union Pacific. In 1898 that property was separated from the Union Pacific and reorganized as the Central Branch Railway in the interest of the Missouri Pacific.

Stock......Par $100........................Authorized, $100,000,000......Issued, $77,802,875

From 1883 to 1887, inclusive, dividends of 7 per cent. per annum were paid on the stock; in 1888, 5½ per cent.; in 1889 and 1890, 4 per cent.; in 1891, 3 per cent. No dividends were paid after the quarterly one of 1 per cent. in July, 1891, until July 20, 1901, when a half yearly dividend of 2½ per cent. was paid. On January 20, 1902, 2½ per cent. was also paid on the stock, and the same rate was also paid July 20, 1902, and January 20, 1903.

The stock outstanding at the end of 1899 was $47,448,650. It was increased in 1901 to present amount by the conversion of $11,628,000 of collateral trust debentures, by sale of $13,495,865 to purchase control of the Denver & Rio Grande, by the issue of $2,983,500 to purchase the Kansas City & Northwestern Railway, by the sale of $846,245 and by the issue of $400,000 in part payment of branch lines.

Stock is transferred by the Treasurer of the company, 195 Broadway, New York. Registrar, Mercantile Trust Co., New York.

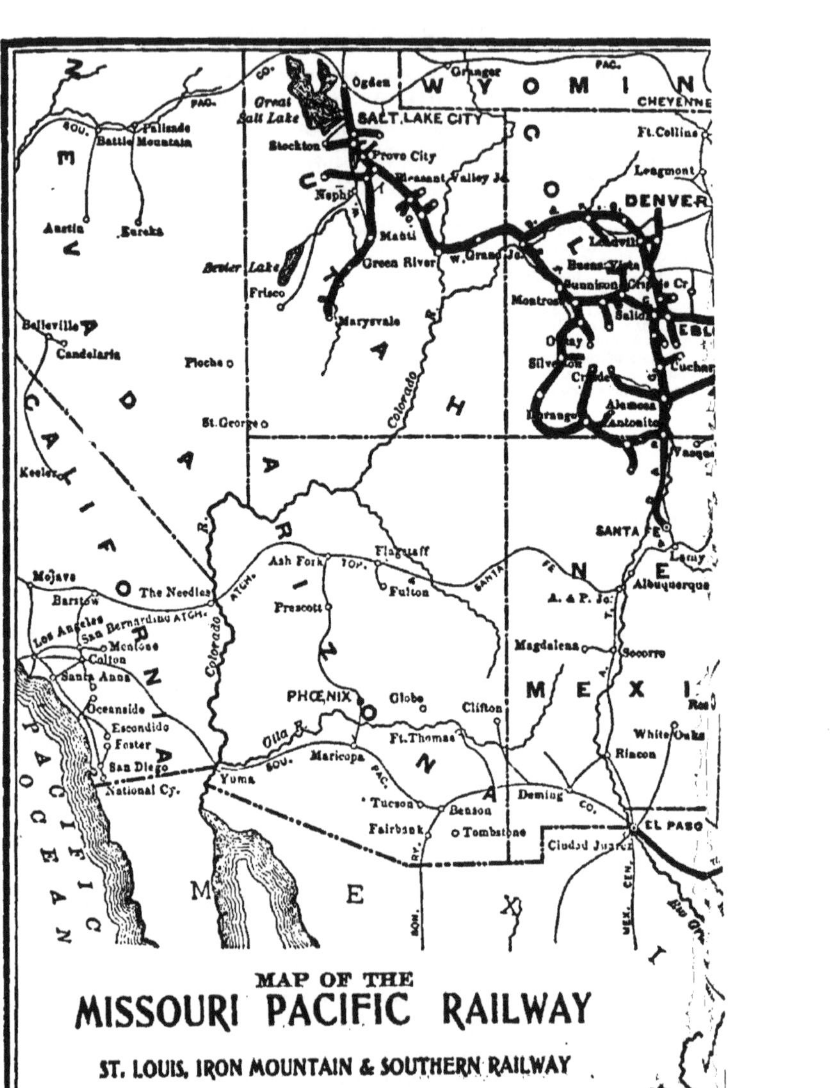


MAP OF THE

# MISSOURI PACIFIC RAILWAY

ST. LOUIS, IRON MOUNTAIN & SOUTHERN RAILWAY

LEASED, OPERATED AND INDEPENDENT LINES AND CONNECTIONS.

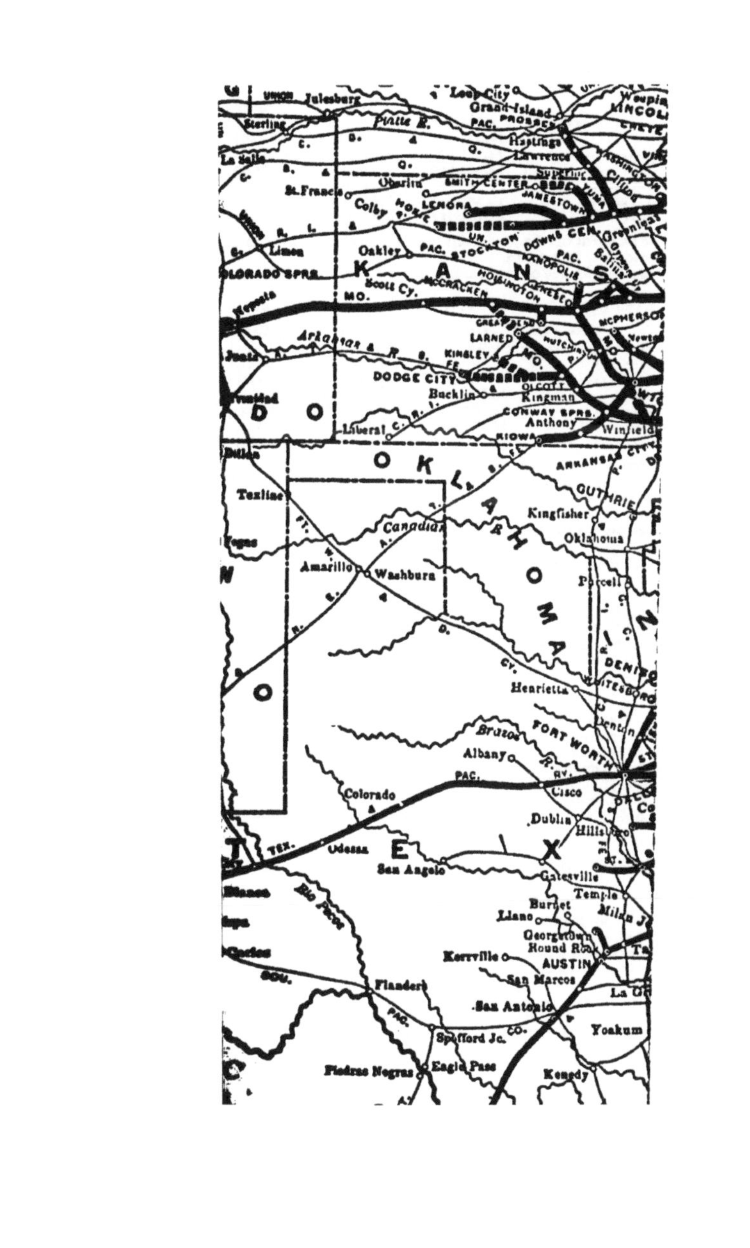

Julesburg
Loup City
Grand Island
Sterling
Platte R.
Hastings
Lawrence
La Salle
St. Francis
Oberlin
Smith Center
Jamestown
Colby
Lenora
Limon
Oakley
Stockton
Downs
Kanopolis
Colorado Sprs.
K
A
N
S
Scott Cy.
McCracken
Hoisington
McPherson
Arkansas R.
Great Bend
Larned
Kingsley
Dodge City
Bucklin
Kingman
Conway Sprs.
Anthony
Kiowa
Winfield
D
O
Liberal
O
K
L
A
H
O
M
A
Arkansas City
Guthrie
Texline
Kingfisher
Canadian
Oklahoma
Amarillo
Washburn
Purcell
Denison
Henrietta
Whitesboro
Denton
Brazos R.
Fort Worth
Albany
Cisco
Colorado
Dublin
Hillsboro
T
E
X
Odessa
San Angelo
Gatesville
Rio Pecos
Temple
Burnet
Llano
Georgetown
Round Rock
Kerrville
Austin
San Marcos
Flanders
San Antonio
Yoakum
Spofford Jc.
Piedras Negras
Eagle Pass
Kenedy

The following are the figures for the Missouri Pacific Railway Co. for a series of years:

EARNINGS (MISSOURI PACIFIC).

| | Gross. | Net. | Charges. | Surplus. |
|---|---|---|---|---|
| 1896 (3,164 miles)................ | $11,065,391 | $2,507,740 | $3,958,355 | Def. $1,450,615 |
| 1897 ( " " )................ | 12,985,165 | 4,034,786 | 3,940,971 | 93,815 |
| 1898 ( " " )................ | 14,111,277 | 4,059,867 | 4,052,212 | 7,655 |
| 1899 ( " " )................ | 14,273,700 | 4,335,402 | 3,935,530 | 399,872 |
| 1900 ( " " )................ | 15,930,276 | 6,930,509 | 4,152,616 | 2,777,893 |
| 1901 (3,408 " )................ | 18,384,077 | 8,699,819 | 3,835,854 | 4,863,965 |
| 1902 (3,489 " )................ | 18,763,317 | 9,260,075 | 3,888,022 | 5,371,953 |

In 1901, after the payment of the dividends on the stock, the surplus was $1,300,163. In 1902, surplus after dividends, $1,516,843.

The following are the figures of the St. Louis, Iron Mountain & Southern for a series of years:

EARNINGS (ST. LOUIS, IRON MOUNTAIN & SOUTHERN).

| | Div. Paid. | Gross. | Net. | Charges. | Surplus. |
|---|---|---|---|---|---|
| 1896 (1,774 miles).......... | .. | $10,946,568 | $3,545,386 | $3,356,533 | $188,853 |
| 1897 ( " " ).......... | .. | 11,820,286 | 4,142,822 | 3,741,518 | 401,304 |
| 1898 ( " " ).......... | .. | 12,633,545 | 4,347,822 | 3,175,578 | 1,172,244 |
| 1899 ( " " ).......... | 2 | 13,806,118 | 6,026,632 | 5,785,577 | 241,055 |
| 1900 ( " " ).......... | 6 | 14,581,036 | 6,432,256 | 5,823,388 | 608,868 |
| 1901 ( " " ).......... | 6 | 16,961,021 | 8,007,520 | 5,423,156 | 2,584,364 |
| 1902 ( " " ).......... | .. | 17,640,578 | 7,908,927 | 6,685,954 | 1,222,973 |

The figures for 1899 include in charges $1,773,690 for premiums and adjustment of interest on bonds exchanged for Iron Mountain general consols. In 1899 the Iron Mountain Co. paid $515,745 in dividends, leaving a surplus of $241,053. In 1900 paid dividends of $1,547,243, in 1901, $1,547,283, and in 1902, $2,578,831.

The following presents the comparative freight traffic statistics of the system:

| | Average Mileage. | Total Tonnage. | Tons Carried One Mile. | Freight Density. | Rate per Ton per Mile. | Earnings per Train Mile. | Av'ge Tons per Train. |
|---|---|---|---|---|---|---|---|
| 1896....... | 4,938 | 7,404,048 | 1,782,413,913 | 360,959 | 0.865c. | $1.70 | 183 |
| 1897....... | 4,938 | 8,438,509 | 2,150,159,677 | 435,431 | 0.843 | 1.75 | 194 |
| 1898....... | 4,938 | 9,431,723 | 2,272,847,374 | 460,277 | 0.844 | 1.76 | 195 |
| 1899....... | 4,938 | 10,206,910 | 2,419,581,821 | 489,992 | 0.827 | 1.87 | 211 |
| 1900....... | 4,938 | 11,126,375 | 2,628,456,522 | 532,291 | 0.834 | 2.14 | 239 |
| 1901....... | 5,554 | 15,479,849 | 3,542,315,399 | 582,322 | 0.825 | 2.30 | 284 |
| 1902....... | 5,613 | 16,649,701 | 3,666,908,434 | 592,299 | 0.807 | 2.45 | 310 |

President, George J. Gould; 1st Vice-President, Frank Jay Gould, New York; 2d Vice-President, Charles G. Warner; 3d Vice-President and General Manager, Russell Harding, St. Louis; Secretary and Treasurer, A. H. Calef; Assistant Secretary, Guy Phillips, New York; General Auditor, S. B. Schuyler, St. Louis.

Directors—George J. Gould, Russell Sage, Fred T. Gates, Edwin Gould, E. Parmalee Prentice, Samuel Sloan, John D. Rockefeller, Jr., James H. Hyde, Howard Gould, Frank Jay Gould, New York; W. K. Bixby, Charles G. Warner, Russell Harding, St. Louis, Mo.

Main office, St. Louis; New York office, 195 Broadway. Annual meeting, second Tuesday in March.

---

## MOBILE & BIRMINGHAM RAILROAD CO.

(Leased to Southern Railway Co.)

Road owned, Mobile to Marion Junction, Ala., 149 miles. Locomotives, 13; passenger cars, 12; freight cars, 308.

This company, incorporated under laws of Alabama July 2, 1895, is a reorganization (1895) of the railway company of same name. Road was connected with the East Tennessee Railroad and the Richmond Terminal system, but was excluded from the reorganization of that property as the Southern Railway. Default took place in 1892 and Receiver appointed. Sold under foreclosure in April, 1895, and purchased by bondholders. In 1899 the road was leased to the Southern Railway for 99 years, from March 1, 1899, lessee guaranteeing a dividend of 1 per cent. on the preferred stock the first year, to be increased by 1 per cent. each year until 4 per cent. is paid, which shall then become the permanent rate.

Stock......Par $100.......Authorized { com., $900,000 / pref., 900,000 } Issued { com., $900,000 / pref., 900,000 } $1,800,000

Transfer Agent, R. D. Lankford, 80 Broadway, New York.

The dividends under the lease are paid half-yearly, January and July.

FUNDED DEBT.

| | |
|---|---|
| Prior lien bonds, 5 per cent., due July, 1945, Jan. and July | $600,000 |
| 1st mort., 4 per cent., due July, 1945, Jan. and July | 1,200,000 |
| Total | $1,800,000 |

The prior lien mortgage is $1,000,000 and may be increased if extension of road to the Cahaba coal district is built. First mortgage bonds were incomes till July, 1899. In 1897 and 1898 2 per cent. was paid on the 1st mortgage income bonds. The lease to the Southern Railway provides for the payment of the full 4 per cent. interest on these bonds.

The earnings of the company are included in those of the lessee.

In 1896-97 surplus over charges on bonds was $15,350; in 1897-98, surplus, $24,593.

President, T. G. Bush, Birmingham, Ala.; Treasurer, H. C. Ansley, Washington, D. C.; Secretary, H. Hammond, Birmingham, Ala.

Main office, Mobile, Ala. Annual meeting, Wednesday after first Tuesday in April.

## MOBILE & OHIO RAILROAD CO.

(Controlled by Southern Railway Co.)

Road owned, Mobile, Ala., to East Cairo, Ky., 493 miles; Montgomery Division, Columbus, Miss., to Montgomery, Ala., 167 miles; branches, 55 miles; total owned, 715 miles; leased, St. Louis & Cairo, 159 miles; total, 874 miles. In 1898-99 the company completed a branch of 39 miles to Port Alabama and Portersville under title of Mobile & Bay Shore Railway. Locomotives, 171; passenger cars, 105; freight cars, 5,189.

Regarding acquisition of control of this company by Southern Railway, see below. The road is operated independently under its own management.

Stock......Par $100..........................Authorized, $10,000,000......Issued, $5,320,600

Stock trust ctfs., 2 to 4 per cent., April and Oct.................................. $4,932,600

In addition to capital stock outstanding given above, $2,359,400 is issued, but is held in the company's treasury.

A dividend of 1 per cent. was paid February 28, 1898. This was the first dividend the company declared.

The dividends on the guaranteed stock certificates of the Southern Railway Co., representing the Mobile & Ohio stock deposited, are payable semi-annually in April and October.

Stock is transferred at the offices of the company, Mobile, Ala., and New York. Registrar, Farmers' Loan & Trust Co., New York.

FUNDED DEBT.

| | |
|---|---|
| 1st mort., 6 per cent., due Dec., 1927, June and Dec | $7,000,000 |
| 1st mort. extension, 6 per cent., due July, 1927, quar., Jan | 1,000,000 |
| Gen. mort., 4 per cent., due Sept., 1938, March and Sept | 9,472,000 |
| Montgomery Div., 1st mort., 5 per cent., due Feb., 1947, Feb. and Aug | 4,000,000 |
| Collateral trust mort., 4 per cent., due May, 1930, quar., Feb | 2,496,000 |
| St. Louis & Cairo, 1st mort., guar. 4 per cent., due Jan., 1931, Jan. and July | 4,000,000 |
| Mobile & Bay Shore, 1st mort., 5 per cent., due May, 1949, May and Nov | 200,000 |
| Car trusts, due 1904-19 | 1,985,000 |
| Total | $30,153,000 |

The 1st mortgage 6s were issued in 1879, when the securities of the company were readjusted under the agreement of October 1, 1876.

The 1st mortgage extension 6s were issued in 1888 to take up a previous issue of Cairo extension bonds.

The general mortgage bonds were issued in 1888 in part to exchange for four series of 7 per cent. income debentures, total issue of which originally amounted to $6,650,000. Of these latter, all but $7,100 have been absorbed by a sinking fund, or are on deposit with the Farmers' Loan & Trust Co. in trust to secure the original issue of $10,500,000 general mortgage bonds. Of these latter 1,028,000 have been cancelled by operation of the sinking fund, leaving outstanding at this date $9,472,000.

In 1899 the Montgomery Division, from Columbus, Miss., to Montgomery, Ala., 167.19 miles, with 21.33 miles of branches, was constructed and became a part of the Mobile & Ohio Railroad system. The construction of this division was provided for by an issue of $4,000,000 5 per cent. bonds, being a first lien upon the division itself, of which issue $500,000 was applied to the purchase of equipment. No stock was issued thereupon.

In 1886 the company leased the St. Louis & Cairo Railroad for 45 years at a minimum rental on a basis of a percentage of certain specified earnings of not less than $165,000 per annum, $160,000 of which rental is paid to the trustee of $4,000,000 of St. Louis & Cairo 1st mortgage 4 per cent. bonds to meet the interest thereon, and any surplus rental is paid to the St. Louis & Cairo Railroad Co. In 1900 the Mobile & Ohio Railroad Co. issued its collateral trust for $2,500,000 to be used for purposes of improvement and also for the absorption of the stock of the St. Louis & Cairo Railroad Co. on the basis of three for one. Total amount of said stock is $6,500,000, and of this, on December 31, 1902, $6,489,000 has become the property of the Mobile & Ohio Railroad Co., having been exchanged and deposited with the Guaranty Trust Co. of New York in trust for the security of said collateral trust issue.

The Mobile & Bay Shore Railway, an extension of the Mobile & Ohio Railroad, from Mobile to the Gulf of Mexico at Portersville, has since June 30, 1902, become an integral part of the Mobile & Ohio system, and its 1st mortgage 5s have been assumed by the Mobile & Ohio Railroad Co.

EARNINGS.

Year ending June 30.

| | Gross. | Net. | Charges. | Surplus. |
|---|---|---|---|---|
| 1892–93 | $3,358,470 | $1,099,281 | $1,044,381 | $54,900 |
| 1893–94 | 3,253,691 | 1,216,972 | 1,037,323 | 179,649 |
| 1894–95 | 3,269,989 | 1,115,502 | 1,034,353 | 81,149 |
| 1895–96 | 3,619,071 | 1,293,869 | 1,059,632 | 234,237 |
| 1896–97 | 3,867,858 | 1,283,895 | 1,060,126 | 223,769 |
| 1897–98 | 4,207,319 | 1,300,745 | 1,074,880 | 225,865 |
| 1898–99 | 4,531,153 | 1,451,630 | 1,144,527 | 307,103 |
| 1899–00 | 5,996,731 | 1,756,273 | 1,418,645 | 337,629 |
| 1900–01 | 6,139,912 | 1,922,012 | 1,555,309 | 366,702 |
| 1901–02 | 6,509,488 | 2,130,667 | 1,589,107 | 541,560 |

There was expended for additions to property and new equipment (not included in operating expenses) in 1890-91, $451,980; in 1891-92, $218,070; in 1892-93, $210,901; in 1893-94, $164,397; in 1894-95, $143,645; in 1896-97, $204,450; in 1897-98, $180,697; in 1898-99, $271,748; in 1899-1900, $314,990; in 1900-01, $389,416, and in 1901-02, $417,510.

Chairman, William Butler Duncan; President, Samuel Spencer, New York; 1st Vice-President, A. B. Andrews, Raleigh, N. C.; 2d Vice-President, William W. Finley, Washington, D. C.; Treasurer and Secretary, Henry Tacon, Mobile, Ala.; Assistant Secretary, A. W. Mackintosh, New York.

Directors—William Butler Duncan, Alexander H. Stevens, C. Sidney Shepard, Adrian Iselin, Jr., W. Emlen Roosevelt, Thomas E. Jevons, E. L. Russell, C. C. Cuyler, James H. Masson, Samuel Spencer, A. B. Andrews, William W. Finley, A. W. Mackintosh.

Main office, Mobile, Ala.; New York office, 80 Broadway. Annual meeting, third Wednesday in February.

## MOBILE, JACKSON & KANSAS CITY RAILROAD CO.

A corporation created under the laws of Alabama and Mississippi. Road owned, Mobile to Hattiesburg, Miss., 70 miles; extension projected to Decatur, Miss. In 1902 the Gulf & Chicago Railway (narrow gauge), Pontotoc, Miss., to Middleton, Tenn., 62 miles, was purchased. Locomotives, 9; passenger cars, 12; freight cars, 131.

Stock......Par $100..........................Authorized, $4,000,000......Issued, $1,918,000

Transfer Agent, Colonial Trust Co., New York.

FUNDED DEBT.

1st mort., 5 per cent., due June, 1946, June and Dec.................................$1,918,000

The 1st mortgage, Central Trust Co., New York, trustee, is for $4,000,000. Bonds can be issued at the rate of $20,000 per mile of road.

EARNINGS.

| Year ending June 30. | Gross. | Net. |
|---|---|---|
| 1898–99 | $53,489 | $26,810 |
| 1899–00 | 114,363 | 56,990 |
| 1900–01 | 140,729 | 76,279 |
| 1901–02 | 167,229 | 79,495 |

President, F. B. Merrill; Vice-President, William H. McIntosh; Secretary and Treasurer, P. C. Butler, Mobile, Ala.

Directors—F. B. Merrill, Joseph C. Rich, William H. McIntosh, J. W. Whiting, H. H. Lane, J. L. Rapier, E. O. Zadek, Mobile, Ala.; Alexander McDonald, Cincinnati; W. D. Stratton, T. L. Chadbourne, Jr., W. A. Stanton, New York.

Main office, Mobile, Ala. Annual meeting, in December, at Mobile, Ala.

## MORGAN'S LOUISIANA & TEXAS RAILROAD & STEAMSHIP CO.

(Leased to Southern Pacific Co.)

Road owned, New Orleans to Cheneyville, La., 205 miles; branches, 95 miles; trackage, Cheneyville to Alexandria, La., 24 miles; total operated, 324 miles. Locomotives, 51; passenger cars, 53; freight cars, 2,618. Also, 8 iron steamships, with ferryboats, tugs, warehouses, etc., the steamship lines extending from New York to New Orleans and Galveston and from New Orleans to Havana and Gulf of Mexico ports.

Stock......Par $100........................Authorized, $15,000,000......Issued, $15,000,000

FUNDED DEBT.

| | |
|---|---|
| 1st mort., 7 per cent., due April, 1918, April and Oct. | $5,000,000 |
| 1st mort., Alexandria extension, 6 per cent., due July, 1920, Jan. and July | 1,494,000 |
| Gen. mort., 5 per cent., due July, 1913, Jan. and July | 1,000,000 |
| Total | $7,494,000 |

In February, 1883, the Southern Pacific purchased entire stock of this company at 150. In 1891 capital stock was increased from $5,000,000 to $15,000,000.

EARNINGS.

| Year ending June 30. | Gross. | Net. |
|---|---|---|
| 1896-97 | $5,490,137 | $1,754,610 |
| 1897-98 | 5,667,419 | 1,738,850 |
| 1898-99 | 6,676,690 | 2,608,200 |
| 1899-00 | 7,031,114 | 2,202,767 |
| 1900-01 | 8,013,138 | 3,017,738 |
| 1901-02 | 7,191,620 | 3,007,481 |

Earnings include receipts from steamships. In 1898-99 the surplus over charges was $1,736,430 in 1899-00, $1,024,846; in 1900-01, $1,038,425, and in 1901-02, $1,897,285.

President, Edward H. Harriman; Treasurer and Secretary, J. B. Richardson, New Orleans.

Main office, New Orleans. Annual meeting, first Monday in April. Books close twenty days previous.

## MORRIS & ESSEX RAILROAD CO.

(Leased to Delaware, Lackawanna & Western.)

Road owned, Hoboken, N. J., to Phillipsburg, 85 miles; branches owned and leased, 72 miles; total, 157 miles.

This road is leased in perpetuity to the Delaware, Lackawanna & Western Co., the latter guaranteeing principal and interest of the bonds and 7 per cent. on the stock, to be increased to 8 per cent. should surplus amount to over 10 per cent. on stock in any year.

Stock.......Par $50........................Authorized, $15,000,000......Issued, $15,000,000

Transfer agency, 26 Exchange place, New York.

Dividends under the lease of 3½ per cent. semi-annually are paid regularly in January (1) and July.

FUNDED DEBT.

| | |
|---|---|
| 1st mort., 7 per cent., due May, 1914, May and Nov. | $5,000,000 |
| Special real estate mort., 4½ per cent., due 1912 | 1,800,000 |
| Consolidated mort., 7 per cent., due June, 1915, June and Dec. | 11,677,000 |
| 1st refunding gold mort., 3½ per cent., due Dec., 2000, June and Dec. | 9,600,000 |
| Total | $28,077,000 |

There is also $221,000 4 per cent. guaranteed stock of the Morris & Essex extension.

The consolidated mortgage is for $25,000,000 and is to include all other debts. On January 1, 1900, $281,000 convertible 7 per cent. bonds matured and were paid off. The refunding mortgage was authorized in 1900 to retire the outstanding bonds at maturity and provide for improvements.

President, William H. Truesdale; Secretary, A. D. Chambers; Treasurer, Fred F. Chambers, New York.

Directors—Samuel Sloan, William H. Truesdale, Fred F. Chambers, E. R. Holden, M. Taylor Pyne, H. A. C. Taylor, Eugene Higgins, James Stillman, Frederic P. Olcott, Richard A. McCurdy, W. F. Halstead, Frederic Cromwell.

Main office, 26 Exchange place, New York.

## MUSCATINE NORTH & SOUTH RAILROAD CO.

Road owned, Muscatine, Ia., to Elrick, Ia., 29 miles. The road connects at Elrick with the Iowa Central Railroad Co.; this company having a traffic contract with the latter.

Stock......Par $100..............................Authorized, $450,000......Issued, $450,000

FUNDED DEBT.

1st mort., 5 per cent., due Jan., 1929, Jan. and July.............................. $398,000

The authorized amount of the 1st mortgage is $450,000. Trustee, New York Security & Trust Co., New York.

President, Walter M. Gorham, Philadelphia; Vice-President, H. F. Balch, Minneapolis; Secretary and Treasurer, Henry Jayne, Muscatine, Ia.

Directors—H. F. Balch, M. J. Peppard, J. A. Nelson, Minneapolis; Walter M. Gorham, Philadelphia; Henry Jayne, P. M. Musser, Muscatine, Ia.; George A. Seevers, Oskaloosa, Ia.

Main office, Muscatine, Ia.

## NASHUA & LOWELL RAILROAD CO.

(Leased to Boston & Lowell Railroad.)

Road owned, Lowell, Mass., to Nashua, N. H., 15 miles. The company leased the Stony Brook, the Wilton and Peterboro roads, but transferred those leases to the Boston & Lowell.

The road is leased to the Boston & Lowell for 99 years from October 1, 1880, at $65,000 a year, lessee assuming bonds and interest thereon. In 1887 lease was transferred to Boston & Maine, and annual rental was raised to $73,000, or 9 per cent. on the stock, and $1,000 per annum for organization expenses.

Stock......Par $100...............................Authorized, $800,000......Issued, $800,000

Stock is transferred by the treasurer of the company, Boston.

Dividends are paid May (1) and November at the rate of 4½ per cent. for each half year.

The company has no funded or other indebtedness.

President, David P. Kimball; Treasurer, John Brooks; Secretary, Alfred S. Hall, Boston.

Main office, 50 State street, Boston. Annual meeting, last Wednesday in May, at Nashua, N. H.

## NASHVILLE, CHATTANOOGA & ST. LOUIS RAILWAY

Road owned, Hickman, Ky., to Chattanooga, Tenn., 320 miles; branches, 484 miles; total owned, 804 miles; leased, Western & Atlantic, Atlanta, Ga., to Chattanooga, Tenn., 137 miles; Paducah & Memphis Division, 254 miles; total leased, 391 miles; total operated, 1,195 miles.

In 1896 the Paducah, Tennessee & Alabama and Tennessee Midland, controlled by Louisville & Nashville, were leased to this company and form the Paducah & Memphis Division. The company has also extensions in progress. Locomotives, 198; passenger cars, 189; freight cars, 6,589.

The Louisville & Nashville Co. owns a majority of the stock.

Stock......Par $100.........................Authorized, $10,000,000......Issued, $10,000,000

Transfer agency, office Louisville & Nashville Railway, 120 Broadway, New York.

For dividends see table of earnings below. Dividends were paid quarterly, February. The February, 1899, dividend was passed in order to pay for additional equipment and reduce the company's floating debt. No dividends have since been paid.

In 1891 $3,331,387 of new stock was sold to stockholders at 50 and proceeds used for construction of extensions.

FUNDED DEBT.

| | |
|---|---|
| 1st mort., 7 per cent., due July, 1913, Jan. and July | $6,300,000 |
| 1st consol. mort., 5 per cent., due April, 1928, April and Oct | 7,432,000 |
| Fayetteville & McM. Branch 1st mort., 6 per cent., due Jan., 1917, Jan. and July | 750,000 |
| Lebanon Branch, 6 per cent., due Jan., 1917, Jan. and July | 300,000 |
| Jasper Branch 1st mort., 8 per cent., due Jan., 1906, Jan. and July | 90,000 |
| Jasper Branch extension, 6 per cent., due Jan., 1923, Jan. and July | 371,000 |
| 1st mort., Centreville Branch, 6 per cent., due Jan., 1923, Jan. and July | 376,000 |
| 2d mort., Duck River Valley Branch, 6 per cent., due Jan., 1909, May and Nov | 22,000 |
| Tracy City Branch bonds, 6 per cent., due Jan., 1903 to 1917, Jan. and July | 380,000 |
| Total | $16,021,000 |

The Western & Atlantic is leased by this company from the State of Georgia for 29 years from December, 1890.

ST. LOUIS
EAST ST. LOUIS
BELLEVILLE
BISMARCK
MO.
ILL.
INDIANA
KENTUCKY
EVANSVILLE
HENDERSON
OWENSBORO
NEW ALBANY
PADUCAH
CAIRO
COLUMBUS
HICKMAN
UNION CY.
MARTIN
McKENZIE
PARIS
HOLLOW ROCK JC.
HOLLOW ROCK
CLARKSVILLE
HOPKINS V.
DICKSON
NASHVILLE
W. NASHVILLE
COLUMBIA
CENTREVILLE
PERRYVILLE
LEXINGTON
JACKSON
SOMERVILLE
MEMPHIS
ALLENS CREEK
FLORENCE
DECATUR
HOLLY SPRS.
ABERDEEN
Tennessee
Mississippi
NASHVILLE, CHATTANOOGA & ST. LOUIS
AGRICULTURE
MOUNTAIN ROUTE

MAP OF THE
NASHVILLE, CHATTANOOGA
& ST. LOUIS RAILWAY
... AND CONNECTIONS ..
Georgetown
Hillsboro
Prestonburg
Pikeville
Booneville
Manchester
Hyden
Hazard
Hindman
Whitesburg
Corbin
Brafford Store
Grundy
Clintwood
Pocahon
Pearyville
Big Stone Gap
Cumberland Gap
Campbellsville
Greensburg
Glasgow
Columbia
Burkesville
Scottsville
Albany
Tateville
Greenwood
Red Boiling Sprs.
Lafayette
Celina
Middlesboro
Jellico
Newcomb
Elk Valley
Caryville
Oakdale
Rockwood
Crossville
Knoxville
Rockford
Maryville
Newport
Rogersville
Jonesboro
Hot Springs
Marshall
Burnsville
Waynesville
Asheville
Dillsboro
Sweet Water
Madisonville
Athens
Tellico Plains
White Cliff Sprs.
Chattanooga
Cleveland
Dalton
Blue Ridge
Ellijay
Talking Rock
Jasper
Kingston
Canton
Dahlonega
Gainesville
Clarksville
Cornelia
Franklin
Walhalla
Easley
Statesville
Murfreesboro
Spencer
Sewanee

Opposition having been made by minority stockholders to the lease of the Paducah, Tennessee & Alabama Railroad and the Tennessee Midland Railway, 253 miles, those properties, which now constitute the Paducah & Memphis Division of the company, were operated separately until July 1, 1900, from which time their earnings are included in those of this company.

The consolidated mortgage is for $20,000,000 at the rate of $20,000 per mile, sufficient of the issue being reserved to retire the other classes of bonds at maturity.

EARNINGS.

Year ending June 30.

| | Div. Paid. | Gross. | Net. | Charges. | Surplus. |
|---|---|---|---|---|---|
| 1892-93 (810 miles)......... | 5 | $5,131,779 | $1,992,374 | $1,483,697 | $508,676 |
| 1893-94 (884 " )......... | 2½ | 4,521,661 | 1,850,482 | 1,468,120 | 382,361 |
| 1894-95 (902 " )......... | 4 | 4,608,501 | 1,882,141 | 1,519,295 | 362,846 |
| 1895-96 (905 " )......... | 4 | 5,074,625 | 1,910,275 | 1,498,481 | 411,793 |
| 1896-97 (904 " )......... | 4 | 5,116,118 | 1,911,446 | 1,508,431 | 403,015 |
| 1897-98 (905 " )......... | 4 | 5,646,548 | 1,982,723 | 1,522,198 | 460,524 |
| 1898-99 (935 " )......... | 1 | 6,081,766 | 2,012,541 | 1,658,005 | 354,535 |
| 1899-00 ( " " )......... | .. | 6,487,317 | 2,272,911 | 1,747,003 | 525,907 |
| 1900-01 (1,195 " )......... | .. | 7,620,127 | 2,531,255 | 1,911,876 | 619,379 |
| 1901-02 ( " " )......... | .. | 7,992,530 | 2,388,546 | 1,863,835 | 524,711 |

The net in 1899 includes $30,482 income from investments; in 1900, $26,177 from the same source; in 1901, $22,253, and in 1901-02, $18,130.

In 1893-94 $100,000 was received from bond sales and $347,682 expended on improvements, etc. In 1894-95 $182,000 consolidated mortgage bonds were sold and in 1895-96 $100,000. In 1896-97 $500,000 more were issued to acquire control of Rome Railroad and other lines. In 1897-98 $619,000 consolidated mortgage bonds were issued to retire old bonds and improve Middle Tennessee & Alabama Railroad.

President, J. W. Thomas; General Manager, J. W. Thomas, Jr.; Secretary and Treasurer, J. H. Ambrose, Nashville.

Directors—J. W. Thomas, A. H. Robinson, J. Hill Eakin, E. C. Lewis, W. R. Cole, E. B. Wesley, E. W. Thompson, J. B. Richardson, J. H. Fall, Nashville; J. E. Washington, Cedar Hill, Tenn.; N. C. Collier, Murfreesboro, Tenn.; J. G. Aydelott, Tullahoma, Tenn.; J. C. Atwater, T. W. Evans, New York; Milton H. Smith, Louisville.

Main office, 1000 Broad street, Nashville. Annual meeting, Wednesday after the second Tuesday in September. Books close ninety days previous.

## NATIONAL RAILROAD CO. OF MEXICO

A corporation formed under the laws of Utah February 24, 1902, to take over the property of the Mexican National Railroad Co., which was reorganized without foreclosure as per plan given in detail below.

Road owned, Nuevo Laredo to City of Mexico, 839 miles; branches, 283 miles; Texas-Mexican Railroad, Laredo to Corpus Christi, and branches, 163 miles; total, 1,285 miles. The gauge of this system was originally 3 feet. Under the reorganization provision was made for changing the main line and principal branches to standard gauge, and this work was in progress during 1902. Locomotives, 131; passenger cars, 124; freight cars, 2,730.

In 1901 the company acquired control of the Mexican International Railroad, 830 miles.

Stock prior to readjustment.......Par $100.....Authorized, $33,350,000.....Issued, $33,350,000

| | | | | |
|---|---|---|---|---|
| Stock under readjustment...... | Par $100..Auth'd | com., $33,350,000<br>pref., 32,000,000 | Issued com., $33,350,000<br>pref., 32,000,000 | $65,350,000 |

The new preferred stock is 4 per cent., non-cumulative.

The voting trust certificates for the new stock are transferred at the office of the company, No. 1 Nassau street, New York.

FUNDED DEBT (PRIOR TO READJUSTMENT).

| | |
|---|---|
| 1st mort., 6 per cent., due June, 1927, June and Dec.............................. | $10,779,000 |
| 2d mort. A, cumulative, 6 per cent., due July, 1917, March and Sept................ | 12,165,000 |
| 2d mort. B, non-cumulative, 6 per cent., due July, 1917, annually, April (1)......... | 12,165,000 |
| 3d mort., non-cumulative, income debentures, due July, 1937, 6 per cent............ | 7,040,000 |
| Total .............................................................. | $42,149,000 |

FUNDED DEBT (UNDER READJUSTMENT).

| | |
|---|---|
| Prior lien mort., 4½ per cent., gold, due 1926, Jan. and July....................... | $20,000,000 |
| 1st cons. mort., 4 per cent., gold, due 1951, April and Oct............................ | 22,000,000 |
| Total.............................................................. | $42,000,000 |

The original company had a subsidy from Mexican Government of $7,000 per kilometer. The total subsidy earned amounted to about $6,000,000 (Mexican currency). Annual payments were originally 6 per cent. of the government customs, but this was reduced in 1893 to 2 per cent., the remaining 4 per cent. being deferred. In 1895 the company received, in full settlement for the subsidy, $4,544,500 of Mexican government 5 per cent. internal bonds, which were deposited with trustee of the 1st mortgage.

The interest due April 1, 1884, and subsequentl was passed. Property was foreclosed and reorganized May, 1887. The stock was held in trust by the Farmers' Loan & Trust Co., New York, until interest had been paid for two consecutive years on the 1st and 2d mortgages, the old stock being represented by the trustee's certificates of a beneficiary interest. Interest was regularly paid on the old 1st mortgage. In March, 1893, 2 per cent. was paid on incomes A and 1 per cent. in April, 1895; in April, 1896, 1½ per cent. was paid; in March, 1897, 3 per cent.; in March, 1898, 3½ per cent.; in April, 1899, 3½ per cent.; in April, 1900, 4½ per cent., and in April, 1901, 4½ per cent.

In 1896 proposition was submitted by certain foreign holders of the old bonds to the holders of A and B incomes to consolidate control of company by turning those classes of securities over to a corporation, the Mexican National Railway Co., Limited, which would issue its own securities in lieu thereof. In July the plan was declared to be operative, and the corporation in question was formed in London. It has received deposits of all but some $3,000,000 of the A and B incomes. In April, 1898 and 1899, that company paid on the A certificates £2 15s. 8d. per cent.; in 1900 paid £3 11s. 8d. per cent., and in 1901 £3 11s. 10d. per cent.

In 1901 control of the Mexican National Railroad Co. was acquired by a syndicate represented by Speyer & Co. of New York, the syndicate taking a large amount of the securities, including the holdings of the Mexican National Construction Co. In October, 1901, Speyer & Co. and Kuhn, Loeb & Co., New York, and Speyer Brothers, London, issued a plan for the financial readjustment of the company. The plan provided for the retirement of the old securities and the providing of sufficient funds to change the line from narrow to standard gauge and furnish adequate equipment, as well as to build needed extensions.

Under the plan the new securities authorized consist of $33,350,000 common stock; $32,000,000,000 4 per cent. non-cumulative preferred stock; $23,000,000 prior lien 4½ per cent. bonds, and $60,000,000 1st consolidated 4 per cent. bonds.

The terms of exchange of old for new securities were as follows:

| Old Stock and Bonds. | Paid. | Received for each $1,000. Prior Lien Bonds. | Cons. Mort. Bonds. | Preferred Stock. | Common Stock. |
|---|---|---|---|---|---|
| 1st mort. 6s | $20.00 | $1,000 | ..... | .... | ..... |
| 2d mort., A | 21.88 | ... | $937.50 | $625 | ..... |
| 2d mort., B | .... | .... | ..... | 900 | ..... |
| 3d mort., income | .... | .... | ..... | 300 | ..... |
| Old stock, each $100 | ... | .... | ..... | .... | $100 |

The plan provided that the new stock should be held in a voting trust for five years, or until 4 per cent. cash dividends had been paid on the new preferred for two successive years. The authorized issue of prior lien 4½ per cent. bonds may be increased to retire at par the Mexican International prior lien bonds, and the 1st consolidated 4 per cent. issue may also be increased to retire at par the Mexican International 1st consols. A syndicate underwrote the plan and provided for cash requirements, the syndicate taking $9,221,000 prior lien bonds, $3,595,000 of the new consols and $1,000,000 of new preferred stock.

In December, 1901, the plan was declared operative, a very large proportion of the old security holders having assented to its provisions. Fixed charges under the plan are about $1,500,000.

EARNINGS.

| | Mexican Currency Gross. | Net. | Extraordinary Expenses. | U. S. Currency not Applicable to Interest. |
|---|---|---|---|---|
| 1892 | $4,756,029 | $1,700,613 | $149,081 | $979,270 |
| 1893 | 4,224,804 | 1,638,438 | 151,612 | 739,353 |
| 1894 | 4,329,079 | 1,891,963 | 93,451 | 720,737 |
| 1895 | 4,513,206 | 2,071,409 | 121,535 | 851,958 |
| 1896 | 5,299,026 | 2,525,958 | 156,586 | 1,090,377 |
| 1897 | 6,080,663 | 2,986,238 | 143,070 | 1,099,083 |
| 1898 | 6,330,920 | 2,991,789 | 161,483 | 1,068,679 |
| 1899 | 7,087,675 | 3,410,402 | 259,461 | 1,212,814 |
| 1900 | 7,866,699 | 3,763,622 | 198,669 | 1,208,635 |
| 1901 | 7,724,526 | 2,923,193 | 167,094 | 1,149,594 |

President, William G. Raoul, New York; 2d Vice-President and General Manager, E. N. Brown, City of Mexico; Treasurer, J. M. Fraser; Secretary and Assistant Treasurer, William Burckel, New York.

Directors—William G. Raoul, Edward H. Harriman, George J. Gould, William B. Leeds, L. F. Loree, Gordon Macdonald, Felix M. Warburg, F. B. Drake, Henry W. Taft, Charles H. Tweed, E. N. Brown, Emilio Velasco, William Landa y Escandon, Jose de Landa y Eacandon, Carl Smith.

Main office, 1 Nassau street, New York. Annual meeting, first Monday in April.

## NEVADA-CALIFORNIA-OREGON RAILWAY

Road owned, Reno, Nev., to Madeline, Cal., 145 miles. An extension to Lake View, Ore., is contemplated. Locomotives, 6; passenger cars, 8; freight cars, 70.

Stock.....Par $100.....Authorized { com., $1,450,000 / pref., 750,000 } Issued { com., $1,450,000 / pref., 750,000 } $2,200,000

The preferred stock is 5 per cent., non-cumulative. Transfer Agents, Moran Brothers, 68 William street, New York.

FUNDED DEBT.

1st mort., 5 per cent., due May, 1919, May and Nov.................................. $450,000

Trustee of the mortgage, Union Trust Co., New York. Interest is paid at the office of Moran Brothers, New York.

This road was originally a private enterprise owned by Moran Brothers of New York. In 1888 the present company was formed and took over the property.

The 1st mortgage is $1,500,000, authorized. In 1901 the old 6 per cent. bonds were exchanged for new 5s.

EARNINGS.—Year ending June 30.

| | Gross. | Net. |
|---|---|---|
| 1900-01 | $152,636 | $55,058 |
| 1901-02 | 159,393 | 55,814 |

President, D. Comyn Moran, New York; Vice-President and General Manager, T. F. Dunaway, Reno, Nev.; Treasurer, Amedee D. Moran, New York; Secretary and Auditor, F. R. Lewis, Reno, Nev.

Directors—D. Comyn Moran, Amedee D. Moran, New York; T. F. Dunaway, Robert L. Fulton, A. H. Manning, Reno, Nev.

Main office, Reno, Nev.; New York office, 68 William street. Annual meeting, Monday preceding the second Tuesday in September, at Reno, Nev.

## NEWBURGH, DUTCHESS & CONNECTICUT RAILROAD CO.

A corporation formed under the laws of New York, January 8, 1877. The road was originally the Dutchess & Columbia Railroad Co., which was foreclosed in 1877.

Road owned, Dutchess Junction, N. Y., to Millerton, N. Y., 58 miles. Locomotives, 9; passenger cars, 12; freight cars, 212.

Stock.....Par $50.......Authorized { com., $500,000 / pref., 600,000 } Issued { com., $500,000 / pref., 600,000 } $1,100,000

Stock is transferred at the office of the secretary, Matteawan, N. Y.

FUNDED DEBT.

| | |
|---|---|
| Collateral trust bonds, 5 per cent., due 1921, May and Nov. | $226,000 |
| Income bonds, 6 per cent., if earned, due 1977 | 1,164,500 |
| Total | $1,390,500 |

EARNINGS.—Year ending June 30.

| | Gross. | Net. | Charges. | Surplus. |
|---|---|---|---|---|
| 1901-02 | $172,016 | $41,361 | $19,794 | $21,567 |

President, John Crosby Brown, New York; Vice-President and General Manager, G. Hunter Brown; Secretary, William A. Wells; Treasurer, H. H. Reed, Matteawan, N. Y.

Directors—John Crosby Brown, William Lummis, James Brown Potter, Clarence Cary, R. Somers Hayes, William C. Le Gendre, W. J. Duane, Thatcher M. Brown, New York; W. B. Lord, Morristown, N. J.; G. Hunter Brown, Garrisons, N.Y.; James Crosby Brown, Philadelphia; S. K. Phillips, Matteawan, N. Y.; William A. Wells, Moore's Mills, N. Y.

Main office, Matteawan, N.Y. Annual meeting, last Thursday in October, at Matteawan, N.Y.

## THE NEW ENGLAND RAILROAD CO.

(Leased to the New York, New Haven & Hartford Railroad Co.)

Road owned, Boston to Hopewell Junction and Fishkill, N. Y., 214 miles; Providence, R. I., to Willimantic, Conn., 58 miles; branches, 88 miles; total owned, 359 miles; leased, Norwich

& Worcester, 72 miles; other branches leased, 75 miles; trackage, 29 miles; total, 535 miles. Company controls, through the lease of Norwich & Worcester Railroad, the Norwich & New York Transportation Co., operating steamer line between Norwich and New London, Conn., and New York.

The company is a reorganization in 1895 of the New York & New England Railroad Co. In the same year it was announced that the New York, New Haven & Hartford had purchased a controlling interest in the stock of the new company and $5,000,000 of the new consolidated mortgage bonds. In February, 1898, it was proposed for minority holders of this company to exchange 2 shares of preferred for 1 share of New Haven and 5 of common stock for 1 share of New Haven stock. This was generally accepted, and on June 30, 1900, only $53,500 common and $74,200 preferred stock were outstanding not held by the New York, New Haven & Hartford. On May 10, 1898, the road was leased to the New York, New Haven & Hartford for 99 years from July 1, 1898.

In 1896 company sold part of its terminal lands at Boston to the Boston Terminal Co. for the new Union Station in that city for $1,923,500. This company uses the South Terminal Station as a passenger terminal and owns one-fifth of its stock.

Stock...Par $100....Authorized { com., $20,000,000; pref., 5,000,000 } Issued { com., $20,000,000; pref., 5,000,000 } $25,000,000

Preferred stock not exchanged receives 3 per cent. annually under the lease.

Stock is transferred at the company's office, South Terminal Station, Boston.

FUNDED DEBT.

| | |
|---|---|
| 1st mort., N. Y. & N. E., 7 per cent., due Jan., 1905, Jan. and July | $6,000,000 |
| " " " 6 per cent., due Jan., 1905, Jan. and July | 4,000,000 |
| Cons. mort., N. E. R.R., 5 per cent., due July, 1945, Jan. and July | 5,000,000 |
| N. Y. & N. E. Boston Term., 1st mort., 4 per cent., due April, 1939, April and Oct. | 1,500,000 |
| Total | $16,500,000 |

The company pays rental of 8 per cent. per annum on the $2,769,200 of Norwich & Worcester stock, and guarantees interest in that road's bonds, 4 per cent., due 1927, for $955,000. The Norwich & Worcester was leased in 1869. Lease modified in December, 1896, and the maturing 6 per cent. bonds for $400,000, together with its floating debt, funded into Norwich & Worcester 4 per cent. bonds.

This road was placed in the hands of a Receiver December 31, 1883. On December 31, 1885, the receivership was closed and the property returned to the stockholders.

In 1893 the company became embarrassed, and Receivers were appointed in January, 1894. It was reorganized in 1895, under a plan the details of which are given in the MANUAL for 1900.

Earnings are included in those of the lessee. The earnings for 1890 to 1897–98, inclusive, were given in the MANUAL for 1902.

President, John M. Hall, New Haven, Conn.; Vice-President, E. D. Robbins, Hartford, Conn.; Secretary, J. W. Perkins; Treasurer, George B. Phippen, Boston.

Main office, Hartford, Conn. Annual meeting, fourth Thursday in October.

## NEW LONDON NORTHERN RAILROAD CO.

(Leased to Central Vermont Railway Co.)

Road owned, New London, Conn., to Brattleboro, Vt., 121 miles; leased, Brattleboro to South Londonderry, Vt., 37 miles; total, 158 miles.

Stock......Par $100..........................Authorized, $1,500,000......Issued, $1,500,000

Stock is transferred at the company's office, New London.

Under the lease 9 per cent. dividends are paid in quarterly payments of 2¼ per cent., in January (2), April, July and October.

FUNDED DEBT.

| | |
|---|---|
| Cons. mort., 5 per cent., due July, 1910, Jan. and July | $812,000 |
| " " 4 per cent., due July, 1910, Jan. and July | 688,000 |
| Total | $1,500,000 |

This road was leased for 99 years from December, 1891, to Consolidated of Vermont for $210,000 per year. Lease was assigned to Central Vermont Railroad and has passed to the Central Vermont Railway Co. Operations are included in those of lessor company.

President and Treasurer, Robert Coit; Secretary, J. A. Southard, New London, Conn.

Main office, New London, Conn. Annual meeting, first Wednesday in February.

## NEW MEXICO RAILWAY & COAL CO.

A corporation formed under the laws of New Jersey May 5, 1897. The company constructed and owns the El Paso & Northeastern Railway, El Paso, Tex., to El Capitan, N. M., 164 miles, and the Alamogordo & Sacramento Mountain Railway, Alamogordo, N. M., to Toboggan, 36 miles; total mileage owned, 200 miles. The El Paso & Rock Island Railway Co., from Carrizosa, N. M., to Santa Rosa, 131 miles, is controlled. This line, which was completed in 1902,, connects with the extension of the Chicago, Rock Island & Pacific, built southwesterly from Liberal, Kan. The Dawson Railway & Coal Company was built in the interest of this company, from Liberty, N. M., to Dawson, 135 miles. Locomotives, 12; passenger cars, 14; freight cars, 328.

The company controls the New Mexico Fuel Co., which owns 3,500 acres of coal lands and operates mines thereon. It has a close traffic contract with the Chicago, Rock Island & Pacific.

Stock....Par $100....Authorized { com., $3,000,000 / pref., 1,000,000 } Issued { com., $3,000,000 / pref., 1,000,000 } $4,000,000

The preferred stock is 5 per cent., non-cumulative.

Stock is transferred at the company's office. Registrar, New York Security & Trust Co.

FUNDED DEBT.

| | |
|---|---|
| 1st cons. mort., 5 per cent., due Oct., 1951, April and Oct. | $1,500,000 |
| Collateral trust mort., gold, 5 per cent., due Oct., 1947, April and Oct. | 3,000,000 |
| Alamogordo & Sac. Mt., 1st mort. guar. 5 per cent., due April, 1928, April and Oct. | 322,000 |
| El Paso & Rock Island, 1st mort. guar. 5 per cent., due Jan., 1951, Jan. and July | 2,500,000 |
| Dawson Ry. & Coal, col. trust 5 per cent. guar., due July, 1951, Jan. and July | 3,000,000 |
| Total | $10,322,000 |

The collateral trust 5 per cent. mortgage, New York Security & Trust Co., trustee, is for $3,000,000, and is secured by the deposit of all the stocks and bonds of the constituent companies. The New Mexico Railway & Coal Co. guarantees the Alamogordo & Sacramento Mountain 1st 5s, principal and interest.

The El Paso & Rock Island 5 per cent. 1st mortgage bond issue is guaranteed by this company. Amount authorized, $2,500,000. The company also guarantees principal and interest of the Dawson Railway & Coal Co.

President, C. D. Simpson, Scranton, Pa.; Vice-President, G. C. W. Lowrey, New York; 2d Vice-President and General Manager, Charles B. Eddy, El Paso, Tex.; Treasurer, H. P. Simpson, Scranton, Pa.; Secretary, B. S. Harmon, New York.

Directors—C. D. Simpson, G. C. W. Lowrey, Charles B. Eddy, H. P. Simpson, B. S. Harmon, J. W. Hollenback, H. M. Boies, L. A. Watres, T. H. Watkins, H. H. Brady, Jr., Kenneth K. McLaren, W. L. Watson, F. H. Ross, J. Howard Ford.

Main office, 68 William street, New York. Annual meeting, second Tuesday in February.

---

## NEW ORLEANS & NORTHEASTERN RAILROAD CO.

Road owned, New Orleans, La., to Meridian, Miss., 196 miles. Locomotives, 45; passenger cars, 37; freight cars 1,965.

Stock......Par $100..........................Authorized, $6,000,000......Issued, $6,000,000

Transfer Agent, Farmers' Loan & Trust Co., New York.

FUNDED DEBT.

| | |
|---|---|
| Prior lien, 6 per cent., due Nov., 1915, April and Oct. | $1,320,000 |
| 1st mort., 6 per cent., due Jan., 1911, Jan. and July | 100,000 |
| General mort., 4½ per cent., due Jan., 1952, Jan. and July | 4,900,000 |
| Income mort., 4½ per cent., non-cum., due July, 1952, Dec. | 1,500,000 |
| Total | $7,820,000 |

This company is controlled by the Alabama, New Orleans, Texas & Pacific Junction Railways Co., Limited.

In 1902 the company readjusted its bonded debt, issuing the general mortgage 4½ per cent. bonds to retire all but $100,000 of the old 6 per cent. 1st mortgage bonds, of which $5,000,000 were outstanding. This reduced the annual fixed charges $98,000. The general mortgage is for $8,000,000, $1,800,000 being reserved for improvements. The income bonds issued at the same time were used to redeem old unpaid coupons and floating debt and acquire additional terminals at New Orleans.

EARNINGS.

Year ending June 30.

| | Gross. | Net. | Interest. | Deficit. |
|---|---|---|---|---|
| 1892–93 | $1,419,963 | $229,004 | $366,871 | $137,867 |
| 1893–94 | 1,293,070 | 228,981 | 373,579 | 144,598 |
| 1894–95 | 1,228,760 | 240,223 | 378,185 | 137,962 |
| 1895–96 | 1,419,720 | 366,971 | 378,185 | 11,114 |
| 1896–97 | 1,313,254 | 298,428 | 377,964 | 79,536 |
| 1897–98 | 1,396,929 | 377,376 | 377,335 | Sur. 41 |
| 1898–99 | 1,545,686 | 399,590 | 388,414 | " 11,176 |
| 1899–00 | 1,856,200 | 519,615 | 380,204 | " 139,411 |
| 1900–01 | 1,929,812 | 475,883 | 385,336 | " 90,547 |
| 1901–02 | 2,030,262 | 535,495 | 342,450 | " 193,045 |

President, C. C. Harvey, New Orleans; Vice-President, Charles Schiff, London, England; Secretary and Treasurer, Henry W. Wenham; Auditor, Larz A. Jones, New Orleans.

Directors—Henry Abraham, C. C. Harvey, Alfred Slidell, B. F. Eshleman, Pearl Wight, J. S. Rainey, H. H. Hall, R. M. Walmsley, New Orleans; Charles Schiff, London, England.

Main office, New Orleans. Annual meeting, first Wednesday in November.

## NEWTON & NORTHWESTERN RAILROAD CO.

A corporation formed under the laws of Iowa in 1902. The company succeeded the Boone, Rockwell City & Northwestern Railway Co.

Road owned, Gowrie to Fraser, Ia., 21 miles. Line projected, Newton, Ia., to Rockwell City, Ia., 104 miles.

Stock......Par $100..........................Authorized, $2,500,000......Issued, $2,500,000

The company has a 1st mortgage, 5 per cent., due October, 1932, April and October. The authorized amount of the 1st mortgage is $2,500,000. Trustee, Old Colony Trust Co., Boston. Bonds are subject to call at 110 and interest.

President, Hamilton Browne; Secretary, William A. Kelley, Boone, Ia.;
Main office, Boone, Ia.

## NEW YORK & CANADA RAILROAD CO.

(Leased to Delaware & Hudson Co.)

Road owned, Whitehall to Rouse's Point, N. Y., 113 miles; branches, 38 miles; total, 151 miles. Equipment furnished by lessee. Road is operated as a division of the Delaware & Hudson Co.'s railroad system, branch lines aggregating 38 miles being included in its returns of earnings.

Stock......Par $100..........................Authorized, $4,000,000......Issued, $4,000,000

FUNDED DEBT.

| | |
|---|---|
| 1st mort., sterling, 6 per cent., due May, 1904, May and Nov. | $4,000,000 |
| Debentures, 4½ per cent., due May, 1904, May and Nov. | 1,000,000 |
| Total | $5,000,000 |

The property is leased to the Delaware & Hudson Co., which owns nearly all the stock and guarantees the bonds, principal and interest. In 1896 company created the 4½ per cent. debentures, which were delivered to Delaware & Hudson for advances.

EARNINGS.

Year ending June 30.

| | Gross. | Net. | Charges, etc. | Loss to Lessee. |
|---|---|---|---|---|
| 1892–93 | $938,936 | $188,271 | $312,729 | Def. $124,458 |
| 1893–94 | 805,327 | 164,604 | 309,867 | " 155,263 |
| 1894–95 | 847,747 | 185,446 | 269,402 | " 83,956 |
| 1895–96 | 915,965 | 274,613 | 274,134 | Sur. 482 |
| 1896–97 | 937,892 | 289,940 | 316,805 | Def. 26,855 |
| 1897–98 | 937,829 | 284,533 | 313,572 | " 29,039 |
| 1898–99 | 976,983 | 372,821 | 319,629 | " 53,192 |
| 1899–00 | 1,146,575 | 417,995 | 319,563 | Sur. 98,432 |
| 1900–01 | 1,183,132 | 458,388 | 317,747 | 140,641 |
| 1901–02 | 1,182,567 | 481,624 | 333,714 | 147,910 |

President, David Willcox; Secretary and Treasurer, Charles A. Walker, New York.
Main office, 21 Cortlandt street, New York. Annual meeting, third Tuesday in June. Books close thirty days before.

## NEW YORK & GREENWOOD LAKE RAILWAY CO.

(Leased to Erie Railroad Co.)

Road owned, New York & Greenwood Junction to Greenwood Lake, N. J., 41 miles; branches, 12 miles; total, 53 miles.

Stock......Par $50..............................Authorized, $100,000......Issued, $100,000

FUNDED DEBT.

Prior lien mort., 5 per cent., due May, 1946, May and Nov............................ $1,500,000

This road was formerly operated by the New York, Lake Erie & Western. In January, 1896, it was decided to readjust the finances of the company and lease it to the Erie Railroad Co. Old 1sts were converted into new prior lien bonds at 50 per cent. of face and old 2ds at 10 per cent. of face. Road was leased from May 1, 1896, to the Erie Railroad Co. at a rental equal to fixed charges, the Erie guaranteeing the prior lien bonds. A fund was also provided for necessary improvements and double tracking a portion of line.
President, (Vacancy); Treasurer, J. W. Platten; Secretary, J. A. Middleton, New York.
New York office, 21 Cortlandt street. Annual meeting, first Monday in May.

## NEW YORK & HARLEM RAILROAD CO.

(Leased to New York Central & Hudson River Railroad Co.)

Road owned, New York to Chatham Four Corners, N. Y., 127 miles; leased, use of Boston & Albany tracks, Chatham Four Corners to Albany, 24 miles. The company also owns 8½ miles of street railroad (Fourth Avenue line) in New York City, which is not included in lease but was leased July, 1896, to the Metropolitan Street Railway Co.

Stock....Par $50....Authorized { com., $8,656,050 / pref., 1,343,950 } Issued { com., $8,656,050 / pref., 1,343,950 } $10,000,000

Stock is transferred at the office of the company, Grand Central Station, New York. Registrar, Union Trust Co., New York.
The regular dividends, on both classes of stock, aggregating 14 per cent. per annum, are paid as follows: From New York Central lease 5 per cent. each in January and July. From Metropolitan Street Railway lease, 2 per cent. each in April and October.

FUNDED DEBT.

Refunding mort., 3½ per cent., due May, 2000, May and Nov...................... $12,000,000

On October 2, 1899, $2,500,000 was distributed to the stockholders from the company's surplus, making $12.50 per share.
The lease to the New York Central & Hudson River Railroad Co. is for 401 years from 1873, the rental being interest on the bonds and 8 per cent. on the stock. In connection with the refunding of the old 7 per cent. bonds into 3½ per cent. in 1900, it was agreed that the lease rental should be increased 2 per cent., making the dividends paid the New York & Harlem stockholders by the New York Central 10 per cent. per annum or 5 per cent. semi-annually, instead of 4 per cent. This increase began with the July, 1900, payment. An additional 3 per cent. yearly was paid from the profits of the Fourth avenue street car line. The lease of this property to Metropolitan Street Railway Co. in 1896 provided for yearly rental of $350,000 for five years and $400,000 thereafter, or 3½ per cent. rising to 4 per cent. on the company's stock.
It was proposed to include this company's 7 per cent. consolidated mortgage bonds, maturing May 1, 1900, in refunding plan of New York Central & Hudson River Railroad formulated in April, 1897. Litigation on the part of stockholders was instituted, and the issue of the 3½ per cent. refunding bonds of the company was finally authorized and issued for the retirement of the old 7s. The trustee of the 3½ per cent. refunding mortgage is the Guaranty Trust Co., New York.
Earnings are not reported separately, being included in the lessees' report.
President, William K. Vanderbilt; Vice-President and Secretary, Edward V. W. Rossiter; Treasurer, Warren S. Crane, New York.
Directors—William K. Vanderbilt, Frederick W. Vanderbilt, Samuel F. Barger, Hamilton McK. Twombly, Chauncey M. Depew, John B. Dutcher, Charles C. Clark, Edward V. W. Rossiter, James D. Layng, James Stillman, J. Pierpont Morgan, William Rockefeller, George G. Haven.
Main office, Grand Central Station, New York. Annual meeting, third Tuesday in May.

## NEW YORK & OTTAWA RAILROAD CO.

Road owned, Tupper Lake, N. Y., to Ottawa, Ontario, 128 miles, including the bridge across the St. Lawrence river at Cornwall, 2½ miles. The Ottawa & New York Railway Co., controlled by this company, owns line from Ottawa to Cornwall and bridge section across the north channel of the St. Lawrence; and the Cornwall Bridge Co., also controlled by this company, owns bridge across south channel of the St. Lawrence.

This company in 1897 acquired the Northern New York Railroad, Moira to Tupper's Lake, N. Y., 56½ miles, and connecting lines from Moira, N. Y., to the St. Lawrence and Ottawa to Cornwall were built in 1897 and 1898.

Stock......Par $100..........................Authorized, $3,000,000......Issued, $2,540,000

Stock is transferred at the company's office, 27 Pine street, New York.

FUNDED DEBT.

| | |
|---|---|
| 1st mort. gold, 4 per cent., due Nov., 1917, May and Nov. | $1,728,000 |
| 2d mort. income, 6 per cent., due July, 1912, May and Nov. | 632,000 |
| Total | $2,360,000 |

There are $535,000 of 6 per cent. Receiver's certificates outstanding.

The 1st mortgage bonds are at a rate of $15,000 per mile and the 2d mortgage bonds at rate of $5,000 per mile. Bonds of the Ottawa & New York Railway Co. ($825,000 1sts at $15,000 a mile and $275,000 2ds at $5,000 a mile), $1,000,000 in all, and the stocks of the Ottawa & New York Railway Co. and Cornwall Bridge Co. are deposited under the mortgages to secure the bonds of the New York & Ottawa Railroad Co.

The May, 1899, coupons on the 1st mortgage were not paid, and in April, 1900, Henry W. Gays was appointed Receiver of the company.

Chairman, George Foster Peabody, New York; President and Receiver, Henry W. Gays, Ottawa, Ont.; Vice-President, Henry Sanger Snow; Secretary, Charles J. Peabody; Treasurer, Acosta Nichols, New York; Auditor, Assistant Secretary and Assistant Treasurer, G. B. Colpas, Ottawa, Ont.

Directors—George Foster Peabody, Henry Sanger Snow, Alexander M. White, Jr., George Barclay Moffat, Spencer Trask, R. Burnham Moffat, Acosta Nichols, Charles J. Peabody, New York; Henry W. Gays, Ottawa, Ont.

Main office, 74 Sparks street, Ottawa, Ont. Treasurer's office, 27 Pine street, New York. Annual meeting, October 1.

---

## NEW YORK, BROOKLYN & MANHATTAN BEACH RAILWAY CO.

(Leased to Long Island Railroad Co.)

Road owned, Fresh Pond Junction to Coney Island and branches, 19 miles. The company is a consolidation of the New York, Bay Ridge & Jamaica and Long Island City & Manhattan Beach Railroad Cos., effected in August, 1885. The road was leased October 1, 1885, to the Long Island Railroad Co. at a guaranteed minimum rental of $95,980 per annum.

Stock......Par $100......Authorized { com., $350,000; pref., 650,000 } Issued { com., $350,000; pref., 650,000 } $1,000,000

The preferred stock is 5 per cent., non-cumulative.

Dividends on the preferred are paid 2½ per cent. each, semi-annually, in April (1) and October.

Stock is transferred at the office of the company, 192 Broadway, New York.

FUNDED DEBT.

| | |
|---|---|
| New York, Brooklyn & Manhattan Beach consol. (new 1st) mort., 5 per cent., due Oct., 1935 (April and Oct.) | $1,726,000 |

The Long Island Railroad Co. guarantees this company's bonds, principal and interest, and dividends of 5 per cent. per annum on the preferred stock.

President, George S. Edgell; Vice-President, Austin Corbin; Secretary, D. S. Voorhees; Treasurer, M. A. Smith, New York.

Main office, 192 Broadway, New York. Annual meeting, third Tuesday in December.

## NEW YORK CENTRAL & HUDSON RIVER RAILROAD CO.

| Road owned: | Miles. | | Miles. |
|---|---|---|---|
| New York to Buffalo | 440 | Branches | 370 |
| Total owned | | | 810 |

Roads leased:

| | Miles. | | Miles. |
|---|---|---|---|
| West Shore Railroad | 479 | Pine Creek Railway | 75 |
| Rome, Watertown & Ogdensburg Railroad and leased lines | 624 | Beech Creek Railroad | 160 |
| | | Walkill Valley Railroad | 33 |
| New York & Harlem Railroad | 136 | Syracuse, Geneva & Corning Railway | 64 |
| New Jersey Junction Railroad | 5 | Troy & Greenbush Railroad | 6 |
| Mohawk & Malone Railroad | 182 | Spuyten Duyvil & Port Morris Railroad | 6 |
| Carthage & Adirondack Railroad | 46 | Tivoli Hollow Railroad | 1¼ |
| Gouverneur & Oswegatchie Railroad | 13 | Boston & Albany Railroad | 393 |
| New York & Putnam Railroad | 59 | Beech Creek Extension Railroad | 59 |
| Fall Brook Railway | 91½ | | |
| Total leased | | | 2,433 |
| Operated under contract | | | 27½ |
| Trackage | | | 107½ |
| Total operated | | | 3,378 |

The company also has trackage rights and contracts on other roads aggregating 134 miles.

The company controls through stock ownership the Lake Shore & Michigan Southern Railroad, 1,411 miles, and the Michigan Central Railroad, 1,658 miles, which roads, together with the New York, Chicago & St. Louis, 512 miles, controlled by the Lake Shore, are operated separately. In addition the company leases the Dunkirk, Allegbeny Valley & Pittsburg Railroad, 91 miles, which is operated under contract by the Lake Shore. It controls the Toronto, Hamilton & Buffalo, 88 miles, and the Pittsburg & Lake Erie, 184 miles, all of which report separately and are not included in the above mileage. In 1900 control of the Lake Erie & Western, 725 miles, was acquired by the Lake Shore, and in the same year this company and the Lake Shore acquired control of the Cleveland, Cincinnati, Chicago & St. Louis, 2,241 miles, but this company's interest in the latter property was transferred to the Lake Shore. In 1901 the Indiana, Illinois & Iowa was acquired in the interest of this system. The whole system operated and controlled by the New York Central is about 10,300 miles. In 1899-1900 this company and the Pennsylvania acquired large interests in the Chesapeake & Ohio and together control that road. This company and the Pennsylvania also have joint interests in the Pittsburg & Eastern Railroad. The St. Lawrence & Adirondack Railway is operated by this company under agreement.

The leases of the Mohawk & Malone and Carthage & Adirondack roads were made in 1893, and the Gouverneur & Oswegatchie was leased in 1894. In the same year this company acquired control of a majority of the securities of the New York & Northern, which was reorganized as the New York & Putnam Railroad and leased. The acquisition of the Lake Shore and the Michigan Central roads, by an exchange of this company's 3½ per cent. collateral trust bonds for their stocks, was effected in 1899. In 1899 leased the Walkill Valley Railroad, the Fall Brook Railway, including the Pine Creek Railway and Syracuse, Geneva & Corning Railway, and in 1900 leased the Boston & Albany, possession of which was assumed November 1, 1900. In 1901 acquired the Beech Creek Extension Railroad, 59 miles.

See separate statements of the New York & Harlem, Lake Shore & Michigan Southern, Michigan Central, Rome, Watertown & Ogdensburg, Boston & Albany and Beech Creek for details regarding leases of those properties.

Locomotives, 1,729; passenger cars, 2,104; freight cars, 61,855; service cars, 1,805. In addition the company owns 194 ferryboats, propellers, barges, canal boats and floats, and 7 grain elevators with an aggregate capacity of 4,925,000 bushels.

Stock......Par $100.... ..................Authorized, $150,000,000......Issued, $131,908,000

The company's capital stock was increased in April, 1893, from $89,428,300 to $100,000,000, stockholders being given privilege of subscribing for 10 per cent. of their holdings, payments on subscriptions to be by instalments; to be completed July 1, 1894.

In November, 1899, the stock was increased $15,000,000 for the purpose of providing additional equipment. The increase was allotted pro rata to stockholders for subscription at par.

In January, 1902, it was decided to increase the stock by $35,000,000, making the amount authorized $150,000,000. It was also decided to offer $17,250,000 of the increase to the stockholders at $125, making the stock outstanding after May 12, 1902, when the new stock was to be issued, $132,250,000. The purpose of this stock issue was to provide for improvements to the company's tunnel under Fourth avenue, New York, and to enlarge the Grand Central Station, accidents occurring in the tunnel and its unhealthy condition having caused a public demand for a radical change.

Stock is transferred at the office of the treasurer, Grand Central Station, New York. Registrar, Union Trust Co., New York. Registrar in London, Union Bank of London.

For dividends paid see table of earnings below. The January, 1900, dividend was an increase of ¼ per cent. from the rate for two previous quarters, thus putting the company on a 5 per cent. dividend basis. The dividends are paid quarterly, 1¼ per cent. each, in January (15), April, July and October.

FUNDED DEBT.

| | |
|---|---|
| Extended debt certificates, 4 per cent., due May, 1905, May and Nov. | $3,610,500 |
| Debentures, 5 per cent., due Sept., 1904, March and Sept. | 4,526,000 |
| " of 1889, 5 per cent., due Sept., 1904, March and Sept. | 649,000 |
| " 4 per cent., due June, 1905, June and Dec. | 5,097,000 |
| Gold (refunding) mort., due July, 1997, 3½ per cent., Jan. and July | 40,426,916 |
| Gold (Lake Shore collat.) bonds, 3½ per cent., due Feb., 1998, Feb. and Aug. | 90,578,400 |
| Gold (Mich. Cent. collat.) bonds, 3½ per cent., due Feb., 1998, Feb. and Aug. | 19,336,445 |
| Debentures, 3½ per cent., due July, 2000, Jan. and July | 5,500,000 |
| Total | $169,724,261 |

FUNDED DEBT OF LEASED LINES GUARANTEED.

| | |
|---|---|
| West Shore, 1st mort., 4 per cent., due Jan., 2361, Jan. and July | $50,000,000 |
| N. Y. & Putnam, cons. mort., 4 per cent., due Oct., 1993, April and Oct. | 4,025,000 |
| N. Y. & Northern, 1st mort., 5 per cent., due Oct., 1927, April and Oct. | 1,200,000 |
| New Jersey Junction, 1st mort., 4 per cent., due Feb., 1986, Feb. and Aug. | 1,700,000 |
| Mohawk & Malone, 1st mort., 4 per cent., due Sept., 1991, March and Sept. | 2,500,000 |
| " " cons. mort., 3½ per cent., due March, 2002, March and Sept. | 3,900,000 |
| Carthage & Adirondack, 1st mort., 4 per cent., due Dec., 1981, June and Dec. | 1,100,000 |
| Gouverneur & Oswegatchie, 1st mort., 5 per cent., due June, 1942, June and Dec. | 300,000 |
| Pine Creek Ry., 1st mortgage, 6 per cent., due Dec., 1932, June and Dec. | 3,500,000 |
| Walkill Valley, 1st mort., 3½ per cent., due Aug., 1917, Jan. and July | 250,000 |
| " " 2d mort. income, 3½ per cent., due Aug., 1917, March and Sept. | 330,000 |
| Syracuse, Gen. & Corn. Ry., 1st mort., 7 per cent., due Nov., 1905, May (15) and Nov. | 417,100 |
| " " " " 2d mort., 5 per cent., due March, 1909, March and Sept. | 600,000 |

See also statements of the New York & Harlem, Rome, Watertown & Ogdensburg, Beech Creek, etc., for funded debts of those companies.

In 1897 company formulated a plan for refunding its bonded debt through an issue of $100,000,000 3½ 100-year gold bonds, due 1997 (Jan. and July), of which $15,000,000 are reserved for additions and improvements after 1903. The $12,000,000 7 per cent. consols of the New York & Harlem Railroad, maturing 1900, were to be included in this arrangement, but controversy with that company's stockholders caused a new arrangement by which the issue was refunded by 3½ per cent. bonds of the New York & Harlem itself. The $18,327,000 of 1st mortgage 7 per cent. bonds and $5,727,094 of 6 per cent. sterling bonds, maturing January 1, 1903, were retired by an additional issue of 3½ per cent. refunding bonds of 1997.

On February 4, 1898, this company authorized a $100,000,000 3½ 50-year gold bond issue to be exchanged for the stock of the Lake Shore & Michigan Southern at 200 for the $50,000,000 of the latter. The offer, it was stated, was accepted in advance by the Vanderbilt interest, and other holders of Lake Shore were given until April 14, 1898, to accept. In December, 1902, $90,578,400 of the bonds had been issued in exchange for $45,289,200 of Lake Shore stock. The bonds are secured by deposit in trust of the Lake Shore stock acquired.

In February, 1898, company authorized $21,550,000 of similar 3½ per cent. bonds to be offered in exchange for the $18,738,000 of stock of the Michigan Central Railroad at 115 for the latter. These bonds are secured by the Michigan Central stock acquired. In December, 1902, $19,336,445 of the bonds had been issued in exchange for some $16,814,300 of Michigan Central stock.

In 1900 the company issued $5,500,000 of 3½ per cent. debentures to acquire property of the Boston & Albany Railroad not included in the lease of that road.

In December, 1885, the West Shore Railroad was leased for 475 years, lessee guaranteeing 4 per cent. interest on $50,000,000 bonds. This company holds the entire capital stock of the West Shore Railroad, and its earnings are included in those of the lessee. The Rome, Watertown & Ogdensburg was acquired in March, 1891, under guarantee of 5 per cent. on its stock and interest on its bonds. Its earnings from March 15, 1891, are included in those of the lessee. The Beech Creek was leased in 1890 for a guarantee of 4 per cent. on $5,000,000 1st mortgage bonds and 4 per cent. dividends on $5,000,000 stock. $500,000 Beech Creek 2ds were also issued and guaranteed by this company. The Beech Creek Extension Railroad was leased in 1901. The Dunkirk, Allegheny Valley & Pittsburg was leased 1873 for a guarantee of 7 per cent. interest on $2,900,000 7 per cent. bonds and 1½ per cent. dividends on $1,300,000 stock. The New Jersey Junction Railroad was leased in 1886 for 4 per cent. interest on its bonds. The New York & Harlem (which see) was leased 1873 for interest on its bonds and 8 per cent. on its stock, the dividends being increased to 10 per cent. in 1900 in consequence of the refunding of the New York & Harlem bonds at 3½ per cent.

In 1899 the company leased the Walkill Valley Railroad, 33 miles, and guaranteed 3½ per cent. on its $330,000 of stock and a like rate on its $580,000 bonds.

In May, 1899, the company leased the Fall Brook Railway for 999 years at an annual rental of $175,000. The leases of the Pine Creek Railway and the Syracuse, Geneva & Corning Railway to the Fall Brook were canceled and new leases to the New York Central executed.

### Earnings.

Year ending June 30.

| | Gross. | Per Cent. Oper. Ex. | Net. |
|---|---|---|---|
| 1892-93 | $47,796,008 | 65.58 | $17,104,005 |
| 1893-94 | 44,229,607 | 65.28 | 16,068,085 |
| 1894-95 | 43,231,849 | 64.93 | 15,841,697 |
| 1895-96 | 46,027,198 | 64.11 | 17,191,051 |
| 1896-97 | 45,199,465 | 62.80 | 17,478,429 |
| 1897-98 | 47,484,633 | 64.00 | 19,344,221 |
| 1898-99 | 48,124,016 | 62.69 | 22,289,111 |
| 1899-00 | 54,562,951 | 62.41 | 25,228,110 |
| 1900-01* | 66,333,110 | 64.20 | 28,275,189 |
| 1901-02* | 70,903,868 | 69.09 | 28,916,402 |

——* Operations of Boston & Albany included.

All miscellaneous receipts are included in net earnings. In 1897-98 they include $2,251,471 in which is comprised dividends on the company's holdings of Lake Shore and Michigan Central stocks. In 1898-99 the miscellaneous income included in net was $4,324,671; in 1900-01 it was $4,530,293, and in 1901-02 $4,876,023. The disposition of net earnings was as follows:

| | Net Earnings. | Charges. | Profits. | Dividends— Amount. | Per Ct. |
|---|---|---|---|---|---|
| 1892-93 | $17,104,005 | $12,318,288 | $4,785,717 | $4,471,415 | 5 |
| 1893-94 | 16,068,085 | 12,502,196 | 3,565,889 | 4,588,826 | 5 |
| 1894-95 | 15,841,697 | 12,679,824 | 3,161,873 | 4,339,990 | 4½ |
| 1895-96 | 17,191,051 | 13,014,304 | 4,176,747 | 4,000,000 | 4 |
| 1896-97 | 17,478,429 | 13,303,537 | 4,174,892 | 4,000,000 | 4 |
| 1897-98 | 19,344,221 | 14,500,587 | 4,843,634 | 4,000,000 | 4 |
| 1898-99 | 22,289,111 | 16,601,236 | 5,687,875 | 4,000,000 | 4 |
| 1899-00 | 25,228,110 | 17,249,083 | 7,979,027 | 4,937,500 | 4¾ |
| 1900-01* | 28,275,189 | 20,533,006 | 7,742,183 | 5,750,000 | 5 |
| 1901-02* | 28,916,402 | 20,899,684 | 8,016,718 | 5,961,411 | 5 |

——* Operations of Boston & Albany included.

The following presents the comparative freight traffic statistics of the company:

| | Average Mileage. | Total Tonnage. | Tons Carried One Mile. | Freight Density. | Rate per Ton per Mile. | Earnings per Train Mile. | Average Tons per Train. |
|---|---|---|---|---|---|---|---|
| 1896-97 | 2,585 | 24,646,457 | 4,171,760,313 | 1,613,833 | 0.65c | $1.85 | 283 |
| 1897-98 | 2,585 | 28,532,357 | 5,014,190,846 | 1,939,725 | 0.58 | 1.82 | 304 |
| 1898-99 | 2,828 | 31,753,584 | 5,255,353,899 | 1,858,328 | 0.56 | 1.88 | 338 |
| 1899-00 | 2,817 | 37,586,496 | 6,117,572,625 | 2,171,554 | 0.56 | 2.03 | 363 |
| 1900-01* | 3,223 | 36,430,820 | 6,606,890,325 | 1,972,047 | 0.60 | 2.09 | 351 |
| 1901-02* | 3,319 | 35,599,689 | 6,407,594,086 | 1,939,620 | 0.63 | 2.17 | 342 |

——* Boston & Albany figures included.

### Monthly Earnings and Average Mileage for Six Years.

| Month. | 1897. 2,396 Miles. | 1898. 2,396 Miles. | 1899. 2,396 Miles. | 1900. 2,396 Miles. | 1901. 2,828 Miles. | 1902. 3,376 Miles. |
|---|---|---|---|---|---|---|
| January | $3,139,942 | $3,505,435 | $3,635,059 | $4,250,319 | $5,182,978 | $3,710,028 |
| February | 3,301,460 | 3,429,304 | 3,275,916 | 4,010,370 | 4,490,269 | 3,296,539 |
| March | 3,692,021 | 3,860,683 | 3,923,838 | 4,340,593 | 5,329,556 | 3,626,029 |
| April | 3,504,807 | 3,806,706 | 3,630,204 | 4,253,361 | 5,188,745 | 4,176,444 |
| May | 3,808,730 | 3,944,946 | 4,006,124 | 4,650,377 | 5,783,868 | 3,813,559 |
| June | 3,894,713 | 3,625,400 | 4,080,897 | 4,526,262 | 5,893,370 | 3,963,766 |
| July | 3,657,753 | 3,298,217 | 4,435,407 | 4,580,047 | 5,940,096 | 6,036,838 |
| August | 4,272,138 | 3,978,837 | 4,905,211 | 5,112,067 | 6,795,467 | 6,737,247 |
| September | 4,483,919 | 4,117,348 | 4,843,781 | 4,981,461 | 6,686,672 | 6,701,579 |
| October | 4,253,118 | 4,252,100 | 5,005,877 | 5,027,623 | 6,915,319 | 6,799,355 |
| November | 3,960,753 | 4,148,197 | 4,795,493 | 4,869,223 | 5,837,015 | 6,427,977 |
| December | 3,674,592 | 3,837,936 | 4,457,413 | 4,720,433 | 5,690,120 | 6,202,785 |
| Totals for year | $45,609,139 | $45,393,773 | $50,995,209 | $55,292,156 | $69,733,475 | $61,492,146 |
| Averages per month | 3,800,761 | 3,782,810 | 4,249,600 | 4,607,679 | 5,811,123 | 5,124,345 |

Chairman, Chauncey M. Depew; President, William H. Newman; 1st Vice-President, Edward V. W. Rossiter, New York; 2d Vice-President, Edgar Van Etten, Boston; 3d Vice-President, W. C. Brown; 4th Vice-President, John Carstensen; 5th Vice-President, William J. Wilgus; Secretary, Edwin D. Worcester; Treasurer, Edward L. Rossiter; Auditor, Marshal L. Bacon, New York.

Directors—William K. Vanderbilt, Frederick W. Vanderbilt, Chauncey M. Depew, Samuel F. Barger, Charles C. Clarke, J. Pierpont Morgan, Hamilton McK. Twombly, William H. Newman, George S. Bowdoin, William Rockefeller, Darius O. Mills, New York; William Bliss, Boston.

General offices, Grand Central Station, New York. Fiscal Agents in London, J. S. Morgan & Co., 22 Old Broad street. Annual meeting, third Wednesday in April.

Books close for meeting, March 15; for dividends, on March 15, July 1, October 1, January 1.

## NEW YORK, CHICAGO & ST. LOUIS RAILROAD CO.

(Controlled by Lake Shore & Michigan Southern Railway Co.)

Road owned, Buffalo, N. Y., to Illinois State line, 495 miles; leased, Illinois line to Grand Crossing (near Chicago), 10 miles; Silver Creek, N. Y., to Dunkirk, 8 miles; trackage, Grand Crossing to Chicago, 9 miles; other, 1½ miles; total operated, 523½ miles. Locomotives, 159; passenger cars, 73; freight cars, 7,425.

In October, 1882, a controlling interest was bought by the Lake Shore & Michigan Southern Railway Co.

Stock..Par $100..Authorized { com., $14,000,000; 1st pref., 5,000,000; 2d pref., 11,000,000 } Issued { com., $14,000,000; 1st pref., 5,000,000; 2d pref., 11,000,000 } $30,000,000

Stock is transferred at the company's office, Grand Central Station, New York. Registrar, Union Trust Co., New York.

Dividends paid on the 1st preferred stock have been as follows: In 1891, 3½ per cent.; in 1892 and 1893, 3 per cent.; in 1894, 4 per cent.; in 1895, none; in 1896, 5 per cent.; in 1897, none; in 1898, 2 per cent.; in 1899, none; in 1900, 1901 and 1902, 5 per cent.; in 1901 a dividend of 2 per cent. was paid on the 2d preferred and in 1902 3 per cent. was paid on that stock. The dividends have all been annual, payable March 1.

FUNDED DEBT.

| | |
|---|---|
| 1st mort., 4 per cent., due 1937, April and Oct. | $19,425,000 |
| Equipment trusts | 655,000 |
| Total | $20,080,000 |

EARNINGS.

| | Gross. | Net. | Charges. | Surplus. |
|---|---|---|---|---|
| 1892 | $6,467,165 | $1,010,889 | $859,853 | $151,036 |
| 1893 | 6,787,748 | 1,222,601 | 968,460 | 254,141 |
| 1894 | 5,629,239 | 872,326 | 863,000 | 9,326 |
| 1895 | 6,317,950 | 1,141,308 | 860,000 | 281,308 |
| 1896 | 5,587,766 | 893,058 | 889,972 | 3,086 |
| 1897 | 5,815,217 | 1,001,197 | 893,541 | 107,656 |
| 1898 | 6,391,421 | 947,854 | 889,391 | 58,462 |
| 1899 | 6,919,985 | 1,213,885 | 885,241 | 328,644 |
| 1900 | 7,023,358 | 1,357,815 | 881,092 | 476,723 |
| 1901 | 7,485,483 | 1,550,149 | 931,217 | 618,931 |

Chairman, Chauncey M. Depew, New York; President, William H. Canniff, Cleveland; Secretary and Treasurer, Charles F. Cox, New York.

Directors—William K. Vanderbilt, Frederick W. Vanderbilt, Hamilton McK. Twombly, John S. Kennedy, Frederic P. Olcott, Chauncey M. Depew, Charles F. Cox, W. Emlen Roosevelt, William H. Newman, New York; Charles M. Reed, Erie, Pa.; William H. Canniff, Samuel E. Williamson, Ralph W. Hickox, Cleveland.

Main office, 185 Euclid avenue, Cleveland; New York office, Grand Central Station. Annual meeting, first Wednesday in May. Books close thirty days previous.

## NEW YORK, LACKAWANNA & WESTERN RAILROAD CO.

(Leased to Delaware, Lackawanna & Western Railroad Co.)

Road owned, Binghamton, N. Y., to Buffalo and International Bridge, 214 miles.

Stock......Par $100........................Authorized, $10,000,000......Issued, $10,000,000

Transfer agency, 26 Exchange place, New York.

Dividends on the stock are paid quarterly, 1¼ per cent. each, in January (2), April, July and October.

FUNDED DEBT.

| | |
|---|---|
| 1st mort., 6 per cent., due Jan., 1921, Jan. and July | $12,000,000 |
| 2d mort., 5 per cent., due Aug., 1923, Feb. and Aug | 5,000,000 |
| Terminal impt., 4 per cent., due May, 1923, May and Nov | 5,000,000 |
| Total | $22,000,000 |

This road is the Delaware, Lackawanna & Western's extension to Buffalo, and is leased to that company for 99 years from October 2, 1882, for interest on bonds and 5 per cent. on stock. The principal of all the bonds is guaranteed by the lessee. In 1890 $5,000,000 4 per cent. bonds were authorized, to reimburse lessee for advances made.

Earnings are included in those of the lessee company.

President, William H. Truesdale; Secretary and Treasurer, Fred F. Chambers, New York.

Main office, 26 Exchange place, New York. Annual meeting, Tuesday before last Friday in February.

## NEW YORK, NEW HAVEN & HARTFORD RAILROAD CO.

Road owned, Woodlawn, N. Y., to Providence, R. I., 174 miles; branches owned, 264 miles; leased and mainly controlled through stock ownership, 1,569 miles; operated under trackage, 29 miles; total operated, 2,036 miles.

In 1893 the Old Colony Railroad (including the Boston & Providence), 616 miles, was leased, giving this company a through line to Boston.

In 1895 the company acquired a controlling interest in the stock of the New England Railroad Company, the reorganized New York & New England.

This company was formed in 1872, by the consolidation of the New York & New Haven and the New Haven & Hartford Railroad Companies, other tributary roads being subsequently leased or amalgamated. The Hartford & Connecticut Valley, 46 miles, and the Shore Line Railroad, 48 miles, were leased and have been merged with this company. It leases the New Haven & Northampton Railroad, 136 miles; Naugatuck Railroad, 61 miles; Boston & New York Air Line Railroad, 55 miles; Harlem River & Port Chester, 11½ miles. In 1892 acquired and leased New York, Providence & Boston Railroad (including Providence & Worcester Railroad), New London, Conn., to Providence, and branches, 136 miles; also acquired and leased the Housatonic system, 190 miles, that company being in 1898 merged with this road. The Hartford & Connecticut Valley, Shore Line and New York, Providence & Boston have also been merged with this company. The company uses New York & Harlem tracks Woodlawn to New York. The company, through the New York, Providence & Boston, controls the Stonington Steamship Line. In 1900 the New Haven Steamboat Co.'s entire capital stock was purchased, and in 1901 that of the New London Steamboat Co. Uses the new station of Boston Terminal Co. at Boston under rental, and has one-fifth interest in its stock. Locomotives, 942; passenger cars, 1,867; freight cars, 12,965

Stock......Par $100......................Authorized, $100,000,000......Issued, $54,685,400

Transfer agencies, company's office, New Haven; Old Colony Trust Co., Boston. Registrar, Farmers' Loan & Trust Co., New York.

Convertible debenture ctfs., 4 per cent., April and Oct., until exchanged April 1, 1903. $16,397,200

Dividends of 2½ per cent. quarterly or 10 per cent. per annum were paid from 1872 till July, 1894, when rate was reduced to 2 per cent. quarterly or 8 per cent. per annum, and have been paid on that basis since. Dividends are paid March (30), June, September and December.

FUNDED DEBT.

| | |
|---|---|
| 1st mort., 4 per cent., due June, 1903, June and Dec | $2,000,000 |
| Currency debentures, not convertible, 4 per cent., due March, 1947, March and Sept. | 5,000,000 |
| " " " " 3½ per cent., due March, 1942, Mar. and Sept. | 5,000,000 |
| New York, Providence & Boston, g. m., 4 per cent., due April, 1942, April and Oct. | 1,000,000 |
| Housatonic, 1st mort., 4 per cent., due April, 1910, April and Oct | 100,000 |
| " cons. mort., 5 per cent., due Nov., 1937, May and Nov | 2,839,000 |
| Shore Line, 1st mort., 4½ per cent., due March, 1910, March and Sept | 200,000 |
| Total | $16,139,000 |

BONDS OF LEASED ROADS, INTEREST PAID BY N. Y., N. H. & H. CO. AS RENTAL.

| | |
|---|---|
| Harlem River & Port Chester, 1st mort., 7 per cent., due Oct., 1903, April and Oct. | $1,000,000 |
| " " 1st mort., 6 per cent., due Oct., 1903, April and Oct. | 1,000,000 |
| " " 2d mort., 4 per cent., due June, 1911, June and Dec. | 1,000,000 |
| Naugatuck R. R., 1st mort., 4 per cent., due June, 1913, June and Dec | 150,000 |

BONDS OF LEASED ROADS—*Continued.*

| | |
|---|---|
| Boston & New York Air Line, 1st mort., 5 per cent., due Aug., 1905, Feb. and Aug.. | $500,000 |
| Colchester R. R., 1st mort., 7 per cent., due July, 1907, Jan. and July............... | 25,000 |
| New Haven & Northampton, con. s. f. mort., 6 p. c., due April, 1909, April and Oct.. | 1,200,000 |
| " " ext. mort., 5 per cent., due April, 1911, April and Oct... | 700,000 |
| " " convertible mort., 5 p. c., due July, 1904, Jan. and July.. | 350,000 |
| Holyoke & Westfield, 1st mort., 4 per cent., due April, 1911, April and Oct........... | 200,000 |
| Providence & Worcester, 1st mort., 6 per cent., due Oct., 1947, April and Oct........ | 1,500,000 |
| New Haven & Derby cons. mort., 5 per cent., due May, 1918, May and Nov.......... | 575,000 |
| Danbury & Norwalk, cons. mort., 6 per cent., due July, 1920, Jan. and July.......... | 100,000 |
| " " cons. mort., 5 per cent., due July, 1920, Jan. and July........ | 400,000 |
| " " gen. mort., 5 per cent., due April, 1925, April and Oct........ | 150,000 |

There are in addition $18,863,000 of bonds of the Old Colony and its leased or controlled lines which this company guarantees or assumes as rental as well as $17,200,000 bonds of the New England Railroad and its leased properties. See statement of the Old Colony and of the New England Railroad. This company also assumed and guarantees $139,500 6 per cent. bonds of the New Haven Steamboat Co. and $225,000 5 per cent. mortgages of that company.

The Harlem River & Port Chester road is leased and the bonds guaranteed; 4 per cent. is also guaranteed on preferred stock, $2,975,500, of Boston & New York Air Line, and 10 per cent. on the Naugatuck Railroad Co.'s stock, $2,000,000.

In December, 1892, company announced that stockholders of leased lines could exchange their stock for shares of the New York, New Haven & Hartford on the following terms, viz.: New York, Providence & Boston, share for share; Hartford & Connecticut Valley, share for share; Housatonic, 8 shares of preferred for 1 of New York, New Haven & Hartford; New Haven & Derby, 13 shares for 4 of this company; Danbury & Norwalk, 4 shares for 1; New Haven & Northampton, 5 shares for 2; Boston & New York Air Line preferred, 5 shares for 2; Naugatuck, share for share; Shore Line Railway, 4 shares for 3 of this company's. There was on January 30, 1901, $14,399,271 of stocks of leased lines outstanding and not exchanged.

In December, 1892, stockholders were invited to subscribe for $15,000,000 4 per cent. convertible debentures at par, to the extent of 4 per cent. of the par value of their holdings. On April 1, 1903, these debentures will become convertible into stock at par. The proceeds of the debentures were for improvement of the property. In February, 1893, authority was granted to increase stock to $100,000,000; this step being taken to provide for exchange of stock of the Old Colony Railroad. In 1895 $3,287,500 additional debentures were authorized. In March, 1897, $10,000,000 50-year non-convertible debentures were authorized to retire floating debt. This company also guaranteed the $15,000,000 of New England Railroad 5 per cent. bonds held in its treasury and authorized their sale.

The lease of the Old Colony was effected in February, 1895, lessee taking possession of the property April 1, 1893. The lease agreement provided that for 6 months, from June 19, 1893, 10 shares of Old Colony stock could be exchanged for 9 of New Haven stock with 7 per cent. annual dividends on Old Colony stock not exchanged. Up to June 30, 1900, 55,190 shares of Old Colony stock, out of a total of 166,089, had been so exchanged.

EARNINGS.—Year ending June 30.

| | Div. Paid. | Gross. | Net. | Charges. | Surplus. |
|---|---|---|---|---|---|
| 1892-93.................... | 10 | $18,113,474 | $5,917,553 | $2,919,554 | $2,997,998 |
| 1893-94.................... | 10 | 25,576,884 | 7,753,655 | 5,379,978 | 2,373,672 |
| 1894-95.................... | 8 | 27,901,735 | 9,072,553 | 5,593,545 | 3,478,987 |
| 1895-96.................... | 8 | 30,345,630 | 10,064,089 | 6,397,197 | 3,666,898 |
| 1896-97.................... | 8 | 29,623,333 | 10,194,147 | 6,315,903 | 3,878,244 |
| 1897-98.................... | 8 | 30,322,737 | 10,032,119 | 6,112,481 | 3,919,638 |
| 1898-99.................... | 8 | 37,143,917 | 12,186,084 | 7,820,113 | 4,365,970 |
| 1899-00.................... | 8 | 40,325,151 | 12,646,432 | 8,023,819 | 4,622,563 |
| 1900-01.................... | 8 | 40,132,311 | 12,646,392 | 7,988,104 | 4,658,282 |
| 1901-02.................... | 8 | 43,521,087 | 12,860,273 | 8,181,414 | 4,678,855 |

In 1896-97 the dividends paid were $3,803,516, and surplus over same $74,728. In 1897-98 surplus over dividends, $109,822. In 1898-99, dividends, $4,158,688; surplus, $207,282. In 1899-1900, dividends, $4,231,278; surplus, $391,335. In 1900-01, dividends, $4,294,738; surplus, $363,549. In 1901-02, dividends, $4,296,568; surplus, $382,290.

The following presents the freight traffic of the company:

| | Average Mileage. | Total Tonnage. | Tons Carried One Mile. | Freight Density. | Rate per Ton per Mile. | Earnings per Train Mile. | Average Tons per Train. |
|---|---|---|---|---|---|---|---|
| 1897-98.... | 1,441 | 11,042,000 | 899,636,294 | 624,313 | 1.511c | $2.831 | 180 |
| 1898-99 ... | 2,047 | 14,375,823 | 1,257,413,624 | 614,271 | 1.411 | 2.938 | 201 |
| 1899-00.... | 2,032 | 15,708,266 | 1,340,289,590 | 657,894 | 1.451 | 3.069 | 204 |
| 1900-01.... | 2,027 | 15,436,435 | 1,292,378,364 | 643,140 | 1.479 | 3.199 | 208 |
| 1901-02.... | 2,027 | 17,145,313 | 1,444,544,216 | 712,651 | 1.455 | 3.294 | 217 |

Since 1893-94 the Old Colony's figures are included.

President, John M. Hall; Vice-Presidents, William F. Merrill, Percy S. Todd, W. E. Barnett, Fayette S. Curtis; Treasurer, William L. Squire, New Haven, Conn.; Secretary, William D. Bishop, Jr., Bridgeport, Conn.

Directors—George J. Brush, John M. Hall, Arthur D. Osborne, New Haven, Conn.; I. De V. Warner, William D. Bishop, Bridgeport, Conn.; Carlos French, Seymour, Conn.; J. Pierpont Morgan, William Rockefeller, Chauncey M. Depew, George Macculloch Miller, New York; D. Newton Barney, Hartford, Conn.; Joseph Park, Rye, N. Y.; William Skinner, Holyoke, Mass.; Charles F. Choate, Nathaniel Thayer, Boston; Royal C. Taft, Providence, R. I.; Charles F. Brooker, Ansonia, Conn.; Frank W. Cheney, South Manchester, Conn.; Edwin Milner, Moosop, Conn.

Main office, New Haven, Conn. Annual meeting, third Wednesday in October. Books close ten days previous.

## NEW YORK, ONTARIO & WESTERN RAILWAY CO.

The company is a reorganization, in 1879, of New York & Oswego Midland.

Road owned, Cornwall, N. Y., to Oswego, 272 miles; branches, 47 miles; leased, Utica, Clinton & Binghamton, 31 miles; Pecksport Connecting Railway, 4 miles; Rome & Clinton 13 miles; Wharton Valley, 7 miles; Ontario, Carbondale & Scranton, 54 miles; Port Jervis, Monticello & Summitville Railroad, 42 miles; Ellenville & Kingston Railroad, 27 miles; total 496 miles.; company uses the West Shore tracks from Cornwall to Weehawken, 53 miles; total operated, 594 miles. In 1902 an extension of the Ellenville, N. Y., branch to Kingston, N. Y. 27 miles, was completed. In 1902 this company acquired the Port Jervis, Monticello & New York Railroad, which was foreclosed, and reorganized it as the Port Jervis, Monticello & Summitville Railroad Co., which will form a part of a through line between Port Jervis, N. Y., and Kingston, N. Y. Locomotives, 144; passenger cars, 147; freight cars, 6,954.

Stock......Par $100........................Authorized, $58,118,982......Issued, $58,113,982

Preferred stock to the amount of $2,000,000 was issued in the reorganization, but all but $5,000 of preferred stock has been exchanged at par for 1st mortgage bonds.

Stock is transferred at the company's office, 56 Beaver street, New York. Registrar, Mercantile Trust Co., New York. Transfer Agent in London, Association of American Bond and Shareholders, Limited.

FUNDED DEBT.

Refunding mort., 4 per cent., g., due June, 1992, March and Sept.................. $16,937,000

BONDS SECURED BY COAL MORTGAGES.

Gold notes, 5 per cent., secured by Scranton Coal Co. 1st mort., due 1899-1911..... $2,150,000
" " 5 per cent., secured by Elk Hill Coal & Iron Co., 1st mort., due 1900-15, June and Dec.......................................................... 3,200,000

Total ........................................................... $22,287,000

The lease of the Utica, Clinton & Binghamton and Rome & Clinton roads is for 35 years, from June 1, 1886, at an annual rental of $75,000.

The Ontario, Carbondale & Scranton was built to afford this company access to the Lackawanna coal region. All its securities are held by the parent company and both its stock and bonds are deposited with the Trustee of the refunding mortgage.

The consolidated mortgage for $10,000,000 was created to pay for the Ontario, Carbondale & Scranton, 54 miles, and additional equipment and retire $4,000,000 old 1st mortgage, 6 per cent. bonds. The refunding mortgage ($20,000,000 authorized) was created in 1892 to retire $4,000,000 old 1st mortgage 6 per cent. bonds, which were redeemable at 110, and not retired with the 5 per cent. issue and the 5 per cent. consols, and to provide for future additions to property. The old 6s and 5s have been retired.

In January, 1899, it was announced that a large coal property and collieries near Scranton had been acquired in the interest of this company, and the transportation of the coal therefrom reserved by contract, the intention being to increase its tonnage of anthracite coal. Five per cent. gold sinking fund notes for $2,500,000, secured by a 1st mortgage of the Scranton Coal Co., were issued in connection with this purchase.

In December, 1900, the Elk Hill Coal & Iron Co. acquired a number of additional collieries, the railway company securing by contract the transportation of all the coal, and 5 per cent. sinking fund gold notes for $3,500,000 were created to finance the transaction. The gold notes are payable in annual instalments.

In 1898-99 the company's coal tonnage was 1,991,987 tons, and the revenue from the same $1,923,502. In 1899-1900 the coal earnings were $2,223,464 and the coal tonnage 2,157,553 tons. In 1900-01, coal earnings, $2,546,918; tonnage, 2,361,026 tons. In 1902, coal earnings, $2,517,338; tonnage, 2,455,355 tons.

EARNINGS.

Year ending June 30.

| | Gross. | Per Ct. of Exp. | Net. | Charges. | Surplus. |
|---|---|---|---|---|---|
| 1892-93 | $3,688,173 | 73.15 | $889,948 | $633,096 | $256,852 |
| 1893-94 | 3,842,119 | 68.40 | 1,109,579 | 690,013 | 419,566 |
| 1894-95 | 3,669,113 | 69.24 | 1,026,700 | 700,318 | 326,382 |
| 1895-96 | 3,779,335 | 68.42 | 1,080,777 | 705,208 | 375,569 |
| 1896-97 | 3,894,402 | 68.20 | 1,113,906 | 713,995 | 399,911 |
| 1897-98 | 3,914,635 | 68.68 | 1,112,992 | 710,532 | 402,460 |
| 1898-99 | 4,346,163 | 65.15 | 1,376,052 | 689,688 | 686,364 |
| 1899-00 | 4,963,482 | 66.07 | 1,548,565 | 689,541 | 859,024 |
| 1900-01 | 5,322,883 | 68.35 | 1,545,746 | 666,514 | 879,231 |
| 1901-02 | 5,456,696 | 73.60 | 1,298,941 | 639,982 | 658,958 |

The following presents the freight traffic statistics of the company:

| | Average Mileage. | Total Tonnage. | Tons Carried One Mile. | Freight Density. | Rate per Ton per Mile. | Earn'gs per Train Mile. | Av'ge Tons per Train. |
|---|---|---|---|---|---|---|---|
| 1899-00 | 480 | 3,416,606 | 486,442,640 | 1,013,422 | 0.816c. | $2.03 | 287 |
| 1900-01 | 480 | 3,508,508 | 516,135,284 | 1,075,281 | 0.827 | 2.12 | 290 |
| 1901-02 | 480 | 3,612,487 | 541,789,449 | 1,128,728 | 0.824 | 2.04 | 285 |

In 1898-99 $62,646 was deducted from surplus for items not charged to operating expenses, making the net surplus for the year $623,718.

President, Thomas P. Fowler, New York; Vice-President, Joseph Price, London, England; Vice-President and General Counsel, John B. Kerr; Secretary and Treasurer, Richard D. Rickard, New York.

Directors—C. Ledyard Blair, Henry W. Cannon, Francis R. Culbert, Thomas P. Fowler, Gerald L. Hoyt, Grant B. Schley, John B. Kerr, Chauncey M. Depew, Albert S. Roe, O. D. Ashley, New York; Charles S. Whelen, Philadelphia; Joseph Price, H. Pearson, London, England.

Main office, 56 Beaver street, New York; London office, 5 and 6 Great Winchester street, E. C. Annual meeting, last Wednesday in September. Books close one month previous.

## NEW YORK, PHILADELPHIA & NORFOLK RAILROAD CO.

Road owned, Delmar, Del., to Cape Charles, Va., 95 miles; branch, 17 miles; total, 112 miles. Also, steam ferry from Cape Charles to Norfolk, 36 miles. Locomotives, 18; passenger cars, 15; freight cars, 603. Floating equipment, 3 steamboats and 4 tugs, 8 floats, etc.

Stock......Par $100.. ........................Authorized, $2,000,000......Issued, $1,714,375

Transfer Agent, Fidelity Insurance Trust & Safe Deposit Co., Philadelphia.

The first dividend on the stock was 2 per cent., payable January 3, 1901; 2 per cent. was paid in June, 1901, and 2 per cent. in December, 1901; in June, 1902, paid 2 ½ per cent.

FUNDED DEBT.

| | |
|---|---|
| 1st mort., 4 per cent., due Jan., 1939,*Jan. and July | $2,600,000 |
| Income bonds, non-cumulative 4 per cent., due Jan., 1939, May and Nov. | 1,000,000 |
| Total | $3,600,000 |

In April, 1898, a committee, Rudulph Ellis, Philadelphia, Chairman, proposed a plan of reorganization involving foreclosure. A large majority of security holders assented to this plan. Of the new 1st mortgage bonds $400,000 are reserved for improvements.

EARNINGS.

Year ending June 30.

| | Gross. | Net. | Charges. | Balance. |
|---|---|---|---|---|
| 1892-93 | $845,402 | $165,935 | $190,738 | Def. $24,803 |
| 1893-94 | 878,857 | 195,387 | 190,495 | Sur. 4,891 |
| 1894-95 | 907,653 | 217,267 | 203,241 | " 14,026 |
| 1895-96 | 941,253 | 202,594 | 193,761 | " 8,833 |
| 1896-97 | 905,372 | 176,299 | 192,328 | Def. 16,029 |
| 1897-98 | 926,311 | 185,731 | 174,039 | Sur. 11,692 |
| 1898-99 | 1,106,152 | 314,507 | 129,851 | " 184,655 |
| 1899-00 | 1,199,842 | 469,420 | 290,105 | " 179,315 |
| 1900-01 | 1,289,967 | 439,266 | 339,470 | " 99,796 |

In November, 1899, 2 per cent. was paid on the income bonds, and in the subsequent years 4 per cent.

President, William A. Patton; Assistant to President, Robert K. Cassatt; Secretary, O. J. DeRousse; Treasurer, J. G. Cassatt, Philadelphia.

Directors—William A. Patton, J. G. Cassatt, A. J. Cassatt, Rudulph Ellis, John Lloyd, Clement A. Griscom, Robert K. Cassatt, Philadelphia.

Main office, Cape Charles, Va.; Philadelphia office, 26 South Fifteenth street. Annual meeting, third Tuesday in March.

## NEW YORK, SUSQUEHANNA & WESTERN RAILROAD CO.

(Controlled by Erie Railroad Co.)

Road owned, Jersey City, N. J., to Gravel Place, Pa., 101 miles; branches, 39 miles; leased, Wilkes-Barre & Eastern, Wilkes-Barre to Stroudsburg, Pa., 65 miles; other leased lines, 30 miles; trackage on Pennsylvania Railroad to Jersey City, 3 miles; total operated, 238 miles. Locomotives, 81; passenger cars, 87; freight cars, 3,822.

This company has a large terminal property of 62 acres at Edgewater, on the Hudson, opposite 110th street, New York.

In January, 1898, it was announced that the Erie Railroad Co., through J. P. Morgan & Co. of New York, had acquired a controlling interest in the stock of this company. In March, 1898, minority holders of this company's stock were offered $90 in Erie 1st preferred for each share of Susquehanna & Western preferred, and par in Erie common for the common. The road is operated in harmony with the Erie system, but through its own organization. The Erie owns $12,357,400 common and $12,882,800 of the preferred stock.

Stock...Par $100..Authorized { com., $13,000,000; pref., 13,000,000 } Issued { com., $13,000,000; pref., 13,000,000 } $26,000,000

Stock is transferred at the company's office, 21 Cortlandt street, New York.

In 1891 1¼ per cent. was paid on the preferred stock; in 1892, 2¼ per cent., and in 1893, 1¼ per cent. No dividends have been paid since the last-named year.

FUNDED DEBT.

| | |
|---|---|
| New 1st mort., 5 per cent., due Jan., 1937, Jan. and July | $3,745,000 |
| Midland of New Jersey, 1st mort., 6 per cent., due April, 1910, April and Oct. | 3,500,000 |
| Paterson extension bonds, 6 per cent., due June, 1910, June and Dec. | 250,000 |
| New 2d mort., 4½ per cent., due Feb., 1937, Feb. and Aug. | 447,000 |
| Gen. mort., 5 per cent., due Aug., 1940, Feb. and Aug. | 2,551,000 |
| Terminal 1st mort., 5 per cent., due May, 1943, May and Nov. | 2,000,000 |
| Wilkes-Barre & Eastern, 1st mort., guar. 5 per cent., due June, 1942, June and Dec. | 3,000,000 |
| Collateral trust bonds, 6 per cent., due May, 1905, May and Nov. | 253,000 |
| Susquehanna Connecting, 1st mort., 6 per cent., due March, 1907, March and Sept. | 250,000 |
| Passaic & New York R. R., 1st mort., 6 per cent., due Dec., 1910, June and Dec. | 70,000 |
| N. Y., Sus. & Wn. Coal Co., 1st mort., 6 per cent., due March, 1912, March and Sept. | 426,000 |
| N. Y. & Wilkes-Barre Coal Co., 1st mort., 6 per cent., due Nov., 1933, May and Nov. | 430,000 |
| Total | $16,922,000 |

There are $56,690 car trusts outstanding, also $44,000 Macopin Railroad 1st mortgage 5s.

The terminal mortgage covers all the new terminals at Weehawken, N. J., the tunnel and connecting tracks. The Wilkes-Barre & Eastern bonds are guaranteed principal and interest by endorsement.

EARNINGS.

Year ending June 30.

| | Gross. | Net. | Charges. | Surplus. |
|---|---|---|---|---|
| 1894-95 | $1,753,353 | $610,374 | $751,751 | Def. $90,313 |
| 1895-96 | 1,836,799 | 863,026 | 772,713 | 90,312 |
| 1896-97 | 1,819,253 | 813,008 | 772,070 | 40,937 |
| 1897-98 | 2,329,119 | 1,051,141 | 931,425 | 119,716 |
| 1898-99 | 2,446,653 | 1,111,936 | 945,146 | 166,790 |
| 1899-00 | 2,582,116 | 1,143,385 | 936,285 | 205,072 |
| 1900-01 | 2,504,887 | 1,076,819 | 930,238 | 146,581 |
| 1901-02 | 2,583,928 | 1,145,967 | 924,608 | 291,359 |

President, F. D. Underwood; 1st Vice-President, George M. Cumming; 2d Vice-President and Secretary, J. A. Middleton; Treasurer, J. W. Platten, New York.

Directors—W. Lanman Bull, George M. Cumming, Amos L. Hopkins, Cyrus J. Lawrence, Samuel Spencer, Francis Lynde Stetson, Eben B. Thomas, James J. Goodwin, Charles Steele, F. D. Underwood, New York; William H. Corbin, Jersey City; John G. McCullough, North Bennington, Vt.

Main office, 21 Cortlandt street, New York. Annual meeting, first Thursday in September. Books close twenty days before.

## NORFOLK & SOUTHERN RAILROAD CO.

Road owned, Berkeley, Va., to Edenton, N. C., and branch, 74 miles; Mackey's Ferry, N. C., to Belle Haven, N. C., 30 miles; Norfolk to Cape Henry, Va., 23 miles; branch, 22 miles; total, 149 miles; operates ferry, 9 miles, across Albemarle Sound, connecting the two sections of road. Locomotives, 16; passenger cars, 33; freight cars, 449; also 11 steamboats and 2 tugs.

Originally the Elizabeth City & Norfolk. Name changed February, 1883, to Norfolk Southern, Road sold in foreclosure 1891 and present name adopted in 1891. In 1899 control of the Norfolk, Virginia Beach & Southern Railroad Co. was acquired.

Stock......Par $100..........................Authorized, $2,000,000......Issued, $2,000,000

Transfer Agent, Metropolitan Trust Co., New York.

Dividends of 4 per cent. per annum have been paid on the stock from July, 1892. Dividends are paid quarterly, 1 per cent. each, in January (10), April, July and October. In 1901 the rate for the year was 5 per cent., an extra dividend of 1 per cent. having been paid on July 10, 1901.

FUNDED DEBT.

1st mort., 5 per cent., due May, 1941, May and Nov................................ $1,380,000

EARNINGS.

Year ending June 30.

| | Gross. | Op. Exp. Per Cent. | Net. | Charges. | Surplus. |
|---|---|---|---|---|---|
| 1892-93 | $440,170 | 67.85 | $145,028 | $31,250 | $114,178 |
| 1893-94 | 438,922 | 67.85 | 141,097 | 33,000 | 108,097 |
| 1894-95 | 438,637 | 64.28 | 156,671 | 37,106 | 119,564 |
| 1895-96 | 458,624 | 70.26 | 136,389 | 38,981 | 87,407 |
| 1896-97 | 460,612 | 71.94 | 129,237 | 38,731 | 90,505 |
| 1897-98 | 531,289 | 70.63 | 159,197 | 38,482 | 120,715 |
| 1898-99 | 555,636 | 68.87 | 175,497 | 40,232 | 135,265 |
| 1899-00 | 745,122 | 71.83 | 209,928 | 69,649 | 140,279 |
| 1900-01 | 817,818 | 78.19 | 178,293 | 68,240 | 110,052 |
| 1901-02 | 828,374 | 80.19 | 164,109 | 68,464 | 95,645 |

Gross earnings include receipts from steamboats and other sources

President, John Carstensen; Vice-President, Alfred Skitt; Secretary and Treasurer, Clarence Morgan, New York.

Directors—John Carstensen, Alfred Skitt, Walter S. Johnston, Henry Sampson, Charles F. Cox, George R. Turnbull, E. V. W. Rossiter, Chauncey M. Depew, New York; M. K. King, Norfolk, Va.

Main office, Norfolk, Va.; New York office, Grand Central Station. Annual meeting, first Thursday in March, at Norfolk, Va.

## NORFOLK & WESTERN RAILWAY CO.

A corporation formed under the laws of Virginia, September 24, 1896, which acquired October 1, 1896, the property of the railroad company of same name, sold under foreclosure and transferred to this company in pursuance of the plan of reorganization of March 12, 1896. For details of the reorganization, see MANUAL for 1898.

Road owned, Lambert's Point, Norfolk, Va., to Columbus, O., 708 miles; Roanoke, Va., to Hagerstown, Md. (Shenandoah Valley Railroad), 238 miles; Cripple Creek Extension, 44 miles; Radford to Bristol, Va.-Tenn., 107 miles; Clinch Valley Extension, Graham to Norton, 100 miles; Lynchburg to Durham, N. C., 115 miles; Roanoke, Va., to Winston-Salem, N. C., 121 miles; Portsmouth Junction, O., to Cincinnatti, 106 miles; branches, 143 miles; Columbus Connecting & Terminal, 3½ miles; total operated, 1,685½ miles. Locomotives, 502; passenger cars, 248; freight cars, 21,009; floating equipment, 7 coal barges.

In December, 1901, the company acquired the Pocahontas Coal & Coke Co., thus securing control of four-fifths of the entire Pocahontas coal field. This company does not engage directly in mining coal but leases its lands to operating companies. See statement of the Pocahontas Coal & Coke Co. in the Industrial Section of MANUAL.

The old company was a reorganization of Atlantic, Mississippi & Ohio. In 1890 acquired the Scioto Valley & New England, and in the same year purchased the Shenandoah Valley Railroad under foreclosure. The Clinch Valley Division, connecting the road with the Louisville & Nashville, was completed in 1891. The Lynchburg & Durham and Roanoke & Southern, Roanoke to Winston, were leased in March, 1892. These roads were foreclosed under the reorganization plan of 1896. In January, 1901, it acquired the Cincinnati, Portsmouth & Virginia Railway, and absorbed that company.

In 1901 the Pennsylvania Railroad Co. acquired a large interest in this company's stock, and representatives of that corporation became members of the board of directors.

| Stock..Par $100...Authorized | com., $66,000,000<br>pref., 23,000,000 | Issued | com., $66,000,000<br>pref., 23,000,000 | $89,000,000 |
|---|---|---|---|---|

The preferred stock is styled the adjustment preferred and is 4 per cent. non-cumulative, with a preference both as to dividends and the distribution of assets.

Transfer Agent, Metropolitan Trust Co., New York. Registrar, Mercantile Trust Co., New York.

Dividends of 1 per cent. on the new preferred stock began November 15, 1897; in August, 1898, 2 per cent. was paid on preferred, and such semi-annual payments at the rate of 2 per cent. have since been regularly made on the preferred in February (20) and August.

An initial dividend of 1 per cent. was paid on the common stock June 20, 1901, and dividends of 1 per cent. each were paid in December, 1902, and June, 1902, the dividend in the common, paid December 19, 1902, being 1½ per cent.

### Funded Debt.

| | |
|---|---|
| Norfolk & Western R. R., general mort., 6 per cent., due May, 1931, May and Nov.. | $7,283,000 |
| New River Division, 6 per cent., due April, 1932, April and Oct.................... | 2,000,000 |
| Improvement and extension mort., 6 per cent., due Nov., 1934, Feb. and Aug....... | 5,000,000 |
| Scioto Val. & N. E., 4 per cent., due Nov., 1989, May and Nov.................... | 5,000,000 |
| Columbus Con. & Term., 1st mort., guar. 5 per cent., due Jan., 1922, Jan. and July. | 600,000 |
| New 1st consols of 1896, 4 per cent., due 1996, April and Oct...................... | 34,210,500 |
| Total....................................................... ....... | $54,093,500 |

### Joint Obligations of this Company and the Pocahontas Coal & Coke Co.

Poca. Coal & Coke Co., 4 per cent. joint guar. bonds., due Dec., 1941, June and Dec. $20,000,000

There are also equipment trusts outstanding for about $3,572,000. Several of the old bond issues, which matured in 1900, were retired by new 4 per cent. consols.

The Pocahontas Coal & Coke Co. purchase money, 4 per cent. bonds, are the joint and several obligations of these corporations, but as between the two companies the debt it to be paid by the Coal & Coke Co. and is treated as the liability of that company.

### Earnings.

| | Dividends. Com. | Pfd. | Gross. | Per Cent. Oper. Exp. | Net. | Charges. | Surplus. |
|---|---|---|---|---|---|---|---|
| 1893 (1,556 miles)........ | .. | .. | $10,032,617 | .... | $2,974,346 | $3,074,089 | Def. $99,742 |
| 1894 (1,567 " )........ | .. | .. | 10,340,452 | 74.41 | 2,782,132 | 3,107,508 | " 325,376 |
| 1895 (1,570 " )........ | .. | .. | 9,662,087 | 77.89 | 2,174,690 | 3,139,649 | " 964,959 |
| 1896 ( " " )........ | .. | .. | 11,055,845 | 75.41 | 2,330,801 | ........ | ...... |
| 1897 (1,569 " )........ | .. | .. | 7,732,159 | 72.79 | 2,120,305 | 1,645,146 | 475,159 |
| 1897-98 (year end. June 30) | .. | 2 | 11,236,123 | 70.18 | 3,382,987 | 2,239,433 | 1,138,948 |
| 1898-99 ( " " ) | .. | 4 | 11,827,139 | 67.13 | 3,911,400 | 2,241,714 | 1,669,686 |
| 1899-00 ( " " ) | .. | 4 | 14,091,004 | 60.33 | 5,663,471 | 2,273,639 | 3,389,832 |
| 1900-01 ( " " ) | 1 | 4 | 15,785,441 | 59.84 | 6,408,599 | 2,249,717 | 4,158,881 |
| 1901-02 ( " " ) | 2 | 4 | 17,552,204 | 57.75 | 7,490,871 | 2,367,777 | 5,123,094 |

In 1901-02 the dividends paid were $2,199,408; deficiency in interest on Pocahontas Coal & Coke Co. joint bonds, $161,229; miscellaneous payments, $80,391; betterment fund, $2,500,000; surplus, $182,075.

The following presents the comparative freight traffic statistics of the company:

| | Average Mileage. | Total Tonnage. | Tons Carried One Mile. | Freight Density. | Rate per Ton per Mile. | Earnings per Train Mile. | Average Tons per Train. |
|---|---|---|---|---|---|---|---|
| 1897-98 .... | 1,565 | 8,276,948 | 2,301,312,744 | 1,470,487 | 0.404c. | $1.435 | 355 |
| 1898-99 .... | 1,555 | 8,837,739 | 2,456,096,895 | 1,579,480 | 0.397 | 1.524 | 384 |
| 1899-00 .... | 1,555 | 10,783,221 | 2,732,536,626 | 1,757,258 | 0.430 | 1.871 | 435 |
| 1900-01 .... | 1,560 | 10,836,512 | 2,864,370,760 | 1,836,135 | 0.461 | 2.125 | 461 |
| 1901-02 .... | 1,677 | 12,268,110 | 3,151,911,924 | 1,879,553 | 0.463 | 2.202 | 476 |

Coal constitutes the largest item in this company's tonnage. The total shipments of coal were in 1896-97, 3,656,967 tons; in 1897-98, 3,664,191 tons; in 1898-99, 4,001,308 tons; in 1899-1900, 4,477,532 tons; in 1900-01, 4,890,317 tons, and in 1901-02, 5,455,286 tons. Coke also supplied 767,418 tons in 1897, 1,120,575 tons in 1898, 1,257,494 tons in 1899, 1,512,045 tons in 1900, 1,386,816 tons in 1901 and 1,484,868 tons in 1902.

Chairman, Henry Fink, New York; President, Frederick J. Kimball, Philadelphia; Vice-President and General Manager, L. E. Johnson; Treasurer, William G. Macdowell, Philadelphia; Secretary, A. J. Hemphill, Philadelphia.

Directors—Henry Fink, Victor Morawetz, New York; Frederick J. Kimball, William H. Barnes, Joseph I. Doran, John P. Green, Sutherland M. Prevost, Samuel Rea, N. Parker Shortridge, Philadelphia; Walter H. Taylor, Norfolk, Va.; James McCrea, Pittsburg.

Main office, Roanoke, Va.; executive office, Arcade Building, Philadelphia. Annual meeting, second Thursday in October. Books close two weeks previously.

## NORTH CAROLINA RAILROAD CO.

(Leased to Southern Railway Co.)

Road owned, Goldsboro, N. C., to Charlotte, 223 miles. The property was leased to the Richmond & Danville, and after reorganization of that company a new lease was made to the Southern Railway Co. In 1897 a new board of directors was appointed by the State and efforts were set on foot to annul the lease. The courts, however, restrained State from annulling the lease, and a satisfactory adjustment was finally reached.

Stock......Par $100..........................Authorized, $4,000,000......Issued, $4,000,000

Stock is transferred at the company's office, Burlington, N. C.

Dividends are paid semi-annually, 3½ per cent. each, in February (10) and August.

The State of North Carolina owns $3,000,000 of the stock.

Former lease was for 30 years from 1871, at a rental of $260,000 a year, which was sufficient to pay 6 per cent. on stock. New lease of 1896 was for 99 years for $266,000 (6½ per cent.) till 1901 and $286,000 (7 per cent.) thereafter, lessee paying taxes.

President, H. G. Chatham, Elkin, N. C.; Secretary and Treasurer, D. H. McLean, Burlington, N. C.

Main office, Burlington, N. C. Annual meeting, second Thursday in July, at Greensboro, N. C.

## NORTH PENNSYLVANIA RAILROAD CO.

(Leased to Philadelphia & Reading Railway Co.)

Road owned, Philadelphia to Bethlehem, 56 miles; branches, 30 miles; total, 86 miles.

Stock......Par $50..........................Authorized, $6,000,000......Issued, $4,720,850

Stock is transferred by the secretary of the company, Philadelphia.

Dividends are paid quarterly, 2 per cent. each in February (25), May, August and November

FUNDED DEBT.

| | |
|---|---|
| 2d, now 1st, mort., extended 4 per cent., due May, 1936, May and Nov.............. | $1,500,000 |
| Gen. mort., extended, 3½ per cent., due Jan., 1953, Jan. and July.................. | 4,500,000 |
| Reg. loan, 6 per cent., due Sept., 1905, March and Sept........................... | 1,200,000 |
| Funding loan, 4 per cent., due Nov., 1928, May and Nov........................... | 318,000 |
| Total.................................................................. | $7,518,000 |

The lease to the Philadelphia & Reading is for 990 years from May 1, 1879. The rental is interest on bonds, 8 per cent. on stock, and $12,000 a year for organization expenses.

Earnings are included in those of lessee.

President, John H. Michener; Secretary and Treasurer, John S. Wise, Philadelphia.

Main office, 240 South Third street, Philadelphia. Annual meeting, second Monday in January.

## NORTH SHORE RAILROAD CO.

A corporation formed under the laws of California in 1902, which acquired and took over the North Pacific Coast Railroad Co.

Road owned, San Francisco to Cazadero, Cal., 87 miles, of which 6 miles are a ferry across San Francisco Bay; branches, 4 miles; leased, San Rafael & San Quentin Railroad, 3½ miles; total operated, 94 miles. Locomotives, 13; passenger cars, 60; freight cars, 340.

In January, 1902, control of the old company was secured by a syndicate of capitalists who were interested in the Bay Counties Power Co. of San Francisco. It was announced that a considerable portion of the lines would be equipped with electric power.

Stock......Par $100..........................Authorized, $6,000,000......Issued, $6,000,000

The amount of stock issued as given above is nominal.

Stock is transferred by the secretary of the company, San Francisco.

FUNDED DEBT.

| | |
|---|---|
| North Pac. Coast general 1st mort., 5 per cent., due Jan., 1912, Jan. and July...... | $1,500,000 |
| North Shore mort., 5 per cent., due May, 1942, May and Nov..... ....... ......... | 850,000 |
| Total ........................................................ | $2,350,000 |

The old 1st mortgage 6 per cent. gold bonds of the North Pacific Coast Railroad Co., of which there were $515,000 outstanding, matured in 1901 and were paid off, the issue of general mortgage bonds being increased for the purpose.

The new mortgage created by the North Shore Railroad Co. in 1902 is $6,000,000 authorized, $1,500,000 of the bonds being reserved to retire the North Pacific Coast general mortgage 5s.

EARNINGS.

| | Gross. | Net. | Charges. | Surplus. |
|---|---|---|---|---|
| 1901........................................ | $426,511 | $102,151 | $83,083 | $19,067 |
| 1902........................................ | 474,602 | 185,646 | 108,412 | 77,233 |

President, John Martin; Vice-President, Eugene de Sabla; Treasurer, Ant. Borel; General Manager, W. M. Rank; Secretary, F. B. Latham; Auditor, E. D. Thomas, San Francisco.

Directors—John Martin, R. R. Colgate, E. J. De Sabla, R. M. Hotaling, W. M. Pierson, C. A. Grow.

Main office, 626 Market street, San Francisco. Annual meeting, third Monday in January, at San Francisco.

---

## NORTHERN CENTRAL RAILWAY CO.

(Controlled by Pennsylvania Railroad Co.)

Road owned, Baltimore, Md., to Sunbury, Pa., 137 miles; branch, 9 miles; leased, Shamokin Branch, 38 miles; Williamsport, Pa., to Sodus Point and Canandaigua, N. Y., 175 miles Lykens Valley Railroad, 19 miles; Rockville Branch, 3 miles; York, Hanover & Frederick Railroad, 56 miles; York Branch Pennsylvania Railroad, Columbia, Pa., to York, Pa., 13 miles; total, 450 miles. Trains also use the Philadelphia & Erie track from Sunbury to Williamsport, 40 miles, and Philadelphia & Erie trains use track of this road from Marysville to Sunbury, 40 miles. Locomotives, 191; passenger cars, 161; freight cars, 9,645; service cars, 330.

A controlling interest is owned by the Pennsylvania Railroad Co., which holds $6,267,950 of the stock.

Stock......Par $50.........................Authorized, $12,000,000......Issued, $11,462,300

Transfer office, Broad Street Station, Philadelphia.

For dividends paid see table of earnings. The January, 1901, dividend was increased from 3½ to 4 per cent., or 8 per cent. per annum, which has since been the regular rate. Dividends are paid semi-annually, in June (15) and July.

In February, 1900, stock was increased from $8,000,000 to $12,000,000 to retire the bonds maturing in that year. The increase included $2,503,983 offered to stockholders at $70 per share and $1,439,350 issued to acquire additional property.

FUNDED DEBT.

| | |
|---|---|
| Maryland State loan, 6 per cent., perpetual, quar., Jan.. ........................... | $1,500,000 |
| Consolidated general mort., A, B, C and D, 6 per cent., due July, 1904, Jan. and July. | 2,394,000 |
| " " " E, 4½ per cent., due April, 1925, April and Oct........ | 1,757,000 |
| 2d general mort., series A, 5 per cent., due 1926, Jan. and July.................... | 2,565,000 |
| " " " series B, 5 per cent., due 1926, Jan. and July.................... | 1,000,000 |
| Total ................. . ........................................ | $9,216,000 |

There are also $110,706 of real estate mortgages and ground rents outstanding.

The consolidated general mortgage is for $10,000,000, to include all prior liens except Maryland State loan. In April, 1882, the company bought from the Canton Company all the stock of the Union Railroad of Baltimore. The company guarantees, jointly with the Pennsylvania Railroad Co., the first authorized mortgage bonds of the Baltimore & Potomac.

EARNINGS.

| | Div. Paid. | Gross. | Net. | Charges. | Surplus. |
|---|---|---|---|---|---|
| 1893..................... | 8 | $6,881,806 | $2,615,629 | $1,453,988 | $1,161,640 |
| 1894..................... | 7 | 6,031,261 | 2,183,480 | 1,547,519 | 635,960 |
| 1895..................... | 7 | 6,506,028 | 2,364,900 | 1,686,775 | 678,125 |
| 1896..................... | 7 | 6,286,602 | 2,015,643 | 1,411,785 | 603,857 |
| 1897..................... | 7 | 6,732,702 | 2,301,124 | 1,378,253 | 922,871 |

EARNINGS.—*Continued.*

| | Div. Paid. | Gross. | Net. | Charges. | Surplus. |
|---|---|---|---|---|---|
| 1898 | 7 | $6,664,028 | $2,356,940 | $1,427,356 | $929,584 |
| 1899 | 7 | 7,233,417 | 2,483,632 | 1,409,555 | 1,074,077 |
| 1900 | 7 | 7,845,411 | 2,980,067 | 1,682,509 | 1,297,557 |
| 1901 | 8 | 8,266,957 | 3,106,275 | 1,088,256 | 2,018,018 |
| 1902 | 8 | 8,456,685 | 2,927,197 | 1,180,651 | 1,746,546 |

In 1902 the surplus over the 8 per cent. dividends was $829,566.

President, Alexander J. Cassatt; Vice-Presidents, John P. Green, Charles E. Pugh, Sutherland M. Prevost, Samuel Rea, Philadelphia; Treasurer, A. W. Hendrix, Baltimore; Secretary, Stephen W. White, Philadelphia.

Directors—Charles E. Pugh, N. Parker Shortridge, John P. Green, Sutherland M. Prevost, Wayne McVeagh, A. Loudon Snowden, Samuel Rea, Philadelphia; Luther S. Bent, Michael Jenkins, Henry Walters, Baltimore; J. Donald Cameron, Harrisburg, Pa.; M. H. Arnot, Elmira, N. Y.

Main office, Baltimore. Annual meeting, fourth Thursday in February.

---

## NORTHERN PACIFIC RAILWAY CO.

(Controlled by Northern Securities Co.)

A company incorporated by special act in Wisconsin, March 15, 1870; amended in 1871 and April 15, 1895. Purchased under foreclosure sales July 25, 1896, and subsequent dates the property of Northern Pacific Railroad Company pursuant to reorganization plan of latter.

The old Northern Pacific Railroad Company had a charter granted by Congress July 6, 1864.

Road owned, main line, St. Paul, Minn., and Ashland, Wis., to Tacoma, Wash., and Portland, Ore., 2,999 miles; branches, 2,365 miles; total owned, 5,364 miles; controlled, 253 miles; mileage, leased or owned jointly, 32 miles; total of system, 5,649 miles. The company also operates 120 miles of water lines. It had under construction at the end of 1902 other branches.

Of the total mileage of the system, 4,989 miles were, on January 30, 1901, operated by the Northern Pacific Railway Co., 254 miles were operated by controlled lines, 367 by other companies, and 39 miles were not operated. In the mileage operated by other companies is included the company's lines in the Province of Manitoba, 354 miles, which in May, 1901, were leased for 999 years to the Province, and have been sub-leased to the Canadian Northern Railway Co. The Province of Manitoba has the option of purchasing these lines at any time for $7,000,000.

In 1900 the stock of the St. Paul & Duluth was acquired and that road, 245 miles, was merged with this company, and is operated as its Duluth Division. For details as to the St. Paul & Duluth, see statement of that company in the MANUAL for 1900.

In 1901 this company, jointly with the Great Northern Railway Co., acquired nearly all the stock of the Chicago, Burlington & Quincy Railroad Co. in exchange for the joint 4 per cent. debenture bonds of the two purchasing companies. For details, see Chicago, Burlington & Quincy Railroad and Great Northern Railway in this edition of the MANUAL.

The Wisconsin Central, 809 miles, was leased to old company, but lease was terminated in September, 1893. Also leased the Chicago & Northern Pacific (in which this company had large stock interest), but that lease was terminated when Wisconsin Central was surrendered. The Seattle, Lake Shore & Eastern, 245 miles, was also controlled, but was separated from it in 1893. The Central Washington also was not included in the reorganization, but in 1898 was leased by present company, which owns all the stock of the reorganized road. In January, 1898, this company again obtained a controlling interest in the Seattle, Lake Shore & Eastern, and also acquired the Washington & Columbia River Railroad, 163 miles. In 1900 this company acquired control of the Everett & Monte Cristo Railway. In January, 1902, this company acquired the Minneapolis & White Bear Line, 14 miles of the Minneapolis & St. Louis Railway.

Locomotives, 704; passenger cars, 622; freight cars, 26,704; also 2 steamboats.

Stock......Par $100......................Authorized, $155,000,000......Issued, $155,000,000

Under the reorganization the company had $80,000,000 common and $75,000,000 preferred stock. Preferred stock was entitled to 4 per cent. non-cumulative dividends out of surplus earnings in each fiscal year. When in any year both preferred and common received 4 per cent. they participated equally in any further division. Preferred stock had the right to elect a majority of board of directors whenever for two successive quarterly periods after July 1, 1897, full quarterly dividends at rate of 4 per cent. per annum are not paid in cash. The company could retire preferred in whole or part at par on any 1st of January prior to 1917. No additional mortgage could be placed on the property without consent of a majority of both stocks.

On November 13, 1901, the directors gave notice that the preferred stock would be retired at par on January 1, 1902. The common stockholders were also given the right to subscribe for 75-80 of their holdings in 4 per cent. certificates of indebtedness at par, said certificates to be convertible in new common stock; the common stock being increased from $80,000,000 to $155,000,000 for this purpose. This arrangement was carried out on January 1, 1902, the preferred stock being retired and the common increased as stated.

In November, 1901, it was announced that the Northern Securities Co. would exchange its shares for the common stock of the Northern Pacific at 115 for the latter, which arrangement was duly carried out on or about January 1, 1902, the Northern Securities Co. acquiring nearly all the stock of this company.

Transfer Agents, J. P. Morgan & Co., New York; Deutsche Bank, Berlin.

The new company in December, 1897, declared a dividend of 1 per cent. on the preferred stock, payable January 15, 1898. Regular quarterly dividends on the preferred were paid at the rate of 4 per cent. per annum, being 1 per cent. each in March (5), June, September and December. At the time the preferred stock was retired on January 1, 1902, an extra dividend of 1 per cent. was declared in addition to the regular December, 1901, dividend on the preferred.

In December, 1898, the first dividend on the common stock was declared, being 1 per cent. payable February 3, 1899. In August, 1899, 1 per cent. was paid on the common, and in December, 1899, a dividend of 1 per cent. and 1 per cent. extra was declared payable February 5, 1900. In August, 1900, 1 per cent. was paid, and 1 per cent. November 30, 1900. The February, 1901, dividend being also 1 per cent., thus putting the common on a 4 per cent. basis, and the dividends on the common have since been paid, 1 per cent. each, in February, May, August and November (5). In May, 1902, the quarterly rate was increased to 1¼ per cent., putting the stock on a 5 per cent. basis.

FUNDED DEBT.

| | |
|---|---|
| Nor. Pac. Ry., prior lien, 4 per cent., due Jan., 1997, quar., Jan. | $100,209,500 |
| " gen. lien, 3 per cent., due 2046, quar., Feb. | 56,000,000 |
| Western R. R. of Minn., 1st mort., 7 per cent., due May, 1907, May and Nov. | 352,000 |
| St. P. & Nor. Pac., gen. mort., 6 per cent., due Feb., 1923, quar., Feb. | 8,021,000 |
| Minn. & Duluth, 1st mort., 7 per cent., due Jan., 1907, May and Nov. | 280,000 |
| St. P. & Duluth Div. pur. mon. mort., 4 per cent., due Dec., 1996, June and Dec. | 8,054,000 |
| " " 1st mort., 5 per cent., assumed, due Aug., 1931, Feb. and Aug. | 1,000,000 |
| " " 2d mort., 5 p. c., c. bds., assumed, due Oct., 1917, April and Oct. | 2,000,000 |
| " " con. mort., 4 per cent., assumed, due June, 1968, June and Dec. | 1,000,000 |
| Taylor's Falls & Lake Sup., 1st mort., 6 p. c., assumed, due Jan., 1914, Jan. and July. | 210,000 |
| Duluth Short Line, 1st mort., 5 per cent., assumed, due Sept., 1916, March and Sept. | 500,000 |
| Total | $177,626,500 |

FUNDED DEBT JOINTLY WITH GREAT NORTHERN RAILWAY.

| | |
|---|---|
| Northern Pac.-Great Northern, joint col. tr. mort., C., Burlington & Q. stock collateral, 4 per cent., due July, 1921, Jan. and July. | $215,154,400 |

No additional mortgage can be placed on property acquired under reorganization except under the conditions provided in plan, nor can amount of such issues outstanding be increased except in conformity therewith.

Of the $130,000,000 prior lien 4s, $25,000,000 were reserved to be used for construction, etc., at rate of $1,500,000 per annum, and of the $60,000,000 authorized general lien bonds, $4,000,000 were reserved for a like purpose.

In November, 1899, the company called for redemption at 110 the remaining $4,490,000 of 1st mortgage 6 per cent. bonds outstanding. The funds for this purpose were obtained by a sale of part of the company's lands.

The St. Paul & Duluth purchase money mortgage is $20,000,000, authorized, of which $9,215,000 was issued to acquire the road, the balance being reserved to retire the St. Paul & Duluth's prior bonds and provide for improvements.

There are $1,538,000 4 per cent. 1st mortgage bonds of the Washington Central Railway, due March, 1948, interest quarterly, March, which are guaranteed under the lease of that property to Northern Pacific.

For securities of old company see MANUAL for 1896.

Both classes of stock were vested for five years from 1896 in a voting trust. Trustees, J. Pierpont Morgan, George von Siemens, August Belmont, Johnston Livingston and Charles Lanier. The trust was dissolved January 1, 1901, and regular stock certificates issued to holders of the trustees' beneficial interest certificates.

A receiver was appointed for the old Northern Pacific Railroad Co. in 1893. Reorganization committee, formed originally to represent old consolidated 5 per cent. mortgage bonds, consisted of Edward D. Adams, Chairman; John C. Bullitt, Louis Fitzgerald, C. H. Godfrey, J. D. Probst, James Stillman and Ernst Thalmann. Committee worked in conjunction with Berlin interests in company's securities, including the Deutsche Bank of that city, and with J. P. Morgan & Co. of New York and the Deutsche Bank's London agency.

Plan of reorganization was issued March 16, 1896. It provided for foreclosure under 2d and subsequent mortgages and transfer of property to new company. For terms of reorganization, see MANUAL for 1900.

The company had a land grant of 43,000,000 acres, of which 20,261,000 acres were unsold June 30, 1901. During 1899 the company made large sales of its lands. Lands east of the Missouri River were not included in the foreclosure sale.

In August, 1898, it was determined to set aside a fund of $3,000,000, equal to one year's 4 per cent. dividends on the preferred stock, taken out of the earnings since reorganization, to constitute a guarantee of preferred dividends.

EARNINGS.

Year ending June 30.

| | Gross. | Net. | Int. Charges. | Surplus. |
|---|---|---|---|---|
| 1892–93 (4,443 miles)........... | $23,920,108 | $9,489,859 | $9,853,255 | Def. $363,395 |
| 1893–94 (4,468 " )........... | 16,547,209 | 4,605,067 | 10,750,337 | " 6,145,269 |
| 1894–95 (4,469 " )........... | 17,434,980 | 5,914,811 | 11,043,597 | " 5,128,785 |
| 1895–96 (4,404 " )........... | 19,863,159 | 7,691,073 | 11,068,850 | " 3,377,726 |
| 1896–97 (4,375 " ) (10 mos.).. | 14,941,818 | 5,612,305 | 5,122,476 | 489,829 |
| 1897–98 (4,379 " )........... | 23,679,718 | 11,977,034 | 6,079,160 | 5,897,874 |
| 1898–99 (4,579 " )........... | 26,048,673 | 13,950,695 | 6,140,793 | 7,809,902 |
| 1899–00 (4,714 " )........... | 30,021,318 | 15,461,620 | 5,977,801 | 9,488,818 |
| 1900–01 (5,100 " )........... | 32,560,983 | 15,744,274 | 6,530,371 | 9,213,903 |
| 1901–02 (5,019 " )........... | 41,387,380 | 19,792,841 | 6,745,609 | 13,047,232 |

From the earnings of 1898-99 $2,176,619 was deducted for betterments, etc., and $4,600,000 paid for dividends, leaving net surplus for the year, $1,033,282. In 1899-1900, betterments, $3,000,000; dividends paid (4 per cent. on preferred and 3 per cent. on common), $5,400,000; balance surplus, $1,083,818. In 1900-01, betterments, $2,011,285; dividends, $6,200,000; surplus, $1,002,618. In 1901-02, betterments, $3,000,000; dividends, $8,499,946; surplus, $1,547,286.

The following presents the freight traffic statistics of the company:

| | Average Mileage. | Total Tonnage. | Tons Carried One Mile. | Freight Density. | Rate per Ton per Mile. | Earnings per Train Mile. | Average Tons per Train. |
|---|---|---|---|---|---|---|---|
| 1897–98 | 4,362 | 4,951,183 | 1,618,170,284 | 370,969 | 1.065c | $2.85 | 264 |
| 1898–99 | 4,579 | 5,816,639 | 1,830,855,264 | 399,836 | 1.047 | 2.95 | 277 |
| 1899–00 | 4,714 | 7,121,655 | 2,205,317,271 | 467,823 | 0.988 | 3.18 | 317 |
| 1900–01 | 5.100 | 8,792,885 | 2,440,662,665 | 478,561 | 0.944 | 3.12 | 324 |
| 1901–02 | 5,019 | 11,080,101 | 3,300,253,137 | 657,551 | 0.900 | 3,172 | 346 |

New company's first year began September 1, 1896. The first annual report, 1896–97, is consequently for the ten months to June 30, 1897.

Earnings for 1891–92 to 1895–96, both inclusive, are as stated and revised by the reorganization committee. Charges are under the old basis. See MANUAL for 1896 for earnings, charges, etc., as stated in company's report and by Receivers.

President, Charles S. Mellen, St. Paul; Vice-President, Daniel S. Lamont, New York; 2d Vice-President, J. M. Hannaford; Comptroller, Henry A. Gray, St. Paul; Secretary and Assistant Treasurer, George H. Earl, New York; Treasurer, Charles A. Clark, St. Paul.

Directors—Samuel Spencer, Hamilton McK. Twombly, Charles Steele, William Rockefeller, Edward H. Harriman, Brayton Ives, D. Willis James, George F. Baker, James Stillman, Eben B. Thomas, Daniel S. Lamont, John S. Kennedy, New York; Charles S. Mellen, William P. Clough, St. Paul; Samuel Rea, Philadelphia.

Executive office, Broadway and Prince street, St. Paul; administration office, 49 Wall street, New York. Annual meeting, third Thursday in October.

---

## NORTHERN PACIFIC TERMINAL CO. OF OREGON

A corporation formed under the laws of Oregon, August 28, 1882. Owns terminal property in Portland, East Portland and Albina, on Willamette River, comprising real estate, 271 acres; trackage, 32 miles; 39 buildings; 7,904 feet of dock frontage, and a large Union passenger station at Portland.

Stock......Par $100..........................Authorized, $3,000,000......Issued, $3,000,000

Stock is transferred by the Secretary of the company, Portland, Ore.

FUNDED DEBT.

1st mort., 6 per cent., due July, 1933, Jan. and July............................. $3,715.000

The Trustee of the 1st mortgage is the Farmers' Loan & Trust Co., New York. Agent for the payment of interest, Winslow, Lanier & Co., New York.

The sinking fund of company holds $405,000 of the bonds. The unfunded debt is about $50,303.

The property of this company is leased for 50 years from January 1, 1883, jointly to the Northern Pacific, Oregon Railway & Navigation and Oregon & California Railway Companies. The guaranteed rental is an amount sufficient to pay interest, taxes and sinking fund (the latter from 1893). The first two of the above companies guarantee each 40 per cent. and the Oregon & California 20 per cent. of the rental. The stock is held in trust in the same proportion for these companies, to be delivered when the same shall have been paid for in cash, at par, and an equal amount of the company's bonds thereby redeemed and cancelled or otherwise paid, as provided in the mortgage.

President, C. A. Dolph, Portland, Ore.; Vice-President, Charles H. Tweed, New York; Secretary, E. E. Mallory; Treasurer and Comptroller, E. L. Brown, Portland, Ore.

Main office, Portland, Ore.; New York office, 49 Wall street. Annual meeting, third Monday in June, in Portland.

## NORTHERN SECURITIES CO.

A corporation formed under the laws of New Jersey, November 13, 1901. The company has power to acquire and hold the stock and securities of railroad and other corporations. It was organized in pursuance of plans to bring under one ownership the stocks of the Great Northern Railway Co. and the Northern Pacific Railway Co., which companies had acquired joint ownership of the stock of the Chicago, Burlington & Quincy Railroad Co.

It was stated in 1902 that this company had acquired about 99 per cent. of the stock of the Northern Pacific Railway and 75 per cent. of that of the Great Northern Railway.

Stock......Par $100......................Authorized, $400,000,000......Issued, $350,000,000

Transfer Agents, Hudson Trust Co., Hoboken, N. J.; Nicholas Terhune, 26 Liberty street, New York.

The amount of stock issued as given above is only approximate.

The first dividend paid on the stock of the company was 1 per cent. quarterly, paid February 1, 1902. And similar dividends were paid in February (1), May, August and November until 1905, when the quarterly dividend was increased to 1⅛ per cent.

In November, 1901, the holders of the preferred stock of the Great Northern Railway, which was $125,000,000 in amount, were offered $180 per share for their stock, payable in stock of this company. In January, 1902, a considerable amount of the Great Northern preferred had been purchased.

In November, 1901, the holders of Northern Pacific common stock, $155,000,000, were offered $115 per share for their stock, payable in stock of this company. In January, 1902, substantially all the stock of the Northern Pacific had been purchased. See statement of the Northern Pacific Railway in this edition of the MANUAL for details regarding the retirement of the $75,000,000 of that company's preferred stock on January 1, 1902, and the increase of its common stock to $155,000,000.

This company has no bonded debt. Its revenues are derived from the income on its investments in the securities of railroad and other companies which it acquired and holds.

It was stated that the managements of the companies whose stocks were acquired by the Northern Securities Co. would be kept separate and distinct, and that no consolidation or merger of those corporations was intended. Opposition to the plan involved in the formation of this company, however, developed in Minnesota and other Northwestern States, and in January, 1902, the Attorney-General of Minnesota made application to the Supreme Court of the United States to enjoin this company from acquiring and holding the stocks of the Great Northern Railway and the Northern Pacific Railway, on the ground that it constituted an infraction of the laws of Minnesota prohibiting the consolidation of parallel and competing lines, and was contrary to the agreements between the companies and the State, whereby the latter granted lands to the companies. This suit was dismissed by the United States Supreme Court for lack of jurisdiction. A similar suit was also brought by the Attorney-General of the State of Washington, which is pending. The State of Minnesota subsequently brought a similar suit in the courts of that State, which was, however, transferred to the United States Circuit Court for the District of Minnesota.

A suit was also brought in the United States Circuit Court by the Attorney-General of the United States to test the legality of the company's formation and its acquisition of interests in other companies under the United States laws.

EARNINGS.—NORTHERN PACIFIC, GREAT NORTHERN AND CHICAGO, BURLINGTON & QUINCY RAILWAY COS.

Year ending June 30.

| | Gross. | Net. | Charges. | Surplus. |
|---|---|---|---|---|
| 1901-02 (18,377 miles)......... | $134,041,137 | $58,261,961 | $20,145,928 | $38,116,033 |

President, James J. Hill, St. Paul; Vice-President, John S. Kennedy; 2d Vice-President, George F. Baker; 3d Vice-President, D. Willis James, New York; 4th Vice-President, William P. Clough, St. Paul; Secretary and Treasurer, E. T. Nichols, New York.

Directors—James J. Hill, William P. Clough, St. Paul; D. Willis James, Samuel Thorne, E. T. Nichols, George F. Baker, Robert Bacon, George W. Perkins, Daniel S. Lamont, Edward H. Harriman, Jacob H. Schiff, James Stillman, John S. Kennedy, George C. Clark, N. Terhune, New York.

Corporate office, 51 Newark street, Hoboken, N. J.; New York office, 26 Liberty street. Annual meeting, second Monday in November.

## NORWICH & WORCESTER RAILROAD CO.

(Leased to New York, New Haven & Hartford Railroad Co.)

Road owned, Groton, Conn., to Worcester, Mass., 71.60 miles. Extension from Allyn's Point to Groton, Conn., was completed in 1899. The company owns all the stock of the Norwich & New York Transportation Co., known as the Norwich Line of Sound steamers.

The road is operated by the New York, New Haven & Hartford Railroad Co. under 99 years' lease, originally made to the New York & New England, from February, 1869, for interest on bonds and 8 per cent. on stock, which lease was assumed by the New York, New Haven & Hartford Railroad on July 1, 1898.

| Stock...Par $100...Authorized | com., $6,600<br>pref., 3,000,000 | Issued | com., $6,600<br>pref., 3,000,000 | $3,006,600 |
|---|---|---|---|---|

In 1899-1900 the stock was increased by issue and sale of $230,800 new stock, and the bond issue by $245,000 new bonds.

Transfer Agent, Second National Bank, Boston.

The dividends on the preferred stock are paid quarterly, 2 per cent. each, in January (1), April, July and October. No dividends are paid on the common.

FUNDED DEBT.

New plain bonds, 4 per cent., due March, 1927, March and Sept...................... $1,200,000

President, A. G. Bullock, Worcester; Secretary and Treasurer, M. Maturin Whittemore, New Haven, Conn.

Main office, Worcester, Mass. Annual meeting, second Wednesday in January, at Worcester.

## OHIO RIVER & WESTERN RAILWAY CO.

A corporation formed under the laws of Ohio, which, on January 1, 1903, took possession of the property of the Bellaire, Zanesville & Cincinnati Railroad Co.

Road owned, narrow gauge, Bellaire, O., to Mill Run, O., 111 miles; trackage to Zanesville, 1 mile. The present management of the company has taken steps to change the road to broad gauge, which work will be completed early in 1903. It is also intended to equip the line with electric power for its passenger service. The International Coal Co., which owns some 25,000 acres of coal lands adjacent to the line, is controlled in the interest of this company. Locomotives, 10; passenger cars, 10; freight cars, 222.

| Stock...Par $100...Authorized | com., $3,000,000<br>pref., 2,000,000 | Issued | com., $3,000,000<br>pref., ........ | $3,000,000 |
|---|---|---|---|---|

The preferred stock is 6 per cent., non-cumulative. Transfer Agent, Farmers' Loan & Trust Co., New York.

FUNDED DEBT.

1st mort., 5 per cent., due Feb., 1933, Feb. and Aug................................ $2,750,000

The authorized amount of the 1st mortgage is $3,750,000. The bonds are the only lien upon the property of the company, all of the old obligations having been retired. They can be called at 110 after 1908. Trustee of the mortgage and agent for the payment of interest on the bonds, Continental Trust Co., New York.

For the year ending June 30, 1901, the old company reported gross earnings $192,772, net $42,057.

President, Arthur E. Appleyard, Boston; Secretary, W. R. Pomerene, Coshocton, O.; Treasurer, W. R. Mitchell, Boston.

Directors—Arthur E. Appleyard, W. R. Mitchell, H. D. Montgomery, Boston; W. R. Pomerene, Coshocton, O.; S. L. Mooney, W. C. Mooney, Woodfield, O.; T. Edward Hambleton, Frank Hambleton, Baltimore; Richard Emory, W. V. Baker, C. A. Alderman, Columbus, O.; Frank Brandon, Lebanon, O.

Main office, 50 State street, Zanesville, O. Annual meeting in January, at Zanesville, O.

## OHIO RIVER RAILROAD CO.

(Controlled by Baltimore & Ohio Railroad Co.)

Road owned, Benwood, W. Va., to Guyandotte River, 208 miles; trackage, Benwood to Wheeling, 4 miles; leased, 11 miles; total, 223 miles. The Ravenswood, Spencer & Glendale, 33 miles, and the Ripley & Mill Creek, 13 miles, are operated, but their operations are not included in those of this company. Locomotives, 45; passenger cars, 47; freight cars, 1,075.

Control of this company was obtained by the Baltimore & Ohio in 1901, and since August, 1901, the road has been operated as part of the Baltimore & Ohio system, $5,880,000 of the stock of this company being deposited under the Baltimore & Ohio, Pittsburg, Lake Erie & West Virginia Division 1st mortgage.

Stock......Par $100..........................Authorized, $6,000,000......Issued, $5,915,430

FUNDED DEBT.

| | |
|---|---|
| 1st mort., 5 per cent., due June, 1936, June and Dec. | $2,000,000 |
| Gen. mort. (for $3,000,000), 5 per cent., due April, 1937, April and Oct. | 2,941,000 |
| Ravenswood, S. & G., 1st mort., guar. 6 per cent., due Aug., 1920, Feb. and Aug. | 376,000 |
| Huntington & Big Sandy, 1st mort., guar. 6 per cent., due July, 1922, Jan. and July | 303,000 |
| Ripley & Mill Creek 1st mort., guar. 6 per cent., due Aug., 1908, Feb. and Aug. | 50,000 |
| Total | $5,670,000 |

The Huntington & Big Sandy, Huntington to Kenova, was leased in 1892. This company owns its capital stock.

EARNINGS.

| | Gross. | Net. | Charges. | Surplus. |
|---|---|---|---|---|
| 1896 | $970,023 | $328,097 | $306,384 | $21,713 |
| 1897 | 965,196 | 341,899 | 315,404 | 26,495 |
| 1898 | 958,449 | 332,436 | 324,823 | 7,613 |
| 1899 | 1,192,596 | 468,998 | 330,285 | 138,713 |
| 1900 | 1,453,018 | 471,124 | 290,069 | 181,055 |

Earnings are now included in those of the Baltimore & Ohio system.

President, L. F. Loree; Vice-President, Oscar G. Murray; Treasurer, J. V. McNeal; Secretary, Custis W. Woolford, Baltimore.

Main office, Baltimore. Fiscal Agent, Central Trust Co., New York. Annual meeting, second Thursday in May.

---

## OLD COLONY RAILROAD CO.

(Leased to New York, New Haven & Hartford Railroad Co.)

Road owned, Boston to Plymouth, Provincetown and Newport, R. I., etc., 277 miles; Fitchburg to New Bedford, 91 miles; branches, 130 miles; total, 507 miles.

March, 1883, the Boston, Clinton, Fitchburg & New Bedford (previously leased) was consolidated with this company. In May, 1884, the Lowell & Framingham (previously leased) was absorbed. November, 1887, the Boston & Providence was leased for 99 years for all charges, 10 per cent. per year on the stock, besides a bonus of $1,300,000. This has been assumed by the New York, New Haven & Hartford Railroad Co.

On February 28, 1893, the stockholders voted to lease the property for 99 years to the New York, New Haven & Hartford Railroad Co. at an annual rental of 7 per cent. per annum, with a privilege to each stockholder to exchange ten shares of Old Colony stock for nine shares of New Haven stock. A dividend of $2.33⅓ was provided in the lease to be paid June 30, 1893, and dividends on unexchanged stock were thereafter to be 7 per cent. quarterly, January. On June 30, 1900, 55,190 shares had been so exchanged.

Stock......Par $100........................Authorized, $20,000,000......Issued, $16,758,900

In 1889 stock was increased from $12,000,000 to $15,000,000, increase to be sold to provide for additions and improvements. Authorized issue was subsequently increased to $20,000,000. In 1891-92 $600,000 new stock was issued, the premiums on which amounted to $391,993. In 1894-95 $600,000 additional stock was sold to make improvements.

Stock is transferred at the office of the company, South Terminal Station, Boston.

Dividends are paid quarterly, 1¾ per cent. each, in January (1), April, July and October.

FUNDED DEBT.

| | |
|---|---|
| Bonds, not mort., 4 per cent., due July, 1904, Jan. and July | $750,000 |
| " " 4 per cent., due Jan., 1938, Jan. and July | 4,000,000 |
| " " 4½ per cent., due April, 1904, April and Oct. | 498,000 |
| " " 4 per cent., due Feb., 1924, Feb. and Aug. | 3,000,000 |
| " " 4 per cent., due Dec., 1925, June and Dec. | 5,100,000 |
| B., C., F. & N. B., mort., 5 per cent., due Jan., 1910, Jan. and July | 1,912,000 |
| Total | $15,260,000 |

There are also $25,500 1st mortgage 6 per cent. bonds of the Chatham Railroad, interest on which is paid by that company from rental received from the New York, New Haven & Hartford Railroad.

Earnings are now included in those of the lessee.

President, Charles F. Choate; Treasurer, Benjamin B. Torrey; Clerk, A. H. Litchfield, Boston.

Directors—Charles F. Choate, Southboro, Mass.; George A. Gardner, J. M. Sears, Boston; T. J. Borden, John S. Brayton, Fall River; C. L. Lovering, Taunton, Mass.; Nathaniel Thayer, Lancaster, Mass.; Thomas Dunn, Newport, R. I.; John M. Hall, New Haven, Conn.

Main office, South Terminal Station, Boston. Annual meeting, last Tuesday in September.

## OREGON & CALIFORNIA RAILROAD CO.

(Leased to Southern Pacific Co.)

Road owned, Portland, Ore., to State line, 367 miles; branches, 305 miles; total, 672 miles. Locomotives, 45; passenger cars, 60; freight cars, 950.

Stock...Par $100...Authorized { com., $7,000,000; pref., 12,000,000 } Issued { com., $7,000,000; pref., 12,000,000 } $19,000,000

The preferred stock is 7 per cent., non-cumulative.

Transfer agency, 120 Broadway, New York.

FUNDED DEBT.

1st mort., 5 per cent., due July, 1927, Jan. and July ............ $19,207,000

Company was reorganized in 1887. The old 2d mortgage 7 per cent. bonds were retired and old 1st mortgage 6 per cents. exchanged for new 5s. Road is leased to Southern Pacific Co. for 40 years from July 1, 1887. Lessee guarantees interest on bonds, surplus earnings up to 7 per cent. on preferred and 6 per cent. on common stock to stockholders. Stock is nearly all owned by the Southern Pacific Co. Company has land grant of about 3,250,000 acres.

EARNINGS.

| Year ending June 30. | Gross. | Net. |
|---|---|---|
| 1895-96 | $1,564,322 | $292,845 |
| 1896-97 | 1,436,037 | 313,201 |
| 1897-98 | 2,107,851 | 780,151 |
| 1898-99 | 2,252,397 | 787,476 |
| 1899-00 | 2,613,591 | 672,620 |
| 1900-01 | 2,930,088 | 778,689 |
| 1901-02 | 3,504,911 | 1,046,095 |

President, Edward H. Harriman, New York; Secretary, G. H. Andrews, Portland, Ore.; Treasurer, N. T. Smith, San Francisco.

Directors—F. S. Douty, W. D. Fenton, George Crocker, H. E. Huntington, San Francisco; G. H. Andrews, W. W. Bretherton, R. Koehler, L. R. Fields, Portland, Ore.

Main office, Portland, Ore. Annual meeting, second Tuesday in April.

## OREGON & SOUTHEASTERN RAILROAD CO.

A corporation formed under the laws of New Jersey in 1901.

Road projected, Cottage Grove, Ore., to Bohemia Mining District, Ore., 36 miles. Completed and in operation in January, 1903, 18 miles. Locomotives, 2; freight cars, 10.

This road connects at Cottage Grove with the Oregon & California Railroad. It is designed to furnish an outlet for a rich agricultural, lumber and mining district.

Stock ......Par $100......Authorized { com., $500,000; pref., 500,000 } Issued { com., $500,000; pref., 500,000 } $1,000,000

The preferred stock is 7 per cent., cumulative, with dividends semi-annually, April (1) and October. It can be redeemed within three years of date of issue at par and accrued dividends.

Stock is transferred at the New York office of the company. Registrar, Corporation Trust Co., New York.

FUNDED DEBT.

1st mort., 5 per cent., due April, 1922, April and Oct.............................. $150,000

The 1st mortgage was created in 1902. It is $300,000, authorized. Trustee and agent for payment of interest, North American Trust Co., New York.

President, George W. Crosby; Vice-President, Albert Hawkins; Secretary and Treasurer, G. B. Hengen; Assistant Secretary, John H. Pearsons, New York.

Directors—George W. Crosby, Albert Hawkins, G. B. Hengen, John H. Pearsons, Kenneth K. McLaren.

Main office, Cottage Grove, Ore. New York Office, 1133 Broadway. Annual meeting, third Thursday in November.

## OREGON RAILROAD & NAVIGATION CO.

(Controlled by Union Pacific Railroad Co.)

A corporation formed July 16, 1896, under the laws of the State of Oregon, as a reorganization of the Oregon Railway & Navigation Co., under plan issued September 6, 1895, and amended February 5, 1896. Properties were sold under foreclosure July 9-13, 1896, this company taking possession August 17, 1896.

The company is controlled by the Union Pacific Railroad Co., and the road is operated as part of its system.

Road owned, Portland, Ore., to Huntington, Ore., 402 miles; branches, 670 miles; total, 1,072 miles, of which 19½ miles are narrow gauge; leased, 2½ miles; total, 1,074½ miles. Steamboat lines are operated on Columbia, Willamette and Snake Rivers, and an ocean steamship line from Portland to San Francisco, 660 miles; total ocean and river lines, 1,035 miles. Locomotives, 120; passenger cars, 82; freight cars, 2,423; steamships, steamboats and barges, 21.

Stock..Par $100..Authorized { com., $24,000,000; pref., 11,000,000 } Issued { com., $24,000,000; pref., 11,000,000 } $35,000,000

The preferred stock is 4 per cent., non-cumulative. All but $38,210 of the common and $16,954 of the preferred stock is owned by the Union Pacific Railroad Co.

Both classes of stock were held under a voting trust, Central Trust Co., New York, trustee, until May, 1906. In July, 1899, Oregon Short Line guaranteed the dividends on preferred and the voting trust was dissolved. In October, 1899, the Union Pacific offered to exchange its own preferred and common stock, share for share, for the preferred and common of this company not owned by the Oregon Short Line. This offer was accepted by a large proportion of the holders of both classes of stock, and a management was elected representing the Union Pacific. On June 30, 1902, the Union Pacific held $9,883,129 of the preferred and $7,679,900 of common stock, the Oregon Short Line Railroad Co. holding at the same date $16,281,400 common and $976,900 preferred.

Transfer agency, 120 Broadway, New York. Registrar, New York Security & Trust Co., New York.

Dividends on the preferred began July 1, 1897, at rate of 1 per cent. quarterly. In 1897 2 per cent. was paid on the preferred; in 1898, 1899 and 1900 4 per cent. The preferred dividends are paid half yearly, January (2) and July. On the common stock a dividend of 1 per cent. was paid July 2, 1898.

FUNDED DEBT.

Oregon Railroad & Nav. Co. cons. mort., 4 per cent., due June, 1946, June and Dec.. $21,482,000

In 1897 holders of old 1st mortgage 6s were offered privilege of converting them into new 4 per cents. There were, on July 1, 1897, $4,451,000 of 6s, which have now all been retired.

EARNINGS.

Year ending June 30.

| | Dividends. Pref. | Com. | Gross. | Net. | Charges. | Surplus. |
|---|---|---|---|---|---|---|
| 1894-95 | .. | .. | $4,340,791 | $1,230,873 | ....... | ....... |
| 1895-96 | .. | .. | 4,329,108 | 712,622 | ....... | ....... |
| 1896-97 | 4 | .. | 4,677,924 | 1,949,454 | $1,197,986 | $751,471 |
| 1897-98 | 4 | 1 | 6,895,393 | 3,019,839 | 1,265,983 | 1,753,855 |
| 1898-99 | 4 | .. | 7,005,979 | 3,214,904 | 1,094,997 | 2,119,907 |
| 1899-00 | 4 | .. | 7,522,392 | 3,680,249 | 1,069,307 | 2,610,939 |

The earnings for 1900-01 and 1901-02 are included in those of the Union Pacific.

In 1898, surplus over dividends, $963,855; in 1899, surplus, $1,679,907; in 1900, surplus, $2,170,939.

The line was extended to a connection with the Oregon Short Line in November, 1884. In April, 1887, the property was leased to the Oregon Short Line for 99 years for interest and 6 per cent. on stock. The lease was transferred in 1889 to Oregon Short Line & Utah Northern, and rental guaranteed by the Union Pacific. After appointment of Receiver of Union Pacific and default in payment of guaranteed dividends and interests, committees of Oregon Railway & Navigation bond and stockholders were formed. In June, 1894, a separate Receiver was appointed for this property on the application of holders of the Oregon Navigation & Railway Co. first consols.

Reorganization plan is given in full in MANUAL for 1900.

The consolidated 4 per cent. mortgage is for $24,500,000, New York Security & Trust Co., trustee, of which $5,390,000 was reserved for the retirement of old company's 1st mortgage bonds, $1,106,000 for betterments and terminals at rate of $250,000 per annum, and $2,830,000 for new construction at not exceeding $20,000 per mile. The amount distributed among holders of old 5 per cent. consols and old 5 per cent. collateral trust bonds was $15,174,000.

Chairman Executive Committee, Edward H. Harriman, New York; President, A. L. Mohler, Portland, Ore.; Vice-President, William D. Cornish, New York; Secretary, W. W. Cotton, Portland; Assistant Secretary, Alexander Millar; Treasurer, Frederic V. S. Crosby, New York; Assistant Treasurer, John W. Newkirk, Portland, Ore.; Comptroller, William Mahl; Assistant Comptroller, Herbert S. Bradt, New York.

Directors—H. W. Corbett, W. M. Ladd, W. W. Cotton, A. L. Mills, E. S. Benson, William Crooks, H. W. Scott, A. L. Mohler, Portland, Ore.; Miles C. Moore, Walla Walla, Wash.; Otto H. Kahn, William D. Cornish, Winslow S. Pierce, Edward H. Harriman, Henry W. Cannon, William L. Bull, New York.

Main office, Portland, Ore.; executive office, 120 Broadway, New York. Annual meeting, first Thursday in September, at Portland.

---

## OREGON SHORT LINE RAILROAD CO.

(Controlled by Union Pacific Railroad Co.)

This company is a reorganization, in 1897, of the Oregon Short Line & Utah Northern Railway.

Road owned, Granger, Wyo., to Huntington, Ore., 541 miles; Pocatello, Idaho, to Silver Bow, Mont., 256 miles; Ogden, Utah, to McCammon, Idaho, 111 miles; Ogden, Utah, to Calienties, Nev., 396 miles; branches, 375 miles; total operated, 1,740 miles. Locomotives, 178; passenger cars, 149; freight cars, 5,333; service cars, 406.

Stock......Par $100........................Authorized, $27,460,100......Issued, $27,460,100

The company has no preferred stock. All but $10,000 of this stock is held by the Union Pacific Railroad Co., which operates the property as part of its system.

Transfer agency, 120 Broadway, New York. Registrar, Central Trust Co., New York.

FUNDED DEBT.

| | |
|---|---|
| 1st mort., Oregon Short Line 6 per cent., due Feb., 1922, Feb. and Aug. | $14,931,000 |
| Utah & Nor., 1st mort., 7 per cent., due July, 1908, Jan. and July | 4,993,000 |
| " " consol. 1st mort., 5 per cent., due July, 1926, Jan. and July | 1,802,000 |
| O. S. L. R. R., new cons. 1st mort., 5 per cent., due July, 1946, Jan. and July | 12,328,000 |
| " " " " income, non-cum. A, 5 per cent., due July, 1946, Sept. | 511,000 |
| " " " " " " B, 3-4 per cent., due July, 1964, Oct. | 153,000 |
| Participating collateral trust, 4 per cent., due Aug., 1927, Feb. and Aug. | 41,000,000 |
| Total | $75,718,000 |

The 5 per cent. income bonds A, were originally $7,185,000 and the income B bonds $14,841,000. The amount given above were those outstanding in the hands of the public, June 30, 1902.

In December, 1898, the Union Pacific increased its own common stock by $27,460,100, in order to effect an exchange of same for the stock of this company. Minority holders of the company's stock were given, in January, 1899, privilege of exchanging same for Union Pacific common on payment of $3 per share. In October, 1899, holders of A bonds were offered right to exchange them for Union Pacific 4 per cent. bonds, and holders of B bonds to exchange them for Union Pacific preferred stock. On June 30, 1902, the Union Pacific held $6,635,500 income A bonds and $14,688,000 income B bonds and $27,310,700 stock of the company, $109,400 being in the treasury of this company.

The participating gold bonds were issued in 1902 and are secured by an equal amount at par of stock of the Northern Securities Co. Besides the regular 4 per cent. per annum, holders are entitled to receive, beginning with February 1, 1904, any amount in excess of 4 per cent. paid as dividends in the preceding year on the Northern Securities stock held against the bonds.

The old company was a consolidation, 1889, of the Oregon Short Line, the Utah Northern and other lines controlled by the Union Pacific. In April, 1887, the old company leased the Oregon Railway & Navigation Co. for 99 years, for charges and 6 per cent. on its stock. The lease was guaranteed by the Union Pacific.

In September, 1894, the Receivers of the Union Pacific were appointed Receivers of this property.

The plan of reorganization, issued February, 1896, is given in full in the MANUAL for 1900. The Oregon Short Line 1st mortgage 6s, Utah & Northern 1st 7s, and Utah & Northern consolidated 5s were not disturbed in reorganization. Series B incomes bore 3 per cent. interest for three years and 4 per cent. thereafter and had appointment of two directors.

The old company's property was sold under foreclosure January 6, 1897, and bought by the reorganization committee. The present company assumed possession March 16, 1897. In January, 1898, the Union Pacific reorganization committee acquired a large interest in this company in addition to $7,558,000 of the stock which was held as security for the Union Pacific collateral trust notes. For exchange of stock for that of Union Pacific in 1899 see above.

EARNINGS.

| | Gross. | Total Income. | Charges. | Surplus. |
|---|---|---|---|---|
| 1891 (1,424 miles) | $7,574,457 | $3,819,565 | $3,101,724 | $717,841 |
| 1892 ( " " ) | 7,201,199 | 3,696,257 | 2,951,598 | 744,659 |
| 1893 ( " " ) | 5,861,634 | 2,776,959 | 3,015,116 | Def. 238,356 |
| 1894 (1,427 " ) | 5,046,682 | 1,249,950 | 2,803,681 | " 1,553,731 |
| 1895 ( " " ) | 5,394,198 | 2,305,482 | 1,746,799 | " 558,683 |
| 1896 ( " " ) | 5,578,873 | 2,261,224 | ........ | ........ |
| 1897–98 (Mar. 16, '97, to June 30, '98) | 8,037,855 | 3,767,226 | 2,516,852 | 1,250,874 |
| 1898–99 (year ending June 30) | 7,577,108 | 4,049,253 | 1,963,883 | 2,085,869 |
| 1899–00 ( " " " ) | 8,518,397 | 4,754,668 | 1,963,883 | 2,790,785 |

The earnings for 1900–01 and 1901–02 are included in those of the Union Pacific Railroad Co. See statement of the latter.

Out of the earnings from March 16, 1897, to June 30, 1898, 5 per cent. was paid on A incomes and 3 per cent. on B incomes, amounting to $1,091,880, leaving a surplus of $158,994.

In 1898–99 paid 5 per cent. on A bonds and 4 per cent. on B bonds, leaving a surplus of $346,363. In 1900 paid 5 per cent. on income A bonds and 4 per cent. on B bonds; surplus for year, $1,838,838. Interest at the full rate is paid on both classes of incomes remaining in the hands of the public.

President, Edward H. Harriman; Vice-President, William D. Cornish, New York; Vice-President and General Manager, W. H. Bancroft, Salt Lake City, Utah; Secretary, Alexander Millar; Treasurer, Frederic V. S. Crosby; Comptroller, William Mahl; Assistant Comptroller, Herbert S. Bradt, New York.

Directors—Samuel Carr, Oliver Ames, T. Jefferson Coolidge, Jr., Gardiner M. Lane, Oliver W. Mink, Boston; Francis S. Bangs, W. E. Glyn, Winslow S. Pierce, George J. Gould, Edwin Gould, Otto H. Kahn, Edward H. Harriman, William D. Cornish, New York; Horace G. Burt, Omaha; Thomas R. Jones, Salt Lake City, Utah.

Main office, Salt Lake City, Utah; executive office, 120 Broadway, New York. Annual meeting, second Wednesday in October.

---

## OZARK & CHEROKEE CENTRAL RAILWAY CO.

Road owned, Fayetteville, Ark., to Muskogee, I. T., 103 miles. The Shawnee, Oklahoma & Missouri Coal & Railway Co., which has a line from Muskogee to Okmulgee, 40 miles, is controlled by this company. The Muskogee City Bridge is leased.

Stock......Par $100..........................Authorized, $2,000,000......Issued, $2,000,000

FUNDED DEBT.

| | |
|---|---|
| 1st mort., 4 per cent., due Oct., 1941, April and Oct. | $2,000,000 |
| Shaw., Okla. & Mo. Coal & Ry., 1st mort., 4 per cent., due July, 1942, Jan. and July | 680,000 |
| Muskogee City Bridge, 1st mort., 5 per cent., due July, 1942, Jan. and July | 100,000 |
| Total | $2,780,000 |

The authorized amount of the 1st mortgage is $2,000,000. Bonds are subject to call at 105 after 1911. The bonds of the Shawnee Co. can be called at par after July, 1907. The Muskogee City Bridge is leased for 99 years for interest and principal of the bonds and taxes. The bonds can be called at 105 in 1907.

President, H. W. Seaman, Clinton, Ia.; Vice-President, E. E. Hughes; Secretary, J. C. Duffin; Treasurer, H. K. Wade, Fayetteville, Ark.

Directors—H. W. Seaman, E. E. Hughes, J. S. Keefe, J. C. Duffin, J. H. McIlroy, W. L. Stuckey, J. J. Baggett.

Main office, Fayetteville, Ark. Annual meeting, second Tuesday in July, at Fayetteville, Ark.

## PANAMA RAILROAD CO.

Road owned, Colon across Isthmus of Panama to Panama, United States of Colombia, 50 miles. Locomotives, 35; passenger cars, 31; freight cars, 904; service cars, 57; also 3 steamers, 2 tugs and 20 lighters.

Stock......Par $100..........................Authorized, $7,000,000......Issued, $7,000,000

Stock is transferred at the company's office, 24 State street, New York.

The company formerly paid regular dividends, but none were paid from 1893 until March 25, 1901, when 2 per cent. was paid on the stock. In 1902 2 per cent. was paid in June and 2 per cent. in September.

FUNDED DEBT.

| | |
|---|---|
| New 1st mort., 4½ per cent., due Oct., 1917, April and Oct. | $2,386,000 |
| Sinking fund subsidy bonds, 6 per cent., due Nov., 1910, May and Nov. | 1,049,000 |
| Total | $3,435,000 |

The company has a subsidy from the Government of Colombia of $225,000 yearly, which is pledged for the subsidy bonds, surplus over interest being applied to purchase and cancel bonds. In 1897 new 1st mortgage was created to retire the 7 per cent. bonds due October, 1897. The authorized 4½ per cent. issue is for $4,000,000.

EARNINGS.

| | Div. Paid. | Gross. | Net. | Charges. | Surplus. |
|---|---|---|---|---|---|
| 1892 | 2 | $1,768,744 | $820,390 | $637,573 | $182,817 |
| 1893 | 2 | 1,414,126 | 497,365 | 515,933 | Def. 18,568 |
| 1894 | .. | 1,376,285 | 631,192 | 500,739 | 130,454 |
| 1895 | .. | 1,706,440 | 552,862 | 489,919 | 62,943 |
| 1896 | .. | 2,271,141 | 1,035,303 | 489,619 | 545,684 |
| 1897 | .. | 2,300,705 | 894,472 | 484,598 | 409,873 |
| 1898 | .. | 2,142,881 | 751,988 | 485,241 | 266,746 |
| 1899 | .. | 2,195,041 | 775,647 | 480,415 | 295,234 |
| 1900 | .. | 2,655,194 | 922,690 | 475,926 | 446,764 |
| 1901 | 2 | 3,190,709 | 756,402 | 496,812 | 259,590 |

In June, 1881, most of the stock was sold to the Panama Canal Co.

In 1892 disputes arose between this company and the Pacific Mail Steamship Co., and this company established a steamship service of its own in opposition to the Pacific Mail line. Litigation between the two companies followed, and a compromise was finally arranged, in December, 1895, by which the line of steamers controlled by the Panama Co. operated on the Atlantic side of the Isthmus and the Pacific Mail on the Pacific, the two companies forming a through line between New York and San Francisco and other Pacific ports, under the title of the Panama route. This arrangement terminated in 1900 and was not renewed, and the Panama Railroad Co. has instituted a steamship service of its own on the Pacific Coast, which was discontinued in July, 1902. The service is now performed by the Pacific Mail Steamship Co.

In 1894 $97,000 subsidy bonds were redeemed out of net earnings; in 1895, $102,000; in 1896, $107,000; in 1897, $114,240; in 1898, $121,000; in 1899, $129,000; in 1900, $136,000, and in 1901, $144,000.

President, J. Edward Simmons; 2d Vice-President and Secretary, E. A. Drake; General Manager, Charles Paine; Treasurer, Sylvester Deming, New York.

Directors—E. A. Drake, Xavier Boyard, Samuel M. Felton, J. Edward Simmons, J. H. Parker, W. Nelson Cromwell, Vernon H. Brown, C. Einseidler, C. B. Comstock, J. G. Buchanan, George Whaley, Robert M. Gallaway, A. L. Hopkins, New York.

Main office, 24 State street, New York. Annual meeting, first Monday in April.

## PECOS VALLEY & NORTHEASTERN RAILWAY CO.

(Controlled by Atchison, Topeka & Santa Fe Railway Co.)

Road owned, Pecos City, Tex., to Amarillo, Tex., 370 miles. Line connects with Atchison system at Amarillo. Locomotives, 18; passenger cars, 14; freight cars, 166.

This company is the successor of the Pecos Valley Railway Co., which was foreclosed in April, 1898, and reorganized under present title. On the line of road between Roswell and

Pecos City are large irrigation systems supplying water to some 250,000 acres of lands in the valley of the Pecos River.

In January, 1901, the Atchison, Topeka & Santa Fe Railway Co. acquired a controlling interest in this company.

Stock.....Par $100....Authorized { com., $3,162,000 / pref., 3,162,000 } Issued { com., $3,162,000 / pref., 3,162,000 } $6,324,000

The preferred stock is 6 per cent. non-cumulative. Transfer Agent, C. A. Diehl, 59 Cedar street, New York.

FUNDED DEBT.

1st mort., gold, 5 per cent., due Jan., 1948, Jan. and July.......................... $2,916,000

Total bond issue authorized is $3,162,000, or $8,545 per mile on complete system, but $256,000 are held by trustee for company's future requirements. Cash required for two years' interest on bonds is deposited in Central Trust Company, trustee under the mortgage.

In reorganization of Pecos Valley Railroad the old 1st mortgage bonds with October, 1895, coupons attached were exchanged for 120 per cent. in new preferred stock.

The Atchison, Topeka & Santa Fe acquired in December, 1900, a large amount of the bonds and a controlling interest in the stock of the company. The road, however, is operated separately.

EARNINGS.

| Year ending June 30. | Gross. | Net. |
|---|---|---|
| 1899–00 | $446,638 | $129,648 |
| 1900–01 | 452,722 | 149,808 |
| 1901–02 | 617,779 | 187,137 |

President, H. U. Mudge; Secretary, Don A. Sweet; Treasurer, J. C. Paul, Amarillo, Tex.; Assistant Secretary, L. C. Deming; Assistant Treasurer, H. W. Gardiner, New York; Auditor, A. L. Conrad, Amarillo, Tex.

Directors—E. P. Ripley, E. D. Kenna, Chicago; H. U. Mudge, Topeka, Kan.; Avery Turner, Don A. Sweet, A. L. Conrad, J. C. Paul, Amarillo, Tex.; E. A. Cahoon, J. W. Poe, J. J. Hagerman, Roswell, N. M.

Main office, Amarillo, Tex. Annual meeting, first Wednesday in October, at Roswell, N. M.

## PENNSYLVANIA & NORTH WESTERN RAILROAD CO.

(Controlled by Pennsylvania Railroad Co.)

Road owned, Belwood, Pa., to Horatio, Pa., 62 miles; branches, 17 miles; total, 79 miles. Locomotives, 37; passenger cars, 11; freight cars, 76.

The company is a consolidation in 1890 of the Bells Gap Railroad and Clearfield & Jefferson Railway.

In January, 1902, it was announced that the Pennsylvania Railroad Co. had offered $1,000,000 of its own stock in exchange for the stock of this company, the management of which and the large stockholders having approved the proposition.

Stock......Par $100......................... Authorized, $2,500,000......Issued, $2,250,000

The company paid no dividends from 1896 to 1898, inclusive; in 1899 paid 4 per cent.; in 1900, 4 per cent., 2 per cent. half-yearly, January (10) and July. In 1901 4 per cent. was paid, being 2 per cent. semi-annually. A dividend of 2 per cent. was also paid January 10, 1902.

FUNDED DEBT.

| | |
|---|---|
| Bells Gap, 1st mort., 6 per cent., due Aug., 1905, Feb. and Aug. | $81,000 |
| " cons. mort., 6 per cent., due April, 1913, April and Oct. | 145,000 |
| Pennsylvania & North Western, gen. mort., 5 per cent., due Jan., 1930, Jan. and July. | 1,021,000 |
| Clearfield & Jefferson, 1st mort., 6 per cent., due Jan., 1927, Jan. and July. | 1,000,000 |
| Total | $2,247,000 |

The general mortgage is for $2,500,000, sufficient of the issue being reserved to retire prior lien bonds at maturity. There is $250,000 stock in company's treasury.

EARNINGS.

| | Gross. | Net. |
|---|---|---|
| 1894 | $465,094 | $181,198 |
| 1895 | 624,814 | 190,681 |
| 1896 | 482,113 | 147,799 |
| 1897 | 505,464 | 179,356 |
| 1898 | 598,641 | 224,767 |
| 1899 | 670,239 | 260,841 |
| 1900 | 701,577 | 277,478 |
| 1901 | 637,627 | 274,500 |
| 1902 | 718,750 | 249,756 |

President, Samuel Rea; Treasurer, Taber Ashton, Philadelphia.
Directors—John P. Green, W. H. Barnes, N. Parker Shortridge, Effingham B. Morris, T. DeWitt Cuyler, W. A. Patton, Philadelphia.
Main office, Broad Street Station, Philadelphia; dividends and interest paid at Guarantee Trust & Safe Deposit Co., Philadelphia. Annual meeting in February.

## PENNSYLVANIA COMPANY

This company was chartered by the State of Pennsylvania, April 7, 1870, for the purpose of operating in the interest of the Pennsylvania Railroad Co., the lines leased and controlled by it west of Pittsburg, viz.:

| Operated directly by the Pennsylvania Company: | Miles. | |
|---|---|---|
| Pittsburg, Fort Wayne & Chicago Railway | 469.89 | |
| New Castle & Beaver Valley Railroad | 14.98 | |
| Massillon & Cleveland Railroad | 12.23 | |
| Erie & Pittsburg Railroad | 101.21 | |
| Cleveland & Pittsburg Railroad | 201.74 | |
| Pittsburg, Youngstown & Ashtabula Railroad | 125.09 | |
| Toledo, Walhonding Valley & Ohio Railroad | 234.00 | |
| Pittsburg, Ohio Valley & Cincinnati Railroad | 15.27 | |
| Rochester, Beaver Falls & Western Railway | 0.55 | |
| Marginal Railroad, Beaver Falls, Pa. | 2.96 | |
| Rolling Mill Railroad, Toledo, Ohio | 0.71 | |
| State Line & Indiana City Railway | 7.56 | |
| Calumet River Railway | 4.43 | |
| South Chicago & Southern Railway | 10.25 | |
| New Castle Branch, Western New York & Pennsylvania Railway | 37.62 | |
| Cleveland & Marietta Railway | 103.13 | |
| Indianapolis & Vincennes Railroad | 133.11 | |
| | | 1,472.73 |
| Operated by the Pittsburg, Cincinnati, Chicago & St. Louis Railway Co.: | | |
| Pittsburg, Cincinnati, Chicago & St. Louis Railway | 1,155.73 | |
| Ohio Connecting Railway | 3.27 | |
| Chartiers Railway | 23.48 | |
| Steubenville Extension | 1.23 | |
| Pittsburg, Wheeling & Kentucky Railroad | 28.04 | |
| Little Miami Railroad | 194.49 | |
| Englewood Connecting Railway | 2.35 | |
| | | 1,408.59 |
| Otherwise operated, being controlled by the Pennsylvania Railroad Co., Pennsylvania Company, Pittsburg, Cincinnati, Chicago & St. Louis Railway Co., or jointly with other companies: | | |
| Cincinnati & Muskingum Valley Railroad | 148.45 | |
| Waynesburg & Washington Railroad | 28.15 | |
| Cincinnati, Lebanon & Northern Railroad | 31.76 | |
| East St. Louis & Carondelet Railway | 13.25 | |
| St. Louis, Vandalia & Terre Haute Railroad | 158.30 | |
| Cleveland, Akron & Columbus Railway | 196.97 | |
| Newport & Cincinnati Bridge Co. | 0.73 | |
| Louisville Bridge Co. | 2.45 | |
| Terre Haute & Logansport Railway | 159.36 | |
| Terre Haute & Indianapolis Railroad | 122.06 | |
| Terre Haute & Peoria Railroad | 145.12 | |
| Cincinnati, Richmond & Fort Wayne Railroad | 85.60 | |
| Pittsburg, Chartiers & Youghiogheny Railway | 18.32 | |
| Wheeling Terminal Railroad | 9.65 | |
| Toledo, Peoria & Western Railway | 230.70 | |
| Grand Rapids & Indiana Railway | 430.21 | |
| Muskegon, Grand Rapids & Indiana Railroad | 40.68 | |
| Traverse City Railroad | 26.00 | |
| | | 1,874.76 |
| Total | | 4,756.08 |
| Trackage | | 150.77 |
| Total of system | | 4,906.85 |

In 1901 the company acquired the Logansport & Toledo Railway, formerly the Eel River Railroad, 44 miles. In 1902 it acquired the Sandusky Division of the former Columbus, Sandusky

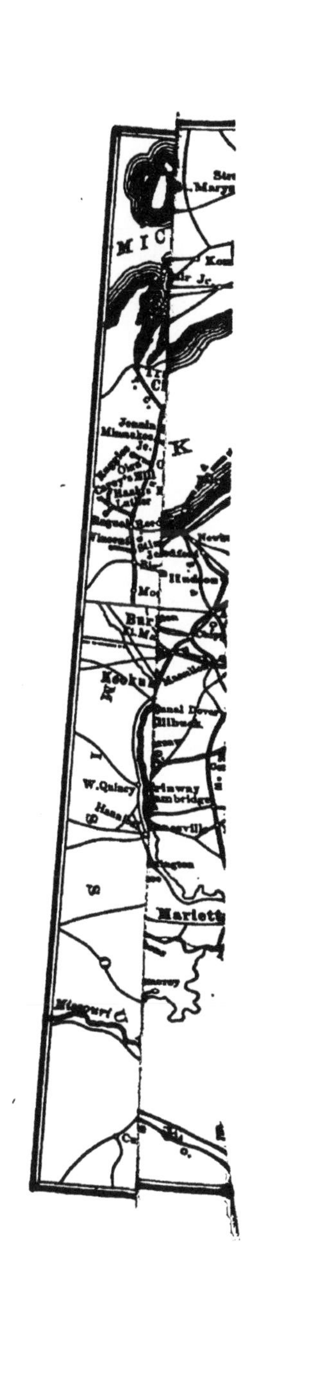

& Hocking Railway, 109 miles, which was consolidated with the Toledo, Walhonding Valley & Ohio Railroad.

Locomotives, 609; passenger cars, 507; freight cars, 50,062.

Statements of the leased and controlled lines will be found under their respective heads.

Stock......Par $50........................Authorized, $40,000,000......Issued, $40,000,000

The stock is all owned by the Pennsylvania Railroad Co. In January, 1902, the stock was increased from $21,000,000 to $40,000,000, the additional $19,000,000 being paid to the Pennsylvania Railroad Co. as consideration for stocks of leased and controlled lines.

No dividends were declared from 1894, when 4 per cent. was paid in May, until 1901, when 3 per cent. was paid on December 30; 3 per cent. was also paid December 30, 1902.

FUNDED DEBT.

| | |
|---|---|
| Bonds of 1881, secured by pledge of stocks and bonds and guaranteed by Pennsylvania R.R. Co., 4½ per cent, due July, 1921, Jan. and July.................. | $19,467,000 |
| Col. tr. ctfs., 3½ p. c., guar. by Pa. R. R., due Sept., 1937, series A, Mar. and Sept. | 4,900,000 |
| " " " " " due Feb., 1941, series B, Feb. and Aug.. | 9,898,000 |
| " " " " " due Nov., 1916, May and Nov........... | 18,666,000 |
| Total ........................................................... | $52,931,000 |

The trust certificates A and B are for $20,000,000. Series A, for $5,000,000, is secured by deposit of an equal amount of guaranteed 7 per cent. stock of the Pittsburg, Fort Wayne & Chicago Railway Co. There are car trusts outstanding amounting to over $3,300,000.

The collateral trust certificates, due November, 1916, have a sinking fund provision of $1,334,000 per annum, bonds to be drawn for the same. They were issued in 1901 to provide for the acquisition of the Pennsylvania Steel Co. and the Cambria Steel Co. They are secured by the deposit of stocks of the Baltimore & Ohio, Norfolk & Western and Pittsburg, Cincinnati, Chicago & St. Louis companies.

INCOME.

| | Gross. | Net. | Charges. | Surplus. |
|---|---|---|---|---|
| 1898 ...................... | $19,561,400 | $7,483,917 | $6,825,342 | $658,574 |
| 1899 ...................... | 23,603,852 | 9,160,130 | 7,013,199 | 2,146,931 |
| 1900 ...................... | 25,407,562 | 9,717,606 | 7,598,004 | 2,119,602 |
| 1901 ...................... | 29,054,544 | 12,247,872 | 8,566,611 | 3,681,261 |
| 1902 ...................... | 33,025,648 | 15,131,202 | 9,347,217 | 5,783,985 |

In 1896 all roads earned gross $42,520,227, and the net profit to this company was $674,587. In 1897, gross, $44,265,450; profit, $2,336,598. In 1898, gross, $46,957,905; profit, $2,518,070. In 1899, gross, $53,924,838; in 1900, $59,970,052; in 1901, $66,445,474.

President, Alexander J. Cassatt, Philadelphia; 1st Vice-President, James McCrea; 2d Vice-President, Joseph Wood; 3d Vice-President, J. J. Turner; 4th Vice-President, Edward B. Taylor; Secretary, S. B. Liggett; Treasurer, T. H. B. McKnight; Comptroller, J. W. Renner, Pittsburg.

Directors—C. Stuart Patterson, W. H. Barnes, George Wood, Charles E. Pugh, Alexander J. Cassatt, Effingham B. Morris, John P. Green, N. Parker Shortridge, Samuel Rea, Philadelphia; J. J. Turner, William Stewart James McCrea, Joseph Wood, Edward B. Taylor, Pittsburg; L. F. Loree, Baltimore.

Main office, Union Station, Pittsburg. Annual meeting, first Tuesday in June.

## *PENNSYLVANIA RAILROAD CO.*

A corporation chartered by the Commonwealth of Pennsylvania, April 13, 1846.

The lines operated directly by this company are its system east of Pittsburg, Buffalo and Erie, Pa., and consist of:

| | Miles. |
|---|---|
| 1. Pennsylvania Railroad Division, Philadelphia to Pittsburg and branches......... | 1,761.32 |
| 2. United Railroads of New Jersey Division, Jersey City to Philadelphia and branches. (Delaware & Raritan Canal, 66 miles, included.) | 535.79 |
| 3. Philadelphia and Erie Railroad Division, Sunbury to Erie, Pa., and branches..... | 599.31 |
| 4. Buffalo & Allegheny Valley Division, including the Allegheny Valley Railway and the Western New York & Pennsylvania Railway................................ | 809.28 |
| Total operated directly................................................... | 3,705.70 |

Of the above mileage, 833.87 miles are owned and 2,871.83 miles are leased or operated under contract.

Locomotives, 2,213; passenger cars, 1,887; freight cars, 95,227; service equipment, 3,309; floating equipment, 275.

The following properties east of Pittsburg and Erie are operated separately, being controlled through ownership of stock:

| | |
|---|---|
| Philadelphia, Baltimore & Washington Railroad | 701.57 |
| West Jersey & Seashore Railroad and branches | 331.52 |
| Northern Central Railway | 449.78 |
| Cumberland Valley Railroad | 163.15 |
| Baltimore, Chesapeake & Atlantic Railway | 87.66 |
| Long Island Railroad | 395.98 |
| Total east of Pittsburg and Erie | 5,836.36 |
| Western lines—Pennsylvania Company | 4,947.60 |
| Total of system | 10,783.96 |

See separate statements of the various leased and controlled companies, including the Pennsylvania Company; Philadelphia & Erie Railroad; United New Jersey Railroad and Canal Cos.; Northern Central Railway; Long Island Railroad; Philadelphia, Wilmington & Baltimore Railroad; Cumberland Valley Railroad; Pennsylvania & Northwestern Railroad; West Jersey & Seashore Railroad; Baltimore & Potomac; Baltimore, Chesapeake & Atlantic; Allegheny Valley Railway; Western New York & Pennsylvania Railway; Belvidere Delaware; Pittsburg, Fort Wayne & Chicago Railroad; Pittsburg, Cincinnati, Chicago & St. Louis Railroad, etc.

In addition operates jointly with Central Railroad of New Jersey the New York & Long Branch Railroad, 38 miles.

The company has a large anthracite property, owned by the Summit Branch, the Lykens Valley, the Mineral Railroad & Mining and the Susquehanna Coal Companies. The Pennsylvania Canal, Columbia to Nanticoke, Pa., and branches, 249 miles, is also controlled. The Allegheny Valley Railway, which this company controlled, was leased in 1900, and in the same year control of the Western New York & Pennsylvania Railway was acquired and the road leased, the two properties being operated since August 1, 1900, as the Buffalo & Allegheny Valley Division. In January, 1902, the Pennsylvania & Northwestern was acquired.

In 1899–1900 the company acquired important interests in the Baltimore & Ohio, Chesapeake & Ohio and Norfolk & Western roads. It also purchased the Erie & Western Transportation Co. In May, 1900, control of the Long Island Railroad was acquired.

The lines owned, leased and controlled west of Pittsburg are operated through the organizations of the Pennsylvania Company and the Pittsburg, Cincinnati, Chicago & St. Louis Railroad Co., and are more fully described under the statements of those companies. The company is also interested in and controls the St. Louis, Vandalia & Terre Haute, the Grand Rapids & Indiana, Terre Haute & Indianapolis, Cleveland, Akron & Columbus, and other roads. This company owns all of the stock of the Pennsylvania Company and a majority of that of the Pittsburg, Cincinnati, Chicago & St. Louis Railroad Co. In 1893 control of the Terre Haute & Indianapolis (in which was included the Terre Haute & Logansport and Terre Haute & Peoria roads), a total of 475 miles, and of the Cleveland & Marietta Railroad, 104 miles, was acquired. In the same year the majority of the stock of the Toledo, Peoria & Western, 247 miles, was purchased. The Logansport & Toledo (formerly the Eel River Railroad) was acquired in 1901.

In the latter part of 1901 the management of this company formulated comprehensive plans for a depot in New York City, with tunnels under the Hudson and East Rivers, connecting the main system with the Long Island Railroad, also to construct a connection between the Long Island Railroad and New England points by a bridge over the East River at Mott Haven, New York. The companies to construct and operate the New York tunnels and terminal are the Pennsylvania, New Jersey & New York Railroad and the Pennsylvania, New York & Long Island Railroad. The New York Connecting Railroad is to furnish the connection with the New York, New Haven & Hartford. In February, 1903, work was begun upon the construction of this extension.

In 1901 the company acquired the minority stock of the Philadelphia, Wilmington & Baltimore with an issue of Pennsylvania Railroad Company's stock, and that company and the Baltimore & Potomac were consolidated under the title of the Philadelphia, Baltimore & Washington Railroad Co. In January, 1902, the stock of the Pennsylvania & Northwestern was acquired by an issue of $1,000,000 of this company's stock.

In 1901 control of the Pennsylvania Steel Co. and the Cambria Steel Co. was acquired.

In 1902 control of the Reading Co. was acquired in the joint interest of this company and of the New York Central, $60,000,000 of the Reading Co.'s stock being vested in the Baltimore & Ohio and the Lake Shore & Michigan Southern as the representatives of the respective parent systems.

Included in the property owned and represented by the capital account are stocks and bonds of other companies having a par value of $317,930,464 and costing $225,948,845. The cash income received from these securities in the form of interest and dividends during 1902 was

$8,118,860. The company has also established a trust for the purchase of the securities of its leased lines, which on December 31, 1902, held securities having a face value of $11,546,230, interest and dividends on which are paid into the trust.

See also statements of leased roads for bonds guaranteed, either directly by the Pennsylvania Railroad or the Pennsylvania Company, including the Pittsburg, Cincinnati, Chicago & St. Louis, the United New Jersey Railroad & Canal Co., etc.

Stock......Par $50......................Authorized, $251,700,000......Issued, $204,374,850

The authorized capital of the company was originally $151,700,000. In January, 1901, the Commonwealth of Pennsylvania, by statute, provided for an increase of $100,000,000 in the stock, making it $251,700,000 authorized, and this increase was approved by the stockholders in March, 1901.

At the annual meeting in 1886 the directors were empowered to issue $15,000,000 of new stock in their discretion. In June, 1887, 8 per cent. of new stock was ordered issued to present stockholders at par, and in May, 1890, 8 per cent. more at the same price. In 1890 $20,000,000 new stock was authorized for improvements, and in 1892 directors were given power to issue $17,456,550 more stock, which amount would complete full amount authorized of $151,700,000. In December, 1899, the directors authorized the issue of $12,930,500 new stock to provide for construction and equipment, and gave stockholders of record December 26, 1899, the right to subscribe for the same at par to the extent of 10 per cent. of their holdings. In April, 1900, $6,700,000 of new stock was issued and sold, making the stock outstanding $151,700,000, or the full amount authorized. At the annual meeting in March, 1901, the stockholders authorized the directors to issue the new stock at their discretion, but at not less than par. The increase was to pay for the company's recent acquisitions of other roads. In March, 1901, stockholders were offered the right to subscribe for new stock, at $60 per share, to the amount of 33⅓ per cent. of their holdings. This involved the issue of $50,500,800 new stock, and increased the amount outstanding to $202,200,800 at the close of 1902. In March, 1902, $1,000,000 of new stock was issued in exchange for the stock of the Pennsylvania & Northwestern Railroad.

See below regarding the convertible 3½ per cent. bonds of 1902 and the offer to convert the same during March and April, 1903.

In January, 1903, it was announced that the stockholders, at the annual meeting on March 10, 1903, would vote on a proposition to increase the authorized stock and funded debt, the issue of the new securities to rest in the discretion of the directors. At the meeting an increase of $150,000,000 in the stock was duly ratified

Transfer agency, Broad Street Station, Philadelphia. Transfer office in New York, 85 Cedar street. Registrars, Girard Trust Co., Philadelphia; American Exchange National Bank, New York.

The company has paid dividends on its stock in every calender year since 1856. Dividends since 1893 are shown below in table of earnings. The dividends are payable May 31 and November 30. The books of the company do not close for the half-yearly dividends. The May, 1900, dividend was 2½ per cent., but the November dividend was 2½ per cent. and 1 per cent. extra, making 6 per cent. for the year 1900. In May, 1901, 2½ per cent. was paid, but the November dividend was again 2½ per cent. and 1 per cent. extra, making 6 per cent. for the year 1901. In 1902 both the May and November dividends were 3 per cent. regular each, or 6 per cent. for the year,

FUNDED DEBT.

| | |
|---|---|
| General mort., 6 per cent., due July, 1910, quar., Jan. | $19,997,820 |
| Consolidated mort., 6 per cent., due June, 1905, quar., March | 1,961,000 |
| " " 6 per cent., due July, 1905, Jan. and July | 22,762,020 |
| " " 6 per cent., due June 19, 1905, June (15) and Dec. | 2,757,000 |
| " " 5 per cent., due Sept., 1919, June and Dec. | 4,998,000 |
| " " 4 per cent., due May, 1943, May and Nov. | 2,853,000 |
| " " 3½ per cent., due July, 1945, Jan. and July | 4,850,000 |
| Convertible certificates, 3½ per cent., due Nov., 1912, May and Nov. | 50,000,000 |
| Trust ctfs. of 1881, reg., P., W. & Balt., 4 per cent., due July, 1921, Jan. and July | 7,702,000 |
| Collateral trust loan, 4½ per cent., due June, 1913, June and Dec. | 9,900,000 |
| Delaware Av. Market, 1st mort., 4 3-10 per cent., due March, 1909, March and Sept. | 300,000 |
| Equip. trust loan, 4 per cent., due Sept., 1914, March and Sept. | 2,728,000 |
| Pennsylvania equip. trust gold certificates, 3½ per cent., due 1903-12, June and Dec. | 9,200,000 |
| Pa. Rolling Stock Trust, 3½ per cent., due 1903-09, quar., Jan. | 3,900,000 |
| Pa. Car Trust, 3½ per cent., due 1903-10, quar., Feb. | 7,000,000 |
| Pa. Steel Car Trust, 3½ per cent., due 1903-12, quar., Jan. | 10,000,000 |
| 1st mort., real estate bonds, 4 per cent., due May, 1923, May and Nov. | 2,000,000 |
| Real estate mortgages and ground rents, various | 5,261,016 |
| Sunbury, Haz. & Wilkes-B., 1st mort., "A," 5 per cent., due May, 1928, May and Nov. | 1,000,000 |
| " " " 2d mort., inc., 6 per cent., due May, 1938, May and Nov. | 1,350,000 |
| Sunbury & Lewisburg, 1st mort., 4 per cent., due July, 1936, Jan. and July | 500,000 |
| Total | $171,019,856 |

In March, 1902, the directors authorized the issue of $50,000,000 10-year 3½ per cent. gold bonds, due November, 1912, with interest May and November. On May 1, 1904, or any subsequent interest period, these bonds are convertible into stock at $70 per share. Beginning May 1, 1904, the bonds may be called at 102½ and interest on 90 days' notice, but if called the holder may nevertheless convert them into stock. Stockholders were offered the right to subscribe for the bonds at par to the extent of 25 per cent. of their holdings. Payments for bonds were in equal installments of 50 per cent. between April 21 and May 1, 1902, and between October 20 and November 1, 1902, respectively, the bonds to be delivered at the latter date. The purpose of this issue was to provide $25,000,000 for additional cars, $20,000,000 for the construction of the New York tunnel and terminal, and $5,000,000 for general purposes. In February, 1903, it was announced that the holders of the convertible bonds could exchange them for stock at $70 per share for the latter between March and April, 1903.

In February, 1903, the company effected a loan of $35,000,000 at 3½ per cent. with a syndicate of one hundred and fourteen banks and bankers running for six months, with the privilege of renewal for a similar period. This was understood to be a temporary arrangement to be replaced by new issues of stock or bonds.

The company had outstanding car trusts on December 31, 1902, to the amount of $31,390,000.

FUNDED DEBT, LEASED AND CONTROLLED LINES.

| | |
|---|---|
| Bald Eagle Valley, 1st mort., 6 per cent., due July, 1910, Jan. and July............ | $316,000 |
| Bedford & Bridgeport, deb. certificates., 5 per cent., due May, 1906, May and Nov... | 1,700,000 |
| Cambria & Clearfield, 1st mort., 5 per cent., due Jan., 1941, Jan. and July.......... | 1,279,000 |
| Camden & Burlington Co., 1st mort., guar., 4 per cent., due Feb., 1927, Feb. and Aug... | 350,000 |
| Columbia & Port Deposit, 1st mort., 4 per cent., due Aug., 1940, Feb. and Aug..... | 1,800,000 |
| Connecting Railroad, 1st mort., 6 per cent., due Sept., 1904, March and Sept........ | 399,000 |
| " " gold mort., 3½ per cent., due Sept., 1930, March and Sept.... | 392,000 |
| Cresson & Irvona, 1st mort., 4 per cent., due July, 1924, Jan. and July... .......... | 500,000 |
| Delaware Riv. R.R. & Bridge, 1st mort., guar., 4 per ct., due Aug., 1936, Feb. and Aug. | 1,300,000 |
| Downington & Lancaster, 1st mort., 4 per cent., due April, 1930, April and Oct..... | 300,000 |
| Ebensburg & Black Lick, 1st mort., 5 per cent., due June, 1943, June and Dec....... | 160,000 |
| Freehold & Jamesburg Ag. R.R., mort., 6 per cent., due July, 1909, Jan. and July..... | 319,000 |
| " " " cons. mort., 4 per cent., due July, 1909, Jan. and July. | 175,000 |
| Genesee Val. Terminal, 1st mort., 6 per cent., due, Nov., 1932, May and Nov....... | 500,000 |
| Girard Point Storage, 1st mort., guar., 3½ per cent., due Oct., 1940, April and Oct.. | 2,214,000 |
| Harrisb., Ports., Mt. Joy & Lanc., 1st mort., ext., 4 p. ct., due July, 1913, Jan. and July. | 700,000 |
| Johnsonburg Railroad, 1st mort., 6 per cent., due March, 1929, March and Sept...... | 200,000 |
| Pa., Schuylkill Valley, 1st mort., 3½ per cent., due Dec., 1935, June and Dec........ | 5,000,000 |
| Perth Amboy & Woodbury, mort., 4 per cent., due Feb., 1918, Feb. and Aug........ | 100,000 |
| Philadelphia & Long Branch, cons. mort., 5 per cent., due Dec., 1913, June and Dec. | 750,000 |
| Phil., Germantown & C.H., 1st mort., guar., 4½ per cent., due May, 1913, May and Nov. | 1,000,000 |
| Pitts., Va. & Charleston, 1st mort., series A, 4½ per ct., due April, 1925, April and Oct. | 3,431,000 |
| Ridgway & Clearfield, 1st mort., 5 per cent., due Nov., 1923, May and Nov.......... | 491,000 |
| River Front, 1st mort., 4½ per cent., due May, 1912, May and Nov................ | 212,000 |
| " " debentures, due Dec. 31, 1903.............................................. | 84,000 |
| Southwest Penna., 1st mort., 7 per cent., due Feb., 1917, Feb. and Aug............ | 900,000 |
| Tyrone & Clearfield, 1st mort., 5 per cent., due Jan., 1912, Jan. and July........... | 1,000,000 |
| Union Terminal Railway, 1st mort., 6 per cent., due June, 1914, June and Dec...... | 1,000,000 |
| West Chester, 1st mort., 5 per cent., due Sept., 1919, March and Sept............... | 75,000 |
| Western Pa., cons. mort., guar., 4 per cent., due June, 1928, June and Dec......... | 4,000,000 |
| York, Hanover & Fredericks., 1st mort., 4 per cent., due May, 1927, May and Nov... | 150,000 |

See also the separate statements in this edition of the MANUAL of funded debts of other controlled and leased lines, including the Philadelphia & Erie, Northern Central, United New Jersey Railroad & Canal Cos., Long Island, Philadelphia, Baltimore & Washington, Allegheny Valley, Western New York & Pennsylvania, etc.

EARNINGS.

| | | Lines East of Pittsburg. | | | Lines West of Pittsburg. | |
|---|---|---|---|---|---|---|
| | Div. Paid. | Gross. | Per Cent. Op. Exp. | Net. | Gross. | Net. |
| 1893.............. | 5 | $66,375,223 | 67.73 | $19,379,206 | $49,012,576 | $14,273,928 |
| 1894.............. | 5 | 58,704,284 | 66.21 | 18,340,538 | 42,669,468 | 12,489,353 |
| 1895.............. | 5 | 64,627,178 | 65.74 | 20,116,522 | 43,574,547 | 12,790,292 |
| 1896.............. | 5 | 62,096,502 | 67.86 | 18,637,175 | 40,027,419 | 10,868,012 |
| 1897.............. | 5 | 64,223,113 | 64.37 | 20,965,486 | 44,265,449 | 15,081,733 |
| 1898.............. | 5 | 65,603,737 | 63.55 | 21,093,722 | 46,957,905 | 14,699,748 |
| 1899.............. | 5 | 72,922,984 | 67.34 | 22,578,351 | 53,924,837 | 17,858,419 |
| 1900.............. | 6 | 88,539,827 | 63.56 | 30,440,621 | 57,658,438 | 18,297,992 |
| 1901.............. | 6 | 132,181,403 | 64.40 | 45,360,557 | 66,445,474 | 19,552,934 |
| 1902.............. | 6 | 145,649,763 | 66.62 | 47,512,859 | 74,200,100 | 20,116,733 |

| *All Lines Operated.* | Gross. | Net. |
|---|---|---|
| 1893 | $134,254,613 | $42,434,953 |
| 1894 | 120,137,054 | 35,105,841 |
| 1895 | 130,319,353 | 39,425,743 |
| 1896 | 123,634,170 | 35,304,790 |
| 1897 | 128,278,087 | 40,637,054 |
| 1898 | 132,869,470 | 39,960,140 |
| 1899 | 152,169,107 | 45,672,655 |
| 1900 | 175,236,353 | 54,738,077 |
| 1901 | 198,626,878 | 64,913,491 |
| 1902 | 219,849,864 | 67,629,592 |

Figures from 1894 are given under a new system of accounting.

The company's condensed income account for four years is as follows:

| | 1899. | 1900. | 1901. | 1902. |
|---|---|---|---|---|
| Gross earnings | $72,922,984 | $88,539,827 | $101,329,795 | $112,663,330 |
| Operating expenses | 50,344,633 | 58,099,206 | 65,259,543 | 75,051,071 |
| Net earnings | $22,578,351 | $30,440,621 | $36,070,252 | $37,612,258 |
| Receipts from other sources | 5,529,283 | 6,491,145 | 8,584,914 | 9,039,876 |
| Gross income | $28,107,634 | $36,931,766 | $44,655,166 | $46,652,135 |
| Interest, rentals, etc | 17,620,163 | 19,654,235 | 22,460,836 | 20,802,172 |
| Net income | $10,487,470 | $17,277,530 | $22,194,330 | $25,849,963 |
| Trust funds and improvements | 1,435,146 | 7,046,815 | 11,336,658 | 13,036,528 |
| Balance | $9,052,324 | $10,230,714 | $10,857,672 | $12,813,434 |
| Dividends | 6,465,266 | 8,781,170 | 10,857,672 | 12,262,491 |
| Surplus | $2,587,058 | $1,449,544 | .......... | $550,943 |

The amount charged to improvements from earnings in 1901 was $10,824,594. The company in that year derived $10,361,928 from premiums on new stock, etc., and charged off $5,000,000 to extraordinary expenditure fund and $3,536,756 for such expenditures in 1901. In 1902 $12,500,000 was charged to extraordinary expenditures.

The condensed balance sheet of the company December 31, 1902, is as follows:

| ASSETS. | | |
|---|---|---|
| Cost of road and equipment | | $152,007,257 |
| Cost of securities owned | | 226,079,635 |
| Securities received with the lease of the U. N. J. R. R. & C. Co. | | 3,283,462 |
| CURRENT ASSETS. | | |
| Due from controlled companies for advances for construction and other purposes | $8,630,097 | |
| Due from agents | 6,245,277 | |
| Bills receivable and miscellaneous assets | 10,500,930 | |
| Materials | 5,421,729 | |
| Cash | 10,228,650 | |
| | | 41,026,685 |
| Sinking Funds, Trust Fund and Insurance Fund | | 11,263,139 |
| Total | | $433,660,178 |

| LIABILITIES. | | |
|---|---|---|
| Capital stock | | $204,374,850 |
| Funded debt (including mortgages and ground rents) | | 140,619,856 |
| Guaranteed stock and bonds of the Harrisburg, Portsmouth, Mt. Joy & Lancaster R. R. Co. | | 1,882,550 |
| Securities received with the lease of the U. N. J. R. R. & C. Co. | | 3,283,462 |
| CURRENT LIABILITIES. | | |
| Pay rolls, vouchers and traffic balances | $16,430,111 | |
| Due controlled companies other than traffic balances | 9,928,703 | |
| Due Saving Fund, Relief Fund, and Insurance Fund | 565,547 | |
| Interest accrued, matured and uncollected, and dividends uncollected | 2,032,631 | |
| Miscellaneous liabilities | 15,283,308 | |
| | | 44,240,701 |
| Sinking Funds and Trust Fund | | 14,516,535 |
| Profit and loss | | 24,742,224 |
| Total | | $433,660,178 |

A detailed statement, by divisions, for the year 1902 is as follows:

| | Main Line and Branches. | New Jersey Division. | Phila. & Erie Division. | Buffalo & Allegheny Valley Division. |
|---|---|---|---|---|
| Gross earnings........ | $68,287,038 | $26,582,639 | $9,299,579 | $8,494,052 |
| Operating expenses.... | 42,884,583 | 18,840,271 | 6,161,419 | 7,164,796 |
| Net earnings.......... | $25,402,474 | $7,742,367 | $3,138,160 | $1,329,256 |

The following presents the comparative freight traffic statistics of the lines east of Pittsburg and Erie:

| | Average Mileage. | Total Tonnage. | Tons Carried One Mile. | Freight Density. | Rate per Ton per Mile. | Earnings per Train Mile. | Average Tons per Train. |
|---|---|---|---|---|---|---|---|
| 1898...... | 2,747 | 84,801,805 | 9,233,924,358 | 3,361,457 | 0.499c | $2.193 | 440 |
| 1899...... | 2,781 | 100,700,037 | 10,875,512,708 | 3,911,279 | 0.473 | 2.221 | 470 |
| 1900...... | 3,716 | 109,471,266 | 11,942,657,794 | 3,213,847 | 0.540 | 2.580 | 480 |
| 1901...... | 3,739 | 122,246,793 | 12,713,626,489 | 3,400,275 | 0.582 | 2.849 | 490 |
| 1902...... | 3,705 | 133,944,161 | 14,040,264,352 | 3,855,238 | 0.586 | 3.039 | 518 |

The aggregate coal and coke shipments on the Pennsylvania Railroad division were 23,241,573 tons in 1896; in 1897, 26,144,836 tons; in 1899, 33,386,356 tons; in 1900, 36,690,041 tons; in 1901, 37,001,478 tons; in 1902, 41,822,988 tons.

GROSS AND NET EARNINGS BY MONTHS FOR THREE YEARS.

| | 1900. | | 1901. | | 1902. | |
|---|---|---|---|---|---|---|
| | Gross. | Net. | Gross. | Net. | Gross. | Net. |
| January ....... | $6,424,271 | $1,776,997 | $7,466,171 | $2,462,697 | $8,000,371 | $2,502,197 |
| February ...... | 6,153,334 | 1,856,601 | 6,636,634 | 1,942,101 | 7,045,034 | 1,960,301 |
| March ......... | 7,014,932 | 2,092,722 | 7,615,132 | 2,445,022 | 8,686,104 | 2,686,919 |
| April.......... | 6,909,372 | 2,141,208 | 7,537,972 | 2,578,208 | 9,099,677 | 3,026,679 |
| May ........... | 7,126,567 | 2,404,497 | 7,770,607 | 2,828,497 | 9,901,838 | 3,795,464 |
| June... ....... | 7,192,835 | 1,971,425 | 7,864,035 | 2,486,425 | 9,596,059 | 3,382,999 |
| July........... | 6,790,095 | 2,214,431 | 7,621,895 | 2,618,631 | 9,771,503 | 3,636,137 |
| August......... | 7,401,961 | 2,832,315 | 8,388,161 | 3,468,815 | 10,106,990 | 3,842,462 |
| September..... | 7,238,539 | 2,821,111 | 7,927,439 | 3,183,311 | 9,822,750 | 3,568,310 |
| October.. ..... | 7,718,578 | 3,039,700 | 8,651,279 | 3,518,000 | 10,546,875 | 3,879,297 |
| November..... | 7,778,524 | 3,229,958 | 8,073,524 | 3,213,158 | 9,465,825 | 2,746,052 |
| December...... | 7,816,904 | 2,921,697 | 7,721,604 | 2,701,297 | 9,529,375 | 2,298,537 |
| Totals......... | $85,565,912 | $29,262,662 | $93,214,612 | $33,446,062 | $111,572,401 | $37,325,354 |
| Aver. per month | 7,130,402 | 2,438,555 | 7,767,884 | 2,784,172 | 9,297,700 | 3,110,446 |

President, Alexander J. Cassatt; Vice-Presidents, John P. Green, Charles E. Pugh, Sutherland M. Prevost, Samuel Rea; Treasurer, Robert W. Smith; Secretary, Lewis Neilson; Assistant Secretaries, A. J. County, Kane S. Green, Philadelphia; Robert H. Groff, New York.

Directors—Alexander M. Fox, N. Parker Shortridge, Alexander J. Cassatt, Clement A. Griscom, Effingham B. Morris, William L. Elkins, William H. Barnes, John P. Green, Amos R. Little, George Wood, Charles E. Pugh, Sutherland M. Prevost, Lincoln Godfrey, T. De Witt Cuyler, Samuel Rea, Philadelphia; James McCrea, Pittsburg.

Main office, Broad Street Station, Philadelphia. Annual meeting, second Tuesday in March. Books do not close for the meeting, but no stock can be voted for directors that has not been qualified by an ownership of sixty days. Directors elected two weeks after annual meeting.

## PEORIA & EASTERN RAILROAD CO.

(Leased to Cleveland, Cincinnati, Chicago & St. Louis Railway Co.)

Road owned, Springfield, O., to Pekin, Ill., 343 miles; trackage leased, Pekin to Peoria, Ill., 10 miles; total, 352 miles. Locomotives, 74; passenger cars, 50; freight cars, 1,908.

Stock......Par $100...................... ..Authorized, $10,000,000......Issued, $10,000,000

Transfer Agents, J. P. Morgan & Co., New York. Registrar, Central Trust Co., New York.

FUNDED DEBT.

| | |
|---|---|
| Ind., Bloom. & W., 1st mort., extended April, 4 per cent., due 1940, April and Oct.. | $981,500 |
| Ohio, Ind. & West., con. 1st mort., 5 per cent., due April, 1938, quar., Jan......... | 500,000 |
| 1st consol. mort., 4 per cent., due April, 1940, April and Oct......................... | 8,500,000 |
| 2d consol. mort., income, 4 per cent., due April, 1990, April....................... | 4,000,000 |
| Total.............. ....................................................... | $13,981,500 |

Leased to Cleveland, Cincinnati, Chicago & St. Louis for 50 years from 1890 for guarantee of interest on 1st consols. If earnings exceed fixed charges and advances made by Cleveland, Cincinnati, Chicago & St. Louis, surplus, as determined by the statements for the calendar year, to go to 2d consols and any further surplus to the Peoria & Eastern. The Cleveland, Cincinnati, Chicago & St. Louis owns one-half the stock. The Indiana, Bloomington & Western 1st mortgage preferred 7 per cent. bonds, which matured January 1, 1900, were refunded and extended at 4 per cent. The company owed the Cleveland, Cincinnati, Chicago & St. Louis $556,228 for advances, and turned over a large amount of its treasury assets to that company to secure the indebtedness. In March, 1901, the Court decided that the company had the right to use a considerable amount of securities reserved at the time of the reorganization. All indebtedness to the Cleveland, Cincinnati, Chicago & St. Louis Railway Co. has now been paid off, and the company had on June 30, 1902, a surplus of $108,472.

The road was formerly the Indiana, Bloomington & Western, which was foreclosed in March, 1887, and reorganized as the Ohio, Indiana & Western. Again reorganized in 1890 under present title.

The first payment on the income bonds was 4 per cent., April 1, 1902.

EARNINGS.

Year ending June 30.

| | Gross. | Net. | Charges. | Surplus. |
|---|---|---|---|---|
| 1892-93 | $1,740,502 | $272,352 | $441,620 | Def. $169,268 |
| 1893-94 | 1,609,806 | 177,190 | 441,620 | " 264,430 |
| 1894-95 | 1,811,739 | 463,937 | 441,620 | 22,317 |
| 1895-96 | 1,902,324 | 457,899 | 441,620 | 16,279 |
| 1896-97 | 1,631,103 | 342,846 | 441,620 | Def. 98,773 |
| 1897-98 | 1,883,107 | 456,782 | 441,620 | 15,162 |
| 1898-99 | 1,903,217 | 453,838 | 441,369 | 12,469 |
| 1899-00 | 2,356,416 | 788,156 | 442,500 | 345,656 |
| 1900-01 | 2,488,303 | 821,949 | 404,075 | 417,874 |
| 1901-02 | 2,518,750 | 654,112 | 564,260 | 89,852 |

Charges for 1901-02 include $160,000, being 4 per cent. paid on the income bonds of the company out of that year's earnings.

President, Melville E. Ingalls; Secretary, J. C. Davie; Treasurer, F. D. Comstock, Cincinnati.

Main office, Central Union Depot, Cincinnati. Annual meeting, second Wednesday in February, at Danville, Ill.

---

## PEORIA & PEKIN UNION RAILWAY CO.

Road owned, 18 miles, extending on both sides of the Illinois River at Peoria, Ill, with double track, sidings and spurs, amounting to an aggregate of about 53 miles of track. Locomotives, 18; passenger cars, 3; freight cars, 253.

This company acquired the Peoria & Springfield Railroad and part of the Peoria, Pekin & Jacksonville Railway.

The stock of the company is owned jointly by the Lake Erie & Western, Toledo, Peoria & Western, Cleveland, Cincinnati, Chicago & St. Louis, Chicago, Peoria & St. Louis and Illinois Central Railroads.

Stock......Par $100..........................Authorized, $1,000,000......Issued, $1,000,000

FUNDED DEBT.

| | |
|---|---|
| 1st mort., 6 per cent., due Feb., 1921, quar., Feb. | $1,495,000 |
| 2d mort., 4½ per cent., due Feb., 1921, May and Nov. | 1,499,000 |
| Total | $2,994,000 |

Trustee of bonds, Central Trust Co., New York.

The proprietary companies pay terminal and switching charges and a yearly rental for the use of this company's facilities. The Chicago & Alton, Rock Island, Iowa Central and Vandalia also rent facilities from this company. In January, 1902, the Chicago & Northwestern purchased half of the $250,000 stock held by the Peoria & Eastern, and became thereby one of the controlling companies.

In 1898-99 the company earned: Gross, $736,000; net, $355,633; surplus over charges, $109,027. In 1899-1900, gross, $770,309; net, $356,362; deficit after charges, $14,656. In 1900-01, gross, $729,181; net, $319,270.

Dividends of 6 per cent. have been paid on the stock each year since 1896.

President, J. A. Barnard, Indianapolis; Vice-President, E. N. Armstrong; Secretary, H. K. Pinkney; Treasurer, J. F. Kiefer, Peoria, Ill.

Main office, Peoria, Ill.

## PERE MARQUETTE RAILROAD CO.

A corporation formed under the laws of Michigan, November 1, 1899, which acquired the Flint & Pere Marquette Railroad Co., the Detroit, Grand Rapids & Western Railroad Co., and the Chicago & West Michigan Railway Co., under an agreement dated May 20, 1899, for that purpose.

Road owned, Toledo to Ludington, Mich., 363 miles; La Crosse, Ind., to Bay View, Mich., 400 miles; Detroit to Grand Rapids, 153 miles; Port Huron, Mich., to Saginaw, 124 miles; Allegan, Mich., to Penwater, 128 miles; branches, 493¼ miles; total owned, 1,661¼ miles; leased, Grand Rapids, Belding & Saginaw, 32 miles; Saginaw, Tuscola & Huron Railroad, 66 miles; trackage, 19¾ miles; spurs, 58 miles; total operated, 1,837 miles. Of this mileage 34 miles are narrow gauge. Locomotives, 250; passenger cars, 265; freight cars, 9,147.

Full details of the constituent companies will be found in the MANUAL for 1899 under their respective titles.

In December, 1902, it was stated that control of this company had been acquired by new interests; also that it had secured the Lake Erie & Detroit River Railroad, 224 miles, and would extend that line from St. Thomas, Ont., to Buffalo.

Stock..Par $100..Authorized { com., $16,000,000 / pref., 12,000,000 } Issued { com., $14,145,500 / pref., 10,512,200 } $24,617,700

The preferred stock is 4 per cent., non-cumulative. The issue of preferred can be increased only with the consent of a majority of each class of stock.

Transfer agencies, 40 Wall street, New York, and 50 State street, Boston. Registrars, Morton Trust Co., New York; International Trust Co., Boston.

The first dividend on the preferred stock of the company was 4 per cent., paid February 11, 1901, out of the profits of the year 1900. On August 15, 1901, a semi-annual dividend of 2 per cent. was paid on the preferred, and a 2 per cent. dividend on February 15, 1902. Regular semi-annual dividends are paid February and August at the same rate.

### FUNDED DEBT.

| | |
|---|---|
| Pere Marquette Railroad cons. mort., due Jan., 1951, 4 per cent., Jan. and July...... | $4,605,000 |
| F. & P. M. new mort. bonds, 6 per cent., due Oct., 1920, April and Oct............ | 4,000,000 |
| " " 4 per cent., due Oct., 1920, April and Oct.............................. | 1,000,000 |
| " " cons. mort., 5 per cent., due May, 1939, May and Nov.................... | 2,850,000 |
| " " Monroe & Toledo 1st mort., 5 per cent., due July, 1937, Jan. and July.... | 400,000 |
| " " Port Huron Div. 1st mort., 5 per cent., due April, 1939, April and Oct... | 3,500,000 |
| Gr. Rap., Newago & Lake Sh. 2d mort., 7 per cent., due June, 1905, June and Dec.. | 19,000 |
| Chicago & W. Mich. cons. mort., 5 per cent., due Dec., 1921, June and Dec........ | 5,758,000 |
| Chicago & N. Mich., 1st mort., guar. 5 per cent., due May, 1931, May and Nov...... | 1,667,000 |
| Detroit, Grand Rapids & W. cons. mort., 4 per cent., due April, 1946, April and Oct. | 5,379,000 |
| Western Equipment Co. mort., 6 per cent., due April, 1909, April and Oct.......... | 93,000 |
| Sag., Tuscola & Huron R. R. 1st mort., 4 per cent., due Aug., 1931, Feb. and Aug... | 1,000,000 |
| Pere Marquette Transportation Co. mort., guar., 6 per cent.......................... | 80,000 |
| Marquette Equipment 1st mort., guar., 5 per cent., due Oct., 1910, April and Oct.... | 797,000 |
| Total.................................................................. | $31,148,000 |

The funded debt given above includes the bonds of the old companies, which were not disturbed at the time of consolidation. The new company was given authority to create a 4 per cent. consolidated mortgage to provide for refunding or retirement of the old bonds, and $1,000,000 of 4 per cent. consols were issued in 1901 for that purpose.

The terms of the consolidation plan and details regarding the constituent companies were given in the MANUAL for 1900.

The revenues given below include the earnings of the three companies in the two years prior to the consolidation.

### EARNINGS.

| | Gross. | Net. | Charges. | Surplus. |
|---|---|---|---|---|
| 1897.................................. | $5,757,460 | $1,428,926 | $1,292,380 | $136,546 |
| 1898.................................. | 6,585,247 | 1,665,081 | 1,308,674 | 296,597 |
| 1899.................................. | 7,207,373 | 1,624,255 | 1,275,343 | 348,912 |
| 1900.................................. | 8,296,112 | 1,965,519 | 1,319,331 | 646,188 |
| 1901.................................. | 9,201,175 | 2,090,963 | 1,508,889 | 582,074 |

President, Frederick H. Prince, Boston; Vice-President, Newman Erb, New York; Vice-President and General Manager, M. J. Carpenter, Detroit; Secretary and Treasurer, Charles Merriam, Boston; Auditor, J. E. Howard, Detroit.

Directors—Thomas H. West, W. K. Bixby, St. Louis; Samuel R. Shipley, Philadelphia; M. J. Carpenter, Chicago; Nathaniel Thayer, Charles Merriam, Walter Hunnewell, Frederick H. Prince, Boston; Mark T. Cox, Thomas F. Ryan, Newman Erb, New York.

Main office, corner Fort and Third streets, Detroit; Boston office, 50 State street. Annual meeting, first Wednesday in May, in Michigan.

## PHILADELPHIA & ERIE RAILROAD CO.

(Leased to Pennsylvania Railroad Co.)

Road owned, Sunbury, Pa., to Erie, 287½ miles; branches, 17 miles. Northern Central trains use 40 miles of this road, from Sunbury to Williamsport. Equipment is furnished by the lessee. Some 380 miles of branch lines controlled or owned by Pennsylvania Railroad are operated for convenience of lessee in connection with this line as Philadelphia & Erie Division of the Pennsylvania, which comprises 702 miles.

Stock...Par $50...Authorized { com., $10,000,000 / special, 2,400,000 } Issued { com., $7,985,000 / special, 2,400,000 } $10,385,000

The special stock is entitled to 7 per cent. per annum, non-cumulative, which is paid annually December 31. It is all owned by the Pennsylvania Railroad Co. Dividends on it have been, in 1888 to 1893 inclusive, 7 per cent.; in 1894 to 1897 inclusive, 2 per cent.; in 1898 and 1899, 4 per cent.; in 1900 and 1901, 7 per cent.

Stock is transferred at the company's office, Broad Street Station, Philadelphia.

Dividends on the common stock have been as follows: In 1892, 2 per cent.; in 1894, 2 per cent.; in 1901, 2 per cent., paid December 31; in 1902, 4 per cent., paid 2 per cent. each in July and December.

FUNDED DEBT.

| | |
|---|---|
| General mort., 6 per cent., coupon, due July, 1920, Jan. and July | $8,680,000 |
| " " 5 per cent., registered, due July, 1920, April and Oct. | 5,263,000 |
| " " 4 per cent., registered, due July, 1920, April and Oct. | 5,880,000 |
| Total | $19,823,000 |

The general mortgage is guaranteed by Pennsylvania Railroad Co. In 1888 $3,000,000 additional general mortgage bonds were issued to retire that amount of maturing 2d mortgage bonds. In 1897 $976,000 maturing Sunbury & Erie 1st mortgage 7s were also retired with the issue of a like amount of general 4s. Pennsylvania Railroad Co. owns $3,501,800 common and all of the $2,400,000 special stock. The city of Philadelphia owned $2,250,000 of the common stock, and in January, 1902, the Pennsylvania Railroad made a proposition for its purchase.

The rental paid by the lessee is the net revenue. Charges include interest on equipment as well as interest paid.

EARNINGS.

| | Gross. | Net. | Charges. | Surplus. |
|---|---|---|---|---|
| 1893 | $5,104,879 | $1,574,350 | $1,198,864 | $375,486 |
| 1894 | 3,965,196 | 1,047,373 | 1,192,555 | Def. 145,182 |
| 1895 | 4,378,574 | 1,238,319 | 1,233,792 | 4,526 |
| 1896 | 4,512,511 | 1,283,522 | 1,275,957 | 7,564 |
| 1897 | 4,601,257 | 1,300,756 | 1,221,034 | 14,153 |
| 1898 | 4,574,443 | 1,378,139 | 1,375,826 | 2,313 |
| 1899 | 5,348,029 | 1,664,234 | 1,503,014 | 101,220 |
| 1900 | 5,824,626 | 2,153,341 | 1,944,640 | 140,366 |
| 1901 | 6,789,689 | 2,797,285 | 2,293,414 | 503,868 |

The earnings are also included in those of the Pennsylvania Railroad lines east of Pittsburg and Erie.

The charges for 1901 include $469,896 for extraordinary expenditure and $600,000 credited to renewal fund and extraordinary expenditure fund.

President, N. Parker Shortridge; Secretary and Treasurer, J. Vanzandt, Philadelphia.

Directors—N. Parker Shortridge, Samuel G. Thompson, Samuel Rea, William L. Elkins, Amos R. Little, J. Bayard Henry, William H. Barnes, John P. Green, John H. Catherwood, George Wood, James Elverson, W. S. P. Shields, Joseph W. Gross.

Main office, Broad Street Station, Philadelphia. Annual meeting, second Monday in February.

---

## PHILADELPHIA, BALTIMORE & WASHINGTON RAILROAD CO.

(Controlled by Pennsylvania Railroad Co.)

This corporation, formed in August, 1902, is a consolidation of the Philadelphia, Wilmington & Baltimore Railroad Co. and the Baltimore & Potomac Railroad Co. It is controlled by the Pennsylvania Railroad Co., which, with its auxiliary, the Northern Central Railway Co., owns practically the entire stock of the company.

Road owned, Philadelphia to Baltimore, 95 miles; Baltimore & Potomac Railroad, 93 miles; branches, 22 miles; total, 210 miles; leased, controlled and worked, Delaware Railroad and branches, 258 miles; Delaware, Maryland & Virginia Railroad, 98 miles; Philadelphia & Baltimore Central Railroad, 80 miles; other branches, 58 miles; total, 703 miles. The Baltimore &

Potomac had been leased to the Philadelphia, Wilmington & Baltimore up to the time of the merger. The Washington Southern Railroad, 35 miles, which this company operated, was transferred to the Richmond-Washington Co. in 1901. Locomotives, 230; passenger cars, 395; freight cars, 3,997.

Stock......Par $50........................Authorized, $28,350,450......Issued, $25,350,450

The stock of Philadelphia, Wilmington & Baltimore was $11,819,350, of which the Pennsylvania Railroad owned $10,890,950, most of which was bought in 1881. In October, 1901, the Pennsylvania offered $100 per share for the minority stock, or to exchange 3 of its own shares for 2 of Philadelphia, Wilmington & Baltimore stock. The stockholders in January, 1902, voted to increase the stock of the company by $8,000,000, to $19,819,350, and when the consolidation with the Baltimore & Potomac was effected the stock of the combined organization was increased by an exchange at par of the $5,531,100 of Baltimore & Potomac stock.

Stock is transferred at the office of the company, Broad Street Station, Philadelphia.

Dividends of 7 per cent. per annum were paid on the stock of the Philadelphia, Wilmington & Baltimore Railroad, 4 per cent. in January and 3 per cent. in July. The first dividend on the stock of the new company was 2 per cent. semi-annual, paid December 31, 1902.

FUNDED DEBT.

| | |
|---|---|
| P., W. & B. plain bonds, 5 per cent., due June, 1910, June and Dec. | $1,000,000 |
| " " plain bonds, 4 per cent., due April, 1917, April and Oct. | 1,000,000 |
| " " plain bonds, 4 per cent., due Nov., 1922, Mar. and Nov. | 1,000,000 |
| " " plain bonds, 4 per cent., due Jan., 1926, Jan. and July | 930,000 |
| " " plain bonds, 4 per cent., due Oct., 1932, April and Oct | 1,000,000 |
| Baltimore & Potomac 1st mort. (tunnel), 6 per cent., due July, 1911, Jan. and July | 1,500,000 |
| " " 1st mort., 6 per cent., due April, 1911, April and Oc | 3,000,000 |
| " " con. mort., 5 per cent., due July, 1929, Jan. and July | 3,000,000 |
| Total | $12,430,000 |

The bonds are simple obligations of the company, not secured by mortgage.

EARNINGS.—Year ending October 31.

| | Div. Paid. | Gross. | Net. | Charges. | Surplus. |
|---|---|---|---|---|---|
| 1892-93 (651 miles) | 7 | $9,868,001 | $3,059,402 | $1,728,762 | $1,330,641 |
| 1893-94 (655 " ) | 6½ | 8,695,959 | 2,767,565 | 1,649,836 | 1,117,728 |
| 1894-95 ( " " ) | 7 | 9,142,532 | 3,124,811 | 1,856,047 | 1,268,764 |
| 1895-96 (669 " ) | 7 | 9,047,131 | 2,904,050 | 1,760,525 | 1,143,525 |
| 1896-97 ( " " ) | 7 | 8,791,436 | 2,846,691 | 1,745,732 | 1,100,958 |
| 1897-98 ( " " ) | 7 | 9,601,563 | 2,911,799 | 1,809,072 | 1,102,726 |
| 1898-99 ( " " ) | 7 | 10,393,806 | 3,614,527 | 2,053,749 | 1,560,778 |
| 1899-00 ( " " ) | 7 | 11,324,531 | 4,095,124 | 2,364,125 | 1,730,998 |
| 1900-01 ( " " ) | 7 | 11,808,649 | 4,361,407 | 2,072,665 | 2,288,742 |
| 1901-02 ( " " ) | 7 | 12,231,194 | 3,989,698 | ........ | ........ |

Earnings include those of Baltimore & Potomac and Washington Southern.

In 1899-1900 the surplus over dividends paid was $903,644; in 1900-01, surplus, $1,461,388.

President, Alexander J. Cassatt; Vice-Presidents, John P. Green, Charles E. Pugh, Sutherland M. Prevost, Samuel Rea; Treasurer, Robert W. Smith; Secretary, Lewis Neilson, Philadelphia.

Directors—William Sellers, John P. Green, N. Parker Shortridge, William H. Barnes, Charles E. Pugh, Alexander J. Cassatt, Samuel Rea, Sutherland M. Prevost, W. A. Patton, Christian C. Febiger, Philadelphia; German H. Hunt, Edward Lloyd, Easton, Md.; E. Tatnall Warner, Preston Lea, Wilmington; John Cassels, Washington.

Main office, Broad Street Station, Philadelphia. Annual meeting, second Monday in January.

## PINE BLUFF & WESTERN RAILWAY CO.

A corporation formed under the laws of Arkansas, May 1, 1900. Road owned, Pine Bluff, Ark., to Sheridan, Ark., 21 miles. An extension of the line to Benton, Ark., was under construction at the end of 1902.

Stock......Par $100..........................Authorized, $1,000,000......Issued, $1,000,000

FUNDED DEBT.

1st mort., 6 per cent., due Oct., 1922, April and Oct.............................. $1,200,000

The 1st mortgage bonds are subject to call at 105 and interest after 1912. Trustee of mortgage, Illinois State Trust Co., East St. Louis, Ill.

President, W. W. Cargill, La Crosse, Wis.; Vice-President, D. A. Kendall, Kansas City; Secretary and Treasurer, John H. McMillan, Pine Bluff, Ark.

Main office, Pine Bluff, Ark.

## PITTSBURG & LAKE ERIE RAILROAD CO.

Road owned, Pittsburg to Youngstown, O., 68 miles; branch, 4 miles; total, 73 miles. From January 1, 1884, leased the Pittsburg, McKeesport & Youghiogheny Railroad, Pittsburg to New Haven, Pa., with branches, 113 miles; total operated, 185 miles. Locomotives, 164; passenger cars, 89; freight cars, 10,592.

The road is operated in harmony with the Vanderbilt system, the Lake Shore & Michigan Southern owning a controlling interest in the property. This company has an interest of $140,000 in the stock and securities of the Pittsburg, Chartiers & Youghiogheny Railroad.

Stock......Par $50............................Authorized, $8,000,000......Issued, $8,000,000

The authorized stock was increased from $4,000,000 to $8,000,000 in January, 1902, to provide for building four tracks and other improvements. Half the new stock was issued in July, 1902, and the remainder in February, 1903, being subscribed for at par by the original holders of stock.

Stock is transferred at the company's office, New Terminal Station, Pittsburg.

Since 1893, inclusive, the company has paid 10 per cent. per annum on its stock, the dividends being semi-annual, 5 per cent. each, in February (1) and August.

FUNDED DEBT (PITTSBURG & LAKE ERIE).

| | |
|---|---|
| 1st mort., 6 per cent., due Jan., 1928, Jan. and July | $2,000,000 |
| 2d mort., 5 per cent., series A, due Jan., 1928, April and Oct. | 1,000,000 |
| " " series B, due Jan., 1928, April and Oct. | 1,000,000 |
| Total | $4,000,000 |

SECURITIES OF PITTSBURG, MCKEESPORT & YOUGHIOGHENY RAILROAD.

| | |
|---|---|
| Pitts., McKeesport & Youg. stock, guar., 6 per cent., Jan. and July | $3,959,650 |
| " " " 1st mort., guar., 6 per cent., due July, 1932, Jan. and July. | 2,250,000 |
| " " " 2d mort., guar., 6 per cent., due July, 1934, Jan. and July. | 900,000 |
| McK. & Belle Vernon, 1st mort., *not* guar., 6 per cent., due July, 1918, Jan. and July. | 600,000 |
| Total | $7,709,650 |

EARNINGS.

| | Gross. | Net. | Charges. | Surplus. |
|---|---|---|---|---|
| 1893 (168 miles) | $4,040,783 | $1,136,072 | $707,454 | $428,617 |
| 1894 ( " " ) | 3,880,175 | 1,224,552 | 700,168 | 524,383 |
| 1895 (174 " ) | 4,704,857 | 1,314,761 | 682,922 | 631,839 |
| 1896 (177 " ) | 4,501,421 | 1,423,581 | 711,550 | 712,031 |
| 1897 ( " " ) | 4,666,686 | 1,442,913 | 714,768 | 728,144 |
| 1898 (180 " ) | 5,071,376 | 1,382,391 | 700,331 | 709,279 |
| 1899 ( " " ) | 5,875,271 | 1,585,142 | 701,576 | 901,348 |
| 1900 ( " " ) | 7,145,023 | 1,699,510 | 799,660 | 880,924 |
| 1901 (184 " ) | 8,047,167 | 1,789,171 | 838,529 | 950,642 |
| 1902 ( ) | 10,098,907 | 2,236,471 | 858,574 | 1,385,806 |

The operations of the Pittsburg, McKeesport & Youghiogheny are included with those of the Pittsburg & Lake Erie from 1884 on, and its rental is included in the charges of the latter company for 1884 and succeeding years.

President, William H. Newman, New York; Vice-President and General Manager, J. M. Schoonmaker; Secretary and Treasurer, John G. Robinson; Auditor, C. H. Bronson, Pittsburg.

Directors—William K. Vanderbilt, Hamilton McK. Twombly, Frederick W. Vanderbilt, Edwin D. Worcester, New York; A. E. W. Painter, D. L. Wilson, M. W. Watson, J. M. Bailey, George E. Shaw, J. M. Schoonmaker, Henry Hice, John G. Robinson, Pittsburg.

Main office, New Terminal Station, Pittsburg. Annual meeting, fourth Tuesday in January.

## PITTSBURG & WESTERN RAILROAD CO.

(Controlled by Baltimore & Ohio Railroad Co.)

A corporation formed under the laws of Pennsylvania January 28, 1902, to take over and operate the road of the Pittsburg & Western Railway Co., which was foreclosed and sold October 9, 1901. The present company was created in pursuance of a plan to reorganize the property and operate the same as part of the Baltimore & Ohio Railroad Co.'s system. The road forms part of the Baltimore & Ohio's Pittsburg, Lake Erie & West Virginia system.

The Baltimore & Ohio owns all the stock and bonds of the present company and a large amount of the underlying bonds. All these securities are deposited as collateral for the Baltimore & Ohio, Pittsburg, Lake Erie & West Virginia system 4 per cent. bonds.

Road owned, Allegheny City to North Sewickley, Pa., 46 miles; Callery to Butler, Pa., 14 miles; Rock Point to New Castle, Pa., 11 miles; branches, 9 miles; Butler to Kane, Pa. (3 feet gauge), 112 miles; branches, 21 miles; leased, Pittsburg, Cleveland & Toledo, New Castle, Pa., to Valley Junction, O., 77 miles; Pittsburg, Painesville & Fairport, 53 miles; branch, 11 miles; total, 354 miles. The narrow gauge division between Foxburg and Ormsby Junction, 104 miles, was leased in November, 1901, to the Bradford, Bordell & Kinzua Railway. Locomotives, 96; passenger cars, 46; freight cars, 4,080.

Stock......Par $100........................Authorized, $13,500,000......Issued, $13,500,000

FUNDED DEBT.

| | |
|---|---|
| Pittsburg & Western Railroad, 1st mort., extended, 4 per cent...................... | $3,500,000 |
| " " " 1st mort., 4 per cent., due 1917, Jan. and July....... | 9,700,000 |
| Total .................................................... | $13,200,000 |

The old company was placed in the hands of Receivers in March, 1885, foreclosed and reorganized in June, 1887. The old company had $8,500,000 common and $5,000,000 preferred 5 per cent. stock. In 1891 a 2d mortgage for $3,500,000 was authorized. The Baltimore & Ohio purchased $6,050,000 of the common stock and incorporated the road in its system, using the main line as part of its through route to Chicago.

In March, 1896, in consequence of the receivership of the parent company, the Baltimore & Ohio, Thomas M. King, president of this company, was appointed Receiver. Interest on the 2ds, due May, 1896, was not paid. In October, 1898, the 2d mortgage committee sold $2,000,000 of these bonds to parties connected with the Lake Erie & Western system. It was thereupon reported that the road would not be reorganized in connection with the Baltimore & Ohio system. In 1899 the Lake Erie & Western's interest in this company's securities was acquired by the Baltimore & Ohio reorganization committee, and a reorganization in the interest of the Baltimore & Ohio followed.

A decree of foreclosure was granted February, 1900, but sale was delayed and did not take place until October, 1901, when the property was bought by representatives of the Baltimore & Ohio.

EARNINGS.

| Year ending June 30. | Gross. | Net. |
|---|---|---|
| 1891-92 | $2,402,595 | $462,326 |
| 1892-93 | 2,586,185 | 532,274 |
| 1893-94 | 2,318,677 | 655,866 |
| 1894-95 | 2,867,892 | 916,663 |
| 1895-96 | 3,091,302 | 981,223 |
| 1896-97 | 2,768,507 | 956,084 |
| 1897-98 | 3,221,407 | 969,416 |
| 1898-99 | 3,309,935 | 1,075,263 |
| 1899-00 | 3,835,033 | 1,337,861 |
| 1900-01 | 4,080,687 | 1,534,029 |

In 1896-97 deficit after charges was $46,286; in 1897-98, deficit, $38,167; in 1889-1900, surplus, $209,935; in 1900-01, surplus, $403,300.

Earnings are now included in those of the Baltimore & Ohio system.

President, William M. Kennedy, Pittsburg; Secretary, C. W. Woolford; Treasurer, J. V. McNeal, Baltimore.

Directors—C. W. Woolford, W. R. Woodford, Henry W. Oliver, T. J. English, J. L. Kirk, Pittsburg; John E. McVey, Youngstown, O.

Main office, 410 Smithfield street, Pittsburg.

## PITTSBURG, BESSEMER & LAKE ERIE RAILROAD CO.

(Leased to Bessemer & Lake Erie Railroad Co.)

Road owned, Bessemer, Pa., to Conneaut Harbor, O., 146 miles; branches, Conneaut Junction to Wallace Junction, Pa., 9 miles; other branches, 43 miles; total, 198 miles; leased, Linesville to Meadville, Pa., 22 miles; trackage, New York, Chicago & St. Louis Railroad, Wallace to Erie, Pa., 13 miles; total operated, 233 miles. Company owns large terminals at Erie, Pa., and Conneaut, O. Locomotives, 75; passenger cars, 37; freight cars, 6,900.

This company is a consolidation, December, 1896, of the Pittsburg, Shenango & Lake Erie Railroad Co. with the Butler & Pittsburg Railroad. The main line of the Pittsburg, Shenango & Lake Erie extended from Butler, Pa., to Wallace Junction, Pa., with branch to Conneaut Harbor, O. The Butler & Pittsburg was incorporated April, 1896, and was controlled by the Carnegie Company. Its line, completed in October, 1897, is from Butler, Pa., to Bessemer, Pa., joining there the Union Railway, a belt line owned by the Carnegie Company and connecting its various industrial establishments along the Monongahela River. The Carnegie Company owned $6,000,000 of the company's stock.

In January, 1901, it was agreed to lease the road for 999 years, from April 1, 1901, to the Bessemer & Lake Erie Railroad Co., which is controlled by the Carnegie Company. Under the terms of lease the lessee guaranteed 6 per cent. per annum on the preferred and 3 per cent. per annum on the common stock in the hands of the public. The Carnegie Company guarantees the lease; and control of this property passed with the control of the Carnegie Company to the United States Steel Corporation.

Stock...Par $50...Authorized { com., $10,000,000 / pref., 2,000,000 } Issued { com., $10,000,000 / pref., 2,000,000 } $12,000,000

The preferred stock is 6 per cent., cumulative. The preferred stock was created in 1899 to provide for the company's floating debt, and $1,500,000 of it was issued in 1899. In December, 1900, the common stockholders were given the right to subscribe for the remaining $500,000 of preferred.

Transfer Agent, United States Trust Co., New York.

Full dividends of 6 per cent. per annum are regularly paid on the preferred stock in semi-annual payments of 3 per cent. each, June 1 and December 1. The guaranteed 3 per cent. dividends on the common are paid, 1½ each, in April and October.

FUNDED DEBT.

| | |
|---|---|
| P., Shenango & L. E., 1st mort., 5 per cent., due Oct., 1940, April and Oct. | $3,000,000 |
| " " consolidated mort., 5 per cent., due July, 1943, Jan. and July. | 658,000 |
| Pitts., Bessemer & L. E., cons. mort., 5 per cent., due Jan., 1947, Jan. and July. | 6,342,000 |
| " " " debentures, 5 per cent., due June, 1919, June and Dec. | 2,000,000 |
| Bessemer equipment trust, due 1902-06, 6 per cent., Jan. and July | 300,000 |
| Conneaut " " due 1902-06, 6 per cent., March and Sept. | 350,000 |
| Shenango " " due 1904-13, 5 per cent., April and Oct. | 725,000 |
| Greenville " " due 1911-20, 5 per cent., May and Nov. | 1,000,000 |
| Butler " " 5 per cent., due April, 1921, April and Oct. | 2,000,000 |
| Total | $16,375,000 |

On the consolidation the stock of the Pittsburg, Shenango & Lake Erie ($4,800,000, par $50) and of the Butler & Pittsburg ($5,20,0000) was retired by exchange, share for share, for common stock of Pittsburg, Bessemer & Lake Erie, making the amount given above.

The Pittsburg, Shenango & Lake Erie consolidated mortgage of 1943 is for $4,800,000, of which $3,000,000 was reserved to retire the 1st mortgage bonds; $1,250,000 was used for retirement and cancellation of indebtedness of the Erie Terminal and Conneaut Terminal companies. There are also $101,416 equipment lease warrants outstanding, the amount including interest on principal.

The consolidated mortgage of the Pittsburg, Bessemer & Lake Erie was created under the terms of the consolidation. The amount of mortgage is $10,000,000, covering all railroad property, docks, franchises and contracts. Of this issue $2,400,000 was to be given to stockholders of Butler & Pittsburg as part consideration for consolidation, $4,800,000 was reserved to retire mortgage indebtedness of Pittsburg, Shenango & Lake Erie at maturity and balance held for corporate purposes under terms of mortgage. The car trusts mature in yearly instalments. The 5 per cent. debentures were created in 1899 and are $2,000,000 authorized.

The company has a contract for 25 years with the Union Railway Co. mentioned above and the Carnegie Company for the transportation of material and products for the latter company, thus assuring a tonnage of about 3,600,000 tons annually. The arrangements include furnishing powerful modern equipment, the reduction of grades on the old portion of the line and construction of extensive new docks at Conneaut Harbor on Lake Erie for handling iron ore and coal. Entire line is laid with 100-pound steel rails, maximum grades are thirty feet to the mile, and 80 per cent. of line is straight track.

The United States & Ontario Steam Navigation Co., in connection with this company, operates boats to carry coal between Conneaut and Port Dover, Ontario.

EARNINGS.

| Year ending June 30. | Gross. | Net. |
|---|---|---|
| 1893-94 | $473,997 | $165,133 |
| 1894-95 | 567,717 | 156,926 |
| 1895-96 | 658,079 | 189,739 |
| 1896-97 | 599,019 | 93,567 |
| 1897-98 | 881,589 | Loss 82,788 |
| 1898-99 | 1,435,070 | 401,891 |
| 1899-00 | 2,179,784 | 1,012,815 |

President, James H. Reed; Vice-President, George W. Kepler; Secretary and Treasurer, D. Heim, Jr., Pittsburg.

Main office, 434 Fifth avenue, Pittsburg. Annual meeting, first Tuesday in April, at Pittsburg.

## PITTSBURG, CINCINNATI, CHICAGO & ST. LOUIS RAILWAY CO.

(Controlled by the Pennsylvania Company.)

This road is known widely as the "Pan Handle."

The company was formed in 1890 by a consolidation of the Pittsburg, Cincinnati & St. Louis, the Chicago, St. Louis & Pittsburg, the Jeffersonville, Madison & Indianapolis and the Cincinnati & Richmond. Road owned and controlled, 1,095 miles; trackage, 61 miles; total, 1,155 miles; leased, Little Miami, 192 miles; Chartiers Railway, 23 miles; Pittsburg, Wheeling & Kentucky, 28 miles; other lines, 10 miles; total leased, 253 miles; total operated 1,408 miles; controlled but operated independently, Cincinnati & Muskingum Valley Railroad, 150 miles; other lines, 47 miles; total of system, 1,605 miles. Locomotives, 452; passenger cars, 368; freight cars, 13,288.

This company is controlled by the Pennsylvania Railroad Co., which, with the Pennsylvania Company, holds $14,555,000 common and $17,761,200 preferred stock.

Stock..Par $100...Authorized { com., $45,000,000 / pref., 30,000,000 } Issued { com., $24,757,107 / pref., 22,698,566 } $47,455,673

Of preferred stock $27,170 and of common $675,630 is represented by scrip or by unexchanged shares of other companies.

The preferred stock is 4 per cent., non-cumulative. After the preferred stock receives 4 per cent. per annum the common receives 3 per cent., then preferred 1 per cent. more, but when the common shall have received 2 per cent. additional, or 5 per cent. in all, subsequent earnings are to be divided equally.

Transfer Agent, Farmers' Loan & Trust Co., New York. Registrar, National Bank of Commerce, New York.

November, 1894, dividend on preferred was passed and none was paid till January, 1896, after which there was another suspension of dividend payments until 1899, when 3 per cent. was paid. The February, 1900, dividend on preferred was increased to 2 per cent., and 2 per cent. was also paid in July, 1900, making 4 per cent. for the year. On January 15, 1901, 2 per cent. was paid on the preferred; 2 per cent. on July 15, 1901, and 2 per cent. on January 15 and July 15, 1902.

The first dividend on the common was 1 per cent., paid August 15, 1901. On February 15, 1902, 1½ per cent. was paid on the common, which is the rate of the subsequent semi-annual dividends, February and August.

### FUNDED DEBT.

| | |
|---|---|
| Consolidated mort., Series A, 4½ per cent., due Oct., 1940, April and Oct. | $10,000,000 |
| " " Series B, 4½ per cent., due April, 1942, April and Oct. | 8,786,000 |
| " " Series C, 4½ per cent., due Nov., 1942, May and Nov. | 1,379,000 |
| " " Series D, 4 per cent., due Nov., 1945, May and Nov. | 4,983,000 |
| " " Series E, 3½ per cent., due Aug., 1949, Feb. and Aug. | 11,254,000 |
| Chic., St. L. & Pitts., cons. mort., 5 per cent., due Oct., 1932, April and Oct. | 1,506,000 |
| Columbus & Ind. Cent., 1st mort., 7 per cent., due Nov., 1904, Jan. and July. | 2,440,000 |
| Jeffersonville, Mad. & Ind., 1st mort., 7 per cent., due Oct., 1906, April and Oct. | 739,000 |
| " " " 2d mort., 7 per cent., due July, 1910, Jan. and July. | 1,975,000 |
| Steubenville & Ind., 1st mort., extended, 5 per cent., due Jan., 1914, Jan. and July. | 3,000,000 |
| Columbus & Ind. Cent., 2d mort., 7 per cent., due Nov., 1904, May and Nov. | 700,000 |
| Union & Logansport, 1st mort., 7 per cent., due Dec., 1905, April and Oct. | 715,000 |
| Total | $47,477,000 |

The consolidated mortgage is for $75,000,000, of which $19,621,000 was reserved to retire underlying bonds.

In 1899 the $8,200,000 of 3½ per cent. consols, series D, were sold to provide for refunding $6,863,000 Pittsburg, Cincinnati & St. Louis consolidated 7s, maturing August 1, 1900, and $1,400,000 Indianapolis & Vincennes 2d 6s, due May 1, 1900.

### EARNINGS.

| | Gross. | Net. | Charges.* | Surplus. |
|---|---|---|---|---|
| 1893 | $15,750,809 | $3,730,224 | $2,905,590 | $824,634 |
| 1894 | 14,247,856 | 3,498,359 | 2,862,867 | 635,492 |
| 1895 (1,150 miles) | 15,439,706 | 4,234,827 | 3,211,930 | 1,022,897 |
| 1896 (1,151 " ) | 14,370,362 | 3,850,049 | 3,421,000 | 429,149 |
| 1897 ( " " ) | 15,144,485 | 4,884,761 | 3,567,792 | 1,316,969 |
| 1898 ( " " ) | 16,236,979 | 4,690,792 | 3,524,785 | 1,166,006 |
| 1899 ( " " ) | 18,104,426 | 5,121,186 | 3,510,105 | 1,711,081 |
| 1900 ( " " ) | 22,264,923 | 5,977,091 | 3,594,741 | 2,382,350 |
| 1901 (1,408 " ) | 24,290,892 | 7,015,568 | 3,494,376 | 3,696,990 |
| 1902 ( " " ) | 26,634,357 | 6,853,262 | 3,831,298 | 3,021,983 |

*Include result of operating leased roads.

President, Alexander J. Cassatt, Philadelphia; Vice-Presidents, James McCrea, Joseph Wood, J. J. Turner, Edward B. Taylor; Treasurer, T. H. B. McKnight; Secretary, S. B. Liggett; Comptroller, John W. Renner, Pittsburg.

Directors—John P. Green, William H. Barnes, Alexander J. Cassatt, Charles E. Pugh, Samuel Rea, N. Parker Shortridge, Philadelphia; Joseph Wood, James McCrea, J. J. Turner, Edward B. Taylor, Pittsburg; George Willard, Chicago; Briggs S. Cunningham, Cincinnati; Samuel S. Dennis, Newark, N. J.; L. F. Loree, Baltimore.

Main office, Union Station, Pittsburg. Annual meeting, second Tuesday in April.

## PITTSBURG, FORT WAYNE & CHICAGO RAILWAY CO.

(Leased to Pennsylvania Railroad Co.)

Road owned, Pittsburg to Chicago, 470 miles; branches leased, 12 miles; total, 482 miles. Locomotives, 353; passenger cars, 310; freight cars, 10,155.

Stock. Par $100.. Authorized { regular, $19,714,286 / special, 24,033,300 } Issued { regular, $19,714,286 / special, 24,033,300 } $43,747,585

The special stock has been issued to lessee from time to time in payment for improvements and additions to property, and is all held by the lessee.

Transfer Agents, Winslow, Lanier & Co., 17 Nassau street, New York.

Dividends of 7 per cent. per annum are paid on both classes of stock in quarterly payments of 1¾ per cent., January (2), April, July and October.

FUNDED DEBT.

| | |
|---|---|
| 1st mort., 7 per cent., due July, 1912, various | $5,250,000 |
| 2d mort., 7 per cent., due July, 1912, " | 5,160,000 |
| 3d mort., 7 per cent., due July, 1912, April and Oct. | 2,000,000 |
| Total | $12,410,000 |

1st mortgage bonds are in six series, A, B, C, D, E, F, of $875,000 each; 2d mortgage bonds in six series, G, H, I, K, L, M, $860,000 each, the only difference being in the months when interest is payable.

EARNINGS.

| | Div. Paid. | Gross. | Net. | Rental. | Profit to Lessee. |
|---|---|---|---|---|---|
| 1892 | 7 | $12,769,831 | $3,576,737 | $3,286,349 | Sur. $189,135 |
| 1893 | 7 | 12,659,668 | 3,712,936 | 3,399,159 | " 231,691 |
| 1894 | 7 | 9,429,859 | 2,268,093 | 3,549,746 | Def. 1,348,638 |
| 1895 | 7 | 11,102,923 | 3,635,894 | 3,693,638 | " 57,743 |
| 1896 | 7 | 10,022,167 | 3,106,897 | 3,620,894 | " 513,996 |
| 1897 | 7 | 10,583,282 | 3,473,442 | 3,342,487 | Sur. 130,955 |
| 1898 | 7 | 11,032,557 | 3,315,222 | 3,260,462 | " 54,760 |
| 1899 | 7 | 13,345,659 | 3,875,630 | 3,312,826 | " 562,804 |
| 1900 | 7 | 14,291,123 | 3,394,933 | 3,045,629 | " 349,304 |
| 1901 | 7 | 16,057,088 | 4,285,327 | 3,454,096 | " 831,230 |

President, Charles Lanier; Treasurer, J. P. Upham, New York; Secretary, John J. Haley, Pittsburg.

Directors—W. C. Egleston, Charles Lanier, John S. Kennedy, George G. Haven, New York; James McCrea, Charles E. Speer, Joseph Wood, Pittsburg; John P. Green, Alexander J. Cassatt, Philadelphia; Charles McCulloch, Fort Wayne, Ind.; Henry C. Urner, Cincinnati; Levi Z. Leiter, Chicago.

Main office, Union Station, Pittsburg. Annual meeting, third Wednesday in May.

## PITTSBURG JUNCTION RAILROAD CO.

(Controlled by Baltimore & Ohio Railroad Co.)

Road owned, Laughlin to Willow Grove, 4½ miles; Ninth street to Forty-third street, Pittsburg, 2½ miles; total, 7 miles. The road affords a connection between the Connellsville Division of the Baltimore & Ohio and the Pittsburg & Western Division. The property is operated as part of the Baltimore & Ohio system.

Stock.....Par $50.....Authorized { com., $1,460,000 / pref., 480,000 } Issued { com., $1,460,000 / pref., 480,000 } $1,940,000

The preferred stock is 7 per cent., cumulative. The last dividend on the preferred was 3½ per cent., paid in May, 1901. The last dividend on the common was 2 per cent., in October, 1900.

Stock is transferred by the secretary of the company, Baltimore.

FUNDED DEBT.

| | |
|---|---|
| 1st mort., 6 per cent., due July, 1922, Jan. and July | $1,440,000 |
| 2d mort., 5 per cent., due July, 1922, Jan. and July | 300,000 |
| Total | $1,740,000 |

The Baltimore & Ohio owns all the preferred stock and $614,850 of the common. It also owns $441,000 of the 1st mortgage bonds and $270,000 of the 2ds. The securities are deposited with the trustees of the Baltimore & Ohio, Pittsburg Junction and Midland Division, 3½ per cent. bonds.

In addition to the bonds given above, this company guarantees $500,000 of Pittsburg Junction Terminal, 5 per cent. bonds, of which issue the Baltimore & Ohio holds $281,000.

The earnings of this company are included in those of the Baltimore & Ohio system.

President, L. F. Loree, Baltimore; Vice-President, W. M. Kennedy, Pittsburg; Secretary, Custis W. Woolford; Treasurer, J. V. McNeal, Baltimore.

Main office, Smithfield and Water streets, Pittsburg. Annual meeting in October.

## PITTSBURG, LISBON & WESTERN RAILROAD CO.

A corporation formed under the laws of Pennsylvania and Ohio, November 12, 1902. The company is a consolidation of the railway company of the same name, the Salem Railroad Co., and the Shenango & Beaver Valley Railroad Co.

Road owned, Lisbon, O., to New Galilee, Pa., 25 miles; Salem, to Washingtonville, O., 7 miles; branch, 3 miles; total, 35 miles. Locomotives, 5; passenger cars, 4; freight cars, 41.

An extension of the line to a connection with the Buffalo, Rochester & Pittsburg Railroad Co. and the Wheeling & Lake Erie Railroad Co. has been planned, also various extensions to points in Ohio.

Stock......Par $100...... ....................Authorized, $5,000,000......Issued, $5,000,000

Transfer Agent, F. S. Requa, New York. Registrar, Bowling Green Trust Co., New York.

FUNDED DEBT.

| | |
|---|---|
| Pitts., Lisbon & West. Ry., 1st mort., 5 per cent., due July, 1920, Jan. and July | $150,000 |
| " " " R. R., 1st mort., 4 per cent., due Dec., 1952, June and Dec. | 600,000 |
| Total | $750,000 |

The new 4 per cent. 1st mortgage of the railroad company was created in 1902, and there has been issued $1,000,000. Trustee of mortgage, Bowling Green Trust Co., New York. Of the bonds $162,000 are reserved to retire the old 5 per cent. bonds and $238,000 are in the company's treasury.

President, N. B. Billingsley, Lisbon, O.; Vice-President, John Slade, New York; Secretary, R. . Tayler, Lisbon, O.; Assistant Secretary, H. R. Wilson; Treasurer, James I. Kernaghan, NeWYork.

Directors—Ira F. Mansfield, Beaver, Pa.; C. H. Akens, New Castle, Pa.; N. B. Billingsley, R. W. Tayler, George B. Harvey, J. W. Clark, Lisbon, O.; John Slade, James I. Kernaghan, William S. Alley, New York.

Main office, Lisbon, O.; New York office, 31 Nassau street. Annual meeting, first Tuesday in October, at Lisbon.

## PITTSBURG, SHAWMUT & NORTHERN RAILROAD CO.

A corporation formed under the laws of New York and Pennsylvania, August 1, 1899. The company was a consolidation of the Buffalo, St. Mary's & Southwestern Railroad Co., Mill Creek Valley Railroad Co., Mt. Jewett, Clermont & Northern Railroad Co., the Smethport & Olean Railroad Co., the Central New York & Western Railroad Co. and the Central New York & Northern Railroad Co. The system as planned will comprise about 350 miles of road, extending from the bituminous coal fields of Elk, Clearfield and Jefferson Counties, Pa., northerly to Macedon, N. Y., on the New York Central & Hudson River Railroad.

Road owned, Wayland, N. Y., to Hydes, Pa., 121.89 miles; leased, Hornellsville Branch, 10.13 miles; Clarion River Branch, 12 miles; proprietary road, 12.54 miles; trackage, 19.87 miles; total, 176.45 miles. New lines under construction to be completed in July, 1903, Bolivar, N. Y., to Angelica, N. Y., 25.2 miles; Clermont to Kasson, 7.76 miles; State Line Junction to Glen Junction, 2.27 miles; total, 33.23 miles; grand total, 209.69 miles. Locomotives, 27; passenger cars, 20; freight cars, 2,934.

The Pittsburg, Shawmut & Northern Railroad Co. is the owner of the capital stock of the Shawmut Mining Co., which owns 13,814 acres of coal land and mineral rights in Elk County, Pa. Also the Kersey Coal Co. property, consisting of 15,000 acres of coal and mineral rights in Elk and

Jefferson counties, Pa. A large timber territory is tributary to the road and on its lines are many industrial establishments.

In addition to the coal lands in Elk County, the company controls extensive coal fields in Jefferson and Armstrong Counties.

Stock......Par $100..........................Authorized, $15,000,000 .....Issued, $6,000,000

FUNDED DEBT.

| | |
|---|---|
| 1st mort., 5 per cent., gold, due Feb., 1949, Feb. and Aug ........................ | $164,000 |
| New mort., 4 per cent., due Feb., 1952, Feb. and Aug..... ........................ | 6,419,000 |
| Total .................... ........................................ | $6,583,000 |

In February, 1902, holders of the 5 per cent. bonds were asked to deposit them with the Central Trust Co. of New York, under a plan to exchange them, dollar for dollar, for bonds of a new issue of $15,000,000 4 per cent. 50-year gold bonds, interest for 2 years on the 5 per cent. bonds to be funded in advance in the new 4 per cent bonds. This plan was decided on in order to provide for the completion of the road, and it has been carried out, all the 5 per cent. bonds being exchanged excepting $164,000 still outstanding. The new $15,000,000 mortgage covers, in addition to the railroad, 13,814 acres of coal land belonging to the Shawmut Mining Co. and about 15,000 acres of coal land belonging to the Kersey Mining Co., all the stock of which companies is owned by the railroad company.

| EARNINGS. | Gross Income. | Net. |
|---|---|---|
| 1902........................................................ | $807,673.41 | $389,141.13 |

The figures include earnings from all sources.

President, John Byrne, New York; Vice-President and General Counsel, Frank Sullivan Smith, Angelica, N. Y.; Vice-President, D. F. Maroney, St. Mary's, Pa.; Treasurer, Harry M. Gough; Secretary, Lewis F. Wilson; Assistant Secretary, Frederic W. Frost, New York; Auditor and Assistant Treasurer, Henry S. Hastings, St. Mary's, Pa.

Directors—John Byrne, Frank H. Davis, George B. Sheppard, Charles E. Barrett, Lewis F. Wilson, Frederic H. Ridgway, George C. Atkins, New York; Frank Sullivan Smith, Angelica, N. Y.; Newell C. Knight, Chicago; Harry M. Gough, Jersey City.; William W. Clark, Wayland, N. Y.; Edwin E. Tait, Bradford, Pa.

Main office, 45 Wall street, New York. Annual meeting in January.

## PORTLAND & RUMFORD FALLS RAILWAY

Road owned, Rumford Junction to Rumford Falls, Me., 54 miles; Canton to Livermore, 10 miles; trackage, Rumford Junction to Lewiston, 4 miles; total operated, 68 miles. This company controls the Rumford Falls & Rangely Lakes Railroad, 31 miles. Locomotives, 11; passenger cars, 10; freight cars, 264.

Stock......Par $100..........................Authorized, $2,000,000......Issued, $2,000,000

Stock is transferred at the company's office, Portland, Me.

Dividends on the stock of the company are paid quarterly, in March, June, September and December. In 1899 6 per cent. was paid on the stock; in 1900 4 per cent.; in 1901 6 per cent., and in 1902 6 per cent.

FUNDED DEBT.

| | |
|---|---|
| Consolidated, new 1st mort., 4 per cent., due Nov., 1926, May and Nov.............. | $992,000 |
| Plain bonds, 4 per cent., due Aug., 1927, Feb. and Aug ............................ | 350,000 |
| Total.............................................................. | $1,342,000 |

There is a sinking fund for the bonds which, on June 30, 1902, held $33,227.

EARNINGS.

Year ending June 30.

| | Gross. | Net. | Charges. | Surplus. |
|---|---|---|---|---|
| 1899-00..... ........................... | $377,177 | $129,729 | $59,127 | $70,602 |
| 1900-01................................ | 461,492 | 175,195 | 76,146 | 99,049 |
| 1901-02 ................................ | 556,686 | 246,513 | 80,656 | 168,856 |

In 1899-00 the dividends were $40,000, and the surplus over same was $30,602; in 1900-01 dividend payments were $65,000, and surplus $34,049; in 1901-02 dividends were $90,000 and surplus $78,856.

President, Hugh J. Chisholm, Portland, Me.; Vice-President, Waldo Pettengill, Rumford Falls, Me.; Treasurer, R. C. Bradford, Portland, Me.

Directors—Hugh J. Chisholm, Fred E. Richards, R. C. Bradford, Portland, Me.; Waldo Pettengill, George D. Bisbee, Rumford Falls; Galen C. Moses, Bath; George C. Wing, Auburn, Me.; Charles D. Brown, Boston; A. N. Burbank, New York.

Main office, Portland, Me. Annual meeting, second Tuesday in September.

## PROVIDENCE & WORCESTER RAILROAD CO.

(Leased to New York, New Haven & Hartford Railroad Co.)

Road owned, Providence, R. I., to Worcester, Mass., 44 miles; branch, 7 miles; total, 51 miles, 5 miles of which is owned jointly with Boston & Providence.

Stock......Par $100........................Authorized, $3,500,000......Issued, $3,500,000

Stock is transferred at the office of the company, Providence, R. I.

Dividends are paid quarterly, 2½ per cent. each, in March (30), June, September and December.

FUNDED DEBT.

1st mort., 4 per cent., due Oct., 1947, April and Oct ................................ $1,500,000

Leased in 1889 to New York, Providence & Boston. That road was leased in 1892 to New York, New Haven & Hartford, which company took a new lease of this road for 99 years, guaranteeing 10 per cent. per annum on stock. The 6 per cent. 1st mortgage, maturing October, 1897, was refunded in 50-year 4 per cent. currency bonds.

President, M. B. I. Goddard; Treasurer, W. A. Leete, Providence, R. I.

Main office, 144 Westminster street, Providence. Annual meeting, second Wednesday in December. Books do not close for meeting.

## THE QUEBEC CENTRAL RAILWAY CO.

A corporation formed under the laws of the Dominion of Canada. Road owned, Sherbrooke to Harlaka Junction, P. Q., 137½ miles; Tring Junction to Megantic, 60 miles; branches, 16 miles; total operated, 213½ miles. Locomotives, 19; passenger cars, 28; freight cars, 554.

Stock......Par $100........................Authorized, $3,381,603......Issued, $3,381,603

Stock is transferred by the secretary of the company, London, England.

FUNDED DEBT.

| | |
|---|---|
| Prior lien bonds, 5 per cent., due Feb., 1908, Feb. and Aug., £152,600 ............. | $742,653 |
| New income bonds, 5 per cent., due 1922........................................... | 1,644,933 |
| Debenture stock, 4 per cent., £338,000 ........................................... | 1,129,733 |
| Total........................................................................ | $3,517,319 |

Interest on the bonds is payable in London. The debenture stock was created to retire prior lien bonds, of which £196,100 have been retired.

In 1899 2¼ per cent. was paid on the new income bonds, in 1900 2¼ per cent and in 1901 1½ per cent.

In 1901 the company created a 3 per cent. 2d debenture stock and gave holders of the income bonds the privilege of exchanging £100 of the latter for £50 of the 2d debenture stock and £50 in a new 7 per cent. income bond.

| EARNINGS. | Gross. | Net. |
|---|---|---|
| 1899........................................................ | $502,409 | $168,171 |
| 1900........................................................ | 537,995 | 109,451 |
| 1901........................................................ | 622,716 | 200,551 |

President, Edward Dent; Secretary, Thomas Lindley, London, England; General Manager, Frank Grundy, Sherbrooke, Canada.

Directors—Edward Dent, Alexander Bremker, Frederick H. Norman, Josepha Price, Samuel G. Sheppard, London, England; Frank Grundy, Sherbrooke, Canada; L. A. Carrier, Levis, Canada.

Main office, 5 Great Winchester street, London, England; operating office, Sherbrooke, Canada. Annual meeting in May, at London.

## QUEBEC SOUTHERN RAILWAY CO.

A corporation formed under the laws of Canada in 1900. The company acquired the franchises and property of the United Counties Railway Co. and the East Richelieu Valley Railway Co.

Road owned, Noyan, P. Q., to Sorel, 89 miles. In 1902 the company acquired the South

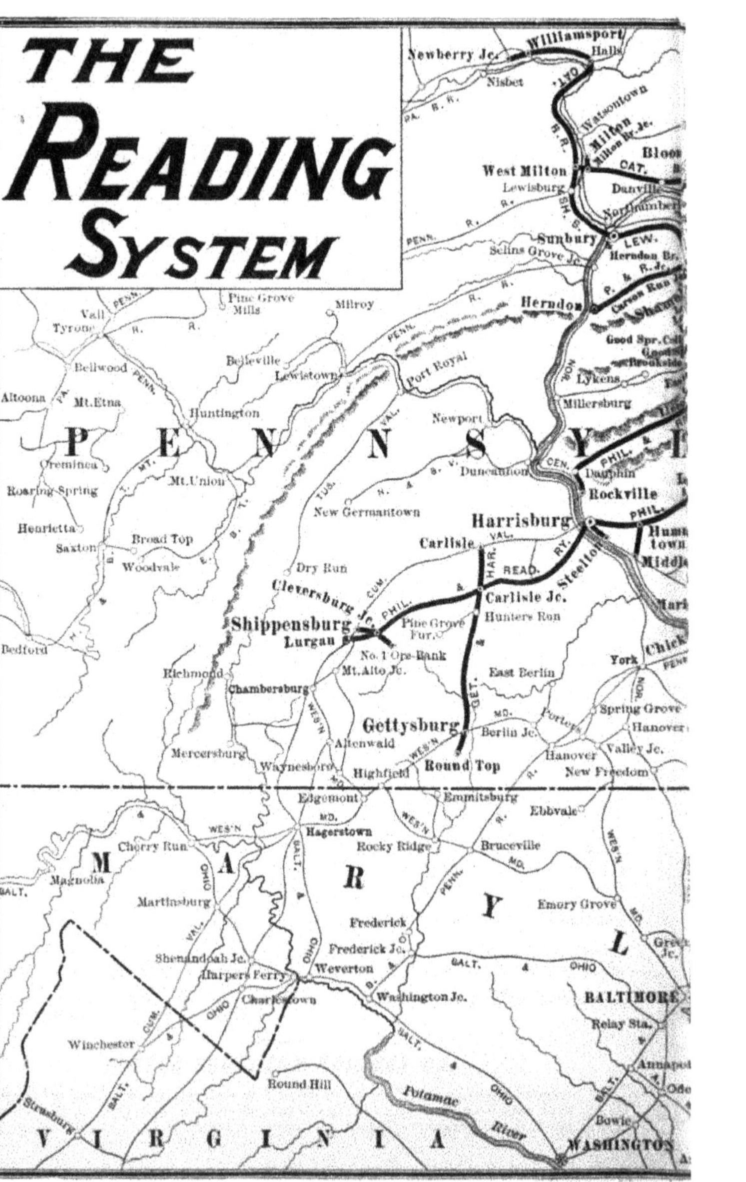
THE READING SYSTEM
Newberry Jc.
Williamsport
Halls
Nisbet
Watsontown
Milton
West Milton
Lewisburg
Bloom
Danville
Northumberland
Sunbury
Selins Grove Jc.
Herndon Br.
Herndon
Lykens
Millersburg
Pine Grove Mills
Milroy
Vail
Tyrone
Bellwood
Belleville
Lewistown
Port Royal
Altoona
Mt. Etna
Huntington
Newport
P E N N S Y L
Oremitea
Mt. Union
Duncannon
Dauphin
Rockville
Roaring Spring
New Germantown
Harrisburg
Henrietta
Broad Top
Saxton
Woodvale
Carlisle
Steelton
Dry Run
Cleversburg Jc.
Carlisle Jc.
Hunters Run
Shippensburg
Lurgan
Pine Grove Fur.
No. 1 Ore Bank
Bedford
York
Richmond
Mt. Alto Jc.
East Berlin
Chambersburg
Spring Grove
Gettysburg
Berlin Jc.
Hanover
Altenwald
Mercersburg
Waynesboro
Highfield
Round Top
Valley Jc.
New Freedom
Edgemont
Emmitsburg
Ebbvale
Hagerstown
Cherry Run
Rocky Ridge
Bruceville
M A R Y L
Magnolia
Martinsburg
Emory Grove
Frederick
Frederick Jc.
Shenandoah Jc.
Harpers Ferry
Weverton
Charlestown
Washington Jc.
BALTIMORE
Relay Sta.
Winchester
Round Hill
Potomac River
Bowie
Strasburg
V I R G I N I A
WASHINGTON

Wilkesbarre
Nanticoke
Lee
Upper
Lehigh
CEN.
Orangeville
White Haven
Drifton
Drifton Jc.
Rock Glen
Roan
Mahanoy
Mauch
Chunk
Saylorsb
Catawissa
Silver Br.
Tamanend
Tamaqua
Mahanoy Jc.
Slatington
Catasauqua
Palo Alto
Rausch's
Mt. Carbon
Schuylkill Haven
Wallner
Crane
Tremont
Lorberry Jc.
Port
Clinton
Lichty
Auburn
Pine Grove
Kutztown
Topton
Alburtis
Leesport
Quarry
Wetzel
V A N I
Muhlenburg
Reading
Birdsboro
Sinking
Spring
Pottstown
Mt. Hope
Adamstown
Manheim
Elverson
St. Peters
Phoenixville
Lancaster Jc.
Suplee
Byers
Lime Kilns
Lancaster
Downingtown
Columbia
Coatesville
West
Chester
PHILA
Strasburg
Pomeroy
Quarryville
Chaddsford Jc.
Avondale
Oxford
Landenburg
Stewartstown
Peach Bottom
Sta.
Delta
Octoraro Jc.
Newark
Porter
Havre de Grace
Delaware
City
Townsend
Bombay
Hook
Spring
Massey
Clayton
Smyrna
Chestertown
Centerville
Susquehanna
River
READ.
PENN.
BALT.
OHIO
WIL.
PHIL.

Shore Railway Co., St. Lambert to Sorel, 55 miles, and operates the same; a consolidation having been arranged between the companies.

Stock......Par, $100........................Authorized, $1,000,000......Issued, $1,000,000

The company has an authorized issue of 1st mortgage 4 per cent. bonds at the rate of $12,000 per mile, and also 5 per cent. income bonds at the rate of $8,000 per mile, but none of the bonds of either class have been sold.

The company received a subsidy from the Government of the Dominion of Canada.

President, H. A. Hodge, Montreal; Vice-President and Treasurer, F. D. White, Rutland, Vt. Main office, 26 St. Sacrament Street, Montreal.

## READING & COLUMBIA RAILROAD CO.

(Controlled by Philadelphia & Reading Railway Co.)

Road owned, Columbia, Pa., to Sinking Spring, 40 miles; Lancaster Branch, 8 miles; Mt. Hope Branch, 6 miles; branch leased, 6 miles; total, 60 miles.

Stock......Par $50..............................Authorized, $958,372......Issued, $958,373

Stock is transferred at the office of the company, Philadelphia.

FUNDED DEBT.

| | |
|---|---|
| 1st mort., extended, 5 per cent., due March, 1912, March and Sept.... .............. | $650,000 |
| 2d mort., extended, 5 per cent., due June, 1904, June and Dec....................... | 350,000 |
| Debenture bonds, 6 per cent., due Dec., 1917, June and Dec......................... | 1,000,000 |
| Total.............................................................. | $2,000,000 |

The Reading Company owns $788,200 of the stock, $9,500 1st mortgage bonds, $35,000 2ds and $1,000,000 debentures.

President, George F. Baer; Treasurer, W. A. Church; Secretary, W. R. Taylor; Comptroller, Daniel Jones, Philadelphia.

Main office, Reading Terminal Building, Philadelphia. Annual meeting, second Monday in January. Books close sixty days previous.

## READING COMPANY

### PHILADELPHIA & READING RAILWAY CO.

### PHILADELPHIA & READING COAL AND IRON CO.

Road owned, Philadelphia to Mount Carbon, 98 miles; branch, Reading to Harrisburg, 54 miles; other branches, 214 miles; total owned, 366 miles; leased, East Pennsylvania Railroad, Reading to Allentown, 36 miles; Mine Hill & Schuylkill Haven Railroad, 42 miles; Little Schuylkill Railroad, 31½ miles; Philadelphia, Germantown & Norristown Railroad, 34 miles; Catawissa Railroad, 103 miles; North Pennsylvania Railroad, 86 miles; Delaware & Bound Brook Railroad, 34 miles; Wilmington & Northern Railroad, 88½ miles; other branches leased, 182 miles; total leased, 637 miles; all lines owned and leased, 1,003 miles; controlled, Central Railroad of New Jersey, 677 miles; Reading & Columbia Railroad, 60 miles; Atlantic City Railroad, 168 miles; Gettysburg & Harrisburg Railway, 34 miles; Northeastern Pennsylvania Railroad, 26 miles; Perkiomen Railroad, 38 miles; Philadelphia & Chester Valley Railroad, 24 miles; Philadelphia, Newtown & New York Railroad, 22 miles; Port Reading Railroad, 21 miles; other branches controlled, 72 miles; total controlled, 1,142 miles; grand total of system, 2,145 miles. Control of the Wilmington & Northern was acquired in interest of this company in 1898. Locomotives, 892; passenger cars, 813; freight cars, 37,571; service cars, 947; also 5 steam colliers, 17 steam tugs, 59 coal barges and 43 car floats, etc.

In January, 1901, a controlling interest in the stock of the Central Railroad of New Jersey was purchased by this company.

The Reading Company is a Pennsylvania corporation, chartered by the Legislature in 1871 as the Excelsior Enterprise Co., afterward the National Company; name changed to Reading Company in 1896 for the purpose of carrying out the reorganization of the Philadelphia & Reading Railroad Co. under plan of December, 1895. This company has power to hold the securities of the Philadelphia & Reading Railway Co. and of the coal companies and other properties, and to carry on the business of the entire system.

The Philadelphia & Reading Railway Co. was organized November 17, 1896, and on November 30, 1896, took possession of the railroad lines, leaseholds and railroad property of the old Philadelphia & Reading Railroad, sold in foreclosure (under the plan of reorganization) September 23, 1896. All the stock of the railway company is owned by the Reading Company.

There is also an auxiliary organization known as the Philadelphia & Reading Coal and Iron Co., whose stock ($8,000,000) is owned by the Reading Company. The Coal and Iron Co. owns and leases an extensive anthracite coal property, on which it operates and leases a large number of collieries. The Reading Company also has a controlling interest in the Reading Iron Co., which owns a rolling mill at Reading and several other iron works and blast furnaces. The property of the Coal and Iron Co. was also sold at foreclosure September, 1896, and transferred to the new organization of the same name, which is controlled by the Reading Company.

The old Philadelphia & Reading Railroad Co. was twice reorganized, in 1887 and 1896 respectively. For details of the receiverships and reorganizations, see MANUAL for 1896 and 1900.

The new company has reduced the rentals paid to owners of a number of the leased branches. Dividends on stock of Catawissa Railroad were reduced from 7 to 5 per cent.; Mine Hill & Schuylkill Haven, from 8 to 6 per cent.; Chestnut Hill Railroad, from 12 to 6 per cent., and Little Schuylkill from 7 to 5 per cent.

| | | | | | | |
|---|---|---|---|---|---|---|
| Stock. Par $50. Authorized | com., | $70,000,000 | Issued | com., | $70,000,000 | $140,000,000 |
| | 1st pref., | 28,000,000 | | 1st pref., | 28,000,000 | |
| | 2d " | 42,000,000 | | 2d " | 42,000,000 | |

The 1st preferred and 2d preferred stock are both 4 per cent., non-cumulative. After 4 per cent. has been paid for two consecutive years on the first preferred, the company may convert the second preferred into one-half common and one-half first preferred stock.

All the stock is held for five years, or until full 4 per cent. has been paid on preferred for two consecutive years, in a voting trust. Trustees: J. Pierpont Morgan, Frederic P. Olcott and C. S. W. Packard.

Transfer Agents, J. P. Morgan & Co., New York.

The first dividend on any of the stocks of the new Reading Company was declared February 8, 1900, when a payment of 1½ per cent. on the 1st preferred was announced, payable March 8, 1900; a second dividend of 1½ per cent. on the 1st preferred was paid September 10, 1900, and on February 6, 1901, 2 per cent. semi-annual was paid on the 1st preferred. On September 10, 1901, and on March 1, 1902, 2 per cent was also paid. But the October, 1902, dividend was 1 per cent. only.

FUNDED DEBT.

| | |
|---|---|
| Reading Co. gen. mort., 4 per cent., due Jan., 1997, Jan. and July | $67,639,000 |
| " " Jersey Central col. trust, 4 per cent., due April, 1951, April and Oct. | 23,000,000 |
| " " Wil. & Northern collat. trust ctfs., 4 per cent., quar., March | 1,295,000 |
| Railway Co. mortgage loan, sterling, 6 per cent., due July, 1910, Jan. and July | 1,512,700 |
| " " mortgage loan, dollar, 6 per cent., due July, 1910, Jan. and July | 954,000 |
| " " mortgage loan, convertible, 4½ per cent., due July, 1910, Jan. and July. | 79,000 |
| " " mortgage loan, coupon, 5 per cent., due Oct., 1933, April and Oct. | 2,696,000 |
| " " consolidated mort., 6 per cent., due June, 1911, June and Dec. | 8,162,000 |
| " " consolidated mort., 7 per cent., due June, 1911, June and Dec. | 10,649,000 |
| " " improvement mort., extended, 4 per cent., due April, 1947, April and Oct. | 9,363,000 |
| " " cons. mort., 1st series, ex., 4 per cent., due March, 1937, March and Sept. | 5,766,717 |
| " " term. mort., guar. by Terml. Co., 5 per cent., due May, 1941, quar., Feb. | 8,500,000 |
| " " Philadelphia subway mort., 3½ per cent., due 1904–23, Jan. and July. | 2,720,000 |
| P. & R. Coal & Iron, coal trust ctfs., 6 per cent., due April, 1904, quar., Jan. | 3,600,000 |
| " " divisional coal land mortgage bonds | 274,500 |
| Reading Co., Del. Riv. terminal ex. mort., 5 per cent., due July, 1942, Jan. and July. | 809,000 |
| " " Del. Riv. terminal mort., 5 per cent., due May, 1942, May and Nov. | 500,000 |
| " " Real estate mortgages, Reading Co. | 1,428,190 |
| Equipment trusts, Series B and C | 4,305,000 |
| Total | $153,253,107 |

For old bonds retired under the reorganization see MANUAL for 1899.

The company has car trust obligations to the amount of $6,296,000, bearing 4½ and 4 per cent. There are real estate mortgages of the railway company for about $630,000.

The $20,000,000 purchase money 6 per cent. mortgage loan of 1896 of the railway company, due 1997, is all held by the Reading Company, and is pledged as security for the latter's general 4 per cent. mortgage. The general mortgage is also secured by deposit of $13,766,686 bonds of other companies and $25,532,875 stocks of other companies.

The new general mortgage of the Reading Company is for $135,000,000, of which $51,109,357 is reserved to take up underlying bonds of the railroad and coal property, and $17,000,000 is reserved to be used for improvements at rate of $1,500,000 per annum. These bonds have a sinking fund operative only when earnings are sufficient to pay the same and dividends on the stock, but cannot be drawn for redemption.

The Reading Company's Jersey Central collateral trust 4 per cent. bonds were created in 1901 to provide for the purchase of control of the Central Railroad of New Jersey. They are secured by deposit with the Pennsylvania Company for Insurances on Lives and Granting Annuities, Philadelphia, trustee, of $14,500,000 stock of the Central Railroad Co. of New Jersey, $1,195,000 stock of the Perkiomen Railroad Co., being all but $5,000 of that stock, and $440,000 stock of the Port Reading Railroad Co. The mortgage provides for the total issue of $45,000,000, but additional bonds can be sold only to acquire further amounts of Jersey Central stock. The bonds can be redeemed at 105 and interest after April 1, 1906, on six months' notice. In February, 1901, $23,000,000 of the bonds were offered for subscription by J. P. Morgan & Co., New York, at 94 and interest.

The Reading Company's Wilmington & Northern collateral trust certificates were created in 1900. They are secured by deposit with Girard Trust Co., Philadelphia, of practically all the $1,500,000 stock of the Wilmington & Northern Railroad Co., which road is leased to the Philadelphia & Reading Railroad Co. under a guarantee of dividends of 3 per cent. per annum on its stock. The bonds have no date of maturity, but are redeemable at 105 and interest.

There were also outstanding purchase money mortgages of the Philadelphia & Reading Coal and Iron Co., secured by different tracts of coal land and endorsed by the railroad company, to the amount of some $1,915,000, which are being retired as they mature out of funds provided in the reorganization plan and with new 4 per cent. general mortgage bonds, only $380,000 remaining outstanding on June 30, 1901.

EARNINGS.

Year ending November 30.

| | Gross. | Net. | Charges. | Sur. or Def. | |
|---|---|---|---|---|---|
| 1892-93 | $22,828,846 | $10,068,495 | $10,675,189 | Def. | $606,694 |
| 1893-94 | 20,344,775 | 9,571,418 | 10,478,824 | " | 907,406 |
| 1894-95 | 21,300,575 | 10,259,253 | 9,922,067 | Sur. | 337,186 |
| 1895-96 | 20,682,676 | 10,104,667 | 10,600,052 | Def. | 495,385 |
| 1896-97 (year ending June 30) | 20,746,864 | 8,898,804 | 9,708,526 | " | 809,722 |
| 1897-98 ( " " " ) | 21,986,834 | 9,600,806 | 9,008,120 | Sur. | 592,686 |
| 1898-99 ( " " " ) | 23,002,581 | 9,122,423 | 8,897,679 | " | 224,744 |
| 1899-00 ( " " " ) | 26,902,987 | 9,649,557 | 8,904,248 | " | 745,309 |
| 1900-01 ( " " " ) | 28,344,169 | 9,777,817 | 9,211,196 | " | 566,620 |
| 1901-02 ( " " " ) | 29,534,156 | 10,745,535 | 9,519,123 | " | 1,226,412 |

The above statement is for the railroad company alone; the charges include all rentals, etc.

The following gives the combined results since reorganization, including the Reading Company, the Philadelphia & Reading Railway Co. and the Coal and Iron Co.:

EARNINGS (ALL COMPANIES).

Year ending June 30.

| | Gross Earnings. | Net. | Charges. | Surplus. | |
|---|---|---|---|---|---|
| 1896-97 (7 months, to June 30) | $22,168,934 | $4,087,294 | $5,330,421 | Def. | $1,243,127 |
| 1897-98 | 45,256,624 | 10,420,364 | 9,043,944 | Sur. | 1,376,420 |
| 1898-99 | 46,882,907 | 10,239,061 | 9,073,852 | " | 1,165,208 |
| 1899-00 | 55,945,015 | 11,088,544 | 9,150,543 | " | 1,938,001 |
| 1900-01 | 58,755,880 | 12,154,842 | 9,491,755 | " | 2,663,087 |
| 1901-02 | 61,347,193 | 16,211,643 | 13,832,817 | | 2,378,826 |

Total coal mined by the company and its tenants, during the year ending November 30, 1890, was 7,338,472 tons; in 1891, 8,080,463 tons; in 1892, 7,749,938 tons; in 1893, 7,879,528 tons; in 1894, 8,658,043 tons; in 1895, 8,633,214 tons, and in 1896-97, during the year ending June 30, 7,128,615 tons; in 1897-98, 7,626,676 tons; in 1898-99, 8,183,644 tons; in 1899-1900, 9,219,764 tons; in 1900-01, 9,253,974 tons; in 1901-02, 8,198,274 tons.

In year 1896-97 (partly under receivership) the Coal and Iron company's total receipts were $21,427,079; profit in operating, $95,366. In 1897-98, receipts, $22,909,553; profit, $476,238. In 1898-99, receipts, $23,643,837; profit, $901,735; surplus over charges, $423,038. In 1899-1900, receipts, $27,884,644; profit, $1,201,912; surplus, $742,065.

The following presents the comparative freight traffic statistics of the railway company:

FREIGHT TRAFFIC.

| | Average Mileage. | Total Tons (2,000 lbs.). | Tons Carried One Mile. | Freight Density. | Rate per Ton per Mile. |
|---|---|---|---|---|---|
| 1896-97 | 913 | 8,324,052 | 554,265,865 | 607,082 | 1.165c |
| 1897-98 | 913 | 9,862,641 | 687,213,585 | 752,968 | 1.420 |
| 1898-99 | 915 | 11,385,928 | 822,615,211 | 899,033 | 0.951 |
| 1899-00 | 1,000 | 14,192,019 | 1,004,500,621 | 1,004,500 | 0.971 |
| 1900-01 | 1,000 | 14,535,083 | 1,026,056,531 | 1,026,056 | 0.982 |
| 1901-02 | 1,003 | 16,413,700 | 1,113,015,544 | 1,109,686 | 0.988 |

COAL TRAFFIC.

| | Average Mileage. | Total Tons (2,240 lbs.). | Tons Carried One Mile. | Freight Density. | Rate per Ton per Mile. |
|---|---|---|---|---|---|
| 1896-97 | 913 | 11,663,176 | 1,154,533,936 | 1,264,548 | 0.826 |
| 1897-98 | 913 | 12,981,667 | 1,390,656,311 | 1,523,162 | 0.714 |
| 1898-99 | 915 | 13,735,315 | 1,468,237,195 | 1,604,630 | 0.687 |
| 1899-00 | 1,000 | 15,212,275 | 1,643,836,143 | 1,643,836 | 0.692 |
| 1900-01 | 1,000 | 15,542,382 | 1,703,914,695 | 1,703,914 | 0.727 |
| 1901-02 | 1,003 | 15,553,041 | 1,710,792,217 | 1,705,575 | 0.726 |

The railway company's report separates the statistics of general freight traffic and coal. The latter includes both anthracite and bituminous coal carried.

RAILWAY CO.—GROSS AND NET EARNINGS BY MONTHS FOR THREE YEARS.

| | 1900. | | 1901. | | 1902. | |
|---|---|---|---|---|---|---|
| | Gross. | Net. | Gross. | Net. | Gross. | Net. |
| January | $2,297,044 | $804,515 | $2,490,817 | $913,767 | $2,630,695 | $1,050,053 |
| February | 1,811,710 | 523,585 | 2,040,166 | 656,643 | 2,174,167 | 823,658 |
| March | 2,091,412 | 610,549 | 2,415,752 | 806,513 | 2,465,274 | 897,065 |
| April | 2,170,343 | 758,320 | 2,222,265 | 674,464 | 2,793,638 | 968,511 |
| May | 2,329,242 | 813,235 | 2,574,734 | 997,840 | 2,274,634 | 718,119 |
| June | 2,461,459 | 764,186 | 2,623,834 | 982,590 | 1,905,764 | 451,035 |
| July | 2,139,748 | 729,416 | 2,239,681 | 758,006 | 1,921,175 | 503,808 |
| August | 2,567,547 | 999,416 | 2,594,250 | 1,019,277 | 1,992,195 | 535,837 |
| September | 2,362,124 | 873,507 | 2,461,900 | 900,984 | 1,939,445 | 377,881 |
| October | 1,878,281 | 364,866 | 2,870,887 | 1,177,033 | 2,244,542 | 713,323 |
| November | 2,476,476 | 869,077 | 2,666,265 | 1,022,184 | 2,887,469 | 1,138,899 |
| December | 2,552,424 | 909,719 | 2,438,434 | 959,610 | 2,861,119 | 1,061,624 |
| Totals | $27,137,810 | $9,020,391 | $29,638,985 | $10,868,911 | $28,090,059 | $9,239,813 |
| Aver. per month | 2,261,484 | 751,697 | 2,469,915 | 905,742 | 2,357,505 | 769,984 |

President, George F. Baer; Vice-Presidents, Theodore Voorhees (Railway Co.), William R. Taylor, C. E. Henderson (Railway Co.); Secretary, W. R. Taylor; Treasurer, W. A. Church; Comptroller, Daniel Jones, Philadelphia.

Directors—Joseph S. Harris, Henry P. McKean, John Lowber Welsh, Samuel Dickson, George C. Thomas, Philadelphia; Charles Steele, Hamilton McK. Twombley, New York; Henry A. Du Pont, Wilmington, Del.

Main office, Reading Terminal Building, Philadelphia. Annual meeting, Reading Company, first Tuesday in June; Philadelphia & Reading Railway Co. and Philadelphia & Reading Coal & Iron Co., second Monday in October.

## RENSSELAER & SARATOGA RAILROAD CO.

(Leased to Delaware & Hudson Co.)

Road owned, Troy, N. Y., to Whitehall, 79 miles; branches owned, 84 miles; branches leased, 30 miles; total, 193 miles.

The lease to the Delaware & Hudson Co. is in perpetuity, the rental being interest on debt and 8 per cent. on stock.

Stock......Par $100........................Authorized, $10,000,000......Issued, $10,000,000

Transfer Agent, National Bank of Commerce, New York.

FUNDED DEBT.

1st mort., consolidated, 7 per cent., due May, 1921, May and Nov.................... $2,000,000

Dividends are paid semi-annually, 4 per cent. each, January (2) and July.

EARNINGS.—Year ending September 30.

| | Gross. | Net. | Rental. | Loss to Lessee. |
|---|---|---|---|---|
| 1893-94 | $2,174,133 | $758,395 | $1,193,173 | $434,778 |
| 1894-95 | 2,273,479 | 788,024 | 1,194,411 | 406,387 |
| 1895-96 | 2,351,545 | 862,484 | 1,210,048 | 347,564 |
| 1896-97 | 2,345,270 | 804,124 | 1,147,405 | 343,281 |
| 1897-98 | 2,470,647 | 833,224 | 1,132,536 | 299,315 |
| 1898-99 | 2,458,032 | 695,183 | 1,029,183 | 334,000 |
| 1899-00 | 2,656,035 | 929,556 | 1,145,016 | 215,460 |
| 1900-01 | 2,636,183 | 714,421 | 1,033,083 | 319,262 |
| 1901-02 | 2,756,720 | 751,104 | 1,034,705 | 283,601 |

President, George B. Warren; Treasurer and Secretary, John H. Neher, Troy, N. Y

Main office, 17 First street, Troy, N. Y. Annual meeting, first Monday in June.

## RICHMOND, FREDERICKSBURG & POTOMAC RAILROAD CO.

(Controlled by Richmond-Washington Co.)

Road owned, Quantico, Va., to Richmond, 80 miles; branch, 3 miles; total operated, 83 miles. Locomotives, 39; passenger cars, 38; freight cars, 199.

In November, 1901, the Richmond-Washington Co. acquired a majority of the capital stock of this company, and the road is operated, in conjunction with the Washington Southern Railway, as part of the through line between Richmond and Washington in the joint interest of the following companies, viz.: Pennsylvania Railroad, Baltimore & Ohio Railroad, Atlantic Coast Line Railroad, Southern Railway, Chesapeake & Ohio Railway, and Seaboard Air Line Railway. Each of these companies owns one-sixth of the Richmond-Washington Co.'s stock.

| Stock. Par $100..Au'd | | Is'd | | |
|---|---|---|---|---|
| com., | $1,316,900 | com., | $1,316,900 | $2,889,300 |
| guar., 7 per cent., | 481,100 | guar., 7 per cent., | 481,100 | |
| " 6 per cent., | 19,300 | " 6 per cent., | 19,300 | |
| div. obligations., | 1,072,000 | div. obligations.. | 1,072,000 | |

Stock is transferred at the office of the company, Richmond.

The company has paid dividends of 6½ or 7 per cent. per annum for a number of years, the same rate being paid on the common and the dividend obligations, the latter, however, possessing no voting power. In 1899-1900 the rate was, however, advanced to 8 per cent. per annum. Dividends on the common and dividend obligations are paid semi-annually, in January (1) and July. On the guaranteed stocks they are semi-annual, in May and November.

FUNDED DEBT.

Consolidated mort., 4½ per cent., due April, 1940, April and Oct.................... 500,000

The guaranteed stocks are secured by a lien on the company's property. The dividend obligations are entitled to receive the same rate of interest as the dividends paid on the common stock, but have no voting power. The State of Virginia owns $275,000 of the common stock.

The company leases the Richmond, Fredericksburg & Potomac and Richmond & Petersburg, guaranteeing 8 per cent. per annum on its $140,000 of stock.

The consolidated mortgage is for $2,000,000. Trustee, Central Trust Co., New York. Maturing prior lien bonds will be retired with consols.

EARNINGS.

Year ending June 30.

| | Dividends. | Gross. | Net. | Charges. | Surplus. |
|---|---|---|---|---|---|
| 1898-99 | 7 | $898,259 | $348,322 | $107,343 | $240,979 |
| 1899-00 | 8 | 993,252 | 439,420 | 104,988 | 334,432 |
| 1900-01 | 8 | 1,066,805 | 398,065 | 109,546 | 288,519 |
| 1901-02 | 8 | 1,168,055 | 457,568 | 71,207 | 386,381 |

President, E. T. D. Myers; Secretary and Treasurer, James B. Winston; Auditor, J. E. Cox, Richmond, Va.

Directors—W. J. Leake, J. T. Ellyson, George W. Stevens, John Skelton Williams, Richmond; Samuel Spencer, New York.

Main office, Canal and Seventh streets, Richmond, Va. Annual meeting, third Monday in November.

---

## RIO GRANDE, SIERRA MADRE & PACIFIC RAILROAD CO.

Road owned, Ciudad Juarez, Mex., to Casas Grandes, 156 miles. Further extensions are proposed.

Stock......Par $100.................... Authorized, $20,000 per mile......Issued, $3,120,000

FUNDED DEBT.

1st mort., 6 per cent., due July, 1977, Jan. and July.............................. $2,000,000

The stock is authorized at the rate of $20,000 per mile and the 1st mortgage bonds at the same rate.

This company is interested in a company under the title of the El Paso Southern Railroad, which built terminals at El Paso and a bridge over the Rio Grande River at that city.

President, A. Foster Higgins; Vice-Presidents, Edwin D. Morgan, A. Gifford Agnew; Secretary, George Rowland, New York.

Directors—A. Foster Higgins, Edwin D. Morgan, A. Gifford Agnew, George Rowland, John T. Terry, Edward M. Shepard, Sidell Tilghman, John B. Lawrence, Jr., W. Morton Grinnell, New York.

Main office, Ciudad Juarez, Mex.; New York office, 100 Broadway.

## RIO GRANDE SOUTHERN RAILROAD CO.

(Controlled by Denver & Rio Grande Railroad Co.)

Road owned, Ridgway to Durango, Col., 162 miles; branches to Telluride, Col., and coal mines, 18 miles; total, 180 miles (3-foot gauge). Locomotives, 22; passenger cars, 15; freight cars, 732.

Stock......Par $100........................Authorized, $5,000,000.....Issued, $4,510,000

FUNDED DEBT.

1st mort., reduced to 4 per cent., due July, 1940, Jan. and July........................ $4,510,000

This road was built in the interest of the Denver & Rio Grande Railroad Co., which owns a majority of the stock. In August, 1893, Receiver was appointed. In February, 1895, the Denver & Rio Grande advanced company $169,839 cash and endorsed $573,498 notes given for this company's floating debt under, arrangement by which all surplus earnings for three years from January 1, 1895, were to be paid to Denver & Rio Grande, which company also received $671,000 Rio Grande Southern 1sts. The Denver & Rio Grande owned $2,277,000 of the bonds, which are guaranteed by that company, but sold $600,000 in 1900.

In 1895 plan was submitted by which interest on 1st mortgage bonds was reduced from 5 per cent. to 3 per cent. during 1896 and 1897, and 4 per cent. after January 1, 1898, all past due coupons being canceled. This arrangement was agreed to by bondholders, floating debt being retired under arrangement of February, 1895, with Denver & Rio Grande, and Receiver was discharged January 15, 1896.

Amount of 1st mortgage authorized is $5,000,000, at rate of $25,000 per mile.

EARNINGS.

Year ending June 30.

| | Gross. | Net. | Charges. | Surplus. |
|---|---|---|---|---|
| 1895-96 | $489,234 | $235,602 | $168,896 | $66,705 |
| 1896-97 | 401,238 | 174,438 | 170,967 | 3,470 |
| 1897-98 | 427,263 | 200,271 | 192,683 | 7,587 |
| 1898-99 | 489,324 | 237,235 | 212,641 | 24,594 |
| 1899-00 | 525,136 | 247,542 | 213,601 | 33,940 |
| 1900-01 | 539,529 | 259,445 | 213,492 | 45,952 |
| 1901-02 | 575,670 | 270,247 | 217,955 | 52,292 |

President, Edward T. Jeffery, Denver; Vice-President, Russell Harding, St. Louis; Treasurer, Joseph W. Gilluly; Secretary, John B. Andrews; Auditor, E. R. Murphy, Denver.

General office, Seventeenth and Stout streets, Denver; New York office, 195 Broadway. Annual meeting, third Monday in October, at Denver. Financial Agents, Maitland, Coppell & Co., New York.

---

## RIO GRANDE WESTERN RAILWAY CO.

(Controlled by Denver & Rio Grande Railroad Co.)

Road owned, Crevasse, Col., to Ogden, Utah, 310 miles; branches, 159 miles; spurs and narrow gauge branches, 20 miles; operates and owns Sevier Railroad, 71 miles; Tintic Range Railroad, 48 miles; total owned, 608 miles; leased, Utah Central, Salt Lake City to Park City, 36 miles; Denver & Rio Grande, Crevasse to Grand Junction, Col., 18 miles; total operated, 662 miles. Locomotives, 94; passenger cars, 74; freight cars, 1,523; other cars, 21.

This company is a reorganization of the Denver & Rio Grande Western Railway.

In 1901 the Denver & Rio Grande acquired all the common stock of this company at $80 per share and also most of the preferred stock, the holders of which were offered 11 shares of Denver & Rio Grande preferred for 10 shares of this company's preferred.

Stock..Par $100...Authorized { com., $15,000,000; pref., 7,500,000 } Issued { com., $10,000,000; pref., 7,500,000 } $17,500,000

The preferred stock is 5 per cent., non-cumulative, and shares with common in any surplus after the common has also received 5 per cent. for any year.

Stock is transferred at the company's office, 195 Broadway, New York.

Dividends on the preferred stock have been as follows: In 1891, 3¾ per cent. and 2½ per cent. in preferred stock; in 1892, 5 per cent.; in 1893, 3¼ per cent.; in 1894, 1895 and 1896, none; in 1897, ¾ per cent. and 4 per cent. in preferred stock; in 1898, 5 per cent.; in 1899, 5½ per cent.; in 1900, 5 per cent. On the common 2 per cent. in preferred stock was paid in 1898 and 1 per cent. in 1899. The first cash dividend on the common was 5 per cent., paid September 1, 1900. Dividends on the preferred are paid quarterly, February (1), May, August and November.

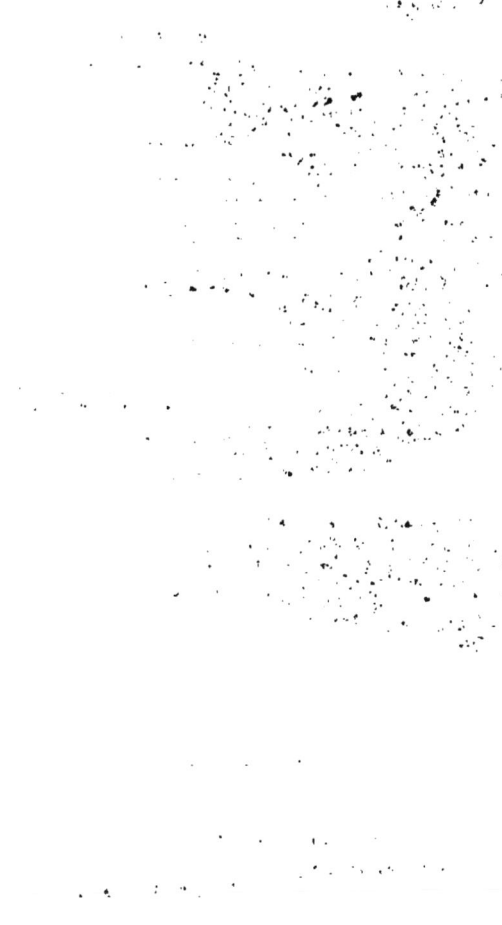

In 1891 preferred stock was increased from $5,000,000 to $6,250,000, stockholders taking new issue at $65 per share, the proceeds being applied to equipment and betterments. In August, 1897, $250,000 in preferred stock was distributed to preferred stockholders as a 4 per cent. dividend on the $6,250,000 of preferred stock then outstanding. In September, 1898, $200,000 preferred was distributed as a 2 per cent. dividend on common stock, and in September, 1899, 1 per cent. in preferred was again paid in common, increasing the preferred by $100,000. In 1900 $700,000 preferred was sold, making the amount outstanding $7,500,000. In 1900 the authorized amount of common stock was increased to $15,000,000 to provide for construction and equipment.

The consolidated mortgage was created in 1899, and is a 1st lien on the Sevier and Tintic Railroads and on new branches.

FUNDED DEBT.

| | |
|---|---|
| 1st mort., 4 per cent., gold bonds, due July, 1939, Jan. and July | $15,200,000 |
| 1st cons. mort., 4 per cent., due April, 1949, April and Oct. | 12,276,000 |
| Utah Central, 1st mort., 4 per cent., due Jan., 1918, April and Oct. | 650,000 |
| Utah Fuel Co., 1st mort., 5 per cent., due March, 1931, March and Sept. | 150,000 |
| Pleasant Valley Coal, 1st mort., 5 per cent., due July, 1928, Jan. and July | 1,227,000 |
| Total | $29,503,000 |

EARNINGS.

Year ending June 30.

| | Gross. | Net. | Charges. | Surplus. |
|---|---|---|---|---|
| 1891-92 | $2,643,924 | $928,571 | $597,121 | $331,450 |
| 1892-93 | 2,496,462 | 822,733 | 596,823 | 225,910 |
| 1893-94 | 2,101,318 | 647,083 | 637,713 | 9,350 |
| 1894-95 | 2,189,691 | 667,092 | 626,831 | 40,261 |
| 1895-96 | 2,457,358 | 870,509 | 629,071 | 241,438 |
| 1896-97 | 2,468,504 | 753,615 | 627,244 | 131,370 |
| 1897-98 | 3,362,288 | 1,182,739 | 637,670 | 545,069 |
| 1898-99 | 3,352,988 | 1,157,123 | 670,279 | 486,844 |
| 1899-00 | 4,510,603 | 1,688,552 | 1,074,569 | 613,983 |
| 1900-01 | 4,907,206 | 1,734,368 | 972,414 | 761,954 |

The earnings for 1901-02 are included in those of the Denver & Rio Grande Railway Co.

Chairman, George J. Gould, New York; President, Edward T. Jeffery, Denver; Vice-President, Russell Harding, St. Louis; Secretary, Stephen Little, New York; Treasurer, Joseph W. Gilluly, Denver.

Directors—George J. Gould, Frank J. Gould, Howard Gould, Jacob H. Schiff, Edward H. Harriman, Winslow S. Pierce, Robert M. Gallaway, New York; Russell Harding, St. Louis; Edward T. Jeffery, Denver.

Main office, Dooly Block, Salt Lake City, Utah; Denver office, Seventeenth and Stout streets; New York office, 195 Broadway. Annual meeting, fourth Monday in October, at Salt Lake City.

## THE ROCK ISLAND CO.

### CHICAGO, ROCK ISLAND & PACIFIC RAILROAD CO.

### CHICAGO, ROCK ISLAND & PACIFIC RAILWAY CO.

The Rock Island Co. is a corporation formed under the laws of New Jersey, July 31, 1902, for the purpose of carrying out the plans for the control and capitalization of the system of railroads owned by the Chicago, Rock Island & Pacific Railway Co. referred to below. The Rock Island Co. is a holding or investment corporation, its charter vesting it with power to acquire and hold, sell or dispose of, mortgage or pledge, the stocks or securities of other corporations, and to exercise the voting powers which may attach to the same.

The company owns all of the outstanding stock of the Chicago, Rock Island & Pacific Railroad Co., which acquired nearly all of the stock of the Chicago, Rock Island & Pacific Railway Co. See below for detailed statements of the railroad and railway companies.

In March, 1903, it was reported that negotiations had been completed by which this company would also acquire control of the St. Louis & San Francisco Railroad Co. and its affiliated lines.

Stock..Par $100...Authorized { com., $96,000,000; pref., 54,000,000 } Issued { com., $67,855,200; pref., 47,497,800 } $115,353,000

The preferred stock is 4 per cent., non-cumulative, from 1903 inclusive until 1910. It then becomes entitled to 5 per cent., non-cumulative, until 1917, and thereafter to 6 per cent. The preferred stock also has a preference up to the par value thereof as to assets of the company in case of a dissolution.

The first quarterly dividend on the preferred stock was 1 per cent., paid February 1, 1903. The quarterly dividend periods for the preferred are February, May, August and November.

Transfer Agent, Commercial Trust Co. of New Jersey, Jersey City. Registrar, United States Mortgage & Trust Co., New York.

The stocks of the Rock Island Co. were issued in pursuance of a plan put forth in August, 1902, by which holders of stock of the old Chicago, Rock Island & Pacific Railway Co. were offered in exchange for each $100 of the old stock the following securities:

$100 in 4 per cent. collateral trust bonds of the Chicago, Rock Island & Pacific Railroad Co.

$100 in common stock of the Rock Island Co.

$70 in preferred stock of the Rock Island Co.

Of the $74,248,100 stock of the old railway company, $67,853,900 had been exchanged for the new securities on November 1, 1902.

The preferred stockholders have the right to elect a majority of the directors, or five of the nine directors provided for in the original incorporation, and should the number of directors be increased, the preferred stock shall still be entitled to choose a majority. This is accomplished by classifying the directors, the first class of five members of the board being those elected by the preferred stockholders. This right can only be surrendered by a two-thirds vote of the preferred stock at a special meeting called for the purpose. The number of directors has been increased to thirteen, the first class elected by the preferred stockholders being seven in number.

It is provided that there shall be a finance committee elected by the directors from their own number, who shall exercise the powers of the board when the latter is not in session.

In the original formation of the Rock Island Co. its directors were given power to buy and sell the stocks of the company at their discretion for its account. This was modified by a by-law providing that the company can only purchase its own stocks for the purpose of retiring and cancelling the same. Furthermore, while the directors have power to make and alter the other by-laws, the above by-law cannot be rescinded or changed except by a vote of the stockholders at an annual or special meeting.

President, William B. Leeds; Chairman of Finance Committee, William H. Moore; Secretary and Treasurer, Daniel G. Reid; Assistant Secretary and Assistant Treasurer, George T. Boggs, New York.

Directors—William H. Moore, William B. Leeds, Daniel G. Reid, F. L. Hine, George G. McMurtry, Anson R. Flower, George S. Brewster, Ogden Mills, New York; Robert R. Cable, James H. Moore, Marshall Field, Chicago; Henry C. Frick, Pittsburg; George T. Boggs, East Orange, N. J.

Finance Committee—William H. Moore, William B. Leeds, Daniel G. Reid, James H. Moore, F. L. Hine, Marshall Field.

Corporate office, 15 Exchange place, Jersey City; New York office, 71 Broadway. Annual meeting, fourth Monday in January, at Jersey City.

CHICAGO, ROCK ISLAND & PACIFIC RAILROAD CO.—A corporation formed under the laws of Iowa, July 31, 1902. The purpose of the company's organization is explained in full above in connection with the Rock Island Co.

Stock......Par $100......................Authorized, $125,000,000......Issued, $113,903,000

The company has no preferred stock. All of its outstanding stock is owned by the Rock Island Co.

FUNDED DEBT.

Collateral trust bonds, gold, 4 per cent., due Nov., 2002, May and Nov............. $67,853,000

The bonds, as stated above, were issued in exchange for the stock of the old railway company. They are secured by the deposit with the Central Trust Co., New York, under a collateral trust agreement, of stock of the Chicago, Rock Island & Pacific Railway Co. equal to the amount of the bonds outstanding. The total amount of bonds to be issued under the agreement is limited to $75,000,000, that being the authorized amount of the old stock. This company also pledges itself to deposit with the trust company, under the said agreement, any additional amount of the old stock which it may acquire.

Coupons are paid at the office of the company, 71 Broadway, New York. Both coupon and registered bonds are provided for, and the one class may be exchanged for the other at the company's office.

President, William T. Rankin; Vice-President, Oliver H. Bogue; Secretary and Treasurer, James H. Mather, Des Moines, Ia.

Main office, Chicago. Annual meeting, third Thursday in October, at Des Moines.

THE CHICAGO, ROCK ISLAND & PACIFIC RAILWAY CO.—This company was formed in 1880, and in June of that year succeeded the railroad company of the same name, the Iowa Southern & Missouri Northern Railroad being consolidated with it.

The main line of this company is from Chicago to Council Bluffs, 500 miles. The system, including leased and controlled roads, extends to Denver, Kansas City, El Paso, Fort Worth and Memphis, with numerous branches and extensions.

The entire system operated at the end of 1902 comprised the following:

| In Operation: | Miles. |
|---|---|
| The Chicago, Rock Island & Pacific Railway Co., owned | 3,731 |
| The Keokuk & Des Moines Railroad Co., leased | 162 |
| Des Moines & Fort Dodge Railroad Co., leased | 144 |
| Peoria & Bureau Valley Railway Co., leased | 47 |
| Burlington, Cedar Rapids & Northern Railway Co., leased | 1,372 |
| Rock Island & Peoria Railway Co., leased | 120 |
| Choctaw, Oklahoma & Gulf Railroad Co., controlled | 1,052 |
| Choctaw, Oklahoma & Texas, controlled | 114 |
| Chicago, Rock Island & Texas Railway Co., controlled | 123 |
| Chicago, Rock Island & El Paso Railway Co., controlled | 111 |
| Chicago, Rock Island & Mexico Railway Co., controlled | 92 |
| Choctaw, Oklahoma & Texas Railroad Co., controlled | 135 |
| Searcy & Des Arc Railroad Co., controlled | 25 |
| Total | 7,228 |

Included in the Chicago, Rock Island & Pacific proper is about 338 miles of trackage.

At the end of 1902 there were under construction the following additional lines:

| | |
|---|---|
| St. Louis, Kansas City & Colorado Railroad Co., St. Louis to Kansas City | 294 |
| Chicago, Rock Island & Texas Railway Co., Jacksboro to Graham | 27 |
| Chicago, Rock Island & Gulf Railway Co., Fort Worth to Houston | 265 |
| Choctaw, Oklahoma & Texas Railroad Co., Amarillo to Texas-New Mexico line, and Chicago, Rock Island & El Paso Railway Co., Texas-New Mexico line to Tucumcari | 125 |
| Choctaw & Chickasaw Railroad Co., Ardmore to Red River, and Chicago, Rock Island & Gulf Railway Co., Red River to Dallas | 113 |
| Choctaw, Oklahoma & Gulf Railroad Co., Guthrie to Chandler | 50 |
| Various branches in Oklahoma and Indian Territory, about | 150 |
| Total under construction | 1,024 |

Locomotives, 822; passenger cars, 605; freight cars, 26,260.

In 1878 this company leased the Keokuk & Des Moines Railroad, and in 1887 the Des Moines & Fort Dodge Railroad was leased (see statement of those companies in this edition of the MANUAL). Between 1886 and 1890 the company built considerable new lines, extending its system into Kansas, Colorado and the Indian Territory. These extensions were mainly built under the titles of the Chicago, Kansas & Nebraska Railway. In 1891 the Chicago, Kansas & Nebraska, all the securities of which were owned by this company, was amalgamated with the parent system. In 1901 completed an extension of 259 miles from Liberal, Kan., to Santa Rosa, N. M., connecting with the New Mexico Railroad & Coal Co.'s lines to El Paso, this company having a close traffic contract with the New Mexico Railroad & Coal Co.

In April, 1902, this company acquired control of the Choctaw, Oklahoma & Gulf Railroad Co. and its affiliated lines. In 1902 it also leased the Burlington, Cedar Rapids & Northern Railway and the Rock Island & Peoria Railway. The St. Louis, Kansas City & Colorado was purchased in 1902 an is to be completed forthwith, thus giving the company a route from Kansas City to St. Louis. d

Stock......Par $100........................Authorized, $75,000,000......Issued, $74,248,100

From 1887 until 1898 the stock authorized and outstanding was $46,156,000. In August, 1898, a 10 per cent. dividend in stock was paid. From the formation of the present company in 1880 until 1887 amount of stock outstanding was $41,960,000, but in 1887 a 10 per cent. allotment at par was made to stockholders. Prior to the consolidation of 1880 the stock of the Chicago, Rock Island & Pacific Railroad Co. was $20,980,000, the increase of the company's stock to double that amount, representing the inclusion of the lines of the Iowa Southern and Missouri Northern Railroad in the system. In July, 1901, the stock was increased from $50,000,000 to $60,000,000, and the stockholders were given the right to take the $10,000,000 of new stock at par, the proceeds being used to build the New Mexico extension and other branches. In 1902 the stock was increased to $75,000,000, the additional amount being to retire minority stock of the Burlington, Cedar Rapids & Northern Railway and the Rock Island & Peoria Railway and purchase the St. Louis, Kansas City & Colorado Railway Co. $9,116,000 was also sold to the stockholders at par.

Commencing November, 1894, dividends were reduced to ½ per cent. quarterly, and remained at that rate until November, 1897, when company again paid 1 per cent. quarterly. In August, 1898, the rate was raised to 1¼ per cent., consisting of a quarterly dividend of 1 per cent. and ¼ per cent. extra, the latter being paid out of the Addition and Improvement account, from which similar extra dividends are to be paid quarterly until the first quarter of 1903 inclusive. The dividends were paid quarterly, February (1), May, August and November, at the rate of 1¼ per cent. Under the new arrangements in 1902 the dividend period was changed, and in January,

1903, 1¼ per cent. was paid as a regular quarterly dividend, with 3 per cent. extra as an advance payment of part of the dividends of the current year.

Transfer agency, 71 Broadway, New York. Registrar, Corn Exchange Bank, New York.

FUNDED DEBT.

| | |
|---|---|
| 1st mort. bonds, 6 per cent., due July, 1917, Jan. and July | $12,500,000 |
| General mort. gold, 4 per cent., due Jan., 1988, Jan. and July | 59,581,000 |
| Col. trust, Choctaw, Okla. & Gulf, 4 per cent., due May, 1903-18, May and Nov. | 23,552,000 |
| Total | $95,633,000 |

Prior to 1898 the company had outstanding (in addition to the 1st mortgage 6 per cent. bonds and $5,000,000 Chicago & Southwestern 7s) $40,394,000 of extension and collateral 5 per cent. bonds, due 1934, and $4,500,000 30-year debentures 5 per cent., due 1921, both of the latter issues being subject to call at 105.

Under date of January 1, 1898, the company executed a mortgage to the Central Trust Co. of New York and George Sherman, as trustees, to secure an issue of $100,000,000 general mortgage gold bonds, to be used in retiring all outstanding bonds and in providing for additions, betterments and extensions, and acquiring connecting roads. The bonds are in coupon and registered forms, coupon bonds being for $1,000 each and registered bonds for $1,000 and $5,000. Coupon bonds may be registered as to principal only, or converted into full registered bonds. The bonds are secured on the entire property and assets of the company now held and on any property which may be acquired hereafter by the proceeds of the bonds. The extension and collateral bonds were called for payment April 30 and the debenture bonds September 1, 1898. The Chicago & Southwestern bonds matured and were paid November 1, 1899. Up to December 31, 1898, there had been issued of the new general mortgage bonds $47,471,000 for the purpose of retiring extension and collateral 5 per cent. and 30-year debenture 5 per cent. bonds at 105, $500,000 for purpose of facilitating issue of general mortgage bonds, and $610,000 for permanent improvements from January 1 to October 31, 1898, and $5,000,000 for retiring Chicago & Southwestern 7 per cent. bonds. In the year ending October 31, 1899, $1,000,000 additional were issued, in the year ending October 31, 1900, $1,000,000 more, and in the year ending October 1, 1901, $1,000,000 more for expenditures for permanent improvements. Total issued to December 31, 1902, $59,581,000.

The collateral trust bonds created in 1902 are $24,000,000 authorized, the unissued balance being held to retire the remaining stock of the Choctaw, Oklahoma & Gulf Railroad. The bonds are in serial form, A to P, maturing annually and redeemable at 101½.

EARNINGS.

Year ending March 31.

| | Div. Paid. | Gross. | Per Cent. Op. Exp. | Net. | Land, etc. | Total Inc. |
|---|---|---|---|---|---|---|
| 1892-93 (3,610 miles) | 4 | $20,971,110 | 68.12 | $5,887,421 | $60,000 | $5,947,421 |
| 1893-94 (3,571 " ) | 4 | 21,039,074 | 67.90 | 6,061,594 | 43,038 | 6,104,632 |
| 1894-95 ( " " ) | 3 | 17,420,816 | 68.00 | 4,738,555 | 1,169,724 | 5,908,279 |
| 1895-96 ( " " ) | 2 | 17,359,653 | 63.23 | 5,493,059 | 38,439 | 5,531,498 |
| 1896-97 ( " " ) | 2 | 17,146,652 | 62.65 | 5,533,825 | 12,242 | 5,546,067 |
| 1897-98 (3,568 " ) | 3 | 19,548,583 | 60.06 | 6,952,617 | 479,785 | 7,432,402 |
| 1898-99 (3,619 " ) | *4¼ | 20,667,915 | 61.75 | 6,991,804 | 710,468 | 7,702,272 |
| 1899-00 (3,646 " ) | 5 | 22,650,604 | 62.18 | 7,668,154 | 701,439 | 8,369,593 |
| 1900-01 (3,819 " ) | 5 | 25,364,695 | 63.96 | 8,199,602 | 701,379 | 8,900,981 |
| 1901-02 (3,910 " ) | 5 | 28,385,845 | 61.06 | 10,131,120 | 948,849 | 11,079,969 |

——*And 10 per cent. in stock.

The disposition of the total net income was as follows:

| | Int. and Rental. | Dividends. | Surplus. |
|---|---|---|---|
| 1892-93 | $3,899,368 | $1,846,232 | $201,821 |
| 1893-94 | 4,049,902 | 1,846,232 | 208,498 |
| 1894-95 | 4,171,058 | 1,384,674 | 352,546 |
| 1895-96 | 4,107,790 | 923,116 | 500,592 |
| 1896-97 | 4,102,471 | 923,116 | 520,480 |
| 1897-98 | 4,110,549 | 1,384,674 | 1,937,179 |
| 1898-99 | 3,929,155 | 1,960,389 | 1,812,728 |
| 1899-00 | 3,907,532 | 1,999,586 | 2,462,475 |
| 1900-01 | 3,803,964 | 1,999,692 | 3,097,325 |
| 1901-02 | 3,859,027 | 2,247,900 | 4,973,040 |

The Addition and Improvement account, referred to above in connection with the payment of extra dividends on the stock, was credited March 31, 1902, with $1,722,917. At the same date the credit to profit and loss was $13,563,838.

GROSS AND NET EARNINGS BY MONTHS FOR THREE YEARS.

| Month. | 1900. Gross. | 1900. Net. | 1901. Gross. | 1901. Net. | 1902. Gross. | 1902. Net. |
|---|---|---|---|---|---|---|
| January | $1,822,536 | $574,626 | $2,194,490 | $672,721 | $2,297,518 | $745,934 |
| February | 1,712,473 | 576,476 | 1,941,881 | 617,763 | 2,283,155 | 1,140,230 |
| March | 1,902,446 | 745,643 | 2,064,950 | 802,276 | 2,214,010 | 1,189,618 |
| April | 1,760,157 | 455,991 | 1,991,110 | 525,755 | 2,119,178 | 510,409 |
| May | 1,795,630 | 479,553 | 2,205,825 | 593,281 | 2,210,114 | 591,929 |
| June | 2,001,490 | 539,996 | 2,127,325 | 585,904 | 2,472,032 | 1,194,311 |
| July | 2,298,928 | 799,259 | 2,790,858 | 1,088,723 | 3,776,308 | 1,573,581 |
| August | 2,600,977 | 1,140,475 | 2,996,672 | 1,333,749 | 3,910,969 | 1,803,110 |
| September | 2,460,515 | 987,419 | 2,703,337 | 1,106,250 | 4,278,680 | 1,910,167 |
| October | 2,615,839 | 1,052,837 | 2,944,491 | 1,365,855 | 4,461,145 | 1,976,531 |
| November | 2,136,266 | 718,650 | 2,489,188 | 810,196 | 3,873,016 | 1,327,605 |
| December | 2,194,951 | 634,041 | 2,291,205 | 594,474 | 3,976,790 | 1,444,837 |
| Totals for year | $25,302,208 | $8,704,966 | $28,741,332 | $10,096,947 | $38,872,915 | $15,408,262 |
| Average per month | 2,108,517 | 725,414 | 2,395,111 | 841,412 | 3,239,409 | 1,284,021 |

Proportionate taxes for each month are deducted from net earnings.

The following presents the comparative freight traffic statistics of the company:

| | Average Mileage. | Total Tonnage. | Tons Carried One Mile. | Freight Density. | Rate per Ton per Mile. | Earnings per Train Mile. | Average Tons per Train. |
|---|---|---|---|---|---|---|---|
| 1896-97 | 3,571 | 5,573,354 | 1,175,517,765 | 329,184 | 0.96c. | $1.51 | 158 |
| 1897-98 | 3,568 | 6,636,129 | 1,421,433,866 | 398,393 | 0.97 | 1.65 | 169 |
| 1898-99 | 3,590 | 7,025,604 | 1,452,386,408 | 404,566 | 0.99 | 1.72 | 174 |
| 1899-00 | 3,646 | 7,538,366 | 1,605,226,704 | 440,273 | 0.99 | 1.75 | 177 |
| 1900-01 | 3,819 | 7,706,535 | 1,789,092,549 | 468,471 | 0.99 | 1.80 | 182 |
| 1901-02 | 3,910 | 8,245,978 | 1,839,027,297 | 470,365 | 1.04 | 1.84 | 178 |

Chairman, Daniel G. Reid, New York; President, William B. Leeds; 1st Vice-President H. A. Parker; 2d Vice-President, Robert Mather; 3d Vice-President, J. M. Johnson; Secretary, George H. Crosby; Treasurer, F. E. Hayne, Chicago; Assistant Secretary and Assistant Treasurer, George T. Boggs, New York; Assistant Treasurer, C. F. Jilson; Comptroller, W. W. Stevenson; Assistant Comptroller, J. L. Cramer, Chicago.

Directors—Alexander E. Orr, Ogden Mills, George S. Brewster, William H. Moore, Daniel G. Reid, William B. Leeds, F. L. Hine, F. S. Wheeler, George G. McMurtry, New York; Marshall Field, James H. Moore, Chicago; R. R. Cable, Rock Island, Ill.

Main office, 144 Van Buren street, Chicago; New York office, 71 Broadway. Annual meeting, first Wednesday in June.

---

## ROME, WATERTOWN & OGDENSBURG RAILROAD CO.

(Leased to New York Central & Hudson River Railroad Co.)

Road owned, Suspension Bridge to Massena Springs, N. Y. (owned, 263.63 miles; leased, 35.40 miles), 299 miles; Richland to Rome, owned, 41 miles; branches owned, 109.68 miles; Utica & Black River R. R., leased, 149.81 miles; branch leased, 29.59 miles; trackage rights to Niagara Falls and Oswego, 14 miles; total mileage, 643.11 miles.

Stock......Par $100........................Authorized, $10,000,000......Issued, $10,000,000

Transfer Agent, Central Trust Co., New York.

Dividends on the stock are paid quarterly, 1¼ per cent. each, February (15), May, August and November.

FUNDED DEBT.

| | |
|---|---|
| Watertown & Rome, 1st mort., extended, 6 per cent., due Sept., 1910, March and Sept. | $417,800 |
| Consolidated mort., 5 per cent., due July, 1922, April and Oct. | 9,076,000 |
| " " 3½ per cent., due July, 1922, April and Oct. | 500,000 |
| 1st mort. Oswego Bridge, 6 per cent., due July, 1915, Feb. and Aug. | 100,000 |
| Syracuse P. & O., 1st mort., 6 per cent., due Feb., 1915, Feb. and Aug. | 175,000 |
| N. & M., 1st mort., 5 per cent., due April, 1916, April and Oct. | 130,000 |
| Oswego & Rome, 1st mort., guar., 7 per cent., due May, 1915, May and Nov. | 350,000 |
| " " 2d mort., guar., 5 per cent., due May, 1915, Feb. and Aug. | 400,000 |
| R. W. & O. Terminal Co., 1st mort., guar., 5 per cent., due May, 1918, May and Nov | 375,000 |
| Utica & Black River, 1st mort., 4 per cent., due 1922, Jan. and July | 1,950,000 |
| Total | $13,473,800 |

The bonds of the Utica & Black River are guaranteed, principal and interest.

Seven per cent. interest is also guaranteed on $2,223,000 stock of the Utica and Black River, $1,120,000 of which is owned by this company.

Of its leased roads the Niagara Falls Branch rental is $17,500 per year, that of the Oswego & Rome $44,500, and that of the Utica & Black River $238,110.

In March, 1891, the road was leased perpetually to the New York Central & Hudson River Railroad, which guarantees debt and rentals and 5 per cent on the stock. The stockholders received a stock dividend of 20 per cent. at the same time. In 1891 the maturing 1st and 2d mortgage 7 per cent. bonds for $2,021,500 were exchanged for 5 per cent. consols, and $500,000 1st mortgages, 7 per cent. bonds of the Syracuse Northern, which matured in 1901, were replaced by $500,000 3½ per cent. consols.

Earnings are included in those of the lessee company.

President, Charles Parsons; Vice-President and Treasurer, Edwin Parsons; Vice-President, Clarence S. Day; Secretary, W. H. Platt, New York; Assistant Secretary, R. W. Parsons, New York.

Directors—Charles Parsons, Clarence S. Day, William Lummis, Edwin Parsons, Walton Ferguson, Chauncey M. Depew, George Parsons, R. W. Parsons, Jefferson Hogan, New York; J. F. Maynard, John M. Crouse, I. N. Maynard, William Pierrepont White, Utica, N. Y.

Main office, 15 Broad street, New York. Annual meeting, December 28. Books close thirty days previously.

## RUTLAND RAILROAD CO.

Road owned, Bellows Falls, Vt., to Ogdensburg, N. Y., 279 miles; Rutland, Vt., to White Creek, N. Y., 59 miles; Chatham, N. Y., to North Bennington, Vt., 57 miles; branches, 21 miles; total owned, 397.33 miles; leased, 19 miles; total operated, 416.33 miles. The Addison Railroad, Leicester Junction, Vt., to Addison Junction, Vt., 16 miles, is leased. The company also has trackage from Noyan Junction to Montreal, 53 miles, over the Quebec Southern and the Canadian Pacific Railways. The company also controls the Rutland Transit Co., which has a fleet of 8 vessels running from Ogdensburg, N. Y., to ports on the lakes. See statement of the company under Industrial Securities. Locomotives, 72; passenger cars, 87; freight cars, 2,706.

This company is a consolidation of the Rutland Railroad, Ogdensburg & Lake Champlain Railroad, Rutland Canadian Railroad, Bennington & Rutland Railway and the Chatham & Lebanon Valley Railroad.

The old Rutland Railroad, Bellows Falls to Burlington, Vt., 120 miles, was leased in 1871 to the Vermont Central, and on the expiration of that lease, in 1891, was again leased to the Central Vermont. In May, 1896, in consequence of the receivership of the lessor, the railroad was returned to the Rutland Railroad Co.'s possession and has since been operated by it. In 1899 the Ogdensburg & Lake Champlain Railroad was acquired, and the construction of the Rutland-Canadian Railroad, between Burlington, Vt., and Rouse's Point, N. Y., to connect the two, was begun. The Bennington & Rutland was acquired in 1900 and the Chatham & Lebanon Valley Railroad in 1901.

Stock....Par $100.....Authorized { com., $2,480,600; pref., 9,075,600 } Issued { com., $199,400; pref., 9,057,600 } $9,257,000

The preferred stock is 7 per cent., cumulative. There was $2,480,600 of common stock, but on June 30, 1902, all but the amount given above had been exchanged for preferred on the basis of ten shares of common for one of preferred.

In November, 1901, $3,578,400 of new preferred stock was offered to the stockholders at $90 per share to provide for improvements.

Transfer Agent, New York Security & Trust Co., New York. Registrar, First National Bank, New York.

Dividends on the preferred stock are paid half-yearly, January (1) and July. Dividends paid on the preferred have been: in 1890, 3 per cent.; in 1891, 2 per cent.; in 1892, 1893, 1894 and 1895, 4 per cent.; in 1896, 2 per cent.; in 1897, 1 per cent.; in 1898 and 1899, 2 per cent.; in 1900, 3 per cent.; in 1901, 4 per cent. The dividend paid January 2, 1902, was 2 per cent.

FUNDED DEBT.

| | |
|---|---|
| 1st mort., 6 per cent., due Nov., 1902, May and Nov. | $1,059,100 |
| Consolidated mort., 4½ per cent., due July, 1941, Jan. and July | 2,440,000 |
| Total | $3,499,100 |

FUNDED DEBT (CONTROLLED ROADS).

| | |
|---|---|
| Rutland Canadian, 1st mort., guar., 4 per cent., due July, 1949, Jan. and July | 1,350,000 |
| Ogdensb'g & Lake Champ., 1st mort., guar., 4 per cent., due July, 1948, Jan. and July | 4,400,000 |
| Bennington & Rutland, 1st mort., 4½ per cent., due Nov., 1927, May and Nov. | 500,000 |
| " " 2d mort., 5 per cent., due March, 1920, March and Sept. | 500,000 |
| Rutland Transit Co., 1st mort., 5 per cent., due Jan., 1920, Jan. and July | 666,000 |
| Chatham & Leb. Valley R. R., 1st mort., 5 per cent., due Nov., 1919, May and Nov. | 500,000 |

The 4½ per cent. consolidated mortgage is for $3,500,000 and was authorized to retire prior liens. In 1898 the outstanding seconds matured and were replaced with consols. The 6 per cent. bonds, maturing November 1, 1902, will be refunded by the issue of an equal amount of consolidated 4½ per cent. bonds, and when this refund is completed the consolidated 4½ per cent. mortgage will be a 1st mortgage on the property.

The Addison Railroad is leased for 3 per cent. on its $500,000 of stock, of which the Rutland owns $435,000.

EARNINGS.

Year ending June 30.

| | Gross. | Net. | Charges. | Surplus. |
|---|---|---|---|---|
| 1896-97 | $713,514 | $305,668 | $216,510 | $89,158 |
| 1897-98 | 738,853 | 294,686 | 207,886 | 86,800 |
| 1898-99 | 803,520 | 427,715 | 275,327 | 152,388 |
| 1899-00 | 1,837,155 | 817,726 | 469,892 | 347,833 |
| 1900-01 | 1,933,136 | 770,947 | 569,578 | 201,369 |
| 1901-02 | 2,134,381 | 923,015 | 659,601 | 263,414 |

President, W. Seward Webb, Shelburne, Vt.; Treasurer, Clarence Morgan, New York.

Directors—W. Seward Webb, Edward V. W. Rossiter, George Bird, Percival W. Clement, Chauncey M. Depew, George H. Ball, John W. Stewart, Samuel R. Callaway, James Lawrence.

Main office, Rutland, Vt. New York office, 51 East Forty-fourth street. Annual meeting in October.

## ST. JOHNSBURY & LAKE CHAMPLAIN RAILROAD CO.

Road owned, Lunenburg to Maquam Bay, Vt., 120 miles; branch, 11 miles; total, 131 miles. Locomotives, 5; passenger cars, 4; freight cars, 160.

Reorganization (1880) of Vermont Division of Portland & Ogdensburg. Controlled by the Boston & Maine.

Stock.....Par $50.....Authorized { com., $2,550,000; pref., 1,298,500 } Issued { com., $2,550,000; pref., 1,298,500 } $3,848,500

Transfer Agent, George W. Cree, St. Johnsbury, Vt.

FUNDED DEBT.

1st mort., 5 per cent., due March, 1944, March and Sept. ........ $2,500,000

1st mortgage was issued in 1894 to retire former bonds and obligations. Amount authorized is $2,500,000. Boston and Maine guarantees $1,328,000 of the issue.

EARNINGS.

Year ending June 30.

| | Gross. | Net. | Charges. | Deficit. |
|---|---|---|---|---|
| 1892-93 | $367,338 | Def. $55,475 | $38,050 | $93,525 |
| 1893-94 | 347,266 | " 21,039 | 47,500 | 68,539 |
| 1894-95 | 358,351 | Sur. 4,191 | 66,400 | 62,209 |
| 1895-96 | 363,173 | Def. 16,666 | 66,400 | 83,066 |
| 1896-97 | 357,259 | " 41,513 | 66,400 | 107,913 |
| 1897-98 | 368,959 | " 31,409 | 66,400 | 97,809 |
| 1898-99 | 379,366 | " 7,505 | 66,400 | 73,905 |
| 1899-00 | 333,569 | Sur. 20,877 | 66,400 | 45,523 |
| 1900-01 | 306,644 | " 2,404 | 66,400 | 78,334 |
| 1901-02 | 316,210 | " 32,564 | 66,400 | 44,832 |

President, H. E. Folsom, Lyndonville, Vt.; Vice-President, H. N. Turner; Treasurer, George W. Cree, St. Johnsbury, Vt.

Directors—Carroll S. Page, Hyde Park, Vt.; Harry Blodgett, Charles H. Stevens, H. N. Turner, St. Johnsbury, Vt.; H. E. Folsom, Lyndonville, Vt.; George W. Hendee, Morrisville, Vt.; Samuel C. Lawrence, Medford, Mass.; Henry R. Reed, Lucius Tuttle, Boston.

Main offices, Boston, and Lyndonville, Vt. Annual meeting, second Thursday in September.

## ST. JOSEPH & GRAND ISLAND RAILWAY CO.

Road owned, St. Joseph, Mo., to Grand Island, Neb., 251 miles; trackage, St. Joseph, Mo., to Kansas City, 61 miles; total operated, 312 miles.

This company is a reorganization of the railroad of same name which was controlled by the Union Pacific. The Union Pacific did not retain its interest in St. Joseph & Grand Island under the latter's reorganization. Locomotives, 29; passenger cars, 20; freight cars, 819.

Stock..Par $100..Authorized { com., $4,600,000; 1st pref., 5,500,000; 2d pref., 3,500,000 } Issued { com., $4,600,000; 1st pref., 5,498,500; 2d pref., 3,430,000 } $13,528,500

The 1st preferred stock is 5 per cent., non-cumulative, the 2d preferred being 4 per cent., non-cumulative.

Transfer Agent, Central Trust Co., New York.

The company paid 5 per cent. on 1st preferred in 1898, 3 per cent. in 1899, and 3 per cent. in 1900. In 1901 paid 5 per cent. Dividends on the 1st preferred are semi-annual, January and July. In January and July, 1902, 2½ per cent. was paid, but the January, 1903, dividend was passed.

FUNDED DEBT.

1st mort., 2-3-4 per cent., due Jan., 1947, Jan. and July.............................. $3,500,000

Company was formerly the St. Joseph & Western. Road sold under foreclosure June 11, 1885, and reorganized as above. In October, 1893, the Union Pacific Receivers were appointed Receivers of this company. Bondholders' committee, with F. P. Olcott of New York as Chairman, was formed. In December, 1895, a decree of foreclosure under 1st mortgage was granted.

Plan of reorganization provided for foreclosure and creation of new company with stocks as above and $5,000,000 1st mortgage bonds, interest 2 per cent. for first 2 years, 3 per cent. for 3 years and 4 per cent. thereafter. Of this issue $1,000,000 was reserved for new mileage at rate of $6,000 per mile and $500,000 for improvements at rate of $100,000 per annum.

The old common stock paid an assessment of 3 per cent., receiving 3 per cent. in 1st preferred and 100 per cent. in common stock. The old 1st mortgage bonds were exchanged for 70 per cent. in 1st preferred, and 25 per cent. in 2d preferred, while the old 2ds were assessed 6 per cent. and received 12 per cent. in 1st preferred and 100 per cent. in 2d preferred. Fixed charges of old company were $420,000 per annum. Under the reorganization they were $80,000 for two first years, ising to $160,000 in five years. Stock was held in a voting trust for five years until January, 1902.

EARNINGS.

Year ending June 30.

| | Gross. | Per Cent. Oper. Exp. | Net. | Charges. | Surplus. |
|---|---|---|---|---|---|
| 1898-99.......................... | $1,261,060 | 72.37 | $272,436 | $98,280 | $174,156 |
| 1899-00.......................... | 1,404,694 | 71.23 | 325,285 | 106,648 | 218,637 |
| 1900-01.......................... | 1,399,954 | 57.98 | 505,812 | 105,528 | 400,284 |
| 1901-02.......................... | 1,349,790 | 63.15 | 415,102 | 122,500 | 292,602 |

In 1899-1900 the dividends paid were $164,928; surplus, $53,709. In 1900-01, dividends, $274,880; surplus, $125,404. In 1901-02, dividends, $274,902; surplus, $17,699.

The following presents the freight traffic statistics of the company:

| | Average Mileage. | Total Tonnage. | Tons Carried One Mile. | Freight Density. | Rate per Ton per Mile. | Earnings per Train Mile. | Average Tons per Train. |
|---|---|---|---|---|---|---|---|
| 1900-01.. | 312 | 677,211 | 79,371,981 | 254,226 | 1.36c | $2.70 | 199 |
| 1901-02.. | 312 | 627,594 | 77,779,000 | 249,126 | 1.32 | 2.64 | 200 |

President, W. T. Van Brunt; Vice-President and General Manager, Raymond Du Puy; Secretary, F. W. Russell; Treasurer, G. G. Lacy, St. Joseph, Mo.

Directors—W. T. Van Brunt, Raymond Du Puy, G. G. Lacy, St. Joseph, Mo.; Townsend Hornor, C. H. Imhoff, Fred G. Reighley, New York; Frank C. Kern, J. V. Lemoine, C. K. Finley, Hiawatha, Kan.

Main office, St. Joseph, Mo. Annual meeting, third Tuesday in October, at Hiawatha, Kan.

## THE ST. LAWRENCE & ADIRONDACK RAILWAY CO.

A corporation formed under the laws of New York, November 18, 1895. The company is a consolidation of the Malone & St. Lawrence Railway Co. and the St. Lawrence & Adirondack Railway Co., a Canadian corporation which had previously absorbed the Southwestern Railway Co.

Road owned, Malone Junction, N. Y., to Valleyfield, Que., 30 miles; Adirondack Junction, N. Y., to Beauharnois, Que., 13 miles; leased, Valleyfield to Beauharnois, 13 miles; trackage over Canadian Pacific, Adirondack Junction to Montreal, 9 miles; total operated, 65 miles. Equipment is furnished by the New York Central & Hudson River Railroad.

Since June, 1898, the road has been operated by the New York Central & Hudson River Railroad, the line connecting the Mohawk & Malone division of that system with Montreal.

Stock......Par $100..........................Authorized, $1,615,000......Issued, $1,615,000

In January, 1902, the stock was increased from $1,300,000 to $1,615,000, the additional $315,000 being subscribed by the stockholders for the purpose of retiring $300,000 of 6 per cent. debentures created to provi e equipment.

Transfer Agent, Claredce Morgan, Treasurer, New York. Registrar, Colonial Trust Co., New York.

San Angelo

MAP OF THE
FRISCO
SYSTEM
ST. LOUIS & SAN FRANCISCO R. R.
AND
ASSOCIATED LINES.

On September 1, 1901, the first semi-annual dividend of 2½ per cent. was paid on the stock; a dividend of 2½ per cent. was also paid March 1, 1902.

FUNDED DEBT.

| | |
|---|---|
| 1st mort., 5 per cent., gold, due July, 1996, Jan. and July | $800,000 |
| 2d mort., 6 per cent., gold, due Oct., 1996, April and Oct | 400,000 |
| Total | $1,200,000 |

The 1st mortgage, Continental Trust Co., New York, trustee, covers all the property of the company, both in New York and Canada. The 2d mortgage covers the same property, subject to the lien of the 1st mortgage. Trustee of the 2d mortgage, Colonial Trust Co., New York.

The company also has equipment trust obligations outstanding for $100,418.

The New York Central & Hudson River Railroad operates the property under agreement, paying over the earnings in excess of cost of operation and maintenance to the St. Lawrence & Adirondack Railway Co.

EARNINGS.

Year ending June 30.

| | Gross. | Net. | Charges. | Surplus. |
|---|---|---|---|---|
| 1898-99 | $169,338 | $91,337 | ...... | ...... |
| 1899-00 | 227,824 | 127,360 | $82,832 | $44,528 |
| 1900-01 | 233,297 | 123,290 | 81,535 | 41,754 |
| 1901-02 | 241,782 | 97,914 | 93,005 | 4,909 |

President, W. Seward Webb, Shelburne, Vt.; Secretary and Treasurer, Clarence Morgan, New York.

Directors—W. Seward Webb, Shelburne, Vt.; Chauncey M. Depew, George Bird, Samuel R. Callaway, Clarence Morgan, New York; Edgar Van Etten, Boston; George T. Jarvis, A. G. Adams, M. E. McClary, Rutland, Vt.

Main office, Board of Trade Building, Montreal; New York office, 51 East Forty-fourth street. Annual meeting, first Wednesday in September.

## ST. LOUIS & NORTH ARKANSAS RAILROAD CO.

A corporation formed under the laws of Missouri, May 25, 1899. The company purchased the property of the Eureka Springs Railway Co.

Road owned, Seligman, Mo., to Gilbert, Ark., 103.62 miles. An extension was in course of construction at the end of 1902. Locomotives, 7; passenger cars, 9; freight cars, 26.

Stock......Par $100.......................Authorized, $3,212,500......Issued, $1,712,500

FUNDED DEBT.

1st mort., 5 per cent.......... $3,212,000

The 1st mortgage is authorized at the rate of $25,000 per mile.

President, John Scullin; Vice-President, G. L. Sands, St. Louis; Secretary, George West, Eureka Springs, Ark.; Treasurer, N. A. McMillan, St. Louis.

Directors—John Scullin, G. L. Sands, F. J. Wade, St. Louis; O. W. Watkins, George West, Eureka Springs, Ark.; J. W. Freeman, Berryville, Ark.; G. J. Crump, Harrison, Ark.

Main office, Eureka Springs, Ark.

## ST. LOUIS & SAN FRANCISCO RAILROAD CO.

"Frisco System."

This company, incorporated June 29, 1896, under the laws of Missouri, took possession June 30, 1896, of the property of the railroad company of same name reorganized and sold under foreclosure June 27, 1896. See below.

Road owned, main line, St. Louis to Oklahoma City, 543 miles; Sapulpa, I. T., to Sherman, Tex., 207 miles; Monett, Mo., to Paris, Tex., 303 miles; Peirce City, Mo., to Ellsworth, Kan., 323 miles; Springfield, Mo., to Kansas City, 189 miles; branches, 471 miles; total, 2,036 miles; the Kansas City, Fort Scott & Memphis and Kansas City, Memphis & Birmingham, 1,140 miles, are controlled; also the Fort Worth & Rio Grande, 146 miles; Paris & Great Northern Railroad, 17 miles; St. Louis, San Francisco & Texas Railway, 16 miles; Red River, Texas & Southern Railway, 87 miles; total of system, 3,442 miles. Locomotives, 228; passenger cars, 156; freight cars, 6,107.

In July, 1897, this company acquired control of the Atlantic & Pacific, Central Division, and in October, 1897, purchased the Kansas City & Southwestern, 61 miles. In March, 1901, control of the Kansas City, Fort Scott & Memphis Railroad and of the Kansas City, Memphis & Birmingham Railroad was acquired.

In 1902 this company acquired the stocks of the Chicago & Eastern Illinois Railroad Co., and arranged for a connection, via St. Louis, between its lines and those of the latter company. In November, 1902, it acquired the St. Louis, Memphis & Southeastern Railway, 300 miles, and the St. Louis & Gulf Railway, 20 miles.

It was reported in February, 1903, that control of this company would be acquired by the Rock Island Co.

| Stock..Par $100..Authorized | | | Issued | | | |
|---|---|---|---|---|---|---|
| | com., | $64,000,000 | | com., | $29,000,000 | |
| | 1st pref., | 5,000,000 | | 1st pref., | 5,000,000 | $50,000,000 |
| | 2d pref., | 31,000,000 | | 2d pref., | 16,000,000 | |

Both preferred stocks are 4 per cent., non-cumulative. All the stock was placed in a voting trust for 5 years from July 1, 1896, and for as long as the 1st preferred should not have received 4 per cent. cash for two consecutive years. The trust was dissolved in 1901. The company can redeem either or both of the preferred stocks at par in cash. The authorized stock was increased to a total of $100,000,000 in 1901.

Transfer Agents, J. Kennedy Tod & Co., New York. Registrar, Mercantile Trust Co., New York.

The company commenced the payment of dividends on 1st preferred with a semi-annual payment of 2 per cent., July, 1897. The first dividend of 1 per cent. was declared on 2d preferred, payable July 6, 1898. In 1899 paid two dividends of 1 per cent. each on 2d preferred. In 1900 also paid 2 per cent. on 2d preferred. In September, 1901, began paying quarterly dividends of 1 per cent. on the 2d preferred, putting it on a full 4 per cent. basis. The dividends were half-yearly, on 1st preferred January, July, and on 2d preferred March and September, but were changed to quarterly in the autumn of 1901.

### Funded Debt.

| | |
|---|---|
| 2d mort. (now 1st), A, B and C, 6 per cent., due Nov., 1906, May and Nov. | $2,051,300 |
| Refunding mort., 4 per cent., due July, 1951, Jan. and July | 40,604,000 |
| Missouri & Western, 1st mort., 6 per cent., due Aug., 1919, Feb. and Aug. | 141,000 |
| St. Louis, Wichita & Western, 1st mort., 6 per cent., due Sept., 1919, March and Sept. | 306,000 |
| Trust bonds, 6 per cent., due Aug., 1920, Feb. and Aug. | 203,000 |
| " " 5 per cent., due Oct., 1987, April and Oct. | 539,000 |
| General mort., 6 per cent., due July, 1931, Jan. and July | 3,715,000 |
| " " 5 per cent., due July, 1931, Jan. and July | 5,802,000 |
| Ft. Smith & Van. B. Bridge, 1st mort., 6 per cent., due April, 1910, April and Oct. | 72,000 |
| St. L. & S. F. R. R., 4 per cent., gold bonds, due July, 1996, Jan. and July | 1,593,000 |
| Southwestern Division, 1st mort., 5 per cent., due Oct., 1947, April and Oct. | 829,000 |
| Central Division, 1st mort., 4 per cent., due April, 1929, April and Oct. | 145,000 |
| Northwestern Div., 1st mort., pur. money, 4 per cent., due April, 1930, April and Oct. | 50,000 |
| Col. tr., St. L., Memphis & Southeastern, 4 per cent., due 1942 | 4,000,000 |
| Trust ctfs., C. & Eastern Illinois, pfd. stock, 6 per cent | 4,055,000 |
| " " " com., 10 per cent | 6,922,000 |
| Total | $71,027,300 |

The refunding mortgage created in 1901 is for $85,000,000. The underlying bonds exchanged for this issue are deposited in trust to secure the refunding mortgage bonds.

In 1897 the company created a new issue of 5 per cent. bonds for $1,500,000, secured by a 1st mortgage on the 112 miles of the Central Division, Atlantic & Pacific, to be known as the Southwestern Division of the company's system. This issue and $300,000 cash were paid for the $2,794,000 old Atlantic & Pacific 1sts, covering that property on completion of foreclosure and transfer of road to this company.

This company guarantees the principal and interest of $11,650,000 of Kansas City, Fort Scott & Memphis 4 per cent. refunding bonds, and has issued and guaranteed $13,510,000 of 4 per cent. certificates against the preferred stock of the Kansas City, Fort Scott & Memphis. See statement of the latter company.

The stock trust certificates against the common and preferred stocks of the Chicago & Eastern Illinois were created in 1902, and are secured by the deposit of the stocks of the latter company which were acquired.

In June, 1901, the stockholders had the right to subscribe, in cash, to the amount of 42½ per cent. of their holdings, and received for each $42.50 paid in $25 in 4 per cent. refunding bonds of the Kansas City, Fort Scott & Memphis Railroad and $29 in 4 per cent. preferred stock trust certificates of the latter company. See statement of Kansas City, Memphis & Birmingham in relation to that company's securities.

See edition of Manual for 1896 and prior for full details of company's finances and its relations to Atlantic & Pacific and Atchison companies. The old company had a half interest with Atchison in Atlantic & Pacific and was joint guarantor of the latter's bonds. In May, 1890, the holders of the old common and 2d preferred stock sold their stock to the Atchison, and received in exchange its stock at the rate of three-quarters of one share for each share of San Francisco common and one and three-eighths shares for each share of San Francisco 2d preferred.

In December, 1893, in consequence of embarrassments of Atchison Co., application was made for a receivership of this company, the same Receivers as those of the Atchison being appointed by United States Court. A bondholders' committee was appointed.

No provision for securities of this company was made in Atchison reorganization plan. Reorganization on an independent basis was determined on and plan issued in April, 1896. In same month Atchison sold its interest in company to the reorganization committee, receiving $1,971,550 cash for its $5,633,000 St. Louis & San Francisco consols. Details of the reorganization are given in the MANUAL for 1899.

New consolidated 4 per cent. mortgage, due 1996, is for $50,000,000. $39,032,000 of this was reserved to retire prior bonds, $1,793,000 reserved to acquire branch lines, and $3,175,000 for construction and improvements at rate of $300,000 per annum, and $500,000 additional for improvements, if deemed advisable.

In 1900 the Northwestern Division 1st purchase money mortgage 4 per cent. bonds were issued to pay for the Kansas Midland road, which the company had acquired. The authorized amount of this issue is $1,300,000.

EARNINGS.

Year ending June 30.

| | Div. Paid. | Gross. | Net. | Charges. | Surplus. |
|---|---|---|---|---|---|
| 1892-93 (1,329 miles)........... | .... | $7,542,657 | $3,253,310 | $2,763,545 | $489,764 |
| 1893-94 (1,327 " )........... | .... | 6,186,667 | 1,671,995 | 2,271,657 | Def. 599,662 |
| 1894-95 ( " " )........... | .... | 6,081,425 | 2,336,787 | 2,948,380 | " 611,593 |
| 1895-96 ( " " )........... | .... | 6,162,055 | 2,200,714 | 2,609,166 | " 408,452 |
| 1896-97 (1,162 " )........... | *2 | 5,993,336 | 2,516,773 | 2,185,706 | 331,066 |
| 1897-98 (1,221 " )........... | *4 †1 | 6,886,467 | 2,926,118 | 2,239,672 | 686,445 |
| 1898-99 (1,333 " )........... | *4 †1 | 7,226,662 | 2,962,631 | 2,377,831 | 584 800 |
| 1899-00 (1,401 " )........... | *4 †2 | 7,983,246 | 3,408,721 | 2,512,361 | 896,360 |
| 1900-01 (1,686 " )........... | *4 †2½ | 10,173,697 | 4,439,859 | 2,810,560 | 1,929,299 |
| 1901-02 (3,252 " )........... | *4 †4 | 21,620,882 | 8,345,572 | 6,068,094 | 2,274,478 |

* On 1st preferred stock. † On 2d preferred stock.

In 1896-97 surplus over 2 per cent. dividend on 1st preferred stock was $231,066; in 1897-98, surplus, after dividends of 4 per cent. on 1st preferred and 1 per cent. on 2d preferred, $326,445; in 1898-99, surplus over dividends, $224,800; in 1899-1900, surplus, $376,360, and in 1900-01, surplus, $1,029,299.

The following presents the comparative freight traffic statistics of the company:

| | Average Mileage. | Total Tonnage. | Tons Carried One Mile. | Freight Density. | Rate per Ton per Mile. | Earnings per Train Mile. | Average Tons per Train. |
|---|---|---|---|---|---|---|---|
| 1896-97.... | 1,162 | 2,098,828 | 403,009,043 | 345,963 | 1.111c | $1.303 | 117 |
| 1897-98.... | 1,282 | 2,526,001 | 485,592,477 | 378,777 | 1.055 | 1.348 | 127 |
| 1898-99.... | 1,333 | 2,587,829 | 506,999,422 | 380,419 | 1.019 | 1.332 | 129 |
| 1899-00.... | 1,400 | 2,865,181 | 521,615,596 | 372,582 | 1.058 | 1.639 | 154 |
| 1900-01 ... | 3,187 | 8,798,261 | 1,540,205,003 | 483,277 | 0.894 | 1.789 | 200 |
| 1901-02.... | 3,414 | 9,068,650 | 1,637,557,119 | 479,659 | 0.953 | 1.781 | 186 |

President and General Manager, B. F. Yoakum; Vice-President and General Auditor, Alexander Douglas; Vice-President and Assistant General Manager, C. H. Beggs; Secretary and Treasurer, Frank H. Hamilton, St. Louis; Assistant Secretary and Assistant Treasurer, Frederick Strauss; Comptroller, C. W. Hillard, New York.

Directors—Isaac N. Seligman, James A. Blair, Henry K. McHarg, Edward C. Henderson, Frederick Strauss, New York; B. P. Cheney, Richard Olney, Nathaniel Thayer, Boston; Samuel C. Eastman, Concord, N. H.; B. F. Yoakum, H. Clay Pierce, Richard C. Kerens, St. Louis.

Main office, St. Louis.

---

## *ST. LOUIS, KANSAS CITY & COLORADO RAILROAD CO.*

(Controlled by Chicago, Rock Island & Pacific Railway Co.)

A corporation formed under the laws of Kansas, December 20, 1884. The company was reorganized in 1899, in December of which year the property came into the possession of the present company. The control of this company was acquired in May, 1902, by the Chicago, Rock Island & Pacific Railway Co.

Road owned, Forest Park, St. Louis, to Belle, Mo., 102 miles; branch, 3 miles; trackage over the Wabash Railroad to St. Louis, Union Station, 4½ miles; total operated, 109½ miles.

An extension from Belle, Mo., to Versailles, Mo., 71 miles, is under construction. Locomotives, 10; passenger cars, 7; freight cars, 86.

Stock......Par $100.................. .......Authorized, $20,000,000......Issued, $1,600,000

FUNDED DEBT.

1st mort., 4 per cent., due July, 1951, Jan. and July................................ $3,030,000

The 1st mortgage bonds authorized are at the rate of $30,000 per mile of road. Trustee of mortgage, Morton Trust Co., New York.

President, W. B. Leeds, Chicago; Secretary, W. P. Kennett, St. Louis; Treasurer, F. E. Hague, Chicago.

Main office, Security Building, St. Louis. Annual meeting, first Thursday in October.

## ST. LOUIS, MEMPHIS & SOUTHEASTERN RAILROAD CO.

(Controlled by St. Louis & San Francisco Railroad Co.)

A corporation formed under the laws of Missouri, January 8, 1902. The company is a consolidation of the St. Louis & Memphis Railway, the Southern Missouri & Arkansas Railroad, Cape Girardeau & Northern Railway, Hoxie, Pocahontas & Northern Railway, and Chester, Perryville & St. Genevieve Railway. Road projected, St. Louis to Luxora, Ark., 420 miles, of which 300 miles were completed in January, 1903. Locomotives, 44; passenger cars, 25; freight cars, 825.

In November, 1902, the St. Louis & San Francisco Railroad Co. acquired control of the company.

Stock......Par $100.........................Authorized, $12,500,000......Issued, $5,000,000

FUNDED DEBT.

1st mort., 4 per cent., due Jan., 1952, Jan. and July................................ $3,800,000

It was stated that the St. Louis & San Francisco Railroad Co. paid 47½ for the stock of this company. It issued to pay for the purchase $4,000,000 of collateral trust 4 per cent. notes secured by the stock.

President, B. F. Yoakum; Vice-President, B. L. Winchell; Secretary and Treasurer, F. H. Hamilton, St. Louis; Assistant Secretary, J. A. Farrell, New York.

Directors—Frederick H. Prince, Frederick Ayer, Boston; Newman Erb, E. Summerfield, New York; George H. Norman, Providence; John Scullin, Hugh McKittrick, Charles Gilbert, St. Louis; E. F. Blomeyer, Cape Girardeau, Mo.

Main office, St. Louis. Annual meeting, second Tuesday in March, at St. Louis.

## ST. LOUIS SOUTHWESTERN RAILWAY CO.

This company is a reorganization of the St. Louis, Arkansas & Texas Railway Co, whose property was sold under foreclosure in October, 1890. Three distinct companies were formed January 12, 1891, the St. Louis Southwestern Railway Co., the St. Louis Southwestern Railway Co. of Texas, and the Tyler Southwestern Railway Co. On October 6, 1899, the Tyler Southwestern Railway Co. was absorbed by the St. Louis Southwestern Railway Co. of Texas. On January 3, 1901, the company purchased at foreclosure sale the Stuttgart & Arkansas River Railroad, extending from Stuttgart to Gillett, Ark., a distance of 34.8 miles, and has operated it as the Stuttgart Branch since January 16, 1901. The company also purchased in 1901 the Dallas, Fort Worth & Gulf Railway, a belt and terminal line around the city of Dallas, Tex. That property has been reorganized, the name of the company being changed to Dallas Terminal Railway & Union Depot Co.

Road owned, Bird's Point, Mo., to Texarkana, Tex., 418 miles; Little Rock branch, 42 miles; Shreveport branch, 59½ miles; Gray's Point branch, 51 miles; other branches, 57 miles; St. Louis Southwestern of Texas, Texarkana to Gatesville, Tex., 304 miles; Sherman branch, 110 miles; Fort Worth branch, 97 miles; Hillsboro branch, 40 miles; Lufkin branch, 89 miles; Dallas branch, 25 miles; the company leases the Gray's Point Terminal Railway, 16 miles; total system, 1,308½ miles, of which 16 miles is leased and 25 miles trackage. Lines in the State of Texas are operated under separate organizations as the St. Louis Southwestern Railway Co. of Texas and the Tyler Southeastern Railway Co. It was stated that an extension to southeastern Texas would be built in 1902. Locomotives, 149; passenger cars, 120; freight cars, 6,711.

Stock..Par $100...Authorized { com., $35,000,000; pref., 30,000,000 } Issued { com., $16,500,000; pref., 20,000,000 } $36,500,000

The preferred stock is 5 per cent., non-cumulative.

Company holds in its treasury $143,900 common stock and $106,350 preferred stock.

Stock is transferred at the company's office, 195 Broadway, New York.

In June, 1902, the authorized amount of the common stock was increased from $16,500,000 to $35,000,000.

**FUNDED DEBT.**

| | |
|---|---|
| 1st mort., 4 per cent., due Nov., 1989, May and Nov. | $20,000,000 |
| 2d mort., income, 4 per cent., due Nov., 1989, Jan. and July | 3,272,000 |
| 1st cons. mort., 4 per cent., due June, 1932, June and Dec. | 12,054,750 |
| Gray's Point Terminal, 1st mort. guar., 5 per cent., due Dec., 1942, June and Dec. | 339,000 |
| Total | $35,665,750 |

There are about $580,000 car trusts outstanding.

The funded debt outstanding on June 30, 1901, consisted of certificates for $20,000,000 1st gold 4s of November 1, 1989, and for $10,000,000 2d income gold 4s of November 1, 1989. The certificates represent 1st mortgage and 2d mortgage bonds of the constituent companies deposited with the trustees—$9,895,000 1st mortgage bonds and $3,947,000 2d mortgage income bonds secured on the St. Louis Southwestern Railway Co.; $9,445,000 1st mortgage bonds and $4,722,500 2d mortgage income bonds of the St. Louis Southwestern Railway Co. of Texas; $660,000 1st mortgage bonds and $330,000 2d mortgage income bonds of the Tyler Southwestern Railway Co. (secured on the Lufkin Branch of the St. Louis Southwestern Railway Co. of Texas.) Interest on 2d mortgage bonds at the rate of not exceeding 4 per cent. per annum, non-cumulative, is declared in October and April, if earned in the preceeding calendar half years, and is payable on January 1 or July 1 following the declaration. In July, 1902, the holders of $6,727,500 of the 2d mortgage income bonds accepted exchange for their bonds, 90 per cent. of their face value in new 1st consolidated mortgage gold bonds, and the bonds thus surrendered have been deposited under the new mortgage.

On June 1st, 1902, and for the purpose outlined, the company executed a mortgage to secure an issue of 1st consolidated mortgage 4 per cent. 30-year gold bonds to the amount of $25,000,000. There have been issued $12,054,000 of the bonds, and the remaining $12,946,000 are reserved—$2,946,000 of them for the retirement of the $2,272,500 2d mortgage income bonds still outstanding, at the rate of exchange of $900 consols for $1,000 income bonds, and $10,000,000 (together with any surplus bonds not used or required for refunding the 2d mortgage income bonds) for the acquisition of branch lines, at a rate not exceeding $20,000 per mile, and for betterments, additions and new equipment. The bonds are secured upon the entire property of the company subject to prior liens and are additionally secured by deposit of the $6,727,500 of 2d mortgage income bonds which have been already exchanged. They are secured by first mortgage on the property formerly owned by the Stuttgart & Arkansas River Railroad Co., including the lines from Stuttgart to Gillett, Ark., 38.8 miles, and will be secured on any additional lines and property acquired with their proceeds, either by direct mortgage or by deposit of the securities representing the ownership of such additional lines and property. By the terms of the mortgage all securities deposited as collateral under it are to be first made non-negotiable, and provision is also made for the cancellation of deposited bonds as fast as the whole of any issue is delivered to the trustee of this mortgage. It is also provided that any income received from securities deposited as collateral shall constitute a sinking fund (a) for the purchase of bonds secured by the mortgage, or of second mortgage income bonds, and (b) for the acquisition of additional property (to be covered by the mortgage); any bonds acquired through the operation of the sinking fund to be deposited under the mortgage as additional security therefor.

The Gray's Point Terminal Railway Co. 1st gold 5s of December 1, 1947, are guaranteed, both as to principal and interest, by the St. Louis Southwestern Railway Co. by endorsement on the back of each bond. They are secured on all of the property of the Gray's Point Terminal Railway Co. The mortgage provides that the bonds may be issued at not exceeding the rate of $15,000 per mile "for each mile of main line and side track or terminal track" whether now owned or hereafter acquired.

**EARNINGS.**

Year ending June 30.

| | Gross. | Per Cent. Op. Exp. | Net. | Charges. | | Surplus. |
|---|---|---|---|---|---|---|
| 1894-95 | $5,217,174 | 76.23 | $1,264,272 | $958,083 | | $306,189 |
| 1895-96 | 4,904,489 | 84.26 | 782,192 | 960,042 | Def. | 177,850 |
| 1896-97 | 4,743,546 | 81.29 | 891,242 | 954,430 | " | 63,188 |
| 1897-98 | 5,279,332 | 79.05 | 1,114,912 | 957,620 | | 157,291 |
| 1898-99 | 5,862,338 | 71.80 | 1,737,707 | 1,329,091 | | 408,617 |
| 1899-00 | 5,908,284 | 70.34 | 1,847,896 | 1,577,604 | | 270,292 |
| 1900-01 | 7,387,174 | 62.72 | 2,836,477 | 1,631,503 | | 1,554,974 |
| 1901-02 | 7,267,259 | 71.18 | 2,183,211 | 1,455,022 | | 728,199 |

The following presents the comparative freight traffic statistics of the company:

| | Average Mileage. | Total Tonnage. | Tons Carried One Mile. | Freight Density. | Rate per Ton per Mile. | Earnings per Train Mile. | Average Tons per Train. |
|---|---|---|---|---|---|---|---|
| 1896-97.... | 1,223 | 1,524,709 | 325,472,192 | 266,126 | 1.130c | $1.818 | 159 |
| 1897-98.... | 1,223 | 1,773,333 | 358,109,737 | 292,812 | 1.160 | 1.907 | 163 |
| 1898-99.... | 1,249 | 1,887,609 | 38c,660,588 | 304,772 | 1.210 | 2.196 | 179 |
| 1899-00.... | 1,258 | 2,101,048 | 412,395,505 | 327,818 | 1.110 | 2.340 | 207 |
| 1900-01.... | 1,275 | 2,399,171 | 468,837,265 | 367,715 | 1.210 | 2.557 | 209 |
| 1901-02.... | 1,293 | 2,586,387 | 514,942,615 | 398,254 | 1.080 | 2.533 | 232 |

President, Edwin Gould, New York; Vice-President and General Manager, F. H. Britton; Treasurer, G. K. Warner, St. Louis; Secretary, George Erbelding, New York.

Directors—Edwin Gould, Thomas T. Eckert, Robert M. Gallaway, Winslow S. Pierce, E. F. Jeffery, William H. Taylor, New York; Murray Carleton, Charles Parsons, F. H. Britton, St. Louis.

Main office, St. Louis; New York office, 195 Broadway. Annual meeting, first Tuesday in October, at St. Louis.

---

## ST. LOUIS, VANDALIA & TERRE HAUTE RAILROAD CO.

(Controlled by Pennsylvania Railroad Co. and leased to Terre Haute & Indianapolis Railroad Co.)

Road owned, Terre Haute to East St. Louis, 158 miles. Locomotives, 124; passenger cars, 96; freight cars, 4,445.

Stock...Par $100....Authorized { com., $2,379,358; pref., 1,544,700 } Issued { com., $2,379,358; pref., 1,544,700 } $3,924,058

Stock is transferred at the office of the secretary, Pittsburg.

The stock of the company is mainly owned by the Pennsylvania and Terre Haute & Indianapolis Railroads.

In September, 1902, suit was instituted by minority holders to set aside the preferred stock, and H. C. Begote, Belleville, Ill., was appointed Receiver of the road.

The $1,899,000 of 1st mortgage bonds and $1,600,000 of the 2d mortgage bonds ($2,600,000) were guaranteed jointly by the lessee and the Pittsburg, Cincinnati, Chicago & St. Louis Co. The 1sts matured January 1, 1897, and were taken up by the Pennsylvania Railroad Co., which created an issue of trust certificates for this purpose and also to retire the 2ds, which matured May 1, 1898.

The rental is 30 per cent. of the gross earnings, the lessee agreeing to advance any deficiency in interest.

EARNINGS.

Year ending October 31.

| | Gross. | Net. | Rental. | Result to Lessee. | |
|---|---|---|---|---|---|
| 1892-93 | $1,884,746 | $536,952 | $565,424 | Loss | $28,492 |
| 1893-94 | 1,649,118 | 374,443 | 494,735 | " | 120,292 |
| 1894-95 | 1,735,950 | 202,022 | 520,785 | " | 310,918 |
| 1895-96 | 1,613,039 | 186,811 | 484,092 | " | 297,281 |
| 1896-97 | 1,507,461 | 259,672 | 452,371 | " | 192,565 |
| 1897-98 | 1,708,639 | 487,806 | 512,592 | " | 24,786 |
| 1898-99 | 1,829,221 | 549,062 | 548,766 | Prof. | 269 |
| 1899-00 | 1,935,786 | 550,371 | 580,736 | Loss | 30,364 |
| 1900-01 | 2,074,928 | 757,059 | 622,478 | Prof. | 134,581 |
| 1901-02 | 2,253,620 | 689,153 | 586,103 | Loss | 103,050 |

In year 1893-94 the lessor company received as rental $494,735. Interest and all expenses, $400,583. Balance surplus, $94,152. In 1895 surplus to lessor was $117,497; in 1896, surplus, $130,673; in 1897, surplus, $96,450; in 1899, surplus, $14,269; in 1900, surplus, $301,581; in 1901, surplus, $348,225.

President, James McCrea; Treasurer, T. H. B. McKnight; Secretary, S. B. Liggett, Pittsburg.

Directors—James McCrea, Joseph Wood, J. J. Turner, E. B. Taylor, J. J. Brooks, Pittsburg; John P. Green, Philadelphia; Robert L. Dulany, Marshall, Ill.; Charles H. Seybt, Highland, Ill.; E. O. Stanard, W. R. Donaldson, St. Louis.

Main office, Greenville, Ill. Annual meeting, second Tuesday in January. Books close ten days previous.

## ST. LOUIS, WATKINS & GULF RAILWAY CO.

A corporation formed under the laws of Louisiana in May, 1902. The company is the successor of the Kansas City, Watkins & Gulf railroad Co., which was sold under foreclosure and reorganized under the present title.

Road owned, Lake Charles, La., to Alexandria, La., 98 miles; branches, 3 miles; total perated, 101 miles. Locomotives, 9; passenger cars, 188; freight cars, 14.

Stock......Par $20........................................................Issued, $993,360

Transfer Agent, J. S. Thomson, Lake Charles, La.

FUNDED DEBT.

1st mort., 5 per cent., due Jan., 1930, Jan. and July.................................. $983,360

The issue consists of $500,000 in $500 bonds and £100,700 in £100 sterling bonds.

Under the plan of reorganization the bondholders of the old company received 50 per cent. of their bonds in new bonds and 50 per cent. in new stock.

President, J. B. Watkins, Lawrence, Kan.; Secretary and Treasurer, J. S. Thomson, Lake Charles, La.

Directors—J. B. Watkins, T. H. Chalkley, Lawrence, Kan.; James Moses, A. H. Kellogg, New York; C. H. Bissell, Lakeville, Conn.; H. B. Kane, A. V. Eastman, Lake Charles, La.

Main office, Lake Charles, La. Annual meeting, January 10, at Lake Charles, La.

## SAN ANTONIO & ARANSAS PASS RAILWAY CO.

(Controlled by Southern Pacific Co.)

Road owned, Kerrville, Tex., to Houston, Tex., 308 miles; Kenedy, Tex., to Corpus Christi, 90 miles; Yoakum to Waco, Tex., 171 miles; Skidmore to Alice, 43 miles; Rockport branch, 21 miles; Austin Junction to Lockhart, 54 miles; total, 687 miles. Locomotives, 59; passenger cars, 57; freight cars, 1,814.

Stock.... .Par $100..........................Authorized, $5,000,000......Issued, $5,000,000

FUNDED DEBT.

1st mort., 4 per cent., due Jan., 1943, Jan. and July............................... $18,900,000

There are equipment trusts for $40,000. The company owes the Southern Pacific Co. $1,927,112 for advances.

Old company defaulted on interest due July 1, 1890. A Receiver was appointed, and in 1892 a reorganization plan was formulated, but in December, 1892, an amended reorganization plan was submitted involving the issue of $21,600,000 1st mortgage 4 per cent. bonds, guaranteed, principal and interest, by the Southern Pacific. The company was successfully reorganized in 1893 under this plan. $2,700,000 of the new bonds were reserved for extensions, making amount authorized on present mileage $18,900,000, there being $1,000,000 in the company's treasury.

EARNINGS.

Year ending June 30.

| | Gross. | Earnings Over Op. Exp's. | Charges. | Deficit. |
|---|---|---|---|---|
| 1896-97 | $2,208,418 | $669,802 | $845,805 | $176,002 |
| 1897-98 | 2,021,835 | 514,430 | 883,788 | 369,358 |
| 1898-99 | 2,046,781 | 454,113 | 913,107 | 458,994 |
| 1899-00 | 2,186,837 | 476,256 | 926,427 | 450,170 |
| 1900-01 | 2,618,377 | 663,197 | 1,037,980 | 370,510 |
| 1901-02 | 2,548,911 | 646,414 | 967,913 | 321,500 |

In 1900-01 $158,059 was expended for betterments and equipments, in 1901-02 $54,882 for the same purpose.

President, William D. Cornish, New York; Vice-President, M. D. Monserrate; Secretary, Reagan Houston; Treasurer, E. C. Tarrant, San Antonio, Tex.

Directors—William D. Cornish, M. D. Monserrate, W. Berry, R. H. Innes, Thomas B. Palfrey, J. W. Terry, Reagan Houston, E. J. Martin, A. W. Houston.

Main office, San Antonio, Tex.; New York office, 120 Broadway. Annual meeting, first Wednesday in September.

## SANFORD & ST. PETERSBURG RAILROAD CO.

(Controlled by Atlantic Coast Line Railroad Co.)

Road owned, Sanford, Fla., to St. Petersburg, Fla., 153 miles. Locomotives, 3; passenger cars, 6; freight cars, 34.

This company was formed in 1893 and acquired the property of the Orange Belt Railway, under foreclosure sale. The road was narrow gauge and has been changed to standard gauge,

The Atlantic Coast Line Railroad Co. owns the control and road is operated as part of its system.

Stock......Par $100..............................Authorized, $600,000......Issued, $600,000

FUNDED DEBT.

| | |
|---|---|
| 1st mort., 4 per cent. guaranteed, due Jan., 1924, Jan. and July | $300,000 |
| " 4 " not guaranteed, due Jan., 1924, Jan. and July | 475,000 |
| Total | $775,000 |

The 1st mortgage is for $1,000,000. Trustee, Pennsylvania Company for Insurance on Lives and Granting Annuities, Philadelphia. The Savannah, Florida & Western guarantees 4 per cent. interest and the principal of $300,000 of the issue.

| EARNINGS. | Gross. | Net. |
|---|---|---|
| 1896-97 | $84,309 | Def. $27,227 |
| 1897-98 | 78,866 | 47,986 |
| 1898-99 | 81,470 | 46,616 |
| 1899-00 | 87,606 | 35,551 |
| 1900-01 | 122,294 | Def. 7,454 |
| 1901-02 | 140,471 | " 795 |

President, Edward T. Stotesbury, Philadelphia; Secretary, Herbert L. Borden, New York; Treasurer, J. F. Post, Wilmington, N. C.

Directors—Edward T. Stotesbury, Philadelphia; R. G. Erwin, Savannah; Michael Jenkins, Henry Walters, Warren G. Elliott, Baltimore.

Main office, Jacksonville, Fla.; New York office, 71 Broadway. Annual meeting, Saturday after second Tuesday in January.

## SAN PEDRO, LOS ANGELES & SALT LAKE RAILROAD CO.

A corporation formed under the laws of Utah in 1900. The company is engaged in building a road from Salt Lake City, Utah, to Los Angeles, Cal., about 1,100 miles. It acquired and owns the Los Angeles Terminal Railway, 49 miles, and in 1902 was engaged in the active construction of its main line. On January 1, 1902, the company had in operation Los Angeles to San Pedro, 27 miles; Los Angeles to Redlands, Cal., 95 miles, and Glendale Junction to Verdugo Park, 7 miles; total operated, 129 miles. Active work is in progress on the sections of road southwest of Salt Lake City. It was reported in September, 1902, that the company had arranged for the lease or purchase of the Southwestern Division of the Oregon Short Line Railway, extending from Salt Lake City to Calientes, Nev. Locomotives, 9; passenger cars, 30; freight cars, 275.

Stock......Par $100..........................Authorized, $25,000,000......Issued, $2,501,600

The agreement for the purchase of the Los Angeles Terminal Railway provided that $2,500,000 should be paid in bonds, but no bonds have been issued, although a 1st mortgage for $20,000,000 has been authorized.

The syndicate, headed by William A. Clark, which is building the road, was understood in January, 1903, to have contributed $6,000,000 cash for the purpose.

President, William A. Clark, Butte, Mont.; 1st Vice-President, Richard C. Kerens, St. Louis; 2d Vice-President, J. Ross Clark; 3d Vice-President, T. E. Gibbon; Secretary, T. F. Miller; Treasurer, H. S. McKee, Los Angeles, Cal.

Directors—William A. Clark, Butte, Mont.; Richard C. Kerens, St. Louis; J. Ross Clark, T. E. Gibbon, T. F. Miller, F. K. Rule, Ross W. Smith, Los Angeles, Cal.; W. S. McCornick, Thomas Kearns, Reed Smoot, E. W. Clark, Salt Lake City; Perry S. Heath, Muncie, Ind.

Corporate office, Salt Lake City, Utah; main office, Los Angeles, Cal. Annual meeting, third Monday in November.

## SANTA FE CENTRAL RAILWAY CO.

A corporation formed under the laws of New Mexico in 1901. Road projected and under construction in 1902, Santa Fe, N. Mex., to Torrance, N. Mex., 117 miles. It is expected that the line will be completed and opened for traffic early in 1903.

Stock......Par $100..........................Authorized, $2,500,000......Issued, $2,500,000

Transfer agency, North American Savings Co., Pittsburg.

FUNDED DEBT.

1st mort., 5 per cent., due 1941, June and Dec.................................. $2,000,000

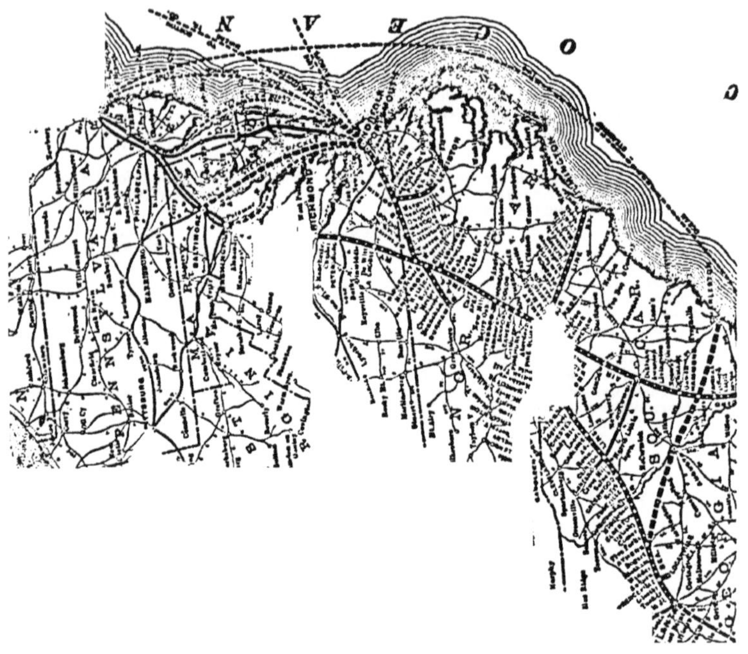

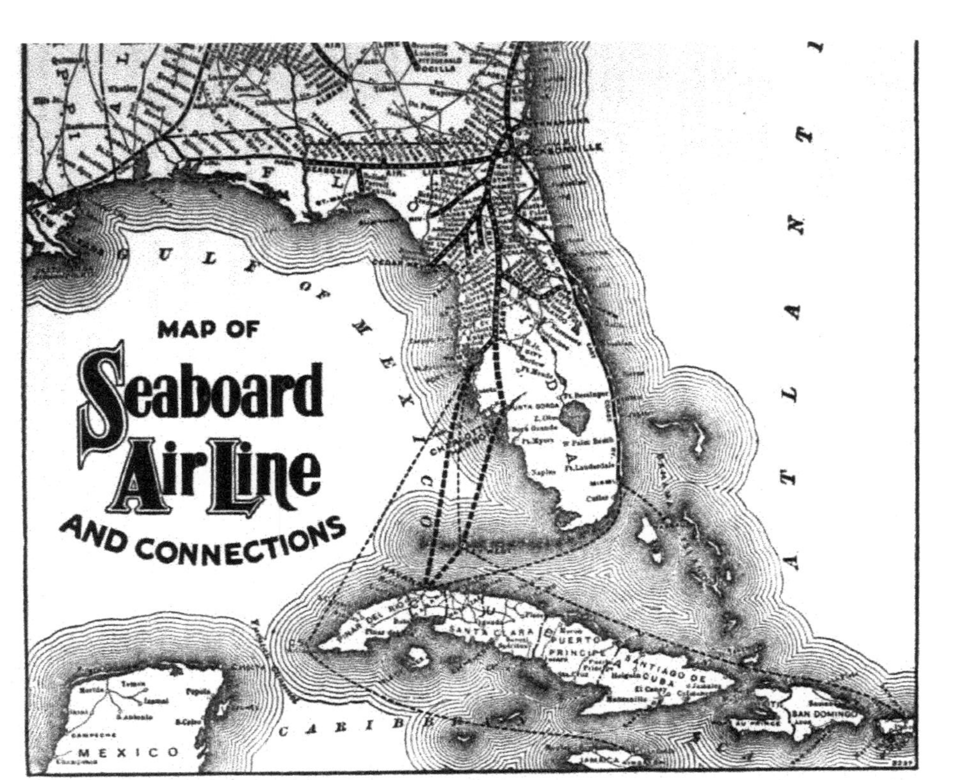
MAP OF
Seaboard Air Line
AND CONNECTIONS
GULF OF MEXICO
ATLANTI
FLORIDA
JACKSONVILLE
CUBA
SANTA CLARA
PUERTO PRINCIPE
SANTIAGO DE CUBA
SAN DOMINGO
MEXICO
CARIBBEAN

The authorized amount of the 1st mortgage is $2,500,000, of which $500,000 is reserved for further extensions and improvements. Trustee of the mortgage and agent for the payment of interest, Pittsburg Trust Co., Pittsburg.

President, W. H. Andrews, Santa Fe, N. Mex.; Chairman, Arthur Kennedy; Vice-President, Francis J. Torrance; Secretary, W. C. Hagan; Treasurer, T. Lee Clark, Pittsburg; General Manager, W. S. Hopewell, Santa Fe, N. Mex.

Main office, Santa Fe, N. Mex.; Pittsburg office, 501 Wood street. Annual meeting, second Tuesday in December, at Pittsburg.

## SANTA FE, PRESCOTT & PHŒNIX RAILWAY CO.

(Controlled by Atchison, Topeka & Santa Fe Railway Co.)

A corporation formed under the laws of Arizona, May 27, 1891.

Road owned, Ash Fork, Ariz., via Prescott to Phœnix, Ariz., 194 miles; branch, 46 miles; total, 240 miles. The line was completed in 1895. The road connects at Ash Fork with the Atchison system and at Phœnix with the Southern Pacific. Locomotives, 12; passenger cars, 12; freight cars, 81.

In 1901 the Atchison, Topeka & Santa Fe acquired control of this company.

Stock.. ...Par $100..........................Authorized, $7,904,000......Issued, $7,903,000

FUNDED DEBT.

| | |
|---|---|
| 1st mort., 5 per cent., due Sept., 1942, March and Sept. | $4,940,000 |
| 2d mort., 5 per cent., due July, 1942, Jan. and July | 2,964,000 |
| Prescott & Eastern 1st mort. guaranteed, due April, 1943, April and Oct. | 339,000 |
| Total | $8,243,000 |

The trustee of the 1st mortgage is the Mercantile Trust Co., New York. The Atchison, Topeka & Santa Fe Railway contracts to pay 5 per cent. of all gross revenue from business interchanged with this company to the trustee to be used for paying interest on the bonds.

EARNINGS.

Year ending June 30.

| | Gross. | Net. | Charges and Rentals. | Surplus. |
|---|---|---|---|---|
| 1895–96 | $584,208 | $311,243 | $218,973 | $1,406 |
| 1896–97 | 656,197 | 343,493 | 247,141 | 4,803 |
| 1897–98 | 764,124 | 399,416 | 247,000 | 33,656 |
| 1898–99 | 875,288 | 430,957 | 258,881 | 23,871 |
| 1899–00 | 987,132 | 555,477 | 264,154 | 143,123 |
| 1900–01 | 956,624 | 525,711 | 413,258 | 112,453 |
| 1901–02 | 1,050,035 | 617,950 | 413,435 | 204,515 |

The amounts derived from contract with Atchison are included in gross earnings. They were as follows: in 1896, $45,263; in 1897, $49,947; in 1898, $52,707; in 1899, $65,139.

President and General Manager, Frank M. Murphy; Secretary and Treasurer, Wallace Fairbank, Prescott, Ariz.

Directors—F. M. Murphy, E. B. Gage, Prescott, Ariz.; Edward P. Ripley, Chicago; Victor Morawetz, E. J. Berwind, T. P. Fowler, R. Somers Hayes, Charles Steele, New York; B. P. Cheney, Boston.

Main office, Prescott, Ariz. Annual meeting, third Wednesday in November, at Prescott, Ariz.

## SEABOARD AIR LINE RAILWAY CO.

A corporation formed under the laws of Virginia, April 1, 1900, succeeding the Richmond, Petersburg & Carolina Railroad Co. The purpose of the company was to combine under one control and management the old Seaboard Air Line system, the Georgia & Alabama Railway Co. and the Florida Central & Peninsular Railroad Co. The mileage of the united system was as follows:

| | Miles. |
|---|---|
| Old Seaboard Air Line system | 1,116 |
| Georgia & Alabama Railway Co. | 467 |
| Florida Central & Peninsular Railroad Co. | 1,017 |
| Total | 2,600 |

| Road owned | Miles. | Proprietary lines | Miles. |
|---|---|---|---|
| Richmond to Savannah............... | 502 | Portsmouth, Va., to Weldon, N. C... | 81 |
| Wilmington, N. C., to Atlanta........ | 437 | Savannah to Jacksonville, Tampa, Fla. | 896 |
| Savannah to Montgomery, Ala........ | 280 | Trackage............................ | 61 |
| Branches........................... | 354 | | |
| Total owned..................... | 1,573 | Total of system.................. | 2,611 |

In 1901 various consolidations were effected by which nearly all the mileage was acquired by this company.

Included in the above mileage is 102 miles from Richmond, Va., to Ridgeway, N. C., the Richmond, Petersburg & Carolina Railroad, built by the present company to give the system an entrance to Richmond, and 91 miles from Cheraw, S. C., to Columbia, to connect the old Seaboard Air Line and the Florida Central & Peninsular systems. These connecting links were completed in 1900. The present company also built 17 miles, Meldrum, Ga., to Savannah, replacing a like mileage formerly leased from the Central of Georgia. An extension from Athens, Ga., to Charleston, S. C., is planned.

The company has a one-sixth interest in the Richmond-Washington Co., which controls and operates the Richmond, Fredericksburg & Potomac Railroad, Richmond to Quantico, Va., and the Washington-Southern, Quantico to Washington, and an arrangement with the Pennsylvania Railroad for its service between Washington and New York.

The Baltimore Steam Packet Co., running steamers between Norfolk, Va., and Baltimore, is controlled by this company, and it also has a large interest in the Old Dominion Steamship Co., which operates a line between New York and Norfolk and Richmond.

This company acquired practically all the stock of the Florida Central & Peninsular Railroad Co. and of the Georgia & Alabama Railway Co. The old Seaboard Air Line system was composed of the Seaboard & Roanoke Railroad Co., Raleigh & Gaston Railroad Co., Raleigh & Augusta Railroad, Georgia, Carolina & Northern Railroad, Carolina Central Railroad, Richmond, Petersburg & Carolina Railroad and other corporations, fourteen in number, in all of which this company holds more than nine-tenths of the capital stocks. For details regarding the companies included in the united system see statement of Seaboard Air Line in MANUAL for 1900, under which head the statements of the separate roads are given at length.

This company has greatly improved the physical condition of the system, and has also made large additions to the equipment. Locomotives, 307; passenger cars, 256; freight cars, 8,161; service cars, 187.

Stock..Par $100..Authorized { com., $37,500,000 / pref., 25,000,000 } Issued { com., $29,000,000 / pref., 19,400,000 } $48,400,000

The preferred stock is 4 per cent., non-cumulative. Both classes of stock are held under a voting trust.

Transfer Agent, common stock, Baltimore Trust Co., Baltimore. Registrar, Continental Trust Co., Baltimore. Transfer Agent, preferred stock, Continental Trust Co., Baltimore. Registrar, Baltimore Trust Co., Baltimore.

FUNDED DEBT.

| | |
|---|---|
| 1st mort., 4 per cent., due April, 1950, April and Oct.............................. | $12,775,000 |
| Collateral trust, 5 per cent., due May, 1911, May and Nov......................... | 10,000,000 |
| Equipment trust, 5 per cent...................................................... | 1,836,813 |
| " " 4½ per cent.................................................. | 638,000 |
| Total ........................................................................ | $25,249,813 |

FUNDED DEBT CONSTITUENT COMPANIES.

| | |
|---|---|
| Seaboard & Roanoke, 1st mort., 5 per cent., due July, 1926, Jan. and July.......... | $2,500,000 |
| " " debentures, 6 per cent., due 1916, Feb. and Aug.............. | 285,000 |
| Raleigh & Gaston, 1st mort., due Jan., 1947, Jan. and July........................ | 1,200,000 |
| Georgia, Carolina & Nor., 1st mort., guar. 5 per cent., due July, 1929, Jan. and July. | 5,360,000 |
| Raleigh & Augusta, 1st mort., guar. 6 per cent., due Jan., 1926, Jan. and July...... | 1,000,000 |
| Georgia & Alabama, 1st cons. mort., 5 per cent., due Oct., 1945, April and Oct...... | 5,405,000 |
| " " Ter. Co., 1st mort., 5 per cent., due Dec., 1948, June and Dec.. | 1,000,000 |
| Florida Central & Peninsular, 1st mort., 5 per cent., due July, 1918, Jan. and July... | 3,000,000 |
| " " " 2d (1st on extensions) mort., 5 per cent., due Jan., 1930, Jan. and July.............................. | 410,000 |
| " " " cons. mort., 5 per cent., due Jan., 1943, Jan. and July. | 4,372,000 |
| South Bound Railroad, 1st mort., 5 per cent., due April, 1941, April and Oct........ | 2,033,000 |
| Carolina Central, 1st cons. mort., 4 per cent., due Jan., 1949, Jan. and July......... | 3,000,000 |
| Roanoke & Tar River, 1st mort., 6 per cent., due 1917, April and Oct................ | 55,000 |
| Durham & Northern, 1st mort., 6 per cent., due Nov., 1928, May and Nov......... | 100,000 |
| Total.......................................................................... | $29,720,000 |
| Total bonds of system ........................................................ | 54,969,813 |

The proprietary companies have car trusts amounting to over $600,000.

The 1st mortgage 4 per cent. bonds are $75,000,000 authorized and are a 1st mortgage on 287 miles. Trustee, Continental Trust Co., Baltimore. Of the total amount $29,725,000 are held to retire underlying bonds of the system; $12,500,000 are reserved for improvements and extensions.

The collateral trust 5 per cent. bonds were created in 1901, and are redeemable at 105. They are secured by the deposit of $20,000,000 of the 1st 4s. The amount authorized is $10,000,000, of which $2,000,000 was reserved to retire the 5 per cent. collateral trust bonds due in October, 1902. The remaining $8,000,000 were issued to retire car trust obligations and to refund $3,400,000 of 6 per cent. 1sts and certificates, as well as to pay for the company's interest in the Richmond-Washington line.

The approximate capitalization of the system per mile is, bonded debt, $19,000; preferred stock, $6,500; common stock, $11,500; total per mile, $37,000.

EARNINGS.

Year ending June 30. All roads and water lines in system.

| | Gross. | Net. | Charges. | Surplus. |
|---|---|---|---|---|
| 1897-98 (2,349 miles) | $7,946,616 | $2,222,261 | .......... | ........ |
| 1898-99 (2,358 " ) | 9,065,461 | 2,499,683 | .......... | ........ |
| 1899-00 ( " " ) | 9,578,286 | 2,618,564 | .......... | ........ |
| 1900-01 (2,591 " ) | 10,929,051 | 2,820,073 | $2,490,414 | $329,659 |
| 1901 (year ending Dec. 31) | 11,579,815 | 3,471,553 | 2,651,296 | 820,256 |

The following presents the freight traffic statistics of the system:

| | Average Mileage. | Total Tonnage. | Tons carried One Mile. | Freight Density. | Rate per Ton per Mile. | Earnings per Train Mile. | Average Tons per Train. |
|---|---|---|---|---|---|---|---|
| 1901-02 | 2,603 | 4,516,072 | 740,169,229 | 284,285 | 1.c68 | $1.87 | 175 |

President, John Skelton Williams, Richmond; 1st Vice-President and General Manager, J. M. Barr, Portsmouth, Va.; 3d Vice-President, J. William Middendorf, Baltimore; 4th Vice-President, V. E. McBee, Portsmouth, Va.; Assistant to President, T. M. R. Talcott, Richmond; Treasurer, John H. Sharp, Portsmouth, Va.; Secretary, D. C. Porteous, New York; Comptroller, T. W. Roby, Portsmouth, Va.

Directors—John Skelton Williams, James H. Dooley, E. B. Addison, Richmond; J. William Middendorf, William A. Marburg, S. Davies Warfield, Robert C. Davidson, Baltimore; Ernst Thalmann, F. R. Pemberton, New York; C. Sidney Shepard, New Haven, Conn.; George W. Watts, Durham, N. C.; J. M. Barr, Portsmouth, Va.

Main office, 922 East Main street, Richmond, Va.; New York office, 15 Wall street. Annual meeting, Friday after the second Thursday in November.

## SHREVEPORT & RED RIVER VALLEY RAILROAD CO.

A corporation formed under the laws of Louisiana, July 23, 1897.

Road owned, Shreveport to Mansura, La., 153 miles. The company is extending its lines, and proposes to build ultimately to New Orleans. Locomotives, 10; passenger cars, 12; freight cars, 310.

Stock......Par $100..........................Authorized, $10,000,000......Issued, $2,210,000

FUNDED DEBT.

1st mort., 4 per cent., due July, 1950, Jan. and July .............................. $3,460,000

The bonds authorized are at the rate of $20,000 per mile, with a reservation of $300,000 of the issue to provide for a bridge over the Red River at Alexandria, La.

President, William Edenborn, New York; Vice-President, P. McIlvreid; Secretary and Treasurer, Clarence Ellerbe; Auditor, H. B. Helm, Shreveport, La.

Main office, Shreveport, La.; President's office, 71 Broadway, New York.

## SIERRA RAILWAY CO. OF CALIFORNIA

A corporation formed under the laws of California in 1896.

Road owned, Oakdale to Tuolumne, Cal., 64 miles; branch, 20 miles; total operated, 84 miles. Locomotives, 9; passenger cars, 5; freight cars, 96.

Stock......Par $100............................Authorized, $5,000,000......Issued, $3,280,000

Stock is transferred at the company's office, San Francisco.

FUNDED DEBT.

| | |
|---|---|
| 1st mort., 6 per cent., due April, 1937, April and Oct. | $1,266,000 |
| Income mort., 6 per cent., due 1937 | 166,000 |
| Total | $2,432,000 |

Interest on the 1st mortgage bonds is paid at the Crocker-Woolworth Bank, San Francisco.
In the year ending December 31, 1902, the company reported total earnings of $303,713.
President, Andre Poniatowki; Vice-President, William H. Crocker; Secretary, S. M. Rickey, San Francisco; Treasurer, S. D. Freshman, Jamestown, Cal.
Directors—Andre Poniatowki, William H. Crocker, Samuel Sussman, Henry J. Crocker, W. F. Pierce, William Angus, San Francisco; S. D. Freshman, Jamestown, Cal.
Main office, 610 Market street, San Francisco. Annual meeting, second Monday in February, at San Francisco.

## SOUTHERN INDIANA RAILWAY CO.

Road owned, Terre Haute to Westport, Ind., 146 miles; branches, 7 miles; leased, 4 miles; total, 158 miles. In 1900 an extension from Linton, Ind., to Terre Haute, 48 miles, was completed. In 1902 other branches were in progress, and a belt line, 8 miles in length, around the City of Terre Haute is to be built in 1903. Locomotives, 20; passenger cars, 20; freight cars, 2,423.
Formerly the Evansville & Richmond, which was owned by the Evansville & Terre Haute. Road sold in foreclosure March, 1897, and present company took possession in December, 1897.

Stock.....Par $100....Authorized { com., $3,000,000 / pref., 500,000 } Issued { com., $3,000,000 / pref., 500,000 } $3,500,000

The preferred stock is 5 per cent., non-cumulative.
In 1901-02 5 per cent. was paid on the preferred stock, and a third semi-annual dividend of 2½ per cent. was paid December 31, 1902.
Transfer Agent, Charles Huntoon, 152 Monroe street, Chicago.

FUNDED DEBT.

1st mort., 4 per cent, due Feb., 1951, Feb. and Aug. ..... $3,160,000

The trustee of the 1st mortgage is the Equitable Trust Co., Chicago.
This company owns the stock of the Bedford Belt Railway Co., which has $350,000 of 5 per cent. bonds outstanding.

EARNINGS.

Year ending June 30.

| | Gross. | Net. | Charges and Taxes. | Surplus. |
|---|---|---|---|---|
| 1897-98 | $136,743 | $41,099 | $10,846 | $30,253 |
| 1898-99 | 324,622 | 121,816 | 74,355 | 47,461 |
| 1899-00 | 363,894 | 149,897 | 96,545 | 53,352 |
| 1900-01 | 439,827 | 145,740 | 112,411 | 33,329 |
| 1901-02 | 630,195 | 277,852 | 158,153 | 119,699 |

In 1901-02 the surplus over the preferred dividends was $94,699.
President, John R. Walsh; Vice-President, James Walsh; Treasurer, L. A. Walton; Secretary and Auditor, Charles F. Weinland, Chicago.
Directors—John R. Walsh, James Walsh, F. D. Meacham, F. M. Trissal, Charles F. Weinland, Chicago.
Main office, Terre Haute; Chicago office, 204 Dearborn street. Annual meeting, third Monday in January, at Bedford, Ind.

## THE SOUTHERN PACIFIC CO.

(Controlled by Union Pacific Railroad Co.)

This company was organized under the laws of the State of Kentucky, March 14, 1884, for the purpose of unifying in management lines of railroad extending from New Orleans, La., to San Francisco, Cal., to Portland, Ore., and to Ogden, Utah.
In February, 1901, the Union Pacific Railroad Co. purchased a controlling interest in the stock of this company, the stock acquired being held as security for the 4 per cent. collateral trust bonds of the Union Pacific.

MAP OF THE
SOUTHERN PACIFIC

The systems of roads leased or controlled comprise the following:

| | Miles. |
|---|---|
| Companies whose capital stocks are principally owned by the Southern Pacific Co.: | |
| Operated under leases: | |
| Southern Pacific Railroad | 3,268 |
| South Pacific Coast Railway | 101 |
| Central Pacific Railway | 1,359 |
| Oregon & California Railroad | 672 |
| Operated by companies owning the lines: | |
| Morgan's Louisiana & Texas Railroad and Steamship Co. | 324 |
| Louisiana Western Railroad | 164 |
| Texas & New Orleans Railroad | 395 |
| Galveston, Harrisburg & San Antonio Railway | 917 |
| Galveston, Houston & Northern Ry. | 54 |
| Houston, East & West Texas Railway | 191 |
| Houston & Shreveport Railroad | 39 |
| New York, Texas & Mexican Railway | 122 |
| Houston & Texas Central Railroad | 669 |
| Carson & Colorado Ry. (narrow gauge) | 299 |
| Companies whose capital stocks are principally owned by Morgan's Louisiana & Texas Railroad and Steamship Co., but which were operated by companies owning the lines: | |
| Iberia & Vermilion Railroad | 16 |
| Gulf, Western Texas & Pacific Ry. | 111 |
| Total of proprietary lines | 8,701 |
| Companies whose capital stocks are owned otherwise than by the Southern Pacific Co., but are operated by the Southern Pacific Co., under leases: | |
| New Mexico & Arizona Railroad | 88 |
| Sonora Railway | 262 |
| Total of leased lines | 350 |
| Affiliated companies: | |
| San Antonio & Aransas Pass Railway | 687 |
| Gila Valley, Globe & Northern Railway | 124 |
| Total mileage, June 30, 1902 | 9,862 |

This company controls the Cromwell Steamship Co., operating 1,800 miles of water lines. Morgan's Louisiana & Texas Railroad and Steamship Co. operates 1,375 miles of steamship lines and the Southern Pacific Co. itself has 1,875 miles of water lines; total water lines, 5,365 miles.

In 1898 the Northern Railway Co. of California, the Northern California Railway and the California Pacific were consolidated with the Southern Pacific Railroad Co. of California.

In March, 1902, the Southern Pacific Railroad of California, the Southern Pacific Railroad of Arizona and the Southern Pacific Railroad of New Mexico were consolidated into a new California company, the Southern Pacific Railroad Co.

The Central Pacific Railroad, 1,359 miles, was formerly leased by this company, but on the readjustment of that company's capital and indebtedness to the United States Government in 1899, the Southern Pacific Company acquired all the stock of the new Central Pacific.

The company operates steamship lines from New York to New Orleans, New Orleans to Havana, and to Bluefields, Nicaragua, as well as ferry, harbor and river lines in Louisiana, Texas and California.

In 1900 the company acquired a controlling interest in the stock of the Pacific Mail Steamship Co.

The Mojave Division of the Southern Pacific Railroad of California, 242 miles, is leased to the Atchison, Topeka & Santa Fe Railway Co. until 1979, at an annual rental of $218,133. The New Mexico & Arizona Railroad and the Sonora Railway, 350 miles, acquired from the Atchison, Topeka & Santa Fe Railway by the company, are operated separately.

Locomotives, 1,388; passenger cars, 1,342; freight cars, 42,224.

Stock......Par $100......................Authorized, $200,000,000......Issued, $197,849,227

Transfer agency, 120 Broadway, New York.

FUNDED DEBT.

| | |
|---|---|
| Steamship, 1st mort. bonds, 6 per cent., due Jan., 1911, Jan. and July | $2,215,000 |
| Gold bonds, Central Pacific, stock collateral, 4 per cent., due Aug., 1949, June and Dec. | 28,818,500 |
| Collateral trust, 4½ per cent. bonds, due Dec., 1905, June and Dec. | 15,000,000 |
| Total | $46,033,500 |

The capital stock authorized was, in 1899, increased from $150,000,000 to $200,000,000, and $67,274,200 of new stock issued in exchange for a like amount of Central Pacific Railway stock.

The 4 per cent. gold bonds were issued in 1899 in connection with the Central Pacific readjustment and purchase. They are secured by a deposit with the Union Trust Co., New York, trustee, of $12,000,000 preferred stock of the Central Pacific Railway and all the common stock of the Central Pacific Railway acquired by the Southern Pacific Co. These bonds were issued in payment to holders of Central Pacific stock at the rate of $25 of bonds to each $100 of stock, in addition to $100 in Southern Pacific stock as noted above.

The 4½ collateral trust bonds are $15,000,000 authorized. They are redeemable at the company's option after December 1, 1902, at par and interest. The bonds are secured by stocks and bonds of the Pacific Mail Steamship Co. and other controlled properties of an aggregate face value of $68,191,000.

This company owns stocks of its proprietary companies of an aggregate par value of $302,767,772.

Physical and financial details of the organizations owned, leased and controlled through ownership of capital stock will be found under their respective heads in this edition of the MANUAL. See Southern Pacific of California, Galveston, Harrisburg & San Antonio, Texas & New Orleans, Louisiana Western, Morgan's Louisiana & Texas Railroad and Steamship Co., Central Pacific, Oregon & California, Houston & Texas Central, Pacific Mail Steamship Co. and others.

### EARNINGS.

| | Gross. | Net. | Charges. | Surplus. |
|---|---|---|---|---|
| 1892 | $48,972,195 | $18,235,814 | $15,625,464 | $2,610,349 |
| 1893 | 48,049,548 | 18,158,790 | 16,162,600 | 1,996,190 |
| 1894 | 44,772,003 | 16,050,950 | 14,824,152 | 1,226,798 |
| 1895 | 50,457,024 | 19,591,474 | 17,406,252 | 2,185,222 |
| 1896 | 48,666,667 | 18,934,105 | 17,144,552 | 1,789,554 |
| 1896-97 (18 ms. ending June 30) | 48,871,900 | 19,533,619 | 17,260,581 | 2,273,038 |
| | **Gross.** | **Expenditure.** | **Betterments.** | **Surplus.** |
| 1897-98 (year ending June 30).. | $58,477,498 | $54,354,895 | $1,299,258 | $2,823,344 |
| 1898-99 ( " " " ).. | 56,951,507 | 53,371,235 | 2,730,407 | 1,747,568 |
| 1899-00 ( " " " ).. | 65,980,430 | 60,874,719 | 3,334,789 | 3,918,630 |
| 1900-01 ( " " " ).. | 81,107,672 | 70,780,162 | 6,870,950 | 3,456,561 |
| 1901-02 ( " " " ).. | 87,161,205 | 76,619,734 | ........ | 10,541,471 |

The following presents the freight traffic statistics of the system:

| | Average Mileage. | Total Tonnage. | Tons Carried One Mile. | Freight Density. | Rate per Ton per Mile. | Earnings per Train Mile. | Average Tons per Train. |
|---|---|---|---|---|---|---|---|
| 1897-98.... | 6,759 | 9,699,814 | 3,142,128,930 | 464,880 | 0.988c | $2.35 | 219 |
| 1898-99.... | 7,174 | 10,084,854 | 3,468,787,286 | 483,522 | 0.952 | 2.33 | 224 |
| 1899-00.... | 7,545 | 12,035,685 | 3,988,460,193 | 501,043 | 0.957 | 2.51 | 241 |
| 1900-01.... | 8,654 | 14,067,162 | 4,873,257,728 | 563,121 | 1.001 | 2.69 | 254 |
| 1901-02.... | 8,757 | 15,736,913 | 4,957,602,303 | 566,244 | 1.021 | 2.79 | 265 |

### GROSS AND NET EARNINGS BY MONTHS FOR THREE YEARS.

| | 1900. | | 1901. | | 1902. | |
|---|---|---|---|---|---|---|
| | Gross. | Net. | Gross. | Net. | Gross. | Net. |
| January | $4,877,138 | $1,352,937 | $6,150,181 | $1,976,496 | $7,148,918 | $2,185,834 |
| February | 4,644,685 | 1,355,284 | 5,735,446 | 1,856,821 | 6,081,412 | 1,540,802 |
| March | 5,234,861 | 1,601,443 | 6,445,785 | 2,012,043 | 6,528,220 | 1,503,160 |
| April | 5,073,488 | 1,725,612 | 6,836,854 | 2,459,058 | 6,810,181 | 1,886,668 |
| May | 5,062,276 | 1,632,289 | 6,941,974 | 2,362,288 | 6,832,856 | 1,770,913 |
| June | 5,085,410 | 1,820,107 | 6,285,246 | 2,342,048 | 6,464,712 | 1,556,826 |
| July | 5,353,453 | 1,992,989 | 6,632,095 | 2,493,916 | 6,926,294 | 2,294,637 |
| August | 5,580,018 | 2,046,839 | 7,184,692 | 2,740,548 | 6,853,384 | 2,186,913 |
| September | 5,780,176 | 2,371,730 | 7,081,319 | 2,558,317 | 8,007,116 | 3,044,136 |
| October | 6,719,600 | 2,726,215 | 7,891,099 | 3,168,194 | 8,279,211 | 2,972,712 |
| November | 6,149,516 | 2,325,795 | 7,484,233 | 2,812,527 | 7,945,320 | 2,401,532 |
| December | 6,167,686 | 2,359,704 | 7,356,403 | 2,554,646 | 7,972,286 | 2,552,974 |
| Totals for year | $65,728,307 | $23,310,944 | $82,031,327 | $29,336,902 | $85,849,910 | $25,897,107 |
| Av. per month | 5,477,359 | 1,942,579 | 6,835,944 | 2,444,741 | 7,154,159 | 2,158,092 |

President, Edward H. Harriman, New York; Vice-President, H. E. Huntington; 2d Vice-President, Charles H. Tweed, New York; 3d Vice-President, John C. Stubbs; 4th Vice-President, J. Kruttschnitt, San Francisco; Secretary, Alexander Millar, New York; Treasurer, Nicholas T. Smith, San Francisco; Assistant Treasurer, Andrew K. Van Deventer, New York; Comptroller, William Mahl, New York.

Directors—Charles H. Tweed, Edward H. Harriman, George J. Gould, James H. Hyde, Otto H. Kahn, William D. Cornish, Darius O. Mills, Winslow S. Pierce, Jacob H. Schiff, James Stillman, James Speyer, Edwin Hawley, New York; H. E. Huntington, San Francisco; T. Jefferson Coolidge, Jr., Boston.

Main office, 4 Montgomery street, San Francisco; New York office, 120 Broadway. Annual meeting, Wednesday after first Monday in April.

## SOUTHERN PACIFIC RAILROAD CO.

(Leased to Southern Pacific Co.)

A corporation formed under the laws of California, March 7, 1902, and was a merger of the Southern Pacific Railroad Co. of California, the Southern Pacific of Arizona and the Southern Pacific of New Mexico.

The Southern Pacific Railroad Co. of California was formed April 12, 1898, by a consolidation of the Southern Pacific Railroad Co. of California with the Northern Railway Co., the Northern California Railway Co. and the California Pacific Railroad Co., all of which were leased to or controlled by the Southern Pacific Co.

Road owned, San Francisco to Tres Pinos, 100 miles; Alcalde, Cal., to Yuma, 551 miles; Colorado River to El Paso, Tex., 560 miles; branches, 1,722 miles; leased, 7 miles; Mojave to the Needles, 242 miles; the latter line is leased to the Atchison, Topeka & Santa Fe until September 1, 1979, at an annual rental of $218,133; total, 3,267 miles. Locomotives, 446; passenger cars, 484; freight cars, 13,042.

The road is leased to the Southern Pacific Co. for ninety-nine years from January 1, 1902, for all charges and interest, and to pay over to the lessor at termination of each year 10 per cent. of the net profit from operation.

The Southern Pacific Railroad Co. of California had a land grant of 10,445,247 acres. Sales of lands to June 30, 1902, amounted to $9,820,547, of which $8,655,500 was applied to redemption of 6 per cent. bonds, $1,165,047 was in fund for that purpose, and $2,036,250 comprised deferred payments in land sale contracts.

Stock......Par $100......................Authorized, $159,455,000......Issued. $128,307,960

The stock is practically all owned by the Southern Pacific Co.

Stock is transferred at the company's office, San Francisco.

FUNDED DEBT.

| | |
|---|---|
| 1st mort., 6 per cent. (A to F), due 1905-06 and 1912, April and Oct ............... | $30,212,500 |
| So. Pac. Br., 1st mort., sinking fd., in Oct., 1937, 6 per cent., due 1937, April and Oct. | 3,533,000 |
| Stockton & Copperopolis, 1st mort., 5 per cent., due Jan., 1905, Jan. and July...... | 500,000 |
| 1st cons. mort. (So. Pac.), guar. 5 per cent., due Nov., 1937, May and Nov......... | 27,125,000 |
| Northern Ry., 1st mort., 6 per cent., due Jan., 1907, Jan. and July................ | 5,156,000 |
| " " " 5 per cent., due Oct., 1938, April and Oct.............. .. | 4,751,000 |
| Nor. California Ry., 1st mort., 5 per cent., due June, 1929, June and Dec........... | 1,074,000 |
| Cal. Pac. R. R., 1st mort., 4½ per cent., due Jan., 1912, Jan. and July............ | 2,232,000 |
| " " 2d mort., 4½ per cent., due Jan., 1911, Jan. and July............. | 1,595,000 |
| " " 3d mort. A, 6 per cent., due July, 1905, Jan. and July............. | 1,998,500 |
| " " " B, 3 per cent., due July, 1905, Jan. and July............. | 1,000,000 |
| So. Pac. of Arizona, 1st mort., 6 per cent., due March, 1909-10, Jan. and July...... | 10,000,000 |
| " " " New Mexico, 1st mort., 6 per cent., due Jan., 1911, Jan. and July...... | 4,180,000 |
| Total.............................................................. | $93,357,000 |

Total amount of 1st mortgage bonds authorized, $46,000,000; series A, $15,000,000; B, C D, E and F, $5,000,000 each. Principal of series E and F mature in 1912; the others in 1905-06.

The Southern Pacific Railroad of California 1st consolidated mortgage, dated 1893 and due 1937, is $30,000,000, authorized, plus amounts needed to retire prior liens. It is a 1st mortgage on 844 miles of road and additional mileage constructe . Of the bonds outstanding $19,168,000 are subject to call at 107½ and interest after April 1, 1905, and are so stamped. The remaining $6,576,000 are unstamped and unaffected by this provision.

The Southern Pacific of Arizona 1st mortgage is in two series, A and B, of $6,000,000 maturing 1909 and $4,000,000 maturing 1910.

EARNINGS.

| YEAR. | Miles Operated.* | Gross. | Net. | Charges. | Surplus. |
|---|---|---|---|---|---|
| 1893........................... | 1,618 | $10,669,222 | $4,603,102 | $2,704,890 | $1,898,211 |
| 1894........................... | 1,634 | 8,999,235 | 3,343,893 | 2,797,842 | 546,051 |
| 1895........................... | 1,678 | 10,470,434 | 4,067,678 | 2,896,347 | 1,171,331 |
| 1896........................... | 1,732 | 9,857,848 | 3,651,393 | 3,109,025 | 542,367 |
| 1896-97 (year ending June 30).. | 1,735 | 9,542,555 | 3,733,094 | 2,969,424 | 763,669 |
| 1897-98 ( " " ).. | 2,300 | 15,078,026 | 6,681,426 | 4,851,187 | 1,830,239 |
| 1898-99 ( " " ).. | 2,571 | 14,628,937 | 5,749,363 | 4,672,634 | 1,077,329 |
| 1899-00 ( " " ).. | 2,670 | 17,514,959 | 6,195,816 | 4,390,150 | 1,975,032 |
| 1900-01 ( " " ).. | 2,471 | 19,635,748 | 7,528,929 | 6,278,222 | 1,250,756 |
| 1901-02 ( " " ).. | 2,725 | 29,481,298 | 12,142,240 | 5,961,793 | 6,180,448 |

* The 242.51 miles Mojave to the Needles are not included in this mileage.

Under terms of the lease there was due this company in 1891 $1,064,496; in 1892, $1,175,180; in 1893, $1,164,740; in 1894, $526,322; in 1895, $916,808; for the 18 months ending June 30,

1897, $719,533; for the year ending June 30, 1898 (including all the consolidated properties), $2,153,130.

President, Edward H. Harriman, New York; Treasurer, Nicholas T. Smith; Secretary, Joseph L. Willcutt, San Francisco.

Directors—Charles H. Tweed, Edward H. Harriman, Nicholas T. Smith, J. Kruttschnitt, Joseph L. Willcutt, J. S. Slauson, I. W. Hellman, A. Hayward, J. K. Wilson, W. F. Herrin, H. S. King.

Main office, 4 Montgomery street, San Francisco; New York office, 120 Broadway. Annual meeting, second Wednesday in April.

---

## SOUTHERN RAILWAY CO.

This company was chartered by the Legislature of Virginia in 1894 to succeed the Richmond & Danville Railroad Co., and purchased the properties of the Richmond & West Point Terminal Railroad and Warehouse Co., which were reorganized under the plan submitted by Drexel, Morgan & Co. in May, 1893, and modified February, 1894.

Road owned or operated June 30, 1902, 6,765 miles, of which 4,365 miles are owned, 1,268 miles controlled by ownership of securities, 818 miles leased, 10 miles operated under agreements and 304 miles represent trackage rights over the lines of other companies. The company also operates 200 miles of steamship routes, controlling the York River Line of boats between Baltimore and West Point, Va., and the Norfolk Line, between Baltimore and Norfolk. The principal lines extend from Washington, D. C., and Richmond, Va., via Danville, Va., and Charlotte, N. C., to Atlanta, Ga.; from Bristol, Tenn., via Knoxville and Chattanooga, to Atlanta; from Atlanta to Brunswick, Ga., and from Atlanta via Birmingham to the Mississippi River at Greenville, Miss.; from Chattanooga, Tenn., to Memphis, Tenn. (the former Memphis & Charleston Railroad), and from Selma, N. C., to Pinner's Point, Norfolk, Va., the latter line by virtue of trackage over the Wilmington & Weldon and Norfolk & Carolina Railroads. Other branches include lines from Richmond to West Point, Va., from Charlotte via Columbia, S. C., to Augusta, Ga.; and from Columbia, S. C., and Augusta to Charleston, S. C.; from Rome, Ga., to Selma, Ala., and Meridian, Miss.; from Greensboro, N. C., to Goldsboro, N. C., and from Salisbury, N. C., via Asheville, N. C., to Murphy and Morristown, Tenn.

The company also owns the former Louisville Southern, Louisville to Lexington and Burgin, Ky., and in June, 1895, purchased the Atlanta & Florida Railway, Atlanta to Fort Valley, Ga., 102 miles. It also acquired in 1895 a controlling interest in the Alabama Great Southern (which is operated separately), and acquired with the Cincinnati, Hamilton & Dayton a joint control of the Cincinnati, New Orleans & Texas Pacific Railway Co., lessee of the Cincinnati Southern. In June, 1896, the Georgia Midland, Columbus to McDonough, Ga., 98 miles, was acquired by lease for 99 years. In 1899 it purchased control of the South Carolina & Georgia Railroad system, 323 miles, which company was, in 1902, combined with the South Carolina & Georgia Extension Railroad, under the title of the Southern Railway, Carolina Division. The same year leased the Mobile & Birmingham Railroad and purchased 166 miles of the Atlantic & Yadkin Railway. In June, 1899, this company and the Louisville & Nashville jointly purchased the Birmingham Southern Railroad from the Tennessee Coal, Iron and Railroad Co., about 70 miles, which property is operated under its own organization. In 1899 this company bought from the State of Georgia the Northeastern Railroad of Georgia.

The Louisville, Evansville & St. Louis, 268 miles, was acquired in 1900 and is operated as the St. Louis Division of that company. In 1902 this company and the Louisville & Nashville Railroad Co. jointly acquired control of the Chicago, Indianapolis & Louisville Railroad Co.

Locomotives, 937; passenger cars, 800; freight cars, 34,684; road car equipment, 715; floating equipment, 121. The latter includes a barge line for coal transportation on the Mississippi River.

The property comprises nearly all the lines of the former Richmond & Danville, East Tennessee, Virginia & Georgia and Georgia Pacific companies, through which the Richmond Terminal Co. controlled the system. That company also controlled the Central Railroad and Banking Co. of Georgia, which, however, was separated from it by legal complications, though provisions were made in the reorganization plan for the future acquisition of that property, and though entirely independent it is operated in harmony with this system. The Memphis & Charleston and Mobile & Birmingham roads included in the old East Tennessee, Virginia & Georgia, were not included in the reorganization, and the Alabama Great Southern and Cincinnati Southern (Cincinnati, New Orleans & Texas Pacific Railway) were also kept out of the new system, though the control of the two latter, as above stated, has since been acquired. In January, 1898, it was announced that the Memphis & Charleston had also been acquired by this company, and in 1899 the Mobile & Birmingham. In 1900 acquired the Louisville, Evansville & St. Louis Consolidated Railway, now operated as the St. Louis Division. In February, 1901, this company acquired control of the Mobile & Ohio Railroad by a purchase of its stock and general mortgage bonds. For further details, reference may be made to the separate statements of the Central of Georgia, Cincinnati, Mobile & Ohio, New Orleans & Texas Pacific Railway, Alabama Great Southern, Georgia Southern & Florida and Mobile & Birmingham in this issue of the MANUAL.

Stock. Par $100.. Authorized { com., $120,000,000; pref., 60,000,000 } Issued { com., $120,000,000; pref., 60,000,000 } $180,000,000

Preferred stock is entitled to 5 per cent., dividends non-cumulative. Both classes of stock were held in a voting trust, J. P. Morgan, George F. Baker and Charles Lanier, trustees, appointed by J. P. Morgan & Co., for five years, or until a dividend of 5 per cent. has been paid in one year on preferred stock. In 1902 nearly all the holders assented to an extension of the voting trust until October, 1907, unless terminated by the action of the trustees.

In 1900 the Legislature of Virginia authorized the company, with the assent of its stockholders, to reduce the amount of the common stock outstanding from $120,000,000 to $60,000,000.

Transfer Agents, J. P. Morgan & Co., New York.

A dividend of 1 per cent. on the preferred stock, the first in company's history, was declared in December, 1896, payable January 4, 1897. In December, 1897, a second dividend of 1 per cent. on the preferred was declared, payable January 20, 1898. In January, 1899, 1 per cent. was paid on the preferred, 1 per cent. in October, 1899, 1½ per cent. April 6, 1900, and 1½ per cent. October 16, 1900, this making 3 per cent. paid on the preferred for the fiscal year 1899-1900. The half-yearly dividend, paid April 9, 1901, was increased to 2 per cent., and the same rate was paid October 16, 1901. The March, 1902, dividend was increased to 2½ per cent., which was also the rate in October, 1902.

### FUNDED DEBT.

| | |
|---|---|
| Southern Railway 1st consolidated mort., 5 per cent., due July, 1994, Jan. and July. | $36,465,000 |
| " " East Tennessee lien, 5 per cent., due March, 1938, March and Sept. | 4,500,000 |
| " " Memphis Div., 1st mort., 4-4½-5 per cent., due July, 1996, Jan. and July | 5,083,000 |
| " " St. Louis Div., 1st mort., 4 per cent., due Jan., 1951, Jan. and July. | 11,250,000 |
| " " Mobile & Ohio col. tr., 4 per cent., due Sept., 1938, March and Sept. | 7,949,000 |
| " " Aiken Branch, 1st mort., 4 per cent., due July, 1998, Jan. and July. | 150,000 |
| " " collateral trust, 4 per cent., due Dec., 1906, June and Dec. | 4,000,000 |
| Richmond & Danville cons. mort., 6 per cent, due Jan., 1915, Jan. and July | 5,997,000 |
| " " debentures, 5 per cent., due April, 1927, April and Oct | 3,368,000 |
| " " equipment trust, 5 per cent., due Sept., 1909, March and Sept. | 490,000 |
| Richmond, York River & Ches., 1st mort., 5 per cent., due Jan., 1910, Jan. and July. | 400,000 |
| " " " 2d mort. ext., due Nov., 1910, 4½ per cent., May and Nov. | 500,000 |
| Washington, Ohio & Western 1st mort., 4 per cent., due Feb., 1924, Feb. and Aug. | 1,025,000 |
| Atlantic, Tennessee & Ohio 1st mort., 6 per cent., due April, 1913, April and Oct | 150,000 |
| Western North Carolina 1st cons. mort., 6 per cent., due July, 1914, Jan. and July. | 2,531,000 |
| Charlotte, Col. & Augusta 1st mort. ext., 5 per cent., due July, 1909, Jan. and July. | 1,480,000 |
| " " " 2d mort., 7 per cent., due 1910, April and Oct. | 500,000 |
| Columbia & Greenville 1st mort., 6 per cent., due Jan., 1916, Jan. and July | 2,000,000 |
| Georgia Pacific 1st mort., 6 per cent., due Jan., 1922, Jan. and July | 5,660,000 |
| " " equip. mort., 5 per cent. call, Feb. and Aug | 690,000 |
| East Tenn., Virginia & Georgia 1st mort., 5 per cent., due July, 1930, Jan. and July | 3,106,000 |
| " " " cons. mort., 5 per cent., due Nov., 1956, May and Nov. | 12,770,000 |
| Knoxville & Ohio 1st mort., 6 per cent., due July, 1925, Jan. and July | 2,000,000 |
| Alabama Central 1st mort., 6 per cent., due July, 1918, Jan. and July | 1,000,000 |
| Spartanburg, Union & Columbia 1st mort., 4 per cent., due Jan., 1995, Jan. and July | 1,000,000 |
| Virginia Midland, series A to F 5 and 6 per cent., due 1906-31, March and Sept | 7,635,000 |
| " " gen. mort., 5 per cent., due May, 1936, May and Nov | 4,859,000 |
| Charlottesville & Rapidan 1st mort., 6 per cent., due July, 1913, Jan. and July | 294,400 |
| Atlantic & Yadkin 1st mort., 4 per cent., due April, 1949, April and Oct | 1,500,000 |
| Total | $128,352,400 |

### BONDS ISSUED JOINTLY WITH LOUISVILLE & NASHVILLE.

| | |
|---|---|
| Collateral trust C. I. & L. stock, 4 per cent, due July, 1952, Jan. and July | $10,000,000 |

### BONDS OF LEASED LINES.

| | |
|---|---|
| Atlanta & Charlotte 1st mort. pref. ex. 4 per cent., due Jan., 1907, April and Oct | $500,000 |
| " " 1st mort., 7 per cent., due Jan., 1907, Jan. and July | 4,250,000 |
| " " incomes, 6 per cent., non-cum., due Jan., 1907, April and Oct. | 750,000 |
| Georgia Midland, 1st mort., 3 per cent., due 1946, April and Oct | 1,650,000 |
| South Carolina & Georgia 1st mort., 5 per cent., due May, 1919, May and Nov | 5,250,000 |
| Spartanburg, Union & Columbia 1st mort., 4 per cent., due Jan., 1995, Jan. and July. | 1,000,000 |
| Southern Ry., Carolina Div., new mort., 4 per cent., due Oct., 1952, April and Oct. | 5,000,000 |

BONDS OF LEASED LINES—*Continued.*

| | |
|---|---|
| Mobile & Birmingham prior lien, 5 per cent., due July, 1945, Jan. and July......... | $600,000 |
| " " 1st mort., 4 per cent., due July, 1945, Jan. and July........ | 1,200,000 |
| Richmond & Mecklenburg 1st mort., 4 per cent., due Nov., 1948, May and Nov..... | 315,000 |
| Sumter & Wateree River 1st mort., 5 per cent., due April, 1919, April and Oct..... | 100,000 |
| Atlantic & Danville 1st mort., 5 per cent., due July, 1950, Jan. and July........... | 3,925,000 |
| Total........................................................ | $24,540,000 |

GUARANTEED STOCKS.

| | |
|---|---|
| Atlanta & Charlotte, 6 per cent., March and Sept................................ | $1,700,000 |
| North Carolina, 6½ to 7 per cent., Jan. and July.................................. | 4,000,000 |
| Mobile & Birmingham preferred stock, 1 to 4 per cent............................ | 900,000 |
| Southern Railway Mobile & Ohio stock trust certificates, 2 to 4 per cent............ | 4,932,600 |

The Southern Railway consolidated 5 per cent. mortgage is for $120,000,000. This issue was provided for in plan and authorized by stockholders in October, 1894. Under plan the amount could be increased with consent of voting trustees, either to acquire the Central Railroad & Banking Co. of Georgia or the Cincinnati Southern or another line as a substitute for it. Of the $120,000,000 now authorized, $78,088,372 were reserved to take up outstanding mortgage and equipment obligations, $21,911,627, including $8,000,000 sold to a syndicate and $3,000,000 for new construction, were to be issued forthwith, and $20,000,000 were reserved for improvements at the rate of $2,000,000 in each year.

The Southern Railway East Tennessee lien bonds for $4,500,000 were created in October, 1894, in pursuance of agreement made with holders of the $6,000,000 of old East Tennessee, Virginia & Georgia improvement and equipment 6 per cent. bonds, by which latter exchanged their holdings for 50 per cent. in Southern Railway preferred stock and 75 per cent. in a bond of equal lien paying 4 per cent. until March, 1898, and 5 per cent. thereafter.

The Memphis Division 1st mortgage bonds were issued in 1898. The amount outstanding, $5,083,000, was issued to retire old Memphis & Charleston bonds. Total authorized issue is $8,000,000, of which $1,000,000 are to be used only to build a line between Stevenson, Tenn., and Chattanooga, if necessary, and $1,417,000 are held for betterments. These bonds bear 4 per cent. until July 1, 1901, then 4½ per cent. until July 1, 1906, and 5 per cent. thereafter. There are also $1,500,000 Memphis Division 2d mortgage 5 per cent. bonds, all owned by the Southern Railway Co. Under terms of purchase of the Memphis & Charleston, the Southern Railway issued $2,990,400 preferred stock to holders of old Memphis & Charleston securities.

The St. Louis Division 4 per cent. 1st mortgage was created in 1900 to acquire the Louisville, Evansville & St. Louis Railroad. The authorized amount is $15,000,000, the bonds being dated January 1, 1901. Of the total, $150,000 were reserved to retire the Venice & Carondelet 1sts, and $5,500,000 were reserved for improvements, etc.

The Mobile & Ohio stock certificates represent the stock of that company acquired in exchange for them and deposited as security for the certificates. The latter draw 2 per cent. for one year following April 1, 1901, 3 per cent. for the second year and 4 per cent. thereafter.

The Southern Railway Mobile & Ohio 4 per cent. collateral trust bonds were created in 1901 and were given in exchange for the Mobile & Ohio general 4 per cents., the bonds acquired being deposited as collateral for the new bonds.

The collateral trust 4 per cent. bonds issued in 1902 for the purchase of the Chicago, Indianapolis & Louisville at 78 for the common and 90 for the preferred stock of that company are a joint obligation of this company and of the Louisville & Nashville Railroad Co. They are secured by the deposit of the acquired stocks.

Full details of the reorganization of the property will be found in the MANUAL for 1899. The plan was issued in May, 1893, and the present company entered into possession of the principal lines July 1, 1894.

EARNINGS.

Year ending June 30.

| | Av. Mileage. | Pref. Div. | Gross. | Per Cent. Op. Exp. | Net. | Charges. | Surplus. |
|---|---|---|---|---|---|---|---|
| 1894-95..... | 4,139 | .. | $17,114,791 | 70.48 | $5,141,615 | $4,245,870 | $895,745 |
| 1895-96..... | 4,574 | .. | 19,082,247 | 70.40 | 5,819,307 | 5,262,828 | 556,478 |
| 1896-97..... | 4,806 | .. | 19,079,499 | 69.35 | 6,133,176 | 5,687,256 | 445,919 |
| 1897-98..... | 4,827 | 1 | 21,095,838 | 68.41 | 6,942,352 | 5,935,339 | 1,007,013 |
| 1898-99..... | 5,254 | 2 | 25,353,686 | 68.46 | 8,325,800 | 6,231,281 | 2,094,519 |
| 1899-00..... | 6,306 | 3 | 31,200,869 | 70.00 | 9,688,228 | 6,770,977 | 2,917,251 |
| 1900-01..... | 6,612 | 4 | 34,660,482 | 69.86 | 10,815,563 | 7,275,062 | 3,540,509 |
| 1901-02..... | 6,743 | 4½ | 37,712,248 | 71.19 | 11,689,920 | 8,089,022 | 3,600,897 |

In 1899-1900 dividends paid $1,800,000; balance surplus, $1,117,251. In 1900-01 dividends, $2,400,000; balance surplus, $1,140,500. In 1901-02 dividends, $1,500,000; balance surplus, $2,100,897.

Earnings of the present system represent a different property from that controlled by the Richmond Terminal. The statements of the latter for some years past were given in the MANUAL for 1900.

APPROXIMATE EARNINGS OF LINES COMPOSING THE SOUTHERN RAILWAY SYSTEM.

For the years ending June 30, 1899, 1900, 1901 and 1902.

| | Year Ending June 30, 1899. 5,254.05 Miles. | | | Year Ending June 30, 1900. 6,300 Miles. | | |
|---|---|---|---|---|---|---|
| MONTH. | Gross Earnings. | Expenses and Taxes. | Net Earnings. | Gross Earnings. | Expenses and Taxes. | Net Earnings. |
| July | $1,971,173 | $1,432,476 | $538,697 | $2,224,394 | $1,578,882 | $645,512 |
| August | 1,993,232 | 1,393,892 | 599,340 | 2,490,130 | 1,695,792 | 794,338 |
| September | 2,204,714 | 1,419,895 | 784,819 | 2,674,595 | 1,688,883 | 985,712 |
| October | 2,259,282 | 1,432,042 | 827,240 | 2,958,593 | 1,854,819 | 1,103,774 |
| November | 2,261,874 | 1,441,154 | 820,720 | 2,805,075 | 1,852,626 | 952,449 |
| December | 2,251,115 | 1,443,818 | 807,297 | 2,749,336 | 1,833,521 | 915,815 |
| January | 2,035,851 | 1,382,292 | 653,559 | 2,630,033 | 1,859,731 | 770,302 |
| February | 1,845,171 | 1,261,184 | 583,987 | 2,553,936 | 1,837,802 | 716,134 |
| March | 2,174,473 | 1,448,835 | 725,638 | 2,855,810 | 1,973,976 | 881,834 |
| April | 1,894,524 | 1,366,019 | 528,505 | 2,386,538 | 1,832,359 | 554,179 |
| May | 2,107,883 | 1,566,759 | 541,124 | 2,465,430 | 1,896,509 | 568,921 |
| June | 2,029,698 | 1,529,420 | 500,278 | 2,407,000 | 1,926,547 | 480,453 |
| Totals | $25,028,990 | $17,117,786 | $7,911,204 | $31,200,870 | $21,831,447 | $9,369,423 |

| | Year Ending June 30, 1901. 6,424.94 Miles. | | | Year Ending June 30, 1902. 6,743.61 Miles. | | |
|---|---|---|---|---|---|---|
| MONTH. | Gross Earnings. | Expenses and Taxes. | Net Earnings. | Gross Earnings. | Expenses and Taxes. | Net Earnings. |
| July | $2,530,351 | $1,887,246 | $643,105 | $2,898,424 | $2,176,398 | $722,026 |
| August | 2,672,586 | 1,826,807 | 845,779 | 3,053,975 | 2,113,515 | 940,460 |
| September | 2,810,942 | 1,815,044 | 995,898 | 3,071,684 | 2,006,205 | 1,065,479 |
| October | 3,223,941 | 2,042,638 | 1,181,303 | 3,555,888 | 2,253,732 | 1,302,156 |
| November | 2,896,805 | 1,884,965 | 1,011,840 | 3,272,444 | 2,152,358 | 1,120,086 |
| December | 2,948,136 | 1,953,304 | 994,832 | 3,142,250 | 2,177,407 | 964,843 |
| January | 2,913,701 | 2,050,879 | 862,822 | 3,259,471 | 2,354,493 | 904,978 |
| February | 2,785,995 | 1,979,750 | 806,245 | 2,957,303 | 2,175,910 | 781,393 |
| March | 3,003,582 | 2,045,458 | 958,124 | 3,212,021 | 2,436,416 | 775,605 |
| April | 2,677,581 | 2,042,943 | 634,638 | 3,119,906 | 2,371,220 | 748,686 |
| May | 2,621,377 | 1,977,227 | 644,150 | 3,152,766 | 2,401,793 | 750,973 |
| June | 2,522,585 | 1,971,291 | 551,294 | 3,016,116 | 2,227,390 | 788,726 |
| Totals | $33,607,582 | $23,477,552 | $10,130,030 | $37,712,248 | $26,846,837 | $10,865,411 |

APPROXIMATE EARNINGS SOUTHERN RAILWAY SYSTEM LAST SIX MONTHS IN 1901 AND 1902.

| | Six Months Ending Dec. 31, 1901. 6,728 Miles. | | | Six Months Ending Dec. 31, 1902. 6,743 Miles. | | |
|---|---|---|---|---|---|---|
| MONTH. | Gross Earnings. | Expenses and Taxes. | Net Earnings. | Gross Earnings. | Expenses and Taxes. | Net Earnings. |
| July | $2,898,424 | $2,176,398 | $722,026 | $3,291,416 | $2,499,443 | $791,973 |
| August | 3,053,976 | 2,113,516 | 940,460 | 3,498,256 | 2,442,689 | 1,055,567 |
| September | 3,071,684 | 2,006,205 | 1,065,479 | 3,620,342 | 2,445,682 | 1,174,660 |
| October | 3,555,888 | 2,253,732 | 1,302,156 | 3,872,389 | 2,590,159 | 1,282,230 |
| November | 3,272,444 | 2,152,358 | 1,120,086 | 3,505,722 | 2,463,188 | 1,042,534 |
| December | 3,142,250 | 2,177,407 | 964,843 | 3,531,964 | 2,515,293 | 1,016,671 |
| Totals | $18,994,665 | $12,879,615 | $6,115,050 | $21,320,089 | $14,956,454 | $6,363,635 |

NOTE.—The above tables are given for purposes of approximate comparison only.

The following presents the comparative freight traffic statistics of the company:

| | Average Mileage. | Total Tonnage. | Tons Carried One Mile. | Freight Density. | Rate per Ton per Mile. | Earnings per Train Mile. | Average Tons per Train. |
|---|---|---|---|---|---|---|---|
| 1896-97 | 4,805 | 7,904,706 | 1,324,015,178 | 275,549 | 0.936c | $1.385 | 148.07 |
| 1897-98 | 4,827 | 8,554,012 | 1,436,673,635 | 297,632 | 0.922 | 1.382 | 150.05 |
| 1898-99 | 5,254 | 10,220,200 | 1,771,925,333 | 337,252 | 0.897 | 1.450 | 161.54 |
| 1899-00 | 6,306 | 13,590,353 | 2,294,257,940 | 363,821 | 0.916 | 1.617 | 176.61 |
| 1900-01 | 6,612 | 15,025,080 | 2,450,220,562 | 364,890 | 0.936 | 1.795 | 191.80 |
| 1901-02 | 6,743 | 16,811,538 | 2,678,308,625 | 397,198 | 0.931 | 1.819 | 195.31 |

The tonnage given above is of revenue freight only.

President, Samuel Spencer, New York; 1st Vice-President, Alexander B. Andrews, Raleigh, N. C.; 2d Vice-President, William W. Finley; 4th Vice-President, J. M. Culp; General Manager, C. H. Ackert, Washington, D. C.; Secretary, R. D. Lankford; Assistant Secretaries, C. E. A. McCarthy, New York, J. H. Drake, Richmond, Va., George R. Anderson; Treasurer, H. C. Ansley; Auditor, A. H. Plant, Washington, D. C.

Directors—Joseph Bryan, Richmond, Va.; Harris C. Fahnestock, Edmund D. Randolph, Charles Lanier, Robert M. Gallaway, Samuel Spencer, Charles Steele, Adrian Iselin, Jr., James T. Woodward, New York; Alexander B. Andrews, Raleigh, N. C.; William W. Finley, Washington, D. C.; Samuel M. Inman, Atlanta, Ga.

Main office, Richmond, Va.; New York office, 80 Broadway; Washington office, 1300 Pennsylvania avenue. Annual meeting, second Monday in October, at Richmond.

## STATEN ISLAND RAILWAY CO.

A corporation formed under the laws of New York in 1873 to take over the property of the Staten Island Railroad Co., which was sold under foreclosure.

Road owned, Clifton, N. Y., to Tottenville, 12¾ miles. Locomotives, 4; passenger cars, 13; freight cars, 7. The company also owns 3 ferryboats.

Stock......Par $75..........................Authorized, $1,050,000......Issued, $1,050,000

Stock is transferred at the office of the company, foot of Whitehall street, New York.

**Funded Debt.**

1st mort., 4½ per cent., due June, 1943, June and Dec............................ $511,000

This road was leased in 1884 to the Staten Island Rapid Transit Railroad Co., but when the latter was foreclosed and reorganized in 1899 this road was separated from it. The Baltimore & Ohio Railroad Co. owns a majority of the stock.

The 1st mortgage was created in 1893 to retire old bonds and is $1,000,000 authorized. In the year ending June 30, 1902, the gross earnings were $167,869; deficit under charges, $374.

President, L. F. Loree; Vice-President, George F. Randolph; Secretary, Custis W. Woolford, Baltimore; Treasurer and Assistant Secretary, Edward Curry, New York.

Main office, foot of Whitehall street, New York. Annual meeting, first Monday in April.

## STATEN ISLAND RAPID TRANSIT RAILWAY CO.

(Controlled by Baltimore & Ohio Railroad Co.)

Road owned, South Beach, N. Y., to Elizabethport, N. J., including the Arthur Kill Bridge, 11 miles. Company has one-half interest in ferry between Staten Island and New York. The Staten Island Railway, Tottenville to Clifton, 13 miles, was formerly leased, but on the reorganization of this company that road was surrendered to its owners. Locomotives, 16; passenger cars, 88; freight cars, 13.

Stock......Par $100. ............................Authorized, $500,000......Issued, $500,000

**Funded Debt.**

| | |
|---|---|
| Staten Island Rap. Tran. R. R. 1st mort., 6 per cent., due Jan., 1913, April and Oct.,.. | $1,000,000 |
| " " " " Ry. 2d mort., 4 per cent. guar., due July, 1904, Jan. and July.. | 2,500,000 |
| Total ............................................................ | $3,500,000 |

Company is controlled through stock ownership by the Baltimore & Ohio Railroad Co., that company also owning a large portion of the 1st mortgage bonds.

The Rapid Transit Ferry Co., operating ferry between St. George, Staten Island, and foot of Whitehall street, New York City, has $1,000,000 5 per cent. bonds, with a sinking fund of $50,000 per annum.

Since the completion of the bridge over Staten Island Sound from Elizabethport, N. J., and line connecting with the Central Railroad of New Jersey, a large part of the New York freight traffic of the Baltimore & Ohio passes over this road to St. George, Staten Island, where the Baltimore & Ohio has terminals, which were enlarged in 1902–03.

In July, 1898, interest on the old 5 per cent. 2d mortgage was defaulted and Receiver was appointed. October, 1898, interest on the 1sts also was not paid.

In January and February, 1899, terms of settlement were announced as follows: 1st mortgage bondholders were offered 126¼ flat for their holdings; 2d mortgage bonds were to be guaranteed at the rate of 4 per cent. per annum by the Baltimore & Ohio for five years, the latter company to have during that period the right to purchase the same at par and interest, and in case of a reorganization of this company during the five years the holders of the 2ds were given an option to take new securities in lieu of the cash price, while if there was a foreclosure new 4 per cent. bonds, with the same lien as at present, were to be created, which would be subject to the same provisions. The income bondholders were offered 7½ for their holdings by Speyer & Co.

Reorganization under this plan was carried out, the old 2d 5 per cent. bonds being exchanged for new 2d 4s. The old income bonds ($4,500,000, due 1945, 6 per cent., non-cumulative) were extinguished in the reorganization.

EARNINGS.

Year ending June 30.

| | Gross. | Net. | Charges. | | Surplus. |
|---|---|---|---|---|---|
| 1892-93 | $1,054,031 | $337,967 | $294,554 | | $43,413 |
| 1893-94 | 1,031,373 | 407,455 | 350,440 | | 57,014 |
| 1894-95 | 875,342 | 386,083 | 326,936 | | 59,147 |
| 1895-96 | 764,455 | 347,912 | 321,467 | | 26,445 |
| 1896-97 | 648,316 | 255,992 | 328,447 | Def. | 72,456 |
| 1897-98 | 680,284 | 304,631 | 327,195 | " | 22,579 |
| 1898-99 | 693,597 | 291,739 | 354,568 | " | 62,831 |
| 1899-00 | 557,731 | 284,761 | 217,798 | | 55,172 |
| 1900-01 | 519,369 | 241,134 | 203,622 | | 37,512 |
| 1901-02 | 583,195 | 261,088 | 202,196 | | 58,892 |

The operations of the Staten Island Railway are included to 1898-99 inclusive. Earnings since 1899-1900 are exclusive of that company's figures.

President, L. F. Loree, Baltimore; Vice-President, C. S. Sims, New York; Treasurer, J. V. McNeal, Baltimore; Assistant Treasurer, Edward Curry, New York; Secretary, Custis W. Woolford, Baltimore.

Directors—L. F. Loree, Custis W. Woolford, Baltimore; C. S. Sims, Lyman McCarty, J. Frank Emmons, James M. Davis, Vernon H. Brown, W. H. Force, Louis L. Stanton, New York.

Main office, foot of Whitehall street, New York. Annual meeting, first Tuesday in April.

## SUFFOLK & CAROLINA RAILWAY CO.

This company was originally the Nansemond Land, Lumber & Railway Co., chartered in 1873, the name being changed to the present title in 1874.

Road owned, narrow gauge, Suffolk, Va., to Edenton, N. C., 50 miles. The present management is changing the road to standard gauge, which will be completed early in 1903. Extension to Elizabeth City, N. C., 25 miles, is under construction. Locomotives, 5; passenger cars, 6; freight cars, 97.

Stock......Par $100..........................Authorized, $1,000,000......Issued, $800,000

The stock was originally $500,000 authorized, and $400,000 of it had been issued, but in 1902 the amount was increased to $1,000,000 and a stock dividend of 100 per cent. was paid in January, 1903, making the outstanding amount $800,000.

Stock is transferred by the secretary of the company, Baltimore.

FUNDED DEBT.

| | |
|---|---|
| 1st mort., 6 per cent., due April, 1911, April and Oct. | $90,000 |
| Cons. mort., 5 per cent., due July, 1952, Jan. and July | 150,000 |
| Total | $240,000 |

The consolidated mortgage was created in 1902 to provide funds for changing the gauge and building extensions. It is for $1,000,000. Trustee of the mortgage and agent for the payment of coupons, International Trust Co., Baltimore. The company also has an issue of $300,000, 4 per cent., non-cumulative, income bonds, all of which are in the treasury.

For the year ending December 31, 1902, the company reported surplus earnings of $39,154

President, William H. Bosley; Vice-Presidents, J. H. Cottman, Charles H. Tilghman; Treasurer, Charles F. Pitt; Secretary, John S. Gittings, Baltimore.

Directors—Charles H. Tilghman, J. H. Cottman, William B. Oliver, A. H. Rutherford, William C. Seddon, John M. Denison.

Main office, Suffolk, Va. Annual meeting, second Tuesday in October.

## SUSQUEHANNA & NEW YORK RAILROAD CO.

A corporation formed under the laws of Pennsylvania, May 24, 1902. The company was a consolidation of the Barclay Railroad Co. and the Binghamton, Towanda & Western Railway Co.

Road owned, Towanda, Pa., to Wheelerville, Pa., 28 miles; Grays Run branch, 9 miles;

trackage, East Laquin to Summit, 7 miles; total operated, 44½ miles. Under construction, Wheelerville to Ralston, 15 miles and branch 7 miles. Line projected, Towanda to Binghamton, 50 miles and Powell to Ansonia, Pa., 75 miles; total projected 125 miles. Locomotives, 7; passenger cars, 5; freight cars, 216.

Stock......Par $100..........................Authorized, $2,000,000......Issued, $1,500,000

The company has no preferred stock. Stock is transferred by the secretary of the company, Williamsport, Pa.

There was no outstanding funded debt at the close of 1902, but in August, 1902, the company authorized an issue of $2,000,000 4½ per cent. 1st mortgage bonds, due 1932, interest June and December, subject to call at par after December 1, 1912.

The outstanding stock and bonds of the Barclay Railroad Co. were retired in exchange for the securities of this company when the consolidation was effected.

The earnings of the company for the six months ending June 30, 1902, covering the operations of 16 miles of road were: gross, $29,305; net, $13,491.

President and General Manager, C. S. Horton, Williamsport, Pa.; Vice-President, E. C. Hoyt; Secretary, M. F. Hammond, New York; Treasurer, A. E. Botchford; Assistant Secretary, A. W. Mallinson; Auditor, R. E. King, Williamsport, Pa.

Directors—C. S. Horton, A. E. Botchford, A. T. Thompson, Williamsport, Pa.; E. C. Hoyt, John J. Lapham, A. Augustus Healy, Eugene Horton, M. F. Hammond, L. H. Lapham, New York; J. A. Hill, Powell, Pa.; F. H. Goodyear, Buffalo.

Main office, Government place, Williamsport, Pa.; operating office, Towanda, Pa. Annual meeting, at Williamsport, Pa., January 12.

---

## SUSQUEHANNA, BLOOMSBURG & BERWICK RAILROAD CO.

A corporation formed under the laws of Pennsylvania, July 31, 1902. The company is a reorganization of the Wilkes-Barre & Western Railroad.

Road owned, Watsontown, Pa., to Orangeville, 31 miles; under construction, Eyersgrove to Berwick, 19½ miles. Locomotives, 6; passenger cars, 6.

Stock......Par $50..........................Authorized, $1,000,000......Issued, $1,000,000

The company has no preferred stock. Stock is transferred by the treasurer of the company, Williamsport, Pa. Registrar, Fidelity Insurance, Trust & Safe Deposit Co., Philadelphia.

FUNDED DEBT.

1st mort., 5 per cent., due Oct., 1952, April and Oct................................ $330,000

The 1st mortgage is for $700,000. The balance of the authorized issue can only be issued at the rate of $15,000 per mile of completed road. Trustee and agent for payment of interest, Fidelity Insurance, Trust & Safe Deposit Co, Philadelphia.

President, J. Henry Cochran, Williamsport, Pa.; Vice-President, Frederick H. Eaton, New York; Secretary and Treasurer, Charles Cochran, Watsontown, Pa.

Directors—J. Henry Cochran, Eugene R. Payne, S. T. McCormick, Williamsport, Pa.; Frederick H. Eaton, New York; J. L. Mitchell, Philadelphia; C. H. Dickerman, Milton, Pa.; Edward B. Tustin, Bloomsburg, Pa.

Main office, Williamsport, Pa. Annual meeting, first Monday in May, at Williamsport, Pa.

---

## SYRACUSE, BINGHAMTON & NEW YORK RAILROAD CO.

(Controlled by Delaware, Lackawanna & Western Railroad Co.)

Road owned, Binghamton, N. Y., to Syracuse, 81 miles.

The Delaware, Lackawanna & Western Railroad Co. owns $1,901,900 of the stock of this company.

Stock......Par $100..........................Authorized, $2,500,000......Issued, $2,500,000

Stock is transferred at the company's office, 26 Exchange place, New York.

Dividends are paid quarterly, 2 per cent each in February (1), May, August and November.

FUNDED DEBT.

Consolidated mort., 7 per cent., due Oct., 1906, April and Oct....................... $1,966,000

The bonds are guaranteed by Delaware, Lackawanna & Western Railroad Co.

President, William H. Truesdale; Secretary and Treasurer, Fred F. Chambers, New York.

Main office, 26 Exchange place, New York. Annual meeting, first Wednesday in December.

## TEMISCOUATA RAILWAY CO.

A corporation formed under the laws of the Dominion of Canada, October 10, 1885.

Road owned, Riviere du Loup, Que., to Connors, N. B., 91 miles. The road connects with the Intercolonial Railway at Riviere du Loup, Que., and with the Canadian Pacific Railway at Edmundston, N. B. Locomotives, 5; passenger cars, 9; freight cars, 101.

This road was completed and opened in 1889. The Province of Quebec guaranteed interest on the bonds for ten years, and when the guarantee lapsed in 1899 the bondholders assumed possession of the property. The bondholders' organization is the Temiscouata Railway Bondholders' Committee, Ltd., H. R. Boyce, Secretary, Winchester House, Old Broad street, London.

Stock......Par $100..........................Authorized, $1,000,000......Issued, $1,000,000

FUNDED DEBT.

1st mort., 5 per cent., due 1908.................................................. $2,258,133

The 1st mortgage is authorized at the rate of $20,000 per mile.

In the year ending June 30, 1902, the gross earnings were $126,027; net, $27,050.

President, Frank Grundy; Vice-President, John H. Walsh, Sherbrooke, Can.; Secretary and General Manager, David B. Lindsay, Riviere du Loup, Can.

Directors—Frank Grundy, John H. Walsh, Andrew Steel, Sherbrooke, Can.; William Cook, Archibald H. Cook, A. Laurie, W. Noble Campbell, Quebec.

Main office, Riviere du Loup, Can. Annual meeting, first Tuesday in December, at company's office, Quebec.

## TENNESSEE CENTRAL RAILROAD CO.

A corporation formed under the laws of Tennessee, April 15, 1902, under the name of the Nashville & Clarksville Railroad Co., and the name was changed to the present title. The company was a consolidation of the Tennessee Central Railway Co., the Nashville & Knoxville Railroad Co., the Cumberland Plateau Railway Co., and the Kingston Bridge & Terminal Co.

Road owned, Nashville to South Harriman, Tenn., 165 miles; branches, 34 miles; total operated, 199 miles. The Nashville Terminal Co. is controlled by this company. Locomotives, 23; passenger cars, 15; freight cars, 911.

Stock......Par $100..........................Authorized, $8,000,000......Issued, $5,000,000

The stock is to be issued at the rate of $25,000 per mile of completed road. The city of Nashville agreed to subscribe for $1,000,000 of stock at par for the completion of the road to Clarksville, Tenn.

FUNDED DEBT.

| | |
|---|---|
| Tenn. Cent. Ry., 1st mort., 5 per cent., due Jan., 1948, Jan. and July............... | $1,550,000 |
| Nashville & Knoxville, 1st mort., 6 per cent., due May, 1918, May and Nov......... | 1,756,000 |
| New 1st mort., 5 per cent., due July, 1952, Jan. and July......................... | 5,000,000 |
| Nashville Terminal, 1st mort., 5 per cent., due Jan., 1932, Jan. and July........... | 1,000,000 |
| Total ................................................................ | $9,306,000 |

The new 1st mortgage was created in 1902, and is for $8,000,000. Trustee of mortgage, Mercantile Trust Co., St. Louis. Bonds can be issued to the amount of $25,000 per mile, and sufficient are reserved to retire the underlying liens.

President, Jere Baxter; Vice-President, N. C. Chapman; Secretary, W. E. Eastman; Treasurer, E. A. Faulhaber, Nashville, Tenn.

Directors—Jere Baxter; N. C. Chapman, E. R. Richardson, J. T. Lellyett, W. C. Collier, R. M. Dudley, Nashville, Tenn.; J. C. Van Blarcom, St. Louis.

Main office, Nashville. Annual meeting, first Monday in October, at Nashville.

## TERMINAL RAILROAD ASSOCIATION OF ST. LOUIS

This company's property comprises the St. Louis bridge and tunnel, the St. Louis Terminal Railway, the St. Louis Merchants' Bridge and Terminal, the new Union Station in St. Louis, completed in 1894, with belt lines and tracks in both St. Louis and East St. Louis, the Madison, Illinois & St. Louis Railway, and valuable real estate. Also owns East St. Louis Electric Street Railroad. Total length of tracks operated, about 50 miles. In March, 1902, assumed the operation of the East St. Louis & Carondelet Railway, 12 miles. In 1902 acquired the property of the Wiggins Ferry Co., also the St. Louis Belt & Terminal Railway and the Interstate Car Transfer Co. Locomotives, 25; passenger cars, 17; freight and mail equipment, 89.

Company was organized in 1889. In 1893 obtained control of the Merchants' Bridge and Terminal Companies. The old St. Louis Bridge Co. and the Tunnel Railroad were leased in

1881 to the Wabash and Missouri Pacific companies in perpetuity. The leases were assigned to this company. The St. Louis Merchants' Bridge Terminal Railway is controlled by ownership of a majority of stock.

The company is owned by the Cleveland, Cincinnati, Chicago & St. Louis, Louisville & Nashville, St. Louis, Iron Mountain & Southern, Baltimore & Ohio Southwestern, Missouri Pacific, Wabash and Pennsylvania companies. The Pennsylvania acquired its interest in the property in 1902. In December, 1902, the Rock Island and the St. Louis & San Francisco also acquired interests in the association.

Stock......Par $100......................Authorized, $50,000,000.. ...Issued, $50,000,000

The authorized amount of stock was $12,000,000, of which $1,441,000 was issued. In December an increase to $50,000,000 was authorized.

FUNDED DEBT.

| | |
|---|---|
| St. Louis Bridge Co., 1st mort., guar. 7 per cent., due April, 1929, April and Oct..... | $5,000,000 |
| Merchants' Br., 1st mort. (int. only), guar. 6 per cent., due Feb., 1929, Feb. and Aug.. | 2,000,000 |
| St. L. Merch. Br. Terminal, 1st mort., guar. 5 per cent., due Oct., 1930, April and Oct. | 3,500,000 |
| Terminal Railroad Association, 1st mort., 4½ per cent., due Oct., 1939, April and Oct. | 7,000,000 |
| " " " cons. mort., 5 per cent., due Aug., 1944, Feb. and Aug. | 4,600,000 |
| " " " new cons. mort., 4 per cent., due 1953 ............... | 8,000,000 |
| Total.................................................................. | $30,100,000 |

Interest only is guaranteed on Merchants' Bridge 1st mortgage. This company also guarantees 6 per cent. dividends on $2,490,000 1st preferred, 3 per cent. on $3,000,000 2d preferred stock of St. Louis Bridge Co., and 6 per cent. on $1,250,000 stock of the Tunnel Railroad of St. Louis.

Consolidated mortgage is for $12,000,000, of which $7,000,000 is reserved to retire 1sts and $3,500,000 was used to retire old 2ds. Trustees of consolidated mortgage hold as additional security all the stock and bonds ($1,200,000 each) of the St. Louis Terminal Railway.

The new consolidated mortgage is for $50,000,000, sufficient being reserved to retire the old bonds. The issue was created in 1902 to provide for the purchase of the Wiggins Ferry Co. and for extensive additions and improvements.

Controlling companies agree in event of deficit to jointly contribute up to $1,000,000 per annum to provide for interest, etc.

EARNINGS.

| | Gross. | Net. | Charges. | | Surplus. |
|---|---|---|---|---|---|
| 1893...................... | $1,862,123 | $1,183,240 | $1,112,554 | | $70,685 |
| 1894...................... | 1,508,912 | 1,099,350 | 1,143,376 | Def. | 144,026 |
| 1895...................... | 1,757,781 | 1,376,070 | 1,370,397 | | 5,673 |
| 1896...................... | 1,799,207 | 1,378,653 | 1,548,756 | Def. | 170,103 |
| 1897...................... | 1,862,228 | 1,520,103 | 1,411,918 | | 108,185 |
| 1898...................... | 1,997,753 | 1,611,814 | 1,375,383 | | 236,430 |
| 1899...................... | 2,119,209 | 1,708,896 | 1,428,343 | | 280,553 |
| 1900...................... | 2,127,090 | 1,677,541 | 1,431,728 | | 245,813 |
| 1901...................... | 2,385,309 | 1,839,956 | 1,402,642 | | 437,314 |

The new Union Station is rented to the various railroad companies entering St. Louis for $325,000 a year, the payments being apportioned on a wheelage basis.

President, Julius S. Walsh; Vice-President and General Manager, W. S. McChesney, Jr.; Secretary, James Hanna, St. Louis; Treasurer, Amos H. Calef, New York.

Directors—Julius S. Walsh, C. G. Warner, Joseph Ramsey, Jr., Russell Harding, St. Louis; E. F. Osborn, W. M. Greene, Cincinnati; Milton H. Smith, Louisville.

Main office, St. Louis. Interest payable at offices of J. P. Morgan & Co., New York, and J. S. Morgan & Co., London. Annual meeting, first Tuesday in March.

## TERRE HAUTE & INDIANAPOLIS RAILROAD CO.

(Controlled by Pennsylvania Railroad Co.)

Road owned, Indianapolis, Ind., to Illinois State line, near Terre Haute, 80 miles; coal branches, 43 miles; total, 123 miles; leased, St. Louis, Vandalia & Terre Haute, 158 miles (on joint account with Pittsburg, Cincinnati & St. Louis, at 30 per cent. of gross earnings and 1st and 2d mortgage bonds guaranteed); controlled, Terre Haute & Peoria, 174 miles. The Indiana & Lake Michigan, 39 miles, was controlled, but was reorganized in 1899 as the St. Joseph, South Bend & Southern Railroad. The Terre Haute & Logansport Railroad, 182 miles, also controlled, was sold under foreclosure in November, 1898, and reorganized as the Terre Haute & Logansport Railway in the interest of the Pennsylvania Railroad. Locomotives, 114; passenger cars, 96; freight cars, 4,445.

The company owns about one-fifth the stock of the St. Louis, Vandalia & Terre Haute. The report includes only the 123 miles owned. In 1892 the Terre Haute & Peoria was leased. In 1893 the Pennsylvania Railroad acquired a large amount of the stock of this company with control of the system.

This road is generally advertised as the Vandalia Line, and is best known by that name.

Stock......Par $50..........................Authorized, $2,000,000......Issued, $1,988,150

Dividends of 8 per cent. per annum were formerly paid on the stock. In 1885 they were reduced to 6 per cent. The semi-annual dividend of 3 per cent. February 1, 1894, was the last paid.

FUNDED DEBT.

| | |
|---|---|
| Consol. mort., now 1st, 5 per cent., due July, 1925, Jan. and July | $1,900,000 |
| New consol. mort., 5 per cent., due July, 1925, Jan. and July | 600,000 |
| Total | $2,500,000 |

Default of interest on leased line bonds occurred in July and September, 1896, the unfavorable traffic conditions, the drain caused by the branches and the accumulation of a floating debt of several hundred thousand dollars embarrassing the company severely. In November, 1896, on complaint of New York bondholders' committee, Volney T. Malott of Indianapolis was appointed Receiver. This step, it was stated, was taken in view of the fact that Terre Haute & Peoria was not earning expenses and rentals and it would be unjust to other creditors to make that company a preferred creditor. Interest on the bonds of this company has been regularly met under the receivership.

EARNINGS.

Year ending October 31.

| | Div. Paid. | Gross. | Net. |
|---|---|---|---|
| 1892-93 | 6 | $1,307,406 | $329,349 |
| 1893-94 | 3 | 1,129,974 | 327,774 |
| 1894-95 | .. | 1,236,526 | 282,758 |
| 1895-96 | .. | 1,213,573 | 196,691 |
| 1896-97 | .. | 1,166,387 | 340,579 |
| 1897-98 | .. | 1,381,453 | 477,020 |
| 1898-99 | .. | 1,501,589 | 588,859 |
| 1899-00 | .. | 1,620,016 | 589,576 |
| 1900-01 | .. | 1,558,216 | 771,967 |
| 1901-02 | .. | 1,779,433 | 682,168 |

In 1893, after payment of fixed charges, dividends and losses on leased lines, the deficit was $93,097; in 1894, deficit after such payments, $50,204; in 1895, deficit $52,266; in 1896, deficit $208,105; in 1897, surplus $49,999; in 1898, surplus $243,839; in 1899, surplus $388,282; in 1900, surplus $336,376; in 1901, surplus $614,030.

Receiver, Volney T. Malott, Indianapolis; President, James McCrea; Vice-President, James J. Turner, Pittsburg; Treasurer, Robert B. Thompson; Secretary, George E. Farrington, Terre Haute, Ind.; Assistant Secretary, W. G. Phelps, Pittsburg.

Directors—William R. McKeen, Herman Hulman, Terre Haute, Ind.; James McCrea, Joseph Wood, James J. Turner, E. B. Taylor, S. B. Liggett, Pittsburg.

Main office, Terre Haute, Ind. Fiscal Agent, Farmers' Loan & Trust Co., New York. Annual meeting, Wednesday after second Tuesday in January.

## TERRE HAUTE & LOGANSPORT RAILWAY CO.

(Controlled by Pennsylvania Railroad Co.)

In November, 1898, road was sold under foreclosure proceedings and purchased by representatives of the Pennsylvania Railroad, in the interest of which the property was reorganized, with a change of name from railroad to railway.

Road owned, South Bend to Rockville, Ind., 159 miles; leased, Rockville to Terre Haute, 23 miles; total operated, 182 miles. Locomotives, 27; passenger cars, 19; freight cars, 1,138.

Stock......Par $50..........................Authorized, $2,000,000......Issued, $2,000,000

FUNDED DEBT.

| | |
|---|---|
| 1st mort., 6 per cent., due Jan., 1910, Jan. and July | $500,000 |
| Convertible debentures, 4 per cent., due 1948, June and Dec | 1,331,500 |
| Total | $1,881,500 |

There was a 4 per cent. mortgage created under the reorganization for $2,000,000, of which $500,000 are reserved to redeem the 1st mortgage bonds. The balance of unissued bonds may be used for improvements. The 4 per cent. debentures given above are convertible into these bonds. The old extension 6 per cent. mortgage bonds under which the road was foreclosed were $1,000,000. They were mostly held by the Pennsylvania Railroad Co. and the Pennsylvania Company.

EARNINGS.

Year ending October 31.

| | Gross. | Rent. and Charges. | Deficit. |
|---|---|---|---|
| 1894-95 | $665,106 | $166,276 | $61,255 |
| 1895-96 | 595,719 | 148,92 | 67,403 |
| 1896-97 | 622,415 | 155,604 | Sur. 1,230 |
| 1897-98 | 686,582 | ...... | ...... |
| 1899 (year ending December 31) | 766,564 | 138,318 | " 9,322 |
| 1900 ( " " " ) | 817,457 | 136,057 | " 22,218 |
| 1901 ( " " " ) | 897,659 | 135,100 | " 56,884 |
| 1902 ( " " " ) | 1,093,746 | 167,388 | " 16,573 |

The Terre Haute & Indianapolis leased the property, paying 25 per cent. of the gross earnings and guaranteeing the 1st mortgage bonds. Interest due July 1, 1896, was defaulted, and road passed into Receiver's hands, foreclosure and reorganization ensuing in 1898.

President, James McCrea, ; Vice-President, James J. Turner, Pittsburg; Treasurer, R. B. Thompson, Terre Haute, Ind.; Secretary, S. B. Liggett, Pittsburg.

Main office, Terre Haute, Ind. Annual meeting, first Monday in February.

## TERRE HAUTE & PEORIA RAILROAD CO.

Road owned and operated, Terre Haute, Ind., to Peoria, Ill., 174 miles, of which 28 miles are leased. Locomotives, 14; passenger cars, 9; freight cars, 480.

Formerly known as the Illinois Midland. Passed into hands of Receiver September, 1875. Sold in foreclosure September 30, 1886, and reorganized March, 1887. In 1892 the Terre Haute & Indianapolis leased the property, agreeing to pay 30 per cent. of gross earnings as rental and to make the amount sufficient to pay all interest charges. In 1892 a new 1st mortgage for $2,500,000 was created, guaranteed by the Terre Haute & Indianapolis. These bonds were to retire existing debt and to provide for equipment. Interest due September, 1896, was defaulted. Bondholders are represented by a committee composed of Mark T. Cox, James A. Blair and James W. Paul, Jr. Depositories, New York Security & Trust Co., New York, and Drexel & Co., Philadelphia. See statement of Terre Haute & Indianapolis above. Litigation concerning the validity of the guarantee was instituted, the United States Circuit Court of Appeals deciding in favor of the guarantee. The case has been appealed.

Stock.....Par $100....Authorized { com., $1,837,400 / pref., 1,926,800 } Issued { com., $1,837,400 / pref., 1,926,800 } $3,764,200

FUNDED DEBT.

| | |
|---|---|
| 1st mort., 5 per cent., due March, 1927, March and Sept. | $33,000 |
| 1st con. mort., 5 per cent., due Sept., 1942, March and Sept. | 2,197,000 |
| Total | $2,230,000 |

The Terre Haute & Indianapolis owns $544,200 of the preferred and $1,388,000 of the common stock.

EARNINGS.

| Year ending October 31. | Gross. | Net. |
|---|---|---|
| 1894-95 | $445,483 | $67,543 |
| 1895-96 | 403,559 | 18,663 |
| 1896-97 | 395,622 | 26,176 |
| 1897-98 | 474,346 | 60,477 |
| 1898-99 | 442,330 | 70,940 |
| 1899-00 | 495,086 | 60,025 |
| 1900-01 | 560,621 | 98,793 |
| 1901-02 | 559,086 | 40,987 |

In 1893 loss to lessee was $102,158; in 1894, $109,630. In 1895 rental was $133,645; loss to lessee, $66,102; 1896, rental, $121,068; loss, $102,405; 1897, rental, $118,686; loss, $92,510; 1898, rental, $142,304; loss, $81,827; 1899, rental, $132,699; loss, $61,759; 1900, rental, $148,556; loss, $88,501; 1901, rental, $168,186; loss, $69,393; 1902, rental, $167,726; loss, $126,739.

President, James McCrea; Vice-President, James J. Turner, Pittsburg; Secretary, George E. Farrington; Treasurer, Robert B. Thompson, Terre Haute, Ind.

Main office, Terre Haute, Ind. Annual meeting in January.

## TEXAS & NEW ORLEANS RAILROAD CO.

Road owned, Houston, Tex., to Sabine River, 112 miles; Sabine Pass to Nacogdoches, Tex., 153 miles; Jacksonville, Tex., to Dallas, Tex., 115 miles; branch, 13 miles; total, 393 miles; owned jointly, ½ mile. In 1899 this company acquired the Louisiana Western Extension Railroad and Texas Trunk Railroad, and authorized the extension to connect latter with the two former roads, making a through line from Dallas, Tex., to Sabine Pass, Tex. The Texas Transportation Company, Houston to Clinton, Tex., 8 miles, was acquired in 1896. Locomotives, 45; passenger cars, 46; freight cars, 2,738.

Stock......Par $100..........................Authorized, $5,000,000......Issued, $5,000,000

Transfer agency, 120 Broadway, New York. Registrar, Mercantile Trust Co., New York.

FUNDED DEBT.

| | |
|---|---|
| 1st mort., 7 per cent., due Aug., 1905, Feb. and Aug. | $915,000 |
| Sabine Division, 1st mort., 6 per cent., due Sept., 1912, March and Sept. | 2,575,000 |
| Consolidated mort., 6 per cent., due July, 1943, Jan. and July | 1,620,000 |
| Dallas Division, 1st mort., 4 per cent., due Aug., 1930, Feb. and Aug. | 2,455,000 |
| State of Texas school fund debt, 6 per cent | 342,232 |
| Total | $7,907,232 |

EARNINGS.

| Year ending June 30. | Gross. | Net. |
|---|---|---|
| 1897-98 | $1,491,831 | $538,910 |
| 1898-99 | 1,864,921 | 766,828 |
| 1899-00 | 1,891,302 | 583,304 |
| 1900-01 | 2,709,185 | 1,007,863 |
| 1901-02 | 3,024,602 | 490,040 |

President, Edward H. Harriman, New York; Vice-President, W. G. Van Vleck; Treasurer, E. C. Cushman; Secretary, C. B. Seger, Houston, Tex.

Main office, Houston, Tex. Annual meeting, second Monday in January.

## TEXAS & PACIFIC RAILWAY CO.

Road owned, New Orleans, La., to Sierra Blanca, Tex., 1,060 miles; Marshall, Tex., via Texarkana Junction, Tex., to Fort Worth, 316 miles; branches, 240 miles; total owned, 1,616 miles; trackage, Sierra Blanca to El Paso, Tex., 92 miles; total operated, 1,208 miles. In 1899 a branch from New Roads to Bougere, La., 25 miles, was built, and in 1900 a branch of 22 miles south from Donaldsonville was built. The company owns all the stock of the New Orleans Pacific, Shreveport to New Orleans, with branches to Baton Rouge and Plaquemine, 344 miles. Locomotives, 277; passenger cars, 158; freight cars, 6,047.

Stock......Par $100...................... ...Authorized, $50,000,000......Issued, $38,760,510

Stock is transferred at the company's office, 195 Broadway, New York.

FUNDED DEBT.

| | |
|---|---|
| 1st mort., Eastern Division, 6 per cent., due March, 1905, March and Sept. | $2,940,000 |
| 1st cons. mort., 5 per cent., due June, 2000, June and Dec. | 21,992,000 |
| 2d cons. income mort. (non-cumulative), 5 per cent., due 2000, March 1 | 24,980,000 |
| Louisiana Division branch, 1st mort., 5 per cent., due Jan., 1931, Jan. and July | 3,161,000 |
| Total | $53,073,000 |

The company defaulted and Receivers were appointed in 1885. The road was foreclosed in 1887 and reorganized 1888, under plan given in detail in MANUAL for 1888. Plan provided for retirement of all bonds subsequent to the Eastern Division 1st mortgage and creation of new firsts and incomes. Stock paid assessment of $10 per share, which, together with net earnings under receivership, was applied to reconstruction and betterment of property. The 2d mortgage trustee, if interest had not been paid on the bonds, had the right to take possession of the property after March, 1892. No interest was paid on the 2ds until March, 1900, when 1½ per cent. was paid out of the earnings of 1899. On March 1, 1901, 4 per cent. was paid on the 2ds out of the earnings of 1900. On March 1, 1902, 5 per cent. was paid on these bonds from the earnings of 1901.

In July, 1899, the St. Louis, Iron Mountain & Southern Railroad Co. offered to holders of the 2d income bonds to exchange same at 65 for new St. Louis, Iron Mountain & Southern Railroad 4 per cent. bonds, a syndicate offering to purchase any of the latter received in exchange at 85. All but $150,000 of the 2ds were exchanged under this arrangement. See statement of Missouri Pacific.

The company's land grant and lands were conveyed to an organization called the Texas Pacific Land Trust for the purpose of retiring the old land grant and income bonds. See statement of that company.

The company has $7,000 of old bonds not yet redeemed under the reorganization and $140,272 of income interest scrip retirable under the provisions of the agreement with the old income bondholders in the reorganization. The outstanding equipment car trust obligations are $1,863,406.

EARNINGS.

| | Gross. | Per Cent. Oper. Ex. | Net. | Charges. | Surplus. |
|---|---|---|---|---|---|
| 1893 | $7,334,294 | 71.14 | $2,030,533 | $1,370,617 | $527,097 |
| 1894 | 7,353,013 | 71.95 | 2,062,639 | 1,588,216 | 474,423 |
| 1895 | 7,015,309 | 73.96 | 1,826,872 | 1,573,732 | 339,463 |
| 1896 | 6,825,145 | 75.51 | 1,567,090 | 1,360,815 | 206,274 |
| 1897 | 7,588,648 | 71.34 | 2,116,197 | 1,410,335 | 705,862 |
| 1898 | 8,006,503 | 71.29 | 2,304,559 | 1,384,085 | 920,474 |
| 1899 | 8,300,186 | 70.47 | 2,581,895 | 2,509,911 | 71,982 |
| 1900 | 9,751,122 | 67.50 | 3,358,668 | 3,150,082 | 208,586 |
| 1901 | 11,769,941 | 68.26 | 4,098,626 | 2,611,648 | 1,486,977 |
| 1902 | 11,236,601 | 68.99 | 3,632,141 | 4,121,377 | 489,256 |

In 1895, $184,491 was expended for betterments, etc., out of income, leaving balance to credit of income for the year $154,971; in 1896, $212,286 was spent for improvements, etc., leaving a deficit of $6,011; in 1897, $237,893 was paid for equipment, etc., and $44,384 of bad debts charged off, leaving a net surplus of $447,969; in 1898, paid for equipment, improvements, etc., $889,320, leaving a net surplus of $31,161; in 1899, surplus over betterments, etc., $71,982; in 1900, surplus, $208,586; in 1901, surplus, $325,071. In 1902, the charges include $2,207,358 for improvements and there was also paid $1,161,900 as interest on the income bonds, making a total deficit for the year of $489,256.

President, George J. Gould, New York; 1st Vice-President, L. S. Thorne, Dallas, Tex.; 2d Vice-President, Frank Jay Gould; Treasurer and Secretary, C. E. Satterlee, New York.

Directors—Russell Sage, A. Lawrence Hopkins, George J. Gould, Edwin Gould, Samuel Sloan, John T. Terry, Charles M. McGhee, C. E. Satterlee, Thomas T. Eckert, Howard Gould, Frank Jay Gould, Louis Fitzgerald, Winslow S. Pierce, John P. Munn, Robert M. Gallaway, New York; L. S. Thorne, Dallas, Tex.

Main office, Dallas, Tex.; New York office, 195 Broadway. Annual meeting, third Wednesday in March. Books close as directors may elect.

---

## TEXAS CENTRAL RAILROAD CO.

Road owned, Waco to Stamford, Tex., 227 miles; total operated, 227 miles. In 1899 an extension from Albany was begun, of which 40 miles was completed in 1900. Locomotives, 15; passenger cars, 18; freight cars, 254.

This road was originally built and controlled by the Houston & Texas Central. Receivers appointed April, 1885. Property sold in foreclosure 1891 and purchased by committee for bondholders. A line 52 miles long, from Garrett to Roberts, formerly included in this road, turned over to the holders of the bonds of that line, and is now known as the Texas Midland.

Stock...Par $100....Authorized { com., $2,675,000 / pref., 1,325,000 } Issued { com., $2,675,000 / pref., 1,325,000 } $4,000,000

Transfer Agent, Farmers' Loan & Trust Co., New York.

Annual dividends were paid on preferred stock at the rate of 3 per cent. in 1896, 1897 and 1898. In 1899-1900 4 per cent. was paid. The annual dividend paid January 15, 1901, was 5 per cent. In July, 1901, the payment of semi-annual dividends of 2½ per cent., January and July, was begun on the preferred. On July 15, 1901, 2½ per cent. was paid on the common and 2½ per cent. in January, 1902. Dividends are paid of 2½ per cent. each in January and July.

FUNDED DEBT.

| | |
|---|---|
| 1st mort., 5 per cent., due April, 1923, April and Oct. | $500,000 |
| 1st mort., 4 per cent., due April, 1923, April and Oct. | 150,000 |
| Total | $650,000 |

The 1st mortgage is for $2,000,000, and was authorized at the rate of $15,000 per mile to retire existing indebtedness and to provide for extensions and improvements. The company holds $650,000 of the bonds in its treasury. The rate on further issues of these bonds can be changed.

| EARNINGS. | Gross. | Net. |
|---|---|---|
| 1895 | $317,162 | $111,786 |
| 1896 | 293,415 | 84,288 |
| 1897 | 344,531 | 133,439 |
| 1897-98 (year ending June 30) | 364,766 | 147,378 |
| 1898-99 ( " " " ) | 394,402 | 165,870 |
| 1899-00 ( " " " ) | 375,573 | 129,615 |
| 1900-01 ( " " " ) | 707,590 | 265,786 |
| 1901-02 ( " " " ) | 593,668 | 160,519 |

In 1895, surplus over charges, $90,786, out of which $63,197 was spent for improvements. In 1896, balance after dividends and $28,790 for improvements was $60. In 1897, improvements, $69,405; balance over dividends, $7,092. In 1897-98, improvements, $64,519; balance over dividends, $19,883; in 1898-99, balance over dividends, $39,814; in 1899-1900, balance over dividends, $29,994. In 1901, balance, $177,314, and in 1902, $1,731.

President, Henry K. McHarg, New York; Vice-President and General Manager, Charles Hamilton; Secretary, H. H. Marache; Treasurer, Edward Rotan, East Waco, Tex.; Assistant Secretary and Treasurer, D. C. Moran, New York.

Directors—Henry K. McHarg, Walton Ferguson, Amedee D. Moran, New York; C. Hamilton, J. S. McLendon, Edward Rotan, Waco, Tex.; George T. Reynolds, Albany, Tex.

Main office, East Waco, Tex.; New York office, 54 William street. Annual meeting, second Wednesday in February.

## TOLEDO & OHIO CENTRAL RAILWAY CO.

Road owned, Toledo to Bremen, O., 173 miles; New Lexington to Corning, O., 13 miles; Whitemore to Thurston, O., 145 miles; Peoria, O., to St. Mary's, O., 58 miles; branch, 11 miles; total owned, 400 miles; used under trackage, 36 miles; total operated, 436 miles. The company also has a controlling interest in the Kanawha & Michigan Railway, Corning, O., to Gauley, W. Va., 154 miles. See statement of the latter company. The Columbus Northwestern Railway, 58 miles, was acquired in 1901, and is now the St. Mary's Division of this company. Locomotives, 85; passenger cars, 39; freight cars, 7,140.

In December, 1899, it was announced that the Hocking Valley Railway had acquired control of this property, capitalists identified with the Chesapeake & Ohio being also interested in the matter. The road is, however, to be operated separately under its own organization. See below for terms of exchange of stocks.

Stock...Par $100....Authorized { com., $6,500,000 / pref., 3,708,000 } Issued { com., $6,500,000 / pref., 3,708,000 } $10,208,000

The preferred stock is entitled to a priority of 5 per cent., non-cumulative, and a further preference of 2 per cent. after the payment of 5 per cent. on common stock.

In 1891 common stock was increased from $1,849,000 to $4,849,000. In 1892 further increase to $6,500,000 was authorized to purchase the Toledo, Columbus & Cincinnati road and to build from Columbus to Ridgeway.

Transfer Agent, J. P. Morgan & Co., New York. Registrar, Central Trust Co., New York.

From 1890 to 1895 5 per cent. per annum was paid on the preferred stock. In 1896 3¾ per cent. was paid, but the July quarterly dividend was the last one paid. On the common stock 2 per cent. was paid in 1891, 4 per cent. in 1892, 2 per cent. in 1893; none since November 25, 1893.

FUNDED DEBT.

| | |
|---|---|
| 1st mort., 5 per cent., due July, 1935, Jan. and July | $3,000,000 |
| Western Division, 1st mort., 5 per cent., due Oct., 1935, April and Oct. | 2,500,000 |
| Gen. mort., 5 per cent., due June, 1935, June and Dec. | 2,000,000 |
| Car trusts, 5, 6 and 7 per cent. | 1,196,000 |
| St. Mary's Div., 1st mort., 4 per cent. due Feb., 1951, Feb. and Aug. | 425,000 |
| " " 1st pref. inc. bds., 4 per cent. non-cum., due Feb., 1951, int. Oct. 1 | 500,000 |
| Total | $9,621,000 |

Company's interest in Kanawha & Michigan stock was acquired in 1890, costing $2,365,000. Company guarantees principal and interest of $2,469,000 4 per cent. 1st mortgage Kanawha & Michigan bonds. The company also guaranteed interest on $300,000 Toledo & Ohio Central Extension Railway Co.'s bonds. This company and the Hocking Valley Railway Co. jointly guarantee the $2,750,000 5 per cent. bonds due 1951, interest January and July, of the Kanawha & Hocking Coal and Coke Co.

In 1899, as above stated, the Hocking Valley Railway Co., which in its reorganization had reserved $5,000,000 each of its preferred and common stock to absorb the Toledo & Ohio Central Railway, acquired a controlling interest in the stock of the latter. The shares purchased were stated in June, 1901, to be all but $54,100 of the common and $11,000 of the preferred. The minority stockholders of the Toledo & Ohio Central were offered the same terms as the majority, namely, to exchange their holdings for Hocking Valley stock of the same class on the basis of $70 of Hocking Valley for $100 of this company's shares.

EARNINGS.

Year ending June 30.

| | Gross. | Per Cent. Op. Exp. | Net. | Charges. | Surplus. |
|---|---|---|---|---|---|
| 1892-93 | $1,963,651 | .... | $704,872 | $320,540 | $384,331 |
| 1893-94 | 1,648,538 | 68.21 | 577,777 | 405,338 | 172,439 |
| 1894-95 | 1,903,990 | 68.19 | 615,005 | 424,265 | 190,740 |
| 1895-96 | 1,944,503 | 68.23 | 627,377 | 469,561 | 157,815 |
| 1896-97 | 1,750,979 | 73.40 | 473,912 | 467,475 | 6,437 |
| 1897-98 | 1,779,615 | 70.00 | 544,174 | 464,536 | 79,637 |
| 1898-99 | 1,897,867 | 72.99 | 626,268 | 497,957 | 128,311 |
| 1899-00 | 2,368,971 | 68.56 | 846,090 | 484,535 | 361,555 |
| 1900-01 | 2,571,721 | 75.30 | 642,513 | 432,158 | 210,355 |
| 1901-02 | 2,877,658 | 79.08 | 616,770 | 477,166 | 139,604 |

The results of the payment of dividends were: in 1892-93, surplus, $57,195; in 1893-94, deficit, $72,243; in 1894-95, surplus, $5,340; 1895-96, deficit, $112,484; total credit income account, June 30, 1896, $588,250. In 1896-97, after paying 1¼ per cent. on preferred, $46,350, and charging off $42,875 for various accounts, the credit balance was $505,463. In 1897-98 no dividends were paid and credit balance was $562,799. In 1898-99 credit balance was reducd by charging off $600,000 to depreciation, making balance $79,273.

Chairman, Decatur Axtell, Richmond, Va.; President, Nicholas Monsarrat, Columbus, O.; 1st Vice-President, Charles G. Hickox, Cleveland; 2d Vice-President and Secretary, J. M. Ferris, Toledo; Treasurer, L. D. Kelley, Toledo, O.

Directors—Decatur Axtell, Richmond, Va.; C. Ledyard Blair, George M. Cumming, Charles Steele, New York; Stevenson Burke, Charles G. Hickox, Ralph W. Hickox, James H. Hoyt, Thomas Johnston, Cleveland; Nicholas Monsarrat, Columbus, O.

Main office, Toledo, O. Annual meeting, first Monday in September. Books close thirty days previous.

## TOLEDO, PEORIA & WESTERN RAILWAY CO.

(Controlled by Pennsylvania Co.)

Road owned, Indiana State line to Warsaw, Ill., 220 miles; branch, 10 miles; trackage, 17 miles; total operated, 247 miles. Locomotives, 34; passenger cars, 29; freight cars, 1,578.

In December, 1893, a controlling interest in this company was acquired by the Pennsylvania and the Chicago, Burlington & Quincy Railroad Cos. jointly.

Stock......Par $100..........................Authorized, $4,500,000......Issued, $4,076,900

Transfer Agent, Farmers' Loan & Trust Co., New York. Registrar, Corn Exchange Bank, New York.

FUNDED DEBT.

| | |
|---|---|
| 1st mort., 4 per cent., due July, 1917, Jan. and July | $4,895,000 |
| Ten-year debenture scrip, due Jan., 1905, 5 per cent | 220,275 |
| Equipment trusts | 150,623 |
| Total | $5,265,898 |

This road was formerly a part of the Wabash system, but was taken possession of by the first mortgage trustees June 11, 1885, foreclosed and reorganized by bondholders.

In July, 1894, interest on the 1st mortgage bonds was defaulted. It was proposed to fund it and two succeeding coupons for $5 cash and $15 in 5 per cent. 10-year scrip, the amount authorized being $220,275. All the bondholders accepted these terms. In January, 1896, payment of coupons in cash was resumed.

EARNINGS.—Year ending June 30.

| | Gross. | Net. | Charges. | Surplus. |
|---|---|---|---|---|
| 1894-95 | $953,238 | $171,094 | $239,722 | Def. $68,627 |
| 1895-96 | 1,010,270 | 220,788 | 211,700 | Sur. 9,088 |
| 1896-97 | 888,881 | 184,475 | 228,847 | Def. 44,372 |
| 1897-98 | 982,650 | 227,388 | 221,821 | Sur. 5,567 |
| 1898-99 | 976,657 | 224,413 | 224,062 | 350 |
| 1899-00 | 1,077,904 | 227,778 | 227,033 | 745 |
| 1900-01 | 1,157,078 | 228,353 | 227,090 | 1,262 |
| 1901-02 | 1,152,033 | 228,303 | 226,048 | 2,255 |

President and Treasurer, E. F. Leonard; Secretary and Auditor, E. D. Usner, Peoria, Ill.
Directors—E. F. Leonard, Peoria, Ill.; W. W. Baldwin, Burlington, Ia.; C. M. Dawes, Franklin H. Head, Chicago; Joseph Wood, Pittsburg.
Main office, Peoria, Ill. Annual meeting, second Wednesday in September. Books close thirty days previous.

---

## TOLEDO, ST. LOUIS & WESTERN RAILWAY CO.

A reorganization of the Toledo, St. Louis & Kansas City Railroad Co., foreclosed in 1900. The present company took possession of the property August 1, 1900.
Road owned, main line, Toledo, O., to East St. Louis, Ill., 451 miles. Locomotives, 82; passenger cars, 33; freight cars, 3,141.

Stock...Par $100...Authorized { com., $10,000,000 / pref., 10,000,000 } Issued { com., $10,000,000 / pref., 10,000,000 } $20,000,000

The preferred stock is 4 per cent., non-cumulative. Both classes of stock are held in a voting trust for five years; trustees, Frederic P. Olcott, Thomas H. Hubbard and William A. Read. Trustees have the right to sell the stock subject to the approval of a majority of the holders of each class of stock..
Transfer Agent, Central Realty Bond & Trust Co., New York. Registrar, Central Trust Co., New York.

FUNDED DEBT.

| | |
|---|---|
| Prior lien mort., 3½ per cent., due July, 1925, Jan. and July | $9,000,000 |
| 1st mort., 4 per cent., due April, 1950, April and Oct. | 6,500,000 |
| Total | $15,500,000 |

The prior lien mortgage is for $10,000,000, of which $1,000,000 was reserved to be used after January 1, 1902, for improvements at the rate of $250,000 per annum. The 1st mortgage bond issue may be increased $10,000,000 to retire the prior lien bonds.
In May, 1893, S. R. Callaway, then president of the old company, was appointed Receiver, and interest due June 1, 1893, was defaulted. Nearly all the old 1st mortgage 6 per cent. bonds, of which there were $9,000,000, were deposited with Continental Trust Co., New York. The old company had $5,805,000 4 per cent. non-cumulative and non-voting preferred stock and $11,250,000 common stock. Preferred stockholders had a committee, of which J. M. Quigley, New York, is Chairman. In 1896 United States Circuit Court decided that preferred stock had no lien. Case was appealed and litigation continued. Foreclosure was ordered in April, 1898, but appeal was taken and final decision was delayed. Sale was finally ordered and made March 27, 1900, the 1st mortgage bondholders' committee being the purchasers. They transferred the property to a new committee, Frederic P. Olcott, New York, Chairman, and a new plan was submitted and carried out for the reorganization.
The plan issued January 12, 1900, provided for a capitalization consisting of $10,000,000 3½ per cent. prior lien bonds; $10,000,000 4 per cent. 1st mortgage bonds; $10,000,000 4 per cent. non-cumulative preferred stock and $10,000,000 common stock. The old bonds were exchanged for 100 per cent. in new prior lien bonds, 62½ per cent. in new 1st mortgage 4s, and 30 per cent. in new preferred stock. The old preferred, on payment of an assessment of $20 per share, was exchanged for 75 per cent. in new preferred and 20 per cent. in new common. The old common, on payment of $12 per share, received 25 per cent. in new preferred and 75 per cent. in new common.

EARNINGS.

Year ending June 30.

| | Gross. | Per Cent. Op. Exp. | Net. | Charges. | Surplus. |
|---|---|---|---|---|---|
| 1899-00 | $1,940,378 | 80.45 | $379,297 | ...... | ...... |
| 1900-01 | 2,490,566 | 72.27 | 696,955 | $614,400 | $82,555 |
| 1901-02 | 2,640,880 | 72.53 | 735,090 | 679,400 | 55,690 |

For earnings under the receivership see MANUAL for 1902.
The following presents the comparative freight traffic statistics of the company:

| | Average Mileage. | Total Tonage. | Tons Carried One Mile. | Freight Density. | Rate per Ton per Mile. | Earnings per Train Mile. | Average Tons per Train. |
|---|---|---|---|---|---|---|---|
| 1900-01... | 451 | 1,600,668 | 349,044,272 | 796,107 | 0.542c | $1.360 | 250 |
| 1901-02... | 451 | 1,665,423 | 357,885,668 | 815,711 | 0.553 | 1.578 | 285 |

Chairman, William A. Read, New York; President, Benjamin Norton, Toledo, O.; Vice-President, Henry Budge; Secretary and Treasurer, Joseph H. Seaman, New York.

Directors—William A. Read, Frederic P. Olcott, Henry Budge, J. Kennedy Tod, John J. Emory, Charles H. Tweed, John Crosby Brown, Alfred R. Pick, Thomas H. Hubbard, New York; C. S. W. Packard, Philadelphia; Benjamin Norton, Toledo, O.

Main office, Frankfort, Ind.; New York office, 44 Pine street. Annual meeting, last Wednesday in October.

## THE TOLEDO, WALHONDING VALLEY & OHIO RAILROAD CO.

(Controlled by the Pennsylvania Company.)

A corporation formed under the laws of Ohio, May 18, 1891. The company was a consolidation of the Northwestern Ohio Railway Co. and the Walhonding Valley Railway Co.

Road owned, Toledo Junction, O., to Toledo, 80 miles; Coshocton, O., to Loudonville, O., 45 miles; Sandusky to Columbus, O., 109 miles; total owned, 234 miles. In October, 1902, the company acquired the northern portion of the former Columbus, Sandusky & Hocking Railway, extending from Columbus to Sandusky, the same having been sold at foreclosure September 24, 1902.

All of the stock is owned by the Pennsylvania Company, and the property is operated as part of the Pennsylvania Railroad's Western system.

Stock......Par $100..........................Authorized, $4,000,000......Issued, $3,000,000

The company has no preferred stock. The outstanding stock, which was $2,500,000, was increased to $3,000,000 in 1902, and the $500,000 additional was sold to the Pennsylvania Company in connection with the purchase of the Columbus, Sandusky & Hocking line.

Stock is transferred by the secretary of the company, Pittsburg.

In 1901 dividends of 4 per cent. were paid on the stock of the company.

FUNDED DEBT.

| | |
|---|---|
| 1st mort., Series A, 4½ per cent., due July, 1931, Jan. and July | $1,500,000 |
| " Series B, 4½ per cent., due July, 1933, Jan. and July | 978,000 |
| " Series C, 4 per cent., due Sept., 1942, March and Sept | 1,492,000 |
| Total | $3,970,000 |

The 1st mortgage, Farmers' Loan & Trust Co., New York, trustee, is for $4,000,000, the three series of bonds issued under it having the same lien. The Series C bonds were created and issued to provide for the acquisition of the Columbus, Sandusky & Hocking line. All the bonds are guaranteed by endorsement as to principal and interest by the Pennsylvania Company. There is a sinking fund of 1 per cent. per annum, bonds to be purchased for the same at or below par, but they cannot be drawn for redemption. The bonds issued are at the rate of $16,936 per mile of road.

The net earnings of all the lines owned by this company, including the part of the Columbus, Sandusky & Hocking which it acquired, were: in 1900, $300,983; in 1901, $357,448; in 1902, $422,838. The annual interest charges on the bonds are $171,190.

President, James McCrea; Vice-President, Joseph Wood; Secretary, S. B. Liggett; Treasurer, T. H. B. McKnight; Auditor, John W. Renner, Pittsburg.

Directors—Joseph Wood, J. J. Brooks, James McCrea, John W. Renner, E. B. Taylor, W. A. Baldwin, W. R. Pomerene, Leander F. McVey, Jesse P. Forbes, J. J. Turner, L. L. Gilbert.

Main office, Pittsburg. Annual meeting, second Friday in March, at Coshocton, O.

## TORONTO, HAMILTON & BUFFALO RAILWAY CO.

Road owned, Welland, Ont., to Hamilton, Ont., 38 miles; Hamilton to Waterford, 43 miles; branches, 7 miles; total, 88 miles. The road was constructed in 1897-98 as a connecting link between the New York Central and the Canadian Pacific systems. Locomotives, 13; passenger cars, 12; freight cars, 115.

Stock.... .Par $100..........................Authorized, $2,500,000......Issued, $2,500,000

Of the capital stock 51 per cent. is held by the New York Central and allied companies and 19 per cent. by the Canadian Pacific.

FUNDED DEBT.

1st mort., 4 per cent., due July, 1946, June and Dec.................................. $3,280,000

The proprietary companies agree to set aside as a guarantee fund for the bonds of this company 25 per cent. of all their earnings and those of their leased and operated lines derived from traffic interchanged with this company. This is equivalent to a traffic guarantee of the bonds by the Canadian Pacific, the New York Central, Michigan Central and Canada Southern.

Trustees of bonds, Charles F. Cox and S. Endicott Peabody.

EARNINGS.

Year ending November 30.

| | Gross. | Net. | Charges. | Surplus. |
|---|---|---|---|---|
| 1898–99 | $370,153 | $111,063 | $131,200 | Def. $20,136 |
| 1899–00 | 400,732 | 146,042 | 131,200 | 14,842 |
| 1900–01 | 493,247 | 194,999 | 131,200 | 63,799 |
| 1901–02 | 479,594 | 178,629 | 131,200 | 47,406 |

The Canadian Pacific pays this company 4 per cent. per annum upon $1,571,770, being half the agreed cost of this company's terminals at Hamilton, Ont., which property is included in the lien of the mortgage.

President, John N. Beckley, Rochester, N. Y.; Vice-President, Sir Thomas G. Shaughnessy, Montreal; Secretary and Treasurer, Charles F. Cox, New York.

Directors—William K. Vanderbilt, William H. Newman, Charles F. Cox, New York; Sir Thomas G. Shaughnessy, Montreal; Henry B. Ledyard, Detroit; S. Endicott Peabody, Boston; John N. Beckley, Rochester, N. Y.

Main office, Hamilton, Ont.; New York office, Grand Central Station. Annual meeting in June.

## THE ULSTER & DELAWARE RAILROAD CO.

A corporation formed under the laws of New York in January, 1902. The company is a consolidation of the old railroad company of the same name, the Delaware & Otsego Railroad Co., Hobart Branch Railroad Co., Kaaterskill Railroad Co. and Stony Cove & Catskill Mountain Railroad Co.

Road owned, Kingston Point, N. Y., to Oneonta, N. Y., 107 miles; branches, 21¾ miles; total operated, 128¾ miles. Locomotives, 20; passenger cars, 34; freight cars, 250.

Stock......Par $100.. ............... ........Authorized, $3,000,000......Issued, $1,900,000

Transfer Agent, Lincoln National Bank, New York. Registrar, Central Trust Co., New York.

FUNDED DEBT.

| | |
|---|---|
| Cons. mort., 5 per cent., due June, 1928, June and Dec. | $1,997,000 |
| Refunding mort., 4 per cent., due Feb., 1952, Feb. and Aug. | 600,000 |
| Total | $2,597,000 |

The authorized issue of consolidated mortgage bonds is $2,000,000. They were issued to take up old 7 per cent. bonds and for extensions. Trustee and agent for payment of interest, Central Trust Co., New York.

Road was formerly New York, Kingston & Syracuse, foreclosed and reorganized in 1875.

The refunding mortgage was created in 1902 and is for $3,000,000. Of the amount outstanding $500,000 was issued to retire a like amount of the old company's 2d mortgage 5 per cent. bonds.

EARNINGS.

| Year ending June 30. | Gross. | Net. |
|---|---|---|
| 1893-94 | $428,053 | $139,846 |
| 1894-95 | 405,227 | 124,276 |
| 1895-96 | 419,354 | 121,148 |
| 1896-97 | 400,757 | 127,757 |
| 1897-98 | 405,267 | 126,065 |
| 1898-99 | 417,193 | 113,752 |
| 1899-00 | 473,663 | 153,776 |
| 1900-01 | 607,423 | 182,661 |

In the six months ending June 30, 1902, the present company earned gross, $273,131; net, $77,778; charges, $80,805; deficit, $3,017.

President, Samuel D. Coykendall; Vice-President, Thomas C. Coykendall; Secretary, Henry C. Soop; Treasurer, Henry S. Coykendall, Rondout, N. Y.

Main office, Rondout, N. Y. Annual meeting, first Tuesday in December.

## UNION PACIFIC RAILROAD CO.

A corporation formed under the laws of Utah, July 1, 1897, to acquire the main line and branches of the former Union Pacific Railway Co., under plan of reorganization of October, 1895.

Road owned, Council Bluffs, Ia., to Ogden, Utah, 1,011 miles; Kansas City, Mo., to Denver, Col., 639 miles; Denver to Cheyenne, 106 miles; Julesburg, Col., to La Salle, 149 miles; branches, 1,041 miles; Leavenworth, Kansas & Western Railway (operated separately), 165½ miles; total, 3,111½ miles. Locomotives, 489; passenger cars, 349; freight cars, 13,325; service cars, 1,824.

The company has acquired practically all of the branch lines which belonged to the former company. For details regarding same see MANUAL for 1899. It also controls through stock ownership the Oregon Short Line, 1,739 miles, and the Oregon Railroad & Navigation Co., 1,074 miles. Total of this system June 30, 1902, 5,929 miles Total equipment, locomotives, 287; passenger cars, 580; freight cars, 21,081; service cars, 2,702; floating equipment, 20 steamers, steamboats, etc.

The Union Pacific, Denver & Gulf Railroad was controlled by the old Union Pacific Railway, but was separated from the system and reorganized as the Colorado & Southern.

The present company took possession of the main line, Council Bluffs to Ogden, on February 1, 1898. The Kansas Pacific Division was purchased at foreclosure in February, 1898. In March, 1898, the Union Pacific, Lincoln & Colorado was acquired. In November, 1898, the company took over a number of the branch lines previously operated by Receivers, and in 1899 assumed possession of the Julesburg branch of the old Union Pacific, Denver & Gulf, La Salle, Col., to Julesburg, 151 miles.

The former Union Pacific Railway Co. was a consolidation, January 24, 1880, of the Union Pacific Railroad Co., the Kansas Pacific and the Denver Pacific. When system was complete, including leaseholds, all controlled lines and one-half mileage of lines owned jointly, it comprised 8,157 miles of road.

In February, 1901, this company acquired a large amount of the stock of the Southern Pacific Co. system of 8,874 miles of railroads and the steamship lines owned and controlled by that corporation, which includes the Pacific Mail Steamship Co. In 1901-02 this company's holdings of Southern Pacific stock were increased from $75,000,000 to $90,000,000.

In 1901 this company acquired, through its controlled property, the Oregon Short Line, large holdings of Northern Pacific stock, which in 1902 were exchanged for $82,491,871 stock of the Northern Securities Co. and $8,900,007 in cash.

Stock..Par $100...Authorized { com., $196,178,700 / pref., 100,000,000 } Issued { com., $108,761,200 / pref., 99,559,500 } $208,320,700

The preferred stock is entitled to 4 per cent., non-cumulative, out of the yearly earnings of the company, and is not entitled to further participation in any surplus.

Common stock was increased $87,460,100 to $88,460,100 in January, 1899, to provide for exchange of same for minority holdings of Oregon Short Line, which were offered the right to convert their stock on payment of $3 a share. In October, 1899, the preferred authorized was increased to $100,000,000 and the common to $97,687,600 in order to provide for acquisition by exchange of the outstanding stocks of the Oregon Railroad & Navigation Co. and the outstanding stock and Income B bonds of the Oregon Short Line Railroad Co. In 1901 the common stock authorized was increased to $200,000,000 in order to provide for the conversion of the collateral trust bonds. See below as to terms of conversion for this issue.

The holders of Oregon Navigation preferred and common stocks outstanding were in October, 1899, offered the right to exchange the same, share for share, for the similar class of Union Pacific stock. The Oregon Short Line Railroad income bonds B were offered the right to exchange their holdings for Union Pacific preferred stock. On June 30, 1902, the Union Pacific had acquired all but $10,000 of the Oregon Short Line stock and $38,210 common and $16,954 preferred stock of the Oregon Railroad & Navigation Co.

Transfer agency, 120 Broadway, New York. Registrar, Mercantile Trust Co., New York.

This company began the payment of dividends on the new preferred stock with 1½ per cent. October 31, 1898. On April 19, 1899, 1½ per cent. was paid, and in October, 1899, company was put on a 2 per cent. semi-annual basis, making the full 4 per cent. to which the preferred is entitled. The preferred dividends are paid 2 per cent. each, April and October. The first dividend of 1½ per cent. on the common was declared in February, 1900, payable April 2, 1900. October 1, 1900, a second dividend of 2 per cent. was paid on the common, putting it on a 4 per cent. basis, and such dividends are paid in April and October.

FUNDED DEBT.

| | |
|---|---|
| 1st mort. and land grant, 4 per cent., due July, 1947, Jan. and July................ | $100,000,000 |
| Collateral trust, convertible bonds, 4 per cent., due May, 1911, May and Nov....... | 87,259,000 |
| Total......... ........................................................ | $187,259,000 |

The 1st mortgage 4 per cent. bonds are $100,000,000 authorized and are a first lien on all lines owned directly and on the securities of branch lines conveyed to the Mercantile Trust Co., New York, trustee, covering a total of 2,150 miles, as well as about 6,500,000 acres of land. The company's interest in Oregon Short Line is not covered by the 1st mortgage.

The collateral trust convertible bonds were created in 1901 and are secured by 859 miles of railroad and the deposit of $15,000,000 stock of the Southern Pacific, $27,334,700 Oregon Short Line stock, $7,663,500 common and $9,876,200 preferred stock of the Oregon Railroad & Navigation Co. and other securities owned by this company and not covered by the 1st mortgage. The authorized amount of the collateral trust bonds is $100,000,000. Prior to May 1, 1906, these bonds can be exchanged for common stock at par, and after May 1, 1896, the company can redeem the bonds at 102½ and interest. Stockholders, both preferred and common, of record, February 23, 1901, had the right to subscribe for $40,000,000 of these bonds at par, at the rate of one $1,000 bond for each 50 shares of either stock.

The funded debts of the Oregon Short Line and Oregon Railroad & Navigation are given under their respective statements.

In 1902 $31,000,000 of 4 per cent. participating bonds were issued by the Oregon Short Line Railroad Co., secured by stock of the Northern Securities Co., and the stockholders of the Union Pacific Railroad Co., both common and preferred, were given the right to subscribe for the same at 92 in the proportion of 15 per cent. of their holdings. See statement of Oregon Short Line.

Details of the funded debt of the old company, its indebtedness to the Government through the issue by the United States of subsidy bonds in aid of the construction of the road, will be found in full in the MANUAL for 1900.

The old company became embarrassed in 1892, and on October 13, 1893, Receivers were appointed.

On January 22, 1897, it was announced that an agreement had been made between the Attorney-General of the United States, representing the Government, and the Union Pacific reorganization committee for the foreclosure of the property under the 1st mortgage and government lien, a syndicate headed by Kuhn, Loeb & Co. of New York guaranteeing a minimum bid of $45,754,000.

Under plan old stock was assessed $15 per share and exchanged for new common, preferred stock being given for amount of assessment. Details as to the exchange of new securities for the old bonds and the arrangements with the Government were given in the MANUAL for 1902.

The earnings of the old company for a score of years prior to the reorganization are given in the MANUAL for 1902.

UNION PACIFIC RAILROAD CO.—EARNINGS.

Year ending June 30.

| | Mileage. | Gross. | Per Cent. Op. Exp. | Net. | Charges. | Surplus. |
|---|---|---|---|---|---|---|
| 1898 (6 months, ending June 30).. | 1,849 | $7,670,579 | .... | $3,742,603 | $1,945,918 | $1,796,685 |
| 1898-99.......................... | 2,421 | 19,811,641 | .... | 9,388,208 | 3,600,000 | 5,788,208 |
| 1899-00.......................... | 2,923 | 23,046,907 | .... | 12,027,810 | 3,890,000 | 8,137,810 |
| 1900-01.......................... | 5,543 | 43,538,181 | 53.62 | 20,010,279 | 7,475,221 | 12,535,057 |
| 1901-02.......................... | 5,710 | 47,500,279 | 50.92 | 26,521,654 | 12,018,396 | 14,503,248 |

In consequence of the different portions of property having been taken over at various times the first report for six months ending June 30, 1898, was necessarily incomplete. In figures given above net includes $606,442 miscellaneous income, part of which accrued prior to January 1, 1898, and charges include $145,918 for adjustment of taxes. The net earnings of branch lines to be included in the system was, for six months ending June 30, 1898, approximately $446,659. In 1898-99 the company received $795,159 from holders of Oregon Short Line stock in payment for privilege of exchange for Union Pacific common stock, making total surplus per year $6,583,367. Dividends on preferred (3½ per cent.), $2,625,000; balance surplus for year, $3,958,367. In 1900 the dividends paid were $7,303,627; balance surplus, $834,183.

The earnings for 1900-01 and 1901-02 include the returns of the Oregon Railroad & Navigation Co. and of the Oregon Short Line Railroad. In 1900-01 dividends were $7,980,970 and the surplus $4,554,087. In 1901-02 dividends, $8,187,288; surplus, $6,315,960. Included in the net for 1901-02 is $4,580,601, being income from investments, of which $4,063,031 was dividends in Northern Pacific stock and Northern Securities shares owned by the system. The figures for 1900-01 and 1901-02 include the statistics of the Oregon Short Line Railroad and the Oregon Railroad & Navigation Co.

The following exhibits the freight traffic statistics of the company for the year ending June 30:

| | Average Mileage. | Total Tonnage. | Tons Carried One Mile. | Freight Density. | Rate per Ton per Mile. | Earnings per Train Mile. | Average Tons per Train. |
|---|---|---|---|---|---|---|---|
| 1898-99... | 2,421 | 4,359,224 | 1,393,205,994 | 575,467 | 1.015c | $2.46 | 309 |
| 1899-00... | 2,923 | 4,872,212 | 1,571,936,786 | 537,782 | 1.049 | 2.62 | 329 |
| 1900-01... | 5,686 | 8,312,371 | ............ | 671,235 | .... | 3.01 | 365 |
| 1901-02... | 5,710 | 8,590,193 | ............ | 751,097 | .... | 3.31 | 417 |

GROSS AND NET EARNINGS BY MONTHS FOR THREE YEARS.

| | 1900. | | 1901. | | 1902. | |
|---|---|---|---|---|---|---|
| | Gross. | Net. | Gross. | Net. | Gross. | Net. |
| January......... | $1,711,098 | $642,114 | $3,207,612 | $1,301,432 | $3,943,208 | $1,942,468 |
| February........ | 1,547,193 | 622,264 | 2,883,422 | 1,091,157 | 3,225,156 | 1,471,264 |
| March........... | 1,869,423 | 875,204 | 3,289,620 | 1,360,593 | 3,476,859 | 1,380,302 |
| April........... | 1,733,335 | 639,211 | 3,418,737 | 1,361,514 | 3,740,374 | 1,497,756 |
| May............. | 1,772,393 | 626,472 | 3,619,341 | 1,403,190 | 3,710,057 | 1,490,440 |

GROSS AND NET EARNINGS BY MONTHS FOR THREE YEARS.—*Continued.*

| | 1900. | | 1901. | | 1902. | |
|---|---|---|---|---|---|---|
| | Gross. | Net. | Gross. | Net. | Gross. | Net. |
| June | $1,898,383 | $764,025 | $3,759,142 | $1,670,256 | $3,860,440 | $1,670,983 |
| July | 2,166,068 | 935,662 | 3,948,692 | 1,897,718 | 4,196,141 | 2,079,085 |
| August | 2,362,940 | 986,945 | 4,123,595 | 1,928,507 | 4,329,598 | 2,092,685 |
| September | 2,398,063 | 991,313 | 4,240,815 | 2,048,941 | 4,637,571 | 2,283,296 |
| October | 4,537,978 | 2,198,004 | 4,797,260 | 2,480,818 | 4,965,951 | 2,485,303 |
| November | 3,824,439 | 1,765,670 | 4,438,497 | 2,303,057 | 4,744,427 | 2,223,535 |
| December | 3,617,732 | 1,663,375 | 3,896,226 | 1,842,995 | 4,158,067 | 1,795,344 |
| Totals for year | $29,439,045 | $12,710,259 | $45,622,959 | $20,690,178 | $47,991,849 | $22,412,461 |
| Aver. per month | 2,469,754 | 1,059,188 | 3,801,913 | 1,724,181 | 3,999,320 | 1,867,705 |

Chairman of Executive Committee, Edward H. Harriman, New York; President, Horace G. Burt, Omaha; Vice-President, William D. Cornish; Secretary, Alexander Millar; Treasurer, Frederic V. S. Crosby; Assistant Secretary, William V. S. Thorne; Comptroller, William Mahl; Assistant Comptroller, Herbert S. Bradt, New York.

Directors—Edward H. Harriman, Winslow S. Pierce, James Stillman, Louis Fitzgerald, James H. yde, Otto H. Kahn, George J. Gould, Jacob H. Schiff, Thomas J. Eckert, Charles A. Peabody, Henry H. Rogers, New York; Marvin Hughitt, Chicago; T. Jefferson Coolidge, Jr., Oliver Ames, Boston; Horace G. Burt, Omaha.

Main office, 120 Broadway, New York. Annual meeting, second Tuesday in October.

## THE UNITED NEW JERSEY RAILROAD AND CANAL COMPANIES

(Leased to Pennsylvania Railroad Co.)

Road owned, Jersey City to Trenton, 57 miles; South Amboy to Camden, 61 miles; branches, 28 miles; leased and almost entirely owned, Trenton to West Philadelphia, 34 miles, and 318 miles of branch lines, making 498 miles. Also owned, Delaware & Raritan Canal, 66 miles. The company owns steam ferries between Jersey City and New York and Philadelphia and Camden.

Consolidation, 1871, of the New Jersey Railroad & Transportation Co., the Camden & Amboy Railroad Co. and the Delaware & Raritan Canal Co. Property leased to Pennsylvania Railroad Co. for 999 years from June 30, 1871, for interest on obligations, fund for maintenance of organization and 10 per cent. on stock.

Stock......Par $100................ ........Authorized, $21,240,400......Issued, $21,240,400

Stock is transferred at the office of the company, Trenton, N. J.

Dividends are paid quarterly, 2½ per cent. each, January (10), April, July and October.

FUNDED DEBT.

| | |
|---|---|
| General 1st mort., 3½ per cent., due March, 1951, March and Sept. | $5,669,000 |
| United Co., gold loan, 6 per cent., due Sept., 1908, March and Sept. | 841,000 |
| " " 4 per cent., due Sept., 1929, March and Sept. | 6,020,000 |
| " " of 1944, 4 per cent., due March, 1944, March and Sept. | 5,646,000 |
| Bonds of 1883, 4 per cent., due Feb., 1923, Feb. and Aug. | 1,824,000 |
| Total | $20,000,000 |

The general, now 1st, 3½ per cent. mortgage bonds were issued in 1901 to retire an equal amount of general mortgage 6 per cent. bonds which matured March 1, 1901. The 3½ per cents. are guaranteed, principal and interest, by the Pennsylvania Railroad Co.

Earnings are reported with those of lessee. A statement of income, etc., is as follows:

EARNINGS.

| | Net Earnings. | Interest on Investments. | Total Income. | Rental. | Profit to Lessee. |
|---|---|---|---|---|---|
| 1892 | $3,865,707 | $517,781 | $4,383,489 | $4,682,688 | Loss $299,198 |
| 1893 | 3,986,607 | 597,977 | 4,584,584 | 4,779,112 | " 194,528 |
| 1894 | 4,796,786 | 526,011 | 5,322,797 | 4,643,336 | 679,460 |
| 1895 | 4,740,603 | 257,100 | 4,997,704 | 4,270,010 | 727,693 |
| 1896 | 4,723,143 | 320,435 | 5,043,579 | 4,604,154 | 439,424 |
| 1897 | 5,101,823 | 231,193 | 5,333,017 | 4,852,297 | 480,720 |
| 1898 | 5,447,814 | 225,630 | 5,673,445 | 5,160,632 | 512,811 |
| 1899 | 5,810,873 | 253,884 | 6,064,757 | 5,910,797 | 153,960 |
| 1900 | 6,956,964 | 245,187 | 7,202,152 | 6,865,017 | 337,135 |
| 1901 | 7,025,358 | 255,170 | 7,280,529 | 7,088,906 | 191,623 |

President, F. Wolcott Jackson, Newark, N. J.; Vice-President, John C. Barron, New York; Secretary and Treasurer, Leroy H. Anderson, Trenton, N. J.

Directors—W. W. Astor, John C. Barron, Joseph D. Bedle, F. Wolcott Jackson, Bayard Henry, Thomas Oakes, J. Lowber Welsh, S. S. Dennis, Henry W. Green, Henry P. McKean, George Henry Warren, M. Taylor Pyne; State Director, Charles Bradley.

Main office, 76 Clinton avenue, Trenton, N. J.; lessee's office, Broad Street Station, Philadelphia. Annual meeting, last Tuesday in May.

## VELASCO, BRAZOS & NORTHERN RAILWAY CO.

A corporation formed under the laws of Texas. Road owned, Velasco, Tex., to Anchor, 20 miles. An extension of the line northward to Dallas is planned. The company succeeded the Velasco Terminal Railway, which was foreclosed in 1901.

Stock......Par $100........................Authorized, $200,000......Issued, $200,000

In 1902 the company obtained authority from the Texas State Railroad Commission to issue $200,000 bonds.

President, C. C. Waller; Vice-President and General Manager, E. P. Speers; Secretary, L. R. Bryan, Velasco, Tex.

Main office, Velasco, Tex.

## VICKSBURG, SHREVEPORT & PACIFIC RAILWAY CO.

This company was organized on April 23, 1901, by the Vicksburg, Shreveport & Pacific Railroad non-assenting 1st mortgage bondholders, who purchased the property of the Vicksburg, Shreveport & Pacific Railroad Co. at foreclosure sale on March 30, 1901, and entered into possession May 1, 1901, retaining as a lien upon the property the Vicksburg, Shreveport & Pacific Railroad Co. prior lien mortgage.

Road owned, Delta, La., to Shreveport, 171 miles, owned but not operated, 17 miles west of Shreveport, La. Locomotives, 20; passenger cars, 22; freight cars, 711.

Stock....Par $100.....Authorized { com., $3,000,000 / pref., 2,200,000 } Issued { com., $2,856,500 / pref., 2,142,800 } $4,999,300

The preferred stock is 5 per cent., non-cumulative.

Transfer Agent, Central Trust Co., New York.

The first dividend on the preferred stock was 5 per cent., paid September 1, 1902.

FUNDED DEBT.

| | |
|---|---|
| Prior lien mort., 6 per cent., due May, 1915, May and Nov. | $1,323,000 |
| General mort., 5 per cent., due May, 1941, May and Nov. | 1,572,000 |
| Total | $2,895,000 |

The new general mortgage was created under the reorganization and is $3,500,000 in amount, $1,323,000 of the bonds being reserved to retire the prior lien bonds and $605,000 for future requirements.

EARNINGS.

Year ending June 30.

| | Gross. | Net. | Charges. | Deficit. |
|---|---|---|---|---|
| 1894-95 | $580,114 | $151,513 | $407,311 | $255,798 |
| 1895-96 | 558,811 | 151,683 | 409,293 | 257,610 |
| 1896-97 | 572,929 | 148,705 | 410,498 | 261,793 |
| 1897-98 | 640,175 | 189,749 | 409,355 | 219,606 |
| 1898-99 | 678,384 | 209,386 | 409,527 | 200,141 |
| 1899-00 | 691,531 | 214,039 | 408,888 | 194,849 |
| 1900-01 | 896,940 | 280,570 | ...... | ...... |
| 1901-02 | 1,080,252 | 315,668 | 149,570 | Sur. 166,098 |

President, C. C. Harvey, New Orleans; Vice-President, Charles Schiff, London, England; Secretary and Treasurer, H. W. Wenham; Auditor, Larz A. Jones, New Orleans.

Directors—Charles Schiff, London, England; C. C. Harvey, H. H. Hall, Larz A. Jones, Henry W. Preston, New Orleans; George T. Bonner, New York; F. P. Stubbs, Jr., Monroe, La.

Offices, New Orleans and Monroe, La. Annual meeting in November, at New Orleans.

## VIRGINIA & SOUTHWESTERN RAILWAY CO.

A corporation formed under the laws of Virginia, January 19, 1899. The company succeeded the South Atlantic & Ohio Railway Co., and was a consolidation of that property, which had been sold under foreclosure, with the Bristol, Elizabethtown & North Carolina Railway Co.

Road owned, Inman, Va., to Mountain City, Tenn., 127 miles; branches, 8 miles; total owned, 135 miles; joint trackage on the Louisville & Nashville, Appalachee to Norton, 15 miles; total operated, 150 miles. Locomotives, 15; passenger cars, 9 freight cars, 440.

Stock......Par $100..........................Authorized, $2,000,000......Issued, $2,000,000

The company has no preferred stock. Transfer Agent, Morton Trust Co., New York. Registrar, The Manhattan Co., New York.

The stock of the company was all owned by the Virginia Iron, Coal & Coke Co., and in 1902, under the plan for the financial readjustment of the latter corporation, its stockholders were given the privilege of taking one-half of the stock of this company. See the statement of the Virginia Iron, Coal & Coke Co. in this edition of the MANUAL.

FUNDED DEBT.

1st mort., guar. 5 per cent., due Jan., 2003, Jan. and July.......................... $3,000,000

The 1st mortgage bonds are a first lien upon 135 miles of main line and branches and upon the equipment of the company. The bonds are in coupon form, but can be registered as to principal only. Trustee of the mortgage, registrar of bonds and agent for the payment of interest, Morton Trust Co., New York.

Under the readjustment plan of the Virginia Iron, Coal & Coke Co. the stockholders of that company were given in 1902 the right of subscribing ratably for the above bond issue, which is guaranteed by endorsement on the bonds, as to both principal and interest, by the Virginia Iron, Coal & Coke Co.

| EARNINGS. | Gross. | Net. |
|---|---|---|
| 1901 | $411,901 | $145,092 |
| 1902 | 535,661 | 210,407 |

President, Henry K. McHarg, New York; Vice-President, Archer A. Phlegar; Secretary and Treasurer, J. W. Cure, Radford, Va.

Directors—Grant B. Schley, Edward J. Berwind, George A. Crocker, Charles B. Squire, Henry K. McHarg, New York; George L. Carter, Bristol, Tenn.; Archer A. Phlegar, Radford, Va.

Main office, Radford, Va. Annual meeting, third Tuesday in May, at Radford.

## WABASH, CHESTER & WESTERN RAILROAD CO.

Road owned, Mt. Vernon, Ill., to Chester, Ill., 65 miles. Locomotives, 6; passenger cars, 5; freight cars, 80.

Stock......Par $100..........................Authorized, $1,250,000......Issued, $1,250,000

Transfer Agent, H. C. Cole, Chester, Ill.

FUNDED DEBT.

| | |
|---|---|
| 1st mort., 5 per cent., due July, 1918, Jan. and July | $300,000 |
| 1st cons. mort., 5 per cent., due Jan., 1928, Jan. and July | 390,000 |
| Total | $690,000 |

In the year ending June 30, 1902, this company reported gross earnings, $97,782; net, $18,509; charges, $34,500; deficit, $15,991.

President, Nathan Cole, St. Louis; Vice-President and Treasurer, Charles B. Cole; Secretary, H. C. Cole, Chester, Ill.

Directors—Nathan Cole, St. Louis; Charles B. Cole, H. C. Cole, J. J. Morrison, H. C. Horner, Chester, Ill.

Main office, Chester, Ill. Annual meeting, first Wednesday in March, at Chester.

## THE WABASH RAILROAD CO.

A corporation formed July 29, 1889, by the consolidation of the Wabash Western Railway Co. with lines east of the Mississippi, both sections having formed part of the Wabash, St. Louis & Pacific Railway Co., which was placed in the hands of Receivers in 1884, the lines west of the Mississippi being reorganizd in 1887 as the Wabash Western Railroad Co. In 1889 the lines east of the Mississippi were foreclosed and the consolidation effected as above.

The Wabash, St. Louis & Pacific was formed in 1879 by a consolidation of the Wabash Railway with the St. Louis, Kansas City & Northern. The Wabash Railway was organized in 1877, succeeding the Toledo, Wabash & Western, which was foreclosed in 1876.

Road owned, 1,936 miles; leased, 110 miles; operated under trackage arrangements, 436 miles; total operated June 30, 1902, 2,482 miles.

The main lines of this system extend from Toledo and Detroit to St. Louis, Chicago, Kansas City, Omaha and Des Moines, with numerous branches.

The company owns one-fifth of the stock of Chicago & Western Indiana and makes use of its terminals at Chicago.

The arrangement with Grand Trunk for joint use of the latter's line from Detroit to Black Rock, N. Y., and Suspension Bridge is for twenty-one years and began March 1, 1898. This company pays its proportion of all expenses of line on a mileage basis according to use made.

The trackage arrangements are: Clarke Junction to Chicago, 26 miles; eight short pieces into Quincy, Detroit, etc., 70 miles. The company also has trackage over the Missouri, Kansas & Texas, Hannibal to Moberly, Mo., 70 miles, and the joint use of the Grand Trunk Railway from Detroit to Suspension Bridge, N. Y., and thence over Erie to Buffalo, N. Y., with use of Lehigh Valley terminals at latter point.

In 1893 the company completed the line from Montpelier, Ind., to junction at Hammond, near Chicago. In 1898 an extension from Moulton to Albia, 28 miles, was completed. The Eel River Railroad, Logansport, Ind., to Butler, Ind., 94 miles, was leased, but in 1900 the courts decided that it could not be leased to the Wabash, and the property was taken out of the system. In 1901 acquired the Omaha & St. Louis, Pattonsburg to Council Bluffs, which has now become the Omaha Division of this com an . The Toledo & Chicago extension, Toledo to Montpelier, 51 miles, was completed in January, 1902.

In 1901 control of the Wheeling & Lake Erie Railroad was acquired by interests identified with this company. In the same year an extension of the Wheeling & Lake Erie to Pittsburg was begun, the purpose being to give the Wabash system a Pittsburg connection. See also the Western Maryland Railroad Co. and the West Virginia Central & Pittsburg Railway Co. for plans set on foot in 1902 to give the Wabash system an outlet at eastern tidewater over those roads.

Locomotives, 490; passenger cars, 396; freight cars, 17,195.

Stock..Par $100...Authorized { com., $28,000,000 / pref., 24,000,000 } Issued { com., $28,000,000 / pref., 24,000,000 } $52,000,000

The preferred stock is 7 per cent., non-cumulative.

Transfer agency, 195 Broadway, New York. Registrar, Mercantile Trust Co., New York.

FUNDED DEBT.

| | |
|---|---|
| 1st mort., 5 per cent., gold bonds, due May, 1939, May and Nov. | $32,381,000 |
| 2d mort., 5 per cent., gold bonds, due Feb., 1939, Feb. and Aug. | 14,000,000 |
| Debenture mort., income, 6 per cent., A bonds, due July, 1939, Jan. and July | 3,500,000 |
| " " " 6 per cent., B bonds, due July, 1939, Jan. and July | 26,500,000 |
| Equipment sinking fund mort., 5 per cent., due March, 1921 | 2,800,000 |
| Detroit & Chicago Extension, 1st mort., 5 per cent., due July, 1941, Jan. and July | 2,349,000 |
| Des Moines Division, 1st mort., 4 per cent., due Jan., 1939, Jan. and July | 1,600,000 |
| Toledo & Chicago Division, 1st mort., 4 per cent., due March, 1941, March and Sept. | 3,000,000 |
| Omaha Division, 1st mort., 3½ per cent., due Oct., 1941, April and Oct. | 3,000,000 |
| St. L., K. C. & N., 1st mort. on St. Ch. Br., 6 per cent., due Oct., 1908, April and Oct. | 568,000 |
| " " 2d mort. on St. Ch. Br., 7 per cent., due Oct., 1903, April and Oct. | 252,500 |
| St. L., Council Bluffs & O., 1st mort., 6 per cent., due July, 1903, Jan. and July | 324,000 |
| Boone County & Booneville, 1st mort., 7 per cent., due May, 1903, May and Nov. | 100,000 |
| K. C., Excl. Springs & N., 1st mort., 4 per cent., due Jan., 1928, Jan. and July | 100,000 |
| Columbia & St. L., 1st mort., 4 per cent., due May, 1942, May and Nov. | 100,000 |
| Brunswick & Chillicothe, 1st mort., 6 to 8 per cent., due Aug., 1903, Feb. and Aug. | 274,500 |
| Total | $90,849,000 |

The 1st mortgage and debentures cover all lines both east and west of the Mississippi owned by the company in 1889. Sufficient 1st mortgage bonds are reserved to provide funds to retire prior liens on lines west of the Mississippi River. The 2d mortgage covers only 1,012 miles, the lines east of the Mississippi, but they are a first lien on rolling stock valued at about $3,000,000. The Detroit & Chicago Extension mortgage was authorized in 1891 and is a first lien upon that section. In 1898 the Des Moines Division mortgage was authorized. This issue was to provide for new branches. The Toledo & Chicago Division bonds and the equipment bonds were issued in 1901. In the same year the 3½ per cent. Omaha Division 1st mortgage was authorized for $3,500,000 at 3½ per cent., of which $3,000,000 were issued in exchange for the old bonds and the retirement of Receiver's indebtedness, as well as for improvements.

The debentures are divided into Series A, $3,500,000, and Series B, $26,500,000. Series A received 6 per cent. for years ending June 30, 1890, 1891, 1892 and 1893; 1 per cent. for the year ending June 30, 1896, and 6 per cent. for the years ending January 30, 1900, 1901 and 1902. Up to January, 1903, no interest had been paid on the B debentures.

### Earnings.

Year ending June 30.

| | Gross. | Per Cent. Op. Exp. | Net. | Charges. | Surplus. |
|---|---|---|---|---|---|
| 1892-93 | $14,220,444 | ..... | $3,233,215 | $3,195,635 | $37,580 |
| 1893-94 | 12,551,448 | 78.32 | 2,684,764 | 3,356,529 | Def. 671,765 |
| 1894-95 | 11,959,839 | 74.59 | 2,803,428 | 3,340,334 | " 542,906 |
| 1895-96 | 12,807,147 | 72.17 | 3,258,278 | 3,221,478 | 31,800 |
| 1896-97 | 11,526,787 | 69.22 | 3,130,962 | 3,102,629 | 28,332 |
| 1897-98 | 13,207,862 | 73.45 | 3,584,252 | 3,182,756 | 401,495 |
| 1898-99 | 14,393,974 | 73.33 | 3,600,368 | 3,452,432 | 147,936 |
| 1899-00 | 16,440,990 | 72.67 | 4,265,769 | 3,845,659 | 420,110 |
| 1900-01 | 17,816,646 | 72.64 | 3,720,463 | 3,627,326 | 93,135 |
| 1901-02 | 19,053,493 | 72.68 | 4,136,746 | 3,935,304 | 261,460 |

Surplus for 1897-98 was devoted to reduction of floating debt, which amounted, in 1897, to $800,000 as a result of payment of interest on 1st and 2d mortgages in fiscal years 1894 and 1895, when operations resulted in a deficit. The charges for 1898-99 include $760,937 for joint track rentals and miscellaneous expenses. Out of the surplus of 1899-1900 $210,110 was paid for the interest on debenture A bonds, making the net surplus for the year $210,000. In 1900-01 the amount paid on the A debenture bonds is included in charges, as well as $656,756 for additions to property. In 1901-02 such additions amounted to $760,547.

The following presents the comparative freight traffic statistics of the company:

| | Average Mileage. | Total Tonnage. | Tons Carried One Mile. | Freight Density. | Rate per Ton per Mile. | Earnings per Train Mile | Average Tons per Train. |
|---|---|---|---|---|---|---|---|
| 1896-97 | 1,936 | 5,954,760 | 1,149,989,024 | 594,003 | 0.661c | $1.407 | 212 |
| 1897-98 | 2,061 | 6,382,831 | 1,365,693,174 | 662,636 | 0.624 | 1.351 | 216 |
| 1898-99 | 2,278 | 6,987,641 | 1,666,830,054 | 731,224 | 0.553 | 1.297 | 234 |
| 1899-00 | 2,358 | 9,563,071 | 1,902,881,000 | 806,989 | 0.557 | 1.500 | 268 |
| 1900-01 | 2,376 | 10,027,358 | 1,978,952,453 | 832,050 | 0.563 | 1.598 | 283 |
| 1901-02 | 2,438 | 10,481,692 | 1,947,404,142 | 798,771 | 0.604 | 1.719 | 284 |

### Gross and Net Earnings by Months for Three Years.

| | 1900. | | 1901. | | 1902. | |
|---|---|---|---|---|---|---|
| | Gross. | Net. | Gross. | Net. | Gross. | Net. |
| January | $1,314,583 | $347,383 | $1,518,685 | $425,793 | $1,660,209 | $507,181 |
| February | 1,209,155 | 305,786 | 1,270,496 | 276,637 | 1,396,171 | 322,691 |
| March | 1,354,261 | 361,554 | 1,467,308 | 404,101 | 1,551,566 | 445,614 |
| April | 1,310,885 | 301,168 | 1,354,535 | 293,734 | 1,481,561 | 367,386 |
| May | 1,292,869 | 323,786 | 1,411,683 | 329,239 | 1,510,760 | 266,735 |
| June | 1,309,579 | 371,415 | 1,406,905 | 384,995 | 1,488,483 | 259,472 |
| July | 1,350,105 | 350,708 | 1,552,340 | 423,064 | 1,721,531 | 475,021 |
| August | 1,527,318 | 476,824 | 1,686,379 | 525,600 | 1,903,705 | 633,698 |
| September | 1,615,570 | 533,652 | 1,661,284 | 565,485 | 1,840,909 | 610,924 |
| October | 1,643,001 | 537,399 | 1,805,700 | 617,654 | 1,970,096 | 606,709 |
| November | 1,431,584 | 379,908 | 1,639,573 | 535,063 | 1,714,999 | 486,471 |
| December | 1,536,238 | 388,394 | 1,592,242 | 402,967 | 1,694,345 | 403,191 |
| Totals for year | $16,895,148 | $4,677,977 | $18,367,230 | $5,184,332 | $19,034,335 | $5,385,093 |
| Aver. per m'nth | 1,407,929 | 389,831 | 1,530,603 | 432,127 | 1,[illegible]1,194 | 448,756 |

Chairman, Ossian D. Ashley, New York; President, Joseph Ramsey, Jr., St. Louis; 1st Vice-President, Edgar T. Welles, New York; 2d Vice-President, Milton Knight; 3d Vice-President, Wells H. Blodgett, St. Louis; Treasurer, F. L. O'Leary; Secretary, J. C. Otteson, New York.

Directors—Ossian D. Ashley, Thomas H. Hubbard, Edgar T. Welles, Joseph Ramsey, Jr., George J. Gould, S. C. Reynolds, John T. Terry, Russell Sage, P. B. Wyckoff, Edwin Gould, Henry K. McHarg, Cyrus J. Lawrence, James H. Hyde.

Main office, Seventh and Chestnut streets, St. Louis; New York office, 195 Broadway. Annual meeting, second Tuesday in October.

## WASHINGTON COUNTY RAILROAD CO.

Road owned, Washington Junction, Me., to Calais, Me., 103 miles; branches to Eastport, Princeton, etc., 34 miles; total operated, 137 miles. Locomotives, 12; passenger cars, 23; freight cars, 276.

Stock....Par $100....Authorized { com., $1,500,000 / pref., 500,000 } Issued { com., $1,500,000 / pref., 500,000 } $2,000,000

The preferred stock is 5 per cent., non-cumulative, and is all held by Washington County, Me., in its Treasury.

FUNDED DEBT.

1st mort., 5 per cent., due Jan., 1948, Jan. and July.............................. $2,142,000

The 1st mortgage is $2,320,000, authorized.

In the year ending June 30, 1900, the road's earnings were, gross, $227,189; net, $29,996. In 1900-01, gross, $226,590; net, $25,164.

President, Frederick W. Whitridge; Vice-President, Grant B. Schley; Treasurer, Frank E. Randall, New York.

Main office, Calais, Me.; New York office, 80 Broadway.

---

## WESTERN MARYLAND RAILROAD CO.

A corporation chartered by the State of Maryland in 1853.

The company became very heavily indebted to the city of Baltimore for guarantees and credits extended to it in aid of the construction of the road and for past due coupons. The city also held a large amount of the stock. Washington County, Md., also had interests in the company, holding the entire issue of $324,000 preferred stock. In 1899 an agitation began for a sale of the city's interest in the road. After delay and litigation bids were invited for the city's interest, and a number were received, including one from the Reading Co. The sale was, however, authorized in May, 1902, to the Fuller syndicate, which had acquired the West Virginia Central & Pittsburg Railway Co. and included capitalists identified with the Wabash Railway Co. and the Wheeling & Lake Erie Railroad Co., their purpose being to make this property the Eastern tidewater outlet of the Wabash system. The price paid for the city's holdings was $8,651,370, and the syndicate also purchased the interests of Washington County in the property. The contract provided that the purchasers should build a connection with the West Virginia Central & Pittsburg and extend the road to tidewater at Baltimore and build extensive terminals. In July, 1902, the agreement was carried out and the syndicate assumed the management of the property. An offer of $35 per share was made by the syndicate for common stock in the hands of other holders, and it acquired nearly all the outstanding stock.

A consolidation of the West Virginia Central & Pittsburg with this company was included in the plan of the syndicate.

Road owned, Baltimore to Williamsport, Md., 93 miles; leased, Baltimore & Cumberland Valley, 34 miles; Baltimore & Harrisburg and branches, 81 miles; Potomac Valley Railroad including the Baltimore & Harrisburg eastern extension, 31 miles; Washington & Franklin Railroad, 19 miles; total, 258 miles. Locomotives, 71; passenger cars, 78; freight cars, 745.

In the autumn of 1902 work was in progress on the tidewater extension and terminals and on a link, 65 miles, to connect with the West Virginia Central & Pittsburg Railway.

Stock...Par $50...Authorized { com., $60,000,000 / pref., 324,000 } Issued { com., $15,685,400 / pref., 324,000 } $16,009,400

At a special meeting on October 14, 1902, the authorized common stock was increased from $685,400 to $60,000,000.

The preferred stock is 6 per cent., non-cumulative.

Stock is transferred at the company's office, Baltimore.

FUNDED DEBT.

| | |
|---|---|
| New 1st mort., 4 per cent., due Oct., 1952, April and Oct. | $25,000,000 |
| Gen. lien and conv. mort., 4 per cent., due Oct., 1952, April and Oct. | 10,000,000 |
| Total | $35,000,000 |

FUNDED DEBT OF LEASED LINES.

| | |
|---|---|
| Balt. & Cumberland Val. Ry. 1st mort., 6 per cent., due July, 1929, Jan. and July.... | $48,500 |
| " " Val. R. R. 1st mort., 6 per cent., due July, 1929, Jan. and July.. | 72,800 |
| " " " ext. 1st mort., 6 per cent., due July, 1931, Jan. and July. | 230,000 |

FUNDED DEBT OF LEASED LINES—*Continued.*

| | |
|---|---|
| Potomac Valley R. R. 1st mort., 5 per cent., due Jan., 1941, Jan. and July.......... | $1,100,000 |
| Washington & Franklin Ry. 1st mort., 5 per cent., due Jan., 1939, Jan. and July.... | 378,000 |
| Baltimore & Harrisburg Ry. 1st mort., 5 per cent., due Nov., 1936, May and Nov.... | 690,000 |
| " " " Wn. ext. 1st mort., 5 p. ct., due May, 1938, May and Nov. | 240,000 |
| Total.......... | $2,959,300 |

EARNINGS.

Year ending September 30.

| | Gross. | Net. |
|---|---|---|
| 1891-92 | $1,083,321 | $392,293 |
| 1892-93 | 1,322,320 | 461,890 |
| 1893-94 | 1,203,174 | 390,735 |
| 1894-95 | 1,277,862 | 439,035 |
| 1895-96 | 1,265,690 | 399,051 |
| 1896-97 | 1,251,238 | 434,907 |
| 1897-98 | 1,468,154 | 494,467 |
| 1898-99 | 1,535,934 | 532,319 |
| 1899-00 | 1,823,740 | 670,528 |
| 1900-01 | 2,119,473 | 784,717 |

The new 4 per cent. 1st mortgage was authorized for $50,000,000 in October, 1902, when a general mortgage was also provided for to the amount of $10,000,000. The new 1sts are secured by the company's property, including its interests in leased and auxiliary lines and about 98 per cent. of the stock of the West Virginia Central & Pittsburg Railroad Co. Of the new 4s, $25,000,000 were sold to a syndicate formed by Vermilye & Co. and George P. Buller & Brother of New York to provide for the purchase of the property, the construction of terminals and a connection with the West Virginia Central & Pittsburg and for additional equipment.

The company guarantees dividends on the stock of leased lines as follows: Baltimore & Cumberland Valley Extension Railroad, 7 per cent. on $270,000 stock, January and July; Washington & Franklin Railway, 5 per cent. on $150,000 stock, January and July; Baltimore & Harrisburg Railway, 5 per cent. on $29,100 preferred stock, May and November.

Chairman, Winslow S. Pierce, New York; President, Joseph Ramsay, Jr., St. Louis; Vice-President, Fairfax S. Landstreet; Secretary, L. F. Timmerman, Baltimore; Treasurer and Assistant Secretary, John T. M. Barnes; Comptroller, H. B. Henson, New York.

Directors—Winslow S. Pierce, George J. Gould, Henry B. Henson, Henry C. Deming, Edwin Gould, Lawrence Greer, William H. McIntyre, New York; Joseph Ramsay, Jr., St. Louis; John W. Gates, Chicago; Fairfax S. Landstreet, John M. Hood, Charles W. Slagle, S. Davies Warfield, Baltimore.

Main office, Hillen and Exeter streets, Baltimore; New York office, 120 Broadway. Annual meeting, third Wednesday in October.

---

## WESTERN NEW YORK & PENNSYLVANIA RAILWAY CO.

(Controlled by Pennsylvania Railroad Co.)

This company was a consolidation, in February, 1883, of the Buffalo, New York & Philadelphia, the Buffalo, Pittsburg & Western, the Oil City & Chicago and the Olean & Salamanca Cos., and is a reorganization (September, 1887) of the company so formed. The present company is a reorganization, 1895, of the railroad company of same name.

In June, 1900, the Pennsylvania Railroad Co. purchased a majority of the stock for $9 per share and of the income bonds at $300 per bond. That company holds $19,402,686 of the stock and $9,123,575 of the incomes. A lease of the road was made to the Pennsylvania Railroad Co. in 1900 and a new lease for 20 years from August 1, 1903, was made in 1903, the same being subject to termination on 30 days' notice.

Road owned, Buffalo, N. Y., to Emporium, Pa., 121 miles; Rochester, N. Y., to Hinsdale, 99 miles; Olean Junction to Bradford, Pa., 17 miles; Bradford to Kinzua, 28 miles; Buffalo to Oil City, Pa., 136 miles; Oil City to Stoneboro, 30 miles; Stoneboro to Mahoningtown, Pa., 38 miles; Olean to Oil City, 116 miles; short coal and oil branches, 64 miles; total, 649 miles, of which 45 miles are leased and 598 miles owned. Locomotives, 128; passenger cars, 103; freight cars, 3,345.

Since its control was acquired by the Pennsylvania the portion of the company's road from New Castle, Pa., to Oil City, 68 miles, has been operated by the Pennsylvania Company as part of its Erie and Ashtabula Division. The balance of the system since August 1, 1900, has been operated by the Pennsylvania as part of its Buffalo & Allegheny Valley Division.

Stock......Par $50........................Authorized, $20,000,000......Issued, $20,000,000

FUNDED DEBT.

| | |
|---|---|
| 1st mort., 5 per cent., due Jan., 1937, Jan. and July........................ | $9,990,000 |
| Gen. mort., 2, 3 and 4 per cent., due April, 1943, April and Oct.................... | 10,000,000 |
| Income mort., due April, 1943, Nov.............................................. | 10,000,000 |
| Total.............................................................. | $29,990,000 |

EARNINGS.

Year ending June 30.

| | Gross. | Net. | Charges. | Surplus. |
|---|---|---|---|---|
| 1891-92 | $3,580,155 | $1,181,796 | $652,740 | $529,055 |
| 1892-93 | 3,716,638 | 1,200,519 | 679,249 | 521,270 |
| 1893-94 | 3,011,901 | 798,257 | 682,606 | 115,651 |
| 1894-95 | 3,282,010 | 1,018,774 | 685,914 | 332,860 |
| 1895-96 | 3,186,031 | 1,008,757 | 688,188 | 320,569 |
| 1896-97 | 2,954,774 | 966,439 | 840,189 | 126,249 |
| 1897-98 | 3,245,937 | 1,111,524 | 921,015 | 190,508 |
| 1898-99 | 3,291,411 | 1,046,234 | 948,216 | 98,017 |
| 1899-00 | 3,803,584 | 938,337 | 920,875 | 17,462 |
| 1900-01 | 4,075,089 | 436,214 | 1,024,209 | Def., 587,995 |
| 1901-02 | 4,764,331 | 705,857 | 1,315,954 | " 610,097 |

President, William H. Barnes; Vice-President, Samuel Rea; Treasurer, Robert W. Smith; Secretary, John M. Harding, Philadelphia.

Main office, Broad Street Station, Philadelphia. Annual meeting, second Monday in January.

## THE WESTERN RAILWAY OF ALABAMA

Road owned, Selma, Ala., to West Point, Ga., 133 miles.

Controlled, through stock ownership, by the Georgia Railroad, the Central of Georgia and the Atlantic Coast Line Co., the road being included in the lease of the Georgia Railroad to the Louisville & Nashville and Atlantic Coast Line.

Stock......Par $100.........................Authorized, $3,000,000......Issued, $3,000,000

Dividends on the stock have in recent years been 5 per cent. in 1899, 4 per cent. in 1900 and 2 per cent. in 1901.

FUNDED DEBT.

Consol. (now 1st) mort., gold, 4½ per cent., due Oct., 1918, April and Oct.......... $1,543,000

EARNINGS.

| Year ending June 30. | Gross. | Net. |
|---|---|---|
| 1896-97 | $636,533 | $258,059 |
| 1897-98 | 603,630 | 214,444 |
| 1898-99 | 668,334 | 261,686 |
| 1899-00 | 739,746 | 244,793 |
| 1900-01 | 821,083 | 288,327 |

President, Charles A. Wickersham; Secretary and Treasurer, F. H. Hill, Atlanta, Ga.

Main office, Atlanta, Ga. Annual meeting in September.

## WEST JERSEY & SEA SHORE RAILROAD CO.

(Controlled by Pennsylvania Railroad Co.)

Road owned comprises the former West Jersey, Camden to Cape May and branches to Bridgeton, Riddleton, Ocean City and Sea Isle, 202 miles; West Jersey & Atlantic, 47 miles; the former Camden & Atlantic and branches, 81 miles; total operated, 330 miles. Locomotives, 69; passenger cars, 312; freight cars, 541.

A controlling interest is vested in the Pennsylvania and the United New Jersey Railroads & Canal Co.

Company is a consolidation, May 4, 1896, of the Camden & Atlantic, West Jersey and West Jersey & Atlantic roads, with their branches, including Philadelphia, Marlton & Medford, Chelsea Branch Railroad and smaller lines. See 1896 edition of MANUAL for other details of Camden & Atlantic and of the West Jersey railroad companies.

Stock..Par $50..Authorized { com., $8,076,000 / spec. guar., 104,000 } Issued { com., $4,952,050 / spec. guar., 104,000 } $5,056,050

Special guaranteed stock is entitled to 6 per cent. per year semi-annual, March and September. It represents a like amount of similar stock of the West Jersey Railroad Co. It may be converted into a 6 per cent. debenture.

The common stock outstanding was issued in the consolidation in exchange for stocks of the various companies, the common stock of West Jersey being exchanged on basis of $60 per share, Camden & Atlantic being at $45 per share for preferred and $20 per share for common, while that of Philadelphia, Marlton & Medford was at $15 per share. Other branch and leased line stocks were also retired in exchange for West Jersey & Sea Shore shares.

Transfer agency, Broad Street Station, Philadelphia.

Dividends on the common stock are paid half-yearly, March (15) and September. In 1896 paid 2½ per cent. on the common. In each year since 5 per cent. per annum has been paid.

FUNDED DEBT.

| | |
|---|---|
| West Jersey, consolidated mort., 6 per cent., due Nov., 1909, May and Nov.......... | $750,900 |
| Woodstown & Swedesboro bonds, 6 per cent., due May, 1912, May and Nov......... | 90,000 |
| Camden & Atlantic, cons. mort., 6 per cent., due July, 1911, Jan. and July.......... | 349,000 |
| " " " 5 per cent., due July, 1911, Jan. and July......... | 650,000 |
| West Jersey & S. S., 1st cons. mort., 4 per cent., due July, 1936, Jan. and July...... | 1,600,000 |
| " " " Series B, 3½ per cent., due July, 1936 Jan. and July.. | 1,500,000 |
| Total.............................................................. | $4,939,900 |

West Jersey & Sea Shore 1st consolidated mortgage was authorized in June, 1896, to arrange the company's indebtedness. Amount is $4,500,000. In July, 1896, bonds aggregating $950,000 were paid off and replaced by new consols. In May, 1898, $600,000 of this issue were sold for improvements, including double tracking the Camden & Atlantic Division. In February, 1899, an issue of 3½ per cent. consols of $1,500,000 was sold to retire the West Jersey 1sts and Camden & Atlantic 2ds maturing during 1899.

For earnings, etc., of the Camden & Atlantic and West Jersey see MANUAL for 1896 under those companies.

EARNINGS (COMBINED COMPANIES).

| | Gross. | Net. | Charges. | Dividends. | Surplus. |
|---|---|---|---|---|---|
| 1892.............. | $2,554,246 | $617,145 | $361,576 | $153,132 | $102,437 |
| 1893.............. | 2,531,371 | 612,452 | 391,540 | 153,017 | 67,895 |
| 1894.............. | 2,440,898 | 649,952 | 416,510 | 248,195 | Def., 14,753 |
| 1895.............. | 2,565,847 | 649,099 | 425,959 | 252,498 | " 29,349 |
| 1896.............. | 2,554,919 | 610,458 | 359,785 | 251,899 | " 1,229 |
| 1897.............. | 2,550,940 | 599,797 | 317,517 | 235,620 | 46,660 |
| 1898.............. | 2,682,121 | 691,845 | 422,561 | 235,650 | 33,634 |
| 1899.............. | 3,008,456 | 891,982 | 562,161 | 253,807 | 76,013 |
| 1900.............. | 3,490,457 | 957,672 | *830,422 | ...... | 127,250 |
| 1901.............. | 3,678,693 | 942,953 | *560,049 | ...... | 382,904 |
| 1902.............. | 3,893,798 | 1,025,581 | *1,023,581 | ...... | ...... |

* Includes both interest and dividends.

President, Alexander J. Cassatt; Vice-Presidents, Charles E. Pugh, Sutherland M. Prevost; Treasurer, R. W. Smith; Secretary, J. M. Harding, Philadelphia.

Directors—Alexander J. Cassatt, John P. Green, W. G. Nixon, Charles E. Pugh, Josiah Wistar, George Wood, N. Parker Shortridge, Samuel Rea, W. H. Barnes, Sutherland M. Prevost, Philadelphia; W. Bettle, B. F. Lee, S. H. Gray, Camden, N. J.; Israel G. Adams, Atlantic City, N. J.; Edward C. Stokes, Millville, N. J.

Main office, Camden, N. J. Annual meeting, first Tuesday in March. Books close thirty days previous.

## WEST SIDE BELT RAILROAD CO.

A corporation formed under the laws of Pennsylvania, July 25, 1895.

Road owned, Pittsburg to Banksville, Pa., 3 miles; Banksville to Bruce Station on the Baltimore & Ohio Railroad, 12 miles. This last mentioned extension was completed in 1902. Total operated, 15 miles. The company also has an extension, Bruce Station to Clairton, 8 miles, under construction, which will be completed in 1903. Locomotives, 5; passenger cars, 1; freight cars, 1,134.

In 1902, a controlling interest in this company was acquired by capitalists identified with the Pittsburg Terminal Railroad & Coal Co., the road being now operated in connection with that corporation, which has extensive coal interests near Pittsburg.

Stock......Par $50............................Authorized, $1,080,000......Issued, $1,080,000

FUNDED DEBT.

1st mort., 5 per cent., due Sept., 1937, March and Sept........................... $461,500

The authorized amount of the bond issue is $1,000,000. Trustee of the mortgage, Union Trust Co., Pittsburg; agent for the payment of interest on the bonds, Colonial Trust Co., Pittsburg.

In the year ending June 30, 1902, the operations of the company covering only the original 3 miles of road, showed a net deficit of $2,602.

President, F. M. Osborne; Vice-President, Charles Donnelly; Treasurer, Joshua Rhodes; Secretary, J. G. Patterson; Assistant Treasurer, W. G. Rock, Pittsburg.

Directors—F. M. Osborne, T. H. Given, M. K. McMullin, F. F. Nicola, S. H. Robbins, Charles Donnelly, J. G. Patterson, J. D. Callery, Joshua Rhodes, T. N. Barnsdall, A. W. Osborne, Pittsburg.

Main office, 345 Fourth avenue, Pittsburg. Annual meeting, May 1.

## WEST VIRGINIA CENTRAL & PITTSBURG RAILWAY CO.

A corporation formed under the laws of West Virginia, February 23, 1881.

In 1902 control of this company was acquired by a syndicate acting in the interest of the Wabash system. The same capitalists also acquired the Western Maryland, and 98 per cent. of this company's stock has been deposited under the new 1st mortgage of the Western Maryland Railroad Co.

Road owned, Piedmont, W. Va., to Elkins, 85 miles; branches, Elkins to Belington, 18 miles; Elkins to Hattonville, 17 miles; other branches, 13 miles; total owned, 132 miles. The company also owns and operates Piedmont & Cumberland Railroad, 29 miles, and controls the Coal & Iron Railway, Elkins to Durbin, W. Va., 47 miles; total operated, 208 miles. In 1900 control of the Piedmont & Cumberland was acquired. The company has about 100,000 acres of coal, iron and timber lands in the Elk Garden mineral district of West Virginia. Locomotives, 43; passenger cars, 22; freight cars, 2,801.

In 1902 an extension to connect this road with the Western Maryland was commenced.

In December, 1899, the company acquired the property of the Davis Coal & Coke Co., which includes 50,000 acres of coal land and 700 coke ovens. For this purpose the stock of the railroad company was increased from $6,000,000 to $10,546,000. The increase of $4,000,000 was used to pay for control of the coal company and for the stock of the Piedmont & Cumberland Railroad. The coal company is operated under its own corporate organization.

Stock......Par $100.........................Authorized, $25,000,000......Issued, $10,546,100

From 1889 to 1894, 1 per cent. per annum was paid on the stock; in 1895, 1896 and 1897, 1½ per cent. was paid; in 1898, ½ per cent.; in 1899, 1 per cent.; in 1900, 2½ per cent.; in 1901, 3 per cent; in 1902, 2 per cent. was paid in March.

FUNDED DEBT.

| | |
|---|---|
| 1st mort., 6 per cent., due July, 1911, Jan. and July | $3,250,000 |
| Piedmont & Cumberland, 1st mort., 5 per cent., due Aug., 1911, Feb. and Aug. | 650,000 |
| Coal & Iron Ry., 1st mort., 5 per cent., due Aug., 1920, Feb. and Aug. | 1,000,000 |
| Total | $4,900,000 |

In 1897-98 $250,000 additional bonds included in the total amount given above were sold to provide for improvements.

EARNINGS.

Year ending June 30.

| | Gross. | Net. | Charges. | Surplus. |
|---|---|---|---|---|
| 1892-93 | $945,948 | $360,650 | $222,817 | $137,833 |
| 1893-94 | 798,238 | 305,165 | 216,588 | 88,577 |
| 1894-95 | 1,060,719 | 322,734 | 222,572 | 104,862 |
| 1895-96 | 1,192,285 | 329,139 | 202,253 | 126,885 |

EARNINGS—*Continued.*

| | Gross. | Net. | Charges. | Surplus. |
|---|---|---|---|---|
| 1896-97 | 604,347 | 274,027 | 180,000 | 94,027 |
| 1897-98 | 660,181 | 284,631 | 183,000 | 101,631 |
| 1898-99 | 697,207 | 320 109 | 109,727 | 120 382 |
| 1899-00 | 1,108,392 | 407,083 | 256,202 | 150,880 |
| 1900-01 | 1,182,181 | 1,038,321 | 170,749 | 867,572 |
| 1901-02 | 1,311,531 | 1,110,212 | 241,846 | 868,366 |

Net includes profits on coal sales In 1898 profit on coal, included in net, $78,457, a loss of $15,415 on Piedmont & Cumberland lease being deducted. In 1899, profit on coal, $70,881; loss on Piedmont & Cumberland, $24,981; dividend (1 per cent.), $55,000; balance surplus, $65,382. In 1900, earnings for coal department, $236,017; total, net, $501,129; betterments, etc., $267,532; dividends, $150,000; net surplus, $83,596. In 1900-01, earnings from coal department, $503,655; real estate department, $100,741. In 1901-02, earnings from coal department, $553,950; from real estate department, $111,529.

Chairman, Winslow S. Pierce, New York; President, Joseph Ramsey, Jr., St. Louis; Vice-President, Fairfax S. Landstreet, Baltimore; Secretary, L. F. Timmerman; Treasurer, J. T. M. Barnes, New York.

Directors—George J. Gould, Howard Gould, Winslow S. Pierce, Henry C. Deming, E. L. Fuller, Lawrence Greer, New York; Fairfax S. Landstreet, Baltimore; Joseph Ramsey, Jr., St. Louis.

Main office, Elkins, W. Va. Annual meeting, second Tuesday in Angurt. Books close twenty days previous.

---

## WHEELING & LAKE ERIE RAILROAD CO.

A reorganization in 1899 of the Wheeling & Lake Erie Railway Co. In 1901 capitalists identified with the Wabash Railway acquired large interests in this company, which is now operated in harmony with the Wabash system, though under its own management.

Road owned, Toledo, O., to Martins Ferry, opposite Wheeling, 218 miles; Cleveland to Zanesville, O., 144 miles; branches, 89 miles; Cleveland Belt Railway, 6 miles; Toledo Belt Railway, 4 miles; total owned, 461 miles; leased, 12 miles; total operated, 473 miles. In 1901 a connection with Pittsburg was begun by capitalists interested in this company under the title of the Pittsburg, Carnegie & Western Railway. Locomotives, 119; passenger cars, 58; freight equipment, 9,312.

In 1899 acquired the Cleveland, Canton & Southern Railroad Co. and Cleveland Belt & Terminal by purchase. For account of the Cleveland, Canton & Southern, see MANUAL for 1889.

| Stock..Par $100..Authorized | | | Issued | | |
|---|---|---|---|---|---|
| | com., $20,000,000 | | | com., $20,000,000 | |
| | 1st pref., 5,000,000 | | | 1st pref., 4,986,900 | $36,980,400 |
| | 2d pref., 12,000,000 | | | 2d pref., 11,993,500 | |

The preferred stocks are 4 per cent., non-cumulative, in their respective order.

Transfer agency, 195 Broadway, New York. Registrar, Mercantile Trust Co., New York.

FUNDED DEBT.

| | |
|---|---|
| 1st mort. (old company) Lake Erie Div., 5 per cent., due Oct., 1926, April and Oct. | $2,000,000 |
| " ( " " ) Wheel. Div., 5 per cent., bonds, due July, 1928, Jan. and July. | 894,000 |
| Extension and imp. mort. (old company), 5 per cent., due Feb., 1930, Feb. and Aug. | 385,000 |
| Toledo Belt Railway, 1st mort., 5 per cent., guar., due 1903, March and Sept. | 24,000 |
| Cons. mort., 4 per cent., due Sept., 1949, March and Sept. | 13,830,000 |
| Equipment trusts | 719,270 |
| Equipment bonds, 5 per cent., due 1922, Jan. and July | 1,927,000 |
| Total | $19,779,270 |

The new 4 per cent. mortgage is for $15,000,000, of which $6,400,000 was reserved to retire prior liens. The purchase of the Cleveland, Canton & Southern and Cleveland Belt & Terminal roads required $3,850,000 of the bonds, being part of $5,600,000 sold in 1899, $1,750,000 being also furnished for improvements and retirement of car trusts, the remaining $3,000,000 being reserved for additional improvements, equipment and terminals. Over one-half of the 5 per cent. bonds of the old company have been refunded into new 4s.

The equipment bonds issued in 1902 may be purchased at 105 or drawn at 108 and interest.

EARNINGS.

Year ending June 30.

| | Gross. | Net. | Charges. | Surplus. |
|---|---|---|---|---|
| 1891-92 (243 miles).................. | $1,371,165 | $513,005 | $320,915 | $192,090 |
| 1892-93 (247 " ).................. | 1,538,645 | 547,884 | 335,635 | 212,249 |
| 1893-94 ( " " ).................. | 1,288,584 | 473,666 | 370,857 | 102,800 |
| 1894-95 ( " " ).................. | 1,353,825 | 412,318 | 378,575 | 33,743 |
| 1895-96 ( " " ).................. | 1,453,917 | 444,890 | 379,778 | 65,112 |
| 1896-97 (243 " ).................. | 1,153,212 | Def. 71,950 | ...... | ...... |
| 1897-98 ( " " ).................. | 1,399,458 | " 633,794 | ...... | ...... |
| 1898-99 (244 " ).................. | 1,549,814 | 153,530 | 53,333 | 100,197 |
| 1899-00 (393 " ).................. | 2,710,095 | 805,102 | 598,866 | 206,236 |
| 1900-01 (442 " ).................. | 2,954,105 | 921,649 | 774,699 | 146,950 |
| 1901-02 ( " " ).................. | 3,537,023 | 943,220 | 871,097 | 72,123 |

The receivership lasted from January 15, 1897, to April 30, 1899. The figures for 1898-99 include two months' operation of the new company.

Chairman, Myron T. Herrick, Cleveland; President, Joseph Ramsey, Jr., St. Louis; Vice-President, Alvin W. Krech, New York; Secretary, James H. Dowland, Cleveland; Treasurer, Henry B. Henson, New York.

Directors—George J. Gould, Edwin Gould, Winslow S. Pierce, Cyrus J. Lawrence, Joseph Ramsey, Jr., Washington E. Connor, Alvin W. Krech, New York; Myron T. Herrick, Robert Blickensderfer, G. A. Garretson, E. W. Oglebay, H. P. McIntosh, W. G. Mather, D. R. Hanna, Cleveland; C. M. Spitzer, Toledo, O.

Main office, Cleveland; New York office, 195 Broadway. Annual meeting, first Wednesday in May.

---

## WHITE PASS & YUKON RAILWAY CO., LIMITED

An English corporation which constructed and operates a line of narrow gauge railroad from Skaguay, Alaska, to White Horse, Yukon Territory, 111 miles. The company also owns the British Yukon Navigation Co., Ltd., which operates steamboats on the Yukon and various rivers and lakes in Yukon Territory and Northern British Columbia. Locomotives, 17; passenger cars, 15; freight cars, 268.

Stock......Par £10....... ..................Authorized, £1,700,000......Issued, £1,375,000

The first dividend paid was 5 per cent., in April, 1901, and in August, 1901, 25 per cent. in stock was paid and 5 per cent. cash in December, 1901.

FUNDED DEBT.

| | |
|---|---|
| Consolidated 1st mort. debenture stock, 5 per cent., due Dec. 31, 1930, Jan. and July.. | £746,702 |
| Mortgage debentures, 6 per cent., due Jan., 1911, Jan. and July..................... | 255,555 |
| Total............................................................... | £1,002,257 |

The authorized amount of the consolidated mortgage debenture stock is £750,000. The 6 per cent. debentures were issued to purchase the fleet of steamboats. This company has reserved £255,555 of its own stock with which to retire the 6 per cent. debentures.

In 1900 the local companies carried, gross, $2,084,331; net, $1,355,201. In 1901, gross, $1,758,065; net, $1,026,966.

EARNINGS.

Year ending June 30.

| | Receipts. | Charges. | Balance. | Dividends. | Surplus. |
|---|---|---|---|---|---|
| 1900-01................. | £321,563 | £60,445 | £261,058 | £55,000 | £206,058 |
| 1901-02................. | 214,828 | 77,861 | 136,967 | 68,750 | 68,217 |

The receipts comprise the dividends and interest on securities of the local companies owned by the parent company.

President, Samuel H. Graves, Chicago; Vice-President and General Manager, A. B. Newell, Skaguay, Alaska; Secretary and Comptroller, Francke C. Elliott; Treasurer, John W. Probert, Chicago; Auditor, A. L. Berdoe, Skaguay, Alaska.

Main office, 138 Washington street, Chicago.

## WILLIAMSPORT & NORTH BRANCH RAILROAD CO.

A corporation formed under the laws of Pennsylvania, September 1, 1882. The company succeeded the Muncy Creek Railroad Co.

Road owned, Halls, Pa., to Satterfield, Pa., 44 miles; branches, 3 miles; total owned, 47 miles; leased, Eagles Mere Railroad, Sonestown to Eagles Mere, Pa., 8 miles; trackage, 5 miles; total operated, 60 miles. Locomotives, 6; passenger cars, 11; freight cars, 6. The company has considerable coal lands.

Stock......Par $50......Authorized { com., $2,000,000 / pref., 400,000 } Issued { com., $923,950 / pref., 400,000 } $1,323,950

The preferred stock is 6 per cent. non-cumulative.

FUNDED DEBT.

1st mort., 4½ per cent., due July, 1931, Jan. and July.............................. $530,000

The 1st mortgage is for $750,000, of which $250,000 was reserved for extensions. It was created to retire the old 5 per cent. bonds. Trustee of the mortgage and agent for the payment of interest, Fidelity Trust Co., Philadelphia.

EARNINGS.

Year ending June 30.

| | Gross. | Net. | Charges. | Surplus. |
|---|---|---|---|---|
| 1901-02.............................. | $121,726 | $47,886 | $33,212 | $14,674 |

President, B. Harvey Welch, Hughesville, Pa.; Vice-Presidents, Horace H. Farrier, Jersey City, C. William Woddrop, Hughesville, Pa.; Secretary and Treasurer, Henry C. Adams, New York; General Manager, S. D. Townsend, Hughesville, Pa.

Directors—B. Harvey Welch, S. D. Townsend, C. William Woddrop, Hughesville, Pa.; Horace H. Farrier, Jersey City, N.J.; Henry C. Adams, New York; Seth T. McCormick, C. La Rue Munson, Williamsport, Pa.

Main office, Hughesville, Pa. Annual meeting, third Wednesday in May.

## WILMINGTON & NORTHERN RAILROAD CO.

(Leased to Philadelphia & Reading Railway Co.)

Road owned, Wilmington, Del., to Highs Junction, below Reading, Pa., 71.50 miles; branches, 16.91 miles; sidings, 32.51 miles; total owned, 121.93 miles; trackage, 3.52 miles. Locomotives, 29; passenger cars, 35; freight cars, 563; service cars, 15.

In October, 1898, control of the property was acquired in the interest of the Reading Company. In 1899 the minority stock was also purchased and the road leased for 999 years from February 1, 1900, to the Philadelphia & Reading Railway, which company has issued $1,300,000 4 per cent. trust certificates secured by this company's stock.

Stock......Par $50............................Authorized, $1,500,000......Issued, $1,500,000

FUNDED DEBT.

| | |
|---|---|
| 1st mort., 5 per cent. bonds, due 1907-27, July and Dec.......................... ... | $354,000 |
| Gen. mort., 5 per cent., due Aug., 1932, quar., Feb.................... ....... . . | 406,000 |
| Total ............................................................ . | $760,000 |

There are also $36,000 of car trust obligations.

The earnings of this company are included in those of the lessee.

President, H. A. Du Pont, Wilmington, Del.; Secretary, E. B. Shurter; Treasurer, W. A. Church; Comptroller, Daniel Jones, Philadelphia.

Main office, Reading Terminal Station, Philadelphia. Annual meeting, first Monday in May.

## WISCONSIN & MICHIGAN RAILWAY CO.

A corporation formed under the laws of Wisconsin in 1893.

Road owned, Fairthorn Junction, Mich., to Peshtigo, Wis., 57 miles; branches, 6 miles; total operated, 63 miles. Freight is transported from Peshtigo to Chicago by a car ferry. An extension to Iron Mountain, Mich., 30 miles, is in progress. Locomotives, 5; passenger cars, 2; freight cars, 200.

Stock......Par, $100............................Authorized, $1,000,000......Issued, $951,000

FUNDED DEBT.

| | |
|---|---|
| 1st mort., 5 per cent., due Jan., 1945, Jan. and July | $951,000 |

The company has been in default as to its interest charges, and plans for a reduction of the same have been proposed, but without definite result.

In the year ending June 30, 1900, the company earned, gross, $115,287; net, $8,139.

President, C. H. Bosworth; Secretary, O. A. Koss; Treasurer, B. Shaw, Chicago.

Directors—J. M. Fairthorn, John R. Walsh, C. H. Bosworth, John C. Ames, Chicago; C. H. Worcester, Marinette, Wis.

Main office, Grand Central Passenger Station, Chicago.

## WISCONSIN CENTRAL RAILWAY CO.

A corporation organized in 1899, and which on July 18, 1899, took possession of the property of the Wisconsin Central Co. and the Wisconsin Central Railroad, which were sold in foreclosure and reorganized under a plan dated April 10, 1899. The property of the present company, besides that which belonged to the two corporations named above, includes that of the Chicago, Wisconsin & Minnesota, Milwaukee & Lake Winnebago Railroad, Central Car Co. and other concerns affiliated with the system, the sole ownership being now vested in this company.

Road owned, Chicago to Trout Brook Junction, Minn., 452 miles; Abbotsford, Wis., to Ashland, Wis., 133 miles; branches, 231 miles; total owned, 816 miles; trackage, Rugby to Milwaukee, 28 miles; other trackage, at Minneapolis, Chicago, etc., 32 miles; spurs to industries, 167 miles, 65 miles of which are not operated; total, 1,043 miles. The company in 1901 purchased the Marshfield & Southeastern Railroad, 33 miles. Locomotives, 157; passenger cars, 141; freight cars, 8,402.

Stock..Par $100...Authorized { com., $17,500,000; pref., 12,500,000 } Issued { com., $16,168,800; pref., 11,276,200 } $27,445,000

The preferred stock is 4 per cent., non-cumulative. Both classes of stock are held in a voting trust for five years or less at trustees' option. The trustees are John Crosby Brown, William L. Bull, Frederick T. Gates and Francis B. Hart.

Transfer Agents, Maitland, Coppell & Co., 24 Exchange place, New York. Registrar, United States Trust Co., New York.

FUNDED DEBT.

| | |
|---|---|
| 1st gen. mort., gold, 4 per cent., due July, 1949, Jan. and July | $24,635,000 |
| Chicago, Wis. & Minn. 1st mort., 6 per cent., due March, 1916, March and Sept. | 776,000 |
| Milwaukee & Lake Winnebago 1st mort., 6 per cent., due July, 1912, Jan. and July. | 604,000 |
| Wisconsin Central R. R. con. mort., 5 per cent., due Jan., 1909, Jan. and July | 664,500 |
| Minneapolis Terminal pur. money mort., 3½ per cent., due Jan., 1950, Jan. and July. | 500,000 |
| Marshfield, S. E. Div., 1st mort., 4 per cent., due May, 1951, May and Nov. | 445,000 |
| Total | $27,624,500 |

There are equipment trusts outstanding for $600,000.

The Wisconsin Central Co. was organized in 1887 to unite the lines affiliated with the Wisconsin Central Railroad Co. The system was leased in April, 1890, to the Northern Pacific.

In September, 1893, the company applied to Court to have the property taken from hands of Northern Pacific Receivers. A decision was rendered dissolving the lease. Receivers were appointed for the company in September, 1893.

The old company leased the Chicago & Northern Pacific, but that property was sub-leased to Northern Pacific and was operated independently of Wisconsin Central lines, and has been reorganized as the Chicago Terminal Transfer Co.

The road was reorganized in 1899 under a plan which is given in full in the MANUAL for 1900.

EARNINGS.

Year ending June 30.

| | Gross. | Per Cent. Op. Exp. | Net. | Charges. | | Surplus. |
|---|---|---|---|---|---|---|
| 1894-95 | $4,090,543 | .... | $1,308,155 | $1,459,958 | Def. | $151,803 |
| 1895-96 | 4,399,511 | .... | 1,715,638 | 1,809,932 | " | 94,294 |
| 1896-97 | 4,179,971 | .... | 1,467,950 | 1,566,561 | " | 98,611 |
| 1897-98 | 4,939,725 | .... | 1,978,739 | 1,469,681 | | 509,058 |
| 1898-99 | 5,118,018 | 59.74 | 2,060,529 | ........ | | ........ |
| 1899-00 | 5,637,416 | 63.52 | 2,064,758 | 1,571,843 | | 402,915 |
| 1900-01 | 5,324,274 | 65.11 | 1,605,615 | 1,419,498 | | 246,117 |
| 1901-02 | 6,041,471 | 64.28 | 1,976,680 | 1,496,575 | | 480,105 |

The following exhibits the comparative freight traffic statistics of the system:

| | Average Mileage. | Total Tonnage. | Tons Carried One Mile. | Freight Density. | Rate per Ton per Mile. | Earnings per Train Mile. | Average Tons per Train. |
|---|---|---|---|---|---|---|---|
| 1896-97.... | 937 | 2,561,980 | 347,666,177 | 372,233 | 0.873c | $1.77 | 201 |
| 1897-98.... | 935 | 3,541,953 | 483,700,402 | 515,187 | 0.755 | 1.84 | 244 |
| 1898-99.... | 939 | 3,636,809 | 513,385,516 | 546,736 | 0.731 | 1.83 | 250 |
| 1899-00.... | 945 | 3,989,032 | 571,086,218 | 604,324 | 0.731 | 1.89 | 258 |
| 1900-01.... | 955 | 3,428,562 | 522,867,887 | 547,505 | 0.742 | 2.03 | 260 |
| 1901-02.... | 977 | 4,004,906 | 636,393,127 | 651,370 | 0.709 | 1.91 | 286 |

Chairman, William L. Bull, New York; President, Henry F. Whitcomb; Treasurer, W. R. Hancock; Secretary, Charles W. Morris, Milwaukee; Assistant Secretary, Joseph S. Dale, New York; Auditor, Robert Toombs, Milwaukee.

Directors—John Crosby Brown, William L. Bull, Frederick T. Gates, Edward W. Sheldon, Joseph S. Dale, Gerald L. Hoyt, James C. Colgate, New York; Francis R. Hart, Boston; Howard Morris, Henry F. Whitcomb, Milwaukee; W. F. Vilas, Madison, Wis.

Main office, Milwaukee; New York office, 38 Broad street. Annual meeting, second Tuesday in October, at Milwaukee.

---

## WORCESTER, NASHUA & ROCHESTER RAILROAD CO.

(Leased to Boston & Maine Railroad.)

Road owned, Worcester, Mass., to Rochester, N. H., 94 miles.

Stock......Par $100..........................Authorized, $3,600,000......Issued, $3,099,800

Transfer Agent, American Loan & Trust Co., Boston.

Dividends are paid semi-annually, in January and July. In 1899 paid 4½ per cent.; in 1900, 4 per cent.; in 1901, 5¼ per cent., and in 1902, 5 per cent. The January, 1903, dividend was reduced to 1¾ per cent.

FUNDED DEBT.

| | |
|---|---|
| Bonds, 4 per cent., due July, 1906, Jan. and July.................................. | $150,000 |
| " " Jan., 1930, Jan. and July. .................................. | 735,000 |
| " " Jan., 1913, Jan. and July.................................. | 511,000 |
| " " Oct., 1934, April and Oct.................................. | 380,000 |
| Total.............................................................. | $1,776,000 |

December 1, 1883, the Nashua & Rochester was consolidated with the Worcester & Nashua, forming the present company. There was no increase in miles worked or bonded debt, and the stock was simply increased by the amount of the Nashua & Rochester, for which new certificates were issued. Stock dividend of 17 per cent. paid November 13, 1885. January 1, 1886, the property was leased for 50 years to the Boston & Maine for $250,000 per year.

President, George G. Haven, New York; Treasurer and Clerk, Charles H. Bowen, Boston.

Main office, Worcester, Mass; treasurer's office, 53 State street, Boston. Annual meeting in January.

---

## THE ZANESVILLE & WESTERN RAILWAY CO.

A corporation formed under the laws of Ohio, October 16, 1902. The company acquired and took over the southern section of the Columbus, Shawnee & Hocking Railroad Co. which was foreclosed, the northern part being taken over by the Toledo, Walhonding Valley & Ohio Railroad Co. The Hocking Valley Railway Co. acquired all the securities of this company.

Road owned, 71½ miles; leased, 11 miles; trackage, 3½ miles; the main line extends from Thurston, O., to Shawnee, 59 miles; branch, Fultonham, O., to Zanesville, 11 miles; other branches, 16 miles. Locomotives, 23; passenger cars, 17; freight cars, 1,836.

Stock ......Par $100.................. .......Authorized, $2,500,000......Issued, $2,500,000

The company has no preferred stock.

FUNDED DEBT.

1st mort., 4 per cent., due Nov. 1, 1952, May and Nov.............................. $2,000,000

The 1st mortgage was created in 1902 and is for $2,000,000. Trustee of mortgage, Standard Trust Co., New York. Agents for payment of interest, J. P. Morgan & Co., New York.

President, Nicholas Monsarrat, Columbus, O.; 1st Vice-President, James H. Hoyt, Cleveland; 2d Vice-President, J. M. Ferris, Toledo; Secretary and Treasurer, W. N. Cott, Columbus, O.

Directors—Nicholas Monsarrat, E. L. McCune, Columbus O.; James H. Hoyt, G. Von den Steinen, Cleveland; R. R. Rogers, New York.

Main office, 50 East Broad street, Columbus, O. Annual meeting, first Tuesday in October, at Columbus, O.

# Comparative Freight Traffic and Rates

## Of the Principal Railroad Systems of the United States

All figures, except as noted below, are for the respective fiscal years ending June 30. The exceptions are as follows: The fiscal year of the Chicago, Rock Island & Pacific ends March 31, the Chicago & Northwestern, May 31, the Pennsylvania, the Missouri Pacific, the Delaware & Hudson and the Chicago, St. Paul, Minneapolis & Omaha December 31.

| RAILROADS. | Year Ending in | Average Mileage. | Total Tonnage. | Tons Carried One Mile. | Freight Density. | Rate per Ton per Mile. | Earnings per Train Mile. | Average Tons per Train. |
|---|---|---|---|---|---|---|---|---|
| | | | | | | Cents. | Dollars. | |
| Ann Arbor | 1901 | 292 | 1,539,270 | 91 ,250,216 | 651,191 | 0.650 | 1.916 | 291 |
| " | 1902 | 292 | 1,594,917 | 200,264,691 | 685,837 | 0.680 | 1.900 | 280 |
| Atchison, Topeka & Santa Fe | 1901 | 7,807 | 11,112,614 | 3,876,793,344 | 496,579 | 1.007 | 2.440 | 242 |
| " " " | 1902 | 7,855 | 11,596,093 | 4,231,748,520 | 538,733 | 0.988 | 2.530 | 247 |
| Baltimore & Ohio | 1901 | 3,220 | 33,528,513 | 7,140,897,00 | 2,217,669 | 0.498 | 1.901 | 381 |
| " " | 1902 | 3,233 | 38,710,216 | 7,495,527,180 | 2,318,443 | 0.515 | 2.012 | 406 |
| Boston & Maine | 1901 | 2,264 | 17,516,571 | 1,538,317,388 | 683,885 | 1.134 | 1.670 | 207 |
| " " | 1902 | 2,265 | 18,183,321 | 1,620,362,196 | 715,391 | 1.119 | .... | ... |
| Central of Georgia | 1901 | 1,678 | 2,708,915 | 437,060,554 | 260,495 | 1.064 | 1.816 | 163 |
| " " | 1902 | 1,845 | 3,258,444 | 491,487,448 | 255,594 | 1.129 | 1.907 | 163 |
| Chesapeake & Ohio | 1901 | 1,506 | 10,125,497 | 3,051,175,642 | 2,026,017 | 0.388 | 1.980 | 511 |
| " " | 1902 | 1,636 | 10,904,165 | 3,194,336,608 | 1,974,250 | 0.402 | 2.046 | 509 |
| Chicago & Eastern Illinois | 1901 | 722 | 5,914,394 | 917,170,653 | 1,263,320 | 0.490 | 2.400 | 487 |
| " " " | 1902 | 737 | 7,411,362 | 1,096,645,035 | 1,487,985 | 0.450 | 2.780 | 605 |

| | | | | | | | | |
|---|---|---|---|---|---|---|---|---|
| Chicago & Northwestern | 1901 | 5,507 | 25,271,726 | 3,701,417,722 | 672,111 | 0.850 | 1.980 | 232 |
| " " | 1902 | [illegible] | 29,321,538 | 4,122,440,480 | 715,825 | 0.810 | 2.030 | 249 |
| Chicago, Burlington & Quincy | 1901 | 7,753 | .......... | 3,870,529,358 | 499,243 | 0.862 | 1.756 | 201 |
| " " " | 1902 | 8,109 | .......... | 4,613,072,546 | 568,881 | 0.772 | 1.967 | 251 |
| Chicago Great Western | 1901 | 929 | 2,651,054 | 833,799,170 | 897,947 | 0.640 | 2.000 | 319 |
| " " " | 192 | 99 | 2,753,675 | 804,613,173 | 865,632 | 0.750 | 2.020 | 269 |
| Chicago, Milwaukee & St. Paul | 1901 | 6,512 | 18,010,683 | 3,639,977,919 | 558,964 | 0.861 | 2.038 | 236 |
| " " " | 192 | 6,604 | 19,885,573 | 3,990,048,676 | 604,186 | 0.840 | 2.136 | 254 |
| Chicago, Rock Island & Pacific | 1901 | [illegible] | 7,706,535 | 1,789,092,549 | 468,471 | 0.990 | 1.800 | 182 |
| " " " | 192 | [illegible] | 8,245,978 | 1,839,027,297 | 470,365 | [illegible] | 1.840 | 178 |
| Chicago, St. Paul, Minneapolis & Omaha | 191 | 1,574 | 5,073,440 | 823,144,727 | 522,328 | 0.961 | 2.370 | 247 |
| " " " " | 1902 | 1,605 | 5,359,509 | 849,645,417 | 529,374 | 0.960 | 2.26 | 234 |
| Cleveland, Cincinnati, Chicago & St. Louis | 1901 | 1,891 | 11,098,315 | 1,909,086,365 | 1,009,511 | 0.610 | 2.030 | 333 |
| " " " " | 1902 | 1,891 | 12,056,981 | 2,012,357,493 | 1,064,192 | 0.592 | 1.970 | 332 |
| Delaware & Hudson | 1901 | 660 | 13,057,958 | 1,274,511,441 | 1,925,653 | 0.755 | 2.681 | ... |
| " " | 1902 | 717 | 10,659,444 | 1,159,831,753 | 1,682,598 | 0.711 | 2.454 | ... |
| Denver & Rio Grande | 1901 | 2,393 | 5,736,062 | 979,498,415 | 409,318 | 1.24 | 2.26 | 182 |
| " " | 192 | [illegible] | 6,507,124 | 998,010,972 | 417,577 | 1.22 | 2.43 | 199 |
| Erie | 1901 | 2,155 | 25,999,602 | 4,989,381,988 | 2,315,351 | 0.587 | 2.201 | 375 |
| " | 1902 | 2,153 | 27,697,159 | 4,756,339,949 | 2,209,169 | 0.635 | 2.389 | 376 |
| Evansville & Terre Haute | 1901 | 162 | 1,708,558 | 101,196,986 | 624,672 | 0.870 | 2.221 | 262 |
| " " | 192 | 162 | 1,810,435 | 109,344,068 | 674,963 | 0.848 | 2.327 | 281 |
| Great Northern | 191 | [illegible] | 11,518,251 | 2,481,751,195 | 477,230 | 0.871 | 3.380 | 381 |
| " " | 192 | 5,247 | 15,099,818 | 3,190,219,482 | 609,776 | 0.859 | 3.640 | 417 |
| Hocking Valley | 1901 | 347 | 6,576,611 | 835,528,765 | 2,402,100 | 0.442 | 2.850 | 645 |
| " " | 1902 | 347 | 8,156,514 | 1,003,371,955 | 2,891,561 | 0.428 | 2.900 | 678 |
| Illinois Central | 191 | [illegible] | 17,735,749 | 4,016,085,602 | 952,826 | 0.619 | 1.456 | 235 |
| " " | 1902 | 4,276 | 19,096,441 | 4,452,073,927 | 1,041,211 | 0.622 | 1.711 | 274 |

## COMPARATIVE FREIGHT TRAFFIC AND RATES—*Continued.*

| RAILROADS. | Year Ending in | Average Mileage. | Total Tonnage. | Tons Carried One Mile. | Freight Density. | Rate per Ton per Mile. | Earnings per Train Mile. | Average Tons per Train. |
|---|---|---|---|---|---|---|---|---|
| | | | | | | Cents. | Dollars. | |
| Iowa Central | 1901 | 506 | 1,667,202 | 252,497,682 | 498,971 | 0.709 | 1.602 | 226 |
| " " | 1902 | 558 | 1,866,971 | 296,184,406 | 530,796 | 0.668 | 1.460 | 218 |
| Kansas City Southern | 1901 | 833 | 1,848,028 | 571,488,288 | 686,060 | 0.687 | 2.060 | 333 |
| " " " | 1902 | 833 | 2,038,843 | 593,113,856 | 712,021 | 0.752 | 2.190 | 327 |
| Lehigh Valley | 1901 | 1,382 | 19,805,624 | 3,805,865,245 | 2,753,882 | 0.542 | 2.536 | 467 |
| " " | 1902 | 1,387 | 18,174,886 | 3,418,884,789 | 2,464,949 | 0.554 | 2.588 | 466 |
| [illegible]ille & Nashville | 1901 | 3,169 | 16,685,466 | 2,655,984,116 | 838,114 | 0.769 | 1.700 | 222 |
| " " | 1902 | 3,320 | 18,320,972 | 3,072,093,936 | 923,813 | 0.741 | 1.710 | 230 |
| Minneapolis & St. Louis | 1901 | 633 | 1,766,287 | 210,799,911 | 333,017 | 1.145 | 3.305 | 288 |
| " " | 1902 | 641 | 1,940,268 | 204,515,108 | 319,056 | 1.235 | 3.160 | 255 |
| Minneapolis, St. Paul & Sault Ste. Marie | 1901 | 1,301 | 2,973,310 | 535,017,533 | 411,235 | 0.617 | 1.942 | 314 |
| " " " | 1902 | 1,396 | 3,234,023 | 617,746,549 | 441,795 | 0.739 | 2.330 | 314 |
| Missouri, Kansas & Texas | 1901 | 2,265 | 4,884,976 | 1,304,[illegible]964 | 576,022 | 0.927 | 1.967 | 212 |
| " " " | 1902 | 2,500 | 5,014,429 | 1,396,710,077 | 558,684 | 0.904 | 1.860 | 206 |
| Missouri Pacific | 1901 | 5,554 | 15,479,849 | 3,542,315,399 | 582,322 | 0.825 | 2.300 | 284 |
| " " | 1902 | 5,613 | 16,649,701 | 3,666,908,434 | 592,299 | 0.807 | 2.450 | 310 |
| New York Central & Hudson River | 1901 | 3,223 | 36,430,820 | 6,606,890,325 | 1,972,047 | 0.60 | 2.090 | 351 |
| " " " " " | 1902 | 3,319 | 35,599,689 | 6,407,594,086 | 1,939,620 | 0.630 | 2.170 | 342 |
| New York, New Haven & Hartford | 1901 | 2,027 | 15,436,435 | 1,292,378,364 | 643,140 | 1.479 | 3.199 | 208 |
| " " " " " | 1902 | 2,027 | 17,145,313 | 1,444,544,216 | 712,651 | 1.455 | 3.294 | 217 |
| Norfolk & Western | 1901 | 1,560 | 10,836,512 | 2,864,370,760 | 1,836,135 | 0.461 | 2.125 | 461 |
| " " | 1902 | 1,677 | 12,268,110 | 3,151,911,924 | 1,879,553 | 0.463 | 2.202 | 476 |

| | | | | | | | | |
|---|---|---|---|---|---|---|---|---|
| Northern Pacific | 192 | 5,100 | 8,792,885 | 2,440,662,665 | 478,561 | 0.944 | 3.120 | 324 |
| " " | 191 | 5919 | 11,080,101 | 3,300,253,137 | 657,551, | 0.900 | 3.172 | 346 |
| Pennsylvania | 191 | 3,739 | 122,246,793 | 12, 6[illegible]89 | 3,400,275 | 0.582 | 2.849 | 490 |
| " | 192 | 3,705 | 133,944,161 | 14,040,264,352 | 5[illegible]238 | 0.586 | 3.039 | 518 |
| Reading (General traffic) | 1901 | 1,000 | 14,535,083 | 1,026,056,531 | 1 96,056 | 0.982 | ..... | ... |
| " " | 192 | 93 | 16,413,700 | 1,113,015,544 | 1,109,686 | 0.988 | ..... | ... |
| Reading (Coal traffic) | 191 | 90 | 15,542,382 | 1,703 9695 | 1, 7914 | 0.727 | ..... | ... |
| " " | 192 | 1,003 | 15 [illegible] | 1,710,792,217 | 1, 5,875 | 0.726 | ..... | ... |
| St. Joseph & Grand Island | 1901 | 312 | 677,211 | 79,371,981 | 254,226 | 1.320 | 2.700 | 199 |
| " " " | 902 | 312 | [illegible]494 | 77,779,000 | [illegible]96 | 1.360 | 2.640 | 200 |
| St. Louis & San Francisco | 1901 | 3,187 | 8,798,261 | 1,540, 913 | 483,277 | 0.894 | 1.789 | 200 |
| " " | 192 | 3,414 | 9,068,650 | 1,637,557,119 | 479,659 | 0.953 | 1781 | 186 |
| St. Louis Southwestern | 1901 | 1,275 | 2,399,171 | 468,837,265 | 367,715 | 1.210 | 2.557 | 209 |
| " " | 192 | 1293 | 2,586,387 | 514,942,615 | 398,254 | 1.080 | 2.533 | 232 |
| Seaboard Air Line | 192 | 2, 63 | 4,516,072 | 740,169,229 | 284,285 | 1.068 | 1.87 | 175 |
| Southern Pacific | 191 | 8,654 | 14,067 162 | 4,873,257,728 | 563,121 | 1.001 | 2.690 | 254 |
| " " | 192 | 8,757 | 15,736 913 | 4,957,602,303 | 566,244 | 1.021 | 2.790 | 265 |
| Southern Railway | 1901 | 6,612 | 15 980 | 2,450,220,562 | 364,890 | 0.936 | 1.816 | 191 |
| " " | 192 | 6,743 | 16,811,538 | 2,678,308,625 | 397,198 | 0.931 | 1.819 | 195 |
| Toledo, St. Louis & Western | 1901 | 451 | 1,600,668 | 349,044, 72 | 796,107 | 0.542 | 1.360 | 250 |
| " " " | 902 | 451 | 1 613 | 357,88 5668 | 815,711 | 0.553 | 1.578 | 285 |
| Union Pacific | 191 | 5,686 | 8,31 ,371 | ........... | 671,235 | ..... | 3.010 | 365 |
| " " | 192 | 5,710 | 8,590,193 | ........... | 751,097 | ..... | 3.310 | 417 |
| Wabash | 191 | 2,376 | 10,027,358 | 1,978,952,453 | 832,050 | 0.563 | 1.598 | 283 |
| " | 1902 | 2,438 | 10,481,692 | 1,947,404,142 | 798,771 | 0.604 | 1.719 | 284 |
| Wisconsin Central | 1901 | 955 | 3,428,562 | 522,867,887 | 547,505 | 0.742 | 2.030 | 260 |
| " " | 902 | 977 | 4,004,906 | 636,393,127 | 651,370 | 0.790 | 910 | 286 |

# General Railroad Statistics

## Record of Construction, Receiverships and Foreclosures

### *RAILROAD CONSTRUCTION*

The following is an estimate of the new railroad construction in the United States by years.

| Year. | Miles. | Year. | Miles. |
|---|---|---|---|
| 871 | 7,379 | 1887 | 12,983 |
| 1872 | 5,878 | 1888 | 7,120 |
| 1873 | 4,097 | 1889 | 5,730 |
| 1874 | 2,117 | 1890 | 6,080 |
| 1875 | 1,711 | 1891 | 4,168 |
| 1876 | 2,712 | 1892 | 4,150 |
| 1877 | 2,280 | 1893 | 2,635 |
| 1878 | 2,629 | 1894 | 1,049 |
| 1879 | 4,746 | 1895 | 1,803 |
| 1880 | 6,876 | 1896 | 1,848 |
| 1881 | 9,796 | 1897 | 1,864 |
| 1882 | 11,568 | 1898 | 3,018 |
| 1883 | 6,741 | 1899 | 4,500 |
| 1884 | 3,825 | 1900 | 4,437 |
| 1885 | 3,608 | 1901 | 5,222 |
| 1886 | 9,000 | 1902 | 5,549 |

### *RAILROADS SOLD UNDER FORECLOSURE IN 1902*

The following is a list of railroad corporations whose property was sold under foreclosure during 1902, with a statement of their mileage, capital stock and funded debt.

| Company. | Miles. | Funded Debt. | Capital Stock. |
|---|---|---|---|
| California & Nevada | 22 | $500,000 | * $500,000 |
| Chicago, Greenville & Southern | 4 | 50,000 | 50,000 |
| Columbus, Lima & Milwaukee | 40 | 545,000 | 1,000,000 |
| Columbus Ry. & Nav. Co. | 3 | 300,000 | 495,000 |
| Columbus, Sandusky & Hocking | 218 | 12,300,000 | 2,500,000 |
| Cumberland Plateau | 9 | *225,000 | *225,000 |
| Duluth Transfer | 14 | 1,180,000 | 2,000,000 |
| Erie & Central New York | 20 | 250,000 | 250,000 |
| Gulf & Brazos Valley | 11 | 88,000 | 10,000 |
| Hogdeville & Elizabethtown | 11 | 150,000 | 123,000 |
| Little Falls & Dolgeville | 10 | 325,000 | 250,000 |
| New Orleans & Northwestern | 101 | 2,500,000 | 4,500,000 |
| New York & Pennsylvania | 52 | 500,000 | 500,000 |
| Omaha, Kansas City & Eastern | 36 | 816,000 | 1,428,000 |
| Pennsylvania Midland | 15 | 513,000 | 1,900,000 |
| Port Jervis, Monticello & N. Y. | 41 | 225,000 | 409,000 |
| Sylvania | 15 | *150,000 | *150,000 |
| Washburn, Bayfield & Iron River | 35 | 235,000 | *500,000 |
| Wilkesbarre & Western | 31 | 620,000 | *620,000 |
| Zanesville Terminal | 5 | 453,000 | 453,000 |
| Total, 18 roads | 693 | $21,925,000 | $17,863,000 |
| Total bonds and stock | .... | ... .... | 39,788,000 |

* Estimated.

## RAILROAD FORECLOSURE SALES IN TWENTY-SEVEN YEARS

| Year. | No. Roads. | Mileage. | Total Stock and Funded Debt. |
|---|---|---|---|
| 1876 | 30 | 3,840 | $217,848,000 |
| 1877 | 54 | 3,875 | 198,984,000 |
| 1878 | 48 | 3,906 | 311,631,000 |
| 1879 | 65 | 4,909 | 243,228,000 |
| 1880 | 31 | 3,775 | 263,882,000 |
| 1881 | 29 | 2,617 | 127,923,000 |
| 1882 | 16 | 867 | 65,426,000 |
| 1883 | 18 | 1,354 | 37,100,000 |
| 1884 | 15 | 710 | 23,504,000 |
| 1885 | 22 | 3,156 | 278,494,000 |
| 1886 | 45 | 7,687 | 374,109,000 |
| 1887 | 31 | 5,478 | 328,181,000 |
| 1888 | 19 | 1,596 | 64,555,000 |
| 1889 | 25 | 2,930 | 137,815,000 |
| 1890 | 29 | 3,825 | 182,495,000 |
| 1891 | 21 | 3,223 | 186,069,000 |
| 1892 | 28 | 1,922 | 95,898,000 |
| 1893 | 23 | 1,410 | 47,264,000 |
| 1894 | 42 | 5,643 | 318,999,000 |
| 1895 | 52 | 12,831 | 761,791,000 |
| 1896 | 58 | 1,373 | 1,150,377,000 |
| 1897 | 42 | 6,675 | 517,680,000 |
| 1898 | 47 | 6,054 | 252,910,000 |
| 1899 | 32 | 4,294 | 267,534,000 |
| 1900 | 24 | 3,477 | 190,374,000 |
| 1901 | 16 | 1,107 | 85,808,000 |
| 1902 | 18 | 693 | 39,788,000 |
| Total, 27 years | 880 | 109,227 | $6,769,567,000 |

## ROADS FOR WHICH RECEIVERS WERE APPOINTED IN 1902

| Road. | Miles. | Funded Debt. | Capital Stock. |
|---|---|---|---|
| Carolina Northern | 40 | $450,000 | $500,000 |
| Chicago & Southeastern | 127 | 395,000 | 2,500,000 |
| Georgetown & Western | 50 | 500,000 | 400,000 |
| Kansas & Southern | 9 | 45,000 | 45,000 |
| New York & Pennsylvania | 52 | 500,000 | 500,000 |
| Total, 5 roads | 278 | $1,890,000 | $3,945,000 |
| Total bonds and stock | .. | ........ | 5,835,000 |

## SUMMARY OF RAILROAD RECEIVERSHIPS FOR TWENTY-SEVEN YEARS

| Year. | Number Roads. | Mileage. | Stocks and Bonds. |
|---|---|---|---|
| 1876 | 42 | 6,662 | $467,000,000 |
| 1877 | 38 | 3,637 | 220,294,000 |
| 1878 | 27 | 2,320 | 92,385,000 |
| 1879 | 12 | 1,102 | 39,367,000 |
| 1880 | 13 | 885 | 140,265,000 |
| 1881 | 5 | 110 | 3,742,000 |
| 1882 | 12 | 912 | 39,074,000 |
| 1883 | 11 | 1,990 | 108,470,000 |
| 1884 | 37 | 11,038 | 714,755,000 |
| 1885 | 44 | 8,286 | 385,460,000 |
| 1886 | 13 | 1,799 | 70,346,000 |
| 1887 | 9 | 1,046 | 90,318,000 |
| 1888 | 22 | 3,270 | 186,814,000 |
| 1889 | 22 | 3,803 | 99,664,000 |
| 1890 | 26 | 2,963 | 105,007,000 |
| 1891 | 26 | 2,159 | 84,479,000 |
| 1892 | 36 | 10,508 | 357,692,000 |
| 1893 | 74 | 29,340 | 1,781,046,000 |
| 1894 | 38 | 7,025 | 395,791,000 |
| 1895 | 31 | 4,089 | 369,075,000 |
| 1896 | 34 | 5,441 | 275,597,000 |
| 1897 | 18 | 1,537 | 92,909,000 |
| 1898 | 18 | 2,069 | 138,701,000 |
| 1899 | 10 | 1,019 | 52,285,000 |
| 1900 | 16 | 1,065 | 78,234,000 |
| 1901 | 4 | 73 | 1,627,000 |
| 1902 | 5 | 278 | 5,835,000 |
| Totals, 27 years | 643 | 114,626 | $6,396,232,000 |

# INDUSTRIAL SECURITIES

## Manufacturing, Street Railway, Electrical, Gas, Mining, Land, Coal, Iron and Steel, Telegraph and Telephone, and Miscellaneous Corporations

### Comprising all Whose Securities are Quoted in the Leading Stock Markets

**Later Information Regarding the Companies Herein Represented and Others, either Organized or in Process of Formation, as well as Those Not of Sufficient Importance to Be Included, will be Furnished Free of Charge to Subscribers to the MANUAL on Application**

### *ABERDEEN CONSOLIDATED GOLD & COPPER CO.*

A corporation formed under the laws of New Mexico in 1901. The company acquired the Aberdeen Copper Co., exchanging its shares for those of the latter company, which owned 40 mining claims near Lordsburg, N. M. Considerable development work has been done on the property, and the new company has proceeded with the erection of a smelter on its property.

Stock......Par $25.......................... Authorized, $1,000,000......Issued, $1,000,000

The stock is full paid and non-assessable. The company has no preferred stock. Stock is transferred at the office of the company, New York.

The Aberdeen Copper Co., of which this company is the successor, paid a dividend of $1 per share in 1901.

President, T. D. Bradford; Secretary, M. Fraser Bolen.

Corporate office, Lordsburg, N. M.; main office, 44 New street, New York.

---

### *ACKER, MERRALL & CONDIT CO.*

A corporation formed under the laws of New York, January 16, 1893. The purpose of the company was to take over and operate the wholesale and retail grocery and cigar business of the firm of Acker, Merrall & Condit, New York. In 1902 the capital of the company was increased and its business extended.

Stock......Par $100..........................Authorized, $5,000,000......Issued, $5,000,000

FUNDED DEBT.

Twenty-year debentures, 6 per cent., due Jan. 10, 1923, Jan. (10) and July ...... .. $3,500,000

Trustee of the mortgage and agent for the payment of interest, United States Mortgage & Trust Co., New York.

President, Harry J. Luce; Vice-Presidents, William J. Merrall, Albert E. Merrall, Frank A. Merrall; Secretary, George J. Smith; Treasurer, Walter H. Merrall; Assistant Treasurer, William B. Merrall.

Directors—Harry J. Luce, Albert E. Merrall, Frank A. Merrall, Walter H. Merrall, Jordan J. Rollins, W. L. Stow, George W. Young, George J. Smith, William J. Merrall, William B. Merrall, Charles F. Merrall, Wilbur K. Matthews, Arthur Turnbull, Charles B. Van Nostrand, George K. McGraw.

Main office, 135 West Forty-second street, New York. Annual meeting, third Monday in January.

---

### *ADAMS EXPRESS CO.*

A joint stock association formed in 1854. The organization operates express routes on some 35,000 miles of railroad, including the Pennsylvania, New York, New Haven & Hartford, Chesapeake & Ohio, Chicago, Burlington & Quincy systems, etc.

Stock is transferred at the company's office, New York. Registrar, Union Trust Co., New York.

Capital......Par $100......................Authorized, 120,000 shares......Issued, $12,000,000

FUNDED DEBT.

Collateral trust debentures, 4 per cent., due March, 1948, March and Sept. ........... $12,000,000

No reports are furnished of this organization's business. In February, 1898, company declared a 100 per cent. dividend in 4 per cent. debenture bonds as a special dividend. The debenture bonds are secured by a deposit with the Mercantile Trust Co., New York, of treasury assets valued at $12,400,000. These collaterals are subject to a right on part of shareholders to indemnification against personal liability.

For many years dividends were 8 per cent. per annum (quarterly 2 per cent.). When the extra dividend in bonds referred to above was paid in 1898, the rate was reduced to 4 per cent., payable half-yearly, 2 per cent. each in June (1) and December. The December 1, 1900, dividend was accompanied by an extra dividend of 2 per cent., which was paid from the revenue on the company's investments, and the same course was followed regarding the subsequent half-yearly dividends. In February, 1903, an extra dividend of 2 per cent. was paid from the sale of property not needed in the conduct of the company's business.

President, Levi C. Weir; Secretary, Horatio H. Gates; Treasurer, B. W. Rowe.

Managers—William B. Dinsmore, Levi C. Weir, William H. Damsel, William M. Barrett, Caleb S. Spencer, Charles Steele.

Executive office, 59 Broadway, New York.

---

## THE ADVENTURE CONSOLIDATED COPPER CO.

A corporation organized under the laws of Michigan, October 17, 1898. The company acquired the Adventure and other mines upon the Mineral Range in Ontonagon County, Mich. The entire property comprises some 2,100 acres. The company since its organization has prosecuted exploration work with vigor.

Stock......Par $25..........................Authorized, $2,500,000......Issued, $2,500,000

Transfer Agent, Old Colony Trust Co., Boston. Registrar, American Loan & Trust Co., Boston. There had been paid in up to January, 1903, $13.50 per share.

Up to December 31, 1902, the receipts of the company had been $1,703,784; expenditures, $1,634,213; balance, $69,570.

President, Charles J. Devereaux, Boston; Secretary and Treasurer, William R. Todd; Assistant Secretary and Treasurer, W. A. O. Paul, New York.

Directors—James S. Dunstan, Charles J. Devereaux, William R. Todd, Henry A. Wyman, Isaac H. Meserve, John Barker.

Main office, 45 Broadway, New York.

---

## ALABAMA CONSOLIDATED COAL & IRON CO.

A corporation formed under the laws of New Jersey, July 19, 1899. The company owns and operates the following iron and coal properties at or near Birmingham, Ala.:

| | |
|---|---|
| Clifton Iron Co., Ironton, Ala. | Jefferson Coal and Ry. Co., Birmingham, Ala. |
| Gadsden Furnace, Gadsden, Ala. | Attala Iron Co. Mines, Etowah County, Ala. |
| Mary Pratt Furnace, Birmingham, Ala. | Mary Lee Coal Mines, Lewisburg, Ala. |
| Gate City Iron Ore Mines, Gate City, Ala. | O'Connor Mining & Manufacturing Co., Jefferson County, Ala. |
| Standard Coal Co., Tuscaloosa County, Ala. | |

These properties include five blast furnaces, nearly 40,000 acres of coal lands, 600 coke ovens, and a large acreage of ore, limestone and timber lands, the mines having a capacity of 500,000 tons of coal per annum, and the coke ovens a product of 225,000 tons of coke yearly. The Jefferson Coal and Railway Co., the Attala Iron Mines and the Mary Lee Coal Mines were acquired in 1901.

Stock....Par $100.....Authorized { com., $2,500,000 / pref., 2,500,000 } Issued { com., $2,500,000 / pref., 2,500,000 } $5,000,000

The preferred stock is 7 per cent., cumulative.

The payment of quarterly dividends on the preferred stock of the company began with the declaration of 1¾ per cent., payable November 1, 1899. Similar quarterly payments have since been regularly made.

Transfer Agent and Registrar, International Trust Co. of Maryland, Baltimore.

In December, 1902, it was announced that a plan would be submitted for the creation of an issue of $3,500,000 5 per cent. bonds and an increase of $1,000,000 in the common stock. The purpose was stated to be to retire the preferred stock in exchange for 100 per cent. of its face in new bonds and 25 per cent. in common stock.

### FUNDED DEBT.

1st mort., 6 per cent., due May, 1911, May and Nov.. ............................. $490,000

The 1st mortgage, 6 per cent., bonds are $500,000 authorized and were created in 1901. Trustee of mortgage, St. Louis Trust Co., St. Louis.

EARNINGS.

Year ending October 31.

| | Gross. | Net. | Charges and Pref. Div. | Surplus. |
|---|---|---|---|---|
| 1899-00 | $1,741,388 | $240,022 | $158,033 | $81,989 |
| 1900-01 | 1,910,782 | 174,961 | 165,703 | 9,258 |
| 1901-02 | 2,873,216 | 448,943 | 200,451 | 248,492 |

President, T. G. Bush, Birmingham, Ala.; Vice-President, Douglas H. Gordon; Secretary and Treasurer, Charles T. Westcott, Baltimore.

Directors—John E. Searles, New York; J. William Middendorf, R. H. Edmonds, Douglas H. Gordon, Summerfield Baldwin, William C. Seddon, Samuel C. Rowland, Baltimore; T. G. Bush, Birmingham, Ala.

Main office, Calvert and Fayette streets, Baltimore.

## ALBANY & HUDSON RAILWAY CO.

A corporation formed under the laws of New York, March 12, 1903. The company is the successor, under the reorganization plan referred to below, of the Albany & Hudson Railway & Power Co. The latter company, which was formed in 1899, acquired the stock and property of the Kinderhook & Hudson Railway, the Hudson Street Railway Co. and Hudson Light & Power Co. of Hudson, N. Y., the Greenbush & Nassau Electric Railway, the Citizens' Electric Light Co., the Kinderhook Power & Light Co., the East Albany Gas Light Co. and the Rensselaer Lighting Co. It also acquired other property, including a water power at Stuyvesant Falls, N. Y., where a large power plant was built by the company. The railroad lines were rebuilt and extended to constitute a continuous third-rail electric line, 35 miles long, from Albany to Hudson, which line was opened for traffic in the latter part of 1900. The cars of the company enter the city of Albany over the lines of the United Traction Co., which it uses under contract. The company also supplies electricity for lighting and power in the cities and towns along its lines.

On Oct. 10, 1902, a receiver was appointed for the old company. A committee, composed of Clinton L. Rossiter, Foster M. Voorhees and Horace M. Andrews, submitted a plan of reorganization, supplementing one which had been formulated some months earlier. See below for details of plan. Depositary of securities under the plan, Colonial Trust Co., New York. The property was foreclosed and bought by the committee on February 11, 1903, the new company taking possession in March, 1903.

Stock.....Par $100....Authorized { com., $1,000,000 / pref., 1,000,000 } Issued { com., $1,000,000 / pref., 1,000,000 } $2,000,000

The preferred stock is 5 per cent., non-cumulative. Transfer Agent, Long Island Trust Co, Brooklyn. Registrar, Colonial Trust Co., New York.

FUNDED DEBT.

1st mort., 4 to 5 per cent., due March, 1943, March and Sept........................ $1,500,000

The new 1st mortgage bears 4 per cent. interest until March 1, 1906, and after that date 5 per cent. Trustee of mortgage, Colonial Trust Co., New York. Authorized amount of bonds, $2,000,000.

The old company had $2,500,000 stock, all common, and $2,500,000 of 5 per cent. bonds, due 1939, March and September.

The reorganization plan submitted in October, 1902, provided for an issue of $2,000,000 bonds, $1,000,000 preferred stock and $1,000,000 common stock. It included the exchange of the old bonds in exchange for 60 per cent. of their face in new bonds and 40 per cent. in new preferred stock on payment of $20 per bond. Of the new bonds, $500,000 were to be reserved for improvements and $500,000 of the new common stock was to be used to settle unsecured claims and $500,000 reserved in the treasury.

EARNINGS.

Year ending June 30.

| | Gross. | Net. | Charges. | Deficit. |
|---|---|---|---|---|
| 1901 | $212,718 | $29,822 | $...... | $...... |
| 1902 | 242,294 | 72,366 | 60,000 | 13,766 |

The charges for 1902 in above table is the interest for one year on $1,500,000 of the new bonds.

President, Clinton L. Rossiter; 1st Vice-President, A. M. Young, New York; 2d Vice-President and General Manager, George T. Blakeslee, Albany N. Y.; Secretary and Treasurer, H. G. Runkle, New York.

Directors—A. M. Young, Henry Siebert, Seth L. Keeney, R. A. C. Smith, Horace E. Andrews, H. G. Runkle, William F. Sheehan, Clinton L. Rossiter, Foster M. Voorhees.

Main office, Rensselaer, N. Y.; New York office, 100 Broadway.

## ALBEMARLE & CHESAPEAKE CANAL CO.

A corporation chartered by both Virginia and North Carolina, 1854-55. It owns and operates a canal 14 miles long, connecting the waters of Chesapeake Bay and Albemarle Sound.

Stock........................................................................ $528,200

FUNDED DEBT.

1st mort., 7 per cent., due July, 1909, Jan. and July.................................. $500,000

Trustee of mortgage, Union Trust Co., New York.

In 1901 bondholders were invited to deposit bonds with a committee with a view to a reduction of the interest rate, but the January, 1902, coupon on bonds was paid in full. The July, 1902, coupons were not paid, and the bondholders' committee has been in negotiation with the company.

In the fiscal year ending September 30, 1900, the earnings of the company were, gross, $35,539; net, $16,512. In 1900-01, gross, $51,906; net, $33,417.

The last dividend payment was 1½ per cent. in 1898.

President, Warren G. Elliott, Baltimore; Vice-President, R. M. Cannon; Secretary and Treasurer, D. S. Burwell, Norfolk, Va.

Directors—Robert M. Cannon, John Vermillion, Norfolk, Va.; J. H. Chapman, New York; Andrew S. White, Syracuse, N.Y.; R. St. P. Lowry, Erie, Pa.; E. G. Richmond, Chattanooga, Tenn.

Main office, Citizens' Bank Building, Norfolk, Va.

## THE ALLEGHENY COAL CO.

A corporation formed under the laws of Pennsylvania in 1901 for the purpose of mining coal. The company acquired about 4,500 acres of coal land on the Allegheny River, fourteen miles from Pittsburg, at the intersection of the West Pennsylvania Railroad and the Bessemer & Lake Erie Railroad. It also holds in fee 1,700 feet of land fronting on the Allegheny River. The tract is some six miles long and four miles wide. Every one hundred acres of the coal land has been drilled, and it has been determined that the company has a continuous vein of coal over its entire property averaging seven feet in thickness.

Stock......Par $100.......Authorized { com., $600,000 / pref., 600,000 } Issued { com., $600,000 / pref., 600,000 } $1,200,000

The preferred stock is 7 per cent., cumulative. Transfer Agent and Registrar, American Trust Co., Cleveland.

FUNDED DEBT.

1st mort. 5 per cent. sinking fund gold bonds, due in three-year periods, ending 1917... $200,000

Trustee of the bonds and agent for the payment of interest, American Trust Co., Cleveland.

President, H. A. Hawgood; Vice-President, J. E. Terry; Secretary, C. L. Terry; Treasurer, Sheldon Parks, Cleveland.

Directors—H. A. Hawgoo , J. E. Terry, U. C. Hatch, W. H. Scriven, Sheldon Parks, Clevelan ; Parks Foster, Elyria, O.; C. F. Perkins, George E. Alter, Pittsburg; M. J. Agan, Springdale, Pa.

Corporate office, Springdale, Pa.; main office, Citizens' Building, Cleveland. Annual meeting, third Tuesday in January.

## ALLEGHENY STEEL & IRON CO.

A corporation formed under the laws of Pennsylvania in 1900. The object of the company is the manufacture of steel sheets. The company has a large plant in Averne, Pa., near Pittsburg. In January, 1903, it had in operation an open-hearth steel furnace department with 50,000 tons capacity, a bar mill with 50,000 tons capacity and a sheet mill with 18,000 tons capacity.

Stock......Par $100................ ............Authorized, $300,000......Issued, $300,000

The company has no preferred stock or funded debt.

Stock is transferred at the office of the company, Pittsburg.

President, Alfred Hicks; Vice-President, George A. McLean; Treasurer, H. M. Brackenridge; Secretary, Robert D. Campbell; General Manager, H. E. Sheldon.

Main office, 357 Fifth avenue, Pittsburg. Annual meeting in July, at Pittsburg.

## THE ALLIANCE REALTY CO.

A corporation formed under the laws of New York in June, 1899. The business of the company is dealing in real estate and buying, selling and mortgaging the same.

Stock......Par $100..........................Authorized, $3,000,000......Issued, $2,000,000

The stock outstanding was $1,000,000, but an additional amount of $1,000,000 was issued early in 1902. The company has no preferred stock or funded debt.

Stock is transferred at the office of the company. Registrar, Standard Trust Co., New York.

A dividend of 1½ per cent. was paid July 15, 1902, and similar dividends in October, 1902, and January 15, 1903.

President, Frederick Southack; Vice-President, Alwyn Ball, Jr.; Secretary, John Carleson; Treasurer, Michael Coleman, New York.

Directors—Frederick Southack, Henry O. Havemeyer, William A. Read, George R. Read, Alwyn Ball, Jr., Edwin M. Bulkley, Walter T. Rosen, F. S. Smithers, John R. Hegeman, James J. Higginson, Charles T. Barney, James H. Post, New York; Charles Francis Adams, 2d, George L. Peabody, Boston.

Main office, 25 Broad street, New York. Annual meeting, third Thursday in February.

## ALLIS-CHALMERS CO.

A corporation formed under the laws of New Jersey, May 1, 1901. The company was organized to manufacture mining machinery, cement mills, rock crushers, steam engines and heavy machinery of various kinds. It acquired the plants of the following concerns, which are largest of their class in the United States:

| | |
|---|---|
| E. P. Allis Co., Milwaukee. | Gates Iron Works, Chicago. |
| Fraser & Chalmers, Incorporated, Chicago. | Dickson Manufacturing Co., Scranton, Pa. |

Stock..Par $100..Authorized { com., $25,000,000; pref., 25,000,000 } Issued { com., $20,000,000; pref., 16,250,000 } $36,250,000

The preferred stock is 7 per cent. cumulative, and has preference as to both dividends and assets in case of the company's dissolution.

Stock is transferred at the office of the company, 25 Broad street, New York. Registrar, Central Trust Co., New York.

The dividend periods for the preferred stock are quarterly, in February (1), May, August and November. The first dividend on the preferred was 1¾ per cent., quarterly, paid July 25, 1901. Since then the regular quarterly payments on the preferred have been made at the periods named above.

The company has no funded debt.

### Earnings.

Year ending April 30.

| | Net. | Pfd. Dividends. | Surplus. |
|---|---|---|---|
| 1901-02 | $1,442,259 | $1,137,500 | $304,759 |

Net is given after deductions for depreciations, etc.

The following is the company's balance sheet, September 30, 1902:

### Assets.

| | | | |
|---|---|---|---|
| Real estate, buildings, plant, machinery, good will, etc | | | $28,331,324 |
| Bills and accounts receivable | | $2,319,058 | |
| Stocks of merchandise, materials and work in progress (at cost) | | 4,082,091 | |
| Cash | | 3,298,539 | |
| | | | 9,699,688 |
| Total | | | $38,031,012 |

### Liabilities.

| | | | |
|---|---|---|---|
| Capital stock: | | | |
| Preferred | | $16,250,000 | |
| Common | | 20,000,000 | |
| | | | $36,250,000 |
| Accounts payable | | $1,064,845 | |
| Dividends accrued | | 189,583 | |
| | | | 1,254,428 |
| Surplus, April 30, 1902 | | 304,759 | |
| Profits, April 30 to October 1, 1902 | $695,783 | | |
| Less dividend on preferred stock, declared and accrued | 473,958 | | |
| Surplus for five months over dividend on preferred stock | | 221,824 | |
| Total surplus | | | 526,584 |
| Total | | | $38,031,012 |

Chairman of Board, Elbert H. Gary, New York; President, Charles Allis; Vice-President and Treasurer, William J. Chalmers; 2d Vice-President, Henry W. Hoyt, Chicago; 3d Vice-President and General Superintendent, Philetus W. Gates, Chicago; 4th Vice-President and Secretary, Joseph H. Seaman; Assistant Secretary, Joseph O. Watkins; Assistant Treasurer, George A. Brewster, New York; Comptroller, James A. Milne, Chicago.

Directors—Edward D. Adams, Elbert H. Gary, William A. Read, James Stillman, Cornelius Vanderbilt, New York; Charles Allis, William J. Chalmers, James H. Eckels, Henry W. Hoyt, Philetus W. Gates, Max Pam, Chicago; William W. Allis, Frank G. Bigelow, Edwin Reynolds, Milwaukee; Mark T. Cox, Orange, N. J.

Executive Committee—Chairman, William J. Chalmers; Edward D. Adams, Charles Allis, James H. Eckels, Henry W. Hoyt, Max Pam, Cornelius Vanderbilt.

Finance Committee—Chairman, William A. Read; Edward D. Adams, William J. Chalmers, Mark T. Cox, Elbert H. Gary.

Corporate office, 15 Exchange place, Jersey City; main office, 205 La Salle street, Chicago; New York office, 25 Broad street. Annual meeting, third Monday in May, at Jersey City.

## ALLOUEZ MINING CO.

A corporation organized under the laws of Michigan. The company owns a large mining property consisting of about 3,500 acres in Keweenaw County, Mich., the portion operated being directly north of the line of the Kearsage Mining Co. In 1898 the company purchased 120 more acres, carrying the underline of the Osceola and other lodes. The outcrop of the Osceola lode, and development work at present is confined to that lode. The shaft in January, 1901, was down 1,150 feet, proving the rock to be very similar to that in the Osceola mine.

Stock......Par $25..........................Authorized, $2,500,000......Issued, $2,500,000

Stock is transferred at the company's office, Boston. Registrar, Old Colony Trust Co., Boston. In 1901, 20,000 shares held in the treasury were distributed *pro rata* to the stockholders.

President, Harry F. Fay; Secretary and Treasurer, Walter B. Mosman; Treasurer, George F. Endicott.

Directors—Harry F. Fay, Walter B. Mosman, Godfrey Morse, H. A. Tucker, Stephen R. Dow, John C. Watson, Boston; Jesse Lewisohn, John Stanton, New York; James Chynoweth, Michigan.

Main office, 60 State street, Boston. Annual meeting, second Tuesday in March.

## ALTON RAILWAY, GAS & ELECTRIC CO.

A corporation formed under the laws of Illinois in 1899. The purposes of the company are owning and operating street railways, gas plants and electric light systems. The company owns the Alton Railway & Illuminating Co., the Alton & East Alton Railway & Power Co., the Alton Gas & Electric Light Co., and the Alton Electric & Service Co., the last two properties having been purchased at foreclosure sales. The Alton Railway & Illuminating Co. has ten miles of street railway and an electric light and power plant. The plant of the Alton Gas & Electric Light Co. is a system of gas works and mains, the electric portion of the plant having been abandoned.

Stock......Par $100....................... .....Authorized, $500,000......Issued, $500,000

The company has no preferred stock. Stock is transferred by the secretary, Alton, Ill.

FUNDED DEBT.

| | |
|---|---|
| 1st mort. 5 per cent., due Oct., 1939, April and Oct. | $250,000 |
| Alton Railway & Illuminating 1st mort., due Oct., 1915, April and Oct. | 236,000 |
| Alton Imp. Co. mort., due Sept., 1904, March and Sept. | 14,000 |
| Total | $500,000 |

The 1st mortgage is for $500,000. Trustee of mortgage and agent for payment of interest, International Banking Trust Co., New York. Of the bonds, $250,000 are reserved to retire underlying liens.

The Trustee of the Alton Railway & Illuminating Co.'s mortgage and agent for payment of interest is the Manhattan Trust Co., New York.

EARNINGS.

Year ending September 30.

| | Gross. | Net. | Charges. | Surplus. |
|---|---|---|---|---|
| 1899-00 | $106,574 | $47,208 | $20,375 | $26,832 |
| 1900-01 | 128,894 | 52,697 | 19,388 | 33,309 |

President and Treasurer, Joseph F. Porter; Vice-President, O. S. Stowell; Secretary, H. S. Baker, Alton, Ill.

Directors—Charles A. Caldwell, George M. Ryrie, Oliver S. Stowell, Henry S. Baker, Joseph F. Porter, Alton, Ill.

Corporate and main office, 205 Market street, Alton, Ill. Annual meeting in January, at Alton, Ill.

## AMALGAMATED COPPER CO.

A corporation formed under the laws of New Jersey, April 27, 1899. The company acquired controlling interests in the Anaconda Copper Co., Parrot Silver & Copper Co., Washoe Copper Co., Colorado Smelting & Mining Co. and other companies. In 1901, acquired the Boston & Montana Consolidated Copper & Silver Mining Co. and the Butte & Boston Consolidated Mining Co.

In a statement made to the New York Stock Exchange in June, 1901, the company stated that it owned the following stocks:

| Companies Whose Stocks are Wholly Owned. | Total Issue. |
|---|---|
| Washoe Copper Co., Butte, Mont | $5,000,000 |
| Colorado Smelting & Mining Co., Butte, Mont | 2,500,000 |
| Diamond Coal & Coke Co., Diamondville, Wyo | 1,500,000 |
| Big Black Foot Milling Co., Bonner, Mont | 700,000 |
| Majority of Stock Owned. | |
| Anaconda Copper Mining Co., Butte, Mont | $30,000,000 |
| Parrott Silver & Copper Co., Butte, Mont | 2,298,500 |
| Hennesey Mercantile Co., Butte, Mont | 1,500,000 |
| Boston & Montana Consolidated Copper & Silver Mining Co., Butte, Mont | 3,750,000 |
| Butte & Boston Consolidated Mining Co., Butte, Mont | 2,000,000 |

The company also acquired $3,447,200 of the Boston & Montana stock and $1,838,500 of that of the Butte & Boston Co.

See separate statements of the Anaconda, Parrott, Boston & Montana and Butte & Boston Cos. in this edition of the MANUAL.

Stock......Par $100......................Authorized, $155,000,000......Issued, $148,540,200

Transfer Agents, National City Bank, New York; Kidder, Peabody & Co., Boston. Registrars, Central Trust Co., New York; Shawmut National Bank, Boston.

The original $75,000,000 stock of this company was offered for public subscription, at par, closing on May 4, 1899, by the National City Bank, New York. It is stated that the total applications amounted to some $412,000,000.

In June, 1901, the authorized stock was increased to $155,000,000, to acquire the stocks of the Boston & Montana and Butte & Boston Cos. Holders of Boston & Montana were offered for each $25 share of that stock 4 shares of Amalgamated Copper and holders of Butte & Boston for each $10 share of its stock received 1 share of Amalgamated Copper stock. The greater part of the stocks of those companies were exchanged under the above terms.

This company has no funded debt, but of the constituent companies the Boston & Montana has $600,000 of 7 per cent. bonds and the Butte & Boston $1,500,000 of 6 per cent. bonds.

No report or statement of the company's finances and operations has been issued. The reductions in the dividend rate on the stock in October, 1901, and January, 1902, were explained as due to heavy decline in the prices of copper.

The net earnings of some of the constituent companies for the years ending June 30, have been reported as follows:

| | 1899. | 1900. | 1901. | 1902. |
|---|---|---|---|---|
| Anaconda | $3,463,700 | $5,365,520 | $5,069,071 | $1,289,610 |
| Boston & Montana | 2,882,955 | 3,701,510 | 7,042,303 | 1,630,695 |
| Butte & Boston | ........ | ........ | 586,053 | 166,136 |
| Parrott | 472,795 | 336,180 | 510,196 | 577,617 |
| Colorado Mining Co | ........ | ........ | 303,619 | 152,495 |
| Total | $6,819,450 | $9,403,210 | $13,511,242 | $3,816,553 |

The first dividend was 1½ per cent. quarterly and ½ per cent. extra was paid October 16, 1899. Similar dividends of 1½ per cent. quarterly and ½ per cent. extra were regularly paid, January (28), April, July and October, until October, 1901, when the rate was made 1½ per cent. without the extra dividend. In January, 1902, 1 per cent. was paid for the quarter, and in May, 1902, only ½ per cent. was paid, the same rate being maintained for the August and November, 1902, and February, 1903, dividends.

President—Henry H. Rogers; Secretary and Treasurer, William G. Rockefeller, New York.

Directors—Frederic P. Olcott, Robert Bacon, James Stillman, William Rockefeller, William G. Rockefeller, Henry H. Rogers, Anson R. Flower, New York; A. C. Burrage, Boston.

Main office, 52 Broadway, New York. Annual meeting, first Monday in June, at Jersey City.

## AMALGAMATED SUGAR CO.

A corporation formed under the laws of Utah, July 5, 1902. The purpose of the company is to manufacture and refine sugar from beets. The company owns three factories, located at Ogden and Logan, Utah, and La Grande, Ore. The Ogden and the La Grande factories have a daily capacity of about 400 tons each and the Logan factory a capacity of about 500 tons.

Stock.... Par $100..... Authorized { com., $1,333,400 / pref., 2,666,600 } Issued { com., $850,500 / pref., 1,701,000 } $2,551,500

The preferred stock is 6 per cent., cumulative.

The first dividend upon the preferred stock was paid October 1, 1902, being 1½ per cent. quarterly; a second quarterly dividend was paid January 1, 1903. The dividends are payable quarterly in January, April, July and October.

Stock is registered and transferred at the office of the company, Ogden, Utah.

The company has no funded debt.

President, David Eccles; Vice-President, Thomas D. Dee; Secretary, Henry H. Rolapp, Treasurer, C. W. Nibley, Ogden, Utah.

Directors—David Eccles, Thomas D. Dee, Henry H. Rolapp, Hiram H. Spencer, Fred. J. Kiesel, Joseph Scowcroft, Adam Patterson, Joseph Clark, Ogden, Utah; Joseph F. Smith, Salt Lake City; Ephraim P. Ellison, Layton, Utah; George Stoddard, Le Grande, Ore.; C. W. Nibley, Baker City, Ore.

Corporate and main office, First National Bank Building, Ogden, Utah. Annual meeting first Monday in March, at Ogden.

## AMERICAN-ABELL ENGINE & THRESHER CO., LIMITED

A corporation formed under the laws of Ontario in 1902 to manufacture engines, separators, etc. The company acquired the business of the John Abell Engine & Machine Works Co., Limited, that was incorporated in 1894. The business was established originally by John Abell in 1845.

Stock...... Par $100.......................... Authorized, $1,000,000...... Issued, $500,000

The company has no preferred stock and no funded debt.

President, A. W. Wright, Alma, Mich.; Vice-President, F. E. Kenaston, West Minneapolis, Minn.; Secretary and Treasurer, W. H. Mason, Battle Creek, Mich.; Assistant Treasurer, Charles J. Agar, Toronto.

Directors—A. W. Wright, Alma, Mich.; F. E. Kenaston, West Minneapolis, Minn.; W. H. Mason, Battle Creek, Mich.; H. C. Akeley, Minneapolis, Minn.; T. A. Rowan, Toronto.

Corporate and main office, 48 Abell street, Toronto; Northwest office, Winnipeg, Manitoba.

## AMERICAN AGRICULTURAL CHEMICAL CO.

A corporation organized under a special charter of the State of Connecticut, June 30, 1893, amended in 1899. The present title was adopted under an order of Court, May 26, 1899. The company was formed in 1899 to combine the principal establishments in the United States engaged in the manufacture of fertilizers and their by-products. The following concerns were acquired:

Acme Fertilizer Co., New York.
Alexander Fertilzer & Chemical Co., Alexander, Va.
Bradley Fertilizer Co., Boston.
Chemical Co. of Canton, Baltimore.
Crocker Fertilizer & Chemical Co., Buffalo,
Cleveland Dryer Co., Cleveland.
Cumberland Bone Phosphate Co., Boston.
L. B. Darling Fertilizer Co., Pawtucket, R. I.
Detrick Fertilizer & Chemical Co., Baltimore.
East India Chemical Works, New York.
Empire Carbon Works, E. St. Louis, Ill.
Lazaretto Guano Co., Baltimore.
Liebig Manufacturing Co., Carteret, N. J., and Wilmington, Del.
Lister's Agricultural Chemical Works, Newark, N. J.
Michigan Carbon Works, Detroit.
Maryland Fertilizing & Manufacturing Co., Baltimore.
Milsom Rendering & Fertilizer Co., E. Buffalo, N. Y.
Moro Phillips Fertilizer Co., Philadelphia.
Nickerson Fertilizer Co., Easton, Md.
Northwestern Fertilizing Co., Chicago.
Preston Fertilizer Co., Brooklyn, N. Y.
Quinnuipac Co, Boston.
Read Fertilizer Co., New York.
Sharpless & Carpenter, Philadelphia.
Suffolk Fertilizer Co., New York.
Susquehanna Fertilizer Co., Baltimore.
Tygert-Allen Fertilizer Co., Philadelphia.
M. E. Wheeler & Co., Rutland, Vt.
Williams & Clark Fertilizer Co., Carteret, N.J.
Zell Guano Co., Baltimore.

The property of the Bowker Fertilizing Co. was acquired in 1902.

Stock.............Authorized { com., $20,000,000 / pref., 20,000,000 } Issued { com., $16,715,200 / pref., 17,153,000 } $33,868,200

The preferred stock is 6 per cent., cumulative, and has preference in the distribution of assets. Transfer Agent, Old Colony Trust Co., Boston. Registrars, Guranty Trust Co., New York; State Street Trust Co., Boston.

The first dividend on the preferred stock was 3 per cent., semi-annual, paid October 2, 1889. Regular semi-annual dividends of 3 per cent. have since been paid on the preferred in April (1) and October.

EARNINGS.

Year ending June 30.

| | Income. | Deductions. | Profits. | Pref. Div. | Surplus. |
|---|---|---|---|---|---|
| 1899-00 (13 months)....... | $2,253,989 | $369,129 | $1,884,860 | $1,516,310 | $368,550 |
| 1900-01.................. | 1,603,746 | 543,954 | 1,059,791 | 1,026,726 | 33,065 |
| 1901-02.................. | 1,605,706 | 462,981 | 1,142,725 | 1,028,754 | 113,971 |

The deductions from income include appropriations for reserve and betterments.

President, John P. Gibbons, New York; Vice-Presidents, Peter P. Bradley, Boston; William H. Grafflin, Philadelphia; Treasurer, Thomas A. Doe; Secretary, Albert French, New York.

Directors—E. A. Becker, Robert S. Bradley, Augustus Brandegee, Peter B. Bradley, John F. Gibbons, James M. Gifford, William H. Grafflin, Deming Jarves, Albert French, John F. Kehoe, M. E. Wheeler, Cord Meyer, J. Edwin Myers, William Prescott, Jesse Stearns, George Beck, H. C. McComas, H. S. Zell, D. Crawford Clark.

Main office, 26 Broadway, New York.

## AMERICAN ALKALI CO.

A corporation organized under the laws of New Jersey, May 6, 1899. The company was formed to manufacture caustic soda and bleaching powder with other by-products by the electrical process covered by the patents of Hermite & Dubosc, John G. A. Rhodin and others. The company owns all these patent rights for the United States and Canada.

A subsidiary company (the Canadian Electro-Chemical Co.) erected an experimental plant at Sault Ste. Marie, Ontario, which was expected to be in operation in the spring of 1903. Half of the interest of this company in the Canadian Electro-Chemical Co. was transferred to the Consolidated Lake Superior Co. in settlement of its claims against the former.

The company having become embarrassed, a reorganization plan was proposed in May, 1902, but was not acceptable to some of the creditors. Receivers were consequently appointed for the company in September, 1902.

Stock...Par $50...Autohrized { com., $24,000,000 / pref., 2,400,000 } Issued { com., $24,000,000 / pref., $2,400,000 } $26,400,000

The preferred stock is 8 per cent., cumulative, and was originally $6,000,000 in amount. On the preferred stock $10 per share was paid in at the time of issue, the preferred being assessable up to the full value. In November, 1901, it was decided to make the preferred full paid by issuing 2 shares full paid for 5 shares of old preferred, on which $20 in cash had been paid in. Quarterly assessments of $2.50 each were called for on the preferred to make it $20 full paid.

The assessments have not been paid in full, and claims against the preferred stockholders for the same complicated the company's position. The common stock was issued full paid and non-assessable in part payment for patent rights, etc. The company has no funded debt.

Receivers—Arthur K. Brown, Philadelphia; Henry I. Budd, Camden, N. J.

President, Arthur K. Brown; Secretary and Treasurer, Clayton E. Platt, Philadelphia.

Directors—Thomas W. Neill, Arthur K. Brown, George P. Brock, Clayton E. Platt, Henry C. Magee, Herbert M. Howe, William M. Kerr.

Main office, 428 Chestnut street, Philadelphia.

## AMERICAN AUTOMATIC WEIGHING MACHINE CO., LIMITED

A corporation formed in London in 1899 under the English General Company's Act. The purpose of the company is the manufacture of automatic weighing machines. It is a consolidation of the following companies incorporated under the laws of New York:

The National Weighing Machine Co.
The National Automatic Machine Co.
The American Automaton Weighing Machine Co.

The company has a practical monopoly of the automatic weighing machine business of the

United States. It owns about 28 patents, including the well known Everitt patent and owns over 7,000 weighing machines placed in railway stations, hotels and other places of public resort.

Stock......Par $5.........Authorized { com., $675,000 / pref., 675,000 } Issued { com., $675,000 / pref., 675,000 } $1,350,000

The preferred stock is 6 per cent., cumulative.

Dividends are payable semi-annually, March 1 and September 1.

The company has no funded debt.

The net profits of the National Automatic Weighing Machine Co., to which this company succeeded, were: In 1895, $66,601; in 1896, $74,288; in 1897, $76,332; in 1898, $81,416.

President, Robert Milburn; Secretary, W. H. Parker, London, England.

Directors—London Board: Robert Milburn, William Graham, Lafayette H. De Friese, LeRoy W. Baldwin, Stanlake Lee.

Corporate and main office, 65 New Broad street, London, E. C. New York office, 62 Murray street.

## AMERICAN BANK NOTE CO.

A corporation formed under the laws of New York in 1858 and reorganized in 1879. Its business is the engraving and printing of bank notes, bonds, stock certificates, etc. It has a large plant in New York, and branch establishments in Philadelphia, Boston and Ottawa, Canada.

Stock......Par $50................ ...........Authorized, $3,600,000......Issued, $3,600,000

The company pays quarterly dividends in March, June, September and December. In 1900, 1901 and 1902 the dividends were 6 per cent. per annum.

The company has no funded debt.

Chairman, Augustus D. Shepard; President, Theodore H. Freeland; Vice-President, Warren L. Green; 2d Vice-President, Jared K. Myers; Secretary and Treasurer, John E. Currier; Assistant Treasurer, F. Rawdon Myers; Assistant Secretary, Daniel E. Woodhull.

Directors—Phineas C. Lounsbury, Augustus D. Shepard, Theodore H. Freeland, Joseph S. Stout, Edmund C. Converse, James B. Ford, Charles A. Moore, Warren L. Green, William Nelson Cromwell, Joseph R. De Lamar, Francis S. Smithers, John Mason Little, Francis L. Hine.

Main office, 86 Trinity place, New York.

## AMERICAN BEET SUGAR CO.

A corporation formed under the laws of New Jersey, March 24, 1899. The object of the company was to acquire the beet sugar growing and manufacturing interests owned by W. Bayard Cutting, Henry T. Oxnard and others. The properties of the company are owned in fee simple, and consist of:

Oxnard Beet Sugar Co., Grand Island, Neb.; capacity, 350 tons of beets per day.
Norfolk Beet Sugar Co., Norfolk, Neb.; capacity, 350 tons of beets per day.
Chino Valley Beet Sugar Co., Chino, Cal.
Pacific Beet Sugar Co., Oxnard, Cal.
Farming land, Southern California, in the immediate vicinity of the Chino Factory and the Pacific Factory, 7,500 acres.

All these factories except the Grand Island Factory are equipped with the Steffens process for extracting sugar from the molasses by-product, and are the only factories in the United States which are so equipped.

During the year 1900 the company erected a 1,000 ton factory in the Arkansas Valley, Colo., with improved modern machinery, at a cost of over $1,000,000. In 1901 it was stated that the company would build a number of additional factories.

Stock..Par $100...Authorized { com., $15,000,000 / pref., 5,000,000 } Issued { com., $15,000,000 / pref., 4,000,000 } $19,000,000

The preferred stock is 6 per cent., non-cumulative. Of the authorized issue of preferred stock, $1,000,000 remains in the treasury as reserve capital. The company has no funded debt.

Transfer Agent, Corporation Trust Co. of New Jersey, New York. Registrar, Morton Trust Co., New York.

On October 1, 1899, the company began the payment of quarterly dividends on the preferred stock, 1½ per cent. Similar quarterly dividends have since been regularly paid in January (2), April, July and October.

EARNINGS.

| | Gross Profit. | Net Profit. | Expense and Interest. | Preferred Div. | Surplus. |
|---|---|---|---|---|---|
| 1900.................... | $668,166 | $425,635 | $130,000 | $240,000 | $55,635 |
| 1901.................... | 854,019 | 481,308 | 225,000 | 240,000 | 26,308 |

Chairman, W. Bayard Cutting, New York; President, Henry T. Oxnard, Oxnard, Cal.; Vice-Presidents, James G. Oxnard, New York; Robert Oxnard, San Francisco; Secretary, James G. Hamilton; Treasurer, John E. Tucker, New York.

Directors—W. Bayard Cutting, R. Fulton Cutting, James G. Oxnard, Dumont Clarke, George Foster Peabody, Edwin M. Buckley, Kalman Haas, James G. Hamilton, J. Archibald Murray, New York; Henry T. Oxnard, Oxnard, Cal.; Robert Oxnard, San Francisco.

Main office, 32 Nassau street, New York. Annual meeting, first Tuesday in April.

---

## AMERICAN BICYCLE CO.

A corporation formed under the laws of New Jersey in 1899. This company was organized to acquire and operate the works of forty-four of the principal manufacturers of bicycles and bicycle parts in the United States.

These concerns represented some fifty-five separate plants, which turned out about 60 per cent. of all the bicycles manufactured in the country.

In November, 1899, it was announced that this company had effected arrangements with the Rubber Goods Manufacturing Cos. involving the sale to that company of the Hartford Rubber Works, the Peoria Rubber & Manufacturing Co., the Indianapolis Rubber Co., and the rubber department of Indiana Bicycle Co., thus disposing of the portion of the property devoted to the making of rubber tires.

During 1900 and 1901 the management of the company pursued a policy of concentrating its different plants, and also of developing the manufacture of automobiles as part of its business.

In December, 1901, two subsidiary companies were incorporated under the titles of American Cycle Manufacturing Co. and International Motor Car Co. to carry on the manufacturing and commercial department of the business. All the stock of these companies is owned by the parent company. Statements of these companies were given in full in connection with that relating to the parent company in the MANUAL for 1902.

In September, 1902, the company defaulted on the interest on its debentures and Receivers were appointed forthwith.

A reorganization committee was appointed, William A. Read, New York, Chairman. Depositary of securities for the committee, Central Trust Co., New York. See below for plan of reorganization submitted by the committee in December, 1902.

In March, 1903, the Pope Manufacturing Co. was incorporated under the laws of New Jersey, to take over the assets of this company under the reorganization plan, the stock of the new company to be $10,000,000 common, $2,500,000 6 per cent. cumulative 1st preferred and $10,000,000 5 per cent., 2d preferred.

| Stock..Par $100...Authorized | com., $17,701,500 | Issued | com., $17,701,500 | $26,996,400 |
|---|---|---|---|---|
| | pref., 9,294,900 | | pref., 9,294,900 | |

The authorized amount of stock was $20,000,000 common and $10,000,000 preferred. In October, 1901, it was decided to reduce the stock to the amount outstanding as above.

The preferred stock is entitled to 7 per cent., cumulative, dividends, and also has a preference in any distribution of assets.

Transfer Agents, Baring, Magoun & Co. Registrar, United States Mortgage & Trust Co., New York.

FUNDED DEBT.

Sinking fund gold debentures, 5 per cent., due Sept., 1919, March and Sept.......... $9,500,000

The debenture bonds were $10,000,000. Holders of the debentures have the option, in case the company shall at any time execute a mortgage on its property, of exchanging their debentures for bonds secured by such mortgage, or declaring the debentures forthwith due and receiving payment for the same at 105 and interest. It is provided that the company shall retire $250,000 of the debentures each year. The debentures were offered for public subscription in September, 1899, by Baring, Magoun & Co., New York, the offering including $6,300,000, the balance of the issue having been taken by the vendors of various plants.

The proceeds of the debentures were used in paying the vendors of plants part of their appraised value in cash.

Receivers' certificates for $500,000 authorized and issued in October, 1902.

The company's report for the ten months ending July 31, 1900, showed net profits after interest on bonds of $605,580. About $1,168,015 had been charged off to depreciation of plants, and $334,746 for property sold. In the year ending July 31, 1901, the profits were $850,682; interest on bonds, $500,000; surplus, $350,682.

The indebtedness of the company and its auxilliary organizations on Nov. 1, 1902, was stated by the Reorganization Committee to be $1,306,608.

The plan of reorganization submitted by the committee referred to above provided for the formation of a new company, with $2,500,000 6 per cent. cumulative first preferred stock, $10,000,000 6 per cent. non-cumulative second preferred stock and $10,000,000 common stock. It also provided that no mortgage should be placed on the company's property without the consent of two-thirds of the first preferred stock. The terms for the exchange of old for new securities were as follows:

| Old Securities. | Pay. | Receives. New 1st Preferred. | New 2d Preferred. | New Common. |
|---|---|---|---|---|
| Debentures, per $1,000 | .. | .. | $1,000 | ... |
| Common stock, per share | $9 | $9 | ...... | $50 |
| Preferred stock, per share | 9 | 9 | ...... | 25 |

The reduction of charges ahead of common stock under the plan is $358,643, and the cash to be provided by the assessments, $2,429,676.

Receivers, Albert A. Pope, R. Lindsay Coleman, John A. Miller.

President, R. Lindsay Coleman; Vice-President and Treasurer, George Pope; Secretary, Paul Walton, New York.

Directors—J. Walter Spalding, Monmouth Beach, N. J.; Albert A. Pope, Gardiner M. Lane, Boston; John W. Kiser, Charles L. Ames, Albert Featherstone, Joseph E. Bromley, Otto Unzicker, Chicago; R. Lindsay Coleman, William Barbour, George W. Young, G. F. Crane, New York; Harry A. Lozier, M. B. Johnson, Cleveland; George Pope, Orange, N. J.

Main office, 13 Park Row, New York. Annual meeting, second Tuesday in October.

## AMERICAN BOOK CO.

A corporation formed under the laws of New Jersey in 1890. The object of the company is the publication and sale of school and college text books and educational works generally. It acquired the copyrights, plates and business in this department of a number of leading publishing firms. It has agencies in various cities and printing and binding plants in New York and Cincinnati.

Stock .....Par $100..........................Authorized, $5,000,000......Issued, $5,000,000

President, Harry T. Ambrose; Secretary, Gilman H. Tucker; Treasurer, Charles P. Batt.

Directors—Alfred C. Barnes, Henry B. Barnes, Charles J. Barnes, William B. Thalheimer, Henry H. Vail, John A. Greene, Harry T. Ambrose, Gilman H. Tucker, Charles P. Batt, L. M. Dillman, A. H. Hinkle.

Corporate office, 15 Exchange place, Jersey City; New York office, 100 Washington Square, East.

## THE AMERICAN BRASS CO.

A corporation formed under a special charter from the State of Connecticut. The purpose of the company is manufacturing and dealing in brass, copper and kindred metals. It acquired the following concerns:

Coe Brass Co., Torrington, Conn., and Ansonia, Conn.
Ansonia Brass & Copper Co., Ansonia, Conn.
Waterbury Brass Co., Waterbury.
Benedict & Burnham Manufacturing Co.
The Holmes, Booth & Haydens Co.
Chicago Brass Co.

Stock.. ...Par $100..... ...................Authorized, $20,000,000......Issued, $10,000,000

The stock of the company was originally $6,000,000, and was increased in 1900 for the purpose of acquiring the Benedict & Burnham Co. The company has no funded debt.

Stock is transferred at the office of the company, Waterbury, Conn. Registrar, Waterbury National Bank, Waterbury.

President, Charles F. Brooker, Ansonia, Conn.; Vice-Presidents, Edward L. Frisbie, Jr., James S. Elton, Waterbury, Conn.; A. A. Cowles, New York; Secretary and Treasurer, John P. Elton, Waterbury, Conn.

Directors—Charles F. Brooker, Ansonia, Conn.; Edward L. Frisbie, Jr., James S. Elton, John P. Elton, Waterbury, Conn.; A. A. Cowles, D. Willis James, C. N. Wayland, William E. Dodge, G. W. Burnham, Thomas B. Kent, John J. Sinclair, Edward Holbrook, T. B. Burnham, New York; James A. Doughty, E. T. Coe, Torrington, Conn.

Main office, Waterbury, Conn. Annual meeting, last Tuesday in February, at Waterbury.

## AMERICAN CAN CO.

A corporation formed under the laws of New Jersey, March 19, 1901. The company was organized to acquire and combine establishments which manufactured 90 per cent. of the tin cans made in the United States. The company has plants in New York, Brooklyn, Boston,

Philadelphia, Baltimore, Chicago, Detroit, Cleveland, and other cities. Interests identified with the American Tin Plate Co. took an active part in the formation of this company.

Stock..Par $100...Authorized { com., $44,000,000 / pref., 44,000,000 } Issued { com., $41,233,300 / pref., 41,233,300 } $82,466,600

The preferred stock is 7 per cent., cumulative.

The company has no funded debt.

The company's profits for the year ending March 31, 1902, were reported as $1,775,564, after charging off about $1,000,000 for depreciation, etc.

President, F. A. Assman; Vice-Presidents, L. Muench, T. G. Cramwell; Secretary, L. H. Landon; Treasurer, F. S. Wheeler; Assistant Secretary, W. F. Dutton; Assistant Treasurers, R. H. Ismon, R. A. Burger.

Directors—William H. Moore, J. H. Moore, D. G. Reid, W. B. Leeds, W. T. Graham, F. S. Wheeler, Warner Arms, Edwin Norton, C. S. Guthrie, James McLean, F. A. Assman, E. P. Breckenridge, F. Rudolph, H. W. Phelps, S. A. Ginna, W. M. Leeds, George G. McMurtrie, L. H. Landon, W. F. Dutton.

Corporate office, Jersey City; main office, 11 Broadway, New York. Annual meeting, in April, at Jersey City.

## AMERICAN CARAMEL CO.

A corporation organized under the laws of Pennsylvania, March 28, 1898. The company manufactures confectionery and owns the plants and business of the Breisch-Hine Co., Philadelphia, the P. C. Weist Co., York, Pa., and the Lancaster Caramel Co., Lancaster, Pa. The company controls about 90 per cent. of the caramel and caramel specialty business of the country and has a large export trade. It owns valuable trademarks.

Stock...Par $100....Authorized { com., $1,000,000 / pref., 1,000,000 } Issued { com., $1,000,000 / pref., 1,000,000 } $2,000,000

The preferred stock is 8 per cent., cumulative.

Transfer Agent, West End Trust Co., Philadelphia. Registrar, Security Title & Trust Co., York, Pa.

FUNDED DEBT.

Sinking fund mort. bonds, 6 per cent., due 1920, June and Dec....................... $500,000

The mortgage is for $600,000, of which $100,000 remains in the treasury for betterments. Trustee, Industrial Trust Co., Providence, R. I. There is a sinking fund for the bonds of $25,000 per annum. The company after December 1, 1901, can retire bonds by lot at 105 and interest, to the amount of $50,000 per annum.

In the year 1898 the earnings of the company were: gross, $355,409 net, $107,768. In 1900 the net was $181,000; in 1901, $161,537, and in 1902, $177,700.

The company pays regular 2 per cent. quarterly dividends on the preferred stock, January, April, July, October. On the common, a dividend of 5 per cent., yearly, was paid January 1, 1899; 4 per cent. being also paid in January, 1900, 3 per cent. in 1901, and 4½ per cent. in 1902.

President, William L. Blair, Lancaster, Pa.; Secretary and Treasurer, Daniel F. Lafean, York, Pa.

Directors—William L. Blair, Milton S. Hershey, Lancaster, Pa.; W. P. Rice, New York; George W. Williams, York, Pa.; Daniel F. Lafean, York, Pa.; Joseph H. Fisher, Philadelphia; Clinton R. Weeden, Providence.

Main office, York, Pa.; Philadelphia office, 12 East Allen street, Philadelphia. Annual meeting, third Tuesday after first Monday in March.

## AMERICAN CAR & FOUNDRY CO.

A corporation formed under the laws of New Jersey, February 20, 1899. It was designed to combine various firms and corporations engaged in the manufacture of freight and passenger cars. The concerns in question were:

Michigan-Peninsular Car Co., Detroit.
Missouri Car & Foundry Co., St. Louis.
Jackson & Woodin Manufacturing Co., Berwick, Pa.
Ohio Falls Car Manufacturing Co., Jeffersonville, Ind.
Union Car Co., Depew, N. Y.
St. Charles Car Co., St. Charles, Mo.
The Wells & French Co., Chicago.
Terre Haute Car & Manufacturing Co., Terre Haute, Ind.
Buffalo Car Manufacturing Co., Buffalo.
Niagara Car Wheel Co., Buffalo.
Ensign Manufacturing Co., Huntington, W. Va.
Pennock Bros., Minerva, O.
Murray, Dougal & Co., Milton, Pa.
Indianapolis Car Co., Indianapolis.

The plants consist of 15 freight car shops, 2 passenger car shops, 13 wheel foundries, 14 casting foundries, 14 iron forging shops, 2 pipe foundries, 2 rolling mills, 2 axle forges, 2 saw mills, 2 malleable foundries, 4 brass foundries, and all the auxiliary shops necessary for the proper conduct of the general car business. The works and store yards cover about 425 acres of ground.

The total annual capacity of the united companies is, in round numbers, 100,000 freight cars, 500 passenger cars, 350,000 tons of wheels, 300,000 tons of forgings, 150,000 tons of castings, 90,000 tons of bar iron, 30,000 tons of pipe. In addition to the general railroad car business, the company furnishes small cars for mines, plantations, contracting work, etc., wheels of all sizes, grey iron castings, pipe, merchant forgings, and miscellaneous railroad supplies. The various plants were taken over by this company on March 1, 1899.

Stock..Par $100...Authorized { com., $30,000,000 / pref., 30,000,000 } Issued { com., $30,000,000 / pref., 30,000,000 } $60,000,000

The preferred stock is 7 per cent., non-cumulative. Transfer Agent, Guaranty Trust Co., New York. Registrar, Central Trust Co., New York.

The company began the payment of regular quarterly dividends of 1¾ per cent. on the preferred stock July 1, 1899. The dividend period was however changed to quarterly, February, May, August and December, and such quarterly payments have since been regularly made.

The first dividend on the common stock was ½ per cent. paid August 1, 1900. Regular quarterly dividends of ½ per cent. have been pai on the common in February (1), May, August and November, until the February, 1903, dividend, which was increased to 1 per cent.

EARNINGS.

Year ending April 30.

| | Dividends. Com. | Dividends. Pref. | Gross. | Net. | Dividends. | Surplus. |
|---|---|---|---|---|---|---|
| 1899–00 (14 months)...... | .. | 7 | $6,831,599 | $5,734,949 | $2,036,300 | $3,698,648 |
| 1900–01 ................ | 2 | 7 | 5,015,394 | 4,055,820 | 2,679,525 | 1,376,301 |
| 1901–02 ................ | 2 | 7 | 5,503,928 | 4,295,602 | 2,700,000 | 1,595,602 |

In the seven months ending November 30, 1902, the net earnings were reported as $4,474,863. The total surplus at that date was $8,970,414.

In October, 1900, it was decided to increase the working capital to $9,000,000. In 1899–00 there was a charge against net earnings of $802,086 for betterments, etc., and in 1900–01 a similar charge of $633,926.

The following is the company's condensed balance sheet of April 30, 1901 and 1902:

| ASSETS. | 1901. | 1902. | LIABILITIES. | 1901. | 1902. |
|---|---|---|---|---|---|
| Cost of properties... | $56,700,720 | $59,118,183 | Preferred stock ..... | $30,000,000 | $30,000,000 |
| Material on hand.... | 7,721,366 | 11,915,129 | Common........... | 30,000,000 | 30,000,000 |
| Accounts receivable. | 6,307,217 | 7,461,951 | Audited vouchers ... | 7,283,153 | 12,925,793 |
| Cash .............. | 1,908,949 | 1,571,458 | Pay-rolls ........... | 280,149 | 470,376 |
| | | | Surplus account .... | 5,074,950 | 6,670,552 |
| Totals ....... | $72,638,252 | $80,066,721 | Totals........ | $72,638,252 | $80,066,721 |

President, Frederick H. Eaton, New York; Chairman Executive Committee, W. K. Bixby; 1st Vice-President, W. J. McBride, St. Louis; 2d Vice-President, W. P. Coleman, New York; 3d Vice-President, E. F. Carry, Chicago; 4th Vice-President, George Hargraves, Detroit; Treasurer, S. S. De Lano; Secretary, D. H. Bixby, St. Louis; Assistant Secretaries, William M. Hager, New York; John F. Robison; 1st Assistant Treasurer, W. S. Avis, St. Louis; 2d Assistant Treasurer, William M. Hager, New York; Auditor, J. M. Buick; Assistant Auditor, N. A. Doyle, St. Louis.

Directors—W. N. McMillan, W. K. Bixby, W. J. McBride, S. S. De Lano, J. M. Buick, St. Louis; F. H. Eaton, Gerald L. Hoyt, J. B. Haggin, Walter G. Oakman, H. R. Duval, William M. Hager, New York; George H. Russell, E. F. Carry, Chicago; W. H. Woodin, Thomas H. West, Adolphus Busch, J. L. Smyser, Louisville.

Main office, Lincoln Trust Building, St. Louis; New York office, 25 Broad street. Annual meeting, last Thursday in June.

---

## AMERICAN CEMENT CO.

A corporation formed under the laws of New Jersey, August 30, 1899, to take over the business of the American Cement Co. of Pennsylvania, the United Building Material Co. of New York, the firm of Lesley & Trinkle, Philadelphia, and a large amount of valuable cement lands. The company has works for the manufacture of Portland and other cements at Egypt and Coplay, Pa., and Jordan, N. Y., and has selling agencies in New York, Philadelphia, Boston and other cities, with a large plant, including wharves, barges, etc.

Stock......Par $10............................Authorized, $2,100,000......Issued, $2,000,000

The company has no preferred stock. Stock is transferred at the company's office. Registrar, The Investment Co., Philadelphia.

The company began the payment of dividends by the declaration of 2 per cent. and 1 per cent. extra for the four months ending December 31, 1899, payable January 15, 1900, and dividends of 3 per cent. and 1 per cent extra have since been paid in January and July.

FUNDED DEBT.

1st mort. 5 per cent., due 1914, April and Oct.................................... $895,000

The 1st mortgage is for $1,000,000, the sinking fund having retired $105,000 of the bonds.

The earnings of the subsidiary companies have been as follows:

| | |
|---|---|
| 1899-00 (16 months, ending Nov. 30) | $372,027 |
| 1909-01 (year, " " ) | 246,334 |
| 1901-02 ( " " " ) | 281,480 |

The surplus of the company December 31, 1902, was $21,853.

President, Robert W. Lesley; Vice-President, George W. Norris; Secretary, Harry B. Warner; Treasurer, Frederick J. Jiggens, Philadelphia.

Directors—Robert W. Lesley, Charles S. Farnum, John W. Eckert, George W. Norris, George H. B. Martin, John H. Catherwood, Alan H. Reed.

Main office, 22 South Fifteenth street, Philadelphia. Annual meeting, second Monday in January.

## AMERICAN CHICLE CO.

A corporation formed under the laws of New Jersey, June 3, 1899. Its name is derived from the Mexican product known as "chicle," which is a principal ingredient of chewing-gum. The companies acquired by this corporation were:

W. J. White, Cleveland.
Adams & Sons Co., Brooklyn, N. Y.
Beeman Chemical Co., Cleveland.
J. P. Primley, Chicago.
Kisme Gum Co., Louisville.
S. T. Britten & Co., Toronto.

Stock....Par $100....Authorized { com., $6,000,000; pref., 3,000,000 } Issued { com., $6,000,000; pref., 3,000,000 } $9,000,000

The preferred stock is entitled to 6 per cent. cumulative dividends. The company has no funded debt.

Transfer Agent, Registrar and Transfer Co. Registrar, United States Mortgage and Trust Co., New York.

The payment of dividends on the stocks of the company was commenced in October, 1899, 1½ per cent. quarterly having been declared on the preferred, and such dividends, which are at the full rate of 6 per cent. per annum, have since been regularly paid each quarter, in January, April, July and October. In October, 1899, 1½ per cent. was paid on the common stock; in January, 1900, 2½ per cent. was paid; in April, 1900, 2 per cent.; in July, 1900, 2½ per cent., and in October, 1900, 2 per cent. In 1901 paid 2½ per cent. in January, 1½ per cent. in April and 2 per cent. in July and October. In January, 1902, also paid 2 per cent. on the common. In April, 1902, 1 per cent. was paid, and monthly dividends of 1 per cent. have since been maintained on the common.

Chairman, Thomas Adams, Jr.; President, W. J. White; Vice-President, George H. Worthington, Cleveland; Secretary and Treasurer, Henry Rowley, New York.

Directors—Thomas Adams, Jr., E. E. Beeman, W. J. White, George H. Worthington, Jonathan P. Primley, T. J. Jefferson, Charles R. Flint, Thomas Adams, Sr., Stephen T. Britten, Henry Rowley, W. B. White, James C. Young, T. L. Jefferson.

Main office, 13 Park Row, New York. Annual meeting in July.

## AMERICAN CIGAR CO.

A corporation formed under the laws of New Jersey, January 11, 1901. The business of the company is the manufacture of cigars, cheroots and all tobacco cigarettes. It acquired the plant and business of Powell, Smith & Co., New York, Chicago, Kingston, N. Y., and Poughkeepsie, N. Y.; the Hummel-Vogt Co., Louisville; S. Levy & Co., New York, and Passaic, N. J.; Harburger, Homan & Co., the Havana-American Co., and has opened factories in various cities. In November, 1901, the company acquired the works of Brown Bros. Co., Detroit, Mich. Various other concerns have since been acquired.

This company was organized by and in the interest of the American Tobacco Co., which is controlled by the Consolidated Tobacco Co.

Stock......Par $100........................Authorized, $10,000,000......Issued, $10,000,000

FUNDED DEBT.

Gold notes, 4 per cent., due March, 1911, March (15) and Sept...................... $10,000,000

The gold notes were created in 1901 and are guaranteed by the American Tobacco Co. and the Continental Tobacco Co.

President, John B. Cobb; Secretary, Robert E. Christie; Treasurer, Benjamin H. Homan, New York.

Main office, 111 Fifth avenue, New York.

## AMERICAN COAL CO.

A Maryland corporation, owning and operating a large bituminous coal property at Barton and Loanaconing, Allegany Co., Md. The company has an interest in the Georges Creek & Cumberland Railroad Co.

Stock......Par $25... ........................Authorized, $1,500,000......Issued, $1,500,000

Stock is transferred at the company's office in New York. Registrar, Metropolitan Trust Co., New York.

Dividends paid have been as follows in the calendar years designated: In 1895, 7 per cent.; in 1896, 8 per cent.; in 1897, 8 per cent.; in 1898, 9 per cent.; in 1899, 10 per cent.; in 1900, 9 per cent. Dividends are paid half-yearly, March 1 and September 1. The March, 1901, dividend was 4 per cent. and 1 per cent. extra, and the same rate was paid in September, 1901. The dividends in 1902 were on the same basis.

President, William De L. Walbridge; Vice-President, Sidney Wintringham, Secretary and Treasurer, George M. Bowlby, New York.

Directors—James A. Alexander, Sidney Wintringham, William De L. Walbridge, J. H. Neher, Joseph E. Gay, Aaron Adams, R. Suydam Grant, John Stanton.

Main office, 1 Broadway, New York. Annual meeting, December 24, at New York.

## AMERICAN COLORTYPE CO.

A corporation formed under the laws of New Jersey in February, 1902. The business of the comp n is color printing, reproducing works of art and merchandise in natural colors for catalogues, calendars, etc. The company is a consolidation of the following corporations:

Osborne Co.
Osgood Art Colortype Co.
American Three Color Co.
Chicago Colortype Co.
National Colortype Co.

Stock....Par $100....Authorized { com., $3,000,000; pref., 1,000,000 } Issued { com., $3,000,000; pref., 900,000 } $3,900,000

The preferred stock is 8 per cent., cumulative.

Stock is transferred at the company's office. Registrar, Merchants' Trust Co., New York.

The company has no funded debt.

President, Edmund B. Osborne; 1st Vice-President, Theodore Regensteiner; 2d Vice-President, Albert D. Sheridan; 3d Vice-President, Max Lau; Treasurer, J. H. Behrens; Secretary, George W. Reynolds.

Directors—Edmund B. Osborne, Albert D. Sheridan, George W. Reynolds, Theodore Regensteiner, Julius Regensteiner, J. H. Behrens, F. S. Osgood, C. D. Beebe, William Nottingham, Max Lau, Francis Lackner, Albert K. Hiscock.

Main office, Broadway and Sixteenth street, New York; branch offices, Chicago and Newark, N. J. Annual meeting, third Monday in February, at 759 Sumner avenue, Newark, N. J.

## AMERIOAN CONSOLIDATED PINE FIBRE CO.

A corporation formed under the laws of New Jersey, October 13, 1900. The purposes of the company comprise the manufacture of a fibre from the needles of the Southern long-leaf pine, suitable for mattresses and upholstery purposes generally. The company has a plant at Cronley, N. C.

Stock....Par $100...Authorized { com., $1,000,000; pref., 1,000,000 } Issued { com., $801,000; pref., 800,000 } $1,601,000

The preferred stock is 7 per cent., non-cumulative.

Transfer Agent and Registrar, North American Trust Co., New York.

The company's balance sheet, May 20, 1901, shows total assets, $1,918,246; surplus, $237,240.

President, H. J. Kaltenbach; Vice-President, Michael Gavin, 2d; Secretary and Treasurer, J. L. Creveling; Assistant Secretary and Treasurer, W. H. Squires.

Directors—H. J. Kaltenbach, Michael Gavin, 2d, Charles P. Phelps, Harmon S. Graves, Frederick W. Whitridge, James I. Raymond.

Corporate office, 15 Exchange Place, Jersey City; main office, 135 Broadway, New York. Annual meeting in May, at Jersey City.

## THE AMERICAN COTTON CO.

A corporation formed under the laws of New Jersey, March 26, 1896. The company controls the patents for machinery and processes involved in making round-lap bales of cotton composed of continuous sheets of the raw staple. The company leases its machinery, which is attached directly to cotton-ginning plants. It also owns and operates many such ginning plants. It had in the season of 1900, 554 presses in operation throughout the South, and 500 are being constructed for 1901. The company owns the Walburn-Swenson Works at Chicago Heights, Ill., where it manufactures its machinery.

Stock....Par $100...Authorized { com., $4,000,000 / pref., 3,000,000 } Issued { com., $4,000,000 / pref., 3,000,000 } $7,000,000

The preferred stock is 8 per cent., cumulative. The common is entitled to 12 per cent., after which both classes share in any surplus. Stock is transferred at the company's office, 25 Broad street, New York. Registrar, Mercantile Trust Co., New York. The company has no funded debt.

In November, 1901, a protective committee (Cornelius N. Bliss, New York, Chairman) was formed, and invited stockholders to deposit their stock with the Central Trust Co., New York, under an agreement by which the committee might sell the deposited stock at 105 and accrued dividends for the preferred and 50 for the common within five months from December 2, 1901.

The payment of dividends on the preferred stock at the full rate of 8 per cent. per annum began in May, 1899. Half-yearly dividends of 4 per cent. were paid in May (2) and November, and none have been paid since.

FUNDED DEBT.

Debentures, 6 per cent., due April, 1905, April and Oct. .......................... $2,000,000

The debentures were created in 1902 to provide for the company's financial requirements. They are secured by its patents and interests in auxilliary organizations. Trustee of debentures, Central Trust Co., New York. Interest is paid at the company's office, New York.

Chairman, James G. Cannon, New York; President, J. P. Cooper, Boston; Vice-President, Frederick Y. Robertson, New York; Vice-President and Treasurer, L. L. Fleming, Boston; Auditor and Assistant Treasurer, John B. Milliken; Secretary, Thomas E. Wing, New York.

Directors—Cornelius N. Bliss, James K. Jones, David R. Francis, Albert W. Smith, Maxwell Woodhull, James G. Cannon, Albert C. Case, Charles Hathaway, Frederick Y. Robertson, Hampden E. Tener, Jr., William H. Porter, J. P. Cooper, L. L. Fleming.

Main office, 25 Broad street, New York. Annual meeting, third Tuesday in June, at Jersey City.

## AMERICAN COTTON OIL CO.

A corporation formed under the laws of New Jersey, October 14, 1889, to succeed the American Cotton Oil Trust. For terms of the conversion and exchange of securities, see previous editions of MANUAL.

The company owns crude oil mills, refineries, lard plants, soap factories, gins, fertilizer works and seed houses, situated in sixteen different States. Also tank and other cars. The appraised cash value of the real estate and machinery is $12,108,723. The total cash assets August 31, 1901, were $18,489,583, against $17,949,863 in 1900. Working capital August 31, 1895, $4,928,204; same date, 1896, $4,534,488; in 1897, $4,972,898; in 1898, $4,809,350; in 1899, $4,917,025; in 1900, $4,828,571; in 1901, $4,830,695; in 1902, $4,648,942.

Stock..Par $100...Authorized { com., $20,237,100 / pref., 14,562,300 } Issued { com., $20,237,100 / pref., 10,198,600 } $30,435,700

The preferred stock is 6 per cent., non-cumulative, and is subject to call at 105.

Transfer Agents, Winslow, Lanier & Co., New York. Registrar, Central Trust Co., New York.

Dividends on the preferred were commenced in June, 1892, at the rate of 6 per cent. per annnm, and have since been regularly continued in half-yearly payments of 3 per cent. each in June and December. In November, 1898, the company also declared a dividend of 3 per cent. on the common stock, payable December 1, 1898. This was the first dividend paid on the common. In November, 1899, the second annual dividend was declared on the common, being 4 per cent., payable December 1, 1899. In 1900 3½ per cent. was paid on the common on December 1. In 1901 2 per cent. was paid on the common on December 2. In 1902 4 per cent. was paid on December 1.

In 1901 a committee (George Austin Morrison, Chairman) called for deposits of both classes of stock with the First National Bank, New York, under an agreement giving the committee power to sell the stock deposited at not less than 105 for the preferred and 60 for the common within three years.

### FUNDED DEBT.

Gold debens., extended, 4½ per cent., due 1915, quarterly, Feb., May, Aug. and Nov. $3,000,000

The authorized issue of 8 per cent. debentures, due November 1, 1900, under the reorganization plan was $5,000,000. In 1891-92, $210,000 of the debentures were retired by the operation of the sinking fund; in 1892-93, $224,000; $240,000 in 1894, and in 1895, $258,000. This left $3,068,000 outstanding. In April, 1900, Winslow, Lanier & Co., New York, published an offer to extend bonds presented before August 1, 1900, at 4½ per cent. for 15 years. The company paid off and retired $68,000 of the debentures at maturity, leaving $3,000,000, which were extended under the above plan.

In 1891 and since the company has published annual reports, distinguished by the full and frank exhibition afforded of its operations and finances.

### EARNINGS.

Year ending August 31.

| | Gross Mfg. Profits. | Expenses and Interest. | Net Profit. |
|---|---|---|---|
| 1892-93 | $1,800,040 | $652,932 | $1,147,107 |
| 1893-94 | 1,428,152 | 731,855 | 696,297 |
| 1894-95 | 1,565,863 | 734,192 | 831,671 |
| 1895-96 | 886,431 | 551,632 | 334,799 |
| 1896-97 | 1,542,673 | 527,592 | 1,015,080 |
| 1897-98 | 1,559,661 | 245,440 | 1,314,221 |
| 1898-99 | 1,883,254 | 245,440 | 1,637,814 |
| 1899-00 | 1,739,449 | 242,266 | 1,497,182 |
| 1900-01 | 1,244,357 | 152,500 | 1,091,857 |
| 1901-02 | 2,373,206 | 135,000 | 2,238,206 |

The company and its auxiliary organizations have no floating debt. In the year 1895-96 the company's results were affected by the depression of general business and depreciation in value of its products. In 1897-98 the company's accounts are stated in a slightly different form. Expenses are deducted from the gross profit and interest comprises only the sum paid on debentures. After dividends of 6 per cent. on preferred and 3 per cent. on common, the surplus balance for 1897-98 was $95,192. In 1897-98 $372,949 was expended for repairs and maintenance of properties. In 1898-99 the surplus after the 6 per cent. dividends on the preferred and 4 per cent. on common stock was $216,414. In the same year $353,238 was devoted to repairs and maintenance. In 1899-1900 the surplus over the dividends, including 3½ per cent. on the common stock, was $176,968. In 1900-01 the surplus over dividends, including 2 per cent. on the common, $75,199. In 1901-02 surplus after 4 per cent. on the common stock, $412,064.

Chairman and President, George Austin Morrison; Vice-President, Robert F. Munro; Secretary and Treasurer, Justus E. Ralph, New York.

Directors—Edmond Urquhart, Robert F. Munro, William Barbour, J. Kennedy Tod, Charles F. Clark, J. R. Maxwell, Richard T. Wilson, George Austin Morrison, Edward D. Adams, Charles Lanier, Harris C. Fahnestock, Joseph Larocque, Bradish Johnson, William Nelson Cromwell, New York; J. F. Chamberlin, Summit, N. J.

Main office, Guttenberg, N. J.; executive offices, 27 Beaver street, New York. Annual meeting, first Thursday in December.

---

## AMERICAN DISTRICT TELEGRAPH CO.

A corporation formed under the laws of New York. In 1892 it absorbed the Mutual District Messenger Co.

The company operates 85 offices in New York City, and a force of over 1,066 messengers, with 1,552 miles of wires and 27,940 instruments. Has also stock interests in Boston District Telegraph Co. and in the American District Telegraph Co. of New Jersey.

Stock......Par $100..........................Authorized, $4,000,000......Issued, $3,844,700

The capital of this company was increased in January, 1892, from $3,000,000 to $4,000,000, to acquire the Mutual District Messenger Co.

The company paid 1 per cent. dividends in 1896, 2 per cent. in 1897 and 1898, 2¼ per cent. in 1899, and 2¼ per cent. in 1900, in these being in the last named year a dividend of 1 per cent. in May and 1¼ per cent. in November; in 1901 paid 2½ per cent., 1 per cent. in May and 1½ per cent. in November; in 1902 paid 2 per cent., 1 per cent. in May and 1 per cent. in November.

| Earnings. | Gross. | Net. |
|---|---|---|
| 1893 | $649,793 | $99,790 |
| 1894 | 552,095 | 68,141 |
| 1895 | 554,957 | 80,635 |
| 1896 | 545,840 | 57,182 |
| 1897 | 548,128 | 75,187 |
| 1898 | 568,156 | 91,335 |
| 1899 | 629,751 | 104,178 |
| 1900 | 590,536 | 86,846 |
| 1901 | 630,701 | 103,419 |
| 1902 | 610,042 | 96,866 |

President, Robert C. Clowry; Vice-President, William H. Taylor; Secretary and Treasurer, J. C. Willever, New York.

Directors—Thomas F. Clark, D. N. Crouse, E. R. Chapman, Thomas T. Eckert, George J. Gould, Edwin Gould, J. F. Patterson, Winslow S. Pierce, Robert C. Clowry, B. Brooks, Charles A. Missing, William H. Taylor, George B. Wilson.

Main office, 6 Dey street, New York. Annual meeting in January.

## AMERICAN EXPRESS CO.

This organization is an association, not an incorporated company, formed under the laws of New York. Its operations are over lines of the Vanderbilt system, Boston & Maine, Illinois Central and various other lines of railroads. It also conducts a foreign forwarding business.

Stock......Par $100......................Authorized, $18,000,000......Issued, $18,000,000

The company pays dividends at the rate of 6 per cent. per annum in half-yearly payments of 3 per cent., January and July. The July, 1901, dividend was 3 per cent. and 1 per cent. extra from the company's investments. Subsequent half-yearly dividends have been at the same rate, or 8 per cent. per annum.

No reports are published of the organization's earnings.

President, James C. Fargo; Vice-President, Francis F. Flagg; Treasurer, James F. Fargo; Secretary, William H. Seward, New York.

Directors—James C. Fargo, Charles G. Clark, William H. Seward, Theodore M. Pomeroy, Charles M. Pratt, Edward B. Judson, Lewis Cass Ledyard, Henry M. Whitney, Francis F. Flagg, Johnston Livingston.

Main office, 65 Broadway, New York.

## AMERICAN FELT CO.

A corporation formed under the laws of New Jersey, in February, 1899. The business of the company is the manufacture and sale of felts and woolen goods, and piano and organ supplies. It acquired and owns the following establishments:

The City Mills, City Mills, Mass.
Dolgeville Mills, Dolgeville, N. Y.
Essex Mills, Picton, N. J.
Franklin Mills, Franklin, Mass.
Glenville Mills, Glenville, Conn.

Stock....Par $100....Authorized { com., $2,500,000; pref., 2,500,000 } Issued { com., $1,627,300; pref., 1,627,300 } $3,254,600

The preferred stock is 6 per cent., cumulative.

Transfer Agent, Registrar & Transfer Co., Jersey City. Registrar, United States Mortgage & Trust Co., New York.

Funded Debt.

1st mort. bonds, 5 per cent., due 1929, Jan. and July ................................ $500,000

President, Charles L. Lovering, Boston; Vice-President, William H. Sweatt, City Mills, Mass.; Secretary, W. S. Armstrong; Treasurer, William Bloodgood, New York.

Directors—S. R. Ingham (chairman), William Bloodgood, Dumont Clarke, Edmund R. Wanckel, New York; William H. Sweatt, City Mills, Mass.; Frederic S. Clark, Charles L. Lovering, Boston.

Corporate office, Picton, N. J.; main office, 110 East Thirteenth street, New York. Annual meeting, last Wednesday in January.

## AMERICAN FIRE ENGINE CO.

A corporation formed under the laws of New York, December 12, 1891. The business of the company is the manufacture and sale of steam fire engines and fire apparatus and supplies. It acquired the properties and business of the following concerns:

Silsby Manufacturing Co., Seneca Falls, N. Y.
Clapp & Jones Manufacturing Co., Hudson, N.Y.
Ahrens Manufacturing Co., Cincinnati.
Button Fire Engine Works, Waterford, N. Y.

Stock......Par $100..............................Authorized, $500,000......Issued, $500,000

Stock is transferred at the company's office, Seneca Falls, N. Y.

FUNDED DEBT.

1st mort., 6 per cent., due Jan., 1912, Jan. and July.................................. $319,000

The trustee of the mortgage is the Farmers' Loan & Trust Co., New York, which institution also pays the interest on the bonds.

On January 1, 1903, the company had a surplus of $196,513.

President and Treasurer, Charles T. Silsby; 1st Vice-President, Charles E. Locke, New York; 2d Vice-President, Christopher Ahrens, Cincinnati; Secretary, William S. Silsby, Seneca Falls, N. Y.

Directors—Christopher Ahrens, William A. Dinsmore, Charles T. Silsby, William S. Taylor, George F. Ahrens, Charles E. Locke, William S. Silsby, George H. Robinson.

Main office, Seneca Falls, N. Y.; branch office, Cincinnati; New York office, 85 Liberty street. Annual meeting, second Tuesday in February at Seneca Falls.

## THE AMERICAN GAS CO.

A corporation formed under the laws of New Jersey, December 12, 1892. The purpose of the company is the ownership, leasing, management and construction of gas works and incidentally of electric light and power plants. The company controls a number of gas organizations operating in various cities and towns throughout the United States.

Stock......Par $100...........................Authorized, $1,000,000......Issued, $1,000,000

Transfer Agent, New Jersey Corporation, Guarantee & Trust Co., Camden, N. J. Registrar, Girard Trust Co., Philadelphia.

The company has paid dividends of 6 per cent. per annum on its stock since 1893. The dividends are paid semi-annually, being 3 per cent. each, June (1) and December.

President, Morris W. Stroud; Secretary and Assistant Treasurer, R. L. Babcock; General Superintendent, S. P. Curtis, Philadelphia.

Directors—Morris W. Stroud, Lewis A. Riley, John C. Lowry, Edward B. Smith, John S. Jenks, Horace C. Jones, E. H. McCullough, Philadelphia; William Carpender, Edmund Penfold, W. R. Beal, New York; C. J. Carpender, New Brunswick.

Corporate office, 419 Market street, Camden, N. J.; main office, 222 South Third street, Philadelphia. Annual meeting, first Tuesday in April at Camden.

## AMERICAN GLUE CO.

A corporation formed under the laws of New Jersey, August 1, 1894. The business of the company is the manufacture and sale of glue, gelatine and similar products, as well as sand paper, emery paper, etc. It has factories at various points and stores in Boston, New York, Philadelphia, Chicago and St. Louis and agencies in other cities. Since 1900 the company has purchased the Union Sand Paper Co., Walpole, Mass.; the factories of Wiggin & Stevens at Malden, Mass., and Dover, N. H.; also the Boston Flint Paper Co., Hallowell, Me.; the Adirondack Garnet Co., North Creek, N. Y.; the Pennsylvania Garnet Co., and the Cape Ann Isinglass Factory, Rockport, Mass.

In November, 1902, it was proposed to form a new organization under the title of the Glue Corporation, but after some controversy a change of the control and management of the original company was effected.

Stock.......Par $100.......Authorized { com., $800,000 / pref., 1,600,000 } Issued { com., $800,000 / pref., 1,300,000 } $2,100,000

The preferred stock is 8 per cent., cumulative. In September, 1900, the preferred stock was increased from $1,000,000 to $1,600,000, the additional $600,000 being offered to stockholders at $133⅓. The new stock was issued to provide for new acquisitions and for working capital. The company has no funded or floating debt.

Stock is transferred at the company's office in Boston. Registrar, Adams Trust Co., Boston.

Since the organization of the company 4 per cent. has been paid semi-annually on the preferred stock, in February (1) and August. On January 31, 1901, 2 per cent. was paid on the common stock, and on November 1, 1901, 2 per cent. was also paid on the common. On April 1 and November 1, 1902, 2 per cent. was paid on the common stock.

In the year ending May 31, 1901, the net earnings were $306,207.

President, Albert N. Parlin; Vice-President, King Upton; Treasurer, Everett J. Stevens; General Auditor, Frank W. Stanley; Assistant Treasurer, D. Webster Dow, Boston.

Directors—Albert N. Parlin, Frank Stearns, Eugene N. Foss, E. P. Carver, Ransom B. Fuller, Kilby Page, King Upton, Frank W. Stanley, D. Webster Dow, Roger Upton, Andrew J. Ward, Everett J. Stevens.

Main office, 419 Atlantic avenue, Boston; New York office, 197 Water street. Annual meeting, third Tuesday in August, at Trenton, N. J.

## AMERICAN GRAPHOPHONE CO.

A corporation formed under the laws of West Virginia, in 1887. The company owns patents covering the manufacture, sale and use of sound records and machines known as graphophones or phonographs. It is the only company in the world engaged in their sole manufacture on an extensive scale. It has a large and admirably equipped factory in Bridgeport, Conn., embraced in which is also the plant of the Burt Co., formerly of Millburn, New Jersey.

The company owns the Columbia Phonograph Co., the Columbia Phonograph Co., General, and the Columbia Phonograph Company M. B. H. of Germany. The Columbia Companies are the selling department of the American Graphophone Co., and have sales depots in London, Paris, Berlin, New York, Philadelphia, Baltimore, Washington, Buffalo, Boston, Pittsburg, Chicago, St. Louis, Minneapolis, Detroit, Milwaukee, Kansas City, Denver, Memphis and San Francisco. It also owns all the capital stock of the Globe Record Co. and a controlling interest in the Burt Co., formerly of Millburn, N. J.

Stock.....Par $10......Authorized { com., $1,500,000 / pref., 1,500,000 } Issued { com., $1,200,000 / pref., 1,191,600 } $2,391,600

The preferred stock is 7 per cent., non-cumulative. After both classes of stock have received 7 per cent. each in any one year they share equally in additional profits.

The company has paid dividends on the preferred at least 7 per cent. annually since 1895. Beginning with 1899, 8 per cent. was paid to August, 1901, after which the rate was reduced to 7 per cent. On the common 4 per cent. was paid in 1896, 6 per cent. in 1897, 7 per cent. in 1898, and 8 per cent. thereafter until September, 1901, after which time it was discontinued. Preferred dividends are paid quarterly, on the 15th of February, May, August and November. Total dividend payments to 1903 over $750,000.

Transfer agencies: 919 Pennsylvania avenue, Washington, D. C.; Columbia Phonograph Co., General, 90 West Broadway, New York.

FUNDED DEBT.

Twenty-year conv. deb., 5 per cent., due 1918 and 1925, May and Nov. or Feb. and Aug. $85,000

The 20-year 5 per cent. debentures are convertible into preferred stock. They are in two series, maturing in 1918 and 1925 respectively. Interest is paid in May and November 1st on the series maturing 1918; in February and August 1st on the series maturing 1925. The company also has a real estate mortgage of $100,000 on its factory real estate at Bridgeport, Conn.

The report of the company for the year ending September 30, 1900, showed an accumulated profit and loss surplus of $271,357. The surplus February 1, 1903, was $605,000.

President and General Manager, Edward D. Easton; Vice-President, Mervin E. Lyle; Executive officer, Herbert A. Budlong; Treasurer, Charles W. Cox; Secretary, E. O. Rockwood; Chairman of the Finance Committee, William E. Bond; General Counsel, W. M. Johnson; Patent Counsel, Philip Mauro; Purchasing Agent, Clement March.

Directors—W. M. Johnson, Andrew Devine, Mervin E. Lyle, Frederick J. Warburton, Edward D. Easton, Mark T. Cox, Philip Mauro, Thomas R. White, Jr., William Herbert Smith, John J. Phelps, William E. Bond, E. V. Murphy, D. C. McEwen.

Main office, 1212 F street, Washington, D. C.; New York office, 141 Broadway. Annual meeting, second Monday in January.

---

## AMERICAN GRASS TWINE CO.

A corporation formed under the laws of Delaware, June 8, 1899. The company acquired the property of the Northwestern Grass Twine Co. and other plants. It owns all the capital stock of the American Furniture and Manufacturing Co., and 55 per cent. of the stock of the Curled Fibre Manufacturing Co. The location, etc., of the several plants are as follows:

Northwest'n Grass Twine Co., St. Paul., Minn.
Wisconsin Grass Twine Co., Oskosh, Wis.
Wisconsin Grass Twine Co., W. Superior, Wis.
American Furn. & Mfg. Co., Brooklyn. N. Y.
Curled Fibre Mfg. Co., St. Paul, Minn.

In November, 1902, acquired the Minnie Harvester Co., St. Paul, which was organized in this company's interest to manufacture harvesters using the binder twine of its make.

The company also owns 15,000 acres of grass lands within 30 miles of its factories, with full equipment for harvesting and handling the grass. Within a radius of 50 miles of the factories the supply of grass is practically unlimited. The company has patents granted in the United States and the leading foreign countries and their colonies.

Stock......Par $100.........................Authorized, $15,000,000......Issued, $14,118,000

The stock is full paid and non-assessable. The company has no preferred stock. There is $1,035,000 stock in the company's treasury and $882,000 remains unissued.

Transfer Agent, Corporation Trust Co., New York. Registrar, Knickerbocker Trust Co., New York.

The first dividend on the stock was 1¼ per cent. quarterly, paid April 1, 1902. Quarterly dividends of the same amount were paid in July and October, 1902. The directors, however, after declaring another quarterly dividend of 1¼ per cent., payable January 2, 1903, rescinded their action and made the dividend ¼ per cent., it being understood that the money was needed for working capital and improvements.

President, Stewart H. Chisholm; Vice-President and Treasurer, Henry E. Howland, New York; 2d Vice-President, M. J. O'Shaughnessy, Jr.; General Manager, Thomas K. Ottis, St. Paul; Secretary, Charles P. Howland, New York.

Directors—Stewart H. Chisholm, J. F. O'Shaughnessy, Henry E. Howland, Jacob Rubino, Robert E. Todd, New York; James J. Hill, M. J. O'Shaughnessy, Jr., St. Paul; Horace G. Knowles, Dover, Del.

Corporate office, Dover, Del.; main office, 35 Wall street, New York.

## THE AMERICAN HAY CO.

A corporation formed under the laws of New Jersey, May 1, 1900. The purpose of the company is to deal in hay. The company acquired the plant and good will of William C. Bloomingdale, with storehouses in Brooklyn and Townley, N. J., and agencies in Boston, Jacksonville, Fla., Havana, Cuba, and St. Johns, Canada.

Stock......Par $100.......Authorized { com., $250,000; pref., 250,000 } Issued { com., $156,600; pref., 110,000 } $266,600

The preferred stock is 8 per cent., non-cumulative. Stock is transferred at the company's office. Dividends of 4 per cent. semi-annual are paid on the preferred stock in January and July.

The company has no funded debt.

President, William C. Bloomingdale; Secretary, William J. Bloomingdale, New York; Treasurer, Joseph Vollkommer, Jr., Brooklyn.

Directors—James Hughes, William C. Bloomingdale, William J. Frederick, Joseph Vollkommer, Jr., William J. Bloomingdale, Jacob F. Ostrander, Roscoe C. Tygert.

Main office, 116 Broad street, New York; branch offices, Louiseville and St. Johns, Canada. Annual meeting, first Monday in May, at Jersey City.

## AMERICAN HIDE & LEATHER CO.

A corporation formed under the laws of New Jersey, in August, 1899. The company acquired the plants and business of twenty-two different establishments engaged in the manufacture and sale of upper leathers, particulars of which are given in the MANUAL for 1901.

The establishments acquired represented 75 per cent. of the business in upper leather in the United States. In each case the properties acquired were taken in fee clear of all encumbrances. The aggregate annual net earnings of the separate concerns before consolidation were $1,585,748.

Stock..Par $100..Authorized { com., $17,500,000; pref., 17,500,000 } Issued { com., $11,274,100; pref., 12,548,300 } $23,822,400

The preferred stock is 7 per cent., cumulative, and has a preference as to assets.

Transfer Agent, Corporation Trust Co. of New Jersey, New York.

FUNDED DEBT.

1st mort., 6 per cent., due Sept., 1919, March and Sept............................ $8,216,000

The first mortgage is for $10,000,000. Of this amount $1,550,000 is reserved for the treasury of the company. Of the bonds outstanding $2,445,000 were accepted by vendors of the properties acquired by the company in payment for same, $3,200,000 were disposed of privately and $2,800,000 were offered in January, 1900, for public subscription by Messrs. J. & W. Seligman, New York, and E. H. Gay & Co., Boston. Of the bonds held in the treasury $1,000,000 can only be issued for the acquisition of new properties which shall become subject to the mortgage. The trustee of the mortgage is the Colonial Trust Co., New York. The mortgage is secured by all the properties of the company. There is a sinking fund of $150,000 par value of bonds per annum. Bonds may be bought for the sinking fund at not over 115, but are not subject to compulsory retirement. On June 30, 1902, there were $309,000 bonds in the sinking fund.

In the year ending June 29, 1901, the surplus over charges was $377,139. In the year ending June 30, 1902, the total profits were $1,411,511; interest and deductions for depreciation, etc., $1,004,634; balance, $406,877.

The following is the company's balance sheet of June, 1902:

| ASSETS. | | LIABILITIES. | |
|---|---|---|---|
| Cost of properties | $26,385,557 | Preferred shares | $13,000,000 |
| Sinking fund: | | Common shares | 11,500,000 |
| Cash and accrued interest | 16,206 | 1st mortgage 6 per cent. bonds | 8,525,000 |
| 309 bonds of the company | 309,000 | Interest accrued | 170,500 |
| Supplies | 6,801,618 | Bills payable | 625,000 |
| Bills and accounts receivable | 1,408,997 | Foreign exchange | 414,602 |
| Sundries, claims, etc | 98,717 | Trade accounts | 244,454 |
| Insurance, unexpired | 67,230 | Wages, etc | 71,436 |
| Cash | 431,389 | Uncompleted construction | 16,000 |
| | | Sinking fund, 1st mortgage | 325,206 |
| | | Surplus | 626,516 |
| Total | $35,518,714 | Total | $35,518,714 |

President, Thomas W. Hall, New York; 1st Vice-President, W. N. Eisendrath, Chicago; 2d Vice-President, Theodore S. Haight; 3d Vice-President, Aaron Hecht; 4th Vice-President, Frank L. Roenitz, Secretary and Treasurer, George A. Hill, New York.

Directors—Thomas W. Hall, W. N. Eisendrath, E. L. White, Theodore S. Haight, Frank L. Roenitz, Matthew Robson, C. H. Buswell, Charles W. Tidd, William Becker, Thomas S. Kiernan, Aaron Hecht, James Skinner, Frederick Strauss, Thomas J. Ryan, George A. Hill.

Main offices, 92 Cliff street, New York, and 17 East street, Boston. Annual meeting, first Monday in September.

## AMERICAN HOMINY CO.

A corporation formed under the laws of New York in April, 1902. The company is a consolidation of the following companies:

| | |
|---|---|
| Indianapolis Hominy Mills, Indianapolis. | Cerealine Manufacturing Co., Indianapolis. |
| The Hudnut Co., Trenton, N. J. | Pratt Cereal Mill Co., Decatur, Ill. |
| M. M. Wright Co., Danville, Ill. | Miami Maize Co., Toledo, O. |
| Hamburg Milling Co., Hamburg, Ia. | Shellabarger Mill & Elevator Co., Decatur, Ill. |

Stock....Par $100.....Authorized { com., $2,500,000; pref., 1,250,000 } Issued { com., $2,500,000; pref., 1,250,000 } $3,750,000

The preferred stock is 6 per cent., cumulative. Transfer Agent, The Merchants Loan & Trust Co., Chicago. Registrar, American Trust & Savings Bank, Chicago.

FUNDED DEBT.

1st mort., 5 per cent., gold, due 1927....$750,000

The authorized amount of the mortgage is $1,250,000; $450,000 remain in the treasury; 2 per cent. of the issue is to be redeemed yearl. Trustee of the mortgage and agent for the payment of interest, American Trust & SavingsyBank, Chicago.

President, Hervey Bates, Jr., Indianapolis; Vice-President, Ralph E. Pratt; Secretary and Treasurer, L. O. Bodman, Indianapolis.

Directors—Hervey Bates, Hervey Bates, Jr., L. O. Bodman, F. W. B. Coleman, Indianapolis; Joy Morton, T. P. Shonts, Ralph E. Pratt, Chicago; B. G. Hudnut, R. G. Jenckes, Terre Haute, Ind.; T. T. Gaff, Cincinnati; George M. Wright, Danville, Ill.; J. H. Bowman, Toledo, O.; Obio C. Barber, Akron, O.; Wendell Wright, Jersey City; D. S. Shellabarger, Decatur, Ill.

Main office, Majestic Building, Indianapolis; corporate office, 15 Exchange place, Jersey City. Annual meeting, fourth Tuesday in March.

## AMERICAN ICE CO.

A corporation formed under the laws of New Jersey, March 11, 1899. The company was organized to bring under one management several large corporations distributing ice in New York, Brooklyn and other eastern cities in combination with ice plants and storage facilities on the Hudson and Kennebec rivers. The company has acquired all the stock of the Consolidated Ice Co. of Maine and of the Knickerbocker Ice Co. of Maine. See statement of Consolidated Ice Co., in the MANUAL for 1899. Through ownership of the above companies this corporation has plants for housing ice on the Hudson river, on the Kennebec and Penobscot rivers and at Booth Bay, Me. It also does an ice business and has plants for manufacturing artificial ice in New York and Brooklyn, and in the cities of Washington, Baltimore and Philadelphia. Also sales depots in New York, Brooklyn, Philadelphia and Baltimore, and depots and distributing facilities, including valuable docks, in the cities of New York, Philadelphia, Baltimore, Washington, Newark, Atlantic City, N. J.; Lakewood, N. J., and Camden, N. J., and is extending its operations. Controls the American Coal Co., which was formed in 1901 to carry on the sale of coal at retail.

Stock..Par $100...Authorized { com., $25,000,000; pref., 15,000,000 } Issued { com., $25,000,000; pref., 15,000,000 } $40,000,000

The preferred stock is 6 per cent., cumulative. The amount of stock authorized was $30,000,000 preferred and $30,000,000 on common, but in March, 1901, a proposal to reduce the authorized stock to $15,000,000 preferred and $25,000,000 common was ratified. Registrar, Central Trust Co., New York.

The company commenced the payment of regular quarterly dividends of 1½ per cent. on the preferred stock in October, 1899, and paid the same in January (15), April, July and October, until April, 1902, inclusive, but the July, 1902, quarterly dividend was deferred, and none have since been paid. Dividends on the common at the rate of 1 per cent. quarterly were commenced in November, 1899, and regularly paid in February (15), May, August and November, until February, 1902, inclusive, but the May, 1902, dividend was passed and none have since been paid.

Stock is transferred at the company's office, New York.

FUNDED DEBT.

Collateral trust bonds, 5 per cent., due April, 1920, April and Oct.................... $2,740,000

The collateral trust bonds are $5,000,000 authorized. They were created in April, 1902, to relieve the finances of the company, the amount issued having been used to retire floating debt.

There are outstanding mortgages of the constituent companies to the amount of $2,200,000.

The directors have power to execute mortgages upon the property of the company without the consent of the stockholders.

For the year ending December 31, 1902, the company showed a profit and loss deficit of $102,492 against a surplus of $658,879 the preceding year.

President, John D. Schoonmaker, Rondout, N. Y.; Vice-Presidents, D. W. Hunt, Philadelphia; Wesley M. Oler, Baltimore; R. W. Hopkins; Treasurer, Eben D. Haley; Secretary, Robert A. Scott, New York.

Directors—Oren Dennett, R. W. Hopkins, Charles W. Morse, New York; D. W. Hunt, Philadelphia; Wesley M. Oler, Baltimore; J. R. Bennett, New Jersey; John D. Schoonmaker, Rondout, N. Y.; I. O. Blake, Eben D. Haley, Henry M. Head, Robert A. Scott.

Main office, Twenty-eighth street and Broadway, New York. Annual meeting in February.

## AMERICAN IRON & STEEL MANUFACTURING CO.

A corporation formed under the laws of Pennsylvania, August 21, 1899. The company acquired and owns the patents and property of the following concerns:

East Lebanon Iron Co., Lebanon, Pa.
Pennsylvania Bolt & Nut Co., Lebanon, Pa.
Lebanon Iron Co., Lebanon, Pa.
J. H. Sternbergh & Son, Reading, Pa.
National Bolt, Nut & Rivet Works, Reading, Pa.

The plants of the company include iron rolling mills and foundries and produce large quantities of nuts, bolts, rivets and similar articles. Their annual capacity is upwards of 150,000 tons of finished material.

Stock...Par $50...Authorized { com., $17,000,000; pref., 3,000,000 } Issued { com., $17,000,000; pref., 3,000,000 } $20,000,000

The preferred stock is 5 per cent., cumulative, with dividends to be paid quarterly, in January, April, July and October. The preferred stock is full paid. On the common stock $5 per share has been paid in.

Stock is transferred at the company's office. Registrar, Provident Life & Trust Co., Philadelphia.

The company has no funded debt.

The company began paying dividends on its preferred stock in January, 1900, at the rate of 5 per cent. per annum, and has regularly paid such dividends in quarterly payments in January, April, July and October.

On the common stock a dividend of 50 cents per share was paid in January, 1900. In May, 1900, 50 cents per share was paid; in January, 1901, 25 cents; in May, 1901, 15 cents; in September, 1901, 15 cents; in January, 1902, 15 cents; in May, 1902, 15 cents.

President, J. H. Sternbergh; Vice-President, H. M. Sternbergh, Reading, Pa.; Treasurer, H. M. M. Richards; Secretary, Charles M. Hallman, Lebanon, Pa.

Directors—J. H. Sternbergh, H. M. Sternbergh, Reading, Pa.; Arthur Brock, H. M. M. Richards, Edward Bailey, James Lord, H. H. Light, Horace Brock, Thomas Evans, Charles M. Hallman, W. H. Wallace, New York.

Main office, Lebanon, Pa. Annual meeting, second Wednesday in February at Lebanon.

## AMERICAN LIGHT AND TRACTION CO.

A corporation formed under the laws of New Jersey, April 6, 1901. The object of the company is to acquire control of other gas, electric and street railway corporations, and to operate gas, electric light and power plants and street railways.

The company has acquired controlling interests in the stocks of the following companies:

Western Gas Co., Milwaukee.
St. Paul Gas Light Co., St. Paul, Minn.
Grand Rapids Gas Light Co., Grand Rapids, Mich.
St. Joseph Gas Co., St. Joseph, Mo.
Madison Gas & Electric Co., Madison, Wis.
Binghamton Gas Works Co., Binghamton, N. Y.
Southern Light & Traction Co., San Antonio, Texas.
Consolidated Gas Co. of New Jersey, Long Branch, N. J.

Statements of the different companies will be found under their respective heads. The constituent concerns were acquired by an exchange of their stocks for stock of this company. The combination was carried out by a committee under the head of Emerson McMillin, New York.

Stock..Par $100..Authorized { com., $15,000,000; pref., 25,000,000 } Issued { com., $4,444,400; pref., 8,570,800 } $13,015,200

The preferred stock is 6 per cent., cumulative, and also has a preference as to assets in case of a dissolution.

The first quarterly dividend of 1½ per cent. on the preferred stock was paid December 1, 1901. Dividends of the same amount have since been regularly paid in February, May, August and November.

Transfer Agents, Emerson McMillin & Co., 40 Wall street, New York. Registrar, The Trust Company of America, New York.

The company has no funded debt. The bonds of the constituent companies are given under their own statements, under their respective titles.

In the 19 months ending January 31, 1903, the net earnings of the company were $1,501,064; dividends on the preferred stock, $748,948; surplus, $752,116.

President, Emerson McMillin, New York; Vice-Presidents, Willard E. Case, Auburn, N.Y.; Philip Lehman; General Manager, Henry L. Doherty; Treasurer, C. T. Scoville; Secretary, A. Lincoln Eglinton, New York.

Directors—William L. Bull, John J. Emery, Ashbel P. Fitch, John S. Foster, Warren W. Foster, Anton G. Hodenpyl, Henry B. Hollins, Thomas H. Hubbard, A. B. Leach, Arthur Lehman, Emerson McMillin, George T. Maxwell, James C. Parrish, George P. Sheldon, Junius M. Stevens, New York; Lewis C. Burnes, St. Joseph, Mo.; James Campbell, St. Louis; Willard E. Case, Auburn, N. Y.; Hugh H. Hamill, Trenton, N. J.; Lewis H. Withey, Grand Rapids, Mich.; Kenneth Clark, St. Paul, Minn.

Corporate office, 245 Washington street, Jersey City; New York office, 40 Wall street. Annual meeting, third Monday in March, at Jersey City.

## *AMERICAN LINSEED CO.*

A corporation formed under the laws of New Jersey, December 5, 1898. The products of the company comprise raw, boiled, bleached, refined and varnish oils, oil cake and oil meal.

The American Linseed Co. has acquired the plants and property of and owns in fee upwards of fifty different companies and properties, which are given in detail in the MANUAL for 1901.

In 1901 control of this company was secured by interests identified with the National Lead Co.

The company has a total of 60 properties equipped for manufacturing purposes in 13 States, comprising, it is estimated, 85 per cent. of the linseed oil production of the United States with elevators, warehouses, tank stations, etc., at various points, and construction and machine shops at Chicago.

Stock...Par $100....Authorized { com., $25,000,000; pref., 25,000,000 } Issued { com., $16,750,000; pref., 16,750,000 } $33,500,000

The preferred stock is 7 per cent., non-cumulative. The common and preferred authorized are each $16,750,000. The company has no bonds, and reserved sufficient stock to provide for certain mortgages on various properties, which have since been paid off.

Stock is transferred at the company's office. Registrar, Central Trust Co., New York.

The company paid quarterly dividends of 1¾ per cent. each, on the preferred stock, from March, 1899, to September, 1900, inclusive. The December, 1900, dividend was, however, passed, the surplus earnings being required for working capital.

The company in February, 1901, issued $6,000,000 of 5 per cent. gold notes, which were called and paid off in August, 1901.

The fiscal year of the company was, in April, 1900, changed to end August 1. The report for the year ending March 1, 1900, showed a gross business of over $14,000,000. Net earnings, $2,028,402. Surplus, over 7 per cent. on the preferred, $911,465. In the year ending July 31, 1901, the operations of the company resulted in a deficiency of $1,109,367, and a total loss of $1,402,492 after the payment of 1¾ per cent. on the preferred stock. No statement of earnings for the year ending June 30, 1902, was published.

President, Frederick T. Gates; Vice-President, L. M. Bowers; Treasurer, John A. McGean; Secretary, William A. Jones; Assistant Treasurer, F. K. Quine; Assistant Secretary, R. H. Adams, New York.

Directors—John D. Rockefeller, Jr., Frederick T. Gates, E. Parmalee Prentice, George Wellwood Murray, L. M. Bowers, John A. McGean, Guy G. Major, R. H. Adams, Homer C. Wise, Augustus N. Eddy, George D. Rogers, Edward V. Cary, Frederick J. Lovatt, William A. Jones, J. W. Hurst.

Corporate office, 243 Washington street, Jersey City; Chicago office, Monadnock Building; New York office, 100 William street. Annual meeting, second Tuesday in September.

## AMERICAN LITHOGRAPHIC CO.

A corporation formed under the laws of New York, December 26, 1895. The company was formed to do a general lithographic business. It acquired the plants, business and good will of the following establishments and companies:

| | | |
|---|---|---|
| The Knapp Co. | Witsch & Schmitt. | F. Heppenheimer's Sons. |
| Donaldson Bros. | Amlico Co. | Lindner, Eddy & Clause. |
| G. H. Buek & Co. | Schumacher & Ettlinger. | The Giles Co. |
| Gies & Co. | George S. Harris & Sons. | |

The company has establishments and offices in New York, Boston, Philadelphia, Chicago, Cincinnati, Buffalo, San Francisco and New Orleans.

Stock......Par $100..........................Authorized, $4,000,000......Issued, $3,785,600

FUNDED DEBT.

| | |
|---|---|
| 1st mort., 5 per cent., due 1921, Jan. and July | $816,600 |
| Debentures, 6 per cent | 2,284,000 |
| Total | $3,100,600 |

The 1st mortgage is $1,000,000 authorized. Trustee of mortgage, Morton Trust Co., New York.

The 6 per cent. debentures are $3,000,000, authorized. The amount given above is that subscribed and paid in. The debentures run for the term of the company's corporate existence.

President, Joseph P. Knapp; Vice-President, R. M. Donaldson; 2d Vice-President, G. H. Buek; Treasurer, Louis Ettlinger; Secretary, Charles Eddy; Auditor, R. N. Asterley, New York.

Directors—Joseph P. Knapp, Bellport, L. I.; H. W. Kupfer, Louis Ettlinger, R. M. Donaldson, John R. Giles, Samuel Untermeyer, Lucien Oudin, New York; G. H. Buek, Brooklyn, N. Y.; Charles Eddy, Montclair, N. J.; Nicholas Witsch, Hoboken, N. J.; F. S. Harris, Philadelphia; William C. Heppenheimer, Jersey City.

Main office, 50 Nineteenth street, New York. Annual meeting, last Tuesday in February.

## AMERICAN LOCOMOTIVE CO.

A corporation formed under the laws of New York, June 10, 1901, for the purpose of building railway locomotives and equipment. The articles of incorporation empower the company to mine, and prepare for use, ores, minerals, metals, and raw materials generally.

The company acquired and owns in fee the following properties:

| | |
|---|---|
| Brooks Locomotive Works, Dunkirk, N. Y. | Rhode Island Locomotive Works, Providence, R. I. |
| Pittsburg Locomotive & Car Works, Pittsburg, Pa. | Schenectady Locomotive Works, Schenectady, N. Y. |
| Dickson Manufacturing Co., Scranton, Pa. | |

The company also owns all the stock of the Richmond Locomotive & Machine Works, Richmond, Va., the Manchester Locomotive Works, Manchester, N. H., the American Locomotive Co. of New Jersey, and the Cooke Locomotive & Machine Co., Paterson, N. J.

Each of the works includes real estate, buildings, machinery and tools, equipped for the manufacture of locomotives. The combined plants occupy about 160 acres, and their aggregate capacity is 2,000 locomotives per annum.

Stock..Par $100...Authorized { com., $25,000,000; pref., 25,000,000 } Issued { com., $25,000,000; pref., 24,100,000 } $49,100,000

The remaining $900,000 of preferred stock is retained in the company's treasury for general purposes.

The preferred stock is 7 per cent. cumulative. The dividends on the preferred are payable quarterly, half yearly or yearly, as the directors may elect. Dividends on the common may be paid only when there shall have been paid, or set apart for payment of preferred stock, dividends at the rate of 7 per cent. from the time of issue to the beginning of the current dividend period. The preferred stock also has preference over the common in any distribution of assets, for its par value and accrued dividends. The preferred stock does not receive any dividends from profits in excess of 7 per cent. per annum, nor any distribution of assets in excess of its par value.

Transfer Agents, Harvey Fisk & Sons, 29 Nassau street, New York. Registrar, The Standard Trust Company of New York.

The first dividend on the preferred stock was 1¾ per cent., paid October 21, 1901, and regular quarterly dividends at that rate have since been paid in January (20), April, July and October.

It is stated that the policy of this company is to devote the surplus over preferred dividends to improvements and increasing its working capital, thus deferring the payment of dividends on the common stock.

FUNDED DEBT.

| | |
|---|---|
| Dickson Manufacturing Co. mort., 5 per cent., due November 1, 1927 | $562,500 |
| Richmond Locomotive Works mort., 6 per cent., due April 1, 1929 | 750,000 |
| International Air Power Co. mort., 4 per cent., due Feb., 1919 | 200,000 |
| Total | $1,512,500 |

The company has no bonded debt of its own and may not mortgage its property except for purchase money mortgage and except upon two-thirds assent of holders of preferred stock. The company assume the above bonds of its constituent companies.

Trustee of the Richmond Locomotive & Machine Works, Central Trust Co., New York. Trustee of the Dickson Manufacturing Co., mortgage, Farmers Loan & Trust Co., New York.* Interest on both bond issues is paid at the office of the American Locomotive Works, New York.

In the twelve and a half months ending June 30, 1902, the gross earnings were $26,398,394; net, $3,107,177; interest, $105,805; preferred dividends, $1,750,000; additions and improvements, $1,027,077; surplus, $224,235.

President, S. R. Callaway; Vice-Presidents, A. J. Pitkin, New York; R. J. Gross, Dunkirk, N. Y.; Secretary, Leigh Best; Treasurer, Charles B. Denny, Comptroller, C. E. Patterson, New York.

Directors—S. R. Callaway, A. J. Pitkin, Pliny Fisk, S. L. Schoonmaker, George R. Sheldon, J. E. French, New York; W. Seward Webb, Shelburne, Vt.; Joseph Bryan, Richmond, Va.; F. H. Stevens, Buffalo, N. Y.; Charles Miller, Franklin, Pa.; G. W. Hoadley, Providence, R. I.

Main office, 25 Broad street, New York. Annual meeting, second Tuesday in October.

## THE AMERICAN LOOM CO.

A corporation formed under the laws of New Jersey, February 20, 1906. The company owns the patents and business of the Universal Loom Co., the Readville Machine Works, and the patents of Henry I. Harriman for automatic shuttle changing looms.

Stock......Par $100..........................Authorized, $1,000,000......Issued, $1,000,000

The company has no preferred stock or funded debt. Registrar, Mercantile Trust Co., New York. The dividend dates for the stock are March 1 and September 1.

President, William C. Lovering, Boston; Vice-President, Hampden E. Tener, Jr., New York; Treasurer, George P. Erhard; Agent, Henry I. Harriman, Readville, Mass.

Directors—William C. Lovering, James G. Cannon, Albert C. Case, Hampden E. Tener, Jr., W. T. Bull, J. Murray Mitchell, George P. Erhard, Henry I. Harriman, S. S. Conover.

Main office, Readville, Mass. Annual meeting, third Tuesday in March.

## AMERICAN LUMBER CO.

A corporation formed under the laws of New Jersey, December 20, 1901. The company owns 292,625.63 acres of timber and other land in New Mexico.

Stock......Par $10..........................Authorized, $8,000,000......Issued, $3,303,770

The company has no preferred stock. Transfer Agent and Registrar, American Trust & Savings Bank, Chicago.

FUNDED DEBT.

1st mort., 5 per cent., due Feb. 1, 1912, Feb. and Aug.............................. $600,000

The outstanding bonds are the full amount authorized.

President, C. A. Ward; Vice-President, E. E. Crepin; Secretary and Treasurer, George O. Harding; Assistant Secretary and Assistant Treasurer, A. E. Trumbull, Chicago; General Manager, Ira B. Bennett, Albuquerque, N. M.

Directors—C. A. Ward, E. E. Crepin, J. H. Lesher, D. W. C. Merriman, Chicago; Ira B. Bennett, C. W. Restrick, Thomas B. Simons, Detroit; E. F. Allen, W. P. Johnson, Cleveland; J. S. Stearns, Ludington, Mich.; W. H. Sawyer, F. M. Stewart, F. A. Roethlisberger, Hillsdale, Mich.; J. H. Wade, Ann Arbor, Mich.; A. F. Freeman, Manchester, Mich.; C. H. Winchester, Elkhart, Ind.; B. S. Spofford, Coldwater, Mich.; H. H. Picking, East Orange, N. J.

Main office, 217 La Salle street, Chicago; branch office, Albuquerque, N. M. Annual meeting, first Monday in December.

---

## AMERICAN MALTING CO.

A company incorporated under the laws of New Jersey, in September, 1897, to acquire and operate a number of the largest and best appointed malt houses in the United States. The properties acquired included plants of the following firms and companies:

Neidlinger & Sons (7 plants), at 63d and 64th streets, Avenue A and East River, New York, 47th street and East River, New York, Brooklyn, South Rondout, N. Y., Cayuga, N. Y., Oswego, N. Y., Sodus Point, N. Y.
C. A. Stadler, New York (two plants), 48th street and East River and 61st street.
New York & Brooklyn Malting Co., Brooklyn.
C. M. Warner Co., Jordan, N. Y.
Miller & Kirby, Weedsport, N. Y.
Fred F. Bullin, Chicago.
John Carden, Jr., Chicago.
L. I. Aaron & Co., Chicago.
W. H. Purcell Co., Chicago.
J. Weil Malting Co., Chicago.
Brand, Bullen & Gund Co., Chicago.
Carden Malting Co., Chicago.
Hales & Curtis Malting Co., Chicago.
Chicago Pneumatic Malting Co., Chicago.
Howard-Northwood Malt Co., Detroit.
Estate of Charles G. Curtis, Buffalo.
Estate of Jacob Wechsler, Erie, Pa.
C. M. Warner Co., Syracuse, N. Y.
Kraus-Merkel Malting Co., Milwaukee.
Hansen Hop & Malt Co., Milwaukee.
Milwaukee Malt & Grain Co., Milwaukee.
Sohngen Malting Co., Hamilton, Ontario.
J. K. Souther & Sons, Clyde, N. Y.
W. D. Matthews Malting Co., Le Roy, N. Y.
W. Buchheit Malting Co., Watertown, Wis.
John W. Moser, Lockport, N. Y.
Scott Malting, Lyons, N. Y.
C. M. Warner Co., Clyde, N. Y.
W. H. Purcell Co., Kensington, Minn.

The establishments of Neidlinger & Sons, New York, were purchased by this company in January, 1899.

Stock...Par $100..Authorised { com., $15,000,000 / pref., 15,000,000 } Issued { com., $14,500,000 / pref., 14,440,000 } $28,940,000

The preferred stock is 7 per cent., cumulative. Transfer Agent, Guaranty Trust Co., New York. Registrar, Chase National Bank, New York.

Dividends of 1¾ per cent., or at the rate of 7 per cent. per annum on the preferred stock were paid quarterly from January, 1898, until October 15, 1899, inclusive. The January, 1900, dividend was passed and none have since been paid.

FUNDED DEBT.

1st mort., 6 per cent., due Dec., 1909, June and Dec. .............................. $3,861,000

The 1st mortgage bonds authorized are $5,000,000. There is a sinking fund which is to be one-half of the amount of each dividend declared on the preferred stock, such sum to be set aside simultaneously with the declaration of any dividend. Bonds may be purchased for sinking fund at not over 105 and interest. The entire issue may be retired at 105 on twelve weeks' notice. Underlying mortgages on the plants amount to $306,000.

EARNINGS.

| | Gross. | Net. | Dividends. | | Balance. |
|---|---|---|---|---|---|
| 1898 | $1,199,013 | $688,387 | $877,800 | Def. | $189,413 |
| 1899 | 702,875 | 177,564 | 977,550 | " | 799,986 |
| 1900–01 (year ending Aug. 31) | 721,977 | 383,261 | ...... | " | 383,261 |
| 1901–02 " " " | 751,470 | 323,754 | ...... | " | 323,754 |

On December 31, 1899, the profit and loss deficit was $1,389,399. In 1900 the fiscal year was changed to end on August 31. The deficit in profit and loss August 31, 1901, was $1,012,426 against $1,395,688 in 1900. On August 31, 1902, the deficit was $688,672. The company had, August 31, 1901, a working capital of $4,889,871, including $1,642,345 cash. Working capital, August 31, 1902, was $5,145,380.

The bond issue was decided on in December, 1899, in consequence of the fact that the company had expended $1,300,000 of its original working capital in the purchase of additional plants, and had for the same purpose issued $1,040,000 preferred and $750,000 common stock.

The floating debt was approximately $3,000,000. A syndicate formed by J. P. Morgan & Co., New York, undertook to finance the company and underwrote the issue of $4,000,000 of the bonds, which were offered to the stockholders at 95, the right being given to subscribe for 15 per cent. on the amount of their holdings of stock.

In December, 1899, the management of the company was also changed, representatives of the syndicate replacing a majority of the old directors.

In March, 1903, a committee—Frederick Uhlman, chairman; Temple Bowdoin, John G. Jenkins and Walter G. Oakman; Secretary, Louis L. Stanton, 25 Broad street, New York—submitted a plan for the readjustment of the company's finances. Holders of the bonds and stock were invited to deposit the same with the Standard Trust Co., New York. It was proposed by the committee that the present company, or a new one to be formed as its successor, should assume the $256,000 of underlying mortgage obligations and the $8,361,000 of the 6 per cent. bonds. The company to have $10,000,000 of cumulative preferred stock, entitled to 4 per cent. per annum until the bonds were reduced to $3,000,000, then 5 per cent until the bonds were reduced to $2,000,000, when 6 per cent. should be paid; and when all the bonds were retired, 7 per cent. The new preferred stock to be given to previous preferred stockholders in the proportion of 35 per cent. of their holdings or $5,054,000, but $3,861,000 more of the new preferred is to be distributed as the bonds are paid off. The common stockholders are to receive 25 per cent. of their holdings, or $3,625,000, with provision for the distribution of $3,861,000 more common when the bonds are retired. There is also provision made for an increased sinking fund to retire the bonds.

President, Charles A. Stadler; Vice-President, Frederick Vullmahn; Treasurer, Louis L. Stanton; Assistant Treasurer, H. Eggerking; Secretary, Faneuil D. S. Bethune; Assistant Secretary, E. A. Short; Chairman of Board, Frederick Uhlmann.

Directors—Charles A. Stadler, Seymour Scott, Charles Sohngen, Charles A. Purcell, Robert M. Gallaway, Frederick Uhlmann, John G. Jenkins, John J. Treacy, Charles W. Goodyear, Louis L. Stanton; Michael Coleman, Frederick Vullmahn, George F. Neidlinger, Albert Tag.

Main office, Sixty-third street and East River, New York. Annual meeting, second Thursday in November.

## AMERICAN NICKEL STEEL CO.

A corporation formed under the laws of Delaware. The plant of the company is located at Pittsburg. The company owns the American rights and patents for the manufacture of nickel steel in the United States.

Stock....Par $50......Authorized { com., $1,450,000 / pref., 50,000 } Issued { com., $1,450,000 / pref., 50,000 } $1,500,000

The preferred stock is 7 per cent., cumulative. The company has no funded debt.

President, B. K. Jamison; Vice-President, Richard H. Rushton; Secretary and Treasurer, John W. Woodside.

Directors—B. K. Jamison, Richard H. Rushton, John W. Woodside, Philip Mauro, J. Parker Crittenden, John F. Anderson, Victor Guillon, F. Rey.

Main office, The Bourse, Philadelphia.

## AMERICAN OIL & REFINING CO.

A corporation formed under the laws of Wyoming in September, 1895, to engage in the business of producing and refining oils. The company owns 40,000 acres of oil and coal land in Wyoming.

Stock. ....Par $100..........................Authorized, $5,000,000......Issued, $5,000,000

The company has no preferred stock and no funded debt.

President, Miguel E. de Aguero, New York; Vice-President, C. B. Richardson; Secretary, Warren Richardson, Jr., Cheyenne, Wyo.; Treasurer, J. W. de Aguero, New York.

Directors—Miguel E. de Aguero, J. W. de Aguero, Frank Williams, New York; C. B. Richardson, Warren Richardson, Jr., Cheyenne, Wyo.

Main office, 52 Broadway, New York. Annual meeting, September 12, at New York.

## AMERICAN PALACE CAR CO.

A corporation formed under the laws of New York, December 14, 1901. The purposes of the company are the construction and operation of palace cars.

Stock......Par $100.....Authorized { com., $4,000,000 / pref., 1,000,000 } Issued { com., $4,000,000 / pref., 1,000,000 } $5,000,000

The preferred stock is 6 per cent., cumulative.

The company has no funded debt.

President, George A. Denham, Boston; Secretary, William M. Hoagland, New York.

Directors—Joseph H. Hoadley, William J. Arkell, Daniel S. Brown, William M. Hoagland, James B. Brady, George E. Bouchie, New York; George H. Worthington, Cleveland; James N. Beckley, Rochester, N. Y.; George A. Denham, Boston; Henry W. Burgett, Brookline, Mass.; William S. P. Melvin, East Orange, N. J.

Main office, 27 William street, New York.

---

## AMERICAN PIG IRON STORAGE WARRANT CO.

A corporation formed under the laws of New Jersey, November 15, 1888. Its business is the storage of pig iron and other forms of iron and steel.

Stock......Par $100.........................Authorized, $1,500,000......Issued, $... .....

No transfers of stock can be made except by consent of the executive committee or the board of directors, and according to the officials of the company none of the stock is issued.

President, George H. Hull; Vice-President and Treasurer, J. C. Maben; Secretary and Assistant Treasurer, Frederick A. Libbey.

Directors—George H. Hull, Tuxedo Park, N. Y.; A. Heckscher, John J. McCook, J. C. Maben, Frederick A. Libbey, New York; Herbert D. Lafferty, Roanoke, Va.

Corporate and main office, 15 Enchange place, Jersey City; branch office, 44 Wall street, New York. Annual meeting, last Wednesday in November, at Jersey City.

---

## THE AMERICAN PIPE MANUFACTURING CO.

A corporation formed under the laws of New Jersey, January 31, 1889, for fifty years. The company's purpose is to act as engineers and contractors for water works, operators of water works and manufacturers of Phipps' hydraulic pipe. It has a plant at Germantown Junction, Philadelphia. The company owns, controls and operates the following water works:

| | |
|---|---|
| Springfield Water Co. | Conshohocken Gas and Water Co. |
| Eddystone Water Co. | Sumter Water Co. |
| Clayton Glassboro Water Co. | Milledgeville Water Co. |
| Wildwood Water Co. | Tallahassee Water Works Co. |
| Westville and Newbold Water Co. | LaGrange Water Works Co. |
| Waukesha Water Works. | Dawson Water Works Co. |
| Paris Mountain Water Co. | East Jersey Coast Water Co. |
| Greenville Water Works Co. | North Springfield Water Co. |
| Opelika Water Works Co. | Norfolk County Water Co. |

Stock..... .Par $100.........................Authorized, $2,000,000......Issued, $2,000,000

The stock was increased from $1,000,000 in 1901. The company has no funded debt.

Stock is transferred at the company's office. Registrar, Columbia Avenue Trust Co., Philadelphia.

The company has paid dividends as follows: 1890, 6 per cent.; 1892, 6 per cent.; 1893, 8 per cent.; 1894, 8 per cent. and an extra 3½ per cent.; 1895, 10 per cent. and an extra 3 per cent.; and from 1896 to 1902, inclusive, 12 per cent.

Dividends are paid quarterly in January (1), April, July and October.

The following gives the balance sheet of the company, December 23, 1902:

| Assets. | | Liabilities. | |
|---|---|---|---|
| Bonds | $2,703,308 | Capital stock paid in | $2,000,000 |
| Stocks | 328,556 | Undivided profits | 1,076,882 |
| Unfinished contracts | 59,934 | Dividend due January 1, 1903 | 60,000 |
| Real estate, clear of incumbrance | 55,119 | Bills payable | 380,000 |
| Book accounts due company | 111,377 | Book accounts owing | 16,204 |
| Bills receivable | 88,883 | | |
| Merchandise on hand | 58,545 | | |
| Cash on hand | 128,364 | | |
| Total | $3,533,086 | Total | $3,533,086 |

| | | | |
|---|---|---|---|
| Net earnings, 1899 | $201,663 | Dividends paid, 1899 | $96,000 |
| Net earnings, 1900 | 266,402 | Dividends paid, 1900 | 96,000 |
| Net earnings, 1901 | 286,500 | Dividends paid, 1901 | 108,000 |
| Net earnings, 1902 | 320,787 | Dividends paid, 1902 | 202,564 |

Not included in the above statement of resources are the factory buildings, machinery, office fixtures, patent rights and bills receivable, and in addition stocks of water companies in the process of development, of the par value of $2,237,100, and sundry bills receivable $112,681.

President and General Manager, Joseph S. Keen, Jr.; Vice-President and Treasurer, George M. Bunting; Secretary and Assistant Treasurer, H. Bayard Hodge; Assistant Secretary, W. H. Roth.

Directors—Joseph W. Hawley, Joseph S. Keen, Jr., George M. Bunting, Howard Watkin, N. B. Cox, H. B. Chambers, George Reynolds, George M. Booth, William H. Miller, William B. Scott, E. Eldridge Pennock.

Main office, 112 North Broad street, Philadelphia. Annual meeting, second Wednesday in January.

## AMERICAN PNEUMATIC HORSE COLLAR CO.

A corporation formed under the laws of New Jersey, June 14, 1901. The objects of the company are to manufacture and deal in pneumatic horse collars, harness and pneumatic and other goods of a similar character. The company is a reorganization of the United States Pneumatic Horse Collar Co. and acquired all its patents and other property.

Stock......Par $1............................Authorized, $2,000,000......Issued, $1,400,000

The company has no preferred stock. Transfer Agent, Lawyers' Incorporation Co., 51 Wall street, New York. Registrar, Continental Trust Co., New York.

The company has no funded debt.

President, Loren N. Downs, St. Louis; Vice-President, Dee Allen, Battle Creek, Mich.; Secretary, A. L. Norman; Treasurer, Charles H. Sewall, New York.

Directors—Loren N. Downs, George J. Kobusch, Z. W. Tinker, St. Louis; Dee Allen, Battle Creek, Mich.; Edward W. Cloud, Philadelphia; A. L. Norman, Charles H. Sewall, New York; George W. Flaacke, Jr., Jersey City.

Corporate office, 1 Montgomery street, Jersey City; main office, 90 West Broadway, New York; Secretary's office, 25 Broad street, New York. Annual meeting, first Tuesday in June, at Jersey City.

## AMERICAN PNEUMATIC SERVICE CO.

A corporation formed under the laws of Delaware in June, 1899. This company took over the business of the International Pneumatic Service Co., the owner of a large number of patents covering pneumatic tube systems for streets. It is also the owner of almost the entire capital stock of the Massachusetts Pneumatic Tube Co., which latter owns and controls the Boston Pneumatic Transit Co. It is also the owner of almost the entire capital stock of the Lamson Consolidated Store Service Co. and about twenty other corporations, owning patents for store service systems and pneumatic tube systems for buildings. See MANUAL for 1899 for details concerning the Lamson Consolidated Store Service Co.

In October, 1902, this company or organizations which it controls obtained contracts from the United States Post Office Department for carrying mails by pneumatic tube service in Boston, Chicago and St. Louis.

Stock par $50........Authorized { com., $10,000,000 / pref., 5,000,000 } Issued { com., $4,586,250 / pref., 4,112,500 } $8,698,750

The preferred stock is 6 per cent., non-cumulative. The present company has no funded or floating debt, but there are $516,000 6 per cent. bonds of the Lamson Consolidated Store Service Co.

The American Pneumatic Service Co. began the payment of regular quarterly dividends at the rate of 6 per cent. per annum on its preferred stock in October, 1899, and has paid such dividends regularly in January (20), April, July and October.

Stock is transferred at the office of the company, Boston. Registrar, Boston Safe Deposit & Trust Co.

The control of its various patents enables the company to engage in the business of installing store service systems or pneumatic tube systems for every variety of use inside buildings and stores, or in streets for the carrying of mail or parcels. The Boston Pneumatic Transit Co. has a franchise for laying tubes in the streets of Boston and has a system between the General Post-Office in Boston and the North Union Station, and one for carrying packages to the Back Bay, South End, and other parts of Boston. It is also the owner of a pneumatic tube system connecting the Associated Press with several of the newspaper offices in Boston, which system is under lease for a long term of years to the newspapers of that city. The company is the owner of patents covering the countries of Europe.

President, W. E. L. Dillaway; Secretary, Wilbur E. Barnard; Treasurer, Arthur S. Temple.

Directors—John Shepard, Benjamin W. Currier, Henry M. Whitney, Arthur S. Temple Ubert K. Pettingill, Oakes Ames, W. E. L. Dillaway, William H. Ames, F. A. Webster.

Corporate office, Wilmington, Del.; main office, 115 Chauncey street, Boston. Annual meeting, first Monday in June.

## AMERICAN PRESS ASSOCIATION

A corporation formed under the laws of New York in 1893. The company was originally incorporated in Illinois in 1882. Its business is the furnishing of matter and illustrations of every description for the use of newspapers throughout the United States, either in the form of patent stereotype plates, matrices, electrotypes, or copy in printed proofs.

Stock......Par $100.................... ......Authorized, $1,600,000......Issued, $1,600,000

The company has no funded debt or floating obligations. Stock is transferred at the company's office. Registrar, Central Trust Co., New York.

Monthly dividends have been regularly paid since 1884. The dividend rate is 6 per cent. per annum or ½ per cent. monthly.

President and General Manager, Orlando J. Smith; Vice-President, George W. Cummings, Secretary and Assistant General Manager, Charles F. Persons; Treasurer, John H. Grant; Auditor, Wayne B. Stowe.

Directors—Orlando J. Smith, George W. Cummings, Charles F. Persons, John H. Grant, Wayne B. Stowe.

Main office, 45 Park Place, New York. The company has branch offices in the various large cities of the United States. Annual meeting, first Monday in February.

## AMERICAN RADIATOR CO.

A corporation formed under the laws of New Jersey February 14, 1899. The company is the successor of an Illinois corporation, also named The American Radiator Co., which controlled fully one-half the steam radiator business in the United States. The present company, in addition to the plant and business of the original company, purchased the radiator department of the Titusville Iron Co., Titusville, Pa., and the plants and business of the St. Louis Radiator & Manufacturing Co., St. Louis; the Standard Radiator Manufacturing Co., Buffalo, N. Y., and the M. Steele Co., Springfield, O. It is stated that the consolidation of these interests gave this company control of 80 per cent. of the entire output of radiators in the United States.

Stock....Par $100.....Authorized { com., $5,000,000; pref., 5,000,000 } Issued { com., $4,893,000; pref., 3,000,000 } $7,893,000

The preferred stock is 7 per cent., cumulative. An amount of $2,000,000 preferred is held in the treasury of the company for the purchase of additional property or the extension of the business.

Transfer Agent, Equitable Trust Co., Chicago. Registrar, Illinois Trust and Savings Bank, Chicago.

The company began paying regular quarterly dividends of 1¾ per cent. on its preferred stock in May, 1899, and has since paid similar dividends in February (15), May, August and November.

EARNINGS.

Year ending January 31.

| | Profits | Pfd. Div. | Surplus. |
|---|---|---|---|
| 1899-00 | $657,162 | $157,500 | $499,662 |
| 1900-01 | 527,998 | 210,000 | 317,998 |
| 1901-02 | 627,614 | 210,000 | 417,614 |
| 1902-03 | 701,094 | 210,000 | 491,094 |

President, Clarence M. Woolley, Chicago; Vice-Presidents, John B. Pierce, Buffalo; Edward A. Sumner, Detroit; Treasurer, Charles H. Hodges, Chicago.

Directors—John B. Pierce, Henry Bond, Chicago; Edward A. Sumner, Clarence Carpenter, Ralph M. Dyar, W. S. Russel, Detroit; Clarence M. Woolley, Charles H. Hodges, Frank O. Lowden, William T. Baker, Chicago; John Fertig, John L. McKinney, Titusville, Pa.; George W. Parker, St. Louis; James B. Dill, East Orange, N. J.

Corporate office, East Orange, N. J.; main office, 40 Dearborn street, Chicago; New York office, 42 East Twentieth street.

## THE AMERICAN RAILWAYS CO.

A corporation formed under the laws of New Jersey, July 2, 1900, and was a consolidation of a company of the same name with the United States Electric Railway & Light Co. The company was formed to acquire and control electric street railway companies. The company owns or controls large amounts of the securities of the following properties of that character:

The Bridgeton & Millville Traction Co., Bridgeton, N. J.
Bridgeton Electric Co., Bridgeton, N. J.
The Springfield Railway Co., Springfield, O.

The Springfield Light & Power Co., Springfield, O.
The Peoples Railway Co., Dayton, O.
Chicago & Joliet Electric Railway.
Chicago & Desplaines Valley Electric Railway Co.
Altoona & Logan Valley Electric Railway.
City Passenger Railway, Altoona, Pa.

In 1902 the company completed the line from Chicago to Joliet.

This company owns $4,263,391 of securities of the constitutent companies, the cost of same being stated as $3,414,850.

Stock......Par $50.........................Authorized, $25,000,000......Issued, $3,902,000

The stock of the company consists of 500,000 shares, of which 98,040 full paid shares have been issued. The remaining shares can only be issued at par. The company has no bonded debt. Stock is transferred at the company's office.

The old American Railways Co. had 500,000 shares, par $50, all issued, on which $7.50 per share had been called and paid in. This was exchanged for 75,000 shares of the present company's stock, fully paid, twenty of the old being given for three new shares.

A dividend of 1 per cent. was paid on the stock December 15, 1900, and quarterly dividends of 1 per cent. were paid in March and June, 1901. The December 15, 1901, dividend was increased to 1¼ per cent. Dividends of the same amount were regularly paid in March (15), June, September and December, until December, 1902, when the quarterly rate was increased to 1½ per cent.

FUNDED DEBT.

Collateral trust, 5 per cent., due Dec., 1911, June and Dec.......................... $2,500,000

The collateral trust bonds were created in December, 1901. They are secured by the bonds and stocks of constituent companies, yielding an annual income of $154,000. They are convertable into stock at par up to November 1, 1904, and after that date can be called at 105 and interest. On June 30, 1902, the company had in its treasury $910,000 of the bonds, which were, however, sold soon after.

EARNINGS.

Year ending June 30.

| | Gross Income. | Net. | Dividends. | Surplus. |
|---|---|---|---|---|
| 1899-00 (15 mos.) | $144,081 | $102,572 | ........ | $94,736 |
| 1900-01 | 274,624 | 226,106 | $112,530 | 113,576 |
| 1901-02 | 370,384 | 302,732 | 178,178 | 124,554 |

President, J. J. Sullivan; Vice-President, William F. Harrity; 2d Vice-President, C. L. S. Tingley; Secretary and Treasurer, Walter W. Perkins; General Manager, H. J. Crowley, Philadelphia; Comptroller and Assistant Treasurer, Frank J. Pryor.

Directors—Richard L. Austin, William F. Harrity, Jeremiah J. Sullivan, William H. Shelmerdine, Samuel R. Shipley, Silas W. Pettit, John S. Bioren, E. Clarence Miller, C. L. S. Tingley, Philadelphia; Heulings Lippincott, Camden, N. J.

Main office, 1321 Walnut street, Philadelphia. Annual meeting, third Thursday in September.

## AMERICAN ROLLING MILL CO.

A corporation formed under the laws of New Jersey, December 27, 1899. The purpose of the company is the manufacture of basic open hearth steel, steel sheet bars, black and galvanized steel sheets, stove pipe sheets and steel sheet building material of all descriptions. The company galvanizes about 50 per cent. of its product and has a manufacturing department formerly owned and operated by the American Steel Roofing Co., of Cincinnati, whose entire plant and business was purchased by this company. This department manufactures sheet metal building material of all kinds. The company's mills and factory are at Middletown, O.

Stock......Par $100.........................Authorized, $400,000......Issued, $325,000

There is also $100,000 7 per cent. cumulative stock authorized, but it was determined not to issue the preferred stock, but to replace it with the bond issue.

Registrar, Central Safe Deposit Co., Cincinnati.

FUNDED DEBT.

1st mort., 6 per cent., due 1910, Feb. and Aug.................................... $150,000

The trustee of the mortgage is the Central Safe Deposit Co., Cincinnati.

President and General Manager, George M. Verity; Vice-President, W. T. Simpson; Secretary, R. C. Phillips; General Superintendent, James B. Strawbridge, Middletown, O.

Directors—George M. Verity, W. T. Simpson, R. C. Phillips, James B. Strawbridge, Middletown, O.; O. H. P. Lloyd, Cincinnati; Jacob Muerer, Brooklyn, N. Y.

Main office, Middleton, O.; branch office, Cincinnati. Annual meeting, February 14, at office of Corporation Trust Co. of New Jersey, Jersey City.

## AMERICAN SCHOOL FURNITURE CO.

A corporation formed under the laws of New Jersey, March 13, 1899. The purpose of the company is the manufacture and sale of seating for public buildings. The company purchased plants and property from companies engaged in this line of business located in a number of cities.

All of the plants were purchased outright, this company not having acquired any of the stocks of the companies whose properties it bought.

Stock....Par $100.....Authorized { com., $5,000,000 / pref., 5,000,000 } Issued { com., $4,883,800 / pref., 4,046,300 } $8,930,100

The preferred stock is 7 per cent., cumulative. Dividends are payable quarterly, in January, April, July and October.

Transfer Agent, Registrar & Transfer Co., Jersey City.

FUNDED DEBT.

1st mort., 6 per cent., due April, 1929, April and Oct.............................. $1,500,000

The 1st mortgage bonds are secured by a lien upon all of the plants acquired by the company. Trustees of the mortgage, Walter G. Oakman and George R. Turnbull, New York. A sinking fund of $60,000 per annum begins in 1904.

In the year 1902, the net earnings were $385,135.

The balance sheet, December 31, 1902, showed total assets, $12,772,371, and surplus, $1,226,147.

President, Thomas M. Boyd; Vice-President, Leo A. Peil; Secretary, F. P. Billmeyer; Treasurer, W. P. Orr.

Directors—Thomas M. Boyd, Leo A. Peil, F. P. Billmeyer, W. P. Orr, F. H. Ray, H. L. Hall, G. W. Perkins, W. F. Spieth, George Faulhaber, J. H. Butler, E. D. Beeghly, James Lynn, M. H. Murphy, E. C. Shafer, E. H. Gates, S. H. Carr, E. W. Irwin, D. D. Bullock, Crawford Fairbanks, E. D. Hubbard, J. F. W. Gatch, W. L. Deckart, H. J. Green, Alexander McDonald, F. E. Naylor.

Main office, 19 West Eighteenth street, New York. Annual meeting, in March at Jersey City.

## AMERICAN SCREW CO.

A corporation formed under the laws of Rhode Island in 1860. The company was a consolidation of the New England Screw Co. and the Eagle Screw Co. It has a large plant at Providence for the manufacture of screws. The company in 1898 sold its foreign properties, viz.: the British Screw Co., Limited, of Leeds, England, and the Canada Screw Co., Limited, of Dundas, Ontario.

In 1902 the company acquired the Massachusetts Screw Co., Holyoke, Mass.; the Boston Screw Co., Fitchburg, Mass., and several other concerns.

Stock......Par $100..........................Authorized, $6,250,000......Issued, $3,250,000

The par value of the stock was $250 per share, there being 13,000 shares, but in 1901 it was decided to change the par value to $100 per share, the outstanding capital of the company, however, remaining unchanged.

Stock is transferred at the company's office. Registrar, Manufacturers' Trust Co., Providence.

The report for 1898 showed quick assets, $1,534,638; total assets, $4,002,996. In 1899 profits were $349,153, and in 1900, $413,956. On December 31, 1899, the surplus was $507,125. On December 31, 1900, surplus was $758,580, and total assets, $4,055,705.

Dividends on the stock in recent years have been as follows: in 1890, 5 per cent.; in 1891, 1892 and 1893, 6 per cent.; in 1894, 5½ per cent.; in 1895 and 1896, 4 per cent.; in 1897 and 1898, none; in 1899, 2 per cent.; in 1900, 5 per cent.; in 1901, 5 per cent.; in 1902, 2 per cent. The 1900 and 1901 dividends were quarterly, being 1¼ per cent. each, in March (31), June, September and December.

President, Samuel M. Nicholson; Vice-President, Marsden J. Perry; Treasurer, George W. Thurston; Secretary, William A. Cranston.

Directors—Charles B. Humphrey, Charles Alexander, Robert W. Taft, George L. Shepley, Samuel M. Nicholson, Marsden J. Perry, Providence; George H. Robinson, New York.

Main office, 21 Stevens street, Providence, R. I. Annual meeting, second Tuesday in February.

## AMERICAN SEWER PIPE CO.

A corporation formed under the laws of New Jersey, February 17, 1900, under the title of The American Clay Manufacturing Co. The company acquired and owns the property or the entire capital stock of the following concerns engaged in the manufacture of vitrified sewer pipe, and other clay products:

Pittsburg Clay Manufacturing Co., New Brighton, Pa.
P. Connor, Elliottsville, O.
Knowles, Taylor & Anderson, E. Liverpool, O.
Jackson Fire Clay, Sewer Pipe & Tile Co., Jackson, Mich.
Uhrichsville Fire Clay Co., Uhrichsville, O.
Kennedy-Kling Co., Toronto, O.
National Sewer Pipe Co., Barberton, O.
Akron Sewer Pipe Co., Akron, O.
Pennsylvania Sewer Pipe Co., Limited, Huntingdon, Pa.
Hill Sewer Pipe Co., Akron, O.
Harry Thompson, Cuyahoga Falls, O.
The Diamond Fire Clay Co., Uhrichsville, O.
The N. U. Walker Clay Manufacturing Co., Walkers, O.
Toronto Clay Manufacturing Co., Toronto, O.
Great Western Fire Clay Co., Toronto, O.
McMahan, Porter & Co., New Cumberland, W. Va.
Columbus Sewer Pipe Co., Columbus, O.
J. J. Mazurie, Uhrichsville, O.
John Francy's Sons Co., Toronto, O.
Ohio Valley Fire Clay Co., Toronto, O.
Empire Fire Clay Co., Empire, O.
Calumet Fire Clay Co., Elliottsville, O.
Goucher, McAdoo & Co., Brazil, Ind.
Freeman Fire Clay Co., Freeman, O.
John Lyth & Sons, Wellsville, O.
Cincinnati Sewer Pipe Co., Cincinnati, O.
Myers-Hartford Clay Mfg. Co., Malvern, O.
Sharon Clay Manufacturing Co., Sharon, Pa.
McElfresh Clay Mfg. Co., West Virginia.
Bennett Sewer Pipe Co., Jackson, Mich.
Grand Ledge Sewer Pipe Co., Grand Ledge, Mich.
United States Clay Mfg. Co., Lisbon, O.

In January, 1903, it was reported that this company might be acquired by the National Fire Proofing Co.

Stock......Par $100........................Authorized, $8,000,000......Issued, $7,805,700

The company has no preferred stock. Transfer Agent, Registrar & Transfer Co., Jersey City. In March, 1903, it was decided to reduce the authorized stock from $10,000,000 to $8,000,000.

FUNDED DEBT.

1st mort. sinking fund, gold bonds, due 1920, March and Sept.................... $1,638,500

The mortgage securing the company's bonds (Knickerbocker Trust Co., New York, trustee), is for $2,500,000. After March 1, 1901, the company can call bonds up to $100,000 per annum at 105.

President, Ulysses D. Eddy, New York; Vice-Presidents, George R. Hill, Akron, O.; R. M. Francy; Treasurer, William B. Goucher, Toronto, O.; Secretary, Thomas D. Brown, New Brighton, Pa.

Directors—William B. Goucher, S. B. Goucher, Robert M. Francy, W. B. Francy, Toronto, O.; George R. Hill, Harry Thompson, Akron, O.; Thomas J. Evans, Uhrichsville, O.; Thomas D. Brown, New Brighton, Pa.; Ulysses D. Eddy, O. C. Barber, Alvah Trowbridge, W. F. Dunspaugh, New York; R. W. Allison, F. N. Klondolf, Pittsburg; Theodore Rhoads, Columbus, O.

Corporate office, 15 Exchange Place, Jersey City; main office, Ninth street and Liberty avenue, Pittsburg. Annual meeting, first Monday in February, at company's principal office in New Jersey.

## AMERICAN SHIPBUILDING CO.

A corporation formed March 16, 1899, under the laws of New Jersey. The company purchased the shipbuilding and dry dock plants of the following companies operating on the great lakes:

Buffalo Dry Dock Co., Buffalo.
The Cleveland Shipbuilding Co., Cleveland and Lorain, O.
The Globe Iron Works Co., Cleveland.
The Ship Owners Dry Dock Co., Cleveland.
Chicago Shipbuilding Co., Chicago.
Detroit Dry Dock Co., Detroit.
Milwaukee Dry Dock Co., Milwaukee.
American Steel Barge Co., shipbuilding plant, West Superior, Wis.
F. W. Wheeler Plant, West Bay City, Mich.
Union Dry Dock Co., Buffalo.

Stock..Par $100...Authorized { com., $15,000,000 / pref., 15,000,000 } Issued { com., $7,600,000 / pref., 7,900,000 } $15,500 0000

Regular quarterly dividends have been paid on the preferred stock at the rate of 7 per cent. per annum, beginning July 15, 1899, the dividend periods being January, April, July and October.

The first dividend on the common stock was 1 per cent., paid December 1, 1902, the directors having declared 4 per cent. on the common, payable December, 1902, and March, June and September, 1903.

The preferred stock is 7 per cent., non-cumulative. Transfer Agent, Corporation Trust Co., New York.

The company has no funded debt except a purchase money mortgage for $150,000 on the Buffalo plant.

In the eighteen months ending June 30, 1900, the company earned, net, $1,100,666; surplus, over preferred dividends, $568,466. In the year ending June 30, 1901, net, $1,998,542; dividends, $553,000; depreciation and maintenance, $271,905; balance surplus, $1,173,638. In the year ending June 30, 1902, the net earnings were $3,507,551 and the surplus $1,184,257.

The following is the company's condensed balance sheet, June 30, 1902:

| ASSETS. | | LIABILITIES. | |
|---|---|---|---|
| Plants and property | $14,993,297 | Preferred stock | $7,900,000 |
| Additions and imp'v'm'ts to plants | 190,414 | Common " | 7,600,000 |
| Materials on hand | 640,560 | Accounts payable | 883,326 |
| Acc'ts and bills receivable and cash | 3,258,888 | Bills payable | 500,000 |
| Work under construction | 1,076,728 | Reserve funds | 350,000 |
| | | Surplus | 2,926,561 |
| Total | $20,159,887 | Total | $20,159,887 |

President, William L. Brown, Chicago; Vice-President, Robert L. Ireland; Secretary and Treasurer, Russell C. Wetmore; General Manager, J. C. Wallace, Cleveland.

Directors—Luther Allen, H. M. Hanna, L. C. Hanna, Robert L. Ireland, L. M. Bowers, J. A. McGean, J. C. Wallace, Robert Wallace, Cleveland; Andrew M. Joys, A. B. Wolvin, Duluth; W. C. McMillan, Alexander McVittie, Detroit; William L. Brown, H. H. Porter, Jr., Chicago; W. T. C. Carpenter, New Jersey.

Main office, 120 Viaduct, Cleveland, O.; New York office, 36 Wall street. Annual meeting, first Wednesday in October, at Jersey City.

## AMERICAN SHOT & LEAD CO.

A corporation formed under the laws of Illinois August 27, 1890, for the purpose of manufacturing shot-lead pipe, sheet lead, bar lead and other articles of like material. The company owns plants at St. Louis, Chicago, Cincinnati, New York, Omaha, St. Paul, Baltimore, New Orleans and Pittsburg.

Stock......Par, $100........................Authorized, $3,000,000......Issued, $2,059,500

The company has no preferred stock and no funded debt. Transfer Agent, N. H. Blatchford, 70 North Clinton street, Chicago. Registrar, Illinois Trust and Savings Bank, Chicago.

President, Alexander Euston, St. Louis; Vice-President, Nathaniel H. Blatchford, Chicago; Secretary and Treasurer, J. R. Wettstein, St. Louis.

Directors—Alexander Euston, G. W. Chadbourne, St. Louis; Nathaniel H. Blatchford, A. W. Bulkley, Chicago; Hugh Merrie, E. H. Murdock, Cincinnati; E. A. Le Roy, New York; W. T. Harvey, Baltimore; John Farrell, Pittsburg.

Main office, 70 North Clinton street, Chicago. Annual meeting, third Thursday in January, at Chicago.

## AMERICAN SMELTING & REFINING CO.

A corporation formed under the laws of New Jersey, April 4, 1899, to combine a number of important establishments engaged in smelting and refining gold, silver, lead and copper and handling the products of those metals. The company acquired the property, rights and assets of the following corporations:

The United States Smelting & Refining Co., Helena and Great Falls, Mont.
National Smelting Co., Chicago.
Omaha & Grant Smelting Co., Omaha and Denver.
San Juan Smelting & Refining Co., Durango, Col.
Pueblo Smelting & Refining Co., Pueblo, Col.
Colorado Smelting Co., Pueblo, Col.
Hanauer Smelting Works, Salt Lake City, Utah.
Pennsylvania Lead Co., Pennsylvania Smelting Co., Salt Lake City, Utah, and Pittsburg, Pa.
Globe Smelting & Refining Co., Denver.
Bi-Metallic Smelting Co., Leadville, Col.
Germania Lead Works, Salt Lake City, Utah.
Consolidated Kansas City Smelting & Refining Co., Kansas City, Mo.; El Paso, Tex.; Leadville, Col., and El Carmen and Sierra Mojada, Mexico.
Chicago & Aurora Smelting and Refining Co., Chicago and Aurora, Ill., and Leadville, Col.
M. Guggenheim Sons' plants at Perth Amboy, N. J., Pueblo, Col., Monterey, Mex., and Aguas Calientes, Mex.

In 1900 the company arranged to acquire the plants of M. Guggenheim Sons at Perth Amboy, N. J., and elsewhere. To carry out this plan the stock was increased to $100,000,000, one half of the increase of $35,000,000 to be preferred and one-half common stock.

Stock..Par $100...Authorized { com., $50,000,000 / pref., 50,000,000 } Issued { com., $50,000,000 / pref., 50,000,000 } $100,000,000.

The preferred stock is 7 per cent. cumulative and has a preference as to assets in case of liquidation.

The authorized capital was originally, preferred stock, $32,500,000; common stock, $32,500,000. Dividends on the preferred stock at the rate of 7 per cent. per annum are payable yearly, half-yearly or quarterly, at the discretion of the directors.

The first dividend on the preferred stock was 1¾ per cent. quarterly, October, 1899. Regular quarterly dividends of the same amount have since been paid in January, April, July and October. April 10, 1900, an additional dividend of seven-eighteenths of 1 per cent. was paid on the preferred, to cover the period from April 11 to April 30, 1899.

Transfer agency, 71 Broadway, New York. Registrar, Chase National Bank, New York.

FUNDED DEBT.

| | |
|---|---|
| Omaha & Grant Smelting Co., 1st mort., 6 per cent., due March, 1911, March and Sept.. | $775,000 |
| Pueblo Smelting & Refining Co. 1st mort., 6 per cent., due March, 1913, March and Sept. | 191,000 |
| Total | $966,000 |

The company paid off on May 1, 1900, the $1,000,000 of 6 per cent. bonds of the Consolidated Kansas City Smelting and Refining Co., which matured at that time. The Omaha & Grant Co. 6s have a sinking fund of $70,000 annually.

At the time of the formation of this company the value of the plants acquired was $19,500,000, and the cash capital provided for the business of the company $7,900,000, a total of $27,400,000, represented by the preferred stock issued and outstanding.

EARNINGS.

Year ending April 30.

| | Gross. | Net. | Dividends on Pfd. | Surplus. |
|---|---|---|---|---|
| 1899-00 | $4,634,027 | $3,524,961 | $1,545,053 | $1,979,908 |
| 1900-01 | 5,988,049 | 3,828,441 | 1,918,000 | 1,910,441 |
| 1901-02 | 7,038,681 | 4,861,619 | 3,500,000 | 1,361,619 |

The earnings for 1900-01 include the operations of the Guggenheim plants for only four months. The net of these plants for the first eight months of the fiscal year were $2,756,662, so that the earnings of the combined properties, after expenses, taxes and interest, but excluding dividends, were $6,585,103 for the full year.

Net earnings for 1900-01 are after deducting $888,409 for betterments and repairs.

The following is a condensed balance sheet, April 30, 1902:

| ASSETS. | | LIABILITIES. | |
|---|---|---|---|
| Property account | $85,869,037 | Capital stock | $100,000,000 |
| Gold, silver, lead and copper in stocks | 20,883,605 | Bonds | 995,000 |
| Material, fuel and flux | 957,878 | Net cash liabilities | *4,755,565 |
| Cash | 992,013 | Profit and loss | 2,951,968 |
| Total | $108,802,533 | Total | $108,702,533 |

* September 2, 1902, reduced to $2,337,000.

President, E. W. Nash; Chairman Executive Committee, Daniel Guggenheim; Vice-President, Barton Sewell; Secretary, Edward Brush; Treasurer, Isaac Guggenheim; Assistant Secretary, W. E. Merriss; Assistant Treasurer, N. Suht.

Directors—E. W. Nash, Daniel Guggenheim, Isaac Guggenheim, Solomon Guggenheim, Murray Guggenheim, Simon Guggenheim, J. B. Grant, Guy C. Barton, Barton Sewell, A. Eilers, M. D. Thatcher, David H. Moffat, Dennis Sheedy, A. R. Meyer, N. Witherell, Grant B. Schley, Herbert L. Terrell, Henry L. Higginson.

Corporate office, 155 Montgomery street, Jersey City; main office, 71 Broadway, New York.

## AMERICAN SNUFF CO.

A corporation formed under the laws of New Jersey, March 12, 1900. The purpose of the company is the manufacture and sale of snuff and dealing in tobacco. It took under control the following properties:

George W. Helme Co., Helmetta, N. J. Atlantic Snuff Co., Philadelphia.

The snuff properties of the Continental Tobacco Co., including the Changewater Branch and the Jersey City (Lorillard) Branch:

The snuff properties of the American Tobacco Co., including the Chicago (Beck) Branch and the Baltimore (Gail & Ax) Branch.

Stock..Par $100. Authorized { com., $12,500,000; pref., 12,500,000 } Issued { com., $11,001,700; pref., 12,000,000 } $23,001,700

The preferred stock is 6 per cent., non-cumulative.

Transfer Agent, Morton Trust Co., New York. Registrar, National Bank of Commerce, New York.

The first dividend of 3 per cent. on the preferred stock was declared in December, 1900, payable January 2, 1901, and quarterly dividends of 1½ per cent. have since been regularly paid on the preferred in January, April, July and October. The first dividend on the common stock was 2½ per cent., paid January 2, 1903.

EARNINGS.

| | Profits. | Div. on Pfd. | Surplus. |
|---|---|---|---|
| 1900 (9 months) | $531,668 | $360,000 | $171,668 |
| 1901 | 1,066,605 | 540,000 | 526,665 |
| 1902 | 1,739,616 | *995,042 | 744,574 |

——* Includes 2½ per cent. paid on the common stock out of the gross earnings.

President, George A. Helme; 1st Vice-President, M. J. Condon; 2d Vice-President, Jonathan Peterson; Secretary, Otis Smith; Treasurer, E. D. Christian; Auditor, E. W. Somers.

Directors—Caleb C. Dula, William C. Ivey, Ernst Schmeisser, E. D. Christian, John W. Woodside, John H. Bowers, Martin J. Condon, Jonathan Peterson, Thomas J. Moloney, John W. Herbert, George A. Helme, James B. Duke, George B. Wilson, Henry D. Moore, Charles E. Halliwell, John B. Cobb, P. S. Hill, Otis Smith.

Main office, 104 First street, Jersey City; New York office, 111 Fifth avenue.

## AMERICAN SODA FOUNTAIN CO.

A New Jersey corporation, formed in 1891 to take over the works and business of the largest manufacturers of soda water apparatus in the United States, including the Tufts and Puffer works at Boston, Matthews at New York, and Lippincott, at Philadelphia.

Stock...Par $100..Authorized { com., $1,250,000; 1st pref., 1,250,000; 2d pref., 1,250,000 } Issued. { com., $1,250,000; 1st pref., 1,250,000; 2d pref., 1,250,000 } $3,750,000

The 1st preferred stock is 6 per cent., cumulative, and the 2d preferred 8 per cent., cumulative.

Stock is transferred at the company's office, Boston. Registrar, Boston Safe Deposit & Trust Co., Boston.

EARNINGS.

| | | Net. | Dividends. | | Surplus. | | Total Surplus Account. |
|---|---|---|---|---|---|---|---|
| 1893 | | $329,055 | $300,000 | | $29,055 | | $250,072 |
| 1894 | | 353,128 | 300,000 | | 53,128 | | 303,141 |
| 1895 | | 321,727 | 300,000 | | 21,727 | | 324,867 |
| 1896 | (loss) | 61,079 | 196,875 | Def. | 257,953 | | 60,913 |
| 1897 (8 months) | " | 37,394 | ...... | " | 37,394 | | 29,519 |
| 1897–98 (year ending Aug. 31) | " | 134,933 | ...... | " | 134,933 | Def. | 105,413 |
| 1898–99 ( " " ) | | 10,083 | ...... | Sur. | 10,083 | " | 95,329 |
| 1899–00 ( " " ) | | 179,006 | ...... | " | 179,006 | Sur. | 83,676 |
| 1900–01 ( " " ) | | 146,418 | 37,500 | | 108,918 | | 192,595 |
| 1901–02 ( " " ) | | 108,589 | 75,000 | | 33,589 | | 226,184 |

There were in 1896 unsecured loans made to company by its managers for $117,730, and additional loans, for which customers' notes were given as collateral, to the amount of $426,134. In 1897 such obligations were $876,768, and in 1896, $1,003,808. During the year 1897–98 the company's obligations were reduced $470,449, in 1899 to $327,586, and in 1900 to $355,947. On August 31, 1898, it held customers' notes for $938,704, and in 1900 the amount was $1,108,191. Impairment of capital, August 31, 1898, was $105,413; August 1, 1899, $95,329. In 1900 this was changed to a profit and loss surplus of $83,676. On August 31, 1902, the company held notes of customers for $1,109,724.

The company paid full dividends on both classes of preferred stock until November, 1896. None were paid from that time to November 21, 1900, when 3 per cent. was paid on the 1st preferred. On November 20, 1901, 6 per cent. was paid on the 1st preferred, and 6 per cent. was also paid November 11, 1902. At that time the unpaid accumulated dividends were 21 per cent. on the 1st preferred and 48 per cent. on the 2d preferred. Dividends on common were formerly paid at the rate of 10 per cent. per annum. In May, 1896, quarterly dividends on common were reduced from 2½ per cent. to 1¼ per cent., and none have been paid since November, 1896.

President, James N. North, Boston; 1st Vice-President, Alfred H. Lippincott; 2d Vice-President, F. Hazard Lippincott, Philadelphia; Treasurer, William T. Jenney; Assistant Treasurer, Leonard Tufts, Boston; Secretary, I. F. North, New York.

Directors—Alfred A. Lippincott, F. Hazard Lippincott, Philadelphia; James N. North, William T. Jenney, Leonard Tufts, Charles Warren, Boston; Charles N. King, Jersey City.

Corporate office, Jersey City; main office, 282 Congress street, Boston; New York office, 449 First avenue. Annual meeting in November, at Jersey City.

---

## AMERICAN STEEL FOUNDRIES

A corporation formed under the laws of New Jersey, June 26, 1902. The purpose of the company is the manufacture of iron, steel, coke and other materials, the acquiring and operating of coal, iron or other mines and timberlands, and the construction and operation of bridges, ships, engines, railroads, water works, gas works, electric works, acqueducts, canals, etc.

The company owns the following properties:

Sargent Co., Chicago.
Franklin Steel Casting Co., Franklin, Pa.
American Steel Foundry Co., Granite City, Ill.
Reliance Steel Casting Co. (Ltd.), Pittsburg.
Leighton & Howard Steel Co., St. Louis, Ill.

The company has also acquired a majority of the stock of the American Steel Casting Co., of New Jersey. The American Steel Casting Co. owns the following plants:

Thurlow Plant, Chester, Thurlow Station, Pa.
Alliance Plant, Alliance, Stark Co., O.
Sharon Plant, Sharon, Pa.

The Steel Casting Co. also owns a plant at Norristown, Pa., leased to the Reconstructed Granite Co.

Stock....Par $100..Authorized { com., $20,000,000 / pref., 20,000,000 } Issued { com., $15,000,000 / pref., 15,500,000 } $30,500,000

The preferred stock is 6 per cent., cumulative. Transfer Agent, The Corporation Trust Co., Jersey City. Registrar, The Colonial Trust Co., New York.

### FUNDED DEBT.

American Steel Casting Co. 1st mort., 5 per cent., gold, due Nov. 1, 1912, May and Nov. $471,000

The full amount of bonds authorized and issued was $490,000, but $19,000 were taken up. Trustee of the mortgage and agent for the payment of interest, Guaranty Trust Co. of New York.

The following is the company's balance sheet, September 30, 1902:

| ASSETS. | | LIABILITIES. | |
|---|---|---|---|
| Real estate, buildings, plant, machinery and other permanent investments | $28,006,846 | Capital stock | $30,500,000 |
| Current assets: | | Bonds of subsidiary companies | 471,000 |
| Merchandise, materials and supplies on hand, partly estimated. | 1,376,629 | Loans, bills and accounts payable. | 1,562,395 |
| Accounts and bills receivable | 1,876,374 | Profit and loss account: Net earnings for two months ending September 30, 1902, subject to provision for depreciation, head office salaries and expenses, and other adjustments to be determined upon | 327,461 |
| Miscellaneous investments | 48,174 | | |
| Real estate not used for business purposes | 310,365 | | |
| Cash and cash assets | 1,228,424 | | |
| Head office expenses | 14,044 | | |
| Total | $32,860,856 | Total | $32,860,856 |

President, Joseph E. Schwab; 1st Vice-President, Daniel Eagan; 2d Vice-President, Clarence H. Howard; Secretary and Treasurer, F. E. Patterson; General Counsel, Max Pam.

Directors—Joseph E. Schwab, George B. Leighton, Max Pam, E. F. Goltra, Arthur J. Eddy, Howard K. Wood, Kenneth K. McLaren, Charles Miller, Donald H. Mann, Daniel Eagan, William K. Bixby, Clarence H. Howard, W. D. Sargent, Lewis Nixon, S. R. Callaway, Alfred Clifford, J. M. Schoonmaker.

Corporate office, Jersey City. New York office, 74 Broadway. Annual meeting, third Tuesday in September.

## AMERICAN STOVE CO.

A corporation formed under the laws of New Jersey, December 26, 1901, for the purpose of consolidating various concerns engaged in the manufacture of gas ranges and gasoline and oil stoves. The properties acquired were:

Ringen Stove Co., St. Louis.
Quick Meal Stove Co., St. Louis.
Twin Burner Stove Co., St. Louis.
George M. Clark & Co., Chicago.
Standard Lighting Co., Cleveland.
Dangler Stove & Man'f'g Co., Cleveland.
Schneider & Trenkamp Co., Cleveland.
National Vapor Stove and Man'f'g Co., Lorain, O.
Monarch Stove and Man'f'g Co., Mansfield, O.

Stock......Par $100..........................Authorized, $5,000,000......Issued, $5,000,000

The company has no preferred stock. Stock is transferred at the company's office. Registrar, Lincoln Trust Co., St. Louis.

FUNDED DEBT.

1st mort. 5 per cent., 1903-1917, Jan. and July......................................$760,000

The bonds fall due $50,000 annually, from January, 1903 to 1917, inclusive, but are subject to call at 105, in whole or in part, on thirty days' notice. The Equitable Trust Co. of Chicago is trustee of the mortgage.

President C. A. Stockstrom, St. Louis; Vice-Presidents, George M. Clark, Chicago; E. K. Stockstrom, F. L. Alcott; Secretary, H. J. Trenkamp, Cleveland; Treasurer, George F. Fisk, St. Louis.

Main office, 410 North Sixth street, St. Louis. Annual meeting in September, at Jersey City.

## AMERICAN STRAW BOARD CO.

A corporation formed under the laws of Illinois in July, 1889. The company manufactures and deals in straw board, wood pulp and their products, having real estate, works and distributing agencies in many parts of the country. Plants, machinery, etc., are valued at over $6,500,000. Capacity of the company's mills is about 400 tons per day.

In 1902 the greater part of this company's stock was acquired by the United Box Board & Paper Co. This company's stockholders received $57.60 in new preferred stock and $55.40 in new common stock for each $100 of the old stock.

Stock......Par. $100..........................Authorized $6,000,000......Issued, $6,000,000

The company has no preferred stock. Stock is transferred at the company's office. Registrar, Merchants' Loan & Trust Co., Chicago.

In June, 1893, 2 per cent. was paid, after which there was no dividend until December, 1898, when 1 per cent. was paid and none after that until June, 1900, when 1 per cent. was paid quarterly, followed by similar dividends of 1 per cent. in September, 1900, and 1 per cent. December 27, 1900. The March, 1901, dividend was passed, and none were paid in 1901.

FUNDED DEBT.

1st mort., 6 per cent., due 1911, Feb. and Aug.................... .................. $516,000

The 1st mortgage bonds were originally $1,250,000. There is a sinking fund containing $734,000. Bonds are subject to call after 1901.

Net profits reported in 1892, $723,201; in 1893, $342,176; in 1894, $52,640; in 1895, $93,473; in 1896, $113,292; in 1897, $89,703; in 1898, $115,862; in 1899, $242,544; in 1900, $292,526.

President, S. H. Emery, Jr., Quincy, Ill.; Vice-President, W. C. Staley; Secretary and Treasurer, E. M. Watkins, Chicago.

Directors—R. F. Newcomb, S. H. Emery, Jr., James A. Roberts, R. B. McEwan, W. C. Staley, T. E. Ellsworth, A. M. Watkins.

Main office, 84 Van Buren street, Chicago. Annual meeting, first Thursday in February.

## AMERICAN SUGAR REFINING CO.

A corporation formed under the laws of New Jersey, January 10, 1891, to succeed the Sugar Refineries Co. or Sugar Trust, which was formed in 1887, a majority of the sugar refineries in the United States being taken into the Trust and its certificates issued to represent the value of their plants. The capital of the Trust represented in certificates was $50,000,000.

Stock..Par $100...Authorized { com., $45,000,000; pref., 45,000,000 } Issued { com., $45,000,000; pref., 45,000,000 } $90,000,000

The preferred stock is 7 per cent., cumulative. Stock is transferred at the office of the company, 117 Wall street, New York. Registrar, Central Trust Co., New York.

The authorized stock was originally $25,000,000 common and $25,000,000 preferred. In 1892 it was increased to $37,500,000 of each class to acquire additional properties. In 1901 both classes were increased to $45,000,000, and the stockholders were given right to subscribe for one share of new stock for each five shares of old held by them. The purpose of this issue was to extend the company's operations in Cuba and elsewhere.

The company has paid 7 per cent. per annum on the preferred stock since the reorganization. On a part of the preferred stock the dividends are semi-annual, 3½ per cent. each, January and July, and part quarterly, 1¾ per cent. each in January, April, July and October.

On the common stock the company paid 4 per cent., half yearly, from July, 1891, till October, 1892, when rate was raised to 2½ per cent. quarterly. In April, 1893, 3 per cent. quarterly and an extra dividend of 10 per cent. was paid, after which it was 3 per cent. quarterly, until April, 1900, when the rate was reduced to 1½ per cent. In July, 1900, 1½ per cent. was also paid. The October, 1900, dividend was 1¾ per cent., or 7 per cent. per annum, and that rate has since been maintained. Dividends on the common are paid quarterly, in January, April, July and October.

Dividends of 2½ per cent. were paid quarterly by the Trust from October, 1887, to July, 1890, amounting to $11,900,992. In consequence of the intended reorganization and the litigation in which the Trust was involved, the October, 1890, dividend was deferred. No statement of earnings was ever rendered by the Trustees, and the operations of the Trust were not made public.

A mortgage on the company's property to secure $10,000,000 6 per cent. bonds, due 1911, was authorized, but the bonds were never issued, and in 1901 the mortgage was cancelled.

The New York Court of Appeals, in June, 1890, decided that the Trust organization was illegal. The Trustees thereupon decided to reorganize the Trust as a corporation, and holders of certificates were asked to deposit them with the Central Trust Co. Litigation was, however, commenced to compel the Trustees to make an accounting, and in November, 1890, the Court appointed Henry O. Havemeyer, S. V. White and Henry W. Slocum Receivers for the property of the Trust.

On January 10, 1891, it being shown that nearly all the certificate holders had assented to the plan, the Court discharged the Receivers and the present company was organized, the old Trust certificates being exchanged, one-half for new preferred and one-half for new common stock, with a cash distribution of $15 per share on the Trust certificates.

In December, 1896, it was announced that interests connected with this company had aquired control of the Woolson Spice Co., of Toledo, O., a corporation engaged in roasting and preparing coffees. The object of this was to meet the competition of Arbuckle Brothers, a large coffee house which was about to build and operate an opposition sugar refinery. Litigation between the Woolson Co. and the Arbuckle Brothers ensued. In the latter part of 1898 the Arbuckle Brothers' refinery began operating, as well as another one completed by Claus Doescher in Brooklyn, in consequence of which the years 1898-99 were marked by severe competition in the business, prices for refined sugar being cut to figures which eliminated any profits to all concerned. At annual meeting of the stockholders in January, 1899, a resolution was approved transferring the accumulated profits or surplus to working capital account.

Net earnings for 1891 were stated to be about $5,073,000. Report for 11 months ending November 30, 1892, stated net earnings to have been $8,615,837, and surplus over dividends, $2,206,380. No annual report or statement has been published since that date.

The company's balance sheets for 1900, and 1901 are as follows:

| ASSETS. | Dec. 31, 1901. | Dec. 31, 1902. | LIABILITIES. | Dec. 31, 1901. | Dec. 31, 1902. |
|---|---|---|---|---|---|
| Real est. and machinery | $34,328,663 | $34,669,190 | Capital stock... | $88,280,370 | $90,000,000 |
| Cash and bills receivable | 36,862,701 | 30,046,750 | Debts.......... | 24,364,026 | 24,958,301 |
| Sugar, raw and refined.. | 12,248,640 | 15,842,924 | Reserve........ | 9,907,491 | 10,871,340 |
| Investm'ts in other cos... | 39,111,882 | 45,270,776 | | | |
| Total.............. | $122,551,888 | $125,829,641 | Total....... | $122,551,888 | $125,829,641 |

President, Henry O. Havemeyer; Secretary, C. R. Heike; Treasurer, Arthur Donner.

Directors—Henry O. Havemeyer, Charles H. Senff, Arthur Donner, W. B. Thomas, John E. Parsons, Lowell M. Palmer, John Mayer.

Main office, Jersey City; New York office, 117 Wall street. Annual meeting, second Wednesday in January.

## AMERICAN TELEGRAPH & CABLE CO.

A corporation formed under the laws of New York, January 18, 1881. The company owns two cables between Sennen Cove, England, and Dover Bay, Nova Scotia. Cables leased to Western Union till 1932, with a guaranty of 5 per cent. per annum on the stock issued.

Stock......Par $100........................Authorized, $20,000,000......Issued, $14,000,000

Stock is transferred at the company's office. Registrar, Mercantile Trust Co., New York.

Dividends are paid quarterly, 1¼ per cent. each, in March (1), June, September, December.

President, Robert C. Clowry; Secretary, Thomas F. Clark; Treasurer, Myron T. Wilbur.

Directors—Robert C. Clowry, Russell Sage, John T. Terry, George J. Gould, Edwin Gould, Thomas F. Clark.

Main office, 195 Broadway, New York. Annual meeting, fourth Wednesday in May, at New York.

## AMERICAN TELEPHONE & TELEGRAPH CO.

A corporation formed under the laws of New York in 1886. The company was organized by the American Bell Telephone Co., a Massachusetts corporation, to build and operate its long-distance telephone system, the Bell Co. owning all the capital stock of this company. See American Bell Telephone Co. in MANUAL for 1900. In March, 1900, the stockholders of the American Bell Telephone Co. decided to turn over to this company all its property and assets, including the stock it owned in operating telephone companies throughout the United States, the arrangement being that holders of the American Bell Telephone stock, of which there was $25,886,300 outstanding, should exchange it for stock of this company, two shares of the latter being given for one share of Bell Telephone Co. stock. The holders of the latter also had the right to subscribe at par for one share additional of this company's stock for every five shares held by them.

The following stocks and bonds were owned by the company October 31, 1902:

| STOCKS. | Total Issue. | Owned by A. T. & T. Co. |
|---|---|---|
| The Bell Telephone Co. of Buffalo | $5,000,000 | $2,511,500 |
| The Bell Telephone Co. of Canada | 5,395,320 | 2,083,220 |
| The Bell Telephone Co. of Missouri | 2,639,160 | 1,752,020 |
| The Bell Telephone Co. of Philadelphia | 9,980,500 | 8,073,450 |
| The Central District & Printing Telegraph Co. | 8,510,520 | 5,689,840 |
| Central New York Telephone & Telegraph Co. | 961,500 | 527,500 |
| Central Union Telephone Co. | 5,437,902 | 3,727,655 |
| The Chesapeake & Potomac Telephone Co. | 2,650,000 | 1,512,100 |
| Chicago Telephone Co. | 11,993,400 | 6,240,000 |
| The City & Suburban Telegraph Association | 3,564,850 | 1,091,450 |
| The Cleveland Telephone Co. | 3,100,000 | 700,000 |
| The Colorado Telephone Co. | 3,400,000 | 1,744,250 |
| Cumberland Telephone & Telegraph Co. | 9,106,000 | 4,629,725 |
| Delaware & Atlantic Telegraph & Telephone Co. | 397,945 | 150,666 |
| Duluth Telephone Co. | 100,000 | 56,650 |
| The Empire State Telephone & Telegraph Co. | 200,000 | 131,880 |
| Hudson River Telephone Co. | 3,613,200 | 1,844,500 |
| Iowa Telephone Co. | 1,423,225 | 471,570 |
| Michigan Telephone Co. | 5,000,000 | 110,400 |
| The Missouri & Kansas Telephone Co. | 3,062,000 | 1,553,200 |
| Nebraska Telephone Co. | 1,800,000 | 918,516 |
| New England Telephone & Telegraph Co. | 19,938,600 | 11,538,600 |
| New York & Pennsylvania Telephone & Telegraph Co. | 1,000,000 | 492,900 |
| New York Telephone Co. | 30,000,000 | 19,329,400 |
| The New York & New Jersey Telephone Co. | 9,979,720 | 934,320 |
| The Northwestern Telephone Exchange Co. | 4,354,300 | 780,000 |
| Pacific States Telephone & Telegraph Co. | 11,000,000 | 5,511,200 |
| The Pennsylvania Telephone Co. | 2,130,866 | 1,162,350 |
| Providence Telephone Co. | 1,600,000 | 480,000 |
| Rocky Mountain Bell Telephone Co. | 2,097,500 | 1,021,100 |
| Southern Bell Telephone & Telegraph Co. | 1,000,000 | 922,500 |
| The Southern New England Telephone Co. | 2,990,000 | 995,400 |
| The Southwestern Telegraph & Telephone Co. | 7,316,000 | 1,200,000 |
| Western Telephone & Telegraph Co. | 32,000,000 | 21,440,200 |
| Western Electric Co. | 10,000,000 | 6,008,400 |
| Wisconsin Telephone Co. | 3,011,100 | 505,100 |
| BONDS. | | |
| The Bell Telephone Co. of Canada | 2,000,000 | 302,500 |
| Central Union Telephone Co. | 6,000,000 | 1,000,000 |
| Iowa Telephone Co. | 750,000 | 350,000 |
| Duluth Telephone Co. | 180,000 | 180,000 |
| New England Telephone & Telegraph Co. | 4,000,000 | 581,000 |

The above statement of the company's interest in other corporations while correct at the date given, is subject to change from the increases in capitalization of the different organizations.

The Western Electric Co., which is controlled by this company, manufactures telephones and telephone supplies, and has factories in New York and Chicago.

The company had no interest in the stock of the Erie Telegraph & Telephone Co. The American Telephone & Telegraph Co., however, had interests in the stocks of the Cleveland Telephone Co., Northwestern Telephone Exchange Co., Southwestern Telegraph & Telephone Co., Michigan Telephone Co. and the Wisconsin Telephone Co., all of which were controlled by the Erie Telegraph & Telephone Co. and operated as parts of its system. In January, 1902, this company acquired a controlling interest in the Western Telephone & Telegraph Co., the successor to the Erie Telegraph & Telephone Co.

The company has interests in various other telephone companies and in different organizations controlled by the operating companies.

Stock......Par $100......................Authorized, $150,000,000......Issued, $114,946,300

The stock of the company was originally $12,000,000. The amount was increased to $20,000,000 in June, 1896; to $25,000,000 in 1898, to $75,000,000 in 1899 and to $100,000,000 in 1900, with a further increase to $150,000,000 in June, 1901. Of the $94,237,500 stock outstanding at the beginning of 1901, $51,772,600 was issued in exchange for the stock of the American Bell Telephone Co., over $10,000,000 was subscribed for at par by the old stockholders, and the balance was issued for the acquisition of other property. In June, 1901, stockholders were given the right to subscribe at par for $20,700,900 of new stock, and in 1902 additional stock to the amount of $21,937,000 was issued and sold to the stockholders. Besides the stock outstanding as given above, $27,110,400 is in the treasury of the American Bell Telephone Co., making the total amount issued $136,826,600.

In March, 1903, it was announced that the authorized stock would be increased to $250,000,000, discretion to be vested in the directors as to the issue of additional amounts of stock.

Stock is transferred at the office of the company's Treasurer in Boston. Registrar, Old Colony Trust Co., Boston.

The Bell Telephone Co. paid dividends on its stocks as follows: In 1892, 15 per cent.; in 1893, 18 per cent.; in 1894, 16½ per cent.; in 1895, 15 per cent., including 3 per cent. extra; in 1896, 15 per cent., including 3 per cent. extra; in 1897, 15 per cent., including 3 per cent. extra; in 1898, 15 per cent., including 3 per cent. extra; in 1899, 15 per cent., including 3 per cent. extra.

The American Telephone & Telegraph Co. paid 2½ per cent. on its stock July 16, 1900, and began the payment of regular quarterly dividends of 1½ per cent. October 15, 1900. The January 15, 1901, dividend was 1½ per cent. and ¾ per cent. extra; in April, 1½ per cent.; in July, 2¼ per cent.; in October, 1½ per cent., making 7½ per cent. in 1901. The same rate was maintained in 1902, the dividend paid January 15, 1902, being 2¼ per cent.

FUNDED DEBT.

| | |
|---|---|
| Collateral trust mort., 4 per cent., due July, 1929, Jan. and July.................... | $28,000,000 |
| American Bell Tel. debentures, 4 per cent., due July, 1908, Jan. and July........... | 10,000,000 |
| Total.............................................................. | $38,000,000 |

The American Telephone & Telegraph 4 per cent. collateral trust mortgage was created in 1899 to provide for extensions. The mortgage secures both the bonds of this company and the American Bell Telephone Co. 4 per cent. debentures. The amount of the bonds may be increased on the deposit of additional collateral, but such additional issue must not exceed 75 per cent. of the estimated value of the securities deposited. The company sold $7,625,000 of the collateral trust bonds in 1899.

In January, 1902, the company issued $13,000,000 additional collateral trust 4s, the new bonds being sold to provide for the acquisition of control of the Western Telephone & Telegraph Co., successor to the Erie Telegraph & Telephone Co.

The American Bell Telephone debenture 4s were created in 1898. In June, 1898, $5,000,000 were sold, of which $2,000,000 were to retire the old 7 per cent. debentures maturing August 1, 1898. The balance of the issue of $10,000,000 was sold in 1898 and 1899 to provide for extensions.

The American Telephone & Telegraph Co. had invested, at the end of 1902, $22,496,191 in constructing and equipping its long-distance lines, which aggregated 13,529 miles of poles and cable lines, 227,725 miles of wires.

The number of telephones in use February 20, 1903, was reported by the company to be 3,293,527, against 2,225,606 December 20, 1901. On January 1, 1902, the licensee companies had 1,411 exchanges, 1,594 branch offices, a total of 1,729,019 miles of wires, and 1,020,647 stations.

EARNINGS.

| (American Bell Telephone Co.) | Gross. | Net. |
|---|---|---|
| 1892.................................................... | $5,100,887 | $3,411,674 |
| 1893.................................................... | 5,781,076 | 3,925,485 |
| 1894.................................................... | 4,848,244 | 3,123,785 |
| 1895.................................................... | 5,124,952 | 3,213,759 |
| 1896.................................................... | 4,327,324 | 3,383,581 |
| 1897.................................................... | 5,130,844 | 4,169,674 |
| 1898.................................................... | 5,448,701 | 4,393,966 |
| 1899.................................................... | 5,760,106 | 4,072,949 |

EARNINGS—(American Telephone & Telegraph Co.)

| | Earnings. | Expenses. | Dividends. | Surplus. |
|---|---|---|---|---|
| 1899.............................. | $7,687,381 | $3,416,873 | $3,882,945 | $387,564 |
| 1900.............................. | 9,534,499 | 4,048,441 | 4,078,601 | 1,407,457 |
| 1901.............................. | 11,606,816 | 4,208,531 | 5,050,023 | 2,348,262 |
| 1902.............................. | 13,277,457 | 5,442,185 | 6,584,403 | 1,250,867 |

The following is the company's balance sheet December 31, 1902:

| Assets. | | Liabilities. | |
|---|---|---|---|
| Construction, equipment and supplies | $22,496,192 | Capital stock | $114,946,500 |
| Telephones | 6,522,106 | Capital instalments | 11,172,472 |
| Real estate | 1,745,280 | Surplus | 3,493,290 |
| Stocks and bonds | 114,864,799 | Bonds | 28,000,000 |
| Patent account | 166,014 | Reserves | 6,079,262 |
| Machinery and tools | 48,127 | Accounts payable | 8,078,169 |
| Cash and deposits | 6,933,364 | Contingent | 18,645,210 |
| Bills and accounts receivable | 15,528,621 | | |
| American Bell Telephone Co | 22,110,400 | | |
| Total | $190,414,903 | Total | $190,414,903 |

President, Frederick P. Fish, Boston; Vice-President, Edward J. Hall, New York; Secretary, Charles Eustis Hubbard; Treasurer, William R. Driver, Boston.

Directors—Alexander Cochrane, Charles W. Amory, Henry S. Howe, Charles P. Bowditch, T. Jefferson Coolidge, Jr., Nathaniel Thayer, W. Murray Crane, Francis Blake, George L. Bradley, J. Malcom Forbes, Frederick P. Fish, Moses Williams, Charles Eustis Hubbard, Charles E. Perkins, Thomas Sanders, Boston; John I. Waterbury, George F. Baker, Theodore N. Vail, New York.

Main office, 125 Milk street, Boston. Annual meeting, last Tuesday in March.

## THE AMERICAN THREAD CO.

A corporation formed under the laws of New Jersey, March 10, 1898, to amalgamate the following manufacturers of spool, crochet, knitting, mending and other cottons, including in some cases the allied businesses of cotton spinning, doubling, twisting, dyeing, bleaching, polishing, spool making, etc.:

| | Established. | Incorporated. |
|---|---|---|
| Barstow Thread Co., Providence, R. I., including good will and trade-marks of Alexander King & Co., in cotton thread business | 1866 | Rhode Island |
| The Glasgo Yarn Mills Co., Glasgo, near Norwich, Conn | 1881 | Connecticut |
| The Glasgo Thread Co., Worcester, Mass | 1883 | Massachusetts |
| Hadley Co., Holyoke, Mass | 1863 | Massachusetts |
| The Kerr Thread Co., Fall River, Mass | 1881 | New Jersey |
| J. O. King & Co., New York City | 1866 | Private Firm |
| Merrick Thread Co., Holyoke, Mass | 1865 | Massachusetts |
| The National Thread Co., Mansfield, Conn | 1873 | Connecticut |
| Morse & Kaley Manufacturing Co., Milford, N. H | 1882 | New Hampshire |
| E. J. W. Morse Co., Boston, Mass., including the patent rights, machinery and good will of the Morse Machine | 1834 | Maine |
| The Ruddy Thread Co., Worcester, Mass | 1891 | Massachusetts |
| The Warren Thread Co., Ashland, Mass | 1865 | Massachusetts |
| The William Clark Co., Westerly, R. I | 1891 | New Jersey |
| Willimantic Linen Co., Willimantic, Conn | 1854 | Connecticut |

The operations of the new company began April 1, 1899, and its fiscal year ends March 31.

Stock....Par $5.....Authorized { com., $6,000,000; pref., 6,000,000 } Issued { com., $4,200,000; pref., 4,890,475 } $9,090,475

The preferred stock is 5 per cent., cumulative. All the common stock is issued, but only $3.50 per share has been paid in on the same. It is understood that the English Sewing Cotton Co. owns practically all the common stock of this company.

Transfer Agent, Guaranty Trust Co., New York. Registrar, First National Bank, New York.

The first regular semi-annual dividend of 2½ per cent. on the preferred stock was paid July 1, 1899. Half-yearly dividends of 2½ per cent. have since been regularly paid in January and July. A dividend of 30 cents per share on the common stock was paid in May, 1900. On July 1, 1901, 35 cents per share or 10 per cent. on the amount paid in was paid on the common. No dividends on the common have been paid since.

**Funded Debt.**

1st mort., 4 per cent., due Jan., 1919, Jan. and July ............................. $6,000,000

The 4 per cent. 1st mortgage is for $6,000,000. The properties formerly owned by the constituent companies are all free and clear of liens and encumbrances. A mortgage for £102,700 on the Kerr Thread Co.'s plant matured and was paid off July 1, 1902. The trustee of the mortgage is the Guaranty Trust Co., New York.

EARNINGS.

Year ending March 31.

| | Profits. | Depreciation. | Charges. | Pref. Div. | Com. Div. | Surplus. |
|---|---|---|---|---|---|---|
| 1900-01 | £254,675 | £62,000 | £53,550 | £50,535 | £86,800 | £1,790 |
| 1901-02 | 160,273 | 62,000 | 54,715 | 50,835 | ...... | def. 6,977 |

The statement for the year ending March 31, 1902, in American currency, is as follows:

| | Profits. | Depreciation. | Charges. | Dividend Pfd. |
|---|---|---|---|---|
| 1901-02 | $754,079 | $300,000 | $264,748 | $244,523 |

The following is the company's balance sheet, March 31, 1902:

| ASSETS. | | LIABILITIES. | |
|---|---|---|---|
| Land, water and steam power, mills, machinery, plant and effects | $12,552,518 | Common stock, $5 each share, $3.50 paid | $4,200,000 |
| Stocks in trade at net cost | 4,133,135 | 5 per cent. preferred shares, $5 each share, fully paid | 4,890,476 |
| Accounts receivable, net | 795,914 | 4 per cent. 1st mortgage bonds | 6,000,000 |
| Cash on hand | 316,117 | Kerr bonds, payable July 1, 1902 | 524,313 |
| Sundry investments | 334,256 | English Sewing Cotton Co., Ltd. | 1,038,827 |
| | | Accounts payable | 323,466 |
| | | Bond interest accrued | 66,137 |
| | | Depreciation fund | 975,000 |
| | | Balance carried forward | 113,721 |
| Total | $18,131,940 | Total | $18,131,940 |

President, Lyman R. Hopkins; 1st Vice-President, Alexander King; 2d Vice-President, Lucius A. Barbour; Secretary and Treasurer, Theodore M. Ives; Assistant Secretary and Assistant Treasurer, I. C. Davis; Auditors, Jones, Crewdson and Youatt.

Directors—Robert K. Clark, James Kerr, Lucius A. Barbour, E. Martin Philippi, Alexander King, Eugene S. Boss, Lyman R. Hopkins, Theodore M. Ives, John E. Lawton, Robert C. Kerr, Elisha A. Still, Algernon Dewhurst.

Executive Committee—Robert C. Kerr, E. Martin Philippi, Elisha A. Still.

Main office, 260 West Broadway, New York. Annual meeting, second Tuesday in May.

## AMERICAN TIE PLATE AND RAIL BRACE CO.

A corporation formed under the laws of New Jersey in June, 1901. The purpose of the company is to manufacture and to license others to manufacture under patents owned by the company the American tie plate and rail brace, a device to prevent the spreading of rails, especially at curves.

Stock......Par $100..........................Authorized, $1,000,000......Issued, $1,000,000

The stock is full-paid and non-assessable. The company has no preferred stock and no funded debt.

Transfer Agent, Corporation Trust Co., Jersey City.

President, Orlando P. Dorman; 1st Vice-President, Hugh L. Fox; 2d Vice-President, George H. Pings; Secretary and Treasurer, W. Arthur Lesser, New York.

Directors—Orlando P. Dorman, George R. Bidwell, Hugh L. Fox, Theodore P. Gilman, George H. Pings, W. Arthur Lesser, New York.

Main office, 220 Broadway, New York.

## AMERICAN TOBACCO CO.

(Controlled by Consolidated Tobacco Co.)

A corporation formed under the laws of New Jersey, January 21, 1890. Its business is manufacturing and dealing in tobacco. It purchased the property and works of the following firms, principally engaged in the manufacture of cigarettes and smoking tobacco: Allen & Ginter, Richmond, Va.; W. Duke Sons & Co., New York and Durham, N. C.; Kinney Tobacco Co., New York and Virginia; W. S. Kimball & Co., Rochester, N. Y., and Oxford, N. C., and Goodwin & Co., New York. In 1898 purchased the Brown Tobacco Co., St. Louis, and the Drummond Tobacco Co., St. Louis. In 1891 the company purchased the works of Marburg Bros. and Gail & Ax of Baltimore. In 1895 bought factories of Thomas H. Hall & Co., Consolidated Cigarette

Co., H.W. Meyer Tobacco Manufacturing Co., New York; J. G. Butler Tobacco Co., St. Louis, and H. Ellis & Co., Baltimore.

This company took an active part in 1898 in the formation of the Continental Tobacco Co., which was to combine the principal manufacturers of plug tobacco in the United States. In 1898 the company sold its plug tobacco manufacturing interests to the Continental Co., and is a large holder of that company's stock. See statement of Continental Co. In regard to the acquisition of the Union Tobacco Co. in 1899, see below. In 1901 purchased the factories of D. H. McAlpin & Co., New York. The company has a large interest in the American Snuff Co.

In December, 1900, it was announced that the American Cigar Co. had been formed in the interest of this company.

In June, 1901, the Consolidated Tobacco Co. offered to purchase the common stock of this company at 200, payable in its own collateral trust 4 per cent. debenture bonds. This offer was accepted by nearly all the stockholders. In January, 1902, it was stated that only about $500,000 of this company's common stock had not been exchanged under this arrangement.

Stock..Par { com., $50 / pref., 100 } Authorized { com., $56,000,000 / pref., 14,000,000 } Issued { com., $54,500,000 / pref., 14,000,000 } $68,500,000

The preferred stock is entitled to 8 per cent. dividends per annum, non-cumulative, paid quarterly, and has a preference as to assets.

In June, 1898, outstanding common stock was increased from $17,900,000 to $21,000,000, and in October, 1898, preferred outstanding was increased from $11,935,000 to $14,000,000, then the authorized limit. In March, 1899, an increase of the common stock from $21,000,000 to $56,000,000 was authorized, of which $21,000,000 was given May 11, 1899, as a 100 per cent. stock dividend to the common stockholders, $12,500,000 was used to acquire the Union Tobacco Co. and $1,500,000 was reserved, making the total common stock outstanding $54,500,000.

Transfer Agent and Registrar, Farmers' Loan & Trust Co., New York.

Dividends of 2 per cent., quarterly, in February, May, August and November, are regularly paid on the preferred stock. It was announced in December, 1895, that February, 1896, dividend on common stock would be passed, but 2 per cent. cash and 20 per cent. in scrip was paid the following May, though August and November, 1896, dividends were passed and none were paid till that of December, 1896. In February, 1897, 3 per cent. was paid; in subsequent quarters, 2 per cent., up to the time of the increase of the common stock and the 100 per cent. stock dividend in May, 1899. The quarterly dividends on the common were then made 1½ per cent., and so continued, until May, 1902, when 2½ per cent. was paid, which has since been the quarterly rate. The dividends on the common are paid quarterly, in February (1), May, August and November.

FUNDED DEBT.

Dividend scrip extended to May 1, 1902, 6 per cent., May and Nov.................. $3,014,490

The dividend scrip was issued in 1896 as a scrip dividend. It was extended in 1899. Interest on it is payable subsequent to the 8 per cent. on the preferred stock. In March, 1902, it was called for payment on May 1, 1902.

This company and the Continental Tobacco Co. jointly guarantee $10,000,000 of 4 per cent. gold notes of the American Cigar Co.

EARNINGS.

| | Net. | Dividends. Pref. | Dividends. Com. | Dividends and Interest. | Surplus. |
|---|---|---|---|---|---|
| 1895 | $3,971,521 | 8 | 9 | $2,569,440 | $1,402,081 |
| 1896 | 3,593,197 | 8 | 9 | 2,729,020 | 864,177 |
| 1897 | 4,179,460 | 8 | 8 | 2,616,160 | 1,563,300 |
| 1898 | 4,957,803 | 8 | 8 | 2,834,120 | 2,123,683 |
| 1899 | 5,202,384 | 8 | 6½ | 4,184,643 | 1,017,741 |
| 1900 | 6,303,498 | 8 | 6 | 4,570,834 | 1,732,694 |
| 1901 | 6,647,114 | 8 | 6 | 4,570,890 | 2,076,224 |
| 1902 | 7,450,575 | 8 | 10 | 3,630,283 | 820,292 |

The following is a condensed balance sheet, December 31, 1901:

| ASSETS. | | LIABILITIES. | |
|---|---|---|---|
| Real estate, etc. | $5,237,110 | Common stock | $54,500,000 |
| Materials and supplies | 13,405,903 | Preferred stock | 14,000,000 |
| Stocks in foreign companies | 13,373,563 | Preferred dividends, due Feb. 1 | 280,000 |
| Stocks in other companies | 15,197,990 | Common dividends, due Feb. 1 | 362,500 |
| Cash | 1,898,725 | Bills and accounts payable | 10,403,738 |
| Bills and accounts receivable | 13,650,303 | Advertisement fund | 683,491 |
| Patents, good-will, trade-marks, etc. | 25,670,743 | Profit and loss surplus | 7,204,608 |
| Total | $88,434,337 | Total | $88,434,337 |

President, James B. Duke; 1st Vice-President, Percival S. Hill; 2d Vice-President, W. R. Harris; 3d Vice-President, R. L. Patterson; Secretary, Charles N. Strotz; Treasurer, B. N. Duke; Assistant Treasurer, J. M. W. Hicks; Auditor, J. Fletcher, Jr., New York.

Directors—Thomas F. Jeffries, Richmond, Va.; George Arents, J. B. Cobb, Oliver H. Payne, C. E. Halliwell, W. R. Harris, Thomas F. Ryan, W. W. Fuller, W. L. Walker, Percival S. Hill, C. C. Dula, R. L. Patterson, New York; James B. Duke, Somerville, N. J.; B. N. Duke, G. W. Watts, Durham, N. C.; Peter A. B. Widener, Philadelphia; Anthony N. Brady, Albany, N. Y.

Corporate office, Jersey City; New York office, 111 Fifth avenue. Annual meeting, second Wednesday in March, at Jersey City.

---

## AMERICAN TYPE FOUNDERS CO.

A corporation formed under the laws of New Jersey in 1892 to acquire and carry on the business of twenty-three of the principal type foundries of the United States.

Stock....Par $100.. ..Authorized { com., $4,000,000 / pref., 2,000,000 } Issued { com., $4,000,000 / pref., 964,300 } $4,964,300

The preferred stock is 7 per cent., cumulative. Stock is transferred at the company's office, New York. Registrar, Mercantile Trust Co., New York.

At annual meeting in October, 1895, it was resolved to fund company's floating debt of about $500,000 and reduce the amount of share capital. The old stock was $4,000,000 preferred and $5,000,000 common, which was converted into $4,000,000 common.

In January, 1902, an issue of preferred stock was authorized, and stockholders were offered the right to subscribe for $1,000,000 of same, the proceeds being to pay the floating debt of company.

Dividends on the common stock began in 1898, with 1 per cent., quarterly, payable October 15, 1898, since which 1 per cent. has been regularly paid quarterly, in January (15), April, July and October. The quarterly dividends of 1¾ per cent. on the preferred stock are also paid at the same periods.

FUNDED DEBT.

Debenture bonds, 6 per cent., due May, 1926, May and Nov......................... $930,800

The 6 per cent. debentures authorized were for $1,000,000, and were created in 1895. Trustee and Registrar of the bonds, Mercantile Trust Co., New York.

There is a sinking fund of $25,000 per annum for the retirement of the debentures, and $69,200 of the bonds have been retired.

EARNINGS.

| Year ending August 31. | Profits. | Charges. | Net Profits. |
|---|---|---|---|
| 1897-98 | $215,446 | $45,632 | $169,811 |
| 1898-99 | 249,563 | 59,511 | 190,054 |
| 1899-00 | 356,156 | 75,915 | 280,241 |
| 1900-01 | 419,037 | 95,568 | 323,469 |
| 1901-02 | 404,656 | 103,129 | 301,527 |

Surplus over dividends in 1898-99 was $30,052; in 1899-1900, $120,241; in 1900-01, $163,469; in 1901-02, $126,302.

The following is the condensed balance sheet, August 31, 1902:

| ASSETS. | | LIABILITIES. | |
|---|---|---|---|
| Plant | $3,266,638 | Capital stock, common | $4,000,000 |
| Merchandise and raw materials | 1,975,302 | Capital stock, preferred | 964,300 |
| Miscellaneous | 244,870 | Accounts payable | 158,884 |
| Stocks and bonds | 266,582 | Bills payable | 685,098 |
| Accounts receivable | 887,856 | Debenture bonds | 930,800 |
| Bills receivable | 364,419 | Miscellaneous | 8,568 |
| Cash | 226,533 | Surplus | 484,550 |
| Total | $7,232,200 | Total | $7,232,200 |

President and General Manager, Robert W. Nelson; Vice-President, Robert M. Janney; Secretary, John T. Murphy; Treasurer, Morris H. Smith, New York.

Directors—G. Frederick Jordan, George Cleveland, J. W. Phinney, Henry Barth, L. Boyd Benton, A. T. H. Brower, Robert M. Janney, Monroe Smith, Robert W. Nelson, Benjamin Kimball, Walter S. Marder, Charles S. Conner, Rudulph Ellis, Charles B. Whiting.

Main office, Jersey City; New York office, 27 William street. Annual meeting in October

## AMERICAN VULCANIZED FIBRE CO.

A corporation formed under the laws of Delaware, December 4, 1901, for the purpose of consolidating the following companies and manufacturing a product known as vulcanized fibre, used chiefly for electrical purposes.

Kartavert Mfg. Co., Wilmington, Del.
Vulcanized Fibre Co., Wilmington, Del.
American Hard Fibre Co., Newark, Del.
Laminar Fibre Co., North Cambridge, Mass.

Stock...Par $100...Authorized { com., $2,500,000 / pref., 900,000 } Issued { com., $1,715,000 / pref., 509,000 } $2,224,000

The preferred stock is 7 per cent., cumulative. Transfer Agent, Security Trust & Safe Deposit Co., Wilmington, Del.

FUNDED DEBT.

1st mort., 6 per cent., due 1921, June and Dec........................................ $424,000

The authorized bond issue is $600,000. These bonds are collateral trust 20-year sinking fund bonds, $100,000 of which are subject to call after 3 years at 105 and accrued interest. Trustee of the mortgage, Security Trust & Safe Deposit Co., Wilmington, Del.

President, Frank Taylor; Secretary, Truman W. Campbell; Treasurer, David W. Masters.

Directors—Frank Taylor, David W. Masters, Wilmington, Del.; George B. Hanford, New York; S. J. Wright, Dover, Del.; C. C. Bell, North Cambridge, Mass.

Main office, 1017 Market street, Wilmington, Del. Annual meeting, first Monday in January.

## AMERICAN WALTHAM WATCH CO.

A corporation formed under the laws of Massachusetts in 1854. The company's factory is at Waltham, Mass. It has agencies in all parts of the United States and foreign countries.

Stock......Par $100.................. ........Authorized, $4,000,000 .....Issued, $4,000,000

The stock in 1899 was increased from $3,000,000 to $4,000,000, the $1,000,000 of new stock being sold at par to the stockholders. The company has no funded debt.

Dividends on the stock are paid half-yearly, March (15) and September (15). Up to September, 1898, 4 per cent. semi-annually, or 8 per cent. per annum, had been regularly paid. In September, 1896, however, the half-yearly dividend was 2 per cent., or 6 per cent. for the year 1898. In 1897 and 1898, paid 6 per cent. In 1899, the regular half-yearly payments were 4 and 5 per cent. each, and in October, 1899, an extra cash dividend of 16⅔ per cent. was paid, making 25⅔ per cent. for 1899. In 1900, the semi-annual dividends were each of 4 per cent., with 2 per cent. extra in September, or 10 per cent. for the year. The dividends in 1901 and 1902 were similar as to dates and amounts.

The following is the company's balance sheet, January 31, 1902:

| ASSETS. | | LIABILITIES. | |
|---|---|---|---|
| Land and Buildings............ | $724,330 | Capital stock.................. | $4,000,000 |
| Machinery...................... | 1,791,678 | Debts.......................... | 45,799 |
| Cash and debts received......... | 569,406 | Profit and loss.. .............. | 1,608,588 |
| Supplies...................... | 2,376,876 | | |
| Patent rights.................. | 192,097 | | |
| Total.................... | $5,654,387 | Total.................... | $5,654,387 |

President, E. C. Fitch; Vice-President, F. R. Appleton; Clerk, P. W. Carter; Treasurer, Royal Robbins.

Directors—A. L. Edmunds, D. F. Appleton, E. C. Fitch, F. R. Appleton, Royal Robbins, H. P. Robbins, A. K. Sloan, B. F. Brown.

Main office, 373 Washington street, Boston. Annual meeting, last Thursday in March.

## AMERICAN WINDOW GLASS CO.

A corporation organized under the laws of Pennsylvania, August 2, 1899. The company was formed to acquire and consolidate the most prominent manufactories of window glass in the States of Pennsylvania, New Jersey, New York and Indiana. The principal plants acquired and their respective locations were:

Chambers & McKee Glass Co., Jeannette, Pa.
Chambers Glass Co., Arnold, Pa.
R. C. Schmertz Glass Co., Bellevernon, Pa.
Thomas Wightman Glass Co., Monongahela City, Pa.
Hartford City Glass Co., Hartford City, Ind.
Maring, Hart & Co., Muncie, Ind.
C. H. Over, Muncie, Ind.
DePauw Glass Co., Alexandria, Ind.
Stewart-Estep Glass Co., Marion, Ind.

Lawrence Glass Co., New Castle, Pa.
Shenango Glass Co., New Castle, Pa.
Cohansey Glass Co., Bridgetown, N. J.
B. N. McCoy Glass Co., Kane, Pa.
Bradford Glass Co., Hazlehurst, Pa.
Hazlehurst Glass Co., Hazlehurst, Pa.
Coudersport Glass Co., Coudersport, Pa.
American Glass Co., Gas City, Ind.
Anderson Glass Co., Anderson, Ind.
Victor Glass Co., Anderson, Ind.
Enterprise Glass Co., Dunkirk, Ind.
Clyde Glass Co., Franklin, Ind.
Bell Glass Co., Fairmont, Ind.

Stock...Par $100....Authorized { com., $13,000,000; pref., 4,000,000 } Issued { com., $13,000,000; pref., 4,000,000 } $17,000,000

The preferred stock is 7 per cent., cumulative.

The company has no bonded debt. No lien or encumbrance can be placed on the property of the company without the consent of 75 per cent. of the preferred stock.

The owners of the various properties took about 80 per cent. of the appraised value of the same in common stock of this company and the balance in cash. To provide funds for this purpose and for working capital, the preferred stock of the company was offered in September, 1899, for subscription at par and interest from September 1, 33 per cent. in common stock being given with each share of preferred stock subscribed for.

The company pays semi-annual dividends on its preferred stock of 3½ per cent. in March and September.

The first dividend on the common was 1½ per cent. in October, 1901; and similar dividends, being at the rate of 6 per cent. per annum, have since been paid on the common in January, April, July and October.

In July, 1902, it was reported that the common stock would be converted into second preferred stock, and new common stock issued for a large amount; the purpose being to acquire valuable property and patents with the proceeds.

The report for 10½ months ending August 31, 1900, showed net profits of $326,687, out of which dividends of 7 per cent. on the preferred stocks were paid. In 1900-01, total profits, $1,712,160; depreciation, $300,000; net profit, $1,412,160. In 1901-02, profits were $1,538,826; other income, $178,334; dividends, $1,000,000; depreciation, $300,000.

President, James A. Chambers; 1st Vice-President, M. K. McMullin; 2d Vice-President, William Loeffler, Pittsburg; 3d Vice-President, Thomas F. Hart, Muncie, Ind.; Treasurer, W. G. McCandless; Secretary, E. I. Phillips, Pittsburg.

Directors—James A. Chambers, M. K. McMullin, William Loeffler, Thomas F. Hart, E. I. Phillips, W. G. McCandless, H. B. Smith, S. L. Bodine, T. H. Given, P. A. B. Widener, W. L. Elkins, T. Wightman, N. T. DePauw, Simon Burns, A. C. Howard, W. J. Carsen.

Main office, 200 Ninth street, Pittsburg.

---

## AMERICAN WOOLEN CO.

A corporation formed under the laws of New Jersey, March 29, 1899. The company acquired and owns the plants and property of the following woolen and worsted manufacturing concerns:

Washington Mills, Lawrence, Mass.
National & Providence Worsted Mills, Providence, R. I.
Saranac Mills, Blackstone, Mass.
Fulton Mills, Fulton, N. Y.
Fitchburg Mills, Fitchburg, Mass.
Beoli Mills, Fitchburg, Mass.
Valley Mills, Providence, R. I.
Riverside Mills, Providence, R. I.
Assabet Mills, Maynard, Mass.
Sawyer Mills, Dover, N. H.
Bay State, Lowell, Mass.
Vassalboro Mills, N. Vassalboro, Me.
Anchor Mills, Harrisville and Pascoag, R. I.
Weybosset Mills, Providence, R. I.
Kennebec Mills, Fairfield, Me.
Puritan Mills, Plymouth, Mass.
Anderson Mills, Skowhegan, Me.
Manton Mills, Manton, R. I.
Chase Mills, Webster, Mass.
Brown Mills, Dover, Me.
Ray Mills, Franklin, Mass.
Baltic Mills, Enfield, N. H.
Moosup Mills, Moosup, Conn.
Lebanon Mills, Lebanon, N. H.
Prospect Mills, Lawrence, Mass.
Globe Mills, Lawrence, Mass.
Beaver Brook Mills, Lowell, Mass.

The plants are all owned in full, except the National & Providence Mills, control of which is held through ownership of all its capital stock. The plants comprise 650 acres—the mills have 7,044,494 feet of floor space. The equipment comprises 463,370 spindles, 606 sets of cards and 6,627 looms.

Stock...Par $100....Authorized { com., $40,000,000; pref., 25,000,000 } Issued { com., $29,501,100; pref., 20,000,000 } $49,501,100

The preferred stock is 7 per cent., cumulative.

Transfer Agents, Guaranty Trust Co., New York; Old Colony Trust Co., Boston. Registrar and Transfer Co., Jersey City. Registrars, Knickerbocker Trust Co., New York; International Trust Co., Boston.

The first quarterly dividend on the preferred was 1¾ per cent. paid July 15, 1899. Regular quarterly dividends have since been paid at the same rate in January (15), April, July and October.

The average annual net earnings of the properties for two years prior to the formation of this company were $2,593,000.

EARNINGS.

| | Total Income. | Net Profits. | Pref. Div. | Depreciation, etc. | Surplus. |
|---|---|---|---|---|---|
| 1900 (21 mos., end. Dec. 31)... | $50,961,205 | $5,523,230 | $2,391,666 | $1,025,912 | $2,105,650 |
| 1901........................ | 34,960,309 | 2,077,758 | 1,400,000 | ........ | 677,758 |
| 1902........................ | 35,522,977 | 3,227,667 | 1,400,000 | ........ | 1,827,600 |

The company has no funded debt, but there is $295,000 unmatured bonds of constituent companies.

The following is the company's balance sheet as of January 3, 1903:

| ASSETS. | | | LIABILITIES. | | |
|---|---|---|---|---|---|
| Cash............................ | | $1,094,407 | Bank Loans.................... | | $6,890,000 |
| Accounts receivable, net.......... | | 8,609,745 | Current vouchers and accounts (33 plants)...................... | | 5,522,056 |
| Inventories: Wool and fabrics, raw, wrought and in process....... | $13,368,707 | | Unmatured bonds of National & Providence Worsted Mills........ | $100,000 | |
| Coal and supplies..... | 563,732 | | Unmatured bonds of Chase Mills.......... | 80,000 | |
| | | 13,932,439 | | | 180,000 |
| Plants, mill fixtures and investments.................. | | 43,067,640 | Capital stock, com... | $29,501,100 | |
| (Including amount expended from surplus earnings for construction, improvements and equipment of plants during the year 1902, viz., $2,205,066.) | | | Capital stock, pref... | 20,000,000 | |
| | | | | | 49,501,100 |
| | | | Sterling credits, per contra....... | | 2,275,876 |
| | | | Undivided profits.............. | | 4,611,076 |
| Surplus wool in warehouses carried under sterling credits to anticipate mill requirements, per contra. ...................... | | 2,275,877 | | | |
| Total............ ...... | | $68,980,108 | Total.................... | | $68,980,108 |

President, Frederick Ayer, Lowell Mass.; Treasurer, William M. Wood, Andover, Mass.; Assistant Treasurer, W. H. Dwelly, Jr.; General Agent, Edward P. Chapin; Secretary, Joseph T. Shaw, Boston; Selling Agent, J. Clifford Woodhull, New York.

Directors—Frederick Ayer, Lowell, Mass.; William M. Wood, John Hogg, Edwin C. Swift, Francis W. Kittredge, James Phillips, Jr., George E. Bullard, Boston; J. Clifford Woodhull, Summit, N. J.; Samuel P. Colt, Providence, R. I.; Edward P. Chapin, Andover, Mass.

Corporate office, Newark, N. J.; main office, Washington and Court streets, Boston; New York office, 66 Leonard street. Annual meeting, first Wednesday in February.

## AMERICAN WRINGER CO.

A corporation formed under the laws of Rhode Island in 1891. The company's business is the manufacture of clothes wringers, rubber rolls, mangles, etc. It has factories at Woonsocket, R. I., and Auburn, N. Y.

Stock....Par $100.....Authorized { com., $1,650,000 / pref., 850,000 } Issued { com., $1,650,000 / pref., 850,000 } $2,500,000

The preferred stock is 7 per cent., cumulative. Quarterly dividends of 1¾ per cent. are paid on the preferred in January, April, July and October. On the common stock, dividends of 8 per cent. per annum are paid.

Dividends at the rate of 7 per cent. per annum have been paid on the preferred stock in each year since the formation of the company. On the common stock the yearly dividends have been: in 1891, 1892 and 1893, 8 per cent.; in 1894 and 1895, 5 per cent.; in 1896, 1897, 1898, 1899 and 1900, 8 per cent.; in 1901 and 1902, 4 per cent.

Registrar, Rhode Island Hospital Trust Co.

President, Walter S. Ballou; Secretary, Stanley G. Smith; Treasurer and General Manager, George Reuter, Jr.

Directors—George Reuter, Jr., Alonzo G. Beardsley, Jr., Walter S. Ballou, William S. Granger, John F. Hemenway, Stanley G. Smith, Lyman A. Mills, John J. Banigan.

Main office, Providence; New York office, 99 Chambers street.

## AMERICAN WRITING PAPER CO.

A company incorporated under the laws of New Jersey, June 30, 1899, for the manufacture of writing paper of all grades. It owns 24 mills in Massachusetts, 3 in Connecticut, 2 in Ohio and 1 each in Wisconsin and Michigan, in all 31 establishments, with a capacity of 350 tons per day, and which produce 84 per cent. of the fine writing paper output of New England and over 76 per cent. of the entire output of the United States. The properties taken over July 25, 1899, are as follows:

Agawam Paper Co., Mittineague, Mass.
Albion Paper Co., Holyoke, Mass.
Beebe & Holbrook Co., Holyoke, Mass.
Chester Paper Co., Huntington, Mass.
Connecticut River Paper Co., Holyoke, Mass.
Crocker Manufacturing Co., Holyoke, Mass.
George R. Dickinson Paper Co., Holyoke, Mass.
Eaton, May & Robbins Paper Co., Lee, Mass.
Esleeck Paper Co., Holyoke, Mass.
G. K. Baird, Paper Co., Lee, Mass.
George C. Gill Paper Co., Holyoke, Mass.
Harding Paper Co., Franklin, O.
Holyoke Paper Co., Holyoke, Mass.
Hurlbut Paper Manufacturing Co., South Lee, Mass.
Hurlbut Stationery Co., Pittsfield, Mass.
Linden Paper Co., Holyoke, Mass.
Massasoit Paper Manufacturing Co., Holyoke, Mass.
Nonotuck Paper Co., Holyoke, Mass.
Norman Paper Co., Holyoke, Mass.
Oakland Paper Co., Manchester, Conn.
Parsons Paper Co., No. 1, Holyoke, Mass.
Platner & Porter Paper Manufacturing Co., Unionville, Conn.
Riverside Paper Co., Holyoke, Mass.
Shattuck & Babcock Co., De Pere, Wis.
Springdale Paper Co., Springfield, Mass.
Syms & Dudley Paper Co., Watervliet, Mich.
Wauregan Paper Co., Holyoke, Mass.
Windsor Paper Co., Windsor Locks, Conn.

In addition the company owns valuable improved real estate in Holyoke, Mass. Most of the properties possess valuable trade-marks, good will, etc.

Stock..Par $100...Authorized { com., $12,500,000 / pref., 12,500,000 } Issued { com., $11,500,000 / pref., 9,500,000 } $21,000,000

The preferred stock is 7 per cent., cumulative, with a preference as to distribution of the company's assets also.

Transfer Agents, New Jersey Registration & Trust Co., East Orange, N. J., and Standard Trust Co., New York. Registrar, United States Mortgage & Trust Co., New York.

FUNDED DEBT.

1st mort. 5 per cent., due July, 1910, Jan. and July.................................. $17,000,000

Trustee of the 1st mortgage is the Old Colony Trust Co., Boston. The bonds are redeemable at 105 after 10 years from date of issue, July 1, 1899.

EARNINGS.

| | Net Income. | Expenses and Charges. | Surplus. |
|---|---|---|---|
| 1900 (17 months) | $1,551,737 | $1,490,056 | $61,680 |
| 1901 | 1,301,742 | 1,087,655 | 214,087 |
| 1902 | 1,605,182 | 958,850 | 646,332 |

The following is the company's balance sheet, January, 1, 1903:

| ASSETS. | | LIABILITIES. | |
|---|---|---|---|
| Investment in 31 paper mills and real estate in Holyoke | $17,105,648 | Capital stock, preferred | $12,500,000 |
| Good-will, trade-marks, etc | 18,010,150 | " " common | 11,500,000 |
| Cash | 927,982 | Bonds, 5 per cent., gold, 20-year sinking fund | 17,000,000 |
| Notes receivable | 221,023 | Accounts payable | 78,805 |
| Accounts receivable | 1,181,876 | Reserve—Balance Jan. 1, 1902 | 275,767 |
| Inventories: Stock and materials | 2,293,551 | Profit and loss. Gain for year | 755,182 |
| $200,000 bonds of this company | 159,924 | | |
| Old Colony Trust Co. Cash held for real estate sold and released | 25,811 | | |
| Miscellaneous | 24,939 | | |
| Sinking fund | 158,850 | | |
| Treasury stock, 20,000 shares common | 2,000,000 | | |
| Total | $42,109,754 | Total | $42,109,754 |

President, W. N. Caldwell; Vice-Presidents, Henry S. Dickinson, Springfield, Mass.; Henry L. Higginson, Boston; O. S. Greenleaf; Treasurer, George B. Holbrook; Assistant Treasurer, William H. Heyward; Secretary, Edward H. Hall, Springfield, Mass.

Directors—C. A. Crocker, O. S. Greenleaf, F. D. Phelon, E. C. Rogers, W. N. Caldwell, Henry S. Dickinson, G. B. Holbrook, B. D. Rising, Springfield, Mass.; Henry L. Higginson, James J. Storrow, Boston; R. F. McElwain, Holyoke, Mass.; N. T. Pulsifer, Manchester, Conn.; A. W. Eaton, Pittsfield, Mass.; Harry H. Picking, East Orange, N. J.; C. H. Harding, Franklin, O.; J. S. Gittins, De Pere, Wis.; Aaron Bagg, Jr., West Springfield, Mass.; Edwin Gould, D. G. Boissevain, New York.

Corporate offices, East Orange, N. J.; main office, Springfield, Mass. Annual meeting, first Tuesday in May.

## AMERICAN ZINC, LEAD & SMELTING CO.

A corporation formed under the laws of Maine, January, 1898, for the purpose of leasing, mining and operating mineral lands, and smelting ores. The company acquired 2,700 acres of zinc lands in fee and holds 500 acres on lease in Joplin, Carterville and Webb City, Missouri.

Stock......Par $25..........................Authorized, $2,500,000......Issued $1,500,000

Transfer Agent, William S. Moller, 4 Post Office Square, Boston. Registrar, National Shawmut Bank, Boston.

The company has no bonded debt and no preferred stock.

President, H. S. Kimball; Secretary, F. Winthrop Batchelder; Treasurer, Rene E. Paine, Boston.

Directors—H. S. Kimball, Edward A. Clark, Edwin P. Brown, William H. Coolidge, Rene E. Paine, Boston.

Main office, 4 Post Office Square, Boston. Annual meeting in October, at Portland, Me.

## AMERICAN ZINC MINING CO.

A corporation formed under the laws of New Jersey, September 1, 1899. The company owns and operates a zinc and lead ore property at Empire City, near Galena, Kan., and about six miles west of Joplin, Mo.

Stock......Par $100..............................Authorized, $50,000......Issued, $50,000

In December, 1902, the authorized stock and amount issued were both reduced from $500,000 to $50,000.

The company has no preferred stock. Transfer Agent, Corporation Trust Co. of New Jersey, Jersey City.

FUNDED DEBT.

1st mort., 6 per cent., due 1910, March and Sept.......................................$90,000

The bond issue was $100,000, and $10,000 of the bonds are to be drawn and redeemed each year. In September, 1900, $10,000 of the issue were retired in accordance with this provision.

In the year ending September 1, 1900, the gross earnings of the company were $62,815; net, $24,329; charges and sinking fund, $16,000; surplus, $8,329.

President, E. Hope Norton, New York; Vice-President, A. F. Nathan, Kansas City; Secretary and Treasurer, Elliott C. Smith, New York.

Directors—E. Hope Norton, Elliott C. Smith, L. H. Hale, Albert T. Kelley, Walter H. Freeman, New York; A. F. Nathan, Kansas City.

Main office, 33 Wall street, New York.

## AMES SHOVEL & TOOL CO.

A corporation formed under the laws of New Jersey, August 16, 1901, to manufacture shovels, spades, scoops and other agricultural, horticultural, farming and garden tools and implements, and also sheet steel for use in such manufacture. The following plants have been acquired:

The Oliver Ames & Sons Corporation.
The T. Rowland's Sons Incorporated.
The H. M. Myers Co.
The Wright Shovel Co.
The St. Louis Shovel Co.
The Elwood Steel Co.
The Elwood Fuel Co.

Stock....Par 100....Authorized { com., $2,000,000; pref., 3,000,000 } Issued { com., $2,000,000; pref., 3,000,000 } $5,000,000

The preferred stock is 7 per cent., cumulative, and has preference as to assets for its face value and unpaid dividends in case of liquidation. The company has no funded debt.

Transfer Agent, Corporation Trust Co. of New Jersey, Jersey City.

President, Hobart Ames, North Easton, Mass.; Vice-President, William J. Alford, Anderson, Ind.; Secretary, William H. Ames, North Easton, Mass.; Treasurer, Oliver W. Mink, Boston.

Directors—Hobart Ames, William H. Ames, North Easton, Mass.; William J. Alford, Anderson, Ind.; Howard Rowland, Cheltenham, Pa.; Charles H. Myers, Beaver Falls, Pa.; Julius C. Birge, St. Louis, Mo.; L. F. Timmerman, Madison, N. J.; Gilmer Clapp, Oliver Ames, Samuel Carr, Oliver W. Mink, Boston.

Main office, Ames Building, Washington and Court streets, Boston. Annual meeting, second Tuesday in April, at Jersey City, N. J.

## AMORY MANUFACTURING CO.

A corporation formed under the laws of New Hampshire in 1879 to manufacture cotton goods. The company absorbed the Langdon Manufacturing Co. in 1887, and its mills are located at Manchester, N. H.

Stock......Par $100..........................Authorized, $2,000,000......Issued, $900,000

The capital stock originally authorized was $1,200,000, of which there was issued $900,000. It was increased to $1,500,000 but only $1,350,000 was issued, and in October, 1900, it was reduced to $900,000.

The company has no preferred stock and no funded debt. Stock is transferred at the office of the company, Boston.

Dividends at the rate of 3 per cent. are paid semi-annually, June 15 and December 15.

President, T. Jefferson Coolidge; Treasurer, Frederic C. Dumaine, Boston.

Directors—T. Jefferson Coolidge, George A. Gardner, Francis I. Amory, C. W. Amory, George von L. Meyer, Frederic C. Dumaine, Boston; Frank P. Carpenter, Manchester, N. H.

Main office, Washington and Court streets, Boston. Annual meeting, first Wednesday in October.

## AMOSKEAG MANUFACTURING CO.

A corporation formed under the laws of New Hampshire in 1831 for the purpose of manufacturing ginghams, denims and cotton flannels. The mills of the company are at Manchester, N. H., and have a capacity of 300,000 spindles.

Stock......Par $1,000..........................Authorized, $4,000,000......Issued, $4,000,000

The company has no preferred stock and no funded debt.

Stock is transferred at the office of the company, Boston.

Dividends, 5 per cent., semi-annually, are paid in February and August.

President, T. Jefferson Coolidge; Treasurer, C. W. Amory, Boston.

Directors—T. Jefferson Coolidge, George A. Gardner, George Dexter, C. W. Amory, George von L. Meyer, Henry F. Sears, J. Lewis Stackpole, George Wigglesworth, Boston; G. Byron Chandler, Manchester.

Corporate office, Manchester, N. H.; main office, Washington and Court streets, Boston. Annual meeting, first Wednesday in October, at Manchester.

## ANACONDA COPPER MINING CO.

A corporation organized under the laws of Montana, June 18, 1895. The company owns the renowned Anaconda Copper Mine at Butte, Montana, and a number of other mines and claims. Those which were lately being worked include the St. Lawrence No. 1 and No. 3, Green Mountain, High Ore No. 2, Diamond, Mountain Consolidated No. 1 and No. 2, Never Sweat, Bell and Buffalo. It has a large amount of practically undeveloped mining property. The company has a large reduction and smelting works at Anaconda, Mont., representing a cost of some $7,000,000. The company has a controlling interest in the Butte, Anaconda & Pacific Railway Co., which road, 27 miles, connects the company's mines with the smelting establishment.

In 1899, a con rolling interest in the stock of this company was purchased by the Amalgamated Copper Co. t

Stock......Par $25........................Authorized, $30,000,000......Issued, $30,000,000

Stock is full paid and non-assessable. Transfer Agent, National City Bank, New York. Registrar, Mercantile Trust Co., New York.

The company up to 1900 had paid over $12,150,000 in dividends on the stock. A half-yearly dividend of $1.25 per share and 75 cents per share extra was paid April 30, 1900, and a similar dividend was paid October 27, 1900, making $4 for the year. The April, 1901, dividend was at the usual rate, but the dividend declared in September, 1901, was $1.25, the extra dividend being omitted. In April, 1902, only 50 cents per share was paid and the same rate was maintained for the dividend paid November 13, 1902.

EARNINGS.

| Year ending June 30. | Gross. | Profit. |
|---|---|---|
| 1896 | $12,057,677 | $4,258,514 |
| 1897 | 17,419,361 | 5,136,048 |
| 1898 | 18,334,233 | 3,551,346 |
| 1900 | 18,730,131 | 5,365,519 |
| 1901 | 18,128,558 | 5,571,816 |

No report for the year 1898-99 was made public.

President, William Scallon, Butte, Mont.; Vice-President, Henry H. Rogers, New York; Secretary, W. H. Dudley, Anaconda, Mont.; Treasurer, William G. Rockefeller; Assistant Treasurer, F. P. Addicks; Assistant Secretary, A. H. Melin, New York.

Trustees—William Scallon, Butte, Mont.; Henry H. Rogers, William Rockefeller, William G. Rockefeller, A. C. Burrage, William L. Bull, E. C. Bogert, New York.

Offices, Anaconda, Mont.; Butte, Mont.; 52 Broadway, New York. Annual meeting in May.

## ANDROSCOGGIN MILLS

A corporation formed under the laws of Maine in 1860, for the purpose of manufacturing sheetings, etc. The mills of the company are at Lewiston, Me.; 71,752 spindles and 2,105 looms.

Stock......Par $100..........................Authorized, $1,000,000......Issued, $1,000,000

The company has no preferred stock and no funded debt. Stock is transferred at the office of the company, Boston.

Dividends are paid semi-annually, January and July, at the rate of 8 per cent. per annum.

President, C. H. Fiske; Treasurer, George F. Fabyan, Boston.

Directors—C. H. Fiske, E. R. Beebe, Lyman Nichols, Grant Walker, George F. Fabyan, C. H. Alford.

Treasurer's office, 100 Summer street, Boston.

## ARCADIAN COPPER CO.

A corporation formed under the laws of New Jersey, March 3, 1899. The company succeeded a corporation of the same name formed under the laws of Michigan in 1898. The original company had a large tract of copper-bearing lands in the upper peninsula of Michigan, adjoining the Quincy and other well-known mines. The present company has added to these holdings, the entire property being now about 4,000 acres, and during 1899 and 1900 prosecuted development work on its property. It has also erected a stamp mill.

Stock......Par $25.. ..........................Authorized, $3,750,000......Issued, $3,750,000

The Michigan Company, to which this is a successor, had a capital of 100,000 shares, par $25, $4 per share paid in. When the present company was organized holders of the original stock were offered the right to exchange it, share for share, for the new. The old stockholders also had the right to subscribe for 50 per cent. of their holdings in new stock at $30 per share.

President, Albert C. Burrage; Vice-President, Sidney Chase; Secretary and Treasurer, Charles D. Burrage.

Directors—Albert C. Burrage, W. Rockefeller, Sidney Chase, Charles D. Burrage, W. A. Paine, Henry H. Rogers, J. H. Rice, Nathan F. Leopold, H. G. Foreman.

Main office, Washington and Court streets, Boston.

## ARIZONA COMMERCIAL CO.

A corporation formed under the laws of New York in 1882 for the purpose of mining, smelting and dealing in copper and other metals. The company has a mining property at Globe, Ariz., near that of the Old Dominion Mining Co. and adjoining the mines operated by Phelps, Dodge & Co. This company's tract comprises 60 acres and a mill site of ten acres a short distance away, with abundant water rights. The property consists of five claims and the company has pursued exploration work, the developments proving very satisfactory.

Stock......Par $10............................Authorized, $1,000,000......Issued, $869,600

The stock of the company consists of 100,000 shares of the par value of $10 each and is full-paid and non-assessable.

Transfer agency, 30 Broad street. Registrar, Continental Trust Co., New York.

The company has no funded debt.

President, Sigourney W. Fay; Secretary and Treasurer, James H. Fay, New York.

Directors—Sigourney W. Fay, James H. Fay, L. E. Whicker, J. Liberman, New York; Frederick Farnsworth, New London, Conn.; W. L. Armster, Boston.

Main office, 30 Broad street, New York. Annual meeting, December 11, at New York.

## ARLINGTON COPPER CO.

A corporation formed under the laws of New Jersey, February 15, 1900. The charter of the company authorizes it to conduct a general mining and smelting business. The company owns 150 acres of valuable copper-bearing lands at North Arlington, Bergen County, N.J., the copper deposits having been thoroughly opened up by means of about 6,000 feet of underground drifts and tunnels and five shafts cutting the ore in different parts of the property. It is estimated that there are 5,000,000 tons of copper ore in sight blocked out ready for mining and milling.

The company in January, 1900, began the construction of a copper reduction works of 150 tons daily capacity.

Stock......Par $10..........................Authorized, $2,500,000......Issued, $1,600,000

FUNDED DEBT.

1st mort., 5 per cent. gold, due 1920, May 17 and Nov. 17.......................... $400,000

The stock is full paid and non-assessable. Registrar, Hobart Trust Co., Passaic, N. J.

The 1st mortgage, Hobart Trust Co., Passaic, N. J., trustee, is for $400,000. The bonds are in denominations of $500 each.

President, William McKenzie, Passaic, N. J.; Vice-President, John Scott, Providence, R. I.; Secretary, H. G. Bott, Arlington, N. J.; Treasurer, Henry G. Bell, Rutherford, N. J.; General Manager, Charles L. Dignowity, Boston; General Counsel, Addison Ely, Passaic, N. J.

Directors—William McKenzie, B. Ward, Addison Ely, Passaic, N. J.; John Scott, Providence, R. I.; Henry G. Bell, William Black, Rutherford, N. J.; Charles L. Dignowity, Boston.

Main office, Arlington, N. J. Annual meeting, February 1, at Arlington, N. J.

## ARLINGTON MILLS

A corporation formed under the laws of Massachusetts in 1865, to manufacture worsted, dress goods and cotton yarns. The mills of the company are at Lawrence, Mass.

Stock......Par $100..........................Authorized, $3,000,000......Issued, $3,000,000

The company has no preferred stock and no funded debt.

Stock is transferred at the office of the company, Boston.

Dividends at the rate of 8 per cent. per annum are paid semi-annually in January and July. The fifty-fifth consecutive semi-annual dividend was paid January 1, 1903.

In the fiscal year ending November 30, 1901, the dividends were $150,000.

The following is the balance sheet of the company, November 29, 1902:

| ASSETS. | | LIABILITIES. | |
|---|---|---|---|
| Land and water power | $230,000 | Capital stock | $3,000,000 |
| Buildings | 1,000,000 | Debts payable | 2,489,514 |
| Machinery | 2,270,000 | Reserve—depreciation | 607,153 |
| Cash and debts receivable | 986,000 | " profit and loss | 2,288,475 |
| Manufactures, merchandise, material and stock in process | 3,819,563 | | |
| Miscellaneous | 79,579 | | |
| Total | $8,385,142 | Total | $8,385,142 |

President, William Whitman; Treasurer, Franklin W. Hobbs, Boston.

Directors—George E. Bullard, William E. Cox, Livingston Cushing, Robert H. Gardiner, Franklin W. Hobbs, Charles W. Leonard, William A. Russell, William Whitman, Boston; William F. Draper, Hopedale, Mass.; George E. Kuhnhardt, Lawrence, Mass.; William M. Whitin, Whitinsville, Mass.

Corporate and main office, 78 Chauncy street, Boston. Annual meeting, last Tuesday in January, at Boston.

## ARMOUR & CO.

A corporation formed under the laws of Illinois, April 14, 1900. The company acquired the plants, property, trade-marks and good will of the firm of Armour & Co., which was established in 1860 by the late Philip D. Armour and his brothers. The properties owned by the company comprise packing houses, glue, soap and fertilizer works, and other establishments. The company also has agencies and branch establishments for the distribution and sale of its products in many cities. It owns valuable trade-marks covering the different classes of its products, which include many well known specialties in meats and foodstuffs, and other classes of goods.

Stock......Par $100..........................Authorized, $20,000,000......Issued, $20,000,000

The company has no funded debt, and its properties are free from encumbrances.

The earnings and the dividends paid on the stock are not reported.

President, J. Ogden Armour; Vice-President and Treasurer, P. Anderson Valentine; Secretary, Charles F. Langdon, Chicago.

Directors—J. Ogden Armour, P. Anderson Valentine, C. M. Favorite, H. P. Darlington, T. J. Connors, Arthur Meeker, George B. Robbins, Chicago.

Main office, 205 La Salle street, Chicago; branch offices, South Omaha, Neb.; Fort Worth, Tex.; East St. Lois, Ill., and Sioux City, Ia. Annual meeting, fourth Monday in November, at Chicago.

## ARNOLD MINING CO.

A corporation formed under the laws of Michigan in 1864. In 1898 the Copper Falls Mining Co. was consolidated with it. The company has a large mineral land property in Keweenaw County, Mich. It has done a large amount of development work upon its mines, which is still being prosecuted, and has a mill on the property.

Stock......Par $25..........................Authorized, $2,500,000......Issued, $1,550,000

Stock is transferred at the company's office in Boston.

The authorized stock of the company consists of 100,000 shares of the par value of $25 each. It was increased to the above amount from 60,000 shares in 1899, but of the additional 40,000 shares only 2,000 have been issued and 38,000 remain in the treasury of the company. On the stock outstanding there has been paid in on calls $8.10 per share.

President, C. Howard Weston; Secretary and Treasurer, John Brooks, Boston.

Main office, 50 State street, Boston. Annual meeting, second Tuesday in May.

## ASH BED MINING CO.

A corporation formed under the laws of Michigan in 1880. The company owns a copper tract in Keweenaw County, Mich. The mine, which is near that of the Arnold Mining Co., was originally known as the Petherick mine, and was reorganized under the present title in 1880. The old company's property was foreclosed and sold, being purchased by the present company. The name is derived from the so-called "ash bed" or amygdaloid vein of copper-bearing ore found in the copper range of upper Michigan.

Stock......Par $25..........................Authorized, $1,000,000 .....Issued, $1,000,000

President, C. Howard Weston; Treasurer, John Brooks, Boston.

Directors—John Brooks, Charles S. Collins, Wesley Clark, C. Howard Weston.

Main office, 50 State street, Boston. Annual meeting, second Tuesday in March.

## ASHLAND EMERY & CORUNDUM CO.

A corporation formed under the laws of New Jersey, November 16, 1901. The purposes of the company are crushing, manufacturing and selling emery and corundum. The company owns the following plants:

Ashland Emery Mills, Perth Amboy, N. J.
Walpole Emery Mills, South Walpole, Mass.
Diamond Mills Emery Co., Frankford, Pa.
Jackson Mills Emery Co., Easton, Pa.
Hampden Emery Mills, Chester, Mass.

Stock....Par $100....Authorized { com., $2,500,000; pref., 500,000 } Issued { com., $1,179,800; pref., 260,000 } $1,385,800

The preferred stock is 6 per cent., cumulative, and has a preference as to the assets of the company in case of dissolution. Stock is transferred at the office of the company, Boston.

Dividends on the preferred stock are payable quarterly, in January, April, July and October. A quarterly dividend of 1½ per cent. was paid January 1, 1902.

FUNDED DEBT.

1st mort., 6 per cent., bonds, due Oct. 1, 1920, April and Oct........................ $360,000

Trustee of the mortgage and agent for payment of interest, Industrial Trust Co., Providence, R. I.

President and Treasurer, Lewis R. Speare, Boston; 1st Vice-President, Ohio C. Barber, Akron, Ohio; 2d Vice-President, C. Albert Sandt, Easton, Pa.; Secretary, E. Ray Speare, Boston.

Directors—Lewis R. Speare, E. Ray Speare, S. L. B. Speare, Boston; Ohio C. Barber, Akron, O.; E. E. Jackson, Jr., New York; C. Albert Sandt, Jr., Easton, Pa.; Sylvester C. Smith, Phillipsburg, N. J.; John A. Way, Walpole, Mass.

Corporate office, 1 High street, Perth Amboy, N. J.; main office, 131 State street, Boston. Annual meeting, first Tuesday in February, at Perth Amboy, N. J.

## THE ASSOCIATED MERCHANTS CO.

A corporation chartered by the Legislature of Connecticut, May 9, 1893, under the title of The Columbian Construction Co. The charter was amended by the Legislature January 25, 1901, the name being changed to the present style. The company has power to conduct any lawful business; may acquire, hold or sell real estate or personal property, and the bonds, stocks, obligations and franchises of other corporations. Under these provisions the company is authorized to deal directly in dry goods or to hold or sell the bonds or stocks of other companies. The company was organized under its present form in 1901 to acquire interests in large wholesale and retail dry goods establishments. The property it acquired consists of:

1. Stocks of the H. B. Claflin Co., New York, as follows: Common, 19,300 shares; 1st preferred, 6,400 shares; 2d preferred, 19,301 shares, or 45,001 shares out of a total of 90,000 shares of the H. B. Claflin Co.'s stock. See separate statement of the latter.

2. Stocks of the Adams Dry Goods Co., as follows: 6,000 shares of common out of 18,000, and 12,000 shares out of 18,000 shares of preferred. The preferred stock of the Adams Dry Goods Co. is 7 per cent., cumulative. This company has a large retail dry goods business at Sixth avenue and Twenty-first and Twenty-second streets, New York.

3. The entire stock and bonded obligations, aggregating $3,600,000 par of James McCreery & Co., a company doing business in dry goods on Twenty-third street, New York.

4. The plant and good-will of Posner Bros., Baltimore. This property was acquired in the latter part of 1901.

The business of H. O'Neill & Co. of New York, was acquired in 1902 in the interest of this company.

The Associated Merchants' Co. transacts no mercantile business directly. Its income is derived from the dividends on the stocks it owns. It began business about April 15, 1901.

| Stock..Par $100..Authorized | | | Issued | | | |
|---|---|---|---|---|---|---|
| | com., | $5,000,000 | | com., | $5,013,000 | |
| | 1st pref., | 10,000,000 | | 1st pref., | 4,932,000 | $15,000,000 |
| | 2d pref., | 5,000,000 | | 2d pref., | 5,055,000 | |

The 1st preferred stock is 5 per cent., cumulative, and has preference for its par value and accrued dividends as to assets in case of the company's dissolution. If any quarterly dividends on the 1st preferred are in arrears they shall be made up in full before anything is paid on the other classes of stock. Holders of the 1st preferred have the right to exchange it at par for either 2d preferred or common stock at any time when the transfer books are open.

The 2d preferred stock is 6 per cent., cumulative, and this stock has preference for its par value and accrued dividends after the 1st preferred and before the common, as to assets, in case of dissolution.

After the respective dividends of the 1st and 2d preferred stocks shall have been paid or set apart the common stock is entitled to all the surplus earnings. The capital stock or any class thereof can be increased or decreased only by a vote of a majority of each class of stock outstanding.

Transfer Agent, F. W. Franklin, 224 Church street, New York. Registrar, Hudson Trust Co., Hoboken, N. J., and New York.

The company has no funded debt or floating obligations.

The income account of the company for nine and one-half months ending February 1, 1902, shows net earnings $701,221, dividends paid and accrued on 1st prererred, stock $180,622, dividends paid and accrued on 2d preferred stock $237,500, balance applicable to dividends on the common stock $283,098; the balance was equivalent to a rate of 7 15-100 per cent. per annum on the common.

The company's balance sheet February 1, 1903, showed total assets, $15,724,451, and surplus, $701,538.

The company paid interest to July 15, 1901, at 5 per cent., on installments paid in on account of subscriptions to the 1st preferred stock, and also interest at 6 per cent. on the 2d preferred from April 15 to July 15, 1901.

On October 15, 1901, the first quarterly dividend of 1¼ per cent. was paid on the 1st preferred, and similar dividends have since been regularly paid, January, April, July and October.

On October 15, 1901, the first quarterly dividend of 1½ per cent. was paid on the 2d preferred, and similar dividends have since been regularly paid in January (15), April, July and October.

The first quarterly dividend on the common stock was 1¼ per cent., paid December 1, 1902, and a similar payment was made March 1, 1903.

The company's fiscal year ends January 31 of each year. A statement of income and balance sheet is regularly published in February and August of each year.

In the six months ending August 1, 1902, the net earnings were reported as $512,788; surplus over preferred dividends, $237,000. In the six months ending February 1, 1903, the net was $543,500, and the surplus over dividends on the preferred stocks and the first quarterly dividend of 1¼ per cent. on the common stock, was $180,660.

President, John Claflin; 1st Vice-President, Edward E. Eames; 2d Vice-President, John C. Eames; Treasurer and Vice-President, Louis Stewart; Secretary, Moses Ely, New York.

Directors—John A. Stewart, Alexander E. Orr, Woodbury Langdon, George F. Crane, Howland Davis, James McCreery, Louis Stewart, John Claflin, New York; Arthur L. Shipman, Hartford, Conn.

Corporate office, Hartford, Conn.; New Jersey office, Hudson Trust Co. Building, Hoboken, N. J. Annual meeting, third Wednesday in April, at Hartford.

## THE ATCHISON & EASTERN BRIDGE CO.

A corporation formed under the laws of Kansas and Missouri in 1898. The company is a reorganization of the Chicago & Atchison Bridge Co. It owns and operates a railway and toll bridge used by the Atchison, Topeka & Santa Fe, the Missouri Pacific and other railroads across the Missouri River from Atchison, Kan., to Winthrop, Mo.

Stock......Par $100..............................Authorized, $700,000......Issued, $700,000

The company has no preferred stock. Transfer Agent, William P. Kelly, Superior and Water streets, Cleveland.

FUNDED DEBT.

1st mort., 4 per cent. gold bonds, due 1928, Jan. and July............................ $600,000

The authorized issue of bonds is $665,000. Trustee of mortgage and agent for the payment of interest, Central Trust Co., New York.

In the year 1901 the gross earnings of the company were $97,883; interest, $24,500; surplus, $44,774; sinking fund charges, $5,500.

President and Treasurer, Howard P. Eells; Vice-President, James H. Hoyt; Secretary, William P. Kelly, Cleveland; Superintendent, N. D. Todd, Atchison, Kan.

Corporate offices, Atchison, Kan., and Winthrop, Mo.; President's office, Superior and Water streets, Cleveland.

## ATLANTA GAS LIGHT CO.

A corporation formed under the laws of Georgia, February 16, 1856. The company owns and operates the gas works in Atlanta, Ga. Control of the company is held by the United Gas Improvement Co.

Stock ....Par $25.....Authorized { com., $1,014,625 / pref., 600,000 } Issued { com., $1,014,625 / pref., 600,000 } $1,614,625

Stock is transferred at the office of the company, Atlanta, Ga.

In 1902 the dividends paid were 1 per cent. annual on the common stock and 7 per cent. annual on the preferred stock.

FUNDED DEBT.

1st mort., 5 per cent., due June 1, 1947, June and Dec.............................$1,150,000

The bonds outstanding are the total amount authorized. Trustee of the mortgage and agent for the payment of interest, New York Security & Trust Co., New York.

President, J. H. Mecaslin; Vice-President, Randal Morgan; Treasurer, Lewis Lillie; Secretary, W. L. Cosgrove.

Directors—Edward C. Peters, J. H. Mecaslin, R. J. Lowry, Jack J. Spalding, Randal Morgan.

Corporate office, Atlanta, Ga. Annual meeting, first Saturday after the second Wednesday in March, at Atlanta.

## ATLANTIC COAST ELECTRIC RAILROAD CO.

A corporation formed under the laws of New Jersey, April 11, 1895. The company acquired control of the following companies:

| | |
|---|---|
| Asbury Park & Sea Girt Railroad Co. | Seashore Electric Railway Co. |
| Atlantic Coast Electric Light Co. | West End & Long Branch Railway Co. |

The company operates an electric trolley road in Asbury Park, N. J., and from Asbury Park to Long Branch, Pleasure Bay, and Belmar, N. J. It has 26 miles of track, a power house and 70 cars. The Atlantic Coast Electric Light Co. supplies electric light to Asbury Park, Allenhurst, Belmar, Ocean Beach, Como and Spring Lake, N. J. The company also controls by lease the Hotel Avenel and grounds at Pleasure Bay, N. J.

Stock......Par $100......................... Authorized, $1,500,000......Issued, $1,500,000

The company has no preferred stock. Transfer Agent and Registrar, Knickerbocker Trust Co., New York.

FUNDED DEBT.

| | |
|---|---|
| 1st mort., 5 per cent., gold, due May, 1945, May and Nov. | $800,000 |
| General mort., 5 per cent., due 1946, Jan. and July | 500,000 |
| Seashore Electric Railway Co. 1st mort., 6 per cent. gold, due 1917, Jan. and July. | 200,000 |
| Atlantic Coast Elec. Light Co. 1st mort., 5 per cent., due June, 1946, June and Dec. | 241,000 |
| Asbury Park & Sea Girt R. R. Co. 1st mort., 5 per cent. gold, due 1918, Mar. and Sept. | 50,000 |
| Total | $1,791,000 |

The authorized amount of the first mortgage is $1,000,000, of which $200,000 was reserved to retire a like amount of Seashore Electric Co.'s bonds. Trustee of the mortgage and agent for the paymen of interest, Knickerbocker Trust Co., New York. The outstanding bonds of the general mortgage are the full amount authorized. Trustee of the bonds and agent for the payment of interest, Guaranty Trust Co., New York. The outstanding bonds of the Seashore Electric Railway Co.'s first mortgage are the full amount authorized. Agent for the payment of interest, Federal Trust Co., Newark, N. J. The authorized amount of the Atlantic Coast Electric Light Trust Co.'s mortgage is $500,000. Bonds are subject to call at 105 after 1901. Agent for the payment of interest, Federal Trust Co., Newark, N. J. The outstanding bonds of the Asbury Park & Sea Girt Railroad Co. are the full amount authorized. Trustee of the bonds and agent for the payment of interest, Monmouth Trust & Safe Deposit Co., Asbury Park, N. J.

The company defaulted on the interest on its 1st mortgage bonds in November, 1901, and on the interest on its general mortgage in January, 1902. A receiver was appointed in February, 1902, and foreclosure proceedings were begun in November, 1902.

EARNINGS.

Year ending September 30.

| | Gross. | Operating Expenses. | Net. |
|---|---|---|---|
| 1889 | $317,425 | $184,035 | $133,390 |
| 1900 | 330,528 | 191,610 | 138,918 |
| 1901 | 290,650 | 144,085 | 146,565 |
| 1902 | 208,895 | 93,743 | 115,152 |

Receiver, James Smith, Jr., Newark, N. J.; President, William E. Benjamin; Vice-President, Daniel O'Day, New York; Treasurer, Albert C. Twining, Asbury Park, N. J.

Directors—William E. Benjamin, Henry H. Rogers, Daniel O'Day, George B. M. Harvey, John P. O'Brien, New York; George F. Kroehl, Albert C. Twining, Asbury Park, N. J.

Main office, Asbury Park, N. J. New York office, 32 Broadway. Annual meeting, third Wednesday in April, at Asbury Park, N. J.

## ATLANTIC COAST LUMBER CO.

A corporation formed under the laws of Virginia, April 25, 1899. The company owns twelve hundred million feet of standing timber. The plant of the company at Georgetown, S. C., consists of three saw mills, a planing mill, foundry, machine shop, car shop, etc. The daily capacity of its mills is 500,000 feet of lumber.

In October, 1902, the company was placed in the hands of receivers, and foreclosure of its 1st mortgage was instituted.

Stock......Par $100..........................Authorized, $10,000,000......Issued, $1,000,000

FUNDED DEBT.

1st mort., 6 per cent ........................................................ $2,000,000

Receivers, Freeman S. Farr, E. J. Hathorne.

President, Freeman S. Farr; Vice-President, E. B. Freeman; Secretary and Treasurer, R. L. Montague.

Directors—Lewis A. Hall, E. B. Freeman, L. R. Freeman, Wallace B. Flint, Freeman S. Farr, W. A. Taft, Alden S. Swan.

Main office, Georgetown, S. C.

## ATLANTIC MINING CO.

A consolidation, December, 1872, of the South Pewabic and Adams Mining Cos. Company's copper mining and milling property is situated in Houghton County, Michigan, and consists of about 3,000 acres of lands, mines, machinery, etc. It is one of the most important mines in upper Michigan

Stock......Par $25............................Authorized, $2,500,000......Issued, $2,500,000

The stock was increased from $1,000,000 to $2,500,000 in March, 1902.

There has been paid in cash on the stock $9.80 per share. Transfer Agent, American Loan & Trust Co., Boston; Registrar, Boston Safe Deposit & Trust Co., Boston.

This company's output in 1893 was 2,771 tons; in 1894, 2,843 tons; in 1895, 3,129 tons; in 1896, 3,224 tons; in 1897, 3,383 tons, yielding 5,109,663 pounds of copper; in 1898, 2,963 tons, yielding 4,369,160 pounds of copper; in 1899, 3,073 tons, yielding 4,675,882 pounds of copper; in 1900, 3,296 tons, in 1901, 3,158 tons. $940,000 has been paid in dividends since formation of company.

In 1899 paid dividends of $2 per share, in 1900 $2; also paid $2 per share in February, 1901.

President, Joseph E. Gay; Treasurer, John Stanton; Secretary, John R. Stanton, New York.

Directors—Joseph E. Gay, John Stanton, John R. Stanton, Samuel L. Smith, J. Wheeler Hardley, William C. Stuart, William A. Paine.

Main office, Atlantic Mines, Houghton Co., Mich.; New York office, 13 William street. Annual meeting, second Tuesday in March.

---

## AUER INCANDESCENT LIGHT MANUFACTURING CO., LIMITED

A corporation formed under the laws of the Dominion of Canada October 8, 1892. The company is engaged in manufacturing the Auer light system in Canada, and controls the local business of the system in Montreal.

Stock......Par $100..............................Authorized, $500,000......Issued, $500,000

The company has no preferred stock. Stock is transferred at the company's office, Montreal.

Dividends on the stock, payable quarterly, April (20), July, October, January, have been as follows, per share: 1897, 50 cents; 1898, $1; 1899, $1.50; 1900, $3; 1901, $4; 1902, $2; 1903, $2.

FUNDED DEBT.

1st mort., 6 per cent. bonds, due 1903, Jan. and July...................... ............ $7,000

The amount of 1st mortgage bonds authorized is $70,500, but all of the issue has been retired except the above and $3,500 will be retired June 1, 1903.

President, A. O. Granger; Vice-President, John Murphy; Treasurer, Thomas Sutton; General Manager and Secretary, W. R. Granger.

Directors—A. O. Granger, John Murphy, W. R. Granger, S. Carsley, F. E. Nelson, J. G. Ross, C. A. Duclos, T. W. Boyd, Hugh Glassford.

Corporate and main office, 1682 Notre Dame street, Montreal. Annual meeting, third Wednesday in April.

---

## THE AURORA, ELGIN & CHICAGO RAILWAY CO.

A corporation formed under the laws of Illinois in 1899 as the Aurora, Wheaton & Chicago Railway Co. to construct and operate a street railway. The company is a consolidation of the above and the Elgin & Chicago Railway Co. and Batavia & Eastern Railway Co., and when its lines are completed it will have 83 miles of track entirely upon private right of way and operated by the third rail electric system. It will connect with the West Side Elevated Railway Co. in Chicago and will pass through the following cities and towns: Aurora, Batavia, Elgin, Wayne, Warrenhurst, Wheaton, Glen Ellyn, Lombard, Elmhurst, Bellwood, Maywood, Harlem, Oak Park and Austin, Ill.

Stock..Par $100......Authorized { com., $3,000,000 / pref., 1,500,000 } Issued { com., $3,000,000 / pref., 1,500,000 } $4,500,000

The preferred stock is 6 per cent., cumulative.

Transfer Agents, The Northern Trust Co., Chicago, and The Cleveland Trust Co., Cleveland. Registrars, Illinois Trust & Savings Bank, Chicago; The Cleveland Trust Co., Cleveland.

FUNDED DEBT.

1st mort., 5 per cent., due 1941, May (15) and Nov.................................. $4,500,000

The outstanding bonds are the total amount authorized. Trustee of the mortgage and agent for the payment of interest, The American Trust & Savings Bank, Chicago.

President, L. J. Wolf, Chicago; Vice-President, M. H. Wilson; Treasurer, M. J. Mandlebaum, Cleveland; Secretary, Warren M. Bicknell, Chicago.

Directors—L. J. Wolf, M. H. Wilson, Fred A. Dolph, Warren M. Bicknell, Harry Greenebaum, W. T. Hapeman.

Main office, 100 Washington street, Chicago; corporate office, 121 Euclid avenue, Cleveland. Annual meeting, second Tuesday in March, at Chicago.

## AUSTIN ELECTRIC RAILWAY CO.

A corporation formed under the laws of Texas, May 29, 1902, as a reorganization of the Austin Rapid Transit Railway Co. The company owns and operates 15½ miles of electric railway in the city of Austin, Tex., serving a population of about 25,000. It has one power plant and 28 cars.

Stock......Par $100........................ . ....Authorized, $200,000......Issued, $200,000

The company has no preferred stock and no funded debt.

President, Ira H. Evans, Austin, Tex.; Vice-President, F. H. Watriss, New York; Secretary, Frank E. Scoville; Treasurer, E. P. Wilmot, Austin, Tex.

Directors—O. C. Fuller, L. J. Petit, Milwaukee, Wis.; F. H. Watriss, New York; Ira H. Evans, E. P. Wilmot, T. B. Cochran, Austin, Tex.

Corporate and main office, 404 Congress avenue, Austin, Tex.; branch office, Milwaukee, Wis. Annual meeting, second Tuesday in June, at Austin, Tex., or Wilwaukee, Wis.

---

## AUTOMATIC WEIGHING MACHINE CO.

A corporation formed under the laws of New York in September, 1901, for the purpose of manufacturing automatic weighing machines, whereby packages of various commodities can be accurately weighed and handled. The company has acquired the entire weighing machine interests of the Pratt & Whitney Co., Hartford, Conn., and the New England Automatic Weighing Machine Co., Boston.

The company owns over 300 patents, controlling this branch of the industry, with all the special plants and machinery of the companies absorbed. Its machines are leased, not sold, the rentals from machines now in service or contracted for amounting to $50,000 per annum.

Stock....Par $100....Authorized { com., $3,000,000; pref., 600,000 } Issued { com., $3,000,000; pref., 502,000 }. $3,502,000

The preferred stock is 6 per cent., cumulative.

Transfer Agent and Registrar, The Trust Co. of America, New York.

The company has no funded debt.

President, Pierre Lorillard; Vice-President, Walter L. Clark; Secretary and Treasurer, C. A. Leonard, New York.

Directors—Pierre Lorillard, Walter L. Clark, W. P. Homans, C. A. Leonard, William Barbour, John H. Hanan, Robert C. McKinney, C. E. Halliwell, New York; S. W. Winslow, George W. Brown, Elmer P. Howe, C. S. Hill, Boston.

Main offices, Green and Bay streets, Jersey City, and 111 Fifth avenue, New York. Annual meeting, in September.

---

## AZTEC GOLD & COPPER MINING CO.

A corporation formed under the laws of Maine, November 10, 1899. The company owns the Aztec and Republic mines and ten other claims in the San Juan district, Needleton, Colo.

Stock......Par $1.......... ....................Authorized, $2,000,000......Issued, $550,000

The company has no preferred stock and no funded debt. Transfer Agent, The George F. Bradstreet Co., 53 State street, Boston. Registrar, American Loan & Trust Co., Boston.

President, David W. Williams, Glastonbury, Conn.; Vice-President, Lyman B. Jordan; Secretary and Treasurer, George F. Bradstreet, Boston.

Directors, David W. Williams, Glastonbury, Conn.; Lyman B. Jordan, George F. Bradstreet, F. E. Chandler, Malden, Mass.; Charles A. Howland, Herbert F. Doble, Quincy, Mass.; W. W. Brookings, N. P. Cummings, Boston; C. W. Davis, Waterville, Me.

Corporate office, Waterville, Me.; main office, 53 State street, Boston; branch office, Needleton, Colo. Annual meeting, second Wednesday in November, at Waterville.

---

## WALTER BAKER & CO., LIMITED

A corporation formed under the laws of Massachusetts, March 5, 1898. The purpose of the company is the manufacture and sale of chocolate and cocoa preparations. The company acquired the real estate, buildings, factories, business and trade-marks of the firm of Walter Baker & Co., which was established at Dorchester, Mass., in 1780.

Stock......Par $100...........................Authorized, $4,750,000......Issued, $2,750,000

The company has no preferred stock. Transfer Agent and Registrar, James H. Perkins, company's office, Boston.

The company paid semi-annual dividends of 2½ per cent. on its stock, beginning in July, 1898, until July, 1900, when the semi-annual rate was raised to 3 per cent., and for the year 1902 extra dividends of ½ per cent. each were paid in addition to the regular 3 per cent. semi-annual dividends. The dividends are paid in January and July.

FUNDED DEBT.

1st mort., 4½ per cent., due 1903, March.............................................. $258,000

The 1st mortgage was $1,500,000 authorized. Interest on the bonds is payable at the company's office.

President, J. Frank Howland; Vice-President, H. C. Gallagher; Treasurer, Herbert Dabney; Clerk, James H. Perkins.

Directors—J. Frank Howland, Boston; Rodolphe L. Agassiz, Hamilton, Mass.; J. Malcolm Forbes, H. C. Gallagher, Nathaniel H. Stone, Ellerton P. Whitney, Milton, Mass.; William L. Putnam, Manchester, Mass.

Main office, 247 Atlantic avenue, Boston; branch offices, 105 Hudson street, New York; 38 Lake street, Chicago; 12 St. John street, Montreal. Annual meeting, fourth Wednesday in January.

## BARNARD MANUFACTURING CO.

A corporation formed under the laws of Massachusetts in 1874, for the purpose of manufacturing cotton cloth. The mills of the company are at Fall River, Mass., and have a capacity of 66,000 spindles.

Stock......Par $100.............................Authorized, $495,000......Issued, $495,000

The company has no preferred stock and no funded debt.

Stock is transferred at the office of the company.

Dividends are paid quarterly, in January, April, July and October. The annual dividend rates in recent years have been as follows: In 1890, 6 per cent.; 1891, 2½ per cent.; 1892, 7 per cent.; 1893, 7½ per cent.; 1894, 5 per cent.; 1896, 7 per cent.; 1897, 1 per cent.; 1898, none; 1899, 3¼ per cent.; 1900, 8 per cent.; 1901, 5¼ per cent; 1902, 6 per cent.

President, Bradford D. Davol; Secretary and Treasurer, Nathaniel B. Borden, Fall River, Mass.

Directors—Bradford D. Davol, Leontine Lincoln, William H. Jennings, William N. McLane, Simeon Borden, Nathaniel B. Borden, Fall River; William H. Gifford, North Westport, Mass.; Stephen A. Jenks, Pawtucket, R. I.

Corporate and main office, Fall River, Mass. Annual meeting, fourth Thursday in October, at Fall River.

## THE BARNEY & SMITH CAR CO.

A corporation formed under the laws of West Virginia, May 31, 1892, which took over the plant and business of the Barney & Smith Manufacturing Co., Dayton, O., one of the largest and most successful car building concerns in the United States. The property owned includes 28 acres of land at Dayton, with over 40 buildings, machinery, etc. The plant is valued on the company's books at $3,226,274. The company manufactures all classes of freight and passenger cars, wheels and car castings, and also cars for electric and street railways and appliances therefor.

Stock....Par $100.....Authorized { com., $1,000,000; pref., 2,500,000 } Issued { com., $1,000,000; pref., 2,500,000 } $3,500,000

Preferred stock is 8 per cent., cumulative. Common stock is entitled after payment of the preferred dividends to up to 12 per cent., and to a further division of net earnings after 4 per cent. has been carried to surplus account. Both classes of stock have equal voting power and share alike in the distribution of assets in case of dissolution.

Transfer Agent, Guaranty Trust Co., New York. Registrar, Union Trust Co., New York.

Dividends on the preferred stock were suspended after March, 1895, until December, 1899, when a quarterly dividend of 2 per cent. was again paid. Quarterly dividends of 2 per cent. have since been regularly paid on the preferred in March (1), June, September and December. The last dividend on common stock was 5 per cent., paid June, 1893.

FUNDED DEBT.

1st mort. 6 per cent., due 1942, Jan. and July........................................ $1,000,000

The 1st mortgage bonds are subject to call at 110 after July 1, 1902. No further issue of bonds can be made without the consent of holders of three-fourths of the preferred stock. Trustee of mortgage, Guaranty Trust Co., New York, which also pays interest thereon.

EARNINGS.

Year ending March 31.

| | Net Income | Charges. | Pref. Div. | Surplus. |
|---|---|---|---|---|
| 1899-00 | $363,198 | $60,299 | $160,000 | $196,844 |
| 1900-01 | 378,192 | 60,380 | 200,000 | 117,812 |
| 1901-02 | 399,991 | 60,026 | 200,000 | 139,967 |

President, James D. Platt; Vice-President, A. M. Kittredge; Superintendent, H. M. Estabrook; Assistant Secretary-Treasurer, J. F. Kiefaber, Dayton, O.

Directors—E. J. Barney, James D. Platt, F. E. Smith, A. M. Kittredge, J. H. Winters, Dayton, O.; W. J. Lippincott, W. H. Doane, Walter St. John Jones, Cincinnati.

Main office, North Keowee street, Dayton, O. Annual meeting, first Tuesday in June, at Dayton.

## BARRETT MANUFACTURING CO.

A corporation formed under the laws of West Virginia, January 1, 1896. The business of the company is the manufacture of coal tar chemicals. It has 15 plants in thirteen cities.

Stock......Par $100..........................Authorized, $5,000,000......Issued, $3,943,700

Stock is transferred at the office of the company, Philadelphia.

FUNDED DEBT.

Debentures, 5 per cent., due 1939.................................................. $2,304,000

The authorized amount of the debentures is $2,500,000.

Regular quarterly dividends of 2½ per cent. are paid on the stock.

The company at the end of 1902 had a surplus of $1,656,129.

Chairman, S. E. Barrett; President, George W. Elkins; Treasurer, T. W. Weeks; Secretary, Edward H. Kidder.

Directors—George W. Elkins, Michael Ehret, George D. Widener, H. S. Ehret, Philadelphia; S. E. Barrett, S. H. Bingham, Chicago; I. D. Fletcher, E. H. Wardwell, W. H. Ellis, Eversley Childs, E. H. Kidder, New York; P. S. Marquis, St. Louis; A. T. Perry, Cleveland.

Main office, Land Title Building, Philadelphia. Annual meeting, third Wednesday in March.

## BAY CITIES CONSOLIDATED RAILWAY

A corporation formed under the laws of Michigan, March 27, 1893, for the purpose of operating a trolley road in Bay City, Mich. The company acquired the Bay City Railroad and West Bay City Railroad, and owns 33 miles of track, serving a population of about 65,000.

In July, 1899, the company was placed in the hands of receivers.

Stock......Par $100..........................Authorized, $1,000,000......Issued, $950,000

The company has no preferred stock.

Registrar, Land, Title & Trust Co., Philadelphia.

FUNDED DEBT.

| | |
|---|---|
| 1st con. mort., 6 per cent., gold, due 1918, March and Sept. | $381,000 |
| 2d mort., 6 per cent., due 1906, March and Sept. | 50,000 |
| Receivers' certificate, 6 per cent. | 290,000 |
| Total | $721,000 |

The authorized amount of the 1st consolidated mortgage is $500,000. Of the issue of receivers' certificates $119,000 was used to retire a like amount of the Bay City Railroad 1st mortgage.

Trustee of the bonds and agent for the payment of interest, Philadelphia Securities Co., Philadelphia.

Receivers, Michael P. Heraty, Philadelphia; J. C. Weadlock, Bay City, Mich.

President, Michael P. Heraty, Philadelphia; General Manager, E. S. Dimmock, Bay City, Mich.

Directors—George E. Shaw, Michael P. Heraty, M. Hipple, L. Johnson, Philadelphia.

Main office, Bay City, Mich. Annual meeting, second Tuesday in March.

## BAY CITIES WATER CO.

A corporation formed under the laws of California. The purpose of the company is to develop and distribute water for municipal and domestic purposes. It has extensive reservoirs and distributing plants in various counties of California.

Stock......Par $100..........................Authorized, $10,000,000......Issued, $10,000,000

Stock is transferred at the company's office. Registrar, Mercantile Trust Co. of San Francisco.

FUNDED DEBT.

1st mort., 5 per cent., due 1945, Jan. and July....................................$276,000

The authorized bond issue is $10,000,000 by the stockholders and $1,000,000 by the directors. The unissued balance of the latter amount being held in readiness for sale when ordered by the directors. Trustee, Mercantile Trust Co., San Francisco. Agents for the payment of interest are the Mercantile Trust Co., San Francisco, and the United States Mortgage & Trust Co., New York.

As the construction work of the company is incomplete, no reports on earnings have yet been made and are not anticipated for at least two years.

President, William S. Tevis, Bakersfield, Cal.; Vice-President, Clinton E. Worden; Secretary, E. G. Wheeler; Treasurer, F. G. Drum; General Manager, Carroll N. Beal; Chief Engineer, Edwin Duryea, Jr., San Francisco.

Directors—William S. Tevis, Bakersfield, Cal.; Clinton E. Worden, E. S. Pillsbury, E. G. Wheeler, F. G. Drum, C. N. Beal, Wakefield Baker, Harry L. Tevis, James W. Byrne, San Francisco.

Corporate and main office, Mutual Bank Building, San Francisco. Annual meeting, third Tuesday in October, at San Francisco.

---

## BAY STATE GAS CO.

A Delaware corporation, formed in 1889, to own the stock of another company of the same name incorporated in 1889 under the laws of New Jersey, with a capital of $1,000,000 of which this company owned $995,000. The purpose of the latter organization was to amalgamate under one management all the companies supplying the city of Boston and its suburbs with gas, comprising 14 companies, including the Bay State Gas Co. of Massachusetts, Boston Gaslight Co., Roxbury Gaslight Co., Dorchester Gaslight Co., South Boston Gaslight Co. The Brookline Gas Co., another Boston concern, was also acquired in 1895. The Bay State of New Jersey held the voting power of the Bay State Co. of Massachusetts, and the Massachusetts company owned the stocks of the companies in question and the large plants and real estate belonging thereto in and around Boston, and made large expenditures for improving same. See below.

On July 7, 1902, in consequence of default in interest and sinking fund payments on the Boston United Gas bonds, the Bay State Gas Co. of New Jersey was placed in the hands of George D. Hallock, as receiver.

Stock......Par $50.........................Authorized, $100,000,000......Issued, $100,000,000

In October, 1895, stock was increased from $5,000,000 to $15,000,000 for the purpose of acquiring the Brookline Gas Co. and other properties. Holders of original stock were then given the right to subscribe for two shares of the new stock at $10 a share for each old share owned. In September, 1897, company increased its stock to $50,000,000, and in October, 1897, offered to pay off its income bonds if $1,950,000 were deposited. The 7 per cent. income bonds, due 1899, were $2,000,000 in amount.

In January, 1899, the stock of the Bay State Gas Co. of Delaware was increased from $50,000,000 to $100,000,000, and in consequence of the absence of information about the purposes of this increase, the Stock Exchanges of New York and Boston struck the stock from their lists.

Transfer Agent, Metropolitan Trust Co., New York.

FUNDED DEBT.

| | |
|---|---|
| Boston United Gas, 1st mort., 5 per cent., due Jan., 1939, Jan. and July........... | $8,159,500 |
| " " " 2d mort., 5 per cent., due Jan., 1939, Jan. and July........... | 3,000,000 |
| Total............................................................ | $11,159,500 |

The 1st and 2d mortgage bonds of the Bay State Gas Co. of Massachusetts, were deposited with the Mercantile Trust Co., New York, which issued Boston United Gas trust certificates, secured by deposit of all the stock of the Bay State Gas Co. of Massachusetts, and of the South Boston, Roxbury and other gaslight companies. Mortgage is for $12,000,000; $3,000,000 of bonds were reserved to provide for improvements. There is a sinking fund of 1 per cent. per annum, and bonds can be drawn at 105. Each registered bond for $1,000 is entitled to five votes at company's meetings.

In October, 1896, an income bondholder brought suit in United States Court at Wilmington, Del., and Receivers were appointed, but were discharged October 31, 1896. In November, 1896, the voting power of the Bay State Gas Co. of New Jersey, in the stocks of the constituent companies in Boston (which stocks were held by the Mercantile Trust Co. of New York, as security for the two issues of Boston United Gas bonds), was transferred to interests connected with the New England Gas & Coke Co. Disputes and litigation ensued in regard to this transaction. In

January, 1903, propositions were made to holders of the Boston United Gas bonds to exchange them for stock of the Massachusetts Gas Companies, the successor of the New England Gas & Coke Co. See statement of the Massachusetts Gas Companies.

President, J. Frank Allee, Dover, Del.; Secretary-Treasurer, W. Harry Miller, Philadelphia. Main office, Wilmington, Del.; Philadelphia office, Chestnut and Broad streets.

## BEAVER VALLEY TRACTION CO.

A corporation formed under the laws of Pennsylvania, June 29, 1891. The company is a consolidation of the following companies:

Beaver Valley Street Railway Co.
Central Electric Street Railway Co.
People's Electric Street Ry. Co. of Rochester.
College & Grand-view Electric Street Ry. Co.
Rochester & Monaca Electric Street Ry. Co.
Beaver & Vanport Electric Street Railway Co.

The company operates 25 miles of track, has a power station in Rochester Township, Beaver County, Pa., and owns 46 motor cars.

Stock......Par $50.... ......................Authorized, $1,500,000......Issued, $1,000,000

The company has no preferred stock. Stock is transferred at the company's office. Registrar, Pennsylvania Co. for Insurance on Lives, Philadelphia.

FUNDED DEBT.

| | |
|---|---|
| 1st mort., 6 per cent. gold, due 1911, Jan. and July | $150,000 |
| 2d mort., 6 per cent. gold, due 1915, April and Oct | 100,000 |
| New 1st con. mort., 5 per cent. gold, due 1950, April and Oct | 675,000 |
| People's Electric Street Railway Co., 1st mort., 6 per cent., May and Nov. | 50,000 |
| " " " " " 2d mort., 6 per cent., Feb. and Aug | 25,000 |
| Total | $1,000,000 |

The outstanding 1st and 2d mortgage bonds are the full amounts authorized. Trustee of both mortgages and agent for the payment of interest, Union Trust Co., Pittsburg. The authorized amount of the new first consolidated mortgage is $1,000,000, of which $325,000 is reserved to retire underlying bonds. Trustee of the mortgage and agent for the payment of interest, Pennsylvania Company for Insurance of Lives and Granting Annuities, Philadelphia. Bonds are redeemable at 110 and accrued interest. Agent for payment of interest on the mortgages of the People's Electric Street Railway Co., Union Trust Co., Pittsburg.

In the fiscal year ending September 30, 1902, the gross earnings were $177,214; net, $80,815; charges, $62,574; surplus, $18,241.

President, John M. Buchanan, Beaver Falls, Pa.; Vice-President, Sydney L. Wright; Secretary and Treasurer, Walter T. Bilyeu, Philadelphia; General Manager, Gaylord Thompson, Beaver Falls, Pa.

Directors—John M. Buchanan, James P. Stone, Theodore P. Simpson, Harry W. Reeves, Gaylord Thompson, Beaver Falls, Pa.; Sydney L. Wright, Walter T. Bilyeu, William R. Wright, W. Frederick Snyder, Howard S. Graham, William Henry Snyder, Philadelphia.

Main office, Beaver Falls, Pa.; Philadelphia office, 308 Chestnut street. Annual meeting, first Saturday in March, at Philadelphia.

## BELL TELEPHONE CO. OF BUFFALO

A corporation organized under the laws of New York in 1879. The company operates a telephone system, under an exclusive license from the American Telephone & Telegraph Co., in the city of Buffalo and the adjacent counties of New York, its territory including Rochester, Niagara Falls, Lockport, Batavia and other large cities and towns. Of the stock $2,507,500 is owned by the American Telephone & Telegraph Co. At the end of 1902 the company had 23,566 stations in operation.

Stock......Par $100.........................Authorized, $10,000,000......Issued, $5,000,000

The authorized stock of the company was increased from $4,000,000 to $5,000,000 in February, 1900, and in November, 1902, a further increase to $10,000,000 was authorized. The directors were empowered to dispose of the increase from time to time, as might be necessary in order to provide for extensions of the company's system. In December, 1900, $1,000,000 of stock was sold at par to the stockholders; in November, 1901, another $1,000,000 of stock was allotted at par to the stockholders, and in November, 1902, $500,000 more of new stock was allotted at par; payments for the same being 50 per cent. on January 15, 1903, and 50 per cent. April 15, 1903.

The company has no funded debt.

Dividends of 6 per cent. per annum have been for some years paid on the stock of the company. The dividends are quarterly, 1½ per cent. each in January, July, April and October.

| EARNINGS. | Gross. | Net. |
|---|---|---|
| 1900 | $704,208 | $217,678 |
| 1901 | 831,200 | 236,100 |
| 1902 | 966,350 | 297,216 |

President, Henry M. Watson; Vice-President, Newcomb Carleton; Secretary and Treasurer, Joseph S. Baecher, Buffalo, N. Y.

Directors—Louis L. Babcock, Joseph P. Bradfield, Newcomb Carlton, Clarence O. Howard, Porter Norton, Thomas T. Ramsdell, Edward M. Hager, Samuel S. Spaulding, Henry M. Watson, Buffalo, N. Y.; Benjamin E. Chase, George Weldon, Rochester, N. Y.; Frederick P. Fish, Boston; Edward J. Hall, New York; Charles M. Helmer, Lockport, N. Y.; William B. Rankine, Niagara Falls, N. Y.

Main office, 14 West Seneca St., Buffalo, N. Y.

## BELL TELEPHONE CO. OF CANADA

A corporation formed under the laws of the Dominion of Canada in 1880. The company owns all the Bell Telephone patents in Canada. Its territory includes the whole of Canada and all its prominent cities, which are connected by a long-distance system of over 6,000 miles of lines. The company had over 277 exchanges at the end of 1902, and a total of 48,481 instruments under rental.

Stock......Par $100... ......................Authorized, $10,000,000......Issued, $6,000,000

Stock is transferred at the company's office.

In June, 1902, $1,000,000 additional stock was allotted at 25 per cent. premium, payments for the same being in five instalments of $25 per share each, in July (2) and October, 1902, and January, April and July, 1903.

The authorized issue of debentures is up to 75 per cent. of the paid-up stock.

The company pays 8 per cent. per annum on its stock, the dividends being quarterly, 2 per cent. each, in January, April, July and October.

FUNDED DEBT.

Debentures, 5 per cent., due April, 1925, April and Oct.............................. $2,000,000

In the year 1902 the company's receipts were: Gross, $2,085,134; net, $504,282.

President, C. F. Sise; Vice-President, Robert Mackay; Secretary and Treasurer, Charles P. Sclater, Montreal.

Directors—C. F. Sise, Robert Mackay, Frederick P. Fish, Robert Archer, William R. Driver, Hugh Paton, Charles Cassils, Thomas Sherwin.

Main office, 1760 Notre Dame street, Montreal. Annual meeting, last Thursday in February.

## BELL TELEPHONE CO. OF MISSOURI

A corporation formed under the laws of Missouri. The company owns and operates a telephone system, under an exclusive license from the American Telephone & Telegraph Co., in the city of St. Louis and the adjoining counties of Missouri, and in East St. Louis and the neighboring districts of Illinois. The American Telephone & Telegraph Co. owns $1,855,600 of this company's stock.

Stock......Par $100...........................Authorized, $4,000,000......Issued, $2,800,000

Stock is transferred at the company's office. Registrar, Boatman's Bank, St. Louis.

The company pays dividends of 8 per cent. per annum on its stock.

President, Frederick P. Fish, Boston; Vice-President, Edwards Whitaker; Secretary and Treasurer, Fritz Nisbet, St. Louis.

Directors—Frederick P. Fish, C. Jay French, Boston; A. Burt, Kansas City; K. Yost, Omaha; James Campbell, G. Drake, W. Duncan, George F. Durant, J. A. Holmes, P. C. Moffitt, E. Whitaker, St. Louis.

Main office, 920 Olive street, St. Louis. Annual meeting, third Thursday in February, at St. Louis.

## BELL TELEPHONE CO. OF PHILADELPHIA

A corporation formed under the laws of Pennsylvania, September 18, 1879. The company operates under an exclusive license from the American Bell Telephone Co., its territory being coextensive with the city of Philadelphia. The Delaware & Atlantic Telegraph & Telephone Co., covering Southern New Jersey and Eastern Pennsylvania, is controlled by this company. The American Telephone & Telegraph Co. owns over 80 per cent. of this company's stock.

Stock......Par $50..........................Authorized, $12,000,000......Issued, $11,972,300

On May 21, 1901, the stock authorized was increased from $6,000,000 to $8,000,000, and $1,000,000 was allotted *pro rata* to the stockholders for subscription at par, payments on such subscription to be completed January 18, 1902. In 1902, the authorized amount was increased to $12,000,000, and $2,000,000 of new stock was allotted to shareholders at par, followed by another issue of $2,000,000 additional in August, 1902.

The company pays 8 per cent. per annum on its stock, the dividends being 2 per cent. quarterly, in January, April, July and October.

The company has no funded debt.

President, James E. Mitchell; Secretary and Treasurer, Winfield S. Piersol, Philadelphia.

Directors—Frederick P. Fish, Thomas Sherwin, C. Jay French, Boston; James E. Mitchell, Thomas E. Cornish, H. S. Huidekoper, Joel J. Baily, Joseph E. Gillingham, Francis B. Reeves, Philadelphia; Edward J. Hall, Edward P. Meany, Joseph M. Brown, New York.

Main office, North Eleventh and Filbert streets, Philadelphia. Annual meeting, third Tuesday in February.

## THE BERGNER & ENGEL BREWING CO.

A corporation formed under the laws of Pennsylvania, January 1, 1879. The company took over the business and plant of Bergner & Engel, of Philadelphia, brewers. The plant at Thirty-second and Masters streets, Philadelphia, covers 12½ acres.

Stock....Par $100 ∴...Authorized { com., $1,650,000 / pref., 1,650,000 } Issued { com., $1,650,000 / pref., 1,650,000 } $3,300,000

The preferred stock is 8 per cent., cumulative. Transfer Agent, Land Title & Trust Co., Philadelphia. Registrar, Union Trust Co., Philadelphia.

Full dividends on the preferred stock were regularly paid, 4 per cent. each, in May and November, until May, 1900, when the dividend was passed, the November, 1900, dividend being also suspended, it being decided to apply the surplus earnings to reducing the company's indebtedness. Regular half-yearly dividends of 4 per cent. in May and November were also paid on the common until May, 1899, inclusive, the November, 1899, dividend on the common being passed.

FUNDED DEBT.

1st mort., 6 per cent., due 1921, Jan. and July....................................$1,500,000

There is no sinking fund provision for the 1st mortgage. Trustee of bonds, Union Trust Co., Philadelphia.

For the year ending September 30, 1902, the company reported gross profits of $135,799.

President, C. William Bergner; Secretary and Treasurer, August W. Woebken, Philadelphia.

Directors—C. William Bergner, August W. Woebken, S. S. Sharp, John F. Stoer, H. F. West, George A. Fletcher, Gustavus A. Muller, Philadelphia.

Main office, Thirty-second and Master streets, Philadelphia.

## BESSEMER COKE CO.

A corporation formed under the laws of Pennsylvania, May 19, 1896. The purposes of the company is the mining of coal and the manufacture of coke. The company acquired and owns the following properties:

Duquesne plant, Bradenville, Pa.
Humphreys plant, Humphreys, Pa.
Martin Plant, New Geneva, Pa.
Empire plant, Ruffsdale and Masontown, Pa.
Griffin plant, Masontown, Pa.

The capacity of these combined plants is 800,000 tons of coke and 150,000 tons of coal per annum.

Stock......Par $25.............................Authorized, $2,500,000......Issued, $850,000

The company has no preferred stock. Dividends of 1½ per cent. were paid on the stock, October 15, 1902, and January 15 and April 15, 1903.

FUNDED DEBT.

1st mort. 5 per cent., due 1921, June and Dec.......................................... $190,000
1st mort., 5 per cent., due 1922, June and Dec.......................................... 200,000

Total.......................................................... $390,000

The bonds outstanding are the full amount authorized. Trustee of the mortgage and agent for payment of interest, The Pennsylvania Trust Co., Pittsburg.

President, William Y. Humphreys; Vice-President, E. H. Jennings; Secretary, William Harris; Treasurer, Hermon Griffin, Pittsburg.

Directors—William Y. Humphreys, Joshua W. Rhodes, Hermon Griffin, William Harris, E. H. Jennings, Dallas C. Byers, B. L. Martin, Pittsburg.

Corporate and main office, 605 Smithfield street, Pittsburg. Annual meeting, third Tuesday in January, at Pittsburg.

## BEST MANUFACTURING CO.

A corporation formed under the laws of Pennsylvania in 1899. The company manufactures valves, fittings and like articles for the piping system of power plants and also bronze and copper specialties for blast furnaces and rolling mills. It owns many patents, particularly on Bosh plates for blast furnace work and standpipes and valves for railroads. The plant of the company consists of an iron foundry of sixty-ton capacity; a brass foundry of seven-ton capacity; a pipe bending and riveting shop and a machine shop.

Stock......Par $100............................ Authorized, $500,000......Issued, $500,000

The company has no preferred stock and no funded debt. Transfer Agent and Registrar, Moreland Trust Co., Pittsburg.

Dividends are paid semi-annually in April and October.

President, George Best; Vice-President, W. H. H. Sheets; Secretary, George H. Danner; Treasurer, Charles H. Rall.

Directors—George Best, W. H. H. Sheets, Charles E. Golden, George H. Danner, Charles R Rall, Joseph K. Smith, William Kretz, Marcellus C. Adams.

Main office, Twenty-fifth and Railroad streets, Pittsburg. Annual meeting, last Tuesday in April, at Pittsburg.

## BIGELOW CARPET CO.

A corporation formed under the laws of Massachusetts, December 9, 1899. The company is a consolidation of the following companies:

Bigelow Carpet Co. Lowell Manufacturing Co.

The mills of the company are located at Clinton and Lowell, Mass.

Stock......Par $100..........................Authorized, $4,030,000......Issued, $4,030,000

Stock is transferred at the office of the company, Boston.

Dividends of 2½ per cent. each are payable semi-annually, January 10 and July 10.

The company has no funded debt.

President, Arthur T. Lyman; Treasurer, Charles F. Fairbanks.

Directors—Arthur T. Lyman, Charles F. Fairbanks, Alexander S. Wheeler, James H. Beal, Edward W. Hutchins, John Sloane, Jacob Rogers.

Corporate and main office, 199 Washington street, Boston; New York office, 141 Fifth avenue. Annual meeting, second Wednesday in March, at Boston.

## BINGHAM CONSOLIDATED MINING & SMELTING CO.

A corporation formed under the laws of Maine, April 5, 1901. This company was the successor to the Bingham Copper & Gold Mining Co., a New Jersey company formed in 1898. See MANUAL for 1901. The present company acquired the $2,000,000 stock and the property of the old company, together with a number of adjoining mines and claims, and the Copper Belt Railway, which connects the Rio Grande Western Railway. The properties are situated near Bingham, Utah, and comprise mines, which though formerly worked for gold comprise large deposits of high grade copper ore.

Stock......Par $50.......................... Authorized, $10,000,000......Issued, $7,500,000

The stock is full paid and non-assessable. Transfer Agent, Federal Trust Co., Boston. Registrar, Massachusetts National Bank, Boston.

The stock of the Bingham Copper & Gold Mining Co. consisted of 200,000 shares, par value $10 each, or $2,000,000. In the formation of the new company $5,000,000 of the new stock was offered in exchange for the old, or 1 of new for 2 shares of old stock. The plan also provided for raising $1,000,000 in cash for improvements and other purposes.

President, Edward L. White; Secretary, Herbert W. Wesson; Treasurer, O. E. Weller, Boston; Superintendent, Duncan McVichie, Bingham, Utah.

Directors—Joseph A. Coram, O. P. Posey, E. L. White, C. K. McCornick, John W. Weeks, O. E. Weller, W. S. McCornick, William Bayly, L. T. Trull, P. S. Kimberly, W. F. Hammett.

Main office, 60 State street, Boston. Annual meeting, third Wednesday in April.

## BINGHAMTON GAS WORKS

(Controlled by the American Light & Traction Co.)

This company owns and operates, under a 50-year franchise, the gas works of Binghamton, N. Y. (population 45,000), and has about 36 miles of mains. Price of gas, $1.40 per 1,000 cubic feet.

This company is controlled by the American Light & Traction Co. See statement of that company.

Stock......Par $100..............................Authorized, $750,000......Issued, $450,000

Transfer Agents, Emerson McMillin & Co., 40 Wall street, New York.

FUNDED DEBT.

1st mort., 5 per cent. gold, due 1938, April and Oct.............................. $528,000

The 1st mortgage is for $750,000. Trustee of mortgage, Central Trust Co., New York.

In August, 1901, the stockholders of this company were offered in exchange for their shares $26.38 in preferred, and $7.91 in common stock of the American Light & Traction Co., a large majority accepting these terms.

President, Emerson McMillin, New York; Vice-President, James W. Manier, Binghamton, N. Y.; Secretary, W. F. Douthirt, New York; Treasurer, Robert W. Manier, Binghamton, N. Y.

Directors—Emerson McMillin, Charles C. Jackson, George F. O'Neil, James W. Manier, C. M. Stone, S. H. Hirshman, G. W. Dunn, W. G. Phelps, Junius M. Stevens.

Main office, Binghamton, N. Y.

## BINGHAMTON RAILWAY CO.

A corporation formed under the laws of New York, September 30, 1901. The company is a consolidation of the Binghamton Railroad Co., Binghamton, Lestershire & Union Railroad, and their constituent companies, comprising all the street railways in the city of Binghamton, N. Y. The company operates 43 miles of electric railways, and serves a population of over 50,000.

Stock......Par $100 ..........................Authorized, $1,150,000......Issued, $700,000

The company has no preferred stock. Stock is transferred at the office of the company. The company paid 2 per cent. on its stock in 1900, 1901 and 1902.

FUNDED DEBT.

1st con. mort., 5 per cent., gold, due Nov., 1931, May and Nov........................ $206,000

Of the consolidated mortgage of the Binghamton Railway Co., $1,301,000 can only be issued against the retirement of corresponding amount of prior lien bonds. Trustee of the mortgage and agent for the payment of interest, Fidelity Trust Co., Buffalo. Interest is also paid by the Seaboard National Bank, New York. After 1911 bonds may be drawn at 110.

EARNINGS.

| | Gross. | Net. | Charges. | Surplus. |
|---|---|---|---|---|
| 1900.................................... | $176,210 | $79,108 | $57,412 | $21,696 |
| 1901.................................... | 204,079 | 93,525 | 62,442 | 31,083 |
| 1902.................................... | 211,127 | 88,967 | 65,647 | 23,314 |

The earnings for 1900 include those of all the constituent companies now merged in this company.

President, George T. Rogers; Vice-President, George E. Green; Secretary, Joseph M. Johnson; Treasurer, H. C. Hardie; General Manager, J. P. E. Clark.

Directors—George T. Rogers, C. J. Knapp, John B. Rogers, Joseph M. Johnson, George E. Green, F. E. Ross, T. J. Keenan, T. S. Rogers, Stoddard Hammond, J. P. E. Clark, Binghamton, N. Y.; J. W. Cunningham, New York.

Main office, Binghamton, N. Y.

## BIRMINGHAM RAILWAY, LIGHT & POWER CO.

A corporation formed in 1899 under a special legislative charter granted by the State of Alabama. The company has full power to acquire, lease and operate railway, gas and electric light and power plants. It has acquired all the facilities of that description in and around Birmingham, Ala. It owns and operates a street railway system of 90 miles connecting Birmingham, Bessemer, Ensley, Pratt City, Avondale and other towns and villages in the vicinity. It has electric light and power plants at Birmingham, Bessemer, Ensley, Woodlawn, Avondale and Pratt City, Ala. It also owns and operates the gas works at Birmingham. The company began to operate the properties July 1, 1901.

Stock....Par $100.....Authorized { com., $3,500,000; pref., 1,500,000 } Issued { com., $3,500,000; pref., 1,500,000 } $5,000,000

The preferred stock is 6 per cent., cumulative, and has a preference in regard to the assets of the company over the common.

Transfer Agents, Old Colony Trust Co., Boston; Commercial National Bank, New Orleans. Registrars, American Loan & Trust Co., Boston; Isidore Newman & Sons, New Orleans.

FUNDED DEBT.

1st mort., 5 per cent., due July, 1951, Jan. and July.............................. $5,561,000

The Old Colony Trust Co., Boston, is trustee of the mortgage and agent for the payment of interest on the bonds. The authorized issue of bonds is $6,000,000. The company had on July 1, 1901, $1,000,000 of bonds in its treasury to be used for improvements and extensions, which in January, 1902, were sold by Ladenburg, Thalmann & Co., New York, by subscription. It also held $1,000,000 more of the funds for improvements up to 75 per cent. of the cost thereof, of which on January 1, 1903, there remained in the company's treasury $439,000.

EARNINGS.

| | Gross. | Net. | Charges. | Pref. Div. | Surplus. |
|---|---|---|---|---|---|
| 1901 (6 months)................. | $479,590 | $237,120 | $138,382 | $45,000 | $53,737 |
| 1902 (year)...................... | 1,076,767 | 493,217 | 293,943 | 90,000 | 109,273 |

The dividend periods for the preferred stock are January and July. The first semi-annual dividend of 3 per cent. on the preferred was paid January 1, 1902.

President, Robert Jemison; Vice-Presidents, W. A. Walker, G. H. Davis; Secretary, Joseph P. Ross; Treasurer and Auditor, C. O. Simpson, Birmingham, Ala.

Directors—Gordon Abbott, Boston; J. K. Newman, New Orleans; H. M. Atkinson, Atlanta, Ga.; A. M. Shook, N. Baxter, Jr., Nashville, Tenn.; W. A. Walker, R. H. Pearson, Alexander T. Lowden, W. H. Kettig, T. T. Hillman, M. V. Joseph, N. E. Barker, B. F. Roden, Robert Jemison, G. B. McCormick, G. H. Davis, Birmingham, Ala.; S. H. Marsh, New York.

Main office, 2104 First avenue, Birmingham, Ala. Annual meeting, first Tuesday in February, at Birmingham.

## BIRMINGHAM REALTY CO.

A corporation formed under the laws of Alabama, December 16, 1899. The purpose of the company is to buy and sell real estate. It acquired the business and property of the Elyton Co. of Birmingham, Ala.

Stock....Par $100....Authorized { com., $1,300,000 / pref., 700,000 } Issued { com., $1,300,000 / pref., 700,000 } $2,000,000

The preferred stock is 4 per cent., non-cumulative, and has a preference as to assets. Stock is transferred at the office of the company. Registrar, Birmingham Trust & Savings Co., Birmingham, Ala.

FUNDED DEBT.

Prior lien, 5 per cent., gold, due 1919, July and Jan.................................. $310,000
1st mort., 5 per cent., gold, due 1930, July and Jan.................................. 400,500

Total.............................................................. ........ $710,500

The authorized amount of the 1st mortgage is $550,000 and of the prior lien $550,000. Trustee and agent for the payment of interest, Union Trust Co., New York.

President, A. Leslie Fulenwider, Birmingham, Ala.; Vice-President, William Halls, Jr., New York; Secretary and Treasurer, Frank Norris; Assistant Secretary and Assistant Treasurer, E. B. Daffin, Birmingham, Ala.

Directors—A. Leslie Fulenwider, James Bowron, A. T. London, David Roberts, Culpepper Exum, John M. Caldwell, Birmingham, Ala.; William Halls, Jr., James T. Woodward, James M. Donald, New York.

Corporate and main office, Birmingham, Ala.

## E. W. BLISS CO.

A corporation formed under the laws of West Virginia in 1892. The company succeeded the E. W. Bliss Co., Limited, an English corporation, which in turn succeeded E. W. Bliss Co., a New York corporation. The business was formerly carried on by E. W. Bliss, Bliss & Williams and Mays & Bliss, the latter having established it some forty years before. The company manufactures dies, presses and other specialties for making sheet metal goods, and is the exclusive manufacturer of the Whitehead torpedo for the United States Government. It also manufactures armor-piercing and semi-armor-piercing projectiles, common shell and shrapnel for the army and navy, and gears, pressed pinions, etc. It has a very large export trade in the various specialties of its manufacture, having agencies in many cities abroad. The different properties of the company cover an area of 185¾ city lots, equal to 9⅝ city blocks of 200 feet square, and include large machine shops, foundries, etc. The plant and other assets, including patents, are valued at over $3,500,000.

In February, 1902, this company acquired the stock of the United States Projectile Co.

Stock....Par $100... Authorized { com., $1,000,000 / pref., 1,000,000 } Issued { com., $1,000,000 / pref., 1,000,000 } $2,000,000

The preferred stock is 8 per cent., cumulative.

Stock is transferred at the company's office, Brooklyn, N. Y. Registrar, Long Island Loan & Trust Co., Brooklyn, N. Y.

Regular quarterly dividends are paid upon both common and preferred, the rate upon the common having been increased in 1899 from 2 per cent., or 8 per cent. per annum, to 2½ per cent., or 10 per cent. per annum, which has since been the regular rate. The dividends are paid quarterly, January, April, July and October.

FUNDED DEBT.

Mort., 6 per cent., due 1932 ........................................................ $750,000

The bonds were issued in 1902 for the purchase of the stock of the United States Projectile Co.

President, Eliphalet W. Bliss; Vice-President, William A. Porter; 2d Vice-President, Arthur T. Porter; Secretary, Howard C. Seaman; Treasurer, Lucian H. Gould.

Directors—Eliphalet W. Bliss, James W. Lane, William A. Porter, Seth L. Keeney, Walter B. Bailey, John J. Flynn, Arthur T. Porter, Frank C. B. Page, Arthur Wilzin, George H. Prentiss, Frederick W. Moss, Chauncey Marshall, Joseph C. Willetts.

Main office, 17 Adams street, Brooklyn, N. Y. Annual meeting, third Monday in July.

## BON AIR COAL & IRON CO.

A corporation formed under the laws of Maine, July 10, 1902. The purpose of the company is to mine ore and coal, make coke and pig iron, operate saw mills and deal in lumber and merchandise. The company acquired the following companies:

Buffalo Iron Co. Bon Air Coal, Land & Lumber Co.

The company owns 75,000 acres of iron ore land, 3 iron furnaces and 40,000 acres of coal land with 2 mining plants and a coke plant, in Tennessee.

Stock....Par $100....Authorized { com., $2,500,000 / pref., 2,500,000 } Issued { com., $1,880,265 / pref., 1,880,265 } $3,760,530

The preferred stock is 6 per cent., cumulative. Transfer Agent and Registrar, Fourth National Bank, Nashville, Tenn.

A quarterly dividend of 1½ per cent. was paid on the preferred stock in October, 1902, and a second quarterly dividend of 1½ per cent. in January, 1903. The original Bon Air Coal, Land & Lumber Co., paid dividends of 6 per cent. annually. Dividend payments are made in January, April, July and October.

FUNDED DEBT.

| | |
|---|---|
| Buffalo Iron Co., 1st mort., 5 per cent., gold, due Oct., 1925, April and Oct......... | $254,733 |
| Bon Air Coal, L. & L. Co., 1st mort., 6 p. c., gold, due July, 1928, Jan. and July... | 180,000 |
| Total................................................................ | $434,733 |

The total authorized 1st mortgage of the Buffalo Iron Co. was $350,000. Trustee of the mortgage, Nashville Trust Co., Nashville, Tenn. Agent for the payment of interest, Fourth National Bank, Nashville, Tenn. The total amount of the authorized 1st mortgage of the Bon Air Coal, Land & Lumber Co., was $200,000. Trustee of the mortgage, Union Bank & Trust Co., Nashville, Tenn. Agent for the payment of interest, Fourth National Bank, Nashville, Tenn.

In the six months ending December 31, 1902, the gross earnings were $92,557; net, $80,209: interest charges, $9,957; dividends, $52,531; surplus, $17,719.

President, John P. Williams; Vice-President and General Manager, J. M. Overton; Secretary and Assistant Treasurer, C. Cooper; Treasurer, William C. Dibrell, Nashville, Tenn.

Directors—John P. Williams, Jesse M. Overton, William C. Dibrell, Samnel J. Keith, Mathew M. Gardner, J. Horton Fall, Thomas M. Steger, Edgar Jones, Augustus H. Robinson, Shade Murray, Nashville, Tenn.; Jacob McG. Dickinson, Chicago.

Corporate and main office, Arcade Building, Nashville, Tenn.; branch offices, Bon Air and Mannie, Tenn. Annual meeting, second Tuesday in March, at Augusta, Me.

## THE BOOKLOVERS LIBRARY

A corporation formed under the laws of New Jersey in June, 1900. The purpose of the company is the establishment and maintenence of circulating libraries in the principal cities of the

United States, Canada and England, also on railway trains of the United States, and on steamships sailing between United States ports and ports of other countries.

Stock......Par $10..........................Authorized, $2,600,000. ....Issued, $1,900,000

The company has no preferred stock and no funded debt.

Registrar, The New Jersey Co-operative Guaranty & Trust Co., Camden, N. J.

Regular quarterly dividends of 2½ per cent. were paid from August 1, 1900, to February, 1902. Semi-annual dividends of 5 per cent were paid August 15, 1902, and February 15, 1903.

President, Seymour Eaton; Vice-President, W. Frank English; Secretary and Treasurer, John E. Bryant, Philadelphia.

Directors—Seymour Eaton, W. Frank English, John E. Bryant, R. G. Kennedy, George W. Warren, R. Thornton Eaton, F. W. Speins, William P. Hood, George H. B. Martin.

Main office, 1323 Walnut street, Philadelphia; New York office, 29 West Thirty-third street. Branch offices, Boston, Chicago, San Francisco, Montreal, and London, England. Annual meeting, second Tuesday in October, at Philadelphia.

## RICHARD BORDEN MANUFACTURING CO.

A corporation formed under the laws of Massachusetts in 1871, for the purpose of manufacturing cotton cloths. The mills of the company are at Fall River, Mass., and have a capacity of 89,328 spindles and 2,602 looms.

Stock......Par $100..............................Authorized, $800,000......Issued, $800,000

The company has no preferred stock and no funded debt.

Dividends in recent years have been at the rate of 6 per cent. per annum and are paid quarterly 1½ per cent. each in January, April, July and October.

President, Edward P. Borden; Clerk, Treasurer and General Manager, Richard B. Borden, Fall River, Mass.

Directors—Edward P. Borden, Philadelphia; Jerome C. Borden, Richard P. Borden, Rufus W. Bassett, Richard B. Borden, Fall River, Mass.

Corporate and main office, Fall River, Mass. Annual meeting, second Tuesday in November, at Fall River, Mass.

## BORDER CITY MANUFACTURING CO.

A corporation formed under the laws of Massachusetts in 1880 for the purpose of manufacturing cotton goods. The mills of the company are at Fall River, Mass., and have 119,812 spindles and 2,937 looms.

Stock......Par $100..........................Authorized, $1,000,000......Issued, $1,000,000

The company has no preferred stock. Stock is transferred and registered at the office of the company.

In 1901 the dividends were 6½ per cent. In 1902 6 per cent. was paid, the dividends being 1½ per cent. quarterly in January, April, July and October.

FUNDED DEBT.

1st mort., 5 per cent., due 1930, Jan. and July........................................$500,000

The bonds outstanding are the total amount authorized. Trustee of the mortgage and agent for the payment of interest, The B. M. C. Durfee Safe Deposit & Trust Co., Fall River, Mass.

President, John S. Brayton; Treasurer, Edward L. Anthony, Fall River, Mass.

Directors, John S. Brayton, Charles J. Holmes, Thomas E. Brayton, Edward L. Anthony, Fall River, Mass; Charles E. Barney, H. C. W. Mosher, New Bedford, Mass.; Francis A. Foster, Boston.

Corporate and main office, Weaver street, Fall River, Mass. Annual meeting, first Wednesday in November, at Fall River, Mass.

## BOSTON & MONTANA CONSOLIDATED COPPER AND SILVER MINING CO.

(Controlled by Amalgamated Copper Co.)

A Montana corporation owning and operating copper mines and smelters at Butte and Great Falls in that State.

Stock .....Par $25............................Authorized, $3,750,000......Issued, $3,750,000

Stock is transferred at the company's office, Boston.

The company has paid dividends since 1888, the total amount thus paid to March, 1901, being $22,475,000. In 1899 paid $36 per share; in 1900 paid $43 per share. In 1901 the dividends were 140 per cent., or $35 per share. In January, 1902, $10 per share was paid, but the April, 1902, was reduced to $2 per share.

FUNDED DEBT.

1st mort., 7 per cent., 3d issue, due 1902-1907, May and Nov........................ $600,000

In June, 1901, the Amalgamated Copper Co. acquired $3,447,200 of this company's capital stock by exchanging 4 shares of its own stock for 1 share of this company's stock.

| EARNINGS. | Gross. | Net. |
|---|---|---|
| 1895 | $4,999,231 | $2,083,542 |
| 1896 | 6,414,347 | 2,674,350 |
| 1897 | 6,949,097 | 2,882,993 |
| 1898 | 7,448,600 | 3,431,843 |
| 1899 | 11,257,280 | 5,979,844 |
| 1900 | 13,242,576 | 7,019,781 |

In 1895 surplus over dividends paid ($1,050,000) amounted to $1,033,542. In 1896, dividends, $1,500,000; surplus, $1,174,350. In 1897, dividends, $1,800,000; maturing bonds and real estate purchased, $338,924; surplus, $744,074. In 1898, dividends, $2,400,000; surplus, $1,031,843. In 1899, dividends ($36 per share), $5,400,000; surplus, $579,844. In 1900 dividends ($43 per share), $6,450,000; surplus, $569,781.

President, Henry H. Rogers.

Directors—Henry H. Rogers, William G. Rockefeller, Frederic P. Olcott, James Stillman, P. J. McIntosh, Anson R. Flower, Robert Bacon, A. C. Burrage.

Main office, Butte, Mont.; Boston office, 199 Washington street. Annual meeting, last Thursday in April, at Butte, Mont.

## BOSTON & PHILADELPHIA STEAMSHIP CO.

A corporation chartered by the State of Massachusetts in 1902 under the title of the Massachusetts Steamship Co., the name being subsequently changed to the present title. The company was formed to recapitalize the old Boston & Philadelphia Steamship Co., also a Massachusetts corporation. See below for organization of the old company. The company operates steamship lines between Boston and Philadelphia and between the latter city and Providence and Fall River. The company has valuable wharf properties in Philadelphia and Providence. Its fleet consists of 7 steamers, aggregating 12,000 tons.

Stock......Par $100..........................Authorized, $1,500,000......Issued, $1,500,000

Stock is transferred at the office of the company, Boston.

The old company had $500,000 of 6 per cent. preferred stock and $212,600 of common stock. The old stockholders subscribed at par for $783,860 of new stock. Dividends on the old preferred were paid semi-annually, 3 per cent. each, in April (1) and October. Dividends of 6 per cent. were paid on the old common stock, the payment being annual, April 1.

The new company began on October 1, 1902, the payment of quarterly dividends of $1.50 per share, or 1½ per cent., being at the rate of 6 per cent. per annum, the dividend periods being January, April, July and October.

President, Alfred Winsor; Treasurer, A. C. Baldwin; General Manager, F. P. Wing.

Main office, 131 State street, Boston. Annual meeting, second Wednesday in April, at Boston.

## BOSTON BELTING CO.

A corporation formed under the laws of Massachusetts in 1845 for the manufacture and sale of mechanical rubber goods. The plant of the company is at Roxbury, Mass.

Stock......Par $100..........................Authorized, $1,000,000......Issued, $1,000,000

The company has no preferred stock and no funded debt. Stock is transferred at the office of the company, Boston.

Dividends at the rate of 8 per cent. per annum are paid quarterly, January, April, July and October.

The following is the company's balance sheet, October 1, 1902:

| ASSETS. | | LIABILITIES. | |
|---|---|---|---|
| Land | $75,000 | Capital stock | $1,000,000 |
| Buildings | 25,000 | Profit and loss | 198,505 |
| Machinery | 50,000 | Reserve for depreciation | 47,623 |
| Cash and debts receivable | 989,319 | Reserve | 700,000 |
| Merchandise, raw and manufactured | 803,258 | | |
| Patent rights | 100 | | |
| Miscellaneous | 3,451 | | |
| Total | $1,946,128 | Total | $1,946,128 |

President, James Pierce; General Manager, James Bennett Forsyth; Assistant Manager, George H. Forsyth; Clerk, Edward Upham; Treasurer, J. H. D. Smith, Boston.

Directors—James Bennett Forsyth, George A. Miner, George H. Forsyth, Charles H. Moseley, J. H. D. Smith, Boston; Lewis M. Crane, Brookline, Mass.; James Pierce, Malden, Mass.

Main office, 256 Devonshire street, Boston. Annual meeting, first Monday in December, at Boston.

## BOSTON ELEVATED RAILWAY CO.

A corporation formed under the laws of Massachusetts, by act of the Legislature, approved June 10, 1897. The company acquired the right to build and operate a large mileage of elevated roads in the vicinity of the city of Boston. The first section of 6 miles was opened in June, 1901. The roads are operated with electric power. In 1902 arrangements were made with the city by which this company is to lease the Washington Street Subway. The company leased the West End Street Railway until June, 1922. See statement of that company. Total operated surface lines, 119 miles; elevated lines, 6.6 miles.

Stock......Par $100........................Authorized, $10,000,000......Issued, $10,000,000

The company has no preferred stock or funded debt.

Transfer Agent, Old Colony Trust Co., Boston. Registrar, American Loan & Trust Co., Boston.

The company began the payment of dividends with 2¼ per cent. in August, 1898. In 1899 5¼ per cent. was paid; in 1900, 4¼ per cent., and in 1901, 5¾ per cent. The dividends in 1902 were 6 per cent., or 3 per cent. each, semi-annual, in February and August.

EARNINGS.

Year ending September 30.

| | Gross. | Net. | Charges. | Surplus |
|---|---|---|---|---|
| 1898-99 | $9,671,440 | $2,928,986 | $2,615,388 | $313,598 |
| 1899-00 | 10,141,209 | 3,408,884 | 2,932,839 | 476,045 |
| 1900-01 | 10,792,993 | 3,532,898 | 2,896,350 | 663,539 |
| 1901-02 | 11,321,030 | 3,458,458 | 2,836,560 | 621,898 |

In 1899-1900 the number of passengers carried was 201,000,000. The surplus over dividends for that year was $138,545. In 1900-01, passengers, 213,700,000; surplus over dividends, $61,539; in 1901-02, passengers, 222,484,811; surplus, $21,898.

President, William A. Bancroft, Vice-President, Charles S. Sergeant; Treasurer, William Hooper; Secretary, John T. Burnett; Auditor, H. L. Wilson.

Directors—W. A. Gaston, F. H. Peabody, W. S. Spaulding, Samuel Carr, Frederick Ayer, J. M. Prendergast, T. Jefferson Coolidge, Jr., William A. Bancroft, Robert Winsor, N. W. Rice, W. S. Swan, John J. Bright.

Main office, 101 Milk street, Boston. Annual meeting, first Monday in January.

## BOSTON STEAMSHIP CO.

The company was originally a voluntary association formed in 1900. It was incorporated by the State of Massachusetts under the same title in 1902, and the old stock, which was $650,000 common and the same amount of preferred, were exchanged share for share for the new stock. The object of the organization is the ownership and operation of ocean steamships. The company at the time of its formation contracted with the Maryland Steel Co. for the construction of two freight steamers of about 11,500 tons capacity each. The company's fleet is operated on the Pacific Ocean, from Puget Sound ports to the Orient, in connection with the Great Northern Railway and the Northern Pacific Railway Cos.

Stock......Par $100.....Authorized { com., $755,000; pref., 755,000 } Issued { com., $755,000; pref., 755,000 } $1,510,000

The preferred stock is 6 per cent., non-cumulative.

Stock is transferred at the office of the company, Boston.

FUNDED DEBT.

1st mort., sinking fund, gold, 5 per cent., due 1922, Jan. (1) and July...... .......... $650,000

The 1st mortgage bonds are subject to call at 110 and interest. The bonds may be registered as to principal.

President, Alfred Winsor; Treasurer, A. C. Baldwin; Managing Agent, Frank Waterhouse.

Main office, 131 State street, Boston.

## BOSTON SUBURBAN ELECTRIC COMPANIES

A voluntary association formed under the laws of Massachusetts in November, 1901. The company holds the entire capital stock of the following companies:

Commonwealth Ave. Street Railway Co.
Lexington & Boston Street Railway Co.
Newton Street Railway Co.
Newton & Boston Street Railway Co.
Wellesley & Boston Street Railway Co.
Waltham Gas Light Co.
Norembega Park Co.

The constituent companies operate about 90 miles of track and numerous extensions and new lines are proposed.

Stock.......Authorized { com., 30,000 shares; pref., 30,000 shares } Issued { com., 29,992 shares; pref., 29,970 shares } 59,962 shares

Neither the common nor the preferred stock of this orgization has any par value.

The preferred shares are cumulative and are entitled to dividends of $4 per share each year, dividend periods being January, April, July and October. In case of liquidation the preferred shareholders are entitled to $100 per share and accrued dividends. The common shareholders participate *pro rata* in the remaining assets.

FUNDED DEBT OF CONTROLLED COMPANIES.

| | |
|---|---|
| Commonwealth Avenue St. Ry., 1st mort., 5 per cent., due Feb., 1916, Feb. and Aug.. | $75,000 |
| Lexington & Boston St. Ry., 1st mort., 4½ per cent., due April, 1920, April and Oct.. | 350,000 |
| Newton St. Ry., 1st mort., cur. 5 per cent. due July, 1912, Jan. and July.............. | 215,000 |
| Newton & Boston St. Ry., 1st mort., 5 per cent., due July, 1912, Jan. and July....... | 200,000 |
| Waltham Gas Light Co., 2d mort., due Sept., 1904, March and Sept................... | 19,500 |
| Total............ | $859,500 |

The authorized bond issue of the Lexington & Boston Street Railway Co. is $500,000, of which $150,000 are reserved for extensions. Trustee of the mortgage and agent for the payment of interest, Beacon Trust Co., Boston. The bonds are subject to call before July 1, 1905, at 110, then until July 1, 1910, and thereafter at 105.

The authorized bond issue of the Newton & Boston Street Railway Co. is $500,000. Trustee of the mortgage and agent for the payment of interest, American Loan & Trust Co., which is also trustee and agent for the Newton Street Railway Co. 1st mortgage.

Trustee of the mortgage of the Commonwealth Avenue Street Railway Co. and agent for the payment of interest, International Trust Co., Boston.

President, Adams D. Claflin; Vice-President, William F. Hammett; Secretary, Jerome C. Smith; Treasurer Frederick H. Lewis.

Directors—Adams D. Claflin, William F. Hammett, Winthrop Coffin, James L. Richards, Sidney Harwood, Newton, Mass.; Alden E. Viles, Frank W. Remick, Boston.

Main office, 797 Washington street, Newtonville, Mass. Annual meeting, Thursday after the first Monday in December.

## THE BOSTON TERMINAL CO.

A company incorporated by Act of Massachusetts Legislature in June, 1896, for the purpose of building and maintaining a passenger station for all the railroads entering Boston on the south, including the Boston & Albany, New York, New Haven & Hartford, Boston & Providence, Old Colony and New England.

Terminal is at the corner of Summer street and Atlantic avenue, occupying the site of the old New England terminal with other property acquired for the purpose, parts of certain streets being closed by the municipality and new ones opened. The whole area covered is some 40 acres. The new train shed is 568 feet wide by 720 in length and contains 28 tracks. There are also four loop tracks on a basement floor for suburban trains. Buildings were opened to use in January, 1899.

Stock......Par $100..............................Authorized, $500,000......Issued, $500,000

The stock is held, one-fifth each, by the five companies, which make use of the new terminal. They agree to pay as rental, in monthly installments, a sum equal to expenses, charges, interest on bonds and 4 per cent. on stock. They also assume joint liability for any deficiency in case of foreclosure.

FUNDED DEBT.

1st mort., 3½ per cent., due Feb., 1947, Feb. and Aug.............................. $14,000,000

The 1st mortgage bonds were originally 2-year 3½ per cent. notes, due August 1, 1898, which were exchanged for present bonds. Interest on registered bonds is payable quarterly, February, May, August and November. Trustee of mortgage, Old Colony Trust Co., Boston.

Terminal company purchased the property of the New England Railroad at foot of Summer street for $1,923,000.

Chairman, John M. Hall, New Haven, Conn.; Vice-Chairman, Samuel Hoar; Treasurer, Austin W. Adams; Clerk, James W. Perkins; Manager, John C. Sanborn, Boston.

Trustees—John M. Hall, Charles L. Lovering, Royal C. Taft, Samuel Hoar, F. S. Curtis.

Main office, Terminal Station, Summer street, Boston.

## BOSTON TOWBOAT CO.

A corporation formed under the laws of Massachusetts in 1873. The purpose of the company is the conduct of a shipping, transportation and towage business. It owns and operates a considerable fleet of steamships, tugs and other vessels. Several of its vessels are engaged in the Pacific trade in conjunction with the steamers of the Boston Steamship Co.

Stock......Par $100..........................Authorized, $1,500,000.... .Issued, $1,250,000

The company has no preferred stock. Transfers of stock are made at the company's office at Boston. The company has no funded debt.

Prior to 1893, 8 per cent. was paid annually on the stock. Since then the annual dividends have been 6 per cent. In 1900-01 an extra dividend of 5 per cent. was paid. Dividends are paid quarterly in January, April, July and October.

In the year ending March 31, 1902, the net earnings of the company were $167,746.46, and the dividends paid $67,500; balance which was credited to depreciation of plant, $100,246.46.

The company's balance sheet, March 31, 1902, showed total assets, $1,416,911; surplus, $40,000.

President, Alfred Winsor; Manager, T. I. Winsor; Superintendent, W. J. Flynn; Treasurer, W. F. Humphrey, Boston.

Directors—Alfred Winsor, A. Davis Weld, Boston; Lincoln N. Kinnicutt, Worcester, Mass.; George H. Allen, Salem, Mass.; W. D. Winsor, Philadelphia.

Main office, 131 State street, Boston; New York office, 70 South street; Philadelphia office, 338 South Delaware avenue; Western agency, Burke Building, Seattle, Wash. Annual meeting, third Tuesday in April, at Boston.

## BOSTON WHARF CO.

A corporation formed under the laws of Massachusetts in 1836. The company owns an extensive and valuable property in Boston, comprising wharves, warehouses, office and other buildings and considerable real estate. The property owned by the company on December 31, 1900, was about 1,854,000 square feet, the assessed valuation of its land in 1900 being $2,873,600, while the valuation of its buildings was $582,000.

Stock......Par $20..........................Authorized, $1,000,000......Issued, $1,000,000

Stock is transferred at 38 State street, Boston.

Dividends of 12 per cent. are paid on the stock, the payments being half-yearly, 6 per cent. each, June 30 and December 31. In 1901 an extra dividend of 1 per cent. was paid, making 13 per cent. for the year and the same was the rate in 1902.

In 1901 the receipts of the company from rentals, wharfage, and storage and interest were $209,584; expenses, insurance and taxes, $64,584; repairs and depreciation fund, $15,000; dividends, $130,000; balance surplus, $250,000. In 1902 the receipts were $181,785.

The company had, on December 31, 1901, a surplus of $2,500,000, a credit to profit and loss account of $250,000, and a repair and depreciation fund of $134,632. It held at that date notes secured by mortgages amounting to $220,000.

President, Edwin F. Atkins; Vice-President, Charles Theodore Russell; Treasurer, Joseph B. Russell; Clerk, Charles Lowell.

Directors—Edwin F. Atkins, Waldron Bates, Edmund D. Codman, Arthur Hobart, Charles Lowell, J. Willard Pierce, Solon O. Richardson, Charles Theodore Russell, Joseph B. Russell, Moses Williams.

Treasurer's office, 114 State street, Boston. Annual meeting, first Tuesday in February.

## BOSTON WOVEN HOSE & RUBBER CO.

'ion formed under the laws of Maine, May 17, 1899. The purpose of the company e of mechanical rubber goods, bicycle tires, cotton and linen hose, cotton belts It has a factory at Cambridgeport, Mass.

o........Authorized { com., $450,000 / pref., 750,000 } Issued { com., $450,000 / pref., 750,000 } $1,200,000

The preferred stock is 6 per cent. cumulative. Dividends are payable semi-annually, in June and December.

The company has no funded debt.

President, J. N. Smith; Vice-President, B. F. Spinney; Secretary, J. Q. Bennett; Treasurer, Henry B. Sprague.

Directors—J. N. Smith, B. F. Spinney, Henry B. Sprague, J. Q. Bennett, W. A. Bullard.

Main office, Hampshire street, Cambridgeport, Mass.

## BRIDGEPORT HYDRAULIC CO.

A corporation formed under the laws of Connecticut in 1857. The original purpose of the company is to supply water to the city of Bridgeport, Conn., and it has extended its operations to Stratford, Fairfield and vicinity. The company owns reservoirs, pipe lines, pumping stations, etc.

Stock......Par $100..........................Authorized, $3,000,000......Issued, $1,500,000

The company has no preferred stock and no funded debt. The authorized stock was increased in 1903 from $1,500,000 to $3,000,000 and it was understood that $750,000 new stock would be issued early in 1903 to retire the company's floating debt.

Stock is transferred at the office of the company.

In 1901 an annual dividend of 8 per cent. was paid. Dividends are payable January 15 and July 15.

In the six months ending November 30, 1901, the gross earnings were $110,518; net earnings, $90,000.

President, Charles Sherwood; Secretary, Walter S. Wilmot; Treasurer, T. B. De Forest, Bridgeport, Conn.

Directors—I. De Ver Warner, L. C. Warner, D. H. Warner, W. B. Hincks, S. H. Wheeler, Charles Sherwood, T. B. De Forest, W. D. Bishop, Jr.

Corporate and main office, 35 John street, Bridgeport, Conn. Annual meeting, second Monday in June, at Bridgeport.

## THE BRITISH COLUMBIA COPPER CO., LIMITED

A corporation formed under the laws of West Virginia in 1898. The company owns copper claims at Greenwood, British Columbia, and is actively engaged in developing them. It has erected a smelter on its property, additions to which with a large converting plant are planned. The Canadian Pacific Railway has built a branch line to this company's mines and smelters.

Stock......Par $5............................Authorized, $2,000,000......Issued, $1,250,000

The stock is full paid and non-assessable. In 1901 the stock was increased by 50,000 shares, which were sold to provide for enlargement of the company's plant and smelter. In 1903 a further increase in the stock to $2,000,000 was authorized, the new stock to be used to defray the cost of additions and improvements.

Transfer Agent, Old Colony Trust Co., Boston. Registrar, The New England Loan & Trust Co., Boston.

President, F. L. Underwood; Vice-President, F. L. Sommer; Secretary, R. H. Eggleston; Treasurer, C. E. Laidlaw, New York.

Directors—F. L. Underwood, P. G. Bartlett, R. H. Eggleston, J. D. Kernan, C. E. Laidlaw, C. H. Ropes, W. H. Thomas, F. L. Sommer, C. A. Starbuck, New York.

Main office, 31 Nassau street, New York. Annual meeting, second Tuesday in February.

## THE BROAD-EXCHANGE CO.

A corporation formed under the laws of New Jersey, May 2, 1900. The company built and owns the Broad-Exchange Building at Broad street and Exchange place, New York, one of the largest office buildings in the city. A controlling interest in the company is held by the Alliance Realty Co.

Stock...Par $100...Authorized { com., $2,000,000 / pref., 2,000,000 } Issued { com., $2,000,000 / pref., 2,000,000 } $4,000,000

The preferred stock is 6 per cent., cumulative; dividends payable quarterly, January (1), April, July and October.

Transfer Agent, Knickerbocker Trust Co., New York.

FUNDED DEBT.

1st mort., 4½ per cent., due 1904, May and Nov.............................. .... $3,500,000

All the bonds are held by the Equitable Life Insurance Company.

President, Walter T. Rosen; Vice-President, H. S. Black; Secretary, Edwin M. Bulkley; Treasurer and Assistant Secretary, John Carlsen.

Directors—Walter T. Rosen, H. S. Black, James J. Higginson, Robert E. Dowling, F. S. Smithers, William A. Read, Edwin M. Bulkley.

Main office, 25 Broad street, New York. Annual meeting, first Monday in May.

## BROADWAY BUILDING CO.

A corporation formed under the laws of New York in 1901 for the purpose of erecting and purchasing buildings and dealing in and renting real estate. The company owns the eighteen-story office building on the southeast corner of Broadway and Maiden lane, New York, covering a lot 78 feet on Broadway and 112 feet on Maiden lane.

Stock......Par $100......Authorized { com., $350,000 / pref., 250,000 } Issued { com., $350,000 / pref., 250,000 } $600,000

The preferred stock is entitled to 6 per cent. dividends, also has preference as to assets. Transfer Agents, Stewart Browne & Co., 170 Broadway, New York.

FUNDED DEBT.

1st mort. 4½ and 5 per cent. bonds, due 1905 and 1911, Aug. and Feb................$2,700,000

The trustee of the mortgage is The Title Guarantee & Trust Co., New York.

President, Stewart Browne; Secretary, W. L. Hoskins; Treasurer, John E. Green, New York.

Directors—Stewart Browne, W. L. Hoskins, John E. Green, James W. Fox, Alexander S. Brown, New York.

Main office, 170 Broadway, New York.

## THE BROADWAY REALTY CO.

A corporation formed under the laws of New York in 1896. The object of the company is owning and renting real estate. It owns the Bowling Green offices, Nos. 5 to 11 Broadway, New York.

Stock......Par $100..............................Authorized, $600,000... ..Issued, $600,000

The company has no preferred stock. Transfer Agents, Spencer Trask & Co., 27 Pine street, New York. Registrar, Morton Trust Co., New York.

FUNDED DEBT.

| | |
|---|---|
| 1st mort., gold, 5 per cent., due Sept., 1926, March and Sept. | $1,800,000 |
| 2d mort., gold, 5 per cent., due June, 1916, June and Dec. | 1,200,000 |
| Total | $3,000,000 |

The 1st and 2d mortgage bonds outstanding are both the full amounts authorized. Trustee of the 1st mortgage, United States Mortgage & Trust Co., New York, at the office of which institution coupons are paid. Trustee of the 2d mortgage, Morton Trust Co., New York, at which institution the 2d mortgage coupons are paid.

President, Spencer Trask, Saratoga Springs, N. Y.; Vice-President, Joseph F. Stier; Secretary and Treasurer, Charles J. Peabody, New York.

Directors—Spencer Trask, Saratoga Springs, N. Y.; Joseph F. Stier, Charles J. Peabody, New York; Gardiner M. Lane, Boston; Edwin M. Bulkley, Englewood, N. J.

Main office, 27 Pine street, New York. Annual meeting in May, at New York.

## BROOKLINE GAS LIGHT CO.

A corporation formed under the laws of Massachusetts, to manufacture and distribute gas in Brookline, Mass., and Boston. The annual output of the company is 740,000,000 feet of gas. The company is controlled by the Massachusetts Gas Companies. See statement of that company.

Stock......Par $100..........................Authorized, $2,000,000......Issued, $2,000,000

The company has no preferred stock. Dividends are payable quarterly, March 31, June 30, September 30 and December 30. Dividends of 10 per cent. were paid in 1900, 1901 and 1902.

FUNDED DEBT.

| | |
|---|---|
| 1st mort., 5 per cent. bonds, due 1911, April and Oct. | $323,000 |
| " 5 per cent. bonds, due 1913, Feb. and Aug. | 677,000 |
| Total | $1,000,000 |

The bonds outstanding are the total amount authorized. Agent for payment of interest, Old Colony Trust Co., Boston.

In the fiscal year ending June 30, 1901, the gross earnings were: $864,610.13; net earnings, $386,795.45; interest charges, $164,320.09; dividends, $200,000; surplus, $22,475.36. In 1902, gross, $920,073; net, $389,068; charges, $169,753; dividends, $200,000; surplus, $19,315.

President, C. A. Stone; Vice-President, John T. Burnett; Secretary, George H. Finn; Treasurer, Frederic Tudor, Boston.

Directors—C. A. Stone, John T. Burnett, C. M. Weld, William M. Butler, William Endicott, Jr., Boston.

Corporate office, Brookline, Mass.; main office, 100 Boylston street, Boston. Annual meeting fourth Wednesday in September, at place appointed by directors.

---

## BROOKLYN FERRY CO. OF NEW YORK

This corporation operates the ferries from Grand, Roosevelt, Twenty-third and Forty-second streets, in the Borough of Manhattan, New York City, to Grand street and Broadway, Brooklyn. It also operates the ferries from Tenth street and Twenty-third street, Manhattan, to Greenpoint, the latter under lease. The company's fleet of ferryboats consists of twenty-three boats, eighteen of which are steel. The company rents the privileges for its various ferry lines from the city of New York for periods of ten years, the annual rental to the city being about $68,750.

Stock......Par $100..........................Authorized, $8,500,000......Issued, $7,500,000

FUNDED DEBT.

| | |
|---|---|
| 1st mort. B. & N. Y. Ferry Co., 6 per cent., due Jan., 1911, Jan. and July........... | $1,000,000 |
| Brooklyn Ferry cons. mort., 5 per cent., due Aug., 1948, Feb. and Aug.............. | 6,500,000 |
| 10th and 23d Street Ferry 1st mort., guaranteed 5 per cent....... ................. | 550,000 |
| Total...................................................................... | $8,050,000 |

The consolidated mortgage bonds of this company are $7,500,000, an amount of $1,000,000 being reserved to retire the Brooklyn & New York Ferry 6s at maturity.

This company leases the Tenth and Twenty-third street ferry for 99 years from December, 1898, guaranteeing interest on the bonds of the latter and 5 per cent. on its $1,000,000 of stock. This company has the right to purchase the property at any time during the lease by assuming the bonds and taking the stock at par.

In the year 1901 the gross earnings were $1,268,302; net, $569,930; charges, $412,500; rentals, $77,500; surplus, $79,930.

President, Joseph J. O'Donohue; Vice-President, H. B. Hollins; General Manager, John Englis; Secretary and Treasurer, Joseph Riley.

Directors, Joseph J. O'Donohue, H. B. Hollins, John Englis, Jacob Hays, B. J. Burke, John G. Jenkins, Theodore F. Jackson, Richard N. Young, George H. Prentiss.

Main office, 392 Kent avenue, Brooklyn; New York office, 101 Front street.

---

## BROOKLYN RAPID TRANSIT CO.

A corporation formed under the laws of New York, January 18, 1896, and acquired all the assets of the Long Island Traction Co., which were sold in foreclosure under its collateral trust mortgage, 1896, and purchased by a reorganization committee. In January, 1899, a controlling interest in the Nassau Electric Railroad Co. was acquired, and the same year the company acquired the Brooklyn Union Elevated Railroad, the Kings County Elevated Railroad Co. and the Brooklyn & Brighton Beach Railroad. The Kings County Elevated Railroad has been merged with the Brooklyn Union Elevated Railroad Co. The Prospect Park & Coney Island Railroad, owned by the Long Island Railroad Co., was leased in 1899.

The Long Island Traction Co. owned the entire capital stock ($200,000) of the Brooklyn Heights Railroad Co. The latter leased the Brooklyn City Railroad Co. and operated the Brooklyn, Queens County & Suburban Railroad Co., the capital stock of which was all owned by the Long Island Traction Co. All these assets passed into the possession of the Brooklyn Rapid Transit Co. The Sea Beach Railway is controlled, and in 1897 the Sea View Railroad was acquired.

The mileage of the various properties owned, controlled and leased, is as follows:

| | Miles. | | Miles. |
|---|---|---|---|
| Brooklyn Heights Railroad........... | 0.59 | Prospect Park & Coney Island Railroad | 9.76 |
| Brooklyn City Railroad.............. | 103.29 | Brooklyn Union Elevated Railroad... | 37.00 |
| Brooklyn, Queens Co. & Sub. Railroad | 24.15 | New York & Brooklyn Bridge Railroad | 1.30 |
| Nassau Electric Railroad............. | 61.77 | Trackage on Coney Island & Brooklyn Railroad.......... ................ | 1.53 |
| Sea Beach Railway.. ...... ........ | 6.17 | | |
| Coney Island & Gravesend Railroad.. | 3.16 | | |
| | | Total............................ | 248.72 |

The company has equipped the elevated railroads with electric power, and arranged a system of transfers of cars from the surface to the elevated tracks, and vice versa. The company has many important franchises.

Included in the different properties are seven power stations, and the equipment comprises 128 locomotives and 3,347 cars of all descriptions.

Stock......Par $100.........................Authorized, $45,000,000......Issued, $45,000,000

The company has no preferred stock. Transfer Agent, Central Trust Co., New York.

The stock was held in a voting trust, which terminated January 1, 1900.

In 1899 the stock was increased from $20,000,000 to $45,000,000 to complete the purchase of the Nassau Electric Railroad and the Brooklyn Union and Kings County Elevated roads.

FUNDED DEBT.

| | |
|---|---|
| Brooklyn Rapid Transit Co., gen. mort., 5 per cent., due Oct., 1945. April and Oct. | $7,000,000 |
| Brooklyn Rapid Transit Co., refund'g mort., 4 per cent., due July, 2002, Jan. and July. | 5,000,000 |
| Brooklyn Heights R. R. 1st mort., 5 per cent., due April, 1941, April and Oct...... | 250,000 |
| Brooklyn City R. R. 1st mort., 5 per cent., due July, 1941, Jan. and July........... | 6,000,000 |
| Brooklyn Crosstown R. R. 1st mort., 5 per cent., due July, 1908, Jan. and July..... | 200,000 |
| New W'msburgh & Flatb'h R.R. 1st mort., 4½ per cent., due July, 1941, Feb. and Aug. | 200,000 |
| Grand Street & Newtown 1st mort., 5 per cent., due April, 1906, April and Oct...... | 200,000 |
| Cal. Cem., Gr'np't & B'klyn R.R. 1st mort., 6 per cent., due June, 1907, June and Dec. | 200,000 |
| Greenpoint & Lorimer Street 1st mort., 6 per cent., due May, 1910, May and Nov... | 125,000 |
| B'klyn, Queens Co. & Sub. R. R. 1st mort., 5 per cent due July, 1941, Jan. and July. | 3,500,000 |
| B'klyn, Queens Co. & Sub. R.R. cons. mort., 5 per cent., due July, 1941, May and Nov. | 2,884,000 |
| Jamaica & Brooklyn 1st mort., 5 per cent., due Jan., 1930, Jan. and July........... | 240,000 |
| Sea Beach Ry. 1st mort., guar. 4 per cent., due Sept., 1916, March and Sept........ | 650,000 |
| Nassau Electric R. R. Co. 1st mort., 5 per cent., due April, 1944, April and Oct. .. | 660,000 |
| Nassau Electric R. R. Co. 1st cons. mort., 4 per cent., due Jan., 1951, Jan. and July. | 10,476,000 |
| Atlantic Avenue 1st cons. mort., 5 per cent., due Oct., 1909, April and Oct......... | 730,000 |
| Atlantic Avenue gen. cons. mort., 5 per cent., due April, 1931, April and Oct........ | 2,241,000 |
| Atlantic Avenue impt. mort., 5 per cent., due Jan., 1934, Jan. and Oct.............. | 220,000 |
| B. Beach & W. End R. R. gen. mort., due Oct., 1933, April and Oct.............. | 121,000 |
| B. Beach & W. End R. R. 1st mort., 5 per cent., due Jan., 1907, Jan. and July..... | 250,000 |
| B. Beach & W. End R. R. 1st mort. B., 5 per cent., due Jan., 1917, April and Oct.. | 250,000 |
| B. Beach & W. End R. R. 2d mort., 5 per cent., due June, 1911, June and Dec..... | 52,000 |
| Brooklyn Union El. R. R. 1st mort., 4 per cent., due Feb., 1950, Feb. and Aug.... | 16,000,000 |
| Kings County El. R. R. 1st mort., 4 per cent., due Aug., 1949, Feb. and Aug....... | 7,000,000 |
| Total.............................................................. .. | $64,449,000 |

The Brooklyn Rapid Transit 1st mortgage is for $7,000,000. Trustee, Central Trust Co., New York. The trustee of the Brooklyn Union Elevated and of the Kings County Elevated 1st mortgage is also the Central Trust Co., New York.

In March, 1902, the stockholders authorized the creation of a new general consolidated and collateral mortgage of $150,000,000 at not to exceed 4 per cent., of which $61,065,000 is to be reserved to retire prior liens. The trustee of the mortgage and agent for the payment of interest is the Central Trust Co., New York. In May, 1902, $5,000,000 of the new bonds were sold.

The trustee of the Nassau Electric Railroad consolidated mortgage is the Guaranty Trust Co., New York.

The company pays, as rental for the Brooklyn City Railroad Co., interest on its bonds and dividends of 10 per cent. per annum on its $12,000,000 of stock.

The company pays, as rental of the Nassau Electric Railroad Co., interest on its bonds and 4 per cent. on its preferred stock, which is $6,500,000, but of which $6,052,000 is owned by the Brooklyn Rapid Transit Co., leaving only $448,000 outstanding.

The Brooklyn Union Elevated Railroad is a reorganization of the Brooklyn Elevated Railway. It has $5,000,000 preferred, and $13,000,000 common stock, nearly all of which is owned by the Brooklyn Rapid Transit Co. In June, 1901, 2 per cent. was paid on the preferred stock. Its 1st mortgage authorized is $16,000,000.

The Kings County Elevated Railroad Co. was a reorganization of the railway company of the same name. Its 1st mortgage is $7,000,000, authorized.

The Nassau Electric Railroad Co. has $6,500,000 preferred and $8,500,000 common stock. The preferred is entitled under the lease to not less than 4 per cent., the dividends being paid at that rate, annually, in December, 1900, and November, 1901. The Brooklyn Rapid Transit owns $6,052,000 of the preferred and $8,499,000 common stock.

The Brooklyn City Railroad Co. consolidated at various times with the Bushwick Railroad, the Brooklyn Crosstown Railroad, Calvary Cemetery, Greenpoint & Brooklyn Railroad, New Williamsburgh & Flatbush Railroad, Greenpoint & Lorimer Street Railroad, Grand Street & Newtown and South Brooklyn Railroad Companies.

The Brooklyn, Queens County & Suburban Railroad was a consolidation of the Jamaica & Brooklyn, Broadway Railroad of Brooklyn and Broadway Ferry & Metropolitan Avenue Railroad Companies, and assumed the bonds of these companies.

EARNINGS—ALL COMPANIES IN SYSTEM.

Year ending June 30.

| | Gross. | Operating Expenses. | Taxes. | Net Fixed Charges. | | Balance. |
|---|---|---|---|---|---|---|
| 1893-94 | $8,811,333 | $5,685,204 | $545,949 | $2,772,778 | Def. | $192,589 |
| 1894-95 | 8,916,896 | 5,961,151 | 549,983 | 3,349,535 | " | 943,773 |
| 1895-96 | 9,576,935 | 5,806,036 | 606,468 | 3,491,259 | " | 326,829 |
| 1896-97 | 9,704,977 | 5,910,942 | 459,922 | 3,747,249 | " | 413,137 |
| 1897-98 | 10,228,768 | 6,400,893 | 416,012 | 3,853,523 | " | 441,660 |
| 1898-99 | 11,316,033 | 7,221,291 | 636,635 | 3,659,988 | " | 201,881 |
| 1899-00 | 11,768,550 | 7,106,373 | 736,721 | 3,398,684 | Sur. | 526,772 |
| 1900-01 | 12,135,559 | 7,444,686 | 754,620 | 3,587,122 | " | 349,125 |
| 1901-02 | 12,788,168 | 8,293,825 | 742,817 | 3,732,633 | " | 18,893 |

The expenses for 1900-01 include $228,678 of special appropriations. In 1901-02 the expenses include $84,424 for the same item.

Chairman, Anthony N. Brady; President, Edwin W. Winter; Vice-Presidents, Horace C. Duval, Timothy S. Williams; Secretary and Treasurer, C. D. Meneely.

Directors—Horace C. Duval; Timothy S. Williams, Edwin W. Winter, John G. Jenkins, Anthony N. Brady, David H. Valentine, Norman B. Ream, H. H. Porter, Edward H. Harriman, Walter G. Oakman, Anson R. Flower, R. Somers Hayes, Henry Seibert.

Main office, 168 Montague street, Brooklyn. Annual meeting, last Friday in January.

## BROOKLYN UNION GAS CO.

A corporation formed under laws of New York, September 9, 1895, and purchased November 4, 1895, subject to existing mortgages, property and franchises of gas companies in Brooklyn, N. Y., viz.: Brooklyn Gaslight Co., Fulton Municipal Gas Co., Metropolitan Gaslight Co., Citizens' Gas Co., Williamsburgh Gaslight Co., People's Gaslight Co. and Nassau Gaslight Co. The property comprises 7 gas plants and systems of mains covering entire Borough of Brooklyn and its suburbs. The company owns all the stock of the Newtown Gas Co., and has acquired the Woodhaven Gas Light, Equity Gas, the Jamaica Gas Light Co., the Richmond Hill & Queens County Gaslight Co. and the Flatbush Gas Co. The rate to private consumers is $1 per 1000 cubic feet.

Stock......Par $100........................Authorized, $15,000,000......Issued, $15,000,000

Transfer Agent, Guaranty Trust Co., New York. Registrar, United States Mortgage & Trust Co.

Dividends paid have been: In 1896, 1897, 1898 and 1899, 6 per cent. In June, 1900, 3 per cent. was paid, but the December dividend was increased to 4 per cent., or 7 per cent. for 1900. In 1901 paid 8 per cent. Dividends were paid semi-annually, on June 1 and December 1, but beginning in September, 1901, were made quarterly, of 2 per cent. each, or at the rate of 8 per cent. per annum.

FUNDED DEBT.

1st cons. mort., 5 per cent., due May, 1945, May and Nov......................... $14,524,000

Consolidated mortgage is for $15,000,000, of which $505,000 was deposited with the Guaranty Trust Co., New York, to retire Citizens' Gas Co. consolidated 5s (February and August) and Union Gaslight consolidated 5s (January and July), which had not yet matured.

President, James Jourdan; Vice-President, Henry H. Rogers; Secretary, W. R. Rossiter; Treasurer, Elverton R. Chapman.

Directors—William Rockefeller, Henry H. Rogers, James Jourdan, David G. Legget, Henry W. Cannon, Elverton R. Chapman, William G. Rockefeller.

Main office, 180 Remsen street, Brooklyn, N. Y. Annual meeting, first Tuesday after the second Monday in November, at Brooklyn, N. Y.

## THE BROWN HOISTING MACHINERY CO., INCORPORATED

A corporation formed under the laws of Delaware, August 16, 1900. The company has a large plant at Cleveland and manufactures hoisting and conveying machinery of every description, cranes, automatic furnace hoists, etc. The company owns the patents under which the hoisting and conveying apparatus and the tramways for the same are built, the various mechanical devices being the inventions of Alexander E. Brown, C. E.

Stock...Par $100....Authorized { com., $1,000,000 / pref., 1,000,000 } Issued { com., $1,000,000 / pref., 1,000,000 } $2,000,000

The preferred stock is 7 per cent., non-cumulative. Stock is transferred at the company's office, Cleveland.

The company has no funded debt.

President, Fayette Brown; Vice-President and General Manager, Alexander E. Brown; Treasurer, Harvey H. Brown; Secretary, George C. Wing; Manager, F. G. Tallman, Cleveland.

Directors—Fayette Brown, Alexander E. Brown, Harvey H. Brown, James Virdin, George C. Wing, Thomas P. Howell, Ralph W. Hickox, H. D. Coffinberry, Leander McBride, Cleveland.

Main office, 1345 St. Clair street, Cleveland; branch offices, New York, Pittsburg, London. Annual meeting first Wednesday in February.

## BRUNSWICK-BALKE-COLLENDER CO.

An Ohio corporation engaged in the manufacture and sale of billiard tables, bowling alleys, refrigerators and bar fixtures. In 1899 the company acquired the Wickes Refrigerator Co.

Stock......Par $100..........................Authorized, $1,500,000......Issued, $1,500,000

FUNDED DEBT.

1st mort., 5 per cent., due July, 1903-13, June and Dec.............................. $600,000

The 1st mortgage was created in 1902, and covers the company's entire property. Beginning July 1, 1903, $60,000 of the bonds fall due each year. Trustee of the mortgage, Union Savings Bank & Trust Co., Cincinnati.

President, Moses Bensinger; 1st Vice-President, B. E. Bensinger, Chicago; 2d Vice-President, B. H. Brunswick, Cincinnati; Treasurer, A. F. Troescher, New York; Secretary, Joseph Wilby, Cincinnati.

Directors—Moses Bensinger, B. E. Bensinger, Chicago; A. F. Troescher, New York; R. F. Balke, R. A. Koehler, B. H. Brunswick, Joseph Wilby, Cincinnati.

Main office, 130 East Sixth street, Cincinnati; New York office, 227 Fourth avenue. Annual meeting, first Monday in March.

## BRUNSWICK DOCK & CITY IMPROVEMENT CO.

A company formed under the laws of Georgia, in 1897, to succeed the Brunswick Co., the property of which was sold in foreclosure and purchased by this corporation. The property consists of 1,500 lots in the city of Brunswick, Ga., with large tracts near that city, much of the land having valuable water fronts.

Stock......Par $100..........................Authorized, $5,000,000......Issued, $5,000,000

The stock outstanding was increased to $5,000,000 in September, 1898, when the company sold 7,302 shares to a syndicate for sufficient to retire the balance of its bonds.

Transfer Agent, Continental Trust Co., New York. Registrar, Morton Trust Co., New York.

The company, as reorganized, had $180,300 5 per cent. 1st mortgage bonds due 1917, the holders of which had the right to elect a majority of the directors for three years from January 1, 1897. The bonds have now been retired as stated above, and voting trust canceled.

President, Henry E. Howland; Vice-President, Edmon Urquhart; Secretary and Treasurer, A. G. Kraetzer, Jr., New York.

Directors—Henry E. Howland, William O. Allison, D. Green, Silas B. Dutcher, F. de L. Hyde, Robert A. Fairbarn, F. Cunningham, Henry P. Condit, Meredith Dryden.

Main office, Brunswick, Ga.; Secretary and Treasurer's office, 8 Bridge street, New York. Annual meeting, second Tuesday in February.

## BUFFALO & SUSQUEHANNA IRON CO.

A corporation formed under the laws of New York, May 17, 1902. The purpose of the company is the manufacture and sale of pig iron and the mining of iron ore and coal, as well as the manufacture of coke and similar products. The company acquired about 50 acres of land in Buffalo, adjoining the terminal of the Buffalo & Susquehanna Railway Co. Two blast furnaces are to be erected with a capacity of from 600 to 800 tons of pig iron per day. The company has also provided for the necessary machinery and equipment, as well as for ore docks, canals, etc. It has acquired iron ore properties in the Mesabi Range, Minnesota, and in Michigan, and coal lands in Pennsylvania.

Stock......Par $100..............................Authorized, $600,000......Issued, $600,000

The company has no preferred stock.

FUNDED DEBT.

1st mort., 5 per cent., due June, 1932, June and Dec............................... $1,500,000

The authorized amount of the 1st mortgage is $3,000,000. Trustee of the mortgage, New York Security & Trust Co., New York. Agents for the payment of interest, Fisk & Robinson, 35 Cedar street, New York.

President, William A. Rogers; 1st Vice-President, F. H. Goodyear; 2d Vice-President, C. W. Goodyear; Secretary and Treasurer, H. D. Carson; General Manager, Hugh Kennedy, Buffalo, N. Y.

Directors—William A. Rogers, F. H. Goodyear, C. W. Goodyear, Hugh Kennedy, Wilson S. Bissell, Buffalo.

Corporate and main office, Erie County Bank Building, Buffalo. Annual meeting, second Thursday in May.

## BUFFALO GAS CO.

A corporation formed under the laws of New York, October 12, 1899, in pursuance of a plan to consolidate the Buffalo City Gas Co. and the Buffalo Gas Light Co. The Buffalo Mutual Gas Light Co. has also been merged into the Buffalo Gas Co.

The Buffalo Gas Co. owns a large majority of the stock and bonds of the People's Gas Light & Coke Co. of Buffalo.

The company controls the gas industry in Buffalo, N. Y. The franchise is perpetual. Rate charged is $1 per 1,000 cubic feet to private consumers and 80 cents to the city.

Stock....Par $100....Authorized { com., $7,000,000 / pref., 1,705,000 }  Issued { com., $7,000,000 / pref., 1,710,000 } $8,710,000

The preferred stock is 6 per cent., non-cumulative. The consolidation plan involved the issue thereof in exchange for 6 per cent. debentures of the Buffalo City Gas Co. The common stock was exchanged for the outstanding stock of the Buffalo City Gas Co.

Transfer Agent, Continental Trust Co., New York. Registrar, New York Security & Trust Co., New York.

FUNDED DEBT.

Buffalo City Gas, 1st mort., 5 per cent., due Oct., 1947, April and Oct................ $5,900,000

The Buffalo City Gas Co. 1st mortgage bonds are secured by a first lien on all the franchises, rights, privileges, plant, machinery, real estate, mains, services and meters now owned by the Buffalo Gas Co. or that may hereafter be acquired by it, and also by the bonds and stock of the People's Gas Light & Coke Co. of Buffalo owned by the Buffalo Gas Co. or that may hereafter be acquired by it. The company has $95,000 of the bonds in its treasury.

EARNINGS.

Year ending September 30.

| | Net. | Charges. | Surplus. |
|---|---|---|---|
| 1899-00 | $288,394 | $290,250 | Def., $1,856 |
| 1900-01 | 303,939 | 290,250 | Sur., 13,689 |
| 1901-02 | 399,137 | 290,250 | " 48,887 |

The following is a condensed balance sheet, September 30, 1902:

| ASSETS. | | LIABILITIES. | |
|---|---|---|---|
| Plant account | $14,613,422 | Common stock, common | $7,000,000 |
| Stock of materials and supplies | 54,497 | Capital stock, preferred | 1,710,000 |
| Treasury bonds | 95,000 | Bonds | 5,900,000 |
| Prepaid accounts | 1,960 | Bench Repair Fund—Credit balance to cover depreciation charged in advance to operating cost | 18,303 |
| Gas bills receivable | 36,007 | Accounts payable | 28,313 |
| City of Buffalo accounts receivable | 18,053 | Consumers' deposits | 68,310 |
| Other accounts receivable | 30,816 | Taxes payable | 49,379 |
| Bills receivable | 8,312 | Accrued wages | 1,846 |
| Construction accounts not closed | 17,818 | Profit and loss | 69,857 |
| Cash | 19,009 | Net profit for current year | 48,886 |
| Total | $14,894,894 | Total | $14,894,894 |

President, Alexander C. Humphreys, New York; Vice-President, Robert L. Fryer; Secretary and Treasurer, William S. Riselay, Buffalo.

Directors—Alexander C. Humphreys, Stephen Peabody, William S. Riselay, Frederick Strauss, Robert C. Pruyn, Robert L. Fryer, Pascal P. Pratt, J. Edward Addicks, Franklin D. Locke, J. Frank Allen, H. L. Clark.

Main office, 186 Main street, Buffalo, N. Y. Annual meeting, first Monday in November, at Buffalo.

## BUFFALO GENERAL ELECTRIC CO.

A corporation formed under the laws of New York in 1892. The company contracts for lighting the city of Buffalo with electric lights, distributes and supplies electricity for lighting and power throughout the city. This company absorbed the Brush Electric Light Co., and the Thompson-Houston Electric Light & Power Co. of Buffalo. The company's electric power is obtained from Niagara Falls.

Stock......Par $100...................... ....Authorized, $2,400,000......Issued, $2,175,000

The company pays 5 per cent. per annum on its stock, the payments being 1¼ per cent. quarterly.

FUNDED DEBT.

1st mort., 5 per cent., due 1939, Feb. and Aug.................................... $2,175,000

The 1st mortgage was created in 1899 and is for $2,400,000. Trustee of mortgage, the Fidelity Trust & Guaranty Co., Buffalo, N. Y. The mortgage was created to retire the old bonds of this company and those of the Thompson-Houston Electric Light & Power Co., both of which issues were exchangeable for the present bonds, the bonds not exchanged being called in and paid, February 1, 1899.

President, Daniel O'Day; 1st Vice-President, George Urban, Jr.; 2d Vice-President and General Manager, Charles R. Huntley; Secretary and Treasurer, Daniel T. Nash.

Directors—Daniel O'Day, Wilson S. Bissell, Eugene Griffin, George Urban, Jr., Charles R. Huntley, H. W. Burt, J. T. Jones, Peter P. Miller, W. C. Warren.

Main office, 40 Court street, Buffalo, N. Y. Annual meeting, second Monday in April.

## BULLOCK ELECTRIC MANUFACTURING CO.

A corporation formed under the laws of New Jersey, April 1, 1899. The purpose of the company is the manufacture and sale of electric apparatus. The company has a large plant at East Norwood, Hamilton County, O., near Cincinnati. The works cover 13 acres of land and comprise an administration building, three machine shops, a power building, service building, brass foundry, pattern storage building and other buildings. In addition, the company controls a foundry plant occupying 7 acres immediately adjoining its main plant. The plant throughout is equipped with every modern appliance and has facilities to manufacture the largest class of electrical apparatus. The works employ about 800 hands.

Stock...Par $100....Authorized { com., $1,000,000 / pref., 1,000,000 } Issued { com., $1,000,000 / pref., 1,000,000 } $2,000,000

The preferred stock is 6 per cent. cumulative. Transfer Agent and Registrar, Union Savings Bank & Trust Co., Cincinnati.

The first dividend on the preferred stock was 1½ per cent., paid April 1, 1901. Since then regular quarterly dividends of 1½ per cent. have been paid in January, April, July and October.

The company has no funded debt.

In the year ending December 31, 1901, the revenues of the company were as follows: Gross profit, $119,167; net, $65,195; interest, $2,737; dividends, $30,000; surplus, $93,665; charged off for depreciation of plant, $53,972. In 1902, gross profits, $190,426; net, $105,287; interest, $9,647; dividends, $44,250; surplus, $127,368; charged off for depreciation, $85,138.

President, George Bullock; Vice-President, Joseph S. Neave; Secretary, James W. Bullock; Treasurer, Stephen R. Burton; Assistant Treasurer, James C. Marshall.

Directors—George Bullock, Joseph Neave, James W. Bullock, Stephen R. Burton, W. S. Roe, Cincinnati; James B. Dill, East Orange, N. J.

Corporate office, New Jersey Registration & Trust Co., East Orange, N. J.; main office, East Norwood, Cincinnati; branch offices, New York, Boston, Baltimore, Philadelphia, Buffalo, Cleveland, Montreal, Chicago, Denver, San Francisco, London. Annual meeting, March 20, at East Orange, N. J.

## BURLINGTON RAILWAY & LIGHT CO.

A corporation formed under the laws of Iowa in 1897, for the purpose of operating street railways and supplying electric light and power in the city of Burlington, Ia. The company is a consolidation of the following companies:

Burlington Electric Railway Co.
Burlington Gas & Fuel Co.
Burlington Electric Light Co.
Burlington Steam Supply Co.

In May, 1899, the company acquired the Burlington Gas Light Co. The company owns 13½ miles of track, operated by electric trolley system, 23 cars, electric light and power plants and a steam heating and gas plant. The population supplied is over 23,000. A new 20-year franchise was granted by the city March 18, 1902.

In 1902 the property and franchises of the company were acquired by the Peoples' Gas & Electric Co.

Stock......Par $100 .......................... Authorized, $1,250,000......Issued, $1,000,000

The company has no preferred stock.

FUNDED DEBT.

1st mort., 5 per cent., due Oct., 1917, April and Oct.................................. $500,000

The authorized amount of bonds is $750,000, of which $125,000 is reserved for extensions to gas plants. The bonds are redeemable after 1902 at 105 and interest, and $500,000 of the same are guaranteed as to principal and interest by the Peoples' Gas & Electric Co. Trustee of the mortgage and agent for the payment of interest, American Loan & Trust Co., Boston.

In the year 1901 the company earned, gross, $169,940; net, $71,210; charges, $31,250 surplus, $39,960.

President, George H. Higbee; Vice-President, E. C. Walsh; Secretary, C. H. Walsh Treasurer, J. T. Remey.

Directors—J. J. Ranson, M. A. Walsh, J. W. Walsh, George H. Higbee, E. C. Walsh, C. H. Walsh, J. T. Remey.

Main office, Burlington, Ia.

## BUTTE & BOSTON CONSOLIDATED MINING CO.

(Controlled by Amalgamated Copper Co.)

A corporation organized under the laws of New York. The company owns a large number of mining claims, including the Silver Bow, Blue Jay, and others. Its mines are situated in the vicinity of Butte, Mont. The property produces copper and silver, the rock also carrying a considerable proportion of gold.

In June, 1901, the quoted part of the stock of this company was acquired by the Amalgamated Copper Co., which offered one share of its stock for each share of this company's stock.

Stock......Par $10............................Authorized, $2,000,000......Issued, $2,000,000

Transfer Agent, International Trust Co., Boston.

A dividend, the first in the company's history, of $5 per share was paid December 10, 1900.

FUNDED DEBT.

1st mort., 6 per cent., due April, 1917, April and Oct.............................. $1,500,000

The stock of the company is full paid and non-assessable.

President, Henry H. Rogers; Secretary and Treasurer, William G. Rockefeller, New York.

Directors—Henry H. Rogers, William G. Rockefeller, Adolph Lewisohn, New York; William G. Riley, James Phillips, Jr., Boston.

Main office, 52 Broadway, New York. Annual meeting, first Monday in April.

## THE BUTTERICK CO.

A corporation formed under the laws of New York, January 16, 1902. The purpose of the company is to print, publish, and to manufacture paper patterns. It owns the following subsidiary companies:

The Federal Publishing Co.
The Butterick Publishing Co., Ltd.
New Idea Publishing Co.
Standard Fashion Co.
New Idea Pattern Co.
Banner Fashion Co.

The company has no preferred stock. Transfer Agent, The City Trust Co., New York, Registrar, Knickerbocker Trust Co., New York.

The first dividend of 1 per cent. was paid March 1, 1902. Dividends at the rate of 4 per cent. annually are paid quarterly in March, June, September and December.

In the fiscal year ending December 31, 1902, the gross earnings were $726,897; net, $426,897; dividends, 300,000; surplus, $2,655,832.

The following is the balance sheet of the company December 31, 1902:

| ASSETS. | | LIABILITIES. | |
|---|---|---|---|
| Cash | $452,412 | Mortgages payable | $245,000 |
| Mortgages | 28,035 | Bills and accounts payable | 271,352 |
| Federal bonds | 535,000 | Federal Publishing Co. bonds | 1,200,000 |
| Stocks | 1,060 | Surplus | 2,655,832 |
| Accounts receivable | 1,531,322 | | |
| Real estate and improvements | 855,360 | | |
| Machinery and plant | 503,696 | | |
| Merchandise, man'f'd and in process | 450,299 | | |
| Patents | 15,000 | | |
| Total | $4,372,184 | Total | $4,372,184 |

President, G. W. Wilder; 1st Vice-President, C. W. Morse; 2d Vice-President, J. F. Birmingham; Secretary, Robert S. O'Loughlin; Treasurer, C. D. Wilder, New York.

Directors—G. W. Wilder, C. W. Morse, C. D. Wilder, B. F. Wilder, H. B. Phinny, New York; Robert S. O'Loughlin, Greenwich, Conn.; J. F. Birmingham, Brooklyn, N. Y.; E. L. Pearsall, Jersey City.

Corporate and main office, 7 West Thirteenth street, New York; branch offices, London, Paris, Toronto, Chicago, St. Louis, San Francisco, Boston. Annual meeting, first Wednesday in February, at New York.

## THE CALIFORNIA COPPER CO.

A corporation organized under the laws of West Virginia. The company owns a copper property in California.

Stock......Par $5..............................Authorized, $1,000,000......Issued, $1,000,000

The stock is full paid and non-assessable. Stock is transferred at the company's office. Registrar, Laidlaw & Co., 14 Wall street, New York.

President, F. L. Underwood; Treasurer, C. E. Laidlaw; Secretary, R. H. Eggleston, New York.

Directors—F. L. Underwood, Henry A. James, C. E. Laidlaw, E. K. Austin, New York.

Main office, 31 Nassau street, New York. Annual meeting, first Tuesday in May.

## CALIFORNIA FRUIT CANNERS' ASSOCIATION

A corporation formed under the laws of California, July 3, 1899. The object of the company is the canning, distribution and sale of fruits and vegetables. The company acquired some twenty-five canneries and plants previously engaged in such business, with their good will, brands and trade-marks, the plants representing an annual output of over 2,000,000 cases of goods. The properties occupy the most favorable positions in the fruit and vegetable growing sections of California. The companies and firms whose properties were acquired control two-thirds of their line of business in California. They embrace the following:

Cutting Fruit Packing Co., San Francisco, Santa Anna, Santa Rosa, Colton.
Fontana & Co., San Francisco, Healdsburg, Hanford.
San Jose Fruit Packing Co., San Jose.
King-Morse Canning Co., San Francisco, San Leandro.
California Fruit Canners' Association, Stockton.
Courtland Canning Co., Sacramento River.
Whittier Cannery, Whittier.
Oakland Preserving Co., Oakland, Milpitas.
Sacramento Packing Co., Sacramento, Visalia, Ventura.
Marysville Packing Co., Marysville.
California Fruit Preserving Co., Oakland, Biggs.
Rose City Canning Co., Santa Rosa.
Hunt Bros. Fruit Packing Co., Santa Rosa.
A. F. Tenney Canning Co., Fresno.
Chico Canning Co., Chico.
Southern California Packing Co., Los Angeles.
Lincoln Fruit Packing Co., Lincoln.
Sutter Canning & Packing Co., Yuba City.

Stock......Par $100.................... ......Authorized, $3,500,000......Issued, $2,891,600

Dividends of 60 cents per share are paid monthly on the stock, this being at the rate of 7 1-5 per cent. per annum.

The association has no funded debt. All the properties are owned in fee simple and are free from mortgage encumbrances.

President, William Fries; Vice-President and Treasurer, Sanford L. Goldstein; 2d Vice-President, Fred Tillman, Jr.; 3d Vice-President, William Thomas; Secretary, Charles B. Carr.

Directors—Francis Cutting, Percy T. Morgan, Sanford L. Goldstein, Henry F. Allen, William Fries, W. C. B. de Fremery, M. J. Fontana, R. I. Bentley, Fred Tillman, Jr., William Thomas, William L. Gerstle.

Main office, 203 California street, San Francisco. Annual meeting, second Tuesday in April.

## CALIFORNIA WINE ASSOCIATION

A corporation formed under the laws of California, August 10, 1894. The business of the association is wine making and dealing in California wines and brandies. The association is a consolidation of the old-established California wine companies and firms of Kohler & Frohling, S. Lachman Co., B. Dreyfus & Co., Kohler & Van Bergen, C. Carpy & Co. and the Napa Valley Wine Co. It also owns interests in the capital stock of a number of other corporations engaged in the manufacture and handling of California wines and brandies, and has wineries and establishments in all the chief wine-producing sections of the State.

Stock......Par $100........................Authorized, $10,000,000......Issued, $4,336,700

Dividends are paid on the stock monthly, being 60 cents per share per month, or at the rate of 7 1-5 per cent. per annum.

The association has no preferred stock, funded debt or mortgage obligations. Transfer Agent, Union Trust Co., San Francisco.

The balance sheet as of December 31, 1902, showed cash assets of $4,331,605, and total assets $8,066,246. Current liabilities were $3,069,295 and the excess of assets over liabilities $4,969.549. The surplus at the above date was $532,849, and the reserve account $100,000.

In 1901 profits were $570,162; dividends paid, $286,255. In 1902, profits $595,679, dividends paid $312,251.

President, Percy T. Morgan; 1st Vice-President and Treasurer, J. Frowenfeld; 2d Vice-President, Albert Lachman; Secretary, William Hanson; Assistant Secretary and Assistant Treasurer, F. Frohman, San Francisco; President of Advisory Board, Edward Frowenfeld; Assistant Treasurer, Carl von Bergen; Assistant Secretary, W. Culman, New York.

Directors—Isaias W. Hellman, H. E. Huntington, Antoine Borel, Percy T. Morgan, J. Frowenfeld, Albert Lachman, H. Van Bergen, J. J. Jacobi, P. C. Rossi, C. Schilling, Isaias W. Hellman, Jr.

Main office, 661 Third street, San Francisco; New York office, 410 West Fourteenth street. Annual meeting, last Thursday in February, at Herculis, Contra Costa County, Cal.

## CALUMET AND ARIZONA MINING CO.

A corporation formed under the laws of Arizona in 1901. The purpose of the company is to mine and smelt ores. The first smelter of the company was blown in in November, 1902.

Stock......Par $10...................... .....Authorized, $2,500,000......Issued, $2,000,000

Stock is transferred at the office of the company, Calumet, Mich. Registrar, Merchants' and Miners' Bank, Calumet, Mich.

The company has no funded debt.

President, Charles Briggs; Vice-President, John S. Dymock; Secretary, Gordon R. Campbell; Treasurer, Peter Ruppe, Calumet, Mich.

Directors—Charles Briggs, John S. Dymock, Peter Ruppe, James Hoatson, Calumet, Mich.; Thomas Hoatson, Laurium, Mich.; George E. Tener, Pittsburg; T. F. Cole, Chester A. Congdon, C. d'Autremont, Jr., Duluth, Minn.

Corporate office, Bisbee, Ariz.; main office, Calumet, Mich. Annual meeting, second Monday in April, at Bisbee, Ariz.

## CALUMET & CHICAGO CANAL & DOCK CO.

A corporation formed under the laws of Illinois, March 10, 1869. The original business of the company was the improvement and docking of the Calumet River and the purchase of real estate. The present business of the company is selling its real estate. It owns lands in South Chicago and in the south part of the city of Chicago.

Stock......Par $100..........................Authorized, $3,495,250......Issued, $3,495,250

Before the reorganization in 1881 the company had $2,000,000 of preferred stock, but that has been paid off and retired. Stock is transferred at the office of the company, Chicago. Registrar, Merchants' Loan & Trust Co., Chicago.

The company has no funded debt.

At the end of the fiscal year, January 31, 1903, the company had a surplus of $599,946.

President, Leslie Carter; Vice-President, William J. Watson; Secretary and Treasurer, Stewart Spalding, Chicago.

Directors—A. C. Bartlett, Henry A. Blair, Leslie Carter, Henry Dibblee, E. A. Hamill, George T. Smith, William J. Watson, Chicago.

Corporate and main office, 135 Adams street, Chicago. Annual meeting, first Wednesday in April, at Chicago.

## CALUMET & HECLA MINING CO.

A Michigan corporation which, in 1900, renewed its charter for thirty years from April 13, 1901.

This company is proprietor of one of the richest copper-producing properties in the world. Its mines are situated at Calumet and Red Jacket, Houghton County, Michigan. It owns several thousand acres of land with stamp mills and smelting works.

Capital stock......Par $25....................Authorized, $2,500,000......Issued, $2,500,000

The company was formed in 1871 by consolidation of Calumet, Hecla, Portland and Scott Copper companies. The stock was increased to the present amount in 1879.

Dividends are usually paid quarterly, in March, June, September and December. In the calendar year 1899 the company paid $100 per share. In 1900, $70 per share; in 1901, $45 per share; in 1902, $25 per share.

The metal produced by the company for a number of years has been, in 1883, 18,561 tons; 1884, 20,236 tons; 1885, 23,623 tons; 1886, 32,214 tons; 1887, 28,558 tons; 1892, 28,247 tons; 1893, 30,213 tons; in 1894, 30,921 tons; in 1895, 38,668 tons; in 1896, 41,981 tons; in 1897, 43,404 tons; in 1898, 41,960 tons; in 1899, 43,879 tons; in 1900, 44,548 tons; in 1901, 36,327 tons; in 1902, 39,982 tons.

The company had returned up to April 30, 1902, dividends to its stockholders amounting to $78,350,000.

President, Alexander Agassiz, Boston; Vice-President, T. L. Livermore; Secretary and Treasurer, George A. Flagg.

Directors—Alexander Agassiz, Quincy A. Shaw, Jr., F. W. Hunnewell, F. L. Higginson, J. N. Wright.

Main office, 12 Ashburton place, Boston. Annual meeting, August, at Boston.

## CAMBRIA STEEL CO.

A corporation formed under the laws of Pennsylvania in 1901 to succeed another company of the same name formed in Pennsylvania, November 14, 1898, for the manufacture and sale of iron, steel and other metals. On December 1, 1898, the old company leased for 999 years the property and franchises of the Cambria Iron Co. The present company was organized with a view to providing for the large annual additions to capital required by the concern and in pursuance of the plans of the Pennsylvania Railroad. The property leased consists of large works, mills and furnaces for the production of steel of all kinds, at Johnstown, Cambria County, Pa., and its vicinity. The proceeds of the calls made on the old stock in 1900–1901 were to be applied to the erection of a new steel plant. In 1902 this company acquired control of the Republic Iron Co., which owns large iron ore properties in Marquette Range, Mich.

In June, 1901, it was announced that the Pennsylvania Railroad Co., in connection with other affiliated roads, had acquired a controlling interest in the stock of this company.

Stock......Par $50..........................Authorized, $50,000,000......Issued, $45,000,000

Stock is transferred at the office of the company, Philadelphia. Registrar, Pennsylvania Co. for Insurance on Lives and Granting Annuities, Philadelphia.

The first dividend on the stock of the new company was 1½ per cent., or 75 cents per share, paid February 15, 1902, and half-yearly dividends of the same amount were paid August 15, 1902, and February 14, 1903.

The $218,000 6 per cent. bonds of the Cambria Iron Co. were retired July 1, 1902.

The stock of the Cambria Iron Co., par $50, is $8,468,000, on which under the lease 4 per cent. per annum is paid, the guaranteed dividends being paid semi-annually, 2 per cent. each in April and October.

The stock of the Cambria Steel Co. of 1898 was $16,000,000 in shares of $50 each. One call of $1.50 per share was made on the old Cambria Steel Co. stock at the time of subscription, and subsequent calls were made to June, 1901, inclusive, making the total amount called and paid per share $13.50.

Under the plan of readjustment of June, 1901, a new corporation was formed with $50,000,000 capital in shares of $50 each. Of this amount $5,000,000 was to be reserved, and $45,000,000 issued under a contract with a company known as the Conemaugh Steel Co., whereby the 320,000 shares of old stock on which $13.50 had been paid were exchanged for $16,000,000 in full-paid shares of the new company and $29,000,000 additional stock of the company on which $27.50 had been paid. Each holder of 10 shares of old stock received 10 shares of new full-paid stock, and had the right to subscribe for the 18 shares of the additional new stock on payment of the $22.50 per share due thereon. This arrangement was carried out under the auspices of Drexel & Co., Philadelphia, and on its completion the new Cambria Steel Co. and the Conemaugh Steel Co. were merged and consolidated under the name of the former company. The arrangement involved the raising of $11,680,000 for the payment of a floating debt of $3,500,000 and for the enlargement and improvement of the plant.

The following is the company's balance sheet, December 31, 1902:

| ASSETS. | | LIABILITIES. | |
|---|---|---|---|
| Property, works, coal, ore lands, etc., subject to payment of rental, under Cambria Iron Co. | $33,090,305 | Capital stock | $45,000,000 |
| Plant additions | 2,145,997 | General depreciation fund | 800,000 |
| Real estate, titles in Cambria Steel Co | 42,247 | Betterment and improvement fund | 1,500,000 |
| Sundry securities | 1,603,569 | Accounts payable, including dividend No. 3 | 2,008,891 |
| Inventory account | 5,134,100 | Bills payable—term notes | 1,955,000 |
| Cash | 5,877,419 | Profit and loss | 1,482,322 |
| Accounts receivable | 4,584,320 | | |
| Bills receivable | 268,256 | | |
| Total | $52,746,213 | Total | $52,746,213 |

EARNINGS.

Year ending October 31.

| | Profit. | Charges, etc. | Dividends. | Surplus. |
|---|---|---|---|---|
| 1898-99 | $2,486,057 | $557,780 | $1,120,000 | $808,377 |
| 1899-00 | 3,943,258 | 850,871 | 2,560,000 | 532,387 |

The fiscal year of the new company has been changed to end December 31. In the 2½ months ending December 31, 1901, gross earnings were $3,987,435; net, $819,391. In the fourteen months ending December 31, 1902, the company's net earnings were $5,084,260; net income, $5,056,962.

President, Powell Stackhouse; Vice-President, John W. Townsend; Secretary and Treasurer, William S. Robinson; Assistant Secretary and Assistant Treasurer, Alexander P. Robinson, Philadelphia.

Directors—Powell Stackhouse, R. Francis Wood, Edward T. Stotesbury, Leonard C. Hanna, Effingham B. Morris, Frank J. Firth, Theodore N. Ely, George F. Baer; John W. Townsend.

Main office, Southeast corner Fifteenth and Market streets, Philadelphia.

## CAMDEN & TRENTON RAILWAY CO.

A corporation formed under the laws of New Jersey, December 15, 1897. Originally the company was called the Monmouth Traction Co., but the present name was adopted in October, 1899. The company has acquired the Cinnaminson Electric Light, Power & Heating Co., Riverton, N. J., and the Bordentown Electric Light & Motor Co., Bordentown, N. J.

The company operates electric light plants, supplying light and power to Riverton, Palmyra, Beverly, Burlington, Bordentown and neighboring villages, and has 30 miles of electric railway between Riverton, and Trenton, N. J., an extension to Camden being in progress in 1902, a traffic arrangement having been made with the Camden & Suburban Railway Co.

Stock......Par $100..........................Authorized, $1,750,000......Issued, $1,750,000

The company has no preferred stock.

FUNDED DEBT.

| | |
|---|---|
| 1st mort., 5 per cent. gold, due Nov., 1929, May and Nov. | $686,000 |
| 1st gen. mort., 5 per cent. gold, due July, 1931, Jan. and July | 200,000 |
| Total | $886,000 |

The authorized amount of the 1st mortgage is $750,000, of which $40,000 is reserved to retire a like amount of bonds of the Cinnaminson Electric Light, Power & Heating Co., and $24,000 is reserved for extensions. The authorized amount of the general mortgage is $1,750,000, of which $750,000 is reserved to retire outstanding liens and $600,000 is held for extensions,

Trustee of both mortgages and agent for the payment of interest, Provident Life & Trust Co., Philadelphia.

In the six months ending November 30, 1901, the company's gross earnings were $42,140; net earnings, $18,205; interest and taxes, $17,950; surplus, $345.

President, Henry V. Massey, Philadelphia; Secretary and Treasurer, Mitchell B. Perkins, Beverly, N. J.

Directors—Henry V. Massey, Merion, Pa.; M. B. Perkins, Beverly, N. J.; Howard Flanders, Burlington, N. J.; John G. Devine, Philadelphia; T. Zurbrugg, Riverside, N. J.; H. C. Horner, Lancaster, Pa.

Main office, Riverside, N. J.; Philadelphia office, 428 Chestnut street.

## CANADA CYCLE & MOTOR CO., LIMITED

A corporation formed under the laws of Ontario in 1899. The company acquired the patents, plants, business and good will of a number of establishments manufacturing bicycles and motor vehicles.

Stock..Par $100..Authorized { com., $3,000,000 / pref., 3,000,000 } Issued { com., $3,000,000 / pref., 2,500,000 } $5,500,000

The preference stock is 7 per cent., cumulative. Stock is transferred at the company's office. Registrar, National Trust Co., Toronto.

The company has no funded debt or mortgages on its properties.

On January 2, 1900, the company began the payment of half yearly dividends on the preference stock at the rate of 7 per cent. per annum, and paid 3½ per cent. in January and July, until January, 1902, when dividends were suspended.

In October, 1902, it was proposed to effect a reorganization of the company.

President, Joseph N. Shenstone; 1st Vice-President, J. W. Flavelle; 2d Vice-President, E. B. Ryckman; Secretary, T. A. Russell.

Directors—E. B. Ryckman, George A. Cox, Lyman M. Jones, J. W. Flavelle, Warren Y. Soper, Joseph N. Shenstone, T. A. Russell.

Main office, 34 King street, West, Toronto. Annual meeting, fourth Thursday in October.

## CANADA FURNITURE MANUFACTURERS, LIMITED

A corporation formed under the laws of Ontario, January 1, 1901. The business of the company is the manufacture and distribution of furniture. It acquired the plants and business of the following concerns:

American Rattan Co., Limited, Walkerton, Ont.
The Anderson Furniture Co., Limited, Woodstock, Ont.
The Anthes Mfg. Co., Limited, Berlin, Ont.
Thomas Bell & Son, Limited, Wingham, Ont.
Broadfoot & Box Furniture Co., Seaforth, Ont.
Burr Bros., Guelph, Ont.
Button & Fessant, Wingham, Ont.
The Hobbs Manufacturing Co., London, Ont.
Lewis Hahn, New Hamburg, Ont.
The Hill Chair Co., Limited, Wiarton, Ont.
Joseph Orr, Stratford, Ont.
Schaefer, Killer & Co., Waterloo, Ont.
Snyder, Roos & Co., Waterloo, Ont.
Siemon & Bros. Mfg. Co., Wiarton, Ont.
The Simpson Furniture Co., Limited, Berlin, Ont.
The Union Furniture Co., Limited, Wingham, Ont.
Zoellner & Co., Mount Forest, Ont.

Stock...Par $100....Authorized { com., $1,000,000 / pref., 2,000,000 } Issued { com., $1,000,000 / pref., 1,241,750 } $2,241,750

The preference stock is 7 per cent., cumulative, with a priority as to both assets and dividends. After providing for a reserve fund and after the common stock shall have received 7 per cent. dividends the preference stock is entitled to divide *pro rata* with the common any remaining surplus for the year.

Transfer Agent and Registrar, National Trust Co., Limited, Toronto and Montreal.

It is provided by the company's charter that after payment of the 7 per cent. dividend on the preference shares and before anything is paid on the common, not less than 25 per cent. of the remaining profits in each year shall be set aside as a reserve fund until such reserve amounts to $500,000.

The company has no funded debt, and no bonds or debentures can be created without the consent of two-thirds in value of the stockholders granted at a special meeting.

Dividends on the preference shares are payable half-yearly, in February and August.

President, Robert Kilgour, Toronto; Vice-President, J. S. Anthes, Berlin, Ont.; Managing Director and Secretary, J. R. Shaw; Treasurer, F. G. Jewell, Toronto.

Directors—J. S. Anthes, Berlin, Ont.; Robert Kilgour, J. R. Shaw, W. R. Hobbs, R. Harmer, A. Hutchison, Toronto; G. H. Meldrum, Montreal.

Main office, 136 King street, East, Toronto.

## THE CANADIAN COLORED COTTON MILLS CO., LIMITED

A corporation formed under the laws of the Dominion of Canada, February 20, 1892, for the purpose of manufacturing cotton cloth and prints. The company runs two mills at Cornwall, one at Merritton, one at Hamilton and one at Milltown, N. B., and controls the Gibson Cotton Mills at Marysville, N. B.

Stock......Par $100..........................Authorized, $5,000,000......Issued, $2,700,000

The company has no preferred stock. Stock is transferred at the company's office, Montreal.

Dividends on the stock are paid at the rate of 4 per cent. annually, dividend periods being January (15), April, July, October.

FUNDED DEBT.

1st mort., 6 per cent. bonds, due April, 1912, April and Oct......................... $2,000,000

The 6 per cent. bonds matured in 1902 and were renewed for 10 years.

Trustee of the mortgage, The Royal Trust Co., Montreal. Agent for the payment of the interest, Bank of Montreal.

In 1900, the net profits of the company were $465,428; in 1901, $328,335; charges, $120,000.

President, David Morrice; Vice-President, C. D. Owen; Secretary-Treasurer, A. Bruce.

Directors—George A. Drummond, E. S. Clouston, T. King, David Morrice, David Morrice, Jr., C. D. Owen.

Main office, 1760 Notre Dame street, Montreal, Que. Annual meeting in May, at Montreal.

## CANADIAN GENERAL ELECTRIC CO., LIMITED

A corporation formed under the laws of the Dominion of Canada in 1892. The purposes of the company are the manufacture and sale of electrical machinery and supplies. It has factories at Montreal, Toronto and Peterboro, Ont. The company in December, 1900, acquired the manufacturing department of the Royal Electric Co., Montreal. In 1900 it also acquired the property of the Canada Foundry Co. The Northey Manufacturing Co. of Toronto, manufacturers of pumps and hydraulic machinery, was acquired in 1902.

Stock....Par $100.....Authorized { com., $1,700,000 / pref., 300,000 } Issued { com., $2,125,000 / pref., 300,000 } $2,425,000

The preferred stock is 6 per cent., cumulative. After January 1, 1902, the company has the right to retire the preferred stock at 105. In February, 1900, the common stock was increased by an issue of $300,000, which was allotted to the stockholders at $125 per share; in 1901 $500,000 additional common stock was issued, and in May, 1902, $425,000 additional common was allotted to the stockholders at $150 per share, making the amount outstanding $2,125,000.

Dividends of 6 per cent. per annum on the preferred and 10 per cent. per annum on the common are paid, the payments being semi-annual in January and July.

The company has no funded debt.

EARNINGS.

| | Net. | Dividends. Com. | Pfd. | Amount of Dividends. | Surplus. |
|---|---|---|---|---|---|
| 1900 | $262,903 | 10 | 6 | $127,623 | $135,280 |
| 1901 | 345,990 | 10 | 6 | 166,750 | 179,240 |
| 1902 | 436,863 | 10 | 6 | 213,739 | 223,123 |

The company's balance sheet December 31, 1902, showed total assets, $4,138,694; reserve fund, $787,000; contingent account, $100,000; profit and loss, $80,722.

President, W. R. Brock; 1st Vice-President, H. P. Dwight; 2d Vice-President, Secretary and Managing Director, Frederic Nicholls.

Directors—W. R. Brock, H. P. Dwight, Frederic Nicholls, George A. Cox, J. K. Kerr, William Mackenzie, Rodolphe Forget, W. D. Matthews, Herbert S. Holt, E. B. Osler, Robert Jaffray, James Ross, H. G. Nicholls, Sir William C. Van Horne.

Corporate and main office, 14 King street, East, Toronto. Annual meeting, in February, at Toronto.

## CANADIAN STEEL & COAL CO.

A corporation formed under the laws of South Dakota in July, 1902, to do a general mining and operating business in coal and iron. The company has acquired 4,000 acres of iron ore property at Natashquan, Province of Quebec, and 9,600 acres of coal property in Cape Breton, N. S. The coal property has been in operation for the past thirty years.

Stock...Par $100....Authorized { com., $5,000,000 / pref., 1,000,000 } Issued { com., $5,000,000 / pref., ...... } $5,000,000

The preferred stock is 7 per cent. cumulative; it remained in the treasury of the company at the beginning of 1903. Transfer Agent and Registrar, Colonial Securities Co., New York.

The company has no funded debt.

Earnings from the coal property amount to about $90,000 net annually.

President, Louis B. Jennings, New York; Vice-President, F. S. Ashley; Secretary, John G. Pearse; Treasurer, J. C. Sinclair.

Directors—J. L. Bittinger, Montreal; F. W. Peck, Chicago; Louis B. Jennings, New York; F. S. Ashley, John G. Pearse, J. C. Sinclair.

New York office, 63 Wall street; Canadian office, Temple Building, Montreal.

## CANTON CO.

A Maryland corporation, incorporated by the State Legislature in 1828-29, which owns some 1800 acres of land in the city of Baltimore and adjoining in Baltimore County, with docks and improvements, etc. The company formerly owned the Union Railroad of Baltimore, but in 1882 sold it to the Northern Central Railway.

Stock......Par $100........................ Authorized, $2,500,000......Issued, $1,330,900

Transfer Agents, Maryland Trust Co., Baltimore.

There was originally 50,000 shares of the company's stock which has been reduced by purchase by the company and cancellation at various times to 23,416 shares in March, 1903.

The sinking fund of the 2d mortgage Union Railroad of Baltimore reverted to the Canton Co., May 1, 1900, when said bonds matured. The bonded debt of the railroad company was assumed by the Northern Central Railway Co., when it purchased the road from the Canton Co. The amount received from the trustees during 1900 and 1901, $583,199.

In the year ending May 31, 1898, the total receipts from all sources were $120,240; payments, $110,403; surplus, $89,845. In 1899, receipts were $112,653; payments, $90,967; surplus, $21,685; total surplus May 31, 1899, $41,822. In 1900, receipts $456,629; surplus, $70,303. In 1901, receipts, $503,291; payments, $548,598; surplus, $24,996. In 1902, receipts, $185,451; payments, $129,492; surplus, $80,955.

On May 10, 1900, a dividend of $10 per share was paid. This was a payment out of the Union Railroad sinking fund. A dividend of $1 per share was paid in July, 1900; 50 cents per share was paid in March, 1901; $1 per share July 15, 1901, and $1 per share March 1, 1902.

President, Walter B. Brooks, Jr.; Vice-President, Alexander Brown; Secretary, William W. Janney; Treasurer, Stuart Kearney.

Directors—Walter B. Brooks, Jr., Alexander Brown, D. D. Mallory, J. W. Middendorf, George C. Jenkins, Baltimore; James B. Colgate, William Baylis, Ferdinand M. Thieriot, John D. Probst, New York.

Main office, Toone and Second streets, Canton, Baltimore County, Md. Annual meeting, second Wednesday in June.

## CAPE BRETON ELECTRIC CO., LIMITED

A corporation formed under the laws of Nova Scotia. The company was organized for the purpose of constructing an electric road in and about Sydney, N. S., and from North Sydney to Sydney mines. It also owns the electric lighting business in Sydney and North Sydney, and a line of ferries across Sydney Harbor between those two places. It is jointly interested with the Dominion Coal Co. in the construction of an interurban line from Sydney to Glace Bay. The road is in process of construction. The franchise of the company expires in 1931.

Stock....Par $100.....Authorized {com., $1,000,000; pref., 1,000,000} Issued {com., $1,000,000; pref., 234,000} $1,234,000

The preferred stock is 6 per cent., non-cumulative. The dividends on the preferred are payable May 1 and November 1.

Transfer Agents, Stone & Webster, 93 Federal street, Boston. Registrar, State Street Trust Co., Boston.

FUNDED DEBT.

1st mort., 5 per cent., due Jan., 1932, Jan. and July................................. $850,000

The 1st mortgage is for $1,500,000. Trustee of the mortgage and agent for the payment of interest, State Street Trust Co., Boston.

In 1902 the earnings of the companies' electric light department were: gross, $46,125; net, $21,276. In the same year the ferry department earned: gross, $33,219; net, $9,549. The railways had been put in operation too recently for any report of earnings

President, E. S. Webster; Vice-President, G. R. Fearing, Jr.; Secretary, H. R. Hayes; Treasurer, H. B. Sawyer; General Managers, Stone & Webster, Boston.

Directors—E. S. Webster, Walter Crowe, W. Wadsworth, J. N. Armstrong, G. R. Fearing, Jr., B. F. Pearson, B. H. Dibblee.

Corporate and main office, Sydney, N. S.; Boston office, 93 Federal street. Annual meeting, first Tuesday in May.

## CAPITAL TRACTION CO.

A corporation formed in 1895. The companyais a consolidation of the Washington & Georgetown Railroad Co. and the Rock Creek Railw y Co. Road operated, 36 miles, equipped with underground trolley system.

Stock......Par $100........................Authorized, $12,000,000......Issued, $12,000,000

Transfer Agent, United States Mortgage & Trust Co., New York. Registrar, Union Trust Co., New York.

The company in 1899 paid 3 per cent. on its stock. In 1900 the dividends were 3¼ per cent. Since April, 1900, 1 per cent. quarterly has been paid in January (1), April, July and October.

An extra dividend of $4 per share was paid on October 1, 1902.

FUNDED DEBT.

1st mort., 4 per cent., due April, 1920, April and Oct.... .......................... $1,080,000

The 1st mortgage 4 per cent. bonds were created in 1900, and were issued to retire the old 5 per cent. bonds. Trustee of mortgage, National Safe Deposit, Savings & Trust Co., Washington.

| EARNINGS. | Gross. | Net. |
|---|---|---|
| 1901 | $1,231,683 | $691,189 |
| 1902 | 1,381,092 | 770,052 |

President, George T. Dunlop; Vice-President, Charles C. Glover; Secretary and Treasurer, Charles M. Koones; Chief Engineer and Superintendent, D. S. Carll.

Directors—George T. Dunlop, Charles C. Glover, Henry Hurt, Edward J. Stellwagen, Maurice J. Adler, John S. Larcombe, Washington, D. C.; William Manice, New York.

Main office, Thirty-sixth and M streets, N. W., Washington, D. C. Annual meeting, second Wednesday in January.

## THE CARIBOO M'KINNEY MINING & MILLING CO., LIMITED

A corporation formed under the laws of the Dominion of Canada for the purpose of operating mining properties in British Columbia. The company was reorganized in 1898. Its mines are at Camp M'Kinney, Yale Mining District, British Columbia.

Stock......Par $1............................Authorized, $1,250,000......Issued, $1,250,000

The stock is full paid and non-assessable and is without personal liability. The company has no preferred stock and no funded debt. Transfer Agent, National Trust Co., Limited, Toronto.

During 1902 two dividends, aggregating 4 per cent., were paid on the company's stock.

President, Robert Jaffray; Vice-President, H. M. Pellatt; Secretary, F. W. Thompson; Treasurer, S. W. McMichael.

Directors—Robert Jaffray, H. M. Pellatt, George B. McAulay, S. W. McMichael, Thomas Long, A. Ansley, G. B. Smith.

Main office, 34 Yonge street, Toronto. Annual meeting, first Tuesday in February, at Toronto.

## THE CARTER-CRUME CO., LIMITED

A corporation formed under the laws of Ontario in 1899. The company was organized to take over the plant and business of the Carter-Crume Co., of Toronto and Niagara Falls, N. Y. The company manufactures merchants' duplicating sales check books and autographic registers and has factories at Toronto, Niagara Falls, and in California. In 1902 the company acquired control of the Kidder Press Co., Dover, N. H.

Stock..Par $100..Authorized { com., $1,250,000 / pref., 750,000 }   Issued { com., $1,250,000 / pref., 725,000 }   $1,975,000

The preferred stock is 7 per cent., cumulative. The company in 1901 purchased and cancelled $25,000 of its preferred stock.

Transfer Agent and Registrar, National Trust Co., Toronto.

The company pays 7 per cent. per annum on the preferred stock, the dividends being quarterly, 1¾ per cent. in January (1), April, July and October.

On the common stock 5 per cent. was paid in 1900, 1901 and 1902. The dividends are 1¼ per cent. each in January (1), April, July and October.

In the fiscal year ending September 30, 1900, the net profits of the company were $170,951. In 1901 net profits, $179,030. In 1902 net Profits, $181,870.

President, Robert Kilgour; Vice-President, J. W. Flavelle; General Manager, S. J. Moore.

Directors—J. W. Flavelle, C. D. Massey, C. H. Duell, W. Caryl Ely, Robert Kilgour, J. L. Morrison, S. J. Moore, A. E. Ames.

Main office, 28 Front street, West, Toronto. Annual meeting, October or November.

## CASEIN COMPANY OF AMERICA

A corporation formed under the laws of New Jersey, March 3, 1900. The object of the company is the manufacture of paint, paper size, glue, food products, milk sugar, etc., from by-products of milk.

The company acquired the plants from the following concerns:

William A. Hall, Bellows Falls, Vt.

National Milk Sugar Co., South New Berlin, Cherry Valley, Rockdale, South Edmeston and Bainbridge, N. Y.; St. Charles, Garden Prairie, Huntley and Union, Ill.

Hayne & Whitaker, Antwerp and Chester, N. Y.

Rosemary Creamery, Mexico and Adams, N. Y.

The united capacities of these stations is about 1,585,000 pounds per month.

Stock..Par...$100...Authorized { com., $5,500,000 / pref., 1,000,000 } Issued { com., $5,492,000 / pref., 1,000,000 } $6,492,000

The preferred stock is 8 per cent., cumulative, and was issued for cash at par.

Transfer Agent, Registrar & Transfer Co., Jersey City. Registrar, Manhattan Trust Co., New York.

The company began the payment of quarterly dividends of 2 per cent., or at the rate of 8 per cent. per annum, on its preferred stock on August 1, 1900, and has continued such quarterly payments regularly in February, May, August and November.

The company has no funded debt, nor any mortgages on its properties except one of $4,320 at Adams, N. Y.

The surplus of the concerns acquired and the amount derived from subscriptions to the preferred stock furnished the company with ample working capital.

In the six months ending December 31, 1900, the gross sales were reported as $196,967. In the year ending December 31, 1901, they were $1,338,230. In 1902 they were $1,615,037. The surplus December 31, 1902, was $205,000.

President, William A. Hall; 1st Vice-President, Isaac L. Rice; 2d Vice-President, Cushing Adams; 3d Vice-President, L. R. Schwerin; Treasurer, Rudolph H. Kissel; Secretary, Maurice Barnett.

Directors—William A. Hall, Cushing Adams, Bellows Falls, Vt.; Isaac L. Rice, William C. Osborn, Rudolph H. Kissel, Maurice Barnett, Louis Stern, Norman Henderson, George J. Gillespie, New York; Albert E. Richardson, Burlington, Vt.

Main office, Bellows Falls, Vt.; branch offices, 11 Broadway, New York; 55 Montgomery street, Jersey City. Annual meeting, second Wednesday in May at Jersey City.

## THE CATARACT POWER & CONDUIT CO.

A corporation formed under the laws of New York in 1897. The business of the company is the transmission and distribution of the electric power generated at Niagara Falls by the Niagara Falls Power Co. This company furnishes currents for electric lighting and power for street railways, motors, elevators, etc.

Stock......Par $100..........................Authorized, $2,000,000......Issued, $2,000,000

Stock is transferred at the office of the company, Buffalo.

FUNDED DEBT.

1st mort., 5 per cent., due 1927........................................ .......... $700,000

The trustee of the mortgage and agent for the payment of interest, Metropolitan Trust Co., New York.

President, Darius O. Mills; 1st Vice-President, George Urban, Jr.; 2d Vice-President and General Manager, Charles R. Huntley; Secretary and Treasurer, DeLancey Rankine.

Directors—Edward D. Adams, John Jacob Astor, Edward A. Wickes, Daniel O'Day, Darius O. Mills, Francis Lynde Stetson, New York; William B. Rankine, Niagara Falls, N. Y.; George Urban, Jr., Charles R. Huntley, Buffalo, N. Y.

Main office, 40 Court street, Buffalo, N. Y. Annual meeting, first Tuesday in July.

## THE CELLULOID CO.

A corporation organized under the laws of New Jersey in 1890. The company was a combination of various concerns engaged in the manufacture of celluloid or artificial ivory and goods made therefrom. The companies acquired included the Celluloid Manufacturing Co., the American Zylonite Co. and other concerns engaged in the same line of business. This company acquired all of the patents, processes and establishments of the constituent companies in exchange for its stock. The company has a large factory at Newark, N. J., and manufactures all varieties of celluloid goods and kindred products, under the trade-mark "Celluloid."

Stock......Par $100..........................Authorized, $6,000,000......Issued $5,925,000

The company has no funded or floating debt of any kind. Stock is transferred at the company's office, New York.

Dividends from the time of organization have been as follows: In 1892, 6 per cent.; in 1893, 5½ per cent.; in 1894, 4 per cent.; in 1895, 4 per cent.; in 1896, 4 per cent.; in 1897, 4 per cent.; in 1898, 5 per cent.; in 1899, 6 per cent., including 1 per cent. extra; in 1900 and 1901, 7 per cent., including 1 per cent. extra, and in 1902, 8 per cent., which includes an extra dividend of 2 per cent. paid December 31, 1902. Dividends are quarterly, January (1), April, July and October.

President, Marshall C. Lefferts; Vice-President, John A. Bartow; Treasurer, Frederic R. Lefferts; Secretary, J. R. Halsey, New York.

Directors—Marshall C. Lefferts, John A. Bartow, Henry C. Hulbert, Joseph Larocque, Frederic R. Lefferts, H. C. Tinker, R. F. Ballantine, W. C. Smith, C. L. Balch, John Eastwood, W. W. Newcomb, John W. Hyatt, W. S. Sillcocks, J. W. Plume, Joseph Larocque, Jr.

Corporate office, 295 Ferry street, Newark, N. J.; New York office, 36 Washington place. Annual meeting, last Tuesday in March, at Newark, N. J.

## CENTENNIAL COPPER MINING CO.

A corporation formed under the laws of Michigan in 1896. The company owns a square mile of mineral land in Houghton County, Mich., located immediately north of the Calumet & Hecla and west of the Wolverine mine. The company also owns a mill site on Torch Lake, opposite the Calumet & Hecla mill.

Stock......Par $25...........................Authorized, $2,500,000......Issued, $2,500,000

The company has 10,000 shares of the stock in its treasury. Stock is transferred at the company's office. Registrar, Old Colony Trust Co., Boston.

President, Harry F. Fay; Secretary, Walter B. Mosman; Treasurer, George G. Endicott, Boston.

Directors—Harry F. Fay, John C. Watson, William Howell Reed, S. R. Dow, Walter B. Mosman, Boston; James Chynoweth, Calumet, Mich.

Main office, 60 State street, Boston. Annual meeting, first Tuesday in April, at Boston.

## CENTENNIAL-EUREKA MINING CO.

A corporation formed under the laws of Utah in 1876. The company owns and operates a large silver and gold mining property near Eureka, Juab County, Utah. Over 99 per cent. of the stock of this company is owned by the United States Mining Co.

Stock......Par $25...........................Authorized, $5,000,000......Issued, $2,500,000

Registrar, National Shawmut Bank, Boston.

At the close of 1900 the company had paid in dividends over $2,400,000. Dividends are paid quarterly. In 1900 paid $1 per share; in 1901 paid $2; on January 10, 1902, 50 cents per share was paid.

President, Robert D. Evans, Boston; Vice-President, C. A. Hight, Portland, Me.; Secretary and Treasurer, F. W. Batchelder, Boston; Managing Director, Albert F. Holden, Cleveland.

Directors—Robert D. Evans, William H. Coolidge, Bradley W. Palmer, Herbert F. Winslow, Boston; C. A. Hight, Portland, Me.; Albert F. Holden, Cleveland.

Main office, 4 Post Office square, Boston. Annual meeting, third Wednesday in April, at Boston.

## CENTRAL & SOUTH AMERICAN TELEGRAPH CO.

A corporation formed under the laws of New York. Owns cable lines and land lines extending from Vera Cruz, Mexico, to the principal ports and cities of Central America and the west coast of South America, as far as Valparaiso, Chili. In 1891 acquired the Trans-Andean line from Valparaiso to Buenos Ayres, Argentine Republic. Cable lines, about 7,318 miles;

land lines, about 1,500 miles. The company has exclusive contracts with the governments of various states of Central and South America; also working agreements with the Mexican Telegraph Co. and the Western Union Telegraph Co.

Stock......Par $100.........................Authorized, $8,000,000......Issued, $7,725,600

In 1890 a stock dividend of 20 per cent. was paid. Stock is transferred at the office of the company. Registrar, Union Trust Co., New York.

| Earnings. | Gross. | Net. |
|---|---|---|
| 1897 | $825,189 | $506,999 |
| 1898 | 937,229 | 537,229 |
| 1899 | 944,086 | 598,971 |
| 1900 | 927,888 | 475,691 |
| 1901 | 982,053 | 549,718 |

From 1888 to 1896 7 per cent. was paid on stock; in 1897, 6¾ per cent.; in 1898, 1899, 1900, 1901 and 1902, 6 per cent. Dividends are paid quarterly, January, April, July and October.

President, James A. Scrymser; Vice-Presidents, Charles Lanier, New York; S. Camacho, City of Mexico; Secretary, J. R. Beard; Treasurer, Clarence Rapkin, New York.

Directors—James A. Scrymser, W. R. Grace, E. D. Adams, W. D. Sloane, Charles Lanier, William G. Hamilton, John L. Riker, New York; T. Jefferson Coolidge, Francis L. Higginson, Boston.

Main office, 66 Broadway, New York. Annual meeting, first Tuesday in June.

## THE CENTRAL CAR TRUST CO.

A corporation organized under the laws of New Jersey in 1884. The company does a large business in connection with car trusts, and under such arrangements leases considerable equipment to various railroad companies.

Stock......Par $100..............................Authorized, $500,000......Issued, $500,000

The company had at the beginning of 1903 car trust bonds outstanding to the amount of about $656,000.

President, E. W. Clark, Jr.; Vice-President, S. W. Colton, Jr.; Treasurer, C. M. Clark; Secretary, C. A. Pearson, Jr.; Assistant Secretary and Assistant Treasurer, H. L. Clark.

Directors—E. W. Clark, E. W. Clark, Jr., C. A. Pearson, Jr., S. W. Colton, Jr., C. M. Clark, Clarence Sill, Philadelphia; George H. B. Martin, Camden, N. J.

Corporate office, Camden, N. J. Financial Agents, E. W. Clark & Co., Philadelphia. Annual meeting, second Wednesday in May.

## CENTRAL COAL & COKE CO.

A corporation organized under the laws of Missouri, April 16, 1893. The company was a consolidation of a number of coal and lumber companies, and operates mines in Missouri, Kansas, Arkansas, the Indian Territory and Wyoming, with large sawmills at Texarkana, Tex., and Keith, La. Its daily output of coal is about 20,000 tons, and of lumber about 600,000 feet.

In February, 1902, this company acquired the Kansas & Texas Coal Co.

Stock....Par $100....Authorized { com., $5,125,000; pref., 1,875,000 } Issued { com., $5,125,000; pref., 1,875,000 } $7,000,000

The preferred stock is 5 per cent., cumulative. The company on June 1, 1901, had assets to the amount of $5,449,527.

Transfer Agent, Nathaniel Norton, 63 Wall street, New York. Registrar, Continental Trust Co., New York.

Regular dividends of 5 per cent. per annum are paid on the preferred stock in quarterly payments of 1¼ per cent. each in January, April, July, October. Dividends of 1½ per cent., or 6 per cent. per annum, are paid on the common stock at the same periods.

| Funded Debt. | |
|---|---|
| Central Coal & Coke Co. gen. con. mort., 6 per cent | $1,250,000 |
| " " " 1st mort., 6 per cent | 650,000 |
| Sweetwater Coal Mining Co., 1st mort., 6 per cent | 204,000 |
| Kansas & Texas Coal Co., 1st mort., 5 per cent | 235,000 |
| " " " 1st mort., 6 per cent | 140,000 |
| Caliente Coal Co., 1st mort., 6 per cent | 20,000 |
| Total | $2,499,000 |

President, Richard H. Keith; Vice-President, Charles Campbell; Secretary and Treasurer, Edward E. Riley, Kansas City, Mo.; Assistant Secretary and Transfer Agent, Nathaniel Norton, New York.

Directors—Richard H. Keith, Charles Campbell, W. C. Perry, C. S. Keith, J. C. Sherwood, Edward E. Riley, Kansas City, Mo.; E. P. Merwin, A. Heckscher, New York; Charles H. Huttig, St. Louis; E. T. Stotesbury, Caleb F. Fox, Philadelphia.

Main office, Keith & Perry Building, Kansas City, Mo.; New York office, 63 Wall street. Annual meeting, fourth Wednesday in July.

## CENTRAL DISTRICT & PRINTING TELEGRAPH CO.

A corporation originally organized under the laws of New York in 1874, and incorporated under an act of the Legislature of Pennsylvania, August 9, 1881. The company operates a telephone system under an exclusive license from the American Bell Telephone Co. in the cities of Pittsburg and Allegheny, Pa., and the adjacent counties of Pennsylvania, Ohio and West Virginia, including the cities of Marietta, O., East Liverpool, O., Wheeling and Parkersburg, W. Va. On January 1, 1903, the company had 41,844 exchange subscribers and 96,145 miles of wire. A controlling interest is owned by the American Telephone & Telegraph Co., which in January, 1903, held $5,856,800 of the stock.

Stock......Par $100..........................Authorized, $10,000,000......Issued, $8,750,000

The stock was increased from $7,500,000 to $10,000,000 in February, 1902. In 1902 the stockholders subscribed for $1,280,000 additional stock at par, making the amount issued $8,750,000.

Transfer Agent, Union Trust Co., Pittsburg.

Dividends of 8 per cent. per annum are paid on the stock of the company, payments being quarterly, 2 per cent. each, in January, April, July and October.

The company has no funded debt.

EARNINGS.

| | Gross. | Net. | Dividends. | Surplus. |
|---|---|---|---|---|
| 1900 | $1,796,400 | $341,724 | $320,000 | $21,724 |
| 1901 | 1,937,732 | 424,752 | 400,000 | 24,752 |
| 1902 | 2,165,981 | 478,050 | 600,000 | Def., 121,950 |

The total surplus of the company December 31, 1902, was $432,047.

President, D. Leet Wilson; Vice-President, D. F. Henry; Secretary, John G. Stokes; Treasurer, F. M. Stephenson, Pittsburg.

Directors—D. Leet Wilson, D. F. Henry, George I. Whitney, Charles E. Speer, J. H. Willock, Daniel H. Wallace, Pittsburg; Frederick P. Fish, C. Jay French, Joseph P. Davis, Boston.

Main office, 416 Seventh avenue, Pittsburg. Annual meeting, second Thursday in February.

## CENTRAL ELECTRIC CO.

A corporation formed under the laws of New Jersey in 1900 for the purpose of supplying electric light, heat and power. The company is a consolidation by merger of the following companies:

Middlesex Electric Co.
Edison Electric Illuminating Co.
Raritan Electric, Light and Power Co.
Rahway Electric Co.
Bound Brook Electric, Light, Heat and Power Co.

The company has perpetual and unlimited franchises to do business in Metuchen, New Brunswick, Perth Amboy, Rahway, Woodbridge, Raritan, Bond Brook, Dunellen, South Plainfield and adjacent territory. It has a power plant at Metuchen and distributing sub-stations at Perth Amboy, New Brunswick, Rahway and Lincoln.

Stock......Par $100.............................Authorized, $750,000......Issued, $750,000

The company has no preferred stock.

FUNDED DEBT.

1st mort., 5 per cent. gold bonds, due 1940.......................................... $750,000

The bond issue is the full amount authorized. The bonds are subject to redemption at 110 per cent. after July, 1905. Trustee of the mortgage, Fidelity Trust Co., Newark, N. J.

President, Philip N. Jackson; Vice-President, Adrian Riker; Treasurer, Percy Ingalls; Secretary, L. D. Howard Gilmour, Newark, N. J.

Directors—Thomas N. McCarter, Chandler W. Riker, Dudley Farrand, Adrian Riker, Philip N. Jackson, Uzal H. McCarter, L. D. Howard Gilmour, Newark, N. J.; W. W. Smalley, Bound Brook, N. J.; Herbert C. Richardson, Metuchen, N. J.

Corporate office, Newark, N. J.; main office, New Brunswick, N. J.

## CENTRAL FIREWORKS CO.

A corporation formed under the laws of New Jersey, June 8, 1896. The business of the company is to manufacture and deal in fireworks, and it has power to purchase, hold and dispose of the stocks or securities of corporations organized for such purposes. The assent of all the directors is necessary for every such purchase. The company owns a majority of the stock of the following concerns:

Detwiller & Street Fireworks Manufacturing Co., New York.
Consolidated Fireworks Co. of America, New York.
The A. L. Due Fireworks Co., Cincinnati, O.
St. Louis Fireworks Co., St. Louis, Mo.
Scharfenberg Fireworks Manufacturing Co., Brooklyn, N. Y.
Pain's Fireworks Co., New York.

Stock....Par $100.....Authorized { com., $1,750,000; pref., 1,750,000 } Issued { com., $1,406,500; pref., 1,267,200 } $2,673,700

The preferred stock is 7 per cent., cumulative. The company has no bonds, funded indebtedness or floating debt.

Transfer Agent, F. L. Hammatt, 9 Park place, New York. Registrar, Corporation Trust Co. of New Jersey, Jersey City.

The company pays semi-annual dividends of 3½ per cent. each on its preferred stock, February 10 and August 10, and semi-annual dividends of 1 per cent. at the same periods on its common stock.

The company's balance sheet of January 28, 1902, showed total assets, $2,734,232; surplus, $59,854.

President, William A. Turner, New York; Vice-President, Jacob J. Detwiller, Jersey City; Secretary and Treasurer, George T. Egbert, New York.

Directors—George T. Egbert, John S. Stanton, A. M. Poole, T. J. Scharfenberg, William A. Turner, New York; C. J. Detwiller, Jacob J. Detwiller, Jersey City; Edmund J. Bingle, St. Louis; Henry Krucker, Cincinnati.

Main office, 15 Exchange place, Jersey City; New York office, 9 Park place. Annual meeting, fourth Tuesday in January, at the company's office, Jersey City. Transfer books close twenty days prior to the annual meeting.

---

## CENTRAL FOUNDRY CO.

A corporation formed under the laws of New Jersey, July 11, 1899. The company manufactures cast-iron soil pipe and fittings. It owns and operates the following establishments for the production of such articles:

A. L. Swett Plant, Medina, N. Y.
Bessemer Plant, Bessemer, Ala.
E. L. Tyler & Co. Plant, Anniston, Ala.
H., B. & W. Plant, Gadsden, Ala.
McShane Plant, Baltimore.
Midvale Plant, Allentown, Pa.
Monitor I. Plant, Newark, N. J.
Phoenix Plant, Lansdale, Pa.
Regester Plant, Baltimore.
Shuster Plant, South Pittsburg, Tenn.
Vincennes Plant, Vincennes, Ind.
Wilmington Plant, Wilmington, Del.
Central Iron & Coal Co., Tuscaloosa, Ala.

Stock...Par $100..Authorized { com., $7,000,000; pref., 7,000,000 } Issued { com., $7,000,000; pref., 7,000,000 } $14,000,000

The preferred stock is 7 per cent., cumulative. There is $350,000 of each class in the company's treasury.

Transfer Agents, Baring, Magoun & Co., New York.

FUNDED DEBT.

Debentures, 6 per cent., due May, 1919, May and Nov. .............................. $3,863,000

In the year ending June 30, 1902, the company reported gross earnings, $378,054; charges, $231,780; betterments, etc., $89,157; surplus, $57,117.

President, Alfred Fowle, Jr.; Vice-President, George F. Ross; 2d Vice-President, Gerard Schumacher; Secretary and Treasurer, Winthrop L. Rogers.

Directors—John Reid, Alfred Fowle, Jr., Robert A. Regester, Gerard Schumacher, Winthrop L. Rogers, A. L. Swett, George F. Crane, Charles F. Smithers, George D. Hallack, James T. Boothroyd, George F. Ross, Joseph Lodge.

Executive Committee—John Reid, Alfred Fowle, Jr., Robert A. Regester, Gerard Schumacher, A. L. Swett, Albert H. Henderson, Charles F. Smithers.

Main office, 116 Nassau street, New York. Annual meeting, last Thursday in July.

## CENTRAL LEAD CO.

A corporation formed under the laws of Missouri in 1874 for the purpose of mining, smelting and refining lead. The company owns 1,600 acres of lead lands at Flat River, Mo. The plant has a capacity of 600 tons per day.

Stock......Par $100..........................Authorized, $1,000,000......Issued, $1,000,000

The company has no preferred stock. Dividends on the common have been regularly paid since June, 1897, the rate being ½ per cent. monthly. Transfer Agent and Registrar, J. C. Howe, 510 Pine street, St. Louis.

President, Arthur Thacher; Vice-President, F. H. Ludington; Secretary and Treasurer, J. C. Howe, St. Louis.

Directors—Arthur Thacher, F. H. Ludington, S. C. Edgar, J. C. Howe, W. E. Guy, F. R. Rice, Allan T. Simpkins, St. Louis.

Main office, 510 Pine street, St. Louis. Annual meeting, second Wednesday in January, at St. Louis.

## CENTRAL LIGHTING CO.

A corporation formed under the laws of New Jersey, December, 1901. The company owns the patents covering an improved form of gas burner. The policy of the company is to form sub-companies in various States to distribute its product.

Stock:...Par $100.....Authorized { com., $500,000 / pref., 500,000 } Issued { com., $500,000 / pref., 500,000 } $1,000,000

The preferred stock is 8 per cent., cumulative. Transfer Agents, Emerson McMillin Co., New York. Registrar, Union Trust Co., New York.

The company has no funded debt.

President, Emerson McMillin; Vice-President, William M. Fleitmann; Treasurer, A. H. Ostrom; Secretary, A. Lincoln Eglinton, New York.

Directors—Emerson McMillin, William M. Fleitmann, Charles N. King, Charles H. Tweed, S. Edward Nash, L. F. Dommerich, Arthur P. Heinze, Reinhard Seidenburg, E. E. Reeve Merritt, New York.

Corporate office, 245 Washington street, Jersey City; main office, 40 Wall street, New York. Annual meeting, third Tuesday in February.

## CENTRAL NEW YORK TELEPHONE & TELEGRAPH CO.

A corporation formed under the laws of New York, December 23, 1882. The company owns and operates a telephone system which extends throughout eleven counties in the central portion of New York, including the cities of Utica and Syracuse. A controlling interest in the stock is owned by the American Telephone & Telegraph Co.

Stock......Par $100............................Authorized, $1,000,000......Issued, $961,500

The company has no preferred stock. Stock is transferred at the office of the company, Utica, N. Y.

Dividends are quarterly, in February, May, August and November. In 1902 the company paid 1 per cent. on its stock.

FUNDED DEBT.

Debentures, 5 per cent., due Dec., 1918, June and Dec.............................. $100,000

The debenture bonds outstanding are the full amount authorized.

President, Lewis H. Lawrence; 1st Vice-President, Joseph Rudd; 2d Vice-President and General Manager, Jeffries Wyman; Secretary and Treasurer, Francis G. Wood, Utica, N. Y.

Directors—Frederick P. Fish, C. Jay French, Boston; Lewis H. Lawrence, Frederick T. Proctor, Frederick G. Fincke, J. F. Maynard, Charles B. Rogers, Joseph Rudd, Francis G. Wood, Jeffries Wyman, George L. Bradford, Utica, N. Y.

Main office, 122 Bleecker street, Utica, N. Y. Annual meeting, second Thursday in February, at Utica.

## CENTRAL OIL CO.

A corporation formed under the laws of Maine, April 11, 1899. The company owned all the stock of the Henry Oil Co. and of the Fearless Oil Co., and took over the property of those companies, which have been dissolved. The company produces a crude petroleum, operating principally in West Virginia and Southern Ohio.

Stock......Par $25..........................Authorized, $2,000,000......Issued, $1,501,250

Stock is transferred at the company's office. Registrar, Mercantile Trust Co., Boston.
The company has no funded debt.
The net earnings in 1899 were $232,628; in 1900, $260,557; in 1901, $160,106.
In October, 1899, the first quarterly dividend of 1½ per cent. was declared, payable November 1, 1899. The company paid regular dividends at the same rate in February, May, August and November, until August, 1901, when the quarterly dividend was deferred to provide for indebtedness and development work. A dividend of 1 per cent. was paid February 1, 1902, and similar dividends in May, August and November, 1902.
In the year 1902 the company's gross earnings were $253,786; net, $151,503.
President, Alfred A. Glasier, Boston; Vice-President, H. C. Speer, Chicago; Secretary and Treasurer, Walter F. Pope, Boston.
Directors—Josiah Q. Bennett, Simon Davis, Alfred A. Glasier, William L. Henry, Walter F. Pope, Boston; H. C. Speer, J. P. Underwood, Chicago; J. P. Morse, Brockton, Mass.; A. B. Bruce, Lawrence, Mass.
Main office, 194 Washington street, Boston. Annual meeting, third Tuesday of February, at Portland, Me.

## CENTRAL RAILWAY & BRIDGE CO.

A Kentucky corporation which owns a bridge nearly 2,000 feet long over the Ohio river between Cincinnati and Newport, Ky., together with the approaches thereto. The bridge is used by street railway lines in the two cities as well as for general traffic.

Stock......Par $100..........................Authorized, $1,500,000......Issued $1,500,000

FUNDED DEBT.

1st mort., 5 per cent., due 1940, Jan. and July.................................... $1,000,000

The bonds are a 1st mortgage upon the bridge and all the property of the company. There is a sinking fund of $5,000 per annum until 1921, when it increases to $10,000 per annum.
President, John A. Williamson; Secretary, L. R. Hawthorne.
Main office, 191 York street, Newport, Ky.

## THE CENTRAL STATION HEATING CO.

A corporation formed under the laws of West Virginia in March, 1900. The business of the company is to construct and operate central heating stations under the patents of Isaac D. Smead. By it it is possible to heat from one to one thousand or more large buildings from a single station by means of hot water mains.

Stock...Par $100....Authorized { com., $1,500,000 / pref., 500,000 } Issued { com., $1,500,000 / pref, 500,000 } $2,000,000

The preferred stock is 6 per cent., non-cumulative. The company has no funded debt. It operates a 300-house station, built by the company.
President and Treasurer, William E. Hutton; Vice-President, Charles E. Prior; Secretary, A. M. Ainslie; General Manager, Isaac D. Smead.
Directors—William E. Hutton, Charles E. Prior, A. M. Ainslie, Isaac D. Smead, A. C. Cassatt, Cincinnati.
Main office, 110 East Fourth street, Cincinnati.

## CENTRAL UNION TELEPHONE CO.

A corporation formed in June, 1883, to consolidate the Western, the Midland and the Central Telephone Cos. It operates telephone systems under exclusive license from the American Bell Telephone Co., its territory covering the States of Ohio, Indiana and Illinois, with the exception of a few counties in each State which contain large cities like Chicago, Cleveland, Cincinnati, etc. The company is controlled by the American Telephone & Telegraph Co., which owns $3,527,655 of the stock. The Iowa Telephone Co., which covers the State of Iowa under a Bell Company's license, was controlled jointly by this company and the American Bell Telephone Co., and in 1900 was merged with this company, the latter issuing its stock in exchange for the $769,000 of the Iowa Co.'s stock. Number of exchanges in operation in 1897, 153; in 1898, 175; in 1899, 192; in 1900, 191; in 1902, 207. Subscribers, in 1896, 32,007; in 1897, 36,331; in 1898, 45,305; in 1899, 59,775; in 1900, 68,997; in 1901, 91,485; in 1902, 98,279.

Stock......Par $100..........................Authorized, $10,000,000......Issued, $5,039,774

The stock was reduced in 1901 by one-half to $3,481,500, and the authorized amount increased to $10,000,000, stockholders being given the right to subscribe for an amount equal to their holdings at par, the proceeds being for improvements.

Stock is transferred by the company's secretary, Chicago. Registrar, Corn Exchange National Bank, Chicago.

Last dividend paid, 1 per cent., April, 1896. No dividends have been paid since, the surplus earnings being devoted to the reconstruction of the company's plant.

FUNDED DEBT.

| | |
|---|---|
| 1st mort., 6 per cent., redeemable 1906-1916, Jan. and July | $2,500,000 |
| Cons. mort., gold, 5 per cent., due 1909-1919, Jan. and July | 3,500,000 |
| Total | $6,000,000 |

The consolidated mortgage (Old Colony Trust Co., Boston, trustee) was created in 1899 to provide for the extension of the company's system. Total issue authorized, $6,000,000, of which $2,500,000 is reserved to retire the 1st mortgage bonds.

EARNINGS.

| | Gross. | Net. | Charges. | Surplus. |
|---|---|---|---|---|
| 1896 | $1,333,082 | $305,767 | $64,557 | $241,209 |
| 1897 | 1,439,001 | 403,047 | 115,247 | 287,799 |
| 1898 | 1,670,899 | 463,228 | 156,415 | 306,813 |
| 1899 | 1,999,312 | 509,709 | 201,150 | 308,559 |
| 1900 | 2,307,743 | 635,075 | 317,567 | 317,508 |
| 1901 | 2,584,780 | 611,288 | 386,761 | 224,527 |

During 1898 there was expended on construction account at exchanges and for additional lines, $866,006. In 1899 the expenditure for same account was $2,093,796; in 1900, $1,525,804, and in 1901, $2,184,415. In most of the large cities the company owns its buildings. It has also constructed many long-distance lines connecting the various exchanges.

President, John I. Sabin; Secretary and Treasurer, Wilson S. Chapman, Chicago.

Directors—C. H. Brownell, Peru, Ind.; W. S. Chapman, L. C. Richardson, John I. Sabin, J. Russell Jones, Robert T. Lincoln, Arthur D. Wheeler, M. J. Carney, Chicago; Frederick P. Fish, Boston; F. H. Griggs, Davenport, Ia.; John F. Wallick, Indianapolis.

Main office, 203 Washington street, Chicago. Annual meeting, third Wednesday in January, at Chicago.

## THE CENTRE STAR MINING CO., LIMITED

A corporation formed under the laws of British Columbia, September 19, 1898. The company owns and operates the Centre Star Gold Mine at Rossland, B. C., which is fully developed and equipped with machinery and buildings at a cost of $250,000.

Stock......Par $1......Authorized, $3,500,000......Issued, $3,500,000

The company has no preferred stock or funded debt. The stock is fully paid and non-assessable. Stock is transferred at the company's office, Toronto.

The first dividend was 1 per cent., paid February 15, 1900. During 1901 the company paid 5 per cent. on its stock, the payments being 1 per cent. each, in January, February, March, April and May.

President, George Gooderham; Vice-President, Thomas G. Blackstock; Secretary and Treasurer, E. J. Kingstone, Toronto.

Directors—George Gooderham, Thomas G. Blackstock, William Henry Beatty, William G. Gooderham, Albert E. Gooderham, Toronto; Charles R. Hosmer, Montreal.

Corporate office, Rossland, B. C.; main office, 49 Wellington street, East, Toronto. Annual meeting, last Tuesday in November, at Toronto.

## CENTURY REALTY CO.

A corporation formed under the laws of New Jersey, March 8, 1901, to deal in selected rea estate in the Borough of Manhattan, New York City.

Stock......Par $100......Authorized, $3,000,000......Issued, $2,000,000

The company has no preferred stock or funded debt.

In September, 1902, the authorized stock was increased from $1,000,000 to $3,000,000.

The company paid 2½ per cent. on its stock in January, 1902; 3 per cent. in July, 1902, and 3 per cent. January 2, 1903.

President, W. H. Cheseborough; Vice-Presidents, George E. Coleman, E. C. Potter; Treasurer, Oakleigh Thorne; Secretary, Oscar T. Roberts, New York.

Directors—Henry B. Hollins, Oakleigh Thorne, E. C. Potter, Henry F. Shoemaker, Charles F. Hoffman, Jr., Charlton T. Lewis, William F. Havemeyer, Warner Van Norden, W. H. Cheseborough, Robert H. McCurdy, George E. Coleman, John C. Tomlinson, Richard G. Park, Ernst Thalmann, Charles T. Barney, John D. Crimmins, Charles W. Morse, August Belmont, Edwin Thorne, John Whalen, New York; James Jourdan, Brooklyn, N. Y.

Main office, 135 Broadway. Annual meeting, first Tuesday in March.

## CHAMPION INTERNATIONAL CO.

A corporation formed under the laws of Maine in 1901. The purpose of the company is the manufacture and sale of pulp and paper. The company acquired the following concerns engaged in that business:

Russell Paper Manufacturing Co., Lawrence, Mass. Champion Card & Paper Co., East Pepperell, Mass.

The Russell Paper Manufacturing Co. was formerly owned by the International Paper Co., which disposed of it to this company in which it has an interest. The assets of the constituent companies were appraised at $1,073,256.

Stock......Par $100..............................Authorized, $650,000......Issued, $650,000

The company has no preferred stock.

A dividend of 1½ per cent. was paid April 10, 1902.

FUNDED DEBT.

1st mort., 6 per cent., gold, due Feb., 1922, Feb. and Aug............................ $300,000

The 1st mortgage is $400,000 authorized. Trustee of mortgage and Agent for the payment of interest, International Trust Co., Boston. The bonds were created and sold to provide the company with additional working capital and to build extensions to the plant at Lawrence, Mass.

President, Charles M. Gage; Vice-President, George F. Russell; Secretary and Treasurer, P. A. Hammond, Lawrence, Mass.

Directors—Charles M. Gage, Charles T. Dole, Tyngsboro, Mass.; George F. Russell, Hugh J. Chisholm, A. N. Burbank, Frederick H. Parks, Lawrence, Mass.; Everett W. Burdett, Boston; P. A. Hammond, Nashua, N. H.

Corporate office, Portland, Me.; main office, 8 Prospect street, Lawrence, Mass. Annual meeting, third Tuesday in January at Portland.

## THE CHAPARRA SUGAR CO.

A corporation formed under the laws of New Jersey, October 17, 1899. The purposes of the company are raising sugar-cane and manufacturing sugar, etc. The company owns a plantation of about 70,000 acres in the province of Santiago, Cuba. It has on its property a railroad system of about 40 miles, with rolling stock and a wharf. The company has a factory with a capacity of 30,000 tons of sugar yearly.

Stock......Par $100...........................Authorized, $2,500,000......Issued, $2,500,000

The company has no preferred stock. Stock is transferred at the office of the company.

FUNDED DEBT.

1st mort., 6 per cent., due 1911, Jan. and July...................................... $1,000,000

President, Robert B. Hawley; Vice-President, Frederick H. Howell; Secretary, Henry A. Clark; Treasurer, James H. Post, New York.

Directors—Robert B. Hawley, Galveston, Tex.; James H. Post, Henry A. Clark, Frederick H. Howell, Hugh Kelly, Frederick D. Mollenhauer, New York; Nathaniel Tooker, Orange, N. J.; Pearl Wight, New Orleans; John Farr, Short Hills, N. J.; Herbert D. Cory, Englewood, N. J.; M. S. Menocal, Chaparra, Cuba.

Corporate office, 15 Exchange place, Jersey City, N. J.; main office, 111 Wall street, New York. Annual meeting, third Tuesday in October.

## CHARLESTON CONSOLIDATED RAILWAY, GAS & ELECTRIC CO.

A corporation formed February 21, 1899, under a special act of the legislature of South Carolina, as a consolidation of the Charleston City Railway and the Charleston & Seashore Railroad. It owns the capital stock of the Charleston Edison Light & Power Co. and the Charleston Gas Light Co., and also the Mount Pleasant & Sullivan Island Ferry Co. and the Middle Street and Sullivan Island Railway Co., which gives it control of all the lighting and transportation facilities in the city. Road operated, 40 miles.

Stock......Par $50............................Authorized, $1,500,000......Issued, $1,500,000

Stock is transferred at the office of the secretary, Charleston, S. C.

FUNDED DEBT.

Consolidated mort., 5 per cent., due March, 1999, March and Sept.... .............. $1,684,000
Charleston City Ry., 1st mort., 5 per cent., due January, 1923, Jan. and July........ 822,000

Total........................................................................... $2,506,000

The consolidated mortgage is $2,500,000 authorized, and sufficient bonds are reserved to retire the Charleston City Railway 1sts. There is an annual sinking fund for the latter issue. Trustee of the 1st mortgage and agent for the payment of interest, Mercantile Trust & Deposit Co., Baltimore. Trustee of the consolidated mortgage and agent for the payment of interest, Baltimore Trust & Guarantee Co., Baltimore.

President, Francis K. Carey, Baltimore; Vice-President, Philip H. Gadsden; Secretary, P. J. Balaguer; Treasurer, Montague Triest; General Manager, S. H. Wilson, Charleston, S. C.

Directors—Francis K. Carey, Robert C. Davidson, Baltimore; Philip H. Gadsden, Samuel H. Wilson, J. S. Buist, George B. Edwards, George W. Williams, Jr., George A. Wagener, William M. Bird, Andrew Simonds, Charleston, S. C.

Main office, 141 Meeting street, Charleston, S. C. Annual meeting, third Monday in March.

## CHARTIERS VALLEY WATER CO.

A corporation formed under the laws of Pennsylvania, July 30, 1896, under a perpetual charter. The company succeeded the St. Clair Water Co., and also acquired the pipe lines of the Monongahela Water Co., outside the city of Pittsburg, except in the boroughs of McKee's Rocks and Esplem. The company supplies water to a territory with a population of 60,000. It owns reservoirs at Mt. Oliver, Whitehall, West Homestead, Crofton and Sheraden, and a pumping station at Beck's Run, on the Monongahela River.

Stock......Par $50..........................Authorized, $1,000,000......Issued, $1,000,000

The company has no preferred stock. Transfer Agent and Registrar, The Union Trust Co., Pittsburg.

2 per cent. dividends were paid in May and December, 1902.

FUNDED DEBT.

| | |
|---|---|
| 1st mort., 6 per cent. gold, due 1927, April and Oct. | $390,000 |
| St. Clair Water Co., 1st mort., guar., 6 per cent. gold, due July, 1914, Jan. and July | 500,000 |
| Total | $890,000 |

The bond issues are the full amounts authorized.

In the fiscal year ending March 31, 1902, the gross earnings were $134,978; net, $93,669; charges, $49,920; surplus, $43,748.

President, J. F. Grimes; Secretary, John L. Sheppard; Treasurer, Daniel Beech; Manager, J. W. Hunter.

Directors—J. F. Grimes, W. W. Murray, Harry Moore, Albert Ernwein, Charles Ott, M. W. Watson, Francis Rawle.

Corporate and main office, 99 Amanda avenue, Knoxville, Pittsburg; branch offices at Carnegie and Crafton. Annual meeting first Monday in May, at Knoxville, Pittsburg.

## CHATEAUGAY ORE & IRON CO.

A corporation formed under the laws of New York. The company has a large iron ore property at Lyon Mountain, Clinton County, N. Y. A readjustment of this company's finances was effected in March, 1902, under the plan described below.

| Stock..Par $100..Authorized | | | Issued | | | |
|---|---|---|---|---|---|---|
| | com. | $1,250,000 | | com., | $1,250,000 | |
| | 1st pref., | 750,000 | | 1st pref., | 750,000 | $2,750,000 |
| | 2d pref., | 750,000 | | 2d pref., | 750,000 | |

The 1st preferred is 4 per cent., non-cumulative, and the 2d preferred is also 4 per cent., non-cumulative.

FUNDED DEBT.

New 1st mort., 4 per cent., due Jan., 1942, Jan. and July...... .................... $1,300,000

The new 1st mortgage is for $1,750,000, of which $600,000 was used to retire underlying bonds and $250,000 is held to provide additional capital. The amount outstanding was issued under the readjustment plan to retire old bonds and provide for payment of floating debt and improvements. The Delaware & Hudson Co. guarantees the new 1st mortgage bonds.

The company, prior to the readjustment, had $1,500,000 stock, $788,000 1st mortgage 6 per cent. bonds and $700,000 consolidated mortgage bonds. Of the latter $400,000 were guaranteed by the Delaware & Hudson Co., and $400,000 of the new bonds are held to retire the same. Holders of the $1,089,000 of unguaranteed old bonds were offered, 40 per cent. cash for the same or 35 per cent. in the new 1st 4s and 65 per cent. in the new 1st preferred stock. The holder of the $1,500,000 of old stock received for the same 50 per cent. in new 2d preferred. The new common stock was given to the Delaware & Hudson Co. as consideration for its guarantee of the new bonds.

President, Smith M. Weed, Plattsburg, N. Y.; Secretary and Treasurer, Talbot Olyphant, New York; General Manager, J. N. Stower, Plattsburg, N. Y.

Main office, Plattsburg, N. Y.; New York office, 21 Cortlandt street.

## CHATTANOOGA ELECTRIC RAILWAY CO.

A corporation formed under the laws of Tennessee in 1896. The company succeeded another road of the same name that was sold under foreclosure. The original road was a consolidation of the City Street Railroad Co. and the Chattanooga Electric Street Railroad Co., of Chattanooga, Tenn. The present company has a power plant, 33 miles of track and 61 cars. The population served is about 35,000.

Stock......Par $100..............................Authorized, $645,000......Issued, $645,000

The company has no preferred stock.

FUNDED DEBT.

1st con. mort., 5 per cent. gold, due Jan., 1919, Jan. and July........................ $576,000

The authorized amount of the 1st consolidated mortgage is $625,000. Of that amount $550,000 has been issued to refund old bonds, bearing 6 per cent. interest, and $49,000 has been reserved for future requirements. The company has a 2d mortgage, 5 per cent., due 1921, but none of the bonds of this issue have been sold, but are used as collateral for advances. Trustee of the 1st mortgage and agent for the payment of interest, Maryland Trust Co., Baltimore. Trustee of the 2d mortgage and agent for the payment of interest, Chattanooga Savings Bank, Chattanooga, Tenn.

President and Treasurer, J. H. Warner; Vice-President and Secretary, Edwin Warner.

Directors—J. H. Warner, Edwin Warner, Percy Warner, Frank Sparlock, W. T. Adams.

Main office, 3 Market street, Chattanooga, Tenn.

## THE CHESAPEAKE & DELAWARE CANAL CO.

A company incorporated in Maryland, December 7, 1799; in Delaware, January 29, 1801; in Pennsylvania, February 19, 1801. The company owns a 14-mile canal from the Delaware River at Delaware City, Del., to Chesapeake City, Md., on a branch of the Elk River, emptying into the head of Chesapeake Bay.

Stock......Par $50............................Authorized, $2,903,238......Issued, $1,903,238

Stock is transferred and registered at the office of the company, 528 Walnut street, Philadelphia.

FUNDED DEBT.

1st mort., 5 per cent. bonds, due July 1, 1916, Jan. and July........................ $2,602,950

Interest payments are made at the office of the company. In 1899 an arrangement was made by which the interest on the bonds was reduced from 5 to 4 per cent. until the contingent fund was increased to $100,000.

In the year ending May 31, 1902, the earnings were: gross, $136,824; net, $93,131; charges, $104,118; deficit, $10,986.

President, Joseph E. Gillingham; Secretary and Treasurer, Coleman L. Nicholson, Philadelphia.

Directors—R. Dale Benson, Hood Gilpin, Andrew Gray, John Cadwalader, William Drayton, George Harrison Fisher, Edward S. Buckley, Bernard Gilpin, Charles Chauncey, Henry Pratt McKean, William Littleton Savage, William Ellis Scull, Archibald R. Montgomery, Emlen Hutchinson, Philadelphia.

Corporate and main office, 528 Walnut street, Philadelphia. Annual meeting, June 1.

## CHESAPEAKE & OHIC ORAIN ELEVATOR CO.

A corporation formed under the laws of New Jersey in July, 1882. It owns a large grain elevator at Newport News, Va., operated in connection with the Chesapeake & Ohio Railway. The latter company owns practically all the stock of this company.

Stock......Par $100..............................Authorized, $500,000......Issued, $500,000

Transfer agents, J. P. Morgan & Co., New York.

FUNDED DEBT.

| | |
|---|---|
| 1st mort., 4 per cent., due 1938, April and Oct. | $830,000 |
| Income mort., 4 per cent., due 1988, Oct. 1 | 450,000 |
| Total | $1,280,000 |

The Chesapeake & Ohio Railway Co. guarantees principal and interest of the 1st mortgage bonds. Trustee of 1st mortgage, Central Trust Co., New York. The income mortgage bonds are non-cumulative, interest being payable only if earned.

In the year ending June 30, 1902, the earnings were; Gross, $70,152; net, $5,559.

President, George W. Stevens; Vice-President, Decatur Axtell; Secretary, C. Edward Wellford; Treasurer, C. E. Potts, Richmond.

Directors—Decatur Axtell, Kenneth K. McLaren, G. W. Stevens, Henry T. Wickham, L. F. Sullivan.

Main office, 805 East Main Street, Richmond, Va. Annual meeting, first Monday in January, at Jersey City.

---

## CHESAPEAKE & POTOMAC TELEPHONE CO.

A corporation formed under the laws of New York, June 30, 1883. The company operates under a license from the American Bell Telephone Co., the territory covered by its system comprising Maryland, including Baltimore; the District of Columbia, including the city of Washington, and adjacent parts of Virginia and West Virginia. A controlling interest in the stock of the company is owned by the American Telephone & Telegraph Co. The company succeeded the National Capital Telephone Co. of Washington and the Telephone Exchange Co. of Baltimore.

Stock......Par $100..........................Authorized, $2,650,000......Issued, $2,650,000

The company paid dividends on its stock at the rate of 4 per cent. per annum, the dividends being 1 per cent. quarterly, in January, April, July and October, but owing to expenditures for additional property and the cost of establishing underground wires in the city of Washington, dividends were suspended in July, 1902.

FUNDED DEBT.

Cons. mort., 5 per cent., due May, 1929, Jan. and July.............................. $1,500,000

The consolidated mortgage is for $1,451,000. Trustee, American Security & Trust Co., Washington. The bonds are subject to call at 105 at the company's option after 1909.

President and General Manager, Union N. Bethell; Vice-President, Horace S. Cummings, Secretary and Treasurer, Charles G. Beebe, Washington, . C.

Directors—Horace S. Cummings, H. A. Willard, C. D Bell, Washington, D. C.; Union N. Bethell, John H. Cahill, Joseph P. Davis, New York; Bernard Carter, Baltimore; Frederick P. Fish, C. Jay French, Boston.

Main office, 619 Fourteenth street, N. W., Washington, D. C. Annual meeting, last Thursday in February.

---

## CHESEBROUGH MANUFACTURING CO., CONSOLIDATED

A corporation organized under the laws of New York in 1880. The company is the sole manufacturer of vaseline and all its preparations, and other specialties.

Stock......Par $100.............................Authorized, $500,000......Issued, $500,000

Stock is transferred at the company's office.

The company pays monthly dividends on its stock. In the last four years the dividends have varied between 21 and 30 per cent. per annum.

President, Robert A. Chesebrough; Vice-President, O. N. Cammann; Secretary and Treasurer, S. A. Drew.

Directors—O. T. Waring, C. C. Burke, James A. Moffett, James Smith, O. N. Cammann, Robert A. Chesebrough, J. J. Almiral, Frederic R. Coudert, Jr., W. H. Chesebrough.

Main office, 17 State street, New York; branch offices, London, Berlin, Montreal. Annual meeting, first Thursday in May.

---

## CHEYENNE LIGHT, FUEL & POWER CO.

A corporation formed under the laws of Wyoming, May 21, 1900. The company was a consolidation of the Cheyenne City Gas Co. and the Brush-Swan Electric Light Co. The company owns an electric plant with a capacity of 160 arc lamps and 6,000 incandescent lamps, and a gas plant with a capacity of 50,000 cubic feet per day. The franchise and contract with the city both run until 1925.

Stock......Par $100.............................Authorized, $600,000......Issued, $250,000

FUNDED DEBT.

1st mort., gold, 5 per cent., due July, 1925, Jan. and July....................... .... $175,000

The trustee of the mortgage and agent for the payment of interest is the American Loan & Trust Co., Boston.

EARNINGS.

Year ending June 30.

| | Gross. | Net. | Charges. | Surplus. |
|---|---|---|---|---|
| 1901-2 | $50,196 | $25,246 | $8,750 | $16,496 |

President, Francis E. Warren; Vice-President, William Sturgis; Secretary and Treasurer, Charles M. Smith.

Trustees—Duane F. Miner, John W. Lacey, William Sturgis, Charles M. Smith, Francis E. Warren.

Main office, Cheyenne, Wyo. Fiscal Agent, American Loan & Trust Co., Boston. Annual meeting, first Tuesday in August.

## CHICAGO & MILWAUKEE ELECTRIC RAILROAD CO.

A corporation formed under the laws of Illinois in May, 1898. The company succeeded the North Shore Interurban Railway Co. of Waukegan, Ill., and acquired by purchase the property of the Bluff City Electric Street Railway Co. It operates 45 miles of electric railway, connecting Evanston, Waukegan and other suburban towns with Chicago.

Stock......Par $100..........................Authorized, $1,000,000......Issued, $1,000,000

The company has no preferred stock.

### FUNDED DEBT.

1st mort., 5 per cent. gold, due July, 1919, Jan. and July.......................... $1,000,000

The authorized amount of the mortgage is $1,500,000, of which $500,000 is held in reserve for extensions and improvements. Bonds may be called on any interest date at three months notice at 105 and accrued interest. A sinking fund of $50,000 annually is provided, to begin July, 1910. Trustees of the mortgage, Cleveland Trust Co., Cleveland, and Royal Trust Co., Chicago. Agent for the payment of interest, Standard Trust Co., New York, and Royal Trust Co., Chicago.

### EARNINGS.

| | Gross. | Net. |
|---|---|---|
| 1900 | $140,684 | $81,169 |
| 1901 | 171,171 | 97,156 |

President, George A. Ball; Vice-President, A. C. Frost; Secretary, George M. Seward; Treasurer, J. W. Mauck.

Directors—George A. Ball, A. C. Frost, George M. Seward, J. W. Mauck.

Main office, 108, LaSalle Street, Chicago. Annual meeting, first Wednesday in August, at Chicago.

## CHICAGO CITY RAILWAY CO.

A corporation formed under the laws of Illinois, February 14, 1859. The company owns and operates 218.71 miles of railway, cable and electric, in the south division of Chicago.

Stock......Par $100......................Authorized, $19,000,000......Issued, $18,000,000

The company has no preferred stock and no funded debt. The entire bonded indebtedness of the company was $4,619,500, which matured and was paid July 1, 1901.

Stock is transferred at the office of the company. Registrar, Northern Trust Co., Chicago.

Dividends on the stock have been paid as follows: 1893, 24 per cent.; 1894, 12 per cent.; 1895 to 1900, inclusive, 12 per cent. per annum; 1901, 12 per cent. on $13,500,000 of stock for six months and 9 per cent. on the capital stock as increased to $18,000,000. Dividends are now 2¼ per cent. quarterly in March (30), June, September and December.

### EARNINGS.

Year ending December 31.

| | Gross. | Net. | Charges. | Dividends. | Surplus. |
|---|---|---|---|---|---|
| 1899 | $5,194,439 | $1,868,762 | $257,877 | $1,449,997 | $160,888 |
| 1900 | 5,543,180 | 1,888,178 | 207,877 | 1,575,000 | 105,301 |
| 1901 | 5,900,271 | 2,031,098 | 283,938 | 1,620,000 | 127,159 |
| 1902 | 6,307,358 | 1,896,677 | 180,000 | 1,620,000 | 276,677 |

The charges for 1902 consist of an item of $180,000 for depreciation.

President, David G. Hamilton; 1st Vice-President, Joseph Leiter; 2d Vice-President, George T. Smith; Secretary and Auditor, C. Nesbitt Duffy; Treasurer, T. C. Pennington; General Manager, Robert McCulloch; Assistant General Manager, Richard McCulloch.

Directors—George T. Smith, David G. Hamilton, Joseph Leiter, S. W. Allerton, Albert W. Goodrich, A. Orr, Lawrence A. Young.

Main office, 2020 State street, Chicago. Annual meeting, first week day after February 15, at Chicago.

## CHICAGO CONSOLIDATED TRACTION CO.

(Controlled by Chicago Union Traction Co.)

A corporation organized under the laws of Illinois in 1899. The company acquired a number of electric trolley roads operating in Chicago and its suburbs. The companies whose stock and property are controlled are: Cicero & Proviso Railway, Chicago Electric Transit Co., North Chicago Electric Co., Chicago North Shore Street Railway Co., Evanston Electric Co., Chicago & Jefferson Transit Co., Ogden Street Railway, and the North Side Electric Street Railway Co. The lines owned and operated by the constituent companies are about 200 miles, extending throughout the western and northern environs of Chicago.

In February, 1900, an arrangement was made by which the company's stock was acquired by the Chicago Union Traction Co., the latter paying for the same $45, in bonds of this company guaranteed by the Chicago Union Traction and $150 in cash for each share of the old stock.

Stock......Par $100........................Authorized, $15,000,000......Issued, $15,000,000

FUNDED DEBT.

| | |
|---|---|
| Chicago Cons. Traction 1st mort., 4½ per cent., due Dec., 1939, June and Dec...... | $6,750,000 |
| Ogden Street Railway 1st mort., 6 per cent., due May, 1916, May and Nov.......... | 750,000 |
| Cicero & Proviso St. Ry. 1st mort., 6 per cent., due Nov., 1904, May and Nov....... | 44,000 |
| Cicero & Proviso St. Ry. cons. mort., 5 per cent., due May, 1915, May and Nov...... | 1,905,000 |
| Chicago & Jefferson 1st mort., 6 per cent., due Nov., 1915, May and Nov........... | 208,000 |
| Chicago Electric Transit 1st mort., 6 per cent., due Aug., 1914, Feb. and Aug....... | 1,097,000 |
| North Side Electric St. Ry. 1st mort., 6 per cent., due Nov., 1915, May and Nov..... | 155,000 |
| North Chicago Electric Railway 1st mort., 6 per cent., due Aug., 1914, Feb. and Aug.. | 868,000 |
| Chicago North Shore Railway 1st mort., 6 per cent., due April, 1913, April and Oct.. | 675,000 |
| Evanston Electric Railway 1st mort., 6 per cent., due Aug., 1916, Feb. and Aug...... | 130,000 |
| Total................................................................ | $12,582,000 |

The 1st mortgage of this company, Equitable Trust Co. of Chicago, trustee, is for $6,750,000. The interest and principal of the bonds are guaranteed by the Chicago Union Traction.

President, John M. Roach; Vice-President, E. S. Harwall; Secretary and Treasurer, Charles F. Marlow, Chicago.

Main office, 444 North Clark street, Chicago.

---

## CHICAGO EDISON CO.

A corporation formed under the laws of Illinois in 1887. The company absorbed the Chicago Arc Light & Power Co. In 1897 it purchased the Chicago Illuminating Co. The Commonwealth Electric Co. is controlled by interests identified with this company. The company rents subway privileges from the Sectional Electric Underground Co. It has four power stations.

Stock......Par $100.........................Authorized, $10,000,000......Issued, $9,866,000

The stock has been increased from time to time to provide for extensions and improvements. In August, 1901, $900,000 of new stock was offered for subscription at par by the stockholders, followed in May, 1902, by another issue of $690,000. On January 24, 1903, stockholders were given the right to February 2, 1903, to subscribe to 30 per cent. of their holdings in new stock at par, the amount of such increase being $2,276,901. The payments on the new stock were to be made, 25 per cent. each, on February 2, May 1, August 1 and November 1, 1903.

Stock is transferred at the company's office. Registrar, Merchants' Loan & Trust Co., Chicago.

The company pays 8 per cent. per annum on its stock, the dividends being quarterly, 2 per cent. each, in February (1), May, August and November.

FUNDED DEBT.

| | |
|---|---|
| 1st mort., 5 per cent., due 1926, April and Oct..................................... | $4,025,000 |
| Debenture bonds, 6 per cent., due 1913, Jan. and July............................... | 1,483,000 |
| Total...................................................................... | $5,508,000 |

The trustee of both the 1st mortgage and the debenture bonds is the Merchants' Loan & Trust Co., Chicago. The debentures are redeemable at par and interest. The 1st mortgage is $6,000,000 authorized, and the bonds are redeemable at par and interest after 1910.

This company guarantees interest and principal of $224,000 4s and $36,000 5 per cent. bonds of the Sectional Electric Underground Co.

EARNINGS.

Year ending March 31.

| | Gross. | Net. | Charges. | Surplus. |
|---|---|---|---|---|
| 1898-99 | $1,954,876 | $740,255 | $262,524 | $477,731 |
| 1899-00 | 2,133,827 | 812,390 | 265,243 | 547,147 |
| 1900-01 | 2,517,219 | 902,959 | 279,791 | 623,168 |
| 1901-02 | 2,806,609 | 1,085,789 | 300,983 | 784,806 |

In 1898-99 the surplus over dividends was $79,659; in 1899-1900, $149,075; in 1900-01, $145,480; in 1901-02, $268,824.

President, Samuel Insull; 1st Vice-President, Robert T. Lincoln; 2d Vice-President, Louis A. Ferguson; Secretary and Treasurer, William A. Fox; Comptroller, W. M. Anthony.

Directors—Samuel Insull, Robert T. Lincoln, John J. Mitchell, Jesse Spaulding, A. A. Sprague, E. M. Phelps, Lambert Tree, Edward L. Brewster, Joseph Leiter.

Main office, 139 Adams street, Chicago. Annual meeting, second Monday in June.

## CHICAGO GENERAL RAILWAY CO.

A corporation formed under the laws of Illinois, October 21, 1893. The company leased the West & South Towns Street Railway Co. in 1894, and in 1896 purchased that road. It operates 21 miles of track in the west side division of Chicago.

Stock......Par $100........................Authorized, $10,000,000......Issued, $772,350

The company has no preferred stock. Stock is transferred at the office of the company. Registrar, Merchants' Loan & Trust Co., Chicago. $272,350 of the stock issued is in litigation.

FUNDED DEBT.

| | |
|---|---|
| General mort., 5 per cent. gold, due Nov., 1935, May and Nov. | $1,438,000 |
| West & South Towns St. Ry. Co., 1st mort., 6 p.c. gold, due Aug., 1902-12, Feb. and Aug. | 290,000 |
| Total | $1,728,000 |

The authorized amount of the general mortgage is $3,000,000. Of this amount, $362,000 were held to retire bonds of the West & South Towns Railway Co.; $75,000 were issued to retire debentures of the Chicago General Railway Co., and $500,000 were issued for the purchase of the West & South Towns Railway Co. The bonds are subject to call after 1905 at 105. Trustee of the mortgage of the Chicago General Railway Co. and agent for the payment of interest, Merchants' Loan & Trust Co., Chicago. The authorized mortgage of the West & South Towns Railway Co. is $500,000. Bonds are redeemable after February, 1902, at 105 and accrued interest. Trustee, Northern Trust Co., Chicago. Agent for the payment of interest, Merchants' Loan & Trust Co., Chicago.

In April, 1900, a Receiver was appointed, the company having defaulted on its coupons. A reorganization committee, consisting of James B. Black, Lyman M. Paine and Glenn E. Plumb, proposed that the bondholders should deposit their bonds, to the amount of one-half or more, with the Real Estate Trust Co., New York, for cancellation, accepting double the amount in stock. A stockholders' committee was formed and committees also represent the General Railway bondholders and those of the West & South Towns Street Railway Co.

Receiver, Edwin J. Zimmer, Chicago.

President, James P. Black; Vice-President, C. L. Bonney; Secretary and Treasurer, Lawton C. Bonney; General Superintendent, Charles P. Hull, Chicago.

Directors—C. L. Bonney, N. D. Lawton, J. P. Black, Lawton C. Bonney, Lyman M. Paine, W. A. Goodman, M. F. Driscoll.

Main office, 1496 West Twenty-second street, Chicago. Annual meeting, second Monday in January, at Chicago.

## CHICAGO JUNCTION RAILWAYS & UNION STOCK YARDS CO.

A corporation formed under the laws of New Jersey. It owns 9,203 shares of the stock of the Chicago Union Stock Yards & Transit Co., the property of which comprises 470 acres of land, cattle yards, sheds, etc., and about 150 miles of railroad tracks and connecting with all railroads entering Chicago. The Transit Company also controls the Chicago & Indiana State Line Railroad Co. In August, 1897, purchased control of the Chicago, Hammond & Western Railroad, Whiting, Ind., to La Grange, Ill., 38 miles. In March, 1898, all the railroads of the company, including the lease of switches and transfer lines at stock yards, were consolidated under the title of Chicago Junction Railway, which operates 297 miles of track. The company owns the $2,199,000 stock of the Chicago Junction Railway. Chicago & Indiana State Line

Co. and the stock yards accounts kept separate. The company has a fifteen-year contract for use of its facilities by the Swift, Armour, and other large slaughtering and packing houses of Chicago.

The number of cars of live stock handled by the companies has been: in year ending June 30, 1893, 284,476; in 1894, 290,985; in 1895, 271,644; in 1896, 281,194; in 1897, 279,662; in 1898, 276,043; in 1899, 269,406; in 1900, 277,205; in 1901, 291,741.

Stock...Par $100....Authorized { com., $6,500,000 / pref., 6,500,000 } Issued { com., $6,500,000 / pref., 6,500,000 } $13,000,000

The preferred stock is 6 per cent., cumulative, and also has a preference as to assets.

Transfer Agents, National Bank of Commerce, New York; Old Colony Trust Co., Boston.

**Funded Debt.**

| | |
|---|---|
| Collateral trust mort., $ and £, 5 per cent., due July, 1915, Jan. and July | $10,000,000 |
| Collateral trust refunding mort., 4 per cent., due April, 1940, April and Oct | 4,000,000 |
| Total | $14,000,000 |

The refunding mortgage is for $14,000,000. It was created and $4,000,000 bonds sold in April, 1900, to retire the $2,465,000 of 5 per cent. income bonds (subject to call) and $400,000 of 5 per cent. notes and to provide for betterments. Of the authorized issue $10,000,000 is held to retire the 5 per cent. collateral trust bonds. The company, in August, 1897, gave a 5 per cent. note of $400,000, payable January, 1903, but subject to call at company's option for the $2,000,000. The Chicago, Hammond & Western Railroad Co. has outstanding $2,090,000 6 per cent. 1st mortgage bonds, due 1927, January and July.

**Earnings.**

| | Gross Income. | Charges. | Net Income. |
|---|---|---|---|
| 1892-93 (year ending June 30) | $1,631,277 | $910,082 | $721,196 |
| 1893-94 ( " " ) | 1,733,005 | 764,946 | 989,894 |
| 1894-95 ( " " ) | 1,700,494 | 756,768 | 944,226 |
| 1895-96 ( " " ) | 1,701,509 | 708,782 | 992,727 |
| 1897 (year ending Dec. 31) | 1,705,796 | 694,403 | 1,011,393 |
| 1898 ( " " ) | 1,699,382 | 724,380 | 1,028,381 |
| 1899 ( " " ) | 1,768,485 | 712,818 | 1,055,667 |
| 1900 ( " " ) | 1,854,310 | 701,447 | 1,152,862 |
| 1901 ( " " ) | 2,054,537 | 777,608 | 1,276,929 |
| 1902 ( " " ) | 1,862,388 | 731,395 | 1,487,932 |

The income of the company is derived from dividends on the Union Stock Yards shares. In 1894-95 an amount of $90,000 was charged off to depreciation; also in 1895-96, 1897, 1898 and 1899. In 1901 the amount thus charged was $55,000, and in 1902 $55,000.

Dividends have been full 6 per cent. yearly on preferred; on common, in 1891, 10 per cent.; in 1892 and since, 8 per cent. per annum. At the February, 1900, meeting it was decided to make the dividend payments on the common stock quarterly, instead of semi-annually, and dividends on both classes of shares have since been paid quarterly at the rate of 2 per cent. on the common and 1½ per cent. on the preferred in January (1), April, July and October.

Chairman and President, Chauncey M. Depew, New York; Vice-President, Nathaniel Thayer, Boston; Treasurer, William C. Lane; Secretary, E. M. F. Miller; Assistant Secretary, William C. Cox, New York.

Directors—Chauncey M. Depew, William D. Guthrie, William C. Lane, New York; George Peabody Gardner, Frederick H. Prince, Nathaniel Thayer, Eugene N. Foss, Boston; John Kean, Jr., Elizabeth, N. J.; Albert H. Veeder, P. A. Valentine, Chicago.

Corporate office, 25 Exchange place, Jersey City; New York office, 40 Wall street. Annual meeting in February, at Jersey City.

## CHICAGO PNEUMATIC TOOL CO.

A corporation formed under the laws of New Jersey, December 23, 1901, for the purpose of consolidating a number of companies engaged in the manufacture of pneumatic tools, air compressors and machinery of like character. The following concerns were acquired:

Chicago Pneumatic Tool Co. of Illinois, Chicago and New York.
Boyer Machine Co., Detroit.
Taite-Howard Pneumatic Tool Co., London, England.
Chisholm & Moore Crane Co., Cleveland.
Franklin Air Compressor Co., Franklin, Pa.

Stock .....Par $100..........................Authorized, $7,500,000......Issued, $6,031,000

The company has no preferred stock.

Transfer Agent, Corporation Trust Co., New York. Registrar, Central Realty Bond & Trust Co., New York.

The dividend periods for the stock are quarterly, January, April, July and October, and they have been regularly paid, beginning April 10, 1902, at the rate of 2 per cent. for each quarter.

FUNDED DEBT.

1st mort., 5 per cent., due 1921, Jan. (2) and July.................................. $2,300,000

The authorized bond issue is $2,500,000, of which $200,000 remains in the company's treasury. There is a sinking fund of $50,000 per annum, and bonds may be drawn for same at 105, or after 1907 can be called at that price.

Trustee of the mortgage, Central Realty Bond & Trust Co., New York. Coupons are paid at the National City Bank, New York.

EARNINGS.

| | Net Profits. | Charges. | Dividends. | Surplus. |
|---|---|---|---|---|
| 1902 | $897,059 | $115,000 | $453,263 | $328,796 |

Out of the surplus earnings $50,000 was transferred to reserve from sinking fund and $165,089 was written off for depreciation, etc., leaving undivided profits for the year of $113,706.

President, John W. Duntley; Vice-President, W. O. Duntley; Secretary and Treasurer, John B. Milliken, Chicago.

Directors—Charles M. Schwab, William B. Dickson, C. H. Matthieson, New York; John A. Lynch, Max Pam, W. O. Duntley, John B. Milliken, Charles Wacker, W. J. Chalmers, John W. Duntley, James H. Eckels, Chicago; John R. McGinley, Pittsburg; Charles A. Miller, Franklin, Pa.; Joseph Boyer, Detroit; Edward Y. Moore, Cleveland; John C. Taite, A. W. Maconochie, London, England.

Corporate office, Corporation Trust Co. Building, Jersey City; main office, 277 Dearborn street, Chicago.

## CHICAGO TELEPHONE CO.

A corporation organized under the laws of Illinois in 1881. The company operates under an exclusive license from the American Bell Telephone Co., covering Chicago, Ill., and the whole of Cook County as well as McHenry, Lake, Kane, Du Page, Kendall, Grundy and Will counties, Ill., and Lake and Porter counties, Ind. The company's system comprises twelve exchanges in the city of Chicago and local exchanges at Joliet, Elgin, Aurora, Waukegan and other places. Telephones in service in January, 1903, 79,043 The American Telephone & Telegraph Co. owns a controlling interest in the stock of this company.

Stock......Par $100......................Authorized, $15,000,000......Issued, $12,000,000

The amount of stock authorized was increased from $5,000,000 to $15,000,000 in January, 1900. This increase was to provide for extensions and improvements. The company has no funded debt. Stock is transferred at the company's office, Chicago. Registrar, Northern Trust Co., Chicago.

Dividends were paid quarterly, 3 per cent. each, in January (1), April, July and October. The April, 1902, dividend was reduced to 2½ per cent., which has since been the regular rate.

EARNINGS.

| | Div. Rate. | Gross. | Net. | Dividends. | Surplus. |
|---|---|---|---|---|---|
| 1896 | 12 | $1,955,829 | $600,205 | $499,224 | $100,985 |
| 1897 | 12 | 2,072,097 | 624,693 | 520,380 | 104,313 |
| 1898 | 12 | 2,307,959 | 633,952 | 520,380 | 113,572 |
| 1899 | 12 | 2,668,714 | 676,559 | 559,550 | 117,009 |
| 1900 | 12 | 3,129,238 | 890,458 | 749,808 | 120,650 |
| 1901 | 12 | 3,775,001 | 1,083,872 | 960,000 | 123,872 |
| 1902 | 10½ | 4,570,805 | 1,202,471 | 1,075,192 | 127,278 |

Chairman, John M. Clark; President, John I. Sabin; 1st Vice-President, Byron L. Smith; 2d Vice-President, Arthur D. Wheeler; Secretary and Treasurer, Charles E. Mosley; Auditor, J. W. Richards.

Directors—John M. Clark, Chauncey Keep, Byron L. Smith, J. Russell Jones, Robert T. Lincoln, Arthur D. Wheeler, Albert A. Sprague, C. E. Perkins, John I. Sabin, Frederick P. Fish, Joseph P. Davis.

Main office 203 Washington street, Chicago Annual meeting, third Wednesday in January.

## CHICAGO UNION TRACTION CO.

A corporation formed under the laws of Illinois, June 3, 1899. The company was organized to absorb and lease the West Chicago Street Railroad Co. and the North Chicago Street Railroad Co., which corporations were leased to this company from July 1, 1899. The West Chicago Street Railway owned 72 miles of double-track road and leased the Chicago West Division Railway Co., 96 miles of double track, and the Chicago Passenger Railway Co., 34 miles of double track; total, 202.70 miles. The North Chicago Street Railroad Co. owned 43¼ miles of double track and leased 51 miles from the North Chicago City Railway Co., a total of 94.33 miles. Total leased by the Chicago Union Traction Co., 297.03 miles. In 1900 the Chicago Consolidated Traction Co. was acquired. Total system, 486.32 miles.

In 1901 and 1902 this company had a controversy with the Chicago municipality concerning its franchises and those of the constituent roads. In February, 1903, a protective committee was formed which requested stockholders to deposit their stock with the Guaranty Trust Co., New York, the purpose of the committee being to bring about a settlement, if possible, on mutually satisfactory terms.

| Stock..Par $100..Authorized | com., $20,000,000<br>pref., 12,000,000 | Issued | com., $20,000,000<br>pref., 12,000,000 | $32,000,000 |
|---|---|---|---|---|

The preferred stock is 5 per cent., cumulative.

Transfer Agents, Illinois Trust & Savings Bank, Chicago; Morton Trust Co., New York; Registrars, Commercial National Bank, Chicago; Central Trust Co., New York.

The company began the payment of dividends of 1¼ per cent. on its preferred stock in October, 1899. Quarterly dividends at that rate, or 5 per cent. per annum, were regularly paid in January, April, July and October, until October, 1900, inclusive, after which they were suspended, and none has since been paid.

FUNDED DEBT.

| | |
|---|---|
| North Chicago St. R. R. 1st mort., 5 per cent., due 1912, Jan. and July............ | $3,171,000 |
| North Chicago St. R. R. refunding mort., 4½ per cent., due April, 1951, April and Oct.. | 1,614,000 |
| North Chicago City Railway 1st mort., 4 per cent., due July, 1907, Jan. and July.... | 500,000 |
| North Chicago City Railway 2d mort., 4½ per cent., due Nov., 1927, May and Nov.. | 2,500,000 |
| West Chicago St. R. R. 1st mort., 5 per cent., due May, 1928, May and Nov........ | 3,864,000 |
| West Chicago St. R. R. cons. mort., 5 per cent., due Nov., 1930, May and Nov...... | 6,136,000 |
| West Chicago St. R. R. debentures, 6 per cent., due Dec., 1914, June and Dec...... | 497,000 |
| West Chicago St. Ry. Tunnel Co. 1st mort., 5 per cent., due Feb., 1928, Feb. and Aug.. | 1,500,000 |
| West Chicago St. Ry. Tunnel Co. power-house mort., 5 per cent., due 1928........ | 184,000 |
| Chicago West Division cons. mort., 5 per cent., due July, 1932, Jan. and July....... | 4,016,000 |
| Chicago Passenger Railway 1st mort., 5 per cent., due Aug., 1903, Feb. and Aug.... | 400,000 |
| Chicago Passenger Railway cons. mort., 5 per cent., due Dec., 1936, June and Dec... | 1,600,000 |
| Total.............................................................. | $25,982,000 |

The company under the lease guarantees 12 per cent. per annum on the $7,920,000 stock of the North Chicago Street Railroad Co., and 6 per cent. per annum on the $13,189,000 stock of the West Chicago Street Railroad. It also assumes and guarantees the bonds and leasehold obligations of the two companies.

This company owns $3,200,000 of the stock of the West Chicago Street Railroad Co. and $2,000,000 of the North Chicago Street Railroad Co. Under the lease agreement there were assigned to it the entire capital stocks of the Chicago West Division Railway Co., the Chicago Passenger Railway Co., and the North Chicago City Railway Co. The Chicago Consolidated Traction Co.'s capital stock, $15,000,000, was purchased for $45 per share in 4½ per cent. bonds of that company, guaranteed by the Chicago Union Traction Co., and $1.50 cash per share.

For earnings of the constituent companies see MANUAL for 1900.

EARNINGS.

Year ending June 30.

| | Div. p. c. | Gross. | Net. | Charges. | Surplus. |
|---|---|---|---|---|---|
| 1899-00.............. | 5 | $7,477,395 | $4,583,951 | $3,979,875 | $604,075 |
| 1900-01.............. | 1¼ | 7,289,139 | 4,216,616 | 4,058,040 | 158,576 |
| 1901-02.............. | .. | 7,825,119 | 3,371,750 | 3,619,228 | Def., 247,528 |

In 1899-1900 the surplus over the 5 per cent. dividends on the preferred stock was $4,075. In 1900-01 the surplus over dividends was $8,576.

Chairman, Henry G. Foreman; President, John M. Roach, Chicago; 1st Vice-President, R. A. C. Smith, New York; 2d Vice-President, Walter H. Wilson; Secretary and Assistant Treasurer, Markham B. Orde; Treasurer, James H. Eckels, Chicago.

Directors—Jesse Spaulding, C. K. G. Billings, C. L. Hutchinson, Walter H. Wilson, J. V. Clark, James H. Eckels, William Dickinson, Chicago; Harry B. Hopkins, R. A. C. Smith, New York; P. A. B. Widener, Philadelphia.

Main office, 444 North Clark street, Chicago. Annual meeting, fourth Tuesday in July.

## THE CINCINNATI GAS & ELECTRIC CO.

A corporation formed under the laws of Ohio, in 1837, under the name of the Cincinnati Gas Light & Coke Co. In 1901 the company absorbed the Cincinnati Edison Electric Co., the Brush Electric Light Co. and the Jones Brothers' Electric Co. of Cincinnati, and assumed its present name. The authorized capital stock was increased from $9,500,000 to $28,000,000, of which the stockholders of the Cincinnati Gas Light & Coke Co. received $19,264,000 in exchange for their holdings; those of the Cincinnati Edison Electric Co., $7,742,000, while the balance went to the stockholders of the other two companies. The company is engaged in supplying gas and electricity for lighting, heating and power to Cincinnati and vicinity.

Stock..... Par $100........................Authorized, $29,000,000......Issued, $29,000,000

The company has no preferred stock and no funded debt.

Transfer Agent, The Union Savings Bank & Trust Co., Cincinnati. Registrar, The Central Trust & Safe Deposit Co., Cincinnati.

The first dividend paid by the company was 12 82-100 per cent. in 1845. The dividend rate is 4 per cent. annually, or 1 per cent. quarterly, and dividend periods are January, April, July and October.

President, Andrew Hickenlooper; Vice-President, Norman G. Kenan; Secretary and Assistant Treasurer, Henry W. Sage; Treasurer and Assistant Secretary, H. A. Barnhorne; Auditor, Harry R. Hooper, Cincinnati.

Directors—Andrew Hickenlooper, Norman G. Kenan, W. A. Goodman, S. R. Burton, R. A. Holden, Jr., M. E. Ingalls, J. G. Schmidlapp, George Bullock, Casper H. Rowe, J. T. Carew, A. Howard Hinkle, Briggs S. Cunningham, M. E. Moch, Charles P. Taft.

Corporate and main offices, Fourth and Plum streets, Cincinnati. Annual meeting, first Monday in May, at Cincinnati.

---

## CINCINNATI, LAWRENCEBURG & AURORA ELECTRIC STREET RAILROAD CO.

A corporation formed under the laws of Ohio in November, 1898, for the purpose of operating an electric railway from Cincinnati to Aurora, Lawrenceburg and Harrison, Ohio. The company operates 42 miles of track.

Stock......Par $100.................. ............Authorized, $750,000......Issued, $750,000

The company has no preferred stock.

FUNDED DEBT.

1st mort., 5 per cent., gold, due July, 1919, Jan. and July............................ $750,000

The bonds outstanding are the full amount authorized. Trustee and agent for the payment of interest, Union Savings Bank and Trust Co., Cincinnati.

President, J. C. Hooven, Hamilton, O.; Secretary, Stanley Shaffer, Cincinnati; Treasurer and General Manager, C. Earle Hooven, Cincinnati.

Directors—J. C. Hooven, Hamilton, O.; J. G. Schmidlapp, A. B. Voorheis, C. Earle Hooven, Stanley Shaffer, Cincinnati.

Main office, Liston avenue and Anderson's Ferry Road, Cincinnati.

---

## THE CINCINNATI, NEWPORT & COVINGTON LIGHT & TRACTION CO.

A corporation formed under the laws of New Jersey March 11, 1902. It acquired all the stock of the Union Light, Heat & Power Co. and of the Cincinnati, Newport & Covington Railway Co. The latter was a corporation formed in 1892 to consolidate the South Covington & Cincinnati Street Railway, Newport & Cincinnati Street Railroad and Cincinnati & Newport Street Railroad. The company also controls, through ownership of stock, the Newport Electric Street Railway, Cincinnati, Covington & Rosedale Railway, Cincinnati, West Covington & Ludlow Street Railway and Covington & Latonia Railway.

The North American Co. has a large interest in the corporation.

Stock..Par $100..Authorized { com., $5,000,000 / pref., 5,000,000 } Issued { com., $3,800,000 / pref., 5,000,000 } $8,800,000

The preferred stock is 4½ per cent., non-cumulative.

FUNDED DEBT.

| | |
|---|---|
| 1st cons. mort., gold, 5 per cent., due Jan., 1922, Jan. and July...................... | $2,500,000 |
| 2d mort., 5 per cent., due July, 1922, Jan. and July.............. ................ | 600,000 |
| South Covington & Cincinnati 1st mort., 6 per cent., due March, 1912, March and Sept.. | 250,000 |
| " " " cons. mort., 6 per cent, due Jan., 1932, Jan. and July.... | 150,000 |

FUNDED DEBT—*Continued.*

| | |
|---|---|
| Newport & Dayton mort., 6 per cent., due Aug., 1917, Feb. and Aug. | 100,000 |
| Union Light, Heat & Power, 1st mort., 4 per cent., due May, 1918, May and Nov... | 1,300,000 |
| Bellevue, W. F. & Gd. mort., 6 per cent. | 100,000 |
| Total | $5,000,000 |

Trustee of consolidated mortgage is Farmers' Loan & Trust Co., New York. The total issue is $3,000,000, of which $500,000 is reserved to retire the underlying bonds given above. The 2d mortgage (same trustee) is for $1,000,000, authorized.

In 1899 dividends of ½ per cent. cash were paid on the old stock of the Street Railway Co. in February and August. In 1900 paid 2 per cent. On February 1, 1901, ¾ per cent. was paid quarterly.

The first dividend on the present company's preferred stock was 1 per cent., October, 1902.

| EARNINGS. | Gross. | Net. |
|---|---|---|
| 1894 | $497,948 | $127,343 |
| 1895 | 624,033 | 205,323 |
| 1897 | 638,477 | 211,197 |
| 1898 | 681,673 | 339,553 |
| 1899 | 713,386 | 427,152 |
| 1900 | 783,588 | 461,949 |

President, James C. Ernst, Covington, Ky.; Vice-President, C. W. Wetmore, New York; Treasurer and Secretary, George M. Abbott, Covington, Ky.

Main office, Fourth and Scott streets, Covington, Ky. Annual meeting, third Wednesday in February.

## THE CINCINNATI TRACTION CO.

A corporation formed under the laws of Ohio, February 19, 1901. The company leased the property of the Cincinnati Street Railway Co., comprising a total of about 210 miles of railway.

In 1896 Cincinnati Street Railway Co. acquired the Mt. Adams and Eden Park Inclined Railway and the Mt. Auburn Cable Railway.

Stock......Par $100..........................Authorized, $2,000,000......Issued, $2,000,000

Stock is transferred at the company's office.

The Cincinnati Street Railway Co. has $18,000,000 of stock, on which, under the lease, beginning February 21, 1901, dividends are 5¼ per cent. for the first year, 5½ per cent. for the second year, 5¾ per cent. for the third year, and 6 per cent. thereafter. The dividends are in quarterly payments in January, April, July and October. The Cincinnati Street Railway Co.'s mortgage bonds for $250,000 were paid at maturity, July 1, 1896.

There are $665,000 bonds of the Mt. Adams & Eden Park Inclined Railway and $200,000 bonds of the Mt. Auburn Cable Railway outstanding.

In 1902 the gross earnings from all sources were $3,559,684.

Chairman Executive Committee, Hugh J. McGowan, Indianapolis; President, W. Kesley Schoepf, Cincinnati; Vice-President, J. B. Foraker, Jr.; Secretary, S. C. Cooper; Treasurer, W. H. MacAlister; Auditor, C. F. Callaway, Cincinnati.

Directors—William L. Elkins, Peter A. B. Widener, Randal Morgan, Philadelphia; W. Kesley Schoepf, J. B. Foraker, Jr., W. T. Irwin, David G. Edwards, Harry M. Levy, William Cooper Procter, William M. Greene, Cincinnati; Hugh J. McGowan, Indianapolis.

Main office, Fifth and Walnut streets, Cincinnati. Annual meeting, second Monday in February.

## THE CINCINNATI UNION STOCK YARDS CO.

A corporation formed under the laws of Ohio, June 1, 1871, to operate stock yards at Cincinnati. The company has a large property in that city.

Stock..Par { com., $100 / pref., 50 } Authorized { com., $1,250,000 / pref., 500,000 } Issued { com., $1,250,000 / pref., 500,000 } $1,750,000

The preferred stock is 5 per cent. and is redeemable at par.

Stock is transferred at the office of the company. Registrar, The Central Trust & Safe Deposit Co., Cincinnati.

Dividends on both the common and the preferred at the rate of 5 per cent. per annum are paid quarterly. Dividend periods for the common stock, March, June, September, December. Dividend periods for the preferred stock, January, April, July, October.

President and Treasurer, N. H. Biggs; Vice-President, W. J. Lippincott Secretary and Assistant Treasurer, B. Frank Davis, Cincinnati.

Directors—W. J. Lippincott, Casimir L. Werk, W. H. Doan, A. J. Mullane, C. D. Kinney, A. Furst, B. Frank Davis, H. L. Breneman, N. H. Biggs.

Corporate office, stock yards, Spring Grove avenue, Cincinnati. Annual meeting, second Monday in March, at Cincinnati.

## CITIZENS TELEPHONE CO.

A corporation formed under the laws of Michigan for the purpose of establishing a telephone system in Grand Rapids, Mich.

Stock......Par $10..........................Authorized, $2,000,000......Issued, $1,125,000

Over 95 per cent. of the stock has been placed in the hands of James M. Bennett, Lester J. Rindge and Ernest A. Stowe, trustees.

The company has no preferred stock or funded debt.

Regular dividends at the rate of 8 per cent. per annum are paid quarterly.

President, Charles F. Rood; Vice-President, E. Fitzgerald; Secretary, E. D. Fisher; Treasurer, W. J. Stuart; Manager, C. E. Tarte.

Main office, 87 Campau street, Grand Rapids, Mich. Annual meeting, third Tuesday in July, at Grand Rapids, Mich.

## THE CITY & SUBURBAN TELEPHONE ASSOCIATION

A corporation formed under the laws of Ohio. The association operates a telephone system under exclusive license from the American Telephone & Telegraph Co., in the cities of Cincinnati, Covington and Newport, Ky., Hamilton, O., and neighboring towns. The American Telephone & Telegraph Co. owns 30 per cent. of the stock. On January 1, 1901, the association had 15,882 stations.

Stock......Par $50..........................Authorized, $4,000,000......Issued, $3,637,250

In November, 1902, the stock was increased by $172,250. The stockholders subscribing for same at par in the proportion of one new share for every twenty old shares held.

The association pays dividends at the rate of 6 per cent. per annum on its stock, in quarterly payments of 1½ per cent. each, in January, April, July and October.

Stock is transferred by the secretary of the association. Registrar, Central Trust & Safe Deposit Co., Cincinnati.

The association has no funded debt.

In the year 1900 the company's gross earnings were $599,064; net earnings, $221,798. In 1902, gross, $811,511; net, $294,014.

President, John Kilgour; Vice-President, C. H. Kilgour; Secretary and Treasurer, W. A. Blanchard; General Manager, Bayard L. Kilgour, Cincinnati.

Directors—Henry Hanna, C. H. Kilgour, George Bullock, John Kilgour, W. A. Blanchard, Charles P. Taft, Bayard L. Kilgour, Cincinnati; C. Jay French, Boston.

Main office, Vine and Baker streets, Cincinnati. Annual meeting, third Wednesday in February.

## CITY GAS CO. OF NORFOLK

A corporation formed under the laws of Virginia in 1851. The company controls all the gas lighting facilities of the city of Norfolk, Va. The yearly output is 116,000,000 cubic feet of gas. In 1899 control of the company was acquired by the Norfolk Railway & Light Co. In May, 1902, that company was acquired by the Norfolk, Portsmouth & Newport News Co. See statement of the latter company.

Stock......Par $100..........................Authorized, $500,000......Issued, $500,000

The company has no preferred stock. Transfer Agents, J. William Middendorf & Co., Baltimore. Registrar, International Trust Co., Baltimore.

FUNDED DEBT.

1st mort., 6 per cent., due 1926, June and Dec.......................................... $500,000

The amount of bonds authorized is $500,000. Trustee of the mortgage and agent for the payment of interest, United States Mortgage & Trust Co., New York.

President, William H. White; Vice-President, E. C. Hathaway; Secretary and Treasurer, F. H. Sawyer; General Manager, H. L. Rice, Norfolk, Va.

Directors—William H. White, C. Brooks Johnston, W. H. Doyle, J. G. Womble, M. T. Cooke, H. Hodges, H. L. Rice, E. C. Hathaway, Norfolk, Va.; R. Lancaster Williams, Richmond Va.; J. William Middendorf, Baltimore; John D. McIlheny, Philadelphia.

Main office, 82 Plume street, Norfolk, Va. Annual meeting, third Monday in January.

## THE H. B. CLAFLIN CO.

A corporation formed under the laws of New Jersey, May 5, 1890, to conduct the wholesale dry goods business of H. B. Claflin & Co. Of the outstanding stock of this company $4,500,000 is held by the Associated Merchants' Co.

| Stock..Par $100..Authorized | | | Issued | | | |
|---|---|---|---|---|---|---|
| | com., | $3,829,100 | | com., | $3,829,100 | |
| | 1st pref., | 2,600,300 | | 1st pref., | 2,600,300 | $9,000,000 |
| | 2d pref., | 2,570,600 | | 2d " | 2,570,600 | |

The 1st preferred stock is entitled to 5 per cent. cumulative dividends, and the 2d preferred to 6 per cent. cumulative dividends. Preferred stock allotted to the public could be converted into common stock to the extent of one-half of its value during the first two years of com any's existence. This option has now expired. By the subscription agreement, members of the firm of H. B. Claflin & Co. subscribed for 60,000 shares of the three classes of stocks, paying therefor $6,000,000 in cash, their preferred stock not being convertible into common. There is no mortgage on any property of the company. Stockholders have no personal liability.

Stock is transferred at the office of the company. Registrar, American Exchange National Bank, New York.

The dividends of 5 per cent. per annum on the 1st preferred and 6 per cent. on the 2d preferred are paid quarterly at the rate of 1¼ and 1½ per cent., respectively, on February 1, May 1, August 1 and November 1. Dividends on common were from date of organization to October, 1892, at rate of 8 per cent. per annum, till July, 1893, 9 per cent. per annum, then 6 per cent. per annum until July, 1899, when the company resumed the payment of 2 per cent. quarterly dividends on the common. Dividends on the common are paid January 15, April 15, July 15 and October 15.

Half-yearly statements are published, and the reports of this company are distinguished by their full and frank exhibition of its affairs.

Profits for the full years have been as follows: 1891, $658,096; 1892, $870,006; 1893, $323,786; 1894, $488,312; 1895, $613,970; 1896, $261,518; 1897, $510,943; 1898, $526,545; 1899, $1,247,851; 1900, $914,353; 1901, $650,554; 1902, $629,562.

EARNINGS.

| | First Six Months. | | | Last Six Months. | | |
|---|---|---|---|---|---|---|
| | Net Earnings. | | Sur. Over Div. | Net Earnings. | | Sur. Over Div. |
| 1895 | $254,697 | Def. | $2,302 | $359,273 | | $102,274 |
| 1896 | 158,114 | " | 98,884 | 103,403 | Def. | 153,596 |
| 1897 | 209,605 | " | 47,393 | 301,338 | | 44,340 |
| 1898 | 241,248 | " | 15,750 | 285,297 | | 28,298 |
| 1899 | 607,032 | Sur. | 330,889 | 640,819 | | 345,530 |
| 1900 | 612,309 | " | 317,020 | 302,045 | | 6,755 |
| 1901 | 303,097 | " | 7,808 | 347,456 | | 52,167 |
| 1902 | 317,377 | " | 22,088 | 312,185 | | 16,895 |

President, John Claflin; Treasurer, D. N. Force; Secretary, George E. Armstrong.

Directors—John Claflin, E. E. Eames, D. N. Force, George E. Armstrong, J. C. Eames, Stewart W. Eames.

Main office, 224 Church street, New York. Annual meeting, January 11, at Elizabeth, N. J.

## CLARKSBURG FUEL CO.

A corporation formed under the laws of West Virginia, September 16, 1901, to engage in mining and selling coal and manufacturing coke. The company has acquired the following properties:

Pursglove mines.
Interstate Coal Co.
Sands and Harner tract.
Park Coal Co.
Colonial Coal and Coke Co.
Clarksburg Coal and Coke Co.
O'Neil Coal and Coke Co.
Pinnickinnick Coal Co.
Dixie Coal Co.
Two Lick Run Coal Co.

These properties are capable of producing about 800,000 tons of coal a year.

Stock......Par $100..........................Authorized, $3,000,000......Issued, $3,000,000

The company has no preferred stock. Transfer Agent, Registrar & Transfer Co., New York. Registrar, Guaranty Trust Co., New York.

FUNDED DEBT.

1st mort., 6 per cent. bonds, due 1931, April and Oct.................................. $2,500,000

The outstanding bond issue is the total amount authorized. Trustee of bonds and agent for the payment of interest, Guaranty Trust Co., New York.

President, Clarence W. Watson, New York; Vice-President, T. M. Jackson, Clarksburg, W. Va.; Secretary, A. K. Bowles, New York; Treasurer, J. E. Sands, Fairmont, W. Va.
Directors—Clarence W. Watson, Walter G. Oakman, W. G. Sharp, T. M. Jackson, L. L. Malone.
Corporate office, Clarksburg, W. Va.; main office, Fairmont, W. Va.; branch office, 1 Broadway, New York. Annual meeting, first Monday in September, at Clarksburg or New York.

## CLEVELAND CITY RAILWAY CO.

A corporation formed under the laws of Ohio in 1893. Road owned, 84 miles.
The company is a consolidation of the Cleveland City Cable Railway and the Woodland Avenue & West Side Street Railroad Co. It is commonly known as the "Little Consolidated."

Stock......Par $100..........................Authorized, $9,000,000......Issued, $7,600,000

Transfer Agent, Cleveland Trust Co. Registrar, Guardian Trust Co., Cleveland.

FUNDED DEBT.

Cleveland City Cable Railway 1st mort., 5 per cent., due July, 1909, Jan. and July... $2,000,000

Prior to 1896 the company paid 4 per cent. annually on stock. In 1896 paid 2 per cent., in 1897 2¼ per cent., in 1898 3 per cent., in 1899 3¼ per cent., in 1900 4½ per cent., in 1901 4 per cent., and in 1902 5 per cent. The January, 1903, dividend was 1¼ per cent. The dividends are paid quarterly, in January, April, July and October.
President, Marcus A. Hanna; Vice-President, C. F. Emery; Secretary and Treasurer, John Ehrhardt.
Directors—Marcus A. Hanna, Christopher F. Emery, Leland W. Prior, Robert R. Rhodes, William B. Sanders, Charles A. Otis, Jr., J. Homer Wade, George G. Mulhern, Horace E. Andrews, Cleveland.
Main office, Superior and Water streets, Cleveland. Annual meeting, third Monday in January.

## CLEVELAND ELECTRIC ILLUMINATING CO.

A corporation formed under the laws of Ohio in 1892. The company succeeded the Brush Electric Light Co. and the Cleveland Electric Light Co. Its corporate title was the Cleveland General Electric Co., the present name being taken in 1895. The company has an unlimited franchise to supply electric light in Cleveland.

Stock...Par $100....Authorized { com., 1,500,000; pref., $1,000,000 } Issued { com., $1,500,000; pref., 800,000 } $2,300,000

The preferred stock is 6 per cent., cumulative, dividends being payable in February, May, August and November. Stock is transferred at the office of the company, Cleveland. Registrar, The Citizens Savings & Trust Co., Cleveland.

FUNDED DEBT.

1st mort., 5 per cent. gold, due Oct. 1, 1927, April and Oct........................ $1,300,000

The total authorized 1st mortgage is $2,500,000. Bonds may be called on or after April 1, 1901, at 110 and accrued interest. Trustee of the mortgage and agent for the payment of interest, The Morton Trust Co., New York.
President, James Parmelee, New York; Vice-President, Samuel Scovil; Secretary, Samuel C. D. Johns; General Superintendent, Robert Lindsay, Cleveland.
Directors—Horace Andrews, Hubbard Cooke, Samuel Scovil, Cleveland; Edwin M. Bulkley, James Parmelee, New York; Howard L. Clark, Providence, R. I.
Corporate and main office, 311 Superior street, Cleveland.

## CLEVELAND ELECTRIC RAILWAY CO.

This company was formed in 1893, and is a consolidation of the Broadway & Newburgh Street Railroad Co., East Cleveland Railroad Co., Brooklyn Street Railroad and South Side Street Railroad. Road owned, 136 miles. It is commonly known as the "Big Consolidated."

Stock......Par $100........................Authorized, $13,000,000......Issued, $13,000,000

Transfer Agent, Savings & Trust Co., Cleveland. Registrar, Guardian Trust Co., Cleveland.

FUNDED DEBT.

| | |
|---|---|
| Cons. mort., 5 per cent., due March, 1913, March and Sept. | $2,450,000 |
| East Cleveland Railroad 1st mort., 5 per cent., due March, 1910, March and Sept. | 1,000,000 |
| Brooklyn Street Railway morts., 6 per cent., due Sept., 1903, March and Sept. | 600,000 |
| South Side Railroad 1st mort., 6 per cent., due Sept., 1903, March and Sept. | 300,000 |
| Total | $4,350,000 |

The authorized issue of consolidated mortgage bonds is $3,500,000. Trustee and agent for payment of interest, Central Trust Co., New York. No more bonds can be issued on present mileage, and new bonds on extensions can only be for 85 per cent. of the cash cost of such extensions. Trustee of mortgage, Central Trust Co., New York.

| EARNINGS. | Gross. | Net. |
|---|---|---|
| 1896 | $1,634,841 | $553,862 |
| 1897 | 1,632,020 | 593,075 |
| 1898 | 1,739,332 | 692,739 |
| 1899 | 1,509,003 | 541,058 |
| 1900 | 2,061,435 | 941,848 |
| 1901 | 2,296,897 | 1,030,944 |
| 1902 | 2,524,949 | 1,087,306 |

In 1897 dividends were 3 per cent.; in 1898, 3¼ per cent.; in 1899, 2¾ per cent. In 1899 the October quarterly dividend was passed. In 1900, paid 3¼ per cent.; in 1901 and 1902, 4 per cent. Dividends are quarterly, January, April, July and October.

President, Horace E. Andrews; Vice-President, R. A. Harman; Secretary, H. J. Davies; Treasurer, George S. Russell.

Directors—Horace E. Andrews, R. A. Harman, John J. Stanley, Myron T. Herrick, Calvary Morris, Charles L. Pack, Cleveland; James Parmalee, New York.

Main office, 154 Prospect street, Cleveland. Annual meeting, third Wednesday in January.

## CLEVELAND, ELYRIA & WESTERN RAILWAY CO.

A corporation formed under the laws of Ohio, June 20, 1900. The company is a consolidation of the following companies:

Cleveland, Berea, Elyria & Oberlin Railway Co.
Lorain County Street Railway Co.
Oberlin & Wellington Railway Co.

The company also controls the Cleveland & Southern Railway Co., and in February, 1902, purchased the Elyria, Grafton & Southern Electric Railway Co. The company has power stations at Elyria and Rockport, O., owns 35 motor cars and operates 69 miles of electric road, extending from Cleveland to Elyria, Berea and Oberlin, O. An extension of 21 miles from Oberlin to Norwalk, O., is under way.

Stock......Par $100..........................Authorized, $2,000,000......Issued, $1,600,000

The company has no preferred stock. Transfer Agent, Cleveland Trust Co., Cleveland.

Dividends to the amount of 3 per cent. were paid in 1901 and a ¾ per cent. dividend in January, 1902.

FUNDED DEBT.

| | |
|---|---|
| 1st mort., 5 per cent. gold, due Aug., 1920 (Feb. and Aug.) | $1,073,000 |
| Cleveland & Elyria El. R.R. Co., 1st mort., 6 per cent, due May, 1915 (May and Nov.) | 200,000 |
| Elyria & Oberlin El. Ry. Co., 1st mort., 6 per cent., due Aug., 1917 (Feb. and Aug.) | 100,000 |
| Cleveland Berea, Elyria & Oberlin Ry. Co., con. mort., 5 per cent. gold, due March, 1919 (March and Sept.) | 127,000 |
| Elyria, Grafton & So. Ry. Co., 1st mort., 5 per cent. gold, due Jan., 1922 (Jan. and July) | 100,000 |
| Cleveland & So. Ry. Co., 1st mort., 5 per cent. gold, due July, 1921 (Jan. and July) | 1,000,000 |
| Total | $2,600,000 |

The authorized mortgage of the Cleveland, Elyria & Western Railway Co. is $1,500,000, of which $427,000 are reserved to retire prior liens. Trustee of mortgage, Western Reserve Trust Co., Cleveland. Agents for the payment of interest, Western Reserve Trust Co. and National Bank of Commerce, New York. Bonds are subject to call after 1910 at 100.

The outstanding bonds of the Cleveland & Elyria Electric Railroad are the full amount authorized. They are subject to call after 1905. Trustee of the mortgage and agent for the payment of interest, Savings & Trust Co., Cleveland.

The outstanding bonds of the Elyria & Oberlin Electric Railway Co. are the full amount authorized. The bonds are subject to call at par after 1907. Trustee of the mortgage and agent for the payment of interest, Cleveland Trust Co., Cleveland.

The authorized mortgage of the Cleveland, Berea, Elyria & Oberlin Railway Co., is $500,000, of which $300,000 are reserved to retire a like amount of the divisional 6s. The bonds are subject to call at par after 1909. Trustee of the mortgage and agent for the payment of interest, Cleveland Trust Co.

The outstanding bonds of the Elyria, Grafton & Southern Electric Railway Co. are the full amount authorized. They are subject to call after 1905. Trustee of the mortgage, Federal Trust Co., Cleveland. Agents for the payment of interest, Federal Trust Co., Cleveland, and Colonial Trust Co., New York.

The 1st mortgage bonds of the Cleveland & Southern Railway Co. are $1,000,000 authorized. Trustees of the mortgage, Western Reserve Trust Co., Cleveland, and Standard Trust Co., New York.

EARNINGS.

| | Gross. | Net. | Charges. | Surplus. |
|---|---|---|---|---|
| 1900 | $179,697 | $77,303 | $34,561 | $42,742 |
| 1901 | 249,259 | 112,394 | 57,023 | 55,371 |

President, A. H. Pomeroy; Vice-President, A. E. Akins; Secretary, E. F. Schneider; Treasurer, F. T. Pomeroy.

Directors—A. H. Pomeroy, A. E. Akins, O. D. Pomeroy, F. T. Pomeroy, Will Christy, M. J. Mandlebaum, M. A. Sprague, D. M. Coe, F. L. Fuller, S. C. Smith, E. S. Schneider.

Main office, 614 Garfield Building, Cleveland. Annual meeting, second Tuesday in January.

## CLEVELAND, PAINESVILLE & EASTERN RAILROAD CO.

A corporation formed under the laws of Ohio, April 25, 1895. The company owns an electric road from Euclid to Painesville and Fairport, O., 23.02 miles, and from Willoughby to Glenville, O., 14.89 miles, with a total trackage of 42.41 miles. It also has trackage over the Cleveland City Railway Co. from Glenville to Cleveland, and over the Cleveland Electric Railway Co. from Euclid to Cleveland. The company owns 32 motor cars, a power-house at Willoughby and three car houses.

Stock......Par $100............................Authorized, $2,000,000......Issued, $1,556,000

The company has no preferred stock. Transfer Agent and Registrar, Cleveland Trust Co., Cleveland.

FUNDED DEBT.

| | |
|---|---|
| 1st mort., 5 per cent gold, due April, 1916, April and Oct. | $500,000 |
| Debentures, 6 per cent., due July, 1907, Jan. and July | 500,000 |
| Con. mort., 5 per cent., due Oct., 1918, April and Oct. | 402,000 |
| Total | $1,402,000 |

The outstanding 1st mortgage bonds and debentures are the full amounts authorized. The authorized amount of the consolidated mortgage is $2,000,000, of which $1,000,000 is reserved to retire the prior liens, and $154,000 is in the company's treasury.

Trustee of the 1st mortgage, Cleveland Trust Co., Cleveland. Agents for the payment of interest, Cleveland Trust Co. and State Trust Co., New York. Trustee of the debentures and the consolidated mortgage, Dime Savings & Banking Co., Cleveland. Agent for payment of interest on the debentures, Dime Savings & Banking Co. Agent for payment of interest on consolidated mortgage, Dime Savings & Banking Co. and Colonial Trust Co., New York.

EARNINGS.

| | Gross. | Net. | Charges. | Surplus. |
|---|---|---|---|---|
| 1901 | $164,971 | $77,869 | $71,296 | $6,573 |
| 1902 | 189,187 | 83,517 | 74,551 | 8,966 |

President, Charles W. Wason, Cleveland; Vice-President, J. A. Biedler, Willoughby, O.; Secretary, Fred S. Barton, Cleveland; Assistant Secretary, George E. Bender; Treasurer, Charles A. Post; Superintendent, J. Jordan, Willoughby, O.

Main office, Willoughby, O.; Cleveland office, 154 Prospect street. Annual meeting, third Wednesday in January, at Cleveland.

## COCHECO MANUFACTURING CO.

A corporation formed under the laws of New Hampshire, June 29, 1827, to manufacture cotton cloth and prints. The print works of the company are at Dover, N. H., and have a capacity of 65,000,000 yards of cloth per year.

Stock......Par $500............................Authorized, $1,500,000......Issued, $1,500,000

The company has no preferred stock nor funded debt. Stock is transferred at the office of the company, Boston.

President, T. Jefferson Coolidge; Treasurer, Arthur B. Silsbee, Boston.

Directors, T. Jefferson Coolidge, George P. Gardner, Charles W. Amory, A. Lawrence, Sumner Wallace, Robert H. Stevenson, Arthur B. Silsbee.

Corporate office, Dover, N. H.; main office, 60 State street, Boston. Annual meeting in June, at Dover, N. H.

## COLONIAL LAND CO.

A corporation formed under the laws of Pennsylvania, June 26, 1901, for the purpose of purchasing and selling real estate at Colonia, near Monaca, Beaver County, Pa. The company acquired about 400 acres, being the town site of Colonia.

Stock......Par $50..............................Authorized, $350,000......Issued, $350,000

The company has no preferred stock and no funded debt.

A dividend of 3 per cent. was paid February 2, 1903. No regular time has been fixed for the payment of future dividends.

Stock is transferred by the treasurer of the company, Pittsburg.

President, J. M. Schoonmaker, Pittsburg; Vice-President, H. C. Fry, Rochester, Pa.; Secretary, B. C. Vaughn; Treasurer, John G. Robinson, Pittsburg.

Directors—J. M. Schoonmaker, B. C. Vaughn, H. C. Fry, L. A. Robinson, J. B. Yoke, John G. Robinson, Pittsburg.

Corporate and main office, 419 Fourth avenue, Pittsburg.

## COLONIAL SUGARS CO.

A corporation formed under the laws of New Jersey, June 20, 1902. The corporation is a merger of the following companies:

Gramercy Sugar Co. Gramercy Finance Co. Damuji Co.

Refinery and sugar plantations at Gramercy, La., and the Constancia sugar estate in the province of Santa Clara, Cuba, are owned by the company.

Stock......Par $100..........................Authorized, $3,000,000......Issued, $2,780,000

The company has no preferred stock.

Transfer Agent, H. W. Poor & Co., 18 Wall street, New York. Registrar, Central Trust Co., New York.

FUNDED DEBT.

1st mort., 5 per cent., gold, due 1952, April and Oct.............................. $2,150,000

The authorized 1st mortgage is $3,000,000. Trustee of mortgage, Central Trust Co., New York. Agent for the payment of interest, H. W. Poor & Co., New York.

President and Treasurer, M. R. Spelman; Vice-President, H. W. Poor; Secretary and Assistant Treasurer, Thomas D. Nesbitt, New York.

Directors—J. C. Atwater, J. W. Doane, Stuyvesant Fish, H. W. Poor, Henry Sanford, M. R. Spelman, A. H. Wiggin, New York; J. W. Hearn, New Orleans; A. H. Larkin, Nutley, N. J.

Corporate office, Jersey City; New York office, 18 Wall street; branch offices, New Orleans and Constancia, Santa Clara, Cuba. Annual meeting, last Tuesday in June, at Jersey City.

## THE COLORADO FUEL & IRON CO.

A corporation formed under the laws of Colorado, October 21, 1892, by the consolidation of the Colorado Coal & Iron Co. and the Colorado Fuel Co. The company owns and operates 28 coal mines in various parts of Colorado and New Mexico, 80,000 acres of coal lands, 3,000 coke ovens, steel and iron mills at Bessemer, Col.; iron mines at Orient, Col.; Sunrise, Wyo., and Fierro, N. M., and considerable undeveloped iron lands, with plants for operating its various properties.

In August, 1896, company leased the coal properties of the Atchison, Topeka & Santa Fe Railway Co., with a capacity of about 600,000 tons of coal per annum.

In September, 1899, the company proposed to largely increase the capacity of its mills and furnaces, raising them from a maximum of 150,000 tons of finished products annually to 550,000 tons, and in connection with this to open new mines, build additional coke ovens and improve the facilities of its plants by the introduction of labor-saving machinery.

In 1902 a contest for the control of the company arose and litigation ensued resulting in a postponement of the annual meeting, which was finally held in December, 1902, under the supervision of a special commissioner of the courts. The contest was finally settled by a compromise in which the Denver & Rio Grande and the Union Pacific interests, as well as the old management, obtained equal representation in the directory of the company.

Stock. Par $100..Authorized { com., $38,000,000; pref., 2,000,000 } Issued { com., $23,932,000; pref., 2,000,000 } $25,932,000

The preferred stock is 8 per cent., cumulative, the dividends being payable in February and August.

The common stock was increased from $11,000,000 to $23,000,000 in September, 1899, for the purpose of providing capital for the additions to plant above referred to. In July, 1901, it was again increased to $38,000,000 to provide for conversion of the 5 per cent. debenture bonds.

Transfer Agents, Knickerbocker Trust Co., New York.

Previous to February, 1900, the last dividend on the preferred had been 4 per cent., February 20, 1897. August, 1894, the dividend on preferred was passed. Dividends were resumed February, 1896, but no dividend was paid until February, 1900, when 8 per cent. was paid on the preferred. In April, September and October further dividends of 8 per cent. each were also paid, and in November, 1900, a dividend of 8 per cent. was declared, payable December 20, 1900, thus completing the 32 per cent. of accumulated dividends on the preferred, amounting to $640,000. The payment of regular semi-annual dividends of 4 per cent. on the preferred began February 15, 1901, and are now 2 per cent. each in February and August.

Prior to 1901 the last dividend paid on the common stock was 1¼ per cent. in May, 1893. On July 15, 1901, 1¼ per cent. quarterly was paid on common, and similar payments were made in October, 1901, January and April, 1902. But the July, 1902, dividend was passed and none have been paid since.

FUNDED DEBT.

| | |
|---|---|
| Colorado Fuel Co. gen. mort., 6 per cent., due May, 1919, May and Nov. | $680,000 |
| Colorado Fuel & Iron gen. mort., 5 per cent., due Feb., 1943, Jan. and July | 5,315,000 |
| Convertible debentures, 5 per cent., due Aug., 1911, Feb. and Aug. | 14,068,000 |
| Grand River C. & C. Co. 1st mort. not guar., 6 per cent., due July, 1919, April and Oct. | 934,000 |
| Rocky Mount. Coal & Iron 1st mort. guar., 5 per cent., due 1951, May and Nov. | 750,000 |
| Total | $21,747,000 |

The convertible debenture 5 per cent. bonds were issued in 1901 to provide for the erection of auxiliary plants for the manufacture of tin-plate hoops, wire, wire nails, etc. The debentures are convertible, at holder's option, into common stock at par from February 1, 1902, to August 1, 1906, after which date the company may redeem them at 105.

The Rocky Mountain Coal & Iron Co's. 1st mortgage 5 per cent. bonds, guaranteed by this company, cover about 258,000 acres of coal and timber lands in Las Animas County, Colo.

There are $673,000 1st mortgage 5 per cent. bonds of the Colorado Coal & Iron Development Co., which are guaranteed by the company. The bonds are redeemable at 105.

See MANUAL for 1901 and preceding years for details regarding the Colorado Coal & Iron Co. and Colorado Fuel Co.

EARNINGS.

Year ending June 30.

| | Gross. | Net. | Charges. | Dividends. | Surplus. |
|---|---|---|---|---|---|
| 1893-94 | $4,375,748 | $562,109 | $435,089 | * $160,000 | $46,843 |
| 1894-95 | 5,667,185 | 678,450 | 513,576 | ...... | 164,874 |
| 1895-96 | 5,587,817 | 720,910 | 559,957 | 160,000 | 74,316 |
| 1896-97 | 5,073,368 | 825,020 | 544,693 | 80,000 | 200,326 |
| 1897-98 | 5,489,115 | 711,543 | 614,907 | ...... | 96,803 |
| 1898-99 | 8,201,392 | 1,094,675 | 817,155 | ...... | 277,530 |
| 1899-00 | 10,350,030 | 2,349,682 | 880,099 | 320,000 | 1,194,577 |
| 1900-01 | 12,246,546 | 2,142,671 | 850,750 | 640,000 | 651,921 |
| 1901-02 | 13,860,593 | 1,801,926 | 1,110,093 | 160,000 | 531,833 |

* In scrip.

Fixed charges include sinking fund provisions. In 1899 the charges were increased by $100,000, set aside to provide for depreciation, and $62,125, reserved for an emergency fund. The dividends paid in 1900 consisted of 32 per cent. of the accumulated dividends on the preferred stock.

Chairman, John C. Osgood, New York; President, Julian A. Kebler; 1st Vice-President, A. C. Cass, Denver; 2d Vice-President and Comptroller, John H. McClement, New York; Treasurer, John L. Jerome; Secretary, D. C. Beaman, Denver.

Directors—John C. Osgood, John L. Jerome, Julian A. Kebler, J. M. Herbert, Frank Trumbull, A. C. Cass, Denver; James H. Hyde, George J. Gould, John H. McClement, Charles H. Butler, Edwin Hawley, Edward H. Harriman, New York; H. E. Huntington, San Francisco.

Main office, Seventeenth and Champa streets, Denver; New York office, 71 Broadway. Annual meeting, third Wednesday in August.

## COLUMBUS & HOCKING COAL & IRON CO.

A company formed under the laws of Ohio, January 26, 1883. The company is a large coal producer. Owns extensive coal, iron ore and furnace properties in Hocking, Perry, Athens and Vinton counties, Ohio. The company was reorganized without foreclosure in 1898.

Stock....Par $100.....Authorized { com., $7,000,000 / pref., 333,499 } Issued { com., $6,978,600 / pref., 21,400 } $7,000,000

In February, 1901, it was decided to increase the authorized common stock from $5,000,000 to $7,000,000 and retire the $333,499 of 5 per cent., non-cumulative, preferred stock, of which all but the amount given above had been retired at the close of 1902.

The last dividend on the preferred stock was 2½ per cent., August 20, 1891. The first dividend on the common stock was ½ of 1 per cent., paid December 1, 1902.

Transfer Agent, Farmers' Loan & Trust Co., New York. Registrar, Central Trust Co., N.Y.

FUNDED DEBT.

1st mort., reduced from 6 to 5 per cent., due Jan., 1917, Jan. and July................ $830,000

The July, 1895, interest was defaulted, and a bondholders' committee, M. S. Scudder, New York, chairman, was formed. A majority of bonds were deposited with Central Trust Co., and foreclosure proposed. Stockholders formed a protective committee to oppose such action. Action for a receivership brought in 1896, but was dismissed in July of that year. 1896 interest was met by assessment of $3 per share on stock, for which preferred stock was to be given. It was then proposed to reduce interest on bonds to 5 per cent. Foreclosure suit was instituted, but in 1898 arrangement was made by which interest on bonds was reduced to 5 per cent. and three past due coupons were redeemed in cash on that basis. Assessment of $3 per share was levied on stock, for which preferred stock was given. Assessment produced over $137,000.

In 1902 a contest for the control of this company was instituted, but litigation ensued, and though the opposition were credited with carrying the election its validity was attacked and the old, or Ziegler, management, remained in control pending a new election.

EARNINGS.

| Year ending March 31. | Gross. | Net. |
|---|---|---|
| 1892-93 | $717,752 | ...... |
| 1893-94 | 412,113 | ...... |
| 1894-95 | 361,920 | ...... |
| 1897-98 | 309,745 | $36,345 |
| 1898-99 | 320,316 | 35,983 |
| 1899-00 | 450,978 | 101,138 |
| 1900-01 | 576,156 | 101,672 |
| 1901-02 | 601,153 | 90,673 |

Deficit after interest in 1894 was $81,702; in 1895, $39,327; in 1898, $23,885; in 1899, $36,487, but in 1900 the surplus was $49,075; in 1901, surplus $49,347, and in 1902, $50,027.

President, William H. Ziegler, New York; Vice-President and Treasurer, S. A. McManigal, Secretary and Auditor, Arthur P. DeVennish, Columbus, O.

Directors—William H. Ziegler, Edwin S. Larchar, New York; S. A. McManigal, Willis P. Bloom, Arthur P. DeVennish, L. G. Addison, Robert Dixon, H. C. Rogers, Charles S. Binns, Columbus, O.

Main office, Wyandotte Building, Columbus, O. Annual meeting, third Wednesday in May.

## COLUMBUS CITIZENS' TELEPHONE CO.

A corporation formed under the laws of Ohio, December 19, 1898, to furnish telephone service in the city of Columbus, O. The number of telephones in service January 1, 1903, was 6,328.

Stock......Par $100..............................Authorized, $750,000......Issued, $750,000

The company has no preferred stock. Transfer Agent, State Savings Bank & Trust Co., Columbus, O.

FUNDED DEBT.

1st mort., 5 per cent. bonds, due 1920, Jan. and July.................................. $650,000

The bond issue is the full amount authorized. Trustee of mortgage and agent for the payment of interest, State Savings Bank & Trust Co., Columbus, O.

EARNINGS.

| | Gross. | Net. | Charges. | Surplus. |
|---|---|---|---|---|
| 1902 | $180,943 | $68,364 | $32,500 | $34,050 |

President, Henry A. Lanman, Columbus, O.; Vice-President, Henry A. Everett, Cleveland; Secretary and Treasurer, Edwin R. Sharp; General Manager, Frank L. Beam, Columbus, O.

Directors—Henry A. Lanman, Edwin R. Sharp, William A. Hordesty, James B. Hanna, Frank A. Davis, Lorenzo D. Hagerty, Columbus, O.; Henry A. Everett, Cleveland; Harry D. Critchfield, Chicago.

Corporate and main office, Long and Third streets, Columbus, O. Annual meeting, second Tuesday in February, at Columbus.

## COLUMBUS EDISON CO.

A corporation organized under laws of New Jersey in December, 1899. The company acquired a controlling interest in the stock of the Columbus Electric Co. and the Columbus Edison Electric Light Co.

In November, 1901, a syndicate offered $35 per share for the common stock and $125 for the preferred, a majority of the stockholders accepting these terms. It was understood that a consolidation of this company with the gas and traction interests of Columbus was intended.

Stock......Par $100.......Authorized { com., $450,000 / pref., 550,000 } Issued { com., $442,762 / pref., 398,175 } $840,937

The preferred stock is entitled to 6 per cent. dividends. In June, 1902, $100,000 additional preferred was authorized and allotted to stockholders at par.

Transfer Agents, Emerson McMillin & Co., 40 Wall street, New York, and Louis Kissewith, Columbus, O. Registrars, Trust Co. of America, New York, and Ohio National Bank, Columbus.

FUNDED DEBT.

| | |
|---|---|
| Columbus Electric Co. 1st mort., 6 per cent., due 1922, May and Nov. | $450,000 |
| Columbus Edison Electric Light 1st mort., 5 per cent., due 1929, April and Oct. | 300,000 |
| Total | $750,000 |

President, Emerson McMillin, New York; Vice-President, A. W. Field; Treasurer, John Siebert, Columbus, O.; Secretary, W. F. Douthirt, New York.

Directors—Emerson McMillin, George W. Bright, A. W. Field, John Siebert, C. H. Lindenberg, E. Kissewith, A. Theobald, Carl J. Horter, W. F. Douthirt.

Main office, 142 East Gay street, Columbus, O.

## THE COLUMBUS GAS LIGHT & HEATING CO.

A corporation formed under the laws of West Virginia, January 9, 1899. The company's business is furnishing natural and artificial gas for heating and lig ting purposes. The company controls the Columbus Gas Co., which owns the artificial gas property in Columbus, O., and the Central Ohio Natural Gas & Fuel Co., owning the natural gas plant in the same city.

Stock....Par $100.....Authorized { com., $1,700,000 / pref., 3,600,000 } Issued { com., $1,700,000 / pref., 3,600,000 } $5,300,000

The preferred stock is 6 per cent., non-cumulative.

Transfer Agents, Thomas & Thomas, 71 Broadway, New York. Registrar, Metropolitan Trust Co., New York.

During 1900 and 1901 the company paid dividends at the rate of 6 per cent. per annum on both classes of stock. In 1902 it paid 6 per cent. on the preferred and 7 per cent. on the common. The same rate was fixed for 1903.

FUNDED DEBT.

| | |
|---|---|
| Columbus Gas Co., 1st mort., 5 per cent., due 1932, Jan. and July | $1,500,000 |

The 1st mortgage bonds of the Columbus Gas Co. are $1,500,000 authorized.

President and Treasurer, John G. Deshler; Vice-President, George W. Sinks, Columbus, O.; Secretary, H. M. Work, New York.

Directors—John G. Deshler, J. O. Johnston, George W. Sinks, E. K. Stewart, F. C. Hubbard, H. D. Turney, C. R. Burton.

Corporate office, Charleston, W. Va.; main office, Long and Front streets, Columbus, O. Annual meeting, third Tuesday in March, at Charleston, W. Va.

## COLUMBUS RAILWAY CO.

A corporation formed under the laws of Ohio in 1899 by a merger and purchase of the entire properties of the Columbus Street Railway Co., Crosstown Street Railway Co. and Columbus Central Railway Co. The company operates 106 miles of track.

Stock....Par $100... .Authorized { com., $3,500,000 / pref., 3,500,000 } Issued { com., $3,000,000 / pref., 3,500,000 } $6,500,000

The preferred stock is 5 per cent., cumulative.

The regular dividends have been paid since February, 1900, dividend periods being February, May, August and November.

Transfer Agents, E. W. Clark & Co., Philadelphia, and the secretary of the company, Columbus, O. Registrars, Provident Life & Trust Co., Philadelphia; State Savings Bank & Trust Co., Columbus, O.

FUNDED DEBT.

| | |
|---|---|
| Columbus Street Railway 1st mort., 5 per cent. gold, due July, 1932, Jan. and July... | $2,384,000 |
| Columbus Con. Street R. R. 1st mort., 5 per cent. gold, due July, 1909, Jan. and July.. | 616,000 |
| Crosstown Street Ry. Co. 1st mort., 5 per cent. gold, due June, 1933, June and Dec... | 572,000 |
| Columbus Railway mort., 4 per cent. gold, due Oct., 1939, Jan. and July............ | 2,338,000 |
| Columbus Street Railway Co. notes, 4 per cent.................................. | 90,000 |
| Total ............................................................ | $6,000,000 |

The authorized mortgage of Columbus Railway Co. is $7,000,000, of which $3,680,000 is reserved to retire prior liens and notes and $1,287,000 is reserved for future extensions and improvements. Trustee of the mortgage, Union Savings Bank & Trust Co., Cincinnati. Agents for the payment of interest, Union Savings Bank & Trust Co., Cincinnati; E. W. Clark & Co., Philadelphia. Interest is also paid at the office of the company. The bonds are redeemable after December 1, 1914, at 105 and interest.

The authorized mortgage of the Columbus Street Railway Co. is $3,000,000, of which $616,000 are now held to retire the 1st mortgage of the Columbus Consolidated Street Railroad Co. Trustee of the mortgage, Knickerbocker Trust Co., Philadelphia. Agent for the payment of interest, E. W. Clark & Co., Philadelphia.

President, Robert E. Sheldon; 1st Vice-President and Treasurer, E. K. Stewart; 2d Vice-President, C. M. Clark; Secretary, P. V. Burington.

Directors—Robert E. Sheldon, E. K. Stewart, George W. Sinks, Theodore Rhodes, Columbus, O.; C. M. Clark, Philadelphia.

Main office, 12 High street, Columbus, O. Annual meeting, first Thursday after January 6.

---

## COMMERCIAL CABLE CO.

A corporation formed under the laws of New York, December 12, 1883. It owns and operates four Transatlantic cable lines known as the Mackay-Bennett system and their connecting cables between Ireland and France and Nova Scotia and New York, a total of 13,000 miles of cables. In January, 1897, purchased the land lines of the Postal Telegraph Cable Co., which company is, however, operated under its own organization and has 170,000 miles of wire. In 1900 this company laid a new cable to the Azores.

The Commercial Pacific Cable Co. is controlled in the interest of this company, which has a large interest in it. See statement of that company in this edition of the MANUAL.

Stock......Par $100.........................Authorized, $25,000,000......Issued, $15,000,000

The stock of this company was increased in 1900 from $10,000,000 to $15,000,000, and $3,333,300 of the increase was allotted for subscription at par by the stockholders. In February, 1903, $1,666,700, being the unissued remainder of the $15,000,000 of authorized, stock was allotted at par, and in March, 1903, it was voted to increase the authorized stock to $25,000,000.

Transfer agency, 253 Broadway, New York. Registrar, Farmers' Loan & Trust Co., New York.

Dividends are paid quarterly at rate of 1¾ per cent. January (1), April, July and October.

In January of each year since 1897 an extra dividend of 1 per cent. was paid in addition to the regular quarterly dividend.

The April, 1903, dividend, declared March 3, 1903, was 2 per cent. for the quarter, the intention being to place the stock on a 2 per cent. quarterly basis.

FUNDED DEBT.

1st mort., 4 per cent. gold bonds and sterling deben., quar., Jan., May, June, Sept...$20,000,000

The bonds authorized are $20,000,000. They were issued in March, 1897, for merger of Postal Telegraph Cable with this company, bearing interest from January 1, 1897. The former company's shares, $15,000,000 in all, were to be exchanged at par for this company's bonds, of which $5,000,000 were reserved for extension of telegraph system. Bonds may be exchanged for sterling debentures at same interest rate at £206 per each $1,000, the debentures having the same lien as the 1st mortgage bonds.

Registrars of the debenture bonds, Farmers' Loan & Trust Co., New York, and Baring Brothers & Co., Limited, London.

The company paid off all its old bonded indebtedness and had no fixed charges until the issue of bonds was made in connection with merger of the Postal Telegraph Cable Co., as stated above.

| Earnings. | Gross. | Net. |
|---|---|---|
| 1897 | $6,685,653 | $1,845,341 |
| 1898 | 7,570,922 | 1,881,740 |
| 1899 | 8,160,451 | 1,863,601 |
| 1900 | 8,818,754 | 2,279,667 |
| 1901 | 9,629,794 | 2,259,896 |
| 1902 | 10,208,293 | 2,383,589 |

In 1900, 1901 and 1902 $500,000 was transferred to the reserve fund for insurance and betterments.

President, Clarence H. Mackay; Vice-President and General Manager, George G. Ward; Vice-Presidents, Charles R. Hosmer, Albert B. Chandler; Treasurer, Edward C. Platt; Secretary, Albert Beck; Assistant Secretary, J. O. Stevens; Assistant Treasurer, Charles E. Merritt.

Directors—William Jay, Gardiner G. Howland, George G. Ward, Edward C. Platt, Clarence H. Mackay, Albert B. Chandler, Dumont Clarke, Edwin Hawley, New York; Lord Strathcona and Mount Royal, Thomas Skinner, London, England; James Gordon Bennett, Paris, France; Sir William C. Van Horne, Charles R. Hosmer, Montreal; W. Seward Webb, Shelburne, Vt.

Executive office, 253 Broadway, New York. Annual meeting, first Monday in March.

## COMMERCIAL PACIFIC CABLE CO.

A corporation formed under the laws of New York, September 23, 1901, for the purpose of laying and operating a submarine cable from San Francisco to the Hawaiian Islands, Midway, Guam, the Philippine Islands and China. The cable was completed and opened for business to the Hawaiian Islands early in 1903, and it is expected that the remaining sections will be completed during the year.

Stock......Par $100........................Authorized, $12,000,000......Issued, $12,000,000

The company has no preferred stock and no funded debt. Stock is transferred at the office of the company, New York.

President, Clarence H. Mackay; Vice-President, Chairman and General Manager, George Gray Ward; Secretary, Albert Beck; Treasurer, Edward C. Platt.

Directors—George Gray Ward, Clarence H. Mackay, Albert B. Chandler, Edward C. Platt, George Clapperton, Albert Beck, W. W. Cook.

Corporate and main office, 253 Broadway, New York. Annual meeting in April at New York.

## COMMONWEALTH ELECTRIC CO.

A corporation formed under the laws of Illinois in May, 1898. The company was a consolidation of a number of companies operating electric lighting and power plants in the environs of Chicago. The consolidation was effected by interests identified with the Chicago Edison Co., and this company has a contract with the latter for power. The company has three power stations.

Stock......Par $100........................Authorized, $10,000,000......Issued, $5,000,000

The authorized amount of stock was increased in December, 1902, from $5,000,000 to $10,000,000. The new stock is to be used for improvemants, etc., and to be issued at the discretion of the directors.

FUNDED DEBT.

1st mort., 5 per cent., due 1943, March and Sept.................................... $4,167,000

The trustee of the mortgage is the Northern Trust Co., Chicago. Additional bonds may be issued for improvements and extensions up to 75 per cent. of the cost of the same. The bonds of the old companies which were consolidated in this company have been retired with the new bonds.

In the year ending March 31, 1899, the surplus over charges was $25,156; in 1900, surplus, $52,969; in 1901, surplus, $81,101.

President, Samuel Insull; 1st Vice-President, Robert T. Lincoln; 2d Vice-President, Lewis A. Ferguson; Secretary and Treasurer, William A. Fox; Comptroller, W. M. Anthony.

Directors—Samuel Insull, Robert T. Lincoln, John J. Mitchell, Edward L. Brewster, Joseph Leiter, Erskine M. Phelps.

Main office, 139 Adams street, Chicago. Annual meeting, third Monday in May.

## COMPOSITE TYPE BAR CO.

A corporation formed under the laws of New Jersey, March 23, 1897. The business of the company is the manufacture of type casting and setting machines, and it owns the patents and inventions for the manufacture of the composite type bar machine. The company has a factory at 86 Madison street, Newark, N. J.

Stock......Par $100.......................Authorized, $10,000,000......Issued, $10,000,000

Transfer Agent, Corporation Trust Co., New York.

In January, 1902, the company reported that it had $15,000 cash and no liabilities.

President, Theodore C. E. Blanchard, Newark, N. J.; Vice-President, J. E. Sayre; Secretary, H. C. McClees, Red Bank, N. J.; Treasurer, T. M. Lloyd, Brooklyn, N. Y.

Directors—Theodore C. E. Blanchard, F. C. Blanchard, T. E. Burke, J. M. Seymore, Newark, N. J.; J. E. Sayre, L. T. Blanchard, H. C. McClees, D. Beebe, Red Bank, N. J.; E. H. Babcock, T. M. Lloyd, G. H. Watson, Brooklyn, N. Y.; I. B. Gilbert, Philadelphia; H. S. Hathaway, S. S. Slater, H. M. Dearborn, New York.

Corporate office, 15 Exchange place, Jersey City; main office, 35 Nassau street, New York. Annual meeting, first Monday in March, at Jersey City.

## COMPRESSED AIR CO.

A corporation formed under the laws of New York, April 19, 1900. The company absorbed the American Air Power Co. of New York and the Compressed Air Motor Co. of Illinois. In January, 1901, it purchased the Rome Locomotive and Machine Works, Rome, N. Y. The company manufactures compressed air, street and railroad cars, engines and motors, including all apparatus necessary for their operation.

The American Air Power Co. had $5,950,600 stock, practically all of which was acquired by this company. A statement of the American Air Power Co. was given in the MANUAL for 1900. The Compressed Air Motor Co. had $2,000,000 stock, which has all been acquired by this company.

Stock....Par $100.....Authorized { com., $7,245,000; pref., 755,000 } Issued { com., $6,401,300; pref., 755,000 } $7,156,300

The preferred stock is 5 per cent., non-cumulative. Stock is transferred at the company's office. Registrar, Morton Trust Co., New York.

FUNDED DEBT.

1st mort., 5 per cent., due April, 1920, April and Oct. .................................. $300,000

The Rome Locomotive and Machine Works Co. had $75,000 of 6 per cent. 1st mortgage bonds, and since its acquirement a new issue of $150,000 consolidated mortgage bonds has been authorized, $75,000 of which are held in trust to retire the $75,000 1st mortgage bonds.

President, H. Monkhouse; Vice-President, Chauncey S. Truax; Secretary and Treasurer, Walter P. D. Hamon.

Directors—Frederic W. H. Huidekoper, Washington, D. C.; D. C. Moorehead, Arthur B. Proal, Chauncey S. Truax, C. H. Duell, Joseph Tate, William E. Nichols, H. H. Benedict, F. W. Devoe, Thomas Clark, Jr., Thomas B. Kent, New York; H. Monkhouse, Edward Comstock, Rome, N. Y.; Newell C. Knight, Alexander C. Soper, Chicago.

Main office, 24 State street, New York. Annual meeting, first Monday after first Friday in March.

## COMSTOCK TUNNEL CO.

A reorganization under foreclosure of the Sutro Tunnel Co. at the Comstock Lode, Nevada.

Stock......Par $2.............................Authorized, $4,000,000......Issued, $4,000,000

FUNDED DEBT.

1st mort. income bonds, 4 per cent. non-cum., due 1919, authorized $3,000,000....... $2,769,000

Out of the surplus earnings $231,000 bonds have been purchased and retired.

In November, 1892, 1½ per cent. was paid on income bonds. No payments thereon since.

President, Franklin Leonard; Vice-President, Avery F. Cushman; Secretary and Treasurer, Franklin Leonard, Jr.

Trustees—Franklin Leonard, C. H. Badeau, Avery F. Cushman, George D. Hilyard, S. Covert, E. B. Smith, Franklin Leonard, Jr.

Main office, 25 Broad street, New York.

## CONCORD ELECTRIC CO.

A corporation formed under the laws of New Hampshire, May 29, 1901, for the purpose of supplying electric light and power in Concord, N. H. The company acquired the property and business of the Concord Land & Power Co. in July, 1901, through foreclosure sale. The company owns 700 acres of real estate with water rights, of which 1,250 horse-power is developed, about half the capacity. It also has an auxiliary steam station of 600 horse-power.

Stock......Par $100.......Authorized { com., $300,000; pref., 100,000 } Issued { com., $300,000; pref., 100,000 } $400,000

The preferred stock is 6 per cent., cumulative, and has preference in the distribution of assets. Stock is transferred at the office of the company.

FUNDED DEBT.

1st mort., 5 per cent. gold bonds, due Jan., 1931, Jan. and July........................ $278,000

The authorized bond issue is $350,000. Trustee of bonds and agent for the payment of interest, American Loan & Trust Co., Boston.

EARNINGS.

Year ending June 30.

| | Gross. | Net. | Charges. | Surplus. |
|---|---|---|---|---|
| 1901-02 | $55,168 | $21,587 | $13,900 | $7,687 |

President, Charles C. Danforth, Concord, N.H.; Treasurer, W. H. Whitney, Boston; Clerk, Allen Hollis, Concord, N. H.

Directors—Robert Treat Payne, 2d, John S. Bartlett, Charles H. Tenney, F. P. Royce, Boston; Charles C. Danforth, F. S. Streeter, Charles T. Page, Concord, N. H.

Corporate and main office, 15 Capitol street, Concord. Annual meeting, last Tuesday in January, at Concord, N. H.

## CONEY ISLAND & BROOKLYN RAILROAD CO.

A corporation formed under the laws of New York, December 10, 1860. The corporation acquired the following companies:

Prospect Park & Flatbush Railroad Co. DeKalb Avenue & North Beach Railroad Co.
Brooklyn City & Newtown Railroad Co.

The company operates over 49.50 miles of track by overhead trolley, of which it owns 26.38 miles, leases 20.86 miles, and has rights over 2.26 miles.

Stock......Par $100........................Authorized, $2,000,000......Issued, $2,000,000

The company has no preferred stock. Transfer Agent and Registrar, Mercantile Trust Co., New York.

Dividends on the stock have been as follows: 1893, 4 per cent. on $500,000 and 3 per cent. on $1,000,000; 1894, 5 per cent.; 1895-6-7, 6 per cent.; 1898, 8 per cent.; 1899, 10 per cent.; 1900, 10 per cent.; 1901, 13⅓ per cent.; in 1902, 16 per cent. Dividend periods are quarterly, February, May, August and November.

FUNDED DEBT.

| | |
|---|---|
| 1st mort., cur. 5 per cent., due July, 1903, Jan. and July | $300,000 |
| Certificates of indebtedness, 5 per cent., due July, 1903, Jan. and July | 400,000 |
| 1st con. mort., 4 per cent., gold, due July, 1948, Jan. and July | 1,300,000 |
| Brooklyn City & Newtown, 1st mort., 5 per cent., due July, 1939, Jan. and July | 2,000,000 |
| Real estate mort | 191,605 |
| Total | $4,191,000 |

The authorized amount of the 1st consolidated mortgage is $2,000,000, of which amount $700,000 is reserved to retire prior liens.

The trustee of the 1st mortgage is the Brooklyn Trust Co. Agent for the payment of interest, The Mechanics' Bank, Brooklyn, N. Y. Trustee of the consolidated mortgage and the Brooklyn City & Newtown mortgage, and agent for the payment of interest on both issues, Mercantile Trust Co., New York.

EARNINGS.

Year ending June 30.

| | Gross. | Net. | Interest, Taxes, etc. | Surplus. |
|---|---|---|---|---|
| 1900 | $1,458,196 | $509,770 | $270,504 | $173,068 |
| 1901 | 1,333,052 | 618,004 | 397,382 | 360,571 |
| 1902 | 1,498,927 | 598,122 | 264,053 | 334,069 |

President, John L. Heins; 1st Vice-President, Louis Fitzgerald; 2d Vice-President, James H. Hyde; Secretary and Treasurer, Duncan B. Cannon; Superintendent, D. W. Sullivan.

Directors—John L. Heins, Louis Fitzgerald, Thomas Clark, Jr., V. P. Snyder, James H. Hyde, William N. Dykman, George H. Prentiss, William H. McIntyre, H. R. Winthrop.

Main office, DeKalb and Central avenues, Brooklyn, N. Y.; New York office, 120 Broadway. Annual meeting, third Monday in October, at Brooklyn.

## CONNECTICUT RAILWAY & LIGHTING CO.

A corporation chartered by the legislature of Connecticut, by act approved July 2, 1895, as the Gas Supply Co. to manufacture and distribute gas in Norwalk, Fairfield, Danbury and other cities and towns. The charter was amended by an act approved March 2, 1899, changing the name to Connecticut Lighting & Power Co., extending the operations of the company to any part of the State, and authorizing it to make electric lighting and power part of its business and giving it power to lease, purchase, hold or sell the stock or bonds of other corporations which manufacture or use gas or electricity. On January 10, 1901, the name was changed to Connecticut Railway & Lighting Co.

The company acquired the property of the following corporations or owns a controlling interest in them:

Norwalk Gas Light Co.
Norwalk & South Norwalk Electric Light Co.
Norwalk Street Railway Co.
Norwalk Tramway Co.
Central Railway & Electric Co.
The Waterbury Traction Co.
Naugatuck Electric Light Co.
Greenwich Gas & Electric Light Co.
Bridgeport Traction Co.
Shelton Street Railway Co.
Milford Street Railway Co.
The Westport & Saugatuck Street Railway Co.
Derby Street Railway Co.
Southington & Plantsville Tramway Co.

The company's plans included the utilization of water power for the generation of electricity through the construction of a large dam in the Housatonic River. The aggregate mileage of the company's railway lines June 30, 1902, was 161 miles; cars in service, 360.

The United Gas Improvement Co. is interested in this company.

Stock..Par $100..Authorized { com., $11,000,000 / pref., 4,000,000 } Issued { com., $11,000,000 / pref., 4,000,000 } $15,000,000

The preferred stock is 5 per cent., being cumulative as to dividends after January 1, 1904.

Transfer Agent, Colonial Trust Co., New York. Registrar, Morton Trust Co., New York.

FUNDED DEBT.

| | |
|---|---|
| 1st and refunding mort., 4½ per cent., due 1951, Jan. and July | $8,482,000 |
| Connecticut Lighting & Power Co., 1st mort., 5 per cent., due 1939, Jan. and July. | 210,000 |
| Bridgeport Traction Co., 1st mort., 5 per cent. gold bonds, due 1923, Jan. and July. | 706,000 |
| Derby Street Railway Co., 1st mort., 6 per cent., due 1914, April and Oct. | 76,000 |
| Total | $9,474,000 |

The trustee of the 1st and refunding 4½ per cent. mortgage is the Colonial Trust Co., New York, at which institution coupons on the bonds are paid.

The authorized amount of the 1st and refunding mortgage is $15,000,000, of which $992,000 is reserved to retire underlying bonds as given above, and $5,526,000 for improvements and additions.

EARNINGS.

Year ending June 30.

| | Gross. | Net. | Charges, etc. | Surplus. |
|---|---|---|---|---|
| 1901-02 | $1,615,384 | $679,083 | $591,270 | $87,813 |

The charges for 1901-02 include: Interest on bonds, $426,556; taxes, $107,080, and betterments, etc., $57,534.

President, Alden M. Young, Branford, Conn.; 1st Vice-President, David S. Plume, New York; 2d Vice-President, George E. Terry, Waterbury, Conn.; Secretary and Treasurer, Lewis Lillie, Philadelphia; Assistant Secretary and Assistant Treasurer, E. W. Poole, Bridgeport, Conn.; Managing Director, Walton Clark, Philadelphia.

Directors—Alden M. Young, M. J. Warner, Branford, Conn.; R. A. C. Smith, H. G. Runkle, New York; Randal Morgan, Walton Clark, Lewis Lillie, Philadelphia; George E. Terry, David S. Plume, B. G. Bryan, Waterbury, Conn.; A. W. Paige, Bridgeport, Conn.

Main office, 623 Water street, Bridgeport, Conn. Annual meeting, second Thursday in March, at Bridgeport, Conn.

## CONSOLIDATED CAR HEATING CO.

A corporation formed under the laws of West Virginia in 1889. The company owns the McElroy, Sewall, and other patents covering apparatus for heating railroad coaches by steam direct from the locomotive. Also owns systems of heating by electricity and car lighting. The company has a large factory at 413 North Pearl street, Albany, N. Y.

Stock......Par $100..............................Authorized, $1,250,000......Issued, $1,131,000

The stock was originally $2,500,000, but was reduced to $1,250,000 in 1893. The company has no bonded or floating debt beyond current accounts.

Stock is transferred at the office of the company, Albany, N. Y.

Dividends upon the stock have been as follows: In 1892, 3 per cent.; in 1893, 3 per cent.; in 1894, 6 per cent.; in 1895, 1 per cent.; in 1896, 3½ per cent.; in 1897, 1½ per cent.; in 1898, 3 per cent.; in 1899, 4 per cent.; in 1900, 7½ per cent. In February, 1900, the company paid a semi-annual dividend of 1½ per cent. and 1 per cent. extra on February 15, and on August 1, 1½ per cent. and 3½ per cent. extra. In February, 1901, paid 1½ per cent. and 1 per cent. extra; in August, 1901, 1½ per cent. and 1½ per cent. extra, and February, 1902, 1½ per cent. and 1½ per cent. extra.

President, Robert C. Pruyn; 1st Vice-President, Charles Tracey, Albany, N. Y.; 2d Vice-President, Daniel D. Sewall, Augusta, Me.; 3d Vice-President, Frederick W. Kelley; Secretary, E. A. Groesbeck; General Manager and Treasurer, Francis C. Green, Albany, N. Y.

Directors—Robert C. Pruyn, Anthony N. Brady, Robert C. Blackall, Charles Tracey, E. A. Groesbeck, James F. McElroy, Frederick W. Kelley, Francis C. Green, Albany, N. Y.; Albion Little, H. S. Osgood, Portland, Me.; Charles J. Peabody, Caleb H. Jackson, New York; Daniel D. Sewall, Augusta, Me.; George Westinghouse, Jr., Pittsburg; James W. Hinkley, Poughkeepsie, N. Y.

Main office, 413 North Pearl street, Albany, N. Y. New York office, Park Row Building. Annual meeting, second Tuesday in June.

## CONSOLIDATED CARIBOO HYDRAULIC MINING CO., LIMITED

A corporation formed under the laws of the Dominion of Canada in 1897, for the purpose of gold mining. The company has mines and works at Bullion, Cariboo District, British Columbia

Stock......Par $5............................Authorized, $5,000,000......Issued, $4,000,000

The company has no preferred stock and no funded debt. Stock is transferred at the office of the company, Toronto.

On December 1, 1902, the company had a credit to profit and loss of $42,657.

President, W. D. Matthews; Vice-President, H. C. Hammond; Secretary, James L. Love, Toronto; Manager, John B. Hobson, Quesnelle Forks, B. C.

Directors—W. D. Matthews, H. C. Hammond, R. B. Angus, Sir Thomas G. Shaughnessy, George F. Hart, E. B. Osler, William Hendrie.

Main office, Board of Trade Building, Toronto. Annual meeting, January 23.

## CONSOLIDATED FRUIT JAR CO.

A corporation formed under the laws of New York in January, 1871. The company is engaged in the manufacture of fruit jar caps and trimmings, metal novelties, sheet metal goods, bronze ornaments, gas fixtures, etc. The company has a plant at New Brunswick, N. J., consisting of six manufacturing buildings and a house for making porcelain-lined glass.

Stock......Par $100............................Authorized, $500,000......Issued, $500,000

The company has no preferred stock and no funded debt. Stock is transferred at the office of the company.

The first annual dividend of 25 per cent. was paid January, 1872. Since then 15 per cent. has been paid annually in three years, 10 to 15 per cent. in sixteen years and from 2 to 7 per cent. in the other years, the dividend rate being 7 per cent. in 1900. Dividends are paid semi-annually in January and July.

In the fiscal year ending December 31, 1901, the dividends were $35,000; surplus, $89,686.

President, George K. Diller; Secretary and Treasurer, H. B. Kent, New Brunswick, N. J.

Directors—John E. McMurtry, Theodore B. Booraem, P. Hampton Wyckoff, New Brunswick, N. J.; Henry McMurtry, Kingston, N. Y.; Charles P. Buckley, Tenafly, N. J.; George K. Diller, Clyde, N. Y.; Henry B. Kent, New York.

Main office, 62 Water street, New Brunswick, N. J.; New York office, 290 Broadway; Chicago office, 59 Dearborn street; Boston office, 131 Tremont street. Annual meeting, third Thursday in January, at 290 Broadway, New York.

## CONSOLIDATED GAS CO. OF BALTIMORE CITY

A corporation formed under the laws of Maryland, May 5, 1888. The company acquired by consolidation the following organizations, controlling under perpetual franchise the entire gas light industry of Baltimore, Md.:

Chesapeake Gas Co. Consolidated Gas Co. Equitable Gas Light Co.

Stock......Par $100........................Authorized, $11,000,000......Issued, $10,770,968

The company pays dividends of 3 per cent. per annum, semi-annually, in June and December. In 1900 paid 2 per cent. in June and an extra dividend of 2½ per cent. in July, with a regular dividend of 1¼ per cent. December 1, 1900, or 5¾ per cent. for the year. In 1901 an extra dividend of ½ per cent. was paid, making 3½ per cent. for the year.

FUNDED DEBT.

| | |
|---|---|
| Cons. Gas (old company) 1st mort., 6 per cent., due July, 1910, Jan. and July....... | $3,584,500 |
| " (new company) 1st mort., 5 per cent., due July, 1939, Jan. and July...... | 3,253,000 |
| " ctfs. of indebtedness, 4½ per cent., due July, 1907-12, Jan. and July..... | 500,000 |
| " " " 4½ per cent., due Jan., 1908-13, Jan. and July.. .. | 500,000 |
| Total.............. | $7,837,500 |

The $1,000,000 of Chesapeake Gas Co.'s 1st 6s, which matured June 1, 1900, were retired by an issue of $1,000,000 of the new consolidated 5s.

The 4½ per cent. certificates of indebtedness were authorized in 1902 for $1,500,000 in three series of $500,000 each. Trustee and agent for the payment of interest on the same, Colonial Trust Co., Baltimore. After five years from date of issue the certificates are redeemable on any interest period on sixty days' notice. The company can issue the remaining $500,000 on July 1, 1903.

Sales of gas have been as follows: In year ending June 30, 1897, 1,321,033,500 feet; in 1897-98, 1,340,156,300 feet; in 1898-99, 1,331,114,200 feet; in 1899-1900, 1,347,678,200 feet.

EARNINGS.

Year ending June 30.

| | Gross. | Net. | Charges. | Surplus. |
|---|---|---|---|---|
| 1896-97.................. ......... | $1,674,687 | $825,981 | $384,170 | $441,811 |
| 1897-98.............................. | 1,709,226 | 851,282 | 386,241 | 465,041 |
| 1898-99.............................. | 1,689,328 | 868,807 | 387,720 | 481,007 |
| 1899-00.............................. | 1,705,916 | 804,403 | 386,887 | 417,516 |
| 1900-01.............................. | 1,639,433 | 720,827 | 377,720 | 343,087 |
| 1901-02.............................. | 1,757,863 | 749,353 | 377,720 | 371,633 |

President, Ferdinand C. Latrobe; Secretary, Edgar T. Powers; Treasurer, Joseph W. Clarke; General Manager, A. S. Miller.

Directors—Ferdinand C. Latrobe, Charles H. Dickey, H. Crawford Black, Michael Stein, Frederick W. Wood, John Whitridge, Townsend Scott, Thomas O'Neill, Daniel C. Ammidon, Ernst Schmisser, Charles T. Crane, James A. Gary, Baltimore.

Main office, 5 Baltimore street, Baltimore.

## CONSOLIDATED GAS CO. OF NEW JERSEY

This company supplies gas to Long Branch, Asbury Park and Red Bank, N. J. It also owns the Long Branch electric light plant and furnishes electric light and power to that place, Elberon, Branchport, Monmouth Beach, etc. Company has 14 local franchises, mostly perpetual. Price of gas, $1.50 per 1,000 feet. Mileage of mains, 63 miles.

In August, 1902, the American Light & Traction Co. offered to purchase $700,000 or more of the company's stock, the offer being to give for each share of stock either $17 in cash, $18 in preferred stock of the American Light & Traction Co. or $49 in the latter's common stock.

Stock......Par $100..........................Authorized, $1,000,000......Issued, $1,000,000

Transfer Agents, Emerson McMillin & Co., 40 Wall street, New York.

FUNDED DEBT.

Cons. mort., 5 per cent., gold, due 1936, Jan. and July.............................. $971,000

The consolidated mortgage, Knickerbocker Trust Co., New York, trustee, is for $1,000,000. Coupons are paid at Emerson McMillin & Co., New York.

President, Emerson McMillin, New York; Vice-President, Emanuel Lehman; Secretary, A. Lincoln Eglinton; Treasurer, C. H. Irwin; General Manager, W. D. Tuttle.

Directors—Emanuel Lehman, Gustavus Maas, Emerson McMillin, Henry B. Wilson, William E. Case, J. G. Beemer, John S. Foster, Jacob Steinbach, F. W. Hope.

Main office, Long Branch, N. J.

## CONSOLIDATED GAS CO. OF NEW YORK

A corporation formed under the laws of New York, November 10, 1884. The company was a consolidation of the New York, Manhattan, Metropolitan, Municipal, Knickerbocker and Harlem Gas Companies of New York City. The company has 1,740 miles of mains, and at beginning of 1903 had 556,300 meters in service.

In December, 1898, this company acquired a large interest in the Mutual Gas Co. In 1899 control of the United Electric Light & Power Co. was obtained in interest of this company. In January, 1900, it was announced that a controlling interest in the New York Gas &

Electric Light, Heat & Power Co. had been acquired, which company controlled the Edison Electric Illuminating Co. of New York and other local electric light and power organizations. In June, 1900, announcement was made of the purchase of a large block of the Standard Gas Light Co.'s stock by this company.

In May, 1900, this company offered to purchase the $12,145,700 common and $9,000,000 preferred stock of the New Amsterdam Gas Co. at $50 for the preferred and $26 for the common, payable in 6 per cent. debenture bonds of the Consolidated Gas Co., said debentures to be redeemable at the option of the latter, prior to May, 1901, in its own stock at 190, which arrangement was carried out. Control of the United Electric Light & Power Co. was also acquired in 1900.

Through these acquisitions the company controls all the gas and electric lighting facilities in the Borough of Manhattan.

It is stated that the company will concentrate the manufacture of gas at the Astoria, L. I., plant of the New Amsterdam Gas Co., which was enlarged for the purpose, and dispose of its large real estate holdings in Manhattan, which would no longer be required.

Stock......Par $100................. .......Authorized, $80,000,000 .....Issued, $72,916,500

In March, 1900, the stock of the company was increased from $39,078,000 to $54,595,200 to carry out the terms of purchase of the New York Gas & Electric Light, Heat & Power Co. An amount of $13,648,800 of stock was subscribed for by the stockholders at $150 per share. To carry out the terms of the purchase of the New Amsterdam Gas Co., the authorized amount of stock was increased to $80,000,000 in July, 1900. The amount given above is the outstanding stock January 31, 1902.

Dividends are paid quarterly, March 15, June, September and December. In June, 1893, dividends were increased from the rate of 6 per cent. to 8 per cent. per annum. In June, 1899, owing to the reduction of gas prices caused by competition, the company reduced the quarterly dividend to 1½ and in the following September to 1 per cent., which rate was maintained until September, 1900, when 2 per cent. was paid, and has since been the regular rate.

Stock is transferred at the office of the company. Registrar, Farmers' Loan & Trust Co., New York.

FUNDED DEBT.

Debenture bonds, 5 per cent., due May, 1908 May and Nov......................... $1,461,000

FUNDED DEBT OF CONTROLLED COMPANIES.

| | |
|---|---|
| Edison Electric Ill., 1st mort., 5 per cent., due March, 1910, March and Sept......... | $4,312,000 |
| " " " 1st cons. mort., 5 per cent., due July, 1995, Jan. and July...... | 2,188,000 |
| Mt. Morris Electric Light, 1st mort., 5 per cent., due Sept., 1940, March and Sept... | 988,000 |
| N. Y. Gas & E. L. H. & Pow., 1st mort., 5 per cent., due Dec., 1948, June and Dec.. | 11,500,000 |
| " " " " pur. mon. mort., 4 pr. ct., due Feb., 1949, Feb. and Aug. | 20,929,391 |
| Equitable Gas Light, cons. mort., 5 per cent., due March, 1932, March and Sept.... | 3,500,000 |
| " " debentures, 5 per cent., due 1906, or on call, March and Sept.. | 500,000 |
| N. Y. & E. River Gas, 1st mort., 5 per cent., due Jan., 1944 Jan. and July.......... | 3,500,000 |
| " " " cons. mort., 5 per cent., due Jan., 1945, Jan. and July....... | 1,500,000 |
| New Amsterdam Gas Co., 1st cons. mort., 5 per cent., due Jan., 1948, Jan. and July. | 10,635,000 |
| Central Union Gas, mort., 5 per cent., due July, 1927, Jan. and July............... | 3,450,000 |
| Northern Union Gas Co., 1st mort., 5 per cent., due Nov., 1927, May and Nov....... | 1,250,000 |
| United Electric Light & P., 1st mort., 5 per cent., due July, 1924, Jan. and July.... | 4,838,000 |
| Brush El. Ill. Co. 1st mort., 5 per cent., Jan. and July............................ | 275,000 |
| Standard G. L., 1st mort., 5 per cent., due May, 1930, May and Nov............... | 1,362,000 |
| Total........................................................................ | $72,188,391 |

The debentures ($3,000,000 authorized) were issued in 1888 to retire maturing bonds and provide for extensions and improvements.

The New York Gas & Electric Light, Heat & Power Co. has $36,000,000 of stock. That company acquired the Edison Electric Illuminating Co. of New York, the stock of which was pledged as security for $21,000,000 of 4 per cent. purchase money bonds and various other electric companies. The purchase money 4s may be called at par prior to February 1, 1902. The Consolidated Gas Co. bought the stock of the New York Gas & Electric Co. with an issue of $36,000,000 of 4 per cent. debentures, redeemable in its own stock at $232 for the latter. All of the debentures have been retired.

President, Harrison E. Gawtry; Vice-Presidents, Samuel Sloan, Walter R. Addicks, Lewis B. Gawtry; Treasurer, James A. Bennett; Assistant Treasurer, Benjamin Whiteley; Secretary, Robert A. Carter; Assistant Secretary, Colin C. Simpson.

Directors—Harrison E. Gawtry, Samuel Sloan, William Rockefeller, M. Taylor Pyne, George F. Baker, James Stillman, Stephen S. Palmer, Frank Tilford, William C. Whitney, Anthony N. Brady, Thomas F. Ryan, John W. Sterling.

Main office, 4 Irving place, New York. Annual meeting, Monday preceding the last Friday in January. Books closed about two weeks before.

## CONSOLIDATED ICE CO.

A corporation formed under the laws of Pennsylvania, April 1, 1899. The business of the company is the harvesting, manufacturing and distribution of ice, natural and artificial. The natural ice plants of the company are located as follows:

| | |
|---|---|
| Lakeville, O. | Stoneboro, Pa. |
| Ligonier, Pa. | Chautauqua Lake, N. Y. |

It owns in the cities of Pittsburg and Allegheny, Pa., eight establishments for the manufacture of ice, together with the necessary plant and facilities for the distribution of the article. The capacity of its plants is about 900 tons of manufactured ice daily and 100,000 tons of natural ice per annum.

Stock....Par $50......Authorized { com., $2,000,000 / pref., 2,000,000 } Issued { com., $2,000,000 / pref., 2,000,000 } $4,000,000

The preferred stock is 6 per cent., cumulative. The company has no funded debt.

Transfer Agent, Union Trust Co., Pittsburg. Registrar, Fidelity Title & Trust Co., Pittsburg.

Dividends on the stocks are paid at the rate of 6 per cent. per annum on the preferred, the payments being quarterly, in January, April, July and October.

President, James McAfee; Secretary and Treasurer, W. F. Melhuish; Manager, T. A. Dunn, Pittsburg.

Directors—James McAfee, T. M. Rees, A. W. Mellon, M. K. McMullin, John S. Craig, W. V. Callery, S. S. Brown, Pittsburg.

Main office, Thirteenth and Pike streets, Pittsburg. Annual meeting, third Monday in February.

---

## THE CONSOLIDATED LAKE SUPERIOR CO.

A corporation chartered by the State of Connecticut, April 18, 1897, under the title of the American Lake Superior Power Co. The name was changed to the present style July 7, 1898, and the charter was amended May 17, 1899, and May 3, 1901. In May, 1901, the company was consolidated with the Ontario Lake Superior Company, and acquired its $14,000,000 of common and $6,000,000 of preferred stock by exchange for its own shares.

The company controls, through stock ownership, the following companies:

1. The Lake Superior Power Co., organized under the laws of Ontario in 1895. Capital stock, preferred, $500,000; common, $1,500,000.

2. The Michigan Lake Superior Power Co., organized under the laws of Michigan in 1897. Capital stock, $500,000; bonded debt, $3,500,000, 5 per cent., fifty-year bonds, secured on the development of water power on the Michigan side.

3. The Sault Ste. Marie Pulp & Paper Co., organized under the laws of Ontario in 1893. Capital stock, preferred, $750,000; common, $1,250,000.

4. Tagona Water & Light Co., organized under the laws of Ontario in 1895. Capital stock, $200,000; bonded debt, $160,000, twenty-year, 5 per cent. bonds.

5. The Algoma Central & Hudson Bay Railway Co., organized under the laws of Canada, August 11, 1899. Capital stock, $10,000,000.

6. The Manitoulin & North Shore Railway Co., organized under the laws of Canada, July 7, 1900. Capital stock, $1,000,000.

7. The International Transit Co., organized under the laws of Canada, May 22, 1888. Capital stock, $150,000.

8. Trans-St. Mary's Traction Co., organized under the laws of Michigan, October 14, 1901. Capital stock, $400,000.

9. The Algoma Commercial Co., Limited, organized under the laws of Ontario, December 27, 1899. Capital stock, $10,000,000.

10. The Algoma Steel Co., Limited, organized under the laws of Ontario, May 10, 1901. Capital stock, $20,000,000.

11. The British America Express Co., Limited, organized under the laws of Ontario, May 29, 1900. Capital stock, $100,000.

The property of the various subsidiary companies embraces the following:

The Algoma Central & Hudson Bay Railway, extending from Sault Ste. Marie, Ont., to the Michipicoten iron ore range and thence to Michipicoten Harbor on Lake Superior, 194 miles. One-half of this line is complete, equipped and in operation. The Manitoulin & North Shore Railway extends 13 miles from Sudbury, Ont., into the nickel district. Its projected line extends from Sudbury to Sault Ste. Marie, Ont., and to Manitoulin Island, and thence by ferry to Bruce Peninsula and to a terminus on Georgian Bay.

On the Michipicoten range, about 120 miles north of Sault Ste. Marie, Ont., the company owns important iron ore properties. The Helen Mine has been shipping for three ears, and its present capacity is about 1,500 tons per day. The Josephine Mine, of bessemergrade ore, is being opened. There are several other large ore deposits on the same range which have been located and prospected, but not developed.

In the Sudbury district, Ontario, the company owns several extensive nickel-copper ore bodies. Two mines, the Gertrude and Elsie, have been developed and have been producing steadily for more than a year. At the Gertrude Mine there is a smelting plant of three furnaces, and a Bessemerizing plant for the concentration of the matte made in these smelters is being constructed at Sault Ste. Marie.

The company's iron and steel works at Sault Ste Marie, Ont., embrace two blast furnaces, Bessemer steel plant and steel rail mill. There is a large installation of retorts for making charcoal and saving by-products. The rail mill has a capacity for rolling about 1,000 tons per day, although the present Bessemer converting capacity is only about 500 tons daily. The company also has a large machine shop, forge and foundry, equipped with modern tools and machinery, building all kinds of machinery for mining and metallurgical purposes, pulp making, etc.

On the Michigan side of the St. Mary's River the company has a canal and power house, capable of utilizing about 60,000 horse-power of hydraulic energy, and a large part of the equipment of the power house has been installed. 20,000 horse-power has been sold to the Union Carbide Co. for a term of twenty-five years, and works for the utilization of this power have been constructed. On the Canadian side of the river a canal yields about 20,000 horse-power, which is utilized in the various works of the company, such as the pulp mills, iron works, steel plant, etc., etc. Electric light and power service and water supply are furnished to the town of Sault Ste. Marie, Ont.

A ground wood mill with capacity of about 100 tons per day, and a sulphite mill with capacity for making about 60 tons per day, are in successful operation, the pulp wood being cut from the company's land grant, and the sulphite mill utilizing chemical by-products from the company's ferro-nickel reduction works.

Extensive lumber operations are conducted upon the company's land grants along the line of the Algoma Central & Hudson Bay Railway, and two saw mills, with a joint capacity of about 175,000 feet per day, are in operation.

Stock..Par $100...Authorized { com., $82,000,000 / pref., 35,000,000 } Issued { com., $72,286,200 / pref., 27,400,000 } $99,686,200

The preferred stock is 7 per cent., non-cumulative. Prior to May, 1901, the capital of the company was $14,000,000 common and $6,000,000 preferred, the amounts being increased in order to acquire the Ontario Lake Superior Co. and to declare a dividend in preferred stock of 25 per cent. on the preferred and of 100 per cent. in common on the common. The proceeds of part of the preferred stock were used in the erection of the steel plant and other industries. The stock was subscribed for with deferred payments, on account of which $9,289,000 was due June 30, 1902.

The company began the payment of quarterly dividends at 1¾ per cent., or 7 per cent. per annum, on its preferred stock, September 15, 1899, and paid the same regularly in December, March, June and September, until September 15, 1902, inclusive. In December, 1902, the action of the Directors in declaring the December dividend was rescinded in consequence of the company's financial embarrassments, and the payment of the same deferred.

Stock is transferred at the company's office, Philadelphia.

In December, 1902, the company became involved owing to its extensive operations and payments for the completion and improvement of its subsidiary properties. The payment of the December, 1902, dividend on the preferred was deferred in consequence. Negotiations were thereupon commenced and a syndicate, headed by Speyer & Co., New York, undertook the financeering of the company. Changes were made in the management and directorate of the company, and part of the plan was the advancing, by the syndicate, of loans amounting to $5,250,000 to pay off floating indebtedness and provide for immediate requirements. These loans to be retired by an issue of bonds, but up to March, 1903, the issue had not been authorized or the amount thereof decided on.

The report for the year ending June 30, 1901, showed receipts from dividends on stocks of subsidiary companies, $684,916; dividends on preferred stock, 7 per cent., $420,000; balance surplus, $8,877. In 1901-02, net income, $1,428,136; expenses and dividends on preferred stock, $1,135,507; surplus, $292,628.

President, (Vacancy); Vice-Presidents, F. H. Clergue, Theodore C. Search, James S. Swartz; Treasurer, J. Parke Hood; Secretary and Assistant Treasurer, Walter P. Douglas; Assistant Treasurer, W. K. Stager; Assistant Secretaries, E. H. Sanborn, Paul W. Farrison.

Directors—E. J. Berwind, C. E. Orvis, Charles H. Tweed, Charles Macdonald, New York; Theodore C. Search, James S. Swartz, H. G. Lloyd, E. V. Douglas, George Philler, Sutherland M. Provost, H. A. Berwind, Samuel Rea, Philadelphia; Lynde Harrison, New Haven, Conn.; F. H. Clergue, Sault Ste. Marie, Ontario, Canada; Gordon Abbott, Boston.

Main office, North American Building, Philadelphia; New York office, 100 Broadway. Annual meeting, fourth Monday in October.

## CONSOLIDATED MERCUR GOLD MINES CO.

A corporation formed under the laws of New Jersey, August 1, 1900. It acquired the following corporations:

Mercur Gold Mining and Milling Co. De La Mar's Mercur Mines Co.

The property of the company includes 79 mining claims, aggregating 944 acres; a 1,000 and a 500-ton cyanide mill, steam electric plant, machine shop, refinery, compressor plants, dwelling houses, electric tramway, a water works system and 20 acres of water right, at Mercur, Utah.

Stock......Par $5..........................Authorized, $5,000,000......Issued, $5,000,000

The company has no preferred stock and no funded debt.

Stock is transferred at the office of the company, Salt Lake City. Registrar, McCornick & Co., Salt Lake City. Transfer Agent, American Loan and Trust Co., Boston. Registrar, State Street Trust Co., Boston.

A dividend of 11 cents per share was paid November 1, 1900. A dividend of 12½ cents per share was paid in May, August and November, 1901, and February, 1902. Beginning with April, 1902, monthly dividends of 3 cents per share have been regularly paid.

The gross earnings for the fiscal year ending June 30, 1902, were $1,458,777; net, $347,263.

The balance sheet of the company June 30, 1902, shows a balance of assets exclusive of real estate, plant construction accounts and supplies in use of $150,395.

President, John Dern; Vice-President, E. H. Airis; Secretary, William M. Thompson; Treasurer and General Manager, George H. Dern, Salt Lake City, Utah.

Directors—John Dern, E. H. Airis, George H. Dern, William M. Thompson, Salt Lake City, Utah; A. W. Chesterton, Boston; Henry A. Bingham, Oradell, N. J.

Corporate office, 15 Exchange place, Jersey City; main office, Dooly Building, Salt Lake City, Utah. Annual meeting first Monday in July, at Jersey City.

## CONSOLIDATED RAILWAY, ELECTRIC LIGHTING & EQUIPMENT CO.

A corporation formed under the laws of New York in 1900, and owned or controlled the following corporations:

Columbian Electric Car Lighting & Brake Co.
American Railway Electric Light Co.
European Railway Electric Lighting Co.
United Electric Co.
Lindstrom Brake Co.
Railway Triplex Ticket Co.
Electric Axle Light & Power Co.

The company owns a system of lighting railway cars generated by the revolving car axle by means of a flexible gear. Cars equipped with this apparatus are in use on many railroads in the United States. It also had a contract with Vickers Sons & Maxim, of England, for the manufacture and sale of its devices in Europe on a royalty basis. The company in addition controls all devices for refrigerating cars by power from the axle.

The American and the European railway electric light companies control valuable patents in this and other countries. The Lindstrom Lever Brake Co. controls the brake of that name which has been adopted by the Pennsylvania Railroad, Pullman Co. and other important organizations. The Railway Triplex Ticket Co. owns and manufactures an improved form of ticket for use in the collection of cash fares.

This company has a manufacturing plant for making its specialties at Derby, Conn.

Stock......Par $100........................Authorized, $22,000,000......Issued, $17,500,000

The stock of the old company was $16,000,000, and its stockholders were given the right to exchange the same for the new stock at par, on payment of $2 per share.

The company has no funded debt.

President, Isaac L. Rice; Secretary and Treasurer, J. L. Watson.

Directors—Walther Luttgen, Norman Henderson, Arthur Turnbull, G. L. Bossevain, Lenord Smith, Lucius H. Beers, Isaac L. Rice, New York; August G. Fromuth, Philadelphia.

Main office, 100 Broadway, New York. Annual meeting in March.

## CONSOLIDATED RUBBER TIRE CO.

A corporation organized under the laws of New Jersey, April 15, 1899. It owns patents covering the manufacture of rubber tires by improved machinery and devices and their attachment to wheels, and sells the same and issues licenses to others.

Stock...Par $100....Authorized { com., $4,000,000 / pref., 1,149,500 } Issued { com., $1,149,500 / pref., 5,149,500 } $6,299,000

The preferred stock is 6 per cent., cumulative.

The authorized stock was originally $5,000,000 of each class, and $4,000,000 each of preferred and common had been issued. In February, 1901, it was proposed to retire $3,000,000 of the preferred with a like amount of the 4 per cent. debentures. In July, 1901, the plan was carried into effect.

Transfer Agent, Colonial Trust Co., New York. Registrar, Hanover National Bank, New York.

The company began paying dividends on its preferred stock September 1, 1899, with 1½ per cent. quarterly, and paid regular quarterly dividends at that rate in March, June, September and December to December, 1900, inclusive. The March, 1901, dividend was postponed in view of the prospective readjustment of the capital, and no dividends have since been paid.

FUNDED DEBT.

Debentures, income 4 per cent.............................................. $2,850,000

On April 1, 1902, 3 per cent. was paid on the debentures out of the earnings of 1901.

Chairman, Isaac L. Rice; President, Van H. Cartmell; Vice-President, Stephen Peabody, New York; Treasurer, William L. Elkins, Jr., Philadelphia; Assistant Treasurer and Secretary, Frederick A. Seaman, New York.

Directors—Frederick A. Seaman, Isaac L. Rice, Stephen Peabody, Emerson McMillin, Van H. Cartmell, New York; Martin Maloney, Philadelphia.

Corporate office, 15 Exchange place, Jersey City; New York office, 40 Wall street. Annual meeting, first Monday in May, at Jersey City.

## THE CONSOLIDATED TELEPHONE CO.

A corporation formed under the laws of Delaware, June 27, 1901, for the purpose of acquiring and controlling telephone exchanges. The company does not operate directly but organizes seperate companies and controls their securities. It controls the Inter-Oceanic Telephone and Telegraph Co., organized in 1901, to build and operate long-distance telephone lines in New York, which has 400 miles built. The latter company has a capital stock of $2,000,000, and has authorized first mortgage bonds to the amount of $1,000,000.

Stock......Par $100.........................Authorized, $10,000,000......Issued, $5,000,000

The company has no preferred stock and no funded debt. Transfer Agent, Corporate Trust Co., New York. Registrar, North American Trust Co., New York.

President, B. G. Hubbell; Vice-President and Treasurer, Charles E. Austin; Secretary, J. B. Ware.

Directors—Luther Allen, R. M. Parmley, H. D. Critchfield, K. F. Gill, Cleveland; B. G. Hubbell, Arthur D. Bissell, Joseph P. Dudley, Charles E. Austin, Martin Carey, Buffalo, N. Y.; Theodore S. Fassett, North Tonawanda, N. Y.

Main office, Buffalo. Annual meeting, second Tuesday in January.

## THE CONSOLIDATED TELEPHONE COMPANIES OF PENNSYLVANIA

A corporation formed under the laws of Pennsylvania, February, 1901, for the purpose of consolidating several existing companies and for operating local and long-distance telephone and telegraph exchanges. The company has acquired the following companies:

Lackawanna Telephone Co., Scranton, Pa.
Peoples' Telephone Co., Wilkes-Barre, Pa.
Anthracite Telephone Co., Hazleton, Pa.
Overland Telephone Co., Lehighton, Pa.
Lehigh & State Belt Telephone Co., Allentown, Pa.
Reading Telephone Co., Reading, Pa.
Interstate Long Distance Line.

The Lackawanna Telephone Co. operated several suburban exchanges, which were acquired by the new company. The service of the consolidated company embraces about 18,500 subscribers.

Stock......Par $100..........................Authorized, $4,000,000......Issued, $4,000,000

The company has no preferred stock. Transfer Agent, C. M. W. Keck, Allentown, Pa. Registrar, Equitable Trust Co., Philadelphia.

FUNDED DEBT.

1st mort., 5 per cent., due 1931, May and Nov.... ................................ $2,600,000

The 1st mortgage, $6,000,000, is authorized. Of this, $1,000,000 has been placed in the hands of the trustee to redeem $820,000 underlying bonds of the companies absorbed.

Trustee of the mortgage and agent for the payment of interest, The Equitable Trust Co., Philadelphia.

President, Robert E. Wright, Allentown, Pa.; Secretary and General Manager, Samuel E. Wayland, Scranton, Pa.; Treasurer, C. W. M. Keck, Allentown, Pa.

Directors—Robert E. Wright, George O. Albright, Thomas Dougherty, Allentown, Pa.; George R. Bedford, Wilkes-Barre, Pa.; William L. Connell, Samuel E. Wayland, E. W. Mulligan, Wilkes-Barre, Pa.; Alvan Markle, C. W. Kline, Hazleton, Pa.; J. P. Helfenstein, Frank H. Green, Shamokin, Pa.

Corporate office, Allentown, Pa.; main office, Scranton, Pa.; branch offices, Carbondale, Wilkes-Barre, Hazleton, Lehighton, Allentown and Reading, Pa. Annual meeting, first Monday in February, at Philadelphia.

## CONSOLIDATED TOBACCO CO.

A corporation formed under the laws of New Jersey, June 5, 1901. The company acquired practically all the common stock of the American Tobacco Co. and the Continental Tobacco Co., in exchange for its own 4 per cent. debenture bonds. See below. Through the constituent companies it has large interests in the American Cigar Co., the Havana Tobacco Co. and other similar corporations. In 1902 it acquired an interest in the Imperial Tobacco Co. of Great Britain, and the British-American Tobacco Co. See separate statements of the American Tobacco Co. and the Continental Tobacco Co.

Stock......Par $100......................Authorized, $40,000,000......Issued, $40,000,000

The stock of the company was originally $30,000,000. In January, 1903, an additional stock issue of $10,000,000 was authorized and subscribed for at par by the shareholders.

A dividend of 20 per cent. on the stock was paid on January 20, 1903.

FUNDED DEBT.

Collateral trust debentures, 4 per cent., due Aug., 1951, Feb. and Aug............ $156,558,400

The 4 per cent. debentures were created and issued to acquire and pay for the common stock of the American Tobacco Co. at $200 per share, payable in the bonds and the common stock of the Continental Tobacco Co. at $100 per share, also payable in the bonds. Practically all the common stocks of the two companies named have been acquired and are deposited as security for the bonds. Trustee and agent for the payment of interest, Morton Trust Co., New York.

The following is the company's report of earnings for the year 1902:

| | |
|---|---|
| Net earnings, after charges and expenses | $13,291,460 |
| Interest on bonds, 4 per cent | 6,376,254 |
| Net | $6,915,206 |
| Surplus Dec. 31, 1901 | 35,010 |
| Total | $6,950,215 |
| 20 per cent. dividend on capital stock | 6,000,000 |
| Surplus Dec. 31, 1902 (after charging off all internal revenue and other taxes and expenses of incorporating and organizing the company).... .......... | $950,216 |

The following is the company's balance sheet December 31, 1902:

| ASSETS. | | LIABILITIES. | |
|---|---|---|---|
| Stocks and bonds, common stock of the American Tobacco Co. and Continental Tobacco, deposited with the Morton Trust Co. to secure bonds of this company | $156,593,400 | Capital stock | $30,000,009 |
| Other stocks and bonds | 19,669,537 | Bonds | 156,593,400 |
| Cash | 3,792,803 | Accrued interest on bonds | 2,609,890 |
| Bills and accounts receivable | 16,526,126 | Accounts payable | 428,412 |
| Office furniture | 51 | Dividend, payable Jan. 20, 1903 | 6,000,000 |
| | | Surplus | 950,216 |
| Total | $196,581,917 | Total | $196,581,917 |

President, James B. Duke; 1st Vice-President, Thomas F. Ryan; 2d Vice-President, James B. Cobb; 3d Vice-President, C. K. Faucette; Treasurer, William R. Harris; Secretary, C. S. Keene.

Main office, 111 Fifth avenue, New York.

## CONSOLIDATED TRACTION CO.

(Controlled by Philadelphia Company.)

A corporation formed July 15, 1895, which acquired control of the Fort Pitt Traction Co., Central Traction, Pittsburg Traction and Duquesne Traction, and of the Citizen's Traction and Allegheny Traction Companies, which were leased to the Fort Pitt Traction Co. Assumed operaion of these properties in 1896. In 1901 control was acquired by the Philadelphia Company. See statement of the latter. The Monongahela Street Railway was leased in January, 1902.

The formation of this company and the exchange or retirement of stocks of old companies undertaken by a syndicate, headed by Messrs. Drexel & Co., Philadelphia, is described in detail in the MANUAL for 1901.

Stock..Par $50...Authorized { com., $15,000,000; pref., 12,000,000 } Issued { com., $15,000,000; pref., 12,000,000 } $27,000,000

The preferred stock is 6 per cent., cumulative, and participates equally with the common in further dividends after the common has also received 6 per cent.

Dividends of 3 per cent. on the preferred stock are paid semi-annually in May and November.

In 1899-1900 the surplus over dividends on the preferred stock was $622. In 1900-01 it was $104,442.

FUNDED DEBT.

| | |
|---|---|
| Central Traction 1st mort., 6 per cent., due July, 1929, Jan. and July | $375,000 |
| Central Pass. Ry. 1st mort., 4 per cent., due Oct., 1924, April and Oct. | 125,000 |
| Duquesne Traction 1st mort., 5 per cent., due July, 1930, Jan. and July | 1,500,000 |
| Citizens' Traction 1st mort., 5 per cent., due April, 1927, April and Oct. | 1,200,500 |
| Penn St. Passenger Ry. 1st mort., 5 per cent., due June, 1922, June and Dec. | 250,000 |
| Allegheny Trac., Millville E. & Sharpsburg mort., 5 p. c., due Nov., 1923, May and Nov. | 750,000 |
| Monongahela Street Ry. 1st mort., due 1928, June and Dec. | 1,000,000 |
| Total | $5,200,500 |

The stock of the Citizen's Traction. $3,000,000, is entitled to guaranteed dividend at 6 per cent. per annum. The Allegheny Traction is guaranteed under lease 5 per cent. per annum on its $500,000 stock.

EARNINGS.

Year ending June 30.

| | Gross. | Interest. | Charges. | Surplus. |
|---|---|---|---|---|
| 1899-00 | $3,014,862 | $1,693,406 | $1,043,009 | $650,397 |
| 1900-01 | 2,919,444 | 1,891,078 | 1,066,636 | 834,442 |

President, James D. Callery; Vice-President, J. H. Reed; Secretary, Winfield B. Carson; Treasurer, C. J. Braun, Jr.; Auditor, C. S. Mitchell.

Directors—James D. Callery, Joshua Rhodes, T. H. Given, J. H. Reed, M. K. McMullin, Benjamin F. Jones.

Main office, 336 Fourth avenue, Pittsburg.

## THE CONSOLIDATED UBERO PLANTATIONS CO.

A corporation formed under the laws of Maine, May 1, 1902. The purpose of the company is to buy, improve and develop lands in Mexico, to operate mills and factories in that country and to conduct a general banking business. The plantations of the company are in Ubero, Mex. The company acquired the following properties:

Mexican Coffee & Rubber Co.
Texas Coffee & Rubber Co.
Littell Plantation, No. 2.
Worrell Plantation, No. 1.
Urbahns, Maxwell & McNeely.
Kent, Maguire, Hand & Strohm.
Hackley & Co.
Mutual Rubber Co.
Estate of W. C. Doak.
Estate of William D. Owen.
Littell Plantation, No. 1.
Bloomington Plantation Co.
Worrell Plantation, No. 2.
J. M. Taylor Development Co.
Coate & Gonzer.
Estate of F. R. Torres.
Estate of Oskar Dunweg.
Zaring Plantation Co.

Stock......Par $5..............................Authorized, $2,500,000......Issued, $2,500,000

Transfer Agent and Registrar, International Trust Co., Boston. Dividends at the rate of 3 per cent. are paid semi-annually.

FUNDED DEBT.

1st mort., 6 per cent., due 1912, Jan. and July.............................. $1,335,000

The authorized 1st mortgage is $2,500,000. Trustee and agent for the payment of interest, International Trust Co., of Boston.

President, Arthur W. Stedman; Vice-President, Frederick C. Hood, Boston; Treasurer, E. H. Nebeker, Indianapolis.

Directors—Arthur W. Stedman, Frederick C. Hood, Boston; E. H. Nebeker, Indianapolis; William D. Owen, Logansport, Ind.; Bernardo Reyes, Thomas Moran, Mexico City, Mex.; Charles A. Muehlbronner, Pittsburg.

Corporate office, Kittery, Me.; Boston office, 89 State street. Annual meeting May 1, at Kittery, Me.

## CONSOLIDATED WIRELESS TELEGRAPH & TELEPHONE CO.

A corporation formed under the laws of Arizona, February 24, 1902. The company is the sole owner of patents for improvements in wireless telegraphy and telephony and was formed to construct, operate, sell or lease such apparatus and lines.

Stock......Par $1..............................Authorized, $7,500,000.... Issued, $3,000,000

The stock of the company is full paid and non-assessable. The company has no preferred stock or funded debt.

Transfer Agent, William J. Moss, 54 North Ninth street, Philadelphia.

President, E. B. Hume; Vice-President and General Manager, G. P. Gehring; Secretary, William J. Moss; Treasurer, R. Leaman; Chief Engineer, Harry Shoemaker.

Directors—G. P. Gehring, M. D.; R. Leaman, Harry Shoemaker, William J. Moss, E. B. Hume.

Corporate office, Phœnix, Ariz.; main office, 1345 Arch street, Philadelphia. Annual meeting, February 15, at Phœnix, Ariz.

## THE CONSOLIDATION COAL CO.

A corporation formed under the laws of Maryland in 1864. The company owns coal property in the George's Creek, Cumberland region, and controls the Cumberland & Pennsylvania Railroad, 55 miles, including branches. The railroad earnings are included in the statements. In 1900 the company acquired coal lands in Somerset County, Pa., and built a railroad line into the new field.

In January, 1903, an alliance was formed between this company and the Fairmont Coal Co. and Somerset Coal Co., representatives of the latter acquiring large interests in the company and taking part in its management.

The Baltimore & Ohio Railroad Co. owns $3,810,000 of the company's stock.

Stock......Par $100.. ......................Authorized, $10,250,000......Issued, $10,250,000

Transfer Agent and Registrar, Guaranty Trust Co., New York.

The company since 1889 has paid 2 per cent. annually on its stock, the last payment being February 1, 1902.

FUNDED DEBT.

| | |
|---|---|
| 1st mort., 4½ per cent., due Jan., 1922, Jan. and July.............................. | $508,000 |
| Cumberland & Penn. Railroad 1st mort., due May, 1921, 5 per cent., May and Nov.. | 1,000,000 |
| Total............................................................................ | $1,508,000 |

The company guarantees the Cumberland & Pennsylvania bonds.

The 6 per cent. 1st mortgage bonds matured January 1, 1897, and were retired with proceeds of sale at par of 4½ per cent. bonds. A sinking fund for 4½ per cent. is provided by royalty on all coal mined, and $55,000 of the bonds have been retired thereby.

EARNINGS.

| | Div. Paid. | Gross. | Net. | Interest. | Surplus. |
|---|---|---|---|---|---|
| 1893...................... | 2 | $2,377,527 | $368,507 | $162,146 | $206,360 |
| 1894...................... | 2 | 2,175,482 | 362,639 | 161,192 | 201,447 |
| 1895...................... | 2 | 2,230,044 | 385,593 | 162,593 | 822,999 |
| 1896...................... | 2 | 1,690,901 | 628,579 | 210,944 | 417,634 |
| 1897...................... | 2 | 1,818,510 | 596,322 | 164,010 | 482,312 |
| 1898...................... | 2 | 1,926,600 | 648,418 | 190,324 | 458,093 |
| 1899...................... | 2 | 2,097,631 | 665,995 | 195,640 | 470,354 |
| 1900...................... | 2 | 2,278,055 | 680,687 | 192,010 | 486,677 |
| 1901...................... | 2 | 3,414,002 | 1,080,571 | 475,812 | 604,860 |

The charges include interest, sinking fund and the royalty on output. In 1901 the company charged $99,565 to depreciation, and the surplus over the dividend was $300,295.

Coal mined, 1892, 938,695 tons; 1893, 907,559 tons; 1894, 892,502 tons; 1895, 923,655 tons; 1896, 1,157,200 tons; 1897, 1,265,846 tons; in 1898, 1,435,418 tons; in 1899, 1,536,468 tons; in 1900, 1,160,155 tons; in 1901, 1,688,384 tons.

Chairman, Charles K. Lord, Baltimore; President, Clarence W. Watson, New York; Secretary, L. G. McPherson, Baltimore; Treasurer, George De Bolt, Fairmont, W. Va.; Assistant Treasurer, Thomas K. Stuart, Baltimore.

Directors—L. F. Loree, Oscar G. Murray, H. Bowdoin, G. M. Schriver, George C. Jenkins, George A. Von Lingen, Baltimore; J. M. Quigley, Clarence W. Watson, Edward R. Bacon, J. H. Wheelwright, New York.

Main office, 44 South street, Baltimore; New York office, 1 Broadway. Annual meeting, third Wednesday in February.

## CONSUMERS' BREWING CO.

A corporation formed under the laws of Pennsylvania, October 26, 1896, and reorganized January 6, 1903, having defaulted on a sinking fund obligation in March, 1900, and in the payment of coupon bonds due April 1, 1900, and having then been put into the hand of a receiver.

Stock......Par $100..........................Authorized, $1,600,000......Issued, $1,600,000.

The company has no preferred stock. Stock is transferred at the office of the company, Philadelphia. Registrar, The Investment Trust Co., Philadelphia.

FUNDED DEBT.

| | |
|---|---|
| 1st mort., 6 per cent. gold, due Jan., 1923, Jan. and July | $400,000 |
| Gen. mort., 4 per cent. gold, due Jan., 1943, Jan. and July | 1,200,000 |
| Total | $1,600,000 |

Trustee of the 1st mortgage and agent for the payment of interest, Fidelity Trust Co. Philadelphia. Interest on the general mortgage is payable at the discretion of the board of directors for three years from January, 1903, and is a fixed charge thereafter. Trustee of the mortgage and agent for the payment of interest, The Investment Trust Co., Philadelphia.

President, H. A. Foster; Secretary, E. Nichols; Treasurer, John J. Collier; Assistant Treasurer, Hirman Birnbrauer.

Corporate and main office, 139 South Fourth street, Philadelphia. Annual meeting, second Tuesday in May, at Philadelphia.

## THE CONSUMERS GAS CO. OF TORONTO

A corporation formed under the laws of Canada in 1848 to supply gas in the city of Toronto The company has a coal gas plant with a daily capacity of 3,000,000 cubic feet, a water gas plant with a daily capacity of 2,000,000 cubic feet. 6 gas holders, 268 miles of mains, and 30,812 meters in use. The output of gas for the year ending September 30, 1902, was 926,749,000 cubic feet.

Stock......Par $50..........................Authorized, $2,000,000......Issued, $1,750,000

The company has no preferred stock. Stock is transferred at the office of the company.

Dividends, ten per cent. annually were paid, 1848–57; eight per cent. annually 1858–1874, and ten per cent. annually since then. Dividend periods are February, May, August and November.

Bonds of the company to the amount of $200,000 have been authorized, but none have been issued.

EARNINGS.

Year ending September 30.

| | Gross. | Net. | Charges. | Dividends. | Surplus. |
|---|---|---|---|---|---|
| 1900–01 | $786,814 | $282,837 | $2,338 | $174,606 | $110,249 |
| 1901–02 | 848,435 | 333,634 | 5,387 | 175,000 | 153,246 |

President, Larratt W. Smith; Vice-President, George R. R. Cockburn; Secretary and General Manager, W. H. Pearson, Toronto.

Directors, A. W. Austin, J. L. Blaikie, Henry Cawthra, George R. R. Cockburn, Isaac C. Gilmor, George Gooderham, James Henderson, Thomas Long, E. B. Osler, Larratt W. Smith, A. J. Somerville, Thomas R. Wood, Toronto.

Main office, 19 Toronto street, Toronto. Annual meeting, last Monday in October, at Toronto.

## CONTINENTAL COTTON OIL CO.

A corporation formed under the laws of New Jersey, April 2, 1899. The company acquired the following cotton oil manufacturing concerns:

| | |
|---|---|
| Paris Oil & Cotton Co., Paris, Tex. | Ladonia Cotton Oil Co., Ladonia, Tex. |
| Corsicana Cotton Oil Co., Corsicana, Tex. | Shreveport Cotton Oil Co., Shreveport, La. |
| Central Texas Cotton Oil Co., Temple, Tex. | Jackson Cotton Oil Co., Jackson, Miss. |
| Waxahachie Cotton Oil Co., Waxahachie, Tex. | Wynnewood Cot. Oil Mfg. Co. Wynnewood, I. T. |
| Chandler Cotton Oil Co., Chandler, Okla. | Decatur Cotton Oil Co., Decatur, Tex. |
| Celeste Oil & Cotton Co., Celeste, Tex. | Arlington Cotton Oil Co., Arlington, Tex. |

Stock...Par $100...Authorized { com., $3,000,000; pref., 3,000,000 } Issued { com., $1,758,679; pref., 1,563,002 } $3,321,681

The preferred stock is 7 per cent., cumulative, and has priority as to assets. Transfer Agent, Registrar & Transfer Co., New York. Registrar, Knickerbocker Trust Co., New York.

For two years prior to the formation of this company its constituent concerns earned an average of $240,000 per annum. The net earnings for the season of 1899–1900 to May, 1900, were $290,822. On March 23, 1900, the company declared 7 per cent. on its preferred, and 6 per cent. on its common stock. In May, 1901, declared 7 per cent. on the preferred and 4 per cent. on the common. On Aprill 29, 1902, declared 7 per cent. on the preferred.

President, A. J. Buston, Liverpool, England; Vice-President, H. L. Scales, Corsicana, Tex.; Secretary and Treasurer, J. J. Culbertson, New York.

Directors—A. J. Buston, Alfred Hood, Liverpool; H. S. Scales, Corsicana, Tex.; R. K. Erwin, Waxahachie, Tex.; J. S. Le Clercq, J. J. Culbertson, W. B. Wise, Paris, Tex.; S. T. Hubbard, New York; W. G. Nunn, Ladonia, Tex.; George McFadden, Philadelphia; Neil P. Anderson, Fort Worth, Tex.

Corporate office, 55 Montgomery street, Jersey City; main office, 45 Cedar street, New York. Annual meeting, first Tuesday in July, at Jersey City.

## CONTINENTAL GIN CO.

A corporation formed under the laws of Delaware, November 27, 1899, for the purpose of the manufacture and sale of cotton ginning and pressing machinery and supplies, engines and boilers, oil-mill machinery, etc. The company acquired the following plants, all of which were manufacturers of cotton gin machinery:

Winship Machine Co., Atlanta, Ga.
Munger Improved Cotton Machine Mfg. Co., Dallas, Tex.
Northington-Munger-Pratt Co., Birmingham, Ala.
Daniel Pratt Gin Co., Prattville, Ala.
Smith Son's Gin & Machine Co., Birmingham, Ala.
Eagle Cotton Gin Co., Bridgewater, Mass.

The company took over the various plants December 1, 1899.

Stock......Par $100..........................Authorized, $3,000,000......Issued, $2,000,000

The company has no preferred stock. The stock outstanding was issued for the purchase of the plants acquired, with their patents, contracts and good-will.

Stock is transferred at the office of the company, Birmingham, Ala.

FUNDED DEBT.

1st mort., 5 per cent., due 1920, Feb. and Aug....................................... $356,000

The bond issue authorized is $750,000, which is covered by a mortgage on all the company's plants. Of the bonds, $24,000 have been purchased and canceled by the sinking fund. The Old Colony Trust Co. of Boston is trustee of the mortgage and agent for payment of interest.

President, S. I. Munger; Vice-President and Treasurer, Arthur W. Smith; Secretary, N. W. Proctor, Birmingham, Ala.

Directors—W. T. Northington, Arthur W. Smith, R. S. Munger, S. I. Munger, D. T. Smith, Birmingham, Ala.; George Winship, C. R. Winship, Atlanta, Ga.; S. P. Gates, F. C. Gammons, Bridgewater, Mass.; Daniel Pratt, J. B. Bell, Prattville, Ala.; Ennis Munger, Dallas, Tex.; James Virdin, Dover, Del.

Main office, Tenth avenue and Thirty-fourth street, Birmingham, Ala. Annual meeting, third Tuesday in January, at Birmingham, Ala.

## CONTINENTAL LAND AND CATTLE CO.

A corporation formed under the laws of Texas for the purpose of engaging in ranching and raising cattle and horses. The company acquired these properties:

The Continental Cattle Co.
The Mill Iron Cattle Co.

The company owns a ranch of 15,360 acres in Val Verde County, Texas; a ranch of 150,000 acres with 12,000 head of cattle in Collingsworth and Wheeler Counties, and one of 225,000 acres with 30,000 head of cattle in Hall, Motley and Cottle Counties. The company also has 2,000 horses on a ranch in Montana.

Stock......Par $100..........................Authorized, $3,000,000......Issued, $2,500,000

The company has no preferred stock and no funded debt. Stock is transferred at the office of the company.

Dividends are paid annually in July. The dividends declared in 1902 was $4 per share.

President and General Manager, William E. Hughes; Vice-President, E. C. Starling; Secretary and Treasurer, John W. Springer, Denver, Col.

Directors—William E. Hughes, John W. Springer, Denver, Col.; E. C. Sterling, Redlands, Col.; R. D. Green, Estelline, Tex.; A. E. Sterling, Wellington, Tex.

Corporate and main office, Dallas, Tex.; branch offices, Continental Building, Denver, Col.; ranch headquarters, Hall County and Collingsworth County, Texas. Annual meeting, first Tuesday in February, at Dallas, Tex., or at ranch headquarters, Collingsworth County, Texas.

## CONTINENTAL TOBACCO CO.

(Controlled by Consolidated Tobacco Co.)

A corporation formed under the laws of New Jersey, December 10, 1898. The company acquired a majority of the plug tobacco manufacturing concerns of the country, including the P. Lorillard Co., Jersey City; P. H. Mayo & Brother, Richmond, Va.; P. J. Sorg Tobacco Co., Middletown, O.; John Finzer & Brother, Louisville; Daniel Scotten & Co., Detroit, Mich., as well as the Drummond Tobacco Co., St. Louis, and other plug tobacco interests controlled hy the American Tobacco Co. In 1899 the company also acquired, among other concerns, the works of Liggett & Meyers Tobacco Co., St. Louis, and of Buchanan & Lyall, Brooklyn, N. Y. The company, jointly with the American Tobacco Co., controls the American Snuff Co. and the American Cigar Co. In January, 1902, this company acquired the Harry Weissinger Tobacco Co. of Louisville, Ky.

In July, 1901, nearly all the common stock was sold to the Consolidated Tobacco Co., which offered stockholders 100 for the same, payable in its own 4 per cent. collateral trust bonds.

The American Tobacco Co. had a large interest in the stock of this company.

Stock..Par $100..Authorized { com., $50,000,000 / pref., 50,000,000 } Issued { com., $48,844,600 / pref., 48,846,100 } $97,690,700

Transfer Agent, Manhattan Trust Co., New York.

The company began the payment of dividends on its preferred stock October 2, 1899, and from that date has made regular quarterly payments of 1¾ per cent., in January (2), April, July and October.

The first dividend on the common stock was 2 per cent., paid January 27, 1902. In April, 1902, paid 2½ per cent., which was made the regular quarterly rate on the common, the dividend periods being January, April, July and October.

FUNDED DEBT.

Debentures, 7 per cent., due 1905, April and Oct....................................$1,581,100

The stock authorized was originally $37,500,000 preferred and $37,500,000 common. In April, 1899, this was increased to $50,000,000 authorized of each class, and additional stock was issued for purchase of other properties. Preferred is 7 per cent., non-cumulative, with dividends payable quarterly.

The 7 per cent. debentures were issued in 1900 to acquire the $2,000,000 8 per cent. preferred stock of the P. Lorillard Co. The authorized issue of debentures is $2,000,000. More than two-thirds of the Lorillard preferred was exchanged for the bonds. This company holds $3,000,000 of the Lorillard common stock, being the entire issue of that company's common shares.

EARNINGS.

| | Net. | Dividends. | Surplus. |
|---|---|---|---|
| 1899 | $2,632,756 | $1,709,561 | $323,195 |
| 1900 | 4,480,858 | 3,419,122 | 1,061,736 |
| 1901 | 7,600,740 | 4,396,044 | 3,204,696 |
| 1902 | 11,776,934 | 9,769,115 | 2,007,819 |

The company's total surplus December 31, 1902, was $6,597,446.

President, James B. Duke; Vice-Presidents, Charles E. Halliwell, Frank H. Ray, C. C. Dula; Treasurer, H. D. Kingsbury; Secretary, W. H. McAlister; Auditor, W. H. Schroder.

Directors—James B. Duke, Oliver H. Payne, John B. Cobb, Grant B. Schley, Pierre Lorillard, Frank H. Ray, Charles E. Halliwell, W. H. McAlister, George A. Helme, Thomas F. Ryan, Anthony N. Brady, C. C. Dula, New York; Thomas Atkinson, Richmond, Va.; Paul Brown, R. B. Dula, St. Louis; William L. Elkins, Thomas Dolan, Philadelphia; R. K. Smith, Louisville.

Corporate office, 104 First street, Jersey City; Executive office, 111 Fifth avenue, New York Annual meeting, second Wednesday in April, at Jersey City.

## CONTINENTAL ZINC CO.

A corporation formed under the laws of Maine, April 4, 1902. The company was organized to succeed the Continental Zinc & Lead Mining & Smelting Co. That company owned in fee the Kohinoor tract, a lead and zinc property of 200 acres at Joplin, Jasper County, Mo.

The stock of the Continental Zinc & Lead Mining & Smelting Co. was $550,000, par value of the shares $5 each. In May, 1902, Hayden, Stone & Co., Boston, requested stockholders of that company to deposit their stock and exchange the same in the proportion of five shares of old stock for one share of this company's stock, par $25.

Stock......Par $25...............................Authorized, $550,000......Issued, $550,000

The stock is full paid and non-assessable.

Transfer Agents, Hayden, Stone & Co., 87 Milk street, Boston. Registrar, Mercantile Trust Co., Boston.

The company pays dividends of 6.4 per annum in quarterly payments of 40 cents per share.

The company has no funded debt.

President, Ernst Thalmann, New York; Vice-Presidents, Galen L. Stone, Edwin H. Mower; Treasurer, Charles Hayden; Secretary, Jeremiah E. Downs, Boston.

Directors—Ernst Thalmann, F. B. Van Vorst, Alfred Kimber, William H. Brearley, New York; Charles Hayden, Edwin H. Mower, William E. Barrett, Galen L. Stone, Boston.

Main office, 87 Milk street, Boston; superintendent's office, Joplin, Mo. Annual meeting, first Tuesday in April.

---

## COPPER RANGE CONSOLIDATED CO.

A corporation formed under the laws of New Jersey, December 2, 1901, to acquire the stocks of the Copper Range Co. and the Baltic Mining Co., both Michigan corporations.

The Copper Range Co. was formed under the laws of Michigan in 1899 to construct and own a railroad in the upper Michigan copper mining district and to acquire and develop the mineral lands lying along the line of the road.

The company acquired the rights and franchise of the Northern Michigan Railroad Co. which was reorganized under the title of the Copper Range Railroad Co. The latter company's road was completed in 1899 from Houghton, Mich., to Range City, Mich., on the Chicago, Milwaukee & St. Paul Railway, a distance of 41 miles. During two succeeding years construction has been going forward, so that the company now has not only a line running to the Baltic, Champion and Trimountain mines, but also one from Mill Mine Junction to the Baltic, Champion, Trimountain and Adventure mills on the shore of Lake Superior, a distance of about 11 miles. The main line has been extended from Houghton to Calumet and Laurium, so that there are now in operation some 120 miles of road.

The railroad company has a large business aside from its general freight and passenger traffic, which consists largely in the hauling of rock to the stamp mills from the Champion, Baltic, Trimountain and Adventure mines, and also in the hauling of timber from the South Range and Wisconsin lumber district to the mines on the North Range.

See below for the capitalization and funded debt of the railroad company.

The Copper Range Co. also owned over 10,000 acres of mineral lands in the Copper Range in Houghton County, Mich. Systematic prospecting and development work has been pursued on the company's property, and very rich discoveries have been made on the lodes which traverse the same. The policy of the company was to organize mining companies to operate the mines which are discovered on its land, but to retain all the stock of such corporations in its own treasury.

The Copper Range Co. organized the Champion Copper Co. in 1899 with a capital of $2,500,000, in shares of $25 each, to develop and operate the Champion Mine. The latter is considered one of the most promising copper properties in the district. Four shafts and an extensive system of drifts were commenced in 1900 to open up the mine, which is equipped with modern machinery. One-half of the stock of the Champion Copper Co. is owned by the Copper Range Co., the other half being held by the St. Mary's Canal Mineral Land Co.

The Copper Range Co. had $2,500,000 stock in shares of $25 par value, on which $23 per share was paid in. See MANUAL for 1901.

The Baltic Mining Co. was formed under the laws of Michigan in 1897. It acquired a copper bearing tract adjoining the Atlantic Mine and developed the same. Its capital was $2,500,000, in shares of $25 par value, on which $8 per share have been paid in.

Stock......Par $100................ .......Authorized, $28,500,000......Issued, $28,500,000

The plan for the formation of the Consolidated Co. was that holders of the old Copper Range Co.'s stock should receive $150 in new stock for each old $25 share and 100,000 shares or $10,000,000 was used to acquire the stock of the Baltic Mining Co. This called for $25,000,000 of the new stock. The remaining $3,500,000 of new stock was offered at $40 per share to the stockholders of the old company.

The Copper Range Railroad Co. has an authorized share capital of $5,000,000, of which $2,605,100 has been issued. All of the outstanding stock of the railroad is owned by the Copper Range Co. The railroad company, in 1899, created a 1st mortgage for $5,000,000 (trustee, American Loan & Trust Co., Boston), secured by its franchise and property. The bonds are 5 per cent., due 1949, April and October and were to be issued at the rate of $20,000 per mile on the main line completed and $15,000 per mile on side track and branches. The bonds outstanding January 1, 1903, were $1,410,000.

| EARNINGS. | Gross. | Net. |
|---|---|---|
| 1901 | $133,201 | $28,803 |
| 1902 | 303,052 | 136,654 |

The first full financial statement of this company was to appear at the time of the annual meeting in May, 1903.

President, William A. Paine; Secretary and Treasurer, Frederic Stanwood, Boston.

Directors—J. Henry Brooks, Charles H. Paine, Frederic Stanwood, William A. Paine, Boston; John Stanton, New York; Samuel L. Smith, Cameron Currie, Detroit, Mich.

Main office, 27 State street, Boston. Annual meeting, first Wednesday in May.

## CORN PRODUCTS CO.

A corporation formed under the laws of New Jersey, February 6, 1902, for the purpose of the manufacture of glucose, starch and other products of corn and the ownership of plants therefor, and the stocks or securities of other companies engaged in such manufacture. The company was organized in pursuance of a plan to combine the Glucose Sugar Refining Co., the National Starch Co., and other concerns of a similar character. The company acquired by an exchange of stock or for cash the majority of the stocks of the following:

Glucose Sugar Refining Co.
National Starch Co.
Charles Pope Glucose Co.
Illinois Sugar Refining Co.
New York Glucose Co.

Statements of the Glucose Sugar Refining Co., the National Starch Co. and the New York Glucose Co., will be found in the MANUAL for 1901.

Stock..Par $100..Authorized { com., $50,000,000 / pref., 30,000,000 } Issued { com., $44,541,700 / pref., 27,097,110 } $71,638,810

The preferred stock is 7 per cent., cumulative.

Transfer Agents, Cuyler, Morgan & Co., New York. Registrar, Guaranty Trust Co., New York.

The company began the payment of quarterly dividends of 1¾ per cent. on the preferred in July, 1902, and has since regularly paid the same, the dividend periods being January (10), April, July and October.

In March, 1903, a dividend of 4 per cent. on the common stock was declared out of the earnings of the preceding year, the same being payable in quarterly payments of 1 per cent. each in April, July, October and January.

FUNDED DEBT OF CONTROLLED COMPANIES.

| | |
|---|---|
| Nat. Starch debentures, 5 per cent., due July, 1925, Jan. and July | $4,137,000 |
| U. S. Sugar Refining, 1st mort., 6 per cent., due Dec., 1921, June and Dec | 778,000 |
| N. Y. Glucose, 1st mort., 6 per cent., due Sept., 1926, March and Sept | 2,400,000 |
| Nat. Starch Mfg., 1st mort., 6 per cent., due May, 1921, May and Nov | 3,002,000 |
| Total | $10,317,000 |

The plan for the formation of this company and the acquisition of the constituent concerns was brought out by Cuyler, Morgan & Co., New York. Under the plan holders of the stock of the Glucose Sugar Refining Co. were approved, $125 in new common for each $100 of old preferred. The stock of the National Starch Co., it was understood, was exchanged for about 95 per cent. of its face in the new common and preferred respectively. The stock of the other companies was acquired partly by cash payments and partly by stock. The syndicate which underwrote the plan furnished $4,500,000 to finance the operation and provide working capital.

President, C. H. Matthiessen; Vice-President, W. J. Calhoun, New York; 2d Vice-President, Joy Morton, Chicago; Secretary, Edward L. Wemple; Treasurer, Benjamin Graham, New York.

Directors—C. H. Matthiessen, W. J. Calhoun, Joy Morton, Edward L. Wemple, Norman B. Ream, E. T. Bedford, F. A. Matthiessen, H. G. Herget, Benjamin Graham, E. A. Matthiessen, Walter G. Oakman; W. H. Nichols.

Main office, 25 Broad street, New York. Fiscal Agents, Cuyler, Morgan & Co., New York.

## WILLIAM CRAMP & SONS' SHIP & ENGINE BUILDING CO.

A corporation formed in 1872 under the laws of Pennsylvania. The company took over the large shipbuilding and machinery plant established at Kensington, Philadelphia, by William Cramp. The present company has greatly enlarged the works, the property covering over 41 acres of ground and embracing a large shipyard, shops, dry dock, etc. In 1900 the company acquired the Hillman plant at Philadelphia, which was transferred to a company controlled by this company, called the Kensington Ship Yard Co.

Stock .....Par $100..........................Authorized, $5,000,000......Issued $4,848,000

In 1892 the company paid a scrip dividend of 20 per cent., in addition to cash dividends of 8 per cent.; in 1893 paid 10 per cent. on stock; in 1894, 18 per cent.; in 1895, 7 per cent. In 1896-97 no dividends were paid on the stock, the entire net earnings being used for additional working capital. Dividend payments were resumed in 1898, 1¼ per cent. being paid in December of that year. In 1899 paid 5 per cent. In 1900 paid 5 per cent., the dividends being quarterly, at the rate of 1¼ per cent. in March (15), June, September and December. The dividends paid in 1901 were also 5 per cent., and in 1902 the quarterly payments were 1¼ per cent. each, including the October dividend. The December, 1902, dividend was, however, passed, owing to the company's requirements for additional working capital.

FUNDED DEBT.

1st mort., 5 per cent., due March, 1929, March and Sept.......................... $1,425,000

The trustee of the 1st mortgage is the Fidelity Insurance Trust & Safe Deposit Co., Philadelphia.

The company had outstanding bonds secured upon the dry dock and shipyard to the amount of about $300,000. At the end of 1898 it was proposed to refund these obligations, and the floating indebtedness of about $500,000, as well as to provide larger working capital, by creating a 5 per cent. 30-year bond issue of $1,500,000. These bonds were authorized at a special meeting held February 21, 1899, and all the indebtedness of the company was funded in them.

In December, 1902, it was proposed to retire the 5 per cent. bonds, the mortgages on the shipyard, and to provide for improvements with a new issue of $5,500,000 5 per cent. bonds.

EARNINGS.

| Year ending April 30. | Gross. | Net applicable for Dividends. |
|---|---|---|
| 1897-98 | $3,982,000 | ...... |
| 1898-99 | 5,254,904 | $400,067 |
| 1899-00 | 7,791,560 | 536,262 |
| 1900-01 | 7,319,000 | 291,772 |
| 1901-02 | 8,202,093 | 385,236 |

In 1899-00 the surplus over dividends was $293,862; in 1900-01, $49,372; in 1901-02, $142,836.

President, Charles H. Cramp; Vice-President and Treasurer, Henry W. Cramp; Secretary, Charles T. Taylor, Philadelphia.

Directors—Charles H. Cramp, Henry W. Cramp, Clement A. Griscom, Thomas Dolan, Morton McMichael, Samuel Dickson, Edwin S. Cramp, William H. Barnes, Philadelphia; Edmund C. Converse, New York.

Main office, corner Beach and Ball streets, Philadelphia.

## THE CRAMP STEEL CO., LIMITED

A corporation formed under the laws of Ontario, May 19, 1900. The company was organized for the purpose of establishing a steel plant and rolling mills at Collingwood, Ont. The plant will have a capacity of 500 tons of product per day. Associate industries in the town consume most of the product. The company is erecting an open-hearth plant with a capacity of 125 tons per day: also rolling mills, and a blast furnace with a capacity of 250 tons per day. The company received from the town of Collingwood a grant of $115,000 in cash and a free site for its plant, fronting on the harbor, tax exemption and other privileges.

Stock....Par $100.....Authorized { com., $3,000,000 / pref., 2,000,000 } Issued { com., $2,000,000 / pref., 1,000,000 } $3,000,000

The preferred stock is 7 per cent., cumulative. No personal liability attaches to the stockholders. The company has no funded debt.

Transfer Agent and Registrar, National Trust Co., Toronto.

President, J. Wesley Allison, New York; Secretary and Treasurer, J. A. Currie, Toronto.

Directors—Charles D. Cramp, William M. Cramp, Philadelphia; Sir Charles Hibbert Tupper, Victoria, B. C.; H. Prentiss Taylor, J. Wesley Allison, New York; J. A. Currie, A. McLean Macdonell, Toronto; H. L. Burrage, Boston; M. Collins, Brazil, Ind.

Main office, Collingwood, Ont.; Toronto office, Temple Building.

## CROCKER-WHEELER CO.

A corporation formed under the laws of New Jersey, December 8, 1891, to engage in electrical engineering and to manufacture electrical machinery and supplies. The company has contracts with the United States government for motors and electrical machinery and an extensive trade in the United States and abroad. The plant is located at Ampere, N. J.

Stock......Par $100..........................Authorized, $1,000,000......Issued, $1,000,900

The company has no preferred stock and no funded debt. Stock is transferred at the company's office. Registrar, Knickerbocker Trust Co., New York.

The first dividend paid by the company was 6 per cent., July, 1892.

President, Schuyler S. Wheeler; Vice-President, Gano S. Dunn; Secretary, A. L. Doremus; Treasurer, W. L. Brownell; Sales Manager, P. A. Bates.

Directors—Charles T. Barney, A. F. Higgins, Schuyler S. Wheeler, Frederick L. Eldridge, Herbert Noble, Gano S. Dunn, F. B. Crocker, J. H. Flagler, A. L. Doremus.

Main office, Ampere, N. J. New York office, 39 Cortlandt street. Annual meeting, second Wednesday in May.

## THE CROW'S NEST PASS COAL CO., LIMITED

A corporation formed under the laws of the Dominion of Canada, April 15, 1897, for the purpose of mining bituminous coal and manufacturing coke. The company owns mines and ovens at Fernie, B. C., with a capacity of over 450,000 tons of coal annually, and has coke ovens producing 1,000 tons of coke per day.

Stock .....Par $25..........................Authorized, $3,500,000......Issued, $2,500,000

The company has no preferred stock and no funded debt. Transfer Agent and Registrar, National Trust Co., Limited, Toronto.

Beginning April, 1901, regular quarterly dividends of 2½ per cent. have been paid, the dividend periods being January, April, July and October.

President, George A. Cox; First Vice-President, Robert Jaffray; Second Vice-President, H. M. Pellatt; Treasurer, E. R. Wood; Secretary, G. G. S. Lindsey; General Auditor, R. W. Macpherson, Toronto; General Manager, John H. Tonkin, Fernie, B. C.

Directors—George A. Cox, Robert Jaffray, E. R. Wood, Elias Rogers, Thomas Walmsley, H. M. Pellatt, James Mason, Frederic Nicholls, G. G. S. Lindsey, Toronto; William Fernie, Victoria, B. C.; David Morrice, Montreal; J. A. Gemmill, Ottawa, Ont., J. D. Chipman, St. Stephen, N. B.

Main office, 24 King street west, Toronto; General Manager's office, Fernie, B. C. Annual meeting, second Friday in March, at Toronto.

## CRUCIBLE STEEL CO. OF AMERICA

A corporation formed under the laws of New Jersey, July 21, 1900. The company purchased the plants and good will of the following concerns engaged in the manufacture of crucible and high-grade steel and products thereof:

Crescent Steel Co.
La Belle Steel Co.
Anderson, Du Puy & Co.
Burgess Steel & Iron Works.
Benjamin Atha & Illingworth Co.
Spaulding & Jennings Co.
Beaver Falls Steel Works.
Aliquippa Steel Co.
Cumberland Steel & Tin Plate Co.
St. Clair Steel Co.
St. Clair Furnace Co.
Clairton Steel Co.

The following establishments are controlled through ownership of their stock:

Park Steel Co.
Howe, Brown & Co., Limited.
Singer, Nimick & Co.
Sanderson Bros. Steel Co.
Consumers' Heating Co.

These companies produce over 90 per cent. of the tool steel made in the United States, their product including many specialties. They also have a large and growing export trade in their manufactures.

In 1901 this company organized the St. Clair Furnace Co. and St. Clair Steel Co., which have built large plants at Clairton on the Monongahela River, the property owned being 175 acres. In 1902 this company formed the Clairton Steel Co., which took over the St. Clair companies and provided funds for the completion and extension of the new plants, the total expenditure on which amounted to $11,000,000. The Crucible Steel Co. owns all the stock of the Clairton Steel Co. In March, 1903, negotiations were commenced for the sale of an interest in the Clairton Steel Co. to the United States Steel Corporation.

Stock ..Par $100...Authorized { com., $25,000,000 / pref., 25,000,000 } Issued { com., $25,000,000 / pref., 25,000,000 } $50,000,000

The preferred stock is 7 per cent., cumulative.

Transfer Agents, Union Trust Co., Pittsburg; Corporation Trust Co. of New Jersey. Registrars, Fidelity Title & Trust Co., Pittsburg; Farmers' Loan & Trust Co., New York.

The first regular quarterly dividend of 1¾ per cent. on the preferred stock of the Crucible Steel Co. of America was paid December 29, 1900, and regular dividends of that amount have since been paid quarterly in March (31), June, September and December.

FUNDED DEBT.

| | |
|---|---|
| St. Clair Furnace, 1st mort., guar., 5 per cent., due Aug., 1910-39, Feb. and Aug... | $3,000,000 |
| " Steel, 1st mort., int. guar., 5 per cent., due Jan., 1904-25, Jan. and July... | 2,250,000 |
| Clairton Steel Co., 1st mort., 5 per cent., due July, 1904-13, Jan. and July.......... | 5,000,000 |
| Total........................................ | $10,250,000 |

• This company guarantees both principal and interest of the Clairton Steel Co.'s 1st mortgage bonds.

When this company was formed a syndicate offered $5,000,000 of the preferred stock for public subscription at par with a share of common stock as bonus for each share of preferred subscribed at that price.

The Park Steel Co. was formed in 1899. Full details of its organization and finances will be found under its own title. This company acquired and owns 94 per cent. of the stock of the Park Steel Co.

EARNINGS.

Year ending August 31.

| | Net. | Dividends. | Surplus. |
|---|---|---|---|
| 1900-01 | $3,521,299 | $1,790,341 | $1,730,958 |
| 1901-02 | 3,552,468 | 1,766,690 | 1,785,778 |

In 1901-02, $1,000,000 was charged off for depreciation, etc., making the net surplus for the year $785,778.

President, W. P. Snyder; Assistant President and General Manager, Frank B. Smith, Pittsburg; 1st Vice-President, Benjamin Atha, Newark, N. J.; 2d Vice-President, Robert E. Jennings, Jersey City; 3d Vice-President, James H. Park; 4th Vice-President, C. E. Clapp, Pittsburg; Secretary, Alexander Thomas; Treasurer, Julius Bieler, Pittsburg.

Directors—Charles H. Halcomb, James W. Brown, Herbert Du Puy, Robert E. Jennings, Reuben Miller, W. H. Singer, Alexander W. Thomas, G. Bruce Harton, James H. Park, Frank B. Smith, L. D. York, H. H. Dickey, James M. May, Benjamin Atha, A. W. Mellon, C. E. Clapp, A. W. Black, W. P. Snyder, Julius Bieler, George E. Shaw.

Main office, Fifth avenue and Grant street, Pittsburg; New York office, 71 Broadway. Annual meeting, third Wednesday in October.

## THE CUBA CO.

A corporation formed under the laws of New Jersey, April 25, 1900. The object of the company is to build, acquire and operate railroad and other properties in the island of Cuba. In 1900 it undertook the construction of a railroad line from San Luis to Santa Clara, which will afford direct railroad communication between Havana and Santiago de Cuba. See statement of Cuba Railroad Co. in this edition of the MANUAL.

Stock......Par $50,000..........................Authorized, $8,000,000......Issued, $8,000,000

The company had an issue of debentures which were called and redeemed December 31, 1902.

President, Sir William C. Van Horne, Montreal; Vice-President, Grenville M. Dodge, New York; Acting Secretary, T. C. Hall; Treasurer, H. M. Francis, New York.

Directors—Sir William C. Van Horne, Montreal; William C. Whitney, Thomas F. Ryan, George G. Haven, Edward J. Berwind, Grenville M. Dodge, New York; W. L. Elkins, Peter A. B. Widener, Philadelphia; H. L. Terry, New Jersey; Henry Walters, Baltimore.

Main office, 80 Broadway, New York. Financial Agent, Morton Trust Co., New York. Annual meeting, third Wednesday in September.

## THE CUBAN-AMERICAN SUGAR CO.

A corporation formed under the laws of New Jersey, May 31, 1899, for the purpose of raising sugar cane and manufacturing sugar, etc. The company owns a plantation of 7,000 acres, a factory and two lines of railroad in the Province of Matanzas, Cuba.

Stock......Par $100..........................Authorized, $1,000,000......Issued, $1,000,000

The company has no preferred stock.

The stock is transferred at the office of the company, New York.

FUNDED DEBT.

1st mort., 6 per cent., due 1910, April and Oct........................................ $500,000

President, Robert B. Hawley, Galveston, Tex.; Vice-President, Nathaniel Tooker; Secretary, Henry A. Clark; Treasurer, James H. Post, New York.

Directors—Robert B. Hawley, Galveston; James H. Post, Henry A. Clark, Frederick D. Mollenhauer, George S. Dearborn, New York; Nathaniel Tooker, Orange, N. J.; Pearl Wight, New Orleans; John Farr, Short Hills, N. J.; Herbert D. Cory, Englewood, N. J.

Corporate office, 15 Exchange place, Jersey City. Main office, 109 Wall street, New York. Annual meeting, third Tuesday in September, at Jersey City.

## CUMBERLAND TELEPHONE & TELEGRAPH CO.

A corporation formed under the laws of Kentucky, June 8, 1883. The company operates under an exclusive license from the American Bell Telephone Co., its territory comprehending all of Kentucky, Tennessee, Mississippi and Louisiana, and the southern parts of Indiana and Illinois. On January 1, 1903, the company had 338 exchanges, with 92,425 subscribers, 11,997 miles of poles and 60,984 miles of toll wires.

In 1899 the company acquired control of the Ohio Valley Telephone Co., the territory of which included the city of Louisville. In 1900 the Ohio Valley Co. was merged with this company.

A controlling interest in this company is owned by the American Telephone & Telegraph Co.

Stock .....Par $100.........................Authorized, $20,000,000......Issued, $9,106,200

The stock was increased in 1899 from $3,600,000 to $4,500,000, and $500,000 of the increase was used to acquire the control of the Ohio Valley Telephone Co. In January, 1900, the authorized stock was increased to $10,000,000; the holders of the Ohio Valley stock, $550,000, received share for share in the new stock. In 1899 the company increased its stock 25 per cent., giving the stockholders the right to subscribe at par for the increase, and further increases were made in 1900 and 1901, bringing the stock outstanding to the above figures. Another increase of $1,871,280, made in December, 1901, provided that the stockholders subscribing for the new stock should pay for the same in instalments extending to January, 1903.

In January, 1903, the authorized stock was increased from $10,000,000 to $20,000,000, and $2,359,075 was offered at par to the stockholders, to be paid for in four instalments of 25 per cent. each on February 2, July 1, October 1, 1903, and January 2, 1904. When the operation is completed the stock issued will be $11,695,375.

Stock is transferred at the office of the company, Nashville, Tenn., or by the American Loan & Trust Co., Boston.

Dividends on the stock are paid quarterly on January (1), April, July and October. Dividend payments began with 1½ per cent. October, 1883, and 1¾ per cent. January, 1884. From April, 1884, to January, 1886, 2 per cent. quarterly was paid; from April, 1886, to April, 1890, 1½ per cent.; in July, 1890, 1¼ per cent.; from October, 1890, to April, 1891, 1½ per cent.; from July, 1891, to January, 1893, 1 per cent.; from April, 1898, to April, 1899, 1¼ per cent.; from July, 1899, to October, 1900, 1½ per cent. From January 1, 1901, until the present time the quarterly rate has been 1¾ per cent.

### FUNDED DEBT.

| | |
|---|---|
| 1st mort., due 1918, 5 per cent., due Jan., 1918, Jan. and July........................ | $894,000 |
| Ohio Valley Telephone Co., 1st mort., 6 per cent., due Jan., 1908, Jan. and July...... | 16,000 |
| Debentures, 5 per cent., Feb., 1920, or on call, April and Oct.......................... | 239,000 |
| Ea. Tenn. Tel. Co., 1st mort., 6 per cent., due July, 1903-18, Jan. and July.......... | 150,000 |
| Total .................................................................. | $1,299,000 |

The trustee of the 1st mortgage and agent for the payment of interest is the Washington Trust Co., New York. Of the bond issue of $1,000,000 there had been retired to January 1, 1901, $106,000 by the sinking fund. The 5 per cent. debentures may be called and paid at any time. Interest is payable at the Fourth National Bank, Nashville, Tenn.

The trustee of the East Tennessee Telephone 1st mortgage and agent for the payment of interest on the bonds is the Nashville Trust Co., Nashville, Tenn. The bonds can be retired after July 1, 1903, at 102½ and accrued interest.

### EARNINGS.

| | Gross. | Net. | Charges and Taxes. | Dividends. | Surplus. |
|---|---|---|---|---|---|
| 1900......................... | $1,884,013 | $678,210 | $162,649 | $399,155 | $176,405 |
| 1901......................... | 2,642,562 | 848,106 | 210,043 | 468,538 | 169,523 |
| 1902......................... | 3,070,162 | 1,001,979 | 219,813 | 623,203 | 158,961 |

On December 31, 1902, the company had assets of $14,114,732. It also had on that date undivided profits, $159,358; reserve for maintenance, $629,351, and reserve for contingent liabilities, $312,260.

President, James E. Caldwell; Vice-Presidents, W. W. Berry, William Litterer; Secretary, Leland Hume; Treasurer, T. D. Webb; Auditor, H. Blair Smith, Nashville, Tenn.

Directors—James E. Caldwell, William Litterer, F. O. Watts, George R. Knox, W. W. Berry, M. J. Smith, V. E. Schwab, W. R. Cole, Nashville, Tenn.; A. G. Sharp, Atlanta, Ga.; E. M. Barton, Chicago; W. H. Woolverton, New York; Frederick P. Fish, Boston.

Corporate office, Hopkinsville, Ky.; main office, 180 North College street, Nashville. Annual meeting, first Thursday in February, at Hopkinsville, Ky.

## CUMBERLAND VALLEY TRACTION CO.

A corporation formed under the laws of Pennsylvania, December 18, 1893. The company leases the Cumberland Electric Passenger Railway Co. It operates 18 miles of electric railway between Carlisle, Boiling Springs, Churchtown and Mechanicsburg, Pa., with a total population of 20,000.

Stock....Par $100..........Authorized { com., $500,000 / pref., 50,000 } Issued { com., $402,900 / pref., 43,500 } $446,400

FUNDED DEBT.

1st mort., 5 per cent. gold, due 1927, April and Oct.................................. $300,000

The bond issue is the total amount authorized. Trustee of the mortgage, Harrisburg Trust Co., Harrisburg, Pa. In the fiscal year ending June 30, 1902, the gross earnings were $25,613.91; net deficit, $1,863.94.

President, G. W. Cumbler; Secretary, F. H. Alleman; Treasurer, W. L. Gorgas, Harrisburg, Pa.

Directors—G. W. Cumbler, F. H. Alleman, W. L. Gorgas, B. F. Myers, S. F. Dunkle, J. J. Baughman, J. D. Landes, S. F. Hertzler, R. H. Moffitt.

Corporate office, Carlisle, Pa.; main office, Harrisburg, Pa. Annual meeting, second Monday in January, at Carlisle, Pa.

## CURTICE BROTHERS CO.

A corporation formed under the laws of New York, June 26, 1901, to carry on the business of preserving and canning articles of food. The company owns the original plant of the Curtice Brothers Co. at Rochester, N. Y., and the plant formerly known as the Curtice Canning Co. at Vernon, N. Y.

Stock......Par $100. .....Authorized { com., $800,000 / pref., 700,000 } Issued { com., $800,000 / pref., 700,000 } $1,500,000

The preferred stock is 7 per cent., cumulative, and also has preference as to assets. Transfer Agent and Registrar, Security Trust Co., Rochester, N. Y. The company has no funded debt.

Dividends were paid January 1, 1902, at the rate of 7 per cent. per annum on the preferred, and $5 per share on the common.

The surplus over dividends in 1902 was $72,000 and the total surplus was about $169,000.

President, Simeon G. Curtice; 1st Vice-President and Treasurer, Edgar N. Curtice; Secretary, Robert A. Badger, Rochester, N. Y.

Directors—Simeon G. Curtice, Edgar N. Curtice, Robert A. Badger, Henry B. McKay, Rufus K. Dryer, William A. Hubbard, Jr., Walter S. Hubbell, Rochester, N. Y.

Corporate and main office, Curtice street, Rochester, N. Y. Annual meeting, the second Tuesday in February, at Rochester.

## THE DALY WEST MINING CO.

A corporation formed under the laws of Colorado in 1902. Its mines are located at Park City, Utah. The company absorbed the Quincy Mining Co. in 1902.

Stock......Par $20..........................Authorized, $3,600,000......Issued, $3,600,000

The company has no preferred stock and no funded debt.

Transfer Agents, American Loan and Trust Co., Boston, and North American Trust Co., New York.

The company paid its first dividend in 1899 of 20 cents per share. In January, 1900, a dividend of 25 cents per share was paid; in January, 1901, 30 cents; in July, 1901, 35 cents; in October, 1901, 40 cents, and in July, 1902, 60 cents. Dividends are now payable monthly on the 15th.

President and General Manager, J. E. Bamberger; Vice-President, J. D. Wood; Treasurer, W. S. McCornick; Secretary, J. Barnett; Assistant Secretary, Arthur W. Mountney.

Directors—J. E. Bamberger, J. D. Wood, W. S. McCornick, J. Barnett, Ezra Thompson, W. H. Dickson.

Corporate office, Denver; main office, 161 South Main street, Salt Lake City. Annua meeting, third Wednesday in February.

## THE DAYTON & WESTERN TRACTION CO.

A corporation formed under the laws of Ohio, in May, 1897. The company owns and operates 25 miles of electric railway, extending from Dayton to Eaton, O., serving a population of 125,000. The plant of the company is located at West Alexandria, O.

Stock......Par $100.......Authorized { com., $400,000 / pref., 400,000 } Issued { com., $400,000 / pref. 400,000 } $800,000

The preferred stock is 5 per cent. It was issued to retire a bond issue of $400,000, due April 1, 1923. Stock is transferred at the company's office.

Dividends are paid quarterly, in January, July, April and October.

President, Treasurer and General Manager, Valentine Winters; Vice-President, Charles B. Clegg; Secretary, J. H. Winters; Assistant Secretary, R. R. Dickey, Jr.

Directors—Valantine Winters, J. H. Winters, C. B. Clegg, R. R. Dickey, Jr., J. E. Lowes.

Corporate office, Dayton, O.; main office, West Alexandria, O. Annual meeting, second Wednesday in January, at Dayton, O.

## DE FOREST WIRELESS TELEGRAPH CO.

A corporation formed under the laws of Maine in January, 1902. The company owns the De Forest Wireless Telegraph patents.

Stock......Par $10..........................Authorized, $3,000,000......Issued, $3,000,000

The company has no preferred stock and no funded debt.

Stock is transferred at the company's office.

President, A. White; First Vice-President, Lee de Forest; Secretary, M. G. Lathrop; Treasurer, James Stewart; General Manager, Clarence G. Tompkins, New York.

Directors—Lee de Forest, A. White, Francis X. Butler, C. C. Galbraith, W. N. Harte, S. S. Bogart, New York; M. M. McRae, Philadelphia; Clarence G. Tompkins, Pittsfield, Mass.

Corporate office, Kittery, Me.; main office, 100 Broadway, New York; branch offices, Chicago, Buffalo, St. Louis, San Francisco, and Providence, R. I. Annual meeting, second Monday in January, at Kittery, Me.

## DE LONG HOOK & EYE CO.

A corporation organized under the laws of West Virginia, May 7, 1900. The company acquired the American and foreign patents and trade-marks, good will, plant and machinery of Richardson & De Long Bros., Philadelphia, manufacturers of the De Long patent "See That Hump" hook-and-eye. The company manufactures not only the De Long patent hooks but other specialties.

Stock......Par $10..........................Authorized, $1,000,000......Issued, $1,000,000

Stock is transferred at the company's office. Registrar, Real Estate Trust Co., Philadelphia.

The company has no funded debt.

Since its organization the company has paid dividends at the rate of 10 per cent. per annum, payments being 2½ per cent. quarterly, in January, April, July and October.

President, Thomas D. Richardson; Vice-Presidents, Edward C. Lee, Frank E. De Long; Secretary and Treasurer, George H. Cliff, Philadelphia.

Directors—Thomas D. Richardson, Frank K. Hipple, Theodore C. Search, Edward C. Lee, E. V. Douglas, George Philler, Frank E. De Long, F. S. Lewis, William F. North, Philadelphia.

Main office, 439 North Twelfth street, Philadelphia. Annual meeting, first Thursday in May.

## DENVER CITY TRAMWAY CO.

A corporation formed March 3, 1899, being a consolidation of the leading street railway lines of Denver, Col., in pursuance of a plan formulated in 1898.

The companies whose property was included in the reorganization and consolidation were the Denver City Railroad, West End Railroad and Denver Consolidated Tramway. Road owned, 143 miles, all operated by electric power.

Stock......Par $100..........................Authorized, $5,000,000......Issued, $5,000,000

The company has no preferred stock. Transfer Agent, Mercantile Trust Co., New York. Registrar, Central Trust Co., New York.

Quarterly dividends of 1 per cent. on the stock were paid, beginning May 15, 1901, in February, May, August and November, but after May, 1902, the payments were suspended.

FUNDED DEBT.

| | |
|---|---|
| Purchase money mort., 5 per cent. gold, due April, 1910, April and Oct. | $2,000,000 |
| Denver Tramway Co., 1st mort., 6 per cent. gold, due July, 1908, Jan. and July | 498,000 |
| " " " cons. mort., 6 per cent. gold, due Jan., 1910, Jan. and July | 1,219,000 |
| Met. St., R. R. Co., 1st. mort., 6 per cent. gold, due Jan., 1911, Jan. and July | 953,000 |
| Denver Con. Tram. Co., cons. mort., 5 per cent. gold, due Oct., 1933, April and Oct. | 1,167,000 |
| Total | $5,837,000 |

The authorized purchase mortgage is $2,000,000. Trustee of mortgage and agent for the payment of interest, Central Trust Co., New York.

The authorized consolidated mortgage of the Denver Consolidated Tramway Co. is $4,000,000. Trustee of the mortgage and agent for the payment of interest, Mercantile Trust Co., New York. The authorized amount of the Denver Tramway Co.'s consolidated mortgage is $2,000,000. Trustee of the mortgage and agent for the payment of interest, Mercantile Trust Co., New York. Interest on all the bonds is also payable at the office of the company.

The purchase money mortgage is a 1st lien on the property of the former Denver City and West End roads, and has a lien, subject to the prior undisturbed mortgages on the Denver Consolidated Tramway Co.'s property.

EARNINGS.

| | Gross. | Net. | Charges. | Surplus. |
|---|---|---|---|---|
| 1900 | $1,302,289 | $579,838 | $374,291 | $205,548 |
| 1901 | 1,507,293 | 688,964 | 383,180 | 305,785 |

Information in regard to the earnings of the company for the year 1902 was refused by the officers.

President, William G. Evans; Vice-President and General Manager, John A. Beeler; Secretary and Treasurer, George E. Ross-Lewin.

Directors—Rodney Curtis, W. G. Evans, George E. Ross-Lewin, Thomas Keely, B. A. Jackson, S. M. Perry, John A. Beeler, Samuel P. Colt, Frederick G. Moffatt.

Main office, 15th and Arapahoe streets, Denver. Annual meeting, third Tuesday in February, at Denver.

## THE DENVER GAS & ELECTRIC CO.

A corporation formed under the laws of Colorado, April 26, 1899. The purpose of the company is supplying gas and electricity. It owns all the facilities for such purposes in Denver. The company consolidated the Denver Consolidated Gas Co. and the Denver Consolidated Electric Co.

The gas plant at Seventh and Wewatta streets, Denver, has a capacity of 2,500,000 cubic feet per day. The company also has a Pintsch gas plant at Eighteenth and Wewatta streets, with a capacity of 30,000 cubic feet of compressed gas per day.

It has two electric plants, at Twenty-first and Wewatta streets, and Sixth and Lawrence streets, with respective capacities of 2,775 and 3,450 horse-power.

Stock......Par $100..........................Authorized, $3,500,000......Issued, $2,650,000

Transfer Agents, Emerson McMillin & Co., 40 Wall street, New York. Registrar, Continental Trust Co., New York.

The company paid semi-annual dividends of 1½ per cent. each, February 15 and August 15, 1900. In February, 1901, the semi-annual dividend was passed in consequence of a threatened competition to the company. No dividends since.

FUNDED DEBT.

| | |
|---|---|
| Denver Cons. Gas, 1st mort., 5 per cent., due Nov., 1911, Jan. and July | $1,500,000 |
| " " debentures, 6 per cent., due Oct., 1911, April and Oct. | 75,000 |
| Denver Cons. Electric, 1st mort., 6 per cent., due Jan., 1910, Jan. and July | 590,000 |
| West. Electrical Con. Co., 1st mort., 6 per cent., due Oct., 1915, April (4) and Oct. | 180,000 |
| Montclair L., H. & Power, 1st mort., 6 per cent., due 1903, Jan. and July | 35,000 |
| Denver Gas & Electric, cons. mort., 5 per cent., due May, 1949, May and Nov. | 2,400,000 |
| Total | $4,780,000 |

The Denver Gas & Electric Co.'s consolidated 5 per cent. mortgage, Continental Trust Co., New York, trustee, is for $5,500,000. Sufficient of these bonds are reserved to retire the underlying issues. Interest payable by Emerson McMillin & Co., New York.

The Denver Consolidated Gas Co.'s 5 per cent. 1st mortgage bonds are $1,500,000 authorized and issued. Emerson McMillin & Co., New York, pay coupons of these bonds. Interest on the debentures is payable by Maitland, Coppell & Co., New York.

The Denver Electric Co.'s consolidated mortgage, 6 per cent., Rollins Investment Co., trustee, is for $600,000. Interest payable at Chemical National Bank, New York.

Interest on the Western Electrical Construction 6 per cent. bonds, is payable by the Massachusetts Loan & Trust Co., Boston, and on the Montclair Light, Heat & Power 6 per cent. bonds by E. H. Rollins & Sons, Boston.

In the fiscal year ending February 28, 1900, the net earnings of the company were $407,286.

Chairman, Emerson McMillin, New York; President and Treasurer, Henry L. Doherty; Vice-President and General Manager, John H. Poole; Secretary, Frank W. Frueauff, Denver, Col.

Directors—Emerson McMillin, W. F. Douthirt, New York; James B. Grant, Andrew S. Hughes, John C. Mitchell, Henry L. Doherty, John H. Poole, George W. Skinner, Harry C. James, Edward W. Rollins, Charles W. Waterman, Frank W. Frueauff, Denver, Col.; Horace K. Devereaux, Colorado Springs, Col.

Main office, 405 Seventeenth street, Denver, Col. Annual meeting, second Tuesday in May, at Denver.

## THE DENVER UNION WATER CO.

A corporation formed under the laws of Colorado, October 14, 1894. The company owns and operates under various franchises extending to 1910, the water works of Denver, Col., and the adjacent towns. The population served is 160,000. The company has a system of about 500 miles of mains and some 3,000 fire hydrants and 26,500 taps.

Stock...Par $100...Authorized { com., $5,000,000 / pref., 2,500,000 } Issued { com., $5,000,000 / pref., 2,500,000 } $7,500,000

The preferred stock is 5 per cent., non-cumulative.

Transfer Agent, Farmers' Loan & Trust Co., New York. Registrar, Continental Trust Co., New York.

FUNDED DEBT.

1st mort., 5 per cent., due July, 1914, Jan. and July.................................. $8,000,000

The 1st mortgage bonds outstanding are the amount authorized. Interest is paid at the Fourth National Bank, New York.

President, Walter S. Cheesman; Vice-President, T. S. Hayden; Treasurer, David H. Moffat; Secretary, Walter P. Miller; Auditor, J. H. Kingwill; Chief Engineer, A. E. Kastle; Manager, W. P. Robinson.

Directors—Walter S. Cheesman, David H. Moffat, T. S. Hayden, J. B. Grant, Moses Hallett, D. C. Dodge, Denver, Col.

Main office, Seventeenth and Glenarm streets, Denver, Col.

## DES MOINES CITY RAILWAY CO.

A corporation formed under the laws of Iowa in 1866. It acquired, by consolidation in 1893, the property of the following companies:

Des Moines Street Railroad Co.
Des Moines Suburban Street Railway Co.

The Des Moines Street Railroad Co. was a consolidation of the following companies:

Des Moines Street Railway Co.
Des Moines Electric Railway Co.
Des Moines Rapid Transit Co.
Des Moines Belt Line Railway Co.
Des Moines Broad Gauge Street Railway Co.
Des Moines & Sevastopol Street Railway Co.

The company controls all the street railway lines in Des Moines, Ia., about 50 miles of track on 31 miles of streets. It owns an electric power plant and 75 motor cars.

Stock....Par $100.....Authorized { com., $3,000,000 / pref., 250,000 } Issued { com., $1,055,000 / pref., 250,000 } $1,305,000

Transfer Agent, Registrar,

FUNDED DEBT.

| | |
|---|---|
| 1st mort., 5 per cent. gold, due April, 1921, April and Oct. | $939,000 |
| Des Moines Street Railroad Co., 1st mort., 6 per cent. gold, due Oct., 1919, April and Oct. | 475,000 |
| Des Moines Suburban Railway Co., 6 per cent. gold, due Jan., 1921, Jan. and July | 272,000 |
| Total | $1,686,000 |

The 1st mortgage of the Des Moines City Railway Co. is for $3,000,000, of which amount $882,000 is reserved to retire underlying bonds. A sinking fund is provided as follows: $10,000 annually, April 1, 1906-10; $15,000 annually, 1911-15, and $25,000 annually, 1916-20. Bonds may be called after April, 1906, at 106 and interest. Trustees of the mortgage and Agents for the payment of interest, Illinois Trust & Savings Bank and W. H. Henkle, Chicago. Interest is also payable at the office of N. W. Harris & Co., New York.

The mortgage of the Des Moines Street Railroad Co. is for $600,000, October, 1899. After October, 1899, the bonds are payable at the rate of $25,000 annually. Trustee of the mortgage and agent for the payment of interest, American Trust & Savings Bank, Chicago.

The authorized amount of the Des Moines Suburban Railway Co. mortgage is $300,000, November, 1890. After January, 1906, the bonds are payable at the rate of $20,000 annually. Trustee of the mortgage, Iowa Loan & Trust Co., Des Moines, Ia. Agents for the payment of interest, Iowa Loan & Trust Co., Des Moines, Ia., and Chemical National Bank, New York.

EARNINGS.

Year ending December 31.

| | Gross. | Operating Expenses. | Net. |
|---|---|---|---|
| 1899 | $299,191 | $203,297 | $95,894 |
| 1900 | 353,034 | 229,722 | 123,312 |
| 1901 | 397,839 | 250,485 | 147,354 |

President, J. S. Polk; Secretary, A. G. Maish; Treasurer and General Manager, George B. Hippee.

Main office, 607 Mulberry street, Des Moines, Ia.

## THE DETROIT & PORT HURON SHORE LINE RAILWAY CO.

(Controlled by the Detroit United Railway.)

A corporation formed under the laws of New Jersey in May, 1900. The company owns the capital stock of the following companies:

Rapid Railway Co.
Detroit, Mount Clemens & Marine City Railway.
Port Huron, St. Clair & Marine City Railway.
Connor's Creek & Clinton Riv. Plank Road Co.
City Electric Railway of Port Huron.
Detroit & Lake St. Clair Railway.
Rapid Railroad.

The Detroit, Mt. Clemens & Marine City Railway owns the Mt. Clemens & Lakeside Traction Co. and the Detroit & River St. Clair Railway.

The consolidated company owns and operates an electric railway known as the Rapid Railway system, extending from Detroit to Port Huron, running through Mount Clemens, New Baltimore, Algonac, Marine City and St. Clair, including all the city electric lines of Mount Clemens and Port Huron and, with a route through the business section of Detroit, a total of 107.97 miles, are serving a population of more than 412,000. The company has a main power station at New Baltimore and five substations. The system is equipped with electric and steam cars for handling freight as well as passengers. The entire capital stock of this company is owned hy the Detroit United Railways.

Stock......Par $100.....Authorized { com., $2,400,000 / pref., 100,000 } Issued { com., $1,900,000 / pref., 100,000 } $2,000,000

FUNDED DEBT.

| | |
|---|---|
| 1st mort., 5 per cent., gold, due 1950, Jan. and July | $1,392,000 |
| Rapid Railway, 1st mort., 5 per cent., due 1915, March and Sept | 300,000 |
| Rapid Railway, 1st consol. mort., 5 per cent., gold, due 1916, May and Nov | 300,000 |
| City Electric Ry. of Port Huron, 1st mort., 6 per cent., gold, due 1913, May and Sept. | 180,000 |
| Detroit & Lake St. Clair Ry. Co., 1st mort., 5 per cent., gold, due 1920, April and Oct. | 290,000 |
| Port Huron, St. Clair & Marine City Ry., 5 per cent., due 1920, March and Sept | 3,000 |
| Total | $2,465,000 |

The amount of authorized bonds of the Detroit & Port Huron Shore Line Railway Co. is $2,500,000. Of that amount $783,000 are reserved for the retirement of divisional liens and $325,000 for acquirement and extensions. Trustee of the mortgage, Union Trust Co., Detroit. Agent for the payment of interest, American Exchange National Bank, New York.

The amount of authorized 1st consolidated mortgage bonds of the Rapid Railway is $600,000, of which $300,000 is reserved to take up the outstanding 1st mortgage bonds of the company. Trustee of the mortgage and Agent for the payment of interest, Finance Co. of Pennsylvania, Philadelphia.

The amount of authorized bonds of the Detroit & Lake St. Clair Railway Co. is $400,000. Trustee of the mortgage and agent for the payment of interest, Union Trust Co., Detroit.

Trustee of the mortgage of the City Electric Railway, Union Trust Co., Detroit. Agent for the payment of interest, Hanover National Bank, New York. Trustee of the mortgage of the Port Huron, St. Clair & Marine City Railway, Union Trust Co., Detroit.

In the year ending December 31, 1902, the gross earnings of the company were $422,070; net, $169,067; fixed charges, $130,068; surplus, $42,848.

President, Jere C. Hutchins; Vice-President, F. W. Brooks; Secretary, Albert E. Peters; Treasurer, George H. Russel.

Main office, 12 Woodward avenue, Detroit.

## DETROIT CITY GAS CO.

A corporation formed under the laws of Michigan, January 17, 1898. It acquired all the gas properties in the city of Detroit, which were combined in 1891 under the title of the Detroit

Gas Co. A reorganization followed under present title, including the Detroit Gaslight Co., the Mutual Gas Co. and the Michigan (Natural) Gas Co.

The company's franchise is 30 years from 1893. It has 262 miles of mains and 93 miles of mains for natural gas, including a pipe line of 51 miles from Toledo, O., to Detroit. The price of gas for illuminating was $1 per 1,000 feet and for fuel-gas 80 cents per 1,000 feet, but in December, 1901, the city passed an ordinance reducing the price of illuminating gas to 70 cents. This company controls and operates by contract two natural gas fields in Canada, supplying fuel-gas to the cities of Detroit and Toledo. In 1902 the company began extensive improvements and new construction work.

Stock......Par $50...................... .....Authorized, $5,000,000......Issued, $4,530,500

Transfer agents, Emerson McMillin & Co., 40 Wall street, New York. Registrar, Continental Trust Co., New York.

Dividends are half-yearly, May and November. The first dividend was 2½ per cent., paid November 15, 1899, and dividends of the same amount were regularly paid until May, 1901, inclusive. The November, 1901, dividend was passed.

FUNDED DEBT.

| | |
|---|---|
| Detroit City Gas prior lien mort., 5 per cent., due Jan., 1923, Jan. and July.......... | $5,055,500 |
| Detroit Gas Co. consolidated 1st mort., 5 per cent., due Feb., 1918, Feb. and Aug..... | 365,000 |
| Income bonds.............................................................. | 16,000 |
| Total.............................................................. | $5,436,500 |

The prior lien mortgage (Continental Trust Co., New York, trustee) is for $6,000,000. Of this amount $365,000 are reserved for exchange for bonds of the Detroit Gas Co. still outstanding, and $921,000 for improvements. The original issue of Detroit Gas Co. consols was $2,000,000 and there were $200,000 of income bonds. All but the amount outstanding have been exchanged for prior liens. The Detroit Gas Co. had $2,117,000 of prior 6 per cent. encumbrance, which have all been discharged by the present company.

| EARNINGS. | Gross. | Net. |
|---|---|---|
| 1896 (year ending Feb. 28)................................. | $570,417 | $247,388 |
| 1897 ( " " " )................................. | ...... | 269,500 |
| 1898 ( " " " )................................. | ...... | 332,715 |
| 1899 ( " " " )................................. | ...... | 427,321 |

President, Emerson McMillin, New York; Vice-President, William C. McMillan; Treasurer, M. W. O'Brien; Secretary and General Manager, Paul Doty, Detroit; Assistant Secretary, W. F. Douthirt, New York.

Directors—Emerson McMillin, Thomas H. Hubbard, John Byrne, F. S. Smith, George H. Russell, W. F. Douthirt, New York; William C. McMillan, M. W. O'Brien, John C. Donnelly, D. M. Ferry, A. C. Angell, Eugene T. Lynch, Detroit.

Main office, 230 Woodward avenue, Detroit. Fiscal and Transfer Agents, Emerson McMillin & Co., 40 Wall street, New York.

## DETROIT, MACKINAC & MARQUETTE RAILROAD LAND GRANT

Land grant 7 per cent. income bonds to the amount of $4,560,000 were created and issued by the Detroit, Mackinac & Marquette Railroad Co., which about 1881 built a line from St. Ignace, Mich., to Marquette, Mich. The company received from the State of Michigan a land grant of some 1,320,000 acres in the upper peninsula, situated in the counties of Chippewa, Mackinac, Marquette and Schoolcraft. These lands, under certain conditions, were pledged as security for the land grant bonds. The Detroit, Mackinac & Marquette Railroad was sold at foreclosure October 20, 1886, and was acquired and reorganized by the syndicate which constructed the Duluth, South Shore & Atlantic Railway. It now forms part of that system. Under the reorganization the holders of the land grant bonds retained their lien upon the lands.

Land grant income bonds, registered, due 1911, April and Oct..................... $2,771,000

Under the instrument securing the bonds only 25 per cent. of the proceeds of lands sold were applicable to the payment of interest, the balance being applied to the expenses of the trust and redemption of bonds. Under this provision and the provision for locating land, with bonds, $1,465,000 of the bonds have been retired by purchase, and $324,000 retired in payment for lands, leaving the above amount outstanding.

Interest payments upon the bonds have been as follows: In 1892, 2 per cent.; in 1893, 2 per cent.; in 1894, 2 per cent.; in 1895, 2 per cent.; in 1896, 2 per cent.; in 1897, 2 per cent.; in 1898, 2 per cent.; in 1899, 2 per cent.; in 1900, 2 per cent.; in 1901, 2 per cent. The payments were semi-annual of 1 per cent. each in April (10) and October at the Central Trust Co., New York. The October, 1902, payment was increased to 1½ per cent.

In August, 1902, a sale was made of 1,000,000 acres for $1,250,000, payable in four instalments, the first payment having been made in December, 1902. This transaction, which will result in the retirement of a further considerable amount of the bonds, left in the trust 180,000 acres in fee and mineral rights in 90,000 acres.

President, Philip H. McMillan; Vice-President, William C. McMillan; Treasurer, Hugh McMillan.

Trustees of Land Grant, Frederick E. Driggs, William W. Heaton; Land Commissioner, E. W. Cotterell; Assistant Land Commissioner, Wetmore Hunt, Detroit.

Main office, 16 Clifford street, Detroit, Mich.

## THE DETROIT UNION RAILROAD DEPOT & STATION CO.

A corporation organized under the laws of Michigan in 1881 to supply station and depot facilities at Detroit to railroads requiring them. The company's property consists of station grounds of about 40 acres in Detroit, along the river front, adjoining the Michigan Central Railroad and terminals, and a railroad through the city and suburbs 3½ miles long. Terminal facilities are leased in perpetuity to the Wabash Railroad Co. and the Pere Marquette Railroad Co. The principal revenues of the company are derived from the rentals of real estate.

Stock......Par $100..........................Authorized, $2,500,000......Issued, $2,250,000

Stock is transferred at the company's office. Registrar, Union Trust Co., Detroit.

The yearly dividends on the stock have been as follows: In 1890, 3 per cent.; in 1891, 4 per cent.; in 1892 and 1893, 5 per cent.; in 1894, 6 per cent.; in 1895, 5½ per cent.; in 1896, 1897, 1898, 1899, 1900, 1901 and 1902, 4 per cent. Dividends are paid quarterly, January (15), April, July and October.

The company has no funded or floating debt.

EARNINGS.

| | Gross. | Net. | Dividends. | Surplus. |
|---|---|---|---|---|
| 1896 | $114,538 | $90,264 | $90,000 | $264 |
| 1897 | 111,408 | 91,334 | 90,000 | 1,334 |
| 1898 | 113,202 | 93,023 | 90,000 | 3,023 |
| 1899 | 123,229 | 97,726 | 90,000 | 7,726 |
| 1900 | 117,563 | 95,393 | 90,000 | 5,393 |
| 1901 | 119,428 | 99,399 | 90,000 | 9,399 |
| 1902 | 115,433 | 93,903 | 90,000 | 3,903 |

President and Treasurer, Henry B. Joy; Vice-President, James Joy; Secretary, James G. Miller.

Directors—James McMillan, Allan Shelden, James Joy, William C. McMillan, Richard P. Joy, Truman H. Newberry, Theodore D. Buhl, Henry B. Joy.

Main office, 68 Griswold street, Detroit. Annual meeting, first Wednesday in February.

## DETROIT UNITED RAILWAY

A corporation formed under the laws of Michigan, December 31, 1900. The company absorbed the Citizens' Traction Co. and thereby secured control of the following companies:

Detroit Citizens' Street Railway Co.
Detroit Electric Railway Co.
Detroit Suburban Railway Co.
Detroit, Ft. Wayne & Belle Isle Railway Co.

The company has also acquired the following companies:

Detroit & Northwestern Railway Co.
Detroit & Pontiac Railway Co.
Wyandotte & Detroit River Railway Co.
Detroit & Flint Railway Co.

The stock of the following companies is owned but they are operated independently:

Sandwich, Windsor & Amherstburg Railway Co., Windsor, Ont.
Detroit & Port Huron Shore Line Railway.
City Electric Railway Co., Windsor, Ont.
People's Electric Light Co., Windsor, Ont.

Through the Detroit & Flint Railway Co., the Detroit United Railway Co. acquired the Detroit, Rochester, Romeo & Lake Orion Railway Co., the North Detroit Electric Railway Co. and the Detroit, Utica & Romeo Railway Co. The company owns and operates all the street railways in Detroit and its suburbs and has extended its operations to Windsor, Ont.

Stock......Par $100........................Authorized, $12,500,000......Issued, $12,500,000

The company has no preferred stock.

Transfer Agents, Kean, Van Cortlandt & Co., New York Registrar, New York Security & Trust Co., New York.

Dividends of 1 per cent. quarterly have been regularly paid since March 1, 1901, in January, April, July and October.

FUNDED DEBT.

| | |
|---|---|
| Detroit United Ry. 1st cons. mort., 4½ per cent., Jan., 1932, Jan. and July......... | $1,775,000 |
| Detroit Citizens' St. Ry. Co. cons. mort., 5 per cent. gold, due July, 1905, Jan. and July. | 6,585,000 |
| Highland Park Railway 1st mort., 5 per cent., due Jan. 1908, Jan. and July........ | 140,000 |
| Detroit Railway Co. 1st mort., 5 per cent. gold, due 1912–1924, June and Dec....... | 1,800,000 |
| Detroit Electric Ry. Co. cons. mort., 5 per cent. gold, due June, 1916, June and Dec.. | 1,000,000 |
| Detroit, Ft. W. & Belle Isle Ry., 1st mort. 5 p. c. gold, due April, 1927, April and Oct. | 1,200,000 |
| Detroit & Northw'n Ry. Co., 1st mort., 4½ per cent. gold, due May, 1921, May and Nov.. | 855,000 |
| Detroit & Pontiac Ry. Co. 1st mort. 5 per cent. gold, due Feb., 1922, Feb. and Aug.. | 500,000 |
| Detroit & Pontiac Ry. 1st con. mort., 4½ per cent. gold, due June, 1926, June and Dec. | 600,000 |
| Wyandotte & Detroit Riv. Ry. Co. 1st mort., 6 p. ct. gold, due June, 1903, June and Dec. | $200,000 |
| Wyandotte & Det. Riv. Ry. 1st cons. mort., 5 p. ct. gold, due Dec., 1918, June and Dec. | 225,000 |
| Detroit & Flint Ry. Co. 1st con. mort., 5 per cent. gold, due Aug., 1921, Feb. and Aug.. | 1,400,000 |
| Detroit, Roch., Romeo & Lake Orion Ry. 1st mort., 5 p. c., due June, 1920, June and Dec. | 1,100,000 |
| Total...................................................................... | $17,380,000 |

In February, 1902, this company authorized the 4½ per cent. consolidated mortgage, due 1932, for $25,000,000, of which $15,880,000 were to be reserved to retire underlying bonds and $3,000,000 would be available for the company's purposes. Trustee of mortgage, New York Security & Trust Co., New York. Agents for the payment of interest, Kean, Van Cortlandt & Co., New York.

The authorized consolidated mortgage of the Detroit Citizens' Railway Co. is $7,000,000. Trustee of the mortgage, New York Security & Trust Co., New York. Agent for the payment of interest, Kean, Van Cortlandt & Co., New York. The Detroit Railway Co.'s 1st mortgage bonds outstanding are the full amount authorized. Trustee of the mortgage, Cleveland Trust Co., Cleveland. The authorized amount of the Detroit Electric Railway Co.'s consolidated mortgage is $2,800,000. Trustee of the mortgage, Cleveland Trust Co., Cleveland. The outstanding bonds of the Detroit, Ft. Wayne & Belle Isle Railway Co. are the full amount authorized. Trustee of the mortgage, New York Security & Trust Co., New York. Agent for the payment of interest, Kean, Van Cortlandt & Co., New York. Bonds are subject to call at 105 and interest.

The authorized 1st mortgage of the Detroit, Rochester, Romeo & Lake Orion Railway Co. was $1,250,000, of which $150,000 have been canceled. Trustee of the mortgage, American Trust & Savings Bank, Chicago. Interest is payable by the trustee and also by the Guaranty Trust Co., New York. The authorized 1st consolidated mortgage of the Detroit & Flint Railway Co. is $3,000,000, of which $1,100,000 is reserved to retire the outstanding bonds of the Detroit, Rochester, Romeo & Lake Orion Railway Co. and $500,000 is unissued. Trustee of the mortgage and agent for the payment of interest, City Trust Co., New York.

EARNINGS.

Year ending December 31.

| | Gross. | Net. | Charges. | Surplus. |
|---|---|---|---|---|
| 1900........................... | $2,575,276 | $1,136,418 | $616,468 | $519,751 |
| 1901........................... | 2,919,171 | 1,345,472 | 652,277 | 670,129 |
| 1902........................... | 3,473,140 | 1,534,221 | 815,003 | 719,218 |

In 1902 dividend payments were $500,000, leaving a surplus of $219,218.

Chairman, H. A. Everett, Cleveland; President and General Manager, Jere C. Hutchins; Vice-President, Arthur Pack, Detroit; Secretary, Edward Henderson, New York; Treasurer, George H. Russel; Assistant Secretary, A. E. Peters, Detroit.

Directors—J. C. Hutchins, George H. Russel, Arthur Pack, Detroit; H. R. Newcomb, H. A. Everett, E. W. Moore, R. A. Harman, Cleveland; R. B. Van Courtlandt, New York; H. S. Holt, Montreal.

Main office, Detroit. Annual meeting in January at Detroit.

---

## DETROIT, YPSILANTI, ANN ARBOR & JACKSON RAILWAY CO.

A corporation formed under the laws of Michigan, January 23, 1901. The company is a combination of the following companies, which were reorganized and merged in the present corporation:

| | |
|---|---|
| Detroit, Ypsilanti & Ann Arbor Railway Co. | Ypsilanti & Saline Electric Ry. Co. |
| Ann Arbor & Ypsilanti Electric Railway Co. | Ann Arbor Street Railway Co. |

The company owns and operates 100 miles of electric road, extending from Detroit to Jackson and Ypsilanti to Saline, Mich., and the Ann Arbor city system. The road serves a population of 405,689. The company owns a power-house at Ypsilanti, repair shops, etc.

Stock......Par $100...........................Authorized, $2,600,000......Issued, 2,600,000

The company has no preferred stock. Stock is transferred at the office of the company.

FUNDED DEBT.

| | |
|---|---|
| 1st mort., 5 per cent. gold, due Feb., 1926, Feb. and Aug. | $1,610,000 |
| Detroit, Ypsilanti & Ann Arbor Ry. Co. 1st mort., 6 p.ct., due Nov., 1917, Nov. and May. | 600,000 |
| Detroit, Ypsilanti & Ann Arbor Ry. 1st con. mort., 6 p.ct., due Feb. 1924, Feb. and Aug. | 330,000 |
| Ypsilanti & Saline Electric Ry. Co. 1st mort., 6 per cent., due July 1919, July and Jan. | 60,000 |
| Total | $2,600,000 |

The authorized 1st mortgage is $2,600,000, of which $990,000 is reserved to retire prior liens. Trustee of mortgage and agent for the payment of interest, Detroit Trust Co.

The outstanding bonds of the Detroit, Ypsilanti & Ann Arbor Railway Co.'s 1st mortgage are the full amount authorized. Trustee of the mortgage and agent for the payment of interest, Union Trust Co., Detroit. The authorized amount of the consolidated mortgage of the Detroit, Ypsilanti & Ann Arbor Railway Co. is $1,000,000, of which $600,000 are reserved to retire the 1st mortgage of the company and $70,000 have not been issued. Trustee of the mortgage and agent for the payment of interest, Union Trust Co., Detroit.

resi ent, James D. Hawks; Vice-President and Treasurer, S. F. Angus; Secretary, Ford A. Hinchman.

Directors—James D. Hawks, S. F. Angus, George M. Crocker, O. Bingham, A. L. C. Henry.

Main office, Dearborn, Mich. Annual meeting, last Monday in January, at Dearborn, Mich.

## THE DEVELOPMENT CO. OF CUBA

A corporation formed under the laws of New Jersey in 1901. The purpose of the company is to engage in the purchase, sale and development of agricultural timber and mining lands in Cuba. The company owns land near Ciego de Avila in Cuba and has established the town site of Ceballos near Ciego. It is largely engaged in citrus culture and makes a specialty of the cultivation of small tracts of lands for investors.

Stock......Par $100.....Authorized { com., $200,000; pref., 150,000 } Issued { com., $200,000; pref., 150,000 } $350,000

The company is a close corporation. It has no funded debt.

President, August Heckscher; Vice-President, J. M. Ceballos, New York; 2d Vice-President, Hugo Lange; Secretary, George H. Gillett; Assistant Secretary, F. J. Atkins; Treasurer, Carl von Pustau.

Directors—L. E. Bomeisler, J. M. Ceballos, George H. Gillett, Arthur Hansl, August Heckscher, Robert Hewitt, Hugo Lange, George W. Mark, Carl von Pustau.

Main office, 27 William street, New York. Fiscal Agents, J. M. Ceballos & Co., 27 William street, New York. Annual meeting in February.

## DIAMOND MATCH CO.

An Illinois corporation, organized 1889, succeeding a company of same name incorporated in Connecticut. Owns and operates match factories in Detroit, Mich.; Barberton, O.; Oswego, N. Y.; and Oskosh, Wis.; has stores in Baltimore and Philadelphia and sawmills at Green Bay, Wis.; Athol, Mass.; Keene, N. H., etc., with timber rights to a considerable tract near last named places. The company owns patents on machinery used in manufacturing matches, and has interests in companies using its processes and machinery in foreign countries. In the summer of 1899 the company acquired the factories of the Continental Match Co. at Detroit, Mich.; Ogdensburg, N. Y.; Kankakee, Ill.; and Passaic, N. J.; and the American Match Co., Aurora, Ind. In 1901 an interest in the Bryant & May Co. of Great Britain was acquired.

Stock......Par $100........................Authorized, $15,000,000..... Issued, $15,000,000

Stock is transferred at the company's office in New York and by the Illinois Trust & Savings Bank, Chicago. Registrars, Merchants' Loan & Trust Co., Chicago; Bowling Green Trust Co., New York.

In February, 1895, stock was increased from $9,000,000 to $11,000,000. Half of increase was distributed as a dividend and stockholders were given right to subscribe for remaining $1,000,000 at par. In 1893 stock was increased from $7,500,000 to $9,000,000 to provide increased facilities, etc. In August, 1899, the stock was increased from $11,000,000 to $15,000,000 to provide for the acquisition of the Continental Match Co. and other properties mentioned above and to pay a floating debt of $1,250,000. Stockholders of record, July 24, 1899, had the right to subscribe at par for $2,750,000 of the increase or 25 per cent. of their original holdings.

Dividends paid were as follows: in 1893, 20 per cent.; in 1894, 10 per cent.; in 1895, 21½ per cent.; in 1896 and subsequently, 10 per cent. Dividends are paid quarterly, at the rate of 2½ per cent., in March, June, September and December.

The company has no funded debt, but in 1902 the Bryant & May Co. authorized a bond issue of about $1,250,000 with which to acquire additional properties.

EARNINGS.

| | Net. | Dividends. | Deductions. | Surplus. |
|---|---|---|---|---|
| 1896 | $1,226,442 | $1,100,000 | ..... .. | ...... |
| 1897 | 1,274,918 | 1,100,000 | ...... | ...... |
| 1898 | 1,155,997 | 1,100,000 | $31,500 | $24,497 |
| 1899 | 1,513,767 | 1,193,750 | ...... | 320,017 |
| 1900 | 2,014,839 | 1,475,000 | 259,856 | 279,983 |
| 1901 | 2,021,072 | 1,482,787 | ...... | 538,285 |
| 1902 | 1,957,674 | 1,500,000 | ...... | 457,674 |

The deductions from income are amounts charged off for depreciation or other accounts. The company on December 31, 1901, had a total surplus of $1,736,919.

President, Ohio C. Barber, New York; Vice-President, James Hopkins, St. Louis; Secretary, Ralph E. Wirt; Auditor, H. C. Cranz; Treasurer, John K. Robinson, New York; Assistant Secretaries, F. Armbruster, John Morava, Chicago; W. C. Findley, New York.

Directors—Ohio C. Barber, A. G. Lindsay, W. M. Graves, C. H. Palmer, John K. Robinson, George T. Smith, James Hopkins.

Main office, 56 Michigan avenue, Chicago; New York office, 27 William street. Annual meeting, first Wednesday in February.

## THE DIAMOND STATE STEEL CO.

A corporation formed under the laws of Delaware, in 1901, to take over the property of the Diamond State Steel Co. The latter leased for 999 years the plant of the Diamond State Iron Co., of Wilmington, Del. This comprised rolling mills, spike works, machine bolt and nut works, rivet works, horse-shoe manufactory, foundry, machine shops, etc. This company also built a large open hearth steel plant of five furnaces with the necessary adjuncts, which is in operation. The lease of the Diamond State Iron Co. property was at an annual rental of $40,000, or 4 per cent. on the $1,000,000 stock of that company.

Stock.....Par $10.....Authorized { com., $2,000,000; pref., 2,250,000 } Issued { com., $2,000,000; pref., 2,250,000 } $4,250,00

The preferred stock is 7 per cent., non-cumulative.

Stock is transferred at the company's office, Philadelphia. Registrar, The Investment Co. of Philadelphia.

The old company paid dividends of 4 per cent. on its stock in January, 1900; July, 1900; January, 1901, and July, 1901, but no dividend was paid in January, 1902.

FUNDED DEBT.

1st mortgage, 4 per cent., due 2000, May and Nov................................ $1,000,000

The fiscal year of the company ends July 1.

President, H. T. Wallace; Treasurer, J. E. McKee, Jr.; Secretary, W. H. Wallace, Wilmington, Del.

Directors—Edward B. Smith, Henry Tatnall, George W. Norris, Edward Wolf, George McCall, Walter M. Graham, Joseph A. Clark, Philadelphia; H. T. Wallace, T. Coleman du Pont, George W. Todd, Wilmington, Del.

Main office, Wilmington, Del.; Philadelphia office, Broad and Chestnut streets; New York office, 29 Broadway.

## DISTILLERS SECURITIES CORPORATION

A corporation formed under the laws of New Jersey, September 18, 1902. The company was organized to acquire the stocks and property of the Distilling Co. of America and to readjust and simplify the capital of that company. See full statement of the Distilling Co. of America and its constituent concerns to the MANUAL for 1902.

The Distillers Securities Corporation acquired 90 per cent. of the preferred stock and 92 per cent. of the common stock of the Distilling Co. of America. The Companies controlled by the Distilling Co. of America are engaged in the manufacture, distribution and sale of spirits, alcohol, Kentucky or Bourbon whiskey, rye whiskey, and their compounding and blending. The spirits and alcohol business is conducted by the American Spirits Manufacturing Co. and the Standard Distilling & Distributing Co. The Bourbon whiskey business is conducted by the Kentucky Distilleries & Warehouse Co., and the rye whiskey business by the Hannis Distilling Co.

Stock......Par $100........................Authorized, $32,500,000......Issued, $29,139,076

The unissued balance of the stock is held to retire the remaining shares of the Distilling Company of America.

The first dividend on the stock was 1 per cent. quarterly, paid January 15, 1903.

FUNDED DEBT.

| | |
|---|---|
| Collateral trust mort., 5 per cent., due Oct., 1927, April and Oct. | $13,116,000 |
| American Spirits Mfg. Co., 1st mort., 6 per cent., due Sept., 1913, March and Sept. | 1,750,000 |
| Distilling Co. of Am., col. trust mort., 5 per cent., due Jan., 1911, Jan. and July.... | 3,800,000 |
| Total | $17,866,000 |

Trustee of the collateral trust mortgage and agent for the payment of interest, Mercantile Trust Co., New York. The stock, both common and preferred, of the Distilling Co. of America acquired by this company is deposited with the trustee as well as $1,208,000 of the Distilling Co. of America's 5 per cent. bonds. There are also deposited with the trustee nearly all the stocks of the different constituent companies. Holders of the Distillers Securities Corporation collateral trust bonds can convert them into stock at par at any time within ten years. These bonds are also redeemable at 105 after 1908, at the company's office.

The Distilling Co. of America had $44,576,117 of common and $29,502,073 of 7 per cent. cumulative preferred stock. The company, which was formed in 1899, had a large amount of accumulated preferred stock dividends. In 1900 a readjustment of its finances was proposed, and in June, 1902, this was undertaken by a committee consisting of Rudulph Ellis, Philadelphia; Crawford Livingston, and Valentine P. Snyder, New York. The securities of the Distilling Co. of America were exchanged for those of the present company on the following terms:

| Each 1,000. | Received: New Stock. | Received: New Bonds. |
|---|---|---|
| Distilling Co. of America, common stock | $170 | .... |
| " " " preferred stock | 700 | $210 |
| " " " 5 per cent. bonds | 200 | 1,000 |
| American Spirits Manufacturing Co. 6 per cent. bonds | .... | 1,000 |

Holders of the preferred stock of the Distilling Co. of America were entitled to subscribe at par to the extent of 13 per cent. of their holdings, receiving also a bonus of 50 per cent. in new stock. An additional $716,000 of the new bonds was offered as a bonus for the exchange of the Distilling Co. of America 5 per cent. bonds for the new bonds at par.

President, E. J. Curley; Vice-President, W. P. Ward; Secretary and Treasurer, Horace S. Gould; Assistant Treasurer, B. W. Jones.

Directors—E. J. Curley, Amory G. Hodges, Russell Murray, W. P. Ward, Horace S. Gould, New York; W. Brentwood Smith, Philadelphia; J. E. Hulshizer, Jersey City.

Executive Committee—E. J. Curley, W. P. Ward, Amory G. Hodges.

Main office, 27 William street, New York.

---

## DOMINION COAL CO., LIMITED

A corporation formed under charter of the Province of Nova Scotia, in 1893, to lease and operate bituminous coal deposits on Cape Breton Island. The company has a grant of same for a term of 99 years under a royalty of 12½c. a ton, graded according to the output.

The company has completed the Sydney & Louisburg Railway, 40 miles, with 57 miles of sidings. Locomotives, 19; passenger cars, 12; freight cars, 1,335. Has extensive shipping facilities and docks at Louisburg and Sydney, together with 5 steamships, 2 tugs and 5 barges.

On September 30, 1897, the company made a contract for 25 years with the New England Gas & Coke Co., but the contract was superseded by an amended contract commencing November, 1902.

In 1899 the company made a further contract with the Dominion Iron & Steel Co. to supply that company with coal for a term of years, the Iron & Steel Co. having a right up to 1903 to lease this company for interest, dividends on preferred stock and 6 per cent. on common. In June, 1902, this company was leased to the Dominion Iron & Steel Co. for 99 years at a rental of $1,600,000 per annum, payable quarterly, and a royalty of 7½c. per ton on all coal mined in excess of 3,500,000 tons per annum.

The coal output of this company has been as follows in the years ending February 28: 1900, 1,739,374 tons; 1901, 2,044,877 tons; 1902, 2,651,263 tons.

Stock...Par $100..Authorized { com., $15,000,000 / pref., 3,000,000 } Issued { com., $15,000,000 / pref., 3,000,000 } $18,000,000

The preferred stock has a preference of 8 per cent. In 1896 $500,000 of preferred stock held in treasury was sold to provide for improvements. In 1900 $1,000,000 more preferred was allotted to stockholders at 110.

The dividends on the preferred stock have been regularly paid, 4 per cent. semi-annually, in January and July.

Dividends on the common stock, under the lease, are 8 per cent. per annum, 2 per cent. quarterly, the dividend periods being January (1), April, July and October.

FUNDED DEBT.

1st mort., 6 per cent., due March, 1913, March and Sept. ........................ $2,571,000

There is a sinking fund of 5c. per ton on all coal shipped to provide for retirement of bonds. March 1, 1902, there was $134,547 in sinking fund.

The company also has real estate debentures amounting to an aggregate of $578,782.

EARNINGS.

Year ending February 28.

| | Gross Profit. | Net. | Interest. | Surplus. |
|---|---|---|---|---|
| 1895-96 | $410,034 | $343,222 | $168,563 | $174,659 |
| 1896-97 | 589,301 | 508,753 | 267,938 | 240,815 |
| 1897-98 | ...... | 540,853 | 242,257 | 279,316 |
| 1898-99 | ...... | 679,304 | 253,518 | 373,259 |
| 1899-00 | ...... | 746,926 | 307,046 | 439,880 |
| 1900-01 | ...... | 787,294 | 310,761 | 476,533 |
| 1901-02 | ...... | 1,551,880 | 374,209 | 1,177,671 |

In fiscal year 1894-95 sinking fund requirements were $32,623, and dividends on preferred, 8 per cent., $120,000. An amount of $105,808 received for railroad subsidy is not included in earnings. In 1896-97 surplus over 8 per cent. dividends on preferred was $80,815. In 1897-98 after 8 per cent. dividends on preferred and $79,547 charged for improvements surplus was $39,769. In 1899 after dividends on preferred and $144,587 charged to improvements, surplus was $68,672. In 1900 $89,741 was charged to extensions and $125,178 for improvements, after which, and the payment of 8 per cent. on the preferred, the surplus was $64,961. In 1901 $104,018 was cleared off, and $213,333 paid for dividends on the preferred, leaving a surplus of $159,182. In 1902 dividends on preferred, $240,000; balance surplus, $937,681.

President, James Ross; Vice-Presidents, L. J. Forget, Montreal; George A. Cox, Toronto; G. H. Duggen, C. Shields, Glace Bay, Cape Breton; Secretary and Treasurer, J. Mackay, Montreal.

Directors—Henry M. Whitney, Boston; J. S. McLennan, Sydney, N. S.; James Ross, Sir William C. Van Horne, R. B. Angus, L. J. Forget, Montreal; George A. Cox, Toronto; Lord Strathcona and Mount Royal, London, England; W. B. Ross, David MacKeen, Halifax, N. S.; H. F. Dimock, F. S. Pearson, New York.

Main office, Liverpool & London & Globe Building, Montreal. Annual meeting, first Thursday in March.

---

## THE DOMINION COTTON MILLS CO., LIMITED

A corporation formed under the laws of the Dominion of Canada in 1890. The business of the company is the spinning of cotton yarns and the manufacture of cotton goods.

Stock......Par $100........................Authorized, $3,033,600......Issued, $3,033,600

Stock is transferred at the company's office.

FUNDED DEBT.

Debentures, 6 per cent., due 1915 ............................................. $3,700,000

President, A. F. Gault; Vice-President, L. J. Forget; Manager, A. B. Mole; Secretary, C. E. Hanna.

Directors—A. F. Gault, J. Grenier, S. H. Ewing, Samuel Finley, L. J. Forget, C. E. Gault, James Wilson.

Main office, 316 St. James street, Montreal. Annual meeting in April.

---

## DOMINION IRON & STEEL CO.

A corporation formed under the laws of Nova Scotia, June 22, 1899. The company has established large iron and steel plants at Sydney, Cape Breton, with a capacity of from 1,000 to 1,200 tons of steel per day. The company has 700 acres of land at Sydney and other real estate. In addition to the steel mills the plant comprises four blast furnaces with a capacity of 1,000 tons daily and 400 coke ovens producing 1,600 tons of coke per day. The company has also acquired the iron ore properties at Belle Island, Newfoundland, at a reported cost of $1,000,000. The works make steel by the open hearth process and will be devoted largely to the production of all forms of structural steel. Construction was begun in the summer of 1899, and the furnaces and other departments began operating in the early part of 1901.

This company has an important contract with the Dominion Coal Co., by which the latter agrees to supply it with coal at $1.24 per ton for its requirements. In June, 1902 this company leased the Dominion Coal Co. for 99 years. See statement of that company.

In December, 1901, a syndicate, headed by James Ross of Montreal, acquired control of this company.

Stock...Par $100...Authorized { com., $20,000,000 / pref., 5,000,000 } Issued { com., $20,000,000 / pref., 5,000,000 } $25,000,000

The preferred stock is 7 per cent., cumulative. It was created in January, 1901, and was issued to provide additional funds for construction work. The preferred stock may be called and retired at 115, or holders may convert it into common stock at any time.

The common stock was increased from $15,000,000 to $20,000,000 in April, 1902. The increase of $5,000,000 being sold to the stockholders at 60.

Transfer Agents, American Loan & Trust Co., Boston, and National Trust Co. of Ontario, Montreal.

The first dividend on the preferred stock was 3½ per cent., October 1, 1901. Dividends on the preferred are semi-annual, in April and October, at the rate of 3½ per cent.

FUNDED DEBT.

1st mort., 5 per cent., due July, 1929, Jan. and July.................................. $7,946,000

The 1st mortgage is $8,000,000, authorized. The trustee is the National Trust Co., Limited, of Montreal. There is a sinking fund of $50,000 per annum for the bonds which are to be drawn at 110 and interest.

President, James Ross; Vice-Presidents, L. J. Forget, Montreal; George A. Cox, Toronto; C. Shields, S. H. Duggan, Sydney, N. S.; Treasurer, J. Mackay; Secretary, W. A. Ross, Montreal.

Directors—James Ross, Sir William C. Van Horne, L. J. Forget, Robert Mackay, R. B. Angus, Montreal; George A. Cox, Elias Rogers, Toronto; H. M. Whitney, Boston; H. F. Dimock, F. S. Pearson, New York; W. B Ross, B. F. Pearson, Halifax; A. H. Paget, J. S. McLennan, Sydney, N. S.

Main office, Liverpool & London & Globe Building, Montreal; operating office, Sydney, Cape Breton. Annual meeting, first Monday in March.

## DOMINION SECURITIES CO.

A corporation formed under the laws of New Jersey in May, 1901. The objects of the company are to acquire properties and securities of railway and other corporations in the Dominion of Canada and elsewhere and to construct and manage the same. It acquired the securities and franchises of the Cape Breton Railway Co., Limited, of Nova Scotia, and was engaged in the construction thereof. See statement of the Cape Breton Railway Co. in the Railway Department of the MANUAL. It also acquired other properties and franchises which are in process of development.

Stock......Par $100.......................... Authorized, $1,500,000......Issued, $1,500,000

The company has no preferred stock or funded debt. The stock is full paid and non-assessable.

Transfer Agent, Continental Trust Co., New York. Registrar, Standard Trust Co., New York.

On January 15, 1902, the company paid its first 2½ per cent. semi-annual dividend out of the earnings for the six months preceding.

President, William A. Prendergast; Vice-President, H. F. Ballantyne; Secretary, H. C. Carson.

Directors—William A. Prendergast, Thomas E. Wing, William C. White, Samuel Wolverton, William H. Porter, James G. Cannon, H. M. Wolfe, Alfred Schiffer, H. C. Carson, H. F. Ballantyne, J. A. Minor.

Corporate office, 15 Exchange place, Jersey City; New York office, 22 Pine street. Annual meeting, first day in June, at Jersey City.

## DOMINION TELEGRAPH CO.

A corporation formed under the laws of the Dominion of Canada in 1871 for the purpose of building and operating telegraph lines. The company owns a telegraph system that extends throughout Canada. Its entire system is leased to the Western Union Telegraph Co., which operates these lines, that are in New Brunswick and Nova Scotia, and sub-lets to the Great Northwestern Telegraph Co. the lines situated west of the Province of New Brunswick.

Stock......Par $50.......................... Authorized, $1,000,000......Issued, $1,000,000

The company has no preferred stock and no funded debt. Stock is transferred at the company's office, Toronto.

Dividends on the stock are paid quarterly at the rate of 6 per cent. per annum, that being the rental paid by the Western Union Co. under the lease.

President, Thomas Swinyard; Vice-President, Thomas R. Wood; Secretary and Treasurer, Fred Roper.

Directors—Thomas Swinyard, Thomas R. Wood, Æmilius Jarvis, Robert C. Clowry, Belvidere Brooks, A. G. Ramsay, Henry Pellatt, Thomas F. Clark, Charles O'Reilly.

Main office, 2 Toronto street, Toronto. Annual meeting, second Wednesday in July, at Toronto.

## DORCHESTER GAS LIGHT CO.

A corporation formed under the laws of Massachusetts to manufacture and sell gas in the Dorchester district of Boston and in Milton. Nearly all the stock of the company is owned by the Massachusetts Gas Companies. See statement of the latter company.

Stock......Par $100.............................Authorized $1,000,000......Issued $519,600

The company has no preferred stock and no funded debt.

Dividends of 10 per cent. annually are paid. Dividend payments are quarterly, March (31), June, September and December.

EARNINGS.

Year ending June 30.

| | Gross. | Net. | Charges. | Dividends. | Surplus |
|---|---|---|---|---|---|
| 1900-01 | $275,793 | $94,348 | $16,993 | $57,156 | $20,198 |
| 1901-02 | 301,045 | 98,332 | 18,913 | 51,960 | 27,459 |

President, John T. Burnett; Vice-President, C. A. Stone; Secretary, George H. Finn; Treasurer, Frederic Tudor, Boston.

Directors—C. A. Stone, John T. Burnett, C. M. Weld, William M. Butler, William Endicott, Jr., Boston.

Corporate office, Freeport street, Dorchester district, Boston; main office, 95 Milk street, Boston. Annual meeting, last Thursday in February, at Boston.

## W. L. DOUGLAS SHOE CO.

A corporation formed under the laws of Maine, September 12, 1902. The company is an incorporation of the manufacturing and wholesale and retail business in boots and shoes of W. L. Douglas. The company has a plant at Brockton, Mass., and has 64 retail stores in 45 American cities.

Stock.....Par $100....Authorized { com., $1,000,000 / pref., 1,000,000 } Issued { com., $1,000,000 / pref., 1,000,000 } $2,000,000

The preferred stock is 7 per cent. non-cumulative and is preferred both as to dividends and assets. The common stock was all retained by W. L. Douglas.

Stock is transferred at the office of the company, Brockton, Mass.

Dividends are payable semi-annually, January 15 and July 15.

The company has no funded debt.

President, W. L. Douglas; Vice-President, Charles F. Richmond; Secretary, A. T. Sweetser; Treasurer and General Manager, Herbert L. Tinkham; Assistant Treasurer, Charles D. Nevins, Brockton, Mass.

Directors—W. L. Douglas, Charles F. Richmond, A. T. Sweetser, Herbert L. Tinkham, Frank L. Erskine, William A. Buchanan, Brockton, Mass.; H. T. Drake, Boston.

Corporate office, Portland, Me.; main office, Brockton, Mass. Annual meeting, second Thursday in January, at Portland, Me.

## DRY DOCK, EAST BROADWAY & BATTERY RAILROAD CO.

(Controlled by Third Avenue Railroad Co.)

A corporation formed under the laws of New York, December 8, 1863. In August, 1897, the Third Avenue Railroad obtained control of the company. The company owns 10½ miles of road and 20¼ miles of track in the city of New York.

Stock .....Par $100...........................Authorized, $1,200,000......Issued, $1,200,000

The company has no preferred stock. Registrar, Washington Trust Co., New York.

The November, 1899, dividend on the stock was passed, and none has been paid since.

FUNDED DEBT.

| | |
|---|---|
| 1st mort., 5 per cent. gold, due Dec., 1932, June and Dec. | $950,000 |
| Certificate of indebtedness, 5 per cent., due Feb., 1914, Feb. and Aug. | 1,100,000 |
| Total | $2,050,000 |

EARNINGS.

Year ending June 30.

| | Gross. | Net. | Charges and Div. | Balance. |
|---|---|---|---|---|
| 1892-93 | $730,517 | $222,254 | $222,120 | Sur., $134 |
| 1893-94 | 642,455 | 191,489 | 205,894 | Def., 14,405 |
| 1894-95 | 719,765 | 197,784 | 136,091 | Sur., 61,163 |
| 1895-96 | 743,474 | 197,324 | 205,509 | Def., 8,185 |
| 1896-97 | 687,646 | 204,898 | 191,626 | Sur., 13,272 |
| 1897-98 | 669,713 | 207,392 | 203,798 | Sur., 3,594 |
| 1898-99 | 630,599 | 168,115 | 189,873 | Def., 16,758 |
| 1899-00 | 632,906 | 179,133 | 131,740 | Sur., 47,393 |
| 1900-01 | 582,124 | 182,053 | 130,140 | Sur., 58,328 |
| 1901-02 | 579,560 | 118,983 | 133,635 | Def., 14,652 |

President, Herbert H. Vreeland; Secretary and Treasurer, Charles E. Warren.
Main office, 621 Broadway, New York. Annual meeting, second Tuesday in January.

## DULUTH-SUPERIOR TRACTION CO.

A corporation formed under the laws of Connecticut in 1900. It is a consolidation of the following companies:

Duluth Street Railway Co.
Superior Rapid Transit Co.
Lakeside Street Railway Co.

The company controls the electric systems of Duluth, Minn., and West Superior, Wis., operating 73 miles of track. It owns an electric power station at Duluth and West Superior and 107 motor cars.

Stock...Par $100...Authorized { com., $3,500,000; pref., 1,500,000 } Issued { com., $3,500,000; pref., 1,500,000 } $5,000,000

The preferred stock is 4 per cent., cumulative. Transfer Agent, Farmers' Loan & Trust Co., New York. Registrar, Central Trust Co., New York.

FUNDED DEBT.

Duluth Street Railway Co., 1st mort., 5 per cent. gold, due May, 1930, May and Nov.... $2,200,000

The authorized amount of the Duluth Street Railway mortgage is $2,500,000, of which $300,000 is reserved for extensions. The mortgage covers all the properties of the Duluth-Superior Traction Co., which were first transferred to the Duluth Street Railway Co. Trustee of the mortgage and agent for the payment of interest, Central Trust Co., New York.

| EARNINGS. | Gross. | Net. |
|---|---|---|
| 1901 | $453,704 | $92,422 |
| 1902 | 538,030 | 133,382 |

President, C. G. Goodrich; Secretary and Treasurer, L. Mendenhall, Duluth, Minn.

Directors—Thomas Lowrey, C. G. Goodrich, Minneapolis; M. D. Munn, St. Paul; L. Mendenhall, G. G. Hartley, Duluth, Minn.; W. J. Hayes, Cleveland; John H. Davis, Walter Hinchman, New York.

Main office, 1108 North Michigan street, Duluth, Minn. Annual meeting, fourth Tuesday in January, at New Haven, Conn.

## JAMES H. DUNHAM & CO.

A corporation formed under the laws of New York, June 14, 1901. The object of the organization was to take over and conduct the wholesale dry goods business of the firm of James H. Dunham & Co., New York.

Stock..Par $100...Authorized { com., $1,250,000; 1st pref., 1,000,000; 2d pref., 500,000 } Issued { com., $1,050,000; 1st pref., 1,000,000; 2d pref., 500,000 } $2,550,000

The 1st preferred stock is 6 per cent., cumulative, and 2d preferred is 5 per cent., cumulative. The preferred stocks have in their respective orders a preference as to assets in case of liquidation.

Stocks are transferred at the company's office, 340 Broadway, New York. Registrar, Knickerbocker Trust Co., New York.

The regular dividends on the 1st and second preferred at their respective rates are paid quarterly, in January, April, July and October.

The company has no funded debt.

The net earnings of the company from its formation to December 31, 1901, were $107,272. Out of which $30,000 was paid for dividends on the 1st preferred and $12,500 and $21,000 were appropriated for dividends on the 2d preferred and common, leaving a balance of $43,000 carried to future dividend account. The total assets of the company December 31, 1901, were $4,007,021.

President, William A. Little; Vice-President, William E. Webb; Secretary, James M. Tappen; Treasurer, John R. Browne.

Directors—William A. Little, William E. Webb, Theodore W. Luling, William B. Goodwin, William C. Engle.

Corporate and main office, 340 Broadway, New York.

## THE DUNLOP TIRE CO., LIMITED

A corporation formed under the Ontario Companies' Act in 1899 for the purpose of manufacturing rubber tires.

Stock......Par $100.......Authorized { com., $700,000 / pref., 300,000 } Issued { com., $700,000 / pref., 300,000 } $1,000,000

The preferred stock is 7 per cent., cumulative, and has a preference as to the assets of the company in liquidation. Transfer Agent and Registrar, National Trust Co., Toronto.

Dividends paid in 1900 were: On the common stock, 6 per cent., and on the preferred, 7 per cent. Dividend periods are January and July.

The company has no funded debt.

President, Warren Y. Soper; Vice-President, E. B. Ryckman; Managing Director, J. Westren.

Directors—Warren Y. Soper, E. B. Ryckman, J. Westren, George A. Cox, W. E. Wellington.

Corporate and main office, 21 Temperance street, Toronto, Ont. Annual meeting, in January, at Toronto.

## DWIGHT MANUFACTURING CO.

A corporation formed under the laws of Massachusetts in 1841 for the purpose of cotton manufacturing. The company owns mills in Chicopee, Mass., and Alabama City, Ala.

Stock......Par $500..........................Authorized, $1,200,000......Issued, $1,200,000

The company has no preferred stock and no funded debt. Stock is transferred at the office of the company, Boston.

Accounts are made up semi-annually and dividends are usually paid in January and July. Dividends of 12 per cent. were paid for the year ending July 1, 1902.

For the year ending July 1, 1902, the quick assets were $1,523,656.40; debts, $245,425.55; surplus, $1,278,230.85.

President, T. Jefferson Coolidge; Clerk, George H. Nutting; Treasurer, J. Howard Nichols, Boston.

Directors—T. Jefferson Coolidge, Amory A. Lawrence, George P. Gardner, Boston; Amos W. Stetson, Braintree, Mass.; Arthur T. Lyman, Waltham, Mass.; J. Howard Nichols, Newton, Mass.

Corporate and main office, 53 State street, Boston; branch offices, Chicopee, Mass., and Alabama City, Ala. Annual meeting, second Monday in July, at Boston.

## EAGLE AND PHENIX MILLS

A corporation formed under the laws of Georgia, May 9, 1898, for the purpose of the manufacture of cotton and woolen goods. The plant covers two city blocks in Columbus, Ga., and is one of the largest textile manufactories in the South. It comprises 4 cotton mills and a woolen mill, warehouses, dye house, an electric plant, office buildings, storage houses, etc. All the buildings are of brick and are equipped with modern machinery and protected by fire sprinklers. Water power is furnished by 10 turbine wheels of about 3,000 horse power. The company operates 2,000 looms and 62,000 spindles.

Stock......Par $100..... .......................Authorized, $2,000,000......Issued, $750,000

The company has no preferred stock. Stock is transferred at the corporate office, 1,237 Front street, Columbus, Ga.

Dividends of 3 per cent. have been paid semi-annually since April 1, 1899, April 1 and October 1.

FUNDED DEBT.

1st mort., 6 per cent. gold, due July 15, 1928, Jan. and July........................$500,000

The bonds are subject to call after five years from July, 1898, at 105 and interest. Trustee, The Trust Co. of Georgia, Atlanta, Ga. Agents for the payment of interest, New York Security & Trust Co., New York, and The Trust Co. of Georgia, Atlanta, Ga.

President, G. Gunby Jordan; Vice-President, W. C. Bradley; Secretary, C. L. Pelrce; Treasurer, E. N. Clemence, Columbus, Ga.

Directors—G. Gunby Jordan, W. C. Bradley, Columbus, Ga.; J. F. Hanson, E. T. Comer, Macon, Ga.; J. W. English, Atlanta, Ga.; George P. Harrison, Opelika, Ala.; Mark W. Munroe, Quincy, Fla.; Henry Buist, Charleston, S. C.; John G. Ruge, Apalachicola, Fla.

Main office, 1,237 Front street, Columbus, Ga. Annual meeting, first Wednesday in July, at Columbus, Ga.

## EAST BOSTON CO.

A corporation formed under the laws of Massachusetts, March 25, 1833, to purchase and improve the island, in the city of Boston, called Noodle's Island, now East Boston. The company owns about 37,500,000 square feet of land, exclusive of 3,500,000 square feet taken by the commonwealth of Massachusetts for dock purposes. Many plans are under way which will enhance the value of the company's property, including the completion of the East Boston tunnel.

Stock......No par value................Authorized, 150,000 shares......Issued, 150,000 shares.

Transfer Agent, Charles E. Adams. Registrar, Old Colony Trust Co., Boston, Mass.

Dividends have been paid at irregular intervals and have consisted of cash, land receipts, ferry stock and Eastern Railroad shares. In all about $2,146,000 has been distributed to the company's shareholders.

At the close of 1902 the company had $350,000 in cash and no indebtedness of any kind.

President, John C. Watson; Treasurer, Charles E. Adams, Boston.

Directors—George B. James, George A. Alden, Henry F. Ross, Charles G. White, Paul H. Kendricken, John C. Watson, Charles E. Adams, Boston.

Main office, 78 Devonshire street, Boston. Annual meeting, first Monday in May, at Boston.

## THE EAST JERSEY WATER CO.

A corporation formed under the laws of New Jersey. The company has a pumping station at Little Falls, N. J., with a daily capacity of 60,000,000 gallons, and in conjunction therewith a filter plant with a daily capacity of 50,000,000 gallons. It has a reservoir on Garret Mount with a capacity of 150,000,000 gallons and a steel conduit from the pumping station to the reservoir and across the Passaic River to Belleville and Kearney in Hudson County, N. J.

Stock......Par $100..............................Authorized, $500,000......Issued, $500,000

The company has no preferred stock and no funded debt. Stock is transferred at the office of the company. The shares of the company are in the hands of a holding company and are not on the market.

President, H. C. Fahnestock, New York; Vice-President, Edmund LeB. Gardiner; Secretary, A. P. Fisher, Paterson, N. J.; Treasurer, F. L. Hine; Assistant Treasurer, S. A. Cunningham, New York.

Directors—George F. Baker, H. F. Fahnestock, E. D. Adams, New York; F. L. Hine, Brooklyn; Edmund LeB. Gardiner, Ridgewood, N. J.

Corporate and main office, 158 Ellison street, Paterson, N. J.; New York office, 2 Wall street. Annual meeting, first Tuesday in August, at Paterson, N. J.

## EASTERN SHIPBUILDING CO.

A corporation formed under the laws of New Jersey in March, 1900. The business of the company is the construction of steamships and steam vessels generally. It has extensive works and yards at New London, Conn.

Stock......Par $100..............................Authorized, $500,000......Issued, $500,000

The company has no funded debt. Transfer Agent, Guaranty Trust Co., New York.

The company commenced operations in the summer of 1900 and has made no report. The two steamers it is building are for the Great Northern Steamship Co. for the Pacific trade and will be the largest in the world, having each a displacement of 33,000 tons and a net tonnage of 20,000 tons, being 630 feet long and 73 feet beam.

President, Charles R. Hanscom; Secretary and Treasurer, Frank W. Allen; Assistant Treasurer, Frank M. Swift, New London, Conn.

Directors—Mason S. Chace, Elizabeth, N. J.; Lewis Nixon, A. C. Gary, New York; Charles R. Hanscom, Frank M. Swift, William C. Besselievre, Frank W. Allen, New London, Conn.

Main office, New London, Conn. Annual meeting, first Monday in March, at Jersey City.

## EASTERN STATES REFRIGERATING CO.

A corporation formed under the laws of New Jersey, May 31, 1900. The company owns and operates the Springfield Cold Storage Co., Springfield, Mass., and the Capital City Cold Storage & Warehouse Co., Albany, N. Y. The united capacity of its warehouses is about 1,000 cars of perishable goods.

Stock......Par $100..............................Authorized, $500,000......Issued, $107,000

Transfer Agent, Corporation Trust Co. of New Jersey, Jersey City.

The company paid an initial dividend of 2 per cent. on its stock, November 20, 1900.

FUNDED DEBT.

1st mort., 5 per cent., May and Nov.............................. .................. $200,000

Trustee of the mortgage, Albany Trust Co., Albany, N. Y.

It is stated that the earnings of the company in the first six months of operation were equal to fully 15 per cent. on its capital.

President, C. H. Parsons, Springfield, Mass.; Secretary, DeWitt C. Becker, Albany, N. Y.; Treasurer, W. H. Parks, Springfield, Mass.; General Manager, H. W. Griswold, Albany, N. Y.

Directors—C. H. Parsons, H. H. Bowman, W. H. Parks, Springfield, Mass.; DeWitt C. Becker, H. W. Griswold, C. R. Sutherland, Richard Stephens, Albany, N. Y.; Louis B. Dailey, Jersey City; F. F. Judd, Boston.

Main offices, Springfield, Mass., and Albany, N. Y.; corporate office, 60 Grand street, Jersey City. Annual meeting, third Tuesday in March.

## EASTMAN KODAK CO.

A corporation formed under the laws of New Jersey, October 24, 1901. The company was organized to combine the ownership of the Eastman Kodak Co. of New York, the General Aristo Co. and Kodak, Limited, the latter being an English company. See MANUAL for 1901 for details regarding the three corporations named above. The business of the company is the manufacture and sale of cameras and photographic materials and supplies. In 1902 the company acquired control of the M. A. Seed Dry Plate Co., St. Louis.

Stock..Par $100...Authorized { com., $25,000,000 / pref., 10,000,000 } Issued { com., $18,797,500 / pref., 6,186,300 } $24,983,800

The preferred stock is 6 per cent., cumulative, and has a preference as to assets.

The company acquired the stocks of the Eastman Kodak Co. and the General Aristo Co., which were merged into one company. It also offered the holders of Kodak, Limited, shares, £1 1s. in new preferred for each £1 of old preferred, and £2 10s. in new common for each £1 of old common, the exchange being on the basis of $4.85 to the £1. In the year 1900 the aggregate earnings of the Kodak Co. were $2,279,082; in 1901, $2,502,702.

The company has no funded debt or other indebtedness beyond current bills payable. Transfer Agent, Alliance Bank, Rochester, N. Y. Registrar, Security Trust Co., Rochester, N. Y.

The dividend periods are January, April, July and October. In 1902 the dividend rate paid on the preferred stock was 6 per cent. and on the common 10 per cent.

President, George Eastman; Vice-President and Treasurer, Henry A. Strong, Rochester, N.Y.; 2d Vice-President, Charles S. Abbott, Jamestown, N.Y.; Secretary, Walter S. Hubbell; Assistant Secretary, A. K. Whitney, Rochester, N. Y.

Directors—George Eastman, Henry A. Strong, Edwin O. Sage, George Elwanger, Walter F. Hubbell, Rochester, N. Y.; Charles S. Abbott, Jamestown, N. Y.; William H. Corbin, Jersey City; Sir James Pender, Lord Kelvin, London, England.

Main office, 343 State street, Rochester, N. Y.; London office, 48 Clerkenwell road, E. C.; New York office, 3 West Twenty-second street; Chicago office, 45 East Randolph street; San Francisco office, 643 Market street. Annual meeting, first Tuesday in April, at Jersey City.

## ECONOMY LIGHT & POWER CO.

A corporation formed under the laws of Illinois in July, 1890. The purpose of the company is to supply electric light and power in Chicago and Joliet, Ill. The plant of the company is at Joliet, 35 miles south of Chicago, where it has a water supply from the Des Plaines River, the Illinois & Michigan Central Canal and the Chicago Sanitary Drainage Canal. The plant consists of a dam and a fire-proof building, and has a maximum capacity of 4,100 horse power. The company has an exclusive franchise for supplying gas and electric light and power in Joliet.

Stock......Par $100............. .................Authorized, $850,000......Issued, $400,000

The company has no preferred stock.

FUNDED DEBT.

1st con. mort., 5 per cent. gold bonds, due 1915, May and Nov.. ...................... $400,000

The total amount of bonds authorized is $800,000. Of that amount $300,000 is held to secure the bonds issued and $100,000 for the future needs of the company. A sinking fund of $35,000 annually is provided.

Trustee of the bonds, Illinois Trust & Savings Bank, Chicago. Agent for the payment of interest, Corn Exchange National Bank, Philadelphia.

President, John L. Norton, Lockson, Ill.; Vice-President, Samuel Insul, Chicago; Secretary and Treasurer, R. L. Allen, Joliet, Ill.

Directors—John L. Norton, Samuel Insul, C. H. Randle.

Corporate and main office, 1 West Madison street, Chicago. Annual meeting, third Monday in May, at Chicago.

## EDISON ELECTRIC ILLUMINATING CO. OF BOSTON

A Massachusetts corporation operating electric light and power plants in the city of Boston. The company has twelve power and distributing stations, and on June 30, 1902, there were connected with its circuits 442,634 incandescent lamps, 8,548 arc lights, and electric motors of a total of 19,130 horse power.

Negotiations for a combination of the company with the Boston Electric Light Co. were on foot in 1900, but were not consummated until June, 1901, when practically all the stock of that company was exchanged for Edison Electric Illuminating, 10 shares of which were given for each 10¼ shares of the Boston company.

Stock......Par $100........................Authorized, $9,500,000......Issued, $8,635,500

The stock of the company has been increased from time to time to provide funds for the extension of the plant and distributive system. In December, 1901, $747,100 of new stock was offered to stockholders at $200 per share. In August, 1902, the stock was increased from $7,850,400 tdhits present amount, the stockholders having the right to subscribe at par for 1 new share for eac 10 shares of old stock, payable 70 per cent. forthwith and 30 per cent. May 3, 1903.

Dividends of 7 per cent. were paid on the stock in 1897; in 1898, paid 8 per cent.; in 1899, 8 per cent., and in 1900, 9 per cent. in quarterly dividends of 2 per cent. each in February, May, August and November, with an extra dividend of 1 per cent. in November. The February, 1901, dividend was also 2 per cent. and 1 per cent. extra. In 1902 the quarterly dividends were 2½ per cent. Transfer Agent, Old Colony Trust Co., Boston.

FUNDED DEBT.

Boston Electric Light consols.................................................... $1,250,000

EARNINGS.

| Year ending June 30. | Gross. | Net. |
|---|---|---|
| 1898-99 | $1,002,261 | $338,243 |
| 1899-00 | 1,131,758 | 406,221 |
| 1900-01 | 1,273,989 | 438,603 |
| 1901-02 | 2,460,158 | 975,712 |

Earnings for 1901-02 include the operations of the combined properties. In the same year charges were $132,269; dividends, $727,345; surplus, $116,098.

President, Charles L. Edgar; Vice-President, Walter C. Baylies; Treasurer, Henry B. Cabot; Clerk, J. Otis Wardwell.

Directors—Walter Charles Baylies, George Dexter, Henry B. Cabot, Charles L. Edgar, T. Jefferson Coolidge, Jr., W. C. W. Amory, Robert Bacon, Isaac T. Burr, Everett W. Burdett, C. M. Wild, E. H. Barnes.

General offices, 3 [illegible] place, Boston. Annual meeting, second Tuesday in October.

## EDISON ELECTRIC ILLUMINATING CO. OF BROCKTON

A corporation formed under the laws of Massachusetts. The purpose of the company is to furnish electric light and power in the city of Brockton, Mass. The company has a perpetual franchise.

Stock......Par $100............................Authorized, $150,000......Issued, $150,000

The company has no preferred stock. Transfer Agents, Stone & Webster, 93 Federal street, Boston.

Dividends at the rate of 5 per cent. annual are payable in May and November.

FUNDED DEBT.

| | |
|---|---|
| 1st mort., 5 per cent., gold, due 1930, June and Dec | $100,000 |
| Coupon notes, 5 per cent., due 1921, March and Sept | 75,000 |
| Total | $175,000 |

The authorized 1st mortgage is $200,000. It is redeemable after 1905 at 110. The authorized coupon notes are $100,000, redeemable after 1904 at 105. A sinking fund of $5,000 per year, beginning March 1, 1906, is provided.

Trustee and Registrar of bonds and Trustee of notes, Boston Safe Deposit & Trust Co., Boston, which also pays coupons.

EARNINGS

Year ending June 30.

| | Gross. | Net. | Fixed Charges. | Net Profit. |
|---|---|---|---|---|
| 1900-01 | $80,849.17 | $25,824.75 | $9,939.61 | $15,885.14 |
| 1901-02 | 90,057.68 | 35,001.47 | 8,960.09 | 26,041.38 |

President—F. B. Howard; Vice-President, E. F. Webster; Treasurer, Henry D. Sawyer Clerk, Henry R. Hayes.

Directors—E. S. Webster, C. A. Stone, W. A. Reed, F. B. Howard, Eliott Wadsworth.

Corporate and main office, Brockton, Mass. Annual meeting, first Tuesday in March.

## THE EDISON PORTLAND CEMENT CO.

A corporation formed under the laws of New Jersey, January 7, 1899, its purposes being the mining, manufacture and sale of cement. This company owns 564 acres of cement land in Warren County, N. J., and has a plant with a capacity of 4,000 barrels per day.

Stock...Par $50....Authorized { com., $9,000,000 / pref., 2,000,000 } Issued { com., $9,000,000 / pref., 1,528,400 } $10,528,400

The preferred stock is 8 per cent. cumulative.

Transfer Agents, New Jersey Corporation Guarantee & Trust Co., Camden, N. J. Registrar, The Real Estate, Title Insurance & Trust Co., Philadelphia.

The company has no funded debt.

President, William H. Shelmerdine, Philadelphia; Vice-President, Walter S. Mallory, Orange, N. J.; Treasurer, William S. Pilling; Secretary, Theron I. Crane, Philadelphia; General Manager, Thomas A. Edison, Orange, N. J.; General Superintendent, Edward A. Darling, Steuartsville, N. J.

Directors—Thomas A. Edison, Walter S. Mallory, Luther S. Bent, Harlan Page, William H. Shelmerdine, E. Clarence Miller, William S. Pilling, Theron I. Crane, Andrew H. McNeal, Robert H. Thompson, Thomas M. Thompson, Williard P. Reid.

Main office, Northeast corner Broad and Chestnut streets, Philadelphia. Annual meeting, second Tuesday in April, at Camden, N. J.

## ELECTRIC BOAT CO.

A corporation organized under the laws of New Jersey, February 25, 1899. The company acquired the property and plant of the Electric Launch Co., which manufactures launches, fenders, ferry-boats and other vessels equipped with electric motive power and which had works for that purpose at Morris Heights, N. Y., but moved its plant in 1899 to Bergen Point, N. J. Also acquired control of the Electro-Dynamic Co., of Philadelphia, which manufactures electrical supplies and has factories at Philadelphia and Newark, N. J. This company also owns the Holland Torpedo Boat Co.

Stock....Par $100....Authorized { com., $5,000,000 / pref., 5,000,000 } Issued { com., $4,999,600 / pref., 2,045,000 } $7,044,600

The preferred stock is 8 per cent., non-cumulative. In the subscription for the shares issued at the formation of the company subscribers for one share of preferred received two and one-half of common as a bonus.

Transfer Agent, Manhattan Trust Co., New York. Registrar, Hanover National Bank, New York.

President, Isaac L. Rice; Secretary and Treasurer, Robert A. Lloyd, New York.

Directors—Isaac L. Rice, William Dulles, Jr., Robert McA. Lloyd, John P. Holland, E. B. Frost, New York; William M. Potts, L. T. Paul, Philadelphia.

Main office, 100 Broadway, New York. Annual meeting, second Tuesday in February, at Jersey City.

## THE ELECTRIC CO. OF AMERICA

A corporation formed under the laws of New Jersey, January 4, 1899, for the purpose of purchasing and operating electric, gas and water plants. The company owns and operates the following companies:

Atlantic Electric Light & Power Co., Atlantic City, N. J.

Bridgeport Electric Light & Power Co., Bridgeport, O.

Electric Light Co. of Atlantic City, Atlantic City, N. J.
Scranton Electric Light & Heat Co., Scranton, Pa.
Suburban Electric Light Co., Scranton, Pa.
Scranton Illuminating, Heat & Power Co., Scranton, Pa.
Columbus Colliery, Scranton, Pa.
Dunmore Electric Light, Heat & Power Co., Dunmore, Pa.
The Wheeling Electrical Co., Wheeling, W. Va.
Rockford Edison Co., Rockford, Ill.
Edison Electric Illuminating Co. (controlling interest), Altoona, Pa.
Canton Light, Heat & Power Co., Canton, O.
Auburn Light, Heat & Power Co., Auburn, N.Y.
Conshohocken Gas Light Co., Conshohocken. Pa.
Conshohocken Electric Light & Power Co., Conshohocken, Pa.

The company has also a large interest in the Atlantic City Gas & Water Co.

A consolidation of this company with the American Railways Co. was proposed in 1901, but the plan was abandoned.

Stock......Par $10..........................Authorized, $5,000,000......Issued, $4,078,600

Stock is transferred at the office of the company, Philadelphia.

The authorized capital stock of the company was originally $50,000,000, par value of shares, $50.

Up to January 1, 1902, there had been called and paid in on the stock $7.50, and $2.50 additional was called July 1, 1902, when the stock was reduced to $5,000,000 and the par value to $10 per share, making the stock full paid to that amount. The company has no funded debt.

The company began the payment of dividends by the declaration of one of 50c. per share paid July 25, 1899. It paid dividends of 50c. each in January (1) and July until July, 1901, when 25c. per share was paid, which has since been the regular rate, but in July, 1902, an extra dividend of $1.50 per share was paid, and a dividend of 25c. per share was paid in August, 1902, and 30 cents per share on January 31, 1903.

In 1901 the net earnings were $281,382. In 1902 they were $352,487.

President, A. Loudon Snowden; Vice-President, John H. Catherwood; 2d Vice-President, H. T. Hartman; Secretary and Treasurer, Frank B. Ball.

Directors—A. Loudon Snowden, H. T. Hartman, John A. Catherwood, George A. Cotton, Samuel G. Thompson, George B. Roberts, Frederick W. Walton, Edward D. Toland, Philadelphia; James E. Hays; Camden, N. J.

Corporate office, 301 Market street, Camden, N. J.; executive office, Land Title Building, Philadelphia. Annual meeting, fourth Tuesday in April.

---

## THE ELECTRIC STORAGE BATTERY CO.

A New Jersey company formed in 1888. Acquired, 1894, all patents and good will of a number of companies for the manufacture and sale of storage batteries, including the Consolidated Electric Storage Co., the General Electric Launch Co., the Electric Launch and Navigation Co., and the Accumulator Co. Also battery patents and rights of the Brush Electric Co., of Cleveland, Ohio, and the patents and good will of the battery branch of the General Electric Co., the Bradbury-Stone Electric Storage Co., the Hopedale Electric Co., the Pumpelly-Sorley Battery Co. and the Plante Co. Also United States and Canadian patents and rights of the Accumulatoren Fabrik Aktiengesellschaft of Hagen, Germany; of le Societe Anonyme pour le Travail Electrique des Metaux, Paris, France; and of the Chloride Electrical Storage Syndicate, Limited, London and Manchester, England. In October, 1902, the company acquired control of the Chloride Electric Storage Syndicate, Limited. The company has factories at Camden, N. J., and Nineteenth street and Allegheny avenue, Philadelphia.

Stock..Par $100...Authorized { com., $15,000,000 / pref., 5,000,000 } Issued { com., $11,749,494 / pref., 4,500,000 } $16,249,494

The preferred stock is 1 per cent., cumulative, and has a preference in case of liquidation. After preferred and common have each received 1 per cent. in dividends they share equally in remaining surplus earnings.

Stock authorized was originally $10,000,000, equally divided into common and preferred. Common stock authorized was increased to $8,500,000 in December, 1894. Preferred stock outstanding was $3,000,000. During 1895 $1,000,000 additional preferred was issued, being oversubscribed for at $50 per share to furnish additional working capital; $500,000 preferred remains in hands of trustees for benefit of company. In May, 1899, the common stock of the company was increased from $8,500,000 to $13,000,000 and $3,375,000 was allotted to stockholders at par. The proceeds of this increase was to increase the facilities of the company and acquire new property and patents, particularly in conection with the electric automobile business.

In December, 1900, the accumulated dividends on the preferred stock were 6 per cent. and a dividend of 6 per cent. on the preferred was paid January 2, 1901. Since then regular quarterly dividends of 1¼ per cent. have been paid on the preferred in January, April, July and October.

The 1st dividend on the common was 1¼ per cent., paid April 1, 1901, since which regular quarterly dividends of the same amount have been paid in the same months as the dividends on the preferred.

The company has no funded debt.

| EARNINGS. | Gross. | Net. |
|---|---|---|
| 1896 | $646,319 | $148,709 |
| 1897 | 842,963 | 223,939 |
| 1898 | 1,163,584 | 320,957 |
| 1899 | 2,122,679 | 924,523 |
| 1900 | 1,447,520 | 1,317,865 |
| 1901 | ...... | 900,243 |
| 1902 | ...... | 1,113,199 |

Dividends paid in 1902 were $812,427, and the surplus $300,772. The company's total surplus December 31, 1902, was $2,084,172.

President, Herbert Lloyd; Secretary and Treasurer, Walter G. Henderson, Philadelphia.

Directors—Herbert Lloyd, P. A. B. Widener, William L. Elkins, Thomas Dolan, Rudulph Ellis, George Philler, George D. Widener, Philadelphia; Grant B. Schley, Thomas J. Regan, New York.

Corporate office, Gloucester, N. J.; executive office, Nineteenth street and Allegheny avenue, Philadelphia; New York office, 100 Broadway; Boston office, 60 State street; Chicago office, Dearborn, Jackson and Van Buren streets; San Francisco office, 825 Market street; Baltimore office, corner Calvert and Fayette streets. Annual meeting in March.

## ELECTRIC VEHICLE CO.

A corporation formed under the laws of New Jersey in 1897. The company was organized to acquire and operate, sell or lease vehicles for propulsion by electric storage batteries or other mechanical means and their accessories and to deal in electric storage batteries.

In 1899 the company united all its patents with those of the Columbia Automobile Co., through a new corporation, the Columbia & Electric Vehicle Co., one-half of the stock of which is owned by this company. The company also bought and owns the entire stock of the Siemens & Halske Electric Co. of America. This company has the exclusive right to purchase the entire output of the Columbia & Electric Vehicle Co., and then to be the sole agent for its disposal. In 1900 the company acquired control of the Riker Motor Vehicle Co.

This company organized companies for the operation of automobiles, among them the New York, the New England and Illinois Electric Vehicle Transportation Cos., and obtained similar control of the Pennsylvania Electric Vehicle Transportation Co.

Stock..Par $100..Auth'd { com., $11,000,000 / pref., 9,000,000 } $20,000,000 Issued { com., $10,450,000 / pref., 8,125,000 } $18,575,000

The preferred stock is 8 per cent., non-cumulative, and also has a preference as to assets of the company. After the preferred has received 8 per cent. out of the earnings of any year the common is entitled to up to 8 per cent., after which both classes of stock share *pro rata* as regards any surplus of net earnings.

Transfer Agent, Morton Trust Co., New York.

In April, 1899, the company paid a first dividend of 8 per cent. on its preferred and 2 per cent., quarterly, on its common stock, and paid similar dividends on the common in July, October and December, 1899, but made no payments since except a 2 per cent. dividend on its preferred, April 16, 1900.

FUNDED DEBT.

Collateral Trust mort., 6 per cent., due Nov. 1, 1904, May and Nov................ $1,675,000

In order to provide for purchase of the Siemens & Halske Electric Co. of America and for the organization and acquisition of this company's interest in the Electric Vehicle Transportation Cos. referred to above, the company, in 1899, increased its preferred stock from $1,000,000 to $5,000,000 and its common stock from $5,000,000 to $7,000,000. In 1900 there was a further increase in both common and preferred to acquire the balance of stock of the Columbia & Electric Vehicle Co. and to purchase the Riker Electric Vehicle Co.

The Electric Storage Battery Co. acquired some $4,000,000 of the company's stocks under the arrangements between the two companies.

The Collateral Trust mortgage was created in January, 1902. Trustee, Morton Trust Co., New York. The bonds are secured by mortgage on the company's manufacturing plant at Hartford, Conn., and by the deposit of stocks of the constituent companies and all the patents owned by this company. Of the bond issue $1,650,000 was used to retire a like amount of old bonds, 6 per cent., due 1904, subject to call, which were issued in early part of 1901.

President, George H. Day; Vice-President, M. J. Budlong; Secretary and Treasurer, A. D. Newton; Assistant Treasurer, H. W. Kyte, Hartford, Conn..

Directors—Isaac L. Rice, Philip T. Dodge, Albert A. Pope, Frederick Vieweg, John Hone, New York; George H. Day, M. Toscan Bennett, M. J. Budlong, A. D. Newton, Hartford, Conn.

Corporate office, 243 Washington street, Jersey City; main office, 1 Laurel street, Hartford,

Conn.; branch offices, 43 Columbus avenue, Boston; 134-138 West Thirty-ninth street, New York; 1421 Michigan avenue, Chicago; Fifteenth street and Ohio avenue, Washington. Annual meeting, third Tuesday in September, at Jersey City.

## ELECTRICAL LEAD REDUCTION CO.

A corporation formed under the laws of Delaware in July, 1899, for the purpose of reducing lead ores by a new electric process, which materially curtails the cost of production. The company acquired the patents covering this process and has a plant at Niagara Falls, N. Y., with a capacity of 10 tons per day.

Stock..Par $100...Authorized { com., $10,000,000 / pref., 2,000,000 } Issued { com., $10,000,000 / pref., 2,000,000 } $12,000,000

The common stock was issued, full paid, for the acquisition of patents and processes. On the preferred stock 10 per cent. or $200,000 was paid in to provide for the erection of the company's plant and working capital.

President, Pedro G. Salom; Vice-President, Henry G. Morris; Secretary and Treasurer, Frederick H. Deacon.

Directors—Pedro G. Salom, Henry G. Morris, Samuel R. Shipley, James Brown, James L. Wilcott, F. H. Deaon.

Main office, The Bourse, Philadelphia; operating office, Niagara Falls, N. Y.; New York office, 71 Broadway.

## THE ELGIN, AURORA & SOUTHERN TRACTION CO.

A corporation formed under the laws of Illinois, May, 1901, as a consolidation of the following companies:

Elgin City, Carpentersville & Aurora Railway Co.
Elgin City Railway Co.
Aurora & Geneva Railway Co.
Aurora Street Railway Co.
Geneva, Batavia & Southern Railway Co.
Aurora, Yorkville & Morris Railway Co.

The company operates 72 miles of track connecting the cities and towns of Aurora, Carpentersville, Dundee, Elgin, South Elgin, Geneva, Batavia, St. Charles, Montgomery, Oswego, Yorkville and Bristol, Ill. The road will reach Chicago by means of the Aurora, Elgin & Chicago Railway. The company also operates an electric lighting plant at Elgin and has a franchise for one at Aurora.

Stock......Par $100..........................Authorized, $2,000,000......Issued, $2,000,000

The company has no preferred stock.

Transfer Agent, Cleveland Trust Co., Cleveland.

FUNDED DEBT.

| | |
|---|---|
| 1st mort., 5 per cent. gold, due June 1, 1916, June and Dec.................... ..... | $1,700,000 |
| Elgin City Railway Co., 1st mort., 5 per cent., due 1907, Feb. and Aug......... ..... | 200,000 |
| Carpentersville, Elgin & Aurora Ry. Co., 1st mort., 5 p. c., due 1907, Jan. and July.. | 100,000 |
| Total.............................................................. | $2,000,000 |

The full amount of the Traction Company's bond issue is $2,000,000, of which $300,000 is reserved to retire the divisional liens. Provision has been made for a sinking fund of $17,000 per annum for the first five years, and $25,000 per annum thereafter.

Trustee and agent for the payment of interest, American Trust & Savings Bank, Chicago. Interest is also payable at First National Bank, New York.

EARNINGS

Year ending February 28.

| | Gross. | Net. | Surplus. |
|---|---|---|---|
| 1901 .......................................... | $361,665 | $155,660 | $55,660 |
| 1902 .......................................... | 410,431 | 166,778 | 66,778 |

President, L. J. Wolf; Secretary and Treasurer, H. C. Lang, Cleveland; Manager, E. C. Faber, Aurora, Ill.

Directors—L. J. Wolf, F. B. Bicknell, M. N. Wilson, E. C. Faber, Harry Greenebaum.

Corporate office, 121 Euclid avenue, Cleveland. General office, Aurora, Ill. Annual meeting, June 2, at Aurora, Ill.

## ELGIN NATIONAL WATCH CO.

A corporation formed under the laws of Illinois, August 27, 1864. The company was organized to manufacture watches, clocks and jewelry, and parts thereof, and materials for the nanufacture of watches, clocks and jewelry. The company's products are known throughout the world and are of the standard in their class. Its factories are at Elgin, Ill.

Stock......Par $1,000................. .......Authorized, $5,000,000......Issued, $4,000,000

The authorized amount of stock was increased from $4,000,000 to $5,000,000 in March, 1903. Registrar, Northern Trust Co., Chicago.

The dividends on the stock are 8 per cent. per annum, payable quarterly, 2 per cent. each, in February (1), May, August and November.

President, Charles H. Hulburd; Vice-President, Ernest A. Hamill; Secretary, William George Prall.

Directors, Charles H. Hulburd, Ernest A. Hamill, George T. Smith, Martin A. Ryerson, George H. Laflin, A. C. Bartlett, H. A. Blair.

Main office, 76 Monroe street, Chicago; branch offices, 11 John street, New York; 206 Kearney street, San Francisco. Annual meeting, second Wednesday in June, at Chicago.

## ELIZABETH, PLAINFIELD & CENTRAL JERSEY RAILWAY CO.

A corporation formed under the laws of New Jersey, November 29, 1900. The company is a consolidation of the following companies:

Plainfield Street Railway Co.
Westfield & Elizabeth Street Railway Co.
Elizabeth City Horse Railroad Co.
Elizabeth Street Railway Co.
Rahway Electric Street Railway Co.
Woodbridge & Sewaren Electric Street Railway Co.

The company operates all the street railway lines in Elizabeth, Plainfield, North Plainfield, Roselle, Cranford, Westfield, Clark, Rahway, Fanwood and Woodbridge, N. J., 59.06 miles of track.

Stock......Par $100..........................Authorized, $3,000,000......Issued, $3,000,000

The company has no preferred stock. Transfer Agent and Registrar, Fidelity Trust Co., Newark, N. J.

FUNDED DEBT.

| | |
|---|---|
| 1st mort., 5 per cent. gold, due Dec., 1950, June and Dec.......................... | $1,400,000 |
| Plainfield Street Railway Co., 1st mort., 5 per cent., due 1942, Jan. and July......... | 100,000 |
| Total............................................................. ....... | $1,500,000 |

The authorized amount of the 1st mortgage is $2,500,000, of which $1,000,000 are held for extensions and $100,000 to retire the Plainfield Street Railway Co.'s bonds, which are subject to call in 1904. Trustee of both mortgages and agent for the payment of interest, Fidelity Trust Co., Newark, N. J.

President, Thomas C. Barr; Vice-President, Thomas A. Nevins; Secretary and Treasurer, Edwin W. Hine; General Manager, John N. Akarman.

Directors—Thomas C. Barr, Thomas A. Nevins, East Orange, N. J.; Edwin W. Hine, Orange, N. J.; U. H. McCarter, C. W. Riker, Thomas H. McCarter, A. R. Kuser, Adrian Riker, Newark, N. J.; S. M. Williams, Roselle, N. J.

Main office, 164 Market street, Newark, N. J. Annual meeting, first Monday in May.

## ELLENVILLE ZINC CO.

A corporation formed under the laws of New Jersey in 1902, for the purposes of mining zinc, lead and other minerals. The company acquired the mineral rights in a tract of about 4,000 acres in the Shawaugunk Mountains, Ulster County, New York. The principal feature of the property is the Ellenville lead mine with a vein of zinc blend. The mine is at Ellenville, 100 miles from New York, on the New York, Ontario & Western Railroad.

Stock......Par $1................ ..............Authorized, $1,000,000......Issued, $100,000

The company has no preferred stock and no funded debt.

President, E. P. Backus, Newark, N. J.; Vice-President, Thomas E. Benedict, Ellenville, N. Y.; Secretary, Thomas E. Provost, Newark, N. J.; Treasurer, Frank B. Hoornbeek; Superintendent, Jacob O. Poole, Ellenville, N. Y.

Directors—E. P. Backus, Joseph Fisch, Philip Lowy, Thomas C. Provost, Newark, N. J.; Jacob O. Poole, Thomas E. Benedict, Frank B. Hoornbeek, Ellenville, N. Y.

Corporate office, Newark, N. J.; main office, Ellenville, N. Y. Annual meeting, fourth Tuesday in January, at Newark, N. J.

## ELMIRA WATER, LIGHT & RAILROAD CO.

A corporation founded under the laws of New York, May 26, 1900. The business of the company is to supply water, electric light and gas, and to operate street railways in the city of Elmira, N. Y., the village of Elmira Heights and the adjoining towns of Horseheads and Southport. It acquired the properties of the Elmira Municipal Improvement Co., and now owns 9 charters and 26 franchises. The companies acquired were

Elmira Water Works Co.
Elmira Gas & Illuminating Co
Elmira Illuminating Co.
West Water Street Railroad Co.
Maple Avenue Railroad Co.
Elmira & Horseheads Railroad Co.
Interstate Fair Association.
Elmira Heights Water Co.
West Side Railroad Co.

The company operates about 27 miles of street railway.

Stock......Par $100..........................Authorized, $1,000,000......Issued, $1,000,000

The company has no preferred stock. Transfer Agent and Registrar, Guaranty Trust Co., New York.

FUNDED DEBT.

| | |
|---|---|
| 1st mort., 5 per cent. gold bonds, due 1949, Jan. and July | $2,000,000 |
| 2d mort., 4 per cent. income bond, due 1949, March | 1,200,000 |
| 1st mort., 6 per cent. bonds, Elmira Water Works Co., due 1913, Jan. and July | 339,000 |
| Total | $3,539,000 |

The issues of both the 1st and 2d mortgage bonds of the Elmira Water, Light & Railway Co., are the full amount authorized. Of the 1st mortgage bond issue, $339,000 is held in the treasury to secure the bonds of the Elmira Water Works Co.

Trustee of the bonds and agent for the payment of interest, United States Mortgage & Trust Co., New York.

The following is the company's balance sheet December 31, 1902:

| ASSETS. | | LIABILITIES. | |
|---|---|---|---|
| Plant and equipment | $2,010,052 | Capital stock | $1,000,000 |
| Franchises and good will | 2,179,622 | First mortgage bonds | 2,000,000 |
| Treasury bonds | 368,000 | Second mortgage income bonds | 1,200,000 |
| Material and supplies | 39,348 | Water works bonds | 339,000 |
| Accounts receivable | 182,198 | Accounts and bills payable | 229,771 |
| Cash | 1,953 | Accrued bond interest | 5,085 |
| | | Profit and loss to balance | 7,317 |
| Total | $4,781,173 | Total | $4,781,173 |

President, Ray Tompkins; Vice-President, W. W. Cole; Secretary, John M. Diven, Elmira, N. Y.; Assistant Secretary, Frank S. Butterworth, New York.

Directors—Ray Tompkins, M. H. Arnot, W. W. Cole, Elmira, N. Y.; S. Reading Bertron, Richard D. Storrs, New York.

Corporate and main office, Realty Building, Elmira, N. Y. Annual meeting, first Thursday in June, at Elmira.

## ELM RIVER COPPER CO.

A corporation formed under the laws of New Jersey in 1899. The company owns 2,360 acres of natural land in Houghton County, Mich., and a mill site on Lake Superior. The Copper Range Railroad now crosses the property. Work on the property during the first year of operation was delayed by the fact that supplies and machinery had to be hauled from Houghton, 20 miles distant. The property is being explored with shafts and other workings, and both the Winona and Shawmut lodes have been located on it.

Stock......Par $12..........................Authorized, $1,200,000......Issued, $1,200,000

The stock is full paid. Stock is transferred at the company's office, Boston. Registrar, Old Colony Trust Co., Boston.

President, Harry F. Fay; Secretary, Walter B. Mosman; Treasurer, George G. Endicott Boston.

Directors—Harry F. Fay, John C. Watson, Walter B. Mosman, S. R. Dow, Boston; Charles N. King, Jersey City.

Main office, 60 State street, Boston. Annual meeting, third Wednesday in April, at Jersey City.

## EL PASO ELECTRIC CO.

A corporation formed under the laws of Texas. The purpose of the company is to construct and operate an electric railway in and about the city of El Paso, Tex., extending across the Rio Grand River to Juarez, Mex. The franchise of the company expires in 1951. The road is now in process of construction.

Stock......Par $100....Authorized { com., $1,000,000 / pref., 250,000 } Issued { com., $1,000,000 / pref., 150,000 } $1,150,000

The preferred stock is 6 per cent., non-cumulative.

Transfer Agent, Stone & Webster, 93 Federal street, Boston. Registrar, State Street Trust Co., Boston.

Dividends on the preferred stock are payable semi-annually in January and July.

FUNDED DEBT.

Collateral Trust mort., 5 per cent., gold, due 1932, January and July................. $600,000

The authorized mortgage is $1,000,000. Trustee and Registrar of bonds, State Street Trust Co., Boston, by whom the coupons are also paid.

President, J. W. Hallowell; Vice-President, J. H. Oakes; Secretary, H. R. Hayes; Treasurer, H. B. Sawyer.

Directors—J. W. Hallowell, J. H. Oakes, H. B. Sawyer, Eliott Wadsworth, Owen D. Young, James B. Dill.

Main office, El Paso, Tex.' Annual meeting, second Monday in January, at

## EMPIRE STATE SUGAR CO.

A corporation formed under the laws of New York, January 24, 1900. The business of the company is the manufacture of beet sugar. It has erected a factory for this purpose at Lyons, N.Y., and produces white granulated sugars.

Stock......Par $100...............................Authorized, $400,000......Issued, $400,000

Transfer Agents, Thomas & Post, 71 Broadway, New York. Registrar, Metropolitan Trust Co., New York.

FUNDED DEBT.

1st mort., 6 per cent., due 1915, Jan. and July........................................ $400,000

The bonds are secured by a mortgage of the company's real estate, plant and other property to the Metropolitan Trust Co., New York, as trustee. The bonds are subject to call at 110 at the option of the company.

President, Orlando F. Thomas, Lyons, N. Y.; Vice-President, William Buckheit; Secretary and Treasurer, Seymour Scott, New York.

Directors—Orlando F. Thomas, J. D. Bashford, Lyons, N. Y.; Seymour Scott, E. N. Post, William Buckheit, New York

Main office, Lyons, N. Y. Annual meeting, first Tuesday in March, at Lyons, N. Y.

## THE EMPIRE STEEL & IRON CO.

A corporation formed under the laws of New Jersey, March 14, 1899. It commenced business April 1, 1899. The company manufactures all grades of basic, low phosphorus, Bessemer, malleable and foundry irons. The capacity of its plants is 1,000 tons daily.

The properties owned are as follows:

Crane Iron Works, Castasauqua, Pa., 4 furnaces.
Allentown Furnances, Allentown, Pa., 2 furnaces.
Macungie Furnaces, Macungie, Pa., 1 furnace.
Topton Furnaces, Topton, Pa., 1 furnace.
Henry Clay Furnaces, Reading, Pa., 2 furnaces.
Oxford Furnace, Oxford, N. J., 1 furnace.
Greensboro Furnace, Greensboro, N. C., 1 furnace.

The company also owns large ore operations at Oxford and Mount Hope, N. J., and Wilsons Mills, N. C., besides controlling many smaller ore operations and many of its own limestone quarries.

The company owned the Goshen and Shenandoah furnaces and the Potts Valley, Boyer, Fox Mountain and Massanutton ore properties in Virginia, but in January, 1902, the Allegheny Ore & Iron Co. was formed for the pur ose of operating these properties, together with the Iron Gate and Buena Vista furnaces and the famous Oriskany ore mine. The Alleghany Co. is controlled by the Empire Co.

The Mount Hope Mineral Railroad, 5 miles, Wharton to Mount Hope, N. J.; Lehigh & Oxford Railroad, 5 miles, Buttsville to Fellows, N. J., and the Catasauqua Bridge & Terminal

Railroad, with about 15 miles of terminal tracks in the town of Catasauqua, Pa., are owned and operated by this company.

Stock.....Par $100....Authorized { com., $5,000,000 / pref., 5,000,000 } Issued { com., $2,281,400 / pref., 2,500,000 } $4,781,400

The preferred stock is 6 per cent., cumulative. Transfer Agent, City Trust Co., New York.

The first dividend of 3 per cent., semi-annual, on the preferred stock was paid July 1, 1899, and similar dividends were regularly paid, January and July, until January 2, 1901, when 1½ per cent. was paid, the reduction being due to expenditure for additions and improvements, and the semi-annual dividends on the preferred have since been at the same rate.

From April 1, 1899, to June 30, 1900, the net earnings were $690,205, and the surplus over preferred dividends $488,837. In the year 1900 the net income was $350,918; surplus over amount charged to depreciation, and 4½ per cent. dividends on the preferred stock was $104,523. In 1901, net, $374,479; charges, $229,095; preferred dividends, 3 per cent., $71,043; balance, surplus, $74,341.

President, Leonard Peckitt; Vice-President, Charles H. Zehnder; Treasurer, J. S. Stillman; Secretary, J. M. Fitzgerald.

Executive Committee—Archer Brown, Chairman; Elverton R. Chapman, Mark T. Cox.

Directors—Leonard Peckitt, Catasauqua, Pa.; F. M. Davis, Archer Brown, Elverton R. Chapman, J. S. Morgan, F. M. Jeffery, Mark T. Cox, Charles H. Zehnder, James W. Fuller, P. Kleesberg, New York.

General office, Catasauqua, Pa.; New York office, 71 Broadway. Annual meeting, fourth Wednesday in February.

## EQUITABLE GAS LIGHT CO.

A corporation formed under the laws of California, February 21, 1898, to supply gas for domestic and manufacturing purposes in the city of San Francisco.

Stock......Par $20..........................Authorized, $5,000,000......Issued, $2,776,400

The company has no preferred stock and no funded debt.

President, Charles L. Ackerman; Vice-President, Leon Blum; Secretary, Samuel H. Tacy; Treasurer, Frank Pauson.

Directors—Charles L. Ackerman, Leon Blum, Samuel H. Tacy, Frank Pauson, F. C. Siebe, Joseph Naphtaly, Albert Cerf.

Corporate and main office, 516 California street, San Francisco. Annual meeting, third Tuesday in January.

## EQUITABLE GAS LIGHT CO. OF MEMPHIS

A corporation formed under the laws of Tennessee in 1885-86. The company is a consolidation of the Memphis Gas Light Co., incorporated in 1853, and the Equitable Gas Light Co. The property of the Memphis Gas Light Co. was purchased from its stockholders in 1899, the sale being sanctioned by an ordinance of the city of Memphis, adopted in December, 1899, in consideration of a payment of $50,000 for the franchise and a reduction in the price of gas. Large extensions of its mains have been made by the company. In 1902 control of the company was acquired by capitalists, who were also interested in the Memphis Light & Power Co., and a consolidation of the two organizations was proposed.

Stock.......Par $100.........................Authorized, $1,000,000......Issued, $1,000,000

Transfer Agent and Registrar, Colonial Trust Co., New York.

FUNDED DEBT.

30-year mort., 5 per cent., due 1929, May and Nov.................................. $1,005,000

The trustee of the mortgage is the Colonial Trust Co., New York.

In the first year after the consolidation the net profits of the company amounted to $85,000.

President, I. Katzenberger; Vice-President, John T. Frost; Secretary and General Manager, William Katzenberger; Treasurer, Frank Jones, Memphis.

Directors—F. G. Jones, John Armistead, Anthony N. Brady, C. K. G. Billings, S. T. Carves, E. J. Kerr.

Main office, 58 Madison street, Memphis.

## THE EQUITABLE ILLUMINATING GAS LIGHT CO. OF PHILADELPHIA

A corporation formed in 1898 under the auspices of the United Gas Improvement Co., to take assignment of the lease of the gas works of Philadelphia from the city to the United Gas

Improvement Co., and to operate the same. Litigation concerning the validity of the lease resulted in its being sustained by the courts.

Stock....Par $100....Authorized { com., $3,125,000 / pref., 3,125,000 } Issued { com., $3,125,000 / pref., 3,125,000 } $6,250,000

Stock is transferred at the company's office. Registrar, Fidelity Trust Co., Philadelphia.

The preferred stock has a preference of 6 per cent. The bulk of the stock is held by the United Gas Improvement Co., which purchases the gas manufactured by this company on terms sufficient to provide for interest and sinking funds on bonds.

FUNDED DEBT.

1st mort., 5 per cent., due Jan., 1928, redeemable 1908, Jan. and July............... $6,969,000

The 1st mortgage bonds, New York Security & Trust Co., trustee, are due in 1928, but are redeemable at 105 in 1908 if the city exercises its option to terminate the lease on payment for improvements and interest on their cost. The bonds can also be drawn for the sinking fund at 105 and interest. Sinking fund is $124,000 per annum plus interest on all bonds bought by the sinking fund. In 1928 the gas works will revert to the city, without payment, when all bonds will have been retired.

Prices for gas authorized by lease are: to the municipality, free; to consumers, $1 per 1,000 cubic feet, until reduced by ordinance of the City Councils, but they shall not be reduced below the following prices: up to December 31, 1907, 90c. per 1,000 feet; up to December 31, 1912, 85c. per 1,000 feet; up to December 31, 1917, 80c. per 1,000 feet; up to December 31, 1927, 75c. per 1,000 feet.

The company paid 4 per cent. on the preferred stock in December, 1898, and 3 per cent. each in July and December since that date. On the common a dividend of 6 per cent. was paid in December, 1899, 1900 and 1901.

President, James Ball; Vice-President, David H. Lane; Treasurer, W. A. McEwen, Philadelphia.

Directors—James Ball, F. H. McMorris, J. A. Pearson, I. W. Morris, David H. Lane.

Main office, Broad and Arch streets, Philadelphia. Annual meeting, first Monday in August.

## THE ERIE & WESTERN TRANSPORTATION CO.

A corporation organized under the laws of Pennsylvania, June, 1865. The company does a general transportation business in freight and passengers on the great lakes, and has docks, grain elevators and other lake terminal facilities at Buffalo, N. Y., Erie, Pa., Chicago, Milwaukee and other lake ports; also has a large fleet of vessels known as the Anchor Line. In 1900 the Pennsylvania Railroad Co. purchased the stock of this company.

Stock......Par $50...... ................ ....Authorized, $3,000,000......Issued $3,000,000

Stock is transferred at the office of the company, Philadelphia.

Dividends are paid yearly, and checks for the same mailed to stockholders. In December, 1900 and 1901, paid annual dividends of 4 per cent.

President, Frank J. Firth; Secretary, Frank Staley; Treasurer, P. R. Perkins; Western Manager, E. T. Evans, Buffalo, N. Y.; Eastern Manager, John E. Payne, Philadelphia; Auditor, William J. Boddy, ; Assistant Auditor, Edward Hare, Philadelphia.

Directors—S. F. Houston, Frank J. Firth, John P. Green, S. M. Prevost, W. H. Barnes.

Main office, 26 South Fifteenth street, Philadelphia. Annual meeting, first Tuesday in June.

## ERIE ELECTRIC MOTOR CO.

A corporation founded under the laws of Pennsylvania, October 8, 1888. The company acquired the following companies:

Erie City Passenger Railway Co. Erie, Reed Park & Lakeside Railway Co.

The company controls all the street railway lines in the city of Erie, Pa., and vicinity, operating 29.79 miles of track. It has a power plant, 76 motor and 10 trail cars.

Stock......Par $100............................Authorized, $1,250,000......Issued, $1,250,000

The company has no preferred stock. Stock is transferred at the office of the company.

FUNDED DEBT.

| | |
|---|---|
| 1st mort., 6 per cent. gold, due Jan., 1919, Jan. and July............................ | $200,000 |
| 2d mort., 6 per cent. gold, due Jan., 1919, Jan. and July.................. ...... .... | 150,000 |
| 1st refunding mort., 5 per cent. gold, due April, 1941, April and Oct.. ............ . | 750,000 |
| Total................................ ............. . ... ............ | $1,100,000 |

The outstanding bonds of the 1st and 2d mortgage are the full amounts authorized; $100,000 have been exchanged and deposited as additional collateral for the refunding mortgage. Trustee of both mortgages and Agent for the payment of interest, Central Trust Co., New York.

The authorized amount of the refunding mortgage is $1,250,000, of which amount $250,000 is reserved to retire the outstanding prior liens and $250,000 for extensions. A sinking fund is provided, calling for 1 per cent. after April, 1906, and 1½ per cent. after April, 1916. Trustee of the mortgage and agent for the payment of interest, New York Security & Trust Co., New York.

EARNINGS.

Year ending December 31.

| | Gross. | Operating Expenses and Taxes. | Net. |
|---|---|---|---|
| 1900 | $183,516 | $110,856 | $72,660 |
| 1901 | 202,631 | ...... | 100,760 |

President, J. S. Casement, Painesville, O.; Vice-President, John C. Brady; Secretary and Treasurer, J. L. Sternberg, Erie, Pa.

Directors—J. S. Casement, Painesville, O.; S. T. Everett, Cleveland; John C. Brady, H. F. Wilbur, J. L. Sternberg, Erie, Pa.

Main office, 202 State street, Erie, Pa. Annual meeting, third Tuesday in January, at Erie, Pa

## ESSEX & HUDSON GAS CO.

A corporation formed under the laws of New Jersey, November 29, 1898. The object of the company is to manufacture, sell and distribute illuminating and fuel gas, etc. The company is controlled by the United Gas Improvement Co. It leases all the property of the Newark Consolidated Gas Co., by virtue of which lease it operates the gas works of Newark, N. J., and the adjacent cities and towns in the county of Essex, N. J. See statement of the Newark Consolidated Gas Co.

Stock......Par $100..........................Authorized, $6,500,000......Issued, $6,500,000

Stock is transferred at the office of the company, 575 Broad street, Newark, N. J.

President, John F. Shanley; 1st Vice-President, George R. Gray; 2d Vice-President, Thomas N. McCarter; Treasurer, Lewis Lillie; Secretary, James P. Dusenberry; General Superintendent, Walton Clark.

Directors—John F. Shanley, George R. Gray, Thomas N. McCarter, James P. Dusenberry, James Smith, 3d; Leslie D. Ward, Peter Hauck, George Spottiswood, Spencer Weart, Halsey M. Barrett, William J. Davis, Uzal H. McCarter, E. B. Gaddis, Newark, N. J.; Randal Morgan, Philadelphia.

Main office, 575 Broad street, Newark, N. J. Registrar, Fidelity Trust Co., Newark. Annual meeting, first Monday in April.

## THE EXPLORATION CO. OF NEW YORK.

A corporation formed under the laws of New Jersey in 1896. The objects of the company are the expert examination of mines and the auditing of mining enterprises. It also finances mining properties of value and promise. The company is the successor of an organization under the title of the Exploration Syndicate, which had pursued the same line of business.

Stock......Par $100............................Authorized, $100,000......Issued, $100,000

Registrar, Knickerbocker Trust Co., New York.

The company has no funded debt. It had in February, 1901, a surplus of $90,000.

President, Frederick G. Corning; Vice-President, Thomas J. Hurley; Secretary and Treasurer, C. Van Rensselaer Cogswell, New York.

Directors—Frederick G. Corning, Thomas J. Hurley, C. Van Rensselaer Cogswell, George A. MacGlone, Charles N. King.

Main office, 15 Broad street, New York; London office, Worcester House, Walbrook, E. C. Annual meeting, first Tuesday in January.

## EXPOSED TREASURE MINING CO.

A corporation formed under the laws of New York. The company owns eight mining claims and an undivided interest in three others, all located at Mojave, Cal. It has a 20-stamp mill with a capacity for crushing 60 tons of ore per day.

Stock......Par $5............................Authorized, $1,500,000......Issued, $1,500,000

The company has no preferred stock and no funded debt. Stock is transferred at the office of the company, New York. Registrar, Knickerbocker Trust Co., New York.

President, Elijah R. Kennedy; 1st Vice-President, Frank Squier; 2d Vice-President, Benjamin Stern; Secretary and Treasurer, M. J. Goodenough, New York.

Directors—Charles F. Bassett, Robert D. Benedict, Z. Taylor Emery, Darwin R. James, Elijah R. Kennedy, Frank Squier, Benjamin Stern, New York; John Landers, San Francisco; M. J. Goodenough, A. M. Roussel, Brooklyn, N. Y.; William J. Nelson, San Andreas, Cal.

Corporate office, Esopus, N. Y.; New York office, 26 Liberty street. Annual meeting, third Wednesday in February, at Esopus, N. Y.

## FAIR HAVEN & WESTVILLE RAILROAD CO.

A corporation formed under the laws of Connecticut, June 20, 1860. The company has acquired the following companies:

New Haven Street Railway Co.
New Haven & Centreville Street Railway Co.
New Haven & North Haven Street Railway Co.

The company operates about 101 miles of electric trolley railway in New Haven, Conn., and vicinity, New Haven, Fair Haven, Westville, Centreville, East Haven and other places. It owns 3 electric power plants and 292 cars. The company controls the Winchester Avenue Railroad Co. The Winchester Avenue Railroad controls, under a 99-year lease, the West Shore Railway Co. The Branford Electric Railway is operated under contract.

Stock......Par $25.............................Authorized, $5,000,000......Issued, $4,426,550

The company has no preferred stock. Stock is transferred at the office of the company.

Dividends on the stock at the rate of 5 per cent. annually were paid in 1899 and subsequently. Dividends are quarterly, 1¼ per cent. each, in January April, July and October.

FUNDED DEBT.

| | |
|---|---|
| 1st purchase mort., 5 per cent., due June, 1914, June and Dec. | $250,000 |
| 1st mort., 5 per cent. gold, due Sept., 1913, March and Sept. | 600,000 |
| New Haven & Centreville St. R. Co., 5 per cent. gold, due Sept., 1933, March and Sept. | 283,000 |
| Total | $1,133,000 |

The outstanding bonds of the 1st purchase mortgage and the 1st mortgage are the full amount authorized. Trustee of the mortgages and agent for the payment of interest, American Loan & Trust Co., Boston.

EARNINGS.

Year ending June 30.

| | Gross. | Net. | Taxes. | Interest. | Dividends. | Surplus. |
|---|---|---|---|---|---|---|
| 1900 | $591,801 | $259,405 | $37,020 | $69,222 | $106,250 | $46,213 |
| 1901 | 644,527 | 264,454 | 40,290 | 62,511 | 125,000 | 36,653 |
| 1902 | 986,334 | 261,202 | 48,758 | 57,738 | 137,500 | 17,206 |

President, James S. Hemingway; Vice-President, John B. Carrington; Secretary and Treasurer, Leverett Candee, New Haven, Conn.

Directors—John B. Carrington, Samuel Hemingway, Hayes Q. Trowbridge, George D. Watrous, James S. Hemingway, Wilbur F. Day, Samuel E. Merwin, New Haven, Conn.

Main office, 902 Chapel street, New Haven, Conn. Annual meeting, second Wednesday in January, at New Haven, Conn.

## FAIRMONT COAL CO.

A corporation formed under the laws of West Virginia, June 19, 1901. The business of the company is the mining and distribution of coal and the ownership of coal lands. The company owns 30,280 acres of bituminous coal lands and holds 24,986 acres under perpetual lease, a total of 55,166 acres of coal lands. The company's property is on both sides of the Monongahela River, adjacent to the lines of the Baltimore & Ohio Railroad, extending from a point south of Clarksburg, W. Va.

It also leased rights from the Monongahela River Railroad Co. and from the Monongahela Co. The company also acquired control of the Northwestern Fuel Co., which has a coal distributing and storage business extending from Chicago to Duluth, with coal yards at St. Paul and

Minneapolis and plants at Milwaukee, Green Bay, Wis.; Washburn, Wis.; West Superior, Wis., and Duluth.

The property of the company embraces 36 operating coal mines, fully equipped, some of which have been in successful operation for twenty-five years; 1,051 coke ovens and 5,300 railroad cars, together with 25 stores at its various mines.

In January, 1903, it was announced that capitalists connected with the company had acquired large interests in the Consolidation Coal Co. and the Somerset Coal Co.

Stock......Par $100........................Authorized, $12,000,000..... Issued, $12,000,000

The company has no preferred stock.

Transfer Agent, Registrar & Transfer Co., New York. Registrar, Guaranty Trust Co., New York.

FUNDED DEBT.

1st mort., 5 per cent., gold, due July, 1931, Jan. and July .......................... $5,525,000

The authorized amount of the 1st mortgage is $6,000,000. There are $475,000 of the bonds reserved to retire obligations outstanding on portions of the properties covered by the mortgage. Trustee of the mortgage, Guaranty Trust Co., New York. Bonds are subject to redemption by the sinking fund on any interest date at 110. There is a sinking fund of 2 cents on each ton of coal mined from the company's property, but the Trustee may use one-half of the proceeds of the sinking fund to acquire additional coal lands.

The operations of the company began July 1, 1901. In the year ending December 31, 1902, the revenues were as follows: Net earnings, after deducting interest charges, $1,400,684; sinking fund, $39,508; balance surplus, $323,324.

Chairman, J. E. Watson; President, Clarence W. Watson; Vice-President, A. B. Fleming; Secretary, George De Bolt; Treasurer, S. L. Watson.

Directors—Clarence W. Watson, J. E. Watson, S. L. Watson, W. H. Baldwin, Jr., Walter G. Oakman, August Belmont, George W. Young, George M. Shriver, Charles T. Barney, A. B. Fleming, Charles Mackall, J. E. Sands, J. H. Wheelwright, Walton Miller, L. L. Malone.

Corporate office, Fairmont, W. Va.; New York office, 1 Broadway. Annual meeting, first Monday in May, at New York or Fairmont, W. Va.

## J. A. FAY & EGAN CO.

A corporation formed under the laws of West Virginia, February 14, 1893. The company is engaged in manufacturing, purchasing and selling wood-working, iron-working and other machinery. It is a consolidation of the J. A. Fay & Co. corporation and the Egan Co. The combined plants are located in Cincinnati, cover three blocks, and give employment to 1,000 men.

Stock....Par $100.....Authorized { com., $1,000,000 / pref., 1,000,000 } Issued { com., $1,000,000 / pref., 1,000,000 } $2,000,000

The preferred stock has no voting power. It is 7 per cent., cumulative.

Stock is transferred at the office of the company, Cincinnati. Registrar, Union Savings Bank & Trust Co., Cincinnati.

Since the organization of the company in 1893 all dividends on the preferred stock have been paid regularly each quarter. Quarterly dividends at the rate of 5 per cent. annually are paid on the common stock.

FUNDED DEBT.

1st mort., 6 per cent. bonds, due 1943, Feb........................................ $500,000

The bond issue is the full amount authorized. Trustee of the mortgage, Union Savings Bank & Trust Co., Cincinnati. Agent for the payment of interest, Ohio Valley National Bank.

In the fiscal year ending January 31, 1902, the gross earnings of the company were $194,022; net earnings, $30,644; interest charges, $30,000; dividends, $87,500; surplus, $127,658. In 1902, net, $310,152; charges, $30,000; dividends, $110,000; surplus, $197,552.

President, Thomas P. Egan; 1st Vice-President, S. P. Egan; 2d Vice-President, A. N. Spencer; Secretary, William M. Green; Assistant Secretary, Parke S. Johnston; Treasurer, Arthur A. Faber, Cincinnati.

Directors—Thomas P. Egan, S. P. Egan, A. N. Spencer, L. G. Robinson, Joseph Rawson, J. E. Bruce, F. H. Simpson, W. H. Doane, Rudolph Kleybolte, Cincinnati.

Corporate and main office, Front and John streets, Cincinnati; branch offices, New York, Chicago, St. Louis, San Francisco, New Orleans, Greensboro, N. C., Seattle, Wash., and Buffalo, N. Y. Annual meeting, third Tuesday in February, at Cincinnati.

## FAYETTE COUNTY GAS CO.

A corporation formed un er the laws of West Virginia in October, 1900, to supply gas to towns in Fayette County, Pa. d

Stock......Par $100..............................Authorized, $1,000,000......Issued, $800,000

FUNDED DEBT.

1st mort., 6 per cent. bonds, May and Nov.......................................... $225,000

The company has a sinking fund to retire $25,000 of the bonds each year. Trustee, Title, Guarantee & Trust Co., Washington, Pa.

President, George W. Crawford; Vice-President and General Manager, John M. Garard; Secretary and Assistant Treasurer, H. C. Reeser; Treasurer, J. W. Donnan.

General offices, 345 Fourth avenue, Pittsburg; branch offices, Uniontown, Connellsville, Scottdale, Mt. Pleasant, Dunbar, Dawson.

## FEDERAL GRAPHITE CO.

A corporation formed under the laws of New Jersey, January 23, 1900. The company owns about 350 acres of graphite-bearing lands in Pikeland Township, Chester County, Pa. The ore in the company's mines is in a soft clay formation, requiring no heavy crushing machinery, and averages about 12½ per cent. of pure flake graphite or plumbago. There are also veins of almost pure graphite on the property. A mill with modern machinery was built in 1901.

Stock......Par $1.........Authorized { com., $100,000 / pref., 100,000 } Issued { com., $100,000 / pref., 80,000 } $180,000

The preferred stock is 6 per cent., non-cumulative. Stock is transferred at the company's office, Boston. Registrar, Federal Trust Co., Boston.

The company has no funded debt.

President, William Grange, Philadelphia; Vice-President, Theodore B. Casey; Secretary and Treasurer, Edwin W. Cates, Boston.

Directors—William Grange, Philadelphia; Theodore B. Casey, F. A. Schirmer, Boston; Charles A. Morse, Jr., New York; Theodore L. Peters, Jersey City.

Corporate office, 243 Washington street, Jersey City; main office, 146 Devonshire street, Boston. Annual meeting, last Tuesday in January.

## FIRTH-STERLING STEEL CO.

A corporation formed under the laws of Pennsylvania, July 11, 1889. The purpose of the company is the manufacture of high-grade steel. The company's office is located at Demmler, Pa., near Pittsburg.

Stock. ....Par $100..............................Authorized, $800,000......Issued, $700,000

The company has no preferred stock or funded debt. Transfers of stock are made at the company's office.

President, Lewis J. Firth, Sheffield, England; Vice-President, Austin A. Wheelock, New York; Secretary, James E. Porter; Treasurer, Eben B. Clarke, Pittsburg.

Directors—Lewis J. Firth, Sheffield, England; Austin A. Wheelock, New York; James H. Willock, James W. Kinnear, Eben B. Clarke, Pittsburg.

Main office, Demmler, Pa.; New York office, 23 Cliff street. Annual meeting at Demmler, Pa., at such time as directors select after the close of the fiscal year, May 31.

## THE FISHERIES CO.

A corporation formed under the laws of New Jersey, May 25, 1900. The company was created as successor to the American Fisheries Co., the property of which was sold under a judicial decree in April, 1900. The assets of the old company were transferred to a company called the United States Menhaden Oil & Guano Co. and assigned to the present company. The business of the company is the manufacture of menhaden oil and fertilizer, the principal plants on the Atlantic coast engaged in that industry having been acquired by the American Fisheries Co. which was formed in 1898.

Stock......Par $100......Authorized { com., $1,000,000 / pref., 2,000,000 } Issued { com., $532,767 / pref., 2,000,000 } $2,532,767

The preferred stock is 7 per cent., non-cumulative.

Transfer Agent, New Jersey Corporation Agency, Jersey City. Registrar, Trust Co. of America, New York.

The company paid an initial half-yearly dividend of 3½ per cent. on its preferred stock January 1, 1901. The preferred dividends were to be semi-annual, January and July, but the July, 1901, dividend was deferred. On January 10, 1903, an annual dividend of 7 per cent. was paid on the preferred.

FUNDED DEBT.

1st mort., 6 per cent., due 1905, Jan. and July.................................... $500,000

It was provided in the reorganization that after payment of interest on the bonds, 7 per cent. on the preferred stock and 5 per cent. on the common, the surplus earnings shall be applied to the redemption of bonds, which are to be drawn at par. When the bonds are all retired surplus earnings are to be divided *pro rata* between the two classes of stock.

The trustee of the mortgage is the United States Mortgage & Trust Co., New York.

The American Fisheries Co. had $2,000,000, 7 per cent., preferred stock and $8,000,000 common, par of each class $5 per share. The company paid 7 per cent. on its preferred in 1898, but became financially embarrassed in 1899. A controlling interest in the old company, as well as in the present one, was held in England. The plan of reorganization carried out in the early part of 1900 provided that each holder of 20 shares of the old preferred stock should receive one share of new preferred on subscribing at par for $25 of the new bonds. Each holder of 160 shares of old common was to pay $5 and receive one share of new common stock.

| EARNINGS. | Gross. | Net. |
|---|---|---|
| 1900 | $747,727 | $143,379 |
| 1901 | 777,408 | 27,770 |

President and General Manager, Nathaniel B. Church; Treasurer, William R. Morse; Secretary, Benjamin P. Clark.

*Directors—Nathaniel B. Church, Brooklyn, N. Y.; Lyman E. Warren, Thomas F. Woodlock, Thomas P. Goodbody, New York; Thomas F. Price, Greenport, L. I.; Robert Goodbody, Haledon, N. J.

Main office, 135 Front street, New York. Annual meeting, second Wednesday in January.

## FISKE WHARF & WAREHOUSE TRUST

A voluntary association formed in Massachusetts under a declaration of trust dated January 1, 1901. The purpose of the trust is to own and operate a wharf and warehouse business at Boston, consisting of Fiske Wharf and Harris Wharf, with adjoining land amounting to about 225,000 square feet. The two wharves possess the docks and necessary equipment for handling merchandise and a new fireproof warehouse, covering 25,000 square feet, seven stories high, with basement, and equipped with modern appliances, has been built. The trustees have also acquired the lease of another wharf at East Boston, with two smaller warehouses, which will be operated in connection with the main plant in Boston.

Stock......Par $100.....Authorized { com., $350,000 / pref., 150,000 } Issued { com., $350,000 / pref., 150,000 } $500,000

The preferred stock is 5 per cent., cumulative, and shares with the common in any surplus earnings after 7 per cent. has been paid on the common stock in any year. The preferred also has a preference as to any distribution of assets in case of dissolution, and is to share *pro rata* in the distribution of the surplus after the common stock has received $150 per share.

Stock is transferred at the company's office, Boston.

FUNDED DEBT.

Gold mort. notes, 4 per cent., due 1921, Jan. and July............................ $500,000

The State Street Trust Co., Boston, is the trustee of the mortgage. The same institution also pays coupons on the bonds.

Trustees—Francis Peabody, Jr., John L. Nichols, Leslie C. Wead, Boston.

Main office, 16 State street, Boston.

## FORT PITT GAS CO.

A corporation formed under the laws of Pennsylvania, December 14, 1899. The business of the company is the production and supplying of natural gas. The company supplies gas in New Castle, Beaver Falls, New Brighton, Rochester, Beaver, Freedom, Sewickley, Avalon, McKee's Rocks, Esplen and other Ohio River towns in Pennsylvania, and in East Liverpool and Wellsville, O., as well as in the cities of Pittsburg and Allegheny, Pa. The lands owned and leased in Pennsylvania and West Virginia are about 645,000 acres. The length of pipe and casing in the company's lines and wells will approximate to 711 miles.

Stock......Par $50..........................Authorized, $2,500,000......Issued, $2,486,400

Stock is transferred at the company's office. Registrar, Union Trust Co., Pittsburg.

FUNDED DEBT.

1st mort., 6 per cent., due 1902 to 1911, June 30 and Dec. 30........................ $900,000

Of the 1st mortgage bonds, $100,000 mature each year from June 30, 1902, to June 30, 1911. Trustee of the mortgage, Union Trust Co., Pittsburg. Interest on the bonds is paid at the office of the Mellon National Bank, Pittsburg.

The company pays 4 per cent. per annum on its stock, the dividends being 1 per cent. quarterly, in March (30), June, September and December.

President, Joseph W. Craig; Vice-President, J. J. Fisher; 2d Vice-President and General Manager, P. L. Craig; Treasurer, E. P. Mellon; Secretary, N. M. McKee.

Directors—Joseph W. Craig, J. J. Fisher, P. L. Craig, A. W. Mellon, E. P. Mellon, Henry C. Frick, John C. Fischer.

Main office, 323 Fourth avenue, Pittsburg. Annual meeting, last Tuesday in November at Pittsburg.

---

## THE FORT STREET UNION DEPOT CO.

A corporation formed under the laws of Michigan, August 24, 1889, for the purpose of furnishing railroads entering Detroit with terminal facilities for freight and passengers. It has expended in securing real estate and right of way, elevated railroad approaches and for the erection of suitable passenger stations, upward of $2,325,000. The length of the double main track from the depot to the end of right of way, where it joins and connects with the Detroit Union Railroad Depot and Station Co., is 1.4 miles, with 1.27 miles of sidings, all laid with seventy-pound steel rails.

This company's property is leased for 999 years from December 10, 1889, to the Wabash, Flint & Pere Marquette, Detroit, Lansing & Northern (Detroit, Grand Rapids & Western Railroad) and Canadian Pacific Railroad Cos. By the terms of the lease the lessees agree to pay as rental to the lessor a sum per annum equal to 5 per cent. on the total cost of the work and the current expenses.

Stock......Par $100........................Authorized, $1,000,000......Issued, $1,000,000

FUNDED DEBT.

| | |
|---|---|
| 1st mort., 4½ per cent., gold, due 1941, Jan. and July.............................. | $1,000,000 |
| 20-year gold bonds, 5 per cent., due 1915, Jan. and July........................... | 294,000 |
| Total .................................................................. | $1,294,000 |

The bonds are secured by mortgage of the property of the company to the Central Trust Co., New York, trustee, at which institution interest on the same is paid.

President, William W. Crapo, New Bedford, Mass.; Vice-President, Charles M. Heald; Secretary and Treasurer, Henry B. Joy, Detroit.

Directors—William W. Crapo, New Bedford, Mass.; Charles M. Heald, J. Ramsey, Jr., St. Louis; Henry B. Joy, Detroit; Thomas Tait, Montreal.

Main office, 68 Griswold street, Detroit.

---

## FORTY-SECOND STREET, MANHATTANVILLE & ST. NICHOLAS AVENUE RAILWAY CO.

(Controlled by Third Avenue Railroad Co.)

A corporation formed under the laws of New York, August 29, 1878. The Third Avenue Railroad Co. purchased controlling interest in this company's stock in November, 1895. The company operates 12 miles of double track by underground electric trolley. A Receiver was appointed in March, 1900, but was discharged in April, 1901.

Stock......Par $100........................Authorized, $2,500,000......Issued, $2,500,000

FUNDED DEBT.

| | |
|---|---|
| 1st mort., 6 per cent., due March, 1910, March and Sept........................... | $1,200,000 |
| 2d mort., 6 per cent., due Jan., 1915, Jan. and July.............................. | 1,500,000 |
| Total .................................................................. | $2,700,000 |

The outstanding bonds of both mortgages are the full amount authorized. Trustee of mortgages and agent for the payment of interest, Union Trust Co., New York. There are also real estate mortgages for $100,000.

EARNINGS.

| Year ending June 30. | Gross. | Net. |
|---|---|---|
| 1897-98 | $703,975 | $77,814 |
| 1898-99 | 571,046 | Def., 9,184 |
| 1899-00 | 340,513 | Def., 67,892 |
| 1900-01 | 697,749 | 225,214 |
| 1901-02 | 815,172 | 372,618 |

President, John Beaver; Secretary, Treasurer and Superintendent, Charles E. Warren. Main office, 177 Manhattan street, New York. Annual meeting, third Thursday in January.

## THE FOUR METALS MINING CO.

A corporation formed under the laws of Colorado, January 17, 1899, to mine, mill and smelt ores. The company owns an operates 47 mining claims with a total acreage of 516.63, at Telluride and Silverton, Col. d

Stock......Par 1..............................Authorized, $2,000,000......Issued, $1,500,000

The company has no preferred stock and no funded debt.

President, W. Frank Carter; 1st Vice-President and Auditor, Charles H. McKee; 2d Vice-President, Patrick Short; Secretary and Treasurer, R. M. Scruggs; Assistant Secretary, William G. McCarty, St. Louis; Superintendent, Joseph H. Shockley, Telluride, Col.

Directors—W. Frank Carter, John Morton, Charles McKee, J. H. Kerr, Patrick Short, R. M. Scruggs, St. Louis; J. M. Galvin, Boston.

Corporate and mine office, Opera House Block, Pueblo, Col.; main office, Equitable Building, St. Louis. Annual meeting, first Saturday in January, at Pueblo, Col.

## THE FRANCISCO SUGAR CO.

A corporation formed under the laws of New Jersey, February 23, 1899. The purpose of the company is to grow cane and manufacture sugar. It owns 16,667 acres of sugar land in the Island of Cuba between Manzanillo and Santa Cruz, and has a factory equipped with machinery with a capacity of grinding 900 to 1,000 tons of sugar cane daily.

Stock......Par $100..............................Authorized, $750,000......Issued, $750,000

The company has no preferred stock.

Stock is transferred at the office of the company, Philadelphia. Registrar, Guarantee Trust & Safe Deposit Co., Philadelphia.

FUNDED DEBT.

1st mort., 6 per cent. gold, due 1911, June and Dec..................................$250,000

The bonds issued are the total amount authorized. Trustee of the mortgage and agent for the payment of interest, Guarantee Trust & Safe Deposit Co., Philadelphia.

President, John F. Craig, Philadelphia; Vice-President, Manuel Rionda, New York; Secretary and Treasurer, Thomas C. McCahan, Philadelphia.

Directors—W. J. McCahan, John F. Craig, Amos R. Little, J. M. McCahan, H. D. Justi, Philadelphia; Manuel Rionda, George R. MacDougall, Joseph I. C. Clarke, New York; Benjamin W. Parker, Boston.

Corporate office, 106 Market street, Camden, N. J.; main office, 143 South Front street, Philadelphia. Annual meeting, second Wednesday in October, at Camden.

## FRANKLIN MINING CO.

A corporation formed under the laws of Michigan, April 3, 1857. It is one of the oldest of the existing Lake Superior copper mining enterprises. The company owns a large copper mining property at Hancock, Houghton County, Mich., upon the same lodes as the Calumet & Hecla and Quincy mines. It has a stamp mill at Portage Lake, and during recent years has prosecuted extensive development work upon its property.

Stock......Par $25..............................Authorized, $2,500,000......Issued, $2,500,000

Stock is transferred at the company's office. Registrar, Mercantile Trust Co., Boston.

In 1898 the capital stock was increased from 40,000 shares to 80,000 shares, the increase being sold to the stockholders at $10 per share. In 1899 the authorized amount was increased to 100,000 shares, this increase being sold at $15 per share. Previous to this stock increase there had been paid in on the old stock $3.20 per share.

The company has paid dividends aggregating about $1,240,000. The last dividend was paid January 1, 1894. During 1896 the company produced 2,746,000 pounds of copper; in 1897,

2,908,000 pounds; in 1898, 2,623,000 pounds; in 1899, 1,230,000 pounds, and in 1900, 3,663,710 pounds; in 1901, 3,759,419 pounds; in 1902, 5,237,400 pounds.

President, Francis H. Raymond; Treasurer and Secretary, Daniel L. Demmon, Boston.

Directors—Daniel L. Demmon, Francis H. Raymond, J. Q. Bennett, George H. Flint, J. D. Hosking.

Main office, 15 Congress street, Boston. Annual meeting, third Wednesday in April.

## THE FRANKLIN STEEL CASTING CO.

A corporation formed under the laws of Pennsylvania, in 1894, for the purpose of manufacturing steel castings of all kinds. The company's plant at Franklin, Pa., consists of three buildings of iron construction, several smaller buildings of brick, for offices, boiler and engine rooms, pattern shops, etc. The property covers about six acres.

The company is controlled by the American Steel Foundries.

Stock......Par $100..............................Authorized, $750,000......Issued, $750,000

Transfer Agent, Franklin Trust Co., Franklin, Pa.

The company has no preferred stock and no funded debt.

The company has paid regular quarterly dividends on its stock at the rate of 6 per cent. per annum, and an extra dividend on several occasions. Dividend payments are January, April, July and October.

President, Charles W. Mackey, New York; 1st Vice-President, Charles Miller; 2d Vice-President, James W. Rowland; Secretary, Robert McCalmont; Treasurer, William J. Bleakley, Franklin, Pa.

Directors—Charles W. Mackey, James W. Rowland, Charles Miller, Robert McCalmont, William J. Bleakley, Joseph E. Schwab, Daniel Eagan, H. B. Heard, F. S. Patterson, New York.

Main office, Franklin, Pa. Annual meeting, third Wednesday in January, at Franklin, Pa.

## THE FRIES MANUFACTURING & POWER CO.

A corporation formed under the laws of North Carolina, February 28, 1891, to furnish electric light and power and to operate an electric railway in Winston-Salem, N. C. The company acquired the franchise and property of the Winston-Salem Railway & Electric Co., which it now operates. It also owns and operates a power-generating plant on the Yadkin river, 13½ miles from Winston-Salem, and a 30-ton refrigerating plant.

Stock.......Par $100........Authorized { com., $600,000; pref., 100,000 } Issued { com., $574,600; pref., 100,000 } $674,600

Stock is transferred at the office of the company, Winston-Salem, N. C.

FUNDED DEBT.

1st mort., 5 per cent., due Jan. 1, 1940, Jan. and July..................................$450,000

The authorized 1st mortgage was $500,000. Trustee of the mortgage and agent for the payment of interest, North American Trust Co., New York.

In the fiscal year ending November 30, 1902, the gross earnings were $103,659; net, $35,315; interest, $2,500; surplus, $12,815.

President, Henry E. Fries; Vice-President, William A. Blair; Secretary and Treasurer, Bernard J. Pfohl, Winston-Salem, N. C.

Directors—Henry E. Fries, John W. Fries, J. C. Bessent, W. A. Whitaker, William A. Blair, J. Jacobs, N. S. Wilson, C. B. Watson, E. E. Gray, W. M. Nissen, J. A. Vance, C. D. Ogburn, Celment Manly, F. C. Brown, J. W. Haines, W. A. Lemly, F. H. Fries, Winston-Salem, N. C.; R. B. Haines, Jr., Philadelphia.

Corporate and main office, Winston-Salem, N. C. Annual meeting, second Tuesday in April, at Winston-Salem.

## GEORGE A. FULLER CO.

(Controlled by United States Realty & Construction Co.)

A corporation formed under the laws of New Jersey, April 1, 1901. The business of the company is building construction. The company has undertaken and carried out the construction of a number of large and important buildings in New York and other cities.

In August, 1902, the stockholders of this company were offered 110 in preferred and 50 in common stock of the United States Realty & Construction Co. for the preferred stock of this company and 45 in preferred and 75 in common stock of the new company for the common stock of this company. A large majority of the stock was exchanged on the above basis.

Stock..Par $100...Authorized { com., $15,000,000; pref., 5,000,000 } Issued { com., $10,000,000; pref., 5,000,000 } $15,000,000

The preferred stock is 7 per cent., cumulative, dividends on the preferred being payable quarterly on the 1st of January, April, July and October. Accumulated unpaid preferred dividends shall be made up before any dividends are paid on the common stock, and the amount of the annual dividend on the preferred shall in each year be reserved before any dividends shall be set apart or paid on the common. In the event of the company's dissolution the preferred shall be entitled to its face value and accrued dividends out of the assets, and the common stock shall be entitled to the entire remaining assets. The preferred stock has no voting power.

Transfer Agent, Central Realty Bond & Trust Co., New York; Registrar, National City Bank, New York.

The company has no funded debt.

The first dividend on the preferred stock was 1¾ per cent. quarterly, paid July 1, 1901. Regular quarterly dividends of the same amount are paid on the preferred at the periods designated above.

President, S. P. McConnell; Secretary, R. G. Babbage; Treasurer, Byron M. Fellows; Assistant Treasurer, D. H. Lanman.

Directors—Harry S. Black, James Stillman, Henry Morgenthau, Hugh J. Grant, S. P. McConnell, New York; P. A. Valentine, John C. Fleming, Chicago; Thorwald Stallnecht, Jersey City.

Corporate office, 15 Exchange place, Jersey City; New York office, 135 Broadway; branch offices: Chicago, Baltimore, Boston, Philadelphia, Richmond, Washington, Pittsburg. Annual meeting, first Tuesday in April, at Jersey City.

---

## FULTON COUNTY GAS & ELECTRIC CO.

A corporation formed under the laws of New York in June, 1900. The purposes of the company are the manufacture of gas and of electric light and power in the cities of Johnstown and Gloversville, Fulton County, N. Y. The company acquired the following companies:

Johnstown & Gloversville Gas Co.
Gloversville Electric Co.
The Johnstown Electric Light & Power Co.

A controlling interest is owned by the United Gas Improvement Co.

Stock......Par $100..........................Authorized, $1,500,000......Issued, $1,500,000

The company has no preferred stock. Stock is transferred at the office of the company, Philadelphia.

FUNDED DEBT.

1st mort., 5 per cent., due June, 1936, June and Dec............................... $1,100,000

The authorized amount of the 1st mortgage is $1,500,000. The trustee of the mortgage is the Morton Trust Co., New York. Coupons of the bonds are paid at that institution.

President, A. M. Young, New York; Vice-President, Randal Morgan; Secretary and Treasurer, Lewis Lillie, Philadelphia.

Directors—A. M. Young, R. A. C. Smith, Samuel H. Hoey, New York; Randal Morgan Walton Clark, Philadelphia.

Main office, Johnstown, N. Y. Annual meeting, second Tuesday in July, at Johnstown, N. Y.

---

## THE GAS & ELECTRIC CO. OF BERGEN COUNTY

A corporation formed under the laws of New Jersey, May 31, 1899. The company is a consolidation of the Hackensack Gas & Electric Co., the Englewood Gas & Electric Co., the Ridgewood Electric Light & Power Co., the New York, Rutherford & Suburban Gas Co. and the Rutherford, Boiling Springs & Carlstadt Electric Co. All the property of the constituent companies was acquired. The company owns three gas plants at Hackensack, N. J., Rutherford, N. J., and Englewood, N. J., respectively. It has about 150 miles of gas mains. Its electric plant at Hackensack supplies the whole district with electricity, there being about 300 miles of pole lines. Its gas franchises are perpetual, as are 90 per cent. of the electric franchises under which it works. Contracts have been made with the authorities of nearly all the municipalities it serves for public lighting. The principal plant is the one at Hackensack, which has been practically rebuilt with modern machinery and appliances. The company's service extends into fifty-four towns and municipal divisions of Bergen County, N. J.

Under date of December 30, 1901, a committee, Edwin Gould, New York, chairman, called for a deposit of the stock of this company with the Bowling Green Trust Co., with a view to a financial readjustment, sale or lease of the company's property. On February 15, 1902, a large majority of the stock had been deposited, and the committee operate the property. Secretary of the committee, William M. Laws, 26 Broadway, New York.

Stock......Par $100..........................Authorized, $2,000,000......Issued, $2,000,000

Transfer Agent, Bowling Green Trust Co., New York. Registrar, Guaranty Trust Co., New York.

FUNDED DEBT.

| | |
|---|---|
| Consolidated mort., 5 per cent., due 1949, June and Dec. | $1,294,000 |
| Debentures, 5½ per cent., due 1920, June and Dec. | 300,000 |
| Hackensack Gas Light Co., gen. mort., 5 per cent., due 1934, Jan. and July | 28,000 |
| Hackensack Gas & Electric Co., gen. mort., 5 per cent., due 1935, Jan. and July | 10,000 |
| " " " " 6 per cent. debentures, A, due 1917, Jan. and July | 5,000 |
| " " " " 6 per cent. debentures, B, due 1918, Jan. and July | 21,000 |
| Bergen Co. Gas Light, 1st mort., 5 per cent., due 1908, March and Sept. | 14,000 |
| Englewood Gas & Electric Co., gen. mort., 5 per cent., due 1939, Jan. and July | 28,000 |
| Rutherford & B. S. Gas Co., gen. mort., 6 per cent., due 1911, March and Sept. | 50,000 |
| N. Y., Ruther. & Subur. Gas Co., con. mort., 6 per cent., due 1911, March and Sept. | 50,000 |
| Total | $1,800,000 |

The consolidated mortgage is for $1,500,000. Of the amount of these bonds outstanding, $206,000 were in January, 1902, held by the Fidelity Trust Co. of Newark, the trustee to retire the outstanding bonds of the constituent companies. There were $412,000 of the underlying bonds, of which $206,000 were retired, with an equal amount of this company's consols.

The debentures are $600,000 authorized, and were created in 1900 to finance the company's floating debt. They are subject to call at 105 after 1905.

Trustee of consolidated mortgage, Fidelity Trust Co., Newark, N. J.

President, David St. John; Vice-President, John J. Phelps; Treasurer and General Manager, Edmund A. Pearce; Secretary, Lemuel Lozier, Hackensack, N. J.

Directors—George W. Conklin, Edmund A. Pearce, D. A. Pell, David St. John, John J. Phelps, Lemuel Lozier, Hackensack, N. J.; William McKenzie, Carlton Hill, N. J.; William N. Coler, New York; John C. Eisele, Newark, N. J.; Addison Ely, Rutherford, N. J.; D. A. Currie, Englewood, N. J.; F. A. E. Cott, Alfred Jaretzki, R. W. Jones, New York; Isaac D. Bogert, Westwood, N. J.

Main office, 114 Main street, Hackensack, N. J.; branch offices, Ridgewood, N. J.; Englewood, N. J., and Rutherford, N. J. Annual meeting, first Monday in June.

## GEARY STREET, PARK & OCEAN RAILROAD CO.

A corporation formed under the laws of California, November 8, 1878. The company owns and operates 7.67 miles of cable street railway in the city of San Francisco. It has a cable power house and 34 cars.

Stock......Par $100........................... Authorized, $1,000,000......Issued, $1,000,000

The company has no preferred stock.

The first dividend was paid May 31, 1880. Annual dividends ranging from 3½ per cent. to 6 per cent. have been annually paid. The present dividend rate is 3½ per cent. annual.

FUNDED DEBT.

1st mort., 5 per cent., due 1921, April and Oct. .......... $671,000

The authorized 1st mortgage was $1,000,000. Trustee of the mortgage, California Safe Deposit & Trust Co., San Francisco. A sinking fund of $10,000 annually after 1911 is provided for.

President, Horace G. Platt; Vice-President, Adam Grant; Secretary, R. Derby; Treasurer, E. O. Wright, San Francisco.

Directors—Horace G. Platt, Adam Grant, W. H. Crocker, R. F. Morrow, N. T. Smith, H. E. Huntington, C. G. Lathrop, San Francisco.

Corporate and main office, 610 Market street, San Francisco. Annual meeting, second Wednesday in April, at San Francisco.

## GENERAL CHEMICAL CO.

A corporation formed under the laws of New York, February 15, 1899, to carry on the business of the manufacture of heavy chemicals. It owns twenty-four plants situated in the East and West. The company began business March 1, 1899.

Stock....Par $100.....Authorized { com., $12,500,000 / pref., 12,500,000 } Issued { com., $7,410,300 / pref., 9,416,000 } $16,826,300

Stock is transferred at company's office, 25 Broad street, New York. Registrar, Title Guarantee & Trust Co., New York.

The preferred stock is entitled to 6 per cent., cumulative, annual dividends. The company has no bonded debt. In October, 1901, new preferred stock to the amount of $856,000 was subscribed at par.

The company began the payment of dividends on its preferred stock July 1, 1899, and has since regularly paid 1½ per cent. quarterly, in January, April, July and October.

In February, 1900, the company began the payment of dividends at the rate of 4 per cent. on the common stock, payable 1 per cent., quarterly, March (1), June, September and December, and has regularly paid such dividends since that time, the dividends for 1902 out of the earnings of 1901 being on that basis. On February 18, 1903, a dividend of 5 per cent. on the common stock out of the earnings of 1902 was declared payable quarterly during 1903.

The accounts of the company, December 31, 1902, certified by Barrow, Wade, Guthrie & Co., public accountants, showed:

| | | |
|---|---|---|
| Surplus on books, December 31, 1901 | | $1,238,437 |
| Net profit for the year 1902 | $1,537,551 | |
| Less fire insurance reserve | 30,000.00 | |
| | | 1,507,551 |
| Total | | $2,745,988 |
| Less dividends paid to stockholders: | | |
| Preferred | $564,960 | |
| Common | 296,412 | |
| | | 861,372 |
| Total | | $1,884,616 |
| Less charged off plant account, etc. | | 269,143 |
| Surplus, December 31, 1902 | | $1,615,473 |
| During the year there has been expended: | | |
| On new construction and betterments | | $706,073 |
| On repairs and reconstruction, charged to expense account | | 415.81 |

The balance sheet, December 31, 1902, was as follows:

| Assets. | | | Liabilities. | | |
|---|---|---|---|---|---|
| Manufacturing investment at cost | | $13,245,006 | Capital stock, preferred | | $9,416,000 |
| Investments in other corporations | | 2,685,760 | " " common | | 7,410,300 |
| Merchandise on hand, at factory cost | | 1,349,674 | Accounts payable: | | |
| Receivable as follows: | | | Sundry accounts | $235,393 | |
| Customers' accounts | $809,244 | | Due to corporations controlled | 24,671 | |
| Due from corporations controlled | 626,141 | | Loans | 350,000 | |
| Loans | 91,772 | | | | 610,065 |
| | | 1,527,158 | Dividends accrued | | 141,240 |
| Cash | | 366,602 | Reserve for fire insurance | | 30,127 |
| Reserved fund for fire insurance | | 30,127 | Surplus | | 1,615,473 |
| Unexpired insurance premiums, etc. | | 18,878 | | | |
| Total | | $19,223,205 | Total | | $19,223,205 |

President, William H. Nichols; 1st Vice-President, Sanford H. Steele; 2d Vice-President, Charles Robinson Smith; Treasurer, James L. Morgan; Secretary, J. Herbert Bagg, Chairman Executive Committee, Edward H. Rising; Consulting Engineer, J. B. F. Herreshoff.

Directors—William H. Nichols, Sanford H. Steele, George W. Kenyon, Charles Robinson Smith, James Speyer, James L. Morgan, J. Herbert Bagg, Edward H. Rising, New York; Eugene Waugh, Highlands, N. Y.; Clarence P. Tiers, Pittsburg; Howard F. Chappell, Henry W. Chappell, Chicago; William M. Johnson.

Main office, 25 Broad street, New York.

## GENERAL ELECTRIC CO.

A corporation formed under the laws of New York, April 15, 1892, to combine the interests of the Edison General Electric and Thomson-Houston Electric Companies. The company owns all the stock of those corporations. It has works at Lynn, Mass.; Schenectady, N. Y., and Harrison,

N. J., for manufacturing machinery and electric supplies. In 1902 the Sprague Electric Co. was acquired.

Stock......Par $100........................Authorized, $45,000,000......Issued, $41,957,100

The company had $2,551,000 preferred stock, which was 7 per cent., cumulative, but had no preference as to assets. In July, 1900, it was decided to increase the common stock, then $18,276,000, by the issue of $4,415,000 to retire the $5,298,000 outstanding 5 per cent. debentures. See below. In 1901 the common stock was increased to $45,000,000 and the preferred stock was all exchanged for common, share for share.

Transfer Agent, Farmers' Loan & Trust Co., New York. Registrar, Guaranty Trust Co. New York.

Last dividend paid on the old preferred stock was 3½ per cent., July 1, 1893; on common, 2 per cent., quarterly, August 1, 1893. The November, 1893, dividend was passed.

Payments on account of the back preferred dividends (on the amount of old stock) were: November 15, 1898, 11⅔ per cent.; December 22, 1898, 17½ per cent.; January 31, 1899, 11⅔ per cent.; March 8, 1899, 19.05⅔ per cent., completing the entire amount of back dividends.

On August 17, 1899, the payment of regular half-yearly dividends of 3½ per cent. on the preferred stock were resumed, and have been paid since in January (31) and July. Dividends on the common stock were resumed by the payment of 1½ per cent. July 15, 1899, and were continued quarterly at the same ratio until October 15, 1900, when 2 per cent. was paid, putting the stock on an 8 per cent. basis, which has been the regular rate since then. The January, 1901, dividend was 2 per cent. regular and 1 per cent. extra. Dividends on the common are paid quarterly, January (15), April, July and October.

FUNDED DEBT.

| | |
|---|---|
| Debentures, 3½ per cent., due Aug., 1942, Feb. and Aug. | $2,049,400 |
| Convertible debentures, 5 per cent., due June, 1922, June and Dec. | 96,000 |
| Total | $2,145,400 |

The 3½ per cent. debentures were issued in 1902, being given in exchange for the stock of the Sprague Electric Co. They are redeemable within ten years at par and afterwards at 105.

The stock was originally $4,252,000 7 per cent., cumulative, preferred stock and $30,468,000 common. The dividends on preferred were unpaid from July 1, 1893, to August, 1898, amounting to $1,527,885. In 1898 it was decided to charge off the debit to the company's profit and loss and impairment of capital by a reduction of the stock to the present figures, making it three-fifths of the old amount. Resolution to this effect was adopted by the stockholders on August 17, 1898. Old stock was exchanged on this basis for the new. There was objection and litigation on part of the old preferred stockholders, but this was settled, and during the autumn and winter of 1898 payment of the accumulated back dividends was liquidated.

On July 15, 1902, the stockholders received a stock dividend of 66⅔ per cent., restoring the 40 per cent. reduction made in 1898. This required $16,812,600 of the new stock.

In 1897 company purchased $750,000 of its 5 per cent. convertible debentures, leaving amount outstanding $8,000,000, and during 1898 $2,300,000 more were retired. In 1902, all but $96,000 of the debentures were retired in exchange for common stock at the ratio of $120 in bonds for $100 in the stock.

In March, 1896, this company entered into agreement with Westinghouse Electric Co., by which patents of the two companies were pooled and opened to their joint use under royalty.

EARNINGS.

| | Gross. | Net. | Charges. | Surplus. |
|---|---|---|---|---|
| 1897 | $12,820,395 | $2,120,441 | $431,250 | $1,689,191 |
| 1898 | 12,524,938 | 2,148,520 | 333,335 | 1,815,185 |
| 1899 | 16,472,022 | 4,166,325 | 290,000 | 3,876,324 |
| 1900 | 23,248,171 | 5,832,464 | 281,667 | 5,550,797 |
| 1901 | 29,829,652 | 6,244,439 | 240,040 | 6,004,399 |
| 1902 | 33,856,363 | 8,598,241 | 42,310 | 8,555,931 |

In 1897 $583,335 was charged for factory extension, reserve and patents. In 1898-99 $269,440 was charged to patents, leaving for dividends $3,606,884. In 1899-1900 $353,334 was charged to patents; surplus for dividends, $5,197,463; dividends, $1,001,004; written off for depreciation, etc., $2,000,000; balance surplus, $2,196,459. In 1901 dividend payments aggregated $1,728,249. In 1902 the surplus over dividends was $6,600,274.

On January 31, 1898, company had $59,422,778 par value of bonds and stocks of other companies carried in books at $7,455,872, a large amount being held at $1 for each lot. In 1899 the same item was $7,226,422. On January 31, 1899, notes and accounts receivable aggregated $5,806,061, and January 31, 1900, $6,978,002. On January 31, 1900, the book value of the securities owned was $6,132,268. On January 31, 1901, it was $6,012,300.

The following is the company's balance sheet, January 31, 1902:

ASSETS.

| | | | |
|---|---|---|---|
| Cash | | | $4,058,448 |
| Stocks and bonds | | $9,825,120 | |
| Real estate (other than factory plants) | | 464,195 | |
| Notes and accounts receivable | | 11,364,345 | |
| Work in progress | | 1,338,258 | |
| Merchandise inventories: | | $22,991,920 | |
| At factories | $7,742,605 | | |
| At general and local offices | 1,037,968 | | |
| Consignments | 96,309 | | |
| | | 8,876,883 | |
| | | | 31,886,803 |
| Factory plants | | $4,000,000 | |
| Patents, franchises and good-will | | 2,000,000 | |
| | | | 6,000,000 |
| Total | | | $41,927,251 |

LIABILITIES.

| | | |
|---|---|---|
| 5 per cent. gold coupon debentures | $372,000 | |
| Accrued interest on debentures | 3,100 | |
| Accounts payable | 1,349,335 | |
| Unclaimed dividends | 4,775 | |
| | | $1,729,211 |
| Capital stock | | 24,910,900 |
| Surplus | | 15,287,140 |
| Total | | $41,927,251 |

In August, 1893, it was arranged to pay off the floating debt of the company by organizing another organization under the title of The Street Railway and Illuminating Properties, to which was turned over $12,000,000 of securities in various local and operating companies held in the treasury of the General Electric. Stockholders of the latter were invited to subscribe for the $4,500,000 preferred stock of the "Illuminating Properties" and the proceeds were to be turned over to this company.

President, C. A. Coffin; Vice-Presidents, Eugene Griffin, E. W. Rice, Jr., Hinsdill Parsons; Treasurer, H. W. Darling; Secretary, M. F. Westover, Schenectady, N. Y.

Directors—J. Pierpont Morgan, Eugene Griffin, George Foster Peabody, J. P. Ord, Charles Steele, New York; C. A. Coffin, T. Jefferson Coolidge, Jr., H. L. Higginson, Oliver Ames, R. T. Paine 2d, Gordon Abbott, George P. Gardner, Frederick P. Fish, Boston.

Main office, Schenectady; New York office, 44 Broad street. Annual meeting, second Tuesday in May at Schenectady, N. Y.

---

## GENEVA, WATERLOO, SENECA FALLS & CAYUGA LAKE TRACTION CO.

A corporation formed under the laws of New York, March 28, 1895. The company is a consolidation of the following companies:

Geneva Surface Railway Co.
Geneva & Waterloo Railway Co.
Seneca Electric Railway Co.
Waterloo, Seneca Falls & Cayuga Lake Railway Co.

The company owns an electric power plant and 31 cars and operates 17.75 miles of track in Geneva, Waterloo and Seneca Falls, N. Y. It also owns the Cayuga Lake Park of 50 acres.

Stock......Par $100.........Authorized { com., $350,000 / pref., 100,000 } Issued { com., $350,000 / pref., 99,500 } $449,500

FUNDED DEBT.

1st mort., 4 per cent. gold, due April, 1920, April and Oct........................... $436,500

The authorized amount of the 1st mortgage is $500,000. Trustee of the bonds and agent for the payment of interest, West End Trust & Safe Deposit Co., Philadelphia.

EARNINGS.

Year ending June 30.

| | Gross. | Net. | Interest and Taxes. | Deficit |
|---|---|---|---|---|
| 1898-99 | $59,856 | $27,103 | $28,647 | $3,768 |
| 1899-00 | 60,370 | 28,787 | 28,879 | 1,389 |
| 1900-01 | 63,576 | 25,888 | 29,376 | 3,152 |
| 1901-02 | 66,043 | 27,325 | 20,542 | Sur. 6,783 |

President, Isaac M. Thomas, Wilkes-Barre, Pa.; Vice-President, W. S. Grant; Secretary and Treasurer, W. C. Gray, Seneca Falls, N. Y.

Directors—Isaac M. Thomas, Wilkes-Barre, Pa.; J. P. Brosius, Merion, Pa.; Robert Wetherill, Chester, Pa.; W. C. Gray, Charles A. Hawley, Seneca Falls, N. Y.; H. A. Doan, W. S. Grant, Jr., Lewis Davis, Philadelphia; L. S. Hoskins, Geneva, N. Y.

Main office, Seneca Falls, N. Y. Annual meeting, second Wednesday in March, at Seneca Falls, N. Y.

## GILCHRIST TRANSPORTATION CO.

A corporation formed under the laws of Ohio, January 21, 1897. The business of the company is general freighting on the lakes, mainly the transportation of grain, coal and iron ore. It owns and operates 80 ships. The company absorbed, in 1903, the following organizations:

| | |
|---|---|
| The Lake Shore Transit Co. | Globe Steamship Co. |
| Inland Star Transit Co. | The Steel Steamship Co. |
| The Merida Steamship Co. | The Tyrone Transportation Co. |
| The Vega Steamship Co. | The Lorain Steamship Co. |

Stock......Par $100........................Authorized, $10,000,000......Issued, $7,000,000

The company has no preferred stock.

FUNDED DEBT.

Bonds, 5 per cent........................................................ $2,902,000

President, J. C. Gilchrist; Vice-President, F. M. Osborne; Secretary, A. J. Gilchrist; Treasurer, F. R. Gilchrist, Cleveland.

Directors—J. C. Gilchrist, F. R. Gilchrist, A. J. Gilchrist, F. M. Osborne, J. A. Gilchrist, F. W. Hart, Cleveland; R. E. Schuck, Sandusky, O.; F. W. Gilchrist, Alpena, Mich.; J. B. Wood, Bellevue, O.

Main office, Mentor Special District, O.; Cleveland office, 103 Superior street. Annual meeting, third Tuesday in January, at Mentor Special District, O.

## THE GINTER GROCERY CO.

A corporation formed under the laws of New York, July 22, 1901, to take over the Ginter Grocery & Produce Co., a New Jersey corporation, and conducting a general grocery business and operating branch stores.

Stock.......Par $10.......Authorized { com., $175,000 / pref., 175,000 } Issued { com., $175,000 / pref., 175,000 } $350,000

The preferred stock is 8 per cent., cumulative, and takes precedence of the common as to assets, payable quarterly. The company has no funded debt.

Transfer Agent and Registrar, International Trust Co., Boston.

Since October 1, 1901, the regular 8 per cent. dividends have been paid on the preferred stock, the payments being 2 per cent. quarterly, in January, April, July and October.

President, Augustus F. Goodwin; Vice-President, Treasurer and Secretary, H. B. Duane, Boston.

Directors—A. F. Goodwin, H. B. Duane, J. C. Duane, E. G. Maturin, Boston; Charles Thorley, New York.

Main office, 236 Tremont street, Boston. Annual meeting, third Monday in June, at New York.

## GOLD & STOCK TELEGRAPH CO.

A corporation formed under the laws of New York in 1867. It has a system of stock, grain and other market reports by means of a ticker service. The company is leased by the Western Union Telegraph Co.

Stock......Par $100......................Authorized, $5,000,000......Issued, $5,000,000

Stock is transferred at the company's office.

The Western Union Telegraph Co. owns $2,555,600 of the company's stock, leaving $2,444,400 outstanding in the hands of the public.

The dividends on the stock are paid quarterly, 1¼ per cent. each, in January, April, July and October.

FUNDED DEBT.

Bonds, not mort., 4½ per cent., due May, 1905, May and Nov........................ $500,000

The lease to the Western Union Telegraph Co. is for 99 years from January 1, 1882, the rental being interest on the bonds and 6 per cent. on the stock.

The bonds of the company are in denominations of $500 each. The present 4½ per cent bond issue replaced one of equal amount bearing 6 per cent. interest, which matured in 1895.

President, Robert C. Clowry; Secretary, A. R. Brewer; Treasurer, M. T. Wilbur.

Directors—Robert C. Clowry, Thomas T. Eckert, Howard Gould, Russell Sage, W. A. Wheelock, John T. Terry, Edwin Langdon, John B. Van Every, George J. Gould, Thomas F. Clark.

Main office, 195 Broadway, New York. Annual meeting, last Tuesday in September.

## THE GOLD BELT CONSOLIDATED ELECTRIC CO.

A corporation formed under the laws of Colorado, November 14, 1899. The company was organized to furnish electric light and power to the towns of the Cripple Creek, Col., district. It purchased outright the properties, business, franchises and contracts of the Victor Light, Water & Motor Co., lighting Victor, Anaconda and Altman; the Gold Belt Electric Co., lighting Goldfield, Independence, Gillett, Cameron and a portion of Cripple Creek; and the Fremont Electric Light & Power Co., lighting the city of Cripple Creek. All the franchises of the above companies have nineteen years to run. The combined population of these towns is about 50,000. The Consolidated Co. abandoned the use of separate stations, and operates the entire district from one power plant, obtaining thereby great economy. The company began business practically on September 1, 1899.

Stock......Par $100............................Authorized, $300,000......Issued, $300,000

Stock is transferred at company's office, Denver, Col.

FUNDED DEBT.

1st mort., 6 per cent., due 1919, Jan. and July.................................... .. $250,000

The bonds are secured by a mortgage of all its property to the International Trust Co., Denver, Col., at which institution the interest is paid. The bonds are in denominations of $500 each.

President—George E. Ross-Lewin; Vice-President, Charles F. Lacombe; Secretary, William F. Jones; Treasurer, Thomas Keely, Denver, Col.

Directors—Sylvester T. Smith, Chicago; Charles F. Lacombe, Thomas Keely, George E. Ross-Lewin, Z. T. Hill, Denver, Col.

Main office, 532 Seventeenth street, Denver, Col.

## GORHAM MANUFACTURING CO.

A corporation formed under the laws of Rhode Island in 1863, the object of the company being to manufacture and sell goods made of gold, silver and other metallic substances. The principal works of the company are located at Providence, R. I.

Stock....Par $100 ... Authorized { com., $3,000,000 / pref., 2,000,000 } Issued { com., $3,000,000 / pref., 1,200,000 } $4,200,000

The preferred stock is 6 per cent., cumulative. Stock is transferred at the company's office, Providence, R. I. Registrar, Rhode Island Hospital Trust Co., Providence, R. I.

The stock of the company was increased to the above figures in 1894. Prior to that time 10 per cent. per annum was paid on the stock. Since 1894 regular dividends of 6 per cent. per annum have been paid on both the preferred and common stocks. Dividends are paid quarterly, 1½ per cent. each, in January, April, July and October.

President and Treasurer, Edward Holbrook, Stamford, Conn.; Vice-President, George H. Robinson, New York; Secretary and Assistant Treasurer, J. F. P. Lawton, Providence, R. I.

Directors—Edward Holbrook, Stamford, Conn.; George H. Robinson, New York; J. F. P. Lawton, William H. Crins, Providence, R. I.; Frederick Grinnall, New Bedford, Mass.

Main office, Elmwood, Providence, R. I.; New York office, Broadway and Nineteenth street Annual meeting, second Wednesday in March.

## THE GOTTLIEB-BAUERNSCHMIDT-STRAUS BREWING CO.

A corporation formed under the laws of New Jersey, August 5, 1901, for the purpose of brewing beer and all other kinds of malt and fermented liquors. The company acquired the property of the Maryland Brewing Co. of Baltimore, which was foreclosed in pursuance of a reorganization plan. See statement of the Maryland Brewing Co. in the MANUAL for 1901.

Stock..... Par $100.......................... Authorized, $5,000,000......Issued, $5,000,000

Transfer Agent and Registrar, Mercantile Trust Co., Baltimore.

FUNDED DEBT.

| | |
|---|---|
| 1st mort., 3 and 4 per cent., due Sept. 1, 1950, March and Sept. | $5,625,000 |
| 2d mort., income, 5 per cent., due Sept. 1, 1951, May and Nov. | 3,500,000 |
| Total | $9,125,000 |

The first mortgage bonds are issued in denominations of $1,000 and $500. Interest on these bonds commenced to accrue from March 1, 1902, at the rate of 3 per cent. for two years from that date, and at the rate of 4 per cent. thereafter.

The second mortgage bonds are incomes and are in denominations of $1,000 and $500. They bear interest up to the rate of 5 per cent., commencing March 1, 1902, non-cumulative and payable out of the net income of the respective interest periods, provided said amount of net income shall have been earned, after providing for interest upon the first mortgage bonds and of the sum of $25,000 in each year, as a sinking fund for the first mortgage gold bonds, and the interest and annual sinking fund of underlying obligations. The November, 1902, coupon on the income bonds was not paid, the surplus earnings being required for working capital.

The Mercantile Trust & Deposit Co. of Baltimore, Md., is trustee and agent for payment of dividends and interest.

The Maryland Brewing Co. had $7,500,000 6 per cent. 1st mortgage bonds, $2,750,000 6 per cent. preferred stock and $2,750,000 common stock. In March, 1901, the company defaulted in its interest payment of the bonds. Receivers were appointed and a committee was formed to represent the bondholders, John Gill of Baltimore being chosen chairman. A reorganization plan was formulated in May providing for the organization of the company to take over the property. Under the plan holders of the old bonds received $750 in new 1st mortgage bonds; $300 in income bonds, and $200 in stock. The old preferred stock was assessed $10 per share and received 20 per cent. in income bonds and 66⅔ per cent. in new stock. The old common stock was assessed $20 per share and received 10 per cent. in income bonds and 33⅓ in new stock. Subsequently the assessments were reduced to $5 on the old preferred, and $2.50 on the old common, the new income bonds they received being also reduced to $10 and $5 respectively. The property was sold under foreclosure July 8, 1901, and was acquired by the present company.

President, George J. Obermann; Vice-President, Frederick H. Gottlieb; Secretary and Treasurer, James Barkley, Baltimore.

Directors—George J. Obermann, Frederick H. Gottlieb, John Bauernschmidt, Joseph H. Straus, Alexander L. Straus, Frank S. Hambleton, Harry A. Orrick, Omer F. Hershey, Baltimore; Peter Hauck, Jr., Newark, N. J.

Main office, Park avenue and Fayette street, Baltimore. Annual meeting, second Monday in May, at Camden, N. J.

---

## GRAND RAPIDS GAS LIGHT CO.

This company, formed in 1895, acquired the property of the Grand Rapids, Mich., Gas Co., and operates the gas works of that city, which has 90,000 population, under a franchise running until 1920. The company has 103 miles of mains.

The American Light & Traction Co. controls this company. See statement of that organization.

Stock......Par $50..........................Authorized, $1,000,000......Issued, $1,000,000

Transfer and Fiscal Agents for payment of coupons, Emerson McMillin & Co., 40 Wall street, New York.

FUNDED DEBT.

1st mort., 5 per cent. gold, due 1915, Feb. and Aug................................ $1,500,000

Trustee of the mortgage, Central Trust Co., New York.

President, H. D. Walbridge; Vice-President, Emerson McMillin; Secretary and Treasurer, H. B. Wales; Assistant Secretary, A. Lincoln Eglinton.

Directors—Emerson McMillin, Arthur D. Meeker, Anton G. Hodenpyl, J. M. Barnett, L. J. Rindge, T. J. O'Brien, Henry Idema, J. Boyd Pantlind, H. D. Walbridge.

Main office, Grand Rapids, Mich.

## THE GRAND RAPIDS, GRAND HAVEN & MUSKEGON RAILWAY CO.

A corporation formed under the laws of Michigan, March 6, 1899. The company owns and operates 45.2 miles of electric railway between the cities of Grand Rapids and Muskegon, Mich., with a branch to Spring Lake and Grand Haven. It owns 19 cars, a power plant and two substations and does a freight business. It has a private right of way over most of its road. The Westinghouse Co. owns 90 per cent. of the stock of the company.

Stock......Par $100........... ..............Authorized, $1,200,000......Issued, $1,200,000

The company has no preferred stock. Stock is transferred and registered at the office of the company, Detroit.

FUNDED DEBT.

1st mort., 5 per cent. gold, due July 1, 1926, Jan. and July........................ $1,250,000

The total amount of the 1st mortgage authorized was $1,500,000. Trustee of the mortgage and agent for the payment of interest, Standard Trust Co., New York. The $250,000 of the bonds remaining in the treasury are held for acquisitions, improvements, etc. Interest on the outstanding bonds is guaranteed for five years by the Security Investment Co., Pittsburg.

In the last eleven months of the fiscal year ending December 31, 1902, the gross earnings were $143,735; net, $44,950; interest and taxes, $44,518; surplus, $432. The operating expenses were 69.22 per cent. of the gross earnings.

President, James D. Hawks, Detroit, Mich.; Vice-President and General Manager, W. K. Morley, Grand Rapids, Mich.; Secretary and Assistant Treasurer, Wallace Franklin, Detroit; Treasurer, Carl M. Vail, New York.

Directors—George C. Smith, Pittsburg; J. D. Hawks, Wallace Franklin, Detroit; W. W. Churchill, New York; Thomas F. Carroll, Grand Rapids, Mich.

Corporate and main office, Grand Rapids, Mich.; branch office, Michigan and Woodward avenues, Detroit. Annual meeting, second Tuesday in February, at Grand Rapids, Mich.

## THE GRATON & KNIGHT MANUFACTURING CO.

A corporation formed under the laws of Massachusetts, January 1, 1872. The business of the company is tanning leather and making leather belting and shoe manufacturers' supplies. The company owns a plant with twenty buildings at Worcester, Mass.

Stock......Par $100.......Authorized { com., $600,000 / pref., 500,000 } Issued { com., $600,000 / pref., 400,000 } $1,000,000

The preferred stock is 6 per cent., cumulative, and has preference as to the distribution of assets in case of liquidation. It is redeemable by the company at its option on any dividend day at $120 per share, after a thirty days' notice. Stock is transferred at the company's office, Worcester, Mass.

The stock was originally $100,000, but has been increased from time to time. The last increase was in 1900, when the amount was raised from $700,000 to $1,000,000.

Since January 1, 1900, quarterly dividends at the rate of 6 per cent. per annum have been paid in January, April, July and October. Since January 1, 1872, dividends have been paid to the amount of $955,119.

The company has no funded debt.

In the year ending December 31, 1901, the gross earnings of the company were $182,278; net earnings, $158,593; interest charges, $23,685; dividends, $60,000; depreciation on merchandise and real estate, $45,000; surplus, $52,907.

President, Joseph A. Knight; Vice-President and Secretary, Walter M. Spaulding; Treasurer, Henry C. Graton, Worcester, Mass.

Directors—Joseph A. Knight, Henry C. Graton, Walter M. Spaulding, George T. Dewey, Worcester, Mass.; Robert Osgood, Boston.

Corporate and main office, 66 Bloomingdale road, Worcester, Mass.; branch offices and stores, New York, Chicago, Philadelphia, Atlanta, Ga.; Portland, Ore.; Seattle. Annual meeting, January 15, at Worcester, Mass.

## GREAT BRITAIN RAILWAYS DEVELOPMENT CORPORATION

A corporation formed under the laws of New Jersey, December 17, 1901. The purposes of the company comprise the purchase and development of electric railways in England and other countries.

Stock......Par $100.................. ........Authorized, $3,300,000......Issued, $3,300,000

The company has no preferred stock or funded debt. Transfer Agent, Corporation Trust Co. of New Jersey, Jersey City.

President, F. R. Pemberton; Vice-President, Ernst Thalmann; Secretary, C. W. King; Treasurer, B. S. Guinness; General Counsel, W. G. McAdoo, New York.

Directors—F. R. Pemberton, Evans R. Dick, Ernst Thalmann, New York; J. Wilcox Brown, J. William Middendorf, Robert C. Davidson, Baltimore; John Skelton Williams, Richmond, Va.; William P. Bonbright, London, England; C. Sidney Shepard, New Haven, N. Y.

Corporate office, 15 Exchange place, Jersey City; main office, 15 Wall street, New York. Annual meeting, second Tuesday in February, at Jersey City.

## THE GREAT LAKES TOWING CO.

A corporation organized under the laws of New Jersey, July 6, 1899. The company acquired and owns the vessels, plants and business of a number of companies and firms engaged in towing, lighterage, wrecking, etc., on the lakes. The company has a large fleet of tugs, lighters, barges, etc. In April, 1901, purchased the properties of another organization engaged in the same business.

Stock....Par $100....Authorized { com., $2,500,000 / pref., 2,500,000 } Issued { com., $1,675,000 / pref., 1,882,850 } $3,557,850

The preferred stock is 7 per cent., non-cumulative.

Quarterly dividends of 1¾ per cent. were paid on the preferred in 1900 in February, May, August and November. The February and May dividends were, however, passed in 1901, but they were resumed in August, 1901.

President and Treasurer, Thomas F. Newman; Vice-President, James Davidson; Secretary, Melville H. Wardwell; General Manager, C. H. Sinclair, Cleveland.

Main office, Superior and Water streets, Cleveland.

## THE GREAT WESTERN CEREAL CO.

A corporation formed under the laws of New Jersey in April, 1901, for the purpose of the manufacture, purchase and sale of grain and grain products. The company owns the plants, good will, trade-marks and patents of the following constituent companies:

The Akron Cereal Co., Akron, O.
Muscatine Oatmeal Co., Muscatine, Ia.
H. R. Heath & Sons, Fort Dodge, Ia.
Pillsbury-Washburn Oatmeal Business, Minneapolis, Minn.
Northwestern Cereal Co., Minneapolis, Minn.
Nebraska City Cereal Mills, Nebraska City, Neb.
Steward & Merriam, Peoria, Ill.
Sioux Milling Co., Sioux City, Ia.
David Oliver, Joliet, Ill.
Cedar Falls Mill Co., Cedar Falls, Ia.

These ten companies have a combined capacity of about 6,000 barrels of cereals per day, 56,000 bushels of grain being used daily. A number of well-known brands of various cereals and food stuffs are manufactured.

Stock......Par $100..........................Authorized, $3,000,000......Issued, $2,509,900

The company has no preferred stock. Transfer Agent, Merchants' Loan & Trust Co., Chicago. Registrar, American Trust & Savings Co., Chicago.

The company paid a dividend of 1½ per cent. on its stock July 1, 1902, but later decided to use the profits to provide for extensions and working capital and to retire its bonds.

FUNDED DEBT.

1st mort., 6 per cent., due 1921, March and Sept.................................. $1,350,000

The authorized bond issue is $1,500,000. Trustee and agent for the payment of interest, The American Trust & Savings Bank of Chicago. The company has retired $150,000 of the bonds.

Chairman, Ohio C. Barber, New York; President, Frank P. Sawyer; 1st Vice-President, Joy Morton, Chicago; 2d Vice-President, Henry L. Little, Minneapolis; Secretary, David Oliver, Jr., Chicago; Treasurer, Lucius C. Miles, Akron, O.

Directors—Ohio C. Barber, New York; David Oliver, Jr., Joliet, Ill.; Joy Morton, W. L. Gregson, Frank P. Sawyer, Chicago; Henry L. Little, Minneapolis; Lucius C. Miles, Akron, O.; H. R. Heath, Fort Dodge, Ia.; Giles W. Brown, Sioux City, Ia.; W. A. Dugane, Cedar Falls, Ia.; S. G. Stein, Muscatine, Ia.; A. P. Stafford, Nebraska City.

Corporate office, 15 Exchange place, Jersey City; main office, 77 Jackson Boulevard, Chicago; branch offices, New York, Boston, Philadelphia, Hamburg and London. Annual meeting, first Wednesday in June, at Jersey City.

## THE GREENE CONSOLIDATED COPPER CO.

A corporation formed under the laws of West Virginia in 1899. The company is the owner of a large copper mining property at Cananea, Sonora, Mexico. The property comprises over 10,000 acres. The mines are fully developed, large ore bodies having been opened up. The company has a smelter with a daily capacity of 1,500 tons, its daily output of copper in February, 1903, averaging 80 tons. The total product in 1901 was 28,826,854 pounds of copper; in 1902 38,268,407 pounds.

Stock......Par $10..........................Authorized, $7,200,000......Issued, $7,200,000

The stock of the company consisted of 600,000 shares, full-paid and non-assessable, all of which is issued. In November, 1902, the stock was increased from $6,000,000 to $7,200,000, the stockholders having the right to take the new stock at $20 per share.

ransfer Agent, North American Trust Co., New York. Registrar, Continental Trust Co., NewIYork.

The company paid a dividend of 2 per cent. in May, 1901; a second dividend, also of 2 per cent., was paid in September, 1901; the third dividend was 2 per cent., January 2, 1903, and the 4th dividend 2 per cent., February 2, 1903.

President, William C. Greene, Bisbee, Ariz.; Vice-President, Mark L. Sperry, Waterbury, Conn.; Secretary, George S. Robbins; Treasurer, Edward B. Tustin; Comptroller, Anson W. Burchard, New York.

Directors—William C. Greene, Mark L. Sperry, George S. Robbins, Edwin Hawley, Anson W. Burchard, Myron W. Parker, Edward C. Rice, Alfred Romer, Edward B. Tustin, A. C. Latimer, J. B. Showalter, A. Bleecker Banks, Thomas H. Anderson, Emil B. Showalter, Henry F. Blount, Henry T. Scott, George Mitchell, Henry Ollesheimer, H. E. Huntington.

Main office, 377 Broadway, New York. Annual meeting, October 10.

## THE GUANAJUATO CONSOLIDATED MINING & MILLING CO.

A corporation formed under the laws of West Virginia in 1898 for the purpose of purchasing and developing a gold and silver mining property in Mexico. The mines of the mother lode of Guanajuato were worked with great profit prior to the Mexican revolution (1810-1812), but were flooded at that time; remained many years idle and required two years in pumping out. Development work is now in progress.

The company owns a large mining property at Guanajuato, Mexico. The plant consists of reduction works, with substantial buildings, the main Sirena tunnel being 5,000 feet, well tracked and walled; the entire water works system of Mata and San Francisco, with aqueducts and Mata dam, and water rights and improvements in connection therewith. A new 20-stamp mill was erected in 1900 and is being trebled in capacity; a tramway through the Sirena mine and tunnel, connecting the same with the works, has also been constructed.

Stock......Par $5..........................Authorized, $2,000,000......Issued, $1,925,000

The unissued 100,000 shares of stock have been set aside for treasury purposes and for retiring the company's bonds. The stock is fully paid and non-assessable.

Transfer Agents, The State Street Trust Co., Boston. Registrar, The Old Colony Trust Co., Boston.

FUNDED DEBT.

1st mort. 6 per cent. bonds, due 1910, May and Nov..................................$200,000

President, William Bouldin, Jr.; Secretary and Treasurer, C. Van Ransselaer Cogswell, New York.

Directors—Donald McLean, R. H. Beach, William Bouldin, Jr., George A. McGlone, E. A. Wiltsee, C. Van Rensselaer Cogswell, New York; A. Bleecker Banks, Albany; Charles N. King, Jersey City; Charles B. Holman, Hopkinton, Mass.

Main office, 35 Wall street, New York.

## THE GUTTA PERCHA & RUBBER MANUFACTURING CO.

A corporation formed under the laws of New York in 1865 to manufacture and sell mechanical rubber goods. The company has a plant in Brooklyn.

Stock......Par $100..........................Authorized, $1,000,000......Issued, $1,000,000

The company has no preferred stock and no funded debt.

Stock is transferred at the office of the company, New York.

President, A. Spadone; Vice-President, Henry Spadone; Secretary, Alfred A. Spadone, New York; Treasurer, Matthew Hawe, New York.

Directors—A. Spadone, Henry Spadone, Alfred A. Spadone, New York; Walter W. Spadone, Brooklyn, N. Y.; Matthew Hawe, Mount Vernon, N. Y.

Corporate and main office, 126 Duane street, New York; branch stores, Chicago, Boston and San Francisco. Annual meeting, first Wednesday in April, at New York.

## HACKENSACK MEADOWS CO.

A corporation formed under the laws of New Jersey, May 25, 1901. The company acquired, for the purpose of reclamation and improvement for commercial purposes, some 5,000 acres of land, lying chiefly between the Hackensack and Passaic rivers, in New Jersey.

Stock......Par $100..........................Authorized, $3,000,000......Issued, $3,000,000

The company has no preferred stock. Transfer Agent, Continental Trust Co., New York. Registrar, Standard Trust Co., New York.

The company acquired the property subject to $1,492,000 at 4½ per cent., due in 1921, interest January and July. Trustee of mortgage, Standard Trust Co., New York.

It was reported in January, 1903, that the company had negotiated a sale of part of its land for $1,000,000, and also that the interest on the mortgage indebtedness due January and July, 1903, would be met.

President, Alfred Schiffer; Vice-President, Frederick P. Voorhees; Treasurer, Edward Barr; Secretary, Thomas P. McKenna.

Corporate office, Jersey City; main office, 25 Broad street, New York. Annual meeting, third Monday in May, at Jersey City.

## HACKENSACK WATER CO.

A corporation formed under the laws of New Jersey in 1881. The company is a reorganization of a corporation of the same name whose property was foreclosed. The company supplies water to the cities of Hoboken and Englewood, and a large number of towns and townships in Hudson and Bergen counties, N. J. It has upward of 250 miles of mains.

Stock...Par $25.....Authorized { com., $3,000,000 / pref., 500,000 } Issued { com., $1,625,000 / pref., 375,000 } $2,000,000

The preferred stock is 6 per cent., cumulative.

The company pays regular dividends of 6 per cent. on the preferred stock. Since 1896 dividends of 6 per cent. have also been paid each year on the common stock.

Stock is transferred at the company's office, Weehawken, N. J.

FUNDED DEBT.

1st mort., 4 per cent., due 1952, Jan. and July.................................... $6,000,000

The 1st mortgage is redeemable at 105 and interest at the company's option since 1896. The general mortgage may also be redeemed at 105 and interest after January 1, 1903.

President, Robert W. De Forest; Vice-President, Myles Tierney, New York; Treasurer and Secretary, William Shippen, Weehawken, N. J.

Directors—Robert W. De Forest, Edwin A. Stevens, Myles Tierney, John H. Kean, William Runkle; William E. Bond; William E. Johnson.

Main office, Weehawken, N. J. Fiscal Agents, First National Bank, Hoboken, and Hudson Trust Co., Hoboken, N. J. Annual meeting, first Monday in April, at New Milford, N. J.

## HALIFAX ELECTRIC TRAMWAY CO., LIMITED

A corporation formed under the laws of Nova Scotia in 1895. The company controls the railways and gas and electric lighting of Halifax, N. S., under a perpetual charter, with exclusive privileges for 21 years. The company acquired the following properties:

Halifax Street Railway Co.
Nova Scotia Power Co.
Halifax Illuminating & Power Co.
People's Heat & Light Co.

The company operates 13 miles of track, and has a power station and 41 cars.

Stock......Par $100..........................Authorized, $1,500,000......Issued, $1,350,000

The company has no preferred stock. Stock is transferred at the office of the company, Halifax, N. S.

Dividends of 5 per cent. per annum were paid in 1901 and 1902; the dividends are quarterly in January, April, July and October, payable at the Bank of Nova Scotia, Halifax, N. S., and Montreal.

FUNDED DEBT.

1st mort., 5 per cent. gold, due Jan. 1, 1916, Jan. and July............................$600,000

The bonds outstanding are the full amount authorized. The bonds may be called after 1900 at 105. Trustee of the mortgage, Eastern Trust Co., Halifax, N. S.

In the fiscal year ending December 31, 1902, the gross earnings were $314,160.72; net earnings, $124,217.92; interest, $30,000; dividends, $47,291.67; surplus, $46,926.25.

President, David MacKeen; Vice-Presidents, John Y. Payzant, W. B. Ross; Secretary and Treasurer, W. J. DeBlois; Manager, F. A. Huntress, Halifax, N. S.

Directors—David MacKeen, John Y. Payzant, W. B. Ross, Henry S. Poole, J. C. MacKintosh, Halifax; Abner Kingham, James Hutchison, W. M. Douall, Montreal.

Corporate and main office, 15 Lower Water street, Halifax, N. S. Annual meeting, second Monday in February, at Halifax.

## THE HALL SIGNAL CO.

A corporation formed under the laws of Maine in October, 1899. The business of the company is the manufacture and installation of automatic railway signals. The company has a large factory plant at Garwood, Union County, N. J., comprising valuable real estate, with buildings, machinery and tools. The company usually carries a large amount of goods on hand. It has a large interest in the Continental Hall Signal Co., which does business on the continent of Europe.

Stock...Par $100....Authorized { com., $1,900,000; pref., 100,000 } Issued { com., $1,585,200; pref., 100,000 } $1,685,200

The preferred stock is 6 per cent., non-cumulative.

The company had 1st mortgage bonds authorized in 1894 for $200,000, of which $116,000 were issued. The company, however, retired the bonds from time to time with surplus earnings, and the $45,000 outstanding at the end of 1900 were retired in 1901.

The following is the company's balance sheet, May 31, 1902:

| Assets. | | Liabilities. | |
|---|---|---|---|
| Cash | $196,371 | Sundry creditors | $21,973 |
| Investments in other companies | 7,448 | Reserve for outstanding bills | 1,784 |
| Inventory | 114,939 | Capital stock | 1,685,200 |
| Real estate, buildings, machinery, etc. | 108,946 | Profit and loss | 429,021 |
| Patents, good will, etc. | 1,710,274 | | |
| Total | $2,137,978 | Total | $2,137,978 |

The company pays 6 per cent. per annum on the preferred stock. On the common stock, 4 per cent. per annum was paid in quarterly dividends of 1 per cent. each, in January, April, July and October, until July, 1902, when the quarterly rates were increased to 1½ per cent.

President, William P. Hall; 1st Vice-President, William H. Lyon; Treasurer and General Manager, Cyrus S. Sedgwick; Secretary, Robert K. Waller.

Directors—William P. Hall, William H. Lyon, T. Gorton Coombe, Thomas M. Waller, Leroy W. Baldwin, Cyrus S. Sedgwick.

Main office, 25 Broad street, New York. Annual meeting, third Wednesday in June, at Portland, Me.

## HAMILTON ELECTRIC LIGHT & CATARACT POWER CO., LIMITED

A corporation formed under the laws of Ontario, in Aug., 1899, for the purpose of operating an electric street railway system and supplying electric light and power in Hamilton, Ont., and vicinity. The company acquired and operates the following properties:

Hamilton Street Railway Co.
Hamilton & Dundas Street Railway Co.
Hamilton Radial Electric Railway Co.
Ontario Light & Power Co.
Hamilton Electric Light & Power Co.
Cataract Power Co.
Electrical Power & Manufacturiug Co.
Dundas Electrical Co.

The company obtains its power at De Cew Falls, above St. Catharines, Ont., two trunk lines carrying the current to Hamilton, Ont. In addition it has three power-houses fully equipped for emergencies. Railways operated, 42 miles.

Stock....Par $100.......Authorized { com., $1,500,000; pref., 2,500,000 } Issued { com., $1,500,000; pref., 2,274,000 } $3,774,400

Stock is transferred at the company's office, Hamilton, Ont.

| Funded Debt. | |
|---|---|
| 1st mort., 5 per cent., due 1929, April and Oct. | $1,250,000 |
| Hamilton Street Railway Co., 1st mort., 4½ per cent., gold, due 1928, June and Dec. | 500,000 |
| Hamilton & Dundas Street Railway Co., 1st mort., 5 per cent., due 1917, Jan. and July. | 100,000 |
| Total | $1,850,000 |

Four per cent. per annum for a sinking fund is provided for the mortgage of the Hamilton Street Railway Co. to begin after the fifteenth year, 1913, to redeem and reduce the bond issue to forty per cent. at maturity.

President, J. M. Gibson; Vice-President, James Dixon; Secretary, William C. Hawkins; Treasurer, J. R. Moodie.

Directors — J. M. Gibson, James Dixon, J. R. Moodie, J. W. Sutherland, William C. Hawkins, Hamilton, Ont.; J. A. Kammerer, Toronto, Ont.

Main office, Hamilton, Ont. Annual meeting, third Monday in February, at Hamilton, Ont.

## THE HAMILTON OTTO COKE CO.

A corporation formed under the laws of West Virginia, 1900, to manufacture coke, tar, ammonia, gas and other products from coal. The company has acquired the following companies:

Hamilton Gas Light & Coke Co. Hamilton Electric Light Co.

The company has a coke plant at Hamilton, O. The two subsidary companies have perpetual franchises in the city of Hamilton, O.

Stock......Par $100..............................Authorized, $500,000......Issued, $300,000

The company has no preferred stock. Stock is transferred at the office of the company, Hamilton, O.

FUNDED DEBT.

1st mort., 5 per cent., due July 1, 1921, Jan. and July................................ $383 000

The authorized 1st mortgage was $500,000. Trustee of the mortgage, Union Saving Bank & Trust Co., Cincinnati. Agents for the payment of interest, Merchants' National Bank, Cincinnati, and Merchants' National Bank, New York.

In the fiscal year 1902, the gross earnings were $293,717; net, $56,393; interest and charges, $26,294; surplus, $30,099.

President, C. W. Andrews, Hamilton, O.; Vice-President, F. L. Garrison, Cincinnati; Secretary, W. E. Bender, Hamilton, O.; Treasurer, R. E. Field, Cincinnati.

Directors—C. W. Andrews, W. E. Bender, Hamilton, O.; F. L. Garrison, R. E. Field, Robert Ramsey, H. S. Rodgers, W. H. Dunham, H. L. Breneman, Joseph S. Trevor, Cincinnati.

Main office, Hamilton, O. Annual meeting, second Tuesday in August, at Hamilton, O.

## THE HAMILTON STEEL & IRON CO., LIMITED

A corporation formed under the laws of Ontario, July 19, 1899. The purpose of the company is the manufacture of pig iron, bar iron and steel, forgings, etc.

The company acquired the following properties:

Hamilton Blast Furnace Co. Limited. Ontario Rolling Mill Co. Limited.

The plants of the company have an annual capacity of about 70,000 tons of pig iron, 36,000 tons of bar iron, 36,000 of ingots, 30,000 tons of steel bars, 50,000 kegs of cut nails, etc.

Stock......Par $100 ..........................Authorized, $2,000,000......Issued, $1,513,600

The company has no preferred stock and no funded debt. Stock is transferred and registered at the office of the company.

Dividends are paid quarterly at the rate of 6 per cent.

President, Charles S. Wilcox; Vice-Presidents, A. E. Carpenter, Charles E. Doolittle; Secretary and General Manager, Robert Hobson; Treasurer, William A. Child, Hamilton, Ont.

Directors—Charles S. Wilcox, A. E. Carpenter, Charles E. Doolittle, William Southam, John Milne, George Lynch Staunton, Hamilton, Ont.; Peter M. Hitchcock, Cleveland.

Corporate office, Barton Township, County of Wentworth, Ont.; main office, Queen and Stuart streets, Hamilton, Ont. Annual meeting, second Wednesday in August, at Hamilton.

## THE G. H. HAMMOND CO.

A corporation formed under the laws of Michigan in 1890. The company owns and operates large packing plants in Chicago and Omaha, Neb.

The entire stock of this company and the control of its business was from 1890 to 1899 owned by an English corporation, the G. H. Hammond Co., Limited. In 1899 the ownership of the company was acquired by American capitalists. See the MANUAL for 1902.

In 1902 interests connected with Armour & Co. acquired large holdings in this company's stock.

Stock......Par $100..........................Authorized, $3,600,000......Issued, $3,600,000

FUNDED DEBT.

1st mort., 6 per cent. bonds, due 1910, Jan. and July ............................... $1,550,000

Trustee of the mortgage, Central Trust Co., New York. Agent for the payment of interest, Fourth National Bank, Boston.

President, Jesse P. Lyman; Vice-President, Arthur Meeker, Chicago; Secretary and Treasurer, James D. Standish, Detroit.

Directors—J. C. Melvin, E. Chapman, Boston; F. B. Comstock, Providence; George Hotchkiss, T. H. W. Wheeler, New York; Jesse P. Lyman, Arthur Meeker, J. F. Meagher, Chicago; James D. Standish, Detroit.

General office, Hammond, Ind.; corporate office, Detroit; Chicago office, 218 La Salle street. Annual meeting, second Wednesday in December.

## THE HAMMOND ICE CO.

A corporation formed under the laws of Delaware, November 2, 1900, for the purpose of manufacturing artificial ice. The plant at Baltimore, employing the Hammond patents, has a capacity of 200 tons per day. The company proposes to extend its operations to New York, Philadelphia, Washington, D. C., Boston and other cities.

Stock......Par $100..........................Authorized, $2,000,000......Issued, $2,000,000

The stock is full-paid and non-assessable. The company has no preferred stock and no funded debt.

President and General Manager, Ormond Hammond; First Vice-President, Charles T. Westcott; Second Vice-President, John L. Blake; Secretary and General Superintendent, Howard Hammond; Treasurer, F. J. Kohler; Consulting Engineer, T. H. Butler; Chief Engineer, Charles Kosenick; General Counsel, Frederick Dallam.

Directors—Ormand Hammond, Charles T. Westcott, John L. Blake, F. J. Kohler, Howard Hammond, Frederick Dallam, W. H. Evans, Patrick Martin, T. H. Butler, James H. Preston, C. H. Basshor, O. E. Robinson, E. T. Wallower, E. E. Jackson, J. A. Sheridan, James Virdin, Ernst Schmeisser, G. W. Gail, Jr., George Miller.

Main office, 12 St. Paul street, Baltimore.

## HARGRAVES MILLS

A corporation formed under the laws of Massachusetts in 1888 to manufacture fine cotton goods. The mills of the company are located at Fall River, Mass., and have a capacity of 101,556 spindles and 3,102 looms.

Stock......Par $100.............................Authorized, $800,000......Issued, $800,000

The company has no preferred stock. Stock is transferred at the office of the company.

The first dividend, 1½ per cent., was paid January 15, 1890. Annual dividends of 6 per cent. have since been paid, the dividend periods being February, May, August and November.

FUNDED DEBT.

1st mort., 5 per cent., due Feb., 1922, Feb. and Aug..........................................$600,000

The bonds outstanding are the total amount authorized. Trustee of the mortgage and agent for the payment of interest, B. M. C. Durfee Safe Deposit & Trust Co., Fall River, Mass.

President, Leontine Lincoln; Clerk, Hilton Reed; Treasurer, Seth A. Borden, Fall River, Mass.

Directors—Leontine Lincoln, Milton Reed, Seth A. Borden, John D. Flint, Fall River, Mass.; Stephen A. Jenks, Fred W. Easton, Pawtucket, Mass.; George C. Silsbury, Salem, Mass.; Walter L. Parker, Lowell, Mass.

Corporate and main office, Fall River, Mass. Annual meeting, last Thursday in October, at Fall River, Mass.

## HARRISON BROS. & CO., INCORPORATED

A corporation formed under the laws of Pennsylvania, March 2, 1898. The objects of the company are the manufacture of white lead, paints, oils, varnishes, acids, chemicals, and kindred articles and products. The company acquired the plant formerly owned by the firm of Harrison Bros. & Co., at Thirty-fifth street and Gray's Ferry Road, Philadelphia, consisting of sixty-five different buildings and covering thirty-five acres of ground. The firm of Harrison Bros. & Co. was founded in 1793.

Stock...Par $100....Authorized { com., $1,000,000 / pref., $1,500,000 } Issued { com., $1,000,000 / pref., $1,500,000 } $2,500,000

The preferred stock is 7 per cent., non-cumulative. The preferred also has priority in respect to distribution of assets in case of a dissolution of the company.
Stock is transferred at the company's office, Philadelphia.
The first dividend on the preferred stock was paid May 2, 1898, being 1¾ per cent. quarterly. From that date full dividends, at the rate of 7 per cent. per annum, have been paid on the preferred, the payments being quarterly, on the first days of February, May, August and November, but the August, 1901, dividend was passed. A special dividend of 2 per cent. was paid on the common stock, November 1, 1899. No dividends on the common since that date.

FUNDED DEBT.

1st mort., 5 per cent., due 1924, May and Nov.......... ........................ $1,300,000

Tustee of the mortgage and agent for the payment of interest, Fidelity Insurance, Trust & Safe Deposit Co., Philadelphia.
In the year ending October 31, 1902, the net earnings of the company were $190,032; charges, $68,686; dividends, $105,000; balance surplus, $121,345.
President and General Manager, Robert S. Perry; Vice-President and Treasurer, C. Leland Harrison; Secretary, J. E. Turner, Philadelphia; Assistant General Manager, James Langmuir, New York.
Directors—Thomas Skelton Harrison, John Harrison, C. Leland Harrison, John H. Barnes, Russell S. Hubbard, Robert S. Perry, Philadelphia; James Langmuir, New York; Gardiner M. Lane, John P. Reynolds, Jr., Boston.
Main office, Thirty-fifth street and Gray's Ferry Road, Philadelphia; branch offices, 117 Fulton street, New York; 27 Lake street, Chicago. Annual meeting, second Wednesday in January.

## HARTFORD & SPRINGFIELD STREET RAILWAY CO.

A corporation formed under the laws of Connecticut, June 21, 1893, as the Enfield & Long Meadow Electric Railway Co. The present name was adopted May 29, 1901. The company owns about 13 miles of electric railway between East Windsor Hill, Conn., and the state line between Massachusetts and Connecticut. At the state line it connects with the Springfield (Mass.) Street Railway and at Windsor Hill, with the Hartford (Conn.) Street Railway, making a through line between Hartford and Springfield. The company also purchased the Windsor Street Railway Co. The company owns a power house and 11 cars.

Stock......Par $100............................Authorized, $600,000......Issued, $400,000

The company has no preferred stock. Stock is transferred by the treasurer of the company.
The company paid its first dividend of 2 per cent. January 1, 1903.

FUNDED DEBT.

1st mort., 5 per cent., gold, due July, 1821, Jan. and July.................. ........$400,000

The total amount of the authorized mortgage was $600,000. Trustee of the mortgage, Treasurer of the State of Connecticut. Agent for the payment of interest, American Loan & Trust Co., Boston.
President, P. L. Saltonstall; Treasurer, Chauncey Eldridge, Boston; Secretary, Arthur Perkins, Hartford, Conn.
Directors—P. L. Saltonstall, Chauncey Eldridge, S. Reed Anthony, Boston; Arthur Perkins, Francis R. Cooley, Hartford, Conn.; Lyman A. Upson, Thompsonville, Conn., Lewis Sperry, South Windsor, Conn.
Corporate office, Warehouse Point, Conn.; main office, 53 State street, Boston. Annual meeting, third Thursday in July, at Hartford, Conn.

## HARTFORD STREET RAILWAY CO.

A corporation formed under the laws of Connecticut, July 1, 1862. Originally the name was the Hartford & Wethersfield Horse Railway Co., the present name being adopted October 4, 1893. The company has acquired the following properties:

East Hartford & Glastonbury Street Ry. Co. Newington Tramway.

The company operates 92.97 miles of electric trolley road, between Hartford, Wethersfield, West Hartford, Windsor, East Windsor, East Hartford and South Glastonbury, Conn., and via the Central Railway & Lighting Co. of New Britain, has a through line from Hartford to New Britain, Conn. It owns an electric power plant and 224 motor cars and 23 freight cars.

Stock......Par $100..........................Authorized, $2,000,000......Issued, $1,000,000

The company has no preferred stock. Stock is transferred at the office of the company, Hartford.

Dividends on the stock have been paid at the rate of 6 per cent. per annum, beginning 1894. The dividend periods are quarterly, in January, April, July and October.

FUNDED DEBT.

| | |
|---|---|
| 1st mort., 4 per cent., gold, due Sept., 1930, May and Sept. | $2,500,000 |
| E. Hartford & Glastonbury St. Ry. Co. deb., 5 per cent., due Dec., 1927, July and Dec. | 200,000 |
| Total | $2,700,000 |

The authorized 1st mortgage is $3,000,000. Trustee and agent for the payment of interest, Connecticut Trust & Safe Deposit Co., Hartford, Conn.

EARNINGS.

Year ending June 30.

| | Gross. | Net. | Interest and Taxes. | Dividends. | Surplus. |
|---|---|---|---|---|---|
| 1899 | $618,913 | $185,206 | $142,763 | $42,000 | $443 |
| 1900 | 682,936 | 248,192 | 142,806 | 75,000 | 30,386 |
| 1901 | 737,871 | 254,057 | 150,294 | 60,000 | 43,133 |
| 1902 | 780,558 | 243,668 | 146,455 | 60,000 | 37,213 |

President, E. S. Goodrich; Vice-President, Samuel G. Dunham; Secretary and Treasurer, Daniel R. Howe; General Manager, N. McD. Crawford, Hartford, Conn.

Directors—James J. Goodwin, New York; George E. Taintor, Charles L. Lincoln, Daniel R. Howe, Atwood Collins, Samuel G. Dunham, E. S. Goodrich, Appleton R. Hillyer, Hartford, Conn.

Main office, 115 State street, Hartford, Conn. Annual meeting in January, at call of directors, at Hartford, Conn.

## HAVANA ELECTRIC RAILWAY CO.

A corporation formed under the laws of New Jersey in 1902. The company acquired the Havana City Railway & Omnibus Co. of the city of Havana, Cuba. It has a franchise running until 1958 and has freight-carrying rights over parts of the system. The company owns and operates about 40 miles of electric railway.

Stock...Par $.......Authorized { com., $7,500,000 / pref., 5,000,000 } Issued { com., $7,500,000 / pref., 5,000,000 } $12,500,000

The preferred stock is 6 per cent., non-cumulative. Stock is transferred by the secretary of the company, New York. Registrar, United States Mortgage & Trust Co., New York.

FUNDED DEBT.

Consolidated mort., 5 per cent. gold, due Feb. 1, 1952, Feb. and Aug. ............... $7,500,000

The authorized amount of the mortgage is $10,000,000. Of the bonds outstanding $6,600,000 were reserved to retire prior liens; $400,000 for floating debt and $500,000 for new properties. A sinking fund of $48,000 per annum, from January 1, 1896, is provided. Bonds may be called for the sinking fund after 1906 at 105, and the entire issue may be called after February, 1907, at 105 and interest. Trustee of the mortgage, Central Trust Co., New York. Interest is payable at the office of the company in New York.

President, Edwin Hanson, Montreal; 1st Vice-President, W. L. Bull, New York; Secretary and Treasurer, Arnold Marcus, New York.

Directors—W. L. Bull, Alexander Laird, Arnold Marcus, H. C. Perkins, Edwin Hanson, William C. Van Horne, Montreal; N. Gelats, Havana, Cuba.

Corporate office, 15 Exchange place, Jersey City; New York office, 52 Broadway.

## HAVANA TOBACCO CO.

A corporation formed under the laws of New Jersey, May 28, 1902. The company was organized in pursuance of a plan to reorganize the Havana Commercial Co., which was formed in 1899, being a consolidation of some of the largest cigar manufacturing interests of Havana, Cuba. See statement of the Havana Commercial Co. in the MANUAL for 1902.

The present company, besides acquiring the properties owned by the Havana Commercial Co., also obtained control of the cigar interests at Havana known as the Bock and the Henry Clay establishments, with their plants, trade-marks and so forth. It also obtained control of the H. de Cabanas y Carvajal Co. The company thus controls about nine-tenths of the Cuban cigar industry. Control of the company is vested in interests identified with the Consolidated Tobacco Co.

Stock...Par $100..Authorized { com., $30,000,000 / pref., 5,000,000 } Issued { com., $30,000,000 / pref., 5,000,000 } $35,000,000

The preferred stock is 5 per cent., non-cumulative.

FUNDED DEBT.

Debentures, 5 per cent., due June, 1922, June and Dec........................... $7,500,000

The authorized amount of the bonds is $10,000,000, and of the amount $2,500,000 remain in the treasury.

Under the terms of the reorganization of the Havana Commercial Co. holders of its common stock received 40 per cent. of their holdings in the common stock of the new company, and the old preferred stock was exchanged for 40 per cent. in new common and 60 per cent. in new preferred. Practically all the old stock was exchanged under this arrangement.

President, J. B. Cobb; 1st Vice-President, Harold Roberts; 2d Vice-President, E. T. Ware; 3d Vice-President, F. H. Ray; Treasurer, H. D. Kingsbury; Secretary, G. M. Gales; Assistant Secretary, J. N. Staples; Auditor, A. R. Haskin.

Directors—L. Carvajal, E. T. Ware, T. A. Corbin, Anthony N. Brady, W. W. Fuller, J. B. Cobb, J. B. Duke, R. R. Govin, Oliver H. Payne, H. W. Cobb, Harold Roberts, Gustavo Bock, Peter A. B. Weidener, F. H. Ray, Robert A. C. Smith, Henry B. Hollins, Thomas F. Ryan, Grant B. Schley.

Main office, 167 Water street, New York.

## THE HAVERSTRAW LIGHT & FUEL CO.

A corporation formed under the laws of New York in 1893 to manufacture and sell gas. The company owns two gas plants in Haverstraw, N. Y.

Stock....Par { com., $10 / pref., 100 } Authorized { com., $100,000 / pref., 500,000 } Issued { com., $100,000 / pref., 100,000 } $200,000

The issue of preferred stock was to take up the common stock. The preferred stock is entitled to all the earnings of the company for 40 years. Stock is transferred at the office of the company, Haverstraw, N. Y.

FUNDED DEBT.

| | |
|---|---|
| 1st mort., 6 per cent., due 1924, May and Nov. | $100,000 |
| 2d mort., 5 per cent., due 1949, June and Dec. | 250,000 |
| Total | $350,000 |

The authorized mortgages are $360,000. Of the 2d mortgage $100,000 is set aside to redeem the 1st mortgage.

Trustee of the mortgages, Morton Trust Co., New York. Interest is paid at the office of the company, Haverstraw, N. Y.

President, Henry Hahn, Haverstraw, N. Y.; Vice-President, B. L. Arbecam; Secretary and Treasurer, S. Victor Constant, New York.

Directors—Henry Hahn, Robert A. Widenmann, Haverstraw, N. Y.; B. L. Arbecam, S. Victor Constant, Nelson Chandler, New York.

Main office, Haverstraw, N. Y.; New York office, 120 Broadway. Annual meeting, second Tuesday in April, at New York.

## HAWAIIAN COMMERCIAL & SUGAR CO.

A corporation formed April 3, 1882, under the laws of the State of California, having a plantation of 40,000 acres and sugar works on the Island of Maui, Hawaiian Islands. The capacity of the plant is 50,000 tons of sugar per annum. Under the laws of California the stockholders of the company are personally liable.

Stock......Par $100......................Authorized, $10,000,000......Issued, $10,000,000

Monthly dividends were paid on the stock at the rate of 6 per cent. per annum, or 50c. per share per month. Dividends were, however, suspended in April, 1901.

Transfer Agent, Farmers' Loan & Trust Co., New York.

FUNDED DEBT.

| | |
|---|---|
| Gold debentures, 5½ per cent., due April and Oct. | $509,328 |
| Gold bonds of 1899, 5 per cent., due 1919, April and Oct. | 1,847,000 |
| Total | $2,356,328 |

It was stated that about $23 per share had been paid in on the stock. The company's balance sheet of date December 31, 1899, showed a surplus of $1,324,471. On December 31, 1900, surplus, $1,937,653.

President, Henry P. Baldwin; Vice-President, Albert Meyer; Secretary, George M. Rolph; Treasurer, Nevada National Bank, San Francisco.

Directors—Henry P. Baldwin, Albert Meyer, Edward Pollitz, S. T. Alexander, Wallace M. Alexander.

Main office, 308 Market street, San Francisco.

## HECKER-JONES-JEWELL MILLING CO.

A corporation formed under the laws of New Jersey in 1892, to combine the principal milling industries in the Metropolitan district. The company acquired the plants and business of the following concerns: G. V. Hecker Co., New York; Jones & Co., New York; Jewell Milling Co., Brooklyn; Kings County Milling Co., Brooklyn; and the Staten Island Milling Co. The capacity of these mills was 2,700,000 barrels of flour per year. The company manufactures various well known cereal specialties. The properties were conveyed clear of encumbrance, and the company acquired all trade-marks, formulas and good will.

Stock....Par $100....Authorized { com., $2,000,000 / pref., 3,000,000 } Issued { com., $2,000,000 / pref., 3,000,000 } $5,000,000

The preferred stock is 8 per cent. cumulative and has a preferential lien on the property of the company.

Full dividends of 8 per cent. were paid on the preferred stock from the formation of the company to December, 1897, inclusive. Ensuing dividends were passed. Last dividend paid on preferred 2 per cent., quarterly, December 1, 1897. Transfer Agent and Registrar, Metropolitan Trust Co., New York.

FUNDED DEBT.

1st mort., 6 per cent., due 1922, March and Sept.. ......................... ....... $2,500,000

The company's 1st mortgage bonds are subject to call at 110 after September, 1902. Trustee, Franklin Trust Co., Brooklyn. Agent for the payment of interest, Metropolitan TrustCo., New York. No additional mortgage can be created without the consent of the holders of 90 per cent. of the preferred stock.

In 1899 the United States Flour Milling Co. acquired by purchase 90 per cent. of the stock of this company, giving holders its own securities in exchange. An amount of $2,500,000 of the United States Flour Milling Co.'s 6 per cent. bonds was deposited with the trustee of the mortgage to exchange for the Hecker-Jones-Jewell bonds, of which in September, 1899, $1,004,000 had been exchanged. The company is now controlled by the Standard Milling Co., the successor of the United States Flour Milling Co.

President, Brayton Ives; Secretary and Treasurer, Scott Tremain.

Directors—Brayton Ives, W. Lanman Bull, Thomas A. McIntyre, New York; William Dick, Brooklyn, N. Y.; Joseph V. Clark, Jersey City.

Main office, Produce Exchange, New York. Annual meeting, third Tuesday in September.

## THE HELENA WATER WORKS CO.

A corporation formed under the laws of New Jersey, June 15, 1898. The purpose of the company is to maintain and operate water works at Helena, Mont. The company acquired the following plants:

Helena Consolidated Water Co. Helena Water Co.

Stock......Par $100...........................Authorized, $1,500,000......Issued, $1,500,000

Transfer Agent, New Jersey Registration & Trust Co., East Orange, N. J.

FUNDED DEBT.

1st mort., 4 per cent., due July, 1928, Jan. and July............................... $1,205,000

The authorized mortgage is $1,350,000. Trustee and Agent for the payment of interest, Old Colony Trust Co., Boston.

President, Charles S. Tuckerman, Boston; Vice-President, John A. Cole, Chicago; Secretary, E. A. Phippen; Treasurer, J. G. Stearns, Boston.

Directors—Charles S. Tuckerman, Edward A. Phippen, John A. Cole, Frederic G. Pousland, James B. Dill.

Corporate office, New Jersey Registration & Trust Co., East Orange, N. J.; main office, Helena, Mont.; branch office, 1 Court street, Boston. Annual meeting, second Wednesday in July, at East Orange, N. J.

## HENDERSON BRIDGE CO.

A corporation formed under the laws of Kentucky in 1880. The company owns the railroad bridge and approaches extending over the Ohio River from Evansville, Ind., to Henderson, Ky., a distance of 10 06 miles. The bridge is operated by the Louisville & Nashville Railroad Co., which, with the other roads making use of the bridge, guarantees tolls to the amount of $200,000 per annum, or sufficient for interest on the bonds of the Bridge Co., sinking fund requirements and 5 per cent. yearly on the stock.

Stock..... Par $100......... ..................Authorized, $1,000,000......Issued, $1,000,000

The Louisville & Nashville Railroad Co. owns a majority of the stock.

Transfer Agent, Louisville & Nashville Railroad Co., 120 Broadway, New York.

FUNDED DEBT.

1st mort., gold, 6 per cent., due Sept., 1931, March and Sept........................ $2,000,000

The bond issue was $2,000,000; $463,000 of the bonds are held operative in the sinking fund. The bonds are drawn at 105.

President, Milton H. Smith; Vice-President, W. D. Hines; Secretary, J. H. Ellis; Assistant Secretary, W. H. Bruce; Treasurer, William W. Thompson, Louisville.

Directors—Brayton Ives, W. Lanman Bull, Thomas McIntyre, New York; William Dick, Brooklyn, N. Y.; Joseph W. Clark, Jersey City.

Main office, Main and Second streets, Louisville. Annual meeting, first Monday in January, at Louisville.

## HERRING-HALL-MARVIN SAFE CO.

A corporation formed under the laws of New Jersey, August 3, 1900, as a reorganization of the Herring-Hall-Marvin Co., a company organized in New Jersey in 1892. The property of that company was foreclosed in 1900 and purchased by the reorganization committee, which transferred them to the present company. The old company took over the business of Herring & Co. New York; Hall's Safe & Lock Co., Cincinnati; the Marvin Safe Co., New York; Farrel & Co., Philadelphia, manufacturers of safes and burglar-proof vaults.

| Stock...Par $100...Authorized | | | Issued | | | |
|---|---|---|---|---|---|---|
| | com., | $1,650,000 | | com., | $1,650,000 | |
| | 1st pref., | 600,000 | | 1st pref., | 600,000 | $3,300,000 |
| | 2d pref., | 1,050,000 | | 2d pref., | 1,050,000 | |

The 1st and 2d preferred are 7 per cent., non-cumulative, dividends paid semi-annually.

Transfer Agent and Registrar, Continental Trust Co., New York.

The old company had $1,500,000 common and $1,800,000 8 per cent. preferred stock.

In December, 1897, Receivers were appointed in New York and all the States where the old company did business. The Receivers were George R. Gray and Wright D. Pownall.

The reorganization committee of security holders (Otto T. Bannard, chairman) submitted in February, 1899, a plan of reorganization. The old common stock was assessed $6 a share, and received $50 in new common and $6 in 1st preferred. The old preferred was assessed $12 a share, receiving $50 in new common, $50 in new 2d preferred and $12 in new 1st preferred. The creditors of the company accepted 25 per cent. in cash and 75 per cent. in new 1st preferred. In November, 1899, the Court directed that the property be sold at public sale. In 1901 the present company paid off the outstanding Receivers' certificates issued prior to the reorganization.

President, H. Allen Tenney; Vice-Presidents, Wright D. Pownall, Richard T. Pullen; Secretary and Treasurer, W. E. Drummond.

Directors—Otto T. Bannard, J. Edward Studley, Richard I. Pullen, Charles U. Carpenter, George R. Gray, Wright D. Pownall, W. E. Drummond, H. Allen Tenney, L. D. York.

Main office, 400 Broadway, New York; branch offices, Hamilton, O.; Philadelphia, San Francisco, St. Louis. Annual meeting, second Thursday of February.

## HEYWOOD BROTHERS AND WAKEFIELD CO.

A corporation formed under the laws of New Jersey, March 17, 1897. The company acquired the property and business of the following firms and corporations engaged in the manufacture and sale of cane and wood seat chairs, reed and rattan furniture, children's carriages, chair cane, car seatings, etc.

Heywood Bros. & Co., Gardner, Mass., established 1826, with branches at Boston, New York, Philadelphia, Baltimore, San Francisco, Los Angeles, Cal.: Portland, Ore.; London and Liverpool, England.

Wakefield Rattan Co., Wakefield, Mass., with branches at Boston, New York, Chicago and San Francisco.

Heywood & Morrill Rattan Co., Chicago.

The company's factories are at Gardner, Mass., Wakefield, Mass., Chicago and San Francisco.

| Stock.....Par $100......Authorized | | | Issued | | | |
|---|---|---|---|---|---|---|
| | com., | $2,000,000 | | com., | $2,000,000 | $6,000,000 |
| | pref., | 4,000,000 | | pref., | 4,000,000 | |

The preferred stock is 6 per cent., cumulative. Stock is transferred at the company's office, Gardner, Mass.

The company has no funded debt.

On January 1, 1898, the surplus was reported as $156,498. On January 1, 1902, it was $1,165,703, and on January 1, 1903, $1,405,160.

In 1898 and 1899 the company paid 4 per cent. per annum on its preferred stock, the dividends being 2 per cent. semi-annually in March and September. In 1900 and 1901 8 per cent. was paid on the preferred, the payments being 3 per cent. in March, 2 per cent. in June and 3 per cent. in September. The dividends on the preferred in 1902 aggregated 6 per cent.

President, Henry Heywood; Vice-Presidents, George Heywood, Louis E. Carlton; Treasurer, C. H. Lang, Jr.; Secretary, Theodore L. Harlow.

Directors—Henry Heywood, George Heywood, L. H. Greenwood, C. H. Hill, J. D. Walsh, C. H. Lang, Jr., Louis E. Carlton, Frank G. Webster, William H. Baxter.

Main office, Gardner, Mass. Annual meeting, third Tuesday in March, at Jersey City.

## HIGGINS OIL & FUEL CO.

A corporation formed under the laws of Texas, April 18, 1901, to develop and operate petroleum oil wells. The company owns oil lands in Jefferson and Harding counties, Texas and other lands in Louisiana. It owns 100 tanks cars, 25 steel tanks, wharves, tugs, barges, pipe lines, and other equipments for pumping and shipping oil.

Stock......Par $100..............................Authorized, $2,500......Issued, $2,105,400

The company has no preferred stock and no funded debt.

The first dividend, 4 per cent., was paid January 6, 1903. Quarterly dividends of 1½ per cent. each were paid in April, July and October, 1902, and January, 1903.

President, John N. Gilbert; Vice-President, H. M. Ernst; Secretary, L. L. Donnelly; Treasurer, W. S. Davidson; General Manager, C. L. Wallis.

Directors—John N. Gilbert, W. S. Davidson, C. L. Wallis, T. H. Franklin, H. M. Ernst, J. H. Eagle, J. H. Broocks.

Corporate and main office, Beaumont, Tex.. Annual meeting, April 18, at Beaumont, Tex.

## HOBOKEN LAND & IMPROVEMENT CO.

A corporation formed under the laws of New Jersey in 1838. The company owns large amounts of real estate in the city of Hoboken, N. J.

Stock......Par $100..........................Authorized, $2,000,000......Issued, $1,473,800

Transfer Agent, William A. Macy, 1 Newark street, Hoboken, N. J.

FUNDED DEBT.

1st mort., 5 per cent., due 1910.................................................. $1,500,000

Agent for the payment of interest, First National Bank, Hoboken, N. J.

President, Edwin A. Stevens; 1st Vice-President, Robert L. Stevens; 2d Vice-President, Richard Stevens; Secretary, William A. Macy; Treasurer and General Manager, Palmer Campbell.

Directors—Edwin A. Stevens, Robert L. Stevens, Richard Stevens, A. S. Alexander, Palmer Campbell, Hoboken, N. J.; S. B. Dod, Orange, N. J.; Lewis H. Hyde, New York; William A. Macy, Montclair, N. J.

Main office, 1 Newark street, Hoboken, N. J. Annual meeting, first Monday in May.

## HOLYOKE STREET RAILWAY CO.

A corporation formed under the laws of Massachusetts, June 1, 1884. The company owns and operates 40 miles of electric railway in and about the city of Holyoke, Mass. It operates under a 25-year lease from June 1, 1897, the Mount Tom Railroad Co., an inclined road running to the summit of Mount Tom. The company has a power house, 107 cars and 191 electric motors.

Stock......Par $100..............................Authorized, $700,000......Issued, $700,000

The company has no preferred stock. Stock is transferred and registered at the office of the company, Holyoke, Mass.

Dividends of 8 per cent. annually have been paid, 1892-1902 inclusive. Dividend periods are January and July.

FUNDED DEBT.

| | |
|---|---|
| Debenture bonds, 5 per cent., due April, 1915, April and Oct | $250,000 |
| Debenture bonds, 5 per cent., due Oct., 1920, April and Oct | 85,000 |
| Total | $335,000 |

Interest on all the bonds is payable at the Holyoke National Bank, Holyoke, Mass. The company pays, under the lease of the Mount Tom Railroad Co., 6 per cent. annually on the $100,000 capital stock of that company.

EARNINGS.

Year ending September 30.

| | Gross. | Net | Charges and Taxes. | Dividends | Surplus. |
|---|---|---|---|---|---|
| 1901 | $296,165 | $99,471 | $51,063 | $48,000 | $408 |
| 1902 | 336,853 | 113,524 | 55,368 | 56,000 | 2,156 |

The operating expenses in 1902 were 66⅓ per cent. of the gross earnings.

At the end of the fiscal year, September 30, 1902, the company had a total surplus of $78,143.

President and General Manager, William S. Loomis; Secretary and Treasurer, William R. Hill, Holyoke, Mass.

Directors—William S. Loomis, J. G. McIntosh, J. F. Sullivan, William R. Hill, Holyoke, Mass.; John Olmstead, Frederick Harris, N. D. Winter, Springfield, Mass.

Corporate and main office, Holyoke, Mass. Annual meeting, third Tuesday in January, at Holyoke, Mass.

## THE HOMESTAKE MINING CO.

A corporation formed under the laws of California, November 5, 1877. The property of the company consists of 154 mining claims, aggregating about 927 acres, located in the White Wood mining district in the Black Hills, near Lead, Lawrence County, S. Dak. The company has a large mining plant for the operation of the gold-bearing veins upon its property, comprising a stamp mill, cyanide works, electric light plant, sawmill, etc. In 1899 the company acquired the Highland Mining Co., the property of which, adjoining the Homestake mine, comprises seventeen mining claims of about 73 acres, with a mill of 140 stamps, hoisting works and other necessary machinery. In the same year this company acquired the Black Hills Canal & Water Co., the property of which consists of forty miles of ditches, flumes, pipe lines, with necessary reservoirs and improvements and water rights covering the water supply of the Deadwood and Lead districts.

This company also owned the Black Hills and Fort Pierre Railroad Co., but sold the same.

Stock......Par $100........................Authorized, $21,000,000......Issued, $21,000,000

Transfer Agents, Lounsbery & Co., 15 Broad street, New York.

The company has no funded debt. Up to January 31, 1901, it had paid in dividends upon its stock, $9,508,750. In November, 1899, the capital stock of the company was increased $8,500,000, in order to provide for the absorption of the Highland Mining Co., Black Hills Canal & Water Co. and Black Hills & Fort Pierre Railroad Co.

The Homestake Mining Co. has paid dividends for many years, usually at the rate of 50 cents a share per month.

President, J. B. Haggin; Vice-President, F. G. Drum; Secretary, Fred Clarke.

Directors—J. B. Haggin, F. G. Drum, Fred Clarke, E. J. McCutchun, E. H. Clark, Thomas Turner, Richard Clark.

General office, Lead, Lawrence County, S. Dak.; secretary's office, 210 Montgomery street, San Francisco; New York office, 15 Broad street.

## HOUGHTON COUNTY STREET RAILWAY CO.

A corporation formed under the laws of Michigan in 1899. The company's line extends through the entire copper belt of Michigan, from Houghton to Hancock, Laurium, Red Jacket and Wolverine, serving a population of about 75,000. The company owns 22 miles of track, much of it being built on a private right of way.

Stock......Par $100......Authorized { com., $750,000 / pref., 200,000 } Issued { com., $750,000 / pref., 200,000 } $950,000

The preferred stock is 6 per cent., non-cumulative, and redeemable at 110. Transfer Agents, Stone & Webster, Boston. Registrar, Boston Safe Deposit & Trust Co., Boston.

FUNDED DEBT.

1st mort., 5 per cent., gold, due July 1, 1920, Jan. and July.......................... $625,000

The authorized amount of the 1st mortgage is $750,000. The bonds are redeemable as a whole after 1905 at 105. Trustee of the mortgage and agent for the payment of interest, Boston Safe Deposit & Trust Co., Boston.

In the year ending June 30, 1902, the gross earnings were $158,580; net, $68,187; charges, $28,310; surplus, $39,877.

President, F. J. Bawden; Vice-President, W. O. Chapman; Treasurer, H. B. Sawyer; Assistant Treasurer, John W. Payne; Secretary, Henry R. Hayes.

Directors—C. A. Stone, B. H. Dibblee, E. S. Webster, W. O. Chapman, F. J. Bawden, Russell Robb, N. H. Stone.

Corporate and main office, Hancock, Mich. Annual meeting, first Tuesday in August.

## HOUSTON OIL CO.

A corporation formed under the laws of Texas, in July, 1901. The purposes of the company are to acquire, deal in and develop oil and lumber lands in Texas. The company acquired about 1,000,000 acres of oil and timber lands in the Beaumont region of Eastern Texas. The company is closely allied with the Kirby Lumber Co., which purchased from it some 8,000,000 feet of standing timber on stumpage contracts.

Stock..Par $100 ..Authorized { com., $20,000,000 / pref., 10,000,000 } Issued { com., $20,000,000 / pref., 7,500,000 } $27,500,000

The company has no funded debt of its own, but guarantees under contract $6,566,000 6 per cent. timber certificates issued in connection with the Kirby Lumber contract. A mortgage on the property of this company forms part of the security for the certificates, which are issued by the Maryland Trust Co., Baltimore, as trustee.

President, Thomas H. Franklin, Houston, Tex.; Secretary, Jesse A. Whittaker, New York.

Directors—J. Wilcox Brown, Baltimore; F. E. Marshall, Henry T. Kent, Nathaniel P. Silsbee, Boston; S. B. Cooper, Beaumont, Tex.; O. C. Drew, W. W. Willson, B. F. Bonner, Joseph H. Eagle, Houston, Tex.

Corporate and main office, Houston, Tex.; New York office, 30 Broad street.

---

## HUDSON COUNTY GAS CO.

A corporation formed under the laws of New Jersey in 1899. The company acquired all the stock of the following gas organizations, which supply all the cities and towns in Hudson County, N. J.:

Hudson County Gas Light Co., Hoboken.
Jersey City Gas Light Co., Jersey City.
Consumers' Gas Co., Jersey City.
People's Gas Light Co., Jersey City.
Bayonne & Greenville Gas Light Co., Bayonne, N. J.

The various companies acquired were, in October, 1899, consolidated and merged into this company.

Stock......Par $100........................Authorized, $10,500,000.. ...Issued, $10,500,000

A controlling interest in the stock of this company is owned by the United Gas Improvement Co. of Philadelphia.

FUNDED DEBT.

| | |
|---|---|
| Consumers' Gas Co., 1st mort., 6 per cent., due 1904, May and Nov.................. | $600,000 |
| Hudson County Gas Co., consolidated 1st mort., gold 5s, due 1949, May and Nov.... | 9,160,000 |
| Total.................................................................. | $9,760,000 |

The 5 per cent. fifty-year mortgage created in 1899 is for $10,500,000. Bonds are in denominations of $100, $500 and $1,000. Of this issue $600,000 is reserved to take up the Consumers' Gas 6s and $740,000 is reserved to provide for improvements and extensions. Trustee of the mortgage, The New Jersey Title Guarantee & Trust Co., Jersey City.

President, Edward F. C. Young, Jersey City; Vice-President, Walton Clark; Treasurer, Lewis Lillie, Philadelphia; Secretary and Assistant Treasurer, P. S. Young; Assistant Secretary, R. D. Miller, Jersey City.

Directors—Edward F. C. Young, P. F. Wanser, E. L. Young, Joseph E. Hulshizer, Joseph D. Bedle, Thomas H. Williams, Cornelius Zabriskie, Elbert Rappleye, William C. Heppenheimer, Mark J. Cox, Jersey City; Randal Morgan, Philadelphia; Hamilton Wallis, East Orange; Myles Tierney, New York; Samuel B. Dod, A. P. Hexamer, Hoboken.

Main office, 1 Montgomery street, Jersey City.

---

## HUDSON RIVER TELEPHONE CO.

A corporation formed under the laws of New York, April 26, 1883. The company operates a telephone system in the counties of New York bordering on the Hudson River. It also controls the Troy Telephone & Telegraph Co., and the Northern New York Telephone Co. It had in January, 1903, 74 exchanges, 20,000 miles of wire and over 18,000 subscribers. The American Telephone & Telegraph Co. owns a majority interest in this company's stock.

Stock......Par $100........................Authorized, $4,000,000.....: Issued, $3,613,200

The company has no funded debt. In 1900, the stock was increased from $2,000,000 to

$3,000,000, and in February, 1900, an increase to $4,000,000 was ratified. In 1902 $400,000 of new stock was sold to the stockholders at par, and in January, 1903, another issue of $386,800 was made.

Stock is transferred at the company's office, Albany, N. Y.

Dividends paid on the stock have been as follows: In 1893, 3 per cent.; in 1894, 3½ per cent.; in 1895, 3½ per cent.; in 1896, 4 per cent.; in 1897, 4 per cent.; in 1898, 4 per cent.; in 1899, 5 per cent.; in 1900, 6 per cent., and in 1901, 6 per cent. Dividends are paid quarterly, in February (1), May, August and November at the rate of 1½ per cent.

| Earnings. | Gross. | Net. |
|---|---|---|
| 1900 | $519,679 | $167,799 |
| 1901 | 672,590 | 225,788 |
| 1902 | 787,330 | 236,564 |

President, James H. Manning, Albany, N. Y.; Vice-President, Jeffries Wyman, Boston; Secretary and Auditor, Walter B. Butler; Treasurer, James J. Fitzsimmons; General Manager, Henry E. Hawley, Albany.

Directors—James H. Manning, D. Cady Herrick, Albany, N. Y.; Joseph P. Davis, New York; Walter C. Humstone, Brooklyn, N. Y.; George P. Ide, Troy; John E. Adriance, Poughkeepsie, N. Y.; Frederick P. Fish, C. Jay French, Jeffries Wyman, Boston.

Main office, Maiden lane and Chapel street, Albany, N. Y. Annual meeting, first Thursday in March.

## HUDSON RIVER WATER POWER CO.

A corporation organized under the laws of New York, November 11, 1899. The company was formed to acquire and develop the water power of the Hudson River between Glens Falls and Palmers Falls, N. Y., and to utilize the same for the creation and distribution of electricity for power, lighting and heating. The company has erected a masonry dam 90 feet high and 1,500 feet long near Glens Falls, which will furnish a minimum of 20,000 horse-power in the driest portion of the year and 50,000 horse-power at other times. The company is also building a large power-house adjoining the dam, and has built transmission lines for conveying its current to Albany, Troy, Saratoga, Schenectady, Ballston, Fort Edward, Glens Falls and Sandy Hill, N. Y. This company has acquired the Saratoga Gas, Electric Light & Power Co. and the Ballston Spa Light & Power Co., and will supply these companies with power from its own plant. Contracts for 10,000 horse-power have been effected with the General Electric Co., Schenectady, N. Y., and for 2,000 horse-power with the Glen Falls Portland Cement Co., which, with the revenue from the company's own properties, will enable it to meet operating expenses and interest upon the entire outstanding bonded debt from the sale of but one-third of its power.

The contracts above referred to with the General Electric Co. and the Glens Falls Portland Cement Co. will bring an additional revenue of about $270,000. The annual operating expenses of the Hudson River Water Power Co., and the Electric Co., a subsidiary organization, are estimated at a maximum of $100,000 per annum. Five per cent. interest on $2,000,000 Water Power Co. and $2,000,000 Hudson River Electric Co. bonds amounts to $200,000, or annual expenses and interest charges of about $300,000 against an assured yearly revenue of about $1,240,000.

Applications have been made to the company from consumers in the cities and towns it will supply for over 6,000 horse-power, calling for additional revenue of about $165,000, and raising the surplus over expenses and charges, applicable to dividends, to over $1,000,000, or 20 per cent. on the $5,000,000 stock of the company.

The Hudson River Electric Co. was organized in 1901 to supply additional power. Its entire capital s o of $3,000,000 is held permanently in the treasury of the Hudson River Water Power Co.ck

Stock......Par $100..........................Authorized, $5,000,000......Issued, $5,000,000

Transfer Agent, D. S. Mills, 149 Broadway, New York.

FUNDED DEBT.

| | |
|---|---|
| 1st mort., 5 per cent., due $50,000 annually, 1914 to 1929, May and Nov. | $2,000,000 |
| Hudson River Electric, 1st mort., 5 per cent., due Dec., 1931, June and Dec. | 2,000,000 |
| Total | $4,000,000 |

The Hudson River Water Power Co.'s bonds are secured by a mortgage to The Trust Co. of America, trustee, of the company's entire property. The authorized amount of bonds is $2,000,000. There is a sinking fund for the bonds of $50,000 per year which becomes operative in 1914.

The Hudson River Electric Co.'s 1st mortgage 5 per cent. bonds are guaranteed, principal and interest, by this company. Trustee, Morton Trust Co., New York.

Contracts for lighting the cities of Albany and Troy, N. Y., were completed in December, 1902, which will produce a large additional revenue.

President, Eugene L. Ashley, Glens Falls, N. Y.; Vice-President, W. H. Trumbull, Salem, Mass.; Secretary, Elmer J. West; Treasurer, Eben H. Gay, Boston; Chief Engineer, William Barclay Parsons, New York.

Directors—Eugene L. Ashley, Elmer J. West, Eben H. Gay, W. H. Trumbull.

Main office, Glens Falls, N. Y.; New York office, 1 Nassau street; Treasurer's office, 131 Devonshire street, Boston. Annual meeting, fourth Tuesday in May.

---

## HUDSON VALLEY RAILWAY

A corporation formed under the laws of New York, August 15, 1901. The company is a consolidation of the following companies:

Glens Falls, Sandy Hill & Fort Edward Street Railway Co.
Warren County Railway Co.
Stillwater & Mechanicsville Street Railway Co.
Greenwich & Schuylerville Electric Railroad Co.
Saratoga Traction Co.
Saratoga Northern Railway Co.

The company owns and operates an electric trolley road for freight and passengers from Albany and Troy, N. Y., to Waterford, Mechanicsville, Stillwater, Schuylerville, Greenwich, Fort Edward, Sandy Hill, Glens Falls, Caldwell, Warrensburg, Round Lake, Ballston and Saratoga. About 133 miles of track is in operation, 85 miles of which is over private right of way. The company also owns Kaydeross Park, at Saratoga Lake; Ondawa Park, between Greenwich and Schuylerville, and Fort William Henry Park and the Fort William Hotel, at Lake George. It has a trackage contract with the United Traction Co. by which its cars enter Albany and Troy.

Stock......Par $100..........................Authorized, $3,000,000......Issued, $2,625,000

The company has no preferred stock. Transfer Agent, Central National Bank, New York. Registrar, Merchants' Trust Co., New York.

FUNDED DEBT.

| | |
|---|---|
| Consolidated mort., 5 per cent., gold, due 1951, Jan. and July | $3,000,000 |
| Glens Falls, Sandy Hill & Ft. Edw. St. Ry. 1st mort., 6 per cent., due 1911, Jan. and July | 100,000 |
| Glens Falls, Sandy Hill & Ft. Edw. St. Ry. 2d m., 6 p. c., due July, 1913, Jan. and July | 50,000 |
| Glens Falls, Sandy Hill & Ft. Edw. St. Ry. 3d m., 5 p. c. due April, 1921, April and Oct. | 81,500 |
| Stillwater & Mechanicsville St. Ry. 1st mort., 6 per cent., due April, 1913, April and Oct. | 47,500 |
| Stillwater & Mechanicsville St. Ry. 2d mort., cons. 6 p. c., due April, 1913, April and Oct | 202,500 |
| Total | $3,481,500 |

The authorized new consolidated mortgage is $4,000,000, of which $1,000,000 is set aside for future requirements and $481,500 is reserved to retire prior liens. Bonds may be called at 110. Trustee and agent for the payment of interest, Merchants' Trust Co., New York.

Trustee of the 1st mortgage of the Glens Falls, Sandy Hill & Fort Edward Street Railway Co. and agent for the payment of interest, Central Trust Co., New York. Trustee of the 2d mortgage and agent for the payment of interest, Merchants' National Bank, Glens Falls, N. Y. The bonds of the 3d mortgage may be called at 100 after April 1, 1902. Trustee of the mortgages of the Stillwater & Mechanicsville Street Railway Co., Union Safe Deposit & Trust Co., Portland, Me. Agents for the payment of interest, Bank of D. Powers & Sons, Lansingburg, N. Y., and Glens Falls Trust Co., Glens Falls, N. Y.

Chairman, Executive Committee, Peter McCarthy, Troy, N. Y.; President, Addison B. Colvin, Glens Falls, N. Y.; Vice-Presidents, J. A. Powers, Troy, N. Y., and George E. Green, Binghamton, N. Y.; Secretary, Thomas O'Connor, Waterford, N. Y.; Treasurer, F. L. Cowles, Glens Falls, N. Y.

Directors—Addison B. Colvin, Glens Falls, N. Y.; J. A. Powers, Frank E. Howe, Peter McCarthy, Troy, N. Y.; George E. Green, G. Tracy Rogers, Binghamton, N. Y.; Thomas O'Connor, Waterford, N. Y.; C. E. Brisbin, Schuylerville, N. Y.; Watson N. Sprague, Greenwich, N. Y.; W. W. Worden, Saratoga Springs, N. Y.; Louis W. Emerson, Warrensburg, N. Y.; J. Ledlie Hees, Fonda, N. Y.; Edwin Langdon, New York; John W. McNamara, Albany, N. Y.; John W. Herbert, Helmetta, N. J.

Main office, Glens Falls, N. Y. Annual meeting, third Wednesday in July, at Waterford, N.Y.

## HUMBOLDT COPPER MINING CO.

A corporation formed under the laws of Michigan in 1863. The company owns a copper property in Houghton County, Mich.

Stock......Par $25.. ........................Authorized, $1,000,000......Issued, $1,000,000

There has been paid on account of the capital, $232,683, including $100,000 represented by real estate.

President, C. Howard Weston, Boston; Secretary and Treasurer, John Brooks, Boston.
Directors—J. D. Huhn, John Brooks, W. C. Fisk, Ashley Watson, Wesley Clark.
Main office, 50 State street, Boston. Annual meeting, fourth Tuesday in March.

---

## ILLINOIS BRICK CO.

A corporation formed under the laws of Illinois, March, 1900, to engage in the manufacture and sale of brick. The company acquired 32 brick-making plants in Cook County, Ill., and vicinity, and now has facilities for making upwards of 750,000,000 bricks annually.

Stock....Par $100.....Authorised { com., $5,000,000; pref., 4,000,000 } Issued { com., $4,350,500; pref., 3,550,500 } $7,901,000

The preferred stock is 6 per cent., cumulative, and has preference as to assets. Stock is transferred at the office of the company, Chicago. Registrar, American Trust & Savings Bank, Chicago.

In the nine months of 1900, after the formation of the company, dividends to the amount of 4½ per cent. were paid. In 1901 and 1902 annual dividends of 6 per cent. were paid. The company has no fixed dates for paying dividends.

The company has a bond issue of $300,000, which is all held in the treasury.

In the fiscal year ending December 31, 1902, the company's gross earnings were $429,116.04; net, $262,708.35; dividends, $213,030.00; surplus, $292,400.27.

The following is the company's balance sheet, December 31, 1902:

| Assets. | | Liabilities. | |
|---|---|---|---|
| Plants | $7,941,000 | Capital stock, preferred | $4,000,000 |
| Bonds unsold | 300,000 | Capital stock, common | 5,000,000 |
| Bills receivable | 49,925 | Bonds | 300,000 |
| Accounts receivable | 299,778 | Bills payable | 141,000 |
| Brick, yard and shop inventories | 216,813 | Accounts payable | 110,330 |
| Preferred stock unissued | 449,500 | Second installment dividend, No. 3 | 106,515 |
| Common stock unissued | 649,500 | Surplus | 292,400 |
| Cash | 43,729 | | |
| Total | $9,950,245 | Total | $9,950,245 |

President, Leonard H. Harland; Vice-President, B. F. Weber; Secretary, William Schlake; Treasurer, C. D. B. Howell; General Superintendent, William H. Weckler, Chicago.

Directors—Frank B. Alsip, Henry Busse, John H. Gray, George C. Prussing, F. W. Labahn, Louis Riemer, A. J. Weckler, William H. Weckler, Chicago; C. D. B. Howell, Evanston, Ill.

Corporate and main office, 138 Washington street, Chicago. Annual meeting, first Monday in February, at Chicago.

---

## INDIANA NATURAL GAS & OIL CO.

A corporation formed under the laws of Indiana, October 5, 1889, for the purpose of developing and distributing natural gas and oil. The company owns pipe lines, gas and oil wells, pumping stations, etc.

Stock......Par $50............................Authorized, $2,000,000......Issued, $2,000,000

The company has no preferred stock.

Stock is transferred at the office of the company, 89 Broadway, New York. Registrar, Central Trust Co., New York.

The first dividend, 1½ per cent., was paid May 5, 1895; since then the dividends have been at the rate of 6 per cent. annually. The dividend periods are February, May, August and November.

Funded Debt.

1st mort., 6 per cent., gold, due July 1, 1910, Jan. and July..........................$4,000,000

The bonds outstanding are the full amount authorized. Trustee of the mortgage and agent for the payment of interest, Central Trust Co., New York.

President and General Manager, Jacob S. Smith; Secretary and Treasurer, Buford T. Kennedy, Chicago; Assistant Secretary, Edward Beers, New York.

Directors—Jacob S. Smith, W. O. Johnson, W. S. McCrea, Buford T. Kennedy, Chicago; Frank S. Hastings, New York.

Corporate office, Hammond, Ind.; Chicago office, 14 East Monroe street; New York office, 80 Broadway. Annual meeting, second Wednesday in June.

## INDIANAPOLIS, COLUMBUS & SOUTHERN TRACTION CO.

A corporation formed under the laws of Indiana in 1895. The company owns an electric railway extending from the limits of the city of Indianapolis, Ind., through Southport, Greenwood and Whiteland to Franklin, Ind., and operates 22 miles of track, 3 miles of which are over the line of the Indianapolis Street Railway Co. The company was formerly the Indianapolis, Greenwood & Franklin Railroad Co. The road has an extension nearly completed from Franklin to Columbus, a distance of 21 miles. Nearly all the track is on private right of way. The company owns a power house and 9 cars.

Stock......Par $100............................Authorized, $600,000......Issued, $285,000

The company has no preferred stock.

FUNDED DEBT.

1st mort., 5 per cent. gold, due Feb. 1923, Feb. and Aug............................ $300,000

The total authorized mortgage is $1,000,000, and $700,000 are reserved for extensions and improvements. Trustee and agent for the payment of interest, Trust Co. of North America, Philadelphia.

In the fiscal year ending June 6, 1902, the gross earnings were $87,002; net, $42,413; in the six months ending Nov. 30, 1902, the gross earnings were $50,535; net, $24,406.

President, Joseph I. Irwin; Vice-President and General Manager, William G. Irwin; Secretary and Treasurer, Hugh T. Miller, Columbus, Ind.

Directors—Joseph I. Irwin, William G. Irwin, Hugh T. Miller, Z. T. Sweeney, L. I. Sweeney, Columbus, Ind.

Corporate and main office, 303 Washington street, Columbus, Ind. Annual meeting, third Tuesday in January, at Columbus, Ind.

## INDIANAPOLIS STREET RAILROAD CO.

A corporation formed under the laws of Indiana, March 7, 1899. The company is a reorganization of the Citizens' Street Railway Co. and the City Railway Co. of Indianapolis. The company acquired a franchise for 34 years from the city, and operates 142 miles of electric road in and about Indianapolis, Ind. The property was leased to Indianapolis Traction & Terminal Co. in December, 1902.

Stock......Par $100.... .....................Authorized, $5,000,000......Issued, $5,000,000

FUNDED DEBT.

1st mort., 4 per cent., gold, due July, 1933, Jan. and July.......................... $6,000,000
Citizens' Street Railway cons. mort., 5 per cent., gold, due May, 1933, May and Nov.. 4,000,000

Total.......................................................... $10,000,000

The authorized 1st mortgage is $6,000,000. Trustee and agent for the payment of interest, Guarantee Safe Deposit Co., Philadelphia. The outstanding bonds of the Citizens' Street Railway Co.'s consolidated mortgage are the full amount authorized. Trustee, Central Trust Co., New York. Agent for the payment of interest, Fourth Street National Bank, Philadelphia.

President, George Brown; Vice-President, J. A. Lemcke; Secretary and Treasurer, Henry Jameson.

Directors—J. A. Lemcke, H. B. Hibben, Henry Jameson, George Brown, Indianapolis; James A. Murdock, Lafayette, Ind.

Main office, Illinois and Washington streets, Indianapolis. Annual meeting, second Wednesday in April.

## INDIANAPOLIS WATER CO.

A corporation formed under the laws of Indiana in 1881. The company's business is the supplying of water in Indianapolis and its suburban towns.

Stock......Par $100............................Authorized, $500,000......Issued, $500,000

FUNDED DEBT.

| | |
|---|---|
| 1st mort., 6 per cent., due 1911, May and Nov. | $500,000 |
| 2d gen. mort., 5 per cent., due 1926, Jan. and July | 1,485,000 |
| 30-year gold bonds, 4½ per cent., due 1930, Jan. and July | 500,000 |
| Total | $2,485,000 |

In the year 1900 the gross receipts were $352,442; in 1901, $351,444; in 1902, $373,193.

President, Thomas A. Morris; Vice-President and Treasurer, F. A. W. Davis; Secretary, Milton A. Morris, Indianapolis.

Directors—E. P. Kimball, Edward Kimball, John K. Bates, Portsmouth, N. H.; Charles H. Payson, Herbert Payson, Portland, Me.; C. S. Andrews, Brazil; Thomas A. Morris, Volney T. Malott, Edward Daniels, Albert Baker, H. McK. Landon, J. L. Ketcham, F. A. W. Davis, Indianapolis.

Main office, 113 Monument place, Indianapolis. Annual meeting, last Thursday in April.

## INDIANA RAILWAY CO.

A corporation formed under the laws of Indiana, March 15, 1899. The company is a consolidation of the following street railway companies:

South Bend Street Railway Co.
General Power & Quick Transit Co.
Elkhart, Goshen & Southern Railway Co.
Indiana Electric Railway Co.
South Bend & Elkhart Railway Co.

The company controls all the local electric railway lines in South Bend, Elkhart, Goshen and Mishawaka, Ind., and an interurban line joining those cities. It operates 50 miles of track and has three power stations and 65 cars. It serves a population of about 75,000.

Stock......Par $50............................Authorized, $1,000,000......Issued, $1,000,000

The company has no preferred stock. Transfer Agent, Northern Trust Co., Chicago.

FUNDED DEBT.

| | |
|---|---|
| 1st mort., 5 per cent. gold, due Jan. 1, 1930, Jan. and July | $900,000 |

The authorized mortgage is $1,000,000. A sinking fund of $10,000 per annum begins January 1, 1905. Bonds for the sinking fund will be bought in the open market. Trustee of the mortgage, Girard Trust Co., Philadelphia. Agent for the payment of interest, Standard Trust Co., New York, and Girard Trust Co., Philadelphia.

President, Arthur Kennedy, Pittsburg; Vice-President and General Manager, J. McM. Smith; Secretary and Treasurer, J. B. McCance, South Bend, Ind.

Directors—Arthur Kennedy, J. McM. Smith, J. B. McCance, Walter Lyon, W. L. Stonex.

Corporate and main office, South Bend, Ind.; Eastern office, 403 Wood street, Pittsburg.

## INTERBOROUGH RAPID TRANSIT CO.

A corporation formed under the laws of New York, May 14, 1902. The company was formed to operate the Rapid Transit Subway in New York City. It acquired all the stock of the Rapid Transit Subway Construction Co. The latter company was a New York corporation, formed in February, 1900. A full statement regarding it was given in the MANUAL for 1902. The Rapid Transit Subway Construction Co. took an assignment of the contract awarded by the Rapid Transit Commission and the municipality of New York in 1900 to John B. McDonald for the construction and operation of the subway in that city.

The subway, when completed, will be a four-track line of road, operated by electricity, extending from the City Hall via Park avenue and Forty-second street and Broadway to 103d street, with two-track extensions, partly viaduct, to Kingsbridge and to Bronx Park. A further extension has also been provided for from the City Hall southward to the Battery and thence by tunnel under the East River to Atlantic avenue, Brooklyn. The total length of the lines will be about 25 miles, with about 65 miles of track.

In January, 1903, this company leased the Manhattan (elevated) Railway Co. See below.

The arrangement with the city, under the contract entered into in January, 1900, which contract was assigned to the Rapid Transit Subway Construction Co. included provisions that the city should issue bonds to the amount of $35,000,000 to pay for the construction of the tunnel, and that the contractor should give a bond of $5,000,000 for the construction and equipment of the road and a continuing bond of $1,000,000, four and a half years being allowed for the completion of the work. Under the terms of the agreement the contractor is to have a lease of the road for fifty years, with the right to renew the same for twenty-five years additional. The rental provided for is the amount of interest paid by the city on its bonds, issued for the purpose, including interest during construction, and in addition 1 per cent. per annum on such cost of construction, there being provisions in regard to an increase of the rental when the gross earnings of the property exceed $5,000,000 per annum. In case of a renewal for twenty-five years, the rental shall be not less than the average amount paid by the company for the last ten years of the original lease.

The company is to provide and pay for the electrical equipment, rolling stock and other accessories of the road, the estimated cost of which is about $16,000,000.

The arrangement in connection with the construction of the tunnel between the City Hall, Manhattan, and Atlantic avenue, Brooklyn, mentioned above, is that the company shall build the same for $3,000,000, supplied by the city, but this part of the work will probably cost considerably more than that sum.

A proposition has also been made to extend the line of the original subway from Fourth avenue and Fourteenth street up Broadway to Forty-second street, connecting there with the main northern portion of the line, thus making a cutoff through the central portion of the city.

The bonds created by the city in connection with the construction of the subway are both 3 per cent. and 3½ per cent., and are being issued as the work progresses, payments by the city to the contractor being made by instalments as the work progresses.

In December, 1902, the company negotiated a lease of the property of the Manhattan Railway Co. for 999 years, from April 1, 1903. The rental under the lease is 6 per cent. per annum on the stock of the Manhattan Railway Co. from the date of the lease to January 1, 1906, and 1 per cent. additional if earned. After January 1, 1906, the rental will be 7 per cent. per annum on the stock of the leased company. See the separate statement of the Manhattan Railway Co. in this edition of the MANUAL.

Stock......Par $100........................Authorized, $35,000,000......Issued, $35,000,000

The company has no preferred stock and no funded debt.

Transfer Agent, August Belmont & Co., New York. Registrar, Guaranty Trust Co., New York.

Of the stock authorized and outstanding, $13,600,000 is full paid. The balance is 80 per cent., full paid, the balance being payable in instalments of 10 per cent. each, May 1 and June 1, 1903, at which latter date all the stock will be full paid.

All the stock of the company is held in a Voting Trust, the Trustees being E. Mora Davison, B. Hamburger and Charles B. Ludlow.

The Rapid Transit Subway Construction Co. had $6,000,000 of stock, all common shares. On this, in May, 1902, 60 per cent. had been paid in in cash. It was then determined to form another company to complete and operate the subway, and the Interborough Rapid Transit Co. was organized to carry out this plan with an authorized capital of $25,000,000.

When the present company was formed the $6,000,000 of stock of the Rapid Transit Subway Construction Co. was exchanged for 160 per cent. of its face, or $9,600,000 of full paid stock, of the Interborough Rapid Transit Co. The stockholders of the Rapid Transit Subway Construction Co. were also given the right to subscribe for 150 per cent. of their original holdings in Interborough Rapid Transit stock at par, being $9,000,000 of the latter, the subscription being payable in instalments.

In August, 1902, the authorized stock of the Interborough Rapid Transit Co. was increased from $25,000,000 to $35,000,000 in order to provide for the construction of the subway extension from the City Hall, Manhattan, to Atlantic avenue, Brooklyn. The additional stock, as well as the amount of the original authorized stock ($6,400,000), which remained unissued when the company was formed, have also, it is understood, been subscribed for by the stockholders.

President, August Belmont; Vice-President, E. P. Bryan; Treasurer, John F. Buck; Secretary, Frederick Evans, New York.

Directors—William H. Baldwin, Jr., M. F. Plant, August Belmont, Andrew Freedman, John B. McDonald, Walter G. Oakman, John Peirce, George W. Young, William A. Read, Cornelius Vanderbilt, New York; James Jourdan, Brooklyn; E. P. Bryan, Yonkers, N. Y.; Gardiner M. Lane, Boston.

Main office, 23 Nassau street, New York. Annual meeting, last Thursday in February.

---

## INTER-COLONIAL COAL MINING CO., LIMITED

A corporation formed under the laws of the Dominion of Canada for the purpose of mining coal. It owns the Drummond Colliery at Westville, Nova Scotia, the property consisting of 2¾ square miles of coal lands, with four workable seams of bituminous coal, only two of which have been worked. The company operates 20 coke ovens, and has a new shipping wharf at Picton under construction connected with a railway line owned and operated by the company.

Stock.....Par $100........Authorized { com., $500,000; pref., 250,000 } Issued { com., $500,000; pref., 219,700 } $719,700

Dividends of 7 per cent. on the preferred stock and 6 per cent. on the common stock were paid in 1902.

FUNDED DEBT.

1st mort., 5 per cent., due 1920, April and Oct. .......... $200,000

The authorized amount of the 1st mortgage is $350,000 and a sinking fund of $3,000 a year is provided.

President, James P. Cleghorn; Vice-President and General Manager, Charles Fergie; Secretary-Treasurer, D. Forbes Angus.

Directors—James P. Cleghorn, Charles Fergie, D. Forbes Angus, W. M. Ramsay, R. MacD. Paterson, A. W. Hooper, F. C. Henshaw.

Main office, 205 St. James street, Montreal. Annual meeting, first Wednesday in March, at Montreal.

---

## INTERNATIONAL ACHESON GRAPHITE CO.

A corporation formed under the laws of New Jersey, May 18, 1900, for the purpose of manufacturing graphite from anthracite coal in the electric furnace. It is claimed that this product, called Acheson Graphite, is identical in physical and chemical characteristics with the natural graphites, and hence can be used in place thereof. The company also manufactures Acheson graphite electrodes, for use in electrolytic or electro metallurgical processes. The electric methods employed are covered by patents granted to E. G. Acheson. The company acquired the plant and property of the Acheson Graphite Co. of Niagara Falls, N. Y., where the present company continues the business. The company controls the foreign patents for the process.

Stock......Par $100.......... Authorized, $500,000......Issued, $500,000

The company had $100,000 7 per cent., non-cumulative, preferred stock and $2,500,000 common stock. In December, 1902, it was decided to retire the preferred with an issue of 5 per cent. bonds and to reduce the common to $500,000, giving the holders of the outstanding common one new share for each six shares of the old. Dividends on the preferred were paid semi-annually, July and January, after the time that stock was retired, with the exception of one dividend, which was passed in order to create a reserve fund. No dividends have been paid on the common stock.

Transfer Agent, Corporation Trust Co. of New Jersey.

FUNDED DEBT.

1st mort., 5 per cent., due 1922, Jan. and July.......... $100,000

The authorized amount of the 1st mortgage is $125,000. Trustee and agent for the payment of interest, North American Trust Co., New York.

President, E. G. Acheson, Niagara Falls, N. Y.; Vice-President, A. W. Mellon, Pittsburg; Secretary, C. L. Collins, 2d, Niagara Falls, N. Y.; Treasurer, C. R. Huntley, Buffalo.

Directors—E. G. Acheson, F. A. J. Fitzgerald, C. L. Collins, 2d, P. P. Pfohl, Niagara Falls, N. Y.; A. W. Mellon, Pittsburg; C. R. Huntley, Buffalo; K. K. McLaren, Jersey City.

Corporate office, 15 Exchange Place, Jersey City; main office, Niagara Falls, N. Y. Annual meeting, fourth Tuesday in January, at Jersey City.

---

## INTERNATIONAL BUTTON-HOLE SEWING MACHINE CO.

A corporation formed under the laws of Maine in 1882. The company controls the Reece button-hole and finishing machine patents in foreign countries. See statement of Reece Button-Hole Machine Co.

Stock......Par $10.......... Authorized, $500,000......Issued, $500,000

Dividends were semi-annual, January (15) and July. In 1900 paid 1 per cent. on January 15, and 1 per cent. was paid January 15, 1901. In 1902, 2 per cent. was paid. The January, 1903, dividend was 1 per cent.

In the year ending April 1, 1899, the earnings of the company were, gross, $15,865; net, $10,113. Dividends paid, 2 per cent. In the year ending April 1, 1900, the gross was $11,948; net, $5,476; dividend, 1 per cent., $5,000. In the year 1900-01, gross, $14,752; net, $7,330; dividend, $5,000.

President and General Manager, Francis A. Shea; Secretary and Treasurer, Frank L. Cady, Boston.

Directors—Francis A. Shea, Frank L. Cady, Theophilus King, Boston; David E. Harding, Mansfield, Mass.; Crawford Ranney, St. Johnsbury, Vt.

Main office, 502 Harrison avenue, Boston.

## INTERNATIONAL ELEVATING CO.

A corporation formed under the laws of New Jersey, May 6, 1891. The business of the company is the handling of grain by means of floating elevators, of which it operates some twenty-five in and about New York harbor.

The company was originally the International Grain Elevating Co., and in 1894 absorbed the Atlantic Elevating Co.

Stock......Par $100..........................Authorized, $2,200,000......Issued, $2,200,000

The stock, which was $1,100,000, was doubled in 1894 to acquire the Atlantic Elevating Co.

President, Edward G. Burgess; Secretary, Charles E. Burgess, New York.

Directors—Thomas A. McIntyre, Edward G. Burgess, Charles E. Burgess, William A. Nash, S. W. Carey, Yale Kneeland, Ernest Pfarrius, Ormsby M. Mitchell, A. D. Pultz.

Corporate office, Jersey City; main office, Produce Exchange, New York.

---

## INTERNATIONAL EXPRESS CO.

A corporation formed under the laws of New York in January, 1899. The company acts as general forwarders to all parts of the world, and issues money orders, drafts, letters of credit, bills of exchange. It has a staff of customs experts in its employ for the handling of export and import express and freight shipments, and depots in New York at 136 Franklin street and 52 Broadway.

Stock......Par $100..........................Authorized, $1,000,000......Issued, $1,000,000

President, George B. Hopkins; Vice-President, William F. Burt; Secretary, Treasurer and General Manager, Walter E. Ogilvie.

Directors—Henry P. Booth, George B. Hopkins, James J. Belden, William F. Burt, H. L. Terry, Spencer P. Smith, Walter E. Ogilvie, Aaron Vanderbilt, John Waldron, Vincent O'Reilly, H. Schrueder.

Main office, 52 Broadway, New York.

---

## INTERNATIONAL FIRE ENGINE CO.

A corporation formed under the laws of New Jersey, December 8, 1899. The purpose of the company is the manufacture and sale of fire apparatus and supplies, etc. The company acquired a controlling interest in the American Fire Engine Co., Seneca Falls, N. Y., and Cincinnati. It acquired the entire properties of the following concerns:

The Fire Extinguisher Mfg. Co., Chicago.
The La France Fire Engine Co., Elmira, N.Y.
Charles T. Holloway & Co., Baltimore.
Gleason & Bailey Mfg. Co., Seneca Falls, N.Y.
Thomas Manning, Jr., & Co., Cleveland.
Rumsey & Co., Limited, Seneca Falls, N. Y. (fire apparatus department).
Waterous Engine Works Co., St. Paul.
The Macomber Chemical Fire Extinguisher Co., Worcester, Mass.

The company began business on August 10, 1900.

Stock...Par $100....Authorized { com., $5,000,000 / pref., 4,000,000 } Issued { com., $5,000,000 / pref., 4,000,000 } $9,000,000

The preferred stock is 7 per cent., cumulative, and also has a preference as to assets.

Stock is transferred at the company's office. Registrar, North American Trust Co., New York.

The company has no funded debt.

The first dividend on the preferred stock was 3½ per cent., semi-annual, paid August 10, 1901. The second semi-annual dividend was also 3½ per cent. March 1, 1902.

President, Julius E. French; 1st Vice-President, William C. Beer, New York; 2d Vice-President, William S. Taylor, Philadelphia; 3d Vice-President, Charles E. Locke; Secretary, William A. Dinsmore; Treasurer, Charles T. Silsby, New York.

Directors—Benjamin P. Cheney, George H. Robinson, John J. McCook, Charles T. Silsby, William C. Beer, William S. Taylor, George R. Bidwell, John H. Flagler, William A. Dinsmore, Horace A. Hutchins, Peter Murray, J. Charles Davis, William B. Plunkett, Charles E. Locke, Wilbur C. Brown, R. Ross Holloway, William J. White, Charles H. Fox, August F. Plate, W. J. Hilands, Charles B. Squire, Julius E. French, Charles H. Horton, Silas Chapman.

Main office, 149 Broadway, New York; branch offices, Chicago, Boston, Elmira, N. Y.; Baltimore. Annual meeting, third Tuesday in October.

## INTERNATIONAL HARVESTER CO.

A corporation formed under the laws of New Jersey, August 12, 1903. The company is a consolidation of the following agricultural machine manufacturing companies:

McCormick Harvesting Machine Co.
Deering Harvester Co.
Plano Manufacturing Co.
The Warder, Bushnell & Glessner Co.
Milwaukee Harvester Co.

The company has warehouses in the large cities of the country and timber land, coal, ore, blast furnaces and steel properties. It also has a plant in Canada under construction at the beginning of 1903.

Stock......Par $100........................Authorized, $120,000,000......Issued, $120,000,000

The company has no preferred stock and no funded debt. The articles of incorporation provide that if an increase of stock shall be voted such increase shall be common stock, while the original stock will become 6 per cent. cumulative preferred.

President, Cyrus H. McCormick; Chairman Executive Committee, Charles Deering; Chairman Finance Committee, George W. Perkins; Vice-Presidents, Harold F. McCormick, James Deering, William H. Jones, John J. Glessner; Secretary and Treasurer, Richard F. Howe.

Directors—Cyrus Bently, Paul D. Cravath, William Deering, Charles Deering, James Deering, E. H. Gary, John J. Glessner, Richard F. Howe, George F. Baker, William H. Jones, Cyrus H. McCormick, Harold F. McCormick, Stanley McCormick, Eldridge M. Fowler, George W. Perkins, Norman B. Ream, Charles Steele, Leslie D. Ward,

Corporate and main office, 7 Monroe street, Chicago. Annual meeting, third Thursday in April.

---

## INTERNATIONAL MERCANTILE MARINE CO.

A corporation formed under the laws of New Jersey, June 6, 1893, under the title of the International Navigation Co., the name having been changed to the present style in 1902. The International Navigation Co. owned and operated the American and the Red Star lines of steamships. See statement of the company given in the MANUAL for 1902. This change of name, together with an accompanying increase in the capitalization of the company, was in pursuance of a plan to unite the ownership and control of a number of the principal companies carrying on a transatlantic steamship service. The plan was financed by a syndicate of American and British capitalists headed by J. P. Morgan & Co., New York.

The properties acquired included: 1. All the shares, being 750 in number of £1,000 each of the Oceanic Steam Navigation Co., together with new vessels building for that company and all rights in the "White Star Line," name, etc.; also the business of Ismay, Imrie & Co., agents of the line, excluding certain properties and rights reserved.

2. All the shares of the Dominion Line (the British & North Atlantic Steam Navigation Co. and the Mississippi & Dominion Steamship Co.), including all new vessels building, name and good will; also the business, etc., of Richards, Mills & Co., agents of the line, except certain properties and rights specified.

3. The capital stock, properties and assets of the International Navigation Co. (American and Red Star lines), including new vessels building.

4. The capital stock and property of the Atlantic Transport Co., including new vessels building.

5. 118,463 ordinary shares and 58,703 preference shares of Frederick Leyland & Co. viz., £1,184,630, being all of the common stock; also £587,030 of the £1,402,030 preferred stock, but none of the £500,000 of the 4 per cent. debentures.

The White Star Line and the Dominion Line were to be taken over as of January 1, 1901, with interest on the purchase prices at 5 per cent. to the date of payment.

The tonnage of all the lines acquired aggregates about 1,000,000 tons. The constituent properties were taken over on December 1, 1902.

A feature of the agreements entered into for the acquisition of the White Star Line properties was that all orders for new vessels and for heavy repairs, requiring to be done at a shipyard of the United Kingdom, were to be given to Harland & Wolff, of Belfast, Ireland, but that this should not prevent placing orders for new steamers and repairs at shipyards in the United States. In return, Harland & Wolff agreed not to build ships for any persons not in the combination, except the Hamburg-American Co., so long as orders from the combination keep their works employed. Harland & Wolff are to be paid the cost of the work plus 5 per cent. on new ships, 10 per cent. on new machinery in old vessels, and 15 per cent. on repairs. This agreement runs for ten years and is terminable thereafter only on five years' notice from either party.

The company is understood to have acquired a large interest in the Holland-American Line.

It also has agreements in regard to rates and competitive service with the North German Lloyd Steamship Co. and the Hamburg American Co.

The company entered into a contract with the British government, for 20 years, renewable on five years notice by either party, according to the terms of which the British vessels belonging to companies, control of which was acquired by this company, shall remain British, not nominally, but in reality. A majority of the directors of the English subsidiary companies shall be of British nationality, the vessels shall fly the British flag, their officers are to be British, and a reasonable proportion of their crews are to be drawn from the same nation.

Stock....Par \$100..Authorized { com., \$60,000,000 / pref., 60,000,000 } Issued { com., \$48,000,000 / pref., 52,000,000 } \$100,000,000

The preferred stock is 6 per cent., cumulative. It is provided that dividends npon the common stock of the company shall be limited to 10 per cent. per annum as long as any of the collateral trust debenture 4½ per cent. bonds described below remain outstanding.

### Funded Debt.

| | |
|---|---|
| Collateral trust debentures, 4½ per cent., due Oct., 1922, April and Oct......... ... | \$50,000,000 |
| Old 1st mort., Int. Nav. Co., 5 per cent., due Feb., 1929, Feb. and Aug............ | 13,686,000 |
| Total...... | \$63,686,000 |

### Funded Debt—Constituent Companies.

Leyland Line debentures, 4 per cent.......................................... £500,000

The 4½ per cent. debentures were created and issued in 1902 in connection with the plan for the formation of this company. Interest on the debentures is paid at the office of the company. The company has the right to redeem the bonds at any time after five years at 105. The debentures were sold to the syndicate, which financed the organization, which is explained below.

The 1st mortgage 5 per cent. bonds were created in 1899. The authorized amount of the bonds is \$20,000,000. Interest on the bonds is paid at the company's office. These bonds are subject to call at par after 1909 and a sinking fund of \$250,000, rising to \$500,000 per annum to retire them, begins May 1, 1905.

The agreements and place in relation to the formation of the company and the distribution of its securities embraced the following details:

The shares of the White Star Line were valued on a basis of capitalizing the net profits for 1900 at 10 per cent. after deducting from profits an amount for depreciation equal to 6 per cent. on the book value of steamers and other items; and the same method was adopted with regard to the firm of Ismay, Imrie & Co. Sums paid on or before December 31, 1900, on vessels building were to be repaid.

The Dominion Line stock was valued on substantially the same basis as the White Star Line, and also the business of Richards, Mills & Co.

The aggregate valuation of the American Line and Atlantic Transport Line was fixed at \$34,158,000, subject to \$13,686,000 5 per cent. bonds of the American Line.

The valuation of the Leyland Line shares was \$11,736,000, there being left outstanding £815,000 5 per cent. preferred shares and £500,000 4 per cent. debentures not being included in the purchase.

For the total valuation of the White Star Line, the business of Ismay, Imrie & Co., and the Dominion Line, with the business of Richards, Mills & Co., the payment was to be made as follows: 25 per cent. in cash., 75 per cent. in preferred stock and 37½ per cent. in common stock of the new company.

For the American Line and the Atlantic Transport Line there was paid \$18,314,000 preferred stock and \$9,157,000 common stock, and for the new tonnage and indebtedness \$15,844,000 cash.

For the stock of the Leyland Line there was paid \$11,736,000 cash, with interest at 6 per cent.

The remainder of the stock of the new company and its collateral trust bonds were sold to a syndicate for \$50,000,000 cash, and there was contributed to the corporation as working capital \$786,000 preferred stock and \$6,643,000 common stock, the syndicate receiving for the \$50,000,000 cash and in full payment for its services the \$50,000,000 debentures and \$2,500,000 of preferred stock and \$25,000,000 common stock.

President, Clement A. Griscom, Philadelphia; Chairman British Committee, Sir Clinton E. Dawkins, London; Vice-President, P. A. S. Franklin; Secretary, Emerson E. Parvin; Treasurer, James S. Swartz.

Directors—Clement A. Griscom, Peter A. B. Widener, Philadelphia; B. N. Baker, Baltimore; John I. Waterbury, Edward J. Berwind, George W. Hawkins, James H. Hyde, Charles Steele, New York.

British Committee—Sir Clinton E. Dawkins, W. J. Pirie, J. Bruce Ismay, Henry Wilding, Charles F. Torrey, London.

Executive Committee—Clement A. Griscom, Peter A. B. Widener, Edward J. Berwind, Charles Steele, George W. Perkins.
Main office, 71 Broadway, New York.

## INTERNATIONAL PAPER CO.

A corporation formed under the laws of New York, January 31, 1898. It owns the following paper manufacturing plants in New York and the New England States, viz.:

Glens Falls Mill, Glens Falls, N. Y.
Fort Edward Mill, Fort Edward, N. Y.
Hudson River Mill, Palmer, N. Y.
Niagara Falls Mill, Niagara Falls, N. Y.
Herkimer Mill, Herkimer, N. Y.
Ontario Mill, Watertown, N. Y.
Lake George Mill, Ticonderoga, N. Y.
Fall Mountain Mill, Bellows Falls, Vt.
Winnepiseogee Mill, Franklin Falls, N. H.
Glen Mill, Berlin, N. H.
Otis Mill, Chisholm, Me.
Piercefield Mill, Piercefield, N. Y.
Solon Mill, Solon, Me.
Lyons Falls Mill, Lyons Falls, N. Y.
Cadyville Mill, Cadyville, N. Y.
Riley Mill, Riley, Me.
Wilder Mill, Wilder, Vt.
Ashland Mill, Ashland, N. H.
Piscataquis Mill, Montague, Me.
Milton Mill, Milton, Vt.
Watertown Mill, Watertown, N. Y.
Wood's Falls Mill, Watertown, N. Y.
Falmouth Mill, Jay, Me.
Umbagog Mill, Livermore Falls, Me.
Rumford Falls Mill, Rumford Falls, Me.
Webster Mill, Orono, Me.
Montague Mill, Turner's Falls, Mass.
Gardiner Mill, South Gardiner, Me.

The company holds title to about 1,000,000 acres of spruce woodlands in New York, New England and Michigan. In 1901 the American Realty Co. was organized in the interest of this company to hold a portion of the company's woodlands in Maine. The plants have a developed water power of 150,000 horse-power, producing about 1,500 tons of news and wrapping and miscellaneous paper per day. The company has available working assets of over $8,000,000.

Stock..Par $100..Authorized { com., $20,000,000 / pref., 25,000,000 } Issued { com., $17,442,800 / pref., 22,406,700 } $39,849,500

The preferred stock is 6 per cent., cumulative. The preferred may be increased $10,000,000 to retire the company's bonds.

Stock is transferred at the company's office. Registrar, Metropolitan Trust Co., New York.

The first regular quarterly dividend of 1½ per cent. on the preferred stock was paid July 11, 1898, and such quarterly dividends have since been regularly paid in January (1), April, July and October. The first dividend of 1 per cent. on the common stock was paid December 31, 1898, and two other quarterly dividends of 1 per cent. each were paid on the common in March and July, 1899, respectively. The October, 1899, dividend on the common was, however, passed, the management stating that the increased business of the company necessitated the use of some $8,000,000 working capital, a larger sum than was originally expected, and no subsequent dividends have been paid on the common stock.

### Funded Debt.

| | |
|---|---|
| 1st cons. mort., 6 per cent., bonds, due Feb., 1918, Feb. and Aug. | $9,866,000 |
| Divisional bonds | 3,087,500 |
| Total | $12,953,500 |

The 1st consolidated 6 per cent. mortgage is for $10,000,000. Bonds are convertible into preferred stock. Of the issue $1,301,000 was reserved to retire prior liens outstanding on various properties of the company, which since its formation has retired $530,000 of such liens, releasing an equal amount of its own bonds originally reserved for that purpose. The bonds are a 1st lien on the plants, water powers and woodlands of the company. Trustee of bonds, United States Trust Co., New York. Registrar of bonds and agent for the payment of interest, Metropolitan Trust Co., New York.

### Earnings.

Year ending June 30.

| | Gross. | Net. | Charges & Taxes. | Dividends. | Surplus. |
|---|---|---|---|---|---|
| 1898-99 | $15,063,568 | $2,845,035 | $596,595 | $1,786,206 | $462,234 |
| 1899-00 | 18,707,635 | 3,125,876 | 842,302 | 1,344,402 | 939,172 |
| 1900-01 | 20,711,902 | 3,961,657 | 907,267 | 1,344,402 | 1,709,988 |
| 1901-02 | 19,719,420 | 2,901,195 | 1,003,740 | 1,344,402 | 553,053 |

The company's balance sheet June 30, 1902, is as follows:

| ASSETS. | | LIABILITIES. | |
|---|---|---|---|
| Mill plants | $41,251,236 | Common stock | $17,442,800 |
| Woodlands | 3,980,433 | Preferred stock | 22,406,700 |
| Securities of sundry corporations | 5,477,523 | 1st mortgage bonds | 9,866,000 |
| Land rights and water powers | 104,502 | Divisional mortgage bonds | 3,087,500 |
| Patents | 12,000 | Accounts payable (since paid) | 1,256,426 |
| Furniture and fixtures | 39,340 | Accrued interest, taxes and water rents not due | 368,015 |
| Sinking funds | ........ | Surplus | 4,073,041 |
| Cash | 566,108 | | |
| Accounts and notes receivable | 3,316,588 | | |
| Inventories of merchandise on hand and advances for wood operations | 3,752,752 | | |
| Total | $58,500,482 | Total | $58,500,482 |

President, Hugh J. Chisholm; 1st Vice-President, F. H. Parks; 2d Vice-President, Thomas T. Waller; Secretary, Elmer W. Hyde; Treasurer, Alonzo N. Burbank.

Directors—F. H. Parks, F. B. Jennings, Alonzo N. Burbank, Warren Curtis, Darius O. Mills, T. S. Coolidge, W. A. Russell, Hugh J. Chisholm, A. Pagenstecher, H. M. Knowles, Anson R. Flower, Samuel R. Callaway, G. F. Underwood.

Offices, Corinth, N. Y., and 30 Broad street, New York. Annual meeting, fourth Wednesday in August.

## INTERNATIONAL POWER CO.

A corporation formed under the laws of New Jersey, January 14, 1899. The original title was The International Air Power Co., which style was changed in March, 1899. The company acquired the patents for the use of compressed air power under the Hoadley-Knight system, except the street car rights in both North and South America. The company is authorized by charter to manufacture, buy, sell and deal in compressed air, electrical machinery and apparatus, locomotives, engines, trucks and cars, and to manufacture all machinery for the supplying of electric, compressed air and other motive powers. It acquired the Rhode Island Locomotive Works at Providence, R. I., where it manufactures compressed air motors, locomotives, stationary engines and other machinery. In February, 1899, the company acquired the Corliss Steam Engine Works, of Providence, R. I., and the American Wheelock Engine Co., Worcester, Mass. It controls the patents for the American Diesel Engine. The company had an interest in the organization of the American Locomotive Co., but is understood to have sold its holdings of that company's stock in 1902.

Stock....Par $100....Authorized { com., $7,400,000 / pref., 600,000 } Issued { com., $6,400,000 / pref., 600,000 } $7,000,000

The preferred stock is entitled to 6 per cent., cumulative dividends. The common stock issued includes $1,353,000 held in the company's treasury.

Transfer Agent, Atlantic Trust Co., New York. Registrar, Guaranty Trust Co., New York.

On March 15, 1900, a dividend at the rate of 6 per cent. per annum for the year 1899 was paid on the preferred stock. On May 15, 1901, 6 per cent. annual was again paid on the preferred, with 1½ per cent. for the first quarter of 1901.

FUNDED DEBT.

1st mort., 4 per cent., due 1919, Feb. and Aug. .......... $200,000

The bonds are secured by the Rhode Island Locomotive Works and the American Wheelock Engine Works, Worcester, Mass. There is also a mortgage of $140,000 on the Corliss Works.

In the year 1900 the profits of the company were $254,151.

In the year 1901 the company reported gross earnings of $513,760 and net $292,796; charges and preferred dividend, $83,328; balance surplus, $209,468.

President, Joseph H. Hoadley, New York; Vice-President and Treasurer, George W. Hoadley, Providence, R. I.; Secretary, George H. Wilson, New York; Chairman of Executive Committee, Joseph Leiter, Chicago.

Directors—Joseph H. Hoadley, James H. Snow, Cyrus Field Judson, Harry E. Knight, Lewis Nixon, New York; Joseph Leiter, Chicago; George W. Hoadley, Alfred H. Hoadley, Providence; Robert I. McKinstry, Camden, N. J.

Main office, 253 Broadway, New York. Annual meeting, second Tuesday in January, at Camden, N. J.

## INTERNATIONAL SALT CO.

A corporation formed under the laws of New Jersey in August, 1901. The company was organized in pursuance of a plan to unite the ownership of the stocks of the National Salt Co. and the Retsof Mining Co. See statements of those corporations in this edition of the MANUAL.

This company has acquired a large majority of the stocks of the National Salt Co. and of the Retsof Mining Co. under the terms mentioned below and issued its own securities in exchange for the stocks of the constituent companies.

Stock......Par $100........................Authorized, $30,000,000......Issued, $18,750,000

The company has no preferred stock. Registrar, Registrar & Transfer Co., Jersey City.

FUNDED DEBT.

1st cons. collateral trust mortgage bonds, 5 per cent., due Oct., 1951, April and Oct....$7,500,000

The collateral trust mortgage bonds, United States Mortgage & Trust Co., New York, trustee, are $12,000,000 authorized. They are secured by a deposit with the trustee of the stocks and securities acquired by the company. The bonds are subject to call at 105 and interest and $200,000 are to be retired each year by a sinking fund. Of the issue $4,500,000 were to remain in the treasury for further acquisitions.

Under the plan for the formation of this company, which was issued in October, 1901, the holders of each 10 shares or $1,000 par value of National Salt preferred were offered $1,000 in this company's bonds, together with one share, or $100 of its stock. Holders of National Salt common were offered one share of this company's stock for each share of National Salt common. Holders of the bonds of the Retsof Mining Co. were offered $1,000 in this company's bonds for $1,000 of Retsof bonds and holders of Retsof Mining Co.'s stock were offered one share of this company's stock for each share of Retsof stock. To acquire all the bonds and stocks of the National Salt Co. and Retsof Mining Co. required $11,350,000 of this company's stock and $7,500,000 of its bonds. A syndicate, headed by Oakleigh Thorne, New York, took $7,400,000 of stock and agreed to finance the operation, the terms including the furnishing of this company with a cash working capital of $1,000,000. There remains in the treasury $11,250,000 of unissued stock, which, with the bonds reserved, can be used only to acquire additional salt properties in this or foreign countries.

President, Edward L. Fuller; Vice-President, M. B. Fuller, Scranton, Pa.; Secretary, Henry S. Fleming; Treasurer, Milo M. Belding, Jr., New York.

Directors—Edward L. Fuller, Milo M. Belding, M. B. Fuller, W. B. Putney, Milo M. Belding, Jr., Archibald S. White, Oakleigh Thorne, F. F. Culver, O. L. Gubelman.

Main office, Scranton, Pa.; New York office, 170 Broadway.

---

## INTERNATIONAL SILVER CO.

A corporation formed under the laws of New Jersey, November 21, 1898. The company was organized to combine the leading manufactories of silver and silver-plated ware in the United States and Canada. The companies included were:

Meriden Britannia Co., Meriden.
Rogers & Brothers, Waterbury.
Barbour Silver Co., Hartford.
William Rogers Manufacturing Co., Hartford.
Manhattan Silver Plate Co., Lyons, N. Y.
Watrous Manufacturing Co., Wallingford, Conn.
Rogers Cutlery Co., Hartford.
Meriden Silver Plate Co., Meriden.
Wilcox Silver Plate Co., Meriden.
Rogers & Hamilton Silver Plate Co., Waterbury.
Norwich Cutlery Co., Norwich.
Standard Silver Plate Co., Toronto.
Holmes & Edwards Silver Co., Bridgeport.
Derby Silver Co., Derby, Conn.
Simpson Nickel Co., Wallingford, Conn.
Simpson, Hall, Miller & Co., Wallingford, Conn.
Middletown Plate Co., Middletown, Conn.

The three last-named concerns were acquired after the organization of the company. The firms and companies represent some 75 per cent. of the total silverware output of the country. The company acquired the trade-marks, etc., of all these establishments.

In 1902 negotiations were on foot between this company and the United States Silver Corporation. Early in 1903 control of the latter organization was obtained by this company. C. Rogers & Brothers, Meriden, Conn., which was controlled by the United States Silver Corporation, also passed under the control of this company.

Stock....Par $100...Authorized { com., $11,000,000 / pref., 9,000,000 } Issued { com., $9,944,700 / pref., 6,607,500 } $16,552,200

The preferred stock is 7 per cent., cumulative. In January, 1903, $1,500,000 additional of preferred stock was issued for the acquisition of the United States Silver Corporation.

Transfer Agent, American Exchange National Bank, New York.

The payment of dividends on the preferred stock was commenced early in 1900, a quarterly dividend on the preferred of 1¾ per cent. being declared, payable April 1, 1900, but no dividends were paid in 1900 or 1901. On January 1, 1902, 1 per cent. was paid on the preferred, and subsequent quarterly payments were on that basis. There was, however, 21¼ per cent. of unpaid cumulative dividends on the preferred on January 1, 1903, and it was decided to settle the claims of the preferred stock by an issue of scrip for the amount of the unpaid dividends.

FUNDED DEBT.

| | |
|---|---|
| 1st mort., 6 per cent., due Dec., 1948, June and Dec. | $3,776,000 |
| Dividend scrip | 1,085,343 |
| Debentures, 6 per cent., due Jan., 1933, Jan. and July | 2,000,000 |
| Total | $6,861,343 |

The authorized amount of the 1st mortgage is $4,500,000. Part of the amount outstanding was sold to a syndicate and proceeds were used for the acquisition of various properties. Continental Trust Co., New York, is trustee and registrar. Additional bonds can only be issued for the purpose of acquiring new property. There are $110,000 of the first mortgage bonds in the company's treasury.

The 6 per cent. debentures were created in 1903 to provide for the acquisition of the United States Silver Corporation. The trustee of the debentures is the Continental Trust Co., New York. The debentures are subject to call at par on sixty days' notice.

There are, in addition to the above, $157,600 of underlying mortgages of the constituent companies.

EARNINGS.

| | Net. | Charges. | Dividends. | Depreciation. | Surplus. |
|---|---|---|---|---|---|
| 1901 | $614,934 | $223,391 | $51,075 | $113,551 | $226,917 |
| 1902 | 881,197 | 220,022 | 204,300 | 242,657 | 214,218 |

President, Samuel Dodd; 1st Vice-President, George H. Wilcox; 2d Vice-President, George C. Edwards; 3d Vice-President, C. A. Hamilton; Treasurer, George M. Curtis; Secretary, George Rockwell.

Directors—Samuel Dodd, George M. Curtis, F. P. Wilcox, George H. Wilcox, George Rockwell, Meriden, Conn.; S. L. Barbour, Hartford; George C. Edwards, Bridgeport; C. A. Hamilton, Waterbury; G. D. Munson, Wallingford, Conn.; Edwin M. Post, E. R. Thomas, New York; C. E. Breckenridge, New Jersey; W. J. Miller, Derby, Conn.

Main office, Meriden, Conn.; New York office, 11 Maiden lane.

## INTERNATIONAL SMOKELESS POWDER & DYNAMITE CO.

A corporation formed under the laws of New Jersey in 1899 to engage in the manufacture of smokeless powder. The company has a contract for supplying its products to the United States Government. The plant is located at Parlin, N. J., and has a capacity of 4,000 pounds per day.

A majority of the stock of this company is owned by The Marsden Co.

Stock....Par $50..... Authorized { com., $9,000,000; pref., 1,000,000 } Issued { com., $9,000,000; pref., 600,000 } $9,600,000

The preferred stock is 8 per cent., cumulative.

Stock is transferred at the office of the company. Registrar, Trust Co. of North America, Philadelphia.

Dividends are paid semi-annually in May and November. The company has no funded debt.

In the fiscal year ending December 31, 1902, the gross sales were $381,186; powder on hand, $210,343; operating expenses, $414,117; net profit, $177,412; dividends, $118,066; undivided profits, $59,345.

President, Carl D. Bradley, Parlin, N. J.; 1st Vice-President, H. C. Watts; 2d Vice-President, E. G. Buckner; Secretary, W. E. Steen; Assistant Secretary, E. H. Seymour; Treasurer, W. E. Steen; Assistant Treasurer, E. H. Seymour, Philadelphia.

Directors—E. G. Buckner, W. W. Gibbs, H. C. Watts, Edward C. Lee, George Philler, Carl D. Bradley, Lewis Nixon, George S. Graham.

Corporate office, Camden, N. J.; main office, Drexel Building, Philadelphia. Annual meeting, first Friday in April, at Camden.

## INTERNATIONAL STEAM PUMP CO.

A corporation formed under the laws of New Jersey, March 24, 1899. The company is a consolidation of several large establishments engaged in the manufacture of steam pumps for all purposes. The plants acquired outright by ownership of at least two-thirds of their stocks embrace the following: Henry R. Worthington Co., Brooklyn, N. Y., and Elizabethport, N. J.; Blake & Knowles Steam Pump Works, Ltd., New York, East Cambridge, Mass., and Warren, Mass.; Deane Pump Works, Holyoke, Mass.; Laidlaw-Dunn-Gordon Co., Cincinnati, O.; Snow Steam Pump Works, Buffalo, N. Y.; Holly Manufacturing Co., Lockport, N. Y.

The above concerns make 90 per cent. of the steam pumps produced in the United States. Their aggregate assets were stated to be $11,981,355, and their combined net profits for 1898 were estimated at $1,200,000.

Stock..Par $100..Authorized { com., $15,000,000 / pref., 12,500,000 } Issued { com., $12,262,500 / pref., 8,850,000 } $21,112,500

The preferred stock is 6 per cent., cumulative.

Of the preferred stock a sufficient amount was set aside to retire the $2,000,000 7 per cent. cumulative preference stock of the Henry R. Worthington Co. and the $1,500,000 6 per cent. debentures and $500,000 8 per cent. preference shares of the Blake & Knowles Co. There are also $700,000 of 5 per cent. 1st mortgage bonds of the Holly Manufacturing Co., due January, 1921.

Transfer Agent, Colonial Trust Co., New York. Registrar, City Trust Co., New York.

The payment of quarterly dividends of 1¾ per cent. on the preferred stock began August 1, 1899, and have been regularly paid at that rate in February (1), May, August and November. A dividend of 4 per cent. on the common was declared out of the earnings of the year ending March 31, 1901, payment to be in quarterly instalments, beginning July 1, 1901, and the same rate was declared for the following year.

FUNDED DEBT.

Convertible debentures, 6 per cent., due Jan., 1913, Jan. and July.................... $2,500,000

The convertable debentures are $3,500,000, and were created in December, 1902, to provide for extensions and improvements. They can be converted into common stock at par. In January, 1903, the stockholders were given the right to subscribe for $2,500,000 of these bonds.

The statement of the company from date of organization to April 1, 1900, showed its net profits derived from the earnings of the constituent companies were $2,049,631. In the year ending March 31, 1901, the net profits were $1,772,632; surplus over charges and preferred dividends, $994,632. In 1901-02 profits, $1,510,486; surplus, $734,436.

The following is a consolidated balance sheet of the company and its affiliated concerns, March 31, 1902:

| ASSETS. | | LIABILITIES. | |
|---|---|---|---|
| Real estate, plants and equipments, good-will, investments, etc..... | $23,939,558 | Capital stocks and bonds authorized, less in treasury........... | $27,279,600 |
| Discounts on bonds............. | 170,625 | Loan ........................... | 156,590 |
| Worthington Pumping Engine Company, London........... | 1,020,984 | Trade accounts.................. | 479,743 |
| Inventories..................... | 3,635,995 | Miscellaneous.................... | 103,556 |
| Bills receivable ................. | 2,606,382 | Dividends ....................... | 132,750 |
| Miscellaneous................... | 190,791 | Associated company balances..... | |
| Associated company balances..... | 26,096 | Surplus account............ .... | 3,614,417 |
| Cash ............................ | 175,226 | | |
| Total .......... ....... | $31,765,657 | Total ............. ...... | $31,765,656 |

President, John W. Dunn; Vice-Presidents, Marcus Stine, Charles L. Broadbent; Secretary, James H. Snow; Treasurer, Max Nathan, New York.

Directors—Max Nathan, Charles L. Broadbent, Marcus Stine, John W. Dunn, Daniel O'Day, James H. Snow, Philip Lehman, Frederick M. Wheeler, Harry B. Hollins, Harry K. Knapp, John E. Borne, Joseph Seep, Edmund C. Converse, Jacob Rubins, Samuel Untermyer.

Corporate office, 243 Washington street, Jersey City; executive office, Van Brunt and Rapalyea streets, Brooklyn; New York office, 120 Liberty street. Annual meeting, first Tuesday in April, at Jersey City.

## INTERNATIONAL TRACTION CO.

A proprietary corporation organized under the laws of New Jersey in 1899. It owns the stock of the International Railway Co., which was formed under the laws of New York in February, 1902, to acquire and combine the street railway lines of Buffalo, N. Y., with the lines extending to and in Niagara Falls, N. Y., Lockport, N. Y., and Tonawanda, N. Y., including the lines on the Canadian side of the Niagara River, at Niagara Falls, and the bridges connecting the trolley lines. The properties comprise:

- Buffalo Railway Co.
- Crosstown Street Railway of Buffalo.
- Buffalo Traction Co.
- Buffalo, Tonawanda & Niagara Falls Electric Railroad.
- Buffalo & Niagara Falls Electric Railway.
- Buffalo, Belleville & Lancaster Railway.
- Buffalo & Lockport Railway.
- Elmwood Avenue & Tonawanda Electric Railway.

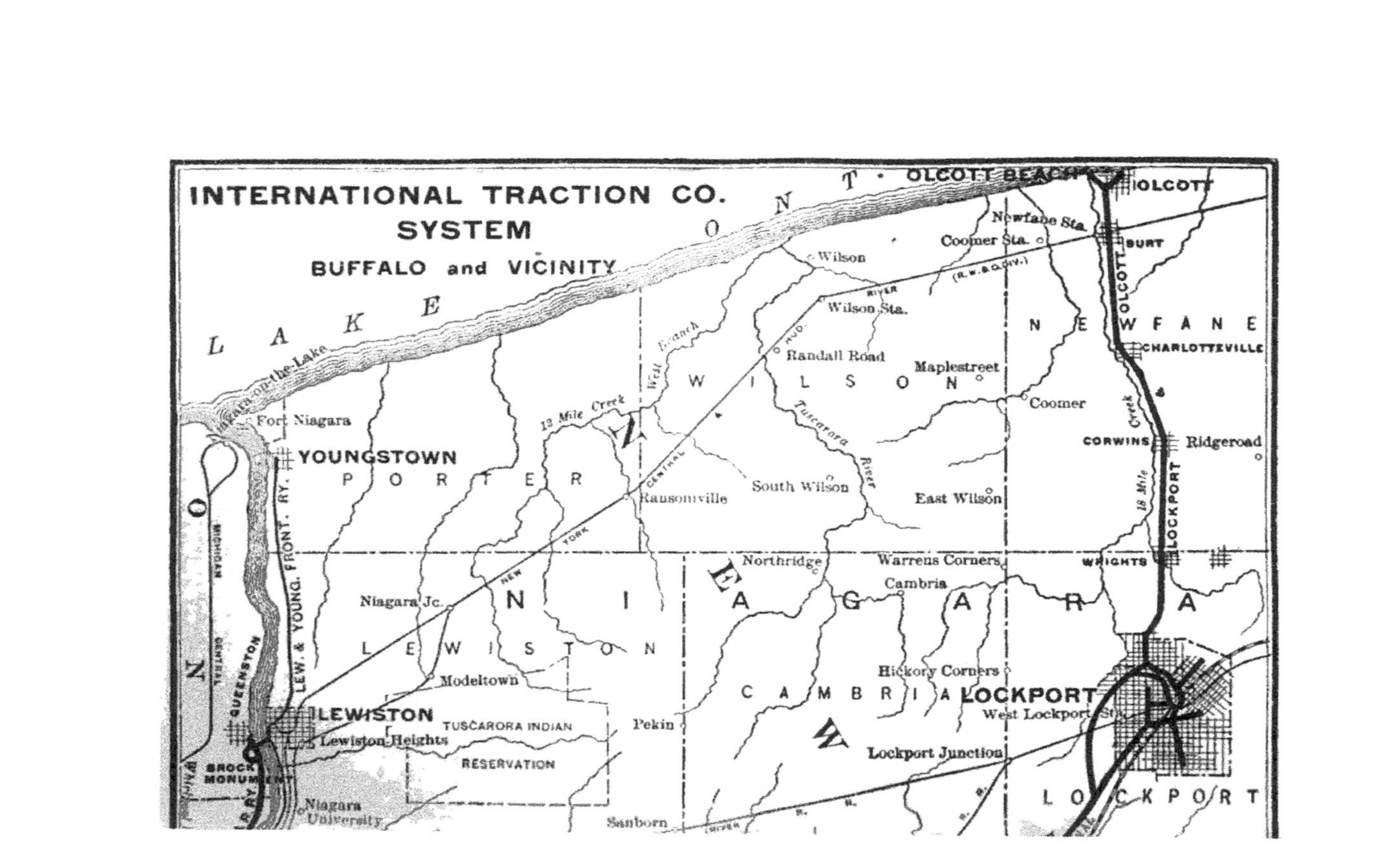

INTERNATIONAL TRACTION CO.
SYSTEM
BUFFALO and VICINITY
LAKE ONT
OLCOTT BEACH
OLCOTT
Newfane Sta.
Coomer Sta.
BURT
Wilson
Wilson Sta.
NEWFANE
CHARLOTTEVILLE
Randall Road
Maplestreet
WILSON
Coomer
Fort Niagara
YOUNGSTOWN
PORTER
18 Mile Creek
West Branch
Tuscarora River
CORWINS
Ridgeroad
South Wilson
Rausonville
East Wilson
LOCKPORT
18 Mile Creek
NEW YORK CENTRAL
Northridge
Warrens Corners
WRIGHTS
Cambria
Niagara Jc.
NIAGARA
LEWISTON
Hickory Corners
Modeltown
CAMBRIA
LOCKPORT
West Lockport Sta.
LEWISTON
TUSCARORA INDIAN
RESERVATION
Pekin
Lewiston Heights
Lockport Junction
BROCK MONUMENT
Niagara University
LOCKPORT
Sanborn
MICHIGAN CENTRAL
QUEENSTON
LEW. & YOUNG. FRONT. RY.

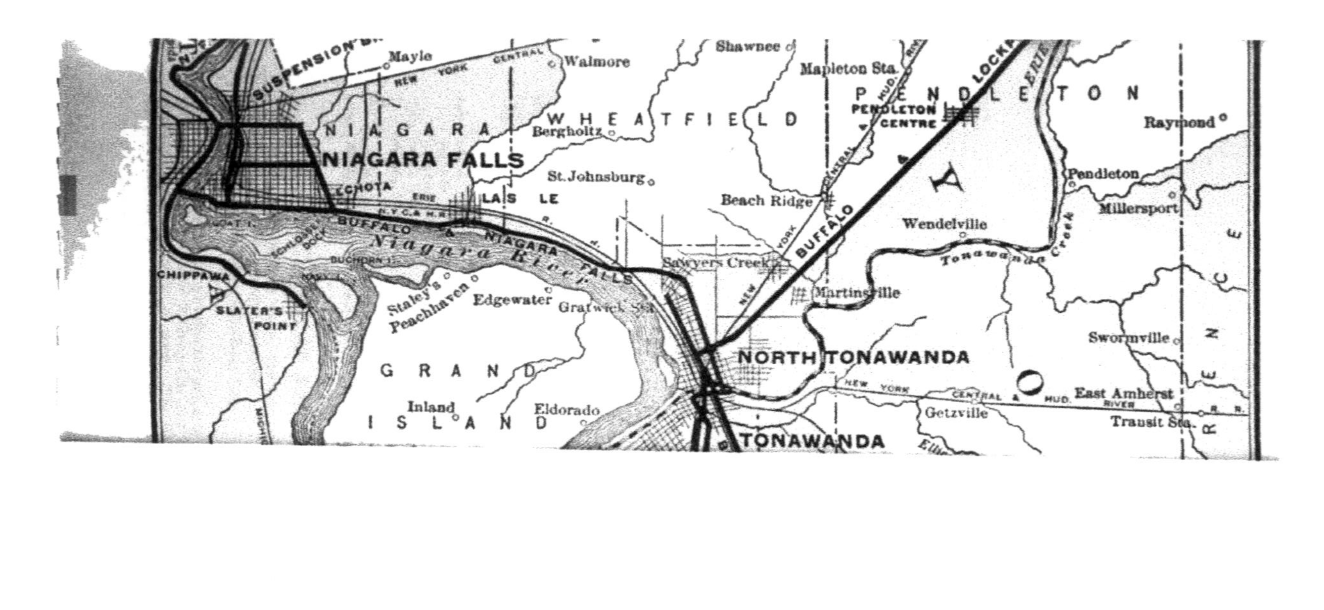

SUSPENSION
Mayle
Walmore
Shawnee
Mapleton Sta.
NEW YORK CENTRAL
NIAGARA
NIAGARA FALLS
ECHOTA
LA SALLE
WHEATFIELD
PENDLETON
PENDLETON CENTRE
Raymond
Bergholtz
St. Johnsburg
Beach Ridge
Pendleton
Millersport
Wendelville
BUFFALO & LOCKPORT
ERIE
BUFFALO & NIAGARA FALLS
Niagara River
Tonawanda Creek
Sawyers Creek
Martinsville
CHIPPAWA
SLATER'S POINT
Staley's
Peachhaven
Edgewater
Gratwick Sta.
GRAND ISLAND
Inland
Eldorado
NORTH TONAWANDA
TONAWANDA
Swormville
East Amherst
Getzville
Transit Sta.
NEW YORK CENTRAL & HUD. RIVER R. R.

Niagara Falls & Suspension Bridge Railway.
Niagara Falls Park & River Railway (Canada).
Clifton Suspension Bridge Co.
Queenstown Heights Bridge Co.
Niagara Falls, Whirlpool & Northern Railway.
Niagara Falls Suspension Bridge Co.
Lewiston Connecting Bridge Co.
Lockport & Olcott Railway Co.

The company purchased all the stocks of the foregoing companies, which are now owned by or merged with the International Railway Co. The united length of the lines is 352.95 miles.

Stock...Par $100....Authorized { com., $10,000,000 pref., 5,000,000 } Issued { com., $10,000,000 pref., 5,000,000 } $15,000,000

The preferred stock is 4 per cent., cumulative. Transfer Agent, Corporation Trust Co. of New Jersey, Jersey City.

FUNDED DEBT.

Collateral trust. mort., 4 per cent., due July, 1949, Jan. and July.................... $15,715,000

FUNDED DEBT OF CONSTITUENT COMPANIES.

| | |
|---|---|
| Buffalo Ry. 1st cons. mort., 5 per cent., due Feb. 1931, Feb. and Aug. | $3,756,000 |
| Buffalo Ry. debentures, 5 per cent., due April, 1917, April and Oct. | 1,000,000 |
| Buffalo Ry. real estate mort., 5 per cent., due June, 1904, June and Dec. | 150,000 |
| Buffalo Street Ry. 2d mort., 6 and 7 per cent., due July, 1905, Jan. and July | 650,000 |
| Buffalo East Side Ry. 1st mort., 7 per cent., due June, 1904, June and Dec. | 300,000 |
| Buffalo East Side Ry. 2d mort., 6 per cent., due Sept., 1912, March and Sept. | 293,500 |
| Crosstown Street Ry. 1st mort., 5 per cent due May, 1930, May and Nov. | 2,974,000 |
| Buffalo Traction 1st mort., 5 per cent., due Dec., 1948, June and Dec. | 673,000 |
| Buffalo & N. F. El. Ry. 1st mort., 5 per cent., due July, 1935, Jan. and July | 750,000 |
| Buffalo & N. F. El. Ry. 2d mort., 5 per cent., due July, 1921, Jan. and July | 175,000 |
| Buffalo & Lockport 1st mort., 5 per cent., due July, 1938, Jan. and July | 500,000 |
| Niagara Falls & Susp. Bridge 1st mort., 6 per cent., due 1903, Jan. and July | 518,000 |
| Niagara Falls Park & River 1st mort., 5 per cent., due Jan., 1914, Jan. and July | 600,000 |
| Niagara Falls Susp. Bridge 1st mort., 5 per cent., due Jan., 1928, Jan. and July | 300,000 |
| Buffalo, Bel. & Lanc. 1st mort., due 1927, June and Dec. | 215,000 |
| Lewistown Con. Bridge, 1st mort., due 1928, April and Oct. | 125,000 |
| Lockport & Olcott Railway, 1st mort., due July, 1920, Jan. and July | 800,000 |
| Niagara Falls, Whirlpool & Nor. 1st mort., 5 per cent., due July, 1903., Jan. and July | 22,500 |
| Total | $13,802,000 |

The collateral trust mortgage is $30,000,000 authorized, an amount of $12,285,000 being reserved to take up previous liens, and $2,000,000 were set aside to provide for improvements, etc.

EARNINGS—ALL COMPANIES.

Year ending June 30.

| | Gross. | Net. | Charges. | Surplus. |
|---|---|---|---|---|
| 1898–99 | $2,333,316 | $1,063,843 | $871,795 | $192,048 |
| 1899–00 | 2,575,921 | 1,275,332 | 925,077 | 350,255 |
| 1900–01 | 3,129,094 | 1,649,773 | 1,121,384 | 528,389 |
| 1901–02 | 4,426,676 | 2,310,021 | 1,174,467 | 1,135,554 |

In 1901–02 the total income of the International Traction Co. was $1,344,471, and its surplus over charges, taxes, etc., was $761,061.

President, W. Caryl Ely; Secretary, Charles MacVeagh; Treasurer, Richard F. Rankine.

Directors—Charles Steele, Francis Lynde Stetson, Temple Bowdoin, Charles MacVeagh, New York: Thomas DeWitt Cuyler, Philadelphia; L. J. Hayden, Park Ridge, N. J.; William B. Rankine, Niagara Falls, N. Y.; W. Caryl Ely, Buffalo, N. Y.; Burt Van Horn, Newfane, N. Y.

Corporate office, 15 Exchange place, Jersey City; Office International Railway Co., 180 Main street, Buffalo, N. Y. Annual meeting, first Monday in April.

## INTERURBAN RAILWAY & TERMINAL CO.

A corporation formed under the laws of Ohio, November 3, 1902. The company is a consolidation of the following companies:

Cincinnati & Eastern Electric Railway Co.
Rapid Railway Co.
Surburban Traction Co.
Interurban Terminal Co.

The company has in operation the property of the Cincinnati Eastern Electric Railway with the properties of the Rapid Railway Co. and the Surburban Traction Co. nearly ready. The company operates 104 miles of track. The Cincinnati & Eastern division between Cincinnati and New Richmond has 36 miles. The Rapid Railway Co. has 38 miles of track between Cincinnati,

Lebanon and Morrow. The Surburban Traction Co. has 30 miles of track between Cincinnati, Bethal and Batavia. The population served, exclusive of the city of Cincinnati, is 59,400. The company owns two power plants and 57 cars.

Stock......Par $100..........................Authorized, $2,500,000......Issued, $2,500,000

The company has no preferred stock. Transfer Agent and Registrar, Cincinnati Trust Co., Cincinnati.

FUNDED DEBT.

1st mort., 5 per cent., gold, due Jan. 1, 1928, Jan., April, July and Oct..............$2,250,000

The 1st mortgage bonds are $2,500,000 authorized. The company holds $250,000 of the issue in its treasury for extensions. Trustee of the mortgage and agent for payment of interest, Cincinnati Trust Co., Cincinnati.

President and General Manager, George R. Scrugham; 1st Vice-President, Lee H. Brooks; 2d Vice-President and General Counsel, E. G. Kinkead; Secretary, William E. Hutton; Assistant Secretary, C. J. Williams; Treasurer, J. M. enne , Cincinnati.

Directors—C. H. Davis, William E. Hutton, J. MKKennedy, G. W. Mallon, E. G. Kinkead, Lee H. Brooks, George R. Scrugham, Cincinnati; G. H. Worthington, Cleveland.

Corporate and main office, Cincinnati. Annual meeting, first Tuesday after the second Monday in November, at Cincinnati.

## IRON STEAMBOAT CO. OF NEW JERSEY

A corporation formed under the laws of New Jersey in August, 1902, and succeeded the company of the same title, the property of the latter having been foreclosed. The company owns seven steamboats and Oscawana Island, on the Hudson, and has an interest in the Long Branch pier.

Stock......Par $10..............................Authorized, $400,000......Issued, $292,790

A dividend of $1 per share was paid in 1892. No dividends have been paid since. Foreclosure proceedings were begun in July, 1901, a Receiver having been appointed in April, 1901. In March, 1902, it was announced that the company would be reorganized.

FUNDED DEBT.

| | |
|---|---|
| New prior lien, 5 per cent., due 1932 | $100,000 |
| " 2d mort., 4 per cent., due 1932 | 500,000 |
| Total | $600,000 |

The 6 per cent. 1st mortgage bonds of the old company fell due in 1901. In the reorganization the holders of the old bonds paid an assessment and received for the same the new prior lien bonds.

EARNINGS.

| Year ending October 31. | Gross. | Surplus. |
|---|---|---|
| 1894 | $263,686 | ...... |
| 1895 | 312,488 | $79,032 |
| 1896 | 255,864 | ....... |
| 1897 | 243,794 | ....... |
| 1898 | 190,646 | ....... |
| 1899 | 224,152 | 21,654 |
| 1900 | 236,935 | 37,176 |

In 1896, deficit after charges, $2,986; in 1897, deficit, $1,954; in 1898, deficit, $13,166.

Receiver, Charles D. Thompson, Jersey City.

President, Allen C. Washington; Treasurer, William H. Wolverton; Secretary, Ambrose I. Harrison, New York.

Main office, 32 Broadway, New York.

## THE ISLE ROYALE COPPER CO.

A corporation formed under the laws of New Jersey in March, 1899. The company was organized to consolidate the Isle Royale Consolidated Mining Co. with the Miners' Copper Co. The Isle Royale Consolidated Mining Co. was a Michigan corporation formed in 1897. The company owns a valuable copper property near Houghton, Mich.

Stock......Par $25..............................Authorized, $3,750,000......Issued, $3,750,000

The company began business with a cash capital of about $1,800,000.

The property of the company includes about two miles or more of what is known as the Isle Royale Lode with about 1,700 acres of land,

The cost of the property to the old company was $1,000,000 in stock ($20 paid). During 1899 and 1900, active development work was in progress on the property. The report for 1900 showed: Expenses, $677,810; cash on hand December 31, 1900, $832,742. In 1901, receipts, $281,269; balance of assets, $406,415. In 1902, receipts, $500,775; balance of assets, $427,255.

President, Albert S. Bigelow; Vice-President, Edgar Buffum; Secretary and Treasurer, W. J. Ladd, Boston.

Directors—Albert S. Bigelow, Edgar Buffum, W. J. Ladd, C. H. Bissell, W. A. I. Chrimes.

Main office, 199 Washington street, Boston. Annual meeting, first Wednesday in April, at Boston.

## JACKSON GAS CO.

A corporation formed under the laws of Michigan, March 17, 1897. The company owns and operates the gas works in the city of Jackson, Mich., under a perpetual franchise. Mileage of mains, 25 miles. Price of gas, $1.00 per 1,000 cubic feet. In 1902 control of this company was acquired by the American Light & Traction Co., which company offered $41.67 in cash or $40 in its own preferred stock with $12 in common for each share of this company's stock.

Stock......Par $50..............................Authorized, $281,000......Issued, $250,000

Dividends on the stock are 4 per cent. per annum, being 2 per cent. semi-annual in June and December.

Transfer Agents, Emerson McMillin & Co., New York.

FUNDED DEBT.

1st mort., 5 per cent., due 1937, April and Oct........................................ $310,000

The 1st mortgage, Illinois Trust & Savings Bank, Chicago, trustee, is for $350,000.

President, Henry D. Walbridge; Vice-President, N. S. Potter; Secretary and Treasurer, W. F. Douthirt; General Manager, W. M. Eaton.

Directors—Emerson McMillin, Henry D. Walbridge, N. S. Potter, W. R. Reynolds, Stephen H. Carroll, Thomas A. Wilson, W. M. Eaton.

Main office, 260 Main street, Jackson, Mich. Annual meeting, third Friday in April, at Jackson.

## JACKSONVILLE ELECTRIC CO.

A corporation formed under the laws of Florida in 1902 as a consolidation of the following companies:

Jacksonville Street Railway Co. — Main Street Railroad Co.
Jacksonville Electric Light Co.

The company operates 15 miles of track electric railway in Jacksonville, Fla., and has an electric lighting franchise.

Stock......Par $100......Authorized { com., $800,000 / pref., 200,000 } Issued { com., $800,000 / pref., 200,000 } $1,000,000

The preferred stock is 6 per cent., non-cumulative. Transfer Agents, Stone & Webster, Boston. Registrar, American Loan & Trust Co., Boston.

The first dividend of 3 per cent. on the preferred stock was paid February 1, 1903.

FUNDED DEBT.

1st mort., authorized, 5 per cent., gold, due May 1, 1927, May and Nov................ $700,000

The total amount of the 1st mortgage is $1,250,000. A sinking fund of 1 per cent. after May 1, 1907, is provided, and may be used for extensions and improvements or for the purchase of bonds. The bond issue may be called as a whole on any interest day at 105 and interest. Trustee of mortgage and agent for the payment of interest, American Loan & Trust Co., Boston.

In the year ending December 31, 1901, the combined gross earnings of the old companies before consolidation were $169,803; net, $69,303.

President, A. Stuart Pratt; Secretary, Henry R. Hayes; Treasurer, H. B. Sawyer; Assistant Treasurer, A. A. Wright; Second Assistant Treasurer, J. Coolidge Coffin; General Managers, Stone & Webster.

Directors—A. Stuart Pratt, Henry R. Hayes, H. B. Sawyer, G. J. Baldwin, C. A. Stone, E. S. Webster, Russell Robb.

Main office, Jacksonville, Fla.

## JACQUES CARTIER WATER POWER CO.

A corporation formed under the laws of Quebec, Canada, in 1898. The company owns and operates a water-power plant on the Jacques Cartier River, about sixteen miles from Quebec, constructed to generate electricity for power and light purposes. The company owns a perpetual franchise for furnishing electric light and power in the city of Quebec, where it has a distributing plant of the most modern type, which has been in operation since April 1, 1899.

Stock......Par $100............................Authorized, $500,000......Issued, $456,500

Transfer Agents, Emerson McMillin & Co., 40 Wall street, New York. Registrar, Continental Trust Co., New York.

FUNDED DEBT.

1st mort., gold, 6 per cent., due 1928, June and Dec.................................. $500,000

The 1st mortgage, Continental Trust Co., New York, trustee, is for $500,000. Coupons are paid at the office of Emerson McMillin & Co., New York.

President, Emerson McMillin; Secretary and Treasurer, C. T. Scoville, New York.

Directors—Emerson McMillin, Russell H. Landale, C. T. Scoville, James B. Taylor, Henry L. Doherty, New York; W. F. Douthirt, Glen Ridge, N. J.; Harold Kennedy, A. H. Cook, Quebec.

Main office, Quebec, Canada. Annual meeting, second Monday in January.

## JEFFERSON & CLEARFIELD COAL & IRON CO.

A corporation organized under the laws of Pennsylvania in May, 1896. The company acquired and owns the extensive coal lands, mines, railroads to mines, about twenty-one miles, and other property in Jefferson and Clearfield counties, Pa., formerly owned by the Bell, Lewis & Gates Coal Mining Co. and other holders. The Rochester & Pittsburg Coal & Iron Co. owns all the common stock and $300,000 of the preferred.

Stock....Par $100....Authorized { com., $1,500,000 / pref., 1,500,000 } Issued { com., $1,500,000 / pref., 1,500,000 } $3,000,000

The preferred stock is 5 per cent. and shares equally with the common in any surplus remaining after the latter has received 5 per cent. per annum.

Transfer Agents, A. Iselin & Co., 36 Wall street, New York. Registrar, Guaranty Trust Co., New York.

Regular semi-annual dividends of 2½ per cent., in February (15) and August, are paid on the preferred stock. The first dividend of 2 per cent. on the common stock was paid August 15, 1900, and in August, 1902, 5 per cent. was paid.

FUNDED DEBT.

1st mort., 5 per cent., gold, due June, 1926, June and Dec.......................... $1,652,000
2d mort., 5 per cent., gold, due June, 1926, June and Dec.......................... 1,000,000

Total............................................................... $2,652,000

The 1st mortgage is $2,000,000, anthorized. Trustee, Guaranty Trust Co., New York. The 2d mortgage is $1,000,000, authorized. Trustee, United States Mortgage & Trust Co., New York. Interest on the bonds is paid at the Guaranty Trust Co., New York.

President, Lucius W. Robinson, Punxsutawney, Pa.; Vice-President, Walter G. Oakman, New York; Treasurer, George H. Clune; Secretary, George L. Eaton, Rochester, N. Y.

Directors—Adrian Iselin, Jr.; Walter G. Oakman, Frederic Cromwell, New York; Arthur G. Yates, Rochester, N. Y.; Lucius W. Robinson, Punxsutawney, Pa.; B. M. Clark, Brookville, Pa.

Corporate office, Reynoldsville, Pa. Main office, West Main and South Fitzhugh streets, Rochester; New York office, 65 Cedar street. Annual meeting, third Tuesday in January, at Reynoldsville, Pa.

## JERSEY CITY, HOBOKEN & PATERSON STREET RAILWAY CO.

A corporation formed under the laws of New Jersey, November 1, 1899. The company operates 140.56 miles of track by trolley system in Jersey City, Hoboken, Weehawken, North Bergen, Passaic, Paterson, N. J., and intermediate towns and villages. It is a consolidation of the following roads:

Jersey City, Hoboken & Rutherford Electric Railway Co.
North Hudson County Street Railway Co.
Palisades Railroad Co.
Paterson Central Electric Railway Co.
Paterson Horse Railroad Co.
Paterson, Passaic & Rutherford Electric Railroad Co.
Paterson Railway Co.
Saddle River Traction Co.
White Line Traction (New Jersey Electric) Co.

The company also controls the Bergen Turnpike Co. A controlling interest in this company is held by the same capitalists who are interested in the North Jersey Street Railway Co.

Stock......Par $100........................Authorized, $20,000,000......Issued, $20,000,000

The company has no preferred stock. Stock is transferred at the office of the company. Registrar, New Jersey Title, Guarantee & Trust Co., Jersey City.

FUNDED DEBT.

| | |
|---|---|
| 1st mort., 4 per cent., due 1949, May and Nov. | $11,575,000 |
| North Hudson County Ry., 1st mort., 6 per cent., due 1914, Jan. and July | 620,000 |
| " " " " 5 per cent. cons. mort., due 1928, Jan. and July | 2,378,000 |
| " " " " 5 per cent. imp. mort., due 1904, May and Nov. | 1,292,000 |
| " " " " 5 per ct. Weehawken ext. mort., due 1915, Feb. and Aug. | 100,000 |
| Paterson Railway Co., 6 per cent. 1st mort., due 1907, Feb. and Aug. | 50,000 |
| " " " 6 per cent. 2d mort., due 1908, June and Dec. | 200,000 |
| " " " 6 per cent. cons. mort., due 1931, June and Dec. | 1,000,000 |
| " " " 6 per cent. 2d gen. mort., due 1914, April and Oct. | 300,000 |
| Total | $17,515,000 |

The company also guarantees an issue of $1,000,000 5 per cent. bonds of the Bergen Turnpike Co., due 1951, January and July. Trustee, New Jersey Title Guarantee & Trust Co.

The authorized amount of 1st mortgage bonds of the Jersey City, Hoboken & Paterson Railway Co. is $20,000,000. Trustee of the mortgage, New Jersey Title, Guarantee & Trust Co., Jersey City. The authorized amount of 1st mortgage bonds of the North Hudson County Railway Co. is $1,000,000. Trustees, W. W. Shippen and S. B. Dod. The authorized amount of consolidated mortgage bonds of the North Hudson County Railway Co. is $3,000,000. Trustees, E. A. Stevens and S. B. Dod. The authorized amount of the improvement mortgage bonds of the North Hudson County Railway Co. is $1,500,000. Trustees, Myles Tierney and W. E. Bond. The authorized amount of the consolidated mortgage bonds of the Paterson Railway Co. is $1,250,000. Trustee, Paterson Savings Bank, Paterson, N. J.

EARNINGS.

| | Gross. | Net. | Charges. | Surplus. |
|---|---|---|---|---|
| 1901 | $1,859,931 | $884,192 | $838,669 | $45,523 |
| 1902 | 1,975,525 | 854,893 | 849,297 | 5,596 |

President, David Young, Hoboken, N. J.; Vice-President, John F. Shanley, Jersey City; Secretary, F. J. Davis; Treasurer, George W. Roe; Auditor, S. C. Stivers; General Superintendent, W. S. Hall, Hoboken, N. J.

Direectors—David Young, A. P. Hexamer, W. C. eppenheimer, Hoboken, N. J.; John F. Shanley, D. McLaughlin, E. F. . Young, Edward H. Young J. L. Hulshizer, Jersey City; C. A. Sterling, Orange, N. J.; WCB. Gourley, John R. Lee, Paterson, N. J.; Randall Morgan, Philadelphia; Chandler W. Riker, W. C. Shanley, Newark, N. J.; Bird W. Spencer, Passaic, N. J.

Main office, 21 Hudson place, Hoboken, N. J. Annual meeting, first Monday in November, at Hoboken.

## JONES & LAUGHLIN STEEL CO.

A corporation formed under the laws of Pennsylvania in 1902, and succeeded Jones & Laughlin, Limited, the latter being a partnership association formed under the laws of Pennsylvania. The establishment of the company, the American Iron & Steel Works, at Pittsburg, is one of the largest in the United States and manufactures a great variety and quantity of forms of iron and steel products. The company in 1901 made large purchases of ore lands, and completed an extensive steel rod mill at its plant.

It was reported in January, 1903, that the company contemplated the construction of a railway line for the transportation of its supplies of ore and its finished product from Pittsburg to some port on Lake Erie.

In March, 1903, it was reported that negotiations for the acquisition of this company by the United States Steel Corporation were in progress.

Stock......Par $100........................Authorized, $30,000,000......Issued, $30,000,000

FUNDED DEBT.

1st mort., 5 per cent........................................................ $10,000,000

The bonds were authorized when the new company was formed to provide for improvements.

President, Benjamin F. Jones, Jr.; Vice-President, W. L. King; Secretary, William C. Moreland; Treasurer, Irwin B. Laughlin; Assistant Treasurer, Thomas K. Laughlin; General Manager, William Larimer Jones; Assistant General Manager, Thomas O'Conor Jones, Pittsburg.

Directors—Benjamin F. Jones, Jr., W. L. King, Irwin B. Laugblin, William C. Moreland, William Larimer Jones, Roland Gerry, J. B. Laughlin, Thomas O'Conor Jones, Benjamin F. Jones, G. M. Laughlin, H. A. Laughlin, James Laughlin, Jr., W. W. Willock, Robert Geddie, Henry S. Kiehl.

Main office, Third avenue and Try street, Pittsburg; branch offices, New York, Philadelphia, Chicago, Boston, Buffalo, Cleveland, Cincinnati, Detroit, St. Louis. Annual meeting, fourth Tuesday in April.

## JOURNEAY & BURNHAM

A corporation formed under the laws of New York in May, 1901, to succeed Journeay & Burnham, a New Jersey corporation formed in 1891, which was reorganized. The old company succeeded to and acquired the property and business of the retail dry goods firm of Journeay & Burnham, established in 1844, in the city of Brooklyn. N. Y.

Stock......Par $10..............................Authorized, $500,000......Issued, $400,000

Stock is transferred at the company's office. Registrar, Williamsburg Trust Co., Brooklyn, N. Y.

The old Journeay & Burnham Co. had $500,000 8 per cent. cumulative preferred stock and $500,000 common. Regular quarterly dividends were paid on the preferred until July, 1898, but no dividends were paid on the common after April, 1896. A reorganization was proposed in June, 1900, the new company to have $500,000 stock of the par value of $10 per share, of which $100,000 was to be held in the treasury, and $400,000 exchanged for the old stock at the rate of $70 in new for each $100 of preferred, and one $10 share of new for each share of old common stock. This arrangement was carried out in 1901. The first dividend on the new preferred stock was 3 per cent. semi-annual, paid April 1, 1902, and dividends have since been paid on this basis.

President, Hugh Boyd; Vice-President, Ethan Allen Doty; Secretary and Treasurer, John L. Russell.

Directors—Hugh Boyd, H. B. Boyd, Ethan Allen Doty, Charles T. Young, Thomas Potts, Frank Harvey Field, Charles M. Allen, John L. Russell.

Main office and stores, Flatbush avenue, near Fulton street, Brooklyn, N. Y. Annual meeting in October.

## KANAWHA & HOCKING COAL & COKE CO.

A corporation formed under the laws of West Virginia in May, 1901, for the purpose of mining coal and manufacturing coke. The company has acquired coal lands, mines, coke ovens and other allied property and a leasehold interest in seven miles of railroad, all in West Virginia, on the line of the Kanawha & Michigan Railway.

Stock......Par $100..............................Authorized, $3,500,000......Issued, $3,500,000

Transfer Agent and Registrar, J. P. Morgan & Co., New York.

FUNDED DEBT.

1st mort., 5 per cent., sinking fund gold bonds, due 1951, Jan. and July.............. $2,750,000

The authorized issue of bonds is $3,500,000. Principal and interest are guaranteed by the Toledo & Ohio Central Railway Co. and the Hocking Valley Railway Co. Trustee of bonds, Morton Trust Co., New York.

EARNINGS.

Year ending June 30.

| | Gross. | Net. | Charges. | Surplus. |
|---|---|---|---|---|
| 1901-02.................................. | $893,887 | $150,822 | $148,027 | $2,795 |

President, Nicholas Monsarrat, Columbus, O.; Vice-President and Counsel, James H. Hoyt, Cleveland; Secretary and Treasurer, William N. Cott; General Manager, J. H. Winder, Columbus, O.

Directors—Nicholas Monserrat, J. H. Winder, Columbus, O.; James H. Hoyt, Cleveland; Charles Steele, Temple Bowdoin, New York.

Main office, Mammoth, West Va.; branch offices, Columbus, O., and Cleveland.

## KANSAS CITY ELECTRIC LIGHT CO.

A corporation formed under the laws of Missouri, December 22, 1884, for the purpose of engaging in the production and distribution of electric light and power. The company controls this field at Kansas City, Mo., and adjacent towns.

Stock......Par $100..........................Authorized, $2,500,000......Issued, $2,100,000

The company has no preferred stock. Stock is transferred at the company's office, 1230 Grand avenue, Kansas City, Mo.

FUNDED DEBT.

1st mort., 5 per cent., due 1915, May and Nov....................................... $750,000

The authorized issue is $1,000,000. Trustees, Farmers' Loan & Trust Co., New York, and Henry C. Flower, Kansas City. Agent for the payment of interest, Blair & Co., 33 Wall street, New York.

President, Bernard Corrigan; Vice-President, L. E. James; Secretary and Treasurer, Walter E. Kirkpatrick, Kansas City, Mo.

Directors—P. Anderson Valentine, L. C. Krauthoff, Chicago; L. E. James, E. F. Swinney, Bernard Corrigan, J. J. Heim, William Huttig, C. W. Armour, Kansas City, Mo.

Main office, 1230 Grand avenue, Kansas City, Mo. Annual meeting, third Thursday in June, at Kansas City, Mo.

## KANSAS CITY, MISSOURI, GAS CO.

A corporation organized under the laws of Missouri in 1897. The company purchased the stock, plant and property of the Kansas City Gas Co. and the Missouri Gas Co. These organizations furnished all the gas facilities of Kansas City, Mo. The system comprises 272 miles of pipe, and the works have a capacity of 4,000,000 cubic feet of gas per day. The franchise is for thirty years from 1898.

Stock......Par $100..........................Authorized, $5,000,000......Issued, $5,000,000

Transfer office, United Gas Improvement Building, Philadelphia.

FUNDED DEBT.

1st mort., gold, 5 per cent., due April, 1922, April and Oct.......................... $4,087,000

The bonds have a sinking fund of $75,000 per annum for ten years, and thereafter of $25,000 per annum, and are subject to call at 105. The trustee of the mortgages is the Guaranty Trust Co., New York.

EARNINGS.

Year ending April 30.

| | Net. | Interest. | Sinking Fund. | Surplus. |
|---|---|---|---|---|
| 1898–99.............................. | $281,320 | $188,920 | $75,000 | $17,400 |
| 1899–00.............................. | 286,357 | 191,100 | 75,000 | 20,257 |
| 1900–01.............................. | 290,310 | 191,783 | 75,000 | 23,527 |
| 1901–02.............................. | 304,428 | 197,100 | 75,000 | 32,328 |

President, Hugh J. McGowan; 1st Vice-President, J. Crawford James; 2d Vice-President, Randal Morgan; Secretary, R. Macmillan; Treasurer, Lewis Lillie; General Superintendent, Walton Clark.

Directors—Randal Morgan, Joseph Bushnell, W. F. Douthirt, E. L. Brundrett, J. Crawford James, Hugh J. McGowan, R. M. Snyder, James T. Holmes, Charles E. Small.

Main office, Kansas City, Mo.

## THE KANSAS CITY STOCK YARDS CO. OF MISSOURI

A corporation which owns and operates extensive stock yards and railroad facilities connected therewith at Kansas City, Mo., the property of the company covering about 175 acres.

Reports were current in 1902 that this company would be included in a combination of packing houses and allied interests, but nothing tangible developed in this connection.

Stock......Par $100..........................Authorized, $8,250,000......Issued, $8,250,000

The stock of the company, which was $7,500,000, was increased in April, 1900, to $8,250,000 authorized, the increase being to provide for the retirement of outstanding bonds. Transfer Agent, Charles Merriam, 50 State street, Boston.

Dividends are paid at the rate of 6 per cent. per annum, the payments being quarterly, 1½ per cent. each, in February (1), May, August and November.

President, Charles F. Morse; Secretary and Treasurer, Elliott E. Richardson, Kansas City, Mo.

Directors, Charles Francis Adams, John A. Burnham, I. P. Dana, F. H. Damon, Walter Hunnewell, Charles Merriam, Wallace Pratt, Nathaniel Thayer.

Main office, State Line, corner Sixteenth street, Kansas City, Mo.; Boston office, 50 State street. Annual meeting, third Wednesday in January.

## THE KENTUCKY & INDIANA BRIDGE & RAILROAD CO.

A corporation formed under the laws of Kentucky, August 8, 1900. The company is the successor to the Kentucky & Indiana Bridge Co., the property of which was sold under foreclosure January 18, 1900, and reorganized under the present title. The bridge is 5 miles long, extending across the Ohio River from Louisville, Ky., to New Albany, Ind. It also has 5 miles of terminal lines in Louisville and important switching facilities. The company has 3 locomotives, a number of cars and a ferry boat.

The company is owned by the Southern Railway Co., the Baltimore & Ohio Southwestern Railroad Co., and the Chicago, Indianapolis & Louisville Railroad Co., each company holding one-third of the stock. The three companies pay rental for the use of the bridge in proportion to the extent of such use and to an amount sufficient to meet operating and maintenance cost, taxes and fixed charges.

Stock......Par $100........ ........................Authorized, $75,000..... Issued, $75,000

FUNDED DEBT.

Kentucky & Ind. Bridge, 1st mort., 5 per cent., due March, 1911, March and Sept... $1,000,000
Ky. & Ind. Bridge & R. R., con. mort., 4 per cent., due April, 1950, April and Oct... 1,069,000

Total.............................................................. $2,069,000

The consolidated 4 per cent. mortgage of the new company is for $2,500,000, of which $1,000,000 is held to retire the old 1st mortgage, and $500,000 is reserved for improvements. Trustee, Standard Trust Co., New York.

President, W. H. McDoel, Chicago; Vice-President, William M. Greene, Cincinnati; Secretary and Treasurer, H. W. Heazlitt; Manager, B. S. Josselyn, Louisville.

Main office, Twenty-ninth and Hyde streets, Louisville.

---

## KEOKUK & HAMILTON BRIDGE CO.

This company owns a bridge across the Mississippi River at Keokuk, Ia. The Wabash Railroad and Toledo, Peoria & Western make use of the bridge under rental. In 1893 an arrangement was made by which the Pennsylvania Company and the Pittsburg, Cincinnati, Chicago & St. Louis were to guarantee a part of any deficiency in meeting interest.

Stock .....Par $100...........................Authorized, $1,000,000......Issued, $1,000,000

FUNDED DEBT.

1st mort., 8 per cent., due April, 1899, April and Oct.............................. $1,000,000

Interest upon the bonds has been in default and payments on account of over-due coupons are made as earnings accumulate, the last payment having been in September, 1902, on account of the April, 1889, coupon. No foreclosure has taken place. There has also been litigation concerning the guarantee of the Pennsylvania and the Pittsburg, Cincinnati, Chicago & St. Louis, referred to above.

President, Andrew Carnegie; Secretary and Treasurer, Theodore Gilman, New York.

Main office, Keokuk, Ia.; New York office, 62 Cedar street.

---

## KEYSTONE TELEPHONE CO.

A corporation formed under the laws of New Jersey, April 4, 1900, for the purpose of installing and operating a telephone system in Philadelphia. Its system, which is designed for 30,000 subscribers, is expected to be completed in 1903.

Stock....Par $50......Authorized { com., $5,000,000; pref., 5,000,000 } Issued { com., $5,000,000; pref., 2,000,000 } $7,000,000

The preferred stock is 6 per cent., cumulative. Stock is transferred at the company's office. Registrar, Provident Life & Trust Co., Philadelphia.

The Keystone Telephone Co., on January 16, 1903, sold to the Keystone Telephone Co. of Philadelphia its entire propert , and in consideration thereof became the owner of all the stock of the Keystone Telephone Co. of Philadelphia, amounting to $2,500,000; also all of the 1st mortgage 5 per cent. gold bonds of the same company, amounting to $2,500,000.

The Keystone Telephone Co. of Philadelphia, under an ordinance granted by the city of Philadelphia, being a perpetual franchise, owns and operates a telephone system in the city, consisting of intersecting conduits, containing trunk cable and lateral lines, wires and other appliances, connecting 8,000 telephones installed in business houses and rivate residences, with six telephone exchanges. The Philadelphia company owns the land, buildings and appurtenances of the six exchanges.

The Keystone Telephone Co. of Philadelphia is also the owner of thirteen letters patent of the United States for telephones, telephonic apparatus, and appliances and switchboards.

President, Robert H. Foerderer; Vice-President, Jacob E. Ridgway; Secretary and Treasurer, William H. Clark; General Manager, Charles E. Wilson.

Directors—Robert H. Foerderer, Jacob E. Ridgway, John M. Mack, Michael Murphy, Norman Grey.

Main office, 135 South Second street, Philadelphia. Annual meeting, second Tuesday in January, at Philadelphia.

## THE KEYSTONE WATCH CASE CO.

A corporation organized under the laws of the State of Pennsylvania, July, 1899. The company took over the plants and business of Keystone Watch Case Co., Philadelphia, and the T. Zurbrugg Co., of Riverside, N. J. The former was incorporated under the laws of the State of Pennsylvania in 1886, succeeding to the business of C. N. Thorpe & Co., formerly Hagstoz & Thorpe, and James Boss, which was established in 1853. The original Keystone Co. was very successful and paid dividends of 6 per cent. per annum and during a portion of the time of 8 per cent. from its incorporation until its amalgamation with the new company in 1899. The T. Zurbrugg Co. was incorporated under the laws of New Jersey in 1899, succeeding to the business of T. Zurbrugg, which was a very profitable one. T. Zurbrugg, in 1898, bought the watch case business of H. Muhr's Sons, of Philadelphia.

The company manufactures all kinds of watch cases, including the celebrated James Boss gold filled case, to which name and trade-mark it owns all of the rights. The plants of the company are among the largest and best equipped in the world. That at Nineteenth and Brown streets, Philadelphia, occupies nearly a block of ground, and consists of three six-story buildings. That at Riverside, N. J., also occupies about a block of ground covered by three and four story buildings. The equipment and labor-saving devices are of the latest. The output of the company is about 4,000 watch cases per day and it employs over 1,500 hands.

Stock......Par \$100......Authorized { com., \$2,000,000 / pref., 2,200,000 } Issued { com., \$2,000,000 / pref., 2,200,000 } \$4,200,000

The preferred stock is 5 per cent., non-cumulative.

Transfer Agents, Drexel & Co., Philadelphia. Registrar, Girard Trust Co., Philadelphia.

The company began the payment of dividends by the declaration in January, 1900, of 2½ per cent. on both preferred and common stock for the first six months of its operations. It paid 5 per cent. per annum on the preferred, payments being 2½ per cent. semi-annually, January and July, but January, 1902, dividend on the common was increased to 3 per cent., or 6 per cent. per annum, which has since been the regular rate.

President, John Lowber Welsh; General Manager, T. Zurbrugg; Treasurer, Howard L. Roberts; Secretary, Charles M. Fogg.

Directors—John Lowber Welsh, Edward T. Stotesbury, Caleb F. Fox, Amos R. Little, Isaac H. Clothier, T. Zurbrugg and Howard L. Roberts.

Main office, corner Nineteenth and Brown streets, Philadelphia. Annual meeting, fourth Friday in July.

## KINGS COUNTY ELECTRIC LIGHT & POWER CO.

A corporation formed under the laws of New York, June 26, 1890. It obtained its franchise from the city of Brooklyn by resolution of the City Council, adopted June 11, 1894. The company was reorganized in 1897. It controls practically all the electric current plants in the Borough of Brooklyn. It acquired the entire stock of the Edison Electric Illuminating Co. of Brooklyn, for which company see MANUAL for 1898. The Edison Electric Illuminating Co. acquired the Citizens' Electric Illuminating Co. in 1895, and in 1898 the Municipal Electric Light Co. The present company has erected a large power station at the foot of Gold street and the East River. Lamp equivalent in service January 1, 1901, about 375,000. The company in 1901 contracted to sell a large amount of power to the Brooklyn Rapid Transit Co.

Stock......Par \$100..........................Authorized, \$2,500,000......Issued, \$5,000,000

In December, 1900, \$520,000 additional stock was sold to extend the system. The existing stockholders had the right to subscribe for this stock at par to the extent of 25 per cent. of their holdings. In March, 1903, another increase of \$1,250,000 in the stock was authorized, the stockholders having the right to subscribe for 50 per cent. of their holdings, the payments to be one-half on or before May 1, 1903, and the balance on November 2, 1903.

The Edison Electric Illuminating Co. paid 6 per cent. dividends, 1896 to 1898 inclusive. At the time of sale to the Kings County Co., it was decided to distribute the Edison Electric Illuminating Co.'s surplus in the form of an extra dividend of 3 per cent., June 30, 1898.

The Kings County Electric Light & Power Co. paid a dividend of 1½ per cent., quarterly, June 1, 1900, and similar dividends have since been paid quarterly in March, June, September and December.

FUNDED DEBT.

| | |
|---|---|
| 1st mort., gold, 5 per cent., due Oct., 1937, ril and Oct. | \$2,500,000 |
| Purchase money mort., 6 per cent., due Oct.Ap997, April and Oct. | 5,176,000 |
| Edison Elec. Ill. of Brooklyn, cons. mort., 4 per cent., due Jan., 1939, Jan. and July | 4,275,000 |
| Total | \$11,951,000 |

The stock of the Edison Electric Illuminating Co. was originally \$1,500,000; in 1893 it was increased to \$2,500,000, in 1894 to \$3,000,000, in 1895 to \$3,750,000, in 1897 to \$4,000,000, and in 1898 to $5,000,000. The latter increase of $1,000,000 was offered to stockholders as a right to subscribe at par for 25 per cent. additional stock at the time of sale of stock to the Kings County Co., in September, 1898, the latter paying for the stock in its 6 per cent. purchase money bonds which are secured by the deposit with the Central Trust Co., New York, trustee, of the Edison shares acquired, a fund of $1,000,000 cash invested in securities being also held by the trustee for the protection of the purchase-money bonds.

The Edison Electric Illuminating consolidated mortgage was authorized in 1898 originally of $5,000,000 at 5 per cent. It was, at the time of the sale of its stock to the Kings County Co., increased to $10,000,000, authorized, at 4 per cent., and $2,000,000 was sold, being to pay for the stock of the Municipal Co. Of the remainder, $1,875,000 was reserved to retire the $1,500,000 of Edison 1st 5s, at 110 in 1900, the Edison stockholders having the right to subscribe for the bonds devoted to this purpose at 88. The balance of the issue may be used to provide for the company's future capital requirements. In 1900 $2,275,000 of the consols were sold, of which $1,875,000 were to retire the Edison 1st mortgage bonds, and $400,000 to provide for extending the Edison Co.'s business.

The trustees of the mortgages and agents for the payment of interest on the different bond issues are as follows:

Kings County Co. 1st mort. 5s, Colonial Trust Co., New York.
Kings County purchase money 6s, Central Trust Co., New York.
Edison Electric Ill. 1st con. 4s, Morton Trust Co., New York.

| EARNINGS (EDISON CO.) | Gross. | Net. |
|---|---|---|
| 1894 | $457,503 | $223,406 |
| 1895 | 651,056 | 267,349 |
| 1896 | 841,414 | 342,348 |
| 1897 | 893,016 | 366,436 |
| 1898 | 1,215,455 | 476,461 |
| 1899 | 1,360,792 | 600,827 |

In 1894 surplus over interest and dividends was $29,656; in 1895, $31,099; in 1896, $67,148; in 1897, $79,327. The net income of the properties combined in the new company was in 1897, $487,000, and the interest charges, $155,000. In 1899 the report showed, net, $625,000.

The following is a condensed balance sheet, September 30, 1902:

| ASSETS. | | LIABILITIES. | |
|---|---|---|---|
| Property | $3,253,862 | Capital stock | $2,500,000 |
| Central Trust Co., trustee | 1,000,000 | 1st mortgage 5s | 2,500,000 |
| Stock in other companies | 5,175,870 | Purchase money 6s | 5,176,000 |
| Bills receivable | 685,000 | Premium on 251 shares sold | 10,542 |
| Accounts receivable | 107,168 | Accounts payable | 337 |
| Cash in banks | 11,267 | Profit and loss | 52,251 |
| Accrued interest on investments | 5,963 | | |
| Total | $10,239,130 | Total | $10,239,130 |

President, Anthony N. Brady; 1st Vice-President, A. M. Young; 2d Vice-President, E. A. Leslie; Secretary, W. W. Freeman; Treasurer, Alfred W. Dater; Assistant Treasurer, A. N. Nielsen.

Directors—A. M. Young, Bernard Gallagher, Anthony N. Brady, Horace C. Duval, Thomas E. Murray, William F. Sheehan, E. A. Leslie, William Berri, Walton Ferguson, Seth L. Keeney, Charles Cooper, Hugh J. Grant, Nicholas F. Brady.

Main office, 360 Pearl street, Brooklyn. Annual meeting, third Monday in February.

---

## KINGSTON CONSOLIDATED RAILROAD CO.

A corporation formed under the laws of New York in July, 1901. The company is a consolidation of the following companies:

Kingston City Railroad Co. Colonial City Traction Co.

The company owns and operates 9.16 miles of electric railway in Kingston, N. Y., serving a population of 30,000. It owns one power station and 40 cars.

Stock......Par $100........Authorized { com., $200,000; pref., 200,000 } Issued { com., $200,000; pref., 200,000 } $400,000

The preferred stock is 4 per cent., cumulative. Transfer Agent and Registrar, Manhattan Trust Co., New York.

FUNDED DEBT.

| | | |
|---|---|---|
| 1st con. mort., 5 per cent. gold, due Jan., 1952, Jan. and July | | $534,000 |
| Kingston City R. R. Co., | 1st mort., 7 per cent., due June, 1909, Jan. and July | 15,000 |
| " " " | debenture bonds, 5 per cent., due 1905, June and Dec. | 10,000 |
| " " " | bond and mort., 6 per cent., on demand quarterly | 6,000 |
| " " " | con. mort., 5 per cent., due March, 1923, March and Sept. | 135,000 |
| Total | | $700,000 |

The authorized amount of the 1st mortgage of the Kingston Consolidated Railroad Co. is $700,000. Of that amount, $166,000 is reserved in the treasury to retire the underlying liens. Trustee of the mortgage and agent for the payment on interest, Manhattan Trust Co., New York.

In the fiscal year ending December 31, 1902, the gross earnings were $112,340.29; net, $44,237.68; interest charges, $35,368.50; surplus, $8,869.18. The operating expenses were 57.50 of the gross earnings.

President, Charles M. Preston, New York; Vice-President and General Manager, C. Gordon Reed, Kingston, N. Y.; 2d Vice-President, A. M. Day, New York; Secretary, Augustus J. Phillips; Treasurer, Abraham Hasbrouck, Kingston, N. Y.

Directors—August Belmont, A. M. Day, New York; Charles M. Preston, G. D. B. Hasbrouck, Abraham Hasbrouck, Luke Loone, Augustus J. Phillips, George Hutton, Noah Wolven, Kingston, N. Y.

Corporate and main office, Kingston, N. Y. Annual meeting, January 9, at Kingston, N. Y.

## KIRBY LUMBER CO.

A corporation formed under the laws of Texas in July, 1901. The company owns and operates about 20 saw-mills in the lumber region of Eastern Texas. It purchased some 8,000,000,000 feet of standing timber from the Houston Oil Co. on stumpage contracts and it is closely identified with that company. In 1902 it acquired a number of other mills and additional timber lands.

Stock....Par $100.....Authorized { com., $5,000,000 / pref., 5,000,000 } Issued { com., $5,000,000 / pref., 5,000,000 } $10,000,000

The preferred stock is 7 per cent., cumulative.

A dividend of 1¾ per cent. on the preferred stock was paid out of the earnings of the six months ending June 30. The dividend periods on preferred are January and July.

The company has no funded debt. In 1902, however, an issue of $6,566,439 of 6 per cent. certificates of beneficial interest, February and August, were created, redeemable in series from A to Q, series A for $100,000 being due August 1, 1903. The certificates are secured by 883,000 acres of land and about 6,000,000,000 feet of timber thereon. The Houston Oil Co. guarantees the contract. Trustee for the certificates, Maryland Trust Co., Baltimore. In December, 1903, a distribution of 10 per cent. was made to the holders of the certificates from the proceeds of sales.

In the six months ending June 30, 1902, the company reported gross earnings $1,798,938; net income, $284,003.

President, John H. Kirby Houston, Tex.; Treasurer, James L. Kirby.

Directors—John H. Kirby, James L. Kirby, John Thomas Kirby, W. W. Willson, Marcellus E. Foster, B. F. Bonner, Frank R. Reichardt, H. Baldwin Rice, Houston, Tex.; S. B. Cooper, Jr., Beaumont, Tex.

Corporate and main office, Houston, Tex.

## THE KNICKERBOCKER ICE CO.

A corporation formed under the laws of Illinois in 1885. Under its charter the company is authorized to deal in ice, building material and merchandise, and to manufacture wagons, tools and machinery. In 1898 the company acquired practically all the ice organizations in and about the city of Chicago, Ill. Its property consists of 39 parcels of land in Chicago, with improvements valued at $1,879,328, property in Illinois, Wisconsin and Indiana, comprising 75 parcels of land, about 3,785 acres, with 87 ice plants and buildings and improvements, a total value of $4,487,269, and personal property, including wagons, machinery, etc., valued at $893,100. The company in 1898, by concentrating operations, greatly reduced expenses of handling. In 1899 the company proposed to dispose of surplus real estate for about $600,000.

Stock....Par $100.....Authorized { com., $4,000,000 / pref., 3,000,000 } Issued { com., $4,000,000 / pref., 3,000,000 } $7,000,000

The preferred stock is entitled to 6 per cent., cumulative dividends. The preferred is convertible into common stock, share for share, and has no priority as to liquidation of the company's assets. Both classes have equal voting power.

Transfer Agents, Walston H. Brown & Bros., 40 Wall street, New York. Registrar, Central Trust Co., New York.

FUNDED DEBT.

1st mort., 5 per cent., gold bonds, due 1928, April and Oct........................ $1,948,000

The 1st mortgage, created in 1898, is $2,500,000 authorized, and was made in pursuance of the consolidation of the various properties. The $512,000 which remain in company's treasury can only be used to acquire additional property by a vote of three-fourths of the entire stock. Trustees under mortgage, Chicago Title & Trust Co. and W. E. Pinney; $43,000 of bonds are reserved to pay off prior liens on various properties.

The company pays regular half-yearly dividends on the preferred of 3 per cent., January and July. It also paid 1 per cent. quarterly on the common, but suspended dividends on the common stock in July, 1900, on account of poor business.

In 1902 the net earnings of the company were $317,525; charges, $97,512; dividends on preferred stock, $179,736; surplus, $40,276.

The following is the company's balance sheet December 31, 1902:

| ASSETS. | | LIABILITIES. | |
|---|---|---|---|
| Plant | $8,952,491 | Common stock | $4,000,000 |
| Bonds in treasury | 512,000 | Preferred stock | 3,000,000 |
| Inventories | 156,093 | Bonds | 2,460,000 |
| Cash on hand | 13,399 | Notes payable | 42,250 |
| Cash in bank | 73,956 | Accounts payable | 64,041 |
| Notes receivable | 13,187 | Pay-rolls | 28,428 |
| Accounts receivable | 275,321 | Interest accrued | 27,226 |
| Ice harvest, 1903 | 42,031 | Surplus | 416,533 |
| Total | $10,038,478 | Total | $10,038,478 |

President, John S. Field; Secretary, William A. Walter; Treasurer, Alexander Dahlman.

Directors—John S. Field, Walston H. Brown, Crawford Livingston, John W. Conley, James Parker Smith, Abner Smith, Charles B. Shedd, John V. Hess, A. D. Joslin, William A. Walter. Charles W. Leaming.

Main office, 171 La Salle street, Chicago.

## KNOXVILLE TRACTION CO.

A corporation formed under the laws of Tennessee, November 15, 1901. It is a consolidation of the following companies:

| | |
|---|---|
| Knoxville Street Railroad Co. | Union Railway Co. |
| Citizen's Railway Co. | West End Street Railroad Co. |

The company also acquired all the securities of the Knoxville Electric Light & Power Co., a consolidation of all the light and power companies in Knoxville. The company now operates all the street railway and electric lighting properties in Knoxville. The company operates 30 miles of electric railway and has one power station and 56 cars; it serves a population of about 40,000.

On November 15, 1901, the Railways & Light Co. of America secured control of this company by the purchase of a majority of its capital stock.

Stock......Par $100..............................Authorized, $750,000......Issued, $750,000

The company has no preferred stock. Transfer Agent and Registrar, Baltimore Trust & Guarantee Co., Baltimore. All the stock is in a pool and is likely to remain so for several years.

Dividends of 1 per cent. are paid semi-annually January 13 and July 15.

FUNDED DEBT.

| | |
|---|---|
| 1st mort., 5 per cent. gold, due April, 1938, April and Oct. | $850,000 |
| 1st debenture, 6 per cent., due July, 1911, Jan. and July | 300,000 |
| Total | $1,150,000 |

The bond issue is the total amount authorized. Trustee of the mortgage, Baltimore Trust & Guarantee Co., Baltimore. Agent for the payment of interest, Baltimore Trust & Guarantee Co., Baltimore. After the stock pays 5 per cent. dividend the bonds will have a sinking fund of $10,000 annually.

President, R. Lancaster Williams; Vice-President, E. L. Bemiss, Richmond, Va.; Secretary, Leon Fender; Treasurer, W. S. Shields; General Manager, C. H. Harvey, Knoxville, Tenn.

Directors—R. Lancaster Williams, E. L. Bemiss, Richmond, Va.; A. H. Rutherford, Baltimore; E. C. Hathaway, Norfolk, Va.; E. E. McMillan, R. M. Rhea, W. S. Shields, Knoxville, Tenn.

Corporate and main office, Knoxville, Tenn. Annual meeting, first Tuesday after the first Monday in July, at Knoxville, Tenn.

## LACKAWANNA & WYOMING VALLEY RAPID TRANSIT CO.

A corporation formed under the laws of New Jersey in October, 1900. The company owns an electric road from Carbondale via Scranton and Pittston to Wilkes-Barre, Pa., about 40 miles. The road was nearly completed at the end of 1902.

Stock......Par $100..........................Authorized, $6,500,000......Issued, $6,500,000

The company has no preferred stock.

FUNDED DEBT.

Col. trust mort., 5 per cent., gold, due Aug., 1951, Feb. and Aug.................... $2,500,000

The authorized amount of the mortgage is $5,000,000. About two-thirds of the bonds had been issued January 1, 1902, the balance being held for issue as the construction of the road is advanced. Trustee of the mortgage and agent for the payment of interest, Standard Trust Co., New York.

President, George C. Smith, Pittsburg; Vice-Presidents, L. A. Watres, T. B. Simpson, E. A. Hancock, Philadelphia; Secretary, Dudley Phelps; Treasurer, C. M. Vail, New York.

Directors—Henry J. Conant, Montclair, N. J.; L. A. Watres, William Connell, T. F. Penman, Scranton, Pa.; Paul D. Cravath, Walter C. Kerr, Dudley Phelps, Frank K. Sturgis, Charles A. Terry, New York; E. A. Hancock, George A. Lee, T. B. Simpson, Philadelphia, Pa.; J. W. Hollenback, Wilkes-Barre, Pa.; Joseph Seep, Oil City, Pa.; George C. Smith, George Westinghouse, Pittsburg, Pa.

Main office, Scranton, Pa. Treasurer's office, 8 Bridge street, New York. Annual meeting, third Wednesday in March, at Camden, N. J.

## LACKAWANNA STEEL CO.

A corporation formed under the laws of New York, February 14, 1902, for the purpose of manufacturing iron and steel, and for more general manufacturing, and other purposes relating thereto. Its property consists of rolling mills, steel works, blast furnaces, coke ovens, open-hearth furnaces, foundry, shops, etc., located at West Seneca, near Buffalo, Erie County, N. Y. The company absorbed, owns or controls the following companies: The Lackawanna Iron & Steel Co., Lackawanna Coal & Coke Co., the South Buffalo Railway Co., Scranton Mining Co., and has interests in other mining properties and companies. The company has erected a large plant at West Seneca, N. Y., near Buffalo, which was nearing completion in March, 1903. The capacity of the works is 1,400,000 tons of finished steel product.

An account of the old Lackawanna Iron & Steel Co. is given in the MANUAL for 1902.

Stock......Par $100........................Authorized, $40,000,000......Issued, $35,000,000

The company has no preferred stock.

Transfer agency, 100 Broadway. Registrar, Farmers' Loan & Trust Co., New York.

FUNDED DEBT.

1st mort., 5 per cent., due April, 1923, April and Oct............................. $15,000,000

The 1st mortgage is for $20,000,000, and was created in March, 1903. Trustee of the mortgage, Farmers' Loan & Trust Co., New York. The issue was made to provide funds for the enlargement of the plant.

The company in March, 1899, paid a dividend of 50 per cent. on its stock from the proceeds of the sale of its coal lands, and in October, 1899, paid another cash dividend of 4 per cent., also from the proceeds of sales of property.

President, Walter Scranton; Vice-President, Moses Taylor Pyne; Treasurer, J. P. Higginson; Assistant Treasurer, F. F. Graham; Secretary, John W. Farquhar; Assistant Secretary, S. B. Cox; Comptroller, Marshall Lapham, New York; Assistant Comptroller, Arja Williams; General Manager, Henry Wehrum, Buffalo; Sales Agent, Joseph H. Scranton.

Directors—Hamilton McK. Twombly, Darius O. Mills, Walter Scranton, Moses Taylor Pyne, William E. Dodge, Warren Delano, Jr., D. C. Blair, Cornelius Vanderbilt, Heber R. Bishop, Adrian Iselin, Jr., Joseph H. Scranton, Moses Taylor, James Speyer, R. B. Van Courtlandt, New York; Henry A. C. Taylor, Newport, R.I.; J. G. McCullough, North Bennington, Vt.; Henry Walters, Baltimore; Samuel Mather, Cleveland; B. H. Buckingham, Lebanon, Pa.; J. J. Albright, Edmund Hayes, Henry Wehrum, Buffalo; B. S. Guinness, G. R. Fearing, Jr., Boston.

Main office, 100 Broadway, New York. Annual meeting, second Wednesday in March.

## LACLEDE GASLIGHT CO.

A corporation formed by a special act of the Legislature of Missouri, March 2, 1857. Its charter is perpetual, and confers upon the company the perpetual right to use the streets of St. Louis for its pipes and any appliance for conducting a substitute for gas. The plant has a capacity of about 6,000,000 feet per day, with about 420 miles of street mains, 65,500 consumers' meters, and 8,000 lamp services and lamp posts. The price for gas is $1 per 1,000 cubic feet for illuminating and 80 cents per 1,000 for fuel. The company also owns and operates a large electric light and power plant.

In March, 1903, control of this company was acquired by the North American Co., which it was understood would combine the company with its other gas and electric properties in St. Louis.

Stock...Par $100....Authorized { com., $8,500,000 / pref., 2,500,000 } Issued { com., $8,500,000 / pref., 2,500,000 } $11,000,000

The preferred stock is 5 per cent., cumulative. The common stock was increased $7,000,000 to $8,500,000 in 1900.

Transfer Agents, H. B. Hollins & Co., 15 Wall street. Registrar, Central Trust Co., New York.

FUNDED DEBT.

| | |
|---|---|
| 1st mort., 5 per cent. gold, due May 1, 1919, quarterly, Feb., May, Aug., Nov...... | $10,000,000 |
| Coupon notes, 5 per cent., due Feb., 1911, Feb. and Aug........................ | 850,000 |
| Total.................................................................. | $10,850,000 |

All the securities of other companies owned by the company are deposited with the Central Trust Co., New York, to secure the company's 1st mortgage bonds. Of the bonds $285,000 were reserved to retire outstanding bonds of the old companies. Coupon notes were created in 1896 to provide for extensions, etc.

Total sales of gas in 1891 were 851,110,000 cubic feet; total receipts, $1,279,196, and net earnings, $582,460. In 1892 sales were 929,611,000 cubic feet, and net earnings $698,090; in 1893 net earnings were $762,785; in 1894, $808,518; in 1895, $883,899; in 1896, $782,213; in 1897, $883,059; in 1898, $939,180; in 1899, $1,021,373; in 1900, $1,000,730; in 1901, $1,054,870; in 1902, $1,153,578.

The dividend of February 8, 1898, on preferred cleared off the cumulative dividends on preferred. The dividends on the preferred are paid semi-annually, 2½ per cent. each, in June (15) and December. The company began paying dividends on its common with one of 1½ per cent., semi-annual, in February, 1898, and it continued such payments on the common at the rate of 3 per cent. per annum in 1898 and 1899. In March, 1900, the semi-annual rate was increased to 2 per cent., putting the common on a 4 per cent. basis, which has since continued. The semi-annual dividends on the common are in March (15) and December.

President, Emerson McMillin, New York; Vice-President, James Campbell; Secretary and General Manager, A. Ross; Treasurer, C. J. Owen, St. Louis; Assistant Secretary, C. L. Horton, New York.

Directors—Emerson McMillin, Frederick Edey, New York; I. H. Lionberger, James Campbell, J. C. Van Blarcom, Harry Scullin, John Scullin, P. J. Doer, St. Louis.

Main office, 716 Locust street, St. Louis; New York office, 40 Wall street. Annual meeting in January.

## LA CROSSE GAS & ELECTRIC CO.

A corporation formed under the laws of Wisconsin, December 2, 1901, for the purpose of furnishing gas and electric light and power in La Crosse, Wis. The company absorbed the following companies:

La Crosse Gas Light Co.
Edison Light & Power Co.
La Crosse Brush Electric Light & Power Co.

In addition to its gas and electric plants it owns a hot-water heating plant. The daily capacity of the gas plant is 240,000 cubic feet, the electric plant having in service 300 arc and 21,000 incandescent lamps.

Stock....Par $100.....Authorized { com., $450,000 / pref., 150,000 } Issued { com., $450,000 / pref., 150,000 } $600,000

The preferred stock is 5 per cent., cumulative. Stock is transferred at the company's office.

FUNDED DEBT.

| | |
|---|---|
| 1st mort., 6 per cent., due July, 1914, Jan. and July.............................. | $75,000 |
| 1st mort., 5 per cent., due Dec., 1921, June and Dec.. .. .......................... | 425,000 |
| Total ................................................................ | $500,000 |

The total of the mortgages is $600,000, authorized, that due in 1914 being on the gas plant only and the other on all the property of the company. Of the bonds $425,000 were issued in payment for the stock of the old companies, $75,000 to retire the La Crosse Gas Light Company's bonds, $50,000 available for immediate and $50,000 reserved for future improvements, but not until the net income of the company is twice the amount of the interest charges.

Trustee of the mortgage and agent for payment of interest, Merchants' Loan & Trust Co., Chicago.

In the year ending November 30, 1901, the gross earnings were $41,179.96.

President, W. W. Cargill; Vice-President and Treasurer, George MacMillan; Secretary, W. S. Cargill, La Crosse, Wis.

Directors—W. W. Cargill, George MacMillan, W. S. Cargill, A. D. Duffus, La Crosse, Wis.; Martin A. Devitt, Chicago.

Corporate and main office, 218 Main street, La Crosse, Wis. Annual meeting, first Tuesday in January, at La Crosse, Wis.

## LAKE SHORE ELECTRIC RAILWAY CO.

A corporation formed under the laws of Ohio in 1901. The company is a consolidation of the following companies:

Lorain & Cleveland Railway Co.
Sandusky & Interurban Railway Co.
Sandusky, Norwalk & Southern Railway Co.
Toledo, Fremont & Norwalk Railroad Co.

The company was placed in the hands of a Receiver in 1902, but a reorganization plan was to be formulated.

The company controls 160 miles of electric trolley railway, connecting Toledo, Norwalk, Sandusky and Lorain, O., with Cleveland.

Stock....Par $100.....Authorized { com., $4,500,000 / pref., 1,500,000 } Issued { com., $4,500,000 / pref., 1,500,000 } $6,000,000

The preferred stock is 5 per cent., cumulative. Transfer Agent, Cleveland Trust Co., Cleveland. Registrar, Dime Savings & Banking Co., Cleveland.

FUNDED DEBT.

| | |
|---|---|
| 1st mort., 5 per cent., due Oct., 1931, April and Oct. | $4,000,000 |
| Lorain & Cleveland Ry. Co., 1st mort., 5 per cent., gold, due July, 1927, Jan. and July. | 750,000 |
| Total | $4,750,000 |

The authorized amount of the 1st mortgage is $6,000,000. Trustee of the mortgage and agent for the pa ment of interest, Western Reserve Trust Co., Cleveland. The authorized amount of the Lorain & Cleveland Railway Co.'s 1st mortgage is $1,000,000. Bonds are subject to call after July 1, 1917. Trustee of the mortgage and agent for the payment of interest, Cleveland Trust Co., Cleveland. Interest is also paid by the Colonial Trust Co., New York.

Receiver, Albion E. Lang.

President, Barach Mahler; Vice-Presidents, W. H. Price, J. B. Hanna; Secretary, F. W. Coen; Treasurer, C. H. Stewart.

Main office, Toledo, O. Annual meeting, third Tuesday in January.

## LANCASTER COUNTY RAILWAY & LIGHT CO.

A corporation formed under the laws of New Jersey, June 15, 1901. Its business is lighting, heating and operating an electric railway. It has 120 miles of electric railway lines. The company acquired the following properties:

Conestoga Traction Co.
Lancaster Gas Light & Fuel Co.
Columbia Electric Light & Power Co.
Edison Electric Illuminating Co., Lancaster, Pa.

Stock....Par $50....Authorized { com., $1,000,000 / pref., 1,000,000 } Issued { com., $1,000,000 / pref., 1,000,000 } $2,000,000

The preferred stock is 5 per cent., cumulative, payable annually. Stock is transferred at the office of the company, Lancaster, Pa.

FUNDED DEBT.

1st mort., 5 per cent., due 1951, Jan. and July.... $1,000,000

The authorized bond issue is $1,000,000. Trustee of the mortgage and agent for the payment of interest, The Lancaster Trust Co., Lancaster, Pa.

President, William B. Given, Columbia, Pa.; Secretary and Treasurer, Oscar M. Hoffman; General Manager, Frank S. Given, Lancaster, Pa.

Directors—William B. Given, Columbia, Pa.; William W. Griest, John Hertzler, R. H. Brubaker, Eckert Slaymaker, John W. B. Bausman, Charles B. Keller, Lancaster, Pa.; Philip B. Shaw, Williamsport, Pa.; Samuel R. Shipley, Philadelphia; Lindley M. Garrison, Jersey City.

Corporate office, 111 Market street, Camden, N. J.; main office, Woolworth Building, Lancaster, Pa. Annual meeting, first Tuesday in June, at Camden, N. J.

## LANSTON MONOTYPE-MACHINE CO.

A corporation formed under the laws of Virginia. The business of the company is the manufacture, sale and rental of machines for typesetting and the casting of type in printing offices, the apparatus for this purpose being covered by the patents of Tolbert Lanston and others which are owned by this company. The company has a factory in Philadelphia for the manufacture of matrices and moulds. The machines are made by William Sellers & Co. At the close of 1901 it had 200 machines in successful use in newspaper and printing offices, including that of the New York Sun. It has contracts for the delivery of many additional machines.

Stock......Par $20..........................Authorized, $5,000,000......Issued, $4,827,240

The amount of stock authorized by law is $10,000,000 and by the stockholders $5,000,000. In 1901 $600,000 new stock was issued.

Stock is transferred at the company's office, New York.

The company has interests in the stock of other companies formed to introduce the Lanston machine in different countries, including the Lanston Monotype Corporation of England and the Colonial Syndicate. These holdings are valued in the company's balance sheet at $515,428.

The report for the year ending February 28, 1900, showed a gross business of $257,187, and cash receipts of $200,239. The profits for the year were $36,543. The balance to the credit of profit and loss on March 31, 1902, was $2,062,332.

President, J. Maury Dove; Vice-President, George E. Hamilton; Secretary and Treasurer, B. F. Cole, Washington.

Directors—B. F. Cole, William H. Hoeke, Tolbert Lanston, J. Maury Dove, George E. Hamilton, Washington; William H. Goadby, William M. Laffan, J. C. Maben, W. E. Strong, New York.

Main office, 1231 Callowhill street, Philadelphia; sales office, 1 Madison street, New York. Annual meeting, third Thursday in April.

---

## THE LAURENTIDE PULP CO., LIMITED

A corporation formed under the laws of the Dominion of Canada for the purpose of manufacturing wood-pulp, paper and paper-board. The mills of the company are located at Grand Mere, Que., and it has timber rights aggregating 1,643 square miles.

Stock......Par $100..........................Authorized, $1,600,000......Issued, $1,600,000

The company pays semi-annual dividends of 4 per cent. each in February and August. The company has no preferred stock.

Transfer Agent and Registrar, Royal Trust Co., Montreal.

FUNDED DEBT.

1st mort., 6 per cent., gold, due Jan., 1920, Jan. and July.......................... $1,200,000

The bonds are in denominations of $1,000 each, and the mortgage covers all the properties of the company, including water power and timber rights.

President, Sir William C. Van Horne, Montreal; Vice-President, George Chahoon, Jr., Grand Mere, Que.; Secretary, E. Alexander, Montreal; Treasurer, Russell A. Alger, Jr., Detroit.

Directors—William C. Van Horne, Richard B. Angus, James Ross, Charles R. Hosmer, Montreal; George Chahoon, Jr., Grand Mere, Que.; Russell A. Alger, Russell A. Alger, Jr., Detroit.

Main office, 4 Hospital street, Montreal, Que. Annual meeting, second Tuesday in October.

---

## LAWRENCE MANUFACTURING CO.

A corporation formed under the laws of Massachusetts, June 7, 1831, for the purpose of manufacturing cotton hosiery and underwear. The company owns mills at Lowell, Mass.

Stock......Par $100..........................Authorized, $1,250,000......Issued, $1,250,000

The company has no preferred stock or funded debt. Stock is transferred at the office of the company.

Dividends of 3 per cent., semi-annual, are paid in June and December.

President, T. Jefferson Coolidge; Treasurer, Clifton P. Baker, Boston.

Directors—T. Jefferson Coolidge, George A. Gardner, Arthur T. Lyman, T. Jefferson Coolidge, Jr., Henry B. Cabot, Charles W. Amory, Clifton P. Baker, Boston.

Corporate and main office, Washington and Court streets, Boston. Annual meeting, second Tuesday in June, at Boston.

## LEHIGH & WILKES-BARRE COAL CO.

(Controlled by Central Railroad Co. of New Jersey.)

A company incorporated in Pennsylvania in 1864. Operates a number of coal mines and owns or leases 28,909 acres of anthracite coal lands in the Wyoming and Lehigh regions.

Stock......Par $50......................Authorized, $10,000,000........Issued, $9,212,500

FUNDED DEBT.

| | |
|---|---|
| Consolidated loan, extended at 4½ per cent., due June, 1910, quar., March......... | $12,175,000 |
| Income bonds, held by Central of New Jersey, if earned, May and Nov............ | 2,353,000 |
| 5 per cent. mort. loan, due 1912.............................................. | 2,691,000 |
| Total.......................................................................... | $17,219,000 |

The Central Railroad of New Jersey owns $6,600,000 of the company's stock, $6,116,000 of consols, $2,353,000 of the incomes, and also held past due coupons of consolidated bonds to the amount of $5,472,000, but canceled the latter. Lehigh Coal & Navigation Company's 6 per cent. bonds for $600,000, due 1894, guaranteed by this company, were paid at maturity. The $500,000 of Lehigh Coal & Navigation 6s, due February 1, 1897, were extended to 1900. The consolidated mortgage bore 7 per cent. interest and matured June 1, 1900, when it was extended at 4½ per cent. until 1910, with the guarantee of principal and interest by the Central Railroad of New Jersey. The Lehigh Coal & Navigation loan of $500,000 at 4½ per cent. matured June 1, 1900, and was paid off.

EARNINGS.—Year ending June 30.

| | Gross. | Net. | Charges. | Surplus. |
|---|---|---|---|---|
| 1900–01...................... | $12,576,247 | $1,567,369 | $1,569,296 | Def. $1,918 |

In 1892 company paid $298,155 interest on the bonds held by Central Railroad of New Jersey. In 1893, $428,120, full 7 per cent., was paid on these bonds. No reports for 1894 to 1896 or since 1897. In 1896 interest and sinking funds, exclusive of interest on consols held by Central of New Jersey, was $973,485.

Company mined 2,245,062 tons of coal in 1883; in 1884, 2,070,264 tons; in 1885, 2,212,220 tons; in 1886, 2,435,552 tons; in 1887, 2,518,692 tons; in 1888, 2,675,386 tons; in 1889, 2,276,052 tons; in 1890, 2,550,000 tons; in 1891, 2,942,956 tons; in 1892, 2,712,641 tons; in 1893, 3,478,242 tons; in 1897, 2,132,042 tons.

President, George F. Baer; Secretary and Treasurer, G. C. Waterman, Philadelphia.

Directors—George F. Baer, Joseph S. Harris, Samuel Dickson, J. Lowber Welsh, Philadelphia; J. Rogers Maxwell, George F. Baker, New York; Andrew H. McClintock, Wilkes-Barre, Pa.

Main office, Reading Terminal, Philadelphia.

## THE LEHIGH COAL & NAVIGATION CO.

A company incorporated in Pennsylvania, February 13, 1822, with a perpetual charter.

This company owns the Lehigh Canal, the Lehigh & Susquehanna Railroad and branches, 163 miles, and the Delaware Division Canal, besides an extensive anthracite coal property. It leases the Nesquehoning Valley Railroad, 17 miles, and the Tresckow Railroad, 7 miles; and Wilkes-Barre and Scranton Railroad, 4 miles; in all, 28 miles leased. These railroads are leased to the Central Railroad Co. of New Jersey at a rental of one-third of gross earnings.

This is the oldest of all the anthracite companies, having been organized in 1822. The first shipments of anthracite coal were made from its property.

Stock......Par $50.......................Authorized, $15,801,300......Issued, $15,801,300

Stock is transferred at the office of the company, Philadelphia.

In 1902 the company issued and sold $1,436,665 of new stock to provide for improvements.

Dividends are paid, semi-annually, in May and November. In May, 1900, the semi-annual rate was increased from 2 to 2½ per cent., and the dividend paid November 27, 1900, was increased to 3 per cent., putting the stock on a 6 per cent. basis, which was the rate in 1901, but the November, 1902, dividend was reduced to 2 per cent., making 5 per cent. on the stock for 1902.

FUNDED DEBT.

| | |
|---|---|
| 1st mort., registered, ext. to July, 1914, 4½ per cent., quarterly, Jan................ | $5,000,000 |
| 1st mort. on railroad, extended, 4 per cent., due April, 1914, quarterly, Feb.......... | 1,992,833 |
| Mort., loan of 1867, extended, 4 per cent., due June, 1914, June and Dec.............. | 1,842,500 |
| Consolidated mort., 7 per cent., due June, 1911, June and Dec...................... | 2,470,750 |
| General mort., 4½ per cent., due May, 1924, quarterly, May......................... | 3,686,000 |
| Collateral trust mort., 4½ per cent., due Sept., 1905, March and Sept.............. | 1,500,000 |
| Funding and impt. mort., 4 per cent., due July, 1948, Jan. and July................ | 1,760,000 |
| Total.......................................................................... | $18,252,083 |

Collateral trust mortgage bonds were issued in 1895. Mortgage is for $1,500,000. 1st mortgage on railroad, 6 per cent., due February 1, 1897, was extended at 4 per cent. The 6 per cent. bonds of 1867 matured in 1897 and were extended at 4 per cent. There were in addition $2,310,000 of this issue assumed by the Central Railroad of New Jersey, and paid off by it December 15, 1897, while $500,000 more assumed by Lehigh & Wilkes-Barre Coal Co. were paid off December 15, 1897. In 1898 this company and the Central Railroad of New Jersey became joint guarantors of $1,062,000 Lehigh & Hudson River Railroad 5 per cent. bonds, of which $1,124,000 were outstanding. In 1898 a new 4 per cent. Lehigh Coal & Navigation mortgage was authorized for $7,500,000. Amount given above was issuable in 1898 on account of the retirement of $800,000 Delaware Division Canal 6s and for other purposes. There are in addition $506,000 of these bonds held in the treasury of the company.

The Delaware Division Canal is leased for interest on its bonds and 4 per cent. on its stock.

EARNINGS.

| | Div. Paid. | Gross. | Int., Rentals and Taxes. | Less Sk. Fd. and Depreciation Property. | Surplus. |
|---|---|---|---|---|---|
| 1895 | 4 | $1,692,878 | $1,253,947 | $95,994 | $438,931 |
| 1896 | 4 | 1,898,279 | 1,339,730 | 95,816 | 558,549 |
| 1897 | 4 | 2,089,735 | 1,329,601 | 92,295 | 667,838 |
| 1898 | 4 | 1,859,783 | 1,300,432 | 87,709 | 559,351 |
| 1899 | 4 | 2,204,123 | 1,299,611 | 83,802 | 820,710 |
| 1900 | 5½ | 2,623,709 | 1,317,799 | 197,576 | 1,108,333 |
| 1901 | 6 | 2,574,928 | 1,325,365 | 187,077 | 1,062,486 |
| 1902 | 5 | 2,353,099 | 1,354,594 | 271,104 | 727,310 |

Earnings include canal tolls and water power, rental of railroad and net receipts from coal sales. Coal production of company in 1892 was 1,293,602 tons; in 1893, 1,445,341 tons; in 1894, 1,386,482 tons; in 1895, 1,521,695 tons; in 1896, 1,549,097 tons; in 1897, 1,530,823 tons; in 1898, 1,450,964 tons; in 1899, 1,807,733 tons; in 1900, 2,098,890 tons; in 1901, 1,905,495 tons.

President, Lewis A. Riley; Vice-President, Charles F. Howell; Secretary and Treasurer, Harry F. Baker, Philadelphia.

Managers—E. W. Clark, Francis R. Cope, Erskine Hewitt, Bayard Henry, Joseph S. Harris, Samuel Dickson, Calvin Pardee, John S. Wentz, James M. Duane, Henry P. McKean, Lewis A. Riley, R. Dale Benson.

Main office, 108 South Fourth street, Philadelphia. Annual meeting, fourth Tuesday in February.

## LEHIGH-NORTHAMPTON GAS & ELECTRIC CO.

A corporation formed under the laws of New Jersey in 1900. The company acquired the plants, contracts and franchises of the Catasauqua Gas Co. and the Catasauqua Electric Light & Power Co. in the Borough of Catasauqua, Pa. The company has obtained franchises from the neighboring townships and boroughs.

Stock......Par $100..............................Authorized, $250,000......Issued, $250,000

FUNDED DEBT.

1st mort., 5 per cent., due 1930, June and Dec........................................ $175,000

The bond issue authorized is $250,000. The bonds are redeemable at the company's option after June 1, 1910. Trustee of the mortgage, The People's Bank, Wilkes-Barre, Pa.

President, M. L. Driesbach, Wilkes-Barre, Pa.; Secretary and Treasurer, C. R. Horn, Catasauqua, Pa.

Directors—M. L. Driesbach, A. A. Sterling, Liddon Flick, Wilkes-Barre, Pa.; C. R. Horn, Catasauqua, Pa.; W. W. Watson, Scranton, Pa.

Main office, Catasauqua, Pa.; Philadelphia office, Fourth and Chestnut streets.

## LEHIGH VALLEY TRACTION CO.

A corporation formed under the laws of Pennsylvania in 1899, and absorbed the Allentown & Lehigh Valley Traction Co., which was a combination of the companies operating lines in Easton, Bethlehem, Slatington, Catasauqua, Allentown and neighboring places, the Easton Consolidated Electric Co., the Slate Belt Electric Street Railway, the Allentown & Slatington Street Railway, the Bethlehem & Nazareth Street Railway and the Coplay, Egypt & Ironton Street Railway. In 1901 it acquired the Philadelphia & Lehigh Valley Traction Co., which was to build a line from Philadelphia to Allentown, Pa. The Quakertown Traction Co. is also leased. Total operated, about 200 miles.

Stock.....Par $50.....Authorized { com., $2,500,000 / pref., 500,000 } Issued { com., $2,500,000 / pref., 500,000 } $3,000,000

FUNDED DEBT.

| | |
|---|---|
| Lehigh Valley Traction mort., 4 per cent., due Dec., 1929, June and Dec. | $3,000,000 |
| Slatington Street Railway 1st mort., 4 per cent., due Dec., 1930, June and Dec. | 500,000 |
| Easton Cons. Electric col. trust, 5 per cent., due May, 1949, May and Nov. | 872,000 |
| Easton Transit Co. 1st mort., 5 per cent., due April, 1922, April and Oct. | 300,000 |
| Easton, Palmer & Bethlehem 1st mort., 5 per cent., due Jan., 1918, Jan. and July | 200,000 |
| Phila. & Lehigh Val. Trac. 1st mort., 4 per cent., due March 1, 1931, March and Sept. | 2,400,000 |
| Quakertown Traction 1st mort., 5 per cent., due 1931 | 300,000 |
| State Belt Elec. 1st mort., guar. 5 per cent., due June, 1930, June and Dec. | 360,000 |
| Total | $7,932,000 |

This company guarantees 3 per cent. dividends on the $1,500,000 stock of the Easton Consolidated Electric Co., and interest on the bonds of that road. The Slate Belt Electric Co. has $360,000 stock, on which 3¼ per cent. dividends are guaranteed, and 5 per cent. is guaranteed on $150,000 stock of the Bethlehem & Nazareth Street Railway and $240,000 stock of the Allentown & Slatington Street Railway.

The trustee of the Lehigh Valley Traction mortgage is the Guarantee Trust Co., New York. Bonds may be called and paid at 105. The same institution is trustee for the Philadelphia & Lehigh Valley Traction 1st mortgage.

The first dividend on the stock was 1 per cent., paid July, 1900, and similar dividends were paid quarterly, in October, 1900, and January, 1901.

President, Robert E. Wright, Allentown, Pa.; Vice-President, Loftin E. Johnson; Secretary and Treasurer, Charles M. Bates, New York.

Main office, Allentown, Pa.

---

## THE LIGHT, HEAT & POWER CORPORATION

A corporation formed under the laws of West Virginia in 1897. The purposes of the company are the manufacturing, selling, purchasing and leasing of machinery and appliances, buildings and real estate; building, equipping, leasing, buying and selling water, light, power, heat and refrigerating plants and pipe lines; furnishing machinery and appliances to be used in connection with the same, and maintaining and operating such plants; also the purchase and sale of the securities of other corporations.

The company controls and operates the following properties:

Milford Electric Light & Power Co., Milford, Mass.
Clinton Gas Light Co. Gas and Electric plants, Clinton, Mass.
The Easton Power Co., Easton, Pa.
The Edison Electric Illum. Co., Easton, Pa.
The Easton Gas Co., Easton, Pa.
The Easton Fuel Gas Co., Easton, Pa.
The Delaware Gas Light Co., Easton, Pa.
The Phillipsburg Electric Lighting, Heating & Power Co., Phillipsburg, N. J.
The Easton Power Co. of New Jersey, Jersey City.

The capacities of the various plants are as follows: Easton, steam, 2,500 horse-power; water, 1,500 horse-power; Clinton, 400 horse-power, steam; Milford, 300 horse-power, steam. The Phillipsburg plant obtains power from Easton. The capacity of the gas plants is as follows: Easton, 60,000,000 cubic feet; Clinton, 25,000,000 cubic feet. The Easton Gas Co. supplies gas to Phillipsburg and to all the Easton gas companies.

Stock.....Par $100......Authorized { com., $1,000,000; pref., 250,000 } Issued { com., $823,000; pref., 101,000 } $924,000

The preferred stock is 5 per cent., non-cumulative. It also has a preference as to assets over the common in case of liquidation.

Transfer Agent and Registrar, Atlas National Bank, Boston.

FUNDED DEBT.

| | |
|---|---|
| Debenture bonds, 5 per cent., due 1918, April and Oct. | $50,000 |
| " " " " 1929, Jan. and July | 50,000 |
| Total | $100,000 |

Interest on the debentures is paid at the National Bank of Redemption, Boston.

EARNINGS.

| | Gross. | Operating Exp. | Charges. | Net. |
|---|---|---|---|---|
| 1900 | $209,501 | $132,299 | $55,667 | $121,535 |
| 1901 | 250,759 | 156,769 | 65,221 | 128,798 |

At the end of 1901 the resources of the company, consisting of cash, securities, accounts receivable and machinery, amounted to $1,321,000.

President and Treasurer, Arthur E. Childs; Vice-President and General Manager, Alfred Clarke; Secretary, C. Frank Whittemore; Assistant Treasurer, Addis M. Whitney, Boston.

Directors—Arthur E. Childs, Alfred Clarke, C. Frank Whittemore, Edward Everett, Boston; George A. Childs, Montreal.

Main office, 131 State street, Boston. Annual meeting, first Tuesday following February 15.

## LINCOLN COAL CO.

A corporation formed under the laws of West Virginia in 1900, for the purpose of mining and selling coal. The property of the company is located at Hadley, Lincoln County, W. Va., and consists of a mine, with a capacity of 1,000 tons daily, about 100 miners' houses, a large company store and a complete mining plant.

Stock......Par $100..............................Authorized, $500,000......Issued, $500,000

The company has no preferred stock and no funded debt.

President and Treasurer, Wilbur C. Brown; Vice-President and Secretary, George G. Hadley; Assistant Secretary and Assistant Treasurer, John W. Perry.

Directors—Wilbur C. Brown, George G. Hadley, Charles M. Howell, C. Fred Reals, John W. Perry.

Main office, Huntington, West Va; New York office, 52 Broadway.

## LIT BROTHERS

A corporation formed under the laws of New Jersey, January 22, 1900. The company was formed to acquire and carry on the department store at the corner of Market and Eighth streets, Philadelphia, established by S. D. & J. D. Lit. The company obtained the leaseholds, improvements, fixtures, machinery, plant, stock, good will, trade-marks and business of the firm.

Stock......Par $10..........................Authorized, $2,500,000......Issued, $2,000,000

Transfer Agent, New Jersey Corporation Guarantee & Trust Co., Camden, N. J.

An amount of $209,140 of the stock is held in the company's treasury. The company began business with a cash working capital of $400,000.

President, Samuel D. Lit; Vice-President, Secretary and Treasurer, Jacob D. Lit; 2d Vice President, R. P. Wedell.

Directors—Samuel D. Lit, Jacob D. Lit, R. P. W. Arnold, Benjamin Wolf, Philadelphia; Charles A. Stimpfheimer, Long Branch, N. J.

Main office, corner Market and Eighth streets, Philadelphia. Annual meeting, third Monday in February.

## LOCKPORT GAS & ELECTRIC LIGHT CO.

A corporation formed under the laws of New York, and owns the gas and electric lighting plants at Lockport, N. Y., which city has a population of 19,000. Gas franchise is perpetual. Price of gas, $1.00 to $1.50 per 1,000 cubic feet. This company is controlled by the United Gas & Electric Co., which see.

Stock......Par $100.............................Authorized, $150,000......Issued, $150,000

Dividends on the stock are paid semi-annually, in January and July, at the rate of 6 per cent. per annum.

Transfer Agents, Bertron & Storrs, 40 Wall street, New York.

FUNDED DEBT.

1st mort., 5 per cent., due 1920, Feb. and Aug....................................... $260,000

The 1st mortgage is for $300,000. Trustee and agent for payment of interest, Trust Co. of America, New York.

In the fiscal year ending June 30, 1900, the net earnings of the company were $29,981; in 1901, net, $32,096.

President, E. E. Witherby; Vice-President, S. C. Lewis; Secretary and Treasurer, A. S. Cook; Assistant Secretary and Assistant Treasurer, Frank S. Butterworth.

Directors—Frank S. Butterworth, H. J. Chadwick, S. C. Lewis, E. E. Witherby, Denman Blanchard, S. R. Bertron, Richard S. Storrs.

Main office, Lockport, New York.

## THE LONDON ELECTRIC CO., LIMITED

A corporation formed under the laws of the Dominion of Canada for the purpose of supplying electric light and power in the city of London, Ont.

Stock......Par $100..............................Authorized, $500,000......Issued, $392,500

The company has no preferred stock.

Dividends at the rate of 6 per cent. per annum were paid in 1898, 1899, 1900 and 1901.

FUNDED DEBT.

1st mort., 5 per cent., due 1905 .................................................. $100,000

The bonds are held by the Canada Life Insurance Co. Agent for payment of interest, Canadian Bank of Commerce, Montreal.

In the fiscal year ending November 30, 1901, the company's net earnings were $26,155; dividends, $19,784; reserve fund, $10,000. In 1901-02 the net profits after charges were $26,790.

President, W. D. Matthews; Vice-President, H. P. Dwight; Secretary, Frederic Nicholls; Manager, Charles B. Hunt.

Directors—W. D. Matthews, H. P. Dwight, W. R. Brock, George A. Cox, Robert Jaffray, J. K. Kerr, Charles B. Hunt, M. J. Kent, Edmund Meredith, Frederic Nicholls, J. C. Judd.

Main office, 359 Richmond street, London, Ont.; Toronto office, 14 King street. Annual meeting in January, at London, Ont.

## LONDON STREET RAILWAY CO.

A corporation formed under the laws of Ontario in 1873, for the purpose of operating a street railway in London, Ont. It operates 30 miles of road under an exclusive franchise granted in 1875 and running for fifty years.

Stock......Par $40...............................Authorized, $750,000......Issued, $450,000

The company has no preferred stock. Transfer Agent and Registrar, Toronto General Trust Co., Toronto.

Dividends are paid semi-annually, at the rate of 4 per cent. per annum.

FUNDED DEBT.

1st mort., 5 per cent., due 1925, March and Sept...................................... $450,000

The total amount of the authorized 1st mortgage is $750,000.

Trustee of the mortgage, Toronto General Trust Co., Toronto. Agent for the payment of interest, Bank of Commerce, Toronto.

EARNINGS.

| | Gross. | Net. | Charges. | Dividends. | Surplus. |
|---|---|---|---|---|---|
| 1901........................... | $141,845 | $57,288 | $23,834 | $16,000 | $7,843 |
| 1902........................... | 154,703 | 61,455 | 16,078 | 32,000 | 13,376 |

President, H. A. Everett, Cleveland; 1st Vice-President, T. H. Smallman; Secretary and Treasurer, C. E. A. Carr, London, Ont.

Directors—H. O. Everett, E. W. Moore, Charles Wason, Cleveland; T. H. Smallman, P. W. D. Broderick, William Spencer, London, Ont.; H. S. Holt, Montreal.

Main office, 410 Richmond street, London, Ont. Annual meeting, second Wednesday in January, at London, Ont.

## THE P. LORILLARD COMPANY

A corporation formed under the laws of New Jersey in 1891 to take over the tobacco manufacturing business of P. Lorillard & Co., at Jersey City, N. J., established in 1760. Real estate and plant owned by company was valued at $1,879,000 and merchandise at about $950,000.

In the autumn of 1898 control of the company had been acquired by the Continental Tobacco Co., which company purchased $3,000,000 common stock of this company. In February, 1900, it was announced that holders of the preferred stock of this company would be given the right of exchanging their stock for an issue of $2,000,000 7 per cent. debentures of the Continental Tobacco Co., and it was stated that two-thirds of the preferred had been so exchanged.

Stock....Par $100.......Authorized { com., $3,000,000 / pref., 2,000,000 } Issued { com., $3,000,000 / pref., 2,000,000 } $5,000,000

Preferred stock is entitled to 8 per cent., cumulative. No mortgage can be created on property without consent of 75 per cent. of preferred stock.

Transfer Agents, Baring, Magoun & Co., New York.

Quarterly dividends of 2 per cent. were regularly paid on the preferred, January (2), April, July and October. On the common stock 2½ per cent. was paid in August, 1898, but no dividend was paid until 1900, when the common received 8 per cent. In 1901 6 per cent. regular was paid on the common with an extra dividend of 10 per cent., declared in December.

On common in 1892, 10 per cent.; in 1893, 5 per cent.; in 1894, 13 per cent.; in 1895, 8 per cent.; in 1896, 3 per cent.; in 1897, 8 per cent.; in 1898, 5 per cent.; in 1899, none; in 1900, 8 per cent.; in 1901, 16 per cent.

Report for year ending June 30, 1892, stated that net profits for the year were $496,313; balance, after payment of dividends, $186,313. No subsequent reports were made public.

President, Thomas J. Maloney; Vice-President and Secretary, William B. Rhett; Treasurer, E. W. Somers.

Main office, 111 First street, Jersey City.

## THE LOS ANGELES ELECTRIC CO.

A corporation formed under the laws of California, October 23, 1882, to furnish electric light, power and heat in the City of Los Angeles, Cal. This company has a franchise running until 1917. It has a steam-power plant and a distributing system of underground conduit and pole lines over a territory of 48 square miles. The company is controlled by the same interests as the Los Angeles Lighting Co., which has a monopoly of the gas-lighting industry in Los Angeles.

Stock......Par $10..............................Authorized, $600,000......Issued, $550,000

The company has no preferred stock. Stock is transferred at the office of the company, Los Angeles, Cal.

FUNDED DEBT.

1st mort., 5 per cent., due Jan. 1, 1928, Jan. and July.......................................... $500,000

The outstanding bonds are the total amount authorized. Trustee of the mortgage and agent for the payment of interest, Union Trust Co., San Francisco. Interest is also payable at the office of the company, Los Angeles, Cal.

President, Walter B. Cline; 1st Vice-President, William M. Van Dyke; 2d Vice-President, Samuel W. Garretson; Secretary, William H. Burns; Treasurer, H. L. Flash; Assistant Treasurer, H. B. Cline.

Directors—Walter B. Cline, William M. Van Dyke, Samuel W. Garretson, Ozro W. Childs, William H. Burns.

Corporate and main office, 451 South Broadway, Los Angeles. Annual meeting, fourth Wednesday in January, at Los Angeles.

## LOS ANGELES LIGHTING CO.

A corporation formed under the laws of California, November 14, 1889, for manufacturing and supplying gas in the city of Los Angeles, Cal. It has a perpetual franchise and owns a plant with a daily capacity of 2,000,000 cubic feet, with 155 miles of mains.

Stock......Par $50..............................Authorized, $1,250,000......Issued, $935,000

The company has no preferred stock.

Dividends are payable monthly.

FUNDED DEBT.

1st mort., 5 per cent., bonds, due 1924, April and Oct.................................. $1,000,000

The outstanding bonds are the full amount authorized.

Trustee of the mortgage, California Safe Deposit & Trust Co., San Francisco. Agent for the payment of interest, Pacific Lighting Co., San Francisco. Interest is also payable at the office of the company.

President, Walter B. Cline; Vice-President, William M. Van Dyke; Secretary, Robert M. Adams; Treasurer, Henry L. Hash, Los Angeles.

Directors—Walter B. Cline, William M. Van Dyke, William A. Cheney, S. W. Garretson, Robert M. Adams, Los Angeles.

Main office, 457 South Broadway, Los Angeles. Annual meeting, fourth Wednesday in January, at Los Angeles.

## LOS ANGELES RAILWAY CO.

A corporation formed under the laws of California, March 30, 1895. The company acquired the following companies:

Los Angeles Consolidated Electric Railway Co.
Main Street & Agricultural Park Railway Co.
Main, Fifth & San Pedro Street Railway Co.

The company also owns a majority of the stock of the Pacific Light & Power Co. of Los Angeles. The company owns and operates 99.86 miles of electric railway in and about the city of Los Angeles, Cal. It has a power plant, 212 motor cars and 16 trailers.

Stock......Par $100..........................Authorized, $5,000,000......Issued, $5,000,000

The company has no preferred stock.

FUNDED DEBT.

1st mort., 5 per cent. gold, due Oct. 1, 1938, April and Oct........................ $4,809,000

The total amount of the authorized mortgage was $5,000,000. Trustee of the mortgage and agent for the payment of interest, Union Trust Co. of San Francisco.

In the fiscal year ending December 31, 1902, the gross earnings were $1,475,211; net, $662,143; fixed charges, $255,206; surplus, $406,937. The operating expenses were 55.11 per cent of the gross earnings.

President, H. E. Huntington, New York; 1st Vice-President, Ch. de Guigne; 2d Vice-President, C. W. Smith; Treasurer, Isaias W. Hellman; Secretary, Edmund B. Holladay, San Francisco; General Manager, J. A. Muir, Los Angeles, Cal.

Directors—H. E. Huntington, New York; Ch. de Guigne, Isaias W. Hellman, Anthony Borel, Edmund B. Holladay, San Francisco; Howard E. Huntingdon, J. A. Muir, Los Angeles, Cal.

Corporate and main office, 609 South Main street, Los Angeles, Cal.

## LOUISVILLE & JEFFERSONVILLE BRIDGE CO.

A corporation formed under the laws of Kentucky in 1892. The company built and owns a railway bridge crossing the Ohio River between Louisville, Ky., and Jeffersonville, Ind. The bridge, which was completed in 1896, is one-half mile long and the approaches are 1½ miles. The company also owns about 100 acres of land on either side contiguous to the approaches of the bridge. The bridge is used by the Chesapeake & Ohio and the Cleveland, Cincinnati, Chicago & St. Louis Railway Companies, in whose interest it was built, control of the Bridge Co.'s stock being held for that purpose.

Stock......Par $100..........................Authorized, $1,425,000......Issued, $1,425,000

FUNDED DEBT.

1st mort., 4 per cent. gold, guaranteed, due 1945, March and Sept.................... $3,500,000

The bonds, principal and interest, are guaranteed by indorsement by the Chesapeake & Ohio and Cleveland, Cincinnati, Chicago & St. Louis Railways. The mortgage is for $5,000,000. Trustees of Mortgage, United States Trust Co., New York, and Union Trust Co., Indianapolis. Interest is payable at the office of J. P. Morgan & Co., New York. In 1902 $500,000 additional bonds were sold to provide for improvements.

President, George J. Long; Secretary, M. L. Akers, Louisville; Treasurer, Frank D. Comstock, Cincinnati.

Directors—Melville E. Ingalls, Cincinnati; George W. Stevens, Richmond, ; George J. Long, A. P. Humphrey, Joseph Huffaker, Louisville.

Main office, Louisville; Treasurer's office, Central Union Depot, Cincinnati. Annual meeting, first Monday in March, at Louisville.

## LOUISVILLE BRIDGE CO.

A company incorporated by a special act of the General Assembly of Kentucky, approved March 10, 1856, entitled "An Act to Incorporate the Louisville Bridge Co." The company owns and operates a railroad bridge crossing the Ohio River between Louisville, Ky., and Jeffersonville, Ind. The bridge is 1 mile and 19 feet in length. The company also owns 1 8-10 miles of railroad track running through Fourteenth street, Louisville. The bridge is used by the Pittsburg, Cincinnati, Chicago & St. Louis Railway, the Chicago, Indianapolis & Louisville Railway, and other companies.

Stock. .....Par $100..........................Authorized, $1,500,000......Issued, $1,500,000

The Pennsylvania Company owns $900,000 of the stock of this company. The company has no funded debt. Stock is transferred at the company's office, Louisville.

Dividends at the rate of 6 per cent. per annum are paid, the payments being half-yearly, 3 per cent. each in January and July.

| EARNINGS. | Gross. | Net. |
|---|---|---|
| 1899 | $249,670 | $92,230 |
| 1900 | 243,286 | 94,424 |
| 1901 | 278,643 | 110,390 |
| 1902 | 306,252 | 154,391 |

President, Charles H. Gibson, Louisville; Treasurer, T. H. B. McKnight, Pittsburg; Secretary, James J. Morris, Louisville; Assistant Treasurer, R. R. Reed, Pittsburg; Superintendent, Bushrod W. Taylor; Assistant Superintendent, J. C. Cox, Louisville.

Directors—Charles H. Gibson, John L. Dodd, Louisville; James McCrea, Joseph Wood, J. J. Brooks, Pittsburg.

Main office, Louisville Trust Building, Louisville. Annual meeting, first Monday in March, at Louisville.

## LOUISVILLE COTTON MILLS CO.

A corporation formed under the laws of Kentucky in 1888 for the purpose of manufacturing cotton goods.

Stock......Par $100.......................... ...Authorized, $500,000......Issued, $300,000

The company has no preferred stock. Stock is transferred at the office of the company.

Dividends are paid semi-annually in January and July. Since 1890 they have been at the rate of 6 per cent., with occasional extra dividends.

FUNDED DEBT.

1st mort., 6 per cent., gold, due 1904, Jan. and July....................................$100,000

This bond issue can be used for purposes of collateral only and no interest on it has ever been paid; all the bonds are now in the treasury of the company and will be retired by limitation when they fall due. Trustee of the mortgage, Fidelity Trust & Safety Vault Co., Louisville.

The company has a surplus of $200,000.

President and Treasurer, Philip S. Tuley; Vice-President, J. B. Speed, Louisville.

Directors—Philip S. Tuley, William A. Robinson, J. B. Speed, George Gaulbert, S. H. Shallcross, G. W. Tarleton, J. W. E. Bayly, E. W. Chamberlain, Louisville.

Main office, 1008 Goss avenue, Louisville. Annual meeting, third Tuesday in December, at Louisville.

## LOUISVILLE GAS CO.

A corporation formed under the laws of Kentucky, January 1, 1889. The purpose of the company is the manufacture, distribution and sale of gas and electric light and power. The company acquired and owns the properties of the old Louisville Gas Co. and of the Louisville Electric Light Co. The capacity of its gas plant is 700,000,000 cubic feet and its electric plant has 7,500 horse-power.

Stock......Par $100............................Authorized, $4,000,000......Issued, $3,600,000

The company has no preferred stock.

The stock is transferred at the office of the company, 729 Fourth avenue, Louisville. Registrar, Fidelity Trust & Safety Vault Co., Louisville.

Dividends on the stock are paid at the rate of 5 per cent. per annum. The dividends are semi-annual, 2½ per cent. each, in January and July.

FUNDED DEBT.

1st mort., 5 per cent., due April, 1918, April and Oct................................. $500,000

The bonds outstanding are the full amount authorized. Trustee, Fidelity Trust & Safety Vault Co., Louisville. Agent for the payment of interest, National Bank of Kentucky, Louisville.

President, Udolpho Snead; Vice-President, John Stites; Secretary, F. A. Nobbe; Treasurer, William P. Lee; Chief Engineer and President of the Louisville Electric Light Co., A. H. Barret, Louisville.

Directors—Udolpho Snead, John Stites, H. V. Loving, D. X. Murphy, K. W. Smith, W. J. Abrams, W. H. Edinger, George Gaulbreck, T. H. Steck.

Main office, 729 Fourth avenue, Louisville. Annual meeting, first Monday in July, at Louisville.

## LOUISVILLE HEATING CO.

A corporation formed under the laws of Delaware in September, 1902. The company was organized to succeed the Kentucky Heating Co., which formed in 1891 and engaged in the business of supplying natural and artificial gas for heating purposes in the city of Louisville. It is proposed to greatly extend the plant and business of the new company.

Stock.....Par $100......Authorized { com., $2,500,000 / pref., 1,600,000 } Issued { com., $2,200,000 / pref., 1,600,000 } $3,800,000

The preferred stock is 5 per cent., cumulative, but has no voting power. Dividends on the preferred are payable quarterly, in January, April, July and October.

Transfer Agent, Delaware Corporation Co., Wilmington, Del.

The old Kentucky Heating Co. had $700,000 of stock, all common shares. In September, 1902, the holders thereof were offered two shares of new preferred stock for each old share, it being provided that of the new preferred $200,000 should be sold at not less than par and the proceeds used to extend the plant of the company.

FUNDED DEBT.

Kentucky Heating Co. 1st mort., 6 per cent., due 1915, June and Dec. ............ ... $100,000

The dividends on the stock of the old company were at the rate of 7 per cent. per annum, and were paid quarterly in January, April, July and October.

President, R. T. Durrett; Vice-President, Daniel E. Doherty; Secretary and Treasurer, Thomas W. Kennedy, Louisville.

Corporate office, Wilmington, Del.; main office, 518 West Green street, Louisville.

## LOUISVILLE HOME TELEPHONE CO.

A corporation formed under the laws of Delaware, March 23, 1901. The company has a telephone plant at Louisville and one at New Albany, Ind.

Stock......Par $100..........................Authorized, $1,500,000......Issued, $1,230,000

The company has no preferred stock. Transfer Agent, Fidelity Trust & Safety Vault Co., Louisville.

FUNDED DEBT.

1st mort., 5 per cent., due July 1, 1922, Jan. and July.............................. $1,230,000

The authorized 1st mortgage is $2,500,000. Trustee of the mortgage and agent for the payment of interest, American Trust & Savings Bank Co., Chicago. Interest is also payable by the First National Bank, New York.

President, John A. Armstrong; Vice-President, C. J. Doherty; Secretary, E. M. Coleman; Treasurer, John P. Starks; General Manager, A. L. Tetu, Louisville.

Directors—C. C. Bickel, John P. Starks, C. J. Doherty, E. M. Coleman, John A. Armstrong, Donald McDonald, W. C. Garland, J. D. Powers, Matt O'Doherty, Louisville; E. L. Barber, Wauseon, O.; J. G. Gray, Wilmington, Del.; E. Rice, Greenville, Ky.; Charles D. Knoefel, New Albany, Ind.

Corporate office, Wilmington, Del.; main office, 627 Fifth street, Louisville. Annual meeting, first Thursday after the first Monday in February.

## LOUISVILLE RAILWAY CO.

A corporation formed under the laws of Kentucky, April 9, 1893. The company owns or controls all the street railway lines in Louisville. It is a consolidation of the following companies:

Louisville City Railway Co.
Kentucky Street Railway Co.
Central Passenger Railway Co.
Beargrass Railway Co.
Crescent Hill Railway Co.

The company has a special perpetual charter, the only condition annexed to grant being to carry public school children at half-fare. It is authorized to use cable or electricity, and operates 140 miles of road by electricity.

Stock....Par $100....Authorized { com., $2,500,000; pref., 3,500,000 } Issued { com., $3,500,000; pref., 2,500,000 } $6,000,000

The preferred stock is 5 per cent., cumulative.

Transfer Agent, Louisville Trust Co., Louisville. Registrar, Fidelity Trust & Safety Vault Co., Louisville.

Dividends on the stock have been paid as follows: preferred, 5 per cent., annually; common, 1896-1897, 2½ per cent.; 1898, 1¼ per cent.; 1900-1901, 4 per cent.; 1902, 4¼ per cent. The January, 1903, dividend was 1¼ per cent. with ½ per cent. extra. Dividends on the common are quarterly, in January, April, July and October.

FUNDED DEBT.

| | |
|---|---|
| Consolidated mort., 5 per cent., gold, due July, 1930, Jan. and July................ | $5,187,000 |
| 2d mort., 4½ per cent., gold, due March, 1940, March and Sept...................... | 800,000 |
| Louisville City Railway mort., 6 per cent., due 1909, Jan. and July................ | 514,300 |
| Central Passenger Ry. Co., 1st mort., 6 per cent., due Nov., 1902, May and Nov..... | 60,000 |
| Central Passenger Ry. Co., 1st mort., 6 per cent., due Nov., 1908, May and Nov..... | 238,000 |
| Total ............................................................. | $6,799,300 |

The authorized amount of the consolidated mortgage is $6,000,000. Trustee of the mortgage, Fidelity Trust Co., Louisville. Agent for the payment of interest, J. & W. Seligman & Co., New York. The authorized amount of the 2d mortgage is $2,000,000, which can be issued for extensions at the rate of not more than $200,000 per annum. Trustee of the mortgage and agent for the payment of interest, Columbia Financial & Trust Co., Louisville.

EARNINGS.

Year ending December 31.

| | Gross. | Net. | Charges. | Surplus. |
|---|---|---|---|---|
| 1898 | $1,297,394 | $458,821 | $309,545 | $149,276 |
| 1899 | 1,436,828 | 482,255 | 308,500 | 173,755 |
| 1900 | 1,520,513 | 582,342 | 314,090 | 268,252 |
| 1901 | 1,617,059 | 593,022 | 320,934 | 272,088 |

In 1900 the surplus over preferred dividends was $3,252; in 1901, $7,083.
President, T. J. Minary; Vice-President, St. John Boyle; Secretary and Treasurer, Samuel G. Boyle.
Directors—Alexander H. Davis, H. H. Littell, J. B. Speed, St. John Boyle, Harry Bishop, Attilla Cox, J. W. Gaulbert, T. J. Minary, John Stites.
Main office, 500 Twelfth street, Louisville. Annual meeting, third Wednesday in February, at Louisville.

## LOWELL & BOSTON STREET RAILWAY CO.

A corporation formed under the laws of Massachusetts, January 25, 1901, to operate street railways in the cities of Lowell and Woburn, Mass., and the towns of Burlington, Billerica and Chelmsford, Mass. The company owns 9.64 miles of track, which was in full operation in September, 1901.

Stock......Par $100..............................Authorized, $90,000......Issued, $90,000

Stock is transferred at the office of the company. The company has no preferred stock.

FUNDED DEBT.

1st mort., 4½ per cent. gold bonds, due 1921, June and Dec.......................... $90,000

The bond issue is the full amount authorized. Trustee of the mortgage and agent for the payment of the interest, Federal Trust Co., Boston.
In the year ending September 30, 1901, the company's gross earnings were $15,402; deficit after expenses, $7,729; charges and taxes, $7,456; deficit for the year, $15,185; total deficit, September 30, 1902, $14,684.
President, Thomas I. Reed, Burlington, Mass.; Vice-President, Frank E. Cotton, Woburn, Mass; Secretary, D. A. Brooks; Treasurer, Edward A. Mead, Boston.
Directors—Thomas I. Reed, Burlington, Mass; Frank E. Cotton, F. A. Partridge, Woburn, Mass.; Edward A. Mead, Boston; Richard Faulkner, Billerica, Mass.
Main office, 53 State street, Boston. Annual meeting in November.

## LUXFER PRISM CO., LIMITED

A corporation formed under the laws of the Dominion of Canada to manufacture prisms and to deal in builders' materials.

Stock......Par $100.......Authorized { com., $300,000; pref., 100,000 } Issued { com., $300,000; pref., 100,000 } $400,000

The preferred stock is 7 per cent., cumulative, and has a preference as to the assets in liquidation. It also ranks equally with the common, for further dividends, after the common shall have received 7 per cent., semi-annually.
The company has no funded debt. Transfer Agents, Osler & Hammond, Toronto.
President, T. W. Horn; Vice-President, E. B. Osler; Secretary and Treasurer, F. W. Barrett.
Directors—T. W. Horn, E. B. Osler, F. W. Barrett, W. R. Brock, W. D. Matthews, William McKenzie, Frederic Nichols, R. H. Warden.
Main office, 100 King street, West, Toronto. Annual meeting, third Friday in January.

## LYMAN MILLS

A corporation formed under the laws of Massachusetts, March 16, 1854. The company was organized for the purpose of manufacturing cotton, woolen, linen or silk goods. It owns four mills in Holyoke, Mass., with 110,000 spindles and 2,200 looms, and sheetings, drills, lawns and fancy cottons are manufactured.

Stock......Par $100..........................Authorized, $2,000,000......Issued, $1,470,000

The company has no preferred stock and no funded debt. Stock is transferred at the office of the company, Boston.

Dividends are paid semi-annually, usually February 1 and August 1. The company paid in 1901 and 1902 4 per cent.

President, J. Howard Nichols; Treasurer, Theophilus Parsons; Clerk of Corporation, George H. Nutting, Boston.

Directors—J. Howard Nichols, Newton, Mass.; Theophilus Parsons, Mattapoisett, Mass.; George Wigglesworth, B. Rodman Weld, Charles W. Amory, Boston.

Corporate office, 53 State street, Boston. Selling Agents, Minot, Hooper & Co., Boston and New York. Annual meeting, first Wednesday in February, at place designated in call for meeting.

## MADISON GAS & ELECTRIC CO.

(Controlled by American Light & Traction Co.)

This company owns and operates the gas and electric plants of the city of Madison, Wis., which has 19,164 inhabitants. The gas franchise is perpetual.

In 1901 the American Light & Traction Co. acquired control through the acquisition of this company's stock in exchange for its own stock, of which 80 per cent. in new preferred and 24 per cent. in new common was offered for each share of the old stock.

Stock......Par $100.........  ....................Authorized, $400,000......Issued, $400,000

Transfer and Fiscal Agents for payment of coupons, Emerson McMillin & Co., New York.

FUNDED DEBT.

| | |
|---|---|
| 1st mort., 6 per cent. gold, due 1926, April and Oct. | $350,000 |
| Debenture, scrip, 6 per cent., due 1910 | 100,000 |
| Total | $450,000 |

The 1st mortgage (Central Trust Co., New York, trustee) is for $400,000, balance of bonds being held in treasury for improvements and additions.

President, Henry L. Doherty; Vice-President, N. B. Van Slyke; Secretary, C. E. Smith, Treasurer and General Manager, John Corscot.

Directors—Henry L. Doherty, N. B. Van Slyke, M. E. Fuller, W. H. Vilas, F. F. Proudfit, H. C. Adams, A. E. Smith.

Main office, 124 East Main street, Madison, Wis.

## MADISON SQUARE GARDEN CO.

A corporation formed under the laws of New York in 1887. It built and owns the Madison Square Garden, covering the block between Twenty-sixth and Twenty-seventh streets, and Madison and Fourth avenues, New York.

Stock......Par $100..........................Authorized, $5,000,000......Issued, $5,000,000

Stock is transferred at the company's office. Registrar, Mercantile Trust Co., New York.

FUNDED DEBT.

| | |
|---|---|
| 1st mort., 5 per cent., due Nov., 1919, May and Nov. | $1,250,000 |
| 2d " 6 per cent., due Nov., 1919, May and Nov. | 750,000 |
| Total | $2,000,000 |

The 2d mortgage coupons have been in default since 1897, and a committee has been appointed to represent the stockholders.

President, Frank K. Sturgis; Vice-President, Stanford White; Secretary and Treasurer, James C. Young.

Directors—Frank K. Sturgis, Stanford White, James C. Young, J. Pierpont Morgan, Darius O. Mills, Henry H. Hollister, Charles Lanier, W. C. Gulliver, W. F. Wharton, James T. Woodward, Frank W. Sanger.

Main office, 51 Madison avenue, New York. Annual meeting, second Tuesday in May.

## MAGNOLIA METAL CO.

A corporation formed under the laws of West Virginia to manufacture Magnolia, Defender, Mystic, Babbitt and other anti-friction metals and special alloys. The Magnolia metal business was established in 1886. The company has offices and factories in New York, Chicago, Montreal, San Francisco and New Orleans.

Stock......Par $100....Authorized { com., $1,000,000 / pref., 200,000 } Issued { com., $1,000,000 / pref., 200,000 } $1,200,000

The preferred stock is 7 per cent., cumulative, and is also preferred as to assets.

The company has no funded debt. Transfer Agent, Trust Co. of the Republic, New York.

In November, 1902, the balance sheet of the company showed a surplus of assets over liabilities, exclusive of good will, patents, trade-marks, etc., of $200,193.

President, Charles B. Miller; Vice-President and General Manager, Edward C. Miller; Secretary and Treasurer, F. Jordan; Assistant Secretary, L. D. Allen.

Directors—Charles B. Miller, Edward C. Miller, L. B. Miller, F. Jordan, L. Allen.

Main office, 511 West Thirteenth street, New York.

## MAGNUS METAL CO.

A corporation formed under the laws of New Jersey in July, 1899. The business of the company is the manufacture of railway supplies. It acquired the property, plans, patents and business of the following concerns:

Brady Metal Co., Jersey City.
Buffalo Brass Co., Depew, N. Y.
Stiles Metal Co., New Haven, Conn.
E. Blunt Manufacturing Co., Newark, N. J.
Fort Pitt Bronze Co., Pittsburg, Pa.

Stock...Par $100....Authorized { com., $1,500,000 / pref., 1,500,000 } Issued { com., $1,400,000 / pref., 1,400,000 } $2,800,000

The preferred stock is 8 per cent., non-cumulative. The company has no funded debt. No report of earnings is made public.

Stock is transferred at the office of the company.

The company since its formation has paid dividends at the rate of 2 per cent. quarterly on the preferred stock in January (18), April, July and October. A yearly dividend of 10 per cent. was paid on the common stock in January, 1900, and a quarterly dividend of 2½ per cent. on February 1, 1901, it being intended to pay such dividends on the common regularly in February, May, August and November.

President, H. H. Hewitt; Vice-President, Julius E. French; Secretary and Treasurer, M. S. Paine, New York.

Directors—Charles Miller, Franklin, Pa.; Julius E. French, W. H. Silverthorn, M. S. Paine, J. B. Brady, H. H. Hewitt, New York; N. H. Haberle, Jersey City.

Main office, 830 Ellicott square, Buffalo; New York office, 170 Broadway; branch offices: Jersey City, New Haven, Newark, Pittsburg, Chicago. Annual meeting, third Wednesday in January, at Jersey City.

## MAMMOTH VEIN COAL & IRON CO.

A corporation chartered in Pennsylvania in 1862. The company owns and operates an anthracite coal property of 1,043 acres in Schuylkill County, Pa. The company is controlled by the Philadelphia & Reading Coal & Iron Co. The company, on June 30, 1900, was indebted to the Reading Company for $72,800.

Stock......Par $10..............................Authorized, $690,000......Issued, $690,000

FUNDED DEBT.

1st mort., 4 per cent., due 1932, Feb. and Aug...................................... $300,000

Trustee of the mortgage, Thomas Hart, Jr., Philadelphia.

President, George F. Baer; Secretary, W. G. Brown; Treasurer, W. A. Church.

Directors—George F. Baer, W. A. Church, Thomas M. Richards, C. E. Henderson, James M. Landis, Philadelphia.

Main office, Reading Terminal, Twelfth and Market streets, Philadelphia. Annual meeting, second Monday in October.

## MANASSAS GAP COPPER MINES

A corporation formed under the laws of New York to engage in mining and smelting gold, copper and silver ores. The company has 700 acres of mining property equipped with machinery and buildings.

Stock......Par $1..............................Authorized, $1,000,000......Issued, $620,000

The company has no preferred stock and no funded debt. Stock is transferred at the office of the company, New York.

Acting President and Vice-President, John S. Wise; Secretary, William Lawrence Clark; Treasurer and General Manager, George Brown Wright, New York.

Directors—John S. Wise, George Brown Wright, William Lawrence Clark, Lionel H. Leadam, Henry P. Porter, Powhatan Weisiger, Arthur L. Root, New York; Walter T. Searing, Tomkins Cove, N. Y.

Corporate and main office, 25 Broad street, New York. Annual meeting, first Monday in October, at New York.

## MANCHESTER STREET RAILWAY

A corporation formed under the laws of New Hampshire, July 20, 1874. The company owns about 35 miles of electric railway tracks in the city of Manchester, N. H., with branches running to Goffstown, Goff Falls and Massabesic Lake, the entire street railway system of Manchester and vicinity. It owns 76 cars.

Stock......Par $100............................Authorized, $520,500......Issued, $520,500

The company has no preferred stock. Stock is transferred by the treasurer of the company.

All the stock of the company is owned by the Manchester Traction, Light & Power Co.

FUNDED DEBT.

1st mort., 5 per cent., due Jan. 1, 1915, Jan. and July.............................. $250,000

The bonds issued are the total amount authorized. Bonds are subject to call after January 1, 1905, at par. Trustee of the mortgage, American Loan & Trust Co., Boston. Agent for the payment of interest, National Bank of Redemption, Boston.

Dividends are paid annually in July at the rate of 6 per cent.

In the fiscal year ending June 30, 1902, the gross earnings were $235,172; net, $46,738; interest charges, $15,057; dividends, $31,330: surplus, $451.

President, S. Reed Anthony, Boston; Secretary, D. A. Taggart, Manchester, N. H.; Treasurer, P. L. Saltonstall, Boston.

Directors—S. Reed Anthony, P. L. Saltonstall, Boston; D. A. Taggart, J. Brodie Smith, Walter M. Parker, Manchester, N. H.

Corporate office, Manchester, N. H.; main office, 53 State street, Boston. Annual meeting, third Wednesday in September, at Manchester, N. H.

## MANCHESTER TRACTION, LIGHT & POWER CO.

A corporation formed under the laws of New Hampshire in 1885, at which time the corporate title was the American Typographic Co. On March 5, 1895, the name was changed to the American Manufacturing Co. and on February 13, 1901, the name was again changed to the present style. The objects of the corporation are indicated by its title. The company owns water plants at Garvin's Falls, Hooksett Falls, Kelly's Falls and Gregg's Falls; all in or near Manchester, N. H. The company owns all the capital stock of the Manchester Street Railway, which operates about 35 miles of street railway by electric power. On March 16, 1901, the company acquired by purchase the following properties:

| | |
|---|---|
| The Manchester Electric Co. | The Garvin Falls Power Co. |
| The Union Electric Co. | Merrimack Electric Light, Heat & Power Co. |

Stock......Par $100.......................Authorized, $5,000,000......Issued, $1,650,000

The company has no preferred stock. The first semi-annual dividend of 3 per cent. was paid July 15, 1901.

Transfer office, 53 State street, Boston. Registrar, American Loan & Trust Co., Boston.

FUNDED DEBT.

1st mort., 5 per cent., due 1921, April and Oct.................................... $1,013,000

The amount of bonds authorized is $2,000,000. Of this, $650,000 are held to retire $150,000 of the Union Electric Co.'s 6 per cent. bonds, which will be called in 1903, $250,000 Manchester Electric Liquid Co.'s bonds and $250,000 for Manchester Street Railway 5 per cent. bonds, to be called in 1905.

The trustee of the mortgage and agent for payment of interest is American Loan & Trust Co., Boston.

President, William A. Tucker, Boston; Secretary, D. A. Taggart, Manchester, N. H.; Treasurer, S. Reed Anthony, Boston.

Directors—William A. Tucker, George H. Hood, S. Reed Anthony, Robert H. Hallowell, Stillman F. Kelley, Boston; Charles M. Floyd, Walter M. Parker, G. Byron Chandler, Roger G. Sullivan, Harry E. Parker, J. Brodie Smith, Manchester, N. H.; Billings P. Learned, New London, Conn.

Main office, 46 Hanover street, Manchester, N. H. Annual meeting, third Wednesday in September, at Manchester, N. H.

## THE MANHATTAN BEACH HOTEL & LAND CO., LIMITED

A corporation formed under the laws of New York, as successor to the Manhattan Beach Improvement Co., Limited, whose property was foreclosed and sold in 1890. The company owns the real estate known as Manhattan Beach, with 416 acres of land, the Oriental and Manhattan Beach Hotels and other improvements.

Stock...Par $100...Authorized { com., $1,500,000 / pref., 500,000 } Issued { com., $1,500,000 / pref., 500,000 } $2,000,000

The preferred stock is 5 per cent., non-cumulative. Stock is transferred at the company's office.

FUNDED DEBT.

| | |
|---|---|
| Gen. mort., 4 per cent., due Nov., 1940, May and Nov. | $1,500,000 |
| Funded coupon scrip, due May, 1904 | 224,700 |
| Total | $1,724,700 |

The coupon scrip was issued in 1894 to fund the interest on the general mortgage 4s for four years.

President, George S. Edgell; Vice-President, Austin Corbin; Secretary, Daniel S. Voorhees; Treasurer, William G. Bosworth.

Directors—Austin Corbin, William G. Bosworth, William J. Kelly, James K. O. Sherwood, George S. Edgell, Daniel S. Voorhees, James G. K. Duer, Charles M. Reynolds, David S. Rogers, Frederick Cook, William F. Brown, R. H. Webber, M. A. Smith.

Main office, 192 Broadway, New York.

## MANHATTAN RAILWAY CO.

(Leased to Interborough Rapid Transit Co.)

A corporation formed November 24, 1875. Road owned, 37¾ miles of double-track elevated road in Manhattan and Bronx Boroughs, New York City. In 1901-02 the road was being equipped with electric power. Locomotives, 292; passenger cars, 1,290; service cars, 41.

By a merger agreement, which was ratified August 1, 1884, new stock was issued for the $13,000,000 of Manhattan stock then outstanding, and $6,500,000 each of Metropolitan and New York Elevated stocks, on the basis of 85 for Manhattan, 120 for New York and 110 for Metropolitan. The present company assumed all liabilities and obligations of the consolidated lines.

In December, 1902, it was decided to lease this road to the Interborough Rapid Transit Co. for 999 years from April 1, 1903. The rental to be 6 per cent. per annum on the stock from April 1, 1903, until January 1, 1906, with 1 per cent. extra if it is earned. After the latter date it shall be 7 per cent. on the stock of the leased road.

Stock......Par $100......................Authorized, $60,000,000......Issued, $55,200,000

Stock is transferred at the office of the company. Registrar, Mercantile Trust Co., New York.

The stock of the company was $48,000,000 authorized, of which $47,999,700 was outstanding. Prior to the lease to the Interborough Rapid Transit Co., the stock was increased to $60,000,000, and $7,200,000 of the same was offered to the stockholders at par, being 15 per cent. of their original holdings. It is provided under the lease that the remaining $4,800,000 of stock may be issued after Jan., 1906, the proceeds to be applied to improvements.

Dividends on the stock are quarterly in January, April, July and October. The January, 1903, dividend was increased from 1 per cent. to 1½ per cent. The April, 1903, dividend was increased to 1¾ per cent. for the quarter with an extra dividend of 1 per cent. out of the surplus revenue of 9 months of the current fiscal year. See above concerning dividends guaranteed under the lease.

FUNDED DEBT.

| | |
|---|---|
| Metropolitan Elevated, 1st mort., 6 per cent., due July, 1908, Jan. and July | $10,818,000 |
| New York Elevated debentures, 5 per cent., due March, 1916, March and Sept. | 1,000,000 |
| Manhattan Railway consol. mort., 4 per cent., due April, 1990, April and Oct. | 28,065,000 |
| Total | $39,883,000 |

The Manhattan Railway consolidated mortgage is for $40,000,000. It was authorized to retire previous issues and provide for extensions. In 1891 $4,000,000 new stock was issued for the acquisition of the Suburban Rapid Transit line.

See below for dividends on the stock of the company. Dividends are paid quarterly, January (1), April, July and October.

On February 1, 1899, it was decided that the motive power of the system should be changed, and $18,000,000 new stock was authorized to meet the expenses of the change of power. Stockholders were offered the privilege of subecribing for the additional stock at par to the extent of 60 per cent. of their holdings.

EARNINGS.

Year ending June 30.

| | Dividends Paid. | Passengers Carried. | Gross. | Net. | Surplus Over Dividends. |
|---|---|---|---|---|---|
| 1892-93 | 6 | 221,407,197 | $11,226,359 | $2,971,292 | $1,171,292 |
| 1893-94 | 6 | 202,751,532 | 10,465,254 | 2,332,647 | 532,647 |
| 1894-95 | 6 | 187,614,985 | 9,684,706 | 1,522,048 | Def. 277,952 |
| 1895-96 | 6 | 184,703,636 | 9,489,454 | 1,118,097 | Def. 681,903 |
| 1896-97 | 5 | 182,964,851 | 9,344,019 | 1,334,651 | Def. 165,349 |
| 1897-98 | 4 | 183,360,846 | 9,395,258 | 1,423,276 | 223,276 |
| 1898-99 | 4 | 174,324,575 | 9,060,096 | 1,120,512 | Def. 259,488 |
| 1899-00 | 4 | 184,164,110 | 9,969,901 | 2,029,516 | 109,516 |
| 1900-01 | 4 | 190,045,741 | 10,253,271 | 2,322,335 | 402,335 |
| 1901-02 | 4 | 215,259,345 | 11,291,711 | 3,073,455 | 1,153,455 |

Gross includes miscellaneous receipts. Net is after deducting interest on bonds.

President, George J. Gould; Vice-President, Alfred Skitt; Secretary and Treasurer, D. W. McWilliams, New York.

Directors—Russell Sage, R. M. Gallaway, Edwin Gould, George J. Gould, Samuel Sloan, G. P. Morosini, Donald Mackay, Howard Gould, Thomas T. Eckert, James H. Hyde, John T. Terry, Alfred Skitt, New York; Eugene N. Foss, Boston.

Main office, 195 Broadway, New York. Annual meeting, second Wednesday in November.

## MANHATTAN STEAMSHIP CO.

A corporation formed under the laws of Delaware in January, 1901. The object of the company was the establishment of lines of steamers to run between New York and Portland; New York, Rockland, Me., and Bangor, Me.; New York, Eastport, Me., and St. John, N. B.; also between New York, Yarmouth and Halifax, N. S. The company has a fleet of six steamships operating on its lines.

Stock.....Par $100.....Authorized { com., $600,000 / pref., 600,000 } Issued { com., $600,000 / pref., 600,000 } $1,200,000

The preferred participating stock is 7 per cent., non-cumulative. After 5 per cent. shall have been paid on the common out of the surplus earnings of any year, the preferred and common share equally in any further division of profits.

The company has no funded debt.

President and General Manager, (Vacancy); Vice-President, George E. Green, Binghamton, N. Y.; Secretary and Assistant Treasurer, Ernst Smith, New York.

Directors—George E. Green, Charles V. Fornes, Ernst Smith, William McKenzie, Richard Morrell, E. R. Bellman, Charles DeHart Brower, Henry McLaughlin, William Pugsley, Walter J. Dunham, Charles S. Hinchman, F. M. Black, William F. Kimber, G. G. Jackson, F. H. Newcomb, Joseph H. Wright.

Main office, 11 Broadway, New York. Annual meeting, first Wednesday in February.

## MANHATTAN TRANSIT CO.

A corporation formed under the laws of New York, May 14, 1902. The company was organized in pursuance of a plan to reorganize the General Carriage Co. A full statement of the latter company is in the MANUAL for 1902.

The company has general powers for manufacturing, operating or dealing in vehicles of all kinds for transporting passengers or freight. It acquired all the stock of the General Carriage Co. and the latter in July, 1902, was merged with this company. The General Carriage Co. was a New York corporation formed in May, 1899, and had under its charter extensive powers in regard to the business of transportation in New York City.

The company acquired the plant and vehicles, about 150 in number, of the General Carriage Co., used in conducting a cab and carriage service in New York City, and now operates the same. It also owns the exclusive rights for the State of New York for the Diesel Engine.

In 1902 the company acquired the franchise of the New York & Brooklyn Tunnel Railroad Co., which has certain rights to construct a tunnel line from Park Row, New York, to the City Hall in Brooklyn. The present company has secured real estate in both New York and Brooklyn for the terminals of the proposed line.

See below for details as to the reorganization of the General Carriage Co.

Stock......Par $20. ........................Authorized, $10,000,000......Issued, $6,000,000

The company has no preferred stock.

FUNDED DEBT.

1st mort., 4 per cent., due 1952 ........ $600,000

The authorized amount of the 1st mortgage is $900,000, of which $300,000 was to be applicable to the retirement of an existing mortgage of $275,000 on the company's real estate at Second avenue and Forty-seventh street, New York.

The General Carriage Co. had $20,000,000 stock, all common, par value $100 per share. In August, 1901, Receivers were appointed for the company and efforts to effect a reorganization at first proved impracticable. In May, 1902, a plan was submitted which was accepted by practically all the old stockholders. The stock of the old company was under the plan exchanged for 10 per cent. of its face of the new stock, an assessment of $2 per share being paid on the old stock. The Atlantic Trust Co. was the depository under the plan, which also involved the providing of $400,000 cash for the new company's general purposes.

President, C. S. Drummond, London; Chairman, William G. Arkell; Secretary, F. W. Curtis, New York; Treasurer, R. G. Macdonald.

Directors—William J. Arkell, W. K. Gillette, Walter H. Knight, James S. Brady, Harold Walker, Walter G. A. Hemming, New York; Patrick H. McCarren, Brooklyn, N. Y.; Lord Kintore, Lord Gray, Sir Charles-Rivers Wilson, C. S. Drummond, London, England.

Main office, 74 Broadway.

## MANUFACTURED RUBBER CO.

A corporation organized under the laws of New Jersey, May 11, 1899. The company owns a patented process for the manufacture of a material resembling pure rubber and which is adapted to all the uses of rubber and other rubber substitutes. The company has a plant at Metuchen, N. J., with a daily capacity of about 5,000 pounds of rubber substitute.

Stock......Par $10......Authorized { com., $1,000,000; pref., 200,000 } Issued { com., $600,000; pref., 200,000 } $800,000

The preferred stock is 6 per cent., non-cumulative.

Stock is transferred at the company's office, Philadelphia. Registrar, Provident Life & Trust Co., Philadelphia.

The company had originally $5,000,000 of full-paid common stock, par $50, and $1,000,000 of 8 per cent. cumulative preferred on which $10 per share had been paid. In September, 1902, it was decided to reduce the par value of the stock to $10 and to exchange the outstanding shares for $600,000 of new common and $200,000 of new preferred, an assessment of $1 per share being levied on the preferred.

President, William W. Gibbs; Secretary and Treasurer, Clayton E. Platt.

Directors—William W. Gibbs, J. Appleton, C. E. Platt, C. W. Sloan, John S. Arndt, Robert B. Baird.

Corporate office, Camden, N. J.; main office, 428 Chestnut street, Philadelphia. Annual meeting, second Wednesday in May.

## THE MANUFACTURERS LIGHT & HEAT CO.

A corporation formed under the laws of Pennsylvania, November 28, 1899, being a consolidation of the Manufacturers Natural Gas Co., the Bellevue & Glenfield Natural Gas Co. and the Peoples Light & Heat Co. The business of the company is the production and supplying of natural gas in Pittsburg, Washington, Pa.; Waynesburg, Pa.; Canonsburg, Pa.; Bellevue, Pa.; Ben Avon, Pa.; Glenfield, Pa.; Coraopolis, Pa., and Castle Shannon, Pa. During the year 1902, this company purchased the entire capital stock of the Waynesburg Natural Gas Co. and the Citizens' Natural Gas Co., of Waynesburg, Pa., and the Tri-State Gas Company, of Pittsburg.

Stock......Par $50........Authorized, $10,000,000......Issued, $6,421,900

The company has no preferred stock. Stock is transferred at the company's office. Registrar, Mercantile Trust Co., Pittsburg.

FUNDED DEBT.

1st mort., 6 per cent., due 1915, Jan. and July........ $597,000

The authorized amount of the 1st mortgage bonds is $750,000. Trustee of the mortgage, Union Trust Co., Pittsburg. Interest on the bonds is also payable at the same institution. Commencing January 1, 1901, $50,000 of the bonds are to be annually retired.

The company paid an initial dividend of two-fifths of 1 per cent. for the month of December, 1899, and after January, 1900, paid regular quarterly dividends at the rate of 6 per cent. per annum, the dividends being 1½ per cent. each, in January, April, July and October. The April and July, 1902, dividends were 2 per cent. each, and that paid in January, 1903, was increased to 2½ per cent.

President, Henry B. Beatty; 1st Vice-President, O. H. Strong; 2d Vice-President, L. A. Meyran; Treasurer, E. H. Myers; Secretary, Henry E. Seibert, Pittsburg.

Directors—O. H. Strong, E. V. Selden, Henry I. Beers, H. M. Nichols, Fred N. Chambers, Oil City, Pa.; Henry B. Beatty, L. A. Meyran, E. H. Myers, George W. Crawford, Pittsburg; David Iseman, Washington, Pa.

Main office, Farmers' Bank Building, Pittsburg; branch offices: Washington, Pa.; Canonsburg, Pa.; Bellevue, Pa.; Waynesburg, Pa.; Coraopolis, Pa. Annual meeting, fourth Wednesday in January, at Pittsburg.

## MANVILLE CO.

A corporation formed under the laws of New Jersey in June, 1901, to manufacture plain and fancy cotton fabrics. The company is a consolidation of the former Manville Co. operating two mills at Manville, R. I., and the Social Manufacturing Co. operating three mills at Woonsocket, R. I. The united plant contains about 230,000 spindles and about 8,000 looms.

Stock....Par $100.....Authorized { com., $4,000,000; pref., 2,000,000 } Issued { com., $4,000,000; pref., 2,000,000 } $6,000,000

The preferred stock is 6 per cent., cumulative. Dividends are payable quarterly, January, April, July and October.

Transfer Agents, Corporation Trust Co., Jersey City.

The company has no funded debt.

President, Eben S. Draper; Treasurer, Charles H. Merriman; General Manager, Henry F. Lippitt.

Corporate office, 15 Exchange place, Jersey City; main office, Market square, Providence, R. I. Annual meeting, first Wednesday in June, at Jersey City.

## MARCONI WIRELESS TELEGRAPH CO. OF AMERICA

A corporation formed under the laws of New Jersey in 1899 to do a general telegraph business and to develop and work the wireless or space system of telegraphy under the patents and inventions of Guglielmo Marconi. The company has acquired all the patents and inventions heretofore taken out or hereafter to be taken out by Signor Marconi for the United States, and also other patents, especially that of Prof. Pupin relating to selective wireless telegraphy.

Stock......Par $100........................Authorized, $6,650,000........Issued, $6,150,000

The company has no preferred stock and no funded debt.

Transfer Agent, Morton Trust Co., New York. Registrar, Continental Trust Co., New York.

Chairman Executive Committee, William H. Bentley; 1st Vice-President, Guglielmo Marconi; 2d Vice-President, Wyllys R. Betts; Secretary and Treasurer, John Bottomley, New York.

Directors—Guglielmo Marconi, London, England; Wyllys R. Betts, William H. Bentley, John W. Griggs, Robert Goodbody, J. D. J. Kelley, Eugene H. Lewis, H. H. McClure, John J. McCook, E. Rollins Morse, Cyrus S. Sedgwick, Loyal L. Smith, Spencer Trask, New York; Samuel Insull, Chicago.

Corporate and main office, Jersey City; New York office, 8 Bridge street. Annual meeting in April, at Jersey City.

## THE MARCONI WIRELESS TELEGRAPH CO. OF CANADA, LIMITED

A corporation formed under the laws of Canada, November 1, 1902, to operate the Marconi system of wireless telegraphy.

Stock......Par $5..........................Authorized, $5,000,000......Issued, $5,000,000

The company has no preferred stock and no funded debt.

Transfer Agents, Montreal Trust & Deposit Co., Montreal, and Security Transfer & Registrar Co., New York. Registrars, The National Trust Co., Montreal, and Knickerbocker Trust Co., New York.

President, F. C. Henshaw; Vice-President, Guglielmo Marconi; General Manager, John D. Oppe; Secretary, Beaumont Shepard.

Directors—F. C. Henshaw, Andrew A. Allen, Rudolph Forget, Willard R. Green, Guglielmo Marconi, John D. Oppe.

Corporate and main office, 1724 Notre Dame street, Montreal. Annual meeting in February, at Toronto.

## MARKEEN COPPER CO.

A corporation formed under the laws of West Virginia in 1899. The company has a valuable copper mining property in Greenlee Gold Mountain Mining District, Graham County, Arizona.

Stock......Par $10..........................Authorized, $1,000,000......Issued, $1,000,000

The stock is full-paid and non-assessable. Stock is transferred at the company's office, New York. Registrar, United States Mortgage and Trust Co., New York.

Leading expert authorities have pronounced the property of this company as presenting a prospect of making a lasting dividend paying copper mine.

President and Treasurer, Thomas A. Lee; Vice-President, Alfred P. Stevenson; Secretary, Thomas E. Warman; General Manager, Leopold Balbach.

Directors—Thomas A. Lee, Charles R. Hedden, Leopold Balbach, James H. Lee, George W. Brown, Alfred P. Stevenson, Thomas E. Warman.

Operating office and mines, Clifton, Ariz.; New York office, 66 Broadway.

## THE MARSDEN CO.

A corporation organized under the laws of New Jersey, February 13, 1897. This company manufactures a variety of products from the cornstalk, such as cellulose for the protection of battleships, for smokeless powder, dynamite, pyroxyline varnish, etc. The fibrous portion of the stalk, together with the leaves and husks, is used for stock feeding; the outer shell, or shives, for the manufacture of paper, etc. The pith, owing to its marked obturative qualities, excludes water from a vessel whose armor has been pierced. The company's plants are located in Illinois, Indiana and Kentucky, eight in all, while various other locations are in contemplation. In 1897 the company acquired the Marsden Development Co. and the Cellulose Co., the former concern being the original owner of the Marsden patents and inventions. In 1899 acquired a controlling interest in the International Smokeless Powder & Dynamite Co., which manufactures smokeless powder and other materials, and has works at Parlin, N. J. In 1901 acquired the American Milling Co., Riverdale, near Chicago.

Stock....Par $100...Authorized { com., $35,000,000 / pref., 15,000,000 } Issued { com., $33,962,200 / pref., 1,547,000 } $35,509,200

Stock is transferred at the company's offices. Registrar, Provident Life & Trust Co., Philadelphia.

The preferred stock is 6 per cent., cumulative. The preferred stock was issued only for cash. Of the common stock outstanding $16,462,200 was issued as a bonus with subscriptions to the preferred; $17,500,000 of the common has been placed in trust by the stockholders.

The report for 1899 showed receipts, $327,124; cash on hand at beginning of year and accounts receivable, $368,753; expenditures, $355,542; balance, $340,335. In 1900 receipts, $385,342; expenditures, $204,898; total surplus, $557,879. The report for 1901 gave no statement of the company's earnings. In 1902 the gross sales were $319,706; profits, $126,381; net profits, $83,841.

President, Edwin G. Buckner; Vice-President, A. G. Winter; Secretary and Treasurer, William E. Steen.

Directors—W. W. Gibbs, George Philler, George S. Graham, Joseph F. Sinnott, Edward C. Lee, J. D. Beacom, Edwin G. Buckner, A. G. Winter, H. C. Watts, George P. Brock.

Executive office, 428 Chestnut street, Philadelphia.

## MARYLAND COAL CO.

A Maryland corporation owning and operating a large bituminous coal property at Lonaconing, Allegany Co., Md. It has an interest in the George's Creek & Cumberland Railroad Co.

Stock......Par $100..........................Authorized, $2,000,000......Issued, $1,885,005

The stock was formerly $4,400,000, but was reduced to $2,000,000, preferred, in 1893. There is $11,100 of the old common still outstanding, and $103,895 of the new preferred in the company's treasury, making up the full $2,000,000 of the new preferred authorized.

Stock is transferred at the company's office, 1 Broadway, New York.

Dividend payments have been as follows: In 1895, 4½ per cent.; in 1896, 3½ per cent.; in 1897, 4 per cent.; in 1898, 4½ per cent.; in 1899, 5 per cent.; in 1900, 5 per cent.; in 1901, 5½ per cent., and in 1902, 7 per cent., including 2½ per cent. July 1, 1902, and 2½ per cent., with 2 per cent. extra, December 31, 1902.

The company's bond issue was paid off and retired in 1900.

The company's coal production in recent years is as follows: In 1896, 359,62 tons; in 1897, 371,233 tons; in 1898, 383,878 tons; in 1899, 480,856 tons; in 1900, 321,558; in 1901, 405,304 tons; in 1902, 373,[illegible] tons.

Surplus earnings over charges have been, in 1898, $112,851; in 1899, $157,248; in 1900, $140,335; in 1901, $150,010; in 1902, $156,874.

President, John E. Knapp; Vice-President, George Hewlett; Secretary and Treasurer Henry B. Nedham, New York.

Dividends from 6 to 10 per cent. annually have been paid. Stock is transferred at the office of the company.

FUNDED DEBT.

1st mort., 5 per cent. bonds, due 1930 .......................................... $1,000,000

The bonds are the full amount authorized. Trustee of the mortgage, Northern Trust Co., Chicago.

President, Samuel T. Carnes; Vice-President, S. H. Brooks; Secretary and Treasurer, Richard H. Allen, Memphis, Tenn.

Directors—Samuel T. Carnes, S. H. Brooks, C. W. Heiskell, Heber Jones, Frank G. Jones, Henry Duffin, Memphis, Tenn.

Main office, 300 Second street, Memphis, Tenn. Annual meeting, third Tuesday in August.

## MERCHANTS' COTTON CO.

A corporation formed under the laws of the Dominion of Canada in 1881, for the purpose of manufacturing cotton cloth. The company owns mills with an equipment of 110,000 spindles and 2,500 looms, employing upwards of 2,000 hands.

Stock......Par $100.......................... .Authorized, $2,000,000......Issued, $1,500,000

The company has no preferred stock.

FUNDED DEBT.

| | |
|---|---|
| 1st mort., 4½ per cent. bonds, due 1909, .......................................... | $400,000 |
| 1st mort., 4½ per cent. bonds, due 1911, .......................................... | 250,000 |
| Total.......................................................................... | $650,000 |

President, James Crathern; Vice-President, W. G. Cheney; Secretary-Treasurer, W. S. Barker.

Directors—A. A. Ayer, James Crathern, R. B. Angus, J. P. Cleghorn, Robert Mackay, Jonathan Hodgson, W. G. Chenay.

Main office, 4 St. Sacrament street, Montreal.

## MERGENTHALER LINOTYPE CO.

A corporation formed under the laws of New York, December 16, 1895. The company is successor to the Mergenthaler Linotype Co. of New Jersey, which had a capital of $5,000,000, and which was a consolidation of several smaller companies. The company owns the patents covering the linotype machine, which does away with the ordinary printer's type and with the old processes of composition and distribution in printing. These machines are now in general use throughout this country. The most important of the patents have some eight to ten years to run. Company has a large factory in Brooklyn, N. Y., for the manufacture of the machines, and both sells and leases them to printers and newspapers, some 967 being leased in this manner. The number of offices where the machines were in use in the United States was 1,721 in October, 1902.

The company sells "Standard" machines at from $3,000 to $3,600 each, and leases them at from $500 to $600 per annum each. It has a large additional business in supplying machine parts and sundries. In 1898 introduced with success a style of machine designed for book composition, and in 1902 a "Junior" machine (price, $1,500) for use in country newspaper offices.

Stock......Par $100........................Authorized, $10,000,000......Issued, $10,000,000

Stock is transferred at the company's office. Registrar, Metropolitan Trust Co., New York

The company has no funded debt.

The following is the company's balance sheet, October 1, 1902:

| ASSETS. | | LIABILITIES. | |
|---|---|---|---|
| Cash.......................... | $863,618 | Capital stock.................... | $10,000,000 |
| Customers' notes received........ | 1,377,606 | Creditors' open accounts......... | 14,100 |
| Open accounts.................. | 264,722 | Dividends unpaid................ | 356 |
| Raw materials, etc....... ...... | 840,539 | Surplus ......................... | 1,619,494 |
| Plant, etc...................... | 978,940 | | |
| Rogers department.............. | 6,700 | | |
| Linotypes ...................... | 1,003,800 | | |
| Office fixtures and furniture...... | 16,889 | | |
| Linotype Co. (Canada) investment | 78,247 | | |
| Rights, privileges, franchises, patents and inventions......... .... | 6,201,580 | | |
| Miscellaneous. ................. | 1,309 | | |
| Total.................... | $11,633,950 | Total.................... | $11,633,950 |

From 1894 to December, 1900, inclusive, the company and its predecessor paid in dividends on the stock $9,865,000. Dividends are paid quarterly, March, June, September and December. In 1897 paid 16¼ per cent., in 1898, 1899 and 1900, 20 per cent., being 10 per cent. regular and 10 per cent. extra. The quarterly dividends were 2½ per cent. regular and 2½ extra each quarter from July, 1897, until December, 1900, inclusive. In 1901 the dividends were 2½ per cent. regular quarterly, and an extra dividend of 3½ per cent. in December. In 1902 15 per cent. was paid, including 5 per cent. extra in December.

President, Philip T. Dodge; Vice-President, Ogden Mills; Secretary and Treasurer, Frederick J. Warburton.

Directors—D. O. Mills, Ogden Mills, Philip T. Dodge, Whitelaw Reid, George L. Bradley, James O. Clephane, Andrew Devine, E. V. Murphy, Robert I. Gammell.

Main office, 154 Nassau street, New York.

## MERIDEN ELECTRIC RAILROAD CO.

A corporation formed under the laws of Connecticut, August 14, 1886, as the Meriden Horse Railroad Co., reorganized and name changed in 1893. The company owns and operates 19.5 miles of road in Meriden, Conn., Wallingford, Conn., and neighboring towns. A controlling interest in the stock of the company has been acquired by the New York, New Haven & Hartford Railroad Co.

Stock......Par $100..........................Authorized, $1,000,000......Issued, $1,000,000

The company has no preferred stock. Stock is transferred at the office of the company. Registrar, John M. Hall, New Haven, Conn.

FUNDED DEBT.

| | |
|---|---|
| Consolidated 1st mort., 5 per cent. bonds, due 1911, Jan. and July.................... | $415,000 |
| Meriden Horse Railroad Co., 1st mort., 5 per cent. bonds, due 1924, April and Oct..... | 85,000 |
| Total........................................................ | $500,000 |

The authorized issue of Meriden Electric Co. bonds is $500,000 and of the Meriden Horse Railroad Co.'s bonds $100,000. Of the Electric Co.'s bonds, $85,000 are held to retire the bond issue of the Horse Railroad Company.

Trustee of both bond issues and agent for the payment of interest, Girard Trust Co., Philadelphia.

EARNINGS.

Year ending June 30.

| | Gross. | Net. | Charges. | Surplus. |
|---|---|---|---|---|
| 1900-01.................................. | $133,153 | $49,667 | $25,508 | $24,159 |
| 1901-02.................................. | 139,283 | 50,026 | 29,139 | 21,887 |

President, Nathan H. Heft; Secretary and Treasurer, W. L. Squire, New Haven, Conn.

Directors—John L. Billard, John C. Bixbee, E. J. Doolittle, Charles L. Rockwell, Meriden, Conn.; John M. Hall, New Haven, Conn.; John W. Mix, Yalesville, Conn.; Nathan H. Heft, Bridgeport, Conn.

Main office, Meadow and Water streets, New Haven, Conn. Annual meeting, second Tuesday in October, at Meriden, Conn.

## MERRIMACK MANUFACTURING CO.

A company incorporated in Massachusetts in 1822. The purpose of the company is the manufacture, bleaching and printing of cotton cloths, corduroy and fancy white goods. The plant of the company at Lowell, Mass., comprises 170,000 spindles, 5,028 looms and 22 printing machines.

Stock......Par $100..........................Authorized, $2,750,000......Issued, $2,750,000

Stock is transferred at company's office, 53 State street, Boston.

The company has no funded debt.

Dividends at the rate of 6 per cent. per annum are paid on the stock, the payments in 1902 being 3 per cent. each, in February and July.

President, Arthur T. Lyman; Treasurer, Charles L. Lovering, Boston.

Main office, 53 State street, Boston. Annual meeting in October.

## METROPOLITAN SECURITIES CO.

A corporation formed under the laws of New York, February 14, 1902. The purpose of the company was to acquire, own or sell the securities of other companies. It owns all the stock of the Interurban Street Railway Co. so far as issued, to which company the Metropolitan Street Railway Co. is leased for 999 years from February 14, 1902. See statement of the latter company.

Stock......Par $100......................Authorized, $30,000,000......Issued, $30,000,000

Up to January, 1903, the entire stock had been subscribed, and there had been paid in on the stock $25 per share.

The plan for the formation of this company provided that the property of the Metropolitan Street Railway should be leased to the Interurban Street Railway, the latter to assume the fixed charges of the Metropolitan Street Railway Co. and guarantee dividends of 7 per cent. per annum on the entire amount of the capital stock. The stockholders of the Metropolitan Street Railway Co. were given the right to buy $25,400,000 of the stock of the Metropolitan Securities Co. at par. This company agreed to pay $23,000,000 cash into the treasury of the Interurban Rapid Transit Co., receiving in return stock of the Interurban Street Railway Co. at par and debentures bearing interest at a rate not exceeding 4 per cent. per annum.

President, Herbert H. Vreeland; Secretary, Edward W. Sayre, New York.

Directors—Herbert H. Vreeland, William H. Baldwin, Jr., Edward J. Berwind, Paul D. Cravath, Thomas P. Fowler, George G. Haven, James H. Hyde, Augustus D. Juilliard, Richard W. Meade, Thomas F. Ryan, Edward W. Sayre, Mortimer L. Schiff, New York.

Main office, 32 Liberty street, New York.

---

## METROPOLITAN STREET RAILWAY CO.

### KANSAS CITY.

A corporation formed under the laws of Missouri, July 19, 1886. The company acquired control of the most important street car lines in Kansas City, including the Kansas City Elevated Railway Co. The other controlled lines are the Kansas City & Independence Railway Co., Kansas City & Rosedale Street Railway Co., Corrigan Consolidated Street Railway, Kansas City Traction Co., West Side Railway Co., South Suburban Railway Co., Kansas City Cable Railway Co., Grand Avenue Railway Co., Central Electric Railway Co. and East Side Electric Railway Co. The company operates electric and cable roads, aggregating 179.24 miles. It owns electric and cable power plants, 382 motor cars, 132 grip cars, 79 cable cars and 224 trail cars. In 1902 it received further extensive franchises from the city covering practically all unoccupied streets, in consideration for which 8 per cent. of the gross earnings shall be set aside and after paying all taxes therefrom the balance shall go to the city.

Stock......Par $100........................Authorized, $8,500,000......Issued, $5,636,800

Dividends on the stock are paid at the rate of 5 per cent. per annum, the payments being quarterly, 1¼ per cent. each, in February, May, August and November.

FUNDED DEBT.

| | |
|---|---|
| Cons. mort., 5 per cent. gold, due May, 1910, May and Nov........................ | $4,244,000 |
| Gen. mort., 5 per cent. gold, due Sept., 1909, March and Sept..................... | 1,000,000 |
| Convertible ten-year notes, 5 per cent. gold, due Jan., 1911, Jan. and July.......... | 2,800,000 |
| Grand Avenue Railway 1st mort., 5 per cent. gold, due July, 1908, Jan. and July.... | 1,200,000 |
| Kansas City Cable Ry. 1st mort., 5 per cent. gold, due April, 1911, April and Oct... | 1,350,000 |
| Kansas City El. Ry. 1st pref. mort., 6 per cent. gold, due July, 1922, Jan. and July. | 600,000 |
| " " " 1st mort., 4 per cent. gold, due July, 1922, Jan. and July... | 2,000,000 |
| Corrigan Street Railway 1st mort, 5 per cent. gold, due July, 1916, Jan. and July... | 706,000 |
| Central Electric Ry. Co. 1st mort., 5 per cent. gold, due May, 1914, May and Nov.... | 2,000,000 |
| East Side Electric Ry. Co. 1st mort., 5 per cent. gold, due July, 1911, Jan. and July.. | 250,000 |
| Park Connecting Railway Co. 1st mort., 6 per cent. gold, due 1908, Feb. and Aug... | 30,000 |
| Total ............................................................ | $16,180,000 |

The authorized consolidated mortgage is $8,500,000, of which $4,256,000 are held to retire the general mortgage, the Corrigan Consolidated Street Railway Co.'s mortgage, the Kansas City Cable Railway Co.'s mortgage and the Grand Avenue Railway Co.'s mortgage. Trustee of the mortgage and agent for the payment of interest, Old Colony Trust Co., Boston. The outstanding bonds of the general mortgage are the full amount authorized. Trustee of the mortgage and agent for the payment of interest, New England Trust Co., Boston. The convertible notes are subject to redemption at the option of the company, or to exchange by holders after January 1, 1903, for the capital stock of the company. Interest is payable at the office of Blair & Co., New York.

The authorized mortgage of the Central Electric Railway Co. is $2,500,000. The outstanding bonds of each of the other constituent companies are severally the full amounts authorized. Trustee of the mortgage of the Kansas City Elevated Railway Co. and agent for the payment of interest, Manhattan Trust Co. Trustee of the mortgage of the Grand Avenue Railway Co. and agent for the payment of interest, Central Trust Co., New York, which also is agent for the payment of the interest on the mortgage bonds of the Corrigan Consolidated Street Railway Co. Interest on the bonds of the Kansas City Railway Co. is payable at the office of Blair & Co., New York. Trustee of the mortgages of the Central Electric Railway Co. and the East Side Electric Railway Co. and agent for the payment of interest, Colonial Trust Co., New York. Interest on the Park Connecting Railway Co.'s bonds is payable at the New England National Bank, Kansas City, Mo.

EARNINGS.

Year ending May 31.

| | Gross. | Net. | Charges. | Surplus. |
|---|---|---|---|---|
| 1895-96 | $1,780,940 | $747,898 | $484,227 | $263,670 |
| 1896-97 | 1,774,892 | 771,206 | 518,047 | 253,159 |
| 1897-98 | 1,942,852 | 853,869 | 616,556 | 162,521 |
| 1898-99 | 2,070,228 | 955,859 | 586,709 | 369,150 |
| 1899-00 | 2,353,267 | ...... | ...... | ...... |
| 1900-01 | 2,666,595 | ...... | ...... | ...... |
| 1901-02 | 2,910,531 | ...... | ...... | ...... |

Surplus over dividends: in 1896-97, 2½ per cent., $6,554; in 1897-98, 2 per cent., $50,785; in 1898-99, 3½ per cent., $173,612. Full reports have not been issued for subsequent years.

Chairman, P. Anderson Valentine, Chicago; President, Bernard Corrigan; Vice-President, L. E. James; Secretary and Treasurer, Walter E. Kirkpatrick.

Directors—P. Anderson Valentine, W. H. Holmes, L. E. James, Wallace Pratt, C. W. Armour, James A. Blair, Norman B. Ream, J. H. Loose.

Main office, 1500 Grand avenue, Kansas City, Mo. Annual meeting, third Tuesday in May.

## METROPOLITAN STREET RAILWAY CO.

### NEW YORK.

A corporation formed under the laws of New York, November 12, 1893.

See above in regard to the Metropolitan Securities Co., and the lease of this company to the Interurban Street Railway Co., which was made in April, 1902, the terms of the lease including the guarantee of 7 per cent. per annum in this company's stock.

The Metropolitan Street Railway Co. controls all the important street railway lines in New York City. An organization known as the Metropolitan Traction Co. was formed in 1891 under the laws of New Jersey to carry out the purchase of the Broadway Surface Railway Co. In September, 1892, the Metropolitan Traction Co. reorganized under the New York law. The Metropolitan Street Railway Co. was chartered in 1893 to operate the roads, and all of its stock was owned by the Metropolitan Traction Co. In 1896 the stock of the Metropolitan Street Railway Co. was increased from $16,500,000 to $30,000,000, and in October, 1897, it was exchanged for the stock of the Metropolitan Traction Co., thus winding up the latter. At the same time the Metropolitan Street Railway Co. purchased the remaining assets of the Traction Co., and paid for the same by an issue of $6,000,000 debenture certificates. These debentures were distributed to the stockholders of the Traction Co. at the time of its dissolution.

In 1898 the Metropolitan Street Railway Co. increased its capital stock to $45,000,000. Out of the increase of $15,000,000 the stockholders were allotted $10,000,000 at par, and of the proceeds $6,000,000 were used to retire the 5 per cent. debentures, the issue being called for payment October 15, 1898. $4,000,000 of the proceeds of stock allotment were devoted to changing the power on various lines to electricity, and the remaining $5,000,000 of stock was sold to stockholders at par in August, 1899. In May, 1900, the stock was increased from $45,000,000 to $52,000,000. In December, 1900, the $7,000,000 additional stock was allotted to the stockholders at 160.

In May, 1900, the company leased the Third Avenue Railroad, and guaranteed its new issue of $50,000,000 4 per cent. bonds. For terms see the Third Avenue Co.'s statement.

The Metropolitan Street Railway Co. was a consolidation of four roads, all the stock of which belonged to the Metropolitan Traction Co., viz.: Broadway Railroad, South Ferry Railway, Houston, West Street & Pavonia Ferry Railroad, and Chambers Street & Grand Street Ferry Railroad Companies. In 1894 and 1895 it also formally absorbed the Columbus & Ninth Avenue Railroad, Metropolitan Crosstown Railway and the Lexington Avenue & Pavonia Ferry Railway Companies. The following companies, in which the Metropolitan Traction Co. had a controlling interest, were also leased to the Metropolitan Street Railway Co.: Broadway & Seventh Avenue Railroad, Sixth Avenue Railroad, Ninth Avenue Railroad, Twenty-third Street Railway (including its leased line, the Bleecker Street & Fulton Street Railroad), Forty-second Street & Grand Street Ferry Railroad, Central Park, North & East River Railroad (Belt Line). Control of the Eighth Avenue Co. was also acquired in November, 1895, and that road was leased to the Metropolitan Street Railway, and in 1896 the Fourth and Madison Avenue surface line of the New York & Harlem Railroad was leased. In 1897 the company acquired a controlling interest in the Central Crosstown Railway Co., including Christopher & Tenth Street, and in the Second Avenue companies, the Second Avenue being leased. The roads leased and controlled through ownership of part or all of their stocks include the Thirty-fourth Street Crosstown Railway, the Twenty-eighth & Twenty-Ninth Street Crosstown Railroad and the Fulton Street Railroad.

Total roads operated by Metropolitan Street Railway Co., 214 miles, of which 47 miles are owned, 149 miles leased and 17¾ miles operated by separate organizations.

Roads equipped with underground electric system, 106 miles; with horse-power, 88 miles. The underground electric system was tested on the Lenox Avenue extension of the Columbus & Ninth Avenue line, where it was installed in 1894. Having proved economical and effective, the same system was installed on the Fourth & Madison Avenue and Second Avenue roads, which were completed in 1897–98. In 1898–99 the Sixth and Eighth Avenue lines were also changed to electric power. In the same year work was begun on the conversion of the Broadway and other cable roads to the electric system, which was completed in 1901. In connection with these plans the company acquired a large water-front property on the East River at Ninety-sixth and Ninety-seventh streets, where it erected a large power station. Some of the lines of the company, particularly the crosstown lines, were equipped with air and electric storage motors, but in 1902, in pursuance of the lease to the Interurban Rapid Transit Co. and the Metropolitan Securities Co., plans were formulated for the electrical equipment of all the roads of the system.

Stock......Par $100..........................Authorized, $52,000,000....Issued, $52,000,000

Stock is transferred at the office of the company. Registrar, Guaranty Trust Co., New York.

Dividends have been as follows: On Metropolitan Traction stock, in 1891, 4 per cent.; in 1892, 3 per cent.; in 1893, none; in 1894, 5 per cent.; in 1895, 5 per cent.; in 1896, 5 per cent.; in 1897, 5 per cent. On Metropolitan Street Railway stock, in 1898, 5 per cent.; in December, 1898, the quarterly dividend, payable January 16, 1899, was increased from 1¼ to 1¾ per cent., putting the stock on a 7 per cent. basis. The dividends are paid quarterly, in January (15), April, July and October.

FUNDED DEBT.

| | |
|---|---|
| Met. St. Ry. col. trust mort., 5 per cent., due Feb., 1997, Feb. and Aug. | $12,500,000 |
| Met. St. Ry. refunding mort., 4 per cent., due April, 2002, April and Oct. | 12,780,000 |
| Broadway Surface R. R. 1st mort., 5 per cent., due 1924, Jan. and July | 1,500,000 |
| Broadway Surface R. R. 2d mort., 5 per cent., due 1905, Jan. and July | 1,000,000 |
| Met. Crosstown 1st mort., 5 per cent., due April, 1920, April and Oct. | 600,000 |
| Lex. Ave. & Pav. Ferry 1st mort., 5 per cent., due Sept., 1993, March and Sept. | 5,000,000 |
| Columbus & Ninth Ave. 1st mort., 5 per cent., due Sept., 1993, March and Sept | 3,000,000 |
| South Ferry R. R. 1st mort., 5 per cent., due April, 1919, April and Oct. | 350,000 |
| Real estate morts. | 950,000 |
| Total | $37,680,000 |

FUNDED DEBT—LEASED AND OPERATED LINES.

| | |
|---|---|
| Twenty-third Street Ry. 1st mort., 6 per cent., due Jan., 1909, Jan. and July | $200,000 |
| Twenty-third Street Ry. debentures, 5 per cent., due Jan., 1906, Jan. and July | 150,000 |
| Forty-second St. & Grand St. 1st mort., 6 per cent., due Jan., 1906, Jan. and July | 186,000 |
| Bleecker St. & Fulton Ferry 1st mort., 4 per cent., due Jan., 1950, Jan. and July | 700,000 |
| Second Ave. 1st mort., 5 per cent., due Nov., 1909, May and Nov. | 1,600,000 |
| Second Ave. debentures, 5 per cent., due Jan., 1909, Jan. and July | 216,000 |
| Second Ave. cons. mort., 5 per cent., due Feb., 1948, Feb. and Aug. | 5,184,000 |
| Broadway & 7th Ave. R. R. 1st mort., 5 per cent., due 1904, June and Dec. | 1,500,000 |
| Broadway & 7th Ave. R. R. 2d mort., 5 per cent., due 1914, Jan. and July | 500,000 |
| Broadway & 7th Ave. R. R. cons. mort., 5 per cent., due Dec., 1943, June and Dec. | 7,650,000 |
| Fulton Street R. R. 1st mort. guar., 4 per cent., due Nov., 1995, May and Nov. | 500,000 |
| Twenty-eighth & Twenty-ninth Sts. Crosstown 1st mort., 5 per cent., due Oct., 1996, April and Oct | 1,500,000 |
| Thirty-fourth Street Crosstown 1st mort., 5 per cent., due April, 1996, April and Oct. | 1,000,000 |
| Total | $20,886,000 |

The general collateral trust mortgage created in 1897 was to provide for changes in motive power, power-houses, etc. Interest is paid at the company's office.

In connection with the formation of the Metropolitan Securities Co. and the lease of this company to the Interurban Street Railway Co., the Metropolitan Street Railway Co. in April, 1902, authorized the creation of a refunding 4 per cent. mortgage, due 2002, with which to retire prior liens and provide for improvements and extensions. The authorized amount of the refunding mortgage is $65,000,000. Trustee, Morton Trust Co., New York. Interest on the bonds is payable at the office of the company. In 1902 bonds of this issue were sold to take up the maturing Central Park, North & East River 7 per cent. bonds for $1,200,000.

Lexington Avenue & Pavonia Ferry Railroad 1st mortgage 5s and the Columbus & Ninth Avenue 5s were authorized in 1894 to provide for extension of cable system. Both issues are guaranteed and assumed by the Metropolitan Street Railway. Of the Broadway Surface Railroad 1st mortgage bonds, $1,125,000 are guaranteed by Broadway & Seventh Avenue Co., and $375,000 by the Twenty-third Street Railway Co.

The company has large stock interests in the various companies leased, stated about June 30, 1901, to be $21,683,428. The following companies are leased upon a guarantee of dividends, the amounts of which and of their respective stocks are as follows:

| | Guarantee. | | Amount of Stock. |
|---|---|---|---|
| *Broadway & Seventh Avenue Railroad | 10 | per cent. per annum | $2,100,000 |
| Sixth Avenue Railroad | 7 | " " | 2,000,000 |
| Ninth Avenue Railroad | 6 | " " | 800,000 |
| *Twenty-third Street Railway | 18 | " " | 600,000 |
| *Forty-second Street & Grand Street Ferry | 18 | " " | 748,000 |
| *Central Park, North & East River Railroad | 9 | " " | 1,800,000 |
| *Bleecker Street & Fulton Ferry | 1½ | " " | 900,000 |
| Eighth Avenue Railroad | | $215,000 rental | 2,000,000 |
| *Second Avenue Railroad | 8 | per cent. per annum | 1,862,000 |

——* Metropolitan Street Railway has a controlling interest in stock of roads thus marked.

The rental of the New York & Harlem Railroad's Fourth Avenue surface road is $350,000 per annum for first five years, and $400,000 per annum thereafter. The Second Avenue lease provides for 8 per cent. dividends for three years from March 1, 1898, and 9 per cent. thereafter.

EARNINGS.

Year ending June 30.

| | Div. | Gross. | Net. | Charges. | Surplus. |
|---|---|---|---|---|---|
| 1893-94 | 5 | $5,398,465 | $2,174,509 | $1,859,791 | $314,538 |
| 1894-95 | 5 | 6,432,933 | 3,043,119 | 2,070,958 | 972,160 |
| 1895-96 | 5 | 8,173,331 | 3,984,186 | 2,517,338 | 1,466,847 |
| 1896-97 | 5 | 9,706,597 | 4,616,581 | 3,226,591 | 1,389,989 |
| 1897-98 | 5 | 11,076,021 | 5,455,536 | 3,609,966 | 1,845,572 |
| 1898-99 | 7 | 13,158,630 | 7,116,812 | 4,477,757 | 2,639,055 |
| 1899-00 | 7 | 13,785,084 | 7,805,880 | 4,445,720 | 3,360,160 |
| 1900-01 | 7 | 14,063,781 | 7,963,635 | 4,534,068 | 3,431,567 |
| 1901-02 | 7 | 14,504,314 | 8,359,501 | 5,551,942 | 2,807,559 |

President, William L. Elkins, Philadelphia; Vice-President, D. B. Hasbrouck; Secretary and Treasurer, D. C. Moorehead, New York.

Directors—Herbert H. Vreeland, P. A. B. Widener, William L. Elkins, Thomas Dolan, D. B. Hasbrouck, Milton G. Starrett, Richard W. Mead, Henry A. Robinson, D. C. Moorehead.

Main office, 621 Broadway New York. Annual meeting, first Monday in December.

## METROPOLITAN WEST SIDE ELEVATED RAILWAY CO.

A corporation formed under the laws of Illinois, January 16, 1899. The company is a reorganization of the railroad company of the same name sold under foreclosure January 4, 1899. It owns an electric railroad, beginning at the Chicago Board of Trade Building and extending westward about six miles, the first two miles being four-tracked, balance double-tracked, making total trackage, with branches, 37.60 miles. The Union Consolidated Elevated, 4.38 miles, is leased. Total operated, 42 miles. The company owns its right of way and makes use of the Union Elevated loop. The charter of the company provides for extensions to towns outside of Chicago.

Stock...Par $100....Authorized { com., $7,500,000; pref., 9,000,000 } Issued { com., $7,500,000; pref., 8,708,100 } $16,208,100

The preferred stock is 5 per cent., non-cumulative.

The common stock is vested for five years, or until 5 per cent. shall have been paid during one year on preferred, in a voting trust. Frederic P. Olcott, Samuel Thorne and Walter G. Oakman, trustees.

Transfer Agents, Central Trust Co., New York, and the secretary of the company. Registrars, Northern Trust Co., Chicago, and Guaranty Trust Co., New York.

Dividends on the preferred stock have been paid as follows: 2½ per cent. for fiscal year ending February, 1900; 3½ per cent. for year ending February, 1901, 3 per cent. in year ending

February 28, 1902, and 3 per cent. in the year ending February 28, 1903. Dividends on the preferred are paid half-yearly, in February (28) and August.

FUNDED DEBT.

| | |
|---|---|
| 1st mort., 4 per cent., gold, due Aug., 1938, Feb. and Aug. | $9,808,000 |
| 1st mort., on extensions, 4 per cent., gold, due July, 1938, Jan. and July | 3,000,000 |
| Total | $12,808,000 |

The authorized amount of the 1st mortgage is $10,000,000. Trustees of the mortgage, Central Trust Co. and G. Sherman, New York. Agent for the payment of interest, Central Trust Co., New York. Interest is also payable at the office of the company.

The authorized amount of the extension bonds is $5,000,000, of which $2,000,000 is reserved for future extensions. Trustee of the mortgage, Northern Trust Co., Chicago. Interest is payable by the Central Trust Co., New York, and at the office of the company. These bonds were issued for the construction of the Garfield Park and Douglas Park branches and to provide a down-town terminal.

The old company had $15,000,000 stock and $15,000,000 5 per cent. 1st mortgage bonds, due 1942, February and August. It defaulted on February, 1897, coupons. January 20, 1897, Receiver was appointed. A reorganization committee, Frederic P. Olcott, New York, chairman, was appointed.

The plan of reorganization, dated June 29, 1898, provided for new securities as given above. The old stock was assessed 4 per cent., and received 50 per cent. in new common and 4 per cent. in new bonds. The old bonds received 60 per cent. in new 1st mortgage bonds and 53½ per cent. in new preferred stock. The assessment yielded some $600,000 cash, and, with cash in Receiver's hands, was expended on improvements. Decree of foreclosure was obtained, and road sold, as stated above.

EARNINGS.

| Year ending February 28. | Gross. | Net. |
|---|---|---|
| 1899-00 | $1,524,114 | $880,805 |
| 1900-01 | 1,628,737 | 933,183 |
| 1901-02 | 1,753,313 | 1,020,743 |
| 1902-03 | 2,040,005 | 1,096,821 |

President, Dickinson MacAllister; Vice-President, Secretary and Treasurer, George Higginson, Jr.

Directors—W. W. Gurley, Dickinson MacAllister, John P. Wilson, Byron L. Smith, F. A. Delano, George Higginson, Jr., Clarence S. Day, James B. Forgan, Benjamin Allen, James J. Higginson, R. Somers Hayes.

Main office, 169 Jackson Boulevard, Chicago. Annual meeting, January 4, at Chicago.

## MEXICAN TELEGRAPH CO.

A corporation formed under the laws of New York in 1878. Owns a cable line from Galveston, Tex., to Vera Cruz and Tampico, Mexico, 738 miles, a land line from Vera Cruz to the City of Mexico, 267 miles, and has a majority of the stock of the direct cable from Galveston to Coatzacoala, Mex. The company has an exclusive concession from the government of Mexico, and working contracts with the Western Union Telegraph Co. and the Central & South American Telegraph Co.

Stock......Par $100..........................Authorized, $2,000,000......Issued, $1,912,600

Stock is transferred at company's office, New York.

Dividends have been as follows: 1882 to 1886, 8 per cent. per annum; in 1887 and since, 10 per cent. per annum. Dividends are paid, quarterly, 2½ per cent., January (15), April, July and October.

President, James A. Scrymser; Vice-Presidents, Edmund L. Baylies, New York; Sebastian Camacho, City of Mexico; Secretary, James R. Beard; Treasurer, Clarence Rapkin, New York.

Directors—James A. Scrymser, J. Pierpont Morgan, Edmund L. Baylies, John E. Alexandre, Charles H. Marshall, William G. Hamilton, W. Emlen Roosevelt, George G. Williams, Percy R. Pyne.

Main office, 60 Broadway, New York.

## MEXICAN TELEPHONE CO.

A corporation formed under the laws of New York in 1882. The company operates under the Bell telephone patents and concessions from the government of Mexico in the Republic of Mexico. It has exchanges in seventeen cities and towns of that country. The company had on February 21, 1903, 4,497 subscribers.

Stock......Par $10..........................Authorized, $2,000,000......Issued, $1,808,710

Transfer Agent, Boston Safe Deposit & Trust Co. Registrar, American Loan & Trust Co., Boston.

EARNINGS.

| Year Ending February 28. | Gross. | Net. |
|---|---|---|
| 1897-98 | $128,364 | $47,571 |
| 1898-99 | 138,937 | 56,440 |
| 1899-00 | 160,640 | 67,388 |
| 1900-01 | 187,466 | 84,830 |
| 1901-02 | 216,060 | 100,910 |

In the ten months ending December 31, 1902, the gross earnings were $203,466; net, $93,916.

Earnings are given in Mexican currency. In 1897-98 the operating department remitted to the United States office $43,713 Mexican, yielding in gold $20,269. In 1898-99 remitted $54,665 Mexican, yielding $25,492 gold. In 1899-1900 remitted $86,911 Mexican, yielding $33,152 gold. In 1900-01 remitted $80,795 Mexican, yielding $39,775 gold. In 1902 $90,815 Mexican, yielding $42,008 in gold.

The company, on February 28, 1902, had a profit and loss surplus of $222,950.

President, Charles H. Rollins; Secretary and Treasurer, W. French Smith, Boston; General Manager, Percival C. Burgess, City of Mexico.

Directors—Orrando P. Dexter, W. C. Carson, New York; William A. Paine, Otis Kimball, Charles H. Rollins, W. French Smith, Boston.

Main office, 4 State street, Boston. Annual meeting, second Wednesday in May, at New York.

## MICHIGAN COPPER MINING CO.

A corporation formed under the laws of Michigan, June 15, 1898. The company acquired the old Minnesota mine in Ontonagon County, Mich., which had been a large producer of copper, and paid dividends on its stock in the early history of copper mining in the Lake Superior district. The Minnesota mine was opened in 1848, but was abandoned in 1870 owing to the unprofitable results from operating it by the crude methods then in vogue. The property consists of some 4,000 acres of mineral and timber land, and is on the line of a branch of the Chicago, Milwaukee & St. Paul Railway. The present company is developing the mine on modern principles, and has installed a complete plant, with hoisting and other machinery, for that purpose.

Stock......Par $25..........................Authorized, $2,500,000......Issued, $2,500,000

The stock of the company consists of 100,000 shares of the par value of $25 each. At the beginning of 1903 there had been paid in $13 on each share.

Transfer Agent, American Loan & Trust Co., Boston. Registrar, Old Colony Trust Co., Boston.

President, John Stanton; Vice-President, Joseph E. Gay; Secretary, J. W. Hardley; Treasurer, John R. Stanton, New York.

Directors—John Stanton, John R. Stanton, Joseph E. Gay, J. W. Hardley, New York; Alfred M. Low, Michigan.

Executive office, 11 William street, New York. Annual meeting, first Tuesday in May, at New York.

## MIDDLESEX & SOMERSET TRACTION CO.

A corporation formed under the laws of New Jersey, in February, 1900. The company succeeded and absorbed the Brunswick Traction Co., New Brunswick City Railway Co., and New York & Philadelphia Traction Co. The company operates 50 miles of electric road in and about New Brunswick, the lines extending to Bound Brook, Metuchen, Raritan and Somerville, N. J., and connecting with the lines in Plainfield, Elizabeth, South Amboy, etc. It owns a power house and has 48 cars.

Stock......Par $100..........................Authorized, $1,500,000......Issued, $1,500,000

The company has no preferred stock.

FUNDED DEBT.

| | |
|---|---|
| 1st mort., 5 per cent., gold, due January, 1950, Jan. and July | $1,000,000 |
| Brunswick Traction Co., 1st mort., 5 per cent., gold, due July, 1926, Jan. and July... | 500,000 |
| Total | $1,500,000 |

The Middlesex & Somerset Traction mortgage is $1,500,000 authorized, of which $500,000 is reserved to retire the Brunswick Traction 5s. Trustee of mortgage and agent for the payment of interest, Fidelity Title and Deposit Co., Newark, N. J.

President, Gottfried Krueger, Newark, N. J.; Vice-President, A. H. Radel, Bridgeport, Conn.; Secretary and Treasurer, Edward H. Radel; General Manager, Thomas F. Walsh, New Brunswick, N. J.

Main office, 392 George street, New Brunswick, N. J. Annual meeting, first Tuesday in February.

## MIDDLESEX COMPANY

A corporation formed under the laws of Massachusetts in 1830 for the purpose of the manufacture of woolen cloths. The company owns mills at Lowell, Mass.

Stock......Par $100.................... ........Authorized, $750,000......Issued, $750,000

Transfer Agent, O. H. Perry, 77 Summer street, Boston.

Semi-annual dividends have been paid in January and July. In January, 1902, 3 per cent. was paid, but no dividend was paid in July, 1902, or January, 1903. The company has no funded debt.

President, Charles P. Curtis; Treasurer, Oliver H. Perry, Boston.

Directors—Charles P. Curtis, Arthur T. Lyman, Robert H. Gardner, Oliver H. Perry Charles Lowell, Boston; Jacob Rogers, Paul Butler, Lowell, Mass.

Main office, 77 Summer street, Boston. Annual meeting, Wednesday after Christmas, at Boston.

## MILFORD & UXBRIDGE STREET RAILWAY CO.

A corporation formed under the laws of Massachusetts, May 14, 1901. The company purchased in 1902 the entire capital stock of the Milford, Holliston & Framingham Street Railway Co. It operates 36 miles of electric railway in South Framingham, Ashland, Holliston, Milford, Hopedale, Mendon, Uxbridge, Bellingham, Medway and Hopkinton, Mass., serving a population of about 30,000. It owns 40 cars.

Stock......Par $100..............................Authorized, $353,000......Issued, $352,000

The company has no preferred stock. Stock is transferred and registered at the office of the company, Milford, Mass.

Dividends are paid quarterly in January, April, July and October.

FUNDED DEBT.

| | |
|---|---|
| 1st mort., 5 per cent., gold, due Jan., 1918, Jan. and July.......................... | $50,000 |
| Milford, Holliston & Framingham Street Railway Co. 1st mort., 5 per cent., gold, due Jan., 1918, Jan. and July .............................................. | 165,000 |
| Total ............................................................ | $215,000 |

The bonds outstanding are the full amounts authorized. Trustee and agent for the payment of interest, American Loan & Trust Co., Boston.

In the fiscal year ending September 30, 1902, the gross earnings ware $142,380; net earnings, $42,366; interest charges, $20,465; dividends, $15,120; deficit, $3,224.

President—John T. Manson, New Haven, Conn.; Vice-President, Arthur R. Taft, Uxbridge, Mass.; Treasurer and General Manager, E. W. Goss, Milford, Mass.

Directors—John T. Manson, Charles E. Graham, Herbert C. Fuller, New Haven, Conn.; Arthur R. Taft, Uxbridge, Mass.; Sydney Harwood, Boston; George A. Draper, Hopedale, Mass.; James E. Walker, Milford, Mass.

Corporate and main office, Milford, Mass.

## MILFORD, ATTLEBOROUGH & WOONSOCKET STREET RAILWAY CO.

A corporation formed under the laws of Massachusetts in 1900. The company owns and operates 31 miles of electric railway in Milford, Hopedale, Mendon, Bellingham, Franklin, Wrentham and Attleborough, Mass., and Woonsocket, R. I. It has entrance to the city of Woonsocket over the tracks of the Woonsocket Street Railway. It serves a population of about 70,000. The company owns a power station and has 26 cars.

Stock......Par $100..............................Authorized, $315,000......Issued, $315,000

The company has no preferred stock. Stock is transferred and registered at the office of the treasurer of the company, Franklin, Mass.

FUNDED DEBT.

1st mort., 5 per cent. gold, due Oct., 1919, April and Oct...... ...................... $165,000

The total amount of the authorized mortgage was $300,000. Trustee of the mortgage and agent for the payment of interest, American Loan & Trust Co., Boston.

EARNINGS.

| Year ending September 30. | Gross. | Net. |
|---|---|---|
| 1900 | $42,131 | $20,018 |
| 1901 | 75,464 | 25,507 |
| 1902 | 75,461 | 32,391 |

President, George W. Wiggen, Franklin, Mass.; Treasurer, Edgar K. Ray, Woonsocket, R. I.; Secretary and Manager, William H. Tyler, Milford, Mass.

Directors—George W. Wiggen, Adelbert D. Thayer, Franklin, Mass.; Edgar K. Ray, Woonsocket, R. I.; William S. Ray, Leominster, Mass.; William H. Tyler, Worcester, Mass.; Charles W. Shippen, Milford, Mass.

Corporate and main office, Milford, Mass.

## MILWAUKEE & CHICAGO BREWERIES, LIMITED

A corporation organized under the laws of Great Britain in 1891. The company acquired the capital stock of the United States Brewing Co., of Chicago, an organization which purchased the M. Brand Brewing Co., Bartholomae & Leicht Brewing Co., Ernst Bros. Brewing Co., Valentin Blatz Brewing Co., K. G. Schmidt Brewery and Bartholemay & Roesing Brewery. The united concerns now have an annual output of 800,000 barrels of beer.

Stock....Par £10.....Authorized { com., £775,000 / pref., 775,000 } Issued { com., £775,000 / pref., 775,000 } £1,550,000

The preferred stock is 8 per cent., cumulative.

Transfer Agent, Illinois Trust & Savings Bank, Chicago.

The company has paid dividends on the preferred stock of the English company, as follows: In 1895-96 (year ending September 30), 8 per cent.; in 1896-97, 10 per cent.; in 1897-98, 5½ per cent.; in 1898-99, none. Dividends on the preferred were resumed in 1900 by the payment of 2 per cent. on September 15, leaving about 18 per cent. of accumulated dividends. Another dividend of 2 per cent. on the preferred was paid December 31, 1900. In 1900-01 paid 5 per cent. on the preferred. No dividends have been paid on the common stock since 1893.

FUNDED DEBT.

U. S. Brewing Co., 1st mort., due 1910, March and Sept........................... $3,500,000

The 1st mortgage issued by the United States Brewing Co. is a 1st mortgage upon the plants and property of that company.

The statement of the American company showed in 1897-98, year ending September 30, a profit of $199,374, ; in 1898-99, a profit of $77,342; in 1899-1900, Profit, $169,769; in 1900-01, $221,227; in 1901-02, $221,829.

Chairman, J. R. Ellerman; Secretary, Daniel Willinck, London, England; President and Treasurer, American company, Rudolf Brand; Vice-President, John Kremer; 2d Vice-President, George W. Kellner; Secretary, James Miles, Chicago.

Directors—J. R. Ellerman, Marquis of Ailesbury, Sir Harry Bullard, J. Akenhead, Reginald Parker, London, England. Directors of the American company—Rudolf Brand, John Kremer, George W. Kellner, John J. Mitchell, F. S. Winston, James Miles, Chicago.

Main office, 35 Copthall avenue, London, E. C.; Chicago office, Monadnock Building. Annual meeting, in December, at London.

## MILWAUKEE ELECTRIC RAILWAY & LIGHT CO.

(Controlled by the North American Co.)

A corporation formed under the laws of Wisconsin in January, 1896, for the purpose of operating street railways and supplying electric light and power in the city of Milwaukee and suburbs. The company succeeded the Milwaukee Street Railway Co. and owns all the stock of the Milwaukee Light, Heat & Traction Co., which owns and operates 79 miles of interurban street railway between Milwaukee, Waukesha, Racine and Kenosha, and the electric light plants formerly belonging to the Badger Electric Co. of Racine, the Belle City Electric Railway Co. and the Racine Gas Light Co. The company has also acquired the following additional companies:

Edison Electric Illuminating Co.
Milwaukee Electric Light Co.
Badger Illuminating Co.
Milwaukee Arc Light & Power Co.
Pabst Light, Heat & Power Co.

The North American Co. owns the capital stock of this company.

Stock...Par $100...Authorized { com., $15,000,000 / pref., 4,500,000 } Issued { com., $7,404,800 / pref., 4,500,000 } $11,904,800

The preferred stock is non-cumulative. Dividends have been paid quarterly on the preferred in February, May, August and November, since February, 1900.

Stock is transferred at the office of the company.

FUNDED DEBT.

| | |
|---|---|
| Milwaukee Electric Ry. & Light Co., cons. mort., 5 per cent., due 1926, Feb. and Aug. | $6,500,000 |
| Milwaukee City Railroad, 1st mort., 5 per cent. gold bonds, due 1908, Jan. and Dec.. | 1,000,000 |
| West Side Street Railway, 1st mort., 5 per cent. gold bonds, due 1909, Jan. and July.. | 500,000 |
| Milwaukee Light, Heat & Traction Co., 1st mort., 5 per cent., due 1929, May and Nov. | 2,526,000 |
| Total | $10,526,000 |

The trustee of the bonds of the Milwaukee Electric Railway & Light Co., and the Milwaukee City Railroad Co., 1st mortgage, is the Central Trust Co., New York, and of the Milwaukee Light, Heat & Traction Co., the City Trust Co. of New York. The interest on the bonds of the Electric Railway & Light Co., the City Railroad and the Traction Co., is paid at the office of the company in New York, and of the West Side Street Railway Co. at the Farmers' Loan & Trust Co. of New York.

The bonds of the Traction Company are subject to call at 110.

EARNINGS.

| | Gross. | Net. | Charges. | Div. Pref. | Surplus. |
|---|---|---|---|---|---|
| 1901 | $2,517,435 | $1,231,901 | $513,396 | $267,431 | $1,006,072 |
| 1902 | 2,302,514 | 1,451,286 | 529,813 | 270,000 | 699,445 |

President and General Manager, John I. Beggs; 1st Vice-President, William Nelson Cromwell; 2d Vice-President, C. W. Wetmore; Secretary, Silas W. Burt; Treasurer, George R. Sheldon.

Directors—Silas W. Burt, C. W. Wetmore, William Nelson Cromwell, Edwin M. Bulkley, George R. Sheldon, F. G. Bigelow, H. C. Payne, John I. Beggs, Charles F. Pfister.

Main office, 451 Broadway, Milwaukee; New York office, 30 Broad street. Annual meeting, third Monday in February, at Milwaukee.

## THE MINE SECURITIES CORPORATION

A corporation formed under the laws of Maine. The purpose of the company is to secure for investors information as to the physical and financial condition of mining properties, to make special examination of mines, to manage mines and to reorganize mining companies and to act as transfer agent for such companies.

Stock......Par $5..........................Authorized, $2,500,000......Issued, $1,300,000

The company has no preferred stock and no funded debt.

Stock is transferred at the office of the company. Registrar, Knickerbocker Trust Co., New York.

President, Thomas J. Hurley; Vice-President, William H. Burger; Secretary, W. Harold Cockcroft; Treasurer, George J. Schermerhorn; Consulting Engineer, Charles P. Perin; General Counsel, Theodore E. Leeds.

Corporate and main office, 35 Wall street, New York. Annual meeting, November 6.

## MINNEAPOLIS GAS LIGHT CO.

A corporation formed under the laws of Minnesota in 1870. The company owns and operates the gas works and gas system in the city of Minneapolis.

Stock......Par $50..........................Authorized, $800,000......Issued, $800,000

The company has no preferred stock. Stock is transferred at the office of the company.

The company pays dividends of 8 per cent. per annum on its stock, the payments being semi-annual, 4 per cent. cash in January and July.

FUNDED DEBT.

1st mort., 6 per cent., due 1910-30, March and Sept..............................$2,900,000

The authorized amount of the 1st mortgage is $3,000,000. Trustee of mortgage, Farmers' Loan & Trust Co., New York. There are $100,000 of the bonds reserved in the hands of the Trustee for extensions, improvements, etc. The bonds fall due in 1930, but are redeemable in 1910, at the company's option.

President, Alonzo T. Rand; Vice-President and Treasurer, Rufus R. Rand; Secretary, William H. Levisgo; Superintendent, Frederick C. Shepard, Minneapolis.

Main office, 530 Hennepin avenue, Minneapolis. Annual meeting, first Monday in March.

## THE MINNEAPOLIS GENERAL ELECTRIC CO.

A corporation formed under the laws of New Jersey in 1892. The purpose of the company is furnishing electric light and power. It has the control of such facilities in the city of Minneapolis and has a perpetual franchise from the city.

Stock...Par $100...Authorized { com., $1,500,000 / pref., 750,000 } Issued { com., $1,500,000 / pref., 750,000 } $2,250,000

The preferred stock is 6 per cent., cumulative, the dividend periods being February (1) and August.

Transfer Agents, Stone & Webster, 93 Federal street, Boston. Registrar, Old Colony Trust Co., Boston.

FUNDED DEBT.

| | |
|---|---|
| 1st mort., gold, 5 per cent., due 1929, Jan. and July | $1,204,000 |
| Underlying bonds due 1908, 6 per cen | 765,000 |
| Total | $1,969,000 |

The 1st mortgage is $2,000,000, authorized. The bonds can be called on any interest day at 105 and interest. There is a sinking fund of $30,000 yearly. Trustee of mortgage, Old Colony Trust Co., Boston.

Of the underlying 6 per cent. bonds, $25,000 mature each year until 1908, when the whole amount outstanding becomes due. There are $765,000 1st 5s reserved to retire the underlying bonds. Trustee of the underlying mortgage, Minnesota Loan & Trust Co., Minneapolis.

EARNINGS.

| | Gross. | Net. | Charges. | Surplus. |
|---|---|---|---|---|
| 1902 | $500,580 | $235,142 | $98,409 | $136,732 |

President, M. B. Koon, Minneapolis; Vice-President, C. A. Stone, Boston; Secretary, B. H. Dibblee, Minneapolis; Assistant Secretary, Henry R. Hayes; Treasurer, Henry B. Sawyer, Boston; Assistant Treasurer, Herbert Dabney, Minneapolis; General Managers, Stone & Webster, Boston.

Directors—C. A. Stone, E. S. Webster, H. K. White, Boston; M. B. Koon, Thomas Lowry, C. G. Goodrich, E. A. Merrill, Minneapolis; James B. Dill, New York; L. S. Cushing, St. Paul.

Corporate office, the Corporation Trust Co. of Jersey City; main office, 15 South Fifth street, Minneapolis; executive office, 93 Federal street, Boston. Annual meeting, first Monday in January, at Jersey City.

---

## MISSOURI & KANSAS TELEPHONE CO.

A corporation formed under the laws of Missouri, July 6, 1899, as successors to a company of the same name. The company operates under an exclusive license from the American (Bell) Telephone & Telegraph Co. The territory covered by its system comprises Missouri, except St. Louis and adjoining counties, all of Kansas, Oklahoma and the Indian Territory. A controlling interest in the stock is owned by the American Telephone & Telegraph Co.

Stock......Par $100..........................Authorized, $5,000,000......Issued, $3,102,000

Transfer Agent, Old Colony Trust Co., Boston.

The authorized amount of stock was increased in January, 1902, to $5,000,000, and in April, 1902, $775,500 additional stock was issued and sold.

The company pays 6 per cent. per annum on its stock, the dividends being 1½ per cent. quarterly, in February (1), May, August and November.

FUNDED DEBT.

1st mort., 5 per cent., due Oct., 1929, April and Oct.................................. $496,000

The 1st mortgage was created in 1899, and is secured by all the property and franchises of the company. The mortgage is for $1,250,000. Trustee and agent for the payment of interest, Old Colony Trust Co., Boston.

President and General Manager, Alonzo Burt; Secretary and Treasurer, Nathaniel R. Ferguson.

Directors—Frederick P. Fish, Boston; John R. Mulvane, Edward Wilder, Topeka, Kan.; Alonzo Burt, J. S. Chick, Nathaniel R. Ferguson, J. F. Downing, Kansas City, Mo.; Casper E. Yost, M. A. Low, Omaha, Neb.

Main office, Sixth and Wyandotte streets, Kansas City, Mo. Annual meeting, fourth Wednesday in January, at Kansas City, Mo.

## MISSOURI EDISON ELECTRIC CO.

A corporation founded under the laws of Missouri, October 4, 1897. The purpose of the company is to carry on a general electric and lighting and power business in St. Louis. It is a consolidation of these companies:

Edison Illuminating Co. of St. Louis. Missouri Electric Light and Power Co.
Municipal Electric Light and Power Co.

Several smaller plants have been purchased since the consolidation. The company owns two stations of about 6,000 horse-power each.

Stock....Par $100.....Authorized { com., $2,000,000 / pref., 2,000,000 } Issued { com., $2,000,000 / pref., 2,000,000 } $4,000,000

The preferred stock is 5 per cent., cumulative. Stock is transferred at the company's office. Registrar, St. Louis Trust Co., St. Louis.

FUNDED DEBT.

| | |
|---|---|
| 1st mort., consolidated, 5 per cent. gold bonds, due 1927, Feb. and Aug. | $3,400,000 |
| Prior lien, 6 per cent. bonds, due 1921, Aug., Nov., Feb. and May | 600,000 |
| Total | $4,000,000 |

Of the consolidated bond issue, $600,000 is reserved for the retirement of the prior lien bonds. Trustee of the 1st mortgage bonds, St. Louis Trust Co., St. Louis. Trustee of the prior lien bond issue, Knickerbocker Trust Co., New York. Agent for the payment of interest on both series of bonds, National Bank of Commerce, St. Louis or New York.

EARNINGS.

| | Gross. | Net. | Charges. | Surplus. |
|---|---|---|---|---|
| 1901 | $792,482 | $261,835 | $206,000 | $55,815 |
| 1902 | 745,209 | 323,770 | 206,000 | 177,776 |

President, S. M. Dodd; Vice-President, James Campbell; Secretary, Sherman B. Pike; Treasurer, John G. Kelley, St. Louis; Assistant Treasurer, C. L. Horton, New York.

Directors—S. M. Dodd, James Campbell, J. C. Van Blarcom, Thomas H. West, R. C. Kerens, Edwards Whitaker, James W. Bell, H. C. Stifel, St. Louis.

Corporate and main office, Broadway and Locust street, St. Louis; branch office, Wall and Broad streets, New York. Annual meeting, second Tuesday in January, at St. Louis.

---

## MOHAWK MINING CO.

A corporation formed under the laws of Michigan in 1898. The company owns a large mineral tract in Keweenaw County, Mich., which is intersected by the same copper-bearing lodes which are found in the Wolverine and Kearsarge mines. It owns a mill site at Traverse Bay, on Lake Superior, and has erected a stamp mill thereon. In 1900 the company acquired and completed the Traverse Bay Railroad, which extends from its mine to the mill.

Stock......Par $25..........................Authorized, $2,500,000......Issued, $2,500,000

In 1900 and 1901 calls for $2.50 were made on the stock; in 1902 $3 was called, and at the beginning of 1903 the amount called and paid in was $18 per share.

Transfer Agent, American Loan & Trust Co., Boston. Registrar, Boston Safe Deposit & Trust Co.

President, John Stanton; Vice-President, Joseph E. Gay; Secretary and Treasurer, John R. Stanton, New York.

Directors—John Stanton, John R. Stanton, Joseph E. Gay, New York; William A. Paine, Boston; Frederick Smith, Kearsarge, Mich.

Executive office, 11 William street, New York. Annual meeting, third Tuesday in March, at New York.

---

## THE MONONGAHELA RIVER CONSOLIDATED COAL & COKE CO.

A corporation formed under the laws of Pennsylvania, October 1, 1899. The company acquired the property and business of a large number of companies and firms engaged in the business of mining and shipping coal by the Ohio and Mississippi rivers. A list of the concerns acquired is given in the MANUAL for 1901.

The amount of coal-bearing lands acquired and owned by the company is about 40,000 acres. It owns practically all the organizations carrying Pittsburg coal upon the Ohio and Mississippi rivers, and has some 100 steamers and 4,000 coal barges. The company also owns facilities for handling Pittsburg coal at Cincinnati, O., Louisville, Ky., Memphis, Tenn., Vicksburg, Miss., Baton Rouge and New Orleans, La. In 1901 it acquired the Corona Coal & Iron Co., Corona

Coal Co., Southern Coal Co., Virginia & Alabama Coal Co. and Alabama Block Coal Co. owning 30,000 acres of coal lands near Birmingham, Ala.

Stock...Par $50...Authorized { com., $20,000,000 / pref., 10,000,000 } Issued { com., $20,000,000 / pref., 9,995,000 } $29,995,000

The preferred stock is 7 per cent., non-cumulative.

Transfer Agent, Union Trust Co., Pittsburg. Registrar, First National Bank, Pittsburg.

The company began the payment of regular semi-annual dividends on the preferred stock of 3½ per cent., July 10, 1900, and has continued to make these payments in January and July.

FUNDED DEBT.

| | |
|---|---|
| 1st mort. bonds, 6 per cent., due 1949, April and Oct. | $9,468,000 |
| Certificates of debt, 5 per cent., due July, 1917, Jan. and July. | 2,060,000 |
| Total | $11,528,000 |

The 1st mortgage is for $10,000,000. Trustee of mortgage, Union Trust Co., Pittsburg. Of the bonds $532,000 have been retired and canceled through the sinking fund.

The certificates of indebtedness are $3,000,000, authorized, and were created in 1902 to refund the floating debt, which was $3,500,000. The certificates are to be retired $300,000 on each 1st of January.

EARNINGS.

| Year ending October 31. | Gross. | Net. |
|---|---|---|
| 1900-01 | $2,503,300 | $1,057,979 |
| 1901-02 | 2,653,809 | 880,037 |

The balance sheet of the company October 31, 1902, was as follows:

| ASSETS. | | LIABILITIES. | |
|---|---|---|---|
| Cash on hand and in banks | $313,892 | Preferred stock | $9,995,000 |
| Accounts and bills receivable | 2,957,168 | Common stock | 20,000,000 |
| Coal on hand | 1,822,971 | Bonds and certificates of indebtedness | 11,528,000 |
| Supplies on hand | 813,475 | | |
| Office furniture | 12,862 | Current debts | 2,467,931 |
| Stocks of other corporations | 422,050 | Undivided profits | 1,037,098 |
| Investments | 38,685,611 | | |
| Total | $45,028,029 | Total | $45,028,029 |

President, John B. Finley; Vice-President and Secretary, George W. Theis; Treasurer, George I. Whitney, Pittsburg.

Directors—John B. Finley, George I. Whitney, H. C. Fownes, S. S. Brown, George W. Theis, Hugh Moren, A. Jutte, John A. Wood, R. H. Boggs.

Main office, 87 Market street, Pittsburg. Annual meeting, third Wednesday in January.

---

## MONONGAHELA WATER CO.

A corporation formed under the laws of Pennsylvania, April 21, 1855. It supplies water to the south side of the city of Pittsburg and neighboring suburbs. The company also supplies the boroughs of McKees Rocks, Esplen and Elliott, comprising a population of over 100,000. The company has two pumping stations with an aggregate capacity of 40,000,000 gallons per day, about double the daily consumption.

Stock......Par $25..............Authorized, $2,300,000......Issued, $2,300,000

In December, 1901, the authorized stock was increased by $200,000, the new stock being issued and sold at par to the stockholders in 1902.

Transfer Agent and Registrar, Safe Deposit & Trust Co., Pittsburg.

FUNDED DEBT.

1st mort., 5 per cent., due Jan., 1912, Jan. and July.......... $100,000

Dividends of 8 per cent. per annum are paid on the stock, 2 per cent. quarterly, in January, April, July and October. The stock was increased by $200,000 in December, 1902, and the additional amount subscribed for by the stockholders at par.

President, Mark W. Watson; Secretary and General Manager, Martin Prenter; Treasurer, F. W. Rudel; Assessor and Collector, H. J. Schneider.

Directors—Mark W. Watson, B. F. Jones, J. R. McGinley, Daniel McKee, James W. Scully, A. W. Mellon, Joseph G. Walter, John Moorhead, Jr., A. Ernwein.

Main office, 1113 Carson street, Pittsburg. Annual meeting, first Tuesday in May.

## MONTANA COAL & COKE CO.

A corporation formed under the laws of New Jersey, April 11, 1899. The company has a coal property at Horr, Park County, Mont., comprising about 3,000 acres, of which 1,500 acres are leased from the Northern Pacific Railway Co. The company has 200 coke ovens.

Stock......Par $25..........................Authorized, $5,000,000......Issued, $5,000,000

The stock of the company consists of 200,000 shares, all full paid. Registrar, Massachusetts Trust Co., Boston.

FUNDED DEBT.

1st mort., 6 per cent., due 1920.................................................. $500,000

The 1st mortgage is $500,000 authorized. It was created in 1900 to provide for improvements and for the purchase of the Butte & Yellowstone Coal & Coke Co. Trustee of mortgage, Central Trust Co., New York.

In 1900 the company paid two dividends of 30 cents each per share in April and October respectively. No dividends were paid in 1901 or 1902.

President, Joseph A. Coram, Lowell, Mass.; Vice-President, Simon H. Stern, New York; Treasurer, H. W. Wesson, Boston; Secretary, H. W. Wesson, Jersey City.

Directors—Joseph A. Coram, Simon H. Stern, T. E. Hopkins, G. L. White, R. W. H. Smith.

Main office, 60 State street, Boston. Annual meeting, third Wednesday in March.

## THE MONTANA ORE PURCHASING CO.

(Controlled by the United Copper Co.)

A corporation formed under the laws of Montana in 1893. The company engages in the business of mining, smelting its own ores and purchasing the ores and concentrates of other mining companies. The company succeeded the private business of the same nature established by F. Aug. Heinze and Stanley Gifford. It owns and operates a smelting and reduction works at Butte, Mont., with a capacity of 5,000,000 pounds of copper per month. It owns and operates the Rarus, Snohomish, Tramway, Mountain Chief, Johnstown, and other valuable copper mines and mineral rights near Butte, and owns the Glengarry mine, which is leased to other parties.

In 1902 control of the compan was acquired by the United Copper Co., which owns practically all its stock and bonds. y

Stock......Par $25..........................Authorized, $2,500,000......Issued, $2,020,825

The capital stock consists of 100,000 shares of the par value of $25 each. Transfers are made at the company's office, New York.

In 1900 the company paid three dividends of $1 each per share on its stock in January, May and September, respectively. In 1902 paid $2 per share each in August and September.

FUNDED DEBT.

1st mort., 6 per cent., due 1917, Jan. and July.................................. $1,000,000

The 1st mortgage bonds are secured by all the property and plant of the company. Trustee of the mortgage, Stephen E. Nash, New York.

President, F. Aug. Heinze, New York; Vice-President, John MacGinniss, Butte; Secretary, Arthur P. Heinze; Treasurer, Stanley Gifford, New York.

Directors—F. Aug. Heinze, Arthur P. Heinze, Otto C. Heinze, John MacGinniss, Stanley Gifford.

Main office, Butte, Mont.; New York office, 31 Nassau street. Annual meeting, third Monday in July, at Butte, Mont.

## MONTREAL & BOSTON COPPER CO.

A corporation formed under the laws of Nova Scotia. The company has a copper property of 115 acres in Kettle River District, British Columbia. It has expended about $500,000 in development work and in 1902 erected a mill and smelter at the mine.

Stock......Par $5..........................Authorized, $3,000,000......Issued, $3,000,000

The company has no preferred stock and no funded debt.

On December 31, 1902, the company reported a surplus of $125,629.

President, H. H. Melville, Boston; First Vice-President, J. N. Greenshields; Second Vice-President, Thomas Crockett; Secretary and Treasurer, A. Munroe, Montreal.

Directors, W. N. Coler, Jr., DeLancy Nicoll, G. Creighton Webb, J. W. Allison, New York; H. H. Melville, W. F. Beal, Boston; J. C. McDiarmid, J. N. Greenshields, William Mitchell, Thomas Crockett, Montreal.

Main office, 189 St. James street, Montreal.

## MONTREAL COTTON CO.

A corporation formed under the laws of the Dominion of Canada for the purpose of manufacturing cotton cloth. The company owns mills at Valleyfield, P. Q., operated by hydraulic-electric power.

Stock......Par $100..........................Authorized, $4,000,000......Issued, $3,000,000

The company has no preferred stock and no funded debt.

Stock is transferred at the office of the company, Montreal.

Dividends on the stock are payable quarterly, March (15), June, September and December.

President, A. F. Gault; Vice-President, Charles Garth; Secretary and Treasurer, D. F. Smith; General Manager, Frederick Lacey.

Directors—A. F. Gault, Charles Garth, R. R. Stevenson, Samuel Finley, J. K. Ward, S. H. Ewing, Jacques Grenier.

Main office, 316 St. James street, Montreal; operating office, Valleyfield, P. Q. Annual meeting, second Tuesday in February.

---

## MONTREAL LIGHT, HEAT & POWER CO.

A corporation formed under the laws of the Province of Quebec, Canada, April 25, 1901, to acquire the stocks of the following companies and engage in the manufacture and distribution of gas and electric light and power. The company controls the entire lighting industry of the city of Montreal.

| | |
|---|---|
| Montreal Gas Co. | Imperial Electric Co. |
| Royal Electric Co. | Montreal & St. Lawrence Light & Power Co. |

Stock......Par $100..........................Authorized, $17,000,000......Issued, $16,977,800

The first quarterly dividend of 1 per cent. was paid August 15, 1901, and similar payments have since been made in August, November, February and May.

Transfer Agents, National Trust Co., Montreal; Lounsbery & Co., New York. Registrars, Royal Trust Co., Montreal; Central Trust Co., New York.

FUNDED DEBT.

| | |
|---|---|
| 1st mort., 4½ per cent., due 1932, Jan. and July | $2,500,000 |
| Montreal Gas Co. mort., 5 per cent., due 1908 | 636,660 |
| Royal Electric Co. 1st mort., 5 per cent., due 1914 | 487,153 |
| Total | $3,623,813 |

The company has no preferred stock.

EARNINGS.

Year ending April 30.

| | Gross. | Net. | Charges. | Dividends. | Surplus. |
|---|---|---|---|---|---|
| 1900-01 | $1,690,706 | $800,377 | $176,670 | $490,404 | $133,303 |
| 1901-02 | 1,760,285 | 821,217 | 91,496 | 587,969 | 141,753 |

President, H. S. Holt; 1st Vice-President, James Ross; 2d Vice-President, Rodolphe Forget; Secretary and Treasurer, H. H. Henshaw, Montreal.

Directors—H. Montagu Allan, L. J. Forget, F. C. Henshaw, Robert Mackay, C. E. L. Porteous, H. B. Rainville, Montreal.

Corporate and main office, 11 Place d'Armes, Montreal. Annual meeting, first week in June, at Montreal.

---

## MONTREAL STREET RAILWAY CO.

A corporation formed under the laws of Canada, May 18, 1861. The company has an exclusive franchise from the city of Montreal, which extends to 1922. The company's system comprises 109 miles of lines, covering Montreal and its immediate environments. In 1901 the company acquired control of the Montreal Park & Island Railway Co.

Stock......Par $50..........................Authorized, $10,000,000......Issued, $6,000,000

The company has no preferred stock. Stock is transferred at the office of the company.

Dividends of 10 per cent. were paid on the stock in 1899, 1900, 1901 and 1902, dividend periods being February, May, August and November.

FUNDED DEBT.

| | |
|---|---|
| Debentures, 1st series, sterling, 5 per cent., due March, 1908, March and Sept......... | $292,000 |
| Debentures, 2d series, sterling, 4½ per cent., due Aug., 1922, Feb. and Aug........... | 681,333 |
| New debentures, 4½ per cent., due May, 1922, May and Nov........................ | 1,500,000 |
| Total.................................................................... | $2,473,333 |

Trustee of the 1st and 2d series of debentures, the Montreal Trust & Deposit Co. They have equal rights. Agent for the payment of interest on the 1st and 2d series, the Bank of Montreal, London. The interest on the new 4½ per cent. debentures issued in 1902 is payable at the Bank of Montreal, Montreal.

EARNINGS.

Year ending September 30.

| | Gross. | Net. | Charges. | Dividends. | Surplus |
|---|---|---|---|---|---|
| 1898-99.................... | $1,660,775 | $747,826 | $116,956 | $478,333 | $152,537 |
| 1899-00.................... | 1,769,904 | 776,979 | 129,733 | 512,500 | 134,746 |
| 1901-01.................... | 1,900,680 | 795,413 | 146,162 | 551,700 | 97,551 |
| 1901-02.................... | 2,046,208 | 911,033 | 210,066 | 600,000 | 100,966 |

President, L. J. Forget; Vice-President, James Ross; Secretary and Treasurer, W. G. Ross; General Manager, Fred L. Wauklyn, Montreal.

Directors—L. J. Forget, Richard B. Angus, James Ross, K. W. Blackwell, F. C. Henshaw, H. M. Allan.

Main office, 574 Craig street, Montreal. Annual meeting, first Wednesday in November, at Montreal.

## MONTREAL TELEGRAPH CO.

A corporation chartered by special act of the Parliament of Canada, in 1847, for the purpose of carrying on a telegraph business in the Dominion of Canada. The company has telegraph lines and cables in Canada and the United States. Its system is operated and maintained by the Great North Western Telegraph Company, of Canada, guaranteed by the Western Union Telegraph Company, under an agreement for ninety-seven years from July 1, 1881.

Stock......Par $40..........................Authorized, $2,000,000......Issued, $2,000,000

The company has no preferred and no funded debt. Stock is transferred at the office of the company.

Since July, 1881, the dividends have been 8 per cent. annually as guaranteed by the companies operating the property. Dividend periods are January (15), April, July, and October. In addition to the regular dividends bonuses of ¼ per cent. each were paid in April, 1902, and April, 1903, out of the revenue derived from the company's contingent fund.

The balance sheet, December 31, 1902, showed total assets $2,287,023.

President, Hugh A. Allan; Vice-President, A. T. Paterson; Secretary and Treasurer, D. Ross-Ross, Montreal.

Directors, Hugh A. Allan, A. T. Paterson, Jesse Joseph, William R. Miller, William McMaster, William Wainwright.

Corporate and main office, 6 St. Sacrament street, Montreal. Annual meeting, second Thursday in January, at Montreal.

## THE MONTVILLE STREET RAILWAY CO.

A corporation formed under the laws of Connecticut, December 20, 1890. The company owns and operates 13 miles of electric railway between Norwich and New London, Conn.

Stock......Par $100..............................Authorized, $300,000......Issued, $250,000

The company has no preferred stock. Stock is transferred at the office of the company, Boston.

A dividend of 3 per cent. was paid in January, 1901. Since then 6 per cent. annually has been paid, the dividend periods being semi-annual in January and July.

FUNDED DEBT.

1st mort., 5 per cent. gold, due May 1, 1920, May and Nov...........................$250,000

The authorized amount of the mortgage is $350,000. The $100,000 unissued is held to be used for improvements or additions. Trustee of the mortgage, Treasurer of the State of Connecticut. Agent for the payment of interest, American Loan & Trust Co., Boston.

In the fiscal year ending June 30, 1902, the gross earnings were $90,037.43; net, $37,628.15; charges, $12,500; dividends, $15,000; surplus, $10,128.15.

President, William A. Tucker, Boston; Secretary, W. A. Briscoe, Norwich, Conn.; Treasurer, P. L. Saltonstall, Boston.

Directors—William A. Tucker, P. L. Saltonstall, Stillman F. Kelley, Boston; B. P. Learned, Walter Learned, New London, Conn.; C. W. Comstock, Montville, Conn.; W. A. Briscoe, Norwich, Conn.

Corporate office, Norwich, Conn.; main office, 53 State street, Boston. Annual meeting, first Monday in October, at Norwich, Conn.

## THE MORGAN ENGINEERING CO.

A corporation formed under the laws of Ohio, February 19, 1900. The company has a large plant at Alliance, O., and manufactures heavy machinery for steel works, rolling mills, blast furnaces, foundries, machine shops and power plants, particularly overhead traveling cranes, steam hammers, presses, punches, shearing and riveting machinery, gun carriages, and all classes of heavy work.

Stock....Par $100....Authorized { com., $1,500,000 / pref., 1,500,000 } Issued { com., $1,500,000 / pref., 1,500,000 } $3,000,000

The preferred stock is 6 per cent., non-cumulative. The company has no funded debt.

President, W. H. Morgan; Secretary and Treasurer, W. H. Ramsey.

Directors—W. H. Morgan, W. H. Ramsey, M. M. Ramsey, A. S. Morgan, J. H. Lloyd, Alliance, O.

Main office, Alliance, O.; branch office, Frick Building, Pittsburg, Annual meeting in May.

## MUNICIPAL GAS CO.

A corporation formed under the laws of New York in July, 1885. The company owns all the gas and electric light facilities of the city of Albany, N. Y. It acquired and consolidated with the Albany Electric Illuminating Co. and the Edison Electric Light & Power Co. of Albany, and owns the West Troy Gas Co.

Stock......Par $100..........................Authorized, $2,000,000......Issued, $2,000,000

FUNDED DEBT.

1st mort., 6 per cent., due 1906, Jan. and July..... ................................. $500,000

The company since 1890 has paid 10 per cent. per annum on its stock, dividends being quarterly, 2½ per cent. each, in February, May, August and November.

President, Anthony N. Brady, New York; Vice-President, Robert C. Pruyn; Secretary and Treasurer, Henry Bronk, Albany.

Directors—Anthony N. Brady, Robert C. Pruyn, William McEwan, Horace G. Young, John G. Myers, John Bowe, John A. Delehanty, William J. Walker.

Main office, 112 State street, Albany, N. Y.

## THE FRANK A. MUNSEY CO.

A corporation formed under the laws of New York in 1902, to publish magazines and newspapers.

Stock......Par $100........................Authorized, $10,000,000......Issued, $10,000,000

The company has no preferred stock and no funded debt.

Stock is transferred by the secretary of the company. Registrar, New York Security & Trust Co., New York.

Three quarterly dividends, at the rate of 5 per cent., have been paid, in July and October, 1902, and January, 1903.

President, Frank A. Munsey; Vice-President, Erman J. Ridgway; Secretary, R. H. Titherington; Assistant Secretary, H. S. Meese; Treasurer, William T. Dewart, New York.

Directors—Frank A. Munsey, Erman J. Ridgway, R. H. Titherington, William T. Dewart, Henry J. Fisher, A. E. Bowers, New York; C. H. Stoddart, Chicago.

Corporate and main office, 111 Fifth avenue, New York. Annual meeting, second Monday in April, in New York.

## MUSKEGON TRACTION & LIGHTING CO.

A corporation formed under the laws of Michigan in February, 1901, for the purpose of operating street railways and furnishing gas and electric light in Muskegon and Muskegon Heights, Mich. The company is a consolidation of the following properties:

Muskegon Street Railway Co.
Muskegon Electric Light Co.
Muskegon Gas Light Co.

It operates 15 miles of street railway. Transfer Agent, Wyoming Valley Trust Co. Wilkes-Barre.

Stock......Par $100..............................Authorized, $600,000......Issued, $600,000

FUNDED DEBT.

1st mort., 5 per cent., due 1931, March and Sept.................................... $600,000

The bond issue is the total amount authorized. The bonds are redeemable at the company's option after March 1, 1911, at 105 and interest.

Trustee and agent for the payment of interest, Wyoming Valley Trust Co., Wilkes-Barre, Pa.

The gross earnings of the railway and electric departments for the year ending April 1, 1902, and of the gas department for that ending, March 1, 1902, were $143,054.11; net, $50,511.85; interest charges, $25,000; surplus, $25,211.85, all of which was applied to extensions and betterments. The gross earnings for the ten months ending December 31, 1902, were $136,500.12; expenses, $86,309.19; net earnings, $50,190.33.

President, F. A. Nims, Muskegon, Mich.; Vice-President, Liddon Flick; Secretary and Treasurer, Theodore S. Barber, Wilkes-Barre, Pa.; Assistant Treasurer, D. D. Erwin, Muskegon, Mich.

Directors—F. A. Nims, Louis Kanitz, J. J. Howden, Muskegon, Mich.; Liddon Flick, John N. Conyngham, E. F. Payne, Theodore S. Barber, Wilkes-Barre, Pa.

Main office, Muskegon, Mich. Annual meeting, first Tuesday in February, at Muskegon.

## NARRAGANSETT ELECTRIC LIGHTING CO.

A corporation formed under the laws of Rhode Island in 1884. In 1889 the company absorbed the Rhode Island Electric Light Co.

Stock......Par $100...........................Authorized, $2,000,000......Issued, $2,000,000

The stock of the company was originally $100,000, and has been increased at various times. In October, 1901, $200,000 debenture certificates were converted into stock.

FUNDED DEBT.

Debenture certificates, convertible into stock April 1, 1905.......................... $1,090,000

The $1,000,000 debentures are redeemable in stock at par at the option of the company.

The company pays 8 per cent. per annum on its stock, the dividends being quarterly, 2 per cent. each, in January, April, July and October.

President and General Manager, Marsden J. Perry; Vice-President, Arthur H. Watson; Secretary and Treasurer, Daniel A. Pierce.

Directors—Marsden J. Perry, Daniel A. Pierce, Fenner H. Peckham, Jr.; Arthur H. Watson, William A. Walton, William W. Douglas, James M. Ripley, George L. Shepley, H. Martin Brown, Isaac M. Potter.

Main office, 170 Westminster street, Providence. Annual meeting, fourth Wednesday in January.

## NATIONAL ASPHALT CO.

A corporation formed under the laws of New Jersey, May 3, 1900. The company absorbed the Asphalt Co. of America, and other companies, including the Pennsylvania Asphalt Paving Co., the Gilson Asphaltum Co., the New Jersey Mexican Asphalt Co., and the Manhattan Trap Rock Co.

The Asphalt Co. of America was a consolidation, July, 1899, of the United Asphalt Co., of New York; the Barber Asphalt Co., of West Virginia; the New Trinidad Lake Asphalt Co., Limited, of London, and the Alcatraz Co., of West Virginia, and a number of other companies. See MANUAL for 1900. The New York & Bermudez Co., a New York corporation owning an asphalt lake at Guanoca, State of Bermudez, Venezuela, was owned by this company.

In December, 1901, in anticipation of a default in the payment of interest, application was made to the courts, and Henry Tatnall, John M. Mack and John F. Shanley were appointed Receivers of the National Asphalt Co.

A committee was appointed to represent the Asphalt Co. of America bondholders; Henry W. Biddle, chairman. Depositaries, Mercantile Trust Co., New York, and Commercial Trust Co., Philadelphia. The National Asphalt bondholders were also represented by a committee; William F. Harrity, chairman. Depositaries, Equitable Trust Co., Philadelphia; Guaranty Trust Co., New York.

A reorganization plan was proposed in July, 1902, the new company to have $17,000,000 of common and $14,000,000 of 5 per cent. cumulative preferred stock. Holders of National Asphalt bonds were to pay $16 on each $1,000 bond and receive $400 in new common stock, while the old common stock was assessed $1.60 per share and was to receive $40 in new common, the old preferred paying $4.40 per share and receiving 110 in new common. The Asphalt Co. of America

5 per cent. bonds were to receive 50 per cent. in new preferred stock. Litigation, however, followed the announcement of the plan, and the affairs of the organization and its constituent companies became legally complicated. It was provided that all the stock of the new company should be held for ten years in a voting trust.

Stock..Par $50....Authorized { com., $12,000,000 / pref., 10,000,000 } Issued { com., $11,551,470 / pref., 8,003,674 } $19,555,144

The preferred stock is 6 per cent., cumulative. In the organization of the company it was provided that $2,250,000 preferred and $900,000 common stock should remain in the treasury for future corporate purposes.

The stock of the Asphalt Co. of America was $30,000,000, par $50, on which $10 per share or 20 per cent. had been paid in. The plan of consolidation issued in September, 1900, offered holders of the Asphalt Co. of America shares $10 per share for their stock in collateral trust 5 per cent. certificates, $7 per share in new preferred, and $10 per share in new common stock. Nearly all the stock in the Asphalt Co. of America was exchanged on these terms, though some dissenting stockholders instituted proceedings to enjoin the merger, but were defeated in the courts.

Transfer Agent, Girard Trust Co., Philadelphia. Registrar, Land Title & Trust Co., Philadelphia.

FUNDED DEBT.

| | |
|---|---|
| Collateral Trust Cfts., 5 per cent., due Jan., 1951, Jan. and July.................... | $5,988,420 |
| Asphalt Co. of America, col. trust, 5 per cent., due April, 1949, April and Oct...... | 29,432,255 |
| Total .................................................................. | $35,420,675 |

The 5 per cent. collateral trust certificates of the National Asphalt Co., Equitable Trust Co., Philadelphia, trustee, are secured by a deposit of the shares of the Asphalt Co. of America. A sinking fund of $50,000 was provided, but payments of interest or principal of these certificates were not to be made until all interest or principal of the 5 per cent. collateral certificates of the Asphalt Co. of America, actually matured, shall have been met.

The collateral trust 5 per cent. certificates of the Asphalt Co. of America, Land Title & Trust Co. of Philadelphia, trustee, are secured by the deposit of securities of the constituent companies of that organization. There is a sinking fund provision of $300,000 per annum. Receivers, Henry Tatnall; John M. Mack, Philadelphia; John F. Shanley, Newark, N. J.

It was stated that in 1900 the net profits of all companies were $483,340, and in 1901 $908,627.

President, (Vacancy); Secretary and Treasurer, Arthur W. Sewall, New York.

Directors—Peter A. B. Widener, George Widener, William L. Elkins, George W. Elkins, John M. Mack, Joseph P. Mack, Robert H. Forderer, Philadelphia; Francis V. Greene, Charles B. Alexander, Amzi L. Barber, Avery D. Andrews, Arthur W. Sewall, August Belmont, New York; Ellis Wainwright, St. Louis; R. J. Wortendyke, Jersey City.

Corporate office, Jersey City; main office, 11 Broadway, New York. Annual meeting, second Wednesday in March.

## NATIONAL BISCUIT CO.

A corporation formed under the laws of New Jersey, February 3, 1898. The company purchased the New York Biscuit Co., American Biscuit & Manufacturing Co., National Cracker Co., Decatur Cracker Co., Hamilton Co., United States Baking Co. Several small companies were controlled by the constituent companies. The present company has 128 different plants in various cities.

Stock..Par $100...Authorized { com., $30,000,000 / pref., 25,000,000 } Issued { com., $29,236,000 / pref., 24,304,500 } $53,540,500

The Preferred stock is 7 per cent., cumulative.

Transfer Agents, Equitable Trust Co., Chicago; Guarantee Trust Co., New York.

The company began the payment of regular dividends on preferred May 31, 1898, at the rate of 1¾ per cent. quarterly, and such dividends are paid February, May, August and November. The first dividend on common was 1 per cent., April 16, 1899. Quarterly dividends of 1 per cent., or 4 per cent. per annum, on the common have since been regularly paid in January, April, July and October.

FUNDED DEBT.

| | |
|---|---|
| New York Biscuit Co. 1st mort., gold, 6 per cent., due 1910, March and Sept......... | $804,000 |
| American Biscuit & Mfg. Co. 1st mort., 6 per cent., due 1911, Feb. and Aug......... | 545,000 |
| " " " bonds, 4½ per cent., due 1900...... .... ............ | 100,000 |
| " " " purchase money mort.............................. | 46,000 |
| Total.................................................................. | $1,495,000 |

EARNINGS.

| | Gross. | Net. | Div. Pref. | Div. Com. | Total Surplus. |
|---|---|---|---|---|---|
| 1898 (thirteen months)... | $34,913,890 | $3,292,143 | $1,214,500 | ......... | $2,077,643 |
| 1899.................... | 35,651,898 | 3,302,155 | 1,647,605 | $584,720 | 3,147,472 |
| 1900.................... | 36,439,160 | 3,318,355 | 1,674,211 | 1,169,440 | 3,622,176 |
| 1901.................... | 38,625,134 | 3,670,445 | 1,647,211 | 1,169,440 | 4,455,424 |
| 1902.................... | 40,291,925 | 3,689,338 | 1,680,511 | 1,169,440 | 5,294,812 |

In November, 1898, the company set aside $1,000,000 from earnings as a cash fund for contingencies. At the February, 1899, meeting of directors it was decided to carry $500,000 additional to reserve account, making $1,500,000 in all.

The following is the balance sheet of the company, January 31, 1903:

ASSETS.

| | | |
|---|---|---|
| Plants, real estate, machinery, patents, etc................ | $51,276,733 | |
| Less depreciation account............. | 300,000 | |
| | | $50,976,733 |
| Cash................ | $1,709,495 | |
| Stocks and securities. | 662,803 | |
| Accounts receivable.. | 3,041,464 | |
| Raw material, supplies and finished product............ | 4,679,603 | |
| | | $10,093,366 |
| Total..................... | | $61,070,099 |

LIABILITIES.

| | | |
|---|---|---|
| Capital stock, preferred............ | $24,304,500 | |
| Capital stock, common.............. | 29,236,000 | |
| | | $53,540,500 |
| Bonds payable and mortgages payable, assumed at formation of company, not yet matured... | $1,814,000 | |
| Less amount paid.... | 319,000 | |
| | | $1,495,000 |
| Accounts payable, including accrued interest............ .... | | $739,787 |
| Balance, Jan. 31, 1902 | $4,455,425 | |
| Earnings, 12 months to Jan. 31, 1903, inclusive............ | 3,689,338 | |
| | $8,144,763 | |
| Less dividends paid, 12 months to Jan. 31, 1903, inclusive.. | 2,849,951 | |
| | | $5,294,812 |
| Total.... ............... | | $61,070,099 |

Chairman, A. W. Green; President, Benjamin F. Crawford; Vice-Presidents, H. F. Vories, Frank O. Lowden; Assistant Treasurer, J. A. Lewis; Secretary, F. E. Bugbee.

Directors—Benjamin F. Crawford, H. F. Vories, Thomas S. Ollive, David F. Bremer, S. S. Marvin, Henry J. Evans, Lewis D. Dozler, Norman B. Ream, William T. Baker, John D. Richardson, C. E. Rumsey, James W. Hazen, Frank O. Lowden, J. B. Vredenburgh, A. W. Green.

Main office, 205 La Salle street, Chicago.

---

## NATIONAL BREAD CO.

A corporation founded under the laws of New Jersey, July 24, 1901. The purpose of the company is to manufacture and sell bread and like food products and the manufacture, sale and leasing of machinery for bread-making.

Stock.....Par $100....Authorized { com., $2,000,000; pref., 1,000,000 } Issued { com., $2,000,000; pref., 1,000,000 } $3,000,000

The preferred stock is 8 per cent., cumulative. Transfer Agent, Corporation Trust Co., New Jersey. Registrar, Corporation Trust Co., New York.

The company has no funded debt.

President, Owen T. Bugg; Vice-President, Henry P. C. Johnston; Secretary, Albert C. Johnson; Treasurer, William H. Meadowcroft, New York.

Directors—Owen T. Bugg, H. A. Lozier, Jr.; Henry P. C. Johnston, New York; Vernon H. Banks, Cleveland; William H. Meadowcroft, Boonton, N. J.

Corporate office, 15 Exchange place, Jersey City; main office, 25 Broad street, New York. Annual meeting, December 15, at Jersey City.

## THE NATIONAL CANDY CO.

A corporation formed under the laws of New Jersey, September 8, 1902, to acquire and operate the following concerns:

O. H. Peckham Candy Mfg. Co., St. Louis.
A. J. Walter Confectionery Co., St. Louis.
F. D. Seward Confectionary Co., St. Louis.
The Pan Confectionery Co., Chicago.
J. K. Farley Manufacturing Co., Chicago.
The P. Echert Co., Cincinnati.
Burt & Sindele, Buffalo.
Frank A. Menne Candy Co., Louisville.
Sibley & Holmwood, Buffalo.
Gray, Toynton & Fox, Detroit.
The Paris Murton Co., Minneapolis.
The Nickols-Krull Co., Indianapolis.
Daggett & Co., Indianapolis.
Putnam Candy Co., Grand Rapids.

| Stock..Par $100...Authorized | | | Issued | | | |
|---|---|---|---|---|---|---|
| | com., | $6,000,000 | | com., | $6,000,000 | |
| | 1st pref., | 1,000,000 | | 1st pref., | 1,000,000 | $8,118,000 |
| | 2d pref., | 2,000,000 | | 2d pref., | 1,118,000 | |

The preferred stock is 7 per cent., cumulative. Registrar, Mississippi Valley Trust Co., St. Louis.

The company has no funded debt.

During the three years ending December 31, 1901, the average annual net profits of the companies absorbed by the corporation were $303,778.38.

President, O. H. Peckham, St. Louis; Vice-Presidents, Peter Echert, Cincinnati; John S. Gray, Detroit; Frank Sibley, Buffalo; V. L. Price, Chicago; Secretary, August J. Walter; Treasurer, Francis D. Seward, St. Louis.

Directors—Osgood H. Peckham, August J. Walter, Francis D. Steward, Breckinridge Jones, St. Louis; Frank A. Menne, Louisville; Charles A. Roach, St. Paul; Vincent L. Price, Jesse K. Farley, Frank F. Reed, Chicago; A. W. Paris, Minneapolis; Frank Sibley, Albert H. Burt, Buffalo; John S. Gray, Detroit; Richard R. Bean, Grand Rapids, Mich.; Peter Echert, Cincinnati; John S. Messick, Indianapolis.

Corporate office, Jersey City; general office, 406 Market street, St. Louis. Annual meeting, in September.

---

## NATIONAL CARBON CO.

A corporation formed under the laws of New Jersey, January 16, 1899. The company manufactures carbons for arc lighting, carbon brushes for electric generators and motors, carbon batteries, carbon diaphragms and back plates for telephones, carbons for electrolytic purposes, and so forth.

| Stock...Par $100....Authorized | | | Issued | | | |
|---|---|---|---|---|---|---|
| | com., | $5,500,000 | | com., | $5,500,000 | $10,000,000 |
| | pref., | 4,500,000 | | pref., | 4,500,000 | |

The preferred stock is 7 per cent., non-cumulative, dividends being payable quarterly in February, May, August and November.

Transfer Agent, Northern Trust Co., Chicago. Registrar, Merchants' Loan and Trust Co., Chicago.

Regular quarterly dividends on the preferred have been paid at the rate of 1¾ per cent. since July 15, 1899, the quarterly dividend periods having been changed in February, 1900, to February, May, August and November.

EARNINGS.

Year ending January 31.

| | Net. | Div. on Pfd. | Additions, Etc. | Surplus. |
|---|---|---|---|---|
| 1899-1900 | $451,687 | (7) $315,000 | $100,742 | $35,945 |
| 1900-1901 | 508,739 | (7) 315,000 | 151,456 | 42,283 |
| 1901-1902 | 586,812 | (7) 315,000 | 217,744 | 54,000 |
| 1902-1903 | 594,371 | (7) 315,000 | 256,637 | 22,734 |

The company's balance sheet, February 1, 1903, was as follows:

| ASSETS. | | LIABILITIES. | |
|---|---|---|---|
| Real estate, plants, machinery, etc. | $9,270,000 | Preferred capital stock | $4,500,000 |
| Merchandise, manufactured and unmanufactured | 448,215 | Common capital stock | 5,500,000 |
| Cash | 162,462 | Fourth dividend on preferred capital stock, payable February 15, 1902. | 78,750 |
| Cash reserved for fourth dividend on preferred capital stock | 78,750 | Accounts payable | 89,278 |
| Bills and accounts receivable | 364,601 | Profit and loss account to balance | 156,000 |
| Total | $10,324,028 | Total | $10,324,028 |

President, James Parmelee; Vice-President, Myron T. Herrick; 2d Vice-President, Webb C. Hayes; Secretary, J. C. Crider; Treasurer, H. E. Hackenberg; General Manager, Daniel D. Dickey.

Directors—James Parmelee, A. M. Young, New York; H. E. Hackenberg, Myron T. Herrick, N. C. Cotabish, Cleveland; Webb C. Hayes, Fremont, O.; John S. Bartlett, Lynn, Mass.; Daniel D. Dickey, J. S. Crider, Pittsburg; Hugh H. Hamill, Trenton, N. J.; J. P. Wilson, Chicago.

Corporate office, Trenton, N. J.; main office, West Madison and Highland avenues, Cleveland. Annual meeting, fourth Monday in February, at Trenton, N. J.

## NATIONAL CASH REGISTER CO.

A corporation formed under the laws of New Jersey, March 31, 1899. The purpose of the company is the manufacture of cash registers and kindred mechanisms. It has a large factory at Dayton, O., with an output of 200 registers per day. The company makes 239 different styles of registers and manufactures 95 per cent. of all the cash registers sold in the United States.

Stock....Par $100.....Authorized { com., $4,000,000 / pref., 1,000,000 } Issued { com., $4,000,000 / pref., 1,000,000 } $5,000,000

The preferred stock is 7 per cent., cumulative. It also has preference as to distribution of the assets in case of dissolution. Transfer Agent, The Corporation Trust Co. of New Jersey.

The company has no funded debt and no mortgages on its property.

The net earnings of the company are stated to have averaged about $300,000 per annum. The dividends on the preferred stock call for $70,000 per annum.

Dividends on the preferred have been regularly paid since the stock was issued, the payments being semi-annual, 3½ per cent. in January and July respectively. The dividends paid on the common stock are not published.

President, John H. Patterson; Vice-President, Robert Patterson; 2d Vice-President and General Manager, Hugh Chalmers; Secretary, Alfred A. Thomas; Treasurer, William Pflum.

Directors—John H. Patterson, Robert Patterson, Hugh Chalmers, Alfred A. Thomas, Andrew J. Lauver, Kenneth K. McLaren, Pearl N. Sigler, Frank H. Bickford, William Pflum, Edward A. Deeds, Julian V. Wright, Frank P. Davis, John H. Dohner, Charles G. Heyne, Gustav H. Wark, Deforest W. Saxe.

Corporate office, 15 Exchange place, Jersey City; main office, Brown and Stewart streets, Dayton, O. Annual meeting, first Tuesday in February.

## NATIONAL ENAMELING & STAMPING CO.

A corporation formed under the laws of New Jersey, January 21, 1899. It is a consolidation of concerns which produce practically all the enamelled ware made in the United States and a large proportion of the tin, galvanized, japanned and copper wares. The plants acquired were those of the St. Louis Stamping Co., St. Louis Tin Plate Co., Granite City Rolling Mills, Granite City Sheet Mills, located at St. Louis, and Granite City, Ill.; Kieckhefer Brothers Co., Milwaukee; Matthai, Ingram & Co., Baltimore, and the Haberman Manufacturing Co., Berlin Village, L. I., and Brooklyn, N. Y.; American Stamping Co., Brooklyn, N. Y.; Eastern Tinware Co., Portland, Conn.; Stewart Enamel Co., Bellaire, O.; Keene & Hagerty Manufacturing Co., Baltimore; H. Haller Manfacturing Co., Limited, New Orleans. The company also acquired the rolling mills of the St. Louis Stamping Co., and its tin plate mills.

Stock..Par $100...Authorized { com., $20,000,000 / pref., 10,000,000 } Issued { com., $15,441,800 / pref., 8,396,600 } $23,838,400

The preferred stock is 7 per cent., cumulative.

Transfer office, 243 Washington street, Jersey City. Registrar, Colonial Trust Co., New York.

The first quarterly dividend of 1¾ per cent. on the preferred stock was paid March 31, 1900, and regular quarterly dividends at the same rate have since been paid, the dividend periods on the preferred now being January (1), April, July and October. The first dividend on the common was 4 per cent., declared in 1901 out of earnings of that year, and payable in four quarterly instalments of 1 per cent. each, beginning January 1, 1902. Dividends at the same rate have since been regularly paid on the common stock in January (1), April, July and October.

The underlying purchase money mortgages on the constituent properties have been paid off.

For the eleven months ending December 31, 1899, the company reported gross profits of $1,635,032, net $1,322,374; dividends on preferred stock, $490,497; balance surplus, $831,877. In the 18 months ending June 29, 1901, profits, $1,127,506; dividends on preferred, $817,068; balance, $310,438. In the year ending June 30, 1902, net profits were $1,720,307 and the surplus over dividends $669,291.

The following is the company's balance sheet June 29, 1902:

| Assets. | | Liabilities. | |
|---|---|---|---|
| Plant, good will, etc. | $22,961,309 | Preferred stock issued | $8,396,600 |
| Materials and supplies | 4,483,456 | Common stock issued | 15,441,800 |
| Accounts and bills receivable | 784,374 | Mortgage debt | 2,335,000 |
| Payments in advance | 38,476 | Bills payable | ........ |
| Miscellaneous | 35,217 | Sundry creditors | 437,084 |
| Cash | 427,634 | Reserve for bad debts | ........ |
| | | Accrued interest | 38,917 |
| | | Dividend payable July 1, 1902 | 301,358 |
| | | Balance | 1,779,707 |
| Total | $28,730,466 | Total | $28,730,466 |

President, Frederick G. Niedringhaus, St. Louis; 1st Vice-President, Ferdinand A. W. Kieckhefer, Milwaukee; 2d Vice-President, Frederick Haberman, New York; Treasurer, James E. Ingram, Baltimore; Secretary, William H. Matthai, Baltimore; Assistant Secretary and Treasurer, Adolph M. Steinhardt, New York.

Directors—Frederick G. Niedringhaus, George W. Niedringhaus, Thomas K. Niedringhaus, Frederick Haberman, Ferdinand A. W. Kieckhefer, James E. Ingram, William H. Matthai, Adolph M. Steinhardt, George W. Knapp, L. C. Bartling, H. August Luddke, Charles W. King, William F. Niedringhaus, Edward H. Schwartzburg, Geoage V. Hagerty, Solomon Richman, Alexander Niedringhaus.

Main office, 81 Fulton street, New York.

---

## NATIONAL FIRE PROOFING CO.

A corporation formed under the laws of Pennsylvania in 1889, with the title of the Pittsburg Terra Cotta Lumber Co. On December 20, 1899, it increased its capital stock for the purchase of additional properties and at the same time changed its corporate title to the National Fire Proofing Co. On February 17, 1902, the stock was again increased to acquire 18 additional plants, the property of 15 different companies.

The company manufactures porous, terra cotta and dense tile fire proofing, plain and ornamental blocks, building, paving and hollow bricks, underground conduits for telegraph, telephone or railway cables and other standard articles and specialties made from clay. The company now has 28 plants located in different States, with considerable real estate, patent rights and other valuable property.

Stock....Par $50....Authorized { com., $4,500,000 / pref., 8,000,000 } Issued { com., $4,500,000 / pref., 8,000,000 } $12,500,000

The preferred stock is 7 per cent., non-cumulative, dividends payable quarterly. The capital stock authorized was originally $1,000,000 preferred and $1,000,000 common. The amounts outstanding were $500,000 common and $623,550 preferred. In July, 1901, it was increased to $2,000,000 common and $3,000,000 preferred, a stock dividend of 12 per cent. on the common being declared. Stockholders had the right to subscribe for 50 per cent. of their holdings in new preferred, at par, with a bonus of 25 per cent. in common, and $500,000 common and $1,000,000 preferred were used to acquire additional properties.

In February, 1902, the stock was increased again by the creation and issue of $2,500,000 common and $5,000,000 additional preferred. The holders of the outstanding stock were invited to subscribe for 50 per cent. of their holdings, such subscriptions covering $1,250,000 of new common and $2,500,000 of new preferred. The balance of the new stock was taken by financial interests identified with the company. The purpose of the new stock issue was to acquire the additional plants referred to above, and to provide $1,000,000 in cash to be added to the company's working capital.

Transfer Agent, Mercantile Trust Co., Pittsburg. Registrar, Union Trust Co., Pittsburg.

The stock of the Pittsburg Terra Cotta Lumber Co. was $500,000. On this regular quarterly dividends of 1½ per cent. were paid.

The company has no funded debt or mortgages on its plant and no obligations beyond current accounts payable.

Regular quarterly dividends of 1¾ per cent. are paid on the preferred stock in January (25), April, July and October. Dividends are paid quarterly on the common stock at the rate of 1½ per cent. each in February, May, August and November.

EARNINGS.

| | Net. | Dividends. | Surplus. |
|---|---|---|---|
| 1902 | $1,126,968 | $554,784 | $572,183 |

| ASSETS. | | LIABILITIES. | |
|---|---|---|---|
| Plants, real estate, properties and equipment, including improvements | $13,226,402 | Capital stock, preferred | $8,000,000 |
| Stocks and bonds of other companies | 89,367 | Capital stock, common | 4,500,000 |
| Accounts and bills receivable | 1,328,306 | Mortgage payable | 44,469 |
| Cash | 445,730 | Mortgages and notes of underlying companies, guaranteed | 251,700 |
| Inventory of manufactured material and supplies | 203,599 | Unpaid dividend, preferred, payable January 25, 1903 | 139,658 |
| | | Unpaid dividends, common, accrued November and December, 1902 | 30,706 |
| | | Accounts and bills payable | 491,115 |
| | | Surplus | 1,835,756 |
| Total | $15,293,404 | Total | $15,293,404 |

Chairman, David F. Henry; President, William D. Henry; Vice-President and Manager of Sales, R. W. Allison, Pittsburg; Vice-President and Eastern Manager, Henry M. Keasbey, New York; Vice-President and Western Manager, E. V. Johnson; Treasurer, William H. Graham; Assistant Treasurer, J. P. Robbins; Secretary, Charles G. Jones, Pittsburg.

Directors—David F. Henry, S. C. Grier, J. J. Booth, William H. Graham, T. J. Hamilton, Adam Wilson, Frederick Gwinner, Jr., W. A. Dinker, T. G. McCutcheon, Henry M. Keasbey, R. W. Allison, A. R. Peacock, H. S. Black, William D. Henry.

Main office, Fifth avenue and Grant street, Pittsburg; Eastern offices, Maiden Lane and Broadway, New York; 73 Tremont street, Boston; Broad and Sansom streets, Philadelphia; Western office, 140 Dearborn street, Chicago.

## THE NATIONAL GAS & CONSTRUCTION CO.

A corporation formed under the laws of New Jersey, September 24, 1897. The purpose of the company is to build and operate gas, electric light and sewer plants and trolley roads. The company has acquired the following companies and their plants:

Capital City Light & Fuel Co., Tallahassee, Fla.
Greenville Gas & Electric Light & Power Co., Greenville, S. C.
Greenville Traction Co., Greenville, S. C.
Selma Lighting Co., Selma, Ala.

Stock......Par $100............. ..............Authorized, $1,000,000......Issued, $500,000

Stock is transferred at the company's office, Philadelphia. Registrar, West End Trust Co., Philadelphia.

The company has no funded debt.

The net profits from the organization of the company to December 31, 1902, were $192,299.

President, Joseph S. Keen, Jr.; Vice-Presdent, J. W. Hawley; Secretary and Assistant Treasurer, H. Bayard Hodge; Treasurer, George M. Bunting; Assistant Treasurer, H. Roth, Philadelphia.

Directors—Joseph S. Keen, Jr., Joseph T. Richards, George M. Bunting, Philadelphia; J. W. Hawley, Media, Pa.; Howard Watkin, Wynnewood, Pa.; George Reynolds, Camden, N. J.; William C. Scott, Haverford, Pa.

Corporate office, 119 Market street, Camden, N. J.; main office, 112 N. Broad street, Philadelphia. Annual meeting, second Wednesday in November, at Camden, N. J.

## NATIONAL GLASS CO.

A corporation formed under the laws of Pennsylvania, November 1, 1899. The company was organized for the purpose of combining under one management the leading American manufacturers of glass tableware. The concerns whose plants and property were acquired are as follows:

Crystal Glass Co., Bridgeport, O.
Canton Glass Co., Marion, Ind.
Central Glass Co., Summitville, Ind.
Cumberland Glass Co., Cumberland, Md.
Beatty-Brady Glass Works, Dunkirk, Ind.
Dalzell, Gilmore & Leighton Wks, Findlay, O.
Fairmont Glass Works, Fairmont, W. Va.
Greensburg Glass Works, Greensburg, Pa.
Indiana Tumbler & Goblet Works, Greentown, Ind.
Keystone Glass Works, Rochester, Pa.
McKee Bros. Glass Works, Jeannette, Pa.
Model Flint Glass Works, Albany, Ind.
Northwood Glass Works, Indiana, Pa.
Ohio Flint Glass Works, Lancaster, O.
Riverside Glass Works, Wellsburg, W. Va.
Robinson Glass Works, Zanesville, O.
Rochester Tumbler Works, Rochester, Pa.
Royal Glass Works, Marietta, O.
West Virginia Glass Works, Martin's Ferry, O.

These properties possessed an aggregate capacity of nearly 600 glass pots and produced a large portion of their class of wares. It was stated that the concerns were acquired strictly on a cash valuation basis, and that all of the properties were at the time of consolidation earning largely.

Stock......Par $50..........................Authorized, $4,000,000......Issued, $2,250,000

In December, 1902, it was proposed to retire $800,000 of the old stock and to create and issue $1,600,000 of 7 per cent., non-cumulative, preferred stock, of which $800,000 was to be exchanged for a like amount of the old common stock and $800,000 sold to provide additional working capital.

Transfer Agent, Union Trust Co., Pittsburg. Registrar, Equitable Trust Co., Pittsburg.

FUNDED DEBT.

| | |
|---|---|
| 1st mort., gold, 6 per cent., due Nov., 1949, May and November...................... | $1,400,000 |
| Gen. mort., 6 per cent., due Nov., 1921, May and Nov............................ | 1,100,000 |
| Total.............................................................. | $2,500,000 |

The 1st mortgage bonds are payable $200,000 per annum in numerical order. The original amount of the bonds was $2,000,000, but $200,000 each, maturing in November, 1900, 1901 and 1902 respectively, were retired.

The general mortgage, Union Trust Co., Pittsburg, Trustee, was created in 1901, and is for $2,500,000, sufficient bonds being reserved to retire firsts. The bonds are subject to call at 105 for a sinking fund, which is to be 5 per cent. of the company's earnings each year.

President, Andrew W. Herron; Vice-President, Frank L. Stevenson; Secretary, Addison Thompson; Treasurer, Myron L. Case, Pittsburg.

Directors—Frank L. Stevenson, George I. Whitney, Andrew W. Herron, Addison Thompson, Myron L. Case, A. L. Strasburger, L. B. Martin, Pittsburg.

Main office, Penn avenue and Eighth street, Pittsburg; commercial business offices in New York, Boston, Philadelphia, Baltimore, Chicago, Denver, San Francisco, Los Angeles, Cal., and London, England. Annual meeting, second Tuesday in August, at Pittsburg.

## NATIONAL LEAD CO.

A corporation formed under the laws of New Jersey, December 7, 1891, to succeed the National Lead Trust, which was organized on the trust plan. The property of the company consists of white-lead works, smelters and refineries in New York, Pennsylvania, Missouri, Ohio, Massachusetts, Illinois, Kentucky, and other States, and comprises 26 large plants. In 1900 purchased a large lead mine in Missouri.

In December, 1902, it was stated that this company and the Union Lead & Oil Co., with other organizations, would be combined.

Stock..Par $100...Authorized { com., $15,000,000; pref., 15,000,000 } Issued { com., $14,905,400; pref., 14,904,000 } $29,809,400

The preferred stock is 7 per cent., cumulative.

Stock is transferred at the company's office, 100 William street, New York. Registrar, Mercantile Trust Co., New York.

The company has no bonded debt, but in 1900 a 5 per cent. mortgage for $1,000,000 was placed on the works of the St. Louis Smelting & Refining Co., one of the constituent concerns, to provide for extensions and improvements, $950,000 of the bonds being held in the treasury.

The reorganization plan of the National Lead Trust also provided $3,000,000 6 per cent. thirty-year debenture bonds, though none of the same have ever been issued so far.

The company commenced paying dividends on preferred stock March, 1892, at the rate of 1¾ per cent., quarterly, and has continued to pay such dividends regularly in March, June, September and December. Three dividends of 1 per cent. each were paid on common in 1894. The October dividend on the common was the only one paid in 1895, after which none was paid until February, 1898, when 1 per cent. was paid, and 1 per cent. was also paid in March, 1899 and 1900.

EARNINGS.

| | Net. | Dividends. | Surplus |
|---|---|---|---|
| 1897........................................ | $1,532,376 | $1,043,280 | $489,096 |
| 1898........................................ | 1,241,838 | 1,192,334 | 49,504 |
| 1899........................................ | 1,373,906 | 1,192,234 | 181,572 |
| 1900........................................ | 1,076,440 | 1,192,334 | 208,847 |
| 1901........................................ | 1,112,140 | 1,043,280 | 68,860 |
| 1902........................................ | 1,202,514 | 1,043,280 | 159,234 |

The following is the company's balance sheet, December 31, 1902:

| Assets. | | Liabilities. | |
|---|---|---|---|
| Plant investment | $13,465,357 | Capital stock, common | $15,000,000 |
| Other investments | 1,219,242 | Capital stock, preferred | 15,000,000 |
| Stock on hand, manufactured, in process and raw | 5,638,617 | Surplus, December 31, 1902 | 1,437,042 |
| Treasury stock, common | 94,600 | Mortgages | 12,603 |
| Treasury stock, preferred | 96,000 | Notes payable | 1,050,000 |
| Cash in banks | 352,343 | Accounts payable | 63,839 |
| Notes receivable | 152,575 | | |
| Accounts receivable | 1,544,750 | | |
| Total | $32,563,484 | Total | $32,563,484 |

President, L. A. Cole, New York; 1st Vice-President, F. W. Rockwell, Chicago; 2d Vice-President, J. A. Stevens; Secretary, Charles Davison, New York.

Directors—W. H. Thompson, E. C. Goshorn, F. W. Rockwell, L. A. Cole, R. R. Colgate, A. P. Thompson, D. B. Shipman, J. A. Stevens, George O. Carpenter, Charles F. Wells, Reginald P. Rowe, Edward F. Beale, Jr., Walter Tufts.

Main office, 100 William street, New York. Annual meeting, third Thursday in February.

## NATIONAL MINING CO.

A corporation formed under the laws of Michigan in 1878. The company owns a copper property in Ontonagon County, Mich., the mine adjoining that of the Michigan Copper Mining Co., formerly the Minnesota mine, one of the most famous of the older mines in the copper range. The National mine has been opened since 1848, and was a large producer of copper, yielding $2,295,231 until it was shut down in 1871. The present company did considerable work upon the mine, but of late years active operations have been suspended.

Stock......Par $25...........................Authorized, $2,500,000......Issued, $1,875,000

Of the stock 25,000 shares remain in the treasury. There has been paid on the outstanding stock $3.20 per share.

President, John C. Watson; Secretary and Treasurer, Daniel L. Denmon, Boston.

Directors—John C. Watson, F. H. Raymond, Daniel L. Denmon, B. F. Chynoweth.

Main office, 15 Congress street, Boston.

## NATIONAL RICE MILLING CO.

A corporation formed under the laws of New Jersey in 1892. The company owns and operates two rice mills at New Orleans and one at Crowley, La., together with warehouses in New Orleans and throughout the State of Louisiana.

In December, 1900, a financial readjustment was proposed, involving a reduction of the authorized common stock of the company and of the par value of shares from $100 to $10 each.

Stock....Par $10........Authorized { com., $500,000; pref., 1,000,000 } Issued { com., $335,220; pref., 669,500 } $1,004,720

The preferred stock is 8 per cent., non-cumulative.

For an account of the old company and of its reorganization, see the MANUAL for 1902.

The dividends on the new preferred stock of the company are 10 per cent. per annum.

President, Henry Kahn; Vice-President, Albert Baldwin, Jr.; Secretary and Treasurer, P. P. Lynch, New Orleans.

Directors—R. E. Craig, A. Katz, Isidore Newman, Sr., Albert Baldwin, Albert Baldwin, Jr., John H. Hanna, P. F. Pescud, Henry Kahn, P. P. Lynch, Simon Pfeifer, T. J. Fableman, New Orleans; Edward Q. Keasby, Newark, N. J.

Corporate office, Newark, N. J.; main office, New Orleans. Annual meeting, first Wednesday in September, at Newark, N. J.

## NATIONAL SALT CO.

(Controlled by International Salt Co.)

A corporation formed under the laws of New Jersey, March 18, 1899. At the time of its organization the company acquired by purchase over 90 per cent. of the salt producing plants in the State of New York.

In October, 1899, the company purchased a number of salt producing plants in the States of Ohio and Michigan, and acquired by contract the salt produced at other plants in those

States, and in January, 1900, the company purchased salt properties in the States of Kansas and Texas.

In the acquisition of the Ohio properties the purchase price was paid in preferred and common stock of the National Salt Co., all of which stock was deposited in escrow with the American Trust Co. of Cleveland, under an agreement whereby the dividends on such stock were assured for a period of five years.

In October, 1901, it was proposed to combine this company with other salt manufacturing concerns under the title of the International Salt Co. The holders of National Salt preferred stock were offered for each 10 shares a $1,000 bond of the International Salt Co. and one share of its stock. The common stock of this company was to be exchanged for stock of the International Salt Co. A majority of the stocks of this company were exchanged on these terms.

In October, 1902, Frank P. McDermott, Jersey City, and N. S. Beardslee, Warsaw, N. Y., were appointed receivers. It was alleged that this action was preparatory to winding up the company.

Stock..Par $100....Authorized { com., $7,000,000; pref., 5,000,000 } Issued { com., $7,000,000; pref., 5,000,000 } $12,000,000

The preferred stock is 7 per cent., non-cumulative, and is preferred as to dividends and assets in the event of dissolution, but the common and preferred stocks have equal voting powers.

The company has no bonded indebtedness, and by its articles of incorporation and by-laws is prohibited from creating any mortgage or other permanent form of indebtedness except with the written consent of at least 75 per cent. of all the preferred and common stock. The Hutchinson Salt Co., one of the constituent concerns, has, however, $260,000 of bonds.

During the year 1900 the net earnings of the company were reported as $1,302,728; in 1901 net was $199,360.

Dividends on the preferred stock are declarable on the fifteenth day of January, April, July, and October, and were paid regularly every quarter in February, May, August and November, from the company's organization, but the February, 1902, dividend on the preferred was not acted on.

There are no fixed dates for the declaration of dividends on common stock. In April, 1900, the common stock was placed on a 6 per cent. basis, and received its first quarterly dividend on August 1, 1900, the second on December 1, 1900, and the third on February 1, 1901. On August 1, 1900, the common received also an extra dividend of one-half of 1 per cent., and 1½ per cent. was paid in November, 1900. In 1900 6 per cent. was paid on the common in quarterly payments of 1½ per cent. in February, May, August and November, and dividends of a like amount were paid in 1901 to November, inclusive.

President, N. S. Beardslee, Warsaw, N. Y.; Vice-President, Joy Morton, Chicago; Secretary and Treasurer, Mortimer B. Fuller, Scranton, Pa.; Assistant Secretary, W. B. Putney, Jr.; Assistant Treasurer, F. W. Relyea, New York.

Directors—N. S. Beardslee, Mortimer B. Fuller, Scranton, Pa.; Joy Morton, Chicago; L. H. Hall, George F. Dominick, Jr.; Frank P. Slade, Westfield, N. J.; H. D. Fuller, Bayonne, N. J.; Robert Maitland, Brooklyn, N. Y.

Corporate office, 15 Exchange place, Jersey City; main office, Ithaca, N. Y.; New York office, 170 Broadway. Annual meeting, fourth Wednesday in March.

## NATIONAL SUGAR REFINING CO. OF NEW JERSEY

A corporation formed under the laws of New Jersey, June 2, 1900. The company acquired and took over the property of the New York Sugar Refining Co., of Long Island City, N. Y., which plant was constructed by Claus Doscher and associates, the refinery of the Mollenhauer Sugar Refinery Co. at Brooklyn, and the National refinery at Yonkers, N. Y. The capacity of these establishments is about 10,000 barrels of refined sugar per day.

It is understood that the constituent concerns were capitalized as follows: National Refining, $1,000,000 stock; Mollenhauer Co., $1,000,000 stock; New York Sugar Refining Co., $600,000 stock, $2,400,000 bonds. These securities were exchanged for stock of the new company.

Stock..Par $100...Authorized { com., $10,000,000; pref., 10,000,000 } Issued { pref., $10,000,000; com., 10,000,000 } $20,000,000

The preferred stock is 6 per cent., cumulative.

Transfer Agent, William H. Corbin, 243 Washington street, Jersey City. Registrar, National City Bank, New York.

The payment of quarterly dividends of 1½ per cent. on the preferred stock began on October 2, 1900, and the same are regularly paid in January, April, July and October.

President, James H. Post; Vice-President and Treasurer, F. D. Mollenhauer; Secretary, Herbert D. Cory, New York.

Directors—James H. Post, F. D. Mollenhauer, H. F. Mollenhauer, J. Henry Dick, Brooklyn, N. Y.; Herbert D. Cory, Englewood, N. J.; George R. Bunker, Yonkers, N. Y.; F. H. Howell, New York.

Main office, 109 Wall street, New York. Annual meeting, second Wednesday in January, at Jersey City.

## THE NATIONAL SUPPLY CO.

A corporation formed under the laws of West Virginia. The business of the company is to manufacture and deal in oil and gas well, plumbers' and steam-fitters' supplies, machinery, cordage and pipe. The plant of the company is located at Toledo, O.

Stock......Par $100........................Authorized, $2,000,000......Issued, $1,666,666

The company has no preferred stock and no funded debt.

Dividends of 2 per cent. quarterly are paid.

President, Henry M. Wilson; 1st Vice-President and Treasurer, William Hardee; 2d Vice-President, W. C. Hillman; Secretary, J. H. Barr, Pittsburg.

Directors—E. C. Converse, A. F. Luke, Edward Worcester, W. C. Hillman, J. H. Barr, Henry M. Wilson.

Main office, Pittsburg.

## NATIONAL TYPEWRITER CO. OF DELAWARE

A corporation formed under the laws of Delaware, April 8, 1899, for the purpose of manufacturing typewriters, supplies and other goods, it being a reorganization of a company of the same name.

Stock......Par $25........................Authorized, $2,000,000......Issued, $2,000,000

The company has no preferred stock and no funded debt. Stock is transferred at the company's office, Philadelphia. Registrar, Guarantee Trust & Safe Deposit Co., Philadelphia.

President, Henry H. Unz; Vice-President, J. Dawson; Secretary and Treasurer, A. K. Clanton, Philadelphia.

Corporate office, Dover, Del.; main office, Lehigh Avenue road and Fifteenth street, Philadelphia.

## THE NATURAL FOOD CO.

A corporation formed under the laws of New York in December, 1900, for the purpose of manufacturing food products and food-making machinery.

Stock....Par $100....Authorized { com., $8,750,000 / pref., 1,250,000 } Issued { com., $8,750,000 / pref., 1,250,000 } $10,000,000

The preferred stock is 6 per cent., cumulative. Stock is transferred at the office of the company, Niagara Falls, N. Y. Registrar, Farmers' Loan & Trust Co., New York.

Dividends are payable quarterly in January, April, July and October.

FUNDED DEBT.

1st mort., 5 per cent., due July, 1912, Jan. and July............................ .... $945,000

Trustee of the mortgage, Fidelity Trust Co., Buffalo. Agent for the payment of interest, Farmers' Loan & Trust Co., New York.

The authorized amount of the bond issue was $1,000,000, but $55,000 have been retired.

President, H. D. Perky; Vice-President, F. D. Locke; Treasurer, A. J. Porter; Secretary and Assistant Treasurer, B. L. Herrick.

Directors—H. D. Perky, W. B. Rankine, F. D. Locke, William Hamlin, Joseph Henderson, T. E. Ellsworth, A. J. Porter.

. Corporate and main office, Niagara Falls, N. Y. Annual meeting, second Tuesday in November, at Niagara Falls.

## NAUMKEAG STEAM COTTON CO.

A corporation formed in Massachusetts in 1839, for the purpose of manufacturing cotton goods. The mills of the company are at Salem, Mass., and have 105,000 spindles and 2,800 looms.

Stock......Par $100........................Authorized, $1,500,000......Issued, $1,500,000

Stock is transferred at the office of the company.

Dividends are paid semi-annually, January and July. In 1901 only 2 per cent. was paid, which was also the rate in 1902, paid in July. In January, 1903, a 2 per cent. dividend was paid.

The quick assets of the company are $1,029,008; liabilities, $585,672; surplus, $443,336.

President, David Pingree; Clerk, J. Foster Smith; Treasurer, Nathaniel G. Simonds, Salem, Mass.

Directors—David Pingree, Nathaniel G. Simonds, William Agge, Salem, Mass.; Grant Walker, Benjamin Phipps, John F. Brooks, S. Parker Bremer, Boston.

Main office, Peabody street, Salem, Mass. Annual meeting, third Wednesday in January, at Salem.

## NEBRASKA TELEPHONE CO.

A corporation formed under the laws of Nebraska in 1883. The company operates a telephone system in Nebraska, Iowa and Black Hills District, S. D., under the Bell patents, the municipalities served including Council Bluffs, Lincoln, Omaha, Nebraska City and South Omaha. The company has 42 exchanges, 133 branch offices and 3,913 miles of toll pole lines, with 15,014 miles of toll line wire. A controlling interest in the company is owned by the American Telephone & Telegraph Co.

Stock......Par $100..........................Authorized, $3,000,000......Issued, $1,800,000

The company has no preferred stock and no funded debt.

Dividends at the rate of 6 per cent. per annum have been paid quarterly, in January, April, July and October, since 1894.

For the fiscal year ending December 31, 1902, the company's gross earnings were $905,660; net, $168,440; dividends, $99,000; surplus, $69,440.

The following is the company's balance sheet, December 31, 1902:

| ASSETS. | | LIABILITIES. | |
|---|---|---|---|
| Construction | $2,039,604 | Capital stock | $1,800,000 |
| Supply department | 73,027 | Surplus | 334,201 |
| Real estate | 158,910 | Reserve | 239,672 |
| Stock and bonds | 2,100 | Bills and accounts payable | 74,272 |
| Accounts receivable | 141,479 | | |
| Cash | 33,025 | | |
| Total | $2,448,145 | Total | $2,448,145 |

President, Casper E. Yost; Vice-President, C. W. Lyman; Secretary and Treasurer, E. M. Morsman; General Manager, H. Vance Lane.

Directors—Alonzo Burt, Guy C. Barton, C. W. Lyman, C. Jay French, George W. Holdrege, E. M. Morsman, W. W. Morsman, Henry W. Yates, Casper E. Yost.

Main office, Omaha, Neb. Annual meeting, second Thursday in February, at Omaha.

---

## NEWARK CONSOLIDATED GAS CO.

A corporation formed under the laws of New Jersey in 1898. The company was a consolidation of the Newark Gas Co., Montclair Gas & Water Co., Summit Gas Co., People's Gas Co., of Irvington, and the Clinton Gas Co. It also owns all the stock of the Orange Gas Light Co. By these acquisitions the company secured control of all the gas facilities of Newark, N. J., and the adjacent cities and towns. The company was organized in the interest of the United Gas Improvement Co. of Philadelphia. The property was leased to that company for 999 years and the lease assigned to another corporation, the Essex & Hudson Gas Co., controlled by the United Gas Improvement Co., the United Gas Improvement being, however, responsible during the first six years of the lease, or to 1905, for all payments under the lease. The terms of lease require as rental the payment of fixed charges, taxes and maintenance, and, beginning in 1900, dividends on the Newark Consolidated Gas Co.'s stock at the rate of 2½ per cent. per annum, increasing ½ per cent. each year until 1908, when such dividends will be 5 per cent. per annum, and so remain.

Stock......Par $100..........................Authorized, $6,000,000......Issued, $6,000,000

FUNDED DEBT.

| | |
|---|---|
| Newark Gas Co., 1st mort., 6 per cent., due April, 1944, quarterly, Jan. | $4,000,000 |
| Montclair Gas & Water, 1st mort., due July, 1903 | 25,000 |
| Newark Consolidated Gas, 1st mort., 5 per cent., due 1948, Jan. and Dec. | 5,274,000 |
| Total | $9,299,000 |

The 1st mortgage of the Consolidated Co. is for $10,000,000, of which $4,025,000 was reserved to retire underlying bonds of old companies and $201,000 for improvements and additions. Trustee of mortgage, Fidelity Trust Co., Newark, which also pays coupons.

President (vacancy); Vice-President, William Scheerer; Secretary and Treasurer, George Barker.

Directors—Ebenezer C. Hay, Adrian Riker, Thomas N. McCarter, William Scheerer, Edgar Ward, Jerome Taylor, Jeremiah O'Rourke and Arthur D. Ball.

Main office, 575 Broad street, Newark, N. J.

## NEW BEDFORD GAS & EDISON LIGHT CO.

A corporation formed under the laws of Massachusetts, April 4, 1850. The purpose of the company is to supply gas and electric light to the city of New Bedford, Mass. The gas plant of the company has a capacity of 750,000 feet per day. The company acquired the following companies:

New Bedford Electric Light Co. Edison Elec. Illuminating Co. of New Bedford

Stock......Par $100..............................Authorized, $845,000......Issued, $650,000

The stock is transferred at the office of the company, New Bedford, Mass.

Annual dividends have been paid as follows: 1890, 8 per cent.; 1891-1898, inclusive, 6 per cent.; 1899-1900, 7 per cent.; 1901-1902, 6 per cent. Dividends are payable quarterly in January, April, July and October.

The company has no funded debt.

In the fiscal year ending June 30, 1902, the gross earnings were: $259,259; net, $119,360; total surplus, $125,993.97.

President and General Manager, George R. Stetson; Clerk and Treasurer, Charles R. Price.

Directors—Horace G. Howland, Thomas H. Knowles, Charles R. Price, George R. Stetson, Charles H. Lawton, Frederic Taber, Andrew G. Pierce, Oliver Prescott, Jr., John S. Perry, Henry M. Knowles, New Bedford, Mass.

Corporate and main office, 125 Middle street, New Bedford, Mass. Annual meeting, second Monday in August, at New Bedford, Mass.

## THE NEWBERRY COTTON MILLS

A corporation formed under the laws of South Carolina in 1882 for the purpose of manufacturing cotton goods, brown sheetings and drills. The company owns mills at Newberry, S. C., equipped with 25,000 spindles and 900 looms.

Stock......Par $100..............................Authorized, $400,000......Issued, $400,000

The company has no preferred stock and no funded debt.

In 1899, 1900, 1901 and 1902 semi-annual dividends of 4 per cent. were paid in January and July.

President and Treasurer, T. J. McCrary; Secretary, George S. Mower, Newberry, S. C.

Corporate and main office, Newberry, S. C. Annual meeting, first Wednesday in May, at Newberry, S. C.

## NEW CENTRAL COAL CO.

A Maryland corporation formed in 1872. It owns and operates a large bituminous coal property in Allegany County, Md., and Marion County, W. Va.

Stock......Par $20...................... .......Authorized, $1,000,000......Issued, $1,000,000

The stock of this company was formerly $5,000,000, par value $100. In 1898 it was reduced to $1,000,000, and the par value of the shares to $20 each.

Stock is transferred at the office of the company, New York.

From 1891 to 1894 inclusive, dividends of 1 per cent. per annum were paid on the $5,000,000 of old stock. No dividends were paid in the three years from 1895 to 1897 inclusive. In October, 1898, an initial dividend of 2 per cent. was paid on the reduced stock of the company. In April, 1899, 2 per cent. was paid and in October 2 per cent., making 4 per cent. for the year. In 1900, 2 per cent. was paid April 2, but the October dividend was passed on account of a strike of the company's miners, and no dividends were paid until March 2, 1903, when 2 per cent. was paid.

President, Henry S. Little; Vice-President and Secretary, Malcolm Baxter, Jr.; Treasurer, Frank W. Cummisky.

Directors—Henry S. Little, Octavius D. Baldwin, David G. Legget, Malcolm Baxter, Jr., William Fairlie, Eugene D. Hawkins, Jose A. Del Valle, Frank W. Cummisky, C. F. Anthony, William Grace, Henry C. Kelcey.

New York office, 1 Broadway.

## THE NEW CENTURY MINING & INVESTMENT CO.

A corporation formed under the laws of Colorado, January 1, 1901. The company acquired the Longfellow group of mines in Jamestown, Boulder County, Col., consisting of 85 acres equipped with a concentrating mill, tramway, motor room, assay office, powder magazines, electric transmission line, etc.

Stock......Par $1..............................Authorized, $1,250,000......Issued, $1,187,000

The company has no preferred stock and no funded debt. Stock is transferred at the office of the company, Denver, Col.

At the close of the fiscal year, December 31, 1902, the company had paid $22,823 in dividends. Dividends are paid quarterly.

President, R. G. Munn; Vice-President, O. B. Nichols; Secretary and Treasurer, R. L. Harper, Denver, Colo.

Directors—R. G. Munn, O. B. Nichols, R. L. Harper, W. D. Watts, Denver, Col.; F. D. Parker, E. L. Knickerbocker, Flint, Mich.; W. H. Duval, New York; F. J. Cook, Fowlerville, Mich.; Andrew Pizzini, Jr., Richmond.

Corporate and main office, 509 Tabor Block, Denver, Col. Annual meeting, second Tuesday in July, at Denver, Col.

## NEW ENGLAND BRICK CO.

A corporation formed under the laws of New Jersey, July 30, 1900. The purpose of the company is the manufacture of bricks and dealing in the same, as well as in building materials generally. It has acquired thirty-seven different plants in Maine, New Hampshire, Massachusetts and New York, being the principal concerns which supply Boston and the best New England markets north of Providence and Springfield. The most important yards of the company are in Cambridge, Belmont, Medford, Taunton, Middleboro, Bridgewater, Greenfield, Turners Falls, East Brookfield and Lancaster, Mass.; East Kingston, Epping and Rochester, N. H.; York and Saco, Me., and Mechanicville, N. Y. Almost without exception the plants were acquired for stock of the new company.

Stock....Par $100.....Authorized { com., $2,000,000 / pref., 3,000,000 } Issued { com., $1,067,500 / pref., 1,738,800 } $2,806,300

The preferred stock is 7 per cent., non-cumulative, and has a preference as to distribution of assets.

Transfer agency, company's office. Registrar, Old Colony Trust Co., Boston.

FUNDED DEBT.

1st mort., 6 per cent., gold, sinking fund bonds, due 1920, Feb. and Aug.............. $732,000

The 1st mortgage is for $850,000; of this amount of bonds $23,000 are held in escrow and $118,000 are in the company's treasury. There is a sinking fund of 3 per cent. of the bonds or $25,000 per annum, and bonds can be drawn at 110 and interest if they cannot be bought for less. Trustee of mortgage, Old Colony Trust Co., Boston, where coupons are also paid.

President, A. E. Locke; Vice-President, Edward W. Capen; Secretary-Treasurer, Thomas Lacey, Boston.

Directors—Charles F. Fairbanks, H. H. Bemis, Edward W. Capen, S. H. Fessenden, A. E. Locke, Thomas Lacey, Boston; M. W. Sands, Joseph Broussard, Cambridge, Mass.; Arthur D. Cady, W. N. Cary, Mechanicville, N. Y.; William A. Sanborn, Somerville, Mass.; Kenneth K. McLaren, Jersey City; W. S. Goodrich, Epping, N. H.; George R. Sampson, Middleboro, Mass.

Main office, 189 Devonshire street, Boston. Annual meeting in April, at Jersey City.

## NEW ENGLAND COTTON YARN CO.

A corporation formed under the laws of New Jersey, July 6, 1899. The company acquired the plants and property of nine leading yarn mills, including the Bennett, Howland, Rotch and New Bedford Spinning Co. Mills at New Bedford, Mass., the Nemasket and Cohanett Mills at Taunton, Mass., and the Globe, Sanford and North Dighton Mills at Fall River, Mass. These concerns operate a total of about 583,000 spindles and have an annual capacity of some 50,000,000 pounds of cotton yarn. The aggregate net earnings of the separate concerns in the year previous to consolidation were $1,106,000.

Stock...Par $100...Authorized { com., $5,000,000 / pref., 6,500,000 } Issued { com., $5,000,000 / pref., 5,000,000 } $10,000,000

The preferred stock is 7 per cent., cumulative, but does not share in surplus in excess of such 7 per cent. After January 1, 1900, the preferred stock may be retired at 140. Before payment of dividends on the preferred a sum equal to 1 per cent. of the outstanding bonds must be paid into a sinking fund for the bonds, and likewise in each year before any dividend is paid on the common stock, an amount equal to 4 per cent. of the outstanding bonds must be set aside either for the sinking fund or for replacements of property as the directors may decide.

Transfer Agents, Kidder, Peabody & Co., 115 Devonshire street, Boston. Registrar, National Shawmut Bank, Boston.

The first dividend on the preferred stock was 3½ per cent. for five and a half months ending December 31, 1899, paid January 1, 1900; on July 2, 1900, paid 3½ per cent., from which time half-yearly dividends of 3½ per cent. have been regularly paid in January and July.

FUNDED DEBT.

1st mort., 5 per cent., due Aug., 1929, Feb. and Aug.................................. $5,523,000

The authorized ssue of bonds is $6,500,000. In 1900 $55,000 of bonds were retired by the sinking fund, and $54,000 in 1901 and in 1902. Bonds and preferred stock in addition to the amounts now outstanding can only be issued for additional property.

In the eleven and a half months ending June 30, 1900, the company earned, net, $1,398,709, and after all charges, dividends and $629,990 for additions, there was a surplus of $119,383. The report for the years ending June 29, 1901, and June 28, 1902, gave no statement of earnings.

The following is the company's balance sheet, June 28, 1902:

| Assets. | | Liabilities. | |
|---|---|---|---|
| Plant, good will, etc. | $13,817,867 | Preferred stock | $5,000,000 |
| Improvements | 420,264 | Common stock | 5,000,000 |
| Material—raw, in process and finished | 3,450,655 | 1st mortgage 5 per cent. bonds | 5,523,000 |
| Accounts and notes receivable | 483,069 | Notes payable | 2,632,500 |
| Investments | 15,950 | Accounts payable | 183,463 |
| Cash | 447,592 | Taxes | 24,930 |
| Suspense account | 45,827 | Interest due August 1 | 115,063 |
| | | Profit and loss | 158,784 |
| | | Reserve for suspense account | 34,475 |
| | | Card clothing account | 9,009 |
| Total | $18,681,224 | Total | $18,681,224 |

President, Andrew G. Pierce; Vice-President and Chairman of Executive Committee, Joseph F. Knowles, New Bedford, Mass.; Agent, James E. Stanton, Jr.; Treasurer, Henry C. Sibley; Assistant Treasurer, J. B. Strongman; Secretary, W. L. Benedict, Boston.

Directors—Andrew G. Pierce, Joseph F. Knowles, James E. Stanton, Jr., Thomas E. Brayton, Eben S. Draper, Charles L. Lovering, C. M. Weld, Robert Winsor, Henry L. Tiffany, George D. Hallock, Alfred Winsor, W. W. Crapo.

Main office, 37 N. Water street, New Bedford, Mass.; branch offices, 346 Broadway, New York; 77 Summer street, Boston; 213 Chestnut street, Philadelphia; 36 State street, Albany, N. Y. Annual meeting, third Tuesday in August at 12 noon, at 1 Exchange place, Jersey City.

## THE NEW ENGLAND GOLD & COPPER MINING CO.

A corporation formed under the laws of Colorado, June 5, 1899, for the purpose of mining, smelting and treating ores and minerals. The company absorbed the Nast Mining & Milling Co. It has mines located at Bingham, Utah, with a complete plant.

Stock......Par $1................................Authorized, $1,000,000......Issued, $761,645

The company has no preferred stock and no funded debt. Transfer Agent, The George F. Bradstreet Co., 53 State street, Boston.

President, David W. Williams, Glastonbury, Conn.; Vice-President, E. M. Gibson, Omaha, Neb.; Secretary and Treasurer, George F. Bradstreet, Boston; Assistant Secretary, R. J. Bardwell, Denver, Col.

Directors—David W. Williams, J. S. Williams, Glastonbury, Conn.; E. M. Gibson, Omaha, Neb.; Frederick Johnson, Auburndale, Mass.; George F. Bradstreet, Malden, Mass.; S. W. West, Salt Lake City; Thomas Kellough, East Boston, Mass.

Corporate office, Denver, Col.; main office, 53 State street, Boston; branch office, Bingham, Utah. Annual meeting, first Monday in June, at Denver.

## NEW ENGLAND TELEPHONE & TELEGRAPH CO.

This company is the sole licensee of the American Telephone & Telegraph Co. for Maine, most of New Hampshire, Vermont and the greater part of Massachusetts. On December 31, 1901, it had 143,958 miles of exchange wire, 84,131 exchange stations, and a total including the controlled companies of 93,822 stations. A majority of the stock is owned by the American Telephone & Telegraph Co.

Stock......Par $100........................Authorized, $30,000,000......Issued, $21,616,700

In May, 1900, the stock authorized was increased from $15,000,000 to $20,000,000, and in May, 1902, to $30,000,000, and the outstanding stock has been increased from time to time to supply requirements for new construction and extensions, the last increase having been of $3,604,700, stockholders having the right to subscribe at par for 20 per cent. of their holdings on July 1, 1902.

Stock is transferred at the office of the company, Boston.

In August, 1897, dividends were increased from 5 per cent. to 6 per cent. per annum, and have since been paid at that rate. The dividends are paid quarterly, February, May, August and November.

FUNDED DEBT.

| | | | | | |
|---|---|---|---|---|---|
| Bonds, 3d series, 6 per cent., due April, 1906, April and October | | | | | $500,000 |
| " 4th " 6 " " " 1907, " " | | | | | 500,000 |
| " 5th " 6 " " " 1908, " " | | | | | 500,000 |
| " 6th " 5 " " " 1915, " " | | | | | 500,000 |
| " 7th " 5 " " " 1916, " " | | | | | 500,000 |
| " 8th " 5 " " " 1919, " " | | | | | 500,000 |
| New bonds, 4 " " Jan., 1930, Jan. and July | | | | | 1,000,000 |
| Total | | | | | $4,000,000 |

The bonds are plain obligations of the company, but are to be secured by any mortgage placed on company's property. The 3d, 4th and 5th series of bonds are subject to call at 102 after 1901, 1902 and 1903 respectively. The 1st and 2d series bonds have been retired at maturity.

| EARNINGS. | Gross. | Net. |
|---|---|---|
| 1892 | $1,801,566 | $436,443 |
| 1893 | 2,042,749 | 482,668 |
| 1894 | 2,172,220 | 498,462 |
| 1895 | 2,430,102 | 557,773 |
| 1896 | 2,780,652 | 604,935 |
| 1897 | 3,097,089 | 660,425 |
| 1898 | 3,425,858 | 690,264 |
| 1899 | 3,946,355 | 783,552 |
| 1900 | 4,518,396 | 896,752 |
| 1901 | 5,177,412 | 1,037,482 |

The net earnings is the amount earned in excess of expenses and interest.

President, Thomas Sherwin; Vice-President, Henry S. Hyde; Treasurer, William R. Driver; Secretary, Edmund M. Longley.

Directors—Charles F. Ayer, John H. Cahill, Alexander Cochrane, Benjamin C. Dean, William H. Elliott, Winfield S. Hutchinson, Henry S. Hyde, David B. Parker, Moses G. Parker, Stephen Salisbury, Thomas Sherwin, Frederick P. Fish.

Main office, 101 Milk street, Boston. Annual meeting, first Monday in May.

## NEW HAVEN IRON & STEEL CO.

A corporation formed under the laws of New Jersey, July 28, 1899. The company acquired the plant at New Haven, Conn., formerly owned by the New Haven Rolling Mill Co. The plant has an annual capacity of 30,000 tons of bar iron and steel.

Stock......Par $5..............................Authorized, $500,000......Issued, $500,000

In the fiscal year ending August 31, 1900, the company paid 16 per cent. on its stock. In 1900-01 and 1901-02 paid 9 per cent. Dividends are semi-annual, March and September.

Transfer Agent, New Jersey Corporation Guarantee & Trust Co., Camden. Registrar, Girard Trust Co., Philadelphia.

The company has no bonded indebtedness.

EARNINGS.

Year ending Aug. 31.

| | Gross. | Net. | Dividends. | Surplus. |
|---|---|---|---|---|
| 1900-01 | $584,805 | $75,629 | $45,000 | $30,628 |
| 1901-02 | 693,195 | 68,023 | 45,000 | 22,385 |

President, Christian C. Kauffman, Columbia, Pa.; Vice-President, A. Loudon Snowden; Secretary and Treasurer, Clarence Kennedy Crossan, Philadelphia.

Directors—Christian C. Kauffman, Columbia, Pa.; A. Loudon Snowden, Kennedy Crossan, L. S. Filbert, Charles A. Porter, Philadelphia; John B. Peddle, Woodbury, N. J.; George D. Watrous, New Haven, Conn.

Corporate office, 419 Market street, Camden; main office, Broad and Chestnut streets, Philadelphia. Annual meeting, first Monday in October.

## NEW HAVEN WATER CO.

A corporation formed under the laws of Connecticut in 1849. The company supplies water in the city of New Haven, Conn., for public and domestic purposes. Water is obtained from Lakes Whitney and Saltonstall and other bodies of water. It has two steam pumping plants with reservoirs and mains, and in 1902 began the construction of important extensions and improvements. A controlling interest in the stock of the West Haven Water Co. is owned by this company.

Stock......Par $50.......................... Authorized, $5,000,000 .....Issued, $2,500,000

The company has no preferred stock or funded debt. Registrar, George W. Curtis, City Bank, New Haven, Conn.

Dividends at the rate of 8 per cent. are paid semi-annually, in January and July.

President and Treasurer, Eli Whitney; Vice-President, James English; Secretary, David Daggett; Assistant Treasurer, A. F. Hemingway, New Haven, Conn.

Directors—Eli Whitney, James English, George D. Watrous, James D. Dewell, Richard M. Everit, Samuel E. Merwin, Charles W. Hemingway, Max Addler, Winston J. Trowbridge.

Main office, 100 Crown street, New Haven, Conn. Annual meeting, first Monday in February.

## NEW JERSEY ZINC CO.

A corporation formed under the laws of New Jersey, October 30, 1880. The title was originally the New Jersey Zinc & Iron Co., which was changed to the present style in 1897. The business of the company is the manufacture of oxide of zinc and similar products. Its chief works are at Newark, N. J.

Stock.. ...Par $100........................Authorized, $10,000,000......Issued, $10,000,000

Dividends at the rate of 12 per cent. per annum have been paid on the stock of the company. The company had a 5 per cent. 1st mortgage, which was withdrawn and canceled when the new 1st mortgage 4 per cent. bonds were created in 1901, the latter being $10,000,000 authorized.

FUNDED DEBT.

1st mort., 4 per cent., due Oct., 1926, April and Oct............................... $4,000,000

President, Stephen S. Palmer; Secretary, A. P. Cobb.

Directors—Stephen S. Palmer, August Heckscher, J. L. Riker, M. Taylor Pyne, D. B. Jones, William P. Hardenbergh, Charles B. Squier, John Price Wetherill, Samuel P. Wetherill.

Main office, Newark, N. J. New York office, 11 Broadway.

## NEW LONDON STREET RAILWAY CO.

A corporation formed under the laws of Connecticut, March 7, 1888. The company was organized as the New London Horse Railway Co., the name having been changed to the present title in June, 1893.

Stock......Par $100.............................Authorized, $500,000......Issued, $250,000

Stock is transferred at the office of the company in Boston. Registrar, International Trust Co., Boston.

The first dividend of 2½ per cent. was paid in July, 1894. Since then dividends have been 6 per cent. in 1895; 7 per cent. in 1896, 1897 and 1898; 5 per cent. in 1899; 4 per cent. in 1900 and 1901; 5 per cent. in 1902. Dividends are paid semi-annually in January and July.

FUNDED DEBT.

1st mort., 5 per cent. gold, due Oct. 1, 1938, April and Oct..........................$140,000

The authorized amount of the mortgage is $150,000. Trustee, Treasurer of the State of Connecticut. Agent for the payment of interest, American Loan & Trust Co., Boston.

In the fiscal year ending June 3, 1902, the gross earnings were $73,228.87; net, $27,270.13; charges, $6,999.70; dividends, $12,500; surplus, $7,770.43.

President and Secretary, Walter Learned, New London, Conn.; Treasurer, William A. Tucker, Boston.

Directors—Walter Learned, Billings P. Learned, James Hislop, Augustus Brandegee, Horace C. Learned, William F. Belcher, New London, Conn.; William A. Tucker, Boston.

Corporate office, New London, Conn.; main office, 53 State street, Boston. Annual meeting, first Wednesday in July, at New London, Conn.

## THE NEW OMAHA THOMSON-HOUSTON ELECTRIC LIGHT CO.

A corporation formed under the laws of Nebraska, September 26, 1885, for the purpose of supplying electric light and power in the city of Omaha.

Stock.....Par $100.....Authorized { com., $600,000 / pref., 500,000 } Issued { com., $600,000 / pref., 303,000 } $903,000

Transfer Agent, Omaha National Bank, Omaha.

The first dividend was paid February 1, 1893, since which date they have been semi-annual, in February and August, at the rate of 6 per cent. per annum.

FUNDED DEBT.

1st mort., 6 per cent. bonds, due 1919, Jan. and Dec. .......... $312,000

The authorized bond issue is $400,000. Trustee of the mortgage and agent for the payment of interest, American Loan & Trust Co., Boston.

President, F. A. Nash; Vice-President, Henry W. Yates; Secretary and Treasurer, S. E. Schweitzer, Omaha.

Directors—F. A. Nash, Henry W. Yates, George W. Holdredge, Guy C. Barton, C. E. Yost, Omaha.

Corporate and main office, 309 South 13th street, Omaha. Annual meeting, first Monday in January, at Omaha.

## NEW ORLEANS LIGHTING CO.

A corporation formed under the laws of New Jersey, April, 1901, for the purpose of acquiring rights and operating gas and electric properties. The company leased on May 1, 1901, from the New Orleans Gas Light Co. its entire property, plant and business. The lease runs until 1925 and includes an option to purchase. The new company is following a plan of expansion and greatly increasing its mains and the efficiency of its service.

The lease of the New Orleans Gas Light Co. is until March 1, 1925. The lessee pays as rental 6 per cent. per annum, dividends semi-annually in January and July, on the $3,750,000 stock of the New Orleans Gas Light Co.

Stock......Par $100..........Authorized, $2,000,000......Issued, $2,000,000

Transfer Agent, New York Security & Trust Co., New York.

FUNDED DEBT.

1st mort., 5 per cent., due 1925, March and Sept. .......... $1,500,000

The authorized amount of bonds is $2,000,000, the balance of $500,000 being held in the treasury. The bonds may be redeemed at 110 and accrued interest. Trustee, New York Security & Trust Co. There is a sinking fund of $40,000 per annum.

President, Abram M. Hyatt; Secretary, Theodore F. Lozier, New York.

Directors—Abram M. Hyatt, Osborn W. Bright, H. W. Whipple, Theodore F. Lozier, New York; Eugene W. Mulligan, Wilkes-Barre, Pa.; Frederick H. Shelton, Philadelphia.

Main office, New Orleans.

## NEWPORT NEWS SHIPBUILDING & DRY DOCK CO.

A Virginia corporation which succeeded the Chesapeake Dry Dock & Construction Co. The company has a large plant at Newport News, Va., for the construction of ocean and river steamers and other craft, with two large dry docks, etc.

Stock..Par $100..Authorized { com., $2,000,000 / pref., 6,000,000 } Issued { com., $2,000,000 / pref., 5,804,200 } $7,804,200

The preferred stock is 5 per cent. cumulative. Stock is transferred at the company's office in New York.

FUNDED DEBT.

| | |
|---|---|
| 1st mort., 5 per cent., due 1990, Jan. 15 and July 15 .......... | $2,000,000 |
| Gen. mort., currency, 5 per cent., due Jan., 1953, Jan. and July .......... | 5,000,000 |
| Chesapeake Dry Dock & Cons., 1st mort., 5 per cent., due 1937, Jan. and July..... | 600,000 |
| Total .......... | $7,600,000 |

The trustee of the 1st mortgage is the Central Trust Co., New York; and of the Chesapeake Dry Dock & Construction mortgage, Metropolitan Trust Co., New York. The latter mortgage is a first lien on the dry dock.

The new general mortgage was created in January, 1903. Trustee, Union Trust Co., New York. None of the new bonds were reserved to retire the old issues.

President, Calvin B. Orcutt; Vice-President and Secretary, Charles Babbidge; Treasurer, Isaac E. Gates, New York.

Directors—Isaac E. Gates, F. H. Davis, Calvin B. Orcutt, Charles H. Tweed, H. E. Huntington.

Main office, Washington avenue and Thirty-ninth street, Newport News, Va.; New York office, 1 Broadway; Treasurer's office, 23 Broad street, New York.

## NEW YORK AIR BRAKE CO.

A corporation formed under the laws of New Jersey in 1890 to manufacture car brakes. The company has a large factory and works at Watertown, N. Y. The plant has been greatly enlarged, and in 1899 the company purchased additional real estate for $50,000. Its working force is over 1,500 men. In 1901 it built a large factory near Moscow, Russia.

Stock......Par $100......................Authorized, $10,000,000......Issued, $8,012,500

The capital stock was $5,000,000. In 1899 an increase to $10,000,000 was authorized and $1,250,000 of the new stock was issued and allotted to stockholders at par, the proceeds being for enlargement of company's business. The balance of new stock is held in the treasury. The company has paid off its 1st mortgage bonds, of which there were $250,000.

In 1896 a dividend of 6 per cent. was paid. In 1899 the payment of dividends was resumed with a quarterly dividend of 2 per cent., paid October 2, 1899, and dividends have since been regularly paid at the rate of 8 per cent. per annum, quarterly in January, May, July and October.

Stock is transferred at company's office, 66 Broadway, New York. Registrar, Knickerbocker Trust Co., New York.

In 1898 a number of prominent New York capitalists acquired an interest in the company and Messrs. Roswell P. Flower and Anthony N. Brady entered the Board of Directors as representatives of such interests. The company was engaged in litigation with the Westinghouse Air Brake Co., of Pittsburg, Pa., which brought suit for alleged infringement of its patents by this company. In 1898 and 1899 decisions of the courts were rendered in favor of this company. The suits were appealed, but the final decisions were in favor of this company, though litigations have since continued. It has been frequently rumored that a plan of consolidation of this company with the Westinghouse Air Brake Co. was contemplated, but no developments of that kind have transpired.

President, Charles A. Starbuck; Vice-Presidents, Thomas C. Purdy, Daniel Magone, George B. Massey; Secretary and Treasurer, John C. Thompson; Assistant Treasurer, Clifford H. Chaffee.

Directors—Charles A. Starbuck, Daniel Magone, John C. Thompson, Frederick Flower, Anthony N. Brady, J. C. Young, H. A. Rogers, George B. Massey, Thomas C. Purdy.

Main office, 66 Broadway, New York.

## NEW YORK & HOBOKEN FERRY CO.

A corporation formed under the laws of New Jersey, November 10, 1898. This company acquired all the property and franchises of the Hoboken Ferry Co. and the New York & New Jersey Ferry Co. The company operates ferries from Barclay, Christopher and West Fourteenth streets, New York, to Hoboken, and has valuable dock property, as well as steam ferry-boats.

In December, 1902, it was announced that a controlling interest in this company had been acquired by capitalists acting presumably in behalf of the Delaware, Lackawanna & Western Railroad Co.

Stock......Par $100..........................Authorized, $3,300,000......Issued, $3,300,000

The company began payment of 1 per cent. quarterly dividends on its stock in December, 1899, and continued to pay at that rate until 1900, the December 1 dividend in that year being increased to 1¼ per cent., putting the stock on a 5 per cent. basis. Dividends are paid in March (1), June, September and December.

FUNDED DEBT.

| | |
|---|---|
| Hoboken Ferry, cons. mort., 5 per cent., due May, 1946, May and Nov.............. | $4,100,000 |
| N. Y. & N. J. Ferry, 1st mort., 4 per cent., due Jan., 1946, Jan. and July........... | 600,000 |
| " " " 2d " 5 " " Jan., 1946, " " "........... | 400,000 |
| N. Y. & Hoboken Ferry, gen. mort., 5 per cent., due May, 1946, June and Dec...... | 3,300,000 |
| Total.............................................................. | $8,400,000 |

The general mortgage of the New York & Hoboken Ferry Co. is for $4,000,000. Trustee, United States Mortgage & Trust Co., New York The unissued $700,000 of these bonds are reserved for improvements. The bonds may be retired at 110.

President, Roswell Eldridge; Secretary, William A. Nash; Treasurer, Lewis A. Eldridge.

Main office, Hoboken, N. J.

## NEW YORK & HONDURAS ROSARIO MINING CO.

A corporation formed under the laws of New York in 1880. The company owns and operates a gold and silver mining property at San Juancito, in the Republic of Honduras, Central America.

Stock......Par $10........ .... ..............Authorized, $1,500,000......Issued, $1,500,000

The stock is full-paid and non-assessable. Stock is transferred at the office of the company.

Up to the end of 1902 the company had paid one hundred and nine dividends on its stock, aggregating $1,770,000. Dividends have generally been monthly. In 1901, it paid 12 per cent.

President, William H. Power; Vice-President, Sidney Abenheimer; Secretary, E. Schernikow; Treasurer, Samuel Heidelsheimer.

Directors—Samuel Heidelsheimer, William H. Power, F. H. Parker, E. J. Swords, W. S. Valentine, H. G. B. Fisher, Sidney Abenheimer, N. Westheimer, P. R. Weiler.

Main office, 18 Broadway, New York. Annual meeting, second Wednesday in December.

---

## NEW YORK & JERSEY RAILROAD CO.

A corporation formed under the laws of New York, February 11, 1902. The company is also incorporated in New Jersey. This company acquired, free from all liens and encumbrances, all the property of the Hudson Tunnel Railway Co., consisting chiefly of two tunnels under the bed of the Hudson River, 18 feet in diameter, and known, respectively, as the North Tunnel and the South Tunnel. A report on the property was made by Charles M. Jacobs, engineer, stating that the completion of the tunnels is entirely feasible, and that they are in all respects suitable and available for the operation of street railway cars. Only 1,200 feet of the North Tunnel remained to be built under the bed of the river at the end of 1902. The entire length of the completed line, including approaches, will be about two miles and it was stated that the tunnel would be in operation before the end of 1904.

The company has acquired real estate for the necessary terminals, consisting of a block in Jersey City, 400 by 200 feet, bounded by 13th and 14th and Henderson and Provost streets, and in New York, of the whole of the west half of the block bounded by Christopher and Tenth and Greenwich and Hudson streets, with the exception of one lot on the southwest corner. Connections will be made at grade at these terminals with the cars of the Metropolitan Street Railway Co., in New York, and with the cars of the North Jersey Street Railway Co. and the Jersey City, Hoboken and Paterson Street Railway Co., in Jersey City.

This tunnel will furnish the only all-rail connection for trolley cars between the contiguous territory of New Jersey, containing a population, by the census of 1900, of 1,078,097, with Manhattan Island.

Contracts have been entered into with the North Jersey Street Railway Co. and the Jersey City, Hoboken and Paterson Street Railway Co., which control all of the surface lines on the Jersey side of the river, providing for adequate and sufficient service to the tunnel over the lines of said companies. A contract for power has also been made with the North Jersey Street Railway Co.

In December, 1902, the company secured the grant of a franchise covering its operations in New York City from the Rapid Transit Commissioners, ratified by the Board of Aldermen and approved by the Mayor, the Sinking Fund Commissioners and the Dock Department.

| Stock...Par $100...Authorized | com., $5,000,000<br>pref., 3,500,000 | Issued | com., $5,000,000<br>pref., 3,500,000 | $8,500,000 |
|---|---|---|---|---|

The preferred stock is 6 per cent., non-cumulative. Stock is transferred at the company's office in New York. Registrar, Continental Trust Co., New York.

FUNDED DEBT.

1st mort., 5 per cent. gold, due Feb., 1932, Feb. and Aug. .......................... $4,500,000

The 1st mortgage is for $7,000,000, of which $2,000,000 is reserved for additional property and $500,000 for corporate purposes. Trustee of the mortgage and agent for the payment of interest, Guaranty Trust Co., New York. The bonds are redeemable at 110, at any interest period.

The $4,500,000 of bonds issued, and all of the preferred and common stock issue of the company, will be used for the acquisition of the property of the Hudson Tunnel Railway Co., which represents an expenditure already made, including interest, of more than $4,000,000 and for the completion of the North Tunnel and the approaches on the New Jersey and New York sides and the equipment of the same with electricity. Provision is made in the financial plan for the ultimate completion of the South Tunnel, 600 feet, or one-ninth, of which is already built, which will greatly enlarge the capacity for business. It is proposed to immediately complete the North Tunnel and the South Tunnel, and to operate the same as a connection between the railway systems of New York and Jersey City. The company is in possession of all necessary public rights and franchises for this purpose.

The Hudson Tunnel Railway Co., which began the construction of the tunnel, failed on account of lack of capital, leaving the work uncompleted. In 1901 the bondholders of the old company co-operated in a plan of reorganization and the property was foreclosed and acquired by the present company.

President, William G. McAdoo; Vice-Presidents, Walter G. Oakman, Edmund C. Converse; Treasurer, Henry A. Murray; Secretary, Charles W. King; Chief Engineer, Charles M. Jacobs, New York.

Directors—Walter G. Oakman, E. H. Gray, Edmund C. Converse, Anthony N. Brady, William G. McAdoo, Frederic B. Jennings, G. Tracy Rogers, Otto T. Bannard, Charles W. King, New York; John Skelton Williams, Richmond; E. F. C. Young, Jersey City; David Young, Newark, N. J.; John G. McCullough, North Bennington, Vt.

Main office, 15 Wall street, New York. Annual meeting, second Wednesday in February.

---

## NEW YORK & KENTUCKY CO.

A corporation formed under the laws of New York, January 25, 1900. The company was organized for the purpose of carrying on the business of manufacturing cologne spirits, alcohol, whiskey, medicinal preparations, etc., and of distributing the same and kindred products among chemists, manufacturers and dealers, and for prosecuting a general distilling, importing and wholesale business.

Stock....Par $100....Authorized { com., $1,000,000 / pref., 1,000,000 } Issued { com., $1,000,000 / pref., 1,000,000 } $2,000,000

The preferred stock is 7 per cent., cumulative, and has also a preference as to assets.

Stock is transferred at the company's office, Rochester, N. Y. Registrar, Union Trust Co., Rochester, N. Y.

The company from its inception has paid regular quarterly dividends of 1¾ per cent. on its preferred stock in January, April, July and October.

The first quarterly dividend of 1½ per cent. on the common was paid February 1, 1901, and dividends on the common were paid at the rate of 6 per cent. per annum, in quarterly payments in February, May, August and November. In 1902 the annual rate on the common was 10 per cent., or 2½ per cent. quarterly.

The company has no funded debt.

President, Walter B. Duffy; Vice-Presidents, Frederick Cook, Rochester, N. Y.; Charles Tracey, Albany, N. Y.; Secretary, William F. Balkam; Treasurer, Frank S. Upton, Rochester, N. Y.

Directors—Walter B. Duffy, Frederick Cook, Eugene H. Satterlee, Benjamin E. Chase, William F. Balkam, Frank S. Upton, Rochester, N. Y.; Charles Tracey, Albany, N. Y.; Walker J. Duffy, Henry M. Naylon, Buffalo.

Main office, 81 Lake avenue, Rochester, N. Y. Annual meeting, fourth Friday in January.

---

## NEW YORK & NEW JERSEY TELEPHONE CO.

A corporation formed under the laws of New York and New Jersey in 1883. The company is the sole licensee of the American Telephone & Telegraph Co. for Brooklyn, N. Y., all of Long Island, Richmond County (Staten Island), N. Y., and the counties of Hudson, Middlesex, Essex, Bergen, Monmouth, Morris, Passaic, Somerset and Union, N. J., including the cities of Jersey City, Hoboken, Newark, Orange, Paterson, Elizabeth, Long Branch, etc. Company has numerous telephone exchanges, and reported January 1, 1903, a total of 53,184 subscribers. The American Telephone & Telegraph Co. and the New York Telephone Co. have large interests in the stock of this company.

Stock......Par $100........................Authorized, $15,000,000......Issued, $12,500,000

The stock authorized was increased in 1898 from $6,000,000 to $8,000,000. On March 1, 1901, the authorized stock was increased to $15,000,000, the new stock to be issued as required, and $1,875,000 of the increase was allotted to stockholders at par. In 1902 stockholders were offered further rights to subscribe for 33⅓ per cent. additional stock at par, payable 40 per cent. November 1, 1902; 30 per cent. May 1, 1903, and 30 per cent. August 1, 1903, thus increasing the outstanding stock to $12,500,000.

Dividends have been paid regularly since 1894 at the rate of 6 per cent., and 1 per cent. extra each year. The dividends are paid quarterly, 1½ per cent. each, in January (15), April, July and October, an extra dividend of 1 per cent. being usually paid in January or April.

FUNDED DEBT.

General, now 1st, mort., 5 per cent., due May, 1920, May and Nov.................. $1,324,000

The general mortgage is $1,500,000 authorized, with a sinking fund provision of $20,000 per annum. $179,000 of these bonds have been purchased for the sinking fund and canceled. The 6 per cent. mortgage bonds of 1885 have been paid, and the mortgage satisfied.

EARNINGS.

| | Gross. | Net. | Charges & Dividends. | Surplus. |
|---|---|---|---|---|
| 1893 | $1,183,832 | $464,791 | $228,620 | $215,276 |
| 1894 | 1,252,509 | 447,942 | 309,892 | 138,050 |
| 1895 | 1,405,882 | 550,607 | 321,628 | 228,979 |
| 1896 | 1,554,585 | 477,731 | 360,633 | 117,098 |
| 1897 | 1,790,287 | 553,467 | 381,726 | 171,741 |
| 1898 | 2,058,477 | 625,001 | 443,305 | 181,696 |
| 1899 | 2,381,369 | 763,177 | 540,407 | 222,770 |
| 1900 | 2,827,481 | 808,878 | 665,381 | 143,497 |
| 1901 | 3,326,432 | 1,081,799 | 790,390 | 291,409 |
| 1902 | 3,962,597 | 1,139,140 | 873,978 | 265,162 |

President, Charles F. Cutler, New York; Vice-President, William D. Sargent; Treasurer, Henry Sanger Snow; Secretary, Waldron Hoppins, Brooklyn, N. Y.

Directors—Charles F. Cutler, Joseph P. Davis, Alexander Cameron, George H. Prentiss, Edward J. Hall, New York; Henry Sanger Snow, William D. Sargent, David H. Powell, Brooklyn, N. Y.; Charles A. Nichols, Springfield, Mass.; Zenas Crane, Dalton, Mass.; Hugh Kinnard, Newark, N. J.

Main office, 81 Willoughby street, Brooklyn, N. Y.

## NEW YORK & PENNSYLVANIA TELEPHONE & TELEGRAPH CO.

A corporation formed under the laws of New York. The company operates under an exclusive license from the American Telephone & Telegraph Co. in the northern tier of counties of Pennsylvania and the southern counties of New York, its system including the telephone facilities of Binghamton, Elmira, Ithaca, Owego, and Jamestown, N. Y., and Erie, Bradford, Montrose, and Tonawanda, Pa. The American Telephone & Telegraph Co. owns a majority of the stock of the company.

Stock......Par $100..........................Authorized, $1,000,000......Issued, $1,000,000

For some years the company paid 6 per cent. dividends on its stock in quarterly payments in January, April, July and October, but no dividends have been paid since 1901.

FUNDED DEBT.

| | |
|---|---|
| 1st mort., 5 per cent. gold, due February, 1926, Feb. and Aug. | $291,500 |
| Gen. mort., 4 per cent. gold, due November, 1929, May and Nov. | 470,000 |
| Total | $761,500 |

The 1st mortgage is for $300,000, but the bonds outstanding have been reduced by the sinking fund to the amount given above.

The general mortgage was created in 1899 and is for $1,000,000. Trustee, Washington Trust Co., New York. Of this issue sufficient is reserved to retire the 1st mortgage bonds and the remainder can be used for improvements and extensions.

President, Charles F. Cutler, New York; Vice-President, W. N. Eastabrook; Treasurer and General Manager, H. F. Stevens; Secretary, W. J. Farquhar.

Directors—Charles F. Cutler, W. N. Eastabrook, Joseph P. Davis, W. T. Bouchelle, Frederick P. Fish, Charles M. Dow, J. L. Sternberg, W. H. Woolverton, U. N. Bethell, Cyrus Strong, W. J. Grandin, Jr.

Main office, Elmira, N. Y.

## NEW YORK & QUEENS COUNTY RAILWAY CO.

A corporation formed under the laws of New York, June 26, 1896. The company is a consolidation of the following companies:

| | |
|---|---|
| Steinway Railway Co. | Riker Avenue Railway Co. |
| Newtown Railway Co. | Long Island City & Newtown Railway Co. |
| Flushing & College Point Railway Co. | Queens Railway Co. |

The company controls the entire street railway system of Long Island City, N. Y., and also has a line to Flushing, N. Y. It owns 74.47 miles of trolley track, a power station at Astoria, L. I., and 224 cars.

The Queens Railway, which was consolidated with this company in 1902, was successor to the New York & North Shore Railway, which was foreclosed.

Stock......Par $100..........................Authorized, $5,000,000......Issued, $3,150,000

The company has no preferred stock. Stock is transferred at the company's office. Registrar, Guarantee Trust & Safe Deposit Co., Philadelphia.

FUNDED DEBT.

| | |
|---|---|
| 1st mort., 4 per cent., gold, due Oct., 1946, April and Oct. | $1,300,000 |
| Flushing & College Point Railway Co., 1st mort., 5 per cent., due 1925, June and Dec. | 50,000 |
| Newtown Railway Co., 1st mort., 5 per cent., due 1924, June and Dec. | 150,000 |
| Steinway Railway Co., 1st mort., 6 per cent., gold, due July, 1922, Jan. and July | 1,500,000 |
| Total | $3,000,000 |

The authorized amount of the 1st mortgage is $3,000,000, of which $1,700,000 have been reserved to retire prior liens. Trustee of the mortgage and agent for the payment of interest, Real Estate Title Insurance & Trust Co., Philadelphia.

The outstanding bonds of the Steinway Railway Co.'s mortgage are the full amount authorized. Trustee of the mortgage and agent for the payment of interest, Morton Trust Co., New York.

EARNINGS.

Year ending June 30.

| | Gross. | Net. | Other Income. | Interest and Taxes. | Surplus. |
|---|---|---|---|---|---|
| 1898-99 | $422,543 | $179,621 | $24,684 | $277,116 | Def. $72,811 |
| 1899-00 | 462,844 | 212,339 | 5,603 | 142,729 | 75,213 |
| 1900-01 | 489,017 | 223,680 | 5,283 | 173,740 | 55,213 |
| 1901-02 | 543,017 | 231,381 | 5,447 | 181,762 | 55,066 |

President, W. H. Shelmerdine, Philadelphia; Vice-President and General Manager, C. D. Simpson; Secretary and Treasurer, I. M. Tritt, Long Island City, N. Y.

Main office, 9 Borden avenue, Long Island City, N. Y. Annual meeting, third Thursday in July.

---

## NEW YORK & QUEENS ELECTRIC LIGHT & POWER CO.

A corporation formed under the laws of New York, July 30, 1900. The company merged with it the New York & Queens Gas & Electric Co., which company acquired and consolidated with the Flushing Gas & Electric Light Co., the New York & Queens Light and Power Co., and the Newtown Light & Power Co. The franchises owned by the company are perpetual and cover Flushing, Newtown, College Point, Ingleside, Winfield, Corona, Whitestone, Ridgewood, and other places in the Borough of Queens, City of New York. The present company also took over the Jamaica Electric Lighting Co. and the Electric Illuminating & Power Co. of Long Island City and retired all the securities of the two latter organizations. The Newtown & Flushing Gas Co. is controlled in the interest of this company.

Stock..Par $100....Authorized { com., $1,250,000; pref., 1,250,000 } Issued { com., $1,250,000; pref., 1,250,000 } $2,500,000

The preferred stock is 5 per cent., non-cumulative.

FUNDED DEBT.

| | |
|---|---|
| 1st cons. mort., 5 per cent., due 1930, Feb. and Aug. | $2,272,000 |
| N. Y. & Queens Gas & Electric, 1st mort., 5 per cent., due Jan., 1949, Jan. and July. | 78,000 |
| Total | $2,350,000 |

The consolidated mortgage is for $2,500,000, and of this $157,000 were reserved to retire the bonds of the Gas & Electric Co., and $150,000 for improvements. Trustee of mortgage, Union Trust Co., New York.

In the year ending August 31, 1902, the earnings were: Gross, $307,669; net, $137,027; charges, $116,775; surplus, $20,252.

President, Frank Tilford; Vice-President, Henry R. Wilson; Secretary and Treasurer, H. L. Snyder.

Directors—Frank Tilford, Harrison E. Gawtry, Lewis B. Gawtry, Thomas W. Stephens, James T. Pyle, Abram M. Hyatt, Henry R. Wilson, New York; Julian D. Fairchild, Brooklyn, N. Y.

Main office, 208 Fifth avenue, New York.

---

## NEW YORK & RICHMOND GAS CO.

A corporation formed under the laws of New York, June 17, 1901, for the purpose of consolidating the various gas companies of the Borough of Richmond, Staten Island. On July 13, 1901, the company consolidated with the former Richmond County Gas Light Co., incorporated in 1856. It owns also, through merger, all the rights of the Consumers' Gas Light Co. of Richmond County. The company owns a plant of the United Gas Improvement Co.'s water gas type at Clifton. The mains extend from South Beach and Fort Wadsworth to Stapleton, Tompkinsville, St. George, New Brighton and Port Richmond.

Stock......Par $100..........................Authorized, $1,500,000......Issued, $1,500,000

Transfer Agency, 36 Wall street, New York. Registrar, Central Trust Co., New York.

FUNDED DEBT.

1st mort., 5 per cent., due 1921, May and Nov......................................$1,000,000

The authorized issue of bonds is $1,500,000. The treasury retains $500,000 for future use. These bonds are redeemable at 110 at any interest period upon three months' notice. Trustee, Central Trust Co., New York.

President, Robert L. Forrest; Vice-President and Treasurer, Charles B. Van Nostrand; Secretary, Thomas O. Horton, New York.

Directors—Robert L. Forrest, Charles B. Van Nostrand, G. Trowbridge Hollister, Thomas D. Holmes, New York; Frederick H. Shelton, Philadelphia.

Main office, 264 Bay street, Stapleton, S. I.; New York office, 36 Wall street. Annual meeting, first Monday in February.

## NEW YORK ARCHITECTURAL TERRA COTTA CO

A corporation formed under the laws of New York in January, 1886. The purpose of the company is to manufacture architectural terra cotta and brick.

Stock......Par $100... ................. .........Authorized, $300,000......Issued, $250,000

The company has no preferred stock. Stock is transferred at the office of the company.

In July, 1887, the first dividend, 6 per cent., was paid and since then an annual dividend of 6 per cent. has been paid. Dividends are paid quarterly, in January, April, July and October.

FUNDED DEBT.

1st mort., 6 per cent., due Jan., 1904, Jan. and July.................................. $150,000

The 1st mortgage bonds are the total amount authorized. Trustee, Title Guarantee & Trust Co., New York. Agent for the payment of interest, Windsor Trust Co., New York.

President, Walter Geer; Vice-President, John Alvin Young; Secretary, Bushnell Danforth; Treasurer, J. R. Owens, New York.

Directors—Walter Geer, John Alvin Young, Frederick Potter, Walter R. Beach, New York; Danforth Geer, Hoosick Falls, N. Y.

Corporate office, 1 Madison avenue, New York; main office, 401 Vernon avenue, Queens Borough, New York. Annual meeting, third Thursday in January, at 401 Vernon avenue, Queens Borough, New York.

## NEW YORK DOCK CO.

A corporation formed under the laws of New York, July 18, 1901. The purposes of the company are to conduct a storage, wharfage, warehousing and forwarding business, including the owning or leasing of docks, wharfs and warehouses, and other real estate, the loaning of money on merchandise and warehouse receipts, and performing all the features of such a business.

The company was created in pursuance of a reorganization of the Brooklyn Wharf & Warehouse Co., the property of which was sold under foreclosure in 1901 and was acquired by this company, the latter taking possession August 1, 1901. A full statement of the Brooklyn Wharf & Warehouse Co. is in the MANUAL for 1901.

The property of the company includes that of the Brooklyn Wharf & Warehouse Co. It also acquired the stocks and property of the Baltic Realty Co. and the Brooklyn Wharf Transfer Co. The property is located on the East River water-front of the Borough of Brooklyn, and extends from the Brooklyn Bridge to the Erie Basin, a frontage of more than 2⅛ miles. The company has constructed a railway terminal yard at the Atlantic Basin.

Stock...Par $100....Authorized { com., $7,000,000; pref., 10,000,000 } Issued { com., $7,000,000; pref., 10,000,000 } $17,000,000

The preferred stock is 5 per cent., non-cumulative. After the preferred and common have received 5 per cent. out of the profits of any fiscal year, beginning August 1, they share equally in any further division of profits.

Transfer Agent, United States Mortgage & Trust Co., New York. Registrar, Guaranty Trust Co., New York.

FUNDED DEBT.

Fifty-year 1st mort., 4 per cent., due Aug., 1951, Feb. and Aug................... $11,580,000

The authorized amount of the 1st mortgage is $13,000,000. In the organization of the company $1,875,000 of the bonds were reserved for the company's general purpose and $1,875,000 of this amount was held on July 31, 1902, in the treasury for extensions and improvements. Trustee of mortgage and agent for the payment of interest, United States Mortgage & Trust Co., New York. The company may redeem the bonds at 105 and interest on any interest date.

For details regarding the Brooklyn Wharf & Warehouse Co. and the terms under which it was reorganized, see the MANUAL for 1902.

EARNINGS.

Year ending July 31, 1902.

| | Gross. | Net. | Charges. | Surplus. |
|---|---|---|---|---|
| 1901-02 | $1,993,496 | $814,534 | $463,200 | $351,334 |

The following is the company's balance sheet July 31, 1902:

| ASSETS. | | LIABILITIES. | |
|---|---|---|---|
| Cash in bank | $857,354 | Preferred stock | $10,000,000 |
| Bonds in treasury | 1,875,000 | Common stock | 7,000,000 |
| Accounts receivable | 146,671 | First mortgage bonds | 13,000,000 |
| Accrued storage, wharfage, etc. | 402,484 | Accounts payable | 64,947 |
| Real estate, wharves and warehouses | 26,534,030 | Due railroads | 1,205 |
| Terminal railroad | 448,165 | Surplus | 351,334 |
| Railroad floats | 90,000 | | |
| Electric plant | 25,000 | | |
| Machinery and tools | 35,741 | | |
| Office furniture and fixtures | 2,726 | | |
| Exchange memberships | 315 | | |
| Total | $30,417,486 | Total | $30,417,486 |

President, David H. King, Jr.; Vice-President, C. O'D. Iselin; Secretary, Richard M. Hurd; Treasurer, George E. Spencer; Assistant Secretary, Henry E. Nitchie.

Directors—Frederic P. Olcott, Walter G. Oakman, George W. Young, Adrian Iselin, Jr., Frederic Cromwell, James Timpson, Samuel Thorne, C. O'D. Iselin, David H. King, Jr., Edwin Thorne, New York; Jacob L. Greene, Hartford, Conn.

Main office, 68 Broad street, New York. Annual meeting, third Tuesday in November.

## NEW YORK MUTUAL GAS LIGHT CO.

A New York corporation which has an extensive system of distributing mains in the southern part of the city of New York. The company also has a large plant. A controlling interest in the company was acquired in 1898 by the Consolidated Gas Co.

Stock......Par $100..........................Authorized, $3,500,000......Issued, $3,500,000

The company has no funded debt.

The charter of the New York Mutual Gas Light Co. prohibits it from consolidating or merging with any other gas organization.

In 1901 and 1902 dividends of 9 per cent. were paid. The dividend periods are semi-annual, January and July.

President, Robert M. Gallaway; Vice-President, Harrison E. Gawtry; Secretary and Treasurer, William C. Besson; Assistant Secretary, W. S. Purdy.

Main office, 36 Union Square, East, New York.

## NEW YORK SHIPBUILDING CO.

A corporation formed under the laws of New Jersey, in October, 1899. The company's purpose is the manufacture and construction of ships, marine engines and boilers. The company has established a large modern shipbuilding plant at Camden, N. J., the property including 141 acres of land with 3,600 feet of water-front on the Delaware River.

Stock......Par $100......................... Authorized, $6,000,000......Issued, $5,000,000

The company has no preferred stock or funded debt. Stock is transferred at the company's office.

President, Henry G. Morse; Secretary, Samuel M. Knox; Treasurer, William G. Randle.

Directors—A. W. Mellon, Pittsburg; Myron C. Wick, J. Craig Smith, Youngstown, O.; Michael Jenkins, Henry Walters, Baltimore; Henry G. Morse, Woodbury, N. J.; William G. Randle, Chester, Pa.

Corporate and main office, Broadway and Fairview street, Camden, N. J.; New York office, 1 Broadway. Annual meeting, second Tuesday in October, at Camden, N. J.

## NEW YORK TELEPHONE CO.

A corporation formed under the laws of New York under the title of the Metropolitan Telephone & Telegraph Co., the name being changed to the present style in 1898. The company operates under an exclusive license from the American Telephone & Telegraph Co. in the Boroughs of Manhattan and the Bronx, city of New York. The American Telephone & Telegraph Co. owns a controlling interest in the stock of the New York Telephone Co., and the Western Union Telegraph Co. also holds $6,164,300 of the stock.

Stock......Par $100........................Authorized, $50,000,000......Issued, $30,000,000

The stock authorized and issued was $16,000,000, but on August 8, 1900, the stockholders voted to increase the amount to $30,000,000. A further increase to $50,000,000 being decided on in December, 1902.

The company pays 6 per cent. dividends on its stock, payments being quarterly, 1½ per cent. each in January, April, July and October.

FUNDED DEBT.

Metropolitan Telephone & Telegraph, 1st mort., due May, 1918, May and Nov...... $1,925,000

The Metropolitan Telephone & Telegraph 1st mortgage, Mercantile Trust Co., New York, trustee, was created in 1888. The bonds outstanding are the full authorized amount. There is a sinking fund of 1 per cent. per annum, the bonds to be purchased at 110 or less. Bonds cannot be drawn for the sinking fund.

President, Charles F. Cutler; Treasurer, William R. Driver; Secretary, John H. Cahill.

Directors—Belvedere Brooks, John H. Cahill, Thomas F. Clark, Robert C. Clowry, Charles F. Cutler, Joseph P. Davis, Frederick P. Fish, George J. Gould, E. J. Hall, Charles Steele, James B. Van Every, W. H. Woolverton.

Main office, 15 Dey street, New York.

---

## NEW YORK TRANSPORTATION CO.

A corporation formed under the laws of New Jersey, February 21, 1899, under the title of New York Electric Vehicle Transportation Co. The name was changed to the present style in January, 1902. The company was organized to operate automobile and other vehicles and to buy, sell or lease the same, to deal in patents and to receive and grant licenses. The company on its formation took over the electric cab service in the city of New York formerly operated by the Electric Vehicle Co., and has a large number of electric vehicles in service. In November, 1899, it acquired the franchise and equipment of the Fifth Avenue Stage Co., operating stages on Fifth avenue, New York. In 1901 acquired the Newport, R. I., plant of the New England Electric Vehicle Co. and of the Metropolitan and Century Express Co.'s in New York City. The company's main station is at 815 Eighth avenue. It has sub-stations at 55 East Eighty-eighth street, 64 Vesey street and 9 West 100th street, New York.

Stock......Par $20...........................Authorized, $5,000,000......Issued, $5,000,000

The stock originally authorized was $25,000,000, par $100. At the formation of the company $5 per share was paid in and a call of $5 per share was made in May, 1899. At the end of 1901 it was decided to call 10 per cent. or $10 per share on the stock, making the latter $20 paid up, and to reduce the capital to $5,000,000, which plan was duly carried out in January, 1902, the name of the company being also changed to the present style.

Transfer Agent, Morton Trust Co., New York. Registrar, Hanover National Bank, New York.

President, Henry Sanderson; Vice-President, S. Herbert Condict; Secretary and Treasurer, William K. Ryan.

Directors—Henry Sanderson, East Orange, N. J.; William K. Ryan, William Jay, G. W. Wesley, W. H. Palmer, Jr.; Harry Payne Whitney, James E. Hays, G. Herbert Condict, New York.

Main office, 815 Eighth avenue, New York. Annual meeting, first Monday in April.

---

## THE NIAGARA FALLS POWER CO.

A corporation formed under the laws of New York in 1886, which has authority by special acts of the State of New York to use the water of Niagara River, and also to transmit any power, heat or light developed from such water to practically any point in the State. Its hydraulic works include 7,200 feet of tunnel, extending from its power-house to the level of the river below the Falls and having a capacity of 105,000 horse-power. Wheel pit No. 1 contains ten 5,000 horse-power turbines connected with ten 5,000 horse-power dynamos in a stone power-house 457 feet long. In wheel pit and power-house No. 2, which have a capacity of eleven 5,000 horse-power turbines connected with eleven 5,000 horse-power dynamos, there are already installed and in operation six 5,000 horse-power turbines and dynamos, and a second installation of five 5,000 horse-power turbines and dynamos has been contracted for, to be completed by September 1, 1903. The completion of this second installation in power-house No. 2 will give the company a capacity of 105,000 electrical horse-power and 8,000 hydraulic horse-power on the American side of the Niagara River.

The company owns 1,071 acres of land in the city of Niagara Falls, N. Y., devoted to sites for manufacturers using its power. The tunnel was opened January 1, 1894. Hydraulic and electrical horse-power is supplied to tenants of the company on its land in the city of Niagara Falls, and to customers in the cities of Niagara Falls, Buffalo, the Tonawandas, and Lockport. The entire output of fifteen generators of 5,000 horse-power each has been sold and is being delivered.

A plant on the Canadian side of the river in the Queen Victoria Niagara Falls park, with a capacity of 100,000 horse-power, is now in course of construction by the Canadian Niagara Power Co. and the first installation of 30,000 horse-power is to be completed in 1903. The first installation in this plant will be three 10,000 horse-power turbines and dynamos, and contracts are being let (April 1, 1903) for a further installation of two 10,000 horse-power turbines and dynamos.

Substantially all the stock of the Canadian Niagara Power Co. is owned by The Niagara Falls Power Co.

Stock......Par $100..........................Authorized, $9,500,000......Issued, $3,331,000

Stock is transferred at the company's office, New York. Registrar, Central Trust Co., New York.

FUNDED DEBT.

| | |
|---|---|
| 1st mort., 5 per cent., due Jan., 1932, Jan. and July.............................. | $10,000,000 |
| Convertible 10 year debentures, 6 per cent., due April, 1910, April and Oct.......... | 2,196,000 |
| " " " 6 per cent., due Oct., 1911, April and Oct.......... | 300,000 |
| Total.............................................................. | $12,496,000 |

The 1st mortgage is $10,000,000 authorized. The coupon bonds are for $1,000 each. Registered bonds are $500 each or multiples of $500. Interest on the bonds is payable at the office of Winslow, Lanier & Co., New York. Trustee of the mortgage, the Central Trust Co., New York. The mortgage securing the company's bonds cover its property in the city of Niagara Falls, and all franchises, transmission lines, etc.; also a majority of the stock of the Cataract Power & Conduit Co. and of the Tonawanda Power Co.

For the construction of power-house and wheel pit No. 2, with connecting tunnel, there was authorized $3,000,000 of 6 per cent. gold coupon convertible debentures, dated April 1, 1900, convertible into stock at the holder's option on or before April 1, 1905. Of these debentures $1,100,000 were outstanding on December 31, 1901.

The stockholders, in July, 1901, subscribed at par to $2,700,000 of an authorized issue of $3,000,000 new 6 per cent. coupon debentures, payable in installments, to build the plant on the Canadian side, these debentures to be secured by debentures of the Canadian Niagara Power Co. in the treasury of the Niagara Falls Power Co., and to be convertible at the holder's option after October 1, 1903, and before October 1, 1908, into stock of the Niagara Falls Power Co.

Subscriptions to first $3,000,000 of debentures are payable at the office of the Metropolitan Trust Co., New York, at which office coupons are also payable. Subscriptions to second $3,000,000 of debentures are payable at the office of the company.

The works of the company were built by the Cataract Construction Co.

President, Darius O. Mills; 1st Vice-President, Edward A. Wickes, New York; 2d Vice-President and Treasurer, William B. Rankine; Secretary, F. L. Lovelace, Niagara Falls, N. Y.; Assistant Secretary and Assistant Treasurer, W. Paxton Little, New York.

Executive Committee—Darius O. Mills, Edward D. Adams, Charles Lanier, Francis Lynde Stetson, Frederick W. Whitridge, John Jacob Astor, Victor Morawetz.

Directors—Edward D. Adams, John Jacob Astor, George S. Bowdoin, Charles F. Clark, Charles Lanier, Joseph Larocque, Darius O. Mills, William B. Rankine, Francis Lynde Stetson, Frederick W. Whitridge, Edward A. Wickes, Daniel O'Day, Victor Morawetz.

Main office, Niagara Falls, N. Y.; New York office, 15 Broad street. Annual meeting, first Tuesday in June.

---

## THE NIAGARA GORGE RAILWAY CO.

A corporation formed under the laws of New York, June 3, 1899. The company succeeded the Niagara Falls & Lewiston Railroad Co. It operates 14.4 miles of electric railway extending from Lewiston, N. Y., along the bank of the Niagara River to the city of Niagara Falls, N. Y., owning a private way for more than 6 miles of its line. The company controls the franchises of the following companies:

Niagara Falls Tower Co.
Niagara Rapids View Co.
Battery Whirlpool Rapids Co.
Niagara Whirlpool Rapids Elevator Co.

By agreement with the Niagara Falls Park & River Railway Co., cars are run across the steel arch bridge to Table Rock and Dufferin's Island. The company has 32 ars. In April, 1903, the company took over the Lewistown & Youngstown Frontier Railway Co.c

Stock......Par $100.........................Authorized, $1,000,000......Issued, $1,000,000

FUNDED DEBT.

Niagara Falls & Lewiston R.R. Co., 1st mort., 5 p ct. gold, due June, 1925, June and Dec. $1,000,000

The total amount of the authorized mortgage is $1,000,000. Trustee of the mortgage and agent for the payment of interest, Knickerbocker Trust Co., New York.

In the fiscal year ending June 30, 1902, the gross earnings were $279,436; net, $225,407; interest charges, $45,849.76.

President—Joseph T. Jones; Vice-President, Herbert P. Bissell; Secretary, Bert L. Jones, Buffalo, N. Y.; Treasurer and General Manager, Bert L. Jones, Niagara Falls, N. Y.

Directors—Joseph T. Jones, Herbert P. Bissell, Bert L. Jones, William H. Hotchkiss, Clarence M. Bushnell, William C. Cornwell, J. Henry Metcalf, Robert R. Hefford, Joseph A. Jones, Robert E. Powers, Buffalo, N. Y.; Francis V. Greene, New York.

Corporate and main office, 38 West Falls street, Niagara Falls, N. Y. Annual meeting, first Saturday in October, at Niagara Falls, N. Y.

## THE NIAGARA, ST. CATHARINES & TORONTO RAILWAY CO.

A corporation formed under the laws of Canada. It is a consolidation of the following companies:

Niagara Central Railway Co.
Port Dalhousie, St. Catharines & Thorold Electric Railway Co.
Niagara Falls, Wesley Park & Clifton Tramway Co.

The company also controls the Niagara, St. Catharines & Toronto Navigation Co. through stock ownership. The company operates 35 miles of electric railway from Port Dalhousie, on Lake Ontario, at the mouth of the Welland Canal, to St. Catharines, Merriton, Thorold, Niagara Falls, Ont., and Niagara Falls, N. Y. The territory served has a population of over 42,000.

Stock......Par $100.............................Authorized, $1,000,000......Issued, $825,000

The company has no preferred stock. Transfer Agent and Registrar, Toronto Safe Deposit & Agency Co., Toronto.

FUNDED DEBT.

1st mort., 5 per cent. gold, due 1929, May and Nov.... ...............................$594,000

The authorized amount of the mortgage is $20,000 per mile. Trustee, The National Trust Co., Toronto. Agent for the payment of interest, Canadian Bank of Commerce, Toronto, and Bank of Scotland, London, England.

The Niagara, St. Catharines & Toronto Navigation Co. has $200,000 of 5 per cent. bonds which are guaranteed by this company.

In the fiscal year ending December 31, 1902, the gross earnings were $172,918.91; net, $46,026.71; interest, $28,000; surplus, $18,026.71.

President, John W. Herbert, New York; Vice-President, Addison B. Colvin, Glens Falls, N. Y.; Secretary-Treasurer, Æmilius Jarvis, Toronto.

Directors—John W. Herbert, Addison B. Colvin, Joseph A. Powers, J. H. Plummer, J. W. Flavalle, Z. A. Lash, Æmilius Jarvis.

Corporate office, St. Catharines, Ont.; main office, Toronto. Annual meeting, first Tuesday in September, at St. Catharines, Ont.

## NICHOLSON FILE CO.

A corporation formed under the laws of Rhode Island in 1864. The company manufactures files and rasps of all kinds. It has large factories at Providence, R. I.; Pawtucket, R. I.; Paterson, N. J.; Kent, O.; Anderson, Ind.; Beaver Falls, Pa., and Port Hope, Ont. The Nicholson plant at Providence is the largest and best equipped establishment in the world devoted to the purpose of manufacturing such specialties.

Stock......Par $100...........................Authorized, $5,000,000......Issued, $2,500,000

The company has no preferred stock or bonded debt and no mortgage indebtedness. The surplus is over $1,100,000.

The average yearly dividends for the past twenty-eight years have been 7 7-10 per cent. per annum. In 1901 the company paid 6 per cent. on its stock. In 1902 10 per cent. was paid, being 2 per cent. quarterly in March (30), June, September and December, and 2 per cent. extra paid December 31.

President and General Manager, Samuel M. Nicholson; Vice-President, Arthur H. Watson; Treasurer, George Nicholson; Assistant Treasurer, Henry W. Harman; Secretary, Robert A. Pearson; Assistant Secretary, W. W. Griffith.

Directors—Samuel M. Nicholson, Marsden J. Perry, Arthur H. Watson, Lewis W. Anthony, John Russet Gladding.

Main office, 23 Acorn street, Providence, R. I.

## NILES-BEMENT-POND CO.

A corporation organized under the laws of New Jersey, August 11, 1899. The company was formed to combine the business of the following manufacturers of machinery and machine tools:

Niles Tool Works Co., Hamilton, O.
Bement, Miles & Co., Philadelphia.
Pond Machine Tool Co., Plainfield, N. J.
Philadelphia Engineering Co., Philadelphia.

In 1900 the Pratt & Whitney Co., of Hartford, Conn., was acquired.

Stock...Par $100....Authorized { com., $5,000,000 / pref., 3,000,000 } Issued { com., $5,000,000 / pref., 2,000,000 } $7,000,000

The preferred stock is 6 per cent., cumulative, and is subject to call at 105 in 1911. Of the preferred an amount of $1,000,000 is held to retire minority stock of the Niles Tool Works Co.

Transfer Agent, Corporation Trust Co. of New Jersey, Jersey City. Registrar, Colonial Trust Co., New York.

The first dividend paid on the preferred stock was 1½ per cent., quarterly, November 29, 1899. Dividends of that amount have since been regularly paid on the preferred, quarterly, February, May, August and November. The first dividend on the common was declared in August, 1900, and was 3 per cent. half-yearly, payable in two installments of 1½ per cent. each on September 20 and December 20, 1900. In 1901 6 per cent. was paid on the common in quarterly payments of 1½ per cent. each in March, June, September and December. In addition to the regular dividend of 1½ per cent. on the common in March, 1902, the company declared an extra 1 per cent. dividend, payable May 15, 1902. The September, 1902, dividend on the common was 2 per cent., which has since been the regular quarterly rate.

The company has no funded debt and acquired all the constituent properties free of encumbrances. There is outstanding $1,225,000 preferred stock of the Pratt & Whitney Co., on which this company guarantees dividends of 6 per cent. per annum, payable quarterly, February, but reserves the right to call the same at par in 1911.

In 1901 the net earnings of the constituent companies were $1,463,571. Surplus over dividends, $865,071. In 1902 the net earnings were $1,627,965; charged for depreciation, $200,000; dividends, $653,500; surplus, $774,465. Total surplus December 31, 1902, $4,413,578.

President, Robert C. McKinney; Vice-Presidents, James K. Cullen, Thomas T. Gaff, A. C. Stebbins, Walter L. Clark; Secretary, E. M'C. Davis; Treasurer, Charles L. Cornell.

Directors—Alexander Gordon, Hamilton, O.; Charles A. Moore, E. M'C. Davis, Walter L. Clark, Robert C. McKinney, New York; Clarence S. Bement, Frederick B. Miles, F. W. Gordon, Philadelphia; Gordon Shillito, Thomas T. Gaff, D. H. Holmes, Cincinnati; James K. Cullen, Hamilton, O.; C. E. Burke, Cleveland; A. C. Stebbins, Plainfield, N. J.; W. S. McKinney, Pittsburg.

Main office, 136 Liberty street, New York. Annual meeting, first Wednesday in February.

## NORFOLK & WASHINGTON STEAMBOAT CO.

A corporation formed under the laws of Virginia, January 31, 1890, for the purpose of operating a line of passenger and freight steamboats between Norfolk, Va., and Washington, D. C., and intermediate points. The company owns three steel vessels, the Newport News, 1,500 tons; Norfolk, 1,300 tons; Washington, 1,300 tons, all of modern style of equpiment and furnishings. It also possesses wharf facilities at Washington, Alexandria and Norfolk.

Stock......Par $100..............................Authorized, $600,000......Issued, $600,000

The company has no preferred stock or funded debt. Stock is transferred by the Secretary of the company at Washington, D. C. Registrar, American Security and Trust Co., Washington, D. C.

The first dividend, 6 per cent. per annum, was paid July 1, 1892. The dividend rate was increased to 8 per cent. per annum, October, 1899, and to 10 per cent. January, 1903. Dividend periods are quarterly, January 15, April, July, and October.

President, Levi Woodbury; Vice-President, Clarence F. Norment; Vice-President and General Manager, John Callahan; Secretary and Treasurer, Odell S. Smith; Assistant General Manager, D. J. Callahan, Washington, D. C.

Directors—John Boyd, John Callahan, Daniel Fraser, D. J. Callahan, Odell S. Smith, Edward Graves, Clarence F. Norment, George W. Pearson, Levi Woodbury.

Corporate office, Norfolk, Va. Main office, Seventh Street Wharf, Washington, D. C.; branch offices, Bond Building, Washington, D. C.; Alexandria, Va.; Norfolk, Va.; Old Point Va. Annual meeting first Wednesday in March, at Washington, D. C.

---

## NORFOLK, PORTSMOUTH & NEWPORT NEWS CO.

A corporation formed under the laws of Virginia in May, 1902, having been formerly known as the Norfolk, Portsmouth & Newport News Railway Co. The company acquired the property and franchises of the following companies:

Berkeley Street Railway Co.
National Gas Co. of Berkeley.
Old Dominion Railway Co.
Portsmouth Electric & Gas Co.
Norfolk Heat, Light & Power Co.

The company owns a majority of the common stock of the Newport News & Old Point Railway & Electric Co. and a majority of the stock of the Norfolk Railway & Light Co. It has franchises for electric railways and electric and gas lighting in Norfolk, Portsmouth and Newport News, Va., in some cases perpetual and in others running from 43 to 47 years. The property of the company includes 7 electric railway systems, 6 ferry lines, 6 electric lighting plants, 3 ice plants, 3 gas companies and 3 seaside resorts, with hotels.

Stock......Par $100........................Authorized, $10,000,000......Issued, $4,000,000

The company has no preferred stock.

FUNDED DEBT.

| | |
|---|---|
| 1st and collateral mort., 5 per cent., gold, due 1942, June and Dec. | $3,000,000 |
| Income bonds, 5 per cent., gold, due 1942, Feb. and Aug. | 2,000,000 |
| Norfolk, Portsmouth & Newport News Ry. Co., con. 1st mort., 5 per cent., gold, due 1950, March and Sept. | 200,000 |
| Norfolk City, 1st mort., 6 per cent., gold, due 1913, Jan. and July | 125,000 |
| Norfolk Street, con. mort., 5 per cent., gold, due 1944, Jan. and July | 915,000 |
| Norfolk Ry. & Light Co., con. mort., 5 p. c., gold, due 1949, May and Nov. | 1,750,000 |
| Newport News & Old Point Ry. & El., 1st mort., 5 per ct., due 1938, May and Nov. | 900,000 |
| Newport News & Old Pt. Ry. & El., gen. mort., 5 p. c., gold, due 1941, Mar. and Sept. | 1,500,000 |
| Citizens Ry., Light & Power Co., 5 per cent., gold, due 1940, May and Nov. | 675,000 |
| Portsmouth St. Ry. Co., 1st mort., 6 per cent., gold, due 1918, Jan. and July | 142,000 |
| " " " " 2d mort., 6 per cent., gold, due 1918, Jan. and July | 100,000 |
| " " " " imp. and ext. mort., 6 p. c., g., due 1920, Jan. and July | 200,000 |
| Total | $11,507,000 |

The authorized 1st and collateral mortgage of the Norfolk, Portsmouth & Newport News Co. is $4,000,000. Of that amount $1,000,000 are reserved for extensions and improvements. The bonds may be called on any interest date at 107 and interest. Trustee of the mortgage and agent for the payment of interest, North American Trust Co., New York. Interest is also payable by Alexander Brown & Sons, Baltimore and New York. The outstanding income bonds of the Norfolk, Portsmouth & Newport News Co. are the total amount authorized. They are convertible until May 1, 1912 into stock at par and may be redeemed at pay and interest on any interest date. Interest is non-cumulative, and payable only if earned. Trustee of the mortgage and agent for the payment of interest, Richmond Trust & Safe Deposit Co., Richmond, Va. Interest is also payable by Alexander Brown & Sons, Baltimore and New York. The authorized mortgage of the Norfolk, Portsmouth & Newport News Railway Co. is $1,000,000, of which $150,000 are reserved for prior liens. A sinking fund of $10,000 is provided, and bonds may be called for this purpose by lot at 110 on any interest day. Trustee of the mortgage and agent for the payment of interest, Fidelity & Deposit Co. of Maryland, Baltimore.

The authorized consolidated mortgage of the Norfolk Railway & Light Co. is $4,000,000. Of that amount $1,040,000 are reserved to retire outstanding bonds and $1,200,000 is held for future acquisitions. A sinking fund of 1 per cent. after November 1, 1909, is provided, and bonds for this purpose may be called at 110 or less. Trustee of the mortgage and agent for the payment f interest, International Trust Co., Baltimore. The authorized Norfolk Street consolidated mortgage is $1,000,000. Trustee of the mortgage and agent for the payment of interest, Merchants Trust & Deposit Co., Baltimore.

The outstanding bonds of the 1st mortgage of the Newport News & Old Point Railway & Electric Co. are the total amount authorized. The bonds may be called on any interest day at 110. The authorized 1st mortgage of the Citizens Railway, Light & Power Co. is $800,000. The bonds may be called on any interest date at 110. Principal and interest are guaranteed by the Newport News & Old Point Railway & Electric Co. The authorized general mortgage of the Newport News & Old Point Railway & Electric Co. is $4,000,000. Of that amount, $1,575,000 are reserved to take up the outstanding 1st mortgage bonds of the Newport News & Old Point Railway & Electric Co. and the Citizens Railway, Light & Power Co., and the remaining $925,000 are reserved for improvements, etc. In addition to the mortgage lien, the bonds are secured by the bonds and stocks of the Citizens Railway, Light & Power Co., Newport News Gas Co., Norfolk & Atlantic Terminal Co., and Danville Electric & Railway Co. Trustee of both mortgages of the Newport News & Old Point Railway & Electric Co. and of the Citizens Railway, Light & Power Co., Maryland Trust Co., Baltimore. Agent for the payment of interest, Alexander Brown & Sons, New York and Baltimore.

The outstanding mortgages of the Portsmouth Street Railway Co. and the River Front Railroad are the full amount authorized. Trustee of the 1st and 2d mortgage of the Portsmouth Street Railway Co. and agent for the payment of interest, United Security Life Insurance & Trust Co., Philadelphia. Trustee of the improvement and extension mortgage of the Portsmouth Street Railway Co. and of the 1st mortgage of the River Front Railroad Co. and agent for the payment of interest, Colonial Trust Co., Philadelphia.

President, R. Lancaster Williams, Richmond; Vice-President, William J. Payne; General Manager, E. G. Hathaway, Norfolk, Va.

Main office, Norfolk, Va.

---

## NORTH AMERICAN CO.

A corporation formed under the laws of New Jersey, June 14, 1890. The company was organized to succeed the Oregon & Transcontinental Co. and purchased the securities owned by the latter.

Stock......Par $100..........................Authorized, $17,000,000......Issued, $17,000,000

On January 23, 1901, the stockholders ratified a reduction of the stock from $50,000,000 authorized to $12,000,000. The amount of old stock outstanding was $39,789,200, which was reduced to the amount given above.

In March, 1903, the stock was increased from $12,000,000 to $17,000,000, the stockholders subscribing at par for the same. The purpose of the increase was to acquire the Laclede Gas Co.

Stock is transferred at the company's office, 30 Broad street, New York. Registrar, Farmers' Loan & Trust Co., New York.

The company purchased considerable stocks of electric companies and of street railroad companies, and owns the entire common stock of Milwaukee Street Railway and Electric Lighting Co., and had over $16,000,000 of that company's bonds, but sold the same in 1897-8 to retire floating debt and collateral notes. It also controls The Detroit Edison Co., which is a consolidation of the Edison Illuminating Co. and the Peninsula Electric Light Co. of Detroit. Has a joint control (with the Mississippi Valley Trust Co.) of the Union Electric Light & Power Co. of St. Louis. In February, 1903, control of the Laclede Gas Co., St. Louis, was acquired.

In December, 1900, the company acquire the Suburban Electric Co. of Covington, Ky., the Covington Gas Co., the Newport, Ky., Gas Co., and other gas and electric companies in Covington, Newport, Ky., and adjacent towns, which were consolidated under the title of the Union Light, Heat and Power Co., the stock of which this company owns.

In 1901-02 the company acquired large electric interests in St. Louis, and formed the Union Electric Light & Power Co. to combine them. It also purchased control of the Detroit Edison. It was interested in a syndicate which in October, 1902, acquired securities of the United States Shipbuilding Co.

The report for May 31, 1896, gave income account as interest, dividends and rentals received, $129,806; taxes, salaries and interest, $172,535. Reports for 1896-97 gave no income account, but stated that company had no liabilities other than an open account for $17,000, against which there were accounts receivable for $222,000; secured loans, $376,206, and cash, $289,759. In 1897-98 receipts were $50,102; surplus, $13,639. In 1898-99, receipts, $119,738; surplus, $85,292. On June 1, 1899, the company had no loans and had cash, $217,015, and accounts receivable, $608,580. In 1899-1900, receipts were $182,147; expenses, $32,398; surplus, $149,749. In the 14 months ending May 31, 1901, the receipts were $90,326. In the year 1901-02 the receipts were $2,103,188; net profits, $1,049,702. The expenses included $1,000,000 charged off the item of good will for the year.

The following is the company's balance sheet, May 31, 1902:

| ASSETS. | | LIABILITIES. | |
|---|---|---|---|
| Good will | $1,000,000 | Capital stock | $12,000,000 |
| Stocks | 8,186,896 | Undivided profits | 1,129,986 |
| Bonds | 1,121,500 | | |
| Loans | 966,900 | | |
| Property | 13,933 | | |
| Bills and accounts receivable | 78,953 | | |
| Cash | 1,761,804 | | |
| Total | $13,129,986 | Total | $13,129,986 |

President, C. W. Wetmore; Vice-President, Charles A. Spofford; 2d Vice-President, William F. White; Secretary, Silas W. Burt; Treasurer, George R. Sheldon, New York.

Directors—C. W. Wetmore, William Nelson Cromwell, Edmund C. Converse, Silas W. Burt, George R. Sheldon, Edward Q. Keasbey, John L. Beggs, Robert Bacon, Charles A. Spofford, Edwin M. Bulkley, New York; Henry C. Payne, Charles F. Pfister, Milwaukee.

Corporate office, Newark, N. J.; main office, 30 Broad street, New York. Annual meeting, third Wednesday in June, at Newark, N. J.

## NORTH AMERICAN TRANSPORTATION & TRADING CO.

A corporation formed under the laws of Illinois in 1892 for the purposes of transportation, mining and merchandising in Alaska, Yukon Territory, and on the Pacific coast. The company owns and operates a large fleet of ocean and river steamers in Alaska and Yukon Territory, with several gold mines in the same localities, and a coal mine and railroad at Cliff Creek, Yukon Territory. The company also owns sawmills, hotels and trading stores at many of the principal points in Alaska and the Yukon Territory.

Stock......Par $100..........................Authorized, $5,000,000......Issued, $4,738,000

The company has no preferred stock and no funded debt. Registrar, Illinois Trust & Savings Bank, Chicago.

President, Michael Cudahy; Vice-President, W. H. Isom, Chicago; Secretary and Treasurer, R. B. Snowden, Seattle, Wash.; Assistant Secretary and Assistant Treasurer, S. E. Graves, Chicago.

Directors—Michael Cudahy, John Cudahy, P. B. Weare, C. H. Walker, H. E. Dick, W. H. Isom, J. C. Dwight, Chicago; August Belmont, Daniel O'Day, New York; Sir Thomas G. Shaughnessy, Montreal.

Corporate and main office, 217 La Salle street, Chicago; branch office, Seattle, Wash. Annual meeting second Tuesday in December.

## NORTH GEORGIA ELECTRIC CO.

A corporation formed under the laws of Georgia, May, 1901. The purpose of the company is to furnish electric light, power and heat in Dahlonega and Gainesville, Ga., and their vicinity. The company acquired several valuable water powers on the Chestatee and Chattahoochee rivers. It operates the electric light plant and street railway system in Gainesville and furnishes power for several industries.

Stock......Par $100............................Authorized, $5,000,000......Issued, $150,000

The company has no preferred stock. Stock is transferred by the secretary of the company.

The company has a first mortgage, securing $200,000 6 per cent. gold bonds, none of which have yet been issued. Trustee of the mortgage, Knickerbocker Trust Co., New York.

President, A. J. Warner, Dahlonega, Ga.; Vice-President, W. A. Carlisle, Gainesville, Ga.; Secretary, J. F. Moore, Dahlonega, Ga.

Directors—A. J. Warner, J. F. Moore, Dahlonega, Ga.; W. A. Carlisle, Gainesville, Ga.; W. H. Slack, Marietta, O.; C. M. Merrick, New Brighton, Pa.

Corporate and main office, Dahlonega, Ga.; branch office, Gainesville, Ga. Annual meeting, first Wednesday in May, at Dahlonega, Ga.

## NORTH JERSEY STREET RAILWAY CO.

### CONSOLIDATED TRACTION CO. OF NEW JERSEY.

A corporation formed under the laws of New Jersey in June, 1894. It absorbed in January, 1898, the Newark & South Orange Railway, and in May, 1898, leased the Consolidated Traction Co. of New Jersey for 999 years. Road owned, 28 miles; leased, 187 miles; total of system, 240 miles. The Jersey City, Hoboken & Paterson Railway is controlled in the same interest.

The Consolidated Traction Co. of New Jersey, organized in 1893, owns the New Jersey Traction Co., Newark Passenger Railway Co., Jersey City & Bergen Railroad, Newark Plank Road, etc., the lines extending from Jersey City to Bergen Point and Newark and Orange, N. J. Line to Elizabeth was completed in 1895. It owns all the stock of the New Jersey Traction Co., to which the Newark Passenger Railway Co. is leased for 999 years, the stock of latter company being owned. Also owns the stock of Jersey City & Bergen Railroad Co., Jersey City, Harrison & Kearney Railroad and Newark Plank Road Co. The Newark Passenger Railway Co. controls the Newark & Bloomfield, Orange & Newark, Belleville & Newark, Essex Passenger Railway and Newark & Irvington Co., and leases the Rapid Transit Street Railway Co.

In May, 1898, a lease of the Consolidated Traction of New Jersey to the North Jersey Traction Co. was made for 999 years, the lessee assuming the lease and guarantee obligations of the lessor company, and guaranteeing dividends on the $15,000,000 of stock as follows: In 1899–1901, inclusive, 2 per cent. per annum; in 1902, 2½ per cent.; in 1903 and 1904, 3 per cent.; in 1905, 3½ per cent.; in 1906 and thereafter, 4 per cent. The dividends are paid semi-annually, January and July.

Stock......Par $100......................Authorized, $15,000,000......Issued, $15,000,000

Transfers of the stocks of both the North Jersey Street Railway Co. and of the Consolidated Traction Co. of New Jersey are made at the office of the companies, 29 Exchange place, Jersey City. Registrar, New Jersey Title Guarantee & Trust Co., Jersey City.

FUNDED DEBT.

| | |
|---|---|
| North New Jersey Street Railway, 1st mort., 4 per cent., due May, 1948, May and Nov.. | $6,500,000 |
| Cons. Traction Co. of New Jersey, 1st mort., 5 per cent., due June, 1933, June and Dec.. | 15,000,000 |
| Orange & Newark, 1st mort., 6 per cent., due April, 1905, April and Oct............ | 496,500 |
| Essex Passenger Railway, cons. mort., 6 per cent., due Nov., 1905, May and Nov..... | 753,500 |
| Newark Passenger Railway, cons. mort., 5 per cent., due July, 1930, Jan. and July... | 4,600,000 |
| Jersey City & Bergen Railroad, 1st mort., 7 per cent., due Jan., 1903, Jan. and July.. | 258,000 |
| Rapid Transit Street Railway, 1st mort., 5 per cent., due April, 1921, April and Oct... | 500,000 |
| Passaic & Newark El. Traction, 1st mort;, guar. 5 per cent., due June, 1937, June and Dec. | 550,000 |
| Total........ | $28,658,000 |

The North Jersey Street Railway 1st mortgage was created in 1898. Amount authorized, $15,000,000. Trustee, Manhattan Trust Co., New York.

The Consolidated Traction Co. of New Jersey 1st mortgage is for $15,000,000. Trustee, Manhattan Trust Co., New York. $7,000,000 of these bonds were set aside to be issued as required for 75 per cent. of cash value of new property betterments, etc. Newark Passenger Railway consolidated mortgage is for $6,000,000, of which $1,600,000 is reserved to retire prior liens. Dividends of 11¼ per cent. per annum are guaranteed on $504,000 stock of Rapid Transit Street Railway.

| EARNINGS. | Gross. | Net. |
|---|---|---|
| 1898........ | $3,472,308 | $1,802,583 |
| 1899........ | 3,757,505 | 1,977,458 |
| 1900........ | 3,992,061 | 2,049,271 |
| 1901........ | 4,172,646 | 2,177,658 |

President, Edward F. C. Young; Vice-President, David Young; Treasurer, E. N. Hill; Secretary, Wilbur F. Johnson, Jersey City.

Main office, 29 Exchange place, Jersey City. Annual meeting, fourth Monday in March.

## NORTH STAR MINES CO.

A corporation formed under the laws of New Jersey, April 10, 1899, for the purpose of acquiring and operating gold mines. The company owns the North Star, Stockbridge, New York Hill and various other mines and claims at Grass Valley, Cal., with water rights and a 40-stamp mill capable of crushing 3,000 tons of ore per month. The mines are equipped with hoisting and pumping plants and other machinery.

Stock......Par $10..........................Authorized, $5,000,000......Issued, $2,500,000

The company has no preferred stock or funded debt.

Transfer Agent, Old Colony Trust Co., Boston. Registrars, Central Trust Co., New York, and American Loan & Trust Co., Boston.

Dividends have been paid by the present company and its predecessor, the North Star Mining Co., to the amount of $600,000. The present company declared a dividend of 2 per cent. on November 20, 1899, since which time it has devoted its resources to the deep development of its property.

In 1902 the company's mines produced $411,147, with an operating profit of $256,920.

President, James D. Hague; Vice-President, William L. Bull; Secretary and Treasurer, W. D. Pagan, New York.

Directors—George B. Agnew, William L. Bull, James D. Hague, Benjamin Strong, New York; Charles G. White, Boston.

Corporate office, 15 Exchange place, Jersey City; main office, 18 Wall street, New York. Annual meeting, second Wednesday in April, at Jersey City.

## NORTH STAR MINING CO., LIMITED

A corporation formed under the laws of the Dominion of Canada for the purpose of engaging in silver mining. The company owns mines at Fort Steele, British Columbia.

Stock......Par $1............................Authorized, $1,500,000......Issued, $1,300,000

The company has no preferred stock and no funded debt. The stock is full-paid and non-assessable.

Dividends on the stock were paid in 1900 at the rate of 9 per cent. annually.

President, D. D. Mann; Vice-President, A. A. Thibaudeau; Secretary, C. E. L. Porteus.

Directors—D. D. Mann, A. A. Thibaudeau, William Mackenzie, H. S. Holt, C. E. L. Porteus.

Main office, 8 Place d'Armes, Montreal. Annual meeting, fourth Wednesday in June, at Montreal.

## NORTH WESTERN FUEL CO.

A corporation formed under the laws of Wisconsin, October 28, 1901, succeeding a Minnesota corporation of the same name that had been in business for about twenty-five years. The business of the company is the forwarding, storage, selling and distributing of coal and the manufacture and sale of coke. The company has a storage and transfer plant at Chicago; docks at Duluth, West Superior, Washburn and Milwaukee; coke ovens at West Superior and yards at St. Paul and Minneapolis. The property comprises 85 acres of dock property, 7 coal docks, 1 rail transfer plant, 10 retail coal yards, coke ovens, etc.

Stock......Par $100..........................Authorized, $2,500,000......Issued, $2,500,000

The company has no preferred stock and no funded debt.

Stock is transferred at the office of the company, St. Paul. Registrar, Guaranty Trust Co., New York.

President, E. M. Saunders, St. Paul; Assistant to President and Treasurer, E. L. Shepley; 1st Vice-President, A. C. Jones, Duluth, Minn.; 2d Vice-President, E. L. Booth, Chicago; Secretary, C. M. Benham; Assistant Treasurer, W. H. Forbes; Assistant Secretary, S. T. Painter, St. Paul.

Directors—E. N. Saunders, E. L. Shepley, C. M. Benham, E. N. Saunders, Jr., St. Paul; C. W. Watson, Baltimore; J. O. Watson, Fairmont; A. C. Jones, Duluth, E. L. Booth, Chicago.

Corporate office, Milwaukee; executive office, St. Paul. Annual meeting, second Tuesday in January, at Milwaukee.

## NORTHAMPTON STREET RAILWAY CO.

A corporation formed under the laws of Massachusetts, April 5, 1865. The company was originally the Northampton & Williamsburg Railway Co., chartered in February, 1873. The company operates an electric railway system in the city of Northampton and the towns of Easthampton and Williamsburg, Mass., serving a population of 28,000. It owns and operates 26.26 miles of road and owns a power plant and 43 cars.

Stock......Par $100.............................Authorized, $300,000... ..Issued, $300,000

The company has no preferred stock. Stock is transferred and registered at the office of the treasurer of the company, Springfield, Mass.

The first dividend, 6 per cent., was paid in October, 1893; in subsequent years the dividends have been: 1894, 8 per cent.; 1895, 7½ per cent.; 1896, 10 per cent.; 1897, 9 per cent.; 1898-1901 inclusive, 8 per cent. Dividends are paid semi-annually in January and July.

FUNDED DEBT.

| | |
|---|---|
| 1st mort., 5 per cent., due April, 1909, April and Oct................................ | $25,000 |
| Coupon bonds, 4½ per cent., due June, 1910, June and Dec......................... | 200,000 |
| Total.............................................. ........................... | $225,000 |

The bonds issued are the total amounts authorized. Trustee of the first mortgage bonds and agent for the payment of interest, Springfield Safe Deposit & Trust Co., Springfield, Mass. Trustee of the coupon bonds and agent for the payment of interest, Third National Bank, Pittsfield, Mass. The coupon bonds can be called at par in 1905.

In the fiscal year ending September 30, 1902, the gross earnings were $144,846; interest charges, $10,250; dividends, $24,000; deficit, $3,492.

President, John Olmsted, Vice-President and Treasurer, Newrie D. Winter, Springfield, Mass.; Secretary, Henry P. Field, Northampton, Mass.

Directors—John Olmsted, Newrie D. Winter, George W. Cook, Frank H. Goldthwait, Springfield, Mass.; John C. Hammond, John A. Sullivan, Henry M. Tyler, Northampton, Mass.

Corporate and main office, Locust and Hatfield streets, Northampton, Mass. Annual meeting, second Tuesday in October, at Northampton, Mass.

## NORTHERN ALABAMA COAL, IRON & RAILWAY CO.

A corporation formed under the laws of New Jersey, June 16, 1899. The original title of the company was the Alabama Coal, Iron & Railway Co. The name was changed to the present style in July, 1899.

This company acquired the property of the Alabama Iron & Railroad Co., which was sold at foreclosure in June, 1899, the property having formerly been the Talladega Iron & Steel Co. The property consists of over 2,000 acres of iron and coal lands in Talladega County, Ala., with blast furnaces and coal mines thereon.

The Birmingham & Atlantic Railroad Co., whose road extends from Talladega to Pell City, Ala., is owned by this company.

Stock......Par $100..............................Authorized, $1,000,000......Issued, $502,000

Transfer Agent and Registrar, Trust Co. of America, New York.

FUNDED DEBT.

1st mort., 5 per cent., due 1940, Jan. and July...................................... $840,000

The 1st mortgage is $1,000,000 authorized. Trustees of mortgage, William A. Underwood and Ashbel P. Fitch. Principal and interest of the bonds are payable at the Trust Co. of America, New York.

President, Walter T. Rosen; Vice-President, S. H. March; Secretary and Treasurer, John Carlsen, New York; Assistant Secretary and Assistant Treasurer, George Dunglinson; General Manager, John C. Soley, Talladega, Ala.

Directors—Eugene Zimmerman, Cincinnati; S. H. March, Richard Limburger, Rush Taggart, Walter T. Rosen, Felix Rosen, New York; Frederick B. Van Vorst, Hackensack, N. J.

Corporate office, 15 Exchange place, Jersey City; Secretary's office, 25 Broad street, New York; operating office, Talladega, Ala. Annual meeting, second Monday in July, at Jersey City.

## NORTHERN COMMERCIAL CO.

A corporation formed under the laws of New Jersey, April 6, 1901, for the purpose o conducting manufacturing, mining and mercantile enterprises in Alaska and Yukon Territory. The company purchased all the interests on Behring Sea, the Yukon River and in Alaska, and Yukon Territory, of the following concerns, with the exception of their steamships, steamboats, etc.:

| | |
|---|---|
| The Alaska Commercial Co. | The Empire Transportation Co. |
| The Alaska Exploration Co. | The Seattle-Yukon Transportation Co. |

The company owns real estate and stores at Nome, Golvin, St. Michaels, Steel Creek, Rampart, Circle, Hamlin and other places in Alaska, and Dawson and Forty Mile, Yukon Territory.

Stock......Par $100...........................Authorized, $2,750,000......Issued, $1,622,800

The company has no preferred stock.

Transfer Agent, New Jersey Title Guarantee & Trust Co., Jersey City.

FUNDED DEBT.

1st mort., 5 per cent, due 1903-1916, Jan. and July.................................. $2,620,000

The authorized bond issue is $4,250,000, and is in series from A to N, inclusive, the bonds being redeemable at various dates; series A, maturing in 1903, and the others yearly until 1916. Trustee of mortgage, The Union Trust Co., San Francisco.

President, Leon Sloss; 1st Vice-President, Isaac Liebes; 2d Vice-President, Louis Sloss, Jr.; Secretary and Treasurer, William L. Gerstle; Assistant Treasurer, George H. Higbee, San Francisco; General Manager, M. L. Washburn.

Directors—Leon Sloss, Lewis Gerstle, G. Niebaum, Isaac Liebes, George H. Higbee, William L. Gerstle, Louis Sloss, Sidney Liebes, Louis Sloss, Jr., Louis H. Phillips, Henry F. Fortmann, Julien Liebes, Martin L. Washburn, Louis Greenbaum, O. H. Greenewald, M. L. Gersth, San Francisco; George H. B. Martin, Camden, N. J.

Corporate office, Camden, N. J.; main office, 645 Market street, San Francisco. Annual meeting, second Tuesday January, at Camden, N. J.

## THE NORTHERN NAVIGATION CO. OF ONTARIO

A corporation formed under the laws of the Province of Ontario in 1899 for the purpose of engaging in the steamship, freight and passenger business on the Georgian Bay. The company is a consolidation of the Great Northern Transit Co. and North Shore Navigation Co.

It also has a controlling interest in the North-West Transportation Co. The company owns 7 steamships. The North-West Transportation Co. has 3 steamships.

Stock......Par $100..............................Authorized, $1,000,000......Issued, $560,000

The company has no preferred stock and no funded debt.

Dividends on the stock are paid semi-annually, in February and August, at the rate of 10 per cent. per annum.

In the fiscal year ending December 31, 1901, the company's net income, above expenses and interest, was $80,967; dividends, $44,085.

President, James Scott, Toronto; Vice-President, John J. Long, Collingwood, Ont.; Secretary, Thomas Long, Toronto; Treasurer, C. E. Stephens, Collingwood, Ont.

Directors—James Scott, Thomas Long, E. B. Osler, Toronto; John J. Long, Charles Cameron, C. E. Stephens, Collingwood, Ont.; W. J. Sheppard, Wanbaushene, Ont.; H. E. Smith, Owen Sound, Ont.

Main office, Collingwood, Ont.

## NORTHERN OHIO TRACTION & LIGHT CO.

A corporation formed under the laws of Ohio, December 29, 1902. The company is a reorganization of the Northern Ohio Traction Co.

The old company was a consolidation in 1899 of the Akron, Bedford & Cleveland Railroad and the Akron Traction & Electric Companies.

Road owned from Cleveland via Cuyahoga Falls to Akron, O., and in the latter city about 98 miles. Has traffic arrangements with Cleveland Electric Railway.

Stock......Par $100..............................Authorized, $7,500,000......Issued, $6,500,000

The company has no preferred stock. Transfer agent, Savings & Trust Co. of Cleveland.

FUNDED DEBT.

| | |
|---|---|
| Ak., Bed. & Cleve. 1st mort., 5 per cent., due 1915, March and Sept.................. | $300,000 |
| Nor. Ohio Traction gen. mort., 5 per cent., due 1919.................................. | 3,000,000 |
| Nor. Ohio Traction & Light mort., 4 per cent., due Jan., 1933, Jan. and July....... | 1,750,000 |
| Total.................................................................. | $5,050,000 |

The authorized amount of the new 5 per cent. bonds is $4,000,000. Trustee, Savings & Trust Co., Cleveland. The latter is agent for the payment of interest, but coupons are also paid at the First National Bank, New York. Of the bonds, $1,000,000 were given to the preferred stockholders of the old company to retire the same.

EARNINGS.

| | Gross. | Net. | Charges. | Surplus. |
|---|---|---|---|---|
| 1900 .................................. | $513,725 | $196,250 | $141,133 | $50,117 |
| 1901 .................................. | 617,011 | 266,166 | 136,162 | 130,004 |
| 1902 .................................. | 745,043 | 334,251 | 155,067 | 179,183 |

President, H. A. Everett, Cleveland; 1st Vice-President, Will Christy; 2nd Vice-President and General Manager, Charles Currie; Secretary, C. F. Moore, Akron, O.; Treasurer, J. R. Nutt, Cleveland.

Directors—H. A. Everett, E. W. Moore, C. W. Wason, B. Mahler, J. R. Nutt, Cleveland; Will Christy, Charles Currie, Akron, O.

Main office, Akron, O.

## NORTHWESTERN ELEVATED RAILROAD

A corporation formed under the laws of Illinois, October 30, 1893. The company owns 6.37 miles of 4-track road in Chicago, making 28 miles single track. The right of way is owned in fee except at street crossings. The company also owns and operates 1.98 miles in the centre of Chicago as the Loop Division of the Northwestern Elevated Railroad Co., formerly the Union Elevated Railroad, which property was purchased by this company in September, 1901, for $6,250,000.

Stock...Par $100....Authorized { com., $5,000,000 / pref., 5,000,000 } Issued { com., $5,000,000 / pref., 5,000,000 } $10,000,000

The preferred stock is 5 per cent., non-cumulative, and preferred only as to dividends.

Transfer Agent and Registrar, Illinois Trust & Savings Bank, Chicago.

Both classes of stock are held in a voting trust. Trustees, John J. Mitchell, Marshall Field and James A. Blair.

FUNDED DEBT.

1st refunding mort., convertible 4 per cent., gold, due 1911, March and Sept.......... $14,000,000
Union Elevated Railroad, 1st mort., 5 per cent., gold, due 1945, April and Oct...... 4,387,000

Total ............................................................ $18,387,000

The 1st refunding mortgage is $25,000,000 authorized. Trustee of mortgage, Illinois Trust & Savings Bank, Chicago, which also pays interest. Agents for the payment of interest in New York, Blair & Co. The refunding mortgage bonds are convertible into preferred stock at par at the holder's option, but the company can call them for redemption at 102½ and interest after September 1, 1906, though when called the holder has the right to take either cash or preferred stock.

The Union Elevated Railroad 1st mortgage is for $5,000,000. Agents for the payment of interest, Illinois Trust & Savings Bank, Chicago; Blair & Co., New York.

EARNINGS.

| | Gross. | Net. | Charges. | Surplus. |
|---|---|---|---|---|
| 1901 ............................. | $1,100,863 | $724,723 | $565,435 | $159,287 |
| 1902 ............................. | 1,410,908 | 946,597 | 757,173 | 189,423 |

President, Clarence Buckingham; Vice-President, Charles Counselman; Secretary and Treasurer, William V. Griffin.

Directors—Clarence Buckingham, Charles F. Ayer, Clarence A. Knight, Charles Counselman, William W. Miller, John B. Dennis, W. V. Griffin.

Main office, 135 Adams street, Chicago. Annual meeting, last Thursday in January, at Chicago.

## NORWICH STREET RAILWAY CO.

A corporation formed under the laws of Connecticut in 1882. The company has a perpetual franchise for an electric railway in Norwich, Conn. It owns about 17 miles of track in Norwich, with a branch extending to Baltic, Conn.

Stock......Par $100..............................Authorized, $600,000......Issued, $250,000

The company has no preferred stock. Stock is transferred at the office of the company in Boston. Registrar, American Loan & Trust Co., Boston.

Dividends at the rate of 5 per cent. annually are paid, the dividend periods being semi-annual in January and July.

FUNDED DEBT.

1st mort., 5 per cent. gold, due Oct. 1, 1923, April and Oct.............................$350,000

The bond issue is the full amount authorized. Trustee of the mortgage, Treasurer of the State of Connecticut. Agent for the payment of interest, American Loan & Trust Co., Boston.

In the fiscal year ending June 30, 1902, the gross earnings were $111,811.47; net, $39,950.28; charges, $18,695.17; dividends, $11,250; surplus, $10,005.11.

President, Billings P. Learned, New London, Conn.; Secretary, W. L. Adams, Norwich, Conn.; Treasurer, William A. Tucker, Boston.

Directors—Billings P. Learned, Walter C. Noyes, New London, Conn.; Costello Lippitt, Stephen B. Meech, Asa Backus, W. A. Briscoe, Norwich, Conn.; William A. Tucker, Boston.

Corporate office, Norwich, Conn.; main office, 53 State street, Boston. Annual meeting, last Wednesday in July, at Norwich, Conn.

## THE NO. 7 MINING CO.

A corporation formed under the laws of West Virginia in September, 1899. The company owns six mining claims in the Kettle River mining division of Yale District, in the Province of British Columbia, about two miles from the United States line. The property is equipped with mining machinery and buildings.

Stock......Par $5............................Authorized, $1,000,000......Issued, $1,000,000

The company has no preferred stock and no funded debt.

Transfer Agent and Registrar, Laidlaw & Co., 14 Wall street, New York.

President, C. E Laidlaw; Vice-President, F. L. Underwood; Treasurer, Charles H. Ropes; Secretary, R. H. Eggleston, New York.

Directors—C. E. Laidlaw, Henry A. James, Charles H. Ropes, R. H. Eggleston, F. L. Underwood, New York.

Corporate and main office, 31 Nassau street, New York. Annual meeting, first Tuesday in October, at New York.

## OCEANIC STEAMSHIP CO.

A corporation formed under the laws of California in 1881. It operates a line of steamships between San Francisco, Honolulu, Samoa, New Zealand, Australta and Tahati, owning a fleet of seven large steamers and one sailing vessel.

Stock......Par $100..........................Authorized, $2,500,000......Issued, $2,500,000

The company has no preferred stock. Stock is transferred at the company's office.

FUNDED DEBT.

1st mort., 5 per cent., gold bonds, due 1924, Jan. and July.......................... $2,405,000

The bonds are subject to call after 1909. A sinking fund of $100,000 per annum is provided.

Trustee of mortgage, Union Trust Co., San Francisco.

For the fiscal year ending December 31, 1901, the gross vessel earnings were $2,002,219; operating expenses, $1,908,036; net vessel earnings. $94,183; assessments, $250,000; overdrafts, $516,834; total receipts, $1,143,306; expenses and fixed charges, $314,436; special disbursement, $828,869. In 1902 the gross receipts were $2,348,571 ; excess of payments, including interest, over receipts, $415,815.

President, John D. Spreckles; Vice-President and Treasurer, Adolph B. Spreckles ; Secretary, H. W. Thomas, San Francisco.

Directors—Claus Spreckels, John D. Spreckels, Adolph B. Spreckels, W. D. K. Gibson, E. F. Preston, George Fritch, F. Tillmann, Jr.

Main office, 327 Market street, San Francisco.

## THE OGILVIE FLOUR MILLS CO.

A corporation formed under the laws of the Dominion of Canada, May 30, 1902, to manufacture and deal in grain and flour.

Stock....Par $100.....Authorized { com., $1,250,000 / pref., 2,000,000 } Issued { com., $1,250,000 / pref., 1,600,000 } $2,850,000

The preferred stock is 7 per cent. Transfer Agent and Registrar, Royal Trust Co., Montreal.

The first dividend of 3½ per cent. was paid September 2, 1902, or at the rate of 7 per cent. per annum on the preferred stock. Dividends are paid semi-annually in September and March.

FUNDED DEBT.

1st mort., 6 per cent., due Dec. and June..........................................$1,000,000

Agent for the payment of interest, Bank of Montreal, Montreal.

President, Charles R. Hosmer ; Vice-President and Managing Director, F. W. Thompson; Secretary, Shirley Ogilvie ; Treasurer, S. A. McMurtry, Montreal.

Directors—George A. Drummond, E. S. Clouston, H. Montagu Allan, Charles R. Hosmer, F. W. Thompson, Montreal.

Corporate and main office, Montreal. Annual meeting, first Wednesday in October, at Montreal.

## OHIO & INDIANA CONSOLIDATED NATURAL & ILLUMINATING GAS CO.

A corporation formed under the laws of New Jersey, December 29, 1899. The company was organized to combine the following organizations and acquired their stock :

Logansport & Wabash Valley Gas Co., Logansport, Ind.; Wabash, Ind.; Peru, Ind., etc.
Indiana Natural and Illuminating Gas Co., Frankfort, Crawfordville, Lebanon, Ind., etc.
Lafayette Gas Co., Lafayette, Ind.
Fort Wayne Gas Co., Fort Wayne, Ind.; Decatur, Ind., etc.
Ohio & Indiana Gas Co., Lima, O.; St. Mary's, O., etc.

The company has over 100,000 acres of gas-producing territory under perpetual lease in Blackford, Wells, Jay, Delaware, Madison, Grant, Howard, Tipton, Clinton and Boone counties, Ind. It has 696 producing gas wells, 996 miles of mains and field lines, 585 miles of city lines, 1,054 miles right of way and 499 miles of telephone lines. It is proposed to extend the lines of the company so as to obtain new sources of supply if necessary.

Stock......Par $100........................ Authorized, $10,000,000......Issued, $9,000,000

Of the authorized stock $1,000,000 is reserved to provide for the purchase of new gas fields or for extensions.

The amount of stock of the old companies and the rate at which each was exchanged for shares of the new company were given in the MANUAL for 1901.

Transfers of stock are made at the company's office, 45 Broadway, New York. Registrar, Central Trust Co., New York.

The company began the payment of dividends on its stock with 1 per cent. paid March 1, 1900, and paid regular quarterly dividends at the same rate, or 4 per cent. per annum, in March (1), June, September and December, until June, 1902, inclusive, after which they were suspended.

FUNDED DEBT.

| | |
|---|---|
| Indiana Nat. & Ill. Gas Co., 1st mort., 6 per cent., due 1908, May and Nov.......... | $820,000 |
| Fort Wayne Gas Co., 1st mort., 6 per cent., due 1925, Jan. and July................ | 1,940,000 |
| Logansport & Wabash Valley Gas, 1st mort., 6 per cent., due 1925, June and Dec.... | 1,690,000 |
| Ohio & Indiana Gas Co., 1st mort., 6 per cent., due 1926, June and Dec.............. | 1,940,000 |
| Lafayette Gas Co., 1st mort., 6 per cent., due 1924, May and Nov.................... | 960,000 |
| Total.............................................................. | $7,350,000 |

The combined earnings and expenditure of the constituent companies for two years prior to the consolidation were as follows: 1898, gross $1,955,758, net $1,420,418, charges $458,285, dividends $495,000, construction $314,873, balance surplus $152,260; 1899, gross $1,961,371, net $1,332,613, charges $454,875, dividends $362,500, construction $486,962, balance surplus $28,276.

The constituent companies from their organization paid 6 and 7 per cent. dividends on their stocks until 1899, when dividends were reduced to 4 per cent. in order to accumulate funds for the purpose of carrying out the plan of consolidation.

It is provided in the organization of the company that the directors cannot sell or dispose of the constituent companies or their stocks which were acquired with its own stock without the consent of 75 per cent. of the outstanding stock.

President, Charles F. Dieterich; Vice-President, J. Bertschmann, New York; Secretary, S. T. Murdock, Lafayette, Ind.; Treasurer, A. B. Proal, New York.

Directors—Charles F. Dieterich, A. E. Dieterich, James H. Benedict, J. Bertschmann, Walton Ferguson, George C. Clark, John Sloane, A. B. Proal, New York; Anthony N. Brady, Albany; Charles H. Mead, New Jersey; James Murdock, Lafayette, Ind.

Main office, 45 Broadway, New York. Annual meeting, first Wednesday in January.

## OLD COLONY COPPER CO.

A corporation formed under the laws of Michigan in 1898. The company acquired over 1,200 acres of copper bearing territory in Houghton County, Mich., lying east of the Calumet & Hecla mine and south of the Mayflower. The property is being explored by shafts, drifts, crosscuts, etc., and also by a tunnel and a diamond drill. By the two latter means nearly all of the underlying lodes from west to east have been intersected, and a number of well-defined lodes have thus been located and are now being thoroughly examined.

Stock......Par $25..........................Authorized, $2,500,000......Issued, $2,500,000

There had been paid in up to March, 1903, $10 per share.

Stock is transferred at the company's office in Boston. Registrar, Old Colony Trust Co., Boston.

President, Henry F. Fay; Secretary, Walter B. Mosman; Treasurer, George G. Endicott, Boston.

Directors—Henry F. Fay, Stephen R. Dow, Walter B. Mosman, William H. Reed, John C. Watson, Rogers L. Barstow, Boston; James Chynoweth, Calumet, Mich.

Main office, 60 State street, Boston. Annual meeting, second Wednesday in December at Boston.

## OLD DOMINION COPPER MINING & SMELTING CO.

A corporation formed under the laws of New Jersey in 1895. The company owns copper mines near Globe, Ariz. The properties have in the past produced considerable amounts of copper and silver. In 1899 arrangements were made to acquire the Continental and other claims adjoining the company's property.

Stock......Par $25..........................Authorized, $5,000,000......Issued, $3,750,000

The stock of the company was increased from 150,000 shares to 200,000 shares in 1899, in order to provide for further acquisitions. The increased amount of stock, 50,000 shares, had not been issued up to January, 1903.

Stock is transferred at the company's office, 35 Congress street, Boston. Registrar, Atlas National Bank, Boston.

The company's statement from its formation to January 1, 1901, showed net receipts from operations, $852,961; from subscriptions, $500,000; total, $1,352,961. Paid for purchase of mines and development work, $951,038; balance on hand January 1, 1901, $401,922. In 1901 the gross receipts were $1,276,979, profits $113,839.

President, A. S. Bigelow; Treasurer, William J. Ladd, Boston.

Directors—Charles S. Smith, Joseph T. Herrick, Charles G. Lavel, Edward F. Newton, J. Waldo Smith, Louis D. Brandeis, George N. Towle.

Main office, 35 Congress street, Boston. Annual meeting, first Wednesday in April, at Jersey City.

## OLD DOMINION LAND CO.

A corporation formed under the laws of Virginia, October 14, 1880. The purpose of the company is to acquire lands, lay out towns and cities and establish, construct, sell, rent and maintain elevators, warehouses, factories, buildings, wharves, docks, etc. The company owns a large amount of land and buildings in the city of Newport News, Va., and vicinity.

Stock......Par $100..........................Authorized, $2,000,000 .....Issued, $1,962,736

Stock is transferred at the office of the secretary of the company, 23 Broad street, New York.

The company has no preferred stock and no funded debt.

Dividends have been paid as follows: November, 1891, 3 per cent.; 1892, 6 per cent.; 1893, 1½ per cent.; 1894, 22 per cent.; 1898, 1 per cent.; 1899, 14 per cent.; 1900, 4 per cent.; 1901, 3 per cent.; 1902, 3 per cent.

There are no regular times for the payment of dividends and no fixed rates.

In the year ending September 30, 1902, the gross earnings of the company were $173,757.60; expenses, $131,041.90; balance, $42,715.70; dividends, $78,500.

President, Calvin B. Orcutt; Vice-President and Treasurer, Isaac E. Gates; Secretary, Charles Babbidge; Assistant Secretary, Vaughn M. Coyne, New York.

Directors—Calvin B. Orcutt, Isaac E. Gates, New York; William G. Low, Charles H. Tweed, John J. Emery, Henry E. Huntington.

Corporate office, Newport News, Va.; New York offices, 1 Broadway and 23 Broad street. Annual meeting, third Tuesday in November, at New York.

## OLD DOMINION STEAMSHIP CO.

A corporation formed under the laws of Delaware in 1875. The company acquired the property of the New York corporation of the same name, which was organized in 1867. The company operates steamship routes, the principal one being between New York, Norfolk, Va., Newport News, Va., Old Point Comfort and Richmond, Va. Its auxiliary lines cover the rivers and bays of Virginia and North Carolina. It leases dock facilities at New York from the city, and owns valuable property of the same kind at Norfolk and Richmond, Va. Its fleet comprises upward of thirty ocean-going steamships and river boats.

Stock......Par $100..........................Authorized, $1,500,000......Issued, $1,500,000

Stock is transferred at the office of the company. Registrar, Farmers' Loan & Trust Co., New York.

FUNDED DEBT.

Gen. mort., 5 per cent., due 1913, March and Sept............... ................. $1,000,000

The bonds are secured by the company's real estate and some of its vessels. Trustee of mortgage, Farmers' Loan & Trust Co., New York.

The company pays 6 per cent. per annum upon its stock. The dividends are semi-annual, being 3 per cent. each in January (2) and June.

President, W. L. Guillaudeu; Secretary, H. B. Walker; Treasurer, J. S. Sammis.

Directors—W. L. Guillaudeu, W. Rowland, Samuel Spencer, F. J. Kimball, F. H. Von Stade, George E. Weed, J. W. Causey, John Skelton Williams, George A. Elliott, George W. Stevens, Henry Walters.

Main office, 81 Beach street, New York. Annual meeting, second Tuesday in February, at New York.

## OMAHA & COUNCIL BLUFFS STREET RAILWAY CO.

A corporation formed under the laws of Nebraska as a successor to the Omaha Street Railway Co. The latter company was a consolidation of the principal street railway companies of Omaha, and acquired other franchises and properties, giving it control of all the cable, horse and electric railway service in the city of Omaha and its suburbs. The company also leased for 99 years from August, 1902, the following properties:

| | |
|---|---|
| The Council Bluffs Street Railway Co. | The Omaha, Council Bluffs & Suburban Street Railway Co. |
| The Omaha & Council Bluffs Ry. & Bdge. Co. | |

The company controls the street railway service between Omaha and Council Bluffs, Ia., and suburbs. The company owns and operates 122.45 miles of railway. It has 257 cars and a complete electric equipment.

Stock....Par $100....Authorized { com., $5,000,000; pref., 5,000,000 } Issued { com., $5,000,000; pref., 4,000,000 } $9,000,000

The preferred stock is 5 per cent., cumulative.

Dividends on the stock of the Omaha Street Railway Co. were paid quarterly at the rate of 4 per cent. per annum.

FUNDED DEBT.

| | |
|---|---|
| 1st con. mort., 5 per cent. gold, due 1928, Jan. and July | $4,850,000 |
| Omaha Street Ry. Co. 1st con. mort., 5 per cent. gold, due May, 1914, May and Nov. | 2,500,000 |
| Omaha & Coun. Bluffs Ry. & Bdge. Co. 1st mort., 6 p. c., due Jan., 1908, Jan. and July. | 400,000 |
| Council Bluffs Street Railway Co. 1st mort., due July, 1909, Jan. and July | 250,000 |
| Total | $8,000,000 |

The total amount of the 1st consolidated mortgage of the Omaha & Council Bluffs Street Railway Co. is $10,000,000, of which amount $2,500,000 are reserved to retire the bonds of the 1st consolidated mortgage of the Omaha Street Railway Co. Trustee of the mortgage and agent for the payment of interest, Morton Trust Co., New York. The outstanding bonds of the Omaha Street Railway Co.'s 1st consolidated mortgage are the total amount authorized. Agent for the payment of interest, Farmers' Loan & Trust Co., New York. Trustee of the 1st mortgage of the Omaha & Council Bluffs Railway & Bridge Co. and the Council Bluffs Street Railway Co. and agents for the payment of interest, Mercantile Trust Co., New York.

President, Frank Murphy; Vice-President, Guy C. Barton; Secretary, R. A. Leussler; Treasurer and General Manager, W. A. Smith; General Superintendent, F. A. Tucker.

Directors—Frank Murphy, Guy C. Barton, C. W. Wattles, W. V. Morse, W. A. Smith, Randal Morgan, Albert Strauss, Hugh McGowan, C. R. Tyler.

Corporate and main office, Merchants' National Bank Building, Omaha.

## OMAHA GAS CO.

A corporation formed under the laws of Nebraska, August 9, 1897, to engage in the business of manufacturing and selling gas. The plant of the company is located at Omaha,. The company is controlled in the interest of the United Gas Improvement Co.

Stock....Par $100.....Authorized { com., $2,500,000; pref., 1,250,000 } Issued { com., $2,500,000; pref., 1,250,000 } $3,750,000

Stock is transferred at the office of the company, Omaha.

A dividend of 6 per cent. was paid in 1902 on the preferred stock.

FUNDED DEBT.

| | |
|---|---|
| 1st consolidated mort., 5 per cent., gold, due Aug. 13, 1917, Feb. and Aug | $1,882,000 |
| Underlying 6 per cent. bonds | 300,000 |
| Total | $2,182,000 |

The total amount of bonds authorized is $2,500,000. Interest on the bonds is payable in London, March and September, and February and August in New York. Trustee of the mortgage and agent for the payment of interest, Guaranty Trust Co., New York.

President, Frank Murphy; Vice-President, George E. Barker; Treasurer, Isaac Battin; Secretary, George W. Clabaugh; Assistant Treasurer, Lewis Lillie.

Directors—Frank Murphy, Samuel T. Bodine, George E. Barker, Randal Morgan, B. B. Wood.

Corporate and main office, 1224 Farnum street, Omaha. Annual meeting, first Monday in January, at Omaha.

## THE OMAHA WATER CO.

A corporation formed under the laws of Maine in 1896. The business of the company is the supplying water for domestic and public uses to Omaha, South Omaha and Florence, Neb.

Stock....Par $50....Authorized { com., $2,500,000; 1st pref., 750,000; 2d pref., 1,000,000 } Issued { com., none.; 1st pref., $750,000; 2d pref., 1,000,000 } $1,750,000

The 1st preferred stock is 5 per cent., non-cumulative. The 2d preferred is 5 per cent., non-cumulative. The preferred stocks can both be called at par. The common stock, although authorized, has not been issued.

The company has paid 5 per cent. per annum on the 1st preferred stock since 1898, inclusive, the dividends being 2½ per cent., semi-annually, in February (10) and August. On the 2d preferred, the initial dividend was 1 per cent., in August, 1899, and half-yearly dividends of 1 per cent. each have since been paid, in February and August.

Transfer Agent, Farmers' Loan & Trust Co., New York.

FUNDED DEBT.

| | |
|---|---|
| Prior lien mort., 5 per cent., due 1916, Jan. and July | $1,093,000 |
| Consolidated mort., 5 per cent., due 1946, Jan. and July | 3,543,000 |
| Total | $4,636,000 |

President, Theodore C. Woodbury, New York; Vice-President, J. M. Woolworth, Omaha; Clerk, H. M. Verrill, Portland, Me.; Treasurer, Stockton Heth, Omaha.

Directors—Theodore C. Woodbury, Ernst Thalmann, Gerald L. Hoyt, Frederick Strauss, H. W. Carpentier, Howard Mansfield, New York; Winthrop Smith, W. R. Nicholson, Philadelphia; F. M. Colston, Baltimore; Albert Stone, Boston; J. M. Woolworth, Omaha.

Main office, Omaha; New York office, 25 Broad street. Annual meeting, third Wednesday in July, at Portland.

## ONTARIO SILVER MINING CO.

A corporation formed under the laws of Utah in 1877. It owns and operates the Ontario and Daly mines, near Park City, Utah. The company owns also the Park City Water Co., the Weber Coal Co., with 811 acres of coal lands, and has considerable interests in other mining properties.

Stock......Par $100........................Authorized, $15,000,000......Issued, $15,000,000

Transfer Agents, Lounsbery & Co., 15 Broad street, New York.

The company's mines are among the largest silver producers in the United States. From its incorporation to December 31, 1901, it paid in dividends $13,737,500. Owing to the low price of silver, it did not pay a dividend from 1897 until April, 1900, when 30c. per share was paid. In July, 1901, 10c. per share was paid; in October, 1901, 10c., and in December, 1901, 30c., making 50c. for the year. In 1902, paid 30c. in March; 30c. in June, and 30c. in September, or 90c. for the year.

President, Frank G. Drum, San Francisco; Vice-President, E. H. Clark; Secretary, Fred Clark; Treasurer, J. B. Haggin; Superintendent, R. C. Chambers.

Directors—J. B. Haggin, Fred Clark, E. H. Clark, Thomas Turner, Frank G. Drum, H. L. Tevis, R. A. Clark.

Main office, 210 Montgomery street, San Francisco. Office of mines, Park City, Utah.

## THE OREGON WATER POWER & RAILWAY CO.

A corporation formed under the laws of Oregon, July 1, 1902, as a successor to the Portland City & Oregon Railway Co. The company owns and operates 33 miles of electric railway between Portland, Sellwood, Milwaukee, Oregon City, Canemah, Mt. Tabor and Gresham, Oregon, serving a population of about 140,000. It has two steam engines, 30 passenger cars and 54 other cars.

Stock......Par $100..........................Authorized, $2,000,000......Issued, $2,000,000

The company has no preferred stock.

FUNDED DEBT.

| | |
|---|---|
| 1st mort., 6 per cent., gold, due July 1, 1932, Jan. and July | $2,500,000 |
| Portland City & Ore. Ry. Co., 1st mort., 6 p. c., gold, due Feb. 15, 1921, Feb. and Aug | 400,000 |
| Total | $2,900,000 |

The total amount of the authorized 1st mortgage of the Oregon Water Power & Railway Co. is $5,000,000, of which $1,000,000 are reserved to retire underlying liens. Bonds may be called after 1912 at 105. A sinking fund of 25 per cent. of net earnings is provided to commence after 1905. The total amount of the authorized 1st mortgage of the Portland City & Oregon Railway Co. is $500,000. Bonds may be called after February 15, 1911, at par and accrued interest. A sinking fund of $5,000 per annum for the first four years and $10,000 per annum thereafter is provided, to commence Feb. 15, 1907.

President, W. H. Hurlburt; Vice-President, J. Frank Watson; Treasurer, Frederick S. Morris; Secretary, William T. Muir, Portland, Ore.

Directors—Frederick S. Morris, A. B. Crossman, J. Frank Watson, W. H. Hurlburt, William T. Muir, Portland, Ore.

Corporate and main office, First and Alder streets, Portland, Ore. Annual meeting, second Tuesday in January, at Portland, Ore.

## OSCEOLA CONSOLIDATED MINING CO.

A corporation formed under the laws of Michigan in 1873. It owns a mineral property near Hancock, Houghton County, Mich., adjoining the famous Calumet & Hecla, the conglomerate lode of which crosses and outcrops on its estate. In 1879 consolidated with the Opechee Mining

Co. Mining began in 1873, and in 1875 the Osceola mill was completed. In 1897 purchased the property of the Kearsarge Mining Co., including the Iroquois Copper Co. and the Tamarack, Jr., Mining Co., paying for the former 25,000 shares and for the latter 16,000 shares.

Stock......Par $25..........................Authorized, $2,500,000......Issued, $2,403,750

The stock is full-paid. Stock is transferred at the office of the company, 199 Washington street, Boston.

In 1897 the company's production was 13,857,373 pounds; gross receipts, $1,338,056; net, $262,401; dividends, $181,000; real estate, $62,611; surplus, $18,789. In 1898, product, 15,848,928 pounds; gross receipts, $1,549,820; net, $371,791; dividends, ($3) $277,250; surplus, $94,541; total surplus, $655,333. In 1899 gross was $1,791,471; net, $534,832; dividends ($6), $558,450; deficit, $23,617; total surplus, $546,867. In 1900, gross, $2,136,253; net, $576,714; dividends, ($6), $571,200; surplus, $5,514; total surplus, $571,427. In 1901, gross, $1,934,437; net, $234,900; dividends, $576,900.

Dividends on the stock are semi-annual, in June and December. In 1899, 1900, and 1901, $6 per share was paid in each year. No dividend was paid in 1902.

President, Albert S. Bigelow; Secretary and Treasurer, W. J. Ladd, Boston; Superintendent, William E. Parnall, Opechee, Mich.

Directors—Albert S. Bigelow, J. Henry Brooks, Edward S. Grew, Leonard Lewishon, Joseph S. Bigelow, W. J. Ladd, William E. Parnall.

Main office, 199 Washington street, Boston. Annual meeting, second Thursday in March.

## OSWEGO TRACTION CO.

A corporation formed under the laws of New York, June 1, 1899. The company succeeded the Oswego Street Railway Co. and The Lake Ontario & Riverside Railway Co., sold at foreclosure. It owns and operates 11 miles of electric railway in the city and town of Oswego, N. Y., and the towns of Scriba and Volney. The company has a perpetual charter. It has 22 cars and rents power from the Oswego Electric Light Co.

Stock......Par $100.......Authorized { com., $200,000; pref., 100,000 } Issued { com., $200,000; pref., 100,000 } $300,000

Transfer Agent and Registrar, Knickerbocker Trust Co., New York.

FUNDED DEBT.

| | |
|---|---|
| 1st mort., 5 per cent. gold, due June 1, 1929, June and Dec. | $97,000 |
| 2d mort., 3 per cent. due June 1, 1929, Mar. and Sept. | 191,000 |
| Total | $288,000 |

Trustee of both mortgages, Knickerbocker Trust Co., New York, which is also agent for the payment of interest.

In the fiscal year ending June 30, 1902, the gross earnings were $41,016; net, $8,393; charges, $13,503; deficit, $5,110.

President, S. M. Coon; Vice-President, Charles A. Tanner; Treasurer, James P. Doyle; Secretary, Daniel A. Williams; General Manager, Frank Arnold, Oswego, N. Y.

Directors—Max B. Richardson, S. M. Coon, David B. Page, Charles A. Tanner, James P. Doyle, Norman S. Bentley, Lawrence Clancy, Daniel A. Williams, Oswego, N. Y.; E. G. Connette, Syracuse, N. Y.; Charles C. Crook, New York; C. Sidney Shepard, New Haven, N. Y.

Corporate and main office, West Bridge street, Oswego, N. Y. Annual meeting, second Thursday in September, at Oswego, N. Y.

## OTIS CO.

A corporation formed under the laws of Massachusetts in 1840, for the purpose of manufacturing cotton dress-goods, cheviots, denims and knit underwear. The company owns mills at Ware, Mass., with a capacity of 61,000 spindles and 1,000 looms, and at Three Rivers, Mass., with a capacity of 32,736 spindles and 936 looms.

Stock......Par $1,000............................Authorized, $800,000......Issued, $800,000

The company has no preferred stock and no funded debt. Stock is transferred at the office of the company.

Dividends are paid in April and October, at the rate of 10 per cent. per annum.

President, Charles H. Fiske; Treasurer, George F. Fabyan, Boston.

Directors—Charles H. Fiske, George F. Fabyan, Robert B. Williams, James C. Davis, Cornelius N. Bliss.

Main office, 100 Summer street, Boston. Annual meeting in February, at Boston.

## OTIS ELEVATOR CO.

A corporation formed under the laws of New Jersey, November 28, 1898, to combine the leading manufacturers of elevators in the United States and about 85 per cent. of the total industry. In January, 1902, the Plunger Elevater Co. of Worcester, Mass., was acquired.

Stock...Par $100....Authorized { com., $6,500,000 / pref., 6,500,000 } Issued { com., $6,350,000 / pref., 5,489,800 } $11,839,800

The preferred stock is 6 per cent., non-cumulative. In September, 1902, the authorized preferred stock was increased from $4,500,000 to $6,500,000 and $1,000,000 of the new stock was offered to stockholders at par to provide additional working capital.

Transfer Agent, New Jersey Registration & Trust Co., New York.

The payment of dividends on the preferred stock began with 1½ per cent. quarterly, April 15, 1899. Regular dividends at the same rate have since been paid quarterly in January, April, July and October. No dividends on the common have been paid, but out of the earnings of 1902 $127,006 was reserved for dividends on the common stock.

FUNDED DEBT.

Gold notes, 4 per cent., 1901-08 .... $1,100,000

EARNINGS.

| | Net. | Dividends. | Charged for Depreciation. | Surplus. |
|---|---|---|---|---|
| 1901 | $842,096 | $267,538 | $274,555 | $300,000 |
| 1902 | 978,410 | 411,835 | 266,575 | 300,000 |

On December 31, 1902, the surplus reserved for working capital was $1,000,000.

In the year 1901 the net earnings were $842,096; dividends, $267,538; charged off for depreciation, $274,558. Surplus added to working capital, $300,000.

Chairman, Norton P. Otis; President, William D. Baldwin; Vice-President, A. G. Mills; Treasurer, Lynde Belknap; Secretary, Albert S. Bard.

Directors—William D. Baldwin, W. H. Baker, Albert B. Chandler, C. G. Comstock, Norton P. Otis, A. G. Mills, Henry R. Reed, F. W. Roebling, John A. Roche.

Main office, 71 Broadway, New York.

## OTTAWA GAS CO.

A corporation formed under the laws of Canada in 1855 for the purpose of erecting and operating gas works and supplying gas in the city of Ottawa. The company has 2,810 meters in use.

Stock......Par $100 ....Authorized, $500,000......Issued, $450,000

The company has no preferred stock. Stock is transferred at the office of company, Ottawa. Dividends at the rate of 6 per cent. per annum are paid quarterly.

FUNDED DEBT.

Debenture bonds, 5 per cent., due 1914, April and Oct.... £20,000

The authorized issue of debenture bonds is £20,000. Trustee of the debentures, C. Magee, Ottawa. Agent for the payment of interest, Par's Bank, London, England.

For the nine months ending December 31, 1901, the profits of the company were $21,324.

President, John Coates; Secretary-Treasurer, David B. Gardner; Superintendent, Thomas Dunderdale, Ottawa.

Directors—John Coates, John Manuel, Thomas Ahearn, George P. Brophy, Ottawa.

Corporate and main office, 23 Sparks street, Ottawa. Annual meeting first week in January, at Ottawa.

## THE PACIFIC COAST CO.

A corporation formed under the laws of New Jersey, November 27, 1897. The company was organized in pursuance of the reorganization of the Oregon Improvement Co. The property and assets of the Oregon Improvement Co. were sold under foreclosure November 6, 1897, and transferred to this company.

Its charter authorizes the company to engage in the business of mining and selling coal and other minerals, to own and operate railroads and tramways in the States of Washington, Oregon and California and in Alaska and adjoining territory, and to build, acquire and operate steamships and other water craft between ports on the Pacific Coast including Alaska and adjacent territory, and also on the tributary waters. The company through the corporations it controls conducts a railway business, a steamship business and a coal mining business.

Property owned includes:

All the stock ($1,000,000) of the Columbia & Puget Sound Railroad Co. The latter has no bonded debt, and its railroad extends from Seattle, Wash., to Franklin. Length of line including branches, 58 miles.

All the stock ($1,370,400), and all the 1st mortgage bonds ($1,370,000) of the Pacific Coast Railway Co., the line of which extends from Port Harford, Cal., to Los Olivas, Cal., 80 miles.

A fleet of 15 steamships of an aggregate tonnage of 21,429 tons.

All the stock ($2,000,000) of the Pacific Coast Steamship Co., which owns 9 steamships of an aggregate tonnage of 10,870 tons. The steamships owned and controlled by the Pacific Coast Co. ply between the ports of Southern California and Northern Mexico, San Francisco, Seattle, Tacoma, Vancouver, Victoria, B. C.; Skagway and all Alaskan ports.

About 5,260 acres of coal lands in King County, Wash., on the line of the Columbia & Puget Sound Railroad, with mines in operation on same. Company also has interests in various selling coal companies organized to market the product of its mines.

Wharf and dock properties at Juneau and Skagway, Alaska.

About 10,000 acres of agricultural and timber lands in Washington and Oregon, and town lots in Seattle, Wash., Portland, Ore., San Francisco and Prescott, Wash.

| Stock...Par $100...Authorized | com., $7,000,000<br>1st pref., 1,525,000<br>2d pref., 4,000,000 | Issued | com., $6,738,800<br>1st pref., 1,502,800<br>2d pref., 3,904,200 | $12,145,800 |
|---|---|---|---|---|

The 1st and 2d preferred stocks are non-cumulative and the 1st is entitled to 5 per cent. and the 2d to 4 per cent. dividends in their order. Then, after 4 per cent. has been paid in any year on the common stock, the 2d preferred and the common share equally in any further surplus earnings.

Transfer Agent, Manhattan Trust Co., New York. Registrar, Chase National Bank, New York.

The payments of dividends on the company's stocks began in June, 1898, with the declaration of 5 per cent. on the 1st preferred and 1 per cent. on the 2d preferred. In 1898 the company paid 5 per cent. on the 1st preferred, 4 per cent. on the 2d preferred and 2 per cent. on the common. In 1899 paid 4¾ per cent. on the 1st preferred, 3½ per cent. on the 2d preferred and 2 per cent. on the common. In November, 1899, the dividend period was changed from half yearly to quarterly. In 1900 the company paid at the rate of 5 per cent. on the 1st preferred, 4 per cent. on the 2d preferred and 4 per cent. on the common. Since August, 1902, the dividends on the common and 2d preferred have been at the rate of 5 per cent. per annum. The quarterly dividends are paid in February (1), May, August and November, and are 1¼ per cent. on 1st preferred, 1¼ per cent. on 2d preferred, and 1¼ per cent. on common.

### Funded Debt.

1st mort., 5 per cent., due June, 1946, June and Dec. .............................. $4,446,000

The authorized issue of 1st mortgage bonds is $5,000,000, an amount of $554,000 of same being reserved for new steamers and improvements.

### Earnings.

Year ending June 30.

| | Gross. | Net. | Interest. | Surplus. |
|---|---|---|---|---|
| 1898 (7 months)..... ............... | $3,081,502 | $693,317 | $129,675 | $563,642 |
| 1898-99 ............................ | 4,893,483 | 1,136,009 | 222,300 | 913,709 |
| 1899-00 ............................ | 5,290,442 | 1,451,853 | 222,300 | 1,229,553 |
| 1900-01 ......... ..... ............. | 5,137,545 | 1,203,719 | 222,300 | 981,419 |
| 1901-02 ............................ | 5,074,207 | 1,129,806 | 222,300 | 1,142,353 |

For the 7 months ending June 30, 1898, after deducting $81,665 for depreciation and dividends of 5 per cent. on 1st preferred, 4 per cent. on 2d preferred and 1 per cent. on common stock, the company showed a surplus of $175,725. In the year 1898-99, after charging $125,000 for depreciation, $21,699 for renewals, $16,656 for "exhaustion fund," and $21,723 for uncollectable assets and paying 5 per cent. on the 1st preferred, 4 per cent. on the 2d preferred and 3 per cent. on the common stock, the company's surplus was $280,506. In 1899-1900 the surplus over all charges, deductions and dividends was $437,177; in 1900-01, surplus $225,361; in 1901-02, surplus $148,951.

President and Chairman, Henry W. Cannon, New York; 1st Vice-President and General Manager, J. C. Ford, Seattle, Wash.; 2d Vice-President and Secretary, Hamilton H. Durand; Treasurer, John Kean; Assistant Treasurer, C. C. Fay, New York; Assistant Treasurer and Auditor, F. C. Ambridge, Seattle, Wash.

Directors—J. D. Farrell, H. A. Tucker, John Kean, Edward H. Harriman, Daniel S. Lamont, Henry W. Cannon, Grant B. Schley, T. Jefferson Coolidge, Jr., Joseph E. Heimerdinger.

Corporate office, 83 Montgomery street, Jersey City; New York office, 10 Wall street; Seattle, Wash., office, Burke Block. Annual meeting, second Wednesday in October, at Jersey City.

## PACIFIC LIGHT & POWER CO.

A corporation formed under the laws of California, March 6, 1902, to supply electric light and power in the city of Los Angeles, Cal., and the adjacent territory. The company acquired the following companies:

San Gabrial Electric Co. Sierra Power Co.

The company has water power, 45 miles of transmission line, distributing pole lines, a steam plant of 4,000 horse power and an underground conduit in the city of Los Angeles, Cal.

Stock......Par $100........................Authorized, $10,000,000......Issued, $10,000,000

The company has no preferred stock. Stock is transferred and registered at the office of the company, Los Angeles, Cal.

The San Gabrial Electric Co. paid dividends at the rate of 6 per cent. per annum, beginning May 1, 1902.

FUNDED DEBT.

| | |
|---|---|
| 1st mort., 5 per cent., due July 1, 1942, July and Jan. | $2,011,000 |
| San Gabrial Electric Co. 1st mort. guar., 6 per cent., due April, 1928, April and Oct. | 500,000 |
| Total | $2,511,000 |

The authorized 1st mortgage of the Pacific Light & Power Co. was $10,000,000. A sinking fund is provided, purchases of bonds to be made at market rates. Trustee of the mortgage and agent for the payment of interest, Union Trust Co., San Francisco. The bonds of the San Gabrial Electric Co. may be called at 104 after April 1, 1903. They are guaranteed by the Pacific Light & Power Co., and will be refunded during the year 1903.

President, William G. Kerckhoff; Vice-President, Epes Randolph; Secretary, Otto Weiss, Los Angeles, Cal.; Treasurer, Isaias W. Hellman, San Francisco; General Manager, A. C. Balch, Los Angeles, Cal.

Directors—William G. Kerckhoff, A. C. Balch, Kaspare Cohn, Epes Randolph, Los Angeles, Cal.; Isaias W. Hellman, Antoine Borel, San Francisco; H. E. Huntington, New York.

Corporate and main office, 254 South Los Angeles street, Los Angeles, Cal.

## PACIFIC MAIL STEAMSHIP CO.

(Controlled by Southern Pacific Co.)

A corporation formed under the laws of New York, April 12, 1848. In November, 1900, a controlling interest in the stock of this company was acquired by Speyer & Co. of New York, who immediately transferred the same to the Southern Pacific Co., which corporation has deposited its holdings in the stock of this company as security for its 4½ per cent. collateral trust bonds.

This company's lines are from Panama to San Francisco and Central American and Mexican ports; from San Francisco to Yokohama and Hong Kong. Under agreement made in 1895 with the Panama Railroad Co., this company withdrew its line between New York and Aspinwall, Colombia, which was to be served by the vessels controlled by the Panama, the latter withdrawing from the Pacific. The contract has been renewed from time to time, the last renewal being in 1902. In 1902 the company completed two new large steamers for its Pacific service. Steamships, 17; tugs, 4, and several launches and lighters.

Capital stock......Par $100.................Authorized, $20,000,000......Issued, $20,000,000

Transfer Agent, Union Trust Co., New York. Registrar, Mercantile Trust Co., New York.

The December, 1898, dividend was increased from 1 to 1½ per cent. No dividend was paid from September 15, 1887, when 1 per cent. was distributed, until December, 1896, when 1 per cent. was paid. In 1897, paid 2 per cent.; in 1898, 2½ per cent.; in 1899, 3 per cent. The last dividend paid was 1½ per cent., December 1, 1899. It was announced that the company would suspend dividends and increase and improve its fleet with the surplus earnings.

EARNINGS.

Year ending April 30.

| | Divs. Paid. | Gross. | | Net. |
|---|---|---|---|---|
| 1892-93 | 0 | $4,118,473 | Def. | $56,742 |
| 1893-94 | 0 | 3,834,093 | | 475,461 |
| 1894-95 | 0 | 4,087,872 | | 712,631 |
| 1895-96 | 0 | 4,222,938 | | 708,381 |
| 1896-97 | 1 | 4,140,149 | | 714,256 |
| 1897-98 | 2 | 4,064,221 | | 620,543 |
| 1898-99 | 2½ | 4,140,713 | | 1,116,336 |
| 1899-00 | 3 | 3,817,620 | | 830,189 |
| 1900-01 | .. | 3,071,166 | | 167,821 |
| 1901-02 | .. | 2,029,346 | Def. | 307,935 |

Gross earnings include revenues other than from steamships, as follows: In 1893, $162,708; in 1894, $433,999; in 1895, $316,172; in 1896, $292,000; in 1897, $380,811; in 1898, $395,744; in 1899, $181,701; in 1900, $207,780; in 1901, $202,197; in 1902, $145,933.

President, Edward H. Harriman, New York; Vice-President and General Manager, R. P. Schwerin, San Francisco; Secretary, Joseph Hellen; Treasurer, A. K. Van Deventer, New York.

Directors—Charles H. Tweed, Edward H. Harriman, James Speyer, Ogden Mills, Russell Sage, George J. Gould, George H. Macy, Edwin Hawley, New York; R. P. Schwerin, San Francisco.

Main office, 120 Broadway, New York. Annual meeting, last Wednesday in May.

## PACIFIC PACKING & NAVIGATION CO.

A corporation formed under the laws of New Jersey, July 20, 1901, for the purpose of operating steamships between Alaska, Seattle and San Francisco, and of canning salmon in Alaska and Puget Sound. The company acquired the following properties:

Pacific American Fisheries Co.
Ainsworth & Dunn.
Seattle Fish Co.
Suadra Packing Co.
Chatham Straits Packing Co.
Western Fisheries Co.
Taku Packing Co.
Thluiket Packing Co.
Pacific Steam Whaling Co.
Fairhaven Canning Co.
Hume Brothers & Hume.
Icy Straits Packing Co.
Chilkoot Packing Co.
Boston Fishing & Trading Co.
Taku Fishing Co.
Arctic Oil Works.

Stock...Par $100....Authorized { com., $12,500,000; pref., 12,500,000 } Issued { com., $6,150,000; pref., 7,100,000 } $13,250,000

The preferred stock is 7 per cent., cumulative. It was increased from $6,500,000 to $7,100,000 in 1902. See below. All the stock was placed in a voting trust for five years.

Transfer Agent, Knickerbocker Trust Co., New York. Registrar, The Registrar & Transfer Co., New York.

FUNDED DEBT.

Debenture bonds, 5 per cent., due Aug., 1922, Feb. and Aug........................ $1,500,000

The company had $3,115,000 of 6 per cent. debentures, due 1908. In 1902 it was agreed to increase the preferred stock and replace the 6 per cent. bonds with $1,500,000 of new 5 per cent. debentures, of which $75,000 per annum will be retired by a sinking fund, beginning January 1, 1904.

President, Charles Counselman, Chicago; Vice-President, Thomas B. McGovern, Seattle, Wash.; Secretary, E. C. Kent; Treasurer, Frederick F. Carey, New York; Assistant Treasurer, F. A. Ross, Seattle, Wash.

Directors—Charles Counselman, Chicago; Stuyvesant Fish, John E. Borne, Richard Delafield, George F. Vietor, Charles R. Flint, Thomas B. McGovern, Frederick F. Carey, New York; Edwin Goodall, San Francisco; D. W. Crowley, Portland, Ore.; Herman Chapin, E. O. Graves, P. F. Kelley, Seattle, Wash.; R. Ouffroy, Whatcom, Wash.; George B. Hanford, Orange, N. J.

Corporate office, Jersey City; main office, Seattle, Wash.; New York office, 95 Hudson street. Annual meeting, first Tuesday in July, at Jersey City.

## PACIFIC STEEL CO.

A corporation formed under the laws of New Jersey, January 18, 1901, for the purpose of operating iron furnaces. The company has a furnace at Irondale, Wash., which went into blast in December, 1901. It has a capacity of about 50 tons. The ores used are from Texada Island and Barclay Sound, B. C.

Stock......Par $100..............................Authorized, $1,000,000......Issued, $700,000

The company has no preferred stock. Registrar, Corporation Trust Co. of New Jersey.

FUNDED DEBT.

1st mort., 6 per cent. gold bonds, due 1921, March and Sept....... .................... $200,000

Trustee of the bonds, Trust Company of America, New York.

President, H. H. Swaney, Irondale, Wash.; Vice-President, Maurice McMicken, Seattle, Wash.; Secretary, H. F. Thomas; Treasurer, M. J. Carrigan, Irondale, Wash.

Directors—H. H. Swaney, Timothy O'Connor, M. J. Carrigan, William Piggott, H. F. Thomas, Irondale, Wash.; Maurice McMicken, Seattle, Wash.; L. J. Devenny, J. C. Smith, McKeesport, Pa.; J. M. Hawthorne, St. Paul; John Irving, Vancouver, B. C.; Frederick E. Day, Elizabeth, N. J.

Corporate office, Corporation Trust Co., Jersey City; main office, Irondale, Wash.

## PAGE WOVEN WIRE FENCE CO.

A corporation formed under the laws of New Jersey, December 11, 1901, for the purpose of manufacturing and selling wire fence. The company acquired the property of the Page Woven Wire Fence Co., with plants at Monessen, Pa., and Adrian, Mich. The business acquired was established in 1889. The plant at Monessen includes furnaces, billet, rod and wire mills, railroad tracks, engines and other accessories. The mills have an aggregate capacity of over 450 tons per da . The plant at Adrian, Mich., includes looms with a capacity of 150 to 200 tons of fence per day.

Stock....Par $100....Authorized { com., $5,000,000 / pref., 1,000,000 } Issued { com., $5,000,000 / pref., 1,000,000 } $6,000,000

The preferred stock is 7 per cent., non-cumulative. Transfer Agent, North American Trust Co., New York. Registrar, Corporation Trust Co., New York.

Dividends at the rate of 7 per cent. have been paid on the preferred stock since the organization of the company, the last semi-annual dividend being paid February 1, 1903. No dividends have been paid on the common stock.

FUNDED DEBT.

1st mort., sinking fund, due April 1, 1922, April and Oct.......................... $1,750,000

The total amount of the authorized 1st mortgage was $2,000,000, of which $250,000 are retained in the treasury of the company. Bonds may be called after July 1, 1905, at 110 and interest. A sinking fund of $100,000 annually, beginning April 1, 1905, is provided for. Trustee of the mortgage and agent for the payment of interest, North American Trust Co., New York.

In the fiscal year ending December 31, 1902, the net earnings of the company were $287,924.

President, J. Wallace Page, Adrian, Mich.; Vice-President, Austin Clement, Chicago; 1st Assistant Vice-President, Charles M. Lamb, Monessen, Pa.; Treasurer, L. B. Robertson, Adrian, Mich.; Secretary, Arthur B. Cody, Chicago.

Directors—J. Wallace Page, L. B. Robertson, John E. Carr, D. M. Baker, Adrian, Mich.; Austin Clement, Arthur B. Cody, David N. Hanson, S. W. McMunn, A. Podrasnik, Chicago; Charles M. Lamb, Monessen, Pa.; Norman Bridge, Los Angeles, Cal.; Charles E. Locke, New York; John Milton Ferry, Jersey City.

Corporate office, 15 Exchange place, Jersey City; Chicago office, 132 Adams street; branch offices, Adrian, Mich., and Monessen, Pa. Annual meeting, third Tuesday in January, at Jersey City.

## THE PALMETTO CO.

A corporation formed under the laws of West Virginia, December 2, 1898. It owns and controls patents and processes for the utilization of scrub palmetto in the manufacture of tannic acid, fibre and other products. The supply of palmetto in the Southern States is practically inexhaustible, and is obtainable at small expense. The company has plants at Wilmington, N. C., and elsewhere. It also manufactures pine products.

Stock......Par $25.......Authorized { com., $650,000 / pref., 350,000 } Issued { com., $650,000 / pref., 350,000 } $1,000,000

The preferred stock is 6 per cent., cumulative, but may be retired at 35 and accrued dividends.

Amount of stock was originally $3,500,000, which in 1901 was increased to $10,000,000. In July and August, 1902, the stock was reduced to $1,000,000, divided into common and preferred, as shown above.

Transfers of stock are made at the company's office. Registrar, Merchants' Trust Co., Philadelphia.

The company has no funded debt.

President, Alfonso A. Rutis; Vice-President, John F. Collins; Secretary, James Warrington; Treasurer, William Mill Butler.

Directors—Alfonso A. Rutis, John F. Collins, William Mill Butler, William Barnet, Jr., James Warrington.

Main office, 428 Chestnut street, Philadelphia. Annual meeting, December 20, at Philadelphia.

## PARA RUBBER PLANTATION CO.

A corporation formed in 1903 to gather and market rubber. The company owns 1,400 square miles of natural rubber forests, carrying over 6,000,000 treees, in Venezuela, situated on both sides of the Casiquian River. It is the intention of the company to own its own line of steamboats on the Casiquian and Rio Negro rivers for the purpose of shipping its rubber and timber.

Stock......Par $10..........................Authorized, $5,000,000......Issued, $5,000,000

Stock is transferred at the office of the company, New York. Registrar, Eastern Trust Co., New York.

President, John Cudahy, Chicago; Vice-President, Allen T. Haight, New York; Treasurer, Elmer B. Martin, Chicago; Secretary, F. M. Crawford, New York.

Directors—J. Wesley Allison, Allen T. Haight, F. M. Crawford, A. H. Bartle, New York; W. J. Hilands, John Cudahy, Elmer B. Martin, Leslie Stavert, Chicago; L. B. Adams, Minneapolis, Minn.

Advisory Board—Andre Michelin, Paris, France; Robert Osterrieth, Armand Grisar, Leon Fuchs, L. C. Van Den Broeck, Antwerp, Belgium; Leon De Bruyn, Brussels, Belgium.

Main office, 52 Broadway, New York.

## PARKER MILLS

A corporation formed under the laws of Massachusetts in 1895, for the purpose of manufacturing cotton goods. The mills of the company are at Fall River, Mass., and at Warren, R. I., with a total of 90,312 spindles and 2,142 looms.

Stock......Par $100.............................Authorized, $800,000......Issued, $800,000

The company has no preferred stock. Stock is transferred at the office of the company, Fall River, Mass.

Dividends paid have been as follows: 1896 and 1897, 3¼ per cent.; 1898, 5 per cent.; 1899, 5¾ per cent.; 1900, 6¼ per cent.; 1901, 8 per cent.; 1902, 8 per cent.

FUNDED DEBT.

1st mort., 5 per cent. coupon bonds, due 1932, Feb. and Aug........................ $600,000

Trustee of mortgage and agent for the payment of interest, B. M. C. Durfee Safe Deposit & Trust Co., Fall River.

Following is the company's balance sheet, September 27, 1902:

| ASSETS. | | LIABILITIES. | |
|---|---|---|---|
| Real estate and machinery........ | $1,010,000 | Capital stock.................... | $800,000 |
| Cash, bills and accounts receivable | 82,995 | Bills payable.................... | 984,872 |
| Stock of cotton cloth............ | 768,204 | Accounts due..................... | 12,000 |
| | | Profit and loss.................. | 64,327 |
| Total....... ....... ........ | $1,861,199 | Total...... ........... | $1,861,199 |

President, Leontine Lincoln; Treasurer, Seth A. Borden, Fall River, Mass.

Directors—Leontine Lincoln, J. E. Osborn, John D. Flint, Milton Reed, Seth A. Borden, Fall River, Mass.; Stephen A. Jenks, Fred W. Easton, Pawtucket, R. I.; George C. Silsbury, Salem, Mass.; George E. Parker, Lowell, Mass.

Corporate and main office, 941 Grinnell street, Fall River, Mass. Annual meeting, last Thursday in October, at Fall River.

## PARK STEEL CO.

A corporation formed under the laws of New York, March 6, 1899. The company acquired the plant and business of Park Brother & Co., Limited, of Pittsburg, manufacturers of merchant steel and copper and proprietors of the "Black Diamond" brand of steel. The establishment of the company in Pittsburg covers about 14 acres, and the business was established over 40 years.

The Crucible Steel Co. of America in 1900 acquired about 94 per cent. of the stock of this company.

Stock....Par $100....Authorized { com., $5,000,000; pref., 5,000,000 } Issued { com., $5,000,000; pref., 5,000,000 } $10,000,000

The preferred stock is 7 per cent., cumulative, and has priority over the common in respect to assets in case of a dissolution.

The first quarterly dividend of 1¾ per cent. on the preferred stock was paid June 1, 1899. Dividends on the preferred have since been regularly paid at the rate of 1¾ per cent., quarterly, in March (1), June, September and December.

President, Reuben Miller; Vice-President, James H. Park; Secretary, Alexander Thomas; Treasurer, Julius Bieler; Assistant Treasurer, John Neeley, Pittsburg.

Corporate office, 1 Exchange place, Jersey City; main office, Fifth avenue and Grant street, Pittsburg; New York office, 71 Broadway.

## PARLIN & ORENDORFF CO.

A corporation formed under the laws of Illinois in 1880. The company is engaged in the business of manufacturing agricultural implements, wagons, etc. It acquired control of the following properties:

Parlin, Orendorff Co. of St. Louis; Dallas, Tex.; Kansas City, Mo.; Portland, Ore., and Denver, Col.; Parlin & Orendorff malleable and gray iron foundries and the Parlin & Orendorff steel wheel works.

Parlin, Orendorff & Martin Co., Omaha.

The annual volume of the company's business is over $5,000,000.

Stock......Par $100..............................Authorized, $100,000......Issued, $100,000

Stock is registered and transferred at the office of the company.

The company has no preferred stock or funded debt.

President, William H. Parlin; Secretary and Treasurer, U. G. Orendorff, Assistant Treasurer, L. H. Gillet, Canton, Ill.

Directors—William H. Parlin, U. G. Orendorff, William H. Orendorff, Mrs. William Parlin, Mrs. W. J. Orendorff, C. E. Parlin.

Main office, Canton, Ill.; branch offices, Kansas City, Mo.; St. Louis; Decatur, Ill.; Denver, Col.; Dallas, Tex.; Des Moines, Ia.; Omaha; Minneapolis and Portland, Ore.

## PARROT SILVER & COPPER CO.

A corporation organized under the laws of Montana in 1880. The company owns a large and valuable mining property near Butte, Mont., and operates the Parrot, Little Minah and Bellona mines. The company also owns and operates copper refining works at Bridgeport, Conn.

In 1899 a controlling interest in the stock of this company was acquired by the Amalgamated Copper Co., and it is now managed and operated under the auspices of that organization.

Stock......Par $10..............................Authorized, $2,300,000......Issued, $2,298,500

The stock of the company consists of 230,000 shares of the par value of $10 each. The stock is full-paid and non-assessable.

During the year 1900 the company paid dividends amounting to $6 per share on its stock, and in 1901 paid $4.50 per share. The dividends were quarterly in January, April, July and October. The July dividend was reduced from $1.50 to $1, and the October, 1901, dividend, as well as that paid in January, 1902, were 50 cents each. No dividends since January, 1902.

The company is one of the large copper producing mines of the country. Its properties also yield considerable silver and gold bullion. In 1897 the output of copper from its mines and smelters was over 14,000,000 pounds of fine copper. In 1898 the output was over 12,000,000 pounds of copper.

President, Charles H. Dickey; Secretary, Charles D. Burrage, Boston.

Main office, Washington and Court streets, Boston.

## PASSAIC WATER CO.

A corporation formed under the laws of New Jersey in 1849, to supply water to the city of Paterson, N. J. The company takes water from the Passaic river and has a plant of 38,000,000 gallons capacity and 130 miles of water mains.

Stock......Par $100..............................Authorized, $750,000......Issued, $750,000

The company has no preferred stock. Stock is transferred and registered at the office of the company.

Dividends have not been regularly paid and are not made public.

FUNDED DEBT.

| | |
|---|---|
| 1st mort., 4 per cent. bonds, due 1920, April and Oct | $359,000 |
| 2d mort., 5 per cent. bonds, due 1937, Jan. and July | 500,000 |
| General mort., 5 per cent. bonds, due 1937, Jan. and July | 2,141,000 |
| Total | $3,000,000 |

Trustee of 1st mortgage, Paterson Savings Institution, Paterson, N. J. Agent for payment of interest, First National Bank, Paterson, N. J. Trustee of 2d mortgage bonds, Paterson Savings Institution, Paterson, N. J. Agent for payment of interest, First National Bank, New York. Trustee of general mortgage bonds, Central Trust Co., New York.

In the year ending January 1, 1902, the gross earnings were $319,940; net earnings, $56,997; interest charges, $145,585; surplus, $56,997.

President, William Barbour; Vice-President, J. Waldo Smith; Secretary, A. P. Fisher; Treasurer, Edmund Le B. Gardiner, Paterson.

Directors—George F. Baker, New York; W. G. Snow, Montclair, N. J.; William Barbour, J. Waldo Smith, R. J. Nelden, Richard Rossiter, Paterson, N. J.; Edmund Le B. Gardiner, Ridgewood, N. J.

Corporate and main office, 158 Ellison street, Paterson, N. J. Annual meeting, second Monday in June, at Paterson, N. J.

## THE PATERSON & PASSAIC GAS & ELECTRIC CO.

A corporation formed under the laws of New Jersey in 1899. The company was a consolidation of the plants which supply lighting facilities in the cities of Paterson and Passaic, N. J. The population of the territory it covers is over 140,000. The company has additional franchises covering adjacent territory. It absorbed the following corporations:

People's Gas Light Co., of Paterson.
The Paterson Gas Light Co.
Edison Electric Illuminating Co., of Paterson.
Passaic Lighting Co.
The Lodi Light, Heat & Power Co.
The Passaic & Bergen Gas Co.

The United Gas Improvement Co. owns a majority of the capital stock of this company.

Stock......Par $100..........................Authorised, $5,000,000......Issued, $5,000,000

Stock is transferred at the office of the company, Paterson, N. J.

FUNDED DEBT.

Consolidated mort., gold, 5 per cent., due March, 1949, March and Sept............. $3,802,000

The consolidated mortgage is $5,000,000, authorized, of which $1,044,000 is reserved to retire the bonds of the constituent companies and $324,000 is reserved for improvements. Trustee of mortgage, Paterson Safe Deposit & Trust Co., Paterson, N. J. Interest on the bonds is paid at the First National Bank, Paterson, N. J.

President, William Barbour; Vice-Presidents, Edward T. Bell, Bird W. Spencer, Paterson, N. J.; Treasurer, Lewis Lillie, Philadelphia; Secretary, W. H. Rogers, Paterson, N. J.

Directors—William Barbour, Edward T. Bell, Bird W. Spencer, Walton Clark, John R. Lee, William B. Gourley, Randal Morgan, John Reynolds, John W. Ferguson, John Agnew, Hobart Tuttle.

Main office, Van Houten and Prospect streets, Paterson, N. J.

## PATTEN VACUUM ICE CO., LIMITED

A corporation formed under the laws of New Jersey, February 19, 1902. The purpose of company is the manufacture of ice by the Patten vacuum process, and to license the process to others. The company controls the Patten patents in the United States and other parts of the world and owns a plant in Baltimore, of 100 tons capacity per day, and a 200-ton plant at New York. Plants are under construction in San Francisco and Porto Rico.

Stock......Par $100......... ................Authorized, $10,000,000......Issued, $2,613,300

Transfer Agent, Corporation Trust Co., Jersey City; Registrar, North American Trust Co., New York.

The company has no funded debt.

President, Herbert R. Limberger; Vice-President, Douglas Henry; Secretary and Acting Treasurer, S. C. Blake, New York.

Directors—Solomon Mehrbach, Charles A. Starbuck, Louis Engelhorn, Herbert R. Limberger, Douglas Henry, Edward N. Rich, Leonard A. Dessar, Spencer C. Blake, New York; John W. Dunn, Orange, N. J.

Corporate office, 15 Exchange place, Jersey City; New York office, 45 Broadway. Annual meeting, first Friday in March, at Jersey City.

## PAYNE CONSOLIDATED MINING CO., LIMITED

A corporation formed under the laws of the Dominion of Canada in June, 1899. The mines operated by the company are in Sandon, British Columbia, the company being the successor of the Payne Mining Co.

Stock......Par $1.............................Authorized, $3,000,000......Issued, $2,600,000

The company has no preferred stock and no funded debt.

Dividends amounting to $1,100,000 were paid by the Payne Mining Co. and $338,000 have been paid by the present company.

President, Fred C. Henshaw; Vice-President, L. J. Forget; Secretary, C. H. Low.

Directors—Fred C. Henshaw, Rudolph Forget, L. J. Forget, William Hanson, F. B. Mathys, W. G. Ross, A. W. McCune, F. E. Sargeant, C. E. L. Porteous.

Main office, 8 Place d'Armes, Montreal. Annual meeting, second Tuesday in May, at Montreal.

## THE PECK, STOW & WILCOX CO.

A corporation organized in 1870 as a joint stock company and in 1880 chartered by an act of the Connecticut Legislature. The company manufactures tinners' machinery, mechanics' tools and general hardware. It has factories at Southington, Plantsville and East Berlin, Conn., and at Cleveland.

Stock......Par $25..........................Authorized, $1,250,000......Issued, $1,250,000

Total assets July 1, 1901, $1,599,980, including $242,000 cash.

President, Augustine R. Treadway, Cleveland; Vice-President, F. L. Wilcox, South Berlin, Conn.; Secretary, Edwin N. Walkley; Treasurer, Stephen Walkley, Southington, Conn.

Directors—Webster R. Walkley, Augustine R. Treadway, Mortimer C. Ogden, Marcellus B. Wilcox, Marcus Holcombe, L. H. Treadway, S. H. Wilcox, S. H. Session, F. Wilcox.

Main office, Southington, Conn. New York salesrooms, 27 Murray street.

---

## PEEKSKILL LIGHTING & RAILROAD CO.

A corporation originally incorporated as the Peekskill Lighting Co. under the laws of New York, July 12, 1900, for the purpose of controlling the gas, electric light and power and street railway systems of the city of Peekskill, N. Y. Its electric and street railway franchises are perpetual. It acquired the following properties:

Peekskill Gas Light Co. Peekskill Traction Co.
Peekskill Electric Light & Power Co.

The company owns and operates 11 miles of street railway in Peekskill and vicinity, and has a gas plant, an electric power house and a storage battery plant.

Stock......Par $100............................Authorized, $500,000......Issued, $350,000

The company has no preferred stock. Stock is transferred by the treasurer of the company at 31 Nassau street, New York.

FUNDED DEBT.

1st mort., sinking fund, 5 per cent. gold, due Oct. 1, 1930, April and Oct.............. $500,000

The total amount of bonds authorized is $750,000. The balance in treasury, $250,000, may be issued for extensions. The bonds may be called at 110 and interest after 1905. Trustee of the mortgage, New York Security & Trust Co., New York.

In the fiscal year ending June 30, 1902, the gross earnings were $86,794; operating expenses, including taxes, $56,392; net, $30,402; interest, $23,125; surplus, $7,277. In the six months ending December 31, 1902, the gross earnings were $56,545; expenses, $33,817; net, $22,728.

President, B. B. Nostrand, Jr., Peekskill, N. Y.; Secretary, Alfred Ely; Treasurer, H. Hobart Porter, Jr., New York.

Directors—B. B. Nostrand, Francis Blossom, William H. Crane, E. N. Sanderson, Richmond Talbot, G. H. Warner, H. Hobart Porter, Jr., Alfred Ely, H. L. Armstrong.

Main office, Peekskill, N. Y. Annual meeting, second Tuesday in February.

---

## PENN-AMERICAN PLATE-GLASS CO.

A corporation formed under the laws of Delaware, December 31, 1900, for the purpose of manufacturing and selling plate-glass. The plant of the company is at Alexandria, Ind.

Stock......Par $100..........................Authorized, $2,000,000......Issued, $1,500,000

The company has no preferred stock and no funded debt. Transfer Agent and Registrar, Farmers' Deposit National Bank, Pittsburg.

Dividends are paid quarterly at the rate of 7 per cent. annually, dividend periods being January 15, April 15, July 15 and October 15. The first dividend was paid January 15, 1901.

In the fiscal year ending December 31, 1901, net earnings were $308,282; dividends, $140,000; surplus, $168,282.

President, W. L. Kann; Vice-President, Emil Wertheimer, Pittsburg; Secretary, Samuel J. Mack, Alexandria, Ind.; Assistant Secretary, W. T. McClarren, Pittsburg.

Directors—W. L. Kann, Emil Wertheimer, Pittsburg; Samuel J. Mack, Anderson, Ind.; J. S. Rosenthal, Baltimore; James Virdin, Dover, Del.

Corporate office, Dover, Del.; main office, 200 Ninth avenue, Pittsburg; branch office, Alexandria, Ind. Annual meeting, second Tuesday in January, at Pittsburg.

## THE PENNSYLVANIA CENTRAL BREWING CO.

A corporation formed under the laws of Pennsylvania, August 23, 1897, for the purpose of carrying on a brewing business. The company acquired the following brewery properties:

Reichard & Weaver, Wilkes-Barre, Pa.
Hughes & Glennon, Pittston, Pa.
Hughes Ale Brewery, Pittston, Pa.
E. Robinson's Sons, Scranton, Pa.
Casey & Kelly Brewing Co., Scranton, Pa.
M. Robinson, Scranton, Pa.
Lackawanna Brewing Co., Scranton, Pa.
Scranton Brewing Co., Scranton, Pa.
Dickson Brewing Co., Dickson, Pa.
John Arnold, Hazleton, Pa.
Peter Krantz, Carbondale, Pa.
A. Hartung, Honesdale, Pa.

Stock....Par $100.....Authorized { com., $2,800,000; pref., 2,800,000 } Issued { com., $2,800,000; pref., 2,800,000 } $5,600,000

The preferred stock is 6 per cent., cumulative.

Stock is transferred at the office of the company. Registrar, Anthracite Savings Bank, Wilkes-Barre, Pa.

FUNDED DEBT.

1st mort., 6 per cent. bonds, due 1927, April and Oct.......... .................... $2,700,000

The authorized bond issue is $2,800,000, but $100,000 has been retired by payment from the sinking fund. Trustee of the mortgage and agent for payment of interest, Fidelity Trust Co., Philadelphia.

In the fiscal year ending September 30, 1900, the gross earnings were $896,421; net earnings, $187,835; interest charges, $162,000; total surplus, $289,859. In the fiscal year ending September 30, 1901, the gross earnings were $918,558; net earnings, $211,613; interest charges, $162,000; total surplus, $339,472.

President, Charles Robinson, Scranton, Pa.; Vice-Presidents, George N. Reichard, Wilkes-Barre, Pa.; William Kelly; Secretary and Assistant Treasurer, W. G. Harding; Treasurer, A. J. Casey, Scranton, Pa.

Directors—Charles Robinson, August Robinson, William Kelly, A. J. Casey, E. J. Robinson, James J. Williams, Scranton, Pa.; George N. Reichard, Wilkes-Barre, Pa.; H. W. Jacobs, Hazleton, Pa.; J. H. Harding, Philadelphia; R. M. Hughes, J. H. Glennon, Pittston, Pa.

General offices, 431 North Seventh street, Scranton, Pa. Annual meeting, second Friday in October, at Scranton, Pa.

---

## PENNSYLVANIA ELECTRIC VEHICLE CO.

A corporation formed under the laws of New Jersey, February 9, 1899, as the Philadelphia Motor Wagon Co., and name changed to present title. The objects of the company are to operate, manufacture, buy, sell and lease self-propelling and other vehicles, to deal in patents therefor, to receive and grant licenses thereunder, and to manufacture machines and appliances connected therewith. This company is the exclusive licensee for the State of Pennsylvania of the Electric Vehicle Co.

The company leases a building, 250-256 North Broad street, Philadelphia, as a central station for the operation of electric vehicles in that city.

Stock....Par $10....Authorized { com., $800,000; pref., 400,000 } Issued { com., $800,000; pref., 400,000 } $1,200,000

The preferred stock is 6 per cent., non-cumulative.

The stock was originally $4,000,000 common and $2,000,000 preferred, the par value of both being $50. The common was issued, full paid, and on the preferred $10 per share was paid in. In December it was reduced to the par value of the stock, from $50 to $10 per share, thus making the preferred full paid, and reducing the capital to the present amount.

Transfer agency, Land Title Building, Philadelphia. Registrar, Provident Life & Trust Co., Philadelphia.

President, Herbert Lloyd; Vice-President, John R. Williams; Secretary and Treasurer, Frank C. Lewin.

Directors—Herbert Lloyd, Henry G. Morris, Pedro G. Salom, John R. Williams, Justus B. Entz, Frank C. Lewin, A. B. Stoughton.

Main office, 250 North Broad street, Philadelphia. Annual meeting, third Tuesday in February.

---

## PENNSYLVANIA FURNACE CO.

A corporation formed under the laws of Pennsylvania in September, 1899. The company was organized to acquire interests in the Cornwall Ore Bank Co., Cornwall, Pa., and the Sheridan Furnaces, Sheridan, Pa. The product of this establishment is a high grade Bessemer pig iron

The capacity of the works was stated to be about 150 tons per day. In the plan of organization of this company about $500,000 was reserved for the erection of new furnaces.

Stock......Par $100..........................Authorized, $3,000,000......Issued, $2,100,000

President, John Reed; Vice-President, J. A. Coram; Treasurer, T. E. Hopkins; Secretary, H. W. Wesson.

Directors—J. A. Coram, T. E. Hopkins, D. M. Anthony, John Reed, William M. Dean, E. C. Hopkins, H. W. Wesson.

Main office, 60 State street, Boston.

## PENNSYLVANIA SALT MANUFACTURING CO.

A corporation formed under the laws of Pennsylvania, September 25, 1850. It was the pioneer concern in the heavy chemical industry in the United States. The company has large plants at Greenwich Point, Philadelphia, Natrona, Allegheny County, Pa., and Wyandotte, Mich. The company imports kryolith, pyrites and nitrate soda, and manufactures Natrona bicarbonate soda, caustic soda, sal soda, pure alumina for aluminum, Natrona porous alum, crystal or lump alum, aluminous ca e, chloride zinc, chloride calcium, salt, bluestone or sulphate of copper, soda ash, aqua ammonia, saponifier, Lewis's 98 per cent. powdered and perfumed lye, potash, copperas, bleaching powder or chloride lime, fluoride calcium, sulphate of iron, refined salt cake for glass makers, Glauber salt, manganese, sulphuric, nitric and muriatic acids, pure ground kryolith for glass makers and hollow ware manufacturers and enamelers, purple ore or blue billy, containing over 67 per cent. metallic iron and free from phosphorus, and other chemicals and specialties which comprise the standard goods in their respective classes.

Stock......Par $50..........................Authorized, $5,000,000......Issued, $3,000,000

The company has no funded debt, having retired the $344,000 5 per cent., 1st mortgage bonds, maturing January 15, 1900. It also has no bills payable of any description.

No report of earnings is made public.

Since 1863 this company has paid dividends of 12 per cent. in half-yearly payments of 6 per cent. each in April (15) and October.

President, Theodore Armstrong; Vice-President and Secretary, Austin M. Purves; Treasurer, Arthur E. Rice.

Directors—Theodore Armstrong, James W. McAllister, Thomas W. Sparks, John S. Jenks, George A. Heyl, J. Tatnall Lea, Joseph Moore, Jr., Philadelphia.

Main office, 115 Chestnut street, Philadelphia. Annual meeting, fourth Wednesday in October.

## PENNSYLVANIA STEEL CO.

A corporation formed under the laws of New Jersey, April 29, 1901. The company acquired and owns the stock of the following companies:

The Pennsylvania Steel Co., of Pennsylvania.
Maryland Steel Co.
Baltimore & Sparrows Point R. R. Co.
The Spanish-American Iron Co.
Half interest in Juragua Iron Co., Limited.

The plant consists of large works at Steelton, Pa., for the manufacture of steel rails, railway material, structural work, railroad crossings and special work, and that of the Maryland Steel Co., at Sparrow's Point, Md. In April, 1901, the company acquired the stock of the Spanish-American Iron Co.; it also owns the Lebanon Blast Furnace, Lebanon, Pa., and has an interest in the Cornwall Ore Banks Co. of Lebanon, Pa., and controls the Cornwall & Lebanon Railroad Co.

The control of this company was acquired in June, 1901, by the Pennsylvania Railroad Co., other allied roads being also interested in the purchase, which involved the acquisition of $10,000,000 each of common and preferred stock.

Stock..Par $100..Authorized { com., $25,000,000; pref., 25,000,000 } Issued { com., $10,750,000; pref., 16,500,000 } $27,250,000

The preferred stock is 7 per cent., non-cumulative.

The stock of the old company consisted of $5,000,000 of common and $1,500,000 of 7 per cent. preferred stock. Under the plan of reorganization a syndicate took $10,000,000 of new common and $10,000,000 of new preferred, and furnished $9,000,000 in cash.

The company paid 1¾ per cent. on the old preferred stock in October, 1899, and paid dividends at the same rate regularly in January, April, July and October.

The payment of regular dividends on the new preferred stock began November 1, 1901, with a half-yearly dividend of 3½ per cent. The dividends on the preferred are May and November.

Stock is transferred at the company's office. Registrar, Girard Trust Co., Philadelphia.

FUNDED DEBT.

| | |
|---|---|
| Pennsylvania Steel Co., of Pa., old 1st mort., due Nov., 1917, 5 p. ct., May and Nov.. | $1,000,000 |
| Maryland Steel Co., 1st mort., 5 per cent., due Feb., 1922, Feb. and Aug........... | 2,000,000 |
| " " car trusts, 5 per cent., due 1903-12, Jan. and July.............. | 800,000 |
| " " consolidated mort., 6 per cent., due Sept., 1925, March and Sept.. | 4,000,000 |
| " " collateral trust loan, 5 per cent., due Oct., 1930, April and Oct.. | 7,500,000 |
| Total.......... | $15,300,000 |

The old 1st mortgage is a prior lien on the plant at Steelton, Pa.

The consolidated mortgage, Girard Trust Co., Philadelphia, trustee, is for $7,000,000, and is secured by the plant and the stock of the Maryland Steel Co. and Juragua Iron Co. Of the issue $3,000,000 is reserved to retire prior bonds, and $3,300,000 was available to settle claims against the company. Interest on the consols was payable in scrip until September, 1898. The scrip is convertible into 2d mortgage 6 per cent. bonds.

The collateral trust bonds were issued in 1902 and are secured by the company's interests in the Cornwall Ore Banks, the Lebanon Furnace and other properties acquired at that time.

EARNINGS—ALL COMPANIES.

| | Gross. | Charges. | Surplus. |
|---|---|---|---|
| 1901 | $3,202,831 | $550,113 | $2,652,718 |

President, Edgar C. Felton; Vice-President, F. W. Wood; Treasurer, Edmund N. Smith; Secretary and Assistant to President, Frank Tenney, Philadelphia.

Directors—Edgar C. Felton, Arthur Brock, Luther S. Bent, Evans R. Dick, George Wood, William D. Winsor, Francis I. Gowen, George H. B. Martin, Effingham B. Morris, Edward T. Stotesbury, George F. Baer, Theodore N. Ely, Frank J. Firth, Philadelphia; F. C. Smirk, Reading, Pa.; John Cassels, Washington, D. C.

Main office, Girard Building, Philadelphia; works, Steelton, Pa.; Lebanon, Pa., and Sparrow's Point, Md.; New York office, 71 Broadway; Boston office, 70 Kilby street. Annual meeting, third Tuesday in April.

## THE PENNSYLVANIA TELEPHONE CO.

A corporation formed under the laws of Pennsylvania in 1882. The company operates a telephone system in Central and Eastern Pennsylvania, under an exclusive license from the American Telephone & Telegraph Co. Its territory includes the cities of Harrisburg, Lancaster, York, Lebanon, Carlisle, Chambersburg, Allentown, Bethlehem, Reading, Pottsville, Mauch Chunk, Easton, Williamsport, Scranton, Wilkes-Barre, Sunbury, Altoona, Clearfield, Pa., and other cities, and it also covers a portion of Western New Jersey. A controlling interest in the stock is owned by the American Telephone & Telegraph Co.

Stock......Par $50.... ......................Authorized, $3,000,000......Issued, $2,130,867

The company pays 6 per cent. per annum on its stock, the dividends being quarterly, 1½ per cent. each in January, April, July and October.

FUNDED DEBT.

| | |
|---|---|
| 1st mort., 5 per cent., due April, 1918, April and Oct.................. | $500,000 |
| 1st mort., 6 per cent., due April, 1925; April and Oct.................. | 158,500 |
| Total.................. | $658,500 |

President, A. R. Shellenberger, Harrisburg, Pa.; Vice-President, H. S. Huidekoper, Philadelphia; Secretary and Auditor, J. H. Crossman, Jr.; Treasurer, W. C. Fink, Harrisburg, Pa.

Directors—A. R. Shellenberger, John E. Fox, Harrisburg, Pa.; H. S. Huidekoper, Philadelphia; Frederick P. Fish, C. Jay French, Boston; W. H. Beck, C. J. Bell, Washington; S. S. Blair, Tyrone, Pa.; Richard O'Brien, Scranton, Pa.; Addison Candor, John A. White, Williamsport, Pa.

Main office, 210 Walnut street, Harrisburg, Pa. Annual meeting, last Wednesday in January.

## PEOPLE'S GAS & ELECTRIC CO. OF OSWEGO

A corporation formed under the laws of New York, April 28, 1900. The company controls the entire gas and electric business of Oswego, N. Y., and furnishes power to the street railways of that city under a 20-year contract. The company is a consolidation of the Oswego Gas Light Co., Home Electric Co. and People's Electric Light and Power Co. Population served, 22,000.

Stock......Par $100................ ...Authorized, $450,000................Issued, $450,000

Transfer Agent, New York Security & Trust Co., New York.

FUNDED DEBT.

1st mort., 5 per cent., gold, due 1930, May and Nov........................... ..... $450,000

The 1st mortgage, New York Security & Trust Co., New York, trustee, is for $450,000. A sinking fund begins in 1910, and bonds may be drawn for same at 105. The 1st mortgage covers the entire property, underlying bonds of the constituent companies having been retired.

The earnings of the three plants combined in this company in 1902 aggregated, gross, $89,148; net, $42,750.

President, William B. Hord; Secretary, Victor Cumberson; Treasurer, Charles F. Street, New York.

Directors—William B. Hord, Hunter Wykes, Charles F. Street, A. M. Hyatt, Osborn W. Bright, New York.

Main office, Oswego, N. Y.; New York office, 44 Wall street. Annual meeting, third Wednesday in June.

## PEOPLE'S GAS LIGHT & COKE CO.

A corporation formed under a special charter granted by the Legislature of Illinois, February 12, 1855, and amended February 7, 1865. It was one of the companies whose stock was owned by the Chicago Gas Trust Co. and the organization known as the Chicago Gas Companies. In July, 1897, an act was passed by the Illinois Legislature allowing the consolidation of all the properties with this company. In addition to the companies which were owned by the old organization, this company, in November, 1897, purchased the property of the Mutual Fuel Gas Co., giving it control of virtually all the gas companies in Chicago. The Mutual and the Hyde Park companies were consolidated with this company in January, 1898. The united properties comprised on December 31, 1902, had 1,866 miles of street mains supplying 342,150 meters and 25,090 public lamps. Control of the Universal Gas Co. was acquired, and in January, 1899, acquired the Calumet Gas Co., operating in South Chicago. In October, 1900, control of the Ogden Gas Co. was obtained by capitalists favorable to this company, and a contract was made by which the latter's property will be taken over by this company when its franchise expires in 1945.

Capital stock......Par $100.................Authorized, $35,000,000......Issued, $32,969,100

In November, 1898, stock was increased from $25,000,000 to $30,000,000 and $3,750,000 offered to stockholders for subscription at par. In September, 1901, there was a further increase to $35,000,000, and $4,300,300 was taken by the stockholders at par.

Transfer Agent, Central Trust Co., New York.

In December, 1892, the dividend on the old stock was increased to 1½ per cent., quarterly. In October, 1893, dividend was declared in scrip redeemable in People's Gas consolidated mortgage bonds. The January, 1894, dividend was declared payable in cash. In April, 1895, dividend period was changed to half-yearly, but in consequence of the litigation and unsettled state of the organization no dividend was paid in October. In autumn of 1896 a compromise was effected with the legal authorities of Illinois and Court orders so modified that a dividend of 1½ per cent. was declared and paid November 25, 1896.

The consolidated company paid its first dividend November 24, 1897, and has since paid regular quarterly dividends at the rate of 6 per cent. per annum in February, May, August and November.

FUNDED DEBT.

| | |
|---|---|
| Chicago Gas Light & Coke, 1st mort., 5 per cent., due July, 1937, Jan. and July.... | $10,000,000 |
| Illinois Light, Heat & Power, 1st mort., 7 per cent., due Nov., 1915, May and Nov.. | 500,000 |
| Lake Gas & Light, 1st mort., 6 per cent., due July, 1915, Jan. and July........... | 300,000 |
| People's Gas Light & Coke, 1st mort., 6 per cent., due Nov., 1904, May and Nov.... | 2,100,000 |
| " " " 2d mort., 6 per cent., due Dec., 1904, June and Dec.... | 2,500,000 |
| " " " cons. mort., 6 per cent., due April, 1943, April and Oct.. | 4,900,000 |
| " " " ref. mort., 5 per cent., due Sept., 1947, March and Sept.. | 2,500,000 |
| Equitable Gas Light & Fuel, 1st mort., 6 per cent., due July, 1905, Jan. and July.... | 2,000,000 |
| Consumers' Gas, 1st mort., 5 per cent., due Dec., 1936, June and Dec............. | 4,246,000 |
| Mutual Fuel Gas, 1st mort., 5 per cent., due Nov., 1947, March and Nov.......... | 5,000,000 |
| Hyde Park Gas, 1st mort., 6 per cent., due Sept., 1904, March and Sept.......... | 200,000 |
| Calumet Gas Co., 1st mort., 6 per cent., due July, 1917, Jan. and July............ | 250,000 |
| Total.............................................................. | $34,496,000 |

The People's Gas Light & Coke Co. refunding mortgage created in 1897 is for $40,000,000, of which $29,046,000 are reserved to retire underlying bonds. The balance may be issued for additional property. Of the reserved amount $2,500,000 was issued to replace Chicago Economic bonds previously held in treasury.

The Chicago Gas Trust Co. was incorporated April 28, 1887, to acquire the controlling interest in all the gas companies supplying the city of Chicago, eight in number, comprising the Chicago Gas Light & Coke Co., the People's Gas Light & Coke Co., the Consumers' Gas Co., Equitable Gas Light & Fuel Co., Suburban Gas Co., Lake Gas Co., Hyde Park Gas Co. and Illinois Light, Heat & Power Co. The Illinois Light, Heat & Power Co. was owned by the People's Co.; the Lake Gas Co. and Hyde Park Gas Co. by the Consumers' Co., and the Suburban Gas Co. by the Chicago Gas Light & Coke Co. The control of the Chicago Economic Fuel Gas Co. was also acquired. For a detailed account of the Chicago Gas Trust Co., see MANUAL for 1900. The charter of that company was surrendered in 1891, and the securities of the various companies were placed in the hands of the Fidelity Insurance Trust & Safe Deposit Co. of Philadelphia, which issued its certificates of an equitable interest in the properties in lieu of the old stock.

In 1895 a committee was formed to carry out a legal reorganization and to effect a consolidation of the separate companies.

The negotiations for passage of an act allowing the companies to consolidate under the present form is referred to above, the act having been passed in July, 1897, and August 3, 1897, the consolidation took place, the old certificates of the Fidelity Insurance Trust & Safe Deposit Co. being exchanged share for share for stock of the present company.

EARNINGS.

| | Gross. | Net. | Charges. | Surplus. |
|---|---|---|---|---|
| 1897 | $7,125,439 | $3,436,463 | $1,842,300 | $1,594,163 |
| 1898 | 7,265,526 | 3,470,225 | 1,842,300 | 1,627,925 |
| 1899 | 8,096,319 | 3,818,872 | 1,857,300 | 1,961,572 |
| 1900 | 9,090,337 | 4,058,374 | 1,857,300 | 2,201,074 |
| 1901 | 9,663,746 | 4,259,469 | 1,857,300 | 2,402,169 |
| 1902 | 11,058,413 | 4,514,616 | 1,857,300 | 2,657,316 |

In 1899 the balance after 6 per cent. dividends on the stock was $241,444. In 1900, surplus over dividends, $480,946; in 1901, surplus, $617,536; in 1902, surplus, $679,170.

The following is the company's balance sheet, December 31, 1903:

| ASSETS. | | LIABILITIES. | |
|---|---|---|---|
| Real estate, franchise, tunnels, street mains, meters, services, etc | $70,305,802 | Capital stock | $35,000,000 |
| Material | 782,582 | Mortgage bonds | 34,496,000 |
| Securities | 2,245,682 | Deposits, security for gas bills | 84,713 |
| Accounts receivable | 369,851 | Accounts payable | 368,193 |
| Deposits with agencies for bond coupons | 350,805 | Coupons past due | 352,715 |
| Gas bills receivable | 851,938 | Bond interest accrued | 217,858 |
| Bills receivable | 104,227 | Profit and loss | 5,427,227 |
| Cash | 935,819 | | |
| Total | $75,946,706 | Total | $75,946,706 |

Chairman, C. K. G. Billings, New York; President, George O. Knapp, Chicago; Vice-Presidents, Anthony N. Brady, Walton Ferguson, New York; C. K. Wooster; Secretary, Lyman A. Wiley; Treasurer, W. S. McCrea, Chicago; Assistant Secretary, H. W. Olcott, New York.

Directors—Anthony N. Brady, Walton Ferguson, Anson R. Flower, C. K. G. Billings, New York; George O. Knapp, Chicago.

Main office, 157 Michigan avenue, Chicago; New York office, 54 Wall street. Annual meeting, February 10.

## PEORIA GAS & ELECTRIC CO.

A corporation formed under the laws of Illinois, March 18, 1899, for the purpose of supplying gas and electricity in Peoria County, Ill. The company erected a new gas plant with a capacity of 500,000 cubic feet per day, and acquired the property of the Peoria General Electric Co., enlarging and reconstructing the latter to its present capacity of 3,000 horse-power.

Stock......Par $100..........................Authorized, $2,000,000......Issued, $2,000,000

The company has no preferred stock and no funded debt. Stock is transferred at the office of the treasurer, 150 Monroe street, Chicago. Registrar, Equitable Trust Co., Chicago.

President, Sumner R. Clarke; Vice-President, F. W. Little; Secretary, Theodore J. Miller, Peoria, Ill.; Treasurer, Lyman A. Walton, Chicago.

Main office, 125 North Jefferson avenue, Peoria, Ill. Annual meeting in March, at Peoria.

# PHILADELPHIA COMPANY

A corporation formed under the laws of Pennsylvania, May 24, 1884. In January, 1899, control was acquired in the interest of a general consolidation of lighting and traction organizations in Allegheny County, Pa., and its environs. The object was to bring under one organization the natural gas interests of this company, together with the electric light and power business of Pittsburg and the surrounding district. See MANUAL for 1902 for a detailed account of the various consolidations and acquisitions.

The company owns or controls by lease the following street railway properties:

The United Traction Co.
Monongahela Street Railway Co.
Pittsburg Railways Co.
Suburban Rapid Transit Street Railway Co.
Tustin Street Railway Co.
Consolidated Traction Co.
Pittsburg & Birmingham Traction Co.
Pittsburg & Charleroi Street Railway Co.
East McKeesport Street Railway Co.

It also owns or controls by lease the following electric and lighting companies:

Allegheny County Light Co.
Southern Heat, Light & Power Co.
South Side Gas Co.
Monongahela Light & Power Co.
Consolidated Gas Co.
Allegheny Illuminating Co.
Ohio Valley Electric Co.

Through its own lines and those of a number of companies controlled by it supplies nearly all the natural gas consumed in Pittsburg and Allegheny and the adjacent towns. The principal fuel gas concerns included in the system are:

Philadelphia Co.
Equitable Gas Co.
Union Gas Co. of McKeesport.
Chartiers Valley Gas Co.
Pennsylvania Natural Gas Co.
Allegheny Heating Co.

The total mileage of the street railways owned and controlled is 409 miles. Statements of the separate traction companies will be found under their own titles in this edition of the MANUAL. For convenience and economy they are all operated, under agreement, by the Pittsburg Railways Co., one of the constituent concerns.

The electric and illuminating gas properties are the only ones supplying the cities of Pittsburg and Allegheny with such facilities.

In connection with its natural gas business the company leases 201,532 acres of gas lands, and in 1902 acquired the gas rights on about 73,917 acres in Pennsylvania and West Virginia, its distributing mains in the cities and towns it serves being connected by larger mains with the sources of supply.

The original business of the company was the supplying of natural gas for light and fuel. The company controlled a large amount of gas territory owned or leased, and had 1,200 miles of pipes, 400 gas wells and 45 oil wells. The distributing territory covered embraced the city of Pittsburg, Allegheny City and suburbs. Completed an extension, 65 miles, to West Virginia gas territory in 1896.

In February, 1898, a circular was issued to the stockholders asking for options on their stock good until July 1, 1898, afterwards extended till January 1, 1899, at $40 per share in view of negotiations for a consolidation of all gas interests in Allegheny County, Pa. This resulted in the sale of the stock to a syndicate headed by Alexander Brown & Sons, Baltimore, Md., the plan of consolidation being carried out as above noted.

Stock...Par $50...Authorized { com., $30,000,000 / pref., 6,000,000 } Issued { com., $28,953,029 / pref., 5,744,812 } $34,697,841

The preferred stock is 5 per cent., non-cumulative. The amount of stock authorized was $6,000,000 preferred and $15,000,000 common, of which there was issued and outstanding $14,752,131 common and $3,998,350 preferred. In December, 1901, the authorized common stock was increased to $30,000,000. This company issued $10,600,000 new common in exchange for the stocks of the Consolidated Traction Co. and the other companies acquired at that time, and also issued for the same purpose, $1,800,000 of the preferred stock held in the treasury.

The stock prior to the consolidation was all common shares of the par value of $50 per share, amounting to $7,500,000.

Transfer Agents, Union Trust Co., Pittsburg; Central Trust Co., New York.

Full 5 per cent. dividends on the preferred stock and on the common at the rate of 5 per cent. per annum have been paid since the consolidation. On the preferred the dividends are 2½ per cent. half-yearly, in March (1) and September. On the common the dividends are 6 per cent. per annum, paid quarterly, 1½ per cent. each, January, April, July and October.

Under the plan for acquiring the Consolidated Traction Co. the company offered 1 share of its common stock for 2 shares of Consolidated Traction common and for each 20 shares of the latter's preferred stock $1,000 in new 50-year 5 per cent. bonds, 3 shares of this company's preferred and 1 share of common with $60 in cash.

FUNDED DEBT.

| | |
|---|---|
| 1st mort. and col. trust 50-year mort., 5 per cent., due March, 1949, March and Sept. | $5,500,000 |
| Cons. mort. and collateral trust, 5 per cent., due Nov., 1951, May and Nov.......... | 11,635,000 |
| Allegheny Co. Light Co. 1st mort., 6 per cent., due 1911, Feb. and Aug............ | 500,000 |
| East End Electric Light Co. 1st mort., 6 per cent., due 1915, Feb. and Aug......... | 500,000 |
| Consolidated Gas Co. 1st mort., 5 per cent., due Feb., 1948, Feb. and Aug......... | 5,000,000 |
| United Traction Co. gen. mort., 5 per cent., due July, 1997, Jan. and July.......... | 4,725,000 |
| Braddock Gas Light 1st mort., 6 per cent., due May, 1908, May and Nov............ | 40,000 |
| East McKeesport 1st mort., 5 per cent., due Dec., 1929, June and Dec.............. | 250,000 |
| Southern H. L. & P. 1st mort., 5 per cent., due Dec., 1949, June and Dec.......... | 200,000 |
| Monongahela L. & P. 1st mort., 5 per cent., due June, 1949, June and Dec....... | 1,700,000 |
| Total.......................................................... | $30,050,000 |

There is outstanding $2,000,000 6 per cent. preferred stock of the Consolidated Gas Co. and $3,000,000 5 per cent. preferred stock of the United Traction Co. on which the regular dividends are paid.

The new 5 per cent. bonds were authorized in February, 1899, for the purposes of carrying out the consolidation. Trustee of mortgage, Maryland Trust Co., Baltimore. Amount authorized is $6,500,000. Of these $1,000,000 are reserved to retire outstanding liens on the property of the Allegheny County Light Co. Bonds are secured by deposit of the securities of constituent companies with the trustee. An amount of $4,000,000 of the bonds was offered for subscription in February, 1899, at 107½ by Brown Bros. & Co., New York, and Alexander Brown & Sons, Baltimore. The 50-year collateral trust was created in 1901 to provide for the acquisition of the Consolidated Traction Co. and other properties. The authorized amount of these bonds is $22,000,000, of which $12,000,000 was to be issued in exchange for the Consolidated Traction securities, $6,500,000 was reserved to take up prior lien bonds, and $3,500,000 was available for extensions and betterments.

The United Traction Co. 5 per cent. mortgage is for $10,000,000, secured by all of that company's property, subject to $5,250,000 prior liens, sufficient of this issue being reserved to retire the latter at maturity.

The United Traction Co. has divisional mortgage bonds outstanding to the amount of $5,250,000 which are not included in the above tabulation of the funded debt of the system.

EARNINGS.—Year ending March 31.

| | Gross. | Net. | Charges. | Surplus. |
|---|---|---|---|---|
| 1899-00......................... | $3,628,167 | $1,952,807 | $1,716,364 | $236,443 |
| 1900-01......................... | 3,810,440 | 1,987,742 | 1,050,112 | 937,629 |
| 1901-02......................... | 4,146,958 | 2,789,399 | 1,400,007 | 1,389,392 |

In 1899 gross of all properties, $5,506,078; net, $2,683,666; surplus, $873,605. In 1899-1900 dividends on common stock were $129,444. Profit and loss credit, March 31, 1900, $803,927.

Last dividend on the old capital stock, 1 per cent., January 10, 1899. October, 1895, dividend was passed. None declared in 1896 or 1897. In 1898 4 per cent. was paid on old stock.

President, James H. Reed; Vice-President, James D. Callery; General Manager, J. F. Guffey; Treasurer, C. J. Braun, Jr.; Secretary, Winfield B. Carson; Auditor, C. S. Mitchell, Pittsburg.

Directors—James H. Reed, James D. Callery, T. H. Given, Joshua Rhodes, M. K. McMullin, Pittsburg; G. H. Frazier, W. L. Elkins, Philadelphia; H. J. Bowdoin, Baltimore; Patrick Calhoun, Atlanta, Ga.

Main office, 435 Sixth avenue, Pittsburg. Annual meeting, first Monday in May.

## PHILADELPHIA ELECTRIC CO.

A corporation formed under the laws of New Jersey, October 6, 1899. The company acquired the stock of the Pennsylvania Manufacturing Light & Power Co. and of the National Electric Co., with the control of practically the entire electric light and power facilities in the city of Philadelphia.

The Pennsylvania Manufacturing Light & Power Co. was a New Jersey corporation formed in 1898, which acquired control of the Pennsylvania Heat, Light & Power Co., a corporation which had acquired the Edison Electric Light Co. of Philadelphia, the Brush Electric Light Co. of Philadelphia, the United States Electric Light Co. and the Philadelphia Electric Light Co. The Pennsylvania Manufacturing Co. and the Heat, Light & Power Co. also acquired a number of smaller electric companies in Philadelphia and its suburbs. See statement of Pennsylvania Manufacturing Co. in the MANUAL for 1899. In 1901 acquired the Kensington Electric Light Co., paying for the same in cash. This completed the company's control of all the electric light facilities of Philadelphia. The company also controls the Electric Light Co. of Chester, Pa.

Stock......Par $25.........................Authorized, $25,000,000......Issued, $25,000,000

An instalment of 10 per cent., or $2.50 per share, was paid on the stock of the Philadelphia Electric Co. at time of issue, and two calls of 5 per cent. each were made in 1900, payable November 21, 1900, and January 21, 1901, respectively. In January, 1902, another call of $2.50 per share was made, payable half March 1 and half September 1, 1902. This made the stock 30 per cent. or $7.50 per share paid in.

The stock of the Pennsylvania Manufacturing Co. was $15,000,000, par $50, on which $5 per share had been paid in. The stock of the National Electric Co. was $4,375,000.

In June, 1902, a dividend of 15c. per share and another of 18¾ per cent. in December, 1902, being at the rate of 2½ per cent. each on the amount paid in.

FUNDED DEBT.

| | |
|---|---|
| Edison Collateral Trust certificates, 5 per cent., subject to call 1946, April and Oct.. | $1,994,300 |
| Pa. H. L. & P. Collateral Trust certificates, 5 per cent., due 1948, April and Oct.... | 11,266,700 |
| Philadelphia Electric Trust certificates, 4 per cent., due Oct., 1949, Jan. and July.... | 14,982,200 |
| Total............ | $28,243,200 |

The Philadelphia Electric Co. 4 per cent. trust certificates are $17,500,000 authorized, of which $15,014,142 were issued, $2,000,000 being held in the company's treasury, having been purchased in the market in 1900. They are secured by the deposit of the shares of the Pennsylvania Manufacturing Light & Power Co. and of the National Electric Co., acquired by this company. Each share of Pennsylvania Manufacturing Co. stock deposited received $35 in the trust certificates and each share of National Electric received $13 in certificates. Only a small amount of each stock now remains outstanding. The balance of the issue, not required for the above purpose, was to be reserved for extension and acquisition of other electric properties.

The Edison collateral trust certificates were issued in 1896 by the Pennsylvania Heat, Light & Power Co., and are secured by the deposit of the stock of the Edison Electric Light Co. of Philadelphia, acquired by the Pennsylvania Heat, Light & Power Co. The Edison company had $2,000,000 stock, and $50 cash and $100 in trust certificates was offered for each $100 share. Nearly all the Edison stockholders accepted these terms.

The Pennsylvania Manufacturing collateral trust certificates, created in 1898, are secured by a deposit of stock of the Pennsylvania Heat, Light & Power Co. and other stocks. The Pennsylvania Heat, Light & Power Co. had $5,000,000 full-paid common stock, par $50, and $5,000,000 6 per cent., cumulative, preferred stock, par $50, on which $35 per share had been paid. The Pennsylvania Manufacturing Light & Power Co. acquired control by exchanging the collateral trust certificates for Pennsylvania Heat, Light & Power stock at the rate of $66 per share for the preferred and $24 per share for the common.

The net earnings of all the controlled companies in 1901 were stated to be $304,160.

President, Joseph B. McCall; Vice-President, William F. Harrity; Treasurer, William P. Conover, Jr.; Secretary, A. V. R. Coe.

Directors—William L. Elkins, Thomas Dolan, Jeremiah J. Sullivan, William F. Harrity, John M. Mack, Joseph B. McCall, J. V. Shoemaker, A. V. R. Coe.

Main office, 117 South Tenth street, Philadelphia. Annual meeting, second Wednesday in April.

## PHILADELPHIA RAPID TRANSIT CO.

A corporation formed under the laws of Pennsylvania, May 1. 1902. The company acquired by lease the Union Traction Railway system, comprising the lines of the Philadelphia Traction Co., the Electric Traction Co. and the Peoples' Traction Co. See statement of the Union Traction Co. It also acquired the capital stock and franchises of the following companies:

Broad Street Rapid Transit Street Railway Co.
Central Rapid Transit Street Railway Co.
Chestnut Hill & Glenside Rapid Transit Street Railway Co.
Eastern Rapid Transit Street Railway Co.
Frankford Elevated Passenger Railway Co.
Germantown Avenue Elevated Passenger Railway Co.
Doylestown & Willow Grove Railway Co.
Market Street Elevated Passenger Railway Co.
Northern Rapid Transit Street Railway Co.
Passyunk Avenue Elevated Passenger Railway Co.
Ridge Avenue Elevated Passenger Railway Co.
Southern Rapid Transit Street Railway Co.
Western Rapid Transit Street Railway Co.

Stock......Par $50..........................Authorized, $30,000,000 .....Issued, $3,000,000

The company has no preferred stock.

Stock is transferred at the office of the company, Philadelphia. Registrar, The Land Title & Trust Co., Philadelphia.

FUNDED DEBT.

Doylestown & Willow Grove Ry. Co., 1st mort., 4 p. c., g., due Jan. 1, 1930, June and Dec. $500,000

The outstanding bonds are the full amount authorized. Trustee of the mortgage and agent or the payment of interest, Land Title & Trust Co., Philiadelphia.

The bonds of the Doylestown & Willow Grove Railway Co. are guaranteed by the Philadelphia Rapid Transit Co., which, however, has no funded debt of its own.

President, John B. Parsons; 1st Vice-President, George D. Widener; 2d Vice-President and General Manager, Charles O. Kruger; Secretary and Treasurer, Robert B. Selfridge; Assistant Secretary and Treasurer, John B. Peddle.

Directors—John B. Parsons, George D. Widener, J. J. Sullivan, William H. Shelmerdine, William L. Elkins, Peter A. B. Widener, John M. Mack, Michael Murphy.

Corporate and main offices, 820 Dauphin street, Philadelphia. Annual meeting, third Wednesday in September, at Philadelphia.

## PHŒNIX GAS & ELECTRIC CO.

A corporation formed under the laws of New Jersey, September 21, 1901, for the purpose of acquiring and operating all the gas, electric and street railway properties in Phœnixville, Royersford and Spring City, Pa. It has acquired and operates the following companies:

Schuylkill Valley Illuminating Co. — Montgomery & Chester Electric Railway Co.
Consolidated Schuylkill Gas Co.

The company has a total of 6½ miles of street railway.

Stock......Par $100............................Authorized, $1,000,000......Issued, $800,000

Stock is transferred at the office of the secretary, Philadelphia.

FUNDED DEBT.

1st mort., 5 per cent., due 1951, April and Oct........................................ $750,000

The authorized bond issue is $1,000,000, and covers all the stock of the constituent companies. The remaining $250,000 is reserved for extensions and improvements. A sinking fund is arranged for, becoming operative in 1907. Trustee of the mortgage and agent for the payment of interest, The Real Estate Trust Co., Philadelphia.

President, L. Knowles Perot; Secretary, Frederick H. Shelton, Philadelphia.

Directors—L. Knowles Perot, George C. Carson, Jr., C. R. Miller, Frederick H. Shelton, Philadelphia; Frank P. Norris, Irvin J. Brower, J. W. Gillette, Phœnixville, Pa.; William P. Snyder, Spring City, Pa.; S. Whittaker Thompson, Mont Clare, Pa.; William D. Lippincott, Camden, N. J.

Main office, Phœnixville, Pa.; Secretary's office, Pennsylvania Building, Philadelphia. Annual meeting, last week in October, at Camden, N. J.

## PHŒNIX GOLD MINING CO.

A corporation formed under the laws of Maine in 1896. The company is a reorganization of the Phœnix Consolidated Gold Mining Co. Its property consists of a large number of claims at Cave Creek, Maricopa County, Arizona, about thirty miles from Phœnix, Ariz. The old company and the preceding owners did considerable development work and there is a mill on the property.

Stock .....Par $1 ......Authorized { com., $750,000 / pref., 750,000 } Issued { com., $750,000 / pref., 750,000 } $1,500,000

The preferred stock is 7 per cent., non-cumulative. The company has a bonded debt of $60,000.

Transfer Agents, Curtis & Romaine, 30 Broad street, New York.

President, Josiah C. Reiff; Vice-President, F. T. Adams, New York; Treasurer, William Christy, Phœnix, Ariz.; Secretary, F. M. Clute, New York.

Directors—Josiah C. Reiff, F. T. Adams, Sidney W. Curtis, E. S. Hatch, New York; William Christy, C. F. Ainsworth, Phœnix, Ariz.; C. Hale, Portland, Me.

Main office, 20 Broad street, New York. Annual meeting, second Wednesday in December.

## THE PILLSBURY-WASHBURN FLOUR MILLS CO., LIMITED

A corporation formed in 1889, under the laws of Great Britain, Companies Acts, 1862–1889. The company owns five of the largest flour mills in the world at Minneapolis, Minn., with an aggregate capacity of 30,000 barrels per day. It owns, in addition, the water power on both sides of the Mississippi River at Minneapolis, with two dams of 45 feet and 20 feet head, respectively. The former furnishes power for the company's mills and other mills located in the city, and the other supplies the street railways of Minneapolis and St. Paul with about 10,000 horse-power for generating electricity. The income derived from the water power is about $250,000 per annum. The company also owns the entire capital stock of the Minneapolis & Northern Elevator Co.

Stock....Par £10.... Authorized { com., £500,000 / pref., 500,000 } Issued { com., £500,000 / pref., 500,000 } £1,000,000

The preference shares are entitled to 8 per cent., cumulative, dividends.

FUNDED DEBT.

| | |
|---|---|
| 1st mort. debentures, 6 per cent., due 1939, May and Nov | £832,000 |
| Preference income certificates | 105,920 |
| Total | £937,920 |

The preference income certificates represent 3½ years' arrears of dividend to February 28, 1895, on the preferred shares. The amount was originally £140,000, but has been reduced to the sum given above out of the profits, the amount annually appropriated for interest and sinking fund on the same being £14,000.

The debentures are secured by a 1st mortgage on the company's property. Trustee, the Trustees', Executors' & Securities Insurance Co., Limited, London. Agent for payment of interest, Morton Trust Co., New York.

EARNINGS.

Year ending August 31.

| | Dividends. Pref. | Com. | Net. | Balance over Charges. | Dividends. | Surplus. |
|---|---|---|---|---|---|---|
| 1898-99 | 8 | 4 | £134,518 | £70,598 | £60,000 | £10,598 |
| 1899-00 | 8 | 4 | 133,934 | 70,014 | 60,000 | 10,014 |
| 1900 01 | 8 | .. | 93,609 | 43,689 | 40,000 | 3,689 |
| 1901-02 | 8 | .. | 104,325 | 40,405 | 40,000 | 405 |

The accounts are converted from American currency to sterling at the exchange of $4.85 to the £.

The Minneapolis & Northern Elevator Co., owned by this company, has $825,000 stock. On August 10, 1900, its aggregate assets were $2,144,079.

The Directors at Minneapolis constitute a Committee of Management in America. All but about 30 per cent. of the stock of this company is held in the United States, but of the debentures some 80 per cent. are held in England.

Chairman, Richard H. Glyn; Secretary, Frank Spencer, London, England; Manager, Henry L. Little; Treasurer, L. P. Hubbard, Minneapolis.

Directors—Richard H. Glyn, J. Flower Jackson, William B. Forwood, Charles T. Fox, London, England; John S. Pillsbury, William D. Washburn, Henry L. Little, C. A. Amsden, W. de La Barre, Minneapolis.

Main office, 20 Broad Street avenue, London, E. C.; operating office, Minneapolis.

## PIONEER MINING CO.

A corporation formed under the laws of Washington, December 27, 1901. The company owns gold, placer and quartz plains in the Cape Nome Mining District, Alaska, aggregating 520 acres, together with office buildings, camp outfits and other mining equipment.

Stock......Par $1..............................Authorized, $5,000,000......Issued, $4,607,672

The company has no pre erre stock and no funded debt. Stock is transferred at the office of the company, New York. f d

In 1902 dividends of 8 per cent. were paid, 2 per cent. on September 25 and 6 per cent. on November 19. The company's surplus assets are estimated at $26,595,000.

President, Jafet Lindeberg, Nome, Alaska; Vice-President, E. O. Lindblom, Berkeley, Cal.; Treasurer, Eugene Chilberg, Seattle, Wash.; Secretary and Assistant Treasurer, J. E. Chilberg, Seattle, Wash., and 25 Broad street, New York.

Directors—Jafet Lindeberg, Nome, Alaska; E. O. Lindblom, Berkeley, Cal.; Eugene Chilberg, J. E. Chilberg, Seattle, Wash.; John Brynteson, San Francisco, Cal.

Corporate and main office, Seattle, Wash.; New York office, 25 Broad street. Annual meeting, in May, at Seattle, Wash.

## PITTSBURG & BIRMINGHAM TRACTION CO.

(Leased to United Traction Co. of Pittsburg.)

A corporation formed in 1889. The company leases the Pittsburg & Birmingham Passenger Railway, South Side Passenger Railway, Pittsburg Inclined Plane Co., and Mount Oliver Incline Plane. All the stock of the Brownsville Avenue Street Railway and the West Liberty Street Railway Co. is owned. In January, 1902, all the property of this company was leased to the United Traction Co.

Road operated, 28 miles.

Stock......Par $50............................Authorized, $3,000,000......Issued, $3,000,000

Dividends on the stock are paid semi-annually, in April and October. In 1898 paid 2 per cent., in 1899 2½ per cent., in 1900 paid 3 per cent., in 1901 1½ per cent.

FUNDED DEBT.

| | |
|---|---|
| 1st mort., 5 per cent., due Nov., 1929, May and Nov. | $1,500,000 |
| Debentures, 5 per cent., April and Oct. | 115,000 |
| Birm., A. &. Knox Traction 1st mort., 6 per cent., due Sept., 1931, March and Sept. | 500,000 |
| Brownsville Avenue Street Ry., 1st mort., 5 per cent., due Oct., 1926, Feb. and Aug. | 300,000 |
| Pittsburg Inclined Plane, 1st mort., 6 per cent., due July, 1919, Jan. and July | 150,000 |
| " " " 2d mort., 6 per cent., due June, 1910, Jan. and July | 100,000 |
| Mt. Oliver Incline Ry. Co., 1st mort., 6 per cent., due 1901 | 44,500 |
| West Liberty St. Ry. Co., 1st mort., 5 per cent., due 1930, Jan. and July | 400,000 |
| South Side Passenger Ry. Co., 1st mort., 5 per cent. | 10,000 |
| Total | $3,119,500 |

Trustee of general mortgage, Fidelity Insurance Trust & Safe Deposit Co., Philadelphia.

EARNINGS.—Year ending June 30.

| | Gross. | Net. | Charges. | Dividend. | Surplus. |
|---|---|---|---|---|---|
| 1898–99 | $483,252 | $242,570 | $198,434 | $60,000 | Def., $16,864 |
| 1899–00 | 632,455 | 398,029 | 246,836 | 90,000 | 61,193 |
| 1900–01 | 661,917 | 404,850 | 267,328 | 90,000 | 47,522 |

President, W. L. Mellon; Secretary and Treasurer, W. H. Rogers.
Main office, 512 Smithfield street, Pittsburg. Annual meeting, second Tuesday in August.

## PITTSBURG BREWING CO.

A corporation formed under the laws of Pennsylvania in 1899. The company acquired the plants and business of the following breweries:

Iron City Brewing Co.
Wainwright Brewing Co.
Eberhardt & Ober.
Keystone Brewing Co.
M. Winter & Bro.
Phœnix Brewing Co.
Straub Brewing Co.
Ober Bros.
Baeuerlein Brewery.
Hauch Brewery.
McKeesport Brewery.
Mt. Pleasant Brewing Co.
Latrobe Brewing Co.
Connellsville Brewing Co.
Uniontown Brewing Co.
Jeannette Brewery.

The aggregate capacity of the above establishments is about 1,500,000 barrels of beer per annum.

Stock....Par $50....Authorized { com., $6,500,000; pref., 6,500,000 } Issued { com., $5,962,250; pref., 6,100,100 } $12,062,350

The preferred stock is 7 per cent., cumulative. There is held in the treasury of the company $399,900 preferred and $537,750 common stock.

Transfer Agent, Union Trust Co., Pittsburg. Registrar, Fidelity Title & Trust Co., Pittsburg.

The company pays dividends at the rate of 7 per cent. per annum on its preferred stock, in quarterly payments of 1¾ per cent. each, in February (20), May, August and November. On the common, 4 per cent. per annum was paid in quarterly payments, which are also in February (20), May, August and November, the quarterly rate being increased to 1¼ per cent. in November, 1902.

FUNDED DEBT.

1st mort., 6 per cent., due 1949, Jan. and July .................... $6,319,000

The 1st mortgage, Fidelity Title & Trust Co., Pittsburg, trustee, is for $6,500,000. Coupons are payable at the office of the trustee. The company holds in its treasury $181,000 of the bonds.

EARNINGS.—Year ending October 31.

| | Gross. | Net. | Charges and Dividends. | Surplus. |
|---|---|---|---|---|
| 1898–99 (9 mos.) | ........ | $1,084,422 | $603,046 | $481,376 |
| 1899–00 | $5,796,144 | 1,830,190 | 1,425,065 | 405,125 |
| 1900–01 | 6,088,692 | 1,617,678 | 1,044,635 | 573,043 |
| 1901–02 | 6,768,538 | 2,123,023 | 1,544,634 | 578,389 |

The charges include taxes and amount charged off for depreciation, which in 1900 was $250,000. The total surplus October 26, 1901, was $1,218,894.

President, Frederick W. Mueller; Vice-President, E. J. Frauenheim; Secretary, William Ruske; Treasurer, J. P. Ober, Pittsburg.

Directors—L. Vilsack, T. F. Straub, H. E. Wainwright, E. J. Frauenheim, Joseph A. O'Neill, Frederick W. Mueller, F. Gwinner, Marcus Aaron.

Main office, 434 Fifth avenue, Pittsburg.

## PITTSBURG COAL CO.

A corporation formed under the laws of New Jersey, September, 1899. The company acquired the mines and property of nearly all the large producers and shippers by rail of steam and gas coal in the Pittsburg district.

A list of the properties included in this company was given in the MANUAL for 1901.

Since its organization the company has purchased undeveloped coal lands adjoining various properties, making the total holdings over 150,000 acres, with 150 operated mines.

The company, from the general character of its business, is known as the "railroad coal combination." The properties acquired and taken over comprised over 80,000 acres of coal land and over 7,000 acres of surface land in Allegheny, Fayette, Washington and Westmoreland counties, Pa. It also has docks and loading plants on the lakes at Chicago, Cleveland, Duluth, Minn., West Superior, Wis., Sault Sainte Marie, Mich., Ashtabula, O., Fairport, O., and Thornburg, O. It also acquired about eleven miles of railroad at the mines, and Northwestern Coal Railway, Allouez Bay, Wis., to St. Louis River, thirteen miles. The company owns 4,500 railroad cars and 17 locomotives.

In January, 1902, the company purchased the New Pittsburg Coal Co. and the Greendale Coal Co., and leased the Shaw Coal Co.'s property for forty years. In 1902 purchased the Pittsburg & Castle Shannon Railroad and mines and acquired an interest in the Milwaukee Western Fuel Co. In January, 1903, the Midland Coal Co. was acquired, together with the National Dock & Fuel Co. of Cleveland and control of the Colonial Coal & Coke Co.

Stock..Par $100..Authorized { com., $32,000,000; pref., 32,000,000 } Issued { com., $32,000,000; pref., 29,710,200 } $61,710,200

The preferred stock is 7 per cent., cumulative.

The company began the payment of regular dividends on the preferred stock at the full rate of 7 per cent. per annum by the declaration of 1¾ per cent., quarterly, payable April 25, 1900, and has since paid same regularly in January (25), April, July and October.

Transfer Agent, Union Trust Co., Pittsburg. Registrar, Fidelity Title & Trust Co., Pittsburg.

The Northwestern Coal Railroad Co. has $794,000 5 per cent. bonds, due 1923, May and November, which are guaranteed by this company.

FUNDED DEBT.

Col. Trust bonds, 5 per cent., due Feb., 1903-08, quarterly, Feb.................... $6,000,000

The bonds were created in 1902, and are secured by stocks of auxiliary companies. They are to be retired in yearly payments of $1,000,000.

EARNINGS.

| | Gross Profits. | Net Profits. | Pref. Dividends. | Surplus. |
|---|---|---|---|---|
| 1900 (16 months ending Dec. 31)...... | $5,480,690 | $4,242,090 | $2,074,709 | $2,167,381 |
| 1901 ................................ | 4,272,209 | 3,099,538 | 2,078,865 | 1,020,673 |
| 1902 ................................ | 5,753,913 | 4,706,587 | 2,427,146 | 2,279,440 |

The deductions from the gross profits consisted in 1900 of $411,684 for depreciation of plants, and $826,915 for a fund to provide for the acquisition of new coal lands. In 1901 these items were $595,824 and $576,847, respectively.

The following is the company's balance sheet December 31, 1902:

| ASSETS. | | LIABILITIES. | |
|---|---|---|---|
| Cash.............................. | $1,325,978 | Preferred stock.................. | $29,701,200 |
| Accounts and bills receivable...... | 6,116,330 | Common stock.................... | 30,308,200 |
| Inventories of coal and other merchandise.................. | 1,933,576 | Undivided earnings (appropriated for additional working capital and dividends on pref. stock, etc.) | 5,467,495 |
| Capital stock of other companies.. | 105,646 | Reserve: | |
| Coal and surface acreage in Pittsburg and Hocking Valley Districts, mine plant and equipments, railways, docks on the lakes, etc...................... | 77,138,406 | Coal royalty fund............ | 2,054,422 |
| | | Depreciation reserve......... | 1,400,051 |
| | | Pittsburg Coal Co. bonds, issue of February 1st, 1902, 5 per cent.. | 6,000,000 |
| | | Bonds of subsidiary corporations.. | 1,565,223 |
| | | Mortgages...................... | 2,237,901 |
| | | Accounts and bills payable....... | 7,885,444 |
| Total.................... | $86,619,936 | Total..................... | $86,619,936 |

Chairman and President, Francis L. Robbins; Vice-President and Treasurer, John D. Nicholson; Secretary, Francis J. Le Moyne.

Directors—Francis L. Robbins, Alexander M. Neeper, Henry C. rick, John A. Bell, Andrew W. Mellon, Henry W. Oliver, John D. Nicholson, Pittsburg; Daniel R. Hanna, William P. Murray, Peter M. Hitchcock, Cleveland; Matthew H. Taylor, Erie, Pa.; Grant B. Schley, New York; John I. Bishop, Philadelphia; C. E. Wales, Minneapolis; L. R. Doty, Chicago.

Main office, 232 Fifth avenue, Pittsburg. Annual meeting, February 11, at Jersey City.

## THE PITTSBURG DRY GOODS CO.

A corporation formed under the laws of Pennsylvania, May 18, 1896. The business of the company is wholesale merchandising and manufacturing.

Stock....Par $100....Authorized { com., $300,000 / pref., 300,000 } Issued { com., $300,000 / pref., 300,000 } $600,000

The preferred stock is 7 per cent., cumulative. The company has no funded debt. Registrar, Fidelity Title & Trust Co., Pittsburg.

On January 1, 1902, the surplus was $260,000, and the undivided profits, $14,000.

The company has paid dividends from the time of its organization. On the preferred stock the full amount of 7 per cent. per annum is paid in semi-annual dividends of 3½ per cent. each, February (1) and August. In 1900 and 1902 the company paid 10 per cent. on its common stock, and in 1901, 9 per cent.

President, Finley H. Lloyd; Vice-President, W. H. Neely; Secretary and Treasurer, William A. Given, Pittsburg; Assistant Treasurer, George H. Fugh.

Directors—J. B. Shea, Allegheny, Pa.; Finley H. Lloyd, Shields Station, Pa.; William A. Given, W. H. Neely, Pittsburg; F. W. Dazell, Bellevue, Pa.

Main office, 933 Penn avenue, Pittsburg; branch office, 42 Leonard street, New York. Annual meeting, third Thursday in January.

## PITTSBURG, M'KEESPORT & CONNELLSVILLE RAILWAY CO.

A corporation formed under the laws of Pennsylvania, December 31, 1900. The company is a consolidation of the following companies:

Connellsville & Uniontown Railway Co.
McKeesport, Wilmerding & Duquesne Railway Co.
McKeesport & Youghiogheny Street Railway Co.

The company owns and operates 55 miles of electric trolley railway in Duquesne, McKeesport, Wilmerding, Connellsville, Uniontown, Scottdale and the neighboring towns near Pittsburg. About 35 additional miles of track are under construction. The company owns and operates its own coal mines adjoining its power-house. It was reported in 1902 that a further consolidation of this and other local companies under the title of the West Pennsylvania Railway & Lighting Co. was in contemplation.

Stock......Par $50..........................Authorized, $3,500,000......Issued, $3,000,000

The company has no preferred stock.

FUNDED DEBT.

1st con. mort., 5 per cent. gold, due Jan., 1931, Jan. and July.................. .... $3,000,000

The authorized amount of the 1st mortgage is $3,500,000, of which $500,000 are reserved for improvements and $231,500 are reserved to retire prior liens. Trustee of the mortgage and agent for the payment of interest, Mercantile Trust Co., Pittsburg.

President, William H. Graham; Secretary, M. K. Salsbury; Treasurer, George I. Whitney.

Directors—Edmund C. Converse, New York; W. H. Graham, M. K. Salsbury, W. S. Kuhn, C. A. Painter, George I. Whitney, J. S. Kuhn, George J. Gorman, Wilson A. Shaw, J. B. Van Wagener, Pittsburg.

Main office, 345 Fourth avenue, Pittsburg.

## PITTSBURGH PLATE GLASS CO.

A corporation organized under the laws of Pennsylvania in 1882. The company owns and operates ten plate glass manufactories, located as follows:

Factory No. 1, Creighton, Pa.
Factory No. 2, Tarentum, Pa.
Factories Nos. 3, 4 and 5, Ford City, Pa.
Factory No. 6, Charleroi, Pa.
Factory No. 7, Elwood, Ind.
Factory No. 8, Kokomo, Ind.
Factory No. 9, Crystal City, Mo.
Factory No. 10, Walton, Pa.

It distributes its product through its own warehouses, located in the following cities:

| | | | | | |
|---|---|---|---|---|---|
| New York | Cleveland | Detroit | St. Louis | St. Paul | Atlanta |
| Boston | Philadelphia | Buffalo | Davenport, Ia. | Milwaukee | Kansas City |
| Minneapolis | Cincinnati | Chicago | Omaha | Brooklyn | |

These establishments are also jobbers of window and art glass, paints, oils and painters' supplies, and are manufacturers of mirrors.

Stock..Par $100...Authorized { com., $12,350,000; pref., 150,000 } Issued { com., $12,350,000; pref., 150,000 } $12,500,000

The preferred stock is 12 per cent., non-cumulative. The dividends on the preferred are payable annually in April.

Stock is transferred at the company's office. Registrar, Union Trust Co., Pittsburg.

Dividends on the common stock are paid quarterly, December 31, April 1, July 1, October 1. In 1899 4 per cent. was paid on the common, and in 1900 and 1901 6 per cent.

The capital of this company was originally $2,750,000. In 1895 the stock was increased to $10,000,000 and $2,500,000 of debenture bonds were issued. The purpose of the latter and of the increase of $7,250,000 in the stock was the acquisition by purchase of the plants of the Diamond Plate Glass Co., Crystal City Plate Glass Co., Charleroi Plate Glass Co. and Duquesne Plate Glass Co. In 1901 an increase of $2,500,000 was made in the preferred for extensions and improvements.

The debenture bonds have been paid off, but there is no funded debt.

EARNINGS.

| | Profits. | Div. Pref. | Div. Com. | Surplus. |
|---|---|---|---|---|
| 1899 | $1,838,806 | $18,000 | $492,492 | $1,328,314 |
| 1900 | 2,026,607 | 18,000 | 591,000 | 1,417,607 |
| 1901 | 1,503,038 | 18,000 | 591,000 | 894,638 |
| 1902 | 1,251,346 | 18,000 | 721,948 | 511,398 |

The following is the company's balance sheet December 31, 1902:

| ASSETS. | | LIABILITIES. | |
|---|---|---|---|
| Investments | $13,602,832 | Capital stock { preferred | $150,000 |
| Stocks, plate and window glass, paints, etc. | 2,924,848 | Capital stock { common | 12,342,600 |
| Material and working accounts | 775,535 | Bills and accounts payable | 2,261,451 |
| Cash, bills and accounts receivable, being quick assets | 4,092,439 | Surplus January 1, 1902 | 6,130,205 |
| | | Passed to surplus | 511,398 |
| Total | $21,395,654 | Total | $21,395,654 |

Chairman and President, John Pitcairn, Philadelphia; Vice-President and Comptroller, Artemas Pitcairn, Pittsburg; Chairman of Commercial Department and General Eastern Agent, W. W. Heroy, New York; General Sales Agent, W. L. Clause; Secretary, Charles W. Brown; Treasurer, Edward Pitcairn; Chief Engineer and Purchasing Agent, W. D. Hartupee, Pittsburg; General Freight Agent, J. M. Belleville.

Directors—John Pitcairn, Philadelphia; W. W. Heroy, New York; Artemas Pitcairn, W. L. Clause, W. D. Hartupee, Charles W. Brown, E. A. Hitchcock, Pittsburg.

Main office, Fifth avenue and Grant street, Pittsburg. Annual meeting, second Tuesday in February.

---

## PITTSBURG RAILWAYS CO.

(Controlled by Philadelphia Company.)

A corporation formed in 1900 under the title of the Southern Traction Co. to take over and extend the system of the West End Traction Co. The latter was formed in 1898, and was a consolidation of the Pittsburg & West End Passenger Railway Co. with other lines. On December 30, 1901, the name was changed to the present style. All of the stock was acquired by the Philadelphia Company in 1901.

The company owns the entire stock of the West End Traction Co., and the stocks of the Virginia Avenue Street Railway, McKees Rocks & Ingraham Street Railway Co., and McKees Rocks & Neville Island Street Railway Co., Crofton & Chartiers Valley Traction Co., and Pittsburg, Banksville & t. Lebanon Street Railway Co.

On January 1, 1902, this company took over and has since operated the properties owned by or leased to the Consolidated Traction Co. and the United Traction Co. of Pittsburg.

Stock....Par $100....Authorized { com., $2,500,000; pref., 2,500,000 } Issued { com., $2,500,000; pref., 2,500,000 } $5,000,000

The preferred stock is 5 per cent., cumulative.

FUNDED DEBT.

| | |
|---|---|
| Southern Traction 1st collateral mort., 5 per cent., due Oct., 1950, April and Oct... | $3,100,000 |
| West End Traction con. mort., 5 per cent., due Jan., 1938, Jan. and July........... | 725,000 |
| Pittsburg & West End Ry. 1st mort., 5 per cent., due July, 1922, Jan. and July...... | 500,000 |
| Pittsburg, Crofton & Mansfield 1st mort., 5 per cent., due July, 1924, Jan. and July.. | 250,000 |
| Total.......... | $4,575,000 |

The Southern Traction Co.'s 1st collateral mortgage is for $900,000. The $900,000 of bonds unissued can be used for betterments and extensions. Trustee and agent for the payment of interest, Union Trust Co., Pittsburg.

The West End Traction consolidated mortgage is for $1,500,000, of which $750,000 are reserved to retire underlying bonds. Trustee and agent for the payment of interest, Union Trust Co., Pittsburg.

President, James D. Callery; Vice-President, J. H. Reed; 2d Vice-President, S. L. Tone; Secretary, Winfield B. Carson; Treasurer, C. J. Braun, Jr.; Auditor, C. S. Mitchell.

Directors—James D. Callery, J. H. Reed, Joshua Rhodes, A. W. Mellon, T. H. Given, Peter A. B. Widener, M. K. McMullin.

Main office, 435 Sixth avenue, Pittsburg.

## PITTSBURG STOVE & RANGE CO.

A corporation formed under the laws of Pennsylvania, August 31, 1899. The company acquired the property and plants of the following manufacturers of stoves, with an annual productive capacity of 80,000 stoves and ranges:

De Haven & Co., Pittsburg.
Walters Stove Co., Sharpsburg, Pa.
Bissel & Co., Pittsburg.
Baldwin & Graham, New Castle, Pa.
Anschutz-Bradberry Co., Allegheny, Pa.
Crea, Graham & Co., Allegheny, Pa.
A. Bradley, Pittsburg.
F. L. Voegtley & Co., Allegheny, Pa.
The Graff Co., Monongahela City, Pa.

Stock...Par $50....Authorized { com., $1,000,000; pref., 1,000,000 } Issued { com., $1,000,000; pref., 1,000,000 } $2,000,000

The preferred stock is 7 per cent., cumulative. The company has no bonded debt.

Transfer Agent, Union Trust Co., Pittsburg. Registrar, Fidelity Title & Trust Co., Pittsburg.

Dividends on the preferred stock were commenced by the payment of 1¾ per cent., quarterly, December 28, 1899.

President, John D. Nicholson; Vice-President, George W. J. Bissell; Secretary and Treasurer, John S. Graham.

Directors—John D. Nicholson, George W. J. Bissell, James F. Mackee, W. S. Huntley, Charles H. Bradley, A. M. Neeper, Pittsburg; John S. Graham, Sewickley, Pa.

Main office, Robinson and Darrah streets, Allegheny, Pa. Annual meeting, first Monday in September.

## PITTSBURG VALVE, FOUNDRY & CONSTRUCTION CO.

A corporation formed under the laws of Pennsylvania, October 31, 1900. The company acquired and operates the establishments of Atwood & McCaffrey, the Shook-Anderson Manufacturing Co., the Pittsburg Valve & Machine Co., Limited, the pipe-fitting department of Wilson-Snyder Manufacturing Co., and the foundry of A. Speer & Sons. The business of these concerns is that of pipe, valve and steam fitting and pipe manipulation for high steam pressure.

Stock......Par $100..........................Authorized, $1,150,000......Issued, $1,150,000

The stock is full paid and non-assessable. The entire amount issued was taken by the companies and firms included in this company, and none was offered for sale. Transfer agent, Union Trust Co., Pittsburg. Registrar, Fidelity Title & Trust Co., Pittsburg.

Chairman, Henry M. Atwood; President, J. T. Speer; Vice-President, Moses Atwood; Secretary, S. G. Patterson; Treasurer, C. A. Anderson.

Directors—Henry M. Atwood, J. T. Speer, C. A. Anderson, R. J. Wilson, John McCaffrey, C. R. Rhodes.

Main office, Duquesne Way and Fifth street, Pittsburg. Annual meeting, fourth Monday in February.

## THE PITTSBURG, WHEELING & LAKE ERIE COAL CO.

A corporation formed under the laws of Ohio, June 22, 1901. The purpose of the company is to mine coal. The company owns 600 acres of coal lands in Jefferson County, Ohio, equipped with electric mining and other machinery. These lands are leased to an operating company, the lease extending to July 1, 1911.

Stock.....Par $100....Authorized { com., $500,000 / pref., 750,000 } Issued { com., $500,000 / pref., 750,000 } $1,250,000

The preferred stock is 4 per cent., non-cumulative. Stock is transferred at the office of the company, Cleveland. Registrar, Mercantile Trust Co., New York.

FUNDED DEBT.

| | |
|---|---|
| 1st mort., 4 per cent., due July, 1921, Jan. and July | $634,500 |
| Prior lien mort., 5 per cent., due July, 1911, Jan. and July | 200,000 |
| Total | $834,500 |

The bonds outstanding are the total amount authorized. Trustee of the 1st mortgage and prior lien mortgage and agent for the payment of interest, Mercantile Trust Co., New York.

President, C. C. Owens; Vice-President, R. F. Denison; Secretary, W. B. Whiting, Cleveland; Treasurer, W. A. Hamilton, New York.

Directors—C. C. Owens, R. F. Denison, W. B. Whiting, G. F. Goss, C. E. Sanders, Cleveland.

Main office, 154 Prospect street, Cleveland. Annual meeting, second Tuesday in July, at Cleveland.

## PLANTERS' COMPRESS CO.

A corporation formed under the laws of Maine, May 24, 1902. The company is a successor to a company of the same name formed in 1897 under the laws of West Virginia and of the Indo-Egyptian Compress Co., the property of both these corporations having been purchased by this company. See below for details of plan. It owns the Lowry patents for compressing cotton, hay, wool, hemp, jute and other commodities into cylindrical bales. The company also owns about 60 ginning plants. The Canadian Baling Co. is controlled.

Stock...Par $100...Authorized { com., $6,750,000 / pref., 3,250,000 } Issued { com., $6,750,000 / pref., 3,250,000 } $10,000,000

The preferred stock is 7 per cent. non-cumulative.

All the common stock is held in a voting trust. Voting Trustees—T. Jefferson Coolidge, Jr., Henry E. Howland, Stephen M. Weld, Walter Hunnewell, Otto T. Bannard.

Transfer Agent, Old Colony Trust Co., Boston. Registrar for the common stock, American Loan & Trust Co., Boston; for the preferred stock, City Trust Co., Boston.

The stock of the old company was $5,000,000, par $100, all common, and was in the hands of trustees who issued trust certificates, par $50, for the same, giving two shares of such certificates for one old share. The stock of the Indo-Egyptian Compress Co. was $12,500,000, par $100. The terms of the exchange of the old securities for new and the assessments were as follows:

| | Paid. | Received. New Pref. | New Com. |
|---|---|---|---|
| Planters' Compress trust certificates, par $50 | $10 | $10 | $25 |
| " " contracts, par $100 | 20 | 20 | 50 |
| Indo-Egyptian Compress Co., par $100 | 2.50 | 2.50 | 6.25 |

In the reorganization plan $968,750 new common and $937,500 new preferred stock was reserved for the acquisition of additional property. The new company began business with a cash working capital of $2,000,000, but $476,700 of the new preferred and $266,000 of the common voting trust certificates were not required for that purpose, and their amounts are now owned by the company.

In May, 1900, the holders of trust shares of the old company were given the right to subscribe for capital stock of the Indo-Egyptian Compress Co., at the rate of $20 per share, in the proportion of one share of the latter company's stock for every five trust shares of the Planters' Compress Co.

Chairman, Stephen M. Weld; President, Arthur R. Marsh; Vice-President, T. Jefferson Coolidge, Jr.; 2d Vice-President, G. T. Francis; Secretary, Frederic S. Goodwin; Treasurer, F. M. Wakefield.

Directors—Arthur R. Marsh, Stephen M. Weld, T. Jefferson Coolidge, Jr., Charles F. Ayer, Albert C. Burrage, Samuel Carr, Stewart H. Chisholm, Amos T. French, Francis R. Hart, Charles Hayden, Walter Hunnewell, James F. O'Shaughnessy, Felix Rackemann, Frank M. Wakefield, Boston; Edward D. Toland, Philadelphia.

Main office, 131 State street, Boston; New York office, Thirty-third street and Twelfth avenue. Annual meeting, third Tuesday in July.

## PLEASANT VALLEY COAL CO.

A corporation formed under the laws of Utah, September 6, 1882. The company owns and operates coal mines at Castle Gate, Winter Quarters and Clear Creek, Utah, with buildings and operating plants, and also has yards at Ogden and Salt Lake, Utah. It owns 15,320 acres of land. The estimated amount of coal contained in its property is 150,000,000 tons. The stock of this company is all owned by the Utah Fuel Co.

Stock......Par $100..........................Authorized, $2,000,000......Issued, $2,000,000

Transfer Agent, Jesse White, 195 Broadway, N. Y.

FUNDED DEBT.

1st mort., 30 years, sinking fund, 5 per cent., gold bonds, due 1928, Jan. and July... $1,174,000

The first mortgage 5 per cent. bonds were issued in 1898, Morton Trust Co., New York, trustee, and are $1,250,000 authorized. The bonds are secured by a 1st mortgage on all the property of the company. There is a sinking fund of 2 cents for each ton of coal mined with which bonds may be redeemed at not over 115. The company can also call and pay the bonds at any interest period at 115 on 90 days' notice.

EARNINGS.

Year ending June 30.

| | Gross. | Net. | Charges. | Surplus. |
|---|---|---|---|---|
| 1900 | $1,082,198 | $207,027 | $75,091 | $131,936 |
| 1901 | 1,235,701 | 240,010 | 97,219 | 142,791 |
| 1902 | 1,517,157 | 305,888 | 111,104 | 194,784 |

President, George W. Kramer, Denver, Col.; Vice-President, Edward T. Jeffery, New York; Secretary and Treasurer, E. A. Greenwood, Salt Lake City, Utah.

Directors—Edward T. Jeffery, George W. Kramer, H. G. Williams, J. F. Evans, E. A. Greenwood.

Main office, Salt Lake City, Utah; New York office, 195 Broadway.

## PNEUMATIC GUN CARRIAGE & POWER CO.

A corporation formed under the laws of West Virginia. The company owns the patent rights covering a system for moving heavy ordnance, battleship turrets, etc., by pneumatic power.

Stock......Par $10..........................Authorized, $1,000,000......Issued, $1,000,000

President, C. Eaton Creecy; Vice-President and Treasurer, Eppa Hutton; Secretary, Charles S. McNeir, Washington.

Main office, Fifteenth and F streets, N. W., Washington.

## PNEUMATIC SIGNAL CO.

A corporation formed under the laws of New York, February 7, 1902, to manufacture and install signal devices for railways. The company is a consolidation of the following companies:

Pneumatic Railway Signal Co.
International Pneumatic Railway Signal Co.
Standard Railroad Signal Co.

The company owns plants at Green Island, Troy, N. Y.; Memands, N. Y., and Rochester, N. Y.

Stock......Par $100..........................Authorized, $3,000,000......Issued, $2,727,600

The company has no preferred stock. Stock is transferred at the office of the company, Rochester, N. Y. Registrar, New York Security & Trust Co., New York.

The company paid its first dividend of 3 per cent. July 1, 1902, and a second dividend of 3 per cent. January 1, 1903. Dividends are payable semi-annually.

FUNDED DEBT.

1st mort., 6 per cent., March and Sept............................................. $400,000

The outstanding bonds are the full amount authorized. Commencing March 1, 1905, $20,000 of the bonds will be drawn and retired each year. Trustee of the mortgage and agent for the payment of interest, Rochester Trust & Safe Deposit Co., Rochester, N. Y.

At the close of the first six months of its first fiscal year, November 1, 1902, the company had a surplus of assets above liabilities of $208,164 and a net profit of $121,584.

President, John N. Beckley; 1st Vice-President, Frederick Cook, Rochester, N. Y.; 2d Vice-President and General Manager, Charles Hansel, New York; Secretary, Thomas A. Smyth; Treasurer, George W. Archer, Rochester, N. Y.; Assistant Treasurer, J. R. Coleman, Troy, N. Y.

Directors—John N. Beckley, George W. Archer, George Weldon, T. A. Smyth, Frederick Cook, A. H. Harris, B. E. Chase, E. M. Upton, J. H. McCartney, George C. Buell, C. H. Palmer, Rochester, N. Y.; William L. Bull, New York.

Corporate and main office, 27 Clinton avenue, South, Rochester, N. Y.; New York office, 25 Broad street; Chicago office, Monadnock Block. Annual meeting, second Tuesday in February, at Rochester, N. Y.

## POCAHONTAS COAL & COKE CO.

A corporation formed under the laws of New Jersey, October 11, 1901. The purpose of the company is to purchase, lease or otherwise acquire coal lands and rights in the Pocahontas coal field of Virginia and West Virgina. The company has acquired about 350,000 acres of such coal lands. One of the principal properties acquired was the Flat Top Coal Land Association. See statement of that organization in the MANUAL for 1901. The syndicate which organized this company paid $170 per share for the $3,714,000 common and $100 per share for the $3,714,000 preferred stock of the Flat Top Coal Land Association.

The Norfolk & Western Railway in December, 1901, acquired the stock of this company. Leases of about 50,000 acres of the coal lands owned by this company have been made to constituent companies of the United States Steel Corporation.

Stock......Par $100..........................Authorized, $1,000,000......Issued, $1,000,000

All of the stock is owned by the Norfolk & Western Railway Co.

FUNDED DEBT.

Norf. & West-Pocahontas joint pur. mon. mort., 4 p. c., due Dec., 1941, June and Dec. $20,000,000

The purchase money 4 per cent. bonds are the joint obligation of the Norfolk & Western Railway Co. and the Pocahontas Coal & Coke Co. The Trustee of the mortgage is the Girard Trust Co., Philadelphia; Agent for the payment of interest and for the registration of bonds, Mercantile Trust Co., New York.

The bonds are secured by all the lands and other property of the company. After December 2, 1906, the bonds are subject to call at 105. There is a provision for a sinking fund, which is to receive 2½ cents on each ton of coal mined from the properties of the company.

President, F. J. Kimball, New York; Secretary, O. Lynn Bottomley; Treasurer, Martin J. Caples, Philadelphia.

Corporate office, 51 Newark street, Hoboken, N. J.; main office, Bramwell, W. Va.; Philadelphia office, Arcade Building. Annual meeting, third Thursday in February, at Hoboken.

## POCASSET MANUFACTURING CO.

A corporation formed under the laws of Massachusetts in 1822, for the purpose of manufacturing print cloths, shirtings and sheetings. The company owns and operates four mills at Fall River, Mass., with a capacity of 77,076 spindles and 1,951 looms.

Stock......Par $100..............................Authorized, $600,000......Issued, $600,000

The company has no preferred stock and no funded debt.

Dividends are payable quarterly, March, June, September and December, at the rate of 6 per cent. per annum.

President, Thomas E. Brayton; Treasurer, W. Frank Shove, Fall River, Mass.

Directors—Edward L. Anthony, Thomas E. Brayton, B. D. Davol, W. Frank Shove, Fall River, Mass.; Joseph F. Knowles, Thomas R. Rodman, Thomas S. Hathaway, New Bedford, Mass.; B. R. Weld, Samuel W. Rodman, Boston.

Main office, Pocasset street, Fall River, Mass. Annual meeting, last Thursday in February, at Fall River, Mass.

## PORTLAND GOLD MINING CO.

A corporation formed under the laws of Iowa. The company owns the Portland mine and other claims and mines on Battle Mountain, Cripple Creek, Colo., the whole property comprising about 200 acres of the most valuable territory in that district. The mine is fully equipped, and the company since its institution has done more than 23 miles of development work.

Stock......Par $1..........................Authorized, $3,000,000......Issued, $3,000,000

The stock outstanding is the amount authorized. The stock is full-paid and non-assessable.

In the year 1899 the company produced gold and silver of a total value of $1,951,219. The total receipts were $1,960,487; expenses, $1,101,471; net profits, $870,907. In 1901 receipts,

$2,439,067; net profits, $719,902. In 1902, receipts, $2,347,216; expenses, $1,875,297; net profits, $471,919.

In 1901 the company paid $720,000 in dividends on its stock. Up to the beginning of 1902 the company had paid in dividends a total of about $4,027,080.

President, James F. Burns; Vice-President, Irving Howbert; Secretary and Treasurer, Frank G. Peck; Assistant Secretary, Charles V. Turner, Colorado Springs, Col.

Directors—James F. Burns, Irving Howbert, Frank G. Peck, R. C. Shannon, Thomas F. Burns.

Main office, Colorado Springs, Col.; corporate office, Council Bluffs, Ia.

## POSTUM CEREAL CO., LIMITED

A corporation formed under the laws of Michigan, October 22, 1896, to manufacture Postum cereal and health foods. The company has a plant at Battle Creek, Mich., consisting of sixteen buildings.

Stock.....Par $10.....Authorized { com., $4,000,000 / pref., 1,000,000 } Issued { com., $4,000,000 / pref., 1,000,000 } $5,000,000

The preferred stock is 4 per cent., cumulative. The company has no funded debt.

Dividends have been paid at the annual rate of 20 per cent. on the common stock and 4 per cent. on the preferred.

Chairman, C. W. Post; Vice-Chairman and Secretary, Carroll L. Post; Treasurer, M. W. Howe, Battle Creek, Mich.

Directors—C. W. Post, Carroll L. Post, Ella L. Post, M. W. Howe, Battle Creek, Mich.

Corporate and main office, Battle Creek, Mich.; branch offices, New York, Boston, Chicago, San Francisco, London, England. Annual meeting, first Monday in October, at Battle Creek, Mich.

## POTSDAM GOLD MINING CO.

A corporation formed under the laws of South Dakota. The company owns 550 acres of mineral bearing land in the Ragged Top district of South Dakota.

Stock......Par $1.......... ..................Authorized, $2,500,000......Issued, $1,500,000

The company has no preferred stock and no funded debt.

President, William Lardner, Deadwood, S. D.; Vice-President, John Gray, Terraville, S. D.; Secretary, William L. McLaughlin; Treasurer, A. J. Malterner; Assistant Secretary, Robert N. Ogden, Deadwood, S. D.

Corporate and main office, Deadwood, S. D. Annual meeting in October, at Deadwood, S. D.

## POTTSVILLE UNION TRACTION CO.

A corporation formed under the laws of Pennsylvania, May 15, 1899, with a perpetual charter. By control of stocks and leaseholds the company operates the following companies:

Schuylkill Electric Railway Co.
Pottsville & Reading Railway Co.
Tamaqua & Pottsville Electric Railroad.
Coal Castle Electric Railway.
Schuylkill Haven & Orwigsburg Street Railway.
Port Carbon & Middleport Electric Railway.
People's Railway Co.

These companies have the only electric railway lines in Pottsville, Schuylkill Haven, Yorkville, Port Carbon, New Philadelphia, Middleport, Pa., and intermediate territory. They operate 45 miles of track.

Stock......Par $50...........................Authorized, $1,250,000......Issued, $1,250,000

The company has no preferred stock. Stock is transferred at the office of the company. Registrar, Real Estate & Trust Co., Philadelphia.

FUNDED DEBT.

1st mort., 5 per cent., gold, due Sept., 1929, March and Sept........................ $1,117,000

The authorized issue of the 1st mortgage bonds is $1,250,000. Of the bonds outstanding $416,000 were deposited to retire outstanding bonds of the leased companies. The $133,000 bonds unissued are reserved for acquiring additional mileage and equipment.

EARNINGS.

| | Gross. | Net. | Charges. | Surplus. |
|---|---|---|---|---|
| 1901 | $173,210 | $79,443 | $74,024 | $5,419 |

President, Clarence P. King; Vice-President, Thomas B. Prosser; Secretary, William C Pollock, Jr.; Treasurer, Joseph B. Hoellman; Superintendent, D. J. Duncan.

Directors—Roland C. Luther, William F. North, Thomas B. Prosser, Frederick H. Treat, William C. Pollock, Jr., Sheldon P. Ritter, C. Berkeley Taylor, Henry H. Pearson, Jr., Marshal S. Collingwood.

Main office, Pottsville, Pa.; President's office, Chestnut and Broad streets, Philadelphia. Annual meeting, second Monday in January, at Pottsville, Pa.

## PRATT & WHITNEY CO.

A corporation formed under the laws of New Jersey, November 12, 1900, succeeding the company of the same name, which was a Connecticut corporation owning and operating the large manufactory at Hartford, Conn., established by the firm of Pratt & Whitney. The company makes machinery and machinists' tools in great variety and has many specialties. The new company was organized to take over the old under an arrangement by which control of the concern was acquired by the Niles-Bement-Pond Co. See statement of the last-named company.

Stock...Par $100...Authorized { com., $1,525,000; pref., 1,225,000 } Issued { com., $1,525,000; pref., 1,225,000 } $2,750,000

The dividends of 6 per cent. on the preferred stock are guaranteed by the Niles-Bement-Pond Co., which owns all the common stock, but the guarantee takes effect only after the full dividends on the preferred stock of the Niles-Bement-Pond Co. have been paid. The preferred dividends are paid quarterly.

Transfer Agent, Corporation Trust Co., Jersey City. Registrars, Cuyler, Morgan & Co., New York.

President, R. C. McKinney; Vice-President, Walter L. Clark; Treasurer, C. L. Cornell; Secretary, F. C. Pratt.

Directors—Amos Whitney, R. C. McKinney, Walter L. Clark, T. T. Gaff, C. L. Cornell, F. W. Gordon, James K. Cullen, F. G. Echols, C. C. Cuyler.

Main office, 136 Liberty street, New York. Annual meeting, first Wednesday after first Monday in February.

## PRESSED STEEL CAR CO.

A corporation formed under the laws of New Jersey, January 12, 1899. The objects of the company are the manufacture of railway cars, including passenger, freight and street cars, pressed steel trucks, bolsters, frames, pressed steel equipments, appliances and specialties for railroad cars, and all the products of steel, iron and other metals or wood; to produce, invest and trade in products and merchandise of any description, and to acquire, hold, mortgage or sell real estate. The company was organized to consolidate the Schoen Pressed Steel Co., of Pittsburg and the Fox Pressed Steel Equipment Co., of Pittsburg and Joliet, Ill. These companies combined controlled the manufacture, use and sale of pressed steel freight cars, steel trucks, truck frames and pressed steel specialties for cars. The company has three large plants in operation—at Pittsburg, Allegheny, McKees Rocks, Pa., and Joliet, Ill., respectively. All the plants are equipped with new machinery, covered to a large extent by patents and designs for the particular work of the company.

Stock..Par $100..Authorized { com., $12,500,000; pref., 12,500,000 } Issued { com., $12,500,000; pref., 12,500,000 } $25,000,000

The preferred stock is 7 per cent., non-cumulative. The preferred stock has a priority as to assets in case of a dissolution.

Transfer Agent, Guaranty Trust Co., New York. Registrar, Central Trust Co., New York.

The company began to pay regular quarterly dividends of 1¾ per cent. on the preferred stock in May, 1899, and has since paid the same regularly in February, May, August and November. The company declared 6 per cent. on its common stock out of the surplus earnings of 1899, this dividend being payable 1½ per cent. each in February (25), May, August and November, 1900. In 1901, the quarterly dividends on the common were reduced to 1 per cent., or 4 per cent. for the year. In 1902 4 per cent. was again paid on the common, but in January, 1903, the directors declared an extra dividend of 1 per cent. on the common out of the profits of 1902 to be paid in four quarterly instalments in addition to the regular 1 per cent. quarterly dividends. This put the common on a 5 per cent. dividend basis.

FUNDED DEBT.

| | |
|---|---|
| 1st mort., 5 per cent. gold notes, due 1902 to 1911, Feb. and Aug. | $3,500,000 |
| McKees Rock purchase money mort., 4 per cent., due 1904 | 235,000 |
| Allegheny Works purchase money morts., 4 per cent., due 1912 | 75,000 |
| Total | $3,810,000 |

The 5 per cent. 1st mortgage gold notes, total amount, $5,000,000, Morton Trust Co., New York, trustee, were created in February, 1901, to provide working capital to meet the growth of the business. Of the notes, $500,000 mature on February 1 of each year, from 1902 to 1911. The notes are secured by a first mortgage on the company's property, subject to a purchase-money mortgage of $235,000 on one of the plants. The notes are redeemable hy the company at any interest period on six weeks' notice.

EARNINGS.

| | Gross. | Net. | Pref. Div. | Surplus |
|---|---|---|---|---|
| 1899 | $13,965,000 | $2,237,000 | $875,000 | $1,362,000 |
| 1900 | 22,540,115 | 2,075,181 | 875,000 | 1,200,181 |
| 1901 | ........ | 1,927,925 | 875,000 | 1,052,925 |
| 1902 | ........ | 4,578,114 | 875,000 | 3,703,114 |

After providing $750,000 for 6 per cent. dividends on the common stock out of the earnings of 1899, there was a surplus of $612,000 added to the working capital. In 1901 $143,635 was charged to depreciation and the common dividends were $500,000, the surplus being $409,290. In 1902, depreciation, $300,000; common dividends, $500,000; surplus, $2,903,114.

The following is the company's balance sheet, December 31, 1902:

| ASSETS. | | LIABILITIES. | |
|---|---|---|---|
| Property and franchise | $25,915,603 | Common stock | $12,500,000 |
| Stocks owned | 1,394,030 | Preferred stock | 12,500,000 |
| Taxes and insurance not accrued | 262 | 1st mortgage gold notes | 4,104,000 |
| Accounts receivable | 1,831,085 | Purchase money mortgage | 310,000 |
| Materials on hand | 4,509,627 | Accounts payable | 3,067,134 |
| Cash | 3,728,569 | Accrued salary and wages | 257,384 |
| | | Accrued dividends, preferred | 218,750 |
| | | Accrued interest | 90,429 |
| | | Surplus | 4,331,479 |
| Total | $37,379,176 | Total | $37,379,176 |

President, Frank N. Hoffstot; Vice-President, J. W. Friend, Pittsburg; Secretary, Adrian H. Larkin, Jersey City; Treasurer, P. G. Jenks; Auditor, S. E. Moore, Pittsburg; Sales Managers, Eastern District, O. C. Gayley, New York; Central District, C. E. Postlethwaite, Pittsburg; Western District, J. H. Mitchell, Chicago; Purchasing Agent, E. E. Porgeus, Allegbeny, Pa.

Directors—J. W. Friend, Frank N. Hoffstot, Henry Phipps, G. E. Macklin, F. G. Ely, James H. Reed, T. H. Given, Pittsburg; Adrian H. Larkin, Jersey City; James A. Blair, New York.

Main office, 248 Fourth avenue, Pittsburg; New York office, 24 Broad street. Foreign Agent, Transportation Development Co., 20 Broad Street House, London. Annual meeting, third Wednesday in February.

## PRESTON COAL & IMPROVEMENT CO.

A corporation chartered in Pennsylvania, in 1864, as the Preston Improvement Co., the name being changed to the present title in 1884. The company owns and operates an anthracite coal property of 2,346 acres in Schuylkill County, Pa. The company is controlled by the Reading Company and the Philadelphia & Reading Coal & Iron Co. On June 30, 1900, it was indebted to the Reading Company for $380,225.

Stock......Par $50........ ....................Authorized, $3,000,000......Issued, $3,000,000

FUNDED DEBT.

Gen. mort., 4 per cent., due 1932, May and Nov.................. ................. $1,097,000

The general mortgage, trustee, Fidelity Insurance, Trust & Safe Deposit Co., Philadelphia, is $1,200,000 authorized. There is a sinking fund of 10 cents per ton on all coal mined from the company's property, the bonds to be purchased at not exceeding par and interest.

President, George F. Baer; Secretary, W. G. Brown; Treasurer, W. A. Church.

Directors—George F. Baer, Joseph S. Harris, E. F. Smith, James M. Landis, Thomas M. Richards, C. E. Henderson, W. A. Church, Philadelphia.

Main office, Reading Terminal, Twelfth and Market streets, Philadelphia. Annual meeting, second Monday in October.

## THE PROCTER & GAMBLE CO.

A corporation formed under the laws of New Jersey in 1890 to purchase and conduct the soap, candle and glycerine business of the firm of Procter & Gamble, Cincinnati.

Stock....Par $100.....Authorized { com., $6,000,000; pref., 2,250,000 } Issued { com., $5,250,000; pref., 2,250,000 } $7,500,000

The preferred stock is 8 per cent., cumulative. The common stock was originally $2,250,000. The company also had $2,000,000 6 per cent. 1st mortgage bonds, due 1940, redeemable after July, 1900, at 110. On January 1, 1901, the bonds were paid in full and the common stock increased $2,250,000, making the amount thereof $4,500,000. In May, 1902, the authorized common stock was increased to $6,000,000, and $750,000 of the new stock was allotted at $150 per share to the stockholders.

Transfer Agents, A. M. Kidder & Co., New York. Registrar, Union Trust Co., New York.

The company has paid 8 per cent. per annum on its preferred stock, the regular dividends being 2 per cent. quarterly, January, April, July and October. The dividends on common were changed from 12 per cent. annual to 6 per cent. semi-annual in January, 1896. In 1898, 1899 and 1900 paid 20 per cent. on the common, the dividends being quarterly, February (15), May, August and November. In 1901 and 1902 the dividends on the common were 12 per cent.

President, William A. Procter; Vice-President, James N. Gamble; Secretary, David B. Gamble; Assistant Secretary, Hastings L. French; Treasurer, J. Henry French; Assistant Treasurer, Herbert G. French; General Manager, William Cooper Procter.

Main office, corner Walnut and Third streets, Cincinnati; corporate office, 1 Exchange place, Jersey City. Annual meeting, second Wednesday in October.

## PROVIDENCE & DANIELSON RAILWAY CO.

A corporation formed under the laws of Rhode Island, April 28, 1898. The company owns and operates an electric railway from Providence, R. I., to East Killingly and Danielson, Conn. It owns 26 miles of track and operates over 7 miles of the Worcester & Connecticut Eastern Railway from East Killingly to Danielson. It owns 40 cars.

Stock......Par $100..............................Authorized, $800,000......Issued, $800,000

The company has no preferred stock. Stock is transferred at the office of the company, Providence. Registrar, Industrial Trust Co., Providence.

FUNDED DEBT.

1st mort., 5 per cent., gold, due May 1, 1931, May and Nov.. ........................$600,000

The outstanding bonds are the total amount authorized. Trustee of the mortgage and agent for the payment of interest, Industrial Trust Co., Providence.

President, James H. Morris, Philadelphia; Vice-President, D. F. Sherman; Secretary, Franklin A. Smith, Jr.; Treasurer, George W. Prentice, Providence.

Directors—James H. Morris, Julius Christensen, D. F. Sherman, James S. Kenyon, Edwin A. Smith, Franklin P. Owen, Franklin A. Smith, Jr., George W. Prentice, John W. Potter.

Corporate and main office, 10 Weybosset st., Providence. Annual meeting, third Wednesday in January, at Providence.

## PROVIDENCE GAS CO.

A corporation formed under the laws of Rhode Island in 1848. In 1877 the company absorbed the Citizens' Gas Co.

Stock......Par $50...........................Authorized, $3,000,000......Issued, $3,000,000

The company pays dividends of 8 per cent. per annum on its stock, the payments being 2 per cent. quarterly, January, April, July and October.

President, John W. Ellis; Vice-President, William Goddard; Secretary and Treasurer, William P. Nye.

Main office, 15 Market square, Providence.

## PROVIDENCE TELEPHONE CO.

A corporation formed under the laws of Rhode Island in 1880. The company operates under an exclusive license from the American Bell Telephone Co., its territory covering most of the State of Rhode Island and Attleboro and North Attleboro, Mass. The American Telephone & Telegraph Co. held in October, 1902, $480,000 of this company's stock.

Stock......Par $50...........................Authorized, $1,600,000......Issued, $1,600,000

In 1899 the stock of the company was increased from $1,000,000 to $1,200,000. In March, 1901, the amount was increased to $1,600,000, the additional stock being taken by the stockholders at par. The company has no funded debt.

The company pays 8 per cent. per annum on its stock, the dividends being 2 per cent. quarterly, in January, April, July and October.

President, Dexter B. Potter; Vice-President, Fenner H. Peckham; Secretary and Treasurer, Charles T. Howard; General Manager, Joseph F. Beck.

Directors—Henry G. Russell, James H. Chase, Rowland G. Hazard, H. F. Barrows, Fenner H. Peckham, Dexter B. Potter, Samuel P. Colt, Frederick P. Fish, W. G. Nightingale, Thomas Sherwin, Nelson W. Aldrich, Robert W. Taft, James M. Scott.

Main office, 110 Union street, Providence. Annual meeting, second Wednesday in February.

## PUEBLO & SUBURBAN TRACTION & LIGHTING CO.

A corporation formed under the laws of Colorado, November 20, 1902, as a consolidation of the following companies:

Pikes Peak Power Co. Pueblo Traction & Lighting Co.

The company owns all the street railway, electric lighting and electric power interests in Pueblo, Col., and vicinity, including a portion of the Cripple Creek District. Its railway franchises expire in 1940 and 1942 and its electric light franchise in 1904. It operates 30 miles of electric railway, owns a steam plant, a water-power plant and electric lighting systems in Pueblo and the Cripple Creek district.

Stock......Par $100..........................Authorized, $3,500,000......Issued, $3,500,000

The company has no preferred stock. Transfer Agent and Registrar, Pueblo Title & Trust Co., Pueblo, Col.

FUNDED DEBT.

| | |
|---|---|
| 1st mort., 5 per cent., gold, due Dec. 1, 1922, April and Oct. | $1,600,000 |
| Pueblo Trac. & Light. Co., 1st mort., 5 per cent., gold, due Jan. 1, 1921, Jan. and July. | 1,100,000 |
| Total | $2,700,000 |

The total amount of the authorized 1st mortgage of the Pueblo & Suburban Traction & Lighting Co. is $3,500,000. Of the bonds outstanding, $1,250,000 are for the redemption of the $1,100,000 bonds of the Pueblo Traction & Lighting Co. and $650,000 are reserved for future extensions. All the bonds may be called after December, 1909, at 104 and interest. A sinking fund to retire at least $50,000 of the bonds per annum commences in 1909. The bonds may be purchased for the sinking fund at not higher than 104, or may be called. All the bonds of the Pueblo Traction & Lighting Co.'s 1st mortgage may be called after January 1, 1906 at 104 and interest. A sinking fund of $10,000 annually commences in 1906.

In the fiscal year ending October 31, 1902, the gross earnings were $410,991; net, $213,690; interest, $135,000; surplus, $78,690.

President, M. D. Thatcher; Vice-President, Warren Woods; Treasurer, H. E. Woods; Secretary, F. M. Woods; General Manager, John F. Vail, Pueblo, Col.

Directors—M. D. Thatcher, John F. Vail, T. H. Devine, H. E. Woods, Pueblo, Col.; F. M. Woods, Warren Woods, Colorado Springs, Col.

Corporate and main office, Pueblo, Col.; branch offices, Victor and Colorado Springs, Col. Annual meeting, last Tuesday in November at Pueblo, Col.

## THE PULLMAN CO.

A corporation formed under the laws of Illinois, February 22, 1867, under the title of Pullman's Palace Car Co. Name changed to The Pullman Co. at a special meeting of the stockholders, December 5, 1899, the change taking effect on December 30, 1899.

In December, 1899, the company purchased the assets and property of the Wagner Palace Car Co., a voluntary association existing under the laws of New York, including its cars, equipments and contracts with various railway companies, and for the purpose of making payment therefor, this company increased its capital stock from $54,000,000 to $74,000,000, the additional 200,000 shares being issued and delivered to the Wagner Palace Car Co.

This company owns or controls 3,417 sleeping, parlor and tourist cars, and owns and operates extensive shops at Pullman, a part of Chicago, and repair shops in St. Louis, Ludlow, Ky., Wilmington, Del., and Denver, Col. The Wagner Co. had extensive works at Buffalo, N. Y., which this company has acquired. The total mileage of railroad covered by this company's operations is 169,830 miles.

Stock......Par $100..........................Authorized, $74,000,000....Issued, $74,000,000

The capital stock was originally $1,250,000, and has been increased at various times until in 1893 it became $36,000,000, all the increases up to that time being cash subscriptions at par by stockholders of record.

Transfer Agents, Farmers' Loan & Trust Co., New York; New England Trust Co., Boston, and company's secretary, Chicago.

The company for years paid dividends, quarterly, at the rate of 8 per cent. per annum, the last payment on that basis being 2 per cent. in November, 1898, on the old capital. In July, 1898, an extra cash dividend of 20 per cent. was declared, payable August 15, and in October,

1898, the capital stock of the company was increased $18,000,000 out of the surplus assets, making the capital stock $54,000,000, upon which a dividend was declared, payable February, 1899, at the rate of 6 per cent. per annum, and the May and August dividends in 1899 were on the same basis, being 1½ per cent. each quarter. In November, 1899, the quarterly dividend rate was, however, restored to 2 per cent., and subsequent dividends have been on that basis, or 8 per cent. per annum. Dividends are paid quarterly, February, May, August and November, about the 15th of each month.

The company paid off $820,000 8 per cent. debentures, which matured in August, 1892, and now has no bonded indebtedness.

EARNINGS.

| Year ending July 31. | Div. Paid. | Gross. | Surplus Applicable to Dividends, etc. |
|---|---|---|---|
| 1892-93 | 8 | $11,389,896 | $6,526,448 |
| 1893-94 | 8 | 9,595,067 | 5,200,417 |
| 1894-95 | 8 | 8,547,625 | 4,290,391 |
| 1895-96 | 8 | 9,244,383 | 4,527,409 |
| 1896-97 | 8 | 8,974,888 | 4,650,850 |
| 1897-98 | 8 | 10,674,868 | 5,273,883 |
| 1898-99 | 7 | 11,478,930 | 5,445,015 |
| 1899-00 | 7½ | 15,022,858 | 8,322,660 |
| 1900-01 | 8 | 17,996,782 | 10,271,822 |
| 1901-02 | 8 | 20,597,903 | 10,844,577 |

In 1898 there was charged against the company's general surplus account $25,200,000 for the cash dividend of 20 per cent and the increase of 50 per cent. in the capital stock of the company. The total surplus, July 31, 1902, was $10,778,030.

The number of passengers carried in company's cars in year 1891-92 was 5,279,020, and the number of miles run was 191,255,656. In 1892-93 the passengers were 5,673,129 and the mileage 206,453,796. In 1893-94 passengers were 5,282,323, and number of miles run 197,409,503. In 1894-95 passengers, 4,788,509; miles run, 179,547,071. In 1895-96, passengers, 5,112,965; mileage run, 191,862,947. In 1896-97 passengers 4,852,398; mileage, 190,562,758. In 1897-98, passengers, 5,356,912; mileage, 201,295,321. In 1898-99, passengers, 6,015,818; mileage, 219,011,905. In 1899-1900, passengers, 7,752,876; mileage run, 274,066,488. In 1900-01, passengers, 9,618,438; mileage run, 335,742,267. In 1901-02, passengers, 10,753,643; mileage run, 360,602,541.

President, Robert T. Lincoln; Vice-President, T. H. Wickes; Secretary, Alfred S. Weinsheimer, Chicago; Eastern Secretary, S. W. Bretzfield, New York.

Directors—Robert T. Lincoln, Marshall Field, Norman B. Ream, O. S. A. Sprague, Frank O. Lowden, Chicago; H. C. Hulbert, William K. Vanderbilt, Frederick W. Vanderbilt, J. Pierpont Morgan, W. Seward Webb, New York; H. R. Reed, Boston.

Main office, Adams street and Michigan avenue, Chicago; New York office, 15 Broad street; London office, London Bridge Station, S. E. Annual meeting, Thursday after second Saturday in October.

## QUAKER OATS CO.

A corporation formed under the laws of New Jersey, September 21, 1901. Its business is milling cereals and manufacturing food products. The company acquired over 95 per cent. of the capital stock of the American Cereal Co., together with several other properties. The American Cereal Co. controls and operates cereal mills in Akron, O.; Cedar Rapids, Ia.; Chicago, and Peterboro, Ont.

Stock...Par $100....Authorized { com., $4,000,000; pref., 8,000,000 } Issued { com., $3,951,750; pref., 7,500,900 } $11,452,650

The preferred stock is 6 per cent., cumulative. Transfer Agent, The Trust Co. of America, New York. Registrar, The Corporation Trust Co., New York.

The first dividend on the preferred stock was paid February 25, 1902.

The company has no funded debt.

The following is the balance sheet of the company, December 31, 1902,

| ASSETS. | | LIABILITIES. | |
|---|---|---|---|
| Investments | $11,149,800 | Capital stock, pref | $7,307,000 |
| Accounts receivable | 90,223 | Capital stock, com | 3,951,750 |
| Bills receivable | 54,600 | Accounts payable | 16,500 |
| Cash | 2,952 | Subscriptions to capital stock other companies | 110,200 |
| Subscription rights | 110,200 | Profit and loss | 22,325 |
| Total | $11,407,775 | Total | $11,407,775 |

President, Henry P. Crowell; Vice-President, Thomas E. Wells; Secretary and Treasurer, Robert Stuart.

Directors—Myron T. Herrick, James Parmelee, George A. Cox, B. E. Walker, Henry P. Crowell, Robert Stuart, Thomas E. Wells, Walter D. Douglas, James H. Andrews, J. G. Schmidlapp, Whiting G. Snow.

Corporate office, 15 Exchange place, Jersey City; main office, Monadnock Building, Chicago. Annual meeting, February, at Jersey City.

## QUEBEC BRIDGE CO., LIMITED

A corporation chartered by the Dominion of Canada with powers to construct a railroad and highway bridge over the St. Lawrence River at Quebec. In 1899 subsidies were granted to the company of $1,000,000 by the Dominion Government; $250,000 by the Province, and $300,000 by the city of Quebec. In 1898 the plans for the structure were approved, and in 1900 contracts were awarded to M. P. Davis for the substructure, and to the Phœnix Bridge Co. for the superstructure. The bridge has a length of 3,300 feet, and consists of one middle cantilever span of 1,800 feet, two anchor spans of 500 feet, and two approach spans of 250 feet each. The erection of the structure was commenced in the summer of 1900, and was completed in the autumn of 1902.

Stock......Par $100..........................Authorized, $1,000,000......Issued, $1,000,000

The stock is the amount authorized. Amount subscribed and paid in at end of 1900 was about $200,000. A bond issue has been authorized.

President, S. N. Parent; Vice-President, Rodolphe Audette; Secretary and Treasurer, Ulric Barthe; Chief Engineer, E. A. Hoare, Quebec; Consulting Engineer, Theodore Cooper, New York.

Directors—H. J. Beemer, Herbert M. Price, Gaspard Le Moine, J. B. Laliberte, John Breakey, N. Rioux, Vesey Boswell, N. Garneau.

Main office, 139 St. Peter street, Quebec. Annual meeting, first Tuesday in September.

## QUICKSILVER MINING CO.

A corporation formed under the laws of New York in 1866. Its mines are located at New Almaden, Cal.

Stock....Par $100....Authorized { com., $5,708,700; pref., 4,291,300 } Issued { com., $5,708,700; pref., 4,291,300 } $10,000,000

The preferred stock is 7 per cent., non-cumulative.

Transfer Agent, Farmers' Loan and Trust Co., New York.

In June, 1891, a dividend of 4 per cent. was paid on the preferred stock. No further dividend was paid on the preferred until May 5, 1899, when ½ per cent. was paid. On July 16, 1900, a dividend of ½ per cent. was paid on the preferred, ½ per cent. was also paid May 10, 1901, and ½ per cent. May 9, 1902. No dividend has been paid on the common stock since the payment of 40 cents per share, June 1, 1882. The preferred stock is entitled to 7 per cent., non-cumulative.

The company has no funded debt.

EARNINGS.

| Year ending April 30. | Gross. | Net. |
|---|---|---|
| 1899-00 | $195,375 | $28,267 |
| 1900-01 | 226,773 | 45,079 |
| 1901-02 | 217,018 | 462,258 |

The cash on hand April 30, 1901, was $47,568.

President, Almon L. Bailey; Vice-President, F. N. Lawrence; Secretary, A. H. Smith; Treasurer, James D. Smith, New York.

Directors—James D. Smith, Edward Brandon, Albert Fries, F. N. Lawrence, Sheppard Gandy, Frank K. Sturgis, Joseph Milbank, Aaron S. Robbins, Almon L. Bailey, A. H. Smith, New York; Henry R. Chace, Providence.

Main office, 20 Nassau street, New York. Annual meeting, third Wednesday in June, at New York.

## QUINCY MINING CO.

A corporation originally formed under a special charter of the State of Michigan, March 30, 1848, and reincorporated under the laws of Michigan, March 6, 1878. The company owns and works one of the richest copper mine properties in the Portage Lake District, Houghton County, Upper Michigan. Company's property comprises over 600 acres mineral lands and 200 acres of timber, stamp mills, etc.

Capital stock......Par $25......................Authorized, $2,500,000......Issued, $2,500,000

Transfer Agent, Old Colony Trust Co., Boston.

The company is a large producer of copper, its output having been in 1895, 16,304,721 pounds; in 1896, 16,863,477 pounds; in 1897, 16,924,618 pounds; in 1898, 16,354,061 pounds; in 1899, 14,301,182 pounds; in 1900, 18,491,749 pounds; in 1901, 20,540,720 pounds; in 1902, 26,425,670 pounds.

| Earnings. | Gross. | Net. |
|---|---|---|
| 1893 | $1,511,039 | $511,213 |
| 1894 | 1,470,272 | 592,587 |
| 1895 | 1,661,446 | 692,074 |
| 1896 | 1,864,198 | 770,064 |
| 1897 | 1,890,238 | 731,278 |
| 1898 | 1,986,117 | 668,104 |
| 1899 | 2,450,178 | 928,666 |
| 1900 | 2,353,416 | 1,054,745 |
| 1901 | 3,327,071 | 1,424,542 |
| 1902 | 2,275,819 | 563,027 |

Dividends are semi-annual, February (15) and August. In 1899, paid dividends of $9.50 per share; in 1900, paid $9 per share. The August, 1900, dividend was reduced to $4 on account of construction and development expenditures. The February, 1901, dividend was $3 per share. In 1902 $4 was paid in February and $3 in August. The February, 1903, dividend was $2.50 per share.

President, William R. Todd, New York; Vice-President, Charles J. Devereaux, Boston; Secretary and Treasurer, W. A. O. Paul, New York.

Directors—Daniel T. Brigham, Charles J. Devereaux, Isaac H. Meserve, Boston; Walter P. Bliss, Cleveland H. Dodge, William R. Todd, New York; Don M. Dickinson, Detroit.

Main office, 45 Broadway, New York.

## RACINE GAS LIGHT CO.

A corporation owning and operating the gas works at Racine, Wis., under an exclusive and perpetual franchise granted by the State of Wisconsin in 1866. In 1887 the company absorbed the Racine People's Gas Light Co. The company has 42 miles of mains.

Stock......Par $100............................Authorized, $500,000......Issued, $500,000

Stock is transferred at the company's office, Milwaukee.

FUNDED DEBT.

1st mort., 5 per cent., due 1930, Jan. and July........................................ $500,000

The consolidated mortgage is for $1,000,000, and was authorized in 1900 for the purpose of erecting a large modern gas plant and extending the plant.

President, John S. Beggs; Secretary, F. G. Bigelow, Milwaukee; Manager and Secretary, Henry H. Hyde, Racine, Wis.

Directors—E. C. Cowdery, F. G. Bigelow, Henry C. Payne, Charles F. Pfister, John I. Beggs, Milwaukee.

Main office, 305 Sixth street, Racine, Wis.; treasurer's office, Milwaukee.

## THE RAILROAD SECURITIES CO.

A corporation formed under the laws of New Jersey in February, 1896, the original title being the American Securities Investment Co. The name was changed to the present style in December, 1900. The company has power to acquire and hold railroad and other securities and to issue its own securities against the same.

Stock...Par $100....Authorized { com., $12,500,000 / pref., 7,500,000 } Issued { com., $3,600,000 / pref., 2,000,000 } $5,600,000

The preferred stock is 4 per cent., cumulative. Stock is transferred at the office of the company, 120 Broadway, New York. Registrar, United States Trust Co., New York.

FUNDED DEBT.

50-year gold bonds, Series A, Ill. Cent. stock col., 3½ p. c., due Jan., 1951, Jan. & July. $8,000,000

The trustee of the Series A 3½ per cent. bonds is the United States Trust Co., New York; agent for the payment of interest on the bonds, Standard Trust Co., New York. The authorized issue is $10,000,000. The bonds outstanding are secured by the deposit with the trustee of an equal amount of stock of the Illinois Central Railroad Co., and the $2,000,000 bonds unissued can only be issued against the deposit of an equal amount of Illinois Central stock in addition to that already in the hands of the trustee. The bonds can be redeemed, in whole or in part, at 105 at any interest date on three months' notice.

President, William C. Lane; Vice-President, Edward H. Harriman; Secretary, J. W. Harriman; Treasurer, C. C. Tegethoff, New York.

Directors—Edward H. Harriman, Otto H. Kahn, William C. Lane, J. W. Harriman, Stuyvesant Fish, F. L. Rodewald, E. M. F. Miller, New York.

Main office, 120 Broadway, New York.

## RAILWAYS & LIGHT CO. OF AMERICA

A corporation formed under the laws of New Jersey, September 7, 1899. The purposes of the company are the financing of electric railway and industrial properties and the purchase, sale and ownership of their securities. The company is interested in a number of electric street railways in Southern cities.

Stock......Par $50........................Authorized, $25,000,000......Issued, $5,000,000

The company has no preferred stock and no funded debt of its own. Transfer Agent and Registrar, International Trust Co. of Maryland, Baltimore.

President, J. William Middendorf, Baltimore; Vice-President, R. Lancaster Williams, Richmond, Va.; Secretary and Auditor, Howard P. Page; Treasurer, A. H. Rutherford; General Manager, E. L. Bemiss, Richmond.

Directors—J. William Middendorf, A. H. Rutherford, Gustavus Ober, F. C. Todd, Baltimore; R. Lancaster Williams, E. L. Bemiss, Richmond, Va.; Kenneth K. McLaren, Jersey City.

Corporate office, 60 Grand street, Jersey City; executive office, Baltimore and Calvert streets, Baltimore; general manager's office, Tenth and Main streets, Richmond. Annual meeting, second Tuesday in March, at Jersey City.

## RAILWAYS COMPANY GENERAL

A corporation formed under the laws of New Jersey, August 25, 1899. The company was organized to operate street railway, gas, electric light and water plants. It has acquired control of the following concerns of the above description:

Lewisburg, Milton & Watsontown Passenger Railway Co.
Montoursville Passenger Railway Co.
Montoursville Electric Light Co.
Michigan Traction Co.
Elmira & Seneca Lake Railway Co.
Milton Electric Light & Power Co.

The company also controls the American Engineering Co.

Stock......Par $10..........................Authorized, $1,200,000......Issued, $1,200,000

Stock is transferred at the company's office. Registrar, Investment Co. of Philadelphia.

The stock was $5 par and $10,000,000 authorized. In October, 1901, the amount authorized was reduced to $1,200,000, par $10, and the $1,500,000 outstanding was reduced to the present figures.

The company has no funded debt.

In the year ending June 30, 1901, the income of company was $50,626; surplus over expenses, $30,330. In the year 1901-02, income, $24,618; surplus, $17,900.

President, Evans R. Dick; Vice-President, Gerald Holsman; Secretary and Treasurer, John J. Collier; General Superintendent, D. A. Hegarty; Consulting Engineer, H. A. Foster, Philadelphia.

Directors—Evans R. Dick, R. H. Rushton, George S. Graham, J. Ogden Hoffman, Jay Cooke, 3d; J. R. McAllister, S. B. Vrooman, Robert I. McKinstry, J. A. Harris, Jr., Gerald Holsman, T. J. Lisman.

Main office, Broad and Sansom streets, Philadelphia. Annual meeting, third Monday in September.

## RAILWAY STEEL SPRING CO.

A corporation formed under the laws of New Jersey, February 25, 1902. The purposes of the company are the manufacture and sale of railway springs, steel-tired wheels and kindred articles. The company acquired the stocks and properties of the following concerns:

A. French Spring Co., Pittsburg.
Spring Department of the Crucible Steel Co. of America, Pittsburg.
Detroit Steel & Spring Co., Detroit.
National Spring Co., Oswego, N. Y.
Pickering Spring Co., Limited, Philadelphia.
Charles Scott Spring Co.
Steel Tired Wheel Co.

The constituent companies represent an output of about 60,000 tons yearly, or about 95 per cent. of the railway car and locomotive springs made in the United States.

The Steel Tired Wheel Co. was acquired in 1902.

Stock...Par $100....Authorized { com., $13,500,000 pref., 13,500,000 } Issued { com., $13,500,000 pref., 13,500,000 } $27,000,000

The stock was originally $10,000,000 each of common and preferred, and was increased in 1902 by $3,500,000 of both issues to provide for the purchase of the Steel Tired Wheel Co.

The preferred stock is 7 per cent., cumulative. Transfer Agent, Metropolitan Trust Co., New York. Registrar, Chase National Bank, New York.

The company has no funded debt.

Chairman, Aaron French; President, Julius E. French; Vice-Presidents, W. H. Silverthorne, Charles Scott, Jr.; Secretary, M. B. Parker; Treasurer, James C. Beach; Assistant Treasurer, Frank Carnahan.

Directors—Julius E. French, Samuel R. Callaway, Charles Scott, Jr., Frank S. Layng, S. L. Schoomaker, W. H. Silverthorn, James C. Beach, Frank S. Barstow, New York; Truman H. Newberry, Detroit, Mich.; Chales Scott, Philadelphia; Frank B. Smith, Philo N French, Pittsburg; Charles Miller, Franklin, Pa.; James W. Fuller, Catasauqua, Pa.; Charles W. Barnum, Lime Rock, Conn.

Main office, 71 Broadway, New York. Annual meeting, first Thursday in March.

## RAPID TRANSIT CO. OF CHATTANOOGA

A corporation formed under the laws of Tennessee and Georgia in 1897, as the Chattanooga Rapid Transit Co. The present name was adopted in 1900. The company has acquired the following companies:

Northside Consolidated Street Railway Co., formerly the Signal Mountain Railway Co.
Chattanooga & Lookout Mountain Railroad Co.

The company also controls, by lease, the mail and express business of the Belt Railway Co. It has an electric power plant and operates 32 miles of track, mostly electric, in Chattanooga, Tenn., and vicinity. The line of the Chattanooga & Lookout Mountain Railroad is operated by steam and cable.

Stock......Par $100..............................Authorized, $350,000......Issued, $350,000

The company has no preferred stock. A controlling interest in the stock is owned by the United Railways, Light & Water Co. of Philadelphia.

FUNDED DEBT.

| | |
|---|---|
| 1st mort., 5 per cent. gold, due Feb., 1925, Feb. and Aug. | $300,000 |
| Chattanooga & Lookout Mtn. R.R. Co., 1st mort., 5 p. c., due Jan., 1926, Jan. and July. | 250,000 |
| Northside Consolidated St. R.R., 1st mort., 5 per cent., gold, due 1920, April and Oct | 110,000 |
| Total | $660,000 |

The authorized amount of the 1st mortgage of the Rapid Transit Co. is $300,000, of which $200,000 were used to retire outstanding bonds and $100,000 for extensions. Trustee and agent for the payment of interest, Real Estate Trust Co., Philadelphia.

President, J. Herbert Jefferis, Philadelphia; Vice-President, Samuel W. Divine; Secretary and Treasurer, J. W. Pittock, Chattanooga, Tenn.

Directors—Samuel W. Divine, G. W. Davenport, W. B. Royster, J. Herbert Jefferis, F. H. Treat, Clarence P. King, J. W. Pittock.

Main office, Chattanooga, Tenn.

## READING IRON CO.

A corporation formed under the laws of Pennsylvania, August 12, 1889. The company owns and operates blast furnaces, rolling mills, forges, foundries, tube mills and other similar establishments at Reading, Pa.; Danville, Pa., Emaus and also has a large bituminous coal property in Somerset County, Pa.

Stock......Par $100..........................Authorized, $1,000,000......Issued, $1,000,000

The company has no preferred stock.

Chairman, George F. Baer, Philadelphia; President, F. C. Smink; General Superintendent, George Schuhmann; Treasurer, George B. Harris; Secretary, George W. Delany, Reading, Pa.

Directors—Joseph S. Harris, J. Lowber Welsh, George F. Baer, F. C. Smink, Samuel R. Seyfert.

Main office, Baer Building, Reading, Pa.

## THE REALTY SYNDICATE

A corporation formed under the laws of California in 1895 for the purpose of buying and selling real estate and other properties. The company owns real estate in Oakland, Cal., and vicinity, a majority of the stock in the Oakland Transit Consolidated, Piedmont Development Co. and Mutual Investment Co., and the entire capital stock of the California Improvement Co., which owns hotel, cottages, quarry and plant.

Stock......Par $100........................Authorized, $5,000,000......Issued, $3,000,000

Stock is transferred at the office of the company, San Francisco.

The company has no preferred stock and no funded debt.

Dividends at the rate of 6 per cent. per annum are payable semi-annually, the first payment being September 30, 1902.

The company has issued at par $2,820,282.11 investment certificates bearing interest at the rate of 5 per cent. and 6 per cent. annually and maturing 10, 15 and 20 years after date.

President, F. M. Smith; Vice-President and Manager, F. C. Havens; Assistant to Manager, John M. Chase; 2d Vice-President, Samuel J. Taylor; 3d Vice-President, W. H. Martin; Secretary, J. C. Winans; Assistant Secretary, Roosevelt Johnson; Auditor, F. M. Nace.

Corporate and main office, 14 Sansome street, San Francisco.

---

## REECE BUTTON-HOLE MACHINE CO.

A corporation formed under the laws of Maine in 1882. The company owns the patents for and manufactures the Reece button-hole machine and the Reece finishing machine. The former cuts, works and bars button-holes of all sizes and shapes, and in any material, each machine having a capacity of from 10,000 to 12,000 button-holes per day. The finishing machine stitches down thrum ends and stay cords on boots and shoes, one machine doing the work of nine hand operatives. The company in recent years has acquired and taken out many new patents and introduced a machine which is equal to two of the old style. On April 1, 1901, it had leased on royalty 4,210 machines. The company has a large factory at 500-514 Harrison avenue, Boston. In 1900 purchased the Consolidated Sewing Machine Co.'s plant, patents and business.

Stock......Par $10.........................Authorized, $1,000,000......Issued, $1,000,000

In 1898-99, the company paid dividends on the stock aggregating 12 per cent., and similar dividends were paid quarterly, in January (15), April, July and October, until July, 1900, when the rate was reduced to 2 per cent. for the quarter to provide for new acquisitions. The subsequent dividends have been at that rate.

The company has paid $1,833,500 in dividends.

Earnings.

Year ending March 31.

| | Royalties. | Merchandise. | Total Receipts. | Net. |
|---|---|---|---|---|
| 1897-98 | $234,437 | $65,090 | $299,528 | $171,837 |
| 1898-99 | 203,249 | 68,391 | 271,640 | 144,760 |
| 1899-00 | 203,345 | 93,508 | 296,853 | 150,967 |
| 1900-01 | 181,547 | 82,111 | 263,658 | 125,277 |
| 1901-02 | 163,875 | 54,703 | 218,578 | 106,374 |

President and General Manager, Francis A. Shea; Secretary and Treasurer, Frank L. Cady, Boston.

Directors—Francis A. Shea, Frank L. Cady, Theophilus King, Boston; David E. Harding, Mansfield, Mass.; James Phelan, Lynn, Mass.

Main office, 502 Harrison avenue, Boston.

---

## THE REECE FOLDING MACHINE CO.

A corporation formed under the laws of Maine in 1900. The company owns valuable patents for machines for manufacturing collars, cuffs and similar articles, performing by automatic machinery, a class of work heretofore considered impracticable for mechanism—viz., to fold and press or inturn the edges of collars, cuffs, etc., whereby the edges are folded with accuracy and precision. The machines are placed with manufacturers on a royalty basis, a number being in operation at factories in Troy, N. Y., and elsewhere.

Stock......Par $10.............................Authorized, $1,000,000......Issued, $1,000,000

The stock is full-paid and non-assessable. The company has no funded debt.

President, Francis A. Shea; Treasurer, Frank L. Cady, Boston.

Directors—Francis A. Shea, Theophilus King, Frank L. Cady, Friend W. Johnston, George Peterson.

Main office, 502 Harrison avenue, Boston.

## REPUBLIC IRON & STEEL CO.

A corporation formed under the laws of New Jersey, May 3, 1899. The company owns and operates the following properties, organized to combine the leading rolling mills and manufacturers of bar and forge iron in the United States. It acquired a number of such establishments, blast furnaces, steel works and large ore, coke and coal properties. The establishments acquired, are as follows:

ORE PROPERTIES.

Cambria Mine, Negaunee, Mich.
Lillie Mine, Negaunee, Mich.
Franklin Mine, Virginia, Mich.
Bessemer Mine, Virginia, Mich.
Victoria Mine, Virginia, Mich.
Pettit Mine, Virginia, Mich.
Kinney Mine, Virginia, Mich.
Mahoning Ore & Steel Co. (3-50 interest) Hibbing, Minn.
Union Ore Co. (½ interest), Virginia, Mich.
Raimund Mine, Birmingham, Ala.
Spaulding Mine, Birmingham, Ala.
Gothite Mine, Birmingham, Ala.
Thompson Mine, Birmingham, Ala.
Washington 6o Steam Coal Lands, Cloakeyville, Pa.

COKE PROPERTIES.

Connellsville Coke Works, Atchison, Pa.
Pioneer Coke Ovens, Thomas, Ala.
Woodside Coking Coal Lands, Nicholson, Pa.

COAL PROPERTIES.

Springfield Mine, Springfield, Ill.
Saggerton Mine, Birmingham, Ala.
Warner Mine, Birmingham, Ala.

LIMESTONE PROPERTIES.

Croton Limestone Works, New Castle, Pa.
Dale Limestone Works, Birmingham, Ala.
Union Limestone Works, Loweville, O.

STEEL PLANTS.

Bessemer Steel Plant, Youngstown, O.
Birmingham Open Hearth Steel Plant, Birmingham, Ala.

BLAST FURNACES.

Pioneer No. 1, Thomas, Ala.
Pioneer No. 2, Thomas, Ala.
Pioneer No. 3, Thomas, Ala.
Atlantic, New Castle, Pa.
Hannah, Youngstown, O.
Haselton, Youngstown, O,
Hall, Sharon, Pa.

RAILROADS AND DOCKS.

Sharon Connecting R. R., Sharon Pa.
Madison County Belt R. R., Alexandria, Ind.
Mahoning & Shenango Dock (2-9th Interest), Ashtabula, O.

ROLLING MILLS.

Alexandria Works, Alexandria, Ind.
Alabama Works, Birmingham, Ala.
Andrews Works, Youngstown, O.
Atlantic Iron & Steel Works, New Castle, Pa.
Birmingham Rolling Mill Works, Birmingham, Ala.
Brown-Bonnell Works, Youngstown, O.
Central Works, Brazil, Ind.
Corns Works, Massillon, O.
Eagle Works, Ironton, O.
Indiano Works, Muncie, Ind.
Inland Works, E. Chicago, Ind.
Mahoning Valley Works, Youngstown, O.
Muncie Works, Muncie, Ind.
Mitchell-Tranter Works, Covington, Ky.
Sharon Works, Sharon, Pa.
Sylvan Works, Moline, Ill.
Springfield Works, Springfield, Ill.
Toledo Works, Toledo, O.
Tudor Works, East St. Louis, Ill.
Terre Haute Works, Terre Haute, Ind.
Wabash Works, Terre Haute, Ind.
Wetherald Works, Frankton, Ind.

These properties include valuable iron and coal mines, and coal and limestone lands in Pennsylvania, Alabama, Michigan and Minnesota, chief among them being the Pioneer properties at Birmingham, Ala., which comprise 26,000 acres, of which 14,000 acres are underlaid with coal of excellent quality, suitable for coking and general steam purposes, and 10,000 acres very rich in brown and red ores; the Franklin group and the Pettit and Kinney Mines on the Mesaba Range; Cambria and Lillie Mines on the Marquette Range, an interest in the Mahoning Ore & Steel Co., and a half interest in the Union Ore Co., all being well known iron ore properties; also some 800 acres of coking coal lands in the Connellsville district.

The company's products are: pig iron, bar iron and steel, steel billets, bolts, nuts, screws, angles, shapes, car axles, T-rails, turnbuckles, harrow tooth, agricultural shapes, etc. The annual capacity of the plants exceeds 1,000,000 tons finished iron and steel and 600,000 tons of pig iron.

| Stock..Par $100...Authorized | com., $30,000,000<br>pref., 25,000,000 | Issued | com., $27,191,000<br>pref., 20,356,000 | $47,547,000 |
|---|---|---|---|---|

The preferred stock is 7 per cent., cumulative, and has a preference up to its par value and any unpaid dividends in any distribution of assets. The company has no funded debt.

The first dividend on the preferred stock was 1¾ per cent. quarterly, paid October 1, 1899. Regular quarterly dividends at that rate have since been paid on the preferred in January, April, July and October.

Transfer agent, City Trust Co., New York. Registrar, Chase National Bank, New York.

EARNINGS.

Year ending June 30.

| | Gross. | Net. | Dividends on Preferred. | | Surplus. |
|---|---|---|---|---|---|
| 1899-1900, 14 months.......... | $5,684,101 | $3,643,728 | $1,421,679 | | $2,222,049 |
| 1900-01...................... | 1,290,444 | 309,099 | 1,421,483 | def., | 1,112,384 |
| 1901-02...................... | 3,260,077 | 2,248,832 | 1,424,107 | sur., | 824,725 |
| 1902, 6 months ending Dec. 31.. | 2,091,887 | 1,384,122 | 712,491 | | 671,631 |

The following is the company's balance sheet December 31, 1902:

ASSETS.

| | | |
|---|---|---|
| Real estate, plants, buildings, machinery, and other permanent investments........ | | $41,234,415 |
| New construction: | | |
| May 1, 1899, to June 30, 1900.............................. | $1,218,203 | |
| July 1, 1900, to June 30, 1901.............................. | 1,164,175 | |
| July 1, 1901, to December 31, 1901.............................. | 1,236,231 | |
| January 1, 1902, to June 30, 1902.............................. | 766,952 | |
| July 1, 1902, to December 31, 1902.............................. | 897,137 | |
| | | 5,282,700 |
| Stocks in sundry companies at cost.............................. | | 309,200 |
| New gas pipe lines, gas leases and oil wells in excess of the amounts charged to operating.............................. | | 92,690 |
| Prepaid royalties on ore and coal, rents and insurance.............................. | | 356,155 |
| Inventories of raw and finished materials.............................. | | 4,195,775 |
| Accounts and bills receivable.............................. | | 3,168,556 |
| Cash.............................. | | 954,588 |
| Total.............................. | | $55,594,079 |

LIABILITIES.

| | | | |
|---|---|---|---|
| Capital stock issued: | | | |
| Preferred.............................. | $20,852,000 | | |
| Less in treasury.............................. | 495,100 | | |
| | | $20,356,900 | |
| Common.............................. | $27,352,000 | | |
| Less in treasury.............................. | 161,000 | | |
| | | 27,191,000 | |
| | | | $47,547,900 |
| Accounts and bills payable.............................. | | | 4,783,430 |
| Preference dividend No. 14, paid January 2, 1903.............................. | | | 356,246 |
| Deferred installments on purchase of coal lands, payable in three annual amounts of $37,000 each.............................. | | | 111,000 |
| Reserve for taxes and insurance.............................. | | | 120,506 |
| Reserve for possible loss in collection of outstanding accounts and bills receivable... | | | 68,977 |
| Profit and loss account: | | | |
| Net profit during six months.............................. | | $1,384,122 | |
| Deduct two quarterly dividends of 1¾ per cent. each on pref. stock... | | 712,491 | |
| Surplus created during the last six months in excess of dividends on preferred stock.............................. | | 671,631 | |
| Add surplus, June 30, 1902.............................. | | 1,934,389 | |
| | | | 2,606,020 |
| Total.............................. | | | $55,594,079 |

President, Alexis W. Thompson; Chairman Executive Committee, G. Watson French; Vice-Presidents, Archibald W. Houston, William H. Hassinger; Vice-President and Treasurer, John F. Taylor; Assistant Treasurer, H. L. Rownd; Secretary, Ysbrand B. Haagsma; Assistant Secretary, Charles E. Graves, Chicago; General Counsel, Harry Rubens; General Sales Agent, George A. Baird; Manager of Rolling Mills, W. L. Simonton; Purchasing Agent, W. L. Lee.

Directors—August Belmont, Grant B. Schley, George R. Sheldon, New York; G. Watson French, Harry Rubens, John F. Taylor, Alexis W. Thompson, Edward N. Ohl, L. C. Hanna, Charles H. Wacker, George A. Baird, John Crerar, Chicago; William H. Hassinger, Birmingham, Ala.; Peter L. Kimberly, Sharon, Pa.; Archibald W. Houston, Cincinnati.

Corporate office, Jersey City; main office, 108 LaSalle street, Chicago; New York sales office, 66 Broadway. Annual meeting, third Wednesday in October, at Jersey City.

## RETSOF MINING CO.

A corporation formed under the laws of New York. The object of the company is the mining and distribution of rock salt and similar products. The Lehigh Salt & Mining Co. and the Livonia Salt Co. were absorbed by this company. It also controls the Greigsville Salt Mining Co. The mines and works of the company are at Livonia and Retsof, Livingston Co., N. Y.

In 1901 control of this company was acquired by the International Salt Co. See statement of the latter company.

Stock........Par $100........................Authorized, $3,600,000......Issued, $3,600,000

FUNDED DEBT.

1st mort., 5 per cent., due 1925, Jan. and July........................................ $2,500,000

President, Edward L. Fuller, Scranton, Pa.; Secretary and Treasurer, Henry D. Fuller, New York.

Directors—Edward L. Fuller, William Connell, M. B. Fuller, Scranton, Pa.; M. M. Belding, M. M. Belding, Jr.; W. B. Putney, Henry D. Fuller, New York; Frank T. Patterson, Philadelphia; J. N. Smith, Boston.

Main office, 115 Broadway, New York; branch office, Scranton, Pa. Annual meeting, third Tuesday in June, at Retsof, N. Y.

## THE RHODE ISLAND CO.

(Controlled by Rhode Island Securities Co.)

A corporation formed under the laws of Rhode Island, April 3, 1902. The company controls by lease the following companies:

Union Railroad Co.
Rhode Island Suburban Street Railway Co.
Pawtucket Street Railway Co.
Interstate Consolidated Street Railway Co.

The consolidation was promoted by the United Gas Improvement Co. of Philadelphia, which guarantees the rentals of the subsidiary companies until $4,000,000 has been expended for extensions and new properties. The Rhode Island Co. is controlled by the Rhode Island Securities Co. The company controls the street railway, gas and electric lighting systems of Providence and Pawtucket, R. I., Attleboro, Mass., and vicinities, serving a population of about 355,000. It owns about 600 cars.

Stock......Par $100...........................Authorized, $2,000,000......Issued, $2,000,000

The company has no preferred stock and no funded debt.

President, Marsden J. Perry, Providence, R. I.; 1st Vice-President, Samuel B. Colt, Bristol, R. I.; 2d Vice-President, Randal Morgan; 3d Vice-President, Walton Clark, Philadelphia; 4th Vice-President, A. T. Potter, Providence, R. I.; Secretary and Treasurer, Lewis Little, Philadelphia; Assistant Secretary and Comptroller, Walter R. Elliott; Assistant Treasurer, C. A. Babcock; General Manager, R. I. Todd, Providence, R. I.

Directors—Marsden J. Perry, Nelson W. Aldrich, William G. Roelker, J. Edward Studley, Howard O. Sturges, Walter F. Angell, Samuel M. Nicholson, Providence; Samuel P. Colt, Bristol, R. I.; Thomas Dolan, Randal Morgan, Walton Clark, Lewis Little, Philadelphia.

Main office, Providence.

## RHODE ISLAND COPPER CO.

A corporation formed under the laws of Michigan, December 9, 1898. The company owns a copper bearing tract in Houghton County, Mich., comprising 800 acres, and has done extensive development work on the same.

Stock......Par $25.................. ........Authorized, $2,500,000......Issued, $2,500,000

Transfer Agent, American Loan & Trust Co., Boston.

The report for 1901 showed total receipts, $84,883; unexpended balance, $31,415. The balance December 31, 1902, was $93,729. There has been paid in on the stock $6 per share. A payment of $1 per share was called in 1902.

President, Charles J. Devereaux, Boston; Secretary and Treasurer, William R. Todd; Assistant Secretary and Assistant Treasurer, W. A. O. Paul, New York.

Directors—Isaac H. Meserve, William R. Todd, Charles J. Devereaux, Henry A. Wyman, John Barker, Thomas B. Dunstan, James S. Dunstan.

Main office, 45 Broadway, New York.

## RHODE ISLAND PERKINS HORSE SHOE CO.

A corporation formed under the laws of New Jersey in 1892. The company acquired the Rhode Island Horse Shoe Co. Property owned is at Valley Falls, R. I., near Providence, and consists of a rolling mill, shops and other buildings, the whole plant covering 6½ acres of land.

Stock......Par $100.....Authorized { com., $1,000,000 / pref., 1,750,000 } Issued { com., $1,000,000 / pref., 1,750,000 } $2,750,000

The preferred stock is 7 per cent., cumulative. The common stock is entitled to 10 per cent. out of surplus, after which any further surplus is divided between preferred and common stock. Company has no bonds or mortgages, and consent of 75 per cent. of stock is necessary for their creation.

In December, 1902, it was proposed to reduce the stock to $1,000,000, all common, the preferred stockholders receiving compensation for the accumulated dividends on their shares.

Transfer Agents, Maitland, Coppell & Co., New York. Registrar, Farmers' Loan & Trust Co., New York.

The company paid 7 per cent. on the preferred from 1892 to 1896, inclusive; in 1897 paid 6¾ per cent.; in 1899, 1900 and 1901, 4 per cent. The January, 1902, dividend was increased to 1¼ per cent., and 5 per cent. was paid in 1902. Dividends on the preferred are quarterly, January (15), April, July and October.

From 1892 to 1895, 10 per cent. per annum was paid on the common stock. In 1896 paid 7 per cent., but the October, 1896, dividend was passed. None paid since on common.

President, F. W. Carpenter; Secretary, R. W. Comstock; Assistant Secretary, G. L. Bowen; Treasurer, Charles R. Stark; General Manager, Charles H. Perkins., Providence.

Directors—F. W. Carpenter, R. W. Comstock, Charles H. Perkins, Fred E. Perkins, Providence; J. Hugh Peters, Englewood, N. J.; George Peabody Wetmore, Newport, R. I.; Gerald L. Hoyt, New York.

Corporate office, Jersey City; main office, 49 Westminster street, Providence. Annual meeting, first Wednesday in October.

---

## RHODE ISLAND SECURITIES CO.

A corporation formed under the laws of New Jersey in June, 1902. The company owns all the stock of the Rhode Island Co. The stockholders of the United Traction Electric Co., which owns the Union Railroad Co., the Pawtucket Street Railway Co. and the Rhode Island Suburban Railway Co., received 25 shares of the Rhode Island Securities Co.'s stock for each share of the shares of Traction stock held.

Stock......Par $100........................Authorized, $20,000,000......Issued, $12,000,000

The company has no preferred stock.

FUNDED DEBT.

Bonds, series A, 4 per cent., due 1932..........................................$3,500,000

The total amount of authorized bonds is $5,000,000. A sinking fund of 1 per cent. annually is provided. An additional bond issue of $15,000,000, with no sinking fund, due 1932, has been authorized, but none of the bonds have been issued.

The outstanding bonds and stock of the company were issued against the lease of the United Traction Co. The remaining stock and bonds may be issued for the acquisition of gas and electric light properties.

President, Marsden J. Perry; Assistant Secretary, Walter R. Elliott.

Main office, Providence.

---

## RICHELIEU & ONTARIO NAVIGATION CO.

A corporation formed under the laws of the Dominion of Canada. The company originated as a private enterprise in 1847 with its head office at St. Charles, P. Q. It subsequently removed its office to Montreal, and placed a line on the St. Lawrence, running between Montreal and Quebec, in competition with the Molson & Torrance line, eventually purchasing the latter's steamers. In 1857 the company was incorporated for the first time. It absorbed various local lines, including the Lake St. Peter Navigation Co., the Terrebonne & Assumption Navigation Co., the Chamblay & Montreal Navigation Co., the Laprairie Navigation Co. and the Longeuil Navigation Co. In 1875 it amalgamated its stock with that of the Canadian Navigation Co., which operated steamers between Toronto and Montreal, and amended its charter, assuming the present title of Richelieu & Ontario Navigation Co. In 1886 it purchased the steamers of the St. Lawrence River Steam Navigation Co. This last purchase completed the control, which the company retains, of the through lake and river passenger and freight business between Toronto, Montreal, Quebec and Chicoutimi, a distance of 800 miles.

The company in 1901 had twenty-seven steamers in commission. Its through passenger business mainly consists of tourist travel and is divided into three main lines: 1st, from Toronto to Montreal, embracing Lake Ontario, the Thousand Isles and the Rapids of St. Lawrence; 2d, from Montreal to Quebec, embracing the river between those points; 3d, from Quebec to Tadousac, and the Saguenay River from Tadousac to Chicoutimi. Its local lines are eleven in number—from Montreal to Hamilton, Laprairie, St. Helen's Island, Longeuil, Boucherville, Contrecœur, Chambly, Berthier, Pierreville, Three Rivers and St. Anne de Beaupre.

The company also owns and operates large modern hotels at Murray Bay and Tadousac.

Stock......Par $100.......................... Authorized, $5,000,000......Issued, $3,738,000

The company since 1894, inclusive, has paid 6 per cent. per annum on its stock, the dividends being semi-annual, 3 per cent. each, in May (2) and November.

Transfer Agent, J. F. Dolan, 128 St. James street, Montreal.

FUNDED DEBT.

1st mort. bonds, sterling, 5 per cent.................................................. $452,113

The 5 per cent. sterling bonds created in 1895 were originally $571,833, but $119,719 of the issue has been canceled through the sinking fund.

EARNINGS.

| | Gross. | Net. | Charges. | Surplus. |
|---|---|---|---|---|
| 1900 | $901,331 | $153,126 | $23,903 | $129,222 |
| 1901 | 1,109,458 | 188,889 | 22,792 | 166,889 |

In 1901 the dividends paid on the stock amounted to $139,952, leaving $26,145 to be carried to surplus account.

President, L. J. Forget; Vice-President, William Wainright; General Manager, C. F. Gildersleeve; Comptroller and Treasurer, J. A. Villeneuve; Traffic Manager, Thomas Henry; Mechanical Superintendent, Gilbert Johnston; Secretary, H. M. Bolger, Montreal.

Directors—L. J. Forget, William Wainright, F. C. Henshaw, William Hanson, George Caverhill, H. M. Molson, Montreal; E. B. Garneau, Quebec; C. O. Paradis, Sorel, P. Q.; J. Kerr Osborne, H. M. Pellatt, Toronto.

Main office, 228 St. Paul street, Montreal. Annual meeting in February.

## THE RICHMOND STREET & INTERURBAN RAILWAY CO.

A corporation formed under the laws of Indiana. The company operates 30 miles of electric railway in Richmond, Ind., including 20 miles to Cambridge City, Dublin and Milton, Ind. The company has a power house and 30 cars.

Stock......Par $100....... ......................Authorized, $500,000......Issued, $500,000

The company has no preferred stock.

FUNDED DEBT.

1st mort., 5 per cent., gold, due 1950, Jan. and July.................................. $500,000

The total amount of the authorized 1st mortgage is $600,000. The bonds may be called at 107½. Trustee of the mortgage and agent for the payment of interest, Lafayette Loan & Trust Co., Lafayette, Ind.

President, H. B. Smith, Hartford City, Ind.; Secretary and Treasurer, C. Murdock, Lafayette, Ind.; Assistant Secretary, J. M. Lontz, Richmond, Ind.

Main office, Richmond, Ind.

## ROCHESTER GAS & ELECTRIC CO.

A corporation formed under the laws of New York in 1892. The purpose of the company is the manufacture and distribution of gas and electricity for light, heat and power. The company was formed as a consolidation of the Rochester Gas Co., the Edison Electric Illuminating Co. of Rochester, and the Rochester Electric Light Co. It also acquired control of the Brush Electric Light Co. and has acquired other valuable properties, including water powers in and about Rochester, N. Y. The company controls the gas and electric facilities of that city.

Stock....Par $100.....Authorized { com., $2,150,000; pref., 2,850,000 } Issued { com., $2,150,000; pref., 2,350,000 } $4,500,000

The preferred stock is 6 per cent., cumulative. Stock is transferred at the office of the company. Registrar, Fidelity Trust Co., Rochester, N. Y.

FUNDED DEBT.

| | |
|---|---|
| 1st mort., 5 per cent., due Nov., 1912, May and Nov | $2,000,000 |
| 2d mort., 4½ per cent., due 1910 or 1920, March and Sept | 1,000,000 |
| Improvement mort., 4½ per cent., due 1911-1921, Jan. and July | 700,000 |
| Total | $3,700,000 |

Trustee of the 1st mortgage and Agent for the payment of interest, Knickerbocker Trust Co., New York.

Trustee of the 2d mortgage and Agent for the payment of interest, Security Trust Co., Rochester.

Dividends of 6 per cent. per annum are paid on both classes of the company's stock. The dividends in each case are semi-annual, 3 per cent. each. On the common stock the dividends are paid in April and October and on the preferred in February and August.

President, George W. Archer; 1st Vice-President, Charles B. Judson, Rochester, N. Y.; 2d Vice-President, William Runkle, New York; Secretary and Assistant Treasurer, Junius R. Judson; Treasurer, W. L. Cole, Rochester, N. Y.

Directors—Frederick Cook, Charles B. Judson, George W. Archer, Junius R. Judson, W. L. Cole, George A. Redman, George C. Hollister, A. H. Harris, Granger A. Hollister, H. L. Brewster, John N. Beckley, Rochester, N. Y.; William Runkle, Walter S. Johnston, New York.

Main office, 84 Andrews street, Rochester, N. Y. Annual meeting, third Wednesday in April, at the company's office.

## ROCHESTER RAILWAY CO.

A corporation formed under the laws of New York, February 25, 1890. The company owns and operates all the passenger lines in Rochester, N. Y. It is a consolidation of the Crosstown Railroad Co., South Park Railroad Co. and the Rochester City & Brighton Railroad Co.

The company owns 86.03 miles of track and operates under lease 17.85 miles additional. It leases the Rochester Electric Railway Co. and a branch of the Rochester & Suburban Railway Co. It also owns a majority of the stock of the Rochester Turnpike Co.

Stock... Par $100....Authorized { com., $2,500,000 / pref., 2,500,000 } Issued { com., $2,500,000 / pref., 2,500,000 } $5,000,000

The preferred stock is 5 per cent., cumulative.

Transfer Agents, E. W. Clark & Co., Philadelphia, and Fidelity Trust & Safety Vault Co., Louisville. Registrars, Trust Co. of North America, Philadelphia, and Columbia Finance & Trust Co., Louisville.

A first dividend of 1 per cent. on the preferred stock was paid January 1, 1902. In April, 1902, 1¼ per cent. was paid and three quarterly dividends have since been paid at that rate, in July July and October, 1902, and January, 1903.

FUNDED DEBT.

| | |
|---|---|
| Cons. mort., 5 per cent., gold, due April, 1930, April and Oct | $2,700,000 |
| 2d mort., 5 per cent., gold, due Dec., 1933, June and Dec | 1,500,000 |
| Collateral trust, 6 per cent., due March, 1905 | 182,000 |
| Rochester City & Brighton 1st mort., 6 per cent., due April, 1919, April and Oct | 175,000 |
| Total | $4,557,000 |

The authorized consolidated mortgage of the Rochester Railway Co. is $3,000,000, of which $300,000 are reserved to retire prior liens. Interest on the consolidated mortgage is paid by Cuyler, Morgan & Co., New York; on the 2d mortgage and on the collateral trust notes at the Security Trust Co., Rochester, and on the Rochester City & Brighton Railroad Co.'s mortgage at the Rochester Trust & Safe Deposit Co.

EARNINGS.

Year ending June 30.

| | Gross. | Net. | Charges. | Surplus. |
|---|---|---|---|---|
| 1899-00 | $953,745 | $376,741 | $291,355 | $86,312 |
| 1900-01 | 981,723 | 394,708 | 304,338 | 90,370 |
| 1901-02 | 1,044,006 | 495,240 | 313,541 | 181,699 |

President, Frederick Cook; Vice-President, T. J. Nicholl; Treasurer, G. L. Estabrook; Secretary, G. G. Morehouse.

Directors—Frederick Cook, T. J. Nicholl, J. N. Beckley, E. W. Clark, Jr., C. M. Clark, A. G. Hodenpyl, G. W. Archer, W. B. Kurtz, Benjamin Graham, J. Richardson, H. Sellers McKee, C. T. Chapin, H. C. Brewster.

Main office, 267 State street, Rochester, N. Y. Annual meeting, third Tuesday in January, at Rochester.

## ROCHESTER TELEPHONE CO.

A corporation formed under the laws of New York in November, 1899, to operate a telephone system in the city of Rochester, N. Y.

Stock.......Par $100.......Authorized { com., $500,000 / pref., 200,000 } Issued { com., $440,000 / pref., 150,000 } $590,000

The preferred stock is 6 per cent. Stock is transferred at the office of the company, Rochester, N. Y. Registrar, Rochester Trust & Safe Deposit Co., Rochester, N. Y.

The first dividends were paid as follows: 1 per cent. on the common stock February 1, 1902, and 1½ per cent. on the preferred January 1, 1902. Dividends are paid quarterly on the preferred stock at the rate of 6 per cent. annually in January, April, July and October, and on the common stock at the rate of 4 per cent. annually, in February, May, August and November.

FUNDED DEBT.

1st mort., 5 per cent., due Jan. 1, 1920, Jan. and July................................$400,000

The authorized amount of the 1st mortgage is $400,000. Trustee of the mortgage and agent for the payment of interest, Rochester Trust & Safe Deposit Co.

In the fiscal year ending December 31, 1902, the gross earnings were $69,814; interest charges, $20,000; dividends, $26,000; surplus, $23,214. The total surplus is $65,024.

President, Frederick Cook; Vice-President, Eugene H. Satterlee; Secretary and Treasurer, George R. Fuller.

Directors—Frederick Cook, Thomas W. Finucane, George W. Archer, Albrecht Vogt, H. Wheeler Davis, Gustave Erbe, George R. Fuller, Jacob Gerling, J. Foster Warren, Edward W. Peck, Horace C. Brewster, Eugene H. Satterlee, Walter B. Duffy, V. Moreau Smith.

Corporate and main office, 59 Stone street, Rochester, N. Y. Annual meeting, fourth Friday in December, at Rochester, N. Y.

---

## THE ROCKY MOUNTAIN BELL TELEPHONE CO.

A corporation formed under the laws of Utah in 1883. The company operates a telephone system under an exclusive license from the American Telephone & Telegraph Co. Its territory comprises the States of Idaho, Montana, Utah and Wyoming. It had in operation December 31, 1902, 75 exchanges, with 13,711 subscribers and 13,487 miles of toll line wires. The American Telephone & Telegraph Co., in March, 1903, owned $1,021,100 of the stock of this company.

Stock......Par $100.........................Authorized, $2,500,000......Issued, $2,200,000

The company has no funded debt. Stock is transferred at the company's office, Salt Lake City, Utah.

Dividends on the stock are 6 per cent. per annum, payments being quarterly, January, April, July and October.

In 1901, gross earnings, $522,984; net, $175,567; in 1902, gross, $707,073; net, $191,819.

President, George Y. Wallace; Vice-President, George M. Downey; Treasurer, W. S. McCornick; Secretary, Harry C. Hill; General Manager, D. S. Murray, Salt Lake City, Utah.

Directors—George Y. Wallace, George M. Downey, Harry C. Hill, Thomas Marshall, W. S. McCornick, James Ivers, Salt Lake City, Utah; Alonzo Burt, Kansas City; C. W. Clark, Butte, Mont.; Frederick P. Fish, Boston.

Main office, 56 South State street, Salt Lake City, Utah. Annual meeting, last Monday in February.

---

## ROCKY MOUNTAIN PAPER CO.

A corporation formed under the laws of New York, December 18, 1900. The business of the company is manufacturing and dealing in paper. It has two paper mills at Denver Mills, and a sulphite mill at Denver, Col.

Stock.....Par $100......Authorized { com., $750,000 / pref., 600,000 } Issued { com., $750,000 / pref., 600,000 } $1,350,000

President, Thomas H. Savery; Vice-President, W. W. Pusey; Treasurer, Louis Dean Speir; Secretary, William H. Savery; General Manager, Thomas H. Savery, Jr.

Directors—Thomas H. Savery, W. W. Pusey, Samuel C. Biddle, Wilmington, Del.; Newell Martin, George W. Kenyon, Charles Robinson Smith, Charles A. Tinker, New York; Thomas Scattergood, Philadelphia.

Main office, 18 Broad street, New York; sales office, Seventeenth and Curtis streets, Denver, Col. Annual meeting, second Monday in January.

## WILLIAM A. ROGERS, LIMITED

A corporation formed under the Ontario Companies' Act of Canada in March, 1901, for the purpose of carrying on the business of manufacturing silver-plated ware. The company is a consolidation of the following companies:

Niagara Silver Co., Niagara Falls, N. Y. William A. Rogers, New York.

The company has also acquired the following properties:

E. E. Wood Cutlery Works, Northampton, Mass. Rogers & Woods Silver-Plating Works. Oneida Silver-Plate Works, Oneida, N. Y.

Stock....Par $100....Authorized { com., $750,000; pref., 600,000 } Issued { com., $750,000; pref., 600,000 } $1,350,000

The preferred stock is 7 per cent., cumulative, and has a preference as to assets in case of liquidation. Before any dividends are paid on the common stock the sum of $15,000 will be annually transferred to the reserve account until that account shall reach $150,000, at which sum it is to be maintained.

Transfer Agent, National Trust Co., Limited, Toronto. The company has no funded debt.

President, Samuel J. Moore; Vice-President, A. E. Ames, Toronto; General Manager, William A. Rogers, New York.

Directors—Samuel J. Moore, A. E. Ames, William A. Rogers, Robert Kilgour, W. Caryl Ely, James L. Morrison, Charles H. Duell.

Main office, 28 Front street, W. Toronto; New York office, 12 Warren street. Annual meeting in February, at Toronto.

---

## ROGERS LOCOMOTIVE WORKS

A corporation formed under the laws of New Jersey, May, 1901, to engage in the business of manufacturing locomotives. The corporation acquired the property of the Rogers Locomotive Co., Paterson, N. J.

Stock....Par $100.........Authorized { com., $800,000; pref., 800,000 } Issued { com., $800,000; pref., 800,000 } $1,600,000

The preferred stock is 6 per cent. cumulative, and is preferred as to assets. After 6 per cent. is paid on the common stock the preferred and common share equally in dividends.

Stock is transferred at the offices of the company, Paterson, N. J., and New York.

FUNDED DEBT.

1st mort., 5 per cent., due May 14, 1921, May and Nov.................................$490,000

The authorized amount of the mortgage is $500,000. Trustee, Colonial Trust Co., New York. Interest is paid at the offices of the company, Paterson, N. J., and New York. Two per cent. of these bonds were redeemed the first year of the issue (1901), 3 per cent. in 1902, 4 per cent. in 1903, and 5 per cent. are to be retired in subsequent years of the issue.

President, John Havron, Paterson, N. J.; Vice-President, E. Hope Norton, New York; Treasurer, Frank P. Holran; Secretary, George E. Hannah, Paterson, N. J.

Directors—John Havron, Passaic, N. J.; Sir William C. Van Horne, Montreal; George Turnure, E. Hope Norton, George B. Hopkins, Stephen Peabody, New York,; Robert C. Pruyn, Albany, N. Y.; Frank P. Holran, John D. Probst, Englewood, N. J., John W. Griggs, R. Wells, Paterson, N. J.

Corporate and main office, Spruce street, Paterson; New York office, 33 Wall street. Annual meeting, second Tuesday in June, at Paterson.

---

## ROYAL BAKING POWDER CO.

A corporation formed under the laws of New Jersey, March 1, 1899. The company is a consolidation of the old Royal Baking Powder Co., Cleveland Baking Powder Co., Price Baking Powder Co., Tartar Chemical Co. and New York Tartar Co.

Stock..Par $100..Authorized { com., $10,000,000; pref., 10,000,000 } Issued { pref., $10,000,000; com., 10,000,000 } $20,000,000

The preferred stock is 6 per cent., cumulative. The preferred elects a new board should the preferential dividends remain unpaid. Otherwise the preferred has no voting power. No mortgage can be placed on the company's property without the assent of 75 per cent. of the preferred stock.

The company has paid regular dividends of 1½ per cent., quarterly, on the preferred stock since its organization, the dividend periods being January (1), April, July and October. It is reported that 8 per cent. per annum is paid on the common. The dividends on the common are also understood to be at the rate of 8 per cent., but no announcement is made regarding them.

Transfer agent for the preferred stock, Central Trust Co., New York.

President, Charles O. Gates; Vice-President, Alfred H. Porter, Jr.; Treasurer, John Morris; Secretary, W. L. Garey.

Directors—Alfred H. Porter, Jr., Charles O. Gates, John Morris, W. R. Peters, William C. Demorest, U. S. Champ, F. J. Boselly.

Main office, 100 William street, New York.

## THE ROYAL ELECTRIC CO.

A corporation formed under the laws of the Province of Quebec, Canada, in 1884. The company furnishes electric light and power in the city of Montreal, under an exclusive franchise. It has power-houses and stations in Montreal and a large plant at Chambly, near that city, for the generation of electricity by water power. In 1901 the stock of this company was acquired by the Montreal Light, Heat & Power Co. See statement of the latter.

Stock......Par $100..........................Authorized, $2,250,000......Issued, $2,250,000

FUNDED DEBT.

Debenture bonds, 4½ per cent.................................................... $449,680

EARNINGS.

Year ending May 31.

| | Gross. | Net. | Charges. | Surplus. |
|---|---|---|---|---|
| 1896–97 | $900,348 | $243,880 | $43,245 | $200,634 |
| 1897–98 | 955,826 | 319,769 | 42,609 | 277,160 |
| 1898–99 | 1,113,770 | 322,284 | 54,600 | 267,684 |
| 1899–00 | 1,519,912 | 597,931 | 41,239 | 556,692 |

Dividends on the stock of the company in recent years have been: in 1896–97, 8 per cent.; in 1897–98, 8 per cent.; in 1898–99, 8 per cent.; in 1899–00, 8 per cent. Dividends are paid, 2 per cent., quarterly.

President, Rodolphe Forget; Vice-President, H. S. Holt; Secretary and Treasurer, H. H. Henshaw.

Directors—Rodolphe Forget, H. B. Rainville, James Wilson, George Caverhill, H. S. Holt, J. Reid Wilson, F. C. Henshaw.

Main office, New York Life Insurance Building, Montreal. Annual meeting, first week in June.

## F. S. ROYSTER GUANO CO.

A corporation formed under the laws of Virginia in 1900. The object of the company is the manufacture and sale of fertilizers. It has three plants, one at Norfolk, Va., with a capacity of 80,000 tons of fertilizer per annum, one at Tarboro, N. C., with a capacity of 15,000 tons, and one at Columbia, S. C., with 40,000 tons capacity. In 1902 the company built a large cotton-seed oil mill at Tarboro, N. C.

Stock.....Par $100........Authorized { com., $500,000; pref., 500,000 } Issued { pref., $500,000; com., 500,000 } $1,000,000

The preferred stock is 6 per cent., cumulative.

Dividends on the preferred stock are payable semi-annually, January and July.

The company has no funded debt or mortgage indebtedness. The consent of a majority of each class of the stock is required for the issuance of bonds.

President and Treasurer, F. S. Royster; Vice-President and Secretary, C. F. Burroughs, Norfolk, Va.

Directors—F. S. Royster, C. F. Burroughs, Charles E. Williams, W. S. Royster, Norfolk, Va.; C. A. Johnson, Tarboro, N. C.

Main office, Withers Building, Norfolk, Va. Annual meeting, first week in July.

## RUBBER GOODS MANUFACTURING CO.

A corporation formed under the laws of New Jersey, January 26, 1899. The plants controlled by this company are engaged in the manufacture of all kinds of rubber goods, except boots and shoes, and of specialties including mechanical goods and tires. The company acquired:

The capital stock of the Mechanical Rubber Co., which owns the plants of the Chicago Rubber Works, Chicago; Cleveland Rubber Works, Cleveland; New York Belting & Packing

Co., Passaic, N. J., and Sandy Hook, Conn.; Fabric Fire Hose Co., Warwick, N. Y.; Stoughton Rubber Co., Stoughton, Mass.

Seventy-five per cent. of the capital stock of Morgan & Wright, Chicago.
The entire capital stock of the Peerless Rubber Manufacturing Co., New York.
The entire capital stock of the India Rubber Co. of Akron, O.
The entire capital stock of the Sawyer Belting Co., Cambridgeport, Mass.
The entire capital stock of the Peoria Rubber & Manufacturing Co., Peoria, Ill.
The entire capital stock of the Indianapolis Rubber Works Co., Indianapolis, Ind.
The entire capital stock of the Hartford Rubber Works Co., Hartford, Conn.
And other valuable properties.

The company began business with a cash working capital of $1,427,820.

In 1900 the company acquired the rubber manufacturing interests of the American Bicycle Co., with valuable patents and contracts.

Stock..Par $100...Authorized { com., $25,000,000 / pref., 25,000,000 } Issued { com., $16,941,700 / pref., 8,051,400 } $24,993,100

The preferred stock is 7 per cent., cumulative.

No bonded debt can be incurred without the consent of two-thirds of the preferred stock and a majority of the common.

The preferred stock was issued only for tangible assets, including real estate, buildings, machinery, plants and all accessories, stocks of raw material and supplies, and goods in process of manufacture, or manufactured goods, as well as accounts and bills receivable approved by this company and guaranteed by the vendors. Where properties could not be acquired directly the company acquired a majority of the stock of the company or companies owning the same. The common stock was issued in payment for good will, patents, secret processes, trade-marks, contracts and other values.

Transfer Agents, Baring, Magoun & Co., New York, and The Corporation Trust Co. of New Jersey, Jersey City. Registrar, United States Mortgage & Trust Co., New York.

FUNDED DEBT—CONSTITUENT COS.

| | |
|---|---|
| Mechanical Rubber Co., 1st mort., 6 per cent., due Jan., 1918, Jan. and July.......... | $845,500 |
| N. Y. Belting & Packing Co., 1st mort., 6 per cent., due Jan., 1918, Jan. and July... | 280,725 |
| American Dunlop Tire, 1st mort., 6 per cent., due 1903.............................. | 19,000 |
| Total........................................................................ | $1,145,225 |

In the three years ending December 31, 1901, the total receipts were $3,350,943; net income, $2,460,657; dividends on preferred, $1,445,548; on common, $811,067; balance surplus, $204,041.

The payment of regular quarterly dividends of 1¾ per cent. on the preferred stock began June 15, 1899, and dividends of the same amount have since been regularly paid, March, June, September and December. A dividend of 1 per cent. on the common was also paid in July (15), 1900, and similar quarterly dividends were paid on the common to July, 1901, inclusive. Action on subsequent dividends on the common was, however, deferred.

In 1902 the board of directors was given authority to borrow $5,000,000 and to pledge the securities owned for this purpose.

President, Alden S. Swan; Vice-Presidents, S. Eugene Underhill, W. R. K. Taylor; Treasurer, James B. Taylor; Secretary, William A. Towner, New York.

Directors—Alvah Trowbridge, Henry Steers, Arthur L. Kelley, Alden S. Swan, William A. Towner, H. S. Burrill, W. R. K. Taylor, H. W. Wilkening, A. G. Whitman, J. Archibald Murray, John B. Morris, H. W. Turnball, Eugene Underhill, Edward Lauterbach, John H. Hammond, New York.

Main office, New Brunswick, N. J.

## RUTLAND TRANSIT CO.

A corporation formed under the laws of the State of Vermont to operate line of steamships between Ogdensburg and the western ports on the Great Lakes, succeeding the Ogdensburg Transit Co. The Rutland Railroad Co. owns all the stock and bonds of this company.

The company owns eight steamships with an average tonnage of 2,200 tons, and the wharf and warehouse property in Chicago.

Stock......Par $100...........................Authorized, $1,000,000......Issued, $1,000,000

FUNDED DEBT.

1st mort., 5 per cent., gold, due Jan., 1920, Jan. and July.......................... $1,000,000

The bond issue is secured by a mortgage of the company's boats and other property to the Old Colony Trust Co. of Boston.

EARNINGS.

| | Gross. | Net. |
|---|---|---|
| 1895 | $345,576 | $51,120 |
| 1896 | 368,948 | 118,017 |
| 1897 | 315,632 | 5,674 |
| 1898 | 308,195 | 49,741 |
| 1899 | 346,268 | 77,747 |
| 1900 | 377,534 | 47,618 |
| 1901 | 347,912 | 93,098 |
| 1902 | 341,703 | 81,297 |

President, W. Seward Webb; Clerk, A. G. Adams, Rutland, Vt.; Treasurer, Clarence Morgan, New York; Auditor, M. H. Chamberlain, Rutland, Vt.

Directors—George R. Bottum, Rutland, Vt.; W. Seward Webb, Shelburne, Vt.; George H. Ball, Boston; Frank R. Wells, Burlington, Vt.

Main office, Rutland, Vt.

## SACRAMENTO ELECTRIC, GAS & RAILWAY CO.

A corporation formed under the laws of California, April 4, 1896, to operate a street railway and supply electric light and power to the city of Sacramento, Cal. The company is a consolidation of the Sacramento Electric Power & Light Co. and the Folsom Water Power Co. It also acquired in July, 1899, the control of the Capital Gas Co. of Sacramento, having a capital stock of $500,000, and 6 per cent. bonds for $150,000. The company has water power at Folsom, Cal., and a street railway system of 24½ miles single track. Its franchises are for 50 years. It also owns East Park and Oak Park. The Capital Gas Co. was consolidated with this company in 1902. A combination of this company with the Bay Counties Power Co. was also reported to be probable.

Stock......Par $100.... ......................Authorized, $2,500,000......Issued, $1,852,000

The company has no preferred stock.

Monthly dividends of 15 cents a share have been paid, beginning January 1, 1901.

FUNDED DEBT.

| | |
|---|---|
| 1st mort., 5 per cent., gold bonds, due 1927, May and Nov. | $1,980,000 |
| Central Electric Ry., 1st mort., 6 per cent., gold, due 1912–1921, June and Dec. | 265,000 |
| Total | $2,245,000 |

The authorized amount of the Sacramento Electric, Gas & Railway Co.'s bonds is $2,500,000, of which $1,685,000 were issued under the terms of the consolidation; $50,000 issued to retire a like amount of the Folsom Water Co.'s 7 per cent. bonds; $265,000 set aside to retire the Central Railway Co.'s bonds, and $400,000 reserved in the treasury.

EARNINGS.

Year ending January 31.

| | Gross. | Net. | Charges. | Profit. | Net Surplus. |
|---|---|---|---|---|---|
| 1901 | $376,970 | $203,572 | $107,185 | $3,206 | $93,180 |
| 1902 | 419,781 | 224,514 | 113,540 | 9,602 | 101,371 |

The total surplus for 1901 was $226,912; dividends paid during the year, $36,103; net surplus, January 31, 1902, $190,808.

President, Albert Gallatin; Vice-President, Alexander McCallum; Secretary-Treasurer and General Manager, Albert Gallatin, Jr.

Directors—John Martin, Albert Gallatin, Alexander McCallum, J. B. Wright, Charles R. Lloyd.

Main office, Market and Third streets, San Francisco; branch office, Sixth and H streets, Sacramento, Cal. Annual meeting, first Tuesday in March, at Sacramento.

## THE SAFETY CAR HEATING & LIGHTING CO.

A corporation formed under the laws of New Jersey in 1887. The company owns the American patents covering the Pintsch compressed oil-gas system for lighting railroad cars. The same system is also employed for lighting buoys and has been adopted by the United States Lighthouse Board for that purpose. Nearly all the leading railroad companies in the United States have placed Pintsch lights in their passenger coaches. This system has been applied to 21,000 cars in the United States. The company has 65 gas works in various cities where cars equipped with its lighting apparatus are charged. The company also controls a system for heating cars by hot water circulation and direct steam with regulating devices.

Stock......Par $100..........................Authorized, $5,000,000.......Issued, $4,849,000

The stock of this company was increased in December, 1899, from $2,500,000 to $5,000,000. The increase being used to provide for additional stations and to extend the company's operations.

Stock is transferred at the office of the company, New York.

The company has paid dividends on its stock as follows: In 1889 to 1892 inclusive, 4 per cent.; in 1893 to 1897 inclusive, 6 per cent.; in 1898, 1899, 1900 and 1901, 8 per cent. In October, 1901, 3 per cent. extra was paid, and on September 2, 1901, 10 per cent. in stock. In October, 1902, and January, 1903, 1 per cent. extra was paid. Dividends are paid quarterly, January (1), April, July and October.

In the year 1902, the earnings were net $626,183. Including the operations of its subsidiary organization, the Pintsch Co., the net was $895,808.

President, Robert Andrews; Vice-President, Robert M. Dixon; Secretary, S. B. Hynes; Treasurer, C. H. Wardwell.

Directors—A. B. Hepburn, Robert Andrews, Thomas C. Platt, Edward Lauterbach, Austin Lathrop, William Barbour, E. M. Bulkley, W. H. Kimball, P. B. Wyckoff, G. F. Baker, Jr., R. M. Dixon, A. C. Soper, J. E. French, William A. Read, Samuel R. Callaway, Randolph Parmley.

Main office, 160 Broadway, New York. Annual meeting, second Tuesday in May, at Jersey City.

## ST. JOSEPH GAS CO.

(Controlled by American Light & Traction Co.)

This company owns and operates the gas works of St. Joseph, Mo., having a perpetual franchise and 52 miles of mains, serving a population of 60,000. Price of gas to consumers, $1 per 1,000 feet.

In 1901 the American Light & Traction Co. acquired practically all the stock of this company, offering $40 in its own preferred and $12 in its common stock for each share of this company's stock. See statement of that company.

Stock......Par $100..........................Authorized, $1,000,000......Issued, $1,000,000

Transfer Agents, Emerson McMillin & Co., 40 Wall street, New York. Registrar, Morton Trust Co., New York.

FUNDED DEBT.

1st mort., 5 per cent. gold, due 1937, Jan. and July................ .................. $752,000

The 1st mortgage, created in 1897, is for $1,000,000.

President, Emerson McMillin, New York; Vice-President, W. A. P. McDonald; Secretary and Treasurer, G. Labrunerie; General Manager, K. M. Mitchell.

Directors—Emerson McMillin, Charles A. Pfeiffer, Milton Tootle, Jr., W. A. P. McDonald, Stephen C. Woodson, Huston Wyeth, H. R. W. Hartwig, James Campbell, L. C. Burnes.

Main office, 516 Francis street, St. Joseph, Mo.

## ST. JOSEPH RAILWAY, LIGHT, HEAT & POWER CO.

A corporation formed under the laws of Missouri in 1895. The company acquired the following companies:

| | |
|---|---|
| The St. Joseph Traction & Lighting Co. | People's Railway, Light & Power Co. |
| Citizens Railway Co. | Union Railway Co. |
| St. Joseph & Lake Railway Co. | Wyatt Park Railway Co. |

The company controls the entire street railway system of St. Joseph, Mo., owning and operating 40 miles of track. It also owns the entire commercial electric lighting and power business of the city, and a pleasure park of 350 acres. Most of its franchises are perpetual, while the others run from 37 to 48 years.

Stock...Par $100.....Authorized { com., $3,500,000 / pref., 2,500,000 } Issued { com., $3,500,000 / pref., 1,500,000 } $5,000,000

The preferred stock is 5 per cent., non-cumulative.

Dividends on the preferred stock at the rate of 5 per cent. per annum have been paid.

FUNDED DEBT.

1st mort., 5 per cent., gold, due Nov. 1, 1937, March and Nov.......................$3,500,000

The authorized amount of the 1st mortgage is $5,000,000, of which amount $1,500,000 are reserved for future betterments, etc. Trustees of the mortgage, Trust Co. of America, New York, and Missouri Valley Trust Co., St. Joseph, Mo. Agent for the payment of interest, Redmond, Kerr & Co., New York.

| EARNINGS. | Gross. | Net. |
|---|---|---|
| 1901 | $455,754 | $220,597 |
| 1902 | 546,275 | 260,193 |

In 1902 the surplus over charges was $105,193.

President and General Manager, W. T. Van Brunt, St. Joseph, Mo.; Vice-President, E. W. Clark, Jr., Philadelphia; Secretary and Treasurer, Charles C. Tegethoff, New York.

Corporate and main office, St. Joseph, Mo.; Secretary and Treasurer's office, 120 Broadway, New York.

## ST. JOSEPH STOCK YARDS CO.

A corporation formed under the laws of Missouri, August 5, 1896. The company's business is the ownership and operation of a stock yard at South St. Joseph, Mo. The property owned consists of 423 acres adjoining the city of St. Joseph, with a Live Stock Exchange, pens for 17,000 hogs, 5,000 cattle and 10,000 sheep, and all needed facilities for the business the company conducts. There are 20 miles of railroad track on the premises and the company owns 6 locomotives.

Stock......Par $100..........................Authorized, $1,650,000......Issued, $1,650,000

The company has no preferred stock. Stock is transferred at the company's office. Registrars, Vermilye & Co., New York.

FUNDED DEBT.

1st mort., 4½ per cent., due Jan., 1930, Jan. and July.............................. $1,250,000

The 1st mortgage bonds are dated Jan. 1, 1900, and are $1,250,000 authorized. Trustees of mortgage, North American Trust Co., New York, and Graham G. Lacey, St. Joseph, Mo. Agent for payment of interest, Vermilye & Co., New York. The company may redeem the bonds in whole or part at 105 and interest at any interest period on or after January 1, 1910, on four weeks' previous notice.

The first dividend on the stock was 3 per cent., paid June 30, 1900. In September, 1900, the company began the payment of regular quarterly dividends of 1½ per cent. on its stock. Dividends at that rate are paid in March (31), June, September and December.

EARNINGS.

| | Gross. | Net. | Charges. | Surplus. |
|---|---|---|---|---|
| 1902 | $409,421 | $276,539 | $134,507 | $142,031 |

President (Vacancy); Vice-President, Treasurer and General Manager, John Donovan; Secretary, Charles Pasche; Assistant General Manager, Horace Wood, St. Joseph, Mo.

Directors—Edward Morris, Albert H. Veeder, J. P. Lyman, Chicago; John Donovan, Horace Wood, J. G. Schneider, St. Joseph, Mo.

Corporate and main office, South St. Joseph, Mo. Fiscal Agents, Vermilye & Co., New York. Annual meeting, second Monday in January, at South St. Joseph, Mo.

## THE ST. LAWRENCE RIVER POWEH CO.

A corporation formed under the laws of New York, July 19, 1902. The company was organized to succeed and take over the property of the St. Lawrence Power Co., which was foreclosed and reorganized as per plan given below.

The company owns 1,800 acres of land and valuable water rights at Massena, N. Y. The company constructed a canal three miles long with a fall of fifty feet connecting the St. Lawrence and Grasse rivers, and has erected a power house having 35,000 horse-power. In March, 1902, the company having unpaid interest charges a reorganization was proposed and bondholders were asked to deposit their bonds with Robert Winthrop & Co., New York, for that purpose.

The plan was carried out and the property sold in July, 1902.

Stock....Par $100.... Authorized { com., $3,500,000 / pref., 3,500,000 } Issued { com., $3,500,000 / pref., 3,000,000 } $6,500,000

The preferred stock is 6 per cent., non-cumulative.

Stock is transferred at the office of the company, 40 Wall street, New York. Registrar, United States Mortgage & Trust Co., New York.

FUNDED DEBT.

1st mort., 5 per cent., due 1913, Jan. and July ...................................... $300,000

The trustee of the mortgage is the United States Mortgage & Trust Co., New York. Interest on the bonds is paid at the office of Robert Winthrop & Co., 40 Wall street, New York.

President, Thomas A. Gillespie, Massena, N. Y.; Vice-President, Mark T. Cox; Secretary and Treasurer, William J. Wilson, New York.

Directors—Mark T. Cox, East Orange, N. J.; Thomas A. Gillespie, Massena, N. Y.; Henry P. Davieson, Englewood, N. J.; Samuel E. Potter, New York.

Main office, Massena, N. Y.; New York office, 40 Wall street. Annual meeting, third Tuesday in January, at Massena, N. Y.

## ST. LOUIS & SUBURBAN RAILWAY CO.

A corporation formed under the laws of Missouri, September 11, 1884. Road operated in St. Louis and suburbs, 40 miles. Extensions are planned of about 30 miles. Company is a reorganization of St. Louis Cable & Western Railway Co. The company absorbed the St. Louis & Kirkwood Railroad.

Stock......Par $100..........................Authorized, $3,000,000......Issued, $2,500,000

Stock is transferred by the secretary of the company in St. Louis.

FUNDED DEBT.

| | |
|---|---|
| St. Louis Cable & Western 1st mort., 6 per cent., due 1914, March and Nov.......... | $600,000 |
| St. Louis & Suburban 1st mort., 6 per cent., due Feb., 1921, Feb. and Aug........... | 1,400,000 |
| Income bonds, 5 per cent., due Feb., 1921, annual, Feb............................ | 300,000 |
| St. Louis & Meramee River Railroad 1st mort., 6 per cent., due May, 1916, May and Nov.. | 1,000,000 |
| Total............................................................. | $3,300,000 |

The St. Louis & Suburban 1st mortgage is for $2,000,000, of which $600,000 are reserved to retire outstanding 5s of old 6s. Trustee and agent for the payment of interest, American Loan & Trust Co., Boston.

President, S. M. Kennard; Secretary and Treasurer, T. C. Kimber, St. Louis.

Directors—Charles H. Turner, S. M. Kennard, Henry Nicolaus, C. Manquard Foster, James Green, Ellis Wainwright, Clark H. Sampson, James P. Dawson, T. M. Jenkins, St. Louis.

Main office, Wainwright Building, St. Louis. Annual meeting, second Monday in January.

## ST. LOUIS BREWING ASSOCIATION

A corporation formed under the laws of Missouri, June 1, 1889, to engage in the business of brewing beer. The association acquired 18 brewery plants in St. Louis and vicinity, and now operates 15 plants. The total production of the plants of the association for 1902 was 695,646 barrels. The association is controlled by the St. Louis Breweries, Ltd., a corporation formed under the English Co.'s Act.

Stock......Par $100..........................Authorized, $5,250,000......Issued, $5,088,624

The association has no preferred stock.

Dividends are declared at the option of the Board of Directors.

FUNDED DEBT.

1st mort., 6 per cent., due 1914, Jan. and July.................................... $4,961,600

The outstanding bonds are the total amount authorized. Trustee of the mortgage, Union Trust Co., St. Louis. Agent for the payment of interest, National Bank of Commerce, St. Louis. Interest is also payable at London.

At the end of the fiscal year, September 30, 1902, the association had in bills receivable, cash and materials, $2,385,329.47, and a balance and surplus of $426,499.

President, Henry Nicolaus; 1st Vice-President, C. Marquard Forster; 2d Vice-President, John G. Grone; Secretary, Philip Stock; Treasurer, William F. Nolker.

Directors—Henry Nicolaus, C. Marquard Forster, John C. Grone, C. Norman Jones, William A. Haren, William F. Nolker, Philip Stock.

Corporate and main office, Seventh and Chestnut streets, St. Louis. Annual meeting, first Monday in October, at St. Louis.

## ST. LOUIS TERMINAL CUPPLES STATION & PROPERTY CO.

A corporation formed under the laws of Missouri, March 18, 1897. The company owns a large union freight station and warehouse building in St. Louis, covering several city blocks adjoining the property and terminal of Terminal Railway Association of St. Louis. The property is operated through the latter company in the interest of the railroads entering St. Louis. Its warehouses are leased to wholesale mercantile houses.

Stock..Par $100 ....Authorized { com., $2,000,000 / pref., 1,000,000 } Issued { com., $2,000,000 / pref., 1,000,000 } $3,000,000

Dividends of 5 per cent. per annum are paid on the preferred stock. On the common, 1 per cent. was paid in May, 1900.

The preferred stock is 5 per cent., cumulative.

FUNDED DEBT.

1st mort. 4½ per cent., due June, 1912, June and Dec............................... $3,000,000

The 1st mortgage bonds are redeemable at 102 after 1902. The trustee of the mortgage is the Union Trust Co. of St. Louis.

EARNINGS.

Year ending May 31.

| | Gross. | Net. | Charges. | Surplus. |
|---|---|---|---|---|
| 1897-98 (13½ months)........................ | $311,740 | $253,648 | $161,854 | $91,794 |
| 1898-99........................................ | 302,970 | 235,794 | 135,000 | 100,794 |
| 1899-00........................................ | 309,639 | 238,183 | 135,000 | 103,183 |
| 1900-01 ........................................ | 314,764 | 228,289 | 135,000 | 93,289 |

President, Robert S. Brookings; Vice-President, Samuel Cupples; Secretary and Treasurer, E. S. Pierce, St. Louis.

Directors—Robert S. Brookings, Samuel Cupples, E. S. Pierce, A. Cupples Scudder, A. W. Benedict.

Main office, corner Seventh and Spruce streets, St. Louis.

## ST. MARY'S MINERAL LAND CO.

A corporation formed under the laws of New Jersey, in March, 1901. The company was organized to succeed the St. Mary's Canal Mineral Land Co. The latter was a New York corporation owning large tracts of mineral land in the copper district of Upper Michigan. The property owned by the present company comprised, on December 31, 1902, 103,335 acres, and the mining rights on 7,806 acres additional in what is known as the Mineral Range. The company sold tracts to various mining companies, receiving in payment for the same cash or securities of the purchasing corporations. The company has large interests in the stocks of the Champion, Mayflower, Trimountain and other copper mining companies.

The St. Mary's Canal Mineral Land Co. had 20,000 shares of $50 par value, or a capital of $1,000,000. Under the plan which was issued in March, 1901, the stockholders of the company were invited to exchange each share of the old stock for six shares of new, and also had the privilege of subscribing at $25 per share in cash for new stock to the amount of their former holdings. The time for deposits of old stock and of subscriptions for new expired March 28, 1901.

Stock......Par $25...........................Authorized, $5,000,000......Issued, $3,484,250

The company's receipts, in 1901, were $626,297; expenditures, $352,561; cash on hand, December 31, 1901, $273,753. In 1902, receipts, $237,043; cash on hand, December 31, 1902, $116,876.

Between 1863 and 1901, the total distribution to each share of old stock included $111 cash, one-quarter share Albany & Boston Mining Company, 1 share Tamarack, 1 share Iroquois, 1½ shares Baltic and ½ share Winona Copper Company. In 1898, the old company paid dividends in cash $8.50 per share. In 1899 paid $29 per share. Last dividend paid, $4, November 28, 1899.

President, Nathaniel Thayer; Vice-President, Charles J. Paine; Secretary and Treasurer, Arthur G. Stanwood, Boston.

Directors—Nathaniel Thayer, Samuel N. Brown, Albert S. Bigelow, J. Henry Brooks, Charles J. Paine, W. Cameron Forbes, George P. Gardner, J. Malcolm Forbes, Walter Hunnewell, Boston; Charles E. Perkins, Burlington, Ia.; Charles N. King, Jersey City.

Main office, 199 Washington street, Boston.

## ST. PAUL GAS LIGHT CO.

(Controlled by American Light & Traction Co.)

A corporation formed under the laws of Minnesota in 1857. The company owns and operates gas and electric light plants of the city of St. Paul, Minn. The gas franchise is exclusive until 1907 and expires 1957. Mileage of mains, 135 miles. Price of gas to consumers is $1.30 per 1,000 feet.

The American Light & Traction Co. acquired nearly all the stock of this company, paying for each share $18.75 in its own common stock and $62 50 in its preferred.

Stock......Par $100................ .........Authorized, $1,500,000......Issued, $1,500,000

Transfer Agent, Emerson McMillin & Co., 40 Wall street, New York. Registrar, New York Security & Trust Co.

FUNDED DEBT.

| | |
|---|---|
| 1st mort., 6 per cent., currency, due 1915, Jan. and July.............................. | $650,000 |
| Consolidated extension mort., 6 per cent., due 1918, Jan. and July.................. | 600,000 |
| General mort., 5 per cent., gold, due 1944, March and Sept......................... | 2,703,000 |
| St. Croix Power Co. mort., guaranteed, due 1929, April and Oct..................... | 750,000 |
| Total ............. ........................................................ | $4,703,000 |

The 1st mortgage and consolidated mortgage bonds outstanding are the full amounts. The general mortgage created in 1894 is for $5,000,000, balance of issue being reserved to retire prior liens and for improvements and extensions. Trustee of general mortgage, New York Security & Trust Co., New York, where coupons on the bonds are paid.

Net earnings for 1897 were $248,853; for 1898, $273,207; for 1899, $278,854.

The company pays dividends of 4 per cent. per annum, in quarterly payments, February (15), May, August and November.

President, A. P. Lathrop; Vice-President, Kenneth Clark; Secretary-Treasurer, J. P. Crowley; Assistant Secretary, H. Lincoln Eglinton.

Directors—A. P. Lathrop, Kenneth Clark, Maurice Auerbach, Elbert A. Young, Emerson McMillin, Crawford Livingston.

Main office, corner Sixth and Jackson streets, St. Paul, Minn. Annual meeting, fourth Monday in January.

## ST. PAUL UNION STOCK YARDS CO.

A corporation formed under the laws of Minnesota, July 1, 1886. The purposes of the company are to construct and operate stock yards, packing houses, elevators, warehouses and to own and deal in real estate and personal property.

The company's main property consists of over 170 acres, situated on the Mississippi River, about five miles south of St. Paul, two-thirds of which is covered by stock yards, pens and inclosures, and by packing plants and other industries, and the whole tract is equipped with a complete sewer and water service and eight miles of track. The yards are on the main line of the Chicago Great Western Railway Co. and Chicago, Rock Island & Pacific Railway Co.

The chief industries located at the company's property in South St. Paul are Swift & Co.'s packing plant, occupying eighteen acres, and a capacity for handling 1,000 cattle, 4,500 hogs and 1,000 sheep per day; three small packing plants, a distillery, a malting establishment and a rendering works.

The company has yards, barns and sheds with a capacity for handling daily 10,000 hogs, 13,000 cattle, and 10,000 sheep; its facilities for sheep feeding, which are leased to sheep feeders from season to season, being sufficient for 100,000 animals.

The property includes a four-story stone and brick office building, in which are located the company's offices, the Stock Yards Bank, the various commission firms, a Cattle Loan Co., the joint railroad agency and other tenants. The company has also on hand a considerable portion of its town site adjacent to the yards.

Stock......Par $100...........................Authorized, $2,000,000......Issued, $2,000,000

The company has no preferred stock. Stock is transferred at the office of the company, St. Paul,. Registrar, Metropolitan Trust Co., New York.

FUNDED DEBT.

| | |
|---|---|
| 1st mort., 5 per cent. gold, due October, 1916, April and Oct.......................... | $1,847,000 |
| Sterling priority loan, £43,714........................................... .......... | 211,950 |
| Total......... ........................................................ | $2,058,950 |

The 1st mortgage is $1,946,000 authorized. Trustees, Robert H. Benson, London, and Metropolitan Trust Co., New York. Agents for payment of interest, Robert Benson & Co., London; Fourth National Bank, New York; company's treasurer, St. Paul.

The 5 per cent. sterling priority loan was created in 1896. It was originally £44,364, or $215,000. The loan is secured by the coupons of the 1st mortgage bonds matured in 1896, 1897 and 1898, which were funded to meet the company's requirements for construction. The Trustee of the priority loan is the Merchants' Trust, Limited, London.

EARNINGS.

| | Gross. | Net. | Charges. | Surplus. |
|---|---|---|---|---|
| 1899 | $128,956 | $80,872 | $82,455 | Def., $1,582 |
| 1900 | 148,418 | 91,708 | 86,458 | 5,249 |
| 1901 | 146,797 | 94,605 | 93,007 | 1,597 |
| 1902 | 184,286 | 118,974 | 98,203 | 20,791 |

The first dividend in the company's stock was 1½ per cent., paid in July, 1888. The company paid 3 per cent. in 1888, 4½ per cent. in 1889 and 4 per cent. in 1890, since which time no dividends have been paid. The above dividends were paid from profit on sales of real estate.

Chairman, C. W. Benson, St. Paul; President, Mark D. Flower, South St. Paul, Minn., Secretary and Treasurer, A. A. McKechnie, St. Paul, ; Superintendent and Assistant Treasurer. H. B. Carroll, South St. Paul, Minn.

Directors—C. W. Benson, Mark D. Flower, Ansel Oppenheim, A. B. Stickney, K. D. Dunlop, R. C. Wight, A. A. McKechnie, St. Paul.

Main office, South St. Paul, Minn. Annual meeting, first Wednesday after the first Tuesday in June.

## ST. REGIS PAPER CO.

A corporation formed under the laws of New York, January 28, 1899, for the purpose of manufacturing pulp and paper. The company owns 700 acres of land near Wilna, Jefferson County, N. Y., and 58,000 acres of timber land in Franklin County, N. Y. The mill has a daily capacity of 120 tons of ground wood, 40 tons of sulphite pulp, and 100 tons of paper. The company owns water power to the extent of 13,000 horse-power.

Stock.....Par $100......Authorized { com., $700,000 / pref., 900,000 } Issued { com., $700,000 / pref., 900,000 } $1,600,000

The preferred stock is 6 per cent., cumulative, and $25,000 per year to be placed to the reserve account before dividends can be declared on the common stock.

The company regularly pays the full annual dividends on the preferred.

Transfer Agent and Registrar, G. C. Sherman, Secretary, Watertown, N. Y.

FUNDED DEBT.

| | |
|---|---|
| 1st mort., 6 per cent., due 1921, June and Dec. | $400,000 |
| 2d mort., 6 per cent., due 1921, due 1921, June and Dec. | 400,000 |
| Total | $800,000 |

The authorized issue of bonds is $800,000. The Colonial Trust Co. of New York is trustee of the mortgage and agent for the payment of interest.

President, George W. Knowlton; Vice-President, William W. Taggart; General Manager, D. M. Anderson; Secretary and Treasurer, G. C. Sherman, Watertown, N. Y.

Directors—George W. Knowlton, William W. Taggart, D. M. Anderson, G. C. Sherman, Watertown, N. Y.; J. Henry Dick, Frederick D. Mollenhauer, Alvah Miller, K. B. Fullerton, A. C. Scrimgeour, Brooklyn, N. Y.

Main office, Watertown, N.Y. Annual meeting, third Wednesday in May, at Watertown, N.Y.

## THE SALEM IRON CO.

A corporation formed under the laws of Pennsylvania, July 29, 1892, for the purpose of manufacturing pig iron. The plant of the company is located at Leetonia, O., and consists of 37 acres of land, one blast furnace stack, four hot-blast stoves, engines, boilers, etc.

Stock. ....Par $50..........Authorized { com., $50,000 / pref., 205,000 } Issued { com., $50,000 / pref., 197,150 } $247,150

FUNDED DEBT.

1st mort., 6 per cent. bonds, due 1911, Jan. and July ...... $200,000

The bonds outstanding are the full amount authorized. Trustee of the mortgage and agent for the payment of interest, The Union Trust Co., Pittsburg.

President, John McKeefrey; Vice-President, W. D. McKeefrey; Secretary and Treasurer, N. J. McKeefrey, Leetonia, O.

Directors—John McKeefrey, W. D. McKeefrey, N. J. McKeefrey, S. R. Fellows, Leetonia, O.; J. W. Renner, George J. Gorman, Pittsburg; J. H. Bartow Cleveland.

Corporate and main office, 217 Fourth avenue, Pittsburg; branch office, Leetonia, O. Annual meeting, fourth Wednesday in July, at Pittsburg.

## SANTA FE GOLD & COPPER MINING CO.

A corporation formed under the laws of New Jersey, January 21, 1899. The company acquired the mines and property of the Santa Fe Copper Co., which was foreclosed in 1892. The property comprises some 40,000 acres of mineral land and claims near San Pedro, Santa Fe County, New Mexico. A large amount of exploration and development work was done by the old company and while the mine was in private hands. It is stated that large quantities of very rich ore have been developed ready for operations. In 1900 the company completed a large smelter at the mine.

Stock......Par $10..........................Authorized, $2,500,000......Issued, $2,250,000

Transfer Agent, Old Colony Trust Co., Boston.

President, J. H. Susmann; Secretary and Treasurer, Edgar Buffum, New York.

Directors—J. H. Susmann, C. S. Henry, Edgar Buffum, J. De Smet Maguire, E. C. Westervelt, E. H. Westlake, A. S. Bigelow, W. A. S. Chrimes.

Main office, 11 Broadway, New York. Annual meeting, fourth Tuesday in January.

---

## THE SAO PAULO TRAMWAY, LIGHT & POWER CO.

A corporation formed under the laws of Ontario in 1899. The company has constructed and operates about 63 miles of electric street railways in the city of Sao Paulo, Brazil. It also supplies the city with electric light and power.

Stock......Par $100..........................Authorized, $7,000,000......Issued, $6,700,000

The company has no preferred stock.

Transfer Agent, National Trust Co., Limited, Toronto.

Dividends have been paid on the stock at the rate of 5 per cent. per annum since July, 1902, the payments being quarterly, 1¼ per cent. each in January, April, July and October.

FUNDED DEBT.

1st mort., 5 per cent., due June, 1929, June and Dec.............................. .. $4,129,000

The authorized issue of 1st mortgage bonds is $6,000,000. Trustee of mortgage, National Trust Co., Limited, Toronto. Interest on the bonds is payable in Toronto or at the office of the Canadian Bank of Commerce, London.

EARNINGS.

| | Gross. | Net. | Charges. | Dividends. | Surplus. |
|---|---|---|---|---|---|
| 1902 | $1,123,285 | $705,369 | $250,000 | $238,978 | $216,391 |

On December 31, 1902, the total surplus of the company was $502,729. The ratio between operating cost and gross earnings in 1902 was 37.2 per cent.

President, William Mackenzie; Vice-President, Frederic Nicholls, Toronto; 2d Vice-President, Alexander Mackenzie, Sao Paulo, Brazil; Secretary-Treasurer, J. M. Smith, Toronto; Assistant Treasurer, D. Mulqueen; General Manager, James Mitchell, Sao Paulo, Brazil.

Directors—William Mackenzie, Frederic Nicholls, George A. Cox, E. R. Wood, J. H. Plummer, A. W. Mackenzie, Toronto; F. S. Pearson, New York; Alexander Mackenzie, Sao Paulo, Brazil.

Main office, Railway Chambers, Toronto; operating office, Rua Direita, No. 7, Sao Paulo, Brazil.

---

## SAULT STE. MARIE BRIDGE CO.

A corporation formed under the laws of Michigan. This company owns the railroad bridge crossing the Sault Ste. Marie used by the Canadian Pacific, Minneapolis, St. Paul & Sault Ste. Marie, and Duluth, South Shore & Atlantic Railways.

Stock......Par $100..........................Authorized, $1,000,000......Issued, $1,000,000

FUNDED DEBT.

1st mort., 5 per cent., due July, 1937, Jan. and July................................. $900,000

The 1st mortgage is for $1,000,000. There is a sinking fund of $5,500 yearly for the bonds. The lessees pay rental equal to the yearly interest charges and sinking fund requirements.

President, Sir Thomas G. Shaughnessy, Montreal; Vice-President, James O. Bloss, New York; Secretary and Treasurer, George H Church, New York.

Main office, 44 Wall street, New York. Annual meeting, fourth Wednesday in June, at Detroit.

## SAVANNAH ELECTRIC CO.

A corporation formed under the laws of Georgia in December, 1901. The company was organized for the purpose of combining the street railway and electric lighting systems of the city of Savannah. It has acquired the following properties:

City & Suburban Railroad.
Edison Electric Illuminating Co.
Savannah, Thunderbolt & Isle of Hope Railway Co.

The Savannah, Thunderbolt & Isle of Hope Railway Co. owned the Suburban & West End Railway and the Savannah Traction Co. The Electric Co. controls and operates 54 miles of track in Savannah and vicinity.

Stock....Par $100.....Authorized { com., $2,500,000; pref., 1,000,000 } Issued { com., $2,500,000; pref., 1,000,000 } $3,500,000

The preferred stock is 6 per cent., non-cumulative, and is subject to call at any time at 120. Transfer Agents, Stone & Webster, 93 Federal street, Boston. Registrar, American Loan & Trust Co., Boston.

FUNDED DEBT.

| | |
|---|---|
| 1st mort., 5 per cent. gold bonds, due Jan., 1952, Jan. & July | $1,500,000 |
| Savannah, Thunderbolt & Isle of Hope Railway Co., 1st mort., 4 per cent. bonds, due 1947, Jan., April, July and Oct. | 1,000,000 |
| Edison Electric Illuminating Co., 1st mort., 5 per cent. bonds, due 1919, April and Oct. | 250,000 |
| City & Suburban R. R., 1st mort., 7 per cent. bonds, due 1907, Feb., May, Aug. and Nov. | 200,000 |
| City & Suburban Railroad, 2d mort., 6 per cent., due 1903, Feb., May, Aug. and Nov. | 50,000 |
| Total | $3,000,000 |

The authorized issue of the Savannah Electric Co.'s bonds is $2,500,000, of which $1,000,000 is retained to retire the outstanding bonds of the Savannah, Thunderbolt & Isle of Hope Railway Co. The authorized issue of the bonds of the Savannah, Thunderbolt & Isle of Hope Railway Co. is $1,250,000, but $250,000 of this issue has been retired. An additional $1,000,000 of bonds may be issued by the Savannah Electric Co. for construction and equipment purposes. The Electric Co. bonds may be called at 110 and accrued interest.

Trustee of the Savannah Electric Co.'s bonds, American Loan & Trust Co., Boston.

Trustee of the Savannah, Thunderbolt & Isle of Hope Railway Co., Central Trust Co., New York.

The earnings of the combined properties in the year ending September 30, 1901, were: Gross, $421,494; net, $197,322; surplus, $185,809. In the year ending June 30, 1902, the gross was $458,365; net, $186,330.

President, George J. Baldwin; Vice-President, A. Stuart Pratt; Secretary, Abram S. Minis; Treasurer, H. B. Sawyer; General Managers, Stone & Webster, Boston.

Directors—George J. Baldwin, Russell Robb, H. D. Stevens, J. S. Bartlett, W. W. Mackall, J. J. Storrow, J. A. G. Garson, Abram S. Minis, E. S. Webster, A. L. Alexander, C. A. Stone, Jacob Paulsen, G. N. Lane, H. B. Sawyer, J. S. Collins.

Main office, 93 Federal street, Boston.

---

## SCHENECTADY RAILWAY CO.

A corporation formed under the laws of New York in February, 1895. The company was organized to succeed the Schenectady Street Railway Co. and absorbed the Schenectady Illuminating Co. It operates the entire street railway, electric light and power system of the city of Schenectady, N. Y., and suburbs. Miles of track operated, 35.

Stock......Par $100 ..............................Authorized, $600,000......Issued, $600,000

The company has no preferred stock. Stock is transferred at the office of the company.

FUNDED DEBT.

1st mort., 4½ per cent. gold bonds, due 1941, March and Sept...................... $2,000,000

The full amount of bonds authorized is $2,000,000. Trustee of mortgage and agent for the payment of interest, Mercantile Trust Co., New York.

EARNINGS.

| Year ending June 30. | Gross. | Net. |
|---|---|---|
| 1900–01 | $93,711 | $75,690 |
| 1901–02 | 288,903 | 128,671 |
| 1902 (year ending Dec. 31) | 573,770 | 187,024 |

President, Hinsdill Parsons; Vice-President and General Manager, E. F. Peck; Secretary and Treasurer, James O. Carr, Schenectady, N. Y.

Directors—Hinsdill Parsons, E. W. Rice, Jr., J. R. Lovejoy, F. O. Blackwell, H. C. Wirt, E. F. Peck, G. E. Emmons, W. L. R. Emmet, A. L. Rohrer, Schenectady, N. Y.

Corporate and main office, 420 State street, Schenectady, N. Y. Annual meeting, first Tuesday in February, at Schenectady, N. Y.

## SCHUYLKILL TRACTION CO.

A corporation formed under the laws of Pennsylvania, September 26, 1892. The corporation has acquired the following companies:

Mahanoy City, Shenandoah, Girardville & Ashland Street Railway Co.
Shenandoah & Pottsville Street Railway Co.
Ashland, Locustdale & Centralia Electric Railway Co.
Lakeside Railway Co.

The company controls the entire electric street railway system in the boroughs of Shenadoah, Mahanoy City, Ashland, Gilberton and Girardville, Pa., with a population of 200,000. It owns 35 cars and operates 38 miles of track.

Stock....Par $100....Authorized { com., $1,500,000 / pref., 500,000 } Issued { com., $1,500,000 / pref., 500,000 } $2,000,000

The preferred stock is 5 per cent., non-cumulative. Stock is transferred at the office of the Secretary, Philadelphia. Registrar, Guarantee Trust Co., Philadelphia.

FUNDED DEBT.

| | |
|---|---|
| 1st mort., 5 per cent., gold, due April, 1943, April and Oct. | $500,000 |
| New con. mort., 4½ per cent., gold, due July, 1951, Jan. and July | 59,000 |
| Lakeside Railway Co., 1st mort., 4 per cent., gold, due Nov., 1923, May and Nov. | 150,000 |
| Total | $709,000 |

The authorized amount of the new consolidated mortgage is $2,000,000. Bonds are subject to call at any time at 105 and interest. A sinking fund of 1 per cent. is provided to take effect August 1, 1907. Trustee of the mortgage and agent for the payment of interest, Fidelity Trust Co., Philadelphia.

The outstanding bonds of the 1st mortgage are the full amount authorized. A sinking fund of $10,000 annually is provided to take effect after April, 1898. Bonds may be purchased for the sinking fund at 105. Trustee of the mortgage and agent for the payment of interest, Equitable Trust Co., Philadelphia.

The outstanding bonds of the Lakeside Railway Co. are the full amount authorized. Trustee of the mortgage and agent for the payment of interest, Equitable Trust Co., Philadelphia.

In the year ending December 31, 1901, the company's gross earnings were: $208,258; net earnings, $56,624; surplus, $23,337.

President, Clarke Merchant; Secretary and Treasurer, J. A. McKee, Philadelphia.

Directors—Dallas Sanders, John F. Finney, Cleaton Newbold, Clarke Merchant, Herman Hoopes, J. A. McKee, Philadelphia.

Main office, Girardville, Pa.; Philadelphia office, 517 Arch street. Annual meeting, second Monday in January, at Girardville.

## SCRANTON RAILWAY CO.

A corporation formed under the laws of Pennsylvania, March 23, 1865, as the People's Street Railway Co. of Luzerne County. When the company adopted its present name the following companies were merged into it:

Scranton Passenger Railway Co.
Scranton Suburban Railway Co.
Dunmore Street Railway Co.
Valley Passenger Railway Co.

The company purchased the assets and assumed the liabilities of the Scranton Traction Co. The company also acquired and operates under leases the following companies:

Scranton & Carbondale Traction Co.
Lackawanna Valley Traction Co.
Pittston & Scranton Street Railway Co.
Carbondale Railway Co.
Scranton & Pittston Traction Co.

The company owns or operates under lease all the street railways in and around the city of Scranton, Pa., including lines to Pittston, Carbondale and other towns. The aggregate of the systems is 76.68 miles and it owns a power house and 140 cars.

It owns the total issue of bonds of the Carbondale Railway Co., $300,000, and 60,000 bonds of the Scranton & Pittston Traction Co. It also owns all of the stock of the Scranton &

Carbondale Traction Co., the Lackawanna Valley Traction Co., the Pittston & Scranton Street Railway Co., the Carbondale Railway Co., and nearly all of the Scranton & Pittston Traction Co.

Stock......Par $50............................Authorized, $6,000,000......Issued, $3,000,000

The company has no preferred stock. Transfer Agents, E. W. Clark & Co., Philadelphia. Registrar, Provident Life & Trust Co., Philadelphia.

The first dividend on the stock was paid September 1, 1900, 1 per cent.

FUNDED DEBT.

| | |
|---|---|
| Scranton Railway, 1st mort., 5 per cent., gold, due Nov., 1932, Jan. and July......... | $900,000 |
| " " col. trust mort., 5 per cent., gold, due Nov., 1932, Jan. and July... | 500,000 |
| Scranton Traction Co., 1st mort., 6 per cent., gold, due Nov., 1932, May and Nov.... | 1,000,000 |
| Scranton Passenger Railway Co., 1st mort., 6 per cent., due May, 1920, May and Nov.. | 100,000 |
| Scranton Suburban Ry., 1st mort., 6 per cent., gold, due May, 1909, May and Nov..... | 200,000 |
| People's Street Railway Co., 1st mort., 6 per cent., gold, due Aug., 1918, Feb. and Aug.. | 200,000 |
| " " " gen. mort., 6 per cent., gold, due Dec., 1921, July and Dec. | 100,000 |
| Carbondale Railway Co., 1st mort., 5 per cent., gold, due June, 1926, July and Dec... | 300,000 |
| Carbondale Traction Co., 1st mort., 6 per cent., gold, due July, 1922, Jan. and July.. | 150,000 |
| Scranton & Carbondale Traction, 1st mort., 6 per cent., due Jan., 1923, Jan. and July. | 150,000 |
| Scranton & Pittston Traction, 1st mort., 6 per cent., due Oct., 1923, April and Oct.... | 355,500 |
| Total.............................................................. | $3,955,500 |

The authorized amount of the 1st consolidated mortgage of the Scranton Railway Co. is $2,500,000, of which $1,600,000 are reserved to retire prior liens. Trustee of the mortgage and agent for the payment of interest, Continental Trust Co., New York. Interest is payable at the company's office or by E. W. Clark & Co., Philadelphia.

The outstanding bonds of the collateral trust mortgage are the full amount authorized. They are subject to call at any time on 30 days' notice at 105 and interest. Trustee of the mortgage, Provident Life & Trust Co., Philadelphia. Interest is payable at the office of the company, in Scranton, and by E. W. Clark & Co., Philadelphia.

The outstanding bonds of the Scranton Traction Co.'s 1st mortgage are the full amount authorized. Interest is payable at the office of the company or by E. W. Clark & Co., Philadelphia. Trustee of the mortgage, Fidelity Trust Co., Philadelphia.

The outstanding bonds of the Carbondale Traction Co.'s 1st mortgage and the Carbondale Railway Co.'s 1st mortgage are the full amount authorized. Trustee of the mortgage of the Carbondale Traction Co. and agent for the payment of interest, Central Trust Co., New York.

The authorized mortgage of the Scranton & Carbondale Traction Co. is $150,000. Agent for the payment of interest, E. W. Clark & Co., Philadelphia. The authorized mortgage of the Scranton & Pittston Traction Co. is $525,000. Trustee of the mortgage and agent for the payment of interest, Union Trust Co., Philadelphia.

In the fiscal year ending June 30, 1901, the company's gross earnings were $614,022; net earnings, $259,564; taxes, $19,200; interest, $200,800; surplus, $38,764.

President, C. M. Clark; Vice-President, E. W. Clark, Jr.; Secretary and Treasurer, C. Ford Stevens, Philadelphia; General Manager, Frank Silliman, Jr., Scranton, Pa.

Directors—C. M. Clark, John M. Burke, E. W. Clark, Jr., G. L. Estabrook, Frank Silliman, Jr., Timothy Burke, C. Ford Stevens.

Main office, 139 South Fourth street, Philadelphia; General Manager's office, Scranton, Pa. Annual meeting, third Tuesday in January, or within sixty days thereafter, at Scranton.

---

## THE SEATTLE ELECTRIC CO.

A corporation formed under the laws of Washington, January 3, 1900. The company controls all the electric light interests and nearly all the street railways in and around the city of Seattle, Wash. The company acquired the following companies:

Seattle Traction Co.
Madison Street Cable Railway Co.
Consumers' Electric Co.
North Seattle Cable Railway Co.
Third Street & Suburban Railway Co.
Burke Block Lighting Plant.
Grant Street Electric Railway Co.
The Seattle Railway Co.
West & North End Electric Railway Co.
Union Trunk Line.
Green Lake Electric Railway Co.
Seattle Steam Heat & Power Co.
Union Electric Co.
First Avenue Cable Railway Co.
James Street Construction Co.

The company owns and operates 82½ miles of railway track.

Stock....Par $100....Authorized { com., $5,000,000; pref., 3,000,000 } Issued { com., $4,600,000; pref., 3,000,000 } $7,600,000

The preferred stock is 6 per cent., non-cumulative, and is redeemable at 120.

Transfer Agents, Stone & Webster, Boston. Registrar, National Shawmut Bank, Boston. Dividends on the preferred stock are payable semi-annually in April and October.

FUNDED DEBT.

| | |
|---|---|
| 1st mort., 5 per cent. gold, due Feb. 1, 1930, Feb. and Aug. | $4,518,000 |
| Seattle Railway Co., 1st mort., 5 per cent. gold, due Nov. 1, 1921, March and Nov. | 500,000 |
| Total | $5,018,000 |

The authorized 1st mortgage of the Seattle Electric Co. was $5,000,000. A sinking fund of 1 per cent. per annum is provided. Bonds may be called at any time at 110 and interest. The outstanding bonds of the Seattle Railway Co's 1st mortgage are the full amount authorized. A sinking fund of 1 per cent. annually is provided. Bonds may be called at 110 and accrued interest at any time. The mortgage is assumed and guaranteed by the Seattle Electric Co. Trustee of both mortgages and Agent for the payment of interest, Boston Safe Deposit & Trust Co., Boston.

In the fiscal year ending December 31, 1901, the gross earnings were $1,499,137; net, $523,737; charges, $221,113; surplus, $302,624.

President, Jacob Furth; Vice-President and Treasurer, H. B. Sawyer; Secretary, George Donworth; Assistant Secretary, Henry R. Hayes; Assistant Treasurer, F. Dabney; General Managers, Stone & Webster, Boston.

Directors—M. H. Young, E. S. Webster, C. A. Stone, C. J. Smith, Jacob Furth, S. E. Furth, G. H. Tarbell, W. C. Forbes, N. McMicken.

Corporate office, Seattle, Wash.; main office, 93 Federal street, Boston. Annual meeting, first Tuesday in April, at Seattle.

---

## SEATTLE-TACOMA INTERURBAN RAILWAY

A corporation formed under the laws of Washington in 1901. The company owns and operates an electric railway, using the third rail, over private-right way, from Seattle to Tecoma, Wash., a distance of 37 miles. It carries both freight and passengers

Stock....Par $100.... Authorized { com., $1,500,000 / pref., 500,000 } Issued { com., $1,500,000 / pref., 500,000 } $2,000,000

The preferred stock is 6 per cent., non-cumulative. Transfer Agents, Stone & Webster, Boston. Registrar, National Shawmut Bank, Boston.

FUNDED DEBT.

1st mort., 5 per cent., gold, due Feb. 1, 1931, Feb. and Aug. ....$2,000,000

The outstanding bonds are the total amount authorized. Bonds may be called at any time at 100 and accrued interest. A sinking fund of 1 per cent. annually is provided after August 1, 1906. Bonds in the sinking fund continue to bear interest. Bonds for the sinking fund may be called when necessary. Trustee of the mortgage and agent for the payment of interest, Old Colony Trust Co., Boston.

President, Jacob Furth; Vice-President, A. Stuart Pratt; Secretary, George Donworth; Treasurer, H. B. Sawyer; Assistant Secretary, H. R. Hays; Assistant Treasurer, F. Dabney; General Managers, Stone & Webster.

Trustees—Jacob Furth, F. K. Struve, C. J. Smith, George Donworth, M. H. Young, E. L. Knapp.

Corporate office, Tacoma, Wash.; main office, 93 Federal street, Boston. Annual meeting, first Tuesday in April, at Tacoma.

---

## SHAMOKIN LIGHT, HEAT & POWER CO.

A corporation formed under the laws of New Jersey, November 6, 1899. The company was organized to purchase and combine the illuminating properties of Shamokin, Pa. The companies acquired were as follows: The Shamokin Gas Light Co., the Edison Electric Illuminating Co., The Shamokin Arc Light Co. and the Shamokin Electric Light & Power Co. The last named company had a contract for a term of nine years, for furnishing power to the Shamokin Street Railway Co., for the operation of its cars, and the illumination of its park and pavilion, during the summer season. The company took over and assumed the operation of the four plants December 1, 1899.

Stock......Par $100..........Authorized, $250,000......Issued, $250,000

Transfer Agent, Guarantee Trust & Safe Deposit Co., Shamokin, Pa.

FUNDED DEBT.

1st mort., 5 per cent., due 1915-29, June and Dec. .... $250,000

The bonds are secured by a mortgage on all the property of this company as well as by the deposit with the trustee, Guarantee Trust & Safe Deposit Co. of Shamokin, Pa., of all the stock of the companies acquired by the corporation. The bonds of the old companies were also acquired and deposited with the trustee.

The companies acquired in 1896, 1897 and 1898 had gross earnings per year in excess of $45,000 and their net was about $20,000 per year.

President, W. C. McConnell; Treasurer, John Mullen; Secretary, George C. Graeber.

Directors—W. C. McConnell, John Mullen, George C. Graeber, H. S. Zimmerman, C. C. Frick, George E. Neff, H. C. Niles, George H. B. Martin, C. C. Leader.

Main office, McWilliams & McConnell Building, Shamokin, Pa.

## SHANNON COPPER CO.

A corporation formed under the laws of Delaware, November 13, 1899, for the purpose of acquiring certain mining properties owned by C. M. Shannon and others near Clifton, Ariz. The property controlled by the company consists of 35 claims, aggregating about 600 acres. The Shannon mine was located in 1872 and patented in 1877. It was worked at various intervals by its owners, but was not properly developed until it was acquired by the present company. The company purchased eleven claims from the Arizona Copper Co. The company has done considerable development work and has erected a smelter and concentrator.

Stock......Par $10..........................Authorized, $3,000,000......Issued, $3,000,000

The company has no preferred stock. Transfer Agent, Boston Safe Deposit & Trust Co., Boston; Registrar, National Shawmut Bank, Boston.

FUNDED DEBT.

1st mort., 7 per cent., due March, 1902, March and Sept .............................. $600,000

President, George C. Gill, Holyoke, Mass.; Vice-President, John F. Alvord, Torrington, Conn.; Secretary, John K. Erskine, Jr., New York; Treasurer, J. W. Hazen, Boston.

Directors—Edwin A. Carter, Springfield, Mass.; John F. Alvord, Torrington, Conn.; John K. Erskine, Jr., New York; Leonard Wheeler, Worcester, Mass.; James Virdin, Dover, Del.; George C. Gill, Holyoke, Mass.; J. W. Hazen, Cambridgeport, Mass.; William B. Thompson, Boston; Charles Kimberly, New Haven, Conn.

Corporate office, Dover, Del.; main office, Clifton, Ariz.; Boston office, 10 Post Office square. Annual meeting, November 27, at Boston.

## SHELBY IRON CO.

A corporation formed under the laws of New Jersey in 1890 for the purpose of manufacturing charcoal, iron and mining ore. The company was formerly known as the Alabama Coal & Iron Co. It owns extensive ore lands, two furnaces and a complete plant at Shelby, Ala.

Stock......Par $100..........................Authorized, $1,000,000......Issued, $1,000,000

The company has no preferred stock and no funded debt.

Transfer Agents, W. S. Gurnee, Jr., & Co., New York. Registrar, Central Trust Co., New York.

Dividends have been paid as follows: August, 1890, 2 per cent.; November, 1892, 3 per cent.; May, 1898, 5 per cent.; May, 1899, 8 per cent.; November, 1899, 5 per cent.; April, 1900, 6 per cent.; June, 1900, 6 per cent.; May, 1901, 5 per cent.; November, 1901, 7 per cent.; May, 1902, 10 per cent.; November, 1902, 6 per cent. There are no fixed dates for the payment of dividends, but the periods will probably be May and November.

President, T. G. Bush, Birmingham, Ala.; Vice-President, W. W. Jacobs, Hartford, Conn.; Treasurer, W. S. Gurnee; Secretary and Assistant Treasurer, B. Y. Frost, New York.

Directors—W. D. Gurnee, E. Lehman, William N. Cromwell, W. S. Gurnee, W. S. Gurnee, Jr., A. C. Gurnee, J. D. Probst, New York; T. G. Bush, Birmingham, Ala.; A. L. Tyler, Anniston, Ala.; W. W. Jacobs, Hartford, Conn.; William J. Curtis, New Jersey; B. Y. Frost, Nyack, N. Y.

Main office, First avenue and Twentieth streets, Birmingham, Ala.; New York office, 80 Broadway. Annual meeting in May.

## THE SHERWIN-WILLIAMS CO.

A corporation formed under the laws of Ohio, July 18, 1884, to manufacture paints and varnishes. The company has manufacturing plants at Cleveland, Chicago, Newark, N. J., and Montreal, and warehouses in Boston, San Francisco, Los Angeles, Kansas City, Minneapolis and Toronto. It also owns a linseed oil plant at Cleveland.

Stock......Par $100..........................Authorized, $2,500,000......Issued, $1,500,000

The company has no preferred stock and no funded debt.

President, Henry A. Sherwin; Vice-President, Edward P. Williams; Secretary and Treasurer, Sereno P. Fenn; General Manager, Walter H. Cottingham.

Directors—Henry A. Sherwin, Edward P. Williams, Walter H. Cottingham, Sereno P. Fenn, William B. Albright, Eugene M. Richardson.

Corporate and main office, 100 Canal street, Cleveland.; New York office, 66 Broadway. Annual meeting, November 1, at Cleveland.

## SIMMONS HARDWARE CO.

A corporation formed under the laws of Missouri in 1873 and 1901. The company conducts an extensive wholesale and retail hardware business in St. Louis.

| Stock..Par $100...Authorized | com., $1,500,000<br>1st pref., 1,500,000<br>2d " 1,500,000 | Issued | com., $1,500,000<br>1st pref., 1,500,000<br>2d " 1,500,000 | $4,500,000 |
|---|---|---|---|---|

The 1st preferred stock is 7 per cent., cumulative. The 2d preferred stock is 8 per cent. non-cumulative.

Stock is transferred at the company's office. Registrar, St. Louis Trust Co., St. Louis.

In 1900 the authorized share capital was increased from $3,000,000 to $4,500,000 by the creation and issue of 2d preferred stock for $1,500,000, which amount was distributed to the common stockholders as a 100 per cent. stock dividend. This amount represents part of the $2,000,000 undivided profits of the company at the time.

Dividends on the 1st preferred stock are paid semi-annually—3½ per cent. each in February and August. On the 2d preferred the semi-annual dividends are 4 per cent. each in March and September. Dividends on the common are paid at the discretion of the directors without any fixed periods.

No statement of the company's earnings is published.

President, Wallace D. Simmons; 1st Vice-President, John E. Pilcher; 2d Vice-President, J. Elwood Smith; Treasurer, Albert E. Dann; Assistant Treasurer, George R. Barclay; Secretary, Archer W. Douglas; Assistant Secretary, Edward H. Simmons, St. Louis.

Directors—Wallace D. Simmons, John E. Pilcher, J. Elwood Smith, Albert E. Dann, George R. Barclay, Archer W. Douglas, Edward H. Simmons, F. N. Johnson, St. Louis.

Advisory Board—Edward C. Simmons, Isaac W. Morton.

Main office, 900 Spruce street, St. Louis. Annual meeting, first Monday in January, at St. Louis.

## SIMPSON-CRAWFORD CO.

A corporation formed under the laws of New York in 1901. The company was organized to acquire and take over the property, good will and business of the retail dry goods firm of Simpson, Crawford & Simpson, New York.

Stock......Par $100..........................Authorized, $2,500,000......Issued, $2,500,000

The company has no preferred stock.

FUNDED DEBT.

Debenture mort., 6 per cent.................................................... $2,500,000

The authorized amount of the debentures is $2,500,000.

President and Treasurer, Henry Siegel; Vice-President, John R. Butler, New York; Secetary, Frank E. Vogel, Chicago; Assistant-Secretary, Robert G. McMeekin; Assistant Treasurer, Joseph J. Murphy, New York.

Directors—Henry Siegel, John R. Butler, Frank E. Vogel, Max Pam, Henry W. Taft, James F. Lowe.

Main office, 311 Sixth avenue, New York.

## THE SINGER MANUFACTURING CO.

A corporation formed under the laws of New Jersey in 1873. The business of the company is the manufacture of sewing machines. It has one of the largest factories in the world devoted to this purpose, at Elizabeth, N. J., and has stores and sales agencies in nearly all the cities of the United States, Europe and other parts of the world.

Stock......Par $100.........................Authorized, $30,000,000......Issued, $30,000,000

In December, 1900, the stock was increased from $10,000,000 to $30,000,000, the stockholders receiving a stock dividend of 200 per cent.

In 1901 and 1902 dividends of 7 per cent. per annum were paid, the payments being 1¾ quarterly, in March, June, September and December.

President, Frederick G. Bourne; 2d Vice-President and Treasurer, Douglas Alexander; 3d Vice-President, E. H. Bennett; Secretary, T. E. Hardenbergh.

Directors—Frederick G. Bourne, D. Alexander, E. H. Bennett, E. S. Clark, T. E. Hardenbergh, Arthur K. Bourne.

Main office, 149 Broadway, New York.

## SLOSS SHEFFIELD STEEL & IRON CO.

A corporation formed under the laws of New Jersey, August 16, 1899. The company was organized in pursuance of a plan to enlarge the business of the Sloss Iron & Steel Co., of Birmingham, Ala. The company owns all the stock of the Sloss Iron & Steel Co.; two-thirds of the stock of the Lady Ensley Furnace at Sheffield, Ala., and owns the Philadelphia Furnace, Florence, Ala.; Hattie Ensley Furnace at Sheffield, Ala., 25,000 acres of coal lands in Walker County, Ala., and the brown ore properties, Russellville, Ala.; it also owns the Lady Ensley Coal, Iron & Railroad Co. The united properties comprise seven large blast furnaces with a yearly capacity of 400,000 tons of pig iron, 1,400 coke ovens with a capacity of 375,000 tons of coke per annum, over 60,000 acres of coal lands with mines operated thereon, and some 31,500 acres of iron ore land, as well as extensive limestone quarries.

Stock....Par $100...Authorized { com., $10,000,000 / pref., 10,000,000 } Issued { com., $7,500,000 / pref., 6,700,000 } $14,200,000

The preferred stock is 7 per cent., non-cumulative.

Transfer Agent, Central Trust Co., New York. Registrar, Guaranty Trust Co., New York.

The company paid its first dividend of 1¾ per cent. on the preferred stock in April, 1900, and has since paid quarterly dividends at the same rate, in March (10), June, September and December.

FUNDED DEBT.

| | |
|---|---|
| Sloss I. & S. Co., 1st mort. deb., 6 per cent., due Feb., 1917, Feb. and Aug. | $2,000,000 |
| " " gen. mort., 4½ per cent., due April, 1918, April and Oct. | 2,000,000 |
| Total | $4,000,000 |

EARNINGS.

Year ending November 30.

| | Net. | Charges. | Pref. Div. | Surplus. |
|---|---|---|---|---|
| 1899-00 | $1,178,313 | $230,463 | $351,750 | $546,000 |
| 1900-01 | 729,120 | 253,751 | 469,000 | Def. 6,369 |
| 1901-02 | 1,350,499 | 240,000 | 456,000 | Sur. 654,499 |

President, John Campbell Maben, New York; 1st Vice-President, Joseph Bryan, Richmond; 2d Vice-President, Secretary and Treasurer, J. W. McQueen; Auditor, C. H. Schoolar, Birmingham, Ala.

Directors—Joseph Bryan, W. H. Goadby, Adrian H. Larkin, John Campbell Maben, Richard Mortimer, Walter G. Oakman, George Parsons, E. W. Rucker, A. E. Ames, J. H. Plummer, W. E. Strong, Moses Taylor, Robert B. Van Cortlandt.

Main office, First avenue and Twentieth street, Birmingham, Ala.

## SOMERSET COAL CO.

A corporation formed under the laws of Pennsylvania in January, 1902. The objects of the company are the ownership of coal mines and coal lands and the mining and sale of coal. The company acquired the following bituminous coal properties in Somerset County, Pa., located on or near the lines of the Baltimore & Ohio Railroad Co.:

| | |
|---|---|
| Cumberland & Elk Lick Coal Co. | Pine Hill Coal Co. |
| Duncombe Mine. | Stuart Coal Co. |
| Cumberland & Summit Coal Co. | Tub Mill Mine. |
| Althouse Mines. | Chapman Mine. |
| Enterprise Coal Co. | Wilmoth Mine. |
| Casselman Coal Co. | Thomas Mine. |
| Listie Mining & Manufacturing Co. | Wilson Creek Coal Co. |

In January, 1903, capitalists connected with this company acquired large holdings in the Consolidation Coal Co. and the Fairmont Coal Co.

Stock......Par $100..........................Authorized, $4,000,000......Issued, $4,000,000

The company has no preferred stock.

Transfer Agent, Registrar & Transfer Co., New York. Registrar, Guaranty Trust Co., New York.

FUNDED DEBT.

1st mort. gold sinking fund, 5 per cent., due Feb., 1932, Feb. and Aug.............. $3,000,000

The 1st mortgage bonds authorized are $4,000,000. Trustee of mortgage, Guaranty Trust Co., New York. The bonds are subject to call on any interest day at 110. In February, 1902, Spencer Trask & Co., New York, offered $1,000,000 of the bonds for subscription at 96 and interest.

President, Clarence W. Watson; Treasurer, W. G. Sharp.

Directors—Walter G. Oakman, August Belmont, W. H. Baldwin, Jr., Acosta Nichols, J. H. Wheelwright, George W. Young, H. J. Bowdoin, T. B. Davis, Jr., G. C. Jenkins, L. F. Loree, G. N. Shriver, Clarence W. Watson.

Corporate office, Somerset, Pa.; New York office, 1 Broadway. Annual meeting, second Tuesday in December.

## SONORA DEVELOPMENT CO.

A corporation formed under the laws of Arizona, September 28, 1900, to develop and work gold, silver, copper and lead mines in Mexico. The company has acquired a mining property in the Moctezuma District, Sonora, Mexico, comprising upward of ten separate mines, the property covering 600 acres. The company has engaged in extensive exploration and development work on its properties, its policy being to demonstrate the value and productive capacity of the different mines with a view to disposing of or retaining the same.

Stock......Par $100..........................Authorized, $1,000,000......Issued, $1,000,000

The stock is full-paid and non-assessable. The company has no preferred stock or funded debt. Stock is transferred at the office of the company, Kansas City, Mo.

President, William Huttig; Vice-President, Alfred Blaker; Treasurer, William A. Rule; Secretary, John W. Amerman, Kansas City, Mo.; General Manager, George F. Woodward, Moctezuma, Sonora, Mexico.

Directors—William Huttig, William A. Rule, John W. Amerman, Kansas City, Mo.; George F. Woodward, Moctezuma, Sonora, Mexico.

Main office, 909 Main street, Kansas City, Mo.; operating office, Moctezuma, Sonora, Mexico. Annual meeting, second Tuesday in January.

## SOUTH CHICAGO CITY RAILWAY CO.

A corporation formed under the laws of Illinois, May 31, 1883. Originally the company was the Ewing Avenue Horse Railway Co., but changed its name in 1885. The company owns and operates two lines of electric street railway extending from Jackson Park, Chicago, to 106th street and the Indiana State line. It owns 34 miles of track and controls the Grand Crossing & Windsor Park Railroad Co. with 3 miles of track. It is operated in connection with the Hammond, Whiting & East Chicago Electric Railway Co., between Chicago and adjacent Indiana towns.

Stock......Par $100..........................Authorized, $2,000,000......Issued, $1,603,800

The company has no preferred stock. Stock is transferred at the office of the company.

FUNDED DEBT.

1st mort., currency, 5 per cent., due July, 1910, Jan. and July...................... $50,000
1st con. mort., 5 per cent., gold, due April, 1913, April and Oct...................... 1,513,000

Total........................................................... $1,563,000

The authorized amount of the consolidated mortgage is $5,000,000. Trustee and agent for the payment of interest, Illinois Trust & Savings Bank, Chicago.

President, D. F. Cameron; Vice-President, D. M. Cummings; Secretary and Treasurer, Otho S. Gaither.

Directors—D. F. Cameron, D. M. Cummings, Otho S. Gaither, Vernon Shaw Kennedy C. R. Corning.

Main office, 164 Dearborn street, Chicago. Annual meeting, first Tuesday in May, at Chicago.

## SOUTHERN CAR & FOUNDRY CO.

A corporation formed under the laws of New Jersey in June, 1899. The business of the company is the construction of freight, mining and cane cars and the manufacture of castings, forgings, wheels, axles, bar iron, malleable castings, etc., for general car purposes. The company acquired and owns plants located as follows:

Anniston, Ala.—Comprising a rolling mill, axle forge, castings, both gray and malleable, and wheel foundries, machine shop, car shops, and wood-working mill.
Gadsden, Ala.—Car works, foundry, forge mill, erecting shops, etc.
Lenoir City, Tenn.—Car works, machine and erecting shops, etc.
Memphis, Tenn.—Car works, wheel and castings foundries, forge mill, machine shops, etc.

The aggregate daily capacity of the company's plants is 50 cars, 120 axles, 100 tons of bar iron, 500 car wheels, 100 tons gray castings and 20 tons malleable castings. The company constructed a street car plant at Easley, Ala., and in 1902 bought the Gadsden Furnace at Gadsden, Ala.

In 1902 it was stated that control of this company had been acquired by capitalists identified with the Standard Steel Car Co.

Stock......Par $100.....Authorized { com., $1,750,000 / pref., 1,750,000 } Issued { com., $750,000 / pref., 750,000 } $1,500,000

Stock to the amount of $500,000 is held in the company's treasury. The preferred stock is 7 per cent., non-cumulative.

Stock is transferred at the company's office, 80 Broadway, New York.

The company has no funded debt, and its properties are held free of all encumbrance.

The net earnings from the date of organization to January 1, 1901, are reported as $355,372. No dividends have been declared, earnings being credited to surplus account.

The following is the company's balance sheet, March 31, 1902:

| ASSETS. | | LIABILITIES. | |
|---|---|---|---|
| Cash | $46,109 | Capital stock | $2,000,000 |
| Book accounts | 335,411 | Bills payable | 294,812 |
| Merchandise and raw material | 136,539 | Bills payable against warrants | 540,968 |
| Material worked and labor paid | 110,352 | Accounts payable | 190,512 |
| Storage warrants | 834,996 | Net credit, loss and gain | 355,372 |
| Office furniture and fixtures, patterns, tools and machinery | 22,981 | | |
| Improvements | 53,776 | | |
| Real estate, improvements, machinery and fixtures | 1,341,500 | | |
| Treasury stock | 500,000 | | |
| Total | $3,381,664 | Total | $3,381,664 |

President, James M. Elliott, Jr., Birmingham, Ala.; 1st Vice-President, G. C. Eikes, New York; 3d Vice-President and Treasurer, W. G. Brockway, Birmingham, Ala.; Secretary, C. L. E. DeGaugue, New York; Assistant Secretary, George W. Bowen, Birmingham, Ala.; Assistant Treasurers, I. Waterhouse, Anniston, Ala.; Samuel Marfield, Lenoir City, Tenn.; W. N. Tumlin, Memphis, Tenn.; J. H. Wragg, Gadsden, Ala.; George W. Bowen, Birmingham, Ala.; H. P. Chilton, New York; Auditor, C. E. Connor, Birmingham, Ala.

Directors—James M. Elliott, Jr., Birmingham, Ala.; E. J. Sanford, Charles M. McGhee, Knoxville, Tenn.; Elverton R. Chapman, G. C. Eikes, H. P. Chilton, C. L. E. DeGaugue, M. D. Chapman, New York.

Main office, Fourth avenue and Nineteenth street, Birmingham, Ala.; New York office, 80 Broadway. Annual meeting, first Tuesday in June, at Jersey City.

---

## SOUTHERN COTTON OIL CO.

A corporation formed under the laws of New Jersey in 1887. The company owns and operates about 100 cotton seed mills, refineries, lard factories, ginneries and similar plants at various Southern points. The crushing capacity of works is about 5,000 tons of seed per day.

In June, 1901, a majority of the stock was acquired by the Virginia-Carolina Chemical Co.

Stock. ....Par $50.........................Authorized, $11,000,000......Issued, $10,000,000

Stock is transferred at the company's office, 11 Broadway, New York. Registrars, Fidelity Insurance Trust & Safe Deposit Co., Philadelphia.

In recent years the company paid dividends of 6 per cent. In 1900 and 1901 paid 8 per cent. Dividends are half-yearly, June (15) and December.

President, Samuel T. Morgan; Vice-President, L. W. Hackett; Secretary and Treasurer, Alan H. Harris.

Corporate office, Corporation Trust Co., New Jersey; main office, 11 Broadway, New York.

## SOUTHERN LIGHT & TRACTION CO.

(Controlled by American Light & Traction Co.)

A corporation formed under the laws of New Jersey, September 6, 1899. The company was organized to combine under one ownership all the gas, electric and street railway facilities of San Antonio, Tex., under a franchise expiring in 1940. The company acquired the San Antonio Gas Co., San Antonio Edison Co., Mutual Electric Light Co. and the San Antonio Street Railway Co. Litigation was, however, instituted by the State of Texas, and the courts decided against the legality of the combination. The litigation, however, was settled, and the San Antonio Gas & Electric Co. was formed to take over the gas and electric properties, the San Antonio Traction Co. acquiring the street railway system. Both the latter companies are controlled in the interest of the Southern Light & Traction Co.

In 1901 the American Light & Traction Co. acquired control of this company through the purchase of its stock, giving $44.28 in preferred and $13.28 in its own common stock for each share of this company's stock.

Stock......Par $100......... ................Authorized, $2,500,000......Issued, $1,805,000

The company began the payment of dividends with 1½ per cent., May 21, 1900. Dividends are semi-annual, at the same rate, May and November.

Transfer Agents, Emerson McMillin & Co., 40 Wall street, New York.

FUNDED DEBT.

Collateral Trust mort., 5 per cent., gold, due 1949, March and Sept...................... $1,985,000

The collateral trust 5 per cent. mortgage, Continental Trust Co., New York, trustee, is secured by a deposit of the bonds and securities of the constituent companies. The authorized amount of bonds is $2,500,000, of which $900,000 were reserved for improvements. The bonds are subject to call at 105 and interest. Coupons are paid at the Continental Trust Co., New York.

President, Emerson McMillin; Secretary and Treasurer, C. T. Scoville, New York.

Directors—Emerson McMillin, Arthur Lehman, J. J. Emery, Philip Lehman, Warren W. Foster, Willard E. Cass, Charles N. King, New York.

Main office, San Antonio, Tex. Annual meeting, first Monday in October.

---

## SOUTHERN NEW ENGLAND TELEPHONE CO.

A corporation formed under the laws of Connecticut in 1881. The company operates under license from the American Telephone & Telegraph Co., in State of Connecticut. The American Telephone & Telegraph Co., in October, 1902, owned $995,400 of this company's stock. At the beginning of 1902 the company had 17,564 stations, and 15,132 subscribers.

Stock......Par $100.........................Authorized, $5,000,000......Issued, $2,990,000

The capital stock was increased in February, 1901, from $2,511,000 to $2,760,000, with a further increase later in the year to $2,990,000. The authorized amount of stock was increased in January, 1902, from $3,000,000 to $5,000,000.

Stock is transferred at the office of the company, New Haven, Conn. Registrar, New Haven Trust Co., New Haven, Conn.

Dividends on the stock are paid quarterly, being 1½ per cent. each, in January (15), April, July and October.

FUNDED DEBT.

1st mort., 5 per cent., gold, due 1948, June and Dec....... ..........................$790,500

EARNINGS.

| | Gross. | Net. | Charges & Rentals. | Dividends. | Surplus. |
|---|---|---|---|---|---|
| 1898.............. | $644,008 | $229,992 | $77,464 | (6) $150,660 | $1,868 |
| 1899.............. | 689,005 | 241,127 | 77,617 | (6) 150,660 | 59,479 |
| 1900..... ....... | 739,392 | 248,835 | 88,036 | (6) 150,660 | 17,238 |
| 1901.............. | 830,301 | 272,740 | 95,194 | (6) 161,865 | 15,680 |
| 1902.............. | 919,556 | 188,424 | 99,050 | (6) 172,500 | 15,924 |

The net earnings are given after the deductions of fixed charges and rentals.

President, Morris F. Tyler; Secretary, Victor Morris Tyler, New Haven, Conn.

Directors—Morris F. Tyler, Max Adler, Lyman B. Jewell, James English, Samuel E. Merwin, A. Heaton Robertson, John W. Alling, New Haven, Conn.; Thomas Sherwin, Frederick P. Fish, Boston.

Main office, 122 Court street, New Haven, Conn. Annual meeting, last Tuesday in January.

## SOUTH JERSEY GAS, ELECTRIC & TRACTION CO.

A corporation formed under the laws of New Jersey, September 1, 1900. The company absorbed by consolidation the following corporations:

| | |
|---|---|
| Camden Gas Light Co. | Consumers' Gas Co. of Woodbury. |
| Camden Gas Light & Fuel Co. | Woodbury Electric Light & Power Co. |
| Camden & Burlington Gas & Electric Co. | Trenton Gas & Electric Light Co. |
| East Side Gas Co. | Bordentown Gas Light Co. |
| Gloucester City Electric Light Co. | Suburban Improvement Co. |

It also controls:

Gloucester City Gas Light Co. Rivershore Gas Co. Burlington Gas Light Co.

The foregoing corporations include the entire gas and electric light interests of Trenton, Camden, Mount Holly, Woodbury and Merchantville, Gloucester, Moorestown, Haddonfield, Burlington, Beverly, Riverton, Bordentown, N. J., and the adjacent towns.

The company also acquired the entire capital stock of the Camden, Gloucester & Woodbury Railway Co. The Bristol (Pa.) Electric Light & Power Co. is controlled by this company.

Stock......Par $100 ........................Authorized, $6,000,000......Issued, $5,889,000

Transfer Agent and Registrar, Fidelity Trust Co., Newark, N. J.

FUNDED DEBT.

| | |
|---|---|
| 1st consolidated mort., 5 per cent., due Sept., 1950, March and Sept................ | $6,000,000 |
| Trenton Gas & El., 1st mort., 5 per cent., due March, 1949, March and Sept..... .. | 2,000,000 |
| Total.............................................................. | $8,000,000 |

The consolidated mortgage is $15,000,000 authorized. Trustee, Fidelity Trust Co., Newark, N. J.

President, Anthony R. Kuser, Newark, N. J.; Vice-President, W. J. Bradley, Camden, N. J.; Treasurer, Charles C. Cook, Trenton, N. J.; Secretary, Forrest F. Dryden, Newark, N. J.; Auditor, James R. Shurtz, Camden, N. J.

Directors—Anthony R. Kuser, Thomas N. McCarter, Uzal H. McCarter, Forrest F. Dryden, Newark, N. J.; Thomas C. Barr, Orange, N. J.; Henry C. Moore, Barker Gummere, Richard Stockton, J. H. Blackwell, John L. Kuser, Trenton, N. J.; Stephen Peabody, New York; William J. Bradley, Charles Watson, J. J. Burleigh, Frank O. Briggs, William J. Thompson, H. W. Johnson, Camden, N. J.; Frank Bergen, Elizabeth, N. J.; Robert C. Pruyn, Albany, N. Y.

Main office, Camden, N. J. Annual meeting, fourth Wednesday in January.

## SOUTH SIDE ELEVATED RAILROAD CO.

A corporation formed under the laws of Illinois in January, 1897. The company is a reorganization of the Chicago & South Side Rapid Transit Railroad Co. which was sold under foreclosure September 16, 1896. It owns an elevated road, operated by electricity, 8.72 miles of double and triple track, a total of 19.44 miles single track, extending from Congress street to Jackson Park, Chicago. The company owns 230 passenger cars.

Stock......Par $100........................Authorized, $10,323,800......Issued, $10,323,800

The company has no preferred stock. Registrar, Northern Trust Co., Chicago.

The first dividend on the stock was one per cent., paid May 1, 1899. In 1899 3 per cent. was paid; in 1900 3 per cent., in 1901 3½ per cent., and in 1902 4 per cent. Dividends are paid quarterly, March (1), June, September and December.

FUNDED DEBT.

1st mort., 4½ per cent. bonds, due July, 1907, Jan. and July........................ $750,000

The authorized amount of the mortgage is $1,500,000, of which $750,000 are reserved for future improvements and additions. The bonds are redeemable after April, 1902, at 102. Trustee of the mortgage and agent for the payment of interest, Illinois Trust & Savings Bank, Chicago.

EARNINGS.

| | Gross. | Net. | Interest. | Dividends. | Surplus. |
|---|---|---|---|---|---|
| 1899.................... | $1,170,381 | $500,448 | $33,750 | $306,672 | $160,026 |
| 1900.................... | 1,286,636 | 538,235 | 33,750 | 306,765 | 197,720 |
| 1901.................... | 1,362,231 | 517,271 | 33,750 | 357,955 | 125,566 |
| 1902.................... | 1,483,843 | 621,505 | 33,750 | 409,124 | 178,631 |

President, Leslie Carter; Vice-President, T. J. Lefens; Secretary and Treasurer, John H. Glade; Auditor, H. F. Hardy; General Manager, M. Hopkins.

Directors—B. L. Smith, C. J. Blair, T. J. Lefens, Leslie Carter, Joseph Leiter, W. B. Walker, George E. Adams, William R. Linn, C. H. Wacker.

Main office, 47 Congress street, Chicago. Annual meeting, last Thursday in January, at Chicago.

## SOUTH WEST MISSOURI ELECTRIC RAILWAY CO.

A corporation formed under the laws of Missouri, August 25, 1892. The company later acquired the following properties:

Jasper County Electric Railroad Co. Joplin & Galena Electric Railway Co.

The company owns and operates 40 miles of electric railway connecting Joplin, Webb City, Carterville, Carthage and Prosperity, Mo., and Galena, Kan., serving a total population of 100,000. It has a central plant at Webb City and an auxiliary plant at Lakeside, Mo.

Stock......Par $100.............................Authorized, $800,000......Issued, $800,000

The company has no preferred stock.

A dividend of 4 per cent. was paid in November, 1901, and 5 per cent. in November, 1902.

FUNDED DEBT.

| | |
|---|---|
| 1st mort., Prosperity to Joplin, 6 per cent., gold, due March 1, 1913, Mar. and Sept..... | $200,000 |
| 1st mort., 6 per cent., gold, Joplin & Galena R. R. prop., due July 1, 1926, Jan. and July | 120,000 |
| 1st mort., 6 per cent., Jasper Co. Electric R.R. Co. prop., due July 1, 1926, Jan. and July | 180,000 |
| 2d mort., 6 per cent., gold, due Nov. 1, 1928, May and Nov.......................... | 300,000 |
| Total.............................................................. | $800,000 |

All the outstanding bonds are the full amounts authorized. The 1st mortgage bonds may be called after 1903. Trustee of the mortgage and agent for the payment of interest, Central Trust Co., New York. The 2d mortgage bonds may be called after 1902 on any November 1st. Trustee and agent for the payment of interest, Mississippi Valley Trust Co., St. Louis. Interest is also payable by the National Bank of Commeree, New York.

In the fiscal year ending August 31, 1902, the gross earnings were $206,799; net, $82,443; interest, $46,963; surplus, $35,480.

President, Treasurer and General Manager, A. H. Rogers, Joplin, Mo.; Vice-President, E. Z. Wallower; Secretary, A. G. Knisely, Harrisburg, Pa.

Directors—Samuel McReynolds, Carthage, Mo.; A. H. Rogers, Joplin, Mo.; E. Z. Wallower, A. G. Knisely, E. S. Herman, H. L. Hershey, Edward Bailey, Harrisburg, Pa.; W. B. Meetch, Millersburg, Pa.; W. S. Chinn, Webb City, Mo.

Corporate and main office, Webb City, Mo.; Eastern office, Harrisburg, Pa. Annual meeting, second Thursday in October, at Webb City, Mo.

## SOUTH YUBA WATER CO.

A corporation formed under the laws of New York in 1880. The company succeeded a California corporation of the same name. The company has a system of 20 storage lakes and reservoirs in the Sierra Nevada Mountains, in Placer, Sacramento and Nevada counties, Cal., 12 distributing reservoirs and some 500 miles of pipe lines and canals. It supplies water to various towns and municipalities for domestic and irrigation purposes. It also has valuable water powers and furnishes electric light and power to the city of Sacramento, Cal. The operations of the company cover an area of 2,000 square miles.

Stock......Par $50........................Authorized, $2,000,000 .. ...Issued, $2,000,000

Stock is transferred at the office of the company, New York.

FUNDED DEBT.

| | |
|---|---|
| 1st mort., 6 per cent., due 1910, April and Oct.................................... | $436,000 |
| Cons. mort., 6 per cent., due 1923, Jan. and July.................................. | 762,000 |
| Total.............................................................. | $1,198,000 |

The consolidated mortgage is for $1,500,000, of which sum $436,000 is reserved to retire the 1st mortgage bonds. Trustee, Farmers' Loan & Trust Co., New York.

President, Warner Van Norden; Secretary, Warner M. Van Norden, New York.

Main office, 751 Fifth avenue, New York; operating office, Nevada City, Cal.

## SPRING BROOK WATER SUPPLY CO.

A corporation formed under the laws of Pennsylvania, March 2, 1896. The company owns and controls an extensive system of water supplies and reservoirs in and adjacent to the Wyoming Valley of Pennsylvania. It owns and controls a number of local companies, including those which supply water to the South Side of Scranton, Wilkes-Barre, Pittstown, Plymouth, and a number of other cities and towns in the same section. The company reservoirs, with an aggregate capacity of nearly 6,000,000,000 gallons, and its mains are upwards of 350 miles.

Stock.......................................Authorized, $5,000,000......Issued, $5,000,000

FUNDED DEBT.

| | |
|---|---|
| 1st mort., 5 per cent., due 1926 | $4,130,000 |
| Divisional morts., various, 5 and 6 per cent | 740,000 |
| Total | $4,870,000 |

The 1st mort. bonds authorized are $5,000,000 in amount, sufficient of the issue being reserved to retire the underlying bonds at maturity.

President, L. A. Watres; Secretary, T. H. Watkins; Treasurer, G. H. Hicks; General Manager, O. M. Lance.

Directors—L. A. Watres, J. W. Hollenback, J. Rogers Maxwell, George F. Baker, T. H. Watkins, C. D. Simpson, Abram Nesbitt, Morgan B. Williams, Samuel T. Peters, Robert C. Adams.

Main office, Wilkes-Barre, Pa.

## SPRINGFIELD STREET RAILWAY CO.

A corporation formed under the laws of Massachusetts March 5, 1868. The company owns a system of lines in and about Springfield, Mass., comprising 86 miles, and has a power station and 219 cars.

Stock .....Par $100.........................Authorized, $2,000,000......Issued, $1,958,000

Dividends of 8 per cent. per annum have been paid in 1893-1902, inclusive.

FUNDED DEBT.

Debentures, 4½ per cent., due April, 1910, April and Oct........................... $100,000

EARNINGS.

Year ending September 30.

| | Gross. | Net. |
|---|---|---|
| 1896 | $521,673 | $200,088 |
| 1897 | 554,312 | 151,587 |
| 1898 | 583,050 | 152,651 |
| 1899 | 626,030 | 192,542 |
| 1900 | 686,050 | 206,204 |
| 1901 | 753,809 | 226,220 |
| 1902 | 644,665 | 250,028 |

President, John Olmstead; Treasurer, Frederick Harris; Clerk, Jonathan Barnes, Springfield, Mass.

Directors—John Olmstead, Frederick Harris, A. W. Damon, George W. Cook, Springfield, Mass.

Main office, North and Main streets, Springfield, Mass. Annual meeting, second Wednesday in January, at Springfield.

## JOHN P. SQUIRE & CO.

A corporation formed under the laws of New Jersey in February, 1901, to take over the assets of the assignee of John P. Squire & Co., a Maine corporation, and to combine with this various allied concerns. The purpose of the company is to conduct a pork-packing business.

The company conducts branches in the following cities and towns in New England: Lynn, Mass.; Fitchburg, Mass.; Worcester, Mass.; Holyoke, Mass.; Lawrence, Mass.; Manchester, N. H.; Portland, Me.; Bath, Me.; Augusta, Me., and Bangor, Me.

Stock ..Par $100....Authorized { com., $6,000,000 / pref., 1,500,000 } Issued { com., $6,000,000 / pref., 519,000 } $6,519,000

Transfer Agent, The Old Colony Trust Co., Boston. Registrar, The State Street Trust Co., Boston.

The preferred stock is entitled to 6 per cent. dividends, and is subject to call, at the option of the Directors, on thirty days' notice at 105.

President, Alvin F. Sortwell; Secretary and Treasurer, Edward D. Whitford, Boston.

Directors—C. Minot Weld, Horatio G. Curtis, Henry L. Burrage, Alvin F. Sortwell, Edward D. Whitford, C. M. Ryder, Boston; Charles Hathaway, New York; Kenneth McLaren, Jersey City.

Main office, 40 North Market street, Boston. Annual meeting, third Tuesday in January.

## STANDARD CHAIN CO.

A corporation formed under the laws of New Jersey, February 2, 1900. The purposes of the company are the manufacture of iron and steel chains of all descriptions and of bar iron and bar steel. The company acquired and consolidated the business of the following manufacturers:

Bower & Mallery Co., Carlisle, Pa.
Baker Chain & Wagon Iron Manufacturing Co., Allegheny, Pa.
Garland Chain Co., Rankin, Pa.
Falls City Chain Works, Jeffersonville, Ind.
Franz Krein Chain Co., St. Mary's, O.
Franz Krein Manufacturing Co., Marion, Ind.
So. Harrisburg Chain Works, Harrisburg, Pa.
Lebanon Chain Works, Lebanon, Pa.
P. Hayden Saddlery Hardware Co., Columbus, O.
Nes Chain Manufacturing Co., York, Pa.
J. C. Schmidt & Co., York, Pa.
H. P. Nail Works of the American Steel & Wire Co., Cleveland.

Stock......Par $100..........................Authorized, $1,500,000......Issued, $1,500,000

The company had $1,500,000 of 7 per cent. non-cumulative preferred stock and $1,500,000 of common stock, of which there had been issued $1,277,200 common and $1,031,400 preferred. In January, 1903, the stock was reduced to $1,500,000, all common, the holders of the old preferred receiving a share of the new stock for each share of preferred, and the holders of the old common one new share for each four shares of the old common.

The first dividend on the preferred stock was 1¾ per cent., May 15, 1901. On November 1, 1901, another dividend of 1¾ per cent. was paid, and no dividends were paid thereafter.

Transfer Agent, Registrar and Transfer Co., Jersey City. Registrar, United States Mortgage & Trust Co.

FUNDED DEBT.

1st mort., 6 per cent., due Feb., 1920, Feb. and Aug.................. ................ $568,000

The 1st mortgage is $700,000 authorized. The trustees of the mortgage are George W. Young and Arthur Turnbull, New York. Agent for the payment of interest, the United States Mortgage & Trust Co., New York. There is a sinking fund for the bonds of $17,500 per annum, which has retired $40,000 of the issue.

The properties owned by this company control about 70 per cent. of the annual production of the United States in their line of goods. Their total sales in 1899 amounted to $1,476,000 and their net profits were over $200,000.

The profits of the company for the year 1902 were reported as being $105,048.

The following is the company's balance sheet, December 31, 1902:

| ASSETS. | | LIABILITIES. | |
|---|---|---|---|
| Real estate, plant, buildings and machinery | $2,461,309 | Capital stock, common | $1,277,200 |
| New construction | 176,506 | Capital stock, preferred | 1,031,400 |
| Common stock in treasury | 10,000 | 1st mortgage bonds | 547,000 |
| Accounts and notes receivable | 261,854 | Accounts payable | 132,369 |
| Materials and supplies, including furniture and interest and insurance paid in advance | 463,944 | Bills payable | 151,000 |
| Cash | 10,376 | Bond interest accrued (not due) | 12,780 |
| | | 1st mortgage bonds, premium account | 6,330 |
| | | Surplus account | 225,910 |
| Total | $3,383,989 | Total | $3,383,989 |

President, John C. Schmidt, York, Pa.; Vice-President, Robert Garland; General Manager, J. T. Davis; Treasurer, William Robertson; Assistant Treasurer, Stanley Mann; Secretary, F. D. Mitchell; General Sales Agent, W. R. Dawson, Pittsburg.

Directors—John C. Schmidt, George S. Schmidt, York, Pa.; A. S. White, Frederick F. Culver, New York; J. T. Davis, Robert Garland, Charles A. Painter, Pittsburg; Charles H. Hayden, F. W. Prentiss, Columbus, O.; Peter Wertz, Carlisle, Pa.; Franz Krein, St. Mary's, O.; Oscar L. Gubelman, Jersey City; Eli Attwood, Lebanon, Pa.

Corporate office, 15 Exchange place, Jersey City; main office, Frick Building, Pittsburg. Annual meeting, third Tuesday in February at Jersey City.

## STANDARD COUPLER CO.

A corporation formed under the laws of New Jersey in January, 1893. The company carries on the business of manufacturing railroad supplies of various kinds. The Standard Steel Platform for passenger cars which is in use on over 100 railroads in the United States, Canada and Mexico is manufactured by this company, also the well-known Standard Car Coupler. The

Sessions-Standard Friction Draft Gear patents are owned by this company which placed it on the market.

Stock....Par $100.....Authorized { com., $1,200,000 / pref., 300,000 } Issued { com., $1,200,000 / pref., 300,000 } $1,500,000

The preferred stock is 8 per cent., cumulative. The company has no bonded debt.

Regular semi-annual dividends, January and July, of 4 per cent., or 8 per cent. per annum, each are paid on the preferred stock. A dividend of 1½ per cent. was paid December 30, 1899, on the common stock; also December 30, 1900; December 31, 1901, and December 31, 1902. On December 31, 1901, 1 per cent. was paid on the common.

President, George A. Post, New York; Vice-President, Henry H. Sessions, Chicago; Secretary and Treasurer, Alfred P. Dennis, New York.

Directors—William Barbour, Alfred P. Dennis, Julius E. French, E. Hawley, Austin Lathrop, D. W. McWilliams, George A. Post, R. Parmly, Henry H. Sessions, A. C. Soper, J. P. Soper.

Main office, 160 Broadway, New York; Chicago office, Dearborn, Jackson and Van Buren streets. Annual meeting, second Tuesday in January at Jersey City.

## STANDARD GAS LIGHT CO.

A corporation formed under the laws of New York in 1886. The mains of the company cover the portion of New York City north of Twelfth street, and are approximately 200 miles in length. It has large works on the East River front at the foot of East One Hundred and Fifteenth street. The Consolidated Gas Co. in 1900 acquired majority of the company's stock.

Stock....Par $100.....Authorized { com., $5,000,000 / pref., 5,000,000 } Issued { com., $5,000,000 / pref., 4,295,700 } $9,295,700

The preferred stock is 6 per cent., non-cumulative.

See MANUAL for 1902 in relation to dividends paid in former years. In 1900 no dividends were paid on the common stock. In 1901 and 1902 6 per cent. was paid on both the common and preferred stock.

FUNDED DEBT.

1st mort., 5 per cent., due 1930, May and Nov........................................ $1,362,000

The amount of bonds authorized is $1,500,000.

President, Frank Tilford; Vice-President and Secretary, W. Greeley Hoyt; Treasurer and Controller, Benjamin Whiteley.

Directors—Frank Tilford, James Tolman Pyle, W. Greeley Hoyt, George F. Dominick, Edwin S. Marston, Abram S. Hyatt, William P. Hardenburgh, William J. Nevins.

Main office, 61 East Fifty-ninth street, New York.

## STANDARD MILLING CO.

A corporation formed under the laws of New Jersey, October 30, 1900. The company was organized in pursuance of a plan for the reorganization of the United States Flour Milling Co. The latter company was formed under the laws of New Jersey, April 27, 1899.

The United States Flour Milling Co. was placed in the hands of a Receiver February 24, 1900. A foreclosure suit was instituted in 1901, the intention being that the properties should be acquired by this company, but the consummation of the plan was delayed by litigation on the part of non-assenting minority interests.

This company proposed to lease certain properties to auxiliary operating companies, and in 1901 the Duluth-Superior Milling Co. was formed to take over the properties at Duluth, Superior, West Superior and other points.

Stock...Par $100...Authorized { com., $4,600,000 / pref., 6,900,000 } Issued { com., $4,600,000 / pref., 6,900,000 } $11,500,000

The preferred stock is 5 per cent., non-cumulative.

The United States Flour Milling Co. had outstanding $3,500,000 common stock, $5,000,000 6 per cent. cumulative preferred stock, and $7,500,000 6 per cent. 1st mortgage bonds.

Transfer Agent, George Macdonald, 37 Wall Street, New York. Registrar, Metropolitan Trust Co., New York.

FUNDED DEBT.

1st mort., 5 per cent., due Nov., 1930, May and Nov............................. $3,447,000

The Trustee of the mortgage and agent for the payment of interest is the Metropolitan Trust Co., New York. The mortgage is for $6,250,000, of which amount $2,261,000 is reserved to retire at par $1,496,000 6 per cent. bonds of the Hecker-Jones-Jewell Co., and $765,000 6 per cent. bonds of the Northwestern Consolidated Milling Co. Under the plan $500,000 of the new bonds could be sold to provide working capital. The bonds not to be sold at less than 95.

Chairman, Brayton Ives; President, (Vacancy); Vice-President, William L. Bull; Secretary and Treasurer, Joseph A. Knox.

Directors—Brayton Ives, William L. Bull, J. Edward Simmons, Warner Van Norden, Thomas A. McIntyre, Edwin Gould, Charles P. Armstrong, T. Howard Latham, James A. Roberts, New York; Joseph V. Clark, Jersey City; A. D. Thomas, Duluth, Minn.

Corporate office, 83 Montgomery street, Jersey City; main office, 37 Wall street, New York. Annual meeting, third Wednesday in October.

## STANDARD OIL CO.

A corporation formed under the laws of New Jersey in 1882. In June, 1899, the company increased its stock from $10,000,000 to $100,000,000 common and $10,000,000 preferred for the purpose of making an exchange of the common for the liquidating trustees' certificates of the Standard Oil Trust.

The property of the company consists of oil refineries, pipe lines, interests in the stock of corporations in various States and, in short, the organization controlling the production, manufacture and distribution of about two-thirds of the output of American petroleum and its products.

Stock......Par $100......................Authorized, $100,000,000......Issued, $97,500,000

Stock is transferred at the company's office, 26 Broadway, New York.

The preferred stock was 6 per cent., non-cumulative. It has been exchanged for common stock and canceled. It cannot be reissued and remains in the company's treasury.

No statements of earnings are published.

Up to 1895 the Standard Oil Trust paid 12 er cent. dividends per annum. The dividends on the Trust certificates and those of the liquidating trustees have been as follows: in 1896, 31 per cent.; in 1897, 33 per cent.; in 1898, 30 per cent.; in 1899, 33 per cent.; in 1900 and 1901 48 per cent. In 1902 the dividends were 45 per cent., and were paid 20 per cent. in March, 10 per cent. in June, 5 per cent. in September and 10 per cent. in December. In March, 1903, 20 per cent. was paid.

President, John D. Rockefeller; Secretary, Charles M. Pratt; Treasurer, W. H. Tilford.

Directors—John D. Rockefeller, William Rockefeller, Henry M. Flagler, John D. Archbold, Henry H. Rogers, W. H. Tilford, Charles M. Pratt, Oliver H. Payne, C. W. Harkness, F. Q. Barstow, J. A. Moffett, E. T. Bedford, Walter Jennings

Main office, 26 Broadway, New York.

## STANDARD ROPE & TWINE CO.

A corporation formed under the laws of New Jersey, November 1, 1896. The company was a reorganization of the United States Cordage Co., which was a reorganization of the former National Cordage Co., a company which controlled a large portion of the cordage and twine industries in the United States and Canada. In 1898–99 a company—the Union Selling Co., with a capital of $500,000—was formed to market this company's manufactured product. At a meeting of the stockholders in September, 1901, the cancellation of the contract was recommended by a committee of stockholders.

For the histories of the National Cordage Co. and United States Cordage Co. see MANUAL for 1898, and for an account of the reorganization and formation of this company under the plan of 1895, see the MANUAL for 1899.

Stock......Par $100........................Authorized, $12,000,000......Issued, $11,916,860

ransfer Agent, Manhattan Trust Co., New York. Registrar, Chase National Bank, New York.

FUNDED DEBT.

| | |
|---|---|
| 1st mort., 6 per cent., due Aug., 1946, Feb. and Aug............................... | $2,740,000 |
| Cons. mort., income, non-cumulative, 5 per cent., due Aug., 1946, Feb. and Aug..... | 6,805,330 |
| Total.................................................................. | $9,545,330 |

The proceeds of 1st mortgage bonds were applied to the extinguishment of underlying liens on the property of United States Cordage Co. and to the furnishing of working capital. The original issue was $3,000,000, of which $215,000 have been retired by the sinking fund.

The consolidated income bonds were $7,500,000. In 1901 the company canceled $694,670 of these bonds held in its treasury.

Trustee of 1st mortgage, Manhattan Trust Co., New York; Trustee consolidated mortgage, Central Trust Co., New York.

In year 1896–97 the sales were $3,542,353; deficit from operation, $169,710; other income, $96,376; charges, $264,212; deficit, $167,836. In 1897–98, sales, $3,100,118; net, $473,428; balance over charges, $223,563. The report for 1898–99 showed current assets, $3,447,030, and accounts and bills payable, $1,827,931, leaving a surplus of assets of $1,619,099. The report for

1899-1900 showed surplus of assets $1,621,141, but gave no details of the year's business. In the year 1900-01 the operations, after payment of interest on bonds and floating debt, resulted in a loss of $630,000. In 1901-02 the surplus over the fixed charges and $59,405 charged off for depreciation, etc., was $28,314.

President, Thomas Russell; Vice-President, Alfred R. Turner, Jr.; Secretary and Treasurer, Joseph G. Taylor, New York.

Directors—William Barbour, William R. Potts, James B. Clews, John Kean, Alfred R. Turner, Jr., Josiah C. Reiff, Thomas Russell, Joseph G. Taylor, E. LeB. Gardiner.

Main office, 17 State street, New York. Annual meeting, third Tuesday in September, at Elizabeth, N. J.

## STANDARD SANITARY MANUFACTURING CO.

A corporation organized under the laws of New Jersey, December 27, 1899. The company has acquired the plants, business and property of the following concerns:

The Ahrens & Ott Manufacturing Co., Louisville.
Buick & Sherwood Manufacturing Co., Detroit.
Cribben & Sexton Co., Sanitary Department, Chicago.
J. J. Vollrath Manufacturing Co., Sanitary Department, Sheboygan, Wis.
Standard Manufacturing Co., Pittsburg.
Pennsylvania Bath Tub Co., Ellwood City, Pa.
Sanitary Manufacturing & Enameling Co., Muncie, Ind.
Victor Manufacturing Co., Allequippa, Pa.
Dawes & Myler, New Brighton, Pa.

The above firms and companies all manufactured plumbers' enameled iron ware, and some of them made, in addition to iron goods, a large line of plumbers' brass work, plumbers' wood work and other goods in the plumbing supply line. The united plants produce about 80 per cent. of all the plumbers' enameled iron ware manufactured in the United States.

Stock...Par $100...Authorized { com., $2,500,000; pref., 2,500,000 } Issued { com., $2,067,400; pref., 1,905,500 } $3,972,900

The preferred stock is 7 per cent., non-cumulative.

Transfer Agent, Union Trust Co., Pittsburg. Registrar, Fidelity Title & Trust Co., Pittsburg.

FUNDED DEBT.

Debentures, 6 per cent., due 1919, Jan. and July.................................... $1,781,000

The authorized amount of bonds is $2,500,000. Trustee, Knickerbocker Trust Co., New York. Interest on the bonds is paid at the National Bank of Commerce, Pittsburg. There is a sinking fund of $50,000 per annum, the bonds being subject to call at 105, and the amount outstanding has been correspondingly reduced, $47,000 of the bonds having been retired in 1901, and $47,000 in 1902.

The plants and businesses of the constituent companies were turned over to the new company free of all incumbrances or liabilities.

None of the stock or bonds were offered to the public, the owners of the constituent concerns taking all themselves.

In February, 1901, a dividend of 3½ per cent. was declared on the preferred stock, payable 1¾ per cent. forthwith and 1¾ per cent. April 15, 1901. On February 10, 1902, 7 per cent. was paid on the preferred stock out of the earnings of 1901. During 1902 quarterly dividends of 1¾ per cent. were paid on the preferred.

President, Theodore Ahrens, Jr., Louisville; 1st Vice-President, Francis J. Torrance, Pittsburg; 2d Vice-President, Henry Cribben, Chicago; Secretary and Treasurer, W. A. Myler, New Brighton, Pa.; General Manager, E. L. Dawes.

Directors—Theodore Ahrens, Jr., Oscar Marschuetz, Junius C. Klein, Louisville; Francis J. Torrance, William Arrott, Charles F. Arrott, W. A. Myler, E. L. Dawes, Pittsburg; A. J. Vollrath, Sheboygan, Wis.; Henry Cribben, Chicago; David Jameson, New Castle, Pa.; Kenneth K. McLaren, Jersey City.

Main office, 403 Wood street, Pittsburg. Annual meeting, second Tuesday in January, at Jersey City.

## STANDARD SCREW CO.

A corporation formed under the laws of New Jersey, March 27, 1900, to manufacture screws machines, etc. The company acquired the plants and consolidated the business of the following companies:

Detroit Screw Works.
Worcester Machine Screw Co.,
Chicago Screw Co.,
Pearson Machine Co.

Stock.......Par $100......Authorized { com., $700,000; pref., 600,000 } Issued { com., $900,000; pref., 400,000 } $1,300,000

The preferred stock is 6 per cent., cumulative, and is preferred both as to assets and dividends.

Transfer Agent and Registrar, Registrar & Transfer Co., 15 Exchange place, Jersey City, N. J.

The company has no funded debt.

President, Charles E. Roberts; 1st Vice-President, W. B. Pearson, Chicago; 2d Vice-President, A. W. Gifford, Worcester, Mass.; Secretary, George Thrall, Detroit; Treasurer, Charles H. Rollins, Chicago.

Directors—Charles E. Roberts, W. B. Pearson, Chicago; A. W. Gifford, E. B. Dulliver, Worcester, Mass.; George Thrall, H. H. Taylor, Detroit; James C. Young, Jersey City.

Corporate office, Jersey City, N. J.; main office, 2 North Canal street, Chicago.

Annual meeting, second Wednesday in May at Jersey City

## STANDARD STEEL CAR CO.

A corporation formed under the laws of Pennsylvania, January 2, 1902. The purpose of the company is the manufacture of railroad equipment. The company has a large plant at Butler, Pa., for the construction of steel railroad cars.

In November, 1902, it was announced that capitalists connected with this company had acquired control of the Southern Car & Foundry Co.

Stock......Par $100..........................Authorized, $3,000,000......Issued, $3,000,000

The company has no preferred stock. Stock is transferred at the office of the company, Pittsburg.

The company has no funded debt.

President, John M. Hansen; Vice-President, James B. Brady; Treasurer, A. R. Fraser; Secretary, Abram S. Valentine, Pittsburg.

Directors—John M. Hansen, A. R. Fraser, W. L. Mellon, Henry Aiken, James B. Brady, L. G. Woods, Henry R. Rea, Pittsburg; Edwin Hawley, Levi C. Weir, New York.

Main office, Fifth avenue and Grant street, Pittsburg. Annual meeting, second Tuesday in February, at Pittsburg.

## STANDARD TABLE OIL CLOTH CO.

A corporation formed under the laws of New Jersey, July 13, 1901. The purposes of the company are the manufacture of table oil cloth, stair and shelf oil cloth, table covers, wall coverings, enameled oil cloths, carriage cloth, tarpaulins, carpet drum cloth coverings, slicker cloth, sign muslin, hatsweats, shoe muslins, lounge coverings, traveling bag coverings and other articles of the same general description. The company acquired and owns the plants and property of the following concerns which were engaged in the above line of business:

Altha & Hughes, Newark, N. J.
Joseph Wild & Co., Astoria, N. Y.
The Ohio Oil Cloth Co., Youngstown, O.
Goodlatte Oil Cloth Co., Passaic, N. J.
Keystone Oil Cloth Co., Norristown, Pa.
The Western Linoleum Co., Akron, O.
A. F. Buchanan & Sons, Montrose, N. Y.

Stock....Par $100.....Authorized { com., $5,000,000 / pref., 5,000,000 } Issued { com., $4,000,000 / pref., 4,000,000 } $8,000,000

The preferred stock is 7 per cent., cumulative, and also has a preference in regard to the assets of the company in case of a dissolution.

Transfer Agent, National Bank of Commerce, New York. Registrar, Morton Trust Co., New York.

The company has no funded debt.

President, H. M. Garlick; 1st Vice-President, G. M. McKelvey, Youngstown, O.; 2d Vice-President, George H. Hughes, New York; Secretary, Alvin Hunsicker, Philadelphia; Treasurer, F. H. Schmidt, New York.

Directors—H. M. Garlick, G. M. McKelvey, C. H. Booth, John Stambaugh, A. E. Adams, Youngstown, O.; Andrew B. Buchanan, George Buchanan, Peekskill, N. Y.; E. A. Oviatt, A. M. Cole, George G. Allen, Akron, O.; George H. Hughes, John H. Berresford, A. Powers Smith, F. H. Schmidt, New York; Benjamin Atha, Newark, N. J.; T. A. R. Goodlatte, Passaic, N. J.; Alvin Hunsicker, Philadelphia; Charles Templeton, Norristown, Pa.

Corporate office, 15 Exchange Place, Jersey City; main office, 320 Broadway, New York. Annual meeting, second Tuesday in May, at Jersey City.

## STANDARD UNDERGROUND CABLE CO.

A corporation formed under the laws of Pennsylvania, in 1889, having previously been incorporated under the laws of New Jersey in 1882. The object of the company is manufacturing cables, underground, submarine and aerial, for all classes of electric work. The company has a large factory at Pittsburg, and branch factories at Perth Amboy, N. J., and Oakland, Cal. In 1902 extensive additions to the Perth Amboy works were completed.

Stock......Par $100... .......................Authorized, $2,000,000......Issued, $2,000,000

The stock of the company, which was originally $1,500,000, was increased to $2,000,000 in 1902 and 1903.

Transfer Agent, Union Trust Co., Pittsburg. Registrar, Fidelity Title & Trust Co., Pittsburg.

Dividends paid have been as follows: In 1890 to 1894, 8 per cent. per annum; in 1895, 6½ per cent.; in 1896, 8 per cent.; in 1897, 7 per cent.; in 1898, 1899, 1900, 1901 and 1902 10 per cent. Dividends are paid quarterly, 2 per cent. each January (10), April, July and October., with 2 per cent. extra at the end of the year.

The surplus, January 1, 1901, was $265,564.

President, Mark W. Watson; Vice-President and General Manager, Joseph W. Marsh; Secretary and Treasurer, Frank A. Rinehart; Auditor, Charles M. Hagen, Pittsburg.

Directors—Mark W. Watson, James H. Willock, John B. Jackson, John Moorhead, Jr., Robert Pitcairn, Benjamin F. Jones, John D. Nicholson, J. N. Davidson, Joseph W. Marsh, Pittsburg.

Main office, 200 Ninth street, Pittsburg; branch offices: New York, 56 Liberty street; Philadelphia, South Broad and South Pennsylvania square; Chicago, 217 LaSalle street; Bost on 101 Milk street; San Francisco, 210 Montgomery street. Annual meeting, fourth Tuesdayin, January.

---

## STANLEY ELECTRIC MANUFACTURING CO.

A corporation formed under the laws of New Jersey in January, 1900. The company has factories for the manufacture of electric plants and appliances at Pittsfield, Mass.

In February, 1903, it was stated that the General Electric Co. had acquired a controlling interest in this company's stock.

Stock......Par $100..........................Authorized, $3,000,000......Issued, $3,000,000

Stock is transferred at the company's office, Trenton, N. J.

The gross business of the company in 1900 was $1,040,904 and in 1901 $1,150,534.

The company declared a dividend on its stock out of the profits of 1900 of 6 per cent., payable, 3 per cent. April 1, 1901, and 3 per cent. October 1, 1901. In April, 1902, it was announced that dividends would be paid quarterly at the rate o 1½ per cent. each in January, A pril, July and October.

The statement for the year 1900 showed on December 31, 1901, a profit and loss surplus of $241,214.

President, F. A. C. Perrine; Treasurer, W. W. Gamwell, Pittsfield, Mass.

Directors—F. A. C. Perrine, W. R. Plunkett, George H. Tucker, W. W. Gamwell, Pittsfield, Mass.; F. W. Roebling, F. O. Briggs, Trenton, N. J.; H. L. Shippy, New York.

Corporate office, Trenton, N. J.; main office and works, Pittsfield, Mass. Annual meeting, second Wednesday in February.

---

## STATEN ISLAND MIDLAND RAILROAD CO.

A corporation formed under the laws of New York, December 1, 1890, and reorganized without a change of name August 19, 1895. The company absorbed the Stapleton and West Brighton branches of the Staten Island Midland Railroad Co. and the Prohibition Park Electric Railroad Co., acquiring in 1898 the Staten Island Traction Co. It owns an electric power plant and operates 28.5 miles of track from Port Richmond to Midland Beach, Staten Island, N. Y., with branches.

Stock......Par $100......... ..................Authorized, $1,000,000......Issued, $1,000,000

The company has no preferred stock.

FUNDED DEBT.

1st mort., 5 per cent., gold, due Jan., 1926, Jan. and July.......................... $1,000,000

The outstanding bonds are the full amount authorized. A sinking fund after 1901 is provided, but bonds cannot be called. Trustee of the mortgage and agent for payment of interest, Farmers' Loan & Trust Co., New York.

In the year ending June 30, 1902, the gross earnings were $137,914; net, $49,672; fixed charges, $69,217; deficit, $19,545.

President and General Manager, Robert Wetherill; Vice-President, Charles L. Spier, New York; Secretary, H. T. Walter, Stapleton, S. I.; Treasurer, H. H. Rogers, Jr., New York.

Directors—Robert Wetherill, Richard Wetherill, James H. Garthwaite, Chester, Pa.; A. F. Dawson, Ridley Park, Pa.; O. G. Paine, G. C. Armstrong, H. T. Walter, New York.

Main office, Stapleton, S. I. Annual meeting, second Monday in January, at Concord, Staten Island, N. Y.

## STERLING WHITE LEAD CO.

A corporation formed under the laws of Pennsylvania, April 17, 1893. The purpose of the company is the manufacture of white lead, dry and in oil; red lead, litharge and other products of lead. The company has works at New Kensington, Pa., on the Allegheny Valley Division of the Pennsylvania Railroad.

Stock......Par $100............................Authorized, $500,000......Issued, $500,000

The company has no preferred stock or funded debt

Stock is transferred at the office of the company, Pittsburg.

President, Gerard C. Smith; Vice-President, William W. Lawrence; Secretary, Charles O. Smith; Treasurer, John J. Lawrence, Jr.

Directors—Gerard C. Smith, William W. Lawrence, John J. Lawrence, Jr.

Main office, 501 Liberty avenue, Pittsburg. Annual meeting, third Monday in January.

## THE JOHN B. STETSON CO.

A Pennsylvania corporation formed May, 1891. The company took over the hat manufacturing business of John B. Stetson, Philadelphia, established in 1865, which is the largest and most complete factory in the world devoted exclusively to the manufacture of fine hats.

Stock...Par $100...Authorized { com., $2,500,000 / pref., 1,500,000 } Issued { com., $2,000,000 / pref., $1,500,000 } $3,500,000

The preferred stock is 8 per cent., cumulative. All the stock is full-paid and non-assessable. The company has no funded debt.

In November, 1902, the common stock authorized was increased from $1,500,000 to $2,500,000, and $500,000 of the new stock was allotted at par to the stockholders. The remaining $500,000 of new issue was to be held in the company's treasury to be used in the discretion of the president and directors for allotment among the employees.

Transfer Agent, Provident Life & Trust Co., Philadelphia. Registrar, Philadelphia Trust, Safe Deposit & Insurance Co., Philadelphia.

In 1891 4 per cent. was paid upon the preferred for six months, and since then 8 per cent. per annum has been paid semi-annually, 4 per cent. each in January (15) and July. Dividends upon the common stock are paid annually, January 15, and have been as follows: In 1891, for six months, 4½ per cent.; in 1892, 6 per cent.; in 1893, 6 per cent.; in 1894 and 1895, 4 per cent.; in 1896, 4 per cent.; in 1897, 5 per cent.; in 1898, 6 per cent.; in 1899, 12 per cent.; in 1900, 15 per cent.; in 1901, 17 per cent.; in 1902, 17 per cent.

Total surplus, November 30, 1901, $898,018; November 30, 1902, $1,264,970.

President, John B. Stetson; 1st Vice-President, William F. Fray; 2d Vice-President, J. Howell Cummings; Treasurer, William K. Krips; Secretary, Harry E. Depuy.

Directors—John B. Stetson, William F. Fray, J. Howell Cummings, John S. Stevens, Paul M. Elsasser, Edwin F. Keen, N. B. Day, Philadelphia.

Main office and factory, Fourth street and Montgomery avenue, Philadelphia; New York office and sales rooms, 750 Broadway. Annual meeting, first Monday in January.

## STONEGA COAL & COKE CO.

A corporation formed under the laws of New Jersey, April 22, 1902. The company leased two tracts of coal land from the Virginia Coal & Iron Co. in Wise County, Virginia. One plant of 666 ovens is in operation, and another plant of 500 ovens is partly constructed.

Stock......Par $100...........................Authorized, $2,000,000. ... Issued, $250,000

The company has no preferred stock and no funded debt. Stock is transferred at the office of the company, Philadelphia.

President, J. S. Wentz; Vice-President, D. B. Wentz; Secretary and Treasurer, W. C. Kent.

Directors—J. S. Wentz, J. L. Wentz, Samuel Dickson, W. Beaumont Whitney, Hazard Dickson, Philadelphia; D. B. Wentz, Big Stone Gap, Va.; Robert H. Sayre, South Bethlehem, Pa.; Samuel Thomas, Catasauqua, Pa.; William D. Lippincott, Camden, N. J.

Corporate office, 33 North Third street, Camden, N. J.; President and Treasurer's office, Girard Trust Building, Philadelphia; operating office, Big Stone Gap, Va. Annual meeting, first Wednesday in March, at Camden, N. J.

## STORAGE POWER CO.

A corporation formed under the laws of West Virginia, in 1898. The company owns the patents covering the storage and transmission of heat and power by means of superheated water. This system is adapted to many uses and its value is said to have been fully demonstrated as motive power for vehicles, being much less expensive than any adaptation of electric storage.

Stock......Par $50...........................Authorized, $5,000,000......Issued, $5,000,000

Transfer Agent, Standard Trust Co., New York.

In May, 1902, a committee, P. Chauncey Anderson, Chairman, was appointed to investigate the position of the company.

President, W. Seward Webb, Shelburne, Vt.; Vice-President, Henry L. Sprague; Secretary and Treasurer, Edward Barr, New York.

Directors—W. Seward Webb, William L. Bull, Andrew G. Blair, Nathan A. Guilford, F. B. Jennings, Henry L. Sprague, J. Wesley Allison, Edward Barr, William E. Prall.

Main office, 30 Broad street, New York. Annual meeting, December 6.

## STREET'S WESTERN STABLE CAR LINE CO.

A corporation formed under the laws of Illinois in 1885. The objects of the company are to build and operate stable cars under the Street patents. The company has 10,000 cars.

Stock...Par $100... Authorized { com., $4,000,000; pref., 1,000,000 } Issued { com., $3,834,800; pref., 776,900 } $4,611,700

The preferred stock is 7 per cent., cumulative.

Stock is transferred at the company's office, Chicago.

The company has paid full 7 per cent. dividends on its preferred stock in half-yearly payments of 3½ per cent., January (1) and July. On the common it paid 4 per cent., from 1890 to 1893, inclusive. In 1894 paid 1 per cent., in 1895 and 1896 no dividend on the common, in 1897 1 per cent., in 1898 1½ per cent., in 1899 2 per cent., and in 1900, 1901 and 1902 2 per cent., the dividends on the common being 50c. per share, or ½ per cent., in January (25), April, July and October.

FUNDED DEBT.

1st mort., 5 per cent., gold, due 1903 to 1908, Feb. and Aug............................ $250,000

The 1st mortgage bonds are secured by the company's cars and by a tract of land near the Union Stock Yards, Chicago. The bonds are payable in instalments of $50,000 per annum, beginning August 1, 1900. On December 31, 1902, the company had outstanding car lease warrants to the amount of $1,966,597.

EARNINGS.

| | Net. | Charges. | Dividends. | Surplus. |
|---|---|---|---|---|
| 1898 | $196,369 | $31,250 | $111,905 | $53,214 |
| 1899 | 179,743 | 23,000 | 131,079 | 25,664 |
| 1900 | 185,675 | 23,679 | 131,079 | 30,917 |
| 1901 | 200,920 | 19,666 | 131,079 | 50,175 |
| 1902 | 398,983 | 91,084 | 131,079 | 176,820 |

President, Herman Grossman; Vice-President and General Manager, F. J. Reichman; Treasurer, Benjamin Rosenberg; Secretary, Howard Hill.

Directors—Franklin H. Head, Herman Grossman, C. G. Bostedo, B. Rosenberg, H. E. Southwell, F. J. Reichman, E. B. Grossman.

Main office, 84 Van Buren street, Chicago. Annual meeting, fourth Tuesday in February.

## THE SUBURBAN RAILROAD CO.

A corporation formed under the laws of Illinois in May, 1895, for the purpose of operating a trolley street railway in Chicago and suburbs. Originally the company was the Suburban Electric Railroad Co. The company owns 57 miles of track and has franchises in Chicago, Cicero, La Grange, Proviso, Grass Dale, River Forest, Harlem and Riverside. It operates, under leases from the Chicago Terminal Transfer Railroad Co., the Chicago, Harlem & Batavia Railroad Co. and the Chicago & Southwestern Railroad to the Harlem race course. A receiver was appointed in July, 1902.

Stock......Par $100...........................Authorized, $1,250,000......Issued, $1,250,000

The company has no preferred stock. Transfer Agent and Registrar, Chicago Title & Trust Co.

FUNDED DEBT.

1st mort., 5 per cent., gold due March, 1916, March and Sept........................ $1,250,000

The authorized amount of the mortgage is $3,000,000, and $1,750,000 may be issued for future extensions and improvements. Trustee of the mortgage and agent for the payment of interest, Chicago Title & Trust Co., Chicago.

Receiver and President, Louis S. Owsley; Vice-President, F. H. Roeschlaub; Secretary and Treasurer, Edwin C. Veasey.

Directors—Louis S. Owsley, F. H. Roeschlaub, William G. Adams, Charles T. Yerkes.

Main office, 135 Adams street, Chicago. Annual meeting, last Thursday in July, at Chicago.

## SUNDAY CREEK COAL CO.

A corporation formed under the laws of Ohio in 1879. It owns about 14,000 acres of coal lands in Perry and Athens counties, Ohio. Operates 4 mines with a total daily capacity of 4,500 tons of coal. Also owns 1,476 feet of valuable dock property at West Superior, Wis.

In 1902 it was stated that the control of the company had been acquired by the Hocking Valley Railway Co.

Stock......Par $10....... Authorized { com., $225,000 / pref., 150,000 } Issued { com., $225,000 / pref., 150,000 } $375,000

The preferred stock is 6 per cent. The stock, which was $100 par and consisted of $2,250,000 common and $1,500,000 preferred, was reduced to $10 par and to the present amounts in October, 1902.

Transfer Agent, Charles B. Van Nostrand, 36 Wall street, New York.

Dividends have been as follows: In 1892, 3 per cent.; in 1893, 1½ per cent.; in 1894, 3 per cent.; in 1895, 3 per cent.; in 1896, 3 per cent.; in 1897, 2 per cent. The company formerly paid 3 per cent. dividends on preferred stock, but suspended same in 1898.

Output of coal was, in 1897, 414,882 tons; in 1898, 489,675 tons; in 1899, 667,123 tons; in 1900, 824,530 tons. In 1902 (year ending June 30), 803,548 tons.

FUNDED DEBT.

1st mort. 6 per cent. sinking fund, due 1912, June and Dec.......................... $350,000

The bonds were issued to retire $200,000 6 per cent. bonds maturing December 1, 1892, and to provide funds for purchase of docks at West Superior, costing $182,000. Bonds carry a sinking fund provision of 2 cents per ton on all coal mined after January 1, 1895, the bonds being subject to redemption at 105 and interest.

EARNINGS.

| | Gross. | Net. | Charges. | Surplus. |
|---|---|---|---|---|
| 1897 | $351,288 | $97,971 | $36,191 | $61,780 |
| 1898 | 394,425 | 75,647 | 37,201 | 38,445 |
| 1899 | 667,123 | 104,391 | 36,695 | 67,696 |
| 1900 | 824,530 | 125,413 | 30,526 | 94,887 |
| 1902 (year ending June 30) | 109,808 | 39,043 | ...... | 70,756 |

President, N. Monsarrat, Columbus, O.; Vice-President, James H. Hoyt, Cleveland; General Manager, John H. Winder; Secretary and Treasurer, W. N. Cott; Auditor, George S. Beeson, Columbus, O.

Directors—N. Monsarrat, G. Vonden Steinen, John H. Winder, F. B. Sheldon, Columbus, O.; J. H. Hoyt, Cleveland.

Main office, 50 East Broad street, Columbus, O.

## SUPERIOR WATER, LIGHT & POWER CO.

A corporation formed under the laws of Wisconsin, August 22, 1889, for the purpose of supplying water, electric light and power, and gas in the city of Superior, Wis. The company owns a water plant with a capacity of 4,500,000 gallons per day, an electric plant equipped for arc and incandescent service, and a gas plant with 18 miles of mains.

Stock......Par $100..........................Authorized, $1,000,000......Issued, $1,000,000

The company has no preferred stock.

Stock is transferred at the office of the secretary, West Superior, Wis.

FUNDED DEBT.

| | |
|---|---|
| 1st mort., 4 per cent., due May, 1931, May and Nov. | $1,400,000 |
| Income bonds, 4 per cent., due 1931 | 350,000 |
| Total | $1,750,000 |

The authorized 1st mortgage is $2,000,000. Of the outstanding bonds $200,000 are held in the company's treasury. Trustee of the mortgage and agent for the payment of interest, United Mortgage & Trust Co., New York.

The authorized issue of income bond is $350,000, $50,000 being held in the company's treasury. Trustee and agent for payment of interest, St. Paul Title & Trust Co., St. Paul.

President, William R. Merriam, Washington, D. C.; Vice-President and Treasurer, Victor M. Watkins, St. Paul; Secretary, William H. Winslow; General Manager, B. F. Ellison, West Superior, Wis.

Directors—William R. Merriam, Washington, D. C.; Kenneth Clark, Robert R. Dunn, Victor M. Watkins, St. Paul; Frank B. Ross, William H. Winslow, B. F. Ellison, West Superior, Wis.

Corporate office, Superior, Wis.; main office, West Superior, Wis. Annual meeting, third Tuesday in November, at West Superior, Wis.

## SUSQUEHANNA COAL CO.

A corporation formed under the laws of Pennsylvania in 1840. The company owns and works mines in an anthracite coal tract at Nanticoke, Luzerne County, Pa. The company is controlled by the Pennsylvania Railroad Co., which owns all the stock.

Stock......Par $100..........................Authorized, $2,136,800......Issued, $2,136,800

FUNDED DEBT.

1st mort., 6 per cent., guaranteed, due Jan., 1911, Jan. and July .................. $1,471,000

The 1st mortgage bonds of this company are guaranteed principal and interest by the Pennsylvania Railroad Co. There is a sinking fund for the bonds, which, however, must be bought in the market, not drawn.

President, A. J. Cassatt; Vice-President, Isaac J. Wister; Secretary, George H. Ross; Treasurer, A. Haviland, Philadelphia.

Main office, Broad Street Station, Philadelphia.

## SUSQUEHANNA IRON & STEEL CO.

A corporation formed under the laws of Pennsylvania in June, 1899. The company acquired the property and plants of the Columbia Rolling Mill, Columbia, Pa.; Vesta Furnace, Lancaster County, Pa.; Columbia Iron Co., Columbia, Pa.; Susquehanna Iron Co., Columbia, Pa.; York Rolling Mill, York, Pa.; Aurora Furnace Co. Wrightsville, Pa., and Janson Iron & Steel Co., Columbia, Pa.

Stock......Par $5............................Authorized, $1,500,000......Issued, $1,500,000

Dividends, at the rate of 6 per cent., are paid semi-annually, in January and July.

FUNDED DEBT.

1st mort., 6 per cent., due 1906................................................... $300,000

The bonds were created in 1902, and were issued to build a pipe mill. After 1903 the bonds can be called at par.

President, Charles A. Porter; Secretary and Treasurer, R. Y. Filbert, Philadelphia.

Directors—L. S. Filbert, Charles A. Porter, H. F. Bruner, J. William Steacy, W. S. Kimball, R. J. Houston, Percy M. Chandler, Henry Clay, W. H. Butler.

Main office, Broad and Chestnut streets, Philadelphia; operating office, Columbia, Pa.

## SWEETSER, PEMBROOK & CO., INCORPORATED

A corporation formed under the laws of New York, November 27, 1901. The company was incorporated to take over the property, business and good will of the wholesale dry goods firm of Sweetser, Pembrook & Co., New York.

Stock......Par $100.......Authorized { com., $750,000 / pref., 750,000 } Issued { com., $750,000 / pref., 750,000 } $1,500,000

The preferred stock is 6 per cent., cumulative, and has a preference as to assets in case of liquidation. Dividends are payable semi-annually in January and July.

Transfer Agent, Merchants' Trust Co., New York. Registrar, Central Trust Co., New York.

The company has no funded debt.

In December, 1901, the Merchants' Trust Co., New York, offered $500,000 of the preferred stock of this company for subscription at par.

President, J. Howard Sweetser,; Vice-President and Treasurer, Howard P. Sweetser, New York; 2d Vice-President, Joseph H. Bumsted, Jersey City; Secretary, Herbert Forrest, New York.

Directors—J. Howard Sweetser, Howard P. Sweetser, Robert Lockhart, Herbert Forrest, Otto J. Frickel, John A. Dingwall, New York; Joseph H. Bumsted, Jersey City.

Corporate and main office, 374 Broadway, New York. Annual meeting, January 20, at the company's office.

## SWIFT AND COMPANY

A corporation formed under the laws of Illinois, April 1, 1885. Its business is the slaughtering and sale of cattle, sheep and hogs and their commercial products. The company has extensive plants in Chicago, Omaha, Kansas City, East St. Louis, St. Joseph, Mo., St. Paul, Minn., and Fort Worth, Tex., and branches and facilities for distributing its products in nearly every large city in the United States, and is represented in every country in the world. In 1900 the Chicago plant of the Chicago Packing & Provision Co. was purchased. The Swift Refrigerator Transportation Co., which owns over 4,000 cars, and the Swift Live Stock Transportation Co., are operated in harmony with this company.

Stock......Par $100........................Authorized, $25,000,000......Issued, $25,000,000

The stock was originally $300,000, and has been increased from time to time, the last increases being to $15,000,000 in 1893, to $20,000,000 in 1899, and to $25,000,000 in February, 1902. These increases were subscribed for by the stockholders at par.

Dividends are 7 per cent. per annum, payable quarterly in January, April, July and October. Since the organization of the company in 1885 to January, 1903, it has paid to stockholders in cash dividends $18,332,931.

Stock is transferred at the company's office, Union Stock Yards, Chicago. Registrar, Illinois Trust & Savings Bank, Chicago.

FUNDED DEBT.

1st mort. bonds, 5 per cent., due July, 1914, Jan. and July........................ .. $5,000,000

The company had $2,500,000 6 per cent. 1st mortgage bonds, due 1910, but on July 1, 1900, they were called and paid off, the company having authorized its new 5 per cent. 1st mortgage bonds for $5,000,000. Trustee of mortgage, American Trust and Savings Bank, Chicago.

Total sales in 1896, $104,000,000; in 1897, $121,500,000; in 1898, $150,000,000; in 1899, $160,000,000; in 1900, $170,000,000; in 1901, $200,000,000; in 1902, $200,000,000.

The following is the company's balance sheet presented at the annual meeting, January 2, 1903:

| ASSETS. | | LIABILITIES. | |
|---|---|---|---|
| Real estate, etc. | $13,718,996 | Capital stock paid in | $25,000,000 |
| Unexpired insurance | 107,319 | Bonds | 5,000,000 |
| Horses, wagons and harness | 113,808 | Bond interest accrued | 62,500 |
| Investments, including branches. | 5,311,089 | Bills payable | 12,538,908 |
| Quick assets: | | Accounts payable | 1,841,783 |
| Sundry stocks and bonds | 2,166,851 | Taxes | 323,664 |
| Cash | 1,659,597 | Surplus | 5,246,006 |
| Accounts receivable | 14,243,632 | | |
| Live cattle, sheep, hogs, dressed beef, etc., on hand | 12,691,569 | | |
| Total | $50,012,861 | Total | $50,012,861 |

President (Vacancy); 1st Vice-President, Edwin C. Swift, Boston; 2d Vice-President, Louis F. Swift; Secretary, D. Edwin Hartwell; Treasurer, Laurence A. Carton; Assistant Treasurer, I. A. Vant,: Assistant Secretary, C. A. Peacock; General Counsel, Albert H. Veeder, Henry Veeder, Chicago.

Directors—Gustavus F. Swift, Louis F. Swift, Laurence A. Carton, Edward F. Swift, Chicago; Edwin C. Swift, Boston; John R. Redfield, Hartford, Conn.; Herbert Barnes, New Haven, Conn.

Main office, Union Stock Yards, Chicago. Annual meeting, first Thursday in January at Union Stock Yards, Chicago.

---

## SYRACUSE GAS CO.

This company owns and operates the gas works system of Syracuse, N. Y., under a perpetual franchise. Miles of mains, 96.

Control of the company was acquired in 1902 by the Syracuse Lighting Co., which exchanged $1,500,000 of its common stock for an equal amount of the company's shares.

Stock......Par $100..........................Authorized, $2,500,000... ..Issued, $1,975,000

Transfer Agent, Colonial Trust Co., New York.

FUNDED DEBT.

1st mort., 5 per cent., gold, due 1946, Jan. and July................................ $2,047,000

The 1st mortgage is for $2,500,000, the balance of issue being reserved for extensions and improvements. Trustee of the mortgage and agent for the payment of interest, Guarantee Trust Co., New York,

President, George A. Wood; Vice-President, Michael Whelan; Secretary, Jerome L. Cheney; Treasurer, John J. Cummins, Syracuse, N. Y.

Directors—Michael Whelan, Frederick J. Baker, Jerome L. Cheney, William E. Tanner, George A. Wood.

Main office, 213 James street, Syracuse.

## SYRACUSE LIGHTING CO.

A corporation formed under the laws of New York, May 23, 1901. The purposes of the company are generating and distributing electricity for light and power. The company acquired and owns the Electric Light & Power Co. of Syracuse, N. Y., and the Underground Electric Wire Co. of the same city. In 1901 it also acquired a majority of the stock of the Syracuse Gas Co., and thus controls the entire gas and electric facilities of the city.

Stock....Par $100.....Authorized { com., $3,000,000 / pref., 1,000,000 } Issued { com., $3,000,000 / pref., 1,000,000 } $4,000,000

The preferred stock is 5 per cent., non-cumulative.

In 1901 the common stock was increased from $1,500,000 to $3,000,000, the increase being made for the purpose of acquiring $1,500,000 of the $1,925,000 stock of the Syracuse Gas Co. by exchanging it for this company's common stock at par.

Transfer Agent, Continental Trust Co., New York. Registrar, Colonial Trust Co., New York.

The first dividend on the preferred stock was 1¼ per cent., paid November 1, 1901. Regular quarterly dividends of the same amount are paid on the preferred in February (1), May, August and November.

FUNDED DEBT.

1st mort., 5 per cent., due June, 1951, June and Dec.................................. $2,000,000

The authorized amount of the 1st mortgage is $2,500,000. Trustee of mortgage, Colonial Trust Co., New York. Agents for the payment of interest, Redmond, Kerr & Co., 41 Wall street, New York.

EARNINGS.

Year ending June 30.

| | Net. | Charges. | Pref. Div. | Surplus. |
|---|---|---|---|---|
| 1901-02 .............................. | $292,132 | $202,350 | $50,000 | $39,782 |

President, Ceylon H. Lewis; Secretary, Louis L. Waters; Treasurer, John J. Cummins, Syracuse, N. Y.

Directors—Stephen Peabody, Henry Seligman, James C. Bishop, New York; Hendrick S. Holden, Louis L. Waters, John Dunfee, John J. Cummins, Syracuse, N. Y.; Robert C. Pruyn, Albany, N. Y.

Main office, 112 East Jefferson street, Syracuse, N. Y. Annual meeting, second Tuesday in October.

## SYRACUSE RAPID TRANSIT RAILWAY CO.

A corporation formed under the laws of New York, May 21, 1896. The company is a consolidation of the Syracuse Street Railroad Co., Syracuse Consolidated Street Railroad Co. and People's Railroad Co.

The company also owns the stock of and has leased the East Side Traction Co. It owns and operates 55.83 miles of track and leases 8.55 miles, a total of 64.38 miles in the city of Syracuse, N. Y. The company has a power house and 125 cars.

Stock.....Par $100......Authorized { com., $2,750,000 / pref., 1,250,000 } Issued { com. $2,750,000 / pref., 1,250,000 } $4,000,000

The preferred stock is 6 per cent., non-cumulative. Transfer Agent and Registrar of Stock, Guaranty Trust Co., New York.

FUNDED DEBT.

| | |
|---|---|
| 1st mort., 5 per cent., gold, due March, 1946, March and Sept.......................... | $2,500,000 |
| 2d mort., 5 per cent., due Jan., 1930, Jan. and July.................................. | 586,000 |
| People's Railroad Co., 1st mort., 5 per cent., due Jan., 1921, Jan. and July........... | 750,000 |
| East Side Traction Co. 1st mort., 5 per cent., gold, due June, 1929, July and Dec...... | 250,000 |
| Total.................................................................. | $4,086,000 |

The authorized amount of the 1st mortgage is $3,250,000, of which $750,000 are reserved to retire the People's Railroad 1sts. Trustee and agent for the payment of interest, Guaranty Trust

Co., New York. The authorized amount of the 2d mortgage is $750,000. Agent for the payment of interest, Savings & Trust Co., Cleveland. The outstanding bonds of the People's Railroad Co. and the East Side Traction Co. are the full amount authorized. Trustee of the East Side Traction Co. mortgage and agent for the payment of interest, Savings & Trust Co., Cleveland.

EARNINGS.

Year ending June 30.

| | Gross. | Net. | Charges. | Surplus. |
|---|---|---|---|---|
| 1898-99 | $481,522 | $194,537 | $191,018 | $7,398 |
| 1899-00 | 548,175 | 229,040 | 216,415 | 16,852 |
| 1900-01 | 615,161 | 274,331 | 223,918 | 56,550 |
| 1901-02 | 687,195 | 309,019 | 228,246 | 80,773 |

President, William P. Gannon, Syracuse, N. Y.; Vice-President and General Manager, Edward G. Connette; Secretary and Treasurer, Theodore H. Conderman.

Directors—William P. Gannon, H. D. Coffinberry, L. K. McClymonds, E. G. Connette, Theodore H. Conderman, H. R. Newcomb, J. L. C. Gooding.

Main office, 109 East Genesee street, Syracuse, N. Y. Annual meeting, second Tuesday in December, at Syracuse.

## TACOMA RAILWAY & POWER CO.

A corporation formed under the laws of New Jersey in February, 1899. The company acquired all the street railroads in Tacoma, Wash., and operates 61 miles of track under franchises which expire in 1939.

In July, 1902, the shareholders voted to sell the property to the Puget Sound Electric Railway Co. for $2,000,000 in the common stock of the latter. The General Electric Co., January 31, 1902, owned $746,400 of the stock and $203,000 bonds of the Tacoma Railway & Power Co.

Stock......Par $100.... . ....................Authorized, $2,000,000......Issued, $2,000,000

The company has no preferred stock. Transfer Agent, Corporation Trust Co., Jersey City. Registrar, Colonial Trust Co., New York.

FUNDED DEBT.

| | |
|---|---|
| 1st mort., 5 per cent., gold, due April 1, 1929, April & Oct. | $1,310,000 |
| 2d mort., 5 per cent., gold, due Jan. 1, 1921, Jan. and July | 114,812 |
| Total | $1,424,812 |

The total amount of the authorized 1st mortgage is $1,500,000, of which amount $393,000 are reserved for improvements and betterments. Trustee of the mortgage and agent for the payment of interest, Old Colony Trust Co., Boston. The total amount of the authorized 2d mortgage is $200,000. The bonds may be called at any time at 103. Trustee of the mortgage and agent for the payment of interest, American Loan & Trust Co., Boston.

In the fiscal year ending December 31, 1901, the gross earnings were $378,920; net, $122,287; charges, $69,730; net balance, $52,557.

President, Robert Treat Paine, 2d; Boston; Vice-President, Leonard H. Hole; Secretary, I. S. Keeler, New York; Treasurer, Ernest L. Carr; Assistant Secretary and Assistant Treasurer, J. S. Simpson; General Managers, Stone & Webster, Boston.

Directors—Robert Treat Paine, 2d., Ernest L. Carr, Bird S. Coler, William H. Whitney, Gordon Abbott, John S. Bartlett, Leonard H. Hole, Charles T. Hughes, Francis R. Hart.

Main office, Tacoma, Wash.; New York office, 44 Broad street. Annual meeting, first Tuesday in February.

## TAMARACK MINING CO.

Owns 1,280 acres of copper lands in Houghton County, Mich. The company was formed in 1882 for the purpose of sinking a shaft to the Calumet lode, which it was believed existed in its property about half a mile below the surface. Shaft was begun February, 1882, and completed June, 1885, when the formation sought was struck at a depth of 2,270 feet. Second, third, fourth and fifth shafts have been constructed, and company has mills, reduction works, etc.

Stock......Par $25..........................Authorized, $1,500,000......Issued, $1,500,000

There has been paid in $13 per share on the stock.

In year ending June 30, 1893, the gross earnings were $1,857,274; net, $721,122. In 1896, gross $1,746,188, mining profit $368,696; in 1897, gross $2,267,340, net $431,530; in 1898, gross $2,381,388, net $518,881; in 1899, gross $2,952,098, net, $740,510; in 1900, gross $3,299,077, net, $1,199,141. In 1901, gross, $2,627,954; net, $526,167. In 1902, gross, $1,947,906; net, $197,308.

During 1893 company paid three dividends amounting to $12 per share; in 1894 paid $8; in 1895, $8; in 1896 $6; in 1897, $6; in 1898, $8; in 1899, $10, and in 1900, $17. The dividends in 1900 were $7 per share June 29, and $10 December 28. In 1901 paid $10 in June and $10 in December. No dividends were paid in 1902.

President, A. S. Bigelow; Secretary and Treasurer, W. J. Ladd, Boston; Superintendent, William E. Parnall, Calumet, Mich.

Directors—A. S. Bigelow, J. Henry Brooks, W. J. Ladd, Edward S. Grew, D. M. Anthony, Joseph S. Bigelow, Boston; William E. Parnall, Calumet, Mich.

Main office, 199 Washington street, Boston. Annual meeting, first Thursday in May.

## TECUMSEH COPPER CO.

A or oration formed under the laws of Michigan in 1880. The company owns a copper mining prpperty in Houghton County, Mich., adjoining the Osceola mine. Considerable exploration and development work has been done on the property.

Stock......par $25..........................Authorized, $2,500,000......Issued, $1,375,000

Registrar, Mercantile Trust Co., Boston.

Of the stock of the company, 44,959 shares remain in the company's treasury. On the stock there had been paid in at the beginning of 1902, $7 per share.

President, John C. Watson; Secretary and Treasurer, Daniel L. Demmon, Boston.

Directors—John C. Watson, F. H. Raymond, Daniel L. Demmon, George H. Flint, Boston; James Chynoweth, Calumet, Mich.

Main office, 15 Congress street, Boston. Annual meeting, second Wednesday in March.

## TEFFT-WELLER CO.

A corporation formed under the laws of New York, April, 1901. The purpose of the company was to take over and conduct the wholesale dry goods business of Tefft, Weller & Co., New York. This firm was founded in 1849.

Stock....Par $100.....Authorized { com., $1,500,000; pref., 1,500,000 } Issued { com., $1,500,000; pref., 1,500,000 } $3,000,000

The preferred stock is 6 per cent., cumulative. The preferred up to July 1, 1903, is convertible into common stock at the option of the holder. It was provided that a reserve fund of $250,000 should be created for the preferred dividends before any dividends in excess of 6 per cent. were paid on the common stock.

Ttransfer Agent, Merchants' Trust Co., New York. Registrar, Central National Bank, New York. h

T e payment of dividends on the preferred is quarterly, in January, April, July and October, and the first dividend of 1½ per cent. was paid October 1, 1901.

The company has no funded debt.

President, George C. Clarke; Vice-President, John N. Beach; Secretary, Morton D. Bogue; Treasurer, Charles M. Allen.

Directors—George C. Clarke, Morton D. Bogue, John N. Beach, Charles M. Allen, William E. Tefft, Edwin Langdon, Stephen S. Palmer, New York.

Corporate and main office, 326 Broadway. Annual meeting, third Wednesday in July.

## TELEPHONE, TELEGRAPH & CABLE CO. OF AMERICA

A corporation formed under the laws of New Jersey, November 9, 1899. As the title indicates, the company has power to build, own, operate, lease or sell telephone, telegraph and cable lines. The object of the company was mainly to extend and perfect a long-distance telephone service throughout the country, connecting the isolated independent local telephone systems with each other and with the large cities.

In 1900 this company acquired a large interest in the Erie Telegraph & Telephone Co. In January, 1901, its holdings of this stock were resold to a Boston syndicate.

Stock......par $15..........................Authorized, $9,000,000......Issued, $7,500,000

Transfer Agent, Registrar & Transfer Co., Jersey City.

The amount of stock originally authorized was $30,000,000, of which $25,000,000 was issued, on which, on February 1, 1901, $15 per share had been paid in. The stockholders at the annual meeting, in February, 1901, adopted a resolution authorizing the Directors to take immediate steps to make the stock full-paid upon the payment of all assessments, thus reducing the share capital to the amount given above.

President, Henry S. Kearney; Secretary, James J. Burke; Treasurer, John E. McDonald.

Directors—Henry S. Kearney, R. L. Edwards, James E. Hays, J. T. Sproull, Miles M. O'Brien, Paul F. Lorzer, R. R. Moore, John E. McDonald, Daniel O'Day.

Main office, 100 Broadway, New York. Annual meeting, second Tuesday in February.

## TEMPLE IRON CO.

A corporation formed under the laws of Pennsylvania in 1873. The company for a number of years operated an iron furnace at Reading, Pa. In March, 1899, it acquired a number of anthracite coal mines near Scranton, Pa., producing about 2,000,000 tons of coal per annum, the property being estimated to contain 45,000,000 tons of unmined coal. The company's charter permits it to manufacture iron and steel, mine coal, and develop the material interests of Pennsylvania. The company is controlled in the interest of the Reading, Central of New Jersey, Lehigh Valley, New York, Susquehanna & Western, Lackawanna and Erie Railroad Companies.

Stock......Par $100........................Authorized, $5,000,000......Issued, $2,500,000

The stock of the company was originally $240,000, and was increased to $5,000,000 authorized in 1899. Dividends of 6 per cent. per annum are guaranteed on the stock by the railroad companies named below. The stock may be called in and retired at par and accrued dividends after January 1, 1904, and becomes payable at par after December 31, 1906. The stock is held in trust by the Guaranty Trust Co., New York, which issues its certificates of a beneficial interest in the same.

Transfer Agent, Guaranty Trust Co., New York.

FUNDED DEBT.

1st mort., guar. gold bonds, 4 per cent., due Jan., 1925, Jan. and July.............. $3,284,000

The 1st mortgage is $15,000,000 authorized, Guaranty Trust Co., New York, trustee. The bonds are guaranteed, principal and interest, by the Delaware, Lackawanna & Western Railway, Central Railroad of New Jersey, Reading Co., Lehigh Valley Railroad Co., Erie Railroad Co., and New York, Susquehanna & Western Railway Co. There is a sinking fund of 15 cents per ton on all coal mined for the redemption of the bonds, which may be drawn for redemption at 110 and interest.

President, George F. Baer, Philadelphia; Secretary and Treasurer, A. F. Law, Scranton, Pa.; Assistant Treasurer, George B. Connard, Reading, Pa.

Directors—George F. Baer, J. Rogers Maxwell, Eben B. Thomas, Joseph H. Harris, Alfred Walter, William H. Truesdale, Thomas P. Fowler, F. D. Underwood, I. A. Stearns.

Main office, Reading, Pa.; Scranton office, Board of Trade Building. Annual meeting, third Tuesday in March, at Reading, Pa.

## TENNESSEE COAL, IRON & RAILROAD CO.

A corporation created in 1860 by the Legislature of Tennessee as the Tennessee Coal & Railroad Co. In 1881 name was changed to the present style. The property of the company consists of 450,000 acres of coal, ore, timber and limestone lands; 20 blast furnaces, with a capaci y of 750,000 tons per annum, and coal mines with a developed capacity of 20,000 tons daily. t In September, 1892, consolidated with the De Bardeleben Coal & Iron Co., and also acquired the Cahaba Coal Mining and Excelsior Coal companies. The Alabama Steel & Shipbuilding Co., organized in 1898, is controlled by this company, and has built a large steel plant at Ensley, Ala., with a capacity of 1,000 tons of steel per day, which is leased to this company. In 1899 the company sold the Birmingham Southern Railroad, 41 miles, connecting its various plants, to the Louisville & Nashville Railroad and the Southern Railway Co.

The Alabama Steel & Shipbuilding Co. was formed in 1898 to build a large steel manufacturing plant at Ensley, Ala. It has $440,000 6 per cent. preferred stock and $1,100,000 6 per cent. bonds. Its common stock is all owned by the Tennessee Coal & Iron Co., which guarantees the bonds and dividends on the preferred stock. Half-yearly dividends of 3 per cent., January and July, are paid on the preferred stock of the Alabama company. The Tennessee Coal & Iron stockholders were, in October, 1898, offered the right to subscribe for the bonds at par, a bonus of $400 Alabama Steel & Shipbuilding preferred stock being given with each $1,000 bond.

Stock..Par $100...Authorized { com., $23,000,000 / pref., 1,000,000 } Issued { com., $22,553,600 / pref., 248,000 } $22,801,600

The preferred stock is 8 per cent., cumulative, and the issue of preferred was $1,000,000. In March, 1900, 54 per cent. of dividends were overdue on the preferred. In March, 1900, the total stock was increased from $20,000,000 to $23,000,000, and $1,800,000 of the issue was reserved to retire the preferred stock and accumulated dividends by giving holders 180 in new common. Most of the preferred accepted the proposal. The remaining $1,200,000 of new common was offered to the stockholders at par.

Until 1900 no dividend had been paid on the preferred since 1893, or on the common since 1887. Payment of the full 54 per cent. of back dividends on the non-assenting preferred stock was made May 1, 1900, and regular quarterly dividends of 2 per cent. each are now paid on the outstanding preferred stock in February (1), May, August and November. A dividend of 2 per cent. on the common was declared payable May 1, 1900, and similar dividends were paid in August and November, 1900. The February, 1901, dividend on the common was passed, and no dividends have since been paid.

Transfer Agent, Hanover National Bank, New York Registrar, Central Trust Co., New York.

FUNDED DEBT.

| | |
|---|---|
| Gen. mort., 5 per cent., due July, 1951, Jan. and July | $3,000,000 |
| Cons. mort., Birm. Div., 6 per cent., due Jan., 1917, Jan. and July | 4,068,000 |
| Tennessee Division, 6 per cent., due Jan., 1917, Jan. and July | 1,206,000 |
| De Bardeleben C. & I. Co., 1st mort. guar. 6 per cent., due Feb., 1910, Feb. and Aug. | 2,741,000 |
| Cahaba Coal Mining Co., 1st mort., 6 per cent., due 1922, June and Dec. | 900,000 |
| Ala. Steel & Shipbuilding, 1st mort., guar. 6 per cent., due July, 1928, Jan. and July | 1,100,000 |
| Total | $13,015,000 |

The general mortgage was created in 1901 and is for $15,000,000, of which $10,653,500 is reserved to retire prior bonds, the balance being for improvements and additional property. In 1901 $3,000,000 of these bonds were sold to provide for the completion of a steel rail mill.

EARNINGS.

Year ending January 31.

| | Net. | Charges. | Surplus |
|---|---|---|---|
| 1892-93 | $923,551 | $553,482 | $370,069 |
| 1893-94 | 685,031 | 739,203 | Def. 54,172 |
| 1894-95 | 561,984 | 630,311 | " 68,327 |
| 1895 (to December 31, eleven months) | 995,794 | 625,826 | 369,968 |
| 1896 (year ending Dec. 31) | 692,333 | 661,270 | 31,063 |
| 1897 ( " " " ) | 623,825 | 663,758 | Def. 39,393 |
| 1898 ( " " " ) | 868,383 | 643,408 | 224,975 |
| 1899 ( " " " ) | 1,865,705 | 654,794 | 1,210,911 |
| 1900 ( " " " ) | 2,347,027 | 703,283 | 1,643,744 |
| 1901 ( " " " ) | 1,725,638 | 862,189 | 863,449 |
| 1902 ( " " " ) | 2,656,746 | 1,223,787 | 1,432,958 |

The charges for 1902 include $419,536 credited to royalty and replacement fund, the same being set aside each month at a fixed rate on each ton of ore coal and coke produced, to cover depletion and depreciation of mines and plants.

The following is the company's balance sheet, December 31, 1902:

| ASSETS. | | LIABILITIES. | |
|---|---|---|---|
| Coal and ore lands and other real estate | $26,131,691 | Capital stock, common | $22,552,800 |
| Plants and equipment | 7,094,024 | Capital stock, preferred | 248,300 |
| Investments | 296,800 | Funded debt | 11,811,616 |
| Treasury securities | 615,000 | Guaranteed securities of proprietary company: | |
| Cash | 277,121 | Bonds of Alabama Steel & Ship Building Co. | 1,100,000 |
| Bills and accounts receivable | 2,019,770 | Preferred stock Alabama Steel & Ship Building Co. | 440,000 |
| Inventory of products and supplies on hand | 1,312,455 | Reserve and provisional funds | 268,940 |
| | | Current liabilities | 1,325,205 |
| Total | $37,746,861 | Total | $37,746,861 |

Chairman, Don H. Bacon; 1st Vice-President, Frank S. Witherbee, New York; 2d Vice-President, Charles McCrery, Birmingham, Ala.; Secretary and Treasurer, Leonard T. Beecher; General Sales Agent, Frank A. Burr, New York.

Directors—Don H. Bacon, James T. Woodward, James H. Smith, William Barbour, Albert B. Boardman, Cord Meyer, Benjamin F. Tracy, Elverton R. Chapman, Frank S. Witherbee, Joseph B. Dickson, S. L. Schoonmaker, New York; Walker Percy, Charles McCrery, Birmingham, Ala.

Main office, First avenue and Twentieth street, Birmingham, Ala.; New York office, 100 Broadway. Annual meeting in May, at Tracy City, Tenn.

## TENNESSEE COPPER CO.

A corporation formed under the laws of New Jersey, April 26, 1899. The company has valuable copper properties in Polk County, Tenn., and during 1899 and 1900 did a large amount of work in developing its mines thereon. A large smelting plant has been erected.

Stock......Par $25 ... ......................Authorized, $5,000,000......Issued, $4,375,000

Transfer Agent, National City Bank, New York. Registrar, Colonial Trust Co., New York.

The company began business with a cash capital of $1,000,000.

The report of the company, covering the period from June 15, 1899, to January 1, 1901, showed receipts, including amount received from stock subscriptions, $1,044,181; expenditures, $780,920; cash on hand, $263,261.

President, J. Park Channing; Vice-President, Frederick Lewisohn; Treasurer, J. H. Susman; Secretary, E. C. Westervelt.

Directors—Albert C. Burrage, James Phillips, Jr., Walter Lewisohn, Edgar Buffum, Frederick Lewisohn, H. H. Rogers, J. H. Susmann, J. Parke Channing, E. C. Westervelt.

Main office, 11 Broadway, New York. Annual meeting, fourth Thursday in February.

## TERMINAL WAREHOUSE CO.

A corporation formed under the laws of New York in 1889. The company owns and operates the Central Stores, foot of Twenty-seventh and Twenty-eighth streets and North River, and the Rosseter Stores, foot of Fifty-ninth and Sixtieth streets and North River, New York. The business of the company includes a general storage, free and bonded, for merchandise, freezing and cold storage and lighterage.

Stock......Par, $100...........................Authorized, $800,000......Issued, $800,000

Transfer Agent and Registrar, New York Security & Trust Co.

FUNDED DEBT.

| | |
|---|---|
| 1st mort., 4 per cent | $700,000 |
| 2d mort., 50 years, 5 per cent., due 1942 | 750,000 |
| Debentures, 10-year, 6 per cent., due 1910 | 200,000 |
| Total | $1,650,000 |

President, John H. Lynch; Secretary, Albro Akin; Treasurer, James Stillman.

Directors—William R. Grace, B. Aymar Sands, James Stillman, George Austin Morrison, George S. Dearborn, John H. Lynch, Alfred Skitt, C. W. Hogan, New York.

Main office, 88 Wall street. Annual meeting, third Wednesday in April.

## TERRE HAUTE ELECTRIC CO.

A corporation formed under the laws of Indiana, June 23, 1899, for the purpose of operating street railway, light, heat and power plants. It succeeded the Terre Haute Electric Street Railway and acquired the Citizens' Electric Light & Power Co. and the Brazil Rapid Transit Street Railway. It controls and operates all the street railway, electric light and power facilities of Terre Haute, Ind., operating 35 miles of street railway.

Stock......Par $100............. .............Authorized, $1,000,000......Issued, $1,000,000

Stock is transferred at the office of the company, Boston. Registrar, Boston Safe Deposit & Trust Co., Boston.

FUNDED DEBT.

1st mort., 5 per cent. gold, due 1929, Jan. and July................................ $1,400,000

The authorized issue of bonds is $1,500,000. Trustees of the mortgage, The Union Trust Co., Indianapolis, and Boston Safe Deposit & Trust Co., Boston. Agent for the payment of interest, Boston Safe Deposit & Trust Co., Boston.

In the fiscal year ending June 30, 1902, the road suffering from strike and boycott, the gross earnings were $307,824; net, $43,214; fixed charges, $68,758; deficit, $25,544. In 1901 the surplus was $12,153.

President, W. R. McKeen; Vice-President, J. G. McNutt; Secretary, John T. Beasley, Terre Haute, Ind.; General Managers, Stone & Webster; Treasurer, Henry B. Sawyer, Boston; Assistant Treasurer, P. P. Thomas, Terre Haute, Ind.

Directors—William R. McKeen, John G. McNutt, John E. Lamb, John T. Beasley, Demas Deming, Terre Haute, Ind.

Main office, Terre Haute, Ind.; executive office, 93 Federal street, Boston. Annual meeting, fourth Thursday in June, at Terre Haute, Ind.

## TEXAS & PACIFIC COAL CO.

A corporation formed under the laws of Texas, in 1888. The company owns over 50,000 acres of coal and other lands in Erath, Palo Alto and Eastland counties, Tex., and operates coal mines and brickyards, and has large mercantile interests at Thurber, Erath County. It owns the water works, electric light plant and all improvements in the town of Thurber, which has 5,000 inhabitants. The company's brick business is the largest in the South, its vitrified product finding a market in Cuba and distant cities, as well as in Texas. This company also owns and operates the Texas Coal & Fuel Co., having a capital of $250,000, with a bonded indebtedness of $100,000, mines being located in Parker County, on line of Mineral Wells and Northwestern Railroad.

Stock......Par $100..........................Authorized, $2,500,000......Issued, $2,250,000

Dividends of 4 per cent. per annum were formerly paid. In 1898 rate was increased to 5 per cent. and to 6 per cent. in 1900. Dividends are paid quarterly, 1½ per cent. each, in January (1), April, July and October.

Transfer Agent and Registrar, Central Trust Co., New York.

FUNDED DEBT.

1st mort., 6 per cent., due 1908, April and Oct...................................... $255,000

The 1st mortgage is for $500,000, the amount having been reduced by the operation of a sinking fund of 8 cents per ton on each ton of coal mined. Trustee, Central Trust Co., New York.

President, Edgar L. Marston, New York; Secretary, S. Mims, Thurber, Tex.

Directors—H. C. Edington, W. H. Newby, Fort Worth, Tex.; S. Mims, E. M. Reardon, Dallas, Tex.; W. K. Gordon, Thurber, Tex.; Joseph Milbank, Joseph Baldwin, John J. Knox, Edgar L. Marston, New York.

Main office, Thurber, Tex.; New York office, 33 Wall street. Annual meeting, third Wednesday in April, at Thurber, Tex.

## TEXAS PACIFIC LAND TRUST.

An unincorporated association formed in 1888 to take over the unsold lands of the Texas & Pacific Railroad Co., which were conveyed to this organization for the purpose of retiring the old Texas & Pacific 7 per cent. Eastern Division land grant and income bonds, of which there were $9,316,000 and scrip for interest on same to the amount of $2,240,000. The lands acquired by the trustees under this arrangement were 3,450,642 acres. At the close of 1902 the trustees held unsold 3,100,139 acres and also town lots at various points on the line of the Texas & Pacific Railway.

Certificates of proprietary interest......Par $100..................................$8,415,540

There is also outstanding $152,512 Eastern Division land scrip, issued by the Texas Pacific Railway Co.

In 1897 the trust sold 6,130 acres of land, and its receipts were $74,256. It had loans and debt in 1896 amounting to $107,333. At the end of 1898 this was reduced to $34,000 due to the Central Trust Co., New York, for advance. In 1898 sales were 18,974 acres for $49,436. In 1899 sold 27,685 acres for $56,061. In 1900 sold 41,781 acres for $99,049. In 1901, 65,371 acres for $163,374. Total collections were: in 1896, $51,144; in 1897, $74,256; in 1898, $93,076; in 1899, $123,418; in 1900, $168,338; in 1901, $211,496. In 1902 the trust sold 29,859 acres for $77,193.

In 1900 the trustees bought and retired $700,000 par value of the Trust certificates for $105,303 cash. In 1901 they retired $500,000 of the certificates for $163,074. In 1902 $300,000 were bought for $118,419.

Trustees, Charles J. Canda, Chairman, Simeon J. Drake, Edwin Einstein, New York. Agent, W. H. Abrams, Dallas, Tex.

Main office, 7 Wall street, New York.

## THIRD AVENUE RAILROAD CO.

(Leased to Metropolitan Street Railway Co.)

A corporation chartered by the State of New York, October 8, 1853.

Road owned, 14 miles, double track. The installation of underground electric power on the company's main line in Third avenue, New York, was completed in 1899, replacing the cable system installed in 1894. In November, 1895, the company acquired control of the Forty-second Street, Manhattanville & St. Nicholas Avenue road, and leased the same. In 1897, acquired control of the Dry Dock, East Broadway & Battery road, and in January, 1898, of the Union Railway Co. of New York. The Yonkers Railroad Co. and the Tarrytown, White Plains & Mamaroneck Railway are also controlled. Total controlled, 188 miles; total of system, 215 miles.

Stock......Par $100.........................Authorized, $16,000,000......Issued, $15,995,800

Transfer Agent, R. L. Anderton, Jr., 621 Broadway, New York. Registrar, Central Trust Co., New York.

The last dividend paid was 1¾ per cent. quarterly in November, 1899. A dividend of 1 per cent., payable February, 1900, was declared, but the payment was postponed in consequence of the proceedings which ended in the receivership.

FUNDED DEBT.

| | |
|---|---|
| 1st mort., 5 per cent., gold, due July, 1937, Jan. and July | $5,000,000 |
| New collateral mort., 4 per cent., due Jan., 2000, Jan. and July | 35,000,000 |
| Total | $40,000,000 |

In January, 1900, the company, in consequence of the acquisition of the Dry Dock, East Broadway & Battery, Forty-second Street, Manhattanville & St. Nicholas Avenue and Union Railway Companies, and the cost of installing electric power on its main line and certain branches, had accumulated a floating debt of about $17,000,000. Propositions for refunding these obligations were made, but syndicates formed to undertake the work, on examination of the company's affairs, abandoned the negotiations. On February 28, 1900, Hugh J. Grant was appointed Receiver.

In April, 1900, control of the company was acquired by the Metropolitan Street Railway Co., and in May the property was leased to that company for 999 years. For the first four years of lease the rental is to be interest and net revenue above the charges. For the next two years 5 per cent. on the company's stock, 6 per cent. for next four years, and 7 per cent. dividends thereafter. The Receiver was discharged May 24, 1900.

The new mortgage, created in 1900, is for $50,000,000, of which $35,000,000 were to be issued forthwith to discharge the $23,000,000 of floating debt and provide for the completion of improvements, $13,443,000 was reserved to retire outstanding bonds of this and the leased companies, and $1,557,000 was reserved for extensions, etc. The bonds are guaranteed by the Metropolitan Street Railway.

EARNINGS.

Year ending June 30.

| | Dividends. | Gross. | Net. | Charges and Dividends. | Surplus. |
|---|---|---|---|---|---|
| 1892-93 | 3 | $1,653,538 | $597,443 | $485,304 | $112,139 |
| 1893-94 | 8 | 2,007,804 | 933,472 | 788,467 | 75,005 |
| 1894-95 | 8 | 2,583,011 | 1,121,594 | 889,500 | 232,004 |
| 1895-96 | 10 | 2,616,161 | 1,269,697 | 1,251,463 | 12,234 |
| 1896-97 | 8¼ | 2,570,842 | 1,173,562 | 1,222,286 | Def. 48,724 |
| 1897-98 | 8 | 2,359,799 | 1,121,650 | 1,169,578 | " 47,928 |
| 1898-99 | 7 | 2,098,871 | 1,387,404 | 1,206,020 | 181,384 |
| 1899-00 | .. | 2,123,834 | 840,016 | 712,325 | 127,691 |
| 1900-01 | .. | 2,206,490 | 1,560,186 | 1,763,296 | Def. 203,110 |
| 1901-02 | .. | 2,259,170 | 1,534,773 | 1,758,309 | " 223,536 |

President, Herbert H. Vreeland; Vice-President, D. B. Hasbrouck; Secretary and Treasurer, John Beaver.

Directors—Robert Charles Remsen, Edward Lauterbach, John D. Crimmins, Herbert H. Vreeland, E. M. Burghard, R. Martin, D. B. Hasbrouck, Charles E. Warren, H. A. Robinson, D. C. Moorehead, Oren Root, Jr., M. G. Starrett.

Main office, 1119 Third avenue, New York. Annual meeting, first Wednesday after the second Monday in November.

---

## THE THOMAS IRON CO.

A corporation originally formed under the laws of Pennsylvania in 1854. At its expiration in 1874 the charter was renewed for twenty years longer, and in 1894 was again renewed in perpetuity. The purpose of the company is the manufacture of iron. It has 10 blast furnaces at Hokendauqua, Hellertown, Alburtis and Island Park, Pa., with an aggregate capacity of about 50,000 tons per annum. A number of iron ore and limestone properties are owned and operated in connection with its furnaces, and the company has interests in several railroad lines operated in connection with its works.

**Stock......Par $50..........................Authorized, $2,500,000......Issued, $2,500,000**

Stock is transferred at the company's office, Easton, Pa.

The company has no funded debt. The company has paid large dividends on its stock, varying, however, as to rate from year to year.

President, B. F. Fackenthal, Jr., Riegelsville, Pa.; Vice-President, William H. Hulick, New York; Secretary and Treasurer, James W. Weaver, Easton, Pa.

Directors—B. F. Fackenthal, Jr., William H. Hulick, Samuel Thomas, W. P. Hardenbergh J. S. Krause, Fred R. Drake, Joseph S. Rodenbough.

Main office, Easton, Pa.; New York agency, 97 Liberty street.

## THORNDIKE CO.

A corporation formed under the laws of Massachusetts in 1836, for the purpose of manufacturing shirtings, denims, cottonades, awnings, etc. The company has mills at Thorndike and West Warren, Mass. The Thorndike plant has 38,864 spindles and 861 looms, and the West Warren plant 30,076 spindles and 736 looms.

Stock......Par $1,000..............................Authorized, $675,000......Issued, $675,000

The company has no preferred stock and no funded debt. Stock is transferred at the office of the company.

Dividends are paid in February and August, at the rate of 8 per cent. per annum.

President, Charles H. Fiske; Treasurer, Pedar Olsen, Boston.

Directors—Charles H. Fiske, George F. Fabyan, Robert B. Williams, J. R. Clark, O. H. Alford, B. L. Young, Cornelius N. Bliss.

Main office, 100 Summer street, Boston. Annual meeting, in February, at Boston.

## TIDE WATER OIL CO.

A corporation formed under the laws of New Jersey in 1888, to refine petroleum oil. The company owns an oil refinery at Bayonne, N. J., with a capacity of 10,000 barrels per day.

Stock......Par $100....Authorized { com., $4,443,200 / pref., 556,800 } Issued { com., $4,443,200 / pref., 556,800 } $5,000,000

President, Samuel Q. Brown; Vice-President, Robert D. Benson; Secretary, W. S. Benson; Treasurer, A. A. Sumner.

Directors—Samuel Q. Brown, Whitehouse, N. J.; Robert D. Benson, W. S. Benson, Passaic, N. J.; A. A. Sumner, John H. Cuthbert, Dickson Q. Brown, New York; Josiah Lombard, Bronxville, N. Y.

Corporate and main office, Bayonne, N. J.; New York office, 12 Broadway. Annual meeting, first Wednesday in May, at Bayonne, N. J.

## TIDEWATER STEEL CO.

A corporation formed under the laws of Pennsylvania, April 6, 1899. The company was organized to acquire and improve the Wellman Iron & Steel Co.'s plant at Chester, Pa. This property comprised 30 acres in direct communication with both the Pennsylvania and the Reading Railroad systems, having a water front on the Delaware River, with piers and docks; a blast furnace, open hearth steel plant, plate and blooming mills, etc. The plant consists of:

A blast furnace equipped with a capacity of 150 tons pig iron per day. By improved equipment the capacity of this furnace has been greatly increased.

Open Hearth Department—Three 45-ton and two 50-ton open hearth furnaces, all in operation, to which two additional 45-ton furnaces are to be added. Total capacity, 350 tons of steel ingots per day.

Mill Department—One 112-inch plate mill, completely equipped with every modern appliance for the economical handling of material. Capacity, 200 tons finished plate per day. One 72-inch plate mill, also thoroughly equipped with modern appliances. Capacity, 75 tons of light weight sheets and plates. One blooming mill, with a capacity of 200 tons per day, of slabs and billets.

The plant also includes a fully equipped laboratory and testing department, a pumping station of large capacity, electric power and light stations, hydraulic and compressed air power stations, and a well equipped machine shop. The products of the company comprise: foundry, forge, and basic pig iron, basic open hearth ingots, billets and slabs; tank, ship, boiler, flange, fire-box and marine steel plates.

Stock....Par $10 ...Authorized { com., $1,500,000 / pref., 600,000 } Issued { com., $1,500,000 / pref., 591,000 } $2,091,000

The preferred stock is 8 per cent., cumulative up to 5 per cent. It was authorized in 1902 to provide for additional facilities. The holders of the original $1,500,000 of common stock were given rights in May, 1902, to subscribe for the preferred at par.

Transfer Agents, Dick Brothers & Co., 435 Chestnut street, Philadelphia. Registrar, Investment Co. of Philadelphia.

A semi-annual dividend of 3 per cent. was paid January 31, 1903, on the preferred stock.

In the six months ending December 31, 1902, the net earnings were $95,814, surplus over preferred dividend, etc., $32,531.

President, C. E. Stafford; Secretary and Treasurer, Paul Lamorelle, Chester, Pa.

Directors—Evans R. Dick, Charles A. Porter, F. W. Wood, Richard H. Rushton, George S. Graham, George McCall, Charles T. Schoen, A. S. L. Shields.

Main office, Broad and Chestnut streets, Philadelphia. General office, Chester, Pa.

## THE TOLEDO & WESTERN RAILWAY CO.

A corporation formed under the laws of Ohio in 1899, to construct and operate an electric railway line in Ohio and Michigan. The company now owns and operates 66 miles of track from Toledo to Fayette, O., and a branch to Adrian, Mich. It carries freight and passengers.

Stock......Par $100.........................Authorized, $1,800,000......Issued, $1,500,000

The company has no preferred stock. Transfer Agent and Registrar, Dime Savings & Banking Co., Cleveland.

FUNDED DEBT.

1st mort., 5 per cent. gold, due 1926, Jan. and July.............................. $1,250,000

The outstanding bonds are the total amount authorized.

Trustee of the mortgage and agent for the payment of interest, Western Reserve Trust Co., Cleveland. Interest is also payable at the National Bank of Commerce, New York.

President and Treasurer, Luther Allen; Vice-President, J. R. Seagrave; Secretary, F. E. Seagrave; Assistant Secretary, E. Bingham Allen, Cleveland.

Directors—Luther Allen, J. R. Seagrave, W. L. Hayes, E. Bingham Allen, Charles M. Stone, F. C. McMillan, Cleveland; C. E. French, F. E. Seagrave, Toledo, O.

Main office, National Union Building, Toledo, O.; President's office, Electric Building, Cleveland. Annual meeting, fourth Saturday in January, at Toledo.

## THE TOLEDO, BOWLING GREEN & SOUTHERN TRACTION CO.

A corporation formed under the laws of Ohio in 1901. The company acquired the following companies:

Findlay Street Railway Co.
Hancock Light & Power Co.
Toledo, Bowling Green & Freemont Railway Co.

The company owns and operates an electric railway of 60 miles, from Toledo to Findlay, O. It also furnishes electric light in Findlay. It has a perpetual lease to operate over 22 miles of the Toledo & Harrisburg Belt Line running to and through Toledo and Harrisburg, O.

Stock......Par $100.........................Authorized, $1,500,000......Issued, $1,500,000

The company has no preferred stock.

The first dividend of 1 per cent. was paid January 1, 1902. In July, 1902, and in January, 1903, dividends of 1½ per cent. were paid.

FUNDED DEBT.

| | |
|---|---|
| 1st mort., 5 per cent., gold, due May 1, 1921, May and Nov.............................. | $1,075,000 |
| Findlay Street Railway Co., 1st mort., 5 per cent., gold, due May, 1911, May and Nov. | 116,000 |
| Findlay St. Ry. Co., 1st con. mort., 5 per cent., gold, due Dec. 1, 1924, June and Dec. | 125,000 |
| Total.............................................................. | $1,316,000 |

The total amount of the authorized 1st mortgage of the Toledo, Bowling Green & Southern Traction Co. is $1,500,000, of which amount $275,000 are held to retire underlying liens and $150,000 for extensions and improvements. Trustee of the mortgage and agent for the payment of interest, Central Trust & Safe Deposit Co., Cincinnati. The total amount of the authorized 1st mortgage of the Findlay Street Railway Co. is $150,000. Trustee of the mortgage and agent for the payment of interest, Central Trust & Safe Deposit Co., Cincinnati. The outstanding bonds of the 1st consolidated mortgage of the Findlay Street Railway Co. are the full amount authorized. Trustee of the mortgage and agent for the payment of interest, Central Trust & Safe Deposit Co., Cincinnati. Interest is also payable by the Atlantic Trust Co., New York.

In the fiscal year ending December 31, 1902, the gross earnings were $246,933; net, $115,166; surplus above fixed charges and 3 per cent. dividends, $12,387.

President, George B. Kerper; Vice-President and Treasurer, Henry Burkhold, Cincinnati; Secretary, J. A. Bope; Assistant Secretary and Assistant Treasurer, A. J. Becht; General Manager, Charles F. Smith, Toledo, O.

Main office, 106 Summit street, Toledo, O.

## TOLEDO RAILWAYS & LIGHT CO.

A corporation formed under the laws of Ohio, July 1, 1901, as a reorganization of the Toledo Traction Co. The company owns all the street railways and the electric lighting and power business of the city of Toledo, O. It operates 102 miles of track and has an electric power plant, and 303 cars. It acquired the following properties:

Toledo & Maumee Valley Railway.
Toledo, Wat. & Southern Railroad.

Stock......Par $100.........................Authorized, $12,000,000......Issued, $12,000,000

The company has no preferred stock. Stock is transferred and registered at the office of the company.

FUNDED DEBT.

| | |
|---|---|
| Con. 1st mort., 4 per cent., gold, due July, 1909, Jan. and July.................... | $4,000,000 |
| Toledo Con. St. Ry. Co., 1st mort., 5 per cent., due July, 1909, Jan. and July...... | 1,066,000 |
| Toledo Elec. St. Ry. Co., 1st mort., 5 per cent., gold, due Feb., 1912, Feb. and Aug.. | 700,000 |
| Toledo Traction Co., 1st. con. mort., 5 per cent., gold, due July, 1909, Jan. and July. | 4,135,000 |
| Toledo & Maumee Val. Ry., 1st mort., 5 per cent., gold, due 1920, March and Sept. | 300,000 |
| Total........................................................ | $10,201,000 |

The authorized amount of the consolidated 1st mortgage of the Toledo Railways & Light Co. is $12,000,000, of which $6,000,000 are reserved to retire all underlying bonds, and $2,000,000 are reserved for extensions and improvements. Bonds are subject to call at 102½ and interest, on 30 days' notice. Trustee of the mortgage, United States Mortgage & Trust Co., New York. Agents for the payment of interest, Kean, Van Cortlandt & Co., New York. Agent for the payment of interest on the bonds of the Toledo Consolidated Street Railway Co. and the Toledo Electric Street Railway Co., Blair & Co., 33 Wall street., New York. Bonds of the Toledo Electric Street Railway Co. are subject to call at 105 and interest, prior to April 1, 1905, and at 102½ and interest after that date. The authorized mortgage of the Toledo Traction Co. is $6,000,000. The unissued bonds have been cancelled. Bonds are subject to call at 105 and interest. Trustee of the mortgage and agent for the payment of interest, Guaranty Trust Co., New York. The outstanding bonds of the Toledo & Maumee Valley Railway are the total amount authorized. Trustee of the mortgage and agent for the payment of interest, Metropolitan Trust Co., New York.

EARNINGS.

Year ending December 31.

| | Gross. | Net. | Fixed Charges. | Surplus. |
|---|---|---|---|---|
| 1900................................ | $1,182,156 | $565,572 | $289,050 | $276,522 |
| 1901................................ | 1,311,084 | 674,677 | 355,167 | 319,510 |

Chairman, Albion E. Lang, Toledo, O.; President, Henry A. Everett, Cleveland; Vice-President and General Manager, L. E. Beilstein; Secretary and Treasurer, E. O. Reed, Toledo, O.

Directors—Albion E. Lang, L. E. Beilstein, Barton Smith, Toledo; Henry A. Everett. E. W. Moore, Cleveland; R. B. Van Cortlandt, New York; H. S. Holt, Montreal.

Main office, Toledo, O. Annual meeting, third Wednesday in January, at Toledo.

## TORONTO ELECTRIC LIGHT CO., LIMITED

A corporation formed under the laws of the Dominion of Canada for the purpose of supplying electric light in the city of Toronto.

Stock......Par $100 ..........................Authorized, $3,000,000......Issued, $2,000,000

Stock is tranferred at the office of the company.

Dividends on the stock have been paid quarterly at the rate of 7 per cent annually, since 1891, dividend periods being January, April, July and October.

FUNDED DEBT.

1st mort., 4½ per cent. bonds, due July, 1916, Jan. and July......................... $1,000,000

| EARNINGS. | Gross. | Net. |
|---|---|---|
| 1901.............................................................. | $457,842 | $195,831 |
| 1902.............................................................. | 525,808 | 182,501 |

The authorized amount of the 1st mortgage is $1,000,000. Trustee, National Trust Co., Toronto. Agent for the payment of interest, Imperial Bank of Canada, Toronto.

President, H. M. Pellatt; Vice-President, W. D. Matthews; Secretary, W. A. Martin; General Manager, J. J. Wright.

Directors—H. M. Pellatt, W. D. Matthews, W. A. Martin, H. P. Dwight, W. R. Brock, George A. Cox, S. F. McKinnon, Thomas Walmesler, Frederic Nicholls, Robert Jeffray, Samuel Trees, Hugh Blain, W. T. Murray.

Main office, 12 Adelaide street, Toronto. Annual meeting, first Tuesday in February, at Toronto.

## THE TORONTO RAILWAY CO.

A corporation formed under the laws of Ontario in 1892. The company's system comprises 99 miles of lines in and around the city of Toronto. The company operates the Toronto

& Scarboro Electric Railway, Light & Power Co., and the Toronto & Mimico Railway & Light Co. It has an exclusive privilege to work the street railways of Toronto until September, 1921. It operates 112 miles of track and has 706 cars.

Stock......Par $100.........................Authorized, $7,000,000......Issued, $6,600,000

The company has no preferred stock. Transfer Agent and Registrar, H. E. H. Vernon, Toronto.

Dividends of 4 per cent. were paid in 1898, 1899 and 1900; 4¼ per cent. in 1901 and 5 per cent. in 1902.

FUNDED DEBT.

1st mort., sterling and $, 4½ per cent., gold, due Aug., 1921, Feb. and Aug......... $2,873,373

The old Toronto Street Railway Co., to which this company was the successor, has outstanding $600,000 6 per cent. bonds, due 1914, to retire which an equal amount of this company's 4½ per cent. bonds are held in escrow. The 1st mortgage is authorized at the rate of $35,000 per mile of single track. Trustees of mortgage, George A. Cox, Toronto, and Richard B. Angus, Montreal.

EARNINGS.

| | Gross. | Net. | Charges. | Dividends. | Surplus |
|---|---|---|---|---|---|
| 1899......................... | $1,333,542 | $683,218 | $217,455 | $240,000 | $128,870 |
| 1900......................... | 1,501,001 | 725,020 | 270,857 | 240,000 | 150,163 |
| 1901......................... | 1,661,017 | 803,405 | 292,679 | 270,000 | 172,726 |
| 1902......................... | 1,834,908 | 819,547 | 325,825 | 302,439 | 133,729 |

President, William MacKenzie, Toronto; Vice-President, James Ross, Montreal; Secretary and Treasurer, J. C. Grace, Toronto.

Directors—William MacKenzie, James Gunn, George A. Cox, W. D. Matthews, H. M. Pellatt, Frederic Nicholls, Toronto; James Ross, Montreal.

Main office, 92 King street, East, Toronto. Annual meeting, third Wednesday in January, at Toronto.

## THE TORRINGTON CO.

A corporation formed under the laws of Maine. The company owns and controls several constituent manufacturing companies, including the Excelsior Needle Co. of Torrington, Conn., and the National Needle Co., and has a majority interest in the stock of the Standard Spoke & Nipple Co. The company also has factories at Coventry, Eng. It has supply houses in New York, Boston, Philadelphia, London, Glasgow and Leicester, Eng.

Stock...Par $25...Authorized { com., A, $1,000,000; " B, 1,000,000; pref., 1,000,000 } Issued { com., A, $1,000,000; " B, 1,000,000; pref., 1,000,000 } $3,000,000

The preferred stock is 7 per cent., cumulative. The common stock A is entitled to 8 per cent. dividends per annum, after which the common B also receives 8 per cent.

Transfer Agents, Kidder, Peabody & Co., Boston. Registrar, New England Trust Co., Boston.

Dividends on the preferred stock are 3½ per cent. semi-annually, and are paid January (1) and July. On the common A, 4 per cent. semi-annually is paid, February (1) and August. On the common B, 8 per cent. annually is paid, September (1).

FUNDED DEBT.

1st mort., 5 per cent., gold, due Sept., 1918, March and Sept......... ...... .......$1,000,000

Trustee of the mortgage and agent for the payment of interest, New England Trust Co., Boston.

EARNINGS.

Year ending September 1.

| | Receipts. | Expenses. | Interest and Dividends. | Surplus. |
|---|---|---|---|---|
| 1899–00..................................... | $312,771 | $12,379 | $280,000 | $20,392 |
| 1900–01..................................... | 285,127 | 11,019 | 280,000 | def., 5,892 |

On September 1, 1900, the cash and cash assets of the company were $198,693. On September 1, 1901, the same item was $192,801.

President, Henry H. Skinner, Springfield, Mass.; Treasurer, W. G. Brooks, Boston.

Directors—Henry H. Skinner, Robert Winsor, J. F. Alvord, Frederick E. Snow, Edwin A. Carter, William Endicott, Jr.

Main office, 115 Devonshire street, Boston. Annual meeting, second Tuesday in September, at Portland, Me.

## TRADE DOLLAR CONSOLIDATED MINING CO.

A corporation formed under the laws of Kentucky in 1891. The purpose of the company is the mining and milling of quartz rock.

Stock......Par $5..............................Authorized, $6,000,000......Issued, $6,000,000

The company has no preferred stock and no funded debt.

Stock is transferred at the office of the company, Pittsburg. Registrar, Pennsylvania Trust Co., Pittsburg.

President, J. M. Guffey; Vice-President, A. W. Mellon; Secretary and Treasurer, Thomas B. McKaig, Pittsburg.

Directors—J. M. Guffey, E. H. Jennings, A. W. Mellon, N. F. Clark, George B. Matheral, M. K. McMullin, Pittsburg; M. Murphy, Philadelphia.

Main office, Fifth avenue and Wood street, Pittsburg.

## TREMONT COAL CO.

A corporation chartered under the laws of Pennsylvania in 1864. The company owns and operates an anthracite coal property of 4,421 acres in Schuylkill County, Pa. The company is controlled by the Reading Co. and the Philadelphia & Reading Coal & Iron Co. On June 30, 1900, it was indebted to the Reading Co. for $255,000.

Stock..... Par $25............................Authorized, $3,000,000......Issued, $3,000,000

FUNDED DEBT.

| | |
|---|---|
| 1st mort., 5 per cent., due 1906, June and Dec.......... | $300,000 |
| General mort., 6 per cent., due 1908, May and Nov.......... | 900,000 |
| Total.......... | $1,200,000 |

The general mortgage is for $1,200,000, $300,000 being reserved to retire the 1st mortgage bonds. Trustee, Guarantee Trust & Safe Deposit Co., Philadelphia.

President, George F. Baer; Secretary, W. G. Brown; Treasurer, W. A. Church.

Directors—George F. Baer, Joseph S. Harris, E. F. Smith, James M. Landis, Thomas M. Richards, G. E. Henderson, W. A. Church, Philadelphia.

Main office, Reading Terminal, Twelfth and Market streets, Philadelphia. Annual meeting, second Monday in October.

## TRENTON & NEW BRUNSWICK RAILROAD CO.

A corporation formed under the laws of New Jersey, December 10, 1901. The company owns and operates 23 miles of electric railway between Trenton and New Brunswick, and is to form part of the New York & Philadelphia Electric Railway. The company owns a 100 feet right of way in fee simple for its line. It has a power station, 6 cars and 1 steam locomotive.

Stock......Par $100...........................Authorized, $1,000,000......Issued, $1,000,000

The company has no preferred stock. Stock is transferred at the office of the company, Philadelphia. Registrar, The Finance Co., Philadelphia.

FUNDED DEBT.

1st mort., 5 per cent. gold, due Jan. 1, 1932, Jan. and July.......................... $750,000

The authorized amount of the mortgage is $1,000,000. There is no sinking fund and the bonds cannot be called. $250,000 are reserved in the treasury for extensions and improvements. Trustee of the mortgage, The Finance Co., Philadelphia.

President, W. A. Stern; Vice-President and Treasurer, I. H. Silverman; Secretary, A. W. From; Assistant Treasurer, L. R. Isenthal, Philadelphia.

Directors—A. N. Chandler, A. S. Chandler, L. R. Isenthal, Thomas S. Phillips, W. A. Stern, I. H. Silverman, Philadelphia; Thomas P. Curley, Frank S. Fithian, James H. Long, Barton Lucas, George H. B. Martin, R. C. Mason, F. L. Mead, C. D. Van Duyn, Camden, N. J.

Corporate and main office, West Windsor Township, N. J.; executive office, Broad and Chestnut streets, Philadelphia. Annual meeting, third Wednesday in December.

## TRENTON GAS & ELECTRIC CO.

A corporation formed under the laws of New Jersey, February 1, 1899. The company controls all the gas and electric facilities of Trenton, N. J., and its suburbs. It acquired the stock and properties of the Trenton Gas Light Co., the City Gas Light Co., the Trenton Light & Power Co., People's Light & Power Co. of Trenton, Trenton Electric Light & Power Co., Edison Electric Light & Power Co. of Trenton, People's Gas Improvement Co. and Delaware

River Improvement Co. The population served is about 75,000. Price of gas, $1 per 1,000 feet.

In December, 1900, control of this company was acquired by the South Jersey Gas, Electric & Traction Co.

Stock......Par $100..........................Authorized, $2,000,000......Issued, $2,000,000

FUNDED DEBT.

1st mort., 5 per cent., due 1949, March and Sept....................................$2,000,000

The 1st mortgage is for $2,000,000, of which $1,500,000 was sold when the company was organized. The balance of the bond issue, $500,000, may be issued for additional property and improvements. Trustee, Colonial Trust Co., New York.

President, Henry C. Moore; Vice-President, Thomas C. Barr; Secretary and Treasurer, Anthony R. Kuser.

Main office, 12 South Warren street, Trenton, N. J.

## TRENTON POTTERIES CO.

A corporation formed under the laws of New Jersey, May 27, 1892, to take over certain sanitary ware factories at Trenton, N. J. It owns and operates six large plants in that city, the chief production being plumbers' earthenware, including porcelain bathtubs, kitchen, pantry and laundry sinks and similar articles, as well as table and toilet ware, druggists' supplies and many miscellaneous goods.

Stock....Par $100.....Authorized { com., $1,750,000; pref., 1,250,000 } Issued { com., $1,750,000; pref., 1,250,000 } $3,000,000

The preferred stock is 8 per cent., non-cumulative. It was originally 8 per cent. cumulative, and on July 1, 1902, 44 per cent. of part due dividends had accumulated in the preferred. At that time the holders of the preferred agreed to exchange it for new non-cumulative preferred and to accept 4 per cent. income certificates for the part due dividends. There was litigation in connection with this plan, but it was sustained in the courts.

Transfer Agents, A. M. Kidder & Co., 18 Wall street, New York. Registrar, Guaranty Trust Co., New York.

In 1900 the company resumed dividends on its preferred, paying 2 per cent. on April 10, 1900, and has since paid regular quarterly dividends of 2 per cent. on the preferred in January (10), April, July and October. The last previous dividends to that of April, 1900, were 2 per cent., quarterly, on preferred, in June, 1894; 5 per cent. on common, in February, 1893. No dividends have been paid on the common since.

FUNDED DEBT.

Income certificates, 4 per cent., Jan. (10) and July.................................. $550,000

The income certificates are subject to call at par for a sinking fund of $25,000 per annum, beginning in 1903.

President, Daniel K. Bayne, New York; Vice-President, William S. Hancock; Secretary-Treasurer, C. E. Lawton; General Manager, J. A. Campbell, Trenton, N. J.

Directors—William S. Hancock, Ferdinand W. Roehling, John A. Campbell, Trenton, N. J.; William Wood, Lewis H. Taylor, Jr., Philadelphia; Edwin Packard, Brooklyn, N. Y.; Horace J. Morse, Daniel K. Bayne, Charles D. Marvin, New York.

Main office, Trenton, N. J. Annual meeting in June.

## TRIMOUNTAIN MINING CO.

A corporation formed under the laws of Michigan in 1899. The company owns 1,120 acres of copper mineral land in Houghton County, Mich. The property lies between the Baltic and the Champion mines. The Copper Range Railroad crosses the property and facilitates operations thereon. Three large modern three-compartment shafts, 1,000 feet apart, are being sunk, and a large amount of ground is opened by connecting drifts, the width of the property allowing for three more shafts at equal distances when needed.

The company also owns a mill site of over 100 acres on Lake Superior. The Copper Range Railroad furnishes a direct connection between the mine and the mill site. In view of the unusually rich quality of the rock encountered in the company's exploration work, the erection of a mill was decided on and its completion is expected at an early date. The company has leased the use, meantime, of facilities at the Arcadian mill.

Stock......Par $25..........................Authorized, $2,500,000......Issued, $2,500,000

Stock is transferred at the company's office, 60 State street, Boston. Registrar, Old Colony Trust Co., Boston.

President, Harry F. Fay; Secretary, Walter B. Mosman; Treasurer, George G. Endicott, Boston.

Directors—Harry F. Fay, John C. Watson, William Howell Reed, Walter B. Mosman, B. Nason Hamlin, S. R. Dow, Boston; James Chynoweth, Calumet, Mich.

Main office, 60 State street, Boston. Annual meeting, second Wednesday in February, at Boston.

## TRINITY COPPER CO.

A corporation formed under the laws of New Jersey in 1900. The company owns copper, gold and silver-bearing property near Kennet, Shasta County, California. The property consists of about 6,000 acres.

The property is equipped with ore compresser, power drills, diamond drills, assay office, also an office building located at Kennet; mess house, hospital building, store house, and there are 22 buildings situated on the possessions of the company.

The underground workings consist of about 8,000 feet of tunnels, upraises, drifts, etc., and enough ore has been blocked out to operate the contemplated smelter for years to come. In 1903 the company opened in one of their drifts one of the largest and highest grade sulphide ore bodies that has been encountered on the property.

Stock......Par $25..........................Authorized, $6,000,000......Issued, $6,000,000

Transfer Agent, American Loan & Trust Co., Boston. Registrar, International Trust Co., Boston.

The company has no funded debt.

President, Thomas W. Lawson; Vice-President, William J. Riley; Treasurer, Allen Arnold; Secretary, H. Albers, Boston. General Manager, Austin H. Brown, Kennet, Cal.

Directors—Thomas W. Lawson, Allen Arnold, William J. Riley, H. Albers, Henry H. Arnold, Louis Auerbach, Arthur P. French, Frank E. Chase, Kenneth K. McLaren.

Main office, Kennet, Cal.; Boston office, 33 State street.

## TRIPLE STATE NATURAL GAS & OIL CO.

A corporation formed under the laws of West Virginia, May 15, 1898. The company supplies natural gas to Huntington, W. Va., Ashland, Ky., Catlettsburg, Ky., Ironton, O., and a number of small towns in the same section.

Stock......Par $100..........................Authorized, $2,000,000......Issued, $2,000,000

FUNDED DEBT.

| | |
|---|---|
| 1st mort., 6 per cent., due 1908, Jan. and July | $500,000 |
| 2d mort., 6 per cent., Jan. and July | 300,000 |
| Total | $800,000 |

The trustee of the 1st mortgage is the Central Trust Co., New York. The trustee of the 2d mortgage is Charles Miller, First National Bank, Franklin, Pa.

President, W. O. Johnson; 1st Vice-President, Otto Germer, Jr.; 2d Vice-President, Thomas Brown; Treasurer, E. H. Sibley; Secretary, J. B. Moorhead.

Directors—Charles Miller, Thomas Brown, Otto Germer, Jr., J. E. French, O. D. Bleakley, W. O. Johnson.

Main office, Franklin, Pa.; business office, Ashland, Ky.

## TRI-STATE GAS CO.

A corporation formed under the laws of West Virginia in 1898 to produce and sell natural gas. The company supplies gas in Pittsburg, West Carnegie, Knoxville and McDonald, Pa.; Wellsburg, W. Va.; Steubenville, Toronto and East Liverpool, O.

Stock......Par $100..........................Authorized, $1,500,000......Issued, $1,500,000

The company has no preferred stock.

The company paid its first quarterly dividend of 2 per cent. April 20, 1900. Dividends at the rate of 12 per cent. annually are now paid quarterly, in January, April, July and October.

FUNDED DEBT.

1st mort., March and September..............................................$254,000

The authorized 1st mortgage was $400,000. Trustee of the mortgage, Fidelity Title & Trust Co., Pittsburg.

President, George W. Crawford; Vice-President and General Manager, F. M. Lowry; Secretary and Treasurer, H. C. Reeser; Assistant Treasurer, J. J. Ormston; Assistant Secretary, Walter S. Hoyt.

Directors—George W. Crawford, F. M. Lowry, H. McSweeney, J. C. McDowell, David Iseman.

Corporate and main office, 248 Fourth avenue, Pittsburg; branch offices, McDonald, Pa., Toronto, O., and Wellsburg, W. Va. Annual meeting, second Tuesday in March at Pittsburg.

## TROW DIRECTORY PRINTING & BOOKBINDING CO.

A corporation formed under the laws of New Jersey, in 1891, to take over the business of the Trow (New York) City Directory Co. and the Trow Printing & Bookbinding Co. The company has an extensive business and a large plant, the aggregate value of its real estate and plant being over $750,000.

Stock......Par $100..............................Authorized, $850,000......Issued, $850,000

Transfer Agent, Fourth National Bank, New York. Registrar, Central Trust Co., New York.

The report for 1896-97, year ending September 30, shows sales of $425,777; for 1897-98, $591,577; for 1898-99, $512,514. In 1899-1900 the company changed a deficit of $16,303 in the preceding year to a surplus of $39,036, and paid a dividend of 2 per cent., October 15, 1900.

President, Robert W. Smith; Vice-President, James G. Cannon; Treasurer, Joseph F. Simmons; Secretary, Walter G. DeWitt.

Directors—Robert W. Smith, Summit, N. J.; James G. Cannon, Joseph F. Simmons Samuel Woolverton, Forrest Raynor, William H. Porter, William C. White, New York.

Main office, 201 East Twelfth street, New York; Directory office, 21 University place, New York. Annual meeting, last Tuesday in October, at 15 Exchange place, Jersey City.

## TROY GAS CO.

A corporation formed under the laws of New York, October 11, 1889. The company controls the electric light and power and gas facilities of Troy, N. Y., and the gas for the neighboring towns of Lansingburg and Waterford.

Stock......Par $100..........................Authorized, $1,000,000......Issued, $1,000,000

Stock is transferred at the office of the company.

FUNDED DEBT.

| | |
|---|---|
| 1st mort., 5 per cent., due 1939, May and Nov. | $400,000 |
| 2d mort., 5 per cent., due 1923, Feb. and Aug. | 500,000 |
| Total | $900,000 |

The 1st mortgage is $500,000 authorized, $100,000 of the bonds being held in the company's treasury. Interest on the bonds is paid at the Manufacturers' National Bank, Troy.

Dividends on the stock are paid at the rate of 8 per cent. per annum, payments being quarterly, 2 per cent. each in March, June, September and December.

President, Edward Murphy, Jr.; Vice-President, William Kemp; Secretary and Treasurer, C. E. Davenport, Troy, N. Y.

Directors—A. Bleecker Banks, Edward Murphy, Jr., A. E. Bonested, Anthony N. Brady, Thomas Breslin, F. E. Draper, James Flemming, S. O. Gleason, G. P. Ide, William Kemp, F. J. Molloy, Robert C. Pruyn, W. A. Thompson.

Main office, Second and State street, Troy, N. Y. Annual meeting, third Wednesday in October.

## TUBULAR DISPATCH CO.

A corporation formed under the laws of New York, May 9, 1874. The objects of the company are the construction and operation of pneumatic tubes for carrying mail packages, etc. The company has in the city of New York 10½ miles of tube, connecting the General Post Office with five branch stations. In 1901, owing to the failure of Congress to make an appropriation for the service, it was discontinued but was renewed in 1902, the contract being awarded to the New York Mail and Newspaper Transportation Co., which is controlled by this company at a price stated to be about $414,000 per annum.

Stock......Par $100..........................Authorized, $2,100,000......Issued, $1,500,000

FUNDED DEBT.

| | |
|---|---|
| 1st mort., 5 per cent., due 1922, Jan. and July | $600,000 |

The 1st mortgage is secured by a lien upon all the property, franchises and contracts of the company. Trustee, Central Trust Co., New York, which is also the agent for the payment of interest.

President, Alfred Skitt; Vice-President and General Manager, W. A. H. Bogardus; Secretary and Treasurer, Guy Phillips, New York.

Directors—Howard Gould, Frank J. Gould, W. A. H. Bogardus, Alfred Skitt, Guy Phillips, Le Roy W. Baldwin, New York; A. Lawrence Hopkins, Williamstown, Mass.

Main office, 195 Broadway, New York. Annual meeting, first Monday in March.

---

## THE TUSCARAWAS TRACTION CO.

A corporation formed under the laws of Ohio in December, 1901. The company was originally the Tuscarawas Railway Co. It absorbed the Tuscarawas Electric Co., and was reorganized under its present name. The company owns and operates 12¾ miles of electric railway between Canal Dover, New Philadelphia, Midvale and Urichsville, O. It has a power-house and 27 cars.

Stock......Par $100..............................Authorized, $350,000......Issued, $250,000

The company has no preferred stock. Stock is transferred at the office of the company. Registrar, Citizens Savings & Trust Co., Cleveland.

A regular dividend of ¾ of 1 per cent. has been paid quarterly, beginning April, 1902.

FUNDED DEBT.

| | |
|---|---|
| Tuscarawas Railway Co., 6 per cent. gold, due June, 1916, June and Dec............. | $100,000 |
| Tuscarawas Electric Co. 5 per cent. gold, due ...., 1910............................ | 100,000 |
| Total.................................................................. | $200,000 |

The total amount of the authorized mortgage is $350,000. Of that amount $200,000 has been issued to take up the underlying liens and $150,000 is reserved for extensions and betterments.

In the fiscal year ending December 31, 1902, the gross earnings of the company were $56,320; interest charges, $11,000; net, $16,685.

President, Fred T. Pomeroy; Vice-President, J. A. Rutherford; Secretary, J. O. Wilson, Cleveland; Treasurer and General Manager, William Akins, New Philadelphia, O.

Directors—Fred T. Pomeroy, J. A. Rutherford, J. O. Wilson, Cleveland; Will Christy, Akron, O.; Theodore Wentz, Canal Dover, O.; George W. Bowers, William Akins, New Philadelphia, O.

Corporate and main office, New Philadelphia, O.; Cleveland office, 121 Euclid avenue. Annual meeting in January, at New Philadelphia, O.

---

## THE TWENTIETH CENTURY MINING CO., LIMITED

A corporation formed under the Ontario Mining Co.'s Incorporation Act, August 23, 1901. The company succeeded the Twentieth Century Trading Co., incorporated under the laws of West Virginia, in 1898. The company owns and operates gold mines on Upper Manitou Lake, Rainy River District, Ontario, and has mining claims in Arizona. Its Canadian mines are fully equipped with stamp mill, rock crusher, power houses, steamboat wharves, saw mill and other accessories.

Stock......Par $10..............................Authorized, $2,000,000......Issued, $2,000,000

The company has no preferred stock and no funded debt. Stock is transferred at the company's office, Boston.

The company paid its first dividend, at the rate of 6 per cent. per annum, June 1, 1900. On January 1, 1902, the dividends were increased to 8 per cent. per annum. Dividends are paid quarterly, in January, April, July and October.

President and General Manager, Anthony Blum; Vice-President and Treasurer, W. K. Smalley; 2d Vice-President, Will R. Stokes; Secretary, John D. Mollath.

Directors—Anthony Blum, William K. Smalley, Augustus Trudo, Boston; John G. Mollath, New York; Will R. Stokes, Coraopolis, Pa.

Corporate office, 59 Yonge street, Toronto; main office, 35 Court street, Boston; branch offices, 220 Broadway, New York; Pittsburg, and London, England. Annual meeting in January, at Boston.

## TWIN CITY RAPID TRANSIT CO.

A corporation formed under the laws of New Jersey, June 3, 1891. It controls and operates all the street railway lines in or connecting the cities of Minneapolis, St. Paul and Stillwater, Minn. Road owned, 252 miles. The franchise is an exclusive one.

Stock...Par $100....Authorized { com., $17,300,000 / pref., 3,000,000 } Issued { com., $16,511,000 / pref., 3,000,000 } $19,511,000

The preferred stock is 7 per cent., cumulative.

In May, 1902, the stockholders had the right to subscribe for $1,501,000 new common stock at par.

Transfer Agent and Registrar, J. Kennedy Tod & Co., New York.

Dividends of 7 per cent. per annum are paid on the preferred stock, in quarterly payments of 1¾ per cent. each, in January, April, July and October.

In August, 1899, the company began the payment of dividends on the common with 1 per cent. In 1900 paid 3 per cent. on the common stock, in 1901, 4 per cent., and in 1902, 5 per cent., the dividends on the common being half-yearly, February and August.

FUNDED DEBT.

| | |
|---|---|
| Minneapolis Street Ry. 1st mort., 7 per cent., due Nov., 1910, May and Nov........ | $230,000 |
| Minneapolis Street Ry. 2d mort., 6 per cent., due Nov., 1913, May and Nov.......... | 600,000 |
| Minneapolis Street Ry. cons. mort., 5 per cent., due Jan., 1919, Jan. and July...... | 4,150,000 |
| St. Paul City Ry. 1st cons. mort., 6 per cent., due Oct., 1932-34, April and Oct.... | 680,000 |
| St. Paul City Ry. cable cons. mort., 5 per cent., due Jan., 1937, Jan. 15 and July 15.. | 3,708,000 |
| Minn. & St. P. Sub. Ry. 1st mort., guar. 5 per cent., due Sept., 1924, March and Sept.. | 500,000 |
| Minn. & St. P. City Ry. 1st. mort., 5 per cent., due Jan., 1911, Jan. and July....... | 1,000,000 |
| Total.................................................................. | $10,868,000 |

The company owns the capital stock of the two operating companies. The St. Paul City Railway cable mortgage is for $4,280,000. The Twin City Co. guarantees $1,120,000 of these bonds. The Minneapolis Street Railway Co. and St. Paul Street Railway Co. each issued in 1893 to the Twin City Co. $1,000,000 of 6 per cent. certificates of indebtedness, to be repaid within three years, the last of which were paid in December, 1897, with proceeds of an increase of $500,000 in the preferred stock.

EARNINGS.

| | Gross. | Per Cent. Op. Exp. | Net. | Charges. | Surplus. |
|---|---|---|---|---|---|
| 1897.......................... | $2,009,121 | 53.18 | $1,007,041 | $692,302 | $314,737 |
| 1898.......................... | 2,170,716 | 49.92 | 1,151,323 | 777,668 | 373,655 |
| 1899.......................... | 2,522,794 | 48.71 | 1,305,822 | 628,243 | 737,579 |
| 1900.......................... | 2,839,356 | 49.16 | 1,534,666 | 624,326 | 910,000 |
| 1901.......................... | 3,173,976 | 48.35 | 1,758,524 | 666,638 | 1,091,486 |
| 1902.......................... | 3,612,210 | 49.30 | 1,982,041 | 711,710 | 1,270,323 |

The preferred stock was created in 1894, and was offered for subscription at par by stockholders. In 1897 $500,000 was issued to pay off guarantee notes.

President, Thomas Lowry; Vice-President, Secretary and Treasurer, C. G. Goodrich; General Manager, W. J. Hield; Auditor, E. S. Pattee, Minneapolis.

Directors—Thomas Lowry, C. G. Goodrich, Clinton Morrison, Minneapolis; John Kean, Elizabeth, N. J.; J. Kennedy Tod, William A. Read, New York; A. E. Ames, Toronto.

Corporate office, Elizabeth, N. J.; main office, Thirty-first and Blaisdell streets, Minneapolis. Annual meeting, first Tuesday in May, at Elizabeth, N. J.

## TWIN CITY TELEPHONE CO. OF MINNEAPOLIS AND ST. PAUL

A corporarion formed under the laws of Minnesota, February 28, 1898, to do a local and long distance telephone business. The company has a main exchange and three branch exchanges in Minneapolis; one main exchange and two branch exchanges in St. Paul, an underground conduit and cable and aerial lines in both cities, and connecting lines with long distance telephone systems.

Stock..Par $100.......Authorized { com., $1,000,000 / pref., 500,000 } Issued { com., $1,000,000 / pref., 470,000 } $1,470,000

The preferred stock is 7 per cent., cumulative.

Since May 1, 1902, dividends of 1¾ per cent., or 7 per cent. per annum, have been paid quarterly on the preferred stock, in February, May, August aud November.

FUNDED DEBT.

1st mort., 5 per cent., due 1912–1926, Jan. and July.................................. $1,000,000

The outstanding bonds are the total amount authorized. Trustee of mortgage and agent for the payment of interest, Royal Trust Co., Chicago. Interest is also paid by Kountze Brothers, New York.

In the fiscal year ending March 31, 1902, the gross earnings were $304,292; net, $154,292; interest charges, $50,000; dividends, $28,900; surplus, $75,392.

President, E. H. Moulton, Minneapolis; Vice-President, Joseph Lockey, St. Paul; Secretary and Treasurer, William M. Kerkhoff; General Manager, Edward E. Webster, Minneapolis.

Directors—E. H. Moulton, William M. Kerkhoff, Edward E. Webster, F. S. Allis, Minneapolis; L. A. Trowbridge, Chicago; J. C. Hubinger, Keokuk, Ia.; Joseph Lockey, St. Paul.

Corporate office, Third avenue, South and Seventh streets, Minneapolis; branch offices, Minneapolis and St. Paul. Annual meeting, first Tuesday in April, at Minneapolis.

---

## UNION BAG & PAPER CO.

A corporation formed under the laws of New Jersey, February 27, 1899. The company is a combination of corporations and firms engaged in the manufacture of paper bags and similar products, the concerns included controlling about 75 per cent. of the entire output of such articles in the United States. The company's plants, including pulp mills, paper mills and bag factories, are at Sandy Hill, N. Y.; Hadley, N. Y.; Ballston Spa, N. Y.; Watertown, Mass., and Kaukauna, Wis.

The company also owns water powers on the Hudson River at Sandy Hill, N. Y., at Hadley Falls, and Kaukauna, Wis. The united concerns also control a number of valuable patents for machinery and processes employed in the industry.

The company has a capacity of 25,000,000 bags a day, making its own paper. It also has wood pulp plants and sulphite plants. The company since its organization has greatly improved the plants and increased their capacity.

It has large tracts of wood lands sufficient to last them many years and directly tributary to its mills.

Stock..Par $100..Authorized { com., $16,000,000 / pref., 11,000,000 } Issued { com., $16,000,000 / pref., 11,000,000 } $27,000,000

The preferred stock is 7 per cent., cumulative. The first dividend on the preferred stock was 1¾ per cent. quarterly, paid July 1, 1899, and similar dividends have since been regularly paid on the preferred in January (1), April, July and October.

Transfer Agent, Manhattan TrustyCo., New York. Registrar, First National Bank, New York.

The company has no bonded debt, and all the properties taken over were acquired free of encumbrance.

EARNINGS.

Year ending March 1.

| | Profits. | Dividends. | Surplus. |
|---|---|---|---|
| 1899-00 | $1,494,160 | $770,000 | $724,169 |
| 1900-01 | 803,063 | 770,000 | 33,063 |
| 1901-02 | 876,470 | 770,000 | 106,470 |

In the year 1900-01 the company paid $967,962 for new construction and additional property.

The following is the company's balance sheet, March 1, 1902:

| ASSETS. | | LIABILITIES. | |
|---|---|---|---|
| Real estate, plant, etc | $26,250,454 | Capital stock | $27,000,000 |
| Cash and stock on hand | 1,789,026 | Profit for year | 876,470 |
| Dividends | 577,500 | Previous surplus | 740,510 |
| Total | $28,616,980 | Total | $28,616,980 |

President, Lucius G. Fisher, Chicago; 2d Vice-President and Secretary, Edgar G. Barratt; Treasurer, George R. Sheldon; Assistant Treasurer, Randolph Rudman, New York.

Directors—M. B. Wallace, St. Louis; Isaac H. Dixon, Baltimore; Charles A. Dean, Boston; Albert H. Chatfield, Cincinnati; Lucius G. Fisher, William H. Moore, Edgar G. Barratt, J. B. Hosford, George R. Sheldon, New York; J. H. Moore, Chicago; L. V. Walkley, Plantsville, Conn.; Douglas W. Mabee, Saratoga Springs, N. Y.; William H. Van Nortwick, Batavia, Ill.; David S. Walton, East Orange, N. J.; John H. Derby, Sandy Hill, N. Y.

Corporate office, 15 Exchange Place, New Jersey; main office, 1 Broadway, New York. Annual meeting, second Tuesday in April, at Jersey City.

## UNION CARBIDE CO.

A corporation formed under the laws of Virginia in April, 1898. The business of the company is the manufacture and sale of calcium carbide for illuminating purposes. It has plants at Niagara Falls, N. Y., and other places.

Stock......Par $100........................Authorized, $6,000,000 .....Issued, $6,000,000

The company pays quarterly dividends of 1 per cent. in January, April, July and October.

Stock is transferred at the company's office, 45 Broadway, New York. Registrar, Central Trust Co., New York.

FUNDED DEBT.

1st mort., 6 per cent., due 1950, Jan. and July.......................... .......... $680,000

The 1st mortgage, Central Trust Co., New York, trustee, is for $2,000,000, and was created in 1900 to provide funds for extensions and improvements to the company's plant.

President, Charles F. Dieterich, New York; Vice-President, George O. Knapp, Chicago; Secretary and Treasurer, Arthur B. Proal, New York; Assistant Secretary-Treasurer, E. J. E. Ward, Chicago.

Directors—Charles F. Dieterich, Arthur B. Proal, Walton Furguson, A. N. Brady, E. N. Dickerson, New York; George O. Knapp, C. K. G. Billings, Chicago.

Main office and transfer agency, 45 Broadway, New York; Chicago office, 157 Michigan avenue. Annual meeting, first Tuesday in April, at Richmond, Va.

## UNION COPPER, LAND AND MINING CO.

A corporation formed under the laws of Michigan in 1863, the charter having been extended in 1893. The company is generally regarded as a land company. Under its charter it is, however, empowered to develop its lands and to operate as a mining company. Its property consists of over 7,000 acres in Keweenaw, Houghton, Ontonagon and Gogebic counties, Mich.

These lands are all located on the so-called "Mineral Range" and extend, in 200 or more parcels, from Eagle Lake on the north to Lake Agogebicon the south, a distance of over 100 miles.

Stock......par $25..........................Authorized, $2,500,000......Issued, $2,000,000

Of the stock 20,000 shares are held in the company's treasury.

Stock is transferred at the company's office, 60 State street, Boston. Registrar, Old Colony Trust Co., Boston.

President, Harry F. Fay; Secretary, Walter B. Mosman; Treasurer, George G. Endicott, Boston.

Directors—Harry F. Fay, John C. Watson, Walter B. Mosman, R. L. Barstow, C. D. Coffin, Boston; R. R. Goodell, Calumet, Mich.

Main office, 60 State street, Boston. Annual meeting, fourth Thursday in March at Boston.

## UNION COPPER MINING CO.

The company owns 1,150 acres of mineral bearing land in Rowan and Carbarrus counties, North Carolina, near Gold Hill. The company has done extensive development work, principally on the Big Cut Copper Vein, which extends the length of the property. It has in sight 1,000,000 tons of 10 per cent. copper ore which also runs high in gold and silver. It claims to have expended some $1,000,000 in work and machinery, including smelters and a concentrating plant.

Stock......Par $10............................Authorized, $3,000,000......Issued, $3,000,000

Transfer Agents, Bowling Green Trust Co., New York.

President, Calvin H. Allen; Secretary, Temple Taylor Berdan; Treasurer, Thomas C. Buck, New York.

Directors—Calvin H. Allen, Vernon C. Brown, Thomas C. Buck, J. L. Drummond, Jacob Field, James Phillipps, Jr., R. P. Doremus, Temple Taylor Berdan, New York; William M. Butler, Boston.

Main office, 11 Broadway, New York. Annual meeting, second Thursday in May.

## UNION ELECTRIC CO.

A corporation formed under the laws of Iowa, August 13, 1900. The company is a consolidation of the Home Electric Co., Star Electric Co., and Dubuque Street Railway Co., the several companies embracing all the electric lighting and traction facilities of Dubuque, Ia.

Stock......Par $100.......Authorized { com., $500,000 / pref., 500,000 } Issued { com., $500,000 / pref., 500,000 } $1,000,000

The preferred stock is 5 per cent., cumulative. The company has no funded debt.

The first dividend on the preferred stock was 2½ per cent., semi-annual, paid January 1, 1901.

President, F. D. Stout; Vice-President, D. D. Myers; Secretary and Treasurer, J. R. Lindsay; Manager, W. J. Brown.

Directors—F. D. Stout, B. W. Lacy, D. D. Myers, W. J. Brown, J. Ellwanger, George W. Kiesel, J. R. Lindsay, W. W. Bonson, Dubuque, Ia.; H. Parsons, New York.

Main office, Sixth and Iowa streets, Dubuque, Ia. Annual meeting, second Tuesday in December.

## UNION ELECTRIC LIGHT & POWER CO. OF ST. LOUIS.

A corporation formed under the laws of Missouri, May 20, 1902. The company was organized in pursuance of a plan to combine the Citizens' Electric Lighting & Power Co., the Imperial Electric Light, Heat & Power Co. and their controlled properties, which included the City Lighting Co., of St. Louis, and The Seckner Contracting Co., both of the latter being controlled by the Imperial Co. A large interest in the company is understood to be owned by The North American Co. The plans of the combination included the construction of another large modern electric light plant in St. Louis.

Stock...Par $100...Authorized { com., $8,000,000; pref., 2,000,000 } Issued { com., $8,000,000; pref., 2,000,000 } $10,000,000

The preferred stock is 5 per cent., non-cumulative.

FUNDED DEBT.

| | |
|---|---|
| 1st mort., 5 per cent., due Sept., 1932, March and Sept. | $2,448,000 |
| Imperial Electric Light 1st mort., 5 per cent., due 1930, April and Oct. | 1,000,000 |
| City Lighting Co. 1st mort., 5 per cent | 552,000 |
| Total | $4,000,000 |

The authorized amount of the 1st mortgage is $10,000,000, sufficient of the issue being reserved to retire the underlying bonds. Trustee of mortgage, Mississippi Valley Trust Co., St. Louis.

President, Julius S. Walsh, St. Louis; Vice-President, C. W. Wetmore, New York; Treasurer, Breckenridge Jones; Secretary, Harold P. G. Coates, St. Louis.

Directors—Adolphus Busch, Samuel M. Kennard, William J. Lemp, Julius S. Walsh, William F. Nolker, John H. Drabelle, Harold P. G. Coates, St. Louis; Chales W. Wetmore, George R. Sheldon, William F. White, New York.

Main office, Tenth and St. Charles streets, St. Louis. Annual meeting,

## UNION FERRY CO.

The company holds franchise for and operates five ferry lines between New York and Brooklyn. It owns real estate and dock property, as well as ferryboats. In 1901 the company made a new arrangement with the city of New York for the ferry franchises on the basis of 3 per cent. of the gross receipts.

Stock......Par $100........................Authorized, $3,000,000......Issued, $3,000,000

The company up to 1898 inclusive paid 4 per cent. per annum on its stock; in 1899 paid 3½ per cent., and in 1900 the rate was reduced to 2 per cent. Dividends are paid quarterly, ½ per cent. each, in January (1), April, July and October.

Stock is transferred at the company's office, foot of Fulton street, Brooklyn, N. Y. Registrar, Central Trust Co., New York.

FUNDED DEBT.

1st mort., gold, due Nov., 1920, May and Nov....................................... $2,200,000

The mortgage covers all the property of the company, including real estate and ferryboats. The bonds are redeemable at 110 since 1895.

President, Julian D. Fairchild; Secretary, George Hyatt; Treasurer and General Manager, H. K. Knapp, New York.

Directors—George W. Quintard, William H. Male, Julian D. Fairchild, Alexander E. Orr, John C. Orr, Lowell M. Palmer, Theodore F. Jackson, William F. Havemeyer, George Hyatt, George N. Gardiner, Charles M. Englis, Roswell Eldridge.

Main office, foot of Fulton street, Brooklyn, N. Y.; New York office, 30 Broad street. Annual meeting, first Tuesday in October.

## UNION RAILWAY CO. OF NEW YORK

(Controlled by Third Avenue Railroad Co.)

A consolidation, July 2, 1892, of the Harlem Bridge, Morrisania & Fordham Railway Co., the North Third Avenue & Fleetwood Park and Melrose & West Morrisania Railroad Co. Leases Westchester Electric Railroad Co. In 1898 purchased the Yonkers Railroad, 10 miles. The

Tarrytown, White Plains & Mamaroneck Railway is also controlled. Road owned, 35 miles; operated, 129 miles.

Stock......Par $100..........................Authorized, $2,000,000......Issued, $2,000,000

Stock is transferred at the office of the company. Registrar, Central Trust Co., New York.

FUNDED DEBT.

| | |
|---|---|
| 1st mort., 5 per cent., due Aug., 1942, Feb. and Aug. | $2,000,000 |
| Westchester Electric R. R. guar. 1st mort., 5 per cent., due July, 1943, Jan. and July. | 500,000 |
| Southern Boulevard Railroad 1st mort., 5 per cent., due July, 1945, Jan. and July... | 250,000 |
| Yonkers Railroad 1st mort., 5 per cent., due April, 1946, April an Oct. | 1,000,000 |
| Tarrytown, W. Plains & Mamaroneck 1st mort., 5 p.c., due March, 1948, March and Sept. | 300,000 |
| Total | $4,050,000 |

The Westchester Electric Railroad was a consolidation of the Mt. Vernon and Eastchester Railway Co. and the New Rochelle Railway & Transit Co. The Southern Boulevard 5 per cent. bonds were guaranteed by this company in 1895. The Yonkers Railroad 1st mortgage is guaranteed by this company and the Third Avenue Co.

EARNINGS.

Year ending June 30.

| | Gross. | Net. | Charges. | Surplus. |
|---|---|---|---|---|
| 1892-93 | $325,181 | $137,657 | $96,924 | $49,732 |
| 1893-94 | 471,926 | 236,582 | 141,218 | 95,364 |
| 1894-95 | 430,165 | 188,579 | 131,168 | 57,411 |
| 1895-96 | 489,668 | 184,886 | 339,886 | 59,826 |
| 1896-97 | 541,855 | 219,822 | 133,431 | 86,391 |
| 1897-98 | 612,831 | 224,867 | 144,709 | 80,157 |
| 1898-99 | 849,324 | 252,154 | 199,019 | 54,135 |
| 1899-00 | 998,691 | 309,153 | 185,280 | 123,873 |
| 1900-01 | 1,153,597 | 349,485 | 192,014 | 157,471 |
| 1901-02 | 1,021,759 | 326,503 | 223,652 | 102,851 |

President, Edward A. Maher; Secretary and Treasurer, Thomas W. Olcott; Superintendent, J. Carrigan, New York.

Main office, 204 East 128th street, New York. Annual meeting, second Monday in January.

## UNION STEEL & CHAIN CO.

A corporation formed under the laws of Delaware in April, 1899. The company owns the capital stock of the Big Stone Gap Iron Co., Big Stone Gap, Va.; the Union Iron & Steel Co., Ironton, O., and the Union Rolling Mill & Foundry Co., Denver, Col. It owns in fee simple the Jefferson Steel Plant, Birmingham, Ala., and the Chatham Furnace, Chatham, N. Y.

It was stated in March, 1902, that the authorized capital of the company would be reduced.

Stock....Par $100.....Authorized { com., $30,000,000; pref., 30,000,000 } Issued { com., $335,100; pref., 766,800 } $1,101,900

The preferred stock is 7 per cent., non-cumulative.

President, William Rotch, Boston; Vice-President and General Manager, E. L. Harper, New York; Treasurer, Thomas S. Holmes, New York; Secretary, E. L. Harper, Jr., Big Stone Gap, Va.

Directors—William Rotch, Boston; Thomas S. Holmes, William F. Carey, E. L. Harper, Herman Cohen, E. L. Harper, Jr., New York; James L. Wolcott, Dover, Del.

Corporate office, Corporation Trust Co., Dover, Del.; New York office, 71 Broadway.

## UNION STORAGE CO.

A corporation formed under the laws of Pennsylvania December 2, 1880. The business of the company includes United States bonded storage, both customs and internal revenue, and general and cold storage. It owns and operates eleven large warehouses in the city of Pittsburg. The company also has ice-making plants, with a capacity of 100 tons per day.

Stock......Par $50.................. ............Authorized, $750,000......Issued, $699,200

e compan has no preferred stock and no funded debt.

Dividends of 3 per cent. are paid on the stock semi-annually in January and July.

The net earnings for eighteen months ending July 1, 1901, were used to liquidate a floating indebtedness.

In 1902 the gross earnings were $170,838; net, $42,274.

President, John L. Porter; 1st Vice-President, Samuel Bailey, Jr.; 2d Vice-President, W. G. McCandless; Secretary and Treasurer, C. L. Criss.

Directors—James M. Schoonmaker, W. G. McCandless, Samuel Bailey, Jr., William M. Kennedy, George E. Painter, John B. Herron, C. L. Criss, John L. Porter.

Main office, Second and Liberty avenues, Pittsburg. Annual meeting, third Wednesday in January.

## THE UNION SWITCH & SIGNAL CO.

A corporation formed under the laws of Pennsylvania in 1882. The company has large works at Swissvale, near Pittsburg, Pa., and manufactures interlocking and signal appliances for railroads. In 1898 the company purchased the entire capital stock ($375,000) of the National Switch & Signal Co., which had large works at Easton, Pa.

Stock......Par $50......Authorized { com., $1,000,000 / pref., 500,000 } Issued { com., $997,950 / pref., 497,600 } $1,495,550

The preferred stock is entitled to 6 per cent. dividends and ½ per cent. additional for every 1 per cent. paid on the common, until both classes of stock receive 12 per cent., above which they share equally.

The company paid 6 per cent. per annum on its preferred stock, but in April, 1900, the quarterly rate was increased to 2 per cent., or 8 per cent. per annum, and has since been paid at that rate quarterly, in January (10), April, July and October. The first dividend on the common was 1 per cent. in April, 1900, and quarterly dividends at that rate have since been regularly paid on the common in January (10), April, July and October.

Transfer Agent, Union Trust Co., Pittsburg.

**FUNDED DEBT.**

New gold bonds, 5 per cent., due 1904-14, Jan. and July.............................. $500,000

In December, 1898, the new 5 per cent. bond issue was authorized for $500,000, with which to purchase the stock of the National Switch & Signal Co. and to provide for improvements and additions to the company's plant; beginning July 1, 1902, $50,000 of the bonds mature each year. The new works, which were completed in 1902, cost $500,000.

| EARNINGS. | Gross. | Net. |
|---|---|---|
| 1897 | $424,190 | $50,947 |
| 1898 | 656,334 | 93,189 |
| 1899 | 979,320 | 146,625 |
| 1900 | 1,688,827 | 389,913 |
| 1901 | 1,605,649 | 297,906 |
| 1902 | 1,774,005 | 353,683 |

The following is the company's balance sheet, December 31, 1902:

| ASSETS. | | LIABILITIES. | |
|---|---|---|---|
| Cash in banks and hands of agents. | $38,043 | Preferred stock | $497,600 |
| Bills and accounts receivable | 459,799 | Common stock | 997,950 |
| Material in stock | 506,732 | Bonds | 530,000 |
| Real estate and buildings | 545,254 | Interest accrued on bonds | 595 |
| Machinery, tools and fixtures | 428,778 | Bills and accounts payable | 280,175 |
| Patents | 800,000 | Surplus | 472,286 |
| Total | $2,778,606 | Total | $2,778,606 |

President, George Westinghouse, Pittsburg; 1st Vice-President and General Manager, H. G. Prout; 2d Vice-President, E. H. Goodman; Secretary and Treasurer, James Johnson, Swissvale, Pa.

Directors—George Westinghouse, William McConway, Robert Pitcairn, H. G. Prout, George C. Smith, James H. Willock, Thomas Rodd.

Main office, Swissvale, Pa.; Pittsburg office, 200 Ninth street; New York office, Liberty and Washington streets; Chicago office, Dearborn, Jackson and Van Buren streets; Boston office, 170 Summer street.

## UNION TALC CO.

A corporation formed under the laws of New York, October 27, 1900. The purpose of the company is the ownership and operation of talc-producing properties. The company acquired and operates the following talc mines, mills and water powers, near Gouverneur, St. Lawrence County, N. Y.:

Columbia Talc Co.
Keller Bros. Talc & Wood Pulp Mills.
American Talc Mill.
Rhodes Water Power.
Wight Talc Mine.

The Balmat and Arnold Talc Mines are also operated under long leases.

The properties of this company constitute the greater part of the only known fibrous talc deposits in the world and are located within a territory of less than five square miles.

Stock......Par $100..........................Authorized, $1,000,000......Issued, $1,000,000

Stoc is transferred at the company's office. Registrar, North American Trust Co., New York. k

FUNDED DEBT.

1st mort., 6 per cent., due 1916, Jan. and July........................................ $370,000

The 1st mortgage is dated January 1, 1901, and is for $600,000. Trustee, North American Trust Co., New York. There is a sinking fund provision for the bonds which becomes operative for their retirement after January 1, 1906.

President, Charles E. Locke; Treasurer, Oakleigh Thorne; Secretary, George H. Hansel, New York.

Directors—Charles E. Locke, Charles C. Deming, Oakleigh Thorne, New York.

Main office, 149 Broadway, New York.

---

## UNION TRACTION CO.

(Leased to Philadelphia Rapid Transit Co.)

A corporation formed under the laws of Pennsylvania, September 6, 1895. The company is a consolidation of the Philadelphia Traction, Electric Traction and People's Traction Companies, and in 1898 acquired and leased the Hestonville, Mantua & Fairmount system, which gave it control of the street railways of Philadelphia. Road operated, 335 miles.

In March, 1902, a proposition was submitted to lease the properties of this company to the Philadelphia Rapid Transit Co. for 999 years, the lessee to guarantee $1.50 per share or 3 per cent. per annum on the stock for the first two years, 4 per cent. for the third and fourth years, 5 per cent. for the fifth and sixth years, and 6 per cent. for the remainder of the lease. The lease began July 1, 1902. The stockholders of this company also had the right to subscribe for 150,000 shares of the Rapid Transit Co.'s stock. It was also proposed to construct elevated roads on certain main streets in Philadelphia.

The Philadelphia Traction Co. was formed in 1883. It leased the Philadelphia City Passenger Railway, Philadelphia & Grays Ferry, Union Passenger Railway, West Philadelphia Passenger Railway, Ridge Avenue Passenger Railway, Thirteenth & Fifteenth Streets, Philadelphia & Darby, Schuylkill River and the Continental Passenger Railway; and owned by a stock control the Empire, Seventeenth & Nineteenth Streets and some small connecting lines, comprising a system of about 210 miles.

The People's Traction Co., formed in 1893, leased the Germantown Passenger Railway, including the Fourth & Eighth Streets and Girard Avenue Railway Companies, and the Greene & Coates Streets Railway. It owned or controlled the People's Passenger Railway (Callowhill street line), the Philadelphia, Cheltenham & Jenkintown Passenger Railway, and other lines. Total mileage, 117 miles.

The Electric Traction Co., formed in 1893, leased the Citizens' Passenger Railway, Frankford & Southwark, including Lombard and South, and Second & Third Streets Passenger Railways, and owned controlling interest in the Lehigh Avenue Passenger Railway and in the Omnibus Co. General. Total mileage, 129 miles.

Stock......Par $50..........................Authorized, $30,000,000.. ...Issued, $30,000,000

There had been paid in on the stock to January 1, 1903, $17.50 share.

The dividends on the stock under the lease are paid half-yearly, in January and July. On January 1, 1903, 1½ per cent. was paid.

Stock is transferred at the office of the company. Registrar, Land, Title & Trust Co., Philadelphia.

STOCKS OF CONSTITUENT AND LEASED COMPANIES (PAR OF ALL STOCKS, $50).

With annual rentals.

| | |
|---|---|
| Philadelphia Traction Co. stock, guar. 8 per cent., $4 per share, April and Oct..... | $20,000,000 |
| Continental Pass. Railway stock, rental $6 per share, 12 per cent.................. | 1,000,000 |
| * Philadelphia & Darby Pass. Railway stock, rental $2 per share, 4 per cent........ | 200,000 |
| Philadelphia City Pass. Railway stock, rental $7.50 per share, 15 per cent.......... | 1,000,000 |
| Philadelphia & Grays Ferry stock, rental $4 per share, 8 per cent.................. | 1,000,000 |
| Ridge Avenue stock, rental $12 per share, 24 per cent.............................. | 750,000 |
| Schuylkill River stock, rental 50 cents per share, 1 per cent........................ | 500,000 |
| Thirteenth & Fifteenth Streets stock, rental, $10 per share, 20 per cent............ | 1,000,000 |
| * Union Pass. Railway stock, rental $9.50 per share, 19 per cent.................... | 1,500,000 |
| * West Philadelphia Pass. Railway stock, rental $10 per share, 20 per cent.......... | 750,000 |
| Germantown Pass. Railway, $5 per share, 10½ per cent........................... | 1,500,000 |
| Greene & Coates Streets stock, rental $6 per share, 12 per cent..................... | 500,000 |
| Citizens' Pass. Railway stock, rental $14 per share, 28 per cent.................... | 500,000 |

STOCKS OF CONSTITUENT AND LEASED COMPANIES—*Continued.*

| | |
|---|---|
| Frankford & Southwark stock, rental $18 per share, 27 per cent | $1,875,000 |
| † Second & Third Streets Pass. Railway stock, $9.50 per share, 19 per cent | 1,060,200 |
| Hestonville, Mantua & Fairmount preferred stock, 6 per cent | 533,900 |
| " " " common stock, 4 per cent | 1,966,100 |
| Fairmount Park & Haddington stock, 6 per cent | 300,000 |
| Total stocks of leased lines | $35,935,200 |

——* Philadelphia Traction owned 705 shares, Philadelphia & Darby, 2,500 shares Union Passenger and 7,8-0 shares West Philadelphia Passenger Railways. The Union Traction Co owns 4,780 shares preferred and 35,294 shares of common stock of the Hestonville, Mantua & Fairmount.† Rental increases until 1903, when it becomes $12 per share.

FUNDED DEBT.

| | |
|---|---|
| Union Trac. Co. col. trust cer., 4 per cent., redeemable after Oct., 1945, April and Oct. | $29,730,114 |
| Phila. Traction Co. col. trust loan, 4 per cent., due Aug., 1917, Feb. 15 and Aug. 15 | 736,000 |
| Catharine & Bainbridge Streets 1st mort., 5 per cent., due April, 1920, April and Oct. | 150,000 |
| Continental Pass. Railway 1st mort., 6 per cent., due July, 1909, Jan. and July | 280,000 |
| Empire Pass. Railway 1st mort., 3½ per cent., due July, 1930, Jan. and July | 200,000 |
| Philadelphia & Darby Railway 1st mort., 4 per cent., due May, 1927, May and Nov. | 100,000 |
| Philadelphia City Pass. Railway 1st mort., 5 per cent., due Jan., 1910, Jan. and July. | 200,000 |
| " " " " debentures, 5 per cent., due March, 1925, March and Sept. | 100,000 |
| 17th and 19th Sts. Pass. Ry. 1st mort. ext., 5 per cent., due July, 1919, Jan. and July. | 100,000 |
| 13th and 15th Sts. Pass. Railway mort., 7 per cent., due Oct., 1903, April and Oct. | 100,000 |
| " " " " " mort., 5 per cent., due Jan., 1934, Jan. and July | 400,000 |
| West Philadelphia Pass. Railway 1st mort., 6 per cent., due April, 1906, April and Oct. | 246,000 |
| " " " " 2d mort., 5 per cent., due May, 1926, May and Nov. | 750,000 |
| Union Pass. Railway 1st mort., 5 per cent., due April, 1911, April and Oct. | 500,000 |
| " " " 2d mort., 5 per cent., due April, 1910, April and Oct. | 250,000 |
| Lombard & South Sts. Pass. Ry. 1st mort., 3½ per cent., due Dec., 1951, June and Dec. | 150,000 |
| West End Pass. Railway 1st mort., 7 per cent., due Oct., 1905, April and Oct. | 132,100 |
| People's Pass. Railway 1st mort., 7 per cent., due Jan., 1905, Jan. and July | 234,000 |
| " " " 2d mort., 5 per cent., due July, 1911, Jan. and July | 285,000 |
| " " " cons. mort., 5 per cent., due March, 1912, March and Sept. | 246,000 |
| Fairmount Park & Del. River mort., 5 per cent., due June, 1904, June and Dec. | 67,500 |
| Hestonville, Mantua & Fairmount cons. mort., 5 per cent., due May, 1924, May and Nov. | 1,250,000 |
| Total | $36,206,714 |

The Union Traction Co. purchased the stock of the People's Traction Co., $10,000,000, par $50, paid in $30, and of the Electric Traction Co., $50 par, full paid, $7,619,000, allotment stock, $30 per share, paid in, $1,131,000, total $8,750,000. It also leased the Philadelphia Traction Co. for 999 years at a net rental of 8 per cent., or $4 per share per annum, payable in gold, half-yearly, free of taxes.

The purchased stock of the People's and Electric Traction Companies was paid for in 4 per cent. collateral trust certificates, not redeemable before October 1, 1945, secured by deposit of purchased stocks with Pennsylvania Company, for Insurances on Lives, etc., trustee. The trust certificates are guaranteed, principal and interest, by the Union Traction Co., and are in denominations of $100 and $1,000. The price paid was $76 in said certificates for each share ($30 paid in) of People's Traction stock, $85 per share for each full paid share of Electric Traction, and $76 per share for the shares of the latter company, on which $30 per share had been paid in.

July 1, 1896, the People's Traction and Electric Traction were leased to this company for all charges, including interest on the 4 per cent. stock trust certificates.

Stockholders of the Philadelphia Electric and People's Traction Companies had the privilege of subscribing for the stock of Union Traction Co. to the extent of 77 per cent. of the number of shares held.

The People's Passenger Railway stock trust certificates were issued when practically all the stock of that company was purchased by People's Traction Co., $75 per share, payable $5 in cash and $70 in trust certificates, being given for the $2,250,000 of People's Passenger Railway stock. Trust certificates are secured by the deposit with Pennsylvania Company for Insurance on Lives, etc., trustee, of 14 2-7 shares of the People's Passenger Railway shares for each $1,000 issued.

EARNINGS.—Year ending June 30.

| | Gross. | Other Earnings. | Net. |
|---|---|---|---|
| 1897–98 | $10,800,542 | ........ | $6,515,062 |
| 1898–99 | 11,793,858 | ........ | 7,242,400 |
| 1899–00 | 12,237,924 | $253,528 | 7,624,920 |
| 1900–01 | 13,269,465 | 162,215 | 7,595,495 |
| 1901–02 | 13,969,233 | 148,725 | 7,715,820 |

In 1897 there was a deficit after charges and rentals of $851,934; in 1898 the surplus ove the same was $24,620; in 1899, surplus $617,073; in 1900, surplus $939,021; in 1901, surplur $861,266; in 1902, surplus $1,078,038.

President, John B. Parsons; 1st Vice-President, George D. Widener; 2d Vice-President, Charles O. Kruger; Secretary and Treasurer, Robert B. Selfridge; Assistant Secretary and Assistant Treasurer, John B. Peddle; Comptroller, Alexander Rennick.

Directors—W. H. Shelmardine, Peter A. B. Widener, William L. Elkins, George D. Widener, Alexander M. Fox, Alexander Balfour, John B. Parsons, George W. Elkins, Charles O. Kruger, John M Mack, Jeremiah J. Sullivan, George H. Earle, Jr.

Main office, 810 Dauphin street, Philadelphia. Annual meeting, third Wednesday in September.

## UNION TRACTION CO. OF INDIANA

A corporation formed under the laws of Indiana in 1899. The company absorbed the street railway lines in Anderson, Muncie, Marion and Elwood, Ind., and the Muncie, Anderson & Indianapolis Street Railway Co. The company has a mileage in the various cities of 60 miles, and its interurban system, extending from Marion and Muncie to Indianapolis, is about 100 miles. In July, 1902, this company leased for 50 years the Indianapolis Northern Traction Co., which is building a line from Indianapolis to Logansport, Peru and Elwood, Ind.

Stock...Par $100...Authorized { com., $4,000,000; pref., 1,000,000 } Issued { com., $4,000,000; pref., 1,000,000 } $5,000,000

The preferred stock of the company is 5 per cent., cumulative. Stock is transferred at the company's office.

In 1902 5 per cent. was paid on the preferred stock, 2½ per cent. each, in April and October.

FUNDED DEBT.

| | |
|---|---|
| Union Traction gen. mort., 5 per cent., due July, 1919, Jan. and July | $4,272,000 |
| Anderson Elect. St. Ry. 1st mort., 6 per cent., due July, 1912, Jan. and July | 150,000 |
| Citizen St. Ry. of Muncie 1st mort., 6 per cent., due Dec., 1927, June and Dec. | 173,500 |
| Marion City Ry. 1st mort., 6 per cent., due May, 1915, May and Nov. | 400,000 |
| Indianapolis Northern Traction 1st mort., 5 per cent., due July, 1932, Jan. and July | 3,500,000 |
| Total | $8,495,500 |

The trustee of the general mortgage is the City Trust Co., New York, which is also agent for the payment of interest. The mortgage is for $5,000,000, sufficient bonds being reserved to retire underlying liens.

The trustee of the Indianapolis Northern Traction and agent for payment of interest on the same is the Colonial Trust Co., New York. The authorized amount of the mortgage is $5,000,000.

EARNINGS.

| | Gross. | Net. | Charges and Pref. Div. | Surplus. |
|---|---|---|---|---|
| 1900 | $447,616 | $200,571 | $177,946 | $22,625 |
| 1901 | 712,524 | 329,849 | 287,239 | 42,610 |
| 1902 | 962,260 | 445,762 | 329,090 | 116,672 |

President and General Manager, George F. McCulloch, Anderson, Ind.; Vice-President, Philip Matter, Marion, Ind.; Secretary, James A. Van Osdol; Treasurer, William C. Sampson, Anderson, Ind.

Directors—Randal Morgan, J. Levering Jones, Philadelphia; W. Kesley Schoepf, Cincinnati; George F. McCulloch, James A. Van Osdol, William C. Sampson, Anderson, Ind.; Philip Matter, Marion, Ind.

Main office, Anderson, Ind. Annual meeting, first Tuesday in March.

## UNION TYPEWRITER CO.

A corporation formed under the laws of New Jersey in 1893. It owns the majority of the stock of the concerns manufacturing and selling typewriter machines, including the Remington, Smith-Premier, Yost, New Century and Densmore typewriters.

Stock...Par $100...Authorized { com., $10,000,000; 1st pref., 4,000,000; 2d pref., 6,000,000 } Issued { com., $10,000,000; 1st pref., 4,000,000; 2d pref., 4,015,000 } $18,015,000

The 1st preferred stock is 7 per cent., cumulative; the 2d preferred 8 per cent., cumulative. Of the 2d preferred an amount of $2,000,000 remains in the company's treasury.

No report of the company's earnings is published. The dividends paid have been as follows: on the 1st preferred, in 1893 3½ per cent., in 1894 and each year since 7 per cent.; on the 2d preferred, in 1895 6 per cent., in 1896 6 per cent., in 1897 8 per cent., in 1898 8 per cent., in 1899 8 per cent., in 1900 8 per cent. and 8 per cent. extra, the latter being on account of past due dividends, which were thus reduced to 8 per cent. In 1901 16 per cent. was paid on the 2d preferred, which completed the overdue dividends. The preferred dividends are paid half-yearly April and October. The first dividend on the common stock was 3 per cent., paid April 1, 1902, a similar dividend being paid in October, 1902.

Stock is transferred at 280 Broadway, New York. Registrar, New York Security & Trust Co.

The company has no funded debt.

President, Clarence W. Seamans; Secretary, George K. Gilluly; Treasurer, Phineas C. Lounsbury, New York.

Directors—Eugene G. Blackford, George K. Gilluly, James M. Gifford, Charles S. Fairchild, Frank L. Babbott, Phineas C. Lounsbury, Clarence W. Seamans, Charles Searle, Wilbert L. Smith, Raymond S. White, Lucius S. Biglow, Clarence F. Wyckoff, Lyman C. Smith, John W. Luggett, John I. McMaster.

Corporate office, 15 Exchange place, Jersey City. Annual meeting, third Wednesday in March.

## UNITED BOX BOARD & PAPER CO.

A corporation formed under the laws of New Jersey, May 28, 1902. The company acquired a majority of the stock of the American Straw Board Co. and all the stock of the Knickerbocker Pulp & Paper Co. In addition it acquired other plants, including the Traders' Paper Co. of Lockport, N. Y., engaged in the manufacture of straw board and box board, and operates or controls in all some 26 plants. These establishments produce about 90 per cent. of the total output of such material in the United States.

Stock..Par $100..Authorized { com., $15,000,000 / pref., 15,000,000 } Issued { com., $14,018,500 / pref., 11,418,000 } $25,436,500

The preferred stock is 7 per cent., cumulative.

The company paid an initial quarterly dividend of 1¾ per cent. on the preferred stock December 15, 1902. The March, 1903, dividend was, however, passed, it being determined to increased the working capital of the company.

FUNDED DEBT.

1st mort., 5 per cent., due Jan., 1904-13, Jan. and July.............................. $2,000,000

The 1st mortgage is for $3,500,000. Trustee and agent for the payment of interest, Morton Trust Co., New York. Beginning January, 1904, $350,000 of the bonds fall due each year to January 1, 1908, inclusive; $250,000 mature January 1, 1909, and $1,500,000 January 1, 1913. Of the authorized issue $1,500,000 were reserved to retire outstanding underlying liens of various constituent companies.

President, James A. Roberts; 1st Vice-President, R. F. Newcomb; 2d Vice-President, Charles D. Brown; 3d Vice-President, Robert B. McEwan; Secretary, W. C. Staley; Treasurer, Eugene M. Ashley.

Directors—W. H. Binnian, D. McCalley, R. C. Clowry, James A. Roberts, W. C. Staley, Robert B. McEwan, R. F. Newcomb, Charles D. Brown, Henry B. Dean, Richard Ruddell, T. E. Ellsworth, Augustus H. Ivins, Charles B. Oglesby, C. S. Merrill, H. Lester Paddock.

Main office, 11 Broadway, New York.

## UNITED BREWERIES CO.

A corporation formed under the laws of New Jersey, in August, 1898, for the purpose of acquiring the property of the following concerns, and conducting a general brewing business:

Blue Island Brewing Co.
Chicago Brewing Co.
Citizens' Brewing Co.
Monarch Brewing Co.
Phœnix Brewing Co.
South Chicago Brewing Co.
Star Brewery.
Carl Corper Brewing Co.
Fecker Brewing Co.
Henn & Gabler Brewing Co.
Northwestern Brewing Co.
William Ruehl Brewing Co.
Sieben Brewery.

The output of these combined plants is about 475,000 barrels annually. The company has greatly improved the plants since acquisition.

Stock......Par $100..........................Authorized, $5,600,000......Issued, $5,463,000

Transfer Agent, Kessler & Co., 54 Wall street, New York. Registrar, Continental Trust Co., New York.

FUNDED DEBT.

1st mort., 6 per cent. gold bonds, due 1928, Feb. and Aug.......................... $3,308,000

The total issue of bonds is $3,500,000, and covers all the property of the company. The sinking fund clause requires that after August 1, 1900, $35,000 each year shall be placed with the Continental Trust Co. of New York, the trustee, to purchase bonds at 105, and after 1908, whenever more than $50,000 accumulates in the sinking fund and bonds are not offered, the trustee may call bonds by lot at 105. The Illinois Trust & Savings Bank, Chicago, and the Continental Trust Co., New York, are agents for payment of interest.

EARNINGS.

Year ending July 31.

| | Gross. | Net. | Surplus. |
|---|---|---|---|
| 1900-01 | $2,394,068 | $431,390 | $10,388 |

Chairman, Isidor Baumgartl; President and Treasurer, Henry C. Bannard; Vice-Presidents, Rudolph E. F. Flinsch, W. O. Tegtmeyer; Secretary, Ernst Hummel.

Directors—Isidor Baumgartl, Henry C. Bannard, Rudolph E. F. Flinsch, Harry Rubens, Rudolf Brand, Ernst Hummel, Charles Stein, North McLean, W. O. Tegtmeyer, Chicago.

Main office, 108 La Salle street, Chicago. Annual meeting, second Tuesday in October, at Chicago.

## UNITED COPPER CO.

A corporation formed under the laws of New Jersey, April 28, 1902. The company acquired nearly all the stock of the following companies:

Montana Ore Purchasing Co.
Nipper Consolidated Copper Co.
Corra-Rock Island Mining Co.
Minnie Healey Mining Co.
Belmont Mining Co.

Stock...Par $100..Authorized { com., $75,000,000; pref., 5,000,000 } Issued { com., $45,000,000; pref., 5,000,000 } $50,000,000

The preferred stock is 6 per cent., cumulative. The company has no funded debt.

The payment of dividends on the preferred stock was begun with a semi-annual dividend of 3 per cent. November 1, 1902.

President, F. Aug. Heinze; Vice-Presidents, Arthur P. Heinze, John MacGinniss; Secretary and Treasurer, Stanley Gifford.

Directors—F. Aug. Heinze, Arthur P. Heinze, John MacGinniss, F. W. Whitridge, Henry Budge, A. A. Brownlee, Stephen E. Nash, G. Reusens, J. Langeroth.

Corporate office, Hoboken, N. J.; main office, 31 Nassau street, New York.

## UNITED ELECTRIC CO. OF NEW JERSEY

A corporation formed under the laws of New Jersey, March 4, 1899. The company was formed to acquire and unite the principal electric light and power concerns in northern New Jersey. It acquired the following companies:

Jersey City Electric Light Co.
Newark Electric Light & Power Co.
Central Power Co.
Thomson-Houston Electric Co.
Newark-Schuyler Electric Co.
Essex County Electric Co.
Montclair Light & Power Co.
Excelsior Electric Co.
Kearny Electric Light & Power Co.
Hudson County Electric Co.
People's Light & Power Co.
Consumers' Electric Light & Power Co.
Suburban Electric Light & Power Co.
Edison Electric Light & Power Co.
Hudson Electric Light Co.
North Hudson Light, Heat & Power Co.
Suburban Electric Co.
Union County Electric Co.
Elizabeth-Schuyler Electric Co.
Consumers' Light, Heat & Power Co.
Morris County Electric Co.

The company has exclusive electric franchises covering Jersey City, Newark, Hoboken, Bayonne, Elizabeth and other cities, towns and divisions of New Jersey.

Stock......Par $100........................Authorized, $20,000,000......Issued, $20,000,000

Registrar, Fidelity Trust Co., Newark, N. J.

FUNDED DEBT.

1st mort., 4 per cent., due June, 1949, June and Dec.............................. $16,110,000

The authorized issue of bonds is $20,000,000, of which $3,760,500 was reserved to retire underlying bonds and to provide for improvements.

The bonds are guaranteed as to interest for five years by the United Gas Improvement Co. Trustee of mortgage, New Jersey Title Guarantee & Trust Co., Jersey City, which institution also pays coupons.

In the year ending January 31, 1902, the gross earnings were $1,677,322; net, $753,414; charges, $698,134; surplus, $55,280.

President, Albert B. Carlton; 1st Vice-President, Gottfried Krueger; 2d Vice-President, E. F. C. Young; 3d Vice-President, Philip N. Jackson; Secretary, L. D. H. Gilmour; Assistant Secretary and Assistant Treasurer, Percy Ingalls; Comptroller and Treasurer, Lewis Lillie; Director-General, Walton Clark; General Manager, Dudley Farrand.

Directors—E. F. C. Young, Joseph D. Bedle, Henry Mehl, William C. Shanley, Hamilton Wallis, Jersey City; Charles A. Sterling, Charles M. Decker, Orange, N. J.; Leslie P. Ward, Philip N. Jackson, Dudley Farrand, J. F. Kehoe, Gottfried Krueger, W. H. Corbin, Peter Hauck, Jr., Albert B. Carlton, Newark, N. J.; John C. Rankin, Jr., Elizabeth, N. J.; A. Philip Hexamer, W. C. Heppenheimer, Hoboken, N. J.; Randal Morgan, Philadelphia; John O. H. Pitney, Morristown, N. J.

Main office, 207 Market street, Newark, N. J.

---

## UNITED ELECTRIC, GAS & POWER CO.

A corporation formed under the laws of California, February 13, 1900, for the purpose of supplying gas and electric light and power. The company has acquired the following plants:

Santa Monica Electric Co.
Long Beach Electric Co.
Redondo Electric Co.
Santa Barbara Electric Co.
San Pedro Electric Co.
Monrovia Electric Co.

These combined plants generate electric current to the extent of about 3,600 horse power, besides supplying a large amount of gas.

Stock......Par $100..........................Authorized, $1,500,000......Issued, $800,000

The company has no preferred stock. Transfer Agent, George I. Cochran, 254 South Broadway, Los Angeles, Cal.

The first quarterly dividend was paid April 1, 1900, at the rate of 2 per cent. per annum. This has been increased to 3 per cent., again to 4 per cent., and is now 5 per cent. Dividend periods are quarterly, January, April, July and October.

FUNDED DEBT.

1st mort., 5 per cent., due 1920, June and Dec.......................................... $500,000

The bonds outstanding are the full amount authorized. Trustee of mortgage and agent for the payment of interest, The Broadway Bank & Trust Co. of Los Angeles, Cal. The Chase National Bank, New York, is also agent for the payment of interest.

President and Treasurer, Halett C. Merritt, Los Angeles, Cal.; Vice-Presidents, Frederick H. Ringe, Santa Monica, Cal.; H. V. Carter; Secretary, George I. Cochran, Los Angeles, Cal.

Directors—H. V. Carter, Los Angeles, Cal.; Frederick H. Ringe, J. J. Davis, Santa Monica, Cal.; Alfred Stedman, Monrovia, Cal.

Main office, 254 South Broadway, Los Angeles, Cal. Annual meeting, second Tuesday in January, at Los Angeles, Cal.

---

## UNITED ELECTRIC LIGHT & POWER CO.

A corporation formed under the laws of New York in 1887. The company acquired the United States Illuminating Co. and the Brush Electric Illuminating Co. Its system is operated under the Brush and Westinghouse patents.

In January, 1900, control of this company was acquired by the Consolidated Gas Co.

Stock....Par $100.....Authorized { com., $4,000,000; pref., 2,000,000 } Issued { com., $4,000,000; pref., 2,000,000 } $6,000,000

The preferred stock is 6 per cent., cumulative.

Stock is transferred at the company's office. Registrar, Union Trust Co., New York.

FUNDED DEBT.

| | |
|---|---|
| 1st mort., 5 per cent., due 1924, Jan. and July.................................... | $5,000,000 |
| Brush Electric Illuminating, 1st mort., 5 per cent., Jan. and July.................. | 275,000 |
| Total .............................................................. | $5,275,000 |

President, Harrison E. Gawtry; Secretary, George H. Church; Treasurer, Benjamin Whiteley; Assistant Secretary, Frank W. Smith.

Directors—Osborn W. Bright, Robert A. Carter, George H. Church, Arthur H. Elliott, Harrison E. Gawtry, Lewis B. Gawtry, Samuel A. Beardsley, Nicholas F. Brady, William Bunker, Thomas E. Murray, Frank W. Smith, Zelah Van Loan, Benjamin Whiteley.

Main office, 55 Duane street, New York. Annual meeting, first Friday in February.

## UNITED ELECTRIC LIGHT CO.

A corporation formed under the laws of Massachusetts in 1887 to supply electric light and power in the city of Springfield, Mass. The company owns and operates a steam power plant and a water power plant and leases an additional water power plant.

Stock......Par $100............................Authorized, $800,000......Issued, $800,000

The company has no preferred stock. Stock is transferred and registered at the office of the company, Springfield, Mass.

Dividends of 8 per cent. per annum are paid quarterly in January, April, July and October.

FUNDED DEBT.

Sinking fund bonds, 5 per cent., due 1917, Jan. and July..............................$200,000

Trustee of the mortgage and agent for the payment of interest, Springfield Safe Deposit & Trust Co., Springfield, Mass.

In the fiscal year ending June 30, 1902, the gross earnings were $251,518; net, $86,736.

President, Robert W. Day; Treasurer, W. A. Lincoln; Manager, Walter A. Mulligan, Springfield, Mass.

Directors, John Olmstead, Charles A. Nichols, A. B. Wallace, Henry J. Beebe, Robert W. Day, George B. Holbrook, Springfield, Mass.

Corporate and main office, 135 State street, Springfield, Mass. Annual meeting, in July, at Springfield, Mass.

## UNITED ELECTRIC SECURITIES CO.

A corporation formed under the laws of Maine, May 20, 1890. The company devotes itself particularly to the purchase of mortgage bonds of corporations operating electric lighting, power and railway plants, and to issuing against them its own collateral trust, 5 per cent., 30-year, gold, sinking fund bonds.

Stock......Par $100.......Authorized { com., $500,000 / pref., 1,000,000 } Issued { com., $500,000 / pref., 1,000,000 } $1,500,000

The preferred stock is 7 per cent., cumulative. Dividends of 3½ per cent. are paid half-yearly on the preferred, May (1) and November.

FUNDED DEBT.

Collateral trust, 5 per cent. bonds, Feb. and Aug.................................. $1,904,000

The total amount of the fourteen series of collateral 5 per cent. bonds issued by the company was $10,000,000. Of these $8,096,000 have, up to February 1, 1903, been redeemed and canceled from the proceeds of sales of the underlying securities, the deeds of trust to the American Loan & Trust Co., Boston, trustee, providing specifically for the application of such proceeds of sales of the securities to that purpose.

Agent for the payment of interest on the company's collateral trust bonds, American Loan & Trust Co., Boston.

The company's balance sheet, February 1, 1903, is as follows:

TRUST ASSETS.

| | | |
|---|---|---|
| Underlying securities, to secure $1,904,000 collateral trust 5 per cent. bonds: | | |
| Par value | $3,284,900 | |
| Appraisal value | | $2,619,196 |
| Cash on hand for the redemption of collateral trust 5 per cent. bonds, being the proceeds from sales of underlying securities | | 7,421 |
| Total | | $2,626,617 |

TRUST LIABILITIES.

| | | |
|---|---|---|
| Collateral trust 5 per cent. bonds outstanding at par | $1,904,000 | |
| Premium payable for retirement of collateral trust 5s | 216 | |
| | | $1,904,216 |
| Surplus of collateral held as security for collateral trust 5s | | 722,401 |
| Total | | $2,626,617 |

GENERAL ASSETS.

| | | | |
|---|---|---|---|
| Brought forward: | | | |
| Surplus of collateral held as security for collateral trust 5s | | | $722,401 |
| Investment securities. Stocks: | | | |
| Par value | $2,681,150 | | |
| Appraisal value | | $877,140 | |
| Bonds: | | | |
| Par value | 205,500 | | |
| Appraisal value | | 156,275 | |
| | | | $1,033,415 |
| Cash, not including funds for the redemption of collateral trust 5 per cent. bonds | | | 93,155 |
| Notes receivable: | | | |
| Face value | 327,608 | | |
| Appraisal value | | | 246,561 |
| Accounts receivable: | | | |
| Face value | 243,469 | | |
| Appraisal value | | | 85,009 |
| Accruedi nterest | | | 29,438 |
| Total | | | $2,209,079 |

GENERAL LIABILITIES.

| | |
|---|---|
| Capital stock: | |
| Preferred | $1,000,000 |
| Common | 500,000 |
| Notes payable | 150,000 |
| Surplus | 559,979 |
| Total | $2,209,979 |

President, Samuel Carr; Vice-President, Robert Treat Paine, 2d; Treasurer, Ernest L. Carr, Boston, General Manager, C. N. Mason.

Directors—Gordon Abbott, Walter Abbott, Samuel Carr, Winthrop Coffin, Philip Dexter, Francis R. Hart, George Von L. Meyer, Robert Treat Paine, 2d, Francis Peabody, Jr., N. W. Rice, W. H. Whitney.

Main office, Washington and Court streets, Boston.

---

## UNITED FACTORIES, LIMITED

A corporation formed under the laws of Ontario in 1901. The purpose of the company is the manufacture of brushes, brooms, woodenware and kindred articles. The company acquired and operates the following plants: Boeckh's factories, Toronto; Bryan's factories, London, Ont.; Cane's factories, Newmarket, Ont.

| Stock....Par $100....Authorized | | | Issued | | | |
|---|---|---|---|---|---|---|
| | com., | $600,000 | | com., | $600,000 | |
| | 1st pref., | 500,000 | | 1st pref., | 400,000 | $1,400,000 |
| | 2d pref., | 400,000 | | 2d pref., | 400,000 | |

The 1st preference stock is 7 per cent., cumulative, and is entitled to annual dividends of that rate, payable quarterly, on March (1), June, September and December. After such dividends on the 1st preference stock are paid, not less than 10 per cent. or more than 20 per cent. of the remaining profits shall be carried to a reserve account to ensure the dividends in question until the reserve amounts to 20 per cent. of the 1st preference stock outstanding, at which sum it must be maintained, and if drawn upon must be restored in the same manner.

The 2d preference stock is 5 per cent., non-cumulative, ranking after the 1st preference and the reserve requirements of the latter. After 5 per cent. has been paid on the 2d preference stock, the three classes of stock share equally in any further profits for the fiscal year.

The 1st preference stock is entitled to be paid in full from assets in case of a dissolution, the 2d preference standing next for payment in full before anything shall be paid on the common.

Transfer Agent and Registrar, Union Trust Co., Toronto.

The company has no funded debt.

In the two fiscal years preceding the formation of this company, the constituent concerns showed average net earnings aggregating $45,669 per annum.

President, Emil C. Boeckh, Toronto; Vice-President, Henry S. Cane, Newmarket, Ont.; Secretary and Treasurer, A. W. Wills, Toronto.

Directors—Emil C. Boeckh, Charles Boeckh, A. W. Wills, William Wilson, George E. Foster, Toronto; Henry S. Cane, Eugene Cane, Newmarket, Ont.; Thomas Bryan, London, Ont.

Main office, 80 York street, Toronto; Montreal office, 143 Debresoles street. Annual meeting, fourth Wednesday in January, at Toronto.

## UNITED FRUIT CO.

A corporation formed under the laws of New Jersey, March 30, 1899. The company was organized for the production, transportation and distribution of tropical fruit from the West Indies and Central America to the United States. It acquired either the whole or a controlling interest in the Boston Fruit Co. and associate fruit companies, also the Tropical Trading & Transportation Co., Limited, together with a line of steamers in service between South and Central America and the West Indies and American ports. The company controls the Fruit Dispatch Co., which is its distributing agent. The fleet of steamers owned or chartered aggregate about sixty. The combined yearly importations of the concerns acquired aggregate 20,000,000 bunches of bananas, and other fruits in proportion. The lands owned in Costa Rica, Cuba, Honduras, Jamaica, San Domingo and Colombia aggregate 248,127 acres, of which 75,035 acres are improved, and it leases 24,273 acres additional, a total of 272,400 acres owned or leased. The company has plantations in Jamaica, Cuba and other West India Islands, and Central and South America. The company owns 112 miles of railways in the countries named above, with 24 locomotives and 515 cars, exclusive of the Northern Railway of Costa Rica. It has a large sugar property in Cuba and erected a sugar mill costing $804,611. It practically controls the importation of fruits into the United States from the countries named.

Stock......Par $100.........................Authorized, $20,000,000......Issued, $12,369,500

In August, 1900, the company offered its stockholders the privilege of subscribing for $1,123,000 of new stock.

Transfer Agent, Old Colony Trust Co., Boston. Registrar, Mercantile Trust Co., Boston.

The company commenced the payment of dividends October 15, 1899, by paying 2½ per cent., and has paid regular dividends at the same rate, quarterly, in January (15), April, July and October, until July, 1901, when the quarterly rate was reduced to 1½ per cent.

FUNDED DEBT.

| | |
|---|---|
| Debentures convertible, 5 per cent., due Sept., 1911, March and Sept................ | $4,000,000 |
| Boston Fruit Co. bonds, 6 per cent ...................... ......................... | 12,500 |
| Nor. Ry. of Costa Rica 1st mort., guar. 5 per cent., due Sept., 1915, March and Sept.. | 1,600,000 |
| Total...................................................................... | $5,612,500 |

There were $3,500,000 of 6 per cent. coupon notes issued in 1899, of which $1,750,000 matured October 1, 1900, and $1,750,000, October 1, 1901.

The debentures are $5,000,000 authorized, and were created in 1901. They are convertible into stock at par, after January 1, 1903, and can be called at 110 and interest after March 1, 1903.

The Northern Railway of Costa Rica 5 per cent. bonds are guaranteed, and are redeemable at 105, and 84,000 of the issue were taken into the sinking fund in September, 1902.

In the year ending August 31, 1901, the company earned gross, $1,251,975; net, $1,098,557; dividends, $1,084,767; balance surplus, $13,789. In the year ending September 30, 1902, net, $2,446,517; charges, $260,699; dividends, $1,051,407; surplus, $1,134,410.

The following is the company's balance sheet September 30, 1902:

| ASSETS. | | LIABILITIES. | |
|---|---|---|---|
| Plantations and equipment....... | $14,531,283 | Capital stock..................... | $12,369,500 |
| Current assets: | | Funded debt: | |
| Cash.......................... | 1,019,316 | Boston Fruit Co. 6 per cent. bonds....................... | 12,500 |
| Accounts collectible............ | 2,345,317 | Convertible 10-year 5 per cent. gold bonds.................. | 4,000,000 |
| Advance payments: | | Current liabilities: | |
| Charters, wharfage, steamship supplies and commissions.... | 57,874 | Accounts payable.............. | 341,079 |
| Investments: | | Sight drafts.................... | 199,770 |
| Stocks of other companies..... | 1,209,225 | Dividend payable Oct. 13, 1902. | 309,238 |
| Miscellaneous................. | 88,174 | Unclaimed dividends............ | 802 |
| | | Due insurance fund (Dr.)......... | 3,555 |
| | | Drawn Boston Fruit Co. bonds... | 1,500 |
| | | Interest accrued, not due......... | 16,979 |
| | | Income account, surplus.......... | 2,003,376 |
| Total..................... | $19,251,189 | Total...... .............. | $19,251,189 |

President, Andrew W. Preston, Boston; Vice-President, Minor C. Keith, New York; Treasurer, Charles A. Hubbard; Secretary, Bradley W. Palmer; Assistant Treasurer, James F. Tilden, Boston.

Directors—Lorenzo D. Baker, T. Jefferson Coolidge, Jr., James A. Jones, Minor C. Keith, Kenneth K. McLaren, Bradley W. Palmer, Andrew W. Preston, John S. Bartlett, Reginald

Foster, Francis R. Hart, Charles A. Hubbard, Hugh Kelly, William S. Spaulding, Harry O. Underwood, Samuel Untermeyer.

Main office, 131 State street, Boston. Annual meeting, second Wednesday in December, at Jersey City.

## UNITED GAS & ELECTRIC CO.

A corporation organized under the laws of New Jersey, December 9, 1901. The purpose of the company is to acquire and operate gas and electric light plants and dispose of the same. The company succeeded the Union Gas & Electric Co., which was formed under the laws of New Jersey in 1899.

The present company controls eight gas and electric properties, valued at $3,983,402, with an annual output of 350,000,000 cubic feet of gas and 4,000,000 kilowatts of electricity, the aggregate populations served being 181,556.

Stock....Par $100.....Authorized { com., $2,500,000 / pref., 1,500,000 } Issued { com., $1,000,000 / pref., 600,000 } $1,600,000

The preferred stock is 5 per cent., cumulative, and also has a preference as to assets in case of dissolution. The dividends on the preferred stock are semi-annual, in January (15) and July.

Transfer Agents, Corporation Trust Co. of New Jersey, Jersey City, and Bertron & Storrs, 40 Wall street, New York.

FUNDED DEBT.

1st mort., collateral trust, 5 per cent., due Jan., 1922, Jan. and July.................. $600,000

Trustee and agent for payment of interest on the bonds, Continental Trust Co., New York. The 1st mortgage is $3,000,000 authorized.

In the year ending February 1, 1902, the constituent companies earned, gross, $512,564; net, $114,037; charges, $30,000; surplus, $84,037. The operating expenses included taxes and interest on the bonds of the constituent companies.

President, S. Reading Bertron; Vice-President, Richard S. Storrs; Secretary and Treasurer, Murray W. Dodge; Assistant Secretary and Treasurer, Frank S. Butterworth, New York.

Directors—S. Reading Bertron, Richard S. Storrs, Abram M. Hyatt, Frank S. Butterworth, Murray W. Dodge, New York; Edward Bailey, Harrisburg, Pa.; Denman Blanchard, Boston; W. C. McMillan, Detroit; E. G. Stoddard, New Haven, Conn.

Corporate office, 15 Exchange place, Jersey City; main office, 40 Wall street, New York. Annual meeting, third Tuesday in December, at Jersey City.

## UNITED GAS IMPROVEMENT CO.

A corporation formed under the laws of Pennsylvania in 1882. Reorganized, 1888, under special charter of Union Contract Co., which was granted power to construct and maintain or manage any work, and furnish all necessary material, labor and implements of any kind, and to hold and own securities in any form, either as collateral or otherwise, and to dispose of the same. The company makes a business of building, purchasing, leasing and operating gas works, and is also interested in electric light and power, as well as in traction enterprises. The following is a list of the companies or works owned or controlled:

Allentown Gas Co., Allentown, Pa.
The Lower Merion Gas Co., Ardmore, Pa.
Atlanta Gas Light Co., Atlanta, Ga.
Burlington Gas Light Co., Burlington, Ia.
Concord Light & Power Co., Concord, N. H.
Capital City Gas Light Co., Des Moines, Ia.
Harrisburg Gas Co., Harrisburg, Pa.
New Gas Light Co. of Janesville, Janesville, Wis.
Hudson County Gas Co., Jersey City.
Fulton County Gas & Electric Co., Johnstown, N. Y.
Wyandotte Gas Co., Kansas City, Kan.
Kansas City (Missouri) Gas Co., Kansas City, Mo.
The People's Gas Light Co., Manchester, N. H.
Essex & Hudson Gas Co., Newark, N. J.
Omaha Gas Co., Omaha, Neb.
The Paterson & Passaic Gas & Electric Co., Paterson, N. J.
Pensacola Gas Co., Pensacola, Fla.
Philadelphia Gas Works, Philadelphia.
Consumers' Gas Co., Reading, Pa.
Mutual Gas Light Co., Savannah, Ga.
Sioux City Gas & Electric Co., Sioux City, Ia.
Sioux Falls Gas Light Co., Sioux Falls, S. D.
St. Albans Gas Light Co., St. Albans, Vt.
St. Augustine Gas & Electric Light Co., St. Augustine, Fla.
Vicksburg Gas Light Co., Vicksburg, Miss.
Waterbury Gas Light Co., Waterbury, Conn.
Northern Liberties Gas Co., Philadelphia.
Connecticut Railway & Lighting Co., Bridgeport, Conn.
Westchester Lighting Co., Mt. Vernon, N. Y.
Wayne Electric Co., Wayne, Pa.

Statements of several of these companies will be found under their own titles in this edition of the MANUAL. The company also has a large interest in the United Electric Co. of New Jersey, and in the gas, electric and street railway properties of Providence, R. I., the latter having been acquired in May, 1902.

The company has a large and perfect organization in all its departments. The operating companies are conducted separately, but with reference to a general policy of management under advice of the central office.

Stock......Par $50........................Authorized, $28,250,000......Issued, $28,250,000

In January, 1896, an extra dividend was paid of 15 per cent. in scrip convertible in stock up to March 2, 1896, after which it was redeemable only in cash. In March, 1898, stock was increased from $11,500,000 to $15,000,000, and increase allotted to stockholders for subscription at par. In 1900 the stock was increased to $22,500,000, the new issue of $7,500,000, or 50 per cent., being offered to stockholders for subscription at par. In January, 1902, the stock was increased to $28,-250,000.

In February, 1903, it was announced that authority would be asked of the stockholders at the annual meeting, May 4, 1903, to increase the stock to $36,725,000.

Dividends of 8 per cent. per annum are paid quarterly, 2 per cent. each, January (15), April, July and October.

Stock is transferred at the company's office. Registrar, Fidelity Trust Co., Philadelphia.

The net earnings of the company have been as follows in the years named:

| | | | |
|---|---|---|---|
| 1897 | $1,424,297 | 1900 | $3,386,771 |
| 1898 | 1,864,129 | 1901 | 2,535,288 |
| 1899 | 4,948,923 | | |

The net for 1899 and 1900 includes premiums on certain securities and also certain outside operations.

President, Thomas Dolan; Vice-Presidents, George Philler, Samuel T. Bodine, Randal Morgan; Secretary and Treasurer, Lewis Lillie, Philadelphia.

Directors—Thomas Dolan, George Philler, William W. Gibbs, Clement A. Griscom, William L. Elkins, Peter A. B. Widener, Samuel T. Bodine.

Main office, Broad and Arch streets, Philadelphia. Annual meeting in May.

## UNITED LIGHTING & HEATING CO.

A corporation formed under the laws of New Jersey, January 5, 1899. The purpose of the company is to manufacture, sell and lease gas and oil machines and other appliances for the production of light, heat and power. The company has street and other lighting contracts.

Stock..Par $100.......Authorized { com., $6,000,000 / pref., 6,000,000 } Issued { com., $6,000,000 / pref., 5,794,800 } $11,794,800

The preferred stock is 6 per cent., non-cumulative. Stock is transferred at the office of the company, Philadelphia. Registrar, The Land Title & Trust Co., Philadelphia.

The company paid its first dividend, 3½ per cent., on the preferred stock, in April, 1901. A dividend of 5 per cent. on the preferred stock was paid April, 1902. Dividends are payable annually, usually in April.

The company has no funded debt.

President, George W. Elkins; Vice-President, William Findlay Brown; Secretary, Arthur E. Shaw; Treasurer, Lewis Lillie; Assistant Treasurer, James Ball, Philadelphia.

Directors—George W. Elkins, William Findlay Brown, Thomas Dolan, Samuel T. Bodine, Randal Morgan, Lewis Lillie, Walton Clark, William L. Elkins, Sidney F. Tyler, M. Ehret, F. W. Hammett, Philadelphia; John M. Devlin, Gloucester, N. J.

Corporate office, Gloucester, N. J.; main office, Broad and Arch streets, Philadelphia. Annual meeting, third Tuesday in April, at Gloucester, N. J.

## UNITED POWER & TRANSPORTATION CO.

A corporation formed under the laws of New Jersey, April 20, 1899. The company is authorized to acquire, construct and operate street railways and electric light and power plants. It acquired a controlling interest in the following companies:

Citizens' Electric Light & Power Co., Delaware County, Pa.
Delaware County & Philadelphia Electric Railway.
Philadelphia & Chester Railway.
Schuylkill Valley Traction Co.
Southwestern Street Railway.
Wilkes-Barre, Dallas & Harvey's Lake Railway.
Edison Electric Illuminating Co., Lebanon, Pa.
Lebanon Valley Street Railway Co.
Holmesburg, Tacony & Frankford Electric Railway Co.
Roxboro, Chestnut Hill & Norristown Railway Co.
Trenton Street Railway.
United Traction Co., Reading, Pa.
Wilkes-Barre & Wyoming Valley Traction Co., Wilkes-Barre.
Wilmington & Chester Traction.
Wilmington (Del.) City Electric Co.

The length of lines owned by the constituent companies is about 425 miles.

Stock......Par $25........................Authorized, $12,500,000......Issued, $3,593,750

Stock is transferred at the office of the company, Philadelphia.

The stock is full paid, the last instalment of $5 per share having been paid in October 1, 1901.

The first dividend on the stock was 50 cents per share, paid in January, 1900. In July, 1900, paid 50 cents; January, 1901, $1; July, 1901, $1; January 20, 1902, $1; July 13, 1902, $1; January 20, 1903, $1.

FUNDED DEBT.

| | |
|---|---|
| United Rys. Trust Cer., 1st series, 4 per cent., due July, 1945, Jan. and July.......... | $7,989,339 |
| United Rys. Trust Cer., 2d series, 4 per cent., due July, 1949, Jan. and July.... ..... | 998,950 |
| Total ........................................................ | $8,988,289 |

FUNDED DEBT CONSTITUENT COMPANIES.

| | |
|---|---|
| Trenton Street Ry., cons. mort., 5 per cent., due July, 1938, Jan. and July........... | $1,000,000 |
| Trenton Pass. Ry., 1st mort., 6 per cent., due 1915-1931, April and Oct............. | 1,000,000 |
| United Tract. Co., Reading, 1st col. mort., 5 per cent., due Jan., 1926, Jan. and July.. | 149,900 |
| Schuylkill Valley Traction, 1st mort., 5 per cent., due Nov., 1945, Feb. and Aug...... | 245,000 |
| Schuylkill Valley Traction income mort., 5 per cent., due Aug., 1949, annual........ | 100,000 |
| Delaware Co. & Phila. Elect. Ry., 1st mort., 6 per cent., due July, 1913, Jan. and July.. | 64,000 |
| Holmesburg, Tacony & F. Elec. Ry., 1st mort., 5 per cent., due May, 1925, May and Nov. | 400,000 |
| Reading & Womelsdorf El. Ry., 1st mort., 5 per cent., due Jan., 1925, Jan. and July.. | 386,000 |
| Reading Traction 1st mort., 6 per cent., due Jan., 1933, Jan. and July............... | 445,000 |
| Reading City Pass. Ry., 1st mort., 5 per cent., due April, 1909, April and Oct........ | 112,000 |
| Reading & Temple, 1st mort., 5 per cent., due 1924, April and Oct.................. | 73,000 |
| Lebanon Valley Street Ry., 1st mort., 5 per cent., due 1929, Jan. and July........... | 500,000 |
| Roxborough, C. H. & Norrist'n Ry., 1st mort., 5 per cent., due June, 1926, June and Dec. | 371,000 |
| Wilkes-Barre & Wyoming Val. T., 1st mort., 5 per cent., due April, 1921, April and Oct. | 1,500,000 |
| Wilkes-Barre & Wyoming col. tr. mort., 5 per cent., due Jan., 1925, Jan. and July... | 317,000 |
| Wilkes-Barre, Dallas & Harvey's Lake Ry., 1st mort., 5 per cent., due Sept., 1925, March and Sept.......................................................... | 150,000 |
| Wilmington & Chester Traction, col. tr., 5 per cent., due April, 1918, April and Oct.. | 2,305,000 |
| Wilmington City Ry., 1st mort., 5 per cent., due 1911, March and Sept............. | 600,000 |
| Union Ry. Co., Chester, 1st mort., 5 per cent., due Jan., 1913, Jan. and July........ | 200,000 |
| Chester Traction Co., 1st mort., 5 per cent., due May, 1914, May and Nov............ | 250,000 |
| Phila. & Chester Ry., 1st mort. 5 per cent., due Nov., 1930, May and Nov........... | 350,000 |
| Southwestern Street Ry., 1st mort., 5 per cent., due 1920, April and Oct............. | 400,000 |
| Citizens' Pass. Ry., 1st mort., 5½ per cent., due Feb., 1955, Feb. and Aug .......... | 80,000 |
| Norristown Pass. Ry., 1st mort., 4½ per cent., due 1923, Jan. and July............ | 75,000 |
| Oley Valley Ry., 1st mort., 4½ per cent., due July, 1931, Jan. and July.............. | 250,000 |
| Pittstown Street Car Co., 1st mort., 6 per cent., due 1918, June and Dec............. | 200,000 |
| Plymouth Branch, 1st mort., 5 per cent., due Oct., 1924, April and Oct.............. | 150,000 |

The United Railways Trust certificates are secured by the deposit of stocks of the constituent companies. The trustee of the 1st series is the New York Security & Trust Co. Trustee of the 2d series, Real Estate Title Insurance & Trust Co., Philadelphia. Interest on both series is paid at the office of the Real Estate Title Insurance & Trust Co., Philadelphia.

There are also outstanding certain small amounts of bonds of the constituent companies.

In the year 1902 the income from securities was $533,09; premium on new stock issued, $187,500; total income for the year, $720,560. Expenses and taxes, $5,396; charges, $359,512; dividends, $268,750; surplus, $86,901. Total surplus, December 31, 1902, $265,954.

President, John A. Rigg; Vice-President, Joseph L. Caven; Secretary and Treasurer, *pro tem.*, Remi Remont.

Main office, 308 Chestnut street, Philadelphia.

---

## UNITED RAILROADS OF SAN FRANCISCO

A corporation formed under the laws of California in 1902. The company was organized to consolidate certain street railways of San Francisco. The following companies were included in the combination:

Market Street Railway Co.
Sutter Street Railway Co.
San Francisco & San Mateo Railway Co.
Sutro Railroad Co.

These companies have an aggregate mileage of 244 miles, of which 56 miles are operated by cable, 176 miles by electric power, 4 miles by horses and 8 miles by steam.

The stocks of the above company were acquired by the United Railways Investment Co. of

San Francisco, a New Jersey corporation with $10,000,000 common and $15,000,000 5 per cent. cumulative preferred stock.

Stock..Par $100..Authorized { com., $20,000,000 / pref., 20,000,000 } Issued { com., $20,000,000 / pref., 20,000,000 } $40,000,000

The preferred stock is 4 per cent., cumulative, and has a preference as to assets.

FUNDED DEBT.

General 1st mort., 4 per cent., due 1927 ........ $20,000,000

FUNDED DEBT OF CONSTITUENT COMPANIES.

| | |
|---|---|
| Market Street Railway Co., cons. mort., 5 per cent., due Sept., 1924, March and Sept. | $6,641,000 |
| Market Street Railway Co., 1st mort., 6 per cent., subject to call | 3,000,000 |
| Omnibus Cable Co., 1st mort., due April, 1918, April and Oct | 2,000,000 |
| Powell Street Railway Co., 1st mort., due March, 1912, March and Sept | 700,000 |
| Ferries & Cliff House Railway Co., 1st mort., due March, 1912, March and Sept | 650,000 |
| Park & Cliff House Railway Co., 1st mort., due Jan., 1913, Jan. and July | 350,000 |
| Park & Ocean Railroad Co., 1st mort., 6 per cent | 250,000 |
| Sutter Street Railway Co., 1st mort., due May, 1908, May and Nov | 1,000,000 |
| Total | $14,591,000 |

The general mortgage is $35,275,000, of which $15,275,000 are reserved to retire prior liens and for improvements.

This company acquired all but $2,620 of the stock of the Sutro Railroad and all the stock of the San Francisco & San Mateo Railway. It acquired $18,341,300 out of $18,617,000 stock of the Market Street Railway and all but $50,000 of the $2,000,000 stock of the Sutter Street Railway.

In the year 1901 the aggregate gross earnings of the constituent companies were $5,125,883; net income, $2,083,155; surplus over charges, $1,275,955.

The organization of the company was financed by Brown Bros. & Co., New York. A part of the arrangement was the furnishing of $1,600,000 cash for immediate improvements, which are under way.

EARNINGS.

| | Gross. | Net. | Charges. | Surplus. |
|---|---|---|---|---|
| 1902 | $5,533,903 | $2,288,680 | $1,438,050 | $850,630 |

President, Arthur Holland; Vice-President, Charles Holbrook; Secretary, George B Willcutt; Treasurer, George E. Starr.

Directors—Antoine Borel, James M. Duane, Isaias W. Hellman, Charles Holbrook, Arthur Holland, Joseph S. Tobin, Alexander B. Williamson, Charles P. Eells, William Alvord.

Corporate and main office, Rialto Building, San Francisco.

## UNITED RAILWAYS & ELECTRIC CO. OF BALTIMORE

A corporation formed in 1899 to consolidate all the street railways of Baltimore, Md. The company acquired the entire capital stock of the Baltimore City Passenger Railway and of the Baltimore Consolidated Railway Co. It also controls of the Baltimore, Sparrow's River & Chesapeake Railway Co.

The United Electric Light & Power Co., comprising all the electric light and power plants of Baltimore, was also acquired by the interests which organized this company, and in November, 1899, this company gave $2,000,000 of its common stock for $1,000,000 of the stock of the United Electric Light & Power Co., but these lighting interests were sold in January, 1903, to a syndicate represented by the Continental Trust Co. of Baltimore for $904,237. Total mileage of railway lines, 359 miles.

Stock..Par $50..Authorized { com., $24,000,000 / pref., 14,000,000 } Issued { com., $15,000,000 / pref., 69,306 } $15,069,306

The preferred stock is 4 per cent., cumulative.

Dividends on the preferred stock were one-half per cent. in June, 1899; 2½ per cent. in December, 1899, and 2 per cent. semi-annually since that time, payments being made in June and December. The dividends on the preferred, but not the interest on the income bonds, are subject to a deduction of one-quarter per cent. for taxes.

Transfer Agent, Maryland Trust Co., Baltimore.

FUNDED DEBT.

| | |
|---|---|
| Consolidated mort., 4 per cent., due 1949, March and Sept | $25,231,000 |
| Income mort., 4 per cent., cumulative, due March, 1949, Jan. and July | 13,934,694 |
| Balt. Traction 1st mort., 5 per cent., due Nov., 1929, May and Nov | 1,500,000 |
| Balt. Traction N. Balt. Div. 1st mort., 5 per cent., due June, 1942, June and Dec | 1,750,000 |
| Balt. Traction convertible bonds, 5 per cent., due May, 1906, May and Nov | 527,000 |
| City & Suburban 1st mort., 5 per cent., due June, 1922, June and Dec | 3,000,000 |

FUNDED DEBT—*Continued.*

| | |
|---|---|
| Balt. & Nor. Electric Ry. 1st mort., 5 per cent., due Nov., 1947 | $139,000 |
| Balt., Catonsville & Ellicott's Mills 1st mort., 5 per cent., due July, 1916, Jan. and July | 500,000 |
| Lake Roland Elev. Ry. 1st. mort., 5 per cent., due Sept., 1942, March and Sept | 1,000,000 |
| Balt. City Pass. Ry. 1st mort., 5 per cent., due 1911, May and Nov | 2,000,000 |
| Balt. City Pass. Ry. certificates of debt, 4½ per cent., due Nov., 1911, May and Nov | 500,000 |
| Central Ry. 1st mort., 6 per cent., due July, 1912, Jan. and July | 41,000 |
| Central Ry. cons. mort., 5 per cent., due May, 1932, May and Nov | 659,000 |
| Central Ry. extension mort., 5 per cent., due March, 1932, March and Sept | 600,000 |
| Total | $51,381,694 |

The income bond issue is $14,000,000, and is cumulative as regards interest. The bonds are payable at the company's option after March, 1949. Nearly all the preferred stock has been exchanged for income bonds. Interest on the income bonds is paid at the office of Alexander Brown & Sons, Baltimore.

The consolidated mortgage is for $38,000,000, of which $12,216,000 are reserved to retire the underlying securities of the City Passenger Railway, the Consolidated Railway and the Baltimore & Northern Railway. Trustee of mortgage, Continental Trust Co., Baltimore. Interest on the bonds is paid at the office of Alexander Brown & Sons, Baltimore.

EARNINGS.

| | Gross. | Net. | Charges. | Surplus. |
|---|---|---|---|---|
| 1901 | $4,718,295 | $2,525,120 | $2,493,001 | $32,119 |
| 1902 | 5,041,275 | 2,789,142 | 2,637,115 | 152,027 |

President, John M. Hood; Vice-President, George C. Jenkins; 2d Vice-President and General Manager, William A. House; Secretary and Treasurer, Harry C. McJilton; Auditor, N. E. Stubbs.

Directors—E. L. Bartlett, H. C. Black, Alexander Brown, John M. Hood, George C. Jenkins, Seymour Mandelbaum, Wesley M. Oler, Henry A. Parr, John B. Ramsey, George R. Webb, Francis E. Waters, Baltimore.

Main office, Baltimore and Calvert streets, Baltimore. Annual meeting, last Wednesday in February.

## UNITED RAILWAYS CO. OF ST. LOUIS

### ST. LOUIS TRANSIT CO.

The St. Louis Transit Co. was formed March 6, 1899, and leased the lines of the United Railway Co. of St. Louis. The United Railway Co. of St. Louis was formerly the Central Traction Co.; in 1899 acquired control of the street railway organizations in St. Louis, except the St. Louis & Suburban, and changed its name to above style.

The companies acquired were the Lindell Railway Co., Missouri Railroad Co., National Railway Co., Union Depot Railroad Co., People's Railway Co. and Southern Electric Railway Co., with their auxiliaries. The total mileage is 360 miles.

Stock..Par $100...Authorized { com., $25,000,000; pref., 20,000,000 } Issued { com., $17,261,300; pref., 16,755,400 } $34,016,700

The preferred stock is 5 per cent., cumulative.

Stock is transferred at the office of the company, St. Louis. Registrar, St. Louis Trust Co., St. Louis.

The St. Louis Transit Co. has $20,000,000 of authorized stock, of which amount $17,264,300 is outstanding.

The St. Louis Transit Co. exchanged its stock for the common stock of the United Railways, the holders of the latter paying $11 per share for the privilege. $17,261,300 of the United Railways' common stock has been exchanged. On the preferred stock of the United Railways the Transit Co. guarantees the payment of the 5 per cent. cumulative dividends. The dividends were paid quarterly, 1¼ per cent. each, in January, April, July and October. The first dividend on the preferred was 1¼ per cent., paid April 10, 1900.

FUNDED DEBT.

| | |
|---|---|
| St. Louis Transit col. notes, 5 per cent., due Nov., 1904, May and Nov | $5,776,000 |
| Jefferson Ave. 1st mort., 5 per cent., due 1905, May and Nov | 277,000 |
| United Railways gen. 1st mort., 4 per cent., due July, 1934, Jan. and July | 28,292,000 |
| Lindell Railway 1st mort., 5 per cent., due Aug., 1911, Feb. and Aug | 1,500,000 |
| Compton H. U. D. & M. T. Co., 1st mort., 6 per cent., due July, 1913, Jan. and July | 1,000,000 |
| Taylor Avenue Railroad 1st mort., 6 per cent., due July, 1913, Jan. and July | 500,000 |
| Cass Avenue & F. G. 1st mort., guar. 5 per cent., due July, 1912, Jan. and July | 1,813,000 |
| Citizens' Railroad 1st mort., 6 per cent., due July, 1907, Jan. and July | 1,500,000 |

Indicate Roads Constructed.
" " Authorized.
City Limits
River des Peres
Watson Road
Gravois
Morgan Ford
Kings Highway
Carondelet Park
Broadway
Eichelberger St.
Nottingham Ave.
Kaiser St.
Flukmag St.
Sharp Ave.
Robert Ave.
Blow St.
Kansas
Insane Asylum
Oak Hill
MISSISSIPPI
MAP OF
ST. LOUIS, MO.
SHOWING THE CITY LINES OF THE
UNITED RAILWAYS COMPANY
OF ST.LOUIS
OPERATED BY THE
ST. LOUIS TRANSIT COMPANY.

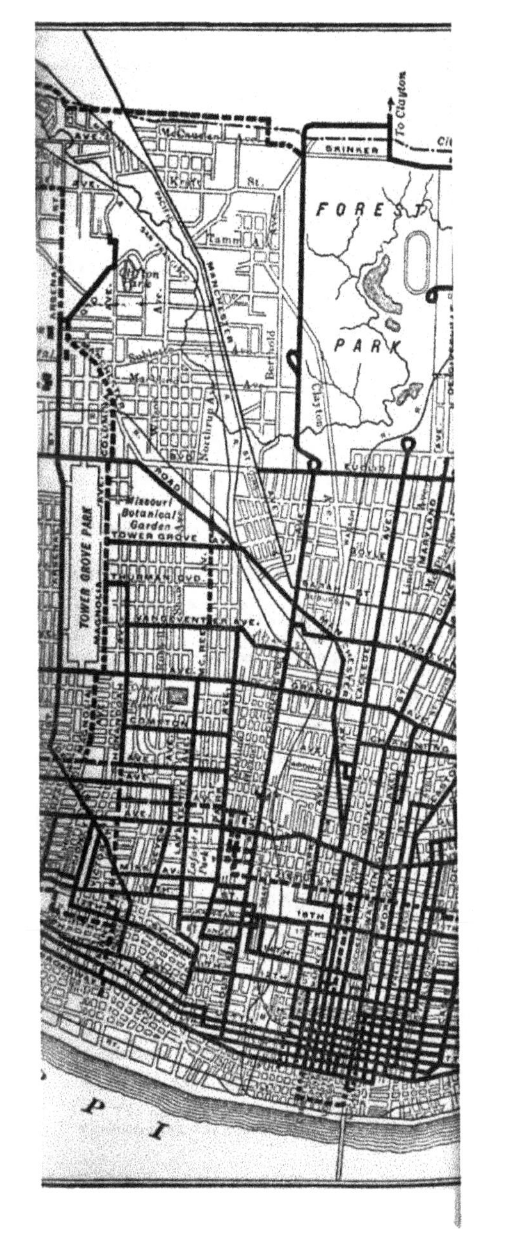
To Clayton
BRINKER
FOREST
PARK
McCausland Ave.
Kraft St.
Tamm Av.
MANCHESTER
Berthold
Clayton
Northrup Av.
TOWER GROVE PARK
Missouri Botanical Garden
TOWER GROVE
THURMAN BVD.
VANDEVENTER AVE.
MARYLAND
GRAND
COMPTON
18TH
P I

FUNDED DEBT—*Continued.*

| | |
|---|---|
| St. Louis Railroad 1st mort. cur., 5 per cent., due May, 1910, call 1900, May and Nov. | $1,948,000 |
| Union Depot Railroad cons. mort., 6 per cent., due June, 1918, June and Dec....... | 3,500,000 |
| Missouri Railroad 1st mort., 5 per cent., due March, 1906, March and Sept.......... | 700,000 |
| Southern Electric 1st mort., 6 per cent., due 1904, March and Nov.................. | 164,000 |
| " " cons. 1st mort., 6 per cent., due 1915, March and Nov............. | 336,000 |
| " " mort., 5 per cent., due Aug., 1916.............................. | 200,000 |
| Baden & St. Louis 1st mort., 5 per cent., due July, 1913, Jan. and July............. | 250,000 |
| Total........................................................................ | $47,756,000 |

The general 1st mortgage is for $45,000,000. Trustee, St. Louis Union Trust Co. Agents for the payment of interest, Brown Brothers & Co., New York and St. Louis Union Trust Co., St. Louis. An amount of $3,000,000 is reserved to acquire the St. Louis & Suburban system, and $13,708,000 is reserved to retire prior liens.

EARNINGS.

| | Gross. | Net. | Charges and Dividends. | Surplus. |
|---|---|---|---|---|
| 1901...................... | $5,777,599 | $2,091,512 | $2,617,142 | Def. $525,630 |
| 1902................. ... | 6,438,788 | 2,484,497 | 2,753,581 | " 268,083 |

The charges include the guaranteed dividends on the preferred stock.

The aggregate number of passengers was, in 1901, 163,995,942, and in 1902, 185,077,940.

President, Murray Carleton; Vice-President, Corwin H. Spencer; 2d Vice-President, A. B. DuPont; Secretary and Treasurer, James Adkins; Auditor, Frank R. Henry.

Directors—James L. Blair, A. D. Brown, James Campbells Murray Carleton, George L. Edwards, F. E. Marshall, H. S. Priest, Corwin H. Spencer, St. Louis; Patrick Calhoun, Eugene Delano, New York; George H. Frazier, Philadelphia.

Main office, St. Louis. Annual meeting, first Monday in March.

## UNITED RAILWAYS INVESTMENT CO. OF SAN FRANCISCO

A corporation formed under the laws of New Jersey, Feb. 17, 1902. The company acquired all the stocks, common and preferred, of the United Railroads of San Francisco, and thus controls and operates the railway system acquired by the latter.

Stock...Par $100... Authorized { com., $10,000,000 / pref., 15,000,000 } Issued { com., $10,000,000 / pref., 15,000,000 } $25,000,00

The preferred stock is 5 per cent., cumulative and is preferred also as to assets. It can be retired at any time after three years from date of issue at 110 and accrued dividends. Transfer Agent, Mercantile Trust Co., New York. Registrar, United States Mortgage & Trust Co., New York.

The first dividend of 1½ per cent. on the preferred stock was paid January 3, 1903.

President—Henry J. Bowdoin, Baltimore, Md.; Vice-President, W. Gerard Vermilye; Secretary and Treasurer, W. J. Duane, New York.

Directors—Henry J. Bowdoin, Baltimore, Md.; W. Gerard Vermilye, Englewood, N. J.; Eugene Delano, Patrick Calhoun, New York; Arthur E. Newbold, Philadelphia, Pa.

Corporate office, 15 Exchange Place, Jersey City; New York office, 59 Wall street. Annual meeting, first Friday in May, at Jersey City.

## UNITED SHOE MACHINERY CO.

A corporation formed under the laws of New Jersey, February 7, 1899. The company is a combination of several large concerns engaged in the manufacture of shoe machinery, among which were the following:

Consolidated & McKay Lasting Machinery Co.
McKay Shoe Machinery Co.
Goodyear Shoe Machinery Co.
Goodyear Shoe Machinery Co. of Canada.
Eppler Welt Machinery Co.
International Eppler Welt Machinery Co.
Davey Pegging Machine Co.

Auxiliary companies have been formed in Canada, Great Britain, France and Germany, known respectively as the United Shoe Machinery Co. of Canada, the British United Shoe Machinery Co., the United Shoe Machinery Co. de France, and the Deutsch Vereinigte Schumaschinen Gesellschaft. A branch office of the company is established in Australia.

Stock...Par $25...Authorized { com., $12,500,000 / pref., 12,500,000 } Issued { com., $10,720,300 / pref., 9,336,450 } $20,056,750

The preferred stock is 6 per cent., cumulative. In April, 1901, $1,829,350 of additional common stock was issued and subscribed for at par by the stockholders.

The International Goodyear Shoe Machinery Co., one of the constituent concerns, has $250,000 of bonds outstanding.

The company began business with a cash working capital of over $500,000.

The company began regular dividends by the payment of ½ per cent. on the preferred and ⅔ per cent. on the common, April 15, 1899. It has since paid regular dividends at the rate of 6 per cent. per annum on the preferred and 8 per cent. on the common. Dividends on both classes of stock are paid quarterly, January (15), April, July and October.

Transfer Agent, American Loan & Trust Co., Boston. Registrar, Old Colony Trust Co., Boston.

President, Sidney W. Winslow, Boston; Vice-Presidents, John H. Hanan, New York; Wallace F. Robinson; Treasurer and General Manager, George W. Brown; Assistant Treasurer, Edward P. Hurd; Secretary, Meylert Bruner, Boston.

Directors—William Barbour, John H. Hanan, John Harsen Rhoades, Samuel Weil, William A. Read, New York; Louis D. Brandeis, George W. Brown, Elmer P. Howe, Edward P. Hurd, Wallace F. Robinson, James J. Storrow, Sidney W. Winslow, Frank Wood, Boston; Joseph C. Kilham, Beverly, Mass.; J. H. Clarke, Worcester, Mass.; George E. Keith, Brockton, Mass.; Rudolph Matz, Chicago; Gordon McKay, Newport, R. I.; Alfred R. Turner, Jr., Paterson, N. J.

Main office, Lincoln and Kneeland streets, Boston. Annual meeting in June.

## UNITED STATES & PORTO RICO NAVIGATION CO.

A corporation formed under the laws of New Jersey in February, 1901, to operate lines of steamships between New York and New Orleans and the ports of Porto Rico. The company acquired the stock and assets of the New York & Porto Rico Steamship Co., including six steamships, wharves, etc.

Stock......Par $100..........................Authorized, $2,000,000......Issued, $2,000,000

The company has no preferred stock. Transfer Agent, George W. Floecke, Jr., 1 Montgomery street, Jersey City.

FUNDED DEBT.

1st mort., 5 per cent. bonds, due March, 1921, March and Sept... .................. $1,335,000

The authorized bond issue is $3,000,000. There is a sinking fund each year of 5 per cent. of the bonds issued.

Trustee of the mortgage and agent for the payment of interest, Continental Trust Co., New York.

President, John E. Berwind; Vice-President, Edward J. Berwind; Secretary, F. Kingsbury Curtis; Treasurer and General Manager, Henry T. Knowlton, New York.

Directors—J. M. Ceballos, Edward J. Berwind, John E. Berwind, F. Kingsbury Curtis, Henry T. Knowlton, Gordon Macdonald, John S. Fiske, Henry P. Booth, Samuel P. Savage.

Corporate office, 1 Montgomery street, Jersey City; main office, 1 Broadway, New York; branch offices, New Orleans and San Juan, Porto Rico. Annual meeting in December, at Jersey City.

## UNITED STATES CAST IRON PIPE & FOUNDRY CO.

A corporation formed under the laws of New Jersey March 13, 1899. The purpose of the organization was to unite the concerns which control the larger part of the cast iron pipe production of the United States. The companies included comprise the following:

Lake Shore Foundry, Cleveland.
McNeal Pipe & Foundry Co., Burlington, N.J.
National Foundry & Pipe Works, Limited, Scottdale, Pa.
Buffalo Cast Iron Pipe Co., Buffalo.
The Ohio Pipe Co., Columbus, O.
Dennis, Long & Co., Louisville.
The Addyston Pipe & Steel Co., Cincinnati, having works at Addyston, O., and Newport, Ky.
American Pipe & Foundry Co., having works at Chattanooga, Tenn.; South Pittsburgh, Tenn.; Bessemer, Ala.; Anniston, Ala., and Bridgeport, Ala.

This company owns the plants of all the concerns enumerated above. The concerns included in this company have a capacity of 450,000 tons per annum out of a total estimated yearly production of 600,000 tons of iron pipe in the United States.

Stock..Par $100..Authorized { com., $15,000,000 / pref., 15,000,000 } Issued { com., $12,500,000 / pref., 12,500,000 } $25,000,000

The preferred stock is 7 per cent., non-cumulative. An amount of $2,500,000 each of preferred and common remains in the treasury of the company for the purchase of additional properties and for contingencies. The company began business with a working capital of $2,000,000.

Transfer Agents, Thomas & Thomas, 71 Broadway, New York. Registrar, Central Trust Co., New York.

The outstanding bonds of the American Pipe & Foundry Co., one of the constituent concerns, are $1,194,000 at 6 per cent., and are provided for by an annual sinking fund for their retirement.

The company began the payment of regular quarterly dividends on the preferred stock with a payment of 1¾ per cent. December 1, 1899, and paid similar dividends in March and June, 1900, but the September, 1900, dividend was passed and none was paid until March 1, 1902, when 1 per cent. was paid on the preferred stock, the same rate on the preferred having since been paid each quarter.

EARNINGS.

Year ending May 31.

| | Gross Profit. | Net. | Dividends, Etc. | Surplus. |
|---|---|---|---|---|
| 1901-02 | $901,949 | $711,184 | $535,890 | $175,294 |

The company's balance sheet May 31, 1902, was as follows:

| ASSETS. | | LIABILITIES. | |
|---|---|---|---|
| Treasury stock | $347,555 | Preferred stock | $15,000,000 |
| Unissued stock | 5,000,000 | Common stock | 15,000,000 |
| Sinking fund | 49,377 | Am. Pipe & F. Co. bonds | 1,500,000 |
| Bonds American Pipe & F. Co. | 306,000 | Anniston mortgage bonds | 87,500 |
| Plant investment | 24,066,167 | Bills and accounts payable | 983,462 |
| Cash | 179,814 | Reserve for addition to working capital | 289,827 |
| Raw and manufactured material | 1,238,372 | Surplus | 671,717 |
| Accounts receivable | 2,345,221 | | |
| Total | $33,532,506 | Total | $33,532,506 |

President, George B. Hayes; 1st Vice-President, George J. Long; 2d Vice-President, A. F. Callahan; Secretary and Treasurer, B. F. Haughton.

Directors—Colgate Hoyt, A. C. Overholt, B. F. Overholt, C. E. Burke, E. C. Fuller, George J. Long, A. F. Callahan, Anthony N. Brady, George B. Hayes, E. R. Thomas, Philip J. Goodhart, David Giles, W. T. C. Carpenter.

Main office, 80 Broadway, New York; Chicago sales office, 217 LaSalle street. Annual meeting, fourth Thursday in June, at Burlington, N. J.

## UNITED STATES COAL & OIL CO.

A corporation formed under the laws of Maine in 1895. The object of the company is operating oil properties in the West Virginia and Ohio oil regions. The company in 1902 acquired the stock and property of the Island Creek Coal Co. It also owns the Island Creek Railroad.

Stock......Par $25..........................Authorized, $6,250,000......Issued, $6,000,000

EARNINGS.

| Year ending September 30. | Gross. | Surplus. |
|---|---|---|
| 1896-97 | $322,021 | $54,801 |
| 1897-98 | 386,523 | 123,927 |
| 1898-99 | 638,162 | 152,132 |
| 1899-00 | 699,079 | 263,861 |
| 1900-01 | 386,151 | 137,930 |
| 1901-02 | 332,245 | 10,370 |

In the year ending September 30, 1900, the company expended $256,296 on construction and improvement work. In 1900-01 it expended $88,806 for the same purpose, and in 1901-02 $167,678.

Up to October 31, 1900, the company had paid $644,250 in dividends. Dividends paid have been in 1897, 6 per cent., 1½ per cent. quarterly; in 1898, 4½ per cent.; in 1899, $3.87½ per share; in 1900, $2.75 per share, being four quarterly payments of 50 cents, with one extra of 75 cents and one of 50 cents. Dividends are quarterly, in January (2), April, July and October. In January, 1901, dividend was passed.

President, Albert F. Holden, Cleveland; Vice-President, Edward R. Andrews; Secretary and Treasurer, F. W. Batchelder, Boston.

Directors—Edward R. Andrews, Edward A. Clark, William H. Coolidge, Benjamin D. Hyde, Boston; F. W. Batchelder, Weston, Mass.; G. Henry Whitcomb, Worcester, Mass.; Henry A. Belcher, Randolph, Mass.; Clarence A. Hight, Portland, Me.; Albert F. Holden, Cleveland; Z. T. Vinson, Huntington, W. Va.

Main office, 4 Post Office square, Boston; corporate office, 36 Exchange street, Portland, Me.; operating office, Parkersburg, W. Va.

## UNITED STATES COTTON DUCK CORPORATION

A corporation formed under the laws of New Jersey, June 4, 1901. The purpose of the company was to acquire the stocks and property of the following concerns engaged in the manufacture of cotton duck:

Mount Vernon-Woodberry Cotton Duck Co.
Stark Mills, Manchester, N. H.
La Grange Mills, La Grange, Ga.
Hogansville Mfg. Co., Hogansville, Ga.

The company also had options running until January 1, 1903, to purchase the properties of the following concerns:

West Point Mfg. Co., West Point, Ga.
Riverdale Cotton Mills, West Point, Ga.
Lanette Bleaching & Dye Works, West Point, Ga.

The three latter, during the term of the option, were operated under contract.

The Mount Vernon-Woodberry Cotton Duck Co. was organized under the laws of Delaware in 1899. A detailed statement is in the MANUAL for 1901.

Stock..Par $100.....Authorized { com., $15,000,000 / pref., 15,000,000 } Issued { com., $10,000,000 / pref., 3,100,000 } $13,100,000

The preferred stock is 6 per cent., cumulative. The outstanding preferred stock included the amount provided for in the plan of consolidation to be exchanged for the Mount Vernon-Woodberry Co.

The amounts of common and preferred stocks authorized under the plan were $25,000,000 each. In January, 1902, it was decided to reduce the amount to $15,000,000 of each class.

Under the plan of consolidation holders of the $9,500,000 stock of the Mount Vernon-Woodberry Co. were offered the right to exchange the same for new common stock in the proportion of two shares of new for three shares of old stock.

Transfer Agent of common stock, Colonial Trust Co., New York. Transfer Agent of preferred stock, Central Trust Co., New York. Registrar of common stock, Central Trust Co., New York. Registrar of preferred stock, Merchants' Trust Co., New York.

A dividend of 3 per cent. was paid on the preferred stock on September 15, 1902.

FUNDED DEBT.

| | |
|---|---|
| Mount Vernon-Woodberry 1st mort., 5 per cent., due Sept., 1949, March and Sept... | $8,000,000 |
| Mount Vernon-Woodberry incomes, 5 p. c., cumulative, due Jan., 1950, Jan. and July. | 6,000,000 |
| Total........ | $14,000,000 |

No interest was paid in January, 1902, on the Mount Vernon-Woodberry incomes. In August, 1902, 2½ per cent. was paid on the bonds in question.

Holders of the bonds of the Mount Vernon-Woodberry Co. were invited to exchange them for preferred stock of the new company, the first mortgage bonds at par and the incomes at 83⅓. This exchange, however, was optional with the bondholders and was not generally accepted by them.

It was stated that the consolidated companies control 400,000 spindles and produce most of both the heavy and light duck made in the United States.

In the ten months ending April 30, 1902, the company reported net earnings, $231,332; charges and expenses, $53,601; dividend on preferred stock, $82,500; surplus, $95,231.

Chairman, S. Davies Warfield; President, Charles K. Oliver, Baltimore; Vice-Presidents, J. Spencer Turner, New York; W. H. Wellington, Boston; Vice-President and Treasurer, H. L. Smith; Assistant Secretary, John R. Dorsey, Baltimore.

Directors—S. Davies Warfield, James E. Hooper, David H. Carroll, Charles K. Oliver, William E. P. Duvall, Thomas J. Hayward, Harry A. Parr, Hugh L. Bond, Jr., J. William Middendorf, J. Southgate Lemmon, John R. Dorsey, Baltimore; Trenor L. Park, E. A. Brinckerhoff, J. Spencer Turner, S. M. Lehman, T. M. Turner, New York; William H. Wellington, Horace S. Sears, Boston; F. P. Carpenter, Manchester, N. H.; Robert S. Green, Elizabeth, N. J.; J. E. Dunson, J. M. Barnard, La Grange, Ga.

Main office, Calvert and German streets, Baltimore. Annual meeting, first Wednesday after second Monday in February, at Jersey City.

## UNITED STATES ENVELOPE CO.

A corporation formed under the laws of Maine in 1898. The company was a combination of the ten concerns which manufacture 90 per cent. of the envelopes made in the United States. The concerns included were the following:

Logan, Swift & Brigham Envelope Co., Worcester, Mass.
United States Envelope Co., Holyoke, Mass.
White, Corbin & Co., Rockville, Conn.
Plimpton Manufacturing Co., Hartford, Conn.
Morgan Envelope Co., Springfield, Mass.
National Envelope Co., Milwaukee, Wis.
P. P. Kellogg & Co., Springfield, Mass.
Whitcomb Envelope Co., Worcester, Mass.
W. H. Hill Envelope Co., Worcester, Mass.
Springfield Envelope Co., Springfield, Mass.

Stock...Par $100...Authorized { com., $1,000,000 / pref., 4,000,000 } Issued { com., $750,000 / pref., 3,750,000 } $4,500,000

The preferred stock is 7 per cent., cumulative.

Transfer Agents, Old Colony Trust Co., Boston; Northern Trust Co., New York. Registrars, American Loan & Trust Co., Boston; Bowling Green Trust Co., New York.

In 1898 the company commenced the payment of dividends at the rate of 7 per cent. per annum on the preferred stock. Dividends on the preferred were paid quarterly, in March (1), June, September and December. Action on the December, 1901, dividend was, however, deferred, and a half-yearly dividend of 2½ per cent., payable March 1, 1902, was declared, which was also the rate paid in September, 1902, and March, 1903.

FUNDED DEBT.

| | |
|---|---|
| 1st mort., 6 per cent., due Aug., 1918, Jan. and July | $2,000,000 |
| Debentures, 5 per cent., due Feb., 1904-12, Feb. and Aug. | 225,000 |
| Total | $2,225,000 |

The 1st mortgage is $2,000,000, authorized, and is secured by a mortgage upon the various plants. Bonds are redeemable after ten years from date of issue in 1898 at 104. A sinking fund of $75,000 per annum began July 1, 1899.

The debentures were issued in 1902 and are payable at 101 at the rate of $25,000 per annum, beginning in 1907.

Trustee and Registrar of bonds, Old Colony Trust Co., Boston.

President, C. H. Hutchins; Vice-Presidents, James Logan, Worcester, Mass.; William H. Prescott, Rockville, Conn.; Treasurer, Robert W. Day; Secretary and Assistant Treasurer, W. M. Wharfield, Springfield, Mass.

Directors—C. H. Hutchins, James Logan, G. Henry Whitcomb, Charles W. Gray, D. Wheeler Swift, Worcester, Mass.; William H. Prescott, Rockville, Conn.; L. B. Plimpton, Hartford; Charles L. Long, Robert W. Day, William O. Day, Frederick T. Kellogg, F. A. Bill, Springfield, Mass.; Felix Rackemann, Boston.

Main office, Hillman and Dwight streets, Springfield, Mass. Annual meeting, first Friday in September, at Portland Me.

## UNITED STATES EXPRESS CO.

An unincorporated association formed under laws of New York in 1854. It operates an express service under contracts over about 30,000 miles of railroads in the United States.

Stock......Par $100 ......Authorized, $10,000,000......Issued, $10,000,000

In September, 1887, company acquired the express business of Baltimore & Ohio Railroad Co., and increased its share capital $3,000,000 to pay for same.

No dividends were paid from November, 1891, until November, 1892, nor were any declared from November, 1894, until May, 1896, when 1½ per cent. was paid. In 1896 3 per cent. was paid on the stock; in 1897, 3 per cent.; in 1898, 3 per cent.; in 1899, 3 per cent.; in 1900, 3 per cent. The November, 1901, dividend was increased to 2 per cent., making 3½ per cent. for the year 1901. In 1902 4 per cent. was paid on the stock. Dividends are semi-annual, May (15) and November.

President, Thomas C. Platt; Vice-President, Secretary and General Manager, C. H. Crosby; Treasurer, Edward T. Platt, New York.

Directors—Thomas C. Platt, F. H. Platt, C. H. Crosby, Levi C. Weir, James C. Fargo, Francis Lynde Stetson, New York; Dan P. Eells, Cleveland.

Main office, 49 Broadway, New York.

## UNITED STATES FINISHING CO.

A corporation formed under the laws of New Jersey, July 1, 1899. The company has establishments at Norwich, Conn., Pawtucket, R. I., and Passaic, N. J. The capacity of the works per day is, bleaching, 80 tons; dyeing, 12,000 pieces; printing, 40 machines. In 1901 control of the Sterling Dyeing & Finishing Co. was acquired. This plant has a capacity of 2,000 pieces per day.

Stock...Par $100...Authorized { com., $1,000,000 / pref., 2,000,000 } Issued { com., $1,000,000 / pref., 2,000,000 } $3,000,000

The preferred stock is 7 per cent., cumulative. Transfer Agent, Bowling Green Trust Co., New York; Registrar, North American Trust Co., New York.

Dividends on the preferred stock at the rate of 7 per cent. per annum are paid quarterly, in January, April, July and October.

FUNDED DEBT.

1st mort., gold, 5 per cent., sinking fund, due 1919, Jan. and July....................$1,750,000

The bonds are secured by a mortgage of the company's property to the Old Colony Trust

Co., Boston. After 1909 they can be retired at 104 and interest at the option of the company. A sinking fund of $50,000 per annum is provided for after July 1, 1901. This sum to be appropriated from the earnings after interest is paid on the bonds and dividends on the preferred stock, but before any dividends for the year are paid on the common stock.

President and General Manager, Joseph H. Wright; Vice-President, Charles Bard; Secretary and Treasurer, J. Hunt Smith; Assistant Treasurer, E. M. Childs; Assistant Secretary, A. S. Bard.

Directors—Peter Reid, Passaic, N. J.; Andrew G. Pierce, New Bedford, Mass.; Joseph H. Wright, New York; J. Hunt Smith, Charles Bard, Norwich, Conn.; James Bryce, Passaic, N. J.

New York office, 320 Broadway; corporate office, 525 Main street, East Orange, N. J. Annual meeting, third Thursday in October.

## UNITED STATES GLASS CO.

A corporation formed under the laws of Pennsylvania, February 12, 1891. The company manufactures pressed and blown glassware of all kinds. It has extensive plants at Pittsburg, Wheeling, Steubenville, O.; Greensburg, Pa.; Findlay, O.; Tiffin, O., and Gas City, Ind.

Stock...Par $100. .Authorized { com., $4,000,000 / pref., 1,000,000 } Issued { com., $3,458,100 / pref., 690,000 } $4,148,100

The preferred stock is 8 per cent., cumulative.

Stock is transfered at the company's office. Registrar, Fidelity Title & Trust Co., Pittsburg.

Dividends on the preferred are half yearly, in March and September. There are about 50 per cent. of accumulated past due dividends on the preferred.

In the year ending June 30, 1902, the net profits of the company were stated to have been about $106,000.

President, Daniel C. Ripley; Vice-President and General Manager, M. M. Anderson; Secretary and Treasurer, William C. King; Assistant Secretary, Ernest Nichol, Pittsburg.

Directors—Daniel C. Ripley, William C. King, Marion C. Bryce, A. L. Brahm, John S. Craig, H. D. W. English, W. J. Crawford, M. M. Anderson, C. H. Schaefer.

Main office, Ninth and Bingham streets, Pittsburg. Annual meeting, third Wednesday in August.

## UNITED STATES GYPSUM CO.

A corporation formed under the laws of New Jersey, December 27, 1901, for the purpose of consolidating the principal gypsum-producing companies of the country. The company acquired the following companies:

The Alabaster Co., Alabaster, Mich.
Durr Plaster Co., Granville, Mich.
Durr Mixing Plant, Granville, Mich.
Midland Plaster Co., Grand Rapids, Mich.
O. B. English Plaster Co., Oakfield, N. Y.
The English Plaster Works, Oakfield, N. Y.
Genesee Stucco Works, Oakfield, N. Y.
Big Four Plaster Co., Oakfield, N. Y.
The Alabaster Co., Chicago.
The Rock Plaster Co., Chicago.
Lieno Wall Finish Co., Chicago.
C. F. Duncombe, Springfield, Ill.
Adamant Mfg. Co., Milwaukee.
Adamant Mfg. Co., West Superior, Wis.
Adamant Mfg. Co., Minneapolis.
Ohio Adamant Co., Cleveland.
Granite Wall Plaster Co., Port Clinton, O.
Granite Wall Plaster Co., Pittsburg.
Granite Wall Plaster Co., Sandusky, O.
Marsh & Co., Sandusky, O.
Buffalo Mortar Works, Buffalo.
Diamond Wall Plaster Co., Indianapolis.
A. J. Baker & Co., Evansville, Ind.
Zenith Wall, Plaster & Finish Co., South St. Paul, Minn.
Cementico Wall Finish Co., St. Paul.
Baker Plaster Co., Omaha.
Wymore Plaster Co., Wymore, Neb.
Blue Valley Plaster Co., Blue Valley, Kan.
Blue Rapids Plaster Co., Blue Rapids, Kan.
Kansas Cement & Plaster Co., Hope, Kan.
Iowa Plaster Association (three mills) Fort Dodge, Ia.
Duncombe Stucco Co., Fort Dodge, Ia.
Carbon Plaster Co., Fort Dodge, Ia.
Okarche Cement & Plaster Co., Okarche, O.T.

Stock....Par $100.....Authorized { com., $3,000,000 / pref., 4,500,000 } Issued { com., $3,000,000 / pref., 4,500,000 } $7,500,000

The preferred stock is 7 per cent., cumulative.

Transfer Agent, North American Trust Co., New York. Registrar, Corporation Trust Co. of New Jersey, at Jersey City.

FUNDED DEBT.

1st mort., 5 per cent., due Sept., 1922, March and Sept ..... ..................... $1,000,000

The 1st mortgage was created in 1902. Trustee, Federal Trust & Savings Co., Chicago.

President, Benjamin W. McCausland; Vice-President, S. O. Fulton, Chicago; Treasurer, Emil Durr, Milwaukee; Secretary, John C. Burch, Chicago; General Counsel, Albert N. Eastman, Chicago.

Directors—W. A. Avery, S. L. Avery, Hewitt Boice, Charles B. Brown, J. C. Burch, N. J. Berkley, J. L. Baker, F. S. Culver, R. W. Crawford, Emil Durr, C. F. Duncombe, George D. Emery, O. B. English, P. A. English, A. E. English, S. Q. Fulton, Percival S. Jones, B. W. McCausland, S. T. Meservey, C. G. Root, George S. Ringland.

Corporate office, Jersey City; main office, 184 La Salle street, Chicago; branch offices, Buffalo, Fort Dodge, Ia., Omaha.

Annual meeting, third Tuesday in January, at Jersey City.

## THE UNITED STATES LEATHER CO.

A corporation formed under the laws of New Jersey, February 25, 1893. It acquired the properties of a large number of companies and firms engaged in the manufacture of leather. The property consists of real estate, tanneries, bark lands, hides, bark, etc. In 1900 acquired the Shaw tanneries in Wisconsin and elsewhere.

Stock..Par $100..Authorized { com., $64,000,000 / pref., 64,000,000 } Issued { com., $62,882,300 / pref., 62,282,300 } $125,164,600

The preferred stock is entitled to 8 per cent. cumulative dividends.

The amount of stock originally authorized was $60,000,000 each of preferred and common. In July, 1895, an increase of $4,000,000 in each class was authorized to provide for purchase of bark lands, etc.

Stock is transferred at the company's office, 26 Ferry street, New York. Registrar, Central Trust Co., New York.

During 1895 6 per cent. was paid on preferred, and in 1896 1 per cent. In 1897 4 per cent. was paid on preferred, and in 1898 4¾ per cent. In April, 1898, dividend was increased from 1 to 1¼ per cent. In 1899 5 per cent. was paid on the preferred. In 1900, 1901 and 1902 6 per cent. was paid. The amount of dividends overdue on the preferred, January 1, 1902, was about 35 per cent. Dividends on the preferred are quarterly, in January (1), April, July and October.

FUNDED DEBT.

Debentures, 6 per cent., due May, 1913, May and Nov. .......... $5,280,000

The issue of debentures was to provide the company with working capital. The bonds are subject to redemption by a sinking fund of 4 per cent. annually, and bonds can be drawn for it at 110.

Report for year ending December 31, 1898, gave profits, $2,619,698; quick assets, $30,738,309, and surplus, $4,027,944. The report for 1899 gave profits, $3,940,243; surplus, $4,855,487. In 1900, surplus, $4,540,870.

The following is the company's balance sheet, December 31, 1902:

| ASSETS. | | LIABILITIES. | | |
|---|---|---|---|---|
| Cash | $1,616,115 | Accrued interest | | $58,530 |
| Due by customers | 5,930,736 | Current accounts | | 328,412 |
| Bills receivable | 90,629 | Bills payable | | 1,557,392 |
| Doubtful debtors, valued at | 16,474 | Exchange, not due | | 1,798,371 |
| Sundry other debtors and book accounts | 117,413 | Bonds | $6,680,000 | |
| | | Less in treasury | 1,400,000 | |
| Hides and leather on hand and in process of tanning | 10,810,369 | | | 5,280,000 |
| Drawbacks due | 462,201 | Reserved for fire insurance | | 383,380 |
| Bark at tanneries | 1,282,097 | Preferred stock | | 62,282,300 |
| Sundry personal property | 291,603 | Common stock | | 62,882,300 |
| Advances to other companies | 14,521,553 | Surplus, January 1, 1903 | | 6,486,325 |
| Tannery plants and lands | 7,197,600 | | | |
| Stock of other companies | 35,678,045 | | | |
| Railroad mortgage | 100,000 | | | |
| Treasury stock | 100,000 | | | |
| Unexpired insurance policies | 9,875 | | | |
| Good wills account and organization expenses | 62,832,300 | | | |
| Total | $141,057,010 | Total | | $141,057,010 |

President, Edward C. Hoyt; Vice-Presidents, A. Augustus Healy, New York; Walter G. Garritt, Boston; John J. Lapham; Treasurer, James R. Plum; Secretary, Josiah T. Tubby, New York.

Directors—James Horton, Edward R. Ladew, James R. Plum, Patrick C. Costello, Jerry Crary, Lewis H. Lapham, Oscar B. Grant, John J. Lapham, Lyman F. Rhoads, Josiah T. Tubby, Samuel P. Davidge, Walter G. Garritt, William H. Humphrey, C. Sumner Horton, A. Augustus Healy, Charles H. Lee, Daniel T. Stevens, George W. Childs, Frank H. Goodyear,

Joseph H. Ladew, George A. Vail, Edward C. Hoyt, Loring R. Gale, James H. Proctor, Edson G. Davidge, Eugene Horton, Theodore R. Hoyt.

Main office, 26 Ferry street, New York. Annual meeting, fourth Wednesday in February, at Jersey City.

## UNITED STATES MINING CO.

A corporation formed under the laws of Maine in 1899. The company acquired the Jordan and Galena copper mines at Bingham, Salt Lake County, Utah, which had been operated for over thirty years, together with the Galena Telegraph and other properties adjoining it, the whole tract being traversed by theHighland Boy and other valuable veins, and contains bodies of high-grade ore. Development work on an extensive scale has been in progress, and a 1,500-ton smelter was completed in November, 1902.

Stock......Par $25..........................Authorized, $6,250,000........Issued, $6,250,000

The stock is full-paid and non-assessable. Stock is transferred at the company's office. Registrar, National Shawmut Bank, Boston.

A large majority of the outstanding stock was, in 1900, deposited with Robert D. Evans and Sidney W. Winslow, trustees, under a voting trust arrangement which expired in March, 1903, and the certificates issued by the Old Colony Trust Co., Boston, representi g the stock so deposited, were then exchanged for regular stock certificates of the company.

FUNDED DEBT.

1st mort., convertible 7 per cent., due 1909. 40 per cent. paid in...................... $320,000

The 1st mortgage is secured by all the company's property. Trustee, American Loan & Trust Co., Boston. The amount of bonds authorized was $1,000,000. It was stated when the bonds were issued in March, 1900, that a fund sufficient to provide for the interest payments for two years had been deposited with the trust company.

The bond issue was created in pursuance of a plan submitted by a stockholders' committee, Charles C. Jackson, chairman, which submitted a report in February, 1900. Under the plan stockholders were given the right to subscribe at par for $500 of the bonds for each 133 shares of stock. Payments on subscriptions for the bonds were to be made 10 per cent. monthly, beginning March 1, 1900. It was further provided that subscribers for the bonds should receive stock of the company to an amount equal to their subscriptions, the stock being taken from an amount of $925,000 of the outstanding stock held in the treasury. Up to December, 1901, only 40 per cent. had been paid in on the $800,000 of bonds subscribed for, and it was decided to issue stock at $15 per share, in place of the remainder of the bond subscriptions.

A sinking fund of 5 per cent. per annum for the bonds begins in 1903. At maturity the bonds may be extended for five years longer, at the holders' option, or may be exchanged for stock at or before maturity, subject, however, to the right of the company to retire them or any part thereof at any time at 105 and interest.

From January 1, 1900, to the end of 1902, $1,706,164 had been expended on the property, of which $813,177 was for the purchase of additional property.

President, Robert D. Evans; Secretary and Treasurer, F. W. Batchelder, Boston; Managing Director, Albert F. Holden, Bingham, Utah.

Directors—Robert D. Evans, Stillman F. Kelley, W. F. Bentinck-Smith, H. F. Winslow, R. A. Parker; William H. Coolidge, Boston; Albert F. Holden, Cleveland; C. A. Hight, Portland, Me; F. W. Batchelder, Weston, Mass.

Main office, 4 Post Office square, Boston; Western office, Salt Lake City, Utah.

## UNITED STATES PLAYING CARD CO.

A corporation formed under the laws of New Jersey in 1894. The object of the company is the manufacture of playing cards and similar merchandise. It acquired the portion of the property and plant of the United States Printing Co., which prior to 1894 was devoted to such purposes.

Stock......Par $100..........................Authorized, $3,600,000......Issued, $3,001,200

Transfer Agent, Corporation Trust Co. of New Jersey, Jersey City.

Since 1896, inclusive, 4 per cent. per annum has been paid on the stock, dividends being 1 per cent. quarterly, in January, April, July and October. The January, 1903, dividend was 1½ per cent.

The company has no preferred stock and no funded debt or floating indebtedness.

President, John Omwake; Vice-President and Treasurer, Robert J. Morgan, Cincinnati; Secretary, R. H. McCutcheon, New York.

Directors—J. C. Armstrong, William R. Polson, Cincinnati; George D. Seih, New York; John Hoge, Zanesville, O.; Robert J. Morgan, John Omwake, S. J. Murray, John F. Robinson, Cincinnati; R. H. McCutcheon, New York.

Main offices, 683 Broadway, New York; Norwood, Cincinnati. Annual meeting, fourth Wednesday in January, at Jersey City.

## THE UNITED STATES PRINTING CO.

A corporation formed under the laws of Ohio, February 1, 1891. The business of the company is color printing and manufacturing of labels, folding boxes, advertising novelties, etc. The company has a six-story printing plant, known as Factory No. 2, at Brooklyn, N. Y.; a seven-story and a six-story printing plants, known as Factories No. 4 and No. 1, at Cincinnati, and a paper plant known as Factory No. 3, at Montclair, N. J. The value of their annual output is about $2,250,000.

Stock......Par $100..........................Authorized, $3,500,000......Issued, $3,376,300

Transfer Agent and Registrar, Central Trust & Safe Deposit Co., Cincinnati.
The company has no bonds or any funded or floating debt beyond current bills.
The quick assets of the company in cash, manufactured stock and bills and accounts receivable are usually from $600,000 to $750,000.
The company has earned in the past nine years about 8 per cent. per annum. Dividends have averaged 5 per cent. per annum. Dividends were 1½ per cent. quarterly, or 6 per cent. per annum, January (15), April, July and October. The April, 1902, dividend, however, was reduced to 1 per cent., or 4 per cent. per annum.
President, John Omwake, Cincinnati; 1st Vice-President, P. F. Downey; 2d Vice-President, George Dan Seib, Brooklyn, N. Y.; 3d Vice-President, Robert J. Morgan; Secretary, Robert W. Doughty, Cincinnati; Treasurer, William R. Polson, Brooklyn, N. Y.; Assistant Treasurer, E. F. Reardon, Cincinnati.
Directors—J. F. Robinson, James C. Armstrong, John Omwake, R. H. McCutcheon, Robert J. Morgan, Robert W. Doughty, S. J. Murray, E. F. Reardon, Cincinnati; William R. Polson, Joseph E. Hinds, Brooklyn, N. Y; George Dan Seib, Richmond Hill, N. Y.; P. F. Downey, New York; John Hoge, Zanesville, O.: W. A. Daniels, Chicago.
Main office, 5th and Lock streets, Cincinnati; New York office, 290 Broadway. Annual meeting, third Wednesday in February, at Cincinnati.

---

## UNITED STATES REALTY & CONSTRUCTION CO.

A corporation formed under the laws of New Jersey, August 2, 1902. The purpose of the company is to deal in real estate and engage in the business of building construction. The company acquired a majority of the stock of the following companies:

George A. Fuller Co. New York Realty Corporation.

The company also acquired in fee several real estate properties in New York city from the Central Realty Bond & Trust Co. and stocks from the Plaza Realty Co.

Stock..Par $100..Authorized { com., $36,000,000; pref., 30,000,000 } Issued { com., $33,198,000; pref., 27,011,100 } $60,209,100

The preferred stock is 6 per cent., cumulative. Transfer Agents, Central Realty Bond & Trust Co., New York, and The Corporation Trust Co., New Jersey. Registrar, Equitable Trust Co, New York.
The company has no funded debt.
President, Bradish Johnson; Chairman Board of Directors, Harry S. Black; Chairman Executive Committee, James Stillman; Vice-Presidents, Albert Flake, Robert E. Dowling, S. P. McConnell; Treasurer, Byron M. Fellows; Secretary and Counsel, R. G. Babbage; Assistant Treasurer, Morris B. Mead.
Executive Committee—James Stillman, Harry S. Black, Charles M. Schwab, Albert Flake, Robert E. Dowling, Hugh J. Grant, Henry Morgenthau.
Directors—James Stillman, Charles M. Schwab, James H. Hyde, Harry S. Black, Albert Flake, Robert E. Dowling, Hugh J. Grant, Henry Morgenthau, James Speyer, Bradish Johnson, William H. McIntyre, Charles H. Tweed, Augustus D. Juilliard, G. G. Haven, Henry Budge, George C. Clarke, Charles F. Hoffmann, Cornelius Vanderbilt, John W. Gates, B. Aymar Sands, S. P. McConnell, Edmund C. Converse, New York; P. Anderson Valentine, Chicago; Henry L. Higginson, Charles Francis Adams, Boston; Kenneth K. MacLaren, Jersey City.
Corporate office, 15 Exchange place, Jersey City; New York office, 137 Broadway. Annual meeting, first Tuesday in July, at Jersey City.

---

## UNITED STATES REDUCTION AND REFINING CO.

A corporation formed under the laws of New Jersey, May 31, 1901. The business of the company is the extraction of gold and other precious metals from ore obtained chiefly from the

Cripple Creek District, Colorado, from Deadwood, S. D., Arizona and New Mexico. The company acquired and owns the following properties:

The Standard Milling and Smelting Co., Colorado City.
The Colorado-Philadelphia Reduction Co., Colorado City.
The Union Gold Extraction Co., Florence, Col.
The Metallic Extraction Co., Florence, Col.
The National Gold Extraction Co., Florence, Col.
Also Ore Sampling Plant of the National Gold Extraction Co., Cripple Creek, Col.
United States Smelting Co., Canon City, Col.

These plants occupy 261 acres and have a monthly capacity of 50,000 tons. The company is not engaged in mining, but has ore contracts which ensure a supply of ore for its plants for two years. The annual output of gold bullion is from $7,000,000 to $9,000,000.

Stock....Par $100....Authorized { com., $6,000,000 / pref., 4,000,000 } Issued { com., $5,918,800 / pref., 3,945,800 } $9,864,600

The preferred stock is 6 per cent., non-cumulative. It has a preference as to the company's assets. Transfer Agents, Kessler & Co., 54 Wall street, New York. Registrar, Continental Trust Co., New York.

The company paid its first quarterly dividend of 1½ per cent. on the preferred stock January 1, 1902, and has since paid at the same rate quarterly, in January, April, July and October.

The first dividend on the common was 1 per cent. quarterly in April, 1902, and dividends of the same amount have since been paid in January, April, July and October.

FUNDED DEBT.

1st mort., 6 per cent., due July, 1931, Jan. and July.................................. $3,000,000

The 1st mortgage is $3,000,000, authorized. Trustee, Continental Trust Co., New York. The bonds are a first lien on all the property owned by the company when the mortgage was created or thereafter acquired. The company sold $500,000 of the bonds to furnish it with a working capital of $500,000. There is a sinking fund of $50,000 per annum and bonds can be drawn at 110, at which figure the bonds can all be retired at any regular interest period after July 1, 1902.

President, Charles L. Tutt; 1st Vice-President and Manager, Charles M. MacNeill, Colorado Springs, Col.; 2d Vice-President, W. K. Gillett, New York; Secretary-Treasurer, Spencer Penrose, Colorado Springs, Col.; Assistant Secretary, J. P. Cobb, New York.

Directors—J. A. Hayes, Charles L. Tutt, Charles M. MacNeill, Spencer Penrose, Colorado Springs, Col.; W. K. Gillett, Rudolph E. F. Flinsch, New York; Kenneth K. MacLaren, Jersey City.

Corporate office, 15 Exchange place, Jersey City; main office, Colorado Springs, Col.; New York office, 54 Wall street. Annual meeting, fourth Wednesday in September, at Jersey City.

---

## UNITED STATES RUBBER CO.

A corporation formed under the laws of New Jersey in April, 1892. Its object is the manufacture of rubber goods, principally boots and shoes. The property of the following concerns was acquired by the company:

American Rubber Co., Boston.
Boston Rubber Co., Boston.
Boston Rubber Shoe Co., Boston.
L. Candee & Co., New Haven, Conn.
Goodyear Metallic Rubber Shoe Co., Naugatuck, Conn.
Goodyear India Rubber Glove Manufacturing Co., Naugatuck, Conn.
Lycoming Rubber Co., Williamsport, Pa.
Meyer Rubber Co., New Brunswick, N. J.
National India Rubber Co., Bristol, R. I.
New Brunswick Rubber Co., New Brunswick, N. J.
New Jersey Rubber Shoe Co., New Brunswick, N. J.
Para Rubber Shoe Co., Boston.
Woonsocket Rubber Co.

Stock..Par $100...Authorized { com., $25,000,000 / pref., 25,000,000 } Issued { com., $23,666,000 / pref., 23,525,500 } $47,191,500

The preferred stock is 8 per cent., non-cumulative.

Stock is transferred at the company's office, 9 Murray street, New York.

The company has paid from 1893 to 1900, inclusive, 8 per cent. per annum on its preferred stock, except in 1897, when 6 per cent. was paid. In January, 1901, the quarterly dividend on the preferred was reduced from 2 to 1 per cent., and no further dividends have been paid since that date. Preferred dividends were quarterly, January (31), April, July and October.

In March, 1895, 2½ per cent. was paid on the common stock, being the only dividend on common to that date. In December, 1896, 2 per cent. more was declared on common, payable February

15, 1897. In July, 1899, 1 per cent. was paid on the common. Three more quarterly dividends of 1 per cent. each on the common were paid, October, 1899, January, 1900, and April 30, 1900, but the July, 1900, dividend was passed and no dividends have since been paid on the common.

FUNDED DEBT.

1st mort., 5 per cent. gold notes, due March, 1905, March (15) and Sept............. $12,000,000

The gold notes were created in March, 1902, their purpose being to fund floating indebtedness of the constituent companies. The notes may be redeemed at the company's office on any interest date.

EARNINGS.

Year ending March 31.

| | Gross Income. | Net. | Dividends. | Surplus. |
|---|---|---|---|---|
| 1894-95 | $2,930,243 | $2,716,370 | $2,056,190 | $660,180 |
| 1895-96 | 2,632,939 | 2,339,791 | 1,552,040 | 787,751 |
| 1896-97 | 2,243,434 | 1,999,612 | 1,955,360 | 44,252 |
| 1897-98 | 2,256,324 | 2,070,751 | 1,552,040 | 518,711 |
| 1898-99 | 3,416,380 | 3,226,513 | 1,882,040 | 1,344,474 |
| 1899-00 | 3,233,773 | 3,007,887 | 2,828,680 | 1 70, 207 |
| 1900-01 | 265,622 | 62,606 | 705,765 | Def., 643,159 |
| 1901-02 | 58,380 | Def., 418,109 | ........ | " 418, 09 |

The following is the company's balance sheets March 31, 1902:

| ASSETS. | | LIABILITIES. | |
|---|---|---|---|
| Cash | $1,418,973 | Preferred stock | $23,525,500 |
| Notes and accounts receivable | 4,919,295 | Common stock | 23,666,000 |
| Merchandise on hand | 1,137,634 | Accounts payable | 419,188 |
| Property, plant and investments | 48,645,770 | Due companies | 3,435,198 |
| Deficit | 1,110,344 | Bills payable | 3,345,000 |
| | | Loans payable | 2,780,356 |
| | | Rebates, not due | 60,774 |
| Total | $57,232,016 | Total | $57,232,016 |

President, Samuel P. Colt, New York; Vice-President, Costello C. Converse; 2d Vice-President, Lester Leland, Boston; Treasurer, James B. Ford,; Secretary, Samuel Norris, Jr.; Assistant Treasurer, H. M. Sadler, Jr.; 2d Assistant Treasurer, John J. Watson, Jr., New York.

Directors—Samuel P. Colt, Providence; E. S. Converse, H. E. Converse, Lester Leland, Costello C. Converse, Boston; James B. Ford, J. Howard Ford, John D. Vermeule, Frederick C. Sayles, Francis Lynde Stetson, Francis L. Hine, Middleton S. Burrell, E. C. Benedict, New York; Henry L. Hotchkiss, Frederick M. Shepard, Orange, N. J.

Main office, 9 Murray street, New York. Annual meeting, third Tuesday in May, at New Brunswick, N. J.

---

## UNITED STATES SHIPBUILDING CO.

A corporation formed under the laws of New Jersey, June 17, 1902, to construct ships and engines and manufacture armor-plate, guns and other iron and steel products. The company has acquired the following properties:

Bath Iron Works, Bath, Me.
Eastern Shipbuilding Co., New London, Ct.
Samuel L. Moore & Sons Co., Elizabethport, N. J.
Bethlehem Steel Co., South Bethlehem, Pa.
Canada Manufacturing Co., Carteret, N. J.
Hyde Windlass Co., Bath, Me.
Crescent Ship Yard Co., Elizabethport, N. J.
Harlan & Hollingsworth Co., Wilmington, Del.
Union Iron Works, San Francisco.

Stock..Par $100.....Authorized { com., $25,000,000 / pref., 20,000,000 } Issued { com., $25,000,000 / pref., 20,000,000 } $45,000,000

The preferred stock is 6 per cent., non-cumulative, has a preference as to assets and has equal voting powers with the common stock. Transfer Agent, Corporation Trust Co., New York. Registrar, Trust Co. of the Republic, New York.

FUNDED DEBT.

1st mort., sinking fund, 5 per cent. gold, due July, 1932, Jan. and July............. $14,500,000
Collateral and mortgage bonds, 5 per cent., due Aug. 1922, Feb. and Aug.......... 10,000,000

Total.............................................................. $24,500,000

The total authorized amount of the 1st mortgage is $16,000,000. Of that amount $1,500,000 are held in the treasury. An annual sinking fund of $200,000 is provided for the retirement of the bonds at not exceeding 110; bonds may be called on any first day of July at 110. Trustee, Mercantile Trust Co., New York. Agent for the payment of interest, Mercantile Trust Co., New York. The outstanding collateral and mortgage bonds are the total amount authorized. Trustee, New York Security & Trust Co.

President, Lewis Nixon; Vice-President, James Duane Livingston; Secretary and Assistant Treasurer, Cyrus C. Wells; Treasurer, A. C. Gary, New York.

Directors—Lewis Nixon, Max Pam, Joseph E. Schwab, Daniel Le Roy Dresser, James Duane Livingston, New York; E. M. McIlvain, Adolph E. Borie, Archibald Johnson, South Bethlehem, Pa.; Charles R. Hanscom, New London, Conn.; Leslie D. Ward, Newark, N. J.

Corporate office, 15 Exchange place, Jersey City; main office, 43 Cedar street, New York. Annual meeting, third Wednesday in October, at Jersey City.

## UNITED STATES STEEL CO.

A corporation formed under the laws of West Virginia, September 5, 1899. The purpose of the organization is the manufacture and sale of steel, steel castings, machinery, tools and kindred products. The company has acquired the patents granted to Andres G. Lundin for making steel and steel castings and the patents of J. H. Neal covering the Neal Duplex brake for electric traction cars.

The company owns 74 acres of land in Everett, Mass., with wharf facilities, where it has a plant which comprises a main foundry building 200 by 130 feet, with two 20-ton open hearth furnaces and traveling electric crane and other machinery, a power-house with 125 kilowatt motor, 200 horse-power boiler, etc. At the beginning of 1902 the company had under contract a further enlargement of the main building, 300 by 130 feet, together with two additional cranes, a power-house to contain three boilers and three 200 kilowatt motors and engines and other machinery.

The plans of the company include the formation in the future of sub-companies for the manufacture of tools and other articles for which Jupiter steel is adapted, such sub-companies' plants to be located on part of the tract of land at Everett, of which the company is the owner.

The main product of the company is Jupiter steel, which title is covered by trade-mark. It is manufactured by the Lundin & Whall process.

The Neal Duplex brake, the patents for which are owned and which is manufactured by this company, is a power brake designed for city and suburban electric cars and is applicable to any form of truck.

Stock......Par $5..........................Authorized, $3,000,000......Issued $1,780,000

There is no preferred stock, all the shares being of one class. The stock is full-paid and non-assessable, without personal liability on the part of stockholders for the debts of the company.

Transfer Agent, the Secretary of the company, 145 Oliver street, Boston.

In December, 1899, the company paid its first dividend of 1 per cent. During 1900 it paid 12 monthly dividends of 1 per cent. each and an extra dividend of 1 per cent. Beginning with a quarterly dividend of 3 per cent., paid January 27, 1901, the dividends have been paid on that basis in January, April, July and October.

The company, in the early part of 1901, sold 10,000 shares by public subscription at their par value of $5 per share, and in December, 1901, offered 40,000 shares of the treasury stock at the same price, the proceeds to be used in extending the works.

The company has no funded debt or mortgages on its property.

President and Treasurer, Charles B. Miller; Vice-President, H. B. Whall; Secretary, Harry R. Bradstreet, Boston; Assistant Treasurer, Louis H. Miller; General Manager, Eugene Edwards, Everett, Mass.

Directors—H. B. Whall, Harry R. Bradstreet, Eugene Edwards, Boston; Thomas H. McDonald, Quincy, Mass.; Henry B. Humphrey, Hyde Park, Mass.; William E. Pearson, Lynn, Mass.; Charles B. Miller, Brookline, Mass.

Main office, 145 Oliver street, Boston, Mass.; branch office, Everett, Mass. Annual meeting, third Tuesday in September.

## UNITED STATES STEEL CORPORATION

A corporation formed under the laws of New Jersey, February 25, 1901, the articles of incorporation having been amended April 1, 1901. The company was organized to acquire the stocks of concerns engaged in the steel industry. The organizations acquired are as follows:

The Carnegie Co.
Federal Steel Co.
American Steel & Wire Co.
National Tube Co.
National Steel Co.
American Tin Plate Co.
American Bridge Co.
American Steel Hoop Co.
American Sheet Steel Co.
Shelby Steel Tube Co.
Lake Superior Consolidated Iron Mines.
Union Steel Co.
Troy Steel Products Co.

The united plants of the organizations owned and controlled comprised in January, 1902, 78 blast furnaces, with an annual capacity of about 6,500,000 tons of pig iron; 149 steel works and 6 finishing plants. Their capacity for steel products is about 9,000,000 tons. The plants include bar mills, structural and bridge steel and plate mills, tin plate works, sheet mills, tube mills, and wire rod and nail mills.

Together with the manufacturing places are Lake Superior iron mines, having an annual output of 12,000,000 tons of ore, together with 18,300 coke ovens, 70,830 acres of coal land and 30,000 acres of other lands, and a lake fleet of 112 vessels. The corporation owns one-sixth interest in the stock of the Oliver Iron Mining Co. and the Pittsburg Steamship Co., the remaining five-sixths being owned by the Carnegie Co. In 1901 constituent companies of the corporation leased from the Pocahontas Coal Co. 50,000 acres of coal land.

In March, 1903, The Carnegie Co., the National Steel Co. and the American Steel Hoop Co. were merged under the title of The Carnegie Co. In April, 1903, the various coke interests of the United States Steel Corporation in the Connelsville region were consolidated with the H. C. Frick Coke Co., a constituent concern of The Carnegie Co.

The Union Steel Co. and its controlled property, the Sharon Steel Co., were acquired in 1902 and the Troy Steel Products Co. was also acquired in the same year.

In March, 1903, it was reported that negotiations were on foot for the acquisition by this corporation of control of, or an interest in, the Clairton (Pa.) Works of the Crucible Steel Co. of America. At the same time the acquisition of Jones & Laughlin, Limited, of Pittsburg, was reported to be under consideration.

The Elgin, Joliet & Eastern Railway, the Pittsburg, Bessemer & Lake Erie Railroad, the Duluth & Iron Range Railroad and the Duluth, Missabe & Northern Railway, with some short railroad lines, are owned or controlled by various constitutent companies acquired by this company.

Stock. Par $100.. Authorized { com., $550,000,000 / pref., 550,000,000 } Issued { com., $508,495,200 / pref., 510,314,100 } $1,018,809,300

Transfer Agent, Hudson Trust Co., Hoboken, N. J., and 71 Broadway, New York. Registrar of preferred stock, Guaranty Trust Co., New York. Registrar of common stock, New York Security & Trust Co.

The following shows the number of stockholders in March, 1903, in comparison with the number at corresponding date in preceding year:

| | 1902. | 1903. | Increase. |
|---|---|---|---|
| Preferred | 25,296 | 31,799 | 6,503 |
| Common | 17,723 | 26,830 | 9,107 |
| Total | 43,019 | 58,629 | 15,610 |

The foregoing does not include subscriptions for preferred stock by 27,379 employes under plan offered them under date of December 31, 1902.

In March, 1902, it was announced that the company would issue $250,000,000 of 5 per cent. bonds with which to retire 40 per cent., or $200,000,000, of its preferred stock and to provide $50,000,000 of additional working capital. Suits were, however, brought to enjoin this plan, and it was not until February, 1903, that the Court of Errors and Appeals in New Jersey finally decided in favor of this company.

On March 3, 1902, J. P. Morgan & Co., New York, acting on behalf of the corporation, submitted the following offer to every holder of preferred stock of record at the close of business March 16, 1903, and during sixty days from and after that date:

(1) The preferential opportunity to subscribe, at par, for ten sixty-year 5 per cent. sinking fund gold bonds of the United States Steel Corporation, in such even amounts (*i. e.*, $500 or multiples thereof) as such holder of preferred stock may desire, in the aggregate not exceeding $200,000,000, nor in any instance exceeding 40 per cent. of the par amount of the preferred stock standing in the name of such holder of preferred stock at the closing of the books on March 16, 1903. Such subscription shall be payable in preferred stock of United States Steel Corporation at par: that is to say, five shares of such preferred stock for each $500 of such bonds; and also

(2) The like opportunity to make an additional subscription, payable in cash, for bonds of such issue, at par and accrued interest, to an even amount approximately equal to 10 per cent. of the par amount of the preferred stock standing in the name of such preferred stockholder on March 16.

The said bonds are to bear date April 1, 1903, and are to be part of an authorized issue of $250,000,000.

The indenture of mortgage, lien or pledge securing said bonds is to bear date April 1, 1903, and is to be next in rank and similar in form to that securing the bonds of the United States Steel Corporation for $304,000,000.

The bonds are to bear interest at the rate of 5 per cent. per annum from their date, April 1, 1903, and every deposit of preferred stock under the offer was to operate as a transfer to the corporation of all right to dividends accruing on such deposited stock after April 1, 1903. The deposited preferred shares will be held in the names in which they are deposited until after the preferred stock books shall have closed for the dividend for the quarter ending April 1, payable

May 15, 1903. The new bonds will be deliverable as soon after the latter date as they can be prepared.

The principal of such bonds will be payable in sixty years, but they will be redeemable at the pleasure of the corporation at any time at the expiration of ten years from the date thereof at 110 and accrued interest. In case less than the whole issue is redeemed at any one time, the bonds to be redeemed are to be designated by lot, and the coupon bonds are to be redeemed first.

An annual sinking fund of $1,010,000 is to be provided for the redemption of the bonds. The bonds will be coupon bonds, each for the principal sum of $1,000 or $5,000, and as registered bonds each for the principal sum of $500, $1,000, $5,000 or of any multiple of $5,000 that may be authorized by the Steel Corporation. The coupon bonds are to be exchangeable at any time for registered bonds, and the registered bonds, when presented in even amounts of $1,000, are to be exchangeable for coupon bonds at the will of the holders, upon terms to be stated in the said indenture.

Under the said bonds and the instrument securing the same, no action or proceeding, either at law or in equity, can be instituted or maintained for the enforcement or collection of interest on the bonds, or for maturing the principal thereof by reason of a default by the Steel Corporation in the payment of any instalment of interest, until after such default in the payment of such instalment shall have lasted for the period of two years continuously.

No subscription paya le in preferred stock would be received from any holder of preferred stock unless he shall deliver certificates for preferred stock duly endorsed for transfer for an amount at par value equal to the portion of his subscription payable in preferred stock.

The preferred stock is 7 per cent., cumulative, with a preference for principal and unpaid dividends in case of a dissolution of the corporation. The charter provides that if in any year dividends amounting to 7 per cent. shall not have been paid on the preferred, the deficiency shall be payable before any dividends shall be payable on the common stock. Whenever all cumulative dividends on the preferred stock for previous years shall have been declared and become payable, and the accrued quarterly instalments for the current year shall have been set aside from surplus or net profits, the Board of Directors may declare dividends on the common stock out of any remaining surplus or profits. The stock may be increased from time to time at the discretion of the directors.

The corporation began the payment of regular quarterly dividends of 1¾ per cent. or at the rate of 7 per cent. per annum on the preferred stock, August 7, 1901, and paid similar dividends on the preferred in November, 1901, and February (13), 1902. The dividend periods on the preferred are quarterly, February, May, August and November. The first quarterly dividend on the common stock was 1 per cent., paid September 14, 1901, and paid similar dividends in December, 1901, and March (21), 1902. The dividend periods on the common stock are quarterly, March, June, September and December.

The amount of stock given in the original articles of incorporation was the nominal amount of $3,000. On April 1, 1901, the amount of stock authorized was formally increased to $550,000,000 preferred and $550,000,000 common. See below for details as to the issue of stocks and bonds for the purchase of constituent companies.

FUNDED DEBT.

| | |
|---|---|
| U. S. Steel Corporation col. trust mort., 5 per cent., due April, 1951, redeemable.... | $153,566,000 |
| " " " " " " 5 " " " " not redeemable | 149,884,000 |
| Ten 60-year bonds, 5 per cent., due April, 1913-1963, April and Oct............... | 250,000,000 |
| Total........ | $553,450,000 |

FUNDED DEBT—CONSTITUENT COMPANIES.

| | |
|---|---|
| Illinois Steel debentures, 5 per cent., due 1910, Jan. and July....................... | $2,872,000 |
| " " A and B debentures, 5 per cent., due 1913, April and Oct............. | 6,900,000 |
| Johnson Co. of Pa., 1st mort., 6 per cent., due 1903-14, March and Sept........... | 1,208,000 |
| American Steamship, 1st mort., 5 per cent., due 1920, May and Nov.... ............ | 4,889,000 |
| Pittsburg Steamship, s. f. mort., 5 per cent., due 1915, Jan. and July.......... .... | 2,437,000 |
| Northern Lakes Steamship 1st mort., 5 per cent., March and Sept.................. | 60,000 |
| Carnegie Co., col. trust mort., 5 per cent., due 2000, April and Oct.................. | 500,000 |
| H. C. Frick Coke Co., s. f. mort., 5 per cent., due 1919, Jan. and July............. | 1,600,000 |
| " " " " pur. money mort., due 1905.................................. | 300,000 |
| Union Steel Co., 1st mort., 5 per cent., due 1952, June and Dec........................ | 37,626,000 |
| New Castle Steel & Tin P. mort., 6 per cent., due 1906, March and Sept........... | 73,000 |
| Am. S. & Wire, Allegheny Furnace mort., 5 per cent., due 1911, Feb. and Aug..... | 78,000 |
| Hostetter, Conn., Coke Co., 1st mort., 5 per cent., due 1942, Feb. and Aug......... | 1,000,000 |
| Continental Coke Co., pur. money mort., 5 per cent., Feb. and Aug............... | 900,000 |
| Ohio Steel Co. 1st mort., 6 per cent., due 1908.................................... | 845,000 |
| King, Gilbert & Warren Co. 6 per cent. bonds, due 1900-1905...................... | 100,000 |
| Bellaire Steel Co. 6 per cent. bonds, due 1906,............................ ....... | 301,000 |
| Buhl Steel Co. 6 per cent. bonds, due 1903........................................ | 200,000 |
| Rosena Furnace Co. 5 per cent. bonds, due 1912, June and Dec...... ............. | 250,000 |
| Total........ | $52,139,000 |

The collateral trust 5 per cent. bonds are $304,000,000 authorized, secured by the deposit with the United States Trust Co., New York, of all the securities of the constituent companies acquired by this company. Series A, C and E of the bonds, aggregating $154,000,000, can be called at 115 in whole or part after April 1, 1911. A sinking fund of $3,040,000 per annum begins June 1, 1902, to purchase bonds at not above 115 and interest, and after April 1, 1911, bonds of the series mentioned above may be drawn for the sinking fund. The purpose of the bond issue was to acquire and retire the $159,450,000 5 per cent. bonds of the Carnegie Co. and to purchase 60 per cent. of the stock of that company.

Coupons of the collateral trust 5 per cent. bonds are payable at the office of J. P. Morgan & Co., New York.

The new 5 per cent. bonds for $250,000 are described in full above. An important feature in this connection was the providing of $50,000,000 for improvements and additional working capital.

The Union Steel Co. 1st mortgage was created in 1902, and is $45,000,000 authorized. Trustee of the mortgage, New York Security & Trust Co. Principal and interest is guaranteed by the United States Steel Corporation. There is a sinking fund of 2 per cent. of the amount of the bonds each year, bonds to be purchased at not above 110 after 1907, the bonds to be redeemable at 110 and interest.

See statements of the separate constituent industrial companies below and also the statements of the Elgin, Joliet & Eastern Railway, the Pittsburg, Bessemer & Lake Erie Railroad, the Duluth & Iron Range Railroad, and the Duluth, Missabe & Northern Railroad, under their respective titles in the railroad section of the MANUAL.

A syndicate, comprising leading American and European financial interests, with subscriptions aggregating $200,000,000, was formed, with J. P. Morgan & Co., New York, as managers, to carry out the plan of acquiring the stocks of the several companies, an agreement to that effect being executed March 1, 1901, between the corporation and the syndicate. J. P. Morgan & Co., under date of March 2, 1901, issued a circular offering the stockholders of the different companies the right until March 20, 1901, to exchange their stocks for those of the United States Steel Corporation on terms which are stated in full in the MANUAL for 1902.

The operations of the company began April 1, 1901, but it was determined that the company's fiscal year, instead of terminating April 1, should correspond with the calendar year.

The statement of the corporation for the year ending December 31, 1902, was as follows:

| | | |
|---|---|---|
| The total net earnings of all properties after deducting expenditures for ordinary repairs and maintenance (approximately $21,000,000 *), also interest on bonds and fixed charges of the subsidiary companies, amounted to.................. | | $133,308,763 |
| Less appropriations for the following purposes, viz: | | |
| Sinking funds on bonds of subsidiary companies................ | $624,064 | |
| Depreciation and extinguishment funds (regular provisions for the year).......... ...................................... | 4,834,710 | |
| Extraordinary replacement funds (regular provisions for the year). | 9,315,615 | |
| Special fund for depreciation and improvements........ ....... | 10,000,000 | |
| | | 24,774,389 |
| Balance of net earnings for the year........ .... ........ ............ | | $108,534,374 |
| Deduct: | | |
| Interest on United States Steel Corporation bonds for year...... | $15,187,850 | |
| Sinking fund on United States Steel Corporation bonds for year. | 3,040,000 | |
| | | 18,227,850 |
| Balance...... ...................................................... | | $90,306,524 |
| Dividends for the year on United States Steel Corporation stocks, viz.: | | |
| Preferred, 7 per cent........................................ | $35,720,178 | |
| Common, 4 per cent........................................ | 20,332,690 | |
| | | 56,052,868 |
| Undivided profits or suplus for the year........................................ | | $34,253,656 |

* The actual expenditures for ordinary repairs and maintenance were $21,230,218.13. It cannot be stated, however, that this specific sum was taken out of the net earnings for the year, because in the manufacturing and producing properties the expenses for repairs and maintenance enter into and form a part of production cost. And as the net earnings of such properties are stated on the basis of gross receipts for product shipped, less the production cost thereof, the income for the year is charged with outlays for repairs and maintenance only to the extent that the production during such period was actually shipped. But as the shipments in 1902 equalled practically the year's production, approximately the entire amount of the expenditures in question has been deducted before stating the net earnings as above.

GENERAL PROFIT AND LOSS ACCOUNT—GROSS RECEIPTS.

| | | |
|---|---|---|
| Gross sales and earnings | | $560,510,479 |
| **MANUFACTURING AND OPERATING EXPENSES.** | | |
| Manufacturing and producing, cost and operating expenses | | *$411,408,818 |
| Balance | | 149,101,661 |
| Miscellaneous manufacturing and operating gains and losses (net) | $2,654,189 | |
| Rentals received | 474,781 | |
| | | 3,128,970 |
| Total net manufacturing, producing and operating income | | $152,230,631 |
| **OTHER INCOME.** | | |
| Proportion of net profits of properties owned but whose operations (gross revenue, cost of product, expenses, etc.) are not included in this statement | $1,972,316 | |
| Interest and dividends on investments and on deposits, etc | 3,454,136 | |
| | | 5,426,452 |
| Total income | | $157,657,083 |
| **GENERAL EXPENSES.** | | |
| Administrative, selling and general expenses (not including general expenses of transportation companies) | $13,202,399 | |
| Taxes | 2,391,465 | |
| Commercial discounts and miscellaneous interest | 1,908,028 | |
| | | 17,501,892 |
| Balance of income | | $140,155,191 |
| **INTEREST CHARGES, ETC.** | | |
| Interest on bonds and mortgages of the subsidiary companies | $3,879,440 | |
| Interest on bills pa able and purchase money obligations of subsidiary companies and miscellaneous interest | 2,234,145 | |
| Rental paid | 732,843 | |
| | | 6,846,428 |
| Net earnings for the year | | $133,308,763 |

* Includes charges for ordinary maintenance and repairs.

MAINTENANCE, RENEWALS AND EXTRAORDINARY REPLACEMENTS.

The physical condition of the properties was fully maintained during the year, the cost of which has been charged to current operations. The amount expended by all properties during the year for maintenance, renewals and extraordinary replacements aggregated $29,157,010.73.

This total is apportioned as follows:

| Expended on | Ordinary Maintenance and Repairs. | Extraordinary Replacements.* | Total. |
|---|---|---|---|
| Manufacturing properties | $16,099,218 | $6,978,230 | $23,077,448 |
| Coal and coke properties | 881,805 | 94,664 | 976,469 |
| Iron ore properties | 355,220 | ....... | 355,220 |
| Transportation properties: | | | |
| Railroads | 3,544,654 | 607,968 | 4,152,622 |
| Steamships and docks | 313,801 | 192,318 | 506,119 |
| Miscellaneous properties | 35,520 | 53,612 | 89,132 |
| Total | $21,230,218 | $7,926,792 | $29,157,010 |

* These expenditures were paid from funds provided from earnings to cover requirements of the character included herein.

The volume of business done by all companies during the year, including sales between the companies, and the gross receipts of transportation and miscellaneous properties, aggregated the total sum of $560,510,479.39.

The production of the several properties for the year 1902 was as follows:

| | Tons. |
|---|---|
| Iron ore mined | 16,063,179 |
| Coke manufactured | 9,521,567 |
| Coal mined, not including that used in making coke | 709,367 |
| Blast furnace products | 7,975,530 |
| Steel ingot production | 9,743,918 |

The rolled and other finished products were as follows:

| | Tons. |
|---|---|
| Steel rails | 1,920,786 |
| Blooms, billets, slabs, sheet and tin plate bars | 782,637 |
| Plates | 649,541 |
| Merchant steel, skelp, shapes, hoops, bands and cotton ties | 1,254,560 |
| Tubing and pipe | 744,062 |
| Rods | 109,330 |
| Wire and products of wire | 1,122,809 |
| Sheets—black, galvanized and tin plates | 783,576 |
| Finished structural work | 481,029 |
| Angle and splice bars and joints | 139,954 |
| Spikes, bolts, nuts and rivets | 42,984 |
| Axles | 136,787 |
| Sundry iron and steel products | 29,177 |
| Total | 8,197,232 |
| Spelter | 23,982 |
| Copperas | 14,224 |
| | Bbls. |
| Cement | 486,357 |

The tonnage of unfilled orders on the books at the close of 1902 equaled 5,347,253 tons of all kinds of manufactured products. At the corresponding date in preceding year the orders booked equaled 4,497,749 tons. In many of the classes of heavier products, like rails, plates and structural material, practically the entire capacity of the mills is sold up until nearly the end of the year 1903.

The following is the company's balance sheet December 31, 1902:

ASSETS.

| | | | |
|---|---|---|---|
| **Property account:** | | | |
| Properties owned and operated by the several companies | | $1,453,635,551 | |
| Less surplus of subsidiary companies at date of acquirement of their stocks by United States Steel Corporation, April 1, 1901 | $116,356,111 | | |
| Charged off to depreciation and extinguishment funds | 12,011,857 | | |
| | | 128,367,968 | |
| | | | $1,325,267,583 |
| **Deferred charges to operations:** | | | |
| Expenditures for improvements, explorations, stripping and development at mines, and for advanced mining royalties, chargeable to future operations of the properties | | | 3,178,760 |
| **Trustees of sinking funds:** | | | |
| Cash held by trustees on account of bond sinking funds | | | 459,246 |
| ($4,022,000 par value of redeemed bonds held by trustees not treated as an assets.) | | | |
| **Investments:** | | | |
| Outside real estate and other property | | $1,874,872 | |
| Insurance fund assets | | 929,615 | |
| | | | 2,804,488 |
| **Current assets:** | | | |
| Inventories | | $104,390,845 | |
| Account receivable | | 48,944,190 | |
| Bills receivable | | 4,153,291 | |
| Agents' balances | | 1,091,319 | |
| Sundry marketable stocks and bonds | | 6,091,340 | |
| Cash | | 50,163,172 | |
| | | | 214,834,157 |
| Total | | | $1,546,544,234 |

LIABILITIES.

| | | |
|---|---|---|
| Capital stock of United States Steel Corporation: | | |
| Common | $508,302,500 | |
| Preferred | 510,281,100 | |
| | | $1,018,583,600 |
| Capital stocks of subsidiary companies not held by United States Steel Corporation, par value: | | |
| Common stocks | $44,400 | |
| Preferred stocks | 72,800 | |
| Lake Superior Consolidated Iron Mines, subsidiary companies | 98,714 | |
| | | 215,914 |
| Bonded and debenture debt: | | |
| United States Steel Corporation bonds | $303,757,000 | |
| Less, redeemed and held by trustee of sinking fund | 2,698,000 | |
| Balance held by the public | $301,059,000 | |
| Subsidiary companies' bonds ... $60,978,900 | | |
| Less, redeemed and held by trustees of sinking funds ... 1,324,000 | | |
| Balance held by the public | 59,654,901 | |
| Debenture scrip, Illinois Steel Co | 40,426 | |
| | | 360,754,327 |
| Mortgages and purchase-money obligations of subsidiary companies: | | |
| Mortgages | $2,901,132 | |
| Purchase-money obligations | 6,689,418 | |
| | | 9,590,550 |
| Current liabilities: | | |
| Current accounts payable and pay-rolls | $18,675,080 | |
| Bills and loans payable | 6,202,503 | |
| Special deposits due employees and others | 4,485,547 | |
| Accrued taxes not yet due | 1,051,605 | |
| Accrued interest and unpresented coupons | 5,398,573 | |
| Preferred stock dividend No. 7, payable February 16, 1903 | 8,929,919 | |
| Common stock dividend No. 7, payable March 30, 1903 | 5,083,025 | |
| | | 49,826,252 |
| Total capital and current liabilities | | $1,438,970,643 |
| Sinking and reserve funds: | | |
| Sinking fund on United States Steel Corporation bonds | $1,773,333 | |
| Sinking funds on bonds of subsidiary companies | 217,344 | |
| Depreciation and extinguishment funds | 1,707,611 | |
| Improvement and replacement funds | 16,566,191 | |
| Contingent and miscellaneous operating funds | 3,413,784 | |
| Insurance fund | 1,539,485 | |
| | | 25,217,748 |
| Bond sinking funds with accretions | | 4,481,246 |
| Represented by cash and by redeemed bonds not treated as assets (see contra). | | |
| Undivided surplus of United States Steel Corporation and subsidiary com anies: | | |
| Capital surplus provided in organization of United States Steel Corporation | $25,000,000 | |
| Surplus accumulated by all companies since organization of United States Steel Corporation | 52,874,597 | |
| | | 77,874,597 |
| Total | | $1,546,544,234 |

In connection with the plan announced in March, 1903, to retire $200,000,000 of the preferred stock and to issue $250,000,000 of new 5 per cent. bonds, of which $50,000,000 would be to provide that amount of additional capital, the following statement was made: "The plan provides for the issuance of $250,000,000 of bonds, $200,000,000 of which are to be exchanged for $200,000,000 of preferred stock. The stock thus retired is entitled to cumulative dividends of 7 per cent. per annum, which represents an outgo of $14,000,000 a year. The $250,000,000 of bonds to be issued bear 5 per cent. interest, which represents an outgo of $12,500,000 a year. There is, therefore, a net saving of $1,500,000 a year, plus the earning capacity of $50,000,000."

The statement outlines the proposed expenditures for extensions and improvements, with their estimated cost and expected increase in annual output (tons), substantially as follows:

| Illinois Steel Co. | Increase in Annual Output (Tons). | Total Estimated Cost. |
|---|---|---|
| At So. Chicago, Ill.—New open-hearth furnace plant, blooming mill and finishing mill (structural steel billets and plates) | 300,000 | $3,000,000 |
| Remodeling 132-inch plate mill train | 70,000 | 650,000 |
| Additional heating capacity at rail mill | Considerable | 200,000 |
| Improvement of Bessemer department | 120,000 | 150,000 |
| New blast furnace blowing engines | 120,000 | 475,000 |
| Repairing stoves at furnaces Nos. 1 to 4 | "Rehabilitation" | 400,000 |
| Addition to machine shop and foundry | ...... | 200,000 |
| At Joliet, Ill.—Remodeling blast furnaces Nos. 1 and 2 (modernizing), increasing output and reducing cost | Not stated | 900,000 |
| Addition to converting mill (will also effect a saving in cost of operation) | 60,000 | 150,000 |
| Sundry improvements at So. Chicago and Joliet | ...... | 420,000 |
| **National Tube Co.** | | |
| At McKeesport, Pa.—Entire rebuilding of rolling mills | 124,000 | |
| Entire rebuilding of tube and pipe mills | 100,000 | |
| One new blast furnace | 166,000 | 9,255,662 |
| Additional Bessemer converter | 140,000 | |
| New water and power plant | ...... | |
| At Lorain, O.—Two additional blast furnaces | 347,000 | |
| Additional rolling mills | 330,000 | 8,646,096 |
| New tube and pipe mill | 300,000 | |
| Also for sun r improvements at Pittsburg, Pa., and at Wheeling, W. Va d y. | ...... | 332,400 |
| **Various Companies.** | | |
| American Steel & Wire Co.—Various additions and improvements to existing facilities | Not stated | 4,535,000 |
| American Sheet Steel Co.—Rebuilding plant at Canal Dover, O. | | |
| Addition to polishing department at Wellsville plant | | |
| Improvement of McKeesport, Pa., works | 44,000 | 355,000 |
| Improvements at Vandergrift works | | |
| Carnegie Steel Co.—At Homestead, Pa., works, additional 140-inch plate mill, improvement of 32-inch mill and of boiler plant | 260,000 | 1,135,000 |
| Edgar Thomson Works, Braddock, Pa.—Addition to steel and iron foundry; modern blowing engines in place of obsolete types. | 116,000 | 275,000 |
| Duquesne Works, Munhall, Pa.—Sundry additions and improvements | ...... | 330,000 |
| National Steel Co.—Additions and improvements at Newcastle, Pa., Bellaire, O., and Youngstown, O. | ...... | 1,592,000 |
| American Steel Hoop Co.—Additions and improvements at Isabella Furnace, Pittsburg, Pa., and at the Upper Union Mills, Youngstown, O. | 30,000 | 285,000 |
| American Tin Plate Co.—At various of its mills modern and improved methods | ...... | 1,000,000 |
| H. C. Frick Coke Co.—Development of coke and steam coal properties, including the erection of additional ovens. | coke, 275,000<br>steam coal, 600,000 | 445,000 |
| Mining Companies.—New crusher plant at Escanaba, Mich. | 510,000 | 143,810 |
| Additional power houses, shafts and mining plants | ...... | 317,000 |
| Duluth, Missabe & Northern Railway.—Additional locomotives, the extension of ore dock at Duluth and improvements at shops | ...... | 543,961 |
| Duluth & Iron Range Railroad.—Sundry improvements to shops, bridges and line of road | ...... | 187,000 |
| Chicago, Lake Shore & Eastern Railway.—Additional steel cars | ...... | 300,000 |
| Pittsburg Steamship Co.—Steam towing machines on bridges and improvement of fleet | ...... | 208,000 |
| Pittsburg & Conneaut Dock Co.—Improvement of unloading machines | ...... | 40,000 |
| Total increase, "all products," about | 2,700,000 | $36,470,929 |

The increase in earnings expected to result from these changes were:

| | From Increased Output. | Reduction in Cost of Production. | Total Gain in Earnings. |
|---|---|---|---|
| National Tube Works at McKeesport, Pa. | $1,553,000 | $1,805,000 | $3,358,000 |
| National Tube Works at Lorain, O. | 1,809,000 | 1,500,000 | 3,309,000 |
| National Tube Works at Pittsburg and Wheeling | 70,000 | 107,000 | 177,000 |
| American Steel & Wire Co. | 1,236,000 | | 1,236,000 |
| Carnegie Steel Co. at Homestead | 1,440,000 | | 1,440,000 |
| Carnegie Steel Co., Edgar Thomson Works | 280,000 | | 280,000 |
| National Steel Co. | 315,000 | | 315,000 |
| All others | 1,885,000 | | 1,885,000 |
| Total of all, about | $7,000,000 | $5,000,000 | $12,000,000 |

On account of the wide interest in this corporation the following summary is given of the charter provisions.

By its articles of incorporation the corporation is empowered to manufacture iron, manganese, coke, copper, lumber and other materials, and all articles consisting or partly consisting of iron, steel, copper, wood or other materials, and all or any products thereof.

To acquire, lease, or occupy, use or develop any lands containing coal, iron, manganese, stone, or other ores, oil or wood lands, to mine and buy and sell these or other materials, and to construct bridges, buildings, machinery, ships, boats, engines, cars and other equipment, railroads, docks, slips, elevators, water, gas and electric works, viaducts, canals and other waterways. It is stipulated, however, that the company shall not maintain or operate any railroad or canal in New Jersey. The company is also empowered to acquire and deal in trade-marks, trade names, patents, inventions, improvements, processes, etc., and to acquire and deal in stocks, bonds and other securities of other companies engaged in the acquisition, manufacture and sale of the products mentioned.

The company is also empowered to engage in other manufacturing, mining, construction or transportation business of any kind or character whatsoever, and to that end to acquire, deal in and dispose of all property, assets, stocks and bonds, and rights of any and every kind, but not to engage in any business hereunder which shall require the exercise of the right of eminent domain within the State of New Jersey.

The company also may acquire by purchase, subscription or otherwise, and hold or dispose of stocks, bonds or other obligations of any corporation formed or engaged in the objects or operations indicated. The company may hold for investment the securities or obligations of any such other corporation and also aid in any manner any corporation whose obligations are held or guaranteed by this company.

The company may conduct its business in any other States or Territories or foreign countries, may have more than one office, and keep the books of the company outside of New Jersey, except as otherwise may be provided by law, and it also may have real estate transactions either in or out of the State.

Without in any particular limiting any of the objects and powers of the company, it is provided that the corporation shall have power to issue bonds and other obligations in payment for property purchased or acquired, or for any other object in or about its business; to mortgage or pledge stocks, bonds or other obligations of any property which may be acquired by it to secure obligations issued or incurred, to guarantee dividends, bonds or contracts, and to make or perform contracts of any description.

It is provided that the number of directors may be increased from time to time as fixed, but if fixed at more than three, by some multiple of three. Directors are to fill one, two and three-year terms.

The directors are authorized to delegate their powers to an executive committee. The board has the power to fix and determine the amount of working capital and to direct and determine the use and disposition of any surplus and net profits over and above the capital stock paid, and to follow out other transactions provided and allowed by law.

By an amendment to the articles of incorporation the company accepted the benefit of the New Jersey statute providing that two-thirds of the stock represented at an annual or special meeting may authorize the directors to create mortgages or pledge the assets of the company.

President, Charles M. Schwab; 1st Vice-President, James Gayley; 2d Vice-President, William B. Dickson; 3d Vice-President, Veryl Preston; General Counsel, Francis Lynde Stetson; Secretary and Treasurer, Richard Trimble; Comptroller, William J. Filbert, New York.

DIRECTORS.

For Three Years Ending 1905.
Marshall Field, Chicago.
Daniel G. Reid, New York.
John D. Rockefeller, Jr., New York.
Alfred Clifford, New York.
Robert Bacon, New York.
Nathaniel Thayer, Boston.
Clement A. Griscom, Philadelphia.

For Two Years Ending 1904.
J. Pierpont Morgan, New York.
John D. Rockefeller, New York.
Henry H. Rogers, New York.
Charles M. Schwab, New York.
Elbert H. Gary, New York.
George W. Perkins, New York.
Edmund C. Converse, New York.
James Gayley.

For One Year Ending 1903.
Francis H. Peabody, Boston.
Charles Steele, New York.
William H. Moore, New York.
Norman B. Ream, Chicago.
Peter A. B. Widener, Philadelphia.
James H. Reed, Pittsburg.
Henry C. Frick, Pittsburg.
William Edenborn, Chicago.

Executive Committee—Elbert H. Gary, Chairman; Daniel G. Reid, William Edenborn, Edmund C. Converse, James Gayley, Charles Steele, Charles M. Schwab, *ex-officio*, George W. Perkins, *ex-officio*.

Finance Committee—George W. Perkins, Chairman; Henry H. Rogers, Norman B. Ream, Peter A. B. Widener, Henry C. Frick, Robert Bacon, Charles M. Schwab, *ex-officio*, Elbert H. Gary, *ex-officio*.

Corporate office, 51 Newark street, Hoboken, N. J.; Executive office, 71 Broadway, New York. Annual meeting, third Monday in April.

The following details are given regarding the constituent companies of the United States Steel Corporation.

AMERICAN BRIDGE CO.—A corporation formed under the laws of New Jersey, April 14, 1900. The business of the company is the manufacture and sale of bridges and bridge and structural work. The properties and plants acquired and owned were given in the MANUAL for 1901.

Stock..Par \$100...Authorized { com., \$35,000,000 / pref., 35,000,000 } Issued { com., \$30,946,400 / pref., 31,348,000 } \$62,294,400

The preferred stock is 7 per cent., cumulative. The company has no funded debt.

Stock is transferred at the company's office, New York. Registrar, Morton Trust Co., New York.

President, Alfred J. Major; Vice-Presidents, Joshua A. Hatfield, William H. McCord, Charles C. Schneider; Treasurer, William H. Connell; Auditor, C. C. Price; Secretary, Henry Schoonmaker; Chief Engineer, Paul L. Wolfel; Purchasing Agent, W. G. A. Miller.

Directors—Elbert H. Gary, Alfred J. Major, Jr., Joshua A. Hatfield, Thomas Murray, Henry Schoonmaker.

Corporate office, 51 Newark street, Hoboken. New York office, 100 Broadway. Annual meeting, last Wednesday in October.

AMERICAN SHEET STEEL CO.—A corporation formed under the laws of New Jersey, March 28, 1900. The company acquired and operates a number of establishments manufacturing steel sheets which were given in full in the MANUAL for 1901.

Stock..Par \$100...Authorized { com., \$26,000,000 / pref., 26,000,000 } Issued { com., \$24,500,000 / pref., 24,500,000 } \$49,000,000

The preferred stock is 7 per cent., cumulative.

Transfer Agent, First National Bank, New York. Registrar, Guaranty Trust Co., New York.

President, George G. McMurtry; Assistant to President, Wallace P. Bache; Vice-President, John A. Topping; Treasurer, F. S. Wheeler; Auditor, I. M. Scott; Secretary, H. B. Wheeler.

Directors, Elbert H. Gary, J. Warner, F. S. Wheeler, George G. McMurtry, Wallace P. Bache, T. M. Day, Jr., Daniel G. Reid, William B. Leeds, W. T. Graham, John A. Topping, Charles M. Schwab.

Main office, 21 State street, New York. Annual meeting third Tuesday in April, at East Orange, N. J.

AMERICAN STEEL & WIRE CO.—A corporation formed under the laws of New Jersey, January 13, 1899, to purchase the American Steel & Wire Co. (of Illinois), together with other establishments, whose principal industries are the manufacture of wire, wire nails, rods, fencing, etc., a list of which was given in the MANUAL for 1901.

The company has acquired various additional properties, including the fleet of the Zerith Transit Co., In November, 1900, the company acquired the American Steamship Co., with its Lake fleet, and guaranteed a bond issue of the Steamship Co.

Stock..Par \$100...Authorized { com., \$50,000,000 / pref., 40,000,000 } Issued { com., \$50,000,000 / pref., 40,000,000 } \$90,000,000

The preferred stock is 7 per cent., cumulative. Of the stock \$21,600,000 common and \$12,000,000 preferred were issued in exchange for the old American Steel & Wire Co.'s shares.

Transfer Agent, Corporation Trust Co., Jersey City. Registrar, Farmers' Loan & Trust Co., New York.

FUNDED DEBT.

American Steamship, 1st mort., guaranteed, 5 per cent., due 1920.................. \$5,530,000

There are mortgages to the amount of \$78,000 secured on properties of the company.

The old American Steel & Wire Co., to which the present company is virtually a successor, was incorporated under the laws of Illinois, April 2, 1898. Its stock consisted of \$12,000,000 7 per cent. cumulative preferred and \$12,000,000 common. The properties it acquired are given above. The bonds on various properties assumed by company were \$392,000.

President, William P. Palmer; 1st Vice-President, J. S. Keefe; Treasurer, F. L. Watson; Secretary, Alonzo F. Allen; Auditor, C. A. Voght; General Counsel, Max Pam.

Directors—Elbert H. Gary, Charles H. Schwab, William Edenborn, William P. Palmer, Alfred Clifford, J. S. Keefe, E. C. Lott, Frank Baackes, F. H. Daniels, C. L. Miller and L. D. Ward.

Main office, 217 La Salle street, Chicago; New York office, 71 Broadway. Annual meeting, third Tuesday in April, at East Orange, N. J.

AMERICAN TIN PLATE CO.—This company, incorporated December 14, 1898, under the New Jersey Corporation Law (revision of 1896), with a perpetual charter, was a consolidation of concerns producing between 90 and 95 per cent. of the tin plate made in the United States. A list of the properties acquired was given in the MANUAL for 1901.

These plants represented a yearly productive capacity of about 8,000,000 boxes of tin plate. The company since its organization has concentrated its operations to a considerable extent at the works which are most advantageously located for that purpose. The company was organized with a cash working capital of about $5,000,000.

Stock..Par $100..Authorized { com., $30,000,000 / pref., 20,000,000 } Issued { com., $28,000,000 / pref., 18,325,000 } $46,325,000

The preferred stock is 7 per cent., cumulative.

Transfer Agent, Guaranty Trust Co., New York. Registrar, First National Bank, New York.

President, W. T. Graham; 1st Vice-President, W. M. Leeds; 2d Vice-President, Frank Dickerson; Treasurer, F. S. Wheeler; Secretary, E. G. Applegate; Auditor, W. P. Beaver.

Directors—Charles M. Schwab, Elbert H. Gary, W. T. Graham, W. P. Beaver, Thomas Murray, E. G. Applegate, George Greer, William B. Leeds, C. A. Robinson, Frank Dickerson.

Corporate office, 525 Main street, East Orange, N. J.; legal agent in New Jersey, New Jersey Registration & Trust Co., East Orange; main office, 21 State street, New York; Chicago office, 204 Dearborn street. Annual meeting, third Tuesday in January.

THE CARNEGIE CO.—A corporation formed under the laws of New Jersey, March 24, 1900. The company owns the stock of a Pennsylvania corporation, the Carnegie Steel Co., formed to carry on the various steel and iron industrial establishments, plants and properties principally in or near Pittsburg, which belonged to Carnegie Bros. & Co., Limited, the firm of Carnegie, Phipps & Co., and the Carnegie Steel Co., Limited. The principal plants or properties owned and controlled are:

Edgar Thomson Furnaces, Bessemer, Pa.
Duquesne Furnaces, Duquesne, Pa.
Carrie Furnaces, Rankin, Pa.
Lucy Furnaces, Pittsburg.
Edgar Thomson Steel Works, Braddock, Pa.
Duquesne Steel Works, Duquesne, Pa.
Homestead Steel Works, Munhall, Pa.
Upper Union Mills, Pittsburg.
Lower Union Mills, Pittsburg.
Keystone Bridge Works, Pittsburg.
Youghiogheny Coke Works, Douglass, Pa.
Lorimer Coke Works, Lorimer, Pa.
Pittsburg, Bessemer & Lake Erie Railroad.

In addition the company controls other important auxiliary properties. Full control of the Pittsburg, Bessemer & Lake Erie Railroad Co. was obtained in 1901, the road being leased for 999 years, from April 1, 1901, with a guaranty of 3 per cent. dividends on its common stock. This road was built to give the plants of this company economical transportation for their supply of ore and for their finished product. The lease is made to the Bessemer & Lake Erie Railroad, a company owned by the Carnegie Co. The Union Railroad, which connects the various plants of the company, is also owned. The H. C. Frick Coke Co., with extensive plants in Fayette and Westmoreland counties, Pa., is also controlled in the interest of this company. In addition it has dock properties at Conneaut and other points on the lakes, and owns a controlling interest in the Oliver Mining Co. It also owns five-sixths of the Pittsburg Steamship Co., which owns a fleet of 90 vessels, and operates under agreement 22 additional, total 112, plying on the Great Lakes, and other iron ore properties in the Lake Superior district and elsewhere.

All the stock of this company was acquired by the United States Steel Corporation.

On March 26, 1903, this company, the National Steel Co. and the American Steel Hoop Co. were consolidated under the title of the National Steel Co., the name being on March 27, 1903, changed to the Carnegie Co. See below.

Stock......Par $25........................Authorized, $63,000,000......Issued, $63,000,000

The stock of the company was originally of a par value of $1,000, the amount authorized and issued being $160,000,000, all common. The National Steel Co. had $32,000,000 of common and $27,000,000 of 7 per cent., cumulative, preferred stock. The American Steel Hoop Co. had $19,000,000 of common and $14,000,000 of 7 per cent. preferred stock. The aggregate capital of the three companies, merged in March, 1903, was $252,000,000. In the merger the par value of the company's stock was reduced to $25 per share, and one share of the new stock was given for each share, both common and preferred, of the three old companies, making the amount authorized and outstanding as above.

Full statements of the National Steel Co. and of the American Steel Hoop Co. were given in the MANUAL for 1902.

The company had an issue of $160,000,000 5 per cent. collateral trust bonds due 2000, of which $159,450,000 were outstanding. These bonds were purchased in March, 1901, by the United States Steel Corporation with part of its own issue of 5 per cent. collateral trust bonds, and all the bonds of the Carnegie Co. have been cancelled except $500,000.

President, W. E. Corey; Secretary and Treasurer, William W. Blackburn; Assistant Treasurer, W. McCausland; Assistant Secretary and Assistant Treasurer, James J. Campbell.

Directors—Charles M. Schwab, Elbert H. Gary, W. E. Corey, William W. Blackburn.

Corporate office, Hoboken, N. J.; main office, 434 Fifth avenue, Pittsburg. Annual meeting, first Monday in April.

FEDERAL STEEL CO.—A corporation formed under the laws of New Jersey, September 9, 1898. The company was organized in pursuance of a plan to acquire the capital stocks of the Illinois Steel Co., Minnesota Iron Co., and Elgin, Joliet & Eastern Railway Co. In addition the company acquired the Duluth & Iron Range Railroad Co., Chicago, Lake Shore & Eastern Railroad Co. and various corporations owned by the constituent companies; see Illinois Steel Co. in MANUAL for 1898. Statements of Elgin, Joliet & Eastern Railway and Duluth & Iron Range Railroad will be found among Railroad Companies in this edition of MANUAL. The company also acquired and owns the entire capital stocks of the Lorain Steel Co. of Ohio, and the Lorain Steel Co. of Pennsylvania, formerly the Johnson Co. Details of the organization of the company and the exchange of old securities for the new, will be found in the MANUAL for 1901.

Stock..Par $100...Authorized { com., $100,000,000; pref., 100,000,000 } Issued { com., $46,484,300; pref., 53,260,900 } $99,745,200

The preferred stock is entitled to 6 per cent., non-cumulative, dividends, and has a preference up to par value as to assets in case of liquidation.

Transfer Agent, Corporation Trust Co. of New Jersey, Jersey City and New York. Registrar, Colonial Trust Co., New York.

FUNDED DEBT.

| | |
|---|---|
| Illinois Steel Co. debentures, 5 per cent., due Jan., 1910, Jan. and July............ | $2,872,000 |
| " " non-conv. debentures, 5 per cent., due April, 1913, April and Oct. | 6,900,000 |
| Elgin, Joliet & Eastern Ry., 1st mort., 5 per cent., due May, 1941, May and Nov.... | 7,852,000 |
| Duluth & Iron Range R. R. 1st mort., 5 per cent., due Oct., 1937, April and Oct.... | 6,732,000 |
| " " " 2d mort., currency, 6 per cent., due Jan., 1916, Jan. & July. | 1,000,000 |
| Lorain Steel Co., formerly Johnson Co., 1st mort., 6 per cent., due 1914, March and Sept............ | 1,200,000 |
| Total ............ | $26,556,000 |

The 5 per cent. convertible debenture bonds of the Illinois Steel Co. were in February, 1899, called for payment on May 3, 1899, holders being offered a waiver of the right to retire same if the privilege of exchanging bonds for stock of the Illinois Steel Co. was surrendered by indorsement on the bonds. The $2,922,000 outstanding are so indorsed.

President, Elbert H. Gary; Vice-President, Charles MacVeagh; Secretary and Treasurer, Richard Trimble; Auditor, William J. Filbert.

Directors—Elbert H. Gary, Charles M. Schwab, Robert Bacon, Charles MacVeagh, James Sim.

Corporate office, 60 Grand street, Jersey City; general office, 71 Broadway, New York; Fiscal agents, J. P. Morgan & Co., New York. Annual meeting, first Monday in April.

LAKE SUPERIOR CONSOLIDATED IRON MINES.—A corporation formed under the laws of New Jersey in 1893. The company owns and operates large iron ore mines on the Missabe Range, Minn., and leases some of its mines to the Carnegie and other iron manufacturing interests; also owns the Duluth, Missabe & Northern Railway, Duluth to Iron Mountain, Minn. See statement of this company in the railroad section of the MANUAL.

Stock......Par $100........................Authorized, $30,000,000......Issued, $29,425,940

Stock is transferred at the company's office, 71 Broadway, New York.

FUNDED DEBT.

| | |
|---|---|
| Duluth, Miss. & Northern Railway, 1st mort., 6 per cent., due Jan., 1922, Jan. and July. | $1,174,000 |
| " " " cons. mort., 6 per cent., due Jan., 1923, Jan. and July. | 2,326,000 |
| " " " 2d mort., 5 per cent., due Jan., 1918, Jan. and July. | 4,823,000 |
| Total ............ | $8,323,000 |

The Lake Superior Consolidated Iron Mines has no mortgage indebtedness of its own, having retired and canceled the last of its bonds in 1898.

President, Thomas F. Cole; Vice-President, D. H. Coble; Treasurer, Charles E. Scheide; Secretary, Charles D. Fraser; General Counsel, Frank B. Kellogg.

Directors—James Gayley, D. H. Coble, Charles P. Coffin, W. M. Jeffery, Thomas F. Cole, Lewis J. Merritt, Charles E. Scheide.

Corporate office, Newark, N. J.; operating office, Duluth, Minn.; New York office, 71 Broadway. Annual meeting, third Tuesday in February, at Newark.

NATIONAL TUBE CO.—A corporation formed under the laws of New Jersey, June 16, 1899. A preliminary incorporation was effected February 15, 1899, under the title of the United States Tube Co. in the same State, the name being changed and the capital enlarged when the present company was organized.

The company has acquired, either by ownership in fee or by ownership of the entire capital stock, the works and property formerly of the following corporations:

National Tube Works, McKeesport and Pittsburg.
Cohoes Tube Works, Cohoes, N. Y.
National Galvanizing Works, Versailles, Pa.
Syracuse Tube Co., Syracuse, N. Y.
Pennsylvania Tube Works, Pittsburg.
Ohio Tube Co., Warren, O.
Allison Manufacturing Co., Philadelphia.
Morris, Tasker & Co., and Delaware Iron Works, New Castle, Del.
Chester Pipe & Tube Co., Chester, Pa.
Oil City Tube Works, Oil City, Pa.
American Tube & Iron Co., Youngstown, O.
American Tube & Iron Co., Middletown, Pa.
Oil Well Supply Co.'s Elba Iron Works and Continental Tube Works, Pittsburg.
Riverside Iron Works, Wheeling, W. Va., Benwood, Va., and Steubenville, O.
Pittsburg Tube Works, Pittsburg.

Stock..Par $100...Authorized { com., $40,000,000 / pref., 40,000,000 } Issued { com., $40,000,000 / pref., 40,000,000 } $80,000,000

The preferred stock is entitled to 7 per cent. annual dividends, cumulative.

Transfer agency, 26 Cortlandt street, New York. Registrar, Colonial Trust Co., New York.

The company has no bonds nor any mortgages or liens of any description upon its properties.

President, William B. Schiller; Vice-Presidents, William H. Latshaw, John D. Culbertson, A. S. Matheson; Secretary and Treasurer, John D. Culbertson; General Counsel, Sullivan & Cromwell.

Directors—Elbert H. Gary, Charles M. Schwab, E. C. Converse, William Nelson Cromwell, John D. Culbertson, William J. Curtis, F. J. Hearne, William H. Latshaw, A. S. Matheson, William B. Schiller, Charles Steele.

Corporate office, 76 Montgomery street, Jersey City; financial office, 26 Cortlandt street, New York; manufacturing and sales offices, Wood and Water streets, Pittsburg. Annual meeting, third Monday of August, at company's office, Jersey City.

SHELBY STEEL TUBE CO.—A corporation formed under the laws of New Jersey, February 9, 1900. The company acquired the plants and business of the following concerns, whose principal occupation is the manufacture of seamless steel tubing. The productive capacity of these establishments is 100,000,000 feet of tubing per annum:

Shelby Steel Tube Co., of Pennsylvania.
Pope Tube Co., Hartford, Conn.
New Castle Tube Co., New Castle, Pa.
Albany Manufacturing Co., Albany, Ind.
Auburn Bolt & Nut Works, Auburn, Pa.
Shelby Steel Tube Co., of Ohio—operating:
Ellwood Works, Ellwood City, Pa.
Greenville Works, Greenville, Pa.
American Weldless Tube Co., Toledo, O.
Shelby Works, Shelby, O.

Stock...Par $100....Authorized { com., $9,000,000 / pref., 6,000,000 } Issued { com., $8,175,000 / pref., 5,000,000 } $13,175,000

The preferred stock is 7 per cent., cumulative.

President, William B. Schiller; Vice-President, William H. Latshaw; Secretary and Treasurer, John D. Culbertson; Auditor, J. M. Shaw; General Counsel, Sullivan & Cromwell.

Directors—Elbert H. Gary, Charles M. Schwab, E. C. Converse, F. J. Hearne, John D. Culbertson, William B. Schiller, William H. Latshaw, A. S. Matheson, William J. Curtis.

Main office, 501 Liberty avenue, Pittsburg. Annual meeting, third Tuesday in August, at Jersey City.

UNION STEEL CO.—A corporation formed under the laws of Pennsylvania, in November, 1902. The company was a consolidation of the Sharon Steel Co. and the Union Steel Co., statements of both these companies were given in the MANUAL for 1902. In December, 1902, the United States Steel Corporation acquired the entire capital stock of the company and guaranteed an issue of $45,000,000 of its bonds.

The Union Steel Co. in 1900-02 completed a large modern steel plant at Donnora, Pa. It also acquired valuable iron ore properties in the Messaba region. The Sharon Steel Co. was organized in 1899 and completed a large plant at Sharon, Pa., for the manufacture of steel and its pro u s. The blast furnaces owned by the Consolidated Co. have a daily capacity of 3,500 tons and the open hearth plans of 4,000 per day. Its coke ovens have a capacity of 3,500 tons per day, and the other auxilliary properties embrace blooming and billet, rod and wire, wire nails, barb wire, tin plate, sheet and skelp, as well as steel rail and other mills.

Stock......Par $100........................Authorized, $45,000,000......Issued, $45,000,000

Stock is transferred at the corporation office, Pittsburg.

FUNDED DEBT.

1st mort., 5 per cent., due 1952, June and Dec.................................. $37,626,000

The authorized amount of the 1st mortgage is $45,000,000. Trustee of the mortgage, New York Security & Trust Co. The bonds are guaranteed by the United States Steel Corporation. The owners of the old companies received the new bonds to the amount they had expended in the construction of the plants, and agreed to furnish $10,000,000 additional cash for extensions and improvements, it being understood that $5,000,000 of the bonds should be held for further extensions. All of the stock of this new company was acquired by the United States Steel Corporation as consideration for the guarantee of the bonds.

Chairman, William Flinn; President, Andrew W. Mellon; Vice-Presidents, W. H. Donner, John Stevenson, Jr.; Secretary and Treasurer, Robert B. Mellon, Pittsburg.

Main office, Fifth avenue and Grant street, Pittsburg.

## THE UNITED STATES WIRE & NAIL CO.

A corporation formed under the laws of Pennsylvania, October 26, 1898. The object of the company is the manufacture of steel and iron rods, wire and wire nails. The works of the company are at Shousetown, near Pittsburg, and extensive additions to the same were begun in 1900.

Stock......Par $100.................. ...........Authorized, $200,000......Issued, $200,000

The capital stock was originally $100,000, but was increased to $200,000 in 1900. The company has no funded debt.

President, Isaac N. De Noon, Pittsburg; Vice-President, E. W. Palmer, Cleveland; Secretary and Treasurer, Joseph C. De Noon, Pittsburg.

Directors—Isaac N. De Noon, Joseph C. De Noon, Pittsburg; E. W. Palmer, Cleveland; Frank Hayes, A. S. Tyler, Chicago.

Main office, 605 Smithfield street, Pittsburg. · Annual meeting, October 26, at Pittsburg.

## UNITED TRACTION & ELECTRIC CO.

### PROVIDENCE-PAWTUCKET-RHODE ISLAND SUBURBAN RAILWAY CO.

(Leased to the Rhode Island Co.)

A corporation formed under the laws of New Jersey in 1893. The company operates 270 miles of electric railway, including all street railways in the cities of Providence and Pawtucket, R. I., and surrounding towns. It owns all the stock of the Rhode Island Suburban Railway Co. and owns practically all the stock and bonds of the Union Railroad Co., Pawtucket Street Railway Co., Providence Cable Tramway Co. and Pawtuxet Valley Street Railway Co.

In 1902 the properties controlled by this company were leased for 999 years to the Rhode Island Co., which is owned by the Rhode Island Securities Co. The rental is fixed charges and 5 per cent. on the stock of the United Traction & Electric Co. The rental is guaranteed for a limited time by the United Gas Improvement Co.

Stock......Par $100.........................Authorized, $8,000,000......Issued, $8,000,000

The company has no preferred stock. Transfer Agent, Central Realty Bond & Trust Co., New York, and the Providence Banking Co., Providence. Registrars, Central Trust Co., New York, and Union Trust Co., Providence.

Dividends on the stock at the rate of 2 per cent. per annum were paid from July, 1897, to January, 1899, since which time 4 per cent. per annum was paid until October, 1902, when the rate was increased to 1¼ per cent., the dividend periods being January, April, July and October.

FUNDED DEBT.

1st collateral trust mort., 5 per cent., due March, 1933, March and Sept............... $8,702,000

The authorized amount of the mortgage is $9,000,000. The bonds are secured by deposit with trustee of all the bonds and stocks of controlled and leased lines. Trustee and agent for the payment of interest, Central Trust Co., New York.

EARNINGS.

| Year ending December 31. | Gross. | Net. |
|---|---|---|
| 1899 | $2,019,009 | $861,738 |
| 1900 | 2,382,258 | 826,836 |
| 1901 | 2,702,383 | 886,026 |

President, Benjamin A. Jackson; Vice-President, Arthur H. Watson; Secretary and Treasurer, Cornelius S. Sweetland, Providence.

Main office, Providence. Annual meeting, second Tuesday in February, at Providence.

## THE UNITED TRACTION CO.

ALBANY, N. Y.

Owns and operates the entire street railway system of Albany, Troy and intermediate places. The total operated, 77 miles. Company is a consolidation, in 1899, of the following companies:

The Albany Railway Co. Troy City Railway Co.
Watervliet Turnpike & Railroad Co.

The Company operates under lease the following companies:

The Troy & Lansingburgh Railroad Co. Lansingburgh & Cohoes Railroad Co.
Troy & Cohoes Railroad Co. Waterford & Cohoes Railroad Co.

The company obtains power under contract with the Hudson River Power Transmission Co.

Stock......Par $100..........................Authorized, $5,000,000......Issued, $4,999,950

Stock is transferred at the office of the company, Albany, N. Y.

Dividends on the stock are paid quarterly, in February, May, August and November. The first quarterly dividend was 1¼ per cent., May 1, 1900, and dividends of that amount, or 5 per cent. per annum, have since been regularly paid.

FUNDED DEBT.

| | |
|---|---|
| United Traction Co. debenture bonds, 4½ per cent., due 1919, May and Nov......... | $567,000 |
| Albany Railway consolidated mort., 5 per cent., due Jan., 1930, Jan. an July........ | 428,000 |
| Albany Railway general mort., 5 per cent., due June, 1947, June and Ddc........... | 496,000 |
| Watervliet Turnpike & Railroad 1st mort., 6 per cent., due May, 1919, May and Nov.. | 350,000 |
| Watervliet Turnpike & Railroad 2d mort., 6 per cent., due May, 1919, May and Nov... | 150,000 |
| Troy City Railway 1st mort., 5 per cent., due 1942, April and Oct.................. | 1,966,000 |
| Troy & Lansingburg 1st mort., 5 per cent., due April, 1903, April and Oct........... | 34,000 |
| Troy City Railway debenture bonds, 5 per cent., due 1904, quarterly, Feb............ | 178,300 |
| Total.......................................................... | $4,169,300 |

There are also outstanding $29,000 Albany Railway 1st 5 per cents., $11,000 4th 6 per cents., and $32,000 5th 5 per cents., to retire which consolidated mortgage bonds are reserved.

Interest on the United Traction 4½ per cent. debentures is paid at the Commercial Bank, Albany.

The Albany Railway consolidated mortgage is for $500,000. Trustee and agent for the payment of interest, Central Trust Co., New York.

The Albany Railway general mortgagewis for $750,000 authorized. Trustee and agent for the payment of interest, Central Trust Co., Ne York.

The Troy City Railway Consolidated mortgage is $2,000,000 authorized. Trustee and agent for payment of interest, Central Trust Co., New York.

EARNINGS.

Year ending June 30.

| | Gross. | Net. | Charges. | Surplus. |
|---|---|---|---|---|
| 1898-99 | $1,241,264 | $454,280 | $252,860 | $201,420 |
| 1899-00 | 1,306,634 | 470,139 | 232,962 | 237,177 |
| 1900-01 | 1,331,879 | 432,683 | 246,551 | 186,132 |
| 1901-02 | 1,461,892 | 474,691 | 272,096 | 202,595 |

Chairman of Board of Directors, Robert C. Pruyn; President, John W. McNamara, Albany, N. Y.; Vice-President, Francis N. Mann, Jr.; Secretary, Charles G. Cleminshaw, Troy, N. Y.; Treasurer, James McCredie; Superintendent, Edgar S. Fassett, Albany, N. Y.

Directors—Robert C. Pruyn, John W. McNamara, A. Bleecker Banks, Anthony N. Brady, James H. Manning, William J. Walker, Albert Hessberg, William McEwan, Albany, N. Y.; William Kemp, Charles Cleminshaw, Francis N. Mann, Jr., William Shaw, James O'Neil, George P. Ide, Troy, N. Y.; Thomas Breslin, Waterford, N. Y.

Main office, Broadway and Columbia street, Albany, N. Y. Registrar, National Commercial Bank, Albany. Annual meeting, third Monday in June.

## UNITED TRACTION CO. OF PITTSBURG

(Controlled by Philadelphia Company and Operated by Pittsburg Railways Co.)

A corporation formed in June, 1897. The company owns the Second Avenue and the North Side Traction Companies in Pittsburg and Allegheny City, Pa., and leases the Pittsburg, Allegheny & Manchester Traction Co. The Federal Street & Pleasant Valley Railway is leased to the North Side Traction Co. In 1899 control of this company was acquired by the Philadelphia Company, which owns $16,994,900 of the common stock. See statement of that corporation.

The roads operated comprise 117 miles.

Stock...Par $50...Authorized { com., $17,000,000 / pref., 3,000,000 } Issued { com., $17,000,000 / pref., 3,000,000 } $20,000,000

There is also $637,350 stock of the Federal Street & Pleasant Valley Railway not owned by this company on which 5 per cent. per annum is paid.

The preferred stock is 5 per cent., cumulative.

Dividends on the preferred stock are paid semi-annually, in January and July. In 1898, 1899 and 1900, 5 per cent. was paid. The January, 1901, dividend on the preferred was 2½ per cent.

FUNDED DEBT.

| | |
|---|---|
| United Traction gen. mort., 5 per cent., due July, 1997, Jan. and July | $4,750,000 |
| Second Avenue Traction mort., 5 per cent., due July, 1933, Jan. and July | 300,000 |
| Second Avenue Traction mort., 5 per cent., due Dec., 1934, June and Dec. | 2,030,000 |
| Second Avenue Pass. Ry. gen. mort., 5 per cent., due July, 1909, Jan. and July | 120,000 |
| Braddock & Tuttle Creek 1st mort., 6 per cent., due April, 1911, April and Oct. | 50,000 |
| Federal St. & Pleasant Valley 1st mort., due 1903, Jan. and July | 74,000 |
| Federal St. & Pleasant Valley mort., due July, 1919, Jan. and July | 98,000 |
| Allegheny St. Ry. 1st mort., 5 per cent., due 1920 | 36,000 |
| Allegheny & Belleville 1st mort., due 1920, Jan. and July | 23,000 |
| Federal St. & Pleasant Val. cons. mort., 5 per cent., due May, 1942, Jan. and July | 873,000 |
| Pittsburg, Al. & Man. Traction Co. 1st mort., 5 p. c., due Oct., 1930, April and Oct. | 1,500,000 |
| People's Park Passenger Ry. Co. 1st mort., 5 per cent., due July, 1912, Jan. and July. | 53,000 |
| Perry Street Passenger Ry. Co. 1st mort., 5 per cent., due Nov., 1920, Jan. and July. | 4,000 |
| Troy Hill Passenger Ry. Co. 1st mort., 5 per cent., due Nov., 1920, Jan. and July | 42,000 |
| Observatory Hill Passenger Ry. Co. 1st mort., 5 per ct., due July, 1917, Jan. and July. | 47,000 |
| Total | $10,000,000 |

The general mortgage is for $10,000,000. Trustee, Maryland Trust Co., Baltimore.

President, J. D. Callery; Vice-President, J. H. Reed; Treasurer, C. J. Braun, Jr.; Secretary, W. B. Carson; Auditor, C. S. Mitchell.

Directors—J. D. Callery; J. H. Reed; M. K. McMullin, Pittsburg; P. Calhoun, Cleveland; H. J. Bowdoin, Baltimore.

Main office, 435 Sixth avenue, Pittsburg. Annual meeting, second Wednesday in October.

## UNITED VERDE COPPER CO.

A corporation formed under the laws of West Virginia, September 11, 1899. The mines and works of the company are located at Jerome, Ariz.

Stock......Par $10..........Authorized, $3,000,000......Issued, $2,999,270

The company has no preferred stock. Stock is transferred at the office of the company, New York. Registrar, ......

FUNDED DEBT.

Income bonds, 4 per cent., due Sept. 30, 1949, April and Oct.... .......... $2,998,800

The total authorized amount of the income bonds is $3,000,000. Interest is paid at the office of the company, New York.

President, William A. Clark; Vice-President, James A. Macdonald; Secretary and Treasurer, J. C. Kennedy, New York.

Directors—William A. Clark, Charles W. Clark, Butte, Mont.; James A. Macdonald, Flushing, N. Y.; H. G. Atwater, Orange, N. J.; James Kitchen, New York.

Main office, Jerome, Ariz.; New York office, 49 Wall street. Annual meeting, third Monday in February, at New York.

## THE UNITED ZINC COMPANIES

A corporation formed under the laws of New Jersey, March 25, 1899, for the purpose of consolidating zinc and lead properties in Missouri. The company has acquired 500 acres of zinc and lead producing lands in the Joplin, Mo., district, on which there are 16 concentrating mills. The daily capacity of these mills is 1,715 tons.

Stock... Par { com., $5 / pref., 25 } Authorized { com., $5,000,000 / pref., 1,000,000 } Issued { com., $374,500 / pref., 375,000 } $749,500

The preferred stock is 8 per cent., cumulative, and also has a preference as to assets in case of liquidation.

Transfer Agent, Corporation Trust Co., Jersey City. Registrar, Beacon Trust Co., Boston.

Beginning in July, 1899, the company has paid regular quarterly dividends of 2 per cent. in January, April, July and October (15).

The company has no funded debt.

In the year ending December 31, 1901, the gross earnings of the company were $91,517; net $82,384; dividends, $29,996; surplus, $52,388.

President, Levi R. Greene; Secretary, James L. Clark; Treasurer, Franklin Playter, Boston.

Directors—Frederick R. Tibbitts, Frederick A. Turner, Franklin Playter, Boston; James L. Clark, Chicago; William L. Lowell, S. D. Whittemore, Newton, Mass.; Levi R. Greene, Joseph A. Allen, Cambridge, Mass.; Kenneth K. McLaren, Jersey City.

Corporate office, Corporation Trust Co., 15 Exchange place, Jersey City; main office, 2 Kilby street, Boston; branch offices, Joplin, Mo., Aurora, Mo. Annual meeting, January 12, at Jersey City.

## UNIVERSAL TOBACCO CO.

A corporation formed under the laws of New Jersey in 1901. The purposes of the company are the manufacture and sale of cigars, cigarettes, plug and other forms of tobacco and the ownership and apparatus of plants and companies identified with the industry. The company acquired the Turco-Egyptian Tobacco Co., of New York, the Kairo Co., and the business and plant of John Anderson & Co. It was also stated that control of the Havana Commercial Co. and of the Harry Weissinger Tobacco Co., of Louisville, Ky., were acquired by interests identified with this company, but in 1902 it was announced that the three properties had been acquired by the Consolidated Tobacco Co.

Stock....Par $100.....Authorized { com., $7,000,000 / pref., 3,000,000 } Issued { com., $7,000,000 / pref., 3,000,000 } $10,000,000

The company has no funded debt.

President, William H. Butler; Secretary, F. W. Galbraith, Jr.; Treasurer, J. Frederick Eagle; Assistant Secretary and Assistant Treasurer, B. M. Cole.

Directors—William H. Butler, Edward A. McAlpin, George R. Sheldon, W. D. Judkins, Edward J. Patterson, New York; J. L. Richards, Boston.

Corporate office, Jersey City; main office, 697 Greenwich street, New York.

## U. S. BOBBIN & SHUTTLE CO.

A corporation formed under the laws of New Jersey, July 31, 1899. The company purchased and operates the bobbin manufacturing plants of the following concerns:

The James Baldwin Co., Manchester, N. H.
Fall River Bobbin & Shuttle Co., Fall River, Mass.
T. J. Hale, Lawrence, Mass.
Frank Parker, Lowell, Mass.
William H. Parker & Sons, Lowell, Mass.
L. Sprague Co., Lawrence, Mass.
Woonsocket Bobbin Co., Woonsocket, R. I.
James Baldwin, Lewiston, Me.

The establishments in question supply about 6,000 textile manufacturers and do about 85 per cent. of the bobbin business of the country.

Stock....Par $100.....Authorized { com., $1,200,000 / pref., 800,000 } Issued { com., $1,001,000 / pref., 650,000 } $1,651,000

Transfer Agent, Corporation Trust Co. of New Jersey, Jersey City. The preferred stock is 7 per cent., cumulative, and has a preference as to assets.

Dividends at the rate of 7 per cent. per annum have been paid on the preferred stock since the formation of the company, the dividend payments on the preferred being 1¾ per cent. quarterly in February (1), May, August and November. The first quarterly dividend on the common was 1½ per cent., paid February 1, 1901.

FUNDED DEBT.

1st mort., 6 per cent. bonds, due 1919, Feb. and Aug.................................. $120,000

The bonds are a first lien on all the assets of the company and were $300,000 in amount. Trustee, Industrial Trust Co., Providence. There is a sinking fund provision by which not over $50,000 per annum can be drawn and retired at 105 and interest. No other bonds can be created without the assent of 75 per cent. of the preferred stock.

President, William H. Perry, Providence; Vice-President, Percy H. Brundage, New York; Secretary, Treasurer and General Manager, H. Martin Brown, Providence.

Directors—William H. Perry, H. Martin Brown, Cyrus P. Brown, Providence; James F. Baldwin, Luther C. Baldwin, Manchester, N. H.; Percy H. Brundage, New York; George B. Hanford, Orange, N. J.; Fred C. Church, Lowell, Mass.

Main office, 123 Westminster street, Providence. Annual meeting, second Tuesday in October, at Jersey City.

## U. S. STANDARD VOTING MACHINE CO.

A corporation formed under the laws of New York, December 14, 1900. The company was organized to manufacture and sell voting machines. It purchased the patents, plant and good will of the Standard Voting Machine Co., Rochester, N. Y., and the United States Voting Machine Co., Jamestown, N. Y. The company now controls the manufacture of the only voting machines ever used in a Presidential election other than in an experimental way, and the only machines that have been used with success in successive elections in the United States. The United States Voting Machine Co. was organized in 1895. The Standard Voting Machine Co. was organized in 1898.

Stock......Par $100..........................Authorized, $1,000,000......Issued, $1,000,000

Stock is transferred at the company's office, Rochester, N. Y. Registrar, Security Trust Co., Rochester, N. Y.

Of the capital stock 6,000 shares or $600,000 were issued to the Standard and the United States Companies in payment for their patents and good will. An amount of 4,000 shares or $400,000 were offered for subscription at par in December, 1900. The company has no funded debt.

President, Arthur C. Wade, Jamestown, N. Y.; Vice-President, Henry A. Strong; Treasurer, Carl F. Lomb; Secretary, Daniel B. Platt, Rochester, N. Y.

Directors—Henry A. Strong, Edward Bausch, Gustav Erbe, Carl F. Lomb, Daniel B. Platt, Charles Van Voorhis, Rochester, N. Y.; Frank E. Gifford, Arthur C. Wade, Jamestown, N. Y.; Alfred J. Gillespie, Atlantic, Ia.

Main office, Wilde Building, Rochester, N. Y.

## UTAH CONSOLIDATED GOLD MINES, LIMITED

A corporation formed under the laws of Great Britain. The company acquired and owns the Highland Boy Mining Co., which has developed a mining property in Salt Lake County, Utah. The ore bears not only copper, but gold and silver. The mine is fully developed, large and valuable ore bodies having been opened, and the property is equipped with hoisting works, a stamp mill, and a smelter with a daily capacity of 450 tons per day.

Stock......par £1..............................Authorized, £300,000......Issued, £300,000

Transfer Agent, International Trust Co., Boston. Registrar, Massachusetts Loan & Trust Co., Boston.

A large proportion of the shares have been deposited with the International Trust Co., Boston, which issues its certificates or receipts against the same. These receipts, which are of the par value of $5 each, corresponding with the par of the English company's shares, are listed at the Boston Stock Exchange and are dealt in in that market.

On January 15, 1903, a dividend of $1.70 per share was paid on the company's stock.

The report of the Highland Boy Gold Mining Co. for fifteen months, from April 1, 1899, to June 30, 1900, gave receipts from sales of gold, $116,385; from silver, $37,224; from copper, $859,308; miscellaneous receipts, $155,541; total receipts, $1,168,459; expenses, $506,832. The company's smelter was in operation for only twelve months of the period covered by the report, and in that time treated 73,331 tons of ore. The gross receipts per ton were $15.93 and the net receipts $9.02 per ton.

Chairman, John E. Dudley Ryder; Secretary, George H. Johnson, London, England; Assistant Treasurer, F. P. Addicks, New York.

Directors—John E. Dudley Ryder, Urban H. Broughton, Charles S. Henry, Jesse Lewisohn, A. P. B. Loftus, Samuel Newhouse.

Main office, 4 Great Winchester street, London, E. C.; New York office, 52 Broadway. Annual meeting in October, at London.

## UTAH LIGHT & POWER CO.

A corporation formed under the laws of Utah, December 30, 1899. The purposes of the company are supplying electric power and lighting and fuel and illuminating gas in Salt Lake City, and Ogden, Utah. The company succeeded the Union Light & Power Co. of Salt Lake City. It owns water-power plants, steam plants, and gas plants and mains in Salt Lake City and Ogden, Utah.

Stock....Par $25....Authorized { com., $1,500,000; pref., 2,000,000 } Issued { com., $1,062,500; pref., 2,000,000 } $3,062,500

The preferred stock is 8 per cent., non-cumulative, and has equal voting power with the common stock.

Transfer Agent, Colonial Trust Co., New York.

FUNDED DEBT.

| | |
|---|---|
| Prior lien, 5 per cent., due Jan. 1. 1930, Jan. and July | $749,000 |
| Consolidated mort., 4 per cent., due Jan. 1, 1930. Jan. and July | 2,250,000 |
| Total | $2,999,000 |

The authorized issue of the prior lien bonds is $750,000, and of the consolidated mortgage bonds, $3,500,000. Trustee of the prior lien bonds, the Central Trust Co., New York; Trustee of the consolidated mortgage bonds, the Colonial Trust Co., New York; Agent for the payment of interest, the Colonial Trust Co., New York.

President, Joseph F. Smith; 1st Vice-President, John R. Winder; 2d Vice-President, T. G. Webber; Secretary, Robert S. Campbell; Assistant Secretary, M. Shepherd; Treasurer, L. S. Hills, Salt Lake City, Utah.

Directors—Joseph F. Smith, John R. Winder, T. G. Webber, William S. McCornick, L. S. Hills, George Romney, Rudger Clawson, Salt Lake City, Utah; William J. Curtis, New York; John J. Banigan, Providence.

Corporate and main office, 7 South Main street, Salt Lake City, Utah; branch office, Ogden City, Utah. Annual meeting, second Tuesday in March, at Salt Lake City.

## UTICA & MOHAWK VALLEY RAILWAY CO.

A corporation formed under the laws of New York, November 27, 1901. The company is a consolidation of the following companies:

Utica Belt Line Street Railroad Co.
Utica & Suburban Railway Co.
Utica & Mohawk Railroad Co.
Frankfort & Utica Street Railway Co.
Deerfield & Utica Railroad Co.
Herkimer, Mohawk, Ilion & Frankfort Electric Railway Co.
Little Falls & Herkimer Street Railway Co.

The company owns and will operate, when extensions are completed, the entire street railway system of Little Falls, Herkimer, Ilion, Frankfort, Utica, Clinton and Rome, N. Y., and intermediate villiages, with the exception of 13 miles of leased road, and a small local line in Rome. When completed the company will have 103.77 miles of track.

Stock.....Par $100....Authorized { com., $2,500,000; pref., 600,000 } Issued { com., $2,500,000; pref., 600,000 } $3,100,000

The preferred stock is 6 per cent., cumulative. Transfer Agent, Utica Trust Co.

FUNDED DEBT.

| | |
|---|---|
| 1st mort., 4½ per cent. gold, due 1941, March and Sept | $1,461,000 |
| Utica Belt Line St. R.R. Co., 1st mort., 5 per cent. gold, due 1939, March and Nov | 500,000 |
| Utica Belt Line St. R.R. Co., 2d mort., 5 per cent., gold, due 1931, Jan. and July | 39,000 |
| Herk., Mohawk, Ilion & Frankfort Elec. Ry., 1st m., 5 p. c., due 1925, Jan. and July | 150,000 |
| Total | $2,150,000 |

The amount of authorized 1st mortgage of the Utica & Mohawk Valley Railroad Co. is $4,000,000, of which amount $689,000 is reserved to retire divisional liens and $1,300,000 to be held for future additions and improvements.

Trustee of the mortgage of the Herkimer, Mohawk, Ilion & Frankfort Electric Railway and agent for the payment of interest, Farmers' Loan and Trust Co., New York. Trustee of all the other bonds and agent for the payment of interest, New York Security & Trust Co. New York.

EARNINGS.

Year ending September 30.

| | Gross. | Net. | Charges. | Surplus. |
|---|---|---|---|---|
| 1901-2 | $471,129 | $195,608 | $115,713 | $79,875 |

President, Horace E. Andrews; Vice-President, John J. Stanley, Cleveland; Secretary, Walter N. Kernan; Treasurer, Charles B. Rogers; Assistant Secretary and Assistant Treasurer, Arthur L. Linn, Utica, N. Y.

Directors—Horace E. Andrews, John J. Stanley, Cleveland; A. M. Young, Branford, Conn.; W. W. Kernan, William E. Lewis, James S. Sherman, Charles B. Rogers, Nicholas E. Devereux, Utica, N. Y.

Main office, corner Bleecker and Charlotte streets, Utica, N. Y. Annual meeting, third Wednesday in January, at Utica.

## UTICA GAS & ELECTRIC CO.

A corporation formed under the laws of New York, May 10, 1902. The company is a consolidation of the Utica Electric Light & Power Co. and the Equitable Gas & Electric Co. It controls the entire gas and electric light and power business of Utica, N. Y., and its vicinity, included in the property being extensive water power with plant at Trenton Falls, N. Y. Electric light and power is transmitted from that point to Utica, a distance of 12 miles.

Stock......Par $100..........................Authorized, $2,000,000......Issued, $2,000,000

The company has no preferred stock. Stock is transferred at the office of the company, Utica, N. Y.

FUNDED DEBT.

| | |
|---|---|
| Utica L. & P., 1st mort., 5 per cent., due 1950, Jan. and July...................... | $1,000,000 |
| Equitable Gas & E. Co., 1st mort., 5 per cent., due April, 1942, April and Oct....... | 850,000 |
| Utica Elec. & Gas Co. mort., 5 per cent., due Aug., 1907, Feb. and Aug............. | 150,000 |
| Total .......................................................... | $2,000,000 |

The 1st mortgage of the Utica Electric Light & Power Co. is for $1,000,000. Trustee, Trust Co. of America, New York. There is a sinking fund of 1 per cent. per annum, bonds to be bought in the market and not drawn.

The Equitable Gas & Electric 1st mortgage is for $1,000,000. Trustee, Central Trust Co., New York. There is $150,000 of the bonds reserved to retire the old 6 per cent. bonds of the Utica Electric & Gas Co., one of the original constituent companies.

President, Anthony N. Brady, Albany, N. Y.; Vice-President, William E. Lewis; Secretary, William J. Cahill; Treasurer, George H. Stack, Utica, N. Y.

Directors—Anthony N. Brady, Albany, N. Y.; William E. Lewis, John F. Maynard, Charles S. Symonds, William T. Baker, Charles B. Rogers, M. Jesse Brayton, Samuel A. Beardsley, Utica, N. Y.

Main office, 219 Genesee street, Utica, N. Y. Annual meeting, first Monday in April, at Utica.

## UTICA STEAM & MOHAWK VALLEY COTTON MILLS

A corporation formed under the laws of New York in August, 1901. The purpose of the company is to manufacture cotton goods, sheetings, shirtings and yarns. The corporation is a consolidation of the following companies:

The Utica Steam Cotton Mills. The Mohawk Valley Cotton Mills.

The company has 130,000 spindles and 2,200 looms.

Stock......Par $100.................. .........Authorized, $2,000,000......Issued, $2,000,000

The company has no preferred stock and no funded debt. Stock is transferred at the office of the company.

A quarterly dividend of 1½ per cent. was first paid in February, 1902, since then dividends at the rate of 6 per cent. annually have been paid, the payment being quarterly in February, May, August and November.

President, John M. Crouse; Vice-President, Francis G. Wood; Secretary and Treasurer, George De Forest, Utica, N. Y.

Directors—John M. Crouse, Thomas R. Proctor, Abram G. Brower, Francis G. Wood, Frank E. Wheeler, Henry F. Mansfield, Israel N. Terry, Rufus P. Birdseye, D. Clinton Murray, George De Forest, Utica, N. Y.; B. Rush Wendell, Cazenovia, N. Y.

Corporate and main office, 45 State street, Utica, N. Y. Annual meeting, fourth Wednesday in January, at Utica.

## VERMILLION RAILWAY & LIGHT CO.

A corporation formed under the laws of West Virginia in September, 1900, for the purpose of doing a general railway and electric light business. It owns the capital stock of the Danville Street Railway & Light Co. and proposes to construct other lines of railway in Vermillion Co., Illinois. The Danville Street Railway & Light Co. was a consolidation of the street railway, electric light, gas and steam-heating interests of Danville, Ill., consisting of a gas works with a perpetual franchise, an electric-light plant with a 99-year franchise and a capacity of 10,000 incandescent and 400 arc lights, and the entire street railway system of the city, with 11½ miles of track.

Stock......Par $100............... .. ........Authorized, $1,000,000......Issued, $1,000,000

The company has no preferred stock.

FUNDED DEBT.

1st mort., col. trust, 5 per cent., due 1918, April and Oct.......... .................... $200,000

The authorized amount of the mortgage is $275,000, the bonds being secured by a deposit of the entire capital stock ($700,000) of the Danville Street Railway & Light Co. The entire issue is subject to call on any interest date, with a compulsory retirement of $15,000 per annum, under which provision $75,000 have been called and cancelled.

Trustee and agent for the payment of the interest, Portland Trust Co., Portland, Me.

President, George F. Duncan; Secretary and Treasurer, Edward Woodman, Portland, Me.

Directors—George Burnham, Jr., George F. Duncan, W. B. McKinley, Philip G. Brown, Edward Woodman, Portland, Me.

Main office, 42 Exchange street, Portland, Me. Annual meeting in January, at Portland, Me.

## *VICTORIA COPPER MINING CO.*

A corporation formed under the laws of Michigan, January 16, 1899. The company acquired a copper mining property in Ontonagon County, Mich., consisting of over 2,000 acres located near the Michigan and Adventure Mines. The company owns a valuable water power on the Ontonagon River. It prosecuted during 1899, 1900, 1901 and 1902 extensive development work at its mine.

Stock......Par $25..........................Authorized, $2,500,000......Issued, $2,500,000

Stock is transferred at the company's office, 53 State street, Boston. Registrar, Massachusetts National Bank.

Up to January 1, 1903, $10 per share had been paid in upon the stock.

The annual report for the first year of the company's existence, ending December 31, 1899, showed payments for development work, $73,732, and cash in hand, $263,845. In 1900, expenditures, $75,271. Cash balance, $188,573. In 1901, expenditures, $94,608. Cash balance, $93,965. In 1902, expenditures, $150,072. Cash balance, $214,648.

President, Calvin Austin; Vice-President, Charles D. Hanchette; Secretary and Treasurer, James P. Graves, Boston.

Directors—Charles D. Hanchette, Boston; F. H. Begole, Marquette, Mich.; Calvin Austin, F. H. Williams, William F. Humphrey, Boston.

Main office, 53 State street, Boston. Annual meeting, third Monday in January, at Boston

## *THE VICTORIA ROLLING STOCK CO., OF ONTARIO, LIMITED*

A corporation formed under the laws of the Dominion of Canada for the purpose of owning and leasing railroad cars.

Stock......Par $5,000......... .................Authorized, $2,000,000... ..Issued, $600,000

The company has no preferred stock.

Dividends are paid semi-annually, June 1 and December 1. A dividend of 12 per cent. was paid for the fiscal year ending February 15, 1902.

FUNDED DEBT.

Debentures.................................................................. $2,605,500

President, John Burns; Vice-President, William Hendrie; Managing Director, H. C. Hammond; Secretary, R. A. Smith.

Directors—John Burns, William Hendrie, H. C. Hammond, R. A. Smith, A. B. Lee, W. D. Matthews, E. B. Osler, H. M. Pellatt, D. R. Wilkie.

Corporate and main office, Toronto. Annual meeting, first Wednesday in March.

## *THE VINDICATOR CONSOLIDATED GOLD MINING CO.*

A corporation formed under the laws of Colorado, November 20, 1866. The mining property of the company is located at Independence, Cripple Creek, Col.

Stock......Par $1...........................Authorized, $1,500,000......Issued, $1,100,000

The company has no preferred stock and no funded debt. Transfer Agent and Registrar, The International Trust Co., Denver, Col.

Dividends to the amount of $253,000 were paid in 1902.

The output of the company in 1902 was 8,661 tons of smelting ore, the average assay value of which was $59.77; net, $49.50, and 8,910 tons of mill ore, the average value of which was $21.66, net, 13.76. The total receipts of the company were $551,831; operating expenses, $233,143; total expenses, including amount paid to lessees, $330,070; net receipts, $210,951; cash on hand January 1, 1903, $126,519.

President, F. L. Sigel; Vice-President, G. S. Wood; Treasurer, Adolph J. Zang; Secretary and Manager, Frank J. Campbell.

Corporate and main office, Denver, Col. Annual meeting, second Thursday in January, at Denver.

## VIRGINIA-CAROLINA CHEMICAL CO.

A corporation formed under the laws of New Jersey, September 12, 1895. The company was formed to consolidate the southern manufactories of fertilizers, sulphuric acid and kindred articles. It has acquired nearly all the most successful establishments and companies of this description from Baltimore, Md., to Florida, together with a large amount of phosphate lands in South Carolina and Tennessee, being the largest owner of phosphate in the world. The company also owns the steamship S. T. Morgan, which is used in the transportation of phosphate. In February, 1901, it acquired control of the Charleston Mining & Manufacturing Co. It also acquired a number of cotton oil plants, and in 1901 bought a controlling interest in the Southern Cotton Oil Co., owning $9,989,550 of the latter's $10,000,000 of stock.

This company also owns and operates large pyrites mines, producing a large portion of the pyrites used by it in manufacturing sulphuric acid, and in addition it has acquired large brimstone deposits in Mexico, which it is developing.

Stock..Par $100..Authorized { com., $38,000,000 / pref., 12,000,000 } Issued { com., $27,984,400 / pref., 12,000,000 } $39,984,400

The preferred stock is 8 per cent., cumulative. The amount of the authorized share capital was in July, 1899, increased to $12,000,000 of each class, and in 1901 the common was increased to $38,000,000 in order to provide for the acquisition of the Southern Cotton Oil Co. and other properties.

Holders of the preferred stock have a preference both as to the payment of dividends and the distribution of the company's assets.

Transfer Agent, Corporation Trust Co. of New Jersey. Registrar, Morton Trust Co., New York.

The payment of the regular quarterly dividends of 2 per cent. on the preferred stock of this company began January 15, 1896, and have been paid each quarter since, in January (15), April, July and October.

The payment of 4 per cent. dividends on the common stock began December 1, 1896, and 1 per cent. has been paid each quarter since, in March (1), June, September and December. The June, 1902, dividend was increased to 1¼ per cent., which has since been the regular rate on the common.

FUNDED DEBT.

Collateral trust, 5 per cent., due Oct., 1912, April and Oct........................ .. $7,000,000

The collateral trust bonds were issued in 1902 to provide working capital and pay for acquisitions. They are secured by $9,881,300 of Southern Cotton Oil stock and $2,219,200 stock of the Charleston Mining & Manufacturing Co. They are subject to call at 105 on any interest day, and beginning in 1904 have a sinking fund of $500,000 per annum at 102½ and interest.

In 1895 and 1896 the output of the company was 175,000 tons of fertilizers; in 1898, 1899 and 1900 it was about 300,000 tons, and in 1900-01 800,000 tons.

The following is the company's balance sheet June 14, 1902:

| ASSETS. | | LIABILITIES. | |
|---|---|---|---|
| Cash in banks and in hands of branch officers | $1,729,401 | Capital stock—preferred | $12,000,000 |
| Accounts receivable | 2,764,096 | " common | 27,984,400 |
| Bills receivable | 4,440,799 | Bills payable | 4,465,380 |
| Inventory, merchandise on hand | 4,029,059 | Accounts payable | 361,033 |
| Insurance (unearned) | 54,235 | Due to subsidiary companies | 2,960,285 |
| Undivided earnings of independent companies | 2,827,786 | Undivided profits | 4,637,838 |
| Investments in other companies, less deferred payments on account of same | 23,637,953 | Contingent fund | 200,000 |
| Floating properties | 157,178 | | |
| Plants, mines and lands, less deferred payments on account of same | 9,619,529 | | |
| Brands, trade-marks, patents, good will, etc | 3,348,900 | | |
| Total | $52,608,936 | Total | $52,608,936 |

EARNINGS.

Year ending June 15.

| | Gross. | Net. | Dividends. | Surplus. |
|---|---|---|---|---|
| 1900-01 | $2,139,509 | $1,783,955 | $1,199,525 | $584,429 |
| 1901-02 | 4,143,471 | 3,481,384 | 1,829,649 | 1,651,735 |

President, Samuel T. Morgan; Vice-Presidents, E. B. Addison and Fortescue Whittle; Secretary, S. Dabney Crenshaw; Treasurer, S. W. Travers; Auditor, E. Thomas Orgain.

Directors—Samuel T. Morgan, E. B. Addison, S. W. Travers, S. Dabney Crenshaw, A. R. Ellerson, Richmond; W. B. Chisolm, Charleston, S. C.; L. A. Carr, Durham, N. C.; Henry Walters, J. William Middendorf, Baltimore; Samuel Spencer, New York; James B. Duke, Summerville, N. J.; Fortescue Whittle, Petersburg, Va.; F. B. Dancy, Atlanta, Ga.

Corporate office, Jersey City; executive office, Crenshaw Building, Richmond. Annual meeting, first Wednesday July 15, at Jersey City.

## VIRGINIA HOT SPRINGS CO.

A corporation formed under the laws of Virginia, for the purpose of acquiring, improving and operating healing and hot springs in Bath County, Va.; to erect and conduct hotels and baths and to sell mineral waters. The principal properties owned by the company are the Hot Springs, the Warm Sulphur Springs, and the Healing rings, containing in all 4,500 acres, located at or near Hot Springs, Va. The company also owns the Homestead and Virginia hotels at Hot Springs.

Stock......Par $100..............................Authorized, $800,000......Issued, $600,000

The company has no preferred stock.

FUNDED DEBT.

| | |
|---|---|
| 1st mort., 5 per cent., due 1941, Jan. and July | $930,900 |
| 2d mort., 5 per cent., due 1941, Jan. and July | 300,000 |
| Total | $1,230,000 |

The authorized amount of the 1st mortgage is $1,000,000. Trustees, Henry T. Wickham and Henry Taylor, Jr., Richmond, Va. Agents for the payment of interest, J. P. Morgan & Co., New York, and the First National Bank, Richmond, Va.

President and Secretary, A. Trevvett, Richmond; Vice-President, G. H. Ingalls, Cincinnati; Treasurer, G. Farintosh, Hot Springs, Va.

Directors—M. E. Ingalls, G. H. Ingalls, E. F. Osborn, N. R. Johnson, Cincinnati; Decatur Axtell, H. T. Wickham, C. E. Wellford, Warner Moore, A. Trevvett, Richmond.

Corporate and main office, Richmond. Annual meeting, last Tuesday in February, at Richmond or Hot Springs, Va.

## VIRGINIA IRON, COAL & COKE CO.

A company formed under the laws of Virginia in February, 1899. The company is a consolidation under one ownership and management of the iron industries of Southwest Virginia. The properties included in the organization comprise thirteen modern blast furnaces having an aggregate productive capacity of 500,000 tons of pig iron per annum, and the lands and property of ten different coal and coke companies which include 130,000 acres of coal lands and five coal mines in active operation, with coking and mining plants and the complete equipment and accessories of such enterprises. The company also acquired about 60,000 acres of iron ore lands and mines with large deposits of limestone, being practically all the available and most valuable ore properties in the entire district.

In addition to the iron and coal properties the company owns the Virginia & Southwestern Railway, 135 miles, which line connects its various properties. See statement of that company on the railroad section of the MANUAL.

The furnaces acquired comprise the following: Dora Furnace Co., Pulaski, Va.; Max Meadows Iron Co., Max Meadows, Va.; Radford-Crane Iron Co., Radford, Va.; Graham Furnace Co., Graham, Va.; Crozer Iron Co., Roanoke, Va.; Bristol Iron & Steel Co., Bristol, Va.; Watts Co., Middleboro, Ky., and others, comprising 11 blast furnaces and 6 charcoal furnaces, the total capacity being from 300,000 to 500,000 tons of iron per year. It also owns the iron mills of the Crescent Horse Shoe & Iron Co., and the Radford Pipe Works, Radford, Va.

The coal, ore and timber properties of the companies are in Washington, Smythe, Wythe, Pulaski, Wise, Dickinson, Russell, Carroll, Montgomery, Roanoke, Bedford and Augusta counties, Va., and Johnson, Carter, Unicoi and Sullivan counties, Tenn. In September, 1899, the company acquired additional coal and ore properties in Wise County, Va., and Alleghany and Craig counties, Tenn. Its total acreage is upwards of 75,000 acres.

Stock.... .Par $100........................Authorized, $10,000,000......Issued, $8,641,600

FUNDED DEBT.

1st mort., 5 per cent., gold, due March, 1949, March and Sept. See below.......... $7,300,000

The 1st mortgage bond issue, Manhattan Trust Co., New York, trustee, is for $10,000,000.

In June, 1900, the company gave a mortgage for $700,000 to the Morton Trust Co., New York, to secure that amount of 6 per cent. notes, due February 1, 1901. This loan has been paid off at maturity to the extent of $575,000.

There are outstanding $585,000 Carter Coal & Iron Co. bonds and $100,000 Virginia & Tennessee Coal & Iron Co. bonds.

The March, 1901, coupons on the bonds were not paid, and in advance of the default receivers were appointed for the company in February, 1901, by the United States Circuit Court in Virginia.

In September, 1902, a plan of readjustment was formulated by a committee which included Levi P. Morton, Edward J. Berwind, Grant B. Schley and Henry K. McHarg. It provided that the bondholders should deposit their bonds with the Morton Trust Co. and would receive amount of the March, 1901, and March, 1902, coupons in cash, but should accept 5 per cent. scrip payable before September, 1907, for the coupons due September, 1901, September, 1902, and September, 1903. The stockholders of the company were also given rights to subscribe for $2,000,000 5 per cent. bonds of the Virginia & Southwestern Railway Co., guaranteed by the Virginia Iron, Coal & Coke Co., with a bonus of $500 in stock for the Railway with each $1,000 bond. The proceeds were to pay off loans and various indebtedness. The security holders generally co-operated in the plan, which was carried out, and the receivers discharged.

President, Henry K. McHarg, New York; Treasurer and Secretary, J. W. Cure, Radford, Va.

Directors—George L. Carter, Pulaski, Va.; W. B. Dickerman, Grant B. Schley, Edward J. Berwind, Henry K. McHarg, George A. Crocker, Charles B. Squier, New York.

Main office, Radford, Va.; New York office, 40 Wall street.

---

## THE VIRGINIA PASSENGER & POWER CO.

A corporation formed under the laws of Virginia in 1901 to operate electric railways and toll roads in Richmond, Manchester and Petersburg, Va., and surrounding territory, and to supply electric light and power. The company acquired the following companies:

Richmond Passenger & Power Co.
South Side Railway & Development Co.
Upper Appomattox Navigation Co.
Brook Turnpike Co.
Manchester Railway Co.
Richmond Traction Co.
Virginia Electrical Railway & Development Co.
Mechanicsville Turnpike Co.
Richmond & Petersburg Electrical Ry. Co.
Westhampton Park Railway Co.

The company controls and operates 118 miles of electric railway, water rights on the St James and Appomattox rivers and toll roads in Henrico County. It owns real essate in Richmond, Manchester and Petersburg, including park properties valued at $1,000,000 and several light and power plants.

Stock...Par $100... Authorized { com., $10,000,000; pref., 5,000,000 } Issued { com., $10,000,000; pref., 4,000,000 } $14,000,000

The preferred stock is 6 per cent., non-cumulative.

FUNDED DEBT.

| | |
|---|---|
| 1st con. mort., 5 per cent., gold, due July 1, 1952, Jan, and July.................... | $7,180,000 |
| South Side Ry. & Dev. Co., 1st mort., 5 p. c., g., due July 1, 1949, March and Sept. | 1,000,000 |
| Virginia Development & Electric Railway Co., 1st mort., due Jan. 1, 1929.......... | 1,500,000 |
| Richmond Pass. & Power Co., con. mort., 5 p. c., g., due Jan. 1, 1925, Jan. and July. | 3,000,000 |
| Richmond Pass. & Power Co., deb. mort., 5 p. c., g., due July 1, 1910, Jan. and July | 1,000,000 |
| Richmond Traction Co., 1st mort., 5 per cent., gold, due July 1, 1925, Jan. and July | 500,000 |
| Total ........... ........................................................ | $14,180,000 |

The total amount of the consolidated mortgage is $15,000,000. Of that amount $7,150,000 are reserved for the underlying bonds of the subsidiary companies. The bonds may be called on any interest date at 110 and interest. The outstanding bonds of subsidiary companies are in each instance the total amount authorized. The debenture bonds of the Richmond Passenger & Power Co. may be called at any time at 102 and accrued interest. The bonds of the Richmond Traction Co. are subject to call at 105 after July 1, 1900. Trustee of the 1st convertible mortgage, the 1st mortgage of the South Side Railway & Development Co., the 1st mortgage of the Virginia Electric & Development Co., and the convertible mortgage of the Richmond Passenger & Power Co., Merchants Trust Co., New York, by whom also interest coupons are paid. Trustee of the debenture mortgage of the Richmond Passenger & Power Co. and agent for the payment of interest, Atlantic Trust Co., New York. Trustee of the mortgage of the Richmond Traction Co., Maryland Trust Co., Baltimore.

President, Fritz Sitterding, Richmond; 1st Vice-President, Frank Jay Gould, New York; 2d Vice-President, Augustus Wright, Petersburg, Va.; Secretary and Treasurer, Guy Phillips, New York; Assistant Secretary and Treasurer, William Northrop, Richmond.

Directors—Frank Jay Gould, Edwin Gould, A. H. Calef, Guy Phillips, Alfred Skitt, New York; Fritz Zieterding, William Northrop, J. D. Payton, Richmond; Augustus Wright, Petersburg, Va.

Corporate office, Richmond; New York office, 195 Broadway. Annual meeting, in March, at New York.

## VIRTUE CONSOLIDATED MINES.

A corporation formed under the laws of Oregon for the purpose of engaging in gold and silver mining. The mines owned by the company are at War Eagle Mountain, Idaho.

Stock......Par $1............................Authorized, $2,000,000......Issued, $2,000,000

The company has no preferred stock and no funded debt.

President, A. F. Gault; Vice-President, Frank J. Hart; Secretary and Treasurer, D. F. Johnson, Montreal.

Directors—A. F. Gault, Frank J. Hart, L. H. Gault, Rodolph Forget, Alphonse Turcotte, C. E. Gault, Montreal; William Smith, Arthur Buckbee, Baker City, Ore.

Main office, Montreal. Annual meeting first Monday in March, at Montreal.

## THE VULCAN CONSOLIDATED COPPER CO.

A corporation formed under the laws of West Virginia, in 1901. The property of the company comprises 49 separate copper mining properties near Sodaville, Esmeralda County, Nev., there being four groups of mines—the Parrot, the New York, the Volcano and the John L.—comprising 980 acres of mineral land. The company has three smelter sites, comprising 160 acres, including the Mt. Diabolo mill at Sodaville. It also has a large tract of coal land adjacent to its mines. Over $250,000 was expended in preliminary and exploration work during 1899, 1900 and 1901, the development of the property including the excavation of 7,000 feet of shafts, tunnels, etc., representing an expenditure of $250,000. It was stated at the beginning of 1902 that in one mine the company had 60,000 tons of ore blocked out and that the company would proceed at once with the erection of a smelting plant.

The company, in January, 1902, offered $500,000 of stock for subscription at $6 per share.

Stock......Par $10..........................Authorized, $5,000,000......Issued, $3,000,000

President, Charles T. Champion, New York; 1st Vice-President, Joseph Siegel, Chicago; 2d Vice-President, John R. Butler; Secretary and Treasurer, Ambrose I. Harrison, New York.

Directors—John R. Butler, Charles T. Champion, Ambrose I. Harrison, New York; F. L. Fisher, Knoxville, Tenn.; Joseph Siegel, F. L. Champion, F. B. Taylor, Chicago.

Main office, 35 Nassau street, New York.

## VULCAN DETINNING CO.

A corporation formed under the laws of New Jersey, April 26, 1902. The company acquired the plant and property of the Vulcan Metal Refining Co. of Sewaren, N. J., and of the Vulcan Western Co. of Streator, Ill. The business of the company is the refining of metals and the reclamation of merchantable tin bars and steel from the scrap tin left from the manufacture of cans and hollow ware. It has large and complete plants at Sewaren, N. J., and Streator, Ill.

Stock......Par $100.....Authorized { com., $2,000,000 / pref., 1,500,000 } Issued { com., $2,000,000 / pref., 1,500,000 } $3,500,000

The preferred stock is 7 per cent., cumulative. Stock is transferred at the office of the company, New York.

The company began the payment of regular quarterly dividends on both the preferred and common stocks at the rate of 1¾ per cent. on the preferred and 1 per cent. on the common on July 20, 1902, and has since paid the quarterly dividends of the same amounts in January, April, July and October.

The company has no funded debt.

The earnings for the six months ending October 1, 1902, were stated to have been: Net, $143,935; betterments, $13,633; dividends, $92,500; balance surplus, $37,802.

President, Joseph B. Bloomingdale; Vice-President, Stephen A. Ginna; Secretary and Treasurer, Meyer Hecht; General Manager, Adolph Kern, New York.

Directors—Joseph B. Bloomingdale, Stephen A. Ginna, Meyer Hecht, Adolph Kern, Samuel R. Beardsley, Lyman G. Bloomingdale, Harry Kraus.

Main office, Sewaren, N. J.; New York office, 157 Cedar street. Annual meeting, first Thursday in May at Sewaren, N. J.

---

## THE WAR EAGLE CONSOLIDATED MINING & DEVELOPMENT CO., LIMITED

A corporation formed under the laws of British Columbia, January, 1897, for the purpose of engaging in gold mining. The mines owned by the company are located at Rossland, British Columbia, and consist of the Crown Point, War Eagle and Richmond group. The company also has a controlling interest in several other important claims.

Stock......Par $1..........................Authorized, $2,000,000......Issued, $1,750,000

The company has no preferred stock and no funded debt.

Monthly dividends of 1½ per cent., were paid from June, 1898, to February, 1900. In 1902 the company loaned $203,249, and had at the end of the year a balance of $308,615.

President, George Gooderham; Vice-President, Thomas G. Blackstock; Secretary, E. J. Kingstone, Toronto.

Directors—George Gooderham, Thomas G. Blackstock, W. G. Gooderham, George T. Blackstock, W. H. Beatty, A. E. Gooderham, C. H. Gooderham, Toronto; Charles R. Hosmer, Montreal.

Main office, Toronto. Annual meeting, last Tuesday in February, at Toronto.

---

## WARWICK IRON AND STEEL CO.

A corporation formed under the laws of Pennsylvania, June 9, 1899. The company is successor to the Warwick Iron Co., and took over the business, contracts, assets and property of the latter. The plant comprised 34 acres of ground at Pottstown, Pa., equipped for the manufacture of superior grade pig iron, the "Warwick" brand having a wide reputation. The furnace had a yearly capacity of about 70,000 tons. The company, in 1901, erected a new furnace with a capacity of 400 tons of pig iron per day, raising the total capacity of the plant to 600 tons per day. Its production in the year was 147,118 tons.

Stock......Par $10..........................Authorized, $1,500,000......Issued, $1,444,740

Of the stock, $1,000,000 was issued, full paid, for the property, consisting of plant, real estate, book accounts, material on hand and cash capital of the old company. The treasury stock, $500,000, was in October, 1899, offered to the stockholders for subscription at par in instalments of $2 each, payable respectively on or before November 15, 1899, and on the 15th of February, May, August and November, 1900.

Stock is transferred at the office of the company. Registrar, Real Estate Title Insurance & Trust Co.

The payments of the dividends on the company's stock began with a quarterly dividend of 2 per cent., paid August 10, 1899. In November, 1899, a second quarterly dividend of 2 per cent. and ½ per cent. extra was paid. In February, 1900, paid 2 per cent., and in May, 1900, 2 per cent. and ½ per cent. extra were paid. Dividends are now paid semi-annually in May and November. In May, 1901, paid 3 per cent. cash, and in November, 1901, 3 per cent. in scrip, convertible into stock at par. In April, 1902, dividends were suspended in order to augment the working capital of the company.

FUNDED DEBT.

1st mort., 5 per cent., due 1921, June and Dec.................................... $300,000

In March, 1901, $300,000 of 5 per cent. 20-year bonds were issued for payments on the new furnace. The bonds have a sinking fund of $15,000 per annum.

In 1902 the earnings were $95,525; charges, $34,001; surplus, $61,524.

The following is the company's balance sheet, December 31, 1902:

| Assets. | | Liabilities. | |
|---|---|---|---|
| Real estate account—No. 1 furnace, including machinery, land (34 acres), equipments, sidings, etc.. | $753,239 | Capital stock.................... | $1,446,740 |
| Construction account—Cost of No. 2 furnace, machinery and equipment.......................... | 868,931 | Bond account.................... | 300,000 |
| New construction account—Dwelling houses, new boiler, ore trestle, and account new casting table No. 1 furnace, etc......... | 57,809 | Profit and loss account. .......... | 42,278 |
| Yarnall Farm (114 acres).......... | 10,013 | Pig iron account................. | 61,524 |
| La Rue Mining Co. payment on 1-20 interest in Lake Ore property ("Mesaba ore") .......... | 2,000 | Relining account — Amount reserved for relining furnaces.... | 22,558 |
| Pig iron on hand December 31, 1902, 336 tons at $20........... | 6,720 | Bills payable..................... | 383,871 |
| General stock at furnace (duplicate parts of machinery, etc.)........ | 19,287 | Accounts payable for book accounts during December............... | 161,851 |
| Bills receivable—Notes for pig iron not discounted................. | 22,091 | | |
| Cash in bank.................... | 44,446 | | |
| Iron-making materials on hand—ore, coke, coal, etc............. | 452,815 | | |
| Pottstown Iron Co., capital stock.. | 4,324 | | |
| Glasgow Iron Co., capital stock... | 1,830 | | |
| Accounts collectable—Shipments of pig iron, November and December | 175,317 | | |
| Total..................... | $2,418,822 | Total..................... | $2,418,822 |

President, Edgar S. Cook, Pottstown, Pa.; Vice-President, Jacob Rech, Philadelphia; Secretary and Treasurer, Gustavus W. Nicolls, Philadelphia.

Directors—William H. Shelmerdine, Edgar S. Cook, Harry C. Francis, Frederick W. Tunnell, W. S. Pilling, Jacob Rech, F. H. Bachman.

Main office, Pottstown, Pa.; Philadelphia office, Broad and Chestnut streets. Annual meeting, third Tuesday in February.

## WASHBURN WIRE CO.

A corporation formed under the laws of Maine in 1900. The object of the company is to manufacture copper and steel wire and kindred products. The company acquired the entire capital stocks of the American Electrical Works, Phillipsdale, R. I., and of the R. H. Wolff & Co., Limited, New York. The company has erected two open hearth steel furnaces and a rolling mill at Phillipsdale.

Stock. ..Par $100.....Authorized { com., $1,250,000 / pref., 2,500,000 }   Issued { com., $1,250,000 / pref., 2,500,000 } $3,750,000

The preferred stock is 7 per cent., cumulative, and has a preference, in case of liquidation, of $130 per share before any payment is made on the common stock; and after the common shall have received $100 per share both classes of stock share equally in the distribution of the remaining assets. The company has the option to call any portion of the preferred stock at 130.

Transfer Agents, Kidder, Peabody & Co., Boston. Registrar, National Shawmut Bank, Boston.

Dividends on the preferred stock are quarterly, in January, April, July and October. The first quarterly dividend on the preferred was 1¾ per cent., paid October 1, 1900, and dividends of the same amount have been paid regularly since then.

The company has no funded debt.

President, Charles G. Washburn, Worcester, Mass.; Treasurer, Joseph Remick, Boston; Clerk, Josiah H. Drummond, Jr., Portland, Me.; General Manager, E. F. Phillips, Phillipsdale, R. I.

Directors—Charles G. Washburn, Worcester; Robert Winsor, Joseph Remick, Boston; Eugene F. Phillips, Edwin A. Smith, Providence.

Main office, Phillipsdale, R. I. Annual meeting, third Tuesday in February, at Portland, Me.

## WASHINGTON & CANONSBURG RAILWAY CO.

A corporation formed under the laws of Pennsylvania, June 3, 1902, as a consolidation of the following companies:

Washington Electric Street Railway Co. Canonsburg Street Railway Co.

The company owns and operates 4 miles of electric railway between Washington and Tylerdale, Pa., and has under construction 9 miles to Canonsburg, Pa. The population served is about 35,000.

Stock......Par $100........................Authorized, $1,000,000......Issued, $1,000,000

The company has no preferred stock.

FUNDED DEBT.

| | |
|---|---|
| 1st mort., 5 er cent., gold, due July 1, 1930, Jan. and July ........ | $550,000 |
| WashingtonpElectric Street Railway Co. mort., due Feb. 1, 1927........ | 125,000 |
| Total........ | $675,000 |

The total amount of the authorized 1st mortgage is $650,000, of which $125,000 are reserved to redeem the underlying lien and $50,000 reserved for improvements. A sinking fund of $5,000 per annum is provided, beginning July 1, 1907.

In the fiscal year ending December 31, 1902, the gross earnings were $62,949.

President, Francis J. Torrance; Vice-President, Arthur Kennedy; Secretary and Treasurer, W. C. Hagan, Pittsburg.

Directors—Francis J. Torrance, Arthur Kennedy, W. C. Hagan, John A. Willson, James Kent, Pittsburg, Pa.

Main office, 403 Wood street, Pittsburg.

## WASHINGTON COPPER MINING CO.

A corporation formed under the laws of Michigan in 1884. The company owns a copper property in Keweenaw County, Mich. During 1902 no operations were conducted on the property.

Stock......Par $25........................Authorized, $2,500,000......Issued, $1,500,000

Of the stock 40,000 shares remain in the company's treasury. The stock outstanding consists of 60,000 shares, on which there has been paid in 25 cents per share.

President, Harry F. Fay, Boston; Secretary and Treasurer, George G. Endicott, Boston.

Directors—Harry F. Fay, J. C. Watson, C. E. Adams, S. R. Dow, Boston; James Chynoweth, Michigan.

Main office, 60 State street, Boston. Annual meeting, fourth Tuesday in March.

## WASHINGTON RAILWAY & ELECTRIC CO.

This company is a reorganization, in 1901, of the Washington Traction & Electric Co., which was sold under foreclosure. The company controls or owns the principal street railways and electric light organizations in Washington, D. C. Total road operated, 100 miles.

Stock....Par $100...Authorized { com., $6,500,000 / pref., 8,500,000 } Issued { com., $6,500,000 / pref., 8,500,000 } $15,000,000

FUNDED DEBT.

| | |
|---|---|
| 1st mort., 4 per cent., due Dec., 1951, June and Dec........ | $8,392,350 |
| Columbia Ry. 1st mort., 6 per cent., due April, 1914, April and Oct........ | 500,000 |
| Columbia Ry. extension mort., 5 per cent., due Oct., 1914, April and Oct........ | 400,000 |
| Metropolitan Ry. 1st mort., 5 per cent., due Feb., 1925, Feb. and Aug........ | 1,850,000 |
| " " cers. of indebtedness, 6 per cent., due 1906-1907........ | 500,000 |
| Anacostia & Potomac Ry. 1st mort., 5 per cent., due April, 1949, April and Oct.... | 2,250,000 |
| Brightwood Railway, 1st mort., 6 per cent., due Oct., 1912, April and Oct........ | 250,000 |
| " " gen. mort., 6 per cent., due 1907, May and Nov........ | 100,000 |
| Total........ | $14,242,350 |

The 4 per cent. 1st mortgage was created in 1901, under the reorganization, and is $17,500,000 authorized, $7,607,000 of the bonds being reserved to retire underlying bonds, and $1,550,000 for improvements. Trustee and agent for the payment of interest, United States Mortgage & Trust Co., New York.

In the reorganization, holders of the old company's bonds received for each $1,000 $550 in new 4s, $550 of new preferred and $200 of new common stock. The old stock paid an assessment of $9 per share and received $9 in new preferred and $30 in new common for each old share.

President, Allen L. McDermott; Vice-President, George H. Harries; Secretary, James B. Lackey; Treasurer, W. F. Ham.

Main office, East Capitol and Fourteenth streets, Washington, D. C.

## THE WASHINGTON WATER POWER CO.

A corporation formed under the laws of Washington, March 14, 1899, October 9, 1890, and May 26, 1899. The company has a broad franchise that gives it the right to own real estate, water powers, mills and manufactories; to own and operate mills, canals, acqueducts, electric power and light plants, street railways, parks, natatoriums, places of amusement, etc. It controls the street railway and electric lighting service of Spokane, Wash., having acquired the following properties:

Edison Electric Illuminating Co.
Spokane Street Railway Co.
Spokane Electric Railway Co.
City Park Transit Co.
Spokane Cable Railway Co.
Falls City Land & Improvement Co.
Spokane Falls Water Power Co.
Spokane Mill Co.
Port Falls Water Power Co.

The water-power of the company is 30,000 horse-power at Spokane and 13,000 horse-power at Port Falls. It develops at Spokane Falls 7,000 horse-power of electric power, and has a 65,000 horse-power plant under construction. It operates 34 miles of street railway under the single trolley system.

Stock......Par $100.......... ..... .........Authorized, $2,600,000......Issued, $2,249,100

The company has no preferred stock.

Transfer Agent, Franklin Trust Co., Brooklyn, N. Y.; Registrar, Spokane & Eastern Trust Co., Spokane, Wash.

Dividends have been paid as follows: 1892, 1 per cent.; 1892, 4 per cent.; 1893, 2 per cent.; 1900, 3 per cent.; 1901, 4 per cent.; 1902, 5 per cent; January 1, 1903, 1¼ per cent. Dividend periods are quarterly, in January, April, July and October.

FUNDED DEBT.

1st cons. mort. and collateral trust, 5 per cent. gold, due 1929, Jan. and July. ........ $1,600,000

The authorized bond issue is $2,000,000. Trustee of mortgage and agent for the payment of interest, Franklin Trust Co., Brooklyn, N. Y.

In the fiscal year ending December 31, 1901, the gross earnings were $556,997; net earnings, $227,249; interest charges, $81,740; dividends, $79,568; surplus, $30,752; depreciation to plant, $34,656; bad assets, $531; total surplus, $143,216.

The following is the company's balance sheet, December 31, 1902:

| ASSETS. | | LIABILITIES. | |
|---|---|---|---|
| Treasury stock | $353,700 | Capital stock | $2,600,000 |
| Real estate, buildings and water power | 1,843,126 | Bonds | 1,600,00 |
| Light and power, property and equipment | 813,924 | Reserve accounts | 1,442 |
| Street railway, property and equipment | 999,286 | Bills payable | 155,000 |
| Merchandise | 91,389 | Accounts payable | 45,492 |
| Stocks in other companies | 296 | Surplus | 224,981 |
| Bills and accounts receivable | 21,244 | | |
| Unfinished plant construction | 127,164 | | |
| Cash | 376,786 | | |
| Total | $4,626,915 | Total | $4,626,915 |

President, Henry M. Richards; 1st Vice-President, A. B. Campbell; 2d Vice-President and General Manager, D. L. Huntington; Treasurer, H. E. Perks; Secretary, H. L. Bleecker.

Directors—W. A. White, George H. Southard, Frank Lyman, Henry M. Richards, A. B. Campbell, D. L. Huntington, J. P. M. Richards, James N. Glover, J. D. Sherwood, Thomas G. Thomson.

Corporate and main office, Spokane, Wash. Annual meeting, first Monday in March, at Spokane, Wash.

## THE WATERLOO & CEDAR FALLS RAPID TRANSIT CO.

A corporation formed under the laws of Iowa in 1895. The company acquired the following companies:

Waterloo Street Railway Co. Cedar Falls & Normal Railway Co.

The company owns and operates 40 miles of electric and steam railway in Waterloo, Cedar Falls, Glasgow and Denver, Ia., serving a population of 50,000. The company has a power-house in Waterloo, stations at Glasgow and Cedar Falls, 29 passenger cars, 35 freight cars, 2 electric locomotives and 2 steam locomotives.

Stock......Par $100..........................Authorized, $1,200,000......Issued, $600,000

The company has no preferred stock. Stock is transferred at the office of the company, Waterloo, Ia.

FUNDED DEBT.

1st mort., 5 per cent., due Oct. 1, 1922, April and Oct...............................$600,000

The total amount of the authorized 1st mortgage is $800,000. Trustees, The Northern Trust Co. and Arthur Heurtley, Chicago. Agent for the payment of interest, First National Bank, Chicago. A sinking fund of $15,000 per annum is provided, commencing in 1907. Bonds may be called at any time.

In the fiscal year ending December 31, 1902, the gross earnings were $86,327; net, $40,226; interest, $17,500; surplus, $22,726; the operating expenses were 53⅓ per cent. of the gross receipts.

President and General Manager, L. S. Cass, Waterloo, Ia.; First Vice-President and Secretary, J. F. Cass, Sumner, Ia.; Treasurer, E. A. Boggs, Waterloo, Ia.

Directors—L. S. Cass, Waterloo, Ia.; J. F. Cass, Sumner, Ia.; E. K. Boisot, Chicago.

Corporate and main office, Waterloo, Ia. Annual meeting, third Tuesday in January, at Waterloo, Ia.

---

## WEAVER COAL & COKE CO.

A corporation formed to mine coal and manufacture coke. Its plants are located in West Virginia, Ohio, Indiana, Illinois and Pennsylvania.

Stock......Par $100..........................Authorized, $3,000,000......Issued, $3,000,000

The company has no preferred stock or funded debt. Transfer Agent, The Illinois Trust & Savings Bank, Chicago.

The company pays 2 per cent. dividends quarterly. It has a surplus of $600,000.

President, Henry E. Weaver; Secretary and Treasurer, Cornelius A. Bickett, Chicago; Assistant Treasurer, H. E. Evans, New York.

Main office, 204 Dearborn street, Chicago; branch offices, New York, Detroit, Pittsburg, Milwaukee, Buffalo, St. Louis.

---

## WELLS FARGO & CO.

A corporation formed under the laws of Colorado, February 5, 1866, but first organized in New York, March 18, 1852. The company has powers to transact both an express and a banking business. It operates an express organization on railroad, steamship and stage lines, aggregating 43,052 miles, with 3,987 offices. It is the only through express line from ocean to ocean, and has agencies in all parts of Europe, South America, China and Japan. It does a general banking business, its bank being in San Francisco, with branches in New York, Salt Lake City and Portland, Ore.

Capital stock......Par $100....................Authorized, $8,000,000......Issued, $8,000,000

Stock is transferred at the company's office, New York.

Dividends on the stock at the rate of 8 per cent. per annum were paid for many years until July, 1894, when the rate was reduced to 6 per cent. The dividends are paid semi-annually, 3 per cent. each, in January (15) and July. In January, 1902, an extra dividend of 2 per cent. was paid and in July, 1902, and January, 1903, extra dividends of 1 per cent. each were paid.

Chairman, Edward H. Harriman, New York; President, Dudley Evans, San Francisco; Vice-President and Secretary, H. B. Parsons, New York; Treasurer, Homer S. King; Assistant Secretary, Nathan Stein, San Francisco.

Directors—Dudley Evans, Homer S. King, H. E. Huntington, George E. Gray, San Francisco; John J. McCook, Edward H. Harriman, F. D. Underwood, W. V. S. Thorne, W. T. Van Brunt, New York.

Main office, corner Second and Mission streets, San Francisco; New York office, 63 Broadway. Annual meeting, second Thursday in August, at New York.

## WELSBACH CO.

A corporation formed under the laws of New Jersey April 28, 1900. It acquired the stocks of the Welsbach Light Co. and the Welsbach Commercial Co., which companies own the patents of Dr. Carl Auer Von Welsbach and others for the manufacture of incandescent and regenerating gas lamps and other improvements. Its factory is at Gloucester, N. J., and its sales agencies in the various cities of the United States.

The Welsbach Commercial Co. had $3,500,000 preferred stock and $3,500,000 common; par of both classes $100. The Welsbach Light Co. had $516,015 stock, par $5. The Welsbach Commercial Co. owned a majority of the stock of the Welsbach Light Co.

The consolidation plan provided that the holders of the outstanding Welsbach Light stock should receive $60 in 5 per cent. bonds of the new company for each $5 share. The preferred stock of the Welsbach Commercial Co. was exchanged at par for bonds of the new company, and the latter's stock was given, share for share, for the Welsbach Commercial Co.'s common.

Stock......Par $100..........................Authorized, $3,500,000......Issued, $3,500,000

In June, 1901, a dividend of 2 per cent. was paid on the stock and another 2 per cent. dividend on June 27, 1902.

FUNDED DEBT.

Collateral Trust mort., 5 per cent., due June, 1930, June and Dec.................. $6,574,940

The collateral trust mortgage is $7,000,000 authorized, Provident Life & Trust Co., Philadelphia, trustee, and is secured by a mortgage of all the property of the company and deposit of the shares acquired in the consolidation. There is an annual sinking fund of $105,000, and bonds are subject to call at par and interest. Of the bonds $409,000 not required to make the above exchanges were reserved for additional property, etc.

President and General Manager, Sidney Mason; 1st Vice-President, Samuel T. Bodine; 2d Vice-President, Randal Morgan; 3d Vice-President, Walton Clark; Secretary and Treasurer, Lewis Lillie, Philadelphia.

Directors—Sidney Mason, Thomas Dolan, Samuel T. Bodine, Randal Morgan, Walton Clark, William W. Gibbs, Lewis Lillie, Philadelphia; B. W. Spencer, Passaic, N. J.

Main office, Broad and Arch streets, Philadelphia.

## THE WERNER CO.

A corporation formed under the laws of New Jersey in January, 1899. It took over the property of an Illinois corporation of the same name. The plant, which is situated at Akron, O., is one of the largest book manufacturing establishments in the world.

Stock...Par $100...Authorized { com., $2,500,000 / pref., 1,000,000 } Issued { com., $2,500,000 / pref., 1,000,000 } $3,500,000

Transfer Agent, Colonial Trust Co., New York. Registrar, New Jersey Registration & Trust Co., East Orange, N. J.

The company has no mortgage debt, but has outstanding $1,600,000 debentures due in ten years, which were given to the creditors of the old Werner Co., of Illinois, in settlement of the debts of that company.

The amount of stock given above is the authorized issue. The preferred stock is entitled to 8 per cent., cumulative. All of the stock is held in trust pending payment of the debentures.

President and General Manager, P. E. Werner; Vice-President, R. M. Werner; Secretary, C. I. Bruner; Treasurer, A. Wagoner; Chairman, H. C. Ellison; Vice-Chairman, U. G. Walker.

Directors—P. E. Werner, R. M. Werner, C. I. Bruner, A. Wagoner, Akron, O.; H. C. Ellison, U. G. Walker, Cleveland; H. H. Picking, East Orange, N. J.

Main office, Akron, O.

## WEST END STREET RAILWAY CO.

(Leased to Boston Elevated Railway Co.)

The company's property was leased to the Boston Elevated Railroad Co. in 1897 until June, 1922. The Elevated Co. took possession January 1, 1898.

This company was formed in 1887 by consolidation of several lines in Boston, including the Metropolitan, Boston Consolidated, Cambridge, South Boston, and Suburban Street Railway Companies. Leases Malden & Melrose Street Railway and Somerville Horse Railroad, and has trackage rights on East Middlesex Street Railway and Lynn & Boston Railroad. It owns 373 miles of road.

This company was a pioneer in the adoption of electricity as a motive power in a city of the first class. All its lines are equipped with electric power.

The company leases the Boston subway from the city for 4⅞ per cent. on cost of same, which was about $5,800,000.

Company has lands and buildings valued at over $10,000,000. The company's franchise empowering it to use electricity in the city of Boston is a comprehensive one.

Stock.....Par $50.....Authorized { com., $9,085,000 / pref., 6,400,000 } Issued { com., $9,085,000 / pref., 6,400,000 } $15,485,000

The preferred stock is 8 per cent., cumulative.

Transfer Agent, American Loan & Trust Co., Boston. Registrar, Old Colony Trust Co., Boston.

The terms of lease to the Boston Elevated include the payment of 7 per cent. per annum on the common stock of the West End Street Railway, and 8 per cent. on the preferred stock, in addition to all charges and rentals.

The dividends under the lease are paid on the preferred stock semi-annually, 4 per cent. each, in January and July. On the common the semi-annual payments are 3½ per cent. each, in April and October.

FUNDED DEBT.

| | |
|---|---|
| Metropolitan Street Railway plain bonds, 5 per cent., due Dec., 1903, June and Dec.. | $500,000 |
| Middlesex Street Railway plain bonds, 5 per cent., due July, 1894, Jan. and July.. | 200,000 |
| Boston Con. Street Railway plain bonds, 5 per cent., due Jan., 1907, Jan. and July.. | 500,000 |
| Cambridge Street Railway 1st mort., 5 per cent., due April, 1903, April and Oct.... | 362,000 |
| Charles River Street Railway 1st mort., 5 per cent., due April, 1904, April and Oct.. | 150,000 |
| South Boston Street Railway plain bonds, 5 per cent., due May, 1905, May and Nov.. | 200,000 |
| West End Street Railway bonds, 4½ per cent., due Nov., 1914, March and Sept.... | 2,000,000 |
| West End Street Railway bonds, 4 per cent., due May, 1916, May and Nov......... | 815,000 |
| West End Street Railway bonds, 4 per cent., due Feb., 1917, Feb. and Aug......... | 2,700,000 |
| West End Street Railway bonds, cur., 4 per cent., due Aug., 1915, Feb. and Aug.... | 4,239,000 |
| West End Street Railway bonds, cur., 4 per cent., due Aug., 1932, Feb. and Aug... | 3,559,000 |
| Total ............................................................ | $15,225,000 |

The company pays as rental for Somerville Horse Railroad 6 per cent. upon $153,000 of that company's stock.

Ten-year bonds, 4 per cent., for $3,000,000 were created in 1893 to pay expense of change to electric power and to discharge floating debt. The issues of West End bonds, due August, 1915 ($4,239,000), and August, 1932 ($3,559,000), were sold to pay for improvements and extensions of the property and for the purpose of refunding the issue of 5 per cent. bonds due November 1st, 1902, as well as some Highland Street Railway Co. bonds that had become due and were paid and some Cambridge Railroad bonds which have been drawn and paid.

Interest on the Cambridge Street Railway 1st mortgage bonds is paid at the New England Trust Co., Boston. Interest on the West End 4s of 1915 is paid at the Old Colony Trust Co., Boston. Agent for the payment of interest on all the other bonds of the system, American Loan & Trust Co., Boston.

The earnings are included in those of the lessee.

President, Joseph B. Russell; Vice-President, John Parkinson; Treasurer, Parkman Dexter.

Directors—Edwin F. Atkins, Charles M. Baker, Parkman Dexter, John Parkinson, Joseph B. Russell, C. Minot Weld, Stephen M. Weld, Charles A. Williams, Moses Williams, Alfred Winsor, Boston; Samuel Spencer, New York.

Main office, 101 Milk street, Boston. Annual meeting, fourth Tuesday in November.

---

## THE WEST INDIA ELECTRIC CO., LIMITED

A corporation formed under the laws of Jamaica, W. I., in 1897. The company has a monopoly of the street railway and electric lighting business in Kingston, Jamaica, on a 30-years franchise with privilege of renewals in 20-year periods. The company owns and operates 25½ miles of electric railway and has a plant consisting of power house, dam, etc., and 26 open cars.

Stock......Par $100..............................Authorized, $800,000......Issued, $800,000

The company has no preferred stock. Stock is transferred at the office of the company in Montreal.

FUNDED DEBT.

1st mort., 5 per cent., due 1928, Jan. and July.................................... $600,000

The bonds outstanding are the full amount authorized. Trustee of the mortgage, Montreal Trust & Deposit Co., Montreal. Agent for the payment of interest, Bank of Montreal, Montreal.

In the fiscal year ending December 31, 1902, the gross earnings were $129,809; net, $64,435; interest and taxes, $35,170; operating expenses were 50.76 per cent. of the gross earnings.

President, F. L. Wanklyn; Vice-President, J. K. L. Ross; Secretary, J. Kitto, Montreal; General Manager, George Lewis, Kingston, Jamaica.

Directors—F. L. Wanklyn, J. K. L. Ross, C. E. L. Porteous, W. B. Chapman, J. R. Wilson, Fayette Brown, James Hutchinson, Montreal.

Corporate office, Kingston, Jamaica: main office, Street Railway Chambers, Montreal. Annual meeting, second Wednesday in March, at Montreal.

## WEST ST. LOUIS WATER & LIGHT CO.

A corporation formed under the laws of Missouri, May 14, 1902. The company has a general distribution plant for water and electric current on the Missouri River, about twelve miles from St. Louis, and 50 miles of water main, pole lines, etc. The company has perpetual franchises from St. Louis County and long-time franchises and contracts with the municipalities in the county.

Stock......Par $100..........................Authorized, $1,000,000. ....Issued, $1,000,000

The company has no preferred stock. Transfer Agent and Registrar, Colonial Trust Co., St. Louis.

The company has an authorized bond issue of $1,000,000, at 5 per cent., due in 5 to 20 years; $500,000 of bonds will be issued in 1903, and the balance will be retained for future extensions and betterments. The bonds may be called after 5 years at 105. Trustee of the mortgage and agent for the payment of interest, Colonial Trust Co. of St. Louis.

President, Thomas W. Crouch; Vice-President and General Manager, J. B. Dingley; Secretary and Treasurer, Edward S. Lewis.

Directors—Thomas W. Crouch, Edward S. Lewis, Sidney M. Phelan, Paul A. Fusz, J. B. C. Lucas, Edgar D. Tilton, N. D. Thompson, St. Louis; J. B. Quigley, John H. Bothwell, Sedalia, Mo.; C. E. Andrews, Boonville, Mo.; L. R. Blackmer, St. Louis.

Corporate and main office, Colonial Trust Building, St. Louis; branch office, St. Louis County, Mo. Annual meeting, second Monday in May, at St. Louis.

## WESTCHESTER LIGHTING CO.

A corporation formed under the laws of New York, November 6, 1900. The company consolidated the companies operating gas and electric-light plants in the Borough of the Bronx, New York City and Yonkers, New Rochelle, Mount Vernon, Rye, Port Chester, Pelham, Mount Kisco, Mamaroneck, and other places in Westchester County, N. Y. The companies acquired were as follows:

Portchester Electric Lighting Co.
East Chester Electric Co.
Larchmont Electric Light Co.
Huguenot Electric Light Co.
Pelham Electric Light & Power Co.
Mount Kisco Lighting Co.
Westchester Gas & Coke Co.
New York Suburban Gas Co.
Municipal Gas Co. of Yonkers.
Yonkers Gas Lighting Co.
Westchester Gas Light Co. of Yonkers.

The population of the territory covered by the company's operations is about 175,000. The present company has consolidated and improved both the gas and electric plants supplying the district.

A controlling interest in the stock is owned by the United Gas Improvement Co.

Stock..Par $100..Authorized { com., $10,000,000; pref., 2,500,000 } Issued { com., $10,000,000; pref., 2,500,000 } $12,500,000

The preferred stock is 5 per cent., at which rate dividends become cumulative after January 1, 1904.

FUNDED DEBT.

1st mort., 5 per cent., due Dec., 1950, June and Dec.......................... ....$4,260,000

The general mortgage is for $10,000,000. Trustee, Colonial Trust Co., New York. Of this amount, $460,000 was reserved to retire underlying bonds of the constituent companies, and $5,280,000 for future acquisitions and extensions.

President, William W. Scrugham; Vice-President, F. A. Stratton; Secretary, B. W. Stilwell; Treasurer, Lewis Lillie; Managing Director, Walton Clark.

Directors—Harold Brown, Lewis Lillie, W. W. Scrugham, Randal Morgan, W. F. Sheehan, R. A. C. Smith, A. M. Young, H. G. Runkle, Walton Clark, George S. Philler, Charles H. Werner.

Main office, Mount Vernon, N. Y.

## WESTCOTT EXPRESS CO.

A corporation formed under the laws of New York in 1894. The Consolidated Transfer Co. was merged with this company. The company transacts a baggage delivery business in New York, Brooklyn, Jersey City, Albany, Utica, Syracuse and Rochester. It has delivery plants, including real estate, stables and delivery wagons, coaches, etc., in the various cities in which it operates.

Stock......Par $100.....Authorized { com., $500,000; pref., 150,000 } Issued { com., $500,000; pref., 150,000 } $650,000

The preferred stock is 7 per cent., cumulative. The company has no funded debt.

The company has paid 7 per cent. on its preferred stock since 1894, the dividends being annual, February 15. On the common stock, a dividend of 2 per cent. was paid in 1896.

President, A. T. Smith, New York; Vice-President, James H. Manning, Albany, N. Y.; Treasurer, W. H. Hollister, New York; Secretary, Theodore T. Wilcox, Albany, N. Y.

Directors—James H. Manning, Albert Hessberg, Frederick Tillinghast, Albany, N. Y.; W. Seward Webb, Shelburne, Vt.; W. H. Hollister, A. T. Smith, Thomas L. James, A. F. Kountze, New York; Eli Weed, Rochester, N. Y.; T. F. Hamilton, Saratoga Springs, N. Y.

Main office, Albany, N. Y.; New York office, 39 East Forty-second street.

## WESTERN GAS CO.

(Controlled by American Light & Traction Co.)

A corporation formed under the laws of New York in 1893. It owns all the stock of the Milwaukee Gas Light Co., the latter being the operating company. The property of the Milwaukee Gas Light Co. consists of 261 miles of mains, with plants, etc., adequate to the supply of a population of over 250,000, and is free from direct encumbrance. The franchise is exclusive and perpetual.

In 1901 control of this company was acquired by the American Light & Traction Co., which offered $100 of its own common and $30 in its preferred for each share of the company's stock.

Stock......Par $100. ........................Authorized, $4,000,000......Issued, $4,000,000

Stock is transferred at the company's office, New York. Registrar, J. & W. Seligman, New York.

Dividends are paid half-yearly, January (20) and July.

FUNDED DEBT.

Milwaukee Gas 1st mort. 4 per cent. gold, due May, 1927, May and Nov.............. $6,000,000

Coupons of bonds are paid at the office of the company, New York.

EARNINGS.

| | Net. | Charges and Dividends. | Surplus. |
|---|---|---|---|
| 1895 | $412,258 | $339,970 | $72,288 |
| 1896 | 434,567 | 388,386 | 46,181 |
| 1897 | 489,211 | ........ | ....... |
| 1898 | 504,821 | ........ | ....... |
| 1899 | 513,530 | ........ | ....... |
| 1900 | 550,875 | ........ | ....... |
| 1901 | 564,849 | ........ | ....... |

Earnings are now included in those of the American Light & Traction Co.

President, Emerson McMillin; Vice-President, Frederick Strauss; Secretary and Treasurer, Robert M. Murray, New York.

Directors—Emerson McMillin, H. B. Wilson, Isaac N. Seligman, Frederick Strauss, George T. Maxwell, New York; Willard E. Case, Junius M. Stevens.

Main office, 17 Broad street, New York.

## WESTERN STONE CO.

A corporation formed under the laws of Illinois in 1889. The company acquired and owns extensive quarries adjacent to the city of Chicago and has real estate used as yards and depots in Chicago, together with a large equipment of canal boats, wagons, teams, etc.

Stock......Par $100..........................Authorized, $2,250,000......Issued, $2,250,000

Stock is transferred at the company's office. Registrar, Northern Trust Co., Chicago.

Dividends on the stock have been in 1890, 10 per cent.; in 1891, 8 per cent.; in 1892, 8 per cent.; in 1893, 4 per cent.; in 1894 and 1895, none; in 1896, 3 per cent.; in 1897, 2 per cent.; in 1898, 1899, 1900 and 1901, none.

FUNDED DEBT.

| | |
|---|---|
| 1st mort., 5 per cent., due 1910, April and Oct. | $200,000 |
| Purchase money mort., 6 per cent., due 1911, May and Nov. | 72,000 |
| Total | $272,000 |

The 1st mortgage, Northern Trust Co., Chicago, trustee, is secured by the company's personalty and all its real estate, except that at Joliet, Ill. The purchase money mortgage is secured by the two last named parcels of real estate. The original issue was $150,000, but $8,000 of the bonds are retired annually.

In 1899 the company earned, net, $36,839. In 1900 the operations showed a loss of $66,458. In 1901 the company completed improvements and preparatory work on its quarries at a cost of $125,000. On December 31, 1902, the company's surplus was $97,818.

President, Martin B. Madden; Vice-President, G. H. Munroe; Secretary, Joseph E. Lindquist; Treasurer, T. A. Heineman.

Directors—C. L. Hutchinson, J. L. Norton, Martin B. Madden, G. H. Munroe, J. H. Dwight, Gustave Stieglitz, H. H. Getty, C. B. Kimbell, A. M. Day, L. C. Huck, C. H. Wacker.

Main office, 138 Washington street, Chicago. Annual meeting, third Wednesday in January.

## WESTERN TELEPHONE & TELEGRAPH CO.

A corporation formed under the laws of New Jersey, January 22, 1902. The company was organized in pursuance of the reorganization of the Erie Telegraph & Telephone Co., which was a New York corporation formed in 1883, and which owned and controlled an extensive system of local and long-distance telephones under licence from the American (Bell) Telephone & Telegraph Co. All the property and franchises of the Erie Telegraph & Telephone Co. were, in January, 1902, sold and acquired by the present company.

The American Telephone & Telegraph Co. owns a controlling interest in the stock of this company.

The principal assets of the Erie Company, which the present company acquired, consisted of a controlling interest of the stocks and other securities of the Cleveland Telephone Co. of Ohio, the Northwestern Telephone Exchange Co. of Minnesota, the Southwestern Telegraph & Telephone Co. of New York, the Michigan Telephone Co. of Michigan, and the Wisconsin Telephone Co. of Wisconsin.

The Cleveland Telephone Co. operates the telephone system under the patents owned by the American Bell Telephone Co. in the county of Cuyahoga, Ohio, which includes the city of Cleveland. The Northwestern Telephone Exchange Co. operates the telephone systems under the patents owned by the American Bell Telephone Co. in Minnesota, North Dakota and South Dakota, excepting the city of Duluth in Minnesota and the Black Hills District in South Dakota. The Southwestern Telegraph & Telephone Co. operates the telephone systems under the patents owned by the American Bell Telephone Co. in Arkansas and Texas. The Michigan Telephone Co. operates the telephone systems under the patents owned by the American Bell Telephone Co. in Michigan. The Wisconsin Telephone Co. operates the telephone systems under the patents owned by the American Bell Telephone Co. in Wisconsin. The Erie Company in 1898, acquired a controlling interest of the stock of the Michigan Telephone Co. In January, 1900, it was announced that the Michigan Telephone Co. had acquired control of the Detroit Telephone Co., the New State Telephone Co. of Michigan, the Central Telephone Co. of Michigan and the Mutual Telephone Co. of Kalamazoo, Mich.

Stock..Par $100..Authorized { com., $16,000,000 / pref., 16,000,000 } Issued { com., $16,000,000 / pref., 16,000,000 } $32,000,000

The preferred stock is entitled to 6 per cent. dividends, if earned, and is to become cumulative after two years from date of issue, and also has a preference for its face value as to assets, in case of liquidation.

In August, 1902, 2 per cent. was paid on the preferred stock and 2 per cent. was also paid on the preferred in February, 1903.

Transfer Agents, Old Colony Trust Co., Boston. Registrar, National Shawmut Bank, Boston.

FUNDED DEBT.

| | |
|---|---|
| Collateral trust, 5 per cent. bonds, due 1932 | $9,835,966 |

The authorized amount of collateral trust bonds is $10,000,000. Trustee, Old Colony Trust Co., Boston. The bonds are secured by the stocks of constituent companies.

FUNDED DEBT—CONTROLLED COMPANIES.

| | |
|---|---|
| Michigan Telephone, 1st mort., 5 per cent., due 1917 | $285,000 |
| " " cons. mort., due Jan., 1929, Jan. and July | 4,715,000 |
| Detroit Tel., 1st mort., 6 per cent., due Feb., 1922, Feb. and Aug. | 594,400 |
| Postal Tel. of Texas, 1st mort., 5 per cent., due Jan., 1928, Jan. and July | 1,189,000 |
| Total | $6,783,400 |

The Erie Telegraph & Telephone Co. had $10,012,800 stock and $19,000,000 of bonds and notes. It paid dividends on its stock as follows: in 1888, 4 per cent.; in 1889, 3¾ per cent.; in 1890, 4 per cent.; in 1891 and 1898, 4 per cent.; in 1899, 4¼ per cent.; in 1900, 5 per cent. The company suspended dividends in April, 1901, having become embarrassed through the necessity of financing the extensions of the constituent companies.

In December, 1901, a plan for the reorganization of the Erie Telegraph & Telephone Co. was submitted by Kidder, Peabody & Co., Boston. The plan included the creation of the new company, with capital as above stated. The following terms were offered to the holders of the old company's securities:

| Per $100 stock, $1,000 bonds. | Paid. | Received: New Bonds. | Received: Com. Stock. | Received: Pref. Stock. |
|---|---|---|---|---|
| Stock ($10,012,800) | $25 | .... | $75 | $25 |
| 5 per cent. bonds of 1928-29, $5,000,000 | .... | $800 | .... | 200 |
| 6 per cent. and 5 per cent. bonds of 1909 and 1926, $5,000,000 | .... | 1,050 | .... | .... |

The $9,000,000 of collateral trust notes of the Erie Company which matured January 10, 1902, were paid off with the proceeds of the assessments. It was provided in the plan that the American Telephone & Telegraph Co. should acquire a majority of the new company's stock. The reorganization plan was duly carried into effect as stated above. The earnings of the Erie Telegraph & Telephone Co. for a series of years were given in the MANUAL for 1901.

President, Frederick P. Fish; Vice-President, W. S. Hutchinson; Treasurer, William R. Driver; Secretary, Charles A. Grant; Auditor, Thomas Sherwin; Assistant Treasurer, John Balch; Assistant Auditor, G. Duthie Strachan, Boston.

Directors—Frederick P. Fish, Charles W. Amory, Alexander Cochrane, T. Jefferson Coolidge, Jr., Philip Dexter, William Endicott, Jr., J. Malcom Forbes, Henry J. Howe, James J. Storrow, Robert Winsor, Boston; Edward J. Hall, New York.

Main office, 125 Milk street, Boston. Annual meeting, third Tuesday in March, at Jersey City.

## WESTERN UNION TELEGRAPH CO.

A corporation chartered by the State of New York. The company in 1856 succeeded another organization entitled the New York & Mississippi Valley Printing Telegraph Co., chartered in 1851.

Stock........Par $100......................Authorized, $100,000,000......Issued, $97,370,000

In October, 1892, the authorized share capital was increased from $86,199,852 to $100,000,000, and a stock dividend of 10 per cent. upon the former amount (the capital then outstanding) was authorized to represent net earnings invested in plant. The stock dividend was made payable December 3, 1892. In July, 1894, $550,000 new stock was issued to pay for the stock of the American Rapid Telegraph Co., theretofore operated under lease, and in June, 1897, $2,000,000 stock was sold for improvements.

Since 1887 the company has paid dividends of 5 per cent. per annum in quarterly payments of 1¼ per cent. each, in January (1), April, July and October.

Stock is transferred at the company's office, 195 Broadway, New York. Registrar, Mercantile Trust Co., New York.

FUNDED DEBT.

| | |
|---|---|
| Collateral trust bonds, Jan., 1938, 5 per cent., Jan. and July | $8,504,000 |
| Funding and Real Estate mort., 4½ per cent., due May, 1950, May and Nov. | 13,000,000 |
| Total | $21,504,000 |

FUNDED DEBT OF LEASED COMPANIES.

| | |
|---|---|
| Mutual Union Telegraph, 1st mort., 6 per cent., due May, 1911, May and Nov. | $1,957,000 |
| Northwestern Telegraph Co., 1st mort., 7 per cent., due Jan., 1904, Jan. and July | 1,180,000 |
| Gold & Stock Telegraph mort. bonds, due May, 1905, May and Nov. | 500,000 |
| Total | $3,637,000 |

The company guarantees also 5 per cent. on the $14,000,000 of stock of the American Telegraph and Cable Co., 6 per cent. upon the $5,000,000 of the Gold & Stock Telegraph Co., 6 per cent. on the $3,000,000 stock of the International Ocean Telegraph Co., 6 per cent. on the stock ($2,500,000) and 7 per cent. on the bonds of the Northwestern Telegraph Co. and 5 per cent. on the stock of the Southern & Atlantic Telegraph Co. The company has $8,502,000 of stocks and bonds of leased companies which are held in its collateral trust, and $9,039,438 of stocks of other companies not leased.

This company in October, 1887, purchased the entire capital stock of the Baltimore & Ohio Telegraph Co. (38,750 shares) for 50,000 shares of Western Union stock, and a rental of $60,000 per year to be paid to the Baltimore & Ohio Railroad Co. for fifty years for the use of the railroad wires. In 1888 the issue of collateral trust bonds was created, to be used in retiring an equal amount of securities of leased companies on which Western Union Co. paid rental.

The 4½ per cent. funding and real estate bonds were authorized and issued in 1900. The total authorized issue is $20,000,000, of which $5,681,000 were to retire the 7 per cent. and 6 per cent. debentures maturing 1900, $2,076,501 to pay for new property and construction, and $2,242,-499 to be issued for like purposes in the future. The remaining $10,000,000 was reserved to take up the $1,158,000 building bonds and for extensions and improvements.

OPERATIONS.

Year ending June 30.

| Years. | Miles of Poles. | Miles of Wire. | Offices. | Messages. | Receipts. | Expenses. | Profits. |
|---|---|---|---|---|---|---|---|
| 1892-93....... | 189,936 | 769,201 | 21,078 | 66,591,858 | $24,978,443 | $17,482,406 | $7,496,037 |
| 1893-94....... | 190,303 | 790,792 | 21,166 | 58,632,237 | 21,852,655 | 16,060,170 | 5,792,485 |
| 1894-95....... | 189,714 | 802,651 | 21,360 | 58,307,315 | 22,218,019 | 16,056,630 | 6,141,389 |
| 1895-96....... | 189,918 | 826,929 | 21,725 | 58,760,444 | 22,612,736 | 16,714,756 | 5,897,980 |
| 1896-97....... | 190,614 | 841,002 | 21,769 | 58,151,684 | 22,638,859 | 16,906,656 | 5,732,203 |
| 1897-98....... | 189,847 | 874,420 | 22,210 | 62,173,749 | 23,915,732 | 17,825,581 | 6,090,151 |
| 1898-99....... | 189,856 | 904,633 | 22,285 | 61,398,157 | 23,954,312 | 18,085,579 | 5,868,732 |
| 1899-00....... | 192,705 | 933,153 | 22,900 | 63,167,783 | 24,758,569 | 18,593,205 | 6,165,363 |
| 1900-01....... | 193,589 | 972,766 | 23,238 | 65,657,049 | 26,354,150 | 19,608,902 | 6,685,248 |
| 1901-02....... | 196,115 | 1,029,984 | 23,567 | 69,374,883 | 28,073,095 | 20,780,766 | 7,292,328 |

EARNINGS.

Year ending June 30.

| | Div. Paid. | Gross. | Rentals and Exp. | Int. and S. F. | Dividends. | Balance. |
|---|---|---|---|---|---|---|
| 1892-93...... | *5 | $24,978,443 | $17,482,406 | $933,377 | $4,631,820 | $1,930,840 |
| 1893-94...... | 5 | 21,852,655 | 16,060,170 | 931,607 | 4,740,064 | 120,814 |
| 1894-95...... | 5 | 22,218,019 | 16,076,630 | 933,813 | 4,767,733 | 439,843 |
| 1895-96...... | 5 | 22,612,736 | 16,714,756 | 933,958 | 4,767,805 | 196,217 |
| 1896-97...... | 5 | 22,638,859 | 16,906,656 | 935,500 | 4,792,855 | 3,847 |
| 1897-98...... | 5 | 23,915,732 | 17,825,581 | 906,545 | 4,867,911 | 315,694 |
| 1898-99...... | 5 | 23,954,312 | 18,085,579 | 897,091 | 4,867,948 | 103,392 |
| 1899-00...... | 5 | 24,758,569 | 18,593,205 | 906,102 | 4,867,983 | 391,277 |
| 1900-01...... | 5 | 26,354,150 | 19,668,902 | 956,160 | 4,868,007 | 861,080 |
| 1901-02...... | 5 | 28,073,095 | 20,780,766 | 992,580 | 4,868,031 | 1,431,717 |

*And 10 per cent. in stock.

The following is the company's balance sheet June 30, 1902:

ASSETS.

| | |
|---|---|
| Telegraph lines, stocks owned of leased telegraph companies that are merged in Western Union Co.'s system, franchises, patents, etc.......... | $108,714,146 |
| Stocks and bonds of leased telegraph companies received in exchange for collateral trust bonds...................... | 8,504,000 |
| Stocks of not leased telegraph companies, and other securities....................... | 9,727,988 |
| Real estate.................... | 4,765,130 |
| Supplies and materials in supply departments............. | 344,775 |
| Sundry accounts receivable, etc. | 2,302,172 |
| Cash in treasury and in hands of agents (since remitted to treasury).................... | 2,665,311 |
| Total.................. | $137,023,522 |

LIABILITIES.

| | |
|---|---|
| Capital stock...................... | $97,370,000 |
| Funded debt.................. | 21,504,000 |
| Gold & Stock Telegraph Co. for stocks of other companies held through lease of that company until 1981.... | 1,956,592 |
| Sundry accounts payable, etc. (including dividend July 15, 1902)...................... | 3,843,743 |
| Surplus of income prior to October 1, 1881, appropriated for construction and acquisition of telegraph lines and property (in excess of the $15,526,590 capital stock distributed in 1881 on account of such appropriations of income during the 15 years preceding).................. | 1,598,184 |
| Surplus of income subsequent to October 1, 1881 ($10,121,-242.91), plus the proportion of surplus of income prior to October 1, 1881 ($629,-759.91), that was not appropriated as above............. | 10,751,003 |
| Total.................. | $137,023,522 |

Chairman, Thomas T. Eckert; President and General Manager, Robert C. Clowry; Vice-Presidents, George J. Gould, J. B. Van Every, Thomas F. Clark; Secretary, A. R. Brewer; Treasurer, M. T. Wilbur; Auditor, J. B. Van Every, New York.

Directors—Thomas T. Eckert, John T. Terry, Russell Sage, Charles Lockhart, George J. Gould, Robert C. Clowry, Edwin Gould, J. Pierpont Morgan, William D. Bishop, Edward H. Harriman, Samuel Sloan, Chauncey M. Depew, Henry M. Flagler, John K. Cowen, James H. Hyde, John Jacob Astor, Oliver Ames, Louis Fitzgerald, C. Sidney Shepard, J. B. Van Every, James Stillman, Jacob H. Schiff, Thomas F. Clark, Howard Gould, John J. Mitchell, Frank Jay Gould, William L. Bull, Morris K. Jesup, Samuel Spencer.

Executive Committee—Thomas T. Eckert, John T. Terry, Samuel Sloan, George J. Gould, Russell Sage, Robert C. Clowry, Edwin Gould, Louis Fitzgerald, Frank Jay Gould, Jacob H. Schiff, James H. Hyde.

Main office, 195 Broadway, New York. Annual meeting, second Wednesday in October.

---

## WESTINGHOUSE AIR BRAKE CO.

A corporation formed under the laws of Pennsylvania. The object of the company is the manufacture of air brakes for railroad locomotives and cars and similar appliances. The company owns the patents of George Westinghouse and others for that class of mechanisms. It has a large plant at Wilmerding, near Pittsburg.

Stock......Par $50...... ............... ...Authorized, $11,000,000 .....Issued, $10,976,950

In November, 1898, acquired the stock of the American Brake Co. which had been leased to this company. The stock of the American company was $2,000,000. To acquire it the Westinghouse gave two of its own shares for each three shares, par value $100, of the American Brake Co. This required about $666,000 of Westinghouse stock. In the autumn of 1898 this company also acquired the property and works of the Boyden Air Brake Co. of Baltimore. These acquisitions increased the stock outstanding to the amount given above.

Transfer Agent, Union Trust Co., Pittsburg. Registrar, Fidelity Title & Trust Co., Pittsburg.

Dividends are paid quarterly, in January (10), April, July and October. On the old stock 20 per cent. per annum was paid. In 1899 paid 25 per cent., 5 per cent. quarterly and 5 per cent. extra on increased capital. In 1900 paid 30 per cent., 2½ per cent. quarterly and 5 per cent. extra. The January, 1901, dividend, however, was 2½ per cent. and 3½ per cent. extra, and the quarterly dividends have since been on that basis.

EARNINGS.

Year ending July 31.

| | Div. Paid. | Gross. | Net. | Dividends. | Surplus. |
|---|---|---|---|---|---|
| 1899–00.............. | 30 | $8,530,905 | $3,519,199 | $3,285,000 | $234,199 |
| 1900–01.............. | 25½ | 7,869,857 | 2,981,342 | 2,792,250 | 189,092 |
| 1901–02.............. | 24 | 8,559,503 | 2,928,696 | 2,634,468 | 294,228 |

The following is the company's balance sheet July 31, 1902:

| ASSETS. | | LIABILITIES. | |
|---|---|---|---|
| Cash on hand.................. | $2,004,419 | Capital stock.................... | $10,976,950 |
| Accounts and bills receivable.... | 2,852,014 | Rebates......................... | 846,651 |
| Railway and other securities.... | 975,836 | Profit.......................... | 3,237,044 |
| Stock in association companies.. | 2,379,655 | | |
| Patents......................... | 2,000,000 | | |
| Wilmerding plant.............. | 1,804,108 | | |
| Real estate..................... | 1,700,000 | | |
| Factory stores, including material | 1,344,613 | | |
| Total.................... | $15,060,645 | Total.................... | $15,060,645 |

President, George Westinghouse; Vice-Presidents, Robert Pitcairn, H. H. Westinghouse, William W. Card; Treasurer,, John Caldwell; Secretary, John F. Miller; General Manager, E. M. Herr, Pittsburg.

Directors—George Westinghouse, H. H. Westinghouse, Robert Pitcairn, John Caldwell, William W. Card, Henry W. Oliver.

Main office, Wilmerding, Pa.; executive office, 820 Penn avenue, Pittsburg. Annual meeting, first Tuesday in October, at Wilmerding.

## WESTINGHOUSE ELECTRIC & MANUFACTURING CO.

A corporation formed under the laws of Pennsylvania in 1872. The company manufactures electric apparatus and appliances for lighting and power plants. It has a plant at Pittsburg, and branches at Newark, N. J., Cleveland, Allegheny, Pa., and Bridgeport, Conn.; factory of the United States Electric Lighting Co., Newark, N. J., and of the Consolidated Electric Light Co., New York. Owns the Tesla patents on alternating currents. In March, 1896, made agreement with General Electric Co. for pooling and joint use under agreed royalties of patents owned by both companies. In September, 1898, the company purchased the Walker Electric Co., which had factories at Cleveland.

In 1899 the British Westinghouse Electric & Manufacturing Co. was incorporated with £1,000,000 preference 6 per cent. stock and £750,000 ordinary stock. The American company acquired all the common as consideration for the right to use its patents in Great Britain and its dependencies, except in North America. The British company has a large plant at Trafford Park, Manchester, England.

| Stock..Par $50..Authorized | | | Issued | | | |
|---|---|---|---|---|---|---|
| | com., | $21,000,000 | | com., | $14,026,701 | |
| | old com., | 3,775 | | old com., | 3,775 | $18,029,176 |
| | 1st pref., | 4,000,000 | | 1st pref., | 3,998,700 | |

The preferred stock has a preference of 7 per cent., cumulative, and participates with the common in further division of profits when the latter has received 7 per cent.

Transfer office, 120 Broadway, New York. Transfer Agents, Union Trust Co., Pittsburg; New England Trust Co., Boston.

The company has paid 7 per cent. on its preferred stock since 1892, the dividends being 1¾ per cent. quarterly, in January, April, July and October. On the common stock the first dividend was 1¼ per cent. quarterly, February 20, 1900. The May 1, 1900, quarterly dividend on common was increased to 1½ per cent., and similar dividends were paid on the common to May, 1901, inclusive. The August, 1901, quarterly dividend on the common was increased to 1¾ per cent., which has been the rate of the subsequent dividends.

FUNDED DEBT.

| | |
|---|---|
| Debentures, 5 per cent. due 1913, Jan. and July .................................... | $3,0[illegible]0,000 |
| Walker Co., 1st mort., 6 per cent., due 1916, Jan. and July ........................ | 890,000 |
| Total ............................................................ | $3,900,000 |

Beginning in July, 1900, $150,000 of the debentures are retired annually.

The company was reorganized in 1891. Stockholders of the United States Electric Light Co. and of Consolidated Electric Light Co. exchanged their stock for stock of this company, which obtained almost the entire share capital of those concerns.

In August, 1898, the 5 per cent. debentures were authorized and issued. Part of issue was used to retire old bonds and part to acquire the Walker Co.

Chairman, Brayton Ives, New York; President, George Westinghouse, Pittsburg; Vice-Presidents, Frank H. Taylor, P. F. Kobbe, L. A. Osborne; Secretary, Charles A. Terry; Treasurer, Theodore W. Siemon; Auditor, James C. Bennett.

Directors—Brayton Ives, August Belmont, George W. Hebard, James H. Hyde, Anthony N. Brady, New York; N. W. Bumstead, Charles Francis Adams, Boston; George Westinghouse, H. H. Westinghouse, George C. Smith, Frank H. Taylor, Pittsburg.

Main office, East Pittsburg; New York office, 120 Broadway. Annual meeting, fourth Wednesday in June.

---

## WESTINGHOUSE MACHINE CO.

A corporation formed under the laws of Pennsylvania in 1881. The company owns large plants at and near Pittsburg, and manufactures gas engines and other machinery.

Stock......Par $50.............................Authorized, $5,000,000..... Issued, $5,000,000

The stock of the company formerly consisted of $500,000 6 per cent., non-cumulative, preferred and $2,500,000 common. In January, 1902, the authorized amount of stock was increased to $5,000,000 and the preferred stockholders surrendered their preferential rights, making the entire stock of the company of one class.

Stock is transferred at the office of the company, Pittsburg.

Dividends on both the common and preferred stock were at the rate of 6 per cent. per annum, and were paid quarterly, in January, April, July and October. The January, 1903, dividend, which was the first one paid after the readjustment of the company's stock, was 2½ per cent. for the quarter, or at the rate of 10 per cent. for the year.

FUNDED DEBT.

| | |
|---|---|
| 1st mort., 6 per cent., due 1914, June and Dec. | $350,000 |
| Debentures, 5 per cent., due 1919, June and Dec. | 1,150,000 |
| Westinghouse Foundry, 1st mort., guar., 5 per cent., due 1907-27, March and Sept. | 1,000,000 |
| Total | $2,500,000 |

The 1st mortgage bonds are payable on call in 1905. The authorized amount of the debentures, which were created in 1899, is $1,500,000, and of this amount $350,000 was reserved to retire the 1st mortgage.

The bonds of the Westinghouse Foundry Co. were created to provide for the construction of a large foundry and are guaranteed by this company.

President, George Westinghouse; Vice-President, E. E. Keller; Secretary and Treasurer, T. L. Brown; Assistant Secretary, Charles Garland; Auditor, T. S. Grubbs.

Main office, East Pittsburg, Pa.

## THE WETZEL GAS CO.

A corporation formed under the laws of West Virginia in 1900 for the purpose of supplying natural gas to towns in West Virginia and Ohio.

Stock......Par $100..............................Authorized, $300,000......Issued, $300,000

The company has no preferred stock.

FUNDED DEBT.

1st mort., 6 per cent ............................................................ $114,000

Trustee of bonds, Title Guarantee & Trust Co., Washington, Pa.

President, George W. Crawford; Vice-President, F. M. Lowry; Secretary and Treasurer, H. C. Reeser; Superintendent, M. E. Lytle.

Main office, 345 Fourth avenue, Pittsburg.

## WHITE KNOB COPPER CO., LIMITED

A corporation formed under the laws of New Jersey, April 24, 1900. The purpose of the company is the mining and smelting of copper. The company is the successor to and acquired the property of a West Virginia company of the same name. Its mine and smelter are at Mackay, Idaho, on the Salmon River branch of the Oregon Short Line Railway.

Stock......Par $10..........................Authorized, $2,000,000......Issued, $1,500,000

The company has no preferred stock. The stock is full paid and non-assessable.

In January, 1903, the stockholders voted to reduce the par value of the stock to $10 per share, authorized an increase in the number of shares of 50,000 shares, confirmed the action of the directors in creating an issue of $500,000 6 per cent. ten-year sinking fund gold debentures and provided that the said debentures shall be convertible, on February 15, 1905, or any interest day thereafter, into stock of the company, at the rate of 80 shares of stock for each $1,000 debenture. The debentures are subject to the provisions of a sinking fund, whereby one-half of the net earnings of the company in the year 1904, and in each year thereafter, shall be applied to the purchase of the outstanding debentures at 115 and interest. Interest on the debentures is due in April and October.

Transfer Agent, Corporation Trust Co., of New Jersey, New York. Registrar, Standard Trust Co., New York.

President, Harry J. Luce; Vice-President, Wilbur K. Mathews; Secretary, Charles G. Funk, New York; Assistant Secretary, Austin M. Poole; Treasurer, Charles B. Van Nostrand; Assistant Treasurer, Austin M. Poole.

Directors—Harry J. Luce, Wilbur K. Mathews, Charles B. Van Nostrand, William L. Stow, Charles G. Funk, E. C. Platt, A. Cass Canfield, Edwin B. Sheldon, E. Roscoe Mather, New York.

Corporate office, 15 Exchange place, Jersey City; New York office, 36 Wall street. Annual meeting, first Wednesday after January 1.

## WILKES-BARRE & HAZLETON RAILROAD CO.

A corporation formed under the laws of New Jersey, May 8, 1901. The company acquired the Wilkes-Barre & Hazleton Railway Co. and the Lehigh Traction Co., Hazelton, Pa.

The Lehigh Traction Co. operates under leases the Hazleton & Suburban Electric Co., the Hazleton & South Side Electric Railway Co. and the Hazleton & North Side Electric Railway

Co. It owns a power plant, 62 cars and 27 miles of electric line, from Hazleton, Pa., to West Hazleton, Yorktown, McAdoo, Freeland, Lattimer and other towns. The Wilkes-Barre & Hazleton Railroad Co. began to operate the Wilkes-Barre & Hazleton Railway from Hazleton to Ashley, March 21, 1903.

Stock....Par $100.....Authorized { com., $2,500,000 / pref., 200,000 } Issued { com., $2,500,000 / pref., 180,720 } $2,680,720

The preferred stock is 6 per cent., non-cumulative. It can be changed at any time at the option of the company into bonds of the company at par, bearing not less than 5 per cent. interest, or may be redeemable at par in cash.

FUNDED DEBT.

| | |
|---|---|
| 1st collateral trust mort., 5 per cent., due May, 1951, May and Nov.................. | $1,900,000 |
| Lehigh Traction Co., 1st mort., 5 per cent., gold, due June, 1923, June and Dec...... | 500,000 |
| Lehigh Traction Co., 5 per cent. certificates of indebtedness, due 1951............... | 140,000 |
| Lehigh Trac. Co., car house bonds, 5 per cent., gold, due March, 1925, March and Sept. | 55,000 |
| Lehigh Trac. Co., Hazle Park bonds, 5 per cent. gold, due April, 1925, April and Oct.. | 30,000 |
| Wilkes-Barre & Hazleton Ry. Co., 1st mort., 5 per cent., due 1951, May and Nov.... | 1,500,000 |
| Total.................................................................. | $4,125,000 |

The authorized issue of the collateral trust mortgage of the Wilkes-Barre & Hazleton Railroad Co. is $2,500,000, of which amount $600,000 are reserved to retire the bonds of the Lehigh Traction Co. The capital stock, $1,500,000, and the bonds, $1,500,000, of the Wilkes-Barre & Hazleton Railway Co., with the $140,000 certificates of indebtedness, and $903,600 of the stock of the Lehigh Traction Co., are deposited as collateral for this mortgage.

President, A. Markle; Vice-President, John B. Price; Secretary, E. S. Doud; Treasurer, N. C. Yost.

Directors—A. Markle, John B. Price, William B. Given, Benjamin Reynolds, A. A. Sterling, E. R. Payne, Kenneth K. McLaren.

Corporate office, Jersey City; main office, Hazleton, Pa. Annual meeting, first Monday in May, at Jersey City.

## WILMINGTON GAS & ELECTRIC CO.

A corporation formed under the laws of Delaware, November, 1901, for the purpose of manufacturing and distributing gas and electricity. The company acquired rights and franchises of the Wilmington Coal Gas Co. and the Universal Conduit Light, Heat & Power Co.

Stock....Par $50...... Authorized { com., $500,000 / pref., 1,000,000 } Issued { com., $500,000 / pref., 650,000 } $1,150,000

The preferred stock is 4½ per cent., cumulative.

Transfer Agent and Registrar, Security Trust & Safe Deposit Co., Wilmington, Del.

FUNDED DEBT.

1st mort., 4½ per cent., due 1931, June and Dec.................................... $1,000,000

Trustee of the mortgage and agent for the payment of interest, the Security Trust & Safe Deposit Co., Wilmington, Del.

President, James Dobson, Philadelphia; Vice-President, Edmund Mitchell; Secretary and Treasurer, William P. Taylor, Wilmington, Del.

Directors—John Dobson, James Dobson, Thomas F. Barry, Philadelphia; George S. Capelle, Thomas Curley, William W. Lobdell, William S. Hilles, Edmund Mitchell, Wilmington, Del.

Corporate and main office, 827 Market street, Wilmington, Del. Annual meeting, first Tuesday in December, at Wilmington, Del.

## WINNIPEG ELECTRIC STREET RAILWAY

A corporation formed under Acts of Parliament in Manitoba, Canada, in 1892. The company has acquired the following companies:

Northwest Electric Co. The Manitoba Electric & Gas Light Co.

The company owns and operates the electric street railway system, the commercial electric lighting and power system and the gas lighting service in the city of Winnipeg, Manitoba.

Stock......Par $100...........................Authorized, $1,250,000......Issued, $1,250,000

The company has no preferred stock.

Dividends at the rate of 6 per cent. per annum have been paid, the dividend periods being January, April, July and October.

FUNDED DEBT.

1st mort., 5 per cent., due Jan. 1, 1927, Jan. and July.......................................... $1,000,000

The outstanding bonds are the total amount authorized.

In six months ending June 30, 1902, the gross earnings were $171,107.

President, William Mackenzie, Vice-President, William Whyte; Secretary, W. Phillips.

Directors—William Mackenzie, William Whyte, William C. Van Horne, D. D. Mann, A. M. Nanton, D. B. Hanna, H. Morton Morse.

Corporate and main office, Winnipeg, Manitoba. Annnal meeting, fourth Tuesday in January, at Winnipeg, Manitoba.

## WINONA COPPER CO.

A corporation formed under the laws of Michigan in 1898. The company owns a mineral property of about 1,500 acres in Houghton County, Mich. Active exploration and development work have been prosecuted on the property since the formation of the company.

Stock......Par $25.............................Authorized, $2,500,000......Issued, $2,500,000

Transfer Agent, American Loan & Trust Co., Boston. Registrar, Boston Safe Deposit & Trust Co.

Up to the beginning of 1903 there had been paid in on the stock $10 per share.

President, John Stanton; Vice-President, Joseph E. Gay; Secretary, J. W. Hardley; Treasurer, John R. Stanton, New York.

Directors—John Stanton, John R. Stanton, Joseph E. Gay, New York; William A. Paine, Boston; James H. Seager, Michigan.

Executive office, 11 William street, New York. Annual meeting, last Monday in March.

## WITHERBEE, SHERMAN & CO.

A corporation formed under the laws of New York in 1901, for the purpose of mining and concentrating iron ores and producing pig iron. The company succeeded to the business interests of Witherbee, Sherman & Co., which had been in existence since 1860. In December, 1901, the Sherman interests in the company were acquired by the Lackawanna Iron & Steel Co. The company owns iron mines and furnaces at Port Henry, N. Y., and in Putnam County, N. Y., with a large annual output of all grades.

Stock......Par $100.............................Authorized, $3,000,000......Issued, $3,000,000

The company has no preferred stock and no funded debt.

President, Frank S. Witherbee, Port Henry, N. Y.; Vice-President, Warren Delano, Jr.; Secretary, L. W. Francis, New York; Treasurer, Walter C. Witherbee, Port Henry, N. Y.

Directors—Frank S. Witherbee, Walter C. Witherbee, Wallace T. Foote, Port Henry, N. Y.; Warren Delano, Jr., L. W. Francis, Moses Taylor, New York.

Corporate and main office, Port Henry, N. Y.; New York office, 71 Broadway. Annual meeting, first Wednesday in February, at Port Henry, N. Y.

## WOLVERINE COPPER MINING CO.

A corporation formed under the laws of Michigan in 1890. The company owns and operates the Wolverine copper mine in Houghton County, Mich.

Stock......Par $25.............................Authorized, $1,500,000......Issued, $1,500,000

The stock of the company consists of 60,000 shares of the par value of $25 each, on which there has been paid up $13 per share.

Transfer Agent, American Loan & Trust Co., Boston.

Dividends are paid half-yearly, in April (1) and October. In 1899 paid $3.50 per share; in 1900 paid $4 per share, and in 1901 and 1902 $4 per share, $2 each half-year.

Production in year ending June 30 was, in 1893, 218,855 pounds of copper; in 1894, 1,611,857 pounds; in 1895, 1,744,070 pounds; in 1896, 1,278 tons; in 1897, 2,316,296 pounds; in 1898, 4,199,961 pounds; in 1899, 4,789,015 pounds; in 1900, 4,796,140 pounds, and in 1901, 4,907,000 pounds.

President, John Stanton; Secretary and Treasurer, J. R. Stanton, New York; Agent, Fred Smith, Allouez, Mich.

Directors—John Stanton, S. L. Smith, Joseph E. Gay, J. R. Stanton, J. W. Hardley.

Main office, 11 William street, New York. Annual meeting, first Monday in August.

## THE WORCESTER & CONNECTICUT EASTERN RAILWAY CO.

A corporation formed under the laws of Connecticut in 1901, under the name of the Thompson Tramway Co. The present name was taken in 1902. The company acquired the following companies:

The Peoples Tramway Co., Webster & Dudley Street Railway Co., The Danielson & Norwich Street Railway Co., Worcester & Webster Street Railway Co.

The company owns and operates 51 miles of electric railway from Worcester, Mass., to Danielson, Conn., Danielson to Central Village, Conn., and Worcester to Webster, Mass. It has a hydraulic water power plant with steam relay at Wauregan, Conn., and a steam plant at Oxford, Mass.

Stock......Par 100..............................Authorized, $900,000......Issued, $500,000

The company has no preferred stock.

FUNDED DEBT.

1st mort., 4½ per cent., gold, due Jan. 1, 1943, Jan. and July........................$1,900,000
The Worcester & Webster Street Ry. Co., 1st mort., 5 per cent. gold, due Nov. 1, 1919 150,000

Total..............................................................$2,050,000

The outstanding bonds of the Worcester & Webster Street Railway Co. are the total amount authorized. A sinking fund of $2,000 annually is provided. Trustee of the mortgage and agent for the payment of interest, International Trust Co., Boston.

President, F. A. Jacobs; Secretary and Treasurer, H. M. Kochersperger.

Directors—Charles F. Brooker, F. A. Jacobs, H. Hobart Porter, Jr., George J. Brush, H. M. Kochersperger, E. D. Robbins, F. S. Curtis, Edward Milner, E. N. Sanderson.

Main office, Worcester, Mass.

## WORCESTER GAS LIGHT CO.

A corporation formed under the laws ot Massachusetts in 1851. The company controls the gas lighting business in the city of Worcester, Mass. Its output aggregates 250,000,000 feet per annum.

Stock......Par $100..............................Authorized, $700,000......Issued, $700,000

The company has no preferred stock and no funded debt.

Dividends to the amount of 10 per cent. were paid in 1902. Dividends are paid quarterly in January, April, July and October.

In the fiscal year ending June 30, 1902, the gross earnings were $341,902; net, $105,124.

President, Charles D. Lamson; Secretary and Treasurer, James P. Hamilton.

Directors—Charles D. Lamson, A. G. Bullock, Josiah H. Clarke, Francis H. Dewey, Albert Wood, Samuel B. Woodward.

Corporate and main office, 240 Main street, Worcester, Mass. Annual meeting, Wednesday next after the tenth of September, at Worcester.

## WORCESTER RAILWAYS & INVESTMENT CO.

A voluntary association formed in Massachusetts in July, 1901. The company is managed by a board of trustees, in whom is vested the ownership of the entire capital stocks, excepting the qualifying shares held by the officers of the constituent corporations, of the Worcester, Mass., Consolidated Street Railway Co., and of certain other companies holding charters under the laws of Massachusetts and engaged in enterprises closely identified with that of street railway transportation. The company also controls other securities of these corporations and valuable property rights.

Stock................Authorized, 71,899 shares.........................Issued, 71,898 shares

The trustees have issued negotiable certificates, or evidence of interest, for 71,898 shares, each share representing a fractional beneficial interest in the property held by the trustees. These shares have no par value.

The shares are non-assessable and holders are relieved from personal liability.

Transfer Agent, Old Colony Trust Co., Boston. Registrar, American Loan & Trust Co., Boston.

Dividends of $2.25 per share were paid in February and August, 1902, and on February 1, 1903.

President, A. George Bullock, Worcester; Secretary, Bentley W. Warren; Treasurer, E. Elmer Foye, Boston.

Trustees — A. George Bullock, Stephen Salisbury, Worcester, Mass.; Samuel Carr, Boston; T. Jefferson Coolidge, Jr., Manchester, Mass.; Frederick W. Kendrick, Cambridge, Mass.

Corporate and main office, Ames Building, Boston. Annual meeting, Wednesday after the first Monday in January.

## HENRY R. WORTHINGTON CO.

A corporation formed under the laws of New Jersey in January, 1892. The company was formed to take over the business of the firm of Henry R. Worthington, of New York, manufacturers of and dealers in steam pumps, meters and other hydraulic machinery, which firm was established in 1845. It has factories in Elizabethport, N. J., and Brooklyn, N. Y. The company owns the Worthington Pumping Engine Co., which operates in Europe.

In 1899 control of this company was acquired by the International Steam Pump Co., through the purchase of the common stock. The International Steam Pump Co. in its organization set aside, unissued, an amount of its stock for the purpose of acquiring the preferred stock of this company, but this arrangement has not been carried out.

Stock....Par $100.....Authorized { com., $5,500,000 / pref., 2,000,000 } Issued { com., $5,500,000 / pref., 2,000,000 } $7,500,000

The preferred stock is 7 per cent., cumulative, and has a preference as to division of assets in case of dissolution. The consent of 75 per cent. of the preferred stock is required for the creation of any mortgage.

Transfer Agent, Colonial Trust Co., New York. Registrar, City Trust Co., New York.

The company has regularly paid the dividends on the preferred stock, dividends being semi-annual, 3½ per cent. each, in May (1) and November.

President, John W. Dunn; Vice-President, Daniel O'Day; Secretary, Theodore L. Herrmann; Treasurer, Max Nathan.

Directors—Max Nathan, John W. Dunn, Marcus Stine, Daniel O'Day, Charles L. Broadbent, Theodore L. Herrmann, William A. Perry.

Main office, 120 Liberty street, New York. Annual meeting, second Tuesday in April.

## WYANDOT COPPER CO.

A corporation formed under the laws of Michigan in 1899. The company owns over 1,000 acres of copper lands in Houghton County, Mich. The property immediately adjoins the Winona, and the company has conducted exploration work on it with a view to determining its capabilities.

Stock......Par $25.......... ................Authorized, $2,500,000......Issued, $2,500,000

The original subscription price for the stock was $8 per share, out of which $3 per share was paid into the treasury of the company, making the stock paid up to that amount.

Stock is transferred at the company's office. Registrar, Old Colony Trust Co., Boston.

President, Henry Stackpole; Treasurer, William O. Gay, Boston.

Directors—Henry Stackpole, William O. Gay, Joseph Darr, I. J. Sturgis, Matthew Van Orden, Boston.

Main office, 4 Liberty street, Boston. Annual meeting, May 1, at Boston.

## THE WYANDOTTE GAS CO.

A corporation formed under the laws of Pennsylvania, June 9, 1899. The company is a consolidation of the following companies:

Bethlehem Gas Co. Fountain Hill Gas Co. West Bethlehem Gas Co.

The company has a perpetual and exclusive franchise in Bethlehem, South Bethlehem, West Bethlehem and Fountain Hill, Pa.

Stock......Par $100..............................Authorized, $600,000......Issued, $600,000

The company has no preferred stock.

FUNDED DEBT.

1st mort., 5 per cent., due July, 1929, Jan. and July............. ....................$500,000

The outstanding bonds are the total amount authorized. Trustee of the mortgage and agent for the payment of interest, Wyoming Valley Trust Co., Wilkes-Barre, Pa.

President, Liddon Flick, Vice-President, Morris Williams; Secretary and Treasurer, R. J. Flick; Superintendent and General Managar, Warren J. Flick, Bethlehem, Pa.

Directors—Liddon Flick, R. J. Flick, Morris Williams, A. L. Williams, E. H. Lawall, Wilkes-Barre, Pa.

Corporate and main office, 74 South Main street, Bethlehem, Pa. Annual meeting, May 1, at Bethlehem, Pa.

## WYOMING VALLEY ELECTRIC LIGHT, HEAT & POWER CO.

A corporation formed under the laws of Pennsylvania, in 1898, for the purpose of supplying electric light, heat and power in the city of Wilkes-Barre, Pa., and vicinity. The company has a perpetual franchise.

Stock......Par $100..............................Authorized, $500,000......Issued, $500,000

The company has no preferred stock. Stock is transferred at the office of the company, Wilkes-Barre, Pa.

FUNDED DEBT.

1st mort., 5 per cent., due 1928, May and Nov........................................$460,000

The total amount of bonds authorized is $500,000. Trustee of the mortgage and agent for the payment of interest, People's Bank, Wilkes-Barre, Pa.

In the fiscal year ending October 31, 1902, the gross earnings were $99,031; net earnings, $38,074; charges, $23,000; surplus, $15,074.

The balance sheet of the company, October 31, 1902, is as follows:

| ASSETS. | | LIABILITIES. | |
|---|---|---|---|
| Plant accounts | $967,339 | Bonds | $460,000 |
| Accounts receivable | 9,445 | Capital stock | 500,000 |
| Cash | 524 | Bills payable | 10,000 |
| Insurance fund | 1,857 | Accounts payable | 3,051 |
| Inventor | 2,445 | Insurance reserve | 600 |
| | | Profit and loss accounts | 7,959 |
| Total | $981,610 | Total | $981,610 |

President, Abram Nesbitt; Vice-President, Charles W. Lee; Secretary and Treasurer, E. W. Mulligan; General Manager, John Flanigan, Wilkes-Barre, Pa.

Directors—Abram Nesbitt, J. W. Hollenback, Charles W. Lee, John Flanigan, E. H. Jones, E. W. Mulligan, A. A. Sterling, Irving A. Stearns, Liddon Flick, Wilkes-Barre, Pa.

Corporate and main office, Wilkes-Barre, Pa. Annual meeting, first Tuesday in December, at Wilkes-Barre, Pa.

## THE YALE & TOWNE MANUFACTURING CO.

A corporation formed under the laws of Connecticut in 1868 for the purpose of manufacturing locks invented by Linus Yale, Jr. The company owns valuable patents, and plants at Stamford and Branford, Conn. It absorbed the Branford Lock Works and the Blount Manufacturing Co. Additional buildings are now in course of construction at Stamford, where it is intended to consolidate the works.

Stock......Par $100..........................Authorized, $1,000,000......Issued, $1,000,000

The company has no preferred stock. The authorized stock was originally $100,000, but was increased to meet business requirements.

FUNDED DEBT.

1st mort., 5 per cent. gold, due 1920............................................ .. .. $292,500

The authorized bond issue is $1,000,000 and was created to retire the floating debt and $251,000 6 per cent. debenture bonds and to provide additional working capital.

The following is the company's balance sheet, January 1, 1901:

| ASSETS. | | LIABILITIES. | |
|---|---|---|---|
| Cash, bills and accounts receivable | $353,615 | Capital stock | $1,000,000 |
| Stock and materials | 814,325 | Bonds | 292,500 |
| Real estate and buildings | 371,250 | Bills and accounts | 542,350 |
| Machinery and tools | 651,477 | Surplus | 450,051 |
| Patents | 20,106 | | |
| Branford plant | 64,128 | | |
| Blount Manufacturing stock | 10,000 | | |
| Total | $2,284,901 | Total | $2,284,901 |

President, Henry R. Towne, New York; Secretary and Treasurer, Schuyler Merritt, Stamford, Conn.; Assistant Treasurer, Edward D. Riker, Boston.

Directors—Henry R. Towne, John H. Towne, New York; Schuyler Merritt, Frederick T. Towne, Albert J. Hatch, Warren H. Taylor, Charles A. Hawley, Stamford, Conn.; Edward E. Magovern, Hoboken, N. J.; Edward D. Riker, Boston.

Corporate office, Stamford, Conn.; main office, 9 Murray street, New York.

## YAQUI COPPER CO.

A corporation formed under the laws of West Virginia. The company acquired 7,723 acres of mineral land in fee and a concession of 108,724 acres at Campo Santo Nino, Sonora, Mexico. About $400,000 has been expended in the development of the property, the installation of machinery, etc.

Stock......Par $10..........................Authorized, $5,000,000..... Issued, $5,000,000

The company has no preferred stock and no funded debt. Transfer Agent, North American Trust Co., New York.

President, W. P. Harlow, New York; Vice-President, William Sauntry, Stillwater, Minn.; Secretary and Treasurer, George E. Green, New York.

Directors—W. P. Harlow, T. S. Coolidge, James R. Branch, New York; William Sauntry, George H. Atwood, Stillwater, Minn.; S. F. Pierce, St. Paul, Minn.; Joseph B. Cotton, Duluth, Minn.; John H. Martin, Tucson, Ariz.; A. E. Magoris, George E. Green, Binghamton, N. Y.; George W. Fairchild, Oneonta, N. Y.; R. B. Brown, John M. Thurston, Washington, D. C.; N. L. Miller, Cortland, N. Y.; William F. Hallstead, Scranton., Pa.; George R. Finch, Glens Falls, N. Y.; C. F. Wright, Susquehanna, Pa.; Thomas O'Connor, Waterford, N. Y.

Corporate office, Charleston, W. Va.; New York office, 170 Broadway. Annual meeting, October 23, at New York.

## YORK COUNTY TRACTION CO.

A corporation formed under the laws of New Jersey, June 30, 1900. The company was organized for the ur ose of controlling street railways and electric light and power and steam heating plants in YprkpCounty, Pa. It acquired the following companies:

York Street Railway Co.
York & Dover Electric Railway Co.
York & Dallastown Electric Railway Co.
York & Manchester Electric Railway Co.
York & Wrightsville Electric Railway Co.
York Light, Heat & Power Co.
Edison Electric Light Co.
Westinghouse Electric Light, Heat & Power Co.
York Steam Heating Co.

The constituent companies operate 27 miles of street railways in York, Pa., and vicinity. The York Steam Heating Co. operates a steam heating plant in York. The York Light, Heat & Power Co. owns all the stock of the Edison Electric Light Co. and the Westinghouse Electric Light, Heat & Power Co., both of which companies own and operate electric light plants in York.

Stock......Par $100..........................Authorized, $1,500,000......Issued, $1,500,000

Stock is transferred at the company's office. Registrar, York Trust Co., York, Pa.

FUNDED DEBT.

1st mort., 5 per cent. bonds, due July, 1950, Jan. and July.......................... $1,112,000

The authorized bond issue is $1,500,000, the bonds being secured by a deposit of the stocks of constituent companies. Trustee of the mortgage and agent for the payment of interest, The Real Estate Trust Co., Philadelphia. Of the bond issue $353,000 is reserved to retire prior liens.

President, W. H. Lanius; Vice-President, George S. Billmeyer; Secretary, George S. Schmidt; Treasurer, Ellis S. Lewis, York, Pa.

Directors—W. H. Lanius, George S. Billmeyer, Grier Hersh, John W. Steacy, George P. Smyser, W. F. Bay Stewart, York, Pa.; W. A. Himes, New Oxford. Pa.

Corporate office, 417 Market street, Camden, N. J.; main office, 27 East Market street, York, Pa. Annual meeting, last Friday in June, at Camden, N. J.

## YORK TELEPHONE CO.

A corporation formed under the laws of Pennsylvania, January 16, 1895. The company owns and operates telephone exchanges in York, Dallastown, Stewartstown, Dillsburg and Wrightsville, Pa. It has 200 miles of pole line, extending from York, Pa., to nearly every point in the county, and about 7 miles of cables. In January, 1903, the company had 1,856 telephone instruments under rental. It connects by toll lines, which it owns, with the Independent Telephone Co., of Lancaster, Pa., Columbia Telephone Co., Hanover Telephone Co., Adams County Telephone Co., Cumberland Valley Telephone Co., Lebanon Telephone Co., Southern Pennsylvania Telephone Co., Maryland Telephone Co., Baltimore; Keystone Telephone Co., Philadelphia, and Frederick Telephone Co., Frederick, Md.

Stock......Par $10............ ...................Authorized, $200,000......Issued, $200,000

FUNDED DEBT.

1st mort., 5 per cent., due 1929, May and Nov........................................ $167,000

The 1st mortgage, Security Title & Trust Co., York, Pa., trustee, is for $200,000. The company has in its treasury $33,000 of these bonds.

The statement of the company of January 1, 1903, showed plant, equipment and franchise valued at $423,745.

President, D. F. Lafean; Vice-President, John McCoy; Secretary, H. H. Weber; Treasurer, C. C. Frick, York, Pa.

Directors—D. F. Lafean, H. H. Weber, C. C. Frick, John McCoy, H. S. Wiest, George B. Rudy, W. S. Eisenhart.

Main office, York, Pa.

## THE YOUNGSTOWN IRON SHEET & TUBE CO.

A corporation formed under the laws of Ohio in November, 1900, for the purpose of manufacturing iron and steel sheets and pipe, black and galvanized. The plant of the company is located at Youngstown, O.

Stock......Par $100..........................Authorized, $4,000,000......Issued, $4,000,000

The company has no preferred stock and no funded debt.

President, George D. Wick; Vice-President and General Manager, James A. Campbell; Secretary, W. H. Foster; Treasurer, Richard Garlick; Auditor, W. C. Reilly, Youngstown, O.

Main office, Federal Building, Youngstown, O.

## YOUNGSTOWN-SHARON RAILWAY & LIGHT CO.

A corporation formed under the laws of New Jersey, December 5, 1900. The purposes of the company are the construction, ownership, control and operation of street railway, gas, water and electric properties. The company acquired the following companies:

Youngstown Consolidated Gas & Electric Co.
The Shenango Valley Electric Light Co.
Sharon Gas & Water Co.
Sharpsville Electric Light Co.
The Valley Street Railway Co.
The Sharon & Wheatland Street Railroad Co.
The Youngstown & Sharon Street Railway Co.

The united properties comprise the lighting franchises and facilities of Youngstown, O., Sharon, Sharpsville, Wheatland and South Sharon, Pa., together with 40 miles of street railway lines. The population of the territory in which the company operates is about 120,000. The company acquired practically all the stocks and bonds of the constituent companies.

Stock......Par $100..........................Authorized, $2,500,000......Issued, $2,500,000

The company has no preferred stock. Transfer Agent, Corporation Trust Co., Jersey City.

FUNDED DEBT.

| | |
|---|---|
| 1st mort., 5 per cent., sinking fund, due Jan., 1931, Jan. and July | $2,468,000 |
| 2d mort., 5 per cent., income, due March, 1927 | 500,000 |
| Total | $2,968,000 |

The authorized amount of the 1st mortgage is $2,500,000 and of the 2d, $1,000,000. Trustee of the mortgages and agent for payment of interest, New York Security & Trust Co., New York.

President, Randall Montgomery, Youngstown, O.; Vice-President, Charles S. Fairchild; Secretary, Leighton Calkins; Treasurer, Osborn W. Bright, New York.

Directors—Abram M. Hyatt, Harlan W. Whipple, G. M. McKelvey, William L. Wallis, Grant Hamilton, Alexander McDowell, Simon Perkins, Leighton Calkins, Myron A. Norris, Caleb B. Wick, J. H. Morris, W. J. Hitchcock, Willis H. Park, George D. Wick, Randall Montgomery, Henry M. Garlick, Peter L. Kimberley, Charles S. Fairchild, Frank B. Medbury, Edwin N. Sanderson, H. Hobart Porter, Jr., Frank R. Battles.

Main office, Youngstown, O. Annual meeting, first Monday in February, at Jersey City.

# GOVERNMENT SECURITIES

## Details of the National Debts and Funded Obligations of the United States and of the Principal Foreign Countries whose Bonds are Known in the American Markets

### Details Regarding the Aggregate Debts and the Separate Bond Issues of the Several Countries

**Later Information Regarding the Debts of Countries Herein Represented and Others whose Securities May Become of Interest to American Investors will be Furnished Free of Charge to Subscribers to the MANUAL on Application**

## *THE UNITED STATES OF AMERICA*

The figures given below as the amount of each class of United States bonds outstanding are taken from the Debt Statement issued y the Treasury Department as of April 1, 1903. The items given in the statement in relatiob to the Government debt bearing no interest and debt on which interest has ceased since maturity are not given herein, as having no relation to the outstanding bonded debt of the Government.

NATIONAL DEBT.

| | |
|---|---|
| Consols of 1930, 2 per cent., due April 1, 1930, quarterly, Jan.................... | $445,940,750 |
| War Loan of 1908–1918, 3 per cent., due Aug. 1, 1918, quarterly, Feb............ | 97,515,660 |
| Funded Loan (consols) of 1907, 4 per cent., due July 1, 1907, quarterly, Jan...... | 233,179,200 |
| Refunding Certificates, 4 per cent., quarterly, Jan.............................. | 30,810 |
| Loan of 1925, 4 per cent., due Feb. 1, 1925, quarterly, Feb...................... | 118,489,900 |
| Loan of 1904, 5 per cent., due Feb. 1, 1904, quarterly, Feb...................... | 19,305,050 |
| Total............................................................ | $914,461,370 |

In addition to the above, there was outstanding of the old debt, which matured prior to January 1, 1861, $1,057,650, interest on which has ceased; $60,750 of the funded loan, which matured September 2, 1891, and $111,700 of the funded loan of 1891, continued at 2 per cent. and called for redemption May 18, 1900, interest having ceased August 18, 1900.

The 2 per cent. consols of 1930 were authorized by the act of March 3, 1900, known as the Currency and Refunding Act. Of the bonds of this issue, $435,436,650 are registered and $10,504,160 coupon. The bonds outstanding were issued in exchange for 3s of 1908, 4s of 1907 and 5s of 1904, under the provisions of the act named above and the terms designated by the Treasury Department in a circular dated March 14, 1900. The act provided that the old bonds named above should be exchangeable for new 2s, provision being made for the payment in cash to holders of the old bonds, making the exchange, of the difference between their par value and their value computed on a basis to yield 2¼ per cent. per annum. The right to exchange the old bonds was suspended by the Treasury Department, under Section 11 of the act, on December 31, 1900. The amount of old bonds refunded under the terms given above was as follows: 3s of 1908, $98,876,700; 4s of 1907, $274,927,650; 5s of 1904, $72,070,300; total, $445,874,650. The aggregate premiums paid on this account were $43,575,209, and the net saving in interest effected was $10,964,797. Under the terms of the act of March 14, 1900, the Secretary of the reasury may change the terms of exchange by requiring a premium upon the 2 per cents., or requiring holders of old bonds to surrender the same in exchange for the new issue at a value to yield more than 2¼ per cent. These bonds are in denominations as follows: Coupon, $50, $100, $500 and $1,000; registered, $50, $100, $500, $1,000, $5,000, $10,000 and $50,000.

The 3 per cent. War Loan of 1908–1918 was authorized by the act of June 13, 1898. The bonds were created and issued to provide for the expenditure caused by the Spanish war. Of the bonds of this issue, $48,963,520 are registered and $48,559,200 coupon. The amount authorized was $200,000,000 and that issued was $198,792,640. There has been retired to December 31, 1900, under the act of March 14, 1900, $98,876,700 of these bonds in exchange for 2 per cent. consols. They are redeemable after August 1, 1908, at the Government's option. The bonds were placed by a public subscription under a Treasury circular dated June 13, 1898, the subscription, which closed July 14, 1900, aggregating $1,325,000,000. Preference in the allotment was given to the small individual subscriptions. These bonds, both coupon and registered, were issued in denominations of $20, $100, $500 and $1,000, and also in registered denominations of $5,000 and $10,000.

The 4 per cent. Funded Loan (consols) of 1907 was authorized by the act of July 14, 1870. Of the bonds of this issue outstanding, $184,987,400 are registered and $51,030,950 coupon. The amount authorized was $1,000,000,000 of thirty-year bonds, and that issued was $740,919,350. The purpose of the issue was to retire the outstanding 5-20 bonds at par. There has been retired to December 31, 1900, under the act of March 14, 1900, $274,927,650 of these bonds in exchange for 2 per cent. consols. A considerable amount have also been retired by purchases by the Treasury for the sinking fund. These bonds are issued in denominations of $50, $100, $500, $1,000, $5,000, $10,000, $20,000 and $50,000 registered and $50, $100, $500 and $1,000 coupon.

The 4 per cent. Refunding Certificates were authorized by the act of February 26, 1879. These certificates were issued at par in denominations of $10, bearing 4 per cent. interest and convertible into 4 per cent. bonds. The entire authorized amount was $40,012,750 when the limit was reached, in October, 1879. Only the amount given above remains outstanding.

The 4 per cent. Loan of 1925 was authorized by the act of January 14, 1875, Resumption Act; and Section 3,700 of the Revised Statutes of the United States, act of March 17, 1862, the latter empowering the Secretary of the Treasury to purchase coin with bonds or notes of the United States. Of the bonds outstanding, $106,622,800 are registered and $31,252,200 coupon. These bonds were issued to replenish the Treasury's gold reserve. An amount of $62,315,400 of the bonds were sold for $65,116,244 in gold to the so-called Belmont-Morgan syndicate under a contract dated February 8, 1895. On January 6, 1896, the Secretary of the Treasury invited bids for $100,000,000 additional of these bonds, payable in gold. The larger part of this amount was allotted to a syndicate, which bid 110.6877 for the whole or part of the issue, the average price obtained for the entire issue being 111⅙. These bonds were issued in denominations of $50, $100, $500, $1,000, $5,000 and $10,000 registered and $50, $100, $500 and $1,000 coupon.

The 5 per cent. loan of 1904 was authorized by the act of January 14, 1875. Of the amount outstanding, $10,744,200 are registered and $8,888,950 coupon. These bonds were issued to replenish the Treasury's gold reserve. An amount of $50,000,000 of the bonds were offered by a Treasury circular dated January 17, 1894, for subscription at not less than 117.223 in gold. Another amount of $50,000,000 of the bonds was offered for subscription by a Treasury circular of November 15, 1894, and was sold to a syndicate at 117.077. The total amount of these bonds originally issued was, consequently, $100,000,000. There had been retired to December 31, 1900, under the act of March 14, 1900, $72,070,300 of these bonds in exchange for 2 per cent. consols. The bonds were issued in denominations of $50, $100, $1,000 and $10,000 registered and $50, $100 and $1,000 coupon.

---

## UNITED STATES OF MEXICO

A Federal Republic consisting of 27 States, 2 Territories and a Federal district. Currency standard, silver. The Mexican peso or dollar is 417.79 grains of silver of the fineness of 902.7. Nominal equivalent in United States currency, 98 cents.

### NATIONAL DEBT.

| | |
|---|---|
| Consolidated external gold loan, 5 per cent., quarterly, Jan., April, July and Oct. | $108,434,748 |
| Internal loans, silver, various | 103,113,051 |
| Total | $211,547,799 |

The Mexican consolidated external 5 per cent. gold loan of 1899 was simultaneously offered in 1899 at London, Berlin, Amsterdam and at New York, at the latter city by J. P. Morgan & Co. In April, 1900, these bonds were listed at the New York Stock Exchange, being the first foreign Government loan to receive that recognition. The quotations for them at the New York Stock Exchange are based on the nominal equivalent of £1=$5.

The above bonds were authorized by a decree of the Congress of Mexico, published June 2, 1899. The issue was created to refund and retire outstanding 6 per cent. and 5 per cent. gold bonds aggregating £16,283,000. A majority of the old bonds were exchanged for the new 5s, the balance being called and paid off.

The principal of the 5 per cent. gold loan was £22,700,000, agreed equivalent in United States currency at $4.85 to the £, or $110,095,000; in German marks, 463,000,000. The bonds are coupon, to bearer, and are without provision for registration. They are issued in fixed denominations of £20, £100, £200, £500 and £1,000, or $97, $485, $970, $2,425 and $4,850, respectively, in United States gold coin of the present standard, also in German marks. Coupons are payable quarterly on January 1, April 1, July 1 and October 1. Each quarterly coupon of the £200 bonds calls for £2 10s., $12.12½, or 51 marks. Coupons on bonds of the other denominations are in proportion to these amounts. Coupons are payable at holder's option either in London by

J. S. Morgan & Co., in New York by J. P. Morgan & Co., in Berlin by S. Bleichroder or the Deutsche Bank, and in Amsterdam. The first coupon matured April 1, 1900.

No period is fixed for the maturity of these bonds. The Mexican government, however, obligates itself to pay from January 1, 1900, a semi-annual sinking fund of 0.31 per cent. of the original amount of the loan. By the operation of the sinking fund it is calculated that the entire issue will be retired within forty-five years. Bonds may be purchased for the sinking fund at below par or drawn and retired at par. After July, 1909, the Mexican government has the right to increase the sinking fund payments or to pay off the loan at par on three months' notice. The bonds and coupons are free from any existing or future Mexican tax. Bonds drawn for the sinking fund are payable at holder's option by any of the firms named above as agents for the payment of coupons at the fixed equivalent amounts in the currencies of the respective countries.

As security for the interest and sinking fund the Mexican Government had pledged 62 per cent. of its combined import and export duties. In the fiscal year 1897-98 these amounted to $22,582,437 Mexican currency or about $14,001,110 gold. The interest and sinking fund requirements for the 5 per cent. gold loan are about $6,200,000 gold per annum.

Fiscal Agents of Mexico in the United States for the 5 per cent. consolidated external gold loan, J. P. Morgan & Co., New York.

---

## THE UNITED KINGDOM OF GREAT BRITAIN AND IRELAND

The figures given below as the amount of each class of British public funds outstanding were taken from the statement of the national debt, March 31, 1902. The British pound sterling consists of 123.27 grains of gold .916⅔ fine, the equivalent of £1 in United States currency being $4.86⅔.

NATIONAL DEBT.

| | |
|---|---|
| Consols, 2½ per cent., due 1923, quarterly Jan. | £499,958,418 |
| Consols of 1901, 2¾ per cent., due 1923, quarterly, Jan. | 60,000,000 |
| Annuity stock, 2¾ per cent., due 1905, quarterly, Jan. | 4,588,291 |
| " " 2½ per cent., due 1905, quarterly, Jan. | 31,394,669 |
| War loan, 2¾ per cent., due 1910, quarterly, Jan. | 30,000,000 |
| Bank of England debt | 11,015,100 |
| Bank of Ireland debt | 2,630,769 |
| Terminable annuities, capitalized values | 63,190,859 |
| Unfunded debt | 20,532,279 |
| Other liabilities | 12,081,478 |
| Exchequer bonds of 1900, 3 per cent., due 1903, quarterly, Jan. | 10,000,000 |
| " " 1901, 3 per cent., due 1905, " " | 11,000,000 |
| Total | £756,391,863 |

In 1902 the National City Bank of New York effected arrangements which the certificates of the bank would be issued against amounts of British consols, to be registered in the joint names of the Union Bank of London and Baring Brothers & Co., Limited, London; all consols so registered to be disposed of only on the joint order of the National City Bank and the Farmers' Loan & Trust Co., New York. Interest on the certificates will be paid in cash by the National City Bank, or checks for the same, mailed to registered holders of certificates on the same day that payment is made by the British government, the same being converted at the current rate of interest at the time, less any income tax imposed by the British government.

There are, in addition to the above, local loan stocks created under authority of act of Parliament and administered by the commissioners of the national debt which amount to about £40,000,000. The total interest charge upon the debt in 1901 was about £19,835,488.

The 2¾ per cent. consols were created in 1888 to refund previous issues. They bear 2¾ per cent. until April, 1903, and 2½ per cent. thereafter, but after 1923 may be redeemed at any time at par, as Parliament may decide. Interest is payable quarterly, January 5, April 5, July 5 and October 5, at the Bank of England. The consols are "inscribed stock," that is, registered, or bonds to bearer.

The consols of 1901 were issued in April, 1901, to provide for the cost of the South African war. The issue price was 94½ and subscriptions were invited in the United States through J. P. Morgan & Co., New York; Baring, Magoun & Co., New York; Drexel & Co., Philadelphia, and Kidder, Peabody & Co., Boston. The American subscriptions aggregated about half the amount of the loan and allotments of 35 per cent were made thereon.

The 2¾ per cent. annuity stock was issued in 1884 to refund 3 per cent. consols. After January, 1905, it may be redeemed as Parliament shall decide. Interest is payable quarterly, January 5, April 5, July 5 and October 5, at the Bank of England. The stock is either "inscribed" or in the form of coupon bonds to bearer.

The 2½ per cent. annuity stock was created in 1853, and various amounts have been issued to refund old obligations. The stock matured in 1895, but was extended to January, 1905, after which it may be redeemed on one month's notice, as Parliament decides. Interest is payable quarterly, January 5, April 5, July 5 and October 5, at the Bank of England.

The 2¾ per cent. national war loan ("Kakhi loan") of £30,000,000 was created in 1900 to provide for the expense of the war in South Africa. The stock matures April 5, 1900. Interest is payable January 5, April 5, July 5 and October 5, at the Bank of England. The stock is "inscribed" or in the form of coupon bonds to bearer. It was issued in denominations of £100, £200, £500 and £1,000. The loan was offered for subscription in March, 1900, at 98½, and considerable allotments were made to American subscribers for the same.

The 3 per cent. Exchequer bonds of 1900 were created and issued in August, 1900, to provide for the further expense of the war in South Africa. The bonds mature August 7, 1903. They are in coupon form, interest being payable quarterly, January 5, April 5, July 5 and October 5, at the Bank of England. The bonds were issued in denominations of £200, £500, £1,000, £5,000 and £10,000. The issue price was 98. In August, 1900, J. P. Morgan & Co. and Baring, Magoun & Co., New York; Drexel & Co., Philadelphia, and Kidder, Peabody & Co., Boston, were authorized by the Bank of England to receive and forward American subscriptions for the issue. Over half of the full amount of bonds was awarded to American subscribers.

The 3 per cent. Exchequer bonds of 1901 were created and issued in February, 1901, for further expenditures caused by the war in South Africa. The bonds mature December 7, 1905. The whole of this issue was subscribed for and allotted in London.

The terminable annuities given in above table represent a description of sinking fund by which a considerable portion of the British national debt is paid off, and, after a certain time, the capitalized sum entirely extinguished. Under various acts of Parliament, the treasury is empowered to grant an annuity for a term of years in exchange for permanent stock. A holder of £1,000 of 2¾ per cent. consols, for example, can surrender them to the treasury in return for a fixed payment for a term of twenty years, the consols being canceled by the operation.

The unfunded debt given in above table is composed of loans made for short periods, usually running not more than twelve months and representing the anticipation of revenue.

The item of other liabilities given in the above table includes contingent or nominal liabilities, such as that to bankrupt estates, unclaimed interest, and other miscellaneous items.

Interest upon the various classes of British funded obligations is subject to the regular income tax of 5 per cent., which is deducted from the coupons at the time of payment thereof.

## GERMAN EMPIRE

The national debt of Germany has been incurred since the formation of the Empire in 1871. The German 20 marks consist of 122.915 grains of gold .900 fine, the equivalent in United States currency for the same being $4.76. The equivalent of the German mark in United States currency is 23.8c.

NATIONAL DEBT.

| | Marks. |
|---|---|
| Imperial converted loan, 3½ per cent., payable 1905, April and Oct. | 450,000,000 |
| Imperial loan, 3½ per cent., payable on call, April and Oct. | 790,000,000 |
| Imperial loan, 3 per cent., payable 1905, Jan. and July | 573,000,000 |
| " " 3 per cent., payable 1905, April and Oct. | 574,500,000 |
| Treasury notes of 1900, 4 per cent., due 1904–05, April and Oct. | 40,000,000 |
| " " " 1900, 4 per cent., due 1904–05, Jan. and July | 40,000,000 |
| Imperial loan of 1901, 3 per cent., April and Oct. | 300,000,000 |
| " " " 1902, 3 per cent, April and Oct. | 115,000,000 |
| " " " 1903, 3 per cent., April and Oct. | 360,000,000 |
| Total | 3,242,500,000 |

The Imperial converted loan was issued under a law of 1897, for the refunding of the old 4 per cent. bonds. The converted bonds cannot be paid off before April 1, 1905. Bonds are in denominations of 200, 500, 1,000, 2,000 and 5,000 marks. Upon compliance with certain conditions these and other issues of German Government bonds can be registered, but checks in payment of registered bond interest will not be remitted abroad. Coupons and principal are payable through the Imperial Bank of Germany at Berlin and its branches. Provision is also made for the payment of coupons in London.

The Imperial 3 per cent. loan of 790,000,000 marks was issued prior to 1890. These bonds may be called for payment at the option of the Treasury on six months' notice. The bonds are in coupon form and are issued in denominations of 200, 500, 1,000, 2,000, 5,000 and 10,000 marks.

The Imperial 3 per cent. loan was issued between 1890 and 1902, interest, as noted in the above table, being payable on a portion thereof, January and July; and on another portion, April 1 and October 1. The bonds may be called for payment after 1905, and are issued in denominations of 200, 500, 1,000, 2,000, 5,000 and 10,000 marks.

The Treasury notes of 1900 were created in that year, the total issue being 80,000,000 marks. They are in four series of 20,000,000 marks each, maturing respectively, April 1, 1904; July 1, 1904; April 1, 1905 and July 1, 1905. The bonds are in coupon form and are issued in denominations of 5,000, 10,000, 25,000, 50,000 and 100,000 marks. These bonds were sold to Kuhn, Loeb & Co. and the National City Bank, New York, and were offered by them for subscription at par and interest in September, 1900, the entire issue being placed in the United States. These bonds are free from the German income tax when in the hands of foreign holders.

The Imperial 3 per cent. loan of 1901, for 300,000,000 marks was created and issued to defray the cost of operations in China and other expenses. This loan was taken by a German syndicate which offered the new bonds in April, 1901, at the price of 87½.

The Imperial 3 per cent. loan of 1902 was also taken by a German syndicate which offered the bonds for subscription at 90. The amount was heavily over-subscribed, but American subscribers received allotments for a small portion of the loan.

The Imperial loan of 1903 was taken by a syndicate of German bankers, the subscription price being 92.

## FRENCH REPUBLIC

The currency system of France is composite but the gold standard is maintained. The value of the franc in United States currency is 19.3 cents. The smallest gold coin is the 5-franc piece, which in United States currency is equivalent to 96.4 cents.

| National Debt. | Francs. |
|---|---|
| Perpetual Rentes, 3 p. c., irredeemable, quarterly, Jan. (1), April, July and Oct.... | 14,661,638,604 |
| Rentes, 3½ per cent., quarterly, Feb. (16), May, Aug. and Nov.................. | 6,789,664,180 |
| Redeem. Rentes, 3 p. c., due March, 1903-1953, quar., Jan. (16), April, July and Oct. | 4,254,146,500 |
| Total............................................................ | 25,705,449,284 |

French Government obligations are either inscribed, that is to say, registered, or in the form of bonds with coupons payable to bearer. The perpetual and the 3 per cent. rentes are also issued, registered as to principal only and coupons payable to bearer.

The title of French Government securities is derived from the rente or income which they yield, and they are dealt in and treated with reference to the interest on or income from a specified amount rather than the principal. The above table, however, gives the principal of each class outstanding. Interest on all the rentes is paid at the Ministry of Finance, Paris, or the branch treasuries in the various departments into which France is divided.

The perpetual 3 per cent. rentes were created under the law of November 7, 1887, for the conversion of the old 4 per cent. and 4½ per cent. rentes. There have been subsequent issues of additional amounts, the last one being for the sum of 265,000,000 francs in December, 1901.

The 3½ per cent. rentes were created under a law of January 16, 1894, by which the 4½ per cent. rentes issued in 1883 and redeemable in August, 1894, were converted.

The 3 per cent. redeemable rentes were created under a law of June 11, 1878. They are redeemable serially by drawings on each March 1, and for that purposes were divided into 175 series. One series was to mature in this way each year from 1879 to 1907 inclusive, two series in each year from 1908 to 1925 and so on, with periodical increases in the number of series redeemed each year until 1953.

## RUSSIAN EMPIRE

The currency system of Russia is a composite one, but its external debt is based on the gold ruble, which is equivalent in United States currency to 77.2 cents. The smallest gold coin is, however, the 5-ruble piece.

NATIONAL DEBT.

LOANS ISSUED TO COVER VARIOUS EXTRAORDINARY EXPENSES OF THE STATE.

| | Amount of Loans Outstanding on 1st of January, 1900. Rubles. | Annual Charges for Payment of Interest (1899). Rubles. | Annual Charges for Sinking Fund (1899). Rubles. |
|---|---|---|---|
| 3 per cent. loans.................. | 452,492,725 | 14,830,224 | 1,192,236 |
| 3½ " " .................. | 29,012,046 | 868,815 | 59,565 |
| 3.79 " " .................. | 61,516,000 | 3,440,410 | ......... |
| 3.8 " " .................. | 85,247,400 | 3,244,132 | 165,000 |
| 4 " " .................. | 2,634,538,077 | 105,097,356 | 9,018,875 |
| 4½ " " .................. | 99,150,000 | 4,467,150 | 160,000 |
| 5 " " .................. | 267,264,838 | 15,745,402 | 3,730,450 |
| 6 " " .................. | 38,483,515 | 2,309,215 | 2,742 |
| Other loans......................... | 55,767,437 | 2,303,243 | 1,602,231 |
| Totals ....................... | 3,723,472,038 | 152,305,947 | 15,931,099 |

LOANS ISSUED FOR THE CONSTRUCTION OF RAILROADS.

| | Amount of Loans Outstanding on 1st of January, 1900. Rubles. | Annual Interest Charges. Rubles. | Annual Charges for Sinking Fund. Rubles. |
|---|---|---|---|
| 3 per cent. loans | 101,754,937 | 3,095,815 | 789,562 |
| 3½ " " " | 125,104,366 | 4,387,090 | 320,121 |
| 4 " " " | 2,126,544,647 | 85,070,738 | 6,484,773 |
| 4½ " " " | 148,220,000 | 6,678,675 | 260,000 |
| Totals | 2,501,623,950 | 99,232,318 | 7,854,458 |
| General totals | 6,274,095,988 | 251,538,266 | 23,785,555 |

In August, 1902, on application of certain New York banking houses acting on behalf of the Imperial Russian Minister of Finance, there were listed at the New York Stock Exchange Imperial Russian Government 4 per cent. Rente to the amount of 2,310,000,000 rubles, which at an agreed equivalent of $51.45 for 100 rubles equals $1,188,495,000 in United States currency.

These bonds were issued in compliance with various Imperial ukases dated from April, 1894, to April, 1901, for the purpose of the conversion of old State loans, bearing higher rates of interest, for the purchase of railroads and for other financial operations.

The Certificates of Rente are of the following denominations: Of 100, 200; 500, 1,000, 5,000 and 25,000 rubles in coupon form to bearer, and, at the option of holders, can be registered as to principal, and are issued in 231 series for 10,000,000 rubles each, aggregating 2,310,000,000 rubles.

The interest is payable quarterly on the 14th of March, June, September and December in each year at the agencies in the United States, being, according to the Russian calendar, the first of those months respectively.

The bonds have coupons attached for ten years from date of issue and also a talon for the delivery of additional coupon sheets thereafter.

The rente are not payable at any fixed date, but the Imperial Russian Government reserves to itself the right to redeem the Certificates of Rente at any time at its option, either by purchases of those certificates in the open market or by payment to the holders thereof of the principal of the certificates at par. Reimbursement will be made only by whole series, drawn by lot not less than three months before the time of reimbursement.

After such drawings are made the State Commission of the Sinking Fund will send printed tables giving the results of the drawings to all the institutions in Russia and also abroad who are authorized to handle the payment of coupons of the 4 per cent. rente. These tables will show the numbers of the series which were drawn at the last drawing, and also those from previous drawings which have not yet been presented for payment. On these tables opposite every drawn series will be indicated the dates when that series is redeemable, and also when the interest ceases to accrue. The places in Russia and other countries where drawn certificates are redeemable will also be stated. Besides the mailing of aforesaid tables of drawings, notice of such drawings will be published in Russia and also in other countries, in daily papers selected for this purpose by the Minister of Finance.

The coupons of the rente will be forfeited if not presented for payment within 10 years after the date when payment is due; the Certificates of Rente of a series, the offer for the reimbursement of which, at par, has been made by the Government, also will be forfeited if not presented for payment within 30 years after the date fixed for payment of the principal.

The coupons are payable: In Russia, by the State Bank, its sub-treasuries and branches; in London, by N. M. Rothschild & Sons, in pounds sterling; in Paris, by De Rothschild Freres, in francs, and in New York by J. P. Morgan & Co., August Belmont & Co., Baring, Magoun & Co., or by the National City Bank, in United States gold dollars.

Payments of coupons are made at the rate of sight exchange on St. Petersburg on the date of payment, but at not less than the equivalent for 100 rubles of £10 11s. 6d., 266 francs, or in American currency, $51.45.

The income tax of 5 per cent. to which the Russian Government subjects the interest of the State Rente is waived in the case of holders who are neither Russians nor reside in Russia. This exemption is secured by registering the certificates in their name according to the rules established by the Minister of Finance. The bankers and bank in New York which are authorized to pay coupons are authorized to exchange Certificates of Rente for receipts carrying such exemption.

## KINGDOM OF SWEDEN

The entire national debt of Sweden was incurred for the construction of railways. The valuation of the roads built and owned by the State is about 343,000,000 kronor, and it has loaned some 43,000,000 kronor to private railways. The Swedish krone consists of 6.914 grains of gold, .900 fine, the equivalent in United States currency being 26.79c.

National Debt.

| | Kronor. |
|---|---|
| Railway loans, various rates and maturities.................................... | 317,000,000 |
| Loan of 1900, 4 per cent., payable 1920, Feb. 15 and Aug. 15..................... | 36,320,000 |
| Total ................................................................... | 353,320,000 |

The 4 per cent. loan of 1900, like the rest of the Swedish national debt, was created and issued for railroad construction purposes. The bonds bear interest at the rate of 4 per cent. from August 15, 1900, to August 15, 1910, and 3½ per cent. thereafter. On or after August 15, 1920, they are redeemable at the option of the government on three months' notice. The principal of the loan is 36,320,000 kronor—£2,000,000, 50,000,000 francs and 40,800,000 marks—principal being payable at the holder's option in any of the above currencies. The bonds are in coupon form, and coupons not presented for redemption within ten years from the date thereof become void. The bonds are issued in denominations of £100, £500 and £1,000, or 1,816, 9,080 and 18,160 kronor. They are also expressed in equivalents of 2,520, 12,600 and 25,200 francs, and in 2,040, 10,200 and 20,400 marks. A large part of this loan was placed in the United States in the autumn of 1900, and provision for the payment of coupons at the National Park Bank, New York, was made.

## INTEREST BEARING DEBT OF THE UNITED STATES, 1891 TO 1903, INCLUSIVE

Year ending June 30.

| Year. | Funded Loan of 1891, 4½ Per Cent. | Funded Loan of 1907, 4 Per Cent. | Refunding Certificates, 4 Per Cent. | Loan of 1904, 5 Per Cent. | Loan of 1925, 4 Per Cent. | Loan of 1908, 3 Per Cent. | Consols of 1930, 2 Per Cent. |
|---|---|---|---|---|---|---|---|
| | $ | $ | $ | $ | $ | $ | $ |
| 1891.......... | 50,869,200 | 559,566,000 | 93,920 | .......... | .......... | .......... | .......... |
| 1892.......... | 25,364,500 | 559,581,250 | 83,580 | .......... | .......... | .......... | .......... |
| 1893.......... | 25,364,500 | 559,604,150 | 68,450 | .......... | .......... | .......... | .......... |
| 1894.......... | 25,364,500 | 559,618,400 | 58,990 | 50,000,000 | .......... | .......... | .......... |
| 1895.......... | 25,364,500 | 559,625,750 | 54,110 | 100,000,000 | 31,157,700 | .......... | .......... |
| 1896.......... | 25,864,500 | 559,636,850 | 47,140 | 100,000,000 | 162,315,400 | .......... | .......... |
| 1897.......... | 25,364,500 | 559,640,100 | 45,130 | 100,000,000 | 162,315,400 | .......... | .......... |
| 1898.......... | 25,364,500 | 559,646,050 | 41,520 | 100,000,000 | 162,315,400 | .......... | .......... |
| 1899.......... | 25,364,500 | 559,652,300 | 37,830 | 100,000,000 | 162,315,400 | 198,678,720 | .......... |
| 1900.......... | 21,979,850 | 355,528,350 | 35,470 | 47,651,200 | 162,315,400 | 128,843,240 | 307,125,350 |
| 1901.......... | .......... | 257,376,050 | 33,320 | 21,854,100 | 162,315,400 | 99,621,420 | 445,940,750 |
| 1902.......... | .......... | 233,177,400 | 31,980 | 19,410,350 | 134,994,200 | 97,515,660 | 445,940,750 |
| 1903 (April 1). | .......... | 233,179,200 | 30,810 | 7,259,800 | 118,489,900 | 97,515,660 | 445,940,750 |

## PUBLIC DEBT OF THE UNITED STATES FROM 1876 TO 1903, INCLUSIVE

Year ending June 30.

| Year. | Principal. | Cash in the Treasury July 1. | Total Debt Less Cash in Treasury. | Annual Interest Charge. |
|---|---|---|---|---|
| 1876 | $2,151,713,667 | $90,788,326 | $2,060,925,340 | $96,104,269 |
| 1877 | 2,163,728,792 | 144,453,360 | 2,019,275,431 | 93,160,643 |
| 1878 | 2,163,561,292 | 164,179,012 | 1,999,382,280 | 94,654,472 |
| 1879 | 2,196,809,422 | 200,394,517 | 1,996,414,905 | 83,773,778 |
| 1880 | 2,085,441,500 | 166,114,752 | 1,919,326,747 | 79,633,981 |
| 1881 | 2,000,139,119 | 180,488,965 | 1,819,650,154 | 75,018,695 |
| 1882 | 1,833,859,164 | 158,835,689 | 1,675,023,474 | 57,360,110 |
| 1883 | 1,699,801,257 | 161,019,431 | 1,538,781,825 | 51,436,709 |
| 1884 | 1,599,939,572 | 161,396,577 | 1,438,542,995 | 47,926,432 |
| 1885 | 1,553,955,087 | 178,602,643 | 1,375,352,443 | 47,014,133 |
| 1886 | 1,509,411,093 | 227,265,253 | 1,282,145,840 | 45,510,098 |
| 1887 | 1,381,492,625 | 206,323,950 | 1,175,168,675 | 41,786,529 |
| 1888 | 1,306,679,062 | 243,674,167 | 1,063,004,894 | 38,991,935 |
| 1889 | 1,185,419,624 | 209,479,874 | 975,939,750 | 33,752,354 |
| 1890 | 1,080,777,474 | 189,993,104 | 890,784,370 | 29,417,603 |
| 1891 | 1,005,806,560 | 153,893,808 | 851,912,751 | 23,615,735 |
| 1892 | 968,218,840 | 126,692,377 | 841,526,463 | 22,893,883 |
| 1893 | 961,431,766 | 122,462,290 | 838,969,475 | 22,894,194 |
| 1894 | 1,016,897,816 | 117,584,436 | 899,313,380 | 25,394,385 |
| 1895 | 1,096,913,120 | 195,240,153 | 901,672,966 | 29,140,782 |
| 1896 | 1,222,729,350 | 267,432,096 | 955,297,253 | 34,387,265 |
| 1897 | 1,226,793,712 | 240,137,626 | 986,656,086 | 34,387,315 |
| 1898 | 1,232,743,062 | 205,657,570 | 1,027,085,492 | 34,387,408 |
| 1899 | 1,436,700,703 | 281,380,468 | 1,155,320,235 | 40,347,872 |
| 1900 | 1,413,416,912 | 305,705,654 | 1,107,711,257 | 33,545,130 |
| 1901 | 1,371,372,244 | 326,833,124 | 1,044,739,119 | 32,317,000 |
| 1902 | 1,328,031,356 | 358,574,115 | 969,457,241 | 25,542,945 |
| 1903 (April 1) | 1,312,325,907 | ........... | 372,921,988 | 23,411,062 |

# Baltimore Stock Exchange

**Quotations for Securities Dealt in on the Stock Exchange, 1901 and 1902**

## STOCKS

### RAILROAD STOOKS

| | Par Value. | 1901. High. | 1901. Low. | 1902. High. | 1902. Low. |
|---|---|---|---|---|---|
| Atlanta & Charlotte | $100 | 160 | 160 | 170¼ | 167¼ |
| Atlantic Coast Line | 100 | 92 | 74 | 183½ | 86¼ |
| " " pref | 100 | 115⅛ | 105½ | 122 | 108½ |
| " " (Conn.) | 100 | 121 | 106 | 357½ | 160 |
| Baltimore & Ohio | 100 | 102 | 90½ | 105⅛ | 105¼ |
| " " pref | 100 | 93⅛ | 85½ | 95⅛ | 95⅛ |
| Charleston Con. Electric | 50 | 12 | 12 | 12 | 10½ |
| Georgia & Alabama | 100 | 35 | 29½ | .. | .. |
| " " pref | 100 | 82½ | 56 | .. | .. |
| Georgia Southern & Florida | 100 | 50 | 45 | 52½ | 48 |
| " " " 1st pref | 100 | 102 | 95 | 102½ | 99 |
| " " " 2d pref | 100 | 80 | 70 | 83½ | 81 |
| Knoxville Traction | 100 | .. | .. | 27 | 15 |
| Lexington Street Railway | 100 | 50 | 33 | 50 | 50 |
| Maryland & Pennsylvania | 100 | 15 | 13 | 32 | 13 |
| Nashville Railway | 100 | 6½ | 2 | 7⅛ | 3 |
| National Railway | .. | .. | .. | 7½ | 3 |
| Newport News & Old Point Street Ry., pref | 100 | 83½ | 78 | .. | .. |
| Norfolk Railway & Light | 100 | 14 | 10 | 14 | 10 |
| Northern Central | 50 | 106½ | 88½ | 125¼ | 104 |
| Richmond Traction | 50 | 56½ | 43 | 46 | 45 |
| Seaboard Air Line | 100 | 31½ | 9¼ | 34¼ | 23⅛ |
| " " pref | 100 | 54 | 24½ | 55⅛ | 40¼ |
| Southern Railway | 100 | 35⅛ | 33¼ | .. | .. |
| " " pref | 100 | .. | .. | 95¼ | 95¼ |
| United Railways & Electric | 50 | 18⅛ | 14 | 17 | 13 |
| " " " pref | 50 | 37½ | 35 | 35 | 33 |
| Western Maryland | 50 | 25 | 11½ | 40 | 20 |

### MISCELLANEOUS STOCKS

| | Par Value. | 1901. High. | 1901. Low. | 1902. High. | 1902. Low. |
|---|---|---|---|---|---|
| Alabama Consolidated Coal & Iron | $100 | .. | .. | 41 | 15½ |
| " " " " pref | 100 | .. | .. | 91 | 81 |
| Atlantic Transport | 100 | 270½ | 201 | 280 | 225 |
| Baltimore Steam Packet | .. | 2,000 | 2,000 | .. | .. |
| Baltimore Warehouse | 20 | 20⅛ | 20 | 23 | 22 |
| Canton | 100 | 100 | 94 | 104 | 06 |
| Consolidated Gas | 100 | 65¼ | 58 | 74⅛ | 62¼ |
| Frederick Turnpike | 20 | 1 | ¼ | 1 | 1 |
| George's Creek Coal Co | .. | 118 | 116 | 116 | 114 |
| Gottlieb-Bauernschmidt-Straus Brewing Co | 100 | 14 | 9⅛ | 20¼ | 10¼ |
| Maryland Brewing | .. | 7¼ | 6 | .. | .. |
| " " pref | .. | 14¼ | 13 | .. | .. |
| M. & M. Transportation Co | .. | 153½ | 145 | 185 | 175 |
| Mount Vernon-Woodbury Cotton Duck | .. | 27½ | 10 | 13½ | 5½ |
| Philadelphia | 50 | 52 | 45 | 50 | 46½ |
| United Electric Light & Power, pref | 100 | 39¼ | 33 | 42 | 32½ |

## INSURANCE STOCKS—BALTIMORE

| | Par Value. | 1901. High. | 1901. Low. | 1902. High. | 1902. Low. |
|---|---|---|---|---|---|
| American Fire | $5 | 5¾ | 4⅛ | 1½ | 1½ |
| Baltimore Fire | 10 | 24¼ | 22⅞ | 23¾ | 22 |
| Firemen's | 18 | 25½ | 22 | 23¼ | 21 |
| German American Fire | .. | 36 | 32½ | 33 | 33 |
| German Fire | 10 | 25 | 23½ | 25 | 23½ |
| Home Fire | 10 | 15½ | 14½ | .. | .. |
| Maryland Fire | 5 | 3½ | 2½ | 3 | 2½ |
| Old Town Fire | .. | .. | .. | 5¾ | 5½ |
| Peabody Fire | 25 | 39½ | 35 | 35 | 35 |
| United Fire | .. | 7 | 6¼ | .. | .. |

# BONDS

## RAILROAD BONDS—BALTIMORE

| | Due. | Interest Payable. | 1901. High. | 1901. Low. | 1902. High. | 1902. Low. |
|---|---|---|---|---|---|---|
| Atlanta con. 5s | .... | ........ | 106¾ | 102 | 108¼ | 105 |
| Anacostia & Potomac 5s | .... | ........ | 99 | 83 | 104 | 92½ |
| Atlanta & Char. 1st 7s. R | 1907 | J. & J. | 118¼ | 114⅜ | 115¼ | 112¼ |
| " pref. 4s | 1907 | A. & O. | 100⅜ | 100⅜ | .. | .. |
| Atlantic Coast Line 5s, certs | .... | ........ | 116 | 115 | 117 | 116½ |
| " " " 4s, certs | .... | ........ | 99¾ | 97½ | 99½ | 98 |
| " " " (Conn.) 4s, certs | .... | ........ | .. | .. | 99½ | 96 |
| " " " " 5s, " | .... | ........ | .. | .. | 117 | 116½ |
| " " " (S. C.) gen. 4s | .... | ........ | 104½ | 102½ | 104⅛ | 102⅝ |
| " " " " 4s, new certs | .... | ........ | .. | .. | 95 | 87 |
| Baltimore & Annapolis Short Line 5s | 1923 | J. & D. | 105 | 102 | 110½ | 102½ |
| Baltimore & Harrisburg 1st 5s. C | 1936 | M. & N. | 125 | 117 | 119½ | 116 |
| " " W. Ex | .... | ........ | 105¼ | 103 | 110¾ | 104 |
| Baltimore & Ohio Southwestern 3½s | 1925 | ........ | .. | .. | 91⅞ | 91⅞ |
| Baltimore & Potomac 1st 6s (Tunnel) | 1911 | J. & J. | 122 | 121¾ | .. | .. |
| " " 6s | 1911 | A. & O. | 122¼ | 120½ | 119 | 118 |
| Baltimore, Catonsville & E. M. 5s | .... | ........ | 113 | 113 | 111¼ | 111¼ |
| Baltimore City Pass. 1st 5s. C | 1911 | M. & N. | 112 | 108¼ | 111⅛ | 105¾ |
| " " " 4½s, deb | .... | ........ | 106¾ | 104½ | 104½ | 102 |
| Baltimore Traction Co. 1st 5s. C | 1929 | M. & N. | 118½ | 116½ | 118½ | 115½ |
| " " " Ex. & Impt. 6s. C | 1901 | M. & S. | 102½ | 100¾ | .. | .. |
| " " " N. Balt. div. 1st 5s. C | 1942 | J. & D. | 123 | 120 | 121½ | 119 |
| " " " convertible 5s. C | 1906 | M. & S. | 103⅛ | 100 | 102 | 100 |
| Carolina Central 4s | 1949 | J. & J. | 97⅛ | 89 | 100 | 95¾ |
| Central Railway con. 5s. C | 1932 | M. & N. | 119⅛ | 118¾ | 116 | 116 |
| " " Ext. and Imp. 5s. C | 1932 | M. & S. | 119 | 118 | 117¾ | 116⅛ |
| Charleston & Western Carolina 5s | 1946 | A. & O. | 112 | 107 | 116 | 109½ |
| Charleston St. Ry. 5s | .... | ........ | 107½ | 105½ | 107½ | 105 |
| " " con. 5s | .... | ........ | 95½ | 90 | 95 | 87½ |
| Charlotte, Columbia & Aug. Extd. 5s. C | 1910 | J. & J. | 116 | 106 | 122¼ | 117¼ |
| " " " 2d 7s. C | 1910 | A. & O. | 109⅛ | 106 | .. | .. |
| Citizens' Ry. Light & Power of Newport News 5s | .... | ........ | 99¼ | 93½ | 100 | 96½ |
| " " " " gen. mort | .... | ........ | 98½ | 98 | .. | .. |
| City & Suburban 1st 5s. C | 1922 | J. & D. | 118¾ | 114 | 116⅛ | 114 |
| " " (Wash.) 5s | .... | ........ | 100 | 85 | 105 | 89¾ |
| Coal & Iron Railway 5s | .... | ........ | .. | .. | 105 | 103¼ |
| Col. & Green 1st 6s. C | 1916 | J. & J. | 124 | 117½ | .. | .. |
| " " 6s | .. | ........ | .. | .. | 122¼ | 118 |
| Georgia & Alabama 1st pref. 5s. C | 1945 | ........ | 108½ | 105¾ | .. | .. |
| " " con. 5s. C | 1945 | ........ | 112 | 107 | 116 | 109¾ |
| Georgia, Carolina & Northern 1st 5s. C | 1929 | J. & J. | 113 | 103½ | 114½ | 110 |
| Georgia Southern & Florida 1st 6s. C | 1927 | J. & J. | 115½ | 112½ | .. | .. |
| " " " 5s | 1945 | J. & J. | .. | .. | 116 | 112¾ |
| Georgia Pacific 1st 6s. C | 1922 | J. & J. | 128⅛ | 124 | 129 | 125¾ |

| | | Due. | Interest Payable. | 1901. High. | 1901. Low. | 1902. High. | 1902. Low. |
|---|---|---|---|---|---|---|---|
| Knoxville Traction 5s | | 1938 | A. & O. | 99¾ | 87 | 102½ | 95 |
| Lake Roland Elev. 1st 5s gtd | C | 1942 | M. & S. | 120½ | 119 | 121½ | 119 |
| Lexington (Ky.) Ry. 5s | | 1949 | J. & D. | 105 | 96⅞ | 104⅞ | 100¾ |
| Metropolitan R. R. (Wash.) 1st 5s | C | 1925 | F. & A. | 121¼ | 118 | 122 | 122 |
| Maryland & Pennsylvania 4s | | 1951 | M. & S. | .. | .. | 99¼ | 96½ |
| " " incomes | | .... | ........ | .. | .. | 70 | 69 |
| Nashville St. Ry. 5s | | .... | ........ | 80 | 60 | 78¼ | 62¾ |
| Newport News & Old Point 5s | | .... | ........ | 108⅝ | 104 | 109¾ | 105½ |
| " " gen'l mort. 5s | | .... | ........ | 98½ | 98 | 96 | 94 |
| Norfolk & Carolina 5s | C | 1930 | A. & O. | 116¾ | 116 | 121 | 118¾ |
| " " 2d 5s | | 1946 | J. & J. | .. | .. | 120½ | 120½ |
| Norfolk Railway & Light 5s | | .... | ........ | 98 | 93½ | 96 | 94 |
| Norfolk St., 1st 5s | C | 1944 | J. & J. | 112½ | 110 | 114½ | 109½ |
| Northern Central 4½s | C | 1925 | A. & O. | 118½ | 116⅛ | 115½ | 112 |
| " 6s | C | 1904 | J. & J. | 109¼ | 106½ | 107⅛ | 104⅜ |
| " 5s (Series A) | C | 1926 | J. & J. | 127 | 123½ | 124¾ | 123½ |
| " 5s (Series B) | C | 1926 | J. & J. | 126 | 125 | 124½ | 123⅜ |
| Petersburg, Class A 5s | C | 1926 | J. & J. | 119½ | 117½ | 119 | 118 |
| " Class B 6s | C | 1926 | A. & O. | 134 | 128½ | 128½ | 128 |
| Pied. & Cumb. 1st 5s | C | 1911 | F. & A. | 110⅜ | 110⅜ | 108½ | 108 |
| Potomac Valley 5s | | 1941 | J. & J. | 114⅛ | 100 | 119 | 144 |
| Raleigh & Augusta 6s | C | 1926 | J. & J. | 125½ | 115¼ | 125½ | 122¾ |
| Raleigh & Gaston 5s | C | 1898 | J. & J. | 115½ | 110¼ | 118½ | 115⅜ |
| Richmond & Danville gold 6s | | 1915 | J. & J. | 123¼ | 122½ | 123 | 120 |
| Richmond Traction | | .... | ........ | 106 | 106 | 109 | 108 |
| " " 5s | | 1925 | J. & J. | .. | .. | 109 | 108 |
| Savannah, Florida & Western 5s | | 1943 | M. & N. | 115¾ | 112 | 116¾ | 114¾ |
| " " " 6s | | 1924 | A. & O. | .. | .. | 130 | 129½ |
| Savannah (St. Johns River Division) 4s | | 1934 | ........ | .. | .. | 98 | 98 |
| Seaboard Air Line 4s | C | 1915 | A. & O. | 86¼ | 68½ | 90 | 82½ |
| " " loan certs 6s | C | 1902 | M. & N. | 102½ | 95¾ | .. | .. |
| " " 10-year 5s | | 1911 | M. & N. | 104 | 101 | 105½ | 101 |
| Seaboard & Roanoke 5s | C | 1926 | J. & J. | 114⅛ | 109 | 116 | 113⅛ |
| " " 6s | | 1916 | F. & A. | .. | .. | 112 | 110½ |
| Second Ave. Traction (Pittsburg) 5s | C | 1934 | J. & D. | 118 | 118 | 118¼ | 118 |
| South Bound 5s | | 1941 | A. & O. | 111 | 100½ | 113 | 109¾ |
| Southern Railway con. 5s | R C | 1994 | J. & J. | 123¼ | 116¼ | 123¼ | 118¼ |
| United Railways & Electric 4s | C | 1949 | ........ | 99½ | 94½ | 98½ | 94¼ |
| " " income 4s | C | 1949 | J. & J. | 77¼ | 66⅜ | 73⅜ | 65½ |
| United Traction (Pittsburg) 5s | | 1997 | J. & J. | 117½ | 113¼ | 117 | 115 |
| Virginia Midland 1st 6s | C | 1906 | M. & S. | 112 | 106½ | 109½ | 104¼ |
| " " 2d 6s | C | 1911 | M. & S. | 120½ | 115 | 117⅝ | 113 |
| " " 3d 6s | C | 1916 | M. & S. | 123 | 119 | 124¼ | 119 |
| " " 4th 3-4-5s | C | 1921 | M. & S. | 110 | 110 | 113 | 110 |
| " " 5th 5s | C | 1926 | M. & S. | 116¼ | 111 | 118 | 114½ |
| " " 6th | | .... | ........ | .. | .. | 117 | 117 |
| " " gen'l mort. 5s | | 1936 | M. & N. | 116⅝ | 116¼ | .. | .. |
| West. Nor. Ca. con. 6s | C | 1914 | J. & J. | 121 | 117¾ | 120½ | 118 |
| West Va. Cent. 1st 6s | C | 1911 | J. & J. | 116½ | 113¼ | 115¼ | 113 |
| Wil. Col. & Aug. 6s | C | 1910 | J. & D. | 117⅛ | 113 | 117 | 113½ |
| Wil. & Weldon 5s | C | 1935 | J. & J. | 123¼ | 120¾ | 123¾ | 120⅛ |
| " 4s | C | 1935 | J. & J. | 105½ | 105½ | 104 | 104 |
| " gen. mort. 7s | | .... | ........ | .. | .. | 170½ | 170½ |

## STATE RONDS—BALTIMORE

| | | Due. | Interest Payable. | 1901. High. | 1901. Low. | 1902. High. | 1902. Low. |
|---|---|---|---|---|---|---|---|
| Maryland 3s (Exch. Loan) | R | 1900 | J. & J. | 103 | 100 | 101½ | 100⅞ |
| North Carolina 4s consols | C | 1909 | J. & J. | 108 | 103½ | 106 | 103 |
| " " 6s | C | 1919 | A. & O. | 137 | 135 | 135⅞ | 131¾ |
| Virginia 3s New | C | 1932 | J. & J. | 100 | 95 | 99⅞ | 95½ |
| " Century, 2-3 | C | 1991 | J. & J. | 100 | 94¼ | 101⅛ | 95⅜ |

## CITY RONDS—BALTIMORE

| | | Due. | Interest Payable | 1901. High. | 1901. Low. | 1902. High. | 1902. Low. |
|---|---|---|---|---|---|---|---|
| City........ ..3½ | per cent | 1952 | ........ | 114⅜ | 114⅜ | 114⅜ | 114⅜ |
| City Hall..................6 | " | 1902 | Jan. Qr. | 103 | 100¼ | .. | .. |
| Court House..............6 | " | 1902 | ........ | .. | .. | 100¼ | 100¼ |
| Exchange..................3½ | " | 1930 | J. & J. | 114 | 109 | 113½ | 109¾ |
| Four Million...............3½ | " | 1945 | M. & S. | 113 | 110¼ | 112½ | 110 |
| Funding....................5 | " | 1916 | M. & N. | 126 | 120 | 123½ | 120 |
| " ....................3½ | " | 1936 | J. & J. | 114 | 112½ | .. | .. |
| Hartford Run..............4 | " | 1904 | J. & J. | 103¾ | 103½ | 102⅛ | 102⅛ |
| " " ...............4 | " | 1920 | J. & J. | 115 | 110½ | 114¼ | 112½ |
| Internal Improvement......3½ | " | 1928 | J. & J. | 113 | 109 | 113 | 109½ |
| Norfolk, Va., Water 8s....C | | 1901 | M. & N. | 103¼ | 102⅜ | .. | .. |
| Public Improvement........3½ | " | 1940 | J. & J: | 114½ | 110 | 114¾ | 111 |
| Water.......................5 | " | 1916 | M. & N. | .. | .. | 123½ | 120 |
| " ..................... 4 | " | 1926 | M. & N. | 116½ | 114⅛ | .. | .. |
| Western Maryland..........6 | " | 1902 | J. & J. | 103¾ | 100¼ | 100¼ | 100¼ |
| " " ..........4 | " | 1925 | J. & J. | 113½ | 113½ | 117½ | 115 |
| " " ..........3¼ | " | 1927 | J. & J. | 100¾ | 99¾ | 105 | 100½ |
| " " ..........3½ | " | 1952 | ........ | 114¼ | 114¼ | 114⅜ | 114⅜ |

## MISCELLANEOUS RONDS—BALTIMORE

| | Due. | Interest Payable. | 1901. High. | 1901. Low. | 1902. High. | 1902. Low. |
|---|---|---|---|---|---|---|
| Consolidated Gas 6s.............................. | 1910 | J. & J. | 116 | 112 | 114¾ | 111¾ |
| " " 5s.............................. | 1939 | J. & J. | 115½ | 111¼ | 117 | 114 |
| " " 4½s.............................. | .... | ........ | .. | .. | 102⅝ | 102⅝ |
| Gottlieb-Bauernschmidt-Straus Brew'g Co. 1st 3 & 4 | 1950 | M. & S. | 50¾ | 45½ | 54⅞ | 48 |
| " " " incomes. | 1951 | M. & N. | 40 | 35 | 48¾ | 34 |
| Great Seaboard certs.............................. | .... | ........ | 131¾ | 111 | .. | .. |
| Maryland Brewing 6s.............................. | .... | ........ | 62¼ | 48 | .. | .. |
| Maryland Steel 5s.............................. | .... | ........ | 104½ | 104½ | 104⅝ | 104⅝ |
| Maryland Telephone 5s.............................. | .... | ........ | 95 | 84 | 94 | 85 |
| Mer. & Mech. P., B. & L.............................. | .... | ........ | 202½ | 195 | 200 | 195 |
| Mt. Vernon Cotton Duck incomes.................. | .... | ........ | 67 | 45 | 50 | 35¾ |
| " " " 5s.................. | .... | ........ | 93 | 81 | 84 | 77 |
| Philadelphia 5s.............................. | .... | ........ | 112½ | 112 | 111¼ | 110¼ |
| United Electric Light & Power 4½s.............. | .... | ........ | 90 | 84 | 88 | 82½ |

# Boston Stock Exchange

## Highest and Lowest Prices Recorded in 1901 and 1902 for Stocks and Bonds on the Exchange and at Public Sales

### STOCKS

### *RAILROAD STOCKS*

| | 1901. | | 1902. | |
|---|---|---|---|---|
| | Highest. | Lowest. | Highest. | Lowest |
| Atchison, Topeka & Sante Fe | 90⅜ | 42⅜ | 96½ | 74⅜ |
| " " " pref | 107½ | 80 | 106 | 95⅜ |
| Berkshire | 170½ | 160 | 176 | 174¼ |
| Boston & Albany | 265 | 251 | 266 | 257 |
| Boston & Lowell | 248 | 238 | 248 | 236 |
| Boston & Maine | 200 | 189 | 209 | 190½ |
| " " pref | 176⅜ | 168 | 190 | 171 |
| Boston & Providence | 307 | 297 | 307 | 297½ |
| Boston, Revere Beach & Lynn | 105 | 78 | 75⅛ | 68⅛ |
| Chicago, Burlington & Quincy | 199¾ | 138½ | .. | .. |
| Chicago Junc. R. R. & Stock Yards | 162 | 143½ | 172 | 150 |
| " " " " pref | 134 | 126 | 136 | 123 |
| Cleveland, Cin., Chicago & St. Louis | 101 | 72½ | 108⅜ | 93 |
| " " " " pref | 124 | 115¾ | 124¼ | 118 |
| Colorado & Southern | 18 | 6⅝ | 35¾ | 14⅛ |
| " " 1st pref | 59¾ | 40 | 79½ | 59¼ |
| " " 2d pref | 28¾ | 16⅝ | 53⅞ | 28 |
| Concord & Montreal, Class 1 | 199¾ | 195 | 200⅛ | 195 |
| " " " 2 | 195 | 195 | 197 | 195 |
| " " " 3 | 198⅜ | 196 | 200 | 196¼ |
| " " " 4 | 203 | 196⅜ | 202⅜ | 194⅞ |
| Concord & Portsmouth | .. | .. | 208¼ | 205 |
| Connecticut & Passumpsic pref | 165¾ | 160 | 167 | 160 |
| Connecticut River | 286 | 275 | 295 | 280 |
| " " scrip, 4s, 1903 | 100½ | 100⅛ | 100¼ | 98⅛ |
| Detroit, Hillsdale & Southwestern | 108 | 107 | .. | .. |
| European & No. American | 137 | 137 | 150 | 150 |
| Fitchburg pref | 148 | 139 | 148 | 141 |
| Granite Railway | 72¾ | 70 | .. | .. |
| Hereford (Me. Cent. Guar.) | 99⅝ | 99½ | 100 | 100 |
| Lowell & Andover | 225 | 225 | 228 | 226⅞ |
| Maine Central | 175 | 166 | 180 | 172 |
| Manchester & Lawrence | 255 | 245¾ | 260½ | 250 |
| Massawippi | .. | .. | 155 | 155 |
| Mexican Central | 28½ | 13¼ | 31⅛ | 22⅜ |
| Nashua & Lowell | 270 | 250 | 265¾ | 262⅜ |
| New York, New Haven & Hartford | 217½ | 201 | 254 | 210 |
| Northern (New Hampshire) | 173 | 163 | 175⅛ | 170 |
| Norwich & Worcester, pref | 232 | 223 | 238 | 230 |
| Old Colony | 212½ | 205 | 217 | 206 |
| Pemigewasset Valley | .. | .. | 155 | 142 |
| Pere Marquette | 95 | 30 | 85¼ | 68 |
| " pref | 89 | 70 | 91 | 79½ |
| " scrip | 80 | 70 | .. | .. |
| Peterboro | 114¾ | 104 | .. | .. |
| Pittsfield & North Adams | 148 | 145 | 150⅛ | 150 |
| Providence & Worcester | 301⅛ | 297 | 306 | 299 |
| Rutland | 13½ | 9 | .. | .. |
| " pref | 120 | 87 | 125¼ | 64⅞ |
| Southern California, pref | 20 | 14½ | .. | .. |
| Stony Brook | 201⅜ | 186 | .. | .. |
| Union Pacific | 132½ | 78½ | 113 | 93⅜ |
| " " pref | 99 | 82 | 94⅛ | 86¾ |

| | 1901. | | 1902. | |
|---|---|---|---|---|
| | Highest. | Lowest. | Highest. | Lowest. |
| Vermont & Massachusetts | 175⅜ | 171¾ | 178 | 172 |
| Wilton | .. | .. | 245 | 245 |
| Wisconsin Central | 24¾ | 17 | 34⅞ | 20⅝ |
| " " pref | 49 | 40⅛ | 53 | 39⅜ |
| Worcester, Nashua & Rochester | 155⅛ | 140¾ | 152⅞ | 145 |

## STREET RAILWAY STOCKS—BOSTON

| | 1901. | | 1902. | |
|---|---|---|---|---|
| | Highest. | Lowest. | Highest. | Lowest. |
| Boston & Chelsea R. R | 80 | 80 | 82¾ | 78 |
| Boston Elevated | 190 | 159¾ | 173½ | 149½ |
| Boston Suburban Electric | .. | .. | 43 | 25¾ |
| " " " pref | .. | .. | 101⅛ | 88⅛ |
| Massachusetts Electric | 45 | 24 | 45⅜ | 33 |
| " " pref | 96 | 77½ | 98¾ | 92 |
| West End Electric Street Ry | 99 | 92½ | 99 | 93 |
| " " " " " pref | 118¾ | 110 | 116⅝ | 111⅛ |

## MISCELLANEOUS STOCKS—BOSTON

| | Par Value. | 1901. Highest. | 1901. Lowest. | 1902. Highest. | 1902. Lowest. |
|---|---|---|---|---|---|
| American Agricultural Chemical | $100 | 34⅞ | 20 | 32½ | 19 |
| " " " pref | 100 | 91 | 79½ | 91 | 77 |
| American Cotton Oil | 100 | 35⅛ | 24½ | 57¾ | 30½ |
| " " pref | 100 | 100 | 85 | 99½ | 86 |
| American Pneumatic Service | 50 | 11 | 3¾ | 9¾ | 4 |
| " " " pref | 50 | 33 | 28½ | 37¾ | 21 |
| American Soda Fountain 1st pref | 100 | 60 | 46¾ | 60¾ | 54¼ |
| American Sugar Refining | 100 | 152⅞ | 103 | 135⅛ | 112⅞ |
| " " " pref | 100 | 130 | 112 | 123 | 115 |
| American Telephone & Telegraph | 100 | 182 | 151 | 185⅛ | 155 |
| American Tobacco Co | 50 | 148⅛ | 99 | .. | .. |
| " " pref | 100 | 150 | 137 | 151½ | 140 |
| American Watch, Waltham | 100 | 215¾ | 162 | 241½ | 215⅜ |
| American Woolen | 100 | 21⅞ | 14⅛ | 17 | 12 |
| " " pref | 100 | 83 | 70⅜ | 80¾ | 73 |
| Amory | 100 | 155 | 132½ | 160½ | 150¾ |
| Amoskeag | 1,000 | 1,775 | 1,650 | 1,940 | 1,751¾ |
| Androscoggin | 100 | 130 | 117⅛ | 125⅝ | 119 |
| Appleton | 100 | 124 | 117 | 116 | 115 |
| Arlington | 100 | 100⅛ | 100 | 120¾ | 100 |
| Atlantic | 100 | 62¾ | 50 | 51 | 39 |
| Bates | 100 | 140¾ | 135 | 169¾ | 141¼ |
| Bigelow Carpet | 100 | 102¾ | 83¾ | 110 | 100 |
| Boott | 1,000 | 862½ | 800 | 626¾ | 575 |
| Boston | 1,000 | 525 | 285 | 505 | 500 |
| " new | 100 | .. | .. | 100 | 100 |
| Boston & Colorado Smelting | 50 | 58⅛ | 54 | 57 | 56 |
| Boston & Philadelphia Steamship | 100 | 165 | 165 | .. | .. |
| " " " pref | 100 | 165 | 165 | .. | .. |
| " " " new | 100 | .. | .. | 140 | 128⅝ |
| Boston Athenæum | 300 | 430 | 390 | 436 | 415 |
| Boston Belting | 100 | 228 | 210⅝ | 235 | 222 |
| Boston Duck | 700 | 1,035 | 1,035 | 1,175 | 1,107½ |
| Boston Tow Boat | 100 | 150⅜ | 130 | 152¾ | 147 |
| Bowker Fertilizer | 100 | 77 | 75¾ | 90½ | 80 |
| Cabot | 100 | 62 | 60 | 71 | 62⅝ |
| Chi., N. Y. & Bos. Rfg. Car | 100 | 35 | 35 | .. | .. |
| Chicopee | 100 | 90 | 62½ | 63 | 42 |
| Cocheco | 500 | 241¾ | 200 | 300 | 200 |
| Continental | 100 | 24¼ | 20 | 40 | 26⅛ |
| Dwight | 500 | 1,060 | 1,000 | 1,025 | 1,000 |

| | Par Value. | 1901. Highest. | 1901. Lowest. | 1902. Highest. | 1902. Lowest. |
|---|---|---|---|---|---|
| Eastern Cold Storage | $100 | 100 | 82½ | 95 | 95 |
| Edwards | 100 | 160 | 160 | 175 | 160 |
| Everett | 100 | 98½ | 94½ | 105 | 100 |
| Fairbanks, E. & T. | 500 | 301 | 282½ | 300 | 285 |
| Franklin | 100 | 101⅛ | 90 | 101⅛ | 99½ |
| Great Falls | 100 | 150¼ | 141 | 167½ | 144 |
| General Electric | 100 | 288½ | 184½ | 332¾ | 171¾ |
| " " pref. | 100 | 263 | 156 | .. | .. |
| Hamilton Cotton | 1,000 | 865 | 750 | 780 | 745 |
| Hamilton Woolen | 100 | 52 | 50¼ | 50 | 45 |
| Heywood Bros. & Wakefield | 100 | 12 | 12 | 15 | 12½ |
| " " " pref. | 100 | 99¾ | 88½ | 97 | 97 |
| Hill | 100 | 41¼ | 37¾ | 50½ | 42½ |
| Indo-Egyptian Compress | 100 | 8 | 4 | 4½ | 1 |
| International Button | 10 | 2¼ | 1 | 3 | 2 |
| Jackson | 1,000 | 1,036¼ | 915 | 950 | 890 |
| Lancaster | 400 | 352½ | 300 | 325 | 290 |
| Lawrence | 100 | 150⅜ | 110½ | 137½ | 118 |
| Lockwood | 100 | 91½ | 88 | 97½ | 90 |
| Lowell Bleachery | 100 | 60 | 46 | 27½ | 25 |
| " " new | 100 | .. | .. | 101⅛ | 98 |
| Lowell Hosiery | 100 | 88 | 85 | .. | .. |
| Lowell Machine Shop | 500 | 810 | 792½ | 810 | 800 |
| Lyman | 100 | 70¼ | 67½ | 66½ | 65 |
| Manchester | 100 | 102⅞ | 95¼ | 100 | 80 |
| Massachusetts | 100 | 101⅜ | 96 | 99⅛ | 95¼ |
| Massachusetts in Georgia | 100 | 107¾ | 102¾ | 108 | 105 |
| Mergenthaler Linotype | 100 | 182¾ | 153 | 190 | 170 |
| Merrimack | 100 | 111¾ | 95¼ | 103⅛ | 90 |
| Middlesex | 100 | 105 | 100 | 90 | 85¼ |
| Nashua | 500 | 682½ | 575 | 600 | 570 |
| National Car | 100 | 25⅛ | 20½ | 30¾ | 22 |
| National Lead | 100 | 25½ | 15 | 32 | 15⅜ |
| " " pref. | 100 | 100⅛ | 74⅜ | 96 | 78⅜ |
| Naumkeag | 100 | 63½ | 60 | 58¼ | 48 |
| New England Cotton Yarn, pref. | 100 | 99 | 88 | 93½ | 87 |
| New England Gas & Coke | 100 | 15 | 4¼ | 7⅝ | 2¾ |
| Otis | 1,000 | 1,852½ | 1,852½ | .. | .. |
| Pacific | 1,000 | 2,125 | 1,950 | 2,175 | 2,100 |
| Pepperell | 500 | 265 | 240 | 266 | 250 |
| Planters' Compress | 100 | 24½ | 12 | 41 | 4 |
| Pullman | 100 | 225 | 198 | 250 | 216 |
| Quincy R. R. Bridge | 100 | 210⅛ | 195 | 200¼ | 196 |
| Reece Buttonhole | 10 | 10½ | 5¾ | 10⅛ | 6½ |
| Salmon Falls | 300 | 170 | 160 | 100 | 100 |
| Swift & Co. | 100 | 110 | 100 | 177 | 100 |
| Swift Refrigerator Transp'n | 100 | 150 | 150 | 154 | 140 |
| Torrington, Class A, 8 per cent., cum. | 25 | 29 | 25½ | 27 | 26 |
| " preferred, 7 " " | 25 | 29 | 27 | 30 | 28 |
| Tremont and Suffolk | 100 | 143½ | 102 | 105 | 85 |
| United Electric Securities, pref. | 100 | 100⅛ | 100⅛ | .. | .. |
| United Fruit, pref. | 100 | 137 | 73 | 116½ | 86 |
| United Shoe Machinery | 25 | 48½ | 31 | 57¼ | 46 |
| " " " pref. | 25 | 30 | 23½ | 33 | 29 |
| United States Leather | 100 | 16¼ | 9 | 15¼ | 11¼ |
| " " pref. | 100 | 83⅛ | 74 | 91 | 80¼ |
| United States Rubber | 100 | 34 | 13½ | 19⅝ | 13½ |
| " " pref. | 100 | 84 | 46¼ | 62¼ | 50 |
| United States Steel | 100 | 54⅝ | 32 | 46¾ | 29¾ |
| " " " pref. | 100 | 101¾ | 86½ | 97½ | 79½ |
| Waltham Bleachery (new) | 100 | .. | .. | 105 | 99 |
| Wamsutta | 100 | 113½ | 108¼ | 120⅛ | 115⅛ |
| Westinghouse Electric | 50 | 89½ | 54 | 115½ | 86⅛ |
| " " pref. | 50 | 91 | 66 | 116½ | 88½ |
| York | 750 | 837½ | 825 | 875 | 825 |

## REAL ESTATE STOCKS AND RONDS—BOSTON

| | Par Value. | Dividends in 1902, Per Cent. | 1901. | | 1902. | |
|---|---|---|---|---|---|---|
| | | | Highest. | Lowest. | Highest. | Lowest. |
| Albany Trust | $100 | $3¼ | 98½ | 97 | 102 | 98 |
| Barristers' Hall Trust | 100 | 1¼ | 108 | 107 | 108 | 103 |
| Beacon Chambers Trust pref. | 100 | 4 | 100 | 85 | 95 | 85 |
| " " com. | 100 | .. | .. | .. | 75 | 50 |
| Bedford Trust | 100 | 4 | 103 | 102 | 103 | 99 |
| Board of Trade Building Trust | 100 | 4 | 104 | 100 | 106 | 100¼ |
| Boston & Roxbury Mill Corporation. | .. | .. | 30 | 30 | .. | .. |
| Boston Co-operative Building Co. | 25 | 5 | 31¼ | 30½ | .. | .. |
| Boston Ground Rent Trust | 1,000 | 3½ | 925 | 900 | 950 | 910 |
| Boston Investment Co. | 100 | .. | 14 | 12 | .. | .. |
| Boston Land Co. | 10 | 25c | 4¾ | 4 | 4½ | 4 |
| Boston Pier or Long Wharf Corp'n. | 100 | 5 | 160 | 160 | 186½ | 185⅛ |
| Boston Real Estate Trust | 1000 | 4½ | 1,450 | 1,410 | 1,440 | 1,390 |
| Boston Storage Warehouse Co. | 100 | 8 | 215 | 201 | 215 | 214 |
| " " " (new). | 100 | .. | .. | .. | 113½ | 110¼ |
| Boston Water Power Co. | 10 | .. | 7½ | 3 | .. | .. |
| Boston Wharf Co. | 20 | 13 | 125 | 120 | 120 | 120 |
| Boylston Street Land Co. | 15 | .. | 5½ | 4 | .. | .. |
| Bromfield Building Trust | 100 | 4½ | 107½ | 105 | 107 | 103 |
| Bromfield Building Trust, receipts | 100 | 4* | 105 | 105 | .. | .. |
| Buckminster Chambers Trust, pref. | 100 | 5 | 100 | 100 | .. | .. |
| Business Real Estate Trust. | 100 | 3½ | 100 | 100 | 100 | 100 |
| Central Building Trust | 100 | 4 | 106 | 103 | 109 | 105 |
| City Associates | $500 | 4½ | 580 | 580 | 590 | 575 |
| Claverly Trust | 500 | 5 | .. | .. | 525 | 525 |
| Congress Street Trust (new) | 100 | 4* | .. | .. | 102½ | 101⅝ |
| Constitution Wharf Trust | 100 | 4½ | 114½ | 113 | 112 | 109 |
| Delta Building Trust | 100 | 4 | 102 | 100 | 102 | 101 |
| Devonshire Building Trust | 100 | 4 | 105 | 102 | 106 | 102 |
| Dwelling House Associates | 1,000 | 3½ | .. | .. | 930 | 900 |
| East Boston Co. | .. | .. | 9⅝ | 7 | 9⅝ | 7 |
| Essex Co. | 50 | 12 | 155½ | 152¼ | 154 | 154 |
| Essex Street Trust | 100 | 3 | 101 | 100 | 100 | 100 |
| Factory Building Trust | 100 | 4 | .. | .. | 116 | 108 |
| Fifty Associates | ... | 120 | 5,175 | 5,050 | 5,275 | 5,175 |
| Fiske Wharf & Wareh'e Trust bds. | 1,000 | 4 | 1,040 | 1,000 | .. | .. |
| " " " " " pref. | 100 | 5 | 102 | 100 | .. | .. |
| Haymarket Trust | 100 | 4 | 103 | 100 | 103 | 101 |
| Hemenway Chambers Trust | 100 | .. | 101 | 100 | .. | .. |
| " " " pref. | 100 | 5 | 105 | 100 | .. | |
| Hotel Bellevue Trust | 100 | .. | 101 | 99 | | |
| Hotel Somerset Trust bonds | 1,000 | 4 | 1,030 | 1,000 | .. | .. |
| " " stock | 100 | 5 | 100 | 90 | .. | .. |
| Hotel Trust (Touraine) | 100 | 5 | 122¼ | 117½ | 122½ | 119 |
| Huntington Chambers Trust | 100 | 3½ | 100 | 90 | .. | .. |
| Improved Dwellings Association | 100 | 2½ | 50 | 30 | .. | .. |
| Journal Building Trust | 100 | 4* | 101 | 100 | 100 | 100 |
| Lenox Hotel 1st mtge. bonds | 1,000 | 4 | 1,010 | 1,010 | .. | .. |
| " " 2d " | 1,000 | 6 | 1,050 | 1,010 | | |
| Lenox Street Buildings Trust | 100 | 3½ | 101 | 99 | .. | .. |
| Lewis Wharf Corporation | 1,000 | 5 | 1,375 | 1,375 | .. | .. |
| Lovejoy's Wharf Trust (new) | 100 | 4* | .. | .. | 101 | 100 |
| Mass. Fire Proof Stge. & W. H. Co. | 100 | .. | 90 | 75 | .. | .. |
| Massachusetts Real Estate Co. | 100 | .. | 14⅝ | 12⅝ | .. | .. |
| Merchants Real Estate Trust | 1,000 | 4* | 1,000 | 1,000 | .. | .. |
| Metropolitan Associates | 100 | .. | 100 | 100 | .. | .. |
| " " pref. | 100 | 5 | 105 | 100 | 105 | 105 |
| Metropolitan Wharf & Stge. Co. bds. | 1,000 | 5 | 1,050 | 1,000 | .. | .. |
| Municipal Real Estate Trust | 100 | 4 | 105 | 104 | 106 | 104 |
| New Eng. Mtge. & Sec. Co. | 100 | .. | 45¼ | 45 | .. | .. |
| New England Real Estate Trust | 100 | 4½ | 110 | 110 | .. | .. |
| Old South Building Trust pref. (new). | 100 | 4* | .. | .. | 101⅞ | 92 |

*During construction.

| | Par Value. | Dividends in 1902. Per cent. | 1901. Highest. | 1901. Lowest. | 1902. Highest. | 1902. Lowest. |
|---|---|---|---|---|---|---|
| Paddock Trust | $100 | 2 | 106 | 105 | 105 | 104 |
| Pemberton Building Trust | 100 | 4 | 103 | 102 | 103 | 100 |
| Post Office Square Trust (new) | 100 | 4* | .. | .. | 106½ | 100 |
| Quincy Market Cold Storage Co | 100 | 6 | 120 | 120 | .. | .. |
| Real Estate Associates | 100 | 4 | 108 | 106 | 110 | 106 |
| Realty Co | 100 | .. | .. | .. | 25 | 25 |
| Revere House Co | 100 | 8 | 209 | 209 | .. | .. |
| Riverbank Court Trust bonds | 1,000 | 5 | 1,030 | 1,030 | .. | .. |
| St. Mary's Mineral Land Co | 25 | .. | 70 | 45 | 55 | 50 |
| Scollay Building Trust | 100 | 4 | 103 | 100 | 100 | 97 |
| Simmons Building Trust (new) | 100 | 3½* | .. | .. | 101 | 100 |
| Somerset Hotel Trust stock | 100 | 5 | 100 | 90 | 108 | 97 |
| " " " bonds | 1,000 | 4 | .. | .. | 1,037½ | 1,037½ |
| South Street Trust | 100 | 4 | 114 | 107 | 114 | 108 |
| South Terminal Trust | 100 | 4* | 107 | 102 | 109 | 103 |
| State Street Exchange | 100 | 4½ | 140 | 135¼ | 138¾ | 130 |
| Suffolk Real Estate Trust | 1,000 | 4 | 1,080 | 1,070 | 1,080 | 1,030 |
| Summer Street Trust | 100 | 4½ | 112½ | 110½ | 112 | 110 |
| Technology Chambers Trust | 100 | 4⅔* | 102 | 100 | .. | .. |
| Terminal Hotel Trust | 100 | 4½ | 95 | 90 | 95 | 90 |
| " " pref | 100 | 4 | 102 | 100 | 100 | 96 |
| Tremont Building Trust | 100 | 4½ | 140 | 140 | 141 | 139 |
| Trimountain Trust (new) | 100 | 3¾* | .. | .. | 102½ | 100 |
| United States Hotel Co | 100 | 6 | 190 | 175 | 185 | 185 |
| West End Land Co | .. | .. | 1¼ | ½ | 1⅛ | ¾ |
| Western Real Estate Trust | 100 | 4 | 101 | 100 | 105 | 100 |
| Winter Street Trust | 100 | 1¾ | 95 | 95 | 90 | 88 |
| Winthrop Shore Land Co | 5 | .. | 35c | 25c | .. | .. |
| Winthrop Building Trust | 1,000 | 4 | 909 | 890 | 900 | 850 |

* During construction.

---

## GAS AND ELECTRIC LIGHT STOCKS AND BONDS—BOSTON

| | Par Value. | 1901. Highest. | 1901. Lowest. | 1902. Highest. | 1902. Lowest |
|---|---|---|---|---|---|
| Boston Electric Light | $100 | 255 | 195 | .. | .. |
| Boston United Gas, 1st 5s | 1,000 | 87 | 78 | 99½ | 83 |
| " " 2d 5s | 1,000 | 68 | 48 | 82½ | 56 |
| Brookline | 100 | 230 | 225 | .. | .. |
| Cambridge | 100 | 243½ | 225½ | 300 | 240 |
| Cambridge Electric | 100 | 240 | 150 | .. | .. |
| Charlestown | 50 | 80 | 74⅜ | 93 | 81 |
| Chelsea | .. | 95¾ | 95¾ | .. | .. |
| East Boston | 25 | 39½ | 35 | 40 | 30 |
| Edison Electric Illuminating (Boston) | 100 | 270 | 217 | 285 | 244 |
| Jamaica Plain | 100 | 130 | 129 | 197 | 140½ |
| Lawrence | 100 | 125 | 111⅜ | 141⅛ | 128⅜ |
| Lowell | 100 | 257¼ | 240¼ | 255¼ | 242½ |
| Massachusetts | 100 | .. | .. | 42⅜ | 36¼ |
| " pref | 100 | .. | .. | 87¾ | 82 |
| Newburyport Gas & Electric | .. | 110¼ | 104½ | .. | .. |
| Newton & Watertown | 100 | 191¼ | 188 | 250¼ | 202⅛ |
| Providence, R. I. | 50 | .. | .. | 102¼ | 102¼ |
| Salem | 100 | 141⅛ | 135⅛ | .. | .. |
| Waltham | 100 | 116½ | 116¼ | .. | .. |
| Worcester | 00 | 210 | 208 | .. | .. |

## TELEPHONE STOCKS AND BONDS—BOSTON

| | Par Value. | 1901. Highest. | 1901. Lowest. | 1902. Highest. | 1902. Lowest. |
|---|---|---|---|---|---|
| American Bell Telephone deb. 4s, 1908 | $1,000 | 101 1/2 | 99 | 100 | 98 |
| American Telegraph & Telephone | 100 | 173 | 151 | .. | .. |
| " " " coll. tr. 4s, 1929 | 100 | 101 1/2 | 98 3/4 | 99 7/8 | 98 |
| Cumberland Telephone & Telegraph | 100 | 140 | 129 1/2 | 130 1/4 | 122 1/2 |
| Erie Telephone | 100 | 98 | 15 | .. | .. |
| Erie Telegraph & Telephone 6s, 1909 | .. | 105 1/4 | 95 5/8 | 110 | 104 1/2 |
| " " " 5s, 1926 | .. | 105 | 100 | 108 1/2 | 105 |
| " " " 5s, 1928 | 100 | 97 | 87 1/2 | 102 | 95 |
| Michigan Telephone | 100 | 50 | 50 | .. | .. |
| " con. mort. 5s, 1929 | .. | 100 | 98 1/4 | .. | .. |
| New England Telephone | 100 | 146 | 127 1/2 | 151 | 135 |
| " " 6s, 1906 | .. | 104 1/8 | 102 | 104 | 103 1/8 |
| " " 6s, 1907 | .. | 104 1/4 | 103 | 105 | 104 |
| " " 6s, 1908–1909 | .. | 105 1/8 | 99 | 105 3/8 | 103 |
| " " 5s, 1915–1916 | .. | 110 | 109 1/4 | 109 | 107 1/4 |
| Western Telephone & Telegraph | 100 | .. | .. | 33 1/2 | 22 |
| " " " pref | 100 | .. | .. | 106 1/8 | 92 |
| " " " 5s, 1932 | .. | .. | .. | 106 | 103 1/2 |

## BONDS—BOSTON

| | Due. | 1901. Highest. | 1901. Lowest. | 1902. Highest. | 1902. Lowest |
|---|---|---|---|---|---|
| Atchison, Topeka & Santa Fe gen. mort. | 4s, 1995 | 103 3/4 | 101 | 104 | 100 |
| " " " scrip | 4s, 1995 | 123 1/2 | 118 1/2 | 126 1/2 | 123 1/2 |
| " " " adj. | 4s, 1995 | 98 1/2 | 87 | 97 | 89 1/4 |
| " " " " scrip | 4s, 1995 | 113 1/4 | 101 1/2 | 115 1/2 | 110 1/4 |
| Baltimore & Ohio prior lien | 3 1/2s, 1925 | 97 3/4 | 94 3/4 | 97 1/4 | 93 |
| Boston & Albany plain | 4s, 1913 | 109 3/8 | 108 | 107 1/2 | 106 1/2 |
| Boston & Lowell plain | 4s, 1932 | 113 | 113 | 113 3/8 | 113 1/8 |
| Boston & Maine imp. sink. fund | 4s, 1905 | 101 | 101 | 99 7/8 | 99 7/8 |
| " " plain | 4 1/2s, 1944 | 128 5/8 | 126 | 125 1/2 | 125 1/2 |
| Boston & Providence plain | 4s, 1918 | .. | .. | 108 1/4 | 108 1/4 |
| Boston, Clinton, Fitch. & New Bed. mort. | 5s, 1910 | .. | .. | 109 | 109 |
| Boston, Concord & Mont. imp. | 6s, 1911 | 120 | 120 | 119 5/8 | 109 1/4 |
| Boston Consolidated (Street) plain | 5s, 1907 | 107 3/8 | 107 1/4 | 105 1/2 | 105 1/2 |
| Boston Terminal (So. Union Depot) | 3 1/2s, 1947 | 115 1/2 | 115 1/2 | 115 5/8 | 115 5/8 |
| Brooklyn Rapid Transit | 5s, 1945 | 106 1/4 | 103 1/2 | 110 1/4 | 102 |
| Burlington & Missouri River exempt. 1st. | 6s, 1918 | 122 7/8 | 119 5/8 | 121 7/8 | 117 5/8 |
| " " expt. $600 pieces | 6s, 1918 | 121 5/8 | 117 5/8 | 120 1/4 | 120 1/4 |
| " " non-expt. 1st. | 6s, 1918 | 106 1/4 | 104 | 105 1/2 | 105 1/2 |
| " " (in Neb.) | 4s, 1910 | 100 1/8 | 100 1/8 | 100 | 99 |
| Burli., Cedar Rapids & Northwestern 1st. | 5s, 1906 | 106 1/2 | 104 | 106 1/4 | 102 1/2 |
| Canada Southern 1st guar | 5s, 1908 | 109 | 106 3/8 | .. | .. |
| Cedar Rapids & Missouri River 1st | 7s, 1916 | 140 1/8 | 138 | .. | .. |
| " " 2d | 7s, 1909 | 124 1/2 | 124 1/8 | .. | .. |
| Central Pacific 1st refunding | 4s, 1949 | 103 1/4 | 100 | 103 1/8 | 100 |
| Central Vermont 1st mort | 4s, 1920 | 90 1/2 | 82 | 90 1/2 | 85 |
| Charles River St. 1st mort | 5s, 1904 | .. | .. | 101 1/2 | 101 1/2 |
| Chicago & North Michigan guar | 5s, 1931 | 109 | 104 | 110 | 107 1/4 |
| " " " scrip | 5s, 1904 | 102 | 98 1/2 | .. | .. |
| Chicago & West Michigan gen. mort. | 5s, 1921 | 110 1/2 | 105 | 110 1/4 | 107 1/2 |
| " " " scrip | 5s, 1904 | 102 | 99 3/4 | .. | .. |
| Chicago, Burl'ton & Quincy, old | 4s, 1919 | 104 5/8 | 104 | .. | .. |
| " " Den. Ex. | 4s, 1922 | 102 | 99 3/4 | 101 1/8 | 100 |
| " " So. W. div. | 4s, 1921 | 100 1/2 | 100 | 100 1/4 | 99 1/4 |
| " " deben | 5s, 1913 | 109 1/4 | 108 | 108 | 108 |
| " Neb. Ex. 1st. | 4s, 1927 | .. | .. | 111 | 106 |
| " con. mort. | 7s, 1903 | 108 3/4 | 105 | 104 3/4 | 101 |
| " joint bonds | 4s, 1921 | 100 1/2 | 94 1/4 | 96 7/8 | 92 3/8 |

| | Due. | 1901. Highest. | 1901. Lowest. | 1902. Highest. | 1902. Lowest. |
|---|---|---|---|---|---|
| Chicago, Burl'ton & Quincy, conv......... | 5s, 1903 | 197½ | 140¾ | .. | .. |
| " " Ill. div. mort.. | 3½s, 1949 | 104 | 101¾ | 102½ | 96¼ |
| Cincinnati, Sandusky & Cleveland 1st.... | 5s, 1928 | 115½ | 113⅝ | 115½ | 113⅝ |
| Connecticut & Passumpsic Rivers 1st.... | 4s, 1943 | .. | .. | 114¼ | 114¼ |
| Current River 1st...................... | 5s, 1927 | 107 | 96½ | 107¼ | 103 |
| Detroit, G. R. & W. 1st gen. mort ...... | 4s, 1946 | 100¼ | 98 | 101 | 98 |
| " " scrip............... | .. 1946 | 107 | 98 | .. | .. |
| Eastern R. R. certificates of indebtedness.. | 6s, 1906 | 114 | 111 | 111 | 107⅛ |
| Fitchburg plain......................... | 4s, 1907 | .. | .. | 102⅞ | 102⅞ |
| " " .... .................... | 5s, 1903 | 104¼ | 104⅛ | 101 | 101 |
| " " ........................ | 4s, 1915 | .. | .. | 106¾ | 106¾ |
| " " ........................ | 4s, 1920 | .. | .. | 110¼ | 110¼ |
| " " ........................ | 5s, 1908 | .. | .. | 107 | 107 |
| Fremont, Elk & Mo. Val. con............ | 6s, 1933 | 137½ | 137¼ | 138½ | 137⅞ |
| " " " unst'p'd... .... | 6s, 1933 | 138¾ | 136 | 138 | 135½ |
| Iowa Falls & Sioux City 1st............ | 7s, 1917 | 136 | 134 | 133½ | 131 |
| Kansas City Belt 1st.................... | 6s, 1916 | 116⅝ | 115 | .. | .. |
| Kansas City, Clin. & Spring............ | 5s, 1925 | 107 | 97 | 106⅛ | 103 |
| Kansas City, Fort Scott& Gulf 1st....... | 7s, 1908 | 116 | 113⅛ | 115½ | 112 |
| Kansas City, Ft. Scott & Memphis...... | 6s, 1928 | 125 | 115 | 126 | 121 |
| Kansas City, Memphis & Birm., new..... | 4s, 1934 | 100⅛ | 98 | 99½ | 98 |
| " " " scrip....... | 4s, ..... | 120 | 113 | 120 | 115 |
| " " " inc.. ...... | 5s, 1934 | 96 | 75 | 97¼ | 84 |
| " " " scrip....... | .. .... | 101 | 80 | 106 | 105 |
| Kansas City, Mem. R. R. & Bridge 1st ... | 5s, 1929 | 108⅛ | 106½ | 111 | 108 |
| Kan. City, St. Joseph & C. B. 1st........ | 7s, 1907 | 118¼ | 115⅛ | 115¼ | 110 |
| Little Rock & Fort Smith L. G. 1st...... | 7s, 1905 | 107 | 105 | 105⅜ | 104 |
| Lynn & Boston (Electric) 1st............ | 5s, 1924 | 114⅛ | 114⅛ | 115 | 114½ |
| Maine Cent. con. mort.................. | 7s, 1912 | 133⅜ | 131½ | 130¾ | 128 |
| " con. mort.................. | 4s, 1912 | 109¾ | 105¾ | 104⅝ | 104⅝ |
| M., Houghton & Ontonagon, M. & W. 1st. | 6s, 1925 | 119⅝ | 119⅝ | 118 | 118 |
| Metropolitan Street plain.............. | 5s, 1903 | 103½ | 103½ | .. | .. |
| Mexican Central 1st..................... | 4s, 1911 | 87¾ | 79 | 84¾ | 73 |
| Mexican Central 1st income.............. | 3s, 1939 | 37⅝ | 27 | 35¾ | 22⅛ |
| " 2d income.............. | 3s, 1939 | 25½ | 14 | 24½ | 20⅞ |
| Middlesex Street........................ | 5s, 1904 | 102¾ | 102¾ | .. | .. |
| Milwaukee & St. Paul, Dubuque div..... | 6s, 1920 | 129 | 128 | 131 | 129¾ |
| " " Wis. Val. div..... | 6s, 1920 | 128½ | 128½ | 128¾ | 128¾ |
| Naumkeag Street con. mort............. | 5s, 1910 | 106½ | 104⅛ | 103¼ | 103¼ |
| N. Y. & N. E 1st....... ............... | 6s, 1905 | 109½ | 107 | 107 | 104 |
| N. Y. & N. E. 1st....................... | 7s, 1905 | 113 | 110 | 109¾ | 106 |
| N. Y., N. H. & H., debenture conv..... | 4s, 1903 | 203 | 203 | 229½ | 204½ |
| Nodaway Valley 1st..... ............... | 7s, 1920 | 111¾ | 111¾ | .. | .. |
| Ogdensburgh (con. 1sts)................. | 4s, 1948 | 104¼ | 98 | .. | .. |
| Old Colony plain........................ | 4s, 1925 | .. | .. | 111⅛ | 111⅛ |
| " " ........................ | 4½s, 1904 | 102 | 102 | .. | .. |
| " " ........................ | 4s, 1938 | 113¾ | 113¾ | .. | .. |
| Oregon Navigation con. mort........... | 6s, 1909 | 110 | 110 | .. | .. |
| " " " ........... | 4s, 1946 | .. | .. | 104¾ | 100 |
| Oregon Short Line 1st......... ......... | 6s, 1922 | 127⅛ | 124¼ | 128¼ | 123½ |
| " " 1st con. mort......... | 5s, 1946 | .. | .. | 119½ | 115 |
| Ports., Gt. Falls & Con. (B. & M. guar.). | 4½s, 1937 | 124⅛ | 124 | 123¾ | 121 |
| Republican Valley West. Div............ | 6s, 1919 | 111 | 106⅝ | 107½ | 105 |
| Rutland 1st mort....................... | 6s, 1902 | 103¾ | 101½ | 101½ | 100 |
| Rutland con. mort.......................... | 4½s, 1941 | 111⅞ | 111⅞ | 113 | 113 |
| St. Johnsbury & Lake C. guar........... | 5s, 1944 | .. | .. | 132½ | 132½ |
| Union Pacific 1st mort., land grant...... | 4s, 1947 | 106⅛ | 103⅜ | 105 | 102¾ |
| " " 1st lien conv............... | 4s, 1911 | 126⅛ | 104½ | 113⅛ | 102¾ |
| Vermont & Mass. (Fitchburg guar.) plain | 5s, 1903 | 103⅜ | 102⅛ | 100 | 100 |
| West End Electric, Street, coupon notes. | 5s, 1902 | 102½ | 100⅞ | 100⅞ | 100⅛ |
| " " " ........................ | 4½s, 1914 | 110 | 108 | 108 | 107⅛ |
| " " " debenture.... ......... | 4s, 1916 | 105¾ | 104½ | 104¼ | 104¼ |
| " " " plain................. | 4s, 1917 | 105¾ | 104 | 103⅝ | 103⅝ |
| Wisconsin Central, 1st gen. mort........ | 4s, 1949 | 92½ | 85¼ | .. | .. |
| Wisconsin Valley 1st.................... | 7s, 1909 | 122 | 122 | 119¾ | 119 |

## MISCELLANEOUS BONDS—BOSTON

| | Due. | 1901. Highest. | 1901. Lowest. | 1902. Highest. | 1902. Lowest. |
|---|---|---|---|---|---|
| American Writing Paper (after 1909)..... | 5s, 1919 | 67 | 67 | 76 | 76 |
| Birmingham Equipment, guar..... .... | 6s, 1903 | .. | .. | 100⅞ | 100⅞ |
| Boston & Montana Mining.............. | 7s, 1904 | 117 | 108½ | 105 | 104 |
| Boston Athletic 2d..................... | 5s, 1908 | 100 | 100 | .. | .. |
| Boston Electric Light............ ...... | 6s, 1908 | 113⅝ | 113⅛ | .. | .. |
| " " " ................... | 5s, 1924 | .. | .. | 114⅝ | 111 |
| Butte & Boston Mining, 1st mort........ | 6s, 1917 | 102 | 94 | .. | .. |
| Chicago Junc. R. R. & Stock Yds.. . .. | 5s, 1915 | 112¼ | 109⅝ | 110 | 105⅝ |
| Dominion Coal 1st..................... | 6s, 1913 | 111½ | 109¼ | 111⅛ | 109 |
| Exchange Club 2d...................... | 5s, 1913 | .. | .. | 88¼ | 88 |
| General Electric conv.................. | 5s, 1922 | 236 | 154 | .. | .. |
| Illinois Steel debentures, conv........... | 5s, 1910 | 101 | 97⅛ | 102 | 100⅞ |
| " " new 5s.................... | 5s, 1913 | 102 | 97 | 102 | 101¼ |
| Lamson Consol. Store Service 1st........ | 6s, 1909 | 102 | 102 | 103 | 100 |
| New England Cotton Yarn.............. | 5s, 1929 | 105¾ | 103 | 104¼ | 102 |
| New England Gas & Coke 1st........... | 5s, 1937 | 71½ | 50 | 69 | 52 |
| New England Mortgage Security........ | 5s, 1902 | 92 | 92 | .. | .. |
| Swift & Co, 1st......................... | 5s, 1914 | 101¾ | 101⅛ | 102⅝ | 101⅝ |
| Torrington 1st.......................... | 5s, 1918 | 108¼ | 108¼ | .. | .. |

# Chicago Stock Exchange

## Quotations for Securities Dealt in on the Stock Exchange, 1901 and 1902

## STOCKS

### RAILROAD STOCKS

| | Dividend Payable. | | 1901. High. | 1901. Low. | 1902. High. | 1902. Low. |
|---|---|---|---|---|---|---|
| Atchison, Topeka & Santa Fe................ | 4 | J. & D. | 79 | 54⅜ | 83 | 76 |
| " " " pref............ | 5 | F. & A. | 99½ | 94¾ | .. | .. |
| Baltimore & Ohio........................ | 4 | M. & S. | .. | .. | 104⅝ | 94 |
| Chesapeake & Ohio........................ | 1 | Oct..... | 40 | 40 | .. | .. |
| Chicago & Alton.......................... | .. | ........ | 41½ | 35 | .. | .. |
| " " pref........................ | 4 | J. & J. | 79⅞ | 76 | 76½ | 72 |
| Chicago, Milwaukee & St. Paul.............. | 6 | A. & O. | 171¾ | 150⅛ | .. | .. |
| Erie ... .................................. | .. | ........ | 40 | 30 | 42½ | 30⅞ |
| Illinois Central............................ | 6 | M. & N. | 144½ | 130 | 139¾ | 139¾ |
| Louisville & Nashville.................... | 5 | F. & A. | 104⅛ | 104⅛ | .. | .. |
| New York Central & Hudson River.......... | 5 | Q., Jan. | 159 | 143 | .. | .. |
| New York, Ontario & Western.............. | .. | ........ | .. | .. | 33⅝ | 33⅝ |
| Pennsylvania.............................. | 6 | M. & N. | .. | .. | 169 | 155¾ |
| Southern Railway.......................... | .. | ........ | .. | .. | 37 | 30 |
| Southern Pacific.......................... | .. | ........ | 60⅛ | 42¾ | .. | .. |
| Union Pacific convert. 4s.................... | .. | M. & N. | .. | .. | 107⅛ | 103¾ |
| " " pref.......................... | 4 | A. & O. | 104½ | 96½ | 103½ | 95⅞ |
| Wabash, pref.............................. | .. | ........ | 42⅜ | 24½ | 49⅞ | 45 |

---

### INDUSTRIAL STOCKS

| | Dividend Payable. | | 1901. High. | 1901. Low. | 1902. High. | 1902. Low. |
|---|---|---|---|---|---|---|
| Amalgamated Copper........................ | .. | ........ | .. | .. | 71⅜ | 69⅞ |
| American Can.. ............................ | .. | ........ | 31½ | 10 | 17 | 8⅝ |
| " " pref.......................... | .. | ........ | 80¾ | 54 | 61½ | 39½ |
| American Linseed.... ...................... | .. | ........ | 5½ | 5¼ | 24½ | 21½ |
| " " pref.................... | 7 | Q., Mar. | 64 | 31½ | 55½ | 55½ |
| American Radiator.......................... | .. | ........ | 43 | 36 | 51½ | 40 |
| " " pref.................... | 7 | Q. Feb. | 116 | 106½ | 121¾ | 116 |
| American Sheet Steel, pref.................... | 7 | Q., Jan. | 82 | 74 | .. | .. |
| American Shipbuilding...................... | 4 | Q., Mar. | .. | .. | 63 | 41¾ |
| " " pref.................... | 7 | Q., Jan. | .. | .. | 106½ | 100 |
| American Steel Hoop. ...................... | .. | ........ | 26½ | 26¼ | .. | .. |
| American Straw Board...................... | .. | ........ | 35 | 23 | 47 | 23 |
| " " " rec...................... | .. | ........ | .. | .. | 49⅛ | 30 |

| | Dividend Payable. | | 1901. High. | 1901. Low. | 1902. High. | 1902. Low. |
|---|---|---|---|---|---|---|
| American Tin Plate | .. | ........ | 70 | 56 | .. | .. |
| " " pref. | 7 | Q., Jan. | 101 | 97 | .. | .. |
| Booth, A., & Co. | 3 | J. & D. | .. | .. | 42½ | 29 |
| " " pref. | 8 | M. & S. | .. | .. | 110 | 91 |
| Calumet & Chicago Canal & Dock | .. | ........ | 77 | 68 | 80⅜ | 66½ |
| Central Union Telephone | .. | ........ | 54 | 34 | .. | .. |
| " " new issue | .. | ........ | 80 | 80 | 90 | 65 |
| Chicago Brewing & Malting | .. | ........ | 2 | 2 | 1 | 1 |
| " " " pref. | .. | ........ | 10 | 8⅞ | 11¾ | 7 |
| Chicago Edison | 8 | Q., Feb. | 180 | 150⅛ | 180 | 160 |
| Chicago Packing & Provision | .. | ........ | 1 | 1 | 2 | ¾ |
| Chicago Pneumatic Tool | 8 | Q., Jan. | .. | .. | 107 | 65 |
| Chicago Telephone | 10 | Q., Mar. | 276 | 218 | 230 | 160 |
| Colorado Fuel & Iron | .. | ........ | 55¼ | 55¼ | 103½ | 86⅝ |
| Diamond Match | 10 | Q., Mar. | 153¾ | 126 | 141 | 130 |
| Federal Steel, pref. | 6 | Quar ... | 89¼ | 89¼ | .. | .. |
| Glucose Sugar | 4 | Q., Mar. | 48 | 43 | .. | .. |
| International Packing & Provision | .. | ........ | 1½ | 1½ | .. | .. |
| Masonic Temple Association | 3 | A. & O. | 57½ | 57½ | 56 | 45 |
| Milwaukee & Chicago Breweries | .. | ........ | 3 | 1 | 3½ | 1⅛ |
| " " " pref. | .. | ........ | 19 | 10 | 20 | 16 |
| National Biscuit | 4 | Q. Jan. | 46⅛ | 36 | 53⅛ | 43¼ |
| " " pref. | 7 | Q., Feb. | 104¼ | 92½ | 109¼ | 101 |
| National Carbon | .. | ........ | 22 | 15¼ | 33¾ | 18½ |
| " " pref. | 7 | Q., Jan. | 89 | 82 | 105 | 82 |
| National Steel | .. | ........ | 40½ | 40½ | .. | .. |
| " " pref. | 7 | Q., Mar. | 102 | 102 | .. | .. |
| People's Gas Light & Coke | 6 | Q., Feb. | 117 | 101 | 106⅜ | 100 |
| Pullman Co. | 8 | Q., Feb. | .. | .. | 220 | 220 |
| Quaker Oats | .. | ........ | .. | .. | 77 | 45 |
| " " pref. | 8 | Q., Feb. | .. | .. | 94 | 83 |
| Republic Iron & Steel | .. | ........ | .. | .. | 21¼ | 21¼ |
| Shelby Steel Tube | .. | ........ | 15 | 6 | 18 | 10 |
| " " pref. | .. | ........ | 58 | 30 | 40¼ | 35½ |
| Street's Western Stable Car Line | 2 | Q., Jan. | 25½ | 19 | 34 | 23½ |
| " " " pref. | 7 | J. & J. | 78 | 67½ | 88 | 73 |
| Swift & Co. | 7 | Q., Jan. | 103½ | 103½ | 177½ | 110 |
| Tennessee Coal & Iron | .. | ........ | .. | .. | 73 | 73 |
| Union Bag & Paper | .. | ........ | 14 | 14 | .. | .. |
| United Box Board & Paper | .. | ........ | .. | .. | 7½ | 7½ |
| " " " pref. | 7 | Q., Mar. | .. | .. | 71 | 50½ |
| United States Steel Corporation | 4 | Q., Sep. | 49 | 39⅝ | 46⅝ | 31¼ |
| " " " " pref. | 7 | Q., Aug. | 92¼ | 90 | 94½ | 94 |
| Western Stone | .. | ........ | 41½ | 20 | 33 | 25 |
| Western Union Telegraph | 5 | Q., Jan. | 93⅝ | 83¼ | .. | .. |

## STREET RAILWAY STOCKS—CHICAGO

| | Dividend Payable. | | 1901. High. | 1901. Low. | 1902. High. | 1902. Low. |
|---|---|---|---|---|---|---|
| Chicago City | 9 | Q., Mar. | 275 | 185 | 229¼ | 187 |
| Chicago Union Traction | .. | ........ | 20¾ | 9½ | 22⅞ | 10 |
| " " " pref. | .. | ........ | 61⅛ | 47 | 59½ | 45 |

| | | Dividend Payable. | 1901. | | 1902. | |
|---|---|---|---|---|---|---|
| | | | High. | Low. | High. | Low. |
| Lake Street Elevated | .. | ........ | 16½ | 9⅝ | 14⅜ | 8 |
| " " trust cer | .. | ........ | 14⅞ | 9¾ | .. | .. |
| Metropolitan Elevated | .. | ........ | 41⅛ | 25 | 43½ | 34½ |
| " " pref | .. | ........ | 93¼ | 78 | 92½ | 83 |
| North Chicago Street | 12 | Q., Jan. | 207 | 180 | 199¾ | 158 |
| Northwestern Elevated | .. | ........ | 55 | 28 | 40 | 31 |
| " " pref | .. | ........ | 97 | 76 | 89½ | 76 |
| South Side Elevated | 4 | Q., Mar. | 119 | 98 | 116 | 105 |
| Union Elevated | .. | ........ | 125 | 87½ | .. | .. |
| West Chicago Street | 6 | Q., Feb. | 108 | 90 | 103¾ | 83 |

# BONDS

## *INDUSTRIAL BONDS—CHICAGO*

| | Interest Payable. | 1901. | | 1902. | |
|---|---|---|---|---|---|
| | | High. | Low. | High. | Low. |
| American Straw Board 6s | F. & A. | 101 | 100⅛ | 100¼ | 98 |
| Chicago Dock, 1st mort. 4s | A. & O. | .. | .. | 100 | 100 |
| Commonwealth Electric 5s, 1943 | M. & S. | 107 | 105 | 107½ | 106½ |
| International Packing, deb., 6s, 1910 | M. & N. | 29 | 24 | 20 | 20 |
| Knickerbocker Ice 5s | A. & O. | 92 | 90¼ | 95 | 92 |
| St. Louis Nat. Stock Yards 4s, 1930 | J. & J. | 99½ | 99½ | 99½ | 99½ |
| United States Brewing 5s | M. & S. | .. | .. | 92 | 92 |
| Western Stone, 5-20 5s | A. & O. | 95 | 95 | 100 | 93 |

## *STREET RAILWAY BONDS—CHICAGO*

| | Interest Payable. | 1901. | | 1902. | |
|---|---|---|---|---|---|
| | | High. | Low. | High. | Low. |
| Cass Ave. & Fair Ground, 5s, 1912 | J. & J. | 102¼ | 102 | 102¼ | 102 |
| Chicago & Milwaukee 5s | J. & J. | .. | .. | 103 | 102 |
| Chicago City, 5-20, 4½s | J. & J. | 100½ | 99½ | .. | .. |
| Chicago Cons. Traction 4½s | J. & D. | .. | .. | 80 | 67 |
| Cicero & Proviso Consol 5s | M. & N. | 105½ | 105¼ | 101 | 101 |
| Lake St. Elevated, deb., 5s | J. & J. | 104½ | 94¾ | 105 | 102½ |
| " " " inc., 5s | February. | 80 | 35 | 60 | 42 |
| " " " 1st mort. 5s | J. & J. | .. | .. | 103 | 99½ |
| Metropolitan Elevated, 1st mort. g. 4s | F. & A. | 102⅜ | 98 | 102 | 99¾ |
| Metropolitan W. S. El. R. R. Extension, 4s | J. & J. | 98⅝ | 98 | 99⅞ | 94⅞ |
| North Chicago City, 4½s, 1927 | M. & N. | 108½ | 105 | 107 | 105 |
| North Chicago Street, 1st m. 5s, 1906 | J. & J. | 104½ | 104 | 103 | 103 |
| " " " 1st m. 5s, 1909 | J. & J. | 106½ | 106 | 104¼ | 104 |
| Northwestern Elevated 5s | J. & J. | 105⅞ | 104½ | .. | .. |
| " " 4s | M. & S. | 96½ | 95 | 99 | 94 |
| Union Elevated Loop 5s | A. & O. | 114¼ | 108 | 114½ | 112 |
| West Chicago Street, deb., 6s | J. & D. | 100¼ | 100 | 100¼ | 99½ |
| " " " 1st m. 5s | M. & N. | 111 | 109½ | 109½ | 104¾ |
| " " " con. gold 5s | M. & N. | 104⅛ | 98⅞ | 101½ | 94 |
| West Division City 4½s | J. & J. | 110 | 108½ | 109½ | 109½ |

## MISCELLANEOUS BONDS—CHICAGO

| | Interest Payable. | 1901. High. | 1901. Low. | 1902. High. | 1902. Low. |
|---|---|---|---|---|---|
| Chicago Board of Trade 4s, 1927 | J. & D. | 103¼ | 101 | 103½ | 103 |
| Chicago Edison, debt 6s | J. & J. | 103 | 101¼ | 104 | 103½ |
| " " " 1st mort. 5s | A. & O. | 108⅛ | 106½ | 108⅛ | 106 |
| Chicago Gas Light & Coke 5s, 1937 | J. & J. | 109½ | 107½ | 109¾ | 108½ |
| Consumers' Gas, 1st m. 5s, 1927 | J. & D. | 107⅜ | 105⅛ | 108⅛ | 106 |
| Hyde Park Gas 6s | M. & S. | 104 | 104 | .. | .. |
| Masonic Temple Association 5s | J. & J. | 102½ | 102¼ | 103¼ | 103 |
| Ogden Gas 5s | M. & N. | .. | .. | 93½ | 87¼ |
| Pearsons-Taft Land Credit 5s | J. & D. | 102 | 101¼ | 102 | 101 |
| " " " " 4s-40 | M. & S. | 100 | 99½ | 100 | 98½ |
| People's G. L. & C. ref'd gold 5s | M. & S. | 107 | 106 | 107¼ | 107¼ |
| " " " 1st con. 6s | A. & O. | .. | .. | 123 | 118 |

# Cincinnati Stock Exchange

## Quotations for Securities Dealt in on the Stock Exchange, 1901 and 1902

### *MISCELLANEOUS STOCKS*

| | 1901. | | 1902. | |
|---|---|---|---|---|
| | High. | Low. | High. | Low. |
| Aurora, Elgin & Chicago | .. | .. | 41½ | 40 |
| " " " pref | .. | .. | 95½ | 90 |
| Barney & Smith Car | .. | .. | 25 | 25 |
| " " " pref | .. | .. | 130 | 126 |
| Central Market | .. | .. | 32¾ | 27½ |
| " " pref | .. | .. | 95¾ | 89 |
| Chambers Coated Paper pref | .. | .. | 116 | 112 |
| Cincinnati & Hamilton | .. | .. | 41½ | 37½ |
| " " pref | .. | .. | 113½ | 112½ |
| Cincinnati Chamber of Commerce certfs | 10 | 10 | 37 | 25 |
| Cincinnati, Dayton & Toledo | .. | .. | 43 | 26¼ |
| Cincinnati Gas & Electric | 105¼ | 96½ | 104⅜ | 98⅜ |
| Cincinnati, Hamilton & Dayton | .. | .. | 70 | 70 |
| " " " pref. Eagle | .. | .. | 90 | 90 |
| " " " " 5s | .. | .. | 108¾ | 105 |
| Cincinnati, Newport & Covington | .. | .. | 39½ | 35 |
| " " " pref | .. | .. | 93 | 86¼ |
| Cincinnati N. O. & T. P | 92 | 40 | 90 | 75 |
| " " " pref | .. | .. | 109½ | 106 |
| Cincinnati Tobacco Warehouse | 102¾ | 85 | 80 | 63½ |
| Cincinnati Street Ry | 147¾ | 133½ | 145 | 130 |
| Cincinnati Union Stock Yards | 98 | 85¾ | 95 | 89½ |
| " " " pref | 105 | 98 | 105 | 100 |
| Columbus & Xenia | 233 | 219 | 224¾ | 219¼ |
| Columbus Gas & Heating | 94 | 45 | 108½ | 89½ |
| " " " pref | 109 | 78 | 111½ | 100½ |
| Columbus Railway | .. | .. | 58½ | 55½ |
| " " pref | .. | .. | 107½ | 104⅞ |
| Dayton & Michigan | .. | .. | 91¾ | 91¾ |
| " " pref | .. | .. | 215¾ | 215 |
| Detroit United Railways | 81½ | 73 | 97 | 55 |
| Elgin, Aurora & Southern | .. | .. | 61 | 51 |
| Farmers & Shippers Tobacco Warehouse | 85¾ | 62½ | 60 | 50 |
| " " " " 1st pref | .. | .. | 110 | 110 |
| " " " " 2d pref | 120 | 120 | .. | .. |
| Fay, J. A., & Egan pref | .. | .. | 110 | 107 |
| Globe-Wernicke pref | .. | .. | 114 | 112½ |
| Hooven, Owens, Rentschler pref | .. | .. | 113¾ | 110½ |
| Jergens, Andrew, pref | .. | .. | 122½ | 116 |
| Kroger Grocery & B. pref | .. | .. | 112½ | 110½ |
| Little Miami | 234 | 223¾ | 231½ | 227 |
| Miami & Erie Canal | .. | .. | 35½ | 27 |
| Niles-Bement-Pond pref | .. | .. | 109½ | 109½ |
| Northern Ohio Traction pref | .. | .. | 97 | 93¼ |
| Ohio Trust, pref | 112⅜ | 96 | 104 | 102 |
| Procter & Gamble | .. | .. | 342 | 337 |
| " " | .. | .. | 205 | 203½ |
| Shillito, John | .. | .. | 115 | 115 |
| " " pref | .. | .. | 112 | 107 |
| Springfield & Xenia | .. | .. | 17¾ | 17¾ |
| Toledo, Bowling Green & Southern | .. | .. | 61 | 58 |
| Toledo Railway & Light | .. | .. | 36⅞ | 30 |
| United States Cast Iron Pipe & Foundry | .. | .. | 16¾ | 15 |
| " " " " " pref | .. | .. | 57 | 50 |
| United States Playing Card | .. | .. | 105 | 95 |
| United States Printing | 100 | 80 | 95 | 75¾ |

## MISCELLANEOUS RONDS

| | Due. | 1901. High. | 1901. Low. | 1902. High. | 1902. Low. |
|---|---|---|---|---|---|
| Barney & Smith 6s | 1942 | .. | .. | 112 | 111 |
| Cincinnati 3s | 1919–1939 | 104 | 103 | 104¼ | 98 |
| " 3½s | 1910 | 104¼ | 104¼ | .. | .. |
| " 3 65s | 1937 | 115 | 111½ | 111½ | 107½ |
| " 4s | 1909 | 105 | 105 | 101¼ | 101¼ |
| " 4s | 1919 | 105¼ | 105¼ | 105 | 105 |
| " 4s | 1936 | 103½ | 103 | 105 | 105 |
| " 3s | 1921–1941 | .. | .. | 104 | 101 |
| " 3½s | 1918–1938 | .. | .. | 134¼ | 134¼ |
| " 3½s | 1911–1921 | .. | .. | 104¼ | 102½ |
| " 3½s | 1922–1952 | .. | .. | 106 | 106 |
| " 4s | 1911–1931 | .. | .. | 106 | 105¼ |
| " 5s | 1910–1930 | .. | .. | 111 | 109½ |
| " 7 3-10s | 1902 | .. | .. | 101½ | 100¼ |
| " 7 3-10s | 1906 | .. | .. | 113 | 112½ |
| Cincinnati & Hamilton Elect. 1st 6s | 1918 | .. | .. | 113 | 113 |
| Cincinnati Chamber of Commerce 4s | 1898–1908 | 100¼ | 100¼ | .. | .. |
| Cincinnati Con. S. F. 3-65s | 1937 | 115 | 111½ | .. | .. |
| Cincinnati, Dayton & Toledo 5s | 1922 | .. | .. | 87½ | 82 |
| Cincinnati, Hamilton & Dayton 4½s | 1937 | 115 | 112¼ | 111⅛ | 109¾ |
| " " " 5s | 1905 | 112 | 105½ | 104 | 102¼ |
| " " " 6s | 1905 | 111 | 109 | 106¼ | 105 |
| " " " 5s | 1942 | .. | .. | 114⅜ | 112¾ |
| Cincinnati, Hamilton & Indianapolis 7s | 1903 | 104¼ | 103¾ | 102½ | 100 |
| Cincinnati, Indianapolis, St. Louis & Chicago 6s | 1920 | .. | .. | 107½ | 107½ |
| Cincinnati Laurenceburg & Aurora 5s | 1919 | .. | .. | 106 | 106 |
| Cincinnati, Newport & Covington 1st 5s | 1922 | .. | .. | 112¼ | 110½ |
| " " " 2d 5s | 1922 | .. | .. | 109 | 107⅞ |
| Cincinnati Pavement 4s | 1901–1911 | 100⅝ | 100⅝ | .. | .. |
| Cincinnati Southern, gold 7 3-10s | 1902 | 106 | 101¾ | .. | .. |
| Cincinnati Water Works 3½s | 1918–1938 | 106½ | 106½ | .. | .. |
| C. L. & W. 5s | 1916 | 113¼ | 113½ | .. | .. |
| Cifton Sewers 4½s | 1917 | 114 | 114 | .. | .. |
| Columbus Gas 1st gold 5s | 1932 | .. | .. | 108¼ | 108 |
| " " 1st guar. 5s | 1922 | 107¼ | 107¼ | .. | .. |
| Columbus Railway 1st coup. 4s | 1914–1939 | .. | .. | 85 | 85 |
| Covington 7-30s | 1906 | 118½ | 118½ | .. | .. |
| " 4s | 1905 | 102 | 102 | .. | .. |
| " 5s | 1910–1920 | 113½ | 113½ | 113 | 113 |
| " 4s | 1928 | .. | .. | 112 | 112 |
| Covington Res. & Water Works 4s | 1930 | 114¾ | 113½ | .. | .. |
| Dayton & Michigan 5s | 1911 | 112⅝ | 109¾ | 109 | 108 |
| Dayton & Union 7s | .... | 121½ | 120¾ | .. | .. |
| Dayton & Western guar. 6s | 1905 | 108 | 108 | 106 | 105 |
| Detroit & Union Railways 5s | 1916 | 105½ | 105½ | .. | .. |
| Fay, J. A., & Egan 6s | 1943 | .. | .. | 110 | 110 |
| Little Miami 5s | 1912 | 117 | 114⅝ | 114½ | 114½ |
| Miami & Erie Canal 5s | 1921 | .. | .. | 79 | 70 |
| Mount Adams & Eden Park Cable 5s | 1906 | 108¼ | 108¼ | 105 | 104 |
| Mount Auburn Cable 1st 5s | 1907 | 110½ | 110½ | 105 | 105 |
| Northern Ohio Traction 5s | 1919 | .. | .. | 100¼ | 100 |
| Sou. Covington & Cincinnati gold 6s | 1932 | 135 | 135 | .. | .. |
| Union Light H. & P. 4s | 1913 | 101½ | 101½ | 101½ | 100¾ |

# Cleveland Stock Exchange

## Quotations for Securities Dealt in on the Stock Exchange, 1901 and 1902

### STREET RAILWAY STOCKS

| | 1901. | | 1902. | |
|---|---|---|---|---|
| | Highest. | Lowest. | Highest. | Lowest |
| Aurora, Elgin & Chicago Traction | .. | .. | 44 | 31½ |
| " " " " pref | .. | .. | 100 | 83½ |
| " " " " receipts | .. | .. | 41 | 35 |
| Cincinnati, Dayton & Toledo Traction | .. | .. | 42 | 23 |
| Cleveland & Eastern | 47 | 30 | . | .. |
| Cleveland City | 123 | 100 | 115 | 99½ |
| Cleveland Electric | 93¼ | 75 | 92½ | 69¾ |
| Cleveland, Elyria & Western | .. | .. | 75 | 70 |
| Cleveland, Painesville & Eastern | .. | .. | 35 | 31 |
| Detroit United Railway | 84 | 71½ | 95¼ | 56½ |
| Eastern Ohio Traction | .. | .. | 30 | 28 |
| Elgin, Aurora & Southern Traction | 45 | 37 | 65 | 35¼ |
| Lake Shore Electric | .. | .. | 22¼ | 10 |
| " " " pref | . | .. | 61 | 45 |
| Lorain & Cleveland | 80 | 58¼ | .. | .. |
| Northern Ohio Traction | 51 | 39¾ | 70 | 20 |
| " " " pref | 92¾ | 83 | 98 | 80 |
| " " " pref., receipts | .. | .. | 96½ | 92½ |
| Southern Ohio Traction | 81 | 68¼ | 83½ | 57 |
| Springfield & Xenia Traction | .. | .. | 30½ | 16¼ |
| Syracuse Rapid Transit | 25 | 13¾ | 32 | 24¼ |
| " " " pref | 68 | 42¼ | 79 | 63½ |
| Toledo Railways & Light | 28 | 28 | 40 | 20 |
| Tuscarawas Railroad | 35 | 30 | .. | .. |
| Western Ohio Railway, receipts | .. | .. | 35 | 19 |

### MISCELLANEOUS STOCKS

| | 1901. | | 1902. | |
|---|---|---|---|---|
| | Highest. | Lowest. | Highest. | Lowest. |
| American Chicle | 86 | 86 | 125 | 79¾ |
| " " pref | .. | .. | 87 | 87 |
| American Linseed | 22 | 8 | .. | .. |
| " " pref | 35⅝ | 33⅞ | .. | .. |
| American Shipbuilding | 39½ | 32½ | 63 | 35½ |
| " " pref | 102 | 94 | 109⅞ | 95½ |
| Brotherton Iron | .. | .. | 5 | 5 |
| Chandler Iron | 80 | 80 | .. | .. |
| Cleveland & Buffalo Transit | 135¼ | 118 | 105 | 101 |
| Cleveland & Sandusky Brewing | 8¼ | 7⅜ | 35⅜ | 8⅝ |
| " " " pref | 37½ | 34¾ | 77⅝ | 40¾ |
| " " " combined | 47½ | 40 | 62½ | 39 |
| Cleveland-Cliffs Iron | 150 | 105 | 148 | 140 |
| Cleveland Steel Canal Boat | 20 | 20 | .. | .. |
| Cleveland Stone | 94¾ | 88¼ | 96¾ | 93 |
| Columbus Citizens' Telephone | .. | .. | 80 | 80 |
| Cuyahoga Telephone | 46 | 19 | 15⅛ | 6⅞ |
| Detroit & Buffalo Steamboat | 51¾ | 50 | 56¼ | 50 |
| Detroit & Cleveland Navigation | 89¼ | 83 | .. | .. |
| Federal Telephone | 40¼ | 4½ | 9 | 1½ |
| Great Lakes Towing | 22 | 6 | 11½ | 8¼ |
| " " pref | 76½ | 55¾ | 75 | 54½ |

| | 1901. | | 1902. | |
|---|---|---|---|---|
| | Highest. | Lowest. | Highest. | Lowest. |
| Lake Superior Consolidated Iron Mines | 175 | 95 | .. | .. |
| Lorain Gas | 51½ | 51½ | .. | .. |
| Massillon Coal & Mining | 103 | 103 | 103 | 86¼ |
| Merchants' Banking & Storage | 52¾ | 48 | 50 | 45 |
| Miami & Erie Canal Transportation | .. | .. | 36 | 15 |
| National Carbon | 21 | 15½ | 27⅝ | 19⅜ |
| " " pref | 88⅛ | 82 | 101¾ | 82 |
| Pittsburg & Lake Angeline Iron | 129 | 129 | .. | .. |
| Pittsburg Coal | 34½ | 25¼ | 25¾ | 24⅝ |
| " " pref | 65 | 50 | 90½ | 90⅛ |
| Republic Iron | 18 | 10½ | 14½ | 10¾ |
| Sandusky Portland Cement | 65 | 50 | .. | .. |
| Shelby Steel Tube | 10 | 10 | .. | .. |
| Union Steel Screw | 100 | 100 | .. | .. |

## RAILWAY BONDS—CLEVELAND

| | 1901. | | 1902. | |
|---|---|---|---|---|
| | Highest. | Lowest. | Highest. | Lowest. |
| A, B & C 1st mort. 5s | 103 | 102¾ | .. | .. |
| Brooklyn Street Railway 1st mort. 6s | 103 | 102¼ | .. | .. |
| Cincinnati & Hamilton 1st mort. 6s | 113 | 110½ | 111⅞ | 111⅞ |
| Cincinnati, Dayton & Toledo 1st con. 5s | .. | .. | 87 | 84 |
| Cleveland & Chagrin Falls 1st 6s | 103¼ | 101¾ | 103 | 99¾ |
| Cleveland & Elyria 1st mort. 6s | 103¾ | 103½ | .. | .. |
| C. B. E. & O. 5s | .. | .. | 100 | 100 |
| Cleveland City Cable 1st mort. 5s | 103¼ | 103¼ | 103 | 103 |
| Cleveland Electric con. 5s | 108 | 105⅞ | 105 | 105 |
| Cleveland, Elyria & Western con. 5s | 100½ | 100 | 98 | 98 |
| Cleveland, Painesville & Eastern 1st mort. 5s | 103½ | 102⅝ | .. | .. |
| Detroit Electric con. 5s | 106½ | 101 | 102¾ | 102¾ |
| Detroit, Fort Worth & B. I. 1st mort. 5s | 103⅜ | 103⅜ | .. | .. |
| Detroit Railway 1st mort. 5s | 108¼ | 108¼ | 109 | 105¾ |
| Elyria & Oberlin 1st mort. 6s | .. | .. | 101 | 101 |
| Lorain & Cleveland 1st mort. 5s | 103 | 101 | 101 | 100½ |
| Northern Ohio Traction con. 5s | 100¾ | 97¾ | 100 | 99½ |
| Southern Ohio Traction 1st con. 5s | 101⅜ | 97¼ | .. | .. |
| South Side 1st mort. 6s | 103 | 103 | .. | .. |
| Syracuse Rapid Transit 1st mort. 5s | 100¾ | 100 | 104 | 104 |
| " " " 2d mort. 5s | 89 | 89 | 89 | 89 |
| Tuscarawas 1st mort. 6s | 100¾ | 100 | .. | .. |
| Western Ohio 1st mort. 5s | .. | .. | 84¾ | 78¼ |

## TELEPHONE BONDS—CLEVELAND

| | 1901. | | 1902. | |
|---|---|---|---|---|
| | Highest. | Lowest. | Highest. | Lowest. |
| Columbus Citizens' Tel. 5s | 101¼ | 101 | .. | .. |
| Cuyahoga Telephone 1st mort. 5s | 87⅝ | 85½ | .. | .. |
| United States Tel. 1st mort. 5s | 85½ | 85 | 77⅜ | 53¼ |

## MISCELLANEOUS BONDS—CLEVELAND

| | 1901. | | 1902. | |
|---|---|---|---|---|
| | Highest. | Lowest. | Highest. | Lowest. |
| Cleveland & Sandusky Brewing 1st mort. 6s | 93¼ | 85½ | 97½ | 85¾ |
| Cleveland Chamber of Commerce 5s | 103⅝ | 101¾ | .. | .. |
| Cleveland Stone 1st mort. 6s | 93¼ | 85½ | .. | .. |
| Lake View Cemetery 4s | 76½ | 74¾ | 76⅛ | 75 |

# Detroit Stock Exchange

### Quotations for Securities Dealt in on the Stock Exchange, 1901 and 1902

## MISCELLANEOUS STOCKS

| | 1901. | | 1902. | |
|---|---|---|---|---|
| | Highest. | Lowest. | Highest. | Lowest. |
| Adventure Copper | .. | .. | 23½ | 23½ |
| American Car & Foundry | .. | .. | 36¼ | 31⅝ |
| American Radiator | .. | .. | 51 | 50 |
| American Shipbuilding | 38½ | 36¾ | 63 | 36¼ |
| " " pref. | 99 | 94½ | 109¾ | 96¼ |
| Belle Isle Scenic Railway | .. | .. | 11½ | 10 |
| Clyde Gold Mining | 24 | 17 | .. | .. |
| Detroit & Buffalo Steamboat | 52½ | 51 | 58 | 50½ |
| Detroit & Cleveland Navigation | 90 | 84 | 88 | 85 |
| Detroit & Deadwood Mining | 21 | 8 | .. | .. |
| Detroit City Gas | .. | .. | 84 | 73 |
| Detroit Club | 250 | 125 | .. | .. |
| Detroit Fire & Marine Insurance | 113¾ | 113¾ | 117½ | 115 |
| Detroit Oil | .. | .. | 110 | 100 |
| Detroit Southern P. R. | .. | .. | 22¾ | 16 |
| Detroit Union Railroad Depot and Station | 93 | 91 | .. | .. |
| Detroit United Railway | 81½ | 76 | 95¾ | 72 |
| Edison Illuminating, pref | 37 | 32 | 55½ | 37 |
| Iola Portland Cement | 20½ | 17½ | 26 | 21 |
| Iron Silver Mining | 65 | 64 | 75 | 65 |
| Michigan Copper Mining | 13¾ | 8½ | 12 | 7 |
| Michigan Fire & Marine Insurance | 70 | 70 | 62 | 60 |
| Michigan Telephone | 51½ | 50½ | .. | .. |
| Mohawk Copper | .. | .. | 46 | 36½ |
| Old Club | 170 | 150 | .. | .. |
| Ophir M. & M. | 52½ | 31 | .. | .. |
| Parke Davis & Co | 70 | 70 | 72½ | 70¼ |
| Peninsular Sugar | 20 | 20 | 16 | 15 |
| Phœnix Consolidated Copper | 8 | 8 | 4½ | 3½ |
| Rhode Island Copper | 7 | 6 | .. | .. |
| Rouge River Salt | 10 | 10 | .. | .. |
| Saginaw City Gas | 43 | 43 | .. | .. |
| Scotten-Dillon Tobacco Co. | 106 | 106 | .. | .. |
| United States Scenic Railway | .. | .. | 25 | 21 |
| Victoria Copper | 9¾ | 7 | 6 | 4¼ |
| Wabash Portland Cement | 65 | 65 | .. | .. |
| Wolverine Copper Mining | .. | .. | 54¾ | 54¾ |

## MISCELLANEOUS BONDS—DETROIT

| | | 1901. | | 1902. | |
|---|---|---|---|---|---|
| | Due. | Highest. | Lowest. | Highest. | Lowest. |
| Bellevue, O., Gas 6s | 1929 | 102½ | 102½ | .. | .. |
| Detroit & Buffalo Steamboat 5s | 1905-1922 | 104¾ | 100⅝ | 102 | 100 |
| Detroit & Pontiac 5s | 1922 | 106¼ | 106 | .. | .. |
| Detroit Citizens 5s | 1905 | 101 | 100 | 100⅝ | 99½ |
| Detroit City Gas 5s | 1923 | 101½ | 98½ | 99½ | 93 |
| Detroit Electric 5s | 1916 | 102½ | 99½ | 103¼ | 102 |
| Detroit Railway 5s | 1912-1924 | .. | .. | 108¼ | 107¾ |
| " " 5s | 1924 | 106¾ | 106¾ | .. | .. |
| Detroit, Rochester, Romeo & L. O. 5s | 1920 | 100 | 100 | 98 | 98 |

| | Due. | 1901. Highest. | Lowest. | 1902. Highest. | Lowest. |
|---|---|---|---|---|---|
| Detroit Suburban Railway 5s........................ | 1908 | 102 | 102 | .. | .. |
| Detroit Telephone 6s....... ........................ | 1922 | 101½ | 98½ | 99 | 99 |
| Detroit, Ypsilanti & A. A. 5s........................ | 1917 | 114 | 112 | 113 | 112½ |
| " " " 6s........................ | 1924 | 108 | 106 | 107½ | 106 |
| Detroit, Ypsilanti, A. A. & Jackson 5s.............. | 1926 | 101½ | 98 | 98 | 98 |
| Joplin, Mo., Gas 6s................................ | 1930 | 103 | 100 | .. | . |
| Michigan Telephone 5s. ............................ | 1929 | 96 | 96 | .. | .. |
| Peoria & Pekin Terminal Railway 5s................ | 1930 | 104½ | 104½ | .. | .. |
| Rapid Railway 5s................................... | 1915 | 105 | 105 | 105 | 102 |
| Wayne County 3½s................................ | 1913 | 105 | 105 | .. | .. |
| Wyandotte & Detroit River 5s............. . ..... | 1918 | 102 | 101½ | 100 | 100 |

# New York Stock Exchange

### Highest and Lowest Prices Recorded in 1900, 1901 and 1902 for all Stocks and Bonds Traded in on the Exchange

## STOCKS

| | 1900. | | 1901. | | 1902. | |
|---|---|---|---|---|---|---|
| | Highest. | Lowest. | Highest. | Lowest. | Highest. | Lowest. |
| Adams Express | 140 | 114 | 199 | 147 | 230 | 199 |
| Albany & Susquehanna | 205 | 204 | .. | .. | .. | .. |
| Allis-Chalmers | .. | .. | .. | .. | 21 | 18 |
| " " pref. | .. | .. | .. | .. | 82½ | 80⅝ |
| Amalgamated Copper | 99½ | 89¾ | 130 | 60½ | 79 | 53 |
| American Agricultural Chemical | .. | .. | 35 | 21 | 32¼ | 21 |
| " " " pref. | .. | .. | 91 | 80 | 91 | 78½ |
| American Beet Sugar | 23 | 23 | 30 | 24 | 30 | 30 |
| " " " pref. | 75 | 75 | 79 | 77 | .. | .. |
| American Bicycle | 25½ | 3 | 8¼ | 1½ | 8½ | ¼ |
| " " pref. | 52 | 18 | 35 | 10 | 26½ | 1½ |
| American Car & Foundry | 25½ | 12½ | 35 | 19 | 37⅝ | 28¼ |
| " " pref. | 72 | 57⅜ | 89¼ | 67 | 93⅜ | 85¾ |
| American Coal | 175 | 150 | 180½ | 180 | 200 | 180¼ |
| American Cotton Oil | 37¾ | 30 | 35½ | 24 | 57¾ | 30½ |
| " " " pref. | 100 | 88¼ | 91½ | 85 | 99½ | 86 |
| American District Telegraph | 37 | 24⅞ | 40 | 32 | 42⅜ | 32½ |
| American Express | 191 | 145 | 210 | 170 | 265 | 210 |
| American Grass Twine | .. | .. | 45 | 39⅝ | 62¼ | 27 |
| American Hide & Leather | .. | .. | .. | .. | 13¼ | 8¼ |
| " " " pref. | .. | .. | .. | .. | 43½ | 34 |
| American Ice | 49½ | 27½ | 41⅜ | 25¾ | 31⅞ | 9½ |
| " " pref. | 78½ | 60½ | 77¼ | 62 | 67 | 32 |
| American Linseed | 16¼ | 6 | 30⅛ | 5⅛ | 28 | 14 |
| " " pref. | 60 | 34½ | 66 | 31 | 58 | 39½ |
| American Locomotive | .. | .. | 33⅞ | 22½ | 36⅞ | 23½ |
| " " pref. | .. | .. | 91¾ | 83⅜ | 100¼ | 89 |
| American Malting | 7¾ | 3 | 8 | 4½ | 7½ | 5 |
| " " pref. | 31½ | 18⅞ | 30 | 22½ | 29 | 21 |
| American Sheet Steel | .. | .. | 42 | 36 | .. | .. |
| " " " pref. | .. | .. | 97½ | 80½ | .. | .. |
| American Smelting & Refining | 56½ | 34½ | 69 | 38½ | 49⅝ | 36⅞ |
| " " pref. | 99 | 85 | 105 | 88 | 100⅛ | 87½ |
| American Snuff | .. | .. | 49⅞ | 26 | 135 | 40½ |
| " " pref. | .. | .. | 90 | 73 | 101 | 85 |
| American Spirits Manufacturing | 4 | 1½ | 2½ | 2 | .. | .. |
| " " " pref. | 14 | 14 | .. | .. | .. | .. |
| American Steel & Wire | 59⅞ | 28½ | 53½ | 38 | .. | .. |
| " " pref. | 95 | 69½ | 112½ | 83¾ | .. | .. |
| American Steel Foundries | .. | .. | .. | .. | 15 | 12 |
| " " " pref. | .. | .. | .. | .. | 70 | 50¼ |
| American Steel Hoop | 50½ | 17 | 49 | 23 | .. | .. |
| " " pref. | 86 | 64¼ | 97½ | 69 | .. | .. |
| American Sugar Refining | 149 | 128¾ | 153 | 103⅛ | 135⅛ | 113 |
| " " " rights | .. | .. | 6 | 2¼ | .. | .. |
| " " " pref. | 118 | 107 | 130 | 111 | 122 | 115 |
| " " " " rights | .. | .. | 3⅛ | 2⅛ | .. | .. |
| American Telegraph & Cable | 96½ | 89 | 100 | 95 | 95 | 84 |
| American Telephone & Telegraph | .. | .. | 167¾ | 157½ | 186 | 160¾ |
| American Tin Plate | 56⅞ | 18 | 80 | 55 | .. | .. |
| " " pref. | 92 | 70¼ | 121 | 87 | .. | .. |
| American Tobacco | 114⅝ | 84½ | 144 | 99 | 300 | 140 |
| " " pref | 140 | 128 | 150 | 137 | 151½ | 140 |

| | 1900. | | 1901. | | 1902. | |
|---|---|---|---|---|---|---|
| | Highest. | Lowest. | Highest. | Lowest. | Highest. | Lowest. |
| American Woolen | 22½ | 21¼ | 21⅞ | 13¾ | 17⅝ | 12 |
| " " pref | 77 | 76 | 82¾ | 70 | 80¼ | 73 |
| Anaconda Copper Mining | 54⅞ | 37⅞ | 54¼ | 28¾ | 146 | 180 |
| Ann Arbor | 25 | 16 | 34 | 20 | 48¾ | 32 |
| " pref | 59 | 40½ | 66 | 50 | 77⅝ | 62½ |
| Associated Merchants, 1st pref | .. | .. | .. | .. | 96 | 95 |
| Atchison, Topeka & Santa Fe | 48¾ | 18⅝ | 91 | 42¾ | 96⅝ | 74¾ |
| " " " pref | 88¾ | 58¼ | 108 | 70 | 106⅛ | 95½ |
| Baltimore & Ohio | 89⅞ | 55¾ | 114½ | 81¾ | 118½ | 92⅝ |
| " " rights | .. | .. | 1½ | ¾ | 3⅜ | 1 |
| " " pref | 90 | 72¾ | 97 | 83⅝ | 99 | 92 |
| " " sub. ctfs | .. | .. | .. | .. | 108⅜ | 96⅝ |
| Beech Creek | .. | .. | .. | .. | 104 | 104 |
| Boston Air Line, pref | .. | .. | .. | .. | 108½ | 108½ |
| Brooklyn Rapid Transit | 88⅞ | 47⅝ | 88⅞ | 55⅞ | 72⅜ | 54¾ |
| Brooklyn Union Gas | .. | .. | 228 | 175 | 253 | 210 |
| Brunswick Dock & City Improvement | 16⅜ | 6½ | 14¾ | 8¾ | 14⅝ | 7⅞ |
| Buffalo, Rochester & Pittsburg | 85 | 52 | 122 | 77 | 128 | 110 |
| " " " pref | 125 | 95¾ | 146 | 116 | 145 | 139 |
| " " " rights | .. | . | .. | .. | 2 | 1⅛ |
| Burlington, Cedar Rapids & Northern | 137¾ | 119 | 136 | 120 | 230 | 139 |
| Butterick Co | .. | .. | .. | .. | 53 | 41 |
| Canada Southern | 61¼ | 47⅝ | 89 | 54⅜ | 97 | 71 |
| Canadian Pacific | 99¾ | 84¾ | 117½ | 87 | 145¼ | 112¼ |
| " " sub. ctfs | .. | .. | .. | .. | 144⅜ | 122 |
| " " rights | .. | .. | .. | .. | 6½ | 3 |
| Capital Traction | 101⅞ | 91¾ | 103¼ | 103¼ | .. | .. |
| Central Railroad of New Jersey | 150½ | 115 | 196⅝ | 145¾ | 198 | 165 |
| Chesapeake & Ohio | 42¾ | 24 | 52⅝ | 29 | 57½ | 42⅝ |
| Chicago & Alton | 42 | 31 | 50½ | 27 | 45⅜ | 29½ |
| " " pref | 78½ | 68½ | 82¼ | 72½ | 79 | 68 |
| Chicago & Eastern Illinois | 109 | 88 | 140 | 91 | 220¼ | 134¾ |
| " " " pref | 125 | 119½ | 136 | 120½ | 151 | 136½ |
| Chicago & Northwestern | 172¾ | 150¼ | 215 | 168½ | 271 | 204⅛ |
| " " pref | 220 | 195⅛ | 248 | 207 | 274½ | 230 |
| Chicago, Burlington & Quincy | 144 | 119⅜ | 199⅞ | 138¼ | 194¾ | 194¼ |
| " " " rights | .. | .. | 4½ | 3¾ | .. | .. |
| Chicago Consolidated Traction | 39⅝ | 37 | .. | .. | .. | .. |
| Chicago Great Western | 18 | 9⅞ | 27 | 16 | 35 | 22 |
| " " 5 per cent., Pref. "A" | 82 | 68½ | 90½ | 75 | 90¼ | 81½ |
| " " 4 " " "B" | 45 | 30 | 56 | 41 | 51¾ | 33 |
| " " debentures | 94¼ | 81 | 94¾ | 90 | 95¼ | 89½ |
| Chicago, Indianapolis & Louisville | 29 | 14 | 52⅞ | 23 | 80 | 49¼ |
| " " " pref | 64 | 45¾ | 77¾ | 58¾ | 91¼ | 75 |
| Chicago, Milwaukee & St. Paul | 148¼ | 108½ | 188 | 134 | 198¾ | 160½ |
| " " " pref | 188 | 169¼ | 200 | 175 | 200¾ | 186 |
| Chicago, Rock Island & Pacific | 122⅛ | 102 | 175¼ | 116⅞ | 206 | 152 |
| " " " rights | .. | .. | 11½ | 6½ | .. | .. |
| Chicago, St. Paul, Minneapolis & Omaha | 126 | 110 | 146¾ | 125 | 170½ | 140 |
| " " " " pref | 175 | 172 | 201 | 180 | 210 | 194⅞ |
| Chicago Terminal Transfer | 14⅞ | 8⅛ | 31 | 10½ | 24⅞ | 15 |
| " " " pref | 39¾ | 36½ | 57½ | 28¾ | 44 | 29 |
| Chicago Union Traction | .. | . | 20¼ | 12 | 23 | 10¾ |
| " " " pref | .. | .. | 60 | 54¾ | 60 | 44¾ |
| Claflin, H. B. Co | 115½ | 105 | 112 | 100 | 102 | 100 |
| " 1st pref | 102½ | 101 | .. | .. | .. | .. |
| " 2d pref | 106 | 106 | .. | .. | .. | .. |
| Cleveland & Pittsburg | 187⅛ | 185⅛ | 195 | 189 | 192 | 189 |
| Clev., Cin., Chic. & St. Louis | 76 | 55 | 101 | 72½ | 108⅜ | 93 |
| " " " " pref | 118 | 103⅛ | 124 | 115¾ | 124⅛ | 118 |
| Cleveland, Lorain & Wheeling | 30 | 14½ | 42½ | 27⅝ | 90 | 35 |
| " " " pref | 72 | 46 | 82 | 67 | 99 | 77½ |
| Colorado & Southern | 8¼ | 5 | 18 | 6⅝ | 35¾ | 14⅛ |
| Colorado & Southern, 1st pref | 47¼ | 36 | 60 | 40 | 79½ | 59¾ |
| " " 2d pref | 20¼ | 14 | 28¾ | 16¼ | 57⅞ | 28 |

| | 1900. | | 1901. | | 1902. | |
|---|---|---|---|---|---|---|
| | Highest. | Lowest. | Highest. | Lowest. | Highest. | Lowest. |
| Colorado Coal & Iron Development...... | 2⅜ | ½ | .. | .. | . | .. |
| " " " pref.. | 3⅜ | ¾ | .. | .. | .. | .. |
| Colorado Fuel & Iron.................. | 56½ | 29¼ | 136½ | 41¾ | 110½ | 73¾ |
| " " " pref.............. | 131½ | 117 | 142½ | 116 | 140 | 130¼ |
| Colorado Midland... ................. | 12⅜ | 9 | .. | .. | .. | .. |
| " " pref.................. | 29⅞ | 21 | .. | .. | .. | .. |
| Columbus & Hocking Coal and Iron...... | 21 | 11½ | 25½ | 12½ | 24⅞ | 14⅛ |
| Commercial Cable...................... | 183 | 158 | 189 | 168½ | 180 | 152 |
| Consolidated Gas...................... | 201 | 164 | 238 | 187 | 230¾ | 205 |
| " " rights................. | 5⅜ | 3½ | .. | .. | .. | .. |
| Consolidation Coal.................... | 60 | 50 | 63 | 56½ | 85 | 80 |
| Continental Tobacco................... | 40¾ | 21½ | 71¾ | 38¾ | .. | .. |
| " " pref.............. | 95 | 70 | 124 | 93¾ | 126½ | 114 |
| Corn Products Co...................... | .. | .. | .. | .. | 38⅛ | 26¾ |
| " " " pref................. | .. | .. | .. | .. | 90 | 79⅝ |
| Crucible Steel........................ | .. | .. | 27⅞ | 23 | 24¾ | 21¾ |
| " " pref...................... | .. | .. | 86½ | 81¾ | 87 | 85¾ |
| Delaware & Hudson..................... | 134½ | 106½ | 185½ | 105 | 184½ | 153½ |
| Delaware, Lackawanna & Western....... | 194¾ | 171½ | 258 | 188¼ | 297 | 231 |
| Denver & Rio Grande................... | 34½ | 16½ | 53½ | 29½ | 51¾ | 35⅛ |
| " " pref............... | 87½ | 64½ | 103¼ | 80 | 96¼ | 86½ |
| " " " rights.......... | .. | .. | ½ | ¼ | .. | .. |
| Denver & Southwestern......... ....... | .. | .. | 71 | 49 | 50 | 40 |
| " " pref............ | .. | .. | 69 | 69 | 64 | 49 |
| Des Moines & Ft. Dodge................ | 21⅜ | 1¼ | 45 | 18 | 53⅝ | 35 |
| " " pref............ | .. | .. | 130 | 123 | 150 | 130 |
| Detroit City Gas...................... | 98½ | 89 | 92 | 72½ | 90 | 65 |
| Detroit Southern...................... | .. | .. | 17 | 14¾ | 25 | 13 |
| " " pref.................. | .. | .. | 40⅞ | 36 | 48¾ | 26 |
| Detroit United Railway................ | .. | .. | 82 | 75 | 97 | 75 |
| Diamond Match......................... | .. | .. | 152½ | 127½ | 139⅞ | 130¼ |
| Distillers' Securities................ | .. | .. | .. | .. | 33 | 27 |
| Distilling Co. of America............. | .. | .. | 10½ | 6⅞ | 10 | 4 |
| " " " pref........... | .. | .. | 34½ | 23¼ | 45 | 33 |
| " " " trust receipts.... | .. | .. | .. | .. | 5⅞ | 4 |
| " " " " " pref. | .. | .. | .. | .. | 39 | 31¾ |
| Duluth, South Shore & Atlantic......... | 6¼ | 4 | 12½ | 4½ | 24 | 10 |
| " " " pref..... | 17⅛ | 12 | 22½ | 13⅛ | 35¼ | 18⅝ |
| Eighth Avenue......................... | 400 | 395 | 405 | 405 | .. | .. |
| Erie.................................. | 27⅛ | 10½ | 45½ | 24½ | 44⅜ | 28⅝ |
| " 1st pref........................... | 63½ | 30⅜ | 75 | 59¼ | 75¾ | 60½ |
| " 2d pref............................ | 43¼ | 15 | 62¾ | 39¼ | 63¼ | 41½ |
| Erie Telegraph & Telephone............ | 122⅜ | 101 | .. | .. | .. | .. |
| " " " Rights... . | 1½ | 1 | .. | .. | .. | .. |
| Evansville & Terre Haute.............. | 54⅜ | 38½ | 68 | 41 | 74⅜ | 50 |
| " " pref........... | 94¾ | 74 | 95 | 81 | 100¼ | 82 |
| Federal Steel................. ........ | 58¼ | 28¾ | 59 | 41 | .. | .. |
| " " pref...................... | 79½ | 60¼ | 105½ | 68 | .. | .. |
| Fort Worth & Denver City.............. | 20 | 14½ | 36 | 17 | 67½ | 30 |
| Fort Worth & Rio Grande............... | .. | .. | 29 | 25 | .. | .. |
| Fuller, George A., Co................. | .. | .. | .. | .. | 64 | 40 |
| " " " pref............... | .. | .. | .. | .. | 108¾ | 92 |
| " " " trust receipts....... | .. | .. | .. | .. | 62¼ | 61 |
| " " " " " pref... | .. | .. | .. | .. | 104½ | 104½ |
| Gas & Electric, Bergen County.......... | 81 | 64 | 101⅝ | 24¾ | 29 | 29 |
| General Chemical.... ................. | .. | .. | .. | .. | 67½ | 60⅛ |
| " " pref.................. | .. | .. | .. | .. | 103 | 98½ |
| General Electric...................... | 200 | 144¾ | 289¼ | 183½ | 334 | 170 |
| Glucose Sugar Refining................ | 60 | 44 | 65 | 37 | 51½ | 39⅛ |
| " " " pref............. | 103 | 92 | 107 | 93¾ | 110 | 90 |
| " " " trust receipts..... | .. | .. | .. | .. | 46⅜ | 43¼ |
| " " " " " pref.. | .. | .. | .. | .. | 112 | 108 |
| Great Northern, pref.................. | 191½ | 144¾ | 208 | 167½ | 203 | 181½ |
| " " " Rights............ | 5¼ | 5½ | .. | .. | .. | .. |
| Green Bay & Western................... | 47 | 40 | 59½ | 50 | 84⅞ | 75 |

| | 1900. | | 1901. | | 1902. | |
|---|---|---|---|---|---|---|
| | Highest. | Lowest. | Highest. | Lowest. | Highest. | Lowest. |
| Hocking Valley | 42⅞ | 30 | 75½ | 40½ | 106 | 66 |
| " " pref | 74¾ | 58 | 88½ | 69¾ | 98⅜ | 81⅛ |
| Homestake Mining | 79½ | 65 | 104 | 75 | 99 | 65 |
| Illinois Central | 133 | 119 | 154¾ | 124 | 173½ | 137 |
| " " leased lines | 103¾ | 99 | 106 | 105 | 105 | 105 |
| " " rights | .. | .. | 8¼ | 7½ | 12⅜ | 8¾ |
| Indiana, Illinois & Iowa | .. | .. | 80 | 77½ | 90 | 90 |
| International Paper | 26½ | 14½ | 28 | 18½ | 23⅝ | 16½ |
| " " pref | 75 | 58 | 81½ | 69 | 77¾ | 70 |
| International Power | 55¾ | 24 | 100½ | 54⅞ | 199 | 49 |
| International Silver | 10⅞ | 3¾ | 11 | 5¼ | 24½ | 6½ |
| " " pref | .. | .. | 51 | 32½ | 65 | 35 |
| International Steam Pump | 29¾ | 28 | 49 | 24⅛ | 57¾ | 40 |
| " " pref | .. | .. | 89 | 74 | 95 | 82 |
| Iowa Central | 27⅜ | 11⅞ | 43¾ | 21 | 51¾ | 35⅛ |
| " " pref | 58 | 39 | 87½ | 48 | 90⅛ | 65 |
| Kanawah & Michigan | 25 | 10 | 41 | 21 | 50½ | 33⅞ |
| Kansas City, Fort Scott & Memphis, pref. | .. | .. | 81¾ | 77½ | 88 | 75 |
| Kansas City, Pittsburg & Gulf | 9 | 8 | .. | .. | .. | .. |
| " " " " trust receipts | 9¾ | 7⅞ | .. | .. | .. | .. |
| " " " " 1st in. paid. | 12¾ | 12 | .. | .. | .. | .. |
| " " " " all in. paid.. | 21½ | 13¾ | .. | .. | .. | .. |
| Kansas City Southern | 17½ | 7 | 25 | 13½ | 39 | 19 |
| " " pref | 43⅜ | 27¾ | 49 | 35 | 62¾ | 44 |
| Keokuk & Des Moines | 6 | 3½ | 18½ | 5¼ | 41 | 13 |
| " " pref | 23 | 14½ | 45½ | 24 | 84 | 45 |
| Kingston & Pembroke | 9¾ | 7 | 11 | 8 | 14 | 8⅜ |
| " " 1st pref | .. | .. | 50 | 45 | .. | .. |
| Knickerbocker Ice, Chicago | 40 | 10 | 29 | 12 | 17½ | 12 |
| " " " pref | 66 | 50 | 62½ | 50½ | 55 | 53 |
| Laclede Gas | 80 | 65 | 95⅛ | 70 | 92 | 88½ |
| " " pref | 100 | 96 | 106½ | 95 | 110 | 100 |
| Lake Erie & Western | 52 | 20⅜ | 76½ | 39¾ | 71½ | 40 |
| " " pref | 115 | 83¾ | 135½ | 108⅛ | 138 | 120 |
| Lake Shore & Michigan Southern | 230 | 206 | 352½ | 230 | 346 | 325 |
| Long Island | 89 | 47½ | 90 | 67 | 91⅞ | 72½ |
| Louisville & Nashville | 89⅛ | 69¾ | 111¾ | 76 | 159½ | 102⅛ |
| Manhattan Beach | 19¾ | 6¾ | 22 | 8 | 19 | 9 |
| Manhattan Elevated | 117 | 84 | 145 | 83 | 158 | 128 |
| Maryland Coal, pref | 81 | 74 | 75 | 67½ | 110 | 72 |
| Mergenthaler Linotype | 210 | 180 | 182½ | 181 | .. | .. |
| Metropolitan Securities | .. | .. | .. | .. | 134½ | 109½ |
| Metropolitan Street Railway | 182 | 143¾ | 177 | 150 | 174 | 135 |
| " " " rights | 37½ | 24½ | 2 | ⅝ | 11 | 5½ |
| Metropolitan West Side El. of Chicago | 37½ | 24½ | 41 | 27 | 43 | 35 |
| " " " " pref | 84⅜ | 76 | 93 | 79½ | 91¾ | 89 |
| Mexican Central | 17⅜ | 10½ | 30 | 12¼ | 31⅛ | 20⅝ |
| Mexican National certificates | 5 | 2⅝ | 15¼ | 3⅝ | 20¾ | 14⅜ |
| Michigan Central | 115 | 105 | 180 | 107 | 192 | 150 |
| Milwaukee Elec. Railway and Light, pref. | .. | .. | 118 | 118 | .. | .. |
| Minneapolis & St. Louis | 71½ | 55½ | 111¼ | 67¾ | 115 | 105 |
| " " pref | 104¼ | 87½ | 124½ | 101¾ | 127¾ | 118½ |
| Minneapolis, St. Paul & Sault Ste. Marie | 27 | 14 | 36¼ | 15 | 84 | 36½ |
| " " " " pref | 69 | 47 | 94¾ | 49 | 139 | 90 |
| Missouri, Kansas & Texas | 17⅜ | 9 | 35½ | 15 | 35¾ | 22½ |
| " " " pref | 47½ | 25⅜ | 68⅜ | 37 | 69¾ | 51 |
| Missouri Pacific | 72½ | 38⅜ | 124½ | 69 | 125½ | 96¼ |
| " " rights | .. | .. | 2⅛ | ¼ | .. | .. |
| Mobile & Ohio | 49 | 35 | 85 | 44 | .. | .. |
| Morris & Essex | 189½ | 184 | 197¼ | 192 | 197 | 195 |
| Nashville, Chattanooga & St. Louis | 50 | 43 | 80 | 75½ | 122 | 80 |
| National Biscuit | 40¼ | 27¾ | 46 | 37 | 53¾ | 40 |
| " " pref | 96 | 79½ | 103⅜ | 92 | 109½ | 101¾ |
| National Lead | 28¼ | 15⅞ | 25½ | 15 | 32 | 15⅜ |
| " " pref | 106½ | 83 | 93⅞ | 74¾ | 96 | 78⅜ |

| | 1900. | | 1901. | | 1902. | |
|---|---|---|---|---|---|---|
| | Highest. | Lowest. | Highest. | Lowest. | Highest. | Lowest. |
| National Linseed Oil | 3¼ | 3⅛ | .. | .. | .. | .. |
| National Railroad of Mexico | .. | .. | .. | .. | 21¾ | 14⅛ |
| " " " pref. | .. | .. | .. | .. | 45⅜ | 31¾ |
| National Salt | 46 | 43 | 50 | 23 | 30 | 15 |
| " " pref. | 76¼ | 69 | 84 | 61¾ | 70 | 61 |
| National Steel | 53½ | 20 | 60⅛ | 37 | .. | .. |
| " " pref. | 97 | 79¾ | 120 | 90 | .. | .. |
| National Tube | 69⅞ | 40⅞ | 70⅛ | 51 | .. | .. |
| " " pref. | 105½ | 86¾ | 121 | 93 | .. | .. |
| New Central Coal | 37 | 30 | 41 | 26⅛ | 45 | 33 |
| New York Air Brake | 175 | 112 | 175 | 133 | 196 | 148 |
| New York & Harlem | 413 | 405 | 430 | 420 | 410 | 405 |
| New York & New Jersey Telephone | .. | .. | 173 | 173 | .. | .. |
| New York Central | 145⅜ | 125⅝ | 174½ | 139⅜ | 168⅜ | 147 |
| New York, Chicago & St. Louis | 24½ | 11 | 57⅞ | 16 | 57⅝ | 40 |
| New York, Chicago & St. Louis, 1st ref. | 110 | 75 | 120 | 97 | 124½ | 110½ |
| " " " 2d pprel.. | 58¼ | 29 | 95 | 47 | 100 | 80 |
| New York Dock | .. | .. | 15 | 13 | 28 | 12 |
| " " pref. | .. | .. | 47¼ | 44 | 64¾ | 39½ |
| New York, Lackawanna & Western | 134 | 130 | 139 | 136 | 141 | 138½ |
| New York Mutual Gas | .. | .. | 295 | 294 | .. | .. |
| New York, New Haven & Hartford | 215½ | 210 | 217 | 210 | 255 | 209½ |
| New York, Ontario & Western | 32¼ | 18¼ | 40½ | 24 | 37⅝ | 25¼ |
| Norfolk & Western | 45¾ | 22⅝ | 61⅜ | 42 | 80¾ | 55 |
| " " pref. | 82½ | 67 | 92¼ | 82 | 98 | 90 |
| North American | 22¾ | 13⅝ | 25 | 19⅛ | 134 | 88 |
| " " new | .. | .. | 109 | 73½ | .. | .. |
| Northern Central | .. | .. | .. | .. | 250 | 235 |
| Northern Pacific | 86½ | 45¾ | 700 | 77¼ | .. | .. |
| " " pref. | 91½ | 67 | 113½ | 84¼ | .. | .. |
| Ohio & Indiana Con. Nat. & Ill. Gas | 31⅞ | 25 | .. | .. | .. | .. |
| Ontario Mining | 9 | 6 | 13 | 6¼ | 9½ | 5½ |
| Pacific Coast | 62 | 46 | 78 | 52 | 81½ | 65 |
| " " 1st pref. | 90¼ | 82½ | 103½ | 89 | 106 | 98 |
| " " 2d pref. | 69½ | 57 | 83 | 63 | 84¾ | 72¼ |
| Pacific Mail | 57 | 25¾ | 49½ | 30½ | 49⅜ | 37 |
| Pennsylvania Coal | 740 | 420 | .. | . | .. | .. |
| Pennsylvania Railroad | 149½ | 124⅜ | 161½ | 137½ | 170 | 147 |
| " " rights | 3 | 2⅛ | 11¼ | 6¾ | 1⅝ | ⅝ |
| " " subscription receipts | 137⅛ | 127¼ | .. | .. | .. | .. |
| People's Gas, Chicago | 111½ | 81⅜ | 120½ | 95¾ | 109½ | 98¼ |
| Peoria & Eastern | 18 | 5 | 50 | 14⅞ | 47½ | 30 |
| Peoria, Decatur & Evansville | 4 | 1¼ | .. | .. | .. | .. |
| Pere Marquette | 35 | 20 | 94 | 33¾ | 85½ | 71 |
| " " pref. | 73½ | 54½ | 86 | 72 | 93 | 80 |
| Philadelphia Co | 74 | 74 | 109 | 90½ | .. | .. |
| Pittsburg & Western, pref. | 24½ | 8 | .. | .. | .. | .. |
| Pittsburg, Cin., Chic. & St. Louis | 80½ | 49¾ | 81 | 57 | 105½ | 80⅛ |
| " " " " pref. | 94 | 78 | 113 | 88 | 128 | 113 |
| Pittsburg, Fort Wayne & Chicago | 188 | 186 | 195 | 188½ | 193¼ | 192⅞ |
| Pressed Steel Car | 58¾ | 32⅛ | 52 | 30 | 63½ | 39 |
| " " " pref. | 89½ | 70¾ | 89 | 72½ | 96½ | 82¾ |
| Pullman | 204 | 176 | 225 | 195½ | 250 | 215 |
| Quicksilver Mining | 2½ | 1⅛ | 5¼ | 1¼ | 4⅜ | 2 |
| " " pref. | 10⅛ | 7¾ | 12¾ | 7 | 11⅞ | 9½ |
| Railroad Securities | .. | .. | .. | .. | 96½ | 92 |
| Railway Steel Spring | .. | .. | .. | .. | 38½ | 24 |
| " " " pref. | .. | .. | .. | .. | 90¼ | 80 |
| Reading | 26 | 15 | 58 | 24½ | 78½ | 52¼ |
| " 1st pref. | 71⅞ | 49 | 82⅞ | 65 | 90¼ | 79⅞ |
| " 2d pref. | 39⅛ | 23⅝ | 64½ | 38 | 80⅞ | 60 |
| Rensselaer & Saratoga | 200 | 193 | 215 | 215 | .. | .. |
| Republic Iron & Steel | 27½ | 8¾ | 24 | 11¾ | 24¾ | 15⅝ |
| " " " pref. | 70¾ | 49 | 82 | 55¼ | 83⅜ | 68 |
| Rio Grande Western | 65 | 43¼ | 85 | 65 | .. | .. |

| | 1900. | | 1901. | | 1902. | |
|---|---|---|---|---|---|---|
| | Highest. | Lowest. | Highest. | Lowest. | Highest. | Lowest. |
| Rio Grande Western, pref | 95¾ | 80 | 108 | 93 | .. | .. |
| Rock Island | .. | .. | .. | .. | 50⅛ | 33½ |
| " " pref | .. | .. | .. | .. | 85½ | 71 |
| Rome, Watertown & Ogdensburgh | 133½ | 131¾ | 140 | 135 | 141 | 138 |
| Rubber Goods Mfg | .. | .. | 38¼ | 18 | 25⅜ | 17¾ |
| " " pref | .. | .. | 90 | 65 | 74 | 63 |
| Rutland, pref | .. | .. | 112¾ | 97 | 125 | 64½ |
| St. Joseph & Grand Island | 8⅞ | 5 | 15¾ | 7⅞ | 24¼ | 10 |
| " " 1st pref | 64½ | 38¾ | 78½ | 55 | 81½ | 49¾ |
| " " 2d pref | 21½ | 11⅜ | 36 | 17 | 42 | 24½ |
| St. Lawrence & Adirondack | .. | .. | 134 | 57 | 141½ | 50 |
| " " rights | .. | .. | .. | .. | 6¼ | 6¼ |
| St. Louis & San Francisco | 24¼ | 8⅜ | 56½ | 21⅛ | 85½ | 55¾ |
| " " 1st pref | 78½ | 64 | 88 | 75 | 90 | 77 |
| " " 2d pref | 55 | 31¼ | 76¾ | 53⅜ | 80⅜ | 65½ |
| St. Louis Southwestern | 18½ | 8¼ | 39½ | 16 | 39 | 24½ |
| " " pref | 45½ | 21⅞ | 71 | 41½ | 80 | 55¼ |
| St. Paul & Duluth | 62 | 50⅛ | .. | .. | .. | .. |
| " " pref | 101 | 99½ | .. | .. | .. | .. |
| Silver Bullion certificates | 66¼ | 59½ | 65½ | 59¾ | 55⅜ | 52⅝ |
| Sloss Sheffield Steel & Iron | 26 | 17½ | 41½ | 19½ | 83 | 29½ |
| " " pref | 71 | 59¼ | 86 | 65½ | 95½ | 80¼ |
| Southern Pacific | 45¾ | 30⅛ | 63⅝ | 29 | 81¼ | 56 |
| Southern Railway | 23⅛ | 10⅝ | 35¾ | 18 | 41⅞ | 31⅞ |
| " " extended | . | .. | .. | .. | 38¾ | 28 |
| " " pref | 73⅛ | 49¾ | 94⅝ | 67¼ | 98½ | 92 |
| " " extended | .. | .. | .. | .. | 97 | 89¼ |
| " " M. & O. stock ctfs | .. | .. | .. | .. | 93 | 90 |
| Standard Rope & Twine | 10¼ | 4½ | 8½ | 3½ | 83 | 4 |
| Tennessee Coal, Iron & Railroad | 104 | 49 | 76⅝ | 49⅞ | 74⅝ | 49½ |
| " " " " pref | 160 | 155 | .. | .. | .. | .. |
| Texas & Pacific | 26¼ | 13⅛ | 52¼ | 23¾ | 54¾ | 37 |
| " land trust | 21¾ | 11½ | 42¼ | 19 | 44½ | 35 |
| Texas Central | 14 | 14 | .. | .. | .. | .. |
| " " pref | 60 | 60 | .. | .. | .. | .. |
| Third Avenue Railroad | 135⅛ | 45¼ | 129½ | 117 | 134 | 122 |
| Toledo, Peoria & Western | 10 | 10 | 10 | 10 | 20 | 20 |
| Toledo Railways & Light | .. | .. | .. | .. | 38 | 32½ |
| Toledo, St. Louis & Western | .. | .. | 25⅛ | 10¾ | 33¼ | 18½ |
| " " " pref | .. | .. | 39½ | 28 | 49¾ | 35 |
| Twin City Rapid Transit | 70¼ | 40¼ | 109⅜ | 65¾ | 129 | 107 |
| " " " pref | 146 | 136 | 160 | 147 | 159½ | 156¼ |
| " " " rights | .. | .. | .. | .. | 1¾ | 1⅜ |
| Union Bag & Paper | 25 | 10 | 19⅜ | 12 | 18¼ | 11½ |
| " " pref | 77¾ | 56¼ | 75¾ | 65 | 85 | 72 |
| Union Pacific | 81⅜ | 44⅜ | 133 | 76 | 113¼ | 93½ |
| " " pref | 85⅜ | 70½ | 99½ | 81⅝ | 95 | 86⅝ |
| " " rights | .. | .. | 1¼ | ½ | .. | .. |
| United New Jersey Railroad & Canal | 272¼ | 268¾ | 282½ | 278 | 280 | 280 |
| United Railways Investment | .. | .. | .. | .. | 24⅞ | 20 |
| " " " pref | .. | .. | .. | .. | 66 | 60 |
| United States Cast Iron Pipe & Fdry | .. | .. | .. | .. | 17 | 10½ |
| " " " " " " pref | .. | .. | .. | .. | 59 | 42 |
| United States Express | 59 | 45¼ | 100 | 54 | 160 | 97 |
| United States Flour Milling | ½ | ¼ | .. | .. | .. | .. |
| " " pref | 13½ | 4 | .. | .. | .. | .. |
| United States Leather | 19 | 7¾ | 16⅝ | 7¾ | 15¼ | 10½ |
| " " pref | 75 | 65 | 83¾ | 69½ | 91¼ | 79⅞ |
| United States Realty & Construction | .. | .. | .. | .. | 32 | 20 |
| " " " " pref | .. | .. | .. | .. | 75½ | 64½ |
| United States Reduction & Refining | .. | .. | .. | .. | 44⅝ | 25 |
| " " " " pref | .. | .. | .. | .. | 68 | 57 |
| United States Rubber | 44 | 21 | 34 | 12½ | 19⅜ | 14 |
| " " pref | 104¾ | 77¾ | 85 | 47 | 64 | 49½ |
| United States Steel | .. | .. | 55 | 24 | 46¾ | 29¼ |

| | 1900. | | 1901. | | 1902. | |
|---|---|---|---|---|---|---|
| | Highest. | Lowest. | Highest. | Lowest. | Highest. | Lowest. |
| United States Steel, pref. | .. | .. | 101⅞ | 69 | 97¾ | 79 |
| Virginia-Carolina Chemical | .. | .. | 72 | 51 | 76⅜ | 54 |
| " " " pref. | .. | .. | 125 | 116 | 134⅞ | 120 |
| Vulcan Detinning | .. | .. | .. | .. | 34½ | 29½ |
| " " pref. | .. | .. | .. | .. | 81½ | 78½ |
| Wabash | 14 | 6½ | 26 | 11⅛ | 38¾ | 21¾ |
| " pref. | 27 | 6½ | 46⅛ | 23¾ | 54½ | 37 |
| Wagner Palace Car | 185 | 185 | .. | .. | .. | .. |
| Wells-Fargo Express | 140 | 123 | 199 | 135 | 250 | 194¾ |
| Western Union Telegraph | 88½ | 77½ | 100¾ | 81 | 97½ | 84¾ |
| Westinghouse Elec. & Manfg. | .. | .. | 180 | 145 | 233 | 169½ |
| " " 1st pref. | .. | .. | 187 | 157 | 234 | 180 |
| Wheeling & Lake Erie | 13½ | 8 | 22 | 11⅜ | 30¾ | 17 |
| " " " 1st pref. | 58½ | 44½ | 60¾ | 45 | 66 | 49½ |
| " " " 2d " | 33⅛ | 21⅛ | 38 | 24 | 42⅜ | 28 |
| Wisconsin Central | 20¾ | 10 | 26 | 14½ | 31 | 19⅛ |
| " " pref. | 57 | 30 | 49¾ | 38½ | 57⅜ | 38½ |

## *MISCELLANEOUS STOCKS.—NEW YORK*

### SALES ON THE CURB AND AT AUCTION.

| | 1900. | | 1901. | | 1902. | |
|---|---|---|---|---|---|---|
| | Highest. | Lowest. | Highest. | Lowest. | Highest. | Lowest. |
| Acme Ball-Bearing Caster Co. | 60 | 40 | .. | .. | .. | .. |
| Adirondack Land & Investment Co. | .. | .. | .. | .. | $1.08 | 50c |
| Adirondack League Club | .. | .. | 585 | 500 | 670 | 510 |
| Aero Pulverizer Co. | .. | .. | 1 | 1 | .. | .. |
| Ætna Fire Ins. Co., Hartford, Conn. | 290½ | 290½ | 289 | 289 | .. | .. |
| Ætna Silk Co. of Norfolk, Conn | .. | .. | 25 | 25 | .. | .. |
| Alabama & Georgia Iron Co. | 10 | 8 | .. | .. | .. | .. |
| " " " pref. | 33 | 21 | .. | .. | .. | .. |
| Aladdin Manufact'ing Co. (364 shares). | .. | .. | .. | .. | $5 lot | |
| Albro, E. D., Co. | .. | .. | .. | .. | 50 | 50 |
| Allegheny & Western R. R. Co., guar. | 123 | 123 | .. | .. | .. | .. |
| Alliance Realty Co. | 110 | 72 | 126½ | 120 | 120 | 90¼ |
| American Bank Note Co. | 54 | 45 | 59⅞ | 50 | 60 | 52 |
| American Brewing Co. of New York. | .. | .. | 30 | 20 | .. | .. |
| American Bridge Co. | 46 | 42 | .. | .. | .. | .. |
| " " pref. | 95¾ | 92 | .. | .. | .. | .. |
| American Can. | .. | .. | 31⅝ | 14¾ | 16¼ | 8¼ |
| " " pref. | .. | .. | 84 | 53⅜ | 60 | 39 |
| American Chicle Co. | 92 | 52 | 89½ | 75 | 135 | 76 |
| " " pref | 85 | 70 | 84 | 76¼ | 96 | 78 |
| American Coal Co. | 148 | 148 | .. | .. | .. | .. |
| American Cotton. | .. | .. | 25 | 13 | 23½ | 5 |
| " " pref. | .. | .. | 66 | 59 | 65 | 40 |
| American Dist. Tel. Co. of Brooklyn. | .. | .. | 35 | 35 | .. | .. |
| American Felt Co., pref. | .. | .. | .. | .. | 80½ | 80½ |
| American Finance Co. | .. | .. | 140 | 140 | .. | .. |
| American Grocer Publishing Co. | .. | .. | 5 | 5 | .. | .. |
| American Hide & Leather Co. | 14½ | 4½ | 12 | 3¾ | .. | .. |
| " " " pref. | 41½ | 25 | 40 | 27 | .. | .. |
| American Horse Exchange, Ltd. | .. | .. | .. | .. | 7 | 7 |
| American Ins. Co., Newark, scrip. | .. | .. | 308 | 308 | .. | .. |
| American Light & Traction. | .. | .. | 28 | 18 | 45 | 24½ |
| " " " pref. | .. | .. | 98 | 87½ | 98 | 86 |
| American Lithographic Co. | .. | .. | .. | .. | 20 | 20 |
| American Machine Co. | .. | .. | .. | .. | 8 1-10 | 8 1-10 |
| American Manufacturing Co. | .. | .. | .. | .. | 120 | 120 |
| American Press Association. | 68 | 66 | .. | .. | 90 | 11 |
| American School Furniture Co., pref. | .. | .. | .. | .. | 40¼ | 40¼ |
| American Soda Fountain, 2d pref. | 7 | 7 | .. | .. | 20¼ | 10 |

| | 1900. | | 1901. | | 1902. | |
|---|---|---|---|---|---|---|
| | Highest. | Lowest. | Highest. | Lowest. | Highest. | Lowest. |
| American Spirits Manufacturing...... | .. | .. | .. | .. | $1.11⅛ | $1.11⅛ |
| American Thread Co., pref .......... | .. | .. | 4½ | 4½ | .. | .. |
| American Type Founders' Co......... | .. | .. | 60 | 51 | 53 | 42 |
| American Waltham Watch Co. ...... | .. | .. | .. | .. | 239 | 230 |
| American Whiting & Putty Co....... | .. | .. | $11.55 | $11.55 | .. | .. |
| American Writing Paper............ | .. | .. | 3 | 1½ | 6⅞ | 1½ |
| " " " pref......... | .. | .. | 15 | 8 | 25⅜ | 8½ |
| Amphion Academy, Brooklyn........ | 20½ | 20½ | 34¾ | 31 | 36 | 36 |
| Anchor Manufacturing Co., Detroit... | .. | .. | 2 | 2 | .. | .. |
| Anniston City Land Co..... ........ | 16¼ | 16 | .. | .. | 15¼ | 15¼ |
| Anniston (Ala.) Invest. & Guar. Co... | 25 | 25 | .. | .. | .. | .. |
| Anthony & Scoville Co.............. | .. | .. | .. | .. | 5½ | 5½ |
| Apollo Incandescent Gas Light Co.... | 13 | 13 | 10 | 10 | .. | .. |
| Arts Realty Co........ ............ | .. | .. | .. | .. | 13 | 13 |
| Asphalt Company of America........ | 91 | 58 | .. | .. | .. | .. |
| Atlanta & Charlotte Air Line Co..... | 129 | 129 | 168½ | 149 | 164 | 164 |
| Atlanta, Knoxville & Northern, pref.. | .. | .. | 35 | 35 | .. | .. |
| Atlantic Dock Co.................... | 95 | 85 | .. | .. | 85 | 85 |
| Atlas Match Co...................... | .. | .. | .. | .. | 1 | 1 |
| Atwater, W. C., & Co. (375 shares)... | .. | .. | .. | .. | $1,000 lot | |
| Audit Co., pref...................... | 176 | 155 | .. | .. | 175¼ | 175¼ |
| Automatic Fire Alarm & Exting. Co.. | .. | .. | .. | .. | 123 | 123 |
| Avon, Geneseo & Mt. Morris R. R. gu. | 73¾ | 73¾ | .. | .. | .. | .. |
| Bailey, A. R., Co.................... | 2 | 2 | .. | .. | .. | .. |
| Baltimore & Annapolis Short Line.... | .. | .. | .. | .. | 116⅛ | 112¼ |
| Bank Clerks' Co-oper. Bldg. & L. Assn | .. | .. | 11 | 11 | .. | .. |
| Bankers' & Mers. Tel. Co. (300 shares). | .. | .. | .. | .. | $3 lot | |
| Bank of Minn., St. Paul (510 shares).. | .. | .. | .. | .. | $11 lot | |
| Barney & Smith Car Co.............. | 21 | 13 | 24 | 21 | 30 | 23 |
| " " pref............ | 122 | 94½ | 125 | 118 | 125 | 120 |
| Batopilas Mining Co., $20 each....... | 1 | 1 | $1.45 | $1.45 | .. | .. |
| Bay State Gas Co.................... | 2½ | ⅞ | 1 | ⅝ | 4¼ | ½ |
| Bay State Seam Face Granite Co..... | .. | .. | .. | .. | ½ | ¼ |
| Beaver Coal Co..................... | .. | .. | 3½ | 3½ | .. | . |
| Bedford Riding Academy............ | 14 | 14 | 2¼ | 2¼ | .. | .. |
| Binghamton R. R. Co............... | 27 | 27 | .. | .. | .. | .. |
| Birmingham Realty.................. | .. | .. | .. | .. | 35¼ | 35¼ |
| " " pref............ | .. | .. | .. | .. | 61 | 55¼ |
| Black Jack Gold Mining Co. (10c par). | .. | .. | 1c | 1c | .. | .. |
| Blanchard, Isaac H., Co., pref........ | .. | .. | 10 | 10 | .. | .. |
| Bliss, E. W., Co..................... | .. | .. | 143½ | 130 | 145¼ | 139 |
| Blooming Grove Park Association..... | 50 | 50 | 37 | 30 | .. | .. |
| Blue Jacket Cons. Copper Co. (par $10). | .. | .. | .. | .. | 5c | 5c |
| Bon Ami Co..... .......... ...... | .. | .. | 176 | 176 | .. | .. |
| Bonanza Dev. Co., Col .............. | 4¼ | 4¼ | .. | .. | .. | .. |
| Bonne Terre Farm. & Cat. Co. (par $10). | .. | .. | .. | .. | 2 | 2 |
| Booklovers' Library.................. | .. | .. | 99⅞ | 99⅞ | .. | .. |
| Bordens' Condensed Milk Co., pref.... | .. | .. | .. | .. | 113¾ | 108 |
| Boston & New York Air Line........ | .. | .. | 5⅜ | 5⅜ | .. | .. |
| " " " pref.... | .. | .. | 109¼ | 109¼ | .. | .. |
| Boston, Hartford & Erie Railroad Co.. | .. | .. | .. | .. | 16½c | 16½c |
| Brearley School, Limited............ | 90 | 80 | .. | .. | .. | .. |
| Bridgeton & Saco River R. R. Co..... | 20 1-5 | 20 1-5 | .. | .. | .. | .. |
| British American Development Co.... | .. | .. | 75 | 75 | .. | .. |
| British Columbia Copper Co......... | .. | .. | .. | .. | 10½ | 5 |
| British Columbia Smelt. & Refin. Co. | .. | .. | 50 | 50 | .. | .. |
| Brooklyn Academy of Music.......... | 113 | 110 | 126 | 107½ | 130 | 119 |
| Brooklyn Athæneum................. | .. | .. | 4 | 4 | .. | .. |
| Brooklyn District Telegraph.......... | .. | .. | 3½ | 3½ | .. | .. |
| Brooklyn Dock & Terminal Co........ | 30 | 30 | .. | .. | .. | . |
| Brooklyn Ferry Co. of New York..... | 30 | 15 | 30 | 15 | 20 | 12 |
| Brooklyn Jockey Co................. | .. | .. | .. | .. | 158 | 158 |
| Brooklyn Real Estate Exchange, Ltd.. | .. | .. | 80 | 80 | .. | .. |
| Brooklyn Hills Pump Co.... ... | .. | .. | 50 | 50 | .. | .. |
| Brooklyn Warehouse & Storage Co... | 120 | 120 | 120 | 115 | 112 | 110⅛ |

| | 1900. | | 1901. | | 1902. | |
|---|---|---|---|---|---|---|
| | Highest. | Lowest. | Highest. | Lowest. | Highest. | Lowest. |
| Brooklyn Wharf Transportation Co... | .. | .. | 10 | 10 | .. | .. |
| Brooklyn Wharf & Warehouse, pref. B | .. | .. | $2 | 13c | .. | .. |
| Buffalo City Gas Co................. | 15 | 3 | 12⅝ | 5 | 15 | 5 |
| " " pref.............. | .. | .. | .. | .. | 29½ | 22 |
| Butchers' Hide & Melting Ass'n (hyp.) | 84 | 80 | .. | .. | .. | .. |
| Campbell, A. S., Art Co............ | .. | .. | .. | .. | 31¼c | 31¼c |
| Canterbury Mining Co. of Leadville, Col. (par 10 cts., 700,000 shares).... | .. | .. | .. | .. | $19 lot | |
| Cayuga & Susquehanna R. R. Co..... | 206¼ | 206¼ | 213 | 213 | .. | .. |
| Celluloid Co........................ | 100 | 80 | 103 | 95 | 121 | 107 |
| Central & South American Tel........ | 112½ | 96 | .. | .. | 110 | 78 |
| Central Arizona Mining Co. (par $10, 100 shares)........................ | .. | .. | .. | .. | $2 lot | |
| Central Fireworks Co................ | 15⅞ | 11⅛ | .. | .. | .. | .. |
| " " " pref........... | 50 | 50 | .. | .. | .. | .. |
| Central Foundry Co.................. | 4 | 1 | 2⅛ | ¾ | 4¾ | ½ |
| " " pref............ | 15 | 8 | 10¾ | 5 | 28 | 5 |
| Central Mining Co................... | $2.70 | $2.70 | $2.50 | $2.50 | .. | .. |
| Central National Bank, Norwalk, Conn. | 101 | 101 | .. | .. | .. | .. |
| Central New England Railway, pref.. | .. | .. | 21 | 21 | .. | .. |
| Central New Jersey Land Imp. Co.... | 4⅛ | 1¾ | .. | .. | 1 | 1 |
| Century Realty Co................... | .. | .. | 101 | 100 | 112 | 100 |
| helsea Realty....................... | .. | .. | .. | .. | 110 | 100 |
| Chesapeake & Potomac Telephone Co. | .. | .. | .. | .. | 72 | 40 |
| Chesebrough Co., Consolidated....... | 346¼ | 346¼ | .. | .. | 456 | 455 |
| Chicago Edison Co.................. | .. | .. | . | .. | 130 | 130 |
| Chicago H'gts Land Assn (480 shares) | .. | .. | $80 | $80 | .. | .. |
| Chicago, Peoria & St. Louis, pref.... | 5¼ | 2½ | .. | .. | 15 | 8 |
| Cincinnati, Sand. & Cleve. R. R., pref. | 128 | 128 | .. | .. | .. | .. |
| Cincinnati Street Railway........... | .. | .. | 138⅞ | 138⅞ | .. | .. |
| Citizens' Nat. Bank, Elizabeth, N. J... | 102½ | 102½ | .. | .. | .. | .. |
| Citizens' National Bank of Yonkers.... | 206 | 206 | 230 | 230 | .. | .. |
| City Bank of New Haven, Ct.......... | .. | .. | .. | .. | 153 | 153 |
| Cleveland Electric Railway........... | .. | .. | 29 1-9 | 29 1-9 | .. | .. |
| Clinton Hall Association............ | 65¼ | 51 | 55¼ | 50 | 56½ | 56⅛ |
| Coale Muffler Safety Valve Co........ | .. | .. | 60¼c | 60¼c | .. | .. |
| Collap. Tube & Metal Co............ | .. | .. | .. | .. | 50c | 50c |
| Colonial Real Estate Association...... | 101 | 101 | .. | .. | .. | .. |
| Col. Coal, Iron & Dev. Co........... | .. | . | .. | .. | 87½c | 16c |
| Columbus & Xenia R. R., guar....... | 221½ | 221½ | .. | .. | 217 | 217 |
| Columbus Gas, L. & Heat. Co........ | 60 | 40 | 96 | 43½ | 108½ | 93½ |
| " " " pref.... | 88 | 70 | 106 | 76 | 110 | 100½ |
| Columbus (O.) Edison Co............ | .. | .. | .. | .. | 66 | 38 |
| " " " pref......... | .. | .. | .. | .. | 112½ | 90 |
| Columbus Railway Co................ | 39½ | 20 | 49 | 36½ | 65 | 46½ |
| " " pref........... | 94 | 80 | 104½ | 92 | 107½ | 100 |
| Commercial Union Telegraph........ | .. | .. | .. | .. | 113 | 113 |
| Compania Metalurgica Mexicana, pref. | 101¼ | 101¼ | .. | .. | .. | .. |
| Composite Type Bar Co.......... ... | 12½ | 12½ | .. | .. | .. | .. |
| Compressed Air..................... | 50 | 18 | 44 | 7½ | 11 | 1¼ |
| Comstock Tun'l Co.(par $2) 1,000 shr's. | .. | .. | .. | .. | $52 lot | |
| Cons. Ry. Elect. Light & Refr. Co.... | .. | .. | .. | .. | 8¼ | 4½ |
| Consolidated Fireworks.......... .. | 9 | 9 | .. | .. | .. | .. |
| Consolidated Gas Co. of Newark, N. J. | 55 | 46 | 56 | 44 | .. | .. |
| Consolidated Gas Co. of N. J........ | 20 | 10 | 14¼ | 9¼ | .. | .. |
| " " " deb. 5s. | 90 | 80 | .. | .. | .. | .. |
| Cons. Ry., Electric Light & Equipment | 18 | 5⅝ | .. | .. | .. | .. |
| Cons. Roll. Stock Co., Bridgeport, Ct. | 24⅜ | 24⅜ | .. | .. | .. | .. |
| Consolidated Rubber Tire Co......... | 10 | 2½ | .. | .. | 5 | 1¼ |
| " " " pref..... | 50 | 23 | 22 | 21½ | 18 | 8 |
| Consolidated Traction Co. of N. J.... | 63 | 56 | 69 | 58 | 71 | 65 |
| Con. Zinc & Lead Mfg & Smelt. Co.. | .. | .. | .. | .. | 20 | 15 |
| Consumers' Gas Co., Newburgh...... | 94 | 94 | .. | .. | .. | .. |
| Consumers' of Jersey City 6s......... | 104 | 104 | .. | .. | .. | .. |
| Cook & Bernheimer Co............... | .. | .. | . | . | 87 | 86 |

| | 1900. | | 1901. | | 1902. | |
|---|---|---|---|---|---|---|
| | Highest. | Lowest. | Highest. | Lowest. | Highest. | Lowest. |
| Cook & Bernheimer Co., pref........ | .. | .. | .. | .. | 87 | 86 |
| Coney Island Jockey Club............ | .. | .. | .. | .. | 175½ | 175½ |
| Copper King Mining Co. of Arizona.. | .. | .. | 5½c | 5½c | .. | .. |
| Cornish Sil. Min. Co. of Can. (350 shares) | .. | .. | .. | .. | $3 lot | |
| Corporation Liquid'n Co. 7 p. c. pref.. | .. | .. | 107½ | 107½ | 107½ | 107½ |
| Cramp, Wm., & Sons' S. & E. Bldg. Co. | 85 | 65 | 85 | 70 | 80 | 60 |
| Cranford Co.......................... | .. | .. | .. | .. | 53 | 53 |
| Crocker-Wheeler Co................. | 98 | 98 | .. | .. | .. | .. |
| Cross, Austin & Ireland Lumber Co... | .. | .. | 42 | 42 | .. | .. |
| Cuba Quarry Co..................... | .. | .. | .. | .. | 1¾ | 1¾ |
| Dan Talmage's Sons, pref....... .... | 100 | 100 | 95 | 95 | .. | .. |
| Detroit & Mackinac, new common.... | .. | .. | .. | .. | 40 | 30 |
| " " " pref........ | .. | .. | .. | .. | 83 | 70 |
| Declat Manufacturing Co............ | .. | .. | 5 | 5 | .. | .. |
| Dennett's Surpassing Coffee Co....... | 18 | 18 | 11 | 11 | .. | .. |
| Denver Gas & Electric Co........... | 45 | 15 | .. | .. | 25 | 5 |
| Denver Union Water Co............. | 7 | 1 | .. | .. | 40 | 9½ |
| " " " pref......... | 15 | 3 | .. | .. | 50 | 25 |
| Detroit, Hills. & S. W.............. | 116¾ | 107⅝ | .. | .. | 108¾ | 108¾ |
| Dobbs Ferry Bank.................. | 130 | 130 | .. | .. | .. | .. |
| Dodd & Childs Ex. Co. (88 shares)... | .. | .. | $10 | $10 | .. | .. |
| Doe Run Lead Co.................. | .. | .. | 126 | 125 | 115 | 115 |
| Donahoe's Magazine Co............. | .. | .. | .. | .. | 1½ | 1½ |
| Dominion Securities................ | .. | .. | 90 | 55 | 120 | 13 |
| Driggs Seabury Gun & Ammunition.. | .. | .. | 2 | 2 | .. | .. |
| Eagle Tile Co...................... | .. | .. | .. | .. | 1-15 | 1-15 |
| East River Mill & Lumber Co........ | .. | .. | .. | .. | 25 | 25 |
| Economy Sewing Machine Co........ | .. | .. | .. | .. | 5 | 5 |
| Edison Elect. Ill. of Boston......... | .. | .. | .. | .. | 260 | 260 |
| Edison, Jr., Elec. Lt. & Pr. Co. (par $10) | .. | . | . | .. | 75c | 75c |
| Electrical Develop. Co. (1,000 shares).. | .. | .. | $50 lot | | .. | .. |
| Electric Boat Co.................... | 34 | 10 | 28½ | 10 | 39 | 15 |
| " " pref................. | 54 | 20 | 52½ | 20 | 50 | 35 |
| Electric Corporation (325 shares)...... | .. | .. | .. | .. | $50 lot | |
| Electric Enameling Co.............. | .. | .. | 1 | 1 | .. | .. |
| Electric Vehicle Co................. | 70 | 14½ | 25 | 1½ | 7½ | 2 |
| " " pref ............. | 90 | 33 | 45 | 3½ | 15⅛ | 4 |
| Electro Gas......................... | 205 | 130 | 190 | 140 | 160½ | 110 |
| Electro Pneumatic Transit Co........ | 4⅛ | 1⅛ | .. | .. | 2⅜ | ⅝ |
| Elizabeth Telephone Co............. | 51 | 51 | .. | .. | .. | .. |
| Empire & Bay States Tel. Co......... | .. | .. | .. | .. | 80 | 80 |
| Empire Consol. Quicksilver & Mining Co., par $10 each............... | .. | .. | .. | .. | 3 | 2½ |
| Empire State Idaho Mining Developing Co., par $10................. | .. | .. | .. | .. | 6¼ | 6¼ |
| Empire Steel Co.................... | 10 | 2½ | .. | .. | 15 | 8 |
| " " pref................. | 70 | 31 | .. | .. | 54 | 40 |
| Empire State Surety Co............. | .. | .. | 200 | 200 | .. | .. |
| Ensley Land Co..................... | 8¼ | 8¼ | .. | .. | .. | .. |
| Equitable Gas Co. of Memphis....... | 10 | 10 | .. | .. | .. | .. |
| Erie Gas Co., Pa., par $50 (149 shares). | .. | .. | .. | .. | $100 lot | |
| Erie & Kalamazoo R. R ............. | 256⅞ | 256⅞ | .. | .. | .. | .. |
| Erie Telephone Co.................. | .. | .. | .. | .. | 2 | 2 |
| Essex & Hudson Gas Co............. | 35 | 35 | .. | .. | 35½ | 26 |
| Evergreen Cemetery Co.............. | .. | .. | .. | .. | 100 | 100 |
| Fair Haven & Westville R. R. Co. of New Haven, Conn............... | 39¾ | 39¾ | .. | .. | .. | .. |
| Farmers' Feed Co. of New Jersey, com. pref., 129 shares of each...... | .. | .. | .. | .. | $500 lot | |
| " Sugar Co.................... | .. | .. | .. | .. | 45 | 35 |
| " " pref............... | .. | .. | .. | .. | 95 | 85 |
| First National Bank, Bridgeport, Conn | .. | .. | 196 | 196 | .. | .. |
| First National Bank, Elizabeth, N. J.. | 162 | 162 | .. | .. | .. | .. |
| First National Bank of Staten Island.. | .. | .. | .. | .. | 177 | 177 |
| First National Bank, Sing Sing, N. Y.. | 111 | 111 | .. | .. | .. | .. |

| | 1900. | | 1901. | | 1902. | |
|---|---|---|---|---|---|---|
| | Highest. | Lowest. | Highest. | Lowest. | Highest. | Lowest. |
| Fitchburg Railroad, pref. | .. | .. | 143½ | 143½ | .. | .. |
| Fleming Coal & Coke Co. (100 shares). | .. | .. | .. | .. | $51 lot | |
| Forest Hotel Co. | 91 | 90 | .. | .. | .. | .. |
| Fort Wayne & Jackson, pref. | .. | .. | .. | .. | 152½ | 152½ |
| Foster Bros. & Chatillon Co. | .. | .. | .. | .. | 100⅛ | 100⅛ |
| Franco-American Chemical Works of Woodridge, N. J. | .. | .. | .. | .. | 10c | 10c |
| Franklin National Bank, hypothecated. | .. | .. | .. | .. | 10 | 10 |
| Fuller, George A. Contruction Co. | .. | .. | 45 | 45 | 29¼ | 29¼ |
| " " " pref. | .. | .. | .. | . | 101 | 92 |
| Garmo, W. A., Co. (par $10) | .. | .. | .. | .. | $1 | $1 |
| Gas Engine Pr. Co. & Charles L. Seabury, con. | .. | .. | 4⅞ | ⅜ | .. | .. |
| Gauley Assn, pref. (10 shs.) $1,000 each | .. | .. | $8,150 lot | | .. | .. |
| General Carriage Co. | 20 | 3¼ | .. | .. | 3⅛ | 3⅛ |
| General Chemical Co., pref. | .. | .. | 103⅛ | 103⅛ | .. | .. |
| Glenwood & Polytechnic St. Ry. Co. | .. | .. | 94⅙ | 94⅙ | .. | .. |
| Globe Buffer Co. | 25 | 25 | .. | .. | .. | .. |
| Gold and Stock Telegraph Co. | 120⅛ | 117¼ | 121¼ | 118 | 122 | 117 |
| Goodwin Car Co. | .. | .. | 9 | 9 | .. | .. |
| Gramercy Sugar Co. | 21¼ | 18⅝ | .. | .. | .. | .. |
| Grand Rapids & Indiana | 33 | 20 | .. | .. | 50 | 30 |
| Grand Rapids Gas Co. | 108 | 95 | .. | .. | .. | .. |
| Grand Rapids Street Ry. | 26 | 24 | .. | .. | 57½ | 31 |
| " " pref. | 78 | 72½ | .. | .. | 98 | 87 |
| Gray National Telautograph Co. | .. | .. | 40 | 22 | .. | .. |
| Great Eastern Casualty and Indem. Co. | .. | .. | 100 | 95 | .. | .. |
| Greene Consolidated Copper Co. | .. | .. | .. | .. | 32¼ | 19 |
| Guarantee Co. of North America | .. | .. | .. | .. | 80 | 80 |
| Haaker, William, Co. | .. | .. | 5 | 5 | .. | .. |
| Hackensack Meadows | .. | .. | 50 | 36 | 79 | 12½c |
| Hackensack Trust Co. | .. | .. | 170½ | 170½ | .. | .. |
| Hall Signal | .. | .. | .. | .. | 51 | 51 |
| Hampshire Paper Co. | .. | .. | .. | .. | 110 | 110 |
| Haug, A., Co. | .. | .. | 2 | 2 | .. | .. |
| " " pref. | .. | .. | 75 | 75 | .. | .. |
| Havana-American Co. | .. | .. | 26 | 26 | 53 | 41½ |
| " " " pref. | 88 | 88 | .. | .. | 70 | 65 |
| Havana Commercial Co. | 20½ | 6 | 14¾ | 6 | .. | .. |
| " " pref. | 60¼ | 30 | 58¼ | 43½ | .. | .. |
| Havana Electric Ry. Co., pref. | 15 | 15 | .. | .. | .. | .. |
| Herring-Hall-Marvin Co., new | .. | .. | 41¼ | 41¼ | 1 1-16 | 1 1-6 |
| " " 1st pref., new. | 13⅝ | 12⅛ | 38½ | 38½ | 25¼ | 25¼ |
| Holland Building Association | .. | .. | .. | .. | 25 | 25 |
| Holmes Electric Protective Co. | 110¼ | 110¼ | .. | .. | .. | .. |
| Home Silver Mining Co. | $1.50 | $1.50 | .. | .. | .. | .. |
| Houston Oil Co. | . | .. | .. | .. | 23¾ | 8 |
| " " pref. | .. | .. | .. | .. | 81½ | 65 |
| Howard & Co. | 110 | 110 | .. | .. | .. | .. |
| Hudson County Gas Co. | .. | .. | .. | .. | 43 | 27 |
| Hudson River Brick Mfg. Co. of Verplanck's Point | .. | .. | .. | .. | 30c | 30c |
| Hudson River Telephone Co. | .. | .. | 104½ | 104½ | .. | .. |
| Illinois Electric Vehicle Trans. Co. | 3 | ¾ | 1¼ | ½ | .. | .. |
| Il Progresso Italo-Americano News Co. | 1 | 1 | .. | .. | .. | .. |
| Imperial Trust Co. of Canada | 25 | 25 | .. | .. | .. | .. |
| Improved Dwellings Association | 95 | 95 | .. | .. | .. | .. |
| Indianapolis Gas Co. | 100 | 50 | .. | .. | 80 | 45 |
| Indianapolis Passenger Ry., new | 30 | 20 | .. | .. | .. | .. |
| Industrial Federation of America | .. | .. | .. | .. | 15 | 15 |
| Industrial Tr. Co. of Providence, R. I. | .. | .. | .. | .. | 288 | 280 |
| Interb. Rapid Transit, 40 p. c. paid | .. | .. | .. | .. | 125 | 101 |
| International Express Co. | 8½ | 8 | .. | .. | .. | .. |
| International Fire Engine Co., pref. | .. | .. | .. | .. | 40 | 40 |
| International Hydraulic Co. | 25½ | 25½ | .. | .. | .. | .. |

| | 1900. | | 1901. | | 1902. | |
|---|---|---|---|---|---|---|
| | Highest. | Lowest. | Highest. | Lowest. | Highest. | Lowest. |
| International Mercantile Marine...... | .. | .. | .. | .. | 21 | 10 |
| " " " pref. | .. | .. | .. | .. | 50 | 46 |
| International Ocean Tel. Co.......... | 117⅛ | 117½ | 330 | 330 | .. | .. |
| International Traction of Buffalo..... | .. | .. | 20 | 20 | 35 | 22½ |
| " " " pref. | .. | .. | 50 | 40 | 70 | 50 |
| International Zinc Co................ | 60 | 60 | .. | .. | .. | .. |
| Interstate Oil Co.................... | .. | .. | 4⅜ | 1 | .. | .. |
| Iron Steamboat Co.................... | 4 | 1 | 4 | 1½ | 60c | 60c |
| Issaquah Coal Co., Seattle, Wash..... | .. | .. | 23 | 22⅝ | .. | .. |
| Jackson, Lansing & Saginaw R. R.... | .. | .. | 95 | 95 | 94⅝ | 94⅝ |
| Jamestown & Newp't Steam Ferry Co. | .. | .. | 101 | 101 | .. | .. |
| Jekyl Island Club ($600).............. | .. | .. | $1,000 | $1,000 | $1,000 | $600 |
| Jer. City, Hob. & Paterson St. Ry. Co. | 21½ | 14 | .. | .. | 26 | 16½ |
| Jewelers' Circular Publishing Co...... | .. | .. | 40 | 40 | .. | .. |
| Joliet & Chicago R. R. Co............ | 191 | 191 | .. | .. | .. | .. |
| Journeay & Burnham.............. | 5 | 2½ | .. | .. | .. | .. |
| " " pref......... | 30 | 25 | .. | .. | .. | .. |
| Kan. City, St. L. & Chi. R.R., pref., gu. | 151½ | 151½ | .. | .. | .. | .. |
| Kings County E. L. & P. Co.......... | 118 | 105 | .. | .. | 215 | 185 |
| Knickerbocker Steamship Co......... | .. | .. | 68c | 68c | $1.44 | $1.44 |
| Krystaleid Water Co. (1,632 shares)... | .. | .. | .. | .. | $250 lot | |
| Lackawanna Iron & Coal Co. of Penn. | .. | .. | 101 | 90¾ | 90 | 90 |
| Lackawanna Iron & Steel Co......... | 101 | 85 | 105 | 100 | 108 | 95 |
| Lackawanna Store Association........ | 41⅛ | 41⅛ | 25 | 4 | .. | .. |
| Ladue, Joseph, Gold Min. & Dev., pref., $10...................... | $1.66 | $1.25 | $1.50 | $1.50 | $1.55 | $1.00 |
| Lady Helen Copper Mining Co........ | 5⅞c | 5c | .. | .. | .. | .. |
| Laflin & Rand Powder Co........... | .. | .. | .. | .. | 236 | 236 |
| Lanston Monotype Mach. Co., par $20. | 15½ | 11½ | 14½ | 11 | .. | .. |
| Lanyon Zinc Co., pref............. .. | .. | .. | 11 | 11 | .. | .. |
| Lawyers' Incorporation Co........... | .. | .. | 60 | 55⅜ | .. | .. |
| Lehigh & New York R.R., pref....... | .. | .. | 30¼ | 30¼ | .. | .. |
| Liberty Silk Co., pref... ............ | 85 | 85 | .. | .. | .. | .. |
| Little Pittsburg Consol. Mining Co... | .. | .. | .. | .. | 4c | 4c |
| Little Schuylkill R.R. Nav. & Coal Co. | .. | .. | .. | .. | 115 | 115 |
| London & New York Invest. Corp., Ltd | .. | .. | 11¼ | 11¼ | .. | .. |
| Long Branch Pier Co............... | .. | .. | $2 | 24c | .. | .. |
| Lorillard, P., Co., pref............... | .. | .. | .. | .. | 126½ | 126½ |
| Louisville Street R.R............... | .. | .. | .. | .. | 107 | 107 |
| " " " pref............ | .. | .. | .. | .. | 122 | 114½ |
| Louisville, Henderson & St. Louis..... | 1⅞ | 1⅞ | .. | .. | 8 | 5 |
| " " " pref | 19⅛ | 16¼ | 21⅝ | 21⅝ | 27 | 20 |
| Lykens Valley Railroad and Coal Co.. | .. | .. | 81 | 16 | 80 | 80 |
| Madison Gas and Electric Co......... | 77½ | 60 | .. | .. | .. | .. |
| Madison Square Garden Co.......... | 7½ | 4 | .. | .. | 15 | 9½ |
| Mahoning Coal R.R. Co............. | .. | .. | 211½ | 211½ | .. | .. |
| " " pref.......... | 175 | 120 | .. | .. | 107¼ | 107¼ |
| Maine Steamship Co................ | .. | .. | .. | .. | 31 | 20 |
| Manhanset Improvement Co.......... | .. | .. | 51 | 51 | .. | .. |
| Manhattan Real Estate Association.... | 101 | 101 | .. | .. | .. | .. |
| Manhattan Telegraph Co............ | 115 | 115 | .. | .. | .. | .. |
| Manhattan Transit, par $20.......... | .. | .. | .. | .. | 9½ | 4 |
| Markeen Copper Co................. | .. | .. | 2⅝ | ¾ | .. | .. |
| Mason, Au & Magenheimer Confectionery & Manufacturing Co...... | 100 | 100 | .. | .. | .. | .. |
| Massachusetts Lighting............... | .. | .. | .. | .. | 42 | 25 |
| " " pref......... | .. | .. | .. | .. | 90 | 82 |
| Meadville Distilling Co., Ltd......... | .. | .. | .. | .. | 75 | 75 |
| Mechanics Bank of New Haven, Conn., par $60......................... | .. | .. | .. | .. | $78 | $78 |
| Mechanical Rubber Co., pref.......... | 97 | 97 | .. | .. | .. | .. |
| Mediterranean & N. Y. SS. Co., Ltd.. | .. | .. | .. | .. | 14 | 14 |
| Menantic Steamship Co., par £125.... | .. | .. | 751 | 646 | .. | .. |
| Merchants' Ins. Co., Newark, N. J.... | .. | .. | .. | .. | 145¼ | 140 |
| Merchants' Refrigerating Co.......... | 93⅜ | 93⅜ | .. | .. | .. | .. |

| | 1900. | | 1901. | | 1902. | |
|---|---|---|---|---|---|---|
| | Highest. | Lowest. | Highest. | Lowest. | Highest. | Lowest. |
| Merriam Realty Co. | .. | .. | .. | .. | 33⅓ | 33⅓ |
| Merritt & Chapman Derr. Wreck. Co. | 135½ | 135½ | .. | .. | 145 | 145 |
| Metropolitan Nat. Bank, 68 per cent. paid in liq. (37 shares) | .. | .. | .. | .. | $55 lot | |
| Metropolitan Steamship Co. of Boston. | .. | .. | 325 | 325 | .. | .. |
| Mexican Nat. Construction Co., pref. | 18 | 7½ | .. | .. | 8⅛ | 6 |
| Mexican Northern R.R. | 56 | 56 | .. | .. | .. | .. |
| Mexican Telegraph Co. | 220 | 195 | .. | .. | 220 | 200 |
| Mexican Trust Co. | .. | .. | .. | .. | 116 | 100 |
| Michigan Telephone Co. | .. | .. | 30 | 30 | .. | .. |
| Middlesex Bank Co., Middletown, Ct. | .. | .. | .. | .. | 21 | 21 |
| Mill Creek & Mine Hill Nav. Ry. Co. | 50 | 50 | .. | .. | .. | .. |
| Minneapolis Trust Co. | .. | .. | 100 | 100 | .. | .. |
| Mission Rock Co. of California | .. | .. | .. | .. | 49½ | 49½ |
| Momand Light Co. | .. | .. | 1 | 1 | .. | .. |
| Mondamin Block Co., Sioux City, Ia. | .. | .. | .. | .. | 60 | 54 |
| Montclair & Bloomfield Telephone Co., par $10 (3,831 shares) | .. | .. | .. | .. | $175 lot | |
| Montreal & Boston Copper Co. | .. | .. | .. | .. | 4½ | 2⅛ |
| Mountain Spring Water Co. of Hillburn, N. Y. | 100½ | 100½ | .. | .. | .. | .. |
| Mt. Hope Cemetery Assn. | .. | .. | 11½ | 11½ | 1 1-5 | 1 1-5 |
| Music Hall Co. of New York | .. | .. | .. | .. | 6 | 6 |
| Mutual Trust Co. of Westchester Co. | .. | .. | .. | .. | 213 | 213 |
| Mutual Union Telegraph Co. | .. | .. | 109 | 109 | .. | .. |
| Napa Quicksilver Co. | .. | .. | 3¼ | 3¼ | .. | .. |
| Nassau Brewing Association | .. | .. | 107 | 107 | .. | .. |
| Nassau Ferry Co. | .. | .. | 200 | 200 | .. | .. |
| National Academy of Design, Fellowship in Perpetuity | .. | .. | .. | .. | 160 | 160 |
| National Asphalt | 11 | 5 | 8 | 1½ | .. | .. |
| National Bank of Cuba | .. | .. | 118 | 118 | .. | .. |
| " " " pref. | 22½ | 10 | 14½ | 2 | .. | .. |
| National Bank of Petersburgh, Va. | .. | .. | .. | .. | 175 | 175 |
| National Blank Book Co. | .. | .. | .. | .. | 162½ | 162½ |
| National Enameling & Stp. Co | 20 | 15 | 35 | 15 | 40½ | 27 |
| " " " pref. | 80 | 70 | 85 | 79½ | 93 | 82 |
| National Exhibition Co. | .. | .. | 5 3-10 | 5 3-10 | .. | .. |
| National Gramophone Co. | 65 | 15 | .. | .. | .. | .. |
| National Machine Co. | .. | .. | .. | .. | 190 | 190 |
| Natural Gas Trust | .. | .. | .. | .. | 305 | 305 |
| New Amsterdam Gas Co. | 47½ | 47½ | .. | .. | .. | .. |
| " " pref. | 47½ | 47½ | .. | .. | .. | .. |
| " " 1st 5s, 1948 | 109⅛ | 107⅞ | .. | .. | .. | .. |
| New England Gas & Coke Co. | 25 | 10 | 13 | 4½ | 5 | 5¼ |
| New Eng. Elec. Vehicle Transportation. | 22½ | 2½ | 3⅛ | ⅜ | 3¼ | 3¼ |
| N. E. Piano Co., Boston, class A, pref. | .. | .. | .. | .. | $5 | $5 |
| New Jersey Steamboat Co. | .. | .. | 38½ | 35 | 40 | 36¼ |
| New Jersey Zinc | 125 | 125 | 245⅛ | 230¼ | .. | .. |
| New Orleans City R. R. | 31 | 17 | .. | .. | 18½ | 11 |
| " " pref. | 108 | 90 | .. | .. | 57 | 45 |
| New Orleans Light Co. | .. | .. | .. | .. | 50 | 50 |
| Newport Casino | .. | .. | 321 | 321 | .. | .. |
| Newport Trust Co. | .. | .. | .. | .. | 350 | 295 |
| New Rochelle & Westchester Tel. Co. (5,998 shares.) | .. | .. | .. | .. | $55 lot | |
| New York & East River 1st 5s | .. | .. | 117¼ | 115¼ | .. | .. |
| " " con. 5s. 1949. | 114 | 106 | .. | .. | .. | .. |
| New York & East River Ferry Co. | 72 | 65 | 71 | 66 | 82 | 70 |
| New York & Hoboken Ferry Co. | 85 | 64 | 83½ | 79 | 100 | 68½ |
| N. Y. & Honduras Rosario Mining Co. | 8¼ | 8¼ | .. | .. | .. | . |
| New York & Java Trading Co. | .. | .. | 50 | 50 | . | .. |
| New York & New Jersey Telephone | 185 | 160 | 180¼ | 160 | 185 | 157 |
| New York & Penn. Telephone Co. | 116 | 110 | 89 | 88 | 80 | 40 |
| New York & Queens Co. E. L. & P. | .. | .. | 75 | 65 | 45 | 28 |

| | 1900. | | 1901 | | 1902. | |
|---|---|---|---|---|---|---|
| | Highest. | Lowest. | Highest. | Lowest. | Highest. | Lowest. |
| N. Y. & Queens Co. E. L. & P., pref. | .. | .. | 40 | 22 | 80 | 70 |
| New York & Rock. Beach R. R. Co... | .. | .. | 3½ | 3⅛ | .. | .. |
| New York & Texas Land Co..... ... | 40⅜ | 40⅜ | 43 | 43 | 81 | 81 |
| N. Y. & Texas Land Syndicate, No. 1. | 7¼ | 7¼ | .. | .. | .. | .. |
| " " " No. 2. | 80c | 80c | .. | | | |
| New York Butchers' Calf Skin Assn... | .. | .. | 41 | 41 | .. | .. |
| New York Cab Co............ ...... | 20 | 20 | .. | .. | .. | .. |
| New York Coffee Exchange.......... | .. | .. | .. | .. | $1,400 | $1,400 |
| New York Elec. Veh. & Tr., $10 pd. in | 15 | 6 | 12¾ | 7 | .. | .. |
| New York House Wrecking Co........ | .. | .. | .. | .. | 20 | 20 |
| N. Y. Ladies' Guide & Vis. B., par. $5. | .. | .. | .. | .. | 6c | 6c |
| New York Law Institute..... ........ | 150 | 145 | 147½ | 123 | 149 | 100 |
| New York Loan & Improvement Co.. | .. | .. | 79¼ | 79¼ | .. | .. |
| New York Mutual Gas................ | 112½ | 100 | . | .. | 336 | 331 |
| New York Mutual (Marine) Ins. Co. (136 p. c. paid in liquidation)....... | .. | | .. | .. | 50c | 50c |
| New York Mutual Telegraph Co..... | .. | .. | 100 | 100 | .. | .. |
| New York News Publishing Co....... | .. | .. | .. | .. | 1,050 | 1,050 |
| New York Produce Exchange......... | 265 | 68 | 180 | 70 | 425 | 151 |
| New York Real Estate Association.... | 101 | 101 | .. | .. | .. | .. |
| New York Realty Corp............... | .. | .. | .. | .. | 180¼ | 142¾ |
| New York Rubber Co................ | 120 | 110¼ | 130¼ | 130¼ | 151 | 151 |
| New York Society Library........... | .. | .. | 80 | 80 | 60 | 50 |
| N. Y. Sus. & West. Coal Co., pref... | .. | .. | .. | .. | $2.91 | $2.91 |
| Niagara Falls Power Co. ............ | 78 | 50 | .. | .. | 100 | 70 |
| Nicaragua Canal Construction Co.... | 6 | 1½ | 4 | 4 | .. | .. |
| Nicaragua Co. (17 shares)............ | .. | .. | .. | .. | $5 lot | |
| Niles-Bement Pond Co., com......... | .. | .. | .. | .. | 120 | 120 |
| Nipper Consolidated Copper Co...... | .. | .. | 65 | 65 | .. | .. |
| Norf. Bk. for Savs. & Trusts, Norfolk, Va. | .. | .. | .. | .. | 231 | 231 |
| Norfolk Natl. Bank, Norfolk, Va. .... | .. | .. | .. | .. | 275¼ | 275¼ |
| North American Lumber & Pulp Co.. | .. | .. | .. | .. | 9½ | 9½ |
| North American Rubber Co.......... | .. | .. | .. | .. | 75 | 75 |
| North Jersey Street Ry............. | 35 | 20 | 30 | 20 | 35½ | 26 |
| North Star Mines Co................ | $3.50 | $3.50 | .. | .. | .. | .. |
| Northern Securities Co.............. | .. | .. | 112 | 100¼ | 118½ | 98⅝ |
| Nor. & N. Brunswick Hos. Co. of N. J. | 37 | 37 | 31 | 31 | 20 | 20 |
| North Ward Natl. Bank, Newark, N. J. | .. | .. | .. | .. | 251 | 251 |
| Northern Improvement Co........... | .. | .. | .. | .. | $1 | $1 |
| Northern Pacific.................... | .. | .. | .. | .. | 126 | 126 |
| Nyack National Bank............... | .. | .. | 151½ | 151½ | .. | .. |
| Old Dominion Land Co............. | 101 | 101 | 95½ | 75 | 75 | 75 |
| Old Dominion S.S. Co.............. | 106 | 82 | 120 | 120 | .. | .. |
| Olympic Club of Bay Shore.......... | .. | .. | .. | .. | 20 | 20 |
| Omaha & St. Louis R. R. Co. (250 shares com. and pref.)............. | 6 | 6 | .. | .. | $3 lot | |
| Omaha Street Ry. Co................ | .. | .. | 73 | 60 | .. | .. |
| Omaha Water Co., 1st pref.......... | 35 | 25 | 35 | 26 | 35 | 28 |
| " " 2d pref.......... | 12 | 6 | 15 | 8 | 15 | 8 |
| Orange Athletic Club, Orange, N. J. (par $25)................ ...... | .. | .. | .. | .. | 50c | 50c |
| Orange Co. Trust & Safe Deposit Co., Middletown, N. Y.................. | .. | .. | 134½ | 134½ | .. | .. |
| Oswego & Syracuse Railroad......... | 223 | 215¼ | 230 | 230 | .. | .. |
| Otis Elevator Co.................... | 33 | 20 | 35 | 27½ | 40½ | 28 |
| " " pref............... | 93 | 85 | 97½ | 90 | 105 | 92 |
| Otis Ry. Co......................... | .. | .. | .. | .. | $3.20 | $3.20 |
| Ottman, J., Lithograph Co........... | .. | .. | .. | .. | 100 | 100 |
| Pacific Pack'g & Nav. Co............ | .. | .. | .. | .. | 20 | 3¼ |
| " " " pref...... | .. | .. | .. | .. | 52½ | 22½ |
| Passaic Print Works................ | .. | .. | 62 | 62 | .. | .. |
| Paterson & Passaic Gas Co.......... | 40 | 30 | .. | .. | 25 | 25 |
| Paterson Safe Deposit & Trust Co.... | 325½ | 325½ | .. | .. | .. | .. |
| Peacock Copper Co. (300 shares)...... | .. | .. | .. | .. | $15 lot | |
| Pearson Publishing Co............... | .. | .. | .. | .. | $2.08 | $2.08 |

| | 1900. | | 1901. | | 1902. | |
|---|---|---|---|---|---|---|
| | Highest. | Lowest. | Highest. | Lowest. | Highest. | Lowest. |
| Peck Bros. & Co. of New Haven, Conn. | .. | .. | .. | .. | 9 2-5 | 9 2-5 |
| Pennsylvania Furnace Co. | .. | .. | 32 | 32 | .. | .. |
| Penn. Knitting Mills, Reading, Pa. | 23 | 23 | .. | .. | .. | .. |
| People's Bank & Trust Co., Passaic, N.J. | .. | .. | 131 | 131 | .. | .. |
| Peoria & Bureau Valley R. R. Co. | 206⅛ | 206⅛ | .. | .. | .. | .. |
| Peru-La Salle Gas, Light & Power Co. | .. | .. | $1.75 | $1.10 | .. | .. |
| Peru Steel Ore Co., Ltd. | .. | .. | 11¾ | 11¾ | .. | .. |
| Phœnix Mining Co. | .. | .. | .. | .. | 2c | 2c |
| Phœnix Silk Mfg Co., of N. J., pref. | .. | .. | 50 | 50 | .. | .. |
| Pittsburg, Lisbon & West | .. | .. | 15 | 15 | .. | .. |
| Pittsburg, Bessemer & L. E., guar. | 31 | 18 | 37 | 28½ | 37½ | 33 |
| Pitts, Bessemer & L. E., pref. | .. | .. | .. | .. | 76 | 70 |
| Pittsburg, McKeesport & Yough., gtd. | .. | .. | 145 | 144 | 142¾ | 140 |
| Planters' Compress Co. | 23½ | 10 | .. | .. | 42 | 25 |
| " " pref. | .. | .. | .. | .. | 90 | 75 |
| Playa De Oro Mining Co. | .. | .. | 1⅛ | 1⅛ | 2¾ | 1 |
| Pneumatic Rolling Co. | .. | .. | 150 | 150 | .. | .. |
| Pocantico Water Works Co. | 1 7-20 | 1 7-20 | .. | .. | .. | .. |
| Port Jefferson Milling Co. | .. | .. | .. | .. | 45 | 45 |
| Portland Gas Co. | 13 | 13 | .. | .. | .. | .. |
| Pratt & Whitney Co. | 10 | 5 | .. | .. | .. | .. |
| " " pref. | 55 | 39 | 93½ | 70 | 95 | 89 |
| Premium Reserve Co. of West Va. | 10 | 6 | .. | .. | .. | .. |
| Primrose Colliery | .. | .. | .. | .. | 5 | 5 |
| Procter & Gamble Co., pref. | 202 | 202 | .. | .. | .. | .. |
| Projected Cannel Coal Mfg. Co. | .. | .. | 40c | 40c | .. | .. |
| Prospect Ice Co. of Shelter Island | .. | .. | 300 | 300 | .. | .. |
| Publishers' Plate Renting Co. | .. | .. | 2 | 2 | .. | .. |
| Railway Automatic Sales Co., pref. | .. | .. | .. | .. | 51 | 51 |
| Ry. Cab Elec. Signal Co. (100 shares). | .. | .. | .. | .. | $2 lot | |
| Randolph Coal & Coke Co. | .. | .. | .. | .. | .. | .. |
| Rapid Safety Filter Co. of New York. | .. | .. | 3¾ | 3¾ | .. | .. |
| Rapid Transit Subway Construction | .. | .. | 215 | 180 | .. | .. |
| Realty Associates (50 per cent. paid) | .. | .. | .. | .. | 117¾ | 116¾ |
| Red River Valley Co. | 47 | 41 | .. | .. | .. | .. |
| Richmond County Gas Light Co. | .. | .. | 117 | 115 | .. | .. |
| Richmond, Fredericksburg & Potomac R. R. Co., 6 per cent. guar. | 200 | 200 | .. | .. | .. | .. |
| Richmond, Fredericksburg & Potomac R. R. Co., 7 per cent. guar. | 200 | 199 | .. | .. | .. | .. |
| Richmond, Fredericksburg & Potomac R. R. Co. div. oblig. | 197 | 196 | .. | .. | .. | .. |
| Richmond & West Point Terminal Ry. & Warehouse Co. (200 shares) | .. | .. | .. | .. | $1 lot | |
| Ridgewood Land & Improvement Co. | .. | .. | 80 | 80 | .. | .. |
| Roane Iron Co. | .. | .. | .. | .. | 62 | 62 |
| Robys & Swart Mfg. Co. (1,398 shares) | .. | .. | .. | .. | $30,000 lot | |
| Rochester Railway, new | .. | .. | 42½ | 25 | 77½ | 42 |
| " " pre | .. | .. | 96 | 80 | 102 | 92 |
| Rock Island & Peoria R. R. Co. | 109¾ | 108 | .. | .. | .. | .. |
| Royal Baking Powder | .. | .. | 130 | 100 | 128 | 110 |
| " " " pref. | .. | .. | 106 | 93 | 106 | 100 |
| Runnymeade Ranch Co. | .. | .. | .. | .. | 35 | 35 |
| Royal Copper Co. | .. | .. | 4 | 4 | .. | .. |
| Royal Specialty Co. | .. | .. | 1 | 1 | .. | .. |
| Rumson Improvement Co. | 25 | 25 | .. | .. | .. | .. |
| Sackett-Wilhelms Litho. & Ptg. Co. | .. | .. | 102 | 102 | .. | .. |
| Safety Car Heating & Lighting Co. | 135 | 110 | 160 | 110 | 185 | 136 |
| Saginaw Steel Steamship Co. | 139 | 132 | .. | .. | .. | .. |
| St. Albans & Boone R. R. (deposited with trustee under pooling agreement) 12,500 shares | .. | .. | .. | .. | $6,450 lot | |
| St. Joseph Electric | .. | .. | .. | .. | 40 | 37 |
| St. Joseph Lead Co., $10 par | .. | .. | .. | .. | 17¾ | 17¾ |
| St. Joseph (Mo.) Gas Co. | 44 | 25 | .. | .. | .. | .. |

| | 1900. | | 1901. | | 1902. | |
|---|---|---|---|---|---|---|
| | Highest. | Lowest. | Highest. | Lowest. | Highest. | Lowest. |
| St. Lawrence Power Co., pref........ | 2 11-17 | 2 11-17 | .. | .. | .. | .. |
| St. Louis, Alton & Terre Haute Co... | .. | . | 68 | 68 | .. | .. |
| St. Louis Transit Co................ | 35 | 16½ | 31½ | 18 | 35 | 25 |
| St. Paul Gas Light Co.............. | 54 | 50 | .. | .. | .. | .. |
| Ste. Marg. Salmon Club, par $1,500.. | .. | .. | .. | .. | $550 | $550 |
| Sand Fork Ex. Oil Co., 1,200 shares.. | .. | .. | .. | .. | $50 lot | |
| San Francisco Dry Dock of California. | .. | .. | .. | .. | 49½ | 49½ |
| Saranac & Lake Placid R. R. Co..... | .. | .. | .. | .. | 49 | 10½ |
| Scoville Mfg. Co...... ............. | .. | .. | .. | .. | 150 | 150 |
| Sav. Inv. & Tr. Co. of E. Orange, N. J. | 75¼ | 75¼ | 80⅛ | 80⅛ | .. | .. |
| Scarsdale Water Co................. | .. | .. | 4 | 4 | .. | .. |
| Seaboard Air Line.................. | .. | .. | 33 | 12⅜ | 34⅞ | 23¼ |
| " " " pref................. | .. | .. | 55 | 28¾ | 55¼ | 39½ |
| Second National Bank of Hoboken, N. J. | .. | .. | 167 | 167 | .. | .. |
| Second Nat. Bank of New Haven.... | .. | .. | .. | .. | 200¼ | 200¼ |
| Securities Co. of New York.......... | 96 | 96 | .. | .. | .. | .. |
| Sheet Steel Co., pref................ | 76¾ | 68 | .. | .. | .. | .. |
| Shelter Island Heights Assn.......... | .. | .. | 61 | 60 | .. | .. |
| Shober-Cornell Pub. Co.............. | .. | .. | .. | .. | 71c | 71c |
| Singer Mfg. Co ..................... | .. | .. | 285½ | 235½ | 789 | 745 |
| Small Hopes Consolidated Mining Co. | .. | .. | 50c | 50c | .. | .. |
| Southern & Atlantic Telegraph Co.... | 100 | 100 | 102⅛ | 102⅝ | 95 | 95 |
| Southern Bank of the State of Georgia, Savannah, Ga...................... | .. | .. | .. | .. | 158 | 158 |
| Southern Cotton Oil Co.............. | 51 | 51 | .. | .. | .. | .. |
| So. New England Telegraph Co...... | .. | .. | .. | .. | 150⅛ | 150⅛ |
| Southern Light & Traction Co ....... | 35 | 26 | .. | .. | .. | .. |
| Spokane & East. Trust Co. of Spokane | 110½ | 110½ | .. | .. | .. | .. |
| Standard Milling Co................ | .. | .. | .. | .. | 10½ | 5 |
| " pref....................... | .. | .. | .. | .. | 30 | 20 |
| Standard Coupler Co................ | 50 | 35 | 28 | 28 | 40 | 27½ |
| " " " pref.......... | 122 | 114 | 115 | 115 | 135 | 125 |
| Standard Gas 1st 5s, 1930............ | 116 | 115¾ | .. | .. | .. | .. |
| Standard Oil Co.................... | 830 | 460 | 843 | 650 | 715 | 615 |
| Steel Tired Wheel Co................ | 45½ | 41 | 81 | 75 | 82¼ | 82¼ |
| " " " pref.......... | 86½ | 84¼ | 95 | 86½ | 82¼ | 82¼ |
| Sterne, L., & Co., Ltd., of London, par £10...................... ..... | .. | .. | .. | .. | $1 | $1 |
| Stetson, J. B., Co............. ..... | 105 | 95 | 152¼ | 116 | 175 | 135 |
| " " pref.............. | 125 | 115 | 140 | 115 | 145 | 120 |
| Syracuse, Binghamton & New York... | .. | .. | 191 | 185¼ | .. | .. |
| Syracuse Chilled Plow Co...... ..... | 100 | 100 | .. | .. | .. | .. |
| Syracuse Gas Co................ ... | 13 | 5 | .. | .. | .. | .. |
| Syracuse Rapid Transit Ry. Co....... | .. | .. | .. | .. | 34½ | 20 |
| " " " pref. | .. | .. | .. | .. | 77½ | 57 |
| Syracuse Lighting Co .............. | .. | .. | .. | .. | 35¼ | 12 |
| " " pref.......... | .. | .. | .. | .. | 90 | 75 |
| Taylor & Fox Realty Co...... ....... | 30 | 30 | .. | .. | .. | .. |
| Tefft-Weller Co..................... | .. | .. | .. | .. | 33¼ | 11 |
| " " pref ......... | .. | .. | .. | .. | 106½ | 90 |
| Tel., T. & Cab. Co. of Amer., $10 pd. | 10 | 2 | .. | .. | .. | .. |
| Tennessee Copper Co................ | 20¼ | 10 | 28⅞ | 9¼ | 18¼ | 10½ |
| Terminal Warehouse Co............. | 2⅛ | 2⅛ | .. | .. | .. | .. |
| Terre Haute and Indianapolis........ | 50 | 50 | .. | .. | 115 | 110 |
| Tex. & Ill. Oil & Fuel Co., 10,000 sh. | .. | .. | .. | .. | $40 lot | |
| Texas & Pacific Coal Co............. | 90 | 70 | 100 | 86 | 90 | 75 |
| Texas Land Co...................... | 10¾ | 10¾ | 10 | 10 | .. | .. |
| " " No. 2 .......... ..... | .. | .. | $2.70 | $2.70 | .. | .. |
| Thomas Iron Co. .................. | 52½ | 52½ | .. | .. | .. | .. |
| Tradesmans' Natl. Bank, 20 per cent. paid in liquidation............ ... | .. | .. | .. | .. | $3 | $1.30 |
| Travelers Ins. Co. Hartford, Conn.... | .. | .. | 395¼ | 395¼ | .. | .. |
| Toledo & Wabash Elevator Co....... | .. | .. | 21 | 21 | .. | .. |
| Trenton Potteries................... | 8 | 4 | 7 | 4 | 25 | 4¾ |
| " " pref............. | 62 | 42 | 75 | 53 | 117 | 80 |

| | 1900. | | 1901. | | 1902. | |
|---|---|---|---|---|---|---|
| | Highest. | Lowest. | Highest. | Lowest. | Highest. | Lowest. |
| Trow Directory, P. & B. Co.......... | 52½ | 45 | 56 | 50 | 75 | 60 |
| Union Coarse Salt Co................ | 12½ | 12½ | .. | .. | .. | .. |
| Union Copper Co.................... | 8 | 8 | .. | .. | 4⅝ | 2¼ |
| Union Debenture Co. ... ........... | 75 | 75 | .. | .. | .. | .. |
| Union Ferry Co................ ..... | 42½ | 29 | 49 | 30 | 48¾ | 40 |
| Union Gas & Elec. Co. of N. J., pref. | 98 98 | | .. | .. | .. | .. |
| Un. Gas L. Co. of B'klyn 6s, 1905.... | 112⅛ | 112⅛ | .. | .. | .. | .. |
| Union Insurance Co. of Philadelphia. | .. | .. | .. | .. | 100 | 100 |
| Union Pacific Tea Co....... ........ | .. | .. | .. | .. | 7 | 7 |
| Union Selling Co.................... | .. | .. | .. | .. | 116½ | 110¾ |
| Union Typewriter Co................ | 31 | 20 | 74 | 35 | 132 | 72 |
| " " 1st pref...... | 112 | 110 | 125 | 110 | 135 | 122 |
| " " 2d pref...... | 124 | 100 | 126 | 110 | 135 | 119 |
| United Copper Co.................... | .. | .. | .. | .. | 36½ | 28 |
| United National Bank, Troy, N. Y... | .. | .. | .. | .. | 301½ | 301½ |
| United Railways of St. Louis, pref.... | 90 | 60 | 91 | 68 | 89 | 79 |
| United Shoe Machinery Co........... | 34 | 28 | 48½ | 21 | 58 | 46 |
| " " pref... | 27 | 22 | 30 | 22 | 32 | 47½ |
| U. S. Butter Extractor Co............ | .. | .. | .. | .. | 31 | 31 |
| U. S. Cast Iron Pipe & Foundry Co... | 9 | 3½ | 11 | 4½ | .. | .. |
| " " " " pref. | 55 | 25½ | 40½ | 26 | .. | .. |
| U. S. Fidelity & Guaranty Co. of Baltimore (12½ shares)...... ...... | ... | .. | .. | .. | 150 | 150 |
| United States Petroleum Co.......... | .. | .. | 2 | 2 | .. | .. |
| United States Playing Card Co.. .... | 70½ | 70½ | .. | .. | .. | .. |
| United States Printing Co........... | 69 | 69 | .. | .. | .. | .. |
| United States Projectile Co........... | .. | .. | 111½ | 111½ | .. | .. |
| United States Reduction & Refining Co. | .. | .. | 43¾ | 26 | .. | .. |
| " " " " pref.. | .. | .. | 68⅜ | 42 | .. | .. |
| United Traction and Elec. Co. of N. J. | 100 | 90 | 110½ | 100 | 120 | 108 |
| United Verde Copper Co............. | .. | .. | 70 | 70 | .. | .. |
| United Verde Extension G. S. & Copper Co. of Arizona (5,000 shares).... | .. | .. | .. | .. | $39 lot | |
| Universal Tobacco................... | .. | .. | .. | .. | 18 | 2 |
| " " pref...... ...... | .. | .. | .. | .. | 63 | 14 |
| Utica, Chen. & Susq. Valley R. R. Co. | 216 | 154⅛ | 159⅞ | 159⅞ | .. | .. |
| Virginia Copper Co.................. | .. | .. | 80½c | 80½c | .. | .. |
| Virginia Iron, Coal & Coke Co....... | 30 | 3 | 12½ | 2 | .. | .. |
| Vulcanized Fibre Co................. | 50 | 50 | .. | .. | .. | .. |
| Vulcan Metal Refining Co............ | .. | .. | .. | .. | 142⅜ | 140⅝ |
| Warburton Hall Ass'n of Yonkers..... | .. | .. | .. | .. | 75 | 75 |
| Warren R. R Co...................... | 184¼ | 184¼ | 197½ | 195⅝ | 194⅛ | 194⅛ |
| Washington D. C., Street Ry......... | .. | .. | .. | .. | 19¼ | 12½ |
| " " " pref...... | .. | .. | .. | .. | 56¼ | 40 |
| Waverly Refining Co. of New York... | .. | .. | .. | .. | 10c | 10c |
| Westchester Trust Co. of Yonkers.... | 170 | 170 | 140 | 133 | 150¼ | 150¼ |
| Western Anth. Coal & Coke Co.. pref. | .. | .. | .. | .. | 20½ | 20½ |
| Western Gas Co...................... | 106 | 89 | .. | .. | .. | .. |
| Westinghouse Air Brake Co.......... | 410 | 350 | 385 | 342 | 400 | 330 |
| West Sh. Ry. Co. of New Haven, Ct... | .. | .. | .. | .. | 125⅛ | 125⅛ |
| White Knob Copper Co............. | .. | .. | .. | .. | 24 | 5½ |
| Wilcox & Gibbs Sewing Machine Co.. | .. | .. | 145 | 145 | .. | .. |
| Winchester Repeating Arms Co... .. | 800 | 800 | .. | .. | 1150 | 1150 |
| Windsor Co., pref., No. Adams, Mass. | 43 | 43 | .. | .. | .. | .. |
| Woodlawn Cemetery................. | 150 | 150 | .. | .. | .. | .. |
| Wood's Motor Vehicle Co............ | 1 | 1 | .. | .. | .. | .. |
| " " " pref...... | 2½ | 2½ | .. | .. | .. | .. |
| Worcester Traction Co .............. | 35 | 25 | .. | .. | .. | .. |
| " " pref........... | 107½ | 100 | .. | .. | .. | .. |
| Workman's St'd Book Co. (55 shares).. | .. | .. | .. | .. | $2 lot | |
| Worthington, H. R., Co., pref........ | .. | .. | .. | .. | 128 | 120 |
| Yale Building Co.................... | .. | .. | 90 | 90 | .. | .. |
| Yale & Towne Manufacturing Co..... | 45 | 45 | .. | .. | .. | .. |
| Yellow Pine Lumber Co............. | 2½ | 2½ | .. | .. | .. | .. |
| Yonkers Publishing Co.............. | 234 | 234 | .. | .. | .. | .. |
| Zeltner, H., Brewing Co.(2,488 shares). | .. | .. | .. | .. | $800 lot | |

## INSURANCE STOCKS—NEW YORK

| | Par Value of Shares. | 1900. Highest. | 1900. Lowest. | 1901. Highest. | 1901. Lowest. | 1902. Highest. | 1902. Lowest. |
|---|---|---|---|---|---|---|---|
| American Surety | $100 | 200 | 170 | 197½ | 180 | 190½ | 150 |
| Bond and Mortgage Guaranty | 50 | 312 | 201 | 472 | 360 | 500 | 356 |
| Brooklyn Life | 100 | 119¼ | 119¼ | .. | .. | .. | .. |
| Citizens' | 20 | 116½ | 116 | 116 | 115 | 96 | 60 |
| Colonial Assurance | 100 | .. | .. | 100 | 100 | .. | .. |
| Continental | 100 | 559 | 535 | 624 | 601 | 730 | 665½ |
| Eagle | 40 | 217½ | 200 | .. | .. | .. | .. |
| Eastern Insurance Co | 100 | 55 | 55 | .. | .. | .. | .. |
| Empire City | 100 | 85½ | 85½ | 90 | 54 | 100 | 100 |
| Equitable Life | 100 | 1,500 | 1,500 | .. | .. | .. | .. |
| Fidelty & Casualty Co | .. | .. | .. | .. | .. | 630 | 630 |
| German Alliance Fire | 100 | .. | .. | 150 | 150 | .. | .. |
| German-American | 100 | 513 | 480¼ | .. | .. | .. | .. |
| Germania | 50 | 280¼ | 280 | 301 | 289½ | 321 | 313 |
| German Real Estate & Title Guar. | .. | .. | .. | 39½ | 30 | 30 | 30 |
| Globe & Rutgers | 50 | 70 | 49½ | 65 | 45 | .. | .. |
| Greenwich | 25 | 162½ | 162½ | 191 | 185½ | 186½ | 171 |
| Hamilton | 15 | .. | .. | 105 | 105 | 105½ | 105½ |
| Hanover | 50 | 140 | 136½ | 134½ | 134 | 138 | 138 |
| Home Fire | 100 | 217½ | 170 | 306⅞ | 253½ | 336½ | 300 |
| Home Life | 100 | 351 | 332⅝ | .. | .. | .. | .. |
| Insurance Co., State of New York | .. | 3½ | 3½ | .. | .. | .. | .. |
| Lawyers' Mortgage | 100 | 122 | 100¼ | 233½ | 150 | 289 | 206 |
| Lawyers' Surety | 100 | 104⅞ | 104⅞ | 100½ | 94 | .. | .. |
| Lawyers' Title | 100 | 165 | 154 | 400¼ | 268¼ | 428 | 325 |
| Manhattan Life | 50 | 413 | 375 | .. | .. | 430 | 410 |
| Metropolitan Plate Glass | 100 | 250 | 250 | .. | .. | .. | .. |
| Nassau | 50 | 152¾ | 152¾ | 170¼ | 164 | 193 | 179 |
| National Surety | .. | 145½ | 145½ | 151 | 151 | 154 | 140 |
| New Amsterdam Casualty Co | 100 | .. | .. | .. | .. | 82¼ | 82¼ |
| New York | 100 | .. | .. | 100 | 100 | 96 | 96 |
| New York Mortgage & Security | 100 | .. | .. | .. | .. | 130 | 130 |
| Niagara | 50 | 167¼ | 167¼ | 200 | 195 | 285¼ | 210 |
| Northern | .. | 56 | 56 | .. | .. | .. | .. |
| North River | 25 | .. | .. | 155 | 152 | .. | .. |
| Pacific | 25 | 140 | 140 | .. | .. | .. | .. |
| Peter Cooper | 20 | 123 | 123 | 151 | 127 | .. | .. |
| Phenix | 50 | 191 | 175 | 205⅛ | 179 | 247 | 230 |
| Stuyvesant | 25 | 71 | 71 | 68½ | 58½ | 61 | 40 |
| Title Insurance Co | 100 | .. | .. | .. | .. | 170 | 155 |
| Traders' | .. | 40 | 40 | .. | .. | .. | .. |
| Travelers' | .. | 365 | 365 | .. | .. | .. | .. |
| United States Casualty | .. | 91¾ | 91¾ | .. | .. | 151½ | 150 |
| United States Fire | 25 | 120 | 120 | 140 | 135 | .. | .. |
| Westchester | 10 | .. | .. | 365 | 360 | .. | .. |
| Williamsburgh City | 50 | 476 | 476 | 562 | 560 | 601 | 601 |

## SAFE DEPOSIT STOCKS—NEW YORK

| | 1900. Highest. | 1900. Lowest. | 1901. Highest. | 1901. Lowest. | 1902. Highest. | 1902. Lowest. |
|---|---|---|---|---|---|---|
| Fifth Avenue | 125 | 125 | .. | .. | .. | .. |
| Lincoln | .. | .. | 185 | 185 | 165½ | 140 |
| Long Island | 31 | 31 | 60 | 50 | 62½ | 62½ |
| Mercantile Safe Deposit | .. | .. | .. | .. | 750 | 750 |
| National | 111 | 111 | .. | .. | .. | .. |
| Produce Ex. Safe Dep. & Stor. Co. | .. | .. | 125 | 117 | 272 | 272 |
| Safe Deposit Co., of New York | 127½ | 127½ | 131 | 124¾ | 134 | 130 |

## STREET RAILWAY STOCKS AND RONDS—NEW YORK

| | 1900. | | 1901. | | 1902. | |
|---|---|---|---|---|---|---|
| | Highest. | Lowest. | Highest. | Lowest. | Highest. | Lowest. |
| Atlantic Avenue 1st mort. 5s, 1934 | .. | .. | 108 | 108 | 103¾ | 100 |
| " con. 5s, 1931 | 115 | 112 | 114¼ | 114¼ | 114¼ | 112 |
| Bleecker Street & Fulton Ferry | .. | .. | 37½ | 35 | 38 | 33 |
| " " 1st mort. | 102 | 100 | .. | .. | 101 | 100 |
| Broadway & Seventh Avenue | .. | .. | 250 | 235 | 255 | 240 |
| " " 1st mort. 5s. | 105½ | 105½ | 103 | 102½ | 102½ | 100 |
| " " 2d mort. 5s. | 114 | 110 | 110½ | 109 | 109 | 106¼ |
| " Surface 5s, 1924 | .. | .. | 105 | 105 | 114¼ | 110¼ |
| " " 2d 5s, 1905 | .. | .. | .. | .. | 102¾ | 101 |
| Brooklyn, Bath & West End gen. mort. 5s, 1933 | 104½ | 100½ | 103½ | 101½ | 104 | 100 |
| Brooklyn City and Newtown | 336 | 330 | 334 | 334 | .. | .. |
| " " 1st 5s, 1939 | 118 | 116 | 117⅛ | 116 | 117 | 114 |
| Brooklyn City | 232 | 229 | 248 | 230 | 252 | 243⅛ |
| " Cal. Cem., Gpt. & Bkn. 6s, 1907 | 108¼ | 108¼ | 113¼ | 113¼ | 109½ | 109½ |
| Brooklyn Heights | 108½ | 106 | 108½ | 106 | 107 | 105½ |
| " 1st 5s, 1941 | .. | .. | .. | .. | 108 | 105¼ |
| Central Cross Town | .. | .. | 116¼ | 116¼ | .. | .. |
| " " gen. 1st 6s, 1922 | .. | .. | .. | .. | 126¾ | 125 |
| Central Park, N. & E. River | 200½ | 200½ | .. | .. | 217½ | 215½ |
| Christopher & Tenth Street | .. | .. | 186 | 168 | 192 | 179 |
| Coney Island & Brooklyn | 325 | 325 | 328 | 326 | .. | .. |
| " " certificates | .. | .. | 100⅛ | 100⅛ | .. | .. |
| " " con. bonds | .. | .. | 100 | 100 | .. | .. |
| Dry Dock, E. B'way & Battery scrip | 103½ | 93 | 102½ | 101 | 105 | 103⅛ |
| Eighth Avenue | .. | .. | 404 | 400 | .. | .. |
| " scrip 6s, 1914 | 108 | 100 | 116¼ | 116¼ | 105 | 105 |
| Forty-second & Grand Street | 405 | 405 | .. | .. | .. | .. |
| Forty-second, M. & St. Nicholas ave | 62 | 60 | .. | .. | 114½ | 110½ |
| " " 1st mort. | 117 | 110 | .. | .. | 105 | 97½ |
| " " 2d income | 100½ | 99 | .. | .. | .. | .. |
| Fulton Street 4s, 1995 | .. | .. | 95 | 95 | .. | .. |
| Grand Street & Newtown 5s, 1906 | 105 | 105 | .. | .. | .. | .. |
| Jamaica & Brooklyn, 1st mort. 5s, 1939 | 106½ | 102½ | .. | .. | .. | .. |
| Long Island City & Flushing 6s, 1911 | .. | .. | .. | .. | 112 | 110⅛ |
| Nassau Electric preferred | 70 | 70 | .. | .. | .. | .. |
| " 1st mort. 5s, 1944 | 114½ | 110½ | 114 | 114 | 112 | 112 |
| " con. mort. 4s | .. | .. | 98 | 98 | 96 | 85 |
| Newtown, W'msburgh & Flatbush bonds. | 97½ | 88 | .. | .. | .. | .. |
| Ninth Avenue | .. | .. | .. | .. | 205¼ | 205¼ |
| Second Avenue | .. | .. | 221 | 217 | 220¾ | 218⅛ |
| " con. 5s, 1909 | 109½ | 105½ | 106⅛ | 106⅛ | 108 | 106 |
| " consols, 1948 | 120½ | 116⅛ | .. | .. | 120½ | 118 |
| Sixth Avenue | .. | .. | 206 | 200 | 185 | 175 |
| Tenth & 23d St. Ferry Co. 1st 5s, 1919 | .. | .. | .. | .. | 105 | 105 |
| Thirty-fourth Crosstown 1st 5s | .. | .. | 115¼ | 115¼ | .. | .. |
| Twenty-eighth & 29th Streets guaranteed. | 115⅛ | 110 | .. | .. | 114 | 110 |
| Twenty-third Street stock | 402 | 402 | .. | .. | .. | .. |

# BONDS

**Highest and Lowest Prices of all Bonds Dealt in on the New York Stock Exchange, Compiled from Quotations of Daily Sales, 1900, 1901 and 1902.**

## GOVERNMENT BONDS

| | Due. | Interest Payable. | Amount Outstanding. | 1900. H. | 1900. L. | 1901. H. | 1901. L. | 1902. H. | 1902. L. |
|---|---|---|---|---|---|---|---|---|---|
| Dist. of Columbia 3.65 | 1924 | A., F. | $14,224,100 | 121 | 121 | 126 | 125 | .. | .. |
| U. S. 2s registered | 1930 | Q., Jan. | 445,940,750 | 107 | 104 | 109⅛ | 105½ | 109⅞ | 108¼ |
| " 2s coupon | 1930 | Q., Jan. | | 106 | 103⅛ | 109½ | 105¼ | 109 | 107¾ |
| " 4s registered | 1907 | Q., J. | 233,177,400 | 117½ | 114 | 114½ | 111⅝ | 112⅝ | 107¼ |
| " 4s coupon | 1907 | Q., J. | | 118½ | 114 | 115¼ | 112 | 113 | 108¾ |
| " 5s registered | 1904 | Q., F. | 19,385,050 | 116½ | 112⅜ | 111⅞ | 110 | 106½ | 103¼ |
| " 5s coupon | 1904 | Q., F. | | 116¼ | 112½ | 113½ | 107¼ | 106½ | 103⅞ |
| " 4s registered | 1925 | Q., F. | 118,489,900 | 139 | 132⅝ | 139¼ | 137 | 139½ | 132 |
| " 4s coupon | 1925 | Q., F. | | 138⅝ | 131¼ | 139⅞ | 136⅞ | 139¾ | 136½ |
| " 3s coupons 10-20 | 1918 | Q., F. | 97,515,660 | 112¼ | 108¾ | 112 | 108¼ | 110 | 105¾ |
| " 3s small 10-20 | 1918 | Q., F. | | 111¾ | 108½ | 112 | 106¼ | 109½ | 106⅛ |
| " 3s registered 10-20 | 1918 | Q., F. | | 112 | 108¾ | 111⅜ | 107½ | 109½ | 105⅞ |
| U. S. of Mexico ex. g. loan of 1899, S. F. 5s | .... | *Q., J. | £22,357,680 | 98 | 96 | 97¼ | 96 | 100 | 96 |
| Frankfort-on-M., 3½, Ser. I | .... | †M. & S. | M14,776,000 | .. | .. | 93 | 91⅛ | 95½ | 94¾ |

* Quotations for these bonds on the basis of £ = $5. †Quotations on the basis of 4M = $1.00.

## STATE BONDS

| | Due. | Interest Payable. | 1900. H. | 1900. L. | 1901. H. | 1901. L. | 1902. H. | 1902. L. |
|---|---|---|---|---|---|---|---|---|
| Alabama, class A, 4 and 5s | 1906 | J. & J. | 116⅛ | 108½ | 109½ | 108 | 107 | 104⅜ |
| " class B, 5s | 1906 | J. & J. | 109¼ | 109¼ | .. | .. | .. | .. |
| " class C, 4s | 1906 | J. & J. | 102¼ | 102 | 103½ | 102 | 102½ | 102½ |
| " Currency Funding 4s | 1920 | J. & J. | .. | .. | 109 | 109 | 111 | 111 |
| Louisiana new con. 4s | 1914 | J. & J. | 108½ | 106½ | 109 | 106½ | 107 | 106 |
| North Carolina con. 4s | 1910 | J. & J. | 106¼ | 104 | 106¼ | 105 | 104½ | 104 |
| " 6s | 1919 | A. & O. | .. | .. | 136½ | 135 | .. | .. |
| South Carolina 4½s, 20-40 | 1933 | J. & J. | 120 | 120 | .. | .. | .. | .. |
| Tennessee new settlement 3s | 1913 | J. & J. | 96⅛ | 93⅝ | 99¼ | 95 | 96⅝ | 95½ |
| " small | .... | J. & J. | 96⅝ | 90 | 96 | 94½ | 95 | 94 |
| Virginia 6s, deferred bonds, trust rcts | .... | ....... | 10 | 6 | 10¼ | 7⅛ | 15⅜ | 7¼ |
| " Fund Debt, 2-3s | 1991 | J. & J. | 96⅜ | 85 | 96¾ | 93½ | 99¾ | 95¼ |

## RAILROAD AND MISCELLANEOUS BONDS

NOTE.—The bonds embraced in brackets are covered by the company directly above the bracket. On all income bonds the interest is payable only as earned, and is not cumulative. In the column showing when interest is payable, "J. & J." denotes January and June, "F. & A.," February and August, etc. "Q., J.," means interest payable quarterly, beginning with January.

| | Due. | Interest Payable. | 1900. H. | 1900. L. | 1901. H. | 1901. L. | 1902. H. | 1902. L. |
|---|---|---|---|---|---|---|---|---|
| Adams Express col. tr. g. 4s | 1948 | M. & S. | 105 | 102 | 109 | 103 | 107½ | 103½ |
| American Bicycle s. f. deb. 5s | 1919 | M. & S. | .. | .. | 82 | 55 | 73 | 38 |
| American Cotton Oil deb. 8s | 1900 | J. & F. | 104 | 100½ | .. | .. | .. | .. |
| " " " extended 4½s | 1915 | ........ | 100½ | 98⅝ | 102 | 99 | 102 | 98 |
| American Hide & Leather 1st s. f. 6s | 1919 | M. & S. | .. | .. | 98 | 90 | 100 | 94 |
| American Spirits Manufacturing 1st 6s | 1915 | M. & S. | 85 | 63 | 85 | 75 | 91½ | 80 |
| American SS. Co. of West Va. 5s, g | 1920 | M. & N. | .. | .. | .. | .. | 101½ | 100¼ |
| American Telep. & Teleg. col. tr. 4s | 1929 | J. & J. | .. | .. | .. | .. | 100⅛ | 97½ |
| American Thread Co. 1st col. tr. 4s | 1919 | J. & J. | .. | . | .. | .. | 83 | 82 |
| Ann Arbor, 1st g. 4s | 1995 | Q., J. | 97 | 90 | 101 | 95 | 100 | 95 |

| | Due. | Interest Payable. | 1900. H. | 1900. L. | 1901. H. | 1901. L. | 1902. H. | 1902. L. |
|---|---|---|---|---|---|---|---|---|
| Atch., Top. & S. Fe gen. gold 4s........ | 1995 | A. & O. | 103 | 98½ | 105¼ | 101⅞ | 105¾ | 100 |
| " " " gen. gold 4s reg.... | 1995 | A. & O. | 101⅛ | 98½ | 104 | 101¾ | 105¼ | 100 |
| " " " adj. gold 4s........ | 1995 | Nov .... | 90 | 78½ | 99 | 86¼ | 97 | 89 |
| " " " adj. gold 4s reg.... | 1995 | Nov .... | .. | .. | 95 | 92 | 94¾ | 93½ |
| " " " adj. gold 4s stpd... | 1995 | M. & N. | .. | .. | 97 | 90 | 95¾ | 88½ |
| " " " deb. 4s, ser. A..... | 1903 | F. & A. | .. | .. | .. | .. | 97 | 97 |
| " " " " " " L..... | 1914 | F. & A. | .. | .. | .. | .. | 95¼ | 92⅞ |
| Atlanta, Knoxv. & Nor. 1st g. 5s........ | 1946 | J. & D. | 106 | 105 | 109 | 108 | 114½ | 114½ |
| Baltimore & Ohio pr. lien gold 3½s...... | 1925 | J. & J. | 98¼ | 92¼ | 97¾ | 94½ | 97¼ | 93 |
| " " pr. lien gold 3½ reg... | 1925 | Q., J. | .. | .. | 97 | 95 | 97 | 96½ |
| " " 1st gold 4s............ | 1948 | A. & O. | 102¾ | 97½ | 105 | 99 | 105 | 99⅞ |
| " " 1st gold 4s reg......... | 1948 | Q. J. | .. | .. | 104 | 100⅛ | 104 | 102 |
| " " convertible deb. 4s.... | 1911 | M. & S. | .. | .. | 110 | 100½ | 118 | 104 |
| Central Ohio reorganization 1st 4½s. | 1930 | M. & S. | .. | .. | 112 | 112 | 108 | 108 |
| Pitts. Junc. & M. D. 1st g. 3½s..... | 1925 | M. & N. | 90 | 85 | 91¼ | 87½ | 93½ | 89 |
| Southwestern Div. 1st g. 3½s....... | 1925 | J. & J. | 92 | 85½ | 92⅝ | 88⅝ | 91⅞ | 88½ |
| Southwestern Div. 1st g. 3½s reg... | 1925 | Q., J. | .. | .. | 91 | 90½ | 90¼ | 90¼ |
| Monongahela River 1st gu. g. 5s.... | 1919 | F. & A. | 112 | 111 | .. | .. | 114¼ | 114¼ |
| P. L. E. & W. Va. sys., ref. 4s....... | 1941 | M. & N. | .. | .. | .. | .. | 101 | 94 |
| Brooklyn Ferry 1st con. g. 5s........... | 1948 | F. & A. | 88¼ | 81¾ | 91¼ | 83 | 85½ | 75½ |
| Brooklyn Rapid Transit gold 5s......... | 1945 | A. & O. | 108 | 100 | 110½ | 103½ | 110¼ | 102 |
| B'yn, Queens Co. & S. con. gen. 5s. | 1941 | M. & N. | 104 | 96 | 105⅛ | 100 | 106½ | 100 |
| Brooklyn Union Elev. 1st g. 4-5s... | 1950 | J. & J. | 100 | 91 | 103 | 98 | 105 | 100 |
| Kings Co. Elev. 1st g. 4s........... | 1949 | F. & A. | 90 | 83¼ | 95 | 88 | 93 | 86 |
| Brooklyn City 1st 5s................ | 1941 | J. & J. | 115 | 113 | 115 | 111 | 114½ | 112½ |
| Brooklyn Union Gas 1st 5s............. | 1945 | M. & N. | 118 | 113½ | 119½ | 115½ | 120½ | 115¼ |
| Brooklyn Wharf & W. 1st g. 5s......... | 1945 | F. & A. | 84 | 68 | 78 | 68 | 76 | 76 |
| Buffalo & Sus. 1st ref. g. 4s............. | 1951 | J. & J. | .. | .. | 101 | 101 | 103 | 102 |
| Buffalo, Roch. & Pitts. gen. gold 5s..... | 1937 | M. & S. | 115½ | 109 | 118¾ | 115 | 119½ | 116 |
| " " " 1st 6s...... .... | 1921 | F. & A. | 131 | 129 | 131 | 127 | 130½ | 128 |
| " " " con. 1st 6s....... | 1922 | F. & D. | 128 | 124 | 130 | 127⅝ | 129½ | 125¾ |
| Burlington, Ced. Rap. & North. 1st m. 5s. | 1906 | J. & D. | 109 | 106 | 108¼ | 103¾ | 106¼ | 102½ |
| Burl., C.R. & N. con. 1st and col. tr 5s. | 1934 | A. & O. | 118⅜ | 115 | 127½ | 119½ | 126¼ | 121¾ |
| " " " con. 1st & col. tr. 5s reg. | 1934 | A. & O. | 118 | 115 | .. | .. | 124¾ | 124⅝ |
| Ced. Rap., Iowa F's & N. 1st mort. 5s. | 1921 | A. & O. | 113½ | 113½ | .. | .. | 118 | 118 |
| Canada Southern 1st mort., int. guar. 5s. | 1908 | J. & J. | 109⅛ | 105 | 109 | 105½ | 107½ | 104⅜ |
| " " 2d mort............... | 1913 | M. & S. | 109½ | 106 | 111 | 107 | 111 | 107 |
| " " 2d mort. 5s reg........ | 1913 | M. & S. | 104 | 104 | 107 | 106¾ | 106⅝ | 106 |
| Central Branch Union Pac. 1st g. 4s..... | 1948 | J. & D. | 92 | 87⅛ | 95 | 91 | 95 | 93 |
| Cent. of Ga. Ry. con. 5s................ | 1945 | M. & N. | 100 | 88½ | 108¾ | 97¾ | 113½ | 104½ |
| " " con. 5s reg............ | 1945 | M. & N. | 96 | 96 | 105½ | 105½ | .. | .. |
| " " 1st g. 5s............... | 1945 | F. & A. | 120 | 117 | 122 | 119 | 123 | 119½ |
| " " 1st pref. inc. g. 5s...... | 1945 | October. | 62 | 32½ | 84½ | 60 | 89½ | 72 |
| " " 2d pref. inc. g. 5s...... | 1945 | October. | 20½ | 9¼ | 36⅞ | 20 | 44½ | 32½ |
| " " 3d pref. inc. g. 5s...... | 1945 | October. | 9¾ | 4½ | 21 | 8 | 31 | 18½ |
| " " M. & Nor. div. 1st g. 5s. | 1946 | J. & J. | .. | .. | .. | .. | 108¼ | 108¼ |
| " " Mobile div. 1st g. 5s... | 1946 | J. & J. | 106 | 105 | .. | .. | 112½ | 106 |
| " " Mid. Ga. & Atl. div. 5s. | 1947 | J. & J. | .. | .. | 105¾ | 105¾ | .. | .. |
| " " Ch'nooga div. pur. my. 4s | 1951 | J. & D. | .. | .. | 92 | 91½ | 93⅜ | 91¾ |
| Central of New Jersey cons. 7s.......... | 1902 | M. & N. | 114¼ | 106¾ | 108 | 102⅝ | 101¼ | 101¼ |
| " " gen. mort. 5s..... | 1987 | J. & J. | 129¼ | 117½ | 137⅛ | 127 | 141 | 132 |
| " " gen. mort. 5s, reg.. | 1987 | Q., J. | 127½ | 116 | 137 | 127 | 139¼ | 131 |
| " " conv. deb. 6s...... | 1908 | M. & N. | 130 | 130 | .. | .. | .. | .. |
| Lehigh & Wilkes. con. ext. guar. 4½s | 1910 | Q., M. | 103½ | 100 | 105½ | 102 | 105 | 100 |
| Lehigh & Wilkes. mort. 5s.......... | 1912 | M. & N. | 105 | 100 | 107 | 103¼ | 106 | 102 |
| American Dock and Imp. bonds 5s.. | 1921 | J. & J. | 117 | 112¼ | 116¾ | 112 | 115 | 112⅝ |
| Central R. & B. of Ga. con. gold 5s....... | 1937 | M. & N. | 96⅜ | 91 | 103½ | 96 | 109¾ | 106½ |
| Chesapeake & Ohio 6s gold, series A..... | 1908 | A. & O. | 117¾ | 113 | 117 | 113 | 115 | 109⅝ |
| " " 6s ................. | 1911 | A. & O. | 119½ | 115¼ | 119 | 115 | 117 | 112 |
| " " 1st con. 5s.......... | 1939 | M. & N. | 121¾ | 115½ | 122 | 119 | 123½ | 116¾ |
| " " " " reg......... | 1939 | M. & N. | 117 | 117 | 121 | 120⅛ | .. | .. |
| " " gen. 4½s........... | 1992 | M. & S. | 104⅜ | 95½ | 108¾ | 104 | 110¼ | 102 |
| " " gen. 4½s reg....... | 1992 | ........ | 96 | 93 | 103 | 103 | .. | .. |
| " " R. & A. div. 1st 4s.. | 1989 | J. & J. | 107¼ | 101 | 107½ | 103 | 105½ | 102½ |
| " " " " 2d 4s | 1989 | J. & J. | 99½ | 92 | 103 | 99 | 100 | 98 |

| | Due. | Interest Payable. | 1900. H. | 1900. L. | 1901. H. | 1901. L. | 1902. H. | 1902. L. |
|---|---|---|---|---|---|---|---|---|
| Chesapeake & Ohio, Craig Val. 1st gold 5s | 1940 | J. & J. | 103 | 100 | .. | .. | 116 | 108½ |
| Elizabethtown, Lex. & Big Sandy 5s. | 1902 | M. & S. | 103 | 100 | 102½ | 100 | 102¼ | 101⅞ |
| Warm Springs Valley 1st g. 5s...... | 1941 | M. & S. | .. | .. | .. | .. | 106½ | 106½ |
| Chicago & Alton sinking fund 6s........ | 1903 | M. & N. | 106½ | 104½ | 105¾ | 102⅜ | 104½ | 101 |
| " ref. gold 3s........... | 1949 | A. & O. | 93 | 92⅞ | 94 | 86 | 88 | 82⅛ |
| " Ry. gold 3½s......... | 1950 | J. & J. | .. | .. | 87½ | 83½ | 86 | 78 |
| " " " reg...... | 1950 | J. & J. | .. | .. | .. | .. | 83¾ | 83⅝ |
| " U. S. Tr. Co., ctfs. 3%. | 1950 | J. & J. | 86 | 81½ | 93⅛ | 91½ | .. | .. |
| Chi. & East Ill. 1st mort. s. f. 6s, cur.... | 1907 | J. & D. | 116 | 112 | 117 | 111½ | 114 | 109⅛ |
| " " 1st con. mort. 6s........ | 1934 | A. & O. | 138 | 133½ | 140 | 135 | 139⅞ | 136 |
| " " gen. con. 1st 5s......... | 1937 | M. & N. | 117 | 112 | 127 | 115 | 126½ | 120 |
| " " gen. con. 1st 5s reg.... | 1937 | M. & N. | 115 | 115 | .. | .. | 124¾ | 120 |
| Chi. & Ind. Coal Rys. 1st mort. 5s... | 1936 | J. & J. | 115½ | 105½ | 125 | 112¾ | 125 | 121½ |
| Chicago & N. W. con. 7s............... | 1915 | Q., F. | 144 | 137½ | 142½ | 139½ | 141 | 134 |
| " coup. gold 7s............. | 1902 | J. & D. | 112¼ | 106½ | 108 | 102⅝ | 104¾ | 101¼ |
| " reg. gold 7s.............. | 1902 | J. & D. | 112 | 106½ | 108 | 102 | 104 | 101¼ |
| " sinking fund 6s ...... | 1879-1929 | A. & O. | 119½ | 114¼ | 116¾ | 113½ | 118 | 115 |
| " sinking fund, reg., 6s. | 1879-1929 | A. & O. | 117 | 111 | .. | .. | .. | .. |
| " sinking fund 5s...... | 1879-1929 | A. & O. | 110 | 107 | 110⅛ | 106¾ | 110 | 106½ |
| " sinking fund, reg., 5s. | 1879-1929 | A. & O. | 107½ | 107 | 107⅜ | 107⅜ | .. | .. |
| " sinking fund deben. 5s.... | 1933 | M. & N. | 125 | 118 | 125¼ | 121½ | 124 | 117½ |
| " sinking fund, registered... | 1933 | M. & N. | 120 | 120 | 123 | 122 | .. | .. |
| " debentures 5s............. | 1909 | M. & N. | 109⅞ | 107 | 110¾ | 108 | 109½ | 105½ |
| " registered.............. | 1909 | M. & N. | .. | .. | 108⅜ | 108 | 105½ | 105½ |
| " gen. gold 3½s........... | 1987 | M. & N. | 110⅞ | 105¼ | 111 | 109¼ | 106⅝ | 102¼ |
| " 30 year debenture 5s...... | 1921 | A. & O. | 119 | 116 | 117¼ | 114¾ | 118½ | 114 |
| " 30 year deb. 5s reg....... | 1921 | A. & O. | .. | .. | 114 | 114 | .. | .. |
| Chicago & N. W. exten. 4s coup.... | 1886-1926 | F. & A. | 111⅛ | 108½ | 112 | 108¼ | 107½ | 105 |
| " exten. 4s reg......... | 1886-1926 | F. & A. | 107 | 107 | .. | .. | 106⅜ | 106⅜ |
| Escanaba & L. Sup'r 1st mort. 6s.... | 1901 | J. & J. | 103¼ | 103¼ | .. | .. | .. | .. |
| W. & St. P. 2d mort. 7s............ | 1907 | M. & N. | 123½ | 120 | .. | .. | 119½ | 116½ |
| Mil. & Madison 1st mort. 6s......... | 1905 | M. & S. | 112⅝ | 112⅝ | 113 | 113 | 106 | 106 |
| Ottum., C. F. & St. P. 5s............ | 1909 | M. & S. | 111¼ | 110 | 111¼ | 110¼ | 107 | 107 |
| Northern Illinois, 1st mort. 5s....... | 1910 | M. & S. | 112¼ | 112¼ | 111 | 110⅞ | 109½ | 108 |
| Mil., L. S. & Western 1st mort. 6s.. | 1921 | M. & N. | 139½ | 133¼ | 141¼ | 135¼ | 137¾ | 131⅛ |
| " " inc.................. | 1911 | M. & N. | .. | .. | 113 | 113 | 114¼ | 110⅛ |
| " " ext. & imp. s. f. g. 5s. | 1929 | F. & A. | 127½ | 122⅜ | 127⅜ | 123½ | 128½ | 123½ |
| " " conv. debentures 5s... | 1907 | F. & A. | 107½ | 105 | 107⅛ | 107⅛ | .. | .. |
| " Mich. Div. 1st m. 6s.......... | 1924 | J. & J. | 137⅛ | 137⅛ | 143 | 138⅝ | 139¾ | 139½ |
| " Ashland Div. 1st gold 6s...... | 1925 | M. & S. | 139½ | 139½ | 143¾ | 143¾ | 142½ | 142¼ |
| Chi. & Western Ind. gen. mort. 6s...... | 1932 | Q., M. | 120 | 118 | 119¾ | 117 | 119 | 116¾ |
| Chicago, Bur. & Quincy con. 7s......... | 1903 | J. & J. | 113¼ | 109¾ | 109⅞ | 106⅜ | 106¼ | 102¾ |
| " " 5s, sinking fund. | 1901 | A. & O. | 103 | 100⅜ | .. | .. | .. | .. |
| " " 5s, debentures.. | 1913 | M. & N. | 112 | 108½ | 112¾ | 108 | 110 | 106½ |
| .. " conv. 5s........ | 1903 | M. & S. | 140⅞ | 120½ | 196¼ | 142¾ | .. | .. |
| " Ill. Div., 3½s.. | 1949 | J. & J. | 105½ | 100¾ | 104¾ | 101¾ | 103½ | 97⅞ |
| " Ia. Div. s. f. 5s. | 1919 | A. & O. | 117 | 113¾ | 115⅞ | 114 | 116¼ | 114¼ |
| " Ia. div. s. f. 4s.. | 1919 | A. & O. | 107 | 103 | 107 | 103⅝ | 106 | 103 |
| " Denver Div. 4s.. | 1922 | F. & A. | 103 | 100½ | 102½ | 101 | 103½ | 100½ |
| " " " 4s.. | 1921 | M. & S. | 102 | 100½ | .. | .. | .. | .. |
| " Neb. ext. 4s.... | 1927 | M. & N. | 113 | 108¾ | 113 | 110 | 111½ | 107 |
| .. " " ext. 4s reg. | 1927 | M. & N. | .. | .. | 112¾ | 109½ | .. | .. |
| " " C. & Ia. div. 5s.. | 1909 | F. & A. | 104¾ | 104¾ | .. | .. | .. | .. |
| Han. & St. Joseph con. 6s.......... | 1911 | M. & S. | 122 | 118½ | 123¼ | 120 | 122 | 116 |
| Southwestern Div. 4s.............. | 1921 | M. & S. | .. | .. | 100⅜ | 100⅜ | 100 | 99¼ |
| Chi., Ind. & Louisv. refunding gold 5s.. | 1947 | J. & J. | 107 | 100 | 116¾ | 106⅞ | 117½ | 113 |
| " " " refunding gold 6s | 1947 | J. & J. | 120 | 111½ | 128 | 115 | 132½ | 126 |
| Louisville, N. Alb. & Chi. 1st mort. 6s | 1910 | J. & J. | 117 | 113 | 117 | 113 | 115 | 113⅜ |
| Chi. Junc. Ry. & Stock Yards col. tr. 5s. | 1915 | J. & J. | 111 | 110 | 111 | 111 | .. | .. |
| Chi., M. & St. Paul 1st mort. 7s, $ gold, R D | 1902 | J. & J. | 179 | 116½ | 192½ | 184 | .. | .. |
| " " 1st mort. 7s, £ g., R S | 1902 | J. & J. | 172⅛ | 172⅛ | .. | .. | .. | .. |
| " " 1st mort. C. & M. 7s... | 1903 | J. & J. | 181 | 166¼ | 190 | 183 | .. | .. |
| " " con. 7s............... | 1905 | J. & J. | 185¾ | 166 | 194 | 180 | 196 | 182½ |
| " " 1st m. 7s, I. & D. ext.. | 1908 | J. & J. | 174½ | 166 | 188 | 185 | 191½ | 182½ |
| " " 1st m. 6s, S'thwest Div. | 1909 | J. & J. | 119⅛ | 116⅝ | 117½ | 113 | 115 | 113¾ |

| | Due. | Interest Payable. | 1900. H. | 1900. L. | 1901. H. | 1901. L. | 1902. H. | 1902. L. |
|---|---|---|---|---|---|---|---|---|
| Chi., M. & St. Paul, 1st m. 5s, La C. & Dav. | 1919 | J. & J. | 119⅝ | 117⅜ | 119 | 117½ | 119 | 116 |
| " " 1st m. So. Min. Div. 6s. | 1910 | J. & J. | 121½ | 117⅜ | 119½ | 114⅞ | 117½ | 114 |
| " " 1st m. H. & D. Div. 7s. | 1910 | J. & J. | 127⅞ | 124¼ | 126½ | 120¾ | 124 | 120⅝ |
| " " 1st m. H. & D. Div. 5s. | 1910 | J. & J. | 111½ | 109 | 110½ | 109 | 110½ | 107⅜ |
| " " Chi. & Pac. Div. 6s... | 1910 | J. & J. | 120⅛ | 117 | 119 | 116 | 118 | 114¾ |
| " " 1st m. C. & Pac. W. 5s. | 1921 | J. & J. | 122¼ | 118 | 122 | 116½ | 121¾ | 116⅞ |
| " " Ch. & Mo. R. Div. 5s.. | 1926 | J. & J. | 124 | 120 | 122¾ | 118 | 124⅛ | 118⅞ |
| " " Min'al P't Div. 5s...... | 1910 | J. & J. | 111⅛ | 110¾ | 110⅝ | 108 | 109⅛ | 108⅜ |
| " " C. & L. Sup'r Div. 5s.. | 1921 | J. & J. | 120¾ | 117⅝ | 121 | 116½ | 120½ | 120½ |
| " " Wis. & Min. Div. 5s... | 1921 | J. & J. | 120¾ | 117 | 120 | 116⅜ | 121⅛ | 116⅛ |
| " " Terminal 5s.......... | 1914 | J. & J. | 116⅜ | 112 | 115⅜ | 111½ | 115 | 112 |
| " " Dak. & G. S. 5s....... | 1916 | J. & J. | 117⅛ | 110½ | 116¼ | 111¾ | 115¾ | 112¼ |
| " " gen. series A 4s....... | 1989 | J. & J. | 114⅝ | 109 | 114½ | 110 | 117 | 110¾ |
| " " gen. 4s, series A 4s reg. | 1989 | Q., J. | .. | .. | .. | .. | 111 | 111 |
| " " gen. g. 3½, series B... | 1989 | J. & J. | .. | .. | .. | .. | 104⅞ | 104¾ |
| Mil. & North. 1st mort. 6s.......... | 1910 | J. & D. | 121 | 118 | 119⅜ | 116 | 117 | 115 |
| " 1st mort. extens. 6s... | 1913 | J. & D. | 122 | 120 | 122 | 118¾ | 123¼ | 120½ |
| Chicago, R. I. & Pacific, 6s, coup....... | 1917 | J. & J. | 134 | 129 | 132¼ | 127¼ | 132 | 128 |
| " " 6s, reg.............. | 1917 | J. & J. | 132⅞ | 127 | 132½ | 126 | 131 | 127⅜ |
| " " gen. gold 4s......... | 1988 | J. & J. | 109¾ | 103½ | 110 | 105⅝ | 113⅛ | 105¾ |
| " " gen. gold registered.. | 1988 | J. & J. | 107⅜ | 105⅞ | 107⅞ | 105½ | 112 | 109 |
| " " col. tr. 4s, series B... | 1904 | M. & N. | .. | .. | .. | .. | 99 | 99 |
| " " col. tr. 4s, series C... | 1905 | M. & N. | .. | .. | .. | .. | 100⅜ | 100¼ |
| " " col. tr. 4s, series H . | 1910 | M. & N. | .. | .. | .. | .. | 99⅞ | 99⅞ |
| " " col. tr. 4s, series M.. | 1915 | M. & N. | .. | .. | .. | .. | 99½ | 99⅜ |
| " " col. tr. 4s, series N... | 1916 | M. & N. | .. | .. | .. | .. | 99⅜ | 99¾ |
| Keokuk & Des Moines 1st mort. 5s.. | 1923 | A. & O. | 114 | 107 | 112½ | 110½ | 110½ | 109¾ |
| Des M. & Ft. Dodge, 1st 4s......... | 1905 | J. & J. | 96 | 96 | 99⅞ | 99⅞ | 99⅛ | 97½ |
| " " 1st 2½s....... | 1905 | J. & J. | 86¾ | 86½ | .. | .. | 93 | 91¼ |
| " " ext. mort. 4s.. | 1905 | J. & J. | 97 | 96 | .. | .. | .. | .. |
| Chicago, R. I. & Pacific R. R. 4s....... | 2002 | M. & N. | .. | .. | .. | .. | 87½ | 82½ |
| " " " " 4s, reg.. | 2002 | M. & N. | .. | .. | .. | .. | 86⅝ | 86⅝ |
| Chic., St. Paul, Minn. & Omaha, con. 6s. | 1930 | J. & D. | 136¾ | 131 | 142 | 134¾ | 142 | 134½ |
| Chic., St. Paul & Minn. 1st mort. 6s. | 1918 | M. & N. | 135 | 131 | 140½ | 134 | 141⅜ | 135 |
| St. Paul & Sioux City 1st mort. 6s... | 1919 | A. & O. | 132½ | 127 | 132 | 127 | 130⅝ | 125¼ |
| North Wis., 1st 6s................ | 1930 | J. & J. | 140 | 140 | 140 | 140 | 140 | 137½ |
| Chi. Ter. Transfer 4s................. | 1947 | J. & J. | 97½ | 91 | 98 | 87 | 90¾ | 85 |
| Choct., Okla. & Gulf, g. 5s............ | 1919 | J. & J. | .. | .. | .. | .. | 114½ | 105 |
| Cincinnati, Hamilton & Dayton 7s...... | 1905 | A. & O. | 117 | 115 | 111½ | 111½ | .. | .. |
| Cincinnati, Hamil'n & Day. 2d gold 4½s | 1937 | J. & J. | 113½ | 112¼ | .. | .. | .. | .. |
| " Day. & Ironton 1st 5s, guar.. | 1941 | M. & N. | 114 | 111 | 115 | 112½ | 115½ | 113½ |
| Cleveland & Mahoning Val. con. 5s..... | 1938 | J. & J. | 132 | 128 | 130½ | 129½ | 128 | 127½ |
| C., C., C. & St. L., Cin. Wab. & Mic. 4s. | 1991 | J. & J. | 100¼ | 93 | 104⅛ | 98¾ | 103¾ | 100 |
| " " Cairo div., 4s....... | 1939 | J. & J. | .. | .. | 99 | 99 | 102 | 101½ |
| " " general gold 4s..... | 1993 | J. & D. | 102 | 94 | 105¼ | 101 | 104⅝ | 98 |
| " " St. Louis div. 1st 4s. | 1990 | M. & N. | 104½ | 100½ | 105⅜ | 102 | 104¾ | 101⅜ |
| " " registered........... | 1990 | M. & N. | .. | .. | .. | .. | 103 | 103 |
| Cin. Ind., St. L. & Chic. 1st gold 4s. | 1936 | Q., F. | 105½ | 105 | 106 | 104 | 106 | 99½ |
| Cin., San. & Cleve. 1st 5s.......... | 1928 | J. & J. | 115¾ | 114 | 115½ | 113⅝ | 115½ | 113⅝ |
| Peoria & Eastern 1st con. 4s........ | 1940 | A. & O. | 95 | 84½ | 100½ | 95 | 102 | 98 |
| " income 4s.......... | 1990 | April... | 50 | 24 | 79½ | 45½ | 82½ | 72 |
| Ind., Bloomington & W. 1st pref. 4s. | 1940 | J. & J. | .. | .. | 104½ | 104½ | .. | .. |
| C., C., C. & Ind. con. mort. 7s.... | 1914 | J. & D. | 136 | 134 | 138 | 130 | 134⅛ | 134⅛ |
| " " " gen. con. 6s...... | 1934 | J. & J. | 137 | 128½ | 138½ | 133 | 138 | 138 |
| Spring & Col. Div. 1st gold 4s...... | 1940 | M. & S. | .. | .. | 100 | 100 | 102 | 101 |
| Cleveland, Lorain & Wheeling 1st 5s.... | 1933 | A. & O. | 111 | 106 | 115 | 115 | 116½ | 114 |
| Colorado & Southern 1st gold 4s........ | 1929 | F. & A. | 87 | 78½ | 90½ | 83 | 97 | 90 |
| Colorado Coal & Iron 1st con. 6s....... | 1902 | F. & A. | 103½ | 100¼ | 104½ | 101 | .. | .. |
| " " " Dev. Co. gu. g. 5s | 1909 | J. & J. | 58 | 55 | .. | .. | .. | .. |
| Colorado Fuel & Iron genr. s. f. g. 5s.... | 1943 | F. & A. | 98 | 90 | 108 | 96¾ | 106¼ | 102¼ |
| " " " conv. deb., g. 5s.. | 1911 | F. & A. | .. | .. | .. | .. | 111¼ | 90½ |
| Colorado Fuel Co., gen., gold 6s........ | 1919 | M. & W. | 108¾ | 102½ | 106¼ | 106¼ | 115 | 110½ |
| Colorado Midland 1st gold 2-3-4s........ | 1947 | J. & J. | 80½ | 63 | 87½ | 78 | 87 | 82 |
| " " 1st gold 4s... ..... | 1947 | J. & J. | 81 | 71½ | 87½ | 77 | 86¾ | 79½ |
| Columbus & Ninth Ave. 1st 5s.......... | 1993 | M. & S. | 125 | 122 | 126 | 121¾ | 124½ | 120 |

| | Due. | Interest Payable. | 1900. H. | 1900. L. | 1901. H. | 1901. L. | 1902. H. | 1902. L. |
|---|---|---|---|---|---|---|---|---|
| Commercial Cable Co. 1st gold 4s | 2397 | Q., J. | 103½ | 101 | 100½ | 100½ | 100½ | 100½ |
| " " " " reg | 2397 | Q., J. | 100½ | 100½ | .. | .. | .. | .. |
| Conn. Ry. & Light, 1st g. 4½s | 1951 | J. & J. | .. | .. | 101 | 100½ | 99⅞ | 98 |
| Consolidated Tobacco, 50 yr. gold 4s | 1951 | F. & A. | .. | .. | 67¼ | 62¼ | 69⅞ | 60 |
| " " 50 yr. g. 4s. 1951, reg | 1951 | ........ | .. | .. | .. | .. | 66½ | 65½ |
| Consumers Gas (Chicago) 1st 5s | 1936 | J. & D. | 109 | 105 | 110 | 104¼ | 109½ | 107¼ |
| Del. & Hud. Canal 1st Pa. Div. coup. 7 | 1917 | M. & S. | 148 | 146⅛ | 147½ | 145½ | 144 | 140¼ |
| " " 1st Pa. Div. 7s, reg | 1917 | M. & S. | 141 | 141 | 150 | 149 | .. | .. |
| Albany & Susq. 1st con. guar. 7s | 1906 | A. & O. | 121 | 116⅞ | 117 | 114½ | 115¼ | 113 |
| " 1st con. guar. 6s | 1906 | A. & O. | 115 | 111⅛ | 111½ | 110⅛ | 109 | 106 |
| " 1st con. guar. 6s, reg | 1906 | A. & O. | 113½ | 112½ | 112½ | 109½ | 111⅜ | 111⅜ |
| Rens. & Sara. 1st mort. coup. 7s | 1921 | M. & N. | 148¾ | 147 | 153½ | 150¼ | 151½ | 143¾ |
| " 1st reg. 7s | 1921 | M. & N. | 148¾ | 148¾ | 151 | 151 | 147½ | 147½ |
| Del., Lack. & Western mort., 7s | 1907 | M. & S. | 124½ | 122⅛ | 123½ | 117¾ | 120⅛ | 114¾ |
| Syracuse, Bing. & N. Y. 1st mort. 7s | 1906 | A. & O. | 122 | 118¾ | 117⅞ | 116 | 117⅜ | 112 |
| Morris & Essex, 1st mort. 7s | 1914 | M. & N. | 142 | 136 | 140 | 136½ | 138 | 132¼ |
| " 7s of 1871 | 1901 | A. & O. | 107½ | 102⅞ | 104⅛ | 101½ | .. | .. |
| " 1st con., guar., 7s | 1915 | J. & D. | 141¼ | 138 | 140½ | 136¾ | 141 | 137 |
| N. Y. Lack. & Western 1st mort. 6s | 1921 | J. & J. | 138 | 133 | 137 | 133½ | 137 | 132⅜ |
| " " " con. 5s | 1923 | F. & A. | 122 | 119 | 119½ | 118½ | 118¼ | 115⅜ |
| Terminal & Impt. 4s | 1923 | M. & N. | 106 | 103½ | 104¾ | 104¼ | 105½ | 102 |
| Warren R. R. 1st ref. gen. 3½s | 2000 | F. & A. | .. | .. | .. | .. | 103½ | 103½ |
| Denver & Rio Grande 1st con. g. 4s | 1936 | J. & J. | 102¾ | 96½ | 104½ | 100 | 104½ | 99½ |
| " " 1st con. g. 4½s | 1936 | J. & J. | 109⅝ | 106 | 114⅛ | 108 | 112 | 105 |
| " " Improve. g. 5s | 1928 | J. & D. | 108 | 101⅛ | 113½ | 107 | 113¼ | 105 |
| Den. Con. Tram. 1st gold 5s | 1933 | A. & O. | 97½ | 95 | .. | .. | .. | .. |
| Denver & Southwestern, gen., s. f., g. 5s | 1919 | J. & D. | .. | .. | 96 | 89½ | 91 | 84½ |
| Detroit & Mack. 1st lien 4s | 1995 | J. & D. | 98½ | 85 | 102 | 102 | 102½ | 101 |
| " " g. 4s | 1995 | J. & D. | 90 | 76½ | 93 | 85 | 95½ | 92½ |
| Detroit & Southern 1st gold 4s | 1951 | J. & D. | .. | .. | 87¼ | 85 | 87¾ | 84½ |
| Ohio Southern Div. 1st gold 4s | 1941 | M. & S. | .. | .. | 95 | 93¼ | 95½ | 91 |
| Detroit Citizens' 1st con. g. 5s | 1905 | J. & J. | .. | .. | 103 | 101½ | .. | .. |
| Detroit City Gas gold 5s | 1923 | J. & J. | 100 | 93 | 103 | 94 | 99½ | 92½ |
| Detroit Gas con. 1st gold 5s | 1918 | F. & A. | .. | .. | 106 | 102 | 104 | 104 |
| Detroit, Mack. & Mar. land grant 3½s S.A. | 1911 | A. & O. | 40 | 19 | 35½ | 29 | 91¼ | 30 |
| Des Moines Union Ry., 1st gold 5s | 1917 | M. & N. | 109 | 108¼ | 111 | 108¾ | .. | .. |
| Distilling Co. of America col tr. g. 5s | 1911 | J. & J. | .. | .. | 88 | 82 | 98 | 86 |
| Duluth & Iron Range 1st 5s | 1937 | A. & O. | 111 | 107 | 116 | 110½ | 115 | 112¼ |
| Duluth, S. S. & Atlantic guar. 5s | 1937 | J. & J. | 115 | 110 | 116 | 112 | 115 | 111 |
| Edison El. Illum. Brooklyn 1st 5s | 1939 | A. & O. | 96½ | 96½ | 97½ | 96 | 99 | 97 |
| Edison El. Illum. N. Y. 1st 5s | 1910 | M. & S. | 110 | 106¼ | 109½ | 105 | 109 | 105⅜ |
| " " " 1st con. gold 5s | 1995 | J. & J. | 120 | 117¾ | 121¾ | 121 | 121¼ | 120 |
| Elgin, Joliet & Eastern, 1st gold 5s | 1941 | M. & N. | 113 | 107½ | 113 | 112½ | 115 | 112 |
| Equitable Gas, N. Y. 1st 5s | 1932 | M. & S. | 118½ | 115⅞ | 118½ | 118½ | 118 | 117 |
| Erie 1st ext. gold 4s | 1947 | M. & N. | 119 | 116½ | 119⅛ | 115 | 118 | 113½ |
| 2d mort., extended, 5s | 1919 | M. & S. | 119⅛ | 119⅛ | 121 | 119 | 122 | 118⅝ |
| 3d mort., extended, 4½s | 1923 | M. & S. | 116⅞ | 113¼ | 118 | 111 | 116⅛ | 115 |
| 4th mort., extended, 5s | 1920 | A. & O. | 123½ | 123½ | 124 | 123¼ | 121¼ | 117 |
| 5th mort., extended, 4s | 1928 | J. & D. | .. | .. | 108 | 107 | 109¼ | 108⅝ |
| 1st con. gold 7s | 1920 | M. & S. | 142 | 134½ | 143½ | 129 | 142 | 137 |
| 1st con. gold fund, coup. 7s | 1920 | M. & S. | .. | .. | 137 | 135¼ | 139 | 136 |
| 1st con. pr. gold 4s | 1996 | J. & J. | 99 | 87 | 101⅜ | 95½ | 102 | 97¼ |
| 1st con. pr. gold 4s reg | 1996 | J. & J. | .. | .. | 99 | 99 | 98½ | 98½ |
| 1st con. gen. l. 3-4s | 1996 | J. & J. | 86½ | 67 | 91½ | 82¼ | 90 | 83 |
| Pennsylvania col. tr. g. 4s | 1951 | J. & D. | .. | .. | 96½ | 92½ | 96 | 91 |
| Long Dock gold 6s | 1935 | A. & O. | 139¼ | 136¼ | 140 | 137 | 137¼ | 134 |
| C. & R. R. Co., 1st cur. guar. 6s | 1922 | M. & N. | .. | .. | .. | .. | 121 | 113¾ |
| D. & Impt. Co., 1st cur. 6s | 1913 | J. & J. | 118 | 118 | 121 | 118½ | 118½ | 118½ |
| Buffalo, N. Y. & Erie 1st mort. 7s | 1916 | J. & D. | .. | .. | 136½ | 136½ | 133 | 127¼ |
| Jefferson R. R. 1st 5s | 1909 | J. & J. | 104½ | 104⅛ | 108 | 105 | 106 | 103¾ |
| Chicago & Erie 1st guar. 4s-5s | 1982 | M. & N. | 123 | 114 | 123¼ | 116 | 125¾ | 118½ |
| New York, Sus. & W'n 1st ref. 5s | 1937 | J. & J. | 111 | 107½ | 119 | 111 | 118 | 114 |
| " " 2d 4½s | 1937 | F. & A. | 99½ | 98 | 94 | 94 | 103 | 102 |
| " " gen. mort. 5s | 1940 | F. & A. | 105½ | 90 | 110¾ | 100 | 110½ | 105 |
| " " term. 1st gold 5s | 1943 | M. & N. | 113 | 108½ | 115½ | 115½ | 116½ | 110 |

| | Due. | Interest Payable. | 1900. H. | 1900. L. | 1901. H. | 1901. L. | 1902. H. | 1902. L. |
|---|---|---|---|---|---|---|---|---|
| Erie, Wilkes. & East. 1st 5s | 1942 | J. & D. | 109 | 104 | 112 | 107½ | 115½ | 110½ |
| Midland of N. J., 1st mort. 6s | 1910 | A. & O. | 120 | 115½ | 118⅝ | 115 | 118 | 112⅛ |
| Evansville & Ind. 1st con. guar. gold 6s | 1926 | J. & J. | 108 | 100 | 114 | 108 | 116 | 114 |
| Evansville & T. H. 1st con. 6s | 1921 | J. J. | 125½ | 120 | 126 | 123 | 126½ | 121 |
| " " 1st gen. gold 5s | 1942 | A. O. | 110 | 102½ | 111 | 107 | 112 | 108⅛ |
| Mt. Vernon 1st 6s | 1923 | A. O. | .. | .. | .. | .. | 112 | 112 |
| Flint & P. Marquette mort. 6s | 1920 | A. O. | 125 | 120 | 127 | 126 | 125 | 121 |
| " " 1st con. 5s | 1939 | M. N. | 108½ | 102 | 114½ | 108 | 115 | 112 |
| " " Pt. Huron div. 1st 5s | 1939 | A. O. | 110 | 105 | 115¼ | 109 | 117 | 111¼ |
| Florida Central & Pen. 1st 5s | 1918 | J. J. | 100 | 100 | .. | .. | .. | .. |
| " " Consol. gold 5s | 1943 | J. J. | .. | .. | .. | .. | 106½ | 106½ |
| Fort Worth & Denver City 1st gold 4-6s | 1921 | J. D. | 84 | 70 | 111 | 76½ | 116½ | 106 |
| Fort Worth & Rio Grande 1st mort. 3-4s | 1928 | J. J. | 69⅛ | 55 | 92 | 67 | 92½ | 86¼ |
| Gal., Har. & Hous. 1st mort. 5s | 1913 | A. O. | 104¼ | 100 | 105 | 101 | 106¼ | 102 |
| Gas & Elec. of Bergen Co., 1st con. g. 5s | 1949 | J. D. | 110¼ | 102⅛ | 102½ | 61½ | .. | .. |
| Georgia & Ala. 1st con. 5s | 1945 | J. J. | .. | .. | .. | .. | 112 | 111 |
| Georgia, Carolina & Northern 1st 5s | 1929 | J. J. | 99½ | 99½ | 109 | 109 | 112 | 109½ |
| General Electric debenture 5s | 1922 | J. D. | 165 | 113 | 185½ | 155 | .. | .. |
| Grand Rapids Gas Light Co., 1st g. 5s | 1915 | F. A. | 107¾ | 107¾ | .. | .. | .. | .. |
| Grand River Coal & Coke 1st g. 6s | 1919 | A. O. | .. | .. | .. | .. | 115 | 108 |
| Great North., Chi., Bur. & Q. col. tr. 4s | 1921 | J. J. | . | .. | 101 | 95 | 97¼ | 94½ |
| " " " " registered | 1921 | J. J. | .. | .. | 98 | 96 | 96⅝ | 93 |
| Hocking Valley 1st con. g. 4½s | 1999 | J. J. | 106¼ | 98 | 110 | 103½ | 112 | 107⅛ |
| Columbus & Hocking Val. 1st ex. g. 4s | 1948 | A. O. | 108 | 102 | 106¾ | 104 | 106 | 105½ |
| Illinois Central 1st gold 4s | 1951 | J. J. | 116 | 114 | 115½ | 115½ | 116 | 113¼ |
| " 1st gold 4s, reg | 1951 | J. J. | 113½ | 113½ | .. | .. | .. | .. |
| " Louisville div., gold 3½s | 1953 | J. J. | 103½ | 100 | 103 | 100½ | 101¼ | 98½ |
| " St. Louis div., gold 3s | 1951 | J. J. | 92¼ | 90 | 91 | 90 | 87½ | 87⅛ |
| " St. L. div., gold 3½ | 1951 | J. J. | 103½ | 99½ | 102¼ | 101¼ | 101 | 98¼ |
| " 1st gold 3½s | 1951 | J. J. | 106½ | 104½ | 107½ | 104 | 105⅜ | 104 |
| " gold 4s | 1952 | A. O. | 105 | 100 | 106 | 104 | 106¾ | 104⅝ |
| " registered | 1952 | A. O. | .. | .. | 102 | 102 | .. | . |
| " gold 4s | 1953 | M. M. | 104½ | 101 | 106 | 102 | 106 | 102½ |
| " registered | 1953 | M. N. | 98 | 98 | .. | .. | 104⅜ | 104¼ |
| " Chic., St. L. & N. O. g. 5s | 1951 | J. D. | 127 | 125 | 130 | 126 | 131 | 127 |
| " Chic., St. L. & N. O. r. g. 5s | 1951 | J. D. | 122 | 122 | 124 | 123⅞ | 126¼ | 126¼ |
| " " gold 3½ | 1951 | J. D. | 103 | 100 | 101¼ | 101⅛ | 104⅝ | 104⅝ |
| " Memphis Div. 1st 4s | 1951 | J. D. | 105½ | 105½ | 107¼ | 106 | 106¾ | 105 |
| " Springfield div., 1st g. 3½s | 1951 | J. J. | 100 | 100 | .. | .. | .. | .. |
| " Western lines 1st 4s | 1951 | F. A. | 114¼ | 111 | 115½ | 112½ | 114¾ | 110 |
| Belle & Caron 1s g. 6s | 1923 | J. D. | 121 | 119¼ | 124 | 124 | .. | .. |
| St. L. South. 1st gu. g. 4s | 1931 | M. S. | 102½ | 102½ | 105 | 105 | 104½ | 101 |
| Illinois Steel deben., non-conv. deb. 5s | 1910 | A. O. | .. | .. | 100½ | 100 | 100 | 100 |
| Indiana, Dec. & West. 1st gtd. 5s | 1935 | J. D. | .. | .. | .. | .. | 107½ | 107½ |
| " " 1st g. 5s | 1935 | J. J. | 105 | 103½ | 109 | 105 | 110 | 105⅝ |
| Indiana, Illinois & Iowa 1st ref. gold 5s | 1948 | M. S. | 110½ | 106½ | .. | .. | .. | .. |
| " " " 1st gold 4s | 1950 | J. J. | .. | .. | 100½ | 98⅝ | 102¾ | 100 |
| Int. & Gt. North. 1st mort. 6s., gold | 1919 | M. N. | 125⅜ | 119½ | 128 | 123 | 127 | 119¼ |
| " " 2d mort. 4½-5s | 1909 | M. S. | 96½ | 83 | 103 | 96 | 103 | 97 |
| " " 3d mort. 4s | 1921 | M. S. | 66 | 54 | 80 | 65 | 80 | 71 |
| International Paper Co. 1st con. 6s | 1918 | F. A. | 109 | 102½ | 112 | 105 | 112 | 107 |
| Iowa Central 1st gold, 5s | 1938 | J. D. | 117¼ | 111 | 119 | 115¼ | 119¼ | 115 |
| " " 1st ref. gold 4s | 1951 | M. S. | .. | .. | 94 | 94 | 97 | 91 |
| Kan. & Hock. Coal & Coke 1st gtd. g. 5s | 1951 | J. J. | .. | .. | .. | .. | 106¼ | 106 |
| Kansas City Southern, 1st g. 3s | 1950 | A. O. | 70 | 61 | 72¾ | 66⅛ | 74 | 68¾ |
| " " 1st g. 3s reg | 1950 | A. & O. | 63¼ | 63¼ | .. | .. | .. | .. |
| Kings Co. Elec. L. & P. Co. pur. my. 6s | 1997 | A. & O. | .. | .. | 126¼ | 123¾ | 124¼ | 120 |
| Knickerbocker Ice Co. (Chic) 1st g. 5s | 1928 | ........ | 95 | 87½ | .. | .. | .. | .. |
| Laclede Gas 1st 5s | 1919 | Q., F. | 111 | 106 | 110 | 107 | 110 | 107½ |
| Lake Erie & Western, 1st mort. 5s | 1937 | J. & J. | 125 | 116½ | 124⅛ | 118¾ | 123 | 119½ |
| " " 2d mort. 5s | 1941 | J. & J. | 120 | 108½ | 120 | 117 | 118¼ | 115 |
| " " N. Ohio 1st gtd 5s | 1945 | A. & O. | 112½ | 110 | 115½ | 110 | 115⅛ | 112½ |
| Lehigh & New York 1st gtd. gold 4s | 1945 | M. & S. | 93 | 91 | 100 | 95 | 97 | 96½ |
| Lehigh Valley Coal 1st 5s | 1933 | J. & J. | .. | – | 109 | 109 | 108½ | 108½ |
| Lehigh Valley of N.Y. 1st 4½s | 1940 | J. & J. | 111½ | 106⅞ | 111⅞ | 108¼ | 112 | 108½ |

| | Due. | Interest Payable. | 1900. H. | 1900. L. | 1901. H. | 1901. L. | 1902. H. | 1902. L. |
|---|---|---|---|---|---|---|---|---|
| Lehigh Valley of N. Y., reg | 1940 | J. & J. | 111 | 109 | 111 | 108⅛ | 109½ | 109½ |
| Lehigh Valley Terminal 1st 5s | 1941 | A. & O. | 115¼ | 112 | 118⅜ | 114⅛ | 120¼ | 117½ |
| Lehigh Valley (Pa.) coll. gold 5s | 1997 | M. & N. | .. | .. | 110½ | 110⅛ | 110½ | 109 |
| Long Island 1st con. 5s | 1931 | Q., J. | 122¼ | 120 | 123 | 121 | 122 | 117½ |
| " gen. mort. 4s | 1938 | J. & D. | 104 | 96 | 105 | 100 | 104¼ | 101¼ |
| " unified gold 4s | 1949 | M. & S. | 99 | 85 | 101 | 97 | 103 | 99 |
| " deb. gold 5s | 1934 | J. & D. | .. | .. | .. | .. | 111 | 111 |
| " Ferry 1st 4½s | 1922 | M. & S. | 105 | 97½ | 105 | 102¼ | 104 | 103 |
| N. Y. & Rockaway Beach 1st 5s | 1927 | M. & S. | 105 | 105 | .. | .. | 112½ | 112½ |
| N. Y., Bklyn & Manhat. Bch. 1st 5s. | 1935 | A. & O. | .. | .. | .. | . | 118 | 112 |
| Brooklyn & Montauk 1st 5s | 1911 | M. & S. | 110 | 106 | 110 | 109½ | .. | .. |
| " North Sh. bch. con. g. 5s. | 1932 | A. & J. | 113 | 105 | .. | .. | 114½ | 112½ |
| Louis. & Jeff. Bridge, guar. gold 4s | 1915 | M. & S. | .. | .. | 100 | 100 | .. | .. |
| Louisville & Nashville, Cecilian Branch 7s | 1907 | M. & S. | 106 | 103½ | .. | .. | .. | .. |
| " N. O. & Mobile 1st mort. 6s | 1930 | J. & J. | 130 | 127 | 131½ | 130 | 130½ | 128½ |
| " " 2d mort. 6s. | 1930 | J. & J. | 117 | 117 | 120 | 119½ | 124⅝ | 122 |
| " E. H. & Nash. 1st mort. 6s. | 1919 | J. & D. | 115 | 111½ | 116 | 113 | 116 | 112 |
| " gen. mort. 6s | 1930 | J. & D. | 122 | 116 | 121 | 112 | 122 | 115½ |
| " Pensacola Div. 6s | 1920 | M. & S. | 115 | 115 | .. | .. | 116⅜ | 115 |
| " St. Louis Div. 1st mort. 6s. | 1921 | M. & S. | 127 | 123 | 126¼ | 124½ | 127½ | 125½ |
| " St. Louis Div., 2d gold 3s | 1980 | M. & S. | 63½ | 63½ | 73½ | 73½ | 77½ | 75 |
| " Pen. & Atlantic 1st mort. 6s. | 1921 | F. & A. | 113⅜ | 110¾ | 117 | 111½ | 117 | 112 |
| " Nash., Flor. & S. 1st guar. 5s | 1937 | F. & A. | 111½ | 109 | 115 | 111 | 114⅞ | 113 |
| " col. trust 5s | 1931 | M. & N. | 111½ | 106¼ | 114¾ | 110½ | 116 | 110½ |
| " L. & N. & Mob. & M. 1s 4½. | 1945 | M. & S. | 111 | 107½ | 112 | 110½ | 110½ | 110¼ |
| " 50 year 5s | 1937 | M. & N. | 112⅛ | 107½ | 114⅛ | 111 | 117 | 111 |
| " unified 4s | 1940 | J. & J. | 102 | 96¼ | 104¼ | 99⅜ | 103¼ | 100⅜ |
| Louisville, Cin. & Lex. g. 4½ | 1931 | M. & N. | .. | .. | .. | .. | 109½ | 109½ |
| " Nash. col. tr. 5-20s, g. 4s | 1903–18 | A. & O. | 100 | 96¼ | 102 | 99 | 101⅛ | 98 |
| " So. & No. Ala. guar. con. 5s. | 1936 | F. & A. | 111 | 107 | 115½ | 110 | .. | .. |
| " S. F. (S. & N., Ala.) 6s | 1910 | A. & O. | .. | .. | .. | .. | 112 | 112 |
| " Ken. Central mort. 4s | 1987 | J. & J. | 99⅜ | 95⅜ | 102 | 96¼ | 101½ | 99 |
| Metropolitan Elevated 1st mort. 6s | 1908 | J. & J. | 118 | 112 | 117⅜ | 114 | 114⅜ | 111 |
| Manhattan R. R. con. 4s | 1990 | A. & O. | 105⅛ | 99 | 107 | 102 | 107½ | 103 |
| " " con. 4s reg | 1990 | A. & O. | .. | .. | 105¼ | 105¼ | 103⅞ | 103⅞ |
| Man. Beach Hotel & Land, ltd., gen. g. 4s | 1940 | M. & N. | .. | .. | .. | .. | 50 | 38 |
| Metropolitan St. Ry. gen. col. tr. gold 5s. | 1997 | F. & A. | 122½ | 116½ | 122½ | 117½ | 122 | 116½ |
| Refunding gold 4s | 2002 | A. & O. | .. | .. | .. | .. | 99 | 96 |
| Broadway & Seventh Ave. 1st 5s | 1943 | J. & D. | 123¼ | 118¾ | 122¾ | 118 | 119⅜ | 116⅜ |
| Registered 1st 5s | 1943 | J. & D. | 119½ | 119½ | .. | .. | .. | .. |
| Lexington Ave. & Pav. F. 1st 5s | 1993 | M. & S. | 125½ | 122 | 123½ | 120 | 124 | 120½ |
| Metropolitan Tel. & Tel. 1st s. f. g. 5s | 1918 | M. & N. | .. | .. | 114 | 114 | 114½ | 114 |
| Metropolitan Wt. Side El. (Chgo.) 1st 4s. | 1938 | F. & A. | .. | . | .. | .. | 103 | 101 |
| Mexican Central consol. 4s | 1911 | J. & J. | 82 | 70 | 90 | 80 | 85 | 74 |
| " 1st con. income gold 3s | 1939 | July | 29⅞ | 20½ | 38¼ | 26½ | 36½ | 21 |
| " 2d con. income gold 3s | 1939 | July | 15¼ | 10 | 27 | 13 | 25½ | 14¼ |
| " col. tr. g., 4½s 1st series. | 1907 | F. & A. | .. | .. | .. | .. | 98⅝ | 96 |
| Mexican International 1st gold 4s | 1977 | M. & S. | 88½ | 83½ | 91⅜ | 82 | .. | .. |
| Mexican National 2d inc. 6s "A" | 1917 | M. & S. | 81 | 81 | 98¼ | 85¼ | .. | .. |
| " 2d inc. 6s "B" | 1917 | August | 18 | 12 | 34½ | 23 | 40¼ | 35 |
| " 1st gold 6s | 1927 | J. & D. | 103⅛ | 103 | 101¾ | 100 | 101 | 100½ |
| Mexican Northern 1st gold 6s | 1910 | J. & D. | 105¼ | 105 | .. | .. | .. | .. |
| Minneapolis & St. Louis 1st mort. 7s | 1927 | J. & D. | 151 | 143½ | 147½ | 147½ | 147½ | 144¼ |
| " 1st con. gold 5s | 1934 | M. & N. | 119 | 111½ | 121¾ | 116½ | 124½ | 120 |
| " 1s and refund gold 4s | 1949 | M. & S. | 99¾ | 93 | 105 | 97 | 106 | 102 |
| " Iowa Ex. 1st mort. 7s | 1909 | J. & D. | 123⅛ | 122½ | 122½ | 119 | 121 | 118 |
| " S'west'n Ex. 1st mort. 7s | 1910 | J. & D. | 123 | 122½ | 122½ | 122½ | 121 | 121 |
| " Pacific Ex. 1st mort. 6s. | 1921 | A. & O. | 128 | 124½ | 123½ | 123½ | 129¼ | 126⅜ |
| Minn. S. S. M. & Atl. 1st g. 4s, stpd., payment of interest guar | 1926 | J. & J. | .. | .. | 103⅛ | 98 | .. | .. |
| Minn., St. P. & S. S. M. con. g. 4s, stpd., payment of interest guar | 1926 | J. & J. | .. | .. | 98 | 98 | . | .. |
| Minn. St. Ry. 1st con. gold 5s | 1919 | J. & J. | .. | .. | 110 | 110 | 110 | 110 |
| Missouri, Kansas & Eastern 1st guar g. 5s. | 1942 | A. & O. | 108 | 102 | 111½ | 107 | 113½ | 109 |
| Missouri, Kansas & Texas 1st 4s | 1990 | J. & D. | 98⅛ | 88⅛ | 100⅞ | 96¼ | 101½ | 97½ |

| | Due. | Interest Payable. | 1900. H. | 1900. L. | 1901. H. | 1901. L. | 1902. H. | 1902. L. |
|---|---|---|---|---|---|---|---|---|
| Missouri, Kansas & Texas 2d 4s........ | 1990 | F. & A. | 77½ | 64 | 87 | 75 | 87¼ | 80 |
| " " 1st 5s....... | 1944 | M. & S. | 98 | 89 | 106 | 97 | 108 | 102½ |
| " K. Cy. & Pac. 1st guar. 4s. | 1990 | F. & A. | 87 | 76 | 91¾ | 87⅛ | 92 | 88 |
| " Dal. & Waco 1st guar. 5s.. | 1940 | M. & N. | 90 | 90 | 100 | 98 | 106¼ | 102 |
| " St. Louis Div., 1st reg. 4s... | 2001 | A. & O. | .. | .. | .. | .. | 88¼ | 85½ |
| " T. of T., 1st 5s ........... | 1942 | M. & S. | 97½ | 88 | 108 | 96 | 108½ | 100 |
| Sherman, Shrevep't & So. 1st gu.g. 5s | 1942 | M. & S. | 99¾ | 92¼ | 105⅞ | 99¾ | 105½ | 101½ |
| Missouri Pacific 1st 7s.................. | 1903 | M. & N. | .. | .. | .. | .. | 114¾ | 110 |
| " 1st con. 6s............ | 1920 | M. & N. | 121⅛ | 114¾ | 125⅝ | 119½ | 126 | 120¼ |
| " 3d mort. 7s ............ | 1906 | M. & N. | 118 | 112 | 117 | 114 | 114¾ | 110 |
| " 1st col. 5s.............. | 1920 | F. & A. | 104 | 90 | 110 | 103 | 109 | 103½ |
| " trust gold 5s........... | 1917 | M. & S. | 103½ | 94 | 109½ | 100½ | 109¼ | 103 |
| Central Bch Ry. 1st guar. g. 4s..... | 1919 | F. & A. | .. | .. | 91 | 89½ | 95⅝ | 91⅛ |
| Leroy & Caney Val. A. L. 1st 5s.... | 1926 | J. & J. | 94 | 92 | 100 | 100 | .. | .. |
| Pacific of Missouri, 1st ex. g. 4s..... | 1938 | F. & A. | 107¼ | 105¾ | 107 | 105 | 107¼ | 104 |
| " 2d mort. extd. 5s. | 1938 | J. & J. | 115¼ | 112½ | 115½ | 113 | 116½ | 114 |
| St.L.& Iron M't'n gen.con. r'y& l. g.5s | 1931 | A. & O. | 114¼ | 108 | 119 | 114 | 120 | 112 |
| " stamped guar. 5s.. | 1931 | A. & O. | 113 | 109 | 116½ | 114½ | 114 | 112½ |
| " Ufd & Ref. 4s....... .. | 1929 | J. & J. | 88 | 76 | 96¼ | 84¼ | 95 | 91 |
| Mobile & Birmingham prior lien gold 5s. | 1945 | J. & J. | 110¼ | 110¼ | .. | .. | .. | .. |
| " " mtg. gold 4s..... | 1945 | J. & J. | .. | .. | .. | .. | 93½ | 93 |
| Mobile & Ohio new mort. 6s............ | 1927 | J. & D. | 130 | 122 | 132 | 127½ | 132 | 128 |
| " 1st mort. ext. 6s......... | 1927 | Q., J. | 124 | 120¼ | 130 | 121 | 128½ | 127 |
| " gen. 4s .................. | 1938 | M. & S. | 87¾ | 83 | 97 | 87½ | 100 | 97 |
| " J. P. Morgan & Co. ctfs.. | .... | ......... | .. | .. | 96 | 94 | .. | .. |
| " St. L. & C. 4s........... | 1931 | J. & J. | 96½ | 96½ | 101½ | 99 | 101½ | 100½ |
| " col. tr. g. 4s............ | 1930 | A. F. | .. | .. | 95¼ | 95¼ | 91 | 91 |
| " Montgomery div. 1st g. 5s. | 1947 | F. & A. | 110 | 106½ | 116¾ | 110 | 118½ | 114 |
| Nash., Chattanooga & St. L. 1st m. 7s... | 1913 | J. & J. | 130⅝ | 126 | 130 | 126½ | 129 | 125¾ |
| " " 2d 6s.............. | 1901 | J. & J. | 100½ | 100½ | .. | .. | .. | .. |
| " " 1st con. gold 5s... | 1928 | A. & O. | 110½ | 104½ | 116 | 111 | 116 | 112¼ |
| " " 1st g. 6s McM. M. W. & Ala....... | 1917 | J. & J. | .. | .. | .. | .. | 116 | 116 |
| National Starch Mfg. Co., 1st 6s........ | 1920 | M. & N. | 108 | 104 | 110 | 105 | 110¼ | 95 |
| National Starch Co. s. f. deb. 5s....... | 1925 | J. & J. | .. | .. | 96 | 91 | 95 | 73 |
| New York & New Jersey Tel., gen. 5s.. | 1920 | M. & N. | .. | .. | 117 | 113¼ | .. | .. |
| New York & Queens Electric Light & Power 1st con. g. 5s.................. | 1930 | F. & A. | .. | .. | 104⅛ | 102 | 108½ | 104½ |
| New York Central & Hud. R. 1st coup. 7s | 1903 | J. & J. | 112 | 108¾ | 108 | 104½ | 104⅞ | 101⅜ |
| " " 1st reg....... | 1903 | J. & J. | 111 | 108⅛ | 107⅞ | 102¾ | 104⅝ | 101⅜ |
| " deb. 5s coup ......... | 1904 | M. & S. | 108 | 102¾ | 106½ | 101 | 104 | 102⅜ |
| " deb. 5s reg........... | 1904 | M. & S. | 107⅞ | 105 | 106¾ | 103 | 103¾ | 101¼ |
| " deb. 4s of 1890....... | 1905 | J. & D. | 103⅜ | 101⅞ | 104⅞ | 102¼ | 101¾ | 100¾ |
| " reg. 4s. 1890......... | 1905 | J. & D. | .. | .. | 102¼ | 99⅞ | 100¼ | 99 |
| " deb. cert. ext. 4s...... | 1905 | M. & N. | 103⅝ | 101 | 103⅜ | 100 | 101⅜ | 100 |
| " deb. cert. ext. 4s reg.. | 1905 | M. & N. | .. | .. | 100⅛ | 100⅛ | 99½ | 99½ |
| " gold mortgage 3½s.. | 1997 | J. & J. | 111½ | 108¼ | 110¾ | 107½ | 109½ | 104 |
| " registered ........... | 1997 | J. & J. | 110 | 110 | 109½ | 109½ | 109 | 106 |
| " Lake Sho. col. g. 3½s | 1998 | F. & A. | 99 | 95½ | 99 | 95 | 98 | 92 |
| " " registered.. | 1998 | F. & A. | 98 | 93 | 97⅛ | 94 | 96¼ | 91 |
| " Mich. Cent. col. g 3½s | 1998 | F. & A. | 98 | 95 | 97⅛ | 93⅞ | 97⅝ | 92 |
| " " registered. | 1998 | F. & A. | 97 | 94 | 97 | 96 | 96 | 91 |
| " Pitts., McK. & Y. 1st 6s | 1932 | J. & J. | .. | .. | 146⅜ | 146⅜ | .. | .. |
| New Jersey Junction, guar., 1st 4s... | 1986 | F. & A. | 102 | 102 | 108 | 108 | 105 | 105 |
| West Shore 1st 4s, guar............. | 2361 | J. & J. | 116¼ | 110 | 116⅛ | 111 | 116 | 112 |
| West Shore 1st 4s, guar., reg......... | 2361 | J. & J. | 114⅛ | 110 | 115⅛ | 110½ | 115½ | 109 |
| New York & Putnam 1st 4s......... | 1993 | A. & O. | .. | .. | 105½ | 104½ | .. | .. |
| Beech Creek 1st gold 4s............. | 1936 | J. & J. | 110½ | 108 | 112⅛ | 111 | .. | .. |
| Rome, Wat. & Ogd. con. 1st m., ext., 5s. | 1922 | A. & O. | 129½ | 125⅜ | 129 | 125¼ | 127½ | 118 |
| U.& B. Riv. gtd. 4s.................. | 1922 | J. & J. | 110 | 108 | 110½ | 110¼ | 109⅞ | 107½ |
| Clearfield Bituminous Coal Corporation 1st s. f. int. gtd. gold 4s ser. A | 1940 | J. & J. | .. | .. | 92½ | 92½ | 95 | 93 |
| Lake Shore & Michigan Southern— | | | | | | | | |
| Detroit, M. & Tol. 1st mort. 7s...... | 1906 | F. & A. | 121 | 119 | 117⅝ | 117 | 114 | 114 |
| Lake Shore Div. con. coup. 2d mort. 7s | 1903 | J. & D. | 116½ | 109⅝ | 113 | 107⅛ | 107⅛ | 102⅜ |

| | Due. | Interest Payable. | 1900. H. | 1900. L. | 1901. H. | 1901. L. | 1902 H. | 1902 L. |
|---|---|---|---|---|---|---|---|---|
| New York Central & Hudson River— | | | | | | | | |
| Lake S. div. con. reg. 2d mort. 7s... | 1903 | J. & D. | 114⅜ | 111¼ | 111 | 107⅛ | 107¾ | 104 |
| " gold 3½s.............. | 1997 | J. & D. | 111⅜ | 109 | 111¼ | 107½ | 109½ | 104 |
| " " reg............. | 1997 | J. & D. | 110½ | 110½ | .. | .. | .. | .. |
| Mahoning Coal, 1st mort. 5s........ | 1934 | J. & J. | 130 | 129 | 128 | 128 | 127½ | 127½ |
| Mohawk & Malone 1st g. gu. g. 4s.. | 1991 | M. & S. | 107½ | 106¾ | .. | .. | .. | .. |
| " " income 5s.. .... | 1992 | Sept.... | .. | | 110¼ | 99¼ | .. | .. |
| Michigan Central 1st con. 7s........ | 1902 | M. & N. | 109¾ | 104½ | 106⅜ | 101⅛ | 102⅝ | 101¾ |
| " con. 5s............ | 1902 | M. & N. | 104¾ | 101⅞ | 103¼ | 100¼ | 101⅜ | 101⅜ |
| " coup. 5s.......... | 1931 | M. & S. | 128 | 126 | 131⅜ | 127 | 132½ | 128 |
| " reg. 5s............ | 1931 | Q., M. | 127½ | 127½ | 125 | 125 | 130 | 127 |
| " con. 6s........... | 1909 | M. & S. | 121 | 119¼ | 119 | 118½ | .. | .. |
| " mort. 4s.......... | 1940 | J. & J. | 105 | 105 | 110 | 110 | .. | .. |
| " mort. 4s, reg...... | 1940 | J. & J. | 106½ | 106½ | .. | .. | .. | .. |
| New York & Harlem g. 3½s........ | 2000 | M. & N. | 115⅞ | 115⅞ | .. | .. | .. | .. |
| New York & Northern 1st gold 5s... | 1927 | A. & O. | 122½ | 121 | 122½ | 121 | 121½ | 119½ |
| New York, Chi. & St. Louis 1st gold 4s.. | 1937 | A. & O. | 108½ | 104⅛ | 109⅛ | 106 | 108 | 104 |
| " " reg........ | 1937 | A. & O. | 106¼ | 103½ | 107 | 105 | 106⅝ | 105 |
| New York Dock 50 year gold 4s......... | 1951 | F. & A. | .. | .. | 94½ | 93⅞ | 100 | 90½ |
| New York G., E. L., H. & P. 1st col. tr. 5s | 1948 | J. & D. | .. | .. | 116 | 108⅛ | 116¼ | 110¼ |
| " " pur. my. col. tr. g. 4s | 1949 | F. & A. | .. | .. | 98¼ | 94⅜ | 98½ | 94 |
| New York, New Hav. & Hart. 1st reg. 4s.. | 1903 | J. & D. | .. | .. | 102 | 100 | .. | .. |
| " " con.deb.certs.$1,000 | .... | A. & O. | 195½ | 185¾ | 206 | 196 | 229½ | 204½ |
| " " " small " $100 | .... | ........ | 189⅛ | 185 | 203 | 195 | 220 | 207 |
| Housatonic con. mort. 5s........... | 1937 | M. & N. | 135½ | 132 | 136 | 134 | 135½ | 135½ |
| New York & New Eng'd 1st mort. 7s | 1905 | J. & J. | 114 | 114 | .. | .. | .. | .. |
| " " 1st mort. 6s | 1905 | J. & J. | .. | .. | 110 | 108 | 106⅞ | 106¼ |
| New York, Ont. & Western refunding 4s. | 1992 | M. & S. | 107¾ | 102 | 108 | 101½ | 105⅛ | 100½ |
| Norfolk & Southern 1st 5s..... ........ | 1941 | M. & N. | 114¼ | 110 | 112½ | 110¼ | 116½ | 116½ |
| Norfolk & Western gen. mort. 6s........ | 1931 | M. & N. | 136 | 129 | 136 | 132 | 135½ | 133 |
| " New River 1st mort. 6s. | 1932 | A. & O. | 133 | 130 | 134 | 131 | 135¼ | 131¾ |
| " imp. and ext. 6s....... | 1934 | F. & A. | 131¾ | 129 | 133½ | 129½ | 136 | 129 |
| " 1st con. g. 4s.......... | 1996 | A. & O. | 100 | 90½ | 104 | 99½ | 104½ | 99½ |
| " 1st con. g. 4s reg...... | 1996 | A. & O. | 97⅜ | 97⅜ | 103 | 103 | 100½ | 100½ |
| " Col.C. & T. 1st gu. g. 5s | 1922 | J. & J. | .. | .. | 107½ | 107½ | .. | .. |
| " Poca. C. & C. joint 4s. | 1941 | J. & D. | .. | .. | .. | .. | 95 | 90 |
| Scioto Val. & N. E. 1st gen. g. 4s... | 1989 | M. & N. | 103 | 95 | 104 | 99 | 104⅛ | 100⅜ |
| Northern Pacific, term. 1st gold 6s....... | 1933 | J. & J. | 120 | 113 | 119 | 115⅛ | 119½ | 115 |
| St. Paul & N. P. gen. 6s............ | 1923 | F. & A. | 132½ | 131½ | 131½ | 128 | 129⅛ | 127¾ |
| Nor. Pac. Ry. prior lien 4s......... | 1997 | Q., J. | 106¼ | 102¼ | 106 | 103 | 106⅛ | 102⅝ |
| " " " registered | 1997 | Q., J. | 105½ | 101 | 105⅞ | 103½ | 105½ | 102 |
| " " gen. lien gold 3s..... | 2047 | Q., F. | 72½ | 63⅞ | 73⅞ | 69½ | 75⅜ | 71⅝ |
| " " gen. lien gold 3s reg. | 2047 | Q., F. | 70¼ | 65½ | 72⅜ | 69 | 75 | 72 |
| Washington Central Ry 1st gold 4s. | 1948 | Q. Mch. | 88¾ | 88¾ | 94⅞ | 94⅞ | 94½ | 94½ |
| St. Paul & Duluth 1st mort. 5s. .. | 1931 | F. & A. | 130 | 124 | 122½ | 122½ | 122 | 118 |
| " 2d mort. 5s...... | 1917 | A. & O | 116½ | 109 | 117 | 110⅜ | 112½ | 110 |
| " 1st con. g. 4s.... | 1968 | J. & D. | 105 | 97½ | 106 | 100 | 100 | 100 |
| St. Paul-Duluth Div. g. 4s.......... | 1996 | J. & D. | .. | .. | 102 | 99¾ | 102½ | 100 |
| Ohio River 1st gold 5s.................. | 1936 | J. & D. | 110 | 109 | 112½ | 112 | 114 | 113 |
| " gen. gold 5s................. | 1937 | A. & O. | 95½ | 90 | .. | .. | 110 | 108 |
| Omaha & St. Louis 1st g. 4s trust cert... | 1901 | J. & J. | 77 | 60 | .. | .. | .. | .. |
| Pacific Coast 1st gold 5s................ | 1946 | J. & D. | 112 | 104¼ | 113 | 108 | 114½ | 108 |
| Panama, 1st s. f. g. 4½................ | 1917 | A. & O. | 105 | 102 | 105 | 102 | 102½ | 101 |
| Panama, S. F. sub. g. 6s.............. | 1910 | M. & N. | 101 | 101 | .. | .. | 102 | 101½ |
| Pennsylvania, guar. 4½s., 1st coup...... | 1921 | J. & J. | 117⅛ | 111½ | 115¼ | 112 | 113½ | 109½ |
| " 1st reg................ | 1921 | J. & J. | 116 | 111½ | 114½ | 110½ | 112¾ | 109½ |
| " gtd. 3½ col. tr. certs. B. | 1941 | F. & A. | .. | .. | 98 | 98 | 99 | 97½ |
| " tr. co.certs., guar. g. 3½ | 1916 | M. & N. | .. | .. | .. | .. | 98 | 96 |
| " real estate 4s, gold....... | 1923 | M. & N. | .. | .. | 109½ | 109½ | 110½ | 105½ |
| " conv. g. 3½............. | 1912 | M. & N. | .. | .. | .. | .. | 112⅝ | 103⅛ |
| " P.C.C.& St.L.con.4½s A | 1940 | A. & O. | 117⅜ | 114 | 118 | 114 | 116½ | 114¾ |
| " " B | 1942 | A. & O. | 117¼ | 113⅞ | 117¾ | 113 | 115½ | 112 |
| " " C | 1942 | M. & N. | .. | .. | 116½ | 116½ | .. | .. |
| " " 4s D | 1945 | M. & N. | 115¾ | 106½ | 106¾ | 106¼ | 106¼ | 106¼ |
| " " 3½ E | 1949 | F. & A. | 101⅞ | 99 | 99¾ | 97 | 97½ | 97 |

| | Due. | Interest Payable. | 1900. H. | 1900. L. | 1901. H. | 1901. L. | 1902. H. | 1902. L. |
|---|---|---|---|---|---|---|---|---|
| Pennsylvania, G.R.& I. ex. 1st gu. g. 4½... | 1941 | J. & J. | 112¼ | 108 | 112½ | 112 | 111½ | 111 |
| " P., Ft. W. & C. 1st m. 7s | 1912 | J. & J. | 139⅛ | 135 | 136½ | 132½ | 132 | 127⅝ |
| " " 2d m. 7s | 1912 | J. & J. | 137¼ | 135½ | 136¼ | 132½ | 131½ | 127¾ |
| " " 3d m. 7s | 1912 | A. & O. | 134 | 131 | 136⅛ | 128¼ | .. | .. |
| " Cle. & Marietta 1st g. 4½ | 1935 | M. & N. | 112¾ | 109 | .. | .. | .. | .. |
| " gen. gu. g. 4½ ser. A.. | 1942 | J. & J. | 121 | 117½ | .. | .. | .. | .. |
| Un. N. J. R. R. & Can. gen. 4s...... | 1944 | M. & S. | 117 | 117 | .. | .. | .. | .. |
| Chicago, St. L. & Pitts. 1st con. 5s.. | 1932 | A. & O. | 124 | 121 | 126⅛ | 121¼ | 123 | 122½ |
| Erie & Pitts. gen. gu. g. 3½ B., ... | 1940 | J. & J. | 102 | 101¼ | .. | .. | .. | .. |
| People's Gas & C., Chicago, 1st gld 6s.. | 1904 | M. & N. | 107 | 107 | .. | .. | 104 | 104 |
| " " " 2d gld. 6s.. | 1904 | J. & D. | 115½ | 102½ | 104 | 102⅛ | 106 | 103 |
| " " " 1st c. g. 6s.. | 1943 | A. & O. | 127 | 116 | 126 | 120 | 126 | 117¾ |
| " " " refund. g. 5s | 1947 | M. & S. | .. | .. | .. | .. | 104 | 104 |
| " Chi. Gas. L. & C., 1st gu. g. 5s. | 1937 | J. & J. | 109½ | 107 | 111½ | 108 | 111¼ | 108½ |
| " Consol. of Chic., 1st gu. g. 5s. | 1936 | J. & D. | 109 | 105 | 110 | 104½ | 109½ | 107¼ |
| " Equit. G. & F., Chi., 1st gu. 6s. | 1905 | J. & J. | 103 | 103 | 105¾ | 102 | 105 | 102½ |
| Mutual Fuel Gas, 1st gu. g. 5s...... | 1947 | M. & N. | 105 | 102 | 106 | 102 | 106 | 105 |
| Peoria & Pekin U'n 1st mort. gold 6s.... | 1921 | Q., F. | 132½ | 130 | 133½ | 133¼ | 130¼ | 130 |
| " 2d mort. gold 4½s...... | 1921 | M. & N. | 101 | 98 | .. | .. | .. | .. |
| Pitts. & Western 1st gold 4s........... | 1917 | J. & J. | 101 | 99⅝ | 101¼ | 99 | 102½ | 100 |
| " " 1st gold 4s J. P. M & Co. certs | .... | ........ | 101½ | 99½ | 101½ | 98 | 101 | 100 |
| Pittsburg Junction 1st 6s.............. | 1922 | J. & J. | .. | .. | 120 | 120 | .. | .. |
| Pitts., Shen. & L. Erie 1st 5s.......... | 1940 | A. & O. | 116½ | 113½ | 118½ | 113⅜ | 121 | 119 |
| Pitts., Young. & Ash. 1st con. 5s....... | 1927 | M. & N. | .. | .. | 121½ | 121 | 120½ | 111 |
| Pleasant Valley Coal 1st s. f. 5s....... | 1928 | J. & J. | 105 | 105 | .. | .. | .. | .. |
| Railroad Securities Co. g. 3½s (Ill. Cen. col.) | 1951 | J. & J. | .. | .. | 91¾ | 91¼ | .. | .. |
| Reading gen. 4s........................ | 1997 | J. & J. | 96⅛ | 83 | 100¾ | 92½ | 101 | 95½ |
| " gen. 4s reg..................... | 1997 | J. & J. | 88 | 87¼ | 92 | 92 | . | .. |
| Jersey Central col. g. 4s............ | 1951 | A. & O. | .. | .. | .. | .. | 98 | 92 |
| Rio Grande Junc. 1st 5s................ | 1939 | J. & D. | 101 | 94¼ | 105 | 105 | 115¼ | 112½ |
| Rio Grande So. 1st 4s.................. | 1940 | J. & J. | 81¼ | 71 | 85 | 80½ | 82½ | 80½ |
| Rio Grande, So., guaranteed 4s......... | 1940 | J. & J. | 94 | 92⅞ | 94¼ | 92½ | 94⅝ | 91 |
| Rio Grande W., 1st g. 4s............ ... | 1939 | J. & J. | 101 | 94¼ | 103¾ | 98½ | 102⅞ | 99 |
| " mtg. & col. tr. g. 4s, ser. A. | 1949 | A. & O. | .. | .. | 96¼ | 93¼ | 95¼ | 91⅛ |
| Utah Cent. 1st gu. g. 4s........... | 1917 | A. & O. | 88¼ | 85 | 90 | 90 | 97 | 97 |
| Rutland, Can., 1st guar. g. 4s.......... | 1949 | J. & J. | .. | | 101¼ | 101¼ | .. | .. |
| St. Jo. & G. I. 1st gold 2-3-4s.......... | 1947 | J. & J. | 92 | 81 | 98 | 89½ | 99½ | 95 |
| St. L. & San F. 2d mort. 6s, class B.... | 1906 | M. & N. | 113¼ | 110⅛ | 114⅛ | 110 | 111½ | 105⅝ |
| " 2d mort. 6s, class C........ | 1906 | M. & N. | 113½ | 110⅛ | 114⅛ | 110 | 110⅛ | 107 |
| " gold 4s..................... | 1996 | J. & J. | 92½ | 79 | 102 | 91¼ | 101 | 96 |
| " Southw'n div. 1st gold 5s.... | 1947 | A. & O. | 100 | 98½ | 106½ | 106½ | 100 | 100 |
| " Central div. 1st gold 4s..... | 1929 | A. & O. | 95 | 90¾ | 100 | 96 | .. | .. |
| " gen. mort. 6s............... | 1931 | J. & J. | 130 | 121¾ | 136½ | 125 | 134 | 130 |
| " gen. mort. 5s............... | 1931 | J. & J. | 115½ | 106 | 119 | 112½ | 118½ | 114 |
| " 1st trust gold 5s........... | 1987 | A. & O. | 104 | 102½ | .. | .. | .. | .. |
| " Northwestern Div. 4s....... | 1950 | ........ | .. | .. | 102¾ | 97 | .. | .. |
| " refunding g. 4s............ | 1951 | J. & J. | .. | .. | 98½ | 97¼ | 98⅛ | 93½ |
| " K.C. F. S. & M. R.R. c. g. 6s | 1928 | M. & N. | .. | .. | 123½ | 123½ | 125⅛ | 125⅛ |
| " K.C. F. S. & M. Ry. ref. g. 4s | 1936 | A. & O. | .. | .. | 90⅛ | 87 | 94¾ | 85¾ |
| St. Louis Southwestern 1st 4s........... | 1989 | M. & N. | 96⅝ | 85 | 101½ | 95¼ | 100½ | 94 |
| " " 2d inc. 4s....... | 1989 | J. & J. | 75 | 53⅞ | 82¼ | 71 | 90½ | 87 |
| " " consol. gold 4s.. | 1932 | J. & D. | .. | .. | .. | .. | 90½ | 80 |
| St. Paul City Cable con. 5s............. | 1937 | J. & J. | 115 | 111 | 114½ | 111½ | .. | .. |
| St. Paul, Minn. & Manitoba 2d mort. 6s. | 1909 | A. & O. | 121 | 116¼ | 118⅞ | 115¼ | 117 | 112 |
| " Dakota Ext. 6s........... | 1910 | M. & N. | 121½ | 117½ | 120½ | 116 | 118⅛ | 113⅛ |
| " 1st con. 6s.............. | 1933 | J. & J. | 143½ | 137 | 142 | 139 | 141½ | 133⅞ |
| " 1st con. 6s reg........... | 1933 | J. & J. | .. | .. | .. | .. | 140 | 139 |
| " 1st con. 6s reduced to 4½s. | 1933 | J. & J. | 117⅛ | 112¼ | 116½ | 113 | 115½ | 112 |
| " registered............... | 1933 | J. & J. | 115¼ | 115¼ | 116⅛ | 116⅛ | .. | .. |
| " Montana ext. 1st gold 4s.. | 1937 | J. & D. | 105 | 102½ | 107⅛ | 102½ | 109 | 102½ |
| " " registered...... | 1937 | J. & D. | .. | .. | 106 | 106 | .. | .. |
| " Mont. Cen. 1st 6s, int. guar. | 1937 | J. & J. | 135½ | 129½ | 140 | 132 | 141¼ | 133½ |
| " " guar. 5s....... | 1937 | J. & J. | 118¾ | 116⅞ | 124 | 121 | 125 | 124⅛ |
| " Minn. Union 1st 6s....... | 1922 | J. & J. | 128 | 128 | .. | .. | .. | .. |
| " Ea. Minn. div. 1st 5s..... | 1908 | A. & O. | 109⅛ | 108 | 110 | 106 | 107½ | 106⅛ |

| | Due. | Interest Payable. | 1900. H. | 1900. L. | 1901. H. | 1901. L. | 1902. H. | 1902. L. |
|---|---|---|---|---|---|---|---|---|
| St. Paul, Minn. & Manitoba, W. & S. F. 1st 5s | 1938 | J. & D. | .. | .. | .. | .. | 125½ | 124⅜ |
| San Fran. & Nor. Pac. 1st s. f. 5s | 1919 | J. & J. | 112 | 112 | 113¼ | 110½ | .. | .. |
| Santa Fe Pres. & Ph. 1st g. 5s | 1942 | M. & S. | .. | .. | 111 | 104 | .. | .. |
| Sav., Fla. & West. 1st 6s | 1934 | A. & O. | 126½ | 125½ | 128 | 128 | 128 | 128 |
| " " 1st g. 5s | 1934 | A. & O. | .. | .. | .. | .. | .. | .. |
| St. Johns div. 1st g 4s | 1934 | J. & J. | 94½ | 94½ | 95¼ | 94 | .. | .. |
| Brunswick & Western 1st gu. g. 4s | 1938 | J. & J. | 85 | 82⅝ | 87 | 87 | .. | .. |
| Alabama Midland 1st g. 5s | 1928 | M. & N. | 106 | 100 | 111 | 106⅛ | 112¼ | 110 |
| Silver Sp., Ocala & Gulf guar. g. 4s | 1918 | J. & J. | .. | .. | 91⅝ | 91¼ | 97 | 89½ |
| Seaboard Air Line g. 4s | 1950 | A. & O. | .. | .. | .. | .. | 90 | 82½ |
| " " col. tr. ref. g. 5s | 1911 | M. & N. | .. | .. | .. | .. | 105⅛ | 100½ |
| Seaboard & Roanoke—Carolina Cent. con. g. 4s | 1949 | J. & J. | .. | .. | .. | .. | 98 | 96¼ |
| Sodus Bay & South. 1st g. 5s | 1924 | J. & J. | .. | .. | 100 | 100 | .. | .. |
| Southern Pacific of Ariz. guar. 1st 6s | 1909 | J. & J. | 114½ | 110 | 114½ | 110½ | 113 | 112⅝ |
| " guar. 6s | 1910 | J. & J. | .. | .. | .. | .. | 114½ | 112½ |
| " of Cal. 1st g. 6s, A | 1905 | J. & J. | 110 | 107 | 111½ | 107 | 108¼ | 105¼ |
| " " 1st g. 6s, B | 1905 | April. | 110⅜ | 110⅜ | 108¼ | 106⅝ | .. | .. |
| " " 1st g. 6s, C and D | 1906 | Oct. | 112 | 110¼ | 109 | 108 | 110⅝ | 110⅝ |
| Southern Pacific 1st gold 6s | 1905-1912 | A. & O. | 119 | 117¾ | 120 | 119 | 119½ | 119½ |
| " 1st con. guar. 5s | 1937 | M. & N. | 107 | 105½ | .. | .. | .. | .. |
| " 1st con. gu. 5s stpd | 1937 | M. & N. | 109½ | 104½ | 111 | 106½ | 111 | 108½ |
| " 2-5 year 4½s | 1905 | J. & D. | .. | .. | 101½ | 95⅜ | 101⅞ | 97¾ |
| " Austin & N.W. 1st 5s | 1941 | J. & J. | 99¼ | 94¾ | 111 | 96 | .. | .. |
| " of New Mexico 1st 6s | 1911 | J. & J. | 116½ | 116⅛ | 114¼ | 110 | 116¼ | 112 |
| Gal., Har'g & S. Ant'o 1st mort. 6s | 1910 | F. & A. | 110½ | 110 | 113½ | 108½ | 113 | 109¾ |
| " " " 2d mort. 7s | 1905 | J. & D. | 106½ | 104½ | 107¾ | 106 | 108 | 108 |
| " " " M.&P. Div. 1st g. 5s | 1931 | M. & N. | 102¾ | 97½ | 107½ | 100 | 110¼ | 109½ |
| Morgan's La. & Texas 1st mort. 6s | 1920 | J. & J. | 120½ | 120½ | 125 | 123 | 123½ | 122 |
| " " 1st 7s | 1918 | A. & O. | .. | .. | 137½ | 136 | 137 | 130 |
| Oregon & California 1st mort. 5s | 1927 | J. & J. | 101⅛ | 98½ | 112½ | 107 | .. | .. |
| Houston & Tex. Cen. 1st guar. 5s | 1937 | J. & J. | 114 | 109 | 113½ | 110 | 112½ | 110 |
| " " con. guar. 6s | 1912 | A. & O. | 113 | 109⅝ | 112 | 110 | 114½ | 110⅜ |
| " " gen. guar. 4s | 1921 | A. & O. | 87 | 81 | 95 | 86¼ | 97 | 90½ |
| " " Waco & N.W. 1st g. 6s | 1930 | M. & N. | .. | .. | 126 | 126 | 127½ | 125¾ |
| Central Pacific, col. g. 4s | 1949 | J. & D. | 85⅜ | 76½ | 95½ | 83 | 96 | 89 |
| " " col. g. 4s reg | 1949 | J. & D. | .. | .. | 89 | 89 | 95 | 94⅜ |
| " " 1st ref. gu. g. 4s | 1949 | F. & A. | 101¾ | 97 | 103¼ | 100 | 104 | 100 |
| " " 1st reg. gu. g. 4s | 1949 | F. & A. | 99⅞ | 99⅞ | .. | .. | .. | .. |
| " " mort. gu. g. 3½ | 1929 | J. & D. | 86¼ | 80⅞ | 89½ | 83¼ | 89¼ | 84¾ |
| Gila Val. G. & Nor. 1st gu. g. 5s | 1924 | M. & N. | 110 | 100 | 108 | 105 | 112 | 108 |
| Nor. of Cal. 1st gu. g. 5s | 1938 | A. & O. | .. | .. | 113 | 113 | .. | .. |
| Texas & N. O., 1st 7s | 1905 | F. & A. | 114¼ | 114¼ | 110¼ | 110 | 108 | 108 |
| " " 1st con. gold 5s | 1943 | J. & J. | 106¼ | 101 | 111⅛ | 103¾ | .. | .. |
| " " Sabine Div., 1st 6s | 1912 | M. & S. | .. | .. | .. | .. | 114½ | 111½ |
| Houst., E. & W. Tex. 1st gold 5s | 1933 | M. & N. | 105 | 100 | 106½ | 106 | 106 | 103 |
| " " " 1st gu. g. 5s | 1933 | M. & N. | .. | .. | .. | .. | 102½ | 102½ |
| San Ant'o & Aransas Pass 1st guar. 4s | 1943 | J. & J. | 81¼ | 73 | 91¾ | 77⅞ | 92 | 85 |
| Southern Railway 1st con. gold 5s | 1994 | J. & J. | 114½ | 106 | 124½ | 111¾ | 124 | 118 |
| " " 1st con. gold 5s reg | 1994 | J. & J. | 108¾ | 107¾ | 120¼ | 116 | 122 | 122 |
| Memphis Division 1st 4-4½-5s | 1996 | J. & J. | 109½ | 108 | 112 | 109 | 115 | 112½ |
| St. Louis Div. 1st gold 4s | 1951 | J. & J. | .. | .. | 101 | 96 | 101½ | 99 |
| Columbia & Greenville 1st mort. 5-6s | 1916 | J. & J. | 115 | 115 | 121 | 119¾ | 120 | 119 |
| East Tenn., Va. & Ga. 1st con. 5s | 1956 | J. & J. | 120 | 115 | 121 | 117 | 122¾ | 118 |
| East Tenn., Va. & Ga. divisional 5s | 1930 | J. & J. | 119 | 114¾ | 120¼ | 117½ | 120½ | 116¾ |
| E. Tenn., reorg. lien 4-5s | 1938 | M. & S. | 112 | 108½ | 116⅛ | 111⅞ | 117½ | 113½ |
| Knox. & Ohio, 1st 6s, gold | 1925 | J. & J. | 124 | 118 | 129 | 124⅛ | 127¾ | 125 |
| Alabama Central, 1st 6s | 1918 | J. & J. | .. | .. | 120 | 120 | .. | .. |
| Georgia Pacific 1st g. 6s.b | 1922 | J. & J. | 125¼ | 119½ | 128⅜ | 124½ | 129 | 125 |
| Richmond & Danville de . 5s stpd | 1927 | A. & O. | 109½ | 104 | 111½ | 109 | 113¾ | 111 |
| " Equip. s. f. gold 5s | 1909 | M. & S. | 101¼ | 101 | .. | .. | .. | .. |
| " W. O. & W. 1st 4s | 1924 | F. & A. | 91½ | 87 | .. | .. | 98 | 98 |
| " con. gold 6s | 1915 | J. & J. | 126 | 119 | 124½ | 121 | 122½ | 119 |
| Virginia Midland gen. mort. 5s | 1936 | M. & N. | 113½ | 109 | 117 | 113 | 117½ | 114 |

| | Due. | Interest Payable. | 1900. H. | 1900. L. | 1901. H. | 1901. L. | 1902. H. | 1902. L. |
|---|---|---|---|---|---|---|---|---|
| Southern Railway— | | | | | | | | |
| Virginia Midland, gen. 5s, stamped.. | 1936 | M. & N. | 113½ | 108 | 116½ | 115 | .. | .. |
| " " ser. B 6s.......... | 1911 | M. & S. | .. | .. | .. | .. | 123 | 123 |
| " " ser. C 6s.......... | 1916 | M. & S. | .. | .. | .. | .. | 113½ | 113½ |
| " " ser. E 5s.......... | 1926 | M. & S. | .. | .. | 114 | 114 | 114 | 114 |
| West North Car. 1st con. 6s........ | 1914 | J. & J. | 119 | 114½ | 120⅝ | 110 | 121 | 117¾ |
| Atlantic & Danville, 1st gold 4s..... | 1948 | J. & J. | 94⅝ | 93¼ | 97 | 93 | 98½ | 94 |
| Mobile & Ohio col. tr. 4s........... | 1938 | M. & S. | .. | .. | 97½ | 95 | 100 | 94½ |
| South Carolina & Georgia 1st 5s.... | 1919 | M. & N. | 109 | 102 | 110 | 106 | 112 | 106 |
| Spring Valley Water Works 1st 6s...... | 1949 | M. & S. | 113½ | 113½ | .. | .. | .. | . |
| Standard Rope & Twine 1st 6s.......... | 1946 | F. & A. | 84 | 66¼ | 72½ | 47 | 74 | 55 |
| Standard Rope & Twine income, gold 5s.. | 1946 | ........ | 24 | 8 | 12 | 5¼ | 19 | 6¾ |
| Staten Island Ry. 1st gu. g. 4½s........ | 1943 | J. & D. | .. | .. | .. | .. | 104½ | 98½ |
| Tenn. C. & I. & R. R., Tenn. Div. 1st g. 6s. | 1917 | A. & O. | 112 | 102 | 110 | 104 | 111½ | 106 |
| " " Birm. Div. 1st con. 6s | 1917 | J. & J. | 112½ | 103 | 112 | 105 | 113 | 108 |
| DeBardeleben C. & I. g. 6s........ | 1910 | F. & A. | 109 | 98 | 104½ | 100 | 104 | 100½ |
| Cah. Coal M.......................... | 1922 | J. & D. | 105 | 105 | .. | .. | .. | .. |
| Term. R. R. of St. Louis 1st 4½s....... | 1939 | A. & O. | .. | .. | 116 | 113½ | 114½ | 111 |
| 1st con. g. 5s....................... | 1944 | F. & A. | 115½ | 113½ | 116½ | 115 | 119 | 116½ |
| St. L. M. Bdge. Term. g. 5s........ | 1930 | A. & O. | 111 | 111 | 115 | 113 | 115½ | 112¾ |
| Texas & Pacific East. Div. 1st mort 6s... | 1905 | M. & S. | 105 | 104⅞ | 104 | 104 | 101¾ | 101¾ |
| " 1st gold 5s............ | 2000 | J. & D. | 117 | 110½ | 120¼ | 115⅛ | 122 | 116 |
| " 2d gold income 5s....... | 2000 | March... | 90 | 53 | 100 | 90 | 102¼ | 96 |
| " La. Div. B. L. 1st g. 5s. | 1931 | J. & J. | .. | .. | 111 | 110½ | .. | .. |
| Third Ave. 1st gold 5s................. | 1937 | J. & J. | 127 | 117⅛ | 126 | 123 | 127⅛ | 120 |
| " 1st con. guar. 4s............ | 2000 | J. & J. | 107 | 106¼ | 105 | 100 | 101⅝ | 97 |
| Toledo & Ohio Cen. 1st mort., gold, 5s.. | 1935 | J. & J. | 116½ | 105 | 117½ | 113 | 114½ | 112½ |
| " gen. gold 5s........ | 1935 | A. & O. | 106¼ | 95 | 108½ | 103 | 110⅜ | 107 |
| " West Div. 1st g. 5s. | 1935 | A. & O. | 114 | 105 | 115¼ | 112½ | 113⅞ | 113⅞ |
| Kanawha & Mich. 4s.............. | 1990 | A. & O. | 92 | 84½ | 99¼ | 95 | 98¾ | 94½ |
| Toledo, Peoria & Western 1st guar. 4s... | 1917 | J. & J. | 86 | 78 | 95 | 86 | 93½ | 91 |
| Toledo, St. L. & K. C. 1st 6s trust rects.. | 1916 | J. & D. | 130¼ | 110 | .. | .. | .. | .. |
| Toledo, St. Louis & West. pr. lien g. 3½s. | 1925 | J. & J. | .. | .. | 93 | 88 | 92¼ | 82¼ |
| Toledo, St. Louis & West. 50-year gold 4s. | 1950 | A. & O. | .. | .. | 85⅝ | 73 | 87 | 75 |
| Toronto, Ham. & Buff. 1st g. 4s........ | 1946 | J. & D. | 100 | 97¾ | 100 | 98 | 99½ | 97 |
| Trenton Gas & Electric 1st g. 5s........ | 1949 | M. & S. | 107 | 107 | 109 | 109 | .. | .. |
| Ulster & Delaware 1st con. 5s.......... | 1928 | J. & D. | 107 | 103 | 109⅛ | 106½ | 114 | 109 |
| Union Pacific 1st R. R. & ld. gt. gold 4s. | 1947 | J. & J. | 108 | 101¾ | 107¼ | 103½ | 106½ | 103¼ |
| " registered................ | 1947 | J. & J. | 106½ | 103¼ | 106¾ | 103½ | 106½ | 103 |
| " 1st lien conv. 4s.......... | 1911 | M. & N. | .. | .. | 129 | 103 | 113⅞ | 103 |
| Oregon Railway & Nav. 1st mort. 6s.. | 1909 | J. & J. | 111 | 110 | 112⅞ | 110 | 109 | 109 |
| " " " con., 4s..... | 1946 | J. & D. | 104⅞ | 100½ | 105¼ | 101½ | 104¾ | 100 |
| Oregon Short Line 1st 6s.......... | 1922 | F. & A. | 130 | 125¾ | 130 | 125 | 129½ | 125 |
| " " 1st con. 5s....... | 1946 | J. & J. | 118¼ | 110½ | 121 | 115 | 119½ | 115 |
| " " 4s & particip...... | 1927 | F. & A. | .. | .. | .. | .. | 96⅛ | 91¾ |
| " " non-cum. inc. A 5s | 1946 | Sept.... | 106 | 106 | 106 | 103½ | .. | .. |
| Utah & Northern 1st 7s.......... | 1908 | J. & J. | .. | .. | 119 | 117 | 115 | 115 |
| " " con. 5s......... | 1926 | J. & J. | 102½ | 102½ | 113 | 113 | 114½ | 114½ |
| United States Leather s. f. deb. 6s.. ... | 1913 | M. & N. | 116½ | 112 | 115⅛ | 112¼ | 116½ | 110½ |
| United States Red. & ref. 1st s. f. g. 6s.. | 1931 | ........ | .. | .. | .. | . | 89¾ | 84½ |
| Wabash R. R. 1st gold 5s.............. | 1939 | M. & N. | 118½ | 113 | 120¼ | 117 | 121 | 115 |
| " " 2d gold 5s.............. | 1939 | F. & A. | 108¼ | 98½ | 115 | 107½ | 114¾ | 107 |
| " " debentures series A...... | 1939 | J. & J. | 99½ | 83 | 102½ | 96⅜ | 104 | 100 |
| " " debentures series B...... | 1939 | J. & J. | 43¼ | 29¾ | 70 | 40 | 89 | 66½ |
| St. L., K. C. & N., St. Chas. B'dge 1st 6s | 1908 | A. & O. | 113 | 109½ | 112 | 110 | 111½ | 109 |
| D. & Chicago Ex. 1st 5s............ | 1940 | J. & J. | 112½ | 108 | 111 | 110 | 111¼ | 109 |
| Des Moines Div. 1st g. 4s.......... | 1939 | J. & J. | 96 | 91 | 98⅛ | 95 | 97 | 95 |
| Omaha Division 1st g. 3½s......... | 1941 | A. & O. | .. | .. | .. | .. | 89 | 83 |
| Toledo & Chicago Division 1s g. 4s. | 1941 | M. & S. | .. | .. | .. | .. | 98 | 98 |
| Western Gas col. tr. g. 5s............... | 1933 | M. & N. | 105½ | 105½ | 107½ | 107½ | .. | .. |
| West. N. Y. & Penna. 1st 5s............ | 1937 | J. & J. | 123 | 110 | 122 | 119 | 121½ | 118 |
| " " " gen. g. 2-3-4s.... | 1943 | A. & O. | 95⅜ | 68¼ | 100½ | 95 | 102 | 98¼ |
| " " " income 5s....... | 1943 | Nov.... | 35 | 22½ | 40 | 31 | .. | .. |
| Western Union col. trust cur. 5s....... | 1938 | J. & J. | 116 | 109 | 115⅞ | 111 | 113½ | 109⅞ |
| " fund & r. est. 4½s g. | 1950 | M. & N. | 107 | 104¼ | 109½ | 105½ | 109¾ | 103⅝ |
| Mutual Union Tel. s. f. 6s.......... | 1911 | M. & N. | 112⅜ | 109 | 116 | 111 | 113¼ | 110¼ |

| | Due. | Interest Payable. | 1900. H. | 1900. L. | 1901. H. | 1901. L. | 1902. H. | 1902. L. |
|---|---|---|---|---|---|---|---|---|
| West Va., Central & Pittsburgh 1st 6s.. | 1911 | J. & J. | .. | .. | 113½ | 113½ | 114½ | 112½ |
| Wheeling & Lake Erie 1st 5s........... | 1926 | A. & O. | 116 | 107 | 117½ | 112 | 115½ | 113 |
| " " Wh'ling Div. 1st 5s | 1928 | J. & J. | 114½ | 99⅞ | 116¼ | 111¼ | 113 | 112½ |
| " " ext. & imp. 5s.... | 1930 | F. & A. | 108 | 98½ | 113 | 112 | 111⅜ | 111⅜ |
| " " 1st con. 4s........ | 1949 | F. & A. | 91 | 84 | 94 | 89 | 97½ | 91 |
| Wheeling, L. E. & Pitts. Coal 1st 5s.... | 1919 | J. & J. | 32 | 32 | .. | .. | .. | .. |
| Wisconsin Central 1st g. 4s............. | 1949 | J. & J. | 93¼ | 82 | 92½ | 85¼ | 95 | 88 |

## MISCELLANEOUS BONDS.—NEW YORK

SALES ON THE CURB AND AT AUCTION.

| | 1900. Highest. | 1900. Lowest. | 1901. Highest. | 1901. Lowest. | 1902. Highest. | 1902. Lowest. |
|---|---|---|---|---|---|---|
| Aetna Iron Mfg. Min. & Oil Co 1st ser., 6s guar..................... | .. | .. | 97½ | 97½ | .. | .. |
| Albany & Hudson Ry.& Pr.Co.,5s,1939 | .. | .. | .. | .. | 60¼ | 60⅛ |
| Alleghany Valley R. R. 1st 7s, 1910.... | .. | .. | .. | .. | 122¾ | 122⅛ |
| Amer. Home Teleph.Co.col. tr. 4s, 1921 | .. | .. | .. | .. | 92 | 50 |
| American Lith. Co. 1st mort. 5s, 1921. | 70 | 29 | 80 | 70 | 80 | 70 |
| " " " deb. 6s.......... | .. | .. | 70 | 25 | 40 | 20 |
| American Malting Co. 6s, 1914........ | .. | .. | 98 | 95 | 100½ | 94¼ |
| American Matting Co. 6s............. | 96 | 87 | .. | .. | .. | .. |
| American Mutoscope of New Jersey 1st 7s, 1906, J. & J................. | 51 | 51 | .. | .. | .. | .. |
| American Thread Co. 1st 4s, 1919...... | 85 | 85 | .. | .. | 84 | 84 |
| American Type Founders deb. 6s, 1926 | 100 | 90 | 102 | 97 | 106 | 100 |
| American Valley Co. 5s, 1911........ | .. | .. | .. | .. | 89½ | 89½ |
| American Writing Paper Co. 1st 5s.... | 72¼ | 71⅜ | 72 | 65 | 79¾ | 67 |
| American Yacht Club 1st 4s ($500)... | .. | .. | .. | .. | 100 | 100 |
| Aperwamis Club, Rye ($250) 5 per cent. certs. of indebt, 1907........ | .. | .. | $105 | $105 | .. | .. |
| Arion Sing. Soc. of Brooklyn 2d 5s, 1908 | 82 | 82 | .. | .. | .. | .. |
| " " " 3d 5s, 1906 | 97 | 97 | .. | .. | .. | .. |
| Asphalt Co. of America bond ctfs., 5s. | 91 | 58 | 72½ | 29 | .. | .. |
| Atlanta & Charlotte Air Line 1st 7s, 1907 | 117¾ | 117¾ | .. | .. | 114 | 114 |
| Atlantic & Gulf R. R. Co. bonds..... | .. | .. | .. | .. | 25 | 25 |
| Atlantic Avenue Imp. 5s, 1934....... | .. | .. | 100 | 97 | 103¾ | 100 |
| " " con. 5s, 1931... | .. | .. | 113½ | 113½ | 114¾ | 112 |
| Atlantic Coast Electric Light Co. 1st 5s | 92½ | 92½ | .. | .. | .. | .. |
| At. Coast Electric Ry. 1st mort. 5s, 1946 | 82⅜ | 72 | .. | .. | 85 | 85 |
| Atlantic Mutual Ins. Co. scrip of 1899. | .. | .. | 105½ | 104¾ | .. | .. |
| " " " " 1901. | .. | .. | 107⅜ | 104¾ | .. | .. |
| " " " scrip 6s 1900 | 107 | 103 | .. | .. | 104⅞ | 103 |
| " " " " of 1897 | .. | .. | .. | .. | 102½ | 102 |
| " " " " " 1902 | .. | .. | .. | .. | 108 | 102 |
| Atlantic Yacht Club 2d 5s, 1903 ($300). | $155 | $155 | .. | .. | .. | .. |
| " " 2d 5s, 1902 ($100). | 100 | 100 | .. | .. | .. | .. |
| Austrian 5s, 500 florins, issued 1860... | .. | .. | .. | .. | $555 | $555 |
| Ballston Ter.R.R. Co. 5s, 1931,($6,000) | .. | .. | .. | .. | $190 lot | |
| Baltimore & Po. R. 1st m. l. 6s, 1911.. | 124⅜ | 124⅜ | .. | .. | .. | .. |
| Bangor & Portland 1st 6s, 1930....... | .. | .. | 124¾ | 124¾ | .. | .. |
| Bankers' & Merchants' Telegraph Co. gen. mort. certs. ($59,000)........ | .. | .. | .. | .. | $25 lot | |
| Barney & Smith Car Co. 1st 6s, 1942... | 105 | 105 | .. | .. | 114 | 110 |
| Bergenfield, Bergen Co., N.J., imp. 5s. | .. | .. | .. | .. | 90 | 85 |
| Bergenfield, N. J., District School 5s, 1906-1907......................... | 100½ | 100½ | .. | .. | .. | .. |
| Berkeley Oval Swimming Bath & Gymnasium 1st 5s, 1903............... | 5 | 5 | 8 | 8 | .. | .. |
| Berkeley School 2d 6s, 1903........... | 50 | 50 | .. | .. | .. | .. |
| Big Muddy Coal & Iron Co. 1st 6s, 1923 (J. & J.).................... | 75 | 75 | .. | .. | . | .. |

| | 1900. | | 1901. | | 1902. | |
|---|---|---|---|---|---|---|
| | Highest. | Lowest. | Highest. | Lowest. | Highest. | Lowest. |
| Binghamton Gas Works 5s.......... | 95 | 90 | .. | .. | 95 | 89¾ |
| Birmingham (Ala.) Wr. Wk's 2d 6s, 1921 | .. | .. | .. | .. | 110¾ | 110¾ |
| Blooming Grove Park Association $50 certificates of indebtedness........ | .. | .. | .. | .. | 40 | 40 |
| Blue Ridge Mining Co. 1st 5s, 1920.... | .. | .. | .. | .. | 24⅝ | 11 |
| Boston United Gas 2d 5s.............. | .. | .. | 58½ | 50½ | .. | .. |
| Bridgeport Brass Co. 1st 4.5s, 1920... | .. | .. | .. | .. | 95 | 95 |
| Brooklyn & Rockaway Beach R. R. Co. con. 6s, 1931.... ........... ... | 51 | 51 | .. | .. | 59¾ | 37½ |
| Brooklyn City Bridge 4s, 1925......... | .. | .. | .. | .. | 112¼ | 112¼ |
| " " Local Imp'ment 3s, 1910. | .. | .. | .. | .. | 98⅛ | 98⅛ |
| " " New York & Brooklyn Bridge 6s, 1912.................. | .. | .. | .. | .. | 125⅝ | 121⅝ |
| Brooklyn City, New York & Brooklyn Bridge 6s, 1911................. | .. | .. | .. | .. | 123½ | 123½ |
| Brooklyn City 7s (park loan), 1917.... | 90 | 81½ | .. | .. | .. | .. |
| " " Perm'n't Water 7s, 1910. | .. | .. | .. | .. | 128¾ | 128¾ |
| " " Public Market 3s, 1904.. | .. | .. | .. | .. | 98⅛ | 98⅛ |
| " " Pub. Park 7s, 1915 (J.&J.) | 145⅝ | 145⅝ | 144¾ | 144¾ | 138 | 138 |
| " " Public Park 6s, 1924... | .. | .. | 147¾ | 147¾ | 144½ | 144½ |
| " " " " 6s, 1915.... | .. | .. | .. | .. | 144⅝ | 144⅝ |
| Brooklyn Ferry Co. 1st mort. 5s, 1948 | 90 | 80½ | 91 | 83 | .. | .. |
| Brunswick & Chillicothe 1st 8s, 1903.. | .. | .. | 103 | 103 | .. | .. |
| Buff. & Niag. Falls El. Ry. Co. 1st mort. | .. | .. | .. | .. | 110½ | 107¾ |
| Buffalo City Gas 1st mort. 5s, 1947.... | 75 | 69 | 81⅛ | 65 | 86 | 70 |
| Buffalo Crosstown 1st 5s, 1932........ | .. | .. | .. | .. | 115 | 110¾ |
| Buffalo General Electric 5s, 1939...... | .. | .. | 108½ | 108 | 109 | 107 |
| Buffalo Railway debenture. ........ | .. | .. | .. | .. | 107 | 105 |
| " " 1st consols.... ...... | .. | .. | . | .. | 117 | 112½ |
| Buffalo Traction Co. 1st 5s, 1948...... | 108 | 105 | 110 | 106 | 109 | 107 |
| Cal. Pac. R. R. 1st 4½, 1912.......... | .. | .. | .. | .. | 103⅝ | 103⅝ |
| California Water & Mining Co. 1st gold 6s, Nov. 1883, coupons on ($30,000) | .. | .. | .. | .. | $100 per bond | |
| Cape Breton Ry. Co. 1st 5s, 2001, $30,000 | .. | .. | .. | .. | $1,610 lot | |
| Carnegie Steel Co. 5s................ | .. | .. | 113⅜ | 113⅜ | .. | .. |
| Central Foundry Co. deb. 6s, 1919..... | 80 | 70 | 75 | 55 | 75 | 45 |
| Central Union Gas Co. of N. Y. 1st.. | 109 | 102 | .. | .. | 110¾ | 105½ |
| Chateaugay O. & Iron 6s 1915 (J. & J.) | 30 | 30 | 13¾ | 13¾ | .. | .. |
| Chattanooga So. Ry. Co. 1st Tr. Co. cer. | 53 | 53 | .. | .. | .. | .. |
| Chesa. & O. Grain Elevator 1st 4s, 1938 | 76½ | 17¾ | .. | .. | 91 | 80 |
| " " " 2d inc. 1938 | 16⅛ | 16⅛ | .. | .. | 25 | 15 |
| Chesa. & Ohio Ry. Co. of Va. and West Va. 6s, 1922....... ............. | .. | .. | .. | .. | 122⅝ | 122⅝ |
| Chesa. Dry D. & Construc. Co. 5s, 1937. | .. | .. | .. | .. | 92¾ | 92¾ |
| Chicago & Northwestern R. R.— | | | | | | |
| Plainview R. R. 1st 7s, 1908...... | 121¼ | 121¼ | .. | .. | .. | .. |
| Menominee R. R. 1st 7s, 1906..... | 119⅝ | 119⅝ | .. | .. | .. | .. |
| Rock & Minn. R. R. 1st 7s, 1908.. | 121⅝ | 121⅝ | .. | .. | .. | .. |
| Madison Ext. 1st 7s, 1911........ | .. | .. | .. | .. | 129⅜ | 129⅜ |
| Chicago, Iowa & Dak. R. R. 1st 4s, 1932 | 50 | 50 | .. | .. | .. | .. |
| Chic., Ind. & Louisv. guar. when iss., 4s. | .. | .. | .. | .. | 97 | 89 |
| Chicago, Milwaukee & St Paul R. R. Dubuque Division 1st 6s, 1920..... | 133⅜ | 130 | 131½ | 131½ | .. | .. |
| Chicago, Peoria & St. Louis 1sts...... | 23 | 23 | .. | .. | .. | .. |
| Chicago, Peoria & St. Louis Ry. 1sts.. | 4⅝ | 4⅝ | .. | .. | .. | .. |
| Chicago, Peoria & St. Louis prior lien, new 4½s, 1930.................. | .. | .. | 107 | 104½ | 107½ | 105 |
| Chicago, Peoria & St. Louis con. mort. 5s, 1930, new.................. | .. | .. | 103 | 86 | 103 | 91 |
| Chicago, Peoria & St. Louis incomes, new, 1930...................... | .. | .. | 32½ | 14 | 36¾ | 27 |
| Chicago Ry. & Term. El. 1st 6s, 1943.. | 67⅝ | 61 | 61¼ | 59½ | 54 | 47 |
| Chicago, Wis. & Minn. inc. 5s, 1916... | .. | .. | 92 | 92 | .. | .. |
| " " " 1st 6s, 1916.... | .. | .. | 122⅞ | 119⅞ | .. | .. |
| Cincinnati (O.) con. S. F. 5s, 1910-1930 | 115⅞ | 115⅞ | .. | .. | .. | .. |

| | 1900. | | 1901. | | 1902. | |
|---|---|---|---|---|---|---|
| | Highest. | Lowest. | Highest. | Lowest. | Highest. | Lowest. |
| Cincinnati 7 3-10s, 1902 (J. & J.)...... | .. | .. | 104⅝ | 104⅝ | .. | .. |
| Citizens' Street R.R.Co.of Ind., 5s,1933 | .. | .. | .. | .. | 111½ | 107¾ |
| Citizen Gas Co., Bdgpt., Ct., 1st 6s, 1935 | .. | .. | 10 | 10 | .. | .. |
| City of Chicago Sanitary Dist. 5s, 1902. | 100 | 100 | .. | .. | .. | .. |
| City of Lincoln (Ills.) Gas Co. 1st 6s.... | .. | .. | .. | .. | 60 | 60 |
| City of Louisv. (E. & P. R. R.) 7s, 1903 | .. | .. | 106¾ | 106¾ | .. | .. |
| City of Mobile, Ala., 4-5s, 1906........ | 100 | 100 | .. | .. | .. | .. |
| City of Montgomery, Ala., 5s, 1907.... | 100 | 100 | .. | .. | .. | .. |
| City of Newark, N. J., 6s, 1908....... | .. | .. | 108¾ | 108¾ | .. | .. |
| City of N. Y. Assented, funded 6s, 1910. | .. | .. | 121½ | 120 | .. | .. |
| " " 6s, con., 1901........... | .. | .. | 101 | 101 | .. | .. |
| " " 3s, con. (Police Dept.)... | .. | .. | 99⅞ | 99⅞ | .. | .. |
| " " 3½s, 1915............... | .. | .. | 103⅛ | 103⅛ | 104¾ | 104¾ |
| City of Yonkers Water 7s, 1906....... | .. | .. | 120¾ | 120¾ | .. | .. |
| Clev., Akron & Col. R. R. 1st 5s, 1927.. | .. | .. | .. | .. | 115⅛ | 115 |
| Clev., Ter. & Val. R. R. 1st g. 4s, 1995. | 95⅛ | 95⅛ | .. | .. | 100 | 100 |
| Colonial Club of N. Y. 2d 5s, 1911.... | .. | .. | .. | .. | 70 | 70 |
| Col. Spring. & Cin. R. R. 1st 7s, 1909 | .. | . | 106 | 106 | .. | .. |
| Col. & Toledo R. R. Co. 7s, 1905..... | .. | .. | .. | .. | 109¾ | 109¾ |
| Columbus Crosstown 1st mort. 5s, 1933 | .. | .. | 112 | 109 | 112 | 110 |
| Columbus Electric Co. 1st mort. 6s.... | .. | .. | 100 | 95 | 103 | 99 |
| Columbus Gas Co. 1st mort. 5s, 1932.. | 106 | 100 | .. | .. | 108 | 105 |
| Columbus Ry. gen. mort. 4s, 1939.... | .. | .. | .. | .. | 97 | 93 |
| Columbus, Sandusky & Hocking R. R. 1st mort. 5s, scrip, tr. rec......... | 36 | 20 | .. | .. | .. | .. |
| Columbus, Sandusky & Hocking 1st 6s, April, 1897, coupons on.......... | .. | .. | 71 | 71 | .. | .. |
| Columbus, Sandusky & Hock'g gens.. | 5½ | 3¾ | .. | .. | .. | .. |
| Columbus Street Ry. 1st 5s, 1932...... | 112½ | 105 | 115 | 111 | 107 | 103 |
| Consolidated Gas Co. of N. J. 1st con.. | .. | .. | 84 | 77½ | 91 | 78 |
| Consolidated Rubber Tire deb. 4s, 1951. | .. | .. | .. | .. | 36 | 10 |
| Consolidated Traction Co. (N. J.) 1st.. | 112 | 105 | 110½ | 108 | 110⅜ | 106½ |
| Consolidated Water Co., Utica, N. Y., 1st 5s, 1930..................... | .. | .. | .. | .. | 100 | 100 |
| Consumers' Gas Co. of N. J. 1st con. 5s | 85 | 75 | 106 | 104 | .. | .. |
| Con. & Lavela R. R. & Imp. Co. 1st 6s | 30 | 30 | .. | .. | .. | .. |
| Continental Tobacco deb. 7s, 1905..... | .. | .. | 107 | 102 | 107 | 102 |
| Cook County, Ill., 4s, 1903.......... | 102 | 102 | .. | .. | .. | .. |
| Corrigan St. Ry. Co. of K. C. 1st 5s, 1916 | 106⅝ | 106⅝ | 106⅝ | 106⅝ | .. | .. |
| Council Bluffs City Water Co. 6s, 1906. | .. | .. | 100 | 61 | .. | .. |
| Coxsackie & Greenville Traction Co. 5s, 1925 ($20,000)................ | .. | .. | .. | .. | $210 lot | |
| Crescent Athletic Club ($500) 5s, 1911. | .. | .. | .. | .. | 90 | 90 |
| Crystal Water Co. of Edgewater 1st 6s | 60 | 60 | .. | .. | .. | .. |
| Dayton & Michigan R. R. con. 5s, 1911 | 114⅜ | 114⅜ | .. | .. | .. | .. |
| Denver Consolidated Gas Co. 1st...... | 102 | 99 | .. | .. | 104 | 99 |
| Denver Gas & Electric 5s, 1949........ | 80 | 55 | 77 | 60 | 75 | 50 |
| Denver Tram. Co. 1st prior lien 5s, 1919 | .. | .. | .. | .. | 108 | 101 |
| " " con. mort. 5s, 1933.. | .. | .. | .. | .. | 108 | 100 |
| Denver Un. Water Co. 1st 20-yr. 5s, 1914 | 95 | 79 | 99½ | 87 | 102 | 95 |
| Detroit & Lima Nor. Ry. 1st 5s, 1947. | 20⅝ | 20⅜ | .. | .. | .. | .. |
| Detroit Citizens Trac. 1st con. 5s, 1905. | .. | .. | .. | .. | 101 | 99 |
| Deutscher Verein, N. Y., 1st 5s, 1911.. | . | .. | .. | .. | 65½ | 62 |
| Diamond State Steel Co. 4s, 2001..... | .. | .. | .. | .. | 83¾ | 83¾ |
| Distillers Securities Co. 5s. .......... | .. | .. | .. | .. | 81 | 65 |
| Ducktown Sulphur, Copper & Iron Co. deb. 5s ($3,300).................. | .. | .. | $10,000 lot | | .. | .. |
| Durland Co. 5s, 1943................ | .. | .. | 60 | 60 | .. | .. |
| " " 2d 5s, 1925.......... ... | .. | .. | 80 | 32 | 60 | 60 |
| Easton & Amboy R. R. 5s, 1920...... | .. | .. | .. | .. | 110⅜ | 110⅜ |
| Elmira Water, Light & R.R.Co. 5s, 1949 | .. | .. | 97 | 97 | .. | .. |
| Equi. Gas Co. of Memphis new 5s, 1927 | .. | .. | 101 | 90 | 103 | 96 |
| Essex Co. Country Club, Orange, N. J., 5s, 1910....................... | .. | .. | .. | .. | 50 | 50 |
| Essex County, N. J. 3.65s Park bds, 1915 | .. | .. | 104½ | 104½ | .. | .. |

| | 1900. | | 1901. | | 1902. | |
|---|---|---|---|---|---|---|
| | Highest. | Lowest. | Highest. | Lowest. | Highest. | Lowest. |
| Eureka Springs 1st mort.............. | .. | .. | .. | .. | .. | .. |
| Ev., T. H. & Chi. R. R. R. inc. 6s, 1920 | 115 | 115 | .. | .. | .. | .. |
| Excelsior Club, Bklyn, 2d 5s ($2,100).. | .. | .. | .. | .. | 90 | 90 |
| Express Coal Line Equip. 13.......... | .. | .. | 7½ | 7½ | .. | .. |
| Fisheries Co. 1st 6s, 1905............. | .. | .. | 60 | 60 | .. | .. |
| Flatbush Water Wks. Co. 1st 6s, 1911.. | .. | .. | .. | .. | 105 | 105 |
| Florida Sou. R.R. 1st mort. gu. 4s, 1945 | .. | .. | .. | .. | 90 | 70 |
| Fort Wayne Gas Co. 1st 6s., 68, 1925.. | 60 | 50 | .. | .. | 60 | 48 |
| Freundschaft Society 1st 4s, 1928 ($60). | .. | .. | $100 | $100 | .. | .. |
| Gainesville, Jeff. & So. 1st 7s guar.... | .. | .. | 101½ | 101½ | .. | .. |
| Galveston, Tex., 5s, 1931............. | .. | .. | .. | .. | 63½ | 63½ |
| Gal., Tx., 40-yr. ltd. dbt. 5s, 1923 (J.&D.) | 94 | 94 | .. | .. | .. | .. |
| Gen. Gas, Electric & Power Co. 1st 5s gold s. f., 1932.................. | .. | .. | .. | .. | 101 | 101 |
| Georgia Midland 3s, 1946............. | .. | .. | 67½ | 67½ | .. | .. |
| German Liederkranz of N. Y. 1st 5s.... | 100 | 100 | .. | .. | .. | .. |
| Grand Rapids Gas Co. 1sts 5s........ | .. | .. | 105½ | 103 | 105 | 104 |
| Grand Rapids Hydraulic Co. of Grand Rapids, Mich., coup. on.......... | .. | .. | .. | .. | 5⅜ | 5⅜ |
| Grand Rapids St. Ry. 1st mtg. 5s, 1916. | .. | .. | 104 | 102 | 104 | 103½ |
| Grand River Coal & C. Co. 1st 6s, 1919 | 103⅝ | 103⅝ | .. | .. | .. | .. |
| Great Southern Gas & Oil Co. of Zanesville, O. 1st 6s, 1905.............. | 50 | 50 | .. | .. | .. | .. |
| Guanajuato Consol. Mining & Milling Co. con. 6s, 1910................ | .. | .. | .. | .. | 5 | 5 |
| Hamilton Club, Brooklyn, 5s......... | 75 | 75 | 92 | 92 | 110⅛ | 110½ |
| Harlem Club 2d 5s, 1909 (F. & A.).... | 30 | 30 | .. | .. | .. | .. |
| Harlem R. & Port. R.R. 7s, guar., 1903 | 113⅝ | 113⅝ | .. | .. | .. | .. |
| " " 1st 7s, 1903... | .. | .. | 108¾ | 108¾ | .. | .. |
| Harlem Riv. & Portches. R. R. 6s, 1903 | 110½ | 109⅜ | .. | .. | .. | .. |
| " " 1st 6s, guar. | 107 | 107 | .. | .. | .. | .. |
| Hav'traw L. & F. Gas Co. gen. 5s, 1949 | 96 | 96 | .. | .. | 93½ | 90 |
| Heb. B. & O. Asyl. Soc. of N.Y. 3d bds. | .. | .. | .. | .. | 75½ | 70 |
| Hecker-Jones-Jewl. Mlg. Co. 1st 6s, 1922 | 84¼ | 84¼ | 98¾ | 98¾ | .. | .. |
| Hoboken Ferry 1st 5s, 1946........... | 112½ | 110 | 113 | 110 | 111 | 104½ |
| Hoboken Land and Improvement Co. | 110⅝ | 110⅝ | .. | .. | . | .. |
| Hudson & Riv. Falls R. R. 1st 8s, 1908 | 121 | 121 | .. | .. | .. | .. |
| Hudson County Gas Co. 5s, 1949..... | .. | .. | .. | .. | 104¾ | 101 |
| Huntington (N. Y.) Gas 1st 5s, 1915... | 75½ | 75½ | .. | .. | .. | .. |
| Ind. & St. L. R.R. 1st 7s, ser. A, 1919 | .. | .. | 136 | 136 | .. | .. |
| Ind. Natural & Ill'g Gas Co. 6s, 1908... | 61 | 45 | 56 | 45 | 56 | 42 |
| Indiana Natural Gas & Oil Co. 6s..... | .. | .. | .. | .. | 84 | 65 |
| Indianapolis Gas Co. 1st mort. 6s.... | 104 | 88¼ | 101 | 89¾ | 106 | 99¾ |
| Indianapolis St. Ry. gen. mort. 4s, 1933 | .. | .. | .. | .. | 89 | 85 |
| Internat. Br. & Tram. Co. $1,000 bds. | .. | .. | .. | .. | $450 | $450 |
| International Kaolin Co. 10-year 5s, 1911, ($5,000).................... | .. | .. | .. | .. | $1,000 lot | |
| International Silver 1st 6s, 1948...... | 100 | 95 | 97¼ | 97¼ | 103 | 95 |
| International Traction Co. 4s......... | .. | .. | .. | .. | 92 | 80½ |
| Iowa & Illinois Coal Co. 1st tr. ctfs... | .. | .. | 29 | 20 | .. | .. |
| Iron Steamboat Co. 6s, assessm't paid | 62 | 45½ | .. | .. | 60 | 40 |
| Jackson Gas Co. 1st mort. 5s, 1937.... | 102½ | 94 | .. | .. | 101½ | 101½ |
| Jacques Cartier Water Co., Quebec, 1st s. f. 6s, 1928..... ...... ...... | .. | .. | 87 | 87 | .. | .. |
| Jamaica (N.Y.) Tp. Water Co. 1st 6s, 1908 | .. | .. | 101 | 101 | .. | .. |
| Jamaica Water Supply 6s, 1907....... | .. | .. | 98 | 98 | .. | .. |
| Jamestown & Chautau. Ry. 1st 5s, 1998 | 91 | 40 | .. | .. | .. | .. |
| Jeff'ville, Mad. & Ind. R. R. 2d 7s, 1910 | 126⅞ | 126⅞ | .. | .. | 122½ | 122½ |
| " " " 1st 7s, 1906 | 113½ | 113½ | .. | .. | .. | .. |
| Jersey City, Hoboken & Paters. con. 4s | 83 | 76 | .. | .. | 81¾ | 78 |
| Jersey City ext. 6s, 1904 (J. & D.).... | .. | .. | .. | .. | 106½ | 106½ |
| " assessm't 5s. 1922 (J. & J.) | .. | .. | .. | .. | 129½ | 113⅓ |
| " Water 7s, 1902 (M. & S.).. | .. | .. | 112 | 112 | .. | .. |
| " " 7 per cent., 1913... | 129¾ | 129¾ | .. | .. | 129½ | 128¾ |
| Jour. of Com. & Com. Bul. s. f. 6s, 1905. | 100 | 100 | .. | .. | .. | .. |

| | 1900. | | 1901. | | 1902. | |
|---|---|---|---|---|---|---|
| | Highest. | Lowest. | Highest. | Lowest. | Highest. | Lowest. |
| Judge Co. pur. mon. 4s, "A," pref., 1909 | 46 | 40½ | 40 | 38¼ | 40 | 37½ |
| Kala. & White Pig. R.R. 1st 5s, 1940. | . | .. | .. | .. | 128⅜ | 128⅜ |
| Kankakee Electric Co. 1sts............ | 60 | 60 | .. | .. | .. | .. |
| Kansas City Elevated R.R. con. gtd. 6s | . | . | .. | .. | 113 | 112 |
| " " " " " ...4s | 89 | 89 | .. | .. | 89 | 85 |
| Kansas City (Mo.) Gas 1st mort. 5s.... | .. | | .. | .. | 102 | 100 |
| Kan. City, St. J. & C. B. R.R. c. 7s, 1907 | 120 | 120 | .. | .. | .. | .. |
| Keene Hgts. Htl. Co. 6s, 1902......... | .. | .. | .. | .. | 50 | 50 |
| Kensington Park Co. 1st 5s, 1914, May, 1902 coupons attached............. | .. | .. | .. | . | 10 | 10 |
| Kewaunee, Gr. B. & W. Ry. 1st 5s, 1921 | .. | . | 106 | 106 | .. | .. |
| Kings Co. Elec. Light & Pw. Co. 1st 5s | 106 | 101½ | 110 | 103 | 110½ | 109 |
| " " " pur. my. 6s | 123 | 116 | 125 | 118 | 125 | 120 |
| Kingston (N. Y.) 3½, 1924........... | .. | .. | .. | .. | 103 | 103 |
| Knickerbocker Steamboat 6s, 1911.... | .. | .. | 31 | 31 | 48⅛ | 48½ |
| Knoxville Water Co. 6s, 1912......... | 95 | 95 | .. | .. | .. | .. |
| Lafayette Gas Co. of Ind. 1st mort. 6s | .. | .. | .. | .. | 58 | 50 |
| Lake Cities Electric Ry. Co. (Michigan City, Ind.) 1st 30-year 6s tr. rects. | 10 | 10 | .. | .. | .. | .. |
| Laredo, Tex., City Imp. 6s, 1913...... | .. | .. | .. | .. | 104¼ | 104¼ |
| Lanyon Zinc Co. 6s.............. | .. | .. | 84 | 81½ | .. | .. |
| Lima Northern Ry. Co. 1st cer. of dep. | .. | .. | .. | .. | 8 | 8 |
| Litchfield & Madison Ry. inc. 5s, 1930. | .. | .. | .. | .. | 45 | 30 |
| Logans. & Wab. Valley Gas Co. 1st.. | 51 | 50 | .. | .. | 56 | 46 |
| Lotos Club 2d mort. 6s, 1902, J. & J.. | 100½ | 84½ | .. | .. | .. | |
| Louisville, Hend. & St. L. 1st 5s, 1946 | 100 | 90 | 106½ | 106½ | 111½ | 98 |
| Louisville Street Ry. 5s, 1930........ | .. | .. | . | .. | 118 | 116½ |
| Lynn & Boston 1st mort. 1st 5s, 1924. | .. | .. | .. | .. | 113 | 112 |
| Madison Gas & Elect. Co. 1st mort., 5s | 107 | 100 | 109 | 107 | 100 | 107½ |
| Maine Steamship Co. 5s, 1931........ | .. | .. | .. | .. | 78 | 75 |
| Manitou & Pikes Peak R. R. 1st 5s, 1909 | .. | .. | 44 | 44 | .. | .. |
| Massachusetts State 3½s, 1923........ | .. | .. | 110¼ | 110¼ | .. | .. |
| Meadow Golf Club Co. of L. I. inc. ($200) 1946...................... | .. | .. | .. | .. | $90 lot | |
| Mechanical Rubber Co. 1st 6s, 1919.... | .. | .. | .. | .. | 95 | 95 |
| " " " 6s, 1918. ..... | .. | .. | .. | .. | 102¾ | 102¾ |
| Medina Gas & Electric Light Co. 1st 6s, April, 1897, coupon on .......... | 3 | 3 | .. | . | .. | .. |
| Memphis & Ohio R. R. 1st 7s, 1901... | 101¾ | 101¾ | .. | .. | .. | .. |
| Meriden Horse R. R. of Conn. 5s, 1924. | .. | .. | .. | .. | 115¾ | 115¾ |
| Metropolitan Ferry Co. 1st 5s, 1937... | 111 | 107 | 110½ | 104 | .. | .. |
| Metropolitan R. R. of Denver 6s, 1911 | .. | .. | 110¼ | 110¼ | .. | .. |
| Metropol. Water Works Co. 1st 4s, 1919 | 65 | 65 | .. | .. | .. | .. |
| Mexican National con. 4s, when issued. | .. | .. | 79⅛ | 76½ | .. | .. |
| Mex. Nat. prior lien 4½, when issued.. | .. | .. | 102½ | 100½ | .. | .. |
| Mex. Northern R. R. 1st mort. 6s, 1910 | .. | .. | .. | .. | 108½ | 108½ |
| Mich. Lake Superior Co. 1st 5s, 1949... | .. | .. | .. | .. | 89½ | 89½ |
| Michigan Peninsular Car Co. 1st mort. | .. | .. | | .. | .. | .. |
| Mil. & Lake Winnebago R. R. 6s, 1912. | .. | .. | 117¾ | 117¾ | .. | .. |
| Mil. Elec. Ry. and L. Co. 5s, 1926.... | .. | .. | 111 | 104½ | .. | .. |
| Milwaukee, Wis., 5s, 1906............ | 103¼ | 103¼ | 108⅜ | 108⅜ | .. | .. |
| Milwaukee, Wis., Public Park 5s, 1903. | .. | .. | .. | .. | 102½ | 102½ |
| Minneapolis Brewing Co. 1st 7s, 1913.. | 108 | 108 | .. | .. | .. | .. |
| Minneapolis East. Ry. 1st mort. 7s, 1909 | .. | .. | .. | .. | 117 | 117 |
| Minneapolis Gas con. 6s, 1910........ | .. | .. | .. | .. | 110 | 110 |
| Minneapolis, Minn., 4½s, 1921........ | 121⅝ | 121⅝ | .. | .. | .. | .. |
| Minneapolis Street Ry. con. 1st 5s..... | .. | .. | 111½ | 108⅛ | 111½ | 110 |
| Minnesota Valley 7s, 1908............ | .. | .. | .. | .. | 117⅝ | 117⅝ |
| Moesmers Brew. Co. 2d 6s, 1919, coups. | .. | .. | 25 | 25 | .. | .. |
| Monongahela River R. R. 1st 5s, 1919. | .. | .. | 112¾ | 112¾ | .. | .. |
| Montauk Club, Brooklyn, 2d 5s ($500). | 26 | 26 | 52 | 52 | .. | .. |
| Montgomery, Ala., corp. 5s, 1907...... | .. | .. | .. | .. | 98⅞ | 98⅞ |
| Mystic Val. Wat. Co. 1st S. F. 5s, 1908 | 92½ | 92½ | .. | .. | .. | .. |
| Nassau Electric 1st 5s, 1944........... | .. | .. | 114½ | 114½ | 112 | 112 |
| " " con. 4s, 1951......... | .. | .. | 97½ | 94½ | 96 | 85 |

| | 1900. | | 1901. | | 1902. | |
|---|---|---|---|---|---|---|
| | Highest. | Lowest. | Highest. | Lowest. | Highest. | Lowest. |
| National Asphalt 5s | .. | .. | 48¾ | 10¼ | 15 | 6 |
| Nat. Mill. Co. of Minneap. 1st 5s, 1907 | .. | .. | 80 | 80 | .. | .. |
| Newark (N. J.) funded debt Water 4s, 1922 (F. & A.) | .. | .. | 112⅝ | 112⅝ | .. | .. |
| Newark Consolidated Gas Co. 5s | .. | .. | .. | .. | 102 | 105 |
| Newark Gas Co. 1st 6s, 1944 | 141¼ | 141¼ | 141¼ | 140½ | 141½ | 141½ |
| Newark Passenger R. R. con. guar. 5s | 119½ | 111½ | 119 | 116¾ | 118 | 115 |
| New Amster. Gas Co. 1st con. 5s, 1948 | .. | .. | .. | .. | 113⅜ | 107¾ |
| Newark (N. J.) New Wat. Sup. 4s, 1922 | .. | .. | .. | .. | 113½ | 113½ |
| Newburg, Dutchess & Conn. bds., 1977 | .. | .. | 20 | 20 | 15½ | 15½ |
| New England Gas & Coke 1st mort. 5s | 77 | 55 | .. | .. | .. | .. |
| New Jersey & New York R. R. 6s, 1910 | 113¾ | 113¾ | .. | .. | .. | .. |
| New Jersey Steamb't Co. con. 5s, 1921 | .. | .. | 95¾ | 95¾ | 97½ | 96¼ |
| New London Gas & Elec. Co. 5s, 1929 | .. | .. | .. | .. | 101¾ | 101¾ |
| New Orleans Brew. Asso. bonds, 1915 | .. | .. | .. | .. | .. | .. |
| New Orleans City & Lake Cons. 1st | .. | .. | .. | .. | 110 | 110 |
| New Orleans City R. R. gen. 4-5s | 96 | 96 | .. | .. | 106 | 106 |
| New Orleans Railway Co. 4½s, 1952 | .. | .. | .. | .. | 91½ | 77 |
| New York 5s con. stock, 1928 | 112 | 112 | .. | .. | .. | .. |
| N.Y. & Bos. R.R. 1st 7s, 1889, ($15,000) | .. | .. | .. | .. | $10 lot | |
| New York & E. River Ferry 1sts, 1922 | 100 | 94 | 99 | 94 | 95 | 90 |
| New York & East River Gas 1st mort. | .. | .. | 114 | 110 | 114 | 110 |
| Con. 1st mort. 5s | .. | .. | .. | .. | 114 | 107 |
| N. York & Hoboken Fy. con. 4s, 1948 | 96 | 92 | 97 | 90 | 98½ | 83 |
| N. Y. & N. J. Ferry 1st mtge. 5s, 1946 | .. | .. | 110 | 106 | 107 | 103 |
| New York & Shawnee Coal Co. 1st S. F. 6s, 1908 | 48½ | 48½ | .. | .. | .. | .. |
| New York & South Brooklyn Ferry & Trans. Co. 5s, 1906 | .. | .. | 80 | 75 | 75 | 75 |
| New York & Westchester Water Co. pr. lien 5s, 1927, A. & O. | 12½ | 12½ | .. | .. | .. | .. |
| N. Y. & White Plains Sub. Water Co. 1st S. F. 30-yr. 6s, My, '96, coup. | 6 | 6 | .. | .. | .. | .. |
| N. Y. & Wilkes-Barre Coal Co. 6s | .. | .. | .. | .. | 60 | 50 |
| N. Y. Athletic Club deb. 6s, 1903 | 110 | 96 | .. | .. | 93½ | 82½ |
| N. Y. Ath. Club 2d 5s, 1910 (A. & O.) | 100 | 80 | 80 | 80 | 85 | 85 |
| N. Y. Belting & Packing Co. 6s, 1918 | 92¾ | 92¾ | .. | .. | .. | .. |
| New York Biscuit Co. 1st mort. 6s, 1911 | 116 | 112 | .. | .. | 116 | 114½ |
| N. Y. City Additional Water 6s, Bridge stock, 1905 | 113⅜ | 113 | .. | .. | .. | .. |
| N. Y. City Addl. Wat. stock 3s, 1907 | .. | .. | .. | .. | 99½ | 98½ |
| " " " " " 3s, 1904 | .. | .. | .. | .. | 98¾ | 98¾ |
| " " Bridge 7s, 1920 | 156½ | 156½ | .. | .. | .. | .. |
| " " Col. City of N.Y. 3½s, 1915 | .. | .. | .. | .. | 104⅞ | 104⅞ |
| " " Consol. Dock 3½s, 1928 | .. | .. | 106⅝ | 106½ | .. | .. |
| " " City Improvement 3s, 1915 | .. | .. | .. | .. | 99¾ | 99¾ |
| " " Croton Water 5s | 110¼ | 110¼ | .. | .. | .. | .. |
| " " Harl. Riv. Drive. 3s, 1920 | .. | .. | .. | .. | 99½ | 99½ |
| " " Imp. Riv'side Prk. 3s, 1914 | .. | .. | .. | .. | 99½ | 99½ |
| " " School House 3s, 1914 | .. | .. | .. | .. | 99⅝ | 99⅝ |
| " " Wash. Br. Park 3s, 1920 | .. | .. | .. | .. | 99½ | 99½ |
| " " 7s, Dock stock, 1902 | .. | .. | 103 | 103 | .. | .. |
| " " 6s, " " 1905 | 127⅞ | 114 | .. | .. | .. | .. |
| " " 3s, " " 1925 | .. | .. | .. | .. | 99½ | 99½ |
| " " 3½s, 1928 | .. | .. | .. | .. | 102¾ | 102¾ |
| " " 3½s, 1940 | .. | .. | .. | .. | 105 | 102¾ |
| " " 4s, 1913 | .. | .. | .. | .. | 106⅛ | 106⅛ |
| " " 6s, Park Imp., 1902 | 104¼ | 104¼ | .. | .. | .. | .. |
| " " 6s, Croton Reservoir, 1907 | 117⅜ | 117⅜ | .. | .. | .. | .. |
| " " 2½ per cent. consols, 1909-1929, ex. ints. | 87¼ | 87¼ | .. | .. | .. | .. |
| N. Y. County Asst. Fund 7s, 1903 | .. | .. | 108¼ | 108¼ | .. | .. |
| " " con. 6s, 1901 | 102⅝ | 102⅝ | .. | .. | .. | .. |
| New York Hygeia Ice Co. 1st 6s, 1902 | .. | .. | .. | .. | .. | .. |
| N. Y., P. & Bos. R. R. Co. gn. 4s, 1942 | 118¼ | 118¼ | .. | .. | .. | .. |

| | 1900. | | 1901. | | 1902. | |
|---|---|---|---|---|---|---|
| | Highest. | Lowest. | Highest. | Lowest. | Highest. | Lowest. |
| N.Y., Ruth. & Sub. Gas Co. 1st 6s, 1911 | 105¼ | 105¼ | .. | . | .. | .. |
| Niagara Falls Power Co. 1st 5s....... | 107 | 102½ | 109 | 103 | 108 | 106 |
| Nipper Consol. Copper Co. 1st 6s, 1921 | .. | .. | .. | .. | 105 | 105 |
| N. Chicago S. & R.R. 5s, 1906 (J. & J.) | .. | .. | .. | .. | .. | .. |
| North Hudson Co. R. R. con. 5s...... | .. | .. | .. | .. | 115 | 112 |
| North Jersey Street Ry. 4s, 1948.... . | 88 | 77 | 82 | 79 | 86½ | 81¼ |
| North. Un. Gas Light Co. 1st mort. 5s | .. | .. | 108½ | 103 | 109 | 105 |
| Northwestern Grand Trunk R. R. Co. 1st 6s, 1910 (J. & J.)............. | 112¼ | 112¼ | .. | .. | .. | .. |
| Nowell Gold Mining Co. 1st 7s, 1914.. | 25 | 25 | .. | .. | .. | .. |
| Ohio & Indiana Gas Co. 1st mort. 6s.. | 62½ | 45 | .. | .. | 55 | 41 |
| Ohio & West Virginia R.R. 1st 7s, 1910 | .. | .. | .. | .. | 116½ | 116½ |
| Ohio Mining & Mfg. Co. inc. 5s, 1949. | .. | .. | 6 | 3 | .. | .. |
| Old Colony R. R. deb. 4s, 1925....... | .. | .. | .. | .. | 110⅜ | 110⅜ |
| Old Dominion S. S. Co. gu. 5s, 1913.... | .. | .. | 104 | 104 | .. | .. |
| Omaha Water Co. con. 4½s......... | 80 | 80 | .. | .. | .. | .. |
| " " 5s.... ..... ...... | .. | .. | .. | .. | 90 | 77½ |
| Orange & Passaic Valley Gas Co. 5s.. | .. | .. | .. | .. | 100 | 92 |
| Otis Ry. Co. 1st 5s, 1910, ($4,000)..... | .. | .. | .. | .. | $3,525 lot | |
| Pacific Packing & Navigation deb. 6s.. | .. | .. | .. | .. | 100 | 80 |
| Park Row Realty Co. 2d 4s, 1919...... | .. | .. | .. | .. | 65 | 57 |
| Passaic Lighting Co. con. 5s, 1925..... | 102⅜ | 102⅜ | .. | .. | .. | .. |
| Paterson & Pas. Gas cn. mort. 5s, 1949 | .. | .. | .. | .. | 103 | 100 |
| Paterson Extension R. R. 1st 6s, 1910. | .. | .. | 117 | 114¾ | .. | .. |
| Paterson Ry. Co. con. 1st 6s......... | .. | .. | .. | .. | 132 | 128 |
| Peekskill (N. Y.) Water 7s, 1904...... | .. | .. | 112¾ | 112¾ | .. | .. |
| Penn Cent. Brewing Co. 1sts, 1927.... | 90 | 90 | 50 | 50 | .. | .. |
| Peoria Water Works 4s, 1948......... | 51 | 50 | 51⅛ | 50 | .. | .. |
| " " " deb. 4s......... | .. | .. | 14¾ | 14¾ | .. | .. |
| Perry R. R. Co. 1st 7s, 1902.......... | 103¼ | 103¼ | .. | .. | .. | .. |
| Peru & La Salle Gas Co. 1st 6s, 1928.. | 60 | 60 | 50 | 50 | .. | .. |
| Pitts. & Con'ville R. R., 1st ex. 4s, 1946 | 113⅛ | 113⅛ | .. | .. | .. | .. |
| Pitts., Lisb. & West. 1sts, Jan., cp. on | .. | .. | 90 | 90 | .. | .. |
| Pittsburg Hiland Sub. School District, 19th Ward, 4s, 1902.............. | 100½ | 100½ | .. | .. | .. | .. |
| Pitts., Shawmut & Nor. R.R. 1st 5s, 1949 | 92⅝ | 92⅝ | 67 | 53½ | 70¼ | 64⅜ |
| Plainview R. R. 7s, 1908........... | .. | .. | .. | .. | 117⅞ | 117⅞ |
| Port Reading 1st 5s, 1941 ............ | .. | .. | 112¼ | 112¼ | .. | .. |
| Progress Club of N. Y. mort. 4s, 1930. | .. | .. | .. | .. | 56½ | 56½ |
| Providence & Pawtucket 1st mort..... | .. | . | .. | .. | 114¾ | 113 |
| Racquet & Tennis Club 2d inc. 6s, 1915 | 51 | 51 | .. | .. | 60 | 60 |
| Railroad Equipment Special Car Trust 6s., 1900, Ser. B 74 A............ | 14 | 14 | .. | .. | .. | .. |
| R.R. Equip. Co. 6s, Oct., 1895, Ser. A.E | 25 | 25 | .. | .. | 2½ | 2½ |
| Raritan River R. R. 1st 5s, 1939...... | .. | .. | 96⅛ | 96½ | .. | .. |
| Republic of Cuba 6s of 1869.......... | .. | .. | .. | .. | 3 | 1⅜ |
| " " 6s of 1896.......... | .. | .. | .. | .. | 50 | 20 |
| Richmond Pass. & Power Co. 5s, 1925 | .. | .. | .. | .. | 90 | 90 |
| Riding & Driving Club 2d 5s, 1911.... | 31½ | 31½ | .. | .. | .. | .. |
| Rid. & Driv. Club of B'klyn 1st 6s, 1905 | 76 | 76 | .. | .. | .. | .. |
| Rio Grande Southern 1st 4s, 1940..... | .. | .. | .. | .. | 84 | 80 |
| Rio Tinto Cop. Mfg. Co. of N. J. 6s, 1917 | .. | .. | .. | .. | 10½ | 10½ |
| Rochester City Water 7s, 1903........ | .. | .. | .. | .. | 100¼ | 100¼ |
| Roch. Gas & Elec. Co. con. 5s, 1912.. | 109 | 107⅝ | .. | .. | .. | .. |
| Rochester Gas & Elect. con. 5s, 1912.. | .. | .. | 105 | 105 | .. | .. |
| Rochester Ry. 1st con. 5s............ | .. | .. | 113½ | 108½ | 112 | 109 |
| " " 2ds 5s................ | .. | .. | 100 | 84 | 106 | 100 |
| St. Joseph Gas Co. 1st mort. 5s, 1937.. | .. | .. | .. | .. | 97 | 95 |
| St. Louis & Hannibal Ry. 1st pur. mon. 5s, 1933, July, 1891, coup. on..... | 5 | 5 | .. | .. | .. | .. |
| St. Louis & Hannibal Ry. 1st pur. mon. 5s, June, 1900, coup. on . ....... | 8 | 8 | .. | .. | .. | .. |
| St. Louis Co., Mo., Park 6s, 1905 ..... | .. | .. | .. | . | 108¼ | 108¼ |
| St. Louis, Mo., 4s, 1905.............. | .. | .. | .. | .. | 103½ | 103¼ |
| " " 3-65s, 1907........... | .. | .. | .. | .. | 103¼ | 103¼ |

| | 1900. | | 1901. | | 1902. | |
|---|---|---|---|---|---|---|
| | Highest. | Lowest. | Highest. | Lowest. | Highest. | Lowest. |
| St. Paul Cable Ry. 5s, 1937 | .. | . | .. | .. | 113 | 113 |
| St. Paul, Stillwater & Taylor Falls R. R. 7s, 1908 | 120 | 120 | 118¾ | 118¾ | .. | .. |
| St. Paul Gas Light Co. ext. 6s, 1918 | 115 | 110 | .. | .. | 115 | 114 |
| " " 1st 6s, 1915 | 115 | 110 | .. | .. | 115 | 114 |
| " " gen. 5s, 1944 | 85 | 75 | .. | .. | 93 | 89 |
| St. Paul Union Depot 1st 6s, 1930 | .. | .. | 120 | 120 | .. | .. |
| San Antonio (Tex.) Refunding School. 5s 1905 (M. & S.) | .. | .. | .. | .. | 101 | 101 |
| San Diego, Guayamaca & East Ry. Co. of Cal. 1st 6s, 1918, Jan. '99, c. on | 5 | 5 | .. | .. | .. | .. |
| San Francisco Ry. subs. ex | .. | . | .. | .. | 50 | 45 |
| Sand., M.& New.R.R. July 7, '09, tr.ctfs | 119¼ | 119¼ | .. | .. | .. | .. |
| Saratoga Gas & Elec. L. Co. inc. bds. | .. | .. | .. | .. | .. | .. |
| Savannah, Ga., 5s, 1913 | .. | .. | .. | .. | 110¼ | 109⅝ |
| " " 5s, 1907 | .. | .. | .. | .. | 107⅜ | 107 |
| Scranton Traction Co. 1st 6s, 1932 | .. | .. | 120 | 116 | .. | .. |
| Sea Beach Ry. Co. con. 4s, 1916, guar. by Brooklyn Rapid Transit | 86 | 86 | .. | .. | .. | .. |
| Seattle Coal & Iron Co. 1st 5s, Trust Co. cer. of dep | 110⅝ | 110⅝ | .. | .. | .. | .. |
| Securities Co. of N. Y. con. ser. C. | .. | .. | 87½ | 80 | .. | .. |
| " " " con. 4s | 60 | 60 | 95 | 85 | 75 | 58¼ |
| Shinnecock Hills Golf Club of L. I., $200 incomes, 1993 | .. | .. | .. | .. | $95 lot | |
| Sloss Iron & Steel Co. 1st m. 6s, 1920 | .. | .. | .. | .. | 111¾ | 111¾ |
| Sloss Iron & Steel Gen. 4½s, 1918 | 85 | 76½ | 84 | 75 | 85 | 83 |
| South Amboy Gas Light Co. 1st 6s, 1924 (J. & D.) | 11 | 11 | .. | .. | .. | .. |
| South Carolina 4½s, 1933 | 110¼ | 110¼ | .. | .. | .. | .. |
| " 4½s, cer. of indbt | 100 | 100 | .. | .. | .. | .. |
| South Car. $20,000 bds. dat. Jan. 1, 1869 | .. | .. | .. | .. | $58 per bond | |
| S. Dak. & Wyo. Town Site Co., Omaha | .. | .. | .. | .. | .. | .. |
| Southern Light & Traction Co. 1st 5s. | 80 | 70 | 86 | 75 | 93 | 84 |
| Southern Ry. Co. (Aiken Br. 4s), 1998 | .. | .. | 83½ | 83½ | .. | .. |
| Southwestern Coal & Imp. 1st 6s | .. | .. | 111 | 111 | .. | .. |
| South Yuba Water 6s, 1910 | .. | .. | 109½ | 109½ | .. | .. |
| Spanish Government indemnity scrip. | 38 | 38 | .. | .. | .. | .. |
| Spring Garden Ins. Co., Philadelphia | 70 | 70 | .. | .. | .. | .. |
| Standard Gas Co. 1st mort. 5s, 1930 | 118½ | 115 | 117½ | 115 | 117 | 115½ |
| Standard Milling Co. 1st 5s, 1930 | .. | .. | 72⅜ | 72½ | .. | .. |
| State of Indiana 3s, 1909 | .. | .. | 100 | 100 | .. | .. |
| Steinway Ry. 1st 6s, 1922 | .. | .. | .. | .. | 118 | 115 |
| Sussex Railroad 7s, 1903 | .. | .. | 104 | 104 | .. | .. |
| Syracuse Gas Light Co. 1st mort. 5s | 91½ | 80 | 92 | 85 | 100 | 90 |
| Syracuse Rapid Transit 1sts 5s, 1946 | 98 | 91½ | 102¼ | 97½ | 105 | 99 |
| Taylor I. & S. bonds, 1899, $1,000 | .. | .. | .. | .. | .. | .. |
| Terminal Warehouse Co. 6s, 1942 | 68 | 68 | .. | .. | .. | .. |
| " " " 6s, 1910 | .. | .. | .. | .. | 71½ | 71½ |
| " " " deb. 8s, 1904 | 65 | 65 | .. | .. | .. | .. |
| " " " 5s | 80 | 80 | .. | .. | .. | .. |
| Ter. Haute & Log'p't R. R. 1st 6s, 1910 | 115¾ | 115¾ | .. | .. | .. | .. |
| Texas Central Railroad 1st 5s, 1923 | .. | .. | 100 | 100 | .. | .. |
| Toledo & Ohio Cent. (St. Mary's Div.) 1st pref. inc., 1951 | .. | .. | .. | .. | 50 | 50 |
| Toledo Rys. & Light Co. consol. 4s, 1909 | .. | .. | .. | .. | 90 | 90 |
| Trinidad, Col., Water 5s, 1912 | .. | .. | .. | .. | 93½ | 93½ |
| Union Ferry Co. 1st 5s, 1920 | 102 | 98 | 100 | 93 | 100 | 93 |
| Union League Club of Bklyn. ($100) | .. | .. | .. | .. | .. | .. |
| Union Ry. Co., 1st 5s, 1942 | 114 | 114 | 117 | 117 | 120 | 115 |
| Union Water Co. col. tr. 6s, 1923 | 5 | 5 | .. | .. | .. | .. |
| United Breweries Co. of Chicago 1st 6s | 80 | 80 | .. | .. | .. | .. |
| United Electric Light & Power Co. 1st | 95 | 90 | .. | .. | .. | .. |
| United Electric Light Co. of N. J. 4s. | 80 | 70 | .. | .. | 70½ | 66½ |
| United Ry. Co. of St. Louis 4s | 95 | 84 | 91½ | 85½ | 91 | 84 |

| | 1900. | | 1901. | | 1902. | |
|---|---|---|---|---|---|---|
| | Highest. | Lowest. | Highest. | Lowest. | Highest. | Lowest. |
| United States Flour Milling Co. 1st 6s, May, 1900, coup. on | 28¾ | 26 | 25 | 20 | .. | .. |
| United States Envelope 1st 6s | 106 | 106 | .. | .. | 106 | 106 |
| United States Reduc. & Refin. Co. 6s | .. | .. | 87 | 85 | .. | .. |
| United States Sugar Refin. Co. 6s, 1921 | 82¾ | 60 | .. | .. | 90 | 90 |
| United Traction & Electric, Providence, 1st 5s, 1933 | .. | .. | 114½ | 114½ | 114 | 114 |
| University Club, New York, 2d 5s | .. | .. | 90 | 90 | 85 | 85 |
| Utica, Clin. & Bin. R. R. 1st g. 5s, 1939 | 123 | 123 | .. | .. | 121 | 121 |
| Verdigris Valley & Independence guar. 5s, 1926 | .. | .. | .. | .. | 108 | 100 |
| Virginia Iron, Coal & Coke 1st m. 5s | 63 | 25 | 56 | 25 | 82½ | 25 |
| Washington Ry. & Electric Co. 4s, temp. rects | .. | .. | .. | .. | 82½ | 82½ |
| Washington Trac. 4s, 1949 | .. | .. | 82 | 77½ | 85 | 79 |
| Washington Traction & Electric Co. col. tr. 4½s, 1949, J. & D | 85 | 85 | .. | .. | .. | .. |
| Westchester Electric 1st guar. 5s, 1943 | 112 | 110 | .. | .. | 110 | 108½ |
| Western Gas Co. 1st mort. 5s | 108 | 102 | .. | .. | .. | .. |
| Western Transit Co. 4½s, 1903 | .. | .. | 102¾ | 102¾ | .. | .. |
| Westinghouse Elect. & Mfg. 5s, 1913 | .. | .. | .. | .. | 103½ | 103½ |
| Westport, Conn., Water Co. 1st 5s, 1922 | 40 | 40 | .. | .. | .. | .. |
| Wisconsin Cen. R. R. 1st ser. 5s, 1909 | .. | .. | 110¾ | 110¾ | .. | .. |
| Wisconsin Valley R. R. 1st 7s, 1909 | 126 | 126 | .. | .. | .. | .. |
| Wladikawkas R. R. Co. 4s, 1957 | .. | .. | .. | .. | 96½ | 96½ |
| Zanesville & Ohio Ry. 1st m. bond cer. | 2 | 2 | .. | .. | .. | .. |

# Philadelphia Stock Exchange

## Quotations for Securities Dealt in on the Stock Exchange, 1901 and 1902

## STOCKS

### RAILROAD STOCKS

| | 1901. | | 1902. | |
|---|---|---|---|---|
| | Highest. | Lowest. | Highest. | Lowest. |
| Allegheny Valley pref | 28½ | 20 | 34¼ | 26 |
| Ann Arbor | 26⅛ | 26⅛ | .. | .. |
| " pref | 61⅞ | 61⅞ | .. | .. |
| Atchison, Topeka & Santa Fe pref | 106¼ | 86 | 103 | 97½ |
| " " " trustees certfs | 89⅝ | 45 | 96¼ | 78⅜ |
| Baltimore & Ohio | 98⅛ | 87⅞ | 118 | 98⅜ |
| Camden & Burlington | .. | .. | 40 | 40 |
| Catawissa Railroad, 1st pref | 60 | 56 | 64¼ | 58 |
| " " 2d pref | 60 | 55 | 65 | 59 |
| Central Railroad of New Jersey | 152⅛ | 152⅛ | 194 | 194 |
| Chesapeake & Ohio | 49⅛ | 37 | 57⅜ | 46 |
| Chicago & Alton | 47⅞ | 47⅞ | 43 | 43 |
| Chicago, Burlington & Quincy | 188¼ | 188¼ | .. | .. |
| Chicago Great Western | 26 | 24½ | 34½ | 28 |
| Chicago, Milwaukee & St. Paul | 176⅛ | 148⅝ | 190¼ | 162½ |
| Chicago Terminal | .. | .. | 22⅜ | 22⅜ |
| " " pref | 42⅛ | 42⅜ | .. | .. |
| Choctaw, Oklahoma & Gulf | 69⅛ | 37½ | .. | .. |
| " " pref | 46½ | 45 | .. | .. |
| " " voting trust cer | 82¼ | 42 | 83½ | 70 |
| " " " " pref | 60 | 45¼ | 60¼ | 53 |
| Cleveland, Cincinnati, Chicago & St. Louis | .. | .. | 96⅛ | 96⅛ |
| Colorado Southern | 11¾ | 8¾ | 31⅜ | 18⅜ |
| " " pref | 46⅞ | 46¼ | 49½ | 48½ |
| Delaware & Bound Brook | 211 | 211 | 211 | 211 |
| Denver & Rio Grande | 40¼ | 30⅜ | 49⅞ | 41½ |
| East Penna | 70 | 68½ | .. | .. |
| Elmira & Williamsport | 57 | 52½ | 52 | 52 |
| " " pref | 70 | 70 | 77½ | 77½ |
| Erie | 44⅝ | 30 | 44⅞ | 29⅜ |
| " 1st pref | 71⅛ | 64⅞ | .. | .. |
| " 2d pref | 48⅞ | 48⅞ | .. | .. |
| Harrisburg, Por., Mt. Joy & Lanc | 110⅛ | 110 | 111 | 106 |
| Hocking Valley, pref | 82 | 75 | .. | .. |
| Hunt. & Broad Top | 28 | 15 | 32 | 22 |
| " " pref | 59 | 48 | 59¾ | 52 |
| Kansas & Texas | .. | .. | 35 | 24⅝ |
| " " pref | .. | .. | 69½ | 55⅜ |
| Kansas City Southern | .. | .. | 30 | 20⅜ |
| " " " pref | 44¾ | 40⅝ | 46⅞ | 46 |
| Lehigh Valley | 39⅜ | 28½ | 38½ | 29¼ |
| " pref | 40 | 40 | .. | .. |
| Little Schuylkill | 60 | 57¾ | 63 | 59½ |
| Louisville & Nashville | 106 | 96¾ | .. | .. |
| Mexican Central | 22 | 4 | 30⅜ | 26⅝ |
| Mexican National | 14⅜ | 14 | .. | .. |
| Minehill & Schuylkill Haven | 65 | 58¾ | 66¼ | 62½ |
| Missouri, Kansas & Texas, pref | 57½ | 57½ | .. | .. |
| Missouri Pacific | 85¼ | 85¼ | 124¾ | 122¾ |

| | 1901. | | 1902. | |
|---|---|---|---|---|
| | Highest. | Lowest. | Highest. | Lowest. |
| Nesquehoning Valley | 54½ | 51 | 52½ | 50½ |
| New York, Ontario & Western | 37⅝ | 27⅞ | 36⅝ | 29¼ |
| Norfolk & Western | 58½ | 43¾ | 79¾ | 56½ |
| " " pref | .. | .. | 91 | 91 |
| North Pennsylvania | 109 | 107 | 110 | 108 |
| Northern Central | 105½ | 91 | 124½ | 104 |
| Northern Pacific voting trust cer | 230 | 79 | .. | .. |
| " " " " pref | 110 | 87½ | .. | .. |
| Pennsylvania & Northwestern | 36 | 26 | 38 | 32½ |
| Pennsylvania | 81 | 69 | 85 | 73¾ |
| " allotments | 16 | 9 | .. | .. |
| " receipts | 76¼ | 70 | .. | .. |
| " rights | .. | .. | ⅜ | ¼ |
| Philadelphia & Erie | 49 | 30 | 72½ | 47 |
| Philadelphia & Trenton | 284 | 280 | .. | .. |
| Philadelphia, Germantown & Norristown | 165 | 158 | 178 | 168¼ |
| Philadelphia, Wilmington & Baltimore | 109⅛ | 87 | .. | .. |
| Pittsburg, Cincinnati, Chicago, & St. Louis | 77⅛ | 77⅛ | 82⅜ | 82⅜ |
| Reading Co., trust cer | 28⅞ | 12¼ | 39¼ | 26½ |
| " " 1st pfd | 41⅜ | 34½ | 45⅞ | 39⅞ |
| " " 2d pfd | 32¾ | 19 | 40¼ | 30 |
| St. Joseph & Rock Island, pref | .. | .. | 61 | 61 |
| St. Louis & San Francisco, 2d pref | 72¼ | 72¼ | 72⅞ | 72⅞ |
| St. Louis & Southwestern | 32⅞ | 27¾ | 36⅛ | 30¼ |
| " " pref | 69⅝ | 49⅝ | 65⅛ | 65⅝ |
| Southern Pacific | 60¼ | 44 | 81 | 56⅞ |
| Southern Railway | 35¼ | 19 | 41¼ | 28⅛ |
| " " pref | 94¼ | 77⅛ | .. | .. |
| Texas & Pacific | 51⅛ | 25½ | 52⅜ | 37¾ |
| Toledo, St. Louis & Southwestern, pref | .. | .. | 35 | 35 |
| Union Pacific | 94¾ | 89 | 112⅞ | 94⅞ |
| " " pref | 96¾ | 85 | .. | .. |
| United Companies of New Jersey | 286 | 274 | 285½ | 280 |
| Wabash | 25 | 12⅜ | 37½ | 22⅞ |
| " pref | 45⅞ | 28⅞ | 48¾ | 42½ |
| Western N. Y. & Pa | 12¼ | 4¾ | 8⅝ | 6 |
| West Jersey & Seashore | 67 | 62½ | 71¾ | 67 |
| Wheeling & Lake Erie | 15⅛ | 15⅛ | . | .. |
| " " pref | 60⅛ | 59⅝ | .. | .. |
| Wisconsin Central | 18 | 18 | 28⅝ | 28⅝ |
| " " pref | 42½ | 42½ | .. | .. |

## CANAL STOCKS—PHILADELPHIA

| | 1901. | | 1902. | |
|---|---|---|---|---|
| | Highest. | Lowest. | Highest. | Lowest. |
| Delaware & Hudson | 148¾ | 148 | 180⅝ | 175 |
| Lehigh Coal & Navigation | 78 | 62½ | 79¾ | 65 |
| " " " allotments | .. | .. | 19½ | 15 |
| " " " receipts | .. | .. | 70⅛ | 69 |
| Morris, pref. guar., 10 per cent | 161 | 160 | 172 | 171 |
| " " 4 per cent | 50 | 50 | 70 | 67 |

## STREET RAILWAY STOCKS—PHILADELPHIA

| | Par Value. | 1901. Highest. | 1901. Lowest. | 1902. Highest. | 1902. Lowest |
|---|---|---|---|---|---|
| American Railways | $50 | 46 | 31½ | 56¾ | 42½ |
| Brooklyn Rapid Transit | 100 | .. | .. | 67 | 64½ |
| Camden & Trenton | 100 | .. | .. | 48¼ | 43¾ |
| " " | 10 | .. | .. | 6¼ | 3½ |
| Citizens' Pass | 50 | 360 | 360 | .. | .. |
| Columbus (O.) Street | 100 | .. | .. | 59¾ | 59¾ |
| " " | 100 | 45¾ | 40 | .. | .. |
| Consolidated Traction, New Jersey | 100 | 69 | 59¾ | 70⅜ | 67 |
| " " Pittsburg | 50 | 28½ | 21 | 23⅞ | 22¾ |
| " " " pref | 50 | 67 | 59 | 64¼ | 63⅞ |
| Continental Pass., $29 paid | 50 | 155 | 155 | 153 | 153 |
| Detroit United | 100 | .. | .. | 79 | 75½ |
| Fairm't Park & Hadingston, rcts. full paid | 50 | 71 | 71 | 75 | 72 |
| " " Transportation, full paid | .. | 28 | 20 | 35 | 20 |
| Frankford & Southwark | 50 | 466 | 465½ | 462 | 460 |
| Germantown Pass | 50 | 150 | 146 | 148 | 145 |
| Green & Coates, $15 paid | 50 | 155 | 155 | 155 | 151½ |
| Hestonville, Mantua & Fairmount | 50 | 48 | 47 | 48½ | 48 |
| " " " pref | 50 | 74¾ | 73 | 75 | 73 |
| Indianapolis Street | 100 | 48 | 25 | 93 | 46 |
| Manhattan | 100 | 125½ | 122¾ | 138¼ | 134 |
| Metropolitan Street | 100 | 173 | 154⅝ | 167¼ | 145⅞ |
| Philadelphia City Pass., $23.75 paid | 50 | 211¼ | 205 | 210⅛ | 210 |
| Philadelphia Rapid Transit | 50 | .. | .. | 18⅞ | 8¼ |
| Philadelphia Traction | 50 | 101½ | 90 | 100¼ | 87 |
| Railways Company, General | 10 | 3¼ | 2 | 6½ | 4 |
| Reading (Pa.) Traction | 50 | 35 | 28½ | 33 | 30 |
| Ridge Avenue Pass., $28 paid | 50 | 310 | 305 | 304½ | 304½ |
| Rochester (N. Y.) | 100 | 84 | 24 | 67 | 43 |
| " " pref | 100 | 95 | 85 | 101¼ | 95 |
| Second & Third | 50 | 306¼ | 303 | 305 | 300 |
| Thirteenth & Fifteenth | 50 | 311 | 307 | 310 | 307 |
| Twin City | 100 | .. | .. | 20⅞ | 20⅞ |
| Union Pass., $30 5-6 paid | 50 | 240 | 246 | .. | .. |
| Union Traction, receipts, $17.50 paid | 50 | 37 | 24¼ | 48¾ | 32 |
| " " warrants | .. | .. | .. | 6 | 3 |
| Union Traction, Chicago | .. | 16½ | 15⅜ | 20 | 20 |
| Union Traction, Indiana | 100 | .. | .. | 54 | 51 |
| " " pref | 100 | .. | .. | 90 | 90 |
| United Power & Transportation, $20 paid | 25 | 47¼ | 32¾ | 52 | 42 |
| " " " rights | .. | .. | .. | 11 | 7 |
| " " " rec., $17.50 pd. | . | .. | .. | 28½ | 25½ |
| United Traction of Pittsburg pref | 50 | 53 | 49¾ | 52¾ | 50⅜ |
| West Philadelphia Pass | 50 | 258 | 258 | .. | .. |

---

## MISCELLANEOUS STOCKS—PHILADELPHIA

| | Par Value. | 1901. Highest. | 1901. Lowest. | 1902. Highest. | 1902. Lowest |
|---|---|---|---|---|---|
| Adams Express | $100 | 175 | 175 | .. | .. |
| American Academy of Music | 100 | .. | .. | 315 | 315 |
| American Alkali | 50 | 2⅜ | ¼ | 1¼ | ⅛ |
| " " pref., $10 paid | 50 | ⅜ | ⅛ | .. | .. |
| American Car & Foundry | 100 | 34 | 34 | 33⅝ | 33⅝ |
| " " pref | 100 | 81 | 81 | .. | .. |
| American Cement | 10 | 8¾ | 6 | 9⅛ | 5½ |
| American Iron & Steel Manufacturing | 50 | .. | .. | 5½ | 4¾ |
| American Steel & Iron, $5 paid | 50 | 10 | 5 | .. | .. |
| American Steel & Wire | 100 | 53 | 39⅛ | .. | .. |

| | Par Value. | 1901. Highest. | 1901. Lowest. | 1902. Highest. | 1902. Lowest. |
|---|---|---|---|---|---|
| American Sugar Ref. | $100 | 150⅝ | 110⅝ | 132½ | 116⅝ |
| " " pref. | 50 | 46 | 46 | .. | .. |
| American Tobacco | 50 | 129 | 68¼ | .. | .. |
| Asphalt of America, receipts, com | .. | .. | .. | ⅝ | ⅝ |
| Bell Telephone of Philadelphia | 50 | 75 | 70 | 77 | 70 |
| Bergner & Engle Brewing pref. | 100 | 41 | 41 | 45 | 41 |
| Bethlehem Iron | 50 | 63¼ | 59 | .. | .. |
| Bethlehem Steel, $1 paid | 50 | 25½ | 17 | .. | .. |
| Brooklyn Gas & Electric Light, $5 paid | 50 | 2½ | 2 | .. | .. |
| Cambria Iron | 50 | 49 | 45¼ | 49½ | 46½ |
| Cambria Steel receipts, $2.50 paid | .. | 4½ | 1⅜ | .. | .. |
| " " " $10.50 " | .. | 24⅞ | 15¾ | .. | .. |
| " " " $13.50 " | .. | 35¼ | 22⅛ | .. | .. |
| " " " $22.50 " | .. | 28⅜ | 23⅛ | .. | .. |
| " " " $50.00 full paid | .. | 27⅜ | 24⅛ | 29⅛ | 23 |
| " " warrants | .. | 6½ | ¾ | .. | .. |
| " " Drexel receipts, $13.50 paid | .. | 28½ | 21½ | .. | .. |
| Camden Land | .. | 3 | ⅜ | 1⅜ | ¼ |
| Central Coal & Coke | 100 | .. | .. | 66 | 66 |
| Consolidated Lake Superior | 50 | 38½ | 28 | .. | .. |
| " " " pref | 50 | 49 | 40 | 80¼ | 33 |
| " " " | 100 | 31½ | 20⅜ | 36 | 6 |
| " " " pref | 100 | 80¼ | 63 | .. | .. |
| " " " warrants | .. | 5½ | 2¾ | .. | .. |
| Continental Tobacco | 100 | 46⅛ | 43⅜ | .. | .. |
| " " pref. | 100 | 118½ | 118½ | 119½ | 119½ |
| Cramp, W. & Son, Ship & Engine Building | 100 | 35½ | 73 | 76¼ | 60 |
| Crucible Steel of America | 100 | 27½ | 24⅛ | .. | .. |
| " " pref. | 100 | 83 | 83 | .. | .. |
| Danville Bessemer | 5 | 1½ | ¼ | ½ | ¼ |
| DeLong Hook & Eye | 10 | 10 | 10 | 10½ | 9½ |
| Diamond State Steel, $5 paid | 10 | 4⅛ | 3 | 2¼ | ⅝ |
| " " " $6.25 paid | .. | 6 | 5⅛ | .. | .. |
| " " " new co., full paid, n. s. | .. | 3¾ | 1½ | .. | .. |
| " " " " pref. | 10 | 7¼ | 4 | 6½ | 3 |
| " " " " D. W. I. | .. | 4¼ | 3 | .. | .. |
| " " " " pref. | .. | 8 | 7 | .. | .. |
| " " " $6.25 paid | .. | 6 | 5⅛ | .. | .. |
| " " " $6.25 " Girard tr. rcpts. | .. | 7½ | 5 | .. | .. |
| Easton Con. Electric, $12.50 paid | 50 | 17½ | 17½ | .. | .. |
| " " " $15 paid | 50 | 22 | 10½ | 20½ | 19½ |
| Electric Co. of Am., $7.50 " | 50 | 10 | 6 | 8 | 5½ |
| " " " $10 " | 50 | .. | .. | 11⅛ | 8½ |
| Electric Storage Battery | 100 | 84 | 61 | 96 | 55¼ |
| " " " pref. | 100 | 88¼ | 53½ | 94¼ | 55¼ |
| Electro-Pneumatic Transit | 5 | 2⅜ | 1½ | 1½ | 1½ |
| Federal Steel | 100 | 75½ | 75½ | .. | .. |
| Harrison Bros., pref. | 100 | 95 | 90 | 20 | 20 |
| Highlander Mill & Mining | 5 | 3¼ | 1¼ | .. | .. |
| Insurance of North America | 10 | 24⅞ | 22 | .. | .. |
| International Paper | 100 | .. | .. | 19⅝ | 19½ |
| Int. Smokeless Powder & Dynamite | 50 | 12½ | 7 | 12⅞ | 8 |
| " " " " pref. $25 paid | 50 | 32½ | 30 | 46½ | 29 |
| John B. Stetson | 100 | .. | .. | 170 | 170 |
| " " pref. | 100 | .. | .. | 150 | 150 |
| " " warrants | 100 | .. | .. | 55 | 42 |
| Lit Brothers | 10 | 10⅞ | 10⅛ | 12½ | 10¼ |
| Manufactured Rubber | 50 | 1⅜ | ¼ | ½ | ⅛ |
| " " pref. $10 paid | 50 | ½ | ¼ | .. | .. |
| Marsden Company | 100 | 7⅝ | 3⅝ | 5¼ | 2½ |
| " " pref. | 100 | 32 | 20 | 40 | 25 |
| Montreal & Boston Copper | 5 | 5¼ | 5 | 4⅜ | 2¾ |
| National Asphalt | 100 | 8½ | ¼ | 1 | ¼ |
| " " pref. | 100 | 15⅝ | 1 | 2⅜ | ¼ |
| " " receipts | .. | .. | .. | ¼ | ¼ |

| | Par Value. | 1901. Highest. | 1901. Lowest. | 1902. Highest. | 1902. Lowest. |
|---|---|---|---|---|---|
| National Asphalt, receipts, pref | .. | .. | .. | 1¾ | ¼ |
| National Tube | $100 | 70 | 70 | .. | .. |
| New Haven Iron & Steel | 5 | 6⅜ | 4⅝ | 6 | 5 |
| North American | 100 | 24⅝ | 21 | .. | .. |
| " " new stock | .. | 90⅛ | 90⅛ | 127⅞ | 105¾ |
| Northern Liberties Gas | 25 | .. | .. | 50 | 50 |
| Overland Telegraph | 10 | 3½ | 3½ | .. | .. |
| Pacific Mail | 100 | 45⅝ | 41⅛ | 47¼ | 40⅝ |
| Palmetto | 25 | 1 | ⅛ | ⅜ | ⅛ |
| Parkside Apartment House | 10 | 2 | 2 | .. | .. |
| Pennsylvania Electric Vehicle | 50 | 2¾ | ⅜ | 2 | ½ |
| " " " pref., $10 paid | 50 | 2 | ½ | 6⅜ | 2¼ |
| Pennsylvania Gas Coal | 50 | 38 | 35 | 50 | 38½ |
| Pennsylvania Salt Manufacturing | 50 | 123 | 110½ | 115 | 110 |
| " " " receipts, $50 paid | .. | 61 | 60 | .. | .. |
| " " " warrants | .. | 15 | 5½ | .. | .. |
| Pennsylvania Steel | 100 | 80⅛ | 42 | 55 | 37 |
| " " pref | 100 | 100 | 82 | 105 | 80¼ |
| " " scrip | .. | 55 | 30 | .. | .. |
| " " " pref | .. | 90 | 80 | .. | .. |
| " " new | .. | 60 | 30 | .. | .. |
| " " " pref | .. | 90 | 80 | .. | .. |
| " " Girard trust receipts | .. | 86 | 77 | .. | .. |
| " " " " " pref | .. | 100⅛ | 94 | .. | .. |
| Pennsylvania Traffic | .. | .. | .. | 7¼ | 6½ |
| People's Gas | .. | .. | .. | 105 | 105 |
| Philadelphia Bourse | 50 | 5 | 5 | 6⅛ | 5 |
| Philadelphia (Pittsburg) | 50 | 54¼ | 40¼ | 50⅜ | 43½ |
| " " pref | 50 | 49¾ | 45 | 50½ | 43⅞ |
| Philadelphia Electric, $3.75 paid | 25 | 6⅜ | 5¼ | .. | .. |
| " " $5.00 " | 25 | 8⅜ | 4¼ | 4¾ | 3⅛ |
| " " $6.25 " | 25 | .. | .. | 6 | 4½ |
| " " $7.50 " | 25 | .. | .. | 9½ | 5½ |
| Pressed Steel Car | 100 | 44⅛ | 44⅛ | .. | .. |
| Republic Iron & Steel | 100 | 13 | 13 | .. | .. |
| " " pref | 100 | 72¾ | 72¾ | .. | .. |
| Southern Cotton Oil | 50 | 70 | 50 | .. | .. |
| Susquehanna Iron & Steel | 5 | 2¾ | 1⅝ | 3 | 1⅝ |
| Tennessee Coal & Iron | 100 | 76 | 63⅛ | 73 | 69¼ |
| Tidewater Steel | 10 | 10 | 5⅛ | 7⅛ | 4¾ |
| " " pref. receipts | .. | .. | .. | 11¼ | 11¼ |
| United Gas Improvement | 50 | 128½ | 113 | 126 | 101½ |
| " " " stk. rcts. $12.50 paid | .. | .. | .. | 68½ | 67¾ |
| " " " " " $25 " | .. | .. | .. | 83 | 83 |
| " " " warrants | .. | .. | .. | 55¾ | 50½ |
| United States Leather | 100 | 15 | 12 | 14⅞ | 11¼ |
| " " pref | 100 | 100 | 72⅝ | 90 | 81¾ |
| United States Steel Corporation | 100 | 54½ | 30 | 46⅝ | 29½ |
| " " " pref | 100 | 101⅞ | 86½ | 98 | 79¾ |
| Warwick Iron & Steel | 10 | 8 | 6¼ | 7 | 4 |
| Warwick Iron & Steel scrip | .. | 6⅜ | 6 | .. | .. |
| Washington (D. C.) Gas | 20 | .. | .. | 85½ | 85½ |
| Welsbach Company | 100 | 55 | 38 | 40½ | 24 |
| Welsbach Incandescent of Canada | 5 | 1¼ | ⅜ | ¾ | ¼ |
| Western Union | 100 | .. | .. | 95⅛ | 88 |
| Westmoreland Coal | 50 | 72 | 68 | 80 | 74½ |

# BONDS

## RAILROAD BONDS—PHILADELPHIA

| | Due. | Interest Payable. | 1901. High. | 1901. Low. | 1902. High. | 1902. Low. |
|---|---|---|---|---|---|---|
| Allegheny Valley 7s, E. Ext. *c* | 1910 | A. & O. | .. | .. | 124½ | 123 |
| " gen. mort. 4s | 1942 | M. & S. | 108½ | 108⅛ | 109 | 107 |
| Allentown Terminal 5s | .... | ........ | 102½ | 102½ | .. | .. |
| " " 1st mort. 4s *r. c.* | 1919 | J. & J. | .. | .. | 104 | 104 |
| Ann Arbor 4s | 1995 | Q., J. | .. | .. | 97 | 97 |
| Ashtabula & Pittsburgh 6s *r. c* | 1908 | F. & A. | 116 | 116 | 114 | 114 |
| Atlantic City 1st 5s | 1919 | M. & N. | 115¾ | 112½ | 115 | 112 |
| Ballston Terminal 1st 5s *r. c* | 1926 | J. & D. | .. | .. | 98 | 94 |
| Baltimore & Ohio 4s | 1948 | A. & O. | 103¼ | 103¼ | 103½ | 100½ |
| " " prior lien 3½s | 1925 | J. & J. | .. | .. | 94½ | 94½ |
| Baltimore & Potomac 6s *c* | 1911 | A. & O. | 120½ | 120½ | 117½ | 117½ |
| " " tunnel 1st mort. 6s | 1911 | J. & J. | .. | .. | 118¼ | 118¾ |
| Belvidere-Delaware 1st 6s coup | 1902 | J. & D. | 104 | 104 | .. | .. |
| Bell's Gap con. mort. 6s *r. c* | 1913 | A. & O. | .. | .. | 121 | 121 |
| " " 1st 6s *r. c* | 1905 | F. & A. | 108 | 108 | .. | .. |
| Catawissa 1st m. 6s *r* | 1902 | F. & A. | 103½ | 102 | 101¾ | 101¾ |
| " 1st con. 4s *r. & r. c* | 1948 | A. & O. | 111½ | 111½ | .. | .. |
| Central Georgia 2d pref. inc. 5s | 1945 | Oct. | 34¼ | 30⅜ | .. | .. |
| " " 3d pref. inc. 5s | 1945 | Oct. | 16¾ | 16½ | .. | .. |
| Chartiers Val. 1st mort. 7s *c* | 1901 | A. & O. | 101 | 101 | .. | .. |
| Chesapeake & Ohio 4s | .... | ........ | .. | .. | 106¾ | 106¼ |
| " " 5s | .... | ........ | .. | .. | 119¼ | 119¼ |
| Choctaw & Memphis 1st mort. 5s *r. c* | 1949 | J. & J. | 118 | 108 | 120 | 115⅜ |
| Choctaw, O. & G. gen. 5s | 1919 | J. & J. | 113 | 107 | 114¾ | 110 |
| Clearfield & Jefferson 1st mort. 6s | 1927 | J. & J. | 120 | 120 | 125 | 125 |
| Colorado & Southern 1st 4s | 1929 | F. & A. | 89¼ | 89¾ | .. | .. |
| Connecting 6s *c* | 1902 | M. & S. | 107 | 107 | 103 | 101 |
| Del. & Bd. Bk. 1st mort. 7s *c* | 1905 | F. & A. | 115 | 114 | 112½ | 109½ |
| Easton & Amboy mort. 5s *r* | 1920 | M. & N. | 117 | 114 | 116½ | 115¾ |
| Elmira & Williamsport 1st mort. 6s *r* | 1910 | J. & J. | 118⅜ | 117 | 118½ | 118½ |
| Erie 1st con. 4s | .... | ........ | 100⅛ | 98⅝ | 90 | 90 |
| " prior lien 4s | 1996 | J. & J. | .. | .. | 99⅞ | 99⅞ |
| Gettysburg & Harrisburg 5s | .... | ........ | 101 | 101 | .. | .. |
| Harrisburg P. Mt. J. & L. 1st U. S. *r* | 1913 | J. & J. | 106⅛ | 106⅛ | 106½ | 106¾ |
| Hunt. & Bd. Top con. mort., 5s *r. c* | 1925 | A. & O. | 110 | 110 | 111 | 111 |
| " " 1st mort., g. 4s *c* | 1920 | A. & O. | 105 | 102½ | 104½ | 104¾ |
| Kansas City & Southern 3s | 1950 | A. & O. | 70⅛ | 67⅝ | 73⅜ | 73 |
| Lehigh Valley 1st extd. 4s, *c* | 1948 | J. & D. | 121¼ | 117½ | 119¾ | 116 |
| " " " 4s, *r* | 1948 | J. & D. | 118 | 117¾ | .. | .. |
| Lehigh Valley 2d mort. 7s *r* | 1910 | M. & S. | 131¼ | 126 | 128¾ | 121¾ |
| " con. mort. 6s *c* | 1923 | J. & D. | 126 | 122 | 127 | 120 |
| " con. mort. 6s *r* | 1923 | J. & D. | 126 | 121½ | .. | .. |
| " annuity 6s *r* | .... | J. & D. | 133½ | 127 | 143⅜ | 139 |
| " con. 4½s *r. c* | 1923 | J. & D. | 106½ | 102½ | 110¾ | 103¾ |
| " con. 4½s *r* | 1923 | J. & D. | .. | .. | 110⅜ | 101½ |
| " annuity 4½s | .... | J. & D. | .. | .. | 111 | 105½ |
| " mort. & cl. trust, 5s *c. & r. c* | 1997 | M. & N. | 109⅞ | 107½ | 112. | 107 |
| " 1st mort. 4½s *c. r* | 1940 | J. & J. | 110⅜ | 109 | 109 | 106 |
| " 1st mort. 4½s *c. & r. c* | 1940 | J. & J. | 111 | 107 | 111½ | 106 |
| " Terminal 5s | 1941 | A. & O. | .. | .. | 118½ | 118½ |
| Mexican Central 2d incomes | 1939 | ........ | 26⅛ | 26⅛ | .. | .. |
| Michigan Central 7s | .... | ........ | 105½ | 105½ | .. | .. |
| Midland of N. J. 1st 6s | 1910 | A. & O. | 115⅞ | 115⅞ | .. | .. |
| Missouri, Kansas & Texas 1st 4s | 1990 | J. & D. | .. | .. | 99 | 99 |
| " " " 2d 4s | 1990 | F. & A. | .. | .. | 85 | 85 |
| New York, Phila. & Norf. 1st mort. 4s *r. c* | 1939 | J. & J. | 105 | 103 | 103½ | 102 |
| " " " inc. 4s *r* | 1939 | M. & N. | 86½ | 85 | 93 | 90 |
| " " " scrip | .... | ........ | .. | .. | 101½ | 101½ |
| Norfolk & Western con. 4s | 1996 | A. & O. | 103⅛ | 103⅛ | 103½ | 103½ |
| North Pennsylvania 1st 4s *c* | 1936 | M. & N. | 117 | 117 | .. | .. |
| " gen. mort. 7s *r* | 1903 | J. & J. | 108½ | 103¾ | 104½ | 101½ |

| | Due. | Interest Payable. | 1901. High. | 1901. Low. | 1902. High. | 1902. Low. |
|---|---|---|---|---|---|---|
| North Pennsylvania gen. mort. 7s *c* | 1903 | J. & J. | 108½ | 105¼ | 104½ | 101½ |
| " deb. 6s *r* | 1905 | M. & S. | 108½ | 108½ | 109 | 109 |
| Northern Central 2d gen. mort. 5s, series A. *c* | 1926 | J. & J. | 122 | 120 | 125½ | 122¾ |
| " 2d gen. mort, 5s, series B, *c* | 1926 | J. & J. | 122¼ | 122¼ | 126¼ | 125½ |
| " con. mort. 6s, series C | 1904 | J. & J. | .. | .. | 107 | 107 |
| " con. mort. 4½s series E, C | 1925 | A. & O. | .. | .. | 117½ | 117 |
| Northern Pacific prior lien 4s | 1997 | Q., J. | 105¼ | 104½ | 105⅝ | 105⅝ |
| " gen. lien 3s *r. c* | 2047 | Q. Feb. | 72⅞ | 70⅝ | 74⅞ | 73½ |
| Pennsylvania & New York Canal 7s *r. c* | 1906 | J. & D. | 117⅛ | 117 | 113½ | 110¾ |
| " " " con. mort. 5s *r* | 1939 | A. & O. | 110 | 108 | 115⅛ | 109½ |
| " " " con. mort. 4s *r* | 1939 | A. & O. | 94½ | 92 | 101½ | 98 |
| " " " con. mort. 4½s *r.* | 1939 | A. & O. | 106½ | 102 | 108 | 107¼ |
| Pennsylvania & Northwestern gen. 5s *c* | 1930 | J. & J. | 103 | 101¼ | 116 | 114½ |
| Pennsylvania gen. mort. 6s *r* | 1910 | A. & O. | 120¾ | 120½ | 122 | 117 |
| " gen. mort. 6s *c* | 1910 | J. & J. | 124¼ | 120¼ | 122½ | 118 |
| " con. mort. 6s *r* | 1905 | Q., June | 111¼ | 107¾ | 109¼ | 106⅝ |
| " con. mort. 6s *c* | 1905 | J. & D. | 112 | 108 | 109¼ | 107¼ |
| " con. mort. 5s *r* | 1919 | Q., S. | .. | .. | 123 | 120½ |
| " con. mort. 5s *c* | 1919 | M. & S. | .. | .. | 122¼ | 118 |
| " trust 4½s *r. c* | 1913 | J. & D. | 111 | 111 | 110½ | 108 |
| " g. 4s *c* | 1943 | M. & N. | 116⅞ | 116⅞ | .. | .. |
| " Equip. tr. g. 4s, Series A | 1914 | M. & S. | 103⅛ | 103½ | 103½ | 103 |
| " conv. 3½s | .... | ........ | .. | .. | 108¾ | 104½ |
| " " 3½s scrip | .... | ........ | .. | .. | 108½ | 104¾ |
| " " war. 3½ bonds, 50 p. c. paid | .... | ........ | .. | .. | 112 | 103 |
| " " right to subsc. to converted bds. | .... | ........ | .. | .. | 6 | 5⅝ |
| Perkiomen 1st ser. 5s *c* | 1918 | Q. Jan. | .. | .. | 115 | 115 |
| Philadelphia & Erie gen'l mort. 4s *r* | 1920 | A. & O. | 111 | 107¾ | 110 | 107 |
| " con. mort. 5s *r* | 1920 | A. & O. | 121⅝ | 120 | 121¾ | 119 |
| " genl. 6s | 1920 | J. & J. | 132 | 132 | 130⅛ | 130 |
| Phila. & Reading 1st mort. 6s *r. c* | 1910 | J. & J. | 123 | 123 | 122¼ | 117 |
| " con. mort. 6s, g, *r* | 1911 | J. & D. | 122⅛ | 119 | .. | .. |
| " 10 yr. s. f. g, 5s *r. c. r* | 1902 | F. & A. | 101¼ | 101¼ | .. | .. |
| " 2d mort. 5s. gen'l *r* | 1933 | A. & O. | 132 | 129½ | 132 | 130 |
| " con. mort. 7s *r* | 1911 | J. & D. | 132 | 127 | 128½ | 122 |
| " con. mort. 7s *c* | 1911 | J. & D. | 132 | 127⅜ | 128½ | 122 |
| " con. mort. 6s, g, *r. c* | 1911 | J. & D. | 123 | 121 | 122 | 118¼ |
| " extd. imp. 4s *r. c* | 1947 | A. & O. | 109 | 107 | 110 | 108½ |
| " 1st series, con. mort. extd, 4s *r. c.* | 1937 | M. & S. | 106¼ | 105¼ | 109¼ | 107½ |
| " terminal 5s *r. c* | 1941 | Q., M. | 126 | 124 | 126½ | 124 |
| " terminal 5s *c* | 1941 | Q., M. | 124¼ | 124 | .. | .. |
| Phila., Wilmington & Balt. deb. 4s *r* | 1917 | A. & O. | .. | .. | 107 | 107 |
| " " " deb. 4s reg. | 1932 | A. & O. | .. | .. | 109 | 109 |
| P. C. C. & St. L. gr. con., series A, gr. 4½s *r. c* | 1940 | A. & O. | .. | .. | 112¼ | 112¼ |
| Pitts., Ft. Wayne & Chic., 2s, 7s | 1912 | ........ | 129¼ | 129¼ | .. | .. |
| Pitts., Youngstown & A. 5s *c* | 1927 | M. & N. | .. | .. | 121 | 121 |
| Port Reading 1st 5s, *r. c.* & *c* | 1941 | J. & J. | 110 | 109½ | .. | .. |
| Reading, Jersey Central col. guar. 4s, *r.* & *r. c* | 1951 | A. & O. | .. | .. | 96¾ | 93 |
| Reading & P. & R. C. & I. gen. mort. 4s *c* | 1997 | J. & J. | 100⅞ | 92½ | 101 | 95⅞ |
| Richmond & Danville con. mort. guar. 6s | 1915 | J. & J. | .. | .. | 121 | 121 |
| Schuylkill Riv., E. Side, 1st 5s *c* | 1935 | J. & D. | 113 | 109½ | 113 | 110 |
| " " " 1st 5s, *r* | 1935 | J. & D. | .. | .. | 112 | 111¼ |
| Seaboard Air Line 1st mort. guar. 4s *r. c* | 1950 | A. & O. | .. | .. | 84 | 84 |
| Seattle & San Francisco 1st 5s | .... | ........ | 61 | 53 | 65 | 50 |
| Sham., Sun. & Lewis. 1st mort. 5s *c* | 1912 | M. & N. | 106 | 106 | .. | .. |
| " " " 2d mort. guar. 6s *c* | 1925 | J. & J. | .. | .. | 116½ | 116½ |
| Sham., Val. & Pottsv. 7s *c* | 1901 | J. & J. | 101⅞ | 101⅞ | .. | .. |
| Southern Pacific 4s | .... | ........ | 92½ | 92½ | . | .. |
| Steubenville & Indiana 1st mort. 5s *r* | 1914 | J. & J. | 115⅛ | 114 | 112 | 111½ |
| Stony Creek 1st mort. 7s *c* | 1907 | A. & O. | 122 | 121¾ | 117¼ | 115 |
| Sun., H. & Wilk. 1st mort. 5s *c* | 1928 | M. & N. | 107½ | 106 | 109 | 106 |
| " 2d mort. 6s *c* | 1938 | M. & N. | 116 | 115 | 117¼ | 116¼ |
| Tex. & Pacific 1st m. 6s E. Div. *r. c* | 1905 | M. & S. | 106¼ | 104 | 103 | 103 |
| Toledo, St. Louis & Western P. L. 3½s | 1925 | J. & J. | 90⅞ | 90⅞ | .. | .. |
| " " " " 4s | 1950 | A. & O. | .. | .. | 84 | 84 |

| | Due. | Interest Payable. | 1901. High. | 1901. Low. | 1902. High. | 1902. Low. |
|---|---|---|---|---|---|---|
| United N. J. gen. mort. 4s, g. *r*.. .. .............. | 1923 | F. & A. | 110½ | 109½ | 111 | 110⅜ |
| " " " guar. 4s. *r*. *c*. & *r*......... | 1929 | M. & S. | .. | .. | 112 | 112 |
| " " gen. 4s............................ | 1944 | M. & S. | 120 | 118⅜ | .. | .. |
| Western N. Y. & Pa. 1st mort. 5s, *r*. *c*............ | 1937 | J. & J. | 122 | 119¼ | 121¾ | 118 |
| " " " scrip............... | .... | ......... | .. | .. | 110 | 110 |
| " " new gen. 4s, *r*. *c*............ | 1943 | A. & O. | 101 | 95 | 102⅜ | 98¼ |
| " " " " scrip........... | .... | .... ... | 115 | 106 | 31 | 30 |
| " " new inc. 5s, *r*. *c*.............. | 1943 | Nov.... | 45 | 45 | .. | .. |
| West Jersey & Seashore 1st con. mort. 4s *r*. *c*...... | 1936 | J. & J. | 114 | 114 | .. | .. |
| West Jersey cons. mort. 6s...................... | 1909 | M. & N. | .. | .. | 116½ | 116½ |
| Western N. Y. & Pa. new inc. 5s scrip........... | .... | ......... | 40 | 27½ | .. | .. |
| West. Penna., g. 4s *c*. & *r*. *c*.......... ......... | 1928 | J. & D. | 113¼ | 112¼ | .. | .. |
| West Shore 1st mort. 4s *r*. *c*........... .......... | 2361 | J. & J. | 113½ | 113½ | .. | .. |

## CANAL BONDS—PHILADELPHIA

| | Due. | Interest Payable. | 1901. High. | 1901. Low. | 1902. High. | 1902. Low. |
|---|---|---|---|---|---|---|
| Ches. & Del. 1st mort. 5s *r*........................ | 1916 | J. & J. | 53¼ | 50 | 53¼ | 50¼ |
| Lehigh Nav. 4½s *r*.... ........................ | 1914 | Q., J. | 114 | 110 | 112¾ | 109 |
| " 4s, *r*. *c*.............................. | 1914 | J. & D. | 108½ | 106¼ | 108 | 105½ |
| " R.R. ext. 4s *r*... .................... | 1914 | Q. Feb. | 108½ | 104 | 104¼ | 104 |
| " con. mort. 7s *r*...................... | 1911 | J. & D. | 129 | 125¾ | 127¾ | 125 |
| " gen. mort. 4½s *r*.................... | 1924 | Q., M. | 109 | 108½ | 112 | 109 |
| " imp. 4s.............................. | 1948 | J. & J. | 107 | 105 | .. | .. |
| " col. trust, 4½s, *r*. *c*.................. | 1905 | M. & S. | 102½ | 102⅛ | 102½ | 102½ |
| Pa. Canal gen. mort. 6s *c*........................ | 1910 | J. & J. | 47 | 43½ | 42 | 39 |

## STREET RAILWAY BONDS—PHILADELPHIA

| | Due. | Interest Payable. | 1901. High. | 1901. Low. | 1902. High. | 1902. Low. |
|---|---|---|---|---|---|---|
| American Railway col. tr. conv. 5s *r*. *c*............ | 1911 | J. & D. | .. | .. | 111¼ | 102¾ |
| Bridgeton & Millville Traction 1st 5s *c*. & *r*. *c*...... | 1930 | J. & J. | 104 | 102¼ | 105 | 101¾ |
| Buffalo City Passenger 5s........... . ......... | 1931 | ........ | . | .. | 118½ | 118⅛ |
| Camden & Trenton 1st mort. 5s *r*. *c*......... .... | 1929 | M. & N. | .. | .. | 101 | 101 |
| Citizens (Indianapolis), 1st con. 5s g. *r*. *c* ........ | 1933 | M. & N. | 111 | 107 | 111 | 108 |
| Consolidated Traction, New Jersey, 5s *c*.......... | 1933 | J. & A. | 111½ | 108½ | 112⅜ | 107 |
| Delaware County Ry. 4s, trust ctfs. *r*.......... ... | 1949 | J. & J. | 86 | 80 | 85 | 85 |
| Electric & Peoples Trac. 4s, trust ctfs *r*............ | 1945 | A. & O. | 103 | 90½ | 101 | 97 |
| Hestonville, M. & F. 2d 6s......................... | 1902 | M. & S. | 102 | 101¾ | .. | .. |
| " con. 5s........................ | 1924 | M. & N. | 121 | 120 | 116 | 116 |
| Indianapolis Street Railway 4s..................... | 1933 | J. & J. | 88 | 78 | 88¼ | 85 |
| " " " 4s scrip ................ | .... | ......... | 71 | 71 | .. | .. |
| Lehigh Valley Traction 1st 4s *r*. *c*................ | 1929 | J. & D. | 89¼ | 89⅜ | 90⅞ | 87 |
| Newark con. 5s *r*. *c*.............................. | 1930 | J. & J. | 118¼ | 116½ | 118⅜ | 115⅝ |
| People's col. tr. 4s *r*......................... .. | 1943 | F. & A. | 108⅛ | 105 | 107½ | 104 |
| Reading Traction 1st mort. 6s........... ......... | 1933 | J. & J. | 126 | 126 | .. | .. |
| Rochester con. 5s g. *r*. *c*.......................... | 1930 | A. & O. | 112 | 109 | 114½ | 111 |
| Scranton 1st con. 5s *r*. *c*.......................... | 1932 | J. & J. | 103 | 103 | .. | .. |
| Scranton Traction 1st 6s *r*. *c*...................... | 1932 | M. & N. | 117 | 117 | 119 | 119 |
| Second Ave. (Pitts.) Traction 1st 5s *r*. *c*........... | 1934 | J. & D. | 119⅛ | 115½ | 119¼ | 117½ |
| Syracuse Rapid Transit 5s........................ | 1946 | M. & S. | .. | .. | 104¾ | 102½ |

| | Due. | Interest Payable. | 1901. High. | 1901. Low. | 1902. High. | 1902. Low. |
|---|---|---|---|---|---|---|
| Union Traction, Indiana, 1st mort. 5s | 1919 | J. & J. | .. | .. | 102½ | 100 |
| United Railways (Baltimore), 1st con. 4s *r. c.* | 1949 | M. & S. | 95 | 95 | .. | .. |
| " " " g., 4s, trust ctfs. | 1949 | J. & J. | 94 | 86½ | 92 | 85¼ |
| United Reading, Pa., mfg. & col. 1st. 5s *c.* | 1926 | J. & J. | .. | .. | 103½ | 103½ |
| United Traction of Pitts. gen. mort. 5s *r. c.* | 1997 | J. & J. | 117¼ | 114 | 117½ | 115⅛ |
| West Philadelphia 2d 5s *c* | 1926 | M. & N. | 118 | 118 | .. | .. |
| Wilmington & Chester Traction 5s | 1918 | A. & O. | 106½ | 105 | 108¼ | 105 |

## STATE AND CITY BONDS—PHILADELPHIA

| | Due. | Interest Payable. | 1901. High. | 1901. Low. | 1902. High. | 1902. Low. |
|---|---|---|---|---|---|---|
| Pennsylvania 4s *r.* | 1912 | F. & A. | 114¼ | 112 | 112½ | 110 |
| " 3½s | 1912 | F. & A. | .. | .. | 103½ | 103½ |
| Philadelphia 6s *r.* | 1902 | J. & J. | .. | .. | 102½ | 100½ |
| " 6s *r.* | 1903 | J. & J. | .. | .. | 105 | 101⅜ |
| " 6s *r.* | 1901 | J. & J. | 102⅜ | 101¼ | .. | .. |
| " 6s *r.* | 1902 | J. & J. | 104¾ | 101¼ | .. | .. |
| " 6s *r.* | 1903 | J. & J. | 108⅜ | 103 | .. | .. |
| " 6s *r.* | 1904 | J. & J. | 109¼ | 109¼ | 107½ | 104½ |
| " 4s *r.* | 1903 | J. & J. | 103¼ | 103¼ | 102 | 102 |
| " 3½s *r.* | 1908 | J. & J. | 103 | 103 | .. | .. |
| " 3½s *r.* | 1905 | J. & J. | 101 | 101 | 100 | 100 |
| " 3½s *r.* | 1906 | J. & J. | 101⅜ | 101⅜ | 103½ | 103 |
| " 3½s *r.* | 1907 | J. & J. | 105 | 101½ | .. | .. |
| " 3½s *r.* | 1915 | J. & J. | 102⅝ | 102⅜ | 105 | 105 |
| " 3½s *r.* | 1916 | J. & J. | 107 | 107 | .. | .. |
| " 3½s. | 1913 | J. & J. | 106 | 102 | 104½ | 104½ |
| " 3½s *r.* | 1926 | J. & J. | 109 | 109 | 106¼ | 106¼ |
| " 3½s *r.* | 1912 | J. & J. | .. | .. | 105 | 105 |
| " 3½s *r.* | 1918 | ........ | .. | .. | 103½ | 103½ |
| " 3½s *r.* | 1931 | ........ | .. | .. | 105⅝ | 105⅝ |
| " 3½s *r.* | 1932 | J. & J. | .. | .. | 108¼ | 108¼ |
| " 3s, *r.* | 1902-1919 | M. & N. | .. | .. | 101 | 99¾ |
| Pittsburg comp. 5s *r. c.* | 1913 | J. & J. | 117⅛ | 117½ | .. | .. |

## MISCELLANEOUS BONDS—PHILADELPHIA

| | Due. | Interest Payable. | 1901. High. | 1901. Low. | 1902. High. | 1902. Low. |
|---|---|---|---|---|---|---|
| American Cement 1st mort. & col. tr. gr. 5s *r. c.* | 1914 | A. & O. | .. | .. | 87½ | 87½ |
| Asphalt Co. of America col. g. 5s *r.* | 1949 | A. & O. | 94 | 85½ | 37½ | 20 |
| " " " trust receipts | .... | ........ | .. | .. | 36½ | 20 |
| Bergner & Engel 1st 6s *c.* | 1921 | J. & J. | 103 | 101½ | 101 | 101 |
| Bethlehem Steel 6s | 1998 | Aug. Q. | 124¼ | 121 | 126 | 124 |
| Borough of Brooklyn Gas 1st 5s | 1938 | M. & S. | 80 | 75 | .. | .. |
| Consumers Brewing 1st mort. trust ctfs. 6s | .... | ........ | 18¾ | 18¾ | .. | .. |
| Delano Land Co. gen. 5s | 1932 | J. & J. | 106 | 106 | .. | .. |
| Delaware River Ferry 5s *r. c.* & *r.* | 1921 | Q. J. | .. | .. | 105 | 105 |
| Eastern Milling & Export 1st 5s | 1931 | J. & J. | 101½ | 101 | .. | .. |
| Easton Cons. Electric 5s *c.* and *r. c.* | 1949 | M. & N. | 107½ | 101 | 106 | 103 |
| Edison Electric Light 5s trust ctfs. | 1949 | M. & N. | 115¼ | 112½ | 113½ | 111 |
| Equitable Illuminating Gas Light 1st 5s | 1908 | J. & J. | 111 | 107¼ | 110 | 107¼ |
| Girard Fruit Storage 1st 3½s | 1940 | A. & O. | 98 | 98 | .. | .. |
| Harrison Bros. 5s | 1924 | M. & S. | 98 | 97 | 90 | 85 |
| International Navigation Co. 6s | 1906 | M. & N. | 107¾ | 107¾ | .. | .. |
| Lehigh Valley Coal 1st 5s *r. c.* | 1933 | J. & J. | 110⅝ | 105½ | 112½ | 108 |
| " " 1st 5s *r. c.* | 1933 | J. & J. | 105 | 104 | 110 | 109 |
| land Steel Co. 1st mort. 5s *r.* | 1922 | F. & A. | 106 | 100 | 106½ | 105 |

| | Due. | Interest Payable. | 1901. High. | 1901. Low. | 1902. High. | 1902. Low. |
|---|---|---|---|---|---|---|
| National Asphalt gold trust 5s | 1951 | J. & J. | 48½ | 10¼ | 15 | 5 |
| " " 5s, trust receipts | .... | ........ | .. | .. | 15 | 5 |
| Newark Consol. Gas con. 5s *r. c.* | 1948 | J. & D. | 107½ | 104 | 109 | 104⅞ |
| Penna. & Maryland Steel, cons. mort., 6s | 1925 | M. & S. | 115½ | 100 | 118 | 114 |
| " " scrip | .... | ........ | 100 | 92½ | .. | .. |
| Pennsylvania Company 4½s *c* | 1921 | J. & J. | 115 | 109¾ | 113½ | 111⅛ |
| " " g. m. 4½ *r* | 1921 | J. & J. | 113 | 113 | .. | .. |
| " " 3½s trust ctfs., series B | .... | ........ | .. | .. | 97½ | 97½ |
| Pennsylvania Steel 1st 5s *r* | 1917 | M. & N. | 110 | 108 | 107⅛ | 104½ |
| Philadelphia Co. 5s *r. c.* | 1949 | M. & S. | 115½ | 112 | 113½ | 110½ |
| " " 5s *r. c.* | 1951 | M. & N. | .. | .. | 108¾ | 104 |
| Phila. Electric 5s, gold trust ctfs | 1948 | A. & O. | 105 | 99½ | 102½ | 93 |
| Philadelphia Electric 4s, trust ctfs | 1950 | J. & J. | 74⅛ | 63 | 73¾ | 55 |
| Phil., Wilm. & Balt. col. trfs. cts 4s | 1921 | J. & J. | 110¼ | 108¼ | 109⅝ | 106½ |
| Susquehanna Coal 6s *c* | 1911 | J. & J. | 118½ | 118½ | .. | .. |
| United Gas Impt. deb. 6s | 1902 | J. & J. | 104½ | 101 | 101½ | 101½ |
| Welsbach col. trust 5s *r. c.* | 1930 | J. & D. | 80¼ | 64 | 75¾ | 60 |
| " col. trust scrip | ... | ........ | .. | .. | 70 | 55 |

# Pittsburg Stock Exchange

## Quotations for Securities Dealt in on the Stock Exchange, 1901 and 1902

### STOCKS

### *MISCELLANEOUS STOCKS*

| | Par Value. | 1901. High. | 1901. Low. | 1902. High. | 1902. Low. |
|---|---|---|---|---|---|
| Amalgamated Copper | $100 | 88⅛ | 62 | 78⅝ | 55¼ |
| American Can | 100 | 28 | 16½ | 15⅞ | 15 |
| " " pref. | 100 | 67⅝ | 65⅝ | 55½ | 55½ |
| American District Telegraph, pref. | 100 | 67⅝ | 65⅝ | 55½ | 55½ |
| American Linseed | 100 | 9¼ | 9¼ | .. | .. |
| American Locomotive, pref. | 100 | .. | .. | 95 | 94½ |
| American Sheet Steel | 100 | 48½ | 20 | .. | .. |
| " " pref. | 100 | 95½ | 73 | .. | .. |
| American Steel & Wire | 100 | 46 | 46 | .. | .. |
| American Steel Hoop | 100 | 36¼ | 26 | .. | .. |
| " " pref. | 100 | 78 | 76¼ | .. | .. |
| American Sugar Refining | 100 | .. | .. | 132¾ | 129 |
| American Tin Plate | 100 | 62⅞ | 56⅜ | .. | .. |
| American Window Glass | 100 | 65 | 36½ | 64⅞ | 45½ |
| " " pref. | 100 | 97¼ | 84½ | 97 | 87 |
| Beaver Coal | 50 | 10 | 8 | 10 | 8¼ |
| " pref. | 50 | 44 | 35 | 43 | 43 |
| Calumet & Arizona Mining | 10 | 23½ | 23½ | 50½ | 50 |
| Carnegie Company | 1,000 | 1,000 | 1,000 | .. | .. |
| Central District & Printing Telegraph | 100 | 125 | 125 | .. | .. |
| " " " " warrants | .. | .. | .. | 2¼ | 2¼ |
| " " " " rights | .. | .. | .. | 10 | 9 |
| Chartiers Land | 50 | $7 | $7 | .. | .. |
| " " pref. | 50 | $10 | $10 | .. | .. |
| Chartiers Valley Water | 50 | 50 | 35 | 50 | 42½ |
| Colonial Land | 50 | 50 | 50 | 55 | 55 |
| Colorado Fuel & Iron | 100 | .. | .. | 108¼ | 104 |
| Columbian Fireproofing | 50 | 45 | 45 | 45 | 44½ |
| Consolidated Bonanza Gold Mining | .. | .. | .. | $2.65 | $2.00 |
| Consolidated Ice | 50 | 24 | 11½ | 16 | 9¼ |
| " " pref. | 50 | 41 | 35¾ | 39½ | 36 |
| Crucible Steel | 100 | 28⅞ | 19 | 24⅝ | 16 |
| " " pref. | 100 | 88⅝ | 75 | 88¼ | 82½ |
| El Socorro Mining & Milling | .. | .. | .. | 5c | 5c |
| Firth-Sterling Steel | 100 | 100 | 100 | .. | .. |
| Franklin Steel Casting | 100 | .. | .. | 82 | 55 |
| Guffy, J. M., Oil | 100 | .. | .. | 79 | 79 |
| Hidalgo Mining | 10 | 10 | 9 | 6 | 6 |
| Keystone Sign & Decorating | 50 | .. | .. | 56 | 56 |
| Lustre Mining | 10 | 10 | 7 | 15 | 10¼ |
| Macbeth-Evans Glass | 50 | 41 | 40 | .. | .. |
| Mansfield Coal & Coke | 50 | 153 | 153 | .. | .. |
| Marsden | 100 | 7⅝ | 3⅛ | 5¾ | 3 |
| Monongahela River Con. Coal & Coke | 50 | 15½ | 10½ | 14½ | 9½ |
| " " " " pref. | 50 | 49 | 42¾ | 45 | 39 |
| Monongahela Water | 25 | 42⅝ | 40 | 42 | 38 |
| " " warrants | .. | .. | .. | 43 | 35 |
| Moss Distilling | 50 | .. | .. | 34 | 34 |
| National Fireproofing | 50 | 49 | 23⅞ | 43 | 23⅛ |
| " " pref. | 50 | 55 | 41½ | 49¾ | 35½ |
| " " receipts | .. | 38 | 22½ | 42 | 22½ |
| " " rights | .. | 8 | 6 | .. | .. |
| " " warrants | .. | .. | .. | 6 | 1½ |
| National Glass | 50 | 27¼ | 15½ | 17¾ | 15¼ |
| National Lead | 100 | .. | .. | 92½ | 92½ |
| National Steel | 100 | 42 | 41 | 42 | 41 |

| | Par Value. | 1901. High. | 1901. Low. | 1902. High. | 1902. Low. |
|---|---|---|---|---|---|
| National Supply | $100 | 122½ | 122½ | .. | .. |
| North Side Bridge | 50 | .. | .. | 16½ | 15 |
| Penn-American Plate Glass | 100 | 145 | 110 | .. | .. |
| Philadelphia Company | 50 | 54⅛ | 40½ | 50⅛ | 43¼ |
| " " pref. | 50 | 50 | 45 | 50 | 44 |
| " " com. scrip | .. | .. | .. | 50 | 45 |
| " " pref. scrip | .. | .. | .. | 48 | 43 |
| Pittsburg & Allegheny Bridge | 50 | 49 | 49 | .. | .. |
| Pittsburg Brewing | 50 | 28⅝ | 23½ | 33⅞ | 24 |
| " " pref. | 50 | 47 | 43 | 48⅝ | 44 |
| Pittsburg Coal | 100 | 35⅛ | 24¾ | 32¼ | 24 |
| " " pref. | 100 | 99¾ | 86 | 92⅞ | 86½ |
| " " com. scrip | .. | .. | .. | 30 | 20 |
| Pittsburg Dry Goods | 100 | 107½ | 107½ | 115 | 115 |
| Pittsburg Plate Glass | 100 | 183 | 149 | 155½ | 126 |
| " " pref. | 100 | 300 | 300 | .. | .. |
| " " rights | .. | 15 | 10½ | 12 | 12 |
| " " warrants | .. | 50 | 42 | 52 | 43 |
| Pittsburg Reduction | 100 | .. | .. | 280 | 280 |
| Pittsburg Stove & Range | 50 | 5¼ | 2 | 4 | 3 |
| " " " pref. | 50 | 35 | 16 | 22 | 18 |
| Pressed Steel Car | 100 | 50 | 31 | 62 | 38 |
| " " pref. | 100 | 88 | 73 | 95½ | 82¼ |
| Railway Steel Spring, pref. | 100 | .. | .. | 87½ | 84 |
| Sheraden Land & Improvement | 25 | $10 | $10 | .. | .. |
| Standard Chain | 100 | 12½ | 10 | 12½ | 9 |
| " " pref. | 100 | .. | .. | 41 | 38 |
| Standard Plate Glass | 100 | 145 | 130 | 135 | 135 |
| Standard Underground Cable | 100 | 225 | 205 | 240 | 210 |
| " " " rights | .. | .. | .. | 120 | 115 |
| " " " warrants | .. | .. | .. | 43 | 33 |
| Suspension Bridge (Sixth street) | 25 | 60 | 60 | 60 | 57 |
| Tennessee Coal & Iron | 100 | .. | .. | 74 | 74 |
| Trade Dollar Cons. Mining | 5 | $3.01¾ | $2.50 | $2.10 | $1.90 |
| Union Storage | 50 | 40 | 31¾ | .. | .. |
| Union Switch & Signal | 50 | 78 | 46¾ | 99 | 74½ |
| " " " pref. | 50 | 91¾ | 75 | 110 | 91 |
| United States Cast Iron Pipe & Foundry | 100 | .. | .. | 56 | 43¼ |
| United States Glass | 100 | 40 | 31¾ | 37½ | 33 |
| " " " pref. | 100 | 141 | 130 | 145 | 138 |
| United States Leather | 100 | .. | .. | 14¾ | 13⅝ |
| United States Steel Corporation | 100 | 54½ | 30 | 47 | 30 |
| " " " " pref. | 100 | 101 | 86¼ | 97½ | 79 |
| Westinghouse Air Brake | 50 | 192 | 166⅛ | 195 | 167 |
| Westinghouse Electric & Manufac., 1st pref. | 50 | 90 | 66 | 118 | 88 |
| " " " 2d pref. | 50 | 90 | 54 | 116½ | 88 |
| " " " receipts | .. | 39 | 30 | . | .. |
| " " " sub. rights | .. | $2.50 | $1.25 | .. | .. |
| Westinghouse Machine | 50 | 75 | 66 | .. | .. |
| Wolfe, J. N., Soap | 50 | 14¾ | 14¾ | 10c | 10c |

## RAILROAD STOCKS—PITTSBURG

| | Par Value. | 1901. High. | 1901. Low. | 1902. High. | 1902. Low. |
|---|---|---|---|---|---|
| Allegheny Valley, pref. | $100 | 28½ | 20½ | 34¼ | 26 |
| " " scrip | .. | 25c | 25c | 34c | 26c |
| Erie & Pittsburg | 50 | .. | .. | 78 | 78 |
| Lehigh Valley | 50 | .. | .. | 34 | 34 |
| Missouri, Kansas & Texas, pref. | 100 | .. | .. | 55⅛ | 55½ |
| Pennsylvania | 50 | 76 | 72 | 83¾ | 74¼ |
| " receipts | .. | 25 | 25 | .. | .. |
| " warrants | 50 | 15½ | 12 | ⅝ | 5-6 |
| Pittsburg & Lake Erie | 50 | 300 | 250 | 250 | 240 |
| Pittsburg, Bessemer & Lake Erie | 50 | 37 | 28 | 36⅝ | 34 |
| " " " pref. | 50 | 75 | 60 | 74½ | 73 |

| | Par Value | 1901. High. | 1901. Low. | 1902. High. | 1902. Low. |
|---|---|---|---|---|---|
| Pittsburg, Bessemer & Lake Erie, rights | .. | $6 | $6 | .. | .. |
| Pittsburg, McKeesport & Youghiogeny | $50 | 73 | 71 | 75 | 74. |
| Pittsburg, Virginia & Charleston | 50 | .. | .. | 115 | 115 |
| Pittsburg, Youngstown & Ashtabula | 50 | 62 | 58 | 75 | 75 |
| Southern | 100 | .. | .. | 39¾ | 38¾ |
| Southern Pacific | 100 | .. | .. | 79¼ | 67⅞ |
| Union Pacific | 100 | .. | .. | 105¾ | 105¾ |
| Wabash, pref | 100 | .. | .. | 47⅝ | 43⅞ |

## STREET RAILWAY STOCKS—PITTSBURG

| | Par Value. | 1901. High. | 1901. Low. | 1902. High. | 1902. Low. |
|---|---|---|---|---|---|
| Allegheny Traction | $50 | 48 | 48 | 51 | 48 |
| Chartiers Ry | 50 | 94⅞ | 92 | 150 | 150 |
| Citizens' Traction | 50 | 73½ | 70 | 71½ | 69 |
| Consolidated Traction | 50 | 29 | 20 | 24 | 23½ |
| " " pref | 50 | 67 | 60 | 65½ | 63 |
| " " receipts | .. | 23⅝ | 23 | 23½ | 23¼ |
| " " " pref | .. | 65¼ | 63¼ | 65¼ | 64 |
| Federal Street & Pleasant Valley | 25 | 27½ | 26½ | 27½ | 26 |
| Pittsburg & Birmingham Traction | 50 | 48½ | 42 | 50 | 45 |
| Pittsburg, Neville Island & Coraopolis Traction | 50 | 42 | 42 | .. | .. |
| United Traction | 50 | 15 | 13½ | .. | .. |
| " " pref | 50 | 53 | 49¾ | 52 | 50 |

## GAS STOOKS—PITTSBURG

| | Par Value. | 1901. High. | 1901. Low. | 1902. High | 1902. Low. |
|---|---|---|---|---|---|
| Consolidated Gas, pref | $50 | 51½ | 45 | 46 | 44 |
| Fayette County Gas | 100 | 80 | 80 | 81 | 80 |
| Fort Pitt Gas | 50 | 57 | 42 | 70 | 54¾ |
| Manufacturers' Light & Heat | 50 | 75 | 65 | 92¼ | 54½ |
| Natural Gas of West Virginia | 100 | 100½ | 97½ | 120 | 110 |
| Ohio Valley Gas | 25 | 40 | 40 | .. | .. |
| People's Natural | 50 | 65 | 65 | .. | .. |
| People's Nat. G. & P. | 25 | 26 | 21 | 26⅛ | 25 |
| South Side | 25 | .. | .. | 5 | 5 |
| Tri-State Gas | 100 | 135 | 130 | .. | .. |
| Wheeling Natural Gas | 25 | 65 | 65 | .. | .. |

## BONDS—PITTSBURG

| | | Due. | Interest Payable. | 1901. High. | 1901. Low. | 1902. High. | 1902. Low. |
|---|---|---|---|---|---|---|---|
| Allegheny City Sewer | 4s | 1923 | J. & J. | .. | .. | 107 | 107 |
| Allegheny County Comp. | 5s | 1913 | J. & J. | 101 | 101 | .. | .. |
| " " Light | 6s | 1911 | F. & A. | .. | .. | 113 | 112 |
| Allegheny Va., ex. 1st m. con. | 7s | 1910 | A. & O. | 125½ | 124 | .. | .. |
| " gen. m. g. | 4s | 1942 | M. & S. | 110 | 110 | .. | .. |
| American Clay Mfg. Co. | 6s | 1920 | S. & M. | 102 | 102 | .. | .. |
| " " " | 5s | 1921 | F. & A. | 95 | 95 | .. | .. |
| Beaver Coal Co. gold | 5s | 1910 | Q. Jan. | 103 | 101½ | 104 | 103 |
| Birmingham, K. & A. Traction. | 6s | 1931 | M. & S. | 118¼ | 112 | 119⅞ | 116 |
| Birmingham Water Works | 5s | 1939 | F. & A. | 100 | 97½ | .. | .. |
| Bloomfield Street | 5s | 1922 | F. & A. | 113¼ | 113¼ | .. | .. |
| Brownsville Avenue Traction | 5s | 1926 | F. & A. | .. | .. | 113 | 113 |
| Carnegie Co. Series B | 5s | 2000 | M. & S. | 110 | 110 | .. | .. |
| " " " C | 5s | 2000 | M. & N. | 113¼ | 106¼ | 113¾ | 113¾ |
| " " " D | 5s | 2000 | J. & D. | 115 | 103 | .. | .. |
| Central Traction | 5s | 1929 | J. & J. | 115 | 115 | .. | .. |
| Chattanooga (Tenn.), Water | 6s | 1908 | J. & J. | 100 | 100 | .. | .. |
| Citizens' Traction | 5s | 1927 | A. & O. | 118¼ | 118¼ | 118¼ | 118 |
| City of Pittsburg | 4s | 1913 | M. & N. | 107¼ | 107¼ | . | .. |
| " " comp. | 5s | 1913 | J. & J. | 117 | 117 | .. | .. |

| | | Due. | Interest. Payable. | 1901. High | 1901. Low | 1902. High. | 1902. Low. |
|---|---|---|---|---|---|---|---|
| City of Pittsburg, imp. | 4s | 1915 | J. & D. | .. | .. | 109 | 109 |
| Conn. Suburban St. Ry. | 5s | 1932 | J. & J. | .. | .. | 98 | 97 |
| Consolidated Gas | 5s | 1948 | F. & A. | 114½ | 111½ | 114½ | 110 |
| Duquesne Traction | 5s | 1930 | J. & J. | 118½ | 117 | 115½ | 115 |
| Federal Street & P. Val. | 5s | 1942 | J. & J. | 115¾ | 115¾ | 116½ | 116½ |
| Fort Pitt Traction | 5s | 1935 | J. & D. | 116¾ | 114¼ | .. | .. |
| Fort Pitt Gas | 6s | 1911 | J. & D. | 105 | 105 | .. | .. |
| Frick, H. C., Coke | 5s | 1919 | J. & J. | 106 | 103½ | 106 | 106 |
| Hostetter Coke Co. | 5s | 1937 | F. & A. | .. | .. | 100 | 100 |
| McKeesport & Bellevernon R.R. | 6s | 1918 | J. & J. | 125 | 125 | .. | .. |
| M. E. & S. Traction | 5s | 1923 | M. & N. | .. | .. | 113½ | 112¾ |
| Monongahela Light & Power | 5s | 1949 | J. & D. | 109¾ | 105½ | 111 | 106½ |
| Monon. River Con. Coal & Coke | 6s | 1949 | A. & O. | 120 | 116 | 120 | 111 |
| Monongahela St. Ry. | 5s | 1928 | J. & D. | 115½ | 115½ | 115½ | 115 |
| National Glass | 6s | 1900-09 | M. & N. | 100 | 100 | 100 | 100 |
| New Castle Traction | 5s | 1927 | M. & N. | 109 | 109 | .. | .. |
| North Side Bridge | 6s | 1915 | J. & J. | 102½ | 102½ | 103⅜ | 103⅜ |
| Northwestern Coal Ry. | 5s | 1923 | M. & N. | .. | .. | 100 | 100 |
| Penn Street Ry. | 5s | 1922 | J. & D. | 110⅛ | 110⅛ | 110½ | 110½ |
| Philadelphia Company | 5s | 1949 | M. & S. | 114½ | 111¾ | 112½ | 110⅝ |
| " " | 5s | 1951 | M. & N. | 105 | 105 | 108½ | 105 |
| " " scrip | .. | .... | ........ | .. | .. | 108 | 105 |
| Philadelphia Electric | 4s | 1949 | J. & J. | 64⅜ | 64⅜ | .. | .. |
| Pittsburg A. & M. Traction | 5s | 1930 | A. & O. | 120 | 116½ | 114½ | 114½ |
| Pittsburg & Allegheny Bridge | 5s | 1929 | J. & J. | 107 | 107 | .. | .. |
| Pittsburg & Birmingham Tract. | 5s | 1929 | M. & N. | 116½ | 113½ | 117½ | 115 |
| Pittsburg & Charleroi St. Ry. | 5s | 1932 | M. & N. | .. | .. | 106 | 105½ |
| Pitts. & McKeesport & Y. R. R. 1st | 6s | 1932 | J. & J. | .. | .. | 142½ | 142½ |
| Pitts. & West End Passenger Ry. | 5s | 1922 | J. & J. | .. | .. | 114¼ | 114½ |
| Pittsburg & Western Ry. | 4s | 1917 | J. & J. | 100 | 100 | .. | .. |
| Pitts., Bessemer & Lake Erie deb. | 5s | 1919 | J. & D. | 106 | 100 | 106 | 106 |
| Pittsburg, Bess. & L. Erie con. | 5s | 1947 | J. & J. | 120 | 114 | 121¼ | 118¼ |
| Pittsburg Brewing | 6s | 1949 | J. & J. | 115 | 109¾ | 114 | 110⅝ |
| Pittsburg Junction R. R. T'rmin'l. | 5s | 1907 | A. & O. | 103¼ | 102½ | 103½ | 101¾ |
| " " " 1st mort. | 6s | 1922 | J. & J. | 130 | 125 | .. | .. |
| Pitts., McK'pt & Con'llsville Ry. | 5s | 1931 | J. & J. | 103 | 100 | 101¾ | 97½ |
| Pittsburg, Shenango & L. E. old | 5s | 1940 | A. & O. | 120 | 120 | 121 | 119 |
| Pittsburg Traction | 5s | 1927 | A. & O. | .. | .. | 120 | 120 |
| St. Clair Furnace | 5s | 1910-39 | F. & A. | .. | .. | 102½ | 100 |
| St. Clair Steel 1st mort. | 5s | 1904-24 | J. & J. | .. | .. | 100¾ | 100¾ |
| St. Clair Water | 6s | 1924 | J. & J. | 125 | 125 | 110 | 110 |
| Second Avenue Passenger Ry. | 5s | 1909 | J. & J. | .. | .. | 105 | 105 |
| Second Avenue Traction | 5s | 1933 | J. & J. | 119 | 118¾ | .. | .. |
| " " con. | 5s | 1934 | J. & D. | 120 | 119 | 119¼ | 118¼ |
| Sharon Steel | 5s | 1941 | J. & J. | 100 | 100 | 100 | 100 |
| Southern Traction | 5s | 1950 | A. & O. | 111½ | 106½ | 108¼ | 106 |
| Suburban Water | 6s | 1913 | M. & N. | .. | .. | 102½ | 102½ |
| Troy Hill Passenger Ry. | 5s | 1920 | A. & O. | 117 | 117 | .. | .. |
| Union Switch & Signal | 6s | 1905 | M. & S. | 102 | 102 | .. | .. |
| " " " | 5s | 1904-13 | J. & J. | .. | .. | 101½ | 101½ |
| U. S. Fire-Proofing Corp'n. | 6s | 1922 | M. & S. | .. | .. | 103¼ | 95 |
| United States Government | 3s | 1908 | Q. Feb. | 111 | 109¾ | 109 | 108⅛ |
| " " | 4s | 1907 | Q. Jan. | 113 | 113 | 111 | 111 |
| " " new | 3s | 1908 | Q. Feb. | 111 | 109¾ | .. | .. |
| U. S. Steel Corp'n, Series A. | 5s | 1951 | J. & J. | 114½ | 113¾ | 115½ | 107½ |
| " " " " B. | 5s | 1951 | F. & A. | 114¼ | 112½ | 115¼ | 114½ |
| " " " " C. | 5s | 1951 | M. & S. | .. | .. | 114 | 114 |
| " " " " D. | 5s | 1951 | A. & O. | 112 | 112 | 115¼ | 114½ |
| " " " " E. | 5s | 1951 | M. & N. | .. | .. | 114 | 114 |
| United Traction | 5s | 1997 | J. & J. | 118½ | 112 | 116½ | 115¼ |
| West End Traction | 5s | 1938 | J. & J. | 118½ | 118½ | 117 | 117 |
| Westinghouse Electric deb. | 5s | 1913 | J. & J. | 104¼ | 103 | 104 | 103½ |
| Westinghouse Machine | 6s | 1905-14 | J. & D. | .. | .. | 100 | 100 |
| " " deb. | 5s | 1920 | J. & J. | 98 | 98 | .. | .. |
| West Side Belt R. R. | 5s | 1936 | M. & S. | .. | .. | 100 | 100 |
| Wilkinsburg & E. Pitts. St. Ry. | 5s | 1929 | M. & S. | 114¼ | 112 | 115 | 112½ |

# St. Louis Stock Exchange

## Quotations for Securities Dealt in on the Stock Exchange, 1901 and 1902

### MISCELLANEOUS STOCKS

| | 1901. | | 1902. | |
|---|---|---|---|---|
| | Highest. | Lowest. | Highest. | Lowest. |
| American Central Insurance | 245 | 43½ | 295 | 232 |
| Bell Telephone of Missouri | 241 | 241 | 145 | 145 |
| Central Coal & Coke Co. | .. | .. | 73 | 59 |
| Chicago Railway Equipment | 6¾ | 6¼ | 8.05 | 7.25 |
| Consolidated Coal | 21 | 12 | 22 | 19½ |
| Ely-Walker Dry Goods, pref. | 129 | 129 | .. | .. |
| Hargadine-McKittrick Dry Goods, 1st pref. | .. | .. | 120½ | 120½ |
| Hydraulic Press Brick | 92 | 89½ | 97 | 88 |
| International Auto Air Brake Coupling | 4⅝ | 3¼ | .. | .. |
| Interstate Transit | .. | .. | 106 | 105 |
| Kennard Carpet | 105 | 103 | .. | .. |
| " " pref. | 110 | 107 | .. | .. |
| Laclede Gas Light | 96 | 73¼ | 91 | 84 |
| " " pref. | 98 | 98 | 108 | 100 |
| Missouri Edison Electric Light | 21¼ | 17 | 18¾ | 15 |
| " " " " pref. | 60 | 50 | 47½ | 38 |
| St. Louis & Missouri Valley Trans. | 110 | 105 | .. | .. |
| St. Louis Cotton Compress | 25 | 10 | 53½ | 50 |
| St. Louis Exposition | 1.80 | 1.50 | 2.50 | 1.00 |
| St. Louis Transfer | 73 | 73 | .. | .. |
| Schultz Belting | 102 | 98 | .. | .. |
| Simmons Hardware | 170 | 165 | 180 | 160 |
| " " pref. | 143½ | 138 | 164 | 139 |
| " " 2d pref. | 143 | 138 | 161 | 145 |
| Union Dairy | 130 | 130 | .. | .. |
| Westinghouse Automatic A. & S. Coupler | 58 | 39 | 52¼ | 47½ |
| Wiggins Ferry | 240 | 230 | .. | .. |

### MINING STOCKS

| | 1901. | | 1902. | |
|---|---|---|---|---|
| | Highest. | Lowest. | Highest. | Lowest. |
| American Gold Mining | $1.50 | $1.02½ | $1.25 | .70 |
| Catherine Lead | 6.00 | 6.00 | .. | .. |
| Central Lead | 133.00 | 130.00 | .. | .. |
| Columbia Lead | .12½ | .12½ | .. | .. |
| Doe Run Mining | 132.00 | 128.00 | .. | .. |
| Granite Bimetallic | 3.15 | 1.80 | 2.95 | .65 |
| Kansas & Texas Coal | .. | .. | 51.50 | 41.00 |
| Renault Lead | 11.00 | 9.50 | .. | .. |
| St. Joseph Lead | .20½ | .16 | 17.50 | 16.00 |
| Scantic Gold M. & M. | .50 | .35 | 40c | 18c |

### STREET RAILWAY STOCKS—ST. LOUIS

| | 1901. | | 1902. | |
|---|---|---|---|---|
| | Highest. | Lowest. | Highest. | Lowest. |
| East St. Louis & Suburban | .. | .. | 58 | 51½ |
| St. Louis & Suburban | 99 | 84½ | 90 | 79 |
| St. Louis Transit | 36¼ | 18¾ | 34⅛ | 25 |
| " " pref. | 90¼ | 68½ | .. | .. |
| United Railways, pref. | .. | .. | 86¾ | 80 |

# BONDS

## MISCELLANEOUS BONDS—ST. LOUIS

| | Due. | 1901. Highest | 1901. Lowest. | 1902. Highest. | 1902. Lowest. |
|---|---|---|---|---|---|
| Alton Bridge 5s | 1933 | 78 | 78 | 75 | 75 |
| Carleton Building | .... | 103 | 103 | .. | .. |
| Century Building 1st 6s | 1916 | 105¼ | 105 | 106 | 106 |
| Commercial Building 6s | 1907 | 102 | 100 | .. | .. |
| Consolidated Coal 6s | 1911 | 95 | 92¼ | .. | .. |
| East St. Louis | 1908 | 109 | 108 | 106 | 106 |
| Hydraulic Press Brick 5s | 1904 | 102 | 100 | .. | .. |
| Imperial Electric Light, Heat & Power | 1930 | 100 | 98 | .. | .. |
| Kinloch Telephone 6s | 1928 | 105½ | 101½ | 108¾ | 108 |
| Laclede Building 5s | 1919 | 104 | 102 | .. | .. |
| Laclede Gas Light 5s | 1919 | 107 | 107 | 109¼ | 107 |
| Little Rock & Hot Springs 4s | 1929 | .. | .. | 94 | 94 |
| Merchants Building 6s | 1929 | 116 | 115½ | .. | .. |
| Merchants Bridge & Terminal Ry 5s | 1930 | 113 | 112½ | 112½ | 112½ |
| Missouri Edison Electric Light 5s | 1927 | 97 | 93 | 95½ | 85 |
| Missouri Electric Light 6s | 1921 | 119 | 116½ | .. | .. |
| St. Louis Agricultural & Mechanical Association 5s | 1901-6 | 100 | 100 | .. | .. |
| St. Louis Brewing Association 6s | 1914 | 102¼ | 91 | 101½ | 92¾ |
| St. Louis Cotton Comp. 6s | 1910 | 91 | 89½ | .. | .. |
| St. Louis Exposition 6s | 1912 | 98 | 98 | .. | .. |
| St. Louis Merchants Bridge 6s | 1929 | .. | .. | 117 | 115¾ |
| St. Louis, Troy & Eastern | .... | 104½ | 104½ | .. | .. |
| Terminal Association of St. Louis 4½s | 1939 | 114 | 113 | .. | .. |
| " " " 5s | 1944 | 116 | 115 | .. | .. |
| Terminal Hotel & Arcade | 1905 | 104 | 102 | .. | .. |
| Union Dairy | 1901 | 101 | 100 | .. | .. |

## STREET RAILWAY BONDS—ST. LOUIS

| | Due. | 1901. Highest. | 1901. Lowest. | 1902. Highest. | 1902. Lowest. |
|---|---|---|---|---|---|
| Baden & St. Louis 5s | 1913 | 103½ | 102½ | .. | .. |
| Cass Avenue & Fair Grounds 5s | 1912 | 102¾ | 102¾ | .. | .. |
| Citizens 6s | 1907 | 110 | 109 | .. | .. |
| Compton Heights, Union Depot, Merchants Ter. 6s | 1913 | 116¼ | 116¼ | 116½ | 116½ |
| East St. Louis & Suburban 5s | .... | .. | .. | 98 | 96¾ |
| Jefferson Avenue 5s | 1915 | 103 | 102 | .. | .. |
| Lindell 5s | 1911 | 106 | 106 | 107 | 106¼ |
| Missouri 5s | 1916 | 106¼ | 105 | .. | .. |
| St. Louis 5s | 1910 | 102 | 100½ | 101¼ | 101¾ |
| St. Louis & Cable Western 6s | 1914 | .. | .. | 116 | 116 |
| St. Louis & Meramec River 6s | 1916 | 116¼ | 115¼ | 113¾ | 112 |
| St. Louis & Suburban 5s | 1911 | 106 | 105½ | 105¼ | 104¾ |
| " " income 5s | 1911 | 94½ | 94½ | .. | .. |
| Southern 6s | 1904 | 106 | 104 | . | .. |
| " 6s | 1909 | 117 | 115 | .. | .. |
| Taylor Avenue 6s | 1913 | 117 | 117 | 116½ | 116½ |
| Union Depot 6s | 1913 | 121½ | 120 | .. | .. |
| " " 6s | 1918 | .. | .. | 120½ | 120½ |
| United Railway 4s | 1919 | 91¾ | 86¼ | 90 | 84½ |

# Washington Stock Exchange

## Quotations for Securities Dealt in on the Stock Exchange, 1901 and 1902

### INSURANCE STOCKS

| | Par Value. | Dividend Period. | Stock Outstanding. | 1901. High. | 1901. Low. | 1902. High. | 1902. Low. |
|---|---|---|---|---|---|---|---|
| Arlington | $10 | M. & N. | $100,000 | 30 | 28 | 32 | 26½ |
| Colonial | 100 | ........ | 200,000 | 119 | 110 | 105 | 100 |
| Columbia | 5 | M. & N. | 100,000 | 11⅞ | 10 | 11¼ | 10½ |
| Commercial Fire | .. | ........ | ...... | .. | .. | 5¼ | 4½ |
| Corcoran | 50 | J. & J. | 100,000 | 62 | 62 | .. | .. |
| Franklin | 25 | M. & N. | 125,000 | 50 | 50 | 51 | 48 |
| Firemen's | 20 | J. & J. | 200,000 | 30 | 27 | .. | .. |
| German-American | 100 | F. & A. | 100,000 | 225 | 225 | .. | .. |
| Metropolitan | 50 | J. & J. | 100,000 | 81 | 81 | 77 | 77 |
| National Union | 5 | J. & J. | 100,000 | 9½ | 7⅛ | 9 | 7¼ |
| People's | 5 | J. & J. | 100,000 | 6½ | 6 | 7 | 6⅜ |
| Potomac | 25 | J. & J. | 200,000 | 72 | 70 | 65 | 65 |
| Riggs | 5 | J. & J. | 100,000 | 7½ | 7⅛ | 8¼ | 7⅛ |

### TITLE INSURANCE STOCKS

| | Par Value. | Dividend Period. | Stock Outstanding. | 1901. High. | 1901. Low. | 1902. High. | 1902. Low. |
|---|---|---|---|---|---|---|---|
| Columbia Title | $5 | Q., J. | $150,000 | 5 | 4¾ | 5 | 4⅜ |
| Real Estate Title | 100 | J. & J. | 200,000 | 96 | 82 | 97 | 86 |
| Washington Title | 10 | ........ | 100,000 | 3⅝ | 2¼ | 3 | 2½ |

### STREET RAILWAY STOCKS

| | Par Value. | Dividend Period. | Stock Outstanding. | 1901. High. | 1901. Low. | 1902. High. | 1902. Low. |
|---|---|---|---|---|---|---|---|
| Capital Traction | $100 | Q., J. | $12,000,000 | 107½ | 101⅞ | 128 | 106⅞ |
| Washington St. Ry., pref | .. | ...... | ........ | .. | .. | 58 | 36 |

### GAS AND MISCELLANEOUS STOCKS

| | Par Value. | Dividend Period. | Stock Outstanding. | 1901. High. | 1901. Low. | 1902. High. | 1902. Low. |
|---|---|---|---|---|---|---|---|
| American Graphophone | $10 | Q., M. | $1,200,000 | 11¼ | 4 | 6⅛ | 3 |
| " " pref | 10 | Q., F. | 800,000 | 11¾ | 7¼ | 10¼ | 6¾ |
| Chesapeake & Potomac Telephone | 100 | Q., J. | 2,650,000 | 75 | 62¼ | 67 | 40 |
| Dove, J. Maury, & Co | .. | ........ | ........ | .. | .. | 115 | 110 |
| Georgetown Gas | 25 | J. & J. | 150,000 | 75 | 62 | 80 | 73 |
| Greene Copper | . | ........ | 6,000,000 | 33½ | 30 | 33¼ | 19½ |
| Lanston Monotype | 20 | ........ | 3,000,000 | 15⅝ | 9¾ | 17 | 9½ |
| Mergenthaler Linotype | 100 | Q., J. | 10,000,000 | 182¼ | 153½ | 190 | 169⅝ |
| Norfolk & Washington Steamboat. | 100 | J. & J. | 300,000 | 185 | 176 | 225 | 188½ |
| Washington Gas | 20 | Q., F. | 2,600,000 | 66¾ | 56½ | 87 | 67⅛ |
| Washington Market | 50 | J. & J. | 1,000,000 | 15½ | 14 | 17½ | 17½ |

## GOVERNMENT AND DISTRICT BONDS—WASHINGTON

| | Due. | Interest Payable. | 1901. High. | 1901. Low. | 1902. High. | 1902. Low. |
|---|---|---|---|---|---|---|
| United States 2s, registered | 1930 | Q., J. | 106 | 105¾ | 109⅞ | 108¼ |
| " 2s, coupon | 1930 | Q., J. | 107¾ | 107¾ | 109 | 107¼ |
| " 3s, registered | 1908–1918 | Q., F. | 111½ | 107⅛ | 109½ | 105⅞ |
| " 3s, coupon | 1908–1918 | Q., F. | 111¼ | 107¾ | 110 | 105¼ |
| " 4s, registered | 1907 | Q., J. | 114⅛ | 111¾ | 112½ | 107¼ |
| " 4s, coupon | 1907 | Q., J. | 115 | 109¼ | 113 | 108¾ |
| " 4s, registered | 1925 | Q., F. | 138 | 138 | 139½ | 132 |
| " 4s, coupon | 1925 | Q., F. | 138¼ | 138¼ | 139¼ | 136½ |
| " 5s, coupon | 1904 | Q., F. | 111½ | 111½ | 106½ | 103⅞ |
| District of Columbia "funding" currency 3.65s | 1924 | F. & A. | 126 | 123 | 126 | 124 |

## MISCELLANEOUS BONDS—WASHINGTON

| | Due. | Interest Payable. | Bonds Outstanding. | 1901. High. | 1901. Low. | 1902. High. | 1902. Low. |
|---|---|---|---|---|---|---|---|
| American Graphophone deb. 5s, reg. | .... | M. & N. | $300,000 | 99 | 90 | 93 | 93 |
| American Security & Trust 4s | .... | ........ | 400,000 | 101⅞ | 101¾ | .. | .. |
| Capital Traction 4s | 1903–1920 | A. & O. | 1,080,000 | 109½ | 106½ | 106⅝ | 100 |
| Chesapeake & Potomac Tel. 5s | 1909–1929 | J. & J. | 1,500,000 | 106¾ | 103 | 106½ | 103⅞ |
| Columbia R. R. 2d mort, 5s | 1914 | A. & O. | 400,000 | 110 | 105 | 108 | 105½ |
| " " 6s | 1914 | A. & O. | 500,000 | 122 | 116 | 124 | 120 |
| Masonic Hall Association 5s, coupon | 1908 | F. & A. | 88,000 | 108 | 105¼ | 107½ | 104 |
| Metropolitan R. R. 5s | 1925 | F. & A. | 1,850,000 | 119 | 116 | 122 | 118¾ |
| " " 6s | 1906–1907 | ........ | ........ | .. | .. | 108½ | 105¼ |
| " " Cert. of Indeb., A. | 1906 | A. & O. | 250,000 | 110 | 104 | 117 | 104⅛ |
| " " " " B. | 1907 | J. & D. | 250,000 | 107⅝ | 105 | 117 | 104⅜ |
| U. S. Elec. L. Certs. of Indebt. 6s. | 1907 | A. & O. | 350,000 | 106¾ | 102 | .. | .. |
| " " Debentures Imp. 6s | 1907 | M. & N. | 300,000 | 107 | 102½ | 108 | 104 |
| Washington Gas, Series A, 6s | 1902–1927 | J. & J. | 300,000 | 115 | 113½ | 117 | 104½ |
| " " " B, 6s | 1901–1929 | J. & J. | 300,000 | 117 | 113½ | 117 | 104⅜ |
| Washington Market 1st 6s* | 1892–1911 | Q., J. | 119,000 | 110⅛ | 108 | .. | .. |
| Washington Trac. & Elec. coll. 4½s. | 1949 | J. & D. | 13,000,000 | 109½ | 106½ | .. | .. |
| " " " 4s | .... | ........ | .... ... | .. | .. | 86 | 79¾ |

* $7,000 retired annually.

# Toronto Stock Exchange

## Quotations for Securities Dealt in on the Stock Exchange, 1901 and 1902

### *MISCELLANEOUS STOCKS AND BONDS*

| | 1901. | | 1902. | |
|---|---|---|---|---|
| | High. | Low. | High. | Low. |
| Bell Telephone of Canada | 175 | 166 | 170 | 162 |
| British America | 114 | 100 | 102½ | 96½ |
| Canada Cycle & Motor, pref. | 81½ | 15 | .. | .. |
| British Columbia Packers Association, A, pref. | .. | .. | 102½ | 98½ |
| " " " " B, pref. | .. | .. | 102 | 95 |
| Canada Life Ins. | 500 | 151 | 171 | 158 |
| Canada North-West Land | 30 | 16 | 150 | 30 |
| " " " pref. | 70½ | 47 | 100 | 69 |
| Canadian General Electric | 235½ | 187 | 227½ | 193 |
| " " " pref. | 110 | 106 | 111 | 106 |
| Canadian Pacific Railway | 116⅝ | 87 | 145¼ | 109½ |
| Carter-Crume, pref. | 107⅝ | 104 | 107¼ | 100 |
| Commercial Cable | 188½ | 165 | 180½ | 148½ |
| " " coupon bonds | 102⅛ | 100¼ | 98½ | 98 |
| " " reg. bonds | 102¾ | 100 | 99 | 95 |
| Confederation Life Ins. | 283 | 272 | 285 | 285 |
| Consumers Gas | 220 | 210 | 216 | 210 |
| Dominion Coal | 51 | 38 | 146 | 53¾ |
| Dominion Iron & Steel | 39 | 23 | 79¼ | 25 |
| " " " pref. | 90½ | 74 | 103¼ | 81 |
| " " " 5 per cent. bonds | .. | .. | 94¼ | 81 |
| Dominion Telegraph | 128 | 121 | 125 | 118 |
| Dunlop Tire | 108⅜ | 100 | 107 | 102 |
| Halifax Electric Tramway | 104½ | 95 | .. | .. |
| Imperial Life Association | 145 | 141 | 147 | 143 |
| London Electric Light | 112¼ | 104 | 108 | 99 |
| London Street Railway | 170 | 170 | 160 | 155 |
| Luxfer Prism, pref. | .. | .. | 65 | 65 |
| Montreal Gas | 247½ | 217½ | .. | .. |
| Montreal Street Railway | .. | .. | 278 | 278 |
| National Trust of Ontario | 135½ | 120 | 142 | 133 |
| Niagara Navigation | .. | .. | 160 | 120 |
| Northern Navigation | 109 | 105 | 173 | 105¾ |
| Ontario & Qu'Appelle Land | 70 | 59⅞ | 90 | 70 |
| Richelieu & Ontario Navigation | 124 | 107¼ | 116 | 90¼ |
| Rogers, W. A., pref. | .. | .. | 106½ | 102 |
| St. Lawrence & Chicago Navigation | .. | .. | 185 | 125 |
| Sao Paulo Tramway, Light & Power | .. | .. | 109 | 50 |
| Toledo Railway & Light | .. | .. | 41⅞ | 34⅝ |
| Toronto Electric Light | 145½ | 132 | 163¼ | 140 |
| Toronto General Trusts | 167 | 150 | 170 | 161 |
| " " " part paid | 156½ | 147 | .. | .. |
| Toronto Railway | 118 | 106¼ | 124½ | 110 |
| Twin City Rapid Transit | 110 | 66 | 128⅜ | 107⅝ |
| Western Assurance, part paid | 123 | 100 | .. | .. |
| " " fully paid | 116 | 100 | 103 | 92¾ |
| Winnipeg Street Railway | .. | .. | 140 | 125½ |

### *MINING STOCKS—TORONTO*

| | 1901. | | 1902. | |
|---|---|---|---|---|
| | High. | Low. | High. | Low. |
| Canadian Salt | .. | .. | 130 | 110 |
| Cariboo Consolidated Mining & Milling | 42¾ | 14 | 33 | 18 |
| Consolidated Lake Superior | .. | .. | 34 | 7 |

| | 1901. | | 1902. | |
|---|---|---|---|---|
| | High. | Low. | High. | Low. |
| Crow's Nest Pass Coal | 331 | 224 | 520 | 312 |
| Golden Star Mining & Express | 8½ | 1⅝ | .. | .. |
| North Star Mining | 89½ | 24½ | 25 | 19½ |
| Nova Scotia Steel & Coal 6 per cent. bonds | .. | .. | 112 | 103 |
| " " " " pref | .. | .. | 140 | 127 |
| " " " " com | .. | .. | 118⅛ | 44 |
| Payne Mining | 61½ | 9 | 33 | 15 |
| Republic Consolidated Gold Mining | 61⅞ | 2½ | 11 | 3½ |
| Virtue Consolidated Mines | 33 | 10 | 21 | 10½ |
| War Eagle Mining | 103½ | 10½ | 28 | 10 |

## *LOAN AND SAVINGS SECURITIES—TORONTO*

| | 1901. | | 1902. | |
|---|---|---|---|---|
| | High. | Low. | High. | Low. |
| British Canadian Loan & Investment | 85 | 50 | 75 | 60 |
| Canada Landed & National Investment | 103 | 76 | 108⅝ | 97 |
| Canada Permanent Loan & Savings | 126 | 106 | 125 | 119 |
| Canadian Savings & Loan | 113 | 113 | 116 | 116 |
| Central Canada Loan & Savings | 135½ | 135½ | 135 | 135 |
| Dominion Savings & Investment | 72 | 70 | 71 | 70 |
| Hamilton Provident & Loan | 120 | 111 | 121 | 117 |
| Huron & Erie Loan & Savings | 186 | 178 | 185½ | 181 |
| Imperial Loan & Investment | 76 | 61 | 80 | 70 |
| " " " 30 per cent | 37½ | 37½ | .. | .. |
| Landed Banking & Loan | 115 | 113½ | 121 | 121 |
| London & Canadian Loan & Agency | 90½ | 61 | 100 | 80 |
| London Loan | 110 | 110 | 115¾ | 115¾ |
| Manitoba & North-West Loan | 60 | 40 | 75 | 60 |
| Ontario Loan & Debenture | 122 | 121 | 123 | 121 |
| People's Loan & Debenture | 35¼ | 26 | 37 | 31½ |
| Real Estate | 75 | 70 | 80 | 65 |
| Toronto Mortgage | 95 | 76 | 94½ | 90 |
| " " partly paid | .. | .. | 72 | 60 |

# Montreal Stock Exchange

## Quotations for Securities Dealt in on the Stock Exchange, 1901 and 1902

## STOCKS

### *RAILROAD STOCKS*

| | 1901. | | 1902. | |
|---|---|---|---|---|
| | High. | Low. | High. | Low. |
| Canadian Pacific | 117¼ | 87½ | 145¼ | 110 |
| " " new stock | .. | .. | 143 | 119 |
| Duluth, South Shore & Atlantic | 12 | 5¾ | 23¾ | 10 |
| " " pref | 22 | 15 | 35½ | 22 |

### *STREET RAILWAY STOCKS*

| | 1901. | | 1902. | |
|---|---|---|---|---|
| | High. | Low. | High. | Low. |
| Detroit United Railways | 77⅝ | 75 | 97 | 77 |
| Halifax Street | 105 | 86 | 115 | 100 |
| Hamilton Electric | 53 | 50 | .. | .. |
| " " pref | 91 | 87½ | 88¼ | 85 |
| Montreal Street | 306½ | 261¼ | 288 | 260 |
| " " new | 304 | 259 | .. | .. |
| St. John Street | 117½ | 113 | 120 | 113 |
| Toledo Street | .. | .. | 43¼ | 29 |
| Toronto Street | 118¼ | 106 | 124 | 110½ |
| Twin City Rapid Transit | 110 | 65¼ | 129 | 107½ |
| " " " pref | 142 | 142 | 157¼ | 157¼ |
| " " " new | .. | .. | 124 | 116 |
| West India | .. | .. | 69 | 50 |
| Winnipeg Street | 117½ | 105 | 140⅛ | 118 |

### *MISCELLANEOUS STOCKS*

| | 1901. | | 1902. | |
|---|---|---|---|---|
| | High. | Low. | High. | Low. |
| Bell Telephone | 175½ | 165¼ | 176 | 160 |
| British Columbia Packers Association, A | .. | .. | 103 | 98 |
| " " " " B | .. | .. | 102¼ | 100¼ |
| Canadian Colored Cotton | 79 | 55 | 64 | 50 |
| Canadian Rubber | .. | .. | 80 | 80 |
| Commercial Cable | 189¼ | 163½ | 180½ | 145 |
| Consolidated Lake Superior | .. | .. | 29½ | 9¾ |
| Diamond Glass | 120 | 120 | 140 | 140 |
| Dominion Coal | 51½ | 33¼ | 148 | 54 |
| " " pref | 121 | 108½ | 118 | 112 |
| Dominion Cotton Mills | 93 | 45 | 64 | 45 |
| Dominion Iron & Steel | 39 | 20 | 79⅜ | 25 |
| " " " pref | 95 | 71 | 104 | 80¼ |
| Intercolonial Coal | 55 | 50 | 80 | 50 |
| " " pref | 54 | 54 | 90 | 75 |
| Lake of the Woods Milling | .. | .. | 175 | 165 |
| Laurentide Pulp | 125 | 95 | 100 | 97 |
| Loan & Mortgage | 136½ | 135 | 138 | 137 |
| Merchants' Manufacturing | 139 | 89 | 86 | 70 |
| Montmorency Cotton | .. | .. | 80 | 80 |

| | 1901. | | 1902. | |
|---|---|---|---|---|
| | High. | Low. | High. | Low. |
| **Montreal & London** | 5½ | 3 | .. | .. |
| **Montreal Cotton** | 146 | 110 | 131 | 115 |
| **Montreal Telegraph** | 175 | 166 | 175 | 163¼ |
| National Salt | 47½ | 37 | .. | .. |
| North Star | .90 | .24 | 25 | 16 |
| **North Western Land** | 30 | 30 | 225 | 130 |
| " " " pref. | 70 | 45 | 99 | 75 |
| Nova Scotia Steel | .. | .. | 110 | 65 |
| " " " pref | . | .. | 138 | 118 |
| " " " new | .. | .. | 114 | 100 |
| Ogilvie Milling, pref | .. | .. | 130½ | 105 |
| Payne Mining | .60 | .14 | 32 | 10 |
| Republic Cons. Gold Mining | .60 | .7 | .12½ | .7 |
| Richelieu & Ontario Navigation | 125 | 105½ | 117 | 89 |
| " " " new | .. | .. | 112½ | 109 |
| Virtue Mining | .32 | .8 | .30 | .8½ |
| War Eagle Mining | 1.05 | .14 | .28 | .10 |
| Windsor Hotel | 85 | 80 | 80 | 72 |

## GAS AND ELECTRIC STOCKS—MONTREAL

| | 1901. | | 1902. | |
|---|---|---|---|---|
| | High. | Low. | High. | Low. |
| Canadian General Electric | 227¼ | 225 | 220¾ | 220¾ |
| Halifax Heat & Light | 3 | 3 | .. | .. |
| Montreal Gas | 250 | 215 | .. | .. |
| Montreal, Light, Heat & Power | 103 | 90 | 105⅛ | 83 |
| Royal Electric | 249 | 207 | .. | .. |

## MISCELLANEOUS BONDS—MONTREAL

| | 1901. | | 1902. | |
|---|---|---|---|---|
| | High. | Low. | High. | Low. |
| Bell Telephone 5s | 112½ | 110 | .. | .. |
| Canadian Colored Cotton 6s | 100 | 98 | 102½ | 99 |
| Canadian Pacific Land 5s | 110½ | 109¼ | 110 | 109½ |
| City of Montreal 4s | 105 | 102½ | .. | .. |
| " " 7s | 190 | 185 | .. | .. |
| Commercial Cable c 4s | 103¼ | 99 | 99½ | 98 |
| " " registered 4s | .. | .. | 100 | 95 |
| Corporation 4s | .. | .. | 103 | 103 |
| Dominion Coal 6s | 111 | 110 | 111 | 110 |
| Dominion Iron & Steel 5s | 89 | 76½ | 94¾ | 81 |
| Halifax Heat & Light 5s | 42 | 15 | 25 | 25 |
| Halifax Street Railway 5s | 104 | 103 | 108 | 102½ |
| Harbour 4s | 102½ | 102½ | .. | .. |
| Intercolonial Coal 5s | .. | .. | 94 | 94 |
| Laurentide Pulp 5s | 105 | 100 | 108 | 103 |
| Montmorency Cotton 5s | 105 | 105 | 100⅛ | 100 |
| Montreal Street Railway 4½s | .. | .. | 107¾ | 104 |
| Nova Scotia Steel 6s | .. | .. | 112 | 108½ |
| Ogilvie Milling 6s | .. | .. | 119 | 109 |
| St. Johns Street Railway 5s | | .. | 112½ | 112½ |
| Winnipeg Street Railway 5s | 109¼ | 108 | .. | .. |

# Mining

## Quotations for Mining Stocks in the Leading Markets. Productions of Precious Metals and of Coal and Iron

### *MINING STOCKS—NEW YORK*

The following gives the highest and lowest quotations of all mining stocks dealt in at the New York Consolidated Stock & Petroleum Exchange in 1901 and 1902, with location of mines, par values and amount of capital stock. G—Gold. S—Silver. C—Copper. L—Lead. I—Iron. Q—Quicksilver.

| Name. | Character. | Location. | Par Value. | Capital. | 1901. High. | 1901. Low. | 1902. High. | 1902. Low |
|---|---|---|---|---|---|---|---|---|
| Acacia | (G.) | Colorado. | $1 | $1,500,000 | .. | .. | .11 | .05 |
| Adams | (S. & L.) | " | 10 | 1,500,000 | .25 | .10 | .45 | .28 |
| Alamo | (G.) | " | 1 | 1,500,000 | .17 | .12 | .15 | .03 |
| Alice | (G.) | Montana. | 25 | 10,000,000 | .84 | .37 | .56 | .25 |
| Amalgamated | (C.) | " | 100 | 75,000,000 | 130.00 | 60.50 | 79.00 | 53.00 |
| Anaconda | (C.) | " | 25 | 30,000,000 | 54.25 | 28.50 | 36.50 | 20.00 |
| " | (G.) | Colorado. | 5 | 5,000,000 | .46 | .20 | .30 | .14 |
| Argentum-Juniata | (G. S. & L.) | " | 2 | 2,600,000 | .29 | .08 | .15 | .02 |
| Belcher | (S. & G.) | Nevada. | 3 | 312,000 | .. | .. | .14 | .07 |
| Best & Belcher | (G. & S.) | " | 3 | 302,400 | .32 | .13 | 1.05 | .08 |
| Breece | (I. & S.) | Colorado. | 25 | 5,000,000 | 1.88 | 1.20 | .75 | .60 |
| British Columbia | (C.) | Br. Columb. | 5 | 1,000,000 | 22.75 | 14.50 | .. | .. |
| Brunswick Con | (G.) | California. | 1 | 500,000 | .40 | .09 | .30 | .05 |
| Cable con | (G.) | Colorado. | 1 | 1,500,000 | .05 | .04 | .. | .. |
| Catalpa | (S. & L.) | " | 10 | 3,000,000 | .15 | .13 | .14 | .10 |
| Chollar | (G. & S.) | Nevada. | 3 | 336,000 | .12 | .05 | .. | .. |
| Chrysolite | (S. & L.) | Colorado. | 50 | 10,000,000 | .10 | .03 | .10 | .04 |
| Comstock Tunnel | (S. & G.) | Nevada. | 2 | 4,000,000 | .08 | .03 | .07 | .05 |
| " " bonds | (S. & G.) | " | 100 | 1,908,000 | .08 | .04 | .07 | .05 |
| Con. Cal. & Va | (G. & S.) | " | 2½ | 540,000 | 2.80 | 1.30 | 1.80 | .80 |
| Creede & Cripple Creek | (G.) | Colorado. | 1 | 800,000 | .12 | .06 | .09 | .03 |
| Crescent | (L. & S.) | " | 10 | 3,000,000 | .13 | .12 | .14 | .08 |
| Cripple Creek Con | (G.) | " | 1 | 2,000,000 | .13 | .06 | .11 | .06 |
| Crœsus | | " | 1 | ........ | .. | .. | .10 | .10 |
| Crown Point | (G. & S.) | Nevada. | 3 | 300,000 | .17 | .04 | .12 | .03 |
| Daly | (G.) | Utah. | 20 | ........ | 1.50 | 1.30 | 1.60 | 1.50 |
| Deadwood Terra | (G.) | S. Dakota. | 100 | 5,000,000 | .60 | .50 | .75 | .65 |
| Dunkin | (G. & S.) | Colorado. | 1 | 200,000 | .15 | .08 | .14 | .07 |
| Elkton Con | (G.) | " | 1 | 1,250,000 | 1.85 | 1.30 | 1.33 | .27 |
| El Paso | | " | 1 | ........ | .. | .. | .73 | .73 |
| Fanny Rawlings | (G.) | " | 1 | 1,000,000 | .21 | .19 | .. | .. |
| Gold Dollar | (G.) | " | 1 | ........ | .28 | .10 | .09 | .05 |
| Golden Fleece | (G. & S.) | " | 1 | 600,000 | .38 | .20 | .45 | .06 |
| Gould & Curry | (G. & S.) | Nevada. | 3 | 324,000 | .12 | .06 | .. | . |
| Greene Con | (C.) | Mexico. | 10 | 7,200,000 | .. | .. | 31.38 | 24.75 |
| Hale & Norcross | (G. & S.) | Nevada. | 3 | 336,000 | .30 | .14 | .42 | .12 |
| Hart | (G.) | Colorado. | 1 | ........ | .14 | .12 | .05 | .05 |
| Homestake | (G.) | S. Dakota. | 100 | 12,500,000 | 104.00 | 75.00 | 99.00 | 65.00 |
| Horn Silver | (G. S. C. Sp. & L.) | Utah. | 25 | 10,000,000 | 2.25 | 1.10 | 2.00 | 1.30 |
| Iron Silver | (I. & S.) | Colorado. | 20 | 10,000,000 | 1.15 | .60 | .95 | .61 |
| Isabella | (G.) | " | 1 | 2,250,000 | .75 | .30 | .41 | .23 |
| Jack Pot | (G.) | " | 1 | 1,250,000 | .64 | .40 | .35 | .10 |
| Justice | (S.) | Nevada. | 1 | ........ | .12 | .02 | .15 | .07 |
| Kingston & Pembroke | (I.) | Ontario. | 10 | .... .. | .25 | .25 | .16 | .16 |
| La Crosse | (G.) | Colorado. | 10 | 1,000,000 | .10 | .10 | .07 | .05 |
| Leadville Con | (G. & S.) | " | 10 | 4,000,000 | .09 | .06 | .12 | .03 |
| Little Chief | (S. & L.) | " | 1 | 10,000,000 | .17 | .12 | .34 | .10 |
| Mexican | (G. & S.) | Nevada. | 3 | 302,400 | .60 | .10 | .87 | .18 |
| Mine Securities | | ...... | 5 | 2,500,000 | .. | .. | 8.00 | 6.50 |
| Mollie Gibson | (S.) | Colorado. | 5 | 5,000,000 | .46 | .18 | .18 | .06 |
| Moon Anchor | (G.) | " | 5 | ........ | .34 | .32 | .21 | .08 |
| Moulton | (G.) | Montana. | 25 | ........ | .40 | .30 | .30 | .20 |
| Mt. Rosa | (G.) | Colorado. | 1 | 1,000,000 | .35 | .35 | .. | .. |

| Name. | Character. | Location. | Par Value. | Capital. | 1901. High. | 1901. Low. | 1902. High. | 1902. Low. |
|---|---|---|---|---|---|---|---|---|
| Occidental | | Nevada. | $1 | ........ | .. | .. | .15 | .15 |
| Ontario | (S. & L.) | Utah. | 100 | $15,000,000 | 13.00 | 6.25 | 9.50 | 5.50 |
| Ophir | (G. & S.) | Nevada. | 3 | 324,000 | 1.20 | .35 | 1.80 | .80 |
| Pharmacist | (G.) | Colorado. | 1 | 1,200,000 | .13 | .06 | .06 | .04 |
| Phœnix Con | (G.) | Arizona. | 1 | 750,000 | .18 | .07 | .08 | .04 |
| Plymouth Con | (G.) | California. | 10 | 1,000,000 | .10 | .09 | .. | .. |
| Portland | (G.) | Colorado. | 1 | 3,000,000 | 3.20 | 2.30 | 3.85 | 1.25 |
| Potosi | (G. & S.) | Nevada. | 3 | 336,000 | .26 | .02 | .38 | .07 |
| Quicksilver | (Q.) | California. | 100 | 5,700,000 | 5.25 | 1.00 | 4.25 | 2.00 |
| " pref | (Q.) | " | 100 | 4,300,000 | 12.75 | 7.00 | 11.88 | 8.00 |
| Savage | (G. & S.) | Nevada. | 2½ | 280,000 | .30 | .03 | .20 | .09 |
| Sierra Nevada | (G. & S.) | " | 3 | 300,000 | .40 | .07 | .46 | .08 |
| Silver Hill | | " | 1 | ........ | .. | .. | .66 | .66 |
| Small Hopes | (S. & L.) | Colorado. | 20 | 5,000,000 | .80 | .45 | .55 | .30 |
| Standard con | (G. & S.) | California. | 10 | 200,000 | 4.35 | 2.65 | 4.00 | 2.50 |
| Syndicate | (G.) | " | 10 | ........ | .12 | .06 | .07 | .04 |
| Tennessee | (C.) | Tennessee. | 25 | 5,000,000 | 28.38 | 14.00 | 19.38 | 10.00 |
| Union Con | (G. & S.) | Nevada. | 2½ | 250,000 | .12 | .10 | .55 | .21 |
| Union Copper | (C.) | N. Carolina. | 10 | 3,000,000 | 8.25 | 3.50 | 5.63 | 2.25 |
| Virginia Mountain | (G.) | Colorado. | 1 | 1,000,000 | .. | .. | .03½ | .02 |
| White Knob | (G. & S.) | Nevada. | 100 | ........ | .. | .. | 27.25 | 9.50 |
| Work | (G.) | Colorado. | 1 | 1,200,000 | .22 | .08 | .18 | .05 |
| Yellow Jacket | (G. & S.) | Nevada. | 3 | 360,000 | .20 | .08 | .27 | .15 |

## *MINING STOCKS—BOSTON*

The following are the highest and lowest quotations for all mining shares on the Boston Stock Exchange in 1901 and 1902, with character of mines, par value and amount of capital stock. C—Copper. G—Gold. S—Silver. I—Iron. Q—Quicksilver.

| Name. | Par Value. | Capital. | 1901. Highest. | 1901. Lowest. | 1902. Highest. | 1902. Lowest. |
|---|---|---|---|---|---|---|
| Adventure Con (C.) | $25 | $2,500,000 | 33.00 | 9.25 | 24.75 | 12.50 |
| Allouez (C.) | 25 | 2,500,000 | 6.25 | 1.75 | 4.75 | 2.25 |
| Amalgamated Copper (C.) | 100 | 75,000,000 | 128.50 | 60.00 | 79.00 | 52.00 |
| Am. Zinc Lead & Smelt | 25 | 2,500,000 | 16.50 | 8.50 | 16.00 | 7.00 |
| Anaconda (C.) | $25 | $30,000,000 | 53.00 | 29.00 | 35.00 | 21.00 |
| Arcadian (C.) | 25 | 3,750,000 | 24.75 | 3.50 | 13.25 | 3.50 |
| Ætna Con (Q.) | 5 | 500,000 | 1.00 | .50 | .80 | .40 |
| Arnold (C.) | 25 | 1,000,000 | 5.75 | .40 | 1.00 | .50 |
| Ash Bed (C.) | 25 | 1,000,000 | .44 | .25 | .22 | .20 |
| Atlantic (C.) | 25 | 1,000,000 | 43.00 | 24.37 | 36.00 | 6.50 |
| Baltic (C.) | 25 | 2,500,000 | 58.00 | 31.00 | 63.00 | 34.00 |
| Bingham (G. & C.) | 10 | 2,000,000 | 43.75 | 15.50 | 39.75 | 20.50 |
| Bonanza Development | 10 | 3,000,000 | 1.89 | .87½ | 1.05 | .50 |
| Boston | 10 | ........ | .. | .. | 5.00 | 2.00 |
| Boston & Montana (C.) | 25 | 3,750,000 | 498.00 | 308.00 | .. | .. |
| Breece (I.) | 25 | 5,000,000 | .. | .. | .50 | .50 |
| British Columbia (C.) | 5 | 1,000,000 | 23.25 | 9.00 | 10.50 | 5.00 |
| Butte & Boston (C.) | 25 | 5,000,000 | 124.50 | 77.00 | .. | .. |
| Calumet & Hecla (C.) | 25 | 2,500,000 | 860.00 | 535.00 | 650.00 | 420.00 |
| Catalpa (S.) | 10 | 3,000,000 | .22 | .15 | .50 | .50 |
| Centennial (C.) | 25 | 2,500,000 | 34.25 | 10.50 | 28.00 | 11.00 |
| Centennial Eureka (G.) | 25 | 5,000,000 | 34.00 | 23.00 | .. | .. |
| Central Oil | 25 | 2,500,000 | 14.00 | 7.50 | 8.89 | 6.25 |
| Cochiti (G.) | 10 | 1,500,000 | 13.25 | 1.75 | 2.00 | .25 |
| Con. Mercur (G.) | 5 | 5,000,000 | 4.00 | 1.25 | 2.25 | 1.89 |
| Continental Zinc & Lead | 10 | 1,500,000 | 3.00 | 1.50 | 4.00 | 2.00 |
| Copper Range (C.) | 25 | 2,500,000 | 83.00 | 34.00 | 65.25 | 43.50 |
| Crescent (S. & I.) | 10 | 3,000,000 | .18 | .10 | .. | .. |
| Daly-West (G.) | 20 | 3,600,000 | 41.50 | 28.00 | 56.00 | 18.00 |
| Dominion (I. & S.) | 100 | ........ | 39.00 | 20.00 | 79.89 | 25.00 |
| Dominion Coal | 100 | 15,000,000 | 53.25 | 32.00 | 146.50 | 52.50 |
| " " pref | 100 | 3,000,000 | 120.00 | 108.00 | 119.50 | 114.50 |
| Elm River (C.) | 12 | 2,500,000 | 7.00 | 1.75 | 5.50 | 1.50 |

| Name. | Par Value. | Capital. | 1901. Highest. | 1901. Lowest. | 1902. Highest. | 1902. Lowest |
|---|---|---|---|---|---|---|
| Franklin .................. (C.) | $25 | $2,500,000 | 25.00 | 11.50 | 16.00 | 7.50 |
| Guanajuato.................(G.) | 5 | 2,000,000 | .. | .. | 5.75 | 2.25 |
| Humboldt...................(C.) | 25 | 1,000,000 | .63 | .10 | .. | .. |
| Isle Royale................(C.) | 25 | 3,750,000 | 56.50 | 18.00 | 25.00 | 10.00 |
| Massachusetts Con.........(C.) | 25 | 2,500,000 | 37.63 | 11.00 | 21.50 | 12.50 |
| Mayflower............(C. & G.) | 25 | 1,000,000 | 5.63 | 1.50 | 3.63 | 1.50 |
| Marced............ ......(G.) | 15 | 2,250,000 | 6.00 | 3.50 | 3.50 | 2.50 |
| Melones....................(G.) | 10 | 2,000,000 | 2.00 | 1.00 | .. | .. |
| Michigan...................(C.) | 25 | 2,500,000 | 20.38 | 5.50 | 13.25 | 7.00 |
| Mohawk............ .....(C.) | 25 | 2,500,000 | 56.25 | 22.00 | 49.25 | 27.00 |
| Mont. Coal & Coke............ | 25 | 5,000,000 | 7.00 | 4.00 | 6.00 | 2.50 |
| Montreal & Boston.........(C.) | 5 | 3,000,000 | .. | .. | 4.75 | 2.00 |
| National ...................(C.) | 25 | 2,500,000 | 5.25 | .50 | 3.75 | 1.00 |
| N. A. Gold Dredging.. ...(G.) | 5 | 1,000,000 | 5.75 | .50 | 3.89 | 1.50 |
| New England Gas & Coke.... | 100 | ... .... | 15.00 | 4.25 | 7.63 | 2.75 |
| New Idria.................(Q.) | 5 | 500,000 | 10.00 | 6.00 | 9.75 | 7.00 |
| Old Colony.................(C.) | 25 | 2,500,000 | 5.63 | 2.00 | 4.50 | .75 |
| Old Dominion............ (C.) | 25 | 3,750,000 | 38.75 | 20.50 | 25.25 | 14.50 |
| Osceola ...................(C.) | 25 | 2,500,000 | 120.00 | 72.00 | 89.75 | 47.50 |
| Parrot................(S. & C.) | 10 | 2,300,000 | 58.50 | 26.50 | 35.00 | 21.00 |
| Phœnix Con................(C.) | 25 | 2,500,000 | 8.75 | 3.50 | 5.00 | 3.25 |
| Quincy......................(C.) | 25 | 2,500,000 | 187.00 | 125.00 | 147.00 | 100.00 |
| Rhode Island..............(C.) | 25 | 2,500,000 | 10.00 | 2.38 | 3.75 | 1.50 |
| Santa Fe............(C. & G.) | 10 | 2,500,000 | 10.13 | 2.25 | 4.00 | 1.50 |
| Santa Ysabel..............(G.) | 5 | 500,000 | 2.50 | .50 | .50 | .50 |
| Shannon...................(C.) | 10 | 3,000,000 | .. | .. | 16.50 | 8.00 |
| Tamarack ..................(C.) | 25 | 1,500,000 | 363.00 | 230.00 | 281.00 | 140.00 |
| Tecumseh ..................(C.) | 25 | 1,500,000 | 3.00 | .50 | 3.50 | .50 |
| Tennessee..................(C.) | 25 | 5,000,000 | 30.00 | 9.13 | 17.75 | 11.75 |
| Tri-Mountain..............(C.) | 25 | 2,500,000 | 60.00 | 19.50 | 125.00 | 34.00 |
| Trinity .....................(C.) | 25 | 6,000,000 | 41.00 | 10.00 | 18.50 | 8.00 |
| Union............(C. L. & Q.) | 25 | 2,500,000 | 4.00 | 2.00 | .. | .. |
| United ....... ............(C.) | 100 | ........ | .. | .. | 35.38 | 27.00 |
| United States........(C. & G.) | 25 | 6,250,000 | 24.00 | 9.25 | 22.89 | 13.00 |
| United States Coal & Oil...... | 25 | ........ | 17.00 | 10.25 | 18.25 | 11.00 |
| Utah Con...........(C. & G.) | 5 | 1,500,000 | 37.50 | 18.50 | 27.25 | 19.50 |
| Victor .....................(G.) | 5 | 1,000,000 | .80 | .25 | .. | .. |
| Victoria....................(C.) | 25 | 2,500,000 | 12.00 | 3.50 | 7.00 | 4.00 |
| Washington ...............(C.) | 25 | 1,500,000 | .80 | .13 | 1.50 | .25 |
| Winona ....................(C.) | 25 | 2,500,000 | 10.00 | 1.50 | 6.00 | 1.00 |
| Wolverine..................(C.) | 25 | 1,500,000 | 73.00 | 44.00 | 64.00 | 42.00 |
| Wyandotte ................(C.) | 25 | 2,500,000 | 3.00 | 1.00 | 1.75 | .75 |

## *MINING STOCKS—COLORADO SPRINGS*

Quotations for all mining shares dealt in on the Colorado Springs Mining Exchange in 1901 and 1902, with character of mines, location, par values and amount of capital stock. G—Gold. S.—Silver. L—Lead.

| Name. | Location. | Par of Shares. | Capital. | 1901. High. | 1901. Low. | 1902. High. | 1902. Low. |
|---|---|---|---|---|---|---|---|
| Acacia ..................(G.) | Cripple Creek. | $1 | $1,500,000 | .30 | .11 | .14 | .05 |
| Alamo ..................(G.) | " | 1 | 1,000,000 | .16 | .11 | .14 | .02⅞ |
| American Con...........(G.) | " | 1 | 2,000,000 | .07 | .03 | .04½ | .01 |
| Anaconda ..............(G.) | " | 5 | 5,000,000 | .50 | .25 | .. | .. |
| Anchor ..................(G.) | " | 1 | 1,250,000 | .03 | .02 | .35 | .12 |
| Antelope.................(G.) | " | 1 | 1,250,000 | .05 | .02 | .. | .. |
| Aola.......................(G.) | " | 1 | 1,000,000 | .06 | .03 | .. | .. |
| Argentum-Juniata. (S. & L.) | " | 2 | 2,600,000 | .34½ | .05 | .. | .. |
| Banner..................(G.) | " | 1 | 1,500,000 | .04 | .02 | .. | .. |
| Battle Mt. Con..........(G.) | " | 1 | 2,500,000 | .28 | .11 | .. | .. |
| Ben Hur..................(G.) | " | 1 | 900,000 | .. | .. | .06 | .01 |
| Black Belle..............(G.) | " | 1 | 1,250,000 | .14 | .07 | .09½ | .01 |
| Blue Bell.................(G.) | " | 1 | 1,000,000 | .22 | .08 | .12 | .03 |
| Buckhorn ...............(G.) | " | 1 | 1,000,000 | .07 | .03 | .. | .. |

| Name. | Location. | Par of Shares. | Capital. | 1900. High. | 1900. Low. | 1901. High. | 1901. Low. |
|---|---|---|---|---|---|---|---|
| Cadillac Con...........(G.) | Cripple Creek. | $1 | $1,500,000 | .03 | .01 | .. | .. |
| Central Con.............(G.) | " | 1 | 1,000,000 | .11 | .05 | .. | . |
| Champion ..............(G.) | " | 1 | 1,250,000 | .07 | .03 | .. | .. |
| Chicolo..................(G.) | " | 1 | 1,500,000 | .03 | .02 | .. | .. |
| Creede & Cripple Creek(G.) | " | 1 | 800,000 | .15 | .04 | .. | .. |
| Cripple Creek Con......(G.) | " | 1 | 2,000,000 | .13 | .07 | .12 | .05 |
| C. C. & Man............(G.) | " | 1 | 1,800,000 | .11 | .05 | .. | .. |
| C. C. Columbia.........(G.) | " | 1 | 1,000,000 | .26 | .11 | .. | .. |
| C. C. G. exts............(G.) | " | 1 | 1,250,000 | .16 | .05 | .. | .. |
| C. K. & N...............(G.) | " | 1 | 1,250,000 | .06 | .01 | .12 | .02 |
| Dante....................(G.) | " | 1 | 1,000,000 | .17 | .04 | .05⅝ | .01½ |
| Doctor-Jack Pot Con...(G.) | " | 1 | 3,000,000 | .. | .. | .50 | .08 |
| Eclipse .................(G.) | " | 1 | 1,250,000 | .17 | .08 | .. | .. |
| Elkton Con..............(G.) | Colorado. | 1 | 1,250,000 | 1.91 | 1.39 | 1.40½ | .30 |
| El Paso...........(G. & C.) | " | 1 | 650,000 | .80 | .36 | .73 | .43¼ |
| Fanny Rawlings..(G. & S.) | Leadville. | 1 | 1,000,000 | .30 | .10 | .15 | .03 |
| Findley .................(G.) | Cripple Creek. | 1 | 1,250,000 | .14 | .07 | .12 | .01 |
| Gold Dollar.............(G.) | " | 1 | 2,000,000 | .. | .. | .09¾ | .02 |
| Golden Fleece..........(G.) | " | 1 | 600,000 | .41 | .20 | .60 | .05 |
| Gold Sovereign .........(G.) | " | 1 | 2,000,000 | .09 | .03 | .06 | .02 |
| Hayden Gold............(G.) | " | 1 | 5,000,000 | .02 | .01 | .. | .. |
| Ingham con..............(G.) | " | 50c | 1,500,000 | .29 | .12 | .. | .. |
| Ironclad.................(G.) | " | 1 | 1,000,000 | .07 | .02 | .06 | .02 |
| Isabella .................(G.) | " | 1 | 2,500,000 | .77 | .35 | .38 | .15 |
| Jack Pot.................(G.) | " | 1 | 1,250,000 | .73 | .34 | .36 | .08 |
| Josephine ...............(G.) | " | 1 | 1,500,000 | .03 | .01 | .. | .. |
| Key West... .........(G.) | " | 1 | 1,250,000 | .03 | .02 | .. | .. |
| Last Dollar................ | " | 1 | ........ | .. | .. | .80 | .40 |
| Lexington...............(G.) | " | 1 | 1,500,000 | .15 | .03 | .08½ | .04 |
| Little Puck.............(G.) | " | 1 | 2,000,000 | .. | .. | .07 | .03 |
| Magnet Rock............(G.) | " | 1 | 1,250,000 | .04 | .02 | .. | .. |
| Margaret................(G.) | " | 1 | 1,250,000 | .04 | .01 | .. | .. |
| Margery.................(G.) | " | 1 | 1,500,000 | .04 | .02 | .. | .. |
| Midway..................(G.) | " | 1 | 1,250,000 | .08 | .02 | .. | .. |
| M. J. T..................(G.) | " | 1 | 1,250,000 | .05 | .02 | .. | .. |
| Mobile ..................(G.) | " | 1 | 1,250,000 | .04 | .02 | .. | .. |
| Mollie Dwyer...........(G.) | " | 1 | 1,500,000 | .08 | .03 | .. | .. |
| Mollie Gibson Con......(S.) | Colorado. | 5 | 5,000,000 | .50 | .13 | .20 | .04 |
| Monarch ... ..........(G.) | Cripple Creek. | 1 | 1,000,000 | .09 | .03 | .. | .. |
| Montreal ................(G.) | " | 1 | 1,000,000 | .05 | .01 | .. | .. |
| Moon-Anchor............(G.) | Colorado. | 1 | 600,000 | .34 | .20 | .30 | .05 |
| Morning Star............(G.) | Cripple Creek. | 1 | 1,250,000 | .05 | .02 | .07 | .01⅜ |
| National ................(G.) | " | 1 | 1,500,000 | .11 | .02 | .04 | .01 |
| Nellie V..................(G.) | " | 1 | 1,500,000 | .08 | .03 | .04⅜ | .01 |
| New Haven..............(G.) | " | 1 | 1,500,000 | .12 | .02 | .05 | .01¼ |
| Olive Branch............(G.) | " | 1 | 1,250,000 | .05 | .02 | .. | .. |
| Oriole....................(G.) | " | 1 | 1,250,000 | .05 | .02 | .. | .. |
| Orphan ..................(G.) | " | 1 | 1,250,000 | .23 | .10 | .. | . |
| Pappoose.................(G.) | " | 1 | 2,250,000 | .. | .. | .03⅛ | .01 |
| Pelican...................(G.) | " | 1 | 1,250,000 | .03 | .02 | .. | .. |
| Pharmacist..............(G.) | " | 1 | 1,200,000 | .14 | .03 | .07 | .03 |
| Pilgrim Con.............(G.) | " | 1 | 1,250,000 | .14 | .03 | .. | .. |
| Pinnacle...... .........(G.) | " | 1 | 2,000,000 | .22 | .05 | .09 | .04 |
| Portland ................(G.) | " | 1 | 3,000,000 | 3.50 | 2.75 | 2.90 | .01¾ |
| Prince Albert...........(G.) | " | 1 | 3,000,000 | .06 | .03 | 1.92 | .01 |
| Princess .................(G.) | " | 1 | 1,000,000 | .06 | .02 | .. | .. |
| Progress .................(G.) | " | 1 | 1,000,000 | .07 | .03 | .. | .. |
| Republic ................(G.) | " | 1 | 1,250,000 | .09 | .02 | .04⅝ | .01 |
| Robert Burns............(G.) | " | 1 | 1,500,000 | .08 | .02 | .. | .. |
| Rose Maud...............(G.) | " | 1 | 1,250,000 | .09 | .03 | .07 | .01 |
| Sunset Eclipse............. | " | 1 | ........ | .. | .. | .13¾ | .01 |
| Uncle Sam................. | " | 1 | ........ | .05 | .02 | .03 | .01 |
| Vindicator Con.........(G.) | " | 1 | 1,500,000 | 1.40 | 1.00 | 1.26 | .85 |
| Virginia Mt.............(G.) | " | 1 | 1,000,000 | .10 | .03 | .. | .. |
| Work ....................(G.) | " | 1 | 1,250,000 | .23 | .09 | .10 | .04⅝ |

## MINING STOCKS—SALT LAKE CITY, UTAH

Following are the highest and lowest quotations of mining stocks dealt in at the Salt Lake Stock & Mining Exchange in 1901 and 1902, with location of mines, par values and amount of capital stock. G—Gold. S—Silver. C—Copper. L—Lead. I—Iron. Z—Zinc.

| Name. | Character. | Location. | Par Value. | Capital. | 1901. High. | 1901. Low. | 1902. High. | 1902. Low. |
|---|---|---|---|---|---|---|---|---|
| Albion | (G. C. S. L. & Z.) | Cotton Wood. | .10 | $15,000 | .70 | .20 | .75 | .25 |
| Alice | (L.) | Montana. | $25.00 | 10,000,000 | .55 | .30 | .50 | .20 |
| Ajax | (C. & S.) | Tintic. | 10.00 | 3,000,000 | 1.65⅞ | .56 | .64½ | .20 |
| Ben Butler | (C. & S.) | Bingham. | .10 | 50,000 | .19¾ | .01⅝ | .13 | .07¼ |
| Boss Tweed | (S. & C.) | Tintic. | 1.00 | 250,000 | .74½ | .08 | .60½ | .22 |
| Bullion Beck | (C. & S.) | " | 10.00 | 1,000,000 | 4.00 | 2.00 | 3.00 | 1.50 |
| Burton | (G.) | Park Valley. | .10 | 20,000 | .. | .. | .. | .. |
| California | (S. L. C. G. & Z.) | Park City. | 1.00 | 500,000 | .57½ | .45⅛ | .72½ | .13 |
| Carisa | (G. S. & C.) | Tintic. | 1.00 | 500,000. | 1.34¾ | .62¾ | .75 | .16 |
| Century | (G.) | Park Valley. | 1.00 | 150,000 | 3.55 | 1.00 | 1.27 | .10¼ |
| Congor | (G. S. & C.) | Bingham. | 1.00 | 200,000 | .30 | .10 | .40 | .10 |
| Con. Mercur | (G.) | Mercur. | 5.00 | 5,000,000 | 3.40 | 1.53½ | 2.09 | 1.71¾ |
| Creole | (G. S. & L) | Park City. | 1.00 | 150,000 | .90 | .25 | .06½ | .28 |
| Dalton | (G.) | Marysville. | 1.00 | 500,000 | .12 | .01½ | .03¼ | .01 |
| Daly | (S. & L.) | Park City. | 20.00 | 3,000,000 | 3.00 | 1.00 | 2.10 | 1.30 |
| Daly-Judge | (S.L.G.Z.I.& C.) | " | 1.00 | 300,000 | .. | .. | 11.85 | 8.15 |
| Daly-West | (S. L. G. C. & Z.) | " | 20.00 | 3,000,000 | 42.00 | 27.15 | 54.00 | 18.30 |
| Dexter | (G.) | Nevada. | 5.00 | 1,000,000 | 1.29 | .40 | .50 | .20 |
| Eagle & Blue Bell | (C. S. & L.) | Tintic. | 1.00 | 250,000 | 1.25 | .72¾ | 1.17 | .70 |
| Emerald | (S. G. & L.) | Tintic. | 1.00 | 300,000 | .15 | .03 | .09 | .04½ |
| Galena | (G.) | Fish Springs. | 10.00 | 1,000,000 | .40 | .05 | .18½ | .06 |
| Golden Eagle | (S. G. & L.) | Nevada. | 1.00 | 400,000 | .03½ | .01¼ | .00½ | .00¼ |
| Golconda | (G. S. & L.) | Park Valley. | .10 | 30,000 | .05 | .01 | .05 | .01 |
| Grand Central | (C. S. & G.) | Tintic. | 1.00 | 250,000 | 7.49 | 2.00 | 6.15 | 3.00 |
| Homestake | (S. & L.) | " | 1.00 | 400,000 | .. | .. | .. | .. |
| Horn Silver | (S.) | Frisco. | 25.00 | 10,000,000 | 2.05 | 1.07½ | 1.60 | 1.10 |
| Ingot | (G.) | Mercur. | .50 | 250,000 | .05 | .01 | .13½ | .05½ |
| Joe Bowers | (S. & L.) | Tintic. | 1.00 | 700,000 | .07 | .01 | .04½ | .02½ |
| La Reine | (G. L. & S.) | " | 1.00 | 300,000 | .40 | .19 | .22¼ | .04 |
| Little Chief | (S. L. C. & G.) | " | .10 | 40,000 | .26½ | .06¼ | .11 | .02½ |
| Lower Mammoth | (C.S.G.& L.) | " | 1.00 | 150,000 | 4.54 | 1.54 | 1.90 | .66 |
| Mammoth | (C. & G.) | " | 25.00 | 10,000,000 | 2.63 | 1.25 | 1.90 | 1.00 |
| Manhattan | (C.) | " | .10 | 100,000 | .01¼ | .00½ | .01½ | .00½ |
| Martha Washington | S.L. & G.) | " | .50 | 150,000 | .48¾ | .01½ | .15¼ | .01¾ |
| May Day | (S. & L.) | " | .25 | 100,000 | 3.00 | .42 | .69 | .16½ |
| New York | (S. G. C. & L.) | Park City. | 1.00 | 300,000 | .. | .. | .65 | .27¼ |
| Northern Light | (G.) | Mercur. | 5.00 | 2,000,000 | .12 | .02½ | .04½ | .001-16 |
| Ontario | (S. L. & G.) | Park City. | 100.00 | 15,000,000 | 12.00 | 6.60 | 9.00 | 5.75 |
| Petro | (C. S. L. & G.) | Bingham. | 5.00 | 1,000,000 | .20 | .06 | .13 | .09 |
| Richmond-Anaconda | (I.) | Tintic. | 1.00 | 300,000 | .35 | .05 | .10 | .05 |
| Rocco Homestake | (L.) | Nevada. | 1.00 | 300,000 | 1.08 | .50 | .75 | .10 |
| Sacramento | (G.) | Mercur. | 5.00 | 5,000,000 | .46 | .12¼ | .31¼ | .17 |
| Shower Con | (S. L. & C.) | Tintic. | 5.00 | 2,000,000 | .18 | .03 | .07 | .02 |
| Silver King | (S. & L.) | Park City. | 20.00 | 3,000,000 | 87.50 | 72.00 | 81.00 | 78.00 |
| Silver Shield | (C. S. & L.) | Bingham. | .20 | 60,000 | .27 | .01½ | .08 | .04¼ |
| South Swansea | (C. L. & G.) | Tintic. | 1.00 | 300,000 | 1.36 | .26 | .70 | .18 |
| Star Con | (G. & C.) | " | 1.00 | 500,000 | .86 | .26 | .37 | .10 |
| Sunshine | (G.) | Mercur. | 10.00 | 2,500,000 | .30 | .05 | .27¾ | .12 |
| Swansea | (S. & L.) | Tintic. | 5.00 | 500,000 | 4.10 | 1.30 | 1.10 | .74 |
| Tetro | (C. & S.) | " | 1.00 | 300,000 | .37 | .05 | .23¾ | .13¾ |
| Uncle Sam Con | (S. L. & G.) | " | 1.00 | 500,000 | 2.38 | .71 | .77 | .21½ |
| United Sunbeam | (S.L.G. & C.) | " | 1.00 | 150,000 | .. | .. | .40 | .10 |
| Utah | (S. L. & G.) | Fish Springs. | 10.00 | 1,000,000 | .80 | .40 | .58 | .4 7 |
| Valeo | (S. & L.) | Park City. | 1.00 | 200,000 | .40 | .16¼ | .14 | .07 |
| Victor | (G. S. L. & C.) | Tintic. | 1.00 | 500,000 | .58 | .19 | .43 | .10 |
| Wabash | (S. S. L. & C.) | Park City. | 1.00 | 300,000 | .. | .. | 2.34 | .54¼ |
| West Morning Glory | (C. & S.) | Tintic. | .10 | 50,000 | .07 | .04 | .05 | .01 |
| White Rock | (G.) | Nevada. | 2.50 | 500,000 | .30 | .26 | .50 | .35 |
| Yankee Con | (S. L. & C.) | Tintic. | 1.00 | 500,000 | 5.50 | .08¼ | 3.10 | .31 |

# COPPER PRODUCTION AND EXPORTS

## COPPER PRODUCTION OF THE UNITED STATES.

(In tons of 2,240 pounds.)

| | 1898. | 1899. | 1900. | 1901. | 1902. |
|---|---|---|---|---|---|
| January | 17,744 | 18,624 | 21,013 | 22,679 | 18,955 |
| February | 17,322 | 19,899 | 20,897 | 21,100 | 20,331 |
| March | 20,381 | 21,918 | 23,283 | 23,384 | 24,035 |
| April | 22,909 | 19,954 | 24,067 | 21,438 | 24,624 |
| May | 22,741 | 22,082 | 22,682 | 22,392 | 25,763 |
| June | 19,390 | 22,010 | 22,635 | 22,401 | 26,740 |
| July | 16,052 | 21,333 | 23,012 | 21,985 | 26,749 |
| August | 19,508 | 22,686 | 21,067 | 22,667 | 25,296 |
| September | 18,764 | 22,715 | 21,386 | 21,580 | 25,788 |
| October | 21,129 | 23,980 | 23,345 | 24,098 | 26,252 |
| November | 19,850 | 23,217 | 23,276 | 21,728 | 25,297 |
| December | 18,482 | 23,788 | 22,124 | 19,803 | *24,000 |

*Estimated.

## EXPORTS OF COPPER FROM THE UNITED STATES.

| | 1898. | 1899. | 1900. | 1901. | 1902. |
|---|---|---|---|---|---|
| January | 12,026 | 7,480 | 12,441 | 9,845 | 15,474 |
| February | 8,161 | 8,068 | 13,653 | 7,589 | 14,001 |
| March | 13,350 | 12,747 | 18,585 | 6,624 | 20,015 |
| April | 10,005 | 7,760 | 12,475 | 4,929 | 16,400 |
| May | 10,626 | 6,769 | 12,569 | 10,910 | 15,493 |
| June | 11,166 | 8,899 | 15,599 | 9,428 | 13,258 |
| July | 13,201 | 6,962 | 10,861 | 7,563 | 11,370 |
| August | 10,971 | 10,318 | 13,849 | 6,408 | 11,814 |
| September | 8,316 | 7,463 | 10,362 | 6,354 | 12,627 |
| October | 8,830 | 10,746 | 13,196 | 7,571 | 12,234 |
| November | 12,052 | 9,974 | 7,627 | 6,367 | 10,829 |
| December | 12,533 | 15,451 | 10,771 | 8,620 | 10,751 |

## EUROPEAN COPPER STOCKS.

| | 1901. | | | 1902. | | |
|---|---|---|---|---|---|---|
| | Supplies During Month. | Deliveries During Month. | Stock at End of Month. | Supplies During Month. | Deliveries During Month. | Stock at End of Month. |
| January | 17,828 | 17,784 | 28,904 | 20,415 | 19,154 | 23,312 |
| February | 19,907 | 19,816 | 28,995 | 25,762 | 25,501 | 23,573 |
| March | 16,536 | 17,300 | 28,234 | 29,145 | 24,594 | 28,124 |
| April | 16,700 | 17,396 | 27,535 | 28,026 | 29,139 | 27,011 |
| May | 22,609 | 22,913 | 27,231 | 22,968 | 25,715 | 24,264 |
| June | 21,415 | 21,184 | 27,462 | 26,702 | 27,747 | 23,219 |
| July | 21,943 | 22,010 | 27,395 | 28,274 | 30,180 | 21,313 |
| August | 19,296 | 20,870 | 25,821 | 18,203 | 19,241 | 20,275 |
| September | 16,043 | 17,099 | 24,765 | 24,430 | 26,464 | 17,245 |
| October | 17,852 | 21,652 | 20,965 | 20,953 | 21,541 | 16,657 |
| November | 17,623 | 18,018 | 20,570 | 22,957 | 22,547 | 16,707 |
| December | 20,200 | 18,700 | 22,051 | 22,100 | 22,200 | 16,570 |
| Total | 227,952 | 234,742 | | 288,939 | 264,623 | |

# COPPER PRODUCTION AND PRICES

## PRODUCTION OF COPPER IN THE UNITED STATES.

| Year | Tons. | Year | Tons. | Year | Tons. |
|---|---|---|---|---|---|
| 1877 | 21,000 | 1886 | 70,430 | 1895 | 170,137 |
| 1878 | 21,500 | 1887 | 81,017 | 1896 | 202,235 |
| 1879 | 23,000 | 1888 | 101,054 | 1897 | 219,481 |
| 1880 | 27,000 | 1889 | 101,239 | 1898 | 235,050 |
| 1881 | 32,000 | 1890 | 115,966 | 1899 | 261,313 |
| 1882 | 40,467 | 1891 | 126,839 | 1900 | 270,588 |
| 1883 | 51,574 | 1892 | 154,018 | 1901 | 266,716 |
| 1884 | 64,708 | 1893 | 147,033 | 1902 | 293,830 |
| 1885 | 74,052 | 1894 | 158,120 | | |

## FLUCTUATIONS IN SPOT COPPER PRICES AT NEW YORK AND LONDON.

| | New York Lake. | | London G. M. B. | | | | | |
|---|---|---|---|---|---|---|---|---|
| | Cents Per Pound. | | £ Per Ton. | | | | | |
| | Highest. | Lowest. | Highest. | | | Lowest. | | |
| | $ | $ | £ | s. | d. | £ | s. | d. |
| 1892 | .1225 | .1050 | 48 | 0 | 0 | 43 | 7 | 6 |
| 1893 | .1220 | .0940 | 46 | 16 | 3 | 40 | 12 | 3 |
| 1894 | .1010 | .0895 | 43 | 0 | 0 | 37 | 17 | 6 |
| 1895 | .1230 | .0925 | 47 | 8 | 9 | 38 | 13 | 9 |
| 1896 | .1200 | .0975 | 50 | 5 | 0 | 40 | 11 | 3 |
| 1897 | .1200 | .1075 | 51 | 15 | 0 | 47 | 0 | 0 |
| 1898 | .1312½ | .1085 | 57 | 8 | 9 | 48 | 5 | 0 |
| 1899 | .1925 | .1337½ | 79 | 5 | 0 | 59 | 17 | 6 |
| 1900 | .1700 | .1625 | 79 | 15 | 0 | 69 | 2 | 6 |
| 1901 | .1700 | .1300 | 72 | 17 | 6 | 47 | 0 | 0 |
| 1902 | .1350 | .1100 | 56 | 17 | 6 | 45 | 10 | 0 |

## PRICES FOR STANDARD COPPER PER TON AT LONDON IN 1902.

| | Highest. | | | Lowest. | | | Average. | | |
|---|---|---|---|---|---|---|---|---|---|
| | £ | s. | d. | £ | s. | d. | £ | s. | d. |
| January | 55 | 2 | 6 | 45 | 10 | 0 | 48 | 7 | 7 |
| February | 56 | 17 | 6 | 52 | 10 | 0 | 55 | 3 | 2 |
| March | 54 | 15 | 0 | 51 | 15 | 0 | 53 | 8 | 2 |
| April | 53 | 12 | 6 | 52 | 0 | 0 | 52 | 16 | 1 |
| May | 55 | 5 | 0 | 52 | 10 | 0 | 54 | 1 | 4 |
| June | 54 | 10 | 0 | 52 | 10 | 0 | 53 | 17 | 6 |
| July | 53 | 7 | 6 | 52 | 7 | 6 | 52 | 17 | 3 |
| August | 53 | 0 | 0 | 51 | 8 | 9 | 51 | 19 | 6 |
| September | 54 | 5 | 0 | 51 | 13 | 9 | 52 | 13 | 9 |
| October | 52 | 10 | 0 | 51 | 10 | 0 | 52 | 4 | 3 |
| November | 52 | 3 | 9 | 49 | 13 | 9 | 51 | 0 | 8 |
| December | 52 | 15 | 0 | 49 | 12 | 6 | 50 | 17 | 8 |
| All 1902 | 56 | 17 | 6 | 45 | 10 | 0 | 52 | 8 | 11 |
| All 1901 | 72 | 17 | 6 | 47 | 0 | 0 | 66 | 17 | 6 |

## AVERAGE DAILY PRICES OF LAKE COPPER FOR SPOT DELIVERY AT NEW YORK DURING 1902

IN CENTS, PER POUND

| Day. | Jan. | Feb. | March. | April. | May. | June. | July. | Aug. | Sept. | Oct. | Nov. | Dec. |
|---|---|---|---|---|---|---|---|---|---|---|---|---|
| 1. | ....... | ....... | ....... | 12.12½ | 11.87½ | ....... | 12.07½ | 11.95 | ....... | 11.65 | ....... | 11.37½ |
| 2. | 13.00 | ....... | ....... | 12.12½ | 11.92½ | 12.42½ | 12.17½ | ....... | 11.45 | 11.65 | ....... | 11.50 |
| 3. | 12.12½ | 13.50 | 12.25 | 12.12½ | 11.95 | 12.37¼ | 12.12½ | ....... | 11.45 | 11.62½ | 11.75 | 11.50 |
| 4. | ....... | 13.00 | 12.30 | 12.12½ | ....... | 12.40 | ....... | 11.85 | 11.62½ | ....... | ....... | 11.65 |
| 5. | ....... | 12.75 | 12.30 | ....... | ....... | 12.37½ | ....... | 11.85 | 11.80 | ....... | 11.75 | 11.65 |
| 6. | 12.12½ | 13.10 | 12.37½ | ....... | 12.05 | 12.40 | ....... | 11.85 | ....... | 11.65 | 11.75 | ....... |
| 7. | 12.12½ | 12.75 | 12.37½ | 12.12½ | 12.00 | ....... | 12.12½ | 11.85 | ....... | 11.70 | 11.70 | ....... |
| 8. | 12.12½ | ....... | ....... | 12.12½ | 12.00 | ....... | 12.02½ | 11.90 | 12.05 | 11.65 | ....... | 11.65 |
| 9. | 12.12½ | ....... | ....... | 12.12½ | 12.00 | 12.42½ | 12.05 | ....... | 12.12½ | 11.57½ | ....... | 11.65 |
| 10. | 12.12½ | 12.55 | 12.37½ | 12.12½ | 12.17½ | 12.45 | 12.07½ | ....... | 12.00 | 11.57½ | 11.62½ | 11.65 |
| 11. | ....... | 12.62½ | 12.37½ | 12.12½ | ....... | 12.42½ | 12.07½ | 11.80 | 12.00 | ....... | 11.60 | 11.65 |
| 12. | ....... | ....... | 12.37½ | ....... | .. | 12.52½ | ....... | 11.75 | 11.95 | ....... | 11.60 | 11.65 |
| 13. | 11.25 | 12.50 | 12.25 | ....... | 12.17½ | 12.40 | ....... | 11.70 | ....... | 11.57½ | 11.60 | ....... |
| 14. | 11.25 | 12.50 | 12.25 | 12.25 | 12.25 | ....... | 12.00 | 11.60 | ....... | 11.62½ | 11.60 | ....... |
| 15. | 11.12½ | ....... | ....... | 12.25 | 12.25 | ....... | 12.00 | 11.60 | 11.95 | 11.62½ | ....... | 11.65 |
| 16. | 11.12½ | ....... | ....... | 12.25 | 12.25 | 12.37½ | 12.00 | ....... | 11.90 | 11.65 | ....... | 11.65 |
| 17. | 11.12½ | 12.50 | 12.25 | 12.25 | 12.37½ | 12.32½ | 12.00 | ....... | 11.80 | 11.85 | 11.60 | 11.65 |
| 18. | ....... | 12.37½ | 12.25 | 12.25 | ....... | 12.22½ | 12.00 | 11.60 | 11.80 | ....... | 11.57½ | 11.65 |
| 19. | ....... | 12.37½ | 12.25 | ....... | ....... | 12.22½ | ....... | 11.60 | 11.70 | ....... | 11.50 | 11.65 |
| 20. | 11.00 | 12.37½ | 12.25 | ....... | 12.37½ | 12.22½ | ....... | 11.62½ | ....... | 12.00 | 11.50 | ....... |
| 21. | 11.00 | 12.37½ | 12.25 | 12.00 | 12.50 | ....... | 12.00 | 11.60 | ....... | 12.00 | 11.50 | ....... |
| 22. | 11.00 | ....... | ....... | 12.00 | 12.57½ | ....... | 11.95 | 11.60 | 11.67½ | 12.00 | ....... | 11.65 |
| 23. | 11.00 | ....... | ....... | 12.00 | 12.60 | 12.20 | 11.95 | ....... | 11.67½ | 11.87½ | ....... | 11.65 |
| 24. | 11.00 | 12.37½ | 12.25 | 12.00 | 12.75 | 12.22½ | 11.90 | ....... | 11.67½ | 11.87½ | 11.50 | 11.65 |
| 25. | ....... | 12.50 | 12.25 | 12.00 | ....... | 12.20 | 11.90 | 11.57½ | 11.62½ | ....... | 11.45 | ....... |
| 26. | ....... | 12.50 | 12.25 | ....... | ....... | 12.12½ | ....... | 11.57½ | 11.62½ | ....... | 11.37½ | 11.75 |
| 27. | 11.12½ | 12.37½ | 12.25 | ....... | 12.50 | 12.07½ | ....... | 11.57½ | ....... | 11.85 | ....... | ....... |
| 28. | 11.50 | 12.37½ | ....... | 12.00 | 12.50 | ....... | 11.85 | 11.52½ | ....... | 11.85 | 11.37½ | ....... |
| 29. | 12.00 | ....... | ....... | 12.00 | 12.42½ | ....... | 11.87½ | 11.52½ | 11.65 | 11.85 | ....... | 11.75 |
| 30. | 12.75 | ....... | ....... | 12.00 | ....... | 12.10 | 11.87½ | ....... | 11.65 | 11.75 | ....... | 11.75 |
| 31. | 13.00 | ....... | 12.25 | ....... | ....... | ....... | 11.92½ | ....... | ....... | 11.75 | ....... | 12.00 |

# PRODUCTION OF GOLD AND SILVER

## PRODUCT OF GOLD AND SILVER FROM MINES IN THE UNITED STATES.

**The following tables are taken from the report of the Director of the Mint.**

| CALENDAR YEARS. | Gold. | | Silver. | | |
|---|---|---|---|---|---|
| | Fine Ounces. | Value. | Fine Ounces. | Commercial Value. | Coining Value. |
| 1879 | 1,881,787 | $38,900,000 | 31,550,000 | $35,430,000 | $40,800,000 |
| 1880 | 1,741,500 | 30,000,000 | 30,320,000 | 34,720,000 | 39,200,000 |
| 1881 | 1,678,612 | 34,700,000 | 33,260,000 | 37,850,000 | 43,000,000 |
| 1882 | 1,572,187 | 32,500,000 | 36,200,000 | 41,120,000 | 46,800,000 |
| 1883 | 1,451,250 | 30,000,000 | 35,730,000 | 39,660,000 | 46,200,000 |
| 1884 | 1,489,950 | 30,080,000 | 37,800,000 | 42,070,000 | 48,800,000 |
| 1885 | 1,538,325 | 31,800,000 | 39,910,000 | 42,500,000 | 51,600,000 |
| 1886 | 1,693,125 | 35,000,000 | 39,440,000 | 39,230,000 | 50,000,000 |
| 1887 | 1,596,375 | 33,000,000 | 41,260,000 | 40,410,000 | 53,350,000 |
| 1888 | 1,604,841 | 33,175,000 | 45,780,000 | 43,020,000 | 59,195,000 |
| 1889 | 1,587,000 | 32,800,000 | 50,000,000 | 46,750,000 | 64,646,464 |
| 1890 | 1,588,880 | 32,845,000 | 54,500,000 | 57,225,000 | 70,464,000 |
| 1891 | 1,604,840 | 33,175,000 | 58,330,000 | 57,630,000 | 75,416,565 |
| 1892 | 1,597,098 | 33,014,981 | 63,500,000 | 55,563,000 | 82,101,000 |
| 1893 | 1,739,323 | 35,955,000 | 60,000,000 | 46,800,000 | 77,576,000 |
| 1894 | 1,910,813 | 39,500,000 | 49,500,000 | 31,422,000 | 64,000,000 |
| 1895 | 2,254,760 | 46,610,000 | 55,727,000 | 36,445,000 | 72,051,000 |
| 1896 | 2,568,132 | 53,088,000 | 58,835,000 | 39,655,000 | 76,069,000 |
| 1897 | 2,774,935 | 57,363,000 | 53,860,000 | 32,316,000 | 69,637,000 |
| 1898 | 3,118,398 | 64,463,000 | 54,438,000 | 32,118,000 | 70,384,000 |
| 1899 | 3,437,210 | 71,053,000 | 54,764,000 | 32,859,000 | 70,806,000 |
| 1900 | 3,829,897 | 79,171,000 | 57,647,000 | 35,741,000 | 74,533,000 |
| 1901 | 3,805,500 | 78,666,700 | 55,214,000 | 33,128,000 | 71,387,800 |
| * 1902 | 3,911,268 | 80,853,070 | 58,566,084 | 31,040,025 | 75,550,248 |

* Estimated.

## PRODUCT OF GOLD AND SILVER IN THE WORLD.

| CALENDAR YEARS. | Gold. | Silver. | | |
|---|---|---|---|---|
| | | Fine Ounces (Troy). | Commercial Value. | Coining Value |
| 1875 | $97,500,000 | 62,262,000 | $77,578,000 | $80,500,000 |
| 1876 | 103,700,000 | 67,753,000 | 78,322,000 | 87,000,000 |
| 1877 | 114,000,000 | 62,648,000 | 75,240,000 | 81,000,000 |
| 1878 | 119,000,000 | 73,476,000 | 84,644,000 | 95,000,000 |
| 1879 | 109,000,000 | 74,250,000 | 83,383,000 | 96,000,000 |
| 1880 | 106,500,000 | 74,791,000 | 85,636,000 | 96,700,000 |
| 1881 | 103,000,000 | 78,890,000 | 89,777,000 | 102,000,000 |
| 1882 | 102,000,000 | 86,470,000 | 98,230,000 | 111,800,000 |
| 1883 | 95,400,000 | 89,177,000 | 98,986,000 | 115,300,000 |
| 1884 | 101,700,000 | 81,597,000 | 90,817,000 | 105,500,000 |
| 1885 | 108,400,000 | 91,652,000 | 97,564,000 | 118,500,000 |
| 1886 | 106,000,000 | 93,276,000 | 92,772,000 | 120,600,000 |
| 1887 | 105,775,000 | 96,141,000 | 94,048,000 | 124,304,000 |
| 1888 | 110,197,000 | 108,827,000 | 102,283,000 | 140,706,000 |
| 1889 | 123,489,000 | 125,420,000 | 117,268,000 | 162,159,000 |
| 1890 | 118,849,000 | 126,095,000 | 132,400,000 | 163,032,000 |
| 1891 | 130,650,000 | 137,171,000 | 135,525,000 | 177,352,000 |
| 1892 | 146,298,000 | 152,940,000 | 133,825,000 | 197,741,000 |
| 1893 | 157,287,000 | 166,092,000 | 129,551,000 | 214,745,000 |
| 1894 | 181,175,000 | 164,610,561 | 104,493,000 | 212,829,200 |
| 1895 | 199,304,100 | 167,288,249 | 109,406,800 | 216,292,500 |
| 1896 | 202,682,300 | 168,178,887 | 113,352,000 | 217,442,000 |
| 1897 | 236,073,700 | 160,421,082 | 96,252,700 | 207,413,000 |
| 1898 | 286,586,500 | 173,227,864 | 102,294,600 | 223,971,500 |
| 1899 | 306,584,900 | 167,224,243 | 100,321,100 | 216,209,100 |
| 1900 | 254,576,500 | 173,591,870 | 107,626,900 | 224,441,200 |
| 1901 | 263,374,700 | 174,998,573 | 104,999,100 | 226,260,700 |
| * 1902 | 304,589,862 | 178,866,084 | 87,529,093 | 392,118,955 |

* Estimated.

## PRODUCTION OF GOLD AND SILVER IN THE UNITED STATES AND THE KLONDIKE.

| State or Territory. | 1901. Gold. | 1901. Silver Commer. Value. | 1901. Total. | *1902. Gold. | *1902. Silver Commer. Value. | *1902. Total. |
|---|---|---|---|---|---|---|
| Alabama | $3,100 | $60 | $3,160 | $2,873 | $50 | $2,923 |
| Alaska | 6,885,700 | 28,740 | 6,914,440 | 7,823,793 | 30,061 | 7,853,854 |
| Arizona | 4,083,000 | 1,687,440 | 5,770,440 | 4,155,039 | 1,680,100 | 5,835,139 |
| California | 16,891,400 | 555,360 | 17,446,760 | 17,124,041 | 480,793 | 17,604,834 |
| Colorado | 27,693,500 | 11,062,680 | 38,756,180 | 27,502,429 | 9,085,714 | 36,588,143 |
| Georgia | 124,500 | 240 | 124,740 | 102,388 | 349 | 102,737 |
| Idaho | 1,869,000 | 3,325,740 | 5,195,040 | 2,067,183 | 3,180,000 | 5,247,183 |
| Maryland | ........ | ........ | ........ | 2,956 | 2 | 2,958 |
| Michigan | 30,800 | 48,600 | 79,400 | 30,800 | 42,930 | 73,730 |
| Missouri | ........ | ........ | ........ | ........ | ........ | ........ |
| Montana | 4,744,100 | 7,879,020 | 12,623,120 | 4,134,365 | 6,890,000 | 11,024,365 |
| Nevada | 2,963,800 | 2,087,500 | 4,051,300 | 3,514,212 | 2,120,000 | 5,634,212 |
| New Mexico | 688,400 | 338,040 | 1,026,440 | 688,400 | 298,602 | 987,002 |
| North Carolina | 55,500 | 12,180 | 67,680 | 91,783 | 11,490 | 103,273 |
| Oregon | 1,818,100 | 96,060 | 1,914,160 | 1,860,465 | 63,600 | 1,924,065 |
| South Carolina | 46,700 | 120 | 46,820 | 147,928 | 152 | 148,080 |
| South Dakota | 6,479,500 | 46,800 | 6,526,300 | 7,398,057 | 182,373 | 7,580,430 |
| Tennessee | ........ | ........ | ........ | 145 | ........ | 145 |
| Texas | 600 | 283,400 | 284,040 | 600 | 250,372 | 250,972 |
| Utah | 3,690,200 | 6,456,480 | 10,146,680 | 3,720,930 | 6,360,000 | 10,080,930 |
| Virginia | 5,300 | 420 | 5,720 | 4,444 | 273 | 4,717 |
| Washington | 580,500 | 206,640 | 787,140 | 434,109 | 360,400 | 794,509 |
| Wyoming | 12,700 | 12,840 | 25,510 | 45,230 | 2,756 | 47,986 |
| Total U. S. | $78,666,700 | $33,128,400 | $111,795,100 | $80,853,070 | $31,040,025 | $111,893,095 |
| Klondike | ........ | ........ | ........ | 14,564,191 | 91,756 | 14,653,947 |
| † Nome | ........ | ........ | ........ | 5,023,256 | 9,540 | 5,032,796 |

* Estimated. † Included in Alaska.

## *SILVER IN LONDON*

THE FOLLOWING SHOWS THE COURSE OF THE LONDON SILVER MARKET IN PENCE PER OUNCE.

| | 1900. Highest. | 1900. Lowest. | 1901. Highest. | 1901. Lowest | 1902. Highest. | 1902. Lowest. |
|---|---|---|---|---|---|---|
| January | 27 11-16 | 27 | 29 9-16 | 27¾ | 26⅛ | 25 7-16 |
| February | 27¾ | 27 5-16 | 28 5-16 | 27⅞ | 25½ | 25⅜ |
| March | 27 11-16 | 27 7-16 | 28 3-16 | 27¼ | 25 7-16 | 24 13-16 |
| April | 27½ | 27 5-16 | 27 15-16 | 26 15-16 | 24⅞ | 23 5-16 |
| May | 27⅝ | 27½ | 27 9-16 | 27¼ | 24⅛ | 23⅜ |
| June | 28 9-16 | 27 9-16 | 27 9-16 | 27¼ | 24 7-16 | 23 15-16 |
| July | 28 9-16 | 27¾ | 27¼ | 26 13-16 | 24 9-16 | 24¼ |
| August | 28 7-16 | 27 15-16 | 27⅛ | 26¾ | 24 7-16 | 24⅛ |
| September | 29¼ | 28 7-16 | 27 | 26 15-16 | 24⅛ | 23 9-16 |
| October | 30 3-16 | 29⅛ | 26⅞ | 26⅜ | 23 9-16 | 23¼ |
| November | 29 15-16 | 29 7-16 | 26 7-16 | 25⅜ | 23¼ | 21 11-16 |
| December | 29⅞ | 29½ | 25¾ | 24 15-16 | 22⅝ | 21⅞ |
| Year | 30 3-16 | 27 | 29 9-16 | 24 15-16 | 26⅛ | 21 11-16 |

## PRICES OF BAR SILVER IN LONDON PER OUNCE, 925 FINE

| YEAR. | Highest | Lowest | YEAR. | Highest | Lowest |
|---|---|---|---|---|---|
| 1850 | 61½d | 59½d | 1877 | 58¼ | 53¼ |
| 1851 | 61⅝ | 60 | 1878 | 55¼ | 49½ |
| 1852 | 61⅞ | 59⅞ | 1879 | 53¼ | 48⅞ |
| 1853 | 61⅞ | 60⅝ | 1880 | 52⅞ | 51⅝ |
| 1854 | 61⅞ | 60⅞ | 1881 | 52⅞ | 50⅞ |
| 1855 | 61⅝ | 60 | 1882 | 52⅜ | 50 |
| 1856 | 62¼ | 60½ | 1883 | 51 3-16 | 50 |
| 1857 | 62⅜ | 61 | 1884 | 51⅜ | 49½ |
| 1858 | 61⅞ | 60¾ | 1885 | 50 | 46⅞ |
| 1859 | 62¾ | 61¾ | 1886 | 47 | 42 |
| 1860 | 62⅜ | 61¼ | 1887 | 47⅜ | 43¼ |
| 1861 | 61⅜ | 60⅛ | 1888 | 44 9-16 | 41⅝ |
| 1862 | 62⅛ | 61 | 1889 | 44⅜ | 41 15-16 |
| 1863 | 61¾ | 61 | 1890 | 54⅝ | 43⅝ |
| 1864 | 62½ | 60⅝ | 1891 | 48¾ | 43½ |
| 1865 | 61⅜ | 60½ | 1892 | 43¾ | 37⅞ |
| 1866 | 62¼ | 60⅜ | 1893 | 38¾ | 30 |
| 1867 | 61¼ | 60⅜ | 1894 | 31¾ | 27 |
| 1868 | 61⅛ | 60⅜ | 1895 | 31⅜ | 27 3-16 |
| 1869 | 61 | 60 | 1896 | 31 15-16 | 29¾ |
| 1870 | 60¾ | 60¼ | 1897 | 29 13-16 | 23¾ |
| 1871 | 61 | 60 3-16 | 1898 | 28 5-16 | 25 |
| 1872 | 61⅛ | 59¼ | 1899 | 29⅞ | 26⅝ |
| 1873 | 59 15-16 | 57⅞ | 1900 | 30 3-16 | 27 |
| 1874 | 59½ | 57¼ | 1901 | 29 9-16 | 24 15-16 |
| 1875 | 57⅝ | 55½ | 1902 | 26⅛ | 21 11-16 |
| 1876 | 58½d | 46¾d | | | |

## ANTHRACITE COAL SHIPMENTS AND PRODUCTION

IN TONS.

| YEAR. | Wyoming Region. | | Lehigh Region. | | Schuylkill Region. | | Total Shipments. |
|---|---|---|---|---|---|---|---|
| | Shipments. | Production. | Shipments. | Production. | Shipments. | Production. | |
| 1873 | 10,309,755 | 11,711,053 | 3,705,596 | 3,801,447 | 7,212,601 | 7,335,333 | 21,227,952 |
| 1874 | 9,504,408 | 10,204,764 | 3,773,836 | 4,139,591 | 6,866,877 | 7,280,793 | 20,145,121 |
| 1875 | 10,596,155 | 11,231,924 | 2,834,605 | 3,004,681 | 6,281,712 | 6,558,615 | 19,712,472 |
| 1876 | 8,424,158 | 8,929,607 | 6,221,934 | 6,595,250 | [illegible] | 4,080,214 | 18,501,011 |
| 1877 | 8,300,377 | 8,798,399 | 8,195,042 | 8,686,744 | 4,332,760 | 4,592,725 | 20,828,179 |
| 1878 | 8,085,587 | 8,570,722 | 6,282,226 | 6,659,159 | 3,237,449 | 3,431,695 | 17,605,262 |
| 1879 | 12,586,293 | 13,341,475 | 8,960,829 | 9,478,478 | 4,595,567 | 4,871,303 | 26,142,689 |
| 1880 | 11,419,279 | 12,104,435 | 7,554,742 | 8,008,026 | 4,463,261 | 4,773,014 | 23,437,242 |
| 1881 | 13,951,383 | 14,784,465 | 9,253,958 | 9,809,195 | 5,294,676 | 5,612,235 | 28,500,017 |
| 1882 | 13,971,371 | 14,809,653 | 9,459,288 | 10,026,845 | 5,689,437 | 6,040,803 | 29,120,096 |
| 1883 | 15,604,492 | 16,540,761 | 10,074,726 | 10,679,209 | [illegible] | 6,480,637 | 31,793,027 |
| 1884 | 15,677,753 | 16,618,418 | 9,478,314 | 10,047,012 | [illegible] | 5,895,959 | 30,718,293 |
| 1885 | 16,236,470 | 17,210,558 | 5,898,634 | 6,252,552 | 9,488,426 | 10,057,731 | 31,623,529 |
| 1886 | 17,031,826 | 18,053,736 | 5,723,129 | 6,066,587 | 9,381,407 | 9,944,291 | 32,136,362 |
| 1887 | 19,684,929 | 20,866,025 | 4,347,062 | 4,607,886 | 10,639,027 | 11,245,569 | 34,641,018 |
| 1888 | 21,852,366 | 23,163,508 | 5,639,236 | 5,977,593 | 10,654,116 | 11,293,462 | 38,145,718 |
| 1889 | 18,654,454 | 19,773,721 | 6,481,159 | 6,870,029 | 10,371,714 | 10,994,017 | 37,567,725 |
| 1890 | 18,657,694 | 19,777,156 | 6,329,658 | 6,709,437 | 10,867,821 | 11,519,910 | 35,855,173 |
| 1891 | 21,325,046 | 22,634,229 | 6,381,198 | 6,689,870 | 12,750,661 | 13,515,701 | 40,414,907 |
| 1892 | 22,815,460 | 25,096,000 | 6,451,076 | 7,096,000 | 12,626,784 | 13,888,000 | 41,893,321 |
| 1893 | 23,839,741 | 26,223,715 | 6,892,352 | 7,581,587 | 12,357,443 | 13,593,187 | 43,089,536 |
| 1894 | 22,650,761 | 24,915,837 | 6,705,433 | 7,375,000 | 12,035,005 | 13,238,000 | 41,391,199 |
| 1895 | 24,943,421 | 27,437,763 | 7,298,124 | 8,027,936 | 14,269,932 | 15,696,925 | 46,510,477 |
| 1896 | 23,589,473 | 25,948,420 | 6,490,441 | 7,139,485 | 13,097,571 | 14,407,328 | 43,177,485 |
| 1897 | 23,207,263 | 25,323,760 | 6,249,540 | 6,848,930 | 12,181,061 | 13,152,590 | 41,637,864 |
| 1898 | 22,775,993 | 25,141,731 | 6,283,050 | 6,911,355 | 12,566,100 | 13,822,710 | 41,625,143 |
| 1899 | 26,792,444 | 29,194,840 | 7,149,750 | 7,784,227 | 13,723,009 | 14,958,079 | 47,665,204 |
| 1900 | 24,686,125 | 27,154,737 | 6,918,627 | 7,610,489 | 13,502,732 | 14,853,005 | 45,107,484 |
| 1901 | 30,337,036 | 33,370,739 | 7,211,974 | 7,933,171 | 16,019,591 | 17,621,550 | 53,568,601 |
| 1902 | 19,258,763 | 21,184,639 | 3,470,736 | 3,817,809 | 8,471,391 | 9,318,530 | 31,200,890 |

## PRODUCTION OF COAL COMPANIES

Shipments of coal by the various companies and their percentages;

| | 1900. | | 1901. | | 1902. | |
|---|---|---|---|---|---|---|
| | Tons. | Per Cent. | Tons. | Per Cent. | Tons. | Per Cent. |
| Reading ........... | 9,338,516 | 20.7 | 10,971,007 | 20.5 | 5,909,401 | 18.94 |
| Lehigh Valley....... | 6,909,442 | 15.3 | 8,310,343 | 15.5 | 4,631,535 | 14.84 |
| Cen. of New Jersey . | 5,309,856 | 11.8 | 6,160,037 | 11.5 | 3,629,986 | 11.63 |
| Del., L. & W....... | 6,013,849 | 13.3 | 7,531,735 | 14.1 | 5,152,408 | 16.51 |
| Del. & Hudson ..... | 3,973,859 | 8.8 | 5,007,622 | 9.3 | 3,090,604 | 9.91 |
| Penn R. R.......... | 5,169,947 | 11.4 | 5,647,125 | 10.5 | 2,610,234 | 8.37 |
| Pennsylvania Coal.. | 2,090,153 | 4.6 | | | | |
| Erie............... | 1,741,069 | 3.8 | 5,841,593 | 10.9 | 3,814,150 | 12.22 |
| N. Y., Sus. & W ... | 1,333,848 | 2.9 | | | | |
| N. Y., Ont. & W... | 1,658,457 | 3.6 | 2,508,277 | 4.7 | 1,627,478 | 5.22 |
| Del., Sus. & Sch.... | 1,568,488 | 3.4 | 1,590,862 | 2.9 | 735,004 | 2.36 |
| Total ... ...... | 45,107,484 | 100.00 | 53,568,601 | 100.00 | 31,200,890 | 100.00 |

Tonnage, 1890........................................ 35,865,174
" 1891........................................ 40,448,336
" 1892........................................ 41,625,143
" 1893........................................ 43,089,536
" 1894........................................ 41,391,199
" 1895........................................ 46,545,670
" 1896........................................ 43,177,485
" 1897........................................ 41,637,864
" 1898........................................ 41,625,143
" 1899........................................ 47,665,203
" 1900........................................ 45,107,484
" 1901........................................ 53,568,601
" 1902........................................ 31,200,890

---

## COMPARATIVE MONTHLY ANTHRACITE SHIPMENTS

| Months. | Tons, 1898. | Tons, 1899. | Tons, 1900. | Tons, 1901. | Tons, 1902. |
|---|---|---|---|---|---|
| January .................. | 3,075,000 | 3,761,760 | 4,482,641 | 5,183,392 | 4,538,138 |
| February ................. | 2,762,000 | 2,810,460 | 3,188,180 | 4,098,968 | 3,741,253 |
| March .................... | 2,700,000 | 3,416,712 | 3,133,896 | 4,964,359 | 3,818,767 |
| April .... ............. .. | 2,228,750 | 3,078,088 | 3,364,482 | 3,685,013 | 4,924,830 |
| May ............ ........ | 2,390,000 | 3,557,694 | 3,833,097 | 4,674,707 | 1,708,892 |
| June ..................... | 3,026,971 | 4,073,364 | 4,676,580 | 4,755,748 | 92,203 |
| July ..................... | 3,770,000 | 4,189,251 | 3,599,720 | 3,698,814 | 250,079 |
| August.................... | 3,783,000 | 4,319,032 | 4,951,166 | 4,710,517 | 300,774 |
| September................. | 4,260,710 | 4,365,649 | 2,972,948 | 4,379,157 | 445,883 |
| October .................. | 4,765,195 | 4,899,303 | 834,786 | 4,938,132 | 1,176,257 |
| November ................. | 4,854,517 | 4,688,859 | 4,994,799 | 4,697,443 | 4,943,384 |
| December ................. | 4,000,000 | 4,505,026 | 5,075,189 | 3,623,423 | 5,260,430 |
| Total, Gross Tons...... | 41,625,143 | 47,665,203 | 45,107,484 | 53,568,601 | 31,200,890 |

## ANTHRACITE COAL TRADE

Shipments commenced from the Lehigh region in 1820, the Schuylkill region in 1825, the Lackawanna region in 1829, the Pittston or upper Lackawanna region in 1850 and the Scranton region in 1856.

The quantity of anthracite coal sent to market from the first shipments to the end of 1902, as reported by the official accountants, has been as follows:

| | Tons. | | Tons. | | Tons. |
|---|---|---|---|---|---|
| 1820 | 365 | 1848 | 3,089,238 | 1876 | 18,906,000 |
| 1821 | 1,073 | 1849 | 3,242,541 | 1877 | 20,824,411 |
| 1822 | 2,240 | 1850 | 3,254,321 | 1878 | 17,306,911 |
| 1823 | 5,823 | 1851 | 4,377,130 | 1879 | 26,142,689 |
| 1824 | 9,541 | 1852 | 4,925,695 | 1880 | 23,437,243 |
| 1825 | 34,893 | 1853 | 5,114,491 | 1881 | 28,485,080 |
| 1826 | 48,047 | 1854 | 5,753,369 | 1882 | 29,305,782 |
| 1827 | 63,434 | 1855 | 6,552,301 | 1883 | 31,793,027 |
| 1828 | 77,516 | 1856 | 6,751,542 | 1884 | 30,718,293 |
| 1829 | 112,083 | 1857 | 6,420,342 | 1885 | 61,637,350 |
| 1830 | 174,734 | 1858 | 6,491,187 | 1886 | 32,136,363 |
| 1831 | 176,820 | 1859 | 7,517,516 | 1887 | 34,341,017 |
| 1832 | 363,871 | 1860 | 8,131,234 | 1888 | 38,145,718 |
| 1833 | 487,748 | 1861 | 7,474,917 | 1889 | 35,510,710 |
| 1834 | 376,636 | 1862 | 7,481,719 | 1890 | 35,855,000 |
| 1835 | 560,758 | 1863 | 8,704,918 | 1891 | 40,448,336 |
| 1836 | 682,428 | 1864 | 9,032,007 | 1892 | 41,893,320 |
| 1837 | 881,476 | 1865 | 9,488,396 | 1893 | 43,089,536 |
| 1838 | 739,293 | 1866 | 13,418,472 | 1894 | 41,391,199 |
| 1839 | 819,327 | 1867 | 12,637,697 | 1895 | 46,292,443 |
| 1840 | 865,414 | 1868 | 14,214,889 | 1896 | 43,177,000 |
| 1841 | 958,899 | 1869 | 13,908,819 | 1897 | 41,637,864 |
| 1842 | 1,108,001 | 1870 | 15,552,380 | 1898 | 41,899,751 |
| 1843 | 1,263,539 | 1871 | 15,610,663 | 1899 | 47,665,204 |
| 1844 | 1,631,669 | 1872 | 20,747,149 | 1900 | 45,107,484 |
| 1845 | 2,023,052 | 1873 | 21,689,959 | 1901 | 53,568,601 |
| 1846 | 2,343,992 | 1874 | 19,805,074 | 1902 | 31,200,890 |
| 1847 | 2,982,303 | 1875 | 20,643,509 | | |

## PIG IRON PRODUCTION OF THE UNITED STATES

1855 to 1872, net tons; 1873 to 1902, gross tons.

| | | | |
|---|---|---|---|
| 1855 | 784,178 | 1879 | 2,741,853 |
| 1856 | 883,137 | 1880 | 3,835,151 |
| 1857 | 798,157 | 1881 | 4,144,254 |
| 1858 | 705,094 | 1882 | 4,623,323 |
| 1859 | 840,627 | 1883 | 4,593,510 |
| 1860 | 919,770 | 1884 | 4,097,868 |
| 1861 | 731,544 | 1885 | 4,044,526 |
| 1862 | 787,662 | 1886 | 5,683,329 |
| 1863 | 947,604 | 1887 | 6,417,148 |
| 1864 | 1,135,996 | 1888 | 6,489,738 |
| 1865 | 931,582 | 1889 | 7,603,642 |
| 1866 | 1,350,344 | 1890 | 9,203,703 |
| 1867 | 1,461,626 | 1891 | 8,279,870 |
| 1868 | 1,603,000 | 1892 | 9,157,000 |
| 1869 | 1,916,641 | 1893 | 7,124,000 |
| 1870 | 1,865,000 | 1894 | 6,657,088 |
| 1871 | 1,911,608 | 1895 | 9,446,308 |
| 1872 | 2,854,558 | 1896 | 8,623,127 |
| 1873 | 2,560,963 | 1897 | 9,652,860 |
| 1874 | 2,401,262 | 1898 | 11,773,934 |
| 1875 | 2,023,733 | 1899 | 13,620,703 |
| 1876 | 1,868,961 | 1900 | 13,789,243 |
| 1877 | 2,066,594 | 1901 | 15,878,354 |
| 1878 | 2,301,215 | 1902 | 17,821,307 |

# Produce

## Grain and Provision Prices in the Chicago and Other Markets for a Series of Years—Statistics of Production, Movement, Supplies and Export

### *PRICES OF GRAIN AND PROVISIONS AT CHICAGO*

| Years | Wheat. | | Corn. | | Oats. | | Pork. | | Lard. | |
|---|---|---|---|---|---|---|---|---|---|---|
| | High. | Low. | High. | Low. | High. | Low. | High. | Low. | High. | Low. |
| 1858...... | $ .97 | $ .53 | $ .66 | $ .30 | $ .50 | $ .20½ | $ 17.50 | $ 12.00 | $ 10.50 | $ 8.00 |
| 1859...... | 1.15 | .50 | .81 | .42 | .56 | .24 | 19.00 | 14.00 | 12.50 | 9.75 |
| 1860...... | 1.13 | .66 | .55 | .27 | .38 | .16 | 20.00 | 13.00 | 13.00 | 9.25 |
| 1861...... | 1.25 | .55 | .45 | .29 | .24 | .13 | 21.00 | 9.00 | 11.50 | 6.12½ |
| 1862...... | .92½ | .64 | .41 | .22 | .43¼ | .16 | 12.25 | 8.00 | 9.75 | 5.75 |
| 1863...... | 1.15 | .80 | .98 | .42 | .72 | .30½ | 18.50 | 10.00 | 12.00 | 7.25 |
| 1864...... | 2.26 | 1.07 | 1.41 | .76 | .81 | .57 | 44.00 | 17.50 | 23.50 | 11.75 |
| 1865...... | 1.55 | .85 | .88 | .38 | .66 | .25 | 38.00 | 22.50 | 30.00 | 16.00 |
| 1866...... | 2.03 | .78 | 1.00 | .33¾ | .44½ | .21¾ | 34.00 | 17.00 | 23.00 | 11.25 |
| 1867...... | 2.95 | 1.55 | 1.12 | .56¾ | .90 | .38½ | 24.50 | 18.00 | 13.75 | 11.25 |
| 1868...... | 2.20 | 1.04½ | 1.02½ | .52 | .74 | .41½ | 30.00 | 19.62½ | 19.50 | 11.75 |
| 1869...... | 2.47 | .76½ | .97½ | .44 | .71 | .35½ | 34.00 | 27.00 | 20.75 | 16.25 |
| 1870...... | 1.31½ | .73¼ | .94½ | .45 | .53½ | .32½ | 30.50 | 18.00 | 17.25 | 11.00 |
| 1871...... | 1.32 | .99½ | .56½ | .39½ | .51½ | .27 | 23.00 | 12.00 | 13.00 | 8.37½ |
| 1872...... | 1.61 | 1.01 | .48⅝ | .29½ | .43¼ | .20¼ | 16.00 | 11.05 | 11.00 | 7.00 |
| 1873...... | 1.46 | .89 | .54¼ | .27 | .40⅝ | .23¾ | 18.00 | 11.00 | 9.37 | 6.50 |
| 1874 ..... | 1.28 | .81½ | .86 | .49 | .71 | .37¼ | 24.75 | 13.75 | 15.00 | 8.20 |
| 1875...... | 1.30½ | .83¼ | .76½ | .45½ | .64½ | .29½ | 23.50 | 17.70 | 15.75 | 11.80 |
| 1876...... | 1.26¼ | .83 | .49 | .38⅝ | .35 | .27 | 22.75 | 15.20 | 13.85 | 9.55 |
| 1877...... | 1.76½ | 1.01⅛ | .58 | .37⅝ | .45¾ | .22 | 17.95 | 11.40 | 11.55 | 7.55 |
| 1878...... | 1.14 | .77 | .43⅝ | .29⅞ | .27⅛ | .18 | 11.35 | 6.02½ | 7.80 | 5.32½ |
| 1879...... | 1.33⅛ | .81⅝ | .49 | .29⅜ | .36¼ | .19½ | 13.75 | 7.27½ | 7.75 | 5.30 |
| 1880...... | 1.32 | .86½ | .43¼ | .31½ | .35 | .22½ | 19.00 | 9.37½ | 7.85 | 6.35 |
| 1881...... | 1.43¼ | .95⅜ | .76⅜ | .35¾ | .47¾ | .29½ | 20.00 | 12.40 | 13.00 | 9.20 |
| 1882..... | 1.40 | .91⅛ | .81½ | .49¼ | .62 | .30½ | 24.75 | 16.00 | 13.10 | 10.05 |
| 1883...... | 1.13½ | .90 | .70 | .46 | .43½ | .25 | 20.15 | 10.20 | 12.10 | 7.15 |
| 1884...... | .96 | .69½ | .87 | .34½ | .34¼ | .23 | 19.50 | 10.55 | 10.00 | 6.45 |
| 1885...... | .91¾ | .73⅜ | .49 | .34⅜ | .36½ | .24⅜ | 13.25 | 8.00 | 7.10 | 5.82½ |
| 1886...... | .84¾ | .69⅜ | .45 | .33⅛ | .35 | .22⅞ | 12.20 | 8.20 | 7.50 | 5.82½ |
| 1887...... | .94¾ | .66⅝ | .51⅛ | .33 | .31½ | .23½ | 24.00 | 11.60 | 7.92½ | 6.20 |
| 1888...... | 2.00 | .71⅛ | .60 | .33½ | .37¾ | .23¼ | 16.00 | 12.90 | 11.20 | 7.25 |
| 1889...... | 1.08⅜ | .75½ | .61 | .29¼ | .26⅜ | .17¾ | 13.37½ | 8.35 | 7.55 | 5.75 |
| 1890...... | 1.08¼ | .74¼ | .53⅞ | .27½ | .45 | .19¼ | 13.62½ | 7.50 | 6.52½ | 5.50 |
| 1891...... | 1.16 | .85 | .75½ | .39⅜ | .57¾ | .26¼ | 13.00 | 7.45 | 7.05 | 5.47½ |
| 1892...... | .91¾ | .69⅛ | 1.00 | .36½ | .35½ | .27 | 15.05 | 9.25 | 10.60 | 6.05 |
| 1893...... | .88 | .54 | .44¾ | .34¼ | .32 | .22 | 21.80 | 10.25 | 13.20 | 6.00 |
| 1894...... | .65¼ | .50 | .59½ | .34 | .50 | .27 | 14.57½ | 10.67½ | 9.05 | 6.45 |
| 1895...... | .85⅜ | .48¾ | .55⅛ | .25 | .31⅛ | .16¾ | 12.87½ | 7.50 | 7.17½ | 5.15 |
| 1896...... | .94⅜ | .53 | .30⅝ | .19½ | .20½ | .14¾ | 10.85 | 5.50 | 5.85 | 3.05 |
| 1897...... | 1.09 | .64⅛ | .32⅝ | .21¾ | .23⅞ | .15⅝ | 9.00 | 7.15 | 4.90 | 3.47½ |
| 1898...... | 1.85 | .62 | .38¼ | .26 | .32 | .19⅜ | 12.30 | 7.65 | 6.82½ | 4.40 |
| 1899...... | .79½ | .64 | .38½ | .30 | .28¼ | .19¼ | 10.45 | 7.85 | 5.77½ | 4.90 |
| 1900...... | .87½ | .61½ | .49½ | .30½ | .26¼ | .20⅞ | 16.00 | 10.35 | 7.35 | 5.65 |
| 1901...... | .79½ | .63⅛ | .67½ | .36 | .48¼ | .23¼ | 16.80 | 12.60 | 10.25 | 6.90 |
| 1902 ..... | .95 | .67½ | .88 | .43¼ | .56 | .25 | 18.70 | 15.00 | 11.60 | 9.07½ |

## WHEAT OPTIONS AT CHICAGO

Highest and lowest quotations per bushel by months for May, July, September and December delivery of No. 2 regular wheat at the Chicago Board of Trade:

| | | 1901. Deliveries | | | | 1902. Deliveries | | | |
|---|---|---|---|---|---|---|---|---|---|
| | | May. | July. | Sept. | Dec. | May. | July. | Sept. | Dec. |
| January | H. | 79¾ | 76½ | .. | .. | 84¼ | 84 | .. | .. |
| | L. | 73¾ | 73¼ | .. | .. | 77 | 76⅞ | .. | .. |
| February | H. | 76¾ | 75⅝ | .. | .. | 79 | 79¼ | 78½ | .. |
| | L. | 74⅛ | 73½ | .. | .. | 75⅜ | 75⅛ | 75 | .. |
| March | H. | 77⅝ | 77⅛ | 76⅜ | .. | 78¼ | 78⅝ | 78 | .. |
| | L. | 74⅝ | 74 | 75 | .. | 70½ | 71⅜ | 71⅝ | .. |
| April | H. | 75⅞ | 76⅝ | 75⅞ | .. | 77 | 78¼ | 78½ | .. |
| | L. | 69⅝ | 70¼ | 70⅜ | .. | 70⅝ | 71 | 70¾ | .. |
| May | H. | .. | 74⅜ | 73⅝ | .. | .. | 77½ | 76¾ | 78 |
| | L. | .. | 70⅜ | 69⅜ | .. | .. | 71¾ | 70¼ | 71½ |
| June | H. | .. | 79¾ | 74⅛ | 71 | .. | 75 | 74 | 74¼ |
| | L. | .. | 65½ | 66 | 67¾ | .. | 70¼ | 69⅜ | 70⅝ |
| July | H. | .. | .. | 73⅜ | 75½ | .. | .. | 75⅝ | 76½ |
| | L. | .. | .. | 63¾ | 65⅝ | .. | .. | 69½ | 68¼ |
| August | H. | 80½ | .. | 74⅝ | 76⅞ | 72⅛ | .. | 72½ | 69½ |
| | L. | 72¾ | .. | 67½ | 69¾ | 68½ | .. | 67⅛ | 65⅝ |
| September | H. | 75⅝ | .. | .. | 72⅛ | 71¼ | .. | .. | 70½ |
| | L. | 73⅜ | .. | .. | 69⅞ | 69 | .. | .. | 67⅜ |
| October | H. | 75⅛ | .. | .. | 71¾ | 75⅜ | .. | .. | 73⅝ |
| | L. | 72 | .. | .. | 68½ | 70 | .. | .. | 65⅝ |
| November | H. | 77⅜ | .. | .. | 73½ | 77⅞ | .. | .. | 77½ |
| | L. | 73¾ | .. | .. | 70⅛ | 72¼ | .. | .. | 70½ |
| December | H. | 83¾ | 83½ | .. | .. | 78⅛ | 74⅞ | .. | .. |
| | L. | 76⅞ | 77⅝ | .. | .. | 74⅝ | 72⅝ | .. | .. |

## CORN OPTIONS AT CHICAGO

Highest and lowest quotations per bushel by months for May, July, September and December deliveries of No. 2 corn at the Chicago Board of Trade:

| | | 1901. Deliveries | | | | 1902. Deliveries | | | |
|---|---|---|---|---|---|---|---|---|---|
| | | May. | July. | Sept. | Dec. | May. | July. | Sept. | Dec. |
| January | H. | 39⅝ | 39⅛ | .. | .. | 68 | 67⅜ | 66½ | .. |
| | L. | 36⅝ | 38⅜ | .. | .. | 59⅞ | 59⅞ | 59⅜ | .. |
| February | H. | 41⅞ | 41⅛ | .. | .. | 64¼ | 64⅜ | 63⅛ | .. |
| | L. | 38½ | 38½ | .. | .. | 59⅛ | 59 | 57⅞ | .. |
| March | H. | 44¾ | 44½ | 44⅞ | .. | 63⅛ | 62⅝ | 60⅝ | .. |
| | L. | 40¼ | 40 | 41¾ | .. | 57½ | 58 | 56⅜ | .. |
| April | H. | 49 | 46 | 45½ | .. | 64½ | 66 | 65 | .. |
| | L. | 40¾ | 41½ | 42¼ | .. | 57½ | 58 | 57⅝ | .. |
| May | H. | .. | 47⅝ | 47⅜ | .. | .. | 64¾ | 62⅞ | 48⅛ |
| | L. | .. | 43 | 42¾ | .. | .. | 60⅝ | 59 | 44½ |
| June | H. | .. | 45¼ | 45⅞ | 44⅝ | .. | 72⅝ | 63⅜ | 49 |
| | L. | .. | 41½ | 42¼ | 39½ | .. | 60¾ | 57¾ | 43⅜ |
| July | H. | .. | .. | 59⅞ | 60¼ | .. | .. | 64¼ | 50 |
| | L. | .. | .. | 45¼ | 44 | .. | .. | 54¾ | 42½ |
| August | H. | 65¾ | .. | 61¼ | 64 | 41⅝ | .. | 60 | 44⅜ |
| | L. | 57⅜ | .. | 53⅛ | 55¼ | 38⅛ | .. | 50 | 39 |
| September | H. | 63 | .. | .. | 61 | 41⅝ | .. | .. | 47 |
| | L. | 58⅛ | .. | .. | 55⅞ | 39 | .. | .. | 42 |
| October | H. | 60½ | .. | .. | 58 | 44⅝ | .. | .. | 53⅞ |
| | L. | 57⅝ | .. | .. | 55 | 41¼ | .. | .. | 45¼ |
| November | H. | 65⅜ | .. | .. | 62⅞ | 44⅝ | .. | .. | 59½ |
| | L. | 59⅝ | .. | .. | 57⅛ | 41⅜ | .. | .. | 49⅞ |
| December | H. | 69¼ | 68⅞ | .. | .. | 45 | 43½ | .. | .. |
| | L. | 64½ | 64⅜ | .. | .. | 42¼ | 41⅜ | .. | |

## OATS OPTIONS AT CHICAGO

Highest and lowest quotations per bushel, by months, for May, July, September and December deliveries of No. 2 Oats at the Chicago Board of Trade.

| | | 1901. Deliveries | | | | 1902. Deliveries | | | |
|---|---|---|---|---|---|---|---|---|---|
| | | May. | July. | Sept. | Dec. | May. | July. | Sept. | Dec |
| January | H. | 25¾ | .. | .. | .. | 47⅜ | 42⅝ | 34¼ | .. |
| | L. | 24⅛ | .. | .. | .. | 39⅛ | 35½ | 31⅜ | .. |
| February | H. | 26 | .. | .. | .. | 44⅞ | 39 | 33⅛ | .. |
| | L. | 25 | .. | .. | .. | 41½ | 34⅛ | 29⅝ | .. |
| March | H. | 26⅝ | 26⅛ | .. | .. | 46½ | 37⅛ | 31 | .. |
| | L. | 24½ | 24⅜ | .. | .. | 41 | 33½ | 28½ | .. |
| April | H. | 27⅛ | 26⅝ | 25½ | .. | 44¾ | 37⅝ | 32⅞ | .. |
| | L. | 24½ | 24½ | 24⅛ | .. | 41¼ | 33⅜ | 28½ | .. |
| May | H. | .. | 29⅜ | 27¼ | .. | .. | 35⅞ | 30½ | 30⅞ |
| | L. | .. | 26 | 24¼ | .. | .. | 33¼ | 27¾ | 28½ |
| June | H. | .. | 28¾ | 27¼ | .. | .. | 43⅛ | 32 | 32⅛ |
| | L. | .. | 26⅜ | 25¼ | .. | .. | 34 | 27½ | 27⅞ |
| July | H. | .. | .. | 38½ | 39 | .. | .. | 34 | 34 |
| | L. | .. | .. | 27⅛ | 31¾ | .. | .. | 28 | 27⅜ |
| August | H. | 40¾ | .. | 37½ | 38⅜ | 32 | .. | 29¼ | 28 |
| | L. | 36⅝ | .. | 33 | 34⅛ | 28¾ | .. | 24¼ | 24½ |
| September | H. | 39½ | .. | .. | 37⅜ | 32½ | .. | .. | 27⅜ |
| | L. | 36⅝ | .. | .. | 34⅜ | 30½ | .. | .. | 25¾ |
| October | H. | 39¼ | .. | .. | 37⅛ | 34½ | .. | .. | 28⅞ |
| | L. | 36⅞ | .. | .. | 34¾ | 31⅜ | .. | .. | 26¼ |
| November | H. | 43½ | .. | .. | 43⅛ | 32¾ | .. | .. | 29½ |
| | L. | 38½ | .. | .. | 36⅜ | 30⅝ | .. | .. | 27½ |
| December | H. | 47⅝ | 42½ | .. | .. | 34⅜ | 32⅝ | .. | .. |
| | L. | 43 | 38½ | .. | .. | 31⅞ | 31⅜ | .. | .. |

——* Old crop, May and July quotations, are for No. 2. New crop are for standard.

## PORK OPTIONS AT CHICAGO

Highest and lowest quotations per barrel, by months, for January, May, July and September deliveries of mess pork at the Chicago Board of Trade.

| | | 1901. Deliveries | | | | 1902. Deliveries | | | |
|---|---|---|---|---|---|---|---|---|---|
| | | Jan. | May | July. | Sept. | Jan. | May. | July. | Sept. |
| January | H. | .. | $14.45 | .. | .. | .. | $17.42½ | .. | .. |
| | L. | .. | 12.72½ | .. | .. | .. | 15.52½ | .. | .. |
| February | H. | .. | 14.35 | $14.05 | .. | .. | 16.07½ | $16.10 | .. |
| | L. | .. | 13.90 | 13.75 | .. | .. | 15.10 | 15.25 | .. |
| March | H. | .. | 17.10 | 15.55 | .. | .. | 16.72½ | 16.90 | .. |
| | L. | .. | 13.97½ | 13.55 | .. | .. | 15.00 | 15.27½ | .. |
| April | H. | .. | 15.65 | 15.35 | $14.87½ | .. | 17.00 | 17.22½ | $17.25 |
| | L. | .. | 14.07½ | 14.22½ | 14.35 | .. | 16.25 | 16.40 | 16.70 |
| May | H. | .. | .. | 15.32½ | 15.15 | .. | .. | 17.60 | 17.65 |
| | L. | .. | .. | 14.50 | 14.25 | .. | .. | 16.62½ | 16.77½ |
| June | H. | .. | .. | 14.90 | 15.10 | .. | .. | 18.40 | 18.70 |
| | L. | .. | .. | 14.47½ | 14.57½ | .. | .. | 17.00 | 17.10 |
| July | H. | .. | .. | .. | 14.85 | .. | .. | .. | 18.87½ |
| | L. | .. | .. | .. | 13.87½ | .. | .. | .. | 16.65 |
| August | H. | 15.72½ | .. | .. | 14.45 | $15.90 | .. | .. | 17.50 |
| | L. | 14.75 | .. | .. | 13.75 | 13.90 | .. | .. | 15.75 |
| September | H. | 16.40 | .. | .. | .. | 15.40 | .. | .. | .. |
| | L. | 15.50 | .. | .. | .. | 14.80 | .. | .. | .. |
| October | H. | 15.95 | .. | .. | .. | 16.15 | .. | .. | .. |
| | L. | 14.82½ | .. | .. | .. | 15.02½ | .. | .. | .. |
| November | H. | 16.40 | .. | .. | .. | 16.10 | .. | .. | .. |
| | L. | 14.62½ | .. | .. | .. | 15.00 | .. | .. | .. |
| December | H. | 17.00 | 17.50 | .. | .. | 17.50 | 16.65 | .. | .. |
| | L. | 15.97½ | 16.32½ | .. | .. | 15.67½ | 14.85 | .. | .. |

## LARD OPTIONS AT CHICAGO

Highest and lowest quotations per 100 lbs., by months, for January, May, July and September deliveries of lard at the Chicago Board of Trade.

| | | 1901. Deliveries. | | | | 1902. Deliveries. | | | |
|---|---|---|---|---|---|---|---|---|---|
| | | Jan. | May. | July. | Sept. | Jan. | May. | July. | Sept. |
| January | H. | .. | $7.62½ | .. | .. | .. | $10.05 | .. | .. |
| | L. | .. | 7.02½ | .. | .. | .. | 9.30 | .. | .. |
| February | H. | .. | 7.60 | $7.65 | .. | .. | 9.60 | $9.67½ | .. |
| | L. | .. | 7.40 | 7.47½ | .. | .. | 9.17½ | 9.27½ | .. |
| March | H. | .. | 8.22½ | 8.12½ | .. | .. | 9.87½ | 9.90 | .. |
| | L. | .. | 7.37½ | 7.45 | .. | .. | 9.27½ | 9.37½ | .. |
| April | H. | .. | 8.60 | 8.32½ | $8.32½ | .. | 10.07½ | 10.20 | $10.30 |
| | L. | .. | 8.00 | 7.95 | 7.95 | .. | 9.40 | 9.50 | 9.60 |
| May | H. | .. | .. | 8.22½ | 8.25 | .. | .. | 10.45 | 10.45 |
| | L. | .. | .. | 7.82½ | 7.85 | .. | .. | 9.92½ | 10.00 |
| June | H. | .. | .. | 8.85 | 8.90 | .. | .. | 10.70 | 10.75 |
| | L. | .. | .. | 8.15 | 8.15 | .. | .. | 10.15 | 10.20 |
| July | H. | .. | .. | .. | 8.77½ | .. | .. | .. | 11.50 |
| | L. | .. | .. | .. | 8.42½ | .. | .. | .. | 10.50 |
| August | H. | $8.95 | .. | .. | 8.97½ | $8.90 | .. | .. | 11.00 |
| | L. | 8.60 | .. | .. | 8.55 | 8.12½ | .. | .. | 10.10 |
| September | H. | 9.77½ | .. | .. | .. | 8.85 | .. | .. | .. |
| | L. | 8.82½ | .. | .. | .. | 8.27½ | .. | .. | .. |
| October | H. | 9.35 | .. | .. | .. | 9.40 | .. | .. | .. |
| | L. | 8.65 | .. | .. | .. | 8.55 | .. | .. | .. |
| November | H. | 9.57½ | .. | .. | .. | 9.60 | .. | .. | .. |
| | L. | 8.47½ | .. | .. | .. | 8.95 | .. | .. | .. |
| December | H. | 10.17½ | 10.22½ | .. | .. | 10.07½ | 9.70 | .. | .. |
| | L. | 9.32½ | 9.40 | . | .. | 9.37½ | 8.72½ | .. | .. |

## RANGE OF PRICES IN THE CHICAGO MARKET

### CASH WHEAT.

| Month. | 1900. | | 1901. | | | 1902. | | |
|---|---|---|---|---|---|---|---|---|
| | Highest. | Lowest. | Highest. | Lowest. | Closing. | Highest. | Lowest. | Closing. |
| January...... | .67⅛ | .61½ | .76⅜ | .71⅜ | .73⅛ | .80½ | .74 | .75⅛ |
| February .... | .67½ | .63⅞ | .74¾ | .72⅛ | .74 | .76½ | .72⅞ | .74⅝ |
| March ... | .67 | .64 | .76¼ | .73¼ | .75 | .76 | .69¾ | .70¼ |
| April........ | .67¾ | .64¾ | .74⅞ | .69½ | .71¾ | .76¾ | .70 | .74¾ |
| May......... | .67½ | .63⅝ | .75⅛ | .70 | .74⅜ | .76¼ | .72¾ | .73⅞ |
| June ....... | .87½ | .65⅞ | .77¼ | .65½ | .65½ | .75¾ | .71¼ | .75½ |
| July......... | .81½ | .74 | .71¾ | .63⅛ | .67⅛ | .79 | .71½ | .76 |
| August ...... | .76¼ | .71¾ | .77 | .66⅝ | .70 | .76 | .68¼ | .74¾ |
| September ... | .79⅜ | .72½ | .71 | .68⅛ | .68⅛ | .95 | .70 | .95 |
| October...... | .77⅜ | .71⅛ | .71½ | .66¼ | .69¾ | .75½ | .67½ | .74 |
| November ... | .74¼ | .69⅝ | .73¼ | .70 | .73 | .77⅜ | .69⅜ | .75 |
| December.... | .74⅝ | .69¼ | .79½ | .73 | .78¼ | .77¾ | .71⅞ | .73¾ |

### CASH CORN.

| Month. | 1900. | | 1901. | | | 1902. | | |
|---|---|---|---|---|---|---|---|---|
| | Highest. | Lowest. | Highest. | Lowest. | Closing. | Highest. | Lowest. | Closing |
| January...... | .31⅝ | .30½ | .37¾ | .36 | .37¼ | .64½ | .56½ | .60¼ |
| February..... | .34¼ | .34½ | .40 | .37¼ | .39¼ | .61¼ | .56⅝ | .59¾ |
| March ...... | .38¼ | .33⅜ | .44 | .39 | .44 | .61⅛ | .56 | .59⅛ |
| April......... | .40⅞ | .38¼ | .48 | .41 | .47¾ | .64½ | .56¾ | .62⅞ |
| May......... | .40½ | .36 | .58½ | .42⅝ | .43¼ | .64¾ | .59⅛ | .61½ |
| June......... | .43½ | .37⅜ | .44⅜ | .41 | .43⅞ | .71½ | .61 | .71½ |
| July......... | .44¾ | .38⅜ | .58¼ | .43½ | .54 | .88 | .56 | .58 |
| August ...... | .41¼ | .37¼ | .59½ | .53¾ | .54⅝ | .60 | .54 | .59 |
| September ... | .43¼ | .38⅞ | .59¼ | 54⅛ | .55¼ | .62½ | .57 | .58 |
| October ...... | .41¾ | .36½ | .58 | .54⅝ | .57½ | .61½ | .55 | .56¼ |
| November.... | .49½ | .35 | .63⅞ | .57⅛ | .62¾ | .58 | .52 | .54½ |
| December... | .49½ | .35¼ | .67½ | 62½ | .63½ | .57¼ | .43¼ | .44¼ |

### CASH OATS.

| Month. | 1900. | | 1901. | | | 1902. | | |
|---|---|---|---|---|---|---|---|---|
| | Highest. | Lowest. | Highest. | Lowest. | Closing. | Highest. | Lowest | Closing. |
| January...... | .23 | .22½ | .24½ | .23¼ | .24 | .46¼ | .38⅜ | .43¾ |
| February .... | .23¾ | .22½ | .25½ | .24⅛ | .25 | .44¼ | .40¾ | .44¼ |
| March....... | .24½ | .23 | .26½ | .24¾ | .26½ | .45½ | .40¼ | .41⅜ |
| April ........ | .25¼ | .23 | .27½ | .25½ | .27 | .44½ | .41 | .42¾ |
| May ........ | .23¾ | .21¼ | .31 | .27⅞ | .28½ | .49½ | .41 | .49½ |
| June ........ | .26¼ | .21¾ | .28¾ | .27 | .28 | .48½ | .39 | .48½ |
| July......... | .24¾ | .21½ | .39 | .27½ | .34 | .56 | .30 | .47 |
| August ...... | .22⅝ | .21 | .37½ | .33½ | .34¾ | .31 | .25 | .26¾ |
| September ... | .22¼ | .21⅛ | .36¾ | .33⅝ | .35¼ | .27¼ | .26⅛ | .27⅛ |
| October...... | .22⅝ | .21⅜ | .37¾ | .34½ | .37¾ | .30 | .27¼ | .28¼ |
| November ... | .22½ | .21¾ | .44⅛ | .37⅛ | .42 | .29½ | .27¾ | .29 |
| December.... | .22¾ | .21¾ | .48¼ | .42 | .44½ | .32 | .29¼ | .31 |

## CASH PORK.

| Month. | 1900. | | 1901. | | | 1902. | | |
|---|---|---|---|---|---|---|---|---|
| | Highest. | Lowest. | Highest. | Lowest. | Closing. | Highest. | Lowest. | Closing. |
| January | $10.90 | $10.35 | $15.00 | $12.60 | $13.70 | $17.00 | $15.50 | $15.65 |
| February | 11.10 | 10.50 | 14.15 | 13.77½ | 13.90 | 15.85 | 15.00 | 15.30 |
| March | 12.75 | 10.50 | 16.80 | 13.90 | 15.35 | 16.65 | 15.00 | 16.55 |
| April | 13.25 | 12.45 | 15.55 | 14.10 | 14.50 | 16.95 | 16.35 | 16.65 |
| May | 12.10 | 11.20 | 15.20 | 14.45 | 14.45 | 17.50 | 16.75 | 17.15 |
| June | 12.85 | 11.05 | 14.90 | 14.50 | 14.62 | 18.45 | 17.20 | 18.30 |
| July | 12.75 | 11.55 | 14.60 | 13.75 | 14.00 | 18.70 | 16.75 | 16.80 |
| August | 12.20 | 10.90 | 14.50 | 13.70 | 14.40 | 17.05 | 15.85 | 17.00 |
| September | 12.30 | 10.85 | 15.05 | 14.35 | 14.70 | 16.85 | 16.10 | 16.20 |
| October | 16.00 | 11.50 | 14.65 | 13.40 | 13.50 | 17.50 | 16.50 | 16.75 |
| November | 11.50 | 10.37½ | 15.25 | 13.75 | 15.15 | 17.00 | 16.50 | 16.87½ |
| December | 11.62½ | 11.00 | 16.10 | 15.10 | 15.80 | 17.25 | 16.62½ | 17.25 |

## CASH LARD.

| Month. | 1900. | | 1901. | | | 1902. | | |
|---|---|---|---|---|---|---|---|---|
| | Highest. | Lowest. | Highest. | Lowest. | Closing. | Highest. | Lowest. | Closing. |
| January | $6.05 | $5.72½ | $7.50 | $6.90 | $7.32½ | $10.00 | $9.17½ | $9.72½ |
| February | 6.07½ | 5.65 | 7.52½ | 7.37½ | 7.40 | 9.40 | 9.07½ | 9.22½ |
| March | 6.55 | 5.70 | 8.35 | 7.35 | 8.30 | 9.75 | 9.12½ | 9.72½ |
| April | 7.35 | 6.45 | 8.62½ | 8.10 | 8.10 | 10.07½ | 9.45 | 10.02½ |
| May | 7.07½ | 6.72½ | 8.27½ | 7.85 | 8.17½ | 10.42½ | 10.05 | 10.15 |
| June | 7.07½ | 6.47½ | 8.85 | 8.15 | 8.62½ | 10.62½ | 10.12½ | 10.55 |
| July | 6.90 | 6.60 | 8.70 | 8.40 | 8.65 | 11.42½ | 10.42 | 10.80 |
| August | 6.90 | 6.60 | 8.97½ | 8.55 | 8.95 | 10.87½ | 10.00 | 10.45 |
| September | 7.20 | 6.67½ | 10.25 | 8.95 | 9.92½ | 11.60 | 10.35 | 11.50 |
| October | 7.40 | 6.77½ | 9.97½ | 8.60 | 8.60 | 11.42½ | 10.15 | 11.00 |
| November | 7.25 | 6.85 | 9.60 | 8.47½ | 9.55 | 11.25 | 10.37½ | 10.80 |
| December | 7.22½ | 6.75 | 10.15 | 9.37½ | 9.95 | 11.00 | 10.00 | 10.02½ |

## CASH SHORT RIBS.

| Month. | 1900. | | 1901. | | | 1902. | | |
|---|---|---|---|---|---|---|---|---|
| | Highest. | Lowest. | Highest. | Lowest. | Closing. | Highest. | Lowest. | Closing. |
| January | $5.95 | $5.40 | $7.30 | $6.40 | $6.85 | $8.62½ | $8.05 | $8.30 |
| February | 6.15 | 5.60 | 7.30 | 6.40 | 6.95 | 8.60 | 8.15 | 8.40 |
| March | 6.90 | 5.65 | 8.20 | 6.90 | 8.00 | 8.90 | 8.10 | 8.90 |
| April | 7.40 | 6.55 | 8.40 | 8.00 | 8.05 | 9.50 | 8.70 | 9.40 |
| May | 6.90 | 6.35 | 9.40 | 7.80 | 7.80 | 9.85 | 9.40 | 9.80 |
| June | 7.30 | 6.30 | 8.25 | 7.75 | 7.95 | 10.95 | 9.75 | 10.72½ |
| July | 7.30 | 6.50 | 8.40 | 7.75 | 7.85 | 10.85 | 10.05 | 10.35 |
| August | 7.40 | 6.75 | 8.45 | 7.70 | 8.25 | 10.55 | 9.40 | 10.25 |
| September | 8.35 | 7.05 | 9.10 | 8.30 | 8.80 | 11.45 | 10.15 | 10.90 |
| October | 8.35 | 6.40 | 8.90 | 7.85 | 7.85 | 12.25 | 10.50 | 11.00 |
| November | 7.75 | 6.50 | 8.45 | 7.75 | 8.25 | 10.87½ | 8.87½ | 9.12½ |
| December | 7.00 | 6.25 | 8.70 | 8.15 | 8.52½ | 9.00 | 8.37½ | 8.62½ |

CASH NO. 2 WHEAT. HIGHEST AND LOWEST PRICES PER BUSHEL, BY MONTHS.

| MONTH. | 1884. | 1885. | 1886. | 1887. | 1888. | 1889. | 1890. | 1891. | 1892. | 1893. | 1894. | 1895. | 1896. | 1897. | 1898. | 1899. | 1900. | 1901. | 1902. |
|---|---|---|---|---|---|---|---|---|---|---|---|---|---|---|---|---|---|---|---|
| January.......... | .95¼<br>.88½ | .81½<br>.76 | .85½<br>.76½ | .80⅛<br>.76⅞ | .78½<br>.76 | 1.01½<br>.92 | .78⅛<br>.74½ | .93¼<br>.89 | .90<br>.84½ | .78⅛<br>.72 | .64<br>.58¼ | .55<br>.48¼ | .68⅞<br>.55¼ | .94<br>.71¼ | 1.10<br>.89½ | .76<br>.66½ | .67⅛<br>.61½ | .76⅜<br>.71⅜ | .80½<br>.74 |
| February......... | .96<br>.90¼ | .79½<br>.74¼ | .81¾<br>.78¼ | .78¼<br>.71⅞ | .78¼<br>.74⅝ | 1.08¼<br>.93¼ | .77<br>.74¼ | .97¼<br>.93 | .91¾<br>.84⅝ | .75⅞<br>.72 | .61<br>.54 | .58⅜<br>.49⅜ | .71¼<br>.62 | .87⅞<br>.71⅜ | 1.08<br>.95 | .74½<br>.69¼ | .67½<br>.63⅞ | .74¾<br>.72⅛ | .76½<br>.72⅞ |
| March............ | .93⅝<br>.82 | .79⅝<br>.73⅜ | .81⅜<br>.75 | .81½<br>.72⅝ | .79⅝<br>.71¼ | 1.04⅞<br>.93⅜ | .80⅞<br>.76¼ | 1.03½<br>.99½ | .91<br>.77¼ | .79¾<br>.72¼ | .60<br>.55⅝ | .62¾<br>.51⅜ | .71<br>.59⅞ | .90¼<br>.70½ | 1.06¾<br>1.00 | .74½<br>.66 | .67<br>.64 | .76¼<br>.73¼ | .76<br>.69¼ |
| April............ | .94½<br>.76 | .91¾<br>.77½ | .80¼<br>.72⅓ | .83¼<br>.77 | .82<br>.71⅝ | .96½<br>.79⅝ | .92¼<br>.77½ | 1.16<br>1.02⅛ | .86<br>.76⅜ | .88<br>.70 | .65¼<br>.57 | .69½<br>.53½ | .71<br>.61¼ | .97<br>.64⅛ | 1.23¾<br>1.01 | .76½<br>.70 | .67¾<br>.64¾ | .74⅞<br>.69½ | .76¾<br>.70 |
| May.............. | .94¾<br>.85 | .90¾<br>.85⅜ | .79<br>.72⅓ | .88¼<br>.80¾ | .89⅞<br>.81¼ | .99¾<br>.80 | 1.00<br>.89¼ | 1.08<br>.98⅞ | .85¼<br>.82¼ | .76¼<br>.68¼ | .60¼<br>.52⅞ | .85⅜<br>.60¼ | .67⅝<br>.57⅛ | .97⅞<br>.68¾ | 1.85<br>1.17 | .79½<br>.68⅜ | .67½<br>.63⅝ | .75⅛<br>.70 | .76¼<br>.72⅜ |
| June............. | .89⅝<br>.83⅞ | .89⅞<br>.83¾ | .78<br>.70⅞ | .94¾<br>.68 | .85½<br>.78¼ | .84½<br>.78 | .93<br>.84 | 1.02<br>.90½ | .87¾<br>.78 | .69<br>.61⅛ | .63⅝<br>.53½ | .84¾<br>.68¾ | .67<br>.53⅝ | .83½<br>.67 | 1.20<br>.75 | .79¼<br>.71¼ | .87½<br>.65⅞ | .77¼<br>.65⅛ | .75¾<br>.71¼ |
| July............. | .84½<br>.79⅞ | .90<br>.85⅛ | .81<br>.73½ | .72<br>.67¾ | .85<br>.79 | .85<br>.76¼ | .94¼<br>.85 | .98<br>.85 | .80½<br>.76 | .66¼<br>.54⅜ | .60½<br>.50⅜ | .74⅞<br>.61⅜ | .62¼<br>.54¼ | .79¾<br>.68¼ | .88<br>.65¾ | .75⅜<br>.68⅝ | .81½<br>.74 | .71⅜<br>.63⅛ | .79<br>.71½ |
| August .......... | .83<br>.76¼ | .89<br>.78 | .79¼<br>.73⅞ | .69½<br>.66⅝ | .94⅜<br>.81½ | .79<br>.75¼ | 1.08¼<br>.89⅝ | 1.13<br>.86⅞ | .80<br>.74⅜ | .63¾<br>.55½ | .58½<br>.51½ | .72<br>.58¾ | .63⅝<br>.53 | 1.07<br>.75¼ | .75<br>.65½ | .74½<br>.69 | .76¼<br>.71¼ | .77<br>.66⅝ | .76<br>.68¼ |
| September ....... | .79¾<br>.73¼ | .86½<br>.76¼ | .76½<br>.72¼ | .71⅜<br>.67½ | 2.00<br>.89¾ | .83<br>.75⅝ | 1.04¾<br>.95½ | .99¼<br>.90¾ | .74⅝<br>.71⅝ | .69¾<br>.62⅜ | .56<br>.50 | .65<br>.55⅛ | .70<br>.55 | 1.01⅛<br>.85½ | .68<br>.62¼ | .75⅛<br>.69⅜ | .79⅜<br>.72½ | .71<br>.68⅛ | .95<br>.70 |
| October.... ..... | .79½<br>.72½ | .91⅝<br>.83⅞ | .74⅜<br>.69⅜ | .72¼<br>.69⅛ | 1.17¼<br>1.04½ | .82⅝<br>.77⅞ | 1.03¼<br>.96 | .99<br>.92½ | .74¾<br>.69⅛ | .66½<br>.60⅓ | .57⅜<br>.50¼ | .64⅛<br>.57½ | .81¼<br>.65½ | .99⅛<br>.87⅞ | .70¼<br>.62 | .74¾<br>.68½ | .77⅜<br>.71⅜ | .71½<br>.66¼ | .75½<br>.67½ |
| November......... | .74⅝<br>.70⅞ | .91<br>.83¼ | .76⅜<br>.73 | .76½<br>.71⅝ | 1.16<br>1.02½ | .81⅜<br>.78 | 1.01⅝<br>88¼ | .97<br>.91¼ | .73⅜<br>.69¾ | .63<br>.58¾ | .61⅝<br>.51⅜ | .62⅜<br>.55⅜ | .94⅜<br>.71 | 1.00½<br>.91 | .69½<br>.64½ | .71½<br>.65 | .74¼<br>.69⅝ | .73¾<br>.70 | .77⅜<br>.60⅞ |
| December......... | .76⅜<br>.69½ | .88⅜<br>.83⅛ | .79½<br>.75⅛ | .79¼<br>.75⅛ | 1.05½<br>.96⅝ | .80¾<br>.76¾ | .93<br>.87½ | .89⅜<br>.93½ | .73<br>.69½ | .64½<br>.59⅛ | .63⅝<br>.52⅞ | .64¾<br>.54 | .93⅜<br>.94⅝ | 1.09<br>.94 | .70<br>.63⅝ | .69½<br>.64 | .74⅝<br>.69¼ | .79½<br>.73 | .77¼<br>.71⅞ |
| Highest ......... | .96 | .91¾ | .85½ | .94¾ | 2.00 | 1.08¼ | 1.08¼ | 1.16 | .91¾ | .88 | .65¼ | .85⅜ | .94⅜ | 1.09 | 1.85 | .79½ | .87½ | .79½ | .95 |
| Lowest .......... | .69½ | .73⅜ | .69⅜ | .66⅝ | .71⅛ | .75¼ | .74¼ | .85 | .69⅛ | .54⅜ | .50 | .48¾ | .53 | .64⅛ | .62 | .64 | .61½ | .63⅛ | .67½ |

## PRICES IN CHICAGO.

CASH NO. 2 CORN. HIGHEST AND LOWEST PRICES PER BUSHEL, BY MONTHS.

| MONTH. | 1884. | 1885. | 1886. | 1887. | 1888. | 1889. | 1890. | 1891. | 1892. | 1893. | 1894. | 1895. | 1896. | 1897. | 1898. | 1899. | 1900. | 1901. | 1902. |
|---|---|---|---|---|---|---|---|---|---|---|---|---|---|---|---|---|---|---|---|
| January... | .57¾<br>.51 | .40<br>.34¼ | .37¼<br>.36 | .37⅜<br>.35⅝ | .49¾<br>.47½ | .35¼<br>.33 | .29⅛<br>.28¾ | .50<br>.47½ | .39⅛<br>.37¼ | .44¾<br>.40½ | .35¾<br>.34 | .46<br>.40 | .28¼<br>.25¼ | .23⅜<br>.21¾ | .28¼<br>.26 | .38⅛<br>.35¼ | .31⅝<br>.30½ | .37¾<br>.36 | .64½<br>.56½ |
| February.. | .55<br>.52 | .38½<br>.36 | .38¼<br>.35⅞ | .37<br>.36 | .49<br>.45⅞ | .35⅞<br>.33 | .29<br>.27½ | .54½<br>.50¼ | .41<br>.39 | .44⅜<br>.39⅝ | .35⅜<br>.34 | .43¼<br>.40½ | .29<br>.27¾ | .23¼<br>.21⅞ | .30⅝<br>.27¼ | .37<br>.33½ | .34¼<br>.31½ | .40<br>.37¾ | .61¼<br>.56⅝ |
| March .... | .54⅝<br>.49½ | .41½<br>.37 | .37½<br>.34½ | .40<br>.33½ | .52½<br>.45½ | .35⅛<br>.34 | .29⅛<br>.28 | .70<br>.54 | .41⅝<br>.37¼ | .41¾<br>.39⅞ | .37⅛<br>.34⅜ | .46<br>.42¼ | .29¾<br>.28 | .24¼<br>.22¼ | .29¼<br>.28⅛ | .36⅛<br>.33 | .38¼<br>.33⅜ | .44<br>.39 | .61⅛<br>.56 |
| April ..... | .56<br>.44¼ | .49<br>.40⅜ | .37⅝<br>.32⅞ | .38⅝<br>.37 | .56¾<br>.47½ | .35¼<br>.33½ | .33¼<br>.29⅜ | .75½<br>.65⅞ | .42¾<br>.38¼ | .42<br>.39½ | .39¼<br>.36½ | .48¼<br>.45⅞ | .30⅝<br>.28⅝ | .25¼<br>.23⅛ | .35¼<br>.28⅞ | .35½<br>.34 | .40⅞<br>.38¼ | .48<br>.41 | .64½<br>.56¼ |
| May...... | .57<br>.52½ | .49<br>.44¾ | .36¾<br>.34¼ | .39⅜<br>.36⅞ | 60<br>.55½ | .35⅞<br>.33⅞ | .35<br>.32¾ | .69½<br>.55 | 1.00<br>.40¾ | .41½<br>.39½ | .38½<br>.36¼ | .55½<br>.47¾ | .29½<br>.27 | .25½<br>.23 | .37<br>.32⅜ | .34⅜<br>.32½ | .40½<br>.36 | .58½<br>.42⅝ | .64¾<br>.59⅛ |
| June...... | .56½<br>.51¼ | .49<br>.43⅞ | .35½<br>.33⅞ | .39<br>.35⅛ | .55⅝<br>.46¼ | .35⅝<br>.33⅛ | .34½<br>.33⅜ | .62<br>.54¼ | .55¼<br>.46¾ | .42<br>.37⅛ | .42½<br>.37⅜ | .53⅛<br>.46⅞ | .28½<br>.26¼ | .25⅜<br>.23¼ | .33¾<br>.31 | .35½<br>.33¼ | .43½<br>.37⅜ | .44⅜<br>.41 | .71½<br>.61 |
| July...... | .56⅜<br>.49¼ | .48<br>.45¾ | .45<br>.34½ | .38½<br>.35⅛ | .50½<br>.45⅛ | .37⅛<br>.34¾ | .36⅝<br>.33⅞ | .66<br>.57 | .51¾<br>.47½ | .41½<br>.35⅞ | .46¼<br>.40¼ | .47½<br>.41¾ | .27¾<br>.24¼ | .28¼<br>.24⅝ | .35½<br>.31¾ | .34⅞<br>.31 | .44¾<br>.38⅜ | .58¾<br>.43½ | .88<br>.56 |
| August ... | .55¾<br>.50¼ | .47½<br>.43 | .44⅜<br>.39⅝ | .42⅛<br>.38¼ | .47¾<br>.43¼ | .36¼<br>.33¼ | .50½<br>.45½ | .67⅞<br>.58½ | .54½<br>.49⅛ | .40<br>.36⅜ | .59½<br>.46⅝ | .44½<br>.36¼ | .25<br>.20½ | .32⅝<br>.26⅛ | .33⅛<br>.29¼ | .33<br>.30½ | .41¼<br>.37¼ | .59½<br>.53¾ | .60<br>.54 |
| September | .87<br>.51¾ | .45½<br>.40⅞ | .41¼<br>.36⅛ | .43<br>.40⅜ | .45⅞<br>.40½ | .34¼<br>.33⅛ | .50⅛<br>.44⅞ | .68¼<br>.48½ | .48¾<br>.43⅜ | .42⅝<br>.37⅛ | .58<br>.48 | .36⅝<br>.31¼ | .22¼<br>.19½ | .32<br>.27¼ | .31⅜<br>.29⅝ | .35<br>.31¼ | .43¼<br>.38⅞ | .59¾<br>.54⅜ | .62½<br>.57 |
| October... | .59½<br>.41 | .44½<br>.40⅛ | .36½<br>.33⅛ | .42¾<br>.40½ | .46⅛<br>.39⅞ | .32¾<br>.30⅛ | .53¾<br>.47¾ | .58½<br>.52 | .44¼<br>.40½ | .40¾<br>.37¼ | .53¼<br>.48⅛ | .32⅛<br>.28½ | .26½<br>.22¼ | .29<br>.24 | .32⅞<br>.28¼ | .33<br>.31 | .41¾<br>.36½ | .58<br>.54⅝ | .61½<br>.55 |
| November | .45½<br>.34⅛ | .47¾<br>.39⅜ | .37⅜<br>.35 | .47⅜<br>.40⅞ | .42½<br>.35⅝ | .33¾<br>.31¾ | .53⅞<br>.49 | .71<br>.53 | .43<br>.40⅝ | .39⅜<br>.34⅞ | .53<br>.47 | .30<br>.26½ | .25½<br>.22¾ | .27⅝<br>.25¾ | .34⅜<br>.31⅝ | .33¾<br>.30¾ | .49½<br>.35 | .63⅞<br>.57⅛ | .58<br>.52 |
| December | .40¼<br>.34½ | .43⅜<br>.35⅞ | .38<br>.35¾ | .51⅛<br>.47 | .35⅞<br>.33½ | .35<br>.30 | .53<br>.47¾ | .59<br>.39⅜ | .42⅞<br>.40 | .36½<br>.34¼ | .47½<br>.44¾ | .26¾<br>.25 | .23¾<br>.22½ | .27½<br>.25 | .38¼<br>.32⅞ | .31½<br>.30 | .40½<br>.35¾ | .67½<br>.62½ | .57¾<br>.43¾ |
| Highest... | .87 | .49 | .45 | .51⅜ | .60 | .37⅛ | .53⅞ | .75½ | 1.00 | .44¾ | .59½ | .55½ | .30⅝ | .32⅜ | .38¼ | .38⅛ | .49½ | .67½ | .88 |
| Lowest.... | .34½ | .34¼ | .32⅞ | .33½ | .33½ | .30 | .27½ | .39⅜ | .37¼ | .34¼ | .34 | .25 | .19½ | .21¾ | .26 | .30 | .30½ | .36 | .43¾ |

## PRICES IN CHICAGO.

### Cash No. 2 Oats. Highest and Lowest Prices per Bushel, by Months.

| Month. | 1884. | 1885. | 1886. | 1887. | 1888. | 1889. | 1890. | 1891. | 1892. | 1893. | 1894. | 1895. | 1896. | 1897. | 1898. | 1899. | 1900. | 1901. | 1902. |
|---|---|---|---|---|---|---|---|---|---|---|---|---|---|---|---|---|---|---|---|
| January... | .33¾ | .29 | .36 | .26½ | .31¾ | .25⅛ | .21¼ | .45 | .30½ | .32 | .29½ | .30 | .19½ | .17 | .24 | .27¾ | .23 | 24½ | .46¼ |
| | .31¼ | .25½ | .28 | .25⅜ | .29 | .24⅛ | .20 | .42½ | .28 | .30 | .27 | .27¾ | .16½ | .15¾ | .21½ | .26¼ | .22½ | .23¼ | .38⅛ |
| February . | .33¼ | .29 | .30¼ | .25¾ | .30 | .25¾ | .21 | .48 | .30½ | .32 | .29 | .29 | .20½ | .16⅝ | .27 | .28¼ | .23¾ | .25½ | .44¼ |
| | .32 | .20¾ | .28⅓ | .23¼ | .27 | .25 | .19½ | .44¼ | .28½ | .29½ | .27¾ | .27½ | .19 | .15⅝ | .24 | .26¼ | .22½ | .24⅛ | .40¼ |
| March .... | .33¾ | .31 | .29½ | .24½ | .31¼ | .25¾ | .22 | .54½ | .30 | .31 | .31⅛ | .30¼ | .20¼ | .17 | .26¾ | .27¾ | .24½ | .26½ | .45½ |
| | .28¾ | .26⅛ | .20½ | .23½ | .26¾ | .24 | .20 | .47 | .27 | .28⅞ | .29 | .28½ | .18¼ | .16 | .24⅞ | .25¾ | .23 | .24¾ | .40¼ |
| April ..... | .34¼ | .36½ | .29⅝ | .28⅝ | .32¾ | .25⅛ | .25 | .57¾ | .30¼ | .29¼ | .34 | .30⅛ | .20 | .18¼ | .31⅞ | .27¾ | .25¾ | .27½ | .44½ |
| | .26⅝ | .27½ | .25½ | .23½ | .27¼ | .21½ | .22¼ | .48¾ | .28 | .26⅝ | .30¼ | .28 | .17⅝ | .16 | .25 | .26⅜ | .23 | .25½ | .41 |
| May ...... | .33¼ | .36 | .29½ | .27¼ | .37¾ | .26⅛ | .29¾ | .54¼ | .33½ | .32 | .36¼ | .31 | .19⅝ | .18¾ | .32 | .27¾ | .33¾ | .31 | .49½ |
| | .30¾ | .31⅜ | .26¼ | .25⅛ | .32¼ | .21⅝ | .24¼ | .45 | .28½ | .29 | .32¾ | .28⅛ | .17½ | .16⅞ | .26 | .24 | .21¼ | .27⅞ | .41 |
| June.. ... | .33½ | .34¾ | .28 | .26½ | .34⅛ | .24 | .29¼ | .46 | .35½ | .31 | .50 | .31½ | .18½ | .18¾ | .26½ | .26¼ | .26¼ | .2 ¾ | .48½ |
| | .30¼ | .31⅞ | .26¼ | .24½ | .30½ | .21⅝ | .26¾ | .33 | .28 | .27¾ | .34 | .24⅞ | .15¼ | .17½ | .21 | .24¼ | .21¾ | .27 | .39 |
| July...... | .28⅛ | .34 | .32 | .27 | .33¼ | .23 | .34½ | .38½ | .34¼ | .30¼ | .48 | .25¼ | .18½ | .18⅛ | .26 | .25 | .24¾ | .39 | .56 |
| | .25½ | .26 | .27 | .24 | .28¼ | .22⅛ | .27⅜ | .27¾ | .29½ | .22⅛ | .28⅜ | .22½ | .15 | .17 | .20¾ | .19⅞ | .21½ | .27½ | .30 |
| August ... | .30½ | .29 | .27⅞ | .26¼ | .31 | .21⅞ | .40¾ | .31¾ | .34¾ | .25 | .33 | .23¾ | .18½ | .20⅛ | .21½ | .22 | .22⅝ | .37½ | .31 |
| | .24⅝ | .24½ | .25⅛ | .24 | .24¼ | .19 | .33½ | .27¾ | .30½ | .22 | .28¼ | .19 | .15¾ | .16¼ | .19⅜ | .19¼ | .21 | .33½ | .25 |
| September | .26¼ | .26¾ | .25¾ | .26¾ | .24½ | .19½ | .39½ | .30 | .34½ | .29¼ | .30⅞ | .20¼ | .17¼ | .20¾ | .22⅜ | .23¼ | .22¼ | .36¾ | .27¼ |
| | .24½ | .24¼ | .24⅝ | .23¾ | .23¼ | .19 | .35 | .26½ | .31¾ | .23⅜ | .27¾ | .18¼ | .14¾ | .18⅞ | .20¼ | .21 | .21⅛ | .33⅝ | .26⅛ |
| October... | .28 | .26¼ | .26½ | .26⅛ | .25¼ | .19⅝ | .45 | .30⅛ | .32 | .28¼ | .29½ | .18¾ | .19⅜ | .19¾ | .25 | .23½ | .22⅝ | .37¾ | .30 |
| | .25⅛ | .24¾ | .24⅛ | .25 | .23⅜ | .17⅞ | .38¼ | .26¼ | .28½ | .26 | .27½ | .17¾ | .17¼ | .17¾ | .21½ | .22 | .21⅜ | .34½ | .27¼ |
| November | .26¾ | .28½ | .27 | .29½ | .27⅜ | .22 | .44½ | .34 | .32¼ | .29¼ | .29¾ | .19 | .19¾ | .22¼ | .27¾ | .24 | .22½ | .44⅛ | .29½ |
| | .25⅛ | .25¾ | .25½ | .25¼ | .24⅜ | .18½ | .41 | .30½ | .30 | .27¼ | .28½ | .18 | .17½ | .19½ | .24¼ | .22½ | .21¾ | .37⅛ | .27¾ |
| December. | .25⅜ | .29⅜ | .27¼ | .31¼ | .27 | .21 | .43½ | .33 | .31½ | .29¼ | .30¼ | .17¾ | .18¾ | .23⅞ | .29 | .23 | .22¾ | .48¼ | .32 |
| | .23 | .27 | .25¾ | .29 | .25 | .20 | .39½ | .11 | .30 | .28 | .29 | .17 | .16½ | .21 | .25½ | .22¼ | .21¾ | .42 | .29¼ |
| Highest... | .34¼ | .36½ | .36 | .31 | .37¾ | .26⅛ | .45 | .57¾ | .35½ | .32 | .50 | .31½ | .20½ | .23⅞ | .32 | .28¼ | .26¼ | .48¼ | .56 |
| Lowest... | .23 | .24¼ | .24⅛ | .23½ | .23¼ | .17⅞ | .19½ | .26½ | .30 | .22 | .27 | .17 | .14¾ | .15⅝ | .19⅜ | .19¼ | .21 | .23¼ | .25 |

## PRICES IN CHICAGO.

### Cash Mess Pork. Highest and Lowest Prices per Barrel, by Months.

| Month. | 1884. | 1885. | 1886. | 1887. | 1888. | 1889. | 1890. | 1891. | 1892. | 1893. | 1894. | 1895. | 1896. | 1897. | 1898. | 1899. | 1900. | 1901. | 1902. |
|---|---|---|---|---|---|---|---|---|---|---|---|---|---|---|---|---|---|---|---|
| Jan... | 16.35<br>14.12½ | 12.45<br>11.30 | 11.15<br>9.95 | 12.60<br>11.60 | 15.37½<br>13.75 | 13.35<br>11.47 | 10.00<br>9.10 | 10.75<br>9.50 | 11.87½<br>10.37½ | 19.87½<br>16.25 | 13.67½<br>12.52½ | 11.75<br>9.42½ | 10.85<br>8.62½ | 8.00<br>7.55 | 10.00<br>9.00 | 10.45<br>9.70 | 10.90<br>10.35 | 15.00<br>12.60 | 17.00<br>15.50 |
| Feb... | 18.37½<br>16.30 | 13.25<br>[illegible] | 11.50<br>10.50 | 17.50<br>12.37½ | 14.50<br>13.55 | 11.47<br>10.95 | 9.90<br>9.65 | 9.75<br>9.25 | 11.87½<br>11.02½ | 19.70<br>17.87½ | 12.92½<br>11.82½ | 10.37½<br>9.62½ | 10.67½<br>9.50 | 8.00<br>7.45 | 11.15<br>9.75 | 10.25<br>9.20 | 11.10<br>10.50 | 14.15<br>13.77½ | 15.85<br>15.00 |
| Mar... | 18.12½<br>17.45 | 12.75<br>11.70 | 10.65<br>9.15 | 20.75<br>18.25 | 14.10<br>13.12½ | 12.07<br>11.05 | 10.62<br>9.80 | 12.62½<br>9.60 | 11.27½<br>9.85 | 18.67½<br>16.92½ | 11.85<br>10.67½ | 12.62½<br>10.15 | 9.85<br>8.25 | 8.90<br>7.95 | 10.65<br>9.35 | 9.35<br>8.75 | 12.75<br>10.50 | 16.80<br>13.90 | 16.65<br>15.00 |
| April. | 17.55<br>16.00 | 1245<br>11.55 | 9.45<br>8.87½ | 21.00<br>20.50 | 14.30<br>13.20 | 11.77<br>11.50 | 13.62<br>10.50 | 12.90<br>12.12½ | 10.30<br>9.25 | 19.25<br>1575 | 13.30<br>11.37½ | 12.60<br>11.87½ | 8.75<br>8.05 | 8.60<br>8.05 | 11.35<br>9.55 | 9.25<br>8.90 | 13.25<br>12.45 | 15.55<br>14.10 | 16.95<br>16.35 |
| May .. | 19.50<br>17.00 | 11.70<br>10.25 | 9.10<br>8.20 | 24.00<br>20.00 | 14.50<br>13.60 | 12.65<br>11.27 | 13.37<br>11.75 | 13.00<br>10.55 | 10.85<br>9.35 | 21.80<br>18.80 | 12.52½<br>11.70 | 12.87½<br>11.75 | 8.10<br>6.95 | 8.70<br>7.95 | 12.30<br>10.75 | 8.85<br>7.85 | 12.10<br>11.20 | 15.20<br>14.45 | 17.50<br>16.75 |
| June.. | 19.50<br>16.00 | 10.65<br>10.05 | 9.80<br>8.25 | 15.00<br>14.00 | 14.15<br>13.40 | 12.17<br>11.37 | 13.25<br>12.00 | 10.62½<br>9.75 | 10.90<br>10.15 | 21.62½<br>18.75 | 12.62½<br>11.65 | 12.65<br>11.70 | 7.20<br>6.85 | 7.95<br>7.30 | 11.20<br>9.40 | 8.32½<br>7.95 | 12.85<br>11.05 | 14.90<br>14.50 | 18.45<br>17.20 |
| July.. | 18.00<br>15.50 | 10.45<br>9.75 | 10.30<br>9.37½ | 17.00<br>14.00 | 14.75<br>13.10 | 11.72<br>10.47 | 12.50<br>11.00 | 11.62½<br>10.00 | 12.20<br>11.15 | 19.77½<br>18.20 | 12.87½<br>12.37½ | 12.30<br>10.00 | 6.95<br>5.95 | 7.95<br>7.40 | 10.05<br>9.30 | 9.20<br>8.15 | 12.75<br>11.55 | 14.60<br>13.75 | 18.70<br>16.75 |
| Aug.. | 19.50<br>15.50 | 10.15<br>8.62 | 10.10<br>9.40 | 15.50<br>14.75 | 14.87½<br>13.20 | 10.72<br>9.45 | 12.00<br>10.10 | 11.40<br>9.87½ | 13.25<br>10.05 | 18.50<br>10.25 | 14.00<br>12.75 | 10.10<br>9.00 | 7.20<br>5.50 | 8.95<br>7.70 | 9.45<br>8.55 | 8.60<br>8.15 | 12.20<br>10.90 | 14.50<br>13.70 | 17.05<br>15.85 |
| Sept.. | 19.00<br>16.25 | 9.10<br>8.20 | 11.40<br>9.25 | 15.50<br>15.00 | 15.35<br>14.00 | 11.65<br>10.60 | 10.45<br>9.25 | 11.10<br>9.80 | 11.20<br>9.95 | 17.05<br>15.00 | 14.57½<br>13.00 | 9.00<br>8.00 | 6.15<br>5.52½ | 9.00<br>8.05 | 8.85<br>8.00 | 8.25<br>7.90 | 12.30<br>10.85 | 15.05<br>14.35 | 16.85<br>16.10 |
| Oct... | 16.50<br>15.50 | 8.50<br>7.95 | 9.30<br>8.50 | 14.75<br>13.00 | 16.00<br>14.50 | 11.50<br>9.60 | 10.50<br>9.55 | 10.12½<br>8.25 | 12.35<br>10.75 | 18.00<br>16.75 | 13.62½<br>11.87½ | 8.65<br>8.00 | 7.50<br>6.35 | 8.20<br>7.55 | 8.10<br>7.65 | 8.25<br>7.85 | 16.00<br>12.60 | 14.65<br>13.40 | 17.50<br>16.50 |
| Nov.. | 15.00<br>10.75 | 9.25<br>8.00 | 10.35<br>9.00 | 14.50<br>13.00 | 15.00<br>13.37½ | 10.00<br>8.90 | 10.25<br>8.62 | 8.80<br>8.20 | 13.87½<br>11.25 | 17.[illegible]<br>12.75 | 12.75<br>11.87½ | 8.37½<br>7.75 | 7.20<br>6.30 | 7.70<br>7.20 | 8.05<br>7.75 | 8.30<br>7.95 | 11.50<br>10.37½ | 15.25<br>13.75 | 17.00<br>16.50 |
| Dec .. | 11.75<br>10.55 | 9.45<br>8.75 | 12.20<br>10.40 | 15.10<br>14.00 | 13.87½<br>12.90 | 9.47<br>8.65 | 8.87<br>7.30 | 8.62½<br>7.50 | 15.05<br>13.70 | 13.25<br>12.22 | 12.37½<br>11.25 | 8.12½<br>7.50 | 7.00<br>6.50 | 8.15<br>7.15 | 9.00<br>7.90 | 9.15<br>8.00 | 11.62½<br>11.00 | 16.10<br>15.10 | 17.25<br>16.62 |
| Highest. | 19.50 | 13.25 | 12.20 | 24.00 | 16.00 | 13.35 | 13.62 | 13.00 | 15.05½ | 21.80 | 14.57½ | 12.87½ | 10.85 | 9.00 | 12.30 | 10.45 | 16.00 | 16.80 | 18.70 |
| Lowest.. | 10.55 | 7.95 | 8.20 | 11.60 | 12.90 | 8.65 | 7.50 | 8.20 | 9.35 | 10.25 | 10.67½ | 7.50 | 5.50 | 7.15 | 7.65 | 7.85 | 10.35 | 12.60 | 15.00 |

## PRICES IN CHICAGO.

### Cash Prime Steam Lard. Highest and Lowest Prices per 100 Pounds, by Months.

| Month. | 1884. | 1885. | 1886. | 1887. | 1888. | 1889. | 1890. | 1891. | 1892. | 1893. | 1894. | 1895. | 1896. | 1897. | 1898. | 1899. | 1900. | 1901. | 1902. |
|---|---|---|---|---|---|---|---|---|---|---|---|---|---|---|---|---|---|---|---|
| Jan.... | 9.17½ | 7.00 | 6.17½ | 6.62½ | 7.87½ | 7.62 | 5.97 | 6.00 | 6.50 | 11.80 | 8.35 | 6.95 | 5.85 | 4.05 | 4.87½ | 5.77½ | 6.05 | 7.50 | 10.00 |
|  | 8.60 | 6.67½ | 6.00 | 6.20 | 7.25 | 6.80 | 5.77 | 5.65 | .07½ | 10.50 | 7.50 | 6.30 | 5.25 | 3.80 | 4.62½ | 5.45 | 5.72½ | 6.90 | 9.17 |
| Feb.... | 10.00 | 7.10 | 6.15 | 7.17½ | 7.87½ | 6.95 | 5.85 | 5.80 | 6.57½ | 12.90 | 7.65 | 6.70 | 5.80 | 4.10 | 5.27½ | 5.67½ | 6.07½ | 7.52½ | 9.40 |
|  | 9.00 | 6.75 | 5.92½ | 6.35 | 7.52½ | 6.50 | 5.70 | 5.47½ | 6.35 | 11.20 | 7.20 | 6.30 | 5.25 | 3.67½ | 4.72½ | 5.15 | 5.65 | 7.37½ | 9.07 |
| March.. | 9.62½ | 6.97½ | 6.05 | 7.85 | 7.75 | 7.05 | 6.20 | 6.87½ | 6.47½ | 13.20 | 7.35 | 7.17½ | 5.40 | 4.25 | 5.22½ | 5.35 | 6.55 | 8.35 | 9.75 |
|  | 9.15 | 6.72½ | 5.77½ | 6.95 | 7.45 | 6.65 | 5.82 | 5.52½ | 6.15 | 10.42½ | 6.45 | 6.37½ | 5.00 | 3.95 | 4.87½ | 5.15 | 5.70 | 7.35 | 9.12 |
| April... | 9.20 | 7.10 | 5.97½ | 7.47½ | 8.17½ | 6.95 | 6.52 | 6.90 | 6.27½ | 10.55 | 8.02½ | 7.05 | 5.07½ | 4.25 | 5.85 | 5.30 | 7.35 | 8.62½ | 10.07 |
|  | 8.15 | 6.72½ | 5.85 | 6.85 | 7.47½ | 6.70 | 6.07 | 6.45 | 6.12½ | 9.40 | 6.77½ | 6.70 | 4.67½ | 4.05 | 5.00 | 5.12½ | 6.45 | 8.10 | 9.45 |
| May ... | 8.60 | 6.87½ | 5.97½ | 6.92½ | 8.70 | 7.02 | 6.40 | 6.75 | 6.42½ | 10.97½ | 7.52½ | 6.75 | 4.80 | 4.12½ | 6.82½ | 5.20 | 7.07½ | 8.27½ | 10.42 |
|  | 7.85 | 6.40 | 5.82½ | 6.37½ | 7.92½ | 6.75 | 6.00 | 6.20 | 6.12½ | 6.95 | 6.70 | 6.50 | 4.10 | 3.55 | 5.75 | 4.90 | 6.72½ | 7.85 | 10.05 |
| June... | 8.20 | 6.67½ | 6.50 | 6.70 | 8.65 | 6.97 | 5.97 | 6.30 | 6.95 | 10.35 | 6.82½ | 6.62½ | 4.27½ | 4.15 | 6.25 | 5.10 | 7.07½ | 8.85 | 10.62 |
|  | 7.07½ | 6.35 | 5.87½ | 6.20 | 8.02½ | 6.65 | 5.62 | 5.95 | 6.30 | 9.35 | 6.57½ | 6.42½ | 3.85 | 3.42½ | 5.32½ | 4.90 | 6.47½ | 8.15 | 10.12 |
| July... | 7.52½ | 6.67½ | 6.90 | 6.70 | 9.00 | 6.47 | 6.15 | 6.75 | 7.35 | 10.20 | 7.00 | 6.55 | 3.92½ | 4.30 | 5.62½ | 5.52½ | 6.90 | 8.70 | 11.42 |
|  | 6.95 | 6.42½ | 6.37½ | 6.37½ | 7.95 | 6.02 | 5.62 | 6.07½ | 6.90 | 9.20 | 6.67½ | 6.12½ | 3.05 | 3.80 | 5.22½ | 5.05 | 6.60 | 8.40 | 10.40 |
| Aug... | 8.00 | 6.55 | 7.45 | 6.60 | 9.52½ | 6.40 | 6.27 | 6.65 | 8.15 | 9.50 | 8.37½ | 6.25 | 3.50 | 4.85 | 5.47½ | 5.45 | 6.90 | 8.97½ | 10.87 |
|  | 7.30 | 6.10 | 6.87½ | 6.35 | 8.60 | 5.90 | 5.97 | 6.40 | 7.27½ | 6.00 | 6.90 | 5.80 | 3.10 | 4.00 | 5.05 | 5.15 | 6.60 | 8.55 | 10.00 |
| Sept... | 7.65 | 6.30 | 7.50 | 6.62½ | 10.92½ | 6.15 | 6.30 | 7.05 | 8.05 | 10.00 | 9.05 | 5.97½ | 3.82½ | 4.90 | 5.05 | 5.52½ | 7.20 | 10.25 | 11.60 |
|  | 7.00 | 6.00 | 5.95 | 6.27½ | 9.52½ | 5.87 | 6.00 | 6.57½ | 7.20 | 7.95 | 8.25 | 5.72½ | 3.17½ | 4.35 | 4.72½ | 5.17½ | 6.67½ | 8.95 | 10.35 |
| Oct.... | 7.75 | 6.15 | 6.10 | 6.60 | 11.20 | 6.85 | 6.45 | 6.82½ | 8.90 | 10.50 | 8.52½ | 5.90 | 4.55 | 4.52½ | 5.15 | 5.60 | 7.40 | 9.97½ | 11.42 |
|  | 6.90 | 5.82½ | 5.57½ | 6.20 | 8.12½ | 5.17 | 6.15 | 5.85 | 8.10 | 9.30 | 6.85 | 5.45 | 3.85 | 4.15 | 4.62½ | 5.20 | 6.77½ | 8.60 | 10.15 |
| Nov.... | 7.25 | 6.27½ | 6.07½ | 7.20 | 8.55 | 6.10 | 6.32 | 6.32½ | 10.50 | 10.00 | 7.35 | 5.62½ | 4.30 | 4.32½ | 5.12½ | 5.20 | 7.25 | 9.60 | 11.25 |
|  | 6.77½ | 5.85 | 5.87½ | 6.30 | 8.42½ | 5.82 | 5.70 | 5.85 | 8.35 | 8.07½ | 6.80 | 5.37½ | 3.70 | 4.15 | 4.80 | 4.95 | 6.85 | 8.47½ | 10.37 |
| Dec.... | 6.95 | 6.05 | 6.60 | 7.92½ | 8.42½ | 5.97 | 5.92 | 6.17½ | 10.60 | 8.42 | 7.05 | 5.37½ | 3.95 | 4.75 | 5.62 | 5.67½ | 7.22½ | 10.15 | 11.00 |
|  | 6.45 | 5.90 | 6.02½ | 7.12½ | 7.60 | 5.77 | 5.50 | 6.07½ | 9.25 | 7.60 | 6.62½ | 5.15 | 3.70 | 4.15 | 4.40 | 5.05 | 6.75 | 9.37½ | 10.00 |
| Highest.. | 10.00 | 7.10 | 7.50 | 7.85 | 11.20 | 7.62 | 6.52 | 7.05 | 10.60 | 13.20 | 9.05 | 1.17½ | 5.85 | 4.90 | 6.82½ | 5.77½ | 7.40 | 10 25 | 11.60 |
| Lowest... | 6.45 | 5.82½ | 5.57½ | 6.20 | 7.25 | 5.17 | 5.50 | 5.47 | 6.07½ | 6.00 | 6.45 | 5.15 | 3.05 | 3.42½ | 4.40 | 4.90 | 5.65 | 6.90 | 9.07 |

# NEW YORK PRODUCE MARKET

## QUOTATIONS ON THE NEW YORK PRODUCE EXCHANGE.

### AVERAGE PRICES, BY MONTHS, OF NO. 2 RED WINTER WHEAT F. O. B. AND AFLOAT.

| | 1897. | 1898. | 1899. | 1900. | 1901. | 1902. |
|---|---|---|---|---|---|---|
| January | 1.02⅜ | 1.03 5-16 | 81⅝ | 75⅜ | 81 7-16 | 90 1-16 |
| February | 97 5-16 | 1.05 7-16 | 84⅝ | 77 13-16 | 81⅝ | 89 13-16 |
| March | 96 | 1.05 1-16 | 82¾ | 78 11-16 | 81 | 87⅛ |
| April | 96 13-16 | 1.10 3-16 | 82½ | 79 11-16 | 80⅝ | 87 3-16 |
| May | 96¼ | 1.54¼ | 83 5-16 | 80⅛ | 82⅞ | 90¾ |
| June | 84 15-16 | 99 3-16 | 82 13-16 | 86⅜ | 79 5-16 | 89⅞ |
| July | 82 13-16 | 85 15-16 | 78 7-16 | 85⅝ | 76 1-16 | 84¾ |
| August | 93 7-16 | 77 3-16 | 76⅝ | 81 5-16 | 77¾ | 76 11-16 |
| September | 99¼ | 73¼ | 75¼ | 82⅛ | 76¼ | 75⅝ |
| October | 98⅜ | 75 5-16 | 76⅜ | 79 13-16 | 77⅜ | 76 7-16 |
| November | 98 3-16 | 76 5-16 | 73⅝ | 79 | 82 9-16 | 77 3-16 |
| December | 98 15-16 | 77⅜ | 74 3-16 | 78⅝ | 87 1-16 | 78⅞ |
| **Annual average** | **95 6-16** | **95 3-16** | 79⅜ | 80⅜ | 80¼ | 83⅝ |
| Range for year: | | | | | | |
| Highest | $1.07¾ | $1.93½ | 87½ | 96⅞ | 89⅜ | 94½ |
| Lowest | 77¾ | 68¾ | 72¼ | 72⅞ | 71⅞ | 73½ |

### AVERAGE PRICES, BY MONTHS, OF NO. 2 MIXED CORN IN STORE AND ELEVATOR AT NEW YORK.

| | 1897. | 1898. | 1899. | 1900. | 1901. | 1902. |
|---|---|---|---|---|---|---|
| January | 30 | 33 5-16 | 42¼ | 40 3-16 | 47 1-16 | 69 |
| February | 29 13-16 | 35⅝ | 43¼ | 41½ | 48 5-16 | 68 3-16 |
| March | 30¼ | 35¼ | 43 | 43 9-16 | 48⅞ | 68¾ |
| April | 30⅞ | 36⅜ | 42 13-16 | 46 13-16 | 50 11-16 | 68¾ |
| May | 30¾ | 39½ | 40 15-16 | 43 1-16 | 51⅝ | 70 |
| June | 30¼ | 36¼ | 40¼ | 45⅝ | 47⅞ | 69⅛ |
| July | 32 13-16 | 36 13-16 | 38 3-16 | 47⅛ | 54⅞ | 69⅞ |
| August | 34¼ | 36½ | 37½ | 44 11-16 | 61 7-16 | 65¾ |
| September | 35⅞ | 34⅝ | 38⅞ | 47¼ | 63⅝ | 70½ |
| October | 32 1-16 | 36⅝ | 40 5-16 | 45 7-16 | 62 | 68 3-16 |
| November | 32⅞ | 38 5-16 | 39 9-16 | 46 | 67 1-16 | 65 |
| December | 33 9-16 | 40½ | 39 7-16 | 45 15-16 | 71 1-16 | 63⅜ |
| Annual average | 31 15-16 | 36¾ | 40⅝ | 44 11-16 | 56 3-16 | 67 15-16 |
| Range for year: | | | | | | |
| Highest | 39 | 43⅝ | 45⅝ | 51⅛ | 74 | 75 |
| Lowest | 28½ | 33 | 35⅝ | 39½ | 45¾ | 58½ |

AVERAGE PRICES, BY MONTHS, OF NO. 2 MIXED OATS IN STORE AND ELEVATOR AT NEW YORK.

| | 1897. | 1898. | 1899. | 1900. | 1901. | 1902. |
|---|---|---|---|---|---|---|
| January | 23⅜ | 28 11-16 | 34 | 29 5-16 | 30⅛ | 50 15-16 |
| February | 22⅝ | 30 11-16 | 35 1-16 | 28 13-16 | 30⅝ | 49¼ |
| March | 22 15-16 | 31 | 33¼ | 28 9-16 | 30 13-16 | 49⅝ |
| April | 23½ | 31 7-16 | 32 15-16 | 28 7-16 | 31 1-16 | 47⅞ |
| May | 23 11-16 | 31 9-16 | 31⅝ | 27 15-16 | 33 3-16 | 46 15-16 |
| June | 22 15-16 | 29⅞ | 30 13-16 | 27⅝ | 32 7-16 | 47½ |
| July | 23 | 27⅜ | 29¼ | 28¼ | 37 | 59 |
| August | 23⅞ | 27 9-16 | 26 11-16 | 25⅞ | 38 15-16 | 48⅞ |
| September | 25⅜ | 25 7-16 | 27 | 25½ | 38 7-16 | 33⅛ |
| October | 24 11-16 | 27 13-16 | 28 13-16 | 25⅜ | 39 13-16 | 33 9-16 |
| November | 26 7-16 | 29¾ | 29¾ | 26 | 45 11-16 | 35 |
| December | 28½ | 32⅜ | 29⅜ | 27 5-16 | 51¼ | 37¼ |
| Annual average | 24 13-16 | 29 11-16 | 30 11-16 | 27 5-16 | 36⅝ | 44⅞ |
| Range for year: | | | | | | |
| Highest | 29¼ | .... | 35½ | 30 | 52½ | 65 |
| Lowest | 21¼ | .... | 25¼ | 25 | 28¼ | 32 |

AVERAGE PRICES, BY MONTHS, OF PORK, LARD AND TALLOW AT NEW YORK.

| | Mess Pork, Old or New, per Bbl. | | Western, Steam Lard, per Lb. | | Tallow, Prime, per Lb. | |
|---|---|---|---|---|---|---|
| | 1901. | 1902. | 1901. | 1902. | 1901. | 1902. |
| January | $13.85 | $16.85 | 7.65c | 9.91c | 5 1-16c | 6⅛c |
| February | 14.20 | 16.42½ | 7.78 | 9.67½ | 4⅞ | 6 3-16 |
| March | 15.25 | 16.13 | 8.08 | 9.80 | 4¾ | 6¼ |
| April | 15.65 | 17.10 | 8.67 | 10.12½ | 4 15-16 | 6 7-16 |
| May | 15.62½ | 18.17 | 8.38 | 10.57 | 4 13-16 | 6 13-16 |
| June | 16.10 | 18.93 | 8.81 | 10.72 | 4⅞ | 6¼ |
| July | 15.87½ | 19.39 | 8.86 | 11.25 | 4 13-16 | 6⅝ |
| August | 15.95 | 18.54 | 9.08 | 10.87½ | 4 15-16 | 6 7-16 |
| September | 16.25 | 18.55 | 10.08 | 10.96 | 5 11-16 | 6 |
| October | 16.05 | 18.62 | 9.76 | 11.11 | 5 11-16 | 6 7-16 |
| November | 15.75 | 18.29 | 9.10 | 11.19 | 5 13-16 | 6¼ |
| December | 16.85 | 18.27 | 10.15 | 10.91 | 6 | 5 15-16 |
| Average for year: | | | | | | |
| 1902 | 17.94 | | 10.59 | | 6 5-16 | |
| 1901 | 15.62 | | 8.87 | | 5 1-5 | |
| 1900 | 12.51 | | 7.75 | | 4⅞ | |
| 1899 | 9.35 | | 5.57 | | 4 9-16 | |
| 1898 | 9.82 | | 5.53 | | 3 9-16 | |
| 1897 | 7.71 | | 4.42 | | 3 5-16 | |
| 1896 | 8.95 | | 4.67 | | 3 7-16 | |
| 1895 | 11.91 | | 6½ | | 4 5-16 | |
| 1894 | 14.13 | | 7.75 | | 4 13-16 | |
| 1893 | 18.35 | | 10.34 | | 5 7-16 | |
| 1892 | 11.52 | | 7.11-16 | | 4⅝ | |
| 1891 | 11.38 | | 6.59 | | 4 13-16 | |
| 1890 | 12.13 | | 6.33 | | 4 19-32 | |
| 1889 | 12.57½ | | 6.87 3-16 | | 4 11-16 | |
| 1888 | 15.10 | | 8.72 | | 4 15-16 | |
| 1887 | 15.02 | | 7.09 | | 4 1-16 | |

# ACREAGE AND CEREAL PRODUCTION

## Acreage Devoted to Cereal Crops in the United States.

Estimates of the United States Department of Agriculture.

| Years. | Wheat Acres. | Corn, Acres. | Oats, Acres. | Rye, Acres. | Barley, Acres. | B'kwheat, Acres. | Totals, Acres. |
|---|---|---|---|---|---|---|---|
| 1877.. | 27,277,546 | 50,369,133 | 12,826,148 | 1,413,852 | 1,614,654 | 649,923 | 93,150,256 |
| 1878.. | 32,108,560 | 51,585,000 | 13,176,500 | 1,622,700 | 1,790,400 | 673,580 | 100,956,260 |
| 1879.. | 35,430,052 | 62,368,869 | 16,144,593 | 1,842,303 | 1,997,717 | 848,389 | 118,631,923 |
| 1880.. | 37,986,717 | 62,317,842 | 16,187,977 | 1,767,611 | 1,843,329 | 822,802 | 120,926,284 |
| 1881.. | 37,709,020 | 64,262,025 | 16,831,000 | 1,789,100 | 1,967,510 | 828,815 | 123,387,470 |
| 1882.. | 37,067,194 | 65,659,546 | 18,494,691 | 2,227,889 | 2,272,103 | 847,112 | 126,568,535 |
| 1883.. | 36,455,593 | 68,301,889 | 20,324,962 | 2,214,754 | 2,379,009 | 857,349 | 130,633,556 |
| 1884.. | 39,475,885 | 69,683,780 | 21,300,917 | 2,343,963 | 2,608,818 | 879,403 | 136,292,766 |
| 1885.. | 34,189,246 | 73,130,150 | 22,783,630 | 2,129,301 | 2,729,329 | 914,934 | 135,876,590 |
| 1886.. | 36,806,184 | 75,630,150 | 23,658,474 | 2,129,918 | 2,652,957 | 917,915 | 141,795,598 |
| 1887.. | 37,641,783 | 72,392,720 | 25,920,906 | 2,053,447 | 2,901,953 | 910,506 | 141,821,315 |
| 1888.. | 37,336,138 | 75,672,763 | 26,998,282 | 2,364,805 | 2,996,382 | 912,630 | 146,281,000 |
| 1889.. | 38,123,859 | 78,319,651 | 27,462,316 | ....... | ....... | ...... | ......... |
| 1890.. | 36,087,000 | 71,970,763 | 26,431,369 | ....... | ....... | ...... | ......... |
| 1891.. | 39,918,897 | 75,204,515 | 25,581,861 | ....... | ....... | ...... | ......... |
| 1892.. | 38,554,430 | 70,626,658 | 27,063,835 | ....... | ....... | ...... | ......... |
| 1893.. | 34,629,418 | 72,036,465 | 27,273,033 | 2,038,485 | 3,220,371 | 815,614 | 140,013,386 |
| 1894.. | 34,882,436 | 62,582,000 | 27,023,553 | 1,944,780 | 3,170,602 | 789,232 | 130,392,603 |
| 1895.. | 34,047,000 | 82,075,000 | 27,878,300 | 1,890,600 | 3,299,400 | 763,000 | 149,953,300 |
| 1896.. | 34,619,000 | 81,627,000 | 27,566,000 | 1,831,000 | 2,951,000 | 755,000 | 149,349,000 |
| 1897.. | 39,465,066 | 80,095,101 | 25,730,375 | 1,703,561 | 2,719,116 | 717,836 | 150,431,035 |
| 1898.. | 44,055,000 | 77,721,000 | 25,777,000 | 1,643,207 | 2,583,125 | 678,332 | 152,457,000 |
| 1899.. | 44,592,516 | 82,108,587 | 26,341,380 | 1,659,308 | 3,381,563 | 670,148 | 158,753,502 |
| 1900.. | 42,495,383 | 83,320,872 | 27,364,995 | 1,591,326 | 2,894,282 | 637,930 | 158,304,588 |
| 1901.. | 45,267,000 | 82,821,000 | 26,325,000 | 1,561,000 | 2,863,000 | 681,000 | 159,518,000 |
| 1902.. | 46,202,424 | 94,043,613 | 23,653,144 | 1,978,548 | 4,661,063 | 804,889 | 171,343,681 |

## Cereal Production of the United States.

| Years. | Wheat, Bus. | Corn, Bus. | Oats, Bus. | Rye, Bus. | Barley, Bus. | B'kwheat, Bus. | Totals, Bus. |
|---|---|---|---|---|---|---|---|
| 1877.. | 364,194,147 | 1,342,558,000 | 406,394,000 | 21,169,500 | 34,441,400 | 10,177,000 | 2,278,934,046 |
| 1878.. | 420,122,400 | 1,388,218,750 | 413,578,560 | 25,842,790 | 42,245,630 | 12,246,820 | 2,302,254,950 |
| 1879.. | 459,591,093 | 1,772,909,846 | 407,970,712 | 19,863,632 | 44,149,479 | 11,851,738 | 2,716,336,500 |
| 1880.. | 498,549,868 | 1,717,434,543 | 417,885,380 | 24,540,829 | 45,165,346 | 14,617,535 | 2,718,193,501 |
| 1881.. | 380,280,000 | 1,194,916,000 | 416,481,000 | 20,704,950 | 41,161,330 | 9,486,200 | 2,063,029,570 |
| 1882.. | 504,185,470 | 1,617,025,100 | 488,250,610 | 29,960,037 | 40,953,926 | 11,019,353 | 2,699,394,496 |
| 1883.. | 421,086,160 | 1,551,066,895 | 571,302,402 | 28,058,583 | 50,137,097 | 7,668,954 | 2,629,319,089 |
| 1884.. | 512,763,900 | 1,795,528,432 | 583,628,000 | 28,637,594 | 61,206,652 | 11,116,922 | 2,992,881,500 |
| 1885.. | 357,112,000 | 1,936,176,000 | 629,409,000 | 21,756,000 | 58,360,000 | 12,626,000 | 3,015,439,000 |
| 1886.. | 457,218,000 | 1,665,441,000 | 624,134,000 | 24,489,000 | 59,428,000 | 11,869,000 | 2,842,579,000 |
| 1887.. | 456,329,000 | 1,456,161,000 | 659,618,000 | 24,000,000 | 55,000,000 | 10,844,000 | 2,660,457,000 |
| 1888.. | 415,868,000 | 1,987,790,000 | 701,735,000 | 28,415,000 | 63,884,000 | 12,050,000 | 3,209,742,000 |
| 1889.. | 490,560,000 | 2,112,892,000 | 751,515,000 | .......... | .......... | .......... | .......... |
| 1890.. | 402,050,000 | 1,568,874,000 | 536,685,000 | .......... | .......... | .......... | .......... |
| 1891.. | 611,780,000 | 2,060,164,000 | 738,394,000 | .......... | .......... | .......... | .......... |
| 1892.. | 515,949,000 | 1,628,464,000 | 661,035,000 | .......... | .......... | .......... | .......... |
| 1893.. | 396,131,725 | 1,619,496,131 | 638,854,850 | 26,555,446 | 69,869,495 | 12,132,311 | 2,763,039,958 |
| 1894.. | 460,267,416 | 1,212,770,000 | 662,086,928 | 26,727,615 | 61,400,463 | 12,668,200 | 2,435,920,622 |
| 1895.. | 467,103,000 | 2,151,139,000 | 824,444,000 | 27,210,000 | 87,573,000 | 15,341,000 | 3,572,610,000 |
| 1896.. | 427,684,000 | 2,283,875,000 | 707,346,000 | 24,369,000 | 69,695,000 | 14,090,000 | 3,527,059,068 |
| 1897.. | 530,149,168 | 1,902,967,933 | 698,767,809 | 27,363,324 | 66,685,127 | 14,997,451 | 3,240,930,812 |
| 1898.. | 675,148,705 | 1,924,184,660 | 730,905,643 | 25,657,522 | 55,792,257 | 11,721,927 | 3,423,410,714 |
| 1899.. | 547,303,486 | 2,078,143,933 | 796,177,713 | 23,961,741 | 71,900,000 | 11,094,473 | 3,528,581,706 |
| 1900.. | 522,229,505 | 2,105,102,516 | 800,125,989 | 23,995,927 | 58,925,833 | 9,567,000 | 3,528,946,770 |
| 1901.. | 675,000,000 | 1,359,000,000 | 763,000,000 | 23,598,000 | 70,491,889 | 12,852,000 | 2,903,941,889 |
| 1902.. | 670,063,008 | 2,523,648,312 | 987,842,712 | 33,630,592 | 134,954,023 | 14,529,770 | 4,364,668,417 |

# *WHEAT CROPS OF THE UNITED STATES*

REPORTED BY THE STATISTICIAN OF THE DEPARTMENT OF AGRICULTURE, BY STATES.

| | 1897. | 1898. | 1899. | 1900. | 1901. | 1902. |
|---|---|---|---|---|---|---|
| Ohio | 38,049,133 | 42,103,173 | 39,998,006 | 8,523,876 | 33,532,551 | 36,333,379 |
| Michigan | 23,700,144 | 34,061,851 | 13,335,193 | 9,271,764 | 13,702,939 | 18,693,218 |
| Indiana | 32,675,201 | 38,426,029 | 25,361,178 | 6,411,702 | 31,932,890 | 35,484,448 |
| Illinois | 11,578,003 | 19,334,348 | 12,665,410 | 17,982,068 | 30,052,053 | 32,601,932 |
| **Missouri** | 14,104,458 | 14,104,454 | 11,398,702 | 18,846,713 | 31,137,097 | 56,266,494 |
| Kansas | 47,998,152 | 64,939,412 | 36,468,044 | 82,488,655 | 99,079,304 | 45,827,495 |
| Kentucky | 12,283,343 | 14,465,436 | 8,201,575 | 12,442,846 | 11,611,196 | 7,511,536 |
| Tennessee | 10,052,448 | 13,980,080 | 8,292,727 | 11,696,088 | 13,094,363 | 6,050,743 |
| New York | 7,374,611 | 8,036,263 | 7,005,765 | 6,496,166 | 7,831,481 | 8,033,693 |
| New Jersey | 2,154,584 | 2,168,318 | 1,788,865 | 2,344,582 | 2,062,049 | 1,696,064 |
| Pennsylvania | 28,259,611 | 26,609,940 | 20,472,923 | 20,281,334 | 28,660,797 | 24,628,171 |
| Delaware | 1,229,520 | 988,762 | 932,557 | 1,479,139 | 2,096,586 | 1,792,890 |
| Maryland | 12,277,056 | 11,739,935 | 10,710,966 | 15,187,848 | 13,315,139 | 11,129,223 |
| Virginia | 8,451,864 | 10,626,112 | 6,330,450 | 9,421,932 | 9,080,192 | 3,635,494 |
| N. Carolina | 4,169,680 | 5,274,645 | 3,495,598 | 5,960,803 | 6,762,118 | 3,055,757 |
| S. Carolina | 757,726 | 1,181,709 | 963,762 | 2,142,828 | 2,280,608 | 1,498,969 |
| Georgia | 1,633,946 | 2,607,360 | 2,021,225 | 5,011,133 | 3,042,167 | 1,707,186 |
| Alabama | 302,860 | 519,708 | 431,186 | 916,351 | 1,155,256 | 632,916 |
| Mississippi | 12,370 | 30,094 | 25,010 | 40,781 | 38,623 | 27,904 |
| Texas | 7,028,251 | 9,348,464 | 9,044,635 | 23,395,913 | 6,062,021 | 8,633,277 |
| Arkansas | 1,783,120 | 2,335,036 | 1,953,361 | 2,689,418 | 3,126,860 | 2,245,889 |
| W. Virginia | 5,883,431 | 5,816,700 | 3,880,751 | 4,452,895 | 4,534,444 | 2,743,233 |
| California | 32,394,020 | 12,224,403 | 33,743,909 | 28,543,628 | 34,743,111 | 22,374,201 |
| Oregon | 18,155,031 | 24,708,260 | 21,949,536 | 16,198,012 | 17,158,065 | 15,512,460 |
| Oklahoma | 10,389,542 | 14,176,799 | 16,202,765 | 18,657,373 | 20,558,761 | 12,073,992 |
| **Indian Territory** | .......... | .......... | .......... | .......... | 2,424,469 | 2,481,574 |
| Winter | 332,698,105 | 379,807,291 | 296,674,096 | 330,883,848 | 429,675,140 | 362,672,138 |
| Minnesota | 59,891,104 | 78,417,912 | 68,223,581 | 51,509,252 | 80,102,627 | 79,752,404 |
| Wisconsin | 7,690,775 | 13,689,972 | 11,773,382 | 13,166,599 | 7,576,874 | 9,655,094 |
| Iowa | 13,153,114 | 22,189,624 | 18,195,489 | 21,798,223 | 21,048,101 | 14,869,245 |
| Nebraska | 27,452,647 | 34,679,309 | 20,791,776 | 24,801,900 | 42,006,885 | 52,726,451 |
| N. Dakota | 28,353,552 | 55,654,445 | 51,758,630 | 13,176,213 | 59,310,669 | 62,872,244 |
| S. Dakota | 21,441,248 | 42,040,923 | 37,728,339 | 20,149,684 | 51,662,307 | 43,973,033 |
| Colorado | 5,117,544 | 6,729,565 | 7,337,781 | 7,207,117 | 7,531,756 | 5,287,860 |
| Washington | 20,124,648 | 23,453,043 | 21,710,394 | 25,096,661 | 34,518,968 | 23,672,187 |
| Nevada | 833,441 | 1,064,271 | 687,006 | 991,196 | 488,195 | 537,637 |
| Idaho | 2,707,672 | 4,196,904 | 3,440,103 | 3,104,629 | 6,241,216 | 6,021,946 |
| Montana | 2,268,240 | 2,100,046 | 1,792,935 | 1,929,963 | 2,353,386 | 2,355,158 |
| New Mexico | 4,282,848 | 4,586,926 | 2,579,855 | 3,847,347 | 952,342 | 780,170 |
| Utah | 3,190,740 | 5,105,184 | 3,73[illegible],451 | 3,697,106 | 3,698,876 | 3,748,669 |
| Arizona | 370,782 | 770,532 | .......... | 365,657 | 567,825 | 350,700 |
| Wyoming | 477,075 | 524,623 | .......... | 366,414 | 515,162 | 543,555 |
| Maine | 24,651 | 35,256 | .......... | 40,755 | 177,314 | 212,000 |
| **New Hampshire** | 8,176 | 9,804 | 8,789 | 8,085 | .......... | .......... |
| Vermont | 59,806 | 87,075 | 78,320 | 81,992 | 32,573 | 32,430 |
| **Connecticut** | 3,000 | 6,000 | 5,490 | 6,864 | .......... | .......... |
| Spring | 197,451,063 | 295,341,414 | 250,629,750 | 191,345,657 | 318,785,008 | 307,390,870 |
| Total crop—bshls | 530,149,168 | 675,148,705 | 547,303,846 | 522,219,505 | 748,460,218 | 670,063,008 |
| Commercial Est. | 590,000,000 | 710,000,000 | 570,000,000 | 540,000,000 | 750,000,000 | 675,000,000 |
| Total area, acres | 39,465,066 | 44,055,278 | 44,592,516 | 42,495,385 | 49,895,514 | 46,202,024 |
| Yield per acre | 13.4 | 15.3 | 12.3 | 12.29 | 15.0 | 14.5 |
| Average price | 80.8 | 58.2 | 58.4 | 62.0 | 62.4 | 63.0 |
| Value | $428,547,121 | $392,770,320 | $319,545,259 | $323,515,177 | $466,039,176 | $422,224,117 |

# CORN CROPS OF THE UNITED STATES

REPORTED BY THE STATISTICIAN OF THE DEPARTMENT OF AGRICULTURE, BY STATES.

| STATES. | 1897. | 1898. | 1899. | 1900. | 1901. | 1902. |
|---|---|---|---|---|---|---|
| Maine ........ | 295,000 | 435,720 | 427,428 | 440,244 | 522,720 | 305,167 |
| New Hamp'ire | 713,000 | 976,743 | 975,546 | 934,768 | 1,025,294 | 670,131 |
| Vermont...... | 1,485,000 | 1,984,106 | 1,710,936 | 1,939,080 | 2,285,880 | 1,258,252 |
| Massachusetts. | 1,268,000 | 1,563,640 | 1,449,504 | 1,545,346 | 1,766,488 | 1,460,771 |
| Rhode Island. | 248,000 | 262,820 | 251,596 | 262,304 | 903,987 | 293,145 |
| Connecticut... | 1,417,000 | 1,657,785 | 1,799,811 | 1,771,180 | 1,911,156 | 1,651,671 |
| New York.... | 16,088,000 | 15,671,535 | 15,605,059 | 17,236,032 | 20,672,421 | 16,130,750 |
| New Jersey... | 8,835,000 | 9,334,841 | 9,937,824 | 8,493,012 | 10,288,790 | 10,100,565 |
| Pennsylvania.. | 44,856,000 | 45,190,135 | 40,255,872 | 32,707,900 | 51,003,330 | 53,658,426 |
| Delaware..... | 5,900,000 | 5,219,600 | 4,547,312 | 5,010,312 | 5,558,430 | 5,239,752 |
| Maryland..... | 20,361,000 | 18,163,985 | 18,562,432 | 15,232,802 | 21,298,187 | 20,379,017 |
| Virginia....... | 31,554,000 | 38,756,564 | 34,880,900 | 28,183,760 | 40,903,456 | 41,345,656 |
| N. Carolina .. | 32,535,000 | 34,070,400 | 31,953,168 | 29,790,180 | 30,641,688 | 37,622,880 |
| S. Carolina... | 17,010,000 | 17,519,070 | 16,713,189 | 13,129,137 | 11,885,167 | 18,988,705 |
| Georgia .. ... | 36,663,000 | 26,586,648 | 32,494,790 | 34,119,530 | 37,857,580 | 35,093,979 |
| Florida....... | 4,998,000 | 4,244,472 | 5,093,370 | 4,156,192 | 5,213,079 | 5,180,640 |
| Alabama...... | 30,528,000 | 39,681,630 | 33,015,120 | 29,355,942 | 27,903,161 | 23,223,623 |
| Mississippi.... | 30,348,000 | 39,931,074 | 39,043,712 | 25,231,998 | 22,473,120 | 24,658,588 |
| Louisiana..... | 22,208,000 | 23,758,470 | 25,896,726 | 24,702,598 | 18,035,392 | 16,784,762 |
| Texas ........ | 72,150,000 | 105,336,700 | 81,151,398 | 81,962,910 | 60,050,996 | 44,867,415 |
| Arkansas..... | 35,584,000 | 45,365,220 | 48,087,140 | 45,225,947 | 18,702,122 | 50,655,042 |
| Tennessee .... | 63,672,000 | 76,467,742 | 59,997,760 | 56,997,880 | 45,129,588 | 73,081,329 |
| West Virginia. | 17,003,000 | 20,328,826 | 18,043,584 | 19,299,708 | 17,118,647 | 20,512,616 |
| Kentucky..... | 64,492,000 | 85,177,243 | 55,392,687 | 69,267,221 | 49,575,178 | 90,093,357 |
| Ohio ......... | 92,170,000 | 102,828,439 | 99,048,816 | 106,890,188 | 80,313,302 | 121,608,512 |
| Michigan ..... | 30,721,000 | 33,340,604 | 20,746,350 | 38,888,460 | 45,536,550 | 35,193,814 |
| Indiana ...... | 102,508,000 | 129,154,572 | 141,852,594 | 153,200,800 | 87,753,541 | 171,332,142 |
| Illinois ....... | 225,761,000 | 199,959,810 | 247,150,332 | 264,176,226 | 198,025,713 | 372,436,416 |
| Wisconsin .... | 34,680,000 | 35,327,425 | 41,686,365 | 49,547,240 | 40,021,152 | 42,425,349 |
| Minnesota .... | 24,850,000 | 30,532,000 | 31,171,272 | 31,794,708 | 35,797,456 | 33,826,559 |
| Iowa ......... | 220,081,000 | 254,999,850 | 242,249,841 | 305,859,948 | 230,264,550 | 297,686,016 |
| Missouri...... | 165,300,000 | 154,731,486 | 162,915,064 | 180,710,404 | 66,436,376 | 264,232,605 |
| Kansas........ | 171,475,000 | 132,842,048 | 237,621,222 | 163,870,630 | 61,506,034 | 222,805,621 |
| Nebraska...... | 233,218,000 | 158,754,666 | 224,373,268 | 210,430,064 | 109,141,840 | 252,520,173 |
| South Dakota. | 23,856,000 | 28,109,956 | 30,017,416 | 32,418,819 | 29,842,659 | 29,812,822 |
| North Dakota. | 575,000 | 461,852 | 553,495 | 381,184 | 1,519,534 | 1,604,380 |
| Montana...... | 10,000 | 44,744 | 36,386 | 23,970 | 77,375 | 81,708 |
| Wyoming..... | 40,000 | 39,632 | 53,944 | 81,702 | 87,176 | 47,203 |
| Colorado...... | 3,344,000 | 3,113,892 | 2,911,488 | 3,188,941 | 1,831,872 | 1,009,000 |
| New Mexico.. | 610,000 | 509,418 | 480,300 | 554,752 | 1,154,790 | 811,998 |
| Arizona....... | 192,000 | ............ | ............ | ............ | 177,678 | 151,540 |
| Utah ......... | ............ | 169,113 | 162,680 | 169,180 | 211,829 | 217,281 |
| Idaho......... | ............ | ............ | ............ | ............ | 117,093 | 127,007 |
| Washington .. | 165,000 | 68,400 | 128,478 | 106,140 | 171,815 | 230,322 |
| Oregon....... | 351,000 | 327,744 | 297,418 | 317,147 | 347,589 | 398,853 |
| California..... | 1,800,000 | 1,184,040 | 1,536,975 | 1,351,975 | 1,850,793 | 1,839,150 |
| Oklahoma .... | ............ | ............ | 10,133,365 | 14,144,052 | 10,324,113 | 40,501,640 |
| Indian Territ'y | ............ | ............ | ............ | ............ | 17,883,204 | 38,591,962 |
| Total....... | 1,891,918,000 | 1,924,184,660 | 2,078,143,933 | 2,105,102,516 | 1,522,519,891 | 2,523,648,312 |
| Total acres.... | 80,072,000 | 77,721,781 | 82,108,587 | 83,320,872 | 91,349,928 | 94,043,613 |
| Yield per acre. | 23.7 | 24.8 | 25.3 | 25.3 | 16.7 | 26.8 |
| Farm price.... | 26.5 | 28.7 | 30.3 | 35.7 | 60.5 | 40.3 |
| Value......... | $501,358,000 | $522,025,428 | $629,210,110 | $751,220,034 | $921,555,768 | $1017017,349 |

## *OATS CROPS OF THE UNITED STATES*

REPORTED BY THE STATISTICIAN OF THE DEPARTMENT OF AGRICULTURE, BY STATES.

| | 1898. | 1899. | 1900. | 1901. | 1902. |
|---|---|---|---|---|---|
| Maine | 5,048,000 | 4,957,000 | 5,257,612 | 4,035,780 | 4,541,979 |
| New Hampshire | 1,008,000 | 1,047,000 | 995,148 | 362,938 | 417,690 |
| Vermont | 4,107,000 | 3,959,000 | 3,719,677 | 2,516,415 | 3,111,200 |
| Massachusetts | 484,000 | 489,000 | 550,786 | 210,428 | 209,815 |
| Rhode Island | 99,000 | 95,000 | 114,484 | 47,305 | 62,336 |
| Connecticut | 563,000 | 525,000 | 578,897 | 295,151 | 351,244 |
| New York | 38,727,000 | 45,402,000 | 44,538,974 | 28,049,587 | 52,982,560 |
| New Jersey | 1,923,000 | 2,285,000 | 2,812,089 | 1,154,928 | 2,184,834 |
| Pennsylvania | 27,099,000 | 39,148,000 | 38,000,872 | 23,555,656 | 45,036,182 |
| Delaware | 387,000 | 320,000 | 332,724 | 101,028 | 113,542 |
| Maryland | 1,527,000 | 1,676,000 | 1,783,416 | 833,780 | 1,124,924 |
| Virginia | 6,881,000 | 5,146,000 | 5,167,568 | 3,717,863 | 3,886,295 |
| North Carolina | 6,339,000 | 4,787,000 | 5,046,117 | 3,648,154 | 3,024,415 |
| South Carolina | 4,208,000 | 3,024,000 | 4,023,149 | 3,718,862 | 2,836,182 |
| Georgia | 7,196,000 | 4,292,000 | 7,010,040 | 4,390,331 | 2,930,544 |
| Florida | 623,000 | 321,000 | 378,211 | 414,392 | 434,506 |
| Alabama | 5,383,000 | 3,012,000 | 4,380,754 | 3,181,880 | 2,320,141 |
| Mississippi | 2,406,000 | 1,366,000 | 2,390,052 | 1,839,975 | 1,808,253 |
| Louisiana | 662,000 | 553,000 | 614,142 | 425,530 | 530,966 |
| Texas | 21,122,000 | 17,068,000 | 28,278,232 | 13,662,578 | 20,807,361 |
| Arkansas | 7,230,000 | 5,964,000 | 7,038,665 | 3,136,131 | 5,048,400 |
| Tennessee | 6,755,000 | 5,326,000 | 5,810,160 | 3,501,330 | 2,219,028 |
| West Virginia | 2,911,000 | 3,159,000 | 2,768,451 | 1,633,651 | 2,448,560 |
| Kentucky | 9,466,000 | 8,195,000 | 9,309,293 | 5,379,046 | 5,758,591 |
| Ohio | 27,724,000 | 32,946,000 | 40,340,534 | 35,217,378 | 46,409,791 |
| Michigan | 27,783,000 | 30,599,000 | 33,689,536 | 28,745,003 | 40,340,137 |
| Indiana | 31,939,000 | 34,301,000 | 44,866,035 | 39,633,022 | 48,565,685 |
| Illinois | 88,304,000 | 127,279,000 | 133,642,884 | 112,531,903 | 153,450,423 |
| Wisconsin | 64,643,000 | 67,687,000 | 61,971,552 | 66,647,381 | 95,037,810 |
| Minnesota | 56,298,000 | 52,688,000 | 41,907,046 | 65,734,027 | 82,259,697 |
| Iowa | 123,428,000 | 126,986,000 | 130,572,138 | 122,304,564 | 124,738,337 |
| Missouri | 15,866,000 | 20,299,000 | 24,695,373 | 10,197,746 | 27,816,165 |
| Kansas | 26,689,000 | 39,129,000 | 43,063,943 | 17,332,410 | 31,529,128 |
| Nebraska | 56,245,000 | 51,474,000 | 37,778,572 | 39,065,222 | 62,121,601 |
| South Dakota | 16,127,000 | 15,332,000 | 12,653,266 | 19,554,451 | 24,100,844 |
| North Dakota | 15,061,000 | 17,988,000 | 6,299,284 | 23,576,548 | 29,437,402 |
| Montana | 2,478,000 | 2,318,000 | 2,568,735 | 6,189,336 | 6,668,553 |
| Wyoming | 414,000 | 442,000 | 630,272 | 1,373,459 | 1,302,444 |
| Colorado | 3,063,000 | 2,449,000 | 3,272,390 | 4,570,571 | 3,660,237 |
| New Mexico | 271,000 | 178,000 | 229,994 | 529,268 | 300,710 |
| Utah | 970,000 | 872,000 | 918,214 | 1,498,992 | 1,596,435 |
| Idaho | 1,282,000 | 1,100,000 | 1,349,845 | 3,014,325 | 3,412,794 |
| Washington | 3,270,000 | 3,032,000 | 3,016,226 | 7,033,942 | 7,115,077 |
| Oregon | 4,954,000 | 5,119,000 | 3,282,770 | 8,971,291 | 8,092,168 |
| California | 1,943,000 | 1,844,000 | 1,477,771 | 4,887,347 | 5,148,583 |
| Oklahoma | ........ | ........ | ........ | 3,957,840 | 13,252,072 |
| Indian Territory | ........ | ........ | ........ | 4,130,150 | 6,032,011 |
| Total bushels | 730,906,000 | 796,178,000 | 809,125,989 | 736,808,724 | 987,842,712 |
| Total acres | 25,777,000 | 26,341,000 | 27,364,795 | 28,541,476 | 28,653,144 |
| Yield per acre | 28.3 | 30.2 | 29.6 | 25.8 | 34.5 |
| Farm price | 25.6 | 24.9 | 25.8 | 39.9 | 30.7 |
| Value | $186,405,000 | $198,168,000 | $208,669,233 | $293,658,777 | $303,584,852 |

## VISIBLE WHEAT SUPPLIES—WEEKLY

### EAST OF ROCKY MOUNTAINS.

| *Week Ending | Bradstreets. | | | Official. | | |
|---|---|---|---|---|---|---|
| | 1900. | 1901. | 1902. | 1900. | 1901. | 1902. |
| January 4 | 89,252,000 | 88,456,000 | 94,900,000 | 57,892,000 | 61,261,000 | 58,929,000 |
| January 11 | 88,992,000 | 89,278,000 | 93,572,000 | 56,533,000 | 61,845,000 | 58,077,000 |
| January 18 | 89,638,000 | 87,958,000 | 93,213,000 | 56,535,000 | 61,196,000 | 59,273,000 |
| January 25 | 88,500,000 | 87,408,000 | 91,331,000 | 55,597,000 | 60,791,000 | 59,371,000 |
| February 1 | 87,473,000 | 86,324,000 | 88,800,000 | 54,363,000 | 59,767,000 | 57,929,000 |
| February 8 | 86,608,000 | 84,712,000 | 87,177,000 | 53,805,000 | 58,494,000 | 56,566,000 |
| February 15 | 85,750,000 | 84,095,000 | 86,594,000 | 53,220,000 | 57,682,000 | 55,502,000 |
| February 22 | 85,093,000 | 82,503,000 | 84,953,000 | 53,445,000 | 57,536,000 | 54,385,000 |
| March 1 | 85,570,000 | 80,704,000 | 84,315,000 | 54,084,999 | 57,536,000 | 54,093,000 |
| March 8 | 84,335,000 | 79,300,000 | 82,790,000 | 53,698,000 | 55,892,000 | 53,156,000 |
| March 15 | 82,807,000 | 77,527,000 | 80,441,000 | 58,911,000 | 55,123,000 | 51,997,000 |
| March 22 | 81,542,000 | 76,350,000 | 78,842,000 | 54,093,000 | 54,714,000 | 50,948,000 |
| March 29 | 79,690,000 | 75,501,000 | 75,598,000 | 54,204,000 | 54,749,000 | 49,565,000 |
| April 5 | 77,113,000 | 73,879,000 | 78,576,000 | 55,412,000 | 53,890,000 | 48,414,000 |
| April 12 | 75,840,000 | 69,967,000 | 70,112,000 | 55,273,000 | 51,873,000 | 46,614,000 |
| April 19 | 74,172,000 | 66,235,000 | 65,162,000 | 54,814,000 | 49,868,000 | 44,282,000 |
| April 26 | 70,764,000 | 63,631,000 | 59,184,000 | 52,472,000 | 48,352,000 | 40,449,000 |
| May 3 | 67,268,000 | 60,298,000 | 54,610,000 | 49,825,000 | 46,668,000 | 38,328,000 |
| May 10 | 63,602,000 | 58,941,000 | 50,476,000 | 47,621,000 | 45,761,000 | 35,302,000 |
| May 17 | 61,079,000 | 54,649,000 | 46,672,000 | 46,263,000 | 42,498,000 | 33,577,000 |
| May 24 | 58,705,000 | 50,963,000 | 41,993,000 | 44,755,000 | 40,064,000 | 30,629,000 |
| May 31 | 57,617,000 | 47,109,000 | 37,676,000 | 44,704,000 | 36,932,000 | 28,204,000 |
| June 7 | 57,311,000 | 45,610,000 | 35,067,000 | 44,407,000 | 35,292,000 | 26,091,000 |
| June 14 | 57,428,000 | 45,043,000 | 32,106,000 | 44,176,000 | 35,130,000 | 23,570,000 |
| June 21 | 58,119,000 | 42,017,000 | 29,047,000 | 45,524,000 | 32,908,000 | 21,035,000 |
| June 28 | 58,523,000 | 39,317,000 | 27,453,000 | 46,442,000 | 30,793,000 | 19,760,000 |
| July 5 | 59,063,000 | 37,819,000 | 26,786,000 | 46,877,000 | 29,688,000 | 19,122,000 |
| July 12 | 58,238,000 | 35,977,000 | 27,793,000 | 46,081,000 | 27,979,000 | 19,808,000 |
| July 19 | 57,613,000 | 36,433,000 | 28,165,000 | 45,631,000 | 27,681,000 | 20,415,000 |
| July 26 | 58,622,000 | 38,851,000 | 29,688,000 | 46,354,000 | 29,264,000 | 21,591,000 |
| August 2 | 60,398,000 | 40,924,000 | 31,436,000 | 47,594,000 | 30,369,000 | 21,973,000 |
| August 9 | 61,504,000 | 38,959,000 | 32,293,000 | 48,218,000 | 28,219,000 | 21,773,000 |
| August 16 | 63,995,000 | 38,097,000 | 31,352,000 | 49,761,000 | 26,769,000 | 20,264,000 |
| August 23 | 65,195,000 | 37,428,000 | 31,558,000 | 49,996,000 | 26,007,000 | 20,689,000 |
| August 30 | 66,240,000 | 39,348,000 | 32,366,000 | 50,286,000 | 27,790,000 | 20,966,000 |
| September 6 | 69,003,000 | 42,242,000 | 33,579,000 | 51,738,000 | 28,440,000 | 21,421,000 |
| September 13 | 72,321,000 | 44,320,000 | 34,977,000 | 53,927,000 | 30,872,000 | 22,056,000 |
| September 20 | 73,852,000 | 48,393,000 | 36,153,000 | 54,993,000 | 32,625,000 | 22,526,000 |
| September 27 | 76,071,000 | 51,442,000 | 40,454,000 | 55,409,000 | 35,304,000 | 24,842,000 |
| October 4 | 75,535,000 | 53,790,000 | 44,217,000 | 55,401,000 | 37,474,000 | 25,624,000 |
| October 11 | 77,408,000 | 55,727,000 | 47,961,000 | 56,978,000 | 38,208,000 | 26,111,000 |
| October 18 | 79,164,000 | 58,227,000 | 54,628,000 | 58,313,000 | 39,393,000 | 27,654,000 |
| October 25 | 81,361,000 | 63,181,000 | 58,815,000 | 59,773,000 | 40,634,000 | 29,918,000 |
| November 1 | 82,238,000 | 64,616,000 | 63,480,000 | 60,032,000 | 41,192,000 | 32,200,000 |
| November 8 | 83,636,000 | 67,100,000 | 67,490,000 | 69,703,000 | 41,959,000 | 36,098,000 |
| November 15 | 85,776,000 | 74,470,000 | 69,630,000 | 62,361,000 | 45,677,000 | 38,092,000 |
| November 22 | 85,064,000 | 80,011,000 | 72,968,000 | 62,261,000 | 48,912,000 | 41,731,000 |
| November 29 | 86,591,000 | 85,631,000 | 77,288,000 | 62,179,000 | 52,396,000 | 45,083,000 |
| December 6 | 86,407,000 | 91,023,000 | 78,352,000 | 61,494,000 | 55,240,000 | 45,940,000 |
| December 13 | 86,939,000 | 94,449,000 | 80,527,000 | 61,082,000 | 59,356,000 | 48,151,000 |
| December 20 | 87,926,000 | 94,849,000 | 81,894,000 | 61,473,000 | 58,805,000 | 48,816,000 |
| December 27 | 87,911,000 | 94,736,000 | 82,209,000 | 61,408,000 | 58,648,000 | 49,678,000 |

* The dates are for 1902. The other columns are for corresponding weeks.

## VISIBLE CORN SUPPLIES—WEEKLY

| *Week Ending | Bradstreets. | | | Official. | | |
|---|---|---|---|---|---|---|
| | 1900. | 1901. | 1902. | 1900. | 1901. | 1902. |
| January 4.... | 19,449,000 | 15,199,000 | 16,825,000 | 12,613,000 | 10,420,000 | 11,703,000 |
| January 11.... | 20,855,000 | 15,803,000 | 16,897,000 | 12,884,000 | 10,630,000 | 11,643,000 |
| January 18.... | 21,630,000 | 17,379,000 | 17,388,000 | 14,144,000 | 11,743,000 | 11,752,000 |
| January 25.... | 22,388,000 | 20,890,000 | 17,114,000 | 14,526,000 | 14,137,000 | 11,632,000 |
| February 1.... | 20,110,000 | 21,950,000 | 17,107,000 | 14,583,000 | 14,825,000 | 11,632,000 |
| February 8.... | 22,348,000 | 23,719,000 | 16,828,000 | 14,709,000 | 16,051,000 | 11,580,000 |
| February 15 .. | 22,837,000 | 24,848,000 | 16,393,000 | 14,814,000 | 17,031,000 | 11,132,000 |
| February 22... | 25,217,000 | 25,809,000 | 15,742,000 | 16,333,000 | 18,218,000 | 10,789,000 |
| March 1..... | 28,340,000 | 27,538,000 | 15,270,000 | 19,666,000 | 19,764,000 | 10,333,000 |
| March 8.. .. | 31,170,000 | 28,800,000 | 15,225,000 | 21,060,000 | 21,014,000 | 10,085,000 |
| March 15..... | 29,747,000 | 29,442,000 | 14,785,000 | 20,542,000 | 22,348,000 | 9,686,000 |
| March 22..... | 31,975,000 | 29,948,000 | 14,229,000 | 21,111,000 | 22,862,000 | 9,108,000 |
| March 29.. .. | 31,883,000 | 28,947,000 | 13,540,000 | 21,588,000 | 22,287,000 | 8,799,000 |
| April 5...... | 33,187,000 | 27,916,000 | 12,899,000 | 23,019,000 | 21,990,000 | 8,508,000 |
| April 12...... | 33,868,000 | 26,773,000 | 11,574,000 | 24,789,000 | 22,026,000 | 7,550,000 |
| April 19...... | 33,453,000 | 26,479,000 | 10,998,000 | 24,114,000 | 21,328,000 | 7,226,000 |
| April 26..... | 30,416,000 | 24,817,000 | 10,087,000 | 21,918,000 | 19,295,000 | 6,888,000 |
| May 3. ..... | 25,725,000 | 24,544,000 | 9,093,000 | 18,137,000 | 18,665,000 | 6,243,000 |
| May 10....... | 23,640,000 | 22,781,000 | 8,492,000 | 16,155,000 | 17,338,000 | 5,697,000 |
| May 17....... | 21,847,000 | 20,457,000 | 7,484,000 | 15,227,000 | 15,913,000 | 4,870,000 |
| May 24....... | 19,380,000 | 20,495,000 | 6,319,000 | 12,687,000 | 15,320,000 | 4,297,000 |
| May 31....... | 18,289,000 | 21,904,000 | 6,317,000 | 12,378,000 | 16,413,000 | 4,227,000 |
| June 7....... | 17,896,000 | 22,565,000 | 6,965,000 | 11,228,000 | 16,049,000 | 4,261,000 |
| June 14....... | 18,977,000 | 23,467,000 | 8,183,000 | 11,430,000 | 17,271,000 | 4,719,000 |
| June 21....... | 20,227,000 | 23,782,000 | 8,137,000 | 12,162,000 | 17,186,000 | 5,189,000 |
| June 28....... | 19,087,000 | 21,522,000 | 8,541,000 | 11,019,000 | 15,158,000 | 5,687,000 |
| July 5....... | 21,426,000 | 21,069,000 | 8,684,000 | 13,188,000 | 14,372,000 | 5,912,000 |
| July 12....... | 21,255,000 | 20,941,000 | 8,484,000 | 13,608,000 | 14,067,000 | 5,836,000 |
| July 19....... | 21,087,000 | 20,149,000 | 9,152,000 | 13,525,000 | 13,242,000 | 6,503,000 |
| July 26....... | 18,635,000 | 20,487,000 | 9,850,000 | 11,692,000 | 13,387,000 | 7,486,000 |
| August 2..... | 18,613,000 | 19,648,000 | 9,013,000 | 12,320,000 | 12,565,000 | 7,281,000 |
| August 9..... | 17,453,000 | 19,823,000 | 7,488,000 | 11,351,000 | 13,296,000 | 6,156,000 |
| August 16..... | 13,795,000 | 19,494,000 | 6,354,000 | 9,102,000 | 12,783,000 | 5,438,000 |
| August 23..... | 11,032,000 | 18,720,000 | 4,246,000 | 7,430,000 | 12,205,000 | 3,423,000 |
| August 30..... | 8,766,000 | 19,476,000 | 3,823,000 | 5,313,000 | 12,676,000 | 3,077,000 |
| September 6.. | 8,751,000 | 20,464,000 | 3,176,000 | 5,357,000 | 13,123,000 | 2,523,000 |
| September 13.. | 9,397,000 | 20,020,000 | 3,115,000 | 5,602,000 | 12,502,000 | 2,264,000 |
| September 20.. | 10,443,000 | 20,614,000 | 3,558,000 | 7,322,000 | 12,930,000 | 2,431,000 |
| September 27.. | 11,106,000 | 21,215,000 | 4,607,000 | 7,492,000 | 13,489,000 | 3,048,000 |
| October 4.... | 11,341,000 | 21,212,000 | 4,919,000 | 7,887,000 | 14,026,000 | 3,075,000 |
| October 11.... | 13,382,000 | 20,586,000 | 3,593,000 | 9,829,000 | 13,414,000 | 2,541,000 |
| October 18.... | 12,153,000 | 19,102,000 | 3,371,000 | 8,914,000 | 13,449,000 | 2,231,000 |
| October 25.... | 11,951,000 | 19,627,000 | 4,184,000 | 8,144,000 | 13,636,000 | 2,488,000 |
| November 1.. | 11,601,000 | 19,137,000 | 4,229,000 | 7,983,000 | 12,900,000 | 2,584,000 |
| November 8.. | 9,947,000 | 18,844,000 | 4,419,000 | 6,785,000 | 12,641,000 | 2,790,000 |
| November 15.. | 12,152,000 | 18,254,000 | 3,709,000 | 8,428,000 | 12,156,000 | 2,105,000 |
| November 22.. | 12,427,000 | 17,345,000 | 3,626,000 | 8,704,000 | 11,464,000 | 2,287,000 |
| November 29.. | 12,791,000 | 16,509,000 | 4,552,000 | 9,442,000 | 11,227,000 | 2,938,000 |
| December 6.. | 12,988,000 | 15,849,000 | 5,681,000 | 8,762,000 | 10,930,000 | 3,895,000 |
| December 13.. | 12,220,000 | 15,757,000 | 7,463,000 | 8,138,000 | 11,187,000 | 5,498,000 |
| December 20.. | 13,844,000 | 15,935,000 | 8,496,000 | 7,564,000 | 11,131,000 | 6,342,000 |
| December 27.. | 14,313,000 | 16,224,000 | 9,540,000 | 9,053,000 | 11,252,000 | 7,112,000 |

* The dates are for 1902. The other columns are for corresponding weeks.

## PRIMARY MARKET RECEIPTS OF WHEAT

REPORTED BY THE CINCINNATI PRICE CURRENT, BY WEEKS.

| *Week Ending. | 1897. | 1898. | 1899. | 1900. | 1901. | 1902. |
|---|---|---|---|---|---|---|
| January 6.... | 1,622,000 | 3,454,000 | 4,107,000 | 2,613,000 | 2,869,000 | 3,501,000 |
| January 13.... | 1,685,000 | 2,447,000 | 4,562,000 | 3,236,000 | 3,778,000 | 3,495,000 |
| January 20.... | 1,542,000 | 2,331,000 | 4,336,000 | 2,619,000 | 3,618,000 | 3,613,000 |
| January 27.... | 1,187,000 | 2,033,000 | 4,257,000 | 2,253,000 | 3,126,000 | 2,882,000 |
| February 3... | 1,503,000 | 2,601,000 | 4,030,000 | 2,225,000 | 2,503,000 | 2,645,000 |
| February 10... | 1,481,000 | 2,563,000 | 3,275,000 | 2,665,000 | 3,225,000 | 2,313,000 |
| February 17... | 1,712,000 | 2,815,000 | 2,784,000 | 3,010,000 | 2,942,000 | 2,316,000 |
| February 24... | 1,538,000 | 2,296,000 | 3,402,000 | 3,517,000 | 2,622,000 | 2,469,000 |
| March 3...... | 1,720,000 | 2,632,000 | 3,320,000 | 3,579,000 | 3,377,000 | 3,810,000 |
| March 10...... | 1,783,000 | 2,857,000 | 4,068,000 | 3,837,000 | 2,880,000 | 2,705,000 |
| March 17...... | 1,479,000 | 2,504,000 | 3,187,000 | 4,168,000 | 3,367,000 | 2,646,000 |
| March 24...... | 1,831,000 | 2,641,000 | 2,736,000 | 4,049,000 | 4,362,000 | 2,979,000 |
| March 31...... | 2,877,000 | 2,052,000 | 2,802,000 | 3,692,000 | 4,139,000 | 2,190,000 |
| April 7....... | 1,717,000 | 1,676,000 | 3,811,000 | 3,531,000 | 3,285,000 | 2,519,000 |
| April 14....... | 1,895,000 | 1,660,000 | 2,061,000 | 2,794,000 | 2,900,000 | 1,703,000 |
| April 21....... | 1,194,000 | 2,161,000 | 1,778,000 | 2,615,000 | 2,366,000 | 1,541,000 |
| April 28....... | 2,051,000 | 3,063,000 | 2,573,000 | 2,045,000 | 2,505,000 | 1,366,000 |
| May 5........ | 2,384,000 | 4,676,000 | 2,365,000 | 2,636,000 | 2,583,000 | 1,623,000 |
| May 12........ | 2,054,000 | 4,305,000 | 2,042,000 | 2,393,000 | 2,371,000 | 1,706,000 |
| May 19........ | 2,628,000 | 6,015,000 | 1,996,000 | 2,195,000 | 2,242,000 | 1,448,000 |
| May 26........ | 2,805,000 | 4,680,000 | 3,053,000 | 2,438,000 | 2,180,000 | 1,482,000 |
| June 2....... | 2,034,000 | 3,774,000 | 4,372,000 | 3,455,000 | 2,606,000 | 1,531,000 |
| June 9....... | 1,633,000 | 1,328,000 | 5,245,000 | 4,133,000 | 3,621,000 | 2,401,000 |
| June 16....... | 1,405,000 | 1,186,000 | 5,219,000 | 3,857,000 | 3,400,000 | 2,096,000 |
| June 23....... | 1,565,000 | 711,000 | 5,766,000 | 3,795,000 | 3,002,000 | 2,525,000 |
| June 30....... | 1,444,000 | 578,000 | 5,622,000 | 2,987,000 | 2,943,000 | 2,724,000 |
| July 7........ | 1,781,000 | 747,000 | 4,049,000 | 2,396,000 | 3,572,000 | 1,987,000 |
| July 14........ | 1,972,000 | 1,181,000 | 4,981,000 | 2,774,000 | 4,865,000 | 3,941,000 |
| July 21........ | 3,316,000 | 2,628,000 | 5,819,000 | 4,737,000 | 6,088,000 | 5,163,000 |
| July 28. ...... | 4,981,000 | 3,863,000 | 4,827,000 | 5,128,000 | 6,527,000 | 6,727,000 |
| August 4..... | 5,541,000 | 3,147,000 | 4,654,000 | 5,714,000 | 6,621,000 | 7,620,000 |
| August 11..... | 5,060,000 | 2,734,000 | 3,727,000 | 6,797,000 | 6,008,000 | 6,887,000 |
| August 18..... | 5,632,000 | 3,895,000 | 3,293,000 | 6,519,000 | 6,174,000 | 6,691,000 |
| August 25..... | 5,939,000 | 5,757,000 | 3,569,000 | 7,035,000 | 6,482,000 | 6,359,000 |
| September 1.. | 6,537,000 | 6,691,000 | 4,410,000 | 7,067,000 | 6,231,000 | 6,076,000 |
| September 8.. | 6,965,000 | 8,030,000 | 6,113,000 | 7,655,000 | 8,678,000 | 6,072,000 |
| September 15.. | 8,102,000 | 7,997,000 | 7,870,000 | 7,050,000 | 9,396,000 | 6,839,000 |
| September 22.. | 8,382,000 | 8,339,000 | 7,934,000 | 6,981,000 | 8,292,000 | 8,721,000 |
| September 29.. | 9,047,000 | 9,628,000 | 7,329,000 | 6,928,000 | 8,279,000 | 8,880,000 |
| October 6.... | 7,690,000 | 11,127,000 | 7,761,000 | 5,944,000 | 8,382,000 | 8,698,000 |
| October 13.... | 8,923,000 | 10,329,000 | 8,091,000 | 6,610,000 | 7,560,000 | 7,750,000 |
| October 20.... | 6,858,000 | 9,719,000 | 7,405,000 | 6,829,000 | 6,014,000 | 8,209,000 |
| October 27.... | 7,131,000 | 9,409,000 | 6,585,000 | 5,889,000 | 6,309,000 | 8,776,000 |
| November 3.. | 7,782,000 | 10,395,000 | 6,060,000 | 6,061,000 | 7,273,000 | 9,857,000 |
| November 10.. | 7,749,000 | 9,800,000 | 6,042,000 | 5,152,000 | 6,699,000 | 9,785,000 |
| November 17.. | 7,945,000 | 10,318,000 | 5,673,000 | 4,566,000 | 7,350,000 | 8,707,000 |
| November 24.. | 6,606,000 | 8,501,000 | 5,128,000 | 4,620,000 | 7,356,000 | 7,920,000 |
| December 1.. | 6,582,000 | 9,682,000 | 6,301,000 | 4,617,000 | 7,122,000 | 8,211,000 |
| December 8.. | 5,195,000 | 10,255,000 | 4,378,000 | 5,380,000 | 7,022,000 | 7,440,000 |
| December 15.. | 6,846,000 | 7,478,000 | 3,497,000 | 4,811,000 | 6,494,000 | 6,101,000 |
| December 22.. | 3,993,000 | 6,210,000 | 3,286,000 | 4,746,000 | 4,084,000 | 5,041,000 |
| December 29.. | 4,693,000 | 6,337,000 | 3,055,000 | 4,114,000 | 3,840,000 | 3,959,000 |

* The dates are for 1902. The other columns are for corresponding weeks.

## PRIMARY MARKET RECEIPTS OF CORN

REPORTED BY THE CINCINNATI PRICE CURRENT, BY WEEKS.

| *Week Ending | 1897. | 1898. | 1899. | 1900. | 1901. | 1902. |
|---|---|---|---|---|---|---|
| January 4 | 2,514,000 | 5,368,000 | 4,982,000 | 3,512,000 | 4,216,000 | 3,613,000 |
| January 11 | 2,764,000 | 4,551,000 | 6,435,000 | 4,445,000 | 5,099,000 | 3,348,000 |
| January 18 | 3,871,000 | 3,838,000 | 5,760,000 | 3,391,000 | 5,287,000 | 3,020,000 |
| January 25 | 3,223,000 | 2,810,000 | 5,685,000 | 2,853,000 | 5,417,000 | 2,856,000 |
| February 1 | 5,221,000 | 4,043,000 | 6,103,000 | 4,256,000 | 4,527,000 | 2,281,000 |
| February 8 | 4,578,000 | 4,548,000 | 6,558,000 | 6,007,000 | 5,764,000 | 1,317,000 |
| February 15 | 4,664,000 | 5,648,000 | 4,974,000 | 4,891,000 | 4,383,000 | 1,469,000 |
| February 22 | 3,067,000 | 4,676,000 | 5,320,000 | 5,420,000 | 4,589,000 | 1,491,000 |
| March 1 | 3,879,000 | 6,302,000 | 4,682,000 | 5,348,000 | 5,717,000 | 2,670,000 |
| March 8 | 3,126,000 | 5,382,000 | 4,342,000 | 4,515,000 | 4,941,000 | 2,073,000 |
| March 15 | 2,277,000 | 4,022,000 | 3,614,000 | 4,668,000 | 3,912,000 | 1,745,000 |
| March 22 | 2,190,000 | 3,405,000 | 2,174,000 | 4,289,000 | 3,113,000 | 1,539,000 |
| March 29 | 1,825,000 | 2,852,000 | 1,802,000 | 5,446,000 | 2,502,000 | 1,977,000 |
| April 7 | 1,369,000 | 2,699,000 | 2,279,000 | 4,142,000 | 2,170,000 | 1,977,000 |
| April 14 | 1,384,000 | 2,790,000 | 1,991,000 | 4,289,000 | 1,908,000 | 1,252,000 |
| April 21 | 1,658,000 | 3,027,000 | 1,987,000 | 4,472,000 | 1,572,000 | 941,000 |
| April 28 | 1,904,000 | 4,026,000 | 2,399,000 | 2,593,000 | 1,602,000 | 1,482,000 |
| May 5 | 2,328,000 | 5,362,000 | 2,558,000 | 2,092,000 | 2,783,000 | 1,984,000 |
| May 12 | 2,366,000 | 5,313,000 | 2,216,000 | 2,202,000 | 3,464,000 | 2,068,000 |
| May 19 | 1,906,000 | 5,122,000 | 1,576,000 | 1,820,000 | 2,696,000 | 1,364,000 |
| May 26 | 4,583,000 | 5,152,000 | 2,463,000 | 1,767,000 | 4,910,000 | 1,353,000 |
| June 2 | 6,553,000 | 7,662,000 | 3,824,000 | 3,084,000 | 4,899,000 | 1,603,000 |
| June 9 | 4,982,000 | 6,595,000 | 5,355,000 | 3,404,000 | 4,701,000 | 3,535,000 |
| June 16 | 3,611,000 | 4,336,000 | 4,842,000 | 4,062,000 | 3,058,000 | 2,876,000 |
| June 23 | 3,138,000 | 2,869,000 | 5,354,000 | 5,042,000 | 2,087,000 | 2,299,000 |
| June 30 | 2,562,000 | 2,363,000 | 6,730,000 | 5,500,000 | 1,865,000 | 2,083,000 |
| July 7 | 2,780,000 | 2,667,000 | 5,810,000 | 5,223,000 | 1,648,000 | 1,245,000 |
| July 14 | 2,752,000 | 2,045,000 | 5,297,000 | 4,260,000 | 2,516,000 | 1,858,000 |
| July 21 | 3,266,000 | 2,238,000 | 4,774,000 | 4,175,000 | 3,337,000 | 3,380,000 |
| July 28 | 4,212,000 | 2,630,000 | 5,322,000 | 3,163,000 | 2,431,000 | 2,397,000 |
| August 4 | 6,038,000 | 3,079,000 | 4,661,000 | 3,243,000 | 2,437,000 | 1,747,000 |
| August 11 | 5,403,000 | 2,598,000 | 3,540,000 | 2,410,000 | 2,345,000 | 1,032,000 |
| August 18 | 5,859,000 | 3,496,000 | 3,199,000 | 2,004,000 | 2,319,000 | 1,194,000 |
| August 25 | 7,880,000 | 4,400,000 | 3,622,000 | 1,986,000 | 2,705,000 | 1,024,000 |
| September 1 | 10,176,000 | 4,568,000 | 4,854,000 | 2,284,000 | 2,838,000 | 1,030,000 |
| September 8 | 8,588,000 | 3,923,000 | 5,478,000 | 3,194,000 | 4,140,000 | 924,000 |
| September 15 | 7,503,000 | 3,515,000 | 5,953,000 | 4,193,000 | 2,965,000 | 1,795,000 |
| September 22 | 4,962,000 | 3,818,000 | 6,938,000 | 4,613,000 | 2,314,000 | 2,475,000 |
| September 29 | 4,135,000 | 4,306,000 | 7,047,000 | 4,786,000 | 3,256,000 | 3,019,000 |
| October 6 | 3,437,000 | 5,534,000 | 7,125,000 | 4,672,000 | 3,501,000 | 1,662,000 |
| October 13 | 6,154,000 | 5,473,000 | 5,897,000 | 4,566,000 | 2,780,000 | 1,170,000 |
| October 20 | 5,569,000 | 4,745,000 | 4,311,000 | 4,741,000 | 2,840,000 | 2,231,000 |
| October 27 | 4,609,000 | 3,177,000 | 4,306,000 | 3,415,000 | 2,505,000 | 2,452,000 |
| November 3 | 3,313,000 | 3,736,000 | 3,719,000 | 3,652,000 | 2,101,000 | 2,501,000 |
| November 10 | 3,247,000 | 4,966,000 | 3,327,000 | 2,589,000 | 1,735,000 | 2,186,000 |
| November 17 | 3,278,000 | 3,889,000 | 2,852,000 | 3,680,000 | 1,761,000 | 2,192,000 |
| November 24 | 3,567,000 | 2,808,000 | 2,402,000 | 3,980,000 | 2,388,000 | 2,761,000 |
| December 1 | 4,452,000 | 3,525,000 | 2,980,000 | 3,670,000 | 2,254,000 | 3,474,000 |
| December 8 | 4,543,000 | 4,121,000 | 3,239,000 | 4,460,000 | 3,027,000 | 3,504,000 |
| December 15 | 4,319,000 | 4,500,000 | 2,823,000 | 4,235,000 | 4,096,000 | 3,783,000 |
| December 22 | 3,152,000 | 4,274,000 | 2,645,000 | 6,333,000 | 2,304,000 | 4,086,000 |
| December 29 | 4,100,000 | 4,855,000 | 3,145,000 | 5,696,000 | 3,128,000 | 3,906,000 |

*The dates are for 1902. The other columns are for corresponding weeks.

## GRAIN IN STORE IN CHICAGO

ON THE FIRST OF EACH MONTH.

Compiled by the Daily Trade Bulletin, Chicago.

### WHEAT.

| Months. | 1897. Bushels. | 1898. Bushels. | 1899. Bushels. | 1900. Bushels. | 1901. Bushels. | 1902. Bushels. |
|---|---|---|---|---|---|---|
| January | 14,350,000 | 11,137,000 | 3,611,000 | 16,891,000 | 11,650,000 | 6,183,000 |
| February | 13,032,000 | 11,244,000 | 3,897,000 | 15,016,000 | 11,488,000 | 7,247,000 |
| March | 12,061,000 | 10,398,000 | 4,534,000 | 14,809,000 | 11,361,000 | 7,039,000 |
| April | 10,237,000 | 7,860,000 | 4,576,000 | 13,631,000 | 11,603,000 | 7,392,000 |
| May | 8,088,000 | 3,327,000 | 5,021,000 | 11,886,000 | 10,654,000 | 6,340,000 |
| June | 5,469,000 | 1,954,000 | 4,678,000 | 9,962,000 | 6,681,000 | 4,444,000 |
| July | 4,102,000 | 795,000 | 5,322,000 | 11,319,000 | 5,140,000 | 2,386,000 |
| August | 3,780,000 | 790,000 | 5,720,900 | 10,884,000 | 3,843,000 | 2,429,000 |
| September | 1,766,000 | 333,000 | 6,000,000 | 11,865,000 | 4,697,000 | 2,915,000 |
| October | 3,182,000 | 1,184,000 | 8,627,000 | 13,065,000 | 4,958,000 | 4,460,000 |
| November | 3,384,000 | 1,844,000 | 11,060,000 | 13,109,000 | 5,172,000 | 6,220,000 |
| December | 5,292,000 | 2,375,000 | 14,788,000 | 11,620,000 | 6,577,000 | 7,431,000 |

### CORN.

| Months. | 1897. Bushels. | 1898. Bushels. | 1899. Bushels. | 1900. Bushels. | 1901. Bushels. | 1902. Bushels. |
|---|---|---|---|---|---|---|
| January | 5,957,000 | 18,320,000 | 5,882,000 | 3,520,000 | 2,084,000 | 4,879,000 |
| February | 6,423,000 | 21,537,000 | 11,349,000 | 6,098,000 | 3,755,000 | 4,615,000 |
| March | 7,345,000 | 23,062,000 | 14,614,000 | 7,978,000 | 5,878,000 | 4,455,000 |
| April | 7,694,000 | 23,587,000 | 12,137,000 | 6,358,000 | 8,189,000 | 4,679,000 |
| May | 7,286,000 | 11,433,000 | 11,307,000 | 7,048,000 | 6,623,000 | 4,280,000 |
| June | 5,625,000 | 6,875,000 | 5,762,000 | 3,790,000 | 6,572,000 | 4,248,000 |
| July | 7,707,000 | 8,386,000 | 4,991,000 | 3,449,000 | 5,762,000 | 3,558,000 |
| August | 6,619,000 | 7,157,000 | 3,100,000 | 2,696,000 | 6,966,000 | 5,397,000 |
| September | 12,779,000 | 5,703,000 | 1,601,000 | 700,000 | 7,278,000 | 1,815,000 |
| October | 18,126,000 | 8,915,000 | 5,415,000 | 2,827,000 | 6,974,000 | 1,599,000 |
| November | 20,621,000 | 11,717,000 | 4,166,000 | 1,820,000 | 7,069,000 | 685,000 |
| December | 17,887,000 | 5,151,000 | 2,564,000 | 1,872,000 | 5,676,000 | 521,000 |

### OATS.

| Months. | 1897. Bushels. | 1898. Bushels. | 1899. Bushels. | 1900. Bushels. | 1901. Bushels. | 1902. Bushels. |
|---|---|---|---|---|---|---|
| January | 5,160,000 | 1,335,000 | 1,419,000 | 1,543,000 | 2,938,000 | 881,000 |
| February | 5,165,000 | 1,446,000 | 1,377,000 | 1,517,000 | 4,015,000 | 531,000 |
| March | 5,901,000 | 1,603,000 | 3,463,000 | 2,016,000 | 4,336,000 | 461,000 |
| April | 5,926,000 | 1,425,000 | 1,435,000 | 2,102,000 | 4,364,000 | 692,000 |
| May | 5,001,000 | 819,000 | 993,000 | 1,868,000 | 3,102,000 | 852,000 |
| June | 2,061,000 | 789,000 | 1,233,000 | 1,277,000 | 3,751,000 | 732,000 |
| July | 1,919,000 | 561,000 | 866,000 | 1,703,000 | 3,348,000 | 112,000 |
| August | 1,473,000 | 724,000 | 1,092,000 | 1,457,000 | 741,000 | 1,312,000 |
| September | 2,905,000 | 466,000 | 989,000 | 2,661,000 | 1,500,000 | 441,000 |
| October | 2,842,000 | 852,000 | 1,323,000 | 3,184,000 | 1,941,000 | 1,558,000 |
| November | 2,174,000 | 939,000 | 1,295,000 | 3,470,000 | 1,607,000 | 2,060,000 |
| December | 1,671,000 | 625,000 | 945,000 | 3,448,000 | 919,000 | 2,056,000 |

## GRAIN RECEIPTS AT CHICAGO

| | Wheat. Bushels. | Corn. Bushels. | Oats. Bushels. | Rye. Bushels. |
|---|---|---|---|---|
| 1880 | 23,541,607 | 97,272,844 | 23,490,915 | 1,869,218 |
| 1881 | 14,824,990 | 78,393,315 | 24,861,538 | 1,363,552 |
| 1882 | 23,008,596 | 49,061,755 | 26,802,872 | 1,984,516 |
| 1883 | 20,364,155 | 74,412,319 | 36,502,283 | 5,484,259 |
| 1884 | 26,397,587 | 59,580,445 | 40,082,362 | 3,327,516 |
| 1885 | 18,909,717 | 62,930,897 | 37,678,753 | 1,892,760 |
| 1886 | 16,771,743 | 62,861,594 | 30,976,215 | 956,247 |
| 1887 | 21,848,251 | 51,578,410 | 45,750,842 | 852,726 |
| 1888 | 13,438,069 | 74,208,908 | 52,184,878 | 2,707,571 |
| 1889 | 18,762,646 | 79,920,691 | 49,901,942 | 2,605,984 |
| 1890 | 14,248,770 | 91,387,751 | 75,150,249 | 3,520,508 |
| 1891 | 42,931,258 | 72,770,304 | 74,402,413 | 9,164,198 |
| 1892 | 50,234,556 | 78,510,385 | 79,827,985 | 3,633,308 |
| 1893 | 33,355,101 | 91,205,154 | 84,289,886 | 1,707,072 |
| 1894 | 25,665,902 | 64,951,815 | 63,144,885 | 1,368,157 |
| 1895 | 20,637,642 | 59,527,718 | 79,890,792 | 1,657,216 |
| 1896 | 19,933,402 | 92,722,348 | 109,725,689 | 2,530,336 |
| 1897 | 28,087,147 | 116,747,389 | 118,086,662 | 3,388,751 |
| 1898 | 33,741,556 | 127,426,374 | 110,293,647 | 4,935,308 |
| 1899 | 30,971,547 | 133,776,350 | 110,775,732 | 2,793,476 |
| 1900 | 48,048,298 | 134,603,456 | 105,226,761 | 1,973,701 |
| 1901 | 51,197,870 | 84,136,637 | 90,632,152 | 3,244,394 |
| 1902 | 37,940,953 | 50,622,907 | 78,879,800 | 3,170,541 |

## CONDITION OF CROPS IN THE UNITED STATES

REPORTED BY THE STATISTICIAN OF THE DEPARTMENT OF AGRICULTURE.

| | 1894. | 1895. | 1896. | 1897. | 1898. | 1899. | 1900. | 1901. | 1902. |
|---|---|---|---|---|---|---|---|---|---|
| **WINTER WHEAT.** | | | | | | | | | |
| April | 86.7 | 81.4 | 77.1 | 81.4 | 86.7 | 77.9 | 82.1 | 91.7 | 78.7 |
| May | 81.4 | 82.9 | 82.7 | 80.2 | 86.5 | 76.2 | 88.9 | 94.1 | 76.4 |
| June | 83.2 | 71.1 | 77.9 | 78.5 | 90.8 | 67.3 | 82.7 | 87.8 | 76.1 |
| July | 83.9 | 65.8 | 75.6 | 81.2 | 85.7 | 65.6 | 80.8 | 88.3 | 77.0 |
| September | *83.7 | *75.4 | *74.6 | *85.7 | *86.7 | *70.9 | *69.6 | *82.8 | *80.0 |
| December | 91.5 | 89. | 81.4 | 99.5 | .... | .... | .... | .... | .... |
| **SPRING WHEAT.** | | | | | | | | | |
| June | 88. | 97.8 | 99.9 | 89.6 | 101.0 | 91.4 | 87.3 | 92.0 | 95.4 |
| July | 68.4 | 102.2 | 93.3 | 91.2 | 95.0 | 91.7 | 55.2 | 95.6 | 92.4 |
| August | 67.4 | 95.9 | 78.9 | 86.7 | 96.5 | 83.6 | 56.4 | 80.3 | 89.7 |
| September | .... | .... | .... | 86.7 | *86.7 | *70.9 | *69.6 | .... | .... |
| **CORN.** | | | | | | | | | |
| July | 95. | 99.3 | 92.4 | 82.9 | 90.5 | 86.5 | 89.5 | 81.3 | 87.5 |
| August | 69.1 | 102.5 | 96. | 84.2 | 87.0 | 59.9 | 87.5 | 54.0 | 86.5 |
| September | 63.4 | 96.4 | 91. | 79.3 | 84.1 | 85.2 | 80.6 | 51.7 | 84.3 |
| October | 64.2 | 95.5 | 90.5 | 77.1 | 82.0 | 82.7 | 78.2 | 52.1 | 79.6 |
| **OATS.** | | | | | | | | | |
| June | 87. | 84.3 | 98.8 | 93.3 | 98.0 | 88.7 | 91.7 | 85.3 | 90.6 |
| July | 77.7 | 83.2 | 96.3 | 87.5 | 92.8 | 90.0 | 85.5 | 83.7 | 92.1 |
| August | 76.5 | 84.5 | 77.3 | 86. | 84.2 | 90.8 | 85.0 | 73.6 | 89.4 |
| September | 77.8 | 86. | 74. | 84.6 | 79.0 | 87.2 | 82.9 | 72.1 | 87.2 |

* Includes Winter and Spring.

## WORLD'S SHIPMENTS OF WHEAT

### FROM EXPORTING COUNTRIES, BY WEEKS.

| * Week Ending | 1898. Bushels. | 1899. Bushels. | 1900. Bushels. | 1901. Bushels. | 1902. Bushels. |
|---|---|---|---|---|---|
| January 4 | 4,850,000 | 7,900,000 | 4,414,000 | 5,238,000 | 7,586,000 |
| January 11 | 7,101,000 | 6,999,000 | 6,057,000 | 8,309,000 | 7,360,000 |
| January 18 | 5,174,000 | 6,407,000 | 4,720,000 | 5,352,000 | 8,374,000 |
| January 25 | 7,346,000 | 7,150,000 | 5,269,000 | 7,807,000 | 7,284,000 |
| February 1 | 5,514,000 | 8,881,000 | 4,933,000 | 7,312,000 | 8,286,000 |
| February 8 | 6,180,000 | 8,333,000 | 5,590,000 | 8,830,000 | 8,900,000 |
| February 15 | 7,373,000 | 4,791,000 | 6,538,000 | 8,463,000 | 6,411,000 |
| February 22 | 7,010,000 | 7,124,000 | 7,549,000 | 5,936,000 | 6,881,000 |
| March 1 | 7,524,000 | 9,724,000 | 8,319,000 | 7,273,000 | 7,142,000 |
| March 8 | 7,205,000 | 7,663,000 | 9,241,000 | 7,742,000 | 8,012,000 |
| March 15 | 6,658,000 | 7,834,000 | 7,186,000 | 7,958,000 | 5,278,000 |
| March 22 | 8,216,000 | 6,627,000 | 8,535,000 | 7,651,000 | 7,399,000 |
| March 29 | 8,439,000 | 7,964,000 | 7,258,000 | 8,575,000 | 6,632,000 |
| April 5 | 8,099,000 | 7,037,000 | 6,997,000 | 8,102,000 | 8,863,000 |
| April 12 | 9,036,000 | 7,360,000 | 6,585,000 | 10,166,000 | 8,062,000 |
| April 19 | 7,432,000 | 6,597,000 | 8,490,000 | 8,286,000 | 7,470,000 |
| April 26 | 9,129,000 | 8,742,000 | 6,596,000 | 7,794,000 | 8,963,000 |
| May 3 | 10,220,000 | 8,820,000 | 9,625,000 | 8,069,000 | 8,656,000 |
| May 10 | 10,187,000 | 8,964,000 | 6,737,000 | 9,415,000 | 7,794,000 |
| May 17 | 11,239,000 | 6,788,000 | 9,116,000 | 7,903,000 | 9,405,000 |
| May 24 | 13,029,000 | 8,934,000 | 7,387,000 | 9,244,000 | 9,673,000 |
| May 31 | 13,336,000 | 7,988,000 | 7,021,000 | 8,419,000 | 7,713,000 |
| June 7 | 12,397,000 | 7,910,000 | 7,414,000 | 10,829,000 | 9,460,000 |
| June 14 | 10,117,000 | 7,735,000 | 8,382,000 | 8,503,000 | 8,122,000 |
| June 21 | 8,647,000 | 7,371,000 | 8,886,000 | 9,481,000 | 7,476,000 |
| June 28 | 7,452,000 | 8,188,000 | 6,804,000 | 8,852,000 | 6,159,000 |
| July 5 | 5,729,000 | 8,159,000 | 7,099,000 | 7,478,000 | 6,563,000 |
| July 12 | 5,582,000 | 6,168,000 | 5,470,000 | 7,064,000 | 7,701,000 |
| July 19 | 5,047,000 | 7,104,000 | 7,973,000 | 7,614,000 | 5,663,000 |
| July 26 | 3,880,000 | 7,470,000 | 5,860,000 | 9,983,000 | 6,941,000 |
| August 2 | 5,671,000 | 7,464,000 | 6,771,000 | 8,397,000 | 6,197,000 |
| August 9 | 5,021,000 | 6,704,000 | 5,647,000 | 10,720,000 | 5,996,000 |
| August 16 | 5,060,000 | 6,816,000 | 6,572,000 | 11,632,000 | 7,304,000 |
| August 23 | 4,923,000 | 6,179,000 | 5,439,000 | 9,743,000 | 8,635,000 |
| August 30 | 4,903,000 | 5,861,000 | 6,648,000 | 9,336,000 | 9,805,000 |
| September 6 | 5,236,000 | 6,610,000 | 5,469,000 | 7,478,000 | 11,276,000 |
| September 13 | 5,355,000 | 7,069,000 | 7,458,000 | 9,281,000 | 10,428,000 |
| September 20 | 7,625,000 | 7,571,000 | 7,960,000 | 9,345,000 | 10,899,000 |
| September 27 | 8,395,000 | 7,056,000 | 8,258,000 | 8,778,000 | 11,477,000 |
| October 4 | 8,035,000 | 8,271,000 | 8,155,000 | 10,148,000 | 13,406,000 |
| October 11 | 7,418,000 | 8,620,000 | 9,269,000 | 7,808,000 | 11,902,000 |
| October 18 | 8,543,000 | 7,777,000 | 6,981,000 | 8,736,000 | 10,977,000 |
| October 25 | 8,457,000 | 7,864,000 | 8,925,000 | 7,268,000 | 12,992,000 |
| November 1 | 10,374,000 | 5,679,000 | 8,396,000 | 10,957,000 | 13,126,000 |
| November 8 | 7,347,000 | 8,611,000 | 9,008,000 | 9,862,000 | 10,835,000 |
| November 15 | 8,335,000 | 6,904,000 | 7,774,000 | 8,972,000 | 11,160,000 |
| November 22 | 7,761,000 | 6,289,000 | 8,003,000 | 10,151,000 | 9,518,000 |
| November 29 | 9,844,000 | 5,435,000 | 5,850,000 | 8,497,000 | 8,276,000 |
| December 6 | 8,391,000 | 7,535,000 | 6,024,000 | 8,497,000 | 9,080,000 |
| December 13 | 7,397,000 | 5,163,000 | 8,418,000 | 7,095,000 | 6,497,000 |
| December 20 | 7,035,000 | 4,716,000 | 7,259,000 | 7,565,000 | 6,120,000 |
| December 27 | 7,899,000 | 5,155,000 | 6,971,000 | 6,612,000 | 6,440,000 |

* The dates are for 1902. The other columns are for corresponding weeks.

## *WORLD'S WHEAT SUPPLY*

ESTIMATED BY DAILY TRADE BULLETIN, CHICAGO.

| | Bushels. 1899. | Bushels. 1900. | Bushels. 1901. | Bushels. 1902. |
|---|---|---|---|---|
| EUROPE. | | | | |
| France | 368,400,000 | 325,600,000 | 304,000,000 | 341,800,000 |
| Russia-Poland | 396,400,000 | 365,600,000 | 361,200,000 | 424,000,000 |
| Caucasia | 56,000,000 | 56,800,000 | 67,000,000 | 60,000,000 |
| Italy | 137,600,000 | 116,800,000 | 147,600,000 | 127,000,000 |
| Spain | 92,000,000 | 100,000,000 | 108,000,000 | 124,000,000 |
| Hungary | 140,800,000 | 141,600,000 | 128,000,000 | 160,000,000 |
| Austria | 42,600,000 | 40,800,000 | 43,200,000 | 45,600,000 |
| Croatia and Slavonia | 9,600,000 | 11,200,000 | 10,400,000 | 16,000,000 |
| Herzogovina | 2,400,000 | 2,400,000 | 2,400,000 | 2,600,000 |
| Germany | 141,600,000 | 140,600,000 | 92,000,000 | 138,000,000 |
| United Kingdom | 69,300,000 | 54,400,000 | 56,000,000 | 58,000,000 |
| Turkey-in-Europe | 15,000,000 | 16,000,000 | 22,000,000 | 30,000,000 |
| Roumania | 25,280,000 | 55,200,000 | 72,400,000 | 75,400,000 |
| Bulgaria | 24,000,000 | 26,400,000 | 24,000,000 | 44,000,000 |
| Eastern Roumelia | 3,200,000 | 5,600,000 | 6,400,000 | 6,400,000 |
| Belgium | 13,600,000 | 12,800,000 | 12,000,000 | 12,000,000 |
| Portugal | 6,400,000 | 8,000,000 | 8,000,000 | 5,600,000 |
| Holland | 5,600,000 | 5,600,000 | 4,800,000 | 6,400,000 |
| Greece | 1,600,000 | 2,400,000 | 3,200,000 | 6,000,000 |
| Denmark | 3,200,000 | 3,200,000 | 2,400,000 | 3,400,000 |
| Servia | 8,800,000 | 9,600,000 | 8,800,000 | 12,000,000 |
| Sweden and Norway | 4,320,000 | 5,360,000 | 4,800,000 | 4,400,000 |
| Switzerland | 4,000,000 | 4,000,000 | 4,400,000 | 4,000,000 |
| Cyprus, Malta, etc. | 2,000,000 | 2,400,000 | 2,000,000 | 3,000,000 |
| Total | 1,573,300,000 | 1,512,360,000 | 1,495,000,000 | 1,709,600,000 |
| AMERICA. | | | | |
| United States | 547,303,000 | 522,229,000 | 748,000,000 | 670,000,000 |
| Canada | 60,000,000 | 44,000,000 | 90,000,000 | 105,000,000 |
| Mexico | 16,000,000 | 16,000,000 | 16,000,000 | 14,000,000 |
| Argentine Republic | 92,000,000 | 72,000,000 | 74,000,000 | 110,000,000 |
| Chili and Uruguay | 20,200,000 | 13,600,000 | 17,600,000 | 17,000,000 |
| Total | 735,503,000 | 667,829,000 | 945,600,000 | 916,000,000 |
| OTHER COUNTRIES. | | | | |
| India | 232,000,000 | 248,000,000 | 248,000,000 | 232,000,000 |
| Algeria | 15,000,000 | 17,600,000 | 23,200,000 | 24,000,000 |
| Egypt | 14,400,000 | 9,600,000 | 12,800,000 | 9,000,000 |
| Australasia | 49,000,000 | 58,400,000 | 56,800,000 | 24,000,000 |
| Turkey-in-Asia | 35,000,000 | 28,000,000 | 30,000,000 | 30,000,000 |
| Persia | 16,000,000 | 16,000,000 | 15,200,000 | 16,000,000 |
| Tunis | 4,800,000 | 5,600,000 | 6,400,000 | 8,000,000 |
| Cape Colony | 2,000,000 | 4,000,000 | 4,000,000 | 4,000,000 |
| Japan | 20,000,000 | 16,000,000 | 20,000,000 | 16,000,000 |
| Total | 388,200,000 | 403,200,000 | 416,400,000 | 363,000,000 |
| Grand total | 2,697,003,000 | 2,583,389,000 | 2,857,000,000 | 2,988,600,000 |

## WORLD'S SUPPLY OF WHEAT AND FLOUR RECKONED AS WHEAT

ON THE FIRST DAY OF EACH MONTH.

Estimated by Daily Trade Bulletin, Chicago.

| | United States and Canada, Bushels. | In Europe and Afloat, Bushels. | Total Bushels. |
|---|---|---|---|
| 1901. | | | |
| January | 129,084,000 | 81,980,000 | 211,064,000 |
| February | 125,121,000 | 83,520,000 | 208,641,000 |
| March | 117,889,000 | 86,464,000 | 204,353,000 |
| April | 109,517,000 | 87,496,000 | 197,013,000 |
| May | 93,394,000 | 86,582,000 | 179,976,000 |
| June | 76,188,000 | 84,310,000 | 160,498,000 |
| July | 61,583,000 | 80,834,000 | 142,417,000 |
| August | 62,269,000 | 75,932,000 | 138,201,000 |
| September | 66,262,000 | 79,768,000 | 146,030,000 |
| October | 84,195,000 | 80,954,000 | 165,149,000 |
| November | 102,335,000 | 75,060,000 | 177,395,000 |
| December | 127,518,000 | 82,506,000 | 210,024,000 |
| 1902. | | | |
| January | 130,680,000 | 77,948,000 | 208,628,000 |
| February | 129,128,000 | 81,366,000 | 210,494,000 |
| March | 119,552,000 | 80,148,000 | 199,700,000 |
| April | 107,729,000 | 75,594,000 | 183,323,000 |
| May | 87,326,000 | 71,406,000 | 158,732,000 |
| June | 62,235,000 | 70,938,000 | 133,173,000 |
| July | 47,851,000 | 57,976,000 | 105,827,000 |
| August | 51,885,000 | 43,088,000 | 94,973,000 |
| September | 56,612,000 | 46,872,000 | 103,484,000 |
| October | 73,085,000 | 62,455,000 | 135,540,000 |
| November | 94,081,000 | 79,954,000 | 174,035,000 |
| December | 108,383,000 | 77,346,000 | 185,729,000 |

## FOREIGN GRAIN QUOTATIONS

London quotes American (Atlantic Coast) wheat in quarters of 480 pounds, or 8 bushels. Fluctuations of 1½d. per quarter are equal to about ⅜c per bushel; of 3d. per quarter to ¾c per bushel, and of 6d. to 1½c per bushel.

Liverpool quotes American (Pacific Coast) wheat in centals of 100 pounds, or 1⅔ bushels. Fluctuations of ¼d. per cental equal .003c per bushel; of ½d., .006c per bushel; of 3¼d. .009c per bushel, and of 1d., 12c.

Berlin quotes wheat in 1,000 kilos or about 36¾ bushels. Fluctuations of 12½ pfennings, equal 3-16 of 1 cent; of 50 pfennings, 32-100c per bushel, and of 1 mark, 64-100c per bushel.

Paris quotes wheat in 100 kilos, equal to 3.67 bushels. Fluctuations of 5 centimes equal 0.26c per bushel; of 10 centimes 0.52c per bushel; of 25 centimes 1.31c per bushel; of 50 centimes 2.63c per bushel, and of 1 franc 5.25c per bushel.

## AVERAGE PRICES OF ENGLISH WHEAT

The following table gives the average price of cash English wheat per quarter (eight bushels), by years, in the home market:

| | s. | d. | | s. | d. | | s. | d. | | s. | d. |
|---|---|---|---|---|---|---|---|---|---|---|---|
| 1780..... | 36 | 0 | 1811..... | 95 | 3 | 1842..... | 57 | 3 | 1873..... | 58 | 8 |
| 1781..... | 40 | 6 | 1812..... | 126 | 6 | 1843..... | 50 | 1 | 1874..... | 55 | 8 |
| 1782..... | 49 | 3 | 1813..... | 109 | 9 | 1844..... | 51 | 3 | 1875..... | 45 | 2 |
| 1783..... | 54 | 3 | 1814..... | 74 | 4 | 1845..... | 50 | 10 | 1876..... | 46 | 2 |
| 1784..... | 50 | 4 | 1815..... | 65 | 7 | 1846..... | 54 | 8 | 1877..... | 56 | 9 |
| 1785..... | 43 | 1 | 1816..... | 78 | 6 | 1847..... | 69 | 9 | 1878..... | 46 | 5 |
| 1786..... | 40 | 0 | 1817..... | 96 | 11 | 1848..... | 50 | 6 | 1879..... | 43 | 10 |
| 1787..... | 42 | 5 | 1818..... | 86 | 3 | 1849..... | 44 | 3 | 1880..... | 44 | 4 |
| 1788..... | 46 | 4 | 1819..... | 74 | 6 | 1850..... | 40 | 3 | 1881..... | 45 | 4 |
| 1789..... | 52 | 9 | 1820..... | 67 | 10 | 1851..... | 38 | 6 | 1882.... | 45 | 1 |
| 1790..... | 54 | 9 | 1821..... | 56 | 1 | 1852..... | 40 | 9 | 1883..... | 41 | 7 |
| 1791..... | 48 | 7 | 1822..... | 44 | 7 | 1853..... | 54 | 3 | 1884. . | 35 | 6 |
| 1792..... | 40 | 3 | 1823..... | 53 | 4 | 1854..... | 72 | 5 | 1885..... | 32 | 10 |
| 1793. .. | 49 | 3 | 1824..... | 63 | 11 | 1855..... | 74 | 8 | 1886..... | 31 | 2 |
| 1794..... | 52 | 3 | 1825..... | 68 | 6 | 1856..... | 69 | 2 | 1887..... | 32 | 6 |
| 1795..... | 75 | 2 | 1826..... | 58 | 8 | 1857..... | 56 | 4 | 1888..... | 32 | 0 |
| 1796..... | 78 | 7 | 1827..... | 58 | 6 | 1858. ... | 44 | 2 | 1889..... | 29 | 9 |
| 1797..... | 53 | 9 | 1828..... | 60 | 5 | 1859..... | 43 | 9 | 1890..... | 31 | 9 |
| 1798..... | 51 | 10 | 1829..... | 66 | 3 | 1860..... | 53 | 3 | 1891..... | 37 | 1 |
| 1799..... | 69 | 0 | 1830..... | 64 | 3 | 1861..... | 55 | 4 | 1892..... | 30 | 4 |
| 1800..... | 113 | 10 | 1831..... | 66 | 4 | 1862..... | 55 | 5 | 1893..... | 26 | 4 |
| 1801..... | 119 | 6 | 1832..... | 58 | 8 | 1863.... | 44 | 9 | 1894..... | 22 | 11 |
| 1802..... | 69 | 10 | 1833..... | 52 | 11 | 1864..... | 40 | 2 | 1895..... | 23 | 0 |
| 1803..... | 58 | 10 | 1834..... | 46 | 2 | 1865..... | 41 | 10 | 1896..... | 26 | 3 |
| 1804..... | 62 | 3 | 1835..... | 39 | 4 | 1866..... | 49 | 11 | 1897..... | 30 | 3 |
| 1805..... | 89 | 9 | 1836..... | 48 | 6 | 1867..... | 64 | 5 | 1898..... | 34 | 2 |
| 1806..... | 79 | 1 | 1837..... | 55 | 10 | 1868..... | 63 | 9 | 1899..... | 25 | 9 |
| 1807..... | 75 | 4 | 1838..... | 64 | 7 | 1869..... | 48 | 2 | 1900..... | 26 | 11 |
| 1808..... | 81 | 4 | 1839..... | 70 | 8 | 1870..... | 46 | 10 | 1901..... | 26 | 11 |
| 1809..... | 97 | 4 | 1840..... | 66 | 4 | 1871..... | 56 | 8 | 1902..... | 28 | 1 |
| 1810..... | 106 | 5 | 1841..... | 64 | 4 | 1872..... | 57 | 0 | | | |

## WEEKLY EXPORTS OF WHEAT AND FLOUR FROM UNITED STATES

Reported by Bradstreets.

| * Week Ending | 1897. Bushels. | 1898. Bushels. | 1899. Bushels. | 1900. Bushels. | 1901. Bushels. | 1902. Bushels. |
|---|---|---|---|---|---|---|
| December 25... | 5,495,061 | 6,292,625 | 3,610,557 | 3,868,165 | 4,291,543 | 3,560,486 |
| December 18... | 4,758,000 | 5,515,231 | 2,813,714 | 4,123,350 | 4,332,832 | 3,256,037 |
| December 11... | 4,604,000 | 6,243,859 | 3,254,649 | 4,785,577 | 3,879,809 | 3,761,047 |
| December 4... | 6,006,000 | 6,868,952 | 5,133,331 | 3,432,159 | 4,604,846 | 5,704,440 |
| November 27.. | 6,700,000 | 7,483,959 | 3,699,400 | 2,497,880 | 5,117,478 | 4,179,685 |
| November 20.. | 5,465,000 | 5,824,726 | 3,688,677 | 3,827,296 | 5,518,930 | 5,277,672 |
| November 13.. | 6,654,000 | 5,679,141 | 4,540,007 | 4,062,020 | 4,983,734 | 4,440,160 |
| November 6.. | 5,446,000 | 3,774,693 | 4,650,842 | 3,555,507 | 5,469,645 | 5,715,555 |
| October 30.... | 5,590,000 | 6,773,643 | 3,046,856 | 3,612,421 | 6,672,888 | 5,997,620 |
| October 23..... | 5,911,000 | 5,560,991 | 4,416,495 | 4,932,978 | 4,952,134 | 7,060,137 |
| October 16..... | 5,552,000 | 4,282,773 | 4,160,618 | 3,796,643 | 5,536,073 | 5,240,688 |
| October 9..... | 6,040,000 | 4,729,995 | 5,265,634 | 4,292,855 | 4,719,898 | 5,645,779 |
| October 2..... | 4,836,000 | 5,497,224 | 5,183,398 | 4,459,168 | 6,195,749 | 6,870,578 |
| September 25.. | 5,834,000 | 5,306,879 | 3,872,455 | 4,242,810 | 6,470,352 | 5,077,070 |
| September 18.. | 5,809,000 | 5,224,927 | 4,630,765 | 3,535,857 | 3,840,574 | 5,435,323 |
| September 11.. | 6,290,000 | 3,675,291 | 4,536,552 | 4,665,982 | 6,648,609 | 5,444,146 |
| September 4.. | 5,462,000 | 3,200,208 | 4,353,906 | 3,373,100 | 4,406,064 | 6,276,299 |
| August 28..... | 6,268,000 | 3,687,040 | 3,613,443 | 3,248,313 | 6,607,611 | 5,436,530 |
| August 21..... | 5,150,000 | 3,563,476 | 3,343,825 | 2,695,168 | 6,606,989 | 5,954,759 |
| August 14..... | 5,317,000 | 3,988,348 | 4,040,009 | 3,113,641 | 9,039,761 | 4,591,805 |
| August 7..... | 4,461,000 | 3,928,606 | 3,616,154 | 3,318,760 | 8,832,199 | 4,244,363 |
| July 31........ | 3,308,000 | 4,111,312 | 4,711,614 | 3,347,003 | 6,463,391 | 4,388,534 |
| July 24........ | 2,343,000 | 2,371,872 | 3,766,432 | 2,363,743 | 6,974,526 | 3,980,969 |
| July 17........ | 1,979,000 | 2,303,469 | 3,408,073 | 3,029,381 | 5,221,880 | 3,775,222 |
| July 10........ | 1,522,000 | 2,910,827 | 3,263,815 | 2,829,910 | 5,016,149 | 4,404,115 |
| July 3........ | 2,503,000 | 2,728,642 | 3,758,972 | 3,018,832 | 3,787,639 | 3,211,215 |
| June 26....... | 2,779,000 | 4,716,401 | 3,268,998 | 3,184,144 | 4,364,147 | 3,382,701 |
| June 19...... | 2,156,000 | 3,799,470 | 3,746,718 | 4,645,180 | 5,520,831 | 3,860,434 |
| June 12....... | 2,547,000 | 4,396,787 | 2,799,471 | 4,678,029 | 5,159,107 | 3,400,314 |
| June 5....... | 1,890,000 | 4,730,982 | 3,158,047 | 4,230,221 | 6,644,644 | 4,600,055 |
| May 29........ | 2,620,000 | 5,248,086 | 3,596,065 | 4,533,140 | 4,138,970 | 3,900,645 |
| May 22........ | 2,081,000 | 4,309,133 | 3,198,319 | 3,698,968 | 4,796,084 | 5,184,839 |
| May 15........ | 2,656,000 | 4,064,832 | 2,212,206 | 5,178,422 | 3,984,968 | 5,172,634 |
| May 8. ...... | 2,184,000 | 3,646,543 | 3,284,182 | 3,480,374 | 4,178,872 | 3,302,240 |
| May 1.... ... | 1,799,000 | 2,923,775 | 3,484,081 | 4,537,022 | 5,100,763 | 5,308,155 |
| April 24....... | 1,156,000 | 4,449,009 | 3,028,403 | 3,683,863 | 4,282,129 | 3,750,589 |
| April 17....... | 1,655,000 | 3,232,106 | 2,932,959 | 3,898,451 | 5,306,217 | 4,118,108 |
| April 10....... | 1,344,000 | 4,425,302 | 1,983,619 | 2,896,653 | 6,405,601 | 3,842,012 |
| April 3....... | 2,037,000 | 3,778,726 | 3,384,800 | 3,836,963 | 4,698,693 | 4,446,917 |
| March 27...... | 2,465,000 | 3,550,664 | 3,988,238 | 2,962,349 | 4,494,635 | 2,904,110 |
| March 20...... | 1,749,000 | 3,896,318 | 3,746,761 | 2,903,495 | 3,256,644 | 4,326,304 |
| March 13...... | 1,629,000 | 3,679,056 | 4,114,046 | 2,727,450 | 4,693,939 | 2,906,280 |
| March 6...... | 1,599,000 | 4,484,761 | 4,398,821 | 4,208,758 | 4,229,528 | 4,095,944 |
| February 27.... | 2,075,000 | 3,252,003 | 5,815,585 | 3,863,387 | 5,333,313 | 3,234,540 |
| February 20.... | 1,372,000 | 3,722,469 | 3,844,359 | 3,660,850 | 3,424,302 | 3,609,435 |
| February 13.... | 2,121,000 | 3,832,744 | 2,454,771 | 3,834,069 | 4,814,878 | 3,175,481 |
| February 6.... | 2,051,000 | 3,419,504 | 5,780,500 | 2,902,357 | 4,997,813 | 4,800,457 |
| January 30..... | 3,169,000 | 3,635,035 | 6,585,418 | 2,724,937 | 3,776,100 | 3,702,368 |
| January 23..... | 2,515,000 | 5,026,024 | 4,997,522 | 3,581,197 | 4,838,678 | 3,639,679 |
| January 16..... | 2,917,000 | 3,726,064 | 5,198,671 | 3,061,026 | 3,336,054 | 4,690,202 |
| January 9.... | 2,948,000 | 5,299,517 | 4,647,071 | 4,248,926 | 5,961,095 | 3,567,710 |
| January 2..... | 3,109,000 | 3,481,576 | 6,860,268 | 2,509,682 | 3,914,301 | 4,818,471 |

* The dates are for 1902 The other columns are for corresponding weeks.

## WEEKLY EXPORTS OF CORN FROM UNITED STATES

Reported by Bradstreets.

| * Week Ending | 1897. Bushels. | 1898. Bushels. | 1899. Bushels. | 1900. Bushels. | 1901. Bushels. | 1902. Bushels. |
|---|---|---|---|---|---|---|
| December 25 .. | 4,086,866 | 3,659,745 | 3,226,259 | 4,011,105 | 424,336 | 1,502,551 |
| December 18 .. | 4,879,000 | 4,103,673 | 3,910,000 | 5,465,578 | 330,941 | 1,526,141 |
| December 11 .. | 4,130,000 | 3,251,936 | 4,017,185 | 4,853,458 | 278,307 | 1,301,286 |
| December 4 .. | 3,069,000 | 4,388,535 | 3,815,699 | 5,371,377 | 362,844 | 1,151,563 |
| November 27.. | 4,586,000 | 4,723,988 | 4,441,514 | 4,801,030 | 630,968 | 255,174 |
| November 20.. | 2,870,000 | 3,993,846 | 4,149,523 | 5,235,568 | 445,351 | 243,381 |
| November 13.. | 3,210,000 | 3,531,724 | 4,603,718 | 3,976,914 | 629,924 | 281,901 |
| November 6.. | 2,652,000 | 2,342,745 | 4,581,447 | 3,287,627 | 708,284 | 130,847 |
| October 30 .... | 2,200,000 | 3,566,640 | 4,503,425 | 3,920,110 | 606,159 | 153,205 |
| October 23 .... | 1,589,000 | 2,424,376 | 4,525,519 | 3,365,651 | 1,188,288 | 84,564 |
| October 16 .... | 1,178,000 | 2,597,191 | 5,058,697 | 2,886,993 | 640,033 | 180,674 |
| October 9 .... | 2,225,000 | 2,706,292 | 3,836,793 | 2,895,037 | 678,246 | 180,358 |
| October 2 .... | 2,110,000 | 3,564,710 | 4,238,749 | 2,364,249 | 907,924 | 141,423 |
| September 25.. | 3,109,000 | 2,530,076 | 3,523,089 | 2,156,171 | 585,706 | 74,952 |
| September 18.. | 4,022,000 | 2,626,290 | 3,794,965 | 2,134,205 | 611,258 | 49,508 |
| September 11.. | 3,901,000 | 2,531,005 | 3,282,751 | 2,402,787 | 777,831 | 91,512 |
| September 4.. | 4,943,000 | 3,868,869 | 4,786,878 | 3,162,271 | 550,876 | 21,196 |
| August 28..... | 3,185,000 | 1,661,700 | 4,167,868 | 3,717,490 | 441,918 | 115,150 |
| August 21..... | 2,682,000 | 2,648,933 | 4,596,097 | 3,493,375 | 523,883 | 51,649 |
| August 14..... | 3,929,000 | 3,196,021 | 5,531,405 | 3,017,089 | 508,807 | 93,423 |
| August 7.. . | 3,276,000 | 3,517,952 | 5,950,361 | 2,890,754 | 990,714 | 70,611 |
| July 31........ | 3,224,000 | 2,856,923 | 5,027,706 | 3,890,005 | 563,604 | 28,405 |
| July 24........ | 1,483,000 | 2,601,821 | 3,700,320 | 3,264,745 | 1,155,276 | 79,611 |
| July 17....... | 2,299,000 | 2,822,128 | 3,666,294 | 4,182,159 | 1,714,081 | 130,679 |
| July 10........ | 2,724,000 | 2,822,248 | 4,553,739 | 4,022,068 | 2,800,738 | 185,131 |
| July 3 ....... | 2,733,000 | 2,411,272 | 4,097,144 | 3,614,294 | 2,240,933 | 127,969 |
| June 26....... | 1,924,000 | 2,601,560 | 4,482,116 | 4,654,000 | 2,455,460 | 130,102 |
| June 19....... | 2,282,000 | 3,902,321 | 2,872,432 | 2,514,593 | 2,435,487 | 110,979 |
| June 12....... | 1,924,000 | 4,106,706 | 3,285,301 | 3,631,205 | 2,569,254 | 94,981 |
| June 5....... | 2,398,000 | 4,774,303 | 3,339,889 | 3,084,474 | 2,455,102 | 86,254 |
| May 29........ | 2,397,000 | 6,605,423 | 3,922,497 | 3,882,294 | 2,037,343 | 71,478 |
| May 22........ | 2,186,000 | 6,164,451 | 3,845,818 | 4,374,145 | 2,204,902 | 90,969 |
| May 15........ | 3,190,000 | 5,550,579 | 2,753,414 | 3,437,994 | 2,704,594 | 82,795 |
| May 8........ | 3,097,000 | 6,077,270 | 2,768,694 | 4,638,140 | 1,583,831 | 126,755 |
| May 1...... | 3,128,000 | 6,185,904 | 2,847,290 | 3,411,015 | 2,371,892 | 128,679 |
| April 24....... | 3,657,000 | 4,216,066 | 2,615,079 | 3,620,664 | 1,344,656 | 376,186 |
| April 17....... | 4,769,000 | 3,363,482 | 3,091,940 | 3,158,747 | 2,136,401 | 400,733 |
| April 10....... | 2,328,000 | 4,661,194 | 2,666,125 | 2,799,443 | 2,623,884 | 158,565 |
| April 3....... | 4,646,000 | 3,557,000 | 3,724,654 | 4,361,591 | 2,990,541 | 330,531 |
| March 27...... | 1,470,000 | 4,507,722 | 2,411,443 | 3,193,638 | 3,582,943 | 139,205 |
| March 20...... | 5,863,000 | 4,496,257 | 3,699,629 | 3,123,848 | 2,605,084 | 339,891 |
| March 13...... | 5,939,000 | 3,941,874 | 4,211,326 | 3,729,291 | 3,246,575 | 183,414 |
| March 6..... | 5,311,000 | 3,285,056 | 3,736,586 | 2,187,824 | 3,956,137 | 352,406 |
| February 27.... | 5,256,000 | 5,054,694 | 5,794,863 | 4,533,730 | 4,185,449 | 312,664 |
| February 20.... | 4,745,000 | 3,692,799 | 2,871,057 | 2,896,157 | 3,267,668 | 247,830 |
| February 13.... | 6,441,000 | 5,056,575 | 1,560,845 | 3,490,335 | 4,760,422 | 527,366 |
| February 6.... | 4,169,000 | 4,508,012 | 3,865,622 | 3,450,909 | 4,171,440 | 169,145 |
| January 30.... | 3,660,000 | 4,104,981 | 3,697,731 | 3,598,962 | 3,007,707 | 427,018 |
| January 23.... | 3,012,000 | 4,962,539 | 3,695,733 | 3,526,834 | 3,972,152 | 179,520 |
| January 16... | 3,520,000 | 3,486,713 | 2,928,101 | 3,199,312 | 5,184,550 | 298,093 |
| January 9.... | 3,757,000 | 4,641,750 | 3,297,072 | 3,314,576 | 4,897,345 | 136,873 |
| January 2.... | 4,819,000 | 3,455,416 | 4,844,288 | 4,019,036 | 4,470,521 | 270,236 |

* The dates are for 1902. The other columns are for corresponding weeks.

## EXPORTS OF WHEAT AND WHEAT FLOUR, WITH DESTINATIONS

Year ending June 30.

### WHEAT.

| | 1899. | 1900. | 1901. | 1902. |
|---|---|---|---|---|
| | *Bushels.* | *Bushels.* | *Bushels.* | *Bushels.* |
| United Kingdom | 74,613,304 | 62,774,870 | 78,574,752 | 77,544,418 |
| Germany | 10,311,450 | 9,065,713 | 10,267,622 | 19,725,674 |
| France | 2,232,190 | 1,237,247 | 1,139,525 | 3,324,015 |
| Other countries in Europe | 41,045,883 | 23,917,926 | 29,814,660 | 39,744,877 |
| British North American Possessions | 8,369,014 | 2,673,154 | 7,066,662 | 7,134,094 |
| Cen. Am. States and Br. Honduras | 39,869 | 16,406 | 41,479 | 38,625 |
| West Indies and Bermuda | 899 | 1,071 | 648 | 663 |
| South America | 259,492 | 534,307 | 1,663,775 | 692,674 |
| Asia and Oceanica | 30,112 | 312,806 | 336,314 | 34,777 |
| Africa | 2,523,219 | 1,414,259 | 3,153,410 | 5,699,803 |
| Other countries | 7,083 | 2,630 | 1,820 | 916,482 |
| Total | 139,432,815 | 101,950,389 | 132,060,667 | 154,856,102 |

### WHEAT FLOUR.

| | 1899. | 1900. | 1901. | 1902. |
|---|---|---|---|---|
| | *Barrels.* | *Barrels.* | *Barrels.* | *Barrels.* |
| United Kingdom | 10,233,360 | 10,257,028 | 10,854,573 | 9,059,722 |
| Germany | 502,874 | 691,782 | 502,933 | 703,470 |
| France | 1,959 | 5,620 | 11,466 | 4,110 |
| Other countries in Europe | 1,861,949 | 1,711,539 | 1,739,264 | 2,059,656 |
| British North American Possessions | 743,463 | 187,752 | 137,544 | 209,512 |
| Mexico | 34,537 | 39,804 | 43,507 | 57,615 |
| Central Am. States & Br. Honduras | 248,956 | 233,433 | 270,432 | 299,557 |
| Cuba | 442,081 | 573,012 | 556,556 | 589,556 |
| Puerto Rico | 152,079 | 244,103 | ......... | ......... |
| Santo Domingo | 34,694 | 35,711 | 43,923 | 57,642 |
| Other West Indies and Bermuda | 739,277 | 871,061 | 838,337 | 829,209 |
| Brazil | 818,816 | 638,591 | 655,300 | 544,145 |
| Colombia | 98,519 | 66,880 | 68,713 | 59,764 |
| Other countries in South America | 382,588 | 450,517 | 574,874 | 499,449 |
| China | 28,526 | 102,436 | 63,953 | 99,624 |
| Other countries in Asia & Oceanica | 1,781,868 | 2,275,554 | 1,982,754 | 2,201,282 |
| Africa | 380,078 | 301,341 | 294,508 | 475,533 |
| Other countries | 17,066 | 13,030 | 12,312 | 9,357 |
| Total | 18,502,690 | 18,699,194 | 18,650,979 | 17,759,203 |

## EXPORTS OF GRAIN AND PROVISIONS FROM THE UNITED STATES

BY YEARS.

| Year Ending June 30. | Wheat and Flour. Bushels. | Corn. Bushels. | Oats. Bushels. | Rye. Bushels. | Barley. Bushels. | Bacon and Hams. Pounds. | Pork. Pounds. | Lard. Pounds. |
|---|---|---|---|---|---|---|---|---|
| 1880 | 177,000,000 | 98,000,000 | 800,000 | 2,900,000 | 1,100,000 | 759,773,000 | 95,949,000 | 374,979,000 |
| 1881 | 185,000,000 | 92,000,000 | 400,000 | 1,900,000 | 900,000 | 746,944,000 | 107,928,000 | 378,142,000 |
| 1882 | 122,598,000 | 43,000,000 | 600,000 | 1,000,000 | 200,000 | 468,026,000 | 80,447,000 | 250,367,000 |
| 1883 | 148,785,000 | 41,000,000 | 460,000 | 2,170,000 | 433,000 | 340,258,000 | 62,116,000 | 224,718,000 |
| 1884 | 111,534,000 | 45,000,000 | 1,760,000 | 220,000 | 720,000 | 389,499,000 | 60,363,000 | 265,094,000 |
| 1885 | 132,570,000 | 51,834,000 | 4,200,000 | 2,950,000 | 629,000 | 400,127,000 | 72,073,000 | 283,216,000 |
| 1886 | 94,565,000 | 63,655,000 | 5,670,000 | 200,000 | 250,000 | 419,788,000 | 87,196,000 | 293,728,000 |
| 1887 | 153,804,000 | 40,307,000 | 400,000 | 300,000 | 1,300,000 | 419,922,000 | 85,869,000 | 321,533,000 |
| 1888 | 119,625,000 | 24,278,000 | 300,000 | ......... | 550,000 | 375,439,000 | 58,836,000 | 297,740,000 |
| 1889 | 88,600,000 | 69,592,000 | 624,000 | 87,252 | 1,440,321 | 400,224,000 | 64,110,000 | 318,242,000 |
| 1890 | 109,430,000 | 101,973,000 | 13,692,000 | 2,257,000 | 1,408,000 | 608,490,000 | 80,068,000 | 471,083,000 |
| 1891 | 106,181,000 | 30,768,000 | 953,000 | 332,000 | 973,000 | 599,086,000 | 82,136,000 | 498,343,000 |
| 1892 | 225,665,000 | 75,451,000 | 9,435,000 | 12,040,000 | 2,800,000 | 584,775,000 | 80,714,000 | 460,045,000 |
| 1893 | 191,912,000 | 46,034,000 | 2,380,000 | 1,477,000 | 3,035,000 | 473,936,000 | 53,372,000 | 365,693,000 |
| 1894 | 164,273,000 | 65,324,000 | 5,740,000 | 231,000 | 5,219,000 | 503,623,000 | 64,741,000 | 447,566,000 |
| 1895 | 144,812,000 | 27,691,000 | 570,000 | 9,000 | 1,563,000 | 558,043,000 | 59,085,000 | 474,895,000 |
| 1896 | 126,443,000 | 99,992,000 | 13,012,000 | 988,000 | 7,680,000 | 554,388,000 | 70,243,000 | 509,534,000 |
| 1897 | 145,122,000 | 176,916,000 | 35,096,000 | 8,560,000 | 19,030,000 | 665,747,000 | 68,075,000 | 568,315,000 |
| 1898 | 217,305,904 | 208,744,939 | 69,130,287 | 15,541,575 | 11,237,077 | 850,294,794 | 100,357,363 | 709,344,045 |
| 1899 | 222,694,920 | 174,089,094 | 30,309,680 | 10,140,876 | 2,267,400 | 788,498,230 | 178,507,564 | 711,259,851 |
| 1900 | 186,096,762 | 209,348,284 | 41,369,415 | 2,355,792 | 23,661,662 | 708,508,141 | 159,146,588 | 661,813,653 |
| 1901 | 215,990,072 | 177,817,965 | 37,146,812 | 2,326,882 | 6,293,207 | 672,694,544 | 169,372,197 | 611,357,514 |
| 1902 | 234,772,215 | 26,636,552 | 9,971,139 | 2,697,863 | 8,724,268 | 610,803,856 | 160,067,949 | 556,840,222 |

## EXPORTS OF PROVISIONS FROM THE UNITED STATES

IN POUNDS.

| Months. | Bacon. | | Hams. | |
|---|---|---|---|---|
| | 1901. | 1902. | 1901. | 1902. |
| January | 44,839,000 | 38,875,342 | 16,468,000 | 16,423,028 |
| February | 39,310,000 | 22,833,044 | 14,668,000 | 13,379,461 |
| March | 41,102,000 | 28,091,234 | 20,120,000 | 19,089,609 |
| April | 32,000,000 | 28,147,566 | 18,858,000 | 19,690,865 |
| May | 31,703,000 | 19,456,354 | 23,271,000 | 23,131,344 |
| June | 32,305,000 | 19,385,709 | 21,276,000 | 20,145,876 |
| July | 38,427,000 | 19,262,871 | 23,954,000 | 21,877,618 |
| August | 43,052,000 | 19,328,159 | 19,126,000 | 10,448,553 |
| September | 40,454,000 | 16,697,223 | 20,314,000 | 17,396,155 |
| October | 44,084,000 | 15,615,541 | 15,915,000 | 18,096,515 |
| November | 32,405,000 | 17,161,828 | 18,776,000 | 17,962,913 |
| December | 37,930,000 | 25,260,516 | 17,693,000 | 21,252,550 |
| Total | 447,620,337 | 270,141,141 | 230,156,004 | 224,982,389 |

| Months. | Pork. | | Lard. | |
|---|---|---|---|---|
| | 1901. | 1902. | 1901. | 1902. |
| January | 16,165,000 | 18,601,879 | 59,421,000 | 41,469,010 |
| February | 15,389,000 | 14,318,140 | 51,900,000 | 46,408,231 |
| March | 18,159,000 | 12,417,882 | 61,746,000 | 58,106,309 |
| April | 13,597,000 | 13,815,111 | 42,971,000 | 48,037,094 |
| May | 11,607,000 | 9,858,512 | 54,955,000 | 38,080,585 |
| June | 9,324,000 | 6,721,828 | 50,027,000 | 38,637,387 |
| July | 10,261,000 | 9,974,225 | 45,312,000 | 33,637,197 |
| August | 12,373,000 | 9,067,650 | 47,546,000 | 30,442,071 |
| September | 12,471,000 | 6,774,857 | 43,704,000 | 32,632,430 |
| October | 12,127,000 | 6,968,705 | 43,723,000 | 34,461,485 |
| November | 14,850,000 | 7,287,642 | 48,975,000 | 38,840,475 |
| December | 21,938,000 | 13,619,931 | 54,992,240 | 63,396,031 |
| Total | 168,212,115 | 129,433,963 | 607,266,176 | 504,153,355 |

## *WHEAT AND CORN IN FARMERS' HANDS*

REPORTED BY THE DEPARTMENT OF AGRICULTURE.

| March 1st. | Wheat. Bushels. | Corn. Bushels. |
|---|---|---|
| 1888 | 132,000,000 | 508,000,000 |
| 1889 | 112,000,000 | 787,000,000 |
| 1890 | 156,000,000 | 970,000,000 |
| 1891 | 112,000,000 | 542,000,000 |
| 1892 | 171,000,000 | 860,000,000 |
| 1893 | 135,000,000 | 627,000,000 |
| 1894 | 114,000,000 | 589,000,000 |
| 1895 | 75,000,000 | 475,000,000 |
| 1896 | 123,000,000 | 1,072,273,700 |
| 1897 | 88,000,000 | 1,164,000,000 |
| 1898 | 121,000,000 | 783,000,000 |
| 1899 | 198,000,000 | 800,500,000 |
| 1900 | 158,745,595 | 773,729,528 |
| 1901 | 128,100,000 | 776,200,000 |
| 1902 | 173,700,000 | 443,456,515 |
| 1903 | 164,000,000 | 1,050,000,000 |

## *STOCKS OF PROVISIONS*

Amounts of contract Pork, Lard and Side Ribs in Chicago on the first of each month.

| Months. | Pork. | | Lard. | | Ribs. | |
|---|---|---|---|---|---|---|
| | 1901. | 1902. | 1901. | 1902. | 1901. | 1902. |
| | *Barrels.* | *Barrels.* | *Tierces.* | *Tierces.* | *Pounds.* | *Pounds.* |
| January | 2,581 | 29,045 | 43,997 | 45,836 | 12,289,722 | 21,430,219 |
| February | 14,914 | 50,788 | 36,711 | 62,851 | 16,982,573 | 23,762,310 |
| March | 28,891 | 50,983 | 44,022 | 58,361 | 18,535,879 | 28,384,581 |
| April | 56,568 | 50,844 | 29,399 | 55,574 | 14,413,328 | 24,352,210 |
| May | 61,608 | 50,976 | 32,214 | 43,378 | 15,403,160 | 19,490,022 |
| June | 62,114 | 51,193 | 25,388 | 45,331 | 20,788,086 | 15,497,151 |
| July | 62,083 | 47,680 | 47,193 | 46,070 | 22,200,213 | 22,861,859 |
| August | 60,818 | 42,401 | 51,166 | 46,529 | 19,178,730 | 21,847,908 |
| September | 51,103 | 36,480 | 47,495 | 45,760 | 21,380,255 | 17,705,823 |
| October | 45,931 | 34,376 | 27,759 | 34,900 | 15,149,498 | 11,038,088 |
| November | 36,126 | 24,423 | 26,193 | 9,567 | 8,005,882 | 2,629,108 |
| December | 39,259 | 16,609 | 21,438 | 9,547 | 10,458,378 | 3,251,770 |

## THE WORLD'S HARVEST BY MONTHS

JANUARY—Australia, New Zealand, Chili and Argentine.

FEBRUARY AND MARCH—East India and Upper Egypt.

APRIL—Lower Egypt, Syria, Cyprus, Persia, Asia Minor, India, Mexico and Cuba.

MAY—Algeria, Central Asia, China, Japan, Morocco, Texas and Florida.

JUNE—Turkey, Greece, Italy, Spain, Portugal, South of France, California, Oregon, Louisiana, Mississippi, Alabama, Georgia, Carolina, Tennessee, Virginia, Kentucky, Kansas, Arkansas, Utah, Colorado and Missouri.

JULY—Roumania, Bulgaria, Austro-Hungary, South of Russia, Germany, Switzerland, France, South of England, Nebraska, Minnesota, Wisconsin, Iowa, Illinois, Indiana, Michigan, Ohio, New York, New England and Upper Canada.

AUGUST—Belgium, Holland, Great Britain, Denmark, Poland, Lower Canada, Columbia, Manitoba, North and South Dakota.

SEPTEMBER AND OCTOBER—Scotland, Sweden, Norway and North of Russia.

NOVEMBER—Peru and South Africa.

DECEMBER—Burmah.

---

## MONEY EQUIVALENTS OF FLUCTUATIONS IN GRAIN AND PROVISIONS

| GRAIN. On 10,000 Bushels. | | PORK. On 250 Barrels. | | LARD. On 250 Tierces. | |
|---|---|---|---|---|---|
| 1/8 cent | — $12.50 | 2½ cents | — $6.25 | 2½ cents | — $21.25 |
| 1/4 " | — 25.00 | 5 " | — 12.50 | 5 " | — 42.50 |
| 3/8 " | — 37.50 | 7½ " | — 18.75 | 7½ " | — 63.75 |
| 1/2 " | — 50.00 | 10 " | — 25.00 | 10 " | — 85.00 |
| 2/3 " | — 62.50 | 12½ " | — 31.25 | 15 " | — 127.50 |
| 3/4 " | — 75.00 | 15 " | — 37.50 | 20 " | — 170.00 |
| 7/8 " | — 82.50 | 17½ " | — 43.75 | 25 " | — 212.50 |
| 1 " | — 100.00 | 20 " | — 50.00 | 50 " | — 425.00 |
| For quantities of 5,000 bushels half the above. | | 25 " | — 62.50 | 100 " | — 850.00 |
| | | 50 " | — 125.00 | | |

# Cotton

## Prices, Production and Visible Supply of Cotton

### *YEARLY PRODUCT OF COTTON IN THE UNITED STATES*

Year ending September 1.

| Year. | Bales. | Year. | Bales. | Year. | Bales. | Year. | Bales. |
|---|---|---|---|---|---|---|---|
| 1841 | 1,688,675 | 1857 | 3,238,902 | 1873 | 4,170,388 | 1889 | 7,313,726 |
| 1842 | 2,394,203 | 1858 | 3,994,481 | 1874 | 3,832,991 | 1890 | 8,655,000 |
| 1843 | 2,108,579 | 1859 | 4,823,770 | 1875 | 4,669,288 | 1891 | 9,035,000 |
| 1844 | 2,484,662 | 1860 | 3,826,086 | 1876 | 4,485,423 | 1892 | 6,700,000 |
| 1845 | 2,170,537 | 1861 | No report | 1877 | 4,811,265 | 1893 | 7,534,730 |
| 1846 | 1,860,479 | 1862 | No report | 1878 | 4,073,534 | 1894 | 9,900,005 |
| 1847 | 2,424,113 | 1863 | No report | 1879 | 5,057,397 | 1895 | 7,157,340 |
| 1848 | 2,808,596 | 1864 | No report | 1880 | 5,789,329 | 1896 | 8,757,964 |
| 1849 | 2,171,706 | 1865 | 2,228,987 | 1881 | 5,435,845 | 1897 | 11,199,994 |
| 1850 | 2,415,257 | 1866 | 2,059,271 | 1882 | 6,992,234 | 1898 | 11,274,840 |
| 1851 | 3,090,029 | 1867 | 2,498,895 | 1883 | 5,714,052 | 1899 | 9,436,416 |
| 1852 | 3,352,882 | 1868 | 2,439,039 | 1884 | 5,669,021 | 1900 | 10,383,422 |
| 1853 | 3,035,027 | 1869 | 3,154,946 | 1885 | 6,550,215 | 1901 | 10,680,680 |
| 1854 | 2,932,339 | 1870 | 4,352,317 | 1886 | 6,513,623 | 1902 | *11,200,000 |
| 1855 | 3,645,345 | 1871 | 2,974,351 | 1887 | 7,017,707 | | |
| 1856 | 3,056,519 | 1872 | 3,930,508 | 1888 | 6,935,032 | | |

* Estimated.

### *NEW YORK COTTON PRICES*

The following table shows the highest and lowest prices in New York for "spot" Middling Upland Cotton from January 1 to December 31, in each of the years named.

| Year. | Highest. | Lowest. | Year | Highest. | Lowest. | Year. | Highest. | Lowest. |
|---|---|---|---|---|---|---|---|---|
| 1831 | 11 | 7 | 1855 | 11 | 7 | 1879 | 13¾ | 9¾ |
| 1832 | 12 | 7 | 1856 | 12 | 9 | 1880 | 13¾ | 10 15-16 |
| 1833 | 17 | 9 | 1857 | 15 | 13 | 1881 | 13 | 10 7-16 |
| 1834 | 16 | 10 | 1858 | 13 | 9 | 1882 | 13 1-16 | 10¾ |
| 1835 | 20 | 15 | 1859 | 12 | 11 | 1883 | 11⅛ | 10 |
| 1836 | 20 | 12 | 1860 | 11 | 10 | 1884 | 11 15-16 | 9¾ |
| 1837 | 17 | 7 | 1861 | 28 | 11 | 1885 | 11 5-16 | 9 |
| 1838 | 12 | 9 | 1862 | 68 | 20 | 1886 | 9 9-16 | 9 1-16 |
| 1839 | 16 | 11 | 1863 | 88 | 54 | 1887 | 11 7-16 | 9 7-16 |
| 1840 | 10 | 8 | 1864 | 1.90 | 72 | 1888 | 11⅜ | 9⅝ |
| 1841 | 11 | 9 | 1865 | 1.22 | 33 | 1889 | 11½ | 9⅜ |
| 1842 | 9 | 7 | 1866 | 52 | 32 | 1890 | 12¾ | 9 5-16 |
| 1843 | 8 | 5 | 1867 | 36 | 15½ | 1891 | 9½ | 7¾ |
| 1844 | 9 | 5 | 1868 | 33 | 16 | 1892 | 10 | 6 11-16 |
| 1845 | 9 | 4 | 1869 | 35 | 25 | 1893 | 9 15-16 | 7⅛ |
| 1846 | 9 | 6 | 1870 | 25¾ | 15 | 1894 | 8 1-16 | 5⅜ |
| 1847 | 12 | 7 | 1871 | 21¾ | 14¾ | 1895 | 9¾ | 5 9-16 |
| 1848 | 8 | 5 | 1872 | 27⅜ | 18⅝ | 1896 | 8⅞ | 7 1-16 |
| 1840 | 11 | 6 | 1873 | 21⅜ | 13⅝ | 1897 | 8¼ | 5 3-16 |
| 1850 | 14 | 11 | 1874 | 18⅞ | 14¾ | 1898 | 6 9-16 | 5 5-16 |
| 1851 | 14 | 8 | 1875 | 17⅛ | 13 1-16 | 1899 | 7 13-16 | 5⅞ |
| 1852 | 10 | 8 | 1876 | 13⅜ | 10⅞ | 1900 | 11 | 7 9-16 |
| 1853 | 11 | 10 | 1877 | 13 5-16 | 10 13-16 | 1901 | 12 | 7 13-16 |
| 1854 | 10 | 8 | 1878 | 12 3-16 | 8 13-16 | 1902 | 9⅛ | 8¼ |

## COTTON FUTURES AT NEW YORK

best and lowest quotations for actual sales of future deliveries each week during the crop
om September 7, 1900, to April 3, 1903, at the New York Cotton Exchange.

| Veek …ing | Deliveries. Sept. | Oct. | Nov. | Dec. | Jan. | Feb. | Mar. | April. | May. | June. | July. | Au |
|---|---|---|---|---|---|---|---|---|---|---|---|---|
| 00. | | | | | | | | | | | | |
| …… | 8.84 | 8.60 | 8.49 | 8.46 | 8.45 | 8.49 | 8.47 | 8.48 | 8.49 | 8.57 | 8.87 | .... |
| | 9.59 | 9.45 | 9.31 | 9.27 | 9.25 | 9.23 | 9.21 | 9.07 | 9.24 | 9.18 | 9.10 | .... |
| …… | 9.45 | 9.31 | 9.17 | 9.07 | 9.05 | 9.61 | 9.04 | 9.03 | 9.05 | 9.08 | 8.98 | .... |
| | 10.55 | 10.52 | 10.31 | 10.20 | 10.20 | 10.14 | 10.15 | 10.04 | 10.17 | 10.14 | 10.04 | |
| …… | 9.89 | 9.75 | 9.46 | 9.36 | 9.35 | 9.32 | 9.33 | 9.34 | 9.33 | 9.34 | 9.35 | |
| | 10.50 | 10.45 | 10.20 | 10.03 | 10.02 | 9.99 | 10.00 | 9.86 | 10.03 | 9.98 | 10.00 | |
| …… | 10.02 | 9.85 | 9.56 | 9.44 | 9.44 | 9.45 | 9.44 | 9.44 | 9.44 | 9.64 | 9.50 | |
| | 10.40 | 10.22 | 9.92 | 9.80 | 9.79 | 9.75 | 9.77 | 9.74 | 9.77 | 9.70 | 9.79 | |
| …… | .... | 10.10 | 9.84 | 9.71 | 9.70 | 9.73 | 9.71 | 9.75 | 9.69 | 9.68 | 9.69 | |
| | .... | 10.46 | 10.13 | 9.98 | 9.98 | 9.98 | 9.98 | 10.00 | 9.99 | 10.00 | 9.98 | |
| …… | .... | 9.83 | 9.60 | 9.56 | 9.56 | 9.55 | 9.56 | 9.62 | 9.56 | 9.64 | 9.53 | |
| | .... | 10.60 | 10.31 | 10.16 | 10.15 | 10.15 | 10.18 | 10.10 | 10.18 | 10.17 | 10.17 | |
| …… | .... | 9.27 | 9.14 | 9.12 | 9.10 | 9.11 | 9.11 | 9.12 | 9.10 | 9.10 | 9.07 | |
| | .... | 9.83 | 9.63 | 9.59 | 9.58 | 9.53 | 9.59 | 9.56 | 9.59 | 9.56 | 9.55 | |
| …… | 8.50 | 8.73 | 8.75 | 8.75 | 8.75 | 8.74 | 8.73 | 8.78 | 8.73 | 8.71 | 8.71 | |
| | 8.50 | 9.43 | 9.33 | 9.29 | 9.29 | 9.27 | 9.29 | 9.27 | 9.28 | 9.27 | 9.23 | |
| …… | 8.00 | 8.80 | 8.83 | 8.85 | 8.85 | 8.86 | 8.86 | 8.88 | 8.87 | 8.88 | 8.84 | |
| | 8.00 | 9.02 | 9.13 | 9.16 | 9.18 | 9.16 | 9.18 | 9.15 | 9.18 | 9.16 | 9.14 | |
| …… | .... | .... | 8.89 | 8.88 | 8.89 | 9.92 | 8.92 | 8.93 | 8.93 | 8.93 | 8.90 | |
| | .... | .... | 9.24 | 9.24 | 9.24 | 9.26 | 9.27 | 9.25 | 9.28 | 9.25 | 9.26 | |
| …… | 8.75 | .... | 9.20 | 9.18 | 9.17 | 9.18 | 9.20 | 9.21 | 9.22 | 9.22 | 9.21 | 9.14 |
| | 8.84 | .... | 9.69 | 9.58 | 9.56 | 9.53 | 9.52 | 9.50 | 9.51 | 9.48 | 9.48 | 9.70 |
| …… | 8.81 | .... | 9.61 | 9.46 | 9.39 | 9.41 | 9.38 | 9.37 | 9.35 | 9.34 | 9.34 | 9.28 |
| | 8.95 | .... | 10.15 | 10.00 | 9.98 | 9.94 | 9.92 | 9.86 | 9.90 | 9.86 | 9.85 | 9.69 |
| …… | 8.78 | .... | 9.77 | 9.62 | 9.58 | 9.59 | 9.54 | 9.55 | 9.50 | 9.49 | 9.49 | 9.32 |
| | 8.85 | .... | 10.15 | 10.00 | 9.95 | 9.91 | 9.90 | 9.87 | 9.86 | 9.85 | 9.83 | 9.67 |
| …… | 8.50 | .... | .... | 9.73 | 9.57 | 9.53 | 9.47 | 9.47 | 9.38 | 9.37 | 9.34 | 9.10 |
| | 8.70 | .... | .... | 9.95 | 9.87 | 9.83 | 9.78 | 9.70 | 9.67 | 9.64 | 9.64 | 9.35 |
| …… | 8.19 | 8.00 | .... | 9.25 | 9.09 | 9.05 | 9.00 | 8.97 | 8.95 | 8.96 | 8.90 | 8.75 |
| | 8.52 | 8.00 | .... | 9.78 | 9.70 | 9.62 | 9.59 | 9.50 | 9.49 | 9.41 | 9.43 | 9.18 |
| …… | 8.33 | 8.00 | .... | 9.55 | 9.35 | 9.25 | 9.21 | 9.15 | 9.12 | 9.20 | 9.08 | 8.87 |
| | 8.46 | 8.11 | .... | 10.25 | 9.70 | 9.53 | 9.50 | 9.45 | 9.13 | 9.39 | 9.35 | 9.11 |
| …… | 8.32 | 8.01 | .... | 9.65 | 9.51 | 9.24 | 9.33 | 9.26 | 9.26 | 9.23 | 9.18 | 8.91 |
| | 8.43 | 8.04 | .... | 10.22 | 9.67 | 9.48 | 9.48 | 9.42 | 9.40 | 9.36 | 9.33 | 9.07 |
| 01. | | | | | | | | | | | | |
| …… | 8.45 | 8.02 | 8.05 | .. . | 9.58 | 9.4 | 9.37 | 9.30 | 9.28 | 9.26 | 9.18 | 8.90 |
| | 8.69 | 8.28 | 8.15 | .... | 9.85 | 9.68 | 9.66 | 9.55 | 9.59 | 9.52 | 9.52 | 9.21 |
| …… | 8.60 | 8.24 | .... | .... | 9.74 | 9.51 | 9.46 | 9.47 | 9.42 | 9.41 | 9.37 | 9.00 |
| | 8.76 | 8.37 | .... | ... | 10.00 | 9.74 | 9.70 | 9.64 | 9.68 | 9.62 | 9.59 | 9.30 |
| …… | 8.45 | 8.12 | 8.10 | .... | 9.51 | 9.27 | 9.25 | 9.22 | 9.22 | 9.22 | 9.20 | 8.91 |
| | 8.60 | 8.28 | 8.15 | .... | 9.81 | 9.53 | 9.51 | 9.46 | 9.47 | 9.42 | 9.41 | 9.12 |
| …… | 8.48 | 8.20 | 8.20 | .... | 9.70 | 9.33 | 9.25 | 9.24 | 9.24 | 9.22 | 9.20 | 8.92 |
| | 8.55 | 8.31 | 8.20 | .... | 10.10 | 9.52 | 9.44 | 9.42 | 9.43 | 9.41 | 9.41 | 9.14 |
| …… | 8.32 | 8.00 | 7.91 | .... | 10.11 | 9.21 | 9.15 | 9.05 | 9.05 | 9.00 | 8.97 | 8.66 |
| | 8.50 | 8.27 | 8.15 | .... | 12.75 | 9.60 | 9.44 | 9.33 | 9.35 | 9.32 | 9.33 | 8.98 |
| …… | 8.35 | 8.13 | 8.00 | 7.95 | .... | 9.21 | 9.20 | 9.17 | 9.18 | 9.15 | 9.15 | 8.82 |
| | 8.46 | 8.22 | 8.07 | 8.03 | .... | 9.40 | 9.35 | 9.25 | 9.32 | 9.27 | 9.28 | 8.94 |
| …… | 8.15 | 7.94 | 7.85 | 7.81 | .... | 8.99 | 9.02 | 9.08 | 9.05 | 9.02 | 9.03 | 8.67 |
| | 8.37 | 8.15 | 8.00 | 7.92 | .... | 9.40 | 9.35 | 9.29 | 9.30 | 9.18 | 9.22 | 8.85 |
| …… | 8.17 | 7.93 | 7.87 | 7.83 | .... | 8.77 | 8.77 | 8.80 | 8.86 | 8.87 | 8.83 | 8.57 |
| | 8.33 | 8.12 | 8.01 | 8.00 | ... | 8.99 | 9.04 | 9.02 | 9.06 | 9.05 | 9.09 | 8.75 |
| …… | 8.11 | 7.89 | 7.80 | 7.82 | .... | 8.88 | 8.81 | 8.82 | 8.82 | 8.83 | 8.45 | .... |
| | 8.38 | 8.14 | 8.03 | 8.02 | .... | 9.06 | 9.09 | 9.16 | 9.14 | 9.17 | 8.84 | .... |
| …… | 7.78 | 7.67 | 7.60 | 7.58 | .... | .... | 7.52 | 7.59 | 7.62 | 8.39 | 8.42 | 8.14 |
| | 8.12 | 7.92 | 7.80 | 7.76 | .... | .... | 10.28 | 10.10 | 10.18 | 8.80 | 8.83 | 8.44 |

## COTTON FUTURES AT NEW YORK—*Continued.*

| For Week Ending. | Deliveries. | | | | | | | | | | | |
|---|---|---|---|---|---|---|---|---|---|---|---|---|
| | Sept. | Oct. | Nov. | Dec. | Jan. | Feb. | Mar. | April | May. | June. | July. | Aug. |
| 1901. | | | | | | | | | | | | |
| March 15....... | 7.72 | 7.61 | 7.51 | 7.50 | 7.50 | .... | 8.24 | 8.24 | 8.24 | 8.28 | 8.31 | 8.04 |
| | 7.92 | 7.84 | 7.73 | 7.70 | 7.54 | .... | 8.68 | 8.62 | 8.65 | 8.64 | 8.68 | 8.34 |
| " 22....... | 7.35 | 7.26 | 7.25 | 7.21 | 7.24 | .... | 7.94 | 7.88 | 7.86 | 7.86 | 7.87 | 7.61 |
| | 7.62 | 7.60 | 7.48 | 7.46 | 7.32 | .... | 8.27 | 8.25 | 8.33 | 8.30 | 8.35 | 8.10 |
| " 29....... | 7.20 | 7.10 | 7.07 | 7.06 | 7.06 | .... | 7.58 | 7.60 | 7.66 | 7.67 | 7.68 | 7.41 |
| | 7.43 | 7.36 | 7.38 | 7.33 | 7.33 | .... | 7.97 | 7.98 | 8.00 | 7.97 | 7.97 | 7.69 |
| April 5....... | 7.25 | 7.19 | 7.18 | 7.15 | 7.17 | .... | .... | 7.62 | 7.68 | 7.68 | 7.68 | 7.41 |
| | 7.56 | 7.47 | 7.40 | 7.40 | 7.40 | .... | .... | 8.18 | 8.30 | 8.15 | 8.17 | 7.77 |
| " 12....... | 7.33 | 7.22 | 7.17 | 7.18 | 7.23 | .... | .... | 7.83 | 7.82 | 7.77 | 7.77 | 7.45 |
| | 7.50 | 7.43 | 7.28 | 7.32 | 7.33 | .... | .... | 7.94 | 8.10 | 7.95 | 8.02 | 7.66 |
| " 19....... | 7.43 | 7.29 | 7.25 | 7.24 | 7.27 | 7.27 | .... | 8.01 | 7.96 | 7.87 | 7.87 | 7.55 |
| | 7.75 | 7.52 | 7.43 | 7.36 | 7.38 | 7.35 | .... | 8.13 | 8.16 | 8.13 | 8.14 | 8.08 |
| " 26....... | 7.35 | 7.26 | 7.21 | 7.20 | 7.21 | .... | .... | 8.05 | 7.98 | 8.03 | 8.03 | 7.70 |
| | 7.52 | 7.44 | 7.32 | 7.33 | 7.33 | .... | .... | 8.25 | 8.29 | 8.27 | 8.34 | 7.92 |
| May 3....... | 7.28 | 7.18 | 7.14 | 7.12 | 7.12 | .... | .... | 8.08 | 7.78 | 7.78 | 7.78 | 7.51 |
| | 7.42 | 7.32 | 7.25 | 7.25 | 7.27 | .... | .... | 8.12 | 8.14 | 8.10 | 8.11 | 7.80 |
| " 10....... | 7.03 | 6.95 | 6.93 | 6.92 | 6.93 | 6.94 | .... | .... | 7.39 | 7.41 | 7.41 | 7.15 |
| | 7.25 | 7.18 | 7.14 | 7.13 | 7.15 | 6.98 | .... | .... | 7.75 | 7.74 | 7.79 | 7.49 |
| " 17....... | 7.08 | 7.00 | 6.98 | 6.95 | 6.97 | 7.03 | 7.10 | .... | 7.45 | 7.49 | 7.52 | 7.22 |
| | 7.24 | 7.20 | 7.17 | 7.16 | 7.18 | 7.03 | 7.10 | .... | 7.73 | 7.76 | 7.84 | 7.47 |
| " 24....... | 7.00 | 6.92 | 6.90 | 6.90 | 6.93 | 6.95 | .... | .... | 7.48 | 7.48 | 7.53 | 7.18 |
| | 7.19 | 7.10 | 7.02 | 7.02 | 7.05 | 7.01 | .... | .... | 7.74 | 7.76 | 7.85 | 7.34 |
| " 31....... | 7.01 | 6.96 | 6.98 | 6.96 | 6.99 | 7.04 | .... | .... | 7.65 | 7.63 | 7.70 | 7.27 |
| | 7.22 | 7.17 | 7.15 | 7.16 | 7.18 | 7.09 | .... | .... | 8.06 | 8.06 | 8.10 | 7.50 |
| June 7....... | 7.07 | 7.01 | 7.03 | 7.02 | 7.03 | 7.11 | 7.13 | .... | .... | 7.78 | 7.78 | 7.28 |
| | 7.35 | 7.29 | 7.28 | 7.29 | 7.31 | 7.22 | 7.33 | .... | .... | 8.11 | 8.15 | 7.66 |
| " 14....... | 7.13 | 7.10 | 7.07 | 7.09 | 7.13 | 7.15 | 7.17 | .... | .... | 7.94 | 7.95 | 7.44 |
| | 7.40 | 7.36 | 7.32 | 7.35 | 7.36 | 7.19 | 7.73 | .... | .... | 8.24 | 8.28 | 7.71 |
| " 21....... | 7.31 | 7.20 | 7.24 | 7.22 | 7.24 | 7.25 | 7.27 | .... | 7.41 | 8.13 | 8.15 | 7.61 |
| | 7.54 | 7.46 | 7.41 | 7.45 | 7.47 | 7.43 | 7.50 | .... | 7.41 | 8.29 | 8.41 | 7.83 |
| " 28....... | 7.37 | 7.31 | 7.31 | 7.32 | 7.34 | 7.42 | 7.40 | .... | .... | 8.43 | 8.35 | 7.72 |
| | 7.80 | 7.71 | 7.67 | 7.70 | 7.73 | 7.67 | 7.72 | .. . | .... | 8.80 | 8.85 | 8.11 |
| July 5....... | 7.49 | 7.44 | 7.43 | 7.49 | 7.47 | 7.53 | 7.50 | 7.71 | .... | .... | 8.45 | 7.75 |
| | 7.76 | 7.69 | 7.68 | 7.69 | 7.74 | 7.68 | 7.72 | 7.75 | .... | .... | 8.72 | 8.05 |
| " 12....... | 7.51 | 7.52 | 7.52 | 7.53 | 7.55 | .... | 7.58 | 7.59 | .... | .... | 8.20 | 7.72 |
| | 7.71 | 7.74 | 7.66 | 7.73 | 7.76 | .... | 7.77 | 7.80 | .... | .... | 8.55 | 7.88 |
| " 19....... | 7.58 | 7.61 | 7.61 | 7.61 | 7.65 | 7.70 | 7.68 | 7.74 | .... | .... | 8.20 | 7.67 |
| | 7.76 | 7.83 | 7.80 | 7.83 | 7.87 | 7.73 | 7.88 | 7.77 | .... | .... | 8.39 | 7.90 |
| " 26....... | 7.17 | 7.70 | 7.26 | 7.29 | 7.32 | 7.44 | 7.37 | 7.38 | .... | .... | 7.25 | 7.28 |
| | 7.66 | 7.71 | 7.69 | 7.72 | 7.76 | 7.66 | 7.78 | 7.69 | .... | .... | 8.25 | 7.77 |
| Aug. 2....... | 7.15 | 7.24 | 7.29 | 7.29 | 7.33 | 7.38 | 7.37 | 7.40 | .... | .... | 7.15 | 7.10 |
| | 7.31 | 7.38 | 7.40 | 7.41 | 7.46 | 7.47 | 7.49 | 7.50 | .... | .... | 8.48 | 7.26 |
| " 9....... | 7.01 | 7.07 | 7.10 | 7.10 | 7.13 | 7.16 | 7.17 | 7.18 | .... | .... | .... | 7.01 |
| | 7.32 | 7.39 | 7.40 | 7.45 | 7.47 | 7.39 | 7.49 | 7.45 | .... | .... | .. | 7.28 |
| " 16....... | 7.07 | 7.16 | 7.19 | 7.20 | 7.23 | 7.31 | 7.26 | 7.33 | .... | .... | .... | 7.05 |
| | 7.25 | 7.34 | 7.33 | 7.40 | 7.44 | 7.34 | 7.44 | 7.39 | .... | ... | .... | 7.22 |
| " 23....... | 7.20 | 7.28 | 7.33 | 7.35 | 7.38 | 7.44 | 7.42 | 7.49 | 7.56 | .... | .... | 7.18 |
| | 7.70 | 7.82 | 7.80 | 7.86 | 7.89 | 7.63 | 7.91 | 7.87 | 7.56 | .... | .... | 7.67 |
| " 30....... | 7.56 | 7.68 | 7.70 | 7.73 | 7.76 | 7.77 | 7.79 | 7.86 | 7.81 | .... | .... | 7.85 |
| | 8.00 | 8.06 | 8.04 | 8.07 | 8.09 | 8.02 | 8.12 | 8.10 | 8.11 | .... | ... | 8.00 |
| Sept. 6....... | 7.52 | 7.55 | 7.54 | 7.60 | 7.63 | 7.72 | 7.66 | 7.75 | 7.68 | .... | .... | .... |
| | 7.84 | 7.90 | 7.82 | 7.90 | 7.91 | 7.88 | 7.92 | 7.86 | 7.93 | .... | .... | .... |
| " 13....... | 7.37 | 7.34 | 7.41 | 7.41 | 7.41 | 7.46 | 7.44 | 7.50 | 7.50 | .... | .... | .... |
| | 7.72 | 7.77 | 7.72 | 7.78 | 7.79 | 7.78 | 7.81 | 7.67 | 7.83 | .... | .... | .... |
| " 20....... | 7.53 | 7.45 | 7.46 | 7.52 | 7.52 | 7.55 | 7.54 | 7.65 | 7.57 | .... | .... | .... |
| | 7.83 | 7.84 | 7.84 | 7.87 | 7.88 | 7.80 | 7.90 | 7.86 | 7.91 | .... | .... | .... |

## COTTON FUTURES AT NEW YORK—*Continued.*

| 'REEK ING | Deliveries. | | | | | | | | | | | |
|---|---|---|---|---|---|---|---|---|---|---|---|---|
| | Sept. | Oct. | Nov. | Dec. | Jan. | Feb. | Mar. | April. | May. | June. | July. | Aug. |
| 01. | | | | | | | | | | | | |
| ........ | 7.60 | 7.53 | 7.54 | 7.59 | 7.61 | 7.75 | 7.61 | 7.62 | 7.63 | 7.65 | .... | .... |
| | 7.75 | 7.80 | 7.77 | 7.79 | 7.82 | 7.76 | 7.81 | 7.72 | 7.83 | 7.65 | .... | .... |
| ........ | 7.84 | 7.65 | 7.63 | 7.66 | 7.63 | 7.66 | 7.63 | 7.65 | 7.64 | .... | .... | .... |
| | 7.85 | 8.03 | 8.03 | 8.10 | 8.12 | 8.08 | 8.10 | 8.08 | 8.11 | .... | .... | ... |
| ........ | .... | 7.82 | 7.81 | 7.86 | 7.87 | 7.89 | 7.86 | 7.88 | 7.86 | .... | .... | .... |
| | .... | 8.08 | 8.06 | 8.10 | 8.09 | 8.07 | 8.06 | 8.04 | 8.07 | .... | .... | .... |
| ........ | .... | 7.99 | 8.00 | 8.04 | 8.02 | 7.99 | 7.94 | 8.00 | 7.92 | .... | .... | .... |
| | .... | 8.21 | 8.20 | 8.25 | 8.23 | 8.18 | 8.17 | 8.12 | 8.15 | .... | .... | .... |
| ........ | .... | 7.69 | 7.67 | 7.70 | 7.69 | 7.71 | 7.65 | 7.70 | 7.65 | 7.73 | 7.69 | .... |
| | .... | 7.96 | 7.97 | 8.01 | 8.00 | 7.94 | 7.93 | 7.91 | 7.90 | 7.75 | 7.77 | .... |
| ........ | .... | 7.42 | 7.39 | 7.40 | 7.37 | 7.40 | 7.33 | 7.37 | 7.29 | 7.47 | 7.29 | 7.15 |
| | .... | 7.72 | 7.73 | 7.81 | 7.81 | 7.78 | 7.78 | 7.78 | 7.76 | 7.65 | 7.75 | 7.20 |
| ........ | .... | .... | 7.36 | 7.39 | 7.35 | 7.34 | 7.30 | 7.33 | 7.26 | 7.31 | 7.25 | 7.12 |
| | .... | .... | 7.75 | 7.70 | 7.66 | 7.60 | 7.61 | 7.60 | 7.56 | 7.54 | 7.50 | 7.36 |
| ........ | .... | .... | 7.40 | 7.39 | 7.41 | 7.37 | 7.34 | 7.35 | 7.31 | 7.33 | 7.30 | 7.22 |
| | .... | .... | 7.53 | 7.58 | 7.60 | 7.55 | 7.56 | 7.56 | 7.56 | 7.55 | 7.56 | 7.48 |
| ........ | .... | .... | 7.50 | 7.50 | 7.50 | 7.49 | 7.48 | 7.54 | 7.48 | 7.48 | 7.47 | 7.38 |
| | .... | .... | 7.7[illegible] | 7.72 | 7.70 | 7.65 | 7.69 | 7.70 | 7.70 | 7.65 | 7.67 | 7.55 |
| ........ | .... | .... | 7.60 | 7.60 | 7.60 | 7.60 | 7.58 | 7.58 | 7.57 | 7.60 | 7.57 | 7.41 |
| | .... | .... | 7.69 | 7.70 | 7.67 | 7.66 | 7.66 | 7.66 | 7.66 | 7.66 | 7.64 | 7.50 |
| ........ | 7.20 | ... | .... | 7.56 | 7.55 | 7.53 | 7.53 | 7.53 | 7.52 | 7.54 | 7.50 | 7.38 |
| | 7.63 | . .. | .... | 8.11 | 8.10 | 8.09 | 8.11 | 8.11 | 8.13 | 8.09 | 8.10 | 7.92 |
| ........ | 7.80 | .... | .... | 8.03 | 8.02 | 8.03 | 8.01 | 8.03 | 8.02 | 8.03 | 7.98 | 7.84 |
| | 7.90 | .... | .... | 8.26 | 8.25 | 8.24 | 8.28 | 8.29 | 8.29 | 8.27 | 8.24 | 8.12 |
| ........ | 7.76 | .... | .... | 8.08 | 8.08 | 8.14 | 8.14 | 8.22 | 8.16 | 8.15 | 8.14 | 8.01 |
| | 7.76 | .... | .... | 8.19 | 8.23 | 8.23 | 8.24 | 8.22 | 8.27 | 8.24 | 8.25 | 8.13 |
| ........ | 7.80 | .... | .... | 8.08 | 8.04 | 8.14 | 8.16 | 8.26 | 8.22 | 8.26 | 8.25 | 8.13 |
| | 7.95 | .... | .... | 8.20 | 8.20 | 8.22 | 8.30 | 8.30 | 8.36 | 8.35 | 8.37 | 8.27 |
| 02. | | | | | | | | | | | | |
| ........ | 7.75 | 7.58 | .... | 8.01 | 7.83 | 7.88 | 7.93 | 7.99 | 8.01 | 8.10 | 8.05 | 7.91 |
| | 7.90 | 7.60 | .... | 8.03 | 8.10 | 8.09 | 8.18 | 8.20 | 8.25 | 8.26 | 8.29 | 8.18 |
| ........ | 7.63 | 7.52 | .... | .... | 7.69 | 7.78 | 7.81 | 7.88 | 7.92 | 7.99 | 7.95 | 7.81 |
| | 7.80 | 7.67 | .... | .... | 7.97 | 7.96 | 8.10 | 8.14 | 8.19 | 8.22 | 8.22 | 8.07 |
| ........ | 7.68 | 7.58 | .... | .... | 7.88 | 8.01 | 7.98 | 8.05 | 8.07 | 8.11 | 8.10 | 7.97 |
| | 7.80 | 7.73 | .... | .... | 8.01 | 8.10 | 8.16 | 8.22 | 8.25 | 8.25 | 8.27 | 8.12 |
| ........ | 7.63 | 7.60 | .... | .... | 7.90 | 7.90 | 7.95 | 8.02 | 8.01 | 8.10 | 8.05 | 7.89 |
| | 7.80 | 7.75 | .... | . .. | 8.06 | 8.10 | 8.16 | 8.17 | 8.22 | 8.22 | 8.26 | 8.09 |
| ........ | 7.69 | 7.65 | .... | .... | 7.94 | 7.99 | 8.02 | 8.06 | 8.07 | 8.11 | 8.12 | 7.95 |
| | 7.75 | 7.74 | .... | .... | 8.06 | 8.06 | 8.12 | 8.15 | 8.18 | 8.18 | 8.22 | 8.05 |
| ........ | 7.70 | 7.65 | .... | .... | .... | 8.02 | 8.05 | 8.10 | 8.10 | 8.17 | 8.12 | 7.97 |
| | 7.97 | 7.90 | .... | .... | .... | 8.20 | 8.40 | 8.34 | 8.40 | 8.41 | 8.41 | 8.27 |
| ........ | 7.82 | 7.78 | .... | .... | .... | 8.25 | 8.27 | 8.33 | 8.26 | 8.29 | 8.29 | 8.13 |
| | 8.00 | 7.91 | .... | .... | .... | 8.62 | 8.75 | 8.70 | 8.55 | 8.53 | 8.55 | 8.35 |
| ........ | 7.93 | 7.80 | .... | ... | .... | .... | 8.54 | 8.52 | 8.45 | 8.46 | 8.44 | 8.24 |
| | 8.02 | 7.90 | .... | .... | .... | .... | 8.73 | 8.73 | 8.65 | 8.65 | 8.64 | 8.36 |
| ....... | 7.94 | 7.80 | .... | .... | .... | 8.53 | 8.50 | 8.48 | 8.36 | 8.35 | 8.34 | 8.19 |
| | 8.12 | 8.00 | .... | .... | .... | 8.58 | 8.72 | 8.69 | 8.55 | 8.50 | 8.55 | 8.40 |
| ........ | 8.14 | 8.00 | 7.99 | .... | .... | .... | 8.75 | 8.72 | 8.56 | 8.56 | 8.57 | 8.40 |
| | 8.48 | 8.24 | 8.14 | .... | .... | .... | 9.08 | 9.06 | 8.92 | 8.91 | 8.96 | 8.81 |
| ........ | 8.28 | 8.08 | 7.96 | 7.97 | .... | .... | 8.85 | 8.82 | 8.70 | 8.72 | 8.75 | 8.59 |
| | 8.40 | 8.19 | 8.09 | 8.06 | .... | .... | 9.03 | 9.02 | 8.80 | 8.91 | 8.93 | 8.75 |
| ........ | 8.24 | 8.05 | 7.97 | 8.00 | 8.00 | 8.02 | 8.88 | 8.88 | 8.76 | 8.80 | 8.78 | 8.59 |
| | 8.34 | 8.14 | 8.04 | 8.04 | 8.00 | 8.02 | 9.00 | 9.00 | 8.90 | 8.91 | 8.94 | 87.4 |
| ....... | 8.04 | 7.91 | 7.88 | 7.88 | .... | .... | 8.60 | 8.57 | 8.48 | 8.54 | 8.52 | 8.32 |
| | 8.23 | 8.06 | 7.98 | 7.97 | .... | .... | 8.90 | 8.86 | 8.77 | 8.79 | 8.81 | 8.61 |
| ....... | 8.23 | 8.09 | 8.03 | 8.02 | 8.05 | .... | 8.82 | 8.78 | 8.68 | 8.76 | 8.75 | 8.56 |
| | 8.35 | 8.20 | 8.08 | 8.09 | 8.05 | .... | 8.84 | 9.00 | 8.96 | 8.95 | 8.94 | 8.74 |

## COTTON FUTURES AT NEW YORK—*Continued.*

| For Week Ending | Deliveries. | | | | | | | | | | | |
|---|---|---|---|---|---|---|---|---|---|---|---|---|
| | Sept. | Oct. | Nov. | Dec. | Jan. | Feb. | Mar. | April. | May. | June. | July. | Aug. |
| 1902. | | | | | | | | | | | | |
| April 11........ | 8.29 | 8.12 | 8.04 | 8.04 | 8.03 | .... | .... | 8.99 | 8.83 | 8.86 | 8.86 | 8.67 |
| | 8.46 | 8.25 | 8.15 | 8.13 | 7.15 | .... | .... | 9.19 | 9.09 | 9.12 | 9.10 | 8.92 |
| " 18........ | 8.33 | 8.13 | 8.06 | 8.04 | 8.05 | .... | .... | 8.98 | 8.86 | 8.93 | 8.88 | 8.73 |
| | 8.47 | 8.20 | 8.11 | 8.10 | 8.12 | .... | .... | 9.27 | 9.25 | 9.26 | 9.18 | 8.96 |
| " 25. ...... | 8.35 | 8.11 | 8.02 | 8.01 | 8.03 | .... | .... | 9.18 | 9.11 | 9.14 | 9.08 | 8.85 |
| | 8.55 | 8.30 | 8.18 | 8.19 | 8.20 | .... | .... | 9.60 | 9.56 | 9.52 | 9.47 | 9.22 |
| May 2........ | 8.50 | 8.23 | 8.13 | 8.14 | 8.14 | .... | .... | 9.56 | 9.31 | 9.30 | 9.28 | 9.11 |
| | 8.65 | 8.38 | 8.26 | 8.27 | 8.27 | .... | .... | 9.67 | 9.70 | 9.68 | 9.65 | 9.40 |
| " 9........ | 8.35 | 8.13 | 8.00 | 8.07 | 8.06 | 8.18 | 8.09 | .... | 9.02 | 9.00 | 8.99 | 8.85 |
| | 8.60 | 8.37 | 8.29 | 8.21 | 8.22 | 8.19 | 8.09 | .... | 9.41 | 9.31 | 9.38 | 9.18 |
| " 16.... ... | 8.10 | 7.95 | 7.90 | 7.89 | 7.88 | 8.09 | 7.94 | .... | 9.08 | 9.00 | 8.84 | 8.58 |
| | 8.46 | 8.26 | 8.13 | 8.15 | 8.18 | 8.09 | 7.94 | .... | 9.36 | 9.28 | 9.22 | 8.97 |
| " 23. ...... | 8.00 | 7.88 | 7.84 | 7.83 | 7.82 | 7.95 | 7.94 | .... | 8.90 | 8.86 | 8.65 | 8.39 |
| | 8.22 | 8.06 | 7.98 | 7.96 | 7.99 | 7.95 | 7.97 | .... | 9.35 | 9.21 | 9.06 | 8.75 |
| " 30........ | 8.03 | 7.89 | 7.81 | 7.79 | 7.79 | .... | 7.91 | .... | 9.02 | 9.00 | 8.87 | 8.58 |
| | 8.21 | 8.05 | 7.95 | 7.95 | 7.96 | .... | 7.94 | .... | 9.30 | 9.15 | 9.05 | 8.78 |
| June 6........ | 7.91 | 7.75 | 7.64 | 7.64 | 7.64 | 7.68 | 7.71 | .... | .... | 8.80 | 8.59 | 8.34 |
| | 8.18 | 7.98 | 7.84 | 7.84 | 7.84 | 7.76 | 7.89 | .... | .... | 8.98 | 9.00 | 8.68 |
| " 13........ | 8.00 | 7.87 | 7.81 | 7.79 | 7.80 | 7.85 | 7.86 | .... | .... | 8.90 | 8.65 | 8.42 |
| | 8.25 | 8.11 | 8.04 | 8.04 | 8.05 | 8.05 | 8.06 | .... | .... | 9.05 | 8.82 | 8.58 |
| " 20....... | 7.91 | 7.80 | 7.74 | 7.74 | 7.75 | 8.00 | 7.76 | .... | .... | 8.75 | 8.45 | 8.15 |
| | 8.19 | 8.06 | 7.95 | 8.00 | 8.00 | 8.00 | 8.00 | .... | .... | 9.05 | 8.81 | 8.53 |
| " 27........ | 7.85 | 7.75 | 7.72 | 7.69 | 7.69 | 7.73 | 7.72 | .... | .... | 8.80 | 8.44 | 8.15 |
| | 8.12 | 8.02 | 7.94 | 7.95 | 7.95 | 7.82 | 7.96 | .... | .... | 9.06 | 8.77 | 8.48 |
| July 4........ | 7.88 | 7.75 | 7.66 | 7.66 | 7.64 | 7.68 | 7.64 | .... | .... | .... | 8.52 | 8.19 |
| | 8.11 | 8.01 | 7.93 | 7.95 | 7.94 | 7.95 | 7.95 | .... | .... | .... | 8.84 | 8.45 |
| " 11........ | 7.94 | 7.84 | 7.76 | 7.77 | 7.77 | 7.79 | 7.78 | .... | .. . | .... | 8.57 | 8.28 |
| | 8.11 | 7.97 | 7.90 | 7.90 | 7.90 | 7.89 | 7.92 | .... | .... | .... | 8.72 | 8.47 |
| " 18........ | 8.05 | 7.85 | 7.74 | 7.75 | 7.75 | 7.80 | 7.74 | .... | .... | .... | 8.65 | 8.43 |
| | 8.17 | 7.97 | 7.86 | 7.86 | 7.87 | 7.84 | 7.85 | . .. | .... | .... | 8.72 | 8.52 |
| " 25........ | 7.76 | 7.67 | 7.61 | 7.61 | 7.61 | 7.70 | 7.63 | .... | .... | .... | 8.15 | 8.03 |
| | 8.22 | 7.98 | 7.88 | 7.87 | 7.88 | 7.83 | 7.86 | .... | .... | .... | 8.80 | 8.54 |
| Aug. 1...... .. | 7.75 | 7.64 | 7.53 | 7.54 | 7.53 | 7.58 | 7.50 | .... | .... | .... | 8.42 | 8.10 |
| | 7.94 | 7.81 | 7.70 | 7.72 | 7.73 | 7.62 | 7.70 | .... | .... | .... | 8.53 | 8.34 |
| " 8........ | 7.75 | 7.64 | 7.58 | 7.56 | 7.56 | 7.59 | 7.55 | 7.58 | 7.72 | .... | .... | 8.10 |
| | 7.95 | 7.82 | 7.74 | 7.75 | 7.76 | 7.73 | 7.73 | 7.70 | 7.72 | .... | .... | 8.50 |
| " 15........ | 7.80 | 7.68 | 7.70 | 7.60 | 7.61 | 7.72 | 7.60 | .... | 7.62 | .... | .... | 8.27 |
| | 8.01 | 7.89 | 7.80 | 7.81 | 7.83 | 7.80 | 7.81 | .... | 7.77 | .... | .... | 8.47 |
| " 22........ | 7.90 | 7.80 | 7.72 | 7.72 | 7.73 | 7.82 | 7.72 | 7.87 | 7.73 | ... | .... | 8.36 |
| | 8.14 | 7.99 | 7.90 | 7.91 | 7.95 | 7.90 | 7.91 | 7.87 | 7.91 | .... | .... | 8.56 |
| " 29.. . ... | 8.13 | 7.97 | 7.91 | 7.90 | 7.92 | 7.92 | 7.90 | 8.13 | 7.90 | 8.25 | .... | 8.41 |
| | 8.56 | 8.50 | 8.41 | 8.45 | 8.46 | 8.32 | 8.35 | 8.38 | 8.35 | 8.25 | .... | 8.79 |
| Sept. 5........ | 8.34 | 8.28 | 8.19 | 8.22 | 8.22 | 8.19 | 8.16 | 8.18 | 8.20 | .... | .... | .... |
| | 8.75 | 8.75 | 8.63 | 8.65 | 8.66 | 8.52 | 8.55 | 8.50 | 8.55 | .... | .... | .... |
| " 12........ | 8.22 | 8.18 | 8.18 | 8.13 | 8.15 | 8.09 | 8.07 | 8.17 | 8.09 | .... | .... | .... |
| | 8.55 | 8.46 | 8.41 | 8.42 | 8.42 | 8.29 | 8.27 | 8.29 | 8.29 | .... | .... | .... |
| " 19........ | 8.50 | 8.39 | 8.24 | 8.35 | 8.36 | 8.22 | 8.19 | 8.45 | 8.21 | .... | .... | .... |
| | 8.78 | 8.80 | 8.80 | 8.83 | 8.86 | 8.63 | 8.64 | 8.60 | 8.65 | .... | .... | .... |
| " 26........ | 8.50 | 8.50 | 8.57 | 8.61 | 8.65 | 8.41 | 8.40 | 8.39 | 8.41 | .... | 8.72 | .... |
| | 8.84 | 8.86 | 8.84 | 8.86 | 8.92 | 8.67 | 8.68 | 8.64 | 8.66 | .... | 8.72 | .... |
| Oct. 3........ | 8.61 | 8.58 | 8.65 | 8.72 | 8.75 | 8.56 | 8.55 | 8.54 | 8.55 | 8.58 | 8.62 | 8.55 |
| | 8.73 | 8.69 | 8.75 | 8.84 | 8.90 | 8.67 | 8.67 | 8.66 | 8.68 | 8.58 | 8.62 | 8.55 |
| " 10........ | .... | 8.45 | 8.46 | 8.54 | 8.60 | 8.43 | 8.42 | 8.49 | 8.43 | 8.54 | 3.50 | .... |
| | .... | 8.72 | 8.75 | 8.83 | 8.90 | 8.70 | 8.72 | 8.70 | 8.74 | 8.54 | 8.71 | .... |
| " 17....... | .... | 8.29 | 8.31 | 8.40 | 8.48 | 8.32 | 8.28 | 8.37 | 8.28 | 8.31 | 8.35 | .... |
| | .... | 8.54 | 8.61 | 8.71 | 8.80 | 8.49 | 8.61 | 8.62 | 8.60 | 8.50 | 8.40 | .... |

## COTTON FUTURES AT NEW YORK—*Continued.*

| For Week Ending | Deliveries. | | | | | | | | | | | |
|---|---|---|---|---|---|---|---|---|---|---|---|---|
| | Sept. | Oct. | Nov. | Dec. | Jan. | Feb. | Mar. | April. | May. | June. | July. | Aug. |
| 1902. | | | | | | | | | | | | |
| Oct. 24........ | .... | 8.32 | 8.34 | 8.41 | 8.50 | 8.39 | 8.31 | 8.38 | 8.33 | 8.37 | 8.32 | .... |
| | .... | 8.50 | 8.47 | 8.59 | 8.72 | 8.44 | 8.45 | 8.42 | 8.46 | 8.43 | 8.45 | .... |
| " 31........ | .... | 8.32 | 8.29 | 8.42 | 8.51 | 8.27 | 8.27 | 8.26 | 8.26 | 8.31 | 8.26 | 8.16 |
| | .... | 8.50 | 8.48 | 8.59 | 8.66 | 8.40 | 8.43 | 8.41 | 8.41 | 8.31 | 8.39 | 8.27 |
| Nov. 7........ | .... | .... | 8.06 | 8.12 | 8.17 | 7.97 | 8.01 | 8.00 | 8.03 | 8.15 | 8.40 | 7.94 |
| | .... | .... | 8.32 | 8.47 | 8.55 | 8.27 | 8.32 | 8.21 | 8.32 | 8.25 | 8.31 | 8.15 |
| " 14........ | .... | .... | 7.87 | 7.90 | 7.90 | 7.83 | 7.84 | 7.90 | 7.87 | 7.95 | 7.91 | 7.80 |
| | .... | .... | 8.10 | 8.22 | 8.29 | 8.12 | 8.13 | 8.12 | 8.16 | 8.06 | 8.17 | 7.92 |
| " 21....... | .... | .... | 7.98 | 7.95 | 7.92 | 7.85 | 7.85 | 7.87 | 7.88 | 7.92 | 7.92 | 7.83 |
| | .... | .... | 8.33 | 8.35 | 8.35 | 8.20 | 8.25 | 8.25 | 8.26 | 8.20 | 8.29 | 8.06 |
| " 28........ | 7.80 | .... | 8.25 | 8.24 | 8.22 | 8.18 | 8.13 | 8.14 | 8.15 | 8.19 | 8.19 | 8.02 |
| | 7.81 | .... | 8.40 | 8.44 | 8.48 | 8.34 | 8.39 | 8.39 | 8.40 | 8.37 | 8.42 | 8.25 |
| Dec. 5........ | .... | .... | .... | 8.17 | 8.13 | 8.04 | 8.05 | 8.19 | 8.05 | 8.10 | 8.06 | 7.88 |
| | .... | .... | .... | 8.37 | 8.37 | 8.26 | 8.29 | 8.30 | 8.30 | 8.26 | 8.32 | 8.13 |
| " 12........ | . .. | 7.73 | .... | 8.19 | 8.18 | 8.12 | 8.10 | 8.22 | 8.12 | 8.18 | 8.14 | 7.99 |
| | .... | 7.75 | . .. | 8.38 | 8.37 | 8.27 | 8.32 | 8.31 | 8.36 | 8.32 | 8.37 | 8.21 |
| " 19........ | 7.95 | .... | .... | 8.30 | 8.30 | 8.21 | 8.23 | 8.25 | 8.26 | 8.29 | 8.27 | 8.10 |
| | 8.01 | .... | .... | 8.57 | 8.59 | 8.34 | 8.38 | 8.36 | 8.42 | 8.40 | 8.43 | 8.28 |
| " 26........ | 7.92 | .. . | .... | 8.46 | 8.49 | 8.28 | 8.30 | 8.34 | 8.31 | 8.31 | 8.30 | 8.16 |
| | 8.00 | .... | .... | 8.59 | 8.58 | 8.34 | 8.40 | 8.34 | 8.40 | 8.39 | 8.40 | 8.22 |
| 1903. | | | | | | | | | | | | |
| Jan. 2........ | 8.00 | .... | .... | 8.50 | 8.53 | 8.35 | 8.38 | 8.49 | 8.39 | 8.54 | 8.39 | 8.21 |
| | 8.17 | .... | .... | 8.69 | 8.82 | 8.73 | 8.79 | 8.74 | 8.80 | 8.80 | 8.82 | 8.67 |
| " 9........ | 8.09 | 8.04 | .... | .... | 8.49 | 9.53 | 8.55 | 8.60 | 8.55 | 8.55 | 8.56 | 8.44 |
| | 8.30 | 8.27 | .... | .... | 8.78 | 8.74 | 8.78 | 8.75 | 8.80 | 8.73 | 8.80 | 8.64 |
| " 16........ | 8.11 | 8.09 | .... | .... | 8.53 | 8.51 | 8.59 | 8.65 | 8.61 | 8.62 | 8.61 | 8.44 |
| | 8.31 | 8.18 | .... | .... | 8.78 | 8.75 | 8.85 | 8.84 | 8.90 | 8.84 | 8.91 | 8.68 |
| " 23. ..... | 8.20 | 8.07 | .... | .... | 8.68 | 8.65 | 8.71 | 8.74 | 8.76 | 8.77 | 8.77 | 8.55 |
| | 8.31 | 8.20 | .... | .... | 8.78 | 8.75 | 8.84 | 8.85 | 8.89 | 8.87 | 8.90 | 8.67 |
| " 30........ | 8.18 | 8.03 | .... | .... | 8.68 | 8.62 | 8.66 | 8.79 | 8.71 | 8.72 | 8.71 | 8.50 |
| | 8.31 | 8.19 | .... | .... | 9.00 | 8.87 | 8.91 | 8.92 | 8.95 | 8.90 | 8.93 | 8.72 |
| Feb. 6........ | 8.19 | 8.05 | .... | .... | .... | 8.68 | 8.71 | 8.75 | 8.79 | 8.78 | 8.77 | 8.58 |
| | 8.29 | 8.17 | .... | .... | .... | 8.83 | 8.97 | 9.00 | 9.03 | 8.86 | 8.96 | 8.75 |
| " 13........ | 8.33 | 8.19 | .... | .... | 8.16 | 9.00 | 8.98 | 9.08 | 9.06 | 9.00 | 9.00 | 8.77 |
| | 8.52 | 8.30 | .. . | .... | 8.18 | 9.41 | 9.44 | 9.46 | 9.53 | 9.40 | 9.40 | 9.07 |
| " 20........ | 8.44 | 8.20 | 8.20 | 8.33 | .... | 9.36 | 9.31 | 9.38 | 9.40 | 9.30 | 9.27 | 8.98 |
| | 8.85 | 8.56 | 8.48 | 8.45 | .... | 9.92 | 9.95 | 9.93 | 9.94 | 9.81 | 9.78 | 9.48 |
| " 27........ | 8.64 | 8.40 | 8.31 | 8.30 | 8.50 | 9.84 | 9.73 | 9.73 | 9.70 | 9.55 | 9.49 | 9.18 |
| | 8.98 | 8.65 | 8.56 | 8.52 | 8.50 | 10.10 | 10.14 | 10.10 | 10.12 | 9.85 | 9.90 | 9.57 |
| Mar. 6........ | 8.78 | 8.46 | 8.38 | 8.33 | .... | .... | 9.61 | 9.66 | 9.60 | 9.45 | 9.40 | 9.12 |
| | 9.08 | 8.72 | 8.60 | 8.59 | .... | .... | 10.26 | 10.16 | 10.17 | 9.94 | 9.92 | 9.60 |
| " 13........ | 8.69 | 8.30 | 8.35 | 8.31 | .... | .... | 9.56 | 9.56 | 9.54 | 9.37 | 9.32 | 9.05 |
| | 9.02 | 8.69 | 8.59 | 8.58 | .... | .... | 10.05 | 9.95 | 10.02 | 9.77 | 9.80 | 9.52 |
| " 20........ | 8.85 | 8.52 | 8.45 | 8.44 | 8.52 | .... | 9.73 | 9.76 | 9.68 | 9.54 | 9.53 | 9.30 |
| | 8.98 | 8.67 | 8.57 | 8.53 | 8.52 | .... | 10.01 | 9.93 | 9.95 | 9.80 | 9.80 | 9.54 |
| " 27........ | 8.74 | 8.40 | 8.30 | 8.29 | 8.34 | .... | 9.79 | 9.82 | 9.80 | 9.64 | 9.63 | 9.32 |
| | 8.98 | 8.68 | 8.57 | 8.53 | 8.40 | .... | 9.95 | 9.94 | 10.00 | 9.78 | 9.82 | 9.52 |
| April 3........ | 8.60 | 8.33 | 8.26 | 8.25 | .... | .... | 9.61 | 9.63 | 9.65 | 9.53 | 9.46 | 9.15 |
| | 8.75 | 8.47 | 8.36 | 8.37 | ... | .... | 9.87 | 9.93 | 10.07 | 9.65 | 9.70 | 9.34 |

## VISIBLE SUPPLY OF COTTON IN THE UNITED STATES, EUROPE, AND AT SEA

BALES.

| * Week Ending | 1899. | 1900. | 1901. | 1902. |
|---|---|---|---|---|
| January 3 | 5,659,902 | 4,343,088 | 4,074,438 | 4,357,003 |
| January 10 | 5,638,727 | 4,278,876 | 4,104,607 | 4,509,562 |
| January 17 | 5,729,255 | 4,217,314 | 4,135,715 | 4,474,738 |
| January 24 | 5,692,925 | 4,143,012 | 4,205,264 | 4,449,791 |
| January 31 | 5,697,559 | 4,167,052 | 4,248,900 | 4,554,815 |
| February 7 | 5,588,562 | 4,176,364 | 4,201,510 | 4,475,305 |
| February 14 | 5,463,055 | 4,118,901 | 4,094,843 | 4,468,123 |
| February 21 | 5,462,101 | 4,043,566 | 4,049,480 | 4,525,077 |
| February 28 | 5,416,326 | 3,952,563 | 4,047,890 | 4,488,065 |
| March 7 | 5,387,801 | 3,868,617 | 4,110,469 | 4,411,276 |
| March 14 | 5,218,727 | 3,710,155 | 4,085,664 | 4,361,479 |
| March 21 | 5,200,420 | 3,604,116 | 4,075,608 | 4,343,418 |
| March 28 | 5,201,715 | 3,477,723 | 4,008,465 | 4,233,233 |
| April 4 | 5,191,148 | 3,303,613 | 3,992,400 | 4,096,800 |
| April 11 | 5,138,798 | 3,165,261 | 3,921,132 | 3,988,007 |
| April 18 | 5,048,183 | 3,124,144 | 3,856,026 | 3,875,517 |
| April 25 | 4,933,708 | 2,986,952 | 3,800,793 | 3,772,869 |
| May 2 | 4,857,198 | 2,828,291 | 3,662,302 | 3,644,991 |
| May 9 | 4,741,734 | 2,696,701 | 3,560,577 | 3,470,889 |
| May 16 | 4,643,758 | 2,563,874 | 3,467,971 | 3,332,811 |
| May 23 | 4,524,070 | 2,481,552 | 3,366,132 | 3,229,170 |
| May 30 | 4,368,616 | 2,369,422 | 3,239,162 | 3,098,463 |
| June 6 | 4,233,806 | 2,230,326 | 3,141,525 | 2,950,904 |
| June 13 | 4,110,670 | 2,135,466 | 3,040,705 | 2,810,150 |
| June 20 | 3,964,388 | 2,012,751 | 2,946,376 | 2,660,164 |
| June 27 | 3,797,592 | 1,869,053 | 2,866,908 | 2,559,053 |
| July 4 | 3,625,246 | 1,722,525 | 2,744,908 | 2,428,272 |
| July 11 | 3,463,739 | 1,581,088 | 2,575,394 | 2,251,849 |
| July 18 | 3,310,014 | 1,500,298 | 2,444,042 | 2,102,462 |
| July 25 | 3,144,925 | 1,405,722 | 2,306,521 | 1,911,570 |
| August 1 | 2,997,210 | 1,342,110 | 2,160,994 | 1,761,192 |
| August 8 | 2,840,323 | 1,273,748 | 2,038,172 | 1,641,988 |
| August 15 | 2,734,884 | 1,198,396 | 1,889,345 | 1,512,777 |
| August 22 | 2,669,836 | 1,124,967 | 1,142,572 | 1,434,627 |
| August 29 | 2,596,864 | 1,048,959 | 1,569,588 | 1,346,468 |
| September 5 | 2,597,415 | 965,999 | 1,460,601 | 1,308,831 |
| September 12 | 2,647,296 | 981,256 | 1,407,763 | 1,394,682 |
| September 19 | 2,751,836 | 1,121,914 | 1,408,453 | 1,539,936 |
| September 26 | 2,899,671 | 1,405,161 | 1,474,825 | 1,755,848 |
| October 3 | 3,103,390 | 1,678,980 | 1,643,309 | 1,951,864 |
| October 10 | 3,277,964 | 1,996,457 | 1,873,161 | 2,154,094 |
| October 17 | 3,414,080 | 2,381,641 | 2,135,159 | 2,315,313 |
| October 24 | 2,553,344 | 2,671,775 | 2,493,759 | 2,494,195 |
| October 31 | 3,630,992 | 2,868,455 | 2,762,595 | 2,734,923 |
| November 7 | 3,789,787 | 2,988,691 | 3,017,100 | 2,852,072 |
| November 14 | 3,908,122 | 3,135,979 | 3,193,111 | 3,028,079 |
| November 21 | 4,039,481 | 3,289,280 | 3,370,287 | 3,196,297 |
| November 28 | 4,072,205 | 3,383,150 | 3,496,534 | 3,255,870 |
| December 5 | 4,121,392 | 3,592,840 | 3,670,497 | 3,445,419 |
| December 12 | 4,220,913 | 3,794,794 | 3,820,394 | 3,556,725 |
| December 19 | 4,297,739 | 3,921,733 | 4,028,143 | 3,689,555 |
| December 26 | 4,340,012 | 4,091,283 | 4,110,852 | 3,752,568 |

* The dates are for 1902. The other columns are for corresponding weeks.

## AMERICAN COTTON CROP MOVEMENT

SHOWING AMOUNT OF CROP COMING IN SIGHT, BY MONTHS, WITH AMOUNT AND PER CENT. OF TOTAL CROP IN SIGHT AT CLOSE OF MONTH.

| | | 1891-2. | 1892-3. | 1893-4. | 1894-5. | 1895-6. | 1896-7. | 1897-8. | 1898-9. | 1899-00. | 1900-1. | 1901-2. | 1902-3. |
|---|---|---|---|---|---|---|---|---|---|---|---|---|---|
| September | Came in sight... | 832,317 | 536,278 | 505,249 | 670,537 | 534,795 | 1,241,427 | 1,069,439 | 960,350 | 1,118,712 | 879,327 | 706,326 | 1,256,691 |
| | Per cent. in sight. | 9.21 | 8.0 | 6.7 | 6.7 | 7.4 | 14.1 | 9.5 | 8.5 | 11.8 | 8.4 | 6.6 | ...... |
| October... | Came in sight... | 2,030,643 | 1,462,798 | 1,647,369 | 2,140,996 | 1,736,152 | 1,911,416 | 1,891,897 | 2,288,141 | 1,742,523 | 2,154,225 | 2,170,142 | 1,960,570 |
| | Total in sight... | 2,862,960 | 1,999,076 | 2,152,618 | 2,811,533 | 2,270,947 | 3,152,845 | 2,961,336 | 3,248,495 | 2,861,235 | 3,033,552 | 2,876,468 | 3,217,261 |
| | Per cent. in sight. | 31.69 | 29.38 | 28.5 | 28.4 | 31.7 | 36.0 | 26.4 | 28.8 | 30.3 | 29.2 | 26.7 | ...... |
| November | Came in sight... | 1,919,272 | 1,482,928 | 1,675,041 | 2,190,795 | 1,312,754 | 1,649,058 | 2,349,751 | 2,352,906 | 1,658,425 | 1,781,510 | 1,966,545 | 1,842,431 |
| | Total in sight... | 4,782,232 | 3,482,004 | 3,827,659 | 5,002,328 | 3,583,701 | 4,801,901 | 5,311,087 | 5,601,397 | 4,519,666 | 4,815,062 | 4,843,013 | 5,059,692 |
| | Per cent. in sight. | 52.93 | 51.97 | 50.7 | 50.5 | 50.6 | 54.8 | 47.4 | 49.6 | 48.8 | 46.3 | 45.3 | ...... |
| December. | Came in sight... | 1,663,854 | 1,308,451 | 1,638,433 | 1,992,345 | 1,360,519 | 1,596,291 | 1,985,446 | 2,124,152 | 1,397,778 | 1,760,281 | 1,846,302 | 1,671,125 |
| | Total in sight... | 6,446,086 | 4,790,455 | 5,466,092 | 6,994,673 | 4,944,220 | 6,398,192 | 7,296,533 | 7,725,549 | 5,917,438 | 6,575,343 | 6,689,315 | 6,730,817 |
| | Per cent. in sight. | 71.34 | 71.49 | 72.5 | 70.6 | 69.0 | 73.0 | 65.2 | 68.5 | 62.6 | 63.3 | 62.6 | ...... |
| January .. | Came in sight.. | 762,339 | 565,752 | 788,080 | 1,019,797 | 626,829 | 728,269 | 1,388,394 | 1,169,983 | 954,679 | 982,128 | 1,341,930 | 1,254,069 |
| | Total in sight... | 7,208,425 | 5,356,207 | 6,254,172 | 8,014,470 | 5,571,049 | 7,126,461 | 8,684,927 | 8,895,532 | 6,872,119 | 7,557,471 | 8,031,245 | 7,984,886 |
| | Per cent. in sight. | 79.78 | 79.94 | 83.1 | 80.9 | 77.8 | 81.3 | 77.6 | 78.8 | 72.7 | 72.8 | 75.1 | ...... |
| February . | Came in sight... | 748,529 | 418,136 | 362,431 | 572,442 | 507,215 | 485,636 | 893,341 | 552,010 | 847,180 | 670,748 | 743,320 | 844,474 |
| | Total in sight... | 7,986,954 | 5,774,343 | 6,616,608 | 8,586,912 | 6,078,264 | 7,612,097 | 9,578,268 | 9,447,542 | 7,719,297 | 8,228,219 | 8,774,565 | 8,829,360 |
| | Per cent. in sight. | 88.6 | 86.17 | 87.8 | 86.7 | 84.9 | 86.9 | 85.5 | 83.7 | 81.8 | 79.2 | 82.1 | ...... |
| March.... | Came in sight... | 437,335 | 295,762 | 300,343 | 608,015 | 379,055 | 401,397 | 701,941 | 639,457 | 586,768 | 646,100 | 625,723 | 710,306 |
| | Total in sight. | 8,394,289 | 6,070,105 | 6,916,951 | 9,194,927 | 6,457,319 | 8,013,494 | 10,280,209 | 10,086,999 | 8,306,065 | 8,874,319 | 9,400,288 | 9,539,666 |
| | Per cent. in sight. | 92.90 | 90.59 | 91.7 | 92.8 | 90.2 | 91.5 | 91.8 | 89.4 | 88.0 | 85.4 | 88.4 | ...... |
| April..... | Came in sight... | 271,576 | 202,437 | 249,450 | 342,728 | 240,638 | 232,735 | 354,902 | 419,660 | 283,297 | 488,925 | 360,693 | ...... |
| | Total in sight... | 8,665,865 | 6,272,542 | 7,166,401 | 9,537,655 | 6,697,957 | 8,246,229 | 10,635,111 | 10,506,659 | 8,589,362 | 9,363,244 | 9,760,981 | ...... |
| | Per cent. in sight. | 95.91 | 93.61 | 95.1 | 96.3 | 93.5 | 94.1 | 95.0 | 93.1 | 91.0 | 90.1 | 91.3 | ...... |
| May..... | Came in sight... | 193,353 | 148,655 | 140,834 | 159,615 | 164,800 | 160,853 | 236,706 | 321,111 | 224,899 | 329,896 | 239,949 | ...... |
| | Total in sight... | 8,861,218 | 6,421,197 | 7,307,235 | 9,697,270 | 6,862,757 | 8,407,082 | 10,871,817 | 10,827,770 | 8,854,261 | 9,693,140 | 10000930 | ...... |
| | Per cent. in sight. | 98.7 | 95.83 | 96.9 | 97.9 | 95.9 | 95.9 | 97.1 | 96.0 | 93.8 | 43.3 | 93.6 | ...... |
| June..... | Came in sight... | 107,377 | 86,694 | 84,774 | 79,735 | 93,896 | 80,809 | 151,519 | 176,285 | 133,185 | 277,826 | 180,849 | ...... |
| | Total in sight... | 8,968,595 | 6,507,891 | 7,392,009 | 9,777,005 | 6,956,653 | 8,487,891 | 11,023,336 | 11,004,055 | 8,947,446 | 9,970,966 | 10181779 | ...... |
| July and August. | Per cent. in sight. | 99.24 | 97.12 | 98.0 | 98.7 | 97.1 | 96.9 | 98.5 | 97.6 | 94.8 | 96.0 | 95.4 | ...... |
| | Came in sight... | 66,784 | 192,474 | 157,808 | 124,246 | 200,693 | 270,073 | 229,913 | 405,385 | 488,970 | 497,207 | 498,910 | ...... |
| | Total in sight.. | 9,035,379 | 6,700,365 | 7,549,817 | 9,901,251 | 7,157,346 | 8,757,964 | 11,199,994 | 11,274,840 | 9,436,416 | 10383422 | 10680689 | ...... |
| Total Crop | ........... | 9,035,379 | 6,700,365 | 7,549,817 | 9,901,251 | 7,157,346 | 8,757,964 | 11,199,994 | 11,274,840 | 9,436,416 | 10383422 | 10680689 | ...... |

## *COTTON CROP MOVEMENT*

UNITED STATES PORTS RECEIPTS.

| * Week Ending. | 1897-98. | 1898-99. | 1899-1900. | 1900-01. | 1901-02. | 1902-03. |
|---|---|---|---|---|---|---|
| 1902. | | | | | | |
| September 6.. | 95,874 | 54,079 | 106,487 | 51,507 | 48,029 | 108,960 |
| September 13.. | 176,114 | 111,475 | 164,394 | 83,307 | 60,994 | 154,680 |
| September 20.. | 241,560 | 197,501 | 201,048 | 150,363 | 111,416 | 209,463 |
| September 27 . | 276,858 | 312,039 | 246,566 | 276,666 | 145,533 | 270,771 |
| October 4..... | 281,926 | 340,635 | 281,718 | 309,098 | 219,062 | 307,618 |
| October 11..... | 291,870 | 385,763 | 251,919 | 339,727 | 277,632 | 295,612 |
| October 18..... | 369,319 | 421,873 | 264,526 | 366,159 | 362,964 | 314,752 |
| October 25..... | 369,040 | 407,281 | 241,361 | 323,795 | 420,225 | 305,362 |
| November 1.. | 368,344 | 446,122 | 231,356 | 296,874 | 414,930 | 317,391 |
| November 8.. | 405,835 | 445,868 | 257,558 | 296,316 | 354,404 | 331,146 |
| November 15.. | 398,985 | 417,434 | 266,715 | 277,197 | 336,555 | 346,583 |
| November 22.. | 398,422 | 422,521 | 263,734 | 280,320 | 318,877 | 323,453 |
| November 29.. | 402,850 | 393,581 | 225,416 | 285,869 | 325,345 | 302,540 |
| December 6.. | 354,950 | 392,070 | 248,036 | 307,058 | 332,817 | 326,071 |
| December 13.. | 389,002 | 326,798 | 228,564 | 310,325 | 312,290 | 261,784 |
| December 20.. | 303,134 | 360,558 | 217,368 | 265,959 | 299,132 | 263,318 |
| December 27.. | 302,267 | 294,159 | 171,448 | 224,768 | 301,721 | 285,231 |
| 1903. | | | | | | |
| January 3.... | 293,849 | 285,520 | 149,249 | 175,720 | 301,113 | 254,256 |
| January 10.... | 266,930 | 209,786 | 144,392 | 174,874 | 289,317 | 275,179 |
| January 17.... | 236,823 | 207,533 | 164,341 | 138,721 | 247,968 | 225,476 |
| January 24.... | 212,823 | 170,097 | 165,571 | 169,000 | 198,160 | 222,177 |
| January 31.... | 215,120 | 176,022 | 215,028 | 173,317 | 193,194 | 184,161 |
| February 7... | 198,039 | 122,880 | 207,311 | 143,842 | 126,307 | 194,161 |
| February 14... | 186,863 | 69,499 | 190,672 | 126,386 | 157,837 | 197,181 |
| February 21... | 155,072 | 81,502 | 181,589 | 100,567 | 166,930 | 152,511 |
| February 28... | 148,760 | 96,681 | 155,901 | 125,927 | 159,007 | 143,947 |
| March 7...... | 143,522 | 88,220 | 155,661 | 135,210 | 121,944 | 146,575 |
| March 14...... | 144,675 | 98,678 | 111,682 | 128,551 | 128,624 | 141,613 |
| March 21...... | 99,363 | 105,169 | 105,213 | 129,963 | 101,881 | 87,724 |
| March 28...... | 82,131 | 101,801 | 80,312 | 108,633 | 75,645 | 89,540 |
| April 4...... | 76,194 | 67,236 | 82,947 | 114,868 | 66,646 | 108,431 |
| April 11....... | 71,158 | 67,540 | 56,242 | 91,373 | 73,911 | ...... |
| April 18....... | 66,710 | 61,559 | 44,244 | 80,135 | 69,024 | ...... |
| April 25....... | 58,774 | 70,955 | 39,679 | 71,660 | 60,384 | ...... |
| May 2....... | 55,143 | 68,461 | 41,064 | 88,844 | 66,871 | ...... |
| May 9....... | 35,040 | 62,575 | 24,812 | 75,054 | 60,967 | ...... |
| May 16....... | 37,121 | 59,894 | 41,654 | 76,742 | 47,842 | ...... |
| May 23....... | 38,340 | 36,675 | 30,764 | 54,906 | 22,002 | ...... |
| May 30....... | 33,873 | 31,520 | 23,244 | 57,102 | 20,564 | ...... |
| June 6....... | 31,363 | 48,057 | 16,095 | 50,227 | 21,085 | ...... |
| June 13....... | 18,082 | 26,360 | 12,412 | 54,139 | 23,984 | ...... |
| June 20....... | 15,065 | 26,791 | 16,572 | 50,004 | 21,866 | ...... |
| June 27....... | 19,571 | 17,474 | 10,782 | 69,345 | 22,960 | ...... |
| July 4........ | 9,928 | 20,178 | 13,383 | 49,610 | 13,050 | ...... |
| July 11........ | 9,347 | 24,006 | 25,531 | 44,232 | 10,828 | ...... |
| July 18........ | 7,837 | 15,259 | 40,016 | 49,790 | 16,719 | ...... |
| July 25........ | 11,916 | 7,063 | 27,437 | 24,590 | 13,687 | ...... |
| August 1..... | 10,365 | 6,868 | 16,640 | 23,024 | 19,341 | ...... |
| August 8..... | 3,909 | 8,100 | 4,411 | 19,791 | 15,715 | ...... |
| August 15..... | 8,857 | 14,999 | 3,349 | 12,019 | 11,410 | ...... |
| August 22..... | 20,212 | 29,131 | 7,998 | 17,279 | 25,347 | ...... |
| August 29..... | 32,250 | 65,270 | 24,273 | 51,816 | 60,004 | ...... |

* Dates are for the weeks in season of 1902-1903. Ports included are: Galveston, New Orleans, Mobile, Savannah, Charleston, Wilmington, N. C.; Norfolk, Va.; Baltimore, New York, Philadelphia, Boston, Brunswick, Ga.; West Point, Velasco, Tex., and other minor points.

# COTTON CROP MOVEMENT

## STOCKS AT UNITED STATES PORTS.

Showing stocks of cotton in bales at the United States shipping ports.

| * Week Ending | 1898-99. | 1899-1900. | 1900-01. | 1901-02. | 1902-03. |
|---|---|---|---|---|---|
| 1902. | | | | | |
| September 6 | 190,356 | 457,549 | 113,499 | 233,583 | 203,057 |
| September 13 | 258,310 | 518,761 | 157,985 | 222,708 | 246,457 |
| September 20 | 350,682 | 549,454 | 216,497 | 269,804 | 304,931 |
| September 27 | 513,862 | 658,407 | 396,631 | 316,324 | 406,863 |
| October 4 | 622,186 | 682,915 | 457,883 | 328,701 | 371,619 |
| October 11 | 771,082 | 772,582 | 513,859 | 430,317 | 490,336 |
| October 18 | 888,204 | 802,962 | 608,137 | 546,158 | 540,201 |
| October 25 | 955,468 | 816,466 | 656,872 | 658,945 | 607,955 |
| November 1 | 1,063,519 | 828,881 | 635,627 | 611,447 | 610,102 |
| November 8 | 1,104,816 | 880,545 | 610,811 | 725,727 | 721,523 |
| November 15 | 1,125,867 | 951,757 | 703,909 | 782,820 | 829,896 |
| November 22 | 1,238,223 | 1,014,789 | 774,928 | 820,968 | 925,465 |
| November 29 | 1,290,938 | 975,206 | 810,726 | 820,851 | 999,043 |
| December 6 | 1,302,074 | 1,055,092 | 818,305 | 829,541 | 1,064,826 |
| December 13 | 1,330,482 | 1,102,156 | 904,464 | 884,437 | 1,023,379 |
| December 20 | 1,336,904 | 1,019,225 | 986,578 | 987,757 | 1,060,893 |
| December 27 | 1,291,603 | 1,122,228 | 1,000,614 | 989,243 | 1,084,269 |
| 1903. | | | | | |
| January 3 | 1,204,075 | 1,011,101 | 971,903 | 1,030,188 | 1,039,425 |
| January 10 | 1,157,974 | 997,309 | 866,101 | 1,038,270 | 1,065,727 |
| January 17 | 1,101,558 | 979,507 | 876,231 | 981,167 | 1,075,458 |
| January 24 | 1,080,948 | 971,507 | 880,750 | 974,657 | 1,089,527 |
| January 31 | 981,779 | 984,722 | 939,442 | 889,749 | 1,019,174 |
| February 7 | 899,339 | 1,028,121 | 906,261 | 841,669 | 953,509 |
| February 14 | 840,812 | 1,087,378 | 919,038 | 919,038 | 940,617 |
| February 21 | 799,834 | 1,017,803 | 873,328 | 787,468 | 895,539 |
| February 28 | 761,915 | 947,935 | 845,238 | 765,413 | 850,284 |
| March 7 | 748,529 | 918,659 | 849,523 | 734,558 | 797,146 |
| March 14 | 754,130 | 873,822 | 808,980 | 717,595 | 634,188 |
| March 21 | 786,613 | 808,850 | 824,444 | 717,328 | 567,129 |
| March 28 | 776,400 | 758,937 | 773,398 | 686,067 | 490,992 |
| April 4 | 791,124 | 644,669 | 784,056 | 639,949 | 389,667 |
| April 11 | 788,077 | 561,769 | 719,418 | 654,404 | ...... |
| April 18 | 797,787 | 500,671 | 680,112 | 628,424 | ...... |
| April 25 | 787,489 | 452,377 | 671,054 | 582,806 | ...... |
| May 2 | 745,713 | 369,685 | 585,523 | 547,536 | ...... |
| May 9 | 743,164 | 345,826 | 543,261 | 537,920 | ...... |
| May 16 | 736,501 | 326,830 | 496,383 | 492,506 | ...... |
| May 23 | 700,176 | 277,263 | 462,437 | 461,452 | ...... |
| May 30 | 657,693 | 256,240 | 455,915 | 424,226 | ...... |
| June 6 | 644,857 | 226,575 | 440,356 | 394,798 | ...... |
| June 13 | 609,997 | 215,398 | 402,134 | 381,972 | ...... |
| June 20 | 573,499 | 198,308 | 414,813 | 359,457 | ...... |
| June 27 | 515,139 | 169,118 | 436,369 | 331,150 | ...... |
| July 4 | 453,499 | 147,686 | 454,442 | 309,187 | ...... |
| July 11 | 422,362 | 157,327 | 397,937 | 280,820 | ...... |
| July 18 | 406,217 | 144,779 | 413,276 | 255,801 | ...... |
| July 25 | 395,412 | 142,944 | 361,955 | 227,059 | ...... |
| August 1 | 363,606 | 112,927 | 334,157 | 207,764 | ...... |
| August 8 | 345,703 | 98,513 | 299,829 | 177,109 | ...... |
| August 15 | 354,409 | 87,652 | 268,056 | 150,087 | ...... |
| August 22 | 363,581 | 83,173 | 253,604 | 145,237 | ...... |
| August 29 | 369,960 | 85,361 | 234,760 | 143,818 | ...... |

* The dates are for 1902–03. The other columns are for corresponding weeks.

## COTTON CROP MOVEMENT.

### TOTAL RECEIPTS AT UNITED STATES PORTS.

Aggregate receipts, in bales, at United States ports.

| *Week Ending | 1897-98. | 1898-99. | 1899-1900. | 1900-01. | 1901-02. | 1902-03. |
|---|---|---|---|---|---|---|
| 1902. | | | | | | |
| August 31 | 20,012 | 11,396 | 9,822 | ...... | ...... | ...... |
| September 6 | 115,886 | 65,475 | 116,507 | 51,507 | 48,029 | 90,148 |
| September 13 | 292,000 | 176,950 | 281,033 | 134,814 | 109,023 | 243,633 |
| September 20 | 533,560 | 374,451 | 482,206 | 285,177 | 220,439 | 453,096 |
| September 27 | 810,418 | 686,490 | 728,772 | 561,843 | 365,971 | 723,867 |
| October 4 | 1,092,544 | 1,028,871 | 1,012,371 | 877,441 | 583,428 | 1,029,946 |
| October 11 | 1,384,414 | 1,414,634 | 1,262,934 | 1,228,034 | 861,488 | 1,322,678 |
| October 18 | 1,753,859 | 1,856,507 | 1,530,539 | 1,596,942 | 1,224,452 | 1,637,430 |
| October 25 | 2,122,899 | 2,243,788 | 1,772,105 | 1,920,737 | 1,644,677 | 1,942,792 |
| November 1 | 2,491,243 | 2,689,949 | 2,004,451 | 2,218,768 | 2,062,223 | 2,260,183 |
| November 8 | 2,897,078 | 3,143,708 | 2,263,063 | 2,512,793 | 2,415,403 | 2,590,669 |
| November 15 | 3,296,063 | 3,561,142 | 2,534,156 | 2,790,626 | 2,751,958 | 2,937,618 |
| November 22 | 3,694,485 | 3,988,443 | 2,798,440 | 3,070,946 | 3,070,475 | 3,261,080 |
| November 29 | 4,097,335 | 4,382,904 | 3,023,856 | 3,356,669 | 3,395,820 | 3,564,072 |
| December 6 | 4,452,285 | 4,774,974 | 3,271,892 | 3,655,168 | 3,728,478 | 3,909,242 |
| December 13 | 4,841,287 | 5,105,652 | 3,525,946 | 3,969,427 | 4,036,003 | 4,171,026 |
| December 20 | 5,204,421 | 5,466,210 | 3,742,314 | 4,235,386 | 4,325,415 | 4,433,491 |
| December 27 | 5,506,688 | 5,764,469 | 3,915,049 | 4,460,154 | 4,627,136 | 4,714,470 |
| 1903. | | | | | | |
| January 3 | 5,800,790 | 6,049,989 | 4,071,970 | 4,636,171 | 4,928,249 | 4,968,726 |
| January 10 | 6,066,195 | 6,259,775 | 4,228,505 | 4,811,333 | 5,213,722 | 5,241,593 |
| January 17 | 6,303,018 | 6,472,808 | 4,421,458 | 4,985,746 | 5,461,342 | 5,467,039 |
| January 24 | 6,515,841 | 6,646,256 | 4,585,181 | 5,154,846 | 5,659,502 | 5,689,216 |
| January 31 | 6,730,961 | 6,831,485 | 4,800,209 | 5,328,163 | 5,852,696 | 5,873,377 |
| February 7 | 6,929,000 | 6,965,060 | 5,020,888 | 5,489,734 | 5,976,678 | 6,076,305 |
| February 14 | 7,115,863 | 7,037,409 | 5,241,714 | 5,623,822 | 6,134,515 | 6,273,486 |
| February 21 | 7,270,935 | 7,118,911 | 5,423,453 | 5,745,499 | 6,301,445 | 6,425,997 |
| February 28 | 7,428,695 | 7,251,909 | 5,579,354 | 5,871,226 | 6,460,452 | 6,569,948 |
| March 7 | 7,572,217 | 7,346,258 | 5,726,877 | 6,006,436 | 6,576,060 | 6,715,273 |
| March 14 | 7,716,892 | 7,457,262 | 5,863,233 | 6,145,093 | 6,702,159 | 6,797,886 |
| March 21 | 7,816,255 | 7,562,631 | 5,986,446 | 6,275,056 | 6,804,040 | 6,885,939 |
| March 28 | 7,898,386 | 7,668,711 | 6,048,258 | 6,383,689 | 6,879,685 | 6,975,479 |
| April 4 | 7,974,580 | 7,735,947 | 6,131,756 | 6,498,557 | 6,944,503 | 7,084,628 |
| April 11 | 8,045,738 | 7,803,487 | 6,232,350 | 6,589,930 | 7,020,334 | ...... |
| April 18 | 8,112,448 | 7,874,299 | 6,289,820 | 6,687,919 | 7,089,858 | ...... |
| April 25 | 8,171,222 | 7,945,254 | 6,329,532 | 6,759,579 | 7,150,242 | ...... |
| May 2 | 8,229,289 | 8,015,028 | 6,372,015 | 6,851,197 | 7,216,876 | ...... |
| May 9 | 8,264,329 | 8,077,603 | 6,396,548 | 6,926,251 | 7,277,850 | ...... |
| May 16 | 8,301,450 | 8,162,902 | 6,450,495 | 6,994,142 | 7,325,642 | ...... |
| May 23 | 8,339,790 | 8,199,577 | 6,480,048 | 7,049,048 | 7,347,644 | ...... |
| May 30 | 8,373,663 | 8,237,771 | 6,493,288 | 7,095,029 | 7,368,208 | ...... |
| June 6 | 8,405,026 | 8,285,828 | 6,511,143 | 7,153,627 | 7,388,198 | ...... |
| June 13 | 8,423,108 | 8,312,188 | 6,536,875 | 7,217,177 | 7,415,410 | ...... |
| June 20 | 8,439,937 | 8,338,979 | 6,553,447 | 7,267,781 | 7,437,276 | ...... |
| June 27 | 8,459,508 | 8,356,451 | 6,564,229 | 7,337,126 | 7,467,241 | ...... |
| July 4 | 8,471,736 | 8,403,241 | 6,577,612 | 7,385,582 | 7,478,946 | ...... |
| July 11 | 8,481,083 | 8,438,827 | 6,603,143 | 7,418,901 | 7,489,774 | ...... |
| July 18 | 8,488,920 | 8,454,086 | 6,643,159 | 7,481,426 | 7,503,230 | ...... |
| July 25 | 8,500,836 | 8,461,149 | 6,672,101 | 7,506,016 | 7,516,917 | ...... |
| August 1 | 8,516,966 | 8,468,017 | 6,688,562 | 7,528,933 | 7,536,258 | ...... |
| August 8 | 8,520,875 | 8,476,117 | 6,692,973 | 7,538,554 | 7,550,016 | ...... |
| August 15 | 8,529,732 | 8,499,902 | 6,697,318 | 7,562,284 | 7,563,318 | ...... |
| August 22 | 8,549,944 | 8,539,662 | 6,705,643 | 7,579,563 | 7,593,710 | ...... |
| August 29 | ...... | ...... | 6,723,395 | 7,634,651 | 7,655,795 | ...... |

* The dates are for 1902-03. The other columns are for corresponding weeks.

## COTTON CROP MOVEMENT

### STOCKS AT NEW YORK.

Amounts of cotton in New York, in bales.

| * Week Ending | 1897-98. | 1898.99. | 1899-1900 | 1900-01. | 1901-02. | 1902-03 |
|---|---|---|---|---|---|---|
| 1902. | | | | | | |
| September 5 | 42,857 | 46,353 | 164,707 | 28,501 | 114,029 | 64,515 |
| September 12 | 45,848 | 47,680 | 166,496 | 26,906 | 103,311 | 41,244 |
| September 19 | 46,876 | 46,828 | 158,633 | 24,561 | 88,177 | 33,428 |
| September 26 | 60,811 | 52,160 | 147,047 | 30,778 | 77,876 | 30,693 |
| October 3 | 57,903 | 52,175 | 134,430 | 33,116 | 79,921 | 29,817 |
| October 10 | 50,216 | 57,458 | 125,474 | 42,887 | 86,619 | 37,035 |
| October 17 | 57,919 | 64,976 | 111,164 | 37,175 | 79,372 | 40,779 |
| October 24 | 57,751 | 72,982 | 109,774 | 36,286 | 75,210 | 43,236 |
| October 31 | 66,925 | 77,255 | 105,629 | 46,432 | 77,560 | 51,172 |
| November 4 | 78,918 | 78,354 | 106,239 | 46,427 | 70,206 | 58,591 |
| November 14 | 80,971 | 92,982 | 103,716 | 42,425 | 76,702 | 68,239 |
| November 21 | 94,638 | 100,579 | 103,719 | 41,861 | 78,997 | 85,813 |
| November 28 | 98,008 | 100,723 | 106,033 | 49,366 | 82,127 | 94,886 |
| December 5 | 93,471 | 106,483 | 106,692 | 61,336 | 97,771 | 116,860 |
| December 12 | 98,869 | 89,943 | 109,705 | 61,721 | 101,778 | 129,566 |
| December 19 | 105,517 | 89,651 | 112,794 | 58,893 | 103,778 | 141,962 |
| December 26 | 123,682 | 88,566 | 119,619 | 80,168 | 121,337 | 147,740 |
| 1903. | | | | | | |
| January 3 | 121,621 | 84,292 | 116,144 | 90,179 | 118,858 | 159,061 |
| January 10 | 138,799 | 108,121 | 118,048 | 94,459 | 122,093 | 169,021 |
| January 17 | 138,606 | 104,923 | 126,162 | 102,912 | 129,578 | 169,461 |
| January 24 | 160,679 | 105,674 | 128,669 | 106,241 | 126,274 | 161,388 |
| January 31 | 176,639 | 98,950 | 116,907 | 147,846 | 119,944 | 160,080 |
| February 7 | 162,812 | 99,201 | 117,840 | 152,122 | 123,204 | 150,092 |
| February 14 | 190,795 | 101,184 | 122,153 | 147,394 | 116,699 | 141,306 |
| February 21 | 203,265 | 102,637 | 129,833 | 151,607 | 124,046 | 122,901 |
| February 28 | 190,955 | 110,500 | 135,908 | 141,460 | 125,046 | 126,777 |
| March 7 | 188,224 | 120,057 | 143,603 | 143,028 | 136,718 | 102,126 |
| March 14 | 179,912 | 131,265 | 141,559 | 146,448 | 155,922 | 88,214 |
| March 21 | 197,035 | 136,386 | 140,631 | 154,782 | 174,223 | 74,644 |
| March 28 | 190,768 | 145,074 | 134,793 | 154,804 | 182,915 | 66,415 |
| April 4 | 196,780 | 153,748 | 135,528 | 156,840 | 186,448 | 62,491 |
| April 11 | 185,521 | 157,817 | 128,055 | 144,662 | 189,814 | ...... |
| April 18 | 188,428 | 160,180 | 118,896 | 140,200 | 197,544 | ...... |
| April 25 | 172,243 | 158,283 | 112,040 | 148,418 | 187,853 | ...... |
| May 2 | 192,923 | 171,104 | 79,010 | 135,652 | 195,976 | ...... |
| May 9 | 180,555 | 170,509 | 78,818 | 128,646 | 195,771 | ...... |
| May 16 | 169,180 | 179,915 | 80,500 | 125,230 | 184,676 | ...... |
| May 23 | 135,237 | 171,055 | 79,066 | 123,096 | 186,412 | ...... |
| May 30 | 135,793 | 173,729 | 76,816 | 128,725 | 180,547 | ...... |
| June 6 | 125,127 | 172,053 | 73,948 | 129,272 | 167,629 | ...... |
| June 13 | 115,369 | 175,221 | 75,298 | 132,579 | 166,482 | ...... |
| June 20 | 105,232 | 178,239 | 66,642 | 142,136 | 159,659 | ...... |
| June 27 | 104,429 | 168,316 | 52,475 | 158,208 | 151,512 | ...... |
| July 4 | 101,592 | 154,136 | 45,427 | 170,332 | 150,052 | ...... |
| July 11 | 103,964 | 150,404 | 41,544 | 180,936 | 141,004 | ...... |
| July 18 | 101,537 | 148,796 | 37,438 | 190,185 | 144,950 | ...... |
| July 25 | 92,698 | 145,065 | 37,057 | 183,635 | 135,486 | ...... |
| August 1 | 82,201 | 145,069 | 27,309 | 171,578 | 127,606 | ...... |
| August 8 | 80,615 | 128,274 | 38,609 | 170,111 | 108,514 | ...... |
| August 15 | 66,880 | 144,048 | 31,815 | 159,895 | 90,634 | ...... |
| August 22 | 53,429 | 144,445 | 24,462 | 149,844 | 77,325 | ...... |
| August 29 | 52,395 | 150,821 | 22,637 | 114,401 | 55,015 | ...... |

* The dates are for 1902-03. The other columns are for corresponding weeks.

## THE AMERICAN COTTON CROP AND ITS DISTRIBUTION

The following gives an account of the movements of the American crop of the season of 1901–02, as compared with the previous two seasons, as reported by the New York "Financial Chronicle" and by Mr. Henry Hester, Secretary of the New Orleans Cotton Exchange, the figures being in 1,000's of bales:

| | "Chronicle." | | | New Orleans Cotton Exchange. | | |
|---|---|---|---|---|---|---|
| | 1899-00. | 1900-01. | 1901-02. | 1899-00. | 1900-01. | 1901-02. |
| Port Receipts | 6,575 | 7,605 | 7,571 | 6,734 | 7,666 | 7,679 |
| Overland | 1,265 | 1,153 | 1,187 | 1,161 | 1,140 | 1,104 |
| Southern Mills | 1,600 | 1,667 | 1,943 | 1,541 | 1,577 | 1,897 |
| Total crop | 9,440 | 10,425 | 10,701 | 9,436 | 10,383 | 10,680 |
| Stock, September 1 | 400 | 96 | 245 | 397 | 88 | 241 |
| Supply | 9,840 | 10,521 | 10,946 | 9,833 | 10,471 | 10,921 |
| Stock, August 31 | 96 | 245 | 172 | 88 | 241 | 165 |
| Deliveries | 9,744 | 10,276 | 10,774 | 9,745 | 10,230 | 10,756 |
| Export, Great Britain | 2,341 | 3,041 | 3,046 | 2,339 | 3,064 | 3,036 |
| " Continent | 3,266 | 3,374 | 3,395 | 3,284 | 3,350 | 3,403 |
| Total, Europe | 5,607 | 6,415 | 6,441 | 5,623 | 6,414 | 6,439 |
| Export, Canada | 109 | 102 | 120 | 110 | 102 | 122 |
| " Mexico, etc. | 19 | 32 | 32 | 18 | 35 | 33 |
| " Japan, etc. | 307 | 90 | 168 | 309 | 90 | 169 |
| " Total | 435 | 224 | 320 | 437 | 227 | 324 |
| Total Export | 6,042 | 6,639 | 6,761 | 6,060 | 6,641 | 6,763 |
| United States, North | 2,086 | 1,970 | 2,064 | 2,068 | 1,967 | 2,050 |
| " South | 1,600 | 1,667 | 1,943 | 1,597 | 1,621 | 1,938 |
| Burnt or Lost | 16 | .... | 6 | 20 | 1 | 5 |
| Total United States | 3,702 | 3,637 | 4,013 | 3,685 | 3,589 | 3,993 |
| Total as above | 9,744 | 10,276 | 10,774 | 9,745 | 10,230 | 10,756 |
| United States Mills | 3,686 | 3,637 | 4,007 | 3,665 | 3,588 | 3,988 |
| Mill Stocks, September 1 | 426 | 185 | 67 | 412 | 180 | 122 |
| Supply | 4,112 | 3,822 | 4,074 | 4,077 | 3,768 | 4,110 |
| Mill Stocks, August 31 | 185 | 67 | 56 | 180 | 122 | 123 |
| Consumption | 3,927 | 3,755 | 4,018 | 3,897 | 3,646 | 3,987 |
| Cotton Imported | 106 | 92 | 200 | 131 | 110 | 181 |
| Total Consumption | 4,033 | 3,847 | 4,218 | 4,028 | 3,756 | 4,168 |

## COTTON ACREAGE OF THE UNITED STATES

Acreage of Cotton in the producing States. Estimated by the United States Department of Agriculture.

| States. | 1899-1900. | 1900-01. | 1901-02. | 1902-03. |
|---|---|---|---|---|
| Alabama | 2,883,000 | 2,998,000 | 3,362,000 | 3,598,908 |
| Arkansas | 1,726,000 | 1,899,000 | 2,089,000 | 1,911,398 |
| Florida | 149,000 | 169,000 | 186,000 | 266,059 |
| Georgia | 3,288,000 | 3,551,000 | 3,870,000 | 3,957,417 |
| Indian Territory | 299,000 | 344,000 | 413,000 | 673,702 |
| Louisiana | 1,179,000 | 1,285,000 | 1,401,000 | 1,662,567 |
| Mississippi | 2,784,000 | 2,896,000 | 3,124,000 | 3,243,025 |
| Missouri | 77,000 | 53,000 | 59,000 | 60,268 |
| North Carolina | 1,220,000 | 1,342,000 | 1,476,000 | 1,092,750 |
| Oklahoma | 199,000 | 246,000 | 308,000 | 366,913 |
| South Carolina | 2,212,000 | 2,367,000 | 2,533,000 | 2,241,777 |
| Tennessee | 816,000 | 801,000 | 913,000 | 759,367 |
| Texas | 6,642,000 | 7,041,000 | 7,748,000 | 8,006,546 |
| Virginia | 47,000 | 44,000 | 52,000 | 37,633 |
| Total | 23,521,000 | 25,034,734 | 27,534,000 | 27,878,330 |

## WORLD'S COTTON CONSUMPTION

BALES OF 500 POUNDS.

| | 1896-97. | 1897-98. | 1898-99. | 1899-1900 | 1900-01. | 1901-02. |
|---|---|---|---|---|---|---|
| Great Britain | 3,224,000 | 3,432,000 | 3,519,000 | 3,334,000 | 3,269,000 | 3,253,000 |
| Continent | 4,368,000 | 4,628,000 | 4,836,000 | 4,576,000 | 4,576,000 | 4,784,000 |
| United States | 2,738,000 | 3,040,000 | 3,553,000 | 3,830,000 | 3,635,000 | 4,005,000 |
| East Indies | 1,019,000 | 1,058,000 | 1,313,000 | 1,139,000 | 1,060,000 | 1,100,000 |
| Total | 11,349,000 | 12,158,000 | 13,221,000 | 12,879,000 | 12,540,000 | 13,142,000 |

## WORLD'S COTTON SPINDLES

| | 1897. | 1898. | 1899. | 1900. | 1901. | 1902. |
|---|---|---|---|---|---|---|
| Great Britain | 44,900,000 | 44,900,000 | 45,200,000 | 45,600,000 | 46,100,000 | 47,000,000 |
| Continent | 30,350,000 | 31,350,000 | 32,500,000 | 33,000,000 | 33,350,000 | 33,900,000 |
| United States | 17,356,000 | 17,570,000 | 18,278,000 | 19,130,000 | 20,870,000 | 21,559,000 |
| East Indies | 4,066,000 | 4,260,000 | 4,728,000 | 4,945,000 | 5,007,000 | 5,200,000 |
| Total | 96,672,000 | 98,080,000 | 100,706,000 | 102,675,000 | 105,327,000 | 107,659,000 |

### AMERICAN SPINDLES.

| | 1897. | 1898. | 1899. | 1900. | 1901. | 1902. |
|---|---|---|---|---|---|---|
| North | 13,900,000 | 13,900,000 | 13,950,000 | 14,050,000 | 14,500,000 | 15,100,000 |
| South | 3,456,537 | 3,670,290 | 3,987,735 | 4,540,000 | 5,400,000 | 6,459,000 |
| Total | 17,356,000 | 17,570,290 | 17,937,735 | 18,590,000 | 19,900,000 | 21,559,000 |

## FALL RIVER COTTON MILLS

Statement of the capital and dividends of the Fall River cotton mills.

| CORPORATIONS. | Par Value. | Capital. 1902. | 1900. Rate. | 1900. Amount. | 1901. Rate. | 1901. Amount. | 1902. Rate. | 1902. Amount. |
|---|---|---|---|---|---|---|---|---|
| American Linen Co | $100 | $800,000 | 6½ | $52,000 | 5 | $40,000 | *8 | $64,000 |
| Arkwright Mills | 100 | 450,000 | 4½ | 20,250 | 5½ | 24,750 | 5 | 22,500 |
| Barnard Mfg. Co. | 100 | 495,000 | 8 | 39,600 | 5½ | 27,225 | 6 | 29,700 |
| Bourne Mills | 100 | 400,000 | 14 | 56,000 | 6½ | 26,000 | 12½ | 50,000 |
| Border City Mfg. Co | 100 | 1,000,000 | 8 | 80,000 | 6½ | 65,000 | 6 | 60,000 |
| Barnaby Mfg. Co. | 100 | ¶500,000 | 3 | 12,000 | 4½ | 18,000 | 4½ | 19,000 |
| Chace Mills | 100 | 750,000 | 6 | 45,000 | 6 | 45,000 | 6 | 45,000 |
| Cornell Mills | 100 | 400,000 | 11 | 52,000 | 6½ | 26,000 | 7 | 28,000 |
| Conanicut Mills | 100 | 120,000 | 8 | 9,600 | 8 | 9,600 | 8 | 9,600 |
| Davol Mills | 100 | 400,000 | 8 | 32,000 | 6½ | 26,000 | 6 | 24,000 |
| F. R. Manufactory | 100 | 240,000 | .. | ...... | .. | ...... | .. | ...... |
| Flint Mills | 100 | 580,000 | 8 | 46,400 | 7 | 40,600 | 6 | 34,800 |
| Granite Mills | 100 | 1,000,000 | 8 | 80,000 | 8 | 80,000 | 8 | 80,000 |
| Hargraves Mills | 100 | 800,000 | 6 | 48,000 | 6 | 48,000 | 6 | 48,000 |
| King Philip Mills | 100 | 1,000,000 | 6 | 60,000 | 6 | 60,000 | †16 | 160,000 |
| Laurel Lake Mills | 100 | 300,000 | 6 | 18,000 | 4½ | 13,500 | 6 | 18,000 |
| Merchants' Mfg. Co. | 100 | 800,000 | 6 | 48,000 | 2½ | 20,000 | 4 | 32,000 |
| Mechanics' Mills | 100 | 750,000 | 6 | 45,000 | 5 | 37,500 | 4½ | 33,750 |
| Narragansett Mills | 100 | 400,000 | 8 | 32,000 | 5½ | 22,000 | 6 | 24,000 |
| Osborn Mills | 100 | 750,000 | 8½ | 54,000 | 3½ | 26,250 | 4 | 30,000 |
| Parker Mills | 100 | 800,000 | 6¼ | 50,000 | 8 | 64,000 | 8 | 64,000 |
| Pocasset Mfg. Co. | 100 | 600,000 | 6 | 36,000 | 6 | 36,000 | 6 | 36,000 |
| R. Borden Mfg. Co. | 100 | 800,000 | 9 | 72,000 | 6½ | 52,000 | 6 | 48,000 |
| Robeson Mills | 100 | 78,000 | 6 | 4,680 | 1½ | 1,170 | .. | ...... |
| Sagamore Mfg. Co. | 100 | 900,000 | 9 | 81,000 | 5 | 45,000 | ‡7½ | 67,500 |
| Seaconnet Mills | 100 | 600,000 | 7 | 42,000 | 5 | 30,000 | 5 | 30,000 |
| Shove Mills | 100 | 550,000 | 4½ | 24,750 | 1½ | 8,250 | 4 | 22,000 |
| Slade Mills | 100 | 300,000 | .. | ...... | .. | ...... | .. | ...... |
| Stafford Mills | 100 | 1,000,000 | 8 | 80,000 | 3 | 30,000 | 4 | 40,000 |
| Stevens Mfg. Co. | 100 | 700,000 | 8 | 28,000 | 8 | 28,000 | 8 | 56,000 |
| Tecumseh Mills | 100 | 500,000 | 7½ | 37,500 | 5 | 25,000 | 6 | 30,000 |
| Troy C. & W. Mfy. | 500 | 300,000 | 27 | 81,000 | 17 | 51,000 | §20 | 60,000 |
| UnionCotton MfgCo | 100 | 1,200,000 | 10 | 93,000 | 6½ | 78,000 | 6 | 72,000 |
| Wampanoag Mills | 100 | 750,000 | 7 | 52,000 | 2½ | 18,750 | 4 | 30,000 |
| Weetamoe Mills | 100 | 550,000 | 6 | 33,000 | 3½ | 19,250 | 4 | 22,000 |
| Total |  | $21,463,000 | 7.25 | $1,551,000 | 5.37 | $1,144,725 | 6.475 | $1,389,850 |

* Two per cent. extra paid from sale of real estate. † 10 per cent. extra paid from surplus. ‡ 3 per cent. extra paid from surplus. § 4 per cent. extra paid from sale of real estate. ¶ Capital increased September 15, 1902, $400,000 to $500,000. An average of 6.475 per cent. plus on above capital for 1902.

## FRACTIONAL DIFFERENCES IN COTTON

The following represents the value of fluctuations in price upon 100 bales of cotton:

| | | | |
|---|---|---|---|
| 1-100c on 100 bales — | $5.00 | 50-100c on 100 bales — | $250.00 |
| 2-100c " " — | 10.00 | 1c " " — | 500.00 |
| 5-100c " " — | 25.00 | 2c " " — | 1,000.00 |
| 25-100c " " — | 125.00 | | |

# Petroleum

## Prices of Petroleum, Crude and Refined, in New York for a Series of Years, with Production, Well Movement, and Other Information

### *PRODUCTION, DELIVERIES AND STOCKS OF BUCKEYE (OHIO) OIL*

IN BARRELS.

| Month. | 1899. Production. Daily Av'ge. | 1899. Deliveries. Daily Av'ge. | 1899. Stocks. | 1900. Production. Daily Av'ge. | 1900. Deliveries. Daily Av'ge. | 1900. Stocks. |
|---|---|---|---|---|---|---|
| January | 46,141 | 55,327 | 14,896,134 | 46,452 | 45,996 | 10,646,120 |
| February | 42,480 | 57,314 | 14,480,779 | 44,687 | 47,747 | 10,668,707 |
| March | 48,319 | 59,797 | 14,126,045 | 46,881 | 48,145 | 10,767,147 |
| April | 46,633 | 59,927 | 13,724,910 | 49,481 | 44,417 | 11,127,633 |
| May | 48,372 | 60,718 | 13,339,157 | 52,173 | 40,281 | 11,659,730 |
| June | 49,402 | 61,515 | 12,974,124 | 53,711 | 37,188 | 12,336,290 |
| July | 47,219 | 62,046 | 12,513,792 | 51,573 | 31,971 | 13,070,577 |
| August | 50,578 | 59,322 | 12,250,598 | 53,330 | 34,424 | 13,843,013 |
| September | 47,512 | 62,351 | 11,705,431 | 50,290 | 44,169 | 14,282,144 |
| October | 47,828 | 64,992 | 11,123,366 | 53,325 | 49,123 | 14,678,274 |
| November | 47,684 | 57,679 | 10,748,516 | 48,477 | 47,355 | 14,900,403 |
| December | 44,055 | 52,006 | 10,545,927 | 48,522 | 49,654 | 14,988,928 |
| Total | 17,183,714 | 21,630,115 | ......... | 18,229,970 | 15,758,184 | ......... |
| Average | 47,185 | 59,416 | ......... | 49,908 | 43,372 | ......... |

| Month. | 1901. Production. Daily Av'ge. | 1901. Deliveries. Daily Av'ge. | 1901. Stocks. | 1902. Production. Daily Av'ge. | 1902. Deliveries. Daily Av'ge. | 1902. Stocks. |
|---|---|---|---|---|---|---|
| January | 49,356 | 47,017 | 15,249,598 | 53,465 | 50,339 | 18,010,335 |
| February | 46,445 | 47,668 | 15,360,256 | 49,480 | 61,315 | 17,824,823 |
| March | 48,012 | 47,387 | 15,548,862 | 52,282 | 60,391 | 17,766,927 |
| April | 50,683 | 46,788 | 15,910,636 | 53,843 | 42,984 | 18,205,702 |
| May | 52,046 | 47,953 | 16,248,382 | 55,144 | 53,269 | 18,439,723 |
| June | 52,147 | 51,783 | 16,403,991 | 55,324 | 64,351 | 18,341,671 |
| July | 51,916 | 45,224 | 16,792,433 | 57,814 | 64,354 | 18,315,974 |
| August | 52,130 | 53,439 | 16,885,807 | 57,310 | 67,950 | 18,153,129 |
| September | 52,907 | 50,272 | 17,136,195 | 57,500 | 66,150 | 18,025,986 |
| October | 54,322 | 53,058 | 17,362,717 | 57,914 | 66,130 | 17,833,537 |
| November | 52,439 | 44,696 | 17,570,319 | 53,970 | 67,912 | 17,565,114 |
| December | 47,853 | 48,470 | 17,760,306 | 52,516 | 61,170 | 17,306,426 |
| Total | 18,570,768 | 17,760,515 | ........ | 19,984,366 | 22,090,471 | ......... |
| Average | 50,855 | 48,548 | ........ | 54,713 | 60,526 | ......... |

## PETROLEUM WELL MOVEMENT

| | Jan. | Feb. | Mar. | April. | May. | June. | July. | Aug. | Sept. | Oct. | Nov. | Dec. | Total. |
|---|---|---|---|---|---|---|---|---|---|---|---|---|---|
| **1895**—No. wells completed | 296 | 213 | 355 | 462 | 658 | 811 | 822 | 814 | 775 | 727 | 637 | 568 | 7,138 |
| No. wells drilling | 417 | 443 | 469 | 625 | 829 | 941 | 895 | 866 | 819 | 796 | 760 | 717 | 8,[illegible]87 |
| No. rigs up and building | 270 | 352 | 377 | 461 | 597 | 564 | 571 | 491 | 487 | 461 | 474 | 476 | 5,581 |
| Total, 1895 | 983 | 1,008 | 1,201 | 1,558 | 2,084 | 2,316 | 2,288 | 2,171 | 2,081 | 1,984 | 1,871 | 1,761 | 21,306 |
| **1896**—No. wells completed | 580 | 555 | 542 | 613 | 728 | 794 | 738 | 639 | 644 | 626 | 670 | 682 | 7,811 |
| No. wells drilling | 699 | 621 | 669 | 756 | 728 | 681 | 640 | 624 | 558 | 589 | 657 | 595 | 7,817 |
| No. rigs up and building | 445 | 451 | 448 | 459 | 438 | 437 | 381 | 360 | 377 | 387 | 390 | 365 | 4,938 |
| Total, 1896 | 1,724 | 1,627 | 1,659 | 1,828 | 1,894 | 1,912 | 1,759 | 1,623 | 1,579 | 1,602 | 1,717 | 1,642 | 20,566 |
| **1897**—No. wells completed | 598 | 440 | 415 | 486 | 549 | 605 | 639 | 601 | 490 | 447 | 426 | 384 | 6,080 |
| No. wells drilling | 514 | 433 | 463 | 474 | 521 | 574 | 548 | 463 | 464 | 415 | 401 | 384 | 5,654 |
| No. rigs up and building | 319 | 323 | 332 | 364 | 322 | 311 | 289 | 272 | 244 | 301 | 271 | 217 | 3,565 |
| Total, 1897 | 1,431 | 1,196 | 1,210 | 1,324 | 1,392 | 1,490 | 1,476 | 1,336 | 1,198 | 1,163 | 1,098 | 985 | 15,299 |
| **1898**—No. wells completed | 326 | 255 | 275 | 329 | 329 | 364 | 391 | 417 | 475 | 533 | 532 | 570 | 4,796 |
| No. wells drilling | 311 | 289 | 325 | 333 | 386 | 404 | 407 | 478 | 511 | 535 | 620 | 589 | 5,188 |
| No. rigs up and building | 191 | 210 | 217 | 195 | 214 | 226 | 263 | 255 | 304 | 297 | 354 | 393 | 3,119 |
| Total, 1898 | 828 | 754 | 817 | 857 | 929 | 994 | 1,061 | 1,150 | 1,290 | 1,365 | 1,506 | 1,552 | 13,103 |
| **1899**—No. wells completed | 583 | 454 | 626 | 616 | 751 | 809 | 751 | 765 | 803 | 886 | 895 | 813 | 8,752 |
| No. wells drilling | 563 | 600 | 559 | 590 | 576 | 643 | 647 | 696 | 693 | 716 | 751 | 665 | 7,699 |
| No. rigs up and building | 385 | 415 | 370 | 357 | 393 | 337 | 353 | 392 | 432 | 504 | 475 | 343 | 4,756 |
| Total, 1899 | 1,531 | 1,469 | 1,555 | 1,563 | 1,720 | 1,789 | 1,751 | 1,853 | 1,928 | 2,106 | 2,121 | 1,821 | 21,207 |
| **1900**—No. wells completed | 633 | 591 | 599 | 797 | 859 | 877 | 814 | 807 | 796 | 766 | 672 | 634 | 8,843 |
| No. wells drilling | 653 | 668 | 673 | 702 | 771 | 754 | 704 | 735 | 759 | 706 | 757 | 651 | 8,483 |
| No. rigs up and building | 459 | 404 | 428 | 482 | 453 | 411 | 390 | 396 | 406 | 464 | 494 | 381 | 5,168 |
| Total, 1900 | 1,745 | 1,663 | 1,700 | 1,981 | 2,083 | 2,042 | 1,908 | 1,938 | 1,961 | 1,936 | 1,873 | 1,666 | 22,496 |
| **1901**—No. wells completed | 589 | 506 | 481 | 589 | 673 | 692 | 655 | 727 | 729 | 712 | 766 | 592 | 7,711 |
| No. wells drilling | 616 | 534 | 553 | 587 | 550 | 601 | 626 | 628 | 620 | 653 | 671 | 635 | 7,274 |
| No. rigs up and building | 327 | 357 | 378 | 370 | 386 | 351 | 308 | 341 | 339 | 378 | 378 | 344 | 4,257 |
| Total, 1901 | 1,532 | 1,397 | 1,412 | 1,546 | 1,609 | 1,644 | 1,589 | 1,696 | 1,688 | 1,743 | 1,815 | 1,571 | 19,242 |
| **1902**—No. wells completed | 582 | 455 | 514 | 579 | 648 | 745 | 685 | 725 | 730 | 713 | 729 | 617 | 7,722 |
| No. wells drilling | 622 | 570 | 572 | 560 | 611 | 590 | 592 | 621 | 624 | 617 | 634 | 582 | 7,195 |
| No. rigs up and building | 337 | 335 | 323 | 312 | 307 | 323 | 304 | 331 | 368 | 352 | 377 | 343 | 4,012 |
| Total, 1902 | 1,541 | 1,360 | 1,409 | 1,451 | 1,566 | 1,658 | 1,581 | 1,677 | 1,722 | 1,682 | 1,740 | 1,542 | 18,929 |

## YEARLY PRODUCTION OF PETROLEUM

| Year. | Grand Total, Barrels. | Daily Average, Barrels. | Year. | Grand Total, Barrels. | Daily Average. Barrels. |
|---|---|---|---|---|---|
| 1867 | 3,347,000 | 9,169 | 1885 | 21,225,203 | 58,145 |
| 1868 | 3,583,176 | 9,816 | 1886 | 26,043,645 | 71,283 |
| 1869 | 4,210,720 | 11,536 | 1887 | 21,819,027 | 59,800 |
| 1870 | 5,673,195 | 15,543 | 1888 | 16,259,977 | 44,429 |
| 1871 | 5,715,900 | 15,660 | 1889 | 21,519,636 | 58,878 |
| 1872 | 6,531,675 | 17,895 | 1880 | 29,130,751 | 79,784 |
| 1873 | 7,878,629 | 21,585 | 1891 | 34,128,951 | 93,488 |
| 1874 | 10,950,730 | 30,005 | 1892 | 32,761,466 | 89,512 |
| 1875 | 8,787,506 | 24,072 | 1893 | 30,936,879 | 84,753 |
| 1876 | 9,175,906 | 25,139 | 1894 | 30,052,989 | 82,337 |
| 1877 | 13,940,171 | 38,192 | 1895 | 30,406,398 | 83,242 |
| 1878 | 15,164,462 | 41,546 | 1896 | 33,455,864 | 91,150 |
| 1879 | 19,741,661 | 54,086 | 1897 | 34,724,682 | 95,152 |
| 1880 | 26,562,000 | 72,772 | 1898 | 31,100,630 | 85,223 |
| 1881 | 28,447,115 | 77,934 | 1899 | 32,207,457 | 88,200 |
| 1882 | 31,059,165 | 85,093 | 1900 | 35,489,582 | 97,179 |
| 1883 | 24,385,968 | 66,809 | 1901 | 32,946,115 | 90,238 |
| 1884 | 23,691,264 | 64,880 | 1902 | 31,360,448 | 85,870 |

## DAILY AVERAGE PRODUCTION OF PETROLEUM

(In Barrels of 42 Gallons. Pipe Line Runs.)

| Month. | 1893. | 1894. | 1895. | 1896. | 1897. | 1898. | 1899. | 1900. | 1901. | 1902. |
|---|---|---|---|---|---|---|---|---|---|---|
| January | 76,952 | 82,149 | 77,754 | 86,329 | 86,151 | 88,571 | 78,067 | 91,511 | 94,676 | 82,534 |
| February | 83,298 | 81,520 | 72,567 | 82,285 | 94,206 | 87,230 | 79,389 | 89,787 | 89,637 | 78,570 |
| March | 87,565 | 83,891 | 79,182 | 86,331 | 93,909 | 90,775 | 85,469 | 95,022 | 92,567 | 82,605 |
| April | 81,901 | 81,108 | 85,469 | 95,986 | 92,985 | 88,418 | 87,274 | 96,033 | 93,064 | 87,684 |
| May | 84,473 | 83,863 | 81,582 | 91,600 | 92,004 | 86,488 | 89,219 | 99,180 | 94,237 | 87,517 |
| June | 88,135 | 85,955 | 81,571 | 96,057 | 97,995 | 85,559 | 91,363 | 100,009 | 90,426 | 84,315 |
| July | 85,023 | 83,175 | 85,280 | 93,851 | 96,537 | 80,248 | 89,564 | 97,838 | 94,059 | 89,602 |
| August | 88,786 | 82,408 | 87,347 | 92,610 | 98,796 | 84,608 | 92,648 | 100,810 | 92,330 | 85,940 |
| September | 88,251 | 80,401 | 88,100 | 92,407 | 100,067 | 84,168 | 92,164 | 97,348 | 86,189 | 90,916 |
| October | 85,295 | 83,085 | 86,204 | 92,211 | 97,518 | 80,253 | 91,400 | 103,128 | 88,881 | 90,050 |
| November | 83,088 | 80,322 | 87,119 | 90,056 | 98,295 | 82,838 | 93,546 | 98,238 | 83,997 | 84,409 |
| December | 84,266 | 80,006 | 86,736 | 94,079 | 93,364 | 83,5 2 | 88,280 | 97,241 | 82,797 | 86,106 |
| Totals | 30,936,879 | 30,052,989 | 30,406,398 | 33,455,864 | 34,724,682 | 31,100,630 | 32,207,457 | 35,489,582 | 32,946,115 | 31,360,448 |
| Daily Averages | 84,753 | 82,337 | 83,242 | 91,150 | 95,152 | 85,223 | 88,200 | 97,179 | 90,238 | 85,870 |

## DAILY AVERAGE SHIPMENTS OF PETROLEUM

(Pipe Line Deliveries. Barrels of 42 Gallons.)

| Month. | 1893. | 1894. | 1895. | 1896. | 1897. | 1898. | 1899. | 1900. | 1901. | 1902. |
|---|---|---|---|---|---|---|---|---|---|---|
| January | 95,220 | 101,063 | 101,136 | 81,696 | 81,718 | 93,671 | 79,855 | 93,160 | 101,152 | 97,198 |
| February | 92,240 | 94,666 | 100,043 | 77,531 | 82,335 | 76,148 | 67,852 | 98,109 | 92,332 | 81,531 |
| March | 91,627 | 93,876 | 84,017 | 78,580 | 89,456 | 84,681 | 85,014 | 90,247 | 93,082 | 84,304 |
| April | 88,843 | 94,840 | 92,641 | 74,103 | 81,791 | 80,713 | 79,249 | 94,816 | 98,473 | 114,910 |
| May | 97,861 | 92,354 | 91,784 | 78,014 | 82,151 | 77,188 | 83,179 | 90,105 | 97,856 | 110,002 |
| June | 102,422 | 97,097 | 93,848 | 74,959 | 85,198 | 81,160 | 84,630 | 96,016 | 94,793 | 90,283 |
| July | 107,042 | 93,735 | 84,996 | 81,941 | 87,332 | 82,690 | 76,055 | 88,909 | 106,048 | 88,409 |
| August | 104,752 | 105,042 | 78,164 | 77,548 | 100,007 | 86,954 | 88,654 | 109,148 | 104,852 | 93,911 |
| September | 99,876 | 98,774 | 77,680 | 84,664 | 98,374 | 86,175 | 90,002 | 101,048 | 102,527 | 93,070 |
| October | 106,731 | 105,232 | 82,845 | 83,694 | 117,050 | 91,596 | 88,360 | 96,845 | 104,665 | 103,829 |
| November | 102,959 | 106,597 | 88,185 | 83,150 | 110,420 | 79,935 | 85,812 | 104,825 | 103,877 | 96,623 |
| December | 101,328 | 105,682 | 77,453 | 83,988 | 88,807 | 75,938 | 83,666 | 99,624 | 97,645 | 100,574 |
| Totals | 36,247,273 | 36,176,523 | 31,984,240 | 29,284,116 | 33,621,058 | 30,345,975 | 30,219,073 | 35,312,440 | 36,439,389 | 35,154,460 |
| Daily averages | 99,242 | 99,113 | 87,773 | 79,989 | 92,053 | 83,070 | 82,694 | 96,904 | 99,775 | 96,220 |

## STOCKS OF PENNSYLVANIA CRUDE OIL, MONTHLY

| Month. | 1895. | 1896. | 1897. | 1898. | 1899. | 1900. | 1901. | 1902. |
|---|---|---|---|---|---|---|---|---|
| January | 5,640,000 | 5,329,566 | 9,709,991 | 10,636,318 | 11,485,578 | 13,104,059 | 12,956,099 | 8,965,706 |
| February | 4,908,000 | 5,576,529 | 10,109,577 | 10,947,778 | 11,793,697 | 12,875,240 | 12,880,603 | 8,880,897 |
| March | 4,780,000 | 5,841,722 | 10,221,000 | 11,142,281 | 11,806,881 | 13,026,480 | 12,865,464 | 8,828,230 |
| April | 4,545,000 | 6,532,233 | 10,556,848 | 11,381,111 | 12,047,444 | 13,063,258 | 12,705,345 | 7,996,776 |
| May | 4,319,000 | 6,983,422 | 10,863,052 | 11,663,837 | 12,234,674 | 13,335,536 | 12,579,958 | 7,299,734 |
| June | 4,109,000 | 7,601,666 | 11,248,710 | 11,798,877 | 12,430,289 | 13,450,582 | 12,466,054 | 7,108,844 |
| July | 4,166,000 | 7,992,636 | 11,582,205 | 11,723,581 | 12,785,273 | 13,729,698 | 12,099,866 | 7,156,040 |
| August | 4,287,000 | 8,477,346 | 11,544,353 | 11,652,126 | 12,868,372 | 13,541,571 | 11,706,816 | 6,896,507 |
| September | 4,635,000 | 8,726,861 | 11,621,548 | 11,592,495 | 12,862,444 | 13,213,778 | 11,147,875 | 6,815,799 |
| October | 4,763,000 | 8,986,207 | 11,013,997 | 11,240,712 | 12,911,389 | 13,358,401 | 10,608,822 | 6,416,556 |
| November | 4,756,000 | 9,215,472 | 10,648,100 | 11,328,284 | 13,043,796 | 13,110,709 | 9,978,928 | 6,087,071 |
| December | 5,161,000 | 9,550,583 | 10,789,652 | 11,512,847 | 13,163,819 | 13,174,717 | 9,420,421 | 5,699,127 |

## PRICES OF REFINED OIL

PER GALLON.

| Month. | 1895. | | 1896. | | 1897. | | 1898. | | 1899. | | 1900. | | 1901. | | 1902. | |
|---|---|---|---|---|---|---|---|---|---|---|---|---|---|---|---|---|
| | High. | Low. | High. | Low. | High. | Low. | High. | Low. | High. | Low. | High. | Low. | High. | Low. | High. | Low. |
| January.... | 5.90 | 5.80 | 8.00 | 7.50 | 6.20 | 6.00 | 5.40 | 5.40 | 7.40 | 7.40 | 9.90 | 9.90 | 7.70 | 7.25 | 7.20 | 7.20 |
| February... | 6.10 | 5.90 | 7.50 | 7.10 | 6.30 | 6.00 | 5.60 | 5.40 | 7.40 | 7.40 | 9.90 | 9.90 | 9.95 | 7.70 | 7.20 | 7.20 |
| March..... | 7.10 | 6.10 | 7.50 | 7.10 | 6.50 | 6.30 | 6.20 | 5.75 | 7.40 | 7.35 | 9.90 | 9.90 | 7.95 | 7.95 | 7.20 | 7.20 |
| April...... | 11.50 | 7.10 | 7.35 | 6.80 | 6.50 | 6.05 | 5.75 | 5.70 | 7.25 | 6.95 | 9.90 | 9.20 | 7.95 | 7.50 | 7.40 | 7.20 |
| May....... | 9.15 | 7.75 | 7.95 | 6.55 | 6.35 | 6.05 | 6.15 | 5.60 | 7.20 | 6.95 | 9.20 | 8.60 | 7.40 | 7.25 | 7.40 | 7.40 |
| June....... | 8.10 | 7.65 | 7.00 | 6.55 | 6.20 | 6.05 | 6.25 | 6.15 | 7.35 | 7.20 | 8.85 | 7.85 | 7.25 | 7.25 | 7.40 | 7.40 |
| July....... | 7.95 | 7.10 | 6.90 | 6.50 | 6.05 | 5.75 | 6.40 | 6.10 | 7.70 | 7.35 | 7.85 | 7.85 | 7.50 | 6.90 | 7.40 | 7.40 |
| August.... | 7.10 | 7.20 | 6.70 | 6.65 | 5.75 | 5.75 | 6.50 | 6.40 | 7.80 | 7.70 | 8.05 | 7.85 | 7.50 | 7.50 | 7.40 | 7.40 |
| September. | 7.10 | 7.10 | 6.90 | 6.70 | 5.80 | 5.70 | 6.65 | 6.50 | 8.80 | 7.80 | 8.05 | 8.05 | 7.50 | 7.50 | 7.40 | 7.40 |
| October.... | 8.25 | 7.10 | 7.00 | 6.90 | 5.80 | 5.40 | 7.40 | 6.65 | 9.10 | 8.95 | 7.45 | 7.25 | 7.50 | 7.50 | 7.40 | 7.40 |
| November. | 8.00 | 7.50 | 7.15 | 6.60 | 5.40 | 5.40 | 7.40 | 7.40 | 9.65 | 9.10 | 7.25 | 7.25 | 7.50 | 7.50 | 7.40 | 7.40 |
| December. | .... | .... | 6.60 | 6.20 | 5.40 | 5.40 | 7.40 | 7.30 | 9.65 | 9.65 | 7.25 | 7.25 | 7.45 | 7.20 | 7.40 | 7.40 |
| Average. | 7.40 | .... | 7.10 | ..... | 5.23 | .... | 6.30 | .... | 7.93 | .... | 8.50 | .... | 7.48 | .... | 7.34 | .... |

# Money

## Banking and General Financial and Commercial Statistics

### *CALL LOANS*

Highest and lowest rates for call loans at the New York Stock Exchange.

| * Week Ending | 1900. | | 1901. | | 1902. | |
|---|---|---|---|---|---|---|
| | Highest. | Lowest. | Highest. | Lowest. | Highest. | Lowest. |
| January 3 | 12 | 3 | 6 | 3½ | 15 | 5 |
| January 10 | 6 | 2 | 5 | 2½ | 7 | 4 |
| January 17 | 4½ | 2 | 5 | 2 | 5½ | 3 |
| January 24 | 4 | 2 | 2½ | 1¾ | 4 | 2 |
| January 31 | 3 | 2 | 2 | 1½ | 3 | 2 |
| February 7 | 2½ | 2 | 2½ | 1¾ | 3 | 2¼ |
| February 14 | 2½ | 2½ | 2½ | 1½ | 3 | 2 |
| February 21 | 2½ | 1½ | 2½ | 1¼ | 2½ | 2 |
| February 28 | 2½ | 2 | 2½ | 1½ | 2½ | 2 |
| March 7 | 4 | 2 | 3 | 2 | 3 | 2¼ |
| March 14 | 7 | 3 | 2½ | 2 | 4½ | 3 |
| March 21 | 6 | 3 | 3 | 2 | 5 | 3½ |
| March 28 | 4½ | 2 | 3 | 2¼ | 5 | 3 |
| April 4 | 5 | 3 | 6 | 2 | 4½ | 2½ |
| April 11 | 4 | 2½ | 7 | 3½ | 7 | 3 |
| April 18 | 4 | 2 | 6 | 2½ | 6 | 3¼ |
| April 25 | 2½ | 2 | 5 | 2½ | 6 | 3½ |
| May 2 | 3 | 1½ | 8 | 3½ | 15 | 3¼ |
| May 9 | 2½ | 2 | 75 | 3 | 25 | 5 |
| May 16 | 2¼ | 1½ | 8 | 2 | 10 | 4 |
| May 23 | 2¼ | 1½ | 7 | 3 | 5½ | 2 |
| May 30 | 2 | 1½ | 4 | 2 | 3½ | 2½ |
| June 6 | 2 | 1½ | 4 | 2½ | 5 | 2½ |
| June 13 | 2 | 1½ | 4½ | 2½ | 3½ | 2½ |
| June 20 | 1¾ | 1 | 5 | 3 | 3 | 2½ |
| June 27 | 2 | 1 | 15 | 3½ | 4 | 2½ |
| July 4 | 2 | 1½ | 25 | 4 | 7 | 3 |
| July 11 | 1¾ | 1½ | 8 | 2 | 6 | 3 |
| July 18 | 1½ | 1 | 5 | 1 | 4 | 2 |
| July 25 | 1½ | 1¼ | 3 | 2 | 3 | 2½ |
| August 1 | 1½ | 1¼ | 4 | 2 | 3 | 2½ |
| August 8 | 1½ | 1 | 2½ | 2 | 3 | 2½ |
| August 15 | 2 | 1 | 3 | 2 | 6 | 3 |
| August 22 | 1½ | 1¼ | 3 | 2 | 5 | 3 |
| August 29 | 1½ | 1¼ | 3 | 2 | 5½ | 3 |
| September 5 | 1½ | 1¼ | 4½ | 3 | 8 | 3½ |
| September 12 | 2 | 1 | 10 | 2 | 20 | 5 |
| September 19 | 2 | 1¼ | 6 | 1½ | 20 | 4 |
| September 26 | 2 | 1½ | 4½ | 2½ | 25 | 2 |
| October 3 | 3 | 2 | 4½ | 2½ | 35 | 3 |
| October 10 | 4 | 1¾ | 4 | 3 | 16 | 3 |
| October 17 | 4 | 2½ | 4 | 3 | 18 | 5 |
| October 24 | 6 | 2 | 4 | 3 | 6½ | 2½ |
| October 31 | 20 | 3 | 5 | 3½ | 7 | 3½ |
| November 7 | 25 | 1 | 4 | 3½ | 6 | 4 |
| November 14 | 6 | 2 | 5 | 3 | 7 | 4 |
| November 21 | 5 | 2 | 5 | 3 | 6 | 2 |
| November 28 | 4½ | 3 | 4½ | 3½ | 6 | 4 |
| December 5 | 6 | 2 | 6 | 3½ | 7½ | 3½ |
| December 12 | 6 | 3 | 12 | 3 | 12 | 3 |
| December 19 | 6½ | 3½ | 10 | 2½ | 10 | 4 |
| December 26 | 6 | 3 | 9 | 2½ | 13 | 5½ |

* The dates are for 1902. The other columns are for corresponding weeks.

## IMPORTS AND EXPORTS OF GOLD BULLION, COIN AND ORE FROM THE UNITED STATES

| Months. | Imports. | | | Exports. | | | | | Excess of | |
|---|---|---|---|---|---|---|---|---|---|---|
| | | | | Domestic. | | Foreign. | | | | |
| | Ore. | Bullion and Coin. | Total. | Ore. | Bullion and Coin. | Ore. | Bullion and Coin. | Total. | Imports. | Exports. |
| 1899. | $ | $ | $ | $ | $ | $ | $ | $ | $ | $ |
| July | 537,934 | 2,237,535 | 2,895,469 | 1,600 | 2,176,512 | ...... | 428,345 | 2,606,457 | 289,012 | ........ |
| August | 2,660,141 | 2,731,270 | 5,391,411 | 2,230 | 2,049,936 | 40,000 | 6,896 | 2,099,062 | 3,292,349 | ........ |
| September | 524,783 | 2,069,111 | 2,593,894 | ...... | 569,432 | ...... | 49,563 | 618,995 | 1,973,899 | ........ |
| October | 2,705,463 | 5,836,791 | 8,542,254 | 3,250 | 373,833 | ...... | 2,669 | 379,752 | 8,162,502 | ........ |
| November | 1,767,083 | 1,156,960 | 2,994,043 | 3,400 | 237,925 | ...... | 22,985 | 264,310 | 2,639,733 | ........ |
| December | 725,005 | 4,895,241 | 5,620,246 | 6,410 | 11,850,283 | ...... | 818 | 11,857,511 | ........ | 6,237,265 |
| 1900. | | | | | | | | | | |
| January | 523,184 | 1,469,508 | 1,992,692 | 2,768 | 5,398,047 | ...... | 290,475 | 5,691,290 | ........ | 3,698,598 |
| February | 388,176 | 1,522,940 | 1,911,116 | 2,152 | 981,428 | ...... | 420,078 | 1,403,658 | 507,458 | ........ |
| March | 327,321 | 1,593,715 | 1,921,036 | 18,770 | 852,446 | ...... | 210,064 | 1,081,280 | 839,756 | ........ |
| April | 394,317 | 2,994,496 | 3,388,813 | 511 | 1,057,068 | ...... | 4,001 | 1,961,580 | 1,427,233 | ........ |
| May | 578,369 | 3,105,265 | 3,683,634 | 4,200 | 12,118,024 | ...... | 87,372 | 12,209,596 | ........ | 8,525,962 |
| June | 2,479,710 | 1,248,866 | 3,728,576 | 3,300 | 8,080,368 | ...... | 9,600 | 8,093,268 | ........ | 4,364,692 |
| Total, twelve months | 13,611,486 | 30,961,698 | 44,573,184 | 48,591 | 46,645,302 | 40,000 | 1,532,866 | 48,266,759 | ........ | 3,693,575 |
| July | 5,760,959 | 5,502,373 | 11,263,332 | 1,952 | 3,262,058 | ...... | 8,729 | 3,272,739 | 7,990,593 | ........ |
| August | 1,798,926 | 2,439,432 | 4,238,358 | 5,112 | 18,074,917 | ...... | 4,909 | 18,084,938 | ........ | 13,846,580 |
| September | 4,371,114 | 3,490,439 | 7,861,553 | 3,840 | 789,971 | ...... | 12,761 | 806,572 | 7,054,981 | ........ |
| October | 1,467,115 | 9,264,260 | 10,731,375 | 6,746 | 253,596 | ...... | 181,620 | 441,962 | 10,289,413 | ........ |
| November | 2,511,906 | 10,130,082 | 12,641,988 | 11,455 | 632,731 | ...... | 33,021 | 677,207 | 11,964,781 | ........ |
| December | 444,731 | 2,941,880 | 3,386,611 | 9,120 | 316,943 | ...... | 84,470 | 410,533 | 2,976,078 | ........ |

| | | | | | | | | | | |
|---|---|---|---|---|---|---|---|---|---|---|
| 1901. | | | | | | | | | | |
| January | 728,409 | 3,537,217 | 4,265,626 | 20,800 | 8,190,682 | ...... | 9,677 | 8,221,159 | ........ | 3,955,533 |
| February | 432,591 | 1,426,683 | 1,859,274 | 13,885 | 305,827 | ...... | 97,100 | 416,812 | 1,442,462 | ........ |
| March | 815,011 | 1,705,444 | 2,520,455 | 14,000 | 371,069 | ...... | 105,200 | 490,269 | 2,030,186 | ........ |
| April | 811,862 | 1,437,176 | 2,249,038 | 34,598 | 4,876,401 | ...... | 5,966 | 4,916,965 | ........ | 2,667,927 |
| May | 902,498 | 870,336 | 1,772,834 | 25,913 | 10,071,858 | ...... | 3,406 | 10,101,177 | ........ | 8,328,343 |
| June | 560,331 | 2,700,412 | 3,260,743 | 63,270 | 5,278,565 | ...... | 3,009 | 5,344,844 | ........ | 2,084,101 |
| Total, twelve months | 20,605,453 | 45,445,734 | 66,051,187 | 210,691 | 52,424,618 | ...... | 549,868 | 53,185,177 | 12,866,010 | ........ |
| July | 2,847,569 | 1,228,544 | 4,076,113 | 40,820 | 2,741,742 | 75,049 | 17,509 | 2,875,120 | 1,200,993 | ........ |
| August | 971,465 | 2,519,063 | 3,490,528 | 37,037 | 105,221 | 7,600 | 1,003 | 150,861 | 3,339,667 | ........ |
| September | 5,241,566 | 6,663,865 | 11,905,431 | 30,750 | 120,487 | 11,120 | 1,005 | 163,362 | 11,742,069 | ........ |
| October | 4,272,633 | 4,866,005 | 9,138,638 | 13,606 | 3,848,747 | 204,304 | 90 | 4,066,747 | 5,071,891 | ........ |
| November | 2,808,888 | 4,622,790 | 7,431,678 | 23,171 | 15,669,841 | 386,373 | 213,115 | 16,292,500 | ........ | 8,860,822 |
| December | 1,131,428 | 1,660,094 | 2,791,522 | 10,293 | 4,623,840 | ...... | 109,990 | 4,744,123 | ........ | 1,952,601 |
| 1902. | | | | | | | | | | |
| January | 653,481 | 752,306 | 1,405,787 | 3,720 | 1,683,455 | 250 | 286,250 | 1,973,675 | ........ | 567,888 |
| February | 758,284 | 938,083 | 1,696,967 | 5,900 | 8,602,046 | 48,193 | 9,341 | 8,665,480 | ........ | 6,968,513 |
| March | 1,068,842 | 1,567,471 | 2,636,313 | 3,610 | 4,033,515 | 48,193 | 347,628 | 4,432,946 | ........ | 1,796,633 |
| April | 965,807 | 898,960 | 1,864,767 | 7,045 | 2,826,325 | ...... | 10,834 | 2,844,204 | ........ | 979,437 |
| May | 771,870 | 725,183 | 1,497,053 | 5,635 | 1,962,372 | ...... | 400 | 1,968,407 | ........ | 471,354 |
| June | 3,323,764 | 762,693 | 4,086,457 | 5,000 | 357,260 | 1,485 | 27,780 | 391,525 | 3,694,935 | ........ |
| Total, twelve months | 24,815,597 | 27,205,657 | 52,021,254 | 186,587 | 46,574,851 | 782,567 | 1,024,945 | 48,568,950 | 3,452,304 | ........ |
| Recapitulation by years. Ending June 30. | | | | | | | | | | |
| 1891 | 214,803 | 18,232,567 | 18,447,370 | 34,542 | 84,939,551 | 209 | 1,423,103 | 86,397,405 | ........ | 67,950,035 |
| 1892 | 249,304 | 49,699,454 | 49,948,758 | 39,325 | 43,321,351 | 13,004 | 6,873,976 | 50,247,656 | ........ | 298,898 |
| 1893 | 894,999 | 21,174,381 | 22,069,380 | 225,524 | 102,068,153 | 16,607 | 6,612,691 | 108,922,975 | ........ | 86,855,595 |
| 1894 | 540,444 | 72,449,119 | 72,989,563 | 146,779 | 64,487,354 | 17,069 | 12,490,707 | 77,141,609 | ........ | 4,152,346 |
| 1895 | 1,238,026 | 35,146,734 | 36,384,760 | 328,012 | 55,890,295 | 9,286 | 10,240,888 | 66,468,481 | ........ | 30,083,721 |
| 1896 | 1,804,578 | 31,720,487 | 33,525,065 | 100,811 | 106,833,525 | ...... | 5,475,611 | 112,409,947 | ........ | 78,884,882 |
| 1897 | 3,603,247 | 81,411,533 | 85,014,780 | 246,848 | 38,905,674 | 10 | 1,209,048 | 40,361,580 | 44,653,200 | ........ |
| 1898 | 5,217,686 | 115,173,988 | 120,391,674 | 81,462 | 10,388,909 | ..... | 4,936,020 | 15,406,391 | 104,985,283 | ........ |
| 1899 | 4,673,929 | 84,280,674 | 88,954,603 | 14,165 | 27,464,247 | 150 | 10,043,524 | 37,522,086 | 51,432,517 | ........ |
| 1900 | 13,611,486 | 30,961,698 | 44,573,184 | 48,591 | 46,645,302 | 40,000 | 1,532,866 | 48,266,759 | ........ | 3,693,575 |
| 1901 | 20,605,453 | 45,445,734 | 66,051,187 | 210,691 | 52,418,578 | ...... | 549,868 | 53,179,137 | 12,872,050 | ........ |
| 1902 | 24,815,597 | 27,205,657 | 52,021,254 | 186,587 | 46,574,851 | 782,567 | 1,024,945 | 48,568,950 | 3,452,304 | ........ |

## NEW YORK CLEARING HOUSE AVERAGES

AT END OF EACH WEEK IN 1902.

| Week Ending. | Loans. | Deposits. | Total Reserve. | Surplus Reserve. |
|---|---|---|---|---|
| January 4 | $869,546,600 | $926,204,100 | $239,066,600 | $7,515,575 |
| January 11 | 864,236,800 | 926,892,600 | 244,704,100 | 12,958,450 |
| January 18 | 867,529,100 | 938,722,200 | 253,742,000 | 19,061,450 |
| January 25 | 869,942,600 | 949,666,800 | 262,740,100 | 25,332,400 |
| February 1 | 889,531,700 | 975,997,000 | 270,622,600 | 26,623,350 |
| February 8 | 918,506,000 | 1,000,681,900 | 268,066,700 | 17,896,225 |
| February 15 | 932,004,700 | 1,015,279,000 | 267,380,600 | 13,560,850 |
| February 22 | 936,575,600 | 1,019,474,200 | 267,325,200 | 12,456,650 |
| March 1 | 938,195,200 | 1,017,488,300 | 264,348,000 | 9,975,925 |
| March 8 | 935,102,100 | 1,005,666,700 | 255,375,100 | 3,958,425 |
| March 15 | 920,730,100 | 984,370,000 | 249,205,400 | 3,112,900 |
| March 22 | 912,953,100 | 973,234,600 | 246,779,900 | 3,471,250 |
| March 29 | 904,074,500 | 965,353,300 | 248,303,900 | 6,965,575 |
| April 5 | 907,223,400 | 964,618,300 | 243,804,100 | 2,649,525 |
| April 12 | 900,381,800 | 957,361,400 | 243,912,100 | 4,571,750 |
| April 19 | 894,491,400 | 952,774,200 | 244,772,200 | 6,578,650 |
| April 26 | 893,394,100 | 954,546,600 | 248,097,700 | 9,461,050 |
| May 3 | 904,162,500 | 968,189,600 | 249,531,400 | 7,484,000 |
| May 10 | 901,938,000 | 960,235,600 | 243,519,900 | 3,461,000 |
| May 17 | 879,029,900 | 936,161,900 | 242,387,000 | 8,346,525 |
| May 24 | 870,483,335 | 931,751,000 | 247,239,200 | 14,301,450 |
| May 31 | 885,592,600 | 948,326,400 | 249,010,600 | 11,929,000 |
| June 7 | 884,266,900 | 945,896,500 | 247,759,700 | 11,285,575 |
| June 14 | 881,074,400 | 932,868,800 | 249,019,500 | 13,302,350 |
| June 21 | 889,015,100 | 950,952,600 | 249,896,400 | 12,158,250 |
| June 28 | 893,871,800 | 955,829,400 | 251,935,700 | 12,978,350 |
| July 5 | 910,883,200 | 958,647,500 | 249,746,600 | 10,084,725 |
| July 12 | 906,776,200 | 942,198,000 | 247,776,400 | 12,226,900 |
| July 19 | 903,327,300 | 940,692,900 | 250,882,500 | 15,709,275 |
| July 26 | 913,294,500 | 952,097,200 | 253,526,700 | 15,502,400 |
| August 2 | 919,671,600 | 957,145,500 | 253,024,500 | 13,738,125 |
| August 9 | 926,494,800 | 959,643,000 | 248,942,000 | 9,031,150 |
| August 16 | 929,148,000 | 960,246,000 | 247,188,100 | 7,126,600 |
| August 23 | 918,687,900 | 948,269,800 | 249,804,850 | 9,743,350 |
| August 30 | 910,040,000 | 935,998,500 | 243,742,400 | 9,742,775 |
| September 6 | 906,374,800 | 923,398,200 | 234,946,600 | 4,097,050 |
| September 13 | 899,498,900 | 908,759,300 | 227,907,400 | 715,075 |
| September 20 | 887,534,400 | 888,871,000 | 220,575,700 | *1,642,650 |
| September 27 | 874,181,800 | 876,519,100 | 222,366,400 | 3,236,625 |
| October 4 | 872,303,700 | 872,176,000 | 219,863,200 | 1,819,200 |
| October 11 | 874,647,900 | 872,340,400 | 219,612,500 | 1,527,350 |
| October 18 | 865,450,800 | 863,125,800 | 221,389,700 | 5,608,250 |
| October 25 | 870,977,600 | 882,685,300 | 238,452,800 | 17,781,475 |
| November 1 | 878,509,000 | 893,791,200 | 244,786,900 | 21,399,100 |
| November 8 | 875,480,600 | 885,882,200 | 239,322,900 | 17,852,350 |
| November 15 | 870,424,200 | 878,219,400 | 237,883,200 | 18,328,350 |
| November 22 | 868,217,200 | 875,706,100 | 238,456,500 | 19,529,975 |
| November 29 | 879,826,000 | 883,836,800 | 236,745,500 | 15,786,300 |
| December 6 | 881,437,000 | 879,762,600 | 229,914,400 | 9,973,750 |
| December 13 | 879,371,500 | 873,731,200 | 226,819,700 | 8,386,900 |
| December 20 | 875,861,300 | 865,856,000 | 225,057,600 | 8,093,600 |
| December 27 | 875,321,500 | 865,953,600 | 223,037,600 | 6,549,200 |

* Deficit.

## SURPLUS RESERVE OF THE NEW YORK BANKS

| *WEEK ENDING. | Surplus Reserves. | | | | |
|---|---|---|---|---|---|
| | 1898. | 1899. | 1900. | 1901. | 1902. |
| January 4 | $22,261,575 | $23,530,375 | $11,757,725 | $14,150,075 | $7,515,575 |
| January 11 | 25,968,775 | 28,263,075 | 16,727,350 | 22,398,050 | 12,958,450 |
| January 18 | 31,275,200 | 34,693,675 | 24,185,675 | 27,256,600 | 19,061,450 |
| January 25 | 35,609,450 | 39,232,025 | 29,277,975 | 30,790,450 | 25,332,400 |
| February 1 | 34,781,625 | 37,452,675 | 30,871,273 | 24,838,825 | 26,623,350 |
| February 8 | 32,437,050 | 35,511,825 | 27,897,575 | 20,362,625 | 17,896,225 |
| February 15 | 25,688,450 | 34,373,825 | 24,015,675 | 12,852,450 | 13,560,850 |
| February 22 | 22,729,125 | 30,334,900 | 19,678,550 | 14,546,675 | 12,456,650 |
| March 1 | 20,823,500 | 24,578,125 | 13,641,550 | 14,801,100 | 9,975,925 |
| March 8 | 22,721,425 | 23,203,000 | 5,676,375 | 10,717,275 | 3,958,425 |
| March 15 | 28,060,050 | 19,074,175 | 2,686,425 | 10,002,000 | 3,112,900 |
| March 22 | 33,851,475 | 18,557,425 | 5,817,300 | 10,272,425 | 3,471,250 |
| March 29 | 35,720,800 | 15,494,850 | 9,836,150 | 7,870,500 | 6,965,575 |
| April 5 | 35,036,475 | 15,018,825 | 7,904,800 | 5,817,975 | 2,649,525 |
| April 12 | 37,346,075 | 19,471,525 | 10,950,275 | 7,938,200 | 4,571,750 |
| April 19 | 43,525,100 | 24,175,900 | 14,894,350 | 14,922,100 | 6,578,650 |
| April 26 | 44,504,675 | 25,524,675 | 17,074,275 | 16,759,775 | 9,461,050 |
| May 3 | 43,916,475 | 19,351,950 | 15,978,475 | 10,980,100 | 7,484,000 |
| May 10 | 46,997,225 | 27,137,625 | 15,332,725 | 8,127,475 | 3,461,000 |
| May 17 | 50,715,250 | 34,631,525 | 16,555,225 | 13,299,925 | 8,346,525 |
| May 24 | 53,704,600 | 43,943,725 | 18,812,325 | 21,288,975 | 14,301,450 |
| May 31 | 52,249,700 | 42,710,600 | 20,122,275 | 21,253,050 | 11,929,000 |
| June 7 | 53,841,100 | 39,323,100 | 18,374,250 | 13,341,500 | 11,285,575 |
| June 14 | 59,272,800 | 30,003,200 | 17,498,750 | 8,782,125 | 13,302,350 |
| June 21 | 62,206,250 | 25,697,800 | 15,526,850 | 6,611,350 | 12,158,250 |
| June 28 | 62,013,550 | 14,274,550 | 16,859,375 | 8,484,200 | 12,978,350 |
| July 5 | 53,345,300 | 5,062,475 | 15,589,200 | 5,211,525 | 10,084,725 |
| July 12 | 49,365,825 | 10,698,750 | 19,960,125 | 12,809,375 | 12,226,900 |
| July 19 | 43,012,000 | 12,055,600 | 24,081,900 | 21,029,375 | 15,709,275 |
| July 26 | 41,904,475 | 10,811,125 | 27,535,975 | 23,128,575 | 15,502,400 |
| August 2 | 39,893,000 | 8,110,600 | 29,144,878 | 22,165,350 | 13,738,128 |
| August 9 | 33,111,850 | 14,395,375 | 28,125,950 | 20,952,950 | 9,031,250 |
| August 16 | 28,839,250 | 15,082,350 | 20,557,050 | 18,421,900 | 7,126,600 |
| August 23 | 21,343,300 | 12,378,525 | 23,888,925 | 18,148,100 | 9,743,350 |
| August 30 | 14,991,050 | 9,191,250 | 27,078,475 | 11,919,925 | 9,742,775 |
| September 6 | 7,076,775 | 2,458,925 | 26,056,250 | 6,915,875 | 4,097,050 |
| September 13 | 4,240,400 | 275,450 | 20,836,175 | 7,110,550 | 715,075 |
| September 20 | 8,252,875 | 9,963,700 | 16,552,325 | 13,654,225 | †1,642,650 |
| September 27 | 15,327,150 | 1,724,450 | 12,942,600 | 16,293,025 | 3,236,625 |
| October 4 | 18,743,600 | 643,200 | 6,241,900 | 15,560,025 | 1,819,200 |
| October 11 | 19,661,550 | 1,177,350 | 4,463,925 | 17,483,175 | 1,527,350 |
| October 18 | 23,412,325 | 1,441,075 | 2,947,700 | 15,465,775 | 5,608,250 |
| October 25 | 26,091,550 | 3,038,525 | 6,031,825 | 14,713,175 | 17,781,475 |
| November 1 | 19,023,050 | †338,350 | 5,950,400 | 10,482,800 | 21,399,100 |
| November 8 | 15,011,800 | †2,788,950 | 4,606,050 | 8,689,925 | 17,852,350 |
| November 15 | 16,637,375 | †312,025 | 7,669,775 | 10,103,825 | 18,328,350 |
| November 22 | 18,357,575 | 6,652,200 | 12,278,275 | 14,486,925 | 19,529,975 |
| November 29 | 17,097,950 | 8,536,700 | 10,865,675 | 13,414,575 | 15,786,300 |
| December 6 | 16,743,300 | 6,859,525 | 5,701,125 | 6,607,675 | 9,973,750 |
| December 13 | 16,973,375 | 7,025,825 | 6,325,375 | 5,455,025 | 8,386,900 |
| December 20 | 19,619,050 | 10,384,075 | 9,497,0[illegible]0 | 5,785,325 | 8,093,600 |
| December 27 | 19,180,975 | 11,168,075 | 11,525,900 | 7,891,350 | 6,549,200 |

* The dates are for 1902. The other columns are for corresponding weeks. † Deficit.

## BANK CLEARINGS STATISTICS

### AGGREGATE EXCHANGES AT VARIOUS CITIES

| Clearing Houses. | Rank in 1902. | 1902. | 1901. | Rank in 1901. | Increase per cent. | Dec. per cent. |
|---|---|---|---|---|---|---|
| New York | 1 | $76,328,189,165 | $79,427,685,837 | 1 | .... | 3.9 |
| Chicago | 2 | 8,394,872,346 | 7,756,372,450 | 2 | 8.2 | .... |
| Boston | 3 | 6,930,016,794 | 7,191,685,110 | 3 | .... | 3.6 |
| **Philadelphia** | 4 | 5,875,328,359 | 5,475,345,188 | 4 | 7.3 | .... |
| **St. Louis** | 5 | 2,506,804,322 | 2,270,737,216 | 5 | 10.3 | .... |
| Pittsburg | 6 | 2,147,969,759 | 2,046,605,962 | 6 | 4.9 | .... |
| San Francisco | 7 | 1,369,058,560 | 1,165,250,091 | 8 | 17.5 | .... |
| Baltimore | 8 | **1,202,803,304** | **1,191,867,587** | 7 | .8 | .... |
| Cincinnati | 9 | 1,080,903,000 | 972,502,450 | 9 | 11.1 | .... |
| Kansas City | 10 | 989,289,157 | 918,198,612 | 10 | 7.7 | .... |
| Cleveland | 11 | 761,356,455 | 702,768,639 | 11 | 8.3 | .... |
| Minneapolis | 12 | 720,762,326 | 626,020,452 | 12 | 15.1 | .... |
| New Orleans | 13 | 677,111,109 | 602,264,116 | 13 | 12.4 | .... |
| Detroit | 14 | 536,613,644 | 575,481,632 | 14 | .... | 6.7 |
| Louisville | 15 | 501,433,130 | 462,060,845 | 15 | 8.5 | .... |
| Omaha | 16 | 362,607,657 | 334,102,066 | 17 | 8.5 | .... |
| **Milwaukee** | 17 | 359,522,615 | 327,533,756 | 18 | 9.8 | .... |
| Providence | 18 | 354,165,000 | 349,328,200 | 16 | 1.3 | .... |
| Buffalo | 19 | 303,929,483 | 302,857,979 | 19 | .3 | .... |
| St. Paul | 20 | 294,097,110 | 260,413,678 | 20 | 12.9 | .... |
| Indianapolis | 21 | 270,409,454 | 215,085,895 | 23 | 25.7 | .... |
| Los Angeles | 22 | 245,516,187 | 162,378,058 | 29 | 51.2 | .... |
| St. Joseph | 23 | 235,617,174 | 240,656,541 | 21 | .... | 2.0 |
| Denver | 24 | 230,269,176 | 229,464,095 | 22 | .3 | .... |
| **Richmond** | 25 | 211,714,144 | 196,561,932 | 24 | 7.7 | .... |
| Columbus | 26 | 207,496,350 | 169,924,350 | 28 | 22.0 | .... |
| Seattle | 27 | 191,948,819 | 144,321,026 | 32 | 32.9 | .... |
| Washington | 28 | 188,315,053 | 143,065,791 | 33 | 31.6 | .... |
| Savannah | 29 | 180,542,044 | 182,261,330 | 25 | .... | 1.0 |
| **Memphis** | 30 | 179,199,927 | 154,482,940 | 30 | 15.9 | .... |
| Albany | 31 | 177,595,045 | 172,101,238 | 27 | 3.1 | .... |
| Salt Lake City | 32 | 175,540,010 | 182,087,896 | 26 | .... | 3.5 |
| **Portland, Ore.** | 33 | 155,344,899 | 122,127,342 | 37 | 27.1 | .... |
| Toledo, Ohio | 34 | 148,310,081 | 122,299,537 | 36 | 21.3 | .... |
| Fort Worth | 35 | 148,068,513 | 148,329,127 | 31 | .... | .1 |
| Peoria | 36 | 146,559,689 | 123,763,884 | 35 | 18.4 | .... |
| Hartford | 37 | 139,646,848 | 135,913,117 | 34 | 2.7 | .... |
| Rochester | 38 | 133,727,503 | 117,251,688 | 38 | 14.0 | .... |
| Atlanta | 39 | 131,200,453 | 116,855,848 | 39 | 12.3 | .... |
| **Des Moines** | 40 | 105,599,446 | 85,483,096 | 40 | 23.5 | .... |
| New Haven | 41 | 89,949,666 | 81,600,959 | 41 | 10.2 | .... |
| **Nashville** | 42 | 89,417,004 | 75,740,943 | 43 | 18.0 | .... |
| Spokane, Wash | 43 | 88,470,841 | 58,856,227 | 54 | 50.3 | .... |
| Grand Rapids | 44 | 82,961,442 | 70,823,914 | 46 | 17.1 | .... |
| Sioux City | 45 | 81,152,977 | 67,796,261 | 49 | 19.7 | .... |
| Springfield, Mass | 46 | 80,762,525 | 74,564,541 | 44 | 8.3 | .... |
| Norfolk | 47 | 77,649,088 | 71,953,047 | 45 | 7.9 | .... |
| Dayton | 48 | 76,463,118 | 61,889,394 | 52 | 23.5 | .... |
| Tacoma | 49 | 75,957,838 | 59,170,231 | 53 | 28.3 | .... |
| Worcester | 50 | 75,890,779 | 79,275,372 | 42 | .... | 4.2 |
| Augusta, Ga | 51 | 73,391,020 | 67,186,451 | 50 | 9.2 | .... |
| Portland, Me | 52 | 73,077,094 | 68,056,835 | 48 | 7.3 | .... |
| Scranton | 53 | 72,193,000 | 68,992,870 | 47 | 4.6 | .... |
| Topeka | 54 | 69,282,215 | 58,088,232 | 55 | 19.2 | .... |
| Syracuse | 55 | 66,696,442 | 61,999,990 | 51 | 7.5 | .... |

BANK STATISTICS—*Continued.*

| Clearing Houses. | Rank in 1902. | 1902. | 1901. | Rank in 1901. | Increase per cent. | Dec. per cent. |
|---|---|---|---|---|---|---|
| Evansville | 56 | $59,822,329 | $49,554,502 | 58 | 20.7 | .... |
| Wilmington, Del. | 57 | 59,370,671 | 52,107,698 | 57 | 13.9 | .... |
| Birmingham | 58 | 56,143,852 | 48,005,339 | 59 | 16.9 | .... |
| Davenport | 59 | 52,709,465 | 53,563,155 | 56 | .... | 1.5 |
| Fall River | 60 | 51,326,747 | 44,916,180 | 60 | 14.2 | .... |
| Knoxville | 61 | 40,730,020 | 32,098,714 | 63 | 26.8 | .... |
| Macon | 62 | 37,342,000 | 34,560,600 | 61 | 8.0 | .... |
| Akron | 63 | 34,578,300 | 28,839,500 | 65 | 19.9 | .... |
| Springfield, Ill | 64 | 31,313,772 | 27,148,786 | 67 | 15.3 | .... |
| Wichita | 65 | 30,906,059 | 27,965,849 | 66 | 10.5 | .... |
| Youngstown | 66 | 30,895,112 | 23,171,375 | 71 | 33.3 | .... |
| Helena | 67 | 29,713,333 | 34,156,320 | 62 | .... | 13.0 |
| Lexington | 68 | 28,146,149 | 26,150,773 | 68 | 7.6 | .... |
| Chattanooga | 69 | 28,021,693 | 23,371,778 | 70 | 19.8 | .... |
| Lowell | 70 | 27,675,362 | 29,927,807 | 64 | .... | 7 5 |
| New Bedford | 71 | 27,239,999 | 24,268,653 | 69 | 12.2 | .... |
| Kalamazoo, Mich | 72 | 27,037,448 | 21,901,830 | 72 | 23.9 | .... |
| Fargo, N. D. | 73 | 24,613,697 | 19,916,732 | 73 | 23.5 | .... |
| Canton, Ohio | 74 | 24,240,973 | 17,950,830 | 78 | 35.0 | .... |
| Jacksonville, Fla. | 75 | 22,605,305 | 16,757,775 | 79 | 34.9 | .... |
| Greensburg, Pa | 76 | 21,936,166 | 19,352,151 | 75 | 13.3 | .... |
| Rockford, Ill | 77 | 20,275,486 | 18,004,884 | 77 | 12.6 | .... |
| Holyoke | 78 | 20,123,276 | 19,640,798 | 74 | 2.4 | .... |
| Springfield, Ohio | 79 | 19,081,594 | 16,464,739 | 80 | 15.8 | .... |
| Binghamton | 80 | 18,797,103 | 19,263,400 | 76 | .... | 2.4 |
| Chester, Pa. | 81 | 18,553,312 | 16,127,755 | 81 | 15.0 | .... |
| Bloomington, Ill | 82 | 16,757,871 | 13,941,900 | 83 | 20.1 | .... |
| Quincy, Ill | 83 | 14,350,721 | 14,241,295 | 82 | .7 | .... |
| Sioux Falls, S. D. | 84 | 13,789,300 | 11,580,352 | 84 | 19.0 | .... |
| Mansfield, Ohio | 85 | 10,657,472 | 3,013,681 | 89 | 253.6 | .... |
| Jacksonville, Ill | 86 | 10,064,419 | 8,673,480 | 85 | 16.0 | .... |
| Jackson, Mich. | 87 | 8,932,648 | 7,653,821 | 88 | 18.0 | .... |
| Frederick, Md | 88 | 8,421,886 | 7,993,860 | 87 | 5.3 | .... |
| Fremont, Neb | 89 | 8,413,220 | 8,167,779 | 86 | 3.0 | .... |
| Totals, U. S. | .. | $117,407,355,919 | $117,969,945,955 | .. | .... | .5 |
| Outside N. Y. | .. | 41,079,166,754 | 38,542,260,118 | .. | 6.5 | .... |
| CANADA. | | | | | | |
| Montreal | 1 | 1,089,976,730 | 889,486,915 | 1 | 22.5 | .... |
| Toronto | 2 | 809,078,559 | 599,385,671 | 2 | 34.9 | .... |
| Winnipeg | 3 | 188,370,003 | 134,199,663 | 3 | 40.3 | .... |
| Halifax | 4 | 88,532,252 | 87,148,064 | 4 | 15.9 | .... |
| Vancouver, B. C. | 5 | 54,223,969 | 46,738,805 | 5 | 16.0 | .... |
| Hamilton | 6 | 45,970,217 | 42,554,033 | 6 | 8.0 | .... |
| St. John, N. B. | 7 | 42,465,684 | 40,941,259 | 7 | 3.7 | .... |
| Victoria, B. C. | 8 | 28,680,679 | 30,607,315 | 8 | .... | 6 2 |
| Totals Canada | .. | $2,347,268,093 | $1,871,061,725 | .. | 25.4 | .... |

## COMPARATIVE MONTHLY TOTALS OF BANK CLEARINGS

[000,000's omitted.]

| Mos. | 1890. | 1891. | 1892. | 1893. | 1894. | 1895. | 1896. | 1897. | 1898. | 1899. | 1900. | 1901. | 1902. |
|---|---|---|---|---|---|---|---|---|---|---|---|---|---|
| | $ | $ | $ | $ | $ | $ | $ | $ | $ | $ | $ | $ | $ |
| Jan... | 5,270 | 4,957 | 5,635 | 5,926 | 4,043 | 4,375 | 4,589 | 4,459 | 5,974 | 8,459 | 7,619 | 10,679 | 10,602 |
| Feb .. | 4,464 | 3,965 | 5,190 | 5,060 | 3,195 | 3,397 | 4,089 | 3,672 | 5,533 | 6,951 | 6,388 | 8,323 | 8,318 |
| March | 4,638 | 4,229 | 5,269 | 5,397 | 3,744 | 4,022 | 4,114 | 4,195 | 5,626 | 8,691 | 7,594 | 9,960 | 8,877 |
| April . | 4,842 | 4,795 | 5,071 | 4,933 | 3,717 | 4,246 | 4,285 | 4,092 | 4,962 | 8,256 | 7,440 | 11,969 | 10,867 |
| May.. | 5,896 | 4,806 | 5,015 | 5,263 | 3,882 | 4,853 | 4,222 | 4,158 | 5,330 | 8,301 | 7,284 | 12,786 | 10,337 |
| June.. | 5,105 | 4,381 | 4,921 | 4,533 | 3,583 | 4,387 | 4,281 | 4,456 | 5,493 | 7,474 | 6,639 | 10,069 | 8,165 |
| July .. | 4,839 | 4,401 | 4,622 | 4,142 | 3,504 | 4,550 | 4,350 | 4,803 | 5,010 | 7,089 | 6,223 | 9,333 | 10,129 |
| Aug. . | 4,801 | 4,161 | 4,508 | 3,343 | 3,545 | 4,118 | 3,530 | 4,810 | 5,585 | 6,903 | 5,675 | 7,950 | 8,894 |
| Sept.. | 4,983 | 5,257 | 4,778 | 3,316 | 3,500 | 4,146 | 3,667 | 5,521 | 5,467 | 7,022 | 5,592 | 7,925 | 10,093 |
| Oct .. | 5,803 | 5,527 | 5,473 | 3,998 | 4,256 | 5,206 | 4,551 | 5,602 | 5,899 | 8,280 | 7,564 | 9,460 | 11,288 |
| Nov .. | 5,252 | 4,935 | 5,447 | 4,062 | 4,140 | 4,702 | 4,567 | 5,361 | 6,452 | 7,852 | 8,702 | 9,792 | 10,027 |
| Dec .. | 4,840 | 5,391 | 5,973 | 4,047 | 4,287 | 5,040 | 4,687 | 5,935 | 7,335 | 8,317 | 9,029 | 9,723 | 9,810 |
| Totals | 60,733 | 56,805 | 61,902 | 54,020 | 45,396 | 53,042 | 50,934 | 57,065 | 68,666 | 93,595 | 85,749 | 117,969 | 117,407 |

## SALES ON NEW YORK STOOK EXCHANGE

| | 1901. | | 1902. | |
|---|---|---|---|---|
| | Total Shares. | Par Value. | Total Shares. | Par Value. |
| January | 30,631,350 | $3,063,135,000 | 14,839,819 | $1,483,981,900 |
| February | 21,681,202 | 2,168,120,200 | 13,021,133 | 1,302,113,300 |
| March | 26,809,533 | 2,680,953,300 | 11,890,781 | 1,189,078,100 |
| April | 42,149,208 | 4,214,920,800 | 25,845,914 | 2,584,591,400 |
| May | 25,322,599 | 2,532,259,900 | 13,564,785 | 1,356,478,500 |
| June | 29,686,629 | 2,968,662,900 | 7,765,977 | 776,597,700 |
| July | 15,673,166 | 1,567,316,600 | 16,240,853 | 1,624,085,300 |
| August | 7,997,420 | 799,742,000 | 14,017,019 | 1,401,701,900 |
| September | 13,779,304 | 1,377,930,400 | 20,921,515 | 2,092,151,500 |
| October | 14,945,056 | 1,654,493,900 | 15,894,385 | 1,589,438,500 |
| November | 18,205,402 | 1,494,505,600 | 16,972,045 | 1,697,204,500 |
| December | 16,544,939 | 1,820,540,200 | 15,630,982 | 1,563,098,200 |
| Total | 263,425,808 | $26,342,580,800 | 186,605,208 | $18,660,520,800 |

| | Stocks, Shares. | State and Railroad Bonds. | Governments. |
|---|---|---|---|
| 1902 | 186,605,208 | $893,652,882 | $1,354,750 |
| 1901 | 263,425,808 | 982,929,300 | 1,820,310 |
| 1900 | 138,380,184 | 571,241,200 | 7,012,080 |
| 1899 | 176,421,135 | 823,722,900 | 10,459,230 |
| 1898 | 112,699,957 | 847,654,000 | 24,129,216 |
| 1897 | 77,248,347 | 529,343,000 | 10,134,030 |
| 1896 | 54,490,643 | 358,815,850 | 27,121,550 |
| 1895 | 66,440,576 | 495,904,950 | 7,046,250 |
| 1894 | 49,275,736 | 352,741,950 | 4,293,300 |
| 1893 | 77,984,965 | 299,372,327 | 2,021,450 |
| 1892 | 86,850,930 | 501,398,200 | 1,662,400 |
| 1891 | 72,725,864 | 389,906,700 | 1,539,900 |
| 1890 | 59,441,301 | 374,342,120 | 2,891,050 |
| 1889 | 61,133,161 | 394,151,406 | 4,287,050 |

## SALES ON NEW YORK CONSOLIDATED EXCHANGE

| | Stocks. | | | Wheat. | | |
|---|---|---|---|---|---|---|
| | No. of Shares. (Clearances.) 1900. | No. of Shares. (Clearances.) 1901. | No. of Shares. (Clearances.) 1902. | Bushels. (Clearances.) 1900. | Bushels. (Clearances.) 1901. | Bushels. (Clearances.) 1902. |
| January | 7,487,700 | 10,648,820 | 8,687,320 | 49,235,000 | 46,626,000 | 45,736,000 |
| February | 6,498,140 | 7,847,940 | 7,685,680 | 45,587,000 | 18,028,000 | 36,784,000 |
| March | 9,054,630 | 9,847,960 | 7,267,480 | 49,814,000 | 24,262,000 | 52,152,000 |
| April | 8,694,050 | 12,633,280 | 9,263,260 | 50,896,000 | 34,868,000 | 64,484,000 |
| May | 7,400,380 | 9,119,380 | 7,567,880 | 29,814,000 | 22,262,000 | 56,924,000 |
| June | 7,453,420 | 7,506,160 | 5,498,500 | 95,002,000 | 29,585,000 | 71,104,000 |
| July | 6,431,720 | 6,234,260 | 7,813,020 | 63,102,000 | 28,600,000 | 54,316,000 |
| August | 4,781,300 | 5,608,940 | 6,686,920 | 55,664,000 | 33,572,000 | 55,442,000 |
| September | 5,440,320 | 6,410,140 | 10,624,220 | 64,072,000 | 16,912,000 | 37,358,000 |
| October | 8,937,220 | 8,081,940 | 8,922,360 | 65,284,000 | 27,884,000 | 55,476,000 |
| November | 10,252,910 | 8,429,240 | 9,067,270 | 53,066,000 | 34,504,000 | 48,390,000 |
| December | 10,228,000 | 8,703,960 | 9,894,360 | 33,812,000 | 37,598,000 | 45,994,000 |
| Totals | 92,659,790 | 101,072,020 | 98,978,270 | 655,348,000 | 354,701,000 | 624,160,000 |

| | Bonds. | | | Mining Stocks. | | |
|---|---|---|---|---|---|---|
| | Values. 1900. | Values. 1901. | Values. 1902. | No. of Shares. 1900. | No. of Shares. 1901. | No. of Shares 1902. |
| January | $279,000 | $436,000 | $403,000 | 235,860 | 146,500 | 119,340 |
| February | 310,000 | 281,000 | 1,098,000 | 186,310 | 96,515 | 131,445 |
| March | 492,000 | 479,000 | 415,000 | 197,630 | 140,938 | 153,083 |
| April | 673,000 | 1,027,000 | 250,000 | 128,050 | 118,990 | 120,290 |
| May | 555,000 | 805,000 | 163,000 | 146,540 | 129,515 | 109,970 |
| June | 342,000 | 329,000 | 245,000 | 132,580 | 122,660 | 85,317 |
| July | 172,000 | 227,000 | 144,000 | 126,568 | 131,135 | 83,730 |
| August | 190,000 | 246,000 | 77,000 | 136,425 | 117,610 | 86,450 |
| September | 188,000 | 254,000 | 70,000 | 142,940 | 109,440 | 88,348 |
| October | 235,000 | 395,000 | 136,000 | 139,000 | 158,425 | 132,500 |
| November | 312,000 | 265,000 | 93,000 | 108,600 | 85,980 | 128,760 |
| December | 386,000 | 402,000 | 140,000 | 96,985 | 103,640 | 157,070 |
| Totals | $4,134,000 | $5,146,000 | $3,234,700 | 1,777,488 | 1,461,348 | 1,396,293 |

# EXPORTS AND IMPORTS OF THE UNITED STATES

Showing the Value of Exports and Imports of the United States annually.

| Fiscal Year Ending June 30. | EXPORTS. | | | | | | | | IMPORTS. | | |
|---|---|---|---|---|---|---|---|---|---|---|---|
| | Cotton Unmanuft'd. | Breadstuffs, Provisions and Vegetables. | Other Domestic Products, Except Coin and Bullion. | Total Export of Domestic Products, Except Coin and Bullion. | Domestic Coin and Bullion. | Foreign Coin and Bullion. | Foreign Merchandise Re-exported | Grand Total of Exports | Imports of Merchandise. | *Coin and Bullion. | Total Imports. |
| 1869.... | $162,633,052 | $80,045,165 | $128,366,932 | $371,045,149 | $42,915,966 | $14,222,414 | $10,951,000 | $343,256,077 | $417,506,379 | $19,807,876 | $437,314,257 |
| 1870.... | 227,027,624 | 98,009,219 | 130,173,498 | 555,208,341 | 43,883,802 | 14,271,864 | 16,155,295 | 450,927,434 | 435,958,408 | 26,419,179 | 462,377,588 |
| 1871.... | 218,327,109 | 118,226,406 | 141,561,777 | 478,115,292 | 84,403,359 | 14,038,629 | 14,421,270 | 541,262,166 | 520,223,684 | 21,270,021 | 541,493,707 |
| 1872.... | 180,684,595 | 144,282,933 | 151,453,950 | 476,421,478 | 72,708,240 | 7,079,294 | 15,690,455 | 524,055,120 | 626,595,077 | 13,743,689 | 640,338,768 |
| 1873.... | 227,243,069 | 176,940,392 | 171,043 556 | 575,227,017 | 73,905,546 | 10,703,028 | 17,446,483 | 607,088,496 | 642,136,210 | 21,480,937 | 663,617,143 |
| 1874.... | 211,223,580 | 239,527,854 | 182,587,934 | 633,339,368 | 59,699,686 | 6,930,719 | 16,849,619 | 652,913,445 | 567,406,342 | 28,454,906 | 595,861,248 |
| 1875.... | 190,038,625 | 192,801,666 | 175,797,347 | 559,237,638 | 83,857,129 | 8,275,013 | 14,158,611 | 605,574,853 | 533,005,436 | 20,900,717 | 553,906,156 |
| 1876.... | 192,659,262 | 221,063,302 | 181,195,151 | 594,917,715 | 50,038,691 | 6,467,611 | 14,802,424 | 596,890,973 | 460,741,190 | 15,936,681 | 476,677,871 |
| 1877.... | 171,118,508 | 232,798,225 | 229,064,121 | 632,980,854 | 43,134,738 | 13,027,499 | 12,804,996 | 618,637,457 | 451,323,126 | 40,774,414 | 492,097,540 |
| 1878.... | 180,031,484 | 305,342,043 | 210,376,403 | 695,749,930 | 27,061,885 | 6,678,240 | 14,156,498 | 728,605,891 | 437,051,532 | 29,821,314 | 466,872,846 |
| 1879.... | 162,304,250 | 327,214,178 | 210,020,314 | 699,538,742 | 17,555,035 | 7,442,406 | 12,098,651 | 735,436,882 | 445,777,775 | 20,296,000 | 466,073,775 |
| 1880.... | 211,535,905 | 415,080,077 | 197,330,371 | 823,946,353 | 9,347,893 | 7,795,026 | 11,692,305 | 852,781,577 | 667,954,746 | 93,034,310 | 760,989,056 |
| 1881.... | 247,695,746 | 421,860,787 | 214,369,414 | 883,925,947 | 14,226,944 | 5,179,903 | 18,451,399 | 921,784,193 | 642,664,628 | 110,575,497 | 753,240,125 |
| 1882.... | 199,812,644 | 303,326,229 | 230,100,859 | 733,239,732 | 43,480,271 | 5,937,208 | 17,302,525 | 799,959,736 | 724,639,574 | 42,472,390 | 767,111,964 |
| 1883.... | 247,328,721 | 315,429,137 | 241,465,774 | 804,223,632 | 21,623,181 | 10,197,152 | 19,615,770 | 855,659,735 | 723,180,914 | 28,489,391 | 751,670,305 |
| 1884.... | 197,015,204 | 278,011,682 | 249,037,966 | 724,964,852 | 50,225,635 | 16,907,748 | 15,548,757 | 807,646,992 | 667,697,693 | 37,426,262 | 705,123,955 |
| 1885.... | 201,962,458 | 268,797,351 | 255,908,271 | 726,682,946 | 24,376,110 | 17,855,415 | 15,506,809 | 784,421,280 | 577,527,329 | 43,242,323 | 620,769,652 |
| 1886.... | 205,085,642 | 254,453,044 | 206,410,748 | 665,950,534 | 51,924,117 | 20,539,293 | 13,563,075 | 751,977,019 | 635,374,532 | 38,593,656 | 673,968,188 |
| 1887.... | 206,222,057 | 296,642,634 | 200,157,664 | 703,022,355 | 22,710,340 | 13,287,351 | 13,160,288 | 752,180,334 | 692,253,350 | 60,170,702 | 753,911,991 |
| 1888.... | 223,016,760 | 221,491,679 | 239,353,797 | 683,862,236 | 33,195,504 | 13,218,679 | 12,092,403 | 695,954,639 | 723,879,813 | 59,337,986 | 783,217,799 |
| 1889.... | 237,775,270 | 229,448,763 | 263,058,455 | 730,282,488 | 80,214,994 | 16,426,530 | 12,118,766 | 839,042,908 | 745,131,665 | 28,963,073 | 774,094,738 |
| 1890.... | 250,968,792 | 292,347,528 | 301,777,508 | 845,293,828 | 34,782,189 | 16,366,231 | 12,531,006 | 909,973,254 | 789,222,228 | 33,976,326 | 823,198,554 |
| 1891.... | 290,712,898 | 268,475,102 | 313,082,283 | 872,270,283 | 98,973,265 | 9,980,377 | 12,210,527 | 884,480,810 | 844,916,196 | 36,259,477 | 881,175 673 |
| 1892.... | 258,461,241 | 441,623,421 | 315,647,349 | 1,015,732,011 | 60,086,418 | 22,919,468 | 14,546,137 | 1,113,284,034 | 827,402,469 | 69,654,540 | 897,057,009 |
| 1893.... | 188,771,445 | 340,612,242 | 301,647,098 | 831,030,785 | 125,627,407 | 23,790,756 | 16 634,409 | 997,083,357 | 866,400,922 | 44,367,633 | 910,768,555 |
| 1894.... | 210,869,289 | 313,777,425 | 344,561,227 | 869,207,941 | 103,556,441 | 23,872,885 | 22,935,606 | 1,019,572,873 | 654,995,151 | 85,735,671 | 740 730,822 |
| 1895.... | 204,900,990 | 249,782,617 | 338,716,005 | 793,397,890 | 95,963,517 | 17,394,983 | 14,145,566 | 920,896,665 | 731,969,965 | 56,595,939 | 788,565,904 |
| 1896.... | 190,056,460 | 274 515,633 | 398,628,390 | 863,200,487 | 139,352,100 | 12,819,992 | 19,406,451 | 1,054,779,030 | 779,724,674 | 62,302,251 | 842,026,925 |
| 1897.... | 230,890,971 | 337,331,227 | 463,777,102 | 1,032,001,300 | 94,531,865 | 6,613,863 | 18,985,953 | 1,152,132,981 | 764,730,412 | 115,548,007 | 880,278,419 |
| 1898.... | 230,442,215 | 501,708,348 | 478,051,534 | 1,210,292,097 | 58,055,878 | 12,211,614 | 21,190,417 | 1,301,750,006 | 616,049,654 | 151,319,455 | 767,369,109 |
| 1899.... | 209,564,774 | 452,307,707 | 542,251,396 | 1,203,931,222 | 78,606,255 | 15,193,800 | 23,092,080 | 1,320,823,366 | 697,148,480 | 119,629,659 | 816,746,513 |
| 1900.... | 241,832,737 | 450,050,411 | 678,634,456 | 1,370,517,604 | 98,924,965 | 5,780,796 | 23,719,511 | 1,498,942,876 | 849,941,184 | 79,829,486 | 929,770,670 |
| 1901.... | 313,673,443 | 475,152,662 | 671,636,701 | 1,460,462,806 | 110,806,801 | 6,056 269 | 27,302,185 | 1,604,628,061 | 823,172,165 | 102,437,708 | 925,609,873 |
| 1902.... | 290,651,819 | 415,542,009 | 649,288,031 | 1,355,481,861 | 92,469 467 | 4,785,375 | 26,237,540 | 1,478,974,743 | 903,326 071 | 80,253,508 | 983,580,579 |

* Includes gold and silver ore since 1895.

## MERCHANDISE AND DRY GOODS IMPORTS AND EXPORTS,

EXCLUSIVE OF SPECIE, PORT OF NEW YORK.

| * Week Ending. | Imports. | | * Week Ending. | Exports. | |
|---|---|---|---|---|---|
| | 1901. | 1902. | | 1901. | 1902. |
| January 3 | $9,932,394 | $10,196,685 | January 6 | $9,033,419 | $8,874,991 |
| January 10 | 11,453,846 | 11,839,801 | January 13 | 12,393,284 | 9,096,671 |
| January 17 | 10,983,276 | 11,027,835 | January 20 | 12,606,364 | 12,704,270 |
| January 24 | 11,100,233 | 9,838,232 | January 27 | 12,081,753 | 5,383,290 |
| January 31 | 8,093,145 | 11,369,309 | February 3 | 10,872,962 | 9,204,493 |
| February 7 | 9,800,815 | 10,234,424 | February 10 | 10,476,608 | 10,456,603 |
| February 14 | 10,364,265 | 10,142,395 | February 17 | 7,929,677 | 8,546,771 |
| February 21 | 9,096,084 | 10,878,824 | February 24 | 8,707,301 | 11,123,537 |
| February 28 | 10,954,867 | 9,679,719 | March 3 | 12,774,866 | 8,292,220 |
| March 7 | 12,844,425 | 12,517,510 | March 10 | 13,649,397 | 8,950,207 |
| March 14 | 10,317,929 | 11,941,688 | March 17 | 9,928,114 | 10,692,792 |
| March 21 | 13,953,210 | 10,548,381 | March 24 | 10,069,656 | 10,279,500 |
| March 28 | 13,874,414 | 12,523,419 | March 31 | 7,683,120 | 7,692,102 |
| April 4 | 9,826,289 | 12,512,747 | April 7 | 7,637,641 | 10,177,645 |
| April 11 | 10,327,550 | 10,838,918 | April 14 | 10,311,773 | 12,563,812 |
| April 18 | 12,534,444 | 10,508,742 | April 21 | 12,729,536 | 9,977,480 |
| April 25 | 10,968,622 | 10,912,084 | April 28 | 11,887,253 | 10,168,984 |
| May 2 | 10,487,539 | 11,742,461 | May 5 | 10,032,340 | 9,637,940 |
| May 9 | 12,590,832 | 10,289,422 | May 12 | 12,990,419 | 9,247,162 |
| May 16 | 11,741,669 | 10,644,783 | May 19 | 8,238,956 | 10,496,643 |
| May 23 | 10,561,463 | 9,524,749 | May 26 | 10,669,557 | 9,344,823 |
| May 30 | 10,078,634 | 9,154,978 | June 2 | 8,145,809 | 8,202,160 |
| June 6 | 12,907,190 | 8,928,492 | June 9 | 11,103,761 | 10,732,865 |
| June 13 | 8,279,183 | 9,754,363 | June 16 | 9,174,216 | 7,736,065 |
| June 20 | 8,885,521 | 10,282,786 | June 23 | 10,264,741 | 9,410,937 |
| June 27 | 11,623,700 | 10,169,248 | June 30 | 9,468,192 | 8,214,191 |
| July 4 | 9,631,531 | 11,384,771 | July 7 | 10,042,061 | 6,560,345 |
| July 11 | 10,126,304 | 8,544,970 | July 14 | 9,450,833 | 8,890,725 |
| July 18 | 11,370,877 | 11,023,640 | July 21 | 9,799,711 | 8,113,502 |
| July 25 | 9,834,164 | 10,428,488 | July 28 | 11,334,522 | 8,990,037 |
| August 1 | 9,744,153 | 10,350,949 | August 4 | 10,849,268 | 7,073,578 |
| August 8 | 8,853,887 | 12,134,705 | August 11 | 8,412,705 | 9,513,910 |
| August 15 | 12,130,062 | 9,735,800 | August 18 | 9,452,826 | 8,236,016 |
| August 22 | 8,995,253 | 11,180,174 | August 25 | 9,908,914 | 9,136,381 |
| August 29 | 9,200,175 | 10,172,369 | September 1 | 8,816,992 | 8,005,511 |
| September 5 | 12,305,962 | 11,865,180 | September 8 | 8,043,568 | 9,756,670 |
| September 12 | 8,560,984 | 11,857,565 | September 15 | 10,952,836 | 9,801,430 |
| September 19 | 11,247,804 | 11,333,073 | September 22 | 7,798,314 | 9,475,701 |
| September 26 | 10,644,214 | 10,471,477 | September 29 | 13,143,080 | 10,004,314 |
| October 3 | 8,504,161 | 12,815,460 | October 6 | 9,128,738 | 10,073,286 |
| October 10 | 10,337,263 | 10,590,700 | October 13 | 9,725,643 | 11,527,177 |
| October 17 | 10,202,797 | 11,258,436 | October 20 | 9,654,939 | 10,170,455 |
| October 24 | 11,687,541 | 11,898,550 | October 27 | 10,637,626 | 10,195,821 |
| October 31 | 11,667,230 | 12,545,452 | November 3 | 9,216,053 | 11,848,571 |
| November 7 | 12,155,331 | 10,627,309 | November 10 | 10,136,698 | 7,613,201 |
| November 14 | 10,062,166 | 12,032,646 | November 17 | 8,758,199 | 11,257,635 |
| November 21 | 9,784,972 | 13,316,671 | November 24 | 10,522,846 | 12,280,317 |
| November 28 | 11,721,829 | 12,255,430 | December 1 | 6,091,449 | 7,298,204 |
| December 5 | 11,229,610 | 11,691,267 | December 8 | 11,569,129 | 13,336,103 |
| December 12 | 11,682,781 | 11,461,020 | December 15 | 11,330,534 | 9,965,393 |
| December 19 | 11,043,341 | 10,332,808 | December 22 | 10,889,581 | 11,117,395 |
| December 26 | 12,330,538 | 14,149,573 | December 29 | 8,638,021 | 8,564,353 |
| Official totals for year | 552,813,578 | 591,619,161 | Official totals for year | 510,936,442 | 491,060,207 |

* The dates are for 1902. The other columns are for corresponding weeks.

# INCOME-YIELDING CAPACITY OF STOCKS

| Purchase Price. | Dividend Rate Per Annum. | | | | | | | | | | |
|---|---|---|---|---|---|---|---|---|---|---|---|
| | 1% | 2% | 3% | 4% | 5% | 6% | 7% | 8% | 9% | 10% | 12% |
| 10 | 10.00 | 20.00 | 30.00 | 40.00 | 50.00 | 60.00 | 70.00 | 80.00 | 90.00 | 100.00 | 120.00 |
| 12½ | 8.00 | 16.00 | 24.00 | 32.00 | 40.00 | 48.00 | 56.00 | 64.00 | 72.00 | 80.00 | 96.00 |
| 15 | 6.67 | 13.33 | 20.00 | 26.67 | 33.33 | 40.00 | 46.67 | 53.33 | 60.00 | 66.67 | 80.00 |
| 17½ | 5.71 | 11.43 | 17.14 | 22.86 | 28.57 | 34.28 | 40.00 | 45.71 | 51.43 | 57.14 | 68.57 |
| 20 | 5.00 | 10.00 | 15.00 | 20.00 | 25.00 | 30.00 | 35.00 | 40.00 | 45.00 | 50.00 | 60.00 |
| 22½ | 4.44 | 8.89 | 13.33 | 17.78 | 22.22 | 26.67 | 31.11 | 35.56 | 40.00 | 44.44 | 53.33 |
| 25 | 4.00 | 8.00 | 12.00 | 16.00 | 20.00 | 24.00 | 28.00 | 32.00 | 36.00 | 40.00 | 48.00 |
| 27½ | 3.64 | 7.27 | 10.91 | 14.55 | 18.18 | 21.82 | 25.45 | 29.09 | 32.73 | 36.36 | 43.64 |
| 30 | 3.33 | 6.67 | 10.00 | 13.33 | 16.67 | 20.00 | 23.33 | 26.67 | 30.00 | 33.33 | 40.00 |
| 32½ | 3.08 | 6.15 | 9.23 | 12.31 | 15.39 | 18.46 | 21.54 | 24.62 | 27.69 | 30.77 | 36.92 |
| 35 | 2.86 | 5.71 | 8.57 | 11.43 | 14.29 | 17.14 | 20.00 | 22.86 | 25.71 | 28.57 | 34.29 |
| 37½ | 2.67 | 5.33 | 8.00 | 10.67 | 13.33 | 16.00 | 18.67 | 21.33 | 24.00 | 26.67 | 32.00 |
| 40 | 2.50 | 5.00 | 7.50 | 10.00 | 12.50 | 15.00 | 17.50 | 20.00 | 22.50 | 25.00 | 30.00 |
| 42½ | 2.35 | 4.70 | 7.06 | 9.41 | 11.76 | 14.12 | 16.47 | 18.82 | 21.18 | 23.53 | 28.23 |
| 45 | 2.22 | 4.44 | 6.67 | 8.89 | 11.11 | 13.33 | 15.56 | 17.78 | 20.00 | 22.22 | 26.67 |
| 47½ | 2.11 | 4.21 | 6.32 | 8.42 | 10.53 | 12.63 | 14.74 | 16.84 | 18.95 | 21.05 | 25.26 |
| 50 | 2.00 | 4.00 | 6.00 | 8.00 | 10.00 | 12.00 | 14.00 | 16.00 | 18.00 | 20.00 | 24.00 |
| 52½ | 1.90 | 3.81 | 5.71 | 7.62 | 9.52 | 11.43 | 13.33 | 15.24 | 17.14 | 19.05 | 22.86 |
| 55 | 1.82 | 3.63 | 5.45 | 7.27 | 9.09 | 10.91 | 12.72 | 14.55 | 16.36 | 18.18 | 21.82 |
| 57½ | 1.74 | 3.48 | 5.22 | 6.96 | 8.70 | 10.43 | 12.17 | 13.91 | 15.65 | 17.39 | 20.87 |
| 60 | 1.67 | 3.33 | 5.00 | 6.67 | 8.33 | 10.00 | 11.67 | 13.33 | 15.00 | 16.67 | 20.00 |
| 62½ | 1.60 | 3.20 | 4.80 | 6.40 | 8.00 | 9.60 | 11.20 | 12.80 | 14.40 | 16.00 | 19.20 |
| 65 | 1.54 | 3.08 | 4.62 | 6.15 | 7.69 | 9.23 | 10.77 | 12.31 | 13.85 | 15.38 | 18.46 |
| 67½ | 1.48 | 2.96 | 4.44 | 5.93 | 7.41 | 8.89 | 10.37 | 11.85 | 13.33 | 14.81 | 17.78 |
| 70 | 1.43 | 2.86 | 4.29 | 5.71 | 7.14 | 8.57 | 10.00 | 11.43 | 12.86 | 14.29 | 17.14 |
| 72½ | 1.38 | 2.76 | 4.14 | 5.52 | 6.90 | 8.27 | 9.65 | 11.03 | 12.41 | 13.79 | 16.55 |
| 75 | 1.33 | 2.67 | 4.00 | 5.33 | 6.67 | 8.00 | 9.33 | 10.67 | 12.00 | 13.33 | 16.00 |
| 77½ | 1.29 | 2.58 | 3.87 | 5.16 | 6.45 | 7.74 | 9.03 | 10.32 | 11.61 | 12.90 | 15.48 |
| 80 | 1.25 | 2.50 | 3.75 | 5.00 | 6.25 | 7.50 | 8.75 | 10.00 | 11.25 | 12.50 | 15.00 |
| 82½ | 1.21 | 2.42 | 3.64 | 4.85 | 6.06 | 7.27 | 8.48 | 9.70 | 10.91 | 12.12 | 14.54 |
| 85 | 1.18 | 2.35 | 3.53 | 4.71 | 5.88 | 7.06 | 8.24 | 9.41 | 10.59 | 11.76 | 14.12 |
| 87½ | 1.14 | 2.29 | 3.43 | 4.57 | 5.71 | 6.86 | 8.00 | 9.14 | 10.29 | 11.43 | 13.71 |
| 90 | 1.11 | 2.22 | 3.33 | 4.44 | 5.56 | 6.67 | 7.78 | 8.89 | 10.00 | 11.11 | 13.33 |
| 92½ | 1.08 | 2.16 | 3.24 | 4.32 | 5.41 | 6.49 | 7.57 | 8.65 | 9.73 | 10.81 | 12.97 |
| 95 | 1.05 | 2.11 | 3.16 | 4.21 | 5.26 | 6.32 | 7.37 | 8.42 | 9.47 | 10.53 | 12.63 |
| 97½ | 1.03 | 2.05 | 3.08 | 4.10 | 5.13 | 6.15 | 7.18 | 8.21 | 9.23 | 10.26 | 12.31 |
| 100 | 1.00 | 2.00 | 3.00 | 4.00 | 5.00 | 6.00 | 7.00 | 8.00 | 9.00 | 10.00 | 12.00 |
| 105 | .95 | 1.90 | 2.86 | 3.81 | 4.76 | 5.71 | 6.67 | 7.62 | 8.57 | 9.52 | 11.43 |
| 110 | .91 | 1.82 | 2.73 | 3.64 | 4.55 | 5.45 | 6.36 | 7.27 | 8.18 | 9.09 | 10.91 |
| 115 | .87 | 1.74 | 2.61 | 3.48 | 4.35 | 5.22 | 6.09 | 6.96 | 7.83 | 8.70 | 10.43 |
| 120 | .83 | 1.67 | 2.50 | 3.33 | 4.17 | 5.00 | 5.83 | 6.67 | 7.50 | 8.33 | 10.00 |
| 125 | .80 | 1.60 | 2.40 | 3.20 | 4.00 | 4.80 | 5.60 | 6.40 | 7.20 | 8.00 | 9.60 |
| 130 | .77 | 1.54 | 2.31 | 3.08 | 3.85 | 4.62 | 5.38 | 6.15 | 6.92 | 7.69 | 9.23 |
| 135 | .74 | 1.48 | 2.22 | 2.96 | 3.70 | 4.44 | 5.19 | 5.93 | 6.67 | 7.41 | 8.89 |
| 140 | .71 | 1.43 | 2.14 | 2.86 | 3.57 | 4.29 | 5.00 | 5.71 | 6.43 | 7.14 | 8.57 |
| 145 | .69 | 1.38 | 2.07 | 2.76 | 3.45 | 4.14 | 4.83 | 5.52 | 6.21 | 6.90 | 8.28 |
| 150 | .67 | 1.33 | 2.00 | 2.67 | 3.33 | 4.00 | 4.67 | 5.33 | 6.00 | 6.67 | 8.00 |
| 155 | .65 | 1.29 | 1.94 | 2.58 | 3.23 | 3.87 | 4.52 | 5.16 | 5.81 | 6.45 | 7.74 |
| 160 | .63 | 1.25 | 1.87 | 2.50 | 3.12 | 3.75 | 4.37 | 5.00 | 5.62 | 6.25 | 7.50 |
| 165 | .61 | 1.21 | 1.82 | 2.42 | 3.03 | 3.64 | 4.24 | 4.85 | 5.45 | 6.06 | 7.27 |
| 170 | .59 | 1.18 | 1.76 | 2.35 | 2.94 | 3.53 | 4.12 | 4.71 | 5.29 | 5.88 | 7.06 |
| 175 | .57 | 1.14 | 1.71 | 2.29 | 2.86 | 3.43 | 4.00 | 4.57 | 5.14 | 5.71 | 6.85 |
| 180 | .56 | 1.11 | 1.67 | 2.22 | 2.78 | 3.33 | 3.89 | 4.44 | 5.00 | 5.56 | 6.67 |
| 185 | .54 | 1.08 | 1.62 | 2.16 | 2.70 | 3.24 | 3.78 | 4.32 | 4.86 | 5.41 | 6.49 |
| 190 | .53 | 1.05 | 1.58 | 2.11 | 2.63 | 3.16 | 3.68 | 4.21 | 4.74 | 5.26 | 6.32 |
| 195 | .51 | 1.03 | 1.54 | 2.05 | 2.56 | 3.08 | 3.59 | 4.10 | 4.62 | 5.13 | 6.15 |
| 200 | .50 | 1.00 | 1.50 | 2.00 | 2.50 | 3.00 | 3.50 | 4.00 | 4.50 | 5.00 | 6.00 |

## INTEREST-YIELDING CAPACITY OF BONDS

Showing the price at which a **three** per cent. bond must be bought to realize from 2 to 6 per cent. per annum.
Interest payable semi-annually.

| Years to Run. | 2 | 2¼ | 2½ | 2¾ | 3 | 3¼ | 3½ | 3¾ | 4 | 4¼ | 4½ | 4¾ | 5 | 5¼ | 5½ | 6 |
|---|---|---|---|---|---|---|---|---|---|---|---|---|---|---|---|---|
| 1.... | 100.99 | 100.74 | 100.49 | 100.24 | 100.00 | 99.76 | 99.51 | 99.27 | 99.03 | 98.79 | 98.55 | 98.31 | 98.07 | 97.84 | 97.60 | 97.13 |
| 2.... | 101.95 | 101.46 | 100.97 | 100.48 | 100.00 | 99.52 | 99.04 | 98.57 | 98.10 | 97.63 | 97.16 | 96.70 | 96.24 | 95.78 | 95.33 | 94.42 |
| 3.... | 102.90 | 102.16 | 101.44 | 100.72 | 100.00 | 99.29 | 98.59 | 97.89 | 97.20 | 96.51 | 95.83 | 95.16 | 94.49 | 93.83 | 93.17 | 91.87 |
| 4.... | 103.83 | 102.85 | 101.89 | 100.94 | 100.00 | 99.07 | 98.15 | 97.24 | 96.34 | 95.45 | 94.56 | 93.69 | 92.83 | 91.98 | 91.13 | 89.47 |
| 5.... | 104.74 | 103.53 | 102.34 | 101.16 | 100.00 | 98.85 | 97.72 | 96.61 | 95.51 | 94.42 | 93.35 | 92.29 | 91.25 | 90.22 | 89.20 | 87.20 |
| 6.... | 105.63 | 104.19 | 102.77 | 101.37 | 100.00 | 98.65 | 97.32 | 96.00 | 94.71 | 93.44 | 92.19 | 90.96 | 89.74 | 88.55 | 87.37 | 85.07 |
| 7.... | 106.50 | 104.83 | 103.19 | 101.58 | 100.00 | 98.45 | 96.92 | 95.42 | 93.95 | 92.50 | 91.08 | 89.68 | 88.31 | 86.96 | 85.64 | 83.06 |
| 8.... | 107.36 | 105.46 | 103.61 | 101.78 | 100.00 | 98.25 | 96.54 | 94.86 | 93.21 | 91.60 | 90.02 | 88.46 | 86.95 | 85.45 | 83.99 | 81.16 |
| 9.... | 108.20 | 106.08 | 104.01 | 101.98 | 100.00 | 98.06 | 96.17 | 94.32 | 92.50 | 90.73 | 89.00 | 87.30 | 85.65 | 84.03 | 82.44 | 79.37 |
| 10.... | 109.02 | 106.68 | 104.40 | 102.17 | 100.00 | 97.88 | 95.81 | 93.79 | 91.82 | 89.90 | 88.03 | 86.20 | 84.41 | 82.67 | 80.97 | 77.68 |
| 11.... | 109.83 | 107.27 | 104.78 | 102.36 | 100.00 | 97.70 | 95.47 | 93.29 | 91.17 | 89.11 | 87.10 | 85.14 | 83.23 | 81.38 | 79.57 | 76.09 |
| 12.... | 110.62 | 107.85 | 105.16 | 102.54 | 100.00 | 97.53 | 95.13 | 92.81 | 90.54 | 88.34 | 86.21 | 84.13 | 82.12 | 80.15 | 78.25 | 74.60 |
| 13.... | 111.40 | 108.41 | 105.52 | 102.72 | 100.00 | 97.37 | 94.81 | 92.31 | 89.94 | 87.61 | 85.36 | 83.17 | 81.05 | 78.99 | 77.00 | 73.18 |
| 14.... | 112.16 | 108.96 | 105.88 | 102.89 | 100.00 | 97.21 | 94.50 | 91.89 | 89.36 | 86.91 | 84.54 | 82.25 | 80.04 | 77.89 | 75.81 | 71.85 |
| 15.... | 112.90 | 109.50 | 106.22 | 103.06 | 100.00 | 97.05 | 94.20 | 91.46 | 88.80 | 86.24 | 83.77 | 81.38 | 79.07 | 76.84 | 74.69 | 70.60 |
| 20.... | 116.42 | 112.03 | 107.83 | 103.83 | 100.00 | 96.34 | 92.85 | 89.51 | 86.32 | 83.27 | 80.35 | 77.57 | 74.90 | 72.34 | 69.90 | 65.33 |
| 25.... | 119.60 | 114.28 | 109.25 | 104.50 | 100.00 | 95.74 | 91.71 | 87.90 | 84.29 | 80.87 | 77.62 | 74.55 | 71.64 | 68.87 | 66.25 | 61.41 |
| 30.... | 122.48 | 116.30 | 110.51 | 105.08 | 100.00 | 95.23 | 90.76 | 86.56 | 82.62 | 78.92 | 75.44 | 72.17 | 69.09 | 66.20 | 63.47 | 58.49 |
| 35.... | 125.08 | 118.10 | 111.62 | 105.60 | 100.00 | 94.80 | 89.96 | 85.45 | 81.25 | 77.34 | 73.69 | 70.28 | 67.10 | 64.13 | 61.35 | 56.31 |
| 40.... | 127.44 | 119.71 | 112.60 | 106.04 | 100.00 | 94.43 | 89.28 | 84.53 | 80.13 | 76.06 | 72.29 | 68.79 | 65.55 | 62.54 | 59.73 | 54.70 |
| 45.... | 129.58 | 121.15 | 113.46 | 106.43 | 100.00 | 94.11 | 88.71 | 83.76 | 79.21 | 75.02 | 71.17 | 67.61 | 64.33 | 61.30 | 58.50 | 53.50 |
| 50.... | 131.51 | 122.44 | 114.23 | 106.77 | 100.00 | 93.84 | 88.23 | 83.12 | 78.45 | 74.18 | 70.27 | 66.68 | 63.39 | 60.35 | 57.56 | 52.60 |
| 60.... | 134.85 | 124.63 | 115.49 | 107.33 | 100.00 | 93.42 | 87.50 | 82.16 | 77.32 | 72.95 | 68.98 | 65.36 | 62.07 | 59.06 | 56.30 | 51.44 |
| 70.... | 137.58 | 126.37 | 116.49 | 107.75 | 100.00 | 93.11 | 86.97 | 81.49 | 76.56 | 72.14 | 68.15 | 64.54 | 61.26 | 58.28 | 55.56 | 50.80 |
| 80.... | 139.82 | 127.77 | 117.26 | 108.07 | 100.00 | 92.89 | 86.60 | 81.02 | 76.05 | 71.61 | 67.62 | 64.02 | 60.77 | 57.82 | 55.14 | 50.44 |
| 90.... | 141.66 | 128.88 | 117.86 | 108.31 | 100.00 | 92.73 | 86.34 | 80.71 | 75.71 | 71.26 | 67.27 | 63.70 | 60.47 | 57.55 | 54.89 | 50.24 |
| 100.... | 143.16 | 129.78 | 118.33 | 108.50 | 100.00 | 92.61 | 86.16 | 80.49 | 75.48 | 71.03 | 67.06 | 63.49 | 60.29 | 57.38 | 54.75 | 50.14 |

## *INTEREST-YIELDING CAPACITY OF BONDS*

Showing the price at which a **three and one-half** per cent. bond must be bought to realize from 2 to 6 per cent. per annum.

Interest payable semi-annually.

| Years to Run. | 2 | 2¼ | 2½ | 2¾ | 3 | 3¼ | 3½ | 3¾ | 4 | 4¼ | 4½ | 4¾ | 5 | 5¼ | 5½ | 6 |
|---|---|---|---|---|---|---|---|---|---|---|---|---|---|---|---|---|
| 1.... | 101.48 | 101.23 | 100.98 | 100.73 | 100.49 | 100.24 | 100.00 | 99.76 | 99.51 | 99.27 | 99.03 | 98.79 | 98.55 | 98.32 | 98.08 | 97.61 |
| 2.... | 102.93 | 102.43 | 101.94 | 101.45 | 100.96 | 100.48 | 100.00 | 99.52 | 99.05 | 98.58 | 98.11 | 97.64 | 97.18 | 96.72 | 96.26 | 95.35 |
| 3.... | 104.35 | 103.61 | 102.87 | 102.15 | 101.42 | 100.71 | 100.00 | 99.30 | 98.60 | 97.91 | 97.22 | 96.54 | 95.87 | 95.20 | 94.54 | 93.23 |
| 4.... | 105.74 | 104.76 | 103.78 | 102.82 | 101.87 | 100.93 | 100.00 | 99.08 | 98.17 | 97.27 | 96.38 | 95.49 | 94.62 | 93.76 | 92.91 | 91.23 |
| 5.... | 107.10 | 105.88 | 104.67 | 103.48 | 102.31 | 101.15 | 100.00 | 98.87 | 97.75 | 96.65 | 95.57 | 94.49 | 93.44 | 92.39 | 91.36 | 89.34 |
| 6.... | 108.44 | 106.98 | 105.54 | 104.12 | 102.73 | 101.35 | 100.00 | 98.67 | 97.36 | 96.06 | 94.79 | 93.54 | 92.31 | 91.09 | 89.90 | 87.56 |
| 7.... | 109.75 | 108.05 | 106.39 | 104.75 | 103.14 | 101.55 | 100.00 | 98.47 | 96.97 | 95.50 | 94.05 | 92.63 | 91.23 | 89.86 | 88.51 | 85.88 |
| 8.... | 111.04 | 109.10 | 107.21 | 105.35 | 103.53 | 101.75 | 100.00 | 98.29 | 96.61 | 94.96 | 93.34 | 91.76 | 90.21 | 88.69 | 87.20 | 84.30 |
| 9.... | 112.30 | 110.13 | 108.01 | 105.94 | 103.92 | 101.94 | 100.00 | 98.11 | 96.25 | 94.44 | 92.67 | 90.93 | 89.23 | 87.58 | 85.95 | 82.81 |
| 10.... | 113.53 | 111.14 | 108.80 | 106.52 | 104.29 | 102.12 | 100.00 | 97.93 | 95.91 | 93.94 | 92.02 | 90.14 | 88.31 | 86.52 | 84.77 | 81.40 |
| 11.... | 114.75 | 112.12 | 109.57 | 107.08 | 104.66 | 102.30 | 100.00 | 97.76 | 95.59 | 93.46 | 91.40 | 89.39 | 87.43 | 85.52 | 83.66 | 80.08 |
| 12.... | 115.93 | 113.08 | 110.31 | 107.62 | 105.01 | 102.47 | 100.00 | 97.60 | 95.27 | 93.01 | 90.81 | 88.67 | 86.59 | 84.56 | 82.60 | 78.83 |
| 13.... | 117.10 | 114.02 | 111.04 | 108.15 | 105.35 | 102.63 | 100.00 | 97.45 | 94.97 | 92.57 | 90.24 | 87.98 | 85.79 | 83.66 | 81.60 | 77.65 |
| 14.... | 118.24 | 114.94 | 111.75 | 108.67 | 105.68 | 102.79 | 100.00 | 97.30 | 94.68 | 92.15 | 89.70 | 87.32 | 85.03 | 82.80 | 80.65 | 76.54 |
| 15.... | 119.36 | 115.84 | 112.44 | 109.17 | 106.00 | 102.95 | 100.00 | 97.15 | 94.40 | 91.74 | 89.18 | 86.70 | 84.30 | 81.99 | 79.75 | 75.50 |
| 20.... | 124.63 | 120.04 | 115.66 | 111.48 | 107.48 | 103.66 | 100.00 | 96.50 | 93.16 | 89.96 | 86.90 | 83.98 | 81.17 | 78.49 | 75.92 | 71.11 |
| 25.... | 129.40 | 123.80 | 118.51 | 113.49 | 108.75 | 104.26 | 100.00 | 95.97 | 92.14 | 88.52 | 85.08 | 81.82 | 78.73 | 75.79 | 73.00 | 67.84 |
| 30... | 133.72 | 127.16 | 121.02 | 115.25 | 109.85 | 104.77 | 100.00 | 95.52 | 91.31 | 87.35 | 83.63 | 80.12 | 76.82 | 73.71 | 70.78 | 65.41 |
| 35.... | 137.62 | 130.17 | 123.23 | 116.79 | 110.79 | 105.20 | 100.00 | 95.15 | 90.63 | 86.40 | 82.46 | 78.77 | 75.33 | 72.10 | 69.08 | 63.60 |
| 40.... | 141.16 | 132.85 | 125.19 | 118.13 | 111.60 | 105.57 | 100.00 | 94.84 | 90.06 | 85.63 | 81.53 | 77.71 | 74.16 | 70.86 | 67.79 | 62.25 |
| 45.... | 144.36 | 135.26 | 126.92 | 119.29 | 112.30 | 105.89 | 100.00 | 94.59 | 89.60 | 85.01 | 80.78 | 76.87 | 73.25 | 69.90 | 66.80 | 61.25 |
| 50.... | 147.26 | 137.41 | 128.45 | 120.31 | 112.91 | 106.16 | 100.00 | 94.37 | 89.23 | 84.51 | 80.18 | 76.20 | 72.54 | 69.16 | 66.05 | 60.50 |
| 60.... | 152.27 | 141.04 | 130.98 | 121.98 | 113.88 | 106.58 | 100.00 | 94.05 | 88.66 | 83.77 | 79.32 | 75.26 | 71.55 | 68.15 | 65.04 | 59.53 |
| 70.... | 156.37 | 143.95 | 132.97 | 123.24 | 114.60 | 106.88 | 100.00 | 93.83 | 88.28 | 83.28 | 78.77 | 74.67 | 70.95 | 67.55 | 64.45 | 59.00 |
| 80.... | 159.73 | 146.28 | 134.52 | 124.20 | 115.13 | 107.11 | 100.00 | 93.67 | 88.03 | 82.96 | 78.41 | 74.30 | 70.58 | 67.19 | 64.11 | 58.70 |
| 90.... | 162.48 | 148.14 | 135.73 | 124.94 | 115.53 | 107.27 | 100.00 | 93.57 | 87.85 | 82.75 | 78.18 | 74.07 | 70.35 | 66.98 | 63.91 | 58.54 |
| 100.... | 164.74 | 149.63 | 136.67 | 125.49 | 115.82 | 107.38 | 100.00 | 93.50 | 87.74 | 82.62 | 78.04 | 73.92 | 70.22 | 66.85 | 63.80 | 58.45 |

# INTEREST-YIELDING CAPACITY OF BONDS

Showing the price at which a **four** per cent. bond must be bought to realize from 2 to 6 per cent. per annum.
Interest payable semi-annually.

| Years to Run. | 2 | 2¼ | 2½ | 2¾ | 3 | 3¼ | 3½ | 3¾ | 4 | 4¼ | 4½ | 4¾ | 5 | 5¼ | 5½ | 6 |
|---|---|---|---|---|---|---|---|---|---|---|---|---|---|---|---|---|
| 1.... | 101.97 | 101.72 | 101.47 | 101.22 | 100.98 | 100.73 | 100.49 | 100.24 | 100.00 | 99.76 | 99.52 | 99.28 | 99.04 | 98.80 | 98.56 | 98.09 |
| 2.... | 103.90 | 103.40 | 102.91 | 102.42 | 101.93 | 101.44 | 100.96 | 100.48 | 100.00 | 99.53 | 99.05 | 98.59 | 98.12 | 97.66 | 97.20 | 96.28 |
| 3.... | 105.80 | 105.05 | 104.31 | 103.58 | 102.85 | 102.13 | 101.41 | 100.70 | 100.00 | 99.30 | 98.61 | 97.93 | 97.25 | 96.57 | 95.00 | 94.58 |
| 4.... | 107.65 | 106.66 | 105.68 | 104.70 | 103.74 | 102.79 | 101.85 | 100.92 | 100.00 | 99.09 | 98.19 | 97.30 | 96.41 | 95.54 | 94.68 | 97.98 |
| 5.... | 109.47 | 108.23 | 107.01 | 105.80 | 104.61 | 103.44 | 102.28 | 101.13 | 100.00 | 98.88 | 97.78 | 96.70 | 95.62 | 94.57 | 93.52 | 91.47 |
| 6.... | 111.26 | 109.77 | 108.31 | 106.87 | 105.45 | 104.06 | 102.68 | 101.33 | 100.00 | 98.69 | 97.40 | 96.12 | 94.87 | 93.64 | 92.42 | 90.05 |
| 7.... | 113.00 | 111.28 | 109.58 | 107.91 | 106.27 | 104.66 | 103.08 | 101.53 | 100.00 | 98.50 | 97.03 | 95.58 | 94.15 | 92.76 | 91.38 | 88.70 |
| 8... | 114.72 | 112.75 | 110.82 | 108.92 | 107.07 | 105.25 | 103.46 | 101.71 | 100.00 | 98.32 | 96.67 | 95.06 | 93.47 | 91.92 | 90.40 | 87.44 |
| 9.... | 116.40 | 114.19 | 112.02 | 109.91 | 107.84 | 105.81 | 103.83 | 101.89 | 100.00 | 98.15 | 96.33 | 94.56 | 92.82 | 91.13 | 89.46 | 86.25 |
| 10.... | 118.05 | 115.59 | 113.20 | 110.86 | 108.58 | 106.36 | 104.19 | 102.07 | 100.00 | 97.98 | 96.01 | 94.08 | 92.21 | 90.37 | 88.58 | 85.12 |
| 11.... | 119.66 | 116.97 | 114.35 | 111.80 | 109.31 | 106.89 | 104.53 | 102.24 | 100.00 | 97.82 | 95.70 | 93.63 | 91.62 | 89.65 | 87.74 | 84.06 |
| 12.... | 121.24 | 118.31 | 115.47 | 112.70 | 110.02 | 107.40 | 104.87 | 102.40 | 100.00 | 97.67 | 95.40 | 93.20 | 91.06 | 88.97 | 86.95 | 83.06 |
| 13.... | 122.80 | 119.63 | 116.56 | 113.59 | 110.70 | 107.90 | 105.19 | 102.55 | 100.00 | 97.52 | 95.12 | 92.79 | 90.52 | 88.33 | 86.20 | 82.12 |
| 14.... | 124.32 | 120.92 | 117.63 | 114.44 | 111.36 | 108.38 | 105.50 | 102.70 | 100.00 | 97.38 | 94.85 | 92.39 | 90.02 | 87.72 | 85.49 | 81.24 |
| 15.... | 125.81 | 122.17 | 118.67 | 115.28 | 112.01 | 108.85 | 105.80 | 102.85 | 100.00 | 97.25 | 94.59 | 92.02 | 89.53 | 87.13 | 84.81 | 80.40 |
| 20.... | 132.83 | 128.06 | 123.50 | 119.13 | 114.96 | 110.97 | 107.15 | 103.50 | 100.00 | 96.65 | 93.45 | 90.39 | 87.45 | 84.64 | 81.94 | 76.89 |
| 25.... | 139.20 | 133.32 | 127.76 | 122.49 | 117.50 | 112.77 | 108.29 | 104.03 | 100.00 | 96.17 | 92.54 | 89.09 | 85.82 | 82.71 | 79.75 | 74.27 |
| 30.... | 144.96 | 138.03 | 131.53 | 125.42 | 119.69 | 114.30 | 109.24 | 104.48 | 100.00 | 95.78 | 91.81 | 88.07 | 84.55 | 81.22 | 78.08 | 72.32 |
| 35.... | 150.16 | 142.23 | 134.85 | 127.98 | 121.58 | 115.61 | 110.04 | 104.85 | 100.00 | 95.47 | 91.23 | 87.26 | 83.55 | 80.07 | 76.81 | 70.88 |
| 40.... | 154.88 | 146.00 | 137.79 | 130.21 | 123.20 | 116.72 | 110.72 | 105.16 | 100.00 | 95.21 | 90.76 | 86.63 | 82.77 | 79.19 | 75.84 | 69.80 |
| 45.... | 159.15 | 149.36 | 140.38 | 132.16 | 124.60 | 117.67 | 111.29 | 105.41 | 100.00 | 95.00 | 90.39 | 86.12 | 82.17 | 78.50 | 75.10 | 69.00 |
| 50.... | 163.02 | 152.37 | 142.68 | 133.85 | 125.81 | 118.47 | 111.77 | 105.63 | 100.00 | 94.84 | 90.09 | 85.72 | 81.69 | 77.97 | 74.51 | 68.40 |
| 60.... | 169.69 | 157.46 | 146.48 | 136.64 | 127.75 | 119.74 | 112.50 | 105.95 | 100.00 | 94.59 | 89.66 | 85.15 | 81.03 | 77.25 | 73.78 | 67.63 |
| 70.... | 175.16 | 161.53 | 149.46 | 138.73 | 129.19 | 120.65 | 113.02 | 106.17 | 100.00 | 94.43 | 89.36 | 84.80 | 80.63 | 76.82 | 73.34 | 67.20 |
| 80.... | 179.64 | 164.79 | 151.78 | 140.34 | 130.26 | 121.32 | 113.39 | 106.33 | 100.00 | 94.32 | 89.21 | 84.58 | 80.39 | 76.57 | 73.08 | 66.96 |
| 90.... | 183.31 | 167.39 | 153.59 | 141.56 | 131.05 | 121.80 | 113.65 | 106.43 | 100.00 | 94.25 | 89.09 | 84.44 | 80.24 | 76.41 | 72.94 | 66.83 |
| 100.... | 186.33 | 169.48 | 154.99 | 142.49 | 131.64 | 122.15 | 113.83 | 106.51 | 100.00 | 94.21 | 89.02 | 84.35 | 80.14 | 76.32 | 72.85 | 66.76 |

## INTEREST-YIELDING CAPACITY OF BONDS

Showing the price at which a **four and one-half** per cent. bond must be bought to realize from 2 to 6 per cent. per annum. Interest payable semi-annually.

| Years to Run. | 2 | 2½ | 2¾ | 3 | 3¼ | 3½ | 3¾ | 4 | 4¼ | 4½ | 4¾ | 5 | 5¼ | 5½ | 5¾ | 6 |
|---|---|---|---|---|---|---|---|---|---|---|---|---|---|---|---|---|
| 1.... | 102.46 | 101.96 | 101.71 | 101.47 | 101.22 | 100.97 | 100.73 | 100.49 | 100.24 | 100.00 | 99.76 | 99.52 | 99.28 | 99.04 | 98.80 | 98.56 |
| 2.... | 104.88 | 103.88 | 103.38 | 102.89 | 102.40 | 101.92 | 101.43 | 100.95 | 100.47 | 100.00 | 99.53 | 99.06 | 98.59 | 98.13 | 97.67 | 97.21 |
| 3.... | 107.24 | 105.75 | 105.01 | 104.27 | 103.55 | 102.82 | 102.11 | 101.40 | 100.70 | 100.00 | 99.31 | 98.62 | 97.94 | 97.27 | 96.60 | 95.94 |
| 4.... | 109.56 | 107.57 | 106.59 | 105.61 | 104.65 | 103.70 | 102.76 | 101.83 | 100.91 | 100.00 | 99.10 | 98.21 | 97.33 | 96.45 | 95.59 | 94.74 |
| 5.... | 111.84 | 109.35 | 108.12 | 106.92 | 105.73 | 104.55 | 103.39 | 102.25 | 101.12 | 100.00 | 98.90 | 97.81 | 96.74 | 95.68 | 94.63 | 93.60 |
| 6.... | 114.07 | 111.08 | 109.62 | 108.18 | 106.76 | 105.37 | 104.00 | 102.64 | 101.31 | 100.00 | 98.71 | 97.44 | 96.18 | 94.95 | 93.73 | 92.53 |
| 7.... | 116.25 | 112.77 | 111.07 | 109.41 | 107.77 | 106.16 | 104.58 | 103.03 | 101.50 | 100.00 | 98.53 | 97.08 | 95.65 | 94.25 | 92.88 | 91.53 |
| 8.... | 118.40 | 114.42 | 112.49 | 110.60 | 108.74 | 106.93 | 105.14 | 103.39 | 101.68 | 100.00 | 98.35 | 96.74 | 95.15 | 93.60 | 92.07 | 90.58 |
| 9.... | 120.50 | 116.03 | 113.87 | 111.75 | 109.69 | 107.66 | 105.68 | 103.75 | 101.85 | 100.00 | 98.19 | 96.41 | 94.68 | 92.98 | 91.31 | 89.68 |
| 10.... | 122.56 | 117.60 | 115.21 | 112.88 | 110.60 | 108.38 | 106.21 | 104.09 | 102.02 | 100.00 | 98.03 | 96.10 | 94.22 | 92.39 | 90.59 | 88.84 |
| 11.... | 124.58 | 119.13 | 116.51 | 113.97 | 111.48 | 109.07 | 106.71 | 104.41 | 102.18 | 100.00 | 97.88 | 95.81 | 93.79 | 91.83 | 89.91 | 88.05 |
| 12.... | 126.55 | 120.62 | 117.78 | 115.02 | 112.34 | 109.73 | 107.19 | 104.73 | 102.33 | 100.00 | 97.73 | 95.53 | 93.38 | 91.30 | 89.27 | 87.30 |
| 13.... | 128.49 | 122.08 | 119.02 | 116.05 | 113.17 | 110.37 | 107.66 | 105.03 | 102.48 | 100.00 | 97.60 | 95.26 | 93.00 | 90.80 | 88.66 | 86.59 |
| 14.... | 130.40 | 123.50 | 120.22 | 117.05 | 113.97 | 110.99 | 108.11 | 105.32 | 102.62 | 100.00 | 97.46 | 95.01 | 92.63 | 90.32 | 88.09 | 85.93 |
| 15.... | 132.26 | 124.89 | 121.39 | 118.01 | 114.75 | 111.59 | 108.54 | 105.60 | 102.75 | 100.00 | 97.34 | 94.77 | 92.28 | 89.88 | 87.55 | 85.30 |
| 20.... | 141.04 | 131.33 | 126.78 | 122.44 | 118.28 | 114.30 | 110.49 | 106.84 | 103.35 | 100.00 | 96.80 | 93.72 | 90.78 | 87.96 | 85.26 | 82.66 |
| 25.... | 149.00 | 137.01 | 131.49 | 126.25 | 121.28 | 116.57 | 112.10 | 107.86 | 103.83 | 100.00 | 96.36 | 92.91 | 89.62 | 86.50 | 83.53 | 80.70 |
| 30.... | 156.19 | 142.03 | 135.59 | 129.54 | 123.84 | 118.48 | 113.44 | 108.69 | 104.22 | 100.00 | 96.02 | 92.27 | 88.73 | 85.39 | 82.23 | 79.24 |
| 35.... | 162.70 | 146.47 | 139.17 | 132.37 | 126.02 | 120.09 | 114.55 | 109.37 | 104.53 | 100.00 | 95.75 | 91.78 | 88.04 | 84.54 | 81.25 | 78.16 |
| 40.... | 168.60 | 150.39 | 142.29 | 134.81 | 127.87 | 121.44 | 115.47 | 109.94 | 104.79 | 100.00 | 95.54 | 91.39 | 87.51 | 83.89 | 80.51 | 77.35 |
| 45.... | 173.94 | 153.85 | 145.02 | 136.91 | 129.45 | 122.58 | 116.24 | 110.40 | 105.00 | 100.00 | 95.37 | 91.08 | 87.10 | 83.40 | 79.96 | 76.75 |
| 50.... | 178.79 | 156.90 | 147.40 | 138.72 | 130.79 | 123.53 | 116.88 | 110.77 | 105.16 | 100.00 | 95.24 | 90.85 | 86.78 | 83.02 | 79.54 | 76.30 |
| 60.... | 187.12 | 161.98 | 151.28 | 141.63 | 132.89 | 125.00 | 117.84 | 111.34 | 105.41 | 100.00 | 95.05 | 90.52 | 86.35 | 82.52 | 78.99 | 75.72 |
| 70.... | 193.95 | 165.95 | 154.23 | 143.79 | 134.42 | 126.05 | 118.51 | 111.72 | 105.57 | 100.00 | 94.93 | 90.32 | 86.09 | 82.23 | 78.67 | 75.40 |
| 80.... | 199.55 | 169.04 | 156.48 | 145.39 | 135.53 | 126.79 | 118.98 | 111.97 | 105.68 | 100.00 | 94.86 | 90.19 | 85.94 | 82.06 | 78.49 | 75.22 |
| 90.... | 204.14 | 171.45 | 158.19 | 146.58 | 136.35 | 127.31 | 119.29 | 112.15 | 105.75 | 100.00 | 94.81 | 90.12 | 85.85 | 81.96 | 78.39 | 75.12 |
| 100.... | 207.90 | 173.33 | 159.50 | 147.46 | 136.92 | 127.68 | 119.51 | 112.26 | 105.79 | 100.00 | 94.78 | 90.07 | 85.79 | 81.90 | 78.34 | 75.07 |

## INTEREST-YIELDING CAPACITY OF BONDS

Showing the price at which a five per cent. bond must be bought to realize from 3 to 7 per cent. per annum.
Interest payable semi-annually.

| Years to Run. | 3 | 3¼ | 3½ | 3¾ | 4 | 4¼ | 4½ | 4¾ | 5 | 5¼ | 5½ | 5¾ | 6 | 6¼ | 6½ | 7 |
|---|---|---|---|---|---|---|---|---|---|---|---|---|---|---|---|---|
| 1.... | 101.96 | 101.71 | 101.46 | 101.22 | 100.97 | 100.73 | 100.48 | 100.24 | 100.00 | 99.76 | 99.52 | 99.28 | 99.04 | 98.81 | 98.57 | 98.10 |
| 2.... | 103.85 | 103.36 | 102.87 | 102.39 | 101.90 | 101.42 | 100.95 | 100.47 | 100.00 | 99.53 | 99.07 | 98.60 | 98.14 | 97.68 | 97.23 | 96.33 |
| 3.... | 105.70 | 104.96 | 104.24 | 103.52 | 102.80 | 102.09 | 101.39 | 100.69 | 100.00 | 99.31 | 98.63 | 97.96 | 97.29 | 96.63 | 95.97 | 94.67 |
| 4.... | 107.49 | 106.51 | 105.55 | 104.60 | 103.66 | 102.73 | 101.81 | 100.90 | 100.00 | 99.11 | 98.23 | 97.35 | 96.49 | 95.64 | 94.79 | 93.13 |
| 5.... | 109.22 | 108.02 | 106.83 | 105.65 | 104.49 | 103.35 | 102.22 | 101.10 | 100.00 | 98.91 | 97.84 | 96.78 | 95.73 | 94.70 | 93.68 | 91.68 |
| 6.... | 110.91 | 109.47 | 108.05 | 106.66 | 105.29 | 103.94 | 102.60 | 101.29 | 100.00 | 98.73 | 97.47 | 96.24 | 95.02 | 93.82 | 92.64 | 90.34 |
| 7.... | 112.54 | 110.88 | 109.24 | 107.63 | 106.05 | 104.50 | 102.97 | 101.47 | 100.00 | 98.55 | 97.13 | 95.73 | 94.35 | 93.00 | 91.67 | 89.08 |
| 8.... | 114.13 | 112.24 | 110.39 | 108.57 | 106.79 | 105.04 | 103.33 | 101.65 | 100.00 | 98.38 | 96.80 | 95.24 | 93.72 | 92.22 | 90.76 | 87.91 |
| 9.... | 115.67 | 113.56 | 111.50 | 109.47 | 107.50 | 105.56 | 103.67 | 101.81 | 100.00 | 98.23 | 96.49 | 94.79 | 93.12 | 91.49 | 89.90 | 86.81 |
| 10.... | 117.17 | 114.84 | 112.56 | 110.34 | 108.18 | 106.06 | 103.99 | 101.97 | 100.00 | 98.07 | 96.19 | 94.36 | 92.56 | 90.81 | 89.10 | 85.79 |
| 11.... | 118.62 | 116.08 | 113.60 | 111.18 | 108.83 | 106.54 | 104.30 | 102.12 | 100.00 | 97.93 | 95.91 | 93.95 | 92.03 | 90.16 | 88.34 | 84.83 |
| 12.... | 120.03 | 117.27 | 114.60 | 111.99 | 109.46 | 106.99 | 104.60 | 102.27 | 100.00 | 97.79 | 95.65 | 93.56 | 91.53 | 89.56 | 87.63 | 83.94 |
| 13.... | 121.40 | 118.43 | 115.56 | 112.77 | 110.06 | 107.43 | 104.88 | 102.40 | 100.00 | 97.67 | 95.40 | 93.20 | 91.06 | 88.99 | 86.97 | 83.11 |
| 14.... | 122.73 | 119.56 | 116.49 | 113.52 | 110.64 | 107.85 | 105.15 | 102.54 | 100.00 | 97.54 | 95.16 | 92.85 | 90.62 | 88.45 | 86.13 | 82.33 |
| 15.... | 124.02 | 120.65 | 117.39 | 114.24 | 111.20 | 108.26 | 105.41 | 102.66 | 100.00 | 97.43 | 94.94 | 92.53 | 90.20 | 87.95 | 85.76 | 81.61 |
| 20.... | 129.92 | 125.59 | 121.45 | 117.48 | 113.68 | 110.04 | 106.55 | 103.20 | 100.00 | 96.93 | 93.98 | 91.15 | 88.44 | 85.84 | 83.34 | 78.64 |
| 25.... | 135.00 | 129.80 | 124.86 | 120.17 | 115.71 | 111.48 | 107.46 | 103.64 | 100.00 | 96.54 | 93.25 | 90.12 | 87.14 | 84.29 | 81.59 | 76.54 |
| 30.... | 139.38 | 133.38 | 127.72 | 122.40 | 117.38 | 112.65 | 108.19 | 103.98 | 100.00 | 96.24 | 92.69 | 89.34 | 86.16 | 83.16 | 80.31 | 75.06 |
| 35.... | 143.15 | 136.42 | 130.13 | 124.25 | 118.75 | 113.60 | 108.77 | 104.25 | 100.00 | 96.01 | 92.27 | 88.75 | 85.44 | 82.32 | 79.38 | 74.00 |
| 40.... | 146.41 | 139.02 | 132.16 | 125.79 | 119.87 | 114.37 | 109.24 | 104.46 | 100.00 | 95.84 | 91.95 | 88.31 | 84.90 | 81.71 | 78.71 | 73.25 |
| 45.... | 149.21 | 141.22 | 133.86 | 127.07 | 120.79 | 114.99 | 109.61 | 104.63 | 100.00 | 95.70 | 91.70 | 87.97 | 84.50 | 81.25 | 78.22 | 72.72 |
| 50.... | 151.62 | 143.10 | 135.30 | 128.13 | 121.55 | 115.49 | 109.91 | 104.76 | 100.00 | 95.59 | 91.51 | 87.72 | 84.20 | 80.92 | 77.87 | 72.34 |
| 60.... | 155.50 | 146.07 | 137.51 | 129.75 | 122.68 | 116.23 | 110.34 | 104.95 | 100.00 | 95.45 | 91.26 | 87.39 | 83.81 | 80.50 | 77.42 | 71.89 |
| 70.... | 158.37 | 148.21 | 139.08 | 130.85 | 123.44 | 116.72 | 110.62 | 105.07 | 100.00 | 95.36 | 91.11 | 87.20 | 83.60 | 80.27 | 77.19 | 71.66 |
| 80.... | 160.51 | 149.76 | 140.19 | 131.62 | 123.95 | 117.04 | 110.80 | 105.14 | 100.00 | 95.31 | 91.03 | 87.10 | 83.48 | 80.15 | 77.06 | 71.54 |
| 90.... | 162.10 | 150.89 | 140.97 | 132.15 | 124.29 | 117.25 | 110.91 | 105.19 | 100.00 | 95.28 | 90.98 | 87.04 | 83.41 | 80.08 | 77.00 | 71.49 |
| 100.... | 163.27 | 151.71 | 141.52 | 132.52 | 124.52 | 117.38 | 110.98 | 105.22 | 100.00 | 95.26 | 90.95 | 87.00 | 83.38 | 80.04 | 76.96 | 71.46 |

## *INTEREST-YIELDING CAPACITY OF BONDS*

Showing the price at which a **six** per cent. bond must be bought to realize from 3 to 7 per cent. per annum. Interest payable semi-annually.

| Years to Run. | 3 | 3¼ | 3½ | 3¾ | 4 | 4¼ | 4½ | 4¾ | 5 | 5¼ | 5½ | 5¾ | 6 | 6¼ | 6½ | 7 |
|---|---|---|---|---|---|---|---|---|---|---|---|---|---|---|---|---|
| 1..... | 102.93 | 102.68 | 102.44 | 102.19 | 101.94 | 101.70 | 101.45 | 101.21 | 100.96 | 100.72 | 100.48 | 100.24 | 100.00 | 99.76 | 99.52 | 99.05 |
| 2..... | 105.78 | 105.28 | 104.79 | 104.30 | 103.81 | 103.32 | 102.84 | 102.36 | 101.88 | 101.41 | 100.93 | 100.47 | 100.00 | 99.54 | 99.08 | 98.16 |
| 3..... | 108.55 | 107.80 | 107.06 | 106.33 | 105.60 | 104.88 | 104.17 | 103.46 | 102.75 | 102.06 | 101.37 | 100.68 | 100.00 | 99.33 | 98.66 | 97.34 |
| 4..... | 111.23 | 110.24 | 109.26 | 108.29 | 107.33 | 106.38 | 105.44 | 104.51 | 103.59 | 102.67 | 101.77 | 100.88 | 100.00 | 99.13 | 98.26 | 96.56 |
| 5..... | 113.83 | 112.60 | 111.38 | 110.17 | 108.98 | 107.81 | 106.65 | 105.51 | 104.38 | 103.26 | 102.16 | 101.07 | 100.00 | 98.94 | 97.89 | 95.84 |
| 6..... | 116.36 | 114.88 | 113.42 | 111.99 | 110.58 | 109.18 | 107.81 | 106.46 | 105.13 | 103.82 | 102.53 | 101.25 | 100.00 | 98.76 | 97.55 | 95.17 |
| 7..... | 118.82 | 117.09 | 115.40 | 113.74 | 112.11 | 110.50 | 108.92 | 107.37 | 105.85 | 104.35 | 102.87 | 101.42 | 100.00 | 98.60 | 97.22 | 94.54 |
| 8..... | 121.20 | 119.24 | 117.31 | 115.43 | 113.58 | 111.76 | 109.98 | 108.24 | 106.53 | 104.85 | 103.20 | 101.59 | 100.00 | 98.44 | 96.92 | 93.95 |
| 9..... | 123.51 | 121.31 | 119.16 | 117.05 | 114.99 | 112.97 | 111.00 | 109.07 | 107.18 | 105.32 | 103.51 | 101.74 | 100.00 | 98.30 | 96.63 | 93.41 |
| 10..... | 125.75 | 123.32 | 120.94 | 118.62 | 116.35 | 114.14 | 111.97 | 109.86 | 107.79 | 105.78 | 103.81 | 101.88 | 100.00 | 98.16 | 96.37 | 92.89 |
| 11..... | 127.93 | 125.26 | 122.68 | 120.13 | 117.66 | 115.25 | 112.90 | 110.61 | 108.38 | 106.21 | 104.09 | 102.02 | 100.00 | 98.03 | 96.11 | 92.42 |
| 12..... | 130.05 | 127.15 | 124.33 | 121.58 | 118.91 | 116.32 | 113.79 | 111.33 | 108.94 | 106.62 | 104.35 | 102.15 | 100.00 | 97.91 | 95.88 | 91.97 |
| 13..... | 132.10 | 128.97 | 125.93 | 122.98 | 120.12 | 117.34 | 114.64 | 112.02 | 109.48 | 107.00 | 104.60 | 102.27 | 100.00 | 97.80 | 95.66 | 91.55 |
| 14..... | 134.09 | 130.73 | 127.48 | 124.33 | 121.28 | 118.32 | 115.46 | 112.68 | 109.98 | 107.37 | 104.84 | 102.38 | 100.00 | 97.69 | 95.45 | 91.17 |
| 15..... | 136.02 | 132.44 | 128.98 | 125.63 | 122.40 | 119.26 | 116.23 | 113.30 | 110.47 | 107.72 | 105.06 | 102.49 | 100.00 | 97.59 | 95.25 | 90.80 |
| 16..... | 137.90 | 134.10 | 130.43 | 126.89 | 123.47 | 120.17 | 116.98 | 113.90 | 110.92 | 108.05 | 105.28 | 102.59 | 100.00 | 97.49 | 95.07 | 90.47 |
| 17..... | 139.72 | 135.70 | 131.83 | 128.10 | 124.50 | 121.03 | 117.69 | 114.47 | 111.36 | 108.37 | 105.48 | 102.69 | 100.00 | 97.41 | 94.90 | 90.15 |
| 18..... | 141.49 | 137.25 | 133.18 | 129.26 | 125.49 | 121.86 | 118.37 | 115.01 | 111.78 | 108.67 | 105.67 | 102.78 | 100.00 | 97.32 | 94.74 | 89.85 |
| 19..... | 143.21 | 138.76 | 134.48 | 130.38 | 126.44 | 122.66 | 119.02 | 115.53 | 112.17 | 108.95 | 105.85 | 102.87 | 100.00 | 97.24 | 94.59 | 89.58 |
| 20..... | 144.87 | 140.21 | 135.74 | 131.46 | 127.36 | 123.42 | 119.65 | 116.02 | 112.55 | 109.22 | 106.02 | 102.95 | 100.00 | 97.17 | 94.45 | 89.32 |
| 25..... | 152.50 | 146.82 | 141.43 | 136.30 | 131.42 | 126.79 | 122.38 | 118.18 | 114.18 | 110.38 | 106.75 | 103.29 | 100.00 | 96.86 | 93.86 | 88.27 |
| 30..... | 159.07 | 152.45 | 146.20 | 140.32 | 134.76 | 129.52 | 124.56 | 119.88 | 115.45 | 111.27 | 107.31 | 103.55 | 100.00 | 96.63 | 93.44 | 87.53 |
| 35..... | 164.73 | 157.24 | 150.22 | 143.65 | 137.50 | 131.73 | 126.31 | 121.23 | 116.45 | 111.96 | 107.73 | 103.75 | 100.00 | 96.46 | 93.13 | 87.00 |
| 40..... | 169.61 | 161.31 | 153.60 | 146.42 | 139.74 | 133.52 | 127.71 | 122.29 | 117.23 | 112.49 | 108.05 | 103.90 | 100.00 | 96.34 | 92.90 | 86.63 |
| 45..... | 173.81 | 164.78 | 156.44 | 148.73 | 141.59 | 134.97 | 128.83 | 123.13 | 117.83 | 112.90 | 108.30 | 104.01 | 100.00 | 96.25 | 92.74 | 86.36 |
| 50..... | 177.44 | 167.73 | 158.83 | 150.64 | 143.10 | 136.15 | 129.73 | 123.80 | 118.31 | 113.22 | 108.49 | 104.09 | 100.00 | 96.18 | 92.62 | 86.17 |

## INTEREST-YIELDING CAPACITY OF BONDS

Showing the price at which a **seven** per cent. bond must be bought to realize from 3 to 7 per cent. per annum.
Interest payable semi-annually.

| Years to Run. | 3 | 3¼ | 3½ | 3¾ | 4 | 4¼ | 4½ | 4¾ | 5 | 5¼ | 5½ | 5¾ | 6 | 6¼ | 6½ | 7 |
|---|---|---|---|---|---|---|---|---|---|---|---|---|---|---|---|---|
| 1 .. | [illegible] | 103.66 | 103.41 | 103.16 | 102.91 | 102.66 | 102.42 | 102.17 | 101.93 | 101.68 | 101.44 | 101.20 | 100.96 | 100.72 | 100.48 | 100.00 |
| 2..... | 107.71 | 107.20 | 106.70 | 106.21 | 105.71 | 105.22 | 104.73 | 104.25 | 103.76 | 103.28 | 102.80 | 102.33 | 101.86 | 101.39 | 100.92 | 100.00 |
| 3..... | 111.39 | 110.64 | 109.89 | 109.14 | 108.40 | 107.67 | 106.94 | 106.22 | 105.51 | 104.80 | 104.10 | 103.40 | 102.71 | 102.02 | 101.34 | 100.00 |
| 4..... | 114.97 | 113.96 | 112.96 | 111.97 | 110.99 | 110.02 | 109.06 | 108.11 | 107.17 | 106.24 | 105.32 | 104.41 | 103.51 | 102.62 | 101.74 | 100.00 |
| 5..... | 118.44 | 117.18 | 115.93 | 114.69 | 113.47 | 112.27 | 111.08 | 109.91 | 108.75 | 107.61 | 106.48 | 105.37 | 104.27 | 103.18 | 102.11 | 100.00 |
| 6..... | 121.82 | 120.29 | 118.79 | 117.32 | 115.86 | 114.43 | 113.02 | 111.63 | 110.26 | 108.91 | 107.58 | 106.27 | 104.98 | 103.71 | 102.45 | 100.00 |
| 7..... | 125.09 | 123.31 | 121.56 | 119.85 | 118.16 | 116.50 | 114.87 | 113.27 | 111.69 | 110.14 | 108.62 | 107.12 | 105.65 | 104.20 | 102.78 | 100.00 |
| 8..... | 128.26 | 126.23 | 124.24 | 122.28 | 120.37 | 118.49 | 116.64 | 114.83 | 113.05 | 111.31 | 109.60 | 107.93 | 106.28 | 104.67 | 103.08 | 100.00 |
| 9..... | 131.35 | 129.06 | 126.82 | 124.63 | 122.49 | 120.39 | 118.33 | 116.32 | 114.35 | 112.42 | 110.54 | 108.69 | 106.88 | 105.10 | 103.37 | 100.00 |
| 10..... | 134.34 | 131.80 | 129.32 | 126.89 | 124.53 | 122.21 | 119.95 | 117.75 | 115.59 | 113.48 | 111.42 | 109.41 | 107.44 | 105.52 | 103.63 | 100.00 |
| 11..... | 137.24 | 134.45 | 131.73 | 129.07 | 126.49 | 123.96 | 121.50 | 119.11 | 116.77 | 114.48 | 112.26 | 110.09 | 107.97 | 105.90 | 103.89 | 100.00 |
| 12..... | 140.06 | 137.02 | 134.06 | 131.17 | 128.37 | 125.64 | 122.99 | 120.40 | 117.88 | 115.44 | 113.05 | 110.73 | 108.47 | 106.27 | 104.12 | 100.00 |
| 13..... | 142.80 | 139.50 | 136.31 | 133.20 | 130.18 | 127.25 | 124.40 | 121.64 | 118.95 | 116.34 | 113.80 | 111.34 | 108.94 | 106.61 | 104.34 | 100.00 |
| 14..... | 145.45 | 141.91 | 138.48 | 135.15 | 131.92 | 128.79 | 125.76 | 122.82 | 119.96 | 117.20 | 114.51 | 111.91 | 109.38 | 106.93 | 104.55 | 100.00 |
| 15..... | 148.03 | 144.24 | 140.58 | 137.03 | 133.59 | 130.27 | 127.06 | 123.94 | 120.93 | 118.01 | 115.19 | 112.45 | 109.80 | 107.23 | 104.75 | 100.00 |
| 16..... | [illegible] | 146.50 | 142.60 | 138.84 | 135.20 | 131.69 | 128.30 | 125.02 | 121.85 | 118.79 | 115.83 | 112.96 | 110.19 | 107.52 | 104.93 | 100.00 |
| 17..... | 152.96 | 148.68 | 144.56 | 140.58 | 136.75 | 133.05 | 129.48 | 126.04 | 122.72 | 119.52 | 116.43 | 113.45 | 110.57 | 107.78 | 105.10 | 100.00 |
| 18..... | 155.32 | 150.80 | 146.45 | 142.26 | 138.23 | 134.35 | 130.62 | 127.02 | 123.56 | 120.22 | 117.00 | 113.90 | 110.92 | 108.04 | 105.26 | 100.00 |
| 19..... | 157.61 | 152.85 | 148.28 | 143.88 | 139.66 | 135.60 | 131.70 | 127.95 | 124.35 | 120.88 | 117.54 | 114.34 | 111.25 | 108.27 | 105.41 | 100.00 |
| 20..... | 159.83 | 154.83 | 150.04 | 145.44 | 141.03 | 136.80 | 132.74 | 128.84 | 125.10 | 121.51 | 118.06 | 114.74 | 111.56 | 108.50 | 105.55 | 100.00 |
| 25..... | 170.00 | 163.85 | 158.00 | 152.43 | 147.14 | 142.09 | 137.29 | 132.72 | 128.36 | 124.21 | 120.25 | 116.47 | 112.86 | 109.42 | 106.14 | 10.000 |
| 30..... | 178.76 | 171.52 | 164.69 | 158.24 | 152.14 | 146.38 | 140.94 | 135.78 | 130.91 | 126.29 | 121.92 | 117.77 | 113.84 | 110.11 | 106.56 | 100.00 |
| 35..... | 186.31 | 178.05 | 170.31 | 163.06 | 156.25 | 149.86 | 143.85 | 138.21 | 132.90 | 127.90 | 123.19 | 118.75 | 114.56 | 110.61 | 106.87 | 100.00 |
| 40..... | [illegible] | 183.61 | 175.04 | 167.06 | 159.62 | 152.67 | 146.19 | 140.12 | 134.45 | 129.14 | 124.16 | 119.49 | 115.10 | 110.98 | 107.10 | 100.00 |
| 45..... | [illegible] | 188.34 | 179.02 | 170.38 | 162.38 | 154.95 | 148.06 | 141.64 | 135.67 | 130.10 | 124.90 | 120.04 | 115.50 | 111.25 | 107.26 | 100.00 |
| 50..... | 203.25 | 192.37 | 182.36 | 173.14 | 164.65 | 156.80 | 149.55 | 142.84 | 136.61 | 130.84 | 125.46 | 120.46 | 115.80 | 111.45 | 107.38 | 100.00 |

# INTEREST LAWS IN THE UNITED STATES

Laws of each State and Territory regarding the Rates of Interest and Penalties for Usury, with the Law or Custom as to Days of Grace on Notes and Drafts.

AUTHORITY OF THE LATEST STATUTES.

| States and Territories. | Legal Rate of Interest. | Rate Allowed by Contract. | Penalties for Usury. | Grace or No Grace. |
|---|---|---|---|---|
| | Per Cent. | Per Cent. | | |
| Alabama | 8 | 8 | Forfeiture of entire interest. | Grace. |
| Arizona | 6 | Any rate. | None. | No grace. |
| Arkansas | 6 | 10 | Forfeiture of principal and interest. | Grace. |
| California | 7 | Any rate. | None. | No grace. |
| Colorado | 8 | Any rate. | None. | No grace. |
| Connecticut | 6 | ‡Any rate. | None. | No grace. |
| Dakota, North | 7 | 12 | Forfeiture of double the interest. | No grace. |
| Dakota, South | 7 | 12 | Forfeiture of interest. | Grace. |
| Delaware | 6 | 6 | Forfeiture of principal. | No grace. |
| District of Columbia | 6 | 10 | Forfeiture of entire interest. | No grace. |
| Florida | 8 | 10 | Forfeiture of interest. | No grace. |
| Georgia | 7 | 8 | Forfeiture of excess of interest. | Grace. |
| Idaho | 7 | 12 | None. | No grace. |
| Illinois | 5 | 7 | Forfeiture of entire interest. | No grace. |
| Indian Territory | 6 | 10 | Forfeiture of principal and interest. | Grace. |
| Indiana | 6 | 8 | Forfeiture of excess of interest. | Grace. |
| Iowa | 8 | 8 | Forfeiture of interest and costs. | Grace. |
| Kansas | 6 | 10 | Forfeit. of double the excess interest | Grace. |
| Kentucky | 6 | 6 | Forfeiture of excess of interest. | Grace. |
| Louisiana | 5 | 8 | Forfeiture of entire interest. | Grace. |
| Maine | 6 | Any rate. | None. | No grace. |
| Maryland | 6 | 6 | Forfeiture of excess of interest. | No grace. |
| Massachusetts | 6 | Any rate. | None. | No grace. |
| Michigan | 5 | 7 | Forfeiture of entire interest. | Grace. |
| Minnesota | 6 | 10 | Contract canceled. | Grace. |
| Mississippi | 6 | 10 | Forfeiture of interest. | Grace. |
| Missouri | 6 | 8 | Judgment for money loaned with 8 per cent. interest. | Grace. |
| Montana | 8 | Any rate. | None. | No grace. |
| Nebraska | 7 | 10 | Forfeiture of all interest and costs. | Grace. |
| Nevada | 7 | Any rate. | None. | Grace. |
| New Hampshire | 6 | 6 | Forfeiture of thrice the excess. | No grace. |
| New Jersey | 6 | 6 | Forfeit. of entire interest and costs. | No grace. |
| New Mexico | 6 | 12 | Usury a misdemeanor. | Grace. |
| New York | 6 | *6 | Misdemeanor. | No grace. |
| North Carolina | 6 | 6 | Loss of double the interest. | Grace. |
| Ohio | 6 | 8 | Forfeiture of excess. | No grace. |
| Oklahoma | 7 | 12 | Forfeiture of interest. | Grace. |
| Oregon | 6 | 10 | Forfeiture of principal and interest. | No grace. |
| Pennsylvania | 6 | 7 | Forfeiture of excess of interest. | No grace. |
| Rhode Island | 6 | Any rate. | None. | No grace. |
| South Carolina | 7 | 8 | Forfeiture of double interest. | Grace. |
| Tennessee | 6 | 6 | Forfeiture of excess of interest. | No grace. |
| Texas | 6 | 10 | Forfeiture of entire interest. | Grace. |
| Utah | 8 | Any rate. | None. | No grace. |
| Vermont | 6 | 6 | Forfeiture of excess of interest. | No grace. |
| Virginia | 6 | 6 | Forfeiture of excess of interest. | No grace. |
| Washington | 6 | 12 | Forfeiture of double the interest. | No grace. |
| West Virginia | 6 | †6 | Forfeiture of excess of interest. | No grace. |
| Wisconsin | 6 | 10 | Forfeiture of triple interest. | No grace. |
| Wyoming | 8 | 12 | Forfeiture of all interest. | Grace. |

* In New York, any rate of interest agreed on is legal on call loans of $5,000 or more, on collateral security. † Corporations may contract for a greater rate. ‡ But no more than 6 per cent. can be recovered after debt becomes payable.

# BANKS AND TRUST COMPANIES

## COMPILED FROM OFFICIAL REPORTS AND DATA FURNISHED BY THE INSTITUTIONS REPRESENTED

**Corrected and Revised to January 1, 1903**

**The quotations in the last two columns are in all cases the prices per share in dollars, not per cent. figures. Where no actual sales occurred in 1902 the quotations are either the last sale, or bid and asked prices**

### ALBANY, N. Y.

| Name. | Established. | Capital. | Surplus and Undivided Profits, Dec. 31, 1902. | Par Value of Stock. | Dividends Paid, Per Cent. 1898 | 1899 | 1900 | 1901 | 1902 | Range of Prices 1902. High. | Low. |
|---|---|---|---|---|---|---|---|---|---|---|---|
| Albany County Bank | 1871 | $250,000 | $117,000 | $100 | 6 | 6 | 6 | 6 | 10 | $225 | $200 |
| First National Bank | 1864 | 200,000 | 78,390 | 00 | 8 | 8 | 6 | 6 | 6 | 125 | 115 |
| Mechanics & Farmers Bank | 1811 | 250,000 | 1,014,66 | 100 | 14 | 14 | 14 | 14 | 14 | 550 | 475 |
| National Commercial Bank | 1825 | 500,000 | 1,106,000 | 100 | 16 | 16 | 16 | 20 | 20 | 450 | 430 |
| National Exchange Bank | 1838 | 300,000 | 127,249 | 100 | 4 | 4 | 4 | 4 | 4 | 180 | 140 |
| New York State National Bank | 1803 | 250,000 | 419,457 | 100 | 8 | 54 | 12 | 12 | 12 | 325 | 300 |
| Albany Trust Co. | 1900 | [illegible] | 232,532 | 100 | .. | .. | . | 6 | 6 | 310 | 250 |
| Union Trust Co | 1902 | 250,000 | 204,818 | 100 | .. | | .. | .. | .. | 250 | 220 |

### ALLEGHENY, PA.

| Name. | Established. | Capital. | Surplus and Undivided Profits, Dec. 31, 1902. | Par Value of Stock. | Dividends Paid, Per Cent. 1898 | 1899 | 1900 | 1901 | 1902 | Range of Prices 1902. High. | Low. |
|---|---|---|---|---|---|---|---|---|---|---|---|
| Bank of Secured Savings | 1895 | [illegible] | $56,600 | $50 | 0 | 6 | 0 | 0 | 0 | $95 | $85 |
| Enterprise National Bank | 1870 | 200,000 | 210,965 | 50 | 8 | 8 | 8 | 8 | 8 | 125 | 115 |
| First National Bank | 1864 | 350,000 | 135,739 | 100 | 6 | 6 | 6 | 6 | 6 | 140 | 140 |
| German National Bank | 1875 | 200,000 | 661,605 | 100 | 12 | 12 | 12 | 16 | 16 | 463 | 463 |
| Ohio Valley Bank | 1899 | 100,000 | 21,600 | 100 | .. | .. | .. | 6 | 6 | 140 | 130 |
| Second National Bank | 1865 | 300,000 | 765,110 | 100 | 12 | 12 | 12 | 12 | 16 | 375 | 350 |
| Allegheny Trust Co. | 1901 | 700,000 | 40,185 | 100 | .. | .. | .. | .. | 6 | 162 | 137 |
| Dollar Savings Fund and Trust Co. | 1890 | 500,000 | 1,042,289 | 100 | 8 | 8 | 8 | 8 | 10 | 290 | 221 |
| Provident Trust Co. | 1902 | 200,000 | 37,225 | 100 | .. | .. | .. | .. | .. | .. | .. |
| Workingman's Savings Bank & Trust Co. | [illegible] | 100,000 | 313,768 | 50 | 12 | 12 | 12 | 12 | 12 | 265 | 245 |

## ALTOONA, PA.

| Name. | Established. | Capital. | Surplus and Undivided Profits, Dec. 31, 1902. | Par Value of Stock. | Dividends Paid, Per Cent. 1898 | 1899 | 1900 | 1901 | 1902 | Range of Prices, 1902. High. | Low. |
|---|---|---|---|---|---|---|---|---|---|---|---|
| Fidelity Bank | 1886 | $50,000 | $23,293 | $100 | 8 | 8 | 8 | 12 | 14 | $140 | $132 |
| First National Bank | 1863 | 150,000 | 212,000 | 100 | 8 | 8 | 8 | 8 | 8 | 260 | 260 |
| Second National Bank | 1894 | 100,000 | 34,000 | 100 | .. | .. | .. | .. | 8 | 125 | 115 |
| Altoona Trust Co. | 1901 | 250,000 | ...... | 100 | .. | .. | .. | .. | .. | 105 | 105 |
| Central Pennsylvania Trust Co. | 1902 | 250,000 | 11,440 | 100 | .. | .. | .. | .. | .. | 120 | 100 |

## ATLANTA, GA.

| Name. | Established. | Capital. | Surplus and Undivided Profits, Dec. 31, 1902. | Par Value of Stock. | 1898 | 1899 | 1900 | 1901 | 1902 | High. | Low. |
|---|---|---|---|---|---|---|---|---|---|---|---|
| Atlanta Banking & Savings Co. | 1901 | $150,000 | $54,000 | $100 | .. | .. | .. | 6 | 6 | .. | .. |
| Atlanta National Bank | 1865 | 150,000 | 651,842 | 100 | 20 | 20 | 20 | 20 | 20 | $600 | $600 |
| Capital City National Bank | 1900 | 250,000 | 95,000 | 100 | .. | .. | 6 | 6 | 6 | 135 | 128 |
| Farmers & Traders Bank | 1900 | 25,000 | 12,500 | 100 | .. | .. | .. | .. | .. | 128 | 120 |
| Fourth National Bank | 1896 | 400,000 | 157,882 | 100 | 5 | 5 | 5 | 5 | 5 | 135 | 35 |
| Lowry National Bank | 1861 | 300,000 | 160,606 | 100 | 8 | 8 | 8 | 8 | 8 | 200 | 165 |
| Maddox-Rucker Banking Co. | 1880 | 200,000 | 115,000 | 100 | 12 | 12 | 12 | 12 | 8 | 200 | 200 |
| Neal Loan & Banking Co. | 1887 | 100,000 | 259,772 | 100 | .. | .. | .. | .. | .. | .. | .. |
| Third National Bank | 1896 | 200,000 | 153,275 | 100 | .. | 4 | 4 | 4 | 5 | 200 | 195 |
| American Trust & Banking Co. | 1890 | 100,000 | 8,429 | 100 | .. | .. | 4 | 4 | 4 | 95 | 80 |
| Georgia Savings Bank & Trust Co. | 1899 | 35,000 | 3,921 | 100 | .. | .. | .. | .. | .. | 100 | 100 |
| Title Guarantee & Trust Co. | 1889 | 500,000 | 191,421 | 100 | 6 | 6 | 6 | 6 | 6 | 90 | 100 |
| Trust Co. of Georgia | 1891 | 250,000 | 90,999 | 100 | 6 | 6 | 6 | 6 | 6 | 105 | 95 |

## AUGUSTA, GA.

| Name. | Established. | Capital. | Surplus and Undivided Profits, Dec. 31, 1902. | Par Value of Stock. | 1898 | 1899 | 1900 | 1901 | 1902 | High. | Low. |
|---|---|---|---|---|---|---|---|---|---|---|---|
| Commercial Bank | 1872 | $150,000 | $35,451 | $100 | 6 | 6 | 6 | 6 | 6 | $100 | $94 |
| Georgia Railroad Bank | 1892 | 200,000 | 144,157 | 100 | 10 | 10 | .. | .. | .. | 200 | 200 |
| Irish-American Bank | 1899 | 15,000 | 13,000 | 25 | .. | .. | .. | .. | .. | 25 | 25 |
| National Bank of Augusta | 1865 | 250,000 | 138,082 | 100 | 7 | 7 | 7 | 7 | 7 | 30 | 20 |
| National Exchange Bank | 1871 | 200,000 | 70,000 | 100 | 6 | 6 | 6 | 6 | 6 | 115 | 110 |
| Planters' Loan & Savings Bank | 1870 | 50,000 | 30,000 | 10 | 7 | 7 | 7 | 7 | 7 | 15 | 15 |
| Equitable Trust Co. | 1901 | 278,700 | 7,002 | 100 | .. | .. | .. | 6 | 6 | 95 | 103 |

## AUSTIN, TEX.

| | | | | | | | | | | | |
|---|---|---|---|---|---|---|---|---|---|---|---|
| American National Bank | 1890 | $200,000 | $153,000 | $100 | 8 | 8 | 8 | 8 | 8 | $175 | $175 |
| Austin National Bank | 1890 | 150,000 | 172,422 | 100 | 8 | 8 | 8 | 8 | 8 | 204 | 190 |
| City National Bank | 1885 | 150,000 | 16,000 | 100 | 6 | 6 | 6 | 6 | 6 | 100 | 100 |
| First National Bank | 1871 | 100,000 | 46,000 | 100 | .. | .. | .. | .. | 6 | 145 | 145 |
| State National Bank | 1882 | 100,000 | 72,208 | 100 | .. | .. | .. | .. | . | 200 | 200 |

## BALTIMORE, MD.

| | | | | | | | | | | | |
|---|---|---|---|---|---|---|---|---|---|---|---|
| Calvert Bank | 1901 | $100,000 | $22,623 | $50 | .. | .. | .. | .. | .. | $60 | $60 |
| Canton National Bank | 1892 | 100,000 | 36,358 | 100 | 4 | 4 | 4 | 4½ | 5 | 106 | 103 |
| Citizens' National Bank | 1849 | 1,000,000 | 1,750,000 | 10 | 8 | 8 | 10 | 13 | 14 | 34 | 32 |
| Commercial & Farmers' National Bank | 1810 | 512,560 | 150,000 | 100 | 6 | 6 | 6 | 6 | 6 | 138 | 120 |
| Commonwealth Bank | 1894 | 100,000 | 35,000 | 50 | 4 | 4 | 4 | 6 | 6 | 80 | 75 |
| Drovers' & Mechanics' National Bank | 1875 | 300,000 | 416,000 | 100 | 6 | 8 | 10 | 12 | 15 | 300 | 300 |
| Farmers' & Merchants' National Bank | 1808 | 650,000 | 472,000 | 40 | 7 | 7 | 7 | 7 | 7 | 71 | 69 |
| First National Bank | 1864 | 1,000,000 | 384,771 | 100 | 5 | 6 | 39 | 7 | 7 | 166 | 138 |
| German-American Bank | 1872 | 300,000 | 35,000 | 100 | 5 | 6 | 6 | 5 | 5 | 110 | 105 |
| German Bank | 1881 | 400,000 | 72,355 | 100 | 5 | 5 | 5 | 5 | 5 | 107 | 95 |
| Manufacturers' National Bank | 1882 | 500,000 | 84,767 | 100 | 4 | 4 | 5 | 4 | 4 | 102 | 101 |
| Maryland National Bank | 1856 | 200,000 | 6,900 | 20 | 3½ | 3½ | 4 | .. | .. | 20 | 18 |
| Merchants' National Bank | 1835 | 1,500,000 | 900,00 | 100 | 6 | 6 | 6 | 8 | 8 | 197 | 190 |
| National Bank of Baltimore | 1795 | 1,210,700 | 393,938 | 100 | 8 | 7½ | 7 | 6½ | 6½ | 130 | 110 |
| National Bank of Commerce | 1854 | 300,000 | 229,510 | 15 | 5 | 5 | 6 | 6 | 6 | 29 | 26 |
| National Exchange Bank | 1865 | 1,000,000 | 548,278 | 100 | 6 | 6 | 6½ | 7½ | 8 | 199 | 193 |
| National Howard Bank | 1848 | 230,000 | 41,751 | 10 | 5 | 5 | 5 | 5 | 5 | 12½ | 10 |
| National Marine Bank | 1810 | 400,000 | 151,000 | 30 | 6 | 6 | 6 | 6 | 6 | 39 | 37 |
| National Mechanics' Bank | 1806 | 1,000,000 | 1,119,853 | 10 | 9 | 11 | 12 | 12 | 12 | 32 | 30 |
| National Union Bank | 1804 | 900,000 | 290,000 | 100 | 4½ | 4½ | 5½ | 5½ | 6½ | 120 | 116 |
| Old Town National Bank | 1871 | 200,000 | 36,849 | 10 | 8 | 8 | 8 | 3 | 3 | 12 | 11 |
| Second National Bank | 1832 | 500,000 | 600,000 | 100 | 7 | 7 | 7 | 7 | 7 | 195 | 195 |
| Third National Bank | 1865 | 500,000 | 152,962 | 100 | 4 | 4½ | 6 | 6 | 7 | 134 | 115 |
| Western National Bank | 1835 | 500,000 | 444,542 | 20 | 8 | 8 | 8 | 8 | 8 | 41 | 39 |
| American Bonding & Trust Co. | 1895 | 1,000,000 | 627,339 | 50 | .. | 3 | 7 | 8 | 8 | 87 | 80 |
| Baltimore Trust & Guarantee Co. | 1889 | 1,000,000 | 2,512 289 | 100 | 6 | 7 | 7 | 10 | 12 | 20 | 310 |

BALTIMORE, MD.—*Continued.*

| Name. | Established. | Capital. | Surplus and Undivided Profits, Dec. 31, 1902. | Par Value of Stock. | Dividends Paid, Per Cent. 1898 | 1899 | 1900 | 1901 | 1902 | Range of Prices, 1902. High. | Low. |
|---|---|---|---|---|---|---|---|---|---|---|---|
| Central Trust Co. | 1899 | $500,000 | $254,000 | $50 | .. | .. | 5 | 5 | 5 | $68 | $57 |
| City Trust & Banking Co. | 1899 | 100,000 | 30,000 | 10 | .. | 4 | 5 | 5 | 5 | 15 | 10 |
| Colonial Trust Co. | 1899 | 600,000 | 300,000 | 25 | .. | .. | .. | .. | .. | 35 | 30 |
| Continental Trust Co. | 1899 | 2,000,000 | 3,340,297 | 100 | .. | .. | 7 | 8 | 8 | 220 | 210 |
| Fidelity & Deposit Co. | 1890 | 2,000,000 | 2,876,234 | 50 | 10 | 14 | 14 | 14 | 14 | 75 | 160 |
| International Trust Co. | 1899 | 2,000,000 | ,84 | 100 | .. | .. | .. | 4 | 4 | 152 | 109 |
| Maryland Trust Co. | 1894 | 2,125,000 | 3,130,655 | 100 | 5 | 6 | 6½ | 8 | 8 | 212 | 195 |
| Mercantile Trust & Deposit Co. | 1884 | 2,000,000 | 33 | 50 | 10 | 15 | 18 | 16 | 12 | 168 | 160 |
| Safe Deposit & Trust Co. | 1864 | 600,000 | 1,200,000 | 100 | 10 | 10 | 15 | 12 | 12 | 460 | 430 |
| Security Storage & Trust Co. | 1894 | 200,000 | 3, 397 | 100 | 5 | 5 | 5 | 5 | 5 | 108 | 108 |
| Southern Trust & Deposit Co. | 1901 | 44,700 | 5,883 | 50 | .. | .. | .. | .. | .. | 50 | 50 |
| Title Guaranty & Trust Co. | 1884 | 200,000 | 25,950 | 00 | .. | .. | .. | .. | .. | 115 | 105 |
| Union Trust Co. | 1899 | 1,000,000 | 382,096 | 50 | .. | .. | .. | 4 | 5 | 76 | 70 |
| United States Fidelity & Guaranty Co. | 1896 | 1,650,900 | 1,301,968 | 100 | .. | .. | 5 | 6 | 7 | 56 | 136 |

## BINGHAMTON, N. Y.

| Name. | Established. | Capital. | Surplus and Undivided Profits, Dec. 31, 1902. | Par Value of Stock. | 1898 | 1899 | 1900 | 1901 | 1902 | High. | Low. |
|---|---|---|---|---|---|---|---|---|---|---|---|
| City National Bank | 1852 | $200,000 | $63,176 | $100 | 4 | 4 | 4 | 4 | 5½ | $115 | $115 |
| First National Bank | 1864 | 400,000 | 240,000 | 100 | 7 | 7 | 7 | 10 | 10 | 200 | 200 |
| Peoples Bank | 1895 | 100,000 | 23,191 | 100 | 4 | 4 | 4 | 4 | 4 | 120 | 103 |
| Binghamton Trust Co. | 1890 | 300,000 | 247,737 | 100 | 8 | 8 | 8 | 8 | 8 | 165 | 155 |

## BIRMINGHAM, ALA.

| Name. | Established. | Capital. | Surplus and Undivided Profits, Dec. 31, 1902. | Par Value of Stock. | 1898 | 1899 | 1900 | 1901 | 1902 | High. | Low. |
|---|---|---|---|---|---|---|---|---|---|---|---|
| Alabama National Bank | 1887 | $200,000 | $38,000 | $00 | 6 | 6 | 6 | 6 | 6 | $130 | $125 |
| First National Bank | 1884 | 300,000 | 330,000 | 00 | 6 | 6 | 6 | 6 | 9 | 250 | 210 |
| Alabama Trust & Savings Co. | 1891 | 100,000 | 18,000 | 100 | .. | .. | .. | .. | .. | 125 | 115 |
| Birmingham Trust & Savings Co. | 1887 | 500,000 | 171,811 | 100 | 6 | 6 | 6 | 6 | 6 | 145 | 135 |
| Peoples Savings Bank & Trust Co. | 1888 | 75,000 | 7,893 | 100 | 4 | 4 | 6 | 6 | 6 | 112 | 110 |

## BOSTON, MASS.

| | | | | | | | | | | | |
|---|---|---|---|---|---|---|---|---|---|---|---|
| American National Bank | 1901 | $200,000 | $12,000 | $100 | .. | .. | .. | .. | .. | $107 | $100 |
| Atlantic National Bank | 1828 | 750,000 | 400,000 | 100 | 6 | 6 | 6 | 6 | 6 | 144 | 128 |
| Atlas National Bank | 1833 | 1,000,000 | 559,554 | 100 | 5 | 5 | 5 | 5 | 5 | 121 | 109 |
| Boylston National Bank | 1845 | 700,000 | 244,600 | 100 | 6 | 5 | 5 | 5 | 5 | 113 | 105 |
| Bunker Hill National Bank of Charlestown | 1825 | 500,000 | 448,764 | 100 | 8 | 8 | 8 | 8 | 8 | 190 | 186 |
| Colonial National Bank | 1898 | 1,000,000 | 80,134 | 100 | .. | 3½ | 7 | 7 | 7 | 150 | 150 |
| Commercial National Bank | 1888 | 250,000 | 131,465 | 100 | .. | .. | .. | 4½ | 5 | 135 | 135 |
| Eliot National Bank | 1853 | 1,000,000 | 897,899 | 100 | 6 | 6 | 6 | 6 | 7 | 171 | 166 |
| Faneuil Hall National Bank | 1851 | 1,000,000 | 525,000 | 100 | 6 | 6 | 6 | 6 | 6 | 139 | 133 |
| First National Bank | 1864 | 1,000,000 | 1,140,000 | 100 | 10 | 8 | 8 | 8 | 8 | 178 | 175 |
| First Ward National Bank | 1873 | 200,000 | 159,452 | 100 | 7 | 7 | 8 | 8 | 8 | 175 | 160 |
| Fourth National Bank | 1875 | 1,000,000 | 405,386 | 100 | 6 | 6 | 6 | 6 | 6 | 130 | 130 |
| Freemans National Bank | 1836 | 500,000 | 181,045 | 100 | 5 | 5 | 5 | 5 | 5 | 110 | 104 |
| Massachusetts National Bank | 1784 | 800,000 | 132,000 | 100 | .. | .. | [illegible] | 4 | 4 | 129 | 125 |
| Mechanics' National Bank | 1836 | 250,000 | 135,000 | 100 | 6 | 6 | 6 | 7 | 7 | 120 | 120 |
| Merchants' National Bank | 1831 | 3,000,000 | 2,500,000 | 100 | 6 | 6 | 6 | 6 | 6 | 196 | 178 |
| Metropolitan National Bank | 1875 | 500,000 | 194,260 | 100 | 5 | 5 | 5 | 5 | 5 | 110 | 103 |
| Monument National Bank of Charlestown | 1855 | 150,000 | 158,344 | 100 | 8 | 8 | 8 | 8 | 8 | 192 | 175 |
| Mount Vernon National Bank | 1860 | 200,000 | 50,348 | 100 | 4 | 4 | 4 | 5 | 5 | 100 | 100 |
| National Bank of Commerce | 1850 | 1,500,000 | 939,000 | 100 | 4 | 4 | 4 | 4 | 4 | 157 | 130 |
| National Bank of Redemption | 1864 | 2,000,000 | 1,010,429 | 100 | 6 | 6 | 6 | 6 | 6 | 173 | 150 |
| National Bank of the Republic | 1860 | 1,500,000 | 1,222,281 | 100 | 7 | 7 | 7 | 7 | 7 | 165 | 150 |
| National Exchange Bank | 1847 | 1,000,000 | 660,000 | 100 | 6 | 6 | 6 | 6 | 6 | 153 | 139 |
| National Hamilton Bank | 1898 | 500,000 | 70,000 | 100 | .. | 2 | 4 | 4 | 4 | 100 | 100 |
| National Market Bank of Brighton | 1856 | 250,000 | 128,309 | 100 | 4 | 4 | 4 | 4 | 4 | 102 | 102 |
| National Rockland Bank | 1853 | 300,000 | 101,722 | 100 | 6 | 6 | 6 | 6 | 6 | 161 | 128 |
| National Security Bank | 1867 | 250,000 | 673,905 | 100 | 12 | 12 | 12 | 12 | 12 | 270 | 200 |
| National Shawmut Bank | 1898 | 3,500,000 | 2,923,749 | 100 | .. | 1¼ | 5 | 6 | 6 | 243 | 230 |
| National Suffolk Bank | 1902 | 1,500,000 | 410,000 | 100 | .. | .. | .. | .. | 4 | 134 | 134 |
| National Union Bank | 1792 | 1,000,000 | 872,000 | 100 | 6 | 6 | 6 | 6 | 6 | 187 | 157 |
| National Webster Bank | 1853 | 1,000,000 | 422,000 | 100 | 4 | 4 | 4 | 4 | 4½ | 121 | 115 |
| New England National Bank | 1813 | 1,000,000 | 755,000 | 100 | 6 | 6 | 6 | 6 | 6 | 160 | 150 |
| Old Boston National Bank | 1803 | 900,000 | 241,174 | 100 | 5 | 5 | 4 | 4 | 4 | 114 | 102 |
| People's National Bank | 1864 | 300,000 | 145,075 | 100 | 6 | 6 | 6 | 6 | 6 | 122 | 118 |
| Second National Bank | 1832 | 1,600,000 | 1,462,812 | 100 | 8 | 6½ | 7 | 7 | 7 | 190 | 185 |
| South End National Bank | 1890 | 200,000 | 15,300 | 100 | 2 | 4 | 4 | 4 | 4 | 86 | 80 |
| State National Bank | 1811 | 2,000,000 | 1,215,560 | 100 | 5 | 5 | 5 | 5 | 6 | 155 | 143 |
| Winthrop National Bank | 1875 | 300,000 | 400,000 | 100 | 6 | 6 | 6 | 6 | 6 | 150 | 150 |

BOSTON—*Continued.*

| NAME. | Established. | Capital. | Surplus and Undivided Profits, Dec. 31, 1902. | Par Value of Stock. | DIVIDENDS PAID, PER CENT. | | | | | RANGE OF PRICES, 1902. | |
|---|---|---|---|---|---|---|---|---|---|---|---|
| | | | | | 1898 | 1899 | 1900 | 1901 | 1902 | High. | Low. |
| Adams Trust Co. | 1902 | $1,000,000 | $278,373 | $100 | .. | .. | .. | .. | .. | $155 | $125 |
| American Loan & Trust Co. | 1881 | 1,000,000 | 1,318,833 | 100 | 6 | 6 | 6 | 6 | 6 | 250 | 165 |
| Bay State Trust Co. | 1887 | 500,000 | 349,948 | 100 | 5 | 5 | 5 | 5 | 5 | 125 | 125 |
| Beacon Trust Co. | 1893 | 300,000 | 120,000 | 100 | 5 | 5 | 6 | 6 | 6 | 150 | 142 |
| Boston Safe Deposit & Trust Co. | 1875 | 1,000,000 | 1,850,489 | 100 | 10 | 10 | 10 | 10 | 12 | 268 | 248 |
| City Trust Co. | 1902 | 1,000,000 | 1,125,000 | 100 | .. | .. | .. | .. | .. | 240 | 240 |
| Columbia Trust Co. | 1895 | 100,000 | 25,000 | 100 | 4 | 4 | 4 | 4 | 4 | 110 | 110 |
| Federal Trust Co. | 1899 | 500,000 | 123,357 | 100 | .. | .. | .. | 4 | 4 | 103 | 101 |
| International Trust Co. | 1879 | 1,000,000 | 3,002,627 | 100 | 10 | 10 | 13 | 16 | 16 | 400 | 390 |
| Massachusetts Trust Co. | 1873 | 1,000,000 | 385,000 | 100 | 6 | 6 | 6 | 5 | .. | [illegible] | 108 |
| Mattapan Deposit & Trust Co. | 1892 | 100,000 | 50,000 | 100 | 4 | 4 | 4 | 4 | 4 | 150 | 150 |
| Mercantile Trust Co. | 1888 | 500,000 | 392,354 | 100 | .. | 5 | 5 | 5 | 6 | 150 | 150 |
| New England Trust Co. | 1871 | 1,000,000 | 914,000 | 100 | .. | .. | .. | .. | .. | 275 | 275 |
| Old Colony Trust Co. | 1890 | 1,000,000 | 3,900,000 | 100 | 6 | 6 | 8 | 12 | 12 | 450 | 450 |
| Puritan Trust Co. | 1895 | 200,000 | 112,000 | 100 | .. | .. | 4 | 4 | 4 | 118 | 118 |
| State Street Trust Co. | 1891 | 600,000 | 365,799 | 100 | 4 | 4 | 4½ | 5 | 6 | 150 | 150 |
| Union Trust Co. | 1899 | 100,000 | 123,340 | 100 | .. | .. | 5 | 8 | 8 | 110 | 100 |
| United States Trust Co. | 1895 | 200,000 | 365,262 | 100 | 5 | 6 | 6 | 8 | 10 | 225 | 225 |

## BRIDGEPORT, CONN.

| NAME. | Established. | Capital. | Surplus and Undivided Profits, Dec. 31, 1902. | Par Value of Stock. | 1898 | 1899 | 1900 | 1901 | 1902 | High. | Low. |
|---|---|---|---|---|---|---|---|---|---|---|---|
| Bridgeport National Bank | 806 | $21 850 | $240,000 | $50 | 8 | 8 | 8 | 7 | 7 | $98 | $90 |
| City National Bank | 1854 | 250,000 | 243,969 | 100 | 8 | 8 | 8 | 7 | 6 | 160 | 155 |
| Connecticut National Bank | 1831 | 332,100 | 202,388 | 100 | 8 | 8 | 8 | 7½ | 7 | 155 | 150 |
| First National Bank | 1864 | 210,000 | 120,674 | 100 | 8 | 8 | 8 | 8 | 7 | 185 | 185 |
| Pequonnock National Bank | 1851 | 200,000 | 21,800 | 100 | 6 | 6 | 6 | 7½ | 6 | 150 | 150 |
| Bridgeport Trust Co. | 901 | 138,600 | 49,384 | 100 | .. | .. | .. | 3 | 6 | 165 | 165 |

## BROOKLYN, N. Y.

| | | | | | | | | | | | |
|---|---|---|---|---|---|---|---|---|---|---|---|
| Borough Bank | 1902 | $100,000 | $32,124 | $100 | .. | .. | .. | .. | .. | $135 | $135 |
| Broadway Bank | 1888 | 100,000 | 210,446 | 100 | 9 | 10 | 10 | 10 | 10 | 300 | 300 |
| Brooklyn Bank | 1832 | 300,000 | 163,573 | 50 | 7 | 7 | 7 | 7 | 7 | 65 | 60 |
| Coney Island & Bath Beach Bank | 1902 | 100,000 | 30,091 | 100 | .. | .. | .. | .. | .. | 125 | 125 |
| Eighth Ward Bank | 1893 | 100,000 | 20,000 | 100 | .. | .. | .. | .. | .. | 100 | 75 |
| First National Bank | 1852 | 300,000 | 544,000 | 100 | 16 | 168 | 16 | 16 | 16 | 404 | 360 |
| Manufacturers' National Bank | 1854 | 252,000 | 483,099 | 30 | 8 | 10 | 10 | 10 | 12 | 105 | 105 |
| Mechanics' Bank | 1852 | 500,000 | 376,325 | 50 | 11 | 10 | 10 | 10 | 10 | 115 | 110 |
| Merchants' Bank | 1895 | 100,000 | 40,687 | 50 | .. | .. | .. | .. | .. | 110 | 110 |
| Nassau National Bank | 1859 | 300,000 | 600,000 | 100 | 12 | 12 | 12 | 16 | 16 | 385 | 385 |
| National City Bank | 1850 | 300,000 | 545,000 | 50 | 14 | 14 | 14 | 14 | 14 | 150 | 150 |
| North Side Bank | 1889 | 100,000 | 158,840 | 100 | 6 | 6 | 6 | 7 | 6 | 210 | 190 |
| People's Bank | 1893 | 100,000 | 149,712 | 50 | 6 | 8 | 8 | 8 | 8 | 250 | 250 |
| Seventeenth Ward Bank | 1889 | 100,000 | 80,886 | 100 | .. | .. | . | 6 | 6 | 140 | 140 |
| Sprague National Bank | 1883 | 200,000 | 260,371 | 100 | 6 | 6 | 6 | 6 | 6 | 210 | 207 |
| Stuyvesant Heights Bank | 1902 | 100,000 | 50,000 | 50 | .. | .. | .. | .. | .. | 80 | 75 |
| Twenty-Sixth Ward Bank | 1889 | 100,000 | 162,991 | 100 | 6 | 6 | 6 | 6 | 6 | 145 | 140 |
| Union Bank | 1893 | 200,000 | 118,000 | 100 | .. | .. | 2½ | 5 | 5 | 170 | 170 |
| Wallabout Bank | 1889 | 100,000 | 66,272 | 100 | 5 | 5 | 5 | 5 | 5 | 140 | 125 |
| Brooklyn Trust Co. | 1868 | 1,000,000 | 1,877,209 | 100 | 16 | 16 | 16 | 16 | 16 | 470 | 425 |
| Flatbush Trust Co. | 1899 | 200,000 | 135,455 | 100 | .. | .. | .. | 5 | 6 | 190 | 190 |
| Franklin Trust Co. | 1888 | 1,000,000 | 1,514,395 | 100 | 8½ | 10 | 10 | 11½ | 12 | 351 | 325 |
| Hamilton Trust Co. | 1891 | 500,000 | 425,500 | 100 | 8 | 8 | 8 | 8 | 8 | 340 | 310 |
| Kings County Trust Co | 1889 | 500,000 | 1,221,941 | 100 | 8 | 10 | 10 | 10 | 10 | 435 | 420 |
| Long Island Loan & Trust Co. | 1834 | 1,000,000 | 1,417,343 | 100 | 8 | 8 | 10 | 10 | 10 | 325 | 290 |
| Nassau Trust Co. | 1888 | 500,000 | 471,395 | 100 | 6 | 6 | 6 | 6 | 6 | 243 | 210 |
| People's Trust Co. | 1889 | 1,000,000 | 1,641,000 | 100 | 10 | 12½ | 12 | 12 | 12 | 380 | 347 |
| Williamsburgh Trust Co. | 1899 | 700,000 | 518,752 | 100 | .. | .. | .3 | 6 | 8 | 250 | 211 |

## BUFFALO, N. Y.

| | | | | | | | | | | | |
|---|---|---|---|---|---|---|---|---|---|---|---|
| Bank of Buffalo | 1873 | $500,000 | $591,919 | $100 | 8 | 10 | 12 | 10 | 12 | $231 | $220 |
| Citizens' Bank | 1890 | 100,000 | 170,000 | 100 | 6 | 6 | 6 | 6 | 7 | 230 | 200 |
| Columbia National Bank | 1892 | 200,000 | 485,000 | 100 | 2 | 4 | 4 | 2 | .. | 340 | 120 |
| German-American Bank | 1882 | 200,000 | 156,959 | 100 | 6 | 6 | 6 | 6 | 6 | 130 | 130 |
| German Bank | 1870 | 100,000 | 518,426 | 1,000 | 10 | 10 | 20 | 20 | 20 | 4,750 | 4,750 |
| Manufacturers & Traders' National Bank | 1856 | 1,000,000 | 1,300,000 | 100 | 6 | 6 | 6 | 6 | 12 | 275 | 225 |

BUFFALO, N. Y.—*Continued.*

| NAME. | Established. | Capital. | Surplus and Undivided Profits, Dec. 31, 1902. | Par Value of Stock. | DIVIDENDS PAID, PER CENT. | | | | | RANGE OF PRICES, 1902. | |
|---|---|---|---|---|---|---|---|---|---|---|---|
| | | | | | 1898 | 1899 | 1900 | 1901 | 1902 | High. | Low. |
| Marine National Bank | 80 | $230,000 | $1,527,702 | $100 | 25 | 30 | 30 | 40 | 40 | $1,200 | $1,200 |
| People's Bank | 1889 | 300,000 | 110,494 | 100 | 3 | .. | 6 | 6 | 6 | 115 | 105 |
| Third National Bank | 85 | 500,000 | 127,706 | 100 | 6 | 6 | 4 | .. | .. | 100 | 88 |
| Buffalo Loan, Trust & Safe Deposit Co. | 1883 | 200,000 | 88,000 | 100 | 6 | 6 | 6 | 6 | 6 | 35 | 135 |
| Fidelity Trust Co. | 93 | 500,000 | 600,000 | 100 | .. | .. | 12 | 12 | 12 | 400 | 400 |

## BURLINGTON, IA.

| NAME. | Established. | Capital. | Surplus and Undivided Profits, Dec. 31, 1902. | Par Value of Stock. | 1898 | 1899 | 1900 | 1901 | 1902 | High. | Low. |
|---|---|---|---|---|---|---|---|---|---|---|---|
| First National Bank | 1864 | $100,000 | $32,425 | $100 | 5 | 6 | 6 | 6 | 6 | $125 | $125 |
| German American Savings Bank | 1874 | 125,000 | 93,300 | 100 | 6 | 6 | 6 | 6 | 6 | 200 | 200 |
| Iowa State Savings Bank | 1874 | 200,000 | 97,820 | 100 | 8 | 8 | 8 | 8 | 10 | 160 | 160 |
| Merchants' National Bank | 1870 | 100,000 | 99,018 | 100 | 8 | 8 | 8 | 8 | .. | 175 | 175 |
| National State Bank | 1842 | 150,000 | 114,640 | 100 | 12 | 12 | 12 | 12 | 12 | 250 | 250 |

## BUTTE, MONT.

| NAME. | Established. | Capital. | Surplus and Undivided Profits, Dec. 31, 1902. | Par Value of Stock. | 1898 | 1899 | 1900 | 1901 | 1902 | High. | Low. |
|---|---|---|---|---|---|---|---|---|---|---|---|
| First National Bank | 1881 | $200,000 | $425,000 | $100 | .. | .. | .. | .. | .. | .. | .. |
| Silver Bow National Bank | 1890 | 100,000 | 18,312 | 100 | .. | .. | .. | .. | .. | .. | .. |
| Ætna Banking & Trust Co. | 1901 | 100,000 | 9,000 | 100 | .. | .. | .. | .. | .. | 110 | 105 |
| Daly Bank & Trust Co. | 1901 | 100,000 | 45,000 | 100 | .. | .. | .. | .. | .. | .. | .. |

## CAMBRIDGE, MASS.

| | | | | | | | | | | | |
|---|---|---|---|---|---|---|---|---|---|---|---|
| Cambridgeport National Bank | 1826 | $100,000 | $39,000 | $100 | 6 | 6 | 4 | 4 | 4 | $105 | $105 |
| Charles River National Bank | 1832 | 100,000 | 98,253 | 100 | .. | 8 | 8 | 8 | 10 | 160 | 152 |
| First National Bank | 1864 | 200,000 | 153,000 | 100 | 9 | 8 | 8 | 8 | 8 | 165 | 165 |
| National City Bank | 1853 | 100,000 | 57,640 | 100 | .. | .. | .. | .. | .. | 131 | 131 |
| Cambridge Trust Co | 1892 | 100,000 | 70,000 | 100 | 4 | 4 | 5 | 5 | 6 | | .. |

## CAMDEN, N. J.

| | | | | | | | | | | | |
|---|---|---|---|---|---|---|---|---|---|---|---|
| Camden National Bank | 1885 | $100,000 | $44,672 | $100 | .. | .. | .. | .. | 2½ | $85 | $85 |
| First National Bank | 1864 | 200,000 | 162,666 | 100 | 8 | 8 | 8 | 8 | 8 | 148 | 135 |
| National State Bank | 1812 | 260,000 | 284,000 | 50 | 6 | 6 | 6 | 6 | 6 | 85 | 82 |
| Camden Safe Deposit & Trust Co | 1873 | 100,000 | 497,798 | 25 | 20 | 20 | 20 | 20 | 24 | 210 | 152 |
| Central Trust Co | 1891 | 100,000 | 123,565 | 25 | 5 | 5 | 5½ | 6 | 6 | 50 | 50 |
| Security Trust Co | 1892 | 100,000 | 115,000 | 100 | .. | . | 5 | 10 | 10 | 200 | 200 |

## CEDAR RAPIDS, IA.

| | | | | | | | | | | | |
|---|---|---|---|---|---|---|---|---|---|---|---|
| Cedar Rapids National Bank | 1887 | $100,000 | $83,140 | $100 | .. | .. | .. | .. | .. | $160 | $150 |
| Cedar Rapids Savings Bank | 1883 | 100,000 | 65,000 | 100 | .. | .. | .. | .. | .. | 165 | 165 |
| Citizens' National Bank | 1898 | 100,000 | 14,892 | 100 | 8 | 8 | 8 | 8 | 8 | 140 | 140 |
| Merchants' National Bank | 1881 | 100,000 | 49,259 | 100 | 8 | 8 | 8 | 8 | 8 | 150 | 140 |
| People's Savings Bank | 1900 | 50,000 | 5,365 | 100 | .. | .. | .. | .. | .. | 125 | 120 |
| Security Savings Bank | 1889 | 100,000 | 42,000 | 100 | 6 | 6 | 6 | 6 | 6 | 160 | 160 |
| American Trust & Savings Bank | 1898 | 80,000 | 19,440 | 100 | .. | .. | 6 | .. | 6 | 150 | 150 |
| Cedar Rapids Loan & Trust Co | 1900 | 50,000 | 2,373 | 100 | .. | .. | .. | .. | .. | 120 | 120 |

## CHARLESTON, S. C.

| | | | | | | | | | | | |
|---|---|---|---|---|---|---|---|---|---|---|---|
| Bank of Charleston | 1834 | $300,000 | $260,000 | $100 | 8 | 8 | 8 | 8 | 8 | $195 | $190 |
| Enterprise Bank | 1894 | 50,000 | 10,000 | 25 | 6 | 6 | 6 | 6 | 6 | 28 | 28 |
| First National Bank | 1865 | 200,000 | 347,679 | 100 | 12 | 12 | 12 | 12 | 12 | 250 | 250 |
| Miners & Merchants' Bank | 1889 | 100,000 | 10,691 | 100 | 6 | 6 | 6 | 6 | 6 | 105 | 102 |
| People's National Bank | 1865 | 300,000 | 165,000 | 100 | 10 | 10 | 10 | 10 | 10 | 170 | 165 |

CHARLESTON—*Continued.*

| Name. | Established. | Capital. | Surplus and Undivided Profits, Dec. 31, 1902. | Par Value of Stock. | Dividends Paid, Per Cent. 1898 | 1899 | 1900 | 1901 | 1902 | Range of Prices, 1902. High. | Low. |
|---|---|---|---|---|---|---|---|---|---|---|---|
| Columbian Banking & Trust Co. | 1893 | $50,000 | $7,277 | $50 | 6 | 5 | 5 | 5 | 5 | $50 | $45 |
| Exchange Banking & Trust Co. | 1891 | 50,000 | 6,002 | 100 | .. | .. | .. | .. | 6 | 105 | 100 |
| Hibernia Trust & Savings Bank | 1884 | 30,000 | 12,000 | 100 | 5 | 5 | 5 | 5 | 5 | 115 | 115 |
| South Carolina Loan & Trust Co. | 1869 | 100,000 | 28,913 | 100 | 6 | 6 | 6 | 6 | 6 | 105 | 105 |

## CHATTANOOGA, TENN.

| Name. | Established. | Capital. | Surplus and Undivided Profits, Dec. 31, 1902. | Par Value of Stock. | 1898 | 1899 | 1900 | 1901 | 1902 | High. | Low. |
|---|---|---|---|---|---|---|---|---|---|---|---|
| Bank of Chattanooga | 1900 | $100,000 | $19,692 | $100 | .. | .. | .. | .. | . | $120 | $115 |
| Chattanooga National Bank | 1887 | 200,000 | 35,039 | 10 | 6 | 6 | 6 | 6 | 6 | 125 | 110 |
| First National Bank | 1865 | 200,000 | 380,000 | 100 | 8 | 8 | 8 | 8 | 9 | 200 | 190 |
| Citizens' Bank & Trust Co. | 1889 | 225,000 | 31,500 | 100 | 6 | 6 | 6 | 6 | 6 | 100 | 100 |
| Hamilton Trust & Savings Bank | 1889 | 50,000 | 26,000 | 100 | 6 | 6 | 7 | 7 | 7 | 140 | 110 |

## CHICAGO, ILL.

| Name. | Established. | Capital. | Surplus and Undivided Profits, Dec. 31, 1902. | Par Value of Stock. | 1898 | 1899 | 1900 | 1901 | 1902 | High. | Low. |
|---|---|---|---|---|---|---|---|---|---|---|---|
| Bankers' National Bank | 1892 | $2,000,000 | $875,000 | $100 | 5 | 5 | 5 | 5 | 6 | $180 | $168 |
| Calumet National Bank | 1884 | 50,000 | 51,500 | 100 | 8 | 8 | 8 | 8 | 8 | 150 | 150 |
| Chicago City Bank | 1893 | 200,000 | 77,539 | 100 | 8 | 8 | 8 | 8 | 8 | 170 | 160 |
| Chicago National Bank | 1882 | 1,000,000 | 318,659 | 100 | 12 | 12 | 12 | 12 | 12 | 400 | 400 |
| Commercial National Bank | 1864 | 2,000,000 | 1,508,026 | 100 | 10 | 10 | 12 | 12 | 12 | 415 | 332 |
| Continental National Bank | 1883 | 3,000,000 | 1,181,000 | 100 | 6 | 6 | 6 | 6 | 6 | 280 | 250 |
| Corn Exchange National Bank | 1870 | 3,000,000 | 2,500,000 | 100 | 12 | 12 | 12 | 12 | 12 | 450 | 420 |
| Drexel State Bank | 1902 | 200,000 | 6,060 | 100 | .. | .. | .. | .. | 6 | 112 | 100 |
| Drovers' Deposit National Bank | 1902 | 600,000 | 180,000 | 100 | . | .. | .. | .. | .. | 125 | 125 |
| First National Bank | 1863 | 8,000,000 | 6,422,993 | 100 | 12 | 12 | 12 | 12 | 12 | 475 | 390 |
| First National Bank of Englewood | 1889 | 100,000 | 59,824 | 100 | 6 | 6 | 6 | 6 | 10 | 210 | 150 |
| Foreman Brothers Banking Co. | 1862 | 500,000 | 650,000 | 100 | .. | .. | .. | .. | .. | .. | .. |
| Fort Dearborn National Bank | 1887 | 500,000 | 120,288 | 100 | 6 | 6 | 6 | 6 | 6 | 150 | 120 |

| | | | | | | | | | | | |
|---|---|---|---|---|---|---|---|---|---|---|---|
| Hibernian Banking Association | 1867 | 500,000 | 424,182 | 100 | 10 | 10 | 10 | 10 | 6 | 230 | 215 |
| Milwaukee Avenue State Bank | 1889 | 250,000 | 150,156 | 100 | 6 | 6 | 6 | 6 | 6 | 118 | 115 |
| National Bank of North America | 1902 | 2,000,000 | 590,960 | 100 | .. | .. | .. | .. | .. | 152 | 135 |
| National Bank of the Republic | 1891 | 2,000,000 | 771,232 | 100 | 5 | 5 | 5 | 5 | 6 | 201 | 158 |
| National Live Stock Bank | 1888 | 1,000,000 | 1,300,000 | 100 | 12 | 12 | 12 | 12 | 12 | 340 | 250 |
| Prairie State Bank | 1869 | 250,000 | 94,000 | 100 | .. | 4 | 4 | 4 | 5½ | 140 | 100 |
| State Bank of Chicago | 1879 | 1,000,000 | 331,414 | 100 | 6 | 6 | 6 | 6 | 6 | 250 | 250 |
| Western State Bank | 1873 | 500,000 | 60,650 | 100 | .. | .. | .. | .. | 6 | 140 | 122 |
| | | | | | | | | | | | |
| American Guaranty Co. | 1892 | 500,000 | 304,500 | 100 | .. | .. | .. | .. | .. | .. | .. |
| American Trust & Savings Bank | 1889 | 2,000,000 | 1,126,886 | 100 | .. | .. | 6 | 6 | 6 | 200 | 200 |
| Central Trust Co. | 1902 | 4,000,000 | 1,101,224 | 100 | .. | .. | .. | .. | .. | 125 | 120 |
| Chicago Loan & Trust Co. | 1897 | 500,000 | 28,375 | 100 | 5 | 7 | 10 | 10 | 10 | 119 | 109 |
| Chicago Title & Trust Co. | 1891 | 5,000,000 | 176,251 | 100 | 4 | 4 | 4 | 6 | 6 | 150 | 106 |
| Colonial Trust & Savings Bank | 1902 | 200,000 | 53,422 | 100 | .. | . | .. | .. | .. | 200 | 175 |
| Drovers' Trust & Savings Bank | 1902 | 200,000 | 20,000 | 100 | .. | | .. | .. | 3 | 140 | 105 |
| Equitable Trust Co. | 1887 | 500,000 | 305,019 | 100 | 6 | 6 | 6 | 6 | 6 | 150 | 150 |
| Federal Trust & Savings Bank | 1902 | 2,000,000 | 570,750 | 100 | .. | .. | .. | .. | .. | 150 | 125 |
| Illinois Trust & Savings Bank | 1873 | 4,000,000 | 5,864,889 | 100 | 12 | 12 | 12 | 12 | 14 | 745 | 725 |
| Merchants' Loan & Trust Co. | 1857 | 2,000,000 | 2,103,857 | 100 | 12 | 12 | 12 | 12 | 12 | 425 | 375 |
| Metropolitan Trust & Savings Bank | 1891 | 750,000 | 169,475 | 100 | 6 | 6 | 6 | 6 | 6 | 126 | 115 |
| Northern Trust Co. | 1889 | 1,000,000 | 1,464,410 | 100 | 6 | 6 | 6 | 6 | 8 | 510 | 500 |
| Royal Trust Co. | 1891 | 500,000 | 365,936 | 100 | 5 | 5 | 5 | 5 | 5½ | 152 | 150 |
| Union Trust Co. | 1869 | 1,000,000 | 300,000 | 100 | .. | .. | | .. | .. | 165 | 165 |

## CINCINNATI, O.

| | | | | | | | | | | | |
|---|---|---|---|---|---|---|---|---|---|---|---|
| Atlas National Bank | 1887 | $400,000 | $360,000 | $100 | 6 | 6 | 6 | 6 | 6 | $290 | $280 |
| Brighton German Bank Co. | 1899 | 100,000 | 31,273 | 100 | .. | .. | .. | .. | 4 | 170 | 162 |
| Citizens' National Bank | 1880 | 1,000,000 | 553,950 | 100 | 10 | 10 | 10 | 12 | 12 | 35 | 95 |
| City Hall Bank | 1893 | 100,000 | 24,500 | 100 | 4 | 4½ | 5 | 5 | 5 | 143 | 138 |
| Equitable National Bank | 1887 | 250,000 | 75,000 | 100 | 5 | 5 | 5 | 5 | 5 | 130 | 25 |
| Fifth National Bank | 1882 | 600,000 | 360,000 | 100 | 5 | 5 | 6 | 6 | 8 | 255 | 255 |
| First National Bank | 1863 | 3,000,000 | 1,000,000 | 100 | 12 | 12 | 12 | 12 | 12 | 25 | 23 |
| Fourth National Bank | 1863 | 500,00 | 730,960 | 100 | 8 | 8 | 8 | 8 | 8 | 290 | 90 |
| German National Bank | 1881 | 500,00 | 575,000 | 100 | 8 | 8 | 8 | 8 | 10 | 288 | 85 |
| Helvetia Savings & Banking Co. | 1902 | 50,00 | 53,500 | 10 | .. | .. | .. | . | .. | 21 | 20 |
| Market National Bank | 1881 | 250,00 | 220,535 | 100 | 6 | 6 | 6 | 6 | 8 | 30 | 30 |
| Merchants' National Bank | 1865 | 600,00 | 234,382 | 100 | 6 | 6 | 6 | 6 | 6 | 166 | 48 |
| National Lafayette Bank | 1865 | 600,00 | 581,776 | 100 | 12 | 12 | 12 | 12 | 12 | 35 | 90 |

CINCINNATI—*Continued.*

| Name. | Established. | Capital. | Capital and Undivided Profits, Dec. 31, 1902. | Par Value of Stock. | Dividends Paid, Per Cent. | | | | | Range of Prices, 1902. | |
|---|---|---|---|---|---|---|---|---|---|---|---|
| | | | | | 1898 | 1899 | 1900 | 1901 | 1902 | High. | Low. |
| North Side Bank | 1892 | $50,000 | $10,950 | $50 | .. | .. | .. | .. | .. | $100 | $100 |
| Ohio Valley National Bank | 1834 | 700,000 | 295,000 | 100 | 6 | 6 | 6 | 7 | 8 | 197 | 181 |
| Second National Bank | 1863 | 200,000 | 229,548 | 100 | 12 | 12 | 12 | 12 | 12 | 290 | 275 |
| Third National Bank | 1863 | 1,200,000 | 565,000 | 100 | 7 | 7 | 8 | 9 | 9 | 228 | 215 |
| Western German Bank | 1882 | 250,000 | 541,568 | 100 | 15 | 15 | 15 | 15 | 18 | 500 | 500 |
| Central Trust & Safe Deposit Co | 1884 | 500,000 | 245,037 | 100 | 4 | 4 | 4 | 4 | 4 | 180 | 160 |
| Cincinnati Trust Co | 1900 | 500,000 | 150,000 | 100 | .. | .. | .. | .. | .. | 132 | 120 |
| Provident Savings Bank & Trust Co | 1901 | 500,000 | 44,200 | 10 | .. | .. | .. | .. | .. | 11 | 11 |
| Southern Ohio Loan & Trust Co | 1890 | 785,947 | 51,306 | 100 | 7 | 7 | 7 | 6 | 6 | 110 | 105 |
| Union Savings Bank & Trust Co | 1890 | 500,000 | 1,085,000 | 100 | .. | 8 | 8 | 8 | 8 | 525 | 500 |
| Unity Banking & Savings Co | 1900 | 50,000 | 600 | 100 | .. | .. | .. | .. | .. | 104 | 102 |

## CLEVELAND, O.

| Name. | Established. | Capital. | Capital and Undivided Profits, Dec. 31, 1902. | Par Value of Stock. | 1898 | 1899 | 1900 | 1901 | 1902 | High. | Low. |
|---|---|---|---|---|---|---|---|---|---|---|---|
| Bankers' National Bank | 1901 | 500,000 | 126,000 | 100 | .. | .. | .. | .. | 3 | 125 | 120 |
| Bank of Commerce | 1899 | 2,000,000 | 1,225,000 | 100 | .. | 4 | 8 | 8 | 8½ | 200 | 195 |
| Broadway Savings & Loan Co | 1884 | 300,000 | 173,730 | 100 | 8 | 8 | 8 | 8 | 8 | 165 | 160 |
| Caxton Savings & Banking Co | 1901 | 200,000 | 56,749 | 100 | .. | .. | .. | .. | 3 | 125 | 125 |
| Central National Bank | 1890 | 800,000 | 327,119 | 100 | 6 | 6 | 6 | 6 | 6 | 175 | 160 |
| Citizens' Savings & Loan Association | 1868 | 1,000,000 | 591,740 | 500 | 10 | 10 | 10 | 10 | 10 | 2,020 | 1,250 |
| Clark Avenue Savings Bank Co | 1901 | 50,000 | 2,800 | 50 | .. | .. | .. | .. | .. | 60 | 55 |
| Cleveland National Bank | 1883 | 500,000 | 119,683 | 100 | 6 | 6 | 6 | 6 | 6 | 125 | 120 |
| Cleveland Savings & Banking Co | 1898 | 50,000 | 7,700 | 50 | 4 | 4 | 4 | 6 | 6 | 60 | 60 |
| Cleveland Savings & Loan Co | 1896 | 220,000 | 14,000 | 100 | 6 | 6 | 6 | 6 | 6 | 105 | 105 |
| Coal & Iron National Bank | 1899 | 1,000,000 | 350,000 | 100 | .. | 6 | 6 | 7 | 7 | 163 | 143 |
| Colonial National Bank | 1898 | 1,500,000 | 630,000 | 100 | 6 | 6 | 6 | 7 | 7 | 158 | 143 |
| Columbia Savings & Loan Co | 1890 | 50,000 | 20,046 | 50 | 3 | 3 | 5 | 5 | 5 | 65 | 62 |
| Commercial National Bank | 1845 | 1,500,000 | 300,000 | 100 | 6 | 6 | 6 | 6 | 6 | 128 | 123 |
| Dime Savings & Banking Co | 1890 | 500,000 | 411,859 | 100 | 6 | 6 | 8 | 8 | 8 | 200 | 120 |
| Dollar Savings & Banking Co | 1901 | 50,000 | 500 | 100 | .. | .. | .. | .. | .. | .. | .. |
| East Cleveland Savings & Loan Co | 1898 | 200,000 | 6,223 | 100 | 7 | 6 | 6 | 6 | 5 | 103 | 80 |

| | | | | | | | | | | | |
|---|---|---|---|---|---|---|---|---|---|---|---|
| Equity Savings & Loan Co. | 1899 | 149,529 | 8,469 | 100 | .. | 7 | 7 | 7 | 13 | 110 | 110 |
| Euclid Avenue National Bank | 1886 | 500,000 | 250,000 | 100 | 7 | 7 | 7 | 7 | 7 | 170 | 160 |
| Farmers & Merchants Banking Co. | 1898 | 50,000 | 6,000 | 50 | 6 | 6 | 6 | 6 | 6 | 70 | 65 |
| First National Bank | 1863 | 500,000 | 114,773 | 100 | 6 | 6 | 6 | 6 | 6 | 129 | 126 |
| Forest City Savings Bank Co. | 1890 | 250,000 | 19,512 | 100 | 6 | 6 | 6 | 6 | 6 | 150 | 150 |
| Garfield Savings Bank Co. | 1892 | 100,000 | 100,000 | 100 | 6 | 6 | 6 | 8 | 8 | 220 | 205 |
| Genesee Savings & Banking Co. | 1900 | 50,000 | 2,461 | 100 | .. | .. | .. | .. | .. | 100 | 100 |
| German-American Savings Bank Co. | 1887 | 50,000 | 15,000 | 50 | 6 | 6 | 6 | 6 | 6 | 82 | 65 |
| Hough Avenue Savings & Banking Co. | 1898 | 25,000 | 800 | 50 | .. | .. | 3 | 6 | 6 | 61 | 58 |
| The Indemnity Savings & Loan Co. | 1895 | 700,000 | 76,662 | 100 | 6 | 6 | 6 | 6 | 6 | 105 | 102 |
| Lake Shore Banking & Savings Co. | 1890 | 200,000 | 46,000 | 100 | 6 | 6 | 6 | 6 | 6 | 140 | 127 |
| Lakewood Savings & Banking Co. | 1902 | 62,000 | ...... | 100 | .. | .. | .. | .. | .. | .. | .. |
| Lorain Street Savings Bank Co. | 1891 | 100,000 | 18,210 | 100 | 6 | 6 | 6 | 6 | 6 | 115 | 115 |
| Market National Bank | 1900 | 250,000 | 18,000 | 100 | .. | .. | .. | .. | 5 | 107 | 104 |
| Mercantile National Bank | 1864 | 600,000 | 216,000 | 100 | 6 | 6 | 6 | 6 | 6 | 137 | 134 |
| National City Bank | 1865 | 250,000 | 327,000 | 100 | 8 | 8 | 8 | 8 | 8 | 200 | 200 |
| Ohio Mutual Savings & Loan Co. | 1891 | 617,349 | 50,389 | 100 | 7 | 6 | 6 | 6 | 6 | 101 | 101 |
| Park National Bank | 1895 | 500,000 | 225,000 | 100 | 6 | 7 | 7 | 7 | 7 | 160 | 152 |
| Pearl Street Savings & Loan Co. | 1890 | 100,000 | 25,000 | 100 | 6 | 6 | 6 | 6 | 8 | 150 | 145 |
| People's Savings & Loan Association | 1871 | 100,000 | 180,000 | 200 | 10 | 10 | 10 | 10 | 10 | 510 | 500 |
| Produce Exchange Banking Co. | 1889 | 100,000 | 55,412 | 50 | 6 | 6 | 6 | 6 | 6 | 63 | 63 |
| Savings, Building & Loan Co. | 1889 | 444,808 | 35,567 | 100 | 6 | 6 | 6 | 6 | 6 | 105 | 105 |
| South Cleveland Banking Co. | 1874 | 150,000 | 35,000 | 100 | 6 | 6 | 6 | 6 | 7 | 120 | 120 |
| State National Bank | 1889 | 500,000 | 131,736 | 100 | 6 | 6 | 6 | 6 | 6 | 135 | 133 |
| Union Bank & Savings Co. | 1900 | 100,000 | 2,195 | 100 | .. | .. | .. | 6 | 6 | 108 | 100 |
| Union National Bank | 1884 | 1,000,000 | 323,779 | 100 | 6 | 6 | 6 | 6 | 6 | 156 | 150 |
| United Banking & Savings Co. | 1886 | 250,000 | 170,000 | 100 | 8 | 8 | 8 | 8 | 8 | 300 | 300 |
| Wade Park Banking Co. | 1890 | 200,000 | 90,349 | 100 | 6 | 6 | 6 | 7 | 8 | 150 | 146 |
| West Cleveland Banking Co. | 1894 | 50,000 | 6,107 | 100 | .. | 4 | 4 | 4 | 4 | 102 | 102 |
| Woodland Avenue Savings & Loan Co. | 1887 | 250,000 | 125,000 | 100 | 8 | 8 | 8 | 8 | 8 | 160 | 160 |
| American Trust Co. | 1898 | 500,000 | 425,000 | 100 | .. | 6 | 6 | 6 | 6 | 290 | 240 |
| Central Trust Co. | 1901 | 1,000,000 | 256,745 | 100 | .. | .. | .. | .. | 6 | 125 | 110 |
| City Trust Co. | 1891 | 312,150 | 37,430 | 100 | 6 | 6 | 6 | 6 | 6 | 102 | 102 |
| East End Banking & Trust Co. | 1886 | 200,000 | 141,600 | 100 | 8 | 8 | 8 | 8 | 8 | 225 | 225 |
| Federal Trust Co. | 1901 | 1,500,000 | 152,000 | 100 | .. | .. | .. | .. | 6 | 120 | 105 |
| Guardian Trust Co. | 1894 | 500,000 | 308,000 | 100 | 5 | 5 | 5½ | 6 | 6 | 213 | 180 |
| Prudential Trust Co. | 1901 | 600,000 | 172,500 | 100 | .. | .. | .. | .. | .. | 132 | 112 |
| Savings & Trust Co. | 1883 | 1,500,000 | 1,200,000 | 100 | 6 | 6 | 6 | 6 | 11 | 300 | 225 |
| State Banking & Trust Co. | 1899 | 300,000 | 60,000 | 100 | .. | .. | .. | 3 | 6 | 130 | 113 |

## COLORADO SPRINGS, COL.

| Name. | Established. | Capital. | Surplus and Undivided Profits, Dec. 31, 1902. | Par Value of Stock. | Dividends Paid, Per Cent. 1898 | 1899 | 1900 | 1901 | 1902 | Range of Prices, 1902. High. | Low. |
|---|---|---|---|---|---|---|---|---|---|---|---|
| El Paso National Bank | 1900 | $200,000 | $65,000 | $100 | .. | .. | .. | .. | .. | .. | .. |
| Exchange National Bank | 1888 | 100,000 | 101,787 | .. | .. | .. | .. | .. | .. | .. | .. |
| First National Bank | 1874 | 100,000 | 388,000 | 100 | . | .. | .. | .. | .. | $560 | $560 |
| Colorado Springs Trust Co. | 1901 | 250,000 | 26,307 | 100 | .. | .. | .. | .. | .. | 130 | 125 |
| Colorado Title & Trust Co. | 1901 | 250,000 | 56,917 | 100 | .. | . | .. | .. | .. | 125 | 115 |

## COLUMBUS, O.

| Name. | Established. | Capital. | Surplus and Undivided Profits, Dec. 31, 1902. | Par Value of Stock. | Dividends Paid, Per Cent. 1898 | 1899 | 1900 | 1901 | 1902 | Range of Prices, 1902. High. | Low. |
|---|---|---|---|---|---|---|---|---|---|---|---|
| American Savings Bank Co. | 1898 | $50,000 | $4,675 | $100 | .. | .. | .. | .. | .. | $108 | $100 |
| Bank of Commerce | 1900 | 200,000 | 30,000 | 100 | .. | .. | .. | 6 | 6 | 130 | 130 |
| Capital City Bank | 1875 | 100,000 | 25,000 | 1,000 | 6 | 6 | 6 | 6 | 6 | .. | .. |
| City Deposit Bank Co. | 1898 | 150,000 | 35,000 | 100 | .. | 6 | 6 | 6 | 6 | 150 | 135 |
| Columbus Savings Bank Co. | 1881 | 50,000 | 12,000 | 100 | 8 | 8 | 8 | 8 | 8 | 150 | 150 |
| Commercial National Bank | 1868 | 200,000 | 198,000 | 100 | .. | .. | .. | .. | .. | 250 | 200 |
| Deshler National Bank | 1891 | 300,000 | 123,050 | 100 | 8 | 6 | 8 | 8 | 8 | .. | .. |
| Hayden-Clinton National Bank | 1892 | 400,000 | 117,000 | 100 | 6 | 6 | 6 | 6 | 6 | 130 | 130 |
| Market Exchange Bank | 1896 | 100,000 | 45,000 | 100 | 8 | 10 | 20 | 6 | 6 | 160 | 160 |
| Merchants' & Manufacturers' National Bank | 1896 | 500,000 | 293,341 | 100 | 6 | 6 | 6 | 6 | 6 | 200 | 185 |
| New First National Bank | 1897 | 500,000 | 210,000 | 100 | 10 | 10 | 10 | 10 | 10 | 200 | 175 |
| Ohio National Bank | 1888 | 400,000 | 144,927 | 100 | 6 | 6 | 6 | 6 | 8 | 200 | 180 |
| Columbus Savings & Trust Co. | 1883 | 500,000 | 46,430 | 100 | 5 | 5 | 5 | 5 | 5 | 117 | 106 |
| Ohio Trust Co. | 1901 | 250,000 | 15,000 | 100 | .. | .. | .. | .. | 8 | 143 | [illegible] |
| State Savings Bank & Trust Co. | 1892 | 200,000 | 92,606 | 100 | .. | 6 | 6 | 6 | 6 | 200 | 200 |

## COUNCIL BLUFFS, IA.

| Name. | Established. | Capital. | Surplus and Undivided Profits, Dec. 31, 1902. | Par Value of Stock. | Dividends Paid, Per Cent. 1898 | 1899 | 1900 | 1901 | 1902 | Range of Prices, 1902. High. | Low. |
|---|---|---|---|---|---|---|---|---|---|---|---|
| Commercial National Bank | 1901 | $100,000 | $5,000 | $100 | .. | .. | .. | .. | . | $120 | $120 |
| Council Bluffs Savings Bank | 1870 | 150,000 | 66,500 | 100 | .. | .. | .. | .. | .. | 150 | 150 |
| First National Bank | 1865 | 200,000 | 50,000 | 100 | 12 | 12 | .. | 3 | 10 | 200 | 200 |
| State Savings Bank | 1898 | 75,000 | 25,000 | 100 | .. | .. | 6 | 6 | 6 | 150 | 135 |

## COVINGTON, KY.

| | | | | | | | | | | | |
|---|---|---|---|---|---|---|---|---|---|---|---|
| Citizens' National Bank | 1890 | $200,000 | $74,306 | $100 | 6 | 6 | 6 | 6 | 7 | $145 | $140 |
| Farmers' & Traders' National Bank | 1882 | 300,000 | 212,000 | 100 | 10 | 10 | 12 | 12 | 12 | 225 | 215 |
| First National Bank | 1865 | 300,000 | 137,042 | 100 | 8 | 8 | 8 | 8 | 8 | 165 | 160 |
| German National Bank | 1871 | 350,000 | 126,973 | 100 | 6 | 6 | 6 | 6 | 6 | 135 | 132 |
| Covington Trust Co | 1891 | 100,000 | 6,800 | 100 | 6 | 4 | 4 | 6 | 6 | 115 | 100 |

## DALLAS, TEX.

| | | | | | | | | | | | |
|---|---|---|---|---|---|---|---|---|---|---|---|
| American National Bank | 1884 | $200,000 | $300,000 | $100 | 12 | 15 | 18 | 15 | 17½ | $350 | $350 |
| City National Bank | 1873 | 200,000 | 323,000 | 100 | 8 | 8 | 12 | 12 | 12 | 318 | 305 |
| National Bank of Commerce | 1889 | 150,000 | 55,699 | 100 | 8 | 8 | 8 | 8 | 10 | 135 | 110 |
| National Exchange Bank | 85 | 500,000 | 600,000 | 100 | .. | .. | .. | .. | 2½ | 250 | 250 |
| Western Bank & Trust Co | 93 | 500,000 | .... | 100 | .. | .. | .. | .. | .. | .. | .. |

## DAVENPORT, IA.

| | | | | | | | | | | | |
|---|---|---|---|---|---|---|---|---|---|---|---|
| Citizens' National Bank | 1867 | $300,000 | $134,253 | $100 | 6 | 6 | 6 | 6 | 9 | $152 | $150 |
| Davenport Savings Bank | 80 | 300,000 | 115,000 | 100 | 10 | 10 | 10 | 10 | 10 | 223 | 210 |
| First National Bank | 1863 | 200,000 | 78,500 | 100 | 6 | 6 | 6 | 6 | 6 | 153 | 150 |
| Iowa National Bank | 1889 | 100,000 | 45,000 | 100 | 6 | 6 | 6 | 6 | 6 | 160 | 150 |
| German Trust Co | 84 | 50,000 | 27,716 | 100 | 6 | 6 | 6 | 6 | 6 | 75 | 70 |

## DAYTON, O.

| | | | | | | | | | | | |
|---|---|---|---|---|---|---|---|---|---|---|---|
| City National Bank | 1883 | $200,000 | $155,000 | $100 | 12 | 12 | 12 | 12 | 12 | $292 | $285 |
| Dayton National Bank | 85 | 300,000 | 130,947 | 100 | 4 | 4 | 4 | 5 | 6 | 160 | 160 |
| Fourth National Bank | 88 | 600,000 | 234,000 | 100 | 5 | 5 | 5½ | 6 | 6 | 167 | 165 |
| Merchants' National Bank | 81 | 200,000 | 64,000 | 100 | 5 | 5½ | 6 | 6 | 6 | 150 | 145 |
| Teutonia National Bank | 89 | 200,000 | 46,974 | 100 | .. | 4 | 4 | 4 | 4 | 130 | 130 |
| Third National Bank | 82 | 400,000 | 196,711 | 100 | 8 | 8 | 8 | 8 | 8 | 221 | 221 |
| Winters National Bank | 87 | 500,000 | 259,900 | 100 | 8 | 8 | 8 | 8 | 8 | 220 | 215 |

## DENVER, COL.

| Name. | Established. | Capital. | Surplus and Undivided Profits. Dec. 31, 1902. | Par Value of Stock. | Dividends Paid, Per Cent. | | | | | Range of Prices, 1902. | |
|---|---|---|---|---|---|---|---|---|---|---|---|
| | | | | | 1898 | 1899 | 1900 | 1901 | 1902 | High. | Low. |
| Colorado National Bank | 1866 | $500,000 | $277,141 | $100 | .. | .. | .. | .. | .. | $143 | $135 |
| Continental National Bank | 1902 | 300,000 | ...... | 100 | .. | .. | .. | .. | .. | 100 | 100 |
| Daniels Bank | 1901 | 50,000 | 1,006 | 100 | .. | .. | .. | .. | .. | 100 | 100 |
| Denver National Bank | 1884 | 500,000 | 368,398 | 100 | 6 | 6 | 9 | 10 | 12 | 225 | 225 |
| First National Bank | 1865 | 1,000,000 | 1,000,000 | 100 | .. | .. | .. | .. | .. | ... | ... |
| National Bank of Commerce | 1890 | 200,000 | 73,581 | 100 | .. | .. | .. | .. | .. | ... | ... |
| Western Bank & Safe Deposit Co | 1892 | 100,000 | 132,924 | 100 | .. | .. | .. | .. | .. | 100 | 95 |
| Central Trust Co | 1891 | 65,000 | ...... | 100 | .. | .. | .. | .. | .. | ... | ... |
| Citizens' Trust & Savings Bank | 1892 | 25,000 | 1,208 | 100 | .. | .. | .. | .. | .. | ... | ... |
| Continental Trust Company | 1902 | 300,000 | 201,173 | 100 | .. | .. | .. | .. | .. | 175 | 167 |
| International Trust Co | 1891 | 250,000 | 211,327 | 100 | 6 | 6 | 6 | 6 | 6 | ... | ... |

## DES MOINES, IA.

| Name. | Established. | Capital. | Surplus and Undivided Profits. Dec. 31, 1902. | Par Value of Stock. | 1898 | 1899 | 1900 | 1901 | 1902 | High. | Low. |
|---|---|---|---|---|---|---|---|---|---|---|---|
| Capital City State Bank | 1878 | $100,000 | $16,188 | $100 | 4 | 6 | 6 | 6 | 6 | $115 | $100 |
| Central State Bank | 1895 | 50,000 | 31,000 | 100 | 8 | 8 | 8 | 8 | 8 | 160 | 160 |
| Citizens' National Bank | 1872 | 200,000 | 119,612 | 100 | 8 | 8 | 8 | 8 | 8 | 165 | 160 |
| Des Moines National Bank | 1881 | 300,000 | 75,000 | 100 | 6 | 6 | 6 | 10 | 9 | 165 | 160 |
| Iowa National Bank | 1875 | 100,000 | 17,937 | 100 | .. | .. | .. | .. | .. | 125 | 110 |
| Iowa State Bank | 1901 | 50,000 | 614 | 100 | .. | .. | .. | 6 | 6 | 100 | 100 |
| Valley National Bank | 1883 | 200,000 | 101,000 | 100 | 8 | 8 | 8 | 8 | 8 | 165 | 150 |
| Iowa Loan & Trust Co | 1872 | 500,000 | 451,379 | 100 | 8 | 8 | 8 | 7 | 7 | 130 | 130 |
| Security Trust & Savings Bank | 1882 | 50,000 | 100,000 | 100 | 8 | 8 | 8 | 8 | 8 | 226 | 220 |

## DETROIT, MICH.

| | | | | | | | | | | | |
|---|---|---|---|---|---|---|---|---|---|---|---|
| American Exchange National Bank | 1865 | $400,000 | $152,554 | $100 | .. | .. | .. | .. | .. | $115 | $105 |
| Commercial National Bank | 1881 | 1,000,000 | 474,722 | 100 | 8 | 8 | 8 | 12 | 8 | 155 | 124 |
| Detroit United Bank, Limited | 1901 | 100,000 | ........ | 80 | .. | .. | .. | .. | .. | ... | ... |
| First National Bank | 1882 | 500,000 | 187,910 | 100 | 6 | 8 | 8 | 8 | 8 | 165 | 160 |
| German-American Bank | 1853 | 100,000 | 45,604 | 100 | 6 | 6 | 6 | 6 | 6 | 130 | 130 |
| Old Detroit National Bank | 1902 | 2,000,000 | 450,000 | 100 | .. | .. | .. | .. | .. | 140 | 131 |
| State Savings Bank | 1883 | 1,000,000 | 750,000 | 100 | 8 | 8 | 8 | 8 | 8 | 225 | 225 |
| Union National Bank | 1886 | 200,000 | 30,000 | 100 | .. | 4 | 4 | 4 | 4 | 92 | 90 |
| Detroit Trust Co. | 1901 | 500,000 | 121,002 | 100 | .. | .. | .. | 6 | 8 | 222 | 212 |
| Union Trust Co. | 1891 | 500,000 | 322,589 | 100 | 4 | 4 | 4 | 4 | 5 | 170 | 170 |

## DUBUQUE, IA.

| | | | | | | | | | | | |
|---|---|---|---|---|---|---|---|---|---|---|---|
| Citizens' State Bank | 1890 | $100,000 | $22,339 | $100 | 5 | 6 | 6 | 6 | 5 | $110 | $100 |
| Dubuque National Bank | 1884 | 100,000 | 27,000 | 80 | 6 | 6 | 6 | 6 | 6 | 125 | 115 |
| First National Bank | 1864 | 200,000 | 56,500 | 100 | 6 | 7 | 8 | 8 | 8 | 130 | 11 |
| German Bank | 1864 | 150,000 | 35,798 | 100 | .. | .. | .. | .. | .. | 115 | 100 |
| Second National Bank | 1876 | 300,000 | 80,000 | 100 | 6 | 6 | 6 | 6 | 6 | 130 | 27 |
| German Trust & Savings Bank | 1887 | 100,000 | 10,000 | 100 | 7 | 6 | 6 | 5 | 5 | 110 | 80 |
| Iowa Trust & Savings Bank | 1884 | 300,000 | 109,000 | 100 | 6 | 6 | 6 | 6 | 6 | 40 | 33. |

## DULUTH, MINN.

| | | | | | | | | | | | |
|---|---|---|---|---|---|---|---|---|---|---|---|
| American Exchange Bank | 1879 | $500,000 | $207,000 | $100 | 6 | 6 | 6 | 6 | 6 | $158 | $135 |
| City National Bank | 1902 | 500,000 | ...... | 100 | .. | .. | .. | . | .. | 100 | 100 |
| First National Bank | 1887 | 500,000 | 549,000 | 100 | 6 | 6 | 6 | 6 | 6 | 225 | 205 |

## ELIZABETH, N. J.

| | | | | | | | | | | | |
|---|---|---|---|---|---|---|---|---|---|---|---|
| Citizens' Bank | 1890 | $100,000 | $28,000 | $50 | 6 | 6 | 6 | 6 | 6½ | $60 | $58 |
| Elizabethport Banking Co. | 1889 | 50,000 | 26,210 | 50 | 10 | 10 | 5 | .. | .. | 88 | 63 |
| National State Bank | 1812 | 350,000 | 613,015 | 50 | 11 | 11 | 11 | 11 | 11 | 127 | 123 |
| Union County Trust Co. | 1902 | 200,000 | 116,186 | 100 | .. | .. | .. | .. | .. | 175 | 165 |

## ELMIRA, N. Y.

| Name. | Established. | Capital. | Surplus and Undivided Profits, Dec. 31, 1902 | Par Value of Stock. | Dividends Paid, Per Cent. 1898 | 1899 | 1900 | 1901 | 1902 | Range of Prices, 1902. High. | Low. |
|---|---|---|---|---|---|---|---|---|---|---|---|
| Chemung Canal Bank | 1833 | $300,000 | $600,000 | $100 | .. | .. | .. | .. | .. | $300 | $300 |
| Merchants' National Bank | 1892 | 100,000 | 14,500 | 100 | 4 | 5 | 6 | 6 | 6 | 110 | 110 |
| Second National Bank | 1863 | 300,000 | 180,000 | 100 | 10 | 10 | 10 | 9 | 9 | 160 | 150 |
| Elmira Trust Co. | 1902 | 200,000 | 102,675 | 100 | .. | .. | .. | .. | .. | 175 | 175 |

## ERIE, PA.

| Name. | Established. | Capital. | Surplus and Undivided Profits, Dec. 31, 1902 | Par Value of Stock. | 1898 | 1899 | 1900 | 1901 | 1902 | High. | Low. |
|---|---|---|---|---|---|---|---|---|---|---|---|
| First National Bank | 1863 | $150,000 | $250,000 | $100 | 10 | 10 | 10 | 10 | 15 | $200 | $200 |
| Marine National Bank | 1865 | 150,000 | 290,000 | 100 | 8 | 8 | 8 | 8 | 8 | 225 | 225 |
| Second National Bank | 1864 | 300,000 | 93,626 | 100 | .. | .. | .. | 5 | 5 | 125 | 110 |
| Erie Trust Co. | 1902 | 200,000 | 100,000 | 100 | .. | .. | .. | .. | .. | 150 | 150 |

## EVANSVILLE, IND.

| Name. | Established. | Capital. | Surplus and Undivided Profits, Dec. 31, 1902 | Par Value of Stock. | 1898 | 1899 | 1900 | 1901 | 1902 | High. | Low. |
|---|---|---|---|---|---|---|---|---|---|---|---|
| Citizens' National Bank | 1874 | $200,000 | $50,400 | $10 | 7 | 7 | 7 | 7 | 7 | $175 | $150 |
| City National Bank | 1902 | 350,000 | 80,756 | 100 | .. | .. | .. | .. | 3 | 130 | 115 |
| Old National Bank | 1834 | 500,000 | 197,446 | 100 | 6 | 6 | 6 | 6 | 7 | 160 | 145 |
| Evansville Trust & Savings Co. | 1902 | 100,000 | 5,237 | 100 | .. | .. | . | .. | .. | ... | ... |
| Ohio Valley Trust Co. | 1899 | 126,100 | .... | 100 | .. | .. | .. | .. | .. | ... | ... |
| Trust & Savings Co. | 1902 | 100,000 | 5,237 | 100 | .. | .. | .. | .. | .. | ... | ... |

## FALL RIVER, MASS.

| | | | | | | | | | | | |
|---|---|---|---|---|---|---|---|---|---|---|---|
| Fall River National Bank | 85 | $400,000 | $138,121 | $100 | 5 | 4¾ | 5 | 5 | 5 | $117 | $112 |
| First National Bank | 1866 | 400,000 | 330,542 | 100 | .. | .. | .. | .. | .. | 150 | 150 |
| Massasoit National Bank | 86 | 300,000 | 47,926 | 00 | 7 | 7 | 7 | 7 | 7 | 168 | 163 |
| Metacomet National Bank | 85 | 500,000 | 174,000 | 00 | 6 | 5½ | 6 | 6 | 6 | 128 | 125 |
| National Union Bank | 1823 | 200,000 | 87,000 | 100 | 4½ | 4½ | 4½ | 5 | 5 | 118 | 108 |
| Pocasset National Bank | 84 | 200,000 | 170,710 | 00 | 7 | 7 | 7 | 7 | 7 | 150 | 150 |
| B. M. C. Durfee Safe Deposit & Trust Co. | 88 | 400,000 | 173,521 | 100 | .. | .. | .. | .. | .. | 138 | 132 |

## FITCHBURG, MASS.

| | | | | | | | | | | | |
|---|---|---|---|---|---|---|---|---|---|---|---|
| Fitchburg National Bank | 1832 | $250,000 | $216,000 | $100 | 6 | 6 | 6 | 6 | 6 | $148 | $140 |
| Rollstone National Bank | 1849 | 250,000 | 10,458 | 100 | 6 | 6 | 6 | 6 | 6 | 133 | 132 |
| Safety Fund National Bank | 1874 | 200,000 | 16,000 | 100 | .. | 4 | 4 | 4 | 4 | 110 | 100 |
| Wachusett National Bank | 1875 | 250,000 | 109,371 | 100 | 8 | 8 | 7 | 6 | 6 | 130 | 120 |
| Fitchburg Trust Co | 1897 | 100,000 | ...... | 100 | .. | .. | . | .. | .. | 100 | 90 |

## FORT WAYNE, IND.

| | | | | | | | | | | | |
|---|---|---|---|---|---|---|---|---|---|---|---|
| First National Bank | 1863 | $300,000 | $153,137 | $100 | 7 | 6 | 6½ | 7 | 7½ | $160 | $150 |
| Hamilton National Bank | 80 | 200,000 | 295,991 | 100 | .. | .. | .. | .. | .. | 250 | 225 |
| Old National Bank | 85 | 350,000 | 162,772 | 100 | .. | .. | .. | .. | .. | 150 | 130 |
| White National Bank | 82 | 200,000 | 95,711 | 100 | 8 | 8 | 8 | 8 | 8 | 165 | 165 |
| Citizens Trust Co | 1900 | 200,000 | 3,500 | 100 | .. | .. | .. | 6 | 6 | 115 | 115 |
| Fort Wayne Trust Co | 1898 | 200,000 | 37,034 | 100 | 6 | 6 | 6 | 6 | 8 | 13[illegible] | 120 |

## FORT WORTH, TEX.

| | | | | | | | | | | | |
|---|---|---|---|---|---|---|---|---|---|---|---|
| American National Bank | 1893 | $150,000 | $43,000 | $100 | .. | .. | 8 | 8 | 8 | $130 | $130 |
| Farmers' and Mechanics' National Bank | 1889 | 200,000 | 70,000 | 100 | 8 | 8 | 10 | 10 | 10 | 150 | 135 |
| First National Bank | 87 | 300,000 | 275,000 | 100 | 10 | 10 | 10 | 10 | 5 | 200 | 200 |
| Fort Worth National Bank | 84 | 300,000 | 285,013 | 100 | 10 | 10 | 10 | 10 | 10 | 200 | 200 |
| State National Bank | 84 | 200,000 | 85,000 | 100 | 8 | 8 | 8 | 8 | 8 | 150 | 130 |
| Traders' National Bank | 82 | 125,000 | 80,000 | 100 | 12 | 12 | 12 | 12 | 9 | 167 | 162 |
| Hunter-Phelan Savings & Trust Co. | 1901 | 100,000 | 21,800 | 100 | .. | .. | .. | .. | .. | ... | ... |
| State National Loan & Trust Co | 1898 | 20,000 | 16,000 | 20 | 8 | 8 | 8 | 8 | 9 | 38 | 38 |

## FREDERICK, MD.

| NAME. | Established. | Capital. | Surplus and Undivided Profits, Dec. 31, 1902. | Par Value of Stock. | Dividends Paid, Per Cent. 1898 | 1899 | 1900 | 1901 | 1902 | Range of Prices, 1902. High. | Low. |
|---|---|---|---|---|---|---|---|---|---|---|---|
| Central National Bank | 1808 | $120,000 | $49,608 | $25 | 7 | 7 | 7 | 7 | 7 | $35 | $33 |
| Citizens' National Bank | 1886 | 100,000 | 238,938 | 100 | 8 | 8 | 8 | 8 | 8 | 350 | 350 |
| Farmers' & Mechanics' National Bank | 1817 | 125,000 | 85,209 | 25 | 6 | 6 | 6 | 6 | 6 | 39 | 39 |
| First National Bank | 1865 | 100,000 | 32,560 | 100 | 3 | 3 | 4 | 4 | 4 | 117 | 117 |
| Frederick County National Bank | 1817 | 150,000 | 77,700 | 15 | 6½ | 6½ | 6½ | 6½ | 6½ | 25 | 24 |

## GRAND RAPIDS, MICH.

| NAME. | Established. | Capital. | Surplus and Undivided Profits, Dec. 31, 1902. | Par Value of Stock. | 1898 | 1899 | 1900 | 1901 | 1902 | High. | Low. |
|---|---|---|---|---|---|---|---|---|---|---|---|
| Fifth National Bank | 1886 | $100,000 | $19,566 | $100 | 6 | 6 | 3 | .. | 6 | $115 | $85 |
| Fourth National Bank | 1882 | 300,000 | 125,000 | 100 | 8 | 8 | 8 | 8 | 8 | 170 | 160 |
| Grand Rapids National Bank | 1880 | 500,000 | 130,000 | 100 | 6 | 8 | 7½ | 7 | 7 | 125 | 118 |
| National City Bank | 1885 | 500,000 | 146,602 | 100 | 6 | 6 | 6 | 7 | 7 | 130 | 120 |
| Old National Bank | 1863 | 800,000 | 330,250 | 100 | 6 | 6 | 6 | 6 | 6 | 145 | 140 |
| State Bank of Michigan | 1892 | 150,000 | 100,000 | 100 | 6 | 8 | 8 | 8 | 8 | 195 | 110 |
| Michigan Trust Co. | 1889 | 200,000 | 154,606 | 00 | 9 | 9 | 9 | 9 | 9 | 70 | 170 |

## HARRISBURG, PA.

| NAME. | Established. | Capital. | Surplus and Undivided Profits, Dec. 31, 1902. | Par Value of Stock. | 1898 | 1899 | 1900 | 1901 | 1902 | High. | Low. |
|---|---|---|---|---|---|---|---|---|---|---|---|
| Commercial Bank | 1901 | $50,000 | $4,344 | $50 | .. | .. | .. | .. | .. | $60 | $55 |
| First National Bank | 1864 | 100,000 | 388,871 | 100 | 20 | 20 | 24 | 24 | 28 | 500 | 430 |
| Harrisburg National Bank | 1814 | 300,000 | 200,000 | 25 | 10 | 10 | 10 | 10 | 10 | 56 | 56 |
| Merchants' National Bank | 1[illegible]7 | 100,000 | 65,670 | 100 | 8 | 8 | 8 | 8 | 8 | 185 | 185 |
| Central Guarantee Trust & Safe Deposit Co. | 84 | 125,000 | 60,200 | 25 | 6 | 6 | 6 | 6 | 8 | 50 | 50 |
| Commonwealth Trust Co. | 83 | 250,000 | 380,195 | 100 | 12 | 12 | 12 | 13 | 14 | 260 | 260 |
| Harrisburg Trust Co. | 83 | 250,000 | 200,000 | 100 | .. | 6 | 6 | 6 | 6 | 120 | 120 |

## HARTFORD, CONN.

| | | | | | | | | | | | |
|---|---|---|---|---|---|---|---|---|---|---|---|
| Ætna National Bank | 1857 | $525,000 | $545,000 | $100 | 8 | 8 | 8 | 8 | 8 | $190 | $185 |
| American National Bank | 1865 | 600,000 | 307,000 | 50 | 8 | 8 | 8 | 8 | 6 | 76 | 70 |
| Charter Oak National Bank | 1853 | 500,000 | 218,450 | 100 | 4 | 4 | 4 | 4 | 4 | 110 | 105 |
| City Bank | 1851 | 440,000 | 90,000 | 100 | 6 | 6 | 6 | 3 | .. | 100 | 90 |
| Connecticut River Banking Co. | 1825 | 150,000 | 113,000 | 30 | 5 | 5 | 5 | 5 | 6 | 50 | 45 |
| Farmers' & Mechanics' National Bank | 1833 | 500,000 | 153,000 | 100 | 6 | 6 | 6 | 6 | 5 | 122 | 120 |
| First National Bank | 1864 | 650,000 | 309,279 | 100 | 6 | 6 | 6 | 6 | 6 | 135 | 130 |
| Hartford National Bank | 1792 | 1,200,000 | 780,569 | 100 | 7 | 7 | 7 | 6 | 6 | 142 | 140 |
| National Exchange Bank | 1834 | 500,000 | 222,638 | 50 | 7 | 7 | 7 | 6½ | 6 | 66 | 62 |
| Phœnix National Bank | 1814 | 1,000,000 | 557,976 | 100 | 7 | 6 | 6½ | 6½ | 5½ | 126 | 122 |
| State Bank | 1849 | 400,000 | 230,000 | 100 | 6 | 6 | 6 | 6 | 6 | 130 | 130 |
| United States Bank | 1872 | 100,000 | 299,000 | 100 | 12 | 12 | 16 | 16 | 20 | 385 | 385 |
| Connecticut Trust & Safe Deposit Co. | 1872 | 300,000 | 328,447 | 100 | 8 | 10 | 10 | 10 | 10 | 195 | 195 |
| Fidelity Company | 1896 | 50,000 | 33,443 | 100 | 6 | 6 | 7 | 7 | 7 | 135 | 125 |
| Hartford Trust Co. | 1868 | 300,000 | 210,000 | 100 | 7½ | 7½ | 7½ | 7½ | 7½ | 185 | 165 |
| Security Company | 1875 | 200,000 | 110,000 | 100 | 6 | 6 | 6 | 6 | 5 | 130 | 130 |

## HAVERHILL, MASS.

| | | | | | | | | | | | |
|---|---|---|---|---|---|---|---|---|---|---|---|
| Essex National Bank | 1851 | $100,000 | $30,235 | $100 | .. | .. | .. | .. | .. | $80 | $80 |
| First National Bank | 1864 | 200,000 | 145,206 | 100 | 7 | 7 | 7 | 7 | 7 | 151 | 146 |
| Haverhill National Bank | 1836 | 200,000 | 212,500 | 100 | 6 | 6 | 6 | 6 | 6 | 175 | 167 |
| Merchants' National Bank | 1893 | 100,000 | 43,359 | 100 | 6 | 6 | 6 | 6 | 6 | 135 | 130 |
| Merrimack National Bank | 1864 | 240,000 | 154,579 | 100 | 8 | 6 | 6 | 6 | 6 | 150 | 142 |
| Second National Bank | 1886 | 150,000 | 63,500 | 100 | 8 | 8 | 8 | 8 | 8 | 166 | 157 |
| Haverhill Safe Deposit & Trust Co. | 91 | 200,000 | 29,480 | 100 | .. | 3 | 6 | 6 | 6 | 125 | 123 |

## HOBOKEN, N. J.

| | | | | | | | | | | | |
|---|---|---|---|---|---|---|---|---|---|---|---|
| First National Bank | 1865 | $110,000 | $505,600 | $5 | 16 | 17 | 20 | 20 | 20 | $35 | $135 |
| Second National Bank | 1887 | 125,000 | 134,596 | 00 | 6 | 7 | 7 | 7 | 7½ | 90 | 167 |
| Hoboken Trust Co. | 1902 | 100,000 | 51,024 | 00 | .. | .. | .. | .. | .. | 60 | 60 |
| Hudson Trust Co. | 1890 | 500,000 | 825,074 | 00 | 8 | 8 | 10 | 10 | 10 | 50 | 85 |
| Trust Co. of New Jersey | 1899 | 200,000 | 230,059 | 100 | .. | .. | .. | .. | .. | 25 | 220 |

## HOLYOKE, MASS.

| Name. | Established. | Capital. | Surplus and Undivided Profits, Dec. 31, 1902. | Par Value of Stock. | Dividends Paid, Per Cent. 1898 | 1899 | 1900 | 1901 | 1902 | Range of Prices, 1902. High. | Low. |
|---|---|---|---|---|---|---|---|---|---|---|---|
| City National Bank | 1879 | $500,000 | $123,703 | $100 | 5 | 5 | 5 | 5 | 5 | $120 | $115 |
| Hadley Falls National Bank | 1865 | 200,000 | 150,000 | 100 | 8½ | 7 | 8 | 8 | 7½ | 131 | 130 |
| Holyoke National Bank | 1872 | 200,000 | 161,060 | 100 | 9 | 9 | 9 | 9 | 9 | 160 | 160 |
| Home National Bank | 1884 | 250,000 | 101,204 | 100 | 5 | 5 | 5 | 5 | 5½ | 125 | 118 |
| Park National Bank | 1892 | 100,000 | 55,000 | 100 | 8 | 8 | 8 | 6 | 6 | 125 | 110 |

## HOUSTON, TEX.

| Name. | Established. | Capital. | Surplus and Undivided Profits, Dec. 31, 1902. | Par Value of Stock. | 1898 | 1899 | 1900 | 1901 | 1902 | High. | Low. |
|---|---|---|---|---|---|---|---|---|---|---|---|
| Commercial National Bank | 1886 | $300,000 | $301,705 | $100 | 10 | 10 | 10 | 10 | 10 | $300 | $250 |
| First National Bank | 1866 | 100,000 | 500,927 | 100 | 35 | 35 | 50 | 50 | 50 | 750 | 750 |
| Houston National Bank | 1889 | 100,000 | 28,300 | 100 | 6 | 6 | 6 | 6 | 6 | 128 | 128 |
| Merchants' National Bank | 1901 | 250,000 | 21,500 | 100 | .. | .. | .. | .. | 6 | 130 | 125 |
| Planters' & Mechanics' National Bank | 1890 | 200,000 | 56,275 | 100 | .. | . | 6 | 6 | 6 | 125 | 115 |
| South Texas National Bank | 1890 | 500,000 | 224,754 | 100 | 6 | 6 | 6 | 6 | 8 | 154 | 150 |
| Houston Land & Trust Co. | 1889 | 200,000 | 68,000 | 100 | 6 | 3 | .. | 6 | 6 | 120 | 108 |

## INDIANAPOLIS, IND.

| Name. | Established. | Capital. | Surplus and Undivided Profits, Dec. 31, 1902. | Par Value of Stock. | 1898 | 1899 | 1900 | 1901 | 1902 | High. | Low. |
|---|---|---|---|---|---|---|---|---|---|---|---|
| American National Bank | 1901 | $1,000,000 | $240,000 | $100 | .. | .. | .. | .. | .. | $140 | $120 |
| Capital National Bank | 1889 | 300,000 | 140,000 | 100 | 5 | 5 | 5 | 5 | 5 | 158 | 149 |
| Columbia National Bank | 1901 | 300,000 | 12,500 | 100 | .. | .. | .. | .. | .. | 120 | 110 |
| Fletcher National Bank | 1898 | 500,000 | 500,000 | 100 | .. | .. | .. | .. | 35 | .. | .. |
| Indiana National Bank | 1865 | 1,000,000 | 1,400,000 | 100 | 12 | 12 | 12 | 4 | 5 | 230 | 165 |
| Merchants' National Bank | 1865 | 1,000,000 | 418,908 | 100 | 6 | 6 | 6 | 6 | 6 | 205 | 194 |
| People's Deposit Bank | 1900 | 25,000 | 2,885 | 100 | .. | .. | .. | 6 | 6 | 110 | 105 |
| Union National Bank | 1902 | 200,000 | ...... | 100 | .. | .. | .. | .. | .. | .. | .. |
| Central Trust Co. | 1900 | 300,000 | 31,352 | 100 | .. | .. | 5 | 5 | 5 | 132 | 125 |
| Commercial Trust Co. | 1903 | 300,000 | ...... | 100 | .. | .. | .. | .. | .. | .. | .. |
| Indiana Trust Co. | 1893 | 1,000,000 | 170,049 | 100 | 5 | 5 | 5 | 5 | 5 | 155 | 133 |
| Marion Trust Co. | 1896 | 300,000 | 79,647 | 100 | 5 | 5 | 5 | 5 | 5 | 222 | 209 |
| Security Trust Co. | 1901 | 600,000 | 9,620 | 100 | .. | .. | .. | .. | .. | 111 | 102 |
| Union Trust Co. | 1893 | 600,000 | 25,064 | 100 | 5 | 5 | 6 | 6 | 6 | 230 | 220 |

## JACKSONVILLE, FLA.

| | | | | | | | | | | | |
|---|---|---|---|---|---|---|---|---|---|---|---|
| Commercial Bank | 1893 | $50,000 | $25,000 | $100 | 6 | 6 | 6 | 6 | .. | $125 | $120 |
| First National Bank of Florida | 1874 | 50,000 | 13,000 | 100 | .. | .. | .. | .. | .. | 150 | 150 |
| Mercantile Exchange Bank | 1889 | 100,000 | 63,467 | 100 | .. | .. | .. | .. | 9½ | 150 | 150 |
| National Bank of Jacksonville | 1888 | 150,000 | 342,679 | 100 | 10 | 10 | 10 | 17 | 20 | 400 | 375 |
| National Bank State of Florida | 1885 | 100,000 | 23,000 | 100 | .. | .. | .. | .. | .. | 110 | 100 |
| State Bank of Florida | 1895 | 50,000 | 21,000 | 100 | 6 | 6 | 6 | 6 | 6 | 125 | 125 |
| Union Savings Bank | 1902 | 25,000 | 5,200 | 100 | .. | .. | .. | .. | 6 | 120 | 120 |

## JERSEY CITY, N. J.

| | | | | | | | | | | | |
|---|---|---|---|---|---|---|---|---|---|---|---|
| First National Bank | 1864 | $400,000 | $1,012,177 | $100 | 12 | 12 | 12 | 12 | 12 | $310 | $300 |
| Hudson County National Bank | 1851 | 250,000 | 633,857 | 100 | 12 | 12 | 12 | 12 | 12 | 366 | 360 |
| Second National Bank | 1865 | 250,000 | 312,360 | 100 | 15 | 14 | 13 | 12 | 8 | 185 | 180 |
| Third National Bank | 1887 | 200,000 | 267,052 | 100 | 6 | 6 | 6 | 6 | 6 | 222 | 200 |
| Bergen & Lafayette Trust Co. | 1902 | 100,000 | 53,400 | 100 | .. | .. | .. | .. | .. | 200 | 150 |
| Commercial Trust Co. | 1900 | 1,000,000 | 1,798,489 | 100 | .. | .. | .. | .. | .. | 335 | 335 |
| Greenville Banking & Trust Co. | 1896 | 100,000 | 34,000 | 100 | .. | .. | .. | .. | .. | 163 | 150 |
| Jersey City Trust Co. | 1902 | 100,000 | 52,118 | 100 | .. | .. | .. | .. | .. | 160 | 160 |
| Lincoln Trust Co. | 1902 | 100,000 | 107,593 | 100 | .. | . | .. | .. | .. | 220 | 200 |
| New Jersey Title Guarantee & Trust Co. | 1868 | 200,000 | 750,000 | 100 | .. | .. | .. | .. | .. | 475 | 475 |
| North American Trust Co. | 1901 | 200,000 | 211,605 | 100 | .. | .. | .. | . | 90 | 200 | 200 |
| People's Safe Deposit & Trust Co. | 1896 | 100,000 | 81,115 | 100 | .. | .. | .. | .. | .. | 150 | 140 |
| Real Estate Trusts Co. | 1874 | 25,000 | 16,970 | 100 | 10 | 10 | 10 | .. | .. | 160 | 160 |

## KANSAS CITY, MO.

| | | | | | | | | | | | |
|---|---|---|---|---|---|---|---|---|---|---|---|
| American National Bank | 1886 | $250,000 | $100,000 | $100 | 6 | 6 | 6 | 6 | 6 | $152 | $148 |
| City National Bank | 1900 | 250,000 | 56,264 | 100 | .. | .. | 3 | 6 | 6 | 128 | 115 |
| First National Bank | 1886 | 250,000 | 750,000 | 100 | 10 | 12 | 12 | 15 | 20 | 600 | 550 |
| German-American Bank | 1884 | 50,000 | 25,000 | 100 | .. | .. | .. | .. | 10 | 150 | 135 |
| Inter-State National Bank | 1890 | 1,000,000 | 681,473 | 100 | 6 | 6 | 6 | 6 | 6 | 152 | 147 |
| Kansas City State Bank | 1888 | 200,000 | 50,000 | 100 | 6 | 6 | .. | .. | 3 | 105 | 100 |
| Missouri Savings Association Bank | 1891 | 50,000 | 35,000 | 100 | 8 | 8 | 8 | 8 | 8 | 200 | 180 |
| National Bank of Commerce | 1887 | 1,000,000 | 1,400,000 | 100 | 8 | 8 | 8 | 10 | 12 | 350 | 300 |
| New England National Bank | 1889 | 300,000 | 200,000 | 100 | 6 | 7 | 7 | 7 | 7 | 225 | 180 |

KANSAS CITY—*Continued.*

| Name. | Established. | Capital. | Surplus and Undivided Profits, Dec. 31, 1902. | Par Value of Stock. | Dividends Paid, Per Cent. | | | | | Range of Prices, 1902. | |
|---|---|---|---|---|---|---|---|---|---|---|---|
| | | | | | 1898 | 1899 | 1900 | 1901 | 1902 | High. | Low. |
| Stock Yards Bank of Commerce | 1897 | $10,000 | $17,000 | $100 | .. | .. | 200 | .. | .. | .. | .. |
| Traders' Bank | 1900 | 100,000 | 17,500 | 100 | .. | .. | .. | 6 | 6 | $130 | $120 |
| Union National Bank | 1887 | 600,000 | 473,754 | 100 | 8 | 8 | 10 | 10 | 10 | 230 | 195 |
| Western Exchange Bank | 1881 | 100,000 | 50,000 | 100 | 8 | 8 | 8 | 8 | 8 | 160 | 145 |
| Fidelity Trust Co | 1899 | 1,000,000 | 563,545 | 100 | .. | . | .. | .. | .. | 165 | 144 |
| Missouri Union Trust Co | 1881 | 100,000 | ........ | 100 | .. | .. | .. | .. | .. | .. | .. |
| Pioneer Trust Co | 1903 | 500,000 | 500,000 | 50 | .. | .. | .. | .. | .. | .. | . |
| South-Western Trust Co | 1901 | 65,000 | 8,443 | 100 | .. | .. | .. | .. | 6 | 100 | 100 |
| Surety Trust Co | 1902 | 100,000 | 1,000 | 100 | .. | .. | .. | .. | .. | 105 | 100 |
| Trust Company | 1903 | 500,000 | 500,000 | 50 | .. | .. | .. | .. | .. | .. | .. |
| United States & Mexican Trust Co | 1901 | 1,000,000 | 108,280 | 100 | .. | .. | .. | .. | 6 | 105 | 100 |

## KNOXVILLE, TENN.

| Name. | Established. | Capital. | Surplus and Undivided Profits, Dec. 31, 1902. | Par Value of Stock. | 1898 | 1899 | 1900 | 1901 | 1902 | High. | Low. |
|---|---|---|---|---|---|---|---|---|---|---|---|
| City National Bank | 1888 | $200,000 | $70,000 | $100 | 10 | 10 | 10 | 11 | 12 | $175 | $175 |
| East Tennessee National Bank | 1873 | 175,000 | 240,356 | 100 | 12 | 12 | 12 | 12 | 12 | 240 | 240 |
| Holston National Bank | 1891 | 100,000 | 13,500 | 100 | 3 | 6 | 6 | 6 | 6 | 105 | 102 |
| Knoxville Banking Co | 1888 | 50,000 | 18,000 | 100 | 6 | 6 | 6 | 6 | 6 | 105 | 102 |
| Marble City Bank | 1899 | 25,000 | 1,964 | 100 | .. | 10 | 10 | 10 | 8 | 100 | 100 |
| Mechanics' National Bank | 1882 | 100,000 | 114,918 | 100 | 7 | 11 | 8 | 9 | 12 | 200 | 200 |
| Merchants' Bank | 1881 | 100,000 | 2,000 | 100 | .. | .. | .. | .. | .. | 100 | 90 |
| Third National Bank | 1887 | 200,000 | 56,000 | 100 | 6 | 6 | 6 | 6 | 6 | 130 | 125 |
| Union Bank | 1895 | 50,000 | 1,500 | 100 | .. | .. | .. | 2 | 4 | .. | .. |
| Knox County Bank & Trust Co | 1890 | 50,000 | 1,000 | 00 | 6 | 6 | 6 | 6 | 6 | 100 | 95 |

## LANCASTER, PA.

| | | | | | | | | | | |
|---|---|---|---|---|---|---|---|---|---|---|
| Conestoga National Bank | 1889 | $200,000 | $228,000 | $100 | .. | .. | .. | .. | 10 | $[illegible] | $220 |
| Farmers' National Bank | 1810 | 450,000 | 334,000 | 50 | 10 | 10 | 10 | 8 | 10 | 115 | 113 |
| First National Bank | 1864 | 210,000 | 175,575 | 100 | 10 | 10 | 10 | 10 | 10 | 212 | 208 |
| Fulton National Bank | 1882 | 200,000 | 96,425 | 100 | 10 | 10 | 10 | 9 | 8 | 196 | 191 |
| Lancaster County National Bank | 1841 | 300,000 | 261,000 | 50 | 10 | 10 | 10 | 10 | 10 | 125 | 124 |
| Northern National Bank | 1885 | [illegible] | 41,000 | 100 | 4 | 5 | 6 | 6 | 6 | 140 | 128 |
| People's National Bank | 1887 | 200,000 | 80,000 | 100 | 5 | 5 | 5 | 5 | 5 | 130 | 130 |
| City Savings Fund & Trust Co | 1899 | 150,000 | 90,000 | 100 | .. | .. | .. | .. | .. | 150 | 140 |
| Lancaster Trust Co | 1889 | 250,000 | 400,000 | 100 | 10 | 10 | 10 | 10 | 12 | 270 | 270 |
| Northern Trust & Savings Co | 1902 | 125,000 | 13,000 | 50 | .. | .. | .. | .. | .. | 58 | 51 |
| People's Trust, Savings & Deposit Co | 1892 | [illegible] | 156,439 | 50 | .. | .. | .. | 5 | 10 | 143 | 143 |
| Union Trust Co | 192 | 150,000 | 12,110 | 100 | .. | .. | .. | .. | .. | 56 | 52 |

## LAWRENCE, MASS.

| | | | | | | | | | | | |
|---|---|---|---|---|---|---|---|---|---|---|---|
| Arlington National Bank | 1890 | $100,000 | $33,000 | $100 | 6 | 6 | 6 | 6 | 6 | $125 | $125 |
| Bay State National Bank | 1847 | 375,000 | 135,000 | 75 | 6⅔ | 6⅔ | 6⅔ | 6⅔ | 6⅔ | 115 | 115 |
| Lawrence National Bank | 1872 | 300,000 | 70,300 | 100 | 6 | 6 | 6 | 6 | 6 | 115 | 115 |
| Merchants' National Bank | 1889 | 100,000 | 90,000 | 100 | 6 | 6 | 6 | 6 | 6 | 126 | 116 |
| Pacific National Bank | 1877 | 150,000 | 24,792 | 100 | 6 | 6 | 6 | .. | .. | 100 | 90 |

## LEXINGTON, KY.

| | | | | | | | | | | | |
|---|---|---|---|---|---|---|---|---|---|---|---|
| Central Bank | 890 | $100,000 | $21,963 | [illegible] | 5½ | 4 | .. | 5 | 5 | $105 | $75 |
| Fayette National Bank | 1870 | 300,000 | 270,374 | 100 | 10 | 10 | 10 | 10 | 10 | 230 | 225 |
| First National Bank | 1865 | 400,000 | 133,899 | 100 | 5 | 5 | 6 | 6 | 6 | 137 | 134 |
| Lexington City National Bank | 1865 | 200,000 | 67,851 | 100 | 8 | 8 | 8 | 8 | 8 | 180 | 175 |
| National Exchange Bank | 1878 | 100,000 | 23,468 | 100 | .. | .. | .. | .. | .. | 125 | 118 |
| Phoenix National Bank | 1888 | 150,000 | 35,000 | 100 | 4 | 4 | 4 | 4 | 4 | 150 | 135 |
| Second National Bank | 1883 | 150,000 | 17,702 | 100 | 2½ | 2½ | 5 | 5½ | 6 | 130 | 120 |
| Third National Bank | 1883 | 100,000 | 15,744 | 100 | .. | .. | .. | .. | .. | 100 | 90 |
| Security Trust & Safety Vault Co | 1887 | 400,000 | 107,840 | 100 | 8 | 6 | 6 | 6 | 6 | 157 | 148 |

## LITTLE ROCK, ARK.

| Name. | Established. | Capital. | Surplus and Undivided Profits. Dec. 31, 1902 | Par Value of Stock. | Dividends Paid, Per Cent. 1898 | 1899 | 1900 | 1901 | 1902 | Range of Prices, 1902. High. | Low. |
|---|---|---|---|---|---|---|---|---|---|---|---|
| Bank of Commerce | 1890 | $100,000 | $50,000 | $25 | 3 | 3 | 3 | 6 | 6 | $50 | $50 |
| Citizens Bank | 1892 | 100,000 | 67,000 | 100 | 8 | 10 | 10 | 10 | 10 | 175 | 150 |
| Exchange National Bank | 1882 | 200,000 | 55,000 | 100 | 7 | 7 | 8 | 8 | 8 | 135 | 130 |
| German National Bank | 1873 | 300,000 | 186,589 | 100 | 10 | 10 | 10 | 10 | 10 | 140 | 140 |
| Little Rock Trust Co | 1889 | 50,000 | 30,637 | 25 | 8 | 8 | 8 | 8 | 8 | 50 | 45 |
| Mercantile Trust Co | 1902 | 62,500 | ...... | 100 | .. | .. | .. | .. | .. | 29 | 25 |
| Union Trust Co | 1902 | 50,000 | 10,786 | 100 | .. | .. | .. | .. | 5 | 125 | 125 |

## LOS ANGELES, CAL.

| Name. | Established. | Capital. | Surplus and Undivided Profits. Dec. 31, 1902 | Par Value of Stock. | Dividends Paid, Per Cent. 1898 | 1899 | 1900 | 1901 | 1902 | Range of Prices, 1902. High. | Low. |
|---|---|---|---|---|---|---|---|---|---|---|---|
| American National Bank | 1903 | $1,000,000 | .. | $100 | .. | .. | .. | .. | .. | .. | .. |
| Bank of Commerce | 1886 | 100,000 | $2,800 | 100 | .. | .. | .. | 40 | 6 | $110 | $100 |
| Central Bank | 1900 | 50,000 | 17,761 | 100 | .. | .. | .. | 6 | 6 | 145 | 135 |
| Citizens' National Bank | 1890 | 200,000 | 8669 | 100 | 8 | 8 | 8 | 8 | 8 | 145 | 135 |
| Farmers' & Merchants' National Bank | 1903 | 1,000,000 | 500,000 | 100 | .. | .. | .. | .. | .. | .. | .. |
| First National Bank | 1875 | 400,000 | 590 | 100 | 10 | 10 | 10 | 10 | 12 | 60 | 240 |
| Los Angeles National Bank | 1883 | 500,000 | 200,000 | 100 | 7 | 7 | 7 | 8 | 8 | 175 | 160 |
| Merchants' National Bank | 1886 | 200,000 | 150 00 | 100 | 8 | 8 | 8 | 8 | 8 | 200 | 200 |
| National Bank of California | 1889 | 200,000 | 86 00 | 100 | 6 | 6 | 6 | 6 | 8 | 135 | 130 |
| Southwestern National Bank | 1901 | 300,000 | 6,136 | 100 | .. | .. | .. | .. | .. | 105 | 100 |
| Broadway Bank & Trust Co | 1891 | 100,000 | 39,000 | 100 | 8 | 8 | 8 | 8 | 8 | 150 | 140 |
| Dollar Savings Bank & Trust Co. | 1902 | 50,000 | 1,000 | 100 | .. | .. | .. | .. | .. | 106 | 106 |
| Los Angeles Trust Co | 1902 | 1,000,000 | ...... | 100 | .. | .. | .. | .. | .. | 105 | 100 |
| State Bank & Trust Co | 1889 | 500,000 | 35 00 | 100 | 6 | 6 | 6 | 6 | 6 | 103 | 101 |

## LOUISVILLE, KY.

| | | | | | | | | | | | |
|---|---|---|---|---|---|---|---|---|---|---|---|
| American National Bank | 1894 | $800,000 | $250,000 | $100 | 6 | 6 | 6 | 6 | 6 | $145 | $140 |
| Bank of Commerce | 1866 | 800,000 | 184,500 | 100 | 10 | 60 | 35 | 9 | 8 | 175 | 170 |
| Citizens' National Bank | 1874 | 500,000 | 294,124 | 100 | 6 | 6 | 6 | 6 | 6 | 175 | 172 |
| First National Bank | 1863 | 500,000 | 261,180 | 100 | 8 | 8 | 8 | 8 | 8 | 185 | 170 |
| German Bank | 1869 | 250,000 | 290,571 | 100 | 12 | 12 | 12 | 14 | 14 | 280 | 275 |
| German Insurance Bank | 1872 | 249,500 | 329,658 | 50 | 10 | 10 | 10 | 10 | 10 | 130 | 130 |
| German Security Bank | 1867 | 179,000 | 50,000 | 100 | 8 | 7 | 6 | 8 | 8 | 150 | 135 |
| Louisville National Banking Co. | 1898 | 250,000 | 36,232 | 100 | .. | 6 | 6 | 6 | 6 | 121 | 120 |
| National Bank of Kentucky | 1834 | 1,645,000 | 1,056,000 | 100 | 8 | 8 | 8 | 8 | 8 | 196 | 187 |
| Southern National Bank | 1899 | 250,000 | 60,000 | 100 | .. | 3 | 6 | 6 | 6 | 133 | 130 |
| Third National Bank | 1872 | 200,000 | 16,500 | 100 | 6 | 6 | 6 | 6 | 2 | 109 | 100 |
| Union National Bank | 1889 | 500,000 | 248,965 | 100 | 6 | 6 | 6 | 6 | 6 | 180 | 165 |
| Western Bank | 1865 | 250,000 | 10,760 | 100 | 6 | 5 | 5 | 6 | 6 | 103 | 100 |
| Columbia Finance & Trust Co. | 1890 | 1,000,000 | 179,692 | 100 | 6 | 6 | 6 | 6 | 6 | 148 | 143 |
| Fidelity Trust & Safety Vault Co. | 1882 | 1,000,000 | 787,010 | 100 | 8 | 8 | 8 | 8 | 8 | 283 | 265 |
| Louisville Trust Co. | 1884 | 806,100 | 61,000 | 100 | 6 | 6 | 6 | 6 | 6 | 142 | 140 |
| National Trust Co. | 1902 | 200,000 | ...... | 100 | .. | .. | .. | .. | .. | 110 | 100 |

## LOWELL, MASS.

| | | | | | | | | | | | |
|---|---|---|---|---|---|---|---|---|---|---|---|
| Appleton National Bank | 1847 | $300,000 | $160,000 | $100 | 5 | 5 | 5 | 5 | 5 | $120 | $115 |
| Old Lowell National Bank | 1828 | 200,000 | 64,563 | 100 | 5 | 5 | 5 | 5 | 5 | 113 | 110 |
| Prescott National Bank | 1850 | 300,000 | 108,000 | 100 | 5½ | 4 | 4 | 4 | 4 | 108 | 104 |
| Traders' National Bank | 1892 | 200,000 | 211,098 | 100 | 5 | 7 | 8 | 8 | 8 | 150 | 134 |
| Union National Bank | 1902 | 350,000 | 182,852 | 100 | .. | .. | .. | .. | 8 | 175 | 165 |
| Wamesit National Bank | 1853 | 250,000 | 75,980 | 100 | 5½ | 5 | 5 | 5 | 5 | 103 | 100 |
| Lowell Trust Co. | 1891 | 125,000 | 40,000 | 100 | 5 | 5 | 5 | 5 | 5 | 110 | 100 |
| Middlesex Safe Deposit & Trust Co. | 1894 | 100,000 | 2,509 | 100 | .. | .. | .. | .. | .. | 65 | 60 |

## LYNN, MASS.

| | | | | | | | | | | | |
|---|---|---|---|---|---|---|---|---|---|---|---|
| Central National Bank | 1849 | $200,000 | $161,603 | $100 | 8 | 6 | 6 | 6 | 6 | $155 | $150 |
| First National Bank | 1814 | 500,000 | 235,980 | 100 | 6 | 6 | 5 | 5 | 5 | 125 | 120 |
| Lynn National Bank | 1885 | 100,000 | 165,179 | 100 | 9 | 9 | 9 | 12 | 12 | 220 | 220 |
| Manufacturers' National Bank | 1891 | 200,000 | 50,000 | 100 | 5 | 4 | 4 | 4 | 4 | 105 | 105 |
| National City Bank | 1854 | 200,000 | 179,163 | 100 | 8 | 8 | 8 | 8 | 8 | 160 | 150 |
| National Security Bank | 1881 | 100,000 | 159,993 | 100 | 10 | 10 | 10 | 10 | 10 | 200 | 175 |
| Lynn Safe Deposit & Trust Co. | 1888 | 100,000 | 114,459 | 100 | 6 | 6 | 6 | 9 | 9 | 200 | 200 |
| Security Safe Deposit & Trust Co. | 1891 | 200,000 | 95,343 | 100 | 6 | 6 | 6 | 6 | 6 | 135 | 135 |

## MACON, GA.

| NAME. | Established. | Capital. | Surplus and Undivided Profits, Dec. 31, 1902. | Par Value of Stock. | DIVIDENDS PAID, PER CENT. | | | | | RANGE OF PRICES, 1902. | |
|---|---|---|---|---|---|---|---|---|---|---|---|
| | | | | | 1898 | 1899 | 1900 | 1901 | 1902 | High. | Low. |
| American National Bank | 1891 | $250,000 | $118,472 | $100 | 6 | 6 | 6 | 6 | 6 | $115 | $110 |
| Central Georgia Bank | 1870 | 100,000 | 3,000 | 100 | 2½ | 5 | 5 | 5 | 5 | 85 | 82 |
| Commercial & Savings Bank | 1897 | 50,000 | 26,381 | 100 | 6 | 6 | 7 | 7 | 7 | 155 | 150 |
| Exchange Bank | 1871 | 500,000 | 100,000 | 100 | 6 | 6 | 6 | 6 | 6 | 95 | 90 |
| First National Bank | 1865 | 200,000 | 72,500 | 100 | 6 | 6 | 6 | 6 | 6 | 130 | 130 |
| Georgia Loan & Trust Co. | 1883 | 121,300 | 25,435 | 100 | .. | .. | .. | .. | 4 | ... | ... |
| Georgia Title & Guarantee Trust Co. | 1902 | 50,000 | ..... | 100 | .. | .. | .. | .. | .. | ... | ... |
| Union Savings Bank & Trust Co. | 1890 | 200,000 | 28,784 | 100 | 6 | 6 | 6 | 6 | 6 | 105 | 85 |

## MANCHESTER, N. H.

| NAME. | Established. | Capital. | Surplus and Undivided Profits, Dec. 31, 1902. | Par Value of Stock. | 1898 | 1899 | 1900 | 1901 | 1902 | High. | Low. |
|---|---|---|---|---|---|---|---|---|---|---|---|
| Amoskeag National Bank | 1864 | $200,000 | $225,544 | $100 | 8 | 8 | 8 | 10 | 10 | $200 | $200 |
| First National Bank | 1865 | 150,000 | 110,000 | 100 | 6 | 6 | 6 | 6 | 6 | 150 | 150 |
| Manchester National Bank | 1865 | 150,000 | 95,856 | 100 | 10 | 10 | 10 | 10 | 10 | 250 | 250 |
| Merchants' National Bank | 1853 | 150,000 | 72,243 | 100 | 6 | 6 | 6 | 6 | 6 | 125 | 125 |
| Second National Bank | 1877 | 100,000 | 48,329 | 100 | 6 | 6 | 6 | 6 | 6 | 125 | 125 |

## MEMPHIS, TENN.

| NAME. | Established. | Capital. | Surplus and Undivided Profits, Dec. 31, 1902. | Par Value of Stock. | 1898 | 1899 | 1900 | 1901 | 1902 | High. | Low. |
|---|---|---|---|---|---|---|---|---|---|---|---|
| First National Bank | 1864 | $250,000 | $50,000 | $100 | 6 | 6 | 13½ | 10 | 10 | $200 | $185 |
| Memphis National Bank | 1887 | 250,000 | 125,000 | 100 | 6 | 6 | 6 | 6 | 10 | 190 | 180 |
| Mercantile Bank | 1883 | 200,000 | 26,631 | 100 | 6 | 7 | 10 | 12 | 12 | 215 | 165 |
| National Bank of Commerce | 1897 | 500,000 | 189,606 | 100 | 8 | 8 | 8 | 8 | 8 | 175 | 170 |
| Security Bank | 1885 | 50,000 | 13,780 | 100 | 6 | 6 | 6 | 6 | 6 | 127 | 127 |
| State National Bank | 1873 | 250,000 | 200,000 | 100 | 10 | 10 | 12 | 12 | 12 | 203 | 195 |
| Union & Planters' Bank | 1869 | 600,000 | 66,253 | 100 | .. | .. | .. | .. | .. | 125 | 115 |

| | | | | | | | | | | | |
|---|---|---|---|---|---|---|---|---|---|---|---|
| American Savings Bank & Trust Co. | 1902 | 25,000 | 6,567 | 100 | .. | .. | .. | .. | .. | 200 | 100 |
| Chickasaw Savings Bank & Trust Co. | 1902 | 25,000 | 707 | 80 | .. | .. | .. | .. | .. | 130 | 130 |
| Manhattan Savings Bank & Trust Co. | 1885 | 30,000 | 78,272 | 25 | 20 | 20 | 20 | 20 | 20 | 125 | 113 |
| Memphis Trust Co. | 1891 | 700,000 | 125,000 | 100 | 8 | 8 | 7 | 6 | 6 | 135 | 130 |
| People's Savings Bank & Trust Co. | 1899 | 30,000 | 4,000 | 50 | .. | .. | 10 | 10 | 11 | 85 | 83 |
| Union Savings Bank & Trust Co. | 1895 | 12,500 | 12,500 | 100 | 10 | 10 | 10 | 15 | 20 | 350 | 300 |

## MILWAUKEE, WIS.

| | | | | | | | | | | | |
|---|---|---|---|---|---|---|---|---|---|---|---|
| First National Bank | 1863 | $1,500,000 | $850,000 | $100 | 10 | 10 | 10 | 10 | 10 | $300 | $300 |
| German-American Bank | 1892 | 200,000 | 46,000 | 100 | 6 | 6 | 6 | 6 | 6 | 150 | 150 |
| Marine National Bank | 1900 | 300,000 | 103,249 | 100 | .. | .. | .. | .. | .. | 140 | 140 |
| Marshall & Ilsley Bank | 1847 | 300,000 | 100,000 | 100 | 8 | 8 | 8 | 8 | 8 | 135 | 135 |
| Milwaukee National Bank | 1853 | 450,000 | 85,000 | 50 | 4 | 4 | 5 | 5 | 5 | 54 | 50 |
| National Exchange Bank | 1854 | 500,000 | 200,000 | 100 | 8 | 8 | 8 | 8 | 8 | 185 | 185 |
| West Side Bank | 1894 | 100,000 | 4,628 | 1,000 | .. | .. | .. | .. | 10 | 3,000 | 3,000 |
| Wisconsin National Bank | 1892 | 1,500,000 | 787,618 | 100 | 5 | 5½ | 6 | 6 | 6 | 240 | 230 |
| Milwaukee Trust Co. | 1894 | 200,000 | 10,000 | 100 | 6 | 6 | 6 | 6 | 6 | 100 | 100 |
| Wisconsin Fidelity, Trust & Safe Deposit Co. | 1901 | 125,000 | 1,928 | 100 | .. | .. | .. | .. | .. | 105 | 105 |

## MINNEAPOLIS, MINN.

| | | | | | | | | | | | |
|---|---|---|---|---|---|---|---|---|---|---|---|
| Clarke National Bank | 1902 | $160,000 | ...... | $100 | .. | .. | .. | .. | .. | ... | ... |
| First National Bank | 1864 | 1,000,000 | $415,000 | 100 | .. | 4 | 4 | 4 | 4 | $185 | $180 |
| German-American Bank | 1886 | 60,000 | 35,122 | 100 | 6 | 6 | 6 | 7 | 8 | 130 | 130 |
| Germania Bank | 1893 | 50,000 | 8,500 | 100 | .. | .. | 4 | 6 | 6 | 108 | 106 |
| National Bank of Commerce | 1884 | 1,000,000 | 285,000 | 100 | 4 | 4 | 4 | 6 | 6 | 145 | 145 |
| Northwestern National Bank | 1872 | 1,000,000 | 525,493 | 100 | 8 | 14 | 8 | 8 | 8 | 195 | 170 |
| People's Bank | 1886 | 60,000 | 4,867 | 100 | .. | .. | .. | .. | 2 | 100 | 80 |
| St. Anthony Falls Bank | 1893 | 125,000 | 42,000 | 100 | .. | 5 | 6 | 6 | 6 | 150 | 150 |
| Security Bank | 1878 | 1,000,000 | 200,000 | 100 | .. | .. | .. | 6 | 6 | 160 | 155 |
| South Side State Bank | 1899 | 50,000 | 17,500 | 100 | .. | .. | 6 | 6 | 6 | 135 | 135 |
| Swedish-American National Bank | 1888 | 250,000 | 93,700 | 100 | 4 | 5 | 5 | 5 | 5 | 125 | 122 |
| Minnesota Title Insurance & Trust Co. | 1885 | 250,000 | 5,000 | 100 | .. | .. | .. | .. | 4 | 110 | 110 |
| Minneapolis Trust Co. | 1889 | 500,000 | 97,528 | 100 | 4 | .. | .. | .. | .. | 140 | 100 |
| Minnesota Loan & Trust Co. | 1883 | 500,000 | 130,800 | 100 | .. | .. | 3 | 4 | 5 | 127 | 100 |

## MOBILE, ALA.

| Name. | Established. | Capital. | Surplus and Undivided Profits, Dec. 31, 1902. | Par Value of Stock. | Dividends Paid, Per Cent. 1898 | 1899 | 1900 | 1901 | 1902 | Range of Prices, 1902. High. | Low. |
|---|---|---|---|---|---|---|---|---|---|---|---|
| First National Bank | 1865 | $300,000 | $570,500 | $100 | 12 | 12 | 12 | 18 | 22 | $400 | $380 |
| Merchants' Bank | 1901 | 150,000 | 17,368 | 100 | .. | .. | .. | .. | 3 | 126 | 125 |
| People's Bank | 1871 | 150,000 | 451,306 | 100 | 16 | 16 | 20 | 20 | 20 | 435 | 435 |
| Central Trust Co | 1902 | 250,000 | 62,500 | 25 | .. | .. | .. | .. | .. | 31 | 31 |
| City Bank & Trust Co | 1903 | 500,000 | 350,000 | 100 | .. | .. | .. | .. | .. | ... | ... |

## MONTGOMERY, ALA.

| Name. | Established. | Capital. | Surplus and Undivided Profits, Dec. 31, 1902. | Par Value of Stock. | Dividends Paid, Per Cent. 1898 | 1899 | 1900 | 1901 | 1902 | Range of Prices, 1902. High. | Low. |
|---|---|---|---|---|---|---|---|---|---|---|---|
| Farley National Bank | 1850 | $100,000 | $80,400 | $100 | 6 | 6 | 6 | 6 | 6 | $185 | $175 |
| First National Bank | 1871 | 225,000 | 80,000 | 100 | 6 | 6 | 6 | 6 | 6 | 123 | 118 |
| Fourth National Bank | 1901 | 100,000 | 18,817 | 100 | .. | .. | .. | 3 | 6 | 120 | 110 |
| Merchants' & Planters' National Bank | 1872 | 250,000 | 139,000 | 100 | 6 | 6 | 10 | 6 | 6 | 175 | 150 |
| Union Trust & Savings Bank | 1901 | 75,000 | 2,500 | 100 | .. | .. | .. | .. | .. | 105 | 100 |

## MONTPELIER, VT.

| Name. | Established. | Capital. | Surplus and Undivided Profits, Dec. 31, 1902. | Par Value of Stock. | Dividends Paid, Per Cent. 1898 | 1899 | 1900 | 1901 | 1902 | Range of Prices, 1902. High. | Low. |
|---|---|---|---|---|---|---|---|---|---|---|---|
| First National Bank | 1864 | $200,000 | $30,597 | $100 | 4 | 4 | 4 | 4 | 4 | $100 | $80 |
| Montpelier National Bank | 1824 | 150,000 | 134,800 | 100 | .. | .. | .. | .. | .. | 130 | 115 |
| Capital Savings Bank & Trust Co | 890 | 100,000 | 6,000 | 100 | 5 | 5 | 5 | 5 | 5 | 104 | 104 |
| Montpelier Savings Bank & Trust Co | 1870 | 50,000 | 62,100 | 100 | 8 | 8 | 8 | 8 | 8 | 250 | 250 |

## NASHVILLE, TENN.

| | | | | | | | | | | | |
|---|---|---|---|---|---|---|---|---|---|---|---|
| American National Bank. | 1883 | $1,000,000 | $60,000 | $100 | 1½ | .. | .. | .. | .. | $98 | $75 |
| First National Bank | 1863 | 400,000 | 80,000 | 100 | 6 | 6 | 6 | 6 | 6 | 138 | 133 |
| Fourth National Bank | 1867 | 600,000 | 405,252 | 100 | 8 | 8 | 8 | 8 | 8 | 178 | 170 |
| Merchants' Bank | 1886 | 200,000 | 40,000 | 100 | 4 | 6 | 6 | 6 | 6 | 120 | 110 |
| Nashville Trust Co | 1889 | 350,000 | 6,100 | 100 | 4 | 4 | 4 | 4 | 4 | 115 | 112 |
| Union Bank & Trust Co | 1891 | 100,000 | 51,479 | 100 | 8 | 8 | 8 | 8 | 8 | 165 | 130 |

## NEWARK, N. J.

| | | | | | | | | | | | |
|---|---|---|---|---|---|---|---|---|---|---|---|
| Essex County National Bank | 1859 | $1,000,000 | $1,245,000 | $50 | 16 | 16 | 21 | 20 | 12 | $500 | $400 |
| Manufacturers' National Bank | 1872 | 250,000 | 151,000 | 100 | 10 | 10 | 10 | 10 | 10 | 215 | 200 |
| Merchants' National Bank | 1871 | 200,000 | 221,607 | 100 | 12 | 12 | 12 | 12 | 12 | 320 | 300 |
| National Newark Banking Co | 1804 | 500,000 | 540,000 | 50 | 10 | 10 | 10 | 10 | 10 | 175 | 150 |
| National State Bank | 1812 | 500,000 | 399,609 | 50 | 10 | 10 | 10 | 10 | 10 | 121 | 116 |
| North Ward National Bank | 1873 | 200,000 | 220,000 | 100 | 10 | 10 | 10 | 10 | 10 | 300 | 300 |
| Union National Bank | 1902 | 1,500,000 | 1,686,128 | 100 | .. | .. | .. | .. | 10 | 440 | 415 |
| City Trust Co | 1901 | 100,000 | 11,230 | 100 | .. | .. | .. | .. | .. | 109 | 108 |
| Federal Trust Co | 1901 | 1,000,000 | 561,082 | 100 | .. | .. | .. | .. | .. | 205 | 205 |
| Fidelity Trust Co | 1887 | 1,500,000 | 3,927,062 | 100 | 5 | 5 | 8 | 8 | 18 | 1,025 | 500 |
| Newark Loan & Trust Co | 1902 | 100,000 | 37,000 | 100 | .. | .. | .. | .. | .. | ... | ... |
| West Side Trust Co | 1902 | 200,000 | 109,492 | 100 | .. | .. | .. | .. | .. | 180 | 150 |

## NEW BEDFORD, MASS.

| | | | | | | | | | | | |
|---|---|---|---|---|---|---|---|---|---|---|---|
| First National Bank | 1864 | $1,000,000 | $275,517 | $100 | 5 | 5 | 5 | 5 | 5 | $133 | $126 |
| Mechanics' National Bank | 1832 | 600,000 | 229,784 | 100 | 6 | 5 | 5 | 6 | 6 | 150 | 148 |
| Merchants' National Bank | 1825 | 1,000,000 | 710,893 | 100 | 8 | 8 | 8 | 8 | 8 | 203 | 196 |
| New Bedford Safe Deposit & Trust Co | 1888 | 200,000 | 45,000 | 100 | 4 | 4 | 4 | 4 | 4¼ | 105 | 85 |

## NEW HAVEN, CONN.

| NAME. | Established. | Capital. | Surplus and Undivided Profits, Dec. 31, 1902. | Par Value of Stock. | Dividends Paid, Per Cent. 1898 | 1899 | 1900 | 1901 | 1902 | Range of Prices, 1902. High. | Low. |
|---|---|---|---|---|---|---|---|---|---|---|---|
| City Bank | 1831 | $500,000 | $137,540 | $100 | 6 | 6 | 6 | 6 | 6 | $142 | $142 |
| First National Bank | 1863 | 500,000 | 282,101 | 100 | 7½ | 10 | 8 | 8 | 8 | 150 | 150 |
| Mechanics' Bank | 1824 | 300,000 | 50,000 | 60 | 5 | 5 | 5 | 5 | 5 | 71 | 71 |
| Merchants' National Bank | 1851 | 350,000 | 142,960 | 50 | 6 | 6 | 6 | 6 | 6 | 65 | 59 |
| National New Haven Bank | 1792 | 464,800 | 332,315 | 100 | 10 | 10 | 10 | 10 | 9 | 200 | 196 |
| National Tradesmen's Bank | 1855 | 300,000 | 280,000 | 100 | 8 | 8 | 8 | 8 | 8 | 160 | 150 |
| New Haven County National Bank | 1834 | 350,000 | 337,401 | 10 | 7 | 7 | 7 | 7 | 6 | 16 | 15 |
| Second National Bank | 1855 | 500,000 | 464,364 | 100 | 10 | 10 | 10 | 10 | 8 | 202 | 196 |
| Yale National Bank | 1853 | 500,000 | 222,505 | 100 | 7 | 7 | 7 | 7 | 6 | 135 | 131 |
| **New Haven Trust Co.** | 1895 | 100,000 | 15,713 | 100 | .. | 5 | .. | 4 | 2 | 115 | 112 |
| **Union Trust Co.** | 1871 | 100,000 | 117,301 | 100 | 6 | 6 | 6 | 6 | 6 | 125 | 125 |

## NEW ORLEANS, LA.

| NAME. | Established. | Capital. | Surplus and Undivided Profits, Dec. 31, 1902. | Par Value of Stock. | Dividends Paid, Per Cent. 1898 | 1899 | 1900 | 1901 | 1902 | Range of Prices, 1902. High. | Low. |
|---|---|---|---|---|---|---|---|---|---|---|---|
| Canal Bank | 1895 | $1,000,000 | $215,000 | $100 | 6 | 6 | 6 | 6 | 7 | $163 | $150 |
| Citizens' Bank of Louisiana | 1833 | 380,200 | 185,000 | 100 | 5 | 5 | 5 | 5 | 6 | 155 | 140 |
| Commercial National Bank | 1901 | 300,000 | 83,000 | 100 | .. | .. | .. | .. | .. | 185 | 185 |
| Germania National Bank | 1865 | 300,000 | 133,679 | 100 | 6 | 6 | 6 | 6 | 6 | 161 | 140 |
| Louisiana National Bank | 1865 | 500,000 | 477,465 | 100 | 8 | 8 | 8 | 8 | 8 | 225 | 205 |
| Metropolitan Bank | 1870 | 250,000 | 21,279 | 100 | 8 | 8 | 8 | 8 | 8 | 151 | 128 |
| Morgan State Bank | 1901 | 100,000 | 3,250 | 50 | .. | .. | .. | .. | .. | 75 | 65 |
| New Orleans National Bank | 1871 | 200,000 | 939,760 | 100 | 30 | 30 | 30 | 30 | 30 | 573 | 550 |
| People's Bank | 1869 | 250,000 | 36,624 | 100 | 6 | 6 | 6 | 6 | 6 | 130 | 110 |
| Provident Bank | 1893 | 100,000 | 15,110 | 100 | .. | .. | 6 | 6 | 6 | 132 | 126 |
| State National Bank | 1818 | 300,000 | 212,727 | 100 | 6 | 6 | 6 | 6 | 6 | 350 | 300 |
| Teutonia Bank | 1893 | 100,000 | 19,535 | 100 | 6 | 6 | 6 | .. | .. | 120 | 94 |
| United States Safe Deposit & Savings Bank | 1893 | 100,000 | 1,092 | 100 | .. | .. | .. | .. | .. | 165 | 150 |
| Whitney National Bank | 1883 | 400,000 | 1,412,314 | 100 | 10 | 15 | 15 | 15 | 15 | 655 | 500 |
| Commercial Trust & Savings Bank | 1902 | 250,000 | ...... | 100 | .. | .. | .. | .. | .. | 126 | 100 |
| Germania Savings Bank & Trust Co. | 1881 | 100,000 | 502,717 | 100 | 16 | 16 | 16 | 25 | 25 | 675 | 500 |
| Hibernia Bank & Trust Co. | 1902 | 1,000,000 | 2,020,000 | 100 | .. | .. | .. | .. | 10 | 465 | 455 |
| nterstate Trust & Banking Co. | 1902 | 1,500,000 | 534,791 | 100 | .. | .. | .. | .. | .. | 167 | 150 |

## NEWPORT, R. I.

| | | | | | | | | | | | |
|---|---|---|---|---|---|---|---|---|---|---|---|
| Aquidneck National Bank | 1854 | $200,000 | $64,968 | $50 | 4 | 5 | 5 | 5 | 5 | $66 | $60 |
| First National Bank | 1856 | 120,000 | 88,507 | 100 | 10 | 10 | 10 | 10 | 9 | 200 | 180 |
| National Exchange Bank | 1834 | 100,000 | 63,510 | 50 | 8 | 8 | 8 | 8 | 8 | 82 | 81 |
| New England Commercial Bank | 1818 | 75,000 | 8,976 | 50 | 5 | 5 | 5 | 5 | 5 | 50 | 50 |
| Newport National Bank | 1803 | 120,000 | 90,000 | 60 | 9 | 9 | 9 | 9 | 9 | 121 | 121 |
| Union National Bank | 1881 | 155,250 | 43,184 | 90 | 5 | 5 | 6 | 5 | 5 | 110 | 102 |

## NEW YORK, N. Y.

| | | | | | | | | | | | |
|---|---|---|---|---|---|---|---|---|---|---|---|
| American Exchange National Bank | 1839 | $5,000,000 | $3,500,000 | $100 | 7 | 7 | 7 | 8 | 8 | $282 | $272 |
| American Surety Co. | 1884 | 2,500,000 | 2,099,790 | 50 | 8 | 8 | 8 | 8 | 8 | 95 | 85 |
| Astor National Bank | 1898 | 350,000 | 478,196 | 100 | .. | .. | .. | . | 20 | 1,000 | 700 |
| Bank of America | 1812 | 1,500,000 | 3,343,138 | 100 | 14 | 14 | 14 | 16 | 18 | 559 | 535 |
| Bank of the Manhattan Co. | 1799 | 2,050,000 | 2,336,761 | 50 | 8 | 8 | 10 | 10 | 10 | 170 | 164 |
| Bank of the Metropolis | 1871 | 1,000,000 | 1,280,000 | 100 | 12 | 12 | 12 | 12 | 12 | 551 | 500 |
| Bank of New York | 1784 | 2,000,000 | 2,300,000 | 100 | 10 | 10 | 10 | 10 | 10 | 350 | 340 |
| Bank of Washington Heights | 1901 | 100,000 | 110,000 | 100 | .. | .. | .. | .. | .. | 200 | 200 |
| Bowery Bank | 1865 | 250,000 | 770,000 | 100 | 12 | 17 | 12 | 12 | 7 | 335 | 310 |
| Bronx Borough Bank | 1893 | 50,000 | 54,289 | 100 | .. | .. | .. | .. | .. | 250 | 250 |
| Central National Bank | 1864 | 1,000,000 | 571,793 | 100 | 8 | 8 | 8 | 8 | 8 | 180 | 170 |
| Century Bank | 1901 | 100,000 | 53,783 | 100 | .. | .. | .. | .. | .. | 180 | 155 |
| Chase National Bank | 1877 | 1,000,000 | 3,522,580 | 100 | 10 | 12 | 12 | 12 | 12 | 750 | 700 |
| Chatham National Bank | 1851 | 450,000 | 1,020,000 | 25 | 16 | 16 | 16 | 16 | 16 | 91 | 85 |
| Chemical National Bank | 1824 | 300,000 | 7,368,173 | 100 | 150 | 150 | 150 | 150 | 150 | 4,355 | 4,200 |
| Colonial Bank | 1892 | 100,000 | 180,000 | 100 | .. | .. | .. | .. | .. | 400 | 400 |
| Columbia Bank | 1883 | 300,000 | 236,750 | 100 | 8 | 8 | 8 | 8 | 8 | 400 | 375 |
| Consolidated National Bank | 1902 | 1,000,000 | 1,021,500 | 100 | .. | .. | .. | .. | .. | 210 | 203 |
| Corn Exchange Bank | 1853 | 2,000,000 | 3,000,000 | 100 | 12 | 12 | 12 | 12 | 12 | 480 | 423 |
| East River National Bank | 1852 | 250,000 | 148,990 | 25 | 8 | 8 | 8 | 8 | 8 | 45 | 40 |
| Equitable National Bank | 1902 | 200,000 | 1,795 | 100 | .. | .. | .. | .. | .. | 112 | 100 |
| Federal Bank | 1902 | 100,000 | ...... | 100 | .. | .. | .. | .. | .. | 120 | 120 |
| Fidelity Bank | 1900 | 200,000 | 105,000 | 100 | .. | .. | .. | .. | .. | 195 | 195 |
| Fifth Avenue Bank | 1875 | 100,000 | 1,591,166 | 100 | 100 | 100 | 100 | 100 | 100 | 3,600 | 3,600 |
| Fifth National Bank | 1864 | 250,000 | 360,000 | 100 | 12 | 12 | 12 | 12 | 12 | 400 | 400 |
| First National Bank | 1863 | 10,000,000 | 12,666,609 | 100 | 100 | 100 | 100 | 1960 | 20 | 845 | 776 |
| Fourteenth Street Bank | 1888 | 100,000 | 92,673 | 100 | 6 | 6 | 6 | 6 | 6 | 300 | 300 |
| Fourth National Bank | 1864 | 3,000,000 | 2,786,863 | 100 | 7 | 7 | 7 | 7 | 7 | 242 | 230 |
| Gallatin National Bank | 1829 | 1,000,000 | 2,089,300 | 50 | 12 | 12 | 12 | 12 | 12 | 440 | 420 |

NEW YORK—*Continued.*

| Name. | Established. | Capital. | Surplus and Undivided Profits. Dec. 31, 1902. | Par Value of Stock. | Dividends Paid, Per Cent. 1898 | 1899 | 1900 | 1901 | 1902 | Range of Prices, 1902. High. | Low. |
|---|---|---|---|---|---|---|---|---|---|---|---|
| Gansevoort Bank | 1889 | $200,000 | $50,820 | $50 | .. | .. | .. | .. | .. | $70 | $65 |
| Garfield National Bank | 1881 | 1,000,000 | 223,703 | 100 | 40 | 40 | 50 | 12 | 20 | 500 | 500 |
| German-American Bank | 1870 | 750,000 | 450,000 | 75 | 6 | 6 | 6 | 6 | 6 | 131 | 109 |
| German Exchange Bank | 1872 | 200,000 | 640,000 | 100 | 10 | 10 | 12 | 12 | 14 | 415 | 400 |
| Germania Bank | 1869 | 200,000 | 837,576 | 100 | 10 | 10 | 16 | 16 | 20 | 600 | 500 |
| Greenwich Bank | 1855 | 200,000 | 211,042 | 25 | 6 | 6 | 6 | 6 | 6 | 100 | 88 |
| Hamilton Bank | 1888 | 200,000 | 105,000 | 100 | 6 | 6 | 6 | 6 | 6 | 175 | 160 |
| Hanover National Bank | 1851 | 3,000,000 | 6,061,671 | 100 | 10 | 10 | 10 | 10 | 10 | 671 | 640 |
| Importers' & Traders' National Bank | 1855 | 1,500,000 | 6,300,186 | 100 | 20 | 20 | 20 | 20 | 20 | 690 | 650 |
| International Banking Corporation | 1902 | 6,000,000 | 783,000 | 100 | .. | .. | .. | .. | .. | 210 | 210 |
| Irving National Bank | 1851 | 1,000,000 | 1,006,000 | 50 | 8 | 8 | 8 | 8 | 8 | 125 | 100 |
| Jefferson Bank | 1902 | 400,000 | 216,000 | 100 | .. | .. | .. | .. | .. | 170 | 155 |
| Leather Manufacturers' National Bank | 1832 | 600,000 | 500,000 | 100 | 10 | 10 | 10 | 10 | 10 | 280 | 270 |
| Liberty National Bank | 1891 | 1,000,000 | 1,800,000 | 100 | .. | .. | .. | .. | 20 | 625 | 600 |
| Lincoln National Bank | 1882 | 300,000 | 1,226,406 | 100 | 12 | 18 | 18 | 18 | 18 | 1,050 | 1,050 |
| Market & Fulton National Bank | 1853 | 900,000 | 1,040,547 | 100 | 10 | 10 | 10 | 10 | 10 | 274 | 260 |
| Mechanics' & Traders' Bank | 1830 | 700,000 | 349,781 | 25 | 3 | .. | .. | 6 | 7 | 40 | 40 |
| Mechanics' National Bank | 1810 | 2,000,000 | 2,600,000 | 25 | 8 | 8 | 8 | 8 | 8 | 75 | 70 |
| Mercantile National Bank | 1850 | 1,000,000 | 1,517,722 | 100 | 6 | 6 | 6 | 6 | 8 | 325 | 293 |
| Merchants' Exchange National Bank | 1829 | 600,000 | 306,500 | 50 | 6 | 6 | 6 | 6 | 6 | 94 | 79 |
| Merchants' National Bank | 1803 | 2,000,000 | 1,250,000 | 50 | 7 | 7 | 7 | 7 | 7 | 96 | 91 |
| Mount Morris Bank | 1880 | 250,000 | 94,802 | 100 | .. | .. | .. | .. | .. | 240 | 200 |
| Mutual Bank | 1890 | 200,000 | 184,455 | 100 | .. | .. | .. | .. | .. | 305 | 190 |
| Nassau Bank | 1852 | 500,000 | 300,000 | 50 | 8 | 8 | 8 | 8 | 8 | 103 | 96 |
| National Bank of Commerce | 1839 | 10,000,000 | 7,700,000 | 100 | 8 | 8 | 8 | 8 | 8 | 390 | 310 |
| National Bank of North America | 1851 | 2,000,000 | 1,985,000 | 100 | 6 | 6 | 6 | 8 | 8 | 225 | 225 |
| National Broadway Bank | 1849 | 1,000,000 | 1,870,674 | 25 | 12 | 12 | 12 | 12 | 12 | 99 | 82 |
| National Butchers' and Drovers' Bank | 1830 | 300,000 | 86,359 | 25 | 6 | 6 | 3 | .. | .. | 43 | 38 |
| National Citizens' Bank | 1851 | 1,550,000 | 590,000 | 100 | 7 | 7 | 7 | 6 | 6 | 243 | 200 |
| National City Bank | 1812 | 25,000,000 | 15,394,495 | 100 | 15 | 15 | 6 | 6 | 6 | 375 | 290 |
| National Park Bank | 1856 | 2,000,000 | 4,407,000 | 100 | 10 | 11 | 12 | 15 | 15 | 653 | 641 |
| National Shoe & Leather Bank | 1853 | 1,000,000 | 323,000 | 100 | 4 | 4 | 4 | 4 | 4 | 200 | 110 |
| New Amsterdam National Bank | 1887 | 500,000 | 546,500 | 100 | .. | .. | 10 | 100 | 32 | 750 | 550 |
| New York County National Bank | 1855 | 200,000 | 622,000 | 100 | 40 | 45 | 50 | 150 | 75 | 1,516 | 1,516 |

| | | | | | | | | | | | |
|---|---|---|---|---|---|---|---|---|---|---|---|
| New York National Exchange Bank | 1851 | 500,000 | 368,340 | 100 | .. | .. | .. | .. | 8 | 275 | 230 |
| New York Produce Exchange Bank | 1883 | 1,000,000 | 463,105 | 100 | 6 | 6 | 6 | 6 | 7 | 178 | 168 |
| Nineteenth Ward Bank | 1884 | 200,000 | 185,000 | 100 | .. | .. | .. | .. | .. | 150 | 150 |
| Northern National Bank | 1902 | 300,000 | 211,228 | 100 | .. | .. | .. | .. | .. | 175 | 175 |
| Oriental Bank | 1853 | 300,000 | 419,201 | 25 | 10 | 10 | 10 | 10 | 10 | 59 | 56 |
| Pacific Bank | 1850 | 422,700 | 554,307 | 50 | 8 | 8 | 8 | 8 | 8 | 126 | 118 |
| People's Bank | 1851 | 200,000 | 369,742 | 25 | 10 | 10 | 10 | 10 | 10 | 75 | 75 |
| Phenix National Bank | 1812 | 1,000,000 | 273,500 | 20 | 6 | 6 | 6 | .. | .. | 27 | 23 |
| Plaza Bank | 1891 | 100,000 | 230,000 | 100 | .. | .. | .. | .. | .. | 600 | 600 |
| Riverside Bank | 1887 | 100,000 | 103,500 | 100 | 6 | 6½ | 8 | 8 | 8 | 350 | 310 |
| Royal Bank | 1902 | 100,000 | 1,500 | 100 | .. | .. | .. | .. | 2½ | 120 | 110 |
| Seaboard National Bank | 1883 | 500,000 | 1,250,000 | 100 | 6 | 6 | 6 | 6 | 6 | 650 | 550 |
| Second National Bank | 1863 | 300,000 | 1,214,832 | 100 | 12 | 12 | 12 | 12 | 12 | 700 | 650 |
| Seventh National Bank | 1833 | 2,500,000 | 168,491 | 100 | .. | 6 | 7 | .. | .. | 165 | 137 |
| State Bank | 1890 | 100,000 | 390,000 | 100 | 6 | 10 | 13 | 20 | 20 | 700 | 700 |
| Thirty-fourth Street National Bank | 1902 | 200,000 | 200,713 | 100 | .. | .. | .. | .. | .. | 210 | 210 |
| Twelfth Ward Bank | 1886 | 200,000 | 84,835 | 100 | 6 | 6 | 6 | 6 | 6 | 137 | 120 |
| Twenty-Third Ward Bank | 1888 | 100,000 | 86,700 | 100 | 5 | 5 | 5 | 5 | 5 | 125 | 125 |
| United National Bank | 1901 | 1,000,000 | 200,000 | 100 | .. | .. | .. | .. | .. | 140 | 125 |
| Varick Bank | 1901 | 100,000 | 67,606 | 100 | .. | .. | .. | .. | .. | 210 | 200 |
| Western National Bank | 1887 | 2,100,000 | 3,348,909 | 100 | .. | .. | .. | .. | .. | 624 | 610 |
| West Side Bank | 1869 | 200,000 | 490,468 | 100 | 12 | 12 | 12 | 12 | 12 | 575 | 575 |
| Yorkville Bank | 1893 | 100,000 | 246,518 | 100 | .. | .. | .. | .. | 6 | 380 | 350 |
| | | | | | | | | | | | |
| Bowling Green Trust Co. | 1900 | 2,500,000 | 2,956,329 | 100 | .. | .. | .. | .. | .. | 238 | 190 |
| Broadway Trust Co. | 1902 | 700,000 | 378,145 | 100 | .. | .. | .. | .. | .. | 174 | 174 |
| Central Realty Bond & Trust Co. | 1899 | 2,000,000 | 7,828,970 | 100 | .. | .. | .. | .. | 16 | 800 | 700 |
| Central Trust Co. | 1875 | 1,000,000 | 13,176,887 | 100 | 50 | 50 | 60 | 60 | 60 | 1,935 | 1,900 |
| City Trust Co. | 1899 | 1,000,000 | 1,666,718 | 100 | .. | .. | .. | .. | 8 | 390 | 370 |
| Colonial Trust Co. | 1897 | 1 [illegible] | 1,379,738 | 100 | .. | .. | 10 | 10 | 10 | 400 | 370 |
| Continental Trust Co. | 1890 | 1,000,000 | 3,150,000 | 100 | 6 | 6 | 6 | 6 | 6 | 680 | 450 |
| Eastern Trust Co. | 1902 | 1,000,000 | 953,391 | 100 | .. | .. | .. | .. | .. | 217 | 186 |
| Empire State Trust Co. | 1902 | 500,000 | 510,140 | 100 | .. | .. | .. | .. | .. | 200 | 190 |
| Equitable Trust Co. | 1902 | 3,000,000 | 8,619,486 | 100 | .. | .. | .. | .. | 3 | 550 | 550 |
| Farmers' Loan & Trust Co. | 1822 | 1,000,000 | 7,007,480 | 25 | 30 | 30 | 30 | 35 | 40 | 371 | 365 |
| Fifth Avenue Trust Co. | 1898 | 1,000,000 | 1,287,436 | 100 | .. | .. | .. | 20 | 17 | 643 | 643 |
| Guaranty Trust Co. | 1864 | 2,000,000 | 5,369,398 | 100 | 12 | 12 | 16 | 16 | 20 | 775 | 725 |
| Guardian Trust Co. | 1902 | 1,000,000 | 1,019,653 | 100 | .. | .. | .. | .. | .. | 195 | 195 |
| International Bank & Trust Co. | 1902 | 1,850,000 | 102,000 | 100 | .. | .. | .. | .. | 8 | 120 | 100 |
| Knickerbocker Trust Co. | 1884 | 1,000,000 | 1, [illegible]5 | 100 | 7 | 7 | 7 | 7 | 7 | 800 | 500 |
| Lincoln Trust Co. | 1902 | 500,000 | 523,510 | 100 | .. | .. | .. | .. | .. | 425 | 375 |
| McVickar Realty Trust Co. | 1902 | 500,000 | 541 69 | 100 | .. | .. | .. | .. | .. | 272 | 200 |

NEW YORK—*Continued.*

| Name. | Established. | Capital. | Surplus and Undivided Profits, Dec. 31, 1902. | Par Value of Stock. | Dividends Paid, Per Cent. 1898 | 1899 | 1900 | 1901 | 1902 | Range of Prices, 1902. High. | Low. |
|---|---|---|---|---|---|---|---|---|---|---|---|
| Manhattan Trust Co. | 1888 | $1,000,000 | $2,092,543 | $30 | 5 | 5 | 6 | 6 | 6 | $156 | $148 |
| Mercantile Trust Co. | 1873 | 2,000,000 | 657,634 | 100 | 16 | 16 | 20 | 25 | 30 | 1,250 | 1,200 |
| Merchants' Trust Co. | 1899 | 500,000 | 1,455,099 | 100 | .. | .. | .. | .. | | 345 | 320 |
| Metropolitan Trust Co. | 1881 | 1,000,000 | 2,369,578 | 100 | 10 | 10 | 10 | 10 | 10 | 725 | 525 |
| Morton Trust Co. | 1899 | 2,000,000 | 5,815,982 | 100 | .. | .. | .. | .. | .. | 1,190 | 1,090 |
| Mutual Alliance Trust Co. | 1902 | 500,000 | 513,026 | 100 | .. | .. | .. | .. | .. | 315 | 285 |
| New York Life Insurance & Trust Co. | 1830 | 1,000,000 | 4,152,432 | 100 | 40 | 40 | 40 | 40 | 40 | 1,300 | 1,175 |
| New York Security & Trust Co. | 1889 | 1,000,000 | 4,044,570 | 100 | 10 | 15 | 20 | 20 | 32 | 1,370 | 1,150 |
| North American Trust Co | 1885 | 2,000,000 | 3,006,671 | 100 | 5 | 5 | 5 | 7 | 7 | 325 | 250 |
| Real Estate Trust Co. | 1890 | 500,000 | 629,841 | 100 | 7 | 8 | 8 | 8 | 10 | 450 | 400 |
| Standard Trust Co. | 1898 | 1,000,000 | 816,763 | 100 | .. | .. | .. | 6 | 6 | 425 | 400 |
| Title Guarantee & Trust Co. | 1883 | 4,375,000 | 3,873,614 | 100 | 8 | 10 | 10 | 12 | 12 | 530 | 530 |
| Trust Co. of America | 1899 | 2,500,000 | 3,150,029 | 100 | .. | .. | 7 | 7 | 7 | 300 | 275 |
| Trust Co. of the Republic | 1902 | 1,000,000 | 595,248 | 100 | .. | .. | .. | .. | .. | 360 | 150 |
| Union Trust Co. | 1864 | 1,000,000 | 7,516,338 | 100 | 32 | 32 | 32 | 32 | 40 | 1,440 | 1,390 |
| United States Mortgage & Trust Co. | 1893 | 2,000,000 | 3,548,518 | 100 | 7 | 10 | 10 | 12 | 13 | 500 | 470 |
| United States Trust Co. | 1853 | 2,000,000 | 11,981,523 | 100 | 40 | 40 | 45 | 50 | 50 | 1,720 | 1,705 |
| Van Norden Trust Co. | 1901 | 1,000,000 | 1,060,928 | 100 | .. | .. | .. | .. | .. | 270 | 225 |
| Washington Trust Co | 1889 | 500,000 | 906,213 | 100 | 8 | 10 | 10 | 10 | 12 | 420 | 420 |
| Windsor Trust Co. | 1902 | 1,000,000 | 512,892 | 100 | .. | .. | .. | .. | .. | 275 | 160 |

## NORFOLK, VA.

| Name. | Established. | Capital. | Surplus and Undivided Profits, Dec. 31, 1902. | Par Value of Stock. | 1898 | 1899 | 1900 | 1901 | 1902 | High. | Low. |
|---|---|---|---|---|---|---|---|---|---|---|---|
| Citizens' Bank | 1867 | $300,000 | $200,000 | $100 | 6 | 6 | 6 | 8 | 8 | $190 | $190 |
| City National Bank | 1892 | 200,000 | 83,516 | 100 | 6 | 6 | 6 | 6 | 7 | 135 | 135 |
| Marine Bank | 1872 | 110,000 | 162,350 | 100 | 12 | 12 | 12 | 12 | 12 | 260 | 260 |
| National Bank of Commerce | 1878 | 500,000 | 280,000 | 100 | 6 | 8 | 8 | 8 | 8 | 175 | 166 |
| Norfolk National Bank | 1885 | 400,000 | 419,000 | 100 | 7 | 7½ | 8 | 8 | 10 | 225 | 200 |
| Atlantic Trust & Deposit Co. | 1902 | 78,900 | 85,917 | 100 | .. | .. | .. | .. | .. | ... | ... |
| Norfolk Bank for Savings & Trust | 1893 | 100,000 | 121,911 | 100 | 7 | 8 | 8 | 9 | 10 | ... | ... |
| Virginia-Carolina Trust Co. | 1903 | 250,000 | ........ | 100 | .. | .. | .. | .. | .. | ... | ... |
| Virginia Savings Bank & Trust Co. | 1902 | 100,000 | 4,380 | 100 | .. | .. | .. | .. | .. | 110 | 105 |

## OAKLAND, CAL.

| | | | | | | | | | | | |
|---|---|---|---|---|---|---|---|---|---|---|---|
| California Bank | 1887 | $100,000 | $4,283 | $100 | .. | .. | .. | .. | .. | $95 | $90 |
| Central Bank | 1891 | 300,000 | 261,000 | 30 | 6⅔ | 6⅔ | 6⅔ | 6⅔ | 6⅔ | 60 | 50 |
| First National Bank | 1875 | 300,000 | 89,557 | 100 | 6 | 6 | 6 | 6 | 6 | 130 | 125 |
| Union National Bank | 1875 | 150,000 | 166,294 | 100 | 8 | 8 | 8 | 8 | 8 | 150 | 150 |

## OGDEN, UTAH

| | | | | | | | | | | | |
|---|---|---|---|---|---|---|---|---|---|---|---|
| Commercial National Bank | 1884 | $100,000 | $17,808 | $100 | 6 | 6 | 6 | 6 | 6 | ... | .. |
| First National Bank | 1881 | 150,000 | 73,696 | 100 | 12 | 12 | 12 | 12 | 16 | $240 | $202 |
| Ogden State Bank | 1889 | 100,000 | 21,750 | 100 | 4 | 4 | 4 | 4 | 4 | 100 | 100 |
| Utah National Bank | 1874 | 100,000 | 24,133 | 100 | 6 | 6 | 6 | 6 | 12 | ... | ... |

## OKLAHOMA, OKLA.

| | | | | | | | | | | | |
|---|---|---|---|---|---|---|---|---|---|---|---|
| American National Bank | 1901 | $100,000 | $10,000 | $100 | .. | .. | .. | .. | 10 | $115 | $110 |
| Bank of Commerce | 1896 | 25,000 | 28,000 | 100 | 10 | 10 | 10 | 10 | 10 | 300 | 100 |
| State National Bank | 1893 | 50,000 | 115,000 | 100 | 12 | 12 | 12 | 12 | 12 | 140 | 140 |
| Western National Bank | 1899 | 100,000 | 72,000 | 100 | .. | .. | .. | 100 | .. | 250 | 250 |
| Oklahoma Trust & Banking Co. | 1902 | 200,000 | ...... | 100 | .. | .. | .. | .. | .. | 110 | 105 |
| Union Trust Co. | 1898 | 100,000 | 7,400 | 100 | .. | .. | 20 | 33 | 22 | 125 | 110 |

## OMAHA, NEB.

| | | | | | | | | | | | |
|---|---|---|---|---|---|---|---|---|---|---|---|
| Commercial National Bank | 1884 | $400,000 | $90,000 | $50 | .. | .. | .. | .. | .. | $110 | $90 |
| First National Bank | 1863 | 500,000 | 210,911 | 100 | 10 | 10 | 10 | 10 | 10 | 160 | 160 |
| Merchants' National Bank | 1882 | 500,000 | 127,765 | 100 | 4 | 4 | 4 | 4 | 4 | 120 | 120 |
| Nebraska National Bank | 1882 | 400,000 | 53,130 | 100 | .. | .. | .. | .. | .. | 115 | 110 |
| Omaha National Bank | 1866 | 1,000,000 | 188,439 | 100 | .. | .. | .. | .. | .. | 110 | 100 |
| Union National Bank | 1886 | 250,000 | 40,000 | 100 | .. | .. | .. | .. | .. | ... | ... |
| United States National Bank | 1856 | 400,000 | 130,000 | 100 | .. | .. | .. | .. | .. | 130 | 120 |
| Equitable Trust Co | 1883 | 200,000 | ....... | 100 | 5 | 5 | 4 | 3 | 3 | 85 | 75 |

## PATERSON, N. J.

| Name. | Established. | Capital. | Surplus and Undivided Profits, Dec. 31, 1902. | Par Value of Stock. | Dividends Paid, Per Cent. 1898 | 1899 | 1900 | 1901 | 1902 | Range of Prices, 1902. High. | Low. |
|---|---|---|---|---|---|---|---|---|---|---|---|
| First National Bank | 1864 | $400,000 | $435,000 | $100 | 11 | 12 | 12 | 13 | 14 | $475 | $450 |
| Paterson National Bank | 1889 | 300,000 | 232,000 | 100 | 6 | 6 | 6 | 6 | 6 | 280 | 275 |
| Paterson Savings Institution | 1869 | 500,000 | 500,067 | 100 | 25 | 15 | 20 | 20 | 10 | 580 | 550 |
| Second National Bank | 1864 | 150,000 | 187,000 | 50 | 10 | 10 | 10 | 10 | 10 | 175 | 175 |
| Citizens' Trust Co. | 1901 | 150,000 | 187,300 | 100 | .. | .. | .. | .. | 5 | 400 | 400 |
| German-American Trust Co. | 1902 | 150,000 | 150,000 | 100 | .. | .. | .. | .. | .. | 225 | 225 |
| Hamilton Trust Co. | 1900 | 150,000 | 250,000 | 100 | .. | .. | .. | .. | 6 | 480 | 400 |
| Paterson Safe Deposit & Trust Co. | 1891 | 100,000 | 188,131 | 100 | 6 | 6 | 8 | 10 | 10 | 800 | 800 |
| Silk City Safe Deposit & Trust Co. | 1893 | 100,000 | 65,220 | 100 | .. | .. | .. | .. | 5 | 300 | 300 |

## PEORIA, ILL.

| Name. | Established. | Capital. | Surplus and Undivided Profits, Dec. 31, 1902. | Par Value of Stock. | Dividends Paid, Per Cent. 1898 | 1899 | 1900 | 1901 | 1902 | Range of Prices, 1902. High. | Low. |
|---|---|---|---|---|---|---|---|---|---|---|---|
| Central National Bank | 1884 | $200,000 | $65,426 | $100 | .. | .. | .. | .. | .. | ... | ... |
| Commercial National Bank | 1885 | 200,000 | 171,000 | 100 | 6 | 6 | 6 | 8 | 8 | $165 | $165 |
| First National Bank | 1863 | 150,000 | 275,110 | 100 | 6 | 6 | 6 | 6 | 6 | 250 | 250 |
| German-American National Bank | 1884 | 300,000 | 92,500 | 100 | 9 | 10 | 8 | 7 | 7 | 150 | 140 |
| Home Savings & State Bank | 1892 | 120,000 | 16,825 | 100 | 3 | 5 | 6 | 5 | 6 | 110 | 107 |
| Illinois National Bank | 1900 | 200,000 | 40,009 | 100 | .. | .. | 3 | 6 | 6 | 105 | 105 |
| Merchants' National Bank | 1884 | 200,000 | 123,422 | 100 | 10 | 11 | 12 | 12 | 12 | 200 | 185 |
| Peoria National Bank | 1883 | 200,000 | 45,000 | 100 | 7 | 7 | 7 | 6 | 6 | 125 | 125 |
| Anthony Loan & Trust Co. | 1866 | 164,300 | 20,000 | 100 | 6 | 6 | 6 | 6 | 6 | 117 | 117 |
| Title & Trust Co. | 1890 | 100,000 | 11,140 | 100 | .. | .. | .. | .. | .. | 100 | 90 |

## PHILADELPHIA, PA.

| Name. | Established. | Capital. | Surplus and Undivided Profits, Dec. 31, 1902. | Par Value of Stock. | Dividends Paid, Per Cent. 1898 | 1899 | 1900 | 1901 | 1902 | Range of Prices, 1902. High. | Low. |
|---|---|---|---|---|---|---|---|---|---|---|---|
| Bank of North America | 1781 | $1,000,000 | $1,988,000 | $100 | 12 | 12 | 12 | 12 | 12 | $281 | $265 |
| Centennial National Bank | 1876 | 300,000 | 293,682 | 100 | 10 | 10 | 10 | 10 | 10 | 186 | 186 |
| Central National Bank | 1865 | 750,000 | 2,298,042 | 100 | 12 | 12 | 12 | 12 | 12 | 390 | 361 |
| Consolidation National Bank | 1855 | 300,000 | 203,500 | 30 | 8 | 8 | 7 | 6 | 6 | 41 | 40 |

| | | | | | | | | | | | |
|---|---|---|---|---|---|---|---|---|---|---|---|
| Corn Exchange National Bank | 1864 | 500,000 | 780,000 | 50 | 7½ | 8 | 8 | 8 | 8 | 110 | 90 |
| Eighth National Bank | 1864 | 275,000 | 660,643 | 100 | 12 | 12 | 12 | 12 | 12 | 254 | 254 |
| Farmers' & Mechanics' National Bank | 1807 | 2,000,000 | 921,000 | 100 | 6 | 6 | 6 | 6 | 6 | 150 | 125 |
| First National Bank | 1863 | 1,000,000 | 780,000 | 100 | 10 | 10 | 10 | 10 | 10 | 210 | 210 |
| Fourth Street National Bank | 1886 | 3,000,000 | 4,252,282 | 100 | 8 | 8 | 8 | 8 | 8 | 258 | 230 |
| Fox Chase Bank | 1898 | 50,000 | 33,594 | 50 | .. | .. | 5 | 5 | 5 | 72 | 72 |
| Franklin National Bank | 1900 | 1,000,000 | 1,341,000 | 100 | .. | .. | .. | 6 | 9 | 320 | 295 |
| Girard National Bank | 1832 | 1,500,000 | 1,924,500 | 100 | 10 | 10 | 10 | 15 | 10 | 263 | 250 |
| Kensington National Bank | 1826 | 250,000 | 215,366 | 50 | 6 | 6 | 6 | 6 | 6 | 68 | 63 |
| Manayunk National Bank | 1871 | 200,000 | 248,866 | 100 | 10 | 10 | 10 | 10 | 10 | 215 | 206 |
| Manufacturers' National Bank | 1832 | 500,000 | 290,463 | 100 | 5 | 5 | 5 | 5 | 5 | 112 | 104 |
| Market Street National Bank | 1887 | 500,000 | 318,000 | 100 | 5½ | .. | 2½ | 5 | 5 | 140 | 118 |
| Merchants' National Bank | 1880 | 600,000 | 625,000 | 100 | 5 | 5 | 5 | 5 | 5 | 175 | 136 |
| National Bank of Germantown | 1814 | 200,000 | 476,000 | 50 | 12 | 12 | 12 | 12 | 12 | 165 | 160 |
| National Bank of the Northern Liberties | 1810 | 500,000 | 790,777 | 100 | 12 | 12 | 12 | 12 | 12 | 262 | 230 |
| National Security Bank | 1871 | 250,000 | 422,403 | 100 | 8 | 8 | 8 | 8 | 8 | 200 | 200 |
| Ninth National Bank | 1885 | 300,000 | 370,000 | 100 | 6 | 7 | 7 | 7 | 8 | 200 | 154 |
| Northern National Bank | 1890 | 200,000 | 17,878 | 100 | 5 | 5 | 6 | 6 | 7 | 126 | 126 |
| Northwestern National Bank | 1886 | 200,000 | 329,300 | 100 | 8 | 8 | 10 | 10 | 10 | 225 | 225 |
| Penn National Bank | 1828 | 500,000 | 838,500 | 50 | 8 | 8 | 8 | 8 | 8 | 105 | 100 |
| Philadelphia National Bank | 1804 | 1,500,000 | 2,085,742 | 100 | 10 | 10 | 10 | 10 | 10 | 310 | 272 |
| Quaker City National Bank | 1889 | 500,000 | 311,000 | 100 | 4 | 5 | 6 | 6 | 6 | 119 | 119 |
| Ridge Avenue Bank | 1899 | 150,000 | 38,270 | 50 | .. | .. | .. | .. | .. | 56 | 56 |
| Second National Bank | 1864 | 280,000 | 323,886 | 100 | 6 | 6 | 6 | 6 | 7 | 153 | 151 |
| Sixth National Bank | 1864 | 150,000 | 215,814 | 100 | 8 | 8 | 8 | 8 | 8 | 176 | 159 |
| Southwark National Bank | 1825 | 250,000 | 150,000 | 50 | 10 | 8 | 8 | 8 | 8 | 70 | 65 |
| Southwestern National Bank | 1886 | 200,000 | 97,000 | 100 | 5 | 5 | 5 | 5 | 5 | 100 | 100 |
| Tenth National Bank | 1886 | 200,000 | 84,130 | 100 | 5 | 5 | 5 | 5 | 5 | 100 | 98 |
| Third National Bank | 1864 | 600,000 | 551,176 | 100 | 5 | 5 | 5 | 6 | 6 | 140 | 122 |
| Tradesmen's National Bank | 1846 | 500,000 | 478,000 | 50 | 6 | 6 | 6 | 6 | 6 | 100 | 80 |
| Union National Bank | 1858 | 500,000 | 579,600 | 50 | 7 | 7 | 7 | 7 | 7 | 85 | 85 |
| Western National Bank | 1832 | 400,000 | 219,867 | 50 | 10 | 10 | 10 | 10 | 10 | 101 | 75 |
| American Trust Co. | 1886 | 200,000 | 53,677 | 50 | 4 | 4 | 4 | 4 | 4 | 40 | 35 |
| City Trust, Safe Deposit & Surety Co. | 1886 | 500,000 | 375,000 | 100 | 6 | 6 | 6 | 6 | 6 | 135 | 133 |
| Colonial Trust Co. | 1899 | 250,000 | 24,099 | 50 | .. | .. | .. | .. | .. | 53 | 53 |
| Columbia Avenue Trust Co. | 1887 | 400,000 | 111,760 | 100 | 5½ | 5 | .. | .. | 5 | 100 | 100 |
| Commercial Trust Co. | 1894 | 1,000,000 | 1,390,725 | 100 | .. | .. | 6 | 8 | 8 | 300 | 300 |
| Commonwealth Title Insurance & Trust Co. | 1886 | 1,000,000 | 1,046,177 | 50 | 12 | 12 | 12 | 12 | 12 | 99 | 73 |
| Continental Title & Trust Co. | 1898 | 500,000 | 164,942 | 50 | .. | .. | .. | .. | 4 | 39 | 37 |
| Equitable Trust Co. | 1890 | 1,000,000 | 242,557 | 100 | 7 | 8 | 8 | 7 | 6 | 125 | 101 |
| Excelsior Trust & Saving Fund Co. | 1900 | 150,000 | 6,609 | 25 | .. | .. | .. | .. | .. | 26 | 26 |

PHILADELPHIA—*Continued.*

| NAME. | Established. | Capital. | Surplus and Undivided Profits. Dec. 31, 1902. | Par Value of Stock. | Dividends Paid, Per Cent. | | | | | Range of Prices, 1902. | |
|---|---|---|---|---|---|---|---|---|---|---|---|
| | | | | | 1898 | 1899 | 1900 | 1901 | 1902 | High. | Low. |
| Fidelity Trust Co. | 1866 | $2,000,000 | $4,630,566 | $100 | 18 | 18 | 18 | 18 | 18 | $646 | $646 |
| Finance Co. of Pennsylvania | 1871 | 3,495,300 | 526,654 | 100 | 6 | 6 | 6 | 6 | 6 | 106 | 103 |
| Frankford Real Estate, Trust & Safe Deposit Co. | 1896 | 125,000 | 48,584 | 50 | 5 | 5 | 5 | 5 | 5 | 63 | 60 |
| German-American Title & Trust Co. | 1885 | 500,000 | 103,628 | 50 | .. | 1½ | 3 | 3 | 3 | 57 | 43 |
| Germantown Trust Co. | 1889 | 600,000 | 450,000 | 100 | 5 | 5 | 5 | 5½ | 6 | 180 | 173 |
| Girard Trust Co. | 1836 | 2,500,000 | 8,324,819 | 100 | 16 | 16 | 19 | 19 | 20 | 685 | 621 |
| Guarantee Trust & Safe Deposit Co. | 1871 | 1,000,000 | 357,874 | 100 | 10 | 10 | 10 | 10 | 10 | 210 | 185 |
| Hamilton Trust Co. | 1901 | 125,000 | 2,500 | 50 | .. | .. | .. | .. | 2 | 56 | 56 |
| Industrial Trust, Title & Savings Co. | 1889 | 350,000 | 370,000 | 50 | 6 | 6 | 6 | 7 | 7½ | 63 | 61 |
| Integrity Title Insurance, Trust & Safe Dep. Co. | 1887 | 500,000 | 531,433 | 50 | 6 | 6 | 6 | 8 | 8 | 102 | 100 |
| Investment Co. | 1871 | 2,000,000 | 1,068,971 | 50 | .. | .. | .. | 6 | 6 | 80 | 70 |
| Land Title & Trust Co. | 1885 | 1,000,000 | 1,074,148 | 100 | 5 | 6 | 6 | 6 | 6 | 305 | 295 |
| Lincoln Savings & Trust Co. | 1895 | 132,000 | 34,500 | 25 | 2 | .. | .. | 4 | 4 | 25 | 25 |
| Manayunk Trust Co. | 1889 | 250,000 | 78,000 | 25 | 5 | 5 | 5 | 6 | 6 | 41 | 40 |
| Merchants' Trust Co. | 1889 | 404,970 | 93,383 | 25 | 5 | 5 | 5 | 5 | 5 | 30 | 16 |
| Mortgage Trust Co. | 1890 | 500,000 | 169,418 | 100 | .. | .. | .. | .. | .. | 20 | 20 |
| Northern Trust Co. | 1871 | 500,000 | 625,000 | 100 | 7 | 7 | 7 | 7 | 8 | 250 | 210 |
| Pennsylvania Co. for Ins. on Lives & Gr. An. | 1812 | 2,000,000 | 2,895,514 | 100 | 18 | 18 | 18 | 20 | 20 | 630 | 526 |
| Pennsylvania Warehousing & Safe Deposit Co. | 1881 | 441,100 | 576,855 | 50 | 8 | 8 | 8 | 8 | 8 | 80 | 80 |
| Philadelphia Mortgage & Trust Co. | 1886 | 1,000,000 | 50,000 | 100 | .. | .. | .. | .. | .. | 45 | 45 |
| Phila. Trust, Safe Deposit & Insurance Co. | 1869 | 1,000,000 | 3,089,033 | 100 | 16 | 16 | 16 | 16 | 16 | 533 | 462 |
| Provident Life & Trust Co. | 1865 | 1,000,000 | 4,457,613 | 100 | 18 | 20 | 21 | 23½ | 24½ | 715 | 700 |
| Real Estate Title Insurance & Trust Co. | 1876 | 1,000,000 | 328,682 | 100 | 5 | 5 | 5 | 5 | 5 | 141 | 140 |
| Real Estate Trust Co. | 1885 | 1,500,000 | 1,300,000 | 50 | 6 | 8 | 8 | 8 | 10 | 200 | 200 |
| Safety Banking & Trust Co. | 1900 | 50,000 | 9,030 | 50 | .. | .. | .. | .. | .. | .. | .. |
| Tacony Trust Co. | 1892 | 127,500 | 72,100 | 100 | 4 | 4½ | 5 | 6 | 6 | 105 | 105 |
| Tradesmen's Trust & Savings Fund Co. | 1890 | 125,00c | 114,839 | 50 | 6 | 6 | 6 | 6 | 6 | 31 | 25 |
| Trust Co. of North America | 1889 | 1,000,000 | 168,924 | 100 | .. | 1½ | .. | .. | .. | 145 | 121 |
| Union Surety & Guaranty Co. | 1899 | 250,000 | 114,401 | 50 | .. | .. | .. | .. | .. | .. | .. |
| Union Trust Co. | 1882 | 500,000 | 250,000 | 50 | 2½ | 5 | 2½ | .. | .. | 44 | 40 |
| United Security Life Insurance & Trust Co. | 1887 | 1,000,000 | 539,428 | 100 | 6 | 5 | 5 | 5 | 5 | 115 | 105 |
| West End Trust Co. | 1891 | 1,000,000 | 835,000 | 50 | 5 | 5 | 5 | 5 | 6 | 111 | 103 |
| West Philadelphia Title & Trust Co. | 1890 | 250,000 | 160,166 | 50 | 6 | 6 | 6 | 6 | 6 | 51 | 45 |

## PITTSBURG, PA.

| | | | | | | | | | | | |
|---|---|---|---|---|---|---|---|---|---|---|---|
| Allegheny National Bank | 1857 | $500,000 | $605,000 | $50 | 6 | 6 | 6 | 6 | 7 | $135 | $115 |
| Allegheny Valley Bank | 1901 | 50,000 | 7,565 | 50 | .. | .. | .. | .. | .. | 65 | 60 |
| Anchor Savings Bank | 1873 | 50,000 | 52,340 | 50 | 5 | 5 | 5 | 5 | 5 | 125 | 115 |
| Arsenal Bank | 1872 | 100,000 | 102,000 | 50 | 8 | 10 | 10 | 10 | 10 | 150 | 140 |
| Bank of Pittsburg | 1810 | 1,200,000 | 858,785 | 50 | 8 | 8 | 8 | 8 | 8 | 141 | 134 |
| City Deposit Bank | 1871 | 200,000 | 348,943 | 50 | 10 | 10 | 10 | 10 | 12 | 204 | 190 |
| Columbia National Bank | 1893 | 600,000 | 1,100,000 | 100 | 6 | 6 | 6 | 6 | 9 | 465 | 360 |
| Commercial National Bank | 1882 | 300,000 | 185,000 | 100 | 5 | 5 | 5 | 5 | 5 | 200 | 145 |
| Cosmopolitan National Bank | 1902 | 200,000 | 4,048 | 100 | .. | .. | .. | .. | .. | 110 | 110 |
| Diamond National Bank | 1875 | 500,000 | 1,265,000 | 100 | 10 | 10 | 14 | 14 | 16 | 455 | 40 |
| Duquesne National Bank | 1901 | 500,000 | 700,000 | 100 | 8 | 8 | 8 | 10 | 10 | 299 | 275 |
| Exchange National Bank | 1836 | 1,200,000 | 740,000 | 50 | 6 | 6 | 6 | 6 | 6 | 100 | 85 |
| Farmers' Deposit National Bank | 1832 | 800,000 | 6,139,630 | 100 | 20 | 20 | 20 | 26 | 30 | 1,400 | 940 |
| Federal National Bank | 1901 | 2,000,000 | 555,000 | 100 | .. | .. | .. | .. | .. | 150 | 121 |
| Fifth Avenue Bank | 1869 | 100,000 | 32,800 | 50 | .. | 5 | 5 | 5 | 6 | 75 | 60 |
| Fifth National Bank | 1873 | 100,000 | 36,413 | 100 | 6 | 6 | 6 | 6 | 6 | 200 | 200 |
| First National Bank | 1852 | 1,000,000 | 2,165,910 | 100 | 8 | 8 | 8 | 8 | 10 | 690 | 497 |
| First National Bank of Birmingham | 1865 | 100,000 | 183,750 | 100 | 16 | 17 | 16 | 16 | 16 | 347 | 347 |
| Fort Pitt National Bank | 1879 | 200,000 | 275,300 | 100 | 6 | 6 | 6 | 6 | 7 | 300 | 250 |
| Fourth National Bank | 1864 | 300,000 | 118,000 | 100 | 6 | 6 | 6 | 6 | 6 | 160 | 150 |
| Freehold Bank | 1870 | 200,000 | 1,004,000 | 50 | 16 | 16 | 18 | 24 | 74 | 350 | 108 |
| Germania Savings Bank | 1870 | 150,000 | 259,882 | 100 | 6 | 6 | 6 | 6 | 8 | 375 | 300 |
| German National Bank | 1864 | 250,000 | 209,555 | 100 | 6 | 3 | 6 | 6 | 6 | 260 | 250 |
| Hill Top German Savings Bank | 1900 | 75,000 | 10,000 | 50 | .. | .. | .. | 4 | 5 | 68 | 60 |
| Iron City National Bank | 1857 | 400,000 | 345,000 | 50 | 8 | 8 | 8 | 8 | 8 | 125 | 115 |
| Keystone Bank | 1884 | 500,000 | 741,181 | 100 | 6 | 6 | 8 | 10 | 10 | 400 | 375 |
| Liberty National Bank | 1890 | 200,000 | 102,600 | 100 | 6 | 6 | 6 | 6 | 6 | 200 | 145 |
| Lincoln National Bank | 1869 | 600,000 | 790,000 | 100 | 6 | 6 | 6 | 6 | 8 | 257 | 252 |
| Manufacturers' Bank | 1889 | 100,000 | 130,140 | 50 | 8 | 8 | 10 | 12 | 12 | 122 | 115 |
| Marine National Bank | 1875 | 300,000 | 75,000 | 100 | 4 | 4 | 4 | 4 | 4 | 118 | 113 |
| Mellon National Bank | 1902 | 2,000,000 | 226,062 | 100 | .. | .. | .. | .. | .. | .. | .. |
| Merchants' & Manufacturers' National Bank | 1833 | 800,000 | 888,000 | 50 | 7 | 7 | 8 | 8 | 8 | 148 | 133 |
| Metropolitan National Bank | 1875 | 200,000 | 129,000 | 100 | 6 | 6 | 6 | 6 | 8 | 185 | 150 |
| Monongahela National Bank | 1888 | 500,000 | 553,468 | 100 | 6 | 6 | 6 | 8 | 8 | 299 | 260 |
| National Bank of Western Pennsylvania | 1893 | 500,000 | 385,000 | 100 | 6 | 6 | 6 | 6 | 6 | 200 | 195 |
| North American Savings Co. | 1901 | 700,000 | 450,000 | 50 | .. | .. | .. | .. | 6 | 135 | 80 |
| Pennsylvania National Bank | 1890 | 200,000 | 140,000 | 100 | 6 | 6 | 6 | 6 | 6 | 170 | 70 |
| People's National Bank | 1864 | 1,000,000 | 1,350,000 | 100 | 8 | 8 | 10 | 10 | 12 | 460 | 40 |
| People's Savings Bank | 1866 | 300,000 | 511,057 | 100 | 8 | 8 | 8 | 8 | 8 | 350 | 35 |
| Pittsburg Bank for Savings | 1862 | 75,000 | 300,000 | 100 | 10 | 10 | 10 | 10 | 10 | 800 | 80 |
| Pittsburg National Bank of Commerce | 1864 | 500,000 | 1,140,000 | 100 | 12 | 12 | 12 | 12 | 12 | 440 | 45 |

## PITTSBURG—*Continued.*

| Name. | Established. | Capital. | Surplus and Undivided Profits. Dec. 31, 1902. | Par Value of Stock. | Dividends Paid, Per Cent. | | | | | Range of Prices, 1902. | |
|---|---|---|---|---|---|---|---|---|---|---|---|
| | | | | | 1898 | 1899 | 1900 | 1901 | 1902 | High. | Low. |
| Republic National Bank | 1902 | $200,000 | $27,200 | $100 | .. | .. | .. | .. | .. | $125 | $115 |
| Second National Bank | 1864 | 600,000 | 3,180,514 | 100 | 12 | 12 | 12 | 12 | 24 | 900 | 850 |
| State Bank of Pittsburg | 1896 | 50,000 | 13,000 | 50 | .. | 2 | 4 | 4 | 4 | 90 | 73 |
| Third National Bank | 1864 | 500,000 | 230,126 | 100 | .. | .. | .. | 6 | 6 | 208 | 190 |
| Traders' & Mechanics' Bank | 1872 | 100,000 | 37,241 | 50 | .. | .. | .. | 4 | 4 | 71 | 58 |
| Tradesmen's National Bank | 1865 | 400,000 | 269,132 | 100 | 6 | 6 | 6 | 6 | 6 | 200 | 175 |
| Union National Bank | 1859 | 250,000 | 1,274,000 | 100 | 16 | 20 | 24 | 24 | 30 | 1,053 | 1,053 |
| Union Savings Bank | 1902 | 1,000,000 | 12,993 | 100 | .. | .. | .. | .. | .. | .. | .. |
| United States National Bank | 1895 | 200,000 | 16,823 | 100 | 6 | 6 | 6 | 6 | 6 | 140 | 140 |
| Washington National Bank | 1903 | 200,000 | 100,000 | 100 | .. | .. | .. | .. | .. | .. | .. |
| West End Savings Bank | 1871 | 62,600 | 103,280 | 50 | 6 | 6 | 8 | 8 | 9 | 125 | 125 |
| Western Savings & Deposit Bank | 1895 | 250,000 | 226,785 | 50 | 5 | 6 | 6 | 6 | 7½ | 115 | 100 |
| American Trust Co. | 1900 | 1,000,000 | 103,879 | 100 | .. | .. | .. | .. | .. | 170 | 118 |
| Colonial Trust Co. | 1902 | 2,000,000 | 3,225,000 | 100 | .. | .. | .. | .. | 9 | 680 | 250 |
| Commonwealth Real Estate & Trust Co. | 1902 | 1,500,000 | 1,071,657 | 100 | .. | .. | .. | .. | .. | 260 | 215 |
| East End Savings & Trust Co. | 1901 | 250,000 | 77,000 | 100 | .. | .. | .. | .. | .. | 135 | 135 |
| Equitable Trust Co. | 1898 | 750,000 | 350,839 | 100 | .. | .. | .. | 6 | 6 | 190 | 170 |
| Fidelity Title & Trust Co. | 1886 | 1,000,000 | 1,048,931 | 100 | 6 | 6 | 6 | 6 | 7½ | 700 | 405 |
| German-American Savings & Trust Co. | 1902 | 1,000,000 | 500,000 | 100 | .. | .. | .. | .. | .. | 175 | 165 |
| Hazelwood Savings & Trust Co. | 1901 | 125,000 | 13,000 | 100 | .. | .. | .. | .. | .. | 112 | 105 |
| Iron City Trust Co. | 1902 | 1,000,000 | 392,306 | 100 | .. | .. | .. | .. | .. | 155 | 129 |
| Mercantile Trust Co. | 1891 | 750,000 | 213,334 | 100 | 8 | 8 | 8 | 8 | 8 | 210 | 175 |
| Merchants' Savings & Trust Co. | 1902 | 500,000 | 100,000 | 50 | .. | .. | .. | .. | .. | 68 | 68 |
| Moreland Trust Co. | 1901 | 200,000 | 40,000 | 100 | .. | .. | .. | .. | .. | .. | .. |
| Pennsylvania Trust Co. | 1895 | 500,000 | 320,000 | 100 | .. | .. | 6 | 6 | 6 | 315 | 220 |
| People's Trust Co. | 1901 | 250,000 | 20,163 | 100 | .. | .. | .. | .. | .. | 110 | 107 |
| Pittsburg Trust Co. | 1893 | 2,000,000 | 4,000,000 | 100 | 6 | 6 | 8 | 13⅓ | 25 | 900 | 450 |
| Prudential Trust Co. | 1901 | 200,000 | 42,000 | 100 | .. | .. | .. | .. | .. | 150 | 145 |
| Public Trust Co. | 1902 | 224,385 | 1,772 | 100 | .. | .. | .. | .. | .. | 100 | 100 |
| Real Estate Trust Co. | 1900 | 2,000,000 | 1,735,650 | 100 | .. | .. | 8 | 8 | 10 | 321 | 280 |
| Safe Deposit & Trust Co. | 1867 | 1,000,000 | 681,896 | 50 | 6 | 6 | 6 | 6 | 7½ | 120 | 102 |
| South Side Trust Co. | 1901 | 300,000 | 15,000 | 100 | .. | .. | .. | .. | .. | 116 | 100 |
| Standard Security Trust Co. | 1902 | 250,000 | 137,000 | 100 | .. | .. | .. | .. | .. | 175 | 170 |
| Union Trust Co. | 1889 | 1,500,000 | 16,000,000 | 100 | 6 | 6 | 6 | 6 | 6 | 2,150 | 730 |

## PORTLAND, ME.

| | | | | | | | | | | | |
|---|---|---|---|---|---|---|---|---|---|---|---|
| Canal National Bank | 1865 | $600,000 | $200,000 | $100 | 6 | 5 | 6 | 6 | 6 | $107 | $103 |
| Casco National Bank | 1824 | 800,000 | 325,900 | 100 | 8 | 8 | 8 | 6½ | 6 | 106 | 103 |
| Chapman National Bank | 1893 | 100,000 | 50,000 | 100 | 6 | 6 | 6½ | 7 | 7 | 110 | 105 |
| Cumberland National Bank | 1812 | 150,000 | 36,722 | 100 | 6 | 6 | 6 | 6 | 6 | 102 | 101 |
| First National Bank | 1864 | 600,000 | 212,225 | 100 | 6 | 6 | 6 | 6 | 6 | 110 | 102 |
| Merchants' National Bank | 1825 | 300,000 | 362,000 | 75 | 10 | 8 | 8 | 8 | 8 | 110 | 104 |
| National Traders' Bank | 1865 | 200,000 | 70,000 | 100 | 6 | 6 | 6 | 6 | 6 | 106 | 100 |
| Portland National Bank | 1889 | 300,000 | 175,000 | 100 | 6 | 6 | 6 | 6 | 6 | 150 | 150 |
| Mercantile Trust Co. | 1898 | 100,000 | 60,090 | 100 | 3 | 6 | 6 | 6 | 6 | 140 | 140 |
| Portland Trust Co. | 1885 | 200,000 | 301,250 | 100 | 8 | 8 | 8 | 14 | 18 | 235 | 200 |
| Union Safe Deposit & Trust Co. | 1894 | 250,000 | 97,248 | 100 | 5 | 5 | 5 | 5 | 5 | 147 | 145 |

## PORTLAND, ORE.

| | | | | | | | | | | | |
|---|---|---|---|---|---|---|---|---|---|---|---|
| First National Bank | 85 | $500,000 | $765,000 | $100 | 24 | 24 | 44 | 26 | 26 | $325 | $325 |
| Merchants' National Bank | 1886 | 250,000 | 95,000 | 100 | .. | .. | .. | .. | 4 | 100 | 80 |
| United States National Bank | 81 | 300,000 | 55,000 | 100 | 5 | 6 | 6 | 6 | 3 | 120 | 90 |
| Portland Trust Co. | 87 | 259,000 | ...... | 100 | .. | .. | .. | .. | .. | .. | .. |
| Security Savings & Trust Co. | 1890 | 250,000 | 50,000 | 100 | 6 | 6 | 6 | 6 | 8 | 117 | 110 |

## PROVIDENCE, R. I.

| | | | | | | | | | | | |
|---|---|---|---|---|---|---|---|---|---|---|---|
| American National Bank | 1834 | $1,000,000 | $173,130 | $50 | 5 | 4 | 4 | 4 | 4 | $53 | $49 |
| Atlantic National Bank | 1853 | 225,000 | 21,650 | 50 | 4 | .. | 4 | 4 | 4 | 45 | 40 |
| Blackstone Canal National Bank | 1831 | 500,000 | 217,000 | 25 | 4 | 4 | 4 | 4 | 4 | 30 | 29 |
| Commercial National Bank | 1833 | 500,000 | 170,000 | 100 | 5 | 5 | 5 | 5 | 4 | 115 | 110 |
| First National Bank | 1863 | 500,000 | 190,000 | 100 | 6 | 6 | 6 | 6 | 6 | 125 | 118 |
| Fourth National Bank | 1864 | 500,000 | 200,000 | 100 | 6 | 6 | 6 | 6 | 6 | 120 | 116 |
| High Street Bank | 1828 | 120,000 | 87,000 | 50 | 8 | 8 | 8 | 8 | 8 | 75 | 75 |
| Mechanics' National Bank | 1823 | 500,000 | 142,000 | 50 | 3 | 4 | 4 | 4 | 4 | 54 | 51 |
| Merchants' National Bank | 1818 | 1,000,000 | 560,000 | 50 | 6 | 6 | 6 | 6 | 6 | 77 | 74 |
| National Bank of Commerce | 1865 | 850,000 | 254,319 | 50 | .. | 4 | 5 | 5 | 5 | 56 | 53 |
| National Bank of North America | 1823 | 500,000 | 235,115 | 50 | .. | .. | 3 | 4 | 4 | 58 | 50 |
| National Exchange Bank | 1801 | 500,000 | 661,028 | 50 | 8 | 8 | 8 | 8 | 8 | 115 | 110 |
| Old National Bank | 1834 | 500,000 | 73,000 | 100 | 5 | 4 | 4 | 4 | 4 | 98 | 95 |

PROVIDENCE—*Continued.*

| Name. | Established. | Capital. | Surplus and Undivided Profits. Dec. 31, 1902. | Par Value of Stock | Dividends Paid, Per Cent. 1898 | 1899 | 1900 | 1901 | 1902 | Range of Prices, 1902. High. | Low. |
|---|---|---|---|---|---|---|---|---|---|---|---|
| Phenix National Bank | 1835 | $450,000 | $485,000 | $50 | 7 | 7 | 8 | 8 | 8 | $100 | $98 |
| Providence Banking Co. | 1896 | 200,000 | 500,000 | 100 | 8 | 8 | 9 | 12 | 10 | .. | .. |
| Providence National Bank | 1791 | 500,000 | 623,898 | 400 | 8 | 8 | 8 | 8 | 8 | 800 | 800 |
| United National Bank | 1901 | 500,000 | 547,846 | 100 | .. | .. | .. | .. | 8 | 203 | 203 |
| Westminster Bank | 1854 | 200,000 | 69,868 | 50 | 6 | 6 | 6 | 6 | 6 | 63 | 60 |
| Weybosset National Bank | 1831 | 500,000 | 133,209 | 50 | 4 | 4 | 4 | 4 | 4 | 58 | 55 |
| Industrial Trust Co. | 1887 | 1,500,000 | 1,561,900 | 100 | 4 | 4 | 5½ | 6 | 6 | 400 | 275 |
| Manufacturers' Trust Co. | 1813 | 500,000 | 485,000 | 100 | 6 | 6 | 6 | 6 | 6 | 200 | 200 |
| Rhode Island Hospital Trust Co. | 1867 | 1,000,000 | 1,300,000 | 1,000 | 8 | 9 | 10 | 10 | 10 | 3,250 | 3,250 |
| Union Trust Co. | 1851 | 250,000 | 870,884 | 100 | 4 | 4 | 4 | 4 | 4 | 353 | 353 |

## PUEBLO, COL.

| Name. | Established. | Capital. | Surplus and Undivided Profits. Dec. 31, 1902. | Par Value of Stock | 1898 | 1899 | 1900 | 1901 | 1902 | High. | Low. |
|---|---|---|---|---|---|---|---|---|---|---|---|
| First National Bank | 1871 | $300,000 | $104,989 | $100 | .. | .. | .. | .. | .. | .. | .. |
| Mercantile National Bank | 1898 | 100,000 | 25,000 | 100 | .. | .. | .. | 6 | 6 | $175 | $100 |
| Western National Bank | 1881 | 100,000 | 17,982 | 100 | .. | .. | .. | .. | .. | 135 | 110 |
| Pueblo Title & Trust Co. | 1902 | 250,000 | ...... | 100 | .. | .. | .. | .. | .. | .. | .. |

## RALEIGH, N C.

| Name. | Established. | Capital. | Surplus and Undivided Profits. Dec. 31, 1902. | Par Value of Stock | 1898 | 1899 | 1900 | 1901 | 1902 | High. | Low. |
|---|---|---|---|---|---|---|---|---|---|---|---|
| Citizens' National Bank | 1871 | $100,000 | $79,000 | $100 | 8 | 8 | 8 | 10 | 10 | $150 | $150 |
| Commercial & Farmers' Bank | 1891 | 100,000 | 52,500 | 50 | 8 | 8 | 8 | 8 | 8 | 70 | 65 |
| National Bank | 1885 | 225,000 | 107,452 | 100 | .. | .. | .. | .. | .. | 120 | 115 |
| Carolina Trust Co. | 1901 | 100,000 | 3,200 | 00 | .. | .. | .. | .. | .. | 104 | 100 |

## READING, PA.

| | | | | | | | | | | | |
|---|---|---|---|---|---|---|---|---|---|---|---|
| Farmers' National Bank | 1814 | $400,020 | $645,576 | $30 | 10 | 10 | 10 | 10 | 12 | $102 | $90 |
| First National Bank | 1863 | 500,000 | 211,064 | 100 | 12 | 6 | 6 | 6 | 6 | 170 | 160 |
| Keystone National Bank | 1872 | 100,000 | 106,245 | 00 | 10 | 10 | 10 | 10 | 10 | 224 | 215 |
| National Union Bank | 1857 | 200,000 | 611,000 | 25 | 12 | 12 | 12 | 14 | 16 | 116 | 116 |
| Neversink Bank | 1901 | 46,719 | 1,532 | 50 | .. | .. | .. | .. | .. | 55 | 50 |
| Penn National Bank | 1883 | 100,000 | 176,764 | 100 | 6 | 6 | 6 | 6 | 6 | 290 | 290 |
| Reading National Bank | 1893 | 200,000 | 24,941 | 100 | 6 | 6 | 6 | 6 | 6 | 210 | 200 |
| Schuylkill Valley Bank | 1890 | 100,000 | 120,000 | 50 | 6 | 6 | 6 | 8 | 8 | 110 | 110 |
| Second National Bank | 1881 | 300,000 | 402,575 | 100 | 6 | 6 | 6 | 6 | 6½ | 227 | 200 |
| Berks County Trust Co. | 1901 | 250,000 | 35,591 | 10 | .. | .. | .. | .. | .. | 15 | 15 |
| Colonial Trust Co. | 1900 | 250,000 | 149,850 | 10 | .. | .. | .. | .. | .. | 18 | 17 |
| Pennsylvania Trust Co. | 1886 | 250,000 | 241,481 | 100 | 5 | 5 | 5 | 5 | 5 | 185 | 185 |
| Reading Trust Co. | 1886 | 500,000 | 166,347 | 100 | 6 | 6 | 6 | 6 | 6 | 145 | 135 |

## RICHMOND, VA.

| | | | | | | | | | | | |
|---|---|---|---|---|---|---|---|---|---|---|---|
| American National Bank | 1899 | $300,000 | $60,000 | $100 | .. | .. | 4 | 4 | 4 | $130 | $110 |
| Broad Street Bank | 1901 | 200,000 | 16,473 | 25 | .. | .. | .. | .. | .. | 27 | 26 |
| City Bank | 1871 | 400,000 | 100,000 | 25 | 6 | 6 | 6 | 6 | 6 | 34 | 33 |
| First National Bank | 1865 | 600,000 | 507,024 | 100 | 9 | 8 | 8 | 8 | 8 | 205 | 175 |
| Merchants' National Bank | 1870 | 200,000 | 628,853 | 100 | 7 | 7 | 7 | 7 | 8 | 300 | 300 |
| Metropolitan Bank of Virginia | 1902 | 125,000 | 7,573 | 25 | .. | .. | .. | .. | .. | 29 | 27 |
| National Bank of Virginia | 1865 | 500,000 | 111,000 | 100 | 5 | 5 | 5 | 5 | 5 | 130 | 125 |
| Planters' National Bank | 1865 | 300,000 | [illegible]91 | 100 | 12 | 12 | 12 | 12 | 12 | 330 | 330 |
| State Bank of Virginia | 1870 | 500,000 | 250,000 | 100 | 7 | 7 | 7 | 7 | 7 | 164 | 161 |
| Union Bank | 1866 | 219,750 | 350,000 | 50 | 12 | 12 | 12 | 12 | 12 | 175 | 165 |
| Richmond Trust & Safe Deposit Co. | 1898 | 1,000,000 | 712,189 | 100 | .. | .. | .. | 3 | 4 | 163 | 136 |
| Southern Trust Co. | 1892 | 100,000 | 17,500 | 100 | .. | 5 | 5 | 5 | 5 | 115 | 108 |
| Virginia Trust Co. | 1892 | 500,000 | 138,537 | 100 | 6 | 6 | 6 | 6 | 6 | 124 | 118 |

## ROCHESTER, N. Y.

| | | | | | | | | | | | |
|---|---|---|---|---|---|---|---|---|---|---|---|
| Alliance Bank | 1893 | $275,000 | $156,269 | $100 | 6 | 6 | 6 | 8 | 8 | $260 | $240 |
| Central Bank | 1888 | 200,000 | 150,000 | 100 | 5 | 5 | 6 | 6 | 6 | 200 | 170 |
| Commercial Bank | 1875 | 200,000 | 42,771 | 100 | 4 | 6 | 6 | 6 | 7 | 155 | 150 |
| Flour City National Bank | 1856 | 300,000 | 175,000 | 100 | .. | .. | 4 | 5 | 5 | 150 | 130 |

ROCHESTER—*Continued.*

| NAME. | Established. | Capital. | Surplus and Undivided Profits. Dec. 31, 1902. | Par Value of Stock. | Dividends Paid, Per Cent. | | | | | Range of Prices, 1902. | |
|---|---|---|---|---|---|---|---|---|---|---|---|
| | | | | | 1898 | 1899 | 1900 | 1901 | 1902 | High. | Low. |
| German-American Bank | 1875 | $200,000 | $300,000 | $100 | 10 | 10 | 10 | 10 | 10 | $275 | $275 |
| Merchants' Bank | 1883 | 100,000 | 80,596 | 100 | .. | .. | .. | .. | 6 | 165 | 135 |
| Traders' National Bank | 1852 | 250,000 | 720,532 | 50 | 12 | 12 | 12 | 12 | 12 | 180 | 170 |
| Fidelity Trust Co | 1898 | 200,000 | 137,817 | 100 | .. | .. | .. | 3 | 6 | 250 | 150 |
| Genesee Valley Trust Co | 1901 | 300,000 | 97,353 | 100 | .. | .. | .. | .. | .. | 195 | 190 |
| Rochester Trust & Safe Deposit Co | 1888 | 200,000 | 770,049 | 50 | 10 | 10 | 10 | 10 | 12 | 350 | 300 |
| Security Trust Co | 1892 | 200,000 | 321,184 | 100 | 6 | 6 | 6 | 8 | 8 | 390 | 375 |
| Union Trust Co | 1898 | 200,000 | 115,152 | 100 | .. | .. | .. | 6 | 6 | 165 | 145 |

## ROCKFORD, ILL.

| NAME. | Established. | Capital. | Surplus and Undivided Profits. Dec. 31, 1902. | Par Value of Stock. | 1898 | 1899 | 1900 | 1901 | 1902 | High. | Low. |
|---|---|---|---|---|---|---|---|---|---|---|---|
| Forest City National Bank | 90 | $100,000 | $64,000 | $100 | 6 | 6 | 6 | 6 | 5 | ... | ... |
| Manufacturers' National Bank | 1889 | 125,000 | 72,065 | 100 | .. | .. | .. | .. | .. | ... | ... |
| Rockford National Bank | 91 | 100,000 | 100,000 | 100 | 8 | 8 | 8 | 8 | 8 | $200 | $150 |
| Third National Bank | 94 | 100,000 | 129,279 | 100 | 4 | 4 | 9 | 5 | 5 | 200 | 200 |
| Winnebago National Bank | 1848 | 100,000 | 181,893 | 100 | 14 | 14 | 14 | 14 | 14 | 250 | 250 |
| People's Bank & Trust Co | 91 | 125,000 | 33,619 | 100 | .. | .. | .. | .. | .. | 115 | 105 |

## RUTLAND, VT.

| NAME. | Established. | Capital. | Surplus and Undivided Profits. Dec. 31, 1902. | Par Value of Stock. | 1898 | 1899 | 1900 | 1901 | 1902 | High. | Low. |
|---|---|---|---|---|---|---|---|---|---|---|---|
| Baxter National Bank | 1870 | $300,000 | $85,833 | $100 | 6 | 6 | 6 | 6 | 6 | $115 | $108 |
| Clement National Bank | 1883 | 100,000 | 95,659 | 100 | 6 | 6 | 6 | 6 | 6 | 50 | 35 |
| Killington National Bank | 1883 | 100,000 | 27,000 | 100 | 6 | 6 | 6 | 6 | 6 | 115 | 115 |
| Rutland County National Bank | 1864 | 300,000 | 123,185 | 100 | 8 | 8 | 8 | 7 | 7 | 35 | 30 |
| Rutland Trust Co | 1883 | 50,000 | 53,759 | 100 | 6 | 6 | 6 | 6 | 6 | 135 | 35 |
| State Trust Co | 1883 | 100,000 | ...... | 100 | .. | .. | .. | .. | .. | 90 | 75 |

## SACRAMENTO, CAL.

| | | | | | | | | | | | |
|---|---|---|---|---|---|---|---|---|---|---|---|
| California State Bank | 1882 | $350,000 | $325,000 | $100 | 6 | 6 | 6 | 6 | 6 | $200 | $200 |
| National Bank of D. O. Mills & Co. | 1850 | 500,000 | 310,840 | ... | .. | .. | .. | .. | .. | ... | ... |
| Sacramento Bank | 1875 | 400,000 | 141,608 | 100 | 6½ | 3 | 5¾ | 3¾ | 3¾ | 90 | 90 |

## ST. JOSEPH, MO.

| | | | | | | | | | | | |
|---|---|---|---|---|---|---|---|---|---|---|---|
| Bank of Commerce | 1901 | $10,000 | $300 | $100 | .. | .. | .. | .. | .. | $100 | $80 |
| First National Bank of Buchanan County | 1894 | 250,000 | 75,000 | 100 | 6 | 8 | 8 | 9 | 8 | 130 | 125 |
| German-American Bank | 1887 | 100,000 | 40.000 | 100 | 6 | 6 | 6 | 6 | 6 | 100 | 100 |
| Merchants' Bank | 1879 | 200,000 | 12,500 | 100 | 6 | 6 | 6 | 6 | 6 | 100 | 93 |
| National Bank of St. Joseph | 1873 | 100,000 | 202,063 | 100 | .. | .. | .. | .. | .. | ... | ... |
| Park Bank | 1889 | 40,000 | 8,000 | 100 | 8 | 8 | 8 | 8 | 12 | 125 | 120 |
| St. Joseph Stock Yards Bank | 1898 | 100,000 | 38,591 | 100 | .. | .. | .. | .. | .. | 250 | 250 |
| Tootle-Lemon National Bank | 1902 | 200,000 | 10,000 | 100 | .. | .. | .. | .. | .. | ... | ... |
| Missouri Valley Trust Co. | 1899 | 100,000 | 25,000 | 100 | .. | .. | .. | .. | .. | 200 | 180 |

## ST. LOUIS, MO.

| | | | | | | | | | | | |
|---|---|---|---|---|---|---|---|---|---|---|---|
| American Exchange Bank | 1864 | $500,000 | $570,303 | $50 | 6 | 6 | 6 | 6 | 6 | $168 | $155 |
| Bank of Webster Groves | 1901 | 25,000 | 4,500 | 100 | .. | .. | .. | .. | .. | 116 | 110 |
| Boatmen's Bank | 1847 | 2,000,000 | 1,114,267 | 100 | 7 | 7 | 7 | 7 | 7 | 254 | 205 |
| Bremen Bank | 1868 | 100,000 | 365,000 | 100 | 12 | 12 | 12 | 16 | 16 | 315 | 315 |
| Fourth National Bank | 1864 | 1,000,000 | 1,122,788 | 100 | 8 | 9 | 10 | 10 | 10 | 350 | 285 |
| Franklin Bank | 1867 | 600,000 | 250,090 | 100 | 8 | 8 | 8 | 8 | 8 | 190 | 190 |
| German-American Bank | 1872 | 150,000 | 958,419 | 100 | 40 | 40 | 40 | 40 | 40 | 975 | 850 |
| German Savings Institution | 1853 | 500,000 | 1,269,726 | 100 | 12 | 12 | 12 | 12 | 16 | 400 | 340 |
| International Bank | 1865 | 200,000 | 102,000 | 100 | 6 | 6 | 6 | 6 | 6 | 181 | 165 |
| Jefferson Bank | 1892 | 200,000 | 110,000 | 100 | 5 | 6 | 6 | 8 | 8 | 250 | 240 |
| Lafayette Bank | 1876 | 100,000 | 700,000 | 100 | 10 | 10 | 10 | 10 | 10 | 600 | 600 |
| Manchester Bank | 1902 | 100,000 | 27,000 | 100 | .. | .. | .. | .. | .. | 145 | 138 |
| Mechanics' National Bank | 1857 | 2,000,000 | 2,403,754 | 100 | 8 | 8 | 8 | 8 | 18 | 330 | 268 |
| Merchants'-Laclede National Bank | 1895 | 1,400,000 | 774,157 | 100 | 6 | 6 | 6 | 6 | 8 | 315 | 240 |
| National Bank of Commerce | 1857 | 7,000,000 | 8,100,000 | 100 | 8 | 8 | 10 | 10 | 12 | 415 | 330 |
| Northwestern Savings Bank | 1873 | 200,000 | 360,000 | 100 | 8 | 8 | 8 | 8 | 8 | 200 | 170 |

ST. LOUIS—*Continued*

| NAME. | Established. | Capital. | Surplus and Undivided Profits. Dec. 31, 1902. | Par Value of Stock. | Dividends Paid, Per Cent. 1898 | 1899 | 1900 | 1901 | 1902 | Range of Prices, 1902. High. | Low. |
|---|---|---|---|---|---|---|---|---|---|---|---|
| Olive Street Bank | 1902 | $100,000 | ...... | $100 | .. | .. | .. | .. | .. | .. | .. |
| Southern Commercial & Savings Bank | 1891 | 100,000 | $33,495 | 100 | .. | 6 | 6 | 6 | 6 | $135 | $110 |
| South Side Bank | 1891 | 200,000 | 63,000 | 100 | 6 | 6 | 6 | 6 | 6 | 145 | 140 |
| State National Bank | 1899 | 2,000,000 | 685,400 | 100 | .. | 6 | 6 | 6 | 6 | 228 | 205 |
| Third National Bank | 1857 | 2,000,000 | 1,300,000 | 100 | 6 | 6 | 6 | 8 | 10 | 348 | 238 |
| Vandeventer Bank | 1902 | 100,000 | 10,850 | 100 | .. | .. | .. | .. | .. | 115 | 110 |
| American Central Trust Co. | 1902 | 1,000,000 | 544,518 | 100 | .. | .. | .. | .. | .. | 188 | 165 |
| Colonial Trust Co. | 1901 | 1,500,000 | 1,572,873 | 100 | .. | .. | .. | .. | .. | 240 | 200 |
| Commonwealth Trust Co. | 1901 | 2,000,000 | 3,500,000 | 100 | .. | .. | .. | 3 | 8 | 330 | 300 |
| Germania Trust Co. | 1901 | 1,000,000 | 1,076,059 | 100 | .. | .. | .. | .. | .. | 230 | 197 |
| Hamilton Trust Co. | 1902 | 500,000 | ...... | 100 | .. | .. | .. | .. | .. | 110 | 100 |
| Lincoln Trust Co. | 1894 | 2,000,000 | 1,676,340 | 100 | 6 | 6 | 6 | 6 | 8 | 299 | 240 |
| Mercantile Trust Co. | 1899 | 3,000,000 | 6,787,610 | 100 | .. | .. | 9 | 9 | 16 | 434 | 408 |
| Mississippi Valley Trust Co. | 1890 | 3,000,000 | 4,974,403 | 100 | 6 | 6 | 10 | 12 | 12 | 470 | 415 |
| Missouri Trust Co. | 1900 | 2,000,000 | 347,532 | 100 | .. | .. | .. | .. | .. | 175 | 107 |
| St. Louis Union Trust Co. | 1890 | 5,000,000 | 4,341,049 | 100 | .. | .. | .. | .. | .. | 395 | 368 |

## ST. PAUL, MINN.

| NAME. | Established. | Capital. | Surplus and Undivided Profits. Dec. 31, 1902. | Par Value of Stock. | 1898 | 1899 | 1900 | 1901 | 1902 | High. | Low. |
|---|---|---|---|---|---|---|---|---|---|---|---|
| American Exchange Bank | 1899 | $25,000 | $1,000 | $100 | .. | .. | .. | .. | .. | .. | .. |
| Capital Bank | 1880 | 100,000 | 42,000 | 100 | 6 | 6 | 6 | 6 | 6 | $120 | $110 |
| First National Bank | 1863 | 1,000,000 | 824,614 | 100 | 12 | 12 | 12 | 15 | 15 | 280 | 252 |
| Merchants' National Bank | 1872 | 1,000,000 | 300,000 | 100 | .. | .. | .. | 5 | 5 | 138 | 125 |
| National German-American Bank | 1833 | 1,000,000 | 214,000 | 00 | .. | .. | .. | .. | .. | 130 | 92 |
| St. Paul National Bank | 1883 | 600,000 | 78,838 | 100 | 2½ | 4½ | 5 | 5 | 5 | 108 | 103 |
| Scandinavian-American Bank | 1887 | 100,000 | 46,734 | 100 | 8 | 8 | 8 | 8 | 8 | 135 | 135 |
| Second National Bank | 1854 | 200,000 | 150,000 | 100 | 10 | 10 | 10 | 10 | 10 | 215 | 215 |
| State Bank | 1891 | 25,000 | 5,000 | 100 | .. | .. | .. | .. | .. | 120 | 100 |
| Union Bank | 1891 | 100,000 | 26,500 | 100 | .. | .. | .. | .. | .. | 120 | 120 |
| St. Paul Title & Trust Co. | 1886 | 250,000 | 27,416 | 50 | .. | .. | .. | .. | .. | 28 | 26 |
| Security Trust Co. | 1891 | 200,000 | 42,281 | 100 | .. | .. | .. | 4 | 4 | 120 | 100 |

## SALEM, MASS.

| | | | | | | | | | | | |
|---|---|---|---|---|---|---|---|---|---|---|---|
| Asiatic National Bank | 1824 | $200,000 | $102,116 | $100 | 4 | 4 | 5 | 5 | 5 | $105 | $103 |
| First National Bank | 1819 | 300,000 | 76,842 | 100 | 4 | 4 | 4 | 4 | 4 | 85 | 70 |
| Mercantile National Bank | 1826 | 200,000 | 31,686 | 100 | 5 | 5 | 5 | 5 | 5 | 103 | 100 |
| Merchants' National Bank | 1811 | 200,000 | 150,801 | 50 | 6 | 6 | 6 | 6 | 6 | 65 | 63 |
| Naumkeag National Bank | 1831 | 500,000 | 338,000 | 100 | 5 | 5 | 5 | 5 | 5 | 127 | 125 |
| Salem National Bank | 1861 | 200,000 | 74,000 | 100 | 4 | 4 | 4 | 4 | 4 | 80 | 80 |

## SALT LAKE CITY, UTAH

| | | | | | | | | | | | |
|---|---|---|---|---|---|---|---|---|---|---|---|
| Bank of Commerce | 1890 | $100,000 | ...... | $100 | .. | .. | .. | .. | .. | $85 | $75 |
| Commercial National Bank | 1889 | 200,000 | $21,504 | 100 | 4 | 5 | 6 | 6 | 6 | 100 | 98 |
| Deseret National Bank | 1872 | 500,000 | 466,886 | 100 | 22 | 12 | 17 | 17 | 17 | 286 | 260 |
| National Bank of the Republic | 1890 | 300,000 | 80,000 | 100 | 6 | 6 | 6 | 6 | 6 | 125 | 125 |
| State Bank of Utah | 1890 | 250,000 | 69,000 | 100 | 8 | 8 | 8 | 8 | 8 | 150 | 140 |
| Utah Commercial & Savings Bank | 1889 | 200,000 | 14,251 | 100 | 8 | 6 | 6 | 6 | .. | 90 | 90 |
| Utah National Bank | 1890 | 100,000 | 15,828 | 100 | .. | .. | .. | .. | .. | 80 | 73 |
| Utah Savings & Trust Co. | 1886 | 150,000 | 35,227 | 1,000 | .. | 7 | 8 | 8 | 6 | 1,000 | 1,000 |
| Zion's Savings Bank & Trust Co. | 1873 | 200,000 | 9,043 | 100 | 8 | 8 | 8 | 8 | 8 | 133 | 132 |

## SAN ANTONIO, TEX.

| | | | | | | | | | | | |
|---|---|---|---|---|---|---|---|---|---|---|---|
| Alamo National Bank | 1891 | $250,000 | $102,386 | $100 | 6 | 6 | 6 | 8 | 8 | $172 | $172 |
| City National Bank | 1899 | 100,000 | 9,000 | 100 | .. | .. | 6 | 6 | 6 | 125 | 120 |
| Frost National Bank | 1899 | 250,000 | 210,000 | 100 | .. | .. | .. | .. | .. | 300 | 300 |
| Lockwood National Bank | 1866 | 100,000 | 44,707 | 100 | .. | .. | .. | .. | .. | 140 | 135 |
| San Antonio National Bank | 1866 | 125,000 | 182,000 | 100 | 180 | 25 | 40 | 20 | 40 | .. | .. |
| San Antonio Loan & Trust Co. | 92 | 100,000 | ...... | 100 | .. | .. | .. | .. | .. | .. | .. |

## SAN FRANCISCO, CAL.

| Name. | Established. | Capital. | Surplus and Undivided Profits, Dec. 31, 1902. | Par Value of Stock. | Dividends Paid, Per Cent. 1898 | 1899 | 1900 | 1901 | 1902 | Range of Prices, 1902. High. | Low. |
|---|---|---|---|---|---|---|---|---|---|---|---|
| American National Bank | 1887 | $500,000 | $40,000 | $100 | 6 | 6 | 6 | 6 | 6 | $130 | $125 |
| Anglo-Californian Bank, Ltd. | 1873 | 1,500,000 | 718,000 | 50 | 6 | 6 | 6 | 6 | 6 | 91 | 83 |
| Bank of California | 1864 | 2,000,000 | 4,197,280 | 100 | 12 | 16 | 16 | 16 | 16 | 455 | 417 |
| City & County Bank | 1902 | 187,500 | 5,700 | 100 | .. | .. | .. | .. | .. | 112 | 112 |
| Columbian Banking Co. | 1893 | 75,100 | 34,368 | 30 | 6 | 6 | 6 | 6 | 3 | 70 | 70 |
| Comptoir National d'Escompte de Paris | 1889 | 30,000,000 | 3,403,932 | 100 | 5¼ | 5¼ | 5½ | 5½ | 5¼ | 115 | 115 |
| Crocker-Woolworth National Bank | 1886 | 1,000,000 | 1,306,159 | 100 | 8 | 8 | 8 | 8 | 8 | 215 | 200 |
| Donahoe-Kelly Banking Co. | 1864 | 650,000 | 75,000 | 100 | 5 | 5 | 5 | 5 | 5 | 110 | 100 |
| First National Bank | 1870 | 1,500,000 | 1,370,000 | 100 | 10 | 12 | 12½ | 14 | 16 | 400 | 335 |
| Hong Kong & Shanghai Banking Corporation | 1865 | 10,000,000 | 17,000,000 | 100 | 30 | 30 | 30 | 30 | 30 | 330 | 320 |
| Italian-American Bank | 1899 | 750,000 | 40,000 | 100 | .. | .. | 6 | 5 | 5 | 110 | 105 |
| London & San Francisco Bank, Ltd. | 1865 | 1,400,000 | 100,000 | 50 | 3½ | 3½ | 6 | 6 | .. | 64 | 60 |
| London, Paris & American Bank, Ltd. | 1884 | 2,000,000 | 1,050,000 | 80 | 7 | 7 | 7 | 8 | 8 | 167 | 163 |
| Nevada National Bank | 1875 | 3,000,000 | 1,464,443 | 100 | 6 | 7 | 7 | 7 | 7 | 150 | 150 |
| San Francisco National Bank | 1897 | 500,000 | 170,000 | 100 | .. | .. | 5 | 6 | 6 | 135 | 135 |
| San Francisco Savings Union | 1862 | 1,000,000 | 796,900 | 250 | 6 | 6 | 6 | 6 | 6 | 500 | 500 |
| Wells Fargo & Co. Bank | 1852 | 8,000,000 | 4,263,315 | 100 | 6 | 6 | 6 | 6 | 8 | 255 | 185 |
| Western National Bank | 1900 | 200,000 | 15,000 | 100 | .. | .. | .. | .. | 5 | 150 | 130 |
| California Safe Deposit & Trust Co. | 1882 | 1,000,000 | 288,000 | 100 | 6 | 6 | 6 | 6 | 6 | 138 | 130 |
| California Title, Insurance & Trust Co. | 1886 | 250,000 | 160,000 | 100 | .. | .. | 6 | 6 | 6 | 130 | 130 |
| Central Trust Co. | 1890 | 1,500,000 | 225,000 | 100 | 4 | 5 | 5 | 5 | 5 | 115 | 100 |
| Columbus Savings & Loan Society | 1893 | 100,000 | 53,000 | 250 | 6 | 6 | 6 | 6 | 6 | 125 | 110 |
| Mercantile Trust Company | 1899 | 1,000,000 | 349,255 | 100 | .. | .. | .. | .. | .. | 210 | 185 |
| Union Trust Co. | 1893 | 1,500,000 | 522,688 | 1,000 | 6 | 6 | 7 | 7 | 7 | 2,000 | 2,000 |

## SAN JOSE, CAL.

| Name. | Established. | Capital. | Surplus and Undivided Profits, Dec. 31, 1902. | Par Value of Stock. | Dividends Paid, Per Cent. 1898 | 1899 | 1900 | 1901 | 1902 | Range of Prices, 1902. High. | Low. |
|---|---|---|---|---|---|---|---|---|---|---|---|
| Bank of San Jose | 1866 | $300,000 | $179,773 | $100 | 6 | 8 | 8 | 8 | 8 | $160 | $150 |
| Commercial & Savings Bank | 1874 | 300,000 | 4,682 | 50 | .. | .. | .. | .. | .. | 50 | 45 |
| First National Bank | 1874 | 300,000 | 176,000 | 100 | 7 | 8 | 8 | 23 | 8 | 160 | 143 |
| San Jose Safe Deposit Bank | 1885 | 300,000 | 330,000 | 30 | .. | .. | .. | .. | .. | 65 | 60 |
| Security State Bank | 1902 | 100,000 | 5,696 | 20 | .. | .. | .. | .. | 2½ | 23 | 22 |
| Garden City Bank & Trust Co. | 1893 | 200,000 | 44,646 | 100 | 6 | 6 | 6 | 6 | 6 | 110 | 105 |

## SAVANNAH, GA.

| | | | | | | | | | | | |
|---|---|---|---|---|---|---|---|---|---|---|---|
| Chatham Bank | 1889 | $150,000 | $27,407 | 100 | 6 | 6 | 6 | 6 | .. | $76 | $63 |
| Citizens' Bank | 1888 | 500,000 | 216,868 | 100 | 6 | 6 | 6 | 6 | 6 | 141 | 137 |
| Commercial Bank | 1902 | 50,000 | ...... | 100 | .. | .. | .. | .. | .. | 105 | 100 |
| Germania Bank | 1890 | 200,000 | 125,000 | 100 | 6 | 6 | 6 | 6 | 7 | 150 | 140 |
| Merchants' National Bank | 1866 | 500,000 | 132,782 | 100 | .. | .. | .. | .. | .. | 120 | 112 |
| National Bank of Savannah | 1885 | 250,000 | 234,861 | 100 | 7 | 7 | 7 | 7 | 7 | 160 | 155 |
| Southern Bank | 1870 | 500,000 | 479,453 | 100 | 7 | 7 | 7 | 7 | 8 | 176 | 158 |
| Oglethorpe Savings & Trust Co. | 1887 | 125,000 | 70,000 | 100 | 6 | 6 | 6 | 6 | 6 | 117 | 117 |
| Savannah Bank & Trust Co. | 1869 | 350,000 | 109,548 | 100 | 6 | 6 | 6 | 6 | 6 | 120 | 110 |
| Savannah Trust Co. | 1902 | 500,000 | 64,950 | 100 | .. | .. | .. | .. | .. | 105 | 100 |

## SCRANTON, PA.

| | | | | | | | | | | | |
|---|---|---|---|---|---|---|---|---|---|---|---|
| Dime Deposit & Discount Bank | 1890 | $100,000 | $175,000 | 50 | 6 | 6 | 6 | 8 | 8 | $205 | $00 |
| First National Bank | 1863 | 200,000 | 1,710,237 | 100 | 32 | 50 | 50 | 50 | 50 | 1,350 | 1,350 |
| Merchants' & Mechanics' Bank | 1871 | 250,000 | 287,502 | 25 | 6 | 6 | 6 | 6 | 6 | 68 | 68 |
| North Scranton Bank | 1901 | 50,000 | 3,900 | 50 | .. | .. | .. | .. | .. | 63 | 60 |
| People's Bank | 1901 | 100,000 | 33,965 | 100 | .. | .. | .. | .. | .. | 178 | 178 |
| Third National Bank | 1872 | 200,000 | 665,000 | 100 | 12 | 12 | 16 | 20 | 20 | 600 | 600 |
| Traders' National Bank | 1890 | 250,000 | 150,000 | 100 | 3 | 3 | 3 | 6 | 6 | 260 | 235 |
| West Side Bank | 1875 | 60,000 | 30,000 | 50 | 8 | 8 | 8 | 12 | 12 | 150 | 150 |
| County Savings Bank & Trust Co. | 1871 | 100,000 | [illegible] | 100 | 8 | 10 | 12 | 14 | 14 | 40 | 400 |
| Lackawanna Trust & Safe Deposit Co. | 1887 | 250,000 | [illegible] | 100 | 6 | 6 | 6 | 6 | 6 | 205 | 200 |
| Title Guaranty & Trust Co. | 1901 | [illegible] | 280,773 | 100 | .. | .. | .. | .. | .. | 180 | 170 |

## SEATTLE, WASH.

| | | | | | | | | | | | |
|---|---|---|---|---|---|---|---|---|---|---|---|
| Boston National Bank | 1889 | $180,000 | $63,000 | $100 | .. | .. | .. | 4 | 4 | $110 | $100 |
| First National Bank | 1882 | 150,000 | 85,000 | 100 | 6 | 6 | 8 | 8 | 8 | 60 | 160 |
| National Bank of Commerce | 1889 | 150,000 | 156,000 | 100 | .. | 10 | 10 | 10 | 10 | 200 | 200 |
| Puget Sound National Bank | 1883 | 300,000 | 130,000 | 100 | .. | 4 | 15 | 16 | 12 | 140 | 140 |
| Scandinavian-American Bank | 1892 | 300,000 | 150,000 | 100 | .. | .. | .. | 55 | 30 | 175 | 175 |
| Seattle National Bank | 1890 | 100,000 | 42,000 | 100 | .. | 8 | 8 | 8 | 8 | 175 | 175 |
| Washington National Bank | 1889 | 100,000 | 295,675 | 100 | 8 | 8 | 10 | 11 | 12 | 400 | 400 |
| American Savings Bank & Trust Co. | 1901 | 200,000 | ...... | 100 | .. | .. | .. | .. | .. | .... | .... |

## SHREVEPORT, LA.

| Name. | Established. | Capital. | Surplus and Undivided Profits, Dec. 31, 1902. | Par Value of Stock. | Dividends Paid, Per Cent. 1898 | 1899 | 1900 | 1901 | 1902 | Range of Prices, 1902. High. | Low. |
|---|---|---|---|---|---|---|---|---|---|---|---|
| Citizens' National Bank | 1901 | $100,000 | $7,594 | $100 | .. | .. | .. | .. | .. | $105 | $105 |
| Commercial National Bank | 1886 | 100,000 | 260,000 | 100 | 10 | 10 | 10 | 10 | 10 | 425 | 400 |
| First Natianal Bank | 1887 | 200,000 | 133,800 | 100 | 4 | 4 | 4 | 4 | 4 | 200 | 200 |
| Shreveport National Bank | 1901 | 100,000 | 20,000 | 100 | .. | .. | .. | .. | .. | 120 | 110 |
| Merchants' & Farmers' Bank & Trust Co. | 1889 | 100,000 | 73,337 | 50 | 8 | 8 | 8 | 8 | 8 | 105 | 100 |

## SIOUX CITY, IA.

| Name. | Established. | Capital. | Surplus and Undivided Profits, Dec. 31, 1902. | Par Value of Stock. | 1898 | 1899 | 1900 | 1901 | 1902 | High. | Low. |
|---|---|---|---|---|---|---|---|---|---|---|---|
| First National Bank | 1870 | $200,000 | $62,156 | $100 | .. | .. | .. | .. | .. | $130 | $120 |
| Iowa State National Bank | 1889 | 200,000 | 40,000 | 100 | .. | .. | .. | .. | .. | 115 | 115 |
| Live Stock National Bank | 1895 | 100,000 | 80,574 | 100 | 6 | 6 | 6 | 6 | 6 | 200 | 200 |
| Merchants' National Bank | 1888 | 100,000 | 28,000 | 100 | 8 | 8 | 8 | 8 | 8 | 125 | 115 |
| Northwestern National Bank | 1891 | 100,000 | 28,509 | 100 | 6 | 6 | 8 | 8 | 8 | 125 | 115 |
| Security National Bank | 1884 | 250,000 | 90,000 | 100 | 4 | 4 | 4 | 4 | 6 | 125 | 125 |
| American Bank Trust Co. | 1890 | 50,000 | 10,000 | 100 | 6 | 6 | 6 | 6 | 6 | 125 | 110 |
| Farmers' Loan & Trust Co. | 1873 | 300,000 | 600,000 | 100 | 12 | 12 | 12 | 12 | 12 | 325 | [illegible] |
| Sioux City Safe Deposit & Trust Co. | 1887 | 100,000 | ...... | 100 | .. | .. | .. | .. | .. | ... | ... |

## SPOKANE, WASH.

| Name. | Established. | Capital. | Surplus and Undivided Profits, Dec. 31, 1902. | Par Value of Stock. | 1898 | 1899 | 1900 | 1901 | 1902 | High. | Low. |
|---|---|---|---|---|---|---|---|---|---|---|---|
| Exchange National Bank | 1889 | $250,000 | $200,000 | $100 | 12 | 12 | 12 | 12 | 16 | $[illegible]0 | $170 |
| Fidelity National Bank | 1882 | 100,000 | 36,896 | 00 | 5 | 5 | 5 | 6 | 6 | 00 | 100 |
| Old National Bank | 1891 | 200,000 | 50,000 | 100 | .. | .. | .. | .. | .. | 100 | 00 |
| Traders' National Bank | 1885 | 200,000 | 72,000 | 100 | .. | 10 | 12 | 24 | 22 | 300 | 30 |
| International Investment & Trust Co. | 1901 | 15,000 | 7,583 | 10 | .. | .. | .. | .. | .. | 16 | 15 |
| Spokane & Eastern Trust Co | 1890 | 100,000 | ...... | 00 | .. | .. | 4 | 4 | 5 | 150 | 130 |
| Washington Safe Deposit & Trust Co. | 1892 | 25,000 | 20,134 | 100 | .. | .. | .. | .. | .. | ... | ... |

## SPRINGFIELD, MASS.

| | | | | | | | | | | | |
|---|---|---|---|---|---|---|---|---|---|---|---|
| Agawam National Bank | 1846 | $300,000 | $7,190 | $100 | .. | .. | .. | .. | .. | $75 | $55 |
| Chapin National Bank | 1879 | 500,000 | 172,098 | 100 | 6 | 6 | 6 | 6 | 6 | 130 | 120 |
| Chicopee National Bank | 1836 | 400,000 | [illegible] | 100 | 8 | 8 | 8 | 8 | 8 | 155 | 152 |
| City National Bank | 1879 | 250,000 | 186,000 | 100 | 7 | 7 | 7 | 7 | 7 | 145 | 140 |
| First National Bank | 1863 | 400,000 | [illegible] | 100 | 5 | 5 | 5 | 5 | 5 | 115 | 115 |
| John Hancock National Bank | 1850 | 250,000 | 80,000 | 100 | 5 | 5 | 5 | 5 | 5 | 107 | 107 |
| Second National Bank | 1814 | 300,000 | 57,000 | 100 | 6 | 6 | 6 | 6 | 6 | 135 | 133 |
| Springfield National Bank | 1893 | 200,000 | 271 ,90 | 100 | 6 | 6 | 6 | 6 | 6 | 200 | 190 |
| Third National Bank | 1864 | 500,000 | 438,800 | 100 | 10 | 10 | 10 | 10 | 10 | 225 | 200 |
| Hampden Trust Co. | 1895 | 100,000 | 75,000 | [illegible] | 5 | 5 | 5 | 5½ | 6 | 145 | 135 |
| Springfield Safe Deposit & Trust Co. | 1886 | 500,000 | 400,675 | 100 | 6 | 6 | 6 | 6 | 6½ | 180 | 165 |

## SYRACUSE, N. Y.

| | | | | | | | | | | | |
|---|---|---|---|---|---|---|---|---|---|---|---|
| American Exchange National Bank | 1897 | $200,000 | $19,968 | $100 | .. | .. | 3 | 5 | 2½ | $115 | $112 |
| Commercial Bank | 1891 | 250,000 | 90,000 | 100 | 6 | 6 | 6 | 6 | 6 | 140 | 130 |
| First National Bank | 1863 | 250,000 | [illegible] | 100 | 14 | 14 | 14 | 14 | 14 | 225 | 225 |
| Merchants' National Bank | 1851 | 180,000 | 240,763 | 100 | 14 | 14 | 14 | 14 | 14 | 250 | 200 |
| National Bank of Syracuse | 1900 | 200,000 | 60,855 | 100 | .. | .. | 6 | 6 | 6 | 125 | 125 |
| Salt Springs National Bank | 1852 | 200,000 | 75,848 | 100 | 8 | 8 | 8 | 8 | 8 | 110 | 100 |
| State Bank of Syracuse | 1873 | 100,000 | [illegible] | 100 | 10 | 10 | 10 | 10 | 10 | 250 | 250 |
| Third National Bank | 1863 | 300,000 | 116,000 | 100 | 10 | 10 | 10 | 10 | 10 | 200 | 200 |
| Trust & Deposit Co. of Onondaga | 1866 | 100,000 | 332,103 | 100 | 10 | 10 | 10 | 13 | 17 | 400 | 325 |

## TACOMA, WASH.

| | | | | | | | | | | | |
|---|---|---|---|---|---|---|---|---|---|---|---|
| Lumberman's National Bank | 1901 | $100,000 | $9,900 | $100 | .. | .. | .. | .. | .. | .. | .. |
| National Bank of Commerce | 1888 | 200,000 | 112,000 | 100 | .. | .. | 10 | 10 | 10 | $150 | $150 |
| Pacific National Bank | 1885 | 200,000 | 28,071 | 100 | .. | .. | .. | .. | .. | 110 | 110 |
| Fidelity Trust Co. | 1888 | 300,000 | 51,002 | 100 | .. | .. | .. | .. | 3 | 100 | 100 |

## TAUNTON, MASS.

| Name. | Established. | Capital. | Surplus and Undivided Profits, Dec. 31, 1902. | Par Value of Stock. | Dividends Paid, Per Cent. 1898 | 1899 | 1900 | 1901 | 1902 | Range of Prices, 1902. High. | Low. |
|---|---|---|---|---|---|---|---|---|---|---|---|
| Bristol County National Bank | 1832 | $500,000 | $179,000 | $100 | 5 | 5 | 5 | 5 | 5 | $120 | $118 |
| Machinists' National Bank | 1847 | 200,000 | 127,000 | 100 | 7 | 7 | 7 | 7 | 7 | 165 | 160 |
| Taunton National Bank | 1812 | 600,000 | 225,251 | 100 | 7 | 6 | 6 | 5½ | 5 | 120 | 116 |
| Taunton Safe Deposit & Trust Co | 1901 | 200,000 | 14,500 | 100 | .. | .. | .. | .. | 5 | 113 | 105 |

## TERRE HAUTE, IND

| Name. | Established. | Capital. | Surplus and Undivided Profits, Dec. 31, 1902. | Par Value of Stock. | 1898 | 1899 | 1900 | 1901 | 1902 | High. | Low. |
|---|---|---|---|---|---|---|---|---|---|---|---|
| First National Bank | 1863 | $300,000 | $250,000 | $100 | .. | 10 | 12 | 12 | 12 | $250 | $250 |
| National State Bank | 1865 | 200,000 | 86,998 | 100 | 6 | 6 | 6 | 6 | 8 | 130 | 115 |
| Vigo County National Bank | 1888 | 150,000 | 61,979 | 100 | .. | .. | .. | .. | .. | 130 | 125 |
| Terre Haute Trust Co | 1894 | 200,000 | 55,000 | 100 | .. | .. | .. | .. | .. | 160 | 150 |
| United States Trust Co | 1903 | 500,000 | 100,000 | 120 | .. | .. | .. | .. | .. | .. | .. |

## TOLEDO, O.

| Name. | Established. | Capital. | Surplus and Undivided Profits, Dec. 31, 1902. | Par Value of Stock. | 1898 | 1899 | 1900 | 1901 | 1902 | High. | Low. |
|---|---|---|---|---|---|---|---|---|---|---|---|
| American Savings Bank Co | 1903 | $35,000 | ...... | $50 | .. | .. | .. | .. | .. | ... | ... |
| Central Savings Bank Co | 1899 | 300,000 | $22,291 | 100 | .. | .. | .. | .. | 10 | $118 | $112 |
| Commercial Savings Bank Co | 1899 | 100,000 | 12,665 | 100 | .. | .. | 4 | 4 | 4 | 115 | 113 |
| Dime Savings Bank Co | 1900 | 71,650 | 8,300 | 100 | .. | .. | .. | .. | .. | 60 | 56 |
| Dollar Savings Bank Co | 1901 | 250,000 | 25,000 | 100 | .. | .. | .. | .. | .. | 124 | 100 |
| East Side Bank Co | 1892 | 50,000 | 20,000 | 100 | 6 | 6 | 6 | 6 | 8 | 140 | 130 |
| First National Bank | 1863 | 500,000 | 865,000 | 100 | 10 | 10 | 10 | 10 | 10 | 275 | 270 |
| Holcomb National Bank | 1891 | 300,000 | 105,119 | 100 | .. | .. | .. | .. | .. | 150 | 145 |
| Home Savings Bank Co | 1894 | 250,000 | 102,696 | 100 | .. | .. | .. | 6 | 6 | 158 | 150 |
| Lucas County Savings Bank Co | 1901 | 50,000 | 4,360 | 100 | .. | .. | .. | .. | .. | 110 | 102 |
| Merchants' National Bank | 1871 | 300,000 | 237,000 | 100 | .. | 6 | 6 | 6 | 6 | 189 | 182 |
| National Bank of Commerce | 1888 | 500,000 | 180,000 | 100 | 5 | 5 | 5 | 5 | 6 | 170 | 150 |
| Northern National Bank | 1865 | 300,000 | 340,000 | 100 | 6 | 6 | 6 | 6 | 6 | 212 | 210 |
| Second National Bank | 1864 | 350,000 | 923,526 | 100 | 8 | 8 | 8 | 8 | 8 | 400 | 360 |

| | | | | | | | | | | | |
|---|---|---|---|---|---|---|---|---|---|---|---|
| Home Safe Deposit & Trust Co. | 1893 | $25,000 | $2,020 | $100 | 5 | 6 | 6 | 6 | 6 | $105 | $100 |
| Ohio Savings Bank & Trust Co. | 1897 | 300,000 | 88,849 | 100 | .. | .. | 50 | .. | .. | 155 | 135 |
| Security Trust Co. | 1898 | 200,000 | 32,400 | 100 | .. | .. | .. | .. | 5 | 117 | 114 |
| Toledo Savings Bank & Trust Co. | 1868 | 100,000 | 210,000 | 100 | 10 | 10 | 10 | 10 | 10 | 365 | 365 |

## TOPEKA, KAN.

| | | | | | | | | | | | |
|---|---|---|---|---|---|---|---|---|---|---|---|
| Bank of Topeka | 1869 | $210,000 | $73,500 | $100 | 6 | 6 | 6 | 6 | 6 | $120 | $110 |
| Central National Bank | 1884 | 250,000 | 34,000 | 100 | 5 | 5 | 5 | 5 | 5 | 113 | 110 |
| Citizens' State Bank | 1898 | 5,000 | 31,650 | 100 | 6 | 6 | 6 | 9 | 14 | 300 | 260 |
| First National Bank | 1882 | 300,000 | 40,700 | 100 | 3 | 2 | 2 | 2½ | 5 | 115 | 115 |
| Merchants' National Bank | 1888 | 100,000 | 12,000 | 100 | 6 | 3 | .. | .. | 3 | 100 | 90 |

## TRENTON, N. J.

| | | | | | | | | | | | |
|---|---|---|---|---|---|---|---|---|---|---|---|
| Broad Street National Bank | 1887 | $250,000 | $131,110 | $100 | 6 | 6 | 6 | 6 | 6 | $125 | $120 |
| First National Bank | 1864 | 500,000 | 265,000 | 100 | 9 | 10 | 10 | 10 | 10 | 164 | 158 |
| Mechanics' National Bank | 1834 | 500,000 | 441,600 | 50 | 10 | 11 | 11 | 11 | 11 | 96 | 90 |
| Trenton Banking Co. | 1804 | 500,000 | 386,805 | 50 | 10 | 10 | 10 | 10 | 10 | 91 | 85 |
| Trenton Trust & Safe Deposit Co. | 1888 | 150,000 | 134,774 | 100 | 6 | 6 | 6 | 6 | 7 | 200 | 180 |

## TROY, N. Y.

| | | | | | | | | | | | |
|---|---|---|---|---|---|---|---|---|---|---|---|
| Central National Bank | 1865 | $200,000 | $136,230 | $100 | 8 | 8 | 8 | 8 | 8 | $160 | $155 |
| Manufacturers' National Bank | 1865 | 150,000 | 256,000 | 100 | 10 | 10 | 10 | 10 | 10 | 305 | 300 |
| Mutual National Bank | 1852 | 250,000 | 202,000 | 100 | 8 | 8 | 8 | 8 | 8 | 175 | 175 |
| National State Bank | 1852 | 250,000 | 261,084 | 100 | 10 | 10 | 10 | 10 | 10 | 200 | 195 |
| People's Bank | 1889 | 50,000 | 53,475 | 100 | 6 | 6 | 6 | 6 | 6 | 150 | 150 |
| Union National Bank | 1865 | 300,000 | 77,093 | 50 | .. | .. | .. | .. | .. | 110 | 100 |
| United National Bank | 1865 | 240,000 | 396,708 | 100 | 10 | 10 | 10 | 12 | 17 | 312 | 305 |
| Security Trust Co. | 1902 | 200,000 | 232,805 | 100 | .. | .. | .. | .. | .. | 245 | 225 |
| Troy Trust Co. | 1901 | 200,000 | 91,505 | 100 | .. | .. | .. | .. | .. | 180 | 180 |

## UTICA, N. Y.

| Name. | Established. | Capital. | Surplus and Undivided Profits, Dec. 31, 1902. | Par Value of Stock. | Dividends Paid, Per Cent. 1898 | 1899 | 1900 | 1901 | 1902 | Range of Prices, 1902. High. | Low. |
|---|---|---|---|---|---|---|---|---|---|---|---|
| First National Bank | 1812 | $800,000 | $765,256 | $60 | 10 | 10 | 10 | 10 | 10 | $126 | $110 |
| A. D. Mathers & Co. Bank | 1866 | 200,000 | 28,925 | 100 | 6 | 6 | .. | 2 | 4 | 115 | 106 |
| Oneida National Bank | 1865 | 500,000 | 532,980 | 100 | .. | .. | .. | .. | .. | 208 | 203 |
| Second National Bank | 1864 | 300,000 | 178,438 | 100 | .. | 5 | 5 | 5 | 5 | 150 | 150 |
| Utica City National Bank | 1865 | 500,000 | 233,948 | 50 | 6 | 6 | 6 | 6 | 6 | 73 | 65 |
| Utica Trust & Deposit Co. | 1899 | 200,000 | 275,061 | 100 | .. | .. | .. | 5 | 10 | 250 | 250 |
| **WASHINGTON, D. C.** | | | | | | | | | | | |
| Central National Bank | 1878 | $200,000 | $123,500 | $100 | 6 | 8 | 8 | 9 | 10 | $295 | $275 |
| Citizens' National Bank | 1871 | 300,000 | 204,927 | 100 | .. | .. | .. | .. | .. | 85 | 75 |
| Columbia National Bank | 1887 | 250,000 | 194,000 | 100 | 6 | 6 | 6 | 6 | 7 | 195 | 190 |
| Farmers' and Mechanics' Nat. Bank, Georgetown | 1814 | 252,000 | 329,000 | 100 | 8 | 8 | 12 | 12 | 12 | 300 | 294 |
| Lincoln National Bank | 1890 | 200,000 | 35,926 | 100 | 6 | 6 | 6 | 6 | 6 | 125 | 120 |
| National Bank of Washington | 1809 | 200,000 | 350,314 | 100 | 10 | 10 | 10 | 10 | 10 | 450 | 400 |
| National Capital Bank | 1889 | 200,000 | 140,000 | 100 | 6 | 6 | 6 | 6 | 6 | 165 | 150 |
| National Metropolitan Bank | 1865 | 300,000 | 576,096 | 100 | 20 | 24 | 28 | 32 | 32 | 750 | 725 |
| Riggs' National Bank | 1896 | 500,000 | 500,343 | 100 | .. | 14 | 20 | 20 | 20 | 800 | 700 |
| Second National Bank | 1872 | 225,000 | 81,509 | 100 | 8 | 8 | 8 | 8 | 8 | 193 | 170 |
| Traders' National Bank | 1890 | 200,000 | 84,214 | 100 | 4½ | 5⅛ | 6 | 6 | 6 | 153 | 140 |
| West End National Bank | 1890 | 200,000 | 84,000 | 100 | 4 | 4 | 4 | 4 | 4 | 150 | 26 |
| American Security & Trust Co. | 1889 | 1,250,000 | 575,000 | 100 | 6 | 6 | 6 | 6 | 7 | 222 | 25 |
| National Safe Deposit, Savings & Trust Co. | 1867 | 1,000,000 | 206,000 | 100 | 6 | 6 | 6 | 6 | 6 | 80 | 30 |
| Union Trust & Storage Co. | 1900 | 1,200,000 | 50,630 | 100 | .. | .. | .. | .. | .. | 110 | 104 |
| Washington Loan & Trust Co. | 1889 | 1,000,000 | 443,318 | 100 | 6 | 6 | 6 | 6 | 6 | 25 | 91 |

## WATERBURY, CONN.

| | | | | | | | | | | | |
|---|---|---|---|---|---|---|---|---|---|---|---|
| Citizens' National Bank | 1853 | $300,000 | $139,600 | $100 | 8 | 7 | 8 | 8 | 7 | $145 | $135 |
| Fourth National Bank | 1887 | 100,000 | 55,000 | 100 | 6 | 6 | 6 | 6 | 5 | 135 | 133 |
| Manufacturers' National Bank | 1880 | 100,000 | 48,000 | 100 | 6 | 6 | 6 | 6 | 5 | 125 | 125 |
| Waterbury National Bank | 1848 | 500,000 | 319,852 | 50 | 8 | 8 | 8 | 8 | 7 | 75 | 75 |
| Colonial Trust Co. | 1899 | 400,000 | 120,589 | 100 | .. | .. | .. | 2½ | 5 | 125 | 125 |

## WHEELING, W. VA.

| | | | | | | | | | | | |
|---|---|---|---|---|---|---|---|---|---|---|---|
| Bank of the Ohio Valley | 1875 | $175,000 | $60,000 | $100 | 6 | 6 | 6 | 6 | 6 | $100 | $95 |
| Bank of Wheeling | 1853 | 200,000 | 20,000 | 100 | 8 | 8 | 8 | 6 | 5 | 136 | 131 |
| City Bank | 1886 | 150,000 | 100,000 | 100 | 8 | 8 | 8 | 8 | 8 | ... | ... |
| Commercial Bank | 1849 | 100,000 | 61,250 | 100 | 6 | 6 | 8 | 8 | 8 | 155 | 135 |
| German Bank | 1870 | 80,000 | 254,700 | 100 | 10 | 16 | 16 | 16 | 16 | 360 | 342 |
| National Bank of West Virginia | 1865 | 200,000 | 78,951 | 100 | 6 | 6 | 6 | 6 | 6 | ... | ... |
| National Exchange Bank | 1899 | 300,000 | 232,562 | 100 | .. | 6 | 7½ | 11 | 10 | 230 | 220 |
| People's Bank | 1861 | 100,000 | 52,250 | 20 | 8 | 8 | 8 | 8 | 8 | 32 | 32 |
| South Side Bank | 1890 | 25,000 | 25,000 | 50 | 6 | 6 | 8 | 8 | 8 | 115 | 105 |
| Dollar Savings & Trust Co. | 1887 | 100,000 | 15,000 | 100 | 6 | 6 | 6 | 6 | 6 | 125 | 115 |
| Security Trust Co. | 1903 | 300,000 | 150,000 | 100 | .. | .. | .. | .. | .. | ... | ... |

## WILKES-BARRE, PA.

| | | | | | | | | | | | |
|---|---|---|---|---|---|---|---|---|---|---|---|
| First National Bank | 83 | $375,000 | $275,000 | $100 | 6 | 6 | 6 | 6 | 6 | $150 | $150 |
| People's Bank | 1872 | 250,000 | 364,614 | 100 | 8 | 10 | 10 | 10 | 10 | 300 | 300 |
| Second National Bank | 1863 | 450,000 | 550,000 | 100 | 8 | 8 | 8 | 10 | 10 | 400 | 350 |
| Wilkes-Barre Deposit & Savings Bank | 1871 | 150,000 | 255,539 | 50 | 6 | 6 | 6 | 6 | 6 | 150 | 150 |
| Wyoming National Bank | 1865 | 150,000 | 470,308 | 50 | 10 | 10 | 12 | 12 | 12 | 265 | 265 |
| Luzerne County Trust Co. | 1902 | 150,000 | 150,000 | 100 | .. | .. | .. | .. | .. | 200 | 200 |
| Wyoming Valley Trust Co. | 1893 | 200,000 | 167,000 | 50 | 5 | 5 | 5 | 5 | 5 | 105 | 102 |

## WILLIAMSPORT, PA.

| Name. | Established. | Capital. | Surplus and Undivided Profits, Dec. 31, 1902. | Par Value of Stock. | Dividends Paid, Per Cent. 1898 | 1899 | 1900 | 1901 | 1902 | Range of Prices, 1902. High. | Low. |
|---|---|---|---|---|---|---|---|---|---|---|---|
| First National Bank | 1863 | $300,000 | $221,710 | $100 | 8 | 8 | 8 | 8 | 8 | $175 | $175 |
| Lycoming National Bank | 1875 | 100,000 | 124,565 | 100 | 6 | 6 | 7 | 8 | 8 | 200 | 200 |
| West Branch National Bank | 1835 | 200,000 | 391,000 | 100 | 12 | 12 | 12 | 12 | 12 | 292 | 275 |
| Williamsport National Bank | 1871 | 100,000 | 72,892 | 100 | .. | .. | .. | .. | .. | 130 | 115 |
| Susquehanna Trust & Safe Deposit Co | 1890 | 300,000 | 53,948 | 50 | 4 | 4 | 4 | 4 | 4 | 53 | 53 |

## WILMINGTON, DEL.

| Name. | Established. | Capital. | Surplus and Undivided Profits, Dec. 31, 1902. | Par Value of Stock. | 1898 | 1899 | 1900 | 1901 | 1902 | High. | Low. |
|---|---|---|---|---|---|---|---|---|---|---|---|
| Central National Bank | 1885 | $210,000 | $64,100 | 100 | 6 | 6 | 6 | 6 | 6 | $122 | $118 |
| Farmers' Bank | 1813 | 200,000 | 51,437 | 50 | 6 | 8 | 8 | 8 | 8 | 123 | 120 |
| First National Bank | 1864 | 500,000 | 198,000 | 100 | 5 | 5 | 5 | 5 | 5 | 122 | 120 |
| National Bank of Delaware | 1795 | 110,000 | 141,829 | 100 | 10 | 10 | 10 | 10 | 10 | 225 | 213 |
| National Bank of Wilmington & Brandywine | 1810 | 200,010 | 255,000 | 30 | 12 | 12 | 12 | 12 | 12 | 90 | 85 |
| Union National Bank | 1839 | 203,175 | 380,000 | 25 | 15 | 15 | 15 | 15 | 15 | 90 | 85 |
| Equitable Guarantee & Trust Co | 889 | 500,000 | 328,000 | 100 | 5 | 5 | 5 | 5 | 5 | 165 | 150 |
| Security Trust & Safe Deposit Co | 1885 | 500,000 | 317,180 | 100 | 6 | 6 | 6 | 6 | 6 | 170 | 155 |

## WOONSOCKET, R. I.

| Name. | Established. | Capital. | Surplus and Undivided Profits, Dec. 31, 1902. | Par Value of Stock. | 1898 | 1899 | 1900 | 1901 | 1902 | High. | Low. |
|---|---|---|---|---|---|---|---|---|---|---|---|
| Citizens' National Bank | 1865 | $100,000 | $43,000 | $100 | 6 | 6 | 6 | 5 | 5 | $110 | $107 |
| National Globe Bank | 1834 | 100,000 | 45,467 | 25 | 8 | 7½ | 7 | 7 | 7 | 37 | 36 |
| National Union Bank | 1805 | 150,000 | 25,332 | 50 | 4 | .. | 4 | 4 | 4 | 43 | 40 |
| Producers' National Bank | 1852 | 200,000 | 97,617 | 20 | 7 | 7 | 7 | 7 | 7 | 30 | 30 |

## WORCESTER, MASS.

| | | | | | | | | | | | |
|---|---|---|---|---|---|---|---|---|---|---|---|
| Central National Bank | 1829 | $300,000 | $120,000 | $100 | 5 | 5 | 5 | 5 | 5 | $120 | $110 |
| Citizens' National Bank | 1836 | 150,000 | 85,840 | 100 | 6 | 6 | 6 | 6 | 6 | 145 | 145 |
| City National Bank | 1854 | 200,000 | 100,000 | 100 | 6 | 5 | 5 | 5 | 5 | 116 | 116 |
| First National Bank | 1863 | 300,000 | [illegible] | 100 | 10 | 10 | 10 | 10 | 10 | 200 | 180 |
| Mechanics' National Bank | 1865 | 200,000 | 76,376 | 100 | 4 | 4 | 4 | 4 | 4 | 103 | 100 |
| Quinsigamond National Bank | 1833 | 250,000 | 190,000 | 100 | 6 | 6 | 6 | 6 | 6 | 138 | 138 |
| Worcester National Bank | 1804 | 250,000 | 279,170 | 100 | 5 | 8 | 8 | 8 | 8 | 185 | 185 |
| Worcester Safe Deposit & Trust Co. | 1868 | 200,000 | [illegible] | 100 | 6 | 6 | 6 | 6 | 6 | 155 | 155 |

## YORK, PA.

| | | | | | | | | | | | |
|---|---|---|---|---|---|---|---|---|---|---|---|
| City Bank | 1887 | $100,000 | $70,000 | $50 | 6 | 6 | 7 | 8 | 8 | $100 | $95 |
| Drovers' & Mechanics' National Bank | 1883 | 100,000 | 47,060 | 10 | 7 | 8 | 8 | 8 | 8 | 184 | 180 |
| Farmers' National Bank | 1875 | 200,000 | 142,702 | 100 | 6 | 6 | 6 | 8 | 8 | 175 | 175 |
| First National Bank | 1864 | 300,000 | 200,000 | [illegible] | 10 | 10 | 10 | 10 | 10 | 220 | 220 |
| Western National Bank | 1875 | 150,000 | 74,000 | 100 | 4½ | 5 | 5½ | 6 | 6 | 153 | 150 |
| York County National Bank | 1845 | 300,000 | 225,000 | 20 | 8 | 8 | 8 | 8 | 8 | 48 | 43 |
| York National Bank | 1810 | 500,000 | [illegible] | 25 | 6 | 6 | 6 | 6 | 7 | 50 | 49 |
| Security Title & Trust Co. | 1893 | 150,000 | 90,000 | 50 | 5 | 5 | 6 | 6 | 6 | 80 | 78 |
| York Trust Co. | 1890 | 150,000 | 45,356 | 50 | 6 | 6 | 6 | 6 | 6 | 79 | 75 |

## YOUNGSTOWN, O.

| | | | | | | | | | | | |
|---|---|---|---|---|---|---|---|---|---|---|---|
| Commercial National Bank | 1880 | $200,000 | $93,000 | $100 | 5 | 5 | 5 | 5 | 5 | $122 | $120 |
| First National Bank | 1863 | 500,000 | 330,000 | 100 | 8 | 8 | 8 | 8 | 8 | 160 | 160 |
| Mahoning National Bank | 1877 | 229,000 | 136,000 | 100 | 6 | 6 | 6 | 6 | 6 | 145 | 140 |
| Second National Bank | 1874 | 200,000 | 200,000 | 100 | 8 | 8 | 8 | 8 | 8 | 250 | 225 |
| Wick National Bank | 1894 | 300,000 | 133,539 | 100 | 6 | 6 | 6 | 6 | 6 | .. | .. |
| Dollar Savings & Trust Co. | 1887 | 1,000,000 | 187,051 | 100 | 6 | 6 | 6 | 6 | 6 | 160 | 140 |

# CANADA

## HALIFAX, NOVA SCOTIA

| Name. | Established. | Capital. | Surplus and Undivided Profits, Dec. 31, 1902. | Par Value of Stock. | Dividends Paid, Per Cent. | | | | | Range of Prices, 1902. | |
|---|---|---|---|---|---|---|---|---|---|---|---|
| | | | | | 1898 | 1899 | 1900 | 1901 | 1902 | High. | Low. |
| Bank of Nova Scotia | 1832 | $2,000,000 | $3,012,025 | $100 | 8 | 8½ | 9 | 9 | 9½ | $272 | $260 |
| Eastern Canada Savings & Loan Co., Ltd. | 1887 | 100,500 | 41,000 | 50 | 6 | 6 | 6 | 6 | 6 | 65 | 64 |
| Halifax Banking Co. | 1825 | 600,000 | 529,339 | 20 | 7 | 7 | 7 | 7 | 7 | 36 | 36 |
| People's Bank of Halifax | 1864 | 700,000 | 329,476 | 20 | 6 | 6 | 6 | 6 | 6 | 28 | 28 |
| Royal Bank of Canada | 1869 | 2,481,000 | 2,599,624 | 100 | 7 | 7 | 7 | 7 | 7½ | 217 | 167 |
| Union Bank of Halifax | 1856 | 1,205,900 | 827,167 | 50 | 7 | 7 | 7 | 7 | 7 | 172 | 172 |

## HAMILTON, ONTARIO

| Name. | Established. | Capital. | Surplus and Undivided Profits, Dec. 31, 1902. | Par Value of Stock. | 1898 | 1899 | 1900 | 1901 | 1902 | High. | Low. |
|---|---|---|---|---|---|---|---|---|---|---|---|
| Bank of Hamilton | 1872 | $2,000,000 | $1,644,732 | $100 | 8 | 8 | 8 | 10 | 10 | $230 | $190 |
| Hamilton Provident & Loan Society | 1871 | 1,100,000 | 305,771 | 100 | 6 | 6 | 6 | 6 | 6 | 122 | 119 |
| Landed Banking & Loan Co | 1877 | 700,000 | 195,000 | 100 | 6 | 6 | 6 | 6 | 6 | 121 | 118 |

## LONDON, ONTARIO

| Name. | Established. | Capital. | Surplus and Undivided Profits, Dec. 31, 1902. | Par Value of Stock. | 1898 | 1899 | 1900 | 1901 | 1902 | High. | Low. |
|---|---|---|---|---|---|---|---|---|---|---|---|
| Canada Trust Co. | 1901 | $200,000 | $15,556 | $100 | .. | .. | .. | .. | .. | .. | .. |

## MONTREAL, QUEBEC

| | | | | | | | | | | | |
|---|---|---|---|---|---|---|---|---|---|---|---|
| Bank of British North America | 1836 | $4,866,666 | $1,776,333 | $243 | 5 | 5 | 6 | 6 | 6 | $348 | $316 |
| Bank of Montreal | 1817 | 12,000,000 | 8,435,698 | 200 | 10 | 10 | 10 | 10 | 10 | 274 | 255 |
| Banque d'Hochelaga | 1874 | 2,000,000 | 1,150,892 | 100 | 7 | 7 | 7 | 7 | 7 | 145 | 135 |
| La Banque Provinciale du Canada | 1900 | 819,000 | 138,000 | 12½ | .. | .. | .. | 3 | .. | ... | ... |
| Merchants' Bank of Canada | 1868 | 6,000,000 | 2,700,000 | 100 | 8 | 7 | 7 | 7 | 7 | 164 | 144 |
| Molson's Bank | 1855 | 2,500,000 | 2,356,905 | 50 | 9 | 9 | 9 | 9 | 9 | 109 | 104 |
| Montreal City & District Savings Bank | 1846 | 600,000 | 750,263 | 120 | 13½ | 15 | 15 | 15 | 16⅔ | 450 | 450 |
| Montreal Trust & Deposit Co | 1892 | 64,715 | 3,394 | 100 | .. | .. | .. | .. | .. | ... | ... |
| Royal Trust Co | 1900 | 500,000 | 250,000 | ... | .. | .. | .. | .. | .. | ... | ... |

## OTTAWA, ONTARIO

| | | | | | | | | | | | |
|---|---|---|---|---|---|---|---|---|---|---|---|
| Bank of Ottawa | 1874 | $2,000,000 | $1,937,851 | $100 | 9 | 9 | 9 | 9 | 9 | $226 | $209 |

## QUEBEC, QUEBEC

| | | | | | | | | | | | |
|---|---|---|---|---|---|---|---|---|---|---|---|
| La Banque Nationale | 1860 | $1,500,000 | $410,000 | $30 | 6 | 6 | 6 | 6 | 6 | $33 | $32 |
| La Caisse d'Economie de Notre Dame de Quebec | 1848 | 250,000 | 290,743 | 400 | 12 | 12 | 12 | 12 | 12 | 250 | 240 |
| Quebec Bank | 1818 | 2,500,000 | 800,000 | 100 | 6 | 6 | 6 | 6 | 6 | 118 | 118 |
| Union Bank of Canada | 1866 | 2,245,000 | 750,000 | 100 | 6 | 6 | 6 | 6 | 7 | 126 | 106 |

## ST. JOHN, NEW BRUNSWICK

| | | | | | | | | | | | |
|---|---|---|---|---|---|---|---|---|---|---|---|
| Bank of New Brunswick | 1820 | $500,000 | $765,000 | $100 | 12 | 12 | 12 | 12 | 12 | $300 | $290 |

## TORONTO, ONTARIO

| Name. | Established. | Capital. | Surplus and Undivided Profits, Dec. 31, 1902. | Par Value of Stock. | Dividends Paid, Per Cent. 1898 | 1899 | 1900 | 1901 | 1902 | Range of Prices, 1902. High. | Low. |
|---|---|---|---|---|---|---|---|---|---|---|---|
| Bank of Toronto | 1855 | $2,500,000 | $2,693,128 | $100 | 10 | 10 | 10 | 10 | 11 | $256 | $229 |
| Canadian Bank of Commerce | 1867 | 8,000,000 | 2,500,000 | 50 | 7 | 7 | 7 | 7 | 7 | 83 | 76 |
| Canada Landed & National Investment Co., Ltd. | 1858 | 1,004,000 | 380,374 | 50 | 6 | 6 | 6 | 6 | 6 | 54 | 49 |
| Central Canada Loan & Savings Co. | 1884 | 1,250,000 | 646,525 | 100 | 6 | 6 | 6 | 6 | 7 | 135 | 135 |
| Dominion Bank | 1871 | 3,000,000 | 3,300,000 | 50 | 12 | 12 | 12 | 10 | 10 | 127 | 118 |
| Imperial Bank of Canada | 1875 | 4,000,000 | 2,829,421 | 100 | 9 | 9 | 9½ | 10 | 10 | 252 | 229 |
| Metropolitan Bank | 1902 | 1,000,000 | 1,001,697 | 100 | .. | .. | .. | .. | .. | 200 | 200 |
| Ontario Bank | 1857 | 1,500,000 | 425,000 | 100 | 5 | 5 | 5 | 5 | 6 | 135 | 126 |
| Sovereign Bank of Canada | 1902 | 1,267,000 | 265,000 | 100 | .. | .. | .. | .. | .. | ... | ... |
| Standard Bank of Canada | 1875 | 1,000,000 | 850,000 | 50 | 8 | 8 | 10 | 10 | 10 | 127 | 117 |
| Traders' Bank of Canada | 1885 | 1,500,000 | 450,000 | 100 | 6 | 6 | 6 | 6 | 6 | 135 | 109 |
| National Trust Co., Ltd. | 1898 | 1,000,000 | 312,443 | 100 | .. | 5 | 5 | 6 | 6 | 142 | 133 |
| Toronto General Trusts Corporation | 1882 | 1,000,000 | 270,000 | 100 | .. | 7½ | 7½ | 7½ | 7½ | 170 | 161 |
| Union Trust Co., Limited | 1901 | 1,000,000 | 220,000 | 100 | .. | .. | .. | 4 | 4 | 125 | 125 |

Lightning Source UK Ltd.
Milton Keynes UK
UKHW010057280219
338009UK00005B/123/P

9 780428 637590